ART AND ARCHITECTURE IN CANADA

ART ET ARCHITECTURE AU CANADA

VOLUME 2

LOREN R. LERNER & MARY F. WILLIAMSON

Art and Architecture in Canada: A Bibliography and Guide to the Literature to 1981

Art et architecture au Canada : bibliographie et guide de la documentation jusqu'en 1981

2

UNIVERSITY OF TORONTO PRESS
Toronto Buffalo London

Canadian Cataloguing in Publication Data

Lerner, Loren R. (Loren Ruth), 1948–
 Art and architecture in Canada =
 Art et architecture au Canada

Prefatory material in English and French;
includes English and French publications.
Includes indexes.
ISBN 0-8020-5856-6 (set)

1. Art – Canada – Bibliography.
2. Architecture – Canada – Bibliography.
3. Decorative arts – Canada – Bibliography.
4. Artists – Canada – Bibliography.
5. Architects – Canada – Bibliography.
I. Williamson, Mary F.   II. Title.   III. Title:
 Art et architecture au Canada.

REF   Z5961.C3L47 1991 Vol   016.709′71   C91-093656-OE
                         2

67432

Données de catalogage avant publication (Canada)

Lerner, Loren R. (Loren Ruth), 1948–
 Art and architecture in Canada =
 Art et architecture au Canada

Texte prélim. en anglais et en français;
comprend des publications en anglais et en français.
Comprend des index.
ISBN 0-8020-5856-6 (ensemble)

1. Art – Canada – Bibliographie.
2. Architecture – Canada – Bibliographie.
3. Arts décoratifs – Canada – Bibliographie.
4. Artistes – Canada – Bibliographie.
5. Architectes – Canada – Bibliographie.
I. Williamson, Mary F.   II. Titre.
III. Titre: Art et architecture au Canada.

Z5961.C3L47 1991   016.709′71   C91-093656-OF

These volumes have been published with the assistance of a grant
from the Canadian Research Tools Programme of the Social Sciences
and Humanities Research Council of Canada.

La publication de ces volumes a été subventionnée par le programme
« Les études canadiennes : outils de recherche » du Conseil de recherche
en sciences humaines du Canada.

Contents / Table des matières

Volume 2

Guide to Using Volume 2

Volume 1 of *Art and Architecture in Canada* is organized for the general reader by topic, geographical area, and chronological period. Volume 2, however, consists of author and subject indexes that direct the reader to specific authors, and to the artists, architects, and works discussed in the publications cited. The indexes refer to entry numbers in Volume 1 rather than to page numbers.

Of the two indexes, the Subject Index (in separate English and French versions) assumes by far the most important role because it provides detailed subject access to the entries in Volume 1 and is in itself an authoritative source for names and dates.

AUTHOR INDEX

The Author Index (beginning on p. 3) lists in one alphabetical sequence all authors whose names appear in the citations as the authors or editors of books, theses, articles and essays, and exhibition catalogues. In the case of exhibition catalogues, all significant contributors – curators, and the authors of essays, introductions, and catalogue descriptions – are listed in the Author Index. Full author indexing makes the Author Index a convenient starting point for the compilation of a list of books, articles, and contributions to exhibition catalogues or collections of writings by a single author.

The Author Index is a name index, not a person index. The names of authors are given in the form in which they appear in the original publications, and as a result the same person may be represented by variant forms of his or her name in the Author Index. Typical name variations are the single and married names of women, and the use of initials rather than complete first names. It is not always possible to determine whether the author of a particular book is the same person as the author of a particular article, but in any case it may be useful for the reader to be aware of variations in authors' names in order to identify other writings by the author that have not been included in *Art and Architecture in Canada*:

Dillow, Nancy #5200
Dillow, Nancy E. #543 1919 1922 1923 1936 5198 5626 6728 6837 7195 7285 7320
Robertson, Nancy E. #490 1915 5823 6370

SUBJECT INDEX

The index terms used in *Art and Architecture in Canada* are based on those developed by *RILA* (*Répertoire de la littérature de l'art*) over the past several years. In *Art and Architecture in Canada* certain topics and areas of concern having significance in the Canadian context have been emphasized. This empha-

sis is reflected in the abstracts for the entries in Volume 1 and in the Subject Index. All artists mentioned in the abstracts appear in the Subject Index, as do all proper names, individual works of art, places, media, styles, and subjects. Some of the encyclopaedic features that have been built into the index terms are described and explained below.

The entries in Volume 1 of the bibliography are arranged by broad subject areas, as the contents pages indicate. These invite general browsing of the volume. The Subject Index, however, is intended to provide further access to names and topics in the publications cited. A book about a single artist may be indexed only under the name of the artist, but up to ten artists appearing in a group exhibition are individually indexed, with further index entries under exhibiting galleries and topics referred to in the abstract. In the case of exhibition catalogues and articles where more than ten artists are discussed, individual names are not mentioned in the abstract or noted in the Subject Index. Instead, the entry is indexed using a broad, overall index term, such as "Saskatchewan, painting" or "sculpture, Canadian (1960s)."

For series or journal entries (e.g. entries for the annual exhibition catalogues published over a number of years by an artists' society, or entries for complete runs of art periodicals), the names of the periodicals and the societies or groups are indexed. But beyond these the majority of index terms refer to artists and other individuals who are associated prominently with the groups or periodicals. Photography journals are even more generously indexed, with entries for individual photographers who are represented by portfolios.

In addition, the Subject Index can be consulted independently as an encyclopaedic reference source for various kinds of information. For example, the personal names used in the Subject Index are as complete and accurate as possible.[1] We have used the most authoritative version of the name that we have been able to establish, and other versions of the name have been cross-referenced to it.

Because it has not always been possible to establish an individual's nationality, we have given the country of birth or principal association. Beginning in the seventeenth century and throughout our period, artists have taken up temporary residence in Canada as explorers; as priests, nuns, and missionaries; as military officers, governors, company agents, and their wives; and as manufacturers, itinerant artisans, teachers, jurors, and winners of international design competitions. Depending on their length of stay in Canada, these artists have been assigned the appropriate nationality with or without the added designation "in Canada," or they have simply been called "Can," i.e. "Canadian."

The years of birth and death, or the years in which the individual flourished, have been established in consultation

with numerous sources, including the publications cited in the entries in Volume 1, biographical dictionaries, library catalogues and artists' files, periodical indexes, artists' and architects' associations, scholars, and the artists themselves.

One encyclopaedic feature of the Subject Index is the list of artists' names that appear under the following entries: "folk artists," "Indian artists," "Inuit artists," "photographers," and "women artists." The purpose of the lists is to introduce artists whose names may be unfamiliar to the reader. All of the artists are also indexed individually by name.

Listings of exhibitions by city and by the names of art galleries and museums that have either sponsored the exhibitions or were included in the itinerary of travelling exhibitions can be found by looking up the city, and then the names of art galleries and museums as subheadings.

In Volume 1 the entries for the catalogue of an exhibition and the reviews of the exhibition are not necessarily found together. This is because the exhibition itinerary may extend over two or three years, with reviews appearing at intervals along the way. To find a catalogue and the exhibition reviews, the reader should look in the Subject Index for the subentries "exhibitions" and "exhibitions (reviews)" under the name of the city and gallery:

London (England), Canada House Gallery
- exhibitions
  ...
  - *Exposition d'estampes en l'honneur de C. Krieghoff, 1815–1872/Exhibition of Prints in Honour of C. Krieghoff, 1815–1872* (1972) #6096
  ...
  - *Jack Chambers: Selection of Paintings and Drawings* (1980) #5080
- exhibitions (reviews)
  - *Exposition d'estampes en l'honneur de C. Krieghoff, 1815–1872/Exhibition of Prints in Honour of C. Krieghoff, 1815–1872* (1972) #6099
  ...
  - *Jack Chambers: Selection of Paintings and Drawings* (1980) #5082

Surveys and retrospective studies, as well as publications on specific media, can be found under comprehensive entries such as "art, Canadian," "painting, Canadian," "graphic arts, Canadian," and "architecture, Canadian." These entries can assist the reader to identify relevant names and places that can be consulted in the Subject Index:

graphic arts, Canadian #925
  ...
- 19th c. #838
  - Volpi, Charles de, collection #3248
- 19th c.–1920s #11 14
- (1792–1850) #839
- (1840s–1920s) #4
  ...
- (1927), Canadian National Exhibition (Toronto, Ont) #295
  ...
- advertising
  ...
  - Art Directors' Club of Toronto #854
  - Burns, Cooper, Hynes Ltd. #905 906
  - Burns & Cooper Ltd. #892 896
  - Burton Kramer Associates #889
  - Carlton Studio (London, England) #843
  ...

- block prints #837
- Brant County (Ont), (1793–1930) #1684
- Canadian Society of Graphic Art #801
- Group of Seven #930
...
- landscapes #132
  - (1970s) #595
...
- Montréal (Qué)
  ...
  - Guilde graphique #1647 1653 1655
  ...
  - Olympic Games (1976) #898 901 902 5858

A single topic can often be approached from several points of view in the Subject Index. A building, for example, may be entered in the index under building type (e.g. banks, churches, courthouses, schools, theatres), the name of the city in which the building is located, and the names of the architects or architectural firms involved:

banks, Canadian
- Montréal (Qué)
  - Bank of Montreal (1918) #9168

Montréal (Qué), Bank of Montreal
- architecture
  - Wells, John; McKim, Mead & White #9168

McKim, Mead & White, Amer architectural firm
- Bank of Montreal (1918) #9168

Wells, John, Can architect, 1789–1864
- Montréal (Qué), Bank of Montreal #9168

Entries in the Subject Index for artists who have exhibited widely and have been much discussed are a micropaedia of these artists' lives and careers. Subentries under an artist's name may refer to the following types of information: where the artist was educated; names of teachers; names of other artists whom the artist has influenced or by whom he/she has been influenced; names of artists, groups of artists, and art movements with which the artist is associated; where the artist has worked and travelled; collections in which the artist's work is found; media in which the artist works; names and locations of solo and group exhibitions; specific works of art; references to writings by the artist:

Baillairgé, François, Can architect, artist, 1759–1830 #1232 1592 4585 4586 4588 4589 4590 4593 6947
- and origins of Québec woodcarving and architecture #1574
- and Québec society #1375
- as brother of Pierre-Florent Baillairgé #4594
- as teacher #1582
- Baie-Saint-Paul (Qué), architecture and sculpture #7849
- exhibitions
  - (1975) #4592
- exhibitions, group
  - (1959) portraits #219
- influence of French painting #1244
- influence on Thomas Baillairgé #8328
- paintings #4587
- Québec (Qué)
  - Chapel of the congrégation Notre-Dame de Québec #8864
  - Church of Saint-Joachim de Montmorency, interior #8880

– Notre-Dame-des-Victoires #8858
- rocking horses #2934
- sculptures #1324
- tabernacles #1613 4591
- use of architectural models #7872

...

Lyle, John MacIntosh, Can architect, 1872–1945
- architectural decorations, Canadian banks (1930s) #8226
- as teacher #8243
- Bank of Nova Scotia buildings #9186 9203
- exhibitions, group
  – (1933) #8224
- Halifax (NS), Bank of Nova Scotia #9182
- Kingston (Ont), war memorial, Royal Military College of Canada #1083
- on Canadian art #329
- plan, northwestern entrance to Hamilton (Ont) #7962
- Toronto (Ont)
  – Bank of Ottawa #9159
  – Dominion Bank #9188
  – Government House, competition #8748
  – Masonic Temple, competition #9062
  – Royal Alexandra Theatre #9059
  – Toronto Stock Exchange, competition #9161
  – Union Station #9531 9536
- use of stucco and brickwork #8052

In the nineteenth and early twentieth centuries, architects usually practised independently. Later in the twentieth century, architectural practices have more often taken the form of partnerships or firms that employ a number of architects and other professionals. Where responsibility for a particular building is given in a publication to a firm, rather than to individual architects, the index terms refer only to the name of the firm, and not to the names of the architects involved.

Research on artists depends to a great extent on what the artists have written about themselves – their lives, working methods, and theories of art – in diaries, journals, correspondence, and articles. Writings by artists are brought together in the Subject Index under "artists' correspondence," "artists' diaries," "artists' writings," and "architectural theory and criticism."

The role of Canadian artists in documenting the participation of Canada in both world wars can be approached in several ways: in Volume 1 in the section "Art and War." in Volume 2 in the Subject Index under "war in art," and in specific entries on "World War I (1914–1918)," and "World War II (1939–1945)," where individual artists are listed.

Art galleries and museums are listed in the Subject Index under the cities in which they are located. Over the years names change, and in the Subject Index cross-references are provided to link the old and new names:

Toronto (Ont), Art Gallery of Ontario
- see also Toronto (Ont), Art Gallery of Toronto; Toronto (Ont), Art Museum of Toronto; Toronto (Ont), The Grange

Many artists have arrived in Canada as immigrants and have contributed to the Canadian cultural mosaic through the production of art works based on traditional styles and motifs from the old country. Other artists have formed ethnic art associations that provide a solid cultural base for the artist members to work independently in contemporary, international styles. The participation of these groups in the artistic life of Canada is traced in the Subject Index through a series of subject entries that refer to the country of origin, e.g. "Chinese in Canada," "Estonians in Canada," "Jews in Canada," "Latvians in Canada," "Norwegians in Canada," "Poles in Canada," "Ukrainians in Canada":

Ukrainians in Canada
- architecture #8085 8127 8713
- art #1843
- Bukovynian shirts and jewellery (1865–1945) #2869
- churches #8768 8912 8915
- churches and decorative arts #2270
- domestic architecture #8691 8704 8709 8710
- Easter eggs #2132
- embroidery #2124 2782
- folk art #968 2117
  – late 18th–20th cs. #961
- Kurelek, William, paintings of #6113 6114 6116
- log buildings #8090 8136
- needlework #2780
- sepulchral monuments #733

The story of all the Canadian artists who have studied, worked, and travelled abroad has barely begun to be told. To assist research into the influences experienced by Canadian artists while outside of Canada there are a number of subject entries that have been developed that are based on the phrase "Canadians in ... [name of country]," e.g. "Canadians in Africa," "Canadians in Europe," "Canadians in France," "Canadians in Great Britain," "Canadians in India," "Canadians in Italy," "Canadians in Jamaica," "Canadians in Japan," "Canadians in Mexico," "Canadians in Spain," "Canadians in Sweden," "Canadians in West Indies," "Canadians in USA":

Canadians in Belgium
- Brault, Maurice #4906
- Jackson, A.Y. #5924
Canadians in Brazil
- (1950s) #413 414
- Rio de Janeiro
  – Pellan, Alfred #6798
  – Tonnancour, Jacques Godefroy de #7381
Canadians in China
- McLaren, Norman #6492
- Onley, Toni #6738

The influence of other countries on art and architecture in Canada may be traced in the Subject Index through the names of individual artistic mediums or artifacts, followed by nationality, for example in entries such as the following: "art, American," "architecture, Scottish," "furniture, American," "pottery, British," "sculpture, French":

pottery, British
- 19th c., influence on Canadian pottery #2281 2339
- 19th c., views of Canada, Minton dessert service #2289
  – for Canadian market #2297
    – 18th–19th cs. #2363
    – 19th c. #2288 2294 2315 2320 2354
    – (1750s–early 19th c.) #2316
    – (1830s–early 20th c.) #2357 2358
    – (1850s–1890s) #2361
    – (1880–1914) #2340
  – Glasgow (Scotland), Britannia Pottery #2326
  – Hudson's Bay Company #2351
  – John Marshall & Co., sporting subjects #2360
  – Portneuf Pottery #2285 2306

The use of "St./Ste." or "Saint/Sainte" in the names of Canadian cities, towns, and churches has varied considerably in practice in different times and places. For example, both "St. John" and "Saint John" have been used for New Brunswick's largest city, although Saint John has become the standard spelling. In *Art and Architecture in Canada* the *Canadian Gazetteer* has been used as an authoritative source for the spelling of names of cities and towns, and the proper use of "St." and "Saint," but cross-references are provided in the Subject Index. However, "St./Ste." in the names of churches has been written out as "Saint" and "Sainte" to bring the churches together in one alphabetical sequence in the Subject Index.

A group of subject headings focusses on the relationship between art and architecture and a number of themes, concepts, topics and disciplines, such as "economics and art," "language and art," "law and architecture," "music and art," "nationalism and art," "perception and art," "regionalism and art," "religion and art," "society and art," "state and architecture," "state and art," "taxation and art," and "theatre and art":

perception and art
- Indians of North America #3487
- Inuit #4294
- Molinari, Guido #6591
- Northwest Coast Indians #4001
- Snow, Michael #7245 7259
- Tousignant, Serge #7404
- use of mirrors and windows #525
- video art #651

There are entries on particular and generic subjects that have been depicted in art, and on Canadian iconographic symbols, for example "airplanes in art," "animals in art," "beaver," "birds in art," "Indians of North America in art," "nude in art," "ships in art," "workers in art," "Wolfe, James, Brit army officer in Canada, 1727/1728–1759, portraits of":

birds in art
- Archambault, Louis #4539
- Canadian architectural decoration (1930s) #8226
- Canadian pottery #2309
  - Goold, F.P., & Co. (Brantford, Ont) #2335
- Carr, Emily #5019
- folk art, Québec #1284 1362
- Grondin, Jean-Luc #5662
- Hood, Robert #5826
- Inuit sculpture #4404 4459
- Lansdowne, James Fenwick #6163 6164 6165
- Loates, Glen #6310
- MacDonald, Thoreau #6381
- Murphy, Burland E. #6663
- Nasmith, Eric Anderson #6685
- Newlan, Emery #6690
- Phinney, Robert #6862
- Picher, Claude #6867
- Pootoogook, Kananginak #6904
- Pope, William #6905 6906
- Pratt, George #6916
- raven
  - Kwakiutl #3883
  - Tlingit #3786
- raven rattles, Northwest Coast Indians #3980 4026
- Roussil, Robert #7090

- Savage, Harry #7133
- Shortt, Terence Michael #506 7200

Art movements and styles originating in Europe have also found their expression in Canada. Among the headings in the Subject Index that address art movements and styles are "abstract art," "Art Deco," "Art Nouveau," "Chippendale style," "Dada," "Impressionism," "Louis XVI style," "Pop art," "Post-Impressionism," "post-modernism," "post-painterly abstraction," "realism," "Surrealism," and "Victorian architecture."

The names of art movements, styles, and media entered in the Subject Index can be used to find the names of artists who are associated with the movements, styles, and media. For example, to identify performance artists in Canada, consult the index entry "performance art" in the index. The artists mentioned under the entry can also be looked up individually by name in the index:

performance art
- (1970s) #634 672 2046
  - and sculpture #654
  - tele-performance #603
- Berman, Michaele #4710
- Canada #1799
  - (1970s) #538 598 669 6676
    - sculpture #658
  - (1978) *Fifth Network/Cinquième réseau* #655
  - (1979–1981) *Impressions* #996
  - (1981) #709 713 718
- Clark, Tim #687
- Dean, Max #687
- Falk, Gathie #5410
- General Idea #5583

The names of art galleries, museums, and buildings in Québec are given in French in both the English and French subject indexes. Some buildings and institutions in Québec have been known over the years by English names. In these instances the English names are given as cross-references:

Montréal (Qué), Montreal Museum of Fine Arts
- *see* Montréal (Qué), Musée des beaux-arts de Montréal/ Montreal Museum of Fine Arts

Local emphasis is brought out in the Subject Index entries for cities and towns. Typical references include the names of art galleries and museums and their exhibitions, architectural history, the names of buildings, art schools, and the city or town as subject matter in art:

Victoria (BC)
- architecture #8146 8149 8173 8176 8177 8178
  - (1843–1929) #8180
  ...
  - Chinatown #8179 8181
  - Hooper, Thomas #8376
  - Rattenbury, Francis Mawson #8400
  - Whiteway, William Tuff #9508
- architecture and decorative arts #2269
- art
  - (1910–1941), Island Arts and Crafts Society #1980
  - (1970s) #1870 2053
- art galleries #442
- domestic architecture #8722
  - (1910s) #8494

– museums #3190
– painting #2000
– photographic views
   – (1850–1900) #1061
   – Dally, Frederick #5249
   – Maynard, Hannah Hatherly #6457
– photography, late 19th c. #2022
Victoria (BC), Alexis Martin House
– architecture, Samuel Maclure #8682
Victoria (BC), Art Gallery of Greater Victoria
– collection #3189
– exhibitions

   ...
   – *Daniel Fowler of Amherst Island, 1810–1894* (1979) #5491
   – *Edward Curtis in the Collection of the Edmonton Art Gallery* (1980) #3480
   – *F.H. Varley: A Centennial Exhibition/F.H. Varley: une exposition centenaire* (1981) #7467
   – *Fired Sculpture* (1974) #774

The cities indexed in the Subject Index are not restricted to Canada. They include cities in other countries where exhibitions of Canadian art have been held, where buildings designed by Canadian architects have been built, and where Canadian artists have studied and worked. See, for example, the entry on New York (NY).

Many publications about Canadian art and architecture focus on a particular province or region, e.g. Arctic; Canadian West, Atlantic Provinces, Prairies, Rocky Mountains. Regional literature is brought together in the Subject Index under the name of the province or region by means of a series of descriptive subentries:

Prairies
– architecture #8080 8083 8088 8089
   – 20th c. #8084 8086
   – (1970s) #8087
   – Jewish #8081
   – Ukrainian #8085
   – use of building and ornamental stones (1910s) #7646 7647
– art
   – 20th c. #145
   – (1920s–1960s) #461
   – (1950s) #429
   – (1960s) #1848 1851
   – (1960s–1970s) #1862
   – (1970s) #1860 1880
– bottles #2431
– decorative arts, Germanic tradition #2140
   ...
– folk art
   – (1960s) #1852
   ...
– grain elevators #9237
   ...
– photographic views
   – Hime, Humphrey Lloyd #5801
   ...

– views
   ...
   – Chester, Donovan T. #1858
   ...
   – Wyers, Jan #1918

Because native arts are not covered in the *RILA* bibliographic service, a separate set of index terms has been developed for the art of the Indians and the Inuit. The new index terms for Indians come under the broad heading "Indians of North America" and refer to artifacts, such as "basketry," "beadwork," "petroglyphs," and "stonework." There are subentries for the names of tribes and direct references to the names of tribes. In this way, multiple access is provided to native artifacts, with principal access by type of artifact and by the name of the tribe:

basketry, Iroquois #3519 3605 3625
– (1760s–early 20th c.) #3633
– and Seneca basketry #3552
– stamp-blocked ornamentation #3562
...

...

Iroquois Indians
   ...
– basketry #3552 3562 3625

A total of seventy periodicals have been selected as having particular importance for the history of art, crafts, decorative arts, graphic arts, photography, native arts, and architecture, in Canada. Each periodical has been given its own entry in Volume 1 of the bibliography, with a lengthy abstract in which the publication history and the contents are outlined and summarized. For the names of the seventy periodicals, consult the Subject Index under "architecture, periodicals," "art, periodicals," and "photography, periodicals."

A list of all theses cited in the bibliography can be found in the Subject Index under "theses, Canadian."

Several major index entries bring together large numbers of documents in areas which to date have seen little published research. Among these are "architectural education," "art education," "art theory and criticism," "collectors and collecting," "art market," "illustration, Canadian," "portraits," and "sculpture, Canadian."

NOTE

1 The most useful published sources that the editors have relied upon for the names of artists are: J. Russell Harper, *Early Painters and Engravers in Canada* (Toronto: University of Toronto Press 1970); André Comeau, *Artistes plasticiens: Canada régime français et conquête, Bas-Canada et le Québec* (Montréal: Editions Bellarmin 1983); Canadian Arctic Producers Co-operative Ltd., *Biographies of Inuit Artists* (Ottawa: Canadian Arctic Producers Co-operative Ltd. 1981, 1982) 2 vols. supp.; National Gallery of Canada, *Artists in Canada: A Union List of Files / Artistes au Canada: une liste collective des dossiers* (Ottawa: National Gallery Association, 1982, 1988); RILA, *Subject Headings 1983* (J. Paul Getty Center for the History of Art and the Humanities 1983).

Guide de l'utilisateur, volume 2

Le volume 1 de *Art et architecture au Canada* a été conçu pour être consulté à partir des sujets, des régions géographiques et des époques chronologiques. Le volume 2, par contre, comprend des index des auteurs et des sujets traités qui guident le lecteur vers des auteurs précis, vers les titres des ouvrages de référence bibliographiques inscrits ainsi que vers les artistes, les architectes et leurs œuvres dont il est question dans les publications citées. Les index font référence aux numéros des entrées du volume 1 plutôt qu'aux numéros des pages.

L'index des sujets traités (en versions française et anglaise distinctes) joue un rôle beaucoup plus important que l'index des auteurs du fait qu'il donne un accès détaillé aux entrées du volume 1 et qu'il constitue en soi un document de référence faisant autorité pour ce qui est des noms et des dates.

INDEX DES AUTEURS

Dans l'index des auteurs (débutant à la p. 3) on trouve, classés dans un même ordre alphabétique, tous les noms des auteurs figurant dans les descriptions bibliographiques en tant qu'auteurs ou directeurs de publication d'ouvrages, de thèses, d'articles, d'essais et de catalogues d'exposition. Dans le cas des catalogues d'exposition, les noms de toutes les personnes ayant contribué de façon importante à leur conception, comme les conservateurs et les auteurs d'essais, d'entrées en matière et de descriptions pour les catalogues, apparaissent dans l'index des auteurs. Ce catalogage complet d'un auteur fait de cet index un outil utile comme point de départ pour la compilation des livres, des articles et des textes pour les catalogues d'exposition et des collections de textes d'un même auteur.

L'index des auteurs n'est pas un index des personnes, mais un index des noms. Les noms des auteurs y sont reproduits tels qu'ils figurent dans les publications originales; c'est ainsi que le nom d'une même personne peut apparaître sous diverses formes dans l'index des auteurs. Le plus souvent il s'agit de femmes artistes dont on retrouve le nom alors qu'elles sont célibataires puis mariées, ou encore d'artistes dont le prénom est cité soit en entier soit par de simples initiales. Il n'est pas toujours possible de savoir si l'auteur d'un livre est aussi l'auteur d'un certain article, mais de toute manière il peut être utile pour le lecteur de connaître les diverses façons dont se présente le nom d'un auteur, afin qu'il puisse découvrir d'autres écrits de cet auteur qui n'auraient pas été inclus dans *Art et architecture au Canada* :

Dillow, Nancy #5200
Dillow, Nancy E. #543 1919 1922 1923 1936 5198 5626 6728 6837 7195 7285 7320
Robertson, Nancy E. #490 1915 5823 6370

INDEX DES SUJETS TRAITÉS

INDEX DES SUJETS TRAITÉS

Les termes utilisés pour les index de *Art et architecture au Canada* ont été établis d'après ceux mis au point par le *RILA* (*Répertoire de la littérature de l'art*) au cours des dernières années. Dans *Art et architecture au Canada*, l'accent a été mis sur certains sujets et secteurs d'intérêt qui revêtent une importance particulière dans le contexte canadien. On peut constater ce fait dans les résumés pour les entrées du volume 1 et dans l'index des sujets traités. Tous les noms des artistes mentionnés dans les résumés figurent dans l'index des sujets traités ainsi que tous les noms appropriés, les œuvres d'art, les lieux, les modes d'expression artistique, les styles et les sujets. Certains termes désignant des particularités d'ordre encyclopédique et qui ont été intégrés dans le vocabulaire de l'index sont décrits et expliqués ci-dessous.

Comme on le constatera en consultant la table des matières, les entrées du volume 1 de la bibliographie sont groupés par domaines d'études généraux. Elles donnent un aperçu global. Par contre, à l'aide de l'index des sujets traités, le lecteur a un accès détaillé aux noms et aux sujets dont il est question dans les publications citées. Il se peut qu'un livre sur un seul artiste ne figure dans l'index que sous le nom de cet artiste; cependant, on peut y retrouver, mentionnés individuellement, jusqu'à dix artistes ayant participé à des expositions de groupe, ainsi que d'autres entrées sous les noms des galeries où se tenaient les expositions et sous les sujets dont il est fait mention dans le résumé. Lorsqu'il s'agit de catalogues d'exposition et d'articles où il est question de plus de dix artistes, les noms de chacun d'eux ne sont pas mentionnés dans le résumé, pas plus que dans l'index des sujets traités. En ce cas on a recours dans l'index à un terme général comme « Saskatchewan, peinture » ou « sculpture canadienne (années 1960) ».

Dans le cas des entrées relatives à des collections ou à des publications, comme les catalogues d'exposition annuelle publiés pendant un certain nombre d'années par une société d'art, ou des séries complètes de revues d'art, les noms des sociétés, groupes et périodiques sont bien évidemment mentionnés, mais, en outre, la plupart des termes utilisés dans l'index font référence à des artistes et à d'autres personnes qui ont eu un lien marqué avec les groupes ou les périodiques en question. Quant aux publications sur la photographie, elles occupent encore plus de place dans l'index, puisqu'on y fait référence à chacun des photographes dont le dossier professionnel a été publié.

En outre, on peut consulter l'index des sujets traités simplement en tant qu'ouvrage de référence encyclopédique pour obtenir divers types de renseignements. Par exemple, les noms de personnes figurant dans l'index des sujets traités

sont aussi complets, aussi exacts que possible et aussi officiels[1]. Nous avons en effet utilisé la version du nom faisant le plus autorité dans la mesure où nous avons pu l'établir, et les variantes de ce nom comportent des renvois au nom officiel.

Comme il n'a pas toujours été possible de déterminer la nationalité d'une personne, nous avons indiqué le pays où elle est née ou celui auquel on l'associe principalement. A partir du XVIᵉ siècle et jusqu'à nos jours, des artistes ont élu temporairement résidence au Canada en tant qu'explorateurs, prêtres, religieuses, missionnaires, officiers militaires, gouverneurs, représentants de compagnie avec leurs épouses, manufacturiers, artisans itinérants, enseignants, jurés et lauréats de concours internationaux de création. Dans l'index des sujets traités, ces artistes se sont vu attribuer leur nationalité propre, avec ou sans la mention « au Canada », ou ils ont simplement été désignés « can », i.e. canadien, selon la durée de leur séjour au Canada.

Pour obtenir les années de naissance et de décès, ou celles où l'artiste était au sommet de son art, il a fallu consulter de nombreuses sources de renseignements, dont les publications citées dans les entrées du volume 1, les dictionnaires bibliographiques, les catalogues des bibliothèques ainsi que les dossiers sur les artistes, les index des périodiques, les associations d'artistes et d'architectes, les chercheurs et les artistes eux-mêmes.

Une des particularités encyclopédiques de l'index des sujets traités se trouve dans les listes des noms d'artistes figurant sous les rubriques suivantes : « artistes traditionnels », « artistes amérindiens », « artistes inuit », « photographes », et « femmes artistes ». Ces listes ont pour but de présenter le nom d'artistes que le lecteur ne connaît peut-être pas. Tous ces artistes figurent aussi individuellement dans l'index sous leur nom.

Pour trouver les listes des expositions désignées par les noms des villes, des galeries d'art et des musées qui les ont commanditées ou qui étaient inclus dans le parcours des expositions itinérantes, on consultera l'index aux noms des villes, puis à ceux des galeries d'art et des musées comme sous-titres. Là où le nom des galeries et des musées ne fait aucunement référence à l'endroit où ils sont situés, ils comportent des renvois aux noms des villes appropriées dans l'index.

Dans le volume 1, les entrées relatives au catalogue d'une exposition et celles se référant aux comptes rendus de la même exposition ne se trouvent pas nécessairement réunies, puisqu'il est possible qu'une exposition se soit déplacée pendant plus de deux ou trois ans et que des comptes rendus aient paru de temps à autre dans l'intervalle. Lorsque le lecteur veut trouver dans l'index des sujets traités un catalogue et un compte rendu d'exposition, il doit se reporter aux sous-rubriques « expositions » et « expositions (critiques) », sous le nom de la ville et de la galerie :

Londres (Angleterre), Canada House Gallery
– expositions

   ...

  – *Exposition d'estampes en l'honneur de C. Krieghoff, 1815–1872/Exhibition of Prints in Honour of C. Krieghoff, 1815–1872* (1972) #6096

   ...

  – *Jack Chambers: Selection of Paintings and Drawings* (1980) #5080
– expositions (critiques)

  – *Exposition d'estampes en l'honneur de C. Krieghoff, 1815–1872/Exhibition of Prints in Honour of C. Krieghoff, 1815–1872* (1972) #6099

   ...

– *Jack Chambers: Selection of Paintings and Drawings* (1980) #5082

Sous des rubriques détaillées comme « art canadien », « peinture canadienne », « arts graphiques. Canada », ainsi que « architecture canadienne », on fait référence aux relevés et aux études rétrospectives ainsi qu'aux publications traitant d'un mode d'expression artistique particulier. Ainsi, il est plus facile pour le lecteur de repérer les noms et lieux pertinents auxquels il peut se reporter dans l'index des sujets traités :

arts graphiques . Canada #925
– (1792–1850) #839

  ...

– (1927), Canadian National Exhibition (Toronto, Ont) #295

  ...

– (années 1840–1920) #4

  ...

– comté de Brant (Ont), (1793–1930) #1684

  ...

– Groupe des Sept #930

  ...

– impression sur cliché #837

  ...

– Montréal (Qué)

   ...

  – Guilde graphique #1647 1653 1655

   ...

  – Jeux olympiques (1976) #898 901 902 5858
– paysages #132
  – (années 1970) #595
– publicité
  – Art Directors' Club of Toronto #854
  – Burns, Cooper, Hynes Ltd. #905 906
  – Burns & Cooper Ltd. #892 896
  – Burton Kramer Associates #889
  – Carlton Studio (Londres, Angleterre) #843

  ...

– Société canadienne des arts graphiques #801
– XIXe s. #838
  – Volpi, Charles de, collection #3248

On peut aborder un même sujet sous divers angles dans l'index des sujets traités. Par exemple, dans le cas d'un bâtiment, il peut être désigné dans l'index sous le type de construction dont il s'agit (par exemple, banques, églises, palais de justice, écoles, théâtres et cinémas), sous le nom de la ville où il est situé et sous le nom des architectes ou des entreprises d'architecture en cause :

banques canadiennes
– Montréal (Qué)
  – Banque de Montréal (1918) #9168

Montréal (Qué), Banque de Montréal
– architecture
  – Wells, John; McKim, Mead & White #9168

McKim, Mead & White, agence amér d'architecture
– Banque de Montréal (1918) #9168

Wells, John, architecte can
– Montréal (Qué), Banque de Montréal #9168

Lorsqu'il s'agit d'artistes dont les œuvres ont été beaucoup

exposées et ont fait l'objet de nombreuses études, les articles les concernant dans l'index des sujets traités fournissent une petite documentation encyclopédique sur leur vie et leur carrière. Les sous-entrées au nom d'un artiste et aux dates pertinentes peuvent faire référence aux catégories d'information suivantes : l'endroit où cet artiste a reçu son éducation, le nom de ses professeurs, le nom d'autres artistes ayant subi son influence ou l'ayant influencé, le nom des artistes, des groupes d'artistes et des mouvements artistiques auxquels on l'associe, les lieux où il a travaillé ou qu'il a visités, les collections renfermant ses œuvres, ses modes d'expression artistique, les noms et lieux des expositions auxquelles il a participé seul ou avec d'autres artistes, les noms de certaines de ses œuvres et des indications sur ses écrits :

Baillairgé, François, architecte et artiste can, 1759–1830 #1232 1592 4585 4586 4588 4589 4590 4593 6947
- Baie-Saint-Paul (Qué), architecture et sculpture #7849
- chevaux à bascule #2934
- emploi de modèles architecturaux #7872
- et origines de l'architecture et de la sculpture sur bois au Québec #1574
- et société québécoise #1375
- expositions
  - (1975) #4592
- expositions de groupe
  - (1959), portraits #219
- frère de Pierre-Florent Baillairgé #4594
- influence de la peinture française #1244
- influence sur Thomas Baillairgé #8328
- peinture #4587
- professeur #1582
- Québec (Qué)
  - chapelle de la congrégation Notre-Dame de Québec #8864
  - église Saint-Joachim de Montmorency, intérieur #8880
  - Notre-Dame-des-Victoires #8858
- sculptures #1324
- tabernacles #1613 4591
...
Lyle, John MacIntosh, architecte can, 1872–1945
- décorations architecturales, banques canadiennes (années 1930) #8226
- édifices de la Banque de Nouvelle-Ecosse #9186 9203
- expositions de groupe
  - (1933) #8224
- Halifax (NE), Banque de Nouvelle-Ecosse #9182
- Kingston (Ont), mémorial, Royal Military College of Canada #1083
- plan, accès nord-ouest de Hamilton (Ont) #7962
- professeur #8243
- réflexion sur l'art canadien #329
- Toronto (Ont)
  - Bank of Ottawa #9159
  - Bourse de Toronto, concours #9161
  - Dominion Bank #9188
  - Government House, concours #8748
  - Masonic Temple, concours #9062
  - Royal Alexandra Theatre #9059
  - Union Station #9531 9536
- utilisation de brique et de stuc #8052

Au XIXe et au début du XXe siècle, les architectes travaillaient seuls la plupart du temps. Plus tard, au cours du XXe siècle, ils se sont associés ou réunis de plus en plus fréquemment pour fonder des entreprises d'architecture employant aussi d'autres professionnels. Lorsque, dans une publication, on attribue la conception d'un bâtiment à une entreprise plutôt qu'à tel ou tel architecte, on ne fait référence dans l'index qu'au nom de l'entreprise, et non à ceux des architectes impliqués.

La recherche sur les artistes s'appuie pour une large part sur ce qu'ils ont eux-mêmes écrit au sujet de leur vie, de leurs méthodes de travail et de leurs théories sur l'art, que ce soit dans un journal intime, dans des notes journalières, dans leur correspondance ou dans des articles. Leurs écrits sont réunis dans l'index des sujets traités sous : « artistes . correspondance », « artistes . notes personnelles », « artistes . écrits » et « architecture . théorie et critique ».

Le rôle joué par les artistes canadiens lorsqu'il s'est agi de relater la participation canadienne aux deux guerres mondiales peut être abordé de diverses façons : dans le volume 1 sous « L'art et la guerre », dans le volume 2 dans l'index des sujets traités sous « Guerre mondiale, 1re (1914–1918) » et sur « Guerre mondiale, 2e (1939–1945) », là où sont mentionnés individuellement les noms des artistes.

Dans l'index des sujets traités, le nom des galeries d'art et des musées apparaissent sous le nom des villes où ils sont situés. Au cours des années les noms changent, et, à cette fin, l'index des sujets traités comporte des renvois établissant les liens entre les anciens noms et les nouveaux.

Toronto (Ont), Musée des beaux-arts de l'Ontario
- *voir aussi* Toronto (Ont), Art Gallery of Toronto; Toronto (Ont), Art Museum of Toronto; Toronto (Ont), The Grange

Des artistes ont immigré au Canada et contribué à enrichir la mosaïque culturelle de notre pays en créant des œuvres d'art qui reflètent les styles et les motifs traditionnels des « vieux pays ». D'autres ont formé des associations d'artistes de groupes ethniques assurant à ses membres un appui culturel solide où ils peuvent créer librement dans des styles contemporains et internationaux. L'index des sujets traités fait référence à la participation de ces groupes à la vie artistique canadienne au moyen d'une série de rubriques désignant les pays d'origine comme : « Chinois au Canada », « Estoniens au Canada », « Juifs au Canada », « Lettons au Canada », « Norvégiens au Canada », « Polonais au Canada », « Ukrainiens au Canada ».

Ukrainiens au Canada
- architecture #8085 8127 8713
- architecture domestique #8691 8704 8709 8710
- art #1843
- art traditionnel #968 2117
  - fin XVIIIe–XXe s. #961
- broderie #2124 2782
- chemises et bijoux bukoviniens (1865–1945) #2869
- construction en bois rond #8090 8136
- églises #8768 8912 8915
- églises et arts décoratifs #2270
- Kurelek, William, peintures #6113 6114 6116
- monuments funéraires #733
- œufs de Pâques #2132
- ouvrages à l'aiguille #2780

On commence à peine à raconter l'histoire de tous les artistes canadiens qui ont étudié, travaillé et voyagé à l'étranger. Pour faciliter la recherche sur les diverses influences subies par les artistes canadiens alors qu'ils se trouvaient à l'étranger, on a conçu un certain nombre de rubriques débutant par les mots « Canadiens en ou au... (nom

du pays) », par exemple : « Canadiens au Japon », « Canadiens au Mexique », « Canadiens aux Antilles », « Canadiens aux Etats-Unis », « Canadiens en Afrique », « Canadiens en Espagne », « Canadiens en Europe », « Canadiens en France », « Canadiens en Grande-Bretagne », « Canadiens en Inde », « Canadiens en Italie », « Canadiens en Jamaïque », « Canadiens en Suède » :

Canadiens en Belgique
– Brault, Maurice #4906
– Jackson, A.Y. #5924
Canadiens en Chine
– McLaren, Norman #6492
– Onley, Toni #6738
Canadiens en Ecosse
– MacKenzie, Robert #6393
Canadiens en Espagne
– Ariss, Herb #473
– Ariss, Margot Phillip #473
– Bonet, Jordi #4784
– Chambers, Jack #473 5070 5071 5073
– Coughtry, John Graham #473

Si on cherche dans l'index des sujets traités de la documentation sur l'influence des pays étrangers sur l'art et l'architecture au Canada, on la trouvera en consultant les noms des différents modes d'expression artistique ou objets façonnés, suivis de la nationalité, par exemple sous des rubriques telles que celles-ci :

poterie anglaise
– Compagnie de la baie d'Hudson #2351
– Glasgow (Ecosse), Britannia Pottery #2326
– John Marshall & Co., scènes sportives #2360
– poterie de Portneuf #2285 2306
– pour le marché canadien #2297
 – (1880–1914) #2340
 – (années 1750–début XIXe s.) #2316
 – (années 1830–début XXe s.) #2357 2358
 – (années 1850–1890) #2361
 – XIXe s. #2288 2294 2315 2320 2354
 – XVIIIe–XIXe s. #2363
– XIXe s., influence sur poterie canadienne #2281 2339
– XIXe s., vues du Canada, service à dessert Minton #2289

Suivant les endroits et les époques, l'utilisation de « St/Ste » ou de « Saint/Sainte » dans les noms des villes, villages et églises du Canada varie considérablement. Par exemple, en ce qui concerne la plus grande ville du Nouveau-Brunswick, on écrit indifféremment « St-Jean » ou « Saint-Jean », même si c'est cette dernière forme qui prévaut aujourd'hui. Dans *Art et architecture au Canada*, on a consulté le Répertoire géographique du Canada comme source de référence faisant autorité pour ce qui est de l'orthographe des noms de villes et de villages et de l'utilisation correcte de « St » et de « Ste », mais l'index des sujets traités comporte néanmoins des renvois. Cependant, dans l'index des sujets traités, on utilise « Saint » et « Sainte » pour les noms d'églises plutôt que « St » et « Ste », afin que les noms soient classés par ordre alphabétique.

Un groupe de vedettes-matières mettent l'accent sur les rapports entre l'art et l'architecture et sur un certain nombre de thèmes, de concepts, de sujets et de disciplines, comme : « économie, art et », « langage, art et », « perception et art », « régionalisme, art et », « religion, art et », « société, art et »,

« Etat, architecture et », « Etat, art et », « fiscalité, art et », « théâtre, art et » :

perception et art
– Amérindiens #3487
– art vidéo #651
– Indiens de la côte nord-ouest #4001
– Inuit #4294
– Molinari, Guido #6591
– Snow, Michael #7245 7259
– Tousignant, Serge #7404
– utilisation de miroirs et fenêtres #525

Il existe des rubriques sur des sujets particuliers et généraux qui ont été représentés dans l'art et sur les symboles iconographiques canadiens, par exemple : « avions dans l'art », « castor », « Amérindiens, dans l'art », « nu dans l'art », « bateaux dans l'art », « classe ouvrière dans l'art », « oiseaux dans l'art », « Wolfe, James, officier de l'armée brit au Canada, 1727/1728–1759, portraits » :

oiseaux dans l'art
– Archambault, Louis #4539
– art traditionnel québécois #1284 1362
– Carr, Emily #5019
– corbeau
 – Kwakiutls #3883
 – Tlingits #3786
– crécelles en forme de corbeau, Indiens de la côte nord-ouest #3980 4026
– décoration architecturale canadienne (années 1930) #8226
– girouettes, Québec #2589
– Grondin, Jean-Luc #5662
– Hood, Robert #5826
– Lansdowne, James Fenwick #6163 6164 6165
– Loates, Glen #6310
– MacDonald, Thoreau #6381
– Murphy, Burland E. #6663
– Nasmith, Eric Anderson #6685
– Newlan, Emery #6690
– Oiseau-Tonnerre
 – Algonquiens #3493
 – Amérindiens #3410
 – Indiens de la côte nord-ouest #3831 3855
 – Indiens des plaines #3758
 – Pieds-Noirs #3676
 – Saulteux/Ojibways #3699
– Phinney, Robert #6862
– Picher, Claude #6867
– Pootoogook, Kananginak #6904
– Pope, William #6905 6906
– poterie canadienne #2309
 – Goold, F.P., & Co. (Brantford, Ont) #2335
– Pratt, George #6916
– Roussil, Robert #7090
– Savage, Harry #7133
– sculpture inuit #4404 4459

Les mouvements et styles artistiques d'origine européenne ont trouvé des voies d'expression au Canada. Parmi les rubriques de l'index des sujets traités faisant référence aux mouvements et styles, notons : « architecture victorienne », « Art déco », « Art nouveau », « Dada », « impressionnisme », « pop'art », « post-modernisme », « réalisme », « style Louis XVI », « surréalisme ».

Dans l'index des sujets traités, les noms des mouvements, styles et modes d'expression artistiques peuvent servir à repérer les noms des artistes auxquels ils sont associés. Par exemple, pour trouver les artistes de performance on consulte l'index à la rubrique : « art de performance ». On peut aussi consulter l'index sous les noms de chacun des artistes mentionnés :

art de performance
- (années 1970) #634 672 2046
  - et sculpture #654
  - tele-performance #603
- Berman, Michaele #4710
- Canada #1799
  - (1978), *Fifth Network/Cinquième réseau* #655
  - (1979–1981), *Impressions* #996
  - (1981) 709 713 718
  - (années 1970) 538 598 669 6676
    - sculpture #658
- Clark, Tim #687
- Dean, Max #687
- Falk, Gathie #5410
- General Idea #5583

Les noms des galeries d'art, des musées et des bâtiments du Québec figurent en français dans les index anglais et français des sujets traités. Certains bâtiments et établissements du Québec sont connus sous une appellation anglaise depuis des années. Dans de tels cas, les noms en anglais y figurent comme renvois :

Montréal (Qué), Montreal Museum of Fine Arts
- *voir* Montreal (Qué), Musée des beaux-arts de Montréal/ Montreal Museum of Fine Arts

Dans l'index des sujets traités, les entrées renvoyant aux villes et villages montrent bien l'importance attachée aux données locales. On y retrouve généralement les noms des galeries d'art, des musées et de leurs expositions, l'histoire de l'architecture, les noms des bâtiments, des écoles des beaux-arts avec la ville ou le village comme sujet traité dans l'art :

Victoria (CB)
- architecture #8146 8149 8173 8176 8177 8178
  - (1843–1929) #8180
    ...
  - Hooper, Thomas #8376
  - quartier chinois #8179 8181
  - Rattenbury, Francis Mawson #8400
  - Whiteway, William Tuff #9508
- architecture domestique #8722
  - (années 1910) #8494
- architecture et arts décoratifs #2269
- art
  - (1910–1941), Island Arts and Crafts Society #1980
  - (années 1970) #1870 2053
- galeries d'art #442
- musées #3190
- peinture #2000
- photographie, fin XIXe s. #2022
- vues photographiques
  - (1850–1900) #1061
  - Dally, Frederick #5249
  - Maynard, Hannah Hatherly #6457
Victoria (CB), Art Gallery of Greater Victoria

- collection #3189
- expositions
  ...
  - *Daniel Fowler of Amherst Island, 1810–1894* (1979) #5491
  - *Edward Curtis in the Collection of the Edmonton Art Gallery* (1980) #3480
  - *F.H. Varley: A Centennial Exhibition/F.H. Varley: une exposition centenaire* (1981) #7467
  - *Fired Sculpture* (1974) #774

L'index des sujets traités ne fait pas seulement référence à des localités canadiennes. On y retrouve les villes d'autres pays où ont eu lieu des expositions d'art canadien, où ont été construits des bâtiments conçus par des architectes canadiens et où des artistes canadiens ont étudié et travaillé. Voir par exemple l'entrée consacrée à New York (NY).

De nombreuses publications sur l'art et l'architecture au Canada portent sur une province ou une région en particulier comme l'Arctique, l'Ouest canadien, les Maritimes, les Prairies ou les Montagnes Rocheuses. Les écrits sur une région donnée sont réunis dans l'index des sujets traités sous le nom de la province ou de la région au moyen d'une série de sous-rubriques descriptives :

Prairies
- architecture #8080 8083 8088 8089
  - (années 1970) #8087
  - tradition juive #8081
  - tradition ukrainienne #8085
  - utilisation de pierre à bâtir et de pierre d'ornement (années 1910) #7646 7647
  - XXe s. #8084 8086
  ...
- art
  - (années 1920–1960) #461
  - (années 1950) #429
  - (années 1960) #1848 1851
  - (années) 1960–1970) #1862
  - (années 1970) #1860 1880
  - XXe s. #145
- art traditionnel
  - (années 1960) #1852
  ...
- arts décoratifs, tradition germanique #2140
- bouteilles et flacons #2431
- élévateurs à grain #9237
  ...
- vues
  - Chester, Donovan T. #1858
  ...
- vue photographiques
  - fin XIXe s. #1949
  - Hime, Humphrey Lloyd #5801

En ce qui concerne l'art des Amérindiens et des Inuit, on a élaboré pour l'index une série de termes distincts qui ne figurent pas dans la liste des vedettes-matières ou rubriques des sujets traités du *RILA*, étant donné que le service bibliographique du *Répertoire* ne s'étend pas aux arts des autochtones. Les nouveaux termes utilisés dans l'index pour les Amérindiens font référence à la rubrique générale « amérindiens », aux objets façonnés comme « vannerie », « ouvrages perlés », « pétroglyphes », et « travail de la pierre », et comprennent des sous-rubriques pour les noms des tribus et des références directes à ces mêmes noms. Ainsi il existe

diverses manières d'aborder le sujet des œuvres façonnées par les autochtones, les principales étant le type d'objet et le nom de la tribu :

vannerie . Iroquois #3519 3605 3625
– (années 1760–début XXe s.) #3633
– et vannerie tsonnontouan #3552
– ornementation estampée #3562
...
Iroquois
– vannerie #3552 3562 3625

On a jugé que 70 périodiques revêtaient une importance particulière en ce qui concerne l'histoire de l'art, les métiers d'art, les arts décoratifs, les arts graphiques, la photographie, les arts des autochtones et l'architecture au Canada. Chacune de ces publications fait l'objet d'une entrée dans le volume 1 de la bibliographie et d'un long résumé où l'on donne un aperçu de son historique et de son contenu. Pour obtenir les noms de ces 70 périodiques, il suffit de consulter l'index des sujets traités sous : « architecture . périodiques », « art . périodiques », « photographie . périodiques ».

La liste de toutes les thèses citées dans la bibliographie figure dans l'index des sujets traités sous : « mémoires et thèses . Canada ».

Diverses rubriques plus importantes de l'index renvoient à un grand nombre de documents dans des domaines pour lesquels jusqu'à présent peu d'ouvrages de recherche ont été publiés. En voici des exemples : « enseignement de l'architecture », « enseignement de l'art », « art . théorie et critique », « collectionneurs et collections », « marché de l'art », « illustration . Canada », « portraits », et « sculpture canadienne ».

NOTE

1 Les ouvrages suivants ont constitué pour les auteurs les sources d'information les plus utiles où ils ont puisé les noms des artistes : J. Russell Harper, *Early Painters and Engravers in Canada*. (Toronto : l'University of Toronto Press 1970); André Comeau, *Artistes plasticiens : Canada régime français et conquête, Bas-Canada et le Québec* (Montréal, Éditions Bellarmin 1983); Canadian Arctic Producers Co-operative Ltd., *Biographies of Inuit Artists* (Ottawa : Canadian Arctic Producers Co-operative 1981, 1982) 2 vol. et suppl.; Musée des beaux-arts du Canada, *Artists in Canada : A Union List of Files / Artistes au Canada : une liste collective des dossiers d'artistes* (Ottawa: Association du Musée des beaux-arts du Canada 1982, 1988); RILA, *Subjects Headings 1983* [Vedettes-matières] (J. Paul Getty Center for the History of Art and the Humanities: 1983).

Abbreviations / Abréviations

VOLUME 2

Ala	Alabama	Alabama
all		allemand-e
Alta	Alberta	Alberta
amér		américain-e
Amer	American	
Ariz	Arizona	Arizona
Aus	Austrian	
autr		autrichien-ne
b.	born	
BC	British Columbia	
Bl	Belgian	
brit		britannique
Brit	British	
c.	century	
ca.	circa	circa
Calif	California	Californie
can		canadien-ne
Can	Canadian	
CB		Colombie-Britannique
Colo	Colorado	Colorado
Conn	Connecticut	Connecticut
cs.	centuries	
d.	died	
Da	Danish	
DC	District of Columbia	District of Columbia
DDR	German Democratic Republic	République démocratique allemande
Del	Delaware	Delaware
esp		espagnol-e
EU		Etats-Unis
fl.	flourished	
Fla	Florida	Floride
Fle	Flemish	
flam		flamand-e
fr		français-e
Fr	French	
Ger	German	
holl		hollandais-e
Ill	Illinois	Illinois
Ind	Indiana	Indiana
IPE		Ile du Prince-Edouard
it		italien-ne
It	Italian	

ja		japonais-e
Ja	Japanese	
Kan	Kansas	Kansas
Ky	Kentucky	Kentucky
La	Louisiana	Louisiane
m.		mort-e
Man	Manitoba	Manitoba
Mass	Massachusetts	Massachusetts
Md	Maryland	Maryland
MEd.	Master of Education	
Mich	Michigan	Michigan
Minn	Minnesota	Minnesota
Mo	Missouri	Missouri
Mon	Montana	Montana
NB	New Brunswick	Nouveau-Brunswick
ND	North Dakota	Dakota du Nord
NE		Nouvelle-Ecosse
Nebr	Nebraska	Nebraska
Nfld	Newfoundland	
NJ	New Jersey	New Jersey
Nl	Netherlandish	
NM	New Mexico	Nouveau-Mexique
no	number	numéro
nos	numbers	numéros
NS	Nova Scotia	
NWT	Northwest Territories	
NY	New York	New York
Okla	Oklahoma	Oklahoma
Ont	Ontario	Ontario
Oreg	Oregon	Oregon
PEI	Prince Edward Island	
Qué	Québec	Québec
RI	Rhode Island	Rhode Island
Ro	Romanian	
roum		roumain-e
Ru	Russian	
s.		siècle
Sask	Saskatchewan	Saskatchewan
SD	South Dakota	Dakota du Sud
Sp	Spanish	
Sw	Swiss	
Tenn	Tennessee	Tennessee
Tex	Texas	Texas
TN		Terre-Neuve
TNO		Territoires du Nord-Ouest
uk		ukrainien-ne
Uk	Ukrainian	
URSS		Union des Républiques socialistes soviétiques
USA	United States of America	
USSR	Union of Soviet Socialist Republics	
Va	Virginia	Virginie
Vt	Vermont	Vermont
Wash	Washington	Washington
Wis	Wisconsin	Wisconsin

INDEXES / LES INDEX

Author Index / Index des auteurs

A

Aarons, Anita #1798 3312 8236 9214
Abbott, Charles C. #3491
Abbott, Donald N. #4048 4049
Abell, Walter #336 354 370 404 737 1086
    1088 1089 1332 3028 5273 5864 5865 7324
    7538 7668
Abra, Marion W. #1889
Abrahamson, C.D. #529
Abrahamson, Una #2121 2122 2591
Abrams, Malcolm #7266
Ackerman, R.F. #8256
Ackerman, Robert E. #4348
Acland, James #9373
Acland, James H. #7700 7705 7707 7779 9048
    9100 9114 9215 9216 9294 9319 9460 9516
Acton, James #2463
Adair, E.R. #1573 8797 8805
Adam, G.Mercer #914
Adam, Leonhard #3809 3824 3843
Adam, Monique #5049
Adam-Villeneuve, Francine #9252
Adamczyk, Georges #9553
Adams, Blaine #2148 8435 8436
Adams, Marian #2590
Adams, Sitney P. #7243
Adamson, A.P.C. #8040
Adamson, Anthony #7666 7696 7981 8005
    8254 8512 8522 8904 9351
Adamson, Arthur #1900 4984
Adamson, Gordon S. #8206
Adamson, Jeremy #266 3147 3163 5734
Addison, Ottelyn #7364
Aer, Naima #991
Affleck, R.T. #8310 9314 9323 9325
Affleck, Ray #7746 8282 9320 9462
Affleck, Raymond T. #8194
Agnew, Herbert R. #9031
Ahlborn, Richard E. #2111
Ahlgren, Dorothy #7738
Aimers, Cotton #6847
Aitchison, Ian A. #9100
Aldred, Diane #7889
Alexander, Stephen #2149
Alexandre, Arsène #4550

Alford, Edward John Gregory #369
Alford, John #32
Algie, Susan #8023
Allaire, Sylvain #159 5883
Allan, D. #7970
Allan, M.F. #9208
Alldritt, Judith #3287
Allègre, Christian #4997
Allen, George X. #3546
Allen, Karyn #708 1906
Allen, Max #2758 2761 2762 2766
Allen, Ralph #523 4725 5489
Alleyn, Edmund #7084
Allison, Carlyle #6857
Allison, Glenn #2059 6696
Allodi, Mary #247 248 263 828 839 1676 4614
    6849 7008
Alloucherie, Jocelyne #6535
Allshouse, John Clayton #3857
Allsop, Brian #8086
Allsopp, Robert #9488
Allward, Hugh L. #9027
Alsitt, Alan D. #8250
Alward, W.W. #1178
Alyluia, Jeanne #2436 2437
Amaya, Mario #1766 5072
Ambrosi, Jean #5365
Amerson, L.Price #4041
Ames, Michael #3996
Ames, Michael M. #3994 4003 4057 4295
Amess, Fred A. #1988
Amos, Robert #837 6841
Amsden, Charles A. #3413
Anderson, Bruce #7728 8287
Anderson, C.Ross #9391 9392 9460
Anderson, Dennis R. #6178
Anderson, J.W. #4397
Anderson, Lawrence B. #8206
Anderson, Pat #6409
Anderson, Patrick #375
Anderson, Richard L. #3377
Anderson, Robert #8200 9396
Andre, John #241 242 4694 4699
Andreae, Janice #3174 5975 9145
Andrews, John #8989 9396 9462
Andrews, Stephen #4527
Andrews, Stewart M. #8577
Andrus, Don #111
Andrus, Donald F.P. #1123 4917 5171 5495

7129
Anglim, Paule Matte #7451
Angrave, James #9397
Angrna'naaq, Ruby #4266 4480
Angus, Harry H. #9028
Angus, Margaret S. #258 259 7989 7996 8655
Annau, Ernest #7379 8671
Annett, Margaret R. #2054 7484
Anselm, Mary #2145
Antik, Richard #118
Anton, Ferdinand #3435
Antonelli, Marylu #2325 2337
Antoniou, Sylvia A. #5999 6210
Antonson, Brian #5992
Appelbe, Alison #5267
Applebaum, Isaac #996 3314
Appleton, Frank M. #5360
Arbec, Jules #1626 5096 6162
Arbour, Rose-Marie #1273 1653
Arbuckle, Mrs. Franklin #5970
Arcand, Jennifer #2298
Arcand, Pierre-André #5196 7482
Archambault, Louis #408
Archambault, Marie #5797
Archibald, Margaret #8367 8368
Archibald, Stephen #2710
Arima, Eugene #4417 4437
Ariss, Herb #1828
Armer, Laura A. #3412
Armitage, Merle #7200 .
Armour, David A. #3635
Armour, Drew #6770
Armstrong, Alan H. #8508 8930 8982
Armstrong, Audrey #4992
Armstrong, C.H.A. #9002
Armstrong, F.H. #8009
Armstrong, Frederick H. #8010 8061
Armstrong, Isabel C. #6790
Arn, Robert #550 577 6969
Arneson, Jeannette #5601
Arnott, Brian #693
Arnott, Gordon #9136 9420 9490
Arrington, Joseph Earl #218
Arrowsmith, F.J. #3079
Arsenault, Adrien #459
Arseneault, Jeanne #2876 2894
Arthur, E.R. #1669 8454 9002
Arthur, Eric #8065

Arthur, Eric Ross #7657 7662 7664 7670 7779
  7958 7959 7960 7962 7963 7964 7966 7968
  7973 7974 7976 7984 8040 8055 8070 8207
  8208 8215 8223 8248 8303 8306 8648 8737
  8758 8901 8943 8981 9003 9079 9088 9103
  9196 9228 9393 9454 9455 9475 9482
Arthur, Paul #859 865 866 870 924 2622
Artibise, Alan F.J. #8060 8714 8996
Artinian, Vrej-Armen #9422
Ashton, Dore #5537
Ashwell, Reg #5294 5872 7375
Ashworth, M.J. #8468 8469
Asi, Harry #7112
Askevold, David #604
Asselin, Edwidge #6124 6335
Asselin, Hedwidge #4996 6347
Assiniwi, Bernard #3374
Asti-Rose, Michael #2439 5458 6605
Astles, Allen Richard #7761
Astroff, Vivian #7708
Atcheson, Dona #3073
Atherton, Ray #7357
Aubé, Suzanne #1281
Aubrey, Irene E. #937
Aubry, Yves #1562
Auclair, Elie-J. #5278
Audet, Bernard #2895
Audet, Louis N. #8816 8824
Audoin, Philippe #3942
Austerer, Walter #4530
Austin, Alvyn J. #2451
Austin, Mary #3412
Ayearst, Morely J. #917
Ayers, Frank #8040
Ayling, Vera #6182
Aylott, J.C. #4304
Ayre, John #5846 6111
Ayre, Robert #376 378 382 389 420 427 820
  852 1138 1246 1278 1279 1400 1842 1890
  1911 2378 2380 2694 3034 3256 3257 4460
  4539 4612 4660 4708 4723 4988 5178 5915
  5995 6118 6294 6517 6653 6654 6799 6928
  7041 7045 7078 7175 7287 8228 9093
Azard-Malurie, Marie-Madeleine #875 7943

B

Babinska, Anna #6980
Bachand, Jacques #3016
Bacso, Jean #2310
Badeau, Edward C. #9368
Badner, Mino #3934
Badone, Donalda #2338
Bagnall, W.A. #8254
Bagnani, Gilbert #5632
Bailey, Melville #8650
Bailey, Robert H. #599 3056 3288 3289 9147
  9148
Baillairgé, Charles #8291
Baillairgé, G.F. #8325
Baillargé, C. #8238
Baillargeon, Richard #4522

Baillie-Scott, M.H. #8494
Baird, Genevieve #4004
Baird, George #7746 7753 7839 8171 8282
  8663
Baird, Irene #4192 4389 4464
Baird, Joseph A. #397 6956
Baird, Nina #3272
Baird, P.B. #5919
Baird, Ron #5122 9146
Baker, F.S. #7648 8294
Baker, Jeremy #9220
Baker, Joseph #8283 8989
Baker, Kenneth #1796
Baker, Marilyn #1877 7441
Baker, R.J. #9396 9505
Baker, Suzanne Devonshire #1967
Baker, Victoria #1296 6210
Bakker, Joost #8663
Baldwin, Edward R. #9511
Baldwin, Martin #355 3030 3136
Baldwin, W.W. #8306
Balfe, Michael #1834
Balfour, Henry #3334
Balfour, Lisa #466 2653 8028 9354
Balharrie, Watson #9455
Balikci, Asen #3379
Balkind, Alvin #588 618 622 2036 2037 2063
  2073 4734 5434 6213 6678 6893 6894 8341
Ballantine, E.B. #5589
Ballantyne, Michael #6302
Ballo, Guido #1420
Bancroft, Brian #7698
Bancroft, Marian Penner #5670
Bancroft-Hunt, Norman #3756 4035
Band, Charles S. #7463
Bandi, Hans Georg #4352
Bandson, Michel #690
Banks, Gail #5505
Banks, Kerry #2076
Bantey, Bill #879 1423 3104 3362 9124 9125
Banting, Bill #7201
Banting, F.G. #5908
Banting, Peter M. #2620
Banwell, Michael #797
Banz, George #8265 9289 9476
Baran, Anna Maria #8915
Barbeau, Marius #23 24 26 56 213 299 1232
  1233 1234 1235 1238 1241 1327 1328 1329
  1330 1331 1334 1335 1392 1574 1575 1576
  1577 1579 1581 1585 1840 2093 2094 2095
  2168 2169 2171 2178 2181 2183 2184 2187
  2189 2192 2279 2280 2281 2629 2630 2631
  2658 2660 2661 2662 2751 2753 2777 2778
  2779 2818 2819 2823 2824 2827 2967 3341
  3419 3422 3543 3791 3827 3828 3834 3852
  3855 3862 3863 3868 3879 3890 3895 3904
  3910 4116 4507 4585 5186 5187 5188 5358
  5910 5964 5965 5966 5967 5983 5984 5985
  6083 6084 6085 6086 6089 6091 6093 6254
  6442 6443 6445 6620 6854 7849 7851 8505
  8795 8796 8802
Barbeau, Victor #4877
Barber, Bruce #683 2073
Barber, Janet #3138

Barber, Steve #8108
Barcelo, L.-J. #6199
Barcelo, Michel #8217 8269
Barclay, John C. #2426
Bardo, Arthur #5368 5369
Barfoot, Joan #5756
Barida, Michael N. #1822
Baril, Marie-Albert #6764
Barker, C.E. #4609
Barker, Charles #6352
Barker, Kent #8035
Barkham, Brian #7854 7855
Barkley, Alan #6042 6044 7597
Barnard, Noël #3975
Barnard, Walter #8250
Barnes, Elliott #4610
Barnes, Robert Money #2835
Barnet, Will #6702
Barnett, Homer G. #3851 3858 3896
Barnett, W.E. #9103
Barnhouse, Dorothy #2392
Barr, Alfred H. #9079
Barras, Henri #1447 1599 3093 3111 6659
  6766 7099 7289 7394
Barrett, A. #8401
Barrett, Harry B. #6906
Barrière, Gérard #3458
Barringer, Bill #5849
Barrio-Garay, José L. #5081
Barrow, Francis J. #3859
Barrow, Susan H.L. #3950
Barss, Peter #1035 2157
Barteaux, Eleanor #5775
Bartlett, William Henry #4615
Barton, Kenneth James #2368 2369
Barwick, Frances Duncan #119
Barz, Sandra #4497
Basile, Jean #5194
Baster, Victoria #684 7269
Bastien, Geneviève G. #7947
Bastien, Jean-Pierre #7253
Bastine, André #5237
Bates, Catherine #5747 5748
Bates, Maxwell #405 1947 4621 4622 6049
  6374
Battcock, Gregory #6267
Batten, Jack #1836
Baudouin, Gustave #8790
Bauer, Nancy #7206
Baumeister, Hans #887
Baxter, Barbara #6451
Baxter, Iain #797 6675
Bayefsky, Aba #151
Bayer, Fern #1728 8943
Bayer, Mary Elizabeth #529
Bazin, Bernard #9255
Bazin, Germain #3164
Bazin, Jean #3098
Bazin, Jules #234 235 2834 5184 6180 6624
Beale, L.B. #8494
Beament, Harold #6872
Bean, Audrey #9537
Beardsley, Ginnie #8356
Beattie, Earle #4577

Beattie, William #4617
Beatty, J.W. #5067
Beatty, Willard W. #3557 3674
Beauchamp, Rhéal #1820 1821
Beaudet, André #6193 6194
Beaudet, Louis #7945
Beaudet, Père Henri #5873
Beaudin, Gaétan #2384
Beaudoin-Ross, Jacqueline #2803 2896 2903
Beaugrand-Champagne, Aristide #3555
Beaulac, Henri #9096
Beaulieu, André #8942
Beaulieu, Christian #1560
Beaulieu, Claude #5239 7760 7862 7910 8573
  9092 9209
Beaulieu, Louis-Jacques #5258
Beaulieu, Michel #1443 4652
Beaupré, Paul #3016
Beauregard, Christiane #8814 8883
Beauregard, Jean Louis #7626
Beauregard, Yves #8873
Bebbington, Julia Marie #3745
Bébout, Richard #9536
Beck, Claudia #1038
Beck, J.Jackson #9184
Beck, J.S.R. #8988
Beck, Jenny #2266
Bédard, Hélène #7866 8596
Bédard, Jean #6815
Bédard, Marc-K. #8362
Bédard, Michel #9253
Bédard, Rodrigue #4875 8604
Beer, G.Frank #8492
Beer, Henry #7827
Beetz, Henry #4654
Beetz, Jeannette #4654
Béland, Luc #1532 4655
Bélanger, Françoise #2883 2884
Bélanger, Léon #8879
Bélanger, Marcel #7867
Béliard, Bernard #2296
Bélisle, Jean #1636 7878 8855 9250 9251 9254
Bélisle, Josée #1475 1622 1651
Bell, Andrew #52 370 387 1100 1746 5110
  5718 6296 6399 6549 6681 6697 6732
Bell, Betty #4455
Bell, H.Poynter #312 328
Bell, Keith #132 7064
Bell, Lynne #3202 6290 7066
Bell, Lynne S. #132
Bell, Margaret L. #148
Bell, Michael #239 240 244 246 1816 3230
  3311 4727 5129 6536 6537 7047 7145
Bell, Peter #1147 1148 1154 4739 5703 6910
Bell-Smith, F.M. #4667
Bella, Leslie #8131
Belleau, Massue #880 8574
Bellefleur, Léon #5595
Bellerive, Georges #1318
Bellman, David #2758 6883 7924
Bellot, Paul #8333
Belluschi, Pietro #8205 8208 8985 8986
Belshaw, Linda #578 1810
Bengle, Céline #6582

Bengough, John Wilson #942 4671 4672 4673
Benham, Mary Lile #6017
Benjamin, S.N. #8278
Benndorf, Helga #3434
Bennett, Holly #4159
Bennett, Paul #2260 5131
Bennett, Peter H. #7758
Benoit, Jehane #7981
Benoit, Luc #5083 5286 5344 5608 5638 6597
  6718 6758
Bentham, Douglas #797
Bentley, Mary #4050
Bentley, Ted #4050
Beny, Roloff #4689
Beny, W.Roloff #808 921
Beny, Wilfred R. #4687
Bérard, Serge #4882
Berczy, William von Moll #4696
Bergeron, René #1393
Bergevin, Hélène #8887 8888
Bergs, Lilita #4424
Bériau, O.A. #2166
Bériau, Oscar A. #2164 2185 2186 2719 2720
  2721 2745 2969
Berkeley, Ellen Perry #9326
Berkson, Bill #4740
Berleur, Paul #1357
Berlin, A.F. #3393
Berman, J. #8514
Bernard, Léon #4772
Bernatchez, Anne #8630
Bernatchez, Michèle #2769
Bernier, André #7879
Bernier, Jacques #8616
Bernstein, William #7746
Berry, Virginia #6348
Berry-Hill, Henry #6177
Berry-Hill, Sidney #6177
Bersianik, Louky #6171
Berton, Pierre #5750 6724 7772 9536
Bertos, Rigas N. #7330
Bertrand, Claude #1443
Bertrand, Jean-Pierre #7926
Berwick, R.A.D. #8142
Best, Alexander #3474 3475
Beszedits, S. #8075
Betcherman, Lita-Rose #4697 4698
Betjeman, John #8761
Betts, Randolph C. #8305 9418
Beveridge, Karl #602 1063
Bice, Clare #86 408 413 414 432 440 6792
  7535
Bickersteth, J.B. #9441
Biegert, Claus #1566
Biéler, André #337 351 356 390 1087 4720
  4721
Bienvenue, Marcella #650
Bies, Ernest #5101
Bigué, Michel #1289
Bilodeau, Irène #2890
Binder, Ingrid #8069
Bingham, Russell #1885 1965
Binning, B.C. #4730 4732 8142
Binyon, Laurence #7552
Biondi, Ferdinand F. #529

Bird, Douglas #2413
Bird, Marian #2413
Bird, Michael #1682 2263
Bird, Michael S. #2135 2140 2254 2255 2259
  5579 5829 6896
Birdsall, Jack #867
Birket-Smith, Kaj #4331
Birkhans, Martin #8410
Birkhill, Frederick #6983
Birmingham, W.H. #8142
Biron, Hervé #5317 5318
Biron, Normand #6132 6166 6188 7486
Birrell, A.J. #1014 1015
Birrell, Andrew #1675 2028
Birrell, Andrew J. #1001 1025 1026 1039 1040
  1058 1113 1865 1874 1875 1876 4598 5249
  5837 5838
Bishop, Hunter #6373
Bismanis, Maija #1939 5199
Bissell, Claude #9456
Black, Leslie Forsyth #5751
Black, Mary E. #1119
Black, Sam #3219
Blackburn, Edna #2742
Blackburn, Robert H. #9044 9046
Blackman, Margaret B. #2029 3979 3995 4167
  4168
Blackstock, C.R. #5676
Blackwell, Walter R.L. #9185
Blair, Wendy #623
Blais, Dominique #7926
Blake, Peter #7901 8215
Blake, Sibley #5389
Blake, Verschoyle Benson #7993
Blakeley, Phyllis #2993
Blakeley, Phyllis R. #2489
Blakeman, Evelyn #5382
Blanchard, Gérard #951
Blanchette, Jean-François #2233 2234
Bland, John #1367 7676 7711 7728 7857 7900
  7920 7924 7940 8040 8206 8208 8245 8247
  8248 8250 8515 8570 8594 8820 8856 9079
  9093 9314 9399 9455
Blaser, Robin #7252
Blessing, Fred K. #3702
Blin, Claude #1442
Bliss, Michael #8667
Blissett, W.F. #5029
Block, Jean Libman #2123
Block-Bolten, Izabella R. #2756
Blodgett, Jean #1294 4267 4268 4274 4278
  4283 4284 4285 4286 4299 4443 4450 4562
  4563 6882
Blodgett, Ruth Jean #4429
Blom, Willem A. #451 469
Blomfield, James #9176
Bloom, Tony #2940
Bloore, Ronald L. #1767 1852 3954 4622 4748
  7620
Blouin, André #7900
Blouin, Anne-Marie #1461 1622 4828
Blouin, Nicole #4858 5896 6997 7083
Blouin, Patrick #769
Blouin, René #2073
Blouin-Sioui, Anne-Marie #1372
Blumenfeld, Hans #8041

Bluteau, M.- A. #2946
Boas, Franz #3333 3348 3764 3768 3770 3771
  3772 3774 3780 3783 3784 3785 3787 3789
  3935 4317 4320
Bobak, Bruno #448
Bobak, Molly Lamb #4762 4766
Bochner, Mel #7059
Bockstoce, J.R. #4369
Boddy, Trevor #8084 8087 8089 8135 8999
  9203 9362
Bodmer, Karl #3738
Bodnar, Diana Lynn #8126 8944 8945
Bodolai, J.S. #1800
Bodolai, Joe #550 561 773 1149 1498 7447
Bogardi, George #637 1512 5205 5627 5841
Bogdanski, Douglas #8965
Boggs, Jean Sutherland #136 137 518 562
  3044 3048 3050 3306 4211 7767
Bohi, Charles W. #9542 9543 9544
Boileau, Andrée #3109
Boily, Lise #2233 2234
Boily, Nicole #1456 4817
Boisclair, Marie-Nicole #3119
Boissay, Pauline #7101
Boivin, L.- I. #2962
Bolanz, Maria #3968
Bolduc, David #5654
Bolt, Ron #4779
Bolus, Malvina #4202
Bon, Antoine #6798
Bond, Eleanor #4450
Bonellie, Janet #5688
Bonito Oliva, Achille #600
Bonner, Mary Graham #2096
Bonneville, Jean-Pierre #5478 5481
Bontinen, Sharon #1801
Book, Sam #1802
Boorne, W.Hanson #4796
Borcoman, J.W. #7429
Borcoman, James #7045
Bordeleau, Henri #4575 4744
Borden, Charles E. #3951
Bordier, Roger #7027
Borduas, Paul-Emile #536 1396 1443 1449
  4799 4803 4804 4818 4839 4840 6197 6199
Bornstein, Eli #536 4854 4855 6506
Borsa, Julianna #1027 3165
Bosworth, Newton #7898
Bouchard, Antoine #2952
Bouchard, Claude A. #6447 7207
Bouchard, Denis #6157
Bouchard, Francine #8636
Bouchard, Georges #2163
Bouchard, Laurent #6144 6534 6999
Bouchard, René #1292 2235 2716 5315 7000
Boucher, Alain #9246
Boucher, Anne A. #4836
Boucher, Maximilien #6888
Boucher, Pierre #6142
Boucher, Roger #2516
Boucher de la Bruère, Montarville #8806
Boudreau, Pierre #7015
Boudreau, Pierre de Ligny #5421 5616 6198
  7030
Boudriot, Jean #276

Bouey, Howard L. #8303
Boulanger, Rolland #1260 1401 1436 1486
  4651 5181 5666 5668 6962 6996 7042
Boulet, François #9255
Boulet, Roger #1790 4668 5658 6052 6741
  6861 6957
Boulizon, Guy #1473 5330 5342 5557
Boultbee, W.M. #6636
Bourassa, André-G. #1443 1464 1466
Bourassa, Anne #4869
Bourassa, Napoléon #1303 1304 4862 4864
  4865 4868 4870 8782
Bourdon, David #6264 6267
Bourgault, Pierre #5287
Bourget, Clermont #1281
Bourget, Jean-Loup #4750 5367 7495
Bourget, Jean-Paul #1542 1543
Bourque, France #2879
Bourque, J.Rodolphe #7804
Bousquet-Mongeau, Martine #7283
Boutin, Pierre #5203
Bouvier, Françoise #2904
Bouwman, Roland J. #8249
Boux, René #1844 7347
Bouyer, Marc #276
Bovay, Emile Henri #7010
Bovey, E.C. #521
Bovey, Edmond C. #3154
Bovey, Patricia E. #503 504 956 2644 2897
  3281 5450
Bowdler, M.C. #8185
Bowe, Martin #8538
Bowen, Donald #633
Bower, Joseph H.W. #9018 9028
Bowering, George #6062
Bowker, Walter B. #8037 8041
Bowland, John A. #9194
Bowser, Sara #5116 8301 8511 8512 8983
  9299
Boyd, James #818
Boyd, Robin #8580
Boyer, Jean-Pierre #604
Boyle, John #1808 4893
Boyle, Terry #8679
Boyles, C.H. #8978 9498
Brace, Irvine A. #4657
Bradbeer, Alan #2423
Bradbeer, Dorothy #2423
Bradfield, Helen Pepall #3149
Bradford, John L. #4895 4896
Bradley, Iris M. #648
Bradley, Jessica #699 1041 7421
Bradshaw, John Rea #3291
Bradshaw, Marion Hahn #74
Bradshaw, Thecla #7125
Braide, Janet #4950 4951 4952 4953 4954 5796
  6346 7132
Brandon, Laura #4957
Brandon, William #3427
Brandtner, Fritz #4902
Brannen, Judy #2936
Brassard, Paul G. #7900
Brasser, T.J.C. #3718
Brasser, Ted J. #3359 3465 3466 3622 3625
  3731 3735 3741 3746

Brault, Jacques #4652
Brault, Lucien #9480 9481
Breeze, Claude #620
Bregzis, Ritvars #9046
Brent, Ursula #6453
Breton, A.C. #3797
Breton, Yvan #1281
Brett, J.E. #9314
Brett, K.B. #2839 2843
Brett, Katharine B. #2723 2784 2847 2849
  2851 2853 2870 2888
Breverman, Harvey #5735
Brickman, Julie #601
Bridge, Kay #4243
Bridges, Marjorie Lismer #6305
Bridgman, L.G. #7665
Bridle, Augustus #1071 1671 1713
Brieger, Peter #370
Brigden, Frederick H. #295 296 300 304 313
  316 320 329 1672
Brind'Amour, Serge #952
Brink, A.W. #7994
Brisebois, Marcel #7396
Britton, Susan #671 687
Brochu, Michel #4405 4406
Brock, Daniel J. #8010
Brock, G.W. #7119
Brody, J.J. #3441
Brodzky, Anne #4626 5562
Brodzky, Michael Ethan #4754 5524 5935
  6710
Bromfield, Abjon #4416
Bronson, A.A. #604 672
Brook, Charles #8108
Brooker, Bertram #305 317 321 330 1734 5677
Brooks, Bill #9249
Brooks, George R. #2110
Brooks, Leonard #4930 4931
Brosseau, Denise #5280
Brosseau, Mathilde #7739 7740 8047 9539
Brothers, Ryan #3929
Broun, Francis #665
Brown, Annora #3675 4934
Brown, David R. #9489
Brown, Elizabeth #1157
Brown, Eric #4 7 200 209 284 299 322 335
  3021 3022 5660
Brown, F.Maud #297 458 3029 3040
Brown, G. Sutton #9080
Brown, Harry Faulkner #7693
Brown, I.D. #7994
Brown, J.A. #4031
Brown, Jeremy #506
Brown, Lynn Hutchinson #5893
Brown, Murray #8737
Brown, R.Craig #82
Brown, Robert #4315
Brown, Rosemary Alicia #6413
Brown, Sheila MacKenzie #2717
Browne, John S.L. #5668
Brownstone, Razie #4456
Bruce, David #2455
Bruce, Harry #1035 5148 9103
Bruce, Herbert A. #4519
Bruce, John #4546

Bruce, Robert #4940
Bruchési, Jean #1239 4590
Bruemmer, Fred #3591 4362 9242 9243
Bruette, Marie #6394
Brunet, Michel #4615
Brunet-Weinmann, Monique #1533 1542
  1543 1557 3318 4678 5335 5529 5943 6183
  6332
Brunette, Michel #7299
Brunt, Michael Hugo #9396
Brunvand, Jan Harold #2273
Bryers, Joanne E. #4481
Brymner, William #4947
Buchan, David #3313
Buchanan, D.W. #433
Buchanan, Donald W. #18 27 33 43 347 352
  370 419 420 423 428 430 814 1844 2467
  2468 2600 2601 2602 2603 2604 2606 2607
  2608 2610 3027 3039 3134 3212 3302 4731
  4985 5238 5517 6312 6397 6490 6544 6550
  6617 6619 6621 6622 6807 6808 7151 7177
  7461 9210
Buck, Charles Spurgeon #7965
Buck, Derek #9351
Buckler, Grant #2154
Buckley, John #2040 5650
Buckman, Edward #338
Buckwold, Sidney #8217
Buggey, Susan #7729 7768 7822 7824 7825
  7826 7838
Bugslag, J. #8154
Bujold, Françoise #4556 5668
Bull, W. #4956
Bull, William Perkins #3208
Bunnell, Peter C. #994
Bunting, Jennifer #2085
Bunyan, D.E. #4023
Burant, James K.P. #1217
Burant, Jim #1211 1226 6426
Burch, E.T. #2614
Burchard, John E. #8112
Bureau, Pierre #7869 7877 7890
Burgess, Helen #4197 4203 4403 4408
Burgoyne, St.George #916
Burke, Edmund #8485
Burke, Mary #2129 2802 5120 6642
Burnett, David #152 579 1069 1518 1837 3315
  5077 5538 6070 6071 6592 6594 7404 7565
Burnett, Mary #2734
Burnham, Dorothy K. #2730 2736 2739 2740
  2747 2748 2797 2844 2849 2873
Burnham, Harold B. #2115 2727 2729 2730
  2731 2736 2754
Burnham, Jack #3003 6262 6266 6267 6272
Burns, Doris W. #2438
Burns, Flora Hamilton #5023 5024
Burns, Florence M. #4701
Burns, James T. #9221
Burns, Robert #888 5174 5457
Burns, Robert J. #258 259 8673
Burns, Vera E. #8125
Burr, Christina #4424
Burrell, Martin #1737 4519
Burrows, Anne #529

Burrows, G.Edmond #2925
Burrows, Tom #4960
Bursill, J.Francis #3180
Burtch, Michael #5852 7238
Burton, Dennis #1773 4961 5676
Bush, Edward F. #9520 9521
Bush, Jack #703 4969
Bushnell, David I. #3396 3397 3398 3400
  6006
Bussy, Jacques #5623
Butler, B.Robert #3903
Butler, Darrel #2484
Butler, Eva L. #3571
Butler, K.J. #4241 4243 4473
Butler, Sheila #4230 4486 4489 4491
Butler, Sheila M. #4241 4473
Button, Billy #6354
Butts, Mary Diamond #2793
Buxton, Judith M. #3955
Buxton, Mary Hancock #4216
Buxton-Keenlyside, Judith #2483
Buzzard, Francis H. #8988
Byers, Mary #8014 8678
Byrne, Richard O. #7777

C

Cadieux, Michel #6229
Cadzow, Donald A. #3661 3662 3663 4077
Caffin, Charles H. #7499
Caillat, François #1562
Calkins, Harry #4041
Callaghan, Barry #7073
Calnan, D.M. #8995
Calvert, Lorna #5250
Calvin, D.D. #9445
Cameron, Ann #4524 5166
Cameron, Christina #5127 5128 7741 7742
  8324 8610 8631
Cameron, D.W. #8250
Cameron, Dorothy #531 766 820 7242 7445
Cameron, Duncan #3283 3284
Cameron, Duncan F. #529 2998
Cameron, Eric #553 580 651 830 4630 4794
  4993 5419 5696 5705 6170 7256 7269 7508
  7635
Cameron, Janice #1797
Cameron, Stanley #3232 8931 8932
Cameron, William #7071
Campbell, Angus J. #7782
Campbell, Betty #8966
Campbell, Dorothy #8074
Campbell, H.C. #91 6905 9044
Campbell, Henry C. #4552 4616
Campeau, Michel #1494 1513
Campell, Kathleen #8708
Candy, Kenneth H. #8514
Cane, Fred #8668
Cane, Frederick W. #2556
Cann, Louise Gebhard #4548
Cannon, Georgina #624
Cantieni, Graham #1282 1296 1533 6595
Cantin, Eugène #3105 3106 3107

Cantin, Raymond #4879
Capling, Arthur James #7902
Capper, S.H. #7955 8240
Card, Raymond #8300 9077
Card, Raymond William George #8299
Cardin, Clarisse #3303
Cardinal, Douglas J. #5937 7746 8340 8342
Cardinal, Marilyn #5937
Careless, J.M.S. #82
Careless, M.S. #7767
Carless, William #2089 7655 8560 8561
Carlu, Jacques #9370
Carman, Milton #529
Carmichael, Ruth #5004
Carolan, Trevor #686
Caron, Fernand #7619
Caron, Robert #8870 8884
Carpenter, Carole Henderson #4052 6647
Carpenter, Edmund #3366 3553 3574 4005
  4184 4185 4198 4244 4294 4391 4465
Carpenter, Edmund S. #4341
Carpenter, Ken #711 722 1786 3061 3312
  4970 4971 4974 5114 5307 5758 6477 6660
Carpentier, André #953
Carpentier, Paul #1619 1637 1640
Carr, Emily #5006 5007 5009 5010 5013 5017
  5018 5019 5025 5030 5031
Carr, Mrs. #7954
Carr, Richard #2617
Carr-Harris, Ian #5047 6472
Carrier, Louis #1330 1331 3076 3077
Carrier, Maurice #234 235
Carrier, Roch #7137
Carrière, Gaston #3264
Carrière, Georges E. #5243
Carrington, Selwyn #8103
Carroll, Joy #5613 6400 6644 7154 7621 8234
Carroll, Luscombe #5133 5134
Carruthers, Clare D. #9027 9028 9192 9208
  9339
Carson, Alan #9115
Carswell, J.B. #9434
Carter, Alexandra E. #5351 6349
Carter, Beverly #1489
Carter, C.N. #2909
Carter, David G. #231 1261 3087 3099 3112
  6029
Carter, J.Purves #3078
Carter, Joseph Cleveland #5119
Carter, Margaret #8183
Carter, Sandra #1204
Carter, Sidney #978
Carter, William Harry #3608
Cartier, Jean #5052
Cartwright, Willena D. #3420
Carufel, Hélène de #2484
Carver, Humphrey #370 3033 7666 8217
  8507 8515 8740
Casagrande, L. #3755
Casgrain, H.R. #5406
Casgrain, Henri Raymond #6308
Casgrain, P.B. #1568
Caso, Paul #430
Cassidy, Appolonia Helen #3414
Casson, A.J. #1790 3136 5055

Casson, Hugh #8212 8389
Casson, Paul W. #2595
Cassou, Jean #6804
Castelli, Mireille D. #8603
Castellon, Rolando #1566
Castonguay, Denis #159
Cathelin, Jean #441 1416 6467 7016 7020
Catlin, George #3384 3478
Cattell, Henry W. #6483
Catto, Douglas #9027
Cauchon, Michel #249 250 258 259 3125 7102
    7103 9255
Cauley, John Stuart #8300 8765
Cavaliere, Barbara #6272
Cavell, Edward #4610
Cawker, Ruth #7746
Cazaly, Laurence #7684
Cazort, Mimi #5927 5928
Cazort-Taylor, Mimi #5926
Celant, Germano #940
Celestino, Mary #5063
Cepka, Ed #9258
Chabot, Line #7950
Challener, F.S. #5066
Chalmers, Floyd S. #529
Chalmers, John W. #4580 5035 5834 5992
    6013 8729
Chamberlain, A.F. #3493
Chamberland, Paul #1444
Chambers, Jack #563 5079
Chambers, John #5071
Chambers, L.B. #9011
Chambers, Merton #2105
Champagne, Edith #2898
Champagne, Jean-Serge #637
Champagne, Michel #1519 6144 6238 6867
    6999
Chandler, John #7544
Chandler, John Noel #94 532 1520 4420 5226
    5526 5566 6391 7251 7543 7556 7559
Chantal, Alma de #4625 4627 5998 6737
Chantraine, Pol #4557
Chapelot, Jean #276
Chapin, Howard M. #2915
Chapman, A.H. #7649
Chapman, Allan #4272
Chapman, Anne #3930
Chapman, Howard D. #7976 8344 9456
Chapman, K.M. #3412
Charbonneau, André #8449
Charbonneau, Roger #1494
Charent, Brian #581 5930
Charland, J.-P. #2946
Charland, Paul-V. #1230
Charlebois, J.P.A. #1319
Charlebois, Roland H. #1094
Charlesworth, Hector #4674 4999 5459 5488
    6004 7529
Charney, Melvin #1530 5091 5093 7731 7746
    7867 7868 7906 7931 9316 9400 9401 9403
Charron, François #1552 7139
Charters, Evan #19
Chartier, Emile #1381
Chartrand, Denis #5472 5577 6717
Chartrand, René #2874 2881 2910 2911

Charyk, John C. #9404
Chassay, Christiane #1627
Chassé, Pierre-E. #4726 6930
Châtigny, Edmond #5097
Chaudron, Bernard #5099
Chaudron, Louise #5099
Chauvin, Jean #302 3258
Cheilan, Marina #4714
Chevalier, Denys #3269 5293
Chevalier, Willie #6994 8346
Chiasson, Herménégilde #7140
Chiasson, Rosemary #5657
Chicoine, Emilia #8597
Chicoine, René #5438 8620
Childs, Sidney #9446
Chipp, Herschel B. #3691
Chisvin, Jack #9087
Chitty, Elizabeth #687
Chivers, C.W.U. #8689
Chopin, Henri #4958
Chopping, George Clifford #2431
Choquette, Claude #1534
Choquette, Gilbert #8931 8932
Chouinard, Gaétan #7882 8874 8875 8893
Chouinard, Yvan #2235 7208
Chrétien, Jean #4222
Christensen, E.M. #9488
Christie, Robert #1940 4683 4685 6836
Cinader, B. #4133
Cinader, Bernard #4150 4156
Cinader, Bernard J. #4143
Ciolkowska, Muriel #6615
Clarens, Henri #6843
Clarizio, Nicolas #5797
Clark, A.McFadyen #4104 4105
Clark, Annette McFadyen #3368
Clark, Brenda #4380
Clark, Dean #8126
Clark, Douglas #1879 5812
Clark, H.M. #9265
Clark, Herbert M. #9264
Clark, Hilary #9141
Clark, Ian Christie #3352 3354 3357
Clark, Jennifer #7728
Clark, Paraskeva #570
Clark, Robert #2149
Clark, Tim #687 5113
Clarke, Alan #7728
Clarke, Andrew #8065
Clarke, Basil Fulford Lowther #8761
Clarke, Ian #9232
Clarkes, Gerard #8235
Claus, Jo Anne #4508 5463 6833 6931
Clayton, Lucy #8530
Clayton, Maurice #7722
Clemson, Donovan #8148 8153
Clerk, Nathalie #4823
Clermont, Ghislain #1127 1165 1542 1543
    5146 5713 7218 7482
Clifford, W.Michael #9194
Climer, J.E. #6285
Climer, John #1916 1927 5590 6284 6288 6579
    7128
Clipsham, Muriel #2587
Close, Patrick #1042

Cloutier, Albert #5255 9286
Cloutier, André #7951
Cloutier, Jean-Pierre #2313
Cloutier, Michel #5790
Cloutier, Nicole #1363 1374 4771 6217 6218
    8604
Cloutier, Normand #1480
Cloutier-Cournoyer, Françoise #2772 4824
    4849
Clowery, Freeman #757 764
Clubb, Sally Potter #8114
Cluff, A.W. #9300
Cluff, P.J. #9300
Cluff, Pamela #8514
Clutesi, George #3956
Coatsworth, E.S. #7346
Cobb, Charles S. #8296
Cobb, Henry N. #9314
Cobb, Myrna #2018 2030 6460
Coburn, Kathleen #5020
Coburn, W.Newlands #2420
Cochran, Bente Roed #1974 1975 5041
Cochrane, William #8532
Codere, Helen #3935
Cody, H.A. #7067
Coe, Ralph T. #3359 3460
Cogswell, Fred #1178
Cohen, Bryna Polonsky #903
Cohen, Nathan #95 96
Cohen, Robin #4152
Cohen, S.J. #8302
Cohen, Sorel #673
Coish, Calvin #2152 7793
Colby, Joy Hakanson #5063
Colchester, Edmund #8712
Colchester, Garry #8712
Cole, Douglas #269 270 2008 2009 2010 2016
    3316 4581
Cole, Jean Murray #8674
Coleman, Bernard #3560
Coley, Curtis G. #98
Colgate, William #28 1714 4537 4713 4929
    5955 5956 5976 6008 6356 6357 6524 6756
    6935 7234 7356 7502 7534
Colgate, William G. #5776
Colgrass, Ulla #2940
Colgrove, R.G.P. #5727
Collard, Edgar Andrew #6725
Collard, Eileen #2852 2854 2860 2862 2863
    2871 2878 2885 2886 2889 2905 2906
Collard, Elizabeth #280 890 1367 2288 2289
    2300 2305 2314 2315 2316 2319 2320 2326
    2327 2332 2339 2340 2341 2360 2361 2370
    2410 2538 5362 5753 7593
Collier, Robert #8699
Collier, Robert W. #9302
Collins, A.Roger #7512
Collins, B.R. #2050
Collins, Bradford R. #2051 4923 5106 6135
Collins, Carole #141
Collins, E.R. #8040
Collins, Henry B. #3366 4327 4336 4338 4340
    4343 4353 4364
Collins, Lewis W. #8317

Collins, Maynard #6498
Collins, Peter #7860 8287 8512 9194 9195 9212 9517
Collinson, Helen #674 3200 4492 5553 5618 7541
Collymore, Peter #7743
Colman, M.E. #5015
Colombo, J.R. #6705
Colombo, John Robert #3265 6706 9536
Colton, Alfred Stanley #2989
Colville, Alex #7767
Colwell, Wayne #8477
Comfort, C.F. #1090
Comfort, Charles #379 394 807 1745 5680 5725
Comfort, Charles F. #391 434 1087 6832
Comfort, Charles Fraser #5157 5158
Condé, Carole #602 1063
Cone, Jane Harrison #6669
Confino, Barbara #7304
Conlon, Patrick #2927
Conn, Richard #3359 3378 3453 3469 3479 3685 3692 3695 3722
Connell, James #2573
Conroy, Mary #2799
Constable, W.G. #3026 3032
Constantine, Mildred #2776
Constantinidi, Mela #911
Cook, Ramsay #109 4677 6114
Cooke, Edwy F. #3096
Cooke, Martha E. #5129
Cooke, W.M.E. #259
Cooke, W.Martha E. #258 269 270
Coon, Burwell R. #8506
Cooper, F.S. #9466
Cooper, H.W. #5173
Cooper, J.I. #9287
Cooper, Russell #2735 8675
Coopersmith, Penina #8999
Coote, Michael #8975
Copeland, Mary #1218 2342 2362
Corbeil, Danielle #825 1485 4545 5534 7401
Corbeil, Gilles #1408 3213 6199 6200 6227 6343 7289
Corbeil, Wilfrid #1402 3100 3101 8876
Corbett, E.A. #6007
Corboz, André #7765
Corey, Albert B. #337
Corke, Charles #1724 2413
Corkin, Jane #1070
Cormier, Bruno #1396 1449
Cormier, Charlotte #938
Cormier, Ernest #8740
Corne, Sharon #596 1877
Corneil, Carmen #8284
Corner, John #3952
Cornu, Marcel #7709
Cornwell, Regina #7254 7259 7260 7261 7264 7575
Corriveau, L.de B. #4857
Cossette, Jean-François #7302
Côté, Georges #8803
Côté, Renaud #8779
Côté, Renée #7877 7890
Côté, Suzanne #8868
Cotton, P. #8158

Cotton, Peter #8146 8173 8174 8757
Coughtry, Graham #867
Couling, Gordon #8011
Coulon, Jacques #6568
Coulthart, Hugh #7728
Courthion, Pierre #4510
Courtney, Alice E. #599 3056
Courtney, Richard #3274
Courtois, Denise #884
Courval, Michel de #4411
Courville, Suzette #1801
Cousineau, Penny #1018 1037 5506
Coutts-Smith, Kenneth #4679
Coutu, Jean #241 242
Couture, A. #3924
Couture, Francine #1514
Couture-Laliberté, Luce #1535
Couturier, Marie-Alain #1436 8397
Couvrette, Paul #1028 1043
Cowan, Harvey #2771 7698
Cowan, John Bruce #5901
Cowan, Susan #4261 4275
Cox, E.C.S. #8508
Cox, Leo #1251 1254
Cox, Richard #7703
Cozic, Yvon #1545
Crabtree, Graham #897
Cragg, Allan #2376
Craick, W.Arnot #9156
Craig, Kate #687 2070
Craig, Mary M. #4483 6105
Crandall, Daniel Taylor #4016
Crane, Charles #7011
Crary, Jonathan #6272
Craven, David #687 7031
Crawford, Lawrence #8516
Crawford, Lee #2775
Crawley, Alice M. #1808
Crean, S.M. #3157 3279
Creelman, Joanne #2785
Creighton, Norman #5868
Creighton, Phyllis #258 259
Creighton, Thomas #9396
Crinion, David #8984
Croes, Dale Ross #4017
Croft, L.Scott #5210
Cromarty, W.D. #8926
Crooker, Mervyn John Arthur #227
Cross, Kenneth M.B. #8389
Crossen, T.W. #8995
Crouch, Richard E. #3133
Crowell, Ivan H. #2492 2979
Cruise, David #9296
Cruise, James E. #3161 3170
Cruise, Stephen #5213
Crysdale, Stewart #8906
Cuciurean, Rick #1566
Cullen, Mary K. #7800 8527 8937 8938 8939
Cullers, Samuel #8989
Cumberland, Barlow #9428
Cumming, Glen E. #569 780 1838 5064
Cumming, Mark #7374
Cummings, Stephen #7601
Cunningham, Robert #2150
Curniski, Savelia #8912

Curnoe, G. #962
Curnoe, Greg #536 607 620 5228 6464
Currelly, Charles Trick #3139
Curry, S.G. #7961 8297
Curtis, Edward S. #3399
Cuthbert, Art #4976
Cutler, M.Ebbitt #7386
Cutler, Maurice #2621 4231 4425
Cutler, May Ebbitt #2696 2990 5560 6494
Cutter, Donald C. #1998
Cutts, Anson Bailey #7977
Cyr, Jacqueline #2877
Cyr, Lise #2235
Czegledy-Nagy, Nina #2395

D

D'Arcy, G.Helmer #9393
D'Argencourt, Louise #5622
Da Roza, Gustavo #8088 8198
Dafoe, Christopher #7305
Dafoe, Elizabeth #9044
Dagenais, Bernard #4661
Dagenais, Pierre #1380
Dagg, Cass #2936
Dagneault, Gabrielle #2791
Dahlberg, Richard E. #3353
Daigneault, Gilles #1536 1542 1543 1665 4572 4663 4664 5285 5322 5426 6309 7290 7405 7606
Dair, Carl #860 920 922 929
Dale, William S. #135 429
Dale, William S.A. #741 959 5784
Daley, Frank #95 96
Daley, Hartwell #6945
Dallas, Margery #2001
Dandurand, Mme #1311
Daniells, Roy #5022
Danzker, Jo-Anne Birnie #655 668 1044 1537 1550 2073 3285 6072 6139 6164 6276 7505 7509
Darroch, Lois #6307
Dault, Gary Michael #2768 5403 5404 5405 5525 6709 7193 7275
David, Michel #7952
David, Robert #7686
Davidialuk #4521
Davidovich, Jaime #671
Davidson, D.S. #4079
Davidson, Edward M. #9420
Davidson, Heather #6690
Davidson, Ian #8146 8158
Davidson, Margaret #1763 1764
Davidson, Ruth #2110
Davidson, True #5923
Davies, Blodwen #1738 6350 7353 7363
Davies, Frank #9547
Davies, Gerald A. #8762
Davies, Hugh M. #6673 7423
Davies, John L. #8305
Davies, Robertson #9460
Davies, Will #867

Davis, Ann #121 500 1472 1774 4141 5450
 6850 6851
Davis, Barbara #3987
Davis, Clark #3965
Davis, Marlene #2785
Davis, Rae #1759
Davis, Richard #3987
Davis, Robert Tyler #3875
Davis, T. #8722
Davis, Val #5132 5134
Davis, Wendy #2460
Davis, William G. #9397
Davison, Keith B. #8142
Davison, Robert L. #9044
Dawson, Joyce Taylor #2788 2789
Dawson, Kenneth #4949 5822 7310
Dawson, Nora #1252
Day, Gordon H. #5363
De Marco, Donald #6112
De Pédery-Hunt, Dora #772 5275
de Tonnancour, Jacques #1413
Deacon, Florence E. #5694
Deacon, William Arthur #317 319 5157
Dean, Max #687
Deans, James #3765 3766
Dearborn, Dorothy #1177 1188 7592
Décarie-Audet, Louise #2218
Deffontaines, Pierre #2832 8581
Degen, Pauline #4536
DeGrow, Donald #1812 1813 1932
Delafosse, Marcel #276
Delaney, Barbara Snow #2110
Deligny, Louis #918 6195
Dellamora, Richard #5643
Dellandrea, Jon S. #2427 2432
Delloye, Charles #1421 4604
DeLormier, Michel #7949
Delroy, Stephen Henry #2484
Delvaux, Paul-Henri #159
Demers, Clément #7766
Demers, Pierre #1283
Demeter, Laszlo #8598 8854
Dempsey, Gwen P. #2455
Dempsey, Hugh A. #958 1962 2585 3194
 3351 3703 3707 7312 7313
Denault, J.-Raymond #7907
Dendy, William #8076 8667 8753
Denhez, Marc #8106
Denhez, Marc C. #7772
Denny, Peter #962
Densmore, Frances #3539 3551
Derome, Gilles #2196 5169
Derome, Robert #269 270 1620 2684 2689
 2692 5277 5321 5879 5880 6147 6216 8814
Des Gagniers, Jean #5311
Desbarats, Guy #7728 8279 8992
Desbarats, Peter #957 6401 7770
Deschênes, Donald #938
Desilets, Alphonse #5105 6846
Desjardins, Pierre #4836
Desjardins, Pierre W. #5284
Deslauriers, Ginette #1665 5089
Desloges, Yvon #8450 8452 8463 8473
Desmarais, Danielle #1059
Desmeules, Raynald #2998

Desrosiers, Hughes B. #8269
Desrosiers, Pierre #6126
Désy, Léopold #1609 1610 1612 1615 1633
 7455 8850
Désy, Louise #2390
Deveau, W.D. #2840
Devereux, H.E. #8468 8469
Devine, Mary #8539
Dewdney, Selwyn #3439 3472 3575 3576
 3583 3600 3602 3626 3706 4122 4154 6643
Dewhirst, John #4025 8456
Déziel, Julien #37 4650 4906 5005 5281 5436
 5856 6446 7344
Déziel, Richard #5396
Diamond, A.J. #7731 9503
Diamond, Billy #1566
Diamond, Jack #7728 7746 8989
Dibble, Charles E. #3375
Dick, Lyle #8723 8724
Dick, Ronald A. #8661
Dick-Lauder, Mrs. #7954
Dickard, David #1722
Dickason, Olive Patricia #4126 4127
Dickenson, Victoria #1158
Dickey, John M. #7703
Dickinson, Donald #1805
Dickinson, Peter #8760
Dickman, Chris #7618
Dickman, Thelma #4121
Dignam, M.E. #2277
Dignam, Mary E. #2958
Dikeakos, Christos #2042
Dille, Lutz #5292
Dillingham, Beth #3459
Dillow, Nancy #5200
Dillow, Nancy E. #543 1919 1922 1923 1936
 5198 5626 6728 6837 7195 7285 7320
Dilworth, Carol #2517
Dilworth, Ira #5007 5011 5012 5013 5017
 5019 5030 5031
Dilworth, Tim #2517
Dimakopoulos, Dimitri #8195
Dimson, Theo #867 908
Dinsmore, Cynthia K. #512
Dion, Thérèse #123
Dionne, Denise #1499
Dionne, N.E. #8785
DiStefano, Lynne Delehanty #4253
Dixon, Anne #3056
Dixon, Brian #599 3056
Dixon, John Morris #9496
Dixon, Penelope #1070
Dixon, Roland B. #3498
Dobson, Barbara #2119 2475
Dobson, Henry #2119 2475
Dobush, Peter #8308
Dockstader, Frederick J. #3343 3359 3435
 3437 3450 3476 3911
Dockstader, John #4123
Dodds, Stanley #7674
Doig, Marion Hales #3034
Dolan, George R. #8453
Dole, W.P. #6532
Donahue, A.J. #8256

Donaldson, Joan #5364
Donaldson, Thomas B. #6481
Donnelly, Frank #8128
Dor, Georges #5668
Dorais, Louis-Jacques #4522
Dorais, Lucie #4836 4841 6632 6633
Doré, Guy #2222
Dorion, Jacques #9424
Dorival, Bernard #4702 6803
Dorsey, Candas Jane #5211
Doucet-Saito, Louise #2387
Doughty, Adam #205
Douglas, Fred #2012
Douglas, Frederic H. #3667
Douglas, Ken #2947
Douglas, R.Alan #6992
Douglass, Susan C. #3973
Douville, Raymond #4782
Dow, Helen J. #5143 5147 5149 5150
Dowling, Eric #8762
Downs, Barry #7746 8146 8150 8159 8199
 8918
Doyle, Arthur #1186
Doyle, Judith #652
Doyon, Charles #6199
Doyon, Hélène #1801
Doyon-Ferland, Madeleine #1258 1259 2828
 2829 2841
Dozol, R.P. #1435
Dragan, Rose #2782
Dragu, Margaret #687
Drahanchuk, Ed #2387
Drapeau, Jean #7900 9139
Draper, Nancy #4305
Drayton, Geoffrey #6358 6802
Drew, F.W.M. #3957
Drew, Leslie #3925 4042
Driedger, Leo #968
Driscoll, Bernadette #4300 4306 4314 4459
Drolet, Jean-Paul #4232
Drouin, J.C. #9168
Drucker, Philip #3880 3897 3931 3966
Drummond, Thomas #2812
Du Berger, Jean #3309
Du Cane, John #7249
Du Toit, Roger #8199
Dubé, Doris D. #7947
Dubé, Philippe #2948
Dubé, Yves #4886
Dubois, Lise #4836
DuBois, Macy #7746 8359 8975 9035 9095
 9104 9199 9345 9468 9479
DuBois, Sally #9035 9047
Ducharme, Gérard #2626
Duff, Donald #688
Duff, Shannie #7788
Duff, Wilson #3344 3351 3884 3900 3906
 3926 3948 4053 4054 4055 4119 6428 6985
Duffus, A.F. #7823
Duffy, Dennis #2030 5957
Duffy, Helen #4904 5576 5577 5656
Dufresne, Michel #7880
Duguay, Raôul #4512
Duguay, Rodolphe #5317
Dumais, François #6325

Dumais, Lynda #2879
Dumas, Antoine #2919 2922
Dumas, Paul #124 482 1353 1397 1760 3113
    4390 4461 4526 5084 5241 5257 5353 5746
    5748 5987 6340 6658 6867 7383 9023
Dumesnil, Thérèse #712 5098
Dumond, Don E. #4370
Dumont, Fernand #1449
Dumont, Jean-C. #4928
Dumont, René #9420
Dumouchel, Jacques #3109 5332
Dumouchel, Suzanne Beaudoin #1648
Dunbar, Nancy J. #257
Duncan, Dorothy #2475 2569 2926 2929 8675
Duncan, Douglas #3218
Duncan, Kate #4107
Duncan, Kate Corbin #4110
Dunn, Brenda #8430
Dunn, Dorothy #3716
Dunn, Josephine Hambleton #3891 4885
Dunn, Marty #575
Dunning, Phil #2476 2559
Dunnington-Grubb, H.B. #8495 8501
Dunton, Davidson #3144
Dupin, Jacques #7021
Duplessis, Jacqueline #5339
Dupont, Jean-Claude #2697 2702 2707 2712
    2713 2764 2953 8624
Dupuis, Pierre #5582 6927
Dupuis-Maillet, Corinne #5342
Duquette, Jean-Pierre #1542 1543 4703 6189
    6190 6191 6192 7425
Durand, A. #4576
Durand, Guy #3016
Durham, Bill #3339
Durnford, A.T. Galt #2100 7900
Durocher, René #1617
Duron, Michèle #276
Dusenberry, Verne #3693
Dusseault-Letocha, Louise #1649
Dutaud, Gustave #5767
Duthuit, Georges #7012
Dutil, Daniel Morency #6238
Duval, Paul #39 48 51 53 110 116 498 573
    925 1755 1790 3172 4248 4578 4901 5056
    5057 5061 5251 5515 5725 6121 6122 6311
    6372 6800 7596 7599
Duviols, Jean-Paul #276
Dwyer, Peter #529
Dwyer, Peter M. #481
Dwyer, Ruth #2267
Dyck, Paul #3732
Dyens, M.Georges #1860
Dyonnet, Edmond #16 1315 5347 5349
Dyson, C.E. Cyril #9450
Dzubak, L. #8995

E

E.S. #201
Eadie, Arthur H. #7969 9043
Eaton, Charlotte #5355 5356

Eaton, Leonard K. #8383 9247
Eber, Dorothy #1428 1429 1431 4224 4299
    4460 4476 4484 4559 6712 6875 6876 6878
    6880 6881 6883
Eber, Dorothy Harley #4496 6879
Eberts, Cynthia #2758
Eckbo, Garrett #7677
Eckenwalder, Susan #4987
Eckhardt, Ferdinand #494 1847 1891 1893
    1895 3192 4402 5390 5447 5448
Ede, Carol Moore #7710
Edgar, Lady #4712
Edinburgh, Arnold #3291
Edison, Margaret E. #6385
Edmonds, Alan #8357
Edwards, J.O. #3924
Efimova, A.K. #4302
Efrat, Barbara S. #4025
Eglington, Guy C. #9438
Eicheberg, Fritz #6450
Elarth, H.A. #8256
Elder, Henry #8146 9503
Elder, Linda #2389
Elie, Robert #2193 4800 4802 4813
Elken, Ants #7723
Ellenwood, Ray #1467
Elliot, Robbins #8305
Elliot, Robert S. #1190
Elliott, George #1748 4423 6551 6680 7462
Elliott, John K. #8003
Ellis, Daphne #3156
Ellsworth, Ralph E. #9046
Ellwood, Michael #8247 9314
Elsasser, Albert B. #3928
Elte, Hans #8282 8518 8583 8657 9033 9109
    9461
Elwood, Marie #1206 1207 1212 2333 2363
    2484 2505 2506 2509 8546
Embleton, Gerry #2867
Emerson, J.N. #8468 8469
Emerson, John Norman #3566
Emery, Anthony #1994 7203 7223
Emery, Anthony M. #7182
Emery, Irene #2873 3469
Emery, Marc #9130
Emery, Tony #6455 7225 7630 8158
Emmons, G.T. #3969
Emmons, George T. #3331 3776 3784 3786
    3794 3795 3798 3804 3815 3825 3853 4074
Emperatori, Arthur #6759
Endicott, Norman #570
Endicott, Norman J. #541
Endres, Robin #3286
Engel, Douglas #9477
Engel, Walter #495
Englesmith, G. #2603
Englesmith, George #7426
Ennals, Peter #8551
Ennals, Peter M. #9227 9229
Ennis, Frances #2155
Enright, Robert #6716
Epivent, Jean-Luc #1563 4544 5381 6714 7029
    7149 7435
Epstein, Anita #7197

Erickson, Arthur #7227 7677 7728 7746 8231
    8354 8355 8356 8361 9098 9358 9470
Erickson, Arthur C. #8158 9505
Erickson, Jon T. #3736
Erland, Anastasia #6387
Ernst, Alice Henson #3867 3885
Errol, Constance #7457
Erskine, Ralph #8186
Espessat, Hélène #2206
Essar, Gary #1928
Etherington, A.Bruce #9193
Ethier-Blais, Jean #1270 1448 4802 4805 4811
    4814 4850 6629
Etook, Tivi #5374 5375
Evans, Clifford #4377
Evans, E.W. #9279
Evans, G.Heberton #3609
Evans, Gladstone #9336
Evans, J.A.S. #7983
Evans, Ron #4307
Everman, Bob #3006
Evrard, Marcel #3351
Ewan, Anne F. #6415
Ewen, Paterson #703
Ewers, John C. #1859 3478 3486 3672 3678
    3679 3686 3704 3721 3757
Ewert, Elinor #689
Ewing, R.D. #974
Ewing, William A. #1507
Eyler, Philip #763
Eyre, Ivan #5394
Eyre, Yvonne #7220

F

Fabre, Hector #4863
Fabre-Surveyer, E. #2663 4769
Fabrycki, William #7075
Fagg, William #4360
Fahey, Curtis #8906
Fainmel, Charles #862
Fairbairn, M.L. #190 7498
Fairbairn, Margaret L. #6976
Fairchild, G.M. #1312 1313
Fairley, Barker #344 380 1075 1731 5402 5405
    7464
Fairn, L.R. #8740
Fairweather, C.Lillian #8529
Falardeau, Emile #1578 4859 5108 5407 5435
    6961 7298
Falconer, Robert #5470
Falconer, Sir Robert #3206
Fales, Dean A., Jr. #2577
Fales, Douglas A. #7990
Falk, Gathie #5410
Falk, Lorne #1045
Falkner, Ann #7716 7771
Farabee, William Curtis #3407 3522 3526
    3658
Fardoulis-Vitant, Anne #276
Farr, Dorothy #117 282 6693 7503
Farr, Dorothy M. #4638

Farrand, Livingston #3773
Farrell, Jon #1095
Farrell-Ward, Lorna #147 5890 6407
Fatouros, A.A. #3347
Faucher, A. #8841
Favrholdt, Ken #8478
Favro, Murray #703
Fecteau, Hélène #7390
Feder, Norman #3372 3431 3432 3442 3697
   3698 3705 3752 3753 3918
Feest, Christian F. #3381 3436
Feindel, Glen #2510
Feindel, Susan #135
Feindel, Susan Tenney #8610
Feldman, Seth #626
Felteau, Cyrille #4946 9252
Felter, James Warren #829 1512 2007 2041
Feltham, Dean #9503
Fentiman, H.G. #7686
Fenton, Terry #507 515 620 1862 1915 1917
   1918 1919 1920 1929 4964 4969 6476
Fenton, William N. #3359 3570 3613 4113
Fenwick, K.M. #813
Fenwick, Kathleen M. #437 486 487 5559
Ferdinands, Frances #1797
Ferguson, Bruce #705 1930 5002 5757 6140
   7142 7143 7219
Ferguson, Bruce W. #5631
Ferguson, Gerald #825
Ferguson, Pamela #5858
Ferguson, Ted #1880
Fergusson, C.Bruce #1119 1196 7834
Fergusson, Charles Bruce #241 242 8374
Ferland, Albert #5278
Ferland-Angers, Albertine #8445
Ferrabee, Lydia #2613 2623 4914 5442 9323
   9516
Ferrari, Corinna #600
Fetherling, Doug #6569 9204
Fetherstonhaugh, H.L. #8562
Fewkes, J.Walter #3494
Fidler, Vera #755 4193
Field, Richard #8549
Field, Richard H. #2507 2508
Field, Robin Wayne #4478
Filey, Mike #9536
Filion, Sylvie #2954
Fillmore, Stanley #7981 8057
Filteau, Pierre #8394
Finch, Robert #570
Finkel, Henry #2612
Finlayson, R.W. #2285 2306
Finley, A.Gregg #2504
Finley, Gerald #5786 8015
Finley, Gerald E. #5787 5788
Firestone, O.J. #3239 5925
Firth, Raymond #3348
Fiset, Edouard #7686 7937 7939 8034 9213
Fisette, Jean #4831
Fisette, Serge #2384
Fish, Michael #8594 9537
Fish, Robert #687
Fisher, Brian #620
Fisher, John W. #5922
Fisher, R.A. #9027
Fisher, Robin #8917

Fisher-Taylor, Gail #1046 1047 1053 1060
   1971 3314
Fiske, Patricia #2873 3469
Fitz, W.G. #983
Fitzgerald, Ed #550
Fitzhugh, William #4377
Flagler, Gordon #7159
Flanders, John #2142 7698
Flanders, Richard E. #3635
Flavelle, Muriel I. #2244
Fleisher, Pat #560 566 1131 1870 3004 3006
   3061 3312 3314 4551 5600 5636 5663 5848
   6733 7399 7634
Fleisher, Ron #4778
Fleming, Allan #932 5455
Fleming, John #7188 9508
Fleming, Marie #6514
Fleming, Marie L. #3011
Fleming, Marnie #5811
Fleming, Marnie Lynn #5810
Fleming, Martha #710
Fleming, Roy F. #6353
Fleming, Roy Franklin #202
Flemming, David #8464 8465
Fletcher, Alan #894
Fleury, W.E. #9394
Fliess, Henry #8254 8508 8511 8514 8515
Floyd, J.Austin #7677
Folch, Jacques #4706 4806 5561 6812 9317
Folch-Ribas, Jacques #1432 1591 4784 4785
   4793 7389
Forbes, J.A. #5757
Forbes, J.Allison #7335
Forbes, Jack #2337 2371
Force, Roland W. #4458
Ford, Harriet #181
Foreman, Richard #7243
Forest, H.J. de #3180
Forest, Michel #7132
Forgey, Benjamin #627
Forgues, Rémi-Paul #1443
Forman, Werner #3947
Forrest, Kevin #6330 6331
Forrest, Kevin A. #5451
Forrest, Linn A. #3873
Forsey, William C. #120
Forster, Henry W. #7905
Forster, J.W.L. #1705 5469
Forster, John Wycliffe Lowes #2960 5467
   5470
Forster, Michael #1403
Forsyth, Leslie Lerena #759 5681
Fortier, André #4575 5312
Fortier, John #8422 8425 8439
Fortier, Margaret #8426
Fortier, Marie-France #8633
Fortier, Yvan #2545 6863 8627
Fortin, Gérald #8217
Fortin, M.Ls de Gonzague #1234
Foss, Charles #2501 2512 6603 7811
Foss, Charles H. #2484 2511
Foss, Charles Henry #7810
Foster, Michael #1012
Foster, Mrs. W.Garland #1981 3864
Fournier, Jacques-Gilles #251

Fournier, Marcel #1443 4832
Fournier, Paul #5487
Fowke, H.Shirley #4595
Fowler, C.A.E. #7684 8305
Fowler, Gordon #9027
Fowler, John #4430
Fowler, Marian #7211
Fox, Arthur #3069
Fox, Howard N. #644
Fox, Hyla #2757 2790
Fox, Hyla Wults #2792
Fox, Mary #775 2452 4006 4018 4142 5850
   7315
Fox, Ross Allan C. #2681 2691
Fox, William #9249
Franca, Celia #9103
Francis, Anne #6751
Francis, J.W. #8187
Francis, Jean #2938 2941
Franck, Claude #9497
Frank, Peter #6272
Franklin, Douglas #9509
Franklyn, Mary Eliza #2887
Fraser, Allan M. #3584
Fraser, Carol #607
Fraser, Don #9053
Fraser, Douglas #3342 3348 3975
Fraser, John Arthur #5509 5510
Fraser, Mary #8024 8029
Fraser, Ted #646 1835 4569 4751 7115 7415
Frayne, Trent #7359
Fréchette, Marie #2773
Frederick, Saradell Ard #4233
Fredk, William #8740
Fredrickson, N.Jaye #3645 3646
Freedman, Adele #628 3312 5112 6418 6941
   7560 7564 7633
Freeman, John Crosby #8175 9405
Freeman, Robert C. #611
French, Diana Elizabeth #4007
French, Gary E. #5863
French, Leigh #1083
Frenkel, Vera #713 2994 5327 5519 5522 5523
Freschi, Bruno #8519
Frey, M.W. #8705
Fried, Frederick #756
Friedman, Martin #3359
From, Dot #5115
Fry, B.W. #7861
Fry, George #4582 4760 5682
Fry, Jacqueline #714 4128 4131 4153 4241
   4427 4428 4493 6271 7569
Fry, Jacqueline Delange #4135 4225
Fry, Lesley #4976
Fry, Philip #699 1897 2272 5002 5139 5195
   5213 5274 5536 5540 5684 6432 6940 7147
   7148
Frye, Helen #353 3301 6295
Frye, Helen Kemp #5845
Frye, Northrop #22 106 215 362 443 444 570
   5719 5727 6547
Fulford, Robert #64 87 129 421 529 567 629
   746 748 750 1749 1787 1798 3290 4511 4707
   4756 4763 4990 5142 5189 5456 5581 5637

5772 5813 5945 5997 6313 6682 6698 6704
6866 7017 7069 7224 7239 7243 7271 7319
7408 7411 7412 7416 7444 7589
Fuller, George #8106
Fulton, David #5766
Furneaux, Patrick #4482
Furnival, A.Stanley #867
Furst, Peter T. #3360
Fyshe, Avis #849

G

Gabeline, Donna #7914
Gaboury, Etienne #7746 8369 8519 8908
Gaboury, Etienne J. #8212 8767
Gadbois, Louise #1433 4877
Gagen, Robert F. #1706
Gagern, Axel von #3423
Gagnon, Antoine #2978
Gagnon, Claire #1350
Gagnon, Clarence A. #299
Gagnon, Claude-Lyse #4644 5667 5668 6223
Gagnon, Ernest #8443
Gagnon, François #1267 1443 1451 1483 2201
3307 4826 5440 5595 6599 7398 7490 7491
Gagnon, François-Marc #281 933 964 1270
1284 1294 1354 1358 1362 1363 1367 1373
1454 1456 1460 1468 1542 1543 1654 3234
3461 4607 4816 4819 4829 4830 4833 4834
4838 4839 4842 4843 4844 4851 4852 5290
5483 5640 6222 6511 6585
Gagnon, G.-U. #8863 8877
Gagnon, Jean-Gilles #1551
Gagnon, Jean-Louis #6119
Gagnon, Lysiane #1480
Gagnon, Maurice #1384 1390 1398 4801 6196
Gagnon, Paul #8595 8625 8881
Gagnon-Fortier, C. #5552
Gagnon-Pratte, France #8632
Gaines, Ruth #3412
Gaitskell, C.D. #2986
Galanti-Amiel, Mireille #7492
Galarneau, Claude #1369 1477
Galarneau, Pierre #7927
Gale, Peggy #575 604 605 630 631 650
654 655 656 672 1832 6439 7277
7514
Gallager, Orovell R. #3682
Galy-Carles, Henry #4606 5941 7024
Gambier-Bousfield, R.W. #8239
Garand, Gilles #1285
Garber, Bram #3247
Garcia-Camarillo, Cecilio #554
Gardiner, E.Norman #6482
Gardiner, Frank G. #9029
Gardiner, J.Rawson #7659 7841 7845
Gareau, A.L. #8554
Gareau, Jean #9395
Garfield, Viola E. #3856 3873 3881 3892
Garfield, Viola Edmundson #6788 6789
Gariepy, Eileen #2909

Garneau, René #3321 5218
Garnet, E. #538
Garon, Rosaire #1505
Garrett, Michael #9090
Garth, Thomas R. #8140
Garver, Thomas #7141
Garver, Thomas H. #2039
Garwood-Jones, Trevor #8200
Gascon, André #5183
Gascon, France #1471 1475 1565 2800 7402
Gascon, Marguerite #1490
Gatrill, Adrian #2637 7728
Gaucher, Yves #1430
Gaudard, Pierre #1494
Gaudet, Michel #7097
Gaudibert, Pierre #558
Gaumond, Michel #269 270 2301 2343 2698
7953 8588 8589 8814 8847
Gauquelin, Michel #1644 6610
Gauthier, Claude-Paul #1628
Gauthier, Lise #1538
Gauthier, Marcel #2545
Gauthier, Monique #4836
Gauthier, Ninon #1293 7233
Gauthier, Raymonde #269 270 1359 1613
6256 6257 7883 8611
Gauthier, Richard #7896
Gauthier-Larouche, Georges #8582 8599 8626
Gauvreau, Claude #1396 1443 1449 4643
4807 6199
Gauvreau, Jean-Marie #1394 1406 2172 2173
2174 2176 2179 2182 2188 2190 2523 2833
2970 2980 4505 4883 5062 5542 5544 5545
7454
Gauvreau, Pierre #5097
Geare, Randolph I. #4175
Gearhart, Edna #6852
Gebhard, David #3359 3710 3730
Gedalof, Robin #5902
General, David #4155 4164
Genest, Bernard #1277 1621 2235 2716 6441
7000
Genêt, Nicole #2218 2352
Genn, Robert #5585
Geoffrion, Hélène Gosselin #8405 9327
Georgas, Nora #3291
George, Hardy #7121
George, John #1294
Gérin-Lajoie, Denyse #885 5248
Gérin-Lajoie, Paul #9397
Gerson, Erika #1864
Gerson, W. #8256
Gerson, Wolfgang #8265 8303
Gervais, Raymond #637 687 5842
Gerver, Elisabeth #7615
Gessler, Trisha #4008 6933 6934
Getty, A.L. #4154
Getty, Ronald #2371 2372
Gheerbrant, Gilles #7489
Giannattasio, Sandra #7542
Gibb, Sandra #2654 2655 3645 3646
Gibbon, J.Murray #2097 2780
Gibbons, Lillian #8692 8702
Gibbs, Betty #5590
Gibson, Edward #5591

Gibson, Edward M. #8172 9360
Gibson, G.D. #7669 8514
Gibson, James A. #5760
Gibson, Marjorie #2102
Giddings, J.Louis #4371
Giddings, Ken #7684
Giedion, S. #4341
Giedion, Sigfried #8983
Gifford, E.W. #3412
Gifford, Hilda #9044
Giguère, Guy #8622
Giguère, Roland #818 5599 7460
Gilbert, B. #6904
Gilbert, Edward James #8312
Gilbert, Gerry #550 2044 6061
Gilhooly, David #1939 2387
Gill, Brendan #8524
Gillese, John Patrick #1949
Gillespie, Bernard #9350
Gillespie, Peter #7643
Gillett, Violet #5605
Gillette, Charles H. #3603
Gillies, Suzanne #1899
Gillmor, R.D. #7747 8256
Gillmor, R.Douglas #8088
Gillon, Michèle #6571
Gilmore, B.C. #2017
Gilmore, Berenice C. #2025 4665 4709 5137
Gilmore, John #2102 7114
Gimpel, Charles #4204
Gingras, Claude #6199
Gingras, Line #9526
Gingras, Marcel #6448
Girard, Henri #306 5179 5216 5982 5986 6341
6616 7294
Girard, Isabelle #2861
Girouard-Décarie, Jeanne #2212
Giroux, André #8604
Giroux, Sylvia #6214
Gjessing, Gutorm #3886
Glackens, Ira #6177
Gladu, Paul #4716 4743 4744 5477 5551 5989
6199 6807
Glasser, Penelope #657 1835
Glassie, Henry #7703
Glatthaar, Trisha Corliss #6932
Glazebrook, G.P. de T. #2851 3206
Glover, Guy #1991
Glover, Patricia E. #1896 1898 5159
Glover, Winifred #3477
Glubok, Shirley #4190
Glyde, H.G. #1943
Glynn, Walter S. #9029
Gobeil-Trudeau, Madeleine #7951 8864 8889
Goble, Paul #3758
Goddard, P.E. #3989
Godenrath, Percy F. #21 1085
Godfrey, Larry #5800
Godin, Deborah #715
Godin, Gérald #3269 6650
Godmer, Gilles #6717
Godsell, Patricia #125
Goetz, Helga #4250 4266 4292 4293 4490
6874
Going, A.M. #9239

Gold, Melanie #5644
Goldberg, Yalta #7327
Goldhamer, Charles #1091
Goldman, R. #8147
Goldring, Philip #8475 8476
Goldsborough, Harriett E. #2282
Goldschmidt, Nicholas #9085
Goldsmith, Catherine #159
Gonyea, Ramon #4163
Good, E.Reginald #2578 4628 7539
Good, Mary Elizabeth #3635
Goodman, Eileen #409 3214
Goodridge, Edythe #1152 2945 7272
Gool, Reshard #1167 1169
Gopnik, Irwin #5564 5792 6754 8590
Gopnik, Myrna #5564 5792 8590
Gordon, J.F. #8974
Gordon, Joleen #2156 2157 2785 2907 2935
Gordon, Tom #5568
Gore, Tom #2061 2071 5659
Goring, Trevor #1529
Goss, Arthur S. #978
Gosselin, Amédée Edmond #8791
Gosselin, Claude #4573 5484 6641 7283
Gosselin, Pierre #1552
Gottschalk, Fritz #898
Gougeon, Diane #685
Gough, Hugh #2518
Gouin, Paul #1247 5062 7942
Gould, Jennifer Chambers #3980
Gould, John #5637
Gould, Joseph #179
Goulding, W.S. #7997 8653 8762
Goulding, William #8764
Goulet, Claude #5639
Goupil, Laval #7089
Gour, Romain #5219 5768 7295
Govan, James #9028
Govier, Katherine #5175
Gowans, Alan #228 229 234 235 5651 7689
    7690 7697 7815 7856 7858 8060 8327 8817
    8821 8826 8828 8832 8837
Gowans, Alan W. #8822 8823 8829
Gowans, Alan Wilbert #8825
Gowers, Harold J. #3888
Goyer, Michelle #4827
Grabert, Garland F. #3950
Graburn, Nelson H. #3355 4214 4215 4223
    4234 4251 4262 4263 4264 4276 4277 4295
Grace, Gregory #6777
Graham, C.E.W. #840
Graham, Charles #9241
Graham, Colin #422 2068 3217 5947 6156
    6827 6839 7180 7601 9091
Graham, Colin David #7443
Graham, Dan #604 8402
Graham, John W. #3006 8095
Graham, Mayo #591 658 783
Graham, R. #8147
Graham, Robert #5592
Graham, W.E. #9091
Grande, John K. #6503
Granek, G. #9087
Grant, Alastair #9350
Grant, Campbell #3433

Grant, Christine #2484
Grant, H.Roger #9543 9544
Grant, Malachy #9510
Grant, Principal #942
Grant, Russ #6390
Granzow, Carl #797
Grattan, Patricia #1153 1155 1156 1159
Gratton, Valmore #7900
Gray, John #4688
Gray, Margaret #5059 5160 7156
Gray, Philip Howard #4252
Gray, Viviane #3630
Grayson, John #776
Green, B.H. #8256
Green, H.Gordon #2107
Green, L.J. #8740
Green, Laura Moss #7202
Green, William #165
Greenaway, Cora #8548
Greenberg, Charles #430 9211
Greenberg, Clement #1848 4978
Greenberg, Reesa #6820 6822 6823 6824 6825
    6826
Greenfield, Val #6408
Greenhalgh, Michael #4282
Greenhill, Ralph #1006 1019 1034 1039 5651
    7993 8006
Greening, W.E. #224 1250 1588 2674 3034
    7479 8838
Greenough, John Joseph #8431 8432 8441
Greenough, Joseph #8433 8479
Greenwood, Michael #143 505 582 606 777
    785 1798 4228 4773 4891 4894 5078 5755
    6079 6289 6314 6672 6912 6920 6925 6926
    7028 7108 7562
Greer, John #5653
Greer, William N. #8280
Greiner, Ruth #3807
Grenier, Jacques #1281
Grenier, Nicole #1364
Grenon, Hector #6440
Gretton, Robert #8198 8200 8216 8282 8311
    8314 8318 8320 8321 8379 8583 8964 8974
    8975 9048 9098 9106 9117 9126 9466 9471
    9494 9552
Grey, William #8772
Greyson, John #687
Gribbon, Michael J. #6860
Grier, E.Wyly #203 303 326
Grier, Edmund Wyly #289
Grier, Eldon #7384
Grier, Sir Wyly #7532
Griffin, James Bennett #3459
Griffiths, Alison #2079
Grigaut, Paul L. #216
Grigsby, Jefferson Eugene #3920
Grinnell, George Bird #3647
Grosbois, Louise de #1285 1562
Grossman, Irving #8231 8370 8512 8520 8903
    8989
Grossman, Peter #9044
Groulx, Lionel #2831
Groves, Naomi Jackson #5918 5919 5920
    5921
Grubar, Francis S. #6486
Guanish, Chief Joseph #4149

Guay, Diane #5574
Gubbay, Aline #1623 7930
Guédon, Marie-Françoise #4129 4130 4488
Gueft, Olga #9324
Guernsey, Betty #6683
Guerra, Jorge #3314
Guerriero, Mary #156
Guest, Patricia #5591
Guest, Tim #940
Guilbault, Nicole #5991 5993
Guillet, Edwin C. #2112
Guillet, Edwin Clarence #9285
Guindon, Vianney #8595 8633
Guinn, Rodger C. #8716
Gundy, H.Pearson #7339
Gunn, Barry #4266
Gunn, Cynthia #1655
Gunn, S.W. #3936
Gunn, S.W.A. #3356 3932
Gunn, Sisvan William #3943
Gunther, Erna #3370 3445 3819 3835 3854
    3901 3908 3919 3921 3937 3970
Gusset, Gérard #2364 2365
Gustafson, Paula #2596 2936 4044 4147
Guthe, Carl E. #3037
Guthe, Grace M. #3037
Guthrie, Gay #2652
Gutstein, Donald #8360
Guttenberg, A.Ch. de #89 6092 6623
Guy, Camil #3601
Gwyn, Sandra #95 96 2103 3263 6917

H

Haas, Robert Bartlett #7107
Haberland, Wolfgang #3346 3349 4036
Habs, Gail J. #1806
Hachey, Paul A. #99 1129 1189
Hack, Gary #7728
Hadlock, Wendell S. #3561 3571
Haeberlin, Herman #3835
Haeberlin, Herman K. #3799 3801
Haeck, Philippe #1443
Haeffely, Claude #5655
Hagan, Frederick #5676
Haggan, Claire #946
Haggert, Ron #9536
Hahn, Emanuel #735
Haider, Gulzar #7728
Haig-Brown, Roderick L. #4907
Hail, Barbara A. #3751
Haines, Fred S. #307
Halas, John #899 909
Haldenby, E.W. #9032
Hale, Barrie #568 1775 5190 5702 6963 7072
Hale, C.A. #9004
Hale, Horatio #3495
Hale, Katherine #6069 7528 8929
Hall, Cheryl #2455
Hall, Edwin S. #4167 4168
Hall, Frank #3578
Hall, H.U. #3664
Hall, John #5202

Hall, Pauline #7998
Hall, Rod #6540
Hallé, Jacqueline #7927
Halliday, Hugh A. #5156
Hallorhan, Joan #8460
Hallowell, Irving A. #3549
Halpin, Marjorie #3996 4056
Halpin, Marjorie M. #3981 4026 4057 4295
    5268
Hambleton, Josephine #739 1395 5088
Hamel, Gilles #8276
Hamel, Marcel #5689 6885
Hamel-Minh, Louise #258 259
Hamelin, Pierre #4514
Hamilton, Alice #2450 2461
Hamilton, Alice B. #2458
Hamilton, Ross #7531 7533
Hamilton, Terry #955
Hamilton, William B. #7780
Hammock, Virgil #1542 1543 5151 5780 6315
    6316 6317 7326
Hammock, Virgil G. #3013 6914 9111
Hammond, Lois #5685 7127
Hammond, M.O. #8 11 7500
Hancock, Macklin L. #7677
Handforth, Robert #691 692
Handy, Arthur #1835
Hanganu, Anca #7911
Hanks, Carole Estelle #1721
Hanlan, J.F. #2682
Hanley, Gary #7840
Hanna, Debbie #6744
Hanna, Martha #1063
Hannibal, Emmett Ronald #3196
Hannon, Leslie F. #5916
Hapgood, Thelma E. #3711
Hara, Hiroko Sue #4109
Harder, Rolf #9104
Hardie, Betty #9044
Harding, S. #6310
Hardman, J.N. #2025
Hardy, Denys #6232
Hardy, Jean-Pierre #2206 2207 2231 2711
Harff, Illi-Maria #1853 1892 4410
Harkness, A.H. #9429
Harland, Sidney #9046
Harmon, Carole #5707
Harner, Michael J. #3928
Harp, Elmer #4346 4354 4365
Harper, J.Russell #65 66 76 77 80 222 223 226
    236 241 242 252 258 259 400 452 742 965
    966 971 1171 1197 1345 1607 1715 1720
    1727 2110 3137 3222 3572 4615 4903 4922
    4939 5171 5725 5805 5806 5807 5808 5809
    6014 6016 6090 6096 6100 6101 6102 6398
    6725 7536
Harper, Jennifer #5298 5299
Harper, Russell #5870 7018
Harrington, Lyn #5138 5815 8002
Harrington, M.R. #3506
Harrington, Michael #7794
Harrington, Michael F. #7783
Harrington, Michael Francis #2988
Harrington, Richard #3429 7217
Harris, Bess #5727

Harris, James F. #9373
Harris, Kenneth D. #7813
Harris, Lawren #363 364 1995 5721
Harris, Lawren P. #1178
Harris, Lawren S. #204 293 308 429 1744
    1747 3031 5008 5012 5446 5714 5715 5722
    6298
Harris, Lawren Stewart #1754 5716 5723
Harris, Marjorie #75 820 1641 8337
Harris, Pam #6474
Harris, Peter #5516
Harris, Robert #185 2573
Harris, Salmon #5745
Harris, W.F. #2428
Harrison, Alexandra Duncan #5370
Harrison, Allan #384 850 4795
Harrison, Elizabeth #351
Harrison, Julia D. #3759
Harrison, Ted #5750
Harrod, Stanley #917 978
Harry, Isobel #550 1498
Hart, William #5725
Hart, William S. #135 2002 5724
Harte, W.Blackburn #178
Hartmann, Ruth Bains #5054
Harvey, Jean-Charles #2167
Harvie, Eric #9088
Harwood, Elizabeth #7364
Hashey, Mary W. #1125
Hassrick, Royal B. #3680
Hathaway, Thomas #693
Hatton, Beth #8612
Hatton, Warwick #8612
Haufschild, Lutz #1934
Haultain, Arnold #3249
Hawkes, E.W. #4321
Hawkins, Elizabeth M. #4027
Haworth, Colin #1424
Hawthorn, Audrey #3899 3994 3996 4037
    4118 4120 4124 4427 6429 6985
Hawthorn, Harry #6985
Hawthorn, Harry B. #3912 3931
Haxby, W.T. #8514
Hay, Norman #4431 4979
Hay, William #7638
Hayden, Elke #550
Hayden, Michael #570
Hayes, Bartlett H. #358
Hayman, Sasha #5756
Hayward, Victoria #733 2794 5962
Hayworth, Arthur #5778
Hazeland, A. #8517
Hazen, William #5161
Healey, William #3327
Healy, Julia Schmitt #1208
Heaman, Elizabeth #7080
Hearn, John #2127 2141 8526
Hearn, Sông-Rijong #6420
Heath, Terrence #1869 1924 4681 5401 5553
    6066 6286 6691 7063
Hébert, Adrien #1387 5761
Hébert, Anne #6232
Hébert, Bruno #1606 5769 5770
Hébert, François #1541
Hébert, Henri #1383 1388
Hébert, Julien #5765

Hébert, Maurice #8568
Hébert, Philippe #5771
Hedrick, Robert #3012
Heideman, Margaret L. #7190
Heinrich, Theodore A. #5305
Heinrich, Theodore Allen #1830 3141 3190
    3340 4752 4753 4845 4972 5191 5376 5379
    5906 6515 6964 6966 7074
Held, Robert #2455
Heller, Jules #833
Hellman, George S. #5357
Helwig, David #693
Helyar, Frank #8302
Hembroff, Edythe #2034
Hembroff-Schleicher, Edythe #5026 5040
Hemingway, Peter #7746 8079 8088 8122
    8123 8203
Hemmerick, William J. #8906
Hemming, Arthur G. #3532
Hénault, Gilles #1440 1443 1542 1543 1564
    1599 3091 3094 5117 5118 5260 5262 5368
    5424 5586 5593 5889 6651 7094 7424
Hénault, Odile #8347
Henderson, Alice C. #3412
Henderson, Tracey #9135
Henderson, V.L. #9087
Hendry, Jean #3588
Hendy, Sir Philip #5378
Hennessey, Catherine G. #2311 2484 7795
    8540
Henrickson, Martha #5781
Henrickson, Thomas #5781
Henriquez, Richard #7746
Herbert, Walter #590 3253 3259 3262
Herbert, Walter B. #9237
Heriot, J.C.A. #5782
Hersey, Dick #855
Herzogenrath, Wulf #671
Hesry, Charles d' #5877
Heusch, Lucio de #1532
Heviz, Judy #5291
Heyer, Paul #668 1507 7473 7476
Hickman, Deborah #4308
Hickman, James #4140
Hide, Peter #797
Higginson, Jean #5894
Highwater, Jamake #3462 3487 4161
Hildebrandt, Walter #8481 8484
Hill, Beth #3988 3997 4058
Hill, Charles C. #275 502 589 592 608 6658
    7459
Hill, Isabel Louise #7803
Hill, Peter #1834
Hill, Ray #3988
Hill, Richard #3004 4163
Hill, Tom #4136 4155
Hill-Tout, Charles #5361
Hilton, Theodor #871
Himel, Susan #2256 2440 2596
Hinds, Barbara #7338
Hinds, Margery #4271
Hinstin, Jérôme #1562
Hinterreiter, Gilda #6303
Hipwell, Frederick W.W. #4600
Hirabayashi, Joanne #3898

Hirsch, Gilah Yelin #5037
Hirsch, John #5394 5395
Hirsh, John A. #1891
Hirsh, Michael #947
Hitzeroth, Connie #7557
Hix, John #9127 9352
Hlynsky, David #3314
Ho, Rosa #2067 4312 4447 5647
Hoad, L.M. #7861
Hoad, Linda #7703
Hoare, Will #2038
Hobart, Cathy #659 6786
Hobbs, Lily #1894
Hobson, Robert W. #3944
Hochbaum, H.Albert #8920
Hockman, John #8102
Hodge, Frederick Webb #3399 3813 3829
Hodgins, George Sherwood #2913
Hodgins, John George #9384
Hodgson, Alan James #8964
Hodgson, John Evan #174
Hodgson, Tom #5814
Hoe, Ban Seng #8137
Hoet, Jan #690
Hoffman, W.J. #3492
Hoffman, Walter James #4319
Hogarth, Paul #931
Hohn, Hubert #8913
Holbek, Kai #7684
Holbrook, J.H. #9025
Holden, John #9420
Holden, Laura #5978
Holdsworth, D.W. #8082
Holdsworth, Deryck #8551
Holdsworth, Deryck W. #8714
Holdsworth, Deryck William #8730
Holford, William #8981 8989
Holgate, Edwin H. #804 5794
Holland, Clive A. #241 242
Hollingsworth, Fred #7698 9136
Hollingsworth, Fred Thornton #8310 8972
Hollis, K.E. #9027
Holm, Bill #3359 3933 3948 3974 3985 3998
    4129 4130 4169 6985
Holman, H.T. #5103
Holmes, Janet #2411 2421 2484 2928
Holmes, Janet C. #159 5828
Holmes, R. #7236
Holmes, Robert #2961
Holmes, Willard #699 706 2046 4912 7506
Holmes, William H. #3388
Holmgren, Eric J. #4935
Holstein, Jonathan #460 6667
Holt, John #7645
Holton, Mark #2129 5120
Holton, Mark B. #6946 7430
Holtved, Erik #4179
Home, Margaret #1770 2248
Home, Ruth M. #2375
Honey, Terrence W. #8003
Honigmann, John J. #4088 4090 4092
Honour, Hugh #255 256 260
Hood, Bryan #4377
Hood, Hugh #6173
Hood, Robert #5825
Hooff, Sally #7930

Hoog, Armand #5668
Hook, Gail #6000 6778 7281
Hookey, Robert #6081
Hoover, Alan L. #4043 4059
Hoover, Dorothy #4637
Hopkins, Elisabeth Margaret #5830
Hopkins, Lloyd W. #7784
Hopkins, Thomas #4162
Horeis, William R. #5836
Horn, Ed #4459
Horne, Cleeve #9190
Horner, Herbert #9013
Hornjatkevyc, A.J. #2940
Hornyansky, Nicholas #5839
Horsman, Joan #583 3268
Horvath, George N. #2151
Horwood, H.W. #8946
Horwood, J.C.B. #7640
Hoskins, Cathleen #1833
Hotz, Gottfried #3455
Hough, Michael #9396
Hould, Claudette #1656 1659 5094 6241
Houle, Alain #5168
Houle, Robert #3604 4155 5938
Hounsom, Eric #9034
Hounsom, Eric W. #8058
House, Maria Newberry #2024
Housser, F.B. #315 1735 1739
Housser, Frederick B. #309
Housser, Yvonne McKague #365
Houston, Alma #3345 4299 4460
Houston, C. Stuart #5825 5826 5827
Houston, James #4186 4211 4235 4267 4299
    4423 4450 4460 4532 5374
Houston, James A. #4183 4383 4384 4386
    4388 4452 4462 4470 4471
Howard, A.H. #977 1702
Howard, Constance #2793
Howard, J. #8007
Howard, James H. #3483 3683 3694 3699
    3747
Howard, John G. #8377
Howard, Sidney H. #4506
Howarth, Glen #6901 6902
Howarth, Thomas #7699 8305 8396 9396
    9457 9502
Howay, F.W. #3800
Howell, David J. #981
Hubbard, R.H. #67 68 106 217 407 411 462
    536 1330 1331 1336 1348 1409 1593 1674
    1747 1912 1992 3035 3038 3041 3049 3227
    3234 5272 6447 7362 7463 7701 8036 8158
Hubbard, Robert H. #249 250 5271 7724 8754
Hubbard, Robert Hamilton #57 60 61 85 126
    221 230 7671 7687 7978 8755 8756
Hudson, Andrew #536 644 1425 1753 1807
    1934 5857
Huet, Bernard #8999
Hughes, Jeanne #2261 2735
Hughes, Kenneth #4635 6942 7328
Hughes, Kenneth J. #4634
Hughes, Kenneth James #4636 5109
Hughes, Lynn #5862
Hugo-Brunt, Michael #7814 9374
Hugolin, R.P. #5503

Huguenin, Madeleine #6155
Hulbert, M.Allen #2090
Hultkrantz, Åke #3725
Hulton, P.H. #228 229 7553
Hume, Andrew #7037
Hume, Anne #9043
Hume, Christopher #717 6648
Hume, R.H. #3045
Hume, R.M. #4399
Hume, Robert M. #1995
Hummel, Charles F. #2481
Humphrey, Jack #1172
Humphrey, Jack Weldon #5866
Humphrey, Ruth #5021
Humphreys, B.A. #8047
Humphreys, Barbara #159
Humphreys, Barbara A. #7719 7727 8008
    8012
Humphries, J.W. #5490
Humphrys, Ruth #7196
Hunchberger, Michael #8064
Hunkin, Harry Preston #1777
Hunt, George #3768
Hunt, J.Doris #4933
Hunter, A.F. #3501
Hunter, E.R. #3031 6293 6366 6381
Hunter, E.Robert #6368
Hunter, Edmund Robert #6382
Hunter, Jacqueline #3313
Hunter, Robert #6051
Huntington, Chris #6720
Hupman, Odessa Lenora #9522
Hurdalek, Marta H. #7428
Hurlich, Susan Marilyn #4245
Hussey, Christopher #6484
Hutchings, Charles #4963
Hutchings, Charles Lee #5687 7594
Hutchings, Patrick #6600
Hutchings, Patrick A.E. #5144
Hutchison, Gail #3004
Hutchison, Rosemary #2484
Huyda, R. #5802
Huyda, Richard #1675 5803 6161
Huyda, Richard J. #1029 1048 5804
Huyghe, René #9139
Hyde, Laurence #806 811 5895
Hymas, Alison #2471 2619 9108 9374
Hynes, James #906

I

Ibbotson, Anthony #4503 7161
Iberville-Moreau, Luc d' #1294 4477 4479
    6231 7400 7915 7916 8617 8618
Iglauer, Edith #4400 8363
Ignatieff, Helen #2638 2656
Ignatieff, Helena #2641
Ihrig, Bob #7448
Iliff, Barbara #4041
Iliu, Joseph #8229
Imredy, Peggy #2026
Ingles, Ernest B. #7730 8740
Inglis, Stephen #3060 7314

Ingolfsrud, Elizabeth #2473 2554 2555 2557 2560 2562 2566 2574 2579 2581
Ingram, David #6677
Ingram, George C. #8456
Ingram, William H. #192
Inkel, Henriette #2213
Innis, Mary Quayle #7210
Inverarity, Robert Bruce #3869 3871 3975
Ionesco, Eugène #5899
Iredale, Randle #8201
Ireland, Willard E. #1995
Ironside, J.A. Sybesma #1872
Irvine, Barbara #2317
Irving, Jean #8064
Irwin, David #220
Isaacs, Av #490 4236
Isaacs, Avrom #5654 6109
Isler, Ariane de Jongh #7917
Isola, Mia #5875
Isserkut, Madeleine #4450
Italiaander, Rolf #6452
Izumi, K. #9029

J

J.D. #8315
J.M.D. #9495
J.R. #8315
J.S. #44
Jack, David Russell #915 7167
Jackman, M.R. #9454
Jacknis, Ira S. #3985
Jackson, A.Y. #40 289 370 1076 1087 1098 3210 4600 5124 5720 5795 5907 5908 5911 5912 5913 5916 5918 6297 6300 6364 6626 7054 7363 7463 7614
Jackson, Anthony #7677 7731 7732 7746 7748 8525 8987 9300
Jackson, Don #8247
Jackson, Henry Alexander Carmichael #5927 5928
Jackson, Marion E. #4500
Jackson, Naomi #5929
Jackson, Richard #5676
Jacob, Arthur #6201
Jacob, Fred #844 845
Jacob, Fred R. #7
Jacobsen, Johan Adrian #3762
Jacques, Lucien #9092
Jacquin, Philippe #276
Jaenen, C.J. #234 235
Jagaku, Bunsho #6450
James, Geoffrey #635 636 1007 7308 7329 8358
James, George Wharton #3446
James, John W. #7068
James, William C. #5102
Jamieson, Jack #2405 2449 2642 8664
Jamieson, Walter #7773
Janes, Gordon #2149
Jannasch, Niels W. #1201
Janneau, Guillaume #2529
Jaque, Louis #4642 5414

Jarvis, Alan #453 461 541 570 754 868 1846 3223 5635 5637 6552 6556 6774 8231
Jarvis, Harold #2290
Jarvis, Kenneth #9010
Jasmin, André #1267 1430 4808
Jasmin, Claude #1479 2198 5532 6167
Jauvin, Sylvie #1560
Jaycocks, T.G. #5950
Jean, Jocelyn #1532
Jean, Suzanne #8613
Jeanneret, Marsh #919
Jefferys, C.W. #28
Jefferys, Charles W. #310 2915 3135 7058 7812
Jekyll, Robert #2455
Jenness, Diamond #3671 4084 4176 4177 4322
Jennings, Jesse D. #3375
Jensen, Robert #9036 9349
Jensen, Vickie #2052
Jenson, L.B. #7816 7827
Jérôme, André #4836
Jessiman, R. #9502
Jobidon, Gilles #1545 6419
Johannesen, S.K. #2570
Johannesen, Stanley #2485
Johns, Robert #1500
Johns, Ted #1808
Johnson, Alice M. #5835 7001
Johnson, Charlotte Buel #3215
Johnson, David #2940
Johnson, E.W. #7214
Johnson, Elden #3375
Johnson, Ellen H. #7598
Johnson, F. #8147
Johnson, F.Henry #3150 3155
Johnson, Frederick #3540 3544 3556
Johnson, Linda #2087
Johnson, M.R. #8256
Johnson, Michael #3717
Johnson, Michael G. #3712 3729
Johnson, Mike #3449 3713
Johnson, Nick #3726 5234 5383 5386 6560 6707
Johnson, Peter #7496
Johnson, Russell #9104
Johnson, Terence #5969
Johnson, W.McAllister #3319 3320
Johnston, E.F.B. #194 205 1703 4571 4937
Johnston, George #7152 7153 7155
Johnston, Jill #6258
Johnston, William R. #233 243 6628
Johnston, William R.M. #2842 6625
Johnstone, Ken #6299
Jonaitis, Aldona #4028 4041 4045 4060 4061
Jonassaint, Jean #1552
Jones, A.R.C. #4412
Jones, Bill #564 7257
Jones, Catherine #6657
Jones, E.Alfred #2627
Jones, Edward #8999
Jones, Elizabeth #7136
Jones, Howard #8657
Jones, Howard M. #9401
Jones, Hugh G. #16 7660 8298

Jones, Joan Megan #3953 4009
Jones, Laura #1049 5554
Jones, P.M. #9314
Jones, S. #2443
Jones, T.E.H. #3714
Jones, Tim Edward Hodgson #3760
Jones, Volney H. #3547
Jonescu-Lisitza, Sylvia #5671
Jongh, Elly de #8131
Jongué, Serge #5443 5664
Jordan, Katharine A. #127
Jordan, William E. #6491
Joris-Zavala, Huguette #276
Josephy, Alvin M. #7009
Joubert, Suzanne #7380
Jouvancourt, Hugues de #5224 5477 5482 5546 5547 5785 6098 6103 6998 7296 7297 7300
Jowitt, Deborah #550
Joyal, Serge #1287 9252
Joyce, T.A. #3805
Joyner, Brooks #4528 5798 5847
Joyner, Geoff #7007
Joyner, Geoffrey #116
Joyner, J.Brooks #1958 6703
Joynes, Jennifer R. #7678
Judah-Daniel, Catherine #5980
Judd, N.M. #3412
Julien, Henri #5981
Julien, Pierre-André #2225
Juneau, André #234 235 249 250 6095 6960
Juneja, Mohan #6033
Junius, Marcel #7870
Jury, Wilfred #8066
Jutras, Albert #372
Jutras, V.P. #2811

K

K.H.H. #9207
Kaellgren, C.Peter #2353 2433 2484
Kagis, Indra #6471
Kahn, Gustave #9261
Kahn, Louis #8040
Kaiser, Bob #5814
Kalavinka, Mia #554 6392
Kallmann, Gerhard #8212
Kalman, Harold #7713 7762 7774 7775 8166 8168 8393 8769 8910 8917 9147 9148 9409 9512
Kalman, Harold D. #8906 9291
Kane, Paul #3386 6002 6011
Kangas, Matthew #2072
Kant, Joanita #3733
Kantaroff, Maryon #144 596 6019
Kapches, Mima #3644
Kardos, Ladislas #6020
Karel, David #4592
Karpiscak, Adeline Lee #6179
Karschti, Mikel #2354
Karsh, Yousuf #486 487 6023 6024 6025 6026 6027 6028 6031 6034 6035

Kasadluak, Paulosie #4267
Kästner, Erich #7428
Kattan, Naïm #529 2998 6448 7767
Katz, John Stuart #664
Katzenberg, Dena S. #4015
Kaufmann, C.N. #4010
Kaufmann, Carole Natalie #3958
Kay, Walter #9439
Keane, Patrick #3064
Keate, Stuart #6722
Keeble, Corey #2461
Keeble, K.Corey #2458
Keen, Dorothy B. #2845 2846
Keenleyside, P.M. #8307 8308 9032
Kehlmann, Robert #2455
Kehoe, Alice B. #3687 3688 3748
Kehoe, Thomas F. #3688 3708 3748
Keirstead, James Lorimer #6037
Keith, Arthur G. #9548
Keith, F.S. #7641
Keithahn, E.L. #3916 3917
Keithahn, Edward L. #3909
Kelly, Gemey #6730
Kelly, Terry #6689
Kelman, Ralf #6038
Kembar, Norah #6527
Kemble, Roger #8079 8146 8169 8379
Kemp, Samuel James #3945
Kendal, Elaine #8130
Kennedy, Anthony A. #8766
Kennedy, D.H. #2422
Kennedy, Don #2415
Kennedy, Garry Neill #550 575 703
Kennedy, Howard #8037
Kennedy, Jan #8014
Kennedy, John F. #3427
Kennedy, Sybil #6046
Kennedy, Warnett #2611 7675 8158 9503
Kenney, G.I. #4226
Kenney, James F. #3023
Kent, H.Harold #9175
Kent, Norman #6384
Keppler, Joseph #3541
Kernighan, R.K. #7954
Kerr, A. #8154
Kerr, Alastair #9134
Kerr, Alastair W. #8151 8179
Kerr, Don #9491
Kerr, Estelle #206
Kerr, Estelle M. #800
Kerr, Illingworth #4620 6049
Kerr, Illingworth H. #6047 6048
Kerr, Judith LeBaron #8628
Kerr, R. #3839
Kerr, Robert #4091
Kert, Monroe #9314
Ketcheson, Blair #2940
Kettle, H.G. #331 2092 2466
Kettle, John #3056 7677 7681 8184 8302 8403
   8971 8987 9241 9373
Kettle, Rik #570
Kew, D. #3989
Kew, Michael #4046
Key, A.F. #1846 1945 9098
Key, Archie F. #3043 3055 3240
Key, Sydney #5720

Key, Sydney J. #3136
Keyser, Barbara #1223
Keziere, Russell #2064 3310 5851 6417 7607
   7629
Khurana, J.S. #9292
Kidd, Kenneth E. #3583 6009 6010
Kidd, Martha Ann #8021
Kieran, Michael R. #652
Kikauka, Talivaldis #475
Kilbourn, Elizabeth #75 95 96 449 450 817
   3219 6107 7407
Kilbourn, William #75 444 2577 7985 8231
   9536
Killan, Gerald #8458
Kincaid, Sheila #2013 2048
King, Arden R. #3375
King, Elizabeth #3469
King, J.C.H. #3470 4038 4062 4064
King, John D. #3593
King, John D.H. #1921
King, Jonathan #9395 9401
King, Jonathan C.H. #4048
King, Richard #4174
Kingsmill, Bob #2391
Kingwatsiak, Iyola #4460
Kinietz, Vernon #3417
Kinton, Ada Florence #6053
Kiopini, Christian #1532 6054
Kirby, William #1809 1873 2060 4981 4982
Kirkconnell, Watson #8533
Kirkwood, Hilda #6336
Kirstein, Lincoln #5141 5150
Kissel, Mary L. #3412
Kissell, Mary Lois #3788 3796 3826 3830
Kiyooka, Roy #536 6055 6060
Klaiman, Ester #2372
Klassen, Henry C. #8121
Klein, Jack #8196
Klepac, Walter #1817 4774 5628 6433 6949
   6951
Kleyn, R. #8147
Klinkhoff, Walter #3247 6307
Klippenstein, Lawrence #8715
Klitina, E.N. #4302
Kluyver-Cluysenaer, Margreet #545
Klymasz, Robert #2117
Klymasz, Robert B. #961 2593
Knell, G.E. #5261
Knott, Leonard L. #8510
Knowles, Valerie #2596
Knowlton, Reynold #9134
Kobayashi, Terry #2140
Kobayashi, Teruko #1681 5817 5840
Koch, Ronald P. #3739
Kodar, Tiit #3313
Koeninger, Kay #3378
Koerner, Walter C. #3994
Koerte, Arnold #8733
Kohler, Arnold #7213
Kolbenhier, Eric #2124
Kollar, Kathryn L. #5511 8610
Kolonel, Valerie #1158
Koltun, L.A. #2580
Koltun, Lilly #1061 1725 2031 7744
Komendant, August E. #8585
Komisar, Elizabeth #5625

Kon, Irene #1410 7480
Köngäs-Maranda, Elli #967
Konody, P.G. #1073 1074
Koolhaas, Rem #8364
Korner, John #6077 7179
Korot, Beryl #616
Kostka, V.J. #8303
Kostyniuk, Ron #6080
Kotin, David B. #935
Kozar, Andrew J. #6486
Kraglund, John #95 96
Kramer, Burton #895
Kramer, Hilton #4977
Kraulis, J.A. #1062
Krause, Aurel #3902
Krause, Eric R. #8427
Krickeberg, Walter #3421
Krieber, Johann #1597
Kritzwiser, Kay #1013 3061 3376 4564 5637
   6787
Kroeber, A.L. #3651
Kroeber, Alfred L. #3810
Krysinsky, Wladimir #6530
Kuh, Hans #882
Kuhn, Bob #6501
Kuhns, William #4853
Kupper, Hans Jüng #7263
Kuprowsky, Helena #2455
Kurath, Gertrude Prokosch #3598
Kurelek, Jean #6115
Kurelek, William #6109 6110 6113 6115 6116
Kuspit, Donald B. #1831
Kutcher, Stanley Paul #4676
Kuthan, George #6117
Kuwabara, Bruce #8071 8663
Kuziw, Irene #8102
Kuzyk, E.Jane #4170
Kuzyk, Jane #6539
Kwasny, Barbara #1959
Kyle, Fergus #1710

L

L'Allier, Jean-Paul #3280
L'Allier, Pierre #2690
L'Archevêque-Duguay, Jeanne #5318
L'Heureux, Jean #4094
La Grenade, Monique #2855 2868
La Grenade-Meunier, Monique #9057
La Palme, Robert #408 949 6120
LaBarge, Dorothy #4269
Labatut, Jean #7971
Labelle, Marie-Dominique #7493
Labelle, Ronald #1629
Laberge, Albert #1382 1391 4658 6143
Laberge, André #7897 8861 8890 8893
Laberge, Craig #2758
Laberge, Marie #7118
Labrecque, Cyrille #8791
Lacelle, Claudette #8449
Lacelle, Nicole #1285
Lachance, André #7884
Lackey, Thomas #2763

Lacombe, C. #6199
Lacombe, Claude #5340
Lacombe, Marthe #269 270 8619
Lacroix, Laurier #153 938 1294 1558 3122
    3123 3233 3321 3322 5310 6204 6208 6209
    6210 7138 7265 8814
Lacroix, Richard #1430 1643
LaFarge, Oliver #3412
Lafleur, Claude #1539
Laforest, Jean #3088
Laforet, Andrea #4063
Laforge, Christiane #6133
Laframboise, Yves #7875 7877 7891 8605
    8606 8607
Lafrance, Marc #7908 8449
Lafrenière, Michel #2201
Laguna, Frederica de #3366 3976 4083 4329
Lahaie, Rose #2890
Lahaise, Robert #7932
Lahoud, Pierre #9255
Lai, Chuen-Yan David #8181
Laidlaw, G.E. #3393
Laidlaw, George E. #3504
Laing, G.Blair #1686
Lajoie, Noël #6199
Lakwete, Angela #3469
Laliberté, Alfred #1580 6145
Lalonde, Jean-Louis #8204 8215 8265 8989
Lamanna, Carmen #594 1811
Lamarche, Gustave #1378
Lamarche, Hélène #1294
Lamarche, Lise #695 5341 7452 7476
Lamarche-Ouellet, Hélène #5311 5994
Lamarre, Denis #8766 9420
Lamb, Frank W. #3447
Lamb, H.Mortimer #208 210 283 982 1982
    7352 7590
Lamb, Harold Mortimer #978
Lamb, Kaye #9088
Lamb, Molly #4761
Lambart, Helen #2283
Lambart, Helen H. #2291 2298 2299 2321
    2322
Lambert, Elaine #2256 2440
Lambert, Margaret Anne May #2856
Lambert, Phyllis #7749 7921 7922 7924 7928
Lambert, Richard Stanton #36
Lamberton, Bob #7241
Lambton, Gwen #3004
Lamonde, Pierre #2225
Lamontagne, J.-G. #2175
Lamontagne, Laurence #6148
Lamontagne, Léopold #1487
Lamontagne, Sophie-Laurence #1298 5319
    6149
Lamothe, Raymonde #1285
Lamoureux, Johanne #718 5584
Lamy, Jean-Paul #6172
Lamy, Laurent #539 540 571 832 1264 1271
    1491 1540 1542 1543 1559 1630 1642 2199
    2226 2533 3312 5424 5539 5887 6137 6187
    6713 7026 7146 7436 9105
Lamy, Suzanne #2199
Lanctôt, Gustave #1325 7521

Landon, Fred #9442
Landry, Armour #5665
Landry, Guy #2879
Landry-Gauthier, Raymonde #4591
Landsberg, Michele #7581
Lane, Barbara S. #3882
Lane, Kimbers #8900
Lanford, Benson L. #3635
Lang, Andrea #4502 5391 5759 6580
Lang, George #2573
Langdale, Cecily #6630
Langdon, John #234 235 249 250 2628 2643
    2645
Langdon, John E. #2110 2633 2635 2676 2931
Langer, Monika #7449
Langford, J.A. #8308
Langford, Martha #4567
Langlois, Jacques #2344
Langlois, Jean #1455
Langlois, William J. #4025 7587
Langmead, L.S. #9047 9048
Langton, W.A. #7591 7955 8922 9439
Lank, David #6501
Lank, David M. #6862
Lanken, Dane #7914
Lanken, Paul #9537
Lansdale, Nelson #1673
Lansdowne, J.Fenwick #6906
Lantis, Margaret #4180
Lapalice, O. #6123
LaPalme, Michel #7481
Lapalme, Pierre #1457
Laperrière, Guy #1295
Lapierre, Diane #7927
Laplante, Robert #4832
Lapointe, Claude #6130
Lapointe, Frank #6169
Lapointe, Paul-Marie #1443
Lapointe, Pierre-Louis #8615
Large, Richard Geddes #3883
Larisey, Peter #5728 5729
Larivière-Derome, Céline #3005
Larmour, W.T. #3350 4188 4210 4213 4246
    4402 4414 6743
Larmour, William T. #4200
Laroche, Jacques #8868
Larocque, Yves-M. #1115
Larose, Gilles #9515
Larose, Jean #4669
Larsen, Helge #4355 4374
Larue-Langlois, Jacques #2236 2995
Lash, Mary Ann #6984 7625
Lasnier, Michelle #5614
Lasnier, Rina #4877 5254
Lasserre, Fred #8141 8142 8157 8246 8247
    8248 8380 9080 9390
Latouche, Daniel #2225
Latour, Thérèse #1276 2737 2937
Lauder, Brian #5731
Laurette, Condon #3062 7087
Laurette, Patrick C. #133
Laurette, Patrick Condon #1136 1221 5654
    6355 6967 7135
Laurin, Clément #5609

Laurin, François #4822 4825 5619 6136 6583
    7117
Laurin, Serge #1494
Laurion, Gaston #5668
Lavallée, Gérard #1435 1592 1614 3089 3090
Lavell, W.S. #8455
Lavoie, Elzéar #3323
Lavoie, Francine #9255
Lavoie, Paul L. #2912
Lavoie, Raymond #685
Lawrence, Richard #7178
Lawson, Cecil C.P. #2848
Lawson, Harold #8740 9283
Lawson, Matthew B.M. #8067
Lax, Gary #6747
Lazore, Melissa #4155 7624
Lazosky, Daniel #9319
Le Bihan, René #5163 6190
Le Bordais, D.M. #5679
Le Franc, Marie #4877
Le Grand, Albert #4722
Le Gris, Françoise #1270 4608 4820
Le Moine, Roger #4870 4871
Le Moyne, Jean #95 96
Le Moyne de Morgues, Jacques #276
Le Roy, Léo #5343
Le Vallée, Thérèse #4219
Leadbetter, Dorothy #3876
Lean, Cheryl #5156
Leaning, John #8042 8964 9480 9481
Learoyd, Eileen #5642 6106 6740 6784 6785
    6859
LeBaron, Anna Van Buskirk #8628
Lebel, Bertrand #1446
Lebensold, Fred #8197 9092 9093
Leber, Germain #5180
Lebeuf, Jean Claude #8723 8724
Leblanc, Louise #6168
Leblanc, Pierre #1469
LeBlanc, Yvon #1178 7086
Leblond, Jean-Claude #1657 3275 5704 5942
LeBourdais, D.M. #5678
LeBreton, Clarence #7805
Lebrun, Roland #857
Lecocq, Thelma #6022
Lecoutey, André #1404 1406 1407 6199
Leduc, Denis #2615 2616
Leduc, Fernand #1396 1413 1449 6193 6194
    6199
Leduc, Maurice #2864
Leduc, Ozias #6199
Leduc, Pierre #1343
Lee, Abel #118
Lee, David #8446 8456 8466 8467
Lee, David E. #8447
Lee, Douglas H. #7684 8301
Lee, Molly #4309
Lee, Roger #1850
Lee, Thomas R. #7056 7057
Lee-Nova, Gary #550 4959 6898 7144
Lee-Whiting, Brenda #1723 2582
Leechman, Douglas #863 3415 3418 3847
    3893 4385 8474 9226

Lefeaux, Stuart S. #9081
Lefebvre, Germain #824 1542 1543 1631 3115
  4998 5789 6816 6817 6818 6819 6868 7341
Lefebvre, Jean-Charles #8633
Lefebvre, Jean-Jacques #3076
Lefolii, Ken #75
Lefrançois, Alexis #5843
Légaré, Jean-Pierre #6577
Legault, Guy R. #9550
Legault, Normand #2879
Legendre, Napoléon #1307
Legendre, Odette #6145 6146 6151
Legendre, Rose-Marie #3018
Léger, Francine #1285
Léger, Jules #5247 8755 8756
Léger, Oliva #2836
Léger, Raymond-Marie #9105
Leggat, Portia #7933
Legrand, Paul #8819 9078
Lehmann, Henry #7282
Lehr, John #8713
Lehr, John C. #8085 8090 8127 8704 8709
  8710
Lehrer, Ruth Fine #613
Lehrman, Jonas #8104 8106 8107 8162 8281
  8908 9117 9137 9301 9315
Leider, Philip #2035
Leier, Carolyn #1868
Leitch, Adelaide #2724 3696 5296
Leleu, J.-M. #8788
Leman, Alexander B. #9046 9472
Lemay, Nicole #6525
LeMay, T.D. #7962
Lemerise, Suzanne #1273 1514 3010
Lemieux, Ernest #1406
Lemieux, Irénée #1506
Lemieux, Jean-Paul #1386 1399 1411 6239
Lemieux, Louis #3051
Lemire, Maurice #3324
Lemire, Robert #7750 7921 7928 7933
Lemire, Suzanne #5888
Lemoine, James MacPherson #1305 1306
  1309
LeMoyne, Roy-E. #8287
Lenssen, Barbera G. #3485
Léonidoff, Georges #8595
Léonidoff, Georges-Pierre #8629
Leonoff, Cyril Edel #8081
Leopold, Charles S. #9339
Lepage, Jacques #7098
LeRoy, Hugh #4936
Lesage, Jules S. #1242
Lesage, Pierre #1501
Leslie, Richard #7031
Leslie, Thomas W. #8951
Lessard, Denis #2879
Lessard, Michel #1274 2202 2203 2208 2219
  2222 2924 8591 8592 8600
Lessard, Pierre #130
Lesser, Gloria #3325
Lesser, Howard #9374
Lester, Marie #3142
Letocha, Louise #1294 1470 1564 3010 4849
  6521 6534
Létourneau, Michel #8854

Leung, F. #2949 2950
Leung, Felicity L. #9259
Lever, Anthony #160
Levesque, Albert #1380
Lévesque, Carole #3631
Lévesque, Eugénie #8870
Lévêsque, Jean-Jacques #7395
Levesque, Jocelyne #1801
Lévesque, Laurentin #4717 7209
Lévesque, René #3599
Lévi-Strauss, Claude #3860 3905 3922 6985
Levin, Ray #900
Levine, Catherine #6267
Levine, Les #604 1507 6259 6263 6265 6268
  6269 6270 6273
Lévy, Bernard #1492 1521 1542 1543 1632
  1658 4704 4737 4745 5242 5415 5558
Lewenstein, Eileen #2455 2940
Lewin, Peter K. #4143
Lewis, Brian W. #4409
Lewis, Brian Wyndham #4199
Lewis, Glenn #2070 2073 6276
Lewis, T.H. #3393
Lewis, Wyndham #373
Lhalungpa, Lobsang Phuntshok #559
Licht, Jennifer #7059
Liebich, C.P. #9183
Light, Douglas W. #3723
Lightbody, Charles W. #5885
Lightfoot, Gordon #7515
Lilly, Weil #4223
Lin, Chien-Shih #7601
Lindberg, E.Theodore #3019
Lindberg, Ted #667 2074 2075 5417 6739
  6842 6903 6995 7187 9129
Lindblom, Gerhard #3844
Lindgren, Charlotte #4310
Lindgren, Edward #4310 7698
Lindsay, Charles S. #8428 8429
Lindsay, Doreen #936
Lindsay, Ian G. #4435
Lindsay, Jim #6291
Lingwood, Rex #2936
Linker, Kate #7419
Lintula, Douglas #9104 9222
Lipman, Louise #694
Lipman, Marci #694
Lippard, Lucy R. #4629
Lippel, Leon #4432
Lipton, Barbara #4272
Liscombe, R.W. #8401
Lismer, Arthur #9 15 311 360 361 370 1077
  1087 1711 2965 2966 2968 2971 2974 2975
  2981 2984 2985 2987 3132 5914 6292 7353
  7354 7358 7360 7363 7463
Lismer, Marjorie #3552
Lister, Ardele #564 7252 7582
Lister, Beverley-Ann #4495
Little, C.H. #1106
Little, R.P. #7361
Little, Robert #2484
Little, William T. #7365
Littman, Sol #3312
Litvack, Isaiah A. #2620
Livermore, J.Daniel #8935 8936

Livingston, Myra C. #429
Livingston, Peggy #6685
Livingston, Peggy Ellis #6163
Lobb, Allan #4029
Lobchuk, Bill #632
Locher, Gottfried W. #3840
Lochhead, Douglas #935 5709 6318
Lochnan, Katharine A. #2373
Lochnan, Katharine Jordan #3061
Lock, Carolyn #2749
Locke, Don #3623
Locke, George H. #9040
Locke, John W. #7250
Long, Don #5708
Long, Jack #7746 8088
Long, John #8518
Loomer, L.S. #1128 1173 1179 2648
Lorcini, Gino #6323
Lord, Barry #83 84 113 480 485 516 533 751
  753 821 834 1122 1133 1484 1791 1856 4626
  4747 4749 4908 4909 4916 5430 5431 5893
  6158 6304 6386 6513 7504
Lord, J.Barry #71 819 4195 4611 4613
Lorimer, James #7728
Lorsley, Elizabeth W. #2825
Lortie, Michel #1421
Lotbinière-Harwood, Susanne de #4653
Lotz, Jim #7637
Loubert, Patrick #947
Loudon, Peter #4115
Love, John B. #8254
Lovell, Don #8409
Lowden, James A. #8040
Lower, A.R.M. #398 944
Lowey, M. #5087
Lowey, Mark #5791
Lowie, Robert H. #3653 3684
Lowndes, Joan #550 1871 2049 4623 5520
  6938 7191 7226 7227 7232 7609 7611
Lownsbrough, John #8680
Lowrey, Carol D. #267 1729
Lubell, Cecil #2739
Luca, Earl de #7349
Lucas, Georgina #8610
Lucien, P.Delean #9393
Lucier, Mary #616
Luckyj, Natalie #117 508 509 796 7453
Lucy, Charles L. #3563
Ludlow, Thomas W. #9065
Lugrin, N.de Bertrand #2278
Luik, Asta #9046
Lumsden, Ian G. #103 142 1130 1180 1182
  4498 4765 5462 5871 7221 7517 7518
Lunden, D. #8147
Lundy, Doris #3481 3484
Lundy, Doris Marion #3999
Lussier, Réal #1470
Lutman, John H. #8018
Lutz, Carrie A. #3557 3559
Lyford, Carrie Alberta #3674
Lyle, John #7665
Lyle, John M. #318 7656 8225 8226 8738 9182
  9186 9188
Lyman, John #348 4809 6347 6618
Lyman, Roswell C. #7754

Lynch, Colleen #2765 2767
Lyndon, B.M. #8951
Lyndon, Donlyn #9504
Lynes, Russell #444
Lynn, Elwyn #6752
Lyon, Barry #9378

M

M.J. #8068
Maas, James B. #6110
Mabie, Don #1968
MacAndrew, Barbara #5427 6900 8371
MacBeath, George #1178 7110
MacBeath, George B. #5821
MacBeth, Madge #207
MacCallum, H.R. #1740
MacCallum, James M. #7351
MacCallum, Spencer H. #3959
MacCarthy, Hamilton #727
MacDermot, Anne #6493
Macdonald, Adrian #6791
Macdonald, Albert E. #9236
Macdonald, Colin S. #81
MacDonald, George #4039 4129 4130
MacDonald, George F. #4011 4065 4148
Macdonald, I.S. #7641
MacDonald, J.E.H. #1733 6360 6361 6362
    6371 6372 6373 7350
MacDonald, J.T. #9403
Macdonald, J.W.G. #1841 7463
Macdonald, Jock #429
MacDonald, R.B. #7861
MacDonald, T.R. #5221 7055
MacDonald, Thomas R. #6872
MacDonald, Thoreau #1743 7364
MacDougall, Heather #8016
MacDowall, Cyndra #1833
MacEwan, J.W.Grant #4125
MacFadden, Patrick #7728
Macfarlane, David #161
MacFarlane, Eddy L. #5323
Macfarlane, Nathalie #7314
MacGregor, James G. #3689
MacHardy, Carolyn Wynne #7371
Machell, Margaret #8666
Machell, Margaret S. #8665
MacInnis, Joseph B. #5754
Mack, Joanne M. #3378
MacKay, Alice #298 2165
MacKay, Allan #588 699 7065
Mackay, Donald #1202
Mackay, Donald C. #258 259 2632 2639 2640
    2646
MacKay, J.Harold #978
Mackay, James #370 2932
MacKeeman, Karl #1209 1210 1213 1214 3072
    5428 5464 6523 6663 7088 7134 7199
MacKenzie, A.Stanley #9408
MacKenzie, D. #1134
Mackenzie, Lois #8672
MacKenzie, Ruth #2498
Mackie, Joan #8393

MacKinnon, Charles #258 259
MacKinnon, Frank #5738 9088
MacKinnon, Joan #2563 2567
Macklem, Michael #693
Mackley, Florence MacDonald #2728
Mackley, M.Florence #2732
MacLachlan, Mary E. #5507
MacLachlan, Mary Evans #5980
MacLaren, George #1198 1200 2307 2308
    2417 2489 2493 2494 2496 2497 2499 3624
    6542
MacLaughlin, Marjorie #2750
Maclellan, David #5102
MacLennan, Hugh #257 4779
Maclennan, Ian #8040 8198 8303 8304 8518
Maclennan, Ian R. #8212
Macleod, Malcolm Donald #8119
MacLeod, Margaret Arnett #7003
MacLeod, Pegi Nicol #6396
Maclure, John #6369
Maclure, S. #8682
MacMillan, C. #277
Macmillan, Duncan #4976
MacMillan, Hugh #3148
Macnab, F.J. #9298
MacNair, Peter #4043
MacNair, Peter L. #4132
MacNeish, Richard S. #3564
MacNutt, W.Stewart #945 1178
MacPherson, Dorothy #4339
Macpherson, Duncan #867
Macpherson, Ken #8006
Macpherson, Mary-Etta #2465
MacRae, Marion #8654 8662 8904
MacSymon, John #7458
MacTavish, Newton #5 13 20 196 285 799
    3205 5214 6339 7109
MacWilliam, David #6045 7507
Madill, H.H. #8245 8248 8249 8254 8737
Madill, Shirley #1908
Magee, Phoebe Anne #8550
Magidson, Debbie #7579 7580
Magidson, Debby #5075
Magnan, Hormidas #1229
Magnan, Hormisdas #5876 6243
Magnan, Myriam #6134 6612
Magrini, Alex #685
Maheux, Arthur #4695
Mahon, Lilette #5014
Mailhot, Carl #1275
Maillard, Charles #2972 2973
Mails, Thomas E. #3727
Main, Kenneth de #9104
Maitland, Leslie #2787 8936
Major-Frégeau, Madeleine #269 270 4647
    7522
Makler, Anita C. #8997
Malcolmson, Harry #1756
Malcolmson, Harry A. #5773
Maley, A.Roy #1891
Malin, Edward #3918 4030
Malkin, Peter #7228 7229 7230 7231
Mallery, Garrick #3390 3392
Mallory, Enid Swerdfeger #3581 3589
Mallory, Gordon #3581

Mandel, Eli #1937 5732
Mandelbaum, David G. #3742
Mandolini, Francesco #6130
Manly, Charles M. #2964
Manning, John #7204
Manning, Peter #8285
Mannion, John J. #8523
Manny, Louise #8390
Manson-Smith, Pamela #3313
Mantle, William #895
Maranda, Lynn #6987
Marani, F.H. #9191 9337
Marceau, Marcel #5637
Marchand #5988
Marchand, Clément #5313 5318
Marchand, Gilles #8307
Marchant, A.Cyril #8222 9309
Marcotte, Gilles #95 96
Marino, Carol #1050
Marion, Francine #5797
Mark, Jimmy Innaarulik #4522
Markham, S.F. #3024
Markle, Jack #1798
Markle, Sam #1798
Markson, Jerome #8065 8191 8387
Marquis, Huguette #1274 2202 2203 2208
    2219 2924 8591 8592
Marquis, Maurice #2194 2209
Marquis, T.G. #7573
Marriott, Adelaide #2118
Marriott, Alice #3456
Marsan, Jean-Claude #7746 7893 7912 7918
    7923 7929 7934 8601 9537
Marsh, Winifred Petchey #4265
Marshall, Ingeborg #3627
Marshall, W.Neil #1803
Marteau, Robert #1541 5597 7397
Martel, Richard #1299 3016
Martell, James Stuart #8750
Martijn, Charles A. #1162 4205 4401
Martin, André #6492 6495 6763
Martin, C. #6929
Martin, Constance #8138
Martin, Denis #3124
Martin, J.Edward #6793 6794 9545
Martin, J.L. #3071
Martin, James Edward #9538
Martin, Lévis #5318
Martin, Louis #2534
Martin, Louise #856
Martin, Margaret Burns #7829
Martin, Michel #1364
Martin, Paul-Louis #2343 2535 2536 2700
Martin, Peter #4466
Martin, Ron #661 703
Martin, Thérèse #4835
Martin, Thomas Mower #6435 6436 6437
Martin-Dubost, Paul #7393
Martin-Méry, Gilberte #63
Martinsen, Hanna E.H. #1788
Martirano, Matthew #2448
Martyn, Lucy Booth #8077 8676
Mary-Rousselière, Guy #4356 4357
Maryon, John #9035
Mason, Bas #7999
Mason, Ellsworth #9052

Mason, J.Alden #4089 4323
Mason, Otis T. #3328 3389 3394 3777
Massé, Ginette #5568 5669 6534 6767
Massey, Geoffrey #9098
Massey, Hart #2142 7976 8984 9344 9455
Massey, John #687
Massey, Vincent #19 3137 8300 9439 9440
Massicotte, E.-Z. #1569 1572 2161 2162 2657
    2813 2814 2821 2826 2830 2914 4768 4780
    5053 5416 6104 6253 6947 7603 7844 8565
Massicotte, Edouard-Zotique #2522 2810
    2815 2816 2817 2820 8567
Massy, Patricia #2940
Mather, Edith #8620
Mathers, A.S. #7972 8037 8245 8739 9032
    9192 9338
Mathews, Zena Pearlstone #3632 3636 3642
Mathiassen, Therkel #4324 4326
Mathieu, Jacques #2953
Mathieu, Jocelyne #2764 2879
Mato, Dan #1878
Matsubara, Naoko #6450
Matthews, Marion #2147
Matthews, Ross M. #3237
Matthews, T.E. #2603
Mattie, Joan I. #973
Mattie, Wesley C. #969 2593 2804
Mattison, David #2021 2022 2027 4583 6456
Maurault, Olivier #1231 1236 1324 1326 1385
    2444 3081 4867 5215 5407 5603 6199 7267
    7899 7900 8818 8839 9415
Maurer, Evan M. #3468
Mavor, James #1707 4517 5212
Maw, Betty #809
Maw, S.H. #8735
Maxwell, E. #8958
Maxwell, W.S. #323 7665 7955 8242 8958
Mayerovitch, Harry #6454
Mayrand, Pierre #234 235 1598 7703 7711
    7885 8419
Mazer, Les D. #8149 8176 8178
McAnn, Aida #2144
McBurney, Margaret #8014 8678
McCabe, Kate #6715
McCann, Edward #6602
McCann, L.D. #8705
McCarthy, Pearl #381 5606
McCarthy, William #9110
McCaw, Audrey Martin #6245
McClean, John #4967
McClellan, Catherine #4106
McClelland, Alan #3471 3474 3475
McClintock, Walter #3669 3676 3681
McConathy, Dale #585 586 587 1522 3236
    3276 3277 5602 6287 6662 6708 7563 7568
McConnell, David #8470 8471 8472
McConnell, John #905
McCormack, W.N. #726
McCormick, Anne #9044
McCoy, Doris #6277
McCraken, Harold #3426
McCrea, Rosalie Smith #6634
McCullough, Norah #1846 4989
McCurry, H.O. #383
McCutcheon, Sarah #936 8348

McDermott, John Francis #7004
McDonald, Gladys Christena #7077
McDonald, R.H. #8437
McDonald, T.H. #4097
McDougall, Anne #5452 6240 7130 7131
McDougall, Clark #962 1682 6464
McDougall, Harry #8457
McDougall, Margery Hadley #7437
McElroy, Guy #5338
McErvel, Judith #2851
McEvoy, Bernard #1708 1709 1979
McEwen, Jean #1415
McEwen, John #797
McFadden, David #1792 1808
McFaddin, Charles E. #5068
McFarlane, Arthur E. #4516
McGhee, Robert #4368 4373 4375 4378
McGibbon, Pauline #3270
McGill, Jean #6487 6488 6638
McGinnis, J.P.Dicken #8121
McGinnis, Janice Dicken #8128
McGinnis, John A. #8659
McGowan, Nancy #2586 8703
McGrath, Antonia #1160 5820
McGrath, Judy #2955 4560 6474
McGreevy, Susan Brown #3485
McIlwraith, Thomas F. #3874
McInnes, G.Campbell #214 332 333 1741
    3025
McInnes, Graham #342 343 345 374 392 415
    4568 5867
McInnes, Graham Campbell #29 45 340
McInnes-Hayman, Sasha #719
McIntyre, John #2486 2571 8352
McIntyre, Maureen #8636
McIntyre, W.John #2575 8351
McIntyre, William John #2564
McJohnston, Clifford #978
McKaskell, Robert #5384
McKay, Alexander G. #7991
McKay, Arthur #1935
McKay, Elsie #8909
McKee, Harley J. #7703
McKellar, James #7728
McKendry, Ruth #2805 2806
McKennan, Robert A. #4095 4096
McKenney, Thomas L. #3488
McKenzie, Karen #3175 3313
McKenzie, R.Tait #6485
McKibbon, Millie #669 1051 1864 4584
McKibbon, Millie Richardson #1033 1901
McKinnon, Sarah M. #8614
McLachlan, R.W. #724
McLaren, Carol Sheehan #4019
McLaren, Norman #6496
McLaren, Walter W. #337
McLean, Carol #2936
McLean, Eric #2110 2532 4553 7919
McLean, J.S. #3228
McLean, R.C. #7641
McLean, Robert Craik #8092
McLean, S. #8007
McLean, Terry #6502
McLeish, John A.B. #6301
McLennan, Gordon #5065

McLeod, Carol #6351
McLeod, Carroll #4932
McLuhan, Elizabeth #4151 4155 4156
McLuhan, Marshall #513 4341
McMahon, Paul #4566
McMann, Evelyn de R. #162
McMann, Robert #9536
McMaster, Susan #1020
McMillan, David #1030 1904
McMonies, J. #7954
McMordie, Michael #7728 7730 7746 7751
    8999
McMullen, William B. #1957
McMurray, A.Lynn #2251
McMurray, Allan Lynn #2565
McNairn, Ian #1995 1997 5725 6020
McNaught, Carlton #846
McNeill, Robin #4561 6877
McPherson, Hugo #82 550 747 1750 1757
    3220 4682 5535 6699 7070 7116 7340 7576
    7691 7692
McQuaig, D.A. #8256
McQueen, Monica #8740
McRae, Constance #7523 7524
McRae, D.G.W. #30
McShine, Kynaston L. #534
McWilliams, Allan #147
Meade, Edward F. #3971
Mechlin, L. #314
Medland, Wendy S. #6899
Megaw, Vincent #4282
Mégret, Frédéric #6021
Meier, Kurt von #6640
Meigs, Mary #6510
Meistrich, Ira J. #913
Mekas, Jonas #7241 7248
Meldgaard, Jorgen #4206 4337 4342 4395
Mellen, Peter #136 137 1768 1784 1789 3226
    5223 5904 6968
Melnick, Norman J.P. #7755
Melnyk, George #1866 7623 8342
Melville, Robert #5145
Ménard, Andrée #1281
Ménard, Jean #5349
Ménard, Johanne #1360
Mendel, David #1638
Mendel, Frederick S. #3187
Mendelsohn, Ala #8246
Mendes, Ross #525
Mendez, Carlos #6459
Menear, David W. #9403
Menzies, T.P.O. #3820
Mercier, H. #8308
Mercier, Pierre #8276
Mèredieu, Florence de #1542 1543
Meredith, H.C. #3393
Mérette, Céline #2880
Merrett, Campbell #9455
Merritt, Fran #2136 2137
Merritt, N.J. #8007
Mertins, Detlaf #8289
Merwin, Bruce W. #3517 3518
Mesley, Roger #4968
Metcalfe, Bruce #978
Metcalfe, Eric #2070

Metcalfe, William #621
Metson, Graham #5156
Meunier, Charles #2995
Mews, J.Ewart #9031
Meyer, David #3615
Meyer, Joyce #6063
Meyers, Leonard #2080
Mezei, Lesley N. #517
Miake, Taizo #9106
Micha, René #145
Michael, Marie #2145
Michaelson, Peter #901
Michaud, Claude #7869 7877 7890
Michelson, Annette #7246
Michener, Mel P. #9393
Michener, Wendy #5637
Middleton, J.E. #4913 6363
Miers, Sir Henry Alexander #3024
Mika, Helma #891 8993
Mika, Nick #891 8993
Miles, Charles #3343
Miles, G.P. #3853
Mill, Richard #6534
Millán, Gonzalo #1552
Millar, Blake #8201
Millard, Peter #4684 5201 6329 7280
Miller, Alfred J. #6536 6537
Miller, J.Jefferson #2294
Miller, Jerry #9219
Miller, Leon Gordon #3946
Miller, Martha #7252
Miller, Muriel #7532
Miller, Polly #3946
Millet, Robert #2381 5423
Millette, Michel #5086
Milligan, Frank #693
Mills, David B. #7785 7791 8541
Mills, Edward #8165 9005 9006
Mills, G.E. #8082
Mills, Karen Keenlyside #5585
Millway, Betty #2077
Milne, David #536 6545 6548 6553
Milne, David, Jr. #6560 6561
Milne, David B. #6546
Milne, Marlene #7520
Milnes, Humphrey #3151 4631 4632 4633
Milnes, Humphrey N. #151
Milot, Jocelyne #1292
Milot, Richard #1288
Milovanovic, P. #1427
Milrod, Glenda #6575
Milrod, Linda #510 7160
Miner, Muriel Miller #6979
Minhinnick, Jeanne #2110 2245 2477 2549
    2552 7981 8013
Minotto, Claude #1021 1031
Minton, Eric #9086 9099
Miron, Gaston #5668
Mitchell, C.H. #9331
Mitchell, E.H. #3350 4413
Mitchell, Eric #4363
Mitchell, Eric H. #7377
Mitchell, Howard T. #8143 8698
Mitchell, John Fletcher #968
Miville-Deschênes, Bertrand #9245
Mochon, Marion Johnson #3938

Moffat, Charles L. #2603
Moffett, Kenworth #4965 4966
Mogelon, Alex #4920 4921 6154
Moir, Gillian #8102
Moisan, Micheline #1542 1543 5090
Moissan, Stéphane #2226
Molesworth, David #8067
Molinari, Guido #620 703 1267 1417 4846
    6584 6586 6590
Molson, Colin J.G. #7871
Monahan, Edward J. #2996
Monette, Pierre #2879
Monk, Lorraine #990 1011 8931 8932
Monk, Philip #787 1052 5961 6950 7561
Monpetit, Raymond #5881
Monroe, Robert D. #6505
Montas, Lise #1531 6412
Montbizon, Réa #7388
Montpetit, Raymond #6150
Moody, Alan #9323
Moody, H.H.G. #8308
Moody, Harry #3573
Moody, Herbert H.G. #8207
Moogk, Peter N. #234 235 249 250 269 270
    2227 3007 8621
Moogk, Peter Nicholas #2214
Moon, Barbara #445 446 570 4538 6554 6555
Moon, Robert #7948
Moor, Simon C. #652
Moore, Charles H. #4533
Moore, David #5637 7283
Moore, Jack #6989 8919 9546
Moore, Mavor #3292
Moore, Tom #8069
Moorehead, Warren K. #3393 3406
Moorehead, Warren King #3401 3499
Moorfield, Catherine #160
Moppett, Carroll #5686
Moppett, George #678 679
Moppett, Ron #5683
Morency, Pierre #8261 8269
Morgan, Carl #2594
Morgan, Earle C. #9087 9372
Morgan, Gerald #7106
Morgan, Lewis H. #3489
Morgan, Norma #2908
Morgan, Patrick #1243
Morgan, Peter #6607
Morgan, Sher #2018
Morgan, W. #7632
Morgan, Wayne #1919
Morgan-Powell, S. #1316
Morice, A.G. #4072 4073
Morin, France #634 660 5630 6587 6598
Morin, Lisette #9118
Morin, Victor #728 3082 3083 7900
Morisette, M.Raymonde #529
Morisset, Denys #5240 6611 6613
Morisset, Gérard #35 219 228 229 393 864
    986 1237 1244 1245 1249 1321 1322 1323
    1333 1337 1338 1339 1340 1405 1406 1582
    2177 2180 2197 2665 2666 2667 2668 2669
    2670 2671 2672 2673 2677 2976 2991 2992
    3207 4586 4587 4588 4589 4594 4646 4781
    5371 5504 5571 5572 6248 6280 6281 6604

6749 6884 6959 7100 7853 7938 8326 8329
8336 8572 8813 8814 8827 8830 8833 8834
8835
Morisset, Jean-Paul #1255 1341 1583 3085
Moriyama, Raymond #8194 8973 9095 9106
    9288
Morris, Edmund #197 6637
Morris, Fred #6508
Morris, J.A. #3186
Morris, Jerrold #101 146 154 155 1110 5637
    6639 7409
Morris, Michael #546 2070 6641
Morris, R.Schofield #9190 9339
Morris, Robert Schofield #8389
Morrisette, Brigitte #4656
Morrison, Ann #643 697
Morrison, Ann K. #760
Morriss, Shirley G. #8905
Morrisseau, Norval #4122
Morrow, Mable #3456
Morse, William Inglis #1193 8775
Mortimer, Ann #2388
Morton, J.Coulson #9391
Moses, Gerry #3241 5064
Mosher, Terry #957 6401
Mossop, Jerry #159
Mothersill, Daniel #941
Motherwell, Elizabeth #3000
Mount, M.J. #195 4948 4991 5279 5497 5799
    6338
Moussette, Marcel #2220 2345 2708
Mowat, Alex S. #1119 1195
Moyer, Stanley G. #7530
Mozino Suarez de Figueroa, José Mariano
    #3966
Muhlstock, Louis #6652
Muir, Allan #9295
Muir, Barbara #3166
Muir, Doris #9295
Muir, Norma Phillips #4738
Mulaire, Bernard #2275 4692 5556
Mulcaster, Wynona #7122
Müller-Wille, Ludger #1566
Mungall, Constance #1758 4597 6848 7052
Munk, Linda #2696
Munro, Susan #2024
Munroe, Doris C. #2005
Murchie, John #5048
Murdoch, John #4316
Murdoch, Peter #5375
Murdoch, Su #1730
Murphy, Achille #7946 8870
Murphy, D.T. #5465
Murphy, E.P. #9027
Murphy, Rowley #1087 6665
Murphy, Sean B. #526
Murphy, Serge #1552
Murray, A.L. #7903
Murray, Charlotte C. #8725
Murray, Ian #671
Murray, James #9503
Murray, James A. #7694 8079 8190 8191 8192
    8193 8194 8195 8196 8197 8198 8199 8200
    8201 8203 8204 8212 8303 8515 8583 8763
    8987 8990 9465

Murray, Joan #102 115 237 254 675 676 698 788 822 930 970 971 1116 1678 1785 1826 2394 2596 3169 3248 3317 4570 4710 4767 4892 4936 4942 4961 5060 5232 5302 5393 5394 5454 5675 6056 6074 6139 6283 6319 6333 6378 6422 6431 6438 6478 6489 6507 6709 6783 6918 6919 6965 6966 6970 7162 7237 7367 7368 7497 7571 7586 7617 9010
Murray, Nancy #7060
Murray, Robert A. #3700
Musiol, Marie-Jeanne #5844
Musson, Patricia D. #2568 2572
Myers, Barbara J. #1199
Myers, Barton #7746 8197 8391
Myers, H.Brad #3614
Myers, Marybelle #4258 4259 4267 4274 4288 4292 4293 4296 4433 4521 5375 7318
Myers, R.M. #2682
Myrand, Ernest #2809

N

Nadeau, Jules #5288
Naftel, William #8700 9537
Nagy, Hendrika G. #4207
Nantais, Lyse #2102 3305 4905 5177 5352 6160
Nantel, Lise #1285
Nasby, David #716
Nasby, Judith #253 3159 3173 3176
Nasby, Judith M. #1685 5518 6040 6041
Nasgaard, Roald #550 617 703 723 790 1814 1818 3167 4910 4973 5570 5905 6043 6075 6076 6434
Nash, Joanna #1553
Nasmith, C. #8007
Nason, Roger #7806
Neal, Carolyn #8408
Neary, Kevin #4043
Needham, Gerald #5095 5569
Needham, Harold G. #3152
Needler, G.H. #5933
Neesham, Robin #488
Neilson, G.A. #8808 8810
Neilson, Gordon A. #8564 8807 8809 9022
Neilson, Gordon Antoine #1324
Nelles, Ann J. #610
Nelson, Carl #8281
Nelson, Carl R. #9488
Nelson, E.W. #4360
Nelson, Edward William #4318
Nelson, Joyce #626 693
Nelson, W.H. de B. #6943
Nemiroff, Diana #696 720 1660 5130 5233 7166 7474 7475 7570
Ner, Naima #3314
Nesbitt, J.Aird #5698
Neuburg, Hans #878
Neumann, Peter #3430
Newcombe, C.F. #4053
Newcombe, W.A. #3831 3836
Newell, Dianne #261 8669

Newfeld, Frank #75
Newlands, David #2323 2334
Newlands, David L. #2328 2329 2330 2335 2336 2346 2347 2348 2349 2355 2356 2374
Newman, Nancy #4314
Newman, Oscar #8575 9464
Newman, Richard #112
Newman, Thelma R. #6260
Newton, Eric #43 399 406
Newton, John #4976
Newton, Neil #6694
Niblack, Albert P. #3763
Nichols, Jack #810 818
Nichols, T.R. #2940
Nicholson, Edward J. #883
Nicholson, R.A.V. #9225
Nickel, Karl #4986
Nicol, F.J. #9420
Nicol, Frank J. #9398
Nicol, Pegi #4915
Nicole, Augustin #5480
Nicolet, R.R. #7684
Nicoll, James #1948 9189
Nicolson, Annabel #555
Niverville, Louis de #5097 6709
Nixon, A.M. #8256
Nixon, Virginia #1510 1624 7278
Nixon, William Z. #2573
Nobbs, Percy #7955
Nobbs, Percy E. #731 1079 2693 2963 7642 7650 7651 7652 7653 7658 7661 7663 7900 8221 8241 8244 9492 9493
Noguez, Dominique #7261
Noppen, Luc #258 259 1369 1618 4592 5610 7872 7874 7892 7951 8328 8394 8622 8814 8851 8857 8858 8864 8869 8870 8880 8888 8893 9056 9057
Norcross, E.Blanche #8695
Norman, Howard A. #3610
Norman, J.A. #4542 8231
Normandeau, Pierre #740 4877
Norrie, Leonard #1722
Norris, J.A. #2743
Notebaert, Gérard #8512
Notman, William #6723
Nowlan, Alden #4759
Nowlan, Jeanne #2872
Nungak, Zebedee #4417 4437
Nurse, Ray #2940
Nute, Grace Lee #5833 7002 7003
Nutt, Elizabeth Styring #6541
Nykor, Lynda Musson #2568 2572
Nymark, Victor #9295

O

O'Brian, John #6567
O'Brien, Kevin #238
O'Brien, Mern #2807
O'Brien, Nancy P. #7728
O'Brien, Paddy #454 1964 5081 5974
O'Bright, Jean #6466

O'Dea, F.A. #1150 8752
O'Dea, Fabian #8751
O'Dea, Shane #2502 7786 7787 7790 7792
O'Donnell, Marguerite #6228
O'Grady, Emmett #95 96
O'Kiely, Elizabeth #8160
O'Leary, France #1434
O'Leary, M.F. #6831
O'Leary, Marie-France #4955 5587 5668 6411 6892
O'Neal, Barbara #6176
O'Neill, Paul #7787
O'Shea, William A. #8442
Oberdorf, Charles #1008 1009 1022 6971 6972
Oberlander, Cornelia #8144
Oberlander, Cornelia Hahn #9136
Oberlander, H.Peter #8142 8158
Oberlander, Peter #8144
Obomsawin, Alanis #3363
Ogilvie, Will #570
Oglesby, Catharine #2191
Ohannesian, Paul B. #8167
Oille, Jennifer #721 1804
Oko, Andrew #4609
Oko, Andrew J. #836 6380 6574 6687
Okulitch, Vladimir J. #2019
Oldham, Evelyn #4134
Oliver, Lucile #2544
Olson, Ronald L. #3832 3845
Olvet, Lydia #6795
Olwyler, Peter #6278
Omand, D.N. #9106
Ondaatje, Kim #2796 2798 8672
Onley, Toni #6738
Opat, Ellen-Jane #902
Orchard, W.C. #3412
Orchard, William C. #3443 3457 3534 3818 3821
Orchinsky, Peter #2869
Oreskovich, Carlie #3291 7733
Orobetz, Christine #1684
Orr, Helen #8102
Orr, Rowland #3520
Orr, Rowland B. #3511 3519 3523
Orrell, John #9143
Osborne, H.C. #732 4519
Osborne, Milton S. #8245 8502
Osborne, Milton Smith #8094
Osborne, T.E. #8657
Osgood, Cornelius #4085 4087 4099 4101
Osgood, Cornelius B. #4081
Osler, Pamela #486 487
Osler, Robert #8975
Osler, Stephen Britton #9010
Ostiguy, J.-R. #85
Ostiguy, Jean-René #97 410 417 424 425 429 436 476 489 518 1265 1371 3307 4662 4810 5314 5316 5320 5324 5333 5473 5474 5476 5548 5762 5764 5878 5882 5884 6153 6200 6202 6203 6205 6206 6631 6813 6814 7301
Ostry, Bernard #3290
Otto, Eberhard #3982
Otto, Stephen #8030
Otto, Stephen A. #8382

Ouellet, Gaétan #5615
Ouellet, Gérard #1608 2209
Ouellet, Jean #7746
Ouellette, Fernand #1541 5960
Ouellette, Gabriel-Pierre #6864
Ouellette-Michalska, Madeleine #4648
Oughton, John #1827
Outram, Richard #666
Ouvrard, Hélène #5192
Owen, Graham W. #9483
Owen, John E. #9031
Owings, Nathaniel A. #9026
Owram, Douglas #8976 8977
Oxhorn, Pearl #4297
Oxley, J.Morrow #9190
Oxley, Loren A. #9420
Ozier, Joyce #2058

P

Paalen, Wolfgang R. #3861
Pacey, Anthony #7752
Pacey, Desmond #4757
Pacey, Elizabeth #5932 7831
Pacey, Mary #7809
Pachter, Charles #6747
Page, Forsey #9087 9393
Page, Frank E. #7533
Pagé, Norman #3057
Page, P.K. #4626
Pagé, Suzanne #558 3267
Pageau, René #4860
Pagnoux, Michèle #276
Pagonis, Illyas #2055
Paikowsky, Sandra #111 1478 4775 7049
Paikowsky, Sandra R. #5432 5433
Pain, Howard #2576 2577
Paine, A.J.C. #8206
Paladin, Vivian A. #6944
Palardy, Jean #2204 2530 2531 2539 2540
    2541 2865 8602 8609 8623
Palchinski, Sylvia #6753
Pallascio-Morin, Ernest #4946
Palmer, Alcy M. #2490
Palmer, Bernard C. #8690
Palmer, E.B. #9416
Paltsits, Victor Hugo #191
Panabaker, Frank #6757
Pandev, Margaret #2899
Panneton, Louise #6172
Pantazzi, Sybille #107 928 1765 3313 5824
Panton, L.A.C. #325 366 395 7113 7595
Pape, Gordon #7914
Paquet, Richard #5099
Paquette, Albert #1801
Paquin, Pierre #6167
Paradis, Andrée #1294 1542 1543 1851 3216
    7090 7091
Paradis, J.-G. #5874
Parashis, Sasedis #8069
Paré, Jean #5531 7925
Parent, Alain #782 1465 1523 1532 4655 5204
    5262 5263 5332 5552 5629 5793 6054 6589
    7403 7487 7489

Parent, Jean-Claude #8019
Parent, Michel #5607 5951
Parent, Omer #5289
Parent-Vidal, Louise #2999
Parfitt, Gilbert #8691
Parinaud, André #1542 1543
Paris, Erna #7303
Parizeau, Alice #3092
Parizeau, Marcel #355 1389 7846 7850
Parker, Arthur C. #3406 3508 3509 3512 3516
Parker, Bruce A. #2350
Parker, Gilbert #180
Parker, Harley #3304
Parker, J.Delisle #6244
Parkin, Jeanne #3009
Parkin, John #7746
Parkin, John B. #8205
Parkin, John C. #610 7682 7714 8112 8195
    8232 8396 9393
Parkin, John Cresswell #8651
Parks, William A. #7646 7647
Parry, B.Evan #9020 9021
Parsons, Bruce #550 1132 6771
Parsons, George #9503
Parsons-Doehler, Joan #7840
Partridge, David #6774
Paskievich, John #6777
Pasnak, Jim #8126
Pasonis, Illyas #774
Pasquill, Frank T. #3268
Paterson, T.W. #6430
Patterson, F.W. #9407
Patterson, Freeman #991 1016 6780 6781
    6782
Patterson, Nancy-Lou #1682 2243 2246 2253
    2265 2268 2572 2709 2801 2942 3364 3373
    3639 4144
Patterson, Nancy-Lou Gellermann #2264
Patterson, Norman #186
Patterson, R.G. #5003
Patterson, W.J. #8063
Pattison, Jeanne L. #1782 1783
Paudrat, Jean-Louis #6981
Paul, Eleanor #8072
Paul, Frances #3865
Paul, Henry #9096
Paulette, Claude #7892 8870 8893
Paxton, Maureen #1819
Payant, René #637 695 1524 1544 4847 5163
    5164 5550 6535 7038 7039 7566 7567
Payette, André #5265
Payette, Maurice #8207
Payment, Diane #8115
Payne, Anne #4715 5936 6082 6529 6701
Payne, Marilyn #1187 2649
Payne, Rodney #8348
Peacock, David #8025
Peacock, Suzanne #8025
Peake, Elaine #1959 6181
Pearce, Robert J. #3640
Pearce, Susan M. #3454
Pearse, Harold #7219
Pearson, Carol #5020
Pearson, Lester B. #570 8933 8934

Pearson, Norman #8184
Peck, John #2487
Peck, M.A. #2091
Peck, Mary #8940 8941
Peck, R.M. #9525
Peddle, Walter #2484
Peddle, Walter W. #2519 2520
Peet, Stephen D. #3391 3395
Pehap, Eric #6795
Pei, I.M. #9136
Pellan, Alfred #5595
Pelletier, Gaby #2943 3628 3634 3637 3641
Pelletier, Gérard #529
Pelletier, Pierre #6152 6762 8592
Péloquin, Claude #4770 4792
Pencier, Honor de #278
Pendergast, James F. #3616
Pendergrast, John #996
Penney, Gerald #4377
Penniman, T.K. #4369
Pepall, Rosalind #2462 4641
Pépin, Yves #637
Pepper, Kathleen Daly #6626
Percival, Robert #1151 1183 1184 1185 1778
    4919 5500 5712 6500 6533 6953
Percy, Vivian #9026
Perdue, Jane #687
Perehudoff, W. #9091
Perkins, G.E. #3393
Perks, W.T. #7728
Perkyns, Dorothy #6174
Perlin, Rae #1142
Perrault, Claude #8608
Perrault, Gérard #851
Perrault, Pierre #3269
Perreault, John #6267 6272
Perreault, Lise #1459
Perrin, Peter #662 5521 6393 7255 7276
Perron, Julien #8836
Perry, Anne Anderson #4518
Perry, Art #6526 6936 6937 7610
Perry, Arthur #2062 2065 3312 5418 6403
    6988 7608
Perry, Mrs.W.F. (Madeline) #1894
Persson, Diane Iona #3990
Petel, Denise #831
Peters, Greg #5487
Peters, Helen #2020
Peters, Helen Bergen #2023
Petersen, Karen Daniels #3585
Peterson, Lester R. #6460
Peterson, Margaret #6839
Peterson, Susan #6274
Pethick, Jerry #6840
Petrello, Vincent M. #3542
Petrie, Isabelle #6719
Petryshyn, J. #8995
Pettit, D.W. #8988
Pfaff, L.R. #5733
Pfaff, Larry #3175
Phaneuf, Gabriel #4574
Phelps, Steven #3369
Philibert, David #1854
Phillips, Carol #638 4686 6729
Phillips, Carol A. #1867 2066 3197 7519

Phillips, David #6858
Phillips, Dorrie #5209
Phillips, Duncan #6176
Phillips, E.J. #3080
Phillips, Fred H. #1174 6479 7333
Phillips, John #996
Phillips, John F. #1794
Phillips, R.A.J. #4504 7763 7767 8017
Phillips, Robert Arthur John #8933 8934
Phillips, W.J. #1888 3848
Phillips, Walter J. #6853 6855
Phillips, Walter Joseph #6854
Phillips-Cleland, Jennifer #7833
Picard, François #8451
Pichard, Joseph #1435
Piché, Maurice #4836
Piché, P.-E. #2170
Piché-Wissell, Aline #4878
Picher, Claude #401 1341 1411 6229
Picken, Harry Belfrage #7992
Pickford, A.E. #4114
Pickwell, F.C. #8687 9277
Piene, Nan R. #767
Pierce, Edith Chown #2396
Pierce, Lorne #2397 2398 2399 2489 3135
    5172 5661 6367 6383 6757
Pierce, Margaret #7079
Pierce, S.D. #8389
Piers, Harry #1191 2632 5429
Pigeon, Danielle #7750 8635
Pilot, R.W. #474
Pilot, Robert #5221 6870
Pilot, Robert W. #1143 5220 7055
Pincus-Witten, Robert #7059
Pinker, Donovan #9314 9375
Pinney, Marguerite #2046
Pinsky, Alfred #1178 7045
Piper, David #4980 6916
Pitseolak, Peter #6876 6880 6881
Place, Jennifer #2808 4718
Plante, Emile #8554
Plaskett, Bill #7837
Plaskett, Joe #402 6805 6889
Plaskett, Joseph #4579 6891 6895
Plasse-Lecaisne, Jacques #4877
Platts, R.E. #8732
Plear, Scott #2459
Pocius, Gerald L. #1163 2158 2159 2484 2744
    2759 2760
Pocock, Jasmine #426
Pocock, Philip #426 988 6775
Pohorecky, Z.S. #3714
Pohrt, Richard A. #3740
Pokorny, G.K. #7669
Polidori, Mario #7547
Poliquin, Jean-Marc #8931 8932
Pollock, Ann #794 2063 6528
Pollock, Jack #6649
Pollock, R.Ann #6375
Pontant, Alain #95 96
Pontbriand, Chantal #634 668 699 709 1495
    1507 1512 1525 5092 6138 6587 7262 7420
Pool, Beekman H. #4191
Poole, Nancy #5080
Pootoogook #4460
Pootoogook, Kananginak #4299

Porteous, John #5154
Porter, Allan #6575
Porter, Don #8171
Porter, James A. #5337
Porter, John #529 6217 6218
Porter, John R. #269 270 1355 1356 1368 1609
    1610 1615 1633 2930 3120 6219 6220 6221
    6887 8850 8851 8853
Porter, McKenzie #7465
Porter, Rosalyn #5891 6480
Poser, Carol #2081
Poser, Steven #7612
Poteet, Susan K. #1516 4596
Pothier, Jean-Paul #1435
Potvin, Damase #5963
Potvin, Danielle #1375
Poulin, Roland #6909
Pouliot, Adrien #8571
Poulos, Ted #2272
Pouyez, Christian #8423
Pov, Johnny #4521
Powell, Louis H. #3682
Powrie, David #8254
Prack, Alvin R. #8300
Prangnell, Peter #8282 8286 8313 8973
Pratt, C.E. #8693 8981 8989
Préfontaine, Fernand #1317
Prescott, Winward #917
Prévost, Antoine #2589
Priamo, Carol #8064 9248 9379
Price, Art #6929
Price, F.Newlin #7501
Price, Frederic Newlin #6175
Price, Linda G. #5633
Price, Patricia #971
Price, Ralph #971
Prince, John B. #2150
Prochazka, Alena #9255
Proctor, Alexander Phimister #6944
Proctor, Hester Elizabeth #6944
Prost, Viviane #1554
Proulx, André #2366
Proulx, Gilles #2857 2866 8423
Proulx, Jean-Pierre #8420 8421
Proulx, Laurent #1601 1602 6572 6573 8859
    8860 8865 8866
Provencher, Paul #6525
Provick, A.M. #2403
Provost, Anne #6897
Provost, Honorius #8844
Prueter, Kenneth F. #9403
Prus, Victor #8191 9101 9112 9552
Pullan, Wendy #8064
Pulsifer, Cameron W. #8438
Purdie, James #1823 3312 6064
Purdy, A.W. #5919

Qitsualik, Rosemarie #4435
Quantrill, Malcolm #5082
Quimby, G.I. #3558
Quimby, George Irving #3579 3594

Quintner, David Richard #5276
Quist, W.G. #9136

R

R.R. #7715
Rabinowitch, David #703 6948
Rabinowitch, Royden #703
Raby, Georges #948
Racette, Gilles #5303
Racine, Yolande #5332
Raczka, Paul #3749
Raczka, Paul M. #3754
Raddall, Thomas H. #9524
Radford, J.A. #182 3299
Radulovich, Mary Lou Fox #4156
Raeburn, Pauline #9233
Raeburn, Ronald #9233
Ragon, Michel #5565 5566
Rahman, Fazlur #2858
Raine, David F. #7317
Raine, Norman Reilly #6952
Rainey, Froelich #4272
Rainville, Alain #9256
Rainville, Paul #359 1240 1248
Rajotte, Yves #6954
Rakhra, A.S. #7776
Raley, George H. #3849
Raley, George W.Henry #3837
Ralston, David #7070
Ralston, William #8516
Rambusch, Viggo B.A. #7778
Rampen, Leo #7440
Ramsay, W.A. #9513 9517
Ramsden, Anne #7584
Ramsey, L.G.G. #2101
Rand, Margaret #5059 5160 5900 7156 7212
Randleson, Sara A. #6053
Rans, Goldie #1067
Ransom, Bernard #4377
Raphael, Shirley #6128
Rapoport, Amos #3353
Rapoport, Janis #4670
Rapson, Ralph #8985 8986 9091
Rasmussen, Knud Johan Victor #4328 4330
Rasmussen, Mark A. #8136
Rasporich, Anthony W. #8121
Rastoul, Pierre #7881
Ravenhill, Alice #3866
Ray, Dorothy Jean #3359 4208 4217 4349
    4398
Ray, Tim #1903
Ray, Verne F. #3841
Raymond, Marie #5235
Raymore, W.G. #8303 8308
Rayner, Gordon #6966
Razutis, Al #550
Read, Charles H. #3767
Read, S.E. #7171
Read, Stanley E. #4907 5434
Reade, R.C. #4938
Real, Susan #6922
Reaney, James #78

Reaney, James Crearar #1891
Rebanks, Leslie #9120
Reddaway, Norman #8652
Redekop, Magdalene #7173
Redgrave, Felicity #1135 5466 5508 5697
    6389 6711 6830 6907
Redier, François #5437
Redpath, William #2548
Reed, Frederick #7641
Reed, T.A. #8056
Rees, Ronald #1872 1882 6050 7807 8717
Reeve, John #2387
Reeves, John #1036 1054 6911
Reeves, Wilfred #317 319 5157
Regensteiner, Else #2776
Reichard, Gladys A. #3808
Reid, Alison #7583
Reid, Bill #1995 3948 4066 6073
Reid, Dennis #108 264 265 271 272 518 536
    1772 3063 3229 3313 4926 5227 5726 5818
    5819 7366 7369
Reid, Dennis R. #6375
Reid, F. #8295
Reid, G.A. #6974 8219
Reid, George Agnew #6973 6975 7438
Reid, J.Addison #984
Reid, Leslie #637
Reid, William #3972 3998
Reid, William A. #8953
Reimer, John C. #8715
Reinblatt, M. #4693
Reitav, Jaan #8069
Reksten, Terry #8400 9134
Rempel, J.G. #7128
Rempel, J.I. #7685
Rempel, John #8677
Rempel, John I. #7745 7979 7987 8658
Renaud, Jacques #1546 2232 4945 5575
Render, Lorne E. #1863 1952 3191 6225 7373
Repentigny, Rodolphe de #1752 5051 6655
Restany, Pierre #5621 6272 7488
Reynald #334
Reynolds, Marilynn #8718
Reynolds, Nila #2258
Rhode, W. #6923
Rhodes, Michael #5300
Richard, Alain #1443 7865
Richard, J.-B. #8811
Richard, Jean #8622
Richard, Robert #6531
Richards, J.M. #9220
Richards, Jean #5588 5641 7540
Richards, Larry #7839 8347 8402 8999
Richardson, A.J.H. #7703 7717 7718 7720
    7863 7907 7941 7944 8521 8615
Richardson, Boyce #1566
Richardson, Douglas #7725 7767 7873 8006
    8064 8069 9512 9536
Richardson, Douglas S. #9049
Richardson, Douglas Scott #5461 8776
Richardson, E.P. #1330 1331
Richardson, J.E. #614
Richardson, Kathleen #1891
Richardson, Kathleen M. #8708
Richer, Claude #1415

Richer, Laurette B. #8885
Richer, Louis-R. #8448
Richmond, Brian #8670
Richmond, Chris #1529
Richmond, Leonard #292 1736
Rickard, Dale #3198
Rickard, Vincent #4168
Riddell, W.A. #1938
Riddell, W.Bruce #8740
Ridgeway, W. #3782
Ridley, Hilda #327
Rienaecker, Victor #5135
Rieth, Eric #276
Riley, Robert #2739
Ringereide, Mabel #7876
Ringheim, M. #3755
Ringland, Mabel Crews #4112
Rink, Henrik #4315
Riordon, Bernard #5654 6282
Rioux, Gilles #639 640 1294 1517 1542 1543
    1547 5167 6726
Rioux, Marcel #2827 4848
Rioux, Paul #2188
Risley, Christine #2793
Ritchie, Carson I.A. #4254 4289
Ritchie, David F. #160
Ritchie, John #3527
Ritchie, T. #7712 7726 7734 7980 8004 8026
    8046 8413 9244
Ritchie, Thomas #2699 7695 7704
Ritchie, William A. #3586
Ritzenthaler, Pat #3605
Ritzenthaler, Robert #3605
Ritzenthaler, Robert E. #3359
Roaf, John #8168
Robb, George #9107 9108 9115 9378
Robbie, Roderick #9403
Robbie, Roderick G. #9401
Robert, Fanny #3424
Robert, G. #3273
Robert, Guy #770 926 1258 1259 1269 1289
    1426 1437 1438 1453 1542 1543 1664 2216
    2701 3086 3102 4513 4543 4555 4619 4645
    4705 4786 4787 4788 4789 4791 4821 4837
    5185 5245 5246 5325 5326 5328 5331 5460
    5479 5512 5645 5931 5940 6065 6234 6235
    6236 6237 6250 6324 6410 6596 6601 6761
    6809 6810 7022 7033 7082 7085 7092 7433
Robert, Jacques #3126 8891
Robert, Jean-Rock #1603
Robert, Luc #1801
Robert, Nicole #1603
Roberts, Barry A. #4279
Roberts, Charles G.D. #319
Roberts, Goodridge #408 6686 7043 7045
    7047
Roberts, Helen H. #3801
Robertson, Anthony #5861
Robertson, Bonnie #9523
Robertson, Bryan #492 5566
Robertson, Clive #650 671 683 1955
Robertson, George #3260
Robertson, Heather #693 1111 1112
Robertson, John K.B. #41 6746

Robertson, Marion #3617 8375
Robertson, Nancy E. #490 1915 5823 6370
Robertson, Peter #1024 1107 1114 1675
Robertson, R.Gordon #4396
Robideau, Henri #1063 5671 5672
Robillard, Claude #9081
Robillard, Jean-Louis #1526
Robillard, Yves #1482 1502 1586 1595 1634
    3016 5264 5345 6129 7268
Robins, Corinne #4741
Robinson, Bart #5707
Robinson, E.S. #9043
Robinson, Francis W. #6993
Robinson, Gerald #8067 8512 9084
Robinson, Jeffrey #7036
Robinson, Noel #1984
Robinson, Willard B. #8415
Robitaille, Adrien #7105
Robitaille, André #8579
Robson, Albert H. #14 5541 5909 5954 6005
    6088 6365 7355
Robson, Scott #1220 1222
Roch, Ernst #4482
Rockburne, Dorothea #7059
Rockman, Arnold #464 467 869 1762 1793
    1798 6416 6990 7061 7240
Rodd, John #2271
Roddis, Mary #2785
Rodee, Howard D. #3709
Rodrigue, Cécile #1370
Rodrigues, Pedro #7477
Rodrik, Paul #5971
Roe, Frank Gilbert #8120 8701
Roedde, W.A. #9044
Rogatnick, Abraham #6059 6078 6735 8163
    8341 8355 8356 8964 9085 9290 9506
Roger, Dieter #7735
Rogers, Edward S. #3382 3595 4100
Rogers, Ernesto N. #8981 8989
Rogers, Irene #2498 7797
Rogers, Irene L. #7796 7802 8399 8544
Rogers, Marion G. #4897
Rogers, Otto #7065
Rogers, Wm.T. #8365
Rolfe, Elaine #138
Rombout, L. #5699
Rombout, Louis #1124 5710 5869 6094
Rombout, Luke #576 779 1126 2923 4758
    5434 5700 7229 9117
Romeo, Claudine #5155
Romer, Tadeusz #149
Rondeau, Clément #8873
Rondeau, Danielle #5948
Ronnefeldt, Karin #3738
Roosevelt, Anna Curtenius #4040
Roosevelt, Theodore #3399
Rose, Albert #8511
Rose, Barbara #6668
Rose, Peter #7746 7933 8999
Rose, T.Bert #8734
Rosenberg, Ann #2074 5301 6736 7391 7392
    7588
Rosenberg, Avis Lang #677 701 3293 4599
    5076 6275 6395 6402 6406 6570 6939
Rosenberg, Pierre #6886

Rosenberg, Tanya #612 6421
Rosenfeld, Roslyn #1376
Rosenfeld, Roslyn Margaret #1377
Rosinski, J. #8537
Rosinski, Maud #8537 9410
Ross, Alexander M. #4617
Ross, David #550 2874 2881 2900 3193
Ross, Donald A. #8950
Ross, Edward Hunter #3425
Ross, John K. #9194
Ross, Judy Thompson #2395
Ross, Leone Mosher #8777
Ross, Marcia #838 2521 6721
Rosser, Donald #2722
Rosshandler, Léo #526 685 789 1548 1564
    3116 4482 4853 7322 7324 7325 7491
Rostecki, R.R. #8101 8103 8331 9007 9008
Rostecki, Randy #8106
Rostecki, Randy R. #9361
Roth, Alfred #8985 8986
Roth, H.Ling #3652 3811
Roth, Mark #7525
Roth, Mark J. #7526
Roth, Moira #2073
Rotstein, Abraham #6747
Rouleau-Ross, Lucille #5528 8610
Rounthwaite, Shelagh #8246
Roussan, Jacques de #2000 2741 4556 4593
    4943 4944 5184 5282 5283 5854 5855 6125
    6127 6184 6207 6242 6247 6684 6844 6845
    7286 7288 7434
Rousseau, Gabriel #2977
Rousseau, Jacques #6645
Rousseau, Madeleine #6645
Roussel, Brigitte #1137
Roussel, Claude #1137 1181 7089
Roussil, Robert #3269 7096 7097
Routledge, Marie #4565
Rouve, Pierre #6776
Roux, Gilles #6199
Rowan, Jan C. #9221
Rowan, Julian #1798
Rowan, Michael #5863
Rowat, Theresa #7616
Rowe, R.C. #9238
Rowland, Douglas #8192
Rowland, Wilbee #9294
Rowley, Graham #4333 4335
Rowley, Graham W. #4358
Roy, Antoine #1320 2526 7859 7936
Roy, Gabrielle #6230
Roy, Guy-André #1361 8878
Roy, Katherine #6869
Roy, Murielle #2836
Roy, Pierre-Georges #1570 2822 7935 8444
    8560 8561 8789 8792 8793 9284
Roy, Raoul #8867
Roy, Sylvie #5334
Royer, Jean #1527
Royle, Stanley #7104
Rozaire, Charles E. #3991
Rozon, René #1003 3054 5674 6497
Rubin, Alex J. #8517
Rubin, B. #9194
Rubin, Norman N. #1604
Ruby, R.H. #4031

Ruddel, David Thiery #2231
Ruddel, Thiery #2206
Rudel-Tessier, J. #95 96
Rueter, Marilyn #935
Ruff, Eric #163
Rule, Carolann #8353
Rule, Jane #5831 6321 7320
Rupp, David W. #2367
Ruryk, Nancy R. #2782
Rusk, William Sener #7847
Russell, D.J. #8256
Russell, G.Leslie #9393
Russell, Hilary #9122 9123 9131
Russell, J.A. #8250
Russell, John #7673 8205 8303 9088
Russell, John A. #1891 8247 8256 8305 8986
    9091 9117 9486 9487
Russell, Loris #2120
Russell, Loris S. #2918 2920
Russell, Norman C.H. #8098
Russell, Paul #771 9473
Russell, Victor L. #5633
Russoli, Franco #7018 7023
Rutsch, Edward S. #3618
Rutstrum, Calvin #6473
Ruttan, Frank N. #8688
Ryan, Fortune #1070
Ryan, L.T. #8001
Ryan, M. #8147
Ryan, Patricia #6769
Ryan, Terrence #4194 6768 6769
Ryan, Terrence P. #4299 4441
Ryan, Terry #4460
Rybczynski, Witold #7728
Rybka, Karel R. #9190 9192
Ryder, Huia #1175 1178 2400
Ryder, Huia G. #2491 2495 2500 2503 2882
    7110 7111 8545 8778

S

S.L.R. #8044
Saarinen, Eero #8981 8989 9079 9080
Sabat, Christina #6835
Sabbath, Lawrence #743 3219 5111 5182 5917
    6342 6656 6871 7469 8233
Safdie, Moshe #8403 8404 8406 8577 8583
Safir, O. #8142
Saint-Germain, Michel #5580
Saint-Martin, Fernande #468 588 1414 1439
    1441 1462 1476 1509 1622 1651 3326 4846
    6470 6765
Saint-Martin, Luc #8854
Saint-Michel, Françoise #3362
Saint-Pierre, Angéline #2209 4887 4888 5069
    5485 8871
Saint-Pierre, Marcel #1496 1564 5595 5596
Sainte-Affrique, Olga de #276
Sala, Marco #9406
Saladin d'Anglure, Bernard #4521 4522
Salaman, Malcolm C. #802
Salomon de Friedberg, Barbara #8862
Salt, Jim #7622
Saltmarche, Kenneth #646 1824 3156

Salzer, Robert #3580 3582
Sampson, Barry #8071
Samuel, Margot #4962 5309
Sanderson, Charles R. #9041
Sandilands, R. #8147
Sandomirsky, Janice R. #5634
Sandori, Paul #9127
Sandwell, B.K. #5736 5950
Sangster, Dorothy #3177
Santana, Hubert de #5252 5949
Sapir, Edward #3659
Sapp, Allen #7125
Sarjeant, William A.S. #8114
Sarrazin, Jean #2228 4273 5425 7434
Sarrazin, Roger #1549
Saucier, Pierre #1418
Saucier, Robert #685
Saunders, Doris #2955
Saunders, Ivan J. #8103 8416
Saunders, Judith #3178 7515
Saunders, Mary #2785
Savard, Félix-Antoine #2223 3303
Savard, Pierre #1820 1821
Savard, Rémi #3351
Savignac, Pierre H. #6512
Savoie, Mme Roméo #2836
Saxe, Henry #661
Sayag, Alain #7258
Scadding, Henry #725
Scarlett, Jean #9044
Schack, Katherine von #4719
Schaefer, Carl #7150
Schaefer, Carl Fellman #7155
Schaefer-Simmern, Henry #4392
Schaeffer, Claude E. #62
Schafer, D.Paul #3270
Schellbach, Louis #3538
Schiff, Marilyn A. #6593
Schiller, E.A. #5897
Schledermann, Peter #4367
Schlesier, Karl H. #1566
Schmeizer, Elizabeth #615 1652
Schmertz, Mildred F. #8846
Schneider, Ira #616
Schneider, Pierre #7013 7014 7018 7019 7021
    7032
Schneider, Richard C. #3448
Schoenauer, Norbert #7728 8287 8517 9315
    9399
Schoenherr, Douglas #159
Schoolcraft, Henry #3490
Schoolcraft, Henry R. #3385
Schoonover, Cortlandt #7163
Schoonover, Frank E. #7163
Schrager, Reissa #665 3241 6878
Schrier, Arnold #8763
Schulze-Thulin, Axel #3451 3737 3750
Schupp, Patrick #4783 5259 6519 7343 8840
    8841
Schürmann, Reiner #5162
Schuster, Carl #4334
Schwartz, Herbert T. #3350
Schwartz, Joan #5373
Schwartz, Joan M. #2014 2031 2032 5411
Schwartz, Joan Marsha #2015
Schwartz, Marjorie #4884

Schwarz, Herbert T. #2528 6646 6731
Schweger, Barbara F. #2837
Schweiger, Karol #5646 6679
Scott, Andrew #4529 4601 5043 6404 7170 7602 8726
Scott, Charles H. #1087 1986 1995 4520 7176
Scott, Duncan Campbell #5542 5543 6856
Scott, Fred #2749
Scott, Sandra #75
Scowen, P.H. #1342
Scully, Vincent #3359
Sealy, Spencer G. #4459
Sears, Henry #8518 9377
Séché, Alphonse #4941
Secord, James E. #9393
Secter, Marcia E. #9488
Segger, M. #8722
Segger, Martin #2269 7736 8149 8152 8178 8180 8384 8385 8967 9134
Séguin, Robert-Lionel #1268 1351 2200 2210 2217 2218 2221 2592 2733 2746 2850 2901 2916 2921 2933 2934 2944 7864 7881 8586 8593 9230 9231
Seidelman, Harold #4523 6873
Seig, Louis #3444
Seitz, William C. #400
Selby, Roger #632
Seline, Janice #938 6210
Semak, Michael #1016 1063 7168
Semchishen, Orest #8913
Semmens, J.N. #9044 9389
Sendey, John #4020
Senécal, Irène #3010
Sens, Karen Linda #5449
Sepp, Eda #784 5752
Sereisky, Jean #1121
Sevier, Gerry #1678
Sewter, A.Charles #2453
Shack, Sybil #4890
Shackleton, Phil #2284 2588
Shackleton, Philip #2477 2553 2558 2561 8038
Shadbolt, Doris #79 429 536 588 3185 4423 4729 4755 5027 5028 5030 5039 5042 5044 5073 5385 5386 5408 5514 5563 5566 5859 5860 6055 6359 6695 6890 6910 7387 7628 8217
Shadbolt, Douglas #7728 7737 8192 8284 8316 8319 8992
Shadbolt, J.L. #1844 1987 1990 5944
Shadbolt, Jack #7181 7183 7185 7186 7192 7510
Shalkop, R.L. #4280
Shane, Audrey Patricia MacKay #4032
Shapiro, Babs #8171 8237
Shapiro, Barbara #9149
Shaul, Sandra #654 761 1970 5207 5208
Shave, Harry #7005
Shaw, Avery #1170 5140
Shaw, Hazel B. #8531
Shaw, Neufville #7044
Shea, Albert A. #3261
Shea, John G. #2543
Sheehan, Carol #4051
Sheeler, John #2434

Sheeler, John R. #2406
Shepherd, Elizabeth #2429 2703
Shepherd, George #8706
Shepherd, Michael #131 702
Shere, Charles #2053
Sherman, Tom #604
Sherwood, Angus #8189
Sherwood, W.A. #183 187
Shih, Hsio Yen #9136
Shine, Anthony #7698
Shipley, Nan #2902 4515 7627
Shoemaker, Dorothy #9044
Shoolman, Regina Lenore #6087
Shore, Leonard E. #8247
Shore, M.V. #9289
Shortt, Adam #205
Shortt, George E. #7900
Shortt, James #8719
Shotridge, Florence #3793
Shotridge, Louis #3793 3802 3803 3806 3833
Shuebrook, Ron #1227 2383 3014 5969 6727 7062
Sibley, C.Lintern #7293
Sibun, Piers Seton #2331
Sicard, Bunny #4155
Siddall, Bob #8158
Sieber, Patricia #4459
Siebert, Erna #3947
Siemens, Gary #5392
Sigurdson, Doug #1899
Sikstrom, Brian #8178
Silcox, D.P. #514
Silcox, David #536
Silcox, David P. #477 519 744 4509 5275 6558 6559 6915 7316 7370 7413
Silver, B.C. #8533
Silverstein, John #1828
Silvester, Reg #7133
Simard, Cyril #1274 2211 2223 2224 2228 2229 3374
Simard, Jean #1291 1292 1365 1412 1625 1662 2948 4899
Simmins, Richard #3046 7387
Simmins, Richard B. #1845 1913 4611 4746 5624 6475
Simmonds, H.H. #8142
Simmonds, Wylie #2389
Simms, Richard #6981
Simon, Wilma #4137
Simond, Raymond #1801
Simpson, B.Napier #8335
Simpson, E.G. #8514
Simpson, Gregg #2045
Simpson, Ruth DeEtte #4382
Simpson, Valerie #2875
Sims, Lowery S. #6674
Sinaiticus #8338 8647 9280 9334 9335 9366 9367 9369 9452
Sinclair, A.T. #3330
Sinclair, Lister #6649
Singer, Taki Blues #550
Sioui, Anne-Marie #1475 5244 7494
Sioui, Christine #4155
Sirotnik, Gareth #5409
Sise, Hazen #6326

Sisler, Rebecca #157 666 758
Sismey, Eric D. #3913
Sitney, P.Adams #7241 7574
Skelton, Robin #2043 7205
Skinner, Alanson #3402 3524 3525 3529 3530 3533 3535 3655
Sladen, Gib #2795
Slaight, Annabel #8065
Slater, Norman #9552
Sloan, John #3412
Sloot, Sylvia #1722
Smart, Leslie #877
Smith, Brydon #518 522 548 557 6670 6671
Smith, C. #9350
Smith, C.Ray #9347
Smith, Cyndi M. #7527
Smith, David M. #6328
Smith, Dennis #9465
Smith, Donald B. #4154
Smith, Dorothy A. #4325
Smith, E.Ann #2441 2442
Smith, Eden #7644 8491
Smith, Elizabeth #2125 2131
Smith, Ernest J. #9487
Smith, Ernest W. #5711
Smith, F.I. #9194
Smith, Frances K. #609 4727 5491 5492 7550 7551
Smith, Francis Drake Llewellyn #8902
Smith, George L. #1776
Smith, Gordon A. #1995
Smith, H.M. Scott #8552
Smith, Harlan I. #3408 3785 3814 3816 3817 3822 3846
Smith, Harold J. #9024
Smith, Henri #6444
Smith, J.G.E. #4453
Smith, J.Harry #1251 5346 5348 7549
Smith, J.Percy #2997
Smith, James #184
Smith, James G.E. #4040
Smith, Jean #2125 2131
Smith, Kenneth B. #9103
Smith, Leslie Victor #5050
Smith, Lillian H. #9043
Smith, M.Aileen #8550
Smith, Maralyn E. #1205
Smith, Marian W. #3870 3872 3876 3888
Smith, Marilyn #9523
Smith, Peter #7985 9119
Smith, R.D. #5354
Smith, R.D. Hilton #9043
Smith, S.K. #2547
Smith, Stuart #7808
Smith, Stuart A. #1178 4764
Smith, Sydney #5717
Smith, Wilfred I. #6453
Smith, William Y. #1119
Smyly, Carolyn #3984 4021 4067 8177 9134
Smyly, John #3983 3984 4021
Smyth, David #8129
Snelgrove, Gordon W. #3187
Snider, Greg #5295
Snider, Gregory #6405

Snider, Mary Adelaide #3204
Snitman, Sharon #1797
Snow, Dean #3467
Snow, Michael #607 703 7241 7243 7244 7261
Snyder, Barbara #2484 5170 8031
Snyder, J.F. #3393
Snyder, Jerome #896 5297
Snyderman, George S. #3567
Sobol, Helen F. #4547
Sobol, Samuel M. #4547
Sobral, Luis de Moura #6131 7332
Soby, Trudy #8124 8711
Socha, Erla #3373 4494
Söderberg, Bertil #3960
Solier, René de #4421
Somers, D. #8147
Somerville, H.A. #5123
Somerville, W.L. #8500 8646
Sommer, Warren #8917
Sommer, Warren Frederick #8916
Soucy, Jean #1347 3095 3103 3108 5471 6095
    7485
Souter, William R. #9024
Southam, Christina #7947
Spalding, Jeffrey #139 684 1961 7636
Spalding, Jeffrey J. #2651 7585
Sparling, Mary #1205 1219 1220 1222 1224
Sparling, Mary Christine #1215
Sparshott, Francis #4454
Spears, Borden #93
Speck, F.G. #3554
Speck, Frank G. #3332 3337 3403 3404 3409
    3510 3513 3514 3515 3521 3528 3531 3537
    3545 3562 4075 4076 4078 4080 4082 4086
    4178 4381
Speck, Henry #4120
Spector, David #9202 9205
Speelman, J.J. #7861
Speirs, Doris Huestis #6371
Spence, Basil #9088
Spence, Hilda #2402
Spence, Kevin #2402
Spencer, Audrey #2726
Spencer, Charles #765
Spencer, Charles S. #5612 5996
Spencer, Robert F. #3375
Spendlove, F.St. George #812 2099 2101 2527
    5125 5126
Speyer, Arthur #3434
Spicer, Malcolm S. #7331
Spicer, Stanley T. #5648
Spier, Leslie #3660 4325
Spinden, H.J. #3412
Spiteris, Tony P. #7432
Spivak, Howard #8289
Spotowski, W.J. #8256
Spraque, Mary #5399
Sproull, Jane #4372
Sproull-Thomson, Jane #4377 4379 4380
Squires, Gerald #7272
Squires, W.A. #2407
Squires, W.Austin #3065
Sramek, Peter #1055
St-Arnaud, Micheline #1450
Stacey, C.P. #5270 5272

Stacey, Robert #910 911 1687 5958 5959 7158
    7274
Stacton, David Derek #5016
Stafford, Jean #1443
Staley, John E. #198 4666 5468 5530 5953
    6977
Staley, John Edgecumbe #943 1712
Stallcop, Emmett A. #3724
Stankiewicz, Audrey #9319
Stankiewicz, Malt #8984
Stankiewicz, Z.M. #9458
Stanley, George F.G. #5990
Stanley-Baker, Joan #6449
Stanners, James #7684
Stanton, James B. #2004
Staples, Barry #8910
Staples, S.M. #9222
Stark, Stuart #9134
Ste-Marie, Michel #2237
Stead, J.W. #7954
Stearns, Kathleen M. Graham #2292
Steele, Harland #7756
Steele, M. #8147
Steen, Lois #5059 5160 7156
Steffa, Emil Paulicek #3378
Steida, Sieglinde #934
Stein, Sam #2455
Steinbrueck, Victor #9503
Steiner, R. #3393
Steinhart, Jim #8043 8045
Steinhauer, Ralph #7767
Stellweg, Carla #6272
Stelter, Gilbert A. #8060 8714
Steltzer, Ulli #4145
Stenzel, Franz R. #1999
Stenzel, Mrs. Franz R. #1999
Stephens, Suzanne #8999
Stephenson, Gordon #8981 8989
Stephenson, H.E. #846
Sterling, J.Craig #6211
Stermer, Dugald #886 904
Stern, Theodore #3375
Stevens, Barry #6958
Stevens, Gerald #2099 2104 2397 2399 2401
    2404 2416 2550 5124
Stevens, Gerald F. #2469
Stevens, John R. #7703 9519
Stevens, Pat #6958
Stevens, Peter #92
Stevenson, Alex #4209
Stevenson, H.A. #8009
Stevenson, Orlando John #10
Stevenson, R.A.M. #172
Stevenson, Sheila #2484 2515
Steward, Gillian #8727
Stewart, Cathy #1904
Stewart, Clair #853 858 2603 7427
Stewart, Don R. #2470
Stewart, Gordon #5992
Stewart, Hilary #4068 4069 5269
Stewart, J.Douglas #1680 8339 8392
Stewart, John #7768
Stewart, John J. #8048
Stewart, Kenneth M. #3375
Stewart, Omer C. #3375
Stewart, Susan J. #6018

Stewart, Susan Jane Hopkins #273
Stewart, Walter P. #5152
Stillman, Terry A. #939
Stinson, Jeff #8284
Stirling, J.Craig #6210
Stocking, John #5892 6058
Stoddart, Hugh #710
Stokes, Charles W. #861
Stokes, John P. #8995
Stokes, John Peter #7769
Stokes, Peter #8511
Stokes, Peter J. #8679
Stokes, Peter John #7759 7767 7986 7992
    8000 8994
Stokes, W.E.H. #8959
Stolow, Nathan #73 527 9223
Stolpe, Hjalmar #3334
Stone, Peter #3366
Story, G.M. #8542
Stott, Margaret A. #4000
Stouck, David #104
Stoughton, A.A. #9171
Stovel, Herbert #8032
Stovel, Rex #980
Strachan, A.Matilda #2632
Straight, Lee #4907
Strasman, James #8203
Strong, Emory #3914
Strong, Judith #9126
Strong, Richard #8989
Strong, Roy #232
Strong, William A. #9466
Strongitharm, D. #8722
Strutt, J.W. #9515
Strutt, James #8984
Strutt, Jim #8512
Stuart, Barry #8910
Stuart, Donald #4237
Stuart, Richard #9380 9381 9383
Stucker, E. #7848 8332 8566
Stucker, Eugène #8815
Stuckey-Norman, Deirdre #3992
Stuewe, Paul #693
Stump, Sarain #3728
Sturman, Larry #2262
Sturtevant, William C. #841 3985
Suche, Anne #1966 8381
Sugino, Shin #996
Sullivan, Alan #8398
Sullivan, Edward J. #4876
Sullivan, Françoise #1396 1449
Sullivan, John #9395
Summers, Jack L. #2910 2911
Surrey, Philip #805 6345
Suscan, Charles #7291
Sussman, Lynne #2351 2357 2358
Sutherland, D.B. #9419
Sutherland, Maxwell #8424
Sutherland, Ruby M. #1985
Sutinen, Paul #3203
Sutnik, Maia-Mari #5054
Suttles, Wayne #4033
Sutton, Carol #620 5413
Sutton, Denys #6627
Sutton, Douglas #4377
Sutton, Richard W. #3592

Swain, Margaret #3629
Swain, Robert #4983 5527 7216
Swan, James G. #3761
Swanick, Lynne Struthers #7235
Swanson, Jean #1909 5886
Swanton, John R. #3780 3781
Swauger, James L. #3596
Swayze, Lucy M. #1068
Sweet, Jean M. #4994
Sweetman, Paul W. #3568
Swettenham, John #1108 1109
Swinton, George #412 416 429 4201 4218
    4227 4238 4240 4247 4257 4274 4281 4282
    4300 4350 4393 4404 4407 4410 4423 4426
    4442 4448 4450 4451 4492 7311 7376 7728
Swinton, George S. #4422
Swinton, Nelda #1206 1207 4070 4311 4376
Sydie, R.A. #164
Sykes, Meredith #7705 7719 7727
Symons, Harry #2917
Symons, R.D. #8113
Symons, Scott #2474
Symons, W.L. #9019
Syrokomla, Mathew #642
Syrotynsky, Ian #1822
Szabo, Zoltan #7306
Szajman, Rena #2936
Szilasi, Gabor #1494

T

Taaffe, Gerald #5475 7093
Taggart, Kathleen M. #8696
Tagoona, Armand #7311
Taillefer, Paulette #1801
Taillibert, Roger #9139
Talirunili, Joe #7318
Tamme, Madli #1797
Tamosaitis, Anastasia #2892
Tamosaitis, Antanas #2892
Tamplin, Illi-Marin #1907
Tanner, Sonja #693
Tanobe, Miyuki #7323
Tardif-Painchaud, Nicole #8334
Tarleton, Derek #7686
Tarrab, Gilbert #6755
Tassé, Gilles #3472
Tassé, Louise #4889
Tatley, Richard #8020
Taylor, A.T. #8220
Taylor, C.J. #8047 9009 9058
Taylor, Colin #3701 3715
Taylor, David #2286
Taylor, Frederick B. #1087
Taylor, Gail #6606
Taylor, H.A. #7334
Taylor, Hugh A. #1225
Taylor, J.Garth #4366
Taylor, John R. #3011 6414 6423
Taylor, Joshua C. #3985
Taylor, Mary C. #497
Taylor, P. #4195
Taylor, Patricia #2286

Taylor, Patricia C. #2293
Taylor, Richard #7337
Taylor, Sheryl #6246
Taylor, William E. #1104 1105 2805 3047
    3351 4292 4293 4345 4347 4350 4351 4359
    4361 4423
Teit, J.A. #4093
Teit, James #3769
Teit, James A. #3801 3823
Teit, James Alexander #3774 3783 3789
Templeman, Frank #2146
Teng, Jaan #2324
Tessier, Albert #9240
Têtu, Henri #8787
Teyssèdre, Bernard #1263 1443 1449 4605
    4815 6185 6584
Thauberger, David #1931
Thayer, B.W. #3677
Théberge, Gleason #950
Théberge, Pierre #88 518 536 541 557 574 661
    962 966 1266 1445 1564 1566 3231 5229
    5231 6581 6586 6588 6590 6675 6779 7248
    7258 7261 7583
Théorêt, France #1443
Thériault, Normand #528 634 696 1501 1528
    1564 5368 5533 5540 5566 5567 6760 7421
Thériault, Yves #5312
Thériault, Yvon #6865
Thériault-Chappaz, Marcia #8589
Thibaudeau, Claudine #5339
Thibault, Claude #1286 1369 3108 3127 4592
    8394
Thibault, Marie-Thérèse #7887 8633 8881
Thiébault-Sisson, Albert #299
Thiery, Jacques #5498
Thivierge, Charles-Edouard #9318
Thivierge, Jean #7881
Thivierge, M. #2946
Thivierge, Martin #1635
Thivierge, N. #2946
Thivierge, Sylvie #7493
Thivolet, Marc #5444
Thom, Ian M. #4736 5001 5549 6057 6516
    6566 7189 7546 7631
Thom, R.J. #8193 8310 8990 8991 9048 9460
    9505
Thom, Ron #4733 8284 8411 8412 9119 9140
    9358 9375 9465 9470 9478 9479
Thom, William Wylie #2003
Thomas, Alan #2033
Thomas, Ann #245 262 268 1056 3061 4880
    4936
Thomas, Audrey #3308 5832
Thomas, Christopher #9054
Thomas, Christopher A. #8366
Thomas, Christopher Alexander #9055
Thomas, Clara #5934
Thomas, Davis #3738
Thomas, Greg #8483
Thomas, Gregory #8480 8482
Thomas, L.G. #8720 8721
Thomas, Sheila W. #778
Thomas, Stephanie #8610
Thomas, Susan Jane Davidson #5359

Thomas, William #9103
Thomas, Wynne #4449
Thompson, A.S. #2287 2675
Thompson, David #90 520 536 5566
Thompson, Don W. #1017
Thompson, Grattan D. #8498
Thompson, J.H. #2725
Thompson, John Beswarick #2418
Thompson, Judy #3465 3466 3473 4102
Thompson, Paul #1820 1821
Thompson, William P. #8106
Thompson, William Paul #8105
Thoms, James R. #3597
Thomson, Callum #4377 4379
Thomson, Don W. #989
Thomson, Una B. #2632
Thorkelsson, Ione #8102
Thorne, W.B. #4724
Thornton, Peter #8142 8158 8208 8308 8985
Thornton, Peter M. #8986
Thrift, Eric #8985
Thrift, Eric W. #8986
Thurlow, Ann #641 7431
Thurman, Sue M. #480
Thuro, Catherine #2139
Tibbetts, D.C. #8535
Tiger, Lionel #9505
Tiley, Jim #7345
Tillemont-Thomason, F. #9411
Tillenius, Clarence #7377
Tilney, Philip V.R. #963
Timperlake, J. #8051
Tinning, Campbell #7378
Tippett, Maria #2007 2009 2010 2011 2016
    5032 5033 5034 5036 5038 5045 5136 6463
Tobias, Alex #9289
Todd, Andrew #793
Todd, Patricia Ann #5336
Todd-Hénault, Dorothy #7728
Toews, Julius G. #8715
Toff, Alan #6388
Toker, Franklin #8848 8849 8892
Toles, Page #736
Toller, Jane #2783
Tolmatch, Elaine #159 6306
Tomczak, Kim #687 2073
Tomlinson, Judy #2941
Tonnancour, Jacques de #385 439 806 4541
    5329 6797 7382 7385
Tonnancour, Jacques G. de #4798 6801 7040
    7381
Tooker, Elisabeth #3606
Toulat, Jean #1435
Toupin, Gilles #637 1503 1504 2774 3312
    6772 7471 7472
Toupin, Juanita #3313
Toupin, Paul #6806
Tourangeau, Jean #681 1552 1555 1661 2769
    4995 5085 5952 7035
Tourbin, Dennis #1808
Tourigny, Josée #1285
Tousignant, Claude #1267
Tousley, Nancy #704 3312 5412 7321 7422
Toutloff, M.B. #7641

Tovell, Rosemarie #7270
Tovell, Rosemarie L. #595 5924 6562 6563
  6564 6565
Toward, Lilias M. #1119
Town, Elke #7048
Town, Harold #536 818 947 5501 7370 7414
Town, Harold Barling #5502 7410
Townley, Fred L. #9024
Townsend, Charlotte #535 536 7247
Townsend, Earl C. #3577
Townsend, William #400 536 7417
Townshend, Nancy #1954
Tracie, Carl J. #8717
Tracz, Orysia #2132
Trafford, Dan #8343
Trafford, Diana #4240 4415
Traquair, Ramsay #1234 1324 2659 2664 2752
  7842 7852 8559 8563 8564 8795 8796 8797
  8799 8800 8801 8802 8804 8805 8807 8808
  8809 8810 8812 9022 9414
Trask, Deborah #2435
Trask, Deborah E. #1216
Trasov, Vincent #2070
Tremblay, Claire #6215
Tremblay, Denis #8819 8831 8845
Tremblay, Elyse #7881 8636
Tremblay, Gaétan #7307
Tremblay, Gynette #2879
Tremblay, Jean-Noël #6239 6651
Tremblay, Jules #4640
Tremblay, Michel #7892 8870
Tremblay-Chamberland, Nicole #1501
Tremblay-Gillon, Michèle #1639 1645 2238
  4535 5308 5441 6249
Trépanier, Jean #1560
Trépanier, Léon #7904
Triggs, Stanley #6725
Triggs, Stanley G. #5777
Tritschler, Thomas #4579
Tritschler, Tom #6576
Troster, Cyrel #5236
Trott, Elizabeth Hay #418 8759
Trotter, Reginald G. #337 341
Trottier, Louise #9257
Trowell, Ian #1679 5380
Trudeau, Charles #9088
Trudeau, Pierre Elliott #529
Trudeau, Yves #1430 7434
Trudel, Jean #234 235 258 259 1346 1355
  1356 1589 1590 1594 1596 1600 1605 1611
  1616 2678 2679 2680 2683 2685 2686 2687
  2688 4700 5127 5128 5968 6217 6218 6960
  8852
Tuchman, Phyllis #791
Tuck, James #4377
Tuck, James A. #3611
Tuck, Robert C. #5744 7798 7799 7801 8372
Tuele, Nicholas #6828
Tuele, Nicholas Craig #6829
Turcot, Henri #2718
Turgeon, Pierre #7081
Turnbull, Margaret E. #8660
Turner, Evan #6343

Turner, Evan H. #70 453 455 745 960 1253
  1419 1463 2110 3084 3219 4189 4467 4809
  4812 4986 5494 6468
Turner, Linda #3004
Turner, Lucien M. #3379
Turner, Lucy W. #2143
Turner, Philip J. #7843 8245 8492 8555 9042
  9166 9412 9417
Turner, Philip John #8798
Tweedie, Katherine #1556 5673 7309
Tweedie, R.A. #1178
Twist, Peter #8069
Twizell, R.P.S. #8142
Tye, Diane #6664
Tyler, Edward B. #3496 3775
Tyrchniewicz, Peggy #2893
Tyrwhitt, Janice #4616 6108 9249
Tyrwhitt, Jaqueline #8983
Tzonis, Alexandre #5093

U

Ullmann, S. #2083
Underhill, Frank H. #447 456
Unitt, Doris #2114 2408 2419 2430 2637 2956
Unitt, Peter #2114 2408 2419 2430 2637 2956
Ure, G.P. #8050
Urquhart, O. #2425
Urquhart, Tony #1682 7448
Ursell, Geoffrey #5398
Ussner, Wilfrid #8512
Uüricke, Madis #6212

V

Vachon, André #3607 3612
Vachon, Auguste #2951
Vachon, G.A. #1270
Vaillancourt, Armand #742
Vaillancourt, Emile #1571 6947
Vaillant, George #3335
Vaizey, Marina #5153
Vallières, Pierre #1507 1511 5573
Van Cortlandt, Edward #8033
Van de Velde, Father #4363
Van Egmond, W.G. #8111
van Ginkel, Blanche #8231
van Ginkel, Blanche Lemco #8218
Van Nostrand, John #8663
Van Raalte, Sharon #4260 4423 4440
van Schendel, Michel #4659
Van Wyk, Dirk William #1855
Vandermeulen, E.G. #8388
Vanderpant, J. #7456
Vanderwall, Judith #3977
Vane, Harriet #3246
VanEvery, Jane #7537
Vanier, Georges P. #8755 8756
VanStone, James W. #4111

Varennes, Marie Thérien de #2230
Varin, François #7766
Varley, Christopher #139 1474 3480 5046
  5979 6055 6062 7157 7466 7467 7468
Varney, Ed #3006
Varry, Jacques #4783 7342 8840 8841 9096
  9421 9551
Vastokas, Joan #3365 4034
Vastokas, Joan M. #3619 4212 4229 6986
  7446 9051 9132 9133
Vastokas, Joan Marie #3939
Vastokas, Romas K. #3619
Vaughan, Colin #8067
Vaughan, Thomas #6015
Vaujean, Marcel #7666
Vauxcelles, Louis #6614
Vazan, William #7470 7473
Veillette, John #8914 8917
Veisse, J. #2738
Veisse, Jeannine #4239 4256 4290 4313 4446
  4474
Veissière, Gabriel #8794
Velde, Franz van der #4221
Venne, Emile #8245 8248 8249
Ventures, Duck #6702
Verbist, P.J. #2957
Vermette, Luce #1646 1647 2218 6908
Vernet, Laurence #1435
Véronneau, Jean #954
Vézina, Raymond #159 241 242 258 259 908
  1280 4872 4873 4874 5690 5691 5692 6097
  6233 6750
Viau, Guy #1256 1262 1422 2195 4406 4602
  4603 4809 5165 5594 6186 6251 6344 6518
  7018 7288 7289 7450 7900
Viau, René #5193 5197 7483 9427
Vickers, G.Stephen #9136 9453
Vickers, Roy Henry #4148
Vidal, Jean-Pierre #3016
Vidler, Virginia #3633
Vidricaire, André #1663 7605
Vienneau, Azor #2409
Vilandré, Gilles #8592 8600
Vilder, Roger #7488
Villemure, Pierre #8634
Villeneuve, Paquerette #1421 3266
Villon, Pierre #1181
Vincelli, Brendan MacLean #9200
Vincent, Elizabeth #8459 8461 8462
Vincent, Jean-Paul #3016
Vincent, Rodolphe #2838
Vischer, Jacqueline C. #8169
Visser, John de #8769
Vivash, A.T. #1742
Voaden, Herman #7613
Vollmer, John E. #2776
Volpi, Charles P. de #927 1145 1203 1342
  1349 1716 1717 1718 2006
Voyer, Louise #8893
Voyer, Pierre #4861
Vroom, Richard #1186
Vroom, William Frederick #8774

W

Wachtel, Eleanor #3195
Wacogne, Catherine #7258
Waddington, George #7222
Waddington, Miriam #7165
Wade, Barbara J. #2714 2715
Wade, Edwin L. #4013 4014 4172
Wade, F.A. #8001
Wade, Jill #8097 8100
Wade, John #8158
Wade, Lorraine Laurel #4014
Wadland, John Henry #7172
Waegemaekers, Simon #2758
Wagar, David #1905 6504
Wagg, Susan #8610 9423
Wagg, Susan W. #9425
Wagland, Keith #9147 9148
Wahl, Kenneth #708
Waite, Deborah #3348 3940
Wakefield, Ian #8999
Waldron, Freda F. #9043
Wales, Shirley #818
Walkem, Charles #8553
Walker, Alan #947
Walker, Dean #619
Walker, Doreen #4734 4735 6255
Walker, Doreen E. #3008
Walker, Doreen Elizabeth #496
Walker, Frank N. #8059
Walker, Frank Norman #241 242
Walker, Harold C. #3136
Walker, Iain C. #8456
Walker, Jean Irvine #1683
Walker, John A. #484
Walker, John Barras #1683
Walker, Robert #1507
Wall, Jeff #7506
Wallace, Arthur #7985
Wallace, Arthur W. #7832 8528
Wallace, Brenda #707
Wallace, Don #766
Wallace, George #457 5487 5652
Wallace, Gordon L. #9028
Wallace, Kenneth #6543
Wallace, Ruby #9044
Wallace, W.T. #843
Wallace, William J. #3375
Wallis, Ruth Sawtell #3569
Wallis, Wilson D. #3569
Wallot, Jacques-Albert #3001 7513
Walls, Gordon #1960
Walmsley, Ann #7263
Walters, J.Allan #5493
Walters, Louise #1926 1928 2424
Wanzel, Grant #7835
Ward, John #7515
Wardell, Michael #3067
Wardle, H.Newell #3792
Wardleworth, Eleanor S. #8805
Wardwell, Allen #3923 3961 3978 4024
Waring, Alexandra #5662
Waring, Dennis #2940
Waring, Stephanie E. #7516

Warkentin, John #8080
Warner, Iris #5749
Warner, Janet #6924
Warner, John Anson #4157 4166 4558 4649
    5445 6322 7123 7124 7125 7126
Warren, Jill #6328
Warren, Sue #9046
Warren, W.R. #1719
Waterman, T.T. #3807 3812 3838
Waterman, Thomas T. #3986
Waters, Mackenzie #8738
Watkins, Frances E. #3548
Watkins, Ragland #1832
Watkins, T.H. #8083
Watson, Albert E. #9027
Watson, Ernest W. #6661 7336
Watson, Jennifer C. #3169 6333 6334 6376
    6424 6425
Watson, Sheila #6279
Watson, W.R. #5222
Watson, William A. #9393
Watson, William R. #1272 5342
Watson, William Ritchie #5217
Watt, Robert D. #2454 2456 2457 2647 2786
    6987
Watt, Virginia #5375
Watt, Virginia J. #4292 4293 4460 4487
Wattenmaker, Richard J. #3158
Watterson, Georgia #7194
Waugh, F.W. #3502
Way, Beryl W. #7982
Way, Ronald #7975
Wayne, Johnny #570
Weaver, Emily P. #3131 7164
Webb, Ken #1779
Webb, Marshall #6461
Webb, Marshall H. #1883
Webb, Peter #8193 9289
Webber, Alika #4108
Webber, Alika Podolinsky #3620 4098 4103
Webber, K.R. #8256
Webster, Donald Blake #2295 2297 2302 2303
    2304 2309 2312 2318 2387 2412 2472 2478
    2479 2480 2481 2482 2488 2542 2584 2634
    2704 3962 7767
Webster, J.C. #3065 3209
Webster, J.Clarence #212
Webster, Judith #621
Wechselberger, Joseph #9153
Weelen, Guy #6955
Weibel, Adele Coulin #2781
Weihs, Ron #3004
Weil, Martin #9537
Weiler, Merike #5230 6913
Weiler, Meriké #6915
Weinreich, Harald #8159
Wellmann, Klaus F. #3482
Wells, Oliver N. #3941 3963
Wells, Oliver Nelson #3964
Welsh, Robert #6591
Weltfish, Gene #3411 3842
Wentzell, Doris #2785
Wernick, Annetta #1797
Wertheimer, Esther #7542
Werthman, William C. #945
Wertscheke, John #8171

Wescher, Herta #5422 5424
West, George A. #3416
West, Ian #3713
West, Ian M. #3743
West, J.Pender #8686
West, Linda #3296
Westbridge, Anthony #158
Westerlund, Mia #797
Westgarth, Ralph Wayne #6037
Wetherell, Margaret #4549
Wheating, Pam #4158
Wheatley, W.S. #7548
Whebell, C.F.J. #8656
Wheeler, Dennis #5366 7252
Whitaker, Frederic #6327
White, Earnest C. #2599
White, Eric W. #2998
White, Gary #8914 8917
White, Michael #1494 1497 6496
White, Norman #7554
White, Peter #684 1961 3312 5206 7545 7636
White, Robin #703
White, S.J. #8247
White, Stan #7555
White, Stephanie #8139
Whiteford, Andrew H. #3485
Whiteford, Andrew Hunter #2739 3359 3638
    3744
Whitehead, Ruth Holmes #3643 6635
Whiten, Tim #607
Whiteway, Louise #1139 7781
Whittaker, Henry #8142
Whittaker, Herbert #472 9087 9115 9120
Whittome, Irene #607
Whyte, Catharine Robb #7572
Whyte, Jon #795 835 1960 5372 5707 6165
    7572
Wickens, Keith #2359
Widerspach-Thor, Martine de #4071
Wiebe, Marcia #8731
Wieland, Joyce #6159 7244 7577 7578
Wiens, Clifford #7746 8088 8196
Wiggs, G.Lorne #9339
Wight, Darlene #279
Wightman, W.R. #8009
Wilcox, Gary #2056
Wildschut, William #3665
Wilford, Nigel #4436
Wilkes, F.Hilton #9177
Wilkin, Karen #105 507 565 588 617 645 653
    792 1458 1857 1858 1861 1884 1953 1970
    3235 4777 5104 5486 5578 6067 6734 6838
    6991 7034 7050 7215 7292
Wilkinson, M. #3393
Wilks, Claire Weissman #6457 6458
Will, John #7585
Willett, Frank #3915
Williams, Jr., Edward H. #3406
Williams, Beverly #2936
Williams, Carl #9420
Williams, D.C. #9396
Williams, H. #8246
Williams, M.P. #3850
Williams, Megan #4298
Williams, Olga M. #8022

Williams, Richard #5676
Williams, Richard E. #5388
Williams, Stephen #3621 7076
Williams, Yvonne #2446
Williamson, Mary F. #3313
Williamson, Moncrieff #62 122 474 481 529
  1164 1166 2108 2109 3053 3222 5740 5741
  5743 6834
Williamson, Robert #4196
Williamson, Robert G. #4314
Willmot, Elizabeth A. #9541
Willmott, Jill A. #3358
Willoughby, C.C. #3412
Willoughby, Charles C. #3507 3550 3621
  3649 3779 3790
Wills, James T. #972 8681
Willson, Beckles #7120
Willson, Nancy #2705
Wilson, A.H. #7776
Wilson, Anne Elizabeth #2464 2583
Wilson, Bruce G. #269 270
Wilson, Clifford #7003 7006
Wilson, Daniel #6003
Wilson, Douglas #4042
Wilson, G.Everett #8303
Wilson, George #3181
Wilson, Ian E. #1680
Wilson, J.D. #8009
Wilson, Jane E. #2153 4680 5121
Wilson, Lois #9454
Wilson, Muriel #653
Wilson, P.Roy #8609 8623
Wilson, Peter #1798
Wilson, R.York #396
Wilson, Renate #3927 4121
Wilson, Stuart #8287 8576
Wilson, William D. #4739
Wilson, William Philip #2252
Wilson, York #7596
Wilthoft, John #3565
Wilton, W.P. #7962
Winchester, Alice #2110 2524 2525
Windeyer, R.C. #8290
Windrow, Martin #2867
Wingert, Paul S. #3428 3877 3878 3881 3887
  3889
Winkworth, Peter #1366 6096 6099
Winrob, Harry #4445
Wintemberg, W.J. #3410 3503 3505 3673 4332
Winter, Fritz G.M. #8454
Winter, Gordon #4394
Winters, Robert #8227
Winters, Robert H. #1119
Wiseman, Nelson #7604
Wissler, Clark #3405 3648 3650 3654 3656
  3657 3666 3668
Wistow, David #274
Witham, John #8047
Withrow, W.J. #471 5377
Withrow, William #499 501 752
Withrow, William J. #453 1678 3158 5378
Witney, Dudley #8524 9228 9524
Wittenborn, Rainer #1566
Wittmer, Marcilene K. #3383

Wodehouse, R.F. #1101 1102 1103 1104 1105
  6557 6832
Wodell, N.E. #7954
Woldt, Adrian #3762
Wolfenden, Madge #8145
Wolff, Hennie #1825
Wolff, Hennie L. #682
Wolin, Judith #8406
Wollheim, Peter #1976
Wolodkowicz, Andrzej #149
Wonders, William C. #8136
Wong, Maureen Lansing #5730
Wong, Paul #671 2073
Wood, Alan #6742
Wood, Edmund #4898
Wood, Edward I. #9081
Wood, Elizabeth Wyn #368 377 738 742 2098
  3251
Wood, Herbert Fairlie #1108 1109
Wood, Kathleen #6012
Wood, Kenneth #7680
Wood, Marianna #8069
Wood, Neil R. #9378
Wood, T.C. #430
Wood, Thomas C. #9211
Wood, Woodruff W. #8972
Woodall, Ronald #8083
Woodcock, George #93 140 150 559 3282
  3894 3907 4022 5395 7184 7600
Woodley, Virginia Anne #4975
Woodman, Ross #4242 5081 5225 6464 6465
Woodman, Ross G. #5070
Woodrough, Yves #8276
Woodrow, Paul #550 5350 6462
Woods, Joanna Marsden #6261
Woods, Kathryn Reid #1769
Woods, Kay #511 670 1771 4776 5972 6320
  7046 7413
Woodsworth, Charles J. #8037
Woodward, Arthur #3440 3536 3949
Woodward, Ashbel #3387
Woodward, John A. #3719
Woodworth, John #8694
Wooll, Gerald Ray #7992
Woolworth, Alan R. #3690
Wowk, Stephanie #5779
Woycenko, Ol'ha #2270
Wray, Charles F. #3587
Wray, John #9097
Wright, Bruce H. #8503 8738
Wright, C.H.C. #9449
Wright, Helen K. #6700
Wright, J.V. #3371
Wright, James V. #3380 7767
Wright, Janet #7741 7742
Wright, Judy #1010 7579 7580
Wright, Robin K. #4047
Wurster, William Wilson #8207
Würtele, Frederick C #8786
Wyczynski, Paul #5604
Wylie, Elizabeth #5453
Wylie, Liz #5496 7478
Wyllie, John #6811

Y

Yacowar, Maurice #6499
Yanover, Shirley #3020
Yapp, Russell K. #9471
Yard, Sally E. #7423
Yates, L.G. #3393
Yates, Sarah #647 1902 5853
Yeager, William #1722 2573
Yolles, M.S. #7684 9087
Yolles, Morden #9465
Yolles, Morden S. #9106 9479
York, Annie #4063
Young, David B. #4160
Young, Dennis #98 521 5304 5420 7243
Young, G.I.M. #8512
Young, Ira #1946
Young, Richard J. #8417 8418 8434 8440
Youngblood, Gene #7245
Youngs, Chris #1057
Yuristy, Russell #7632

Z

Zack, David #5397
Zazelenchuk, Stanley #4284 4314 6036
Zdriluk, Deborah #2573
Zeckendorf, William #9314
Zeeh, Thecla #7122
Zeidler, E.H. #9035 9113
Zeidler, Eberhard #9115 9378 9382
Zeidler, Eberhard H. #7746 9037 9114 9420
Zeldin, Gerry #550
Zemans, Joyce #550 4927 6377 6379 6509
  6748 6921 7558
Zemel, Carol #550
Zerafa, Boris #8204
Zervos, Christian #3351
Zimbel, George S. #7439
Zrudlo, Leo #7728
Zuk, Radoslav #8287 8768
Zwarun, Suzanne #3017 5400 8132 8133 8728
Zweite, Armin #1566

Subject Index

A

A.J. Diamond Associates
- see Diamond, A.J., Associates
Aarons, Anita, Can curator, art critic, artist, 1912-
- as director, Art Gallery at Harbourfront (Toronto, Ont) #3166
- jewellery #2696
Abbott, A.C., Can collector, fl. 20th c., and Eileen, Can collector, 1896-1980
- collection, Inuit art #4306
Abenaki Indians
- basketry #3596
- wampum #3526
Abernethy (Sask), Lanark Place
- architecture #8700
Abernethy (Sask), W.R. Motherwell Farmstead National Historic Park #8723 8724 9232
Abitibi (Qué)
- photographic views
  - Szilasi, Gabor #7309
About Arts and Crafts/L'Art et l'artisanat, Can periodical #4269
Abram, George S., Can architect, 1923-
- Winnipeg (Man), City Hall, competition #8985 8986
Abram & Ingleson, Can architectural firm
- Scarborough (Ont), Stephen Leacock Educational Complex #9476
Absil, Mickey, Can photographer, ca. 1950-
- portfolio of photographs #1023
abstract art
- see also geometric abstraction; modernism
- and Canadian art (1950s) #422
- and Painters Eleven #1785
- Borduas, Paul-Emile, on #4803
- British Columbia (1950s) #1990
- Canada #498
  - (1930s) #338
  - (1940s) #151
  - (1950s) #416 417
- Harris, Lawren Stewart, on #5714 5721 5723 5724 5725
- Masson, Henri L., on #6444
- Montréal (Qué), (1940s) #1395
- Non-Figurative Artists' Association of

Montreal #1415 1469
- Prairies (1960s) #1848 1862
- Québec
  - (1940s) #1468
  - (1950s) #1414
  - (1950s-1960s) #1441
  - (1970s) #1544
- Taçon, Edna Jeanette, on #7310
- Toronto (Ont)
  - (1953-1965) #1772 1773
Abstract-expressionism
- see also Tachism
- and Emma Lake Workshops (Emma Lake, Sask) #1929
- and Gordon Appelbe Smith #7225
- and John Graham Coughtry #5191
- and Norman McLaren #6497
- and Paterson Ewen #5384
- and Paul-Emile Borduas #4826 4829 4830
- and Pierre Gendron #5582
- and Robert Percival #6835
- Borduas, Paul-Emile, on #4838
- Canada #52 489
  - drawings #638
  - landscapes #496
- compared with automatism #1476
- Ontario #1748
- Québec #1487
- Toronto (Ont) #1773
Abverdjar (Foxe Basin, NWT)
- Dorset artifacts #4333 4358
academies of art
- 19th c., and Royal Canadian Academy of Arts #16 153 181
- 19th c.-1930s, Canada, criticism of #343
- 20th c., and Royal Canadian Academy of Arts #326
- (1950s), and Royal Canadian Academy of Arts #434
Acadian Village (Caraquet, NB)
- architecture #7805
Achard, Maurice, Can ceramicist, 1942-
- exhibitions, group
  - (1968) #2382
Achim, André, Can sculptor, 1793-1843 #1578
Achim, Normand, Can photographer, ca. 1948- #1534
Achtemichuk, Robert Brian, Can artist, 1948-

- exhibitions, group
  - (1977) #1901
  - (1978) #669
ACID
- see Association of Canadian Industrial Designers (ACID)
acoustics
- Montréal (Qué), Place des Arts #9092 9096
- Ottawa (Ont), National Arts Centre. Opera Hall #9104
Acs, Joe, Can artist, 1936- #1880
ACT
- see Artists' Cooperative Toronto (ACT) (Toronto, Ont)
Adams, Loren Dean, Can artist, 1945-
- exhibitions
  - (1979) #4501
Adamson, Anthony, Can architect, 1906-
- Edmonton (Alta), Canada Packers Limited #7973
Adamson, Gerald (Jerry), Can designer, 1937- #2487
- chairs #2471
Adamson Associates, Can architectural firm
- Toronto (Ont), Hydro Place #9352
Adaskin, Gordon, Can artist, 1931- #4502
Adelaide, Mary Ann, Can artist, 1910-1973
- exhibitions (reviews) #1210
Adelaide (Australia), Art Gallery of South Australia
- exhibitions
  - *Contemporary Canadian Painters* (1957) #423
Adirondack Mountains (NY)
- views
  - Browne, Joseph Archibald #4939
Adoian, Vosdanig Manoog
- see Gorky, Arshile (Vosdanig Manoog Adoian)
adornment
- see also brooches; gorgets; jewellery; neck halters; neck rings; necklaces; silver
adornment, Algonquian #3605 3633
- beadwork #3635
- shellwork #3505
- trade silver #3594 3608
- wampum #3521
adornment, Assiniboine #3653 3739
adornment, Athapaskan #4073

adornment, Blackfoot #3654 3739
adornment, Blood #3739
adornment, Caribou Eskimo #4265
adornment, Coast Salish #3896
adornment, Cree #3402 3739 3742
adornment, Dogrib #4089
adornment, Haida #3763
adornment, Indians of North America #3453
– beadwork #3457
– prehistoric #3393
– shellwork #3388
– trade silver #2631
adornment, Ingalik #4087
adornment, Iroquois #3605 3633
– beadwork #3635
– combs #3587
– shellwork #3505
– trade silver #3645 3646
– wampum #3521
adornment, Kwakiutl #3787
adornment, Maliseet #3641
adornment, Micmac #3569 3641
adornment, Mistassini #4080
adornment, natives of North America #3334
   3341
adornment, Neutral
– stonework #3503
adornment, Ojibwa #3539 4089
adornment, Plains
– metalwork #3698
– secret societies #3727
– wampum #3521
adornment, Sarcee #3739
adornment, Saulteaux #3402
adornment, Seneca
– combs #3587
adornment, Skokomish #3835
adornment, Slavey #4089
adornment, Snuqualmi #3835
adornment, Tagish #4106
adornment, Tahltan
– (1910s) #4074
adornment, Tanana #4095
adornment, Tête de Boule #4079
adornment, Tlingit #3763 3976 4106
adornment, Tsimshian #3763
adornment, Tutchone #4106
adornment, Woodlands #3633
– beadwork #3635
– shellwork #3505
advertising
– see also posters
– and architecture
   – (1950s) #8302
   – (1960s) #8267
– Arthur, Paul, on #859
– Elbaz, André, on #5365
– use of photography #1024
advertising, Canadian
– (1890-1940) #846
– (1940s) #850 851 853 2603
– (1950s) #855 858 860 861 865
– (1960s) #867 868 870
– (1965-1968) #874
– (1970s) #886 888 894 907
– (1981) #941

– Art Directors' Club of Toronto #854
– Art Directors' Club of Winnipeg
   (1964-1970) #872
– Burns, Cooper, Donahue, Fleming &
   Company Ltd. #904
– Burns, Cooper, Hynes Ltd. #905 906
– Burns & Cooper Ltd. #892 896
– Burton Kramer Associates #889
– Bush, Jack Hamilton #4963
– Cooper and Beatty Ltd. #5297
– Design Collaborative Montreal Ltd. #878
   882 885
– Gerald Bern Agency #871
– Gottschalk & Ash #879 887
– Jacques Guillon Designers Inc. #2623
– newspapers, St. John's (Nfld), (1806-1900)
   #1158
– newspapers and magazines, late 19th-early
   20th cs. #891
– Paul Arthur and Associates #873
– posters #903 910
– use of photographs to promote British
   Columbia (1890-1914) #2030
aerial photography, Canadian #1017
aesthetics
– see also art theory and criticism; beauty;
   sublime; taste (aesthetics)
aesthetics, Indians of North America #3487
– (1970s) #4137
aesthetics, Inuit #4263 4282 4295 4297 4420
   4422 4426 4442
aesthetics, natives of North America #3351
Affleck, Desbarats, Dimakopoulos, Leben-
   sold, Michaud, Sise, Can architectural firm
– Montréal (Qué)
   – Place des Arts #9083 9092 9093 9096
   – Place Ville-Marie #9314 9315
– Vancouver (BC)
   – Queen Elizabeth Theatre #7679 9085
   – Vancouver Civic Auditorium, competi-
      tion #9080
Affleck, Desbarats, Dimakopoulos, Leben-
   sold, Sise, Can architectural firm
– Charlottetown (PEI)
   – Confederation Centre #9094
– Chomedey (Qué)
   – City Hall #8990
– Montréal (Qué) #8322
   – Expo '67 theme pavilions #7686 9215
   – Place Bonaventure #7694 9292 9319 9320
      9321 9322 9323 9325
   – Saint George's Greek Orthodox Cathe-
      dral #8841 8846
   – Tifereth Jerusalem Synagogue #8846
– Osaka (Japan)
   – Expo '70. Canadian Pavilion, competi-
      tion #9217
– Ottawa (Ont)
   – National Arts Centre #9104 9105
– Wolfe County (Qué)
   – Church of Saint-Gérard Majella #8846
Affleck, Desbarats, Dimakopoulos, Leben-
   sold, Sise & Schoenauer, Can architectural
   firm
– Charlottetown (PEI)
   – Confederation Centre #7683

– competition #9088 9089
Affleck, Raymond Tait (Ray), Can architect,
   1922-
– Montréal (Qué), Town of Mount Royal
   Post Office #7857
– on architecture #7746
Afikpo (Africa)
– masks #3945
Agawa River region (Ont)
– pictographs, Algonquian #3589
Agnew, Ludlow & Scott, Can architectural
   firm
– Welland (Ont), Welland County General
   Hospital #9031
agricultural implements, Canadian #2095
– (1886-1930), Eaton's catalogues #2851
– as folk art #2139
– wooden, Ontario, 18th-19th cs. #2588
Ahrens, Carl Henry, Can artist, 1863-1936
– and Homer Ransford Watson #7533
Ahrens, Jacob Henry, Can ceramicist,
   1828-1905
– as founder of Ahrens Pottery, Paris (Ont)
   #2328
Ahrens Pottery (known also as Paris Pottery), ceramic manufacturer (Paris, Ont)
   #2328
Ahvakana, Ulaaq (Laurence Reynold), Amer
   artist, 1946- #4272
Aicher, Otl, Ger artist, 1922-
– designs, Olympic Games (Munich, West
   Germany) #898
Aide-Créquy, Jean-Antoine, Can priest,
   artist, 1749-1780 #269 270 1233 1323
Aipelee, Oshaweetuk, Can artist, 1923-
– ceremonial mace, Northwest Territories
   Council #4386
Aird, Neil Carrick, Can jeweller, 1945- #4503
airplanes in art #147
– aviation paintings, Canadian War Museum (Ottawa, Ont) #1104 1105 1110
– Bennett, Geoffrey #4680
– Pattle, Colin #6784
airports, Canadian
– (1950s) #9513 9514 9515
– (1960s) #9517
– Mirabel (Qué), Montreal International
   Airport #9518
– Toronto (Ont), Toronto International Air-
   port #9516
Ajax (Ont), Ajax Municipal Building
– architecture, Craig, Zeidler & Strong #7694
Akeeaktashook
– see Akeeaktashuk
Akeeaktashuk, Can sculptor, 1896-1954
   #4504
Akkanarshoonak
– see Arnasungnaaq, Barnabus
Akulukjuk, Malaya, Can artist, 1941-
– weaving designs #4298
Alabama
– photographic views, Walker Evans #1513
Alary, Zénon, Can sculptor, 1894-1974 #2179
– interview #4505
Alaska
– Inuit

– art #4208 4280 4424
  – (1970s) #4233
  – early 19th c. #4369
  – bonework #4319
  – culture #4272 4318
  – graphic arts #4217
  – ivory carving #4382 4398
  – prehistoric artifacts #4327 4348
– views
  – Jackson, A.Y. #5911
Alaska Native Arts and Crafts Association
  #4208
Albany (NY), Albany Institute of History
  and Art
– exhibitions
  – *Les arts du Canada français, 1613-1870*
    (1946) #1331
  – *Painting in Canada: A Selective Historical
    Survey* (1946) #35
  – *The Arts of French Canada, 1613-1870*
    (1946) #1330
Albany (NY), New York State Museum
– art, Iroquois #3586
– wampum, Woodlands #3603
Albers, Josef, Amer artist, 1888-1976
– use of colour #468
Albert County (NB)
– views, Joan Steeves Gregory #5657
Alberta
– architecture #8083
  – (1900-1930s) #8126
  – (1950s) #8119
  – (1970s) #8087
  – Chinatowns #8137
  – Ukrainian #8127
  – wooden #8120 8136
– art #1953 1967 1972
  – (1920s-1980s) #1941
  – (1930s-1940s) #1943
  – (1930s-1970s) #1942
  – (1940s) #350 1841
  – (1940s-1960s) #1944
  – (1950s) #1946 1947
  – (1950s-1970s) #1884
  – (1970s) #1860 1868 1963
  – (1980) #1969
  – (1981) #1974
  – Hutterite tradition #1962
  – Norwegian tradition #2273
  – realism #1954
– art education (1940s) #2981
– ceramic sculpture (1970s) #1864
– churches #8913
– courthouses (pre-1930) #9005
– domestic architecture
  – ranch houses, late 19th-early 20th cs.
    #8720 8721
  – Ukrainian #8704 8709
– drawing #1968
– graphic arts
  – (1959-1973) #815
  – (1970s) #1958
– painting #1948 1970
– photographic views
  – Biggs, Hugh Beynon #4728
  – Horetzky, Charles George #5838

– Warren, Mary Schaffer #7526
– photography
  – (1930s-1940s) #985
  – (1970s) #1879 1952
  – (1980) #1971 1976
– pottery #2337 2371 2372 2386 2393
– public art #1973
– schools (1950s) #9392
– views #1965 1970
  – Anderton, T.George #4525
  – Barker, Charles Edward #4609
  – Brown, Annora #4933
  – Hind, William George Richardson #5807
  – Kerr, Illingworth Holey #6049
  – Savage, Harry #7133
  – Warren, Mary Schaffer #7527
  – Weber, George #7540
Alberta. Alberta Department of Education
– school designs #9404
Alberta. Department of Public Works
  – Edmonton (Alta), Alberta Government
    Administrative Building #8963
  – Jubilee Auditoriums (1957) #9084
Alberta Art Foundation/Fondation des arts
  de l'Alberta
– collection #1963
Alberta Association of Architects
– headquarters, Duggan House (Edmonton,
  Alta) #8729
Alberta Community Arts Clubs Association
– travelling art exhibition program (1980)
  #1972
Alberta Culture. Historic Sites Service
– conservation of architecture, Calgary (A-
  lta), (1974-1980) #8134
Alberta Potteries, ceramic manufacturer
  (Alta)
– (ca. 1930-1938) #2371
Alberta Potters' Association
– (1980) #2393
Alberta Society of Artists
– and Alfred Crocker Leighton #6225
– exhibitions
  – (1931-) #1942
– periodical, *Highlights, Quarterly Newsletter
  of the Alberta Society of Artists* #1944
Albright, Ivan Le Lorraine, Amer artist,
  1897-
– influence on Tom La Pierre #6122
Aldridge Point (BC)
– petroglyphs, Northwest Coast Indians
  #3814
Aldworth, Roger, Can artist, 1941-
– sculptures #1151
Alert Bay (BC)
– community house and totem poles, Kwakiutl Indians #3936
Alert Bay (BC), U'Mista Cultural Museum
– art, Kwakiutl #4052
– exhibitions
  – *The Art of Nunstins/L'art de Nunstins*
    (1981) #6934
Aleut
– art #3370 4360
– culture, 18th c. #3445
– jade #3331

– prehistoric artifacts #4340
Alexander, William Walker, Can artist,
  1869-1948
– bookplates #917 4506
Alexie, Frederick (Fred), Can artist,
  1853-1939 #4507
– exhibitions
  – (1928) #3827
Alfred (NY), New York State College of
  Ceramics
– McKinley, Donald Lloyd, as student #6489
Algoma (Ont)
– views
  – Group of Seven #1768 1789
  – Jackson, A.Y. #5907
  – MacDonald, J.E.H. #6366 6370
Algonkian Indians
– *see* Algonquian Indians
Algonquian Indians
– art #3374 3385 3403 3404 3434 3558 3574
  3605 3621 3633
  – 19th c. #3737 3750
  – 20th c. #4143 4150
  – (1970s-1980s) #4139
  – (1980) #4159
– basketry #3562 3625
– beadwork #3582 3635
– birchbark #3483 3510 3571
– birdstones #3499 3511 3577
– containers #3507 3638 3744
– costume #3580 3739
– culture #3490 3529 3631 4097
– equestrian trappings #3405
– headgear #3417
– leatherwork #3456
– masks #3337
– mats #3561
– Midewiwin, scrolls #3702
– moccasins and containers #3544
– moose hair embroidery #3513
– painting #3672
  – 20th c. #4144 4157
– petroglyphs #3619
– pictographs #3575 3576 3583 3589 3600
– pipes #3463
– pottery #3502 3530 3545
– quillwork #3443 3471 3474 3475 3652
– serigraphy #4151 4158
– shamanism and tree of life #3365
– shellwork #3505
– silver #2101
– snowshoes #2812 3523
– stonework #3406
– Thunderbird #3493
– trade silver #3594 3608
– tree myths and symbols #3516
– wampum #3521 3541 3567 3603
Algonquin Indians
– art #3601
– containers #3542 4078
– moccasins #3554
Algonquin Legend Painters
– and Jackson Beardy #4161
– and Norval Morrisseau #4161
Algonquin Park (Ont)
– memorial to Tom Thomson #7350

– views, Tom Thomson #7351 7364

Allain, Marie-Hélène, Can sculptor, 1939-
– interview #4508

Allan, George & Moorhouse, Can architectural firm
– Toronto (Ont), domestic architecture #8493

Allan, George William, Can collector, 1822-1901
– as patron of Paul Kane #6004

Allan, Marguerite Buller, Can artist, fl. 1905-1919
– illustrations #916

Allen, Gladys W., Can stained glass artist, fl. 1920s-1940s
– stained glass
– Oshawa (Ont), Saint George's Anglican Church #8899
– Ottawa (Ont), Parliament Buildings. Memorial Tower. Soldiers' Memorial Windows #2445

Allen, Gower, Huggins & Meiklejohn, Can architectural firm
– Vernon (BC), Vernon Civic Centre #8972

Allen, Ralph, Can artist, 1926-
– concept of space #4509

Alleyn, George Edmund, Can artist, 1931- #1542 1543 4510 4511 4513
– exhibitions
– (1974) #4512
– exhibitions, group
– (1962) #1420
– in Paris (France) #426 1434
– interview #1527

alleys
– see streets

Alliance graphique internationale (AGI)
– (1970s) #897

Allison, Frank Drummond, Can artist, 1883-1951
– exhibitions, group
– (1940) #350

Alloucherie, Jocelyne, Can artist, 1945-
– interview #4514

Allukpik, John, Can artist, 1935- #4202

Allward, John Raphael, Can stained glass artist, 1856-1929 #2450 4515

Allward, Walter Seymour, Can sculptor, 1876-1955 #10 1231 1713 4517
– as member, Canadian Art Club #193
– Battle of Ypres war memorial (Ypres, France) #4518
– exhibitions (reviews) #204
– monuments #4516
– Vimy Memorial (France) #4519

Allward & Gillies, Can architectural firm
– Saint John (NB), Saint John General Hospital #9031

Allward & Gouinlock, Can architectural firm
– Toronto (Ont), Sunnybrook Hospital #9027

Allward and McCormick, stained glass studio (Winnipeg, Man) #2450

Almanach du peuple, L', Can periodical
– illustrations, Henri Julien #5987

Alpert, Laura, Can artist, 1948-
– exhibitions, group

– (1975) #1867

Alpine Club of Canada
– and A.Y. Jackson #5919
– and Byron Harmon #5707

Alps
– views, Robert Ford Gagen #5530

altar cloths, Canadian
– embroidery, Ursulines #2777

altarpieces, Canadian
– Baillairgé, François, Church of Notre-Dame de Québec (Québec, Qué) #4591
– Baillairgé, Thomas, Charlesbourg (Qué) #8851
– Bolvin, Gilles #4782 8874
– Gauthier, Amable #8874
– Levasseur, Pierre-Noël, Ursuline Convent. Chapel (Québec, Qué) #8852
– Liébert, Philippe #6280 6281
– Lorretteville (Qué), Church of Notre-Dame-de-la-Jeune-Lorette #8804
– Montréal (Qué), Couvent des récollets #8855
– Nicolet (Qué), Church of Saint-Grégoire de Nicolet #1636
– Pépin, Joseph #8874
– Québec (1650-1925) #1592
– Quévillon, Louis-Amable #8874

Altman, Gerry, Can photographer, fl. 1976
– portfolio of photographs #1023

aluminum, Canadian
– 20th c., and decline of copperware #2704

Amarook, Michael, Can sculptor, 1941-
– exhibitions (reviews) #4403 4408

Amarouk
– see Amarook, Michael

amateur art
– see also Art Brut

amateur art, Canadian
– (1750-1850), Public Archives of Canada (Ottawa, Ont) #239
– (1900-1920s) #309
– compared with folk painting #960
– Newfoundland #1154
– Ontario, art societies, 19th c. #343
– Royal Canadian Air Force (1940s) #1091
– Saint John Art Club (Saint John, NB) #286

amautik, Inuit
– in art #4300

Amaya, Mario, Can curator, 1933-
– and Realism(e)s exhibition, Montreal Museum of Fine Arts (Montréal, Qué) #533

ambrotypes, Canadian
– Halifax (NS) #1211
– portraits, Maritimes #1171
– Toronto (Ont) #1725

America
– in art
– 16th-19th cs., by European artists #255 256 260
– (1564-1867) #231 233

American Institute of Architects (AIA)
– survey of architectural profession (1960s) #8307

American Turf Register, Amer periodical
– illustrations, Peter Rindisbacher #7002

American West
– art
– (1804-1930) #5783
– Kane, Paul, and George Catlin #1845
– late 18th-early 20th c. #1859
– Pacific Northwest region, 19th-early 20th cs. #1999
– periodical illustrations (1857-1900) #931

Americans in Canada
– (1750s-1970s) #126

Amess, Frederick Arthur, Can artist, 1909-1971
– watercolours #4520

Amherst (Mass), University of Massachusetts. University Gallery
– exhibitions
– George Trakas: Log Mass: Mass Carving (1980) #7423

Amittu, Davidialuk Alasua, Can artist, 1910-1976 #4468 4522 4523
– (1977) #4521

Amos, Louis A., Can architect, 1869-1948
– Montréal (Qué), Court House Annex #9001

amulets, Algonquian
– birdstones #3499 3511 3577
– stonework #3406
– trade silver #3608

amulets, Canadian
– Ottawa (Ont), National Museum of Man. Canadian Centre for Folk Culture Studies #963

amulets, Dorset
– bone and ivory #4354
– copper #4365

amulets, Indians of North America #3329

amulets, Inuit #4453

amulets, Micmac #3556

amulets, Mistassini
– hunting #4075

amulets, Montagnais #4075 4082

amulets, Naskapi #4082

amulets, Northwest Coast Indians
– soul catchers #3853

amulets, Ojibwa #3539

amulets, Seneca
– mask images #3533

amulets, Tlingit #3976
– land otter #4028

amulets, Woodlands #3491

Amundsen, Roald Engelbert Gravning, Norwegian explorer, 1872-1928
– expedition, King William Island #4366

Amundson, Dale, Can artist, 1940-
– and public art #4524

amusement parks
– see also recreation buildings

amusement parks, Canadian
– Montréal (Qué), Expo '67. La Ronde #9212 9214

Amyot, Laurent, Can silversmith, 1764-1839 #2660 2662
– analysis of silver composition #2682
– and François Ranvoyzé #2658 2679 6959
– and François Sasseville #2672
– censers #2665

– influence of French silver #1244
– pax #2666
– works
 – Cap-Santé (Qué), church #8814
 – Detroit (Mich), Detroit Institute of Arts #2681 2691
 – Québec (Qué), Musée du Québec #2678
ancestry
– see genealogy
Anchorage (Alaska), Anchorage Historical and Fine Arts Museum
– exhibitions
 – *The Far North: 2000 Years of American Eskimo and Indian Art* (1973) #3366
Anchorage (Alaska), University of Alaska. Native Arts Center
– Anghik, Abe, as student #4530
Anderson, Carol, Can jeweller, fl. 1975 #2706
Anderson, Laurie, Amer artist, 1947-
– *United States: Part II: A Performance* #718
Anderson, Robert William, Can architect, 1924-
– Toronto (Ont), University of Toronto. Engineering Building #9459
Anderson, Tobey C., Can artist, 1946-
– on Jack Chambers #700
Anderton, T.George, Can photographer, fl. 1870s-1890s #4525
Andover (Mass), Phillips Academy. Addison Gallery of American Art
– exhibitions
 – *Aspects of Contemporary Painting in Canada* (1942) #355
– exhibitions (reviews)
 – *Aspects of Contemporary Painting in Canada* (1942) #358
André, Paul, Can artist, 1933- #4526
Andrew Malcolm Furniture Co., furniture-making firm (Kincardine and Listowel, Ont) #2463
Andrew Malcolm Furniture Co., furniture-making firm (Kincardine and Southampton, Ont)
– (1920s) #2547
Andrews, John Hamilton, Can architect, 1933-
– Toronto (Ont)
 – City Hall and Civic Square, competition #8981
 – University of Toronto. Scarborough College #9396 9462 9463 9464
– Vancouver (BC)
 – University of British Columbia. Student Union, competition #9503
Andrews, Stephen, Can artist, 1922- #4528
– on studying in London #4527
Andrews, Sybil, Can artist, 1898- #4529
Angelis, Joseph R. (Joe) de, Can artist, 1939-
– exhibitions, group
 – (1978) #1824
Anghik, Abraham Apakark (Abe), Can artist, 1951- #4530
Angiju, Peter Nauja, Can artist, 1932- #4202 4531
Anglicans

– needlework, Sisters of St. John #2780
Angokwazhuk (Happy Jack), Can sculptor, b. 1873 #4398
Angotiawak, Can artist, fl. 1956
– drawing of "kaitemayoh" gathering #4532
Anguhadluq, Luke, Can artist, 1895-
– exhibitions, group
 – (1976) #4268
– prints (1969-1977) #4533
animals
– as artists, Arnold Rockman on #7061
– livestock, Québec, from Europe #2221
animals in art
– see also birds in art; hunting in art
– Alary, Zénon #4505
– amulets, Montagnais and Mistassini Indians #4075
– animal style
 – Indians of North America #3460
 – Inuit #4334
– bear
 – Blackfoot Indians #3746
 – Inuit #4355
– beaver
 – Canadian and Indian art #56
 – Canadian art #23
 – Canadian pottery #2302 2312
– Beetz, Johan #4654
– Bella Coola Indians #3772
– Bradford, John Locke #4897
– buffalo
 – Blood Indians #3711
 – Canadian and American art, late 18th–20th cs. #62
– Canadian and American stoneware pottery #2309
– Canadian architectural decoration (1930s) #8226
– Canadian art #549
– Carr, Emily #5010 5019
– Clarke, Fred #5115
– Côté, Jean-Baptiste #5187 5188
– devilfish, Tlingit #4045
– dogs, Sandy Haeseker #5675
– European artists in America, 16th-19th cs. #260
– Fafard, Joe #5397
– fish, Tommy Brayshaw #4907
– Fournier, Paul #5487
– French artists in America, 16th-18th cs. #276
– frogs, David James Gilhooly #5601 5602
– headgear, Tlingit Indians #3803
– Hood, Robert #5825 5826 5827
– horses
 – Cameron, Walter Graham #4992
 – horse sticks, Plains #3743
 – Kenyon, J.J. #1681
 – Richard, Wilfrid #7000
 – Todd, Robert Clow #258 259
 – Wickson, Paul Giovanni #7573
– Inuit sculpture #4404
– Kerr, Illingworth Holey #6049
– land otters, amulets, Tlingit #4028
– large animals, Joe Fafard and students #1924

– Loates, Glen #6310
– Lougheed, Robert Elmer #6327
– MacDonald, Thoreau #6381
– maps of New France (1542-1550) #831
– McLean, George E. #6501
– Muhlstock, Louis #6656
– Northwest Coast Indians #3770 3890 4036
– Ontario, 19th c. #1727
– Parr, Nuna #6768
– pipes, Iroquois and Huron #3504
– Plains Indians #3758
– Pope, William #6906
– Pratt, George #6916
– primitive art #3333
– Proctor, Alexander Phimister #6943 6944
– Québec woodcarving (1940s) #1579
– Riopelle, Jean-Paul #7029
– Roussil, Robert #7090
– Savage, Harry #7133
– sepulchral monuments, Ontario, 19th c.-1910s #1723
– serpents
 – Indians of North and Central America #3391
 – Kwakiutl Indians #3840
– Seton, Ernest Thompson #7171 7172 7173
– Tillenius, Clarence #7377
– turtles, Plains Indians #3708
– Waldmann, Oscar #7511
– whales, Northwest Coast Indians #3831 3883
animated cartoons
– see animation (cinematography)
animation (cinematography)
– Canada (1940s) #370
– Doray, Audrey Capel #5301
– McLaren, Norman #6490 6491 6492 6493 6494 6495 6496 6497 6499
– Price, Art #6928
Annacis Island (BC), Annacis Industrial Estate
– architecture, Francis Donaldson #7679 9241
Annapolis Royal (NS), Banks House
– architecture #7823
Annau, Ernest, Can architect, 1931-
– Toronto (Ont), Bedford Glen housing #8078
Annecy (France), Journées internationales du cinéma d'animation (1965)
– exhibitions
 – *Norman McLaren* (1965) #6495
ANNPAC
– see Association of National Non-Profit Artists' Centres (ANNPAC)
Annunciation
– see Mary, Virgin, annunciation
Antigonish (NS), Saint Francis Xavier University
– conference, on handicraft movement in Nova Scotia (1942) #2145
Antiquarian and Numismatic Society of Montreal (Montréal, Qué)
– (1887) #173
– and château de Ramezay (Montréal, Qué) #3076 3077 3083

antlerwork, Copper Eskimo
– sculpture #4412
antlerwork, Iroquois
– carved spoons #3524
– small human effigies #3553
antlerwork, Northwest Coast Indians #3817
– implements #4068
APAC
– see Atlantic Provinces Art Circuit (APAC)
apartment houses
– Safdie, Moshe, on #8403 8404 8406
apartment houses, Canadian
– (1907) #8486
– (1950s) #8508 8514
– (1960s) #8517 8518
  – for the aged #8516
– (1970s) #8512
  – low-income housing #8520
– (1972), Canadian Housing Design Council
  awards #8744
– (1974), Canadian Housing Design Council
  awards #8746
– Calgary (Alta)
  – (1875-1914) #8711
– Manitoba
  – 19th-early 20th cs. #8102
– Montréal (Qué) #7933
  – Chateau Apartments #8558
  – Habitat '67 #8574 8575 8578 8580 8584
    8585 8590 9215
  – Nun's Island #8587
– Toronto (Ont)
  – (1910s) #8640
  – (1920s) #8644
  – Diamond & Myers #8071
– Vancouver (BC)
  – (1960s) #8699
– Winnipeg (Man)
  – (1910s) #8686
  – Assiniboine Block #9361
Appel, Brian, Can photographer, fl. 1970s
– exhibitions, group
  – (1979) #1904
Applebaum-Hébert Commission
– see Canada. Federal Cultural Policy
  Review Committee (Applebaum-Hébert
  Commission)
appliances, Canadian
– (1940s) #2603
applied arts
– see decorative arts
apprentices
– Ontario, 19th c. #2261
– Québec #2222
  – 17th-18th cs. #2214
  – 17th-19th cs. #2236
  – (1660-1815) #2231
  – (1740s) #6253 6255
  – blacksmiths, 17th-19th cs. #2697
  – furniture-makers, 17th-18th cs. #2530
    2531
  – potters
    – (1655-1916) #2344
    – (1850s-1920s) #2345
– Québec (Qué), 17th-19th cs. #2207
April, Raymonde, Can photographer, 1953-

– compared with Suzy Lake #1059
– exhibitions, group
  – (1980) #1063
– photographs as personal expression #1556
APT Bulletin
– see Association for Preservation
  Technology/Association pour
  l'avancement des méthodes de
  préservation. Bulletin (APT Bulletin)
Aqiggaaq, Mathew, Can sculptor, 1940-
– exhibitions
  – (1979) #4534
aquatint, Canadian
– Cotton, John Wesley #822
Arab art
– see Islamic art
Arapaho Indians
– beadwork and quillwork #3414
– moccasins #3554
Arbour, Léo, Can sculptor, 1912- #2174 2179
Arbour, Madeleine, Can artist, 1923- #4535
– interview #4536
Arbuckle, Frances-Anne Johnston, Can
  artist, 1910-
– exhibitions, group
  – (1972) #5972
  – on her art #5970
– reminiscences #4538
Arbuckle, Franklin, Can artist, 1909- #4537
– as husband of Frances-Anne Johnston
  #5970
– reminiscences #4538
Arcadia: A Journal devoted exclusively to Music,
  Art and Literature, Can periodical #179
Archaeological Report, Can periodical #3329
archaeology
– in art, Frank Allen Nulf #6727
Archambault, Louis, Can artist, 1915- #1504
  4539 4541 4543 4544
– and architecture #8231
– and Montréal (Qué) painting (1950s) #1403
– compared with Jacques Godefroy de
  Tonnancour #1412
– exhibitions, group
  – (1977) #1622
– interview #4542
– mural, Canadian Pavilion, Universal and
  International Exhibition of 1958 (Brussels,
  Belgium) #419
– on studying in Europe #408
– Royal Architectural Institute of Canada
  Allied Arts Medal winner (1958) #4540
– Winged Personnages, Place des Arts
  (Montréal, Qué) #8233
Archambault, Pierre, Can artist, 1943- #4545
Archibald, John Smith, Can architect,
  1872-1934
– Ottawa (Ont)
  – Château Laurier #9282
Archipenko, Alexander, Russ sculptor in
  USA, 1887-1964
– as teacher of Sybil Kennedy #6046
architects #8303
– see also women architects
– (1749-1973), emergence as professional
  group, Halifax (NS) #8317

– (1835), proposal for a society of architects
  #8306
– (1870s) #8290
– (1880s-1930s), as members of Royal
  Canadian Academy of Arts #8298
– (1880s-1950s), Ontario #8300
– (1888-1908), obituaries #7639
– (1901-1912) #7956
– (1910s) #8294
  – competition from American architects
    #8296
– (1911-1912) #8295
– (1920s), professional standards for
  admission #8244
– (1940s), opportunities for graduates #8247
– (1945), recommendations #8380
– (1950s)
  – (Don Mills, Ont), and builders #8301
  – on school design #9393
– (1960s) #8267 8307
  – and artists #8234
  – and builders and clients #8310
  – and city planning #8304
  – and housing #8513
  – and society #8279 8280
  – compared with architects, Great Britain
    #7693
  – on architecture #8311
– (1970s) #7728 7835 8315
  – attitudes toward profession #8316
– (1974), criticism of Royal Architectural
  Institute of Canada #8319
– architects' houses (1970s) #8525
– architects' offices
  – (1940s) #9297
  – (1960s) #9346
– Canadian Architect surveys
  – (1958) #8302
  – (1972) #8314 8316
  – (1974-1976) #8320
  – (1976) #8321
– Royal Architectural Institute of Canada
  survey
  – (1965) #8308
  – (1966) #8309
– Toronto (Ont), late 19th-early 20th cs.
  #8070
architects' correspondence
– Harris, William Critchlow #8372
– Rattenbury, Francis Mawson #8401
architects' diaries
– Thomas, William #9103
architects' writings
– Bellot, Dom #8333
– Cardinal, Douglas Joseph #8340 8342
– Chapman, Alfred Hirschfelder #8344
– Demers, Jérôme #7874
– Erickson, Arthur Charles #8354 8356 8361
– Myers, Barton #8391
– Plaw, John #8399
– Richards, Larry Wayne #8402
– Safdie, Moshe #8403 8406
– Taillibert, Roger #9139
– Thom, Ron #8412
– Zeidler, Eberhard Henrich #9037
architectural conservation
– see conservation of architecture

architectural decoration
– *see also* balustrades; fences
architectural decoration, Canadian
– Canadian motifs
  – (1930s) #8225
  – Bank of Nova Scotia buildings (1930s) #9186
– Montréal (Qué)
  – 19th c. #8612
  – domestic architecture #8620
– Ontario, gingerbread, 19th c. #8002 8005
– Québec (1650-1925) #1592
– Toronto (Ont), storefronts (1920s) #9364
– use of bronze and ironwork (1910s) #8222
– use of Canadian motifs (1930s) #8226
– use of paint, Ontario, 19th c. #8013
– use of plasterwork, early 20th c. #8221
– Winnipeg (Man), Birks Building #9355
Architectural Draughtsmen's Club (Toronto, Ont)
– (1886-1889) #8299
– (1886-1896) #8300
architectural drawing
– and monuments, Melvin Charney on #5091 5092
– Montréal (Qué), Canadian Centre for Architecture #7749
– Nobbs, Percy Erskine, on #8241
architectural drawing, Canadian
– (1850s) #1692
– (1927-1939), *Exhibition of Architecture and the Allied Arts* (Toronto, Ont) #8224
– (1930), Canadian National Exhibition (Toronto, Ont) #313
– (1960s) #7984
– Baillairgé, Charles #8324
– Calgary (Alta), University of Calgary. Canadian Architectural Archives #7730 7751
– exhibitions
  – Independent Art Association #1379
  – *Spring Exhibition*, Montreal Museum of Fine Arts (Montréal, Qué), (late 19th-early 20th cs.) #1228
– Harris, William Critchlow #8372
– Montréal (Qué)
  – Archives nationales du Québec à Montréal #8604
  – Ecole des beaux-arts (1930s) #2973
– Ottawa (Ont), private collections #8049
– Rattenbury, Francis Mawson #8401
– Toronto (Ont), Archives of Ontario. John Charles Batstone and Eric Crompton Horwood Collection of Architectural Drawings #8028 8030
– Toronto Society of Arts #1689
architectural education
– Baillairgé, Thomas #8325
– British Columbia (1950s) #8142
– Canada
  – (1880s), recommendations #8238
  – (1890s) #8239
  – (1900-1920s) #7652
  – (1901), recommendations #8240
  – (1902-1908) #7955
  – (1908) #8292

– (1909) #8242
– (1920s) #8244
– (1930s) #7658
– (1940s) #8245 8246 8247 8248
– (1950s) #7670 8249 8250 8252
– (1950s-1960s) #7682
– (1960s) #8265 8280
  – Royal Architectural Institute of Canada survey #8309
– (1970s) #7728 8316
  – survey of architects #8314
– (1980) #8289
– conservation training (1970s) #7773
– Demers, Jérôme #7874
– Halifax (NS), Nova Scotia Technical College. School of Architecture (1970s) #8285
– Montréal (Qué)
  – 19th c. #7900
  – Ecole des beaux-arts
    – (1952) #8251
    – (1953) #8253
    – (1954) #8255
    – (1955) #8257
    – (1956) #8259
    – (1957) #8260 8261
  – McGill University. School of Architecture
    – (1953) #8253
    – (1954) #8255
    – (1955) #8257
    – (1956) #8259
    – (1957) #8260
    – (1958) #8262
    – (1959) #8263
    – (1960) #8264
    – (1961) #8266 8267
    – (1962) #8268
    – (1963) #8270
    – (1964) #8271
    – (1965) #8273
    – (1966) #8274
    – (1967) #8275
    – (1968) #8277
    – (1970s) #8287
  – Université de Montréal. Ecole d'architecture #8269
    – (1958) #8262
    – (1959) #8263
    – (1960) #8264
    – (1961) #8266
    – (1962) #8268
    – (1963) #8270
    – (1964) #8271
    – (1965) #8273
    – (1966) #8274
    – (1967) #8275
    – (1968) #8277
– Ontario
  – (1970s) #8288
– Ottawa (Ont), Carleton University. School of Architecture (1970s) #8284
– Québec
  – (1960s) #8307
  – and domestic architecture (1960s) #8279
– Québec (Qué), Université Laval. Ecole

d'architecture #8271
– (1965) #8273
– (1966) #8274
– (1967) #8275
– (1968) #8277
– Toronto (Ont)
  – (1910s), and John MacIntosh Lyle #8243
  – University of Toronto. School of Architecture
    – (1950s) #8254
    – (1960s) #8282
    – (1967-1975), experimental curriculum program #8286
    – (1968), operational gaming teaching technique #8278
    – (1970) #8313
– Vancouver (BC), University of British Columbia. School of Architecture (1950s) #8258
– Winnipeg (Man), University of Manitoba. School of Architecture
  – (1950s) #8256
  – (1960s) #8272
  – (1968), Environmental Studies program #8281
architectural engineering
– *see* building
Architectural Guild of Toronto (Toronto, Ont)
– (1887-1898) #8297 8299 8300
Architectural Historical Survey of Manitoba
– *see* Manitoba. Architectural Historical Survey of Manitoba
architectural history
– Canada #7699
Architectural Institute of British Columbia #3186 8142
Architectural League of America
– and Toronto Society of Architects #7956
architectural materials
– *see also* brick; cast-iron; cements, mortars, and plasters; concrete; masonry; stone; stucco; wood
– Calgary (Alta), (1875-1914) #8121
– Canada
  – (1867-1967) #7695
  – early 20th c. #7652
– Charlevoix (Qué), houses #8629
– Halifax (NS), 19th c. #7822
– Kingston and Frontenac County (Ont), 19th c. #8015
– Manitoba, 19th-early 20th cs. #8102
– National Research Council. Division of Building Research #7715
– Nova Scotia, 18th c. #7815
– Ontario
  – (1831-1861) #8009
  – houses (1920s) #8646
– Québec
  – 19th-20th cs. #7926
  – (1800-1870) #7947
  – houses, 17th-18th cs. #8581 8603 8621
  – houses, 17th-19th cs. #8614
– Québec and Ontario (1763-1860), travellers' descriptions #8527
– roofs, 17th-19th cs. #7703

– Trois-Rivières (Qué), Forges of
   Saint-Maurice #7878
architectural models, Canadian
– (1927-1939), *Exhibition of Architecture and
   the Allied Arts* (Toronto, Ont) #8224
– (1969) #7700
– (1970) #7702
– New Brunswick churches #7873
– Québec
   – 17th-19th cs. #7872
      – churches, 17th-18th cs. #8869
– Québec (Qué) #7936
architectural pattern books
– *see* pattern books, architecture
architectural periodicals, Canadian #3313
– *Architecture concept* #7667
– *Canadian Architect* #7672
– *Canadian Architect & Builder* #7639
– *Canadian Heritage* #7764
– *Construction: A Journal for the Architectural
   Engineering and Contracting Interests of
   Canada* #7641
– *Royal Architectural Institute of Canada.
   Journal* #7654
– *Selected Papers from the Society for the Study
   of Architecture in Canada* #7721
– *Trace: A Canadian Review of Architecture*
   #7753
architectural photography #7922
– Canadian cities (1850-1900) #7744
– Canadian historic buildings #7688
Architectural Record, Amer periodical
– awards, Record Houses of 1975 #8745
architectural theory and criticism
– Bellot, Dom #8333
– Charney, Melvin #5095
– Cormier, Ernest #8346
– Demers, Jérôme #7874
– Gaboury, Etienne J. #8369
– Nobbs, Percy Erskine #7642
– Safdie, Moshe #8403 8404 8406
architecture #7959
– *see also* Art Deco architecture; banks;
   barns; Baroque architecture; beaux-arts
   architecture; breweries; building;
   Byzantine architecture; castles and
   country houses; churches; city halls; civic
   centres; commercial architecture;
   courthouses; destruction of architecture;
   domestic architecture; exhibition
   buildings; façades; factories; farm
   buildings; gasoline stations; Georgian
   architecture; Gothic revival architecture;
   grain elevators; Greek architecture; Greek
   revival architecture; historic sites;
   hospitals; hotels; igloos; industrial
   architecture; Italianate style architecture;
   libraries; lighthouses; lodges
   (architecture); military architecture; mills;
   mine buildings; monasteries; naval
   architecture; Neo-Baroque architecture;
   Neo-classical architecture; Norman
   architecture; office buildings; oratories;
   palaces; pattern books, architecture;
   performing arts centres; police stations;
   prefabricated buildings; prisons; public

buildings; railroad stations; recreation
   buildings; resorts; restaurants;
   Romanesque revival architecture; roofs;
   schools; shopping centres; skyscrapers;
   spires; stadiums; stores; synagogues;
   taverns; theatres; tipis; towers; Tudor
   architecture; vernacular architecture;
   Victorian architecture; villas; warehouses
– and art
   – (1890s) #8220
   – (1950s) #8227
   – (1960s) #8232 8236
   – (1980s) #8237
   – British American Oil Company
      buildings #8230
   – Clerk, Pierre Jean, on #5116
   – Harris, Lawren Stewart, on #5721
   – Iliu, Josef, on #8229
   – Korner, John Michael Anthony, on
      #6077
   – Reid, George Agnew, on #8219
   – Thomas, Lionel Arthur John, on #7349
– and ceramics, Claude Vermette #7480
– and documentary photography #1019
– and habitation sculpture, Robert Roussil
   #7094 7095 7096 7098
– and mural painting
   – (1930s) #15
   – (1950s), western Canada #1844
architecture, Algonquian
– birchbark #3571
architecture, American
– 17th-19th cs., influence on Canadian
   architecture #7687
– 18th c., influence on Nova Scotia
   architecture #7815
– 18th c., national style, compared with
   Canadian national style (1860-1890) #7697
– 19th c., influence on Québec architecture
   #7850
– 19th-early 20th cs., influence on Canadian
   architecture #7652
– (1850s), influence on Montréal (Qué)
   architecture #7920
– (1880-1914), influence on Montréal (Qué)
   architecture #7928 7929
– (1901-1909), Toronto Society of Architects
   exhibitions #7956
– (1910s), influence on Canadian
   architecture #7648
– (1920s), influence on Canadian
   architecture #7653
– (1930s), influence on Canadian
   architecture #7658 7661
– (1960s-1970s), compared with Canadian
   architecture #8315
– beaux-arts, influence on Québec
   architecture #7923
– early 19th c., influence on Government
   House (Halifax, NS) #8750
– late 19th-mid 20th cs., influence on
   Canadian architecture #7724
– Pacific northwest (pre-1860) #8140
– Second Empire, influence on Canadian
   architecture #7741 7742
– use of concrete (1910s) #7643

– western USA #8083
– wooden, 17th-18th cs. #7717
architecture, Assiniboine #3653
architecture, Athapaskan #4073
architecture, Blackfoot #3654
architecture, British #8494
– 17th-19th cs., influence on Canadian
   architecture #7687
– 18th c., influence on Nova Scotia
   architecture #7815
– 19th c., influence on Canadian architecture
   #7650 7652
– 19th c., influence on Manitoba architecture
   #8097
– 19th c., influence on Québec architecture
   #7850 7892
– (1880-1914), influence on Montréal (Qué)
   architecture #7929
– Gothic revival, national style, compared
   with Canadian national style (1860-1890)
   #7697
– late 19th-mid-20th cs., influence on
   Canadian architecture #7724
– Second Empire, influence on Canadian
   architecture #7741 7742
architecture, Canadian #30 57 58 59 61 129
   7668 7688 7689 7714 7728 8523
– 17th-19th cs. #67 68
   – European and American influences
      #7687
– 17th c.-1910s #7650
– 17th c.-1920s #7651 7652
– 17th c.-1930s #7661
– 17th c.-1940s #7676
– 17th c.-1970s #7711
– 17th-early 19th cs. #7841
– 18th c. #249 250
– 18th c.-1930s #45
– 18th-early 20th cs. #7719 7727
– 19th c. #258 259 7974
– 20th c.
   – and society #7732
   – as cultural expression #7690
   – concept of space #7748
– (1608-1867) #2120
– (1608-1930) #7659
– (1850-1900) #7744
– (1850s), recommendations #7638
– (1867-1967) #7695
– (1870s) #8290
– (1880-1914) #7736
– (1880s), recommendations #8238
– (1880s-1930s), Royal Canadian Academy of
   Arts exhibitions #8298
– (1890-1900) #190
– (1890s) #7640 8291
   – compared with American architecture
      #7640
– (1900-1940) #28
– (1910s) #7644 7648 7649 8294
– (1918-1920s) #7958
– (1919), competition from American
   architects #8296
– (1920s) #7653 7656 7657 7960 7964 8223
– (1927-1939), *Exhibition of Architecture and
   the Allied Arts* (Toronto, Ont) #8224

– (1930s) #1 340 7658 7663 7967 7969 7971 7972 7973
– (1938-1942) #7666
– (1940s) #370 7669
– (1940s-1960s), immigrant architects #465
– (1945), recommendations #8380
– (1945-1960s) #7682
– (1945-1970s) #7737
– (1950s) #388 7670 7673 7675 7680
– (1959-1969) #7700
– (1960-1970) #7710
– (1960s) #7683 7691 7692 7698 8311 9400
– (1960s-1970s), compared with American architecture #8315
– (1967) #7694
– (1967-1970) #7709
– (1970), building designs #7702
– (1970s) #610 7731
    – architects on #7733
– (1981), architects on #7746
– Acadian Village (Caraquet, NB) #7805
– Alberta
    – 18th-19th cs., fur trade posts #8129
    – (1900-1930s) #8126
    – (1950s) #8119
    – (1970s) #1951
    – Chinatowns #8137
    – Ukrainian #8127 8713
    – wooden #8136
– and art
    – (1960s) #753 8235
– and decorative arts (1960s) #8231
– and Heritage Canada #7770
– and landscape architecture, late 19th c.-1950s #7677
– and public art, Vancouver (BC) #2005
– and sculpture
    – (1970s) #773
    – Québec #1234
– and stained glass (1940s) #2446 2447
– and transportation, 19th c. #9512
– and woodcarving (1890s) #726
– archival and historical sources #7729
– Arctic #8184 8185 8186 8187
    – mid-19th–mid-20th cs., wooden #8189
– Association for Preservation Technology #7757
– Aultsville region (Ont) #7980
– Aylmer (Qué), (1800-1921) #7889
– Barkerville (BC) #8151
– Batoche (Sask) #8115
– Beauport (Qué) #7880
– Bedeque Bay (PEI) #7798
– Bellechasse County (Qué) #1281
– bibliographies (1960s-1970s) #7713
– Boucherville (Qué), 17th-19th cs. #7890
– British Columbia #8142 8146
    – (1895-1914) #8152
    – (1899-1901) #1977
    – (1940s) #8141
    – (1950s) #8144
    – (pre-1860) #8140
    – and Royal Engineers #8150
    – Chinese #8154
    – Fraser Valley region #8147
    – Whiteway, William Tuff #9508

– wooden #8153
– Calgary (Alta) #8124 8134
    – (1875-1914) #8121 8128
    – (1880-1980) #8138
    – (1909) #8116
    – (1910) #8118
    – downtown area (1970s) #8122
    – high-level walkways #8132 8135 8139
    – sandstone buildings #8133
– Calgary (Alta), University of Calgary. Canadian Architectural Archives #7730 7751
– Calixa-Lavallée (Qué) #7877
– Canadian Architect awards #8190 8191 8192 8193 8194 8195 8196 8197 8198 8199 8200 8201 8202 8203 8204
– Canadian Inventory of Historic Building #7707 7708 7716
    – computerized inventory #159
– Canadiana Village (Rawdon, Qué) #7876
– Charlottetown (PEI) #7797 7802
– conservation #7767 7772
– Cormier, Ernest #8345
– Dawson City (Yukon), (1897-1903) #8183
– Denison's Mills (Qué) #7884
– Dundas (Ont), (1813-1850s) #7994
– Edmonton (Alta)
    – (1800-1914) #8130
    – (1909) #8117
    – (1910s) #8131
    – downtown area (1970s) #8123
– Estonian #7723
– Expo '67 #483
– Fredericton (NB) #7809
    – 19th c. #7803
– Georgetown (PEI) #7799
– Georgian #8522
– Germanic tradition #2140 7735
– Gothic revival #7671 7724 7739 7740
– Guelph (Ont), 19th c. #7970
– Haliburton County (Ont), John H. Billing #8335
– Halifax (NS) #7816 7833 8317
    – 18th-19th cs. #7818
    – 19th c. #7826
    – (1750s-1930s) #7839
    – Barrington Street #7840
    – Granville Street #7817
    – Lang, George Macdonald #7838
    – waterfront buildings, 19th c. #7822 7834
– Hamilton (Ont) #7978 7985
    – (1910s) #7957
    – Victorian #7991
– Heritage Park (Alta) #8125
– île d'Anticosti (Qué) #7869
– île d'Orléans (Qué) #1252
– influence of climate #7701
– inventory of architectural records before 1950, Ottawa (Ont) private collections #8049
– Kings Landing (NB) #7810 7811
– Kingston (Ont) #1680
    – 19th c. #7995
    – (1673-1867) #7989
    – Browne, George #8339
– Kingston and Frontenac County (Ont),

19th c. #8015
– Kingston and Toronto (Ont), 19th c.-1920s #7961
– Kingston Mills (Ont) #8020
– Laterrière (Qué), 19th c. #7882
– London (Ont) #8018
    – 19th c. #8003 8007 8010
– Lunenburg (NS) #7836 7837
– Manitoba #8094 8098
    – 19th-early 20th cs. #8102
    – (1812-1870) #8097
    – (1980) #1906
    – Stechesen, Leslie #8409
– Maritimes #1119 7779
    – 18th-19th cs. #7780
– Massey Awards for Excellence in the Urban Environment #8217 8218
– Massey Medals for Architecture #8205 8206 8207 8208 8209 8210 8211 8212 8213 8214 8215 8216
– Montréal (Qué) #7906 7909 7913 7927 7930 7931 7933
    – 16th c.-1840s #7898
    – 17th-19th cs. #7899
    – 17th c.-1950s #7900
    – 19th c. #7915 7916
    – 19th-early 20th cs. #7914
    – (1642-1970s) #7918 7934
    – (1850s) #7920
    – (1880-1914) #1367 7928
    – (1880-1915) #7921
    – (1960s) #9220
    – downtown area (1950s-1960s) #7901
    – downtown area (1960s-1970s) #7925
    – greystone buildings #7922
    – Old Montréal #7904 7905 7910 7911 7919
– Montréal (Qué) and Québec (Qué), (1870s-1920s) #7843
– Montréal (Qué) and Toronto (Ont), (1960s) #7693
– Moose Factory (Ont) #7976 8032
– Nelson (BC) #8155
– Neuville (Qué) #7875
– New Brunswick #1178 2150
    – 18th-19th cs. #7808
    – Murray, William #8390
– Newfoundland #7792
    – 16th-19th cs. #7781
– Newfoundland and Labrador #7782
– Niagara-on-the-Lake (Ont)
    – 19th c. #7986 7992 8655
    – late 18th-early 19th c. #8000
– Norwegian tradition #2273
– Nova Scotia #7820
    – 17th-19th cs. #7814
    – 18th-19th cs. #7829
    – 18th c. #7815
    – 19th c. #7832
    – (1605-1850) #1196
– Oakville (Ont) #8025
– Ontario #8017 8024
    – 19th c. #7959 7993 8006 8023 8672
    – (1800-1850) #7965
    – (1800-1855) #8014
    – (1831-1861) #8009
    – and Ontario Heritage Foundation #8001

– hollow-wall construction, 19th c. #8004
– influence of Scottish architecture, 19th c.
  #7977
– Jerome Markson Architects #8386 8387
– Neo-classical #7983
– Ontario Association of Architects #7955
– pioneer villages #8063
– polygonal buildings, 19th c. #7987
– Thomas, William #8413
– views, Charles William Jefferys #5959
– Ordre des architectes du Québec prix
  d'excellence en architecture #7886
– Ottawa (Ont) #8036
  – (pre-1914) #8047
  – early 19th c. #8038
  – Glebe district #8042
  – La Salle Academy #9480 9481
  – National Capital Region #8035 8037 8039
    8043 8044
  – Noffke, Werner Ernest #8393
  – Public Archives of Canada, architectural
    archives #7738
– Ottawa Valley (Ont), log buildings #8029
– periodicals
  – Architecture concept #7667
  – Canadian Architect #7672
  – Canadian Architect & Builder #7639
  – Canadian Heritage #7764
  – Construction: A Journal for the
    Architectural Engineering and Contracting
    Interests of Canada #7641
  – Royal Architectural Institute of Canada.
    Journal #7654
  – Selected Papers from the Society for the
    Study of Architecture in Canada #7721
  – Trace: A Canadian Review of Architecture
    #7753
– Peterborough (Ont), (pre-1890) #8021
– Pictou County (NS) #7821 7827
– Polish-Canadian architects #149
– Pontiac County (Qué) #7894 7895
– Prairies #8080 8088 8089
  – (1970s) #8084 8086 8087
  – Jewish #8081
– precast concrete (1960s) #7684
– prefabricated buildings, western Canada
  (1904-1910) #8082
– Prince Edward Island, 17th c.-1930s #7796
– Québec #1233 1235 1237 1249 1258 1259
  1265 1327 1596 2183 2184 7850 7851 7867
  7868 7887
  – 17th-18th cs. #1320 2181 7844 7845
  – 17th-19th cs. #1334 1335 1341 7842 7852
    7858 7859
    – European influences #2221
  – 17th c. #228 229
  – 17th c.-1940s #7853
  – 18th-19th cs. #1338
  – 18th c. #234 235 269 270 7861
  – 18th c.-1820s #1300
  – 18th-early 20th cs. #1339
  – (1640-1840) #1329
  – (1760-1790) #1369
  – (1780-1850) #1232 1574
  – (1870s) #1307
  – (1880-1914) #7929

– (1925-1950) #1405
– (1930s), influence of French architecture
  #1381
– (1940s) #7846
– (1950s) #7857
– (1960s) #7862
– (1980) #7893
– and art (1970s-1980) #1561
– and land settlement #7855
– and nationalism #7848
– and sculpture (1970s) #1628
– archival sources #7863
– as folk art #1291
– Baillairgé, François #4586
– Baillairgé, Thomas #8326 8328
– Baillif, Claude #8329
– Confrérie des menuisiers de madame
  Sainte-Anne #1241
– influence of Ecole des beaux-arts #8265
– ministère des Affaires culturelles du
  Québec. Service de l'Inventaire des
  biens culturels #1277
– Morisset, Gérard #8891
– Parizeau, Marcel #8397
– recollets #8855
– Roussil, Robert, on #7097
– use of architectural models, 17th-19th cs.
  #7872
– use of plaster #1618
– Québec (Qué) #7892 7938 7939 7940 7942
  7945
  – 17th-18th cs. #7935
  – 17th-19th cs. #1306 1309 7936 7949 7950
  – 17th c. #1352
  – 18th c. #7943
  – (1608-late 19th c.) #7944
  – Baillairgé, Charles #8324
  – Baillairgé, Thomas #8325
  – destruction by fire (late 17th c.-1920s)
    #7952
  – place Royale #7948
– Québec (Qué) and île d'Orléans (Qué)
  #7847
– Regina (Sask)
  – (1909) #8109
  – (1910s) #8111
– Repentigny (Qué) #7888
– Rideau Canal region (Qué and Ont) #8012
– Rideau Corridor (Ont), (pre-1880) #8008
– Royal Architectural Institute of Canada
  awards #7660 7662 7664 7665
– Royal Canadian Academy of Arts #2
– Saint John (NB) #7807
– Saint-Roch-de-l'Achigan (Qué) #7854
– Saskatchewan
  – (1880s-1920s) #8113
  – (1960s) #8112
– Saskatoon (Sask) #8114
  – (1909) #8110
– Second Empire #7741 7742
– shell truss structural system, Québec and
  British Columbia (1950s) #7674
– Sillery (Qué), 17th-19th cs. #7879
– St. Andrews (NB) #7806 8550
– St. John's (Nfld) #7783 7787 7789 7790
  7793 7794

– (pre-1900) #7786
– steel construction (1960s) #7686
– Tignish (PEI) #7801
– Toronto (Ont) #5651 8060 8065 8067
  – 19th c. #8051 8056 8059 8073 8075
  – 19th c.-1930s #8076
  – (1794-1977) #8074
  – (1810) #8058
  – (1834-1934) #8055
  – (1849) #8061
  – (1850s) #8050
  – (1890-1928) #8069
  – (1950s) #8057
  – Archives of Ontario. John Charles
    Batstone and Eric Crompton Horwood
    Collection of Architectural Drawings
    #8028 8030
  – Baker, Francis Spence #8330
  – brickwork and stucco (1910s) #8052
  – Brown, Murray #8338
  – Chapman, Alfred Hirschfelder #8344
  – Diamond & Myers #8071
  – Howard, John George #8378
  – late 18th-early 20th cs. #8070
  – Martin, Arthur N. #6423
  – Romanesque revival #8064
  – Smith, Eden #8408
  – Todmorden Mills #8072
– Toronto Society of Architects #7956
– Toronto Society of Arts #1690
– Trois-Rivières (Qué), (1630s-1910s) #7883
– Truro (NS) #7828
– Ukrainian #8085
– Upper Canada Village (Morrisburg, Ont)
  #7981 7982 7988 8031
– use of building and ornamental stones
  (1910s) #7646 7647
– use of concrete
  – (1910s) #7643
  – Concrete Awards Program #7706
– use of decorative concrete (1903-1920s)
  #7734
– use of terra cotta (1809-1930) #7704
– Vancouver (BC) #7761 8159 8161 8164 8166
  8168 8170
  – (1886-1914) #8165
  – (1914) #8156
  – (1950s) #1992 8157
  – (1959-1961) #8158
  – (1970s) #8162
  – Downs, Barry Vance #8353
  – downtown area #7762 8171
  – Erickson, Arthur Charles #8357
  – Gastown #8160 8163
  – Kemble, Roger #8379
  – Robson Square #8172
– Victoria (BC) #2269 8149 8173 8176 8177
  8178
  – (1843-1929) #8180
  – (1843-1960s) #8174
  – (1872-1912) #8175
  – Chinatown #8179 8181
  – Rattenbury, Francis Mawson #8400
– Victorian #7697 7725 7769
– Waterloo County (Ont), stone buildings,
  19th c. #8011

– Wentworth County (Ont) #7954
– Whitby (Ont) #8016
– Williamstown (Ont) #7997
– Winnipeg (Man) #1891 8092 8096 8105 8256
    – 19th c.-1909 #8093
    – 19th c.-1910s #8099
    – (1831-1960) #8095
    – (1870-1914) #8103
    – (1881-1912) #8101
    – (1970s) #8104
    – Barber & Barber #8331
    – downtown area #8108
– women architects #7678
– wooden
    – 17th-18th cs. #7717
    – 19th c., Hudson's Bay Company, Red River Settlement #8100
architecture, Chilkat #3793 3798
architecture, Coast Salish #3851 3896
– McClallum site (BC) #3872
architecture, competitions
– see competitions, architecture
architecture, Cree #3402 3742
architecture, Dogrib #4089
architecture, domestic
– see domestic architecture
architecture, fictive
– see architecture in art
architecture, French
– 17th-19th cs., influence on Canadian architecture #7661 7687
– 19th c., influence on Québec architecture #7850
– (1930s), influence on Québec architecture #1381
– influence on Canadian architecture #7650 7652 7658
– influence on Québec architecture #7843 7892
– Second Empire, influence on Canadian architecture #7741 7742
architecture, German
– 19th-20th cs., influence on Canadian architecture #7735
architecture, Haida #3763 3982 4021
– H'Kusam #3913
– influence on Arthur Charles Erickson #8359
– longhouses #3979
– reconstruction, Totem Park (Vancouver, BC) #4118
architecture, Han #4101
architecture, Indians of North America
– and Douglas Joseph Cardinal #8341
– conservation #7767
– Manitoba #8102
architecture, Ingalik #4087
architecture, Japanese
– influence on Arthur Charles Erickson #8359
architecture, Kwakiutl #3787
– community house, Alert Bay (BC) #3936
architecture, Métis #8102
architecture, Micmac #3569
architecture, natives of North America #3353

architecture, naval
– see naval architecture
architecture, Northwest Coast Indians #3866
– and pre-Columbian architecture #3810
– house pits #3812
– log buildings #8148
architecture, Ojibwa #4089
architecture, Quinault #3845
architecture, Salish #3807
architecture, Sallirmiut #4324
architecture, Saulteaux #3402
– Island Lake (Man) #3549
architecture, Scandinavian
– log buildings, influence on British Columbia architecture #8148
architecture, Scottish
– 19th c., influence on Manitoba architecture #8097
– 19th c., influence on Ontario architecture #7977
architecture, Slavey #4089
architecture, Tagish #4106
architecture, Tahltan
– (1910s) #4074
architecture, Tanaina #4085
architecture, Tanana #4095
architecture, Thompson Indians
– winter dwellings #4063
architecture, Thule #4324
architecture, Tlingit #3763 4106
– gravehouses #4007
– potlatch #4012
architecture, Tsimshian #3763
architecture, Tutchone #4106
architecture and law
– see law and architecture
architecture and politics
– see politics and architecture
architecture and religion
– see religion and architecture
architecture and society
– see society and architecture
architecture and state
– see state and architecture
architecture and technology
– see technology and architecture
Architecture-Bâtiment-Construction, Can periodical #7667
Architecture Canada, Can periodical #7654
Architecture Canada Newsmagazine, Can periodical #7654
Architecture concept, Can periodical #7667
architecture in art
– Canada, humble dwellings #104
archives, Canadian
– Calgary (Alta), University of Calgary. Canadian Architectural Archives #7730 7751
– Montréal (Qué), Canadian Centre for Architecture #7749
– Ottawa (Ont), private collections of architectural records before 1950 #8049
– Ottawa (Ont), Public Archives of Canada, architectural archives #7738
– photography collections #1029 1040
– Toronto (Ont), Archives of Ontario. John

Charles Batstone and Eric Crompton Horwood Collection of Architectural Drawings #8028 8030
Arctic
– architecture #7728 8185 8186 8187
– art
    – (1960s) #441
– churches #8920
– domestic architecture
    – (1960s) #8732
    – (1970s) #8733
– photographic views
    – Mitchell, Thomas, and George White #240
– prehistoric artifacts #4371 4373
– views
    – 18th-19th cs. #278
    – Angiju, Peter Nauja #4531
    – Back, George #241 242 4580
    – Banting, Frederick Grant #4600
    – Bouchard, Lorne Holland #4858
    – Bradford, Robert William #4898
    – Bruce, Robert Donald #4940
    – Constantineau, Fleurimond #5168
    – Cresswell, Samuel Gurney #258 259
    – Harris, Lawren Stewart #308 1779 5732 5734
    – Haycock, Maurice Hall #5754
    – Hood, Robert #5825 5827
    – Jackson, A.Y. #1779 5907 5919
    – Kudluk, Thomassie #6105
    – McCarthy, Doris Jean #6461
    – McGrath, Judy #6474
    – Paterson, Robert Allen #6778
    – Richard, René-Jean #6997
    – Shortt, Terence Michael #506
    – Varley, Frederick Horsman #506 1779 7461 7466 7467
ARG
– see Québec (Qué), Atelier de réalisations graphiques (ARG)
Argosy, Can periodical
– on John A. Hammond, Owens Art Gallery, and Sackville (NB) #5699
Ariss, Herbert Joshua (Herb), Can artist, 1918-
– exhibitions, group
    – (1965) #473
Ariss, Margot Phillips, Can artist, 1929-
– exhibitions, group
    – (1965) #473
– use of words #4546
Arkell, Robin, Can artist, fl. 1980s
– illustrations #941
Arluk, George, Can sculptor, 1949-
– exhibitions
    – (1979) #4547
arm bands, Micmac #3572
Armington, Caroline Helena, Can artist, 1875-1939 #4548 4549
– as wife of Franklin Milton Armington #4550
Armington, Franklin Milton, Can artist, 1876-1941 #4548
– exhibitions
    – (1921) #4550

armoires, Canadian
- Ontario
  - (1780-1900) #2577
- Québec
  - 17th-18th cs. #2525 2530 2531
arms, coats of
- *see* heraldry
Armstrong, Beere & Hime, printing firm
  (Toronto, Ont)
- album, Toronto (Ont) views #7744
Armstrong, Geoffrey, Can artist, architect,
  1928- #4551
Armstrong, James G., Can artist, fl.
  1879-1890
- exhibitions (reviews) #1692
Armstrong, W.J., Ltd., furniture-making firm
  (Guelph, Ont)
- (1920s) #2547
Armstrong, William, Can artist, engineer,
  1822-1914 #4552
Armstrong, William Walton, Can artist,
  1916- #4553
Armstrong & Molesworth, Can architectural
  firm
- Toronto (Ont), Bruce House #8746
Arn, Robert, Can artist, 1942-
- colour xerography #614
Arnapik site (Mansel Island, NWT)
- pre-Dorset artifacts #4351
Arnasungnaaq, Barnabus, Can sculptor,
  1924- #4554
- exhibitions (reviews) #4403 4408
Arnault, Jean-Marie, Fr medal engraver in
  Canada, fl. 1830s-1840s
- temperance medals #724
Arnold, J., Can artist, fl. 1852
- exhibitions (reviews) #1692
Arnoldi, Charles, Can watchmaker, jeweller,
  1779-1817 #2663
Arnoldi, Johann Peter, Can silversmith,
  1769-1808 #2663
Arnoldi, Michael, Can silversmith, 1763-1807
  #2663
Arsenault, Réal, Can artist, 1931- #4555 4556
  4557
- in Paris (France) #1434
art
- *see also* abstract art; amateur art; Art Brut;
  Byzantine art; children's art; commercial
  art; conservation and restoration, art;
  fantastic art; folk art; kinetic art; minimal
  art; monumental art; Oriental art; Pop art;
  pre-Columbian art; prehistoric art;
  primitive art; Renaissance art; street art;
  Victorian art
- 19th c., Art Association of Montreal
  exhibition (Montréal, Qué), (1865) #1304
- (1905-1938), Canadian National Exhibition
  (Toronto, Ont) #107
- (1970s) #696
  - by younger artists #534
- and architecture
  - (1960s) #8232 8236
  - (1980) #8237
  - Clerk, Pierre Jean, on #5116
  - Iliu, Josef, on #8229

- Ottawa (Ont), National Science Library
  #9049
- and photography (1910s) #982
- Calgary (Alta), Glenbow-Alberta Institute
  #3194
- Charlottetown (PEI), Confederation Centre
  Art Gallery and Museum #3070
- Cobourg (Ont), Art Gallery of Cobourg
  #3162
- early 20th c., Canadian National
  Exhibition (Toronto, Ont) #1
- European
  - Québec (Qué), religious institutions
    #1352
  - views of America, 16th-19th cs. #255 256
    260
- Guelph (Ont), University of Guelph #3173
- Halifax (NS), Mount Saint Vincent
  University #3072
- Hamilton (Ont), Art Gallery of Hamilton
  #3142 3160
- Joliette (Qué), Musée d'art de Joliette
  #3100 3101
- Kingston (Ont), Queen's University. Agnes
  Etherington Art Centre #3145
- London (Ont), London Public Library and
  Art Museum #3153
- Montréal (Qué)
  - Church of Notre-Dame. Museum #3081
  - Concordia University. Sir George
    Williams Art Galleries #3096
  - Dominion Gallery #1293
  - Expo '67 Art Gallery #9223
  - Montreal Museum of Fine Arts #1343
    3104 3112 3117 3118 9133
- Oshawa (Ont), Robert McLaughlin Gallery
  #3169
- Ottawa (Ont)
  - Carleton University #3144
  - National Gallery of Canada #3061
- Québec (Qué)
  - Musée du Québec #3107 3111 3121
  - Université Laval #3080
- Saint-Laurent (Qué)
  - Collège de Saint-Laurent. Galerie Nova
    et Vetera #3089
- Saskatoon (Sask)
  - Mendel Art Gallery #72 3187
  - University of Saskatchewan #3202
- Toronto (Ont)
  - Art Gallery of Ontario #3136 3158
  - Royal Ontario Museum #3139 3141 3170
    - from Educational Museum of Upper
      Canada #3155
- Vancouver (BC)
  - Vancouver Art Gallery #3184 3185 3186
  - Vancouver Museum #3180
    - (1917) #3182
- Victoria (BC)
  - Art Gallery of Greater Victoria #3189
  - University of Victoria. Maltwood Art
    Museum and Gallery #3199
- Windsor (Ont), Art Gallery of Windsor
  #3156
- Winnipeg (Man), Winnipeg Art Gallery
  #3188 3192

art, African
- compared with Inuit art #4225
art, Aleut
- 18th c. #3445
- London (England), British Museum #4360
- Sitka (Alaska), Sheldon Jackson Museum
  #3370
art, Algonquian #3385 3605 3621
- 20th c. #4143 4150
- (1760-1860) #3434
- (1970s-1980s) #4139
- (1980) #4159
- birchbark #3571
- compared with art, Hopewell #3558
- double-curve motif #3403 3404 3409
- floral motif #3543
- Serpent Mound, Rice Lake (Ont) #3574
- Stuttgart (West Germany), Linden
  Museum #3737 3750
- tree myths and symbols #3516
art, Algonquin
- formal properties #3601
art, American
- 18th-19th cs., influence on Nova Scotia art
  #1220 1222
- (1870-1910), compared with Canadian art
  #196
- (1910s), compared with Canadian art #203
- (1950-1970), influence on Canadian art #98
- (1950s), compared with Canadian art #397
- (1960s), influence on Canadian art #515
  519
- (1970s), influence on Toronto (Ont) art
  #1796
- (1970s), influence on western Canadian art
  #1857
- Los Angeles (Calif), compared with
  Vancouver (BC) art #2035
- New York (1980s), compared with Toronto
  (Ont) art #1837
art, Assiniboine
- floral motif #3731
art, Athapaskan #3366 4104 4105
- 18th c. #3445
- Sitka (Alaska), Sheldon Jackson Museum
  #3370
art, Australian
- (1888) #175
- (1890) #177
- compared with Canadian art #44
art, Bella Coola
- Ottawa (Ont), National Museum of Man
  #4000
art, Beothuk
- burial sites, Port-au-Choix (Nfld) #3611
- Red Indian Lake (Nfld) #3623
- St. John's (Nfld), Newfoundland Museum
  #3627
art, Blackfoot
- bear motif #3746
- water monster motif #3757
art, British
- 18th-19th cs., influence on Nova Scotia art
  #1215 1220 1222
- (1928), Canadian National Exhibition
  (Toronto, Ont) #300

– (1929), Canadian National Exhibition
   (Toronto, Ont) #304
– war subjects #1082 1084
Art, Can periodical #560
art, Canadian #5 19 24 29 30 45 58 59 63 79
   80 85 369
– 17th-19th cs., French influences #2180
– 17th c.-1890s #185
– 17th c.-1910s #205
– 17th c.-1940s #40
– 17th c.-1960s #67 68
– 18th-19th cs. #812
– 18th c. #249 250
– 19th-20th cs. #136 137
– 19th c. #241 242 258 259
   – and Napoléon Bourassa #4872 4876
   – World's Fairs #261
– 19th c.-1970s #100
– 20th c. #567
   – influence of decorative arts, 17th-19th
   cs. #2093
– (1564-1867) #233
– (1760-1943) #31
– (1815-1965) #122
– (1820-1940) #28
– (1840s-1920s) #4
– (1850s) #1692
– (1860s) #1302
– (1867-1930) #13
– (1870s-1910s) #196 200
– (1879-1961), Canadian National Exhibition
   (Toronto, Ont) #1
– (1880-1930s) #20
– (1880s) #175
– (1880s-1920s) #10
– (1890-1900) #190
– (1890s) #177 188
– (1890s), advice to Canadian artists #182
– (1901), Pan-American Exposition (Buffalo,
   NY) #189
– (1907), criticism of #3299
– (1909) #194
– (1910s) #203 1713
– (1910s-1960s) #494
– (1920s) #288 289 298 299
– (1920s-1930s) #322
– (1920s-1940s), *Canadian Forum* coverage
   #3301
– (1920s-1960s) #461
– (1924), British Empire Exhibition
   (Wembley, England) #287 288 291 458
   5546 5547
– (1925), British Empire Exhibition
   (Wembley, England) #290 291 292
– (1926-1933) #294
– (1928), Canadian National Exhibition
   (Toronto, Ont) #300
– (1928-1929) #307
– (1929), Canadian National Exhibition
   (Toronto, Ont) #304
– (1930-1980) #151
– (1930s) #22 339 340
– (1930s-1940s) #395
– (1935) #333
– (1938-1939) #345
– (1938-1948) #379

– (1939), New York World's Fair (New York,
   NY) #346
– (1940s) #363 380 381 385 3250 5866
   – and National Gallery of Canada
   (Ottawa, Ont) #3027
– (1940s-1960s) #451 485 536
   – immigrant artists #465
– (1940s-1970s) #571
– (1950-1960) #511
– (1950-1970) #98
– (1950s) #387 388 389 406 415 420 429 432
   433 439
   – compared with American art #397
– (1950s-1960s) #455
– (1950s-1970s) #54 131 6586
– (1952), Venice Biennale (Venice, Italy) #399
– (1958), Universal and International
   Exhibition (Brussels, Belgium) #428 430
– (1960s) #87 441 443 456 469 477 478 480
   481 490 493 514 515 518 519 529
   – by artists in New York (NY) #460
   – conservation #527
– (1960s-1970s) #3274
– (1967) #488
– (1968-1970) #1481
– (1970s) #531 552 555 558 594 610 619 621
   637 680 696 702 703 707
   – artists on #648
   – by artists under 30 #584
   – eastern Canada #543
   – excluding Ontario #569
   – large-scale works #644
   – Marlborough Godard Gallery, Toronto
   (Ont) and Montréal (Qué) #572
– (1975), predictions #585
– (1975-1976) #627 645
– (1980) #690 691 699
   – 11e Biennale de Paris (Paris, France)
   #687
– (1980s) #912
– Acadian #1137 1181
   – (1960s-1980) #1136
– Alberta #1947 1953 1967 1972
   – (1920s-1980s) #1941
   – (1930s-1940s) #1943
   – (1950s) #1946
   – (1970s) #1963
   – (1980) #1969
   – (1981) #1974
   – Edmonton (Alta), Alberta Art
   Foundation #1957
   – periodicals
   – *Highlights, Quarterly Newsletter of the
   Alberta Society of Artists* #1944
– Alberta Society of Artists #1942
– and abstract art (1950s) #422
– and architecture (1960s) #753 8231 8235
– and Arthur Lismer #6292 6293 6297 6300
– and Canadian identity #327
– and collecting (1960s) #3219
– and fashion (1882-1910) #2897
– and history, John Bernard Boyle on #4893
– and John Russell Harper #3317
– and Lenore Crawford #112
– and nationalism #102 143
– and photography (1970s) #635

– Art Association of Newfoundland and
   Labrador #1144
– Art in Living Group (Vancouver, BC)
   #1988
– Arts and Letters Club (Toronto, Ont)
   #1671
– Arts Club of Montreal (Montréal, Qué)
   #1254
– Atlantic provinces #1123
   – (1960s) #1124
   – (1960s-1970s) #1130
   – (1970s) #1127 1131 1132 1133 1135
   – Atlantic Provinces Art Circuit
   (1964-1971) #3053
   – periodicals
   – *ArtsAtlantic* #128
– automatistes #1443
– avant-garde (1960s) #600
– aviation subjects #147
– Banff (Alta) #1964
– Bank of Nova Scotia Fine Art Collection
   #3245
– Bellechasse County (Qué) #1281
– biographical sources #81
– Boucherville (Qué), Church of
   Sainte-Famille #8868
– British Columbia #1986 1987 1995 2010
   3827
   – (1793-1886) #2025
   – (1910s) #1979
   – (1930s) #1982
   – (1932-1968) #1983
   – (1950s) #1994
   – (1950s-1970s) #2013
   – (1970s) #2047 2050 2053 2060 2063 2067
   2068 2078
   – Okanagan region #2048
   – (1970s-1980) #2082
   – (1981) #2084
   – women artists (1970s) #2054
– British Columbia Society of Artists #1978
– Calgary (Alta)
   – (1970s) #1966
   – Glenbow-Alberta Institute #3191 3194
– Canadian Art Club (Toronto, Ont) #193
   204 211
– Canadian museum and gallery collections
   #3320
– Charlottetown (PEI), Confederation Centre
   Art Gallery and Museum #3070
– Châteauguay (Qué), Church of
   Saint-Joachim #8861
– Chicoutimi (Qué), Université du Québec
   (1970s) #3016
– Cobourg (Ont), Art Gallery of Cobourg
   #3162
– compared with Australian art #44
– computerized inventory standards for
   works of art #159
– corporate collections #3243 3259 3291
– *Création* (Montréal, Qué) #1492
– Duncan, Douglas M., collection #119 3218
   3232
– Durham region (Ont), (1970s) #1826
– Eastern Townships (Qué)
   – (1970s) #1282 1535

– Regroupement des artistes des Cantons
de l'Est (RACE) #1539
– Edmonton (Alta)
– (1960s-1980s) #1975
– Edmonton private collections #105
– University of Alberta #3200
– Emma Lake (Sask), Emma Lake
Workshops #1921 1923
– Essex County Artists #1668
– Estonian #118 1761
– Expo '67 #483
– Federation of Canadian Artists #360 364
376
– Fredericton (NB)
– 19th c. #1174
– private collections #142
– Fredericton Art Club (Fredericton, NB)
#1176
– Fusion des arts (Montréal, Qué) #1482
– General Idea #5583 5584
– Group of Seven #375 1732 1780 1790
– Guelph (Ont)
– (1850s-1970s) #1685
– University of Guelph #3173
– guide for collectors #2104
– Halifax (NS)
– (1749-1949) #1195
– (1830s) #1226
– (1980) #1227
– Mount Saint Vincent University #3072
– Hamilton (Ont) #1674 7978
– Art Gallery of Hamilton #3138 3142
3160
– annual exhibition (1948-) #38
– Women's Art Association of Hamilton
#1701
– Hampton Group (Hampton, NB) #1177
– île d'Orléans (Qué) #1238
– imaginary works #530
– Imperial Oil Ltd. #3241
– Independent Art Association #1379
– Island Arts and Crafts Society (Victoria,
BC) #2034
– Jewish artists #435
– Joliette (Qué), Musée d'art de Joliette
#3100 3101
– Kingston (Ont), Queen's University. Agnes
Etherington Art Centre #3145
– Kleinburg (Ont), McMichael Canadian
Collection #3172
– Labor Arts Guild (Vancouver, BC) #1985
– Latvian #49 475
– Limners (Victoria, BC) #2043
– Loeb, Mr. and Mrs. Jules, collection #3231
– London (Ont)
– (1947-1979) #1828
– (1960s) #1759 1791
– late 19th c. #1726
– London Public Library and Art Museum
#3153
– Manitoba #1895 1896
– (1964-1978), Red River Exhibition #1903
– (1970s) #1899 1900
– (1980) #1906
– Maritimes #1119
– 18th-19th cs. #7780

– (1930s-1960s) #1125
– (1950s) #1172
– (1959-1965) #1120
– (1960s) #1122 1126
– McLean, James Stanley, collection #3210
3226
– Millen, Walter H., collection #21
– Montréal (Qué)
– 17th-18th cs. #1325
– (1840s) #1301
– (1910s) #1317
– (1922-1935) #2972
– (1940s-1960s) #1437
– (1950), exhibitions #1400
– (1960s) #1430 1479 1480 1484
– (1968-1969) #1514
– (1970s) #1489 1495 1504 1541 1555
– Art Association of Montreal #1246 1308
1310 1316
– château de Ramezay #3076 3077 3083
– Church of Notre-Dame #8849 8892
– Concordia University. Sir George
Williams Art Galleries #3096
– Ecole des beaux-arts (1925-1932) #2973
– McGill University. McCord Museum
#1366
– Métro stations #1531
– Montreal Museum of Fine Arts #3104
3112 3114 3117 3118
– Bronfman, Saidye and Samuel,
collection #526 3087
– Musée d'art contemporain #3086 3091
3093 3094
– Place des Arts #8233 9092 9093 9096
– Queen Elizabeth Hotel #8228
– Société d'électrolyse et de chimie Alcan
Ltée (Sécal), collection #3246
– *Spring Exhibition*
– (1880-1965) #1228
– (1895) #1311
– (1908-1965) #1261
– (1964) #1423
– Véhicule Art #1503
– New Brunswick #1183
– 20th c. #1182
– New York (NY), 49th Parallel #712
– Newfoundland #1147 1154
– (1867-1967) #1142
– (1970s) #1146 1149
– (1980s) #1161
– late 19th c.-1940s #1138
– women artists (1970s) #1152
– Newfoundland Society of Art #1141
– Niagara (Ont), (1970s) #1795
– Nova Scotia #1191 1202
– (1749-1848) #1215 1220 1222 1224 1225
– (1900-1945) #1194
– (1970s) #1208
– Nova Scotia Talent Trust #1199
– women artists
– (1830s-1840s) #1219
– (1850-1950) #1204
– (1970s) #1205
– Nova Scotia Society of Artists #1192
– Ontario #8943
– (1850s) #1691

– (1881), Art Union #1698
– (1940s-1970s) #1670
– (1970s) #590 1814 1816 1825
– (1979-1981), northern Ontario #1829
– (1981) #1838
– French-speaking Ontario (1970s) #1820
1821
– Government of Ontario Art Collection
(1873-1914) #1728
– periodicals
– *Art Views* #1806
– Ontario and Québec (1960s) #492
– Ontario Society of Artists #1666 1672 1679
1693 1695 1697 1700 1703 1707 1708 1709
1710 1731 1748
– Oshawa (Ont), Robert McLaughlin Gallery
#3169
– Ottawa (Ont)
– Canada Council #90 3266
– Canada Council. Art Bank #576 3276
– Canadian Medical Association
Headquarters #138
– Carleton University #3144
– National Arts Centre #9104 9105 9108
– National Gallery of Canada #3044
– Duncan, Douglas M., collection and
Milne-Duncan bequest #541
– National Science Library #9049
– Owen Sound (Ont), Tom Thomson
Memorial Gallery and Museum of Fine
Art #3146
– Paris (France), Centre culturel canadien
#537 647
– Pen and Pencil Club (Montréal, Qué)
#1251
– periodicals
– *Arcadia: A Journal devoted exclusively to
Music, Art and Literature* #179
– *Artists Review* #1815
– *Artmagazine* #560
– *Arts Bulletin* #551
– *Arts West* #1868
– *Artscanada* #25
– *Ateliers* #1493
– *Canadian Collector* #74
– *Canadian Museums Association. Gazette*
#3042
– *Canadian Review of Music and Art* #357
– *CAR/FAC News* #625
– *Collectioneur, Le* #134
– *Communiqué* #542
– *Craftsman, The/L'Artisan* #2113
– *Criteria* #564
– *Culture vivante* #1257
– *Fuse: The Cultural News Magazine* #603
– *Journal of Canadian Art History/Annales
d'histoire de l'art canadien* #111
– *Lamps* #1667
– *M* #3097
– *Maritime Art* #349
– *National Gallery of Canada. Annual
Bulletin/Galerie nationale du Canada.
Bulletin annuel* #69
– *Only Paper Today* #1799
– *Parachute* #593
– *Parallelogramme* #612

– *RACAR (Revue d'art canadienne/Canadian Art Review)* #114
– *Vanguard* #547
– *Vie des arts* #55
– Peterborough (Ont), Artspace #1836
– Picture Loan Society (Toronto, Ont) #1746
– Polish-Canadian artists #149 642
– Prairies
– (1950s-1970s) #1884
– (1960s) #1848 1851
– (1960s-1970s) #1862
– (1970s) #1860 1880
– women artists (1970s) #1867
– Prince Edward Island #1164 1166
– (1970s) #1165
– women artists (1970s) #1168
– Québec #1233 1234 1237 1239 1271 1294 1444
– 17th-19th cs. #1245 1305 1332 1334 1335 1341 1347 1581
– 17th c. #228 229 1365
– 17th c.-1930s #1235 2169 2171
– 17th c.-1967 #1260
– 18th c. #234 235 269 270
– 18th c.-1820s #1300
– 18th-early 20th cs. #1339
– 19th c.-1920s #1231
– 19th c.-1940s #1242
– 20th c. #1391
– (1520-1880) #216
– (1613-1870) #1330 1331
– (1825-1850) #1368
– (1900-1934) #8334
– (1925-1950) #1405
– (1930s-1970s) #1299
– (1940s) #1383 1386 1387
– (1940s-1960s) #1462
– (1940s-1970s) #1269 1473 1521
– (1950s) #425
– (1960s) #1487
– (1960s-1970s) #1496
– (1962-1972) #1500 1502
– (1963-1980) #1564
– (1966-1976) #1527
– (1970-1975) #1515
– (1970s) #1486 1488 1490 1491 1506 1508 1509 1511 1517 1525 1526 1528 1545 3115
– by artists under 35 #1501
– (1975) #1518
– (1977) #1532
– and Gérard Morisset #3305
– and women (1930s-1970s) #1273
– Corbeil, Maurice and Andrée, collection #3233
– cultural centres #3088
– illustrations of folk legends #1290
– images of the Devil, 17th c.-1840 #1357
– ministère des Affaires culturelles du Québec. Service de l'Inventaire des biens culturels #1277
– ministère des Travaux publics et de l'Approvisionnement #1561
– revolutionary subjects (1759-1914) #1351
– use of plastics (1960s) #1442
– women artists (1930s) #1380

– Québec (Qué) #1399
– 17th-19th cs. #1306 1309
– Church of Notre-Dame de Québec #8791
– Musée du Québec #3085 3092 3095 3107 3111 3121 3122
– National Assembly #8942
– Séminaire de Québec #8842
– Université Laval #3080
– realism #694
– (1970s) #606
– Regina (Sask)
– (1950s) #6284
– University of Regina. Norman Mackenzie Art Gallery #3197
– Royal Canadian Academy of Arts #2 16 152 153 157 162 166 168 171 181 184 186 195 202 210 280 283 296 303 310 312 318 323 325 326 328 329 361 366 434 474 500 686
– Sackville (NB), Mount Allison University #3068
– Saguenay-Lac-Saint-Jean (Qué) #1549
– (1970s) #1538 1540 1546 1547
– Saint-Basile-le-Grand (Qué), Centre communautaire catholique Tour de David #1510
– Saint John (NB)
– 20th c. #1188
– (1940s) #1170
– New Brunswick Museum. John Clarence Webster Canadiana Collection #3073 3209
– Saint John Art Club (Saint John, NB) #286
– Saint-Laurent (Qué)
– Collège de Saint-Laurent. Galerie Nova et Vetera #3089 3090
– Collège de Saint-Laurent. Musée d'art #3123
– Sarnia (Ont), Sarnia Public Library and Art Gallery #3179
– Saskatchewan #1919
– (1945) #1909
– (1950-1964) #1910
– (1950s) #1912
– (1950s-1970s) #1935
– (1960s) #1916
– (1970s) #1926 1930 1937
– Saskatchewan Arts Board #1914
– (1950s) #1911
– collection #1936
– Saskatoon (Sask)
– (1960s) #1917
– (1970s) #1932
– Mendel Art Gallery #72 3187
– private collections #679
– women artists (1970s) #1928
– Shell Canada Ltd., collection #3238 3240
– Society of Artists and Amateurs of Toronto (Toronto, Ont) #1688 1729
– Sudbury (Ont), (1970s) #1801
– synagogues (1950s) #8763
– Toronto (Ont)
– (1890s) #1699
– (1910s) #1712
– (1950s) #1750
– (1960s) #1757

– (1970s) #1804 1809 1818
– (1980) #1832
– (1980s), compared with New York (NY) art #1837
– Art Gallery of Ontario #3149 3158 3163 3167 3171
– Art Gallery of Toronto #3132
– Metro Toronto Public Library #3143
– John Ross Robertson Historical Collection #3130 3131 3204
– Ontario Heritage Foundation. Firestone Art Collection #3239
– Ontario Place #9113
– Royal Ontario Museum #3139 3141
– University of Toronto. Hart House #3134
– women artists (1970s) #1797
– Toronto Art Students' League (Toronto, Ont) #1714 2959 2961
– Toronto Society of Arts (Toronto, Ont) #1689 1690
– Ukrainian #1843
– use of oral documentation #608
– Vancouver (BC)
– (1886-1930) #2003
– (1901) #1977
– (1950s-1960s) #2039
– (1960s) #2035 2036 2038 8158
– (1970s) #2040
– (1980) #2076
– Vancouver Art Gallery #3184 3185 3186
– Vancouver School of Art (1925-1939) #3019
– Vanier, Georges and Pauline, collection #3216
– Vaudreuil (Qué), Musée de Vaudreuil #3109
– Victoria (BC)
– (1970s) #2055
– Art Gallery of Greater Victoria #3189
– Island Arts and Crafts Society #1980
– Victorian #237
– W.O.R.K.S. #1955
– Walker, Sir Byron Edmund, collection #3205
– war subjects #1082 1084 1088 1094 1098 1116 1117
– Ottawa (Ont), Canadian War Museum #1106
– western Canada
– (1970s) #1857 1866 1869 1870 1871 1883
– influence of Hans Hofmann #1850
– Windsor (Ont), Art Gallery of Windsor #3156
– Winnipeg (Man)
– (1960s-1980s) #1907
– Legislative Building #8948 8949 8950
– Winnipeg Art Gallery #3188 3192
– Dobush, Peter, collection #3221
– Winnipeg Sketch Club (Winnipeg, Man) #1887
– Women's Art Association of Canada #176
– women artists #95 96
– (1910s) #207
– (1940s) #377
– (1960s-1970s) #677

– (1960s-1980s) #717
– (1970s) #579 591 659 675 698 1877
    – Montréal (Qué), Powerhouse Gallery
      #1557
– Yukon (1970s) #2086 2088
art, Chinese
– compared with Northwest Coast Indian
   art #3843 3975
– protruding tongue and related motifs
   #3934
art, Chukchi
– Moscow (USSR), Zagorsk History and Art
   Museum #4302
– Siberia (USSR)
    – (1900-1980) #4303
art, Cree
    – (1830-1930) #3734
– floral motif #3731
art, Dakota
– New York (NY), Brooklyn Museum #3705
– protective designs #3650
– St. Paul (Minn), Science Museum of
   Minnesota #3755
art, Danish
– (1929), Canadian National Exhibition
   (Toronto, Ont) #304
art, Delaware #3506
art, Dogrib #4089
art, erotic
– *see* erotic art
art, French
– 17th-19th cs., influence on Canadian art
   #2180
– 17th c.-1920s, influence on Canadian art
   #1244
– views of the New World, 16th-18th cs.
   #276
art, Greek
– compared with Northwest Coast Indian
   prehistoric art #3861
art, Haida #3946
– and Tom Price #6934
– attributions #4169
– influence on Bill Reid #6986
– Montréal (Qué), McGill University.
   McCord Museum #4011
– moon image #4059
– representations of Caucasians #4070
– Washington (DC), Smithsonian Institution
   #3763
Art, Historical and Scientific Association of
   Vancouver (Vancouver, BC)
– (1894-1944) #1984
– (1910s) #1979
art, Hopewell
– compared with art, Algonquian #3558
– Serpent Mound, Rice Lake (Ont) #3574
art, Huron
– (1600-1760) #3579
art, Indians of Central America #3427 3435
– serpents #3391
art, Indians of North America #136 137 3351
   3352 3354 3357 3359 3366 3395 3412 3418
   3422 3427 3428 3442 3448 3452 3458 3467
   4126 4127 4146 4692
– 19th c., emergence of named artists #3486

– 20th c. #4163 4172
– (1960s) #4125 4136
– (1970s) #3376 4140 4155
– (1972-1974) #4138
– (1980) #4161
– (1980s) #4171
– (pre-1850) #3431
– and shamanism #3361 3383
– as motif in Canadian architectural
   decoration (1930s) #8225
– Belfast (Northern Ireland), Ulster Museum
   #3477
– Berlin (West Germany), Berliner Museum
   für Völkerkunde #3421 3423
– Berne (Switzerland), Historisches Museum
   #3400 3473
– Calgary (Alta), Glenbow-Alberta Institute
   #3438
– Cincinnati (Ohio), Cincinnati Art Museum
   #3459
– conservation #7767
– dot motif #3332 4325
– Dresden (East Germany), Indianer
   Museum Radebeul #3430
– Exeter (England), Royal Albert Memorial
   Museum #3454
– influence on British Columbia sculpture
   (1970s) #2066
– Italian collections #3396
– legal protection #3347
– London (England), British Museum
   – Sloane, Sir Hans, collection #3397
– Malaspina collection #3372
– Montréal (Qué), Montreal Museum of Fine
   Arts #3117 3118
– New York (NY), American Museum of
   Natural History #3414
– New York (NY), Museum of the American
   Indian. Heye Foundation #3437 3450
– Newark (NJ), Newark Museum #3425
– Offenbach (West Germany), Deutsches
   Ledermuseum #3464
– Ottawa (Ont), National Museum of Man
   #3408 3465 3466 3622
– serpents #3391
– therapeutic symbolism #3356
– Thunderbird #3410
– Toronto (Ont), Royal Ontario Museum
   #3382
– Tulsa (Okla), Philbrook Art Center #4165
– Vienna (Austria), Museum für
   Völkerkunde #3436
– Wentworth County (Ont) #7954
– Williamstown (Ont), Nor'westers Museum
   #3148
– Zurich (Switzerland), Feldstrasse
   Secondary School #3455
art, Indians of South America #3412 3427
art, Inuit #25 136 137 3351 3352 3354 3357
   3366 3374 3377 4179 4181 4182 4188 4190
   4216 4223 4231 4238 4254 4255 4278 4295
   4317 4338 4368
– (1950s-1970s) #4246
– (1960s) #4193 4204
– (1970s) #3376 4247 4256 4263
   – women artisans #4258

– Alaska #4208 4280
– and aesthetics #4282 4297
– and James Archibald Houston #4449 4452
   5846 5847
– and shamanism #4243 4283
– and society #4232
– biographical sources #4252 4301
   – Pelly Bay (NWT) #4221
– Cambridge (Mass), Harvard University.
   Peabody Museum #4191
– Canadian Arctic Producers #4222 4291
– Canadian Guild of Crafts Quebec #4292
   4293
– Cape Dorset (NWT)
    – (1960s) #4187
    – Levine, Les, on #6270 6271
– Churchill (Man), Eskimo Museum #4227
   4313
– concept of space #4341
– concept of space and time #4244
– dot motif #3332 4325
– Eurasiatic animal style #4334
– European influences #4176
– fantastic art #4240
– Frobisher Bay (NWT), The Museum of
   Things from the Land #4224
– Greenland #4206 4315
– in Arctic churches and public buildings
   #4304
– influence on Art Price #6930
– influence on K.J. Butler #4982
– Kleinburg (Ont), McMichael Canadian
   Collection #3172
– late 18th c.-1940s #4286
– legal protection #3347
– London (England)
    – British Museum #4360
    – museum collections #4289
– Malaspina collection #3372
– Montréal (Qué), Montreal Museum of Fine
   Arts #3117 3118
– Moscow (USSR), Zagorsk History and Art
   Museum #4302
– nalunaikutanga #4264
– Offenbach (West Germany), Deutsches
   Ledermuseum #3464
– Oxford (England), Oxford University. Pitt
   Rivers Museum #4369
– periodicals
    – *About Arts and Crafts/L'Art et l'artisanat*
     #4269
    – *Arts and Culture of the North* #4270
– Povungnituk (Qué) #4274
– prehistoric #3380 4339
– Québec #4296
– research methodology #4225
– Rochester (NY), Rochester Museum #4424
– Sea Goddess #4312 4376
– Sitka (Alaska), Sheldon Jackson Museum
   #3370
– social and economic influences #4215 4245
   4277
– Southampton Island (NWT), (1950s) #4184
– wall hangings #4253
    – Baker Lake (NWT) #4230 4266
    – Pangnirtung (NWT) #4237

– Winnipeg (Man), Winnipeg Art Gallery #3188 4284 4306

art, Iroquois #3559 3566 3605
– 20th c. #4143 4150 4164
– (1760-1860) #3434
– (1970s-1980s) #4139
– (1980) #4159
– Albany (NY), New York State Museum #3586
– formal properties #3601 3639
– Midwinter ceremony #3606
– Rochester (NY), Rochester Museum #3590
– tree myths and symbols #3516

art, Japanese
– influence on Paterson Ewen #5383
– influence on Walter Joseph Phillips #6856

art, Kwakiutl #3935 4037
– Ottawa (Ont), National Museum of Man #3060
– Vancouver (BC), University of British Columbia. Museum of Anthropology #3996

art, Maliseet
– Saint John (NB), New Brunswick Museum #3634

art, Maori
– protruding tongue and related motifs #3934

art, Métis
– floral motif #3731

art, Micmac
– Saint John (NB), New Brunswick Museum #3634

art, Mistassini #4080 4100

art, Montagnais #4082
– double-curve motif #3409

art, municipal
– see public art

art, Naskapi #3554 4082 4149
– double-curve motif #3409

art, natives of North America #3334 3335 3336 3342 3346 3349 3364 3369 3377 3381 3435 3463 3468
– (1980s) #4170
– and shamanism #3360
– Claremont (Calif), Claremont College #3378
– Copenhagen (Denmark), Nationalmuseet #3338
– Denver (Colo), Denver Art Museum #3479
– prehistoric #3375

art, New Zealand
– (1888) #175
– (1890) #177

art, Nootka #3908 4025

art, Northwest Coast Indians #19 299 1995 3333 3342 3799 3809 3827 3854 3869 3871 3907 3911 3919 3921 3923 3928 3933 3942 3948 3950 3959 3969 3970 3989 3992 3998 4022 4034 4036 4043 4049 4055
– 18th c. #3445
    – Vancouver, George, expedition #3767
– (1940-1943), BC Society for the Furtherance of Indian Arts and Crafts #4114
– (1960s) #4117 4119 4121
– (1970s) #4132 4145
– Anchorage (Alaska), Alaska International Art Institute #3987
– and pre-Columbian art #3810
– and Wilson Duff #4003
– animal motifs #3770
– Asiatic sources #3359
– Berlin (West Germany), Berliner Museum für Völkerkunde #3762
– California collections #4041
– Carr, Emily, on #5006
– compared with Chinese art #3843 3975
– Denver (Colo), Denver Art Museum #3918
– influence on Canadian art #24
– influence on Elford Bradley Cox #5202
– influence on Jack Leonard Shadbolt #7184 7189 7191
– influence on Margaret Peterson #6839
– influence on Nancy-Lou Patterson #6783
– Kleinburg (Ont), McMichael Canadian Collection #3172
– London (England), British Museum #4062 4064
– New York (NY), American Museum of Natural History #3860 4024
– Portland (Oreg), Portland Art Museum #3875 3937
– prehistoric #3861 4039
– Reid, Bill, on #6985
– research methodology (1930s-1970s) #4060
– Seattle (Wash), Washington State University. Thomas Burke Museum. Sidney Gerber Memorial Collection #3974
– Sitka (Alaska), Sheldon Jackson Museum #3370
– split representation #3905 3922
– Toronto (Ont), Royal Ontario Museum #4002
– Vancouver (BC), University of British Columbia. Museum of Anthropology #3994
– Victoria (BC), University of Victoria. Maltwood Art Museum and Gallery #3199
– woman subjects #3348

art, Ojibwa #3539 3557 3610 4089
– 20th c. #4173
– (1600-1760) #3579
– (1930s) #4112
– designs #3560
– St. Paul (Minn), Science Museum of Minnesota #3755

art, Ottawa
– (1600-1760) #3579

art, Piegan
– late 19th-early 20th cs., Glenbow-Alberta Institute (Calgary, Alta) #3759

art, Plains #3359 3463 3691 3720 3725 3730
– (1760-1860) #3434
– Bismarck (ND), State Historical Society of North Dakota #3690
– Providence (RI), Brown University. Haffenreffer Museum of Anthropology #3751
– shield motif #3710
– Stuttgart (West Germany), Linden Museum #3737 3750

art, Plateau Indians #3774

art, Potawatomi
– (1600-1760) #3579

art, Roman
– compared with Northwest Coast Indian prehistoric art #3861

art, Sarsi
– bear motif #3746

art, Scandinavian
– (1912-1913), Scandinavian Art Exhibition, influence on Group of Seven #1788
– influence on J.E.H. MacDonald #6370

art, Siouan #3725
– (1760-1860) #3434
– Boston (Mass), Harvard University. Peabody Museum #3649
– floral motif #3731
– Stuttgart (West Germany), Linden Museum #3737 3750

art, Slavey #4089

art, Spanish
– (1928), Canadian National Exhibition (Toronto, Ont) #300

art, Tagish #4106

art, Tahltan
– (1910s) #4074

art, Tanaina #4085

art, Tête de Boule #4079

art, Thompson Indians #3774

art, Tlingit #3946
– devilfish motif #4045
– Russian museum collections #3947 3978
– Washington (DC), Smithsonian Institution #3763

art, Tsimshian #3926
– moon image #4059
– Washington (DC), Smithsonian Institution #3763

art, Tutchone #4106

art, Woodlands #3359
– 20th c. #4143 4150
– (1760-1860) #3434
– (1970s-1980s) #4139
– (1980) #4159
– formal properties #3639
– Kleinburg (Ont), McMichael Canadian Collection #3172

art academies
– see academies of art

art and Communism
– see Communism and art

art and economics
– see economics and art

art and ethics
– see ethics and art

art and history
– see history and art

art and language
– see language and art

art and law
– see law and art

art and literature
– see literature and art

art and mathematics
– see mathematics and art

art and music
– see music and art

art and poetry
- *see* poetry and art
art and politics
- *see* politics and art
art and religion
- *see* religion and art
art and socialism
- *see* socialism and art
art and society
- *see* society and art
art and state
- *see* state and art
art and taxation
- *see* taxation and art
art and technology
- *see* technology and art
art and theatre
- *see* theatre and art
art and war
- *see* war and art
art appreciation
- Borduas, Paul-Emile, on #4799 4821 4839
- Brooker, Bertram Richard, on #317
- Lismer, Arthur, on #311 2965
Art Association of Montreal
- *see* Montréal (Qué), Art Association of
  Montreal
Art Association of Newfoundland and
  Labrador
- (1967-1979) #1144
Art Association of Ottawa (Ottawa, Ont)
- (1890s) #188
Art Association of Vancouver (Vancouver,
  BC)
- (1889-1894) #1981
Art Bank
- *see* Ottawa (Ont), Canada Council. Art
  Bank/Conseil des Arts du Canada.
  Banque d'oeuvres d'art
Art Brut
- *see also* amateur art
- and Francine Simonin #7213
art censorship
- *see* censorship of art
art cooperatives
- *see* artists' cooperatives
art critics
- *see* art historians and critics
art dealers
- *see* art market
Art Deco
- and Paul-Emile Borduas #4828
- Canada #505
- Canadian posters #911
Art Deco architecture
- Montréal (Qué), Cormier House #8347
- Vancouver (BC) #8167
Art Directors' Club of Montreal (Montréal,
  Qué)
- exhibitions
  - (1965) #874
- exhibitions (reviews)
  - (1952) #860
Art Directors' Club of Toronto (Toronto,
  Ont)
- (1940s) #853

- (1950s) #858
- exhibitions
  - (1949-) #854
  - (1968) #874
- exhibitions (reviews)
  - (1952) #860
  - (1973) #894
  - (1974) #888
Art Directors' Club of Winnipeg (Winnipeg,
  Man)
- exhibitions
  - (1964-1970) #872
art education
- *see also* academies of art
- (1894), recommendations #2960
- (1910s), women artists abroad #206
- Alberta #1946 1953
- Askevold, David, on #4566
- Atlantic provinces
  - (1960s) #1124
  - (1960s-1970s) #1130
  - (1970s) #1127 1131
- Banff (Alta), Banff School of Fine Arts
  #3000
- Beaudin, Gaétan #2381
- Benjamin-Constant, Jean-Joseph, as teacher
  of Canadian artists #243
- Biéler, André Charles #4725 4726
- Binning, B.C. #4730
- Borduas, Paul-Emile #2990 3001 4803 4811
  4818 4821 4827 4836 4843
- Bourassa, Napoléon #4864 4875
- Braitstein, Marcel #4899
- Brandtner, Fritz #4904
- British Columbia (1960s) #2989
- Brooker, Bertram Richard #317
- Brymner, William #4949 4953
- Calgary (Alta), Calgary Art Centre (1947)
  #1945
- Cameron, Donald #3000
- Canada
  - 17th c.-1940s, decorative arts #2097 2979
  - 19th c. #343
  - 20th c. #470
  - (1890-1900) #190
  - (1890s) #182 184
    - Canadian artists in Paris (France) #180
  - (1908), recommendations #2963
  - (1930s) #7658
  - (1938-1948) #379
  - (1940s) #370
    - and Royal Canadian Academy of Arts
      #361
    - Canadian artists in Paris (France) #384
    - pottery #2375
  - (1940s-1980s) #2983
  - (1960s) #448
  - (1970s) #542 625 682 2998 3270
    - artists on #648
    - western Canada #3006
  - (1970s), and women #701
  - (1975), predictions #585
- Canadian Handicrafts Guild #2090
- Carr, Emily #5014
- Chabert, Joseph #3005
- Chicoutimi (Qué)

- Ecole d'arts et métiers #2175
- Université du Québec (1970s) #3016
- Couturier, Pierre Charles Marie-Alain
  #1407
- crafts for children (1970s) #2136 2137
- Cruikshank, William #5212
- Cullen, Maurice Galbraith #5219 5220
- Dignam, Mary Ella #2958
- Dumouchel, Albert #3001 5325 5330 5333
- Dyonnet, Edmond #5346 5347 5349
- Eagar, William H. #5351
- Edmonton (Alta), University of Alberta.
  Department of Extension (1930s-1940s)
  #1943
- Emma Lake (Sask), Emma Lake
  Workshops #1921 1923
- Foulis, Robert #258 259
- Frenkel, Vera #5519
- Gaitskell, Charles #2986
- graphic arts (1960s) #867
- Halifax (NS), Nova Scotia College of Art
  and Design #2993 3003 3014
- Hofmann, Hans, as teacher of Canadian
  artists #1850
- Holgate, Edwin Headley #5818 5819
- Holmes, Robert #5822
- Jérôme, frère #6761 6762 6763
- Jones, William Harris #1226
- Kinton, Ada Florence #6053
- Leighton, Alfred Crocker #6225
- Leighton, Barbara #3017
- Lemieux, Jean-Paul #6227 6228 6235 6236
- Lismer, Arthur #9 311 2965 2966 2968 2971
  2974 2975 2981 2984 2985 2987 6293 6295
  6296 6297 6298 6299 6301 6302 6303 6305
- Macdonald, Jock #2990 6375 6378
- MacLeod, Pegi Nicol #6397
- Manitoba (1940s) #1889 1890
- Maritimes (1950s) #1119
- May, Karl #6453
- Miller, Maria Frances Ann Morris #6541
- Montréal (Qué)
  - (1940s) #1395
  - Ecole des beaux-arts #2973 2995
    - (1922-1935) #2972
  - Ecole du meuble (1935-1950) #2980
  - Institut national des beaux-arts, sciences,
    arts et métiers et industrie #3005
- New Brunswick #1137
  - decorative arts (1940s) #2144
  - schools (1960s) #1177
- Newfoundland #1142 1147
  - (1970s) #1146
- Nutt, Elizabeth Styring #6730
- Ontario
  - (1856) #3128
  - (1970s) #3004
  - French-speaking Ontario #1820 1821
- Ontario Society of Artists (1940s) #1666
- Pulford, Edward Berwyn #6945
- Québec #1231
  - (1872-1939), decorative arts #2977
  - (1930s), decorative arts #2166 2969
  - (1930s-1940s), decorative arts #2185
  - (1940s) #1390
  - and women (1930s-1970s) #1273

– Council of Arts and Manufactures, late 19th c. #2598 2962
– Québec (Qué), Ecole des arts domestiques de Québec #2167 2186
– Rimouski (Qué), Séminaire de Rimouski. Ecole d'arts et métiers de Rimouski #2978
– Roberts, Goodridge #7041 7048
– Royal Canadian Academy of Arts #275
– Sackville (NB), Mount Allison University (1893-1977) #3013
– Saint-Joachim (Qué), Ecole des arts et métiers de Saint-Joachim #1233 1327 1363 2967 2991 2992 3007 3008
– Saskatchewan #1919 1935
– Savage, Anne Douglas #7129 7130 7132
– Schaefer, Carl Fellman #7154 7155
– Scott, Charles Hepburn #3019
– Senécal, Irène #2999 3010
– Smith, Gordon Appelbe #7228 7230
– Suzor-Coté, Marc-Aurèle de Foy #7293
– Teitelbaum, Mashel #7340
– Tonnancour, Jacques Godefroy de #3018 7386
– Toronto (Ont)
    – (1910s) #1712
    – (1960s) #1757
    – (pre-1912) #2964
    – Art Gallery of Toronto #3020
    – New School of Art #2994
    – Ontario College of Art
        – (1876-1976) #3009 3011 3012
        – (1960s) #2996 2997
        – (1971-1972) #3002
– Toronto (Ont) and Montréal (Qué), (1960s) #2990
– Toronto Art Students' League
    – (1886-1893) #2959
    – (1886-1894) #2961
– Tully, Sydney Strickland #7438
– Vancouver (BC), Vancouver School of Art (1925-1939) #3019
– Verbist, P.J. #2957
– Winnipeg (Man), Winnipeg Art Gallery #3196
Art Gallery Association of Newfoundland #1142
art historians and critics
– Canada
    – (1907) #3299
    – (1940s) #380
    – (1970s) #3312
– MacDonald, J.E.H., on #6360
art history
– Canada
    – (1930s-1960s) #3306
    – (1980) #3316
    – and sociology of art #164
– methodology
    – Inuit art #4205 4225 4282 4401 4426 4442
    – Northwest Coast Indians #4041 4060
– Québec #1255
    – Morisset, Gérard #3322
– women artists #144
Art in Living Group (Vancouver, BC) #1841
– (1940s) #1988
art market

– and Max Stern #1293 1431
– and Mira Godard #161
– and William R. Watson #1272
– Bush, Jack Hamilton #4975
– Calgary (Alta), (1970s) #1966
– Canada
    – (1950s) #151 409 3214 3260
    – (1960s) #445 446 448 529
        – art dealers #3219
        – art galleries #442
    – (1960s-1970s) #123
    – (1970-1974) #91
    – (1970s) #619 625 682 693 3236 3291 3293
        – and women #562
        – Canadian Artists' Representation #632
    – (1972-1974) #552
    – (1975), predictions #585
    – (1976), survey #599
    – (1980) #688
    – (1980s) #603
– Canadian and European paintings (1950s) #418
– Canadian antiques #2114 2127 2252 2271
– Canadian art prices
    – (1968-1975) #116
    – (1975-1980) #160
    – (1980) #158
– Canadian furniture (1970s) #7081
– Canadian photographs (1970s) #1038
– Canadian toys and games #2928
– Collectionneur, Le periodical on #134
– commercial galleries, Robert Percival on #6834
– decorative arts, Thunder Bay (Ont) #2266
– French-Canadian antiques #2226 2237
– Harris, Lawren Stewart, on #5722
– Indians of North America
    – art #6539
        – (1970s) #4155
    – baskets #3625
    – textiles (1970s) #3476
– Indians of North America and Inuit art (1970s) #3376
– Inuit art #3377 4189 4200 4218 4231 4236 4238 4242 4262 4270 4276 4305 4388 4466 6270
    – Canadian Arctic Producers #4222 4291
– Inuit prints #4483
– Inuit sculpture #4396 4397 4455
    – and Alma Houston #4425
– Iroquois decorative arts (1960s) #4123
– Laing, G.Blair, on #1686
– legal protection of Inuit and Indian arts and crafts #3347
– Montréal (Qué), galleries
    – (1945-1970) #1264
    – (1970s) #1495
– Montréal (Qué) and Québec (Qué), (1970s) #1509
– Muhlstock, Louis, on #6657
– Newfoundland furniture #2520
– Northwest Coast Indians art (1960s) #4121
– Nova Scotia country furniture #2521
– Ontario (1970s) #1825
– Ontario furniture, 19th c. #2564
– Québec #1269 1340

– and religion (1950s) #1406
– Québec (Qué), galleries (1970s) #1519
– Québec paintings #1289
– Québec prints (1970s) #1656
– Québec sculpture (1970s) #1628
– Toronto (Ont)
    – (1970s) #1803
    – and Artists' Union of Toronto #1742
Art moderne
– see Art Deco
Art Nouveau
– and Bruno Joseph Bobak #4756
– and Canadian tapestry #2774
– and Katharine Emma Maltwood #3242
– and Kenneth Campbell Lochhead #6314
– Montréal (Qué) #1367
Art Nouveau interior decoration
– Canada, trains and railway hotels #3281
art objects
– see decorative arts
art patronage
– see patronage of art
art periodicals
– (1950s-1960s), influence on Toronto (Ont) painting #1773
art periodicals, Canadian #3313
– (1970s) #707 3310
    – and art criticism #3308
– Arcadia: A Journal devoted exclusively to Music, Art and Literature #179
– Archaeological Report #3329
– Artisan #2133
– Artists Review #1815
– Artmagazine #560
– Arts Bulletin #551
– Arts West #1868
– ArtsAtlantic #128
– Artscanada #25
– ArtViews #1806
– Ateliers #1493
– Canada Crafts #2126
– Canadian Antiques and Art Review #141
– Canadian Collector #74
– Canadian Design/Design canadien #2625
– Canadian Museums Association. Gazette #3042
– Canadian Review of Music and Art #357
– CAR/FAC News #625
– Collectionneur, Le #134
– Communiqué #542
– Craft Dimensions Artisanales #2116
– Craftsman, The/L'Artisan #2113
– Creative Source #912
– Criteria #564
– Culture vivante #1257
– File #544
– Fuse: The Cultural News Magazine #603
– Highlights, Quarterly Newsletter of the Alberta Society of Artists #1944
– Impulse #538
– Journal of Canadian Art History/Annales d'histoire de l'art canadien #111
– Lamps #1667
– M #3097
– Maritime Art #349
– National Gallery of Canada. Annual

Bulletin/Galerie nationale du Canada. Bulletin annuel #69
- *Only Paper Today* #1799
- *Ontario Craft* #2257
- *Parachute* #593
- *Parallelogramme* #612
- *RACAR (Revue d'art canadienne/Canadian Art Review)* #114
- *Vanguard* #547
- *Vie des arts* #55
art periodicals, Inuit
- *About Arts and Crafts/L'Art et l'artisanat* #4269
- *Arts and Culture of the North* #4270
art property
- *see* copyright
Art Students' Club (St. John's, Nfld) #1142
Art Students' League (Hamilton, Ont)
- (1890s) #1706
art theory and criticism
- *see also* aesthetics
- Barbeau, Charles Marius #3309
- Bates, Maxwell Bennett #405 4621
- Bellot, Dom #8333
- Bloore, Ronald Langley #4748
- Borduas, Paul-Emile #4799 4803 4839
  - press reaction to *Projections libérantes* #4819
  - press reaction to *Refus global* and *Projections libérantes* #1452
- Bourassa, Napoléon #4869 4871
- Bourbeau, Géraldine #4877
- Brooker, Bertram Richard #330 4927
- Brymner, William #4947
- Buchanan, Donald William #3325
- Bush, Jack Hamilton #4975
- Caiserman-Roth, Ghitta #4989
- Canada
  - (1890s) #1705
  - (1907) #3299
  - (1910s) #3300
  - (1920s) #1231
  - (1920s-1940s), *Canadian Forum* #3301
  - (1940s) #380 3302 3304
  - (1960s) #87
  - (1970s) #598 620 3308 3312 6747
    - Canadian art periodicals #3310
    - exhibition catalogues #3311
  - (1980) #3315 3316
- Carr, Emily #5030 5032
- Colville, Alex #5140
- Comfort, Charles Fraser #5157
- Coombs, Edith Grace #5172
- Cosgrove, Stanley Morel #3307
- Crawford, Lenore #112
- exhibition catalogues #3319
- Frenkel, Vera #5522 5523
- Group of Seven #1739 1744
- Harper, John Russell #3317
- Harris, Lawren Stewart #5714 5721 5722 5724 5725 5726 5729
- Hodgson, Tom #5814
- Hofmann, Hans #1850
- Impressionism (1881) #169
- Laliberté, Alfred #6145
- Leduc, Ozias #6211

- Levine, Les #6260
- Lindsay, Jim #6291
- Lyman, John Goodwin #6343 6346 6347
- Martin, Thomas Mower #6437
- Milne, David Brown #6548 6556
- Molinari, Guido #6586 6587
- Montréal (Qué), (1940s-1950s) #1426
- Morisset, Gérard #3305 3321 3324 3326
- Morrice, James Wilson, press reaction (1886-1916) #6634
- non-objective art (1950s) #421
- Peterson, Margaret #6839
- Plamondon, Antoine-Sébastien #1348
- Plaskett, Joe #6889 6891
- Québec #1255 7117
  - (1920-1945) #1456
- Reid, George Agnew #6973
- Repentigny, Rodolphe de #1465 3318
- Rockman, Arnold #7061
- Shadbolt, Jack Leonard #7181 7185 7186 7188 7192
- Swinton, George #7305
- Tonnancour, Jacques Godefroy de #385 7381
- Vaillancourt, Armand #7452
- Villeneuve, Arthur #7492
- Wertheimer, Esther #7542
Art Union of Canada
- (1870s) #1706
- exhibitions (reviews)
  - (1874) #1694
  - (1881) #1698
Arthabaska (Qué)
- views, Marc-Aurèle de Foy Suzor-Coté #7301
Arthur, Eric Ross, Can architect, 1898-
- Edmonton (Alta), Canada Packers Limited #7973
- influence on Ontario domestic architecture #8646
- Ottawa (Ont)
  - Carleton University #9455
- Toronto (Ont)
  - University of Toronto. University College, restoration #7776
Arthur, Paul, Can artist, 1924-
- and *Canadian Art* #25
- as partner of Paul Arthur and Associates #873
- on advertising #859 865
Arthur, Sandy, Can artist, 1947-
- exhibitions, group
  - (1978) #2067
Arthur Pequegnat Clock Company, clockmaking firm (Kitchener, Ont) #2912 2927 2956
Artisan, Can periodical #2133
Artisan News/Artisan nouvelles, Can periodical #2133
artisans
- *see also* apprentices
- Louisbourg (NS) #2148
- Ontario, 19th c. #2261
- Québec #2208 2222 2229
  - 17th-18th cs. #2200 2214
  - 17th-19th cs. #2236

  - 18th-19th cs. #2206
  - (1660-1815) #2231
  - (1810-1819) #8616
  - (1940s) #2190
  - houses, 17th-18th cs. #8621
  - late 19th-early 20th cs. #2235
  - luxury items, late 17th-early 18th cs. #2162
- Québec (Qué) (1608-1950), shoemakers #2946
artists
- *see also* architects; folk artists; immigrant artists; Indian artists; Inuit artists; photographers; women architects; women artists
- (1920s) #305
- (1940s) #380
  - Federation of Canadian Artists #360
- (1941), Conference of Canadian Artists #351
- (1950s)
  - and public art galleries #3031
  - Royal Commission on National Development in the Arts, Letters and Sciences (Massey Report) #3254 3255 3261
- (1960s) #448
  - financial aid #3265
  - young artists #440
- (1960s-1970s), Canadian Artists' Representation #563
- (1970s) #587 3157
  - and Canadian Artists' Representation #632
  - financial aid #3267
  - on marketing Canadian art #599
- (1978), survey #648
- and architects
  - (1960s) #8234
  - British Columbia (1950s) #8142
  - Canada (1960s) #476
- and dealers, G.Blair Laing on #1686
- and workers, Labor Arts Guild (1940s) #1985
- as art critics #3308
- in Canadian fiction (1892-1908) #277
- Montréal (Qué), (1970s) #1505
- Québec
  - (1780-1840) #1375
  - (1970s) #1446
artists' books
- *see also* livres d'artistes
artists' books, Canadian #940
- Editions Erta (Montréal, Qué) #1641
- Guilde graphique (Montréal, Qué) #1647
- Leclair, Michel, and Michel Tremblay #6183
- Morris, Michael William #6640
- Snow, Michael #7254
  - *Cover to Cover* #7255 7256
- Wieland, Joyce #7577
- women artists, Canada (1970s) #936
Artists' Cooperative Toronto (ACT) (Toronto, Ont)
- periodical, *Artists Review* #1815
artists' cooperatives, Indians of North

America
- 'Ksan (Hazelton, BC) #4129 4130
- Garden Hill (Man), Ministic Carvers Co-op #4153
- Island Lake (Man), Garden Hill Cooperative #4135
- Red Lake (Ont), Triple K Co-operative #4151 4158
artists' cooperatives, Inuit #4231 4288
- and commercial art #4262
- Baker Lake (NWT), Sanavik Cooperative #4480 4481
- Belcher Islands (NWT), Metiq Co-operative #4459
- Cape Dorset (NWT) #4187 4464 6270
  - West Baffin Eskimo Co-operative #4192 4299 4460
- Inoucdjouac (Qué) #4267
- Povungnituk (Qué) #4274
artists' correspondence
- Ayotte, Léo #4574
- Baillairgé, François #4585
- Baillairgé, Jean #4585
- Bates, Maxwell Bennett #6376
- Beatty, John William #4638
- Bell-Smith, Frederic Marlett #4668
- Berczy, William von Moll #4696 4701
- Borduas, Paul-Emile #1443 4834 4838
  - and Claude Gauvreau #4804 4805 4807
  - and Robert Elie #1270
- Bourassa, Napoléon #4868 4870
  - and Théophile Hamel #4874
- Bourgault, Médard #4887 4888
- Brayshaw, Tommy #4907
- Brooker, Bertram Richard #503 504
- Carr, Emily #5025
  - and Edythe Hembroff-Schleicher #5026
  - and Ruth Humphrey (1937-1944) #5029
- Cartier, Jean Bernard #5052
- Eaton, Wyatt #5356
- FitzGerald, Lionel LeMoine #503 504
- Fowler, Daniel #5491 5492
- Hamel, Théophile #1348
- Harris, Robert #5737 5741
- Hurley, Robert Newton #5886
- Jameson, Anna Brownell #5934
- Kane, Paul #6014
- Kinton, Ada Florence #6053
- Krieghoff, Cornelius #6091
- Leduc, Fernand #6194
- Levasseur, Pierre-Noël, and François Filiau-Dubois #6253 6255
- Lismer, Arthur #6305
- Luke, Alexandra #6376
- Lyman, John Goodwin #6347
- MacDonald, J.E.H. #6371 6372
- Macdonald, Jock #6376
- mail art, in File periodical #544
- McGrath, Judy #6474
- McKenzie, Robert Tait #6488
- Milne, David Brown #536 6550 6553 6559 6560 6561 6562 6563 6564 6566
- Morris, Michael William, and Vincent Trasov #546
- Nicoll, James McLaren #6376
- Nicoll, Marion F.S. Mackay #6376

- Plamondon, Antoine-Sébastien #1348
- Savage, Anne Douglas, and A.Y. Jackson #7130
- Semak, Michael William, and Freeman Patterson #1016
- Thomson, Tom, and J.E.H. MacDonald #7356
- Varley, Frederick Horsman #7468
- Watson, Homer Ransford #7532
  - and Arthur Lismer #7536
  - and James Spooner #7534
  - and Mrs. Homer Watson #7533
- Whyte, Catharine Robb #7572
artists' diaries
- Baillairgé, François #4590 4592
- Baltzly, Benjamin #4598
- Banting, Frederick Grant #4600
- Borduas, Paul-Emile #4838
- Bourgault, Médard #4887 4888
- Brayshaw, Tommy #4907
- Catlin, George #1845
- Colville, Alex #5156
- Dally, Frederick #5250
- Field (Fish), Robert #5434
- Fowler, Daniel #5491
- Hind, William George Richardson #5807
- Hood, Robert #5825 5827
- Howard, John George #8377
- Jackson, Henry Alexander Carmichael #5927 5928
- Kane, Paul #1845 3386 6014
- Kinton, Ada Florence #6053
- Lapointe, Frank #6169
- Lyman, John Goodwin #6347
- McKenzie, Robert Tait #6488
- Milne, David Brown (1920-1921) #6560
- Onley, Toni #6738
- Pope, William #6905 6906
- Schoonover, Frank Earle #7163
- Simcoe, Elizabeth Posthuma Gwillim #7210 7211 7212
- Warre, Henry James (1845-1846) #7522
- Whyte, Catharine Robb #7572
artists' houses
- Falk, Gathie #5408
- Morash, Barbara #6606
- Norris, Joe #6721
artists' journals
- see artists' diaries
artists' marks, Inuit #4250 4431 4462
- igloo trademark #4213
artists' sketchbooks
- see sketchbooks
artists' studios
- Ayotte, Léo #4574
- Campbell, Ted #4994
- Carr, Emily #5020
- Chaudron, Bernard #5099
- Chaudron, Bernard and Louise #5098
- Jobin, Louis #5962 5964
- Lemieux, Jean-Paul #6238
- Muhlstock, Louis #6658
- Plaskett, Joe #6890 6895
- Watson, Homer Ransford #7528
Artists' Union of Toronto (Toronto, Ont)
- (1930s) #1742

artists' writings
- Andrews, Stephen #4527
- Arbuckle, Frances-Anne Johnston #5970
- Archambault, Louis #408
- Ayotte, Léo #4574
- Baltzly, Benjamin #4598
- Barker, Charles Edward #4609
- Bates, Maxwell Bennett #405 4621 4622 4624
- Baxter, Iain #490 6675
- Beardy, Jackson #4635
- Béland, Luc #4655
- Bell-Smith, Frederick Marlett #4667
- Belzile, Louis #1465
- Bengough, John Wilson #4671 4672 4673
- Beny, Wilfred Roloff #4687
- Berczy, William von Moll #4699
- Beveridge, Karl John #602
- Bice, Clare #408
- Biéler, André Charles #349 4720 4721
- Binning, B.C. #4730 4732
- Blazeje, Zbigniew #490
- Bloore, Ronald Langley #4748
- Bobak, Molly Lamb #4761 4762 4766
- Bogardi, George #637
- Boorne, William Hanson #4796
- Borduas, Paul-Emile #1270 1396 1443 1449 4799 4803 4809 4818 4819 4821 4831 4834 4837 4838 4839 4840 4843 4850 6197
- Bornstein, Eli #490 536 4855
- Bourassa, Napoléon #4862 4865 4868 4869 4870 4871
- Bourgault, Médard #4888
- Boyle, John Bernard #4893
- Bradford, John Locke #4895
- Braitstein, Marcel #4899
- Brandtner, Fritz #4902 4903 4904
- Brittain, Miller Gore #4915
- Britton, Susan #687
- Brooker, Bertram Richard #4927
- Brooks, Leonard #4930 4931
- Brown, Annora #4934
- Bruce, Robert Donald #4940
- Brymner, William #4950
- Bull, W. #4956
- Burrows, Tom #4960
- Burton, Dennis Eugene Norman #1773
- Bush, Jack Hamilton #490 703
- Carr, Emily #92 5007 5009 5010 5013 5017 5018 5019 5025 5030 5031 5044
- Carr-Harris, Ian #5047
- Catlin, George #3384 3478
- Celestino, Mary #5063
- Chambers, Jack #5071 5074 5079 5081
- Champagne, Jean-Serge #637
- Charney, Melvin #5091 5093
- Chitty, Elizabeth #687
- Clark, Tim #687 5113
- Cloutier, Albert-Edouard #9286
- Cohen, Sorel #673
- Colville, Alex #490 5150
- Comfort, Charles Fraser #1090 5158
- Condé, Carole #602
- Cooper, H.W. #5173
- Copithorne, Judith #5176
- Couturier, Pierre Charles Marie-Alain

#1407
- Craig, Kate #687
- Craven, David #687
- Croft, Lewis Scott #5210
- Curnoe, Greg #490 536 5228
- Curtis, Edward Sheriff #3399
- Davies, Thomas #5272
- De Pédery-Hunt, Dora #5275
- Deacon, Peter #1961
- Dean, Max #687
- Deichmann, Kjeld #349
- Dragu, Margaret #687
- Duguay, Rodolphe #5317
- Dyonnet, Edmond #5347 5349
- Eagar, William H. #5351
- Edson, Aaron Allan #5363
- Ewen, Paterson #703
- Eyre, Ivan Kenneth #5394
- Fairley, Barker #344 5405
- Falk, Gathie #5410
- Fauteux, André Lucien #5413
- Favro, Murray #594 703
- Field (Fish), Robert #687 5434
- Fisher, Brian Richard #490
- FitzGerald, Lionel LeMoine #5448 5449
- Forster, John Wycliffe Lowes #5467 5469 5470
- Fowler, Daniel #5488 5489 5491 5492
- Fraser, John Arthur #5509 5510
- Freifeld, Eric #5515
- Frenkel, Vera #5519 5522 5523 5525
- Gadbois, Louise Landry #1433
- Gagnon-Fortier, C. #5552
- Gaucher, Yves #5561
- Gauvreau, Claude #1396 1443 1449
- Genn, Robert #5585
- Gervais, Raymond #637 687
- Giguère, Roland #4831 5593 5595 5596 5599
- Gnass, Peter #5620
- Godwin, Ted #1922
- Goldhamer, Charles #1091
- Gougeon, Diane #685
- Goulet, Claude #5639
- Greyson, John #687
- Harris, Lawren Stewart #92 293 308 1744 1747 1754 5715 5716 5721 5723 5725 5726 5727
- Harris, Robert #5737
- Harris, Salmon #5745
- Harrison, Ted #5750
- Hébert, Adrien #5761
- Hébert, Julien #5765
- Hébert, Louis-Philippe #5771
- Henrickson, Thomas Elton, and Martha Charlotte Henrickson #5781
- Heward, John #5792
- Hodgson, Tom #5814
- Hornyansky, Nicholas #5839
- Hudson, Andrew #5857
- Hughes, Lynn #5862
- Humphrey, Jack Weldon #5866
- Hurley, Robert Newton #5886
- Hushlak, Gerald #1961
- Iliu, Josef #8229
- Jackson, A.Y. #92 5907 5908 5911 5912 5913 5916 5918 5920 5923
- Jameson, Anna Brownell #5934
- Jaycocks, T.G. #5950
- Jérôme, frère #6761
- Jérôme, Jean-Paul #1465
- Johnson, Terence #5969
- Kane, Paul #92 3386 6002 6014 6015
- Kantaroff, Maryon #596 6019
- Karsh, Yousuf #6023 6024 6025 6026 6027 6029 6031 6034 6035
- Keirstead, James Lorimer #6037
- Kelman, Ralf #6038
- Kennedy, Garry Neill #703
- Kennedy, Sybil #6046
- Kerr, Estelle Muriel #206
- Kerr, Illingworth Holey #6047 6048 6049
- Kiopini, Christian #6054
- Kiyooka, Roy Kenzie #6062
- Korner, John Michael Anthony #6077
- Kostyniuk, Ron #6080
- Kurelek, William #6109 6110 6113 6115
- Kuthan, George #6117
- La Palme, Robert #408
- Laliberté, Alfred #6145
- Lasnier, Raymond #6172
- Lavoie, Raymond #685
- Lawson, Ernest #6177
- Leduc, Fernand #1396 1449 6189 6193 6194
- Leduc, Ozias #6196 6199
- Lemieux, Jean-Paul #6239
- Leroy, Hugh Alexander #490
- Levine, Les #6259 6263 6265 6268 6269 6270 6273
- Lewis, Glenn Alun #6276
- Lindgren, Charlotte #6282
- Lindsay, Jim #6291
- Lyman, John Goodwin #6340 6343 6346 6347
- Lynn, Washington Frank #6348
- MacDonald, J.E.H. #1733 6361 6362 6363 6366 6371 6372
- Magrini, Alex #685
- Mars, Tanya #6421
- Martin, Ron #661
- Martin, Thomas Mower #6435 6437
- Massey, John #687
- Masson, Henri L. #6444
- Mayerovitch, Harry #6454
- McDougall, Clark Holmes #6464
- McKay, Arthur Fortescue #490
- McKenzie, Robert Tait #6484 6485
- McLean, Terry #6502
- Meigs, Mary #6510
- Meredith, John #6514
- Metson, Graham #6523
- Miller, Alfred Jacob #6536 6537
- Milne, David Brown #6545 6546 6548 6552 6556 6562 6563 6564
- Molinari, Guido #490 703 6586
- Morisset, Denys #6611 6613
- Morris, Jerrold #6639
- Morris, Michael #6641
- Morrisseau, Norval #6649
- Morton, Douglas Gibb #490
- Murphy, Rowley Walter #6665
- Murray, Robert Gray #490
- Newton, Neil #6694
- Niverville, Louis de #6709
- Nokony, Denis #6716
- Notman, William #6723
- Ondaatje, Kim #2798
- Onley, Toni #6741
- Palchinski, Sylvia Scott #6753
- Panabaker, Frank Shirley #6757
- Patterson, Freeman #6780 6781 6782
- Pehap, Eric Konstantin #6795
- Perrault, Gérard #851
- Peterson, Margaret #6839
- Pethick, Jerry #6840
- Phillips, Walter Joseph #6853 6854 6855 6856
- Pilot, Robert Wakeham #6870
- Pitseolak, Peter #6876
- Poulin, Roland #6909
- Proctor, Alexander Phimister #6944
- Rabinowitch, David George #703 6948
- Rajotte, Yves #6954
- Rayner, Gordon #6966
- Reid, Bill #6985
- Reid, George Agnew #6973
- Reid, Leslie Mary Margaret #637
- Reitzenstein, Reinhard #594
- Repentigny, Rodolphe de #1465
- Riopelle, Jean-Paul #1396 7033
- Roberts, Goodridge #408 7043 7045 7047
- Rockman, Arnold #7061
- Rogers, Otto Donald #7065
- Roussel, Claude #1181 7089
- Roussil, Robert #7096
- Royle, Stanley #7104
- Saucier, Robert #685
- Sawyer, William #7145
- Saxe, Henry #661
- Schaefer, Carl Fellman #349 7150 7155
- Semak, Michael William #7168 7169
- Senécal, Irène #3010
- Seton, Ernest Thompson #7172
- Shadbolt, Jack Leonard #92 7181 7182 7183 7185 7186 7192
- Siebner, Herbert Johannes Joseph #7205
- Snow, Michael #490 7241 7243 7244
- Squires, Gerald Leopold #7272
- Sullivan, Françoise #1396 1449
- Suscan, Charles #7291
- Szabo, Zoltan #7306
- Taçon, Edna Jeanette #7310
- Tanobe, Miyuki #7323
- Thorne, Joseph Bradshaw #7374
- Tillenius, Clarence #7377
- Tinning, George Campbell #7378
- Tomczak, Kim #687
- Tonnancour, Jacques Godefroy de #7381 7382 7385 7387
- Toupin, Fernand #1465
- Town, Harold Barling #92 490 947 7410 7414
- Turner, Richard Julian #490
- Urquhart, Tony #7448
- Vazan, Bill #7470 7473
- Vilder, Roger #7488
- Wall, Jeff #7506
- Wallot, Jacques-Albert-François-Joseph

#7513
- Waring, Stephanie E. #7516
- Warren, Emily Mary Bibbens #7524
- Watson, Homer Ransford #7537
- Wertheimer, Esther #7542
- Wheatley, Willis Sifton #7548
- White, Norman #7554
- White, Stan #7555
- Whyte, Catharine Robb #7572
- Will, John #7585
- Wilson, Ronald York #7596
- Wiseman, Nelson #7604
- Yuristy, Russell #7632
- Zelenak, Ed #594
artists and models
- Mollise, Mâli Christianne Paul, as model #6635
- Whiten, Colette, use of male models #7556 7557 7558
Artists Review, Can periodical #1815
Artmagazine, Can periodical #560 3314
- (1970s) #3310
Arts, Can periodical #551
Arts and Crafts Association (Hamilton, Ont)
- (1890s) #1706
- exhibitions (reviews)
    - (1895) #2239
Arts and Crafts movement
- and George Selkirk Gibson #5591
- and Katharine Emma Maltwood #3242 6413
- California, influence on Vancouver (BC) domestic architecture (1910-1920s) #8730
- Canada #189
- Montréal (Qué) #1367
- Vancouver (BC) #1977
- Victoria (BC) #1980 2269
Arts and Crafts Society of Canada
- exhibitions
    - (1904) #2241
Arts and Culture of the North, Amer periodical #4270
Arts and Letters Club (Toronto, Ont)
- (1908-1944) #1671
- periodical, *Lamps* #1667
- support of Group of Seven #1763
Arts Bulletin, Can periodical #551
Arts Club of Montreal (Montréal, Qué) #1254
- renovation of house, 51 Victoria Street #1314
Arts West, Can periodical #1868 3310
ArtsAtlantic, Can periodical #128
Artscanada, Can periodical #25
- (1970s) #3310
- sculpture symposium (1974) #773
ArtViews, Can periodical #1806
Arvida (Qué), Shipshaw powerhouse
- mural, André Charles Biéler #4721
Ascott, Roy, Brit artist, educator in Canada, 1934-
- as principal, Ontario College of Art (Toronto, Ont) #3002
Ash, Samuel, Can artist, 1951- #4157 4161
- paintings of Algonquian legends #4558
Ash, Stuart B., Can artist, 1942-

- prints #897
- typographic designs #932
Ashcan School
- *see* Eight, The (American group)
Ashevak, Johnniebo, Can artist, 1923-1972 #4559 4563
Ashevak, Karoo, Can artist, 1940-1974 #4560 4561
- exhibitions
    - (1977) #4562
Ashevak, Kenojuak, Can artist, 1927- #4260 4460 4563
- and Johnniebo Ashevak, misattributions #4559
- interview #4564
Ashkewe, Delmer (Del), Can artist, 1947- #6648
- exhibitions, group
    - (1980) #4159
Ashley, Benedict, Amer priest, fl. 1971
- on the sacred in art #94
Ashoona, Kiawak, Can artist, 1933-
- exhibitions
    - (1980) #4565
Askevold, David Marius, Can artist, 1940-
- and avant-garde art #600
- exhibitions, group
    - (1970) #534
    - (1980) #690
- interview #4566
- video art #605
Askren, Patricia Alice (Pat), Can artist, 1951-
- exhibitions, group
    - (1979) #674
- travelling art exhibition program, Alberta (1980) #1972
Aspell, Peter Noel Lawson, Can artist, 1918-
- exhibitions, group
    - (1959) #1997
Assekikuk, Chief
- *see* Assiginack, Jean-Baptiste
Asselin, Denis, Can artist, 1943- #1524 1544
- exhibitions, group
    - (1981) #1565
Assiginack, Jean-Baptiste, Indian Chief, ca. 1768-1865
- wampum belts representing peace treaties (1764-1852) #3501
Assiniboine
- photographic views
    - Hime, Humphrey Lloyd #5801 5802 5803 5804
Assiniboine and Saskatchewan Exploring Expedition (1858)
- and Humphrey Lloyd Hime #1014 1015 1865 5801 5802 5803 5804
Assiniboine Indians
- art #3731
- bows and arrows #3693
- costume #3739
- culture #3653
- gun cases #3713
- petroglyphs #3673
- photographic views
    - Curtis, Edward Sheriff #3399
- tattooing #3723

Association des architectes de la province de Québec (AAPQ)
- (1960s) #8307
Association des artisans de Saint-Jean-Port-Joli
- woodcarvings #1608
Association des métiers d'art du Québec
- (1970s) #1490
Association for Preservation Technology/Association pour l'avancement des méthodes de préservation. Bulletin (APT Bulletin), Can periodical #7757
Association of Canadian Etchers
- exhibitions
    - (1885) #798
Association of Canadian Industrial Designers (ACID)
- (1948-1958) #2612
- (1949) #2604
Association of National Non-Profit Artists' Centres (ANNPAC) #683
- (1976-1981) #598
- and Artspace (Peterborough, Ont) #1836
- periodical, *Parallelogramme* #612
associations, Canadian
- 18th c.-1930s #343
- 19th c. #153 185 275
- 19th c.-1920s #11
- (1860-1890) #264
- (1860s-1930s) #28
- (1870s-1910s) #200
- (1880-1914) #265
- (1880s-1930s) #45
- (1890-1900) #190
- (1890s) #187 188
- (1910s) #205
- (1930s) #502
- (1940s) #363
    - and Royal Canadian Academy of Arts #361
- (1949-1951), Royal Commission on National Development in the Arts, Letters and Sciences (Massey Report) #3254 3255 3256 3261
- (1960s) #447
- (1970s) #682 707 3278 3279
- and museums
    - 19th c.-1970s #3055
    - (1960s) #3043
- British Columbia
    - (1880s-1940s) #1986
    - (1890s-1930s) #2007
    - (1910s) #1979
    - (1940s) #1987
    - (1960s) #2989
    - (1970s) #3272
- craftsmen's associations, Québec #2227
- national association of architects, recommendation for (1897) #8291
- Newfoundland #1138 1142 1147
    - (1950s) #2146
- Nova Scotia (1900-1945) #1194
- Ontario
    - 19th c. #1706
    - (1870s) #1693
    - (1970s) #1802 1825

– Québec
– 17th-18th cs. #2214
– (1825-1850) #1368
– (1940s-1970s) #1269
– Saskatchewan, late 19th c.-1950s #1919
– Toronto (Ont)
– 19th c. #7956
– (1880s) #3129
– Vancouver (BC) #1977
– (1886-1930) #2003
– (1889-1894) #1981
– western Canada (1940s) #1841
Assumption
– see Mary, Virgin, assumption
Astman, Barbara Anne, Can artist, 1950-
#4567
– colour xerography #614
– compared with Fern Helfand #1010
– exhibitions, group
– (1980) #1063
– on Jack Chambers #700
Astous, Roger d'
– see D'Astous, Roger
Atchison, John Danley, Can architect,
1870-1959
– Moose Jaw (Sask), City Hall, competition
#8978
– Winnipeg (Man)
– Bank of Hamilton #9171
– City Hall, competition #8979
– domestic architecture #8493
Atelier libre de recherches graphiques
(Montréal, Qué) #1653
Ateliers, Can periodical #1493
Athabaskan Indians
– see Athapaskan Indians
Athapaskan Indians
– art #3366 3370 4091 4104 4105
– beadwork #4107
– costume #4102 4111
– culture #4072 4073 4097
– 18th c. #3445
– decorative arts (1970s) #3367
– embroidery #4110 4152
– masks #4083
– quillwork #3471 3474 3475
– snowshoes #2812
athletes in art
– Clarke, Fred #5115
– McKenzie, Robert Tait #6481
Atkins, Caven Ernest, Can artist, 1907-
#4568 4570
– exhibitions
– (1979) #4569
Atkins, Gordon L., Can architect, 1937-
– Lake Windermere (BC), Melchin summer
houses #7694
Atkinson, William Edwin, Can artist,
1862-1926 #4571
– as member, Canadian Art Club #193
– exhibitions (reviews) #204 211 1703
Atlantic coast (Canada)
– views #139
Atlantic provinces
– art #128 1123
– (1960s) #1124

– (1970s) #1127 1131 1132 1133 1135
– painting
– (1970s) #588
– silver #2640
Atlantic Provinces Art Circuit (APAC)
– (1960s) #1124
– (1964-1971) #3053
Atlantic Woodcarver's Guild #1194
atrium, Canadian
– (1970s-1980) #7743
Aubin, Ernest, Can artist, 1893-1963
– and Montée Saint-Michel #1236
Aubin, Régine, Can basketmaker, fl. 1981
#2954
Auclair, André, Can sculptor, 1803-1865
#1301 1578
auctions
– see art market
Audet, Louis-Napoléon, Can architect,
1881-1971
– and Ozias Leduc #6204
– Valleyfield (Qué)
– Cathedral of Salaberry-de-Valleyfield
#8843
Audubon, John James, Amer artist,
ornithologist, 1785-1851
– exhibitions
– (1944) #12
– influence on Glen Loates #6310
– Lansdowne, James Fenwick, compared
with #6163
– Pope, William, compared with #6905
Augustinians
– Québec (Qué), Hôtel-Dieu #1352 3119
– tabernacles, Québec #1359
Aultsville region (Ont)
– architecture, 19th c. #7980
Austin (Texas), University Art Museum
– exhibitions
– Canadian Landscape Painting, 1670-1930:
The Artist and the Land (1973) #106
authors, Canadian
– portrait photographs, John Reeves #1065
1066
automatism #1467
– and Alfred Pellan #6815
– and Christian Marcel Barbeau #4602 4606
– and Fernand Leduc #6187 6189 6190 6191
6194
– and Guido Molinari #6591
– and Jean-Paul Armand Mousseau #6650
6651
– and Jean-Paul Riopelle #7012 7022 7031
– and Jock Macdonald #6377 6379
– and Léon Bellefleur #4660
– and Louis Jaque #5942
– and Marcelle Ferron #5421 5424 5425
– and Paterson Ewen #5384
– and Paul-Emile Borduas #1270 1417 1453
1455 4809 4810 4811 4815 4821 4829 4830
4832 4833 4843 4849 7026
– and Pierre Gauvreau #5575 5576 5577 5578
– and Pierre Gendron #5582
– and René Derouin #5285
– and Rita Letendre #6251
– and Roland Giguère #5598

– Canada #6586
– literary works #4831
– Montréal (Qué) #1398 1420 1426 1437 1448
1449 1475 1476
– (1954-1955) #1408
– Québec #1294
– Québec, prints #1650
automatistes (Montréal, Qué) #512 1472 1475
– and Alfred Pellan #1451
– and Paul-Emile Borduas #1462
– and Refus global #1396 1447 1466
– and Surrealism #1458 1464 1467
– compared with plasticiens #7398
– exhibitions (reviews)
– (1950) #1400
– writings #1443
automobile service stations
– see gasoline stations
Avalon Peninsula (Nfld)
– Irish settlements #8523
aviaries (books)
– see bestiaries
awards
– Canadian Design Index-NIDC #2605 3033
– Design Awards #2609
– Jessie Dow Prize, Art Association of
Montreal (1908-1965) #1261
– National Industrial Design Council #2608
2610
– Red River Exhibition (1964-1978) #1903
awards, architecture
– Canadian Architect #7672
– (1968) #8190
– (1969) #8191
– (1970) #8192
– (1971) #8193
– (1973) #8195
– (1974) #8196
– (1975) #8197
– (1976) #8198
– (1977) #8199
– (1978) #8200
– (1979) #8201 8202
– (1980) #8203
– (1981) #8204
– Canadian Housing Design Council
– (1957-) #8741
– (1972) #8744
– (1974) #8746
– (1979) #8747
– Central Mortgage and Housing
Corporation (1960) #8040
– Concrete Awards Program (1971) #7706
– Dominion Housing Act Small House
Competition (1936) #8736
– Eaton, T., Company Architectural
Competition for House Designs (1936)
#8738
– International Calvert House Competition
(1954) #8510
– Massey Awards for Excellence in the
Urban Environment
– (1971) #8217
– (1975) #8218
– Massey Medals for Architecture
– (1952) #8205

– (1955) #8206
– (1958) #8207
– (1961) #8208 8209 8210
– (1962), survey of architects on #8305
– (1964) #8211
– (1967) #8212 8213 8214
– (1970) #8215 8216
– National Awards for Residential Design
  (1969) #8743
– Ontario Government Housing
  Competition (1936) #8737
– Ontario Housing Corporation Design
  Competition (1972) #8663
– Ordre des architectes du Québec (1978)
  #7886
– Prix nationaux aux constructeurs de
  maisons unifamiliales (1960) #8742
– Royal Architectural Institute of Canada
    – (1931) #7660
    – (1937) #7664
    – (1940) #7665
– Royal Institute of British Architects Royal
  Gold Medal
    – Darling, Frank (1915) #8349 8350
    – Morris, Robert Schofield (1958) #8389
Awasatlas
– see Smith, Russell (Awasatlas)
Axangayu
– see Shaa, Aqjangajuk
Aycock, Alice, Amer sculptor, 1946-
– exhibitions, group
    – (1980) #8237
Ayerst, McKenna and Harrison, chemists'
  firm (Montréal, Qué)
– collection, Canadian art #852
Aylmer (Qué)
– architecture (1800-1921) #7889
Ayot, Pierre, Can artist, 1943- #4572
– as director, Graff (Montréal, Qué) #1645
– engravings #1654
– exhibitions
    – (1980) #4573
– exhibitions, group
    – (1981) #1564
– Pop art #1497
Ayotte, Léo, Can artist, 1909-1976 #1393
  4574 4575
Ayr (Ont), Molsons Bank
– architecture #9173
Ayre, Robert, Can art critic, 1900-
– on Albert Henry Robinson #7056
– on Marc-Aurèle Fortin #5475
Aziz, Philip John Andrew Ferris, Can artist,
  1923- #4577
– exhibitions
    – (1957) #4576

B

Baber, Jack, Can photographer, fl. 1960s
– portfolio of photographs #987
Bach, Johann Christian, Ger musician,
  composer, 1735-1782
– La Toccata, influence on Michèle

Cournoyer #5193
Bachelard, Gaston, Fr philosopher,
  1884-1962
– influence on Albert Dumouchel #5333
Bachinski, Walter Joseph Gerard, Can artist,
  1939-
– exhibitions
    – (1977) #4578
    – (1981) #4579
Back, George, Brit naval officer, artist in
  Canada, 1796-1878 #241 242 279 4580
– and Franklin Arctic expedition (1819-1821)
  #5825
Back, Süzel, Can artist, 1956-
– batik #2741
Bacon, Francis, Brit artist, 1909-
– Bates, Maxwell Bennett, compared with
  #4623
– Cohen, Sorel, compared with #5130
– influence on Joe Plaskett #6889
– influence on Louis de Niverville #6711
– Markgraf, Waltraud Erna Else, compared
  with #6416
– Niverville, Louis de, compared with #6707
Bacstrom, Sigismund, Ger artist, physician,
  scientist in Canada, fl. 1763-1795
– views, northwest coast #4581
Baczynski, George, Can photographer, ca.
  1951-
– portfolio of photographs #1023
Badani, Pat, Can artist, 1951- #4582
badges, Canadian
– military #2900
Baffin Island (NWT)
– culture #4320
    – (1920s) #4326
– drawings (1964) #4194
– graphic arts #4499
– photographic views, Peter Pitseolak #6876
– sculpture (1970s) #4420
– views, A.Y. Jackson #5919
bag handles, Inuit
– Washington (DC), Smithsonian Institution
  #4319
Baha'i
– influence on Otto Rogers #7063 7064
Bahamas
– views
    – Gagen, Robert Ford #5530
    – Panabaker, Frank Shirley #6756
Baich, Paul von
– see Von Baich, Paul
Baie-Comeau (Qué), Centre sportif
– exhibitions
    – Un siècle et demi d'art canadien (Collection
      du Musée de la province de Québec)/A
      Century and a Half of Canadian Art
      (Collection of the Museum of the Province
      of Quebec) (1951) #1248
Baie-Saint-Paul (Qué)
– views
    – Bolduc, Blanche #4772
    – Gagnon, Clarence Alphonse #5545
    – Richard, René-Jean #6996 6999
Baie-Saint-Paul (Qué), church
– architecture and interior, François

Baillairgé #7849
Bailey, Charles S., Can photographer,
  1869-1896 #4583
– exhibitions, group
    – (1976) #2012
Bailey, Clayton George (Cal), Can
  photographer, 1947- #1879
– exhibitions
    – (1978) #4584
– exhibitions, group
    – (1977) #1033
Bailey, William, Can photographer,
  1865-1936/1937
– exhibitions, group
    – (1976) #2012
Baillairgé, Charles Philippe Ferdinand, Can
  architect, 1826-1906
– and André-Raphaël Giroux #5610
– Cap-Rouge (Qué), Henry Howison Pottery
  #2301
– exhibitions
    – (1979) #8324
– Québec (Qué)
    – maison mère Mallet #8884
    – Plains of Abraham Prison #9057
Baillairgé, François, Can architect, artist,
  1759-1830 #1232 1592 4585 4586 4588 4589
  4590 4593 6947
– and origins of Québec woodcarving and
  architecture #1574
– and Québec society #1375
– as brother of Pierre-Florent Baillairgé
  #4594
– as teacher #1582
– Baie-Saint-Paul (Qué), architecture and
  sculpture #7849
– exhibitions
    – (1975) #4592
– exhibitions, group
    – (1959), portraits #219
– influence of French painting #1244
– influence on Thomas Baillairgé #8328
– paintings #4587
– Québec (Qué)
    – Chapel of the congrégation Notre-Dame
      de Québec #8864
    – Church of Saint-Joachim de
      Montmorency, interior #8880
    – Notre-Dame-des-Victoires #8858
– rocking horses #2934
– sculptures #1324
– tabernacles #1613 4591
– use of architectural models #7872
Baillairgé, Jean, Can sculptor, 1726-1805
  #4585
– as father of François Baillairgé #4590
– as father of Pierre-Florent Baillairgé #4594
– as teacher #1582
– as teacher of Pierre Emond #5371
– interior, Church of Saint-Jean-Baptiste
  (Saint-Jean-Port-Joli, Qué) #8812
– sculptures #1324
– tabernacles #1613
Baillairgé, Pierre-Florent, Can sculptor,
  1761-1812 #1324 4594
– as teacher #1582

– interior, Church of Saint-Jean-Baptiste
    (Saint-Jean-Port-Joli, Qué) #8812
– interior, Church of Sainte-Famille (île
    d'Orléans, Qué) #8795
– tabernacles #1613
– works, churches, Charlesbourg (Qué)
    #8851
Baillairgé, Thomas, Can architect, sculptor,
    1791-1859 #1232 1324 1592 8325 8326 8327
    8328
– and Québec church architecture #8821
– as teacher #1582
– as teacher of André-Raphaël Giroux #5610
– Charlesbourg (Qué), church #8851
– interior, Church of Saint-Joachim de
    Montmorency (Québec, Qué) #8880
– interior, Church of Sainte-Famille (île
    d'Orléans, Qué) #8795
– Québec (Qué), Episcopal Palace #8787
– supper at Emmaus theme #1615
– tabernacles #1613
– use of architectural models #7872
Baillairgé family, Can architects, sculptors,
    18th-19th cs. #1233 1300
– influence on Québec architecture #7851
– woodcarvings #1573 1575 1576
Baillargé
– see Baillairgé
Baillif, Claude, Can builder, 1635-1698 #228
    229 8329
– as teacher, Ecole des arts et métiers de
    Saint-Joachim (Saint-Joachim, Qué)
    #2992
– Québec (Qué), Notre-Dame-des-Victoires
    #8858
Bailly, Evern Earl, Can artist, 1903-1977
    #4595
Bailly (dit Lafleur), François, Fr builder in
    Canada, ca. 1627-1690 #228 229 7844
Bain, Freda Guttman, Can artist, 1934-
– prints #4596
Baird, George, Can architect, 1939-
– on Toronto architecture #7746
Baird, Nini, Can arts administrator, fl. 1977
– interview, on Canada Council Twenty Plus
    Five green paper #3285
Baird, Ronald Arnott (Ron), Can sculptor,
    1940-
– architectural sculptures #4597
– on Canadian art (1960s) #478
Baker, Francis Spence, Can architect,
    1867-1926
– Toronto (Ont) #8330
    – Graphic Arts Building #9330
Baker, Isaac Bennett, Can builder,
    furniture-maker, 1833-1925 #2581
Baker Lake (NWT)
– art #4266
– graphic arts #4473
    – (1959-1972) #4478
    – (1959-1976) #4490
    – (1969-1973) #4481
    – (1970-) #4472
    – (1975-1977) #3373
    – and Sheila and Jack Butler #4486
– sculpture #4402 4403 4408 4434

– (1950s-1960s) #4400
– wall hangings #4230 4253
– women artists (1970s) #4260
Baker Lake (NWT), Sanavick Co-operative
– prints from drawings by Luke
    Anguhadluq #4533
Bakken, Haakon, Can jeweller, 1932- #2706
Bakuba (Africa)
– masks, compared with masks, Kwakiutl
    Indians #3920
Balboa (Calif), Newport Harbour Art
    Museum
– exhibitions
    – The New Art of Vancouver (1969) #2039
Balch, Reg, Can photographer, 1894-
– portfolio of photographs #991
baldachins
– see canopies
Baldwin, Edward R., Can architect, 1935-
– Toronto (Ont), CN Tower #9511
Baldwin, Lee, Can stained glass artist, fl.
    1975
– stained glass #2452
Baldwin, William Warren, Can architect,
    1775-1844
– proposal for a society of architects (ca.
    1835) #8306
Baldwin & Greene, Can architectural firm
– Toronto (Ont), Ashley & Crippen Building
    #9367
Balharrie, James Watson, Can architect,
    1910-
– Ottawa (Ont), Carleton University #9455
Balint, Gerrie, Can ceramicist, 1928- #2394
ballet
– see also scenography
– Canada #129
– influence on Norman McLaren #6497
– Winnipeg (Man) #1891
balloons
– as sculpture, Royal Canadian Aerial
    Theatre (RCAT) #2058
Balshine, Lorne, Can collector, 20th c.
– collection, Inuit art #4312 4447
Baltimore (Md), Baltimore Museum of Art
– exhibitions
    – "And Eagles Sweep Across the Sky": Indian
        Textiles of the North American West,(1977)
        #4015
    – An Exhibition of Paintings by
        Contemporary Canadian Artists: Catalogue
        (1930) #315
Baltzly, Benjamin, Can photographer,
    1835-1883
– photographs and journals, British
    Columbia expedition (1871) #4598
– survey photographs #1014 1015 1865 1876
balustrades
– see also railings
balustrades, Canadian
– Québec #2702
Bancroft, Marian Penner, Can photographer,
    1947- #2018 2071 4599
– exhibitions, group
    – (1979) #2069
Band, Charles Shaw, Can collector,

1885-1969
– interview #3219
Band, Charles Shaw, Can collector,
    1885-1969, and Helen, Can collector, 20th
    c.
– collection, Canadian paintings and
    drawings, 20th c. #3215
Band, Helen, Can collector, 20th c.
– on Alex Simeon Janvier #5936
Band, Percy, Can collector, 20th c.
– collection, games and toys, 19th c. #2917
Banff (Alta)
– architecture
    – (1920s) #7656
– art #1964
    – (1970s) #1870 1960
– city planning, Thomas Hayton Mawson
    #9405
– photographic views
    – Harmon, Byron #5707
Banff (Alta), Banff Centre. School of Fine
    Arts
– (1970s) #3006
– exhibitions
    – Dennis Burton Retrospective (1978) #4961
Banff (Alta), Banff Centre. Walter Phillips
    Gallery
– exhibitions
    – Artisan '78: The First National Travelling
        Exhibition of Contemporary Canadian
        Crafts/Artisan '78: première exposition
        nationale itinérante d'artisanat canadien
        contemporain (1978) #2134
    – Enns, Evans & Ulrich (1977) #1956
    – Joe Fafard: Recent Sculpture (1980) #5401
    – Louis de Niverville (1980) #6709
    – Sylvain P. Cousineau: Photographs and
        Paintings (1980) #5195
    – The Banff Purchase: An Exhibition of
        Photography in Canada (1979) #1037
– exhibitions (reviews)
    – Andrews, Stephen #4528
    – The Banff Purchase: An Exhibition of
        Photography in Canada (1979) #1046 1060
– photography exhibitions (1970s) #1879
Banff (Alta), Banff School of Fine Arts
– (1940s) #1841
– Cameron, Donald, as director #3000
– Tailfeathers, Gerald, as student #7312
– Townsend, William, as teacher #7418
Banff (Alta), Peter Whyte Gallery
– exhibitions
    – A Tribute to William Townsend: 1909 to
        1973 (1974) #7418
    – Beyond Exceptional Pass (1978) #1960
    – Canadian Political Cartoons (1977) #956
    – H.G. Glyde in Canada (1975) #5618
    – The Group of Seven in the Rockies (1974)
        #1861
    – The Railway: Patron of the Arts in Canada
        (1976) #3281
    – The Temptation of Aquarius: Paintings by
        Robert Ralph Carmichael (1972) #5002
Banff (Alta), Peter Whyte Gallery. Archives
    of the Canadian Rockies
– exhibitions

- *Joe Plaskett and His Paris: In Search of Time Past* (1972) #6893
- *Joe Plaskett et son Paris: à la recherche d'un temps passé* (1972) #6894
- Harmon, Byron, photographs #5707
Banff National Park (Alta), Village Lake Louise development project
- architectural proposal, Arthur Charles Erickson #8360
Banfield, A.F., & Company, Can furniture-making firm
- furniture, Deer Lodge (Winnipeg, Man) #9260
Bank of Montreal
- banks (1930s) #9183
Bank of Nova Scotia
- banks
    - (1920s) #9174
    - (1930s) #9186
- collection, Canadian art #3245
Bank of Toronto
- banks (1930s) #9185
banks, Canadian
- (1867-1967) #9196
- (1910s) #9156 9166 9169
- (1911-1912) #8295
- (1912) #7645
- (1930s) #9184
- (1940s-1950s) #9191
- (1950s) #9193
- Bank of Montreal (1930s) #9183
- Bank of Nova Scotia
    - (1920s) #9174
    - (1930s) #9186
    - and John MacIntosh Lyle #9203
- Bank of Toronto (1930s) #9185
- Canadian Bank of Commerce
    - (1920s) #9172
    - (1930s) #9189
- Dominion Bank (1870s-1930s) #9188
- Edmonton (Alta), Imperial Bank of Canada #9154
- Halifax (NS), Bank of Nova Scotia #9182
- Hamilton (Ont), Bank of Hamilton #9160
- London (Ont), 19th c. #8010
- Molsons Bank (1920s) #9173
- Montréal (Qué)
    - (1845-1933) #9201
    - Bank of British North America #9164
    - Bank of Montreal (1846) #9200
    - Bank of Montreal (1918) #9168
    - Bank of Toronto #9167
    - Canadian Bank of Commerce #9153
    - Canadian Imperial Bank of Commerce #9194
    - Royal Bank of Canada #7933 9176
- Ontario (1915-1919) #9170
- Ottawa (Ont)
    - Bank of Canada head office (1938) #9337
    - Bank of Canada head office (1978) #9199
- restoration (1980s) #9204
- Toronto (Ont)
    - 19th c.-1930s #8076
    - (1910s) #9159
    - (1930s) #9181
    - Bank of British North America #9150

- Bank of Montreal (1910) #9155
- Bank of Montreal (1949) #9190
- Bank of Nova Scotia #9192
- Bank of Toronto (1908) #9151
- Bank of Toronto (1913) #8293 9162
- Canadian Bank of Commerce #9178 9180 9351
- Dominion Bank #9163
- Royal Bank (1908) #9152
- Royal Bank (1915) #9165
- Royal Bank Plaza #9198 9353
- Standard Bank #9158
- Toronto-Dominion Centre #9197 9348
- use of Canadian motifs as architectural decoration (1930s) #8226
- Vancouver (BC), Royal Bank #9179
- Victorian #7769
- western Canada, prefabricated buildings, early 20th c. #8082
- Windsor (Ont), Imperial Bank of Canada #9175
- Winnipeg (Man)
    - (1898-1914) #9205
    - (1910s) #9202
    - Bank of Hamilton #9171
    - Bank of Nova Scotia #9157
banners and flags #2939
- Laliberté, Norman #6154
- Wainwright, Ruth #7497
Bannister, Edward M., Can artist in USA, 1833-1901
- exhibitions, group
    - (1969) #1180
Banting, Frederick Grant, Can physician, artist, 1891-1941 #4600
- paintings, Canadian Medical Association Headquarters (Ottawa, Ont) #138
Banwell, Michael (Mike), Can sculptor, 1943-
- exhibitions, group
    - (1981) #797
- installation work #4601
baptismal fonts
- *see* fonts
Barbeau, Charles Marius, Can anthropologist, 1883-1969 #3303 3309
- and Emily Carr #5021 5024 5034 5040
- and Gordon Edward Pfeiffer #6847
- influence on Tony Law #6174
- on Tsimshian Indians #3981
- revival of *ceinture fléchée* #2833 2864
Barbeau, Christian Marcel, Can artist, 1925- #1282 1453 4606
- and Optical art #1445
- and plasticiens #1439
- exhibitions, group
    - (1967) #480
    - (1968) #1263
- exhibitions (reviews) #4607
- interview #4604
- paintings (1950s-1961) #4602 4603
Barbeau, Jean-Guy, Can artist, 1925- #1549 1551
Barbeau, Marius
- *see* Barbeau, Charles Marius
Barber, Charles Arnold, Can architect, 1848-1915 #8331

Barber, Earle William, Can architect, 1855-1915
- Winnipeg (Man) #8331
Barber & Barber, Can architectural firm
- Winnipeg (Man) #8331
    - City Hall #8996
Barber & Ellis, publishing firm (Toronto, Ont)
- Christmas greeting cards #890
Barbin, Raoul, artist, fl. 1925
- interior, Château Frontenac (Québec, Qué) #9278
Barbizon school
- and Canadian landscape drawings, early 20th c. #497
- and Canadian landscape painting (1880-1910) #214
- and Clarence Alphonse Gagnon #5548
- and Horatio Walker #7503 7504
- and J.E.H. MacDonald #6370
- and Marc-Aurèle de Foy Suzor-Coté #7299 7302
- and Robert Harris #5739
- and Tom Forrestall #5466
- paintings, in Canadian private collections #194
Barbour, Carl, Can artist, 1908- #1155
- exhibitions, group
    - (1977) #1156
Barbour, David, Can photographer, 1952- #1879
    - (1979) #1904
Bardon, Lynn, Can writer, 1947-
- Suttles and Seawinds cottage industry (New Germany, NS) #2154
Bareket, Nir, Can photographer, 1939-
- portfolio of photographs #1023
Baril, Marcel, Can artist, 1929- #4608
Barker, Charles Edward, Can artist, 1900-1974
- exhibitions
    - (1975) #4609
Barker, Sydney Herbert, Can artist, 1893-1970
- exhibitions, group
    - (1958) #1846
Barkerville (BC)
- architecture #8151
Barnard, Henry, Amer educator, 1811-1900
- model books on school architecture #9384
Barnes, Elias Paul, Amer artist, 1840-1865
- panorama of Saint Lawrence River and Great Lakes #218
Barnes, Elliott Chappel, Can photographer, fl. 1905-1919 #4610
Barnes, Robert Percy, Can architect, 1857-1926
- Edmonton (Alta), Imperial Bank of Canada #9154
Barnet, Will, Amer artist, 1911-
- and Marion F.S. Mackay Nicoll #6701 6703
Barnett, David, Can artist, 1933-
- exhibitions, group
    - (1979) #674
barns
- *see also* stables

barns, American #9228
barns, Canadian #9228
– (1608-1867) #2120
– Abernethy (Sask), W.R. Motherwell
  Farmstead National Historic Park #9232
– Acadian #7804
– Alberta #8120
– British Columbia #8148 8153
– Manitoba #8098
  – 19th-early 20th cs. #8102
– Mennonite #8715
– Niagara-on-the-Lake (Ont), 19th c. #7986
– Ontario
  – 19th c. #7745 9227 9229
  – polygonal buildings, 19th c. #7987
– Prairies #8080
– Québec
  – 17th-18th cs. #2217
  – 17th-19th cs. #9230 9231
  – roofs, 17th-18th cs. #7881
– Winnipeg (Man) #8096
Barnsley, James Macdonald, Can artist,
  1861-1929 #4612
– exhibitions
  – (1964) #4611
– influence of Impressionism #227
– works, National Gallery of Canada
  (Ottawa, Ont) #4613
Baroque architecture
– Québec, churches #8817 8821
Baroque furniture
– Ontario (1860s), by Polish settlers #2565
Baroque revival architecture
– Québec, churches #7856
Barot, Cécile, Can weaver, d. 1958
– ceinture fléchée #2833
Barott, Blackader & Webster, Can
  architectural firm
– Montréal (Qué)
  – Bank of British North America #9164
  – St. Denis Theatre #9068
– Vancouver (BC), Canadian Pacific Railway
  Station #9534
Barott & Blackader, Can architectural firm
– Lake Louise (Alta), Château Lake Louise
  #9279
– Montréal (Qué)
  – Aldred Building #9313
  – Bell Canada #9310
Barr, David John, Amer artist, 1939-
– relief structures #777
barracks
– see also fortifications
barracks, Canadian
– Fort Malden (Amherstburg, Ont) #8456
– Louisbourg (NS), King's Bastion #8435
  8436
– Québec (Qué), Artillery Park. Saint-Jean
  Barracks #8449
Barraud, Cyril, Can artist, 1877-1965
– and Walter Joseph Phillips #6856
barrels, Canadian
– Newfoundland, 20th c. #2151
– Newfoundland and Labrador, 20th c.
  #2155
Barrett, Joel, Can architect, fl. 1956

– Vancouver (BC), Vancouver Civic
  Auditorium, competition #9080
Barrett, Samuel A., Amer collector, 20th c.
– collection, masks, Kwakiutl #3938
Barrington (NS), Meeting House
– architecture #7823
Barry, James, Irish artist, 1741-1806
– painting of death of Wolfe #220
Barry, John, Can silversmith, b. 1815, fl.
  1838-1857 #2649
bars
– see taverns
Bartlett, Bob, Brit naval officer in Canada,
  1875-1946
– residence, Brigus (Nfld) #8539
Bartlett, William Henry, Brit artist in
  Canada, 1809-1854 #812 1323
– art and writings #4617
– Canadian Scenery #4615 4616
  – views on pottery #2282 2288 2362
– forgeries #4614
– Windsor, Nova Scotia #1218
Barton Myers Associates, Can architectural
  firm
– Edmonton (Alta), Citadel Theatre #9140
– Los Angeles (Calif), Bunker Hill
  redevelopment #8364
Bartram, Edward John (Ed), Can artist, 1938-
– exhibitions
  – (1979) #4618
Basel (Switzerland), Kunsthalle
– exhibitions
  – General Idea's Reconstructing
    Futures/General Idea: reconstruction de
    l'avenir (1978) #5583
– exhibitions (reviews)
  – Snow, Michael #7263
Basin Head (PEI)
– restoration of fishing shacks #7795
basketry, Abenaki #3596
basketry, Algonquian #3374 3605 3625
– (1760s-early 20th c.) #3633
– stamp-blocked ornamentation #3562
basketry, Canadian #2089
– grasswork, Labrador, 20th c. #2945
– Nova Scotia #2157
– Québec, 20th c. #2954
– splintwood, Nova Scotia #2935
– women's work baskets, 19th c.-1970s #2943
basketry, Carrier
– (1970s) #4145
basketry, Chilcotin #3789
basketry, Coast Salish #3896
basketry, Columbia River Indians
– prehistoric #3842
basketry, Cowichan #4027
basketry, Delaware #3506
basketry, Dogrib #4089
basketry, Great Basin Indians #3986
basketry, Haida
– Santa Ana (Calif), Charles W. Bowers
  Memorial Museum #3991
basketry, Huron #3519
basketry, Indians of North America #2739
  3394 3447
– 20th c. #2143

– Coachella Valley (Calif) #3378
– technique #3446
– Washington (DC), Smithsonian Institution
  #3389
basketry, Inuit #4307
– compared with Tlingit basketry #4309
– Nunivak Island (Alaska) #4180
basketry, Iroquois #3519 3605 3625
– (1760s-early 20th c.) #3633
– and Seneca basketry #3552
– stamp-blocked ornamentation #3562
basketry, Klikitat #3778
– coiled #3777
basketry, Kootenay
– coiled #3788
basketry, Kwakiutl #3787
basketry, Lillooet #3773 3783 3927
basketry, Maliseet #2144 3628 3637
basketry, Menomine
– birchbark #3620
basketry, Micmac #3569 3628 3630 3643
basketry, Mistassini #4080
basketry, natives of North America #3411
basketry, Nootka #3880 4025
– Santa Ana (Calif), Charles W. Bowers
  Memorial Museum #3991
basketry, Northwest Coast Indians #3888
  3953 4009 4015 4029 4142
– and pre-Columbian art #3810
– prehistoric #4017
– Pullman (Wash), Washington State
  Historical Society Museum #4004
– winter count motif #3728
basketry, Ojibwa #3539 3557 4089
– use of sweet grass #3547
basketry, Ottawa
– use of sweet grass #3547
basketry, Quinault #3773 3778
basketry, Salish #3876 4027
– (1970s) #4145
– coiled #3777 3801
– Santa Ana (Calif), Charles W. Bowers
  Memorial Museum #3991
basketry, Seneca #3552
basketry, Shuswap #3789
basketry, Skokomish #3835
basketry, Slavey #4089
basketry, Snuqualmi #3835
basketry, Thompson Indians #3773
basketry, Tlingit #3776 3792 3806 3865 3976
  4027
– compared with Pacific Eskimo basketry
  #4309
– Santa Ana (Calif), Charles W. Bowers
  Memorial Museum #3991
basketry, Woodlands #3625
– (1760s-early 20th c.) #3633
– stamp-blocked ornamentation #3562
Bastien, Jean-Marie, Can artist, 1934- #2769
Bastin, Michèle, Can artist, 1944-
– exhibitions (reviews) #4619
Bates, Maxwell Bennett, Can artist, architect,
  1906-1980 #4620 4625
– as member of Limners #2043
– correspondence, Jock Macdonald #6376
– exhibitions

– (1960) #4622
– (1973) #4624
– exhibitions, group
   – (1962) #1847
– exhibitions (reviews) #4623
– on art #1944
– on art, literature, and photography #4621
– on printmaking #817
– portraits #715
Bates, Patricia (Pat) Martin, Can artist, 1927-
   #4627
– exhibitions
   – (1972) #4626
– exhibitions, group
   – (1967) #821
Bath (England), Bath Festival. Holburne of
   Menstrie Museum
– exhibitions
   – *James Wilson Morrice 1865-1924* (1968)
      #6627
bathers in art
– Alleyn, George Edmund #4512
– Peel, Paul, *After the Bath* paintings #6790
   6794
Bathurst (NB), Nepisiguit Centennial
   Library
– exhibitions
   – *Colville, Pratt, Forrestall* (1974) #1129
   – *The Beaverbrook Art Gallery Presents Nine
      New Brunswick Artists/La Galerie d'art
      Beaverbrook présente neuf artistes du
      Nouveau-Brunswick* (1973) #1182
Bathurst Island (NWT)
– Dorset artifacts #4375
Batiscan (Qué), Old Presbytery
– architecture and interior #8807
Batoche (Sask)
– architecture and land use #8115
Battleford (Sask), Fort Battleford
– architecture #8481 8484
Baturin, Jon, Can photographer, fl. 1980-
– portfolio of photographs #1023
Baudot, Jean, Can artist, 1929-
– computer art #528
Baudry (*dit* Des Butes), Guillaume, Can
   silversmith, 1657-1732 #234 235
Bauhaus
– influence on Canadian architecture #7735
– influence on Canadian tapestry #2774
– influence on Fritz Brandtner #4904
Bauman, Joseph, Can fraktur artist,
   1815-1899 #2255 4628
Baxter, Brian, Can stained glass artist, fl.
   1981 #2460
Baxter, Iain, Can artist, 1936- #4629 4630
– and George Sawchuk #7143
– and N.E. Thing Co. Ltd. #535
– exhibitions, group
   – (1967) #490
   – (1971) #98
   – (1974) #574
   – (1979) #2069
   – (1980) #703
   – (1981) #797
– exhibitions (reviews) #520
– imaginary works #530

– on N.E. Thing Co. Ltd. #6675
– use of photography #1057
Baxter, Ingrid (Elaine) Hieber, Can artist,
   1938-
– and George Sawchuk #7143
– exhibitions, group
   – (1974) #574
Baxter, Robert W., Can architect, 1936-
– Vancouver (BC), University of British
   Columbia. Student Union, competition
   #9503
Bayefsky, Aba, Can artist, 1923-
– exhibitions
   – (1967) #4633
– in India #4631
– mural, *Out of Bondage*, Beth-El Synagogue
   (Don Mills, Ont) #4632
Bayfield, Fanny Amelia Wright, Can artist,
   1814-1891 #1164
Baykal, Erol, Can curator, fl. 1975
– and Gallery of Photography (Vancouver,
   BC) #2052
Bayley, W.B., Can photographer, 1857-1939
   #977
Bazaine, Jean-René, Fr artist, 1904-
– influence on Fernand Leduc #6186
BC Photographer, Can periodical #998
BC Society for the Furtherance of Indian
   Arts and Crafts
– (1940-1943) #4114
Beach, William Godkin, Can glassmaker,
   1839-1902 #2396
Beaconsfield (Qué), Church of Saint
   Edmund of Canterbury
– architecture, Roger D'Astous #8840
beadwork, Algonquian #3374 3582 3605 3635
– (1760s-early 20th c.) #3633
– Albany (NY), New York State Museum
   #3603
– double-curve and floral motifs #3409
beadwork, Arapaho
– New York (NY), American Museum of
   Natural History #3414
beadwork, Assiniboine #3653 3739
beadwork, Athapaskan #4107 4110
beadwork, Blackfoot #3651 3654 3678 3686
   3739
beadwork, Blood #3739
beadwork, Carrier
– (1970s) #4145
beadwork, Chippewa #4089
beadwork, Cree #3651 3729 3739 4077
– (1960s) #3719
– Lac La Ronge (Sask) #3696
beadwork, Delaware #3506
beadwork, Dogrib #4089
beadwork, Gros Ventre #3651
beadwork, Huron
– wampum belts #3495
beadwork, Indians of North America #2739
   3329 3420
– 20th c. #2143
– floral motifs #3449
– New York (NY), Museum of the American
   Indian. Heye Foundation #3457
– Ottawa (Ont), National Museum of Man

#3465 3466
– shellwork #3388
– trade goods #3440
beadwork, Iroquois #3559 3605 3635
– (1760s-early 20th c.) #3633
– Albany (NY), New York State Museum
   #3603
– wampum belts #3496
beadwork, Maliseet #3628 3641
beadwork, Métis #3677 4110
beadwork, Micmac #3624 3628 3641
beadwork, Montagnais
– natutshikan #4103
– plant and animal motifs #4076
beadwork, Nahani #4077
beadwork, Naskapi
– natutshikan #4103
– plant and animal motifs #4076
beadwork, natives of North America #3341
beadwork, Ojibwa #3539 3551 3557
beadwork, Plains #3651 3682 3684 3751
– 19th c. #3722
– moccasins #3666
– New York (NY), American Museum of
   Natural History #3668
beadwork, Salish
– (1970s) #4145
beadwork, Sarcee #3739
beadwork, Siouan #3651 3674
– 19th c. #3722
– moccasins #3666
   – (1880s-1910s) #3740
beadwork, Slavey #4089
beadwork, Tanana #4095
beadwork, Thompson Indians #3808
beadwork, Woodlands #3635
– (1760s-early 20th c.) #3633
– Albany (NY), New York State Museum
   #3603
– moccasins #3554
Bealy, Allan, Can artist, 1951- #1512
Beam, Carl, Can artist, 1943-
– exhibitions, group
   – (1981) #4173
– interview #4155
Beamsville (Ont), high school
– architecture, Walter W. Lachance #9387
Beamsville (Ont), Nipponia Home for the
   Aged
– architecture, Henry Fliess, and Yamazaki
   & Ridpath #8516
Bear Mother, Haida #3868
– argillite carving #3862 3901
Bear Mother, Tsimshian #3868
Beardsley, Aubrey Vincent, Brit artist,
   writer, 1872-1898
– influence on James Frederic McCulloch
   #6463
– influence on Louis de Niverville #6705
Beardy, Jackson, Can artist, 1944- #4157 4161
   4634 4635 4636
– exhibitions (reviews) #1866
   – (1972) #4128
– exhibitions, group
   – (1972) #4131

Beatty, John William, Can artist, 1869-1941
#4637
- and Edith Grace Coombs #5172
- as teacher of Addison Winchell Price
#6935
- as teacher of Alice A. Innes #5900
- as teacher of Frederick Nicholas Loveroff
#6329 6330
- as teacher of Joseph Sydney Hallam #5687
- correspondence, J.E.H. MacDonald #6371
- exhibitions
 - (1981) #4638
- exhibitions, group
 - (1942) #359
- exhibitions (reviews) #1710
Beau, Henri, Can artist, 1863-1949 #1382
- *La dispersion des Acadiens* (1900) #4639
Beau, Paul, Can metalsmith, 1871-1949 #2693
4640 4641
Beauce (Qué)
- crosses and calvaries #1292
- female costume (ca. 1875) #2828
Beauchemin, Micheline, Can artist, 1930-
#2102 4642 4643 4644 4645
- exhibitions, group
 - (1978) #2772
- *La chute d'Icare* tapestry and stage curtain,
Place des Arts (Montréal, Qué) #8233
- theatre curtain, National Arts Centre
(Ottawa, Ont) #9108
Beaucour, Paul
- *see* Mallepart de Grand Maison (*dit*
Beaucour), Paul
Beaucourt, François Malepart de, Can artist,
1740-1794 #269 270 1300 4646 4647
- and Québec society #1375
- exhibitions, group
 - (1959) #219
- influence of French painting #1244
Beaucourt, Josué de Boisberthelot
- *see* Boisberthelot de Beaucours, Josué
Beaudin, Denise, Can artist, 1930-
- exhibitions, group
 - (1978) #2772
Beaudin, Gaétan, Can ceramicist, 1924-
#2395
- as teacher #2381
Beaudoin-Hansen, Kéro-Claire (Kéro), Can
photographer 1940- #4648
Beaudry, Henry, Can artist, 1921- #4649
Beaugrand, Gilles, Can silversmith, 1906-
#2179 2693 4650
- and Québec religious art (1950s) #1250
Beaugrand, Honoré, Can statesman,
1849-1906
- portrait, Alfred Boisseau #4769
Beaugrand-Champagne, Claire, Can
photographer, 1948- #1556 1562
- photographic views, Disraeli (Qué), (1972)
#1513
Beaulac, Henri, Can artist, designer, 1914-
#2174
- and Simone Marie Yvette Hudon-Beaulac
#5856
- Christmas greeting cards #856
- interior, Place des Arts (Montréal, Qué)

#8233
Beaulac, Simone Marie Yvette Hudon
- *see* Hudon-Beaulac, Simone Marie Yvette
Beaulieu, Jean-Louis, Can architect, 1943-
- Montréal (Qué), métro. Angrignon Station
#9555
Beaulieu, Paul Vanier, Can artist, 1910-
#4651 4652
- book illustrations #926
Beaumont, Serge, Can sculptor, 1951-
- Symposium international de sculpture
environnementale de Chicoutimi (Qué),
(1980) #1639
- use of stone #1634
Beaumont (Qué), Church of Saint-Etienne
- architecture and interior #8809
Beauport (Qué)
- architecture (1625-1975) #7880
Beauport (Qué), Quebec Lunatic Asylum
- view of, 19th c., on earthenware bowl
#2342
Beaupré (Qué)
- domestic architecture, 18th-19th cs. #8582
Beauregard, Andrée, Can tapestry artist,
1927- #4653
beauty
- and art
 - Borduas, Paul-Emile, on #4799
 - Harris, Lawren Stewart, on #5716
Beauvais, René
- *see* St-James (*dit* Beauvais), René
beaux-arts architecture
- Canada #7740
 - and Gothic revival architecture #7724
7739
 - railroad stations #9539
- Lyle, John MacIntosh, Bank of Nova Scotia
buildings #9203
- Prairies, legislative buildings #8944 8945
- Québec #7923 8265
- Toronto (Ont) #8069
beaver
- Canadian art #23
- Canadian emblem #56
- Canadian pottery #2302
Beaver Flint Glass Co., glass manufacturer
(Toronto, Ont) #2401
Beaver Hall Group #589 592
- and Anne Douglas Savage #7131 7132
- and Edwin Headley Holgate #5818 5819
Beaverbrook, William Maxwell Aitken,
baron, Can publisher in England, 1879-
1964
- and Beaverbrook Art Gallery (Fredericton
NB) #3067
- and Canadian War Memorials Collection
#1102
- portrait of, Yousuf Karsh #6022
Beck, Hélène Boily (Claire), Can artist, 1932-
#1551
Beck & Eadie, Can architectural firm
- Toronto (Ont), Bank of Nova Scotia #9192
Beckett, Samuel, Irish writer, 1906-
- Kennedy, Garry Neill, compared with
#6043
Beckett, Samuel G., Can architect, 1869-1917
- Toronto (Ont), houses #8639

Beckington, Alice J., Amer artist, 1868-1942
- as teacher of Mary Evelyn Wrinch #7617
7618
Beckmann, Max, Ger artist, 1884-1950
- influence on Ivan Kenneth Eyre #5394
Bédard, Jean-Baptiste, Can carpenter,
surveyor, 1761-1818 #1300
Bedeque Bay (PEI)
- architecture #7798
Bedford, Michael, Can photographer, fl.
1970s
- portfolio of photographs #995
Bedford (Ont), Molsons Bank
- architecture #9173
Bedini, Cajetan, It priest in Canada, fl. 1850s
- *L'album des costumes de communautés
religieuses de femmes au Canada en 1853*
#2834
beds, Canadian #2473
- crewelwork bed hangings, late 18th c.
#2784
- Norfolk County (Ont), Normandale Iron
Works #2699
- Ontario
 - 19th c. #2562
 - (1780-1900) #2577
 - (1790s-1857) #2558
- Québec
 - 17th-18th cs. #2530 2531
Bedwell, Edward Parker, Brit naval officer,
artist in Canada, fl. 1851-1862, d. 1919
#2020
- exhibitions, group
 - (1979) #2023
Beechey, Frederick William, Brit naval
officer, artist in Canada, 1796-1856
- expedition, northwestern Alaska #4369
Beetz, Johan, Can artist, 1874-1949 #4654
Beggs, Neil G., Can architect, 1871-1935
- Toronto (Ont), theatres #9067
Beil, Charlie, Can sculptor, 1894-
- travelling art exhibition program, Alberta
(1980) #1972
Béland, Luc, Can artist, 1951- #1544
- exhibitions
 - (1976) #4655
- exhibitions, group
 - (1977) #1532
 - (1981) #1565
- symposium, Musée du Nouveau-Monde
(La Rochelle, France), (1980) #1559
Bélanger, Gérard, Can artist, 1932-
- interview #1527
Belbin, Louise, Can artist, 1898-
- exhibitions
 - (1978) #2759
Belcher, Edward, Brit naval officer, artist in
Canada, 1799-1877
- expedition, northwestern Alaska #4369
Belcher Islands (NWT)
- sculpture #4459
Belfast (Northern Ireland), Ulster Museum
- art, Indians of North America #3477
Belkin, Arnold, Can artist, 1930- #4656
Bell, Alistair Macready, Can artist, 1913-
- on printmaking #817

Bell, Bert, Can photographer, 1938- #1036
Bell, Clive, Brit critic, 1881-1964
– on James Wilson Morrice #6619
Bell, George Kenneth (Ken), Can
   photographer, 1914-
– interview #4657
– photographs of World War II #1107
– portfolio of photographs #995
Bell, Leland, Can artist, 1953-
– exhibitions, group
   – (1981) #4173
Bell, Mathew, Can ironmaster, fl. 1793-1845
– and Forges of Saint-Maurice
   (Trois-Rivières, Qué) #2698
Bell, W. & D., Pottery, ceramic manufacturer
   (Québec, Qué)
– (1850s-ca. 1900) #2291 2298 2322
– Thomas views #2287
Bell-Irving, Henry Ogle, Can artist, architect,
   1856-1931
– exhibitions, group
   – (1980) #4665
Bell-Smith, Frederic Marlett, Can artist,
   1846-1923 #221 4666
– and British Columbia Society of Fine Arts
   #1978
– and Thomas Mower Martin #6435 6438
– exhibitions
   – (1977) #4668
– exhibitions, group
   – (1978) #1726
– exhibitions (reviews) #174
– on Rocky Mountains and Selkirk
   Mountains sketching trips (1887-1889)
   #4667
Bella Bella Indians
– containers #3985
Bella Coola Indians
– culture #3874
– masks #4000
– mythology #3772
– petroglyphs #3816
– rattles #4026
Belle, Charles Ernest de, Can artist,
   1873-1939 #1382 4658
– compared with Georges Delfosse #1385
Belleau, Charles, Can ceramicist, 1799-1889
   #2366
Bellechasse County (Qué)
– art and architecture #1281
Bellechasse County (Qué), Church of
   Saint-Charles-Borromée
– architecture and interior #8803
Bellefleur, Léon, Can artist, 1910- #1541 1542
   1543 4659 4660 4661
– and Montréal (Qué) painting (1950s) #1403
– exhibitions
   – (1968) #4662
– exhibitions, group
   – (1962) #1420
– in Paris (France) #1434
– influence on Janine Leroux-Guillaume
   #6247
– interview #4663
Bellerive, Marcel, Can artist, 1934- #4664
Belleval, Jean Fournier de, Can designer,

1922-
– stage designs and costumes, Montreal
   Theatre Ballet #1410
Belleville, Alexis Charles
– see Boucher (dit Belleville), Alexis Charles
Belleville, François
– see Guernon (dit Belleville), François
Belleville (Ont)
– brick houses, early 19th c. #8521
– pottery, 19th c. #2286
Belleville (Ont), Belleville Public Library
– exhibitions
   – Quinte Arts Council: Survey 1977 (1977)
      #1816
Belleville (Ont), Institution for the Deaf and
   Dumb
– architecture #8968
Belley, René, Can artist, 1951-
– as member of Centre communautaire
   catholique Tour de David
   (Saint-Basile-le-Grand, Qué) #1510
Belli, Flavio, Can artist, 1950-
– colour xerography #614
Bellingham (Wash), Whatcom Museum of
   Natural History and Art
– exhibitions
   – Arts of a Vanished Era: An Exhibition of
      the Whatcom Museum of History and Art,
      Bellingham, Washington (1968) #3950
Bellot, Paul (Dom), Can priest, architect,
   1878-1944
– churches #8838
– influence on Québec church architecture
   #8334 8820 8831
– Magog (Qué), Monastery of
   Saint-Benoît-du-Lac #8332
– on art and architecture #8333
bells, Canadian
– Newfoundland #2717
Belzile, Louis, Can artist, 1929- #4669
– exhibitions, group
   – (1959) #1414
   – (1977) #1465
   – (1981) #1471
Bemi, Murray & Associates, Can
   architectural firm
– Ottawa (Ont), Saint Basil's Roman
   Catholic Church #8765
Bendahan, Raphael, Can photographer,
   1944- #4670
Bengough, John Wilson, Can artist,
   1851-1923 #4674 4676 4677
– art and writings #4671
– autobiography #4673
– in Québec (1887) #4675
– on his art #4672
– political cartoons #942 957
   – The Grip #943
Bénic, Lorraine, Can artist, 1937- #4678
Benjamin, Anthony, Can artist, 1931- #4679
Benjamin, Max, Can artist, 1928-
– exhibitions, group
   – (1979) #2075
– exhibitions (reviews) #2072
Benjamin-Constant, Jean-Joseph, Fr artist,
   1845-1902

– as teacher of Canadian artists #243
Benjamin Lent Pottery, ceramic
   manufacturer (Lincoln County, Ont)
– (1836-1841) #2367
Bennet & Co., publishing firm (Montréal,
   Qué)
– greeting cards
   – Christmas motif #890
   – sporting subjects #2360
Bennett, Arnold, Brit writer, 1867-1931
– on James Wilson Morrice #6619
Bennett, Geoffrey, Can artist, fl. 1960s-
– interview #4680
Benoît, Jacques, Can artist, 1946-
– and RACE #1536
Benoît, Jean, Can artist, 1922-
– in Paris (France) #426
Benoît, Mimi Parent
– see Parent-Benoît, Mimi
Benoît (dit Livernois), Jules-Isaïe, Can
   photographer, 1830-1865 #258 259 1275
Benson and Hedges Company, tobacco firm
– murals, Montréal (Qué) and Toronto (Ont)
   #539
Bentham, Douglas, Can sculptor, 1947- #145
   4681 4682 4684
– compared with André Fauteux #785
– exhibitions
   – (1973) #1858
   – (1976) #4683
   – (1979) #4685
   – (1980) #4686
– exhibitions, group
   – (1975) #1926
   – (1977) #782
   – (1981) #797
– interview, at Emma Lake Workshops
   (Emma Lake, Sask) #1934
– techniques #792
Bentley, Percy, Can photographer, 1882-1968
– exhibitions, group
   – (1976) #2012
Beny, Wilfred Roloff, Can artist, 1924- #4688
– exhibitions
   – (1971) #4690
– on art #4687
– on book design #921
– photographs, University of Calgary. Art
   Gallery (Calgary, Alta) #4691
Benzie & Bow, Can architectural firm
– Lethbridge (Alta), Saint Michael's General
   Hospital #9021
Beothuk Indians
– art #3528 3611 3623 3627
– costume #3584
– culture #3597
– in art #1162
Bequette, Jean-Baptiste, Can silversmith, fl.
   ca. 1817-ca. 1846
– works, Detroit Institute of Arts (Detroit,
   Mich) #2691
Bérard, François, Can carriage-maker, fl.
   1842 #1301
Bérard, Réal, Can artist, 1935-
– exhibitions
   – (1975) #4692

Bercovitch, Aleksandre (Alexander), Can artist, 1891-1951 #4693

Berczy, Jean-Charlotte Allamand, Can artist, 1760-1839
- as mother and teacher of William Bent Berczy #4694
- correspondence with her husband (1798-1812) #4696

Berczy, William Bent, Can artist, 1791-1873 #241 242 4694
- correspondence, with his father #4700

Berczy, William von Moll, Can artist, 1748-1813 #4695 4697 4698 4699 4701
- as father and teacher of William Bent Berczy #4694
- correspondence, with his wife (1798-1812) #4696
- paintings, Université Laval (Québec, Qué) #3078
- portrait of Hertel de Rouville family member #1345
- *Woolsey Family*, National Gallery of Canada (Ottawa, Ont) #4700

Bergeron, André, Can artist, 1937- #4703
- lithographs, *Le Cantique spirituel* #4702

Bergeron, Fernand, Can artist, 1942-
- engravings, *Pour les nuits blanches de Nini de Saint-H la petite* #4704

Bergeron, Germain, Can sculptor, 1933- #4705

Bergeron, Jean-Baptiste, Can sculptor, enameller, 1919- #2378

Bergeron, Suzanne, Can artist, 1930- #4706 4707
- in Paris (France) #426

Berggren, Nels, Can artist, 1910- #1852

Bergman, Henry Eric, Can artist, 1893-1958 #4708
- exhibitions
  - (1980) #4709
- woodcuts #802
- works, Ayerst, McKenna and Harrison chemists' firm #852

Bériau, Oscar-Alphonse, Can arts administrator, b. 1883
- as director, Ecole des arts domestiques de Québec (Québec, Qué) #2186
- as director, Quebec School of Handicrafts (Québec, Qué) #2969

Bering Strait (Alaska)
- Inuit culture #4318

Berkeley (Calif), University of California. Robert H. Lowie Museum of Anthropology
- exhibitions
  - *Art of the Northwest Coast* (1965) #3928
- masks, Inuit #4349

Berlin (West Germany), Akademie der Künste
- exhibition
  - *Group of Seven: Kanadische Landschafts-Maler: Eine Wanderausstellung der McMichael Canadian Collection, Kleinburg, Ontario, Kanada* (1977) #1781

Berlin (West Germany), Berlin Free University

- architecture #9464

Berlin (West Germany), Berliner Museum für Völkerkunde
- art, Indians of North America #3421 3423
- art, Northwest Coast Indians #3762

Berlin (West Germany), Nationalgalerie
- architecture, Ludwig Mies van der Rohe #9348

Berlinguet, Louis-Thomas, Can architect, sculptor, 1790-1863 #6947
- île d'Orléans (Qué), Church of Saint-Jean #8801
- supper at Emmaus theme #1615

Berman, Michaele, Can artist, 1947-
- interview #4710

Bernatchez-Rousseau, Michèle, Can tapestry artist, 1939- #2769

Berne (Switzerland), Historisches Museum
- art, Indians of North America #3400 3473

Bernini, Gian Lorenzo, It artist, 1598-1680
- baldachin, Saint Peter's Cathedral, Rome (Italy), influence on baldachin, church, Neuville (Qué) #8826

Berry, Martha, Amer collector, 1866-1942
- collection, quill-decorated birchbark boxes, Ottawa Indians #3548

Bersudsky, Sid, Can designer, 1913- #4711

Berthier (Qué), Church of Sainte-Elisabeth
- architecture and interior, Amable Gauthier #241 242

Berthier-en-Haut (Qué), church
- woodcarvings, Gilles Bolvin #4781

Berthierville (Qué), church
- architecture #8833
- architecture and art #8874

Berthierville (Qué), Cuthbert Chapel
- architecture #8881

Berthon, George Theodore, Can artist, 1806-1892 #1705 4713
- portrait, Sir Isaac Brock #4712

Bertounesque, André, Can artist, 1937- #4714

Bérulle, Cardinal Pierre de, Fr priest, 1575-1619
- writings, influence on Canadian art, 17th c. #1365

Besant, Derek Michael, Can artist, 1950- #4715
- exhibitions (reviews) #1883

Besner, Jacques, Can sculptor, 1919- #4716 4717
- use of plastics #1442

Bessonett, Cecilia Augusta, Can artist, fl. 1850s #1118

Betteridge, Lois Etherington, Can silversmith, 1928- #4718

Beube, Douglas S. (Doug), Can photographer, 1950-
- portfolio of photographs #991

Beug, Lorne, Can artist, 1948- #2076
- ceramic sculpture #795
- exhibitions, group
  - (1977) #781

Beull, Vincent, Can artist, 1953- #4719

Beuys, Joseph, Ger artist, 1921-
- Frenkel, Vera, on #713

Bevan & Moore, Can architectural firm
- Toronto (Ont), Government House, competition #8748

Beveridge, Eleanor, Can ceramicist, 1920- #1199

Beveridge, Karl John, Can artist, 1945-
- exhibitions, group
  - (1971) #98
  - (1977) #782
  - (1980) #1063
- *Maybe Wendy's Right* #1052
- on politics and art #602

Beynon, William, Can ethnologist, 1888-1958
- on Tsimshian Indians #3981

Bice, Clare, Can artist, 1909-1976
- on studying in Europe #408

Bick, Walter, Can collector, 20th c.
- glass pickle cruets #2405

Bidner, Michael Thomas, Can artist, 1944-
- colour xerography #614

Biederman, Charles Joseph, Amer artist, 1906-
- and Structurism #6079
- relief structures #777

Biegert, Claus, Ger writer, 1947-
- on James Bay (Qué) #1566

Biéler, André Charles, Can artist, 1896- #1392 4722 4726 4727
- and genre painting #392
- and Gordon Edward Pfeiffer #6847
- exhibitions
  - (1963) #4723
  - (1970) #4725
- exhibitions, group
  - (1977) #1278 1279
- on Canadian art (1941-1951) #390
- on his art #349
- on his techniques #4720 4721
- on nationalism in Canadian art (1930s) #337
- relief prints #4724
- wood engravings #804

Bieler, André Charles Théodore (Ted), Can sculptor, 1938-
- clay sculptures (1960s) #743
- on art and architecture #8235
- sculptures (1960s) #1793

Bieler, Ted A.
- *see* Bieler, André Charles Théodore (Ted)

Bierk, David, Can artist, 1944-
- on Jack Chambers #700

Bierstadt, Albert, Amer artist, 1830-1902
- and Thomas Mower Martin #6435
- in western Canada #1859

Bierwagen, Ottmar, Can photographer, fl. 1970s
- portfolio of photographs #995

Bigger, Charles A., Can photographer, 1853-1923
- survey photographs #1014 1015

Biggs, Hugh Beynon, Can photographer, 1876-1941 #4728

Bill, Edward B., Can artist, fl. 1885-1903
- as teacher of Georges Delfosse #5279

billboards, Canadian #910

Billing, John H., Can stonemason, fl.
1880s-early 20th c.
– Haliburton County (Ont) #8335
binding of books
– see bookbinding
Bingham, John, Can photographer, fl. 1979
– portfolio of photographs #1032
Binning, Bertram Charles (B.C.), Can artist,
1909-1976 #1996 4731
– as teacher of Donald Alvin Jarvis #5947
– drawings #4729
– exhibitions
– (1973) #4734
– (1979) #4736
– exhibitions, group
– (1958) #431
– exhibitions (reviews) #4735
– on his mosaic mural, Imperial Bank,
Vancouver (BC) #4732
– on teaching drawing #4730
– residence, West Vancouver (BC) #8694
– Royal Architectural Institute of Canada
Allied Arts Medal winner (1962) #4733
birchbark, Algonquian #3571 3605
– containers #3510 3544
– cutouts #3483
– double-curve and floral motifs #3409
– Midewiwin, scrolls #3702
birchbark, Algonquin
– containers #3542 4078
birchbark, Cree #3573
birchbark, Dakota
– cutouts #3483
birchbark, Indians of North America
– and pottery, Indians of North America
#3545
– designs #3429
– moose hair embroidery on #3629
birchbark, Iroquois #3605
birchbark, Menomine
– basketry #3620
birchbark, Micmac #3643
– containers #3569
birchbark, Montagnais
– containers #4086
birchbark, Ojibwa #3539 3551 3557
– scrolls #3492 3583 3626
birchbark, Ottawa
– containers, Southwest Museum (Los
Angeles, Calif) #3548
birchbark, Penobscot #3537
– containers #3510
birchbark, Saulteaux
– Island Lake (Man) #3549
birchbark, Siouan
– Midewiwin, scrolls #3702
birchbark, Tête de Boule
– containers #4079 4108
birchbark, Woodlands
– (1760s-early 20th c.) #3633
– drawings on trees #3527
Bird, Eustace Godfrey, Can architect,
1870-1950
– Montréal (Qué), Transportation Building
#9307
– Toronto (Ont)

– Bank of Toronto #8293 9162 9185
– Royal Bank #9152
– Windsor (Ont), Dominion Bank #9188
Bird, John, Can architect, 1923-
– LaSalle (Qué), Saint John Brébeuf Parish
Church #8766
– Montréal (Qué), Saint Gabriel's Church
#8766
Bird, Wallace S., Can collector, 1917-
– collection, Canadian art from Atlantic
provinces, 20th c. #1130
birdhouses, Canadian #2593
birds in art
– Archambault, Louis #4539
– Canadian architectural decoration (1930s)
#8226
– Canadian pottery #2309
– Good, F.P., & Co. (Brantford, Ont)
#2335
– Carr, Emily #5019
– folk art, Québec #1284 1362
– Grondin, Jean-Luc #5662
– Hood, Robert #5826
– Inuit sculpture #4404 4459
– Lansdowne, James Fenwick #6163 6164
6165
– Loates, Glen #6310
– MacDonald, Thoreau #6381
– Murphy, Burland E. #6663
– Nasmith, Eric Anderson #6685
– Newlan, Emery #6690
– Phinney, Robert #6862
– Picher, Claude #6867
– Pootoogook, Kananginak #6904
– Pope, William #6905 6906
– Pratt, George #6916
– raven
– Kwakiutl #3883
– Tlingit #3786
– raven rattles, Northwest Coast Indians
#3980 4026
– Roussil, Robert #7090
– Savage, Harry #7133
– Shortt, Terence Michael #506 7201
– Thorburn, Archibald #7373
– Thunderbird
– Algonquian Indians #3493
– Blackfoot Indians #3676
– Indians of North America #3410
– Northwest Coast Indians #3831 3855
– Ojibwa Indians #3699
– Plains Indians #3758
– weathercocks, Québec #2589
Birdsall, Pam, Can ceramicist, fl. 1980 #2395
birdstones
– see also stonework
birdstones, Algonquian #3406 3491 3499
3511 3577
birdstones, Ojibwa #3546
Birkbeck, George, Brit physician, 1776-1841
– influence on mechanics' institutes,
England and Canada #3064
Birks, Henry Gifford, Can silversmith,
1892-1979
– collection, silver, National Gallery of
Canada (Ottawa, Ont) #2653

Birmingham & Wood, Can architectural firm
– restoration, Chinatown, Vancouver (BC)
#8159
Birmingham (Ala), Birmingham Festival of
the Arts
– exhibitions
– Eskimo Narrative (1979) #4285
Birmingham (England), Ikon Gallery
– exhibitions
– Canada in Birmingham (1981) #710
– Jack Bush: Paintings and Drawings,
1955-1976 (1980) #4976
Birnie, Ian, Can curator, fl. 1974
– interview, on Videoscape exhibition, Art
Gallery of Ontario (Toronto, Ont), (1974)
#566
Birnirk
– prehistoric artifacts #4327 4345
Birnstihl, Adam, Can ceramicist, d. 1900
#2356
Bischoff, Elmer Nelson, Amer artist, 1916-
– as teacher of Gordon Appelbe Smith #7225
– influence on Gordon Appelbe Smith #7232
Bishop, G., Can medal engraver, fl. 1878
– temperance medals #724
Bismarck (ND), State Historical Society of
North Dakota
– art, Plains Indians #3690
Bissett, Bill, Can artist, 1939-
– exhibitions, group
– (1971) #2042
Bissonette, Héliodore, Can artist, 1890-1966
#1428 1429
Bittdorf-Holland-Christianson Architects,
Can architectural firm
– restoration, Duggan House (Edmonton,
Alta) #8729
Black Creek Pioneer Village (Toronto, Ont)
#8063
– doctor's home #8675
– weaver's shop #2735
Blackburn, Jacques, Can tapestry artist,
1945- #4737
Blackfeet Indians
– see Blackfoot Indians
Blackfoot Indians
– art #3654 3678 3686 3754 3757
– bear motif #3746
– boulder monuments #3688
– costume #3414 3695 3739
– (1910-1960) #3712
– culture #3651 3667
– gun cases #3713
– lodges #3647
– Medicine Pipe ceremony #3681
– Minipoka #3749
– pipes #3704
– pipes and pipe bundles #3665
– pottery, 18th-19th cs. #3679
– quillwork #3703 3745
– rites and ceremonies #3721
– Soumak necklaces #3685
– tipis #3669 3676 3718 3735 3741
– winter counts #3707
blacksmithing
– see also ironwork

blacksmithing, Canadian
– Québec #2697 2705 2707 2711
– shops, in woodcarvings, Walter Graham
   Cameron #4992
Blackstock, Hattie, Can artist, 1894-
– interview #4738
Blackwood, David Lloyd, Can artist, 1941-
– exhibitions
   – (1967) #4739
Bladen, Ronald, Can sculptor, 1918- #4741
– interview #4740
– on living in New York (1960s) #460
Blahut, John, Can photographer, 1950- #1007
Blais, Marie-Claire, Can writer, 1939-
– and Mary Meigs #6510
Blake, William, Brit artist, poet, 1757-1827
– influence on Bertram Richard Brooker
   #4925
– influence on Graham Metson #6523
Blakey, Richard Palin, Can architect,
   1879-1963
– Edmonton (Alta), Legislative Buildings
   #8944 8945
Blanchette, Pierre, Can artist, 1953-
– Ispaham #1563
Blanck, Nora, Can artist, 1947-
– exhibitions, group
   – (1978) #663
– exhibitions (reviews) #2081
– natural constructions (1970s) #2065
Bland, John, Can architect, 1911-
– Charlottetown (PEI), Confederation
   Centre, competition #9088
– Ottawa (Ont), Carleton University #9455
Bland, Lemoyne, Edwards, Shine, Can
   architectural firm
– Montréal (Qué), métro. Jarry Station #9549
Bland, Lemoyne & Edwards, Can
   architectural firm
– Charlottetown (PEI), Confederation
   Centre, competition #9089
– Ottawa (Ont), Northern Electric Research
   and Development Laboratories #9344
Bland, Salem Goldworth, Can physician,
   1859-1950
– portrait of, Lawren Stewart Harris #5733
blankets, Carrier
– (1970s) #4145
blankets, Chilkat #3333 3784 3821 3826 3898
   3973
blankets, Coast Salish
– dog hair #3800
blankets, Cowichan
– (1970s) #4145
blankets, Crow
– rosette motif #3752
blankets, Kwakiutl #3973
blankets, Salish #3830
– 19th c. #3790
– New York (NY), Museum of the American
   Indian. Heye Foundation #3818
blankets, Tlingit #3826
blankets, Tsimshian #3826
Blankstein, Coop & Gillmor, Can
   architectural firm
– Saskatoon (Sask), Mendel Art Gallery,

competition #9091
Blatherwick, Kater R., Can architect, 1890-
– Toronto (Ont), Bank of Montreal #9190
Blatter, Caron & Côté, Can architectural
   firm
– Sainte-Foy (Qué), Church of
   Saint-Louis-de-France #8841
Blatter, Robert, Can architect, 1899-
– Québec (Qué), La Solidarité insurance
   building #7939
Blazeje, Zbigniew, Can sculptor, 1942-
– exhibitions, group
   – (1967) #490
– sculptures (1960s) #1793
– use of light #767
Bleyenberg, Harry, Can photographer, ca.
   1947-
– portfolio of photographs #1023
– Woman and World series #4742
Blier, Jean-Marc, Can artist, 1921- #4743 4744
Blin, Claude, Can artist, 1931- #4745
Bloch, Martin, Brit artist, 1883-1954
– influence on Stephen Andrews #4527
Blomfield (né Bloomfield), James Jerris, Can
   stained glass artist, 1872-1951
– stained glass #1977
   – Hamilton (Ont), Hamilton Mausoleum
      #8900
   – Vancouver (BC) #2456
   – Victoria (BC), British Columbia
      Parliament Buildings #8966
Blood Indians
– costume #3414 3739
– painted buffalo hide #3711
Bloomfield, Charles Ernest, Can stained
   glass artist, 1877-1954
– stained glass, Vancouver (BC) #2456
Bloomfield, James Jerris
– see Blomfield, James Jerris
Bloomfield Hills (Mich), Cranbrook
   Academy of Art
– Betteridge, Lois Etherington, as student
   #4718
– Pachter, Charles, as student #6748
Bloomfield Hills (Mich), Cranbrook
   Academy of Art. Museum
– exhibitions
   – Beads: Their Use by Upper Great Lakes
      Indians (1977) #3635
   – Eight from Toronto (1975) #1809
Bloore, Ronald Langley, Can artist, 1925-
   #4753
– aesthetics #4746
– and formalist criticism (1960s) #4747
– drawings #532
– exhibitions
   – (1961) #1913
   – (1975) #4751
– exhibitions, group
   – (1962) #1847
   – (1964) #462
   – (1967) #490
– exhibitions (reviews) #4750 4752 4754
– influence on Arthur Fortescue McKay
   #6476
– interview #4749

– on art #4748
– on Canadian art (1960s) #478
– on the sacred in art #94
– uses and transformation of history #577
Blouin, André, Can architect, 1920-
– churches #7857
– Pointe-aux-Trembles (Qué), Church of
   pèlerinage de-la-Réparation #8840
Blue Eagle, Acee, Amer artist, 1907-1959
– use of water monster motif #3757
Bluenose (ship)
– photographic views, Wallace R. MacAskill
   #6351
Bluesinger, Taki, Can photographer, 1943-
– and Glenn Alun Lewis #6275 6276
– exhibitions, group
   – (1979) #2069
– portfolio of photographs #996
Blum, Michel, Can artist, fl. 1977
– and Marcelle Ferron #5422
Blunden Harbour (BC)
– views, Emily Carr #5036
Boas, Franz, Amer anthropologist, 1858-1942
– influence on Charles Marius Barbeau
   #3309
boats
– see also canoes; kayaks; umiaks
boats, Canadian
– Nova Scotia, views
   – Gray, John Warren #5648
   – Lismer, Arthur #6294
– sail-making, Nova Scotia #2157
Bobak, Bruno Joseph, Can artist, 1923- #1996
   4756 4757 4758
– and Molly Lamb Bobak #4759 4762 4766
– and Vancouver (BC) painting (1950s)
   #1992
– as husband of Molly Lamb Bobak #4764
– compared with Molly Lamb Bobak #4755
– exhibitions, group
   – (1966) #1123
   – (1973) #1182
– figurative works #4760
– on Canadian art (1960s) #448
– on printmaking #817
Bobak, Molly Lamb, Can artist, 1922- #1996
   4763 4767
– and Bruno Joseph Bobak #4759
– and Vancouver (BC) painting (1950s)
   #1992
– as juror, Saskatchewan Arts Exhibition (1955)
   #1910
– autobiography #4766
– compared with Bruno Joseph Bobak #4755
– exhibitions
   – (1977) #4765
– exhibitions, group
   – (1966) #1123
   – (1973) #1182
– interview #4764
– on army life #4761
– on stay in England (1957-1958) #4762
Bodmer, Karl, Sw artist in Canada,
   1809-1893
– and emergence of named Indian artists
   #3486

– watercolours, Plains Indians #3738
Bodolai, Joseph Stephen (Joe), Can artist, 1947-
– and video art #550
Bodor, Andrew Steven, Can sculptor, 1947-
– interview #788
body art
– Canada #6676
– Sullivan, Françoise #7282
body works
– *see* body art
Boehler, Valentine, Can ceramicist, 1852-1876 #2323
Boehler, Xavier, Can ceramicist, fl. 1851-1874 #2348
Boer War
– and John Innes #5901
Bogardi, George, Can artist, 1943-
– exhibitions, group
– (1977) #637
– on Québec art (1940s-1970s) #1521
Boggs, Jean Sutherland, Can curator, art historian, 1922-
– as director, National Gallery of Canada (Ottawa, Ont) #3049 3050 3058
– on Louis Muhlstock #6657
Bohar, Dick, Can photographer, fl. 1970s
– portfolio of photographs #998
Boiestown (NB), Upper Miramichi Regional High School
– exhibitions
– *The Beaverbrook Art Gallery Presents Nine New Brunswick Artists/La Galerie d'art Beaverbrook présente neuf artistes du Nouveau-Brunswick* (1973) #1182
Boileau, Philip, Can artist, 1863-1917
– illustrations #916
Bois-Francs (Qué)
– churches, Protestant, 19th c. #8888
– views, Alfred Laliberté #6151
Boisberthelot de Beaucours, Josué, Fr army officer, architect in Canada, 1662-1750 #7844 8336
Boisseau, Alfred, Can artist, 1823-1901 #4768 4769
Boisvert, Gilles, Can artist, 1940- #1479 1480 1542 1543
– exhibitions
– (1975) #4770
– exhibitions, group
– (1981) #1564
– interview #1485
– Pop art #1497
Boisvert, Paul, Can photographer, fl. 1977
– portfolio of photographs #1023
Boisvert, Pierre, Can artist, fl. 1950
– Christmas greeting cards #856
Boivin, François, Fr architect in Canada, 1612/1616-ca. 1675 #228 229
Boivin, Joseph, Can artist, 1874-1960
– *Ex-voto de Dorval*, Musée de l'Historial de Sainte-Anne-de-Beaupré (Qué) #4771
Boivin, Louis-Philippe, Can silversmith, fl. 1842-1857
– works, Detroit Institute of Arts (Detroit, Mich) #2691

Bokwus, Kwakiutl #3990
Boland, Con, Can photographer, ca. 1948-
– portfolio of photographs #1023
Bolduc, Blanche, Can artist, 1907- #4772
Bolduc, David, Can artist, 1945- #1803 1807 4773 4776
– exhibitions
– (1979) #4775
– exhibitions, group
– (1974) #565
– (1977) #637
– (1981) #722
– paintings (1976-1981) #4777
– paintings (1977-1979) #4774
– participant, Symposium on 20th Century Canadian Culture (Washington, DC), (1977) #621
Boller, Harry, Amer artist in Canada, 1938-
– and Paul Arthur and Associates #873
Bollivar, Samuel, Can artist, b. 1884
– exhibitions (reviews) #1210
Bolt, Beranek & Newman, Can engineering firm
– acoustics, Place des Arts (Montréal, Qué) #9092
Bolt, Ron, Can artist, 1938- #4778 4779
Bolvin, Gilles, Can sculptor, 1711-1766 #249 250 1324 4780 4781
– altarpiece, church, Berthierville (Qué) #8874
– altarpieces, Church of L'Assomption (L'Assomption, Qué) #4782
– baldachins, Parish Church (Neuville, Qué) and church (Trois-Rivières, Qué) #8826
– influence on Philippe Liébert #6281
– sculptures, Church of Saint-Charles (Lachenaie, Qué) #8808
– tabernacles #1613
Bonan, Mino, Can artist, 1943-
– television graphics #909
Bonavista (Nfld)
– architecture #7792
Bond, Eleanor, Can artist, 1948-
– exhibitions, group
– (1981) #1908
Bond & Smith, Can architectural firm
– Toronto (Ont)
– Hermant Building #9332
– Mason & Risch Company Building #9328
Bonet, Jordi, Can artist, 1932-1979 #4783 4784 4786 4787 4791 4792
– exhibitions
– (1974) #4790
– (1980) #4793
– interview #1527
– murals, Grand Théâtre (Québec, Qué) #4788 4789
– murals, Place des Arts (Montréal, Qué) #8233
– winner, Royal Architectural Institute of Canada Allied Arts Medal (1965) #4785
bonework, Cayuga #3525
bonework, Dorset
– Cape Dorset (NWT) #4322
bonework, Indians of North America

– beads #3457
bonework, Inuit
– Washington (DC), Smithsonian Institution #4319
bonework, Iroquois #3525 3566
– small human effigies #3553
bonework, Micmac #3643
bonework, Northwest Coast Indians
– arrows and spearheads #3785
– implements #4068
bonework, Penobscot #3537
bonework, Tagish #4106
bonework, Tlingit #4106
bonework, Tutchone #4106
bonework, Woodlands #3491
Bonham, Don, Can sculptor, 1940-
– theme of human body and machine #4794
Bonin, Raoul, Can artist, 1904-1949 #4795
Bonn (West Germany), Rheinisches Landesmuseum
– exhibitions
– *Michael Snow* (1979) #7258
– *Michael Snow: Works 1969-1978, Films 1964-1976/Michael Snow: Werke 1969-1978, Filme 1964-1976* (1979) #7261
Bonnard, Pierre, Fr artist, 1867-1947
– influence on Alfred Pellan #6811
– Morrice, James Wilson, compared with #6631
Bonnat, Léon-Joseph-Florentin, Fr artist, 1834-1923
– as teacher of Robert Harris #5739
Boogaerts, Pierre, Can photographer, 1946-
– exhibitions, group
– (1976) #1529
– exhibitions (reviews) #1018
book art
– *see* artists' books
book illustration
– *see* illustration
book labels
– *see* bookplates
book trade
– *see* publishing
bookbinding, Canadian
– (1850s) #1692
– (1964-1967) #2108 2109
– Montréal (Qué), (1930s-1940s) #1648
– Ontario (1970s) #935
– Québec #2183 2228
– 17th-18th cs. #2187
bookplates, Canadian #917
– 18th-early 20th cs. #28
– Alexander, William Walker #4506
– Carter, Alexander Scott #5050
– Maritimes, 18th-19th cs. #915
– Smith, Leslie Victor #7234
books
– *see also* artists' books; children's books; conservation and restoration, books; guidebooks; pattern books
– Holmes, Robert, collection, Ontario College of Art (Toronto, Ont) #5824
books, Canadian
– beaver motif #56
– guide for collectors #2104

- on Canadian art (1967) #488
- Ontario (1970s) #935
- Toronto (Ont), Royal Ontario Museum.
  Sigmund Samuel Collection #3140
Boorne, William Hanson, Can photographer,
  1859-1945 #1950
- and Boorne and May #4797
- on photographing Indians #4796
Boorne and May, photographic firm
  (Calgary, Alta) #4797
- (1886-1889) #1950
- and Charles Wesley Mathers #6451
Bordeaux (France), Académie de Bordeaux
- Beaucourt, François Malepart de, as
  student #269 270
Bordeaux (France), Musée de Bordeaux
- exhibitions
  - L'art au Canada (1962) #63
border life
- see frontier and pioneer life
Borduas, Paul-Emile, Can artist, 1905-1960
  #97 1270 1294 1432 4800 4801 4806 4810
  4811 4813 4814 4817 4821 4829 4830 4837
  4843 4845 4849 4850
- Abstraction verte #4852
- Alleyn, George Edmund, compared with
  #4511
- and Alfred Pellan #1451
- and Art Deco #4828
- and automatism #1417 1453 1455 1476
  4832
- and automatistes #1447
- and Contemporary Arts Society #1459
- and frère Jérôme #6761
- and Guy Viau #7485
- and internationalism in art #567
- and Jacques Godefroy de Tonnancour
  #4798
- and Montréal (Qué) art (1940s-1960s)
  #1437
- and nationalism in art #495
- and Paraskeva Clark #5112
- and Pierre Gauvreau #5576 5578
- and Québec separatism #4834 4848
- and Surrealism #1464 1467
- as teacher #1395 2990 3001 4827
- as teacher of André Jasmin #4808
- Bush, Jack Hamilton, compared with
  #1753
- chronology #4842
- concept of space #1441 4816
  - paintings, Paris (1955-1960) #4824
- correspondence, Claude Gauvreau #4804
  4805 4807
- correspondence, Fernand Leduc #6194
- debate with Fernand Leduc #6586
- Dumouchel, Albert, compared with #5332
- exhibitions
  - (1962) #4809
  - (1967) #4812
  - (1971) #1449
  - (1977) #4836 4838
- exhibitions, group
  - (1955) #411 1409
  - (1958) #431
  - (1962) #1420

- (1964) #462
- (1976) #1462
- (1978) #508 509
- (1979) #1472
- (1981) #1471
- exhibitions (reviews) #428
- Gagnon-Fortier, C., compared with #5552
- gouaches (1942) #4822 4825
- in New York (NY), (1953-1955) #4835
- in Paris (France) #426 4846
- influence of American painting (1950s)
  #4826
- influence on Christian Marcel Barbeau
  #4607
- influence on Fernand Leduc #6186
- influence on Jean Albert McEwen #6470
  6471
- influence on Jean-Paul Armand Mousseau
  #6651
- influence on John Meredith #6516
- influence on Marcelle Ferron #5421 5426
- influence on Québec abstract art #1468
- influence on Québec painting #145
- influence on Rita Letendre #6251
- international recognition (1950s) #425
- interview #4802
- La cité absurde #4833
- Molinari, Guido, compared with #6584
- on art #4799 4803
- on nationalism in art #4851
- on Ozias Leduc #6197 6199
- paintings
  - (1930s) #1460
  - (1941-1948) #4823
  - (1953-1956) #1454
  - (1955-1960) #4844
  - (to 1946) #4841
  - Ottawa (Ont), National Gallery of
    Canada #1266
- Projections libérantes #4818 4819
- Refus global #1396 1466 1475 4840
  - compared with other automatistes'
    literary works #4831
  - influence on Françoise Sullivan #7282
  - influence on Le Manifeste des plasticiens
    #1465
  - Leduc, Fernand, on #6189
  - Mousseau, Jean-Paul Armand, on #6650
- Refus global and Projections libérantes, press
  reaction (1948-1949) #1452
- religious paintings #1384
  - (1922-1932) #4820
- Riopelle, Jean-Paul, on #7026
- sign images #4847
- Sous le vent de l'île, National Gallery of
  Canada (Ottawa, Ont) #4815
- writings #92 1443 4839
Borenstein, Sam, Can artist, 1908-1969 #4853
- exhibitions, group
  - (1977) #1278 1279
Borges, Jorge Luis, Argentinian writer, 1899-
- A Personal Anthology, influence on John
  Heward #5793
- influence on Michael Brodie #4923
Bornstein, Eli, Can sculptor, 1922-
- exhibitions

- (1975) #4856
- exhibitions, group
  - (1967) #490 1916
- on art and technology #4855
- on serigraphy #4854
- on structuralism in art #536
- relief structures #777
- sculptures (1960s) #746
Borremans, Guy, Can photographer, 1934-
- portfolio of photographs #997 999
Bosch, Hieronymus (Hieronymus van
  Aken), Nl artist, ca. 1450-1516
- influence on Tom La Pierre #6122
- influence on Tony Urquhart #7446
Boston (Mass), Boston Museum of Fine Arts
- exhibitions
  - Forty Years of Canadian Painting: From
    Tom Thomson and the Group of Seven to
    the Present Day (1949) #383
  - Jack Bush (1972) #4966
- Humphrey, Jack Weldon, as student #5865
- McMurtie, William Birch, views,
  Vancouver Island (BC) #6505
Boston (Mass), Institute of Contemporary
  Art
- exhibitions
  - Nine Canadians (1967) #480
Boszin, Andrew (Endre), Can sculptor, 1923-
- exhibitions, group
  - (1971) #772
Bot, Marten, Can photographer, fl. 1978 #995
botanical illustration
- see also flowers in art; plants in art
botanical illustration, Canadian
- British Columbia #2024
- Jackson, Henry Alexander Carmichael
  #5927 5928
- Miller, Maria Frances Ann Morris #241
  242
botanical illustration, French
- New World, 16th-18th cs. #276
bottles
- see also cruets
bottles, Canadian #2425 2427
- (1825-1931) #2419
- medicine bottles #2432
- milk bottles #2412
- Nova Scotia #2409 2428
- Prairies (1880-1920s) #2431
- Saint-Jean (Qué), Canada Glass Works
  #2420
- Silver, Mr. and Mrs. Stanley S., collection,
  19th-20th cs. #2414
Bouchard, Edith, Can artist, 1924- #1428
  1429
Bouchard, Laurent, Can artist, curator, 1931-
- interview, on Musée du Québec (Québec,
  Qué) #3122
Bouchard, Lorne Holland, Can artist,
  1913-1978 #1393 4857 4858
Bouchard, Marie-Cécile, Can artist,
  1920-1973 #1428 1429
Bouchard, Mary Simone, Can artist,
  1912-1945 #1428 1429
Bouchard, Maurice René, Can architect,
  1909-

– Québec (Qué), école secondaire
  Marie-de-l'Incarnation #7939
Boucher, Maximilien, Can priest, artist,
  1918-1975 #4860
Boucher, Wayne, Can artist, 1943-
– exhibitions, group
  – (1980) #1221
Boucher (dit Belleville), Alexis Charles, Can
  artist, 1808-1885 #4859
Boucherville (Qué)
– architecture, 17th-19th cs. #7890
Boucherville (Qué), Church of Sainte-Famille
– architecture and interior #8868
– tabernacle, Gilles Bolvin #249 250 4781
Boudreau, Pierre de Ligny, Can artist, 1923-
– in Paris (France) #426
Bougie, Louis-Pierre, Can artist, 1946-
– exhibitions
  – (1978) #4861
Bouguereau, Adolphe William, Fr artist,
  1825-1905
– as teacher of John Wycliffe Lowes Forster
  #5469
– as teacher of William Blair Bruce #4941
Boultbee, Alfred, Can artist, 1863-1928 #2085
Boulton, D'Arcy, Jr., Can lawyer, 1785-1846
– residence, The Grange (Toronto, Ont)
  #8680
Boundary Bay (BC)
– antler carvings, Northwest Coast Indians
  #3817
Bourassa, Anne, Can, 1906-
– interview, on Napoléon Bourassa #4873
  4874
Bourassa, Napoléon, Can artist, architect,
  writer, 1827-1916 #1231 1315 1318 1323
  4863 4866 4867 4869 4870 4871 4874 4875
  4876
– and Québec painting #1353
– as teacher of Louis-Philippe Hébert #5768
  5769 5771
– exhibitions
  – (1976) #4872
– exhibitions, group
  – (1880) #1308
– influence of Théophile Hamel #5690
– on his mural paintings #4862
– on taste in art #4864
– oral history sources #4873
– paintings, Chapel of
  Notre-Dame-de-Lourdes (Montréal, Qué)
  #4865 8784 8836
– works, Art Association of Montreal
  (Montréal, Qué) #3075
– writings #4868
Bourassa, Robert, Can statesman, 1933-
– and Olympic Stadium (Montréal, Qué)
  #9139
Bourbeau, Géraldine, Can artist, art critic,
  1906-1953 #4877 4878
Bourdeau, Micheline, Can artist, fl. 1969
  #4879
Bourdeau, Robert Charles John, Can
  photographer, 1931- #4880 4881 4882
– exhibitions, group
  – (1973) #1002

– (1979) #1037
– (1981) #1069 1070
– exhibitions (reviews) #1018 1046 1060
– portfolio of photographs #987 1023
Bourdieu, Pierre, Fr professor of social
  sciences, 1930-
– mentioned, in relation to Montréal (Qué)
  art (1968-1969) #1514
Bourgault, André, Can sculptor, 1898-1958
  #4884 4886
Bourgault, Jean-Julien, Can sculptor, 1910-
  #2194 2209 4884 4886
Bourgault, Médard, Can sculptor, 1897-1967
  #2174 2179 2194 2209 4883 4884 4885 4886
  4887 4888
– and Québec religious art (1950s) #1250
Bourgault, Pier, Can sculptor, 1942- #4889
– and woodcarving school,
  Saint-Jean-Port-Joli (Qué) #1597
– Symposium international de sculpture
  environnementale de Chicoutimi (Qué),
  (1980) #1639
Bourgault family, Can sculptors, 20th c.
– and Québec religious art (1950s) #1250
– influence on Zénon Alary #4505
Bourgeau, Victor, Can architect, 1809-1888
– and Québec Baroque revival architecture
  #7856
– Laval (Qué), Church of Sainte-Rose #8854
– Montréal (Qué)
  – Church of Notre-Dame #8849 8892
  – Church of Saint-Jacques #8782
  – Hôpital-Général #8862
Bourgeault, Victor
– see Bourgeau, Victor
Bourgeois, Albéric, Can artist, 1876-1962
  #1382
Bourgeois, Hélène and Joseph-Romain
  (Roma), Cans, 19th c.
– residence, Grand Digue (NB) #8547
Bourgeois, Marguerite
– see Bourgeoys, Marguerite
Bourgeoys, Marguerite, Can nun, 1620-1700
  #2212
– and Notre-Dame-de-Bon-Secours
  (Montréal, Qué) #8788
– portrait of, Pierre Le Ber #1333 6180
Bourne, Adolphus, Can artist, 1795-1886
– engraving of Robert Auchmaty Sproule's
  View of Montreal from St. Helen's Island
  #2370
Bourque, Célestin, Can, b. 1786
– residence, Memramcook (NB) #8543
Boutilier, Ralph, Can artist, 1906-
– exhibitions (reviews) #1210
Bouzonnet-Stella, Claudine, Fr artist,
  1636-1697
– influence on Antoine-Sébastien
  Plamondon #6886
Bow, Douglas Scott, Can architect, fl. 1913
– Vancouver (BC), University of British
  Columbia, competition #9498
Bowen Island (BC)
– landscapes, Lionel LeMoine FitzGerald
  #5446
Bowers, Robert, Can artist, 1943-

– map images #561
bowls
– see also containers
bowls, American
– glass, 19th-early 20th cs. #2430
bowls, Canadian
– glass, 19th-early 20th cs. #2430
– wooden, Ontario, 18th-19th cs. #2588
bowls, Northwest Coast Indians
– prehistoric stonework #3900
Bowmanville (Ont)
– furniture, 19th c. #2556
Bowmanville (Ont), Bowmanville Public
  Library
– exhibitions
  – Arthur A. Drummond, 1975 (1975) #5309
Bowmanville (Ont), The Photography
  Gallery
– exhibitions
  – Neil Newton Retrospective (1978) #6694
Bowmanville Furniture Manufacturing Co.,
  furniture-making firm (Bowmanville, Ont)
  #2556
bows and arrows, Assiniboine #3693
bows and arrows, Huron #3519
bows and arrows, Inuit #4316
bows and arrows, Iroquois #3489 3519
bows and arrows, natives of North America
  #3328
Boyce, Eleanor, Can quilt-maker, 1918-1980
– interview #4890
Boyd, Douglas, Can silversmith, fl. 1960s
  #2638
Boyd, James Henderson, Can artist, 1928-
– and Ontario printmaking (1960s) #1756
– on printmaking #817 818
Boyd, Jerry, Can photographer, fl. 1979
– portfolio of photographs #1023
Boyd, W.H., Can photographer, fl. 1927
– use of survey camera #989
Boyer, Jean-Pierre, Can artist, 1950-
– videos, Musée d'art contemporain
  (Montréal, Qué) #1498
Boyer, Michel, Can photographer, fl. 1977
– portfolio of photographs #1023
Boyle, John Bernard, Can artist, 1941- #4891
– and nationalism in art #102 143
– and regionalism in art #567
– Elsinore Editions #834
– exhibitions (reviews) #4894
– interview #4892
– on Canadian history and art #4893
– on Jack Chambers #700
Boylen, M.J., Can collector, 1907-1970
– collection, Cornelius Krieghoff paintings
  #1
Bradford, John Locke, Can sculptor,
  1897-1919 #4897
– on woodcarving #4895 4896
Bradford, Robert William, Amer artist, 1923-
  #4898
Bradley, Randy, Can photographer, 1948-
  #2071
Braitstein, Marcel, Can sculptor, 1935-
– sculptures (1959-1969) #4899
– welded sculptures (1960s) #745

Brancusi, Constantin, Ro artist, 1876-1957
- influence on Douglas Bentham #4686
- Westerlund, Mia, compared with #7545
Brandl, Eva, Can artist, 1951- #1512
- exhibitions, group
    - (1976) #1529
Brandon (Man), Brandon Allied Arts Centre
- exhibitions
    - *Canadians: A National Photography Show about People/Canadiens: exposition nationale de photographie ayant les gens comme thème* (1980) #1035
Brandon (Man), Brandon Art Club
- (1950s) #3034
Brandon (Man), Brandon University
- exhibitions
    - *Doig Collection of Canadian Paintings, Featuring the Group of Seven* (1968) #3224
Brandon (Man), Canadian National Railway Station
- architecture, Pratt & Ross #9266
Brandon (Man), Hospital for the Insane
- architecture, Victor William Horwood #9014
Brandon (Man), Prince Edward Hotel
- architecture, Pratt & Ross #9266
Brandtner, Fritz, Can artist, 1896-1969 #1294 4900 4901 4904
- exhibitions
    - (1971) #4903
- exhibitions, group
    - (1977) #1278 1279
- influence on Caven Ernest Atkins #4570
- on linoleum carving #4902
Brangwyn, Frank, Brit artist, 1867-1956
- mural, Manitoba Legislative Building (Winnipeg, Man) #8952
Bransom, Paul, Amer artist, 1885-1979
- influence on George E. McLean #6501
Brant County (Ont)
- art (1793-1930) #1684
- pottery and textiles #2249
Brantford (Ont)
- domestic architecture, post-World War I #8495
Brantford (Ont), Art Gallery of Brant
- exhibitions
    - *Alan C. Collier Retrospective* (1971) #5131
    - *Ed Bartram: 10 Years* (1979) #4618
    - *Four Ontario Realists: D.P. Brown, Ken Danby, Bruce St. Clair, Gerald Zeldin; Paintings, Drawings and Prints* (1976) #1810
    - *Grand River Pottery and Textiles, Past and Present* (1974) #2249
    - *Graphex* (1973-1979, 1981-) #827
    - *Heritage of Brant: A Retrospective Exhibition of Paintings, Maps and Prints from Brant County Selected to Commemorate Brantford's Centennial* (1977) #1684
    - *The Figure: A Sensual Response* (1975) #578
- exhibitions (reviews)
    - Whale, Robert Reginald (1969) #7547
Brantford (Ont), Bell Memorial

- Allward, Walter Seymour #4516
Brantford (Ont), Brantford and District Civic Centre
- architecture, Brooks & Van Poorten #9101
Brantford (Ont), Evangel Pentecostal Church
- architecture, Mark/Musselman/McIntyre/Combe #8766
Brantford (Ont), Woodland Indian Cultural Educational Centre
- exhibitions
    - *Indian Art* (1975-1981) #4139
Brantford Pottery, ceramic manufacturer (Brantford, Ont) #2302 2335
- (1849-1907) #2295
Braque, Georges, Fr artist, 1882-1963
- Borduas, Paul-Emile, compared with #4813
- Brooker, Bertram Richard, on #4927
- East, Benoît, compared with #5353
- influence on Robert La Palme #6119
Brassard, Thérèse Tanguay, Can enameller, 1930- #2102 4905
Brault, Maurice, Can silversmith, enamelist, 1930-1958 #4906
Brauner, Victor, Ro artist, 1902-1966
- influence on Francis Coutellier #5196
Brayshaw, Thomas (Tommy), Can artist, ca. 1886-1967 #4907
Brazil
- views by French explorers, 16th c. #276
Brazilia (Brazil), Canadian Embassy
- exhibitions
    - *Lacos de tradiçao: uma exibiçao de arte canadense indigena contemorânea/Links to a Tradition: An Exhibition of Contemporary Canadian Indian Art/Liens du passé: une exposition d'art contemporain des Indiens du Canada* (1977) #4146
bread
- ovens, Québec #2233 2234
Breeze, Claude Herbert, Can artist, 1938- #145
- *Canadian Atlas* series #4910
- drawings #532
- exhibitions
    - (1978) #4911
- exhibitions, group
    - (1977) #636
- exhibitions (reviews) #520 4909
- figurative works #71
- on art institutions (1970s) #620
- *Sunday Afternoon (from an Old American Photograph)* #4908
Bregman, Sidney (Sid), Can architect, 1922-
- and Bregman & Hamann #8337
Bregman & Hamann, Can architectural firm
- Calgary (Alta), office buildings #9362
- Toronto (Ont) #8337
    - Eaton Centre #9377 9378 9382
    - Olympia Square #9301
    - Toronto-Dominion Centre #7694 9197 9301 9345
Brener, Roland, Can sculptor, 1942-
- interview #4912
Breslau (Poland), Academy of Art
- Kupczynski, Stanislav, as student #6106

Brest (France), Musée municipal de Brest
- exhibitions
    - *Fernand Leduc: microchromie gris, puissance 6* (1977) #6190
    - *Louis Comtois: 4 tableaux récents grand format* (1978) #5163
Breton, André, Fr writer, 1896-1966
- and Alfred Pellan #6821
- and Fernand Leduc #6189
- and Roland Giguère #5598
- correspondence, Fernand Leduc #6194
- influence of Kwakiutl Hawk mask #3361
- influence on Jean-Paul Riopelle #7014 7027
- influence on Paul-Emile Borduas #4814 4850
- influence on Québec painting #1270
- Riopelle, Jean-Paul, on #7026
Breukelman, Jim, Can photographer, 1941- #2071
breweries, Canadian
- glass bottles (1825-1931) #2419
- Nova Scotia (1836-1947) #2428
Briand, Jean-Olivier, Can bishop, 1715-1794
- chapel, Séminaire de Québec (Québec, Qué) #5371 8800
Briansky, Rita, Can artist, 1925-
- on printmaking #817
brick
- *see also* masonry
- and stucco design, Toronto (Ont), (1910s) #8052
- dichromatic, Ontario (1870s-1880s) #8026
- industry
    - Canada (1885-1915) #7726
    - Québec (1650-1837) #2313
- polychromatic, Yorkville Town Hall (Toronto, Ont) #8997
- Toronto (Ont), The Grange #8680
- use in Aultsville (Ont) region architecture, 19th c. #7980
- use in Canadian architecture (1867-1967) #7695
- use in Manitoba architecture, 19th-early 20th cs. #8102
- use in Ontario architecture (1831-1861) #8009
- use in Ontario domestic architecture
    - 19th c. #8677
    - (1920s) #8646
bridges, Canadian
- 19th c. #9512
- Montréal (Qué), Jacques-Cartier Bridge #7933
- Québec, 17th-18th cs. #1320
- railroad bridges (1880-1914) #7736
- wooden
    - British Columbia #8153
    - Ontario, 19th c. #7745
bridges, Huron #3519
bridges, Iroquois #3519
Bridgewater (NS), DesBrisay Museum/National Exhibition Centre
- Hebb, Howard D., furniture exhibited (1977) #2510
Bridgman, John Wesley, Can artist, fl. 1861-1907 #5469

– as teacher of Tomtu H. Roberts #7051
Brief Concerning the Cultural Aspects of Canadian Reconstruction
– *see* Canada. Brief Concerning the Cultural Aspects of Canadian Reconstruction
Brien (*dit* Desrochers), Urbain, Can artist, 1780-1860
– calvary, Varennes (Qué) #1585
Brigden, Frederick, Can artist, 1841-1917
– as founder of Brigdens Limited (Toronto, Ont) #883
Brigden, Frederick Henry (Fred), Can artist, 1871-1956 #4913
– and Frank Shirley Panabaker #6757
– exhibitions (reviews) #1710
– on Walter Joseph Phillips #6856
Brigdens Limited, publishing firm (Toronto, Ont) #883
– and Robert Elmer Lougheed #6327
Brighton (Ont), Union School
– architecture, Ellis & Ellis #9387
Brigus (Nfld)
– architecture #7792
Brigus (Nfld), Hawthorne Cottage
– architecture and interior #8539
Brisbane (Australia), Queensland National Art Gallery
– exhibitions
– *Contemporary Canadian Painters* (1957) #423
Briscoe, Barrie, Can designer, fl. 1960s #4914
Brisley, Stuart, Brit artist, 1933-
– *The one and the other in the attic of poverty* #718
Bristol's Hope (Nfld)
– architecture #7792
Bristol porcelain
– American, imported into Canada, early 20th c. #2346
Britannia metal
– *see* pewter
Britannia Pottery, ceramic manufacturer (Glasgow, Scotland)
– views of Québec #2306 2326
British American Oil Company
– buildings, interior decoration, Canadian decorative arts #8230
British Arctic Expedition (1875-1876)
– Mitchell, Thomas and George White, photographs and watercolours #240
British Columbia
– architecture #8083 8142 8146
– (1895-1914) #8152
– (1940s) #8141
– (1950s) #8144
– (pre-1860) #8140
– Chinese #8154
– Fraser Valley region #8147
– use of building and ornamental stones (1910s) #7646 7647
– Whiteway, William Tuff #9508
– wooden #8148 8153
– art #547 1986 1987 1995 2010
– 20th c. #3199
– (1793-1886) #2025
– (1870s-1940s) #28

– (1909-1967) #1978
– (1910s) #1979
– (1920s-1960s) #461
– (1930s) #1982
– (1932-1968) #1983
– (1940s) #350 1841
– (1950s) #429 1994
– (1950s-1970s) #145
– (1970s) #1868 2040 2047 2050 2053 2063 2067 2068 2078
– (1970s), Okanagan region #2048
– (1970s-1980) #2082
– (1981) #2084
– art education (1960s) #2989
– botanical illustration #2024
– bungalows (1910s) #8684
– canneries #9258
– ceramic sculpture (1970s) #1864
– churches
– (1789-early 20th c.) #8918
– (1858-1925) #8916
– commercial architecture (1970s) #9360
– courthouses (1849-1930) #9006
– decorative arts #2271
– (1970s) #2274 2276
– domestic architecture #8143 8698
– 19th c.-1920s #8690
– (1850s-early 20th c.) #8712
– (1910s) #8685
– (1940s) #8693
– government houses (1849-1871) #8757
– Maclure, Samuel #8385
– summer homes, 20th c. #8524
– furniture (1920s) #2463
– graphic arts (1970s) #2059
– hospitals (1950s) #9029
– jewellery (1950s) #2695
– libraries (1950s) #9044
– open-air sculpture
– (1956-1960) #1993
– (1977) #2057
– painting #2011
– (1848-1890s) #2004
– (1894-1932) #2007
– (1930s) #589 592
– (1940s) #1989
– (1940s-1950s) #412
– (1950s) #1990
– (1960s) #489
– photographic views #1039
– (1858-1871) #2014
– (1858-1888) #2015
– (1890-1914) #2030
– Bailey, Charles S. #4583
– Baltzly, Benjamin #4598
– Brock, J.A., & Co. (1886-1888) #2021
– Dally, Frederick #5249 5250
– Gunterman, Mattie #5670 5672
– Horetzky, Charles George #5837 5838
– Trueman, Richard H. #7437
– photography
– 19th c., Great Eastern Photographic and Advertising Company #2022
– (1858-1900) #2028
– (1858-1914) #2032
– (1860-1978), women photographers

#2018
– (1890-1940) #2012
– (1930s-1940s) #985
– (1970s) #990 996 998 2041 2056 2071
– pottery (1970s) #2391
– samplers #2786
– schools
– (1920s) #9389
– (1950s) #9391 9392
– schools and universities (1960s) #9401
– sculpture
– (1960s) #1849 2001
– (1970s) #2049 2062 2065 2066
– sepulchral monuments #733
– stained glass #2452
– stores (1940s) #9372
– views
– 18th c.-1930s #2008
– (1513-1891) #2006
– (1778-1793), Northwest Coast #2017
– (1840s-1970s) #2016
– (1845-1871) #2020 2023
– Carr, Emily #5033 5045
– Hind, William George Richardson #5807 5810 5811
– Innes, John I. #5901
– Kipling, Ann #6057
– McCall, Helen #6460
– Varley, Frederick Horsman #7462
– Weber, George #7540
– Weston, William Percival #7546
– Wood, Alan #7608 7609
– women artists (1970s) #2054
British Columbia Art Collection
– acquisitions (1974-1980) #2078
British Columbia Ballet (Vancouver, BC)
– stage designs and costumes (1953) #1991
British Columbia Mills Timber and Trading Company (Vancouver, BC)
– prefabricated buildings (1904-1910) #8082
British Columbia Society of Artists
– (1949-1967) #1978
British Columbia Society of Fine Arts #1841 2003
– (1909-1948) #1978
– (1910s) #1979
British in Canada
– 18th-19th cs. #231 244
– Nova Scotia #1215 1220 1222
Brittain, Miller Gore, Can artist, 1912-1968 #1121 1128 1173 1179 1184 4915 4919 4920 4921
– and genre painting #392
– and Saint John (NB) art (1940s) #1170
– exhibitions
– (1968) #4917
– (1972) #4918
– (1981) #4922
– exhibitions, group
– (1966) #1123
– (1973) #1182
– mural cartoons, Saint John General Hospital (Saint John, NB) #4916
Britton, Susan, Can artist, 1952-
– exhibitions, group
– (1977) #631

– (1978) #650
– (1980) #687 1832
broadcasting, Canadian #129
– (1950s), and Royal Commission on
    National Development in the Arts, Letters
    and Sciences (Massey Report) #3254 3255
    3261
– (1970s) #583 3279
broadsheets, Canadian #910
broadsides
– see broadsheets
Brochard, Armand, Can jeweller, 1931-
    #2701 2706
Brock, J.A., & Co., photographic firm
    (Vancouver, BC)
– views of Vancouver (1886-1888) #2021
Brock, John Allan, Can photographer, fl.
    1886-1889
– and J.A. Brock & Co. (Vancouver, BC)
    #2021
Brock, Sir Isaac, Brit statesman and army
    officer in Canada, 1769-1812
– portrait of, George Theodore Berthon
    #4712
Brockville (Ont), Idlewild
– architecture, James P. Johnston #8671
Brockville (Ont), Saint Peter's Anglican
    Church
– architecture, Arthur McClean #8382
Brockville (Ont), Sherwood Park Manor
    Nursing Home
– architecture, Jerome Markson Architects
    #8386
Brodie, F.Neil, Can architect, ca. 1870-1926
– Moncton (NB), Aberdeen School #9387
Brodie, Michael, Can artist, ca. 1950- #4923
Bromley, Valentine Walter, Brit artist in
    Canada, 1848-1877
– views, western Canada #931
Brompton (Qué)
– petroglyphs, Iroquois #3599
Bromsgrove Guild (Montréal, Qué)
– medallions and statuettes #1
Bromsgrove Guild (Worcestershire,
    England)
– works, Victoria College. Library (Toronto,
    Ont) #9038
Bronfman, Samuel, Can collector, 1891-1971
– works commissioned for exhibition, The
    Seagram Collection of Paintings of Cities of
    Canada (1953) #403
Bronfman, Samuel, Can collector, 1891-1971,
    and Saidye, Can collector, 1896-
– donation, Montreal Museum of Fine Arts,
    for purchase of Canadian art, 20th c. #526
    3087
Bronson, A.A., Can artist, 1946-
– exhibitions, group
    – (1977) #5583
bronze
– Toronto (Ont), storefronts (1920s) #9364
bronzes, Canadian
– (1910s) #6141
– British Columbia (1980s) #2083
brooches
– see also adornment

brooches, Algonquian
– silver #3608
brooches, Haida
– Reid, Bill #6984
brooches, Iroquois
– silver #3509 3512 3645 3646
brooches, Scottish
– Luckenbooth, influence on Iroquois
    brooches #3509 3512
Brooke, Arthur Adair, Can artist, 1874-1959
– sketchbook #4924
Brooker, Bertram Richard, Can artist,
    1888-1955 #309 4926 4928
– exhibitions
    – (1971) #4925
– exhibitions, group
    – (1929) #1666
    – (1975) #503 504
– landscapes (1930s) #338
– on art and society #330
– on nudes in art #317
– works (1920s-1940s) #4927
Brooks, Leonard, Can artist, 1911-
– interview #4929
– on his art #4930
– on Mexico #4931
Brooks & Van Poorten, Can architectural
    firm
– Brantford (Ont), Brantford and District
    Civic Centre #9101
Broomfield, Adolphus George, Can artist,
    1906- #4932
Brossard, Urbain, Can builder,
    1633/1634-1710 #234 235 7844
Brossin, Jean-François, Can, fl. 1968
– and Ecole des beaux-arts (Montréal, Qué),
    (1968) #2995
Brothers Glass, ceramic manufacturer
    (London, Ont) #2350
Broughton Island (NWT), wood and
    styrofoam dome house
– architecture, T.Bert Rose #8734
Brown, Alisen, Can photographer, fl. 1977
– portfolio of photographs #1023
Brown, Annora, Can artist, 1899- #4933
– autobiography #4934
– on art #1944
Brown, Arthur William, Can artist,
    1881-1966
– illustrations #916
Brown, Bert, Can photographer, fl. 1979
– portfolio of photographs #995
Brown, Charles, Amer sculptor, fl. 1890s
– totem pole #3856
Brown, Daniel Price Ericksen (D.P.), Can
    artist, 1939-
– and realism #110
– exhibitions, group
    – (1974) #573
    – (1976) #1810
Brown, Douglas, Can photographer, ca.
    1956-
– portfolio of photographs #1023
Brown, E.B., Can artist, fl. 1898 #2085
Brown, Eric, Can curator, 1877-1939
– and British Empire Exhibition (Wembley,

England), (1924) #458
– and Emily Carr #5021 5034
– as director, National Gallery of Canada
    (Ottawa, Ont) #3021 3022 3029 3032 3040
    3041 3049 3050
Brown, Ernest, Can photographer, 1877-1951
    #4935
– and Charles Wesley Mathers #6451
– collection, photographs #1949
Brown, Francis Bruce, Can architect,
    1899-
– Hamilton (Ont), McMaster University
    #9451
Brown, Gordon F., Can photographer, 1943-
– exhibitions, group
    – (1972) #1952
– portfolio of photographs #991
Brown, Huntley, Can artist, 1932-
– illustrations #941
Brown, John Francis, Can architect,
    1866-1942
– Hamilton (Ont), McMaster University
    #9451
Brown, Murray, Can architect, 1885-1958
    #8338
Brown, Peter, Can sculptor, 1947-
– exhibitions
    – (1976) #4936
Brown, Randy, Can photographer, 1943-
– portfolio of photographs #1023 1032
Brown, Thomas, Can photographer, 1945-
    #1000
Brown & Vallance, Can architectural firm
– Montréal (Qué), McGill University.
    Medical Building #9412
– Regina (Sask), War Memorial Museum,
    competition #9073
– Saskatoon (Sask), University of
    Saskatchewan #9489 9491
– Winnipeg (Man)
    – City Hall, competition #8979
    – Legislative and Executive Building,
      competition #8946
Browne, George, Can architect, 1811-1885
– Kingston (Ont) #8339
– Québec (Qué), Chalmers-Wesley Church
    #7873
Browne, Joseph Archibald, Can artist,
    1864/1866-1948 #302 1713 4937 4938 4939
– and Homer Ransford Watson #7533
– as member, Canadian Art Club #193
– exhibitions (reviews) #204 211
Brownell, Peleg Franklin, Can artist,
    1857-1946
– as member, Canadian Art Club #193
– as teacher of Pegi Nicol MacLeod #6397
– exhibitions, group
    – (1935) #17
– exhibitions (reviews) #186 211
Browning (Mon), Museum of the Plains
    Indian
– exhibitions
    – The Buffalo in Western American Art: An
      Exhibition from the Collections of the
      Glenbow Foundation, Calgary (1961) #62
Bruce, Brad, Can artist, ca. 1952-

- exhibitions (reviews) #1227
Bruce, David, Can photographer, fl. 1979
    #2071
Bruce, Robert Donald, Can artist, 1911-
- on Exercise Muskox expedition (1946)
    #4940
Bruce, William Blair, Can artist, 1859-1906
- exhibitions
    - (1907) #4941
    - (1975) #4942
Bruce Brown & Brisley, Can architectural
    firm
- Hamilton (Ont), McMaster Divinity
    College #8765
Bruce County (Ont)
- cemeteries, German-Alsatian crosses #2709
Brücke, Die
- and Karl May #6452
- and Philip Henry Surrey #7290
Bruegel, Pieter, the elder, Fle artist, d. 1569
- Eyre, Ivan Kenneth, compared with #5394
Bruenner, Ralph, Can photographer, fl.
    1970s-
- portfolio of photographs #991
Bruneau, Kittie, Can artist, 1929- #4943 4944
    4945
- Entre chien et loup #1647
Brunet, Joseph, Can sculptor, b. 1899
- sepulchral monuments,
    Notre-Dame-des-Neiges cemetery,
    Montréal (Qué) #1567
Bruni, Umberto, Can artist, 1914- #4946
Bruno, Anthony, Can photographer, fl.
    1970s
- portfolio of photographs #995
Brussels (Belgium), Ambassade du
    Canada/Canadian Embassy
- exhibitions
    - Exposition d'estampes en l'honneur de C.
        Krieghoff, 1815-1872/Exhibition of Prints
        in Honour of C. Krieghoff, 1815-1872
        (1972) #6096
Brussels (Belgium), Centre culturel et
    d'information canadien
- exhibitions
    - D.P. Brown, Ken Danby, Tom Forrestall,
        Christopher Pratt (1974) #573
    - Ozias Leduc: peinture symboliste et
        religieuse/Ozias Leduc: Symbolist and
        Religious Painting (1974) #6206
    - Peter Gnass: installation-Chantier interdit
        au public (1981) #5621
    - Richard Mill: 5 tableaux récents (1980)
        #6535
Brussels (Belgium), galerie Isy Brachot
- exhibitions
    - Exposition d'art esquimau: sculptures
        (1977) #4444
Brussels (Belgium), Palais des beaux-arts
- exhibitions
    - Canada: art d'aujourd'hui (1968) #518
    - Yves Trudeau: "murs fermés et ouverts";
        sculptures et pliages (1976) #7434
Brussels (Belgium), Universal and
    International Exhibition of 1958. Canadian
    Pavilion

- architecture #9209
    - Greenberg, Charles #9211
- architecture and art #419 430
- art #428
- mural, Louis Archambault #4541 4542
- mural, Mario Virgilio Merola #6518 6521
Brute, Dr.
- see Metcalfe, Eric W. (Dr. Brute)
Bry, Theodore de, Nl engraver, 1528-1598
- America, engravings of North American
    Indians and Eskimos after John White
    #7552
Brymner, William, Can artist, 1855-1925
    #178 4948 4952
- and Edmond Dyonnet #5347 5349
- and Royal Canadian Academy of Arts
    #152
- as conservative artist (1930s) #322
- as member, Canadian Art Club #193
- as teacher #4949
- as teacher of Anne Douglas Savage #7130
    7132
- as teacher of Arthur George Racey #6952
- as teacher of Edwin Headley Holgate
    #5818 5819
- as teacher of Lilias Torrance Newton
    #6693
- as teacher of Sarah Margaret Armour
    Robertson #7054
- exhibitions
    - (1979) #4953
- exhibitions, group
    - (1935) #17
    - (1978) #133
- exhibitions (reviews) #174 186 204 211
- female subjects #4954
- in Martigues (France), (1908) #4950
- influence of Impressionism #227
- influence on Robert Wakeman Pilot #6872
- mural paintings, Charles Porteous House,
    île d'Orléans (Qué) #4951
- on art #4947
Bryson, Joseph Vincent, Can photographer,
    1953-
- portfolio of photographs #1032
Buchan, David, Can artist, 1950-
- exhibitions, group
    - (1980) #1832
- exhibitions (reviews) #1067
- performance art #655
Buchan, John, 1st Baron Tweedsmuir, Brit
    writer, governor general in Canada,
    1875-1940
- as patron of Peter Pitseolak #6875 6877
Buchanan, Donald William, Can art
    historian, curator, 1908-1966 #3325
- as critic of art in the Prairies #1851
- correspondence, David Brown Milne #6550
    6553
Bucke, Richard Maurice, Can psychiatrist,
    writer, 1837-1902
- mystical beliefs in Cosmic Consciousness,
    influence on Lawren Stewart Harris #5731
Buckhan, Robert Marshall, Can artist, 1918-
- exhibitions, group
    - (1981) #1117

Budden, John Sherring, Can auctioneer,
    1825-1918
- as patron of Cornelius Krieghoff #6092
Buell, Katrina S.D., Can artist, fl. 1890-1926
    #309
Buff, Richard, Can artist, 1947-
- on Jack Chambers #700
buffalo
- Canadian and American art, late 18th-20th
    cs. #62
Buffalo (NY), Albright-Knox Art Gallery
- views of Niagara Falls exhibited (1964)
    #1673
Buffalo (NY), Buffalo Fine Arts Academy.
    Albright Art Gallery
- exhibitions
    - Exhibition of Paintings by Canadian Artists
        (1928) #301
    - The Collection of Mr. and Mrs. Charles S.
        Band: Contemporary Canadian Painting
        and Drawing (1958) #3215
Buffalo (NY), Pan-American Exposition
    (1901)
- and Laura Adeline Muntz Lyall #6337
- exhibitions (reviews)
    - Canadian art #189
buffalo hair
- bags, Indians of North America #3398
Buffalo National Park (Sask)
- photographic views, John Henry Gano
    #5555
building
- see also walls
- and architecture
    - (1960s) #8310
    - Canadian Architect survey (1974-1976)
        #8320
    - Don Mills (Ont) housing (1950s) #8301
    - Royal Architectural Institute of Canada
        survey (1960s) #8309
- British Columbia #8142
- Canada. National Research Council.
    Division of Building Research #7715
- curtain wall designs, office buildings
    (1950s-1960s) #9300
- Dawson City (Yukon), (1897-1903) #8183
- grain elevators (1920s) #9236
- hollow-wall construction, Ontario, 19th c.
    #8004
- industrial buildings (1950s) #9241
- Lindsay, Jeffrey, "shell truss" structural
    system #7674
- log buildings
    - Alberta, late 19th-early 20th cs. #8120
    - French-Canadian settlers in Ontario,
        19th c. #7685
    - Ontario, 19th c. #7979
    - Ottawa Valley (Ont) #8029
- Louisbourg (NS) #8426 8427 8435 8436
- Ontario houses, 19th c. #8677
- plankwall framing #7712
    - Ontario, 19th c. #8046
- prefabricated buildings, western Canada
    (1904-1910) #8082
- Québec
    - 17th-19th cs. #7864

– 19th-20th cs. #7926
– Québec houses (1960s) #8279
– roofing materials and methods, 17th-19th cs. #7703
– Saskatchewan houses, late 19th-early 20th cs. #8696
– stone
    – Ottawa region (Ont), 19th c. #8033
    – Terrebonne (Qué), (1816-1820s) #7907
    – Waterloo County (Ont), 19th c. #8011
– timber framing
    – Canada and USA, 17th-18th cs. #7717
    – comparison of two houses (1650 and 1836) #8658
– Trois-Rivières (Qué), Forges of Saint-Maurice #7878
– Vancouver (BC), (1888-1913) #8165
– wood construction #7722
    – Ontario, 19th c. #7745
– wood-processing industry
    – 18th-19th cs. #7720
    – Canada and USA (1607-1623) #7718
building materials
– see architectural materials
buildings, prefabricated
– see prefabricated buildings
buildings, public
– see public buildings
Bujold, Françoise, Can artist, 1933-1981
– interview #4955
Bukovyna (Ukraine)
– costume, Peter Orchinsky collection #2869
Bull, Edward Claxton, Can artist, d. 1886
– as member, Toronto Society of Arts #1689
Bull, Perkins, Can collector, 1870-1948
– collection, Canadian painting #3208
Bull, W., Can photographer, fl. 1894
– on photo trip #4956
Bulman, Bessie, Can collector, 1915-1971
– collection, Inuit sculpture #4306 4428
bundles, Blackfoot
– medicine #3754
– pipe #3665
bundles, Ojibwa #3699
bungalows
– see also domestic architecture
bungalows, American
– California
    – (1910s) #8685
    – influence on Vancouver (BC) houses (1910-1920s) #8730
bungalows, Canadian
– (1908) #8487
– British Columbia (1910s) #8684 8685
Bunyard, Richard Geoffrey, Can architect, 1883-1973
– Regina (Sask), War Memorial Museum, competition #9073
Burchfield, Charles Ephraim, Amer artist, 1893-1967
– Schaefer, Carl Fellman, compared with #7157
– Schaefer, Carl Fellman, on #7158
Burden, Eve, Can goldsmith, ca. 1953- #4957
Burden, John, Can goldsmith, fl. 1960s- #4957

Bureau, Monique, Can artist, fl. 1937 #2174
Buren, Daniel, Fr artist, 1938-
– museum theme #714
Burgess, Catherine, Can sculptor, 1953- #717
Burgess, Cecil Scott, Can architect, 1870-1971
– Edmonton (Alta), Alberta Government Administrative Building #8963
Burgess, William, Can photographer, fl. 1856-1867 #1724
burial sites, Algonquian
– Redbank (NB) #3561
burial sites, Beothuk
– Port-au-Choix (Nfld) #3611
burial sites, Huron
– pottery #3520
burial sites, Iroquois
– pottery #3520
– sculpture #3553
burial sites, Ojibwa
– Red Deer River (Man) #3615
Burka, Jan, Can artist, 1924-
– art and poetry #4958
– on his art education #470
Burke, Horwood & White, Can architectural firm
– Calgary (Alta), Hudson's Bay store #8118
– domestic architecture #8496
– Toronto (Ont), domestic architecture #8493
Burke, Rebecca, Can artist, 1946- #717
Burlington (Ont), Burlington Cultural Centre #1806
– exhibitions
    – Ed Bartram: 10 Years (1980) #4618
    – Goodridge Roberts: Paintings from the 1950s and 60s (1981) #7048
    – Ivan Eyre Exposition (1982) #5394
    – Lillian Freiman: Paintings and Drawings (1978) #5518
    – Métiers d'art Ontario-Québec, 1979/1980/Quebec-Ontario Crafts, 1979/1980 (1981) #2138
    – Realism: Structure and Illusion: Toward a Definition of Representational Art (1981) #716
    – The Heritage of Jack Bush: A Tribute (1982) #722
    – Water Colours by E.May Martin (1980) #6424
Burlington Glass Works, glass manufacturer (Hamilton, Ont) #2401 2406 2416 2421 2434
Burman, Irving, Can artist, 1928-
– on Canadian art (1960s) #478
– woodcarvings (1960s) #744
Burnaby (BC)
– views
    – Lamb, Harold Mortimer #6156
Burnaby (BC), Burnaby Art Gallery
– exhibitions
    – 10th Anniversary Show: Burnaby Art Gallery, (1977) #2013
    – A Terrible Beauty: The Art of Canada at War (1979) #1111
    – A Tribute to William Townsend: 1909 to 1973 (1974) #7418
    – Artists from the Sea 1778-1793: A Visual

Documentation of British Columbia (1978) #2017
    – Artists Overland: A Visual Record of British Columbia 1793-1886 (1980) #2025
    – Beauté tragique: les deux conflits mondiaux vus par des artistes canadiens (1979) #1112
    – Bill Koochin (1980) #6073
    – Burnaby Print Show (1967-1977) #816
    – Carol Fraser Paintings and Drawings: 1967-1977 (1977) #5507
    – Charles John Collings, 1848-1931 (1978) #5137
    – David Marshall Sculpture (1978) #6420
    – E. Lindner: Drawings, 1969-1972 (1972) #6285
    – Eskimo Fantastic Art (1972) #4240
    – H.Eric Bergman, 1893-1958 (1980) #4709
    – Jock Macdonald: Retrospective Exhibition/Jock Macdonald: rétrospective (1970) #6375
    – Ken Wallace 1980 (1980) #7510
    – Mountain: A Lithograph by James B. Spencer/Montagne: une lithographie de James B. Spencer (1974) #7270
    – Mystic Circle (1973) #559
    – Northwest Renaissance (1980) #4160
    – Okanagan Energy, An Exhibition of the Work of a Selected Group of Okanagan Artists (1974) #2048
    – Richard Prince: Figure Structures (1979) #6939
    – Ronald: 25 Years (1976) #7073
    – The Bell-Irvings of British Columbia (1980) #4665
    – Three Poet Artists (1978) #649
    – Tom La Pierre: Paintings, Drawings, Prints (1976) #6121
    – Watercolour Painters from Saskatchewan/Aquarellistes de la Saskatchewan (1972) #1920
– Hushlak, Gerald, computer art #5891
Burnaby (BC), Burnaby Centennial Pavilion
– exhibitions
    – Burnaby National Print Show (1961, 1963) #816
Burnaby (BC), Simon Fraser University
– architecture
    – Erickson/Massey #8360 9396 9467 9504 9505 9506
        – competition #9501
    – Erickson, Arthur Charles #8358 8361 9406
– art education (1970s) #3006
– interior design (1960s) #9402
Burnaby (BC), Simon Fraser University. Centre for Communication and the Arts
– exhibitions
    – Kenneth Lochhead: Recent Works on Paper (1972) #6316
Burnaby (BC), Simon Fraser University. Library
– architecture, Robert F. Harrison #9046
Burnaby (BC), Simon Fraser University. Simon Fraser Gallery
– exhibitions
    – Artists' Stamps and Images: An

International Invitational Exhibition (1974)
#829
- *Canadians: A National Photography Show
  about People/Canadiens: exposition
  nationale de photographie ayant les gens
  comme thème* (1980) #1035
- *Changing Visions: The Canadian
  Landscape/Aperçus divers: le paysage
  canadien* (1977) #617
- *Contemporaries of Emily Carr in British
  Columbia* (1974) #2007
- *Dessins de Lionel LeMoine FitzGerald et
  Bertram Brooker* (1975) #503
- *Esther Warkov Drawings* (1977) #7519
- *Images of the Inuit from the Simon Fraser
  Collection* (1979) #4495
- *J.Frederic McCulloch 1905-1932: Works on
  Paper* (1978) #6463
- *Jack Wise: A Decade of Work* (1978) #7601
- *Lionel Lemoine FitzGerald, Bertram
  Brooker: Their Drawings* (1975) #504
- *The Art of the Eskimo* (1971) #4223
- *Vehicle Art: In Transit* (1975) #1512
- *White Sculpture of the Inuit* (1977) #4445
- exhibitions (reviews)
  - British Columbia photographers
    exhibition
    - (1971) #2041
    - (1974) #2056
Burnaby (BC), Simon Fraser University.
  Theatre
- exhibitions
  - *Burnaby National Print Show* (1966) #816
Burnaby Art Gallery Association (Burnaby,
  BC) #2013
Burnaby Art Society (Burnaby, BC) #2013
- (1961-1977), *Burnaby National Print Show*
  #816
Burne-Jones, Edward, Brit artist, 1833-1898
- influence on Graham Metson #6523
- influence on Ozias Leduc #6206
Burnett, Moyra Theresa, Can stained glass
  artist, 1927-
- stained glass #2452
Burnett, William Dudley, Can artist,
  1879-1935
- illustrations #916
Burns, Cooper, Donoahue, Fleming &
  Company Ltd., Can graphic design firm
  #904
Burns, Cooper, Hynes Ltd., Can graphic
  design firm #905
- exhibitions
  - (1979) #906
Burns, Robert, Can artist, 1942-
- and Burns, Cooper, Donoahue, Fleming &
  Company Ltd. #904
- as cofounder of Burns, Cooper, Hynes Ltd.
  #905
- prints #897
Burns, T.M., Can ceramicist, fl. 1862-1865
- as founder of Spring Park Pottery
  (Charlottetown, PEI) #2311
Burns & Cooper Ltd., Can graphic design
  firm #892 896
Burnt Cove (Nfld), Print Shop #1148

Burr, Saxton, Can builder, fl. 1831
- Niagara-on-the-Lake (Ont), Saint
  Andrew's Church #8901
Burr, William, Amer artist, 1810-1875/1876
- panorama of Saint Lawrence River and
  Great Lakes #218
Burritt's Rapids (Ont), Christ's Church
- architecture, Arthur McClean #8382
Burrows, Thomas Carl (Tom), Can artist,
  1940-
- exhibitions, group
  - (1974) #2050
- *Gas Works* #4960
- interview #4959
Burston, Wells & Tampold, Can
  architectural firm
- Toronto (Ont), Holly-Dunfield Apartments
  #7683 8514
Burt, Leonard, Can artist, ca. 1928- #1155
- exhibitions, group
  - (1976) #1153
  - (1977) #1156
Burton, Dennis Eugene Norman, Can artist,
  1933- #1762
- exhibitions
  - (1977) #4961
- exhibitions, group
  - (1979) #510
- interview #4962
- on Frederick Hagan #5676
- on Gordon Rayner #6965
- on his art education #470
- on Toronto painting (1953-1965) #1773
Burton Kramer Associates, Can graphic
  design firm #889
Burwash, Lachan T., Can army officer,
  1874-1940
- on the Inuit (1928) #1021
Bury (England), Corporation Art Gallery
- exhibitions
  - *Exhibition of Canadian Art* (1926) #290
burying-grounds
- *see* cemeteries
Bush, Jack Hamilton, Can artist, 1909-1977
  #1803 4963 4970 4973
- and internationalism in art #567
- and Toronto (Ont) art
  - (1960s) #1753
  - (1970s) #1796
- exhibitions
  - (1972) #4966
  - (1976) #4969
  - (1980) #4976 4978
- exhibitions, group
  - (1967) #480 490 491
  - (1971) #98
  - (1980) #703
  - (1981) #722
- exhibitions (reviews) #4965 4967 4968 4971
  4972 4974 4977
- influence on Douglas Hector Haynes
  #5758
- influence on Toronto (Ont) painting #1807
- interview #536
- support of #123 4975
- use of colour #4964

Bush, Robin B., Can designer, 1921- #4979
  4980
- and architecture #8231
- chairs #2471
- on furniture design #2468
business
- and art
  - Levine, Les #6262
  - Lorcini, Gino #6323
busts
- *see* portrait sculpture
Butcher, Mark, Can builder, fl. 1867
- Charlottetown (PEI), market building
  #7800
Butler, Jack
- *see* Butler, Kenneth John (Jack/K.J.)
Butler, K.J.
- *see* Butler, Kenneth John (Jack/K.J.)
Butler, Kenneth John (Jack/K.J.), Can artist,
  1937- #4981
- and Sanavik Cooperative, Baker Lake
  (NWT) #4480
- collection, Inuit art #4243
- exhibitions
  - (1977) #4982
  - (1981) #4983
- exhibitions, group
  - (1977) #1901
- introduction of printmaking, Baker Lake
  (NWT) #4241 4486
Butler, Sheila, Can artist, 1938-
- exhibitions (reviews) #4984
- introduction of printmaking, Baker Lake
  (NWT) #4241 4486
Butterfield, William, Brit architect, 1814-1900
- Fredericton (NB), cathedral #8770
- St. Stephen (NB), Christ Church #8774
Button Point (Bylot Island, NWT)
- Dorset artifacts #4359 4361
- Dorset mask #4356 4357 4362
buttons, Canadian
- military #2874 2882
Byzantine architecture
- influence on Alberta churches #8913
- influence on Saskatchewan Ukrainian
  Orthodox churches #8912
Byzantine art
- influence on icons and frescoes, Church of
  Saint Nicholas (Toronto, Ont) #1822
- influence on John Bernard Boyle #4894

C

C.A. Fowler and Company
- *see* Fowler, C.A., and Company
C.D. Davidson & Co.
- *see* Davidson, C.D., & Co.
Cabanel, Alexandre, Fr artist, 1823-1889
- as teacher of Charles Edouard Huot #5878
  5884
cabinets, Canadian
- Nova Scotia, 17th-19th cs. #2489 2499
- Ontario
  - 19th c. #2573

– Québec, 17th-18th cs. #2530 2531
cabins
– *see* log cabins
Cadillac Fairview Corporation, Can
   architectural firm
– Los Angeles (Calif), Bunker Hill
   redevelopment, competition #8364
Cage, John, Amer composer, 1912-
– and Max Dean #5274
Cahén, Oscar, Can artist, 1916-1956
– exhibitions
   – (1968) #4986
– exhibitions (reviews) #860
– illustrations #855
– interview #4985
Caiboiosai, Lloyd, Can artist, 1947-1975
   #4157
Cain, Maryanne, Can sculptor, ca. 1948-
   #4987
Caiserman-Roth, Ghitta, Can artist, 1923-
   #4988 4989 4990
– as cofounder of Graphia (Montréal, Qué)
   #1660
Calder, Alexander, Amer sculptor, 1898-1976
– Cowin, Jack I., compared with #5198
Caldwell, Atha Haydock, Can artist, b. 1872
   #4991
Caldwell, Dorothy, Can artist, 1948-
– on Jack Chambers #700
Caledon, Earl of, James Du Prés, Brit army
   officer in Canada, 1812-1888
– collection, art, Indians of North America
   #3465 3466
calendars
– Toronto Art Students' League #1714
calendars, Blackfoot
– winter counts #3707
calendars, Dakota
– winter counts #3747
calendars, Plains
– medicine wheels #3748
Calgary (Alta)
– architecture #8124 8134
   – (1875-1914) #8121 8128
   – (1880-1980) #8138
   – (1909) #8116
   – (1910s) #8118
   – (1920s) #7656
   – Chinatown #8137
   – downtown area (1970s) #8122
   – high-level walkways #8132 8135 8139
   – Myers, Barton #8391
– art
   – (1950s-1970s) #131
   – (1960s) #1848
   – (1970s) #1870 1966
– art galleries (1960s) #442
– city planning, Thomas Hayton Mawson
   #9405
– domestic architecture
   – (1875-1914) #8711
   – (1975-1980) #8728
   – Long, Jack #8381
– graphic arts (1970s) #1958
– office buildings (1970s-1980s) #9362
– photographic views

– Pollard, Harry #6899
– public art #1959 1973
– sculpture (1960s) #1853
– views
   – Nicoll, Jim #6701
Calgary (Alta), 8th Avenue Mall
– restoration #8133
Calgary (Alta), Alberta College of Art
– exhibitions
   – *Lithographs/Lithographies* (1971) #825
– Janvier, Alex Simeon, as student #5936
   5938
Calgary (Alta), Alberta College of Art.
   Gallery
– exhibitions
   – *Alan Wood* (1977) #7608
   – *Another Dimension/Une autre dimension*
      (1977) #783
   – *Calgary Graphics Exhibition* (1959-1974)
      #815
   – *Changes: 11 Artists Working on the
      Prairies* (1976) #1867
   – *Clay as Sculpture* (1977) #781
   – *Clive Robertson: Television: Adjusting the
      Hold* (1977) #7053
   – *Esther Warkov Drawings* (1977) #7519
   – *H.G. Glyde in Canada* (1975) #5618
   – *Illingworth Kerr: Fifty Years a Painter*
      (1973) #6049
   – *Liz Magor* (1981) #6408
   – *Maxwell Bates in Retrospect, 1921-1971*
      (1973) #4624
   – *Mountain: A Lithograph by James B.
      Spencer/Montagne: une lithographie de
      James B. Spencer* (1974) #7270
   – *Peter Kolisnyk* (1980) #6076
   – *Some Drawings by Some Albertans: A
      Major Survey of Drawing in Alberta*
      (1980) #1968
   – *The Canadian Canvas: A Travelling
      Exhibition of 85 Recent Paintings/Peintres
      canadiens actuels: exposition itinérante de
      85 oeuvres récentes* (1976) #588
   – *The History of Ceramics in Alberta* (1975)
      #2386
– exhibitions (reviews)
   – Kiyooka, Harry Mitsuo #6058
   – *The Canadian Canvas: A Travelling
      Exhibition of 85 Recent Paintings/Peintres
      canadiens actuels: exposition itinérante de
      85 oeuvres récentes* (1976) #582
Calgary (Alta), Arton's Gallery
– exhibitions
   – *The 1978 Canadian Video Open* (1978)
      #650
Calgary (Alta), Bank of Nova Scotia
– architecture
   – Lyle, John MacIntosh #8226 9186 9203
   – Sharp & Brown #8118
Calgary (Alta), Bishop Pinkham's College
– architecture #8116
Calgary (Alta), Brae Glen
– architecture, Garden McMillan #8746
Calgary (Alta), Burns Building
– architecture, Hodgson, Bates & Beattie
   #8118

Calgary (Alta), Calgary Allied Arts Centre.
   Coste House
– exhibitions
   – *Jubilee Exhibition of Alberta Paintings*
      (1955) #1948
Calgary (Alta), Calgary Art Centre
– (1947) #1945
Calgary (Alta), Clouds n' Water
– exhibitions
   – *Vehicle Art: In Transit* (1975) #1512
Calgary (Alta), Dominion Bank
– architecture, George W. Northwood #9188
Calgary (Alta), Glenbow-Alberta Institute
   #3194
– art, Indians of North America #3438
– artifacts, Piegan Indians #3759
– exhibitions
   – *A Terrible Beauty: The Art of Canada at
      War* (1979) #1111
   – *Alberta Art Foundation* (1977) #1957
   – *Alberta Society of Artists exhibition*
      (1977) #1942
   – *Archibald Thorburn* (1974) #7373
   – *Art in Alberta: Paul Kane to the Present*
      (1973) #1953
   – *Aspects of Canadian Painting in the
      Seventies* (1980) #684 704
   – *Beauté tragique: les deux conflits mondiaux
      vus par des artistes canadiens* (1979) #1112
   – *C.E. Barker Memorial Exhibition* (1975)
      #4609
   – *Canadian Painting in the Thirties* (1975)
      #592
   – *Canadian Political Cartoons* (1977) #956
   – *Canadian Tapestries, 1977* (1977) #2770
   – *Certain Traditions: Recent British and
      Canadian Art* (1978) #653
   – *Changing Visions: The Canadian
      Landscape/Aperçus divers: le paysage
      canadien* (1977) #617
   – *David Milne: The New York Years,
      1903-1916* (1981) #6567
   – *Deacon/Hushlak: Paintings and Drawings
      by Peter Deacon and Gerald Hushlak*
      (1978) #1961
   – *Dorothy Knowles* (1973) #6067
   – *E. Lindner: Drawings, 1969-1972* (1972)
      #6285
   – *Enns, Evans & Ulrich* (1978) #1956
   – *Focus: Photographic Essays* (1972) #1952
   – *Frederic Marlett Bell-Smith (1846-1923)*
      (1977) #4668
   – *George Sawchuk* (1980) #7142
   – *Gift from the Douglas M. Duncan
      Collection and the Milne-Duncan
      Bequest/Le Don provenant de la collection
      Douglas M. Duncan et le legs
      Milne-Duncan* (1972) #541
   – *Glenbow Collects: An Exhibition* (1969)
      #3191
   – *Greg Curnoe: rétrospective/Greg Curnoe:
      Retrospective* (1981) #5231
   – *Haynes at Glenbow* (1974) #5757
   – *J.W. Beatty, 1869-1941* (1982) #4638
   – *Jack Wise: A Decade of Work* (1978) #7601
   – *Janet Mitchell* (1977) #6574

- *Jim Nicoll: Painting and Poetry* (1977) #6700
- *Joe Fafard: Recent Sculpture* (1979) #5401
- *Joe Plaskett and His Paris: In Search of Time Past* (1972) #6893
- *Joe Plaskett et son Paris: à la recherche d'un temps passé* (1972) #6894
- *John Will: A Catalogue of the Complete Graphic Works to Date Published on the Occasion of an Exhibition of His Prints at the Glenbow Museum* (1980) #7585
- *Kostyniuk: Relief Structures, 1969-1972* (1972) #6079
- *Louis de Niverville* (1979) #6709
- *Marion Nicoll: A Retrospective, 1959-1971* (1975) #6702
- *National Ceramics Exhibition Calgary/Exposition nationale de céramique de Calgary* (1976) #2387
- *New Paintings by Otto Rogers* (1973) #7062
- *Otto Rogers: New Paintings and Sculpture, 1977-78* (1978) #7065
- *Peinture canadienne des années trente* (1975) #589
- *Pipes that Won't Smoke, Coal that Won't Burn: Haida Sculpture in Argillite* (1981) #4051
- *Takao Tanabe, 1972-1976: The Land* (1977) #7320
- *The Contemporary Arts Society: Montreal 1939-1948/La Société d'art contemporain: Montréal 1939-1948* (1980) #1474
- *The Hutterite Diamond Jubilee: An Exhibition of Photographs by Spiteri and Artifacts from the Collections of the Glenbow Museum, Calgary/Le Jubilee [sic] de diamant des Huttérites: une exposition de photographies de Spiteri et d'objets d'artisanat huttérite des collections du Musée de Glenbow, à Calgary* (1978) #1962
- *The Image of Man in Canadian Painting: 1878-1978/L'image de l'homme dans la peinture canadienne: 1878-1978* (1978) #135
- *The Railway: Patron of the Arts in Canada* (1976) #3281
- *The Work of Art: Six Artists* (1979) #665
- *Through Canadian Eyes: Trends and Influences in Canadian Art, 1815-1965* (1976) #122
- *Tim Zuck: Paintings* (1980) #7636
- *Western Untitled* (1976) #1869
- *William Perehudoff* (1977) #6836
- *Yves Gaucher: A Fifteen-Year Perspective, 1963-1978/Yves Gaucher: une perspective de quinze ans, 1963-1978* (1979) #5570
- exhibitions (reviews)
  - *National Ceramics Exhibition Calgary/Exposition nationale de céramique de Calgary* (1976) #2388
  - *Western Untitled* (1976) #1871
- Finlay, George E., drawings #5439
- landscapes, western Canada #1863
- Moodie, Geraldine, photographs #6602
- Phinney, Robert, bird sculptures #6862

Calgary (Alta), Hotel Palliser
- architecture, Edward Maxwell and William Sutherland Maxwell #9271
Calgary (Alta), Hudson's Bay store
- architecture, Burke, Horwood & White #8118
Calgary (Alta), Ian McDougall House
- architecture, Ian McDougall #8727
Calgary (Alta), Institute of Technology and Art
- Leighton, Alfred Crocker, as director #6225
Calgary (Alta), Kelvin Grove Patio Apartments
- architecture, Jack Long #8518
Calgary (Alta), Lancaster Building
- restoration #8133
Calgary (Alta), Lougheed Building
- architecture, R. Wardrop #8118
Calgary (Alta), McKay farm house
- restoration #8133
Calgary (Alta), Mira Godard Gallery
- and Mira Godard #161
- Ashevak, Kenojuak, works exhibited #4564
- exhibitions
  - *Ed Bartram: 10 Years* (1981) #4618
Calgary (Alta), Off Centre Centre
- exhibitions
  - *John Hall: Paintings and Auxiliary Works 1979-1980* (1981) #5686
Calgary (Alta), T. Eaton Company Department Store
- architecture, Ross & Macdonald; Sproatt & Rolph, Consulting Architects #9365
Calgary (Alta), University of Calgary
- architectural education
  - (1980) #8289
- planning, Thomas Hayton Mawson #9405
Calgary (Alta), University of Calgary. Art Gallery
- Beny, Wilfred Roloff, photographs, Siebens Collection #4691
- exhibitions
  - *Drawings and Pastels c. 1930-1967 by Miller Gore Brittain* (1969) #4917
  - *Ron Kostyniuk: Relief Structures, 1972-1977* (1978) #6080
  - *Roy K. Kiyooka: 25 Years* (1976) #6062
Calgary (Alta), University of Calgary. Canadian Architectural Archives #7730 7751
Calgary (Alta), University of Calgary. Faculty of Environmental Design
- architectural education
  - (1976) #7728
- symposium on architectural conservation training in Canada (1979) #7773
Calgary (Alta), University of Calgary. Nickle Arts Museum
- exhibitions
  - *Inuit Art in the 1970's: A Travelling Exhibition/L'Art inuit actuel, 1970-79: exposition itinérante* (1979) #4287
  - *Roger Savage* (1980) #7135
  - *The Paintings of Frederick Nicholas Loveroff/Les peintures de Frederick Nicholas*

Loveroff (1981) #6331
- *William Perehudoff: Ten Years, 1970-1980/William Perehudoff: une décennie, 1970-1980* (1983) #6838
California
- bungalows, influence on British Columbia bungalows #8685
- performance art #2073
Calixa-Lavallée (Qué)
- architecture #7877
Callière, Louis-Hector de, Fr governor general of Canada, 1698-1703
- residence, château de Callière #8565
calligraphy, Chinese
- influence on Chuck Wing Yip #7625
- influence on David Bolduc #4776
- influence on Dennis Eugene Norman Burton #4961 4962
- influence on Emily Carr #5046
- influence on Jack Marlowe Wise #7600 7601 7602
- influence on Raymonde Godin #5623
- influence on Toni Onley #6741
calligraphy, Japanese
- influence on Gaston-Pierre Petit #6843 6844 6845
- influence on Takao Tanabe #7320
Calnen, Robert F., Can photographer, ca. 1946-
- portfolio of photographs #995
Calonne, abbé de, Fr priest and collector in Canada, 1742-1822
- collection, paintings #1323
calvaries
- see also Stations of the Cross
calvaries, Canadian
- Oka (Qué), Calvary at Oka #1355 1356 8853
- Québec #1292 1320 1569 1609
- Varennes (Qué) #1585
Calzetta, Tony, Can artist, 1945-
- compared with Paul Fournier #670
Cambridge (England), Cambridge University. Museum of Archaeology and Ethnology
- carvings, Dorset #4358
Cambridge (England), Cambridge University. Senate House
- statue of George II #725
Cambridge (Mass), Harvard University
- Charney, Melvin, on works exhibited (1977) #5091
Cambridge (Mass), Harvard University. Peabody Museum
- artifacts, Siouan Indians, 19th c. #3649
- carvings and prints, Inuit, Hudson Bay region #4191
- hats, Nootka Indians #3779
Cambridge (Mass), Massachusetts Institute of Technology. Hayden Gallery
- exhibitions
  - *Seven Montreal Artists* (1968) #1263
Cambridge (Ont), Cambridge Public Art Gallery
- exhibitions
  - *Ed Bartram: 10 Years* (1980) #4618

Camera Canada, Can periodical #3314
– criticism of #1016
camera lucida
– use in Canadian painting and
   photography, 19th c. #268
– use in portraits, Maritimes, 19th c. #1171
– use of, James Pattison Cockburn #5125
camera obscura
– use in Canadian painting and
   photography, 19th c. #268
cameras
– Deville, Edouard Gaston Daniel, survey
   camera #989 1874 1875
Cameron, Alex, Can artist, 1947- #1807
– exhibitions, group
   – (1981) #722
– exhibitions (reviews) #639
Cameron, Alexander W., Can businessman,
   fl. 1906-1909
– and Edmonton (Alta) theatres (1906) #9143
Cameron, Donald, arts administrator, 1901-
– as director, Banff School of Fine Arts
   (Banff, Alta) #3000
Cameron, Duncan, Can photographer, 1930-
– exhibitions, group
   – (1970) #1675
Cameron, Eric, Can artist, 1935-
– exhibitions, group
   – (1977) #631
   – (1978) #667
– exhibitions (reviews) #656
– on video art #580 616 651
Cameron, Walter Graham, Can sculptor,
   blacksmith, 1894- #4992
Cameron & Ralston, Can architectural firm
– Hamilton (Ont), Hamilton Mausoleum
   #8900
Camillis, Laurie de, Can artist, 1951-
– exhibitions, group
   – (1979) #2075
– exhibitions (reviews) #2072
Camp, Garry, Can furniture-maker, fl. 1818
   #2571
Campbell, Colin, Can artist, 1942-
– exhibitions, group
   – (1977) #631
   – (1980) #690 705
– *Peripheral Blur* #718
– video art #605 630 4993
Campbell, Daniel Edwin (Ted), Can artist,
   1904- #1173 1184
– influence on Saint John (NB) art #1188
– studio #4994
Campbell, John, Can weaver, fl. 1860s #2723
Campbell, Keith Thomas, Can ceramicist,
   1947- #2395
Campbell, Paul, Can photographer, 1949-
– exhibitions, group
   – (1980) #1832
– exhibitions (reviews) #1067
Campbell, Ted
– *see* Campbell, Daniel Edwin (Ted)
Campbell, William, Can builder, fl.
   1840s-1870s
– St. John's (Nfld), house #8542
Campbell, William, Can Chief Justice,
   1758-1834

– residence, Toronto (Ont) #8661
Campbell-Smith, Struan, Can photographer,
   fl. 1979 #995
Campbellton (NB), galerie
   Restigouche/Restigouche Gallery
– exhibitions
   – *Canadians: A National Photography Show*
      about People/Canadiens: exposition
      nationale de photographie ayant les gens
      comme thème (1978) #1035
   – *Diversité: Diane Gougeon, Raymond Lavoie,*
      Alex Magrini, Robert Saucier (1980) #685
   – *George Rackus: Anodized Aluminum Works*
      & Prints (1973) #6953
   – *Miller Brittain - Painter* (1981) #4922
   – *Roger Savage* (1980) #7135
   – *The Beaverbrook Art Gallery Presents Nine*
      New Brunswick Artists/La Galerie d'art
      Beaverbrook présente neuf artistes du
      Nouveau-Brunswick (1973) #1182
Campbellton (NB), Restigouche Gallery
– *see* Campbellton (NB), galerie
   Restigouche/Restigouche Gallery
Campbellton (NB), Restigouche Senior High
School
– exhibitions
   – *Colville, Pratt, Forrestall* (1974) #1129
Campeau, Michel, Can photographer, 1948-
   #997
– interview, on Groupe d'action
   photographique #1494
– photographic views, Disraeli (Qué), (1972)
   #1513
– portfolio of photographs #997 999
Campeau Corporation (Calgary, Alta)
– restoration of the McKay farm house for
   sales office #8133
Campus, Peter, Amer artist, 1937-
– video art #651
Canada
– in British sculpture (1880s) #725
– maps
   – 17th-18th cs. #875
   – 17th c. #841
– photographic views
   – Jaycocks, T.G. #5950
   – Notman, William #6725
– political cartoons
   – 19th c.-1970s #957
   – Canadian East-West discord (1874-1946)
      #958
   – Union of 1841 #942
– views
   – 16th-19th cs., by European artists #255
      256 260
   – 17th-19th cs. #231
   – 18th-19th cs. #12 222 223 239 244 246
      247 812 828 839 1220 1222 1224 1225
      1366 3230
   – 18th c. #269 270
   – 18th c.-1910s #3130 3131 3143 3204
   – 18th c.-1940s #26
   – 19th c. #224 241 242 266 840 1326 1337
      2362
   – 19th c.-1970s #132
   – 20th c. #41

– (1750-1850) #279
– (1890s) #6436
– (1890s), State dinner service of Canada
   #2333
– (1910s) #1710
– (1950s) #403
– Bartlett, William Henry #4615 4616
– Davies, Thomas #5270 5271
– folk art #965 966
– Group of Seven #1744 1774
– Heriot, George #5785
– Hind, William George Richardson #5807
   5808 5809
– Hopkins, Frances Ann Beechy #5835
– Julien, Henri #5983
– Krieghoff, Cornelius #6091 6101
– Martin, Henry Byam #6426
– Martin, Thomas Mower #6438
– Minton dessert service #2289
– Morrice, James Wilson #6622
– Portneuf Pottery #2285
– pottery, 19th c. #2288 2294 2309
– Roper, Edward #7077
– Russell, Edward John #7111
– Simcoe, Elizabeth Posthuma Gwillim
   #7210
– Staffordshire ware #2099 2282
– Volpi, Charles de, collection #3248
– Warre, Henry James #7522
– White, George Harlow #7551
Canada. Brief Concerning the Cultural
   Aspects of Canadian Reconstruction
   (1944)
– reactions #3250
– report on #3251
Canada. Canadian Broadcasting Corporation
   (CBC)
– and Louis de Niverville #6704 6706
– and the Canadian public #447
– television graphics
   – (1950s) #866 869
   – (1950s-1970s) #909
   – (1970s) #899
Canada. Canadian Film Institute
– McLaren, Norman, films #6498
Canada. Canadian Inventory of Historic
   Building #7707 7708 7716 7771
– computerized survey #159
Canada. Canadian Women's Army Corps
– and Molly Lamb Bobak #4761 4766
Canada. Central Mortgage and Housing
   Corporation
– (1940s) #8507
– Demonstration Program (1970s) #7728
– housing designs (1950s) #8509
– public housing (1960s) #8518
– Roussil, Robert, habitation sculpture #7096
– Smyth Road Development Competition
   (1960) #8040
Canada. Defence Research Board
– military building research (1950s) #8414
Canada. Department of External Affairs
– Murray, Robert Gray, *Haida* #6672
Canada. Department of Indian Affairs and
   Northern Development
– collection, Inuit art #4246

- Inuit sculpture exhibitions for visually handicapped #4430
Canada. Department of National Defence
- collection, photographs #1024
- military architecture (1950s) #8414
Canada. Department of Northern Affairs
- Arctic housing
  - (1950s) #8184
  - (1960s) #8732
Canada. Department of Public Works
- (1840-1960s) #8976 8977
- and Art Bank (1970s) #3277
- and National Gallery of Canada (Ottawa, Ont) competition (1975-1977) #9126
- architecture
  - (1950s) #8227 8971
  - (1954-1959) #7681
  - (1970s) #7728
  - Second Empire #7741 7742
- Fine Art Program (1970s) #9049
- Fort Battleford (Battleford, Sask) #8484
- Fuller, Thomas, as chief architect #8366 9055
- Fuller, Thomas William, as chief architect #8367 8368
- report to Royal Architectural Institute of Canada (1966) #8309
Canada. Department of Transport
- air terminal buildings
  - (1950s) #9514
  - (1960s) #9517
Canada. Federal Cultural Policy Review Committee (Applebaum-Hébert Commission)
- Canadian Conference of the Arts brief
  - (1980) #3294 3295
  - (1981) #3297 3298
- Canadian women artists brief (1980) #719
- on photography #1068
Canada. Federal District Commission
- and National Capital Region (Ottawa, Ont) #8037
Canada. Legislative Council of Canada
- Krieghoff, Cornelius, petition to paint Canadian views (1856) #6091
Canada. Ministry of Culture and Recreation
- support of art (1950s-1970s) #3278
Canada. National Capital Commission
- (1960s) #7683
- and National Capital Region (Ottawa, Ont) #8039 8045
Canada. National Design Council
- (1961-1973) #2624
- Concrete Awards Program
  - (1971) #7706
Canada, National Film Board of Canada #626
- and Jean-Philippe Dallaire #5238 5239
- and Norman McLaren #6492 6493 6498
- and Royal Commission on National Development in the Arts, Letters and Sciences (Massey Report) #3254 3255 3261
- film graphics (1970s) #899
- Minden, Robert, photographs #6570
- publications, Image series (1967-1971) #990
- support of Canadian photography (1970s) #1038

Canada. National Industrial Design Committee
- (1940s) #2604
- (1948-1953) #2609
- (1951) #2606
Canada. National Industrial Design Council
- (1944), recommendation for #2600
- (1950s) #2605 2609
- awards, criticism of
  - (1951) #2608
  - (1958) #2610
- conference on furniture design (1954) #2468
- report on furniture-making (1950) #2467
Canada. National Museums Corporation
- museum design specifications #9129
Canada. National Parks Service
- recreation buildings #9081
Canada. National Research Council
- (1916-1961), and the Canadian public #447
- building research (1960s) #7683
Canada. National Research Council. Division of Building Research #7715
Canada. Parks Canada
- habitation reconstruction policy #7758
Canada. Royal Canadian Air Force
- and Charles Goldhamer #1091
- military architecture (1950
  - unemployment subjects, Atlantic provinces (1970s) #8414
- war artists, World War II #4761
Canada. Royal Canadian Navy
- and Rowley Walter Murphy #6665
- war artists, World War II #4761
Canada. Royal Commission on National Development in the Arts, Letters and Sciences (Massey Report) #3254 3255
- and Alberta Society of Artists #1944
- and Canada Council (1951-1960s) #3264
- and Conference of Canadian Artists (1941) #390
- and Couchiching Conference of the Canadian Institute on Public Affairs (1976) #619
- and Exhibition of Contemporary Canadian Arts (1950) #387
- and Québec artists #1401
- and Vincent Massey #3258
- criticism of #398
- extracts #3256
- influence on Canadian culture (1950s-1970s) #3278 3290
- Milne, David Brown, on #6550
- on architecture #7670 7673
- on art market #3260
- on building of performing arts centres #9086
- on Canadian painting (1920-1950) #391
- on Québec art (1925-1950) #1405
- press reaction #3257
- summary of recommendations #3261
Canada. Société Radio-Canada
- collection, Canadian art #3273
Canada Clock Company, clockmaking firm (Whitby and Hamilton, Ont) #2927
Canada Council

- "Directors' Choice" project (1962-1967) #481
- 1974 proposal on business support for the arts by 1980 #3271
- (1950s-1960s) #3264
- (1960s) #529
- (1970s) #586 693 3278 3293
- and Royal Commission on National Development in the Arts, Letters and Sciences (Massey Report) #3254 3255 3261
- collection, Canadian art #90 3266
- funding policy (1978) #3287
- support of photography (1970s) #1038
- Twenty Plus Five green paper (1977) #3285
Canada Crafts, Can periodical #2126
Canada Foundation
- (1946-1959) #3262
Canada Glass Works, glass manufacturer (Saint-Jean, Qué) #2420
Canada Glass Works, glass manufacturer (Vaudreuil, Qué) #2418
Canada Publishing Co., publishing firm (Toronto, Ont)
- Christmas greeting cards #842
Canada Stained Glass Works, glass manufacturer (Toronto, Ont)
- (1850s-1960s) #2449
Canada Steamship Lines
- Coverdale, William H., Collection of Historical Canadiana #12 3230
Canadian Antiques and Art Review, Can periodical #141
Canadian Antiques Collector, Can periodical #74
Canadian Architect, Can periodical #7672
- as organizer, community art gallery competition (1957) #9082
- awards
  - (1968) #8190
  - (1969) #8191
  - (1970) #8192
  - (1971) #8193
  - (1972) #8194
  - (1973) #8195
  - (1974) #8196
  - (1975) #8197
  - (1976) #8198
  - (1977) #8199
  - (1978) #8200
  - (1979) #8201 8202
  - (1980) #8203
  - (1981) #8204
- surveys of architects
  - (1958) #8302
  - (1972) #8314 8316
  - (1974-1976) #8320
  - (1976) #8321
Canadian Architect & Builder, Can periodical #7639
Canadian Architect Yearbook, Can periodical #7672
Canadian Architectural Students' Association #8250
Canadian Arctic Cooperative
- (1977-1980) #4269
Canadian Arctic Producers

– (1977-1980) #4269
– and Inuit art #4222 4231 4291
Canadian Art, Can periodical #25 349
Canadian Art Club (Toronto, Ont) #14 28
– (1907-1915) #193
– and James Wilson Morrice #6634
– and Laura Adeline Muntz Lyall #6339
– exhibitions (reviews)
  – (1909) #194
  – (1913) #204
  – (1916) #211
– influence on Canadian art (1907-1910) #214
Canadian Art Glass Limited, stained glass
  firm (Calgary, Alta) #2455
Canadian Art Review
– see RACAR (Revue d'art
  canadienne/Canadian Art Review)
Canadian Artists' Representation/Front des
  artistes canadiens (CAR/FAC)
– (1970s) #632 1804 3278
– and Jack Chambers #563 5081
– and Michel Lambeth #6159
– and Niagara Artists' Co-operative #834
– influence on public attitudes (1970s) #6748
– membership policies (1978) #3287
– periodical, *CAR/FAC News* #625
Canadian Arts Council
– founding (1945) #379
Canadian Association of Photographers and
  Illustrators in Communications
– (1981), brief, Federal Cultural Policy
  Review Committee #1068
Canadian Association of University
  Teachers (CAUT)
– and Ontario College of Art (1968) #2997
Canadian Bank of Commerce
– architecture
  – (1920s) #9172
  – (1930s) #9189
  – Horsburgh, V.D. #9169
– prefabricated buildings, western Canada,
  early 20th c. #8082
Canadian Broadcasting Corporation
– see Canada. Canadian Broadcasting
  Corporation (CBC)
Canadian Collector, Can periodical #74
Canadian Conference of the Arts
– (1960s) #447
– (1961) #444
– (1970s) #3270
– brief, Federal Cultural Policy Review
  Committee
  – (1980) #3294 3295
  – (1981) #3297 3298
– periodicals
  – *Arts Bulletin* #551
  – *Communiqué* #542
Canadian Correspondent, Can newspaper
– letters on Society of Artists and Amateurs
  of Toronto exhibition (1834) #1729
Canadian Council of the Environmental Arts
– (1965) #2105
Canadian Crafts Council
– periodical, *The Craftsman/L'Artisan* #2113
  2133
Canadian Craftsmen's

Association/Association des artisans du
  Canada
– periodical, *The Craftsman/L'Artisan* #2113
Canadian Creative Music Collective (CCMC)
– exhibitions
  – (1980) #690
Canadian Design/Design canadien, Can
  periodical #2625
Canadian Design Index-NIDC
– (1950-1957) #2605
– (1953-1954) #3033
– and National Gallery of Canada (Ottawa,
  Ont) #2604 2606
Canadian Dimension, Can periodical
– illustrations, Kelly Clark #5109
Canadian Embroiderer's Guild (London,
  Ont)
– exhibitions
  – (1981) #2793
Canadian Film Institute
– see Canada. Canadian Film Institute
Canadian Forum, Can periodical
– and Barker Fairley #5403 5404 5405
– and Thoreau MacDonald #6381 6383
– illustrations (1920-1951) #930
– on Canadian art (1920s-1940s) #3301
– on Group of Seven #1739 1763
Canadian Group of Painters
– (1930s) #336 502 589 592 1768 1789
– (1933-1970) #498
– (1940s) #382
– exhibitions
  – (1939) #346
– exhibitions (reviews)
  – (1936) #331
  – (1940) #348
  – (1942) #356
  – (1944) #365
  – (1962) #456
Canadian Guild of Crafts
– forerunner, Canadian Handicrafts Guild
  #2118
– periodical, *Craft Dimensions Artisanales*
  #2116
Canadian Guild of Crafts (Ontario)
– and Visual Arts Ontario #1806
Canadian Guild of Crafts (Québec)/Guilde
  canadienne des métiers d'art (Québec)
– Inuit art #4292 4293
Canadian Guild of Potters
– exhibitions (1955-1971) #2379
– exhibitions (reviews)
  – (1957) #2380
Canadian Handicrafts Guild
– (1894-1929) #2090
– (1920s) #2089
– (1929-1967) #2118
– (1930s) #2091
– (1950s) #7900
– (1960s) #2103
– exhibitions (reviews)
  – (1957) #2380
– Inuit art #4397
Canadian Heritage, Can periodical #7764
Canadian Heritage of Quebec
– and conservation of architecture #7871

Canadian Housing Design Council
– awards
  – (1957-) #8741
  – (1972) #8744
  – (1974) #8746
  – (1979) #8747
Canadian Illustrated News, Can periodical
  #5990
– illustrations
  – Julien, Henri #5992
  – Kroupa, Bohuslar #6104
  – Russell, Edward John #7110
  – Taylor, George Thomas #7334
– photographs #1006
Canadian Industrial Photography, Can
  periodical #995
Canadian Inventory of Historic Building
– see Canada. Canadian Inventory of
  Historic Building
Canadian Journal, Can periodical
– and Paul Kane #6003
Canadian Journal of Photography, Can
  periodical #974
Canadian Magazine, Can periodical
– illustrations
  – Brigden, Fred #4913
  – Julien, Henri #5987
Canadian Museums Association
– (1960s) #3045
– (1970s) #3054
– and Harry Orr McCurry #3036
– periodical, *Canadian Museums Association.
  Gazette* #3042
Canadian National Railways
– and Allan Robb Fleming #5457
– château style railway hotels #9290 9291
– Montréal (Qué), Queen Elizabeth Hotel
  #8228 9286
– railroad stations #9542 9545
  – Montréal (Qué), Central Station #9535
Canadian Nature Federation
– exhibitions
  – (1973-) #549
Canadian Northern Railway
– railroad stations #9542 9545
  – Manitoba #9543
Canadian Pacific Railway
– and Alfred Crocker Leighton #6225
– and Charles George Horetzky #1014 1015
  5837 5838
– and Edward Roper #7077
– and Frederic Marlett Bell-Smith #4668
– and Harry Pollard #6899
– and John A. Hammond #5698
– and John Colin Forbes #5459
– and Nick Morant #6605
– and Richard H. Trueman #7437
– architecture
  – Victoria (BC) #8175
    – Crystal Gardens #9146
– architecture and art #3281
– château style railway hotels #9290 9291
– railroad stations #9538 9539 9545
  – Manitoba #9543
  – Saskatchewan #9544
  – Vancouver (BC) #9546

- survey photographs (1870s) #1876
Canadian Photo Journal, Can periodical #1032
Canadian Photographer, Can periodical #987
Canadian Photographic Journal, Can periodical #976
Canadian Photography, Can periodical #995
Canadian Professional Indian Artists Association
- and Alex Simeon Janvier #5936
Canadian Professional Photography, Can periodical #995
Canadian Review of Music and Art, Can periodical #357
Canadian Rock Art Research Associates
- conference, Victoria (BC), (1977) #3481
Canadian Shield
- views, 18th-20th cs. #156
Canadian Small House Competition
- (1946) #8740
Canadian Society for Creative Leathercraft
- (1970s) #2936
Canadian Society of Graphic Art
- (1904-1976) #801
- (1931), yearbook #803
- and Society of Canadian Painter-Etchers and Engravers #3
- and Visual Arts Ontario #1806
- as forerunner of Print and Drawing Council of Canada #835
- exhibitions
  - (1939) #346
  - (1971) #824
- exhibitions (reviews)
  - (1947) #809
Canadian Society of Painters in Water Colour
- (1925-) #6
- (1926-1936) #332
- and Visual Arts Ontario #1806
- exhibitions
  - (1939) #346
  - (1951) #394
  - (1976) #127
- works, to encourage Royal Canadian Air Force amateur artists (1940s) #1091
Canadian West
- architecture #8083
- art
  - (1940s) #381
  - late 18th-early 20th cs. #1859
- folk painting, 20th c. #1846
- painting
  - (1933-1970) #498
  - (1970s) #588
- periodical illustrations (1857-1900) #931
- photographic views
  - (1850s-1890s) #1865
  - (1858-1900) #1014 1015
  - (1870s) #1876
  - (1880s-1890s) #1874
  - Barnes, Elliott Chappel #4610
  - Boorne and May #1950 4797
  - Curtis, Edward Sheriff #3480
  - Hime, Humphrey Lloyd #5801
- views
  - 19th c.-1970s #1863

- 19th-early 20th cs. #1999
- (1804-1930) #5783
- Julien, Henri #5990
- Kane, Paul #6007 6009 6011 6014 6016 6018
- Kane, Paul, and George Catlin #1845
- late 19th c. #271 272
- McCarthy, Doris Jean #6461
- McLean, Terry #6502
- Nevitt, Richard Barrington #6687 6688
- Phillips, Walter Joseph #6857
Canadian Women's Army Corps
- *see* Canada. Canadian Women's Army Corps
Canadiana Village (Rawdon, Qué)
- architecture #7876
Canadians in Africa
- Morrice, James Wilson #6617 6623 6626 6629
- Phillips, Walter Joseph #6857 6860
Canadians in Asia
- Currelly, Charles Trick #3139
- Hammond, John A. #5700
- Mah, Tom #6409
- Wolfe, Robert #7606
Canadians in Belgium
- Brault, Maurice #4906
- Jackson, A.Y. #5924
Canadians in Brazil
- (1950s) #413 414
- Rio de Janeiro
  - Pellan, Alfred #6798
  - Tonnancour, Jacques Godefroy de #7382
Canadians in China
- McLaren, Norman #6492
- Onley, Toni #6738
Canadians in England
- Fowler, Daniel #5491
Canadians in Europe
- 19th c. #197
- 19th c.-1920s #14
- (1930s) #13
- Archambault, Louis #408
- Arthur, Paul #859
- Barnsley, James Macdonald #4612
- Berczy, William von Moll #4699
- Bice, Clare #408
- Bourassa, Napoléon #4868 4875
- Broomfield, Adolphus George #4932
- Bruni, Umberto #4946
- Brymner, William #4948
- Carlyle, Florence #207 5000
- Carr, Emily #5023
- Cormier, Ernest #8345
- Cullen, Maurice Galbraith #5220
- Currelly, Charles Trick #3139
- Dumouchel, Albert #5325
- Dyonnet, Edmond #5347 5349
- Eaton, Wyatt #5356
- Forster, John Wycliffe #5469
- Fowler, Daniel #5491
- Gagen, Robert Ford #5530
- Gagnon, Clarence Alphonse #5546 5547
- Glass, Alan Frank #5614
- Grier, Edmund Wyly #5660
- Hamel, Théophile #5690

- Hamilton, Mary Riter #5694 5695
- Hammond, John A. #5700
- Harris, Robert #5737
- Harrison, Allan #5746
- Humphrey, Jack Weldon #5865
- Kane, Paul #6003 6005 6007 6010
- Kerr, Estelle Muriel #207
- Knowles, Elizabeth Annie McGillivray #207
- Krieghoff, Cornelius #6093
- La Palme, Robert #408
- Leduc, Ozias #6209
- Lemieux, Jean-Paul #6227 6230
- LeMoine, Edmond #6243
- Lismer, Arthur #6301
- Livernois, Jules-Benoît #6308
- Lyall, Laura Adeline Muntz #207 6339
- Lyman, John Goodwin #6347
- Macdonald, Jock #6376
- MacLaughlan, Donald Shaw #6394
- McCulloch, James Frederic #6463
- McNicoll, Helen Galloway #6507
- Mercier, Monique #6512
- Molinari, Guido #6588
- Morrice, James Wilson #6617 6619 6628
- Morris, Jerrold #6639
- Mulcaster, Wynona Croft #6660
- Palchinski, Sylvia Scott #6753
- Parizeau, Marcel #8397
- Peel, Paul #6792
- Pflug, Christiane Sybille #6849
- Pilot, Robert Wakeham #6869
- Plaskett, Joe #6889
- Reid, Leslie Mary Margaret #6980
- Reid, Mary Hiester #207
- Roberts, Goodridge #408
- Ryerson, Adolphus Egerton #3150 3155
- Sandham, J.Henry #7121
- Shadbolt, Jack Leonard #7180
- Smith, William St. Thomas #7236
- Suzor-Coté, Marc-Aurèle de Foy #7295 7297 7298 7300
- Tanobe, Miyuki #7324 7325
- Wheeler, Orson Shorey #7549
- Wrinch, Mary Evelyn #207
Canadians in France
- (1880s), and Jean-Joseph Benjamin-Constant #243
- (1950s) #413 414
- Allward, Walter Seymour #4519
- Amyot, Laurent #1244
- Arsenault, Réal #4556
- Ayotte, Léo #4575
- Baillairgé, François #1244
- Beaucourt, François Malepart de #269 270 1244
- Bergeron, André #4703
- Bruce, William Blair #4941
- Carr, Emily #5027 5028 5044
- Dallaire, Jean-Philippe #5241 5244 5246 5247
- Daoust, Sylvia Marie Emilienne #5257
- Duguay, Rodolphe #5317
- Eaton, Wyatt #5355 5357
- Ferron, Marcelle #5423
- Hamilton, Mary Riter #5693

– Harris, Alfred Peter #5735
– Holgate, Edwin Headley #5818 5819
– Jackson, A.Y. #5924
– Lamarche, Ulric #6155
– Leduc, Ozias #6200
– Lemieux, Jean-Paul #6237
– Lyall, Laura Adeline Muntz #6337 6338
– Macdonald, Jock #6376
– Martigues
  – Brymner, William #4950
– Morisset, Gérard #3126
– Morrice, James Wilson #6626
– Muhlstock, Louis #6655
– Paris #6977
  – (1867-1914) #274
  – (1890-1920) #115
  – (1890s) #180
  – (1910s), women artists #206
  – (1940s) #384
  – (1940s-1960s), Québec printmakers #1641
  – Alleyn, George Edmund #426 1434 4510
  – Armington, Caroline Helena #4548 4549
    4550
  – Armington, Franklin Milton #4548 4550
  – Arsenault, Réal #1434
  – Baillairgé, François #4587 4588 4591 4592
  – Baril, Marcel #4608
  – Barnsley, James Macdonald #227 4612
  – Beaugrand, Gilles #4650
  – Beaulieu, Paul-Vanier #4651 4652
  – Bell-Smith, Frederic Marlett #4666
  – Bellefleur, Léon #1434
  – Benoît, Jean #426
  – Bergeron, Suzanne #426
  – Biéler, André Charles #4725
  – Boisseau, Alfred #4768
  – Borduas, Paul-Emile #426 4802 4810
    4820 4824 4829 4830 4839 4843 4844
    4846 4849
  – Boudreau, Pierre #426
  – Brymner, William #227 4953
  – Carlyle, Florence #4999 5000
  – Caron, Roger #5005
  – Carr, Emily #5024 5045
  – Chabert, Joseph #3005
  – Champeau, André #426
  – Christin, Léopold #5105
  – Coburn, Frederick Simpson #5124
  – Cullen, Maurice Galbraith #227 5217
    5219 5221
  – Duguay, Rodolphe #5313 5316 5320
  – Duquet, Georges-Henri #5343
  – Edson, Aaron Allan #5362
  – Fauteux-Massé, Henriette #5415
  – Ferron, Marcelle #426 1434 5421
  – Forster, John Wycliffe Lowes #5468
  – Franchère, Joseph-Charles #5497
  – Freiman, Lillian #5517
  – Gagnon, Clarence Alphonse #5544 5546
    5547 5549
  – Giguère, Denise #5598
  – Giguère, Roland #5598
  – Gilson, Jacqueline Marie-Charlotte #5606
  – Glass, Alan Frank #426
  – Godin, Raymonde #426 5622
  – Hamel, Théophile #1348

– Harris, Robert #5739
– Hébert, Louis-Philippe #5768
– Hill, George William #192 5799
– Horvat, Miljenko #5842
– Humphrey, Jack Weldon #5870
– Huot, Charles Edouard #5876 5879 5883
– Kerr, Estelle Muriel #206
– Laliberté, Madeleine #6153
– Leduc, Fernand #1434
– Leduc, Ozias #6206
– Legros, Enid Sharon #6223
– Lotbinière, Pierre-Gustave Joly de #6326
– Lyman, John Goodwin #6344
– Maltais, Marcelle #1434 6412
– Marchand, Joseph-Omer #7923
– McEwen, Jean Albert #6468
– Morrice, James Wilson #192 6617 6620
  6623 6627 6630 6632
– Muhlstock, Louis #6657 6658
– Newton, Lilias Torrance #6692 6693
– Nichols, Jack #426
– Parent, Mimi #426
– Parizeau, Marcel #8397
– Peel, Paul #6791
– Pellan, Alfred #1416 6801 6803 6808
  6809 6811 6812 6818 6819 6821 6824
  6825
– Pemberton, Sophia Theresa #6828
– Perron, Germain #1434
– Pflug, Christiane Sybille #6850
– Plamondon, Antoine-Sébastien #1348
  6884
– Plaskett, Joe #6890 6892 6893 6894 6895
– Rapin, François-Xavier Aldéric #6961
– Reid, George Agnew #6979
– Richard, René-Jean #6998
– Riopelle, Jean-Paul #7016 7018 7026 7029
– Robinson, Albert Henry #7057
– Russell, John Wentworth #7109
– Scovil, James Noel #7167
– Sole, Stelio #7265
– Steinhouse, Tobie Thelma #7278
– Suzor-Coté, Marc-Aurèle de Foy #227
  7296
– Tully, Sydney Strickland #7438
– Vanier, Bernard #426
– Walker, Horatio #227
– Wallis, Katherine Elizabeth #7511 7512
– Watson, Homer Ransford #227
– Pépin, Arthur #6831
– Plamondon, Antoine #1244
– Provence
  – Cardinal, Marcel #4997
  – Reid, Leslie Mary Margaret #6981
– Roy, Mario #7099
– Rulofson, William Herman #7107
– Saint-Jean, Michel #1562
– Suzor-Coté, Marc-Aurèle de Foy #7302
– Tourette-sur-Loup
  – Roussil, Robert #7091 7098
– Tousignant, Claude #7400
– Vanier, Bernard #7460
– Vence
  – Archambault, Louis #4539
Canadians in Germany
– Coburn, Frederick Simpson #5124

– Dresden
  – Wallis, Katherine Elizabeth #7512
– Harris, Lawren Stewart #5734
– Hümme, Joseph Julius #5863
– Munich
  – Humphrey, Jack Weldon #5870
Canadians in Ghana
– Semak, Michael William #990
Canadians in Great Britain
– (1950s) #413 414
– Bell-Smith, Frederic Marlett #4668
– Beveridge, Eleanor #1199
– Bobak, Bruno Joseph #4762
– Bobak, Molly Lamb #4762
– Bourdeau, Robert Charles John #4881
– Carr, Emily #5011 5024
– Cooke, Edwy Francis #5171
– Daglish, Peter William #5235
– Duguay, Rodolphe #5313
– Dyonnet, Edmond #5347 5349
– Eaton, Wyatt #5355
– Eyre, Ivan Kenneth #5391
– Field, Robert #5429 5433
– Forbes, John Colin #5459
– Fraser, John Arthur #5511
– Karsh, Yousuf #6022
– Kerr, Illingworth Holey #6049
– Kilpin, Legh Mulhall #6052
– Kurelek, William #6110
– Lismer, Arthur #6301
– London
  – Andrews, Stephen #4527
  – Carr, Emily #5018 5022 5045
  – Coburn, Frederick Simpson #5124
  – Cruikshank, William #5212
  – Pemberton, Sophia Theresa #6828
  – Tully, Sydney Strickland #7438
  – Verner, Frederick Arthur #7484
  – Wallis, Katherine Elizabeth #7512
  – Watson, Homer Ransford #7534
  – Wrinch, Mary Evelyn #7618
– McCulloch, James Frederic #6463
– Morris, Jerrold #6639
– Onley, Toni #6741
– Palchinski, Sylvia Scott #6753
– Phillips, Walter Joseph #6857 6860
– Rulofson, William Herman #7107
– Sandham, J.Henry #7120 7121
– Wallis, Katherine Elizabeth #7511
– Watson, Homer Ransford #7533
Canadians in Greece
– Maltais, Marcelle #6412
Canadians in Guyana
– Morris, Jerrold #6639
Canadians in India
– Bayefsky, Aba #4631
– Chambers, Jack #5077
– Shadbolt, Jack #7192
Canadians in Israel
– Odjig, Daphne #6731
Canadians in Italy
– Allain, Marie-Hélène #4508
– Bourassa, Napoléon #4863
– Farlardeau, Antoine-Sébastien #5407
– Florence
  – Armstrong, William Walton #4553

– Guité, Suzanne #5667
– Lui, Andrew #6332
– Rhéaume, Jeanne Leblanc #6994
– Hamel, Théophile #1348
– Kane, Paul #6011
– Kiyooka, Harry Mitsuo #6058
– Kleyn, Robert #6063
– Morrice, James Wilson #6617 6623 6632
– Peterson, Margaret #6839
– Sole, Stelio #7265
– Sullivan, Françoise #7282
– Venice
  – Binning, B.C. #4732
Canadians in Jamaica
– Field, Robert #5429 5432
Canadians in Japan
– Cassidy, Eugene Haanel #5054
– Knudsen, Chris #6070
– Kyoto
  – Beauchemin, Micheline #4644
– Ngan, Wayne G. #6695
– Onley, Toni #6738
– Petit, Gaston-Pierre #6843 6844 6845
Canadians in Mexico
– (1950s) #413 414
– Brooks, Leonard #4931
– Cosgrove, Stanley Morel #5178 5180 5181
  5184
– Glass, Alan Frank #5614
– Lewis, Stanley #6278
– Mulcaster, Wynona Croft #6660
– Onley, Toni #6740 6741
– Reppen, Jack #6990
– Svarre, Grace #7303
– Wilson, Ronald York #4931 7595
Canadians in Middle East
– Currelly, Charles Trick #3139
Canadians in Near East
– Kane, Paul #6005
– Lotbinière, Pierre-Gustave Joly de #6326
Canadians in Netherlands
– Coburn, Frederick Simpson #5124
– Hammond, John A. #5699
– Jackson, A.Y. #5924
Canadians in Norway
– Brault, Maurice #4906
Canadians in Scandinavia
– Brassard, Thérèse Tanguay #4905
Canadians in Scotland
– MacKenzie, Robert #6393
Canadians in South America
– Bruni, Umberto #4946
– Harrison, Allan #5746
Canadians in Spain
– Ariss, Herb #473
– Ariss, Margot Phillips #473
– Bonet, Jordi #4784
– Chambers, Jack #473 5070 5071 5073
– Coughtry, John Graham #473
– Gould, John Howard #473
– Hedrick, Robert Burns #473
– Lafleur, Pierre #6132
– Lambart, Evelynn #6498
– McLaren, Norman #6498
– O'Brien, Paddy Gunn #473
– Rayner, Gordon #473

– Saltmarche, Kenneth Charles #473
– Urquhart, Tony #473
Canadians in Sweden
– Cartier, Jean Bernard #5052
– Janvier, Alex Simeon #5938
– Stacey, Harold #7273
– Stockholm
  – Bruce, William Blair #4941
Canadians in Switzerland
– Arthur, Paul #865
– Bergeron, André #4703
Canadians in Taiwan
– Onley, Toni #6738
Canadians in Tunisia
– Tunis
  – Pflug, Christiane Sybille #6850
Canadians in USA
– (1759-1970s) #126
– (1850s), Montréal (Qué) architects #7920
– (1890s), architects #7640
– (1910s), graphic artists #916
– (1940s-1960s) #485
– Boisseau, Alfred #4768
– Boston (Mass)
  – Harris, Lawren Phillips #5713
  – Harris, Robert #5737
  – Karsh, Yousuf #6026
  – Miles, John Christopher #6533
  – Sandham, J.Henry #7121
  – Wilson, William F. #7593
– California
  – Levine, Marilyn Ann #6274
  – Rulofson, William Herman #7107
  – Zuck, Tim #7635
– Carlyle, Florence #5000
– Carr, Emily #5023
– Cassidy, Eugene Haanel #5054
– Christin, Léopold #5105
– Cincinnati (Ohio)
  – Meanwell, Jack #646
– Colorado
  – Proctor, Alexander Phimister #6944
– Cooke, Edwy Francis #5171
– Cranbrook (Mich)
  – Betteridge, Lois Etherington #4718
  – Pachter, Charles #6748
– Day, Mabel Killam #5273
– Duncanson, Robert Stuart #241 242
– Eaton, Wyatt #5355
– Field, Robert #5429 5432 5433
– Fraser, John Arthur #5511
– Garnier, Hubert #5556
– Gordon, Hortense Mattice #1850
– Hammond, John A. #5700
– Harrison, Allan #5746
– Humphrey, Jack Weldon #5865 5870
– Jarvis, Donald Alvin #1850
– Kane, Paul #6005
– Kennedy, Sybil #6046
– Lawson, Ernest #6176 6177 6178 6179
– Levine, Les #6262
– Livernois, Jules-Benoît #6308
– Luke, Alexandra #1850
– Macdonald, Jock #1850
– McKenzie, Robert Tait #6482 6484 6485
  6486 6487 6488

– New York (NY)
  – (1910s), women artists #206
  – (1960s) #460
  – (1970s) #555
  – Barnsley, James Macdonald #4612
  – Bladen, Ronald #4741
  – Borduas, Paul-Emile #4803 4810 4826
    4835 4839 4843 4846 4849
  – Brittain, Miller Gore #4917
  – Cardinal, Marcel #4997
  – Clerk, Pierre Jean #5118
  – Coburn, Frederick Simpson #5124
  – Cruikshank, William #5212
  – Dumouchel, Albert #5325
  – Fauteux-Massé, Henriette #5415
  – FitzGerald, Lionel LeMoine #5449
  – Freiman, Lillian #5517
  – Gagnon, Charles #5533 5540
  – Harrison, Allan #862 5747
  – Hümme, Joseph Julius #5863
  – Jarvis, Donald Alvin #5947
  – Jefferys, Charles William #5953 5956
  – Jobin, Louis #5962
  – Kahane, Anne #5998
  – Kerr, Estelle Muriel #206
  – Laliberté, Madeleine #6153
  – Lawson, Ernest #6175
  – MacAskill, Wallace R. #6350
  – MacLeod, Pegi Nicol #6397
  – Maggs, Arnaud #862
  – Milne, David Brown #6554 6555 6560
    6566 6567
  – Morris, Edmund Montague #6636
  – Mousseau, Jean-Paul Armand #6650
  – Nicoll, Marion F.S. Mackay #6703
  – Ogilvie, Will #6732
  – Oliver, Bobbie #675
  – Pavelic, Myfanwy Spencer #6785
  – Riopelle, Jean-Paul #7029
  – Roberts, Goodridge #7044
  – Steinhouse, Tobie Thelma #7278
  – Taylor, Richard #7336 7337
  – Tousignant, Claude #7400
  – Tully, Sydney Strickland #7438
  – Westerlund, Mia #675
  – Wrinch, Mary Evelyn #7618
– Parsons, F.R. #6773
– Philadelphia (Penn)
  – Reid, George Agnew #6977 6979
  – Reid, Mary Hiester #6982
– Plaskett, Joe #1850
– Provincetown (Mass)
  – Borduas, Paul-Emile #4843
  – Stacey, Harold #7274
– Ringness, Charles #7011
– San Francisco (Calif)
  – Carr, Emily #5045
  – Hammock, Virgil #5696
  – Smith, Gordon Appelbe #7225
  – Suzor-Coté, Marc-Aurèle de Foy #7297
    7300
– Tanabe, Takao #1850
– Thomas, Lionel Arthur John #1850
Canadians in USSR
– Semak, Michael William #7169
Canadians in West Indies

– MacDonald, J.E.H. #6371
– Morrice, James Wilson #6617 6626
– Suzor-Coté, Marc-Aurèle de Foy #7297 7300
canals, Canadian
– buildings, Ottawa (Ont) #8019
– canal locks and bridges, 19th c. #9512
Canberra (Australia), Belconnen Government Office Complex
– architecture, John Andrews Architects #8323
Canberra (Australia), National Gallery of Australia
– exhibitions
  – *Contemporary Canadian Painters* (1957) #423
candleholders
– *see* candlesticks
candlesticks, Canadian
– Ontario, 18th-19th cs. #2918
– Ontario and Atlantic provinces, 18th-19th cs. #2475
Candy, Kenneth H., Can architect, 1914-
– Toronto (Ont), Hydro Place #9352
Cannard, Pierre
– *see* Renaud (*dit* Cannard), Pierre
canneries, American
– western USA #8083
canneries, Canadian
– British Columbia #9258
– western Canada #8083
Cannon, John R., Can photographer, 1861-1931 #1724
Cannon, Thomas, Can photographer, 1832-1899 #1724
canoes
– *see also* boats
– canoe voyage scenes, Frances Ann Beechy Hopkins #5834
canoes, Algonquian #3571
canoes, Coast Salish #3851 3896
canoes, Haida
– ceremonial canoe wings #3825
canoes, Indians of North America
– on maps, 17th c. #841
canoes, Nootka
– compared with Inuit umiaks #3344
canoes, Northwest Coast Indians #3339
canoes, Quinault #3845
canopies, Canadian
– Québec
  – 17th-19th cs. #8826
  – (1650-1925) #1592
Cantieni, Graham, Can artist, 1938- #4996
– and RACE #1536
– exhibitions (reviews) #4995
Cantin, Jean-François, Can artist, 1958-
– performance art #655
Cap-Rouge Pottery, ceramic manufacturer (Québec, Qué) #2302
– (1860-1890) #2296 2298 2301 2322
– presentation jug, Philip Pointon #2332
Cap-Santé (Qué)
– churches #8814
Cap-Santé (Qué), church
– architecture, Pierre Renaud (*dit* Cannard)

#269 270
– paintings, Paul Malepart de Grand Maison (*dit* Beaucour) #249 250
Cap-Santé (Qué), Church of Sainte-Famille #8883
Cap-Tourmente (Qué), Ecole du Cap-Tourmente
– *see* Saint-Joachim (Qué), Ecoles des arts et métiers de Saint-Joachim
Cape Bonavista (Nfld), lighthouse #9523 9525
Cape Breton (NS)
– tartan weaving #2724
– textiles #2732
– weaving #2728
Cape Breton (NS), Gaelic College of St. Ann's
– tartan weaving #2724
Cape Dorset (NWT)
– art #6904
  – (1960s) #4187
  – (1970s) #6270 6271
– artists' colony, Peter Pitseolak on #6880 6881
– Dorset artifacts #4322
– graphic arts #4461 4466 4476 4477 4484 4500
  – (1959-1972) #4478
  – (1959-1974) #4483
  – (1959-1976) #4490
  – (1960-) #4460
  – (1960s) #4464
  – (1976-1977) #4491
  – and James Archibald Houston #4186 4462 4470
  – Burnaby (BC), Simon Fraser University. Simon Fraser Gallery #4495
– graphic arts and sculpture #4200 4299
  – (1957-1967) #4211
  – (1960s) #4192
– sculpture #4425 4441
  – mining quarries #4409
– sculpture and drawing (1960s) #4189
– society, Les Levine on #6269
– views
  – Pitseolak, Peter #6883
– women artists (1970s) #4260
Cape Mudge (BC), Cape Mudge Kwakiutl Museum
– art, Kwakiutl #4052
Cape Spear (Nfld), lighthouse #9525
Cappello, Luigi, It artist in Canada, fl. 1874-1892
– paintings, Church of Sainte-Anne (Yamachiche, Qué) #8783
CAR/FAC
– *see* Canadian Artists' Representation/Front des artistes canadiens (CAR/FAC)
CAR/FAC News, Can periodical #625
CAR News/RAC Journal, Can periodical #625
Caraquet (NB), école Polyvalente Louis Mailloux
– exhibitions
  – *Colville, Pratt, Forrestall* (1974) #1129
Caraquet (NB), école polyvalente Louis Mailloux

– exhibitions
  – *The Beaverbrook Art Gallery Presents Nine New Brunswick Artists/La Galerie d'art Beaverbrook présente neuf artistes du Nouveau-Brunswick* (1973) #1182
Carbonear (Nfld)
– architecture #7792
Carcy, Jacques
– *see* Pagé (*dit* Quercy or Carcy), Jacques
Cardero, José (Pepe), Sp artist, 1768-after 1808
– expedition, Northwest Coast #1998
Cardi, Ludovico
– *see* Cigoli
Cardinal, Douglas Joseph, Can architect, 1934- #8084 8341 8343
– Edmonton (Alta), house #8091
– Indian Education Centre #9494
– on architecture #7746
– on his architecture #8340
– writings #8342
Cardinal, Marcelin (Marcel), Can artist, 1920- #4997 4998
Carey, David, Canadian photographer, ca. 1947-
– portfolio of photographs #1023
Caribou Eskimo
– culture #4265
caricature
– *see also* political cartoons
– La Palme, Robert, on #6120
caricature, Canadian #925 946
– 18th-19th cs. #812
– 18th-20th cs. #949
– (1792-1850) #839
– Art Directors' Club of Toronto #854
– Bengough, John Wilson #4671 4673 4675 4676 4677
– Côté, Jean-Baptiste #5186 5187 5188
– Fay-Génot, Jean-Etienne-Achille #5416
– Fiorucci, Vittorio #5442
– Forrestall, Tom #5464
– Hudon, Normand #5854
– Innes, John I. #5901
– Julien, Henri #5981 5983 5986 5987 5990 5993
– La Palme, Robert #6119
– Macpherson, Duncan Ian #6400
– Millikin, William #6543
– Robinson, Albert Henry #7056
– Scovil, James Noel #7167
– Taylor, Richard #7337
– Trier, Walter #7428
Carillon (Qué)
– monument, Dollard des Ormeaux #1591
Carleton Martello tower
– architecture #8437
Carli, Thomas, Can sculptor, 1838-1906
– annunciation theme #1633
– supper at Emmaus theme #1615
Carlton Studio, graphic design firm (London, England)
– (1903-1915) #843
Carlu, Jacques, Fr architect, 1890-1976
– on interior, T. Eaton Company department stores #9370

Carlu, Natacha, Fr artist, fl. 1931
- murals, T. Eaton Company department
  stores #9370
Carlyle, Florence, Can artist, 1864-1923 #207
  4999
- exhibitions
  - (1925) #5000
- exhibitions (reviews) #186
Carmichael, Franklin, Can artist, 1890-1945
- and Alfred Joseph Casson #5056
- and Group of Seven #1732
- book illustration and design #939
- exhibitions
  - (1981) #5001
Carmichael, Maurice
- see Carmichael, William Maurice
Carmichael, Robert Ralph, Can artist, 1938-
- exhibitions
  - (1972) #5002
- exhibitions (reviews) #1866
Carmichael, William John, Can architect,
  1867-1927
- Montréal (Qué), Northern Electric #9234
Carmichael, William Maurice, Can
  silversmith, 1892-1954 #5003 5004
Caro, Anthony, Brit sculptor, 1924-
- influence on Alan Wood #7610 7611
- influence on André Lucien Fauteux #5413
- influence on Douglas Bentham #4684 4686
- influence on Robert Murray #6669
- interview, at Emma Lake Workshops
  (Emma Lake, Sask) #1934
Caron, G.Fernand, Can architect, 1905-1963
- Québec (Qué), La Solidarité insurance
  building #7939
Caron, Louis, Can architect, 1848-1917
- Saint-Eugène (Qué), Church of
  Saint-Eugène-de-Grantham #8873
Caron, Paul Archibald, Can artist, 1874-1941
- woodcuts #802
Caron, Roger, Can tapestry artist, 1925-
  #5005
CAROT, Can periodical #625
Carpenter, Edmund Snow, Can
  anthropologist in USA, 1922-
- on the sacred in art #94
carpets
- see rugs
Carr, Emily, Can artist, 1871-1945 #309 461
  1986 2011 5008 5016 5021 5022 5024 5026
  5033 5034 5035 5037 5040 5045
- and British Columbia painting (1894-1932)
  #2007
- and British Columbia Society of Fine Arts
  #1978
- and Canadian painting #18
- and her sisters #5015
- and Max Stern #1431
- art and writings #5019 5044
- as art critic #3308
- as modernist #507
- as teacher #5014 5020
- autobiography #5009 5010 5013 5017
- Blunden Harbour, National Gallery of
  Canada (Ottawa, Ont) #5036
- compared with Jack Weldon Humphrey

#404
- correspondence, Ruth Humphrey
  (1937-1944) #5029
- exhibitions
  - (1945) #5012
  - (1962) #5023
  - (1971) #5027 5028
  - (1977) #5039
  - (1979) #5042 5046
- exhibitions, group
  - (1928) #294 3827
  - (1940) #350
  - (1947) #377
  - (1958) #1995
- exhibitions (reviews) #1982
- Hughes, Edward John, compared with
  #5861
- influence on British Columbia art #2003
- influence on Jack Leonard Shadbolt #7178
- Klee Wyck #5038
- landscapes #140 2016
  - compared with James Wilson Morrice
    #352
- MacLeod, Pegi Nicol, compared with
  #6398
- oil on paper works (1930s-1940s) #5041
- on art #5030
- on Northwest Coast Indian art #5006
- on Northwest Coast Indians #5007 5031
- on stay (1902-1903), at Sunhill Sanatorium
  (London, England) #5018
- paintings (1930s) #502
- paintings of Northwest Coast Indians
  #1840
- pottery, Indian motifs #2278
- public support of #5032
- reminiscences #5011 5043
- residence, Victoria (BC) #8176 8177
- Shadbolt, Jack Leonard, compared with
  #7191
- works, McMichael Canadian Collection
  (Kleinburg, Ont) #3172
- works, Venice Biennale (1952) #399
- writings #92
  - (1927-1941) #5025
Carr-Harris, Ian, Can artist, 1941-
- exhibitions, group
  - (1974) #574
  - (1981) #710
- exhibitions (reviews) #697 794
- interview #5048
- on his art #5047
- performance sculpture #658
- use of photography #1057
Carrere & Hastings, Amer architectural firm
- Montréal (Qué), Transportation Building
  #9307
- Toronto (Ont)
  - Bank of Toronto #8293 9162 9185
  - Royal Bank #9152
- Windsor (Ont), Dominion Bank #9188
Carrier, Louis, Can collector, b. 1898
- collection, Québec silver #3213
Carrier, Louise, Can artist, 1925-1976 #5049
Carrier Indians
- 'Ksan artists' cooperative #4129 4130

- art
  - (1970s) #4145
- pictographs #3965
Carroll, Jane, Can photographer, fl. 1850s
  #1211
Carrothers, Lewis E., Can architect, b. 1878
- London (Ont), Riverview School #9388
Carruthers, Alan, Can photographer, fl. 1980
- portfolio of photographs #995
Carter, Alexander Scott, Can artist, architect,
  1881-1968 #5050
Carter, Gerald Gordon, Can sculptor, 1930-
- garden sculpture #1849
Cartier, Jean Bernard, Can ceramicist, 1915-
  #5051
- correspondence from Sweden #5052
Cartier, Sir Georges-Etienne, Can statesman,
  1814-1873
- monument, George Hill #1623
Cartierville (Qué),
  Notre-Dame-du-Bel-Amour
- architecture, Roger D'Astous #8763
cartography
- see maps
Cartoon, The, Can periodical
- and Edward John Russell #7110
cartoons, animated
- see animation (cinematography)
Carufel, René de
- see De Carufel, René
Cassan, Vital, Can artist, b. 1852 #5053
Cassidy, Eugene Haanel, Can photographer,
  1903-1980
- exhibitions
  - (1981) #5054
Casson, Alfred Joseph, Can artist, 1898-
  #5057 5059 5061
- and Group of Seven #1732 1774
- book illustration and design #939
- exhibitions
  - (1975) #5058
  - (1978) #5060
- exhibitions, group
  - (1940) #350
- influence on Alan Caswell Collier #5131
- on serigraphy #5055
cast iron
- facade, Cauchon Block (later Empire
  Hotel) (Winnipeg, Man) #9361
casting
- see plaster casts
Castle, William Ivor, Brit photographer, b.
  ca. 1877
- photographs of World War I #1113 1114
Castle and Sons, stained glass artists
  (Montréal, Qué)
- stained glass #2462
Castlegar (BC), hospital
- architecture, Smith & McCulloch #9031
Castlegar (BC), National Exhibition Centre
- exhibitions
  - Canadians: A National Photography Show
    about People/Canadiens: exposition
    nationale de photographie ayant les gens
    comme thème (1980) #1035
  - Looking South (1978) #4278

castles and country houses
– see also palaces; villas
– French, influence on Canadian château
  style hotels #9291
Castonguay, J.Alex, Can photographer,
  1877-after 1949
– exhibitions, group
  – (1970) #1675
Castro, Robert de, Can sculptor, 1923-
– as member of Limners #2043
Caswell, Thomas Jefferson, Can
  furniture-maker, 1806-1894 #2511
catalogues
– exhibition catalogues
  – (1970s) #3311
  – Ontario #3319
– mail-order catalogues, T. Eaton Company
  Limited (1886-1930) #2851
Catchers Society, Blackfoot
– pipe bundles #3665
Catlin, George, Amer artist, 1796-1872
– and emergence of named Indian artists
  #3486
– art and writings #3384 3426
– drawings of tobacco pipes, British
  Museum (London, England) #3478
– exhibitions, group
  – (1955) #1845
– Kane, Paul, compared with #6004 6013
Caton, Peter, Can photographer, fl. 1970s
– on portraiture #624
Cauchon, Alfred, Can carriage-maker, fl.
  1933 #5062
Cauchon, Henri, Can metalworker, fl. 1933
  #5062
Cauchon, Joseph, Can metalworker, ca.
  1856- #5062
Cauchon, Robert, Can artist, 1897-1969
  #1428 1429
– exhibitions (reviews) #964
Caughnawaga (Qué)
– see Kahnawake (Qué)
CAUT
– see Canadian Association of University
  Teachers (CAUT)
Cavoukian (Cavouk), Artin, Can
  photographer, 1915-
– on portraiture #624
Cayley, William, Can statesman, 1807-1890
– Toronto (Ont), The Grange #8637
Cayuga Indians
– culture #3525
– war clubs #3535
CBC
– see Canada. Canadian Broadcasting
  Corporation (CBC)
CCMC
– see Canadian Creative Music Collective
  (CCMC)
ceinture fléchée
– see sashes
celebrations
– see festivals; rites and ceremonies
Celestino, Mary, Can artist, 1935-
– exhibitions
  – (1980) #5063

Celle (West Germany), Schloss Celle
– exhibitions
  – Indianer Nordamerikas (1956) #3423
cements, mortars, and plasters
– see also masonry
– plaster, use in Québec sculpture #1618
cemeteries
– see also sepulchral monuments
cemeteries, Canadian
– Montréal (Qué), Mount Royal cemeteries
  #7933
– Québec (Qué), 17th-19th cs. #1306
– World Wars I and II #1108 1109
censers, Canadian
– silver, Québec, 17th-18th cs. #2665
censorship of art
– and Mark Prent #6922 6924
– Canada (1970s) #625 693
– Montréal (Qué), destruction of Corridart
  street exhibition (1976) #1530
– nudes in art #317 6652
Centerfold, Can periodical #603
Central Mortgage and Housing Corporation
– see Canada. Central Mortgage and
  Housing Corporation
Centrale d'artisanat du Québec #2213 2238
Century, Amer periodical
– illustrations, Henri Julien #5984
Century Pioneer Village (Ont) #8063
ceramic sculpture
– see also terra cotta
ceramic sculpture, American
– California, compared with Regina (Sask)
  ceramic sculpture (1960s-1970s) #1939
ceramic sculpture, Canadian
– 20th c. #795
– (1970s) #781
– figurative works (1970s) #774
– miniatures #2302
– porcelain bust of Colonel de Charette, St.
  Johns Stone Chinaware Company
  (Saint-Jean, Qué) #2314
– Regina (Sask)
  – (1960s-1970s) #1939
  – (1970s) #1924
– western Canada (1970s) #1864
ceramic sculpture, Inuit
– Rankin Inlet (NWT) #4203
ceramics
– see pottery
Cercle des fermières
– encouragement of domestic arts #2212
ceremonial maces, Inuit
– Northwest Territories Council #4304 4386
  4389
ceremonial paddles, Tlingit
– use of human hair #3917
ceremonies
– see rites and ceremonies
Cetin, Anton, Can artist, 1936- #5065
– exhibitions
  – (1978) #5064
Cézanne, Paul, Fr artist, 1839-1906
– Bates, Maxwell Bennett, compared with
  #4623
– Carr, Emily, on #5030

– East, Benoît, compared with #5353
– influence on David Brown Milne #6567
– influence on Goodridge Roberts #7046
– influence on Lawren Phillip Harris #5711
– influence on Lionel LeMoine FitzGerald
  #5450
– influence on Louise Landry Gadbois #5529
– influence on Paraskeva Clark #5110
– influence on Paul-Emile Borduas #1468
  4841
– influence on Paul Fournier #5486
– influence on Pierre Jean Clerk #5118
Chabert, Joseph, Can priest, artist, 1832-1894
– as director, Institut national des
  beaux-arts, sciences, arts et métiers et
  industrie (Montréal, Qué) #3005
– as teacher of François-Xavier Aldéric
  Rapin #6961
Chaboillez, Charles
– see Chaboulié (Chaboillez), Charles
Chabot, J.E., Can photographer, 1897-1976
  #1283
Chaboulié (Chaboillez), Charles, Can
  sculptor, ca. 1638-1708 #234 235 1572
Chadwick & Beckett, Can architectural firm
– Toronto (Ont)
  – Chapman & Walker Building #9332
  – domestic architecture #8493
  – Government House, competition #8748
  – houses #8639
Chagall, Marc, Russ artist, 1887-
– influence on Walter Joseph Gerard
  Bachinski #4578
Chagnon, Alain, Can photographer, 1948-
– portfolio of photographs #997 999
chairs
– see also rocking chairs; Windsor furniture
– sculptures, Les Levine #6258
chairs, American
– 18th-19th cs., influence on Québec rocking
  chairs #2536
– 19th c., influence on Canadian chairs
  #2553 2564
chairs, British
– 19th c., influence on Canadian chairs
  #2553
– Windsor, influence on Québec rocking
  chairs #2536
chairs, Canadian
– 17th-19th cs. #2489
– (1790s-1850) #2553
– (1960s) #2471
– Acadian #2492
– Green, Daniel #2517
– Hébert, Julien #5766
– Mailloux, Joseph #2184
– Manitoba, 19th c. #2584
– Montréal (Qué), (1800-1850) #2538
– New Brunswick, 18th-19th cs. #2500
– Nova Scotia #2496
  – 18th-19th cs. #2493 2499 2509
  – (1740s-1850s) #2497
– Ontario #2560
  – 19th c. #2575
  – (1780-1900) #2577
  – (1790s-1857) #2558

– (1790s-1870s) #2564
– arrow-back chair, as subject for paintings #1770
– Québec #2534
– 17th-18th cs. #2529
– Rogerson, John, for president, St. Andrew's Society (Saint John, NB) #7067 7068
– sketch of, attributed to Pierre-Noël Levasseur #6257
– Toronto (Ont), (1800-1865) #2563
– Windsor #2476
chairs, Scottish
– 19th c., influence on Canadian chairs #2553
chalices, Canadian
– Québec, 17th-19th cs. #2681
– Ranvoyzé, François #2658 2673 2679 2680
Chalitmiut (Alaska)
– bonework, Okvik #4340
Chalke, John, Can sculptor, ceramicist, 1940- #2395
Challener, Frederick Sproston, Can artist, 1869-1959 #4638 5067
– exhibitions, group
– (1935) #17
– mural paintings #5068
– on mural painting #5066
Chalmers, John, Can engineer, fl. 1909
– Edmonton (Alta), Legislative Buildings #8962
Chamard, Emélie, Can weaver, b. 1887 #2194 2209 5069
Chambellan, François, Can silversmith, ca. 1688-1747 #2667
Chambers, John Richard (Jack), Can artist, 1931-1978 #5073 5078
– and art criticism #3315
– and realism #110 533
– autobiography #5079
– death theme #1759
– drawings #532 5077
– exhibitions
– (1970) #5074
– (1980) #700 5080 5081
– exhibitions, group
– (1965) #473
– (1971) #98
– (1979) #674
– exhibitions (reviews) #5082
– films #626
– Hart of London #5076
– influence on Brian Rendel Jones #5974
– influence on London (Ont) art (1960s) #1791
– interview #5070 5075
– on Canadian Artists' Representation #563
– on perceptual realism #5071
– on visual perception #525
– regionalism, compared with Greg Curnoe #5225
– use of light #516
– use of photography #5072
– writings #92
Champagne, Claire
– see Beaugrand-Champagne, Claire
Champagne, Jean-Serge, Can sculptor, 1947- #5083
– exhibitions, group
– (1977) #637 782
Champagne, Louis
– see Foureur (dit Champagne), Louis
Champagne, Michel, Can artist, 1940- #5084 5085

Champagne, Pierre
– see Foureur (dit Champagne), Pierre
Champaign (Ill), University of Illinois
– architecture #9464
Champeau, André, Can artist, 1934-
– in Paris (France) #426
Champlain, Samuel de, Fr explorer in Canada, 1567-1635
– illustrations, Les voyages du sieur de Champlain (1613) #933
– Port Royal Habitation (Granville Ferry, NS) #7655 7813
– portraits #191
– view of Nova Scotia (ca. 1605) #1202
Champlain (Qué), church
– woodcarvings, Gilles Bolvin #4781
chance
– in art
– Hudson, Andrew #5857
– Rockman, Arnold #7061
Chandler Kennedy Architectural Group, Can architectural firm
– Calgary (Alta), office buildings #9362
Chaplin, Carl, Can artist, 1946- #5086
Chaplin, Millicent Mary, Can artist, fl. 1838-1844 #1219
Chapman, Alfred Hirschfelder, Can architect, 1879-1949 #8344
Chapman, Evadna, Can artist, 1933-
– interview #5087
Chapman, Isaac, Can sculptor, ca. 1880-ca. 1908
– argillite carving #5088
Chapman, Oxley & Bishop, Can architectural firm
– Toronto (Ont), Sunnyside #8054
Chapman, Oxley & Facey, Can architectural firm
– Toronto (Ont), Bank of Montreal #9190
Chapman & McGiffin, Can architectural firm
– domestic architecture #8494
– Toronto (Ont)
– Toronto Stock Exchange, competition #9161
– University of Toronto. Knox College #9435 9449
– competition #9432
Chapman & Oxley, Can architectural firm
– Toronto (Ont), Toronto Star Building #9334
Chapnick, Karen, Can artist, 1950-
– exhibitions, group
– (1978) #663
– exhibitions (reviews) #2081
Chaput, Yves, Can photographer, fl. 1973
– portfolio of photographs #997 999
Charbonneau, Jean-Guy, poet, fl. 1978
– poems, for drawings by Louis-Pierre Bougie #4861
Charbonneau, Monique, Can artist, 1928- #5089
– exhibitions
– (1978) #5090
Charbonneau, Roger, Can photographer, 1947- #1556
– interview, on Groupe d'action photographique #1494
– photographic views, Disraeli (Qué), (1972) #1513
– portfolio of photographs #997 999
Chardin, Jean Baptiste Siméon, Fr artist, 1699-1779
– Leduc, Ozias, compared with #6200

Charette, Colonel Athanase-Charles-Marie de, Fr army officer, 1832-1911
– porcelain portrait bust, St. Johns Stone Chinaware Company (Saint-Jean, Qué) #2314
Charlebois, Alyne Gauthier
– see Gauthier-Charlebois, Alyne
Charlebois, Joseph Charles Théophile, Can artist, 1872-1935 #1382
Charles Pachter Graphics, publishing house (Toronto, Ont)
– and Charles Pachter #834
Charlesbourg (Qué)
– churches #8851
Charlevoix (Qué)
– art and architecture #1233
– blankets #2738
– costume
– 19th c. #2829
– late 19th-early 20th cs. #2890
– domestic architecture #8629
– dyes and dyeing, 17th-19th cs. #2733
– folk art #1243
– photographic views
– Szilasi, Gabor #7308
– views
– (1750s-1970s) #1280
– Jackson, A.Y. #5910
– weaving #1327
Charlottetown (PEI)
– architecture #7797 7802
– market buildings (1813-1958) #7800
Charlottetown (PEI), Bank of Nova Scotia
– architecture, Sharp & Horner #9174
Charlottetown (PEI), Confederation Centre
– architecture
– Affleck, Desbarats, Dimakopoulos, Lebensold, Sise #9094
– Affleck, Desbarats, Dimakopoulos, Lebensold, Sise & Schoenauer #7683
– competition for #9088 9089
Charlottetown (PEI), Confederation Centre Art Gallery and Museum
– (1960s) #1122
– collection #3070
– exhibitions
– A Century of Colonial Painting: The Seven Years War to Confederation: An Exhibition Organized for the Inauguration of the Fathers of Confederation Building, Charlottetown, P.E.I./Un siècle de peinture, l'époque coloniale: de la guerre de Sept Ans à la Confédération: exposition organisée pour l'inauguration de l'edifice des Pères de la Confédération, I.P.E. (1964) #226
– A Country Painter's Harvest: Lindee Climo: Paintings and Drawings (1978) #5120
– A Nineteenth Century Look: The Victorian Parlour (1976) #2129
– A Terrible Beauty: The Art of Canada at War (1978) #1111
– André Biéler 50 Years: A Retrospective Exhibition 1920-1970 (1970) #4725
– Annie D. Savage: Drawings and Watercolours (1975) #7129
– Beauté tragique: les deux conflits mondiaux vus par des artistes canadiens (1978) #1112
– Canadian Political Cartoons (1977) #956
– Canadian Tapestries, 1977 (1977) #2770
– Carl Schaefer in Hanover (1980) #7157
– Carol Fraser Paintings and Drawings: 1967-1977 (1977) #5507
– Charles Fraser Comfort: Fifty Years (1973) #5159

– *Christopher Pratt* (1971) #6910
– *Claude Tousignant* (1974) #7401
– *David Bolduc: Recent Work* (1980) #4775
– *Directors' Choice* (1967) #481
– *Douglas Bentham "Enclosures and Opens" 1975/76* (1977) #4683
– *Drawings and Pastels c. 1930-1967 by Miller Gore Brittain* (1969) #4917
– *Drawings by Jack Weldon Humphrey: A Travelling Exhibition Organized by the Beaverbrook Art Gallery, Fredericton, New Brunswick, Canada, 1977-1979* (1979) #5871
– *Esther Warkov* (1971) #7517
– *Felicity Redgrave* (1979) #6967
– *Fritz Brandtner 1896-1969: A Retrospective Exhibition* (1971) #4903
– *Goodridge Roberts: A Retrospective Exhibition/Goodridge Roberts: une exposition rétrospective* (1969) #7045
– *Goodridge Roberts: Selected Works/Goodridge Roberts: oeuvres choisies* (1982) #7050
– *Henry Purdy: A Personal Decade 1968-1978* (1978) #6946
– *Impressionism in Canada, 1895-1935* (1974) #115
– *J.M. Barnsley (1861-1929), Retrospective Exhibition* (1964) #4611
– *Jack Shadbolt* (1970) #7182
– *Jack Wise: A Decade of Work* (1978) #7601
– *Joe Fafard: Recent Sculpture* (1980) #5401
– *John Fox: 10 New Paintings* (1980) #5495
– *L'art de Tom Thomson* (1972) #7367
– *Lithographs/Lithographies* (1972) #825
– *Louis de Niverville* (1979) #6709
– *Manitoba Mainstream: People's Art/Fine Art/Le Grand Courant du Manitoba: arts populaires, beaux-arts* (1973) #1897
– *Metamorphosis, Memories, Dreams and Reflections: The Work of Florence Vale* (1981) #7453
– *Miller Brittain - Painter* (1982) #4922
– *Plains and Northwest Coast Indians: Indian Art and Crafts from Glenbow-Alberta Institute, Calgary* (1970) #3438
– *Robert Harris, 1849-1919* (1967) #5739
– *Robert Harris (1849-1919)* (1973) #5743
– *Robert Young: Prints/Robert Young: gravures* (1981) #7631
– *Roger Savage* (1980) #7135
– *Ronald: 25 Years* (1975) #7073
– *Sunshine and Shadows: A Look at Island Quilts and Quilting* (1978) #2802
– *Terence Johnson: Forts* (1981) #5969
– *The Academy in Retrospect* (1966) #474
– *The Art of Tom Thomson* (1972) #7368
– *The J.S. McLean Collection of Canadian Painting* (1968) #3228
– *The Murray and Marguerite Vaughan Inuit Print Collection/Collection d'estampes inuit* (1982) #4498
– *The Poole Collection: An Exhibition of Canadian Paintings from Krieghoff to Riopelle* (1965) #3222
– *The Queen Comes to New Brunswick: Paintings and Drawings by Molly Lamb Bobak* (1978) #4765
– *The Railway: Patron of the Arts in Canada* (1976) #3281
– *The Saidye and Samuel Bronfman Collection of Canadian Art/La collection Saidye et Samuel Bronfman* (1967) #3087
– *The Society of Canadian Painter-Etchers and Engravers in Retrospect/La Société des peintres-graveurs canadiens: vue rétrospective* (1981) #836
– *The Trowell Touch, 1965-1980* (1980) #7430
– *The Work of Art: Six Artists* (1979) #665
– *William Perehudoff: Recent Paintings* (1979) #6837
– *Women Artists of P.E.I.: A Survey of Female Artistic Activity on the Island* (1977) #1168
– exhibitions (reviews)
    – *Three Painters of Prince Edward Island* (1976) #1167
– influence on Prince Edward Island art (1964-1974) #1165
Charlottetown (PEI), EPTEK National Exhibition Centre
– exhibitions
    – *Looking South* (1978) #4278
Charlottetown (PEI), Government House
– architecture #8754
Charlottetown (PEI), Holland College School of Visual Arts
– Purdy, Henry Carl, as director #6946
Charlottetown (PEI), Islander Motor Inn
– mural, Gwen Johnston Fichaud #5428
Charlottetown (PEI), Prince Edward Island Heritage Foundation
– furniture #2484
Charlottetown (PEI), Province House
– architectural plans #8939
– architecture #8937
– furniture (1864) #8938
Charlottetown (PEI), Saint Dunstan's University
– exhibitions
    – *Contemporary Sacred Art in Canada/L'art sacré contemporain au Canada* (1964) #459
Charney, Melvin, Can architect, artist, 1935- #5094 5095
– as organizer, *Corridart* street exhibition, Montréal (Qué), (1976) #1522 1530
– exhibitions
    – (1972) #7906
    – (1979) #5093
– exhibitions, group
    – (1980) #8237
– interview #5092
– on architecture #7746
– on Canadian architecture (1960s) #9400
– on his architectural designs as monuments #5091
Charpentier, Louis, Can artist, 1947- #1511
Charron, Amable, Can sculptor, 1785-1844
– interior, Church of Saint-Jean-Baptiste (Saint-Jean-Port-Joli, Qué) #8812
Charron, François, Can artist, 1952-
– on his art #1552
charterhouses
    see monasteries
Chartier, Gilles, Can artist, 1940- #1504 5096
Chartrand (*dit* Vincennes), Vincent, Can artist, fl. 1822-1863 #6947
Chase, Wellington, Can photographer, fl. 1860-1870 #1211
Châteauguay (Qué), Church of Saint-Joachim
– architecture and interior #8861
Châteauguay (Qué), Lepailleur McFarlane House
– and Canadian Heritage of Quebec #7871
châteaux
– *see* castles and country houses
Chater, Leslie, Can artist, 20th c.
– and Albert Angus Macdonald #6354
Chatham (NB), James M. Hill Memorial High School
– exhibitions
    – *Colville, Pratt, Forrestall* (1974) #1129
    – *The Beaverbrook Art Gallery Presents Nine New Brunswick Artists/La Galerie d'art Beaverbrook présente neuf artistes du Nouveau-Brunswick* (1973) #1182
Châtigny, Edmond, Can sculptor, 1895- #5097
Chauchetière, Claude, Can priest, artist, 1645-1709 #234 235 1363
– and nationalism in art #1373
– devotional images #1354 1358
Chaudron, Bernard, Can metalsmith, jeweller, 1931- #5098 5099
Chaudron, Louise, Can metalsmith, fl. 1960s-1970s #5098
Chaulette brothers, Can sculptors, 18th c.
– statue of General James Wolfe, Québec (Qué) #1568 1600
Chauvin, Jean, Can writer, 1895-1958
– on Ozias Leduc #6211
Chavignaud, George, Can artist, 1865-1944
– as principal, Nova Scotia College of Art (Halifax, NS) #2993
Chechik, Jeremiah, Can artist, 1951- #992
Chee Chee, Benjamin, Can artist, 1944-1977 #5100 5101 6648
Cheney, Gordon Lewis, Can architect, 1934-
– Charlottetown (PEI), Confederation Centre, competition #9088 9089
Cheney, Nan Lawson, Can artist, 1897-
– on Emily Carr #5043
Cheng, James K.M., Can architect, 1947-
– Vancouver (BC), Chinese Cultural Centre, competition #9144
Chequamegon Bay (Ont)
– views
    – Fraser, John Arthur #5509
Chernavitch, Ken, Can sculptor, 1945-
– ceramic sculpture #795
Cherria, François, Can priest, fl. 1792
– and church, Saint-Denis-sur-Richelieu (Qué) #8811
Cherry, Sheldon, Can, 20th c.
– interview, on projected move of Vancouver Art Gallery (Vancouver, BC) #3198
Chester, Donovan T. (Don), Can artist, 1940-
– exhibitions
    – (1973) #1858
– exhibitions, group
    – (1974) #565 1925
    – (1975) #1926
Chesterfield, Albert A., Can photographer, 1877-1959 #5102
chests, Canadian
– blanket chests
    – Ontario #2554
    – Prince Edward Island #2507 2508
– Ontario #2557
    – (1780-1900) #2577
    – (1790s-1857) #2558
– Québec
    – 17th-18th cs. #2529 2530 2531
    – convex chests #2528
chests, Haida
– London (England), British Museum #3805
chests, Tsimshian
– London (England), British Museum #3805
Chewett, James Grant, Can architect,

1793-1862 #258 259
- Toronto (Ont), City Hall #8993
Chicago (Ill), Art Institute of Chicago
- exhibitions
  - *The Native American Heritage: A Survey of North American Indian Art* (1977) #3468
  - *Yakutat South Indian Art of the Northwest Coast* (1964) #3923
- Loring, Frances Norma, as student #758
- Wyle, Florence, as student #758
Chicago (Ill), Chicago Tribune Building
- Toronto Star Building (Toronto, Ont), compared with #9334
Chicago (Ill), Field Museum of Natural History
- costume, Athapaskan Indians #4111
- masks, Haida #3961
Chicago (Ill), Museum of Contemporary Art
- exhibitions
  - *49th Parallels: New Canadian Art* (1971) #98
Chicoutimi (Qué), Ecole d'arts et métiers
- (1930s) #2175
Chicoutimi (Qué), Hôtel-Dieu Saint-Vallier
- paintings, Charles Edouard Huot #5878 5884
Chicoutimi (Qué), Musée du Saguenay-Lac-Saint-Jean
- exhibitions
  - *James Bay Project - A River Drowned by Water/Projet de la baie James - une rivière qui se noie* (1982) #1566
Chicoutimi (Qué), Societé des arts de Chicoutimi
- exhibitions
  - *De la figuration à la non-figuration dans l'art québécois* (1978) #1461
Chicoutimi (Qué), Université du Québec
- art education (1960s) #3016
Chiendent, Can comic strip artists #948 952 1502
Chignecto (NB)
- architecture and decorative arts #2150
Chigot, Francis, Fr stained glass artist, fl. 1932
- stained glass, Church of Notre-Dame (Montréal, Qué) #2444
Chigot de Limoges, Fr stained glass studio (Limoges, France)
- stained glass, Church of Notre-Dame (Montréal, Qué) #8839
Chilcotin Indians
- culture #3789
childhood
- *see* children
children
- childhood subjects, Canadian art (1970s) #674
- clothing (1780-1930) #2862
- use of language, and N.E. Thing Co. Ltd. #6677
children's art
- and art education
  - Borduas, Paul-Emile #4827
  - Brandtner, Fritz #4901
  - British Columbia #1995
  - Fredericton (NB), Fredericton Art Club #1176
  - Lismer, Arthur #2966 2968 2971 2974 2975 2981 2984 2985 2987 6301 6302 6303
  - Vancouver (BC), Vancouver Art Gallery #3186
- and frère Jérôme #6761

- Rockman, Arnold, on #7061
- Ruhman, Walter, drawings as a child #7106
children's books, Canadian
- illustrations
  - 19th-20th cs. #934 937
  - Houston, James Archibald #5846
  - Newfeld, Frank #6689
  - Odjig, Daphne #6731
children in art
- Heward, Efa Prudence #5796
- Kupczynski, Stanislav #6106
- Lyall, Laura Adeline Muntz #6339
- Ontario art #1687
- Peel, Paul #6790
- Wallis, Katherine Elizabeth #7511 7512
Chilkat Indians
- architecture #3793
- architecture and totem poles #3798
- blankets #3784 3821 3826 3898 3973
- blankets and basketry #3333
- quillwork #3811
Chillas, Robert, Can furniture-maker, fl. 1780s-1820s #2511
Chilliwack (BC)
- architecture #8147
chimneypieces
- *see* fireplaces
China
- photographic views
  - Hinton, John Henry #5812
china painting
- Canada
  - 19th c. #2288
  - (1850s-1890s) #2305
  - (1890s) #2277
- Montréal (Qué), Montreal Museum of Fine Arts, *Spring Exhibition* #1228 1311
- State dinner service of Canada (1898) #2333
chine de commande
- *see* Chinese export porcelain
Chinese export porcelain
- (1610-1790), Susannah Anne Weldon Collection, King's College (Windsor, NS) #2363
Chinese in Canada
- Alberta, architecture #8137
- British Columbia, architecture #8154
- Victoria (BC), architecture #8179 8181
Chipewyan Indians
- *see also* Athapaskan Indians
- petroglyphs #3439
- photographs of
  - Curtis, Edward Sheriff #3399
Chippendale style
- furniture
  - Newfoundland #2502
  - Québec #2542
Chirico, Giorgio de, It artist, 1888-1978
- Colville, Alex, compared with #1115
- influence on Alfred Pellan #6820 6822
- influence on Kenneth Campbell Lochhead #6319
Chisasibi (Qué), Chisasibi School
- exhibitions
  - *James Bay Project - A River Drowned by Water/Projet de la baie James - une rivière qui se noie* (1981) #1566
Chitty, Elizabeth, Can artist, 1953-
- exhibitions, group
  - (1980) #687
- video art #655
Chodorow, Neil, Can artist, 1946-

- interview #5103
cholera
- Légaré, Joseph, *Le choléra à Québec* #6214
Chomedey (Qué), Church of Saint-Pie X
- architecture, Des Rochers & Dumont #8840
Chomedey (Qué), City Hall
- architecture, Affleck, Desbarats, Dimakopoulos, Lebensold, Sise #8990
Chrismas, Lawrence, Can photographer, 1941-
- portfolio of photographs #991
Christensen, Dan, Can artist, 1942-
- exhibitions
  - (1973) #5104
- exhibitions, group
  - (1981) #722
Christie, Robert E., Can artist, 1946-
- exhibitions, group
  - (1974) #565
  - (1975) #1926
  - (1981) #722
Christin, Léopold, Can artist, musician, b. 1877 #5105
Christl, Rudi, Can photographer, ca. 1946-
- portfolio of photographs #1023
Christmas
- Canadian greeting cards
  - (1880s) #842
    - Bennet & Co. #2360
  - (1880s-1890s) #890
  - (1920s) #845
    - *Canadian Artists' Series* #844
  - (1920s-1950s) #863
  - (1940s), Avis Selina Fyshe, on #849
  - (1960s) #868
  - Editions Lacia (1950s) #857
  - Québec (1950) #856
- in art
  - Canadian paintings #864
  - Julien, Henri #5982
Christopher, Ken, Can artist, 1942-
- exhibitions, group
  - (1981) #1885
Chu, T.K., Can photographer, fl. 1977
- portfolio of photographs #1023
Chukchi
- art #4302 4303
church bells
- *see* bells
church furnishings
- *see also* altarpieces; balustrades; tabernacles
church furnishings, Canadian
- Joliette (Qué) #1287 8876
- L'Islet (Qué), Church of Notre-Dame-de-Bon-Secours #8879
- Lockport (Man), Saint Andrew's Church #8909
- Montréal (Qué), Church of Notre-Dame #8839
- Québec (1650-1925) #1592
- Sainte-Anne-de-Beaupré (Qué), Saint Ann's Basilica #1601 1602
Church Point (NS), Saint Mary's Parish Church
- architecture, Léo Melanson #8779
church vestments
- *see* vestments
churches
- *see also* meeting houses
churches, American
- 18th c., influence on Canadian churches #8904
- western USA #8083
churches, British

– 18th-19th cs., influence on Québec
   churches #8821 8870
– 19th c., influence on Frederic William
   Cumberland #8905
churches, Canadian #8769
– 17th c.-1867, European and American
   influences #7687
– 17th c.-1960s #7689
– 17th-early 19th cs. #7841
– (1880-1914) #7736
– (1920s) #7656
– (1950s) #8758 8759 8760 8762 8763 8764
– (1960s) #8765 8766 8767
– (1960s-1970s) #7710
– Acadian #1137
– Alberta
   – (1900-1930s) #8126
   – Byzantine #8913
– Anglican #8761
– Arctic #8920
– Beaumont (Qué), Church of Saint-Etienne
   #8809
– Bellechasse (Qué), Church of
   Saint-Charles-Borromée #8803
– Berthierville (Qué) #8833 8874
   – Cuthbert Chapel #8881
– Boucherville (Qué), Church of
   Sainte-Famille #8868
– British Columbia
   – (1789-early 20th c.) #8918
   – (1858-1925) #8916
   – Indian, wooden #8914 8917
   – wooden #8148 8153
– Cap-Santé (Qué) #8814
   – Church of Sainte-Famille #8883
– Charlesbourg (Qué) #8851
– Châteauguay (Qué), Church of
   Saint-Joachim #8861
– Church Point (NS), Saint Mary's Parish
   Church #8779
– Fredericton (NB) #8770
– Fuller, Thomas (1858-1867) #8366
– Gothic revival #7739 7740
– Guelph (Ont), 19th c. #7970
– Halifax (NS)
   – 18th-19th cs. #7818
   – All Saints' Cathedral #8773
– Hamilton (Ont)
   – Church of Saint John the Evangelist
      #730
   – Victorian #7991
– île d'Orléans (Qué) #1238
   – Church of Saint-François-de-Sales #8796
   – Church of Saint-Jean #8801
   – Church of Saint-Pierre #8802
   – Church of Sainte-Famille #8795
– île Perrot (Qué)
   – Church of
      Sainte-Jeanne-Françoise-de-Chantal
      #8805
– Joliette (Qué) #1287 8876
– Kahnawake (Qué), Church of
   Saint-François-Xavier #8890
– Kingston (Ont)
   – 17th-19th cs. #7989
   – 19th c. #7995
   – Newlands, William #8392
– L'Acadie (Qué) #8830
– L'Islet (Qué), Church of
   Notre-Dame-de-Bon-Secours #8879
– Lac Bouchette (Qué), Marial Chapel #8832
– Lachenaie (Qué), Church of Saint-Charles
   #8808
– Laterrière (Qué), 19th c. #7882

– Laval (Qué), Church of Sainte-Rose #8854
– Lévis (Qué), Church of
   Notre-Dame-de-la-Victoire #8789
– Lockport (Man), Saint Andrew's Church
   #8909
– London (Ont), 19th c. #8007 8010
– Loretteville (Qué), Church of
   Notre-Dame-de-la-Jeune-Lorette #8804
– Lotbinière (Qué) #8835
– Manitoba #8098
   – 19th-early 20th cs. #8102
   – (1812-1870) #8097
   – stained glass windows #2450
– Midland (Ont), Sainte-Marie among the
   Hurons #7999
– Montréal (Qué) #8886
   – 17th-19th cs. #7899
   – architectural drawings, Archives
      nationales du Québec à Montréal #8604
   – Chapel of l'Invention-de-la-Sainte-Croix
      #8862
   – Chapel of Notre-Dame-de-Lourdes
      #8784 8836
   – Christ Church Cathedral #8798
   – Church of Notre-Dame #8780 8828 8839
      8848 8849 8892
   – Church of Saint-Jacques #8781 8782
   – Church of Sainte-Catherine #8407
   – Church of Sainte-Catherine-d'Alexandrie
      #8867
   – Notre-Dame-de-Bon-Secours #8788
   – Saint Joseph's Oratory #8794
   – stained glass windows #2462
– New Brunswick
   – Medley, Edward Shuttleworth #8776
   – use of architectural models, 19th c.
      #7873
– Newfoundland #8772
– Niagara-on-the-Lake (Ont)
   – 19th c. #7986
   – Saint Andrew's Church #8901
– Nicolet (Qué), Saint-Grégoire de Nicolet
   #1636
– Nova Scotia
   – 18th c. #7815
   – late 18th-19th cs. #8775
– Oka (Qué)
   – church #8818 8885
   – Church of the Annunciation #1355 1356
– Ontario #8906
   – 19th c. #8006 8672
   – (1800-1855) #8014
   – (pre-1867) #8904
   – Cumberland, Frederic William #8905
   – influence of Scottish architecture, 19th c.
      #7977
   – McClean, Arthur #8382
   – polygonal buildings, 19th c. #7987
   – wooden, 19th c. #7745
– Oshawa (Ont), Saint George's Anglican
   Church #8899
– Prairies #1852 8080
– Prince Edward Island #8777
– Québec #1233 1324 8816 8819
   – 17th-18th cs. #1320 2181 7655 7845 8790
      8827 8869
   – 17th-19th cs. #1305 7852 7866
   – 17th c. #228 229 8817 8823
   – 17th c.-1940s #7853
   – 17th-early 20th cs. #8821
   – 18th-19th cs. #1338 8893
   – 18th c. #269 270 7861 7865 8799
   – (1600-1850) #8870
   – (1608-1760s) #8825 8837

– (1615-1665) #8822 8823
– (1647-1800) #8792 8793
– (1820s-1880s), Baroque revival #7856
– (1880-1914) #7929
– (1900-1934) #8334
– (1930-1952) #8831
– (1930s) #1381
– (1940s) #8820
– (1940s-1950s) #8838
– (1950s-1960s) #8845
– (1960s) #1435 7862 8840 8841 8846
– Baillairgé, Thomas #8327 8328
– Borduas, Paul-Emile #4836
– Conefroy, Pierre #8834
– interiors, Quévillon School #1571
– Morisset, Gérard #8891
– Ouellet, Joseph-Pierre #8394
– Protestant #8887 8888
– review of literature #1295
– use of clapboarding and whitewashing
   #8829
– woodcarving and interior decoration,
   late 17th-19th cs. #1588
– Québec (Qué)
– Cathedral of the Holy Trinity #8786
– Chapel of the congrégation Notre-Dame
   de Québec #8864
– Church of Notre-Dame de Québec #8791
   8857
– Church of Notre-Dame-des-Anges #9022
– Church of Saint-Augustin-de-Desmaures
   #8889
– Church of Saint-Joachim de
   Montmorency #8880
– Notre-Dame-des-Victoires #8858
– Séminaire de Québec. Chapel of Mgr
   Jean-Olivier Briand #8800
– Ursuline Convent. Chapel #8852
– Quidi Vidi (Nfld), Christ Church #7788
– Red Deer (Alta), Saint Mary's Church
   #8343
– Regina (Sask), RCMP Chapel #8911
– Repentigny (Qué) #7888
– Rimouski (Qué) #1361 8872
– Rivière-du-Sud (Qué), Church of
   Saint-Pierre de la Rivière-du-Sud #8875
– Saint-Boniface (Man), Precious Blood
   Church #8908
– Saint-Denis-sur-Richelieu (Qué) #8811
– Saint-Eugène (Qué), Church of
   Saint-Eugène-de-Grantham #8873
– Saint-Jean-Port-Joli (Qué)
   – Church of Saint-Jean-Baptiste #8812
   – Church of Saint-Jean-Port-Joli #8871
– Saint-Joachim (Qué), Church of
   Saint-Joachim #7953
– Saint John (NB), stone church #8778
– Saint-Laurent (Qué), Collège de
   Saint-Laurent. Chapel #8815
– Saint-Mathias-de-Rouville (Qué), Church
   of Saint-Mathias-de-Rouville #8878
– Sainte-Anne-de-Beaupré (Qué) #8863 8877
   – Saint Ann's Basilica #1601 1602 6572
      6573 8824 8859 8860 8865 8866
– Sainte-Anne-de-Bellevue (Qué), church
   #8336
– Sainte-Anne-de-la-Pocatière (Qué) #8882
– Saskatoon (Sask), Saint John's Episcopal
   Church #8907
– Sault-au-Récollet (Qué), Church of the
   Visitation #8797
– St. John's (Nfld), Saint John's Cathedral
   #8771
– St. Stephen (NB), Christ Church #8774

– Toronto (Ont)
  – 19th c.-1930s #8076
  – Cathedral of Saint Alban the Martyr
    #8896
  – Church of Saint Paul's #8897 8902
  – Saint Anne's Church #1733
  – Thomas, William #8413
  – Timothy Eaton Memorial Church #8898
– Trois-Rivières (Qué) #8806
  – (1630s-1910s) #7883
– Ukrainian #8085 8768
  – Alberta #8704
  – Manitoba #2270
  – Saskatchewan #8912 8915
– Valleyfield (Qué), Cathedral of
  Salaberry-de-Valleyfield #8843
– Vancouver (BC)
  – Christ Church Cathedral #8910
  – Saint Paul's Indian Mission Church
    #8919
– Varennes (Qué) #8813
– western Canada #8083
– Winnipeg (Man) #8096 8105
  – (1831-1960) #8095
  – (1880s-1910s) #8101
  – University of Manitoba. Chapel of
    Christ the King #9486
– Yamachiche (Qué), Church of Sainte-Anne
  #8783
churches, French
– 17th-18th cs., influence on Québec
  churches #8821 8869 8870
– (1930s), influence on Québec churches
  #1381
churches, Indians of North America
– British Columbia #8914 8917 8918
– Ontario #8904
Churchill (Man), Eskimo Museum #4290
  4313
– Inuit art and artifacts #4227
– Inuit walrus tusk sculptures #4446
churchyards
– see cemeteries
ciboria (vessels), Canadian
– 17th-19th cs.
  – Québec #2681
  – Québec and Ontario #2627
Cicansky, Victor (Vic), Can sculptor,
  ceramicist, 1935- #1937
– ceramic sculpture #795
– exhibitions, group
  – (1976) #1930
  – (1977) #781
– exhibitions (reviews) #2383
Ciccimarra, Richard Matthew, Can artist,
  1924-1973 #5106
– as member of Limners #2043
– exhibitions
  – (1974) #5107
Cigoli (Ludovico Cardi), It artist, 1559-1613
– influence on Antoine-Sébastien
  Plamondon #6886
CIL Inc., chemical manufacturing and
  marketing company
– collection, Canadian painting #124
Cinader, Bernard, Can collector, 1919-
– collection, art, Woodlands Indians #4150
Cincinnati (Ohio), Cincinnati Art Museum
– exhibitions
  – Art of the First Americans (1976) #3459
  – Robert S. Duncanson: A Centennial
    Exhibition (1972) #5338
cinema
– see films, theatres

Cinq-Mars, Alonzo, Can artist, 1881-1969
  #1391
circles
– in North American art #559
Cirier, Antoine, Can sculptor, 1718-1798
  #269 270 5108
– influence on Philippe Liébert #6281
Cirier, Martin, Can builder, sculptor,
  1678-1751 #5108
cities and towns, American
– historic and architectural preservation,
  19th c.-1970s #7761
– western USA #8083
cities and towns, Canadian
– folk paintings #965 966
– historic and architectural preservation,
  19th c.-1970s #7761
– photographic views (1850-1900) #1058
  1061 7744
– views
  – 18th-19th cs. #839
  – (1950s) #403
– western Canada #8083
city gates, Canadian
– Québec (Qué) #8444
city halls, British #8944
city halls, Canadian
– (1950s) #8982
– (1960s) #8990
– Cobourg (Ont), Victoria Hall #8994 8995
– Edmonton (Alta), City Hall #8998 8999
  9000
– Hamilton (Ont), City Hall and Civic
  Square #8988
– Leaf Rapids (Man), Town Centre #8974
– Montréal (Qué), City Hall #1231 8980
– Moose Jaw (Sask), City Hall #8978
– Niagara-on-the-Lake (Ont), 19th c. #7986
– Ottawa (Ont), City Hall #8984
– Scarborough (Ont), Scarborough Civic
  Centre #8973
– Toronto (Ont)
  – City Hall and Civic Square #8981 8983
    8989 8991 8992
  – Yorkville Town Hall #8997
– Vernon (BC), Vernon Civic Centre #8972
– Victorian #7769
– Winnipeg (Man)
  – (1876-1962) #8996
  – City Hall (1883-1886) #8331
  – City Hall (1960) #8985 8986 8987
  – City Hall, competition (1913) #8979
city planning
– see also squares (cities); urban development
– Arctic
  – (1950s) #8184
  – (1960s) #8186
  – (1970s) #8187
– British Columbia, late 19th c. #8150
– Calgary (Alta), (1970s) #8122
– Canada
  – (1867-1967) #7695
  – (1880-1914) #7736
  – (1950s) #7675
  – (1960s) #7682 8304
  – early 20th c. #7955
  – Mawson, Thomas Hayton #9405
– Edmonton (Alta), (1970s) #8123
– Halifax (NS) #1119
– Maritimes #7779
– Montréal (Qué) #7931
– Nova Scotia, 17th-19th cs. #7814
– Ontario #8024
– Ottawa (Ont), National Capital Region

#8035 8037
– Québec, 17th-18th cs. #1320 7885 8603
– St. John's (Nfld) #7786
– Toronto (Ont), City Hall and Civic Square
  #8983
– Vancouver (BC)
  – (1886-1929) #8730
  – (1914) #8156
  – (1960s) #8158
– Winnipeg (Man) #1891
  – (1970s) #8104
civic centres, Canadian
– Faro (Yukon), Faro Townsite Recreation
  Centre #8182
– Leaf Rapids (Man), Town Centre #8409
  8974
– Scarborough (Ont), Scarborough Civic
  Centre #8973
– Vancouver (BC), Britannia Community
  Services Centre #9116
– Vernon (BC), Vernon Civic Centre #8972
Cizek, Albert Franz, Austrian sculptor,
  metalworker, 1866-1943
– works, British Columbia Parliament
  Buildings (Victoria, BC) #8967
Cizek, Franz, Czech artist, 1865-1946
– influence on Fritz Brandtner #4904
Claire, Lorna, Can artist, fl. 1920s-
– murals, Jarvis Collegiate Institute
  Auditorium (Toronto, Ont) #6978
Clairrou, Jacques, Can photographer, fl.
  1972
– portfolio of photographs #997 999
Clallam Indians
– culture
  – (1870s) #4031
  – (1920s) #3819
Clam Harbour (NS)
– views, Charlotte Wilson Hammond #5697
Clapp, William Henry, Can artist, 1879-1954
– as member, Canadian Art Club #193
Claremont (Calif), Claremont College
– exhibitions
  – Native American Art from the Permanent
    Collection (1979) #3378
Clark, John Arthur, Can artist, 1943- #1227
Clark, Kelvin William David (Kelly), Can
  artist, 1935- #5109
Clark, Paraskeva, Can artist, 1898- #5110
  5112
– interview #5111
Clark, Tim, Can artist, 1945-
– exhibitions, group
  – (1980) #687
– on his photographs #5113
– photographs as personal expression #1556
Clarke, Ann, Can artist, 1944- #5114
– exhibitions, group
  – (1974) #565
  – (1975) #1867
  – (1980) #698
  – (1981) #722
– on Edmonton (Alta) art (1981) #1975
Clarke, Fred, Can sculptor, ca. 1902- #5115
Clarke, James, Amer artist, 1885-1969
– correspondence, David Brown Milne #6560
Clarke, Stanley, H. (Stan), Can artist, 1914-
– jewellery #2695
Clarke, W.J., & Co., publishing firm
  (Montréal, Qué)
– Christmas greeting cards #890
Class, Gerhard Hans, Can sculptor, 1924-
– fountain, Vancouver (BC) #2077
– garden sculpture #1849

– sculpture, Vancouver (BC) #2080
Claude Neon Ltd., electric sign firm
   (Montréal, Qué)
– corporate graphic image, Gottschalk &
   Ash #887
Clayton, Edith, Can basketmaker, 1920-
   #2935
Clayton & Bond, Can architectural firm
– Vancouver (BC), Vancouver Civic
   Auditorium, competition #9080
Clazie, John, Can artist, fl. 1956
– jewellery #2695
Clemens, Isaac, Can artist, fl. 1770s-1790s
– engravings #1198
Clément, Serge, Can photographer, 1950-
– portfolio of photographs #991
Clemesha & Portnall, Can architectural firm
– Winnipeg (Man)
   – City Hall, competition #8979
   – Legislative and Executive Building,
      competition #8946
Clerk, Pierre Jean, Can artist, 1928- #5117
– exhibitions
   – (1981) #5118
– interview #5116
Cleveland, Xenophon, Can artist, 1839-1899
   #5119
Cleveland (Ohio), Cleveland Museum of Art
– exhibitions
   – L'Amérique vue par l'Europe (1976) #255
   – Les arts du Canada français, 1613-1870
      (1946) #1331
   – Objects of Bright Pride: Northwest Coast
      Indian Art from the American Museum of
      Natural History (1978) #4024
   – The Arts of French Canada, 1613-1870
      (1946) #1330
   – The European Vision of America (1976)
      #256
Cleverdon, Thomas A., Can photographer,
   fl. 1840s-1850s #1211
climate
– influence on Canadian architecture #7648
   7652 7658 7701
– influence on Prairie domestic architecture
   #8717
– influence on Québec domestic architecture
   #8592
Climo, Lindee, Can artist, 1948- #5121
– exhibitions
   – (1978) #5120
clocks
– see also watches
clocks, American
– 19th c., exported to Canada #2927
clocks, Canadian
– 19th c. #2927
– (1700-1900), clockmakers #2931
– (1730s-mid 19th c.) #2925
– Arthur Pequegnat Clock Co. #2912 2956
– by Québec silversmiths, 17th-18th cs.
   #2657
– Filiau (dit Dubois), Jean Baptiste #5435
– guide for collectors #2101
– île aux Coudres (Qué) #2178
– Montréal (Qué), Church of Notre-Dame
   #8839
– Nova Scotia
   – 17th-19th cs. #2489 2499
   – 18th-19th cs. #2496 2497
– Ontario
   – (1780-1900) #2577
   – (1790s-1857) #2558
– Québec

– 17th-18th cs. #1320 2530 2531 2914
Clodion (Claude Michel), Fr sculptor,
   1738-1814
– influence on François Baillairgé #4589
Closse, Lambert, Can army officer, d. 1662
– household furnishings #2522
Cloutier, Albert-Edouard, Can artist,
   1900-1965
– exhibitions, group
   – (1981) #1117
– mural, Queen Elizabeth Hotel. Salle
   Bonaventure #9286
– mural, Queen Elizabeth Hotel (Montréal,
   Qué) #8228
Cloutier, Eugène, Can writer, 1921-
– Blanc-seing, prints by Claude Vermette
   #7482
Cloutier, Marcel, Can photographer, 1949-
   #1283
Cloutier, Pierre, Can sculptor, 1945-
– and woodcarving school,
   Saint-Jean-Port-Joli (Qué) #1597
Cloverdale (BC), Dogwood Gardens
– architecture, Thompson, Berwick, Pratt &
   Partners #8744
Clow, Clephen John, Can artist, fl. 1831-ca.
   1850
– portraits #1171 1211
clowns
– as imagery, Brian Porter #6907
clubs, Canadian
– Montréal (Qué), Montreal Club #9306
– Vancouver (BC), Terminal City Club #9061
clubs, Cayuga
– war clubs #3535
clubs, Iroquois #3489 3519 3538
clubs, Kwakiutl
– whalebone war club #3813
clubs, Northwest Coast Indians #3785
clubs, Skeena #4053
clubs, Tsimshian #4053
– London (England), British Museum #4048
Clutesi, George C., Can artist, 1905- #5122
– on potlatch ceremony #3956
Clyde, John Edward, Can builder, fl. 1831
– Niagara-on-the-Lake (Ont), Saint
   Andrew's Church #8901
Clyde River (NS)
– stonework, Micmac Indians #3531
Clymer, John Ford, Can artist, 1907-
– exhibitions, group
   – (1961) #62
Coach House Press, publishing firm
   (Toronto, Ont)
– (1960s) #488
– (1970s) #1804
Coade firm (London, England)
– and Coade stone, Bank of Montreal
   (Montréal, Qué) #7908
Coade stone
– use for plaques and monuments, Montréal
   (Qué) #7908
Coast Salish Indians
– architecture #3872
– blankets #3800
– culture #3851 3896
– painting #3878
– petroglyphs #3870
– sculpture #4046
Coastal Constructivists
– and Alan Wood #7608 7610
Coaticook (Qué), Church of Saint-Edmond
– paintings, Ozias Leduc #6204
coats of arms

– see heraldry
Cobb, Andrew Randall, Can architect,
   1876-1943
– Halifax (NS)
   – Bank of Nova Scotia #9182
   – Dalhousie University #9408
Cobb, Charles Sherman, Can architect,
   1882-1964
– Moose Jaw (Sask), City Hall, competition
   #8978
– Toronto (Ont)
   – Fairweather's Store #9363
   – houses #8496
   – Registry Office #8969
– Windsor (Ont), Imperial Bank of Canada
   #9175
Cobb, Henry N., Amer architect, 1926-
– Montréal (Qué) #7901
Cobourg (Ont), Art Gallery of Cobourg
– collection #3162
– exhibitions
   – Alan C. Collier Retrospective (1971) #5131
   – Arthur N. Martin, 1889-1961 (1977) #6423
   – C.M. Manly A.R.C.A., 1855-1924 (1973)
      #6414
   – Goodridge Roberts: Paintings from the
      1950s and 60s (1980) #7048
   – Neil Newton Retrospective (1978) #6694
Cobourg (Ont), Ontario Military
   Convalescent Hospital (formerly Old
   Victoria College)
– architecture #9016
Cobourg (Ont), Victoria Hall
– architecture, Kivas Tully #8994 8995
– Thomas, William, as contractor for
   decorative sculpture #8413
Cobra
– and Albert Dumouchel #5325
Coburn, Frederick Simpson, Can artist,
   1871-1960 #302 5124
– drawings, Art Gallery of Cobourg
   (Cobourg, Ont) #3162
– illustrations #916 5123
   – Farmer's Magazine #1765
Cockburn, James Patterson
– see Cockburn, James Pattison
Cockburn, James Pattison, Brit army officer,
   artist in Canada, 1779-1847 #812 5125 5126
– exhibitions
   – (1978) #5129
– landscapes #26
– views, Québec (Qué) #5127 5128
– winter landscapes #1298
coffers
– see chests
Cohen, Lynne, Can photographer, 1944-
– exhibitions, group
   – (1979) #1037
– exhibitions (reviews) #1018 1046 1060 1067
– portfolio of photographs #1053
Cohen, Sorel, Can artist, 1936-
– interview #5130
– on feminist art #673
Cohn, Norman, Can artist, 1946-
– exhibitions, group
   – (1979) #1157
Cohos Evamy & Partners, Can architectural
   firm
– Calgary (Alta), office buildings #9362
coins and medals
– gorgets #2634 2655
– Indian medals #728 763 2101 3645 3646
coins and medals, American
– Toronto (Ont), Royal Ontario Museum.

Sigmund Samuel Collection #3135
coins and medals, Canadian
- 17th-19th cs. #232
- (1680s-1830s) #2628
- beaver motif #23 56
- Colville, Alex #5145 5148 5150
- De Pédery-Hunt, Dora #5275
- Governors General of Canada, medals
  #764
- guide for collectors #2104
- Hahn, Emanuel Otto #5680
  - 1935 silver dollar #5681
- imagery on money #759
- Lieutenant-Governors of Canada, medals
  #757
- MacAskill, Wallace R., *Bluenose* coin
  design #6351
- McKenzie, Robert Tait #6483 6484 6487
- military medals #2900
  - Canadian Militia #2874
- Olympic coins (1976) #778
- Ottawa (Ont), Public Archives of Canada.
  National Medal Collection #772
- temperance medals (1870s) #724
- Toronto (Ont), Royal Ontario Museum.
  Sigmund Samuel Collection #3135
coins and medals, French
- portraits, Louis XIV and Louis XV #1598
Colborne, Lew, Can artist, 1952-
- exhibitions, group
  - (1981) #1908
Colchester County (NS)
- furniture, 19th c. #2515
Cole, James, Can furniture-maker, fl.
  1816-1827 #2493
Coleman, M.E., Can bishop, 1902-
- pectoral cross and episcopal ring, William
  Maurice Carmichael #5003
Colgate, William George, Can writer, art
  historian, b. 1882
- on Canadian architecture #7697
collage
- Bourdeau, Micheline #4879
- British Columbia (1970s) #2042
- Canada (1955-1965) #510
- Craven, David #5206 5208
Collectionneur, Le, Can periodical #134
collectors and collecting
- *see also* corporate collections; patronage of
  art
- 18th-20th cs., art, Northwest Coast Indians
  #4005
- (1880-1912), Montréal (Qué) #1343
- (1890-1900), Canada #190
- (1930s-1970s), Toronto (Ont) #1686
- Abbott, Inuit art #4306
- Balshine, Lorne, Inuit art #4312 4447
- Band, Charles S., Canadian art #3219
- Band, Charles S. and Helen, Canadian art
  #3215
- Band, Percy, toys and games, 19th c. #2917
- Bick, Walter, glass pickle cruets #2405
- Bird, Wallace S., art, Atlantic provinces,
  20th c. #1130
- Boylen, M.J., Cornelius Krieghoff paintings
  #1
- Bronfman, Samuel, Canadian art #403
- Brown, Ernest, Canadian photographs, late
  19th c. #1949
- Bull, Perkins, Canadian painting #3208
- Bulman, Bessie, Inuit sculpture #4306 4428
- Butler, Jack/K.J., Inuit art #4243
- Carr, Emily, pottery, Northwest Coast
  Indians #3827

- Carrier, Louis, Québec silver #3213
- Collison, W.H., art, Northwest Coast
  Indians #3996
- Cook, Ferna and George, argillite carvings
  #4006
- Corbeil, Maurice and Andrée, Québec
  painting #3233 3234
- Coverdale, William H., Canadiana #12
  3230
- Currelly, Charles Trick, art and artifacts
  for Royal Ontario Museum (Toronto, Ont)
  #3139
- Dobush, Peter, Canadian art #3221
- Doig, Mr. and Mrs. D.R., Canadian
  painting #3224
- Duncan, Douglas M., Canadian art, 20th c.
  #119 541 570 3218 3219 3232
- Firestone, Jack, Canadian art #3239
- Fleming, Sandford, Canadian survey
  photographs #1876
- Garber, Bram, Canadian painting, 20th c.
  #3247
- Gerber, Sidney, art, Northwest Coast
  Indians #3974
- Gibb, Benaiah, European and Canadian art
  #3075 3110
- Hooper, James, art, natives of Pacific
  region, Africa, and America #3369
- Howard, John George, paintings #3129
- Jaffe, Lilly Weil, Inuit art #4223
- Jutras, Albert, Canadian painting #372
- Koerner, Walter and Marianne, art,
  Northwest Coast Indians #3994
- Kolbenhier, Eric, Ukrainian Bukovinian
  embroidery #2124
- Larouche-Villeneuve, Jeanne, prints of
  devotional images #130 1662
- Lee, Clifford E., Inuit prints #4492
- Livernois, Jules-Benoît, photographs #6308
- Loeb, Mr. and Mrs. Jules, Canadian art
  #3231
- Luke, Alexandra, Canadian art #3169
- MacAulay, John, Canadian and European
  art #3212
- MacCallum, James Metcalfe, Tom
  Thomson and Group of Seven #3229
- Mackenzie, Norman, European, Asian,
  and Canadian art #1912 3197
- MacMillan, Harvey Reginald, art,
  Northwest Coast Indians #3996
- Maltwood, Katharine Emma, Canadian,
  European, and Oriental art #3242 6413
- Manuge, Robert, Canadian art #3244
- Massey, Vincent, Canadian painting #3220
  3227
- Mavor, James #1713
- McCord, David Ross, Canadian art #222
  223
- McGowan, John, Canadian glass #2424
- McKendry, Ruth, Ontario quilts, 19th c.
  #2804
- McKendry, Ruth and Blake, furniture
  #8681
- McLean, James Stanley, Canadian art, 20th
  c. #3210 3226 3228
- Mendel, Frederick Salomon, European and
  Canadian art #72 1912 3187
- Millen, Walter H., Canadiana #21
- Morgan, D., Canadian textiles #2747 2748
- Mulders, Gerard and Anne, Inuit
  sculpture #4443
- Newcombe family, works, Emily Carr
  #5023
- Orchinsky, Peter, Bukovynian shirts and

jewellery #2869
- Osipov, Lou, Inuit sculpture #4447
- Pierce, Edith Chown, Canadian glass
  #2397 2398 2399
- Poole, Ernest Edward, Canadian and
  European paintings #3217 3222 3235
- Price, Ralph and Patricia, Canadian folk
  art #970 971 972
- Raley, G.H., art, Northwest Coast Indians
  #3996
- Robertson, John Ross, Canadiana #1713
  3130 3131 3204
- Rosenberg, Gloria, quilts #2808
- Ryerson, Adolphus Egerton, art and
  artifacts for Educational Museum of
  Upper Canada (Toronto, Ont) #3150
- Samuel, Sigmund, Canadiana and
  Americana #247 3135 3140
- Schlombs, Wolfgang, Canadian furniture
  #2485
- Sharpe, Nettie, Québec folk sculpture
  #1607
- Shepley, Canadian souvenir spoons #2652
- Shumiatcher, Jacqui and Morris, Inuit art
  #4311
- Silver, Mr. and Mrs. Stanley S., Canadian
  and British glass bottles, 19th-20th cs.
  #2414
- Sloane, Sir Hans, art, Indians of North
  America #3397
- Smith, Jean and Elizabeth, Canadian
  decorative arts #2125 2131
- Stevens, Gerald, Canadian glass #2397
  2398 2399
- Swinton, George, Inuit art #4306
- Twomey, Jerry, Inuit art #4306
- Van Horne, Sir William Cornelius #1713
- Vanier, Georges and Pauline, Canadian art
  #3216
- Viger, Jacques, Canadian art #1326 1337
  2834 4695 8445
- Volpi, Charles de, Canadiana #3248
- Walker, Sir Byron Edmund, Canadian and
  European art #1713 3205 3206
- Webster, John Clarence, Canadiana #3073
  3209
- Weldon, Susannah Anne, British and
  Chinese ceramics, 17th-19th cs. #2363
- Winrob, Harry, Inuit art #4312 4445 4447
- Zazelenchuk, Stanley and Patricia Jean,
  Inuit art #4284 4306
Collier, Alan Caswell, Can artist, 1911-
- exhibitions
  - (1971) #5131
Collings, Charles John, Can artist, 1848-1931
  #2011 5132 5135 5136
  - (1912) #5133
  - (1914?) #5134
  - (1978) #5137
- landscapes #2016
Collison, Louis, Can sculptor, b. 1898
- argillite carvings #5138
Collison, W.E., Can missionary and
  collector, fl. 1890s
- 1950s #3996
Collison, W.H., Can missionary and
  collector, 1847-1922
- collection, art, Northwest Coast Indians
  #3996
Collyer, Robin John, Can artist, 1949- #5139
- exhibitions, group
  - (1973) #557
  - (1977) #782
  - (1980) #1832

Cologne (West Germany),
  Rautenstrauch-Joest-Museum
– exhibitions
  – *Indianer Nordamerikas: Schätze des
    Museum of the American Indian - Heye
    Foundation - New York* (1969) #3437
Cologne (West Germany),
  Wallraf-Richartz-Museum
– exhibitions
  – *Zeitgenössische Kunst in Kanada* (1959)
    #433
colonization
– British in Canada
  – and Joseph Légaré #6216
  – and William George Richardson Hind
    #5811
Colonna, Edward, Amer architect, 1862-1948
– Montréal (Qué), Sir William Van Horne
  Mansion #8594
Colophon, The, Brit periodical
– Milne, David Brown, *Painting Place* #6562
colour
– Bush, Jack Hamilton #4964
– Comtois, Louis #5163 5164
– Gaucher, Yves #5570
– Giguère, Roland, on #5599
– Lindner, Ernest #6286
– Molinari, Guido #6590 6591
– Montréal (Qué) painting (1950s-1960s)
  #1425
– symbolism and cosmology, Indians of
  North America #3498
Colour and Form Society (Toronto, Ont)
– support of Estonian art #118
colour printing
– Milne, David Brown, on #6546 6552 6563
  6564
Columbia River (BC)
– petroglyphs #3870 3903
– prehistoric basketry #3842
– prehistoric sculpture #3914
Colville, Alexander (Alex), Can artist, 1920-
  #5141 5142 5146 5148 5150 5151 5152 5155
– and magic realism #5143
– and realism #110
– compared with Nicolas Poussin #5147
– exhibitions
  – (1977) #5153
  – (1979) #5145
– exhibitions, group
  – (1958) #431
  – (1959) #438
  – (1964) #462
  – (1966) #1123
  – (1967) #490
  – (1974) #1129
  – (1977) #633
  – (1978) #665
  – (1979) #147
  – (1980) #1221
– Forrestall, Tom, compared with #5462
  5466
– *Horse and Train*, Art Gallery of Hamilton
  (Hamilton, Ont) #38
– imagery #5149
– *Infantry near Nijmegen* #1115
– influence on Jim McKenzie #6480
– interview #5154
– nudes #5140
– on printmaking #817
– paintings, National Gallery of Canada
  (Ottawa, Ont) #5144
– Prévost, Antoine, compared with #6927
– prints #1214

– World War II drawings and prints #5156
Combe, Lawrence W., Can architect, 1932-
– winner, Ontario Hydro Golden Medallion
  "All Electric Home" Competition (1961)
  #8514
combs, Iroquois #3587
combs, Seneca #3587
Comfort, Charles Fraser, Can artist, curator,
  1900- #5160
– as director, National Gallery of Canada
  (Ottawa, Ont) #3049 3050
– as teacher of Gerald Tailfeathers #7312
  7313
– *Dieppe Raid* #1115
– exhibitions
  – (1972) #5159
– exhibitions, group
  – (1978) #133
– on art #5157
– on Louis Muhlstock #6657
– on portraiture #624
– on World War II, Italian campaign
  (1943-1944) #1090 5158
– *Parliament Buildings*, Canadian Club of
  New York (New York, NY) #3211
– woodcuts #802
comic strips
– and Greg Curnoe #5233
comic strips, Canadian
– (1939-1945) #947
– Eastern Townships (Qué), (1970s) #1535
– Québec #948 952 953 954
  – (1970s) #950 951 1502
– Vancouver (BC), (1970s) #955
Comingo, Joseph Brown, Can artist, b. 1784,
  fl. to 1820
– portrait, William Hazen's children #5161
commemorative monuments
– *see* monuments
commercial architecture, Canadian
– 17th c.-1960s #7689
– (1880-1914) #7736
– (1910s) #9332
– (1911-1912) #8295
– (1920s) #7656
– (1938-1942) #7666
– (1960-1970) #7710
– British Columbia
  – (1970s) #9360
  – Hooper, Thomas #8376
– Calgary (Alta)
  – (1909) #8116
– Gothic revival #7739 7740
– Halifax (NS) #7819
  – 18th-19th cs. #7818
  – Prince and Hollis streets buildings, 19th
    c. #7831
– Hamilton (Ont)
  – Victorian #7991
– John B. Parkin Associates #8395
– Kingston (Ont)
  – 19th c. #7995
  – (1670s-late 19th c.) #7989
– London (Ont)
  – 19th c. #8007
– Manitoba
  – 19th-early 20th cs. #8102
– Montréal (Qué)
  – architectural drawings, Archives
    nationales du Québec à Montréal #8604
– Nova Scotia
  – 17th-19th cs. #7814
– Ontario
  – 19th c. #8006

– prefabricated buildings, western Canada,
  early 20th c. #8082
– Québec
  – (1960s) #7862
– Regina (Sask)
  – (1909) #8109
– Second Empire #7741 7742
– St. John's (Nfld)
  – (pre-1900) #7786
– Toronto (Ont)
  – 19th c. #8059
  – (1920s) #9335 9367
– Trois-Rivières (Qué)
  – (1630s-1910s) #7883
– Winnipeg (Man) #8105 8106
  – (1831-1960) #8095
  – (1880s-1910s) #8101
commercial art
– Fleming, Allan Robb, on #5456
commercial art, Canadian
– (1930s) #340
– Halifax (NS), Nova Scotia College of Art
  #2993
Commercial Gazette, Can newspaper
– and James Lovell Wiseman #7603
Committee to Strengthen Canadian Culture
– (1970s), and Michel Lambeth #6159
commodes
– *see* chests
communication, mass
– *see* mass media
communication and art
– *see* mass media
Communiqué, Can periodical #542 551
Communism and art
– *see also* socialism and art
– Canada #1393
– Sawchuk, George #7143
Community Design Workshop
– assistance for residents of low-income
  housing, Montréal (Qué), (1970s) #8283
Community Planning Association of Canada
– housing designs (1950s) #8509
Comox (BC), Filberg House
– architecture and interior, Arthur Charles
  Erickson #8355
Compagnie-des-Indes porcelain
– *see* Chinese export porcelain
Compagnons, Les, Can theatre company
– Pellan, Alfred, costume and stage design
  for *La nuit des rois* #6799
competitions, architecture
– 20th c., Canada #7747
– (1950s-1960s), Canada #7682
– (1960s), Canada #7683
– (1970s), survey of architects #8314
– Burnaby (BC), Simon Fraser University
  #9501
– *Canadian Architect* community art gallery
  competition (1957) #9082
– Canadian Small House Competition (1946)
  #8740
– Charlottetown (PEI)
  – Confederation Centre #9088 9089 9094
  – Province House #8937
– Dominion Housing Act Competition
  – (1938) #8739
– Edmonton (Alta), City Hall #8998 8999
  9000
– Hamilton (Ont), northwestern entrance to
  city #7962
– Los Angeles (Calif), Bunker Hill
  redevelopment #8364
– Montréal (Qué), McGill University.

Athletic buildings #9417
– Moose Jaw (Sask), City Hall #8978
– Ontario Hydro Golden Medallion "All
 Electric Home" Competition (1961) #8514
– Osaka (Japan), Expo '70. Canadian
 Pavilion #9217
– Ottawa (Ont)
 – Departmental and Justice Buildings
  #8921
 – National Gallery of Canada
  – (1954) #9079
  – (1975-1977) #9126 9136 9142
 – Parliament Buildings #8922 8923 8924
– Regina (Sask)
 – Legislative Buildings #8954 8955 8956
  8961
 – War Memorial Museum #9073
– Saskatoon (Sask), Mendel Art Gallery
 #9091
– T. Eaton Company Ideal Ontario Home
 Competition (1930) #8735
– Toronto (Ont)
 – Bank of Toronto #8293
 – City Hall and Civic Square #8981 8983
  8989
 – Government House (1911) #8748
 – John Ross Robertson and Glenholme
  schools #9437
 – Masonic Temple #9062
 – Parliament Buildings #8943
 – Toronto Stock Exchange #9161
 – University of Toronto. Knox College
  #9432
– Vancouver (BC)
 – Chinese Cultural Centre #9144
 – elementary school design (1970) #9507
 – University of British Columbia #9498
  9500 9509
  – Student Union #9503
 – Vancouver Civic Auditorium #9080
– Winnipeg (Man)
 – City Hall (1913) #8979
 – City Hall (1960) #8985 8986 8987
 – Legislative Buildings #8946 8949 8950
 – Winnipeg Art Gallery #9102
competitions, sculpture
– Canadian battlefields memorials
 competition, World War I #731 732
– Hamilton (Ont), Art Gallery of Hamilton
 (1976) #780
– Lethbridge (Alta), University of
 Lethbridge (1980-1981) #797
computer art
– (1960s), Canada #517
– (1960s), Québec #528
– Duquet, Suzanne #5344
– Hushlak, Gerald #1961 5891 5892
computers
– and art, Arnold Rockman on #7061
– and inventories of Canadian art and
 architecture #159
– and library architecture (1960s) #9046
Comtois, Louis, Can artist, 1945- #1544 5162
– exhibitions
 – (1978) #5163
 – (1980) #5164
– exhibitions, group
 – (1981) #1565
Comtois, Ulysse, Can artist, 1931- #5165
 – (1955) #1408
 – (1968) #522
 – (1973) #556
– interview #1489
Conacher, John, Can artist, fl. 1919

– illustrations #916
concentration camps
– views
 – Menses, Jan #6511
 – Saarniit, John #7112
 – Shadbolt, Jack Leonard #7189
Conception Bay (Nfld)
– wood-processing mill (ca. 1620) #7718
conceptual art
– amd Tim Zuck #7636
– and Bill Vazan #7473
– and Garry Neill Kennedy #6043
– and George Sawchuk #7143
– and Thomas Elton Henrickson and Martha
 Charlotte Henrickson #5781
– Canada #540 574
 – landscapes #617
– W.O.R.K.S. #1955
concrete
– Concrete Awards Program (1971) #7706
– precast
 – (1960s) #7684 9401
 – Montréal (Qué), Habitat '67 #8578
– Toronto (Ont), Roman Stone Company
 (1903-1920s) #7734
– use in Canadian and American
 architecture (1910s) #7643
– use in Canadian architecture (1867-1967)
 #7695
– use in Hamilton Terminal Station
 (Hamilton, Ont) #9527
– use in Jacobs Building (Montréal, Qué)
 #9305
– use in Manitoba architecture, 19th-early
 20th cs. #8102
Concrete Awards Program
– (1971) #7706
concrete poetry
– Copithorne, Judith #5176
– Frenkel, Vera #5521
– Palchinski, Sylvia Scott #6753
Condé, Carole, Can artist, 1940-
– exhibitions, group
 – (1980) #1063
– Maybe Wendy's Right #1052
– on politics and art #602
Conder, Charles, Brit artist, 1868-1909
– influence on James Wilson Morrice #6630
Condon, Wanda, Can artist, 1951-
– exhibitions, group
 – (1978) #669
 – (1980) #698
– exhibitions (reviews) #5166
Condron, Brian, Can photographer, 1949-
– portfolio of photographs #1053
Conefroy, Pierre, Can priest, architect,
 1752-1816 #8834
– church plan
 – Berthierville (Qué) #8833
 – L'Acadie (Qué) #8830
Conference of Canadian Artists
– (1941) #351 379
– (1941-1951) #390
conferences
– 20th Century Canadian Culture: A
 Symposium (Washington, DC) (1977) #621
 627
– Canadian Conference of the Arts (1961)
 #444
– Conference of Canadian Artists (1941)
 #351 379 390
– Conference on Canadian-American Affairs
 (Kingston, Ont) (1937) #337
– Couchiching Conference of the Canadian

Institute on Public Affairs (Lake
 Couchiching, Ont) (1976) #619
– Federation of Canadian Artists (1941 and
 1947) #376
– Painters' Symposium (Kingston, Ont)
 (1977) #620
– Preserving the Canadian Heritage/La
 préservation du patrimoine canadien
 (1975) #7767
Confrérie des menuisiers de madame
 Sainte-Anne #1241 5965
Conger, Wilson S., Can politician, d. 1864
– portrait of, Paul Kane #6008
congresses
– see conferences
Conner, Bruce, Amer artist, 1933-
– and Gary Lee-Nova #6213
Conner, Scott, Can photographer, ca. 1952-
– portfolio of photographs #1032
Connolly, Reynald, Can artist, 1944- #1479
 5167
Conseil de la sculpture du Québec/Quebec
 Sculpture Council
– (1978-1979) #1628
Conseil des arts et manufactures
– see Council of Arts and
 Manufactures/Conseil des arts et
 manufactures
conservation and restoration
– Canada #7767
– Québec
 – (1970s) #3015
 – and Gérard Morisset #3125 3127 3305
– Québec (Qué), Musée du Québec #3092
conservation and restoration, architecture
– see conservation of architecture
conservation and restoration, art
– (1960s), artists' materials #527
conservation and restoration, books #935
conservation and restoration, decorative arts
 #2252
conservation and restoration, furniture
– Québec, 17th-18th cs. #2530 2531
conservation and restoration, glass
– window glass #7777 7778
conservation and restoration, landscape
 architecture #7768
conservation and restoration, mural painting
– Granville Ferry region (NS), Hall-Croscup
 House #1223
conservation and restoration, musical
 instruments
– Morisset, Gérard #2952
conservation and restoration, petroglyphs
– Indians of North America #3481
– Northwest Coast Indians #3988
conservation and restoration, rugs
– hooked rugs #2756
conservation and restoration, sculpture
– (1970s), recommendations for #793
conservation and restoration, textiles
– Indians of North America #3476
conservation and restoration, totem poles
 #3884 3925 4119
conservation of architecture
– Acadian Village (Caraquet, NB) #7805
– architects' offices (1950s) #9299
– Association for Preservation Technology
 #7757
– banks #9204
– Barkerville (BC) #8151
– British Columbia, wooden Indian churches
 #8917
– Brockville (Ont), Idlewild #8671

– Calgary (Alta) #8121 8133 8134 8138
– Canada #7767 7772
   – (1880s) #7754
   – (1930s-1940s) #7666
   – (1950s), law and legislation #7755
   – (1959), Royal Architectural Institute of
      Canada. Committee on the Preservation
      of Historic Buildings #7756
   – (1960s) #7759
   – (1970s) #7705 7765 7771 8964
      – architectural conservation training
         #7773
   – (1970s-1980s) #7764
   – (1980) #7776
   – conversion of public buildings to
      cultural facilities #9147 9148
– Canada and USA, 19th c.-1970s #7761
– Canadian Inventory of Historic Building
   #7707 7708 7716
– Canadiana Village (Rawdon, Qué) #7876
– Charlottetown (PEI), Province House
   #8938 8939
– Cormier, Ernest, on #8346
– Dawson City (Yukon), Palace Grand
   Theatre #9090
– Edmonton (Alta) #8131
   – Duggan House #8729
   – Holgate House #8718
– facades #7766
– Fanshawe Pioneer Village (Ont) #8066
– Fort George (Niagara-on-the-Lake, Ont)
   #8459
– Fort Langley (BC) #8474
– Fort Saint James (BC) #8478
– Fort William (Ont) #8460
– Granville Ferry (NS), Port Royal
   Habitation #7812 7813
– guide #7774 7775
– Halifax (NS) #7830 7834
   – downtown area #7819
   – Granville Street #7817
   – Halifax Citadel #8430 8434 8440
   – heritage conservation system #7833
   – Neptune Theatre #9097
   – Nova Scotia College of Art and Design
      #9409 9410
   – Prince and Hollis streets buildings #7831
   – waterfront buildings #7822 7824 7825
   – West House, Brunswick Street #8537
– Heritage Canada #7763 7770
– Heritage Park (Alta) #8125
– Kings Landing (NB) #7810 7811
– Kingston (Ont) #7995
– Lake Louise (Alta), Skoki Lodge #9296
– Laval (Qué), André B. Papineau House
   #8625
– log houses #8526
– Louisbourg (NS) #8423 8425 8439 8442
– Lunenburg (NS), Soloman House #8549
– Midland (Ont), Sainte-Marie among the
   Hurons #7999
– mills #9248
– Montréal (Qué) #7911 7914
   – Bigot House #8567
   – château Dufresne #8617 8618
   – Church of Sainte-Catherine-d'Alexandrie
      #8867
   – low-income housing (1970s) #8283
   – Old Montréal #7905 7910 7919
   – Saint Gabriel House #8597
– Moose Factory (Ont) #7998
– Nelson (BC) #8155
– Oka (Qué), Calvary at Oka #8853
– Ontario #8024

   – (1930s) #7966
   – (1971), government preservation
      program #7996
   – churches #8906
   – Local Architectural Conservation
      Advisory Committees (LACAC) #8022
   – log cabins #7990
   – wooden buildings, 19th c. #7745
– Ontario Heritage Foundation #8001
– Ottawa (Ont) #8935
   – Glebe district #8042
   – La Salle Academy #9480 9481
   – National Capital Region #8043 8044
– Peterborough (Ont) #8021
   – Hutchison House #8674
– Pontiac County (Qué) #7894 7895
– Prince Edward Island Heritage
   Foundation #7795
– Québec #1324 7870 8595
   – and Gérard Morisset #7897
   – Canadian Heritage of Quebec #7871
   – churches #1247
   – domestic architecture #7760 8592 8600
      8624
   – ministère des Affaires culturelles du
      Québec. Service de l'Inventaire des
      biens culturels #1277
– Québec (Qué) #7936 7937 7938 7940 7941
   7942
   – Hôpital-Général. Windmill #9245
   – place Royale #7948 7951
   – Royal Battery #8451
– Quidi Vidi (Nfld), Christ Church #7788
– Rimouski (Qué), Musée régional de
   Rimouski #9118
– Saint John (NB) #7807
– Saskatoon (Sask) #8114
– St. Andrews (NB) #8550
– St. John's (Nfld) #7789 7790 7793 7794
– theatres #9131
– Toronto (Ont) #8073
   – Canadian Bank of Commerce #9351
   – central residential areas (1970s) #8068
   – Chief Justice Sir William Campbell
      House #8661
   – Colborne Lodge #8659
   – Fort York #8458
   – Osgoode Hall #9003
   – St. Lawrence Hall #9103
   – St. Lawrence Neighbourhood #8079
   – Stewart Building #9354
   – The Grange #8665 8666 8680
   – Todmorden Mills #8072
   – Toronto Board of Trade
      recommendations (1979) #8027
   – University of Toronto. University
      College #9482
   – Yorkville Village #9376
– Trois-Rivières (Qué), Deschenaux House,
   also known as manoir de Tonnancour
   #8633
– Tunis Snook Farm (near Kingston, Ont)
   #8681
– Upper Canada Village (Morrisburg, Ont)
   #7981 7982 7988 8031
– Vancouver (BC) #7762 8161 8164 8166
   – (1970s) #8162
   – Gastown #8163
   – Hodson Manor #8707
   – Orpheum Theatre #9135
   – rehabilitation of inner city buildings for
      residential use (1980) #8725
– Victoria (BC) #8149 8173 8176 8177 8178
   – British Columbia Parliament Buildings

      #8965 8966
   – domestic architecture #8722
– Victorian #7769
– Village Jacques de Chambly (Qué) #8573
– Winnipeg (Man) #8103 8108
   – warehouses and office buildings #8106
      8107
Constable, John, Brit artist, 1776-1837
– influence on Homer Ransford Watson
   #7531
– influence on J.E.H. MacDonald #6370
Constantineau, Fleurimond, Can artist,
   1905-1981 #5168
construction
– see building
Construction: A Journal for the Architectural
   Engineering and Contracting Interests of
   Canada, Can periodical #7641
Constructivism
– and Lawren Phillips Harris #5711
– and Peter Henry Kolisnyk #6075 6076
– and Robert Gray Murray #6668
– and Roger Vilder #7489
– and Structurism #777
– and Tim Zuck #7636
– and video art #654
– Canadian open-air sculpture (1970s) #784
consumers
– Canada (1885-1925) #2851
containers
– see also bowls
– in art
   – Lee-Nova, Gary #6213
   – McWilliams, Allan #6508
   – Prince, Richard #6938
   – Urquhart, Tony #7448
containers, Algonquian
– beadwork #3635
– birchbark #3571
– fibre bags #3638 3744
– Lac Barrière (Qué) #3544
– shellwork #3505
– wooden, 18th c. #3507
containers, Algonquin
– birchbark #3542 4078
containers, Athapaskan #4104 4105
containers, Bella Bella
– carved wooden bowls and boxes, 19th c.
   #3985
containers, Beothuk #3528
containers, Blackfoot #3654
containers, Canadian
– grasswork, Labrador, 20th c. #2945
– leather (1970s) #2936
– wooden, 18th-19th cs. #2594
containers, Cree #3402 3655 3742
– splint bark #4078
containers, Delaware
– shamanic medicine bags #3506
containers, Dogrib #4089
containers, Great Basin Indians #3986
containers, Haida
– carved wooden bowls and boxes, 19th c.
   #3985
– New York (NY), American Museum of
   Natural History #4066
containers, Huron #3514 3519
containers, Indians of North America
– buffalo hair bags #3398
containers, Ingalik #4087
containers, Iroquois #3519
– beadwork #3635
– fibre bags #3638 3744
– shellwork #3505

containers, Micmac #3528 3569
containers, Mistassini #4080
containers, Montagnais
– birchbark #4086
– splint bark #4078
containers, Naskapi
– splint bark #4078
containers, Northwest Coast Indians #3866 4015
– copper #4071
containers, Ojibwa #3488 3557 4089
containers, Osage
– fibre bags #3744
containers, Penobscot
– birchbark #3510
containers, Plains
– New York (NY), American Museum of Natural History #3668
containers, Saulteaux #3402
– birchbark #3549
containers, Slavey #4089
containers, Tanaina #4085
containers, Tête de Boule
– birchbark #4079 4108
containers, Tlingit
– carved wooden bowls and boxes, 19th c. #3985
containers, Tsimshian
– carved wooden bowls and boxes, 19th c. #3985
containers, Woodlands
– beadwork #3635
– fibre bags #3638 3744
– shellwork #3505
Contant, Gabriel, Can artist, 1931- #5169
Contemporary Arts Society (Montréal, Qué) #589 592 1393 1451 1459 1474
– and Louise Landry Gadbois #1433
– and Paul-Emile Borduas #4809 4843
– influence on Alberta landscape painting #1965
convents
– see also monasteries
convents, Canadian
– Montréal (Qué) #7932
– maison mère des Soeurs Grises #8862
– Québec
– 17th-18th cs. #7845
– 17th-early 19th cs. #7841 7853
– Québec (Qué)
– Hôpital-Général #9022
– maison mère Mallet #8884
– Ursuline Convent #8810
– Trois-Rivières (Qué), (1630s-1910s) #7883
convicts
– see prisoners
Cook, Ferna and George, Can collectors, 20th c.
– collection, argillite carvings #4006
Cook, James, Brit navigator, explorer in Canada, 1728-1779
– collection, art, Northwest Coast Indians #4005
– expedition, Arctic #278
– expedition, Northwest Coast Indians #269 270 3445 4062 4064
Cook, Mrs. Nelson, Can artist, fl. 1830s-1850s #5170
Cook, Nelson, Can artist, 1817-1892
– portraits of Dickinson family #5170
Cooke, Edwy Francis, Can artist, 1926-
– exhibitions
– (1977) #5171
cooking utensils

– see kitchen utensils
Cooksville (Ont), Applewood United Church
– architecture, James A. Murray #8763
cool realism
– see Photo-realism
Coombs, Edith Grace, Can artist, 1890- #5172
Coon, S.B., & Son, Can architectural firm
– Sarnia (Ont), public school #9387
Cooper, H.W., Can artist, fl. 1914-1919
– art and writings, World War I #5173
– illustrations #916
Cooper, Heather, Can artist, 1945- #5175
– and Burns, Cooper, Donoahue, Fleming & Company Ltd. #904
– as cofounder of Burns, Cooper, Hynes Ltd. #905
– paintings and illustrations #5174
– prints #897 941
Cooper, Kenneth R., Can architect, 1928-
– Toronto (Ont), Hydro Place #9352
Cooper, Lynda, Can artist, 1952-
– design, Olympic coins (1976) #778
Cooper and Beatty Ltd., Can graphic design firm
– and Jim Donoahue #5297
– exhibitions (reviews) #860
Coopération des petits dessins, Can comic strip artists #952
Cooperstown (NY), New York State Historical Association
– exhibitions
– The Marine Collection (1943) #12
Copenhagen (Denmark), Ethnografish Samling
– artifacts, Thule #4372
Copenhagen (Denmark), Nationalmuseet
– art, natives of North America #3338
– exhibitions
– Sculpture of the Inuit: Masterworks of the Canadian Arctic/La sculpture chez les Inuit: chefs-d'oeuvre de l'Arctique canadien (1972) #4423 4440
Copithorne, Judith, Can artist, 1939-
– on graphic poems #5176
Copley, John Singleton, Amer artist, 1738-1815
– portraits of Nova Scotians #1197
copper, Canadian
– 19th c. #2704
– guide for collectors #2252
– storefronts (1920s) #9364
copper engraving
– see engraving
Copper Eskimo
– antlerwork #4412
– culture
– (1903-1905) #4366
– (1920s) #4330
coppers, Haida
– Great Killer Whale Copper #4054
– sea monster #3821
coppers, Indians of North America
– prehistoric #3401
coppers, Northwest Coast Indians #4065 4071
– Ottawa (Ont), National Museum of Man #3924
coppers, Skeena
– pictograph, Skeena River (BC) #3822
coppers, Tagish #4106
coppers, Tlingit #3812 4106
coppers, Tutchone #4106

copy art
– Canada (1970s) #614
– Eastcott, Robert Wayne #5354
– Jackson, Sarah Jeanette #5932
– N.E. Thing Co. Ltd. #524
– use of telefacsimile unit #652
– Walker, Robert #668
copyright
– Canada
– and Canadian Artists' Representation #563 632
– artists' rights (1970s) #682
Corbeil, Maurice and Andrée, Can collectors, 20th c.
– collection, Québec painting #3233 3234
Corbeil, Wilfrid, Can priest, architect, artist, 1893-1979
– churches #8838
– on Québec painting (1950s) #1402
Cordeau, Bagbaria, Can architect, fl. 1980s
– Edmonton (Alta), City Hall #8998
Cordner, Andrew, Can stained glass artist, 1935- #2450
Corkan, Juan (Corky), Can architect, 1927-
– restoration, Duggan House (Edmonton, Alta) #8729
Corman, Don, Can photographer, 1951-
– exhibitions, group
– (1980) #1063
Cormier, Bruno M., Can psychiatrist, writer, 1919-
– Refus global #1396
– writings #1449
Cormier, Ernest, Can architect, artist, 1885-1980 #302 8345
– exhibitions, group
– (1933) #8224
– interview #8346
– Montréal (Qué)
– Cormier House #8347 8348
– Court House Annex #9001
Cormon, Fernand Anne Piestre, Fr artist, 1845-1924
– influence on Charles Edouard Huot #5878 5884
Corne, Sharon Joy, Can artist, 1936-
– on Woman as Viewer exhibition, Winnipeg Art Gallery (Winnipeg, Man), (1975) #596 1877
Corneil, Carmen, Can architect, 1933-
– Ottawa (Ont), Carleton University. School of Architecture #8284
Corneil & McBain, Can architectural firm
– Toronto (Ont), Girl Guides of Canada headquarters #7984
Cornell, Joseph, Amer sculptor, 1903-1972
– influence on Alan Frank Glass #5616
Cornellier, Pierre, Can artist, 1943- #1479 1480
Cornwall (Ont), Inverarden (John McDonald of Garth Residence)
– architecture #8673
Cornwall (Ont), Transport Canada Training Institute
– architecture, Thom Partnership #8412
Cornwallis Valley (NS), Acacia Grove House
– architecture #8528
Corot, Jean Baptiste Camille, Fr artist, 1796-1875
– East, Benoît, compared with #5353
– influence on Robert Wakeham Pilot #6869
corporate collections
– Ayerst, McKenna and Harrison #852
– Bank of Nova Scotia #3245

– Canada #3243
  – (1950s) #3259
  – and Art Bank #3286
– Canadian Medical Association #138
– CIL Inc. #124
– Henry Birks and Sons Ltd. #2636 2637
  2650 2651 2656
– House of Seagram #403
– Imperial Oil Ltd. #3241
– International Business Machines
  Corporation (IBM) #350
– Macdonald-Stewart Foundation #2203 2204
– Metro Toronto Board of Trade #3291
– Rothmans of Pall Mall Canada #4257
– Shell Canada Ltd. #1966 3238 3240
– Société d'électrolyse et de chimie Alcan
  Ltée (Sécal) #3246
– Toronto-Dominion Bank #3225 4201 4216
  4427
correspondence
– see artists' correspondence
correspondence art
– see mail art
Corriveau, Jeanne d'Arc, Can tapestry artist,
  1931- #2102 2769 5177
Corsault, Share, Can photographer, 1947-
  #2071
– exhibitions, group
  – (1981) #2084
Cosgrove, Stanley Morel, Can artist, 1911-
  #5180 5182 5183 5184 5185
– and art criticism #3307
– works
  – (1940s) #5179
  – (1944) #5178
  – (1944-1950) #5181
Coshof, Karen, Can photographer, 1945-
  #995
– portfolio of photographs #1023
cosmology, Haida #3780
cosmology, Indians of North America
– cardinal points #3498
cosmology, Northwest Coast Indians
– petroglyphs #3988
cosmology, Plains
– medicine wheels #3748
Cossette, Marie Andrée, Can photographer,
  fl. 1970s #1556
costume
– see also arm bands; buttons; fashion; hats;
  headgear; helmets; military uniforms;
  pattern books, costume; religious costume;
  sashes; shoes; Victorian costume
– Pellan, Alfred #6804
  – La nuit des rois #6799
costume, Algonquian #3374 3605 3672
– (1760s-early 20th c.) #3633
– beadwork #3582 3635
– bustles #3580
– moose hair embroidery #3513
– wampum #3521
costume, Assiniboine #3653 3739
costume, Athapaskan #4073 4102 4104 4105
– 19th c. #4111
costume, Beothuk #3528 3584
costume, Blackfoot #3654 3686 3739
– (1910-1960) #3712
– female #3695
– Minìpoka #3749
– New York (NY), American Museum of
  Natural History #3414
costume, Blood #3414 3739
costume, Canadian #2730
– 17th-19th cs. #2825

– 18th c. #2868
– (1608-1867) #2120
– (1780-1967) #2849
– (1848-1868) #2887
– (1867) #2844
– (1870s) #2854 2859
– (1886-1930), Eaton's catalogues #2851
– (1890-1910), Montréal (Qué) #2861
– Acadian
  – 18th-19th cs. #2836 2876 2894
  – 19th c. #2877
  – (1870s) #2840
– Bukovynian shirts (1865-1945) #2869
– children's clothing
  – (1780-1930) #2862
  – (1820-1890) #2853
  – late 19th c.-1930s #2932
– country clothing
  – Ontario, 19th c. #2888
  – Québec, 17th-18th cs. #2217
– Dugald (Man), Dugald Costume Collection
  #2902
– Edmonton (Alta), University of Alberta
  #3200
– ethnic groups #2893
– female
  – 18th-19th cs. #2903
  – 19th c. #2846 2875 2908
  – (1713-1758), Louisbourg (NS) #2855
  – (1780-1867), Ontario #2839
  – (1800-1821) #2860
  – (1800-1867), underclothing #2886
  – (1803), Québec #2830
  – (1822-1839) #2863
  – (1830s-1880s) #2870
  – (1840-1866) #2885
  – (1840-1965), evening dresses, Montréal
    (Qué) #2842
  – (1840s-1850s) #2847
  – (1867-1898) #2889
  – (1867-1907), Ontario #2843
  – (1870s) #2829 2878
    – Beauce (Qué) #2828
  – (1890s), northwest North America #2856
  – (1909-1919) #2905
  – (1920s) #2906
– General Idea #5583
– île d'Orléans (Qué)
  – 17th-19th cs. #1252
  – 17th c. #2895
– illustrations #1326
– illustrations, Public Archives of Canada.
  Picture Division (Ottawa, Ont) #2883 2884
  2904
– influence of costume, Indians of North
  America #2841
– Lithuanian #2892
– male
  – 17th c., Montréal (Qué) #2821
  – 19th c. #2845
    – Québec #2896
  – (1605-1963), Québec #2838
– Marshall, Pat #6422
– Mennonite #2264
– Montréal (Qué), 19th c. #2837
– Montreal Theatre Ballet (1950s) #1410
– Norwegian #2273
– Ontario
  – (1784-1867) #2852
  – (1867-1907) #2871
– Ottawa (Ont), National Museum of Man.
  Canadian Centre for Folk Culture Studies
  #963
– Pellan, Alfred #6816

– Québec #2879
  – 17th-18th cs. #2850
  – 17th-19th cs. #2822
    – European influences #2221
  – 18th c. #2200
  – (1840-1900) #2899
  – (1850s) #2834
  – as folk art #1291
  – in French-Canadian folk songs #2898
  – muff #2817
  – tailors, 18th c. #2820
– Québec (Qué), Séminaire de Québec #2809
– sports and games, 19th c. #257
– travellers and coureurs de bois, 18th-19th
  cs. #2826
– Ukrainian #2117
– wedding dresses, gowns, and suits,
  Peterborough (Ont), (1810-1938) #2909
– winter clothing
  – 19th c. #2891
  – Charlevoix (Qué), late 19th-early 20th cs.
    #2890
costume, Caribou Eskimo #4265
costume, Chilkat #3811
costume, Coast Salish #3851 3896
costume, Cree #3402 3739 3742
costume, Dakota
– St. Paul (Minn), Science Museum of
  Minnesota #3755
costume, Dogrib #4089
costume, French
– female, nobility (1659) #2830
costume, Gros Ventre #3753
costume, Haida
– Washington (DC), Smithsonian Institution
  #3763
costume, Han #4101
costume, Huron #3514
– moose hair embroidery #3513
costume, Indians of North America #2849
  3453
– 17th-19th cs. #2825
– beadwork #3449
– illustrations, Public Archives of Canada.
  Picture Division (Ottawa, Ont) #2883 2884
– influence on Canadian costume #2841
– paintings of, George Catlin #3384
costume, Ingalik #4087
costume, Inuit
– amautik #4300
costume, Iroquois #3489 3559 3605
– (1760s-early 20th c.) #3633
– beadwork #3635
– Six Nations Reserve (Ont) #3598
– wampum #3521
costume, Kutchin #4102
costume, Kwakiutl #3787
costume, Maliseet #3641
costume, Métis #4110
costume, Micmac #3528 3569 3641 3643
costume, Mistassini #4080 4100
costume, Mohawk
– 18th c. #3550
costume, Naskapi
– painting on #4098
costume, Northwest Coast Indians
– leggings, quillwork #3811
costume, Ojibwa #3488 3539 3557 4089
– Midewiwin shaman buffalo robes #3517
– St. Paul (Minn), Science Museum of
  Minnesota #3755
costume, Piegan
– leggings #3715
– New York (NY), American Museum of

Natural History #3414
costume, Plains #3656 3657 3672 3684 3716
  3717
– bustles #3692
– dance #3694
– female #3658
– leggings #3697
– New York (NY), American Museum of
  Natural History #3668
– secret societies #3727
– wampum #3521
costume, Salish #4013
costume, Sarcee #3739
costume, Saulteaux #3402
– Island Lake (Man) #3549
costume, Shuswap #3789
costume, Siouan #3672
costume, Skokomish #3835
costume, Slavey #4089
costume, Snuqualmi #3835
costume, Tagish #4106
costume, Tahltan
– (1910s) #4074
costume, Tanaina #4085
costume, Tanana #4095
costume, Tête de Boule #4079
costume, Thompson Indians
– beadwork and embroidery #3808
costume, Tlingit #3976 4106
– Washington (DC), Smithsonian Institution
  #3763
costume, Tsimshian #3763 3795
costume, Tutchone #4106
costume, Woodlands
– (1760s–early 20th c.) #3633
– beadwork #3635
costume technique
– see media and techniques, costume
Côté, Dom Claude-Marie, Can priest,
  architect, 1908-
– Québec churches #8334
Côté, Jean-Baptiste, Can sculptor, 1834-1907
  #1334 1335 2169 2171 5186 5187 5188
– animal subjects #1579
– influence on Henri Julien #5993
– Jobin, Louis, compared with #5968
– statue of General Wolfe, Québec (Qué)
  #1600
– supper at Emmaus theme #1615
– woodcarvings #756 1577
    – Québec (Qué), Musée du Québec #1612
    – Sharpe, Nettie, collection #1607
Cotton, John Wesley, Can artist, 1869-1931
– prints #822
Cotton, Michel, Can silversmith, shoemaker,
  1700-after 1747 #249 250
Coubertin, Baron Pierre de, Fr educator,
  1863-1937
– and the Olympic Games #1364
Couchiching Conference of the Canadian
  Institute on Public Affairs (Lake
  Couchiching, Ont)
– (1976), conference papers #619
Coughtry, John Graham, Can artist, 1931-
– and Toronto (Ont) painting
    – (1950s) #1749
    – (1960s) #1753
– exhibitions
    – (1976) #5190
– exhibitions, group
    – (1964) #462
    – (1965) #473
– exhibitions (reviews) #5191
– on Gordon Rayner #6965

– on his art education #470
– paintings (1957-1959) #5189
– paintings and sculptures #449
Coulombe, Jacques, Can sculptor, 1941-
  #1630
Coulson, Harry W., Can artist, fl. 1894-1897
– china painting #2277
Council of Arts and Manufactures/Conseil
  des arts et manufactures
– Quebec, late 19th c. #2962
– report on industrial arts education (1876)
  #2598
Council of Ontario Universities
– recommendations for architectural
  education in Ontario (1970s) #8288
country houses
– see castles and country houses
Coupey, Pierre, Can artist, 1942-
– exhibitions, group
    – (1979) #2075
– exhibitions (reviews) #2072
Courbet, Gustave, Fr artist, 1819-1877
– Boyle, John Bernard, compared with #4891
– influence on Marc-Aurèle de Foy
  Suzor-Coté #7297 7300
Courchesne, Edgar, Can architect, 1903-1979
– Québec, churches #8334
Courcy, Michael John de, Can artist, 1944-
– exhibitions, group
    – (1976) #2060
    – (1979) #2069
– map images #561
coureurs de bois
– clothing #2826 2841
Cournoyer, Georget, Can ceramicist, 1931-
  #5192
Cournoyer, Michèle, Can artist, 1943- #5193
Cournoyer, Serge, Can sculptor, 1943-
– interview #1485
– machine works #5194
– use of light #767
courthouses, Canadian
– Alberta (pre-1930) #9005
– British Columbia (1849-1930) #9006
– Manitoba (pre-1930) #9007
– Montréal (Qué), Court House Annex
  #9001
– New Brunswick (pre-1914) #9004
– New Westminster (BC) #9011
– Newfoundland (1830-1903) #9008
– Ontario
    – 19th-early 20th cs. #9010
    – influence of Scottish architecture, 19th c.
      #7977
– Prince Edward Island (pre-1914) #9009
– Toronto (Ont), Osgoode Hall #9002 9003
– Vancouver (BC), Courthouse #8362 9149
Cousineau, Sylvain P., Can artist, 1949-
– exhibitions
    – (1980) #5195
– exhibitions (reviews) #1018 1067
Coutellier, Francis, Can artist, 1945- #5196
– exhibitions, group
    – (1973) #1182
– portfolio of photographs #996
– prints #1185
Couturier, Pierre, Can builder, fl. 1700-1715,
  d. 1715 #7844
Couturier, Pierre Charles Marie-Alain, Fr
  priest, artist in Canada, 1897-1954 #1407
– and Québec art (1940s) #1402 1436 1474
– influence on Paul-Emile Borduas #4850
– Québec, churches #8838
Couvreur, Daniel, Can sculptor, 1944- #5197

Coverdale, William H., Can engineer,
  collector, 1801-1865 #258 259
– collection, Public Archives of Canada
  (Ottawa, Ont) #12 3230
coverlets
– see also quilts
coverlets, Canadian
– 17th-19th cs. #2730 2736
– Cape Breton (NS) #2728
– Charlevoix (Qué) #2738
– île aux Coudres (Qué) #2178
– Nova Scotia (1820-1930) #2807
– Ontario #2729
    – 19th c. #2805
    – Jacquard weavers #2740
– Québec
    – 17th-19th cs. #2221 2746
coverlets, Salish #3469 4018
coverlets, Tlingit #4018
Covit, Linda, Can artist, curator, 1948-
– interview, on Powerhouse Gallery
  (Montréal, Qué) #1557
Cowichan (Vancouver Island, BC), Marshall
  House
– architecture #8695
Cowichan Indians
– knitting #3882 3929
– knitting and basketry #4027
– spinning #3796
Cowin, Jack I., Can artist, 1947- #5199
– exhibitions
    – (1975) #5198
Cowley, Reta Madeline, Can artist, 1910-
  #5200 5201
– exhibitions, group
    – (1971) #1920
Cox, Elford Bradley, Can sculptor, 1914-
  #5202
– as teacher of George Pratt #6916
– on art and architecture #8235
Cox, George Albertus, Can statesman,
  1840-1914
– Senator Cox's Mausoleum, Mount Pleasant
  Cemetery (Toronto, Ont) #8894
Cox, Palmer, Can artist in USA, 1840-1924
– illustrations #916
Coyne, Michael, Can artist, 1950-
– exhibitions, group
    – (1980) #1221
Cozic, Yvon, Can artist, 1942-
– exhibitions
    – (1974) #5203
    – (1977) #5204
– exhibitions, group
    – (1981) #1564
– interview #1485
cradles, Canadian
– Ontario
    – (1780-1900) #2577
    – (1790s-1857) #2558
– Québec, 17th-18th cs. #2530 2531
cradles, Huron #3519
cradles, Indians of North America #3407
  3485
cradles, Ingalik #4087
cradles, Iroquois #3519
– Montréal (Qué), château de Ramezay
  #3593
cradles, Northwest Coast Indians
– prehistoric #4017
cradles, Saulteaux
– Island Lake (Man) #3549
cradles, Tagish #4106
cradles, Tête de Boule #4079

cradles, Tlingit #4106
cradles, Tutchone #4106
Craft Dimensions Artisanales, Can periodical
#2116
crafts
– see decorative arts
Craftsman, Can periodical #2257
Craftsman, The/L'Artisan, Can periodical
#2113
craftsmen
– see artisans
Craig, John, Can artist, 1804-1854
– as member, Toronto Society of Arts #1689
Craig, Kate, Can artist, 1947-
– exhibitions, group
– (1979) #1157 2070
– (1980) #687
Craig, Zeidler & Strong, Can architectural
firm
– Ajax (Ont), Ajax Municipal Building #7694
– Hamilton (Ont), McMaster University
Health Sciences Centre #9035 9036 9037
– Toronto (Ont)
– Harbour City #8062
– Ontario Place #9113 9114 9115
Craig & Kohler, Can architectural firm
– Ottawa (Ont), Ottawa Civic Centre #9101
Cram, Goodhue & Ferguson, Amer
architectural firm
– Halifax (NS), All Saints' Cathedral #8773
Cram, Ralph Adams, Amer architect,
1863-1942
– influence on Gothic revival architecture in
Canada #7724
Crane, C.Howard, Amer architect, 1885-1952
– Toronto (Ont)
– Allen Theatre #9069
– New Princess Theatre #9069
– Winnipeg (Man), Allen Theatre #9074
Crang & Boake, Can architectural firm
– Toronto (Ont), Holt Renfrew Store #8078
– Waterloo (Ont), University of Waterloo.
Student residence #9467
Cranmer, Doug, Can sculptor, 1927- #4121
– carvings, Totem Park (Vancouver, BC)
#4118 4124
Craven, David, Can artist, 1946-
– collages #5208
– exhibitions
– (1977) #5205
– (1978) #5206
– exhibitions, group
– (1975) #1809
– (1977) #637
– (1980) #687 708
– (1981) #710
– exhibitions (reviews) #639
– works (1975-1978) #5207
Crawford, Julia Tilley, Can artist, 1896-1968
#1173
Crawford, Lenore, Can art critic, 1909-
– on Canadian art #112
Création (Montréal, Qué) #1492
Creative Source, Can periodical #912
creativity
– Canadian artists, 20th c. #594 665
– Frenkel, Vera, on #5522
– Harris, Lawren Stewart, on #5715 5722
– Hodgson, Tom, on #5814
– Shadbolt, Jack Leonard, on #7181
Cree Indians
– art #3731 4141
– (1830-1930) #3734
– beadwork #3696 3719 3729 4077

– birchbark #3573
– boulder monuments #3688
– containers #4078
– costume #3739
– culture #3402 3651 3655 3742
– gun cases #3713
– Manitou effigy #3724 3726
– musical instruments #3363
– painting, 20th c. #4154
– painting and sculpture (1970s) #4133
– paintings of, Sanford Fisher #5445
– petroglyphs #3439
– photographs of, Edward Sheriff Curtis
#3399
– pictographs #3760
– pipes #3662
– quillwork #3745
– snowshoes #2812
– tattooing #3723
– tipis #3663 3735
Crespin, Antoine, Can priest, 18th c.
– inventories of île d'Orléans houses
(1761-1767) #8613
Cresswell, Samuel Gurney, Brit naval
officer, artist in Canada, 1827-1867 #258
259
Cresswell, William Nichol, Can artist,
1822-1888
– exhibitions, group
– (1978) #1726
crests, Haida #3780
– moon image #4059
crests, Northwest Coast Indians #3791 3858
3863 3928
crests, Tsimshian #3795 3981
Crête, Alphida, Can photographer, fl. 1981
#1562
crewelwork, Canadian
– bed hangings, Royal Ontario Museum
(Toronto, Ont) #2784
Crichton, Daniel, Can glassmaker, 1946-
– and Sheridan College School of Crafts and
Design (Mississauga, Ont) #2440
Crisp, Arthur Watkins, Can artist, 1881-
1974
– exhibitions (reviews) #211
– illustrations #916
Crist, Lela Gurnee, Can artist, fl. 1950s-
#5209
Criteria, Can periodical #564
– (1970s) #3310
criticism of art
– see art theory and criticism
Croft, Lewis Scott, Can artist, 1911-
– on his art #5210
Crone-Findlay, Noreen, Can artist, fl. 1981
– interview #5211
Cross, John, Can artist, 20th c. #4169
crosses
– see also calvaries; crucifixes
crosses, Canadian
– iron funeral crosses
– Ontario #2709
– Québec #2716
– Montréal (Qué), Mount Royal #7899
– Ottawa (Ont), National Museum of Man.
Canadian Centre for Folk Culture Studies
#963
– pectoral cross, William Maurice
Carmichael #5003
– Québec #1292 1569 1609 1619 1637 1640
– 17th-18th cs. #1320
– ironwork #2702
– votive offerings #1621

– Québec, New Brunswick, Manitoba, by
French-Canadians #1625
– Rimouski (Qué) #8872
Crow, James, Amer sculptor, fl. 1940
– False Face masks #4113
Crow Indians
– blankets #3752
Crowell, Ivan Herbert, Can weaver, fl.
1940s-1960s
– *Legends on Tapestries* program #5296
Croydon, Peter, Can photographer, 1924-
#1036
crucifixes
– see also crosses
crucifixes, Canadian
– Montréal (Qué), Church of Notre-Dame
#6123
– Québec #1585 1638
– 19th c. #1605
crucifixion
– see Jesus Christ, crucifixion
cruets, Canadian
– glass pickle casters, Walter Bick collection
#2405
Cruickshank, Robert, Can silversmith,
1748-1808
– works, Detroit Institute of Arts (Detroit,
Mich) #2681 2691
Cruikshank, William, Can artist, 1849-1922
#178 5212
– as teacher of Frederick Nicholas Loveroff
#6329
– exhibitions, group
– (1978) #133
– exhibitions (reviews) #186
Cruise, Stephen, Can artist, 1949-
– exhibitions
– (1976) #5213
– exhibitions, group
– (1975) #1809
Crystal, N.B., Glass Co., glass manufacturer
(Saint John, NB) #2400
Crystal Glass Co., glass manufacturer
(Sapperton, BC) #2423
Cubism
– and Alfred Pellan #6815
– and Bertram Richard Brooker #4925
– and Canadian paintings, World War I
#1075
– and David Craven #5207
– and Jack Leonard Shadbolt #7188
– and Jean-Philippe Dallaire #5238
– and Jock Macdonald #6379
– and Lawren Phillips Harris #5711
– and Paul-Vanier Beaulieu #4652
– and Pierre Gendron #5581
– and Raymonde Godin #5623
– and Robert Gray Murray #6668
– and video art #654
Cubist-Realism
– see Precisionism
Cuhaci, Edward J., Can architect, 1930-
– Ottawa (Ont), Saint Michael and All
Angels Church #8766
Cullen, Garry, Can photographer, 1954-
– exhibitions, group
– (1978) #2067
Cullen, Maurice Galbraith, Can artist,
1866-1934 #302 1143 1382 5215 5217 5218
5219 5220 5222 5224
– and Arts Club (Montréal, Qué) #1314
– and Canadian painting #18
– and Edmond Dyonnet #5347 5349
– and Marc-Aurèle de Foy Suzor-Coté #7295

– and modernism #27 383
– and nationalism in art #143
– and Robert Wakeham Pilot #6869
– and Royal Canadian Academy of Arts
   #152
– as member, Canadian Art Club #193
– as teacher of Anne Douglas Savage #7130
– exhibitions
   – (1956) #5221
– exhibitions, group
   – (1935) #17
   – (1977) #1278 1279
– exhibitions (reviews) #204 211 306 1316
   5216
– influence of Impressionism #227
– influence on André Charles Biéler #4725
– influence on Group of Seven #5223
– influence on Robert Wakeman Pilot #6872
– Morrice, James Wilson, on #6622
– winter landscapes #285 5214
cultural centres, Canadian
– Québec (1960s) #3088
Culture Hero, Can newspaper
– and Les Levine #6267
Culture vivante, Can periodical #1257
Cumberland, Frederic William, Can
   architect, 1821-1881
– Ontario, churches #8905
– Toronto (Ont) #8056 8059 8075
   – University of Toronto. University
      College #7697 9428 9429 9449 9453 9475
      9482
Cumberland & Storm, Can architectural
   firm
– Ottawa (Ont), Parliament Buildings #8930
– Toronto (Ont) #8055
   – Osgoode Hall #9002 9003
Cumberland Sound (NWT)
– Inuit culture #4320
– Thule artifacts #4367
cupboards, Canadian
– Ontario #2574
   – (1780-1900) #2577
   – (1790s-1857) #2558
– Prince Edward Island #2508 2518
Cupit, William Henry, Can photographer,
   1946- #2071
cups, Canadian
– silver alms cups, Québec, 17th-18th cs.
   #2671
Curnoe, Gregory Richard (Greg), Can artist,
   1936- #5226
– and nationalism in art #102 143
– and regionalism in art #567 5225
– death theme #1759
– exhibitions
   – (1969) #5227
   – (1975) #5228
   – (1976) #5229
   – (1981) #5231
– exhibitions, group
   – (1967) #490
   – (1979) #510
– exhibitions (reviews) #520 5233
– influence on London (Ont) art (1960s) #1791
– interview #5230
– map images #561
– on Canadian art
   – (1960s) #478
   – (1970s) #620
– on his art education #470
– on visual perception #525
– use of oral documentation #608
– verbal images #78

– works (1960s-1980s) #5232
– writings #92 536
Currelly, Charles Trick, Can curator,
   1876-1957
– as director, Royal Ontario Museum
   (Toronto, Ont) #3170
– autobiography #3139
Currelly, Judith, Can artist, 1946- #5234
currency
– *see* money
Curry & Sparling, Can architectural firm
– Toronto (Ont), G.J. Foy Company Building
   #9332
curtains
– *see* drapery
Curtin, Walter, Can photographer, 1911-
   #1054
Curtis, Edward Sheriff, Amer photographer,
   1868-1952
– exhibitions
   – (1979) #3480
– photographs and writings, Indians of
   North America #3399
Cusack, Stephen, stained glass artist, fl.
   early 1900s
– stained glass, Gregory House (Saint John,
   NB) #8545
Cuthbert, James, Can, d. 1798
– Berthierville (Qué), Cuthbert Chapel #8881
Cuthbertson, George Adrian, Amer artist,
   1900-1969
– paintings of ships and naval engagements
   on the Great Lakes (1680-1835) #12
cutlery
– Roma Site (PEI) #2714 2715
Cutter and Power, furniture-making firm
   (NS) #2493
Cutting, Lorna, Can artist, 1933-
– exhibitions, group
   – (1977) #1933
Czechoslovakia, *Second Triennial of Naive Art*
– Patterson, Dan, Carnation Milk cans
   construction #6779

D

D'Astous, Roger, Can architect, 1926-
– Beaconsfield (Qué), Church of Saint
   Edmund of Canterbury #8840
– Cartierville (Qué),
   Notre-Dame-du-Bel-Amour #8763
– Laval-sur-le-lac (Qué), house #7857
– Montréal (Qué)
   – Church of Saint-Rémi #8841
   – métro. Beaubien Station #9549
   – Olympic Village #9127
Dada
– and David Craven #5207
– and Greg Curnoe #5232 5233
– and Jan Burka #4958
– and Ulysse Comtois #5165
Daglish, Peter William, Can artist, 1930-
   #1418 5235
daguerreotypes, Canadian #1039
– Lotbinière, Pierre-Gustave Joly de #6326
– portraits
   – Halifax (NS) #1211
   – Maritimes #1171
– Québec #1374
– Toronto (Ont) #1725
– views of cities #1061

Dahl, Chris, Can artist, 1948-
– exhibitions, group
   – (1979) #2069
Dahlstrom, Eugene W., Can artist, 1885-1971
– exhibitions, group
   – (1958) #1846
Dair, Carl, Can artist, 1912-1967
– on Canadian industrial typography (1947)
   #920
Dakota Indians
– art #3650 3705 3755
– birchbark #3483
– dolls #3733
– moccasins #3648
– shields #3670
– winter counts and pictographs #3747
Dale, Archibald (Archie), Can artist,
   1882-1962
– political cartoons #957
Dale, Jack, Can artist, 1928-
– interview #5236
– sculptural photographs #994
Dale, William S.A. (Bill), Can curator, 1921-
– as director, National Gallery of Canada
   (Ottawa, Ont) #3049
Dali, Salvador, Sp artist, 1904-
– Comfort, Charles Fraser, compared with
   #1115
– influence on Alfred Pellan #6811 6822
– influence on Fernand Leduc #6186
Dallaire, François, Can artist, 1947- #5237
Dallaire, Jean-Philippe, Can artist, 1916-1965
   #97 5238 5242 5245 5246 5247
– and Canadian painting #5240
– as father of François Dallaire #5237
– exhibitions
   – (1968) #5241
   – (1979) #5244
– exhibitions, group
   – (1958) #431
– interview #5239
– religious paintings (1936-1937) #5243
– wall hanging, Queen Elizabeth Hotel
   (Montréal, Qué) #8228
Dallas (Tex), Dallas Museum for
   Contemporary Arts
– exhibitions
   – *A Canadian Portfolio: The Dallas Museum
      for Contemporary Arts Looks at Art in
      Canada* (1958) #429
Dallégret, François, Can sculptor, 1938-
   #1502 5248
– use of light #767
Dally, Frederick, Can photographer,
   1838-1914 #5249
– and the Victoria Theatre Photographic
   Gallery (Victoria, BC) #2027
– photographs, Northwest Coast Indians
   #2033 5250
Damoreau, Charles F., Amer artist in
   Canada, fl. 1856-1871
– animal portraits #1727
Danby, Kenneth Edison (Ken), Can artist,
   1940- #5251
– and realism #110
– athletes #5252
– design, Olympic coins (1976) #778
– exhibitions
   – (1980) #5253
– exhibitions, group
   – (1974) #573
   – (1976) #1810
dance
– *see also* ballet

– and Bruce Parsons #6772
– Canada
    – and art (1970s) #6676
    – and performance art (1970s) #634
    – folk-dance costumes #2893
– Québec #1258 1259 2879
dance, Algonquian
– Dream Dance #3580
dance, Iroquois
– Six Nations Reserve (Ont) #3598
dance, Northwest Coast Indians
– sun dance, photographs, William Hanson
  Boorne #4796
Daniel Knechtel, furniture-making firm
  (Hanover, Ont) #2463
Danis, Monique Laguerre, Can artist, 1948-
  #1547
Danson, Andrew, Can photographer, 1945-
– portfolio of photographs #1053
Daoust, André, Can architect, 1919-
– Montréal (Qué), Olympic Stadium #9127
Daoust, Sylvia Marie Emilienne, Can
  sculptor, 1902-1974 #739 1380 5254 5257
– and Simone Marie Yvette Hudon-Beaulac
  #5856
– influence on René Thibault #7344
– interview #5255
– Royal Architectural Institute of Canada
  Allied Arts Medal winner (1961) #5256
Daquin, Pierre, Fr tapestry artist, 1936-
– influence on Andrée Beauregard #4653
Darling, Frank, Can architect, 1850-1923
– and John Andrew Pearson #8398
– Edmonton (Alta), University of Alberta
  #9493
– Halifax (NS), Dalhousie University #9408
– Royal Institute of British Architects Royal
  Gold Medal winner (1915) #8349 8350
  8389
– Toronto (Ont) #8055
    – Holwood Mansion #8667
    – University of Toronto. Trinity College
      #9446 9483
Darling & Pearson, Can architectural firm
– Montréal (Qué)
    – Canadian Bank of Commerce #9153
    – Sun Life Building #9308 9309
– Ottawa (Ont)
    – Departmental and Justice Buildings,
      competition #8921
    – Parliament Buildings #8926
– Toronto (Ont)
    – Art Gallery of Toronto #9076
    – Art Museum of Toronto #9070
    – Bank of Montreal #9155
    – Canadian Bank of Commerce #9178
      9180 9189 9351
    – Canadian Pacific Railway Building
      #9329
    – Dominion Bank #9163 9188
    – Standard Bank #9158
    – Toronto General Hospital #9012 9013
    – Toronto General Hospital. Private
      Patients' Building #9020
    – University of Toronto #9444 9449
      – Convocation Hall #9430
      – Trinity College #9446 9483
– Waterloo (Ont), Mutual Life Assurance
  Company Building #9331
– Winnipeg (Man)
    – Bank of Commerce #9202
    – Bank of Nova Scotia #9157 9202
    – Dominion Bank #9188
Darmstadt (West Germany), Hessisches

Landesmuseum
– art, Indians of North America #3464
Dartmouth (NS), Dartmouth Heritage
  Museum
– exhibitions
    – Albert Franck (1899-1973) in Retrospect: A
      Small Selection from the Artist's Collection
      (1974) #5500
    – Annie D. Savage: Drawings and
      Watercolours (1975) #7129
Daubigny, Charles François, Fr artist,
  1817-1878
– Walker, Horatio, compared with #306
Daudelin, Charles, Can artist, 1920- #1541
  5259 5260 5263
– exhibitions
    – (1974) #5262
– exhibitions, group
    – (1977) #1622
– interview #1527
– sculpture, National Arts Centre (Ottawa,
  Ont) #5261 9108
– sculptures, Saint-Jean Parish Church
  (Pointe-Saint-Charles, Qué) #5258
Daudelin, Eric, Can photographer, 1920-
– interview #5264
Daudelin, Fernand, Can artist, 1920- #5265
Davenport, Sumner Godfrey, Can architect,
  1877-1956
– Montréal (Qué), Royal Bank of Canada
  #9176
– Ottawa (Ont), Bank of Canada head office
  #9337
– Vancouver (BC), Royal Bank #8171 9179
David, Athanase, Can public servant,
  1882-1953
– as founder, Ecole des beaux-arts #2973
David, Barott, Boulva, Associated Architects,
  Can architectural firm
– Montréal (Qué), Habitat '67 #7694 8575
David, Charles, Can architect, 1890-1962
– Montréal (Qué), école Louis-Hébert #7664
David, David Fleury, Can sculptor,
  1780-1841
– compared with Noël Levasseur #1596
David, Jacques, Can sculptor, 1946-
– Octa #1627
– use of plastics #1603
David, Joseph (Joe), Can artist, 1946-
– exhibitions
    – (1978) #5266
– silkscreen prints #4148
David, Louis Basile, Can sculptor, fl. 1812
– interior, Church of Saint-Jean (île
  d'Orléans, Qué) #8801
David, Théophile, Can artist, fl. 1842 #1301
David & David, Can architectural firm
– Montréal (Qué), David & David architects'
  office #9299
David Burns Pottery, ceramic manufacturer
  (Holmesville, Ont)
– moulds #2334
Davidialuk
– see Amittu, Davidialuk Alasua
Davidson, Beatrice, Can collector, 20th c.
– interview #3219
Davidson, C.D., & Co., Can architectural
  firm
– Halifax (NS), Halifax International
  Airport. Air Terminal Building #9515
Davidson, Robert, Can artist, 1923- #4132
  4162 5267 5269
– and Bill Reid #6987
– argillite carvings, Vancouver Centennial

Museum (Vancouver, BC) #4006
– exhibitions
    – (1979) #5268
Davidson, Robert Charles, Can artist, 1946-
– silkscreen prints #4148
Davies, Archibald, artist, fl. 1925
– interior, Château Frontenac (Québec, Qué)
  #9278
Davies, Barbara, Can photographer, fl. 1970
  #993
Davies, Thomas, Brit army officer, artist in
  Canada, 1737-1812 #279 812 5270 5271
– exhibitions
    – (1972) #5272
Davis, Leonard, Can photographer, 1906-
– portfolio of photographs #991
Davis, Olea Marion Montgomery, Can
  sculptor, 1899-
– garden sculpture #1849
Davis, Theodore Russell, Amer artist in
  Canada, 1840-1894
– in western Canada #1859
Davis, William L., Can collector, 1905-
– as patron of Albert Henry Robinson #7057
Davis (Calif), University of California.
  Richard L. Nelson Gallery
– exhibitions
    – Northwest Coast Indian Art from California
      Collections (1980) #4041
Davison, Betty, Can artist, 1909-
– exhibitions, group
    – (1979) #674
Davison & Porter, Can architectural firm
– Vancouver (BC), Porter House #7679
Dawson, George Mercer, Can photographer,
  1849-1901
– collection, art, Haida Indians #4011
– survey photographs #1014 1015 1865
Dawson City (Yukon)
– architecture
    – (1897-1903) #8183
    – Fuller, Thomas William #8367 8368
Dawson City (Yukon), Madame Tremblay's
  Store
– architecture #9380 9381
Dawson City (Yukon), Palace Grand Theatre
– architecture #9090
Dawson City (Yukon), Winaut's Store
– architecture #9383
Dawson-Watson, John, Brit artist in Canada,
  fl. ca. 1900 #1312
Day, Bill, Can artist, fl. 1973
– video art #2044
Day, Mabel Killam, Can artist, 1884-1961
  #5273
– exhibitions, group
    – (1940) #350
De Angelis, Joseph R. (Joe)
– see Angelis, Joseph R. (Joe) de
De Appel Foundation
– support of General Idea, Test Tube
  videotape (1979) #692
De Beaucourt, François Malepart
– see Beaucourt, François Malepart de
De Beaucourt, Josué Boisberthelot
– see Boisberthelot de Beaucours, Josué
de Belle, Charles Ernest
– see Belle, Charles Ernest de
De Belleval, Jean Fournier
– see Belleval, Jean Fournier de
de Bry, Theodore
– see Bry, Theodore de
De Camillis, Laurie
– see Camillis, Laurie de

De Carufel, René, Can photographer, 1954-
#1562
De Casson, Dollier
- see Dollier de Casson
De Champlain, Samuel
- see Champlain, Samuel de
De Charette, Colonel
Athanase-Charles-Marie
- see Charette, Colonel
Athanase-Charles-Marie de
De Chirico, Giorgio
- see Chirico, Giorgio de
De Courcy, Michael John
- see Courcy, Micheal John dc
De Fer, Nicholas
- see Fer, Nicholas de
De Heer, Louis-Chrétien
- see Heer, Louis-Chrétien de
De Heusch, Lucio
- see Heusch, Lucio de
De Jong, Simon Leendert
- see Jong, Simon Leendert de
de Kooning, Willem, Amer artist, 1904-
- Ronald, William S., compared with #7076
De La Joue, François
- see La Joue, François de
De Lery, Gaspard Chaussegros
- see Lery, Gaspard Chaussegros de
De Ligny Boudreau, Pierre
- see Boudreau, Pierre de Ligny
De Lotbinière, Pierre Gustave Joly
- see Lotbinière, Pierre Gustave Joly de
Dc Maisonneuve, Paul de Chomedey
- see Maisonneuve, Paul de Chomedey de
De Morée, Michael
- see Morée, Michael de
De Nevers, Edmond
- see Nevers, Edmond de
Dc Niverville, Louis
- see Niverville, Louis de
De Passillé-Sylvestre, Micheline
- see Passillé-Sylvestre, Micheline de
De Pédery-Hunt, Dora, Can sculptor, 1913-
#5275
- design, Olympic coins (1976) #778
- exhibitions, group
- (1971), medals #772
De Ramezay, Claude
- see Ramezay, Claude de
De Repentigny, Marie Favery
- see Repentigny, Marie Favery de
De Repentigny, Rodolphe
- see Repentigny, Rodolphe de (Jauran)
De Rouville, Hertel
- see Rouville, Hertel de
De Stijl
- see Stijl, de
De Suria, Tomás
- see Suria, Tomás de
De Tonnancour, Jacques Godefroy
- see Tonnancour, Jacques Godefroy de
De Vasarely, Victor
- see Vasarely, Victor de
De Visser, John
- see Visser, John de
Dc Volpi, Charles
- see Volpi, Charles de
Deacon, Peter, Can artist, 1945-
- exhibitions, group
- (1978) #1961
dealers
- see art market
Dean, Max, Can artist, 1949- #5274
- A Work and Pass It On #714

- exhibitions, group
- (1977) #1901
- (1978) #669 2066
- (1980) #687
Dean, Tom, Can artist, 1947-
- interview #1489
Deane-Drummond, Sophie
- see Pemberton, Sophia Theresa
Dearle, Duncan W., Brit stained glass artist,
d. 1954
- stained glass windows, Vancouver (BC)
#2458
Dearle, John Henry, Brit stained glass artist,
1860-1932
- stained glass windows, Vancouver (BC)
#2458
death
- death scenes of commanders, Canada,
18th-19th cs. #812
- Dickson, Jennifer, Sweet Death and Other
Pleasures #5291
- London (Ont) paintings (1960s) #1759
Debassige, Blake, Can artist, 1956- #4157
- exhibitions, group
- (1981) #4173
decorative arts
- see also conservation and restoration,
decorative arts; liturgical objects
- household objects, and Les Levine #6258
decorative arts, Canadian #30 45 57 58 59 61
63 485 2089 2094 2096 2097 8228
- 17th-19th cs. #2112
- 19th c. #2099
- 20th c. #2121 2142
- (1608-1867) #2120
- (1750s-1890s) #221
- (1850s) #1692
- (1901-1912), Toronto Society of Architects
exhibitions #7956
- (1904), Arts and Crafts Society of Canada
#2241
- (1910-1961), Canadian National Exhibition
(Toronto, Ont) #1
- (1920s) #2160 7960 8223
- (1920s-1930s) #8224
- (1920s-1940s) #28
- (1930s) #340
- (1940s) #370 374 2601 2603
- and industry #2092
- eastern Canada #2098
- household objects #2604
- (1950s) #387 388 2100
- (1960s) #2102 2103 2105 2106 2196
- (1964-1967) #2108 2109
- (1967-1969) #2115
- (1970s) #2123 2130 2134
- (1979), recommendations #2136 2137
- (1979-1980) #2138
- Acadian #1137
- Alberta (1970s) #1951
- and architecture
- (1950s) #8227
- (1960s) #8231
- British American Oil Company buildings
#8230
- British Columbia #2271
- (1970s) #2274 2276
- Canadian Handicrafts Guild #2090 2118
- (1930s) #2091
- Cap-Santé (Qué), Church of Sainte-Famille
#8883
- Chicoutimi (Qué), Ecole d'arts et métiers
#2175
- Eastern Townships (Qué), (1970s) #1535

- education (1639-1940s) #2979
- ethnic traditions #2122
- Germanic tradition #2140
- Nova Scotia and Ontario #2135
- Ontario #2251 2263
- Group of Seven #1774
- guide for collectors #2101 2114 2119 2125
2127 2131 2141 2252
- Haliburton (Ont) #2258
- Halifax (NS), Nova Scotia Museum #3071
- Hamilton (Ont), Arts and Crafts
Association (1895) #2239
- Hutterite #1962
- île aux Coudres (Qué) #2168 2178
- île d'Orléans (Qué) #1252
- 18th c. #8613
- Independent Art Association #1379
- influence on Canadian art, 20th c. #2093
- Kingcrafts (King City, Ont) #2244
- Kingston (Ont) #1680
- London (Ont), (1970s) #2260
- Lotbinière (Qué), churches #8835
- Louisbourg (NS) #2148
- Manitoba, Franco-Manitoban #2275
- Maritimes
- 19th c. #2147
- 20th c. #1119
- Mennonite #2246 2253
- Ontario #2250 2267
- Waterloo County (Ont) #2243
- Montréal (Qué)
- (1740-1760) #2218
- (1840s) #1301
- (1880-1914) #1367
- (1950s) #389 7900
- Macdonald-Stewart Foundation #2203
2204
- Wiser's Museum #2469
- Murray Bay (Qué), (1930s) #2172
- New Brunswick #1178 2150
- (1940s) #2144
- and Pegi Nicol MacLeod #6398
- Newfoundland #2146 2158 2159
- (1970s) #1149 2152
- Newfoundland and Labrador
- 20th c. #2155
- (1970s), recommendations #2149
- Norwegian #2273
- Nova Scotia #2156 2157
- (1942), proposal for arts and crafts
league #2145
- (1970s) #2154
- Ontario
- 19th c. #2245
- (1800-1850) #7965
- (1850s) #1691
- (1900) #2240
- (1970s) #2247
- artisans, 19th c. #2261
- artisans and sales outlets (1970s) #2256
- Ottawa (Ont), National Museum of Man.
Canadian Centre for Folk Culture Studies
#963 969
- periodicals
- Artisan #2133
- Canada Crafts #2126
- Canadian Antiques and Art Review #141
- Canadian Collector #74
- Canadian Review of Music and Art #357
- Construction: A Journal for the
Architectural Engineering and Contracting
Interests of Canada #7641
- Craft Dimensions Artisanales #2116
- Craftsman, The/L'Artisan #2113

– *Ontario Craft* #2257
– Prince Edward Island #2153
– Québec #1235 1237 1249 1258 1259 1265
    1276 1297 1327 2183 2184 2197 2202 2208
    2219 2222 2223 2228 2229 2237 5069
    – 17th-18th cs. #1320 2181 2217
    – 17th-19th cs. #1334 1335 2128
        – European influences #2221
    – 18th-19th cs. #2206
    – 18th c.-1930s #2177
    – 18th-early 20th cs. #1339
    – 19th c., craft education #343
    – 20th c. #2179 2198
    – (1613-1870), French provincial style
        #2191
    – (1640-1840) #1329
    – (1872-1939), handicrafts schools #2977
    – (1875-1915) #1364
    – (1908) #1313
    – (1920s-1940s) #2189
    – (1930s) #2163 2164 2167 2173 2174 2176
    – (1930s-1940s) #2186
    – (1940s) #2188 2199
    – (1940s-1970s) #1269
    – (1950s) #2193
    – (1960s) #2195
    – (1970s) #1490 2205 2211 2215 2216 2224
        – and predictions to 2001 #2225
        – biographical sources #2230
    – and Gérard Morisset #3305
    – apprentices (1660-1815) #2231
    – artisans, 17th-18th cs. #2214
    – as folk art #1291
    – Centrale d'artisanat du Québec #2213
        2238
    – Confrérie des menuisiers de madame
        Sainte-Anne #1241
    – eastern Québec, late 19th-early 20th cs.
        #2235
    – guide for collectors #2226
    – ironwork #2712
    – luxury items, late 17th-early 18th cs.
        #2162
    – motifs #1274
    – Provincial School of Handicrafts
        – (1930s) #2166
    – Quebec School of Handicrafts
        – (1930s-1940s) #2185
    – Quebec School of Handicrafts (1930s)
        #2969
    – women artisans, 17th-18th cs. #2200
– Québec (Qué)
    – 17th c. #1352
– Royal Canadian Academy of Arts #2
– Saint-Basile-le-Grand (Qué), Centre
    communautaire catholique Tour de David
    #1510
– Saint-Hilaire (Qué), Centre artisanal de
    Saint-Hilaire #2182
– Saint-Jean-Port-Joli (Qué) #2194 2209
– Sherbrooke (Qué), (1970s) #2232
– Society of Applied Arts (1905) #2242
– Thunder Bay (Ont) #2266
– Toronto (Ont), Ontario College of Art
    #3009
– treenware #2591
– Ukrainian, Manitoba #2270
– use of wood (1970s) #2596
– Vaudreuil (Qué), Musée de Vaudreuil
    #3109
– Victoria (BC) #2269
    – Island Arts and Crafts Society #1980
– Victorian parlour (1870-1890) #2129
– Washington (DC), Smithsonian Institution

#2111
– Women's Art Association of Canada #176
– women artists (1970s) #1877
decorative arts, French
– 17th-18th cs., influence on Québec
    decorative arts #2191
decorative arts, Indians of North America
    #2089 2107
– 20th c. #2143
– (1964-1967) #2108 2109
– guide for collectors #2104 2125 2131
– influence on Canadian art, 20th c. #2093
– Québec, biographical sources #2230
decorative arts, Inuit #2089
– (1964-1967) #2108 2109
– (1977-1980) #4269
decorative arts, Iroquois
– (1960s) #4123
decorative arts, Scandinavian
– (1940s), influence on Québec decorative
    arts #2186
decorative arts, Swedish
– influence on Jean Bernard Cartier #5052
decoys (hunting), Canadian
– guide for collectors #2595
– Price, Ralph and Patricia, collection #971
Defence Research Board
– *see* Canada. Defence Research Board
Degas, Hilaire Germain Edgar, Fr artist,
    1834-1917
– influence on Lillian Freiman #5517
DeGeay, Jacques, Can priest, 1717-1774
– correspondence, Gilles Bolvin #4782
Deguise (*dit* Flamand), Jacques, Can builder,
    1697-1780 #269 270
Deichmann, Erica, Can ceramicist, 1914-
    #2144 2376 2377 2380
– and Saint John (NB) art (1940s) #1170
Deichmann, Kjeld, Can ceramicist, 1900-1963
    #1170 2144 2376 2377 2380
– on his art #349
Del Mistro, Walter
– *see* Mistro, Walter del
Delacroix, Eugène, Fr artist, 1798-1863
– influence on Marc-Aurèle de Foy
    Suzor-Coté #7297 7300
Delahaye, Guy
– *see* Lahaise, Guillaume
Delamarre, Elzéar, Can priest, ca. 1854-1925
– and Charles Edouard Huot #5877
Delaroche, Paul, Fr artist, 1797-1856
– as teacher of Alfred Boisseau #4768 4769
Delaunay, Jules Elie, Fr artist, 1828-1891
– as teacher of Maurice Galbraith Cullen
    #5217
Delaunay, Robert, Fr artist, 1885-1941
– Curnoe, Greg, compared with #5233
– Pellan, Alfred, compared with #6814
DeLauro, Joseph Nicola, Can sculptor, 1916-
– exhibitions
    – (1981) #5276
Delavalle, Jean-Marie, Can artist, 1944-
– exhibitions, group
    – (1973) #557
– interview #1485
Delaware Indians
– art #3506
– leatherwork #3554
Delay, Emile E., Can architect, 1875-1939
– Regina (Sask), War Memorial Museum,
    competition #9073
Delbuguet, René, Can photographer, ca.
    1931-
– portfolio of photographs #1023

Delezenne, Ignace-François, Can silversmith,
    1718-1790 #269 270 5277
– as teacher of François Ranvoyzé #1620
– works, compared with French silver #2688
Delfosse, Georges, Can artist, 1869-1939 #302
    5279 5280
– compared with Charles de Belle #1385
– paintings, Cathedral of
    Saint-Jacques-le-Majeur (Montréal, Qué)
    #5278
Delor, Jean-Baptiste-Antoine
– *see* Levasseur (*dit* Delor),
    Jean-Baptiste-Antoine
Delrue, Georges, Can jeweller, 1920- #2694
    2701 5281 5282
Delta (BC)
– architecture #8147
Delvaux, Paul, Bl artist, 1897-
– influence on Alex Colville #5151
Delville, Jean, Bl artist, 1867-1953
– influence on Graham Metson #6523
Demaine, Martin, Can glassmaker, ca. 1943-
    #2440
Demasso, Michel-François, Fr artist,
    1654-1679/1702
– influence on Antoine-Sébastien
    Plamondon #6886
Demers, Claude, Can photographer, fl. 1981
– photographs and poem #1065 1066
Demers, Jean-Antoine, Can artist, 1931-
    #5283
Demers, Jérôme, Can priest, artist, 1774-1853
    #1231
– influence on Québec architecture #7874
– influence on Thomas Baillairgé #8327 8328
– writings, influence on François and
    Thomas Baillairgé #8880
Demers, Maurice, Can artist, 1936-
    #1502 5284
Denault, Pierre, Can artist, fl. 1974
– as member of Centre communautaire
    catholique Tour de David
    (Saint-Basile-le-Grand, Qué) #1510
Denéchaud, Simone, Can artist, 1905-1974
    #1380
– exhibitions, group
    – (1940) #350
Denis, Maurice, Fr artist, writer, 1870-1943
– as teacher of André Charles Biéler #4725
– as teacher of Paul-Emile Borduas #4841
    4843 4850
– mentioned, in relation to Québec religious
    painting (1940s) #1384
Denison's Mills (Qué)
– architecture #7884
Denison & Stephenson, Can architectural
    firm
– Toronto (Ont), Temple-Pattison Building
    #9332
Dennis, Eva A., Can artist, 1904- #1881
– exhibitions, group
    – (1975) #1927
Dennis, Wesley Clare (Wes), Can artist,
    1899- #1881 1927
Denniston, Stan, Can photographer, 1953-
– exhibitions (reviews) #1067
Denny, Marion, Can jeweller, fl. 1975 #2706
Dent, J.M., publishing firm
– illustrations, Illingworth Holey Kerr #6048
Denver (Colo), Denver Art Museum
– art, natives of North America #3479
– art, Northwest Coast Indians #3918
– exhibitions
    – *American Indian Art Before 1850* (1965)
        #3431

– *Objects of Bright Pride: Northwest Coast Indian Art from the American Museum of Natural History* (1978) #4024
– *Robes of White Shell and Sunrise* (1974) #3453
Department of External Affairs
– *see* Canada. Department of External Affairs
Department of Indian Affairs and Northern Development
– *see* Canada. Department of Indian Affairs and Northern Development
Department of Indian and Northern Affairs
– *see* Canada. Department of Indian and Northern Affairs
Department of National Defence
– *see* Canada. Department of National Defence
Department of Northern Affairs
– *see* Canada. Department of Northern Affairs
Department of Public Works
– *see* Canada. Department of Public Works
Department of Transport
– *see* Canada. Department of Transport
Derouin, René, Can artist, 1936- #5285
Déry, François, Can artist, 1941-
– use of light #767
Des Butes, Guillaume
– *see* Baudry (*dit* Des Butes), Guillaume
Des Rochers & Dumont, Can architectural firm
– Chomedey (Qué), Church of Saint-Pie X #8840
Desaulniers, Gilles, Can glassmaker, 1935- #5286
Desbarats Company, printing firm (Montréal, Qué)
– and Henri Julien #5985 5990
DesBarres, Joseph Frederick Wallet, Brit army officer, artist in Canada, 1722-1824 #812
Descartes, René, Fr philosopher, 1596-1650
– Kennedy, Garry Neill, compared with #6043
Deschevery (*dit* Maisonbasse), Jean-Baptiste, Can silversmith, ca. 1695-ca. 1745 #249 250
– works, compared with French silver #2688
DesClayes, Berthe, Can artist, 1877-1968
– exhibitions, group
– (1978) #133
DesClayes, Gertrude, Can artist, 1879-1949
– exhibitions, group
– (1978) #133
design
– *see also* pattern
– Buchanan, Donald William, on #3325
– Fleming, Allan Robb, on #5456
design, Canadian
– (1920s), and art, Indians of North America #3408
– (1940s) #851 2604
– (1950s) #2607
– (1960s) #867 2613 2619 9324
– (1970s) #907 2620 2622
– advertising #904
– (1950s) #860
– (1960s) #868
– and Donald William Buchanan #3325
– Art Directors' Club of Toronto #854
– periodicals
– *Canadian Design/Design canadien* #2625
– Québec (1970s) #2205 2211
– textiles (1940s) #2722

– Toronto (Ont), Ontario College of Art #3009
design, industrial
– *see* industrial design
Design Awards, Can periodical
– (1953-1958) #2609
Design Collaborative Montreal Ltd., Can graphic design firm #878 882 885
Désilets, Antoine, Can photographer, 1927- #5287 5288
Desjardins collection
– and Joseph Légaré #6217 6218
– in Québec religious institutions and private collections #3207
– influence on Jean-Baptiste Roy-Audy #7103
– influence on Québec painting, 19th c. #1244 7102
desks, Canadian
– Ontario #2579
– (1780-1900) #2577
– (1790s-1857) #2558
– Québec
– 17th-18th cs. #2530 2531
Desmarais, Gabriel (Gaby), Can photographer, 1927-
– on portraiture #624
Desmoulins, Jean-Baptiste
– *see* Maillou (*dit* Desmoulins), Jean-Baptiste
Desnoyers, Charles, Can sculptor, 1806-1902 #1578
Desnoyers, Maurice, Can architect, 1927-
– Montréal (Qué), Expo Stadium #9101
Desrochers-Drolet, Françoise, Can ceramicist, enameller, 1921- #2378 5289
Desrosiers, Madeleine, Can artist, fl. 1936 #1380
Dessailliant (*dit* Richeterre), Michel, Can artist, fl. 1701-1723 #234 235 1323 1363 5290
– portraits of clergy #1333
destruction of architecture
– Calgary (Alta), (1875-1914) #8121
– Montréal (Qué)
– (1960s) #8576
– (1970s) #7914
– Sir William Van Horne Mansion #8594 8601
– Ottawa (Ont), Parliament Buildings. Central Block (1916) #8925
– Québec, churches #8790 8893
– Québec (Qué), fires, late 17th c.-1920s #7952
– Toronto (Ont)
– (1849) #8061
– Government House #8753
Desvallières, Georges, Fr artist, 1861-1950
– influence on Paul-Emile Borduas #4850
Desy, Louis Arsene, Can architect, 1856-1924
– Winnipeg (Man), Cauchon Block #9361
detention camps
– *see* concentration camps
Detheridge, Allan, Can artist, 1943-
– exhibitions (reviews) #622
Detroit (Mich), Detroit Institute of Arts
– exhibitions
– *Les arts du Canada français, 1613-1870* (1946) #1331
– *The Arts of French Canada, 1613-1870* (1946) #1330
– *The French in America, 1520-1880* (1951) #216
– *Traditional Arts of French Canada* (1975) #2128

– exhibitions (reviews)
– *The Arts of French Canada, 1613-1870* (1946) #1332
– Québec silver, 17th-19th cs. #2691
– Trakas, George, *Passage* installation work (1972) #7419
Deutscher Werkbund
– influence on Canadian architecture #7735
Devenyi, Denes, Can photographer, ca. 1932-
– portfolio of photographs #987
Devil
– in Québec art, 17th c.-1840 #1357
devilfish, Tlingit #4045
Deville, Edouard Gaston Daniel, Can photographer, 1849-1924
– photogrammetric surveying techniques #989 1874 1875
– survey photographs #1014 1015 1865
Devine, Harry Torkington, Can photographer, 1865-1938
– and J.A. Brock & Co. (Vancouver, BC) #2021
Devlin, Joyce, Can artist, 1932-
– on portraiture #624
Devor, Holly, Can photographer, fl. 1970s #2018
devotional images
– Québec
– 17th c. #1322 1354 1365
– Québec (Qué), Université Laval. Jeanne Larouche-Villeneuve collection #130 1662
– work themes #1662
Dewar & Stirling, Can architectural firm
– and William Critchlow Harris #8371
Dewdney, Edgar, Can statesman, collector, 1835-1916
– collection, art, Indians of North America #3454
Dewdney (BC)
– architecture #8147
Dewey, E.H., Can artist, 19th c.
– animal portraits #1727
Diamond, A.J., Associates, Can architectural firm
– Toronto (Ont), Ontario Medical Association #8078
Diamond, Jack, Can architect, 1932-
– on architecture #7746
Diamond & Myers, Can architectural firm
– Edmonton (Alta)
– University of Alberta #9495
– University of Alberta. Students' Union Housing #9496
– Toronto (Ont) #8071
– Ontario Medical Association #9349
– renovation of central core residential areas (1970s) #8068
– York Square #9347
Diamond Glass Co., glass manufacturer (Montréal, Qué)
– glass patterns (1902-1930s) #2411
– takeover of glass firms #2429
Diamond Glass Co., glass manufacturer (NS) #2409 2416
Diaz de la Pena, Narcisse Virgile, Fr artist, 1807-1876
– influence on Homer Ransford Watson #7531
Dickey, Estelle, Can photographer, b. ca. 1898 #2018
Dickinson, Anson, Can artist, 1779-1852
– miniatures #1377
Dickinson, Peter Allgood Rastall, Can

architect, 1923-1961
- Montréal (Qué), Canadian Imperial Bank
  of Commerce #9194
- Toronto (Ont) #8057
Dickinson family, Can, 19th c.
- portraits, Nelson Cook #5170
Dickson, Alan, Can sculptor, 1937-
- exhibitions, group
  - (1978) #786
Dickson, Jennifer, Can artist, 1936- #5291
dictionaries and encyclopedias
- Canadian artists #81
- Canadian painters and engravers,
  17th-19th cs. #236
- Inuit artists #4252 4301
  - Pelly Bay (NWT) #4221
- Inuit graphic artists #4497
Dieudonné, Jacques, Can sculptor, 1949-
  #1626
Dignam, Mary Ella, Can artist, 1860-1938
- china painting, State dinner service of
  Canada (1898) #2333
- on art education #2958
- on views, Peel County (Ont), William
  Perkins Bull Collection #3208
Dikeakos, Christos, Can artist, 1946-
- exhibitions, group
  - (1971) #2042
Dille, Lutz, Can photographer, 1922- #990
  5292
- portfolio of photographs #987
Dillon, Gera, Can photographer, 1945-
- portfolio of photographs #1023 1032
Dilworth, Ira, Can writer, 1894-1962
- and Emily Carr #5045
Dimson, Theo, Can artist, 1930-
- on his art education #470
- typographic designs #932
Dine, Jim, Amer artist, 1935-
- Ayot, Pierre, compared with #4572
Dineen Construction Ltd.
- Halifax (NS), West House, Brunswick
  Street #8537
Dinel, Pierre Rolland, Can sculptor, 1919-
- sculptures, Place des Arts (Montréal, Qué)
  #5293
Dinsmore, Edward Jackson, Can artist,
  1885-1936
- illustrations #916
Dion, Antoine, Can ceramicist, fl.
  1850s-1890s #2345
Dion, Daniel, Can artist, 1958-
- performance art #655
Dion, Jean-Baptiste, Can ceramicist, fl.
  1850s-1890s #2345
Dion family, Can ceramicists, 1850s-1920s
- and Dion Pottery (L'Ancienne-Lorette,
  Qué) #2298 2322 2345
Dionne, Rose, Can artist, fl. 1936 #1380
dishes
- see tableware
Disney, Walt, Amer filmmaker, 1901-1960
- influence on Glen Loates #6310
Disraëli (Qué)
- photographic views #1513
Disraëli (Qué), Comité culturel de Disraëli
- exhibitions
  - De la figuration à la non-figuration dans
    l'art québécois (1977) #1461
dissertations
- see theses
Division of Building Research
- see Canada. National Research Council.
  Division of Building Research

Dixon, Pat, Can sculptor, fl. 1978
- interview #5294
Doan, Ebenezer, Can builder,
  furniture-maker, 1772-1866 #8351 8352
Doan, John, Can builder, furniture-maker,
  1768-1852 #8351 8352
Dobereiner, John Philip, Can artist, 1920-
- exhibitions
  - (1978) #5295
Dobush, Peter, Can collector, 1908-
- collection, Winnipeg Art Gallery
  (Winnipeg, Man) #3221
Dobush, Stewart, Bourke, Can architectural
  firm
- Montréal (Qué), McGill University.
  McLennan and Redpath Library #9046
documentary photography
- Minden, Robert, on #6570
- views of buildings #1019
documentary photography, Canadian
- (1850s-1910s) #1034
- (1950s-1970s) #1056
- Alberta (1980) #1971
- British Columbia (1858-1871) #2014
- city views (1850-1900) #1061
- early 20th c. #1039
documents, Canadian
- 17th-19th cs. #232
Dodgson, Campbell, Brit art historian,
  museum administrator, 1867-1948
- on Walter Joseph Phillips #6856
Doerrié, Gerhard, Can artist, 1936-
- as partner of Paul Arthur and Associates
  #873
- on his art education #470
Dogrib Indians
- culture #4089
  - (1920s) #4081
- pipes #4077
dogs in art
- Haeseker, Sandy #5675
- Krieghoff, Cornelius, The Pets and the
  Materials #6102
Doig, Mr. and Mrs. D.R., Can collectors,
  20th c.
- collection, Canadian painting #3224
Dojc, Yuri, Can photographer, 1946-
- portfolio of photographs #1023
Dollard des Ormeaux, Adam, Fr army
  officer in Canada, 1635-1660
- monument, Alfred Laliberté #1623
- monument, Carillon (Qué) #1591
Dollier de Casson, François, Can priest,
  historian, 1636-1701
- and Claude Baillif #8329
- and history of Montréal (Qué) #7899
dolls
- late 19th c.-1930s #2932
dolls, Algonquian
- (1760s-early 20th c.) #3633
dolls, Canadian
- (1886-1930), Eaton's catalogues #2851
- guide for collectors #2938 2941
- Mennonite #2264 2942
- Québec (1800-1925) #2937
dolls, Dakota #3733
dolls, Indians of North America
- 20th c. #2143
dolls, Iroquois
- (1760s-early 20th c.) #3633
dolls, Woodlands
- (1760s-early 20th c.) #3633
domestic architecture
- see also apartment houses; bungalows;

hunting lodges; log cabins; public
  housing; row houses; workers' housing
- Erickson, Arthur Charles, on #8354
- Safdie, Moshe, on #8406
domestic architecture, American
- 17th-18th cs., influence on Nova Scotia
  architecture #7823
- 18th-19th cs., influence on Québec
  domestic architecture #8592
- 20th c., influence on Québec domestic
  architecture #8591
- (1745-1845), influence on Canadian
  domestic architecture #8522
- (1908), Spanish-American, influence on
  Canadian domestic architecture #8638
- (1910s), California bungalows, influence
  on British Columbia bungalows #8685
- (1950s) #8509
- Georgian #8498
- summer homes, 20th c. #8524
domestic architecture, Beothuk #3528
domestic architecture, British
- 18th-19th cs., influence on Québec
  domestic architecture #8592
- 19th c., influence on Canadian banks and
  country houses #9200
- 19th c., influence on Prince Edward Island
  domestic architecture #8552
- (1900-1930), Tudor cottages and
  farmhouses, influence on Vancouver (BC)
  houses #8730
- (1950s) #8509
- country houses, influence on Canadian
  houses (1910s) #8490
domestic architecture, Canadian
- 17th-18th cs. #8586
- 17th-19th cs. #7687
- 17th c.-1960s #7689
- 17th-early 19th cs. #7841
- 19th c. #7974
- 19th c.-1960s #8515
- (1608-1867) #2120
- (1770s-1870s) #7696
- (1880-1914) #7736
- (1890s) #8485
- (1909) #8488
- (1910s) #8489 8491 8492 8493 8494
  - suburban houses #8490
- (1920s) #7656 8499
- (1930s) #8500 8502
  - and gardens #8501
  - small houses #8503 8504
- (1938-1942) #7666
- (1940s), small houses #8507
- (1950s) #8227 8508 8509 8510 8512
  - row houses #8511
- (1960-1970) #7710
- (1960s) #8231 8513 8517 8519
- (1970s) #8525
- Abernethy (Sask)
  - Lanark Place #8700
  - W.R. Motherwell Farmstead National
    Historic Park #8723 8724 9232
- Acadian #7804
- Alberta
  - (1900-1930s) #8126
  - ranch houses, late 19th-early 20th cs.
    #8720 8721
  - Ukrainian #8713
  - wooden #8120
- architects' houses
  - (1950s) #9299
- Architectural Record Record Houses (1975)
  #8745

- Arctic
  - (1960s) #8732
  - (1970s) #8733
- awards
  - Canadian Housing Design Council
    - (1957-) #8741
    - (1972) #8744
    - (1974) #8746
    - (1979) #8747
  - Canadian Small House Competition (1946) #8740
  - Dominion Housing Act Competition (1938) #8739
  - Dominion Housing Act Small House Competition (1936) #8736
  - National Awards for Residential Design (1969) #8743
  - Ontario Government Housing Competition (1936) #8737
  - Ontario Housing Corporation Design Competition (1972) #8663
  - Ontario Hydro Golden Medallion "All Electric Home" Competition (1961) #8514
  - Prix nationaux aux constructeurs de maisons unifamiliales (1960) #8742
  - T. Eaton Company Architectural Competition for House Designs (1936) #8738
  - T. Eaton Company Ideal Ontario Home Competition (1930) #8735
- Brigus (Nfld), Hawthorne Cottage #8539
- British Columbia #8143
  - 19th c.-1920s #8690
  - (1850s-early 20th c.) #8712
  - (1910s), bungalows #8685
  - (1940s) #1987 8693
  - Maclure, Samuel #8383 8384 8385
  - summer houses #8698
  - wooden #8153
- Brockville (Ont), Idlewild #8671
- Broughton Island (NWT), wood and styrofoam dome house #8734
- bungalows (1908) #8487
- Calgary (Alta)
  - (1875-1914) #8711
  - (1909) #8116
  - (1975-1980) #8728
  - Ian McDougall House #8727
  - Jenkins, Dan #8726
  - Long, Jack #8381
- Calixa-Lavallée (Qué) #7877
- cement stucco finishes (1908) #8638
- Charlevoix (Qué) #8629
- Comox (BC), Filberg House #8355
- Cornwall (Ont), Inverarden #8673
- Cowichan (Vancouver Island, BC), Marshall House #8695
- doctors' residences, Ontario, 19th c. #8675
- Don Mills (Ont), relationship of architects and builders (1950s) #8301
- Edmonton (Alta)
  - (1900-1914) #8130
  - (1920s-1970s), two-storey houses #8705
  - Duggan House #8729
  - Holgate House #8718
- Erickson, Arthur Charles #8356
- Fanshawe Pioneer Village (Ont) #8066
- Fredericton (NB), 19th c. #7803
- Georgeville (Qué), Joshua Copp House #8628
- Georgian #8498 8522
- Gothic revival #7739 7740
- government houses

- (pre-1867) #8754
- British Columbia (1849-1871) #8757
- Halifax (NS), Government House #8750
- Montréal (Qué), château de Ramezay #3076 3077 8566
- Niagara-on-the-Lake (Ont), Navy Hall #8464 8465
- Ottawa (Ont)
  - Earnscliffe #8652
  - Rideau Hall #8755 8756
- St. John's (Nfld) #8751 8752
- Toronto (Ont)
  - Chorley Park #8749
  - Government House (1866) #8753
  - Government House (1911) #8748
- Grand Digue (NB), Hélène and Roma Bourgeois House #8547
- Guelph (Ont), 19th c. #6040 7970
- Halifax (NS)
  - 18th-19th cs. #7818
  - Black-Binney House #8548
  - West House, Brunswick Street #8537
- Hamilton (Ont)
  - Dundurn Castle #8650 8662
  - Victorian #7991
  - Whitehern #8664
- île d'Orléans (Qué) #1252
  - (1761-1767) #8613
- Irish tradition, 19th c. #8523
- Kings Landing (NB) #7810 7811
- Kingston (Ont)
  - 17th-19th cs. #7989
  - 19th c. #7995
  - Newlands, William #8392
- Kingston Mills (Ont) #8020
- La Canardière (Qué), Garneau House #8615
- LaSalle (Qué), manoir Ogilvie #8636
- Laval (Qué), André B. Papineau House #8625
- Liverpool (NS), Simeon Perkins House #8536
- Lockport (Man), Saint Andrew's Parsonage #8716
- London (Ont)
  - 19th c. #8007 8010
  - Eldon House #8660
- Longueuil (Qué), Lamarre House #8608
- Louisbourg (NS) #8419 8422 8427
- Lunenburg (NS), Soloman House #8549
- Manitoba
  - 19th c. #8098 8692
  - 19th-early 20th cs. #8102
  - (1812-1870) #8097
  - (1907-1927) #8689
- Maritimes
  - 19th c. #8528
  - (pre-1900) #8551
- Memramcook (NB), Célestin Bourque House #8543
- Mennonite #2268 2572 8715
- Meteghan (NS), Vieille Maison #8531
- Montréal (Qué) #8576 8620
  - 19th c. #8612
  - (1698-1940s) #8570
  - (1880s-1890s) #8610
  - (1910s) #8556
  - (1910s), small houses #8555
  - (1920s) #8562
  - (1970s), assistance of McGill University architecture students to residents #8283
  - architectural drawings, Archives nationales du Québec à Montréal #8604
  - Arts Club #1314

- Bigot House #8567
- château de Callière #8565
- château Dufresne #8617 8618
- Cormier House #8347 8348
- George-Etienne-Cartier House #8619
- Nun's Island #8587
- Saint Gabriel House #8597
- Simon McTavish House #8564
- Sir William Van Horne Mansion #8594 8601
- stone building #8598
- Mount Uniake (NS), Uniake House #8534
- Neuville (Qué) #7875 8607
- New Brunswick, late 18th-early 19th cs. #8529
- Newfoundland tilt #8535
- Niagara-on-the-Lake (Ont)
  - 19th c. #7986 8655
  - late 18th-early 19th cs. #8000
- Norfolk County (Ont), 19th c. #8656
- Nova Scotia #7820
  - 17th-18th cs. #7823
  - 17th-19th cs. #7814
  - 18th c. #7815
- Ontario #7968 8654
  - 19th c. #2245 8005 8006 8672 8677 8678
  - 19th-early 20th cs. #8002
  - (1784-1840) #7966
  - (1800-1855) #8014
  - (1850s-1950s), terrace houses #8653
  - (1910s) #8642
  - (1920s) #8646
  - (1930s) #8647
  - Georgian #8648
  - influence of Scottish architecture, 19th c. #7977
  - plankwall framing, 19th c. #8046
  - polygonal buildings, 19th c. #7987
  - southern Ontario, 19th c. #8679
  - summer houses (1940s) #8651
- Ontario and Québec
  - (1910s) #8496
  - (1920s) #8497
  - brick houses (1790s-1810s) #8521
- Ontario and Québec, travellers' descriptions (1763-1860) #8527
- Perth (Ont)
  - 19th c. #8669
  - Matheson House (now Perth Museum) #8670
- Peterborough (Ont), Hutchison House #8674
- Prairies #8080 8717
  - sod houses #8701 8706
- prefabricated buildings, western Canada, early 20th c. #8082
- Prince Edward Island
  - 18th-19th cs. #8530
  - (1880s-1930s) #8544
  - sandstone houses, early 19th c. #8552
- Québec #7868 8568 8591 8592 8599 8600 8603
  - 17th-18th cs. #2217 7655 7845 8602 8605 8606 8621
  - 17th-19th cs. #7852 7866 8505 8559 8579 8593 8596 8609 8623
  - 17th c.-1940s #7853
  - 18th-19th cs. #8560 8561 8582
  - 18th c. #7861 7865
  - (1880-1914) #7929
  - (1960s) #7862
  - and Canadian Heritage of Quebec #7871
  - artisans' houses (1810-1819) #8616
  - country houses #8572

– farmhouses (1910s) #8554
– rural houses
  – 17th–18th cs. #8581
  – 17th–19th cs. #8624
  – (1600–1800) #8614
– seigneuries #8611
– use of stone, 17th–19th cs. #7891
– villas, 19th c. #8632
– Québec (Qué) #8631
  – 17th–19th cs. #7941
  – Fornel House #7953
  – Intendant's Palace #8553
  – Merchant's House, No. 92 Saint Peter
    Street #8563
  – place Royale #8588 8589
  – place Royale. Hazeur House #8626
– rectories
  – Batiscan (Qué), Old Presbytery #8807
– Regina (Sask)
  – (1909) #8109
  – (1910s) #8687
– Repentigny (Qué) #7888
– restoration guide #7760
– Saanich Peninsula (BC), Miraloma #8731
– Saint John's (Nfld) #8542
– Saint John (NB), Gregory House #8545
– Saint-Thomas de Montmagny (Qué),
  Bernatchez House #8630
– Sainte-Foy (Qué), 18th c. #8627
– Sandwich (Ont), Banwell House #7685
– Saskatchewan, pioneer houses, late
  19th–early 20th cs. #8696
– Second Empire #7741 7742
– Sillery (Qué), Maison des jésuites #8571
– St. Catharines (Ont), (1920s) #8645
– St. John's (Nfld)
  – (pre-1900) #7786
  – Commissariat House #8538
– summer homes, 20th c. #8524
– Summerside region (PEI), Green Park
  #8540
– Toronto (Ont)
  – 19th c.–1930s #8076
  – 19th–early 20th cs. #8077
  – (1791–1882) #8676
  – (1910s) #8639 8641
  – (1920), Harold R. Watson #8643
  – (1970s), renovation of central core
    residential areas #8068
  – Casa Loma #8649
  – Chief Justice Sir William Campbell
    House #8661
  – Flemingdon Park #8370 8657
  – Harbour City #8062
  – Holwood Mansion #8667
  – The Grange #8637 8665 8666
  – Thom Partnership #8412
– Trinity Bay (Nfld) #7785 7791 8541
– Trois-Rivières (Qué)
  – (1630s–1910s) #7883
  – Deschenaux House, also known as
    manoir de Tonnancour #8633
– Trois-Rivières (Qué), Forges of
  Saint-Maurice #8634 9250 9254
– Tunis Snook Farm (near Kingston, Ont)
  #8681
– Ukrainian #8085 8691 8704 8709 8710
– Vancouver (BC)
  – (1886–1929) #8714 8730
  – (1950–1960) #8697
  – (1950s) #1992
  – B.C. Binning House #8694
  – Erickson, Arthur Charles #8357 8361
  – False Creek #8169

– Hodson Manor #8707
– rehabilitation proposal for inner city
  buildings (1980) #8725
– Thom, Ron #8411
– Verchères (Qué) #8635
– Victoria (BC) #8722
  – Alexis Martin House #8682
– Village Jacques de Chambly (Qué) #8573
– Wartime Housing Limited, World War II
  #8506
– Whitby (Ont), Lynde House #8668
– Windsor (NS), Shand House #8546
– Winnipeg (Man) #8096 8105
  – 19th c. #8702
  – (1831–1960) #8095
  – (1880s–1910s) #8101
  – (1910s) #8688
  – Dalnavert #8708
  – Rugh, Herbert Bell #8683
  – Seven Oaks House (now Seven Oaks
    Museum) #8703
– Wolfville (NS) #8533
– wooden #7722
– workers' housing, post-World War I #8495
domestic architecture, East Main Cree
– sod houses #3609
domestic architecture, French
– 17th–18th cs., influence on Québec
  domestic architecture #8581 8592 8602
– 18th c., influence on île d'Orléans (Qué)
  domestic architecture #8613
domestic architecture, Huron #3519
domestic architecture, Indians of North
  America
– wooden #7722
domestic architecture, Inuit #7728
– (1950s) #8184
– wooden #7722
domestic architecture, Iroquois #3519
domestic architecture, Micmac #3528
domestic architecture, Ojibwa
– Parry Island Reservation (Ont) #3540
domestic architecture, Potawatomi
– Parry Island Reservation (Ont) #3540
Dominicans
– and Jean-Philippe Dallaire #5243 5247
Dominion Bank
– banks (1870s–1930s) #9188
Dominion Glass Co., glass manufacturer
  (Wallaceburg, Ont) #2401
Dominion Grocery and Fruit Journal, Can
  periodical
– and James Lovell Wiseman #7603
Dominion Housing Act Competition
– awards (1938) #8739
Dominion Housing Act Small House
  Competition
– awards (1936) #8736
Dominion Textile Co., textile manufacturer
  (Montréal, Qué)
– textile designs, Claire Miron #6571
Domville, Paul, Can architect in USA, fl.
  1914–1922
– domestic architecture #8496
Don Bridge Pottery, ceramic manufacturer
  (Toronto, Ont) #2310
Don Mills (Ont)
– housing, relationship of architects and
  builders (1950s) #8301
Don Mills (Ont), Beth-El Synagogue
– architecture, Mendelow & Keywan and
  Henry Fliess #8903
– mural, Out of Bondage, Aba Bayefsky #4632
Don Mills (Ont), Chatham Village

– architecture, James A. Murray and Henry
  Fliess #8511
Don Mills (Ont), Ortho Pharmaceutical plant
  and offices
– architecture, John B. Parkin Associates
  #7679
Don Mills (Ont), shopping centre
– architecture, John B. Parkin Associates
  #7679
Don Mills (Ont), South Mills Village
– architecture, James A. Murray and Henry
  Fliess #7679
Donaldson, Francis, Can architect, 1921–
– Annacis Island (BC), Annacis Industrial
  Estate #7679 9241
Donaldson, Margery Rogers, Can artist,
  1926–
– Legends on Tapestries program #5296
Donoahue, James Thomas (Jim), Can artist,
  1934–
– and Burns, Cooper, Donoahue, Fleming &
  Company Ltd. #904
– as Creative Director of Cooper and Beatty
  Ltd. #5297
– typographic designs #932
Donoghue, Lynn, Can artist, 1953–
– exhibitions, group
  – (1978) #665
Donovan, Duncan, Can photographer,
  1857–1933 #5298 5299
Doon (Ont), Doon School of Art
– Onley, Toni, as student #6741
Doon Pioneer Village (Ont) #8063
doors
– in art
  – Laporte, Lucie, and Joseph Marcil #1663
doors, Canadian
– Halifax (NS), Halifax Citadel #8441
– Ontario (pre-1840) #7963
– Québec, 17th–18th cs. #2530 2531
Doray, Audrey Capel, Can artist, 1931–
  #5300
– interview #5301
Dorion, Isaac, Can contractor, fl. 1835
– La Canardière (Qué), Garneau House
  #8615
Dorrance, David, Can ceramicist, sculptor,
  1946–
– exhibitions, group
  – (1977) #781
Dorset
– amulets
  – Gulf Hazard (NWT) #4365
  – Port-au-Choix (Nfld) #4354
– artifacts #4238 4331 4336 4342 4346 4347
  4351 4373 4377 4378
  – Abverdjar (Foxe Basin, NWT) #4333
  – and shamanism #4361
  – Bathurst Island (NWT) #4375
  – Button Point (Bylot Island, NWT) #4359
  – Cape Dorset (NWT) #4322
  – Igloolik (NWT) #4337
  – Newfoundland #4332
  – Pingerqalik (Foxe Basin, NWT) #4335
  – Point Spencer (Alaska) #4374
  – therapeutic symbolism #3356
– carvings #4350 4358 4364
– culture #4379 4380
– petroglyphs #4344 4362
– wooden mask, Button Point (Bylot Island,
  NWT) #4356 4357
Dorsey, Frances (Fran), Can tapestry artist,
  1948–
– interview #5302

Dorval (Qué), Club 230
– restoration, Tolchinsky & Goodz #7776
Dorval (Qué), La Lanterna Verde Restaurant
– mural, Giuseppe Fiore #5440
Dorval (Qué), Montreal International
  Airport. Air Terminal Building
– architecture #9517
    – Illsely, Templeton & Archibald; Larose
      & Larose; William Alexander Ramsay
      #9515
– mural, Greg Curnoe #5227
Dostaler, Martin d'Angeville, Can architect,
  1846-1915 #1319
Doucet, Louise, Can ceramicist, 1938- #5303
Doukhobors in Canada
– and Frederick Nicholas Loveroff #6330
– furniture #2585
– needlework #2780
– photographs of, Robert Minden #6570
– sepulchral monuments #733
Doull, Mary Allison, Can artist, 1866-1953
  #1164
Douville, Raymond, Can writer, 1905-
– on Gérard Morisset #3305
Dowler & Michie, Can architectural firm
– Calgary (Alta) #8116
Downing, Andrew Jackson, Amer architect,
  1815-1852
– and Calvert Vaux #8048
Downing, Claire, Can photographer, b. 1887
– exhibitions, group
  – (1976) #2012
Downing, Robert James, Can sculptor, 1935-
  #5305
– exhibitions
  – (1969) #5304
  – (1972) #5306
Downs, Barry Vance, Can architect, 1930-
– interview #8353
– on architecture #7746
– West Vancouver (BC), Woyat-Bowie
  Building. Architects' offices #9346
Downs & Archambault, Can architectural
  firm
– Vancouver (BC) #8353
    – Chinese Cultural Centre, competition
      #9144
    – F.P. 18 (Champlain Place) #8744
    – lodge for paraplegics #8744
Dr. Brute
– see Metcalfe, Eric W. (Dr. Brute)
Dragu, Margaret, Can artist, 1953-
– exhibitions, group
  – (1980) #687
Drapeau, Jean, Can statesman, 1916-
– and Olympic Stadium (Montréal, Qué)
  #9139
– on restoration of Old Montréal (Montréal,
  Qué) #7905
Drapell, Joseph, Can artist, 1940- #711 5307
– exhibitions, group
  – (1981) #722
Draper, Edward, Can furniture-maker, fl.
  1749 #2488
Draper site (Ont)
– pottery, Woodlands #3640
drapery, Canadian #2725
drawing
– see also graffiti; sketchbooks
– Ottawa (Ont), National Gallery of Canada
  #3061
drawing, American
– (1960s-1970s) #532
drawing, Canadian

– 17th-19th cs. #232
– 18th-19th cs. #246
– 19th-20th cs. #48 154 155
– 19th c.-1920s #11
– 20th c. #146
– (1850s) #1692
– (1890s-1940s) #367
– (1950s) #429
– (1960s) #464 486 487
– (1960s-1970s) #532
– (1970s) #595 607 638
– Alberta #1954 1968
– British Columbia (1845-1871) #2020 2023
– early 20th c., compared with Barbizon
  school #497
– Group of Seven #1736 1755
– Montréal (Qué)
  – (1960s) #1427
  – McGill University. McCord Museum
    #222 223
– Ottawa (Ont), Public Archives of Canada.
  William H. Coverdale Collection #12 3230
– Prairies #1855
– Québec
  – 20th c. #1520 1523
  – (1975-1980) #1565
  – Surrealism #1470
– Québec (Qué), Séminaire des jésuites
  #2982
– realism #1810
– Saskatchewan (1970s) #1933
– Toronto (Ont), Royal Ontario Museum,
  18th-19th cs. #247
– war subjects #1092 1093 1096 1097 1099
  1111 1112
– Winnipeg Sketch Club #1887
drawing, Inuit
– (1960s), Cape Dorset (NWT) #4189
– (1964), Baffin Island (NWT) #4194
drawing, Plains #3709
drawing technique
– see media and techniques, drawing
Dream Dance, Algonquian #3580
dreams
– in art
  – Crone-Findlay, Noreen #5211
  – Giguère, Roland #5596
  – Granirer, Pnina #5644
  – Lodge, Judy #6321
  – Pellan, Alfred #6808 6815
Drenters, Yosef G., Can sculptor, 1929-
– sculptures (1960s) #744 746
Dresden (East Germany), Indianer Museum
  Radebeul
– art, Indians of North America #3430
dress
– see costume; fashion
Drewry, W.S., Can photographer, fl.
  1880-1890
– survey photographs, Rocky Mountains
  (1880s-1890s) #1874
Drolet, Françoise Desrochers
– see Desrochers-Drolet, Françoise
Drouin, Michèle, Can artist, 1933- #5308
Drué, Juconde, Fr priest, architect, artist in
  Canada, 1664-ca. 1739 #234 235
drugs
– influence on Arthur Fortescue McKay
  #6475 6477
Druik, Don, Can artist, 1945-
– exhibitions, group
  – (1977) #631
– video art #605
Drum, Sydney Maria, Can artist, 1952-

– exhibitions, group
  – (1980) #698
Drummond, Arthur Alexander, Can artist,
  1891-
– exhibitions
  – (1975) #5309
Drummond, George Fairly, Can architect,
  1891-
– Montréal (Qué), Queen Elizabeth Hotel
  #9286
Drummond, William Henry, Can poet,
  1854-1907
– illustrations of poetry, Frederick Simpson
  Coburn #5123
drums, Iroquois #3489
drums, Kwakiutl
– Thunderbird Dance #3867
drums, Micmac #3556
drums, Ojibwa #3539
drums, Tlingit #3976
Drury, Charles Mills, Can politician, 1912-
– and National Gallery of Canada (Ottawa,
  Ont) competition (1975-1977) #9126
Du Mond, Frank Vincent, Amer artist,
  1865-1951
– as teacher of Robert Elmer Lougheed
  #6327
Du Toit, Roger, Can architect, 1939-
– Toronto (Ont)
    – CN Tower #9511
    – Union Station #9540
Dub, Eugene N. (Gene), Can architect, 1943-
– Edmonton (Alta), City Hall #8998
– Edmonton (Alta), City Hall, competition
  #8999 9000
Dubois, Jean Baptiste
– see Filiau (dit Dubois), Jean Baptiste
DuBois, Macy, Can architect, 1929-
– on architecture #7746
– Toronto (Ont), Central Technical School
  Art Centre #7684
Dubois, Marius, Can artist, 1944- #5310
– exhibitions
  – (1979) #5311
Dubois, Pierre Gilles, Can artist, 1938- #5312
DuBois, Strong, Bindhart, Can architectural
  firm
– Toronto (Ont), Joseph E. Shephard
  Government of Canada Building #8975
Dubreuil, Michel, Can photographer, 1953-
  #1562
Dubuc, Jacques, Can artist, fl. 1974
– as member of Centre communautaire
  catholique Tour de David
  (Saint-Basile-le-Grand, Qué) #1510
Dubuffet, Jean, Fr artist, 1901-
– Simonin, Francine, compared with #7213
Duburou, Can priest, 18th c.
– portrait of, François Malepart de
  Beaucourt #4646
Duchamp, Marcel, Fr artist, 1887-1968
– influence on Alan Frank Glass #5616
Duck, Adele, Can artist, 1948- #717
Ducornet, Louis-Joseph-César, Fr artist,
  1806-1856
– portrait of Samuel de Champlain #191
Duff, Wilson, Can ethnologist, 1925-1976
– Festschrift #4049
– on Northwest Coast Indians #4003
Dufferin, Lady Harriot Georgiana, Brit in
  Canada, 1843-1902
– collection, Canadian photographs, 19th c.
  #1048
Dufferin and Ava, Frederick Temple

Blackwood, 1st Marquess of, Brit statesman in Canada, 1826-1902
– plans for Québec (Qué) fortifications (1875) #7946
Duffus, Allan, Can architect, 1915-
– Halifax (NS) #7733
Duffus, Romans, Kundzins & Rounsefell, Can architectural firm
– Halifax (NS), Nova Scotia Technical College. Student residence #9467
Dufour, Claude, Can artist, 1925- #1546 1551
Dufour, Gisèle Trottier
– see Trottier-Dufour, Gisèle
Dufour, Marcellin, Can artist, 1946- #1547
Dufresne, Adrien, Can architect, 1904-
– Québec churches #8334
Dufresne, Hélène Gagné
– see Gagné-Dufresne, Hélène
Dufresne, Marius, Can engineer, surveyor, 1883-1945
– Montréal (Qué), château Dufresne #1294 8617 8618
Dufresne, Oscar, Can manufacturer, 1875-1935/1936
– Montréal (Qué), château Dufresne #1294 8617
Dugald (Man), Dugald Costume Collection #2902
Dugas, Marc, Can artist, 1945-
– as founder of Atelier de réalisations graphiques (Québec, Qué) #1661
Duguay, Raoul, Can musician, 1939-
– poems, for drawings by Louis-Pierre Bougie #4861
Duguay, Rodolphe, Can artist, 1891-1973 #1393 5313 5315 5316 5319 5320
– and Marcel Baril #4608
– autobiography (1907-1927) #5317
– exhibitions
– (1979) #5318
– woodcuts #5314
Dukes, Caroline, Can artist, 1929-
– exhibitions, group
– (1975) #1867
Dulongpré, Louis, Can artist, 1754-1843 #1323
– and Québec society #1375
– exhibitions, group
– (1959) #219
– influence of French painting #1244
– paintings, church, Berthierville (Qué) #8874
– portraits
– Hertel de Rouville family member #1345
– McGill, James #5321
Dumas, Antoine, Can artist, 1932- #5322
Dumouchel, Albert, Can artist, 1916-1971 #824 1453 1665 5323 5324 5325 5326 5329 5331 5333
– and Jean-Paul Lemieux #5328
– and Montréal (Qué) painting (1950s) #1403
– and Serge Tousignant #7405
– as teacher #1641 3001 5327
– Institut des arts graphiques (Montréal, Qué) #1648
– as teacher of Robert Wolfe #7606
– Dallaire, Jean-Philippe, compared with #5238
– engravings #1654
– exhibitions
– (1974) #5332
– (1979) #5334
– exhibitions, group
– (1967) #821

– exhibitions (reviews) #860 5330
– influence on Janine Leroux-Guillaume #6247
Dumouchel, Suzanne, Can artist, 1920- #5335
Dunbar, Frederick Alexander Turner, Can artist, 1849-1921
– Wilde, Oscar, on #238
Duncan, Douglas M., Can artist, art dealer, collector, 1902-1968 #570 3232
– and Picture Loan Society (Toronto, Ont) #1746 1758
– collection, Canadian art, 20th c. #119 541 3223
– interview #3219
– on collecting Canadian art #3218
Duncan, Helen, Can ceramicist, fl. 1950s-1960s #2102
Duncan, James D., Can artist, 1806-1881 #5336
– illustrations, L'album des costumes de communautés religieuses de femmes au Canada en 1853 #2834
– relation of photography and painting #245
Duncan (BC), public school
– architecture, William Tuff Whiteway #9508
Duncan McNab & Partners, Can architectural firm
– Vancouver (BC), Raymur Place Housing #8520
Duncan S. McNab & Associates, Can architectural firm
– Burnaby (BC), Simon Fraser University, competition #9501
Duncanson, Robert Stuart, Can artist, 1821-1872 #241 242 5337
– exhibitions
– (1972) #5338
Dundas (Ont)
– (1813-1850s) #7994
dungeons
– see prisons
Dunington, Lorrie Alfreda, Can landscape architect, d. 1945
– plan, northwestern entrance to Hamilton (Ont) #7962
Dunington-Grubb, Howard Burlingham, Can landscape architect, 1880-1965
– plan, northwestern entrance to Hamilton (Ont) #7962
Duplessis, Jacqueline, Can textile artist, 1920-
– batik #5339
Dupond, Marcel Jules René, Can enamelist, 1907-1954 #5340
Dupont, Chantal, Can artist, 1942-
– exhibitions
– (1979) #5341
Dupont, Marcel, Can artist, fl. 1974
– as member of Centre communautaire catholique Tour de David (Saint-Basile-le-Grand, Qué) #1510
Dupras, Robert, Can artist, 1928-
– exhibitions, group
– (1955) #1408
Dupré, Jules, Fr artist, 1811-1889
– as teacher of Atha Haydock Caldwell #4991
Dupuis, Luce, Can sculptor, 1940- #1632
Dupuis-Maillet, Corinne, Can artist, 1895- #5342
Duquet, Georges-Henri, Can artist, b. 1889 #5343
Duquet, Suzanne, Can artist, 1916- #5344

– and Ecole des beaux-arts (Montréal, Qué), (1968) #2995
– as teacher of Aline Piché-Whissell #6865
Durand, Luc, Can architect, 1929-
– Montréal (Qué), Olympic Village #9127
Durham (Ont), Durham Art Gallery
– exhibitions
– The Prints of Mary Wrinch (1980) #7618
Durham region (Ont)
– art (1970s) #1826
Durocher, Gabriel, Can photographer, fl. 1973
– portfolio of photographs #997 999
Düsseldorf (West Germany), Kunsthalle
– exhibitions
– Alex Colville: Paintings and Drawings, 1970-1977/Alex Colville: Bilder und Zeichnungen, 1970-1977 (1977) #5153
Dutkewytch, Andrew, Can artist, 1944- #1512
– exhibitions, group
– (1976) #1529
Dyens, Georges, Can sculptor, 1932- #5345
dyes and dyeing, Canadian
– (1608-1867) #2120
– Cape Breton (NS) #2732
– Charlevoix (Qué), 17th-19th cs. #2733
– Newfoundland #2744
– Nova Scotia #2749
– Ontario #2742
– Québec #2745
– (1820s) #165
dyes and dyeing, Hurons
– 19th c. #165
dyes and dyeing, Inuit
– and Judy McGrath #4249 4255 6474
dyes and dyeing, Northwest Coast Indians #3415
Dyky, Ivan, Can artist, fl. 1918-
– frescoes, Church of Saint Nicholas (Toronto, Ont) #1822
Dynes, Joseph, Can artist, 1825-1897
– and Samuel C. Hawksett #5753
– as member, Toronto Society of Arts #1689
Dyonnet, Edmond, Can artist, 1859-1954 #302 1240 5346 5348
– and Pen and Pencil Club (Montréal, Qué) #1251
– as teacher of Orson Shorey Wheeler #7549
– autobiography #5347 5349
Dyson, Brian, Can artist, 1944- #5350
– museum theme #714

E

E.B. Eddy Company
– see Eddy, E.B., Company
E.J. Gaboury and Associates
– see Gaboury, E.J., and Associates
E.W. Morris Company
– see Morris, E.W., Company
Eadie, Arthur Hunter, Can architect, 1897-1956
– Toronto (Ont), Bank of Nova Scotia #9193
Eagar, William H., Can artist, 1796-1839 #5351
Eakins, Thomas, Amer artist, 1844-1916
– sporting subjects #5252
earthenware
– see pottery
earthworks, Algonquian #3463

earthworks, Northwest Coast Indians
– 13th c. #3955
earthworks (sculpture)
– Canada #617
– Sawchuk, George #7141 7143
– Vazan, Bill #7477
East, Benoît, Can artist, 1915- #5352 5353
East India porcelain
– see Chinese export porcelain
East Main Cree
– sod houses #3609
Eastcott, Robert Wayne, Can artist, 1943-
– exhibitions
    – (1976) #2059
– interview #5354
Easter
– eggs
    – Ottawa (Ont), National Museum of
      Man. Canadian Centre for Folk Culture
      Studies #963
    – Ukrainian #2132
Eastern Townships (Qué)
– art
    – (1800-1950) #1296
    – (1815-1940) #1288
    – (1970s) #1282 1535 1539
– churches, Protestant, 19th c. #8888
– photographic views
    – (1970s) #1534
– views
    – (1832-1881) #1342
    – Edson, Aaron Allan #5362
Eastlake, Charles Locke, Brit designer,
    writer, 1836-1906
– influence on Jacques & Hay Co. #2559
eating utensils
– see tableware
Eaton, T., Company Limited, Can
    department store
– Architectural Competition for House
    Designs (1936) #8738
– dolls #2941
– Ideal Ontario Home Competition (1930)
    #8735
– mail-order catalogues #2851
    – illustrations, Fred Brigden #4913
– stores (1920s) #9365
Eaton, Timothy, Can businessman,
    1834-1907
– Eaton Mausoleum, Mount Pleasant
    Cemetery (Toronto, Ont) #8895
Eaton, Wyatt, Can artist, 1849-1896 #5355
    5356 5357
Eberhardt, Nicholas, Can ceramicist, b. 1834,
    fl. 1863-1879 #2310
Ebring, Axel, Can ceramicist, 20th c. #2391
Eby, William, Can ceramicist, 1831-1910
    #2356
Ecanada Art Pottery, ceramic manufacturer
    (Hamilton, Ont) #2359
– (1945-1952) #2353
ecclesiastical vestments
– see vestments
Echalook, Thomasee, Can artist, 1935-
– stonecut prints #4487
Echaluk, Thomassie
– see Echalook, Thomasee
Echeverria y Godoy, Atanasio, Sp artist in
    Canada, fl. 1780s-1790s
– expedition, Northwest Coast #1998
Eckerman, Oscar A., Amer architect,
    1873-1950
– John Deere Plow Company warehouses
    #9247

Eco, Umberto, It writer, 1932-
– and Max Dean #5274
Ecole des arts domestiques de
    Québec/Quebec School of Handicrafts
– (1930s) #2969
Ecole des arts et métiers de
    Québec/Provincial School of Handicrafts
– (1930s) #2166
ecology
– and art, Canada (1970s) #617
– Seton, Ernest Thompson, on #7172
economics and art
– Canada
    – (1940s) #353
    – (1960s) #529 3265
    – (1970s) #586 619 682 3267 3275 3278
      3286 3293
        – and Canadian Artists' Representation
          #632
    – (1974), Canada Council proposal on
      business support for the arts by 1980
      #3271
– Inuit #3345 4215 4245 4262 4276 4277 4288
– Ontario (1970s) #1802
– Québec (1970s) #2211 2224
Eddy, E.B., Company, printing firm (Hull,
    Qué)
– typography (1940s) #922
Eden Smith & Sons, Can architectural firm
– Toronto (Ont)
    – D.O. Roblin Warehouse #9234
    – University of Toronto. Men's residence
      #9431
Edenshaw, Albert Edward, Can artist, 19th
    c.
– silver #5358
Edenshaw, Charles, Can artist, 1839-1920
    #4042 4169 5359 5360
– argillite carvings, Vancouver Centennial
    Museum (Vancouver, BC) #4006
– carving, Vancouver Art Gallery
    (Vancouver, BC) #3820
– influence on Bill Reid #6985 6987
– influence on Robert Davidson #5269
– silver #5358
– tombstone crest carvings #3995
Edenshaw, Charles, Can artist, 20th c. #5358
Edenshaw, Henry, Can sculptor, early 20th
    c.
– argillite caskets #5361
Edinburgh (Scotland), Edinburgh
    International Festival (1968)
– exhibitions
    – Canada 101 (1968) #514
– exhibitions (reviews)
    – Canada 101 (1968) #519 520
Edinburgh (Scotland), Edinburgh
    International Festival (1980)
– exhibitions
    – The Legacy: Continuing Traditions of
      Canadian Northwest Coast Indian Art
      (1980) #4043
Edinburgh (Scotland), Royal Scottish
    Academy
– Cruikshank, William, as student #5212
Edinburgh (Scotland), Royal Scottish
    Museum
– artifacts, Athapaskan #4091
– exhibitions
    – Les Athabascans, ces étrangers du Nord:
      une exposition itinérante formée des
      collections du Musée national de l'Homme
      (Canada) et du Royal Scottish Museum
      (1974) #4104

    – The Athapaskans: Strangers of the North;
      An International Travelling Exhibition
      from the Collection of the National
      Museum of Man, Canada, and the Royal
      Scottish Museum (1974) #4105
– totem poles, Niska #3839
Editions Erta, publishing firm (Montréal,
    Qué) #926
– and Roland Giguère #1641
Editions Formart, publishing firm (Montréal,
    Qué)
– exhibitions (reviews)
    – (1970) #1490
Editions Goglin, publishing firm #926
Editions Lacia, publishing firm (Québec,
    Qué)
– Christmas greeting cards #857
Edmond, Pierre, Can sculptor, 1738-1800
– tabernacles #1613
Edmonton (Alta)
– architecture
    – (1800-1914) #8130
    – (1909) #8117
    – Chinatown #8137
    – downtown area (1970s) #8123
    – Myers, Barton #8391
– art
    – (1920s-1980s) #1941
    – (1950s-1970s) #131
    – (1960s) #441 1848
    – (1960s-1980s) #1975
    – (1970s) #1856
– domestic architecture, two-storey houses
    (1920s-1970s) #8705
– graphic arts (1970s) #1958
– photographic views, Ernest Brown #4935
– public art #1973
– sculpture (1960s) #1853
– theatres (1906) #9143
Edmonton (Alta), Alberta Art
    Foundation/Fondation des arts de
    l'Alberta #1957
– exhibitions
    – An Exhibition to Commemorate the XI
      Commonwealth Games/Exposition
      commémorative des XIe Jeux du
      Commonwealth (1978) #1963
Edmonton (Alta), Alberta Government
    Administrative Building
– architecture, Department of Public Works
    of the Province of Alberta; Cecil S.
    Burgess, Consulting Architect #8963
Edmonton (Alta), Canada Packers Limited
– architecture, Eric Ross Arthur and
    Anthony Adamson #7973
Edmonton (Alta), Canadiana Galleries
– exhibitions
    – Holman: Recent Sculpture (1981) #4457
Edmonton (Alta), Citadel Theatre
– architecture, Barton Myers; Rick L. Wilkin
    #8091 9140
Edmonton (Alta), City Hall
– architecture, competition for #7747 8998
    8999 9000
Edmonton (Alta), Dominion Bank
– architecture, George W. Northwood #9188
Edmonton (Alta), Duggan House
– restoration, Juan Corkan and Mickey
    Holland #8729
Edmonton (Alta), Edmonton Art Gallery
– exhibitions
    – Alberta '73 (1973) #1942
    – Alberta Now (1980) #1969
    – Alberta Realists (1974) #1954

– Art in Alberta: Paul Kane to the Present (1973) #1953
– Baker Lake Prints/Estampes (1970) #4473
– Canada X Ten (1974) #565
– Canadian Painting in the Thirties (1975) #592
– Carl Schaefer in Hanover (1980) #7157
– Certain Traditions: Recent British and Canadian Art (1978) #653
– Changing Visions: The Canadian Landscape/Aperçus divers: le paysage canadien (1976) #617
– Chester & Bentham: An Exhibition of Recent Paintings by D.T. Chester and Recent Sculpture by Douglas Bentham (1973) #1858
– Christopher Pratt (1971) #6910
– Claude Tousignant (1974) #7401
– Conceptual Decorative: Prints by Les Levine, 1965-1970/Conceptuel décoratif: estampes de Les Levine, 1965-1970 (1972) #6265
– Dan Christensen: Recent Paintings (1973) #5104
– David Craven: Recent Works (1978) #5205
– David Milne: The New York Years, 1903-1916 (1981) #6567
– Diversity: Canada East (1972) #543
– Dorothy Knowles (1973) #6067
– Drawings and Pastels c. 1930-1967 by Miller Gore Brittain (1969) #4917
– Drawings by Jack Weldon Humphrey: A Travelling Exhibition Organized by the Beaverbrook Art Gallery, Fredericton, New Brunswick, Canada, 1977-1979 (1979) #5871
– Edmonton Collects: 1: Canadian Art (1973) #105
– Edward Curtis in the Collection of the Edmonton Art Gallery (1979) #3480
– Emily Carr: Oil on Paper Sketches (1979) #5046
– Environment '70 (1970) #1951
– F.H. Varley: A Centennial Exhibition/F.H. Varley: une exposition centenaire (1981) #7468
– Gift from the Douglas M. Duncan Collection and the Milne-Duncan Bequest/Le Don provenant de la collection Douglas M. Duncan et le legs Milne-Duncan (1972) #541
– H.G. Glyde in Canada (1974) #5618
– Impressionism in Canada, 1895-1935 (1974) #115
– J.B. Taylor: Landscapes (1973) #7335
– Jack Bush: A Retrospective/Rétrospective: Jack Bush (1977) #4969
– Jack Shadbolt (1970) #7182
– Jock Macdonald: Retrospective Exhibition/Jock Macdonald: rétrospective (1969) #6375
– Jock Macdonald: The Inner Landscape: A Retrospective Exhibition/Jock Macdonald: le paysage intérieur: rétrospective (1981) #6379
– Joe Fafard: Recent Sculpture (1979) #5401
– Kenneth Lochhead: Recent Works on Paper (1972) #6316
– Looking South (1978) #4278
– Marion Nicoll: A Retrospective, 1959-1971 (1975) #6702
– Maxwell Bates: Retrospective Exhibition (1961) #4622
– Modern Painting in Canada: A Survey of Major Movements in Twentieth Century Canadian Art (1978) #507
– Oonark/Pangnark (1970) #4220
– Otto Rogers: New Paintings and Sculpture, 1977-78 (1979) #7065
– Painting in Alberta: An Historical Survey (1980) #1970
– Peinture canadienne des années trente (1975) #589
– Plains Indian (1971) #3720
– Robert Harris (1849-1919) (1974?) #5743
– Ronald: 25 Years (1975) #7073
– Saskatchewan: Art and Artists (1971) #1919
– Takao Tanabe, 1972-1976: The Land (1977) #7320
– The Alberta Landscape (1979) #1965
– The Big Picture: Large Scale Landscape Painting on the Prairies (1981) #1885
– The Canadian Canvas: A Travelling Exhibition of 85 Recent Paintings/Peintres canadiens actuels: exposition itinérante de 85 oeuvres récentes (1975) #588
– The Collective Unconscious: American and Canadian Art, 1940-1950 (1975) #1458
– The Contemporary Arts Society: Montreal 1939-1948/La Société d'art contemporain: Montréal 1939-1948 (1980) #1474
– The Group of Seven in the Rockies (1974) #1861
– The History of Ceramics in Alberta (1975) #2386
– The J.S. McLean Collection of Canadian Painting (1969) #3228
– The John Henry Hinton Photographs: China 1894-1918 (1977) #5812
– William Kurelek: A Retrospective (1970) #6109
– William Perehudoff: Ten Years, 1970-1980/William Perehudoff: une décennie, 1970-1980 (1983) #6838
– Yves Gaucher (1969) #5563
– exhibitions (reviews)
– Burgess, Catherine #717
– Carl Schaefer in Hanover (1980) #7158
– Emily Carr: Oil on Paper Sketches (1979) #5041
– Reynolds, Alan #6991
– Savage, Harry #7133
– Sinclair, Robert #7215
– The Canadian Canvas: A Travelling Exhibition of 85 Recent Paintings/Peintres canadiens actuels: exposition itinérante de 85 oeuvres récentes (1975) #582
– photography collection #1051
– photography exhibitions (1970s) #1879
– Poole, Ernest Edward, collection #3235
– support of Edmonton (Alta) art #1975
Edmonton (Alta), Edmonton International Airport
– architecture #9517
Edmonton (Alta), Government House
– architecture #8131
Edmonton (Alta), Holgate House
– restoration #8718
Edmonton (Alta), Hotel Macdonald
– architecture, Ross & Macdonald #9270
Edmonton (Alta), Imperial Bank of Canada
– architecture, Robert Percy Barnes #9154
Edmonton (Alta), Legislative Buildings
– architecture
– Jeffers, Allan Merrick, and John Chalmers #8962
– Jeffers, Allan Merrick, and R.P. Blakey #8944 8945
Edmonton (Alta), Mathers' Art Gallery
– and Charles Wesley Mathers #6451
Edmonton (Alta), McCauley Plaza
– architecture and urban development #9302
Edmonton (Alta), McDougall United Church
– architecture #8131
Edmonton (Alta), McLeod Building
– architecture #8131
Edmonton (Alta), Muttart Conservatory
– architecture, Peter Hemingway #8091
Edmonton (Alta), Northern Alberta Jubilee Auditorium
– exhibitions
– The Ernest E. Poole Foundation Collection (1966) #3222
Edmonton (Alta), Provincial Archives of Alberta
– photographs, 19th c., Ernest Brown collection #1949
Edmonton (Alta), René le Marchand Mansion Apartments
– architecture #8131
Edmonton (Alta), Ring House Gallery
– see Edmonton (Alta), University of Alberta. Ring House Gallery
Edmonton (Alta), University of Alberta
– architecture #8131
– Diamond & Myers #9495
– Nobbs & Hyde #9492 9493
– collections #3200
– exhibitions
– Tom Forrestall Exhibition (1972) #5461
Edmonton (Alta), University of Alberta. Art Gallery and Museum
– exhibitions
– Childhood: Eight Canadian Artists (1979) #674
– J.Frederic McCulloch 1905-1932: Works on Paper (1978) #6463
– Roger Savage (1981) #7135
Edmonton (Alta), University of Alberta. Department of Anthropology
– painted buffalo hide #3711
Edmonton (Alta), University of Alberta. Department of Art
– exhibitions
– Younger Vancouver Sculptors (1968) #2037
Edmonton (Alta), University of Alberta. Department of Extension
– art education (1930s-1940s) #1943
Edmonton (Alta), University of Alberta. Ring House Gallery
– exhibitions
– A Tribute to William Townsend: 1909 to 1973 (1974) #7418
– Tommie Gallie: In Place (1981) #5553
Edmonton (Alta), University of Alberta. Students' Union Art Gallery
– exhibitions
– Artisan '78: The First National Travelling Exhibition of Contemporary Canadian Crafts/Artisan '78: première exposition nationale itinérante d'artisanat canadien contemporain (1979) #2134
– Eskimo Fantastic Art (1972) #4240
– Lithographs/Lithographies (1972) #825
Edmonton (Alta), University of Alberta. Students' Union Housing
– architecture, Diamond & Myers; Rick L. Wilkin #9496
Edmonton (Alta), Upstairs Gallery
– exhibitions
– Arthur F. McKay (1979) #6478

Edmonton Art Club (Edmonton, Alta)
– exhibitions
  – (1921-) #1941
Edmundston (NB), collège Saint-Louis
– exhibitions
  – *George Rackus: Anodized Aluminum Works & Prints* (1973) #6953
  – *The Beaverbrook Art Gallery Presents Nine New Brunswick Artists/La Galerie d'art Beaverbrook présente neuf artistes du Nouveau-Brunswick* (1973) #1182
Edmundston (NB), collège Saint-Louis. Galerie Coline
– exhibitions
  – *Annie D. Savage: Drawings and Watercolours* (1974) #7129
Edmundston (NB), collège Saint-Louis. Galerie d'art
– exhibitions
  – *Albert Franck (1899-1973) in Retrospect: A Small Selection from the Artist's Collection* (1974) #5500
Edmundston (NB), galerie Coline
– see Edmundston (NB), collège Saint-Louis. Galerie Coline
Edmundston (NB), Madawaska Museum
– exhibitions
  – *The Murray and Marguerite Vaughan Inuit Print Collection/Collection d'estampes inuit* (1982) #4498
Edson, Aaron Allan, Can artist, 1846-1888 #5362 5363
– exhibitions, group
  – (1888) #175
  – (1969) #1180
education
– see also architectural education; art education
– Canada (1970s), American influences #3279
– Ontario, 19th c. #3152
Edwards, Roger, Can designer, 1948- #2487
Edwards & Saunders, Can architectural firm
– domestic architecture #8494
Edwin S. Kent and Geo. W. White Associates, Amer architectural firm
– Lucerne (Qué), Château Lucerne #9283
Eells, Myron, Amer missionary and ethnologist, 1843-1907
– on Salish Indians #4031
effigies
– see portrait sculpture; sepulchral monuments
Egan, Alice Mary, Can artist, b. ca. 1872
– china painting, Canadian State dinner service (1898) #2333
Egmondville Pottery, ceramic manufacturer (Huron County, Ont) #2329
  – (1852-1910) #2323
Eight, The (American group)
– influence on David Brown Milne #6567
– influence on Ernest Lawson #6178
Eisenhauer, Collins, Can sculptor, 1898- #5364
– exhibitions (reviews) #1210 1213
El Al Airlines
– Odjig, Daphne, commissioned work #6731
Elbaz, André, Can artist, 1934- #5365
Eleanor Le Maire Associates, Can interior design firm
– Toronto (Ont), Holt Renfrew Store #8078
electric lighting
– see lighting
electricity in art

– neon signs (Vancouver, BC) #2079
– sculptures, Electric Gallery (Toronto, Ont) #1800
electrographics
– see copy art
electronic art
– see video art
Elgin County (Ont), Hall-Baker-Stewart House
– architecture, Isaac Bennett Baker #2581
Elie, Robert, Can writer, arts administrator, 1915-1973
– correspondence, Paul-Emile Borduas #1270 4834
Elizabeth II, Queen of Great Britain and Northern Ireland, 1926-
– paintings of visit to New Brunswick (1976), Molly Lamb Bobak #4765
Ellingson, William John, Amer artist, 1929-
– as teacher of Charles Ringness #7011
Elliot Lake (Ont)
– development project (1950s) #8184
Elliot Lake (Ont), Centre for Continuing Education
– Frenkel, Vera, as teacher #5519
Elliott, Alfred J., Can artist, fl. 1977
– typographic designs #932
Ellis, Francis Dean, Can artist, 1948- #5366
– exhibitions, group
  – (1976) #2060
– natural constructions (1970s) #2065
Ellis, James E., Can silversmith, fl. 1848-1871 #2638
Ellis & Connery, Can architectural firm
– Toronto (Ont), Bank of British North America #9150
Ellis & Ellis, Can architectural firm
– Brighton (Ont), Union School #9387
– Lambton Mills (Ont), school #9388
– Toronto (Ont), John Ross Robertson and Glenholme schools, competition for #9437
Elmsdale Pottery, Can ceramic manufacturer (Halifax, NS)
– Staffordshire ware #2339
Elora (Ont)
– photography (1856-1867) #1724
Eloul, Kosso, Can sculptor, 1920- #5370
– *Canadac*, Art Gallery of Hamilton (Hamilton, Ont) #780
– exhibitions
  – (1973) #5368
  – (1980) #5369
– *Now*, Fanshawe College (London, Ont) #5367
– ritual and cult elements #789
Elsinore Editions, publishing house (Elsinore, Ont)
– and John Bernard Boyle #834
Eluard, Paul, Fr poet, 1895-1952
– poems, drawings of, Alfred Pellan #6824 6825
emblems and mottoes
– see also heraldry
emblems and mottoes, Canadian #2939
– beaver #56
embroidery
– see also beadwork; crewelwork; needlework
embroidery, Algonquian
– beadwork #3635
– moose hair #3513
embroidery, Athapaskan #4110
embroidery, Canadian
– 20th c. #2121

– (1608-1867) #2120
– Brown, Annora #4933
– Canadian Embroiderer's Guild #2793
– influence on Canadian art, 20th c. #2093
– Le Ber, Jeanne #2778
– Mennonite #2267 2729
– moose hair, 18th c. #3629
  – influence on European embroidery #2783
– Nova Scotia #2731
– Québec #1235 1324 1327 2169 2171 2183 2184
  – 17th-18th cs. #1320 2181 2200 2779
– Ukrainian #2782
– Ukrainian Bukovinian #2124
– Ursuline #1581 2777 2781 2783 2788 2789 2791
embroidery, Huron
– moose hair #3513
embroidery, Indians of North America
– 18th c. #2169 2171
– moose hair #2783 3629
embroidery, Inuit #4259
embroidery, Iroquois
– beadwork #3635
– moose hair #3559
embroidery, Métis #4110
embroidery, Montagnais
– floral motifs #4076
embroidery, Naskapi
– floral motifs #4076
embroidery, Penobscot #3537
embroidery, Thompson Indians #3808
embroidery, Woodlands
– beadwork #3635
Emerging Arts West, Can periodical #1868
Emerson, Ralph Waldo, Amer writer, 1803-1882
– Atkins, Caven Ernest, compared with #4570
Emery, Alban S., Can furniture-maker, fl. 1910- #2511
Emery, George E., Can ceramicist, 1881-1959
– as founder, Ecanada Art Pottery (Hamilton, Ont) #2353 2359
Emilson, Bruce, Can artist, 1944-
– video art #605
Emma Lake (Sask), Emma Lake Workshops #507
– (1950s-1970s) #145
– (1955-1970) #1921
– (1955-1973) #1923
– and Anthony Caro #1934
– and Douglas Bentham #4686
– and Ernest Lindner #6284
– and Judith Allsopp #717
– and Kenneth Campbell Lochhead #6317 6319
– and Marion F.S. Mackay Nicoll #6701 6703
– hard-edge prints #832
– influence on Saskatchewan art #1862 1915 1932 1935
– landscapes #1855
Emmons, George Thornton, Amer collector, 1852-1945
– collection, art, Northwest Coast Indians #4005
Emond, Philippe, Can artist, 1930-
– exhibitions, group
  – (1955) #1408
Emond, Pierre, Can sculptor, 1738-1808 #5371
enamel, Canadian
– (1950s) #2378

– (1964-1967) #2108 2109
– Brassard, Thérèse Tanguay #4905
– Brault, Maurice #4906
– Dupond, Marcel Jules René #5340
– Passillé-Sylvestre, Micheline de #2216
– Québec
    – (1950s) #2193
    – (1970s) #2228
encyclopedias
– see dictionaries and encyclopedias
engineering
– see also masonry
– and architecture (1960s) #8234
– photographs of constructions, compared
    with Canadian art #471
engines (railroad)
– see locomotives
engraving
– see also wood engraving
– colour drypoint, David Brown Milne on
    #6563 6564
engraving, Canadian
– early 20th c. #28
– Nova Scotia (1784-1897) #1198
– Québec (1958-1965) #1654
– Society of Canadian Painter-Etchers and
    Engravers (1885-1976) #836
Enns, Maureen, Can artist, 1943- #5372
– exhibitions, group
    – (1977) #1956
Ens, Frank, Can sculptor, fl. 1978 #2596
Ense, Don, Can artist, 1953- #4155
    – (1981) #4173
Enukso Point (NWT)
– inukshuks and inunguaks, Inuit #4199
environment
– see ecology
environmental art
– Canada #617
– Demers, Maurice #5284
– Senft, Douglas #7170
– Thibert, Patrick #7345
– Vazan, Bill #7478
– Waring, Stephanie E. #7516
envois
– see mail art
episcopal palaces, Canadian
– Québec (Qué), Episcopal Palace #8787
equestrian trappings, Algonquian #3405
equestrian trappings, Plains #3405
equestrian trappings, Siouan #3405
Erb, Isaac, Can photographer, 1846-1924
    #1186
Erdesz, Otto, Can violin-maker, fl. 1979
    #2940
Erickson/Massey, Can architectural firm
    #8360
– Burnaby (BC), Simon Fraser University
    #9396 9504 9505 9506
    – competition #9501
    – student residence #9467
– Osaka (Japan), Expo '70. Canadian
    Pavilion #9224
    – competition #9217
– Vancouver (BC)
    – elementary school design award (1970)
        #9507
    – Hauer House #8519
    – Nelson Towers #8744
Erickson, Arthur Charles, Can architect,
    1924- #8356 8358 8359 8360 8363
– Burnaby (BC), Simon Fraser University
    #9406
– Comox (BC), Filberg House #8355

– interview #8357
– Lethbridge (Alta), University of
    Lethbridge #9406 9497
– Los Angeles (Calif), Bunker Hill
    redevelopment #8364
– on architecture #7746
– on Gordon Appelbe Smith #7227
– on his architecture #8361
– on house design #8354
– Ottawa (Ont), Bank of Canada head office
    #9199
– Vancouver (BC) #7733
    – Eppich House #8745
    – MacMillan Bloedel Building #9358
    – University of British Columbia. Museum
        of Anthropology #8170 9132 9137 9138
Erindale (Ont), Adamson House
– architecture #7959
Erkoolik, Tuna, Can sculptor, 1935- #4407
Ernst, Max, Ger artist, 1891-1976
– influence on Alfred Pellan #6803 6821
– Lee-Nova, Gary, compared with #2051
– Letarte, Jean-Paul, compared with #6249
– Pellan, Alfred, compared with #6820
erotic art
– see also love in art; nude in art; sex in art
– Burton, Dennis Eugene Norman #4961
    4962
– Canada #467
– female fantasies #601
– Hall, Joice #717
– Town, Harold Barling #7410
Esenwein & Johnson, Amer architectural
    firm
– Hamilton (Ont), Royal Connaught Hotel
    #9274
Eskimo Point (NWT)
– Caribou Eskimo culture #4265
– tapestry #4253
Eskimos
– see Inuit
Esler, Annemarie Schmid
– see Schmid-Esler, Annemarie
Esler, John Kenneth, Can artist, 1933-
– exhibitions, group
    – (1967) #821
Essex, Margaret Mary, Can artist, b. 1891
– illustrations #916
Essex County (Ont)
– art #1668
Essex County Artists (Windsor, Ont)
– (1940-) #1668
Esson, James, Can photographer, 1854-1933
– stereo views #5373
estates
– see castles and country houses
Estevan (Sask), National Exhibition Centre
– exhibitions
    – Edward Curtis in the Collection of the
        Edmonton Art Gallery (1981) #3480
    – The Paintings of Frederick Nicholas
        Loveroff/Les peintures de Frederick Nicholas
        Loveroff (1981) #6331
esthetics
– see aesthetics
Estonians in Canada
– architecture #7723
– art #118 1761
etching, Canadian
– (1885), Association of Canadian Etchers
    #798
– (1910), Canadian National Exhibition
    (Toronto, Ont) #1
– (1910s) #799 800

– early 20th c. #28
– Manitoba (1910-1940) #1898
Etherington, A.Bruce, Can architect, 1924-
– on his bank design #9193
ethics and art
– Harris, Lawren Stewart #5731
– Prent, Mark #6924
ethnic groups in Canada
– Alberta, log buildings #8136
– barns #9228
– basketry #2943
– churches #8769
– costume #2893
– decorative arts #2107
– folk art #2122
– furniture, late 19th-early 20th cs. #2585
– needlework #2780
– spinning and weaving #2747 2748
Etobicoke (Ont), Martin Grove Estate
– architecture, Jerome Markson #8744
Etook, Tivi, Can artist, 1928- #5374 5375
– interview #4468
Etrog, Sorel, Can sculptor, 1933- #5377 5378
    5380 5381
– exhibitions
    – (1964) #5376
– painted constructions (1952-1960) #5379
– ritual and cult elements #789
– sculptures (1960s) #1793
Etungat, Abraham, Can sculptor, 1911-
    #5382
eucharistic vessels
– see liturgical objects
Evans, David, Can photographer, 1948-
– exhibitions (reviews) #1018
Evans, Emrys, Can bookbinder, 1944- #2936
Evans, John, Can architect, 1872-1944
– Galt (Ont), public school #9387
Evans, John, Can photographer, fl. 1940s
– portfolio of photographs #995
Evans, Roger T., Can artist, 1940-
– exhibitions, group
    – (1977) #1956
Evans, Walker, Amer photographer,
    1903-1975
– photographic views, Alabama (1936) #1513
Eve
– Cetin, Anton, symbols of #5064
– Lodge, Judy, The Walls of Eden series #6321
Ewen, Paterson, Can artist, 1925-
– and plasticiens #1439
– exhibitions
    – (1976) #5384
    – (1977) #5386
– exhibitions, group
    – (1955) #1408
    – (1977) #636
    – (1980) #703
– exhibitions (reviews) #5385
– interview #5383
– on Jack Chambers #700
– paintings (1960s) #1484
Ewing, Bill, Can curator, fl. 1973
– as director of Centaur Galleries (Montréal,
    Qué) #1004
ex libris
– see bookplates
ex-votos
– see votive offerings
excavations
– see archaeology
Exeter (England), Royal Albert Memorial
    Museum

- art, Indians of North America #3454
exhibition buildings
- Montréal (Qué), Expo '67 #9212 9213 9214 9218 9219 9221 9222
exhibition buildings, Canadian #9211
- Brussels (Belgium), Universal and International Exhibition of 1958. Canadian Pavilion #430 9209
- Montréal (Qué), Expo '67 #9215 9216 9220
- Osaka (Japan), Expo '70 #8356 9217 9224
- Toronto (Ont)
  - Canadian National Exhibition #1 9206
    - Automotive Building #9207
  - Ontario Place #9115
- Vancouver (BC), Crystal Gardens #9146
- Venice (Italy), 19th Biennale #9210
- Victoria (BC), Crystal Gardens #9134
exhibitions
- Art Association of Newfoundland and Labrador (1967-1979) #1144
- Art Directors' Club of Toronto (Toronto, Ont), (1949-) #854
- Brantford (Ont), Art Gallery of Brant. *Graphex* (1973-1979, 1981-) #827
- British Columbia Society of Artists (1909-1967) #1978
- Burnaby Art Society. *Burnaby National Print Show* (Burnaby, BC), (1961-1977) #816
- Calgary (Alta), Alberta College of Art. Art Gallery. *Calgary Graphics Exhibition* (1959-1974) #815
- Canada
  - (1928-1929) #307
  - (1970s) #682
  - (1972-1974) #552
  - (1976-), nonprofit artists' centres #612
  - (1978) #114
  - women artists (1960s-1970s) #677
- Canadian Art Club (1908-1915) #193
- Canadian Group of Painters (1933-1968) #324
- Canadian Guild of Potters (1955-1971) #2379
- Canadian Handicrafts Guild #2090
- Canadian National Exhibition (1879-1961) #1
- Canadian Society of Painters in Water Colour (1926-) #6
- Ecole des beaux-arts (Montréal, Qué), (1925-1932) #2973
- Edmonton Art Club (Edmonton, Alta), (1921-) #1941
- Essex County Artists (1940-) #1668
- Exhibition of Architecture and Allied Arts (Toronto, Ont), (1927-1939) #8224
- Group of Seven (1920-1922, 1925-1926, 1928, 1930-1931) #1732
- Hamilton (Ont), Art Gallery of Hamilton, annual exhibition (1948-) #38
- Independent Art Association (Montréal, Qué), (1932-1963) #1379
- Island Arts and Crafts Club (Victoria, BC), (1910-1941) #1980
- London (Ont), London Art Gallery, *Young Contemporaries/Jeunes contemporains* (1975-1979) #584
- Maritime Art Association (1959-1965) #1120
- Montréal (Qué), Montreal Museum of Fine Arts
  - *Spring Exhibition* (1880-1965) #1228
  - *Survey/Sondage* (1968-1970) #1481

- non-Canadian art, Canadian National Exhibition (Toronto, Ont), (1905-1938) #107
- *Norart* (northern Ontario), (1979-) #1829
- Nova Scotia (1830-1913) #1191
- Nova Scotia Society of Artists (1923-1972) #1192
- Ontario Society of Artists (1873-) #1666
- Ottawa (Ont), National Gallery of Canada
  - (1882-1979) #3063
  - (1926-1933) #294
  - (1953-1968. Biennial) #400
- Québec, 19th c.-1940s #1242
- Quebec Sculptors Association (1961-1977) #1584
- Royal Canadian Academy of Arts
  - (1880-1971) #2
  - (1880-1979) #162
- *Saskatchewan Art Exhibition* (1950-1964) #1910
- Sculptors' Society of Canada (1928-) #734
- Société des artistes professionnels du Québec (1971-1975) #1488
- Society of Canadian Painter-Etchers and Engravers (1919-1974) #3
- Society of Typographic Designers of Canada (1958-1964) #923
- *The Winnipeg Show* (Winnipeg, Man), (1955-1970) #54
- Toronto (Ont), (1977-1980), galleries and artist-run spaces #1815
- Toronto (Ont), Art Gallery of Ontario (1906-1966) #3175
- Toronto Camera Club (Toronto, Ont), (1891-) #975
- Toronto Society of Architects (Toronto, Ont), (1901-1912) #7956
- Toronto Society of Arts (Toronto, Ont), (1847-1848) #1689
- Upper Canada Agricultural Society (1846-1867) #1715
- Vancouver (BC), Vancouver Art Gallery (1932-1968) #1983
- *Western Ontario Exhibition* (London, Ont), (1941-1978) #1670
- Winnipeg Sketch Club (Winnipeg, Man), (1914-) #1887
- Women's Art Association of Hamilton (Hamilton, Ont), (1894-) #1701
- World's Fairs, 19th c., Canadian participation #261
expositions
- *see* exhibitions
Eyetoaq, Ada, Can artist, 1934-
- exhibitions
  - (1979) #5387
Eyre, Ivan Kenneth, Can artist, 1935- #1856 5388 5391 5395
  - (1969) #5389
  - (1974) #5390
  - (1980) #5394
- exhibitions, group
  - (1981) #1885
- exhibitions (reviews) #1883
- interview #5392 5393

F

Fablo, Serge Ventadour, Can artist, 1937-
- interview #5396

fabrics
- *see* textiles
facades, Canadian
- conservation #7766
factories
- *see also* mills
factories, Canadian
- (1910s) #9234
Fafard, Joseph (Joe), Can sculptor, ceramicist, 1942- #1937 5397 5398 5400
- and students, ceramic sculptures #1924
- exhibitions
  - (1979) #5401
- exhibitions, group
  - (1976) #1930
  - (1979) #674
- exhibitions (reviews) #2383 5399
faience
- *see* pottery
Fairfield & DuBois, Can architectural firm
- Peterborough (Ont), Trent University. Student residence #9467
- Scarborough (Ont), Albert Campbell Library #9047
- Toronto (Ont)
  - Dow Corning Silicones Ltd. head office building #9301
  - George Brown College of Applied Arts & Technology. Casa Loma Campus #9479
Fairley, Barker, Can artist, writer, 1887- #5403
- correspondence, Norman I. Gurd #1776
- drawings, Georgian Bay (Ont) #5402
- exhibitions
  - (1980) #5404
- on Canadian art #380
- on Canadian Group of Painters (1940) #348
- on human figure in Canadian art #344
- portraits #5405
Fairn, Leslie Raymond, Can architect, 1875-1971
- Wolfville (NS), Acadia University #9407
Fairy Lake (NS)
- pictographs, Micmac #3494
Fakir Art Club (Windsor, Ont)
- (1930-1940) #1668
Falardeau, Antoine-Sébastien, Can artist, 1822-1889 #1318 1323 5406 5407
- exhibitions, group
  - (1880) #1308
- paintings, Université Laval (Québec, Qué) #3078
- works, Art Association of Montreal (Montréal, Qué) #3075
Falardeau, Pierre, Can artist, 1946-
- exhibitions, group
  - (1979) #1157
  - (1980) #705
- on video art #1537
Falk, Gathie, Can artist, 1928- #5408
- ceramic sculptures (1970s) #2065
- exhibitions, group
  - (1968) #2382
  - (1969) #2039
  - (1975) #591
  - (1976) #2060
  - (1977) #781
- exhibitions (reviews) #579 622 2081
- interview #5409
- on performance art #5410

- performance sculpture #658
False Creek (BC), apartment building
- architectural proposal, Arthur Charles
  Erickson #8360
False Face Society, Iroquois #3595
- masks #3337 3588 3604 7346
False Face Society, Seneca
- masks #3533 3636 4113
fans, Micmac #3500
Fanshawe, Hubert Valentine, Can artist,
  1878-1940
- woodcuts #802
Fanshawe Pioneer Village (Ont) #8063 8066
fantastic art
- Inuit #4240
- landscapes, British Columbia #2045
fantasy
- Milne, David Brown, on #6556
Fardon, George Robinson, Can
  photographer, 1807-1886 #5411
farm buildings
- see also barns; grain elevators; stables
farm buildings, American
- western USA #8083
farm buildings, Canadian
- (1938-1942) #7666
- British Columbia #8153
- Charlevoix (Qué) #8629
- Irish tradition, 19th c. #8523
- Mennonite #8715
- Nova Scotia, 18th c. #7815
- Ontario #9225
- Prairies, painted decorations #1852
- Québec #8572
  - 17th-18th cs. #2217 8581
  - (1910s) #8554
- Tunis Snook Farm (near Kingston, Ont)
  #8681
- western Canada #8083
Farmer's Magazine, Can periodical
- illustrations (1910-1921) #1765
farming
- see rural subjects
Farmington (Conn), Gleason House
- timber framing, compared with Fisher
  House (Toronto, Ont) #8658
Farnsworth, Miss, Can photographer, fl.
  1894 #977
Faro (Yukon), Faro Townsite Recreation
  Centre
- architecture, Thompson, Berwick, Pratt &
  Partners #8182
Farrar family, Can ceramicists, fl. 1840s-1927
  #2288 2299 2321
fashion
- see also costume
- (1870s)
  - in magazines #2878
  - in newspapers #2859
- (1882-1910) #2897
- (1920s), in magazines and sales catalogues
  #2906
- (1920s-1930s), *Eaton's Weekly News* #2851
Fat, Dulcie Foo, Can artist, 1946-
- exhibitions, group
  - (1975) #1867
- interview #5412
Faucher, Paul, Can architect, fl. 1960s-
- Sherbrooke (Qué), Chapelle universitaire
  chrétienne #8841
Faugeron, Jean, Fr architect, fl. 1960s-
- Montréal (Qué), Expo '67. Pavillon de la
  France #1435
Fauteux, André Lucien, Can sculptor, 1946-

#1817
- compared with Douglas Bentham #785
- exhibitions
  - (1976) #5413
- exhibitions, group
  - (1975) #1809
  - (1977) #782 784
  - (1978) #786
  - (1981) #797
- interview #788
- techniques #792
Fauteux-Massé, Henriette, Can artist, 1924-
  #5414 5415
Fauvism
- and Clark Holmes McDougall #6464
- and David Brown Milne #6552 6567
Favro, Murray, Can artist, 1940-
- exhibitions, group
  - (1973) #557
  - (1977) #783
  - (1980) #703
- influence on Ron Martin #6431
- on art #594
- regionalism, compared with Greg Curnoe
  #5225
- works, Carmen Lamanna Gallery
  (Toronto, Ont) #1811
Fawcett, George, Can artist, 1877-1944
- etchings #800
Fay-Génot, Jean-Etienne-Achille, Fr actor
  and artist in Canada, 1823-1879 #5416
Fear, Jeffery, Can designer, fl. 1981 #2487
feather work, Blackfoot #3654
- bonnets #3678
feather work, Plains
- bonnets #3683
Featherston, William (Bill), Can artist, 1927-
- exhibitions
  - (1979) #5417
- paintings, Squamish workers #5418
Federal Cultural Policy Review Committee
  (Applebaum-Hébert Commission)
- see Canada. Federal Cultural Policy
  Review Committee (Applebaum-Hébert
  Commission)
Federal District Commission
- see Canada. Federal District Commission
Fédération des caisses Desjardins
- as art patron (1970s) #3275
Fédération des coopératives du Nouveau
  Québec
- (1977-1980) #4269
Federation of Canadian Artists #390 502
- (1940s) #360 363 376 386
- (1941), founding #379
- Harris, Lawren Stewart, on #364
Feininger, Andreas, Amer photographer,
  1906-
- on Wilfred Roloff Beny #4690
Feist, Harold Elmer, Can artist, 1945-
- exhibitions, group
  - (1974) #565
  - (1975) #1926
Feldman, Isadore, Can architect, 1887-1919
- Toronto (Ont), Cooper Cap Company
  Building #9332
Felter, James Warren, Can artist, 1943-
- exhibitions
  - (1976) #2059
feminism
- and art, Canada (1970s) #121 601 673
- and Freda Guttman Bain #4596
- and Maryon Kantaroff #6019
- and Maureen Paxton #6786

fences, Canadian #9226 9233
- British Columbia, wooden, 19th-20th cs.
  #8148
- Québec, ironwork #2702
- wooden, 18th-19th cs. #2594
Fenton, Terry, Can artist, curator, 1940-
- exhibitions, group
  - (1967), photographs #8113
- influence on Douglas Bentham #4683
- interview, at Emma Lake Workshops
  (Emma Lake, Sask) #1934
- participant, Symposium on 20th Century
  Canadian Culture (Washington, DC),
  (1977) #621
- support of Edmonton (Alta) art #1975
Fer, Nicholas de, Fr cartographer, 1646-1720
- view of Newfoundland #1150
Fergus (Ont)
- photography (1856-1867) #1724
Ferguson, Gerald, Can artist, 1937- #5419
- exhibitions
  - (1977) #5420
- exhibitions, group
  - (1970) #534
Ferguson, Mary, Can photographer, fl.
  1970s-
- portfolio of photographs #991
Fernandes, Michael, Can artist, 1944-
- prints #1214
Ferraro, Robert (Bob), Can artist, 1936-
- exhibitions, group
  - (1978) #1824
Ferron, Marcelle, Can artist, 1924- #5421
  5422 5423 5425 5426
- and Création #1492
- exhibitions
  - (1970) #5424
- exhibitions, group
  - (1962) #1420
- in Paris (France) #426 1434
- on printmaking #817
Ferron, Monique Bourbonnais, Can
  ceramicist, 1924- #2395
Ferryland (Nfld)
- architecture #7792
Ferryland Downs (Nfld)
- views
  - Squires, Gerald Leopold #7272
Ferryland Head (Nfld), lighthouse #9523
festivals
- see also theatre
- Norwegian #2273
- Nova Scotia, Joseph Howe Festival #2887
- Toronto (Ont), Latvian Song Festival #49
- Vancouver (BC)
  - Living Art Performance Festival (1979)
    #2073
  - *Pacific Vibrations* (1973) #2046
fêtes
- see festivals
Fetherstonhaugh, Harold Lea, Can architect,
  1887-1971
- Montréal (Qué), Chateau Apartments
  #8558
fibrework
- see also textiles
fibrework, Canadian
- 20th c. #2142
- (1970s) #2771
- (1979-1980) #2138
- (1980) #2257
- Mennonite #2264
- Vancouver (BC), (1980s) #2775
Fichaud, Gwen Johnston, Can artist, 1915-

#5427 5428
– exhibitions (reviews) #1167
fictive architecture
– see architecture in art
Fieguth, Menno, Can photographer, ca. 1952-
– portfolio of photographs #1023
Field, Robert, Can artist, 1769-1819 #1191 5429 5433
– engravings #1198
– exhibitions
– (1978) #5432
– influence on Maria Frances Ann Morris Miller #6541
– portraits, Provo William Parry Wallis, National Gallery of Canada (Ottawa, Ont) #5430 5431
Field (Fish), Robert, Can artist, 1948-
– exhibitions
– (1978) #5434
– exhibitions, group
– (1980) #687
Fiertel, Neil, Can sculptor, 1941-
– exhibitions, group
– (1978) #2066
figure painting
– see human figure in art
figureheads of ships
– Canada, 18th-19th cs. #1604
– Côté, Jean-Baptiste #1577 5186
– Nova Scotia, 19th c. #1200
– Rogerson, John #7067 7068
File, Can periodical #544
– (1970s) #3310
Filer, Mary Harris, Can glassmaker, 1920- #2440
Filiau (dit Dubois), Jean Baptiste, Can clockmaker, 1699-1772 #5435
Filiau-Dubois, François, Can builder, b. 1700
– correspondence, Pierre-Noël Levasseur (1745) #6253 6255
Filion, Armand, Can sculptor, 1910- #5436 5437 5438
Filipovic, Augustin, Can sculptor, 1931-
– clay sculptures (1960s) #743
films
– see also animation (cinematography)
– (1970s) #634
– autobiographical, Canada and USA (1970s) #664
films, Canadian #2 129 626
– (1940s) #374
– (1960s) #521
– (1970s) #555 598 610 3279
– (1980s) #690 912
– Berman, Michaele #4710
– Chambers, Jack #5072 5074 5076 5081
– Cournoyer, Michèle #5193
– Dallaire, Jean-Philippe #5238 5239
– Doray, Audrey Capel #5301
– Fiorucci, Vittorio #5442
– Gagnon, Charles #5533 5534 5535 5537
– Gordon, Lee #993
– Gould, John Howard #5636
– graphics
– (1950s) #866
– (1970s) #899
– Harmon, Byron #5707
– Lee-Nova, Gary #6213
– McLaren, Norman #6491 6492 6493 6494 6495 6496 6497 6498 6499
– Niverville, Louis de #6704 6706
– Price, Art #6928
– Québec

– (1970-1975) #1515
– women filmmakers #1064
– Snow, Michael #568 7241 7243 7245 7246 7247 7249 7250 7252 7253 7255 7256 7257 7260 7261 7263
– Wieland, Joyce #568 7574 7575 7576 7577 7578 7579 7580 7581 7582 7583
Finlay, George E., Brit army officer, artist in Canada, fl. 1834-1848 #5439
Fiore, Giuseppe, Can artist, 1931- #5441
– mural, La Lanterna Verde Restaurant (Dorval, Qué) (1963) #5440
Fiorucci, Vittorio, Can artist, 1932- #5442
– exhibitions
– (1981) #5444
– posters #5443
fire stations, Canadian
– Toronto (Ont), (1930s) #8970
– Vernon (BC), Vernon Civic Centre #8972
firearms
– see also weapons
firearms, Canadian
– 19th c. #2099
– guide for collectors #2104
– Québec, 17th-19th cs. #2221
firearms, Plains
– gun cases #3713
fireplaces, Canadian
– implements, Québec, 17th-18th cs. #2210
– ironwork #2703 2705
– mantelpieces, Québec, 17th-18th cs. #2530 2531
Firestone, Otto John (Jack), Can collector, 1913-
– collection, Canadian art, Ontario Heritage Foundation (Toronto, Ont) #3239
Fischer, Hervé, Fr artist, 1941-
– museum theme #714
Fischl, Eric, Amer artist in Canada, 1948-
– performance sculpture #658
– use of words #662
Fiset, Edouard, Can architect, 1910-
– Montréal (Qué), Expo '67 #9213
fish
– in art, Tommy Brayshaw #4907
Fish, R.
– see Field (Fish), Robert
Fisher, Bob, Can photographer, ca. 1945- #995
Fisher, Brian Richard, Can artist, 1939-
– drawings #532
– exhibitions, group
– (1967) #490
– (1969) #2039
– (1971) #98
– exhibitions (reviews) #520
– on Canadian painting (1970s) #620
Fisher, Jeff, Amer photographer, fl. 1970s #1000
Fisher, Sanford, Can artist, 1927- #5445
Fisher, Tom, Can photographer, fl. 1970s
– photographs as personal expression #1556
Fiske, John, Can builder, fl. 1977
– restoration, Nova Scotia College of Art and Design (Halifax, NS) #9409
FitzGerald, Lionel LeMoine, Can artist, 1890-1956 #309 1896 5449 5453
– and Bertram Richard Brooker #4925 4926
– and children's art education (1940s) #1889 1890
– and Douglas M. Duncan, as patron #119 541
– as member, Canadian Group of Painters #324

– as member, Winnipeg Sketch Club #1887
– as teacher of Stephen Andrews #4528
– exhibitions
– (1958) #5448
– (1978) #5450
– exhibitions, group
– (1962) #1847
– (1975) #503 504 589 592
– influence on Caven Ernest Atkins #4570
– landscapes #1855
– Bowen Island (BC) #5446
– paintings
– (1930s) #502
– Winnipeg (Man), Winnipeg Art Gallery #3188
– prints #5451
– technique #5447 5452
Fitzgerald, Owen, Can photographer, fl. 1970s-
– portfolio of photographs #991
Fitzmaurice, J.Ben, Can artist, ca. 1873-1924
– cartoons, Montreal Herald #943
Fitzpatrick, Francis W., Amer architect, 1864-1931 #8365
flags
– see banners and flags
Flaherty, Robert, Amer photographer, 1884-1951
– collection, Inuit sculpture #4185
Flamand, Jacques
– see Deguise (dit Flamand), Jacques
Flandrin, Jean Hippolyte, Fr artist, 1809-1864
– influence on Napoléon Bourassa #4874
flasks
– see bottles
Flat River Crafts Studio (PEI) #2153
flats
– see apartment houses
Flavelle, Sir Joseph Wesley, Can businessman, 1858-1939
– residence, Holwood Mansion (Toronto, Ont) #8667
Fleisher, Pat, Can artist, art critic, 1930- #5454
– as editor, Artmagazine #560
Fleming, Allan Robb, Can artist, 1929-1977 #5456
– and Burns, Cooper, Donoahue, Fleming & Company Ltd. #904
– graphic designs #897 5457
– on typography #5455
Fleming, Erik, Swedish designer, 1894-
– as teacher of Harold Stacey #7273 7274
Fleming, John, Can artist, fl. 1976
– video art #616
Fleming, John, Can photographer, 1836-1876
– survey photographs #1865
Fleming, Sandford, Can engineer, scientist, artist, 1827-1915
– and Charles George Horetzky #5837
– collection, survey photographs, Canadian Pacific Railway #1876
Fleming & Smith, Can architectural firm
– Montréal (Qué), Jewish General Hospital #9031
Fletcher, Kenneth, Can photographer, fl. 1970- #992
Fleury, Arthur & Barclay, Can architectural firm
– Hamilton (Ont), City Hall and Civic Square #8988
Fleury & Arthur, Can architectural firm
– Toronto (Ont), University of Toronto. Victoria College. Wymilwood #9454

Fliess, Henry, Can architect, 1921-
– Beamsville (Ont), Nipponia Home for the
   Aged #8516
– Don Mills (Ont)
   – Beth-El Synagogue #8903
   – Chatham Village #8511
   – South Mills Village #7679
– Toronto (Ont), Clintwood Maisonette
   Project #8514
Flomen, Michael, Can photographer, 1952-
– exhibitions (reviews) #1018
floors, Canadian
– Ontario, use of paint, 19th c. #8013
Florence (Italy), Museo nazionale di
   antropologia ed etnologia
– art, Indians of North America #3396
Florida (USA)
– views by French explorers, 16th c. #276
flour mills
– see mills
flowers
– artificial flowers
   – Québec, 18th c. #1320
   – Québec (Qué), Hôtel-Dieu, 18th-19th cs.
      #1350
flowers in art
– see also plants in art
– Algonquian Indians #3543
– Brown, Annora #4933
– Canadian and American stoneware
   pottery #2309
– Canadian architectural decoration (1930s)
   #8225 8226
– Ciccimarra, Richard Matthew #5107
– Gillett, Violet Amy #5605
– Griffiths, James, and John Howard #2305
– Holmes, Robert #5822
– Miller, Maria Morris Ann Morris #241
   242 1219 6542
– natives of North America #3378
– Pellan, Alfred #6818 6819
– Rakine, Marthe #6956
– sepulchral monuments, Ontario, 19th
   c.-1910s #1723
– Warren, Mary Schaffer #7526 7527
Fogo (Nfld)
– architecture #7792
Foisy, Dennis, Can furniture-maker, 1946-
   #5458
Foisy, Gilles, Can artist, 1948-
– exhibitions, group
   – (1971) #2042
   – (1973) #2045
– exhibitions (reviews) #2051
Folch-Ribas, Jacques, Can architect, 1928-
– Carillon (Qué), Dollard des Ormeaux
   #1591
– Sherbrooke (Qué), Chapelle universitaire
   chrétienne #8841
Foley, Herbert C., Can artist, 1935-
– as member of Hampton Group #1177
foliage
– see leaves in art
folk architecture
– see vernacular architecture
folk art, American
– barn decorations #9228
– decorated stoneware pottery #2309
– woodcarvings #756
folk art, Canadian #369 966 1562 2094
– 19th-20th cs. #973
– (1970s) #962
– Acadian (1960s-1980) #1136
– barn decorations #9228

– beaver motif #23
– birdhouses #2593
– Charlevoix (Qué), (1940s) #1243
– compared with provincial art #959
– decorated stoneware pottery #2309
– decoys #2595
– ethnic traditions #2122
– Germanic tradition #2140
– heraldry #2951
– hooked rugs #2757
   – Bluenose #2763
– Labrador, grasswork, 20th c. #2945
– Latvian #49
– Manitoba, 20th c. #1897
– Mennonite #2243 2246 2264 2268
– Newfoundland #1155
   – (1970s) #1146 1153 1156
   – and Patrick J. Murphy #6664
– Newfoundland and Labrador, 20th c.
   #2155
– Norwegian tradition #2273
– Nova Scotia
   – 20th c. #1206 1207 1210 1212 1213
   – furniture #2514
– Ontario
   – (1960s) #1792
   – (1970s) #1682
   – German-Alsatian iron funeral crosses
      #2709
– Ottawa (Ont), National Museum of Man.
   Canadian Centre for Folk Culture Studies
   #963 969
– painting #964 965
– Prairies #1852
   – (1970s) #1881
– Price, Ralph and Patricia, collection #970
   971 972
– Québec #1235 1268 1276 1285 1297 2183
   2184
   – (1875-1915) #1364
   – (1920s-1940s) #2189
   – (1960s) #1428 1429 2195
   – bird motif #1284
   – compared with literature #967
   – crucifixes #1638
   – folk sculpture
      – 17th-19th cs. #1589 1611
      – Sharpe, Nettie, collection #1607
   – inventory #1291
   – iron funeral crosses #2716
   – ironwork #2702 2712
   – Montréal (Qué), McGill University.
      McCord Museum #1362
   – motifs #1274
   – review of literature #1295
   – weather vanes #2589
   – women artisans, 17th-18th cs. #2200
   – wooden models in bottles #2944
– Saint-Marc-des-Carrières (Qué), stone
   sculpture #1629
– Saskatchewan, 20th c. #1927 1931
– tools and utensils #2139
– Ukrainian #2117 2270
   – Easter eggs #2132
   – late 18th-20th cs. #961
   – painted decorations on buildings #8090
– Ukrainian and Latvian traditions
   compared #968
– use of oral documentation #608
– western Canada, 20th c. #1846
– woodcarvings #756
folk artists, Canadian
– Barbour, Carl #1155 1156
– Barker, Sydney Herbert #1846

– Berggren, Nels #1852
– Bissonette, Héliodore #1428 1429
– Bouchard, Edith #1428 1429
– Bouchard, Marie-Cécile #1428 1429
– Bouchard, Mary Simone #1428 1429
– Burt, Leonard #1153 1156
– Cauchon, Robert #964 1428 1429
– Côté, Jean-Baptiste #1607
– Dahlstrom, Eugene W. #1846
– Dennis, Eva A. #1881 1927
– Dennis, Wes #1881 1927
– Eisenhauer, Collins #1213
– Harbuz, Ann Alexandra #1881 1927
– Hopkins, Elisabeth Margaret #5830 5831
   5832
– Hudson, Tom #1155 1156
– Jost, Edward R. #964
– Keevil, Roland #1846
– Lachapelle, Edouard #6124
– Laithwaite, George #1792
– Leblanc, Leo B. #6182
– Lefebvre, Oliver #1607
– Lenhardt, Molly #1881
– Lewis, Maude #6277
– MacDonald, Charles William #6355
– Macdonald, John A. #964
– McCargar, William C. #1881
– McInnes, Harvey A. #1881
– McLaughlin, Agnes #6500
– Moulding, Fred #1881
– Murphy, Patrick J. #6664
– Norris, Joe #6720 6721
– Panko, William #964 1846
– Patterson, Dan #962
– Pieroway, Percy #1153 1155 1156
– Rhéaume, Damase #1607
– Richard, Wilfrid #7000
– Spencer, Sam A. #1881 1927
– St. Germain, Arthème #962
– Stansell, Walter H. #1792
– Stewart, W.N. #1846
– Stryjek, Dmytro #1927 7280
– Themarat, Jeanne Aline #1881
– Tremblay, Georges-Edouard #1428 1429
– Turgeon, Adélard #1607
– Villeneuve, Arthur #1428 1429 7490 7491
   7492
– Williams, Arch #1153 1155 1156
– Wyers, Jan G. #1846 1852 7620
folk songs, Canadian #2096
– île d'Orléans (Qué) #1238
– illustrations, Joseph-Charles Franchère
   #5497
– Norwegian tradition #2273
– Québec #1234 1258 1259
   – illustrations #938
   – references to costume #2898
folk tales
– see folklore; legends
folklore
– see also legends; mythology
folklore, Canadian
– Québec #2169 2171
   – and Georges Saint-Pierre #7118
fonts, Canadian
– Québec (1650-1925) #1592
food
– bread and pastry, Québec #2187
– decoration, Mennonite #2264
– decoration, Ukrainian Easter eggs #2132
– domestic manufacture, 18th-19th cs. #2112
– moulds, National Museum of Man.
   Canadian Centre for Folk Culture Studies
   (Ottawa, Ont) #963

– Ontario, 19th c. #2245 7981
– Québec, European influences #2221
Forbes, John Colin, Can artist, 1846-1925
    #5459
Forbes, Kenneth Keith, Can artist, 1892-1980
– exhibitions (reviews) #432
Forest, Fred, Fr artist, 1933-
– museum theme #714
forgeries
– Canadian antiques #2127
forgeries, drawing
– Bartlett, William Henry #4614
forgeries, painting
– Canadian paintings #64 70 73
– Krieghoff, Cornelius #6101
– Québec paintings, early 20th c. #1313
forges, Canadian
– Jones Falls (Ont) #8019
– Norfolk County (Ont), Normandale Iron
    Works #2699
– Trois-Rivières (Qué), Forges of
    Saint-Maurice #2698 2708 2711 7878 9238
    9240 9250 9251 9253 9254 9256 9257
Forget, Robert, Can artist, 1943-
– and Vidéographe (Montréal, Qué) #1498
– on video art #1537
Forget, Sylvain, Can artist, 1962- #5460
formalism
– and Canadian landscape (1960s) #496
– and Canadian painting (1970s) #620
– and David Bolduc #4774
– and David Craven #5207
– and Michael Snow #7260
– and Ronald Langley Bloore #4747
Forrest, Charles Ramus, Brit army officer,
    artist in Canada, fl. 1821-1823, d. 1827
    #279
Forrest, Nita Osborne, Can artist, 1926-
– as member of Limners #2043
Forrestall, Thomas De Vany (Tom), Can
    artist, 1936- #5464 5465 5466
– and realism #110
– compared with Alex Colville #5462
– exhibitions
    – (1971) #5461
– exhibitions, group
    – (1966) #1123
    – (1974) #573 1129
    – (1980) #1221
– Shaped by This Land #5463
Forster, John Wycliffe Lowes, Can artist,
    1850-1938 #5469
– as teacher of Tomtu H. Roberts #7051
– interview #5468
– on art education #2960
– on portrait painting #5467 5470
– on views, Peel County (Ont), William
    Perkins Bull Collection #3208
Forsyth, Douglas, Can artist, fl. 1970s-
– prints #1214
Fort Amherst (Nfld), lighthouse #9523
Fort Anne (NS)
– architecture, South Magazine #8424
Fort Battleford (Sask)
– architecture #8481 8484
Fort Beauséjour (NB)
– shoes and boots (1750s-1830s) #2858
Fort Chambly (Qué)
– architecture
    – Boisberthelot de Beaucours, Josué #8336
    – Guard House #8446
Fort Erie (Ont), Mather Park
– and Niagara Parks Commission #7975
Fort Frontenac (Ont)

– architecture #8454
Fort Garry (Man)
– interior decoration #7758
– views
    – Hind, William George Richardson #5807
Fort Garry (Man), University of Manitoba
– works, Tony Tascona #7326
Fort George (Niagara-on-the-Lake, Ont)
– and Niagara Parks Commission #7975
– architecture #8454 8457 8463 8472 8473
    – guardhouse #8459 8461 8462
Fort Henry (Kingston, Ont)
– architecture #8454 8455 8457
Fort Langley (BC)
– architecture #8477
– interior decoration #7758
– restoration #8474
Fort Lennox (Qué)
– architecture #8447
Fort Malden (Amherstburg, Ont)
– architecture #8456
– interior decoration #7758
Fort Mississauga (Toronto, Ont)
– architecture #8454 8457 8472
Fort Niagara (Youngstown, NY)
– architecture #8454 8457
Fort Ontario (Oswego, NY)
– architecture #8457
Fort Portchartrain (Qué)
– recommended for conservation (1881)
    #7754
Fort Prince of Wales (Man)
– architecture #8094
Fort Rouille (Ont)
– architecture #8457
Fort Saint James (BC)
– architecture #8478
Fort Saint Joseph (Ont)
– architecture #8468 8469
Fort Simpson (NWT)
– men's house #8482
Fort Smith (NWT), Northern Life Museum
    and National Exhibition Centre
– exhibitions
    – Images of the Inuit from the Simon Fraser
        Collection (1980) #4495
Fort Ste Marie (Ont)
– architecture #8454
Fort Toronto (Ont)
– architecture #8454
Fort Wellington (Ont)
– architecture #8454 8466 8467
– interior decoration #7758
Fort William (Ont)
– architecture #8460
Fort William (Ont), Thunder Bay Historical
    Society
– exhibitions
    – The Far West (1943) #12
Fort Worth (Tex), Amon Carter Museum of
    Western Art
– exhibitions
    – The Artist was a Young Man: The Life
        Story of Peter Rindisbacher (1970) #7009
    – The Far North: 2000 Years of American
        Eskimo and Indian Art (1973) #3366
Fort York (Toronto, Ont)
– architecture #8457
Fortier, Ivanhoë, Can sculptor, 1931- #5471
– exhibitions
    – (1979) #5472
Fortier, Michel, Can artist, 1943-
– Pop art #1497
fortifications

– see also city gates; Martello towers
– in art, Terence Johnson #5969
fortifications, Canadian
– 17th-early 19th cs. #7841
– Alberta, 18th-19th cs. #8129
– blockhouses (1749-1841) #8417 8418
– Boisberthelot de Beaucours, Josué #8336
– Fort Anne (NS) #8424
– Fort Battleford (Sask) #8481 8484
– Fort Chambly (Qué) #8446
– Fort George (Niagara-on-the-Lake, Ont)
    #8461 8462 8463 8473
    – guardhouse #8459
– Fort Henry (Kingston, Ont) #8455
– Fort Langley (BC) #8474
– Fort Lennox (Qué) #8447
– Fort Malden (Amherstburg, Ont) #8456
– Fort Rodd Hill (Victoria, BC), upper and
    lower batteries #8479
– Fort Saint James (BC) #8478
– Fort Saint Joseph (Ont) #8468 8469
– Fort Wellington (Ont) #8466 8467
– Fort William (Ont) #8460
– Fort York (Toronto, Ont) #8458
– Halifax (NS), Halifax Citadel #8430 8431
    8432 8433 8434 8438 8440 8441
– Kingston (Ont)
    – (1759-1838) #8453
– Kingston Mills (Ont) #8020
    – blockhouse #8019
– Lake Ontario #8457
– Louisbourg (NS) #8419 8422 8423 8425
    8426 8439 8442
    – guardhouses #8428 8429
– Lower Fort Garry (Man) #8475 8476 8480
    8482 8483
– Manitoba #8094
– Montréal (Qué), citadel #8445
– Niagara-on-the-Lake (Ont)
    – (1814-1837) #8470
    – (1871-1978) #8472
    – Navy Hall #8464 8465
– Ontario #8454
– Placentia (Nfld), (1662-1811) #8420 8421
– Québec, use of mills as fortresses #9242
– Québec (Qué) #269 270 1306 8450
    – Artillery Park #8449
    – Artillery Park. Redoute Dauphine #8448
        8452
    – fort and château Saint-Louis #8443
    – Royal Battery #8451
Fortin, Marc-Aurèle, Can artist, 1888-1970
    #302 1391 1392 1393 1432 5473 5477 5479
    5480 5482
– exhibitions
    – (1964) #5474
    – (1968) #5478
– exhibitions, group
    – (1977) #1278 1279
– exhibitions (reviews) #5475
– in Gaspé #5481
– paintings of houses #5476
Fortin, Yvan, Can artist, 1950- #1526
Forton, Michel, Can silversmith, 1754-ca.
    1816
– works, Detroit Institute of Arts (Detroit,
    Mich) #2691
fortresses
– see military architecture
Fosbery, Ernest George, Can artist,
    1874-1958
– criticism of Canadian art exhibition (1927)
    #298
Foster, Janet Green, Can photographer,

1940-
– exhibitions (reviews) #1009
– portfolio of photographs #991
Foster, John, Can photographer, 1933-
– exhibitions (reviews) #1009
– portfolio of photographs #991
Foster, Stuart, Can photographer, ca. 1953-
– portfolio of photographs #1023
Foster Brothers Glass Works, glass
    manufacturer (Saint-Jean, Qué)
– and Canada Glass Works #2420
Foulem, Leopold L., Can sculptor, 1945-
– exhibitions, group
    – (1977) #781
Foulis, James, Can architect, 1882-1932
– Ottawa (Ont), Parliament and
    Departmental Buildings, competition
    #8923
Foulis, Robert, Can artist, 1796-1866 #258
259
– engravings #1198
– portraits #1171
fountains, Canadian
– Laliberté, Alfred #6141
– San Francisco (Calif), Embarcadero Plaza,
    Armand Vaillancourt #7451
– Toronto (Ont), Memorial to Dr. D.W.
    Young #729
– Vancouver (BC) #2077
Fouré, Raoul-Jean, Can dress designer, fl.
1956
– costumes, *Piano Concerto*, Montreal Theatre
    Ballet #1410
Foureur (*dit* Champagne), Louis, Can
    furniture-maker, sculptor, 1720-1789 #269
270
Foureur (*dit* Champagne), Pierre, Can
    silversmith, 1756-ca. 1795
– works, Detroit Institute of Arts (Detroit,
    Mich) #2691
Fournelle, André, Can sculptor, 1939- #5483
5484
Fournier, Arthur, Can furniture-maker,
    sculptor, collector, 1863-1931 #5485
Fournier, François-Marie, Can sculptor,
    1790-1864
– influence of Baillairgé family #1582
Fournier, Paul, Can artist, 1939- #1807 5486
5487
– compared with Tony Calzetta #670
Fowler, C.A., and Company, Can
    architectural firm
– Halifax (NS), Saint Mary's University.
    Library #9046
Fowler, Daniel, Can artist, 1810-1894 #1705
5488 5490
– correspondence and will #5492
– exhibitions
    – (1964) #5489
    – (1979) #5491
– exhibitions (reviews) #5493
Fowler, Orson Squire, Amer writer,
    phrenologist, 1809-1887
– polygonal buildings #7987
Fox, John Richard, Can artist, 1927- #5494
5496
– exhibitions
    – (1980) #5495
Fox River (Wis)
– views, Paul Kane #6009
fractur
– *see* fraktur
fraktur
– Bauman, Joseph #4628

– Hoover, Christian #5829
– Ontario #2250 2253 2254 2255 2264 2267
– Ontario and Pennsylvania #2259
– Weber, Anna #7539
Frame, Statira Elizabeth, Can artist,
    1870-1935 #2011
– landscapes #2016
frames, Canadian
– guide for collectors #2252
– shaped
    – Forrestall, Tom #5461 5465
    – Zellinger, Jean #7634
Francastel, Pierre, Fr art historian, 1900-1970
– sociology of art theories, applied to
    Canadian art (1760-1860) #251
Franchère, Joseph-Charles, Can artist,
    1866-1921 #1315 1391 5497 5498
– and François-Xavier Aldéric Rapin #6961
Francis, Sam, Amer artist, 1923-
– influence on Claude Tousignant #7401
– influence on Jean Albert McEwen #6471
Francis Clementson & Co., ceramic firm
    (Saint-John, NB) #2361
Franck, Albert Jacques, Can artist, 1899-1973
    #5502
– and Florence Gertrude Vale #5499
– as husband of Florence Gertrude Vale
    #7453
– exhibitions
    – (1973) #5500 5501
François, Claude (frère Luc), Fr artist in
    Canada, 1614-1685 #228 229 1323 1363
    5503 5504
– and Claude Baillif #8329
– and Québec painting #1353
– *La France apportant la Foi aux Sauvages de la
    Nouvelle-France* #1328
– paintings, Saint Ann's Basilica
    (Sainte-Anne-de-Beaupré, Qué) #1321
Frank, Leonard, Can photographer,
    1871-1944
– exhibitions, group
    – (1976) #2012
Frank, Robert Louis, Amer photographer in
    Canada, 1924- #5506
– exhibitions (reviews) #5505
– interview #664
Frankford (Ont)
– photographic views, Lizzy Wadsworth
    #7496
Frankfurt am Main (West Germany),
    Städtische Museum für Völkerkunde
– art, Indians of North America #3464
Franklin, David Randall, Can architect,
    1882-1948
– Toronto (Ont), John Ross Robertson and
    Glenholme schools #9437
Franklin, Sir John, Brit naval officer,
    explorer in Canada, 1786-1847
– Arctic expedition #278
    – and George Back #241 242 4580
    – and Robert Hood #5825 5826 5827
Franks, Rhonda, Can artist, 1959-
– exhibitions, group
    – (1980) #4159
Franquelin, Jean-Baptiste-Louis, Fr
    cartographer, artist in Canada,
    1651/1653-1718
– maps of Canada #875
Fraser, Carol Lucille Hoorn, Can artist,
    1930- #5508
– exhibitions
    – (1977) #5507
– exhibitions, group

– (1966) #1123
Fraser, John Arthur, Can artist, 1838-1898
    #178 5511
– and Canadian painting #18
– and Ontario Society of Artists #1666
– exhibitions (reviews) #174
– on trip to Chequamegon Bay (Ont) #5509
– on trip to Rocky Mountains (Canada)
    #5510
Fraser, Judith Margaret Williams, Can artist,
    1940-
– on collage #2042
Fraser Valley region (BC)
– architecture #8147
Fréchette, Louis Honoré, Can poet,
    1839-1908
– Wilde, Oscar, on #238
Frédéric, Frédéric, Can artist, 1938- #5512
Fredericks, Beany, Can weaver, fl. 1966
    #5513
Fredericton (NB)
– architecture #7809
    – 19th c. #7803
– art (1960s) #441
– photographic views
    – Smith, Madge #7235
    – Taylor, George Thomas #7334
– views, 19th c. #1174
Fredericton (NB), Beaverbrook Art Gallery
    #1178
– (1960s) #1122
– acquisitions (to July 1959) #3066
– exhibitions
    – *Canadian Painting: Yesterday and Today,
        1800-1960: From the Collection of the
        Beaverbrook Art Gallery/La peinture
        canadienne hier et aujourd'hui, 1800-1960:
        collection de la Galerie d'art Beaverbrook*
        (1972) #99
    – *Carol Fraser Paintings and Drawings:
        1967-1977* (1977) #5507
    – *Claude Tousignant* (1973) #7401
    – *Colville, Pratt, Forrestall* (1974) #1129
    – *Conceptual Decorative: Prints by Les
        Levine, 1965-1970/Conceptuel décoratif:
        estampes de Les Levine, 1965-1970* (1971)
        #6265
    – *David Bolduc: Recent Work* (1979) #4775
    – *Dennis Burton Retrospective* (1977) #4961
    – *Drawings and Pastels c. 1930-1967 by
        Miller Gore Brittain* (1968) #4917
    – *Drawings by Jack Weldon Humphrey: A
        Travelling Exhibition Organized by the
        Beaverbrook Art Gallery, Fredericton, New
        Brunswick, Canada, 1977-1979* (1978)
        #5871
    – *E. Lindner: Drawings, 1969-1972* (1972)
        #6285
    – *Edwy Cooke: aquarelles, 1942-1977* (1978)
        #5171
    – *Esther Warkov* (1970) #7517
    – *Fernand Leduc* (1971) #6186
    – *Fredericton Collects* (1979) #142
    – *Goodridge Roberts: Selected
        Works/Goodridge Roberts: oeuvres choisies*
        (1981) #7050
    – *Gordon Rayner Retrospective* (1980) #6966
    – *Greg Curnoe: rétrospective/Greg Curnoe:
        Retrospective* (1982) #5231
    – *Inuit Art in the 1970's: A Travelling
        Exhibition/L'Art inuit actuel, 1970-79:
        exposition itinérante* (1979) #4287
    – *Ivan Eyre Exposition* (1981) #5394
    – *Jack Humphrey: A Retrospective*

Exhibition/Jack Humphrey: une exposition (1970) #5870
- *Joe Plaskett and His Paris: In Search of Time Past* (1972) #6893
- *Joe Plaskett et son Paris: à la recherche d'un temps passé* (1972) #6894
- *John Fox: 10 New Paintings* (1980) #5495
- *Kostyniuk: Relief Structures, 1969-1972* (1973) #6079
- *L'art du paysage au Québec, 1800-1940/Landscape Painting in Québec, 1800-1940* (1978) #1286
- *Maritime Art Exhibition* (1959-1965) #1120
- *Miller Brittain - Painter* (1981) #4922
- *Painters Eleven in Retrospect* (1981) #1785
- *Ronald: 25 Years* (1975) #7073
- *The Beaverbrook Art Gallery Presents Nine New Brunswick Artists/La Galerie d'art Beaverbrook présente neuf artistes du Nouveau-Brunswick* (1973) #1182
- *The Figure in Canadian Painting: From the Collection of the Beaverbrook Art Gallery/La peinture figurative canadienne: collection de la galerie d'art Beaverbrook* (1972) #103
- *The Image of Man in Canadian Painting: 1878-1978/L'image de l'homme dans la peinture canadienne: 1878-1978* (1978) #135
- *The J.S. McLean Collection of Canadian Painting* (1969) #3228
- *The Mr. and Mrs. Jules Loeb Collection/La collection M. et Mme Jules Loeb* (1971) #3231
- *The Murray and Marguerite Vaughan Inuit Print Collection/Collection d'estampes inuit* (1981) #4498
- *The New Brunswick Landscape Print: 1760-1880* (1980) #1189
- *The Queen Comes to New Brunswick: Paintings and Drawings by Molly Lamb Bobak* (1977) #4765
- *The Railway: Patron of the Arts in Canada* (1976) #3281
- *The Saidye and Samuel Bronfman Collection of Canadian Art/La collection Saidye et Samuel Bronfman* (1966) #3087
- *The Society of Canadian Painter-Etchers and Engravers in Retrospect/La Société des peintres-graveurs canadiens: vue rétrospective* (1981) #836
- *The Work of Art: Six Artists* (1979) #665
- *Tom Forrestall Exhibition* (1971) #5461
- *Wallace S. Bird Memorial Collection: An Exhibition of the Work of Artists from Atlantic Canada* (1975) #1130
- *William G.R. Hind (1833-1888): A Confederation Painter in Canada* (1967) #5806
- *William Perehudoff: Recent Paintings* (1979) #6837
Fredericton (NB), cathedral
- architecture, William Butterfield #8770
Fredericton (NB), chapel
- architecture, Frank Wills #8770
Fredericton (NB), Fredericton National Exhibition Centre
- exhibitions
  - *Canadians: A National Photography Show about People/Canadiens: exposition nationale de photographie ayant les gens comme thème* (1979) #1035
Fredericton (NB), Government House
- architecture #8754

- Woolford, John Elliott #258 259
Fredericton (NB), Kings Landing Historical Settlement
- furniture #2484
Fredericton (NB), Legislative Building
- architecture #8940 8941
Fredericton (NB), New Brunswick Provincial Archives
- exhibitions
  - *George Thomas Taylor, 1838-1913: An Exhibition of Photographs, Paintings, and Memorabilia to Mark the Official Opening of the New Brunswick Provincial Archives on May 29th, 1968* (1968) #7334
- Smith, Madge, photographs #7235
Fredericton (NB), University of New Brunswick
- Bobak, Bruno Joseph, as resident artist (1960-1961) #4757
- Taylor, George Thomas, photographs #7333
Fredericton (NB), University of New Brunswick. Art Centre
- exhibitions
  - *Albert Franck (1899-1973) in Retrospect: A Small Selection from the Artist's Collection* (1974) #5500
  - *Annie D. Savage: Drawings and Watercolours* (1975) #7129
  - *Fritz Brandtner 1896-1969: A Restrospective Exhibition* (1971) #4903
  - *George Rackus: Anodized Aluminum Works & Prints* (1973) #6953
Fredericton (NB), University of New Brunswick. King's College
- architecture, John Elliott Woolford #258 259
Fredericton Art Club (Fredericton, NB)
- (1936-1961) #1176
Fredericton Society of Artists (Fredericton, NB) #1176
Freedman, Adele, Can art critic, 1946-
- winner, critical writing on art competition (1979) #3312
Freifeld, Eric, Can artist, 1919- #5515
- and realism #110
- exhibitions
  - (1968) #5514
- interview #5516
Freiman, Lillian, Can artist, 1908- #336 5517
- exhibitions
  - (1978) #5518
Frémont (Qué)
- city planning #7728
French in Canada
- (1520-1880) #216
- (1564-1867) #231
Frenière, F. Daunais, Can artist, fl. 1833-1843 #1301
Frenière, F.X., Can artist, fl. 1842 #1301
Frenkel, Vera, Can artist, 1938- #5521 5526
- as student of Albert Dumouchel #5327
- as teacher of Ed Bartram #4618
- exhibitions
  - (1978) #5525
- exhibitions (reviews) #5520
- on art #5523
- on art, love, and politics #5522
- on performance and video art #713
- on teaching art to high school students (1969) #5519
- video, *No Solution - A Suspense Thriller* #5524
frescoes

- *see* mural painting
Freud, Sigmund, Aus psychiatrist, 1856-1939
- theories
  - applied to Northwest Coast Indian prehistoric art #3861
  - influence on Surrealism #1466
Frick, Joan, Can artist, 1942-
- exhibitions (reviews) #5527
Friend, Ray, Can stained glass artist, fl. 1980
- stained glass, Coquitlam Centre (Vancouver, BC) #2459
Friend, Washington, Amer artist, ca. 1820-ca. 1886
- exhibitions, group
  - (1888) #175
  - (1890) #177 1839
Fringe Research Inc., photographic firm (Toronto, Ont)
- exhibitions
  - (1979) #1905
- holograms #1827
Fripp, Charles Edward, Brit artist in Canada, 1854-1906
- views, western Canada #931
Fripp, Robert Mackay, Can architect, 1858-1917
- Vancouver (BC), houses #8685
Fripp, Thomas William, Can artist, 1864-1931 #1986 2011
Frise, James Llewellyn, Can artist, 1891-1948
- illustrations #855
Frobisher, Sir Martin, Brit explorer in Canada, 1535-1594
- Eskimos captured, portraits of, John White #7553
- expedition, Arctic #228 229
Frobisher Bay (NWT)
- development project (1950s) #8184
Frobisher Bay (NWT), Frobisher Bay Academic and Occupational School
- architecture, Papineau, Gérin-Lajoie, LeBlanc, Edwards #8188
Frobisher Bay (NWT), The Museum of Things from the Land
- Inuit art #4224
frogs in art
- Fafard, Joe, and students #1924
- Gilhooly, David James #5601 5602
Frontenac County (Ont)
- architecture, 19th c. #8015
frontier and pioneer life
- Black Creek Pioneer Village (Ont) #8675
- Canada #2112 2120
- Canadiana Village (Rawdon, Qué) #7876
- Fanshawe Pioneer Village (Ont) #8066
- Heritage Park (Alta) #8125
- Kings Landing (NB) #7810 7811
- Louisbourg (NS) #8442
- Ontario, 19th c. #2245
- pioneer village museums, southern Ontario #8063
- Québec #2217
  - 17th-18th cs. #2200
  - women #2212
- Upper Canada Village (Morrisburg, Ont) #7981 7982 8031
Fry, George, Can artist, fl. 1960s
- as member of Hampton Group #1177
Fry, Samuel, Can weaver, 1812-1881 #2723
Fuertes, Louis Agassiz, Amer artist, 1874-1927
- Lansdowne, James Fenwick, compared with #6165
Fuller, Richard Buckminster, Amer architect,

1895-
– Montréal (Qué), Expo '67. American Pavilion #9218
Fuller, Thomas, Can architect, 1823-1898 #8366
– as father of Thomas William Fuller #8367 8368
– Ottawa (Ont), Parliament Buildings #7671
– post offices #9054 9055
Fuller, Thomas William, Can architect, 1865-1951 #8367 8368
Fuller & Jones, Can architectural firm
– Ottawa (Ont), Parliament Buildings #8922 8930
Fulton, Christopher, Can photographer, fl. 1862-1864
– and the Victoria Theatre Photographic Gallery (Victoria, BC) #2027
fur trade
– and *ceinture fléchée* #2818 2824 2827
– and Edmonton (Alta) architecture (1800-1870) #8130
– and Indian trade goods #3440
– and Indian trade silver #2659 3594 3608 3645 3646
– artifacts, Nor'westers Museum (Williamstown, Ont) #3148
– trading posts
  – Alberta, 18th-19th cs. #8129
  – Canada, 17th c. #7655
  – Fort Langley (BC) #8477
  – Hudson's Bay Company #8100
Furihata, Ja artist, 20th c.
– as teacher of Gaston-Pierre Petit #6844
furniture
– *see also* armoires; beds; cabinets; chairs; chests; Chippendale style; conservation and restoration, furniture; cradles; cupboards; desks; garden ornaments and furniture; Georgian furniture; mirrors; Sheraton style furniture; sofas; tables; upholstery; Victorian furniture; Windsor furniture; woodwork
– in Canadian museum collections #2484
– nursery furniture, late 19th c.-1930s #2932
furniture, American
– 18th-19th cs., exported to Niagara (Ont) #2569
– 18th-19th cs., influence on Ontario furniture #2550
– 19th c., exported to Ontario #2575
– 19th c., influence on Ontario furniture #2549 2552 2576
– (1760-1840), influence on Canadian furniture #2477
– (1780-1900), influence on Ontario furniture #2577
– (1780s), influence on New Brunswick furniture #2495
– (1970s), compared with Québec furniture #2533
– Georgian, compared with Canadian furniture #2479 2481 2482
– late 18th c., influence on Québec furniture #2537 2543
furniture, British
– 18th-19th cs., brought to Niagara (Ont), by military officers #2569
– 18th-19th cs., influence on Ontario furniture #2550 2576
– 19th c., influence on Ontario furniture #2552
– (1760-1840), influence on Canadian furniture #2477

– (1780-1900), influence on Ontario furniture #2577
– (1810s), influence on New Brunswick furniture #2495
– Georgian, compared with Canadian furniture #2481
– late 18th c., influence on Québec furniture #2537 2543
furniture, Canadian #63 2107
– 17th-19th cs. #2464
– 17th c.-1867 #2110
– 18th-19th cs. #2474 2594
– 19th c. #2099
– 19th c.-1920s #2463
– (1608-1867) #2120
– (1837-1887) #253
– (1850s) #1692
– (1910-1961), Canadian National Exhibition (Toronto, Ont) #1
– (1920s) #2465 2547
– (1930s) #2466
– (1940s) #2602 2603 2604
– (1950s) #2467 2468 2610
  – and National Industrial Design Committee #2606
– (1967-1969) #2115
– (1970s) #2224 7081
– (1980s) #2487
– (pre-1867), English Canada #2470
– Acadian #7804
  – 18th-19th cs. #2516
  – chairs #2492
– Baker, Isaac Bennett #2581
– Barker, Charles Edward #4609
– beaver motif #56
– Bersudsky, Sid #4711
– Bowmanville (Ont), 19th c. #2556
– Bush, Robin B. #4979 4980
– Charlottetown (PEI), Province House #8937 8938
– Colchester County (NS), 19th c. #2515
– Cormier, Ernest #8347
– Côté, Jean-Baptiste #5187 5188
– Doan, John and Ebenezer #8351 8352
– Foisy, Dennis #5458
– Fournier, Arthur #5485
– Gemeinhardt, John #5579
– Georgian #2477 2479 2480 2481 2482 2488
– Germanic tradition #2140 2251
– Graham, Kent #2596
– Green, Daniel #2517
– guide for collectors #2101 2104 2125 2131 2252 2486
– Hamilton (Ont), Whitehern #8664
– Hebb, Howard D. #2510
– Hébert, Julien #5766
– Holder, Thomas Cook, and Henry Arthur #2505 2506
– île aux Coudres (Qué) #2168
– île d'Orléans (Qué) #1252
– Jacques & Hay Co. #2546 2559
– James, Ralph #2583
– Kingston (Ont) #1680
  – (1800-1867) #2567
– Kleyn, Robert #6063
– Levasseur (*dit* Delor), Jean-Baptiste-Antoine, and François-Noël Levasseur #269 270
– Lower Fort Garry (Man), men's house #8482
– MacGregor, John #6388
– Manitoba, 19th c. #2584 2586
– Maritimes, 19th c. #2147
– McKinley, Donald Lloyd #6489

– Mennonite #2568 2572
– Montréal (Qué)
  – 17th-18th cs. #2522
  – (1800-1850) #2538
  – Cormier House #8347
  – Ecole du meuble (1930s) #2976
  – Grey Nuns #8862
  – Place des Arts #9092
  – Saint Gabriel House #8597
– Moore, John Warren #2512 6603
– Mount Uniake (NS), Uniake House #8534
– museum identification techniques #2478
– National Parks Branch habitation reconstruction policy #7758
– New Brunswick #2150 2491 2503
  – 18th-19th cs. #2495 2500
    – Saint John (NB), New Brunswick Museum #2504
  – 19th c. #2501
  – (1760s-1920s) #2511
– Newfoundland #1155 2520
  – 18th c.-1850s #2502
  – 19th-early 20th cs. #2519
– Niagara (Ont) #2569 2571
– Nova Scotia #2521
  – 17th-19th cs. #2489
  – 17th c.-1840s #2494
  – 18th-19th cs. #2496 2499
  – 19th c. #2513
  – decorations #1206 1207 2514
– Ontario #2570
  – 19th c. #2245 2552 2561 2573 2576
  – (1780-1900) #2577
  – (1790s-1850s) #2550
  – (1790s-1857) #2558
  – (1800-1837), Upper Canada Village (Morrisburg, Ont) #2549
  – (1850-1900) #2551
  – Germanic tradition #2263
  – use of paint, 19th c. #8013
– Ontario and Atlantic provinces, 18th-19th cs. #2475
– Ottawa (Ont)
  – Earnscliffe #8652
  – National Museum of Man. Canadian Centre for Folk Culture Studies #963
– Perth (Ont), Matheson House (now Perth Museum) #8670
– Ploethner, Frederick K. #6896
– Prince Edward Island, 18th-19th cs. #2498 2508 2518
– Québec #1327 2237 2544
  – 17th-18th cs. #1320 2181 2217 2526 2529 2530 2531 2539 2543
  – 17th-19th cs. #2128 2524 2541
    – European influences #2221
  – 18th-19th cs. #2532 2536
    – English #2542
  – 18th c. #2545
  – (1613-1870), French provincial style #2191
  – (1660-1760) #2540
  – (1700-1820) #2537
  – (1875-1915) #1364
  – (1930-1935), Ecole technique de Montréal (Montréal, Qué) #2970
  – (1940s) #2523
  – (1970s) #2533
  – late 17th-mid 19th cs. #2527
– Québec (Qué)
  – Hôpital-Général #9022
  – Ursuline Convent #8810
– Saskatchewan, late 19th c.-1921 #2587
– Schlombs, Wolfgang, collection #2485

- Spencer, Hugh #2551
- Tonnancour, Jacques Godefroy de #2608
- Toronto (Ont), (1800-1865) #2563
- Tunis Snook Farm (near Kingston, Ont) #8681
- use of lacquer decorations #2548
- Victoria (BC) #2269
- Victorian #2472
- western Canada, ethnic traditions, late 19th-early 20th cs. #2585
- Wilno furniture, Renfrew County (Ont), (1860s) #2565
- Windsor (NS), Shand House #8546
- Winnipeg (Man)
  - Deer Lodge #9260
  - Legislative Building #8951
- Witmer, Joseph #2578
- Zadow, J. Albert #2582
furniture, French
- 17th-18th cs., compared with Québec furniture #2530 2531
- 17th-18th cs., influence on Québec furniture #2529 2539 2543
- 19th c., influence on Ontario furniture #2549
- (1660-1760), influence on Québec furniture #2540
furniture, German
- 19th c., influence on Ontario furniture #2576 2577
furniture, Italian
- (1970s), compared with Québec furniture #2533
furniture, Polish
- 19th c., influence on Ontario furniture #2576 2577
furniture, Swedish
- (1970s), compared with Québec furniture #2533
Furse, Barbara, Can artist, fl. 1960s
- as member of Hampton Group #1177
Furse, Peter Reynolds, Can cartographer, d. 1970
- as member of Hampton Group #1177
Fuse: The Cultural News Magazine, Can periodical #603
Fusion des arts (Montréal, Qué) #1483 1502
- (1964-1968) #1482
- and Richard Lacroix #6126
- use of plastics #1442
Futurism
- and video art #654
- Canada (1910s) #1071
Fyshe, Avis Selina, Can artist, b. 1886
- on Canadian Christmas cards #849

G

Gabo, Naum, Russ sculptor, 1890-1977
- use of plastics #768
Gaboury, E.J., and Associates, Can architectural firm
- Saskatoon (Sask), Mendel Art Gallery, competition #9091
Gaboury, Etienne J., Can architect, 1930- #8084
- on architecture #7746 8369
- Regina (Sask), Saint Anne's Church and Rectory #8767
- Saint-Boniface (Man), Precious Blood Church #8091 8908

- stained glass windows #2450
- Winnipeg (Man), Etienne Gaboury House #8519
Gabriel, Pier, Can sculptor, fl. 1979 #1626
Gabriola Island (BC)
- petroglyphs, Northwest Coast Indians #4050
Gadbois, Louise Landry, Can artist, 1896- #5529
- exhibitions
  - (1979) #5528
- on Montréal (Qué) painting (1939-1950) #1433
Gaddi, Taddeo, It artist, ca. 1300-1366
- influence on David Brown Milne #6567
Gadois (dit Mauger), Jacques, Can silversmith, 1686-1750 #249 250
Gaettens, Marianne, Can photographer, fl. 1970 #993
Gagen, Robert Ford, Can artist, 1847-1926
- correspondence, John William Beatty (1918) #4638
- exhibitions, group
  - (1978) #1726
- interview #5530
Gagné, Andrée, Can photographer, 1951-
- portfolio of photographs #1023
Gagné, Marc-André, Can photographer, 1939- #991 997 999 1000
Gagné, Marcel, Can architect, 1926-1973
- Osaka (Japan), Expo '70. Canadian Pavilion, competition #9217
Gagné-Dufresne, Hélène, Can sculptor, ceramicist, 1931- #5531
- and Ecole des beaux-arts (Montréal, Qué), (1968) #2995
Gagnier, H., Ltd., publishing firm (Toronto, Ont)
- headquarters, Graphic Arts Building #9330
Gagnon, Charles, Can artist, 1934- #1007 1484 1542 1543 5533 5535
- and art criticism #3315
- and minimal art #1483
- collages (late 1950s) #5532
- exhibitions
  - (1979) #5540
- exhibitions, group
  - (1977) #636
  - (1979) #510 1037
- exhibitions (reviews) #1018 1046 1060 5537 5538 5539
- interview #5534
- paintings and photographs #5536
- participant, Symposium on 20th Century Canadian Culture (Washington, DC), (1977) #621
- photographs as personal expression #1556
- portfolio of photographs #997 999
Gagnon, Clarence Alphonse, Can artist, 1881-1942 #302 1315 1392 5541 5543 5544 5546 5547
- and Albert Henry Robinson #7057
- and Canadian painting #18
- and Québec painting #1270
- as member, Canadian Art Club #193
- Boeufs au labeur/Oxen Ploughing Beaupré #5548
- etchings #799
- exhibitions
  - (1942) #5542
  - (1981) #5549
- exhibitions, group
  - (1942) #359
- illustrations, Maria Chapdelaine #1

- in Baie-Saint-Paul (Qué) #5545
- influence on René-Jean Richard #6997 6998 6999
- on Maurice Galbraith Cullen #5221
- works, McMichael Canadian Collection (Kleinburg, Ont) #3172
Gagnon, Edmond, Can basketmaker, fl. 1981 #2954
Gagnon, Maurice, Can writer, 1904-
- and Paul-Emile Borduas #4814
- writings #1393
Gagnon, Pnina, Can artist, 1940- #5550
Gagnon, René, Can artist, 1927- #5551
Gagnon, Yvonne Tremblay
- see Tremblay-Gagnon, Yvonne
Gagnon-Fortier, C., Can artist, 1938
- exhibitions
  - (1978) #5552
Gaitskell, Charles Dudley, Can educator, artist, 1908-
- on art in Canadian schools #2986
Gallagher, Chris, Can photographer, 1951-
- exhibitions, group
  - (1979) #2069
Gallie, Tommie J., Can artist, 1946-
- exhibitions
  - (1981) #5553
- exhibitions, group
  - (1978) #2066
Gallop, John Frederick, Can architect, fl. 1960s
- chairs #2471
- Osaka (Japan), Expo '70. Canadian Pavilion, competition #9217
Gallozzi, Chuck, Can photographer, fl. 1977
- portfolio of photographs #1023
Galt (Ont), Gore District Mutual Fire Insurance Company building
- architecture, Marani, Lawson & Morris #7973
Galt (Ont), public school
- architecture, John Evans #9387
Gambioli, Joan, Can sculptor, 1920-
- The Family, Van Dusen Gardens (Vancouver, BC) #775
Gamble, Eric, Can artist, 1950-
- exhibitions (reviews) #639
Gamble, Millie, Can photographer, b. 1887 #5554
games
- see also Olympic Games
- 19th-early 20th cs., imported into Canada #2928
- Band, Percy, collection #2917
- children's games, late 19th c.-1930s #2932
- in art, David Askevold #4566
games, Canadian
- 19th-early 20th cs. #2928
- board games, 19th-20th cs. #2597
- Labrador #2955
- Québec, as folk art #1291
games, Cree #3402
games, Ingalik #4087
games, Inuit
- prints #4492
games, Iroquois #3489
games, Micmac #3500
games, Ojibwa #3539
games, Saulteaux #3402
Gammon, George, Can furniture-maker, fl. 1830s-1859 #2493
Gano, John Henry, Can photographer, 1873-1947 #5555
GAP

– *see* Groupe d'action photographique (GAP)

Garber, Bram, Can collector, 20th c.
– collection, Canadian painting, 20th c. #3247

Gard, Thomas Dapleton, Can silversmith, fl. 1856-1877 #2649

Gard, W.Tremaine, Can silversmith, 1867-1914 #2649

Garden Hill Cooperative (Island Lake, Man) #4135

Garden McMillan, Can architectural firm
– Calgary (Alta), Brae Glen #8746

garden ornaments and furniture, American
– late 19th c., Halifax (NS) parks #2710

garden ornaments and furniture, British
– late 19th c., Halifax (NS) parks #2710

garden ornaments and furniture, Canadian
– garden sculpture, British Columbia (1960s) #1849
– Ottawa (Ont), National Museum of Man. Canadian Centre for Folk Culture Studies #963
– Québec, as folk art #1291

gardens
– *see also* garden ornaments and furniture; landscape architecture
– and domestic architecture, Moshe Safdie on #8406
– in art
– Pellan, Alfred #6815 6818 6819
– Sawyer, Walter Michael #7144
– Vivenza, Francesca #7495

gardens, Canadian
– (1950s), and architecture #7677
– (1970s), rooftop gardens and architecture #7728
– Ontario, 19th c. #2245

Gardet, Georges, Fr sculptor, 1863-1939
– sculpture, Legislative Building (Winnipeg, Man) #8948 8949 8952

Gardiner, Frederick, Can artist, fl. 1898-1905 #2085

Gardiner, Thornton, Gathe, Davidson, Garrett, Masson & Associates, Can architectural firm
– Osaka (Japan), Expo '70. Canadian Pavilion, competition #9217

Gardiner, Thornton, Gathe & Associates, Can architectural firm
– Surrey (BC), Surrey Memorial Hospital #9032
– Winnipeg (Man), University of Manitoba. Saint Paul's College and Chapel of Christ the King #9486

Gardiner & Mercer, Can architectural firm
– Vancouver (BC), Saint Paul's Hospital. Surgical Wing #9021

Garneau, François-Xavier, Can historian, 1809-1866
– residence, Garneau House (La Canardière, Qué) #8615

Garnier, Hubert, Can sculptor, 1903-
– exhibitions
– (1976) #5556

Garnier, Jacques, Can ceramicist, 1943- #5557

Garrett, R.Michael, Can architect, 1931-
– Vancouver (BC), University of British Columbia. Student Union, competition #9503

Garstang-Hodgson, Wilfred, Can sculptor, 1885-1971 #5815

Garthwaite, Ernest Paul, Can artist, 1946-

– exhibitions (reviews) #5558

Garwood-Jones, Trevor Patrick, Can architect, 1928-
– Hamilton (Ont), Art Gallery of Hamilton #3165

Gascon, Michel, Can photographer, 1948- #1562

gasoline stations, Canadian
– (1919) #9235

Gaspé (Qué)
– log cabins #7896
– photographic views
– Karnick, Irwin #1008
– views
– Fortin, Marc-Aurèle #5481

Gathe, Asbjorn R., Can architect, 1921-
– Vancouver (BC), University of British Columbia. Student Union, competition #9503

Gaucher, Yves, Can artist, 1934- #536 1542 1543 5561 5562 5564 5567 5568
– and minimal art #1483
– and Optical art #1445
– and Québec printmaking (1960s) #1641
– as juror, *B.C. Artists Annual Exhibition,* Vancouver Art Gallery (Vancouver, BC), (1967) #1983
– drawings #532
– exhibitions
– (1969) #5563
– (1976) #5566
– exhibitions, group
– (1967) #480 490 821
– (1977) #643
– exhibitions (reviews) #5569 5570
– interview #5560
– on his art education #470
– paintings (1963-1973) #5565
– prints (1960s) #1654 5559
– support of #123

Gaudard, Pierre Raymond, Can photographer, 1927-
– documentary photographs #1556
– photographs of workers #990

Gaudin, Jean, Fr artist, 1879-1954
– mosaics, Saint Ann's Basilica (Sainte-Anne-de-Beaupré, Qué) #8859 8860 8865 8866

Gaudin (*dit* Lapoterie), Louis-Nicolas, Can silversmith, 1725-1809 #5571

Gaudin (*dit* Lapoterie), Nicolas, Can silversmith, ca. 1695-ca. 1743 #5572
– as father of Louis-Nicolas Gaudin (*dit* Lapoterie) #5571

Gauguin, Paul, Fr artist, 1848-1903
– influence on Mary Evelyn Wrinch #7617

Gauthier, Amable, Can sculptor, architect, 1792-1873 #241 242 6947
– interior, church, Berthierville (Qué) #8874

Gauthier, Claude-Paul, Can sculptor, 1951- #1630

Gauthier, Michel, Can photographer, fl. 1970s #1283

Gauthier, Paul, Can architect, 1935-
– Québec (Qué) #7733
– Jardins Mérici #7886

Gauthier, Robert, Can artist, 1951- #5573

Gauthier & Guité, Can architectural firm
– Québec (Qué), church #8766

Gauthier-Charlebois, Alyne, Can artist, fl. 1932 #1380

Gauthier Guité Roy, Can architectural firm
– Québec (Qué), Jardins Mérici #8746

Gauthier-Mitchell, Louisette, Can artist,

1941- #1511
– exhibitions
– (1980) #5574

Gautier, Théophile, Fr writer, 1811-1872
– on art #405

Gauvreau, Claude, Can artist, writer, 1925-1971 #1502
– correspondence, Paul-Emile Borduas #4804 4805 4807 4834
– on Ozias Leduc #6199
– *Refus global* #1396
– writings #1449
– writings and correspondence #1443

Gauvreau, Jean-Marie, Can furniture-maker, 1903-1970
– and Centrale d'artisanat du Québec #2238
– as director, Ecole du meuble (Montréal, Qué) #2176 2976

Gauvreau, Pierre, Can architect, 1813-1884
– Québec (Qué), National Assembly #8942

Gauvreau, Pierre, Can artist, 1922-
– and automatism #5575
– and Montréal (Qué) painting (1950s) #1403
– exhibitions
– (1979) #5577
– (1981) #5578
– exhibitions, group
– (1955) #1408
– interview #5576

Geisel, Albert, Can artist, 1889-1973
– exhibitions, group
– (1975) #1682

Gelin, Denis, Fr sculptor, fl. 1931
– works, T. Eaton Company department stores (Montréal, Qué, and Toronto, Ont) #9370

Gemeinhardt, John, Can furniture-maker, 1826-1912 #5579

Gendron, Ernest, Can artist, 1912- #5580

Gendron, Pierre, Can artist, 1934- #5581 5582
– on printmaking #817

genealogy
– *see also* heraldry
– Bourassa, Napoléon #4872 4874
– Bourgault family #4886
– Hamel, Théophile #5692
– use of samplers #2790

General Idea (Toronto, Ont) #5584
– and avant-garde art #600
– books #940
– *Conversation Pierre: Three Booths for the Miss General Idea Pavilion* #714
– correspondence, on 1971 Miss General Idea Pageant #546
– exhibitions
– (1977) #5583
– (1980) #690
– exhibitions, group
– (1977) #631
– (1980) #705 1063 8237
– performance art #655
– periodical, *File* #544
– *Test Tube* #692
– use of photography #1057
– video art #605 630

Généreux, Marie Arline, Can artist, 1897- #1380

Genn, Robert, Can artist, 1936-
– autobiography #5585

Génot, Achille
– *see* Fay-Génot, Achille

genre, Canadian
– 18th-19th cs. #812

– Montréal (Qué), McGill University. McCord Museum #222 223 1366
– (1890s) #183
– (1950s) #392
– Hébert, Louis-Philippe #5767
– Hind, William George Richardson #5811
– Krieghoff, Cornelius #6097
– Québec, 17th c.-1960s #1344
– Reid, George Agnew #6973
Gentile, Charles, Can photographer, 1835-1893
– and the Victoria Theatre Photographic Gallery (Victoria, BC) #2027
Geoffrey Massey/E.J. Watkins/R.B. Archambault/C.D. Rowett, Can architectural firm
– *Canadian Architect* community art gallery competition (1957) #9082
Geoffroy, André, Can sculptor, 1946-
– Symposium international de sculpture environnementale de Chicoutimi (Qué), (1980) #1639
geography
– and Canadian landscape #26 41
Geological Survey of Canada
– (1871), and Benjamin Baltzly #1014 1015 4598
– (1875-1900), and George Mercer Dawson and Joseph Burr Tyrrell #1014 1015
geology
– and Paterson Ewen #5383
geometric abstraction
– and Guido Molinari #6591
– Canada (1950s) #832
– Montréal (Qué), (1950s-1960s) #1437
– Québec (1955-1965) #1471
geometry
– in art
– Bloore, Ronald Langley #4749
– Dubois, Marius #5310
– Rockburne, Dorothea #7060
George & Moorhouse, Can architectural firm
– Toronto (Ont), Toronto Stock Exchange #9187
George II, king of Great Britain and Ireland, 1683-1760
– statue of, Cambridge University. Senate House (Cambridge, England) #725
George River (Qué)
– graphic arts (1972-1975) #4475
Georgetown (PEI)
– architecture #7799
Georgeville (Qué), Joshua Copp House
– architecture and interior #8628
Georgian architecture
– Canada #7661 7687 7696 8522
– Canada and USA #8498
– Nova Scotia #7839
– Ontario #7959 8648 8654 8677
– Perth (Ont), Matheson House (now Perth Museum) #8670
– Saint John (NB) #2490
– St. John's (Nfld), Commissariat House #8538
– Toronto (Ont) #5651 8060
– The Grange #8637
– Whitby (Ont), Lynde House #8668
Georgian Bay (Ont)
– views
– Fairley, Barker #5402
– Group of Seven #1745
– Jackson, A.Y. #5919
– Lismer, Arthur #6304

Georgian Bay (Ont), F.S. Eaton summer residence
– architecture, Blake Millar #8519
Georgian Bay (Ont), summer residence
– architecture, Blake Millar #8745
Georgian furniture
– Canada #2477 2479 2480 2481 2482 2488
– Ontario, chairs #2553
– Saint John (NB) #2490
Gerald Bern Agency, Can graphic design firm #871
Gerald Hamilton & Associates, Can architectural firm
– Ottawa (Ont), Ottawa Civic Centre #9101
Gerber, Sidney, Amer collector, d. 1965
– collection, art, Northwest Coast Indians #3974
Gérin-Lajoie, Guy, Can architect, 1928-
– Montréal (Qué), métro. Peel Station #9553
Gérin-Tétreault, Denyse, Can artist, 1940- #1282
– and RACE #1536
Germans in Canada
– Alberta, log buildings #8136
– architecture, 19th c.-1970s #7735
– Maritimes, Ontario, and Prairies, decorative arts #2140
– Nova Scotia and Ontario, decorative arts #2135
– Ontario
– decorative arts #2243
– Mennonites, decorative arts #2250 2251 2263 2264 2267
– pottery #2318 3962
Gérôme, Jean-Léon, Fr artist, 1824-1904
– as teacher of François-Xavier Aldéric Rapin #6961
– as teacher of Joseph-Charles Franchère #5497
– as teacher of Wyatt Eaton #5357
Gervais, Lise, Can artist, 1933- #5586
– interview #5587
Gervais, Raymond, Can artist, 1946-
– exhibitions, group
– (1977) #637
– (1980) #687 696
– performance sculpture #658
Geske, Allan, Can artist, 1945-
– exhibitions, group
– (1981) #1908
gesture
– in painting, Gordon Appelbe Smith #7223
Ghana
– photographic views
– Semak, Michael William #990
Ghent (Belgium), Museum van Hedendaagse Kunst
– exhibitions
– *Prospekt 80/2: Canada; CCMC, David Askevold, Colin Campbell, Dan Graham, Noel Harding, General Idea, Michael Snow* (1980) #690
ghost dance, Plains #3736
Giacometti, Alberto, Sw artist, 1901-1966
– influence on Joe Plaskett #6889
Gibb, Benaiah, Can collector, d. 1877
– and Art Association of Montreal (Montréal, Qué) #3075 3110
Gibbard, W.T., furniture-making firm (Beauharnois, Qué) #2463
Gibbs, Leonard (Len), Can artist, 1929- #5589 5590
– interview #5588
Gibson, Carol, Can photographer, 1945-

– exhibitions (reviews) #1018
Gibson, George, Can sculptor, 1915-
– works, British Columbia Parliament Buildings (Victoria, BC) #8967
Gibson, George Selkirk, Can artist, 1867-1942 #5591
Gibson, Susan, Can artist, 1947-
– exhibitions, group
– (1980) #1221
Gibson, Thomas Kent Hamilton (Tom), Can photographer, 1930- #5592
– (1979) #1037
– exhibitions (reviews) #1018 1046 1060
– portfolio of photographs #997 999
Gibson's Landing (BC), Elphinstone Pioneer Museum
– McCall, Helen, photographs #6460
Giddings, J.Louis, Amer archaeologist, 1909-1964
– expedition, Arctic #4371
Giguère, Denise, Can ceramicist, 1926-
– interview #5598
Giguère, Roland, Can artist, writer, 1929- #1541 5594 5595
– and Editions Erta #926 1641
– dream images #5596
– exhibitions
– (1966) #5593
– interview #1527
– on his art #5598
– on Léon Bellefleur #4662
– on printmaking #817 818
– paintings and poems #5597 5599
– writings #4831
Gilbert, Albert, Can photographer, 1920-
– portfolio of photographs #995
Gilbert, André, Can architect, 1919-
– Saint-Nicolas (Qué), Church of Saint-Nicolas #8766
Gilbert, Bradford Lee, Amer architect, 1853-1911
– Ottawa (Ont), Central Station and Château Laurier #9528 9529
Gilbert, Cass, Amer architect, 1858-1934
– Regina (Sask), Legislative Buildings, competition #8954
Gilbert, Henry Byran, Can architect, 1885-
– Toronto (Ont), Union Bank of Canada #9159
Gilbert, Ina Elaine, Can artist, 1932- #5600
Gilbert, William Herbert (Herb), Can artist, 1926-
– exhibitions, group
– (1959) #1997
– (1974) #2050
gilding, Canadian
– Québec #2930
Giles, William, Brit artist, b. 1872
– and Walter Joseph Phillips #6860
Gilhooly, David James, Can sculptor, ceramicist, 1943- #538 5601 5602
– and Joe Fafard #5398
– and Toronto (Ont) art (1970s) #1796
– exhibitions, group
– (1977) #781
– exhibitions (reviews) #2383
Gill, Charles Ignace Adélard, Can artist, writer, 1871-1918 #89 1231 1382 5603
– and François-Xavier Aldéric Rapin #6961
– exhibitions
– (1971) #5604
Gill, Dennis, Can artist, 1950-
– exhibitions (reviews) #1227
– prints #1214

Gillam, William Charles Frederick, Can
architect, b. 1867
– Victoria (BC), Provincial Normal School
#9386
Gilleland & Strutt, Can architectural firm
– Halifax (NS), Halifax International
Airport. Air Terminal Building #9515
– Ottawa (Ont), Ottawa International
Airport. Air Terminal Building #9515
Gilles, Albert, Can artist, 1895-1979
– and Québec religious art (1950s) #1250
Gillespie, J.H., Can artist, b. 1793, fl.
1820s-1840s #1171
Gillett, Violet Amy, Can artist, 1898- #1173
5605
Gilson, Jacqueline Marie-Charlotte, Can
artist, 1912- #5606
Gingras, André, Can sculptor, 19th c.
– interior, Church of Saint-Jean-Baptiste
(Saint-Jean-Port-Joli, Qué) #8812
Gingras, Micheline, Can artist, 1947- #5607
Gingras, Ulric-Louis, Can poet, 1894-1954
– *Du soleil sur l'étang noir*, illustrations,
Rodolphe Duguay #5320
Girard, Claude, Can artist, 1938- #5608
Girouard, Jean-Joseph, Can statesman, artist,
1795-1855 #5609
Giroux, André-Raphaël, Can sculptor,
architect, 1815-1869 #258 259 5610
– influence of Baillairgé family #1582
– interior, Cap-Santé (Qué) #8814
– Québec (Qué), Notre-Dame-des-Victoires
#8858
– use of architectural models #7872
Giroux, Raphäel
– *see* Giroux, André-Raphäel
Gitksan Indians
– 'Ksan artists' cooperative #4134
– totem poles #3797 3815 3828 3834 3884
3925 4032
Gjoa Haven (NWT)
– sculpture, Inuit #4435
Glackens, William James, Amer artist,
1870-1938
– influence on James Wilson Morrice #6626
Gladstone, Gerald, Can sculptor, 1929- #5612
– exhibitions
– (1962) #5611
– interview #5613
– on relationship of artists and architects
#8234
– on visual perception #525
– sculptures (1960s) #745 746
Gladu, Arthur, Can artist, 1918-
– exhibitions (reviews) #860
Glasgow (Scotland), Glasgow School of Art
– McLaren, Norman, as student #6492 6493
glass
– *see also* bottles; conservation and
restoration, glass; glass painting
– bottles (1600-1903) #2427
– Louisbourg (NS), Dugas House #2441 2442
– Roma Site (PEI)
– 19th c. #2436 2437
Glass, Alan Frank, Can artist, 1932- #5614
5615 5616
– in Paris (France) #426
glass, Algonquian
– beadwork #3635
glass, American
– 19th c., influence on Canadian glass #2434
– (1800-1940), in Canada #2433
– pressed #2430
glass, British

– (1800-1940), in Canada #2433
– bottles, Mr. and Mrs. Stanley S. Silver
collection #2414
glass, Canadian #2402 2408
– 19th c. #2099 2421
– 20th c. #2121 2142
– (1800-1940) #2433
– (1825-1920) #2399
– (1825-1925) #2404
– (1837-1887) #253
– (1940s) #2601
– (1960s-1980s) #2440
– (1970s) #2224
– (1979-1980) #2138
– and silver tableware #2637
– Beach, William Godkin #2396
– Beauséjour (Man), Manitoba Glass Works
#2415
– bottles #2425
– 19th -early 20th cs. #2427
– (1825-1931) #2419
– Nova Scotia #2409 2428
– Prairies (1880-1920s) #2431
– Silver, Mr. and Mrs. Stanley S.,
collection #2414
– Calgary (Alta), Skookum Art Glass #2439
– Desaulniers, Gilles #5286
– fruit jars #2413 2426
– guide for collectors #2104 2252 2422 2429
– Hamilton (Ont), Burlington Glass Works
#2406 2434
– Hookway, Elmer John #5828
– McGowan, John, collection #2424
– medicine bottles #2432
– milk bottles #2412
– Montréal (Qué), St. Lawrence Glass Co.
#2410
– New Brunswick #2150 2400
– Nova Scotia #2114 2398 2417
– Ontario
– 19th c. #2416
– (1825-1948) #2401
– (1970s) #2262
– paperweights (1880-1925) #2438
– patterns (1902-1940) #2411
– pickle cruets, Walter Bick collection #2405
– Pierce, Edith Chown, and Gerald Stevens,
collection #2397
– pressed #2407 2430
– Québec #2226 2228 2237
– 19th c. #2418
– 20th c. #2198
– Québec (Qué), place Royale #2201
– Saint-Jean (Qué), Canada Glass Works
#2420
– Sapperton (BC), Crystal Glass Co. #2423
– Schantz, Karl #7159
– Trenton (NS), Nova Scotia Glass Co. #2435
– window glass, 19th-20th cs. #7752
glass, Iroquois
– beadwork #3635
glass, Woodlands
– beadwork #3635
glass painting, Canadian #2455
– (1880s) #2443
– (1901-1912), Toronto Society of Architects
exhibitions #7956
– (1910-1961), Canadian National Exhibition
(Toronto, Ont) #1
– (1940s)
– Plamondon, Marius Gérald, on #2447
– Williams, Yvonne, on #2446
– (1960s) #2106
– Allward, John Raphael #4515

– and architecture (1960s) #8236
– Blomfield, James Jerris #1977 8900 8966
– British Columbia #2452
– churches, influence of French glass
painting #1435
– Ferron, Marcelle #5422 5423 5424 5425
5426
– Horwood, H. #2111
– Huot, Charles Edouard #5876
– Lockport (Man), Saint Andrew's Church
#8909
– Louy, Pierre #1177
– Manitoba #2450
– May, Karl #6452 6453
– mid 19th-early 20th c. #2399
– Milne, Eleanor #6569
– Ottawa (Ont), Parliament Buildings
#6568
– Montréal (Qué) #2448
– Bibliothèque Saint-Sulpice #9039
– Church of Notre-Dame #2444 8839
– late 19th c. #2462
– Morris, William #2453
– Murphy, Rowley Walter #6666
– Oshawa (Ont), Saint George's Anglican
Church #8899
– Ottawa (Ont), Parliament Buildings. Peace
Tower and Memorial Chamber #8929
– Patterson, Nancy-Lou #6783
– Pellan, Alfred #1442 8233
– Piché-Whissell, Aline #6865
– Plamondon, Marius Gérald #1404 6888
– Québec (1940s) #2199 8820
– Reid, Stuart #6983
– Toronto (Ont)
– (1880s-1890s) #2451
– City Hall (1898) #2449
– Trinity College Chapel #2461
– Vancouver (BC)
– (1890-1940) #2456
– heraldic motifs #2454
– use of pattern books #2457
– Coquitlam Centre #2459
– Dearle, John Henry and Duncan W.
#2458
– Victoria (BC) #2269
– western Canada (1980s) #2460
– Williams, Yvonne #7589
– Winnipeg (Man), Marlborough Hotel
#9277
– women artists (1920s-1940s) #2445
glass painting, French
– influence on Canadian glass painting
#1435
Gleason, Herbert Wendell, Amer
photographer, 1855-1937
– photographic views, western Canada and
USA #5617
Glengarry (Ont)
– log cabins #7990
Globe and Mail, Can newspaper
– headquarters, William H. Wright Building
(Toronto, Ont) #9338
Glyde, Henry George, Can artist, 1906-
– as teacher of Gerald Tailfeathers #7312
– exhibitions
– (1974) #5618
– travelling art exhibition program, Alberta
(1980) #1972
Gnass, Peter, Can sculptor, 1936- #5619
– *Chantier interdit au public* #1563
– exhibitions
– (1977) #5620
– (1980) #5621

Gnosill, Albert E., Can artist, 1895-
– exhibitions
– (1960) #1668
Gobeil, Lucien, Can sculptor, 1946-
– use of plastics #1603
Gobelins tapestry
– Jaworska, Tamara Hans #5949
goblets, American
– pressed #2430
goblets, Canadian
– pressed #2430
Goblin, Can periodical
– cartoons, Richard Taylor #7336
Godard, Mira, Can art dealer, 1932- #161
Godin, Raymonde, Can artist, 1930-
– exhibitions
– (1979) #5623
– in Paris (France) #426
– interview #5622
Godwin, Ted, Can artist, 1933- #5624
– exhibitions
– (1961) #1913
– exhibitions, group
– (1962) #1847
– (1967) #1916
– (1972) #1922
– (1981) #1885
– interview, on Royal Canadian Academy of
Arts #689
Goethals, Gregor, Amer artist, art historian,
1926-
– on the sacred in art #94
Gogh, Vincent van, Nl artist, 1853-1890
– influence on Alfred Pellan #6803
– influence on Emily Carr #5046
– influence on John Bernard Boyle #4894
Goguen, Jean, Can artist, 1927-
– exhibitions, group
– (1959) #1414
– (1968) #1263
– (1981) #1471
gold mines and mining
– photographic views, British Columbia,
Charles Wesley Mathers #6451
– views
– British Columbia
– (1860s) #2004
– Hind, William George Richardson
#5811
– Klondike Gold Rush of 1898 #2085
Goldberg, Michael (Mike), Can filmmaker,
1945-
– interview, on videos #5625
Goldhamer, Charles, Can artist, 1903-
– exhibitions, group
– (1981) #1117
– on his post as administrative artist, Royal
Canadian Air Force #1091
goldsmithing
– *see also* gilding; jewellery
goldsmithing, Canadian
– Burden, Eve and John #4957
– Nova Scotia
– 17th-19th cs. #2639
– 18th c.-1940s #2632
– Québec
– 17th-18th cs. #1327 2181 2664
– 18th c. #2673
– use of coins #2628
Gomez, Ricardo Vincente José (Ric), Can
sculptor, 1942-
– exhibitions
– (1977) #5626
Gonor, Allan B., Can physician, 20th c.

– and Allen Sapp #7123
Goodridge, Harold Barwick, Can artist,
1901-
– mural, Confederation Building (St. John's,
Nfld) #1140
Goodwin, Betty Roodish, Can artist, 1923-
#1504
– exhibitions
– (1976) #5629
– interview #5630
– *Passage in a Red Field* #714
– performance sculpture #658
– Rue Mentana project #1558 5631
– *Vest* and *Tarpaulin* series #5627 5628
Goold, F.P., & Co., ceramic manufacturer
(Brantford, Ont)
– bird designs #2335
Gordon, Hortense Mattice, Can artist,
1889-1961
– as student of Hans Hofmann #1850
Gordon, John Sloan, Can artist, 1868-1940
– illustrations #916
Gordon, Lee, Can filmmaker, 1926- #993
Gordon, Mary, Can artist, fl. 1955
– jewellery #2695
Gordon, Ronald, Can artist, fl. 1956
– stage designs and costumes, *Pantomime*,
Montreal Theatre Ballet #1410
Gordon S. Adamson & Associates, Can
architectural firm
– Toronto (Ont)
– St. Lawrence Centre for the Arts #9109
– William Wrigley Junior Co. Ltd.
Building #9343
– York University #9396 9469
– Winnipeg (Man), Winnipeg Art Gallery,
competition #9102
Gore, Tom, Can photographer, 1946- #2071
gorgets
– *see also* adornment
gorgets, Algonquian
– stonework #3406
gorgets, Indians of North America
– shellwork #3388
– trade silver #3440
gorgets, Iroquois
– trade silver #3536
gorgets, Seminole
– trade silver #3536
Gorin, Jean, Fr artist, 1899-
– relief structures #777
Goring, Trevor, Can artist, 1949-
– exhibitions, group
– (1976) #1529
Gorky, Arshile (Vosdanig Manoog Adoian),
Amer artist, 1904-1948
– influence on John Meredith #6516
– influence on Walter Tandy Murch #6662
Gorman, Richard Borthwick, Can artist,
1935- #5632
– and Ontario printmaking (1960s) #1756
– exhibitions, group
– (1967) #821
– on Gordon Rayner #6965
Goss, Andrew, Can jeweller, 1944- #2706
Goss, Arthur S., Can photographer,
1911-1940 #5634
– exhibitions
– (1980) #5633
Goss, Sandra, Can jeweller, 1946- #2706
Gosselin, F.Xavier, Can metalsmith, fl. 1842
#1301
Gosselin, Félix, Can metalsmith, fl. 1842
#1301

Gosselin, Gabriel, Can metalsmith, fl. 1842
#1301
Gosselin, Gabriel, Can silversmith,
1690-1769
– sculptures, Church of Saint-Pierre (île
d'Orléans, Qué) #8802
Gosselin, Gérard, Can artist, fl. 1974
– as member of Centre communautaire
catholique Tour de David
(Saint-Basile-le-Grand, Qué) #1510
Gosselin, Pierre, Can artist, 1953-
– on his art #1552
Gothic revival architecture
– Battleford (Sask), Fort Battleford #8484
– Belleville (Ont), Institution for the Deaf
and Dumb #8968
– Canada #7652 7668 7671 7724 7739 7740
– churches, Ontario #8904
– domestic architecture
– Canada #7696
– Ontario #8677
– Fuller, Thomas #8366
– Harris, William Critchlow #8372
– Kingston and Frontenac County (Ont)
#8015
– London (Ont), University of Western
Ontario #9442
– Medley, Edward Shuttleworth #8776
– Montréal (Qué) #1367
– Church of Notre-Dame #8828 8848
– New Brunswick #7808
– Ottawa (Ont) #8036
– Parliament Buildings #8921 8922 8925
– Regina (Sask), Legislative Buildings #8954
– Saint John (NB), stone church #8778
– Saskatoon (Sask), University of
Saskatchewan #9491
– St. Stephen (NB), Christ Church #8774
– Toronto (Ont)
– Cathedral of Saint Alban the Martyr
#8896
– Church of Saint Paul's #8897 8902
– University of Toronto
– Hart House #9433 9438
– Knox College #9435
– Yorkville Town Hall #8997
Gottlieb, Adolph, Amer artist, 1903-1974
– influence on Douglas Hector Haynes
#5758
– influence on Jack Hamilton Bush #4972
Gotto, Basil, Brit sculptor, 1866-1954
– St. John's (Nfld), Fighting
Newfoundlanders' Memorial #7783
Gottschalk, Fritz, Can artist, 1937-
– designs, Olympic Games (1976) #898
– prints #897
– typographic designs #932
Gottschalk & Ash, Can graphic design firm
#879 886
– corporate graphic image for Claude Neon
Ltd. #887
Gougeon, Diane, Can sculptor, 1955-
– concept of space #1631
– exhibitions
– (1980) #685
Gouinlock, George Wallace, Can architect,
1861-1932
– Toronto (Ont)
– Canadian National Exhibition buildings
#1 9206
– Gayety Theatre #9060
– Government House, competition #8748
– John Ross Robertson and Glenholme
schools, competition for #9437

Gould, John, Brit artist, ornithologist,
1804-1881
– Lansdowne, James Fenwick, compared
with #6163
Gould, John Howard, Can artist, 1929- #5635
– exhibitions
– (1979) #5637
– exhibitions, group
– (1965) #473
– (1978) #665
– films and drawings #5636
Gould & Harvey, Amer architectural firm
– Toronto (Ont), Masonic Temple,
competition #9062
Goulet, Claude, Can artist, 1925- #1542 1543
5638 5640
– exhibitions
– (1971) #5639
Goulet, Michel, Can sculptor, 1944-
– exhibitions
– (1980) #695
– *Leur instable XVI* #1627
– Symposium international de sculpture
environnementale de Chicoutimi (Qué),
(1980) #1639
Gouthro, Frederick Stephen (Steve), Can
artist, 1951-
– exhibitions, group
– (1981) #1908
Govan, Ferguson, Lindsay, Kaminker, Maw,
Langley, Keenleyside, Can architectural
firm
– Toronto (Ont), Hospital for Sick Children
#9028
government buildings
– *see* public buildings
Government of Ontario Art Collection
– *see* Ontario. Government of Ontario Art
Collection
Governors General of Canada
– medals #764
Gow, Isobel Dowler, Can artist, 1933- #1512
– exhibitions, group
– (1976) #1529
Gowans, Kent and Co., glass manufacturer
(Toronto, Ont)
– glass patterns (ca. 1914) #2411
Goya y Lucientes, Francisco José de, Sp
artist, 1746-1828
– Chambers, Jack, compared with #516
– influence on Tony Urquhart #7446
– influence on Walter Joseph Gerard
Bachinski #4578
Graff, Leslie Frederick (Les), Can artist,
1936-
– interview #5641
graffiti
– on sculptures, Yves Trudeau #7435
Grafton (Ont), Barnum House
– architecture #7959
Graham, Albert W., Can engraver, fl.
1858-1871
– print of portrait of James McGill #5321
Graham, Colin, Can artist, curator, 1915-
#5642
Graham, Dan, Can artist, 1942-
– exhibitions, group
– (1977) #631
– (1980) #690
Graham, John, Can sculptor, fl. 1827-1880
– woodcarvings, New Brunswick Museum
(Saint John, NB) #1187
Graham, Kay M., Can artist, 1913- #1803
1807 5643

– exhibitions, group
– (1974) #565
– (1981) #722
Graham, Kent, Can furniture-maker, fl. 1978
#2596
Graham, Robert, Can sculptor, fl. mid
19th-late 19th c.
– woodcarvings, New Brunswick Museum
(Saint John, NB) #1187
Graham, Robert, Jr., Can sculptor, fl. late
19th-early 20th c.
– woodcarvings, New Brunswick Museum
(Saint John, NB) #1187
grain elevators, Canadian #9237
– (1880-1914) #7736
– (1920s) #7657 9236
– in art, Robert Newton Hurley #5885
– Manitoba, 19th-early 20th cs. #8102
Granby (Qué), art gallery
– (1950s) #3034
Granche, Pierre, Can sculptor, 1948-
– concept of space #1631
– Symposium international de sculpture
environnementale de Chicoutimi (Qué),
(1980) #1639
Grand Bank (Nfld)
– architecture #7792
Grand Digue (NB), Hélène and Roma
Bourgeois House
– architecture #8547
Grand Falls (NB), Thomas Albert Senior
High School
– exhibitions
– *The Beaverbrook Art Gallery Presents Nine
New Brunswick Artists/La Galerie d'art
Beaverbrook présente neuf artistes du
Nouveau-Brunswick* (1973) #1182
Grand Falls (Nfld), Newfoundland
Government Centre
– architecture #7782
Grand Maison, Paul Mallepart de
– *see* Mallepart de Grand Maison (*dit*
Beaucour), Paul
Grand Pré (NS), Old Covenanter's House
– architecture #7823
Grand Rapids (Mich), Grand Rapids Public
Museum
– exhibitions
– *Beads: Their Use by Upper Great Lakes
Indians* (1977) #3635
Grand Trunk Pacific Railway
– railroad stations #9542 9545
– railroad stations, Manitoba #9543
Grand Trunk Railway
– Ottawa (Ont), Central Station and Château
Laurier #9528
– railroad stations #9538 9539
Grandbois, Alain, Can poet, 1900-1975
– influence on Alfred Pellan #6826
Grande Prairie (Alta)
– architecture, Douglas Joseph Cardinal
#8341
Granirer, Pnina, Can artist, 1935- #5644
– exhibitions
– (1976) #2059
Gransow, Helmut, Can artist, 1921- #5645
Grant, George William, Can architect,
1852-1925
– New Westminster (BC), Courthouse #9011
Grant, Ted, Can photographer, 1929-
– portfolio of photographs #995
Grant, Thomas J., Can army officer, fl.
1860s-1870s
– collection, photographic views of Canada,

19th c. #1048
Granville (NS), Amberman House
– architecture #7823
Granville Ferry (NS), Hall-Croscup House
– mural paintings, restoration #1223
Granville Ferry (NS), Port Royal Habitation
#7655
– architecture #7823 7849
– restoration #7812 7813
Graphic, Brit and Amer periodical
– illustrations, Henri Julien #5983 5984
graphic arts
– *see also* aquatint; colour printing;
commercial art; engraving; etching;
lithography; naval prints; posters;
printing; wood engraving
– (1970s) #824
– Arthur, Paul, on #859
– Fleming, Allan Robb, on #5456
– Ottawa (Ont), National Gallery of Canada
#3061
– Québec (Qué), Séminaire de Québec #3124
graphic arts, American
– television graphics (1980) #913
– Toronto (Ont), Royal Ontario Museum.
Sigmund Samuel Collection #3135
graphic arts, Canadian #925
– 17th-19th cs. #236
– 18th-19th cs. #812 828
– 19th-20th cs. #48
– 19th c. #838
– Volpi, Charles de, collection #3248
– 19th c.-1920s #11 14
– (1792-1850) #839
– (1840s-1920s) #4
– (1880s) #170
– (1900-1940) #28
– (1910-1960s), Canadian National
Exhibition (Toronto, Ont) #1
– (1910s) #916
– (1927), Canadian National Exhibition
(Toronto, Ont) #295
– (1930), Canadian National Exhibition
(Toronto, Ont) #313
– (1930s) #340
– (1931), Canadian Society of Graphic Art
#803
– (1938-1948) #379 809
– (1939), Canadian Society of Graphic Art
#346
– (1940s) #374 806 808 851
– (1950s) #429 437 813 814 855 860 869
– (1950s-1960s) #821
– (1960s) #486 487 817 818 819 820 867 868
– (1960s-1970s) #816
– (1965-1968) #874
– (1966-1968) #881
– (1967) #877
– (1969-1974) #823
– (1970s) #610 827 833 895 897 907
– (1980s) #912
– advertising
– 1880s-early 20th cs. #891
– (1890-1940) #846
– (1940s) #850 853
– (1950s) #858 861 865
– (1960s) #870
– (1970s) #886 888 894
– Art Directors' Club of Toronto #854
– Burns, Cooper, Hynes Ltd. #905 906
– Burns & Cooper Ltd. #892 896
– Burton Kramer Associates #889
– Carlton Studio (London, England) #843
– Cooper and Beatty Ltd. #5297

– Gerald Bern Agency #871
– Gottschalk & Ash #879 887
– Jacques Guillon Designers Inc. #884 2623
– Paul Arthur and Associates #873
– Alberta
  – (1950s-1973) #815
  – (1970s) #1951 1958
  – Edmonton (Alta), Alberta Art Foundation #1957
– beaver motif #23
– block prints #837
– Brant County (Ont), (1793-1930) #1684
– Canadian Society of Graphic Art #801
– Group of Seven #930
– guide for collectors #2101 2252
– Halifax (NS), (1749-1949) #1195
– hard-edge #832
– Kingston (Ont) #1680
– landscapes #132
  – (1970s) #595
– London (Ont), (1970s) #1812
– Manitoba #1895
– Montréal (Qué)
  – 20th c. #1648
  – (1940s-1960s) #1641
  – (1960s-1970s) #1652
  – atelier Arachel #1657
  – Atelier libre de recherches graphiques #1642
  – Design Collaborative Montreal Ltd. #878 882 885
  – Graff #1645 1658
  – Graphia #1660
  – Groupe Média Gravures et Multiples #1646
  – Guilde graphique #1647 1653 1655
  – McCord Museum. McGill University #840
  – Olympic Games (1976) #898 901 902 5858
– Montréal (Qué), Expo '67 #876
– New Brunswick
  – (1760-1880) #1189
  – (1970s) #1185
– Newfoundland
  – 19th c.-1950s #1139
  – (1970s) #1148 1149
  – (1980) #1159
– Nova Scotia (1970s) #1214
– Ontario
  – 19th c. #1720
  – (1960s) #1756
  – (1970s) #1806
– Ottawa (Ont), Public Archives of Canada. William H. Coverdale Collection #12 3230
– Print and Drawing Council of Canada #835
– Québec #1249 1258 1259
  – 17th-18th cs. #1320 1649
  – (1940-1980) #1665
  – (1940s-1970s) #1269
  – (1960s) #1643
  – (1967-1977), livres d'artistes #1659
  – (1970s) #1644 2228
    – figurative works #1651
  – (1974-1981), Société des graphistes du Québec #893
  – (1977-1981) #1533
  – and Albert Dumouchel #5325
  – and Rodolphe Duguay #5320
  – art market (1970s) #1656
  – as folk art #1291
  – automatism and Surrealism #1650

– Québec (Qué), Atelier de réalisations graphiques #1661
– realism #716 1810
– Society of Canadian Painter-Etchers and Engravers #3
– television and film graphics (1970s) #899
– television graphics
  – (1950s) #866
  – (1950s-1970s) #909
  – (1980) #913
– Toronto (Ont)
  – (1980) #1830
  – Brigdens Limited #883
  – Graphic Arts Club of Toronto #1711
  – Metro Toronto Public Library #3143
    – John Ross Robertson Historical Collection #3130 3131
  – Open Studio #1819 1833
  – Royal Ontario Museum. Sigmund Samuel Collection #3135 3140
– unlimited print editions (1970s) #834
– Val-David (Qué), Atelier de l'île #1664
– views of British Columbia (1513-1891) #2006
– views of Eastern Townships (Qué), (1832-1881) #1342
– views of Montréal (Qué), 16th-19th cs. #927
– views of Newfoundland
  – 18th-19th cs. #1150
  – (1497-1887) #1145
– views of Niagara Peninsula (Ont), (1697-1880) #1718
– views of Nova Scotia (1605-1878) #1203
– views of Ottawa (Ont), (1807-1882) #1716
– views of Québec (Qué), (1608-1875) #1349
– views of Toronto (Ont), (1813-1882) #1717
– western Canada
  – (1964-1970) #872
  – (1970s) #2059
– Winnipeg (Man)
  – (1970s) #1901
  – (1981) #1908
  – Grand Western Canadian Screen Shop #1902
– women artists (1970s) #936 1877
graphic arts, Carrier
– 'Ksan artists' cooperative #4129 4130
graphic arts, Gitksan
– 'Ksan artists' cooperative #4134
graphic arts, Haida
– and Tom Price #6932
graphic arts, Indians of North America #3381
– (1975-1977) #3373
graphic arts, Inuit #1294 3374 4200 4214 4229 4239 4465 4482 4493
– (1950s) #4311
– (1959-1968) #4479
– (1959-1969) #4471
– (1959-1972) #4478
– (1959-1976) #4490
– (1959-1980) #4498
– (1960s) #4463 4467
– (1970s) #4287
– (1977-1980) #4269
– Alaska #4217
– amautik subject #4300
– and Robert Allen Paterson #6778
– and shamanism #4488
– Baffin Island (NWT), Iqutaq Group, Clyde River #4499
– Baker Lake (NWT) #4241 4266 4473 4480
  – (1969-1973) #4481

– (1970-) #4472
– (1975-1977) #3373
– and Sheila and Jack Butler #4486
– biographical sources #4497
– Cape Dorset (NWT) #4192 4211 4299 4460 4461 4466 4476 4477 4483 4484 4500
  – (1960s) #4464
  – (1976-1977) #4491
  – and James Archibald Houston #4186 4462 4470
  – Burnaby (BC), Simon Fraser University. Simon Fraser Gallery #4495
– game and contest subjects #4492
– Holman (NWT) #3350 4197 4469
  – (1960s) #4195
– Inoucdjouac (Qué) #4267 4279 4487
– Montréal (Qué), Montreal Museum of Fine Arts #4474
– Pangnirtung (NWT), (1973-) #4485
– Povungnituk (Qué) #4219 4494 4496
  – (1962-) #4468
  – (1976) #4489
– Québec #4475
– symbolism #4234
– Toronto (Ont), York University. Art Gallery of York University #4228
– Toronto-Dominion Bank collection #4201 4248
– Winnipeg (Man), Winnipeg Art Gallery #4285
– women artists (1970s) #4260
graphic arts, Northwest Coast Indians #5269
– (1950s-1970s) #4162
– (1960s-1970s) #4166
Graphic Arts Club of Toronto (Toronto, Ont)
– and Canadian National Exhibition (Toronto, Ont), (1913) #1711
graphic arts technique
– see media and techniques, graphic arts
Graphica Club of Montreal (Montréal, Qué)
– exhibitions
  – (1967) #874
Graphis, Sw periodical
– and Paul Arthur #865
Graser, Toby, Can artist, 1937-
– interview #5646
Grassby, Percy, Brit artist in Canada, fl. 1915
– etchings #799
grasses
– as artistic medium, Labrador (Nfld), 20th c. #2945
grates
– see fireplaces
Grauer, Sherry, Can artist, 1939- #2053
– exhibitions
  – (1980) #5647
– exhibitions, group
  – (1975) #591
  – (1976) #2060
– exhibitions (reviews) #579
Grauerholz, Angela, Can photographer, 1952-
– exhibitions (reviews) #1067
Gravel, Charles, Can sculptor, 18th c.
– works, churches, Charlesbourg (Qué) #8851
Gravelot, Hubert François, Fr artist, 1699-1773
– maps of Canada #1323
graves
– see cemeteries
gravestones
– see sepulchral monuments

graveyards
– see cemeteries
Gray, John Warren, Can artist, 1824-1912 #5648
– exhibitions, group
  – (1969) #1180
– marine paintings #5649
Gray & Betts, ceramic manufacturer
  (London, Ont) #2350
Great Basin Indians
– culture #3986
Great Eastern Photographic and Advertising
  Company (Vancouver, Nanaimo, and
  Victoria, BC)
– (1880s) #2022
Great Lakes (Ont and Mich)
– lighthouses #9519
– pictographs, Algonquian #3583
– views
  – 18th-19th cs., Ottawa (Ont), Public
    Archives of Canada. William H.
    Coverdale Collection #12
  – Armstrong, William #4552
Great Whale River (Qué)
– graphic arts (1972-1975) #4475
Gréber, Jacques, Fr architect, 1917-1962
– plan, National Capital Region, Ottawa
  (Ont) #8034 8035 8039 8041 8045
Greco, El, Greek artist in Spain, 1541-1614
– influence on Jacques Godefroy de
  Tonnancour #7388
Greek architecture
– influence on William Perehudoff #6837
Greek revival architecture
– Ontario, churches #8904
Greek sculpture
– athletes, Robert Tait McKenzie on #6485
Green, Art, Can artist, 1941- #2053
– interview #5650
Green, Blankstein, Russell & Associates, Can
  architectural firm
– Ottawa (Ont), National Gallery of Canada
  #3035
  – competition #9079
– Winnipeg (Man)
  – City Hall, competition #8985 8986 8987
  – Green, Blankstein, Russell & Associates
    architects' office #9299
  – University of Manitoba. Saint Paul's
    College and Chapel of Christ the King
    #9486
Green, Daniel, Can furniture-maker, fl.
  1813-1821 #2517
Green, Frederick Walter, Can architect,
  1821-1877
– Victoria (BC) #8145
Green, Harold, Can photographer, 1917-
– portfolio of photographs #991 1032
Greenberg, Charles, Can architect, 1922-
– Brussels (Belgium), Canadian Pavilion,
  Universal and International Exhibition of
  1958 #419 430 9209 9211
Greenberg, Clement, Amer critic, 1909-
– and Emma Lake Workshops (Emma Lake,
  Sask) #1929 6317 6319
– and Painters Eleven #1785
– and William S. Ronald #7072
– influence on Jack Hamilton Bush #123
  4970 4972 4975
– Luke, Alexandra, on #6334
– on Marion F.S. Mackay Nicoll #6702
– on Red River Exhibition (1978) #1903
– theory of imagination, and Canadian art
  (1960s) #515
Greene, Thomas Garland, Can artist,

1875-1955
– illustrations #916
Greenhill, Ralph, Can photographer, 1924-
– photographic views, Toronto (Ont) #5651
Greenhow family, Can artists, 20th c.
– exhibitions, group
  – (1961) #1668
Greenland
– Inuit
  – culture #4315
  – sculpture #4206
Greenshields, Charles Glass, Can collector,
  1882-1974
– as founder of Elizabeth T. Greenshields
  Memorial Foundation #466
Greensides, Harold C., Can architect,
  1904-1969
– Montréal (Qué), Queen Elizabeth Hotel
  #9286
– winner, Ontario Government Housing
  Competition (1936) #8737
Greenspoon, Freedlander & Dunne, Can
  architectural firm
– Montréal (Qué)
  – Place Victoria #9195
  – Temple Emmanu-El #8840
Greenspoon, Henry Eli, Can architect, 1909-
– Montréal (Qué) and Toronto (Ont), Odeon
  theatres #9078
Greenstone, Marion, Can artist, 1925- #5652
Greer, John Sydney, Can artist, 1944-
– exhibitions
  – (1974) #5653
  – (1981) #5654
– exhibitions, group
  – (1974) #574
– exhibitions (reviews) #1208 1227
– prints #1214
greeting cards, Canadian
– (1920s) #4
– Christmas motifs
  – (1920s) #845
    – Canadian Artists' Series #844
  – (1920s-1950s) #863
    – nativity theme #393
  – (1940s), Avis Selina Fyshe, on #849
  – late 19th c. #842 890
– sporting subjects, Bennet & Co. #2360
Grégoire, Normand, Can photographer,
  filmmaker, 1944- #990 997 999 1556 1562
  5655
– portfolio of photographs #987
Gregor, Helen Frances, Can tapestry artist,
  1921- #5656
– exhibitions, group
  – (1981) #2776
– exhibitions (reviews) #2771
Gregory, J.Fraser, Can lumber merchant, b.
  ca. 1841
– residence, Saint John (NB) #8545
Gregory, Joan Steeves, Can artist, fl. 1977
– drawings, Albert County (NB) landmarks
  #5657
Gregson, Sally, Can artist, 1939-
– exhibitions
  – (1976) #5658
– exhibitions, group
  – (1979) #2075
– exhibitions (reviews) #2072
Grey Glass, ceramic manufacturer (London,
  Ont) #2350
Grey Nuns
– Montréal (Qué), architecture and art #8862
Greyson, John, Can artist, 1960-

– books #940
– exhibitions, group
  – (1980) #687
Grice, Arthur D. (Art), Can photographer,
  1942- #5659
– portfolio of photographs #991 996 998
Grice, Emily, Can photographer, fl. 1976
  #5659
grids
– in art
  – Knudsen, Chris #6070
  – Martin, Ron #6432
  – Smith, Gordon Appelbe #7227
Grier, Edmund Wyly, Can artist, 1862-1957
  #17 1713 5660 5661
– debate with A.Y. Jackson, Empire Club
  (Toronto, Ont) #5923
– exhibitions (reviews) #1703 1710
– on views, Peel County (Ont), William
  Perkins Bull Collection #3208
Grier, Eldon Brockwill, Can artist, 1917-
– exhibitions, group
  – (1978) #649
Grierson, John, Can filmmaker, 1898-1972
– and documentary photography #1056
– influence on Norman McLaren #6493
Grierson & Walker, Can architectural firm
– Charlottetown (PEI), Confederation
  Centre, competition #9088
– Toronto (Ont), Grierson & Walker
  architects' office #9299
Griffith, Julius Edward Lindsay, Can artist,
  1912-
– on printmaking #817
Griffiths, James, Can artist, 1814-1896 #2305
Griffiths, John Howard, Can artist,
  1826-1897 #2305
Grimsby (Ont), Grimsby Public Library and
  Art Gallery
– exhibitions
  – Of Human Bondage (1976) #611
Grip, Can newspaper
– and John Wilson Bengough #942 943 4673
  4674 4677
– illustrations #14
Grip Limited, publishing firm (Toronto,
  Ont)
– and Group of Seven #1766
– headquarters, Graphic Arts Building
  (Toronto, Ont) #9330
gristmills
– see mills
Grizzly Bear Dance, Blackfoot #3681
Grobb, John, Can furniture-maker, b. 1800
  #2571
Grobb, Moses, Can weaver, b. 1806, fl.
  1853-1872 #2723
Grondin, Jean-Luc, Can artist, 1938- #5662
Groningen (Netherlands), Groningen
  Museum
– exhibitions
  – Moderne canadese schilderkunst (1959) #431
Gros Ventre Indians
– costume #3753
– culture #3651
Grossman, Irving, Can architect, 1926-
– Montréal (Qué), Administration and Press
  Building, Expo '67 #9301
– Toronto (Ont)
  – architect's office and apartment
    residence #9299
  – Edgeley in the Village #8520
  – Flemingdon Park #7683 8370 8514 8657
  – synagogues #8903

grotesque in art
– Prent, Mark #6920
Group of Seven #5 14 24 28 45 52 66 97 289
   374 412 461 507 1667 1735 1738 1740 1743
   1760 1766 1768 1774 1777 1784 1789 1790
– (1920s) #309 1737
– (1924), British Empire Exhibition
   (Wembley, England) #458
– (1930s) #336 502 1234
– and A.Y. Jackson #5912 5915 5917 5918
   5923
– and Alan Caswell Collier #5131
– and Alexandra Luke #6333 6334
– and Alfred Joseph Casson #5056 5058 5060
– and Alice A. Innes #5900
– and Anne Douglas Savage #7131
– and Arthur Lismer #6293 6296 6298 6300
   6301
– and Barker Fairley #5404 5405
– and Bertram Richard Brooker #4925 4926
   4927
– and Canadian art (1940s) #375
– and Canadian Art Club #214
– and Canadian Group of Painters #324
– and Canadian painting #456
– and Carl Fellman Schaefer #7155 7156
– and Catharine Robb Whyte and Peter
   Whyte #7571
– and Charles William Jefferys #5956 5958
– and David Brown Milne #6551
– and Emily Carr #5025 5030 5034
– and Franklin Carmichael #5001
– and Frederick Horsman Varley #7462 7463
– and Goodridge Roberts #7050
– and Impressionism #227
– and J.E.H. MacDonald #6361 6369
– and Jock Macdonald #6375 6379
– and Lawren Stewart Harris #1744 1754
   5720
– and Lionel LeMoine FitzGerald #5450
– and Marion F.S. Mackay Nicoll #6703
– and Maurice Galbraith Cullen #5223
– and modernism #319
– and National Gallery of Canada (Ottawa,
   Ont) #3025
– and nationalism in art #102 109 327 338
   354 378 495
– and nature in art #496
– and Picture Loan Society (Toronto, Ont)
   #1758
– and Québec painting (1930s) #1460
– and Robert Gray Murray #613
– and Thoreau MacDonald #6384
– and Tom Thomson #7357 7363 7369
– and Toni Onley #613
– Arctic trips #1779
– Bergeron, Suzanne, compared with #4707
– book illustration and design #928 939
– Carr, Emily and Morrice, James Wilson,
   compared with #352
– drawings #1736 1755
– Ewen, Paterson, compared with #5385
– exhibitions
   – (1920) #286
   – (1920-1922, 1925-1926, 1928, 1930-1931)
      #1732
   – (1954) #1747
   – (1958) #429
   – (1969) #3229
   – (1974) #1861
   – (1976) #1778
   – (1977) #1780 1781 1782
   – (1980) #156
– exhibitions (reviews)

– (1920) #1767
– (1926) #1734
– (1927) #298
– (1932) #1739
– forgeries, Ward-Price Galleries (Toronto,
   Ont), (1962) #64
– Heidelberg (Australia) artists, compared
   with #44
– illustrations
   – Canadian Forum #930
   – Farmer's Magazine #1765
– influence of Scandinavian art #1788
– influence on Canadian painting #57 300
   342 345 379 380 397 406 424
– Lecor, Tex, compared with #6184
– Loveroff, Frederick Nicholas, compared
   with #6331
– MacCallum, James Metcalfe, as patron
   #3237
– McLean, Tom, compared with #6503
– Milne, David Brown, compared with
   #6549
– Phillips, Walter Joseph, compared with
   #6858
– posters #911
– support of #1763 1764
   – Gurd, Norman I., and Sarnia Art
      Movement #1776
– use of colour #347
– views
   – Charlevoix (Qué) #1280
   – Georgian Bay (Ont) #1745
– works
   – Doig Art Collection of Manitoba #3224
   – Kleinburg (Ont), McMichael Canadian
      Collection #1783 3164
   – McLean, J.S., collection #3228
   – Poole, Ernest Edward, collection #3217
   – Toronto (Ont)
      – Ontario Heritage Foundation.
         Firestone Art Collection #3239
      – University of Toronto. Hart House
         #3134 3137
      – University of Toronto. University
         College #3151
Groupe d'action photographique (GAP)
   (Montréal, Qué)
– (1970s) #1003 1494
Groupe Média Gravures et Multiples
   (Montréal, Qué)
– (1969-1973) #1646
– exhibitions (reviews)
   – (1970) #1490
Groupes du Nouvel-Age #1502
Grünewald, Matthias, Ger artist, ca.
   1480-1528
– influence on Tom La Pierre #6122
Guderna, Ladislav, Can artist, 1921- #5663
Guelph (Ont)
– architecture, 19th c. #7970
– art #1685
– photography (1856-1867) #1724
– views
   – Kennedy, David Johnston #6040 6041
Guelph (Ont), City Hall
– architecture, William Thomas #8413
Guelph (Ont), Guelph General Hospital
– architecture #9029
Guelph (Ont), Guelph Military Convalescent
   Hospital (formerly Ontario Reformatory)
– architecture #9016
Guelph (Ont), Macdonald Consolidated
   School (now Macdonald Stewart Art
   Centre)

– architecture, George Martel Miller #3176
Guelph (Ont), Macdonald Stewart Art
   Centre
– architecture, George Martel Miller;
   renovation, Raymond Moriyama #3176
– exhibitions
   – Ivan Eyre Exposition (1981) #5394
   – Painters Eleven in Retrospect (1981) #1785
   – Realism: Structure and Illusion: Toward a
      Definition of Representational Art (1981)
      #716
   – Water Colours by E.May Martin (1980)
      #6424
Guelph (Ont), University of Guelph
– exhibitions
   – Lithographs/Lithographies (1972) #825
Guelph (Ont), University of Guelph. Art
   Gallery
– collection #3173
– exhibitions
   – Canada in the Victorian Image, 1837-1887
      (1975) #253
   – Centennial Exhibition of Quebec and
      Ontario Contemporary Painters, 1967
      (1967) #484
   – Ed Bartram: 10 Years (1980) #4618
   – Five Years of Robert Downing, 1966-1971
      (1972) #5306
   – Imprint '76 (1977) #833
   – Lillian Freiman: Paintings and Drawings
      (1978) #5518
   – Realism: Emulsion and Omission (1972)
      #545
   – The Ontario Community Collects: A Survey
      of Canadian Painting from 1766 to the
      Present (1976) #120
   – Trésors d'art populaire québécois/Folk Art
      Treasures of Quebec (1981) #1297
   – Visitors, Exiles and Residents: Guelph
      Artists Since 1827 (1977) #1685
– video art, by faculty and students (1973)
   #553
Guelph (Ont), University of Guelph. Arts
   Building
– architecture, Hancock, Little, Calvert
   Associates; Sert, Jackson #9468
Guelph (Ont), University of Guelph. Library
   Building
– architecture, Hancock, Little, Calvert
   Associates; Sert, Jackson #9468
Guelph (Ont), University of Guelph.
   McLaughlin Library
– exhibitions
   – 19th and 20th Century Canadian Paintings
      from the Art Gallery of Hamilton (1974)
      #3159
   – Video Circuits: An Exhibition on the Theme
      of Videotape as Art (1973-1974) #553
Guernon (dit Belleville), François, Can
   sculptor, ca. 1755-ca. 1789
– woodcarvings, Calvary at Oka (Oka, Qué)
   #1355 1356
guidebooks
– Quebec and Its Environs (1831), attributed
   to James Pattison Cockburn #5129
Guilde canadienne des métiers d'art Québec
– see Canadian Guild of Crafts
   Quebec/Guilde canadienne des métiers
   d'art Québec
Guillaume, Janine Leroux
– see Leroux-Guillaume, Janine
Guillon, Jacques S., Can designer, 1922-
   #2471
– and Jacques Guillon Designers Inc. #884

Guimond, Daniel, Can artist, fl. 1978
– performance art #655
Guimond, Pierre, Can photographer, 1946-
#5664
Guimons, Jean, Can photographer, fl. 1971
#997
Guindon, Arthur, Can artist, 1864-1923
– paintings of Iroquois legends #5665
Guité, Suzanne, Can sculptor, 1927-1981
#5666 5668
– exhibitions
– (1977) #5669
– exhibitions (reviews) #1400
– mural, palais de justice, New Carlisle
(Qué) #5667
Guité, Thérèse, Can artist, 1930-1981
– batik #2741
Gulf Hazard (NWT)
– copper amulet, Dorset #4365
Gundry & Langley, Can architectural firm
– Toronto (Ont), Government House #8753
Gunnlogsson & Nielsen, Danish
architectural firm
– Toronto (Ont), City Hall and Civic Square,
competition #8981
guns
– see firearms
Gunterman, Ida Madeline Warner (Mattie),
Can photographer, 1872-1945 #2018 5670
5672
– exhibitions
– (1977) #5671
– exhibitions, group
– (1976) #2012
Gurd, Norman I., Can art patron, 1870-1943
– and Sarnia Art Movement #1776
Gurdjieff, Georgei Ivanovitch, Russ mystic,
ca. 1877-1949
– influence on Alexandra Luke #6334
Gurnett, George, Can politician, magistrate,
ca. 1792-1861
– portrait, Paul Kane #3178
Gusella, Ernest, Can artist, 1941-
– video art #616
Gustafson, Anna, Can artist, 1952-
– exhibitions, group
– (1978) #2067
– stained glass, Coquitlam Centre
(Vancouver, BC) #2459
Gutiérrez, José, Mexican artist, 1900-1968
– as teacher of Réal Bérard #4692
Gutsche, Clara, Can photographer, 1949-
– documentary photographs #1556
– exhibitions
– (1980) #5673
– portfolio of photographs #1053
Guyana
– views by French explorers #276
Guyon, Jean, Fr priest, artist in Canada,
1659-1687 #228 229 1363
Gwaytihl, Can sculptor, d. 1912 #3862 4169
gypsoteche
– see plaster casts

H

H. Gagnier Ltd.
– see Gagnier, H., Ltd.
H.H. Martyn & Co.
– see Martyn, H.H., & Co.
H'Kusam (BC)

– architecture and totem poles, Haida
Indians #3913
Haacke, Hans Christoph, Ger artist, 1936-
– museum theme #714
habit
– see religious costume
Haddon, Jim, Can photographer, fl. 1981
– portfolio of photographs #1023
Hadley, Glen, Can architect, 1934-
– Charlottetown (PEI), Confederation
Centre, competition #9088
Haeffely, Claude, Can photographer, 1927-
#5674
– poems, for drawings by Louis-Pierre
Bougie #4861
Haeseker, Alexandra (Sandy), Can artist,
1945-
– exhibitions, group
– (1975) #1867
– (1979) #674
– (1980) #698
– interview #5675
Hagan, Frederick, Can artist, 1918- #5676
Hagarty, Clara Sophia, Can artist, 1871-1958
– exhibitions (reviews) #1703
Hahn, Emanuel Otto, Can sculptor,
1881-1957 #5677 5679 5680
– and Canadian sculpture #741
– as husband of Elizabeth Wyn Wood #5678
– design, 1935 Canadian silver dollar #5681
Haida Indians
– architecture #4021
– architecture and totem poles #3913 3979
3982 4118
– argillite carving #3419 3868 3890 3901 3958
4006 4010 4016 4042 4051 5088 5138 5361
– art #3946 3966 4011 4169
– 19th c. #4070
– (1970s) #4145
– moon image #4059
– canoes #3825
– containers #4066
– 19th c. #3985
– coppers #3821 4054
– culture
– (1870s) #3761
– (1880s) #3763
– (1905-1909) #3780
– funerary art #3995
– gambling pegs, 19th c. #3915
– graphic arts #6932
– headgear #4019
– masks #3794 3961
– photographs of, Edward Sheriff Curtis
#3399
– pipes #4047
– pipes and spoons #3782
– rattles #4026
– sculpture #3904 4040 4041 4116
– late 19th c. #3862
– silver #5358
– totem poles #3765 3766 3775 3943 4008
4067 4124
hair
– human, in Tlingit shamanic art #3917
Hale, Catherine, Can sculptor, 1927-
– fibreworks #5682
Haliburton, Thomas Chandler, Can writer,
judge, 1796-1865
– on Maritimes household wares and
furnishings #2147
Haliburton (Ont)
– decorative arts #2258
Haliburton (Ont), Haliburton School of Fine

Arts #2258
Haliburton County (Ont)
– architecture, John H. Billing #8335
Halifax (NS)
– architecture #7816 8317
– 18th-19th cs. #7818
– 19th c. #7826
– (1750s-1930s) #7839
– (1960s) #7698
– downtown area #7819
– Granville Street #7817
– Hydrostone area (1920s) #7839
– Lang, George Macdonald #7838
– Prince Street and Hollis Street buildings,
19th c. #7831
– waterfront buildings, 19th c. #7822 7824
7825 7834
– architecture and historic sites #7830
– art
– (1749-1949) #1195
– (1830s) #1226
– (1950s-1970s) #131
– (1970s) #1208
– (1980s) #1227
– art galleries (1960s) #442
– bottles (1836-1947) #2428
– city planning #1119
– conservation of architecture #7833
– Martello towers #8416
– painting (1815-1867) #1217
– photographic views (1850-1900) #1061
– photography (1830s-1860s) #1211
– urban development #7835
– video art #605
– views
– Lyttleton, Westcott Whitchurch Lewis
#6349
– Short, Richard #249 250
Halifax (NS), All Saints' Cathedral
– architectural proposal, William Critchlow
Harris #8371
– architecture, Cram, Goodhue & Ferguson
#8773
Halifax (NS), Anna Leonowens Gallery
– see Halifax (NS), Nova Scotia College of
Art and Design. Anna Leonowens Gallery
Halifax (NS), Art Gallery of Nova Scotia
– exhibitions
– Acadia Nova – 15 Artists (1980) #1136
– An Exhibition of Canadian Gameboards of
the 19th & 20th Centuries from Ontario,
Quebec & Nova Scotia (1981) #2597
– Annapolis Valley; Seven Artists 1980
(1980) #1221
– Art populaire de la Nouvelle-Ecosse: une
exposition itinérante d'art populaire de la
Nouvelle-Ecosse du XXe siècle (1977)
#1206
– Charles Wm. MacDonald: Seaman,
Labourer, Artist, Manufacturer (1874-1967)
(1980) #6355
– Charlotte Lindgren: Fibre Structures (1980)
#6282
– Claude Breeze (1978) #4911
– David Bolduc: Recent Work (1980) #4775
– Don Pentz: An Exhibition of Paintings and
Drawings (1979) #6830
– Felicity Redgrave (1979) #6967
– Folk Art of Nova Scotia: A Travelling
Exhibition of 20th Century Folk Art of
Nova Scotia (1976) #1207
– Joe Sleep Retrospective (1981) #7219
– John Greer: Sculptural Objective,
1968-1981; Everything Always Changes

but Something Still Remains (1981) #5654
- Looking South (1978) #4278
- Miller Brittain - Painter (1981) #4922
- Painters Eleven in Retrospect (1981) #1785
- Robert Field 1769-1819 (1978) #5432
- Roger Savage (1979) #7135
- Scottish Painting Canada (1978) #133
- The Murray and Marguerite Vaughan Inuit
  Print Collection/Collection d'estampes inuit
  (1982) #4498
- The New Brunswick Landscape Print:
  1760-1880 (1980) #1189
- Yves Gaucher & Christopher Pratt (1977)
  #643
- exhibitions (reviews)
  - Folk Art of Nova Scotia: A Travelling
    Exhibition of 20th Century Folk Art of
    Nova Scotia (1976) #1210 1213
  - MacKeeman, Karl (1977) #6389
Halifax (NS), Bank of Nova Scotia
- architecture #7839
  - Lyle, John MacIntosh #8226 9186 9203
  - Lyle, John MacIntosh; Cobb, Andrew
    Randall, Associate Architect #9182
Halifax (NS), Barrington Street
- architecture #7840
Halifax (NS), Black-Binney House
- architecture and interior #8548
Halifax (NS), Cambridge Library
- architecture #7839
Halifax (NS), Centennial Art Gallery
- exhibitions
  - A Selection of Works by Women Artists in
    Nova Scotia, 1850-1950 (1975) #1204
  - Adrien Hébert: trente ans de son oeuvre,
    1923-1953/Adrien Hébert: Thirty Years of
    His Art, 1923-1953 (1972) #5763
  - Albert Franck (1899-1973) in Retrospect: A
    Small Selection from the Artist's Collection
    (1973) #5500
  - Watercolour Painters from
    Saskatchewan/Aquarellistes de la
    Saskatchewan (1972) #1920
Halifax (NS), Crimean Memorial
- architecture #7839
Halifax (NS), Dalhousie Art Gallery
- see Halifax (NS), Dalhousie University.
  Dalhousie Art Gallery
Halifax (NS), Dalhousie University
- architecture #7830
  - Darling, Frank, Thomas Hayton
    Mawson, Andrew Randall Cobb #9408
  - planning, Thomas Hayton Mawson #9405
Halifax (NS), Dalhousie University.
  Dalhousie Art Gallery
- exhibitions
  - Bruce Parsons: A Model of Reality/Bruce
    Parsons: un modèle de la réalité (1976)
    #6772
  - Carl Schaefer in Hanover (1980) #7157
  - Carol Fraser Paintings and Drawings:
    1967-1977 (1977) #5507
  - Claude Tousignant (1974) #7401
  - Dalhousie Drawing Exhibition (1976-) #607
  - Daniel Fowler of Amherst Island,
    1810-1894 (1979) #5491
  - Decorated Nova Scotia Furnishings (1978)
    #2514
  - Douglas Bentham "Enclosures and Opens"
    1975/76 (1976) #4683
  - Drawings by Jack Weldon Humphrey: A
    Travelling Exhibition Organized by the
    Beaverbrook Art Gallery, Fredericton, New
    Brunswick, Canada, 1977-1979 (1979)

#5871
- Early Nova Scotia Quilts and Coverlets
  (1981) #2807
- Elizabeth S. Nutt: Heart and Head and
  Hand; Paintings from Nova Scotia
  Collections (1981) #6730
- Frank Nulf (1975) #6727
- Fritz Brandtner 1896-1969: A Retrospective
  Exhibition (1971) #4903
- Gerald Ferguson: Paintings (1977) #5420
- Gift from the Douglas M. Duncan
  Collection and the Milne-Duncan
  Bequest/Le Don provenant de la collection
  Douglas M. Duncan et le legs
  Milne-Duncan (1971) #541
- Graham Coughtry: Retrospective (1976)
  #5190
- In Video (1977) #631
- J.W. Beatty, 1869-1941 (1981) #4638
- Joe Norris: Paintings and Furniture (1978)
  #6720
- Joe Plaskett and His Paris: In Search of
  Time Past (1973) #6893
- Joe Plaskett et son Paris: à la recherche d'un
  temps passé (1973) #6894
- Kostyniuk: Relief Structures, 1969-1972
  (1973) #6079
- Lawren P. Harris 37/72 (1972) #5711
- Louis Comtois: Paintings, 1974-1979 (1980)
  #5164
- Louis de Niverville (1978) #6709
- Messages from Southern Saskatchewan
  (1976) #1930
- Metamorphosis, Memories, Dreams and
  Reflections: The Work of Florence Vale
  (1981) #7453
- Peter Kolisnyk (1977) #6075
- Sceptical Art Works at the Killam (1974)
  #5653
- Stephen Cruise (1976) #5213
- Susan Schelle: Recent Work (1981) #7160
- Terence Johnson: Forts (1981) #5969
- The Canadian Canvas: A Travelling
  Exhibition of 85 Recent Paintings/Peintres
  canadiens actuels: exposition itinérante de
  85 oeuvres récentes (1975) #588
- The Contemporary Arts Society: Montreal
  1939-1948/La Société d'art contemporain:
  Montréal 1939-1948 (1981) #1474
- exhibitions (reviews)
  - Fischl, Eric #662
  - Hammock, Virgil (1978) #5696
  - Lawren P. Harris 37/72 (1972) #5712
  - Louis de Niverville (1978) #6711
  - Shirley, James #1208
  - Six from Halifax (1981) #1227
  - The Canadian Canvas: A Travelling
    Exhibition of 85 Recent Paintings/Peintres
    canadiens actuels: exposition itinérante de
    85 oeuvres récentes (1975) #582
Halifax (NS), Dalhousie University. Killam
  Library
- architecture, Leslie R. Fairn & Associates
  #9052
- exhibitions (reviews)
  - Sleep, Joseph #1208
Halifax (NS), Eye Level Gallery
- (1975-1976) #1209
- exhibitions (reviews)
  - Cohen, Sorel #5130
Halifax (NS), Gorsebrook House
- architecture #8528
Halifax (NS), Government House
- architecture #7839

- Hildrith, Isaac #8374 8750 8754
Halifax (NS), Grand Parade
- architecture #7839
Halifax (NS), Halifax Citadel
- architecture #8431 8432 8438 8440
  - (1906-1951) #8430
  - doors and windows #8441
  - south magazine #8433
  - west front #8434
Halifax (NS), Halifax International Airport.
  Air Terminal Building
- architecture, Gilleland & Strutt; C.D.
  Davidson & Co.; William Alexander
  Ramsay #9515
Halifax (NS), Halifax Memorial Library
- exhibitions
  - Nova Scotia Society of Artists #1192
  - The Development of Canadian Painting: As
    Illustrated by Pictures Lent by Individuals
    and Institutions (1951) #47
Halifax (NS), Halifax Public Gardens
- decorative ironwork, late 19th c. #2710
Halifax (NS), Little Dutch Church
- architecture #7839
Halifax (NS), Lord Nelson Hotel
- exhibitions
  - Nova Scotia Society of Artists #1192
Halifax (NS), Manuge Gallery
- (1975-1979) #3244
Halifax (NS), Maritime Museum of the
  Atlantic #3074
Halifax (NS), Mechanics' Institute
- and Nova Scotia Museum #3071
Halifax (NS), Mount Saint Vincent
  University. Art Gallery
- collection #3072
- exhibitions
  - A Terrible Beauty: The Art of Canada at
    War (1978) #1111
  - Ann Kipling: Recent Landscapes (1980)
    #6057
  - Beauté tragique: les deux conflits mondiaux
    vus par des artistes canadiens (1978) #1112
  - Canadian Political Cartoons (1977) #956
  - Canadians: A National Photography Show
    about People/Canadiens: exposition
    nationale de photographie ayant les gens
    comme thème (1978) #1035
  - De grandes espérances: la vision européenne
    en Nouvelle-Ecosse, 1749-1848 (1980)
    #1220
  - Great Expectations: The European Vision in
    Nova Scotia, 1749-1848 (1980) #1222
  - L'art du paysage au Québec,
    1800-1940/Landscape Painting in Québec,
    1800-1940 (1978) #1286
  - Manitoba Mainstream: People's Art/Fine
    Art/Le Grand Courant du Manitoba: arts
    populaires, beaux-arts (1973) #1897
  - Some Nova Scotia Women Artists (1975)
    #1205
  - Survival Atlantic Style: Works by 16
    Artists from the Atlantic Provinces (1979)
    #1133
  - The Portrait Sculpture of Doris M. Judah
    (1980) #5980
  - Tim Zuck: Paintings (1981) #7636
- exhibitions (reviews)
  - Canadians: A National Photography Show
    about People/Canadiens: exposition
    nationale de photographie ayant les gens
    comme thème (1978) #1055
  - Great Expectations: The European Vision in
    Nova Scotia, 1749-1848 (1980) #1224 1225

– Greer, John #1208
– *Survival Atlantic Style: Works by 16 Artists from the Atlantic Provinces* (1979) #1135
Halifax (NS), Mount Uniacke House
– architecture, John Merrick #8528
Halifax (NS), Neptune Theatre (formerly Garrick Theatre)
– architecture and restoration, John Wray #9097
Halifax (NS), Nova Scotia College of Art
– (1880s-1960s) #2993
– exhibitions
– Nova Scotia Society of Artists #1192
– Nutt, Elizabeth Styring, as principal #1194
– Savage, Roger, as student #7136
Halifax (NS), Nova Scotia College of Art and Design
– (1887-1977) #3014
– (1970s) #3003
– and Art Green #5650
– architecture #9409 9410
– Askevold, David, as teacher #4566
– conference session, on Canadian art funding (1979) #3293
– exhibitions
– *Conceptual Decorative: Prints by Les Levine, 1965-1970/Conceptuel décoratif: estampes de Les Levine, 1965-1970* (1971) #6265
– *Lithographs/Lithographies* (1972) #825
– *Trans VSI Connection NSCAD-NETCO* (1969) #524
– Lithography Workshop #830
– photography (1970s) #1134
– video art #550
– (1970s) #575
– (1973), faculty and students #553
Halifax (NS), Nova Scotia College of Art and Design. Anna Leonowens Gallery
– exhibitions
– *The Canadian Canvas: A Travelling Exhibition of 85 Recent Paintings/Peintres canadiens actuels: exposition itinérante de 85 oeuvres récentes* (1975) #588
– exhibitions (reviews)
– *The Canadian Canvas: A Travelling Exhibition of 85 Recent Paintings/Peintres canadiens actuels: exposition itinérante de 85 oeuvres récentes* (1975) #582
Halifax (NS), Nova Scotia Museum #3071
– exhibitions
– *Elitekey: Micmac Material Culture from 1600 A.D. to the Present* (1980) #3643
– furniture #2484
– Holder, Thomas Cook, and Henry Arthur, furniture #2505
Halifax (NS), Nova Scotia Technical College. School of Architecture
– architectural education (1970s) #8285
Halifax (NS), Nova Scotia Technical College. Student residence
– architecture, Duffus, Romans, Kundzins & Rounsefell #9467
Halifax (NS), Point Pleasant Park
– decorative ironwork, late 19th c. #2710
Halifax (NS), Prince's Lodge. Music Room
– architecture #7839
Halifax (NS), Province House
– architecture #7839
Halifax (NS), Queen Elizabeth High School
– exhibitions
– *200 Years of Art in Halifax: An Exhibition Prepared in Honour of the Bicentenary of the Founding of the City of Halifax, N.S., 1749-1949* (1949) #1195
Halifax (NS), Royal Artillery Park
– architecture #7839
Halifax (NS), Saint George's Church
– architecture #7839
Halifax (NS), Saint Mary's University. Art Gallery
– exhibitions
– *George Rackus: Anodized Aluminum Works & Prints* (1973) #6953
– exhibitions (reviews)
– Society of Canadian Artists (1976) #1208
Halifax (NS), Saint Mary's University. Library
– architecture, C.A. Fowler and Company #9046
Halifax (NS), Saint Mary's University. Student residence
– architecture, Tampold & Wells #8744
Halifax (NS), Saint Paul's Burial Ground
– architecture #7839
Halifax (NS), Scotia Square
– architecture and urban development #9302
Halifax (NS), State Building of Nova Scotia
– exhibitions (reviews)
– Royal Canadian Academy of Arts (1881) #168
Halifax (NS), Technical University of Nova Scotia
– architectural education (1980) #8289
Halifax (NS), Victoria School of Art and Design
– and Nova Scotia College of Art (Halifax, NS) #2993
– and Nova Scotia College of Art and Design (Halifax, NS) #3014
Halifax (NS), West House, Brunswick Street
– architecture #8537
Halifax Monthly Magazine, Can periodical
– exhibition reviews (1830-1831) #1226
Hall, Benjamin, Can photographer, fl. 1856-1867 #1724
Hall, Hezekiah, Can photographer, fl. 1856-1867 #1724
Hall, John, Can artist, 1943-
– exhibitions
– (1979) #5683
– (1981) #5686
– exhibitions (reviews) #5684
– interview #5685
– Lindner, Ernest, compared with #1860
Hall, Joice, Can artist, 1943- #717
– exhibitions, group
– (1975) #1867
Hall, Sydney Prior, Can artist, 1842-1922
– views, western Canada #931
Hall, William, Brit naval officer in Canada, fl. 1804
– Québec (Qué), Cathedral of the Holy Trinity #8786
Hallam, Joseph Sydney, Can artist, 1889-1953 #5687
hallmarks
– on Indian trade silver #2629
hallmarks, Canadian
– on silver #2627 2633 2635
– Atlantic provinces #2640
– Québec #2664
– on silver and gold, Nova Scotia #2632
Hamada, Shoji, Ja ceramicist, 1894-1978
– influence on Wayne G. Ngan #6695
Hamann, George Frederick, Can architect, 1928-
– and Bregman & Hamann #8337
Hamasaki, Kazuo, Can artist, 1925- #5688
Hambidge, Jay, Can artist, 1867-1924
– illustrations #916
Hamburg (West Germany), Ernst Barlach Haus-Stiftung Reemtsma
– exhibitions
– *Group of Seven: Kanadische Landschafts-Maler: Eine Wanderausstellung der McMichael Canadian Collection, Kleinburg, Ontario, Kanada* (1977) #1781
Hamburg (West Germany), Galerie der Buchhandlung Berens
– exhibitions
– *Skulpturen Kanadischer Inuit* (1980) #4451
Hamburg (West Germany), Museum für Völkerkunde
– exhibitions
– *Donnervogel und Raubwal: Die Indianische Kunst der Nordwestküste Nordamerikas,*(1979) #4036
Hamel, Eugène, Can artist, 1845-1932
– influence of Théophile Hamel #5690
– paintings, Université Laval (Québec, Qué) #3078
Hamel, Théophile, Can artist, 1817-1870 #258 259 1315 1318 1323 1336 5689 5690 5691
– and Napoléon Bourassa #4874
– and Québec painting #1353
– and Québec society #5692
– exhibitions, group
– (1880) #1308
– (1959) #219
– (1970) #1348
– paintings, Université Laval (Québec, Qué) #3078
– portrait of Samuel de Champlain #191
– works, Art Association of Montreal (Montréal, Qué) #3075
Hamilton, Gerald, Can architect, 1923-
– Vancouver (BC), Imperial Bank of Canada #9193
Hamilton, Mary Riter, Can artist, 1873-1954 #5694
– and British Columbia Society of Fine Arts #1978
– as member, Winnipeg Sketch Club #1887
– exhibitions
– (1906) #5693
– (1978) #5695
Hamilton, Ron, Can artist, 1950- #4132
– silkscreen prints #4148
Hamilton (Ont)
– architects' offices (1940s) #9297
– architecture #7985
– (1910s) #7957
– Thomas, William #8413
– Victorian #7991
– architecture and art #7978
– art #1674
– decorative arts (1890s) #2239
– domestic architecture (1910s) #8494 8496
– photographic views (1867-1900) #1719
– pottery #2347
– schools (1910s) #9436
– views (1890s) #6436
Hamilton (Ont), Art Gallery of Hamilton
– (1950s) #3138
– architecture, Trevor Patrick Garwood-Jones #3165
– Brymner, William, *Summer Landscape Martigues* #4950

- Canadian paintings, 19th-20th cs. #3159
- collection #3142
- exhibitions
  - *11th Annual Exhibition of the Latvis Society of Artists* (1966) #475
  - *7 West Coast Painters* (1959) #1997
  - *9 Out of 10: A Survey of Contemporary Canadian Art* (1974) #569
  - *Adrien Hébert: trente ans de son oeuvre, 1923-1953/Adrien Hébert: Thirty Years of His Art, 1923-1953* (1971) #5763
  - *Albert H. Robinson: Retrospective Exhibition* (1955) #7055
  - *André Biéler 50 Years: A Retrospective Exhibition 1920-1970* (1971) #4725
  - *Annual Exhibition of Contemporary Canadian Art* (1971) #38
  - *Annual Winter Exhibition* (1948-1970) #38
  - *Anton Cetin: Etchings, Lithographs, Collages, Aquatints, Paintings, Drawings* (1978) #5064
  - *Carl Schaefer: Retrospective Exhibition; Paintings from 1926 to 1969* (1969) #7155
  - *Certain Traditions: Recent British and Canadian Art* (1979) #653
  - *Charles Fraser Comfort: Fifty Years* (1973) #5159
  - *Daniel Fowler* (1965) #5489
  - *Dennis Burton Retrospective* (1978) #4961
  - *Goodridge Roberts: A Retrospective Exhibition/Goodridge Roberts: une exposition rétrospective* (1969) #7045
  - *Goodridge Roberts: Selected Works/Goodridge Roberts: oeuvres choisies* (1982) #7050
  - *Guido Molinari: Works on Paper* (1981) #6594
  - *Hamilton Camera Club: A Retrospective of Hamilton, Ontario and Metropolitan Areas from Confederation, 1867 to 1900* (1967) #1719
  - *Irene Whittome, 1975-1980* (1980) #7569
  - *J.M. Barnsley (1861-1929), Retrospective Exhibition* (1964) #4611
  - *J.W. Beatty, 1869-1941* (1981) #4638
  - *Joe Fafard: Recent Sculpture* (1980) #5401
  - *John Lyman* (1963) #6343
  - *Ken Danby: The Graphic Work, Lithographs and Serigraphs* (1980) #5253
  - *Kosso Eloul: "Celebration of the Arch"* (1980) #5369
  - *Maurice Cullen, 1866-1934* (1956) #5221
  - *Metamorphosis, Memories, Dreams and Reflections: The Work of Florence Vale* (1981) #7453
  - *Miller Brittain - Painter* (1982) #4922
  - *Ontario Now I* (1976) #38
  - *Ontario Now II* (1977) #38
  - *Ontario Society of Artists: 100 Years* (1972) #1678
  - *Otto Rogers: New Paintings and Sculpture, 1977-78* (1979) #7065
  - *Ozias Leduc: peinture symboliste et religieuse/Ozias Leduc: Symbolist and Religious Painting* (1974) #6206
  - *Robert W. Pilot Retrospective/Rétrospective Robert W. Pilot* (1969) #6872
  - *Some Artists Who have Lived and Worked in Hamilton: "Centennial Exhibition"* (1967) #1674
  - *Some Paintings, Drawings and Prints from the Douglas Duncan Collection* (1968) #3223
  - *Surrealism in Canadian Painting* (1964) #463
  - *T.R. MacDonald, 1908-1978* (1980) #6380
  - *The Ontario Community Collects: A Survey of Canadian Painting from 1766 to the Present* (1976) #120
  - *The Paintings of Frederick Nicholas Loveroff/Les peintures de Frederick Nicholas Loveroff* (1982) #6331
  - *The Saidye and Samuel Bronfman Collection of Canadian Art/La collection Saidye et Samuel Bronfman* (1966) #3087
  - *The Society of Canadian Painter-Etchers and Engravers in Retrospect/La Société des peintres-graveurs canadiens: vue rétrospective* (1978) #836
  - *Trésors d'art populaire québécois/Folk Art Treasures of Quebec* (1981) #1297
  - *Viewpoint: Twenty-nine by Nine; An Exhibition of Twenty-nine Works by Ontario Artists, Selected by Nine Curators* (1981) #1838
  - *Walter Bachinski: Sculpture & Drawing* (1981) #4579
  - *William Blair Bruce* (1975) #4942
- exhibitions (reviews)
  - *Ecanada Art Pottery* (1979) #2359
  - *Hastenteufel, Dieter* #5752
- sculpture competition (1976) #780
- Women's Committee (1950-1968) #3160
Hamilton (Ont), Bank of Hamilton
- architecture, Charles Mills #9160
Hamilton (Ont), Beckett Gallery
- exhibitions
  - *Dorothy Knowles* (1973) #6067
Hamilton (Ont), Church of Saint John the Evangelist
- architecture, Witton & Walsh #730
Hamilton (Ont), Church of the Ascension
- architecture, Frederic William Cumberland #8905
Hamilton (Ont), City Hall and Civic Square
- architecture, Stanley M. Roscoe; Fleury, Arthur & Barclay, Consulting Architects #8988
Hamilton (Ont), Dundurn Castle
- architecture, Robert Charles Wetherell #8650 8662
Hamilton (Ont), First Methodist Church
- architecture, William E.N. Hunter #7957
Hamilton (Ont), Hamilton Art School
- Robinson, Albert Henry, as teacher and director #7056
Hamilton (Ont), Hamilton Mausoleum
- architecture #8900
Hamilton (Ont), Hamilton Public Library
- architecture, Alfred W. Peene #7957
Hamilton (Ont), Hamilton Technical School
- architecture #9436
Hamilton (Ont), Hamilton Terminal Station
- architecture, Charles Mills #9527
Hamilton (Ont), Loew's Theatre
- architecture, Thomas White Lamb #9069
Hamilton (Ont), McMaster Divinity College
- architecture, Bruce Brown & Brisley #8765
Hamilton (Ont), McMaster University
- architecture, W.L. Somerville; John Francis Brown and Francis Bruce Brown, Associated Architects #9451
- Canadian art history instruction (1933) #3306
- exhibitions
  - *David Blackwood: Paintings, Drawings, Prints* (1967) #4739
Hamilton (Ont), McMaster University. Art Gallery
- exhibitions
  - *A.J. Casson: Retrospective* (1975) #5058
  - *Anne Kahane: Sculpture, Prints and Drawings, 1953-1976* (1981) #5999
  - *Gift from the Douglas M. Duncan Collection and the Milne-Duncan Bequest/Le Don provenant de la collection Douglas M. Duncan et le legs Milne-Duncan* (1971) #541
  - *Mennonite Decorative Art* (1981) #2267
Hamilton (Ont), McMaster University. Student Centre
- architecture, John Andrews Architects #8323
Hamilton (Ont), McMaster University Health Sciences Centre
- architecture, Craig, Zeidler & Strong #9035 9036 9037
Hamilton (Ont), Memorial School
- architecture #9436
Hamilton (Ont), Molsons Bank
- architecture #9173
Hamilton (Ont), Royal Connaught Hotel
- architecture, Esenwein & Johnson; Alfred W. Peene, Associate Architect #9274
Hamilton (Ont), Whitehern
- architecture and furniture #8664
Hamilton (Ont), YWCA building
- architecture, Mills & Hutton #7957
Hamilton Camera Club (Hamilton, Ont)
- exhibitions
  - (1967) #1719
- exhibitions (reviews) #978
Hamilton Glass Works, glass manufacturer (Hamilton, Ont) #2401
Hamilton Pottery, ceramic manufacturer (Hamilton, Ont) #2347
Hammock, Virgil, Can artist, 1938- #5696
Hammond, Charlotte Wilson, Can artist, 1941- #1169 5697
Hammond, John A., Can artist, 1843-1939 #178 5698 5700
- exhibitions
  - (1967) #5699
- exhibitions, group
  - (1969) #1180
- exhibitions (reviews) #186
Hampton Group (Hampton, NB)
- (1960s) #1177
Han Indians
- culture #4101
Hance, James B., Can artist, 1847-1915 #1312
Hancock, Little, Calvert Associates, Can architectural firm
- Guelph (Ont), University of Guelph. Arts and Library buildings #9468
Hand, Harris & Merritt, Can architectural firm
- Toronto (Ont), Bowles Lunch Room #9269
hands
- drawings, Ernest Lindner #6287
- Inuit sculpture #4439
Handy, Arthur, Can artist, 1933- #5701 5702
- on Canadian art (1960s) #478
- sculptures (1960s) #1793
Hanford, Robert Gilmore, Can architect, b. 1885, fl. 1911-1914
- Winnipeg (Man), domestic architecture #8493
Hankes, Jarvis, Amer artist in Canada, b. 1799, fl. 1827-1834 #1377
Hannaford, Edmund Phillips, Can architect, 1834-1902

– Montréal (Qué), Bonaventure Station #9538

Hanover (NH), Dartmouth College. Hopkins Center. Jaffe-Friede Gallery
– exhibitions
– *Paul-Emile Borduas, 1905-1960: A Loan Exhibition* (1967) #4812

Hanover (NH), Dartmouth College. Hopkins Center Art Galleries
– exhibitions
– *Canadian Landscape Painting, 1670-1930: The Artist and the Land* (1973) #106
– *Eleven Canadian Printmakers* (1967) #821

Hanover (NH), Hopkins Center Art Galleries
– *see* Hanover (NH), Dartmouth College. Hopkins Center Art Galleries

Hanover (NH), Jaffe-Friede Gallery
– *see* Hanover (NH), Dartmouth College. Hopkins Center. Jaffe-Friede Gallery

Hanover (Ont)
– views
– Schaefer, Carl Fellman #7153 7157

Hansen, Folmer, Can ceramicist, 1930-
– interview, on Hansen-Ross Pottery (Fort Qu'Appelle, Sask) #2389

Hansen, James Colin, Can artist, 1939- #5703

Hansen, Kéro-Claire
– *see* Beaudoin-Hansen, Kéro-Claire (Kéro)

Hansen-Ross Pottery, ceramic manufacturer (Fort Qu'Appelle, Sask) #2389

Hanuse, Roy James, Can artist, 1943-
– silkscreen prints #4148

Haohao, Bella Coola
– petroglyph of #3816

Harbour Grace (Nfld)
– architecture #7792

Harbour Grace (Nfld), lighthouse #9523

harbours, Canadian
– Montréal (Qué) #7917
– waterfront buildings, Halifax (NS), 19th c. #7822 7824 7825 7834

Harburn, Flora, Can artist, fl. 1955
– jewellery #2695

Harbuz, Ann Alexandra, Can artist, 1908- #1881
– exhibitions, group
– (1975) #1927

hard-edge
– and Gordon Appelbe Smith #7226 7227 7229
– and Pierre Jean Clerk #5118
– Canada, prints (1960s-1970s) #832

Harder, Rolf, Can artist, 1929- #5704
– and Design Collaborative Montreal Ltd. #878 882
– prints #897

Hardie, Martin, Brit artist, 1875-1952
– on Walter Joseph Phillips #6856

Harding, James Duffield, Brit artist, 1798-1863
– as teacher of Daniel Fowler #5491

Harding, Noel, Can artist, 1945-
– exhibitions, group
– (1977) #631
– (1978) #667
– (1980) #687 690
– exhibitions (reviews) #656
– performance sculpture #658
– video art #651 5705

Hardman, Jack Nelson, Can sculptor, 1923-
– garden sculpture #1849

Hardman, Trish, Can artist, fl. 1973
– video art #2044

hardware
– *see also* tools

hardware, Canadian
– architectural, 17th-19th cs. #2705
– late 18th-mid 19th cs. #2703

Hardy, Jean-Baptiste, Can sculptor, 1731-after 1758 #1592

Hare Indians
– culture
– (1920s) #4081
– (1960s) #4109

Harman, Jack Kenneth, Can sculptor, 1927- #5706
– foundry for bronze casting (Vancouver, BC) #2083

Harmer, William Morell, Can photographer, 1859-1949
– exhibitions, group
– (1970) #1675

Harmon, Byron, Can photographer, 1880-1942 #5707

Harold, Alexander, Can artist, d. ca. 1923
– exhibitions, group
– (1978) #133

Haroutiun, Georges, Can photographer, 1945-
– interview #5708

Harper, John, Brit naval officer in Canada, 19th c.
– portrait, wrongly identified #5430 5431

Harper, John Russell, Can art historian, 1914- #3317
– book, *Painting in Canada* #488

Harper's, Amer periodical
– illustrations, Henri Julien #5984

Harpignies, Henri Joseph, Fr artist, 1819-1916
– influence on James Wilson Morrice #6626

Harris, Alfred Peter, Can artist, 1932-
– exhibitions
– (1977) #5735

Harris, Bess Larkin Housser, Can artist, 1890-1969
– and G.Blair Laing #1686
– exhibitions, group
– (1928) #301

Harris, James Edward, Can architect, 1886-1954
– and William Critchlow Harris #8372

Harris, Lawren Phillips, Can artist, 1910- #5709 5710 5712 5713
– *Battleground before Ortona* #1115
– exhibitions
– (1972) #5711
– exhibitions, group
– (1966) #1123
– (1973) #1182

Harris, Lawren Stewart, Can artist, 1885-1970 #24 1996 5719 5727 5730 5732
– abstract art theories #5724
– and A.Y. Jackson #5912
– and Bertram Richard Brooker #4925 4926
– and Brief Concerning the Cultural Aspects of Canadian Reconstruction (1944) #3251
– and G.Blair Laing #1686
– and Group of Seven #1732
– and nationalism in art #143 5729
– Arctic trips #1779
– book illustration and design #939
– Breeze, Claude Herbert, compared with #4910
– exhibitions
– (1948) #5720
– (1963) #5725
– (1978) #5734
– exhibitions, group
– (1968) #3224
– (1975) #589 592
– (1979) #147
– exhibitions (reviews) #1710 5717 5718
– influence of Scandinavian art #1788
– influence on Alan Caswell Collier #5131
– influence on Alberta landscape painting #1965
– influence on Emily Carr #5021 5044
– landscapes (1908-1930) #5728
– McCarthy, Doris Jean, compared with #6461
– mystical influences #5726 5731
– on A.Y. Jackson #5925
– on abstract art #5721 5723
– on art criticism #3300
– on Arthur Lismer #6298
– on Canadian art and creativity #5715
– on Canadian North in art #308
– on Canadian painting #293
– on Emily Carr #5012
– on Federation of Canadian Artists #364
– on Group of Seven #1744 1747 1754
– on modern art #5714
– on society and art #5722
– on theosophy and art #5716
– portraits #5733
– Schaefer, Carl Fellman, compared with #7157
– winter landscapes #285
– writings #92

Harris, Pamela, Can photographer, 1940-
– portfolio of photographs #996

Harris, Peter
– *see* Harris, Alfred Peter

Harris, Robert, Can artist, 1849-1919 #178 221 5738 5741 5744
– exhibitions
– (1967) #5739
– (1973) #5743
– exhibitions, group
– (1976) #3281
– (1978) #665
– exhibitions (reviews) #174 186
– lost portraits and sketches #5742
– portraits #1698
– relation of photography and painting #245
– *The Fathers of Confederation* #5736 5740
– writings #5737

Harris, Robert Harold, Can artist, 1878-1948
– linocuts, covers of exhibition catalogues, Winnipeg Sketch Club #1887

Harris, Salmon, Can artist, 1948- #2053
– exhibitions
– (1978) #5745

Harris, William Critchlow, Can architect, 1854-1913 #8372
– and Dewar & Stirling (Halifax, NS) #8371
– Charlottetown (PEI), market building #7800
– Prince Edward Island, churches #8777

Harris family, 19th-20th cs.
– residence, Eldon House (London, Ont) #8660

Harrison, Allan, Can artist, 1911- #5746 5747
– exhibitions
– (1978) #5748
– record covers #862

Harrison, Birge Lovell, Can artist, 1854-1911 #1312

Harrison, Mark Robert, Can artist, 1819-1894
– as member, Toronto Society of Arts #1689

Harrison, Robert F., Can architect, 1925-
– Burnaby (BC)
  – Simon Fraser University, competition #9501
  – Simon Fraser University. Library #9046
Harrison, Ted, Can artist, 1926- #5750 5751
– interview #5749
Hart, Ernest H., Can furniture-maker, 20th c. #2493
Hart Pottery, ceramic manufacturer (Picton and Belleville, Ont)
– (1848-1914) #2286 2293
Hartung, Hans, Ger artist, 1904-
– and Mario Roy #7099
Hastenteufel, Dieter, Can artist, 1939- #5752
hats
– see also costume; headgear
hats, Canadian
– (pre-1736) #2831
– Huppé (dit Lagroix), Joseph #269 270
– Montréal (Qué), 19th c. #2837
– Nova Scotia, late 18th-19th cs. #2907
– Québec, 17th-19th cs. #2815
– straw hats, 18th c. #2200
hats, Nootka
– Cambridge (Mass), Harvard University. Peabody Museum #3779
– worn by chiefs #3829
hats, Tlingit #3865
Hauer, Jacob, Can artist, fl. 1847
– as member, Toronto Society of Arts #1689
Haufschild, Lutz, Can artist, 1943- #2460
– fountain, Vancouver (BC) #2077
– stained glass, Coquitlam Centre (Vancouver, BC) #2459
Havre-Aubert (îles de la Madeleine), Musée des îles
– exhibitions
  – De la figuration à la non-figuration dans l'art québécois (1977) #1461
Hawes, James, Can furniture-maker, fl. 1820s-1850s #2511
Hawksett, Samuel C., Can artist, 1837-1910 #5753
– paintings, Université Laval (Québec, Qué) #3078
– relation of photography and painting #245
Haworth, Peter, Can stained glass artist, 1889-
– stained glass, Montréal (Qué) #2448
Hawthorn, Audrey, Can collector, 20th c.
– and University of British Columbia. Museum of Anthropology (Vancouver, BC) #3195
Hawthorn, Harry Bertram, Can anthropologist, 1910-
– and University of British Columbia. Museum of Anthropology (Vancouver, BC) #3195
Hawthorn, Henry Gilbert John, Can architect, 1939-
– Queen Charlotte Islands (BC), Queen Charlotte Islands Museum #9129
– Vancouver (BC), renovation, Canadian Pacific Railway station for office/retail complex #9546
Hawthorn Mansfield Towers, Can architectural firm #8373
Hawthorne, Charles Webster, Amer artist, 1872-1930
– as teacher of Jack Weldon Humphrey #5865
Hay, Pierre, Can sculptor, 1661-1708 #1572 1578

Hay, Robert, Can furniture-maker, 1808-1890 #2463
Hay, William, Can architect, 1818-1888
– on Toronto (Ont) architecture #8050
– Toronto (Ont) #8055 8056 8059
  – Yorkville Town Hall #8997
Haycock, Maurice Hall, Can artist, 1900- #5754
Hayden, Michael, Can sculptor, 1943-
– and Intersystems #767
– colour xerography #614
– Escalator Piece #5755
– exhibitions, group
  – (1970) #771
– sculptures (1960s) #1793
Hayman, Sasha, Can tapestry artist, 1947- #5756
Haynes, Douglas Hector, Can artist, 1936- #5758
– exhibitions
  – (1974) #5757
– exhibitions, group
  – (1981) #722
– on Edmonton (Alta) art (1981) #1975
Hayter, Stanley William, Brit artist, 1901-
– as teacher of David Silverberg #7206
– as teacher of Québec printmakers #1641
– influence on Canadian printmaking (1960s) #820
Hayward, William B., Amer architect, fl. 1950s
– Toronto (Ont), City Hall and Civic Square, competition #8981
Hazelgrove, Nancy Ann, Can artist, 1945-
– exhibitions, group
  – (1980) #1835
Hazelton (BC)
– totem poles, Gitksan #3797
Hazelton (BC), 'Ksan
– exhibitions
  – 'Ksan, Breath of our Grandfathers: An Exhibition of 'Ksan Art (1972) #4130
  – 'Ksan: le souffle des ancêtres, une exposition de l'art de 'Ksan (1972) #4129
Hazen, William, Can, 18th c.
– portrait of his children, Joseph Comingo #5161
Head, George Bruce, Can artist, 1931- #5759
– exhibitions, group
  – (1962) #1847
  – (1981) #1907
Head, Lady Anna Maria Yorke, Brit artist in Canada, 1808-1890
– exhibitions, group
  – (1978) #5760
Head, Sir Edmund Walker, Brit statesman, artist in Canada, 1805-1868
– and architecture of Parliament Buildings (Ottawa, Ont) #8930
– and architecture of University of Toronto. University College (Toronto, Ont) #9453
– exhibitions, group
  – (1978) #5760
headdresses
– see headgear
headgear
– see also hats; helmets
– antlerwork, Asia and North America #3460
headgear, Algonquian
– roach headdress #3417
headgear, Assiniboine #3739
headgear, Blackfoot #3739
headgear, Blood #3739

headgear, Cree #3739
headgear, Haida #4019
headgear, Indians of North America #3453
headgear, Northwest Coast Indians #3977
– prehistoric #4017
headgear, Ojibwa #3539
headgear, Plains
– feathered headdress #3683
– secret societies #3727
headgear, Sarcee #3739
headgear, Tlingit #4019
– Philadelphia (Penn), University of Pennsylvania. Museum #3803
headgear, Tsimshian #4019
heads
– Inuit and Dorset sculpture, multiple human images #4429
Heakes, Francis Riley, Can architect, 1858-1930
– Toronto (Ont), Chorley Park #8749
Heaps, Mr. and Mrs. Leo J., Brit collectors, 20th c.
– collection, J.Henry Sandham artworks #7121
Heaviside, Mary (Lady Love), Can artist, 1806-1866 #258 259
– New Brunswick lithographs (1830) #1175
Hebb, Howard D., Can furniture-maker, 1860-1939 #2510
Hébert, Adrien, Can artist, 1890-1967 #302 1392 1393
– exhibitions
  – (1971) #5763
– on his art #5761
– Port de Montreal #5762
– works (1909-1923) #5764
Hébert, Anne, Can writer, 1916-
– Prévost, Antoine, compared with #6927
Hébert, Henri, Can sculptor, 1884-1950 #302 1315
– on Québec art (1940s) #1383
Hébert, Jeannine Tardif
– see Tardif-Hébert, Jeannine
Hébert, Julien, Can artist, 1917- #5766
– bronze elevator doors, Queen Elizabeth Hotel (Montréal, Qué) #8228
– fountain, National Arts Centre (Ottawa, Ont) #9108
– on sculptural themes #5765
– works, Place des Arts (Montréal, Qué) #8233
Hébert, Louis-Philippe, Can sculptor, 1850-1917 #1315 5767 5768 5769 5770 5771
– as teacher of Maurice Galbraith Cullen #5217
– exhibitions (reviews) #204
– Laliberté, Alfred, compared with #6142
– monument to Paul de Chomedey de Maisonneuve, Montréal (Qué) #1623
– sculptures, Montréal (Qué) and Ottawa (Ont) #727
– tombstone, cemetery, L'Acadie (Qué) #8830
– works, Art Association of Montreal (Montréal, Qué) #3075
Hébert, Marie Pollet, Can, 17th c.
– and household crafts #2212
Hébert, Philippe
– see Hébert, Louis-Philippe
Hébert, Pierre, Can artist, 1944-
– computer art #528
Hedges, Jack, Can metalsmith, fl. 1944 #2693
Hedrick, Robert Burns, Can artist, 1930- #5772 5774

- exhibitions, group
  - (1965) #473
- exhibitions (reviews) #5773
- on Canadian art (1960s) #478
- on Gordon Rayner #6965
- paintings and sculptures #449
Heer, Louis-Chrétien de, Can artist, 1755-1807 #1323
- and Québec society #1375
- exhibitions, group
  - (1959) #219
- influence of French painting #1244
Held, Robert D.M., Can glassmaker, 1943-
- and Sheridan College School of Crafts and Design (Mississauga, Ont) #2440
- as founder of Skookum Art Glass (Calgary, Alta) #2439
Helena (Mon), Montana Historical Society
- exhibitions
  - An Art Perspective of the Historic Pacific Northwest (1963) #1999
Helfand, Fern, Can photographer, 1952-
- compared with Barbara Anne Astman #1010
Heller, Mary Ida Clair, Can sculptor, 1909- #5775
Helmcken, John S., Can physician, fl. 1857
- presentation silver tea service #2647
Helmer Associates, Can architectural firm
- Ottawa (Ont), La Salle Academy #9480 9481
helmets
- see also costume; headgear
helmets, Tlingit
- shark helmet, Kaguanton Clan, University of Pennsylvania. Museum (Philadelphia, Penn) #3833
Helsinki (Finland), Institute of Crafts and Design
- McKinley, Donald Lloyd, as student #6489
Hembroff-Schleicher, Edythe, Can artist, 1906-
- correspondence, Emily Carr (1930-1940) #5026
- on Emily Carr #5043
Heming, Arthur Henry Howard, Can artist, 1870-1940
- exhibitions
  - (1934) #5776
- illustrations #916
Hemingway, Peter, Can architect, 1929- #8084
- Edmonton (Alta) #7733
- Edmonton (Alta), Muttart Conservatory #8091
- on Alex Simeon Janvier #5936
- on architecture #7746
- Sherwood Park (Alta), County of Strathcona Building #5937
Hémon, Louis, Fr writer in Canada, 1880-1913
- Maria Chapdelaine, illustrations
  - Gagnon, Clarence A. #1
  - Lemieux, Jean-Paul #6239
Hénault, Gilles, Can poet, curator, art critic, 1920-
- on Charles Daudelin #5262
- on Léon Bellefleur #4662
Hendershot, Janet, Can artist, 1945- #675 717
- exhibitions, group
  - (1980) #698
Henderson, Alexander, Can furniture-maker, fl. 1866-1906 #2511
Henderson, Alexander, Can photographer,

1831-1913 #5777
- survey photographs, Canadian Pacific Railway (1870s) #1876
Henderson, D'Arcy S., Can artist, 1940-
- exhibitions, group
  - (1978) #2067
Henderson, J.T., printing firm (Montréal, Qué)
- Christmas greeting cards #890
Henderson, James, Can artist, 1871-1951 #5778
- exhibitions
  - (1969) #5779
- exhibitions, group
  - (1928) #294
  - (1978) #133
Henderson, Tom, Can sculptor, 1936- #5780
Hendery, Robert, Can silversmith, 1820-after 1895 #2638
- and Québec silver #2675
- hallmarks #2635
- works, Detroit Institute of Arts (Detroit, Mich) #2691
Hennessey, Frank Charles, Can artist, 1894-1941
- influence on Tony Law #6174
- landscapes, for hooked rugs #2750
Henri, Robert, Amer artist, 1865-1929
- as teacher of Mabel Killam Day #5273
- influence on James Wilson Morrice #6626 6630 6633
Henrickson, Martha Charlotte, Can photographer, 1944-
- Awakenings #5781
Henrickson, Thomas Elton, Can photographer, 1944-
- Awakenings #5781
Henriquez, Richard G., Can architect, 1941-
- on architecture and art #7746
Henriquez & Todd, Can architectural firm
- Vancouver (BC), elementary school design award (1970) #9507
Henry Birks and Sons Ltd.
- collection, Canadian silver #2636 2637 2650 2651 2656
Henry Bloomfield and Sons, stained glass studio (Vancouver, BC)
- stained glass, British Columbia Parliament Buildings (Victoria, BC) #8966
Hepplewhite style
- furniture, Québec #2542
heraldry
- see also badges; emblems and mottoes; genealogy
heraldry, Canadian #2913 2915 2939
- Alexander, William Walker #4506
- as folk art and kitsch #2951
- beaver motif #56
- Carter, Alexander Scott #5050
- on stained glass windows, Vancouver (BC), (1890-1940) #2454
Heriot, George, Brit postmaster, artist in Canada, 1766-1844 #279 5782 5785 5787 5788 5789
- exhibitions
  - (1978) #5786
- paintings of Indians #5783
  - Windsor (Ont), Willistead Art Gallery #5784
Heritage Canada
- and architectural preservation #7771
- conservation of architecture
  - (1973) #7763
  - (1973-1977) #7770

- periodical, Canadian Heritage #7764
Heritage Canada/Héritage Canada, Can periodical #7764
Heritage Ottawa
- inventory, architectural records before 1950 in Ottawa (Ont) private collections #8049
Heritage Park (Alta)
- architecture #8125
Herman, Jack, Can ceramicist, 1927- #2395
Herman, Josef, Brit artist, 1911-
- influence on Stephen Andrews #4527
Herman, Lorraine, Can ceramicist, 1929- #2395
heroes and heroines, Canadian
- Boyle, John Bernard #4892 4893 4894
- Hébert, Louis-Philippe #5767
- Jefferys, Charles William #5957
heroines
- see heroes and heroines
Héroux, Yvon, Can artist, fl. 1972
- exhibitions
  - (1972) #5790
Herreilers, John, Can artist, fl. 1975
- interview #5791
Herring, John, Can glassmaker, 1818-1898 #2396
Herring Glass Works, glass manufacturer (Mallorytown, Ont)
- and John Herring #2396
Hersey, John A., Can silversmith, fl. 1823-1850 #2649
Hertel, François, Jesuit priest, educator, writer, 1905-
- and Paul-Emile Borduas #4814
Herzog, Fred, Can photographer, 1930-
- portfolio of photographs #998
Herzog, Saul, Can architect, 1933-
- Red Deer (Alta), City Hall #8990
Hesse, Eva, Amer artist, 1936-1970
- Westerlund, Mia, compared with #7545
Hesse, Hermann, Ger writer, 1877-1962
- influence on Vera Frenkel #5526
Heusch, Lucio de, Can artist, 1946- #1544
- exhibitions, group
  - (1977) #1532
  - (1981) #1565
- symposium, Musée du Nouveau-Monde (La Rochelle, France), (1980) #1559
Heuvel, Francis van den, Can photographer, 1949-
- portfolio of photographs #997 999
Heward, Efa Prudence, Can artist, 1896-1947 #5794
- exhibitions
  - (1948) #5795
  - (1980) #5796
Heward, John, Can artist, 1934- #5792
  - (1977) #5793
Hewett, M., Brit physician, collector, 18th c.
- collection, artifacts, Northwest Coast Indians #3767
Hewton, Randolph Stanley, Can artist, 1888-1960
- and Albert Henry Robinson #7057
- and Group of Seven #1732
- as member, Canadian Group of Painters #324
Heyer, Paul, Can anthropologist, 1946-
- on conceptual art #7473
Heyvaert, Pierre, Can sculptor, 1934-1974 #5797
Hicklin, Barbara Jane, Can artist, 1918- #5798

Hicks, Bill, Can photographer, ca. 1945-
- portfolio of photographs #995
Hidai, Nankoku, Ja artist, 20th c.
- as teacher of Gaston-Pierre Petit #6844
Hidatsa Indians
- quillwork #3701
Hide, Peter, Can sculptor, 1944-
- exhibitions, group
  - (1981) #797
- techniques #792
Higgins, Steve, Can artist, 1946-
- exhibitions, group
  - (1977) #1901
Highlands (Scotland)
- views, Robert Ford Gagen #5530
Highlights, Quarterly Newsletter of the Alberta
  Society of Artists, Can periodical #1944
Hildred, Philip, Can photographer, fl. 1971
- portfolio of photographs #998
Hildrith, Isaac, Can architect, 1741-1807
  #8374 8375
- Halifax (NS), Government House #8750
Hill, George William, Can sculptor,
  1862-1934 #192 5799
- monument to Sir Georges-Etienne Cartier,
  Montréal (Qué) #1623
Hill, James Thomas, Can artist, 1930-
- illustrations #941
Hill, Stanley R. (Stan), Can sculptor, 1921-
  #5800
Hill, Tom, Can artist, 1943-
- interview #4155
Hilst, Robert van der, Can photographer, ca.
  1940-
- portfolio of photographs #1023
Hilton, Charles, Can sculptor, ceramicist,
  1937- #2392
Hime, Humphrey Lloyd, Can photographer,
  1833-1903 #5802 5803
- photographs, Assiniboine and
  Saskatchewan Exploring Expedition (1858)
  #1865 5801 5804
- survey photographs #1014 1015
Hind, William George Richardson, Can
  artist, 1833-1888 #5805 5808 5809
- as expedition artist of Overlanders journey
  (1862) #5807
- as Victorian artist #5810
- British Columbia gold rush scenes #5811
- exhibitions
  - (1967) #5806
- exhibitions (reviews) #1692
- landscapes #1855
Hines, Sherman, Can photographer, ca.
  1942-
- portfolio of photographs #995
Hinge (Vancouver, BC) #2040
Hinton, John Henry, Can photographer,
  1875-1948
- exhibitions
  - (1977) #5812
Hiroshige, Ja artist, 1797-1858
- Tanobe, Miyuki, compared with #7322
Hirschberg, Martin, Can sculptor, 1937-
- sculptures (1960s) #1793
- use of light #767
historic sites
- see also war memorials
historic sites, Canadian
- and conservation (1880s) #7754
- Halifax (NS) #7830
- London (Ont) #8010
- Québec #7887
- Toronto (Ont) #5651

historical monuments
- see monuments
history, natural
- see natural history
history and art
- Boyle, John Bernard, on #4893
- Shadbolt, Jack Leonard, on #7185
history painting, Canadian
- 17th-19th cs. #187
- 18th-19th cs. #247 812
- Beau, Henri #4639
- Berczy, William Bent #241 242
- Bourassa, Napoléon #4872 4874
- Delfosse, Georges #5280
- Harris, Robert #5736 5740
- Huot, Charles Edouard #5876 5878 5880
  5881 5884
- Innes, John I. #5901
- Jefferys, Charles William #5954 5956
- Légaré, Joseph #6214 6216 6219
- Montréal (Qué), Ecole des beaux-arts
  #2972
- Morrison, Alfred L. #6642
- Québec #1344
- Reid, George Agnew #6978
- Rindisbacher, Peter #7006 7009
- stained glass windows, Church of
  Notre-Dame (Montréal, Qué) #2444
Hlynsky, David, Can photographer, 1947-
- and Image Nation #992
- exhibitions, group
  - (1979) #1905
  - (1981) #1070
- holograms, Fringe Research Inc. (Toronto,
  Ont) #1827
Hobart (Australia), Tasmanian Museum and
  Art Gallery
- exhibitions
  - Contemporary Canadian Painters (1957) #423
Hobden, Mark D., Can photographer, 1947-
- exhibitions, group
  - (1972) #1952
- portfolio of photographs #991
Hobson Pottery, ceramic manufacturer
  (Sainte-Angèle, Qué)
- (1890s) #2298 2322
Hodge, Albert Hemstock, Brit sculptor,
  1875-1918
- sculpture, Legislative Building (Winnipeg,
  Man) #8948 8949
Hodgins, John George, Can educator,
  1821-1912
- on school architecture #9384
Hodgkinson, Edward Allen, Can artist,
  1918-
- exhibitions
  - (1963) #1668
- exhibitions, group
  - (1977) #646
Hodgson, Alan James, Can architect, 1928-
- Victoria (BC), British Columbia Parliament
  Buildings, restoration #8964 8965 8966
Hodgson, Bates & Beattie, Can architectural
  firm
- Calgary (Alta), Burns Building #8118
Hodgson, Thomas Sherlock (Tom), Can
  artist, 1924- #5813
- art and writings #5814
Hodgson, Wilfred Garstang
- see Garstang-Hodgson, Wilfred
Hodler, Ferdinand, Sw artist, 1853-1918
- influence on John Bernard Boyle #4894
Hoey, Elizabeth Wilkes, Can artist, fl. 1930s-
  #5816

- and Albert Angus Macdonald #6354
Hoferichter, Bert, Can photographer, ca.
  1939-
- portfolio of photographs #991
Hoffman, F.Burrall jr., Amer architect, fl.
  1914-1946
- Winnipeg (Man), Bank of Hamilton #9171
Hoffman, Fred G., Can sculptor, 1845-1926
  #5817
Hoffman, Louis, Can furniture-maker,
  1818-1900 #2573
Hofmann, Hans, Amer artist, 1880-1966
- as teacher of Alexandra Luke #6333
- as teacher of Canadian artists #402 1850
- as teacher of Donald Alvin Jarvis #5947
- as teacher of Ruth Wainwright #7497
- influence on Jack Hamilton Bush #4970
Hogle & Davis, Can architectural firm
- Montréal (Qué), Bank of Toronto #9167
Holbrook, Elizabeth M. Bradford, Can
  sculptor, 1913-
- exhibitions, group
  - (1971) #772
Holder, Henry Arthur, Can furniture-maker,
  1853-1935 #2505 2506
Holder, Thomas Cook, Can furniture-maker,
  1821-1894 #2505 2506
Holgate, Bidwell A., Can real estate
  promoter, b. 1878
- residence, Edmonton (Alta) #8718
Holgate, Edwin Headley, Can artist,
  1892-1977 #302 309 5818 5819
- and Albert Henry Robinson #7057
- and Group of Seven #1732 1774
- as teacher of Jean-Paul Lemieux #6228
- book illustration and design #939
- Cullen, Maurice Galbraith, compared with
  #5216
- exhibitions, group
  - (1977) #1278 1279
- woodcuts #802
Holiwell, Charles E., Brit army stationer in
  Canada, fl. 1870s
- views of Québec #2326
Holland, Michael (Mickey), Can architect,
  1929-
- restoration, Duggan House (Edmonton,
  Alta) #8729
Hollett, John, Can cooper, 1888- #2151
Hollingsworth, Fred Thornton, Can
  architect, 1917-
- West Vancouver (BC), Woyat-Bowie
  Building. Architects' offices #9346
Hollister, F.S.J., Can stained glass artist, fl.
  1924-
- Oshawa (Ont), Saint George's Anglican
  Church #8899
- Ottawa (Ont), Parliament Buildings.
  Memorial Tower. Soldiers' Memorial
  Windows #2445
Holloway, Elsie, Can photographer, fl.
  1908-1946 #5820
Holm, Bill, Can anthropologist, 1925-
- and Bill Reid #6987
- influence on Pat Dixon #5294
Holman, Donald (Don), Can artist, 1946-
- and James Burton Spencer, collaboration
  on a lithograph #7270
Holman, James Henry, Can artist, 1821-1891
- exhibitions
  - (1959) #5821
Holman (NWT)
- graphic arts #4197
  - (1959-1972) #4478

– (1959-1976) #4490
– (1960s) #4195
– (1966-) #4469
– graphic arts and sculpture #3350 4200
– whalebone carving #4457
Holmes, Robert, Can artist, 1861-1930 #5822
– and Charles MacDonald Manly #6414
– and Mary Evelyn Wrinch #7617
– books from his library #5824
– Coombs, Edith Grace, compared with #5172
– exhibitions
– (1964) #5823
hologram
– see holography
holography
– Canada (1970s) #1827
– Pethick, Jerry #6840 6841
Holownia, Thaddeus, Can photographer, 1949-
– exhibitions, group
– (1981) #1070
Holt, Elizabeth Russell, Can artist, fl. 1920s-1960s
– and Saint John Art Club (Saint John, NB) #1173
Holy Family
– Jobin, Louis #5968
Holyoke, Rich, Can composer, fl. 1970s
– and W.O.R.K.S. #1955
Homemaker's, Can periodical
– Haroutiun, Georges, as art director #5708
homesteading
– see frontier and pioneer life
Honsberger, Henry, Can, fl. 1850
– house, St. Catharines (Ont) region #2485
Hood, Robert, Brit naval officer, artist in Canada, 1796-1821 #5826
– journal of Franklin Arctic expedition (1819-1821) #5825 5827
hooked rugs
– see rugs
Hooker, Marion Hope Nelson, Can artist, 1886-1946
– Indian portraits #1896
Hookway, Elmer John, Can glassmaker, 1889-1974 #5828
Hooper, James, Brit collector, 20th c.
– collection, art, natives of North America #3369
Hooper, John, Can sculptor, 1926-
– as member of Hampton Group #1177
Hooper, Katherine B. (Kathy), Can artist, 1934-
– as member of Hampton Group #1177
– exhibitions, group
– (1973) #1182
Hooper, Thomas, Can architect, 1859-1935 #8376
– Vancouver (BC), University of British Columbia, competition #9509
Hoover, Christian, Can fraktur artist, 1835-1918 #5829
Hope, William R., Can artist, 1865-1931
– as member, Canadian Art Club #193
Hopewell Indians
– art #3558 3574
Hopkins, Edward Martin, Brit, employee of Hudson's Bay Company in Canada, 1820-1893
– collection, leggings, Piegan Indians #3715
– travels through Canada #5835
Hopkins, Elisabeth Margaret, Can artist, 1894- #5831 5832

– exhibitions (reviews) #1883
– on Frances Ann Beechy Hopkins #5830
Hopkins, Frances Ann Beechy, Brit artist in Canada, 1838-1918 #5830 5833 5834 5835
– exhibitions, group
– (1888) #175
Hopkins, Lawson & Nelson, Can architectural firm
– Toronto (Ont), Osgoode Hall #9002 9003
Hopper, Robin, Can ceramicist, 1939- #2395
Horeis, William Richard, Can photographer, 1945-
– exhibitions, group
– (1981) #1070
– interview #5836
Horetzky, Charles George, Can photographer, 1838-1900 #5838
– portfolio of photographs #995
– survey photographs, Canadian Pacific Railway (1870s) #1014 1015 1865 1876 5837
Horne, Cleeve, Can artist, 1912-
– on portraiture #624
Horne, David Ernest, Can architect, 1929-
– Toronto (Ont), City Hall and Civic Square, competition #8981
Horning, Isaac, Can photographer, fl. 1850-1870
– views, Simcoe (Ont) #1722
Hornyansky, Nicholas, Can artist, 1896-1965
– on etching #5839
Horsburgh, Victor D., Can architect, 1866-1947
– Canadian Bank of Commerce banks #9169
– Toronto (Ont), Canadian Bank of Commerce #9181
horse hair, Hidatsa
– quillwork #3701
horse hair, Mandan
– quillwork #3701
horse sticks, Plains #3743
horse trappings
– see equestrian trappings
horses in art
– Cameron, Walter Graham #4992
– Hill, George William #5799
– Kenyon, J.J. #1681
– Richard, Wilfrid #7000
– Todd, Robert Clow #258 259
– Wickson, Paul Giovanni #7573
Horsfall, Arthur, Can artist, 1915-
– exhibitions, group
– (1981) #1907
Horst, David B., Can sculptor, 1873-1965 #5840
Horvat, Miljenko, Can artist, 1935- #5841
– exhibitions
– (1980) #5843
– interview #5842
Horvath, Tibor, Can photographer, fl. 1950s-
– portfolio of photographs #995
Horwood, Eric Crompton, Can architect, 1900-1984
– architectural drawings, Archives of Ontario (Toronto, Ont) #8028 8030
Horwood, Harold A., Can stained glass artist, fl. 1867-1890s
– animal portraits #1727
– stained glass, Smithsonian Institution (Washington, DC) #2111
Horwood, John Charles Batstone, Can architect, 1864-1938
– architectural drawings, Archives of Ontario (Toronto, Ont) #8028 8030

– on Canadian architecture #7640
Horwood, Victor William, Can architect, 1878-1939
– Brandon (Man), Hospital for the Insane #9014
Horwood & White, Can architectural firm
– Toronto (Ont), Northway Department Store #9366
hospitalières de l'Hôtel-Dieu
– embroidery #2779
hospitals, Canadian
– 18th c. #7861
– (1911-1912) #8295
– (1914-1917), military hospitals #9016
– (1919-1920) #9018
– (1920s), military hospitals #9019
– (1930s) #9020 9021
– (1940s) #9024 9026
– sanatoriums #9025
– (1950s) #9029 9031
– (1960s) #9032
– Brandon (Man), Hospital for the Insane #9014
– Hamilton (Ont), McMaster University Health Sciences Centre #9035 9036 9037
– Kingston (Ont), (pre-1867) #7989
– Montréal (Qué)
– Hôtel-Dieu. Pavillon Jérôme Le Royer de la Dauversière #9023
– Montreal General Hospital #9030
– Royal Victoria Hospital. Ross Pavilion #9017
– Sainte-Justine Hospital #8407
– Sault Ste Marie (Ont), Group Health Centre #9033
– Toronto (Ont)
– Hospital for Sick Children #9015
– Provincial Lunatic Asylum #8378 9034
– Sunnybrook Hospital #9027
– Toronto General Hospital #9012 9013
hotels
– see also motels
hotels, American
– 19th c., inns #9285
hotels, Canadian
– 19th c. #9512
– inns #9285
– (1880-1914) #7736
– and Canadian railway companies #3281
– Brandon (Man), Prince Edward Hotel #9266
– Calgary (Alta)
– (1875-1914) #8711
– Hotel Palliser #9271
– château style railway hotels #7652 9290 9291
– Edmonton (Alta), Hotel Macdonald #9270
– Guelph (Ont), 19th c. #7970
– Hamilton (Ont), Royal Connaught Hotel #9274
– Lake Louise (Alta), Skoki Lodge #9296
– Lucerne (Qué), Château Lucerne #9283
– Manitoba #8098
– Montebello (Qué), Château Montebello #9295
– Montréal (Qué)
– 17th c.-1950s #9287
– Mount Royal Hotel #9276
– Place Bonaventure #9292 9319 9320 9321 9322 9323 9325
– Queen Elizabeth Hotel #8228 9286
– Ritz-Carlton Hotel #9267
– Ottawa (Ont), Château Laurier #9264 9265 9282 9528 9529

– Québec (Qué)
 – Château Frontenac #9261 9278
 – Hôtel Union #9284
– Saskatoon (Sask), Flanagan Hotel #9263
– Toronto (Ont)
 – Four Seasons Sheraton Hotel #9294
 – Hotel Mossop #9262
 – Hyatt Regency Hotel #9293
 – Inn on the Park #9289
 – Royal York Hotel #9280 9281
 – St. Charles Hotel #9269
 – Toronto Hilton Hotel #9292
– Vancouver (BC), Hotel Vancouver #9272
  9273
– Winnipeg (Man)
 – (1831-1960) #8095
 – Deer Lodge #9260
 – Empire Hotel #9361
 – Fort Garry Hotel #9268
 – Hotel at Silver Springs #9263
 – Marlborough Hotel #9277
 – Royal Alexandra Hotel #2599
Houle, Robert James, Can artist, curator,
 1947-
– interview #5844
hourglasses, Canadian
– 17th-18th cs. #2914
House of Liechtenstein
– see Liechtenstein, House of
houses
– see domestic architecture
housing projects
– see public housing
Housser, Frederick Broughton, Can writer,
 1889-1936
– correspondence, Norman I. Gurd #1776
Housser, Muriel Yvonne McKague, Can
 artist, 1898- #309 5845
– on Alexandra Luke #6333
Houston, James Archibald, Can artist, 1921-
 #5846
– and Inuit sculpture #4392 4449
– and Kenojuak Ashevak #4564
– and Peter Pitseolak #6880 6881
– interview #5847
– introduction of printmaking to the Inuit
 #4186 4201 4461 4462 4470
– support of Inuit art #4397 4452
Houston (Tex), Museum of Fine Arts
– exhibitions
 – The Eskimo (1969) #4216
Hovadik, Jaroslov, Can artist, 1935- #5848
Howard, Barbara, Can artist, 1926-
– exhibitions, group
 – (1978) #666
Howard, Jemima Frances Meikle (Mrs.
 John), Can artist, d. 1877 #3129
– (1834) #1688
Howard, John, Can farmer, photographer,
 furniture-maker, b. 1877 #2587
Howard, John George, Can architect, artist,
 collector, 1803-1890
– as member, Toronto Society of Arts #1689
– exhibitions
 – (1979) #8378
– paintings, Colborne Lodge (Toronto, Ont)
 #3129
– Toronto (Ont) #8056 8075
 – Colborne Lodge #8659
 – Provincial Lunatic Asylum #9034
– writings #8377
Howard, Ronald, Can architect, 1933-
– Vancouver (BC), Caulfield Cove
 Townhouses #8746

Howard, Sidney, Can sculptor, 1913- #2596
– exhibitions (reviews) #1210
Howarth, Edward J., Can artist, 1943-
– Stratoscape (Woodsworth Building,
 Winnipeg, Man) #5853
Howarth, Glenn, Can artist, 1946- #2053
 5849 5850 5851
Howarth, Thomas, Can architect, 1914-
– Toronto (Ont), York University. Glendon
 Hall #9457
Howe, John Donallen, Can furniture-maker,
 b. ca. 1841 #2511
– sideboard and staircase, Gregory House
 (Saint John, NB) #8545
Howe, Jonas, Can furniture-maker, b. ca.
 1844 #2511
Howe, Joseph, Can statesman, 1804-1873
– Joseph Howe Festival (NS), costumes for
 #2887
Hower, Else, Can artist, fl. 1925
– interior, Château Frontenac (Québec, Qué)
 #9278
Howison, Henry, Can ceramicist, fl. 1860s
 #2301
Howlin, John, Can artist, 1941-
– exhibitions
 – (1979) #5852
HP (Anonymous), Can silversmith, 19th c.
 #2691
Hudon, Normand, Can artist, 1929- #5854
 5855
Hudon-Beaulac, Simone Marie Yvette, Can
 artist, 1905- #1380 5856
– Christmas greeting cards #857
– exhibitions (reviews) #806
Hudson, Andrew, Can artist, art critic, 1935-
– on his art #5857
– selection of works, 14 Canadians: A Critic's
 Choice (1977) #623 627 645
Hudson, Susan Mary, Can artist, 1941-
– as cofounder of Graphia (Montréal, Qué)
 #1660
Hudson, Thomas (Tom), Can artist, 1886-
 #1155
– exhibitions, group
 – (1977) #1156
Hudson's Bay Company
– and Edward Hopkins #5835
– architecture
 – Alberta, trading posts #8129
 – Fort Langley (BC), trading post #8477
 – Lower Fort Garry (Man) #8483
  – men's house #8482
 – Manitoba #8094
 – Moose Factory (Ont) #7976 7998 8032
 – plankwall framing #7712
 – Red River Settlement (Man) #8097 8100
 – Victoria (BC) #8175
 – warehouses #8480
– ceinture fléchée #2818 2819 2824 2827
– imports of Spode and Copeland pottery
 #2300 2357 2358
– pottery #2351
– stained glass windows, John Allward
 #4515
– support of Canadian artists (1821-1860)
 #273
Hudson River School
– and Aaron Allan Edson #5362
– and Robert Stuart Duncanson #5338
Huel, Georges, Can artist, 1930- #5858
– designs, Olympic Games (1976) #898 901
 902
Hughes, Edward John, Can artist, 1913-

#1996 5859 5861
– and realism #110
– exhibitions
 – (1976) #5860
Hughes, Lynn, Can sculptor, 1941-
– ceramic sculptures (1970s) #2065
– Rank Beginnings #5862
Hughto, Darryl, Amer artist, 1943-
– exhibitions, group
 – (1981) #722
Huguet (dit Latour), Pierre, Can silversmith,
 1748-1817
– as teacher of Paul Morand #6604
– pax #2666
– works, Detroit Institute of Arts (Detroit,
 Mich) #2691
Hull (Qué)
– recreation buildings #9081
Hull (Qué), National Capital Region
– statues and monuments #762
human figure in art
– see also hands; heads; nude in art;
 skeletons in art; women in art
– art, Haida Indians #4070
– Bobak, Bruno Joseph #4760
– Bonham, Don #4794
– Brooker, Bertram Richard #317
– Canada #71 103
 – 19th-20th cs., sculpture #760
 – (1878-1978), painting #135
 – (1940s) #380
 – (1960s), woodcarving #744
 – (1970s) #578 611 6676
  – ceramic sculpture #774
 – (1980s), sculpture #796
– Coughtry, John Graham #5190
– Cox, Elford Bradley #5202
– Fairley, Barker #344
– Lemieux, Jean-Paul #6233
– MacEachern, Ian #6386
– Montréal (Qué)
 – (1940s-1950s) #1426
 – (1950s-1960s) #1438
– Nichols, Jack #6698
– Pellan, Alfred #6822
– Québec (1970s), prints #1651
– Saint John (NB), 20th c. #1184
– sculpture, Inuit #4404
Humberstone Potteries, ceramic
 manufacturer (north of Toronto, Ont)
 #2288
– (1798-1918) #2338
Hume, Clare, Can photographer, fl. 1970s-
– portfolio of photographs #991
Humeston, Jay, Can furniture-maker, fl.
 1798-1815 #2493
Humlebaek (Denmark), Louisiana Museum
 of Modern Art
– exhibitions
 – 10 Canadian Artists in the 1970s (1980)
  #703
Hümme, Joseph Julius, Can artist, 1825-1889
 #5863
Hummer Sisters
– performance art #655
Humphrey, Jack Weldon, Can artist,
 1901-1967 #336 1121 1128 1173 1179 1184
 5864 5865 5867 5868
– and Maritime painting (1960s) #1122
– as member, Canadian Group of Painters
 #324
– compared with Emily Carr #404
– exhibitions
 – (1970) #5870

– (1978) #5871
– exhibitions, group
  – (1966) #1123
  – (1973) #1182
– interview #5869
– on Canadian art (1940s) #5866
– on Maritime art (1950s) #1172
Humphrey, Ruth, Can educator, 1898-
– correspondence, Emily Carr (1937-1944)
  #5029
Humphreys Glass Works, glass
  manufacturer (Trenton, NS) #2398 2400
  2409 2417
Humphries, Henry, Brit naval officer, artist
  in Canada, d. 1799
– views, Nootka Sound, Vancouver Island
  (BC) #2002
Hunsicker, Isaac, Can fraktur artist,
  1803-1870 #2255
Hunt, Henry, Can sculptor, 1923- #4132 5872
– totem pole, Beacon Hill Park (Victoria, BC)
  #4115
Hunt, Richard, Can artist, 1951- #4148
Hunt, William Edward, Can artist, fl. 1916
  #1391
Hunter, Samuel, Can artist, 1858-1939
– cartoons, Toronto Star #943
Hunter, William E.N., Amer architect,
  1868-1947
– Hamilton (Ont), First Methodist Church
  #7957
hunting in art
– see also sporting subjects
– Etook, Tivi #5375
– Parr, Nuna #6768
hunting lodges, Canadian
– Gaspé (Qué), log cabins #7896
Huntress, Judith Allsopp, Can artist, 1943-
  #717
– exhibitions, group
  – (1975) #1867
Huot, Charles Edouard, Can artist,
  1855-1930 #302 1312 1315 1323 5873 5875
  5876 5878 5884
– and Elzéar Delamarre #5877
– as teacher of Edmond LeMoine #6243
– as teacher of Georges-Henri Duquet #5343
– Débats sur les langues de 1793, National
  Assembly (Québec, Qué) #5880 5881
– Je me souviens, National Assembly
  (Québec, Qué) #5874
– paintings
  – (1873) #5879
  – Chapel of l'Ermitage (Lac Bouchette,
    Qué) #5882
  – Church of Saint-Sauveur (Québec, Qué)
    #5883
Huppé (dit Lagroix), Joseph, Can builder,
  hatter, 1696-after 1776 #269 270
Huret, Grégoire, Fr artist, 1606-1670
– and nationalism in art #1373
Hurlbut, Spring, Can artist, 1931-
– exhibitions, group
  – (1981) #723
Hurley, Robert Newton, Can artist,
  1894-1980 #5885 5886
– Cowley, Reta Madeline, compared with
  #5200
– exhibitions, group
  – (1970) #1918
  – (1971) #1920
Hurni, Jean-Claude, Can photographer,
  1936-
– portfolio of photographs #997 999

Huron Indians
– art
  – (1600-1760) #3579
  – culture (1910s) #3514
  – dyes and dyeing #165
  – pipes #3504 3632
  – pottery #3502 3520
  – wampum #3495 3526
  – woodwork #3519
Huron Pottery, ceramic manufacturer
  (Egmondville, Ont)
– moulds #2334
Hurst, Patrick Russell, Can artist, 1947-
– exhibitions, group
  – (1977) #781
Hurtubise, Jacques, Can artist, 1939- #1418
  1542 1543 5887 5889
– and minimal art #1483
– and Optical art #1445
– and plasticiens #1439
– exhibitions
  – (1981) #5890
– exhibitions, group
  – (1965) #469
  – (1967) #480 491
  – (1968) #1263
– Gagnon-Fortier, C., compared with #5552
– paintings (1960-1980) #5888
– symposium, Musée du Nouveau-Monde
  (La Rochelle, France), (1980) #1559
Hushlak, Gerald, Can artist, 1944- #5892
– exhibitions, group
  – (1978) #1961
– interview #5891
Hutchinson, Leonard, Can artist, 1896-1980
– prints (1930-1940) #5893
Hutchinson, Mrs. Richard Ernest, Can artist,
  fl. 1850s #1118
Hutchinson, Peter, Can photographer, 1946-
– portfolio of photographs #991
Hutchison, Alexander Cowper, Can
  architect, 1838-1922
– LaSalle (Qué), manoir Ogilvie #8636
Hutchison, Wood & Miller, Can
  architectural firm
– Montréal (Qué), houses #8556
– Toronto (Ont), Masonic Temple,
  competition #9062
Hutchison & Wood, Can architectural firm
– Montréal (Qué), Canadian Express
  Company Building #9304
– Toronto (Ont), John Ross Robertson and
  Glenholme schools, competition for #9437
Hutner, Paul, Can artist, 1948- #1807
– exhibitions, group
  – (1974) #565
  – (1975) #1809
Hutterites in Canada
– art #1962
– decorative arts #2140
  furniture #2585
Hutton, Gordon Johnston, Can architect,
  1881-1942
– domestic architecture #8496
Hutton, John, Brit artist, 1906-
– engraved glass panels, lobbies, National
  Library of Canada and Public Archives of
  Canada (Ottawa, Ont) #5894
Hyde, C., Can artist, fl. 1847-1848
– as member, Toronto Society of Arts #1689
Hyde, Laurence, Can artist, 1914-
– on stamp design #811
– on wood engraving #5895
Hynes, Feldman & Watson, Can

architectural firm
– Oak Ridge (Ont), De La Salle Training
  School #9386
– Toronto (Ont)
  – Allen's Bloor Street Theatre #9071
  – Allen's Danforth Theatre #9072
  – Allen Theatre #9069
  – Saint Charles Hotel #9269
Hynes, James Patrick, Can architect,
  1868-1953
– Toronto (Ont), Hotel Mossop #9262

I

I.M. Pei & Associates
– see Pei, I.M., & Associates
Iacurto, Francesco, Can artist, 1908- #5896
IBM
– see International Business Machines
  Corporation (IBM)
Iceland
– (1946), Carl Fellman Schaefer on #7150
icons
– Schlieper, Heiko #7161
Igloolik (NWT)
– Dorset artifacts #4337 4342
igloos #4213 4271 8733
Iglulik
– culture
  – (1920s) #4326
  – early 20th c. #4366
Ikoy Partnership, Can architectural firm
– Winnipeg (Man), Ikoy Partnership
  Architects' office #8091
Iksik, Francis, Can sculptor, 1920- #5897
Ikutaaq, David, Can sculptor, 1929- #4407
– exhibitions
  – (1981) #5898
île à la Crosse (Sask), school and community
  centre
– architecture, Douglas Joseph Cardinal
  #8341
île aux Coudres (Qué)
– decorative arts #2178 2184
  – (1930s) #2168
île Bélair (Qué)
– views
  – Hébert, Adrien #5764
île d'Anticosti (Qué)
– architecture #7869
île d'Orléans (Qué)
– architecture #7847
– art #1323
– art and architecture #1233 1238
– costume, 17th c. #2895
– domestic architecture #8624
  – 18th-19th cs. #8582
  – (1761-1767) #8613
– rugs #2764
– weaving #1327
île d'Orléans (Qué), Charles Porteous House
– mural paintings, William Brymner #4951
île d'Orléans (Qué), Church of
  Saint-François
– architectural model #8869
île d'Orléans (Qué), Church of
  Saint-François-de-Sales
– architecture and interior #8796
île d'Orléans (Qué), Church of Saint-Jean
– architecture and interior #8801
île d'Orléans (Qué), Church of Saint-Pierre

– architecture and interior #8802
île d'Orléans (Qué), Church of
  Sainte-Famille
– architectural model #8869
– architecture and interior #8795
– sculptures, Lauréat Vallière #7455
– woodcarvings #1612
île de Qikertaaluk (Qué)
– petroglyphs #4344
île Perrot (Qué), Church of
  Sainte-Jeanne-Françoise-de-Chantal
– architecture and interior #8805
îles de la Madeleine (Qué)
– barns, 19th c. #9230
– domestic architecture #8624
– photographic views
  – Beaudoin-Hansen, Kéro #4648
– quilts (1920s) #2794
Iliu, Josef, Fr artist, 1914- #5899
– on his art #8229
Illsely, Templeton & Archibald, Can
  architectural firm
– Dorval (Qué), Montreal International
  Airport. Air Terminal Building #9515
illumination
– see lighting
Illustrated London News, Brit periodical
– illustrations, Edward John Russell #7110
illustration, book
– see illustration
illustration, botanical
– see botanical illustration
illustration, Canadian #925
– 18th-19th cs. #246 812
– 19th-20th cs., children's books #934 937
– 19th c.-1940s, and Québec folk songs #938
– 19th c.-1960s #925
– (1759-1914), Québec, revolutionary subjects
  #1351
– (1880s-1940s) #28
– (1890s-1940s) #928
– (1910-1921), *Farmer's Magazine* #1765
– (1910s) #205 916
– (1930), Canadian National Exhibition
  (Toronto, Ont) #313
– (1940s) #374
  – Beny, Wilfred Roloff, on #921
– (1945), textbooks #919
– (1950s) #855 860
– (1960s) #867 868
  – Québec #926
– (1965-1968) #874
– (1967) #877
– (1970s) #907
– (1980s) #912
– (1981) #941
– advertising
  – (1940s) #850
  – (1960s) #870
  – (1970s) #888 894
– Art Directors' Club of Toronto #854
– Barnsley, James Macdonald #4612
– Béraréal #4692
– Brigden, Fred #4913
– Bush, Jack Hamilton #4963
– Cain, Maryanne #4987
– Cassan, Vital #5053
– Clark, Kelly #5109
– Coburn, Frederick Simpson #5123
– Cooper, Heather #5174 5175
– costume illustrations, Public Archives of
  Canada. Picture Division (Ottawa, Ont)
  #2904
– Cruikshank, William #5212
– Curnoe, Greg #5230

– Duguay, Rodolphe #5314 5316
– Duncan, James D. #2834
– Eager, William H. #5351
– Franchère, Joseph-Charles #5497
– Gagnon, Clarence Alphonse #1 359 5541
  5543 5546 5547
– Group of Seven #939 1774
– Innes, John I. #5901
– Jefferys, Charles William #5954 5955 5957
  5959
– Jopling, Frederick Waistell #822
– Julien, Henri #5981 5983 5984 5985 5986
  5987 5988 5990 5991
– Kerr, Illingworth Holey #6047 6048
– Kroupa, Bohuslar #6104
– Kurelek, William #6111
– Leduc, Ozias #918
– Lemieux, Jean-Paul #6239
– Macdonald, Evan Weekes #6356
– MacDonald, Thoreau #6381 6382 6383 6384
  6385
– Massicotte, Edmond-Joseph #6441
– Millen, Walter H., collection #21
– Murphy, Rowley Walter #6666
– Phillips, Walter Joseph #6856
– *Picturesque Canada: The Country As It Was
  and Is* (1882) #914
– Price, Art #6929
– Robinson, Albert Henry #7056
– Russell, Edward John #7110 7111
– Sandham, J.Henry #7121
– Seton, Ernest Thompson #7172 7173
– Suzor-Coté, Marc-Aurèle de Foy #7299
– Thomson, Tom #7367 7368
– Tillenius, Clarence #7377
– Tremblay, Jean-Jacques #7425
– Trier, Walter #7428
– Varley, Frederick Horsman #7466 7467
– Wiseman, James Lovell #7603
Illustration, L', Fr periodical
– illustrations, Henri Julien #5983 5984
illustration, medical
– see medical illustration
illustration, periodical
– see periodical illustration
illustration, topographical
– see topographical illustration
illustration, Woodlands
– (1970s-1980s) #4139
Image Bank (Vancouver, BC) #2040
– correspondence, on 1971 Miss General
  Idea Pageant #546
– postal cards #826
Image et Verbe #1502
Image Nation, Can periodical #992 3314
imagery
– Shadbolt, Jack Leonard, on #7183 7192
imagination
– see also creativity; fantasy
– in Canadian art and literature #104
Immaculate Conception
– see Mary, Virgin, Immaculate Conception
Immaculates
– see Precisionism
immigrant artists in Canada
– (1940s-1960s) #465
– (1970s) #3287
– Ontario, 19th c. #2261
immigrants in art
– photographs of, Québec (1908-1910) #1031
Imperial Oil Ltd.
– collection, Canadian art #3241
– Jefferys, Charles William, paintings and
  drawings #5956

Imperial Oil Review, Can periodical #924
– illustrations #3241
implements, Algonquian #3529
– beadwork #3635
implements, Athapaskan #4073 4104 4105
implements, Beothuk
– Red Indian Lake (Nfld) #3623
implements, Blackfoot #3654
implements, Dogrib #4089
implements, Dorset
– Cape Dorset (NWT) #4322
implements, Great Basin Indians #3986
implements, Han #4101
implements, Huron #3514
implements, Indians of North America
– prehistoric #3393 3401
– shellwork #3388
– trade goods #3440
implements, Ingalik #4087
implements, Inuit
– ivory carving #4453
implements, Iroquois
– beadwork #3635
implements, Micmac #3569
implements, Mistassini #4080
implements, Netsilik #4363
implements, Northwest Coast Indians #4068
implements, Ojibwa #4089
– Parry Island Reservation (Ont) #3540
implements, Plains
– New York (NY), American Museum of
  Natural History #3668
implements, Potawatomi
– Parry Island Reservation (Ont) #3540
implements, Quinault #3845
implements, Slavey #4089
implements, Tanaina #4085
implements, Tanana #4095
implements, Tlingit #3976
implements, Woodlands #3491
– beadwork #3635
Impressionism
– and Albert Henry Robinson #7055
– and Alfred Pellan #6815
– and Donald Shaw MacLaughlan #6394
– and Ernest Lawson #6176 6178
– and Group of Seven #354
– and Helen Galloway McNicoll #6507
– and J.E.H. MacDonald #6366
– and James Wilson Morrice #6618 6622
  6633
– and John Wentworth Russell #7109
– and Lionel LeMoine FitzGerald #5450
– and Marc-Aurèle de Foy Suzor-Coté #7297
  7299 7300 7301
– and Maurice Galbraith Cullen #5214 5218
  5224
– and Ozias Leduc #6200
– Canada #39
  – (1890-1900) #190
  – (1895-1930s) #227
  – (1895-1935) #115
– Canada and France (1867-1914) #274
– criticism of (1881) #169
Impressions, Can periodical #996 3314
– (1970s) #3310
Impulse, Can periodical #538 3310
Imredy, Elek, Can sculptor, 1912-
– exhibitions, group
  – (1971), medals #772
– garden sculpture #1849
INCA
– see International Native American Council
  of Arts (INCA)
Incite, Can periodical #992

Independent Art Association (Montréal, Qué)
– (1932-1963) #1379
Indian artists
– Alexie, Fred #3827 4507
– Ash, Samuel #4161 4558
– Ashkewe, Del #4159 6648
– Beam, Carl #4155 4173
– Beardy, Henry #4649
– Beardy, Jackson #1866 4128 4131 4161 4634 4635 4636
– Bell, Leland #4173
– Brown, Charles #3856
– Chapman, Isaac #5088
– Chee Chee, Benjamin #5100 5101 6648
– Clutesi, George C. #3956 5122
– Cranmer, Doug #4121
– Cross, John #4169
– Crow, James #4113
– David, Joe #4148 5266
– Davidson, Robert #4006 4132 4162 5267 5268 5269
– Davidson, Robert Charles #4148
– Debassige, Blake #4173
– Dixon, Pat #5294
– Edenshaw, Albert Edward #5358
– Edenshaw, Charles #3820 3995 4006 4042 4169 5358 5359 5360 6985
– Edenshaw, Henry #5361
– Ense, Don #4155 4173
– Fisher, Sanford #5445
– Franks, Rhonda #4159
– Gwaytihl #3862 4169
– Hamilton, Ron #4132 4148
– Hanuse, Roy James #4148
– Hill, Stan #5800
– Hill, Tom #4155
– Houle, Robert James #5844
– Hunt, Henry #4115 4132 5872
– Hunt, Richard #4148
– James, Charlie #3848
– Janvier, Alex Simeon #1866 4128 4131 5936 5937 5938 5939
– John, Chauncey Johnny #4113
– Kakegamic, Goyce #4151 4155 4158 4159 4161
– Kakegamic, Joshim #4151 4158 4161
– Kakige, Francis #4159
– King-ego #3862
– Laford, John #4173
– Lonechild, Michael #6322
– Lorenzetto, Adeline #3941
– Madahbee, Mel #4173
– Marks, Gerald Yanders #2706 4148
– Martin, David #4115
– Martin, Mungo #3912 4054 4115 5872 6427 6428 6429 6430 6984
– McGrath, Jim #554
– McGuire, Pat #5294
– Miller, Gary #6538 6539
– Moody, Rufus #4006
– Morris, Christina #6635
– Morrisseau, Norval #3350 4122 4144 4151 4154 4155 4156 4161 6643 6644 6645 6646 6647 6649
– Neel, Ellen #4121
– Odjig, Daphne #1866 4128 4131 4154 4173 6731
– Panamick, Martin #4173
– Peel, Bryan #6788 6789
– Peters, Barry #4151
– Peters, Mary #3941
– Peters, Paddy #4151
– Price, Art #6928 6929 6930

– Price, Tom #4169 6932 6933 6934
– Ravenhill, Alice #4114
– Ray, Carl #4161 6648
– Reid, Bill #2695 4121 4155 4162 6984 6985 6986 6987 6988 6989
– Restoule, Tim #4159 4173
– Robson, John #4169
– Ross, Rosie #4121
– Sapp, Allen #4125 4161 7122 7123 7125
– Seaweed, Willie #4054
– Shaughnessy, Arthur #5872
– Shilling, Arthur #4154 7198
– Smith, Awasatlas #4148
– Speck, Henry #4121
– Tailfeathers, Gerald #4125 7312 7313
– Tait, Norman #7314
– Thomas, Jacob #7346
– Trudeau, Angus #4173
– Trudeau, Randy #4159 4173
– Vickers, Roy Henry #4148
– Vincent, Zacharie #7493 7494
– Williams, Francis #4148 7587
– Williams, Saul #4151
– Yerxa, Leo #4140 7624
Indian Carry, Saranac Lake (NY), Habitat
– architecture, Moshe Safdie #8404
Indian Education Centre (Alta)
– architecture and interior, Douglas Joseph Cardinal #9494
Indians of Central America
– and Northwest Coast Indians #3810
– art #3435
– in art #3427
– serpents #3391
– weaving #3832
Indians of North America
– see also Abenaki, Algonquian, Algonquin, Arapaho, Assiniboine, Athapaskan, Bella Coola, Boethuk, Blackfoot, Blood, Carrier, Cayuga, Chilcotin, Chilkat, Chipewyan, Clallam, Coast Salish, Cowichan, Cree, Crow, Dakota, Delaware, Dogrib, East Main Cree, Flathead, Gitksan, Great Basin, Gros Ventre, Haida, Han, Hare, Hidatsa, Huron, Ingalik, Interior Salish, Iroquois, Kaska, Klikitat, Kootenay, Koyukon, Kutchin, Kwakiutl, Lillooet, Lummi, Makah, Maliseet, Mandan, Menomine, Micmac, Mistassini, Mohawk, Montagnais, Nahani, Naskapi, Neutral, Nez Percé, Niska, Nootka, Northwest Coast, Ojibwa, Oneida, Onondaga, Osage, Ottawa, Passamaquoddy, Penobscot, Piegan, Plains, Plateau, Potawatomi, Quinault, Salish, Sarcee, Saulteaux, Sekani, Seneca, Shuswap, Siouan, Skeena, Skokomish, Slavey, Snuqualmi, Squamish, Tagish, Tahltan, Tanaina, Tanana, Tête de Boule, Thompson, Tlingit, Tsimshian, Tutchone, Twana, Woodlands, Yellowknife Indians
– aesthetics #3487
– (1970s) #4137
– and religion, 17th c. #1354 1358
– architecture #7722
– and Douglas Joseph Cardinal #8341
– influence of climate #7701
art #5 45 63 129 136 137 485 2093 2096 3117 3118 3148 3329 3351 3352 3354 3355 3357 3359 3366 3372 3382 3395 3397 3400 3408 3412 3418 3421 3422 3423 3425 3428 3430 3431 3436 3438 3442 3448 3450 3452 3454 3455 3458 3459 3460 3463 3464 3465 3466 3467 3473 3477 4126 4127 4146 4165
– 19th c. #3486

– 20th c. #4163 4172
– (1950s) #151
– (1960s) #4125 4136
– (1970s) #3376 4138 4140 4155
– (1980s) #4161 4171
– and Inuit art #3332 4325
– therapeutic symbolism #3356
– basketry #2943 3389 3394 3446 3447 3991
– 20th c. #2143
– beadwork #2143 3420 3449 3457
– beaver motif #23 56
– Cardinal, Douglas J.H., on #8342
– conservation of architecture and art #7767
– cosmology #3498
– costume #3453
– 17th-19th cs. #2825
– influence on Canadian costume #2841 2849
– cradles #3407 3485
– culture #3343
– decorative arts #2089 2104 2107 2125 2131
– 20th c. #2143
– (1964-1967) #2108 2109
– Québec (1970s) #2230
– dolls, 20th c. #2143
– embroidery #2783
– 18th c. #2169 2171
– facial painting #3461
– footwear #2814 3424
– graphic arts (1970s) #3373
– implements, prehistoric #3393
– in art #12
– 16th-18th cs. #276
– 16th-19th cs. #255 256 260
– 17th-19th cs. #3427
– 17th c. #1363
– Armstrong, William #4552
– Brown, Annora #4933
– Carr, Emily #5011
– Catlin, George #1845 3384 3426
– Chauchetière, Claude #234 235
– headless figures #281
– Hébert, Louis-Philippe #5767
– Henderson, James #5778 5779
– Heriot, George #5783 5784
– Hooker, Marion Hope Nelson #1896
– Housser, Muriel Yvonne McKague #5845
– images of women #121
– Jefferys, Charles William #5953
– Kane, Paul #1845 3386 6002 6003 6004 6005 6006 6011 6012 6014 6015 6016 6018
– Krieghoff, Cornelius #6091 6093 6097 6436
– late 19th c. #1839
– Légaré, Joseph #6222
– Lynn, Washington Frank #6348
– Miller, Alfred Jacob #6536 6537
– Morris, Edmund Montague #6636 6637 6638
– Nicolas, Louis #1372
– Phillips, Walter Joseph #6854
– Proctor, Alexander Phimister #6943 6944
– Rindisbacher, Peter #7003 7005 7006 7007
– Roper, Edward #7077
– Shilling, Arthur #7197
– Simcoe, Elizabeth Posthuma Gwillim #7210
– Thornton, Mildred Valley Stinson #7375
– Verner, Frederick Arthur #7484
– Vincent, Zacharie #7493
– White, John #7552

– Indian motifs, on pottery (1920s) #2278
– jewellery, 20th c. #2143
– law and art #3347
– looms #3413
– moccasins #2241 2872
– musical instruments #3363
– painting #165 3432 3451 3462
  – 20th c. #3441
  – (1970s) #6648
– photographs of
  – Boorne, William Hanson #4796
  – Boorne and May #1950 4797
  – Chesterfield, Albert A. #5102
  – Curtis, Edward Sheriff #3399 3480
  – Hime, Humphrey Lloyd #5801 5803
  – Jauvin, Serge #1562
  – Mathers, Charles Wesley #6451
  – Moodie, Geraldine #6602
  – Pollard, Harry #6899
– pictographs #3390 3392
– pipes #3470 3700
  – drawings of, George Catlin #3478
– pipes and tobacco #3416 3444
– prehistoric artifacts #3371 3380 3401
  – Arctic region #4373
– quillwork #3474 3475
– quilts #2799
– religious articles from Jesuit missionaries
  #2192
– rock art #3433 3472 3481 3482 3484
– sculpture #761 3362
– sepulchral monuments #733
– serpents #3391
– shamanism #3361 3383
– shellwork #3388
– silver #2630
– snowshoes #2812 3515
– textiles #2727 2739 3469
– Thunderbird #3410
– toys #2917 2934
– trade goods #3440
– trade silver #269 270 728 2101 2628 2629
  2631 2633 2634 2651 2653 2654 2655 2659
  2664
– treaty medals #763
– wampum #3387 3522 3612
– weaving #2747 2748 3476
  – ceinture fléchée #2818 2823 2824 2827
    2873
Indians of South America
– art #3355 3412
– in art #3427
– weaving, influence on Canadian weaving
  #2774
industrial architecture
– see also breweries; factories; mills;
  warehouses
industrial architecture, Canadian
– (1938-1942) #7666
– (1950s) #9241
– (1960-1970) #7710
– Alberta (1900-1930s) #8126
– Montréal (Qué)
  – (1950s) #7900
  – architectural drawings, Archives
    nationales du Québec à Montréal #8604
– Nova Scotia, 17th-19th cs. #7814
– Ontario, 19th c. #8006
– Québec (1960s) #7862
– Rideau Canal region (Qué and Ont) #8019
– Winnipeg (Man) #8105
industrial design, Canadian
– (1940s) #2600 2601 2603 2604
  – recommendations #353

– (1947) #2602
– (1948-1958) #2611
  – Association of Canadian Industrial
    Designers #2612
– (1950s) #2605 2606 2607 2608 2609 2610
– (1960s) #2614 2615
  – household objects #2619
  – influence of National Gallery of Canada
    (Ottawa, Ont) #3039
– (1961-1973), National Design Council
  #2624
– (1967), Canada Design '67 program #2616
  2617
– (1970), Design Centre, closures (Montréal,
  Qué, and Toronto, Ont) #2621
– (1970s) #610 2620 2622 2626
– Alberta (1970s) #1951
– and architecture (1960s) #8231
– and Donald William Buchanan #3325
– Bersudsky and Associates #4711
– Montréal (Qué), Expo '67 #2618
– Ottawa (Ont), National Gallery of Canada.
  Design Centre (1953-1954) #3033
– Québec #2190
  – (1960s) #2195
  – late 19th c. #2598
– Royal Canadian Academy of Arts #2
industrial housing
– see workers' housing
Infonie #1502
Ingalik Indians
– culture #4087
– masks #4083
Ingalls, Harry Creighton, Amer architect,
  1876-1936
– Winnipeg (Man), Bank of Hamilton #9171
Inglis, James, Can photographer, fl.
  1864-1884
– and Frederic Marlett Bell-Smith #4666
Inkster, John, Can merchant, farmer,
  1799-1874
– residence, Seven Oaks House (Winnipeg,
  Man) #8703
Innes, Alice A., Can artist, 1890-1970 #5900
Innes, John I. (Jack), Can artist, 1863-1941
  #5901
– cartoons, Vancouver Sun #943
– exhibitions, group
  – (1961) #62
Inoucdjouac (Qué)
– art #4452
– graphic arts
  – (1970s) #4487
  – (1972-1975) #4475
– graphic arts and sculpture #4267 4279
insects in art
– Berczy, William Bent #241 242
insignia
– see also badges; ceremonial maces;
  emblems and mottoes
insignia, Canadian
– military #2900
installation works
– (1980), Canada #691 699
– (1980), Toronto (Ont) #1834
– Banwell, Mike #4601
– Cameron, Eric #656 667
– Carr-Harris, Ian #710
– Craven, David #687 710
– Cruise, Stephen #5213
– Dean, Max #5274
– Fish, Robert #687
– Frenkel, Vera #5521 5525
– Gallie, Tommie J. #5553

– Gervais, Raymond #687
– Gnass, Peter #1563 5620 5621
– Goodwin, Betty Roodish #5631
– Grauer, Sherry #5647
– Harding, Noel #656 667
– Hughes, Lynn #5862
– Johnson, Nancy #710
– Johnson, Terence #5969
– Levine, Les #6263
– Massey, John #687 723 6439
– Murray, Ian #710
– Singleton, Becky #723
– Trakas, George #7419 7420 7421
– Wall, Jeff #7506
– Whiten, Colette #7556
– Whittome, Irene #710 7565 7568 7569 7570
– Wood, Alan #7611
Institut des artisans
– and Québec art (1830) #1368
Institut des artisans et association
  bibliophile du comté de Drummond
  (L'Avenir, Qué)
– (1856-1890) #1360
Instruments of the Passion
– see Jesus Christ, passion
Insurrection Art Co.
– and Robert Walker #7505
intaglio printing
– see also printing
intaglio printing, Canadian
– Montréal (Qué), McGill University.
  McCord Museum #840
Interdesign Ltd., Can design firm
– and Robin B. Bush #4980
interior decoration
– see also Art Nouveau interior decoration;
  drapery; upholstery; Victorian interior
  decoration; wallpaper
interior decoration, Canadian
– (1890-1900) #190
– (1920s) #7960
– (1960s), interior designers and
  manufacturers #9324
– British Columbia, houses #8712
– National Parks Branch habitation
  reconstruction policy #7758
– trains and hotels #3281
– universities (1960s) #9402
Interior Salish Indians
– architecture #3872
– jade #3331
Intermedia (Vancouver, BC) #2040
– and Glenn Alun Lewis #6275
International Boundary Commission
– surveys (1886-1900) #1014 1015
International Business Machines
  Corporation (IBM)
– collection, Canadian art, 20th c. #350
International Calvert House Competition
– (1954) #8510
International Grenfell Association
– support of Newfoundland handicrafts
  (1950s) #2146
International Native American Council of
  Arts (INCA) #4163
International Silver Company,
  silversmithing firm (Hamilton, Ont)
– (1922-1960s) #2642
International Style (architecture, 20th c.)
– Canada #7680
  – banks #9196
  – domestic architecture #8502
– Prairies #8084 8086
internment camps

– *see* concentration camps
Intersystems (Toronto, Ont)
– sculptures, use of light #767
Inuit
– *see also* Birnirk, Caribou Eskimo, Chukchi,
  Copper, Dorset, Iglulik, Ipiutak, Labrador,
  Netsilik, Okvik, Old Bering Sea, Punuk,
  Sarqaq, Sallirmiut, Thule
– aesthetics #4282 4297
– architecture
  – (1950s) #8184
  – (1970s) #7728
  – influence of climate #7701
  – wooden #7722
– art #25 63 136 137 1294 3117 3118 3172
  3188 3329 3351 3354 3355 3357 3366 3370
  3372 3374 3377 3463 3464 4179 4181 4182
  4188 4190 4193 4200 4216 4218 4223 4224
  4227 4231 4232 4235 4245 4255 4258 4262
  4264 4276 4278 4284 4289 4290 4292 4293
  4295 4296 4302 4306 4313 4338 4339 4360
  4368
  – 18th c.-1940s #4286
  – (1940s-1970s) #4277
  – (1950s) #151
  – (1950s-1970s) #4246
  – (1960s) #4204 4215
  – (1970s) #3376 4247 4256 4263 4270 4281
    4287
  – Alaska #4208 4280 4369 4424
    – (1970s) #4233
  – and James Archibald Houston #4452
    5846 5847
  – and perception #4294
  – and shamanism #4283
  – and values #4251
  – Baker Lake (NWT) #4266
  – bear cult #4355
  – biographical sources #4221 4252 4301
  – Canadian Arctic Producers #4222 4291
  – Cape Dorset (NWT) #4187 6270 6271
    6880 6881
  – concept of space #4341
  – concept of space and time #4244
  – dot motif #3332 4325
  – Eurasiatic animal style #4334
  – European influences #4176
  – in Arctic churches and public buildings
    #4304
  – Povungnituk (Qué) #4274
  – research methodology #4205 4225 4401
  – Southampton Island (NWT) #4184
  – symbolism #4234
  – therapeutic symbolism #3356
  – tree of life motif #3365
– art market #4236 4238 4242 4305 4396 4397
– artists' cooperatives #4288
– artists' marks #4250
– basketry #4180 4307 4309
– bonework #4319
– bows #4316
– ceremonial mace, Northwest Territories
  Council #4386 4389
– culture #3343 3368 4254 4317 4320
  – 18th c. #4097
  – (1840s) #4174
  – (1880s) #3379
  – (1930s) #4185
  – (1960s) #4399
  – Alaska #4272
  – Bering Strait (Alaska) #4318
  – Greenland #4315
  – Labrador (Nfld), (1910s) #4321
  – Levine, Les, on #6269

– Pitseolak, Peter, on #6876
– decorative arts #2089
  – (1964-1967) #2108 2109
  – (1970s) #3367
– drums #3363
– dyes and dyeing #4249
– embroidery #4259
– engraved artifacts #4323
– fantastic art #4240
– graphic arts #451 3345 4465 4466 4471 4474
  4482 4493 4500
  – (1959-1968) #4479
  – (1959-1972) #4478
  – (1959-1976) #4490
  – (1959-1980) #4498
  – (1960-) #4460
  – (1960s) #4463 4467
  – (1970s) #3373
  – (1972-1975) #4475
  – Alaska #4217
  – and shamanism #4488
  – and Terrence Ryan #4194
  – Baffin Island (NWT) #4499
  – Baker Lake (NWT) #4241 4472 4473 4480
    4481 4486
  – biographical sources #4497
  – Cape Dorset (NWT) #4461 4462 4464
    4470 4476 4477 4483 4484 4491 4495
  – game and contest subjects #4492
  – Holman (NWT) #4197
  – Inoucdjouac (Qué) #4487
  – Povungnituk (Qué) #4468 4489 4494
    4496
– graphic arts and sculpture #4191 4201 4228
  4229 4239 4285
  – (1950s) #4311
  – (1960s) #4189
  – amautik subjects #4300
  – Cape Dorset (NWT) #4192 4211 4299
  – Holman (NWT) #3350
  – Inoucdjouac (Qué) #4267 4279
  – Povungnituk (Qué) #4219
– graphic arts collections
  – Toronto-Dominion Bank #4248
– igloos #4213 4271 8733
– in art
  – Back, George #4580
  – Bruce, Robert Donald #4940
  – Constantineau, Fleurimond #5168
  – images of women #121
  – Rindisbacher, Peter #7005
  – White, John #228 229 7552 7553
– inukshuks and inunguaks #4199
– kayaks and umiaks #3339
– law and art #3347
– masks #3337 3340 3940 4178 4212 4349
– painting #4202
– photographs of
  – (1920s) #1021
  – Chesterfield, Albert A. #5102
  – Mathers, Charles Wesley #6451
  – Pitseolak, Peter #6879
– pottery, Rankin Inlet (NWT) #4226
– prehistoric artifacts #3371 3380 4331 4336
  4343 4364 4352 4370 4371 4373 4378
  – Alaska #4340 4348
  – compared with Paleolithic artifacts
    #4329
  – Greenland #4206
  – Newfoundland and Labrador #4377
– sculpture #761 3359 3362 4183 4198 4257
  4261 4275 4381 4388 4390 4394 4395 4404
  4406 4410 4414 4418 4419 4423 4426 4427
  4428 4430 4431 4432 4433 4440 4442 4443

  4444 4446 4447 4449 4451 4455 4456
  – (1940s-1960s) #4392
  – (1950s) #4383 4384 4385 4387 4393
  – (1960s) #4407
  – (1970s) #4273 4420 4422 4448
  – Baker Lake (NWT) #4400 4402 4403 4408
    4434
  – Belcher Islands (NWT) #4459
  – Cape Dorset (NWT) #4425 4441
  – hands #4439
  – ivory carving #4175 4391 4438 4453 4458
  – Keewatin (NWT) #4196
  – Maricourt (Qué) #4405
  – mining quarries #4409
  – Povungnituk (Qué) #4411 4415 4417
    4421 4437
  – Rankin Inlet (NWT) #4203 4207 4210
    4314
  – Repulse Bay (NWT) #4450
  – soapstone carving #4214
  – Spence Bay (NWT) #4416 4454
  – whalebone carving #4413 4436 4445 4457
– Sea Goddess #4312 4376
– snowshoes #2812 3515
– string figures #4177
– tattooing #4209
– umiaks #3344
– wall hangings #4253
  – Baker Lake (NWT) #4230
– weaving, Pangnirtung (NWT) #4237 4298
  4308 4310
– women artists (1970s) #4260
Inuit artists
– Aipelee, Oshaweetuk #4386
– Akeeaktashuk #4504
– Akulukjuk, Malaya #4298
– Allukpik, John #4202
– Amarook, Michael #4403 4408
– Amittu, Davidialuk Alasua #4468 4521
  4522 4523
– Anghik, Abe #4530
– Angiju, Peter Nauja #4202 4531
– Angokwazhuk #4398
– Angotiawak #4532
– Anguhadluq, Luke #4268 4533
– Aqiggaaq, Mathew #4534
– Arluk, George #4547
– Arnasungnaaq, Barnabus #4403 4408 4554
– Ashevak, Johnniebo #4559 4563
– Ashevak, Karoo #4560 4561 4562
– Ashevak, Kenojuak #4260 4460 4563 4564
– Ashoona, Kiawak #4565
– Echalook, Thomasee #4487
– Erkoolik, Tuna #4407
– Etook, Tivi #4468 5374 5375
– Etungat, Abraham #5382
– Eyetoaq, Ada #5387
– Iksik, Francis #5897
– Ikutaaq, David #4407 5898
– Inukpuk, Daniel #4487
– Ipellie, Alootook #5902
– Iquliq, Tuna #5903
– Ishulutaq, Elisapee #4260
– Kavik, John #6036
– Kiakshuk #4460
– Kudluk, Thomassie #6105
– Malkauskas, Algie #4436
– Morgan, Peter #6607
– Nuna, Noah #6712
– Oonark, Jessie #4220 4242 4260 4460 6743
  6744
– Osuitok, Ipeelee #6745
– Osuitok, Tuqiqi #6746
– Parr, Nuna #6768 6769 6770

– Piqtoukun, David Ruben #775 6873
– Pitseolak, Mary #4260
– Pitseolak, Peter #4202 4242 4460 6874 6875
  6877 6880 6881 6883
– Pitsiulak, Lypa #4386
– Pootoogook, Kananginak #4460 6904
– Pudlat, Pudlo #4460
– Qinnuayuaq, Lucy #4260 4460
– Saila, Pauta #4460
– Shaa, Aqjangajuk #7174
– Sivuarapik, Charlie #7217
– Smith, Levi Alasua Pirti #4421
– Tagoona, Armand #7311
– Takrik, Bobby #7317
– Talirunili, Joe #7318
– Tatty, Robert #3350
– Teevee, Jamasie #4460
– Tiktak, John #4407 7376
– Tunnillie, Ikayukta #4460
– Tuu'luq, Marion #4255 4268 7441 7442
Inukpuk, Daniel, Can artist, 1942-
– stonecut prints #4487
inukshuks, Inuit
– Enukso Point (NWT) #4199
inukshuks, Netsilik #4363
inunguaks, Inuit
– Enukso Point (NWT) #4199
inventories
– Canadian art and architecture #159
Invermere (BC), hospital
– architecture, Smith & McCulloch #9031
Iowa City (Iowa), University of Iowa.
  Museum of Art
– exhibitions
  – *The Art of the Shaman* (1973) #3361
Ipellie, Alootook, Can artist, 1952-
– interview #5902
Ipiutak
– artifacts
  – compared with Dorset artifacts #4361
  – Point Spencer (Alaska) #4374
Iquliq, Tuna, Can sculptor, 1935-
– exhibitions
  – (1979) #5903
Iqutaq Group, Clyde River (Baffin Island,
  NWT)
– graphic arts #4499
Ireland, Denise, Can artist, 1949-
– on Jack Chambers #700
Irish in Canada
– 19th c. #8523
iron
– industry, Québec and Ontario, late
  18th-mid 19th cs. #2703
– use in Canadian architecture #7695
ironwork
– *see also* blacksmithing; cast iron
ironwork, American
– late 19th c., Halifax (NS) parks #2710
ironwork, British
– late 19th c., Halifax (NS) parks #2710
ironwork, Canadian
– 17th-19th cs. #2705
– 18th-19th cs. #2703
– architectural (1910s) #8222
– Beau, Paul #4640 4641
– Cauchon family #5062
– facade, Cauchon Block (later Empire
  Hotel) (Winnipeg, Man) #9361
– guide for collectors #2252
– New Brunswick #2150
– Norfolk County (Ont), Normandale Iron
  Works #2699
– Ontario, German-Alsatian funeral crosses

#2709
– Price, Ralph and Patricia, collection #971
– Québec #2226 2228 2702 2711 2712
  – 17th-18th cs. #2530 2531
  – as religious art #2713
  – funeral crosses #2716
– Trois-Rivières (Qué), Forges of
  Saint-Maurice #2698 2708 9238 9240
Iroquois Indians
– and Arthur Guindon #5665
– antler spoons #3524
– art #3434 3559 3566 3586 3601 3605 3633
  3639
  – 20th c. #4143 4150 4164
  – (1970s-1980s) #4139
  – (1980) #4159
– artifacts #3616
– basketry #3552 3562 3625
– beadwork #3635
– brooches #3509 3512
– combs #3587
– containers #3638 3744
– cradles #3593
– culture #3489 3490 3525 3631
– dance and song rituals #3598
– decorative arts (1960s) #4123
– gorgets #3536
– masks #3337 3570 3588 3595 3604 3613
  7346
– Midwinter ceremony #3606
– musical instruments #3363
– painting, 20th c. #4144
– painting and sculpture (1970s) #4133
– petroglyphs #3599
– pipes #3504 3618 3642 3644
– pottery #3502 3520 3545 3555 3564
– sashes #3534
– sculpture #3553
– shellwork #3505
– snowshoes #3523
– trade silver #3645 3646
– tree myths and symbols #3516
– wampum #3496 3518 3521 3532 3567 3603
  3607
– war clubs #3538
– woodwork #3519
Irving, Daphne, Can artist, 1933-
– exhibitions (reviews) #1167
Irving, Mary, Can, 19th c.
– samplers (1860s) #2786
Irving, Susan, Can, 19th c.
– samplers (1860s) #2786
Irving, William, Can architect, 1830-1883
– Toronto (Ont) #8059
  – Dominion Bank #9188
Isaacs, Avrom (Av), Can art dealer, 1926-
– on Inuit art market #4236
Ishulutaq, Elisapee, Can artist, 1925- #4260
Iskowitz, Gershon, Can artist, 1921- #5905
– exhibitions, group
  – (1972) #548
  – (1973) #556
  – (1977) #636
– exhibitions (reviews) #5906
– interview #5904
Islamabad (Pakistan), Canadian Embassy
– Kahane, Anne, *The Sea* #5998
Islamic art
– influence on Pat Bates #4627
Island Arts and Crafts Club (Victoria, BC)
– (1912-1922) #1980
Island Arts and Crafts Society (Victoria, BC)
– (1910-1941) #1980
– (1930s) #2034

Island Arts Club (Victoria, BC)
– (1910-1912) #1980
– (1910s) #1979
Island Lake (Man)
– culture, Saulteaux #3549
– Garden Hill Cooperative #4135
Isle of Man (England), Douglas School of
  Art
– Onley, Toni, as student #6741
Islet (Qué)
– *see* L'Islet (Qué)
Istanbul (Turkey), Hagia Sophia
– murals, J.E.H. MacDonald on #6362
Italianate style architecture
– Albernethy (Sask), Lanark Place #8700
– Canada
  – domestic architecture #7696
  – railroad stations #9539
– Ontario, churches #8904
Itter, Carole, Can artist, 1939- #2053
Ives, R.E., Can photographer, fl. 1970s-
– portfolio of photographs #991
Iveson, Robert, Can sculptor, 1951-
– exhibitions, group
  – (1978) #2066
ivories, Canadian
– Québec, 17th-18th cs. #1320
ivories, Inuit #4453
Ivujivik (Qué)
– graphic arts (1972-1975) #4475
Izumi, Arnott & Sugiyama, Can
  architectural firm
– Saskatoon (Sask), University of
  Saskatchewan #9490

J

J. McCausland & Co.
– *see* McCausland, J., & Co.
J.A. Brock & Co.
– *see* Brock, J.A., & Co.
J.M. Dent
– *see* Dent, J.M.
Jack, Richard, Can artist, 1886-1952
– *Mount Eisenhower*, Canadian Club of New
  York (New York, NY) #3211
Jack Klein & Henry Sears, Can architectural
  firm
– Toronto (Ont)
  – Don Valley Wood/Phase 1 project #8518
  – Whitburn Apartments #8514
  – Yorkwoods Village/Phase 1 project
    #8518
Jackson, Alexander Young (A.Y.), Can artist,
  1882-1974 #24 309 373 5909 5915 5919 5922
  5923 5925
– and Albert Henry Robinson #7057
– and Canadian silkscreen prints, World
  War II #805
– and Group of Seven #1732
– and Louis Jobin #5964
– and Maurice Hall Haycock #5754
– and Molly Lamb Bobak #4766
– and Paraskeva Clark #5112
– and Tom Thomson #7351 7352
– Arctic trips #1779
– art and writings #5908
– as art critic #3308
– at studio of Louis Jobin (1925) #5966
– autobiography #5916 5918
– book illustration and design #939

– correspondence, Anne Douglas Savage #7130
– drawings #5920
   – Sainte-Louise (Qué) #5921
– exhibitions
   – (1953) #5914
– *Georgian Bay, November,* University of Toronto. Hart House (Toronto, Ont) #3134
– interview #5917
– on army life #5913
– on Arthur Lismer #6297 6300
– on Canadian War Memorials exhibition, Burlington House (London, England) #1076
– on Frederick Grant Banting #4600
– on Frederick Horsman Varley #7463
– on J.E.H. MacDonald #6364
– on James Wilson Morrice #6622 6626
– on Lawren Stewart Harris #5720
– on Maurice Galbraith Cullen #5221
– on sketching in Algoma (Ont) #5907
– on sketching on the Alaska Highway #5911
– on war art #1098
– paintings, Canadian War Memorials Collection #1077
– reminiscences #5912
– sketchbook (1909), National Gallery of Canada (Ottawa, Ont) #5924
– views, Charlevoix (Qué) #5910
– writings #92
Jackson, George, Can furniture-maker, 1822-1901 #2573
Jackson, Henry, Can silversmith, 1837-1869 #2638
Jackson, Henry Alexander Carmichael, Can artist, 1877-1961 #5926
– watercolours of mushrooms, National Gallery of Canada (Ottawa, Ont) #5927 5928
Jackson, J.Anthony, Can architect, 1940-
– on architecture #7746
Jackson, John, Can furniture-maker, 1818-1898 #2573
Jackson, Naomi, Can artist, 1910-
– on children's art, Finland (1946) #5929
Jackson, Sarah Jeanette, Can artist, 1924- #5931
– copy art #5932
– interview #5930
– prints #1214
Jackson, William H., Amer artist in Canada, b. 1832 #1164
Jacobsen, Johan, Ger explorer, 1853-1947
– on material culture, Northwest Coast Indians #3762
Jacovleff, Alexandre, Russ artist in France, 1887-1938
– as teacher of Lilias Torrance Newton #6692 6693
Jacquard weaving
– Ontario, 19th c. #2740
Jacques, John, Can furniture-maker, 1804-1880 #2463
Jacques, Louis, Can sculptor, 1664-1735
– works, churches, Charlesbourg (Qué) #8851
Jacques, Sylvie, Can basketmaker, fl. 1981 #2954
Jacques & Hay Co., furniture-making firm (Toronto, Ont)
– (1835-1880s) #2463 2546 2559
Jacques Guillon Designers Inc., Can graphic design firm #884 2623

Jacquet, François, Can ceramicist, ca. 1731-after 1777 #269 270
Jacquiés (*dit* Leblond), Jean, Can artist, 1688-1724 #234 235 1572
– tabernacle of Saint-Maurice, Chapel of the Recollets (Trois-Rivières, Qué) #8850
Jacson (*dit* Jolybois), Antoine, Can sculptor, 1725-ca. 1805
– sculptures, Church of Saint-Charles (Lachenaie, Qué) #8808
– sculptures, Church of Saint-Pierre (île d'Orléans, Qué) #8802
jade, Aleut #3331
jade, Interior Salish #3331
jade, Salish #3331
jade, Tlingit #3331
Jaffe, Lilly Weil, Can collector, 20th c.
– collection, Inuit art #4223
jails
– *see* prisons
Jakobshavan (Greenland)
– prehistoric artifacts #4342
Jamaica
– views, Charles William Jefferys #5958
James, Ann, Can artist, 1925-
– exhibitions (reviews) #2383
James, Charlie, Can sculptor, ca. 1870-1938
– totem poles #3848
James, Percy Leonard, Can architect, 1880-1970
– Victoria (BC), Crystal Gardens #9134 9146
James, Ralph, Can furniture-maker, fl. 1926 #2583
James Bay (Qué)
– photographic views
   – Turcot, Guy #1562
– views (1981) #1566
James Campbell & Son, publishing firm (Toronto, Ont)
– Christmas greeting cards #842 890
James Chisolm & Son, Can architectural firm
– Winnipeg (Man), Marlborough Hotel #9277
James Secord & Saul Herzog, Can architectural firm
– Charlottetown (PEI), Confederation Centre, competition #9088
Jameson, Anna Brownell, Brit artist, writer in Canada, 1794-1860 #5934
– art and writings #5933
Janitch, Mary, Can artist, 1949- #5935
– works, Carmen Lamanna Gallery (Toronto, Ont) #1811
Janosi, Paul, Can photographer, ca. 1954-
– portfolio of photographs #1032
Janson (*dit* Lapalme), Pierre, Can builder, d. 1743 #7844
Janvier, Alex Simeon, Can artist, 1935- #4136 5936 5938
– exhibitions
   – (1978) #5939
– exhibitions, group
   – (1972) #4131
– exhibitions (reviews) #1866 4128
– paintings, County of Strathcona Building (Sherwood Park, Alta) #5937
Jaque, Louis, Can artist, 1919- #1542 1543 5940 5941
– exhibitions
   – (1977) #5942
   – (1978) #5943
Jarden, Richard, Can artist, 1947-
– exhibitions, group

– (1970) #534
– imaginary works #530
Jarvis, Alan, Can arts administrator, 1915-1972
– as director, National Gallery of Canada (Ottawa, Ont) #3049 3050
– correspondence, David Brown Milne #6563 6564
Jarvis, Donald Alvin (Don), Can artist, 1923- #5945
– and Vancouver (BC) painting (1950s) #1992
– as student of Hans Hofmann #402 1850
– exhibitions
   – (1977) #5947
– exhibitions, group
   – (1959) #1997
– exhibitions (reviews) #2074
– interview #5946
– notebooks #5944
Jarvis, Joan D., Can ceramicist, fl. 1980s #2394
Jarvis, Nathan Sturges, Amer collector, 1801-1862
– collection, art, Dakota Indians #3705
Jarvis, Samuel J., Can photographer, 1863-1952
– exhibitions, group
   – (1970) #1675
Jasmin, André, Can artist, 1922- #5948
– as student of Paul-Emile Borduas #4808
– on printmaking #817
Jasmin, Claude, Can writer, 1930-
– on Marc-Aurèle Fortin #5475
Jauran
– *see* Repentigny, Rodolphe de (Jauran)
Jauvin, Serge, Can photographer, fl. 1981 #1562
Jaworska, Tamara Hans, Can tapestry artist, 1926- #5949
– exhibitions (reviews) #2771
Jaycocks, T.G., Can photographer, b. 1889
– photographs and writings #5950
Jean, Jocelyn, Can artist, 1947-
– exhibitions, group
   – (1977) #1532
Jean, Marcel, Can artist, 1937- #5952
– columns, Grand Théâtre de Québec (Québec, Qué) #5951
Jean-Louis, Donald (Don), Can artist, 1937- #1762
Jeffers, Allan Merrick, Can architect, 1875-1926
– Edmonton (Alta), Legislative Buildings #8944 8945 8962
Jefferson Glass Co., glass manufacturer (Toronto, Ont) #2401
– glass patterns (1915-1940s) #2411
Jeffery, Alicia Anne, Can artist, b. 1808 #1219
Jefferys, Charles William, Can artist, 1869-1951 #10 5953 5954 5955 5956 5957
– exhibitions
   – (1976) #5958
– exhibitions, group
   – (1935) #17
– exhibitions (reviews) #1703 1710
– illustrations #916
   – *Farmer's Magazine* #1765
   – Ontario historic buildings #5959
– on views, Peel County (Ont), William Perkins Bull Collection #3208
Jenkins, Dan, Can architect, 1948-
– Calgary (Alta) #8726

Jensen, Vicki, Can photographer, fl. 1970s
– portfolio of photographs #998
Jenson, L.B., Can artist, 1921-
– drawings of Halifax (NS) buildings #7816
– drawings of Pictou County (NS) buildings #7827
Jérôme, frère
– see Paradis, Jérôme (frère Jérôme)
Jérôme, Jean-Paul, Can artist, 1928- #1541 5960
– exhibitions, group
    – (1977) #1465
    – (1981) #1471
Jerome Markson Architects, Can architectural firm
– Ontario #8386 8387
Jerusalem (Israel), Habitat Israel
– architecture, Moshe Safdie #8404
Jesuits
– Midland (Ont), Sainte-Marie among the Hurons #7999
– Montréal (Qué), buildings (1692-1791) #7932
– Québec, 17th c. #1354 1358 1363 2192
– Québec (Qué), Séminaire de Notre-Dame-des-Anges #8785
– Sillery (Qué), Maison des jésuites #8571
Jesup North Pacific Expedition #3771 3772 3773 3774 3780 3783 3785 3787 3789 3969
Jesus Christ
– crucifixion, Québec sculpture #1638
– Good Shepherd, Québec sculpture, 17th-19th cs. #1594
– Last Supper, Jean Baptiste Côté #5188
– Leduc, Ozias #6195
– nativity
    – Canadian art #393
    – Canadian painting #864
    – Côté, Jean-Baptiste #5188
– passion, in bottles, Québec #2944
– Québec art, 17th c. #1365
– redemption, with Virgin Mary, Ozias Leduc #6204
– supper at Emmaus, Québec sculpture, 19th-20th cs. #1615
Jewell, Milton, Can artist, 1938- #5961
jewellery
– see also brooches; rings; silver
jewellery, Canadian
– 20th c. #2142
– (1837-1887) #253
– (1960s) #2696
– (1964-1967) #2108 2109
– (1970s) #2706
– (1979-1980) #2138
– Aird, Neil Carrick #4503
– Alberta (1970s) #1951
– Arnoldi, Charles #2663
– British Columbia (1950s) #2695
– Delrue, Georges #2694 5281 5282
– Gaudin (dit Lapoterie), Nicolas #5572
– guide for collectors #2125 2131
– Leadbeater, Roy #6181
– Letarte, Jean-Paul #6249
– Nicoll, Marion F.S. Mackay #6702
– Nordbeck, Peter #258 259
– Ottawa (Ont), National Museum of Man. Canadian Centre for Folk Culture Studies #963
– Picard, Louis-Alexandre #269 270
– Price, Art #6928
– Québec #2228
    – 17th-18th cs. #2657
    – (1950s) #2193

– (1970s) #2701
– in French-Canadian folk songs #2898
– Reid, Bill #6985 6987
– Toronto (Ont), Ontario College of Art #3009
– Ukrainian (1865-1945) #2869
– Varin (dit La Pistole), Jacques #269 270
– Vidal, Guy #2216
jewellery, Indians of North America
– 20th c. #2143
– trade silver #2634
Jews in Canada
– art #435
– Prairies, architecture #8081
Jobin, Gilles, Can artist, 1942- #1551
Jobin, Louis, Can sculptor, 1845-1928 #24 1233 1334 1335 1600 5962 5963 5965 5966 5967
– Côté, Jean-Baptiste, compared with #5186 5187
– crucifixes #1585 1605
– interview #2169 2171 5964
– The Holy Family #5968
– use of plaster #1618
– woodcarvings #756 1576 1577
Joe, Mathilde, Can basketmaker, fl. 1976 #4142
Johansen, John M., Amer architect, 1916-
– Worcester (Mass), Clark University. Goddard Library #9046
John, Augustus Edwin, Brit artist, 1878-1961
– Varley, Frederick Horsman, compared with #7463
John, Chauncey Johnny, Amer sculptor, fl. 1940
– False Face masks #4113
John Andrews Architects, Can architectural firm #8323
John Andrews International, Can architectural firm
– Toronto (Ont)
    – CN Tower #9511
    – Union Station #9540
John B. Parkin Associates, Can architectural firm #8395 8396
– Charlottetown (PEI), Confederation Centre, competition #9088 9089
– Don Mills (Ont)
    – Ortho Pharmaceutical plant and offices #7679
    – shopping centre #7679
– Malton (Ont), Toronto International Airport #9516
– Niagara Falls (Ont), Greater Niagara General Hospital #9031
– Oshawa (Ont), 45 Hillsdale Manor Home for the Aged #8516
– Ottawa (Ont), National Capital Region, proposals #8041
– Toronto (Ont)
    – City Hall and Civic Square #8990 8991 8992
        – competition #8989
    – Four Seasons Sheraton Hotel #9294
    – hotel on Queen Street, proposal #9292
    – Ontario Association of Architects headquarters #7679 8300 9341
    – Sun Life Building #9342
    – Toronto-Dominion Centre #7694 9197 9301 9345
    – York University #9396 9469
John C. Spence and Sons, stained glass studio (Montréal, Qué)
– stained glass #2399 2462

John Deere Plow Company
– warehouses #9247
John E. Garrett Co., pattern makers (NS)
– Bluenose hooked rugs #2763
John M. Dayton & Roy Jessiman, Can architectural firm
– Winnipeg (Man), City Hall, competition #8985 8986 8987
John M. Moore & Company, Can architectural firm
– London (Ont), University of Western Ontario #9442 9448
John Marshall & Co., ceramic manufacturer (Bo'ness, Scotland)
– Canadian Sports Series #2306 2360
Johnniebo
– see Ashevak, Johnniebo
Johns, Jasper, Amer artist, 1930-
– influence on Arthur Fortescue McKay #6476
Johnson, Bruce Henderson, Can artist, 1926-
– illustrations #941
Johnson, Burton Glenwood, Can photographer, 1912-1965
– photographs of World War II #1107
Johnson, Esther, Can stained glass artist, fl. 1920s-1940s
– stained glass #2445
Johnson, Joanne Jackson, Can photographer, 1936-
– exhibitions, group
    – (1977) #1033
Johnson, Johnson & Roy, Amer architectural firm
– Montréal (Qué), Nun's Island #8587
Johnson, Lloyd, Can architect, 1767-1842
– Saint John (NB), stone church #8778
Johnson, Nancy, Can artist, 1951-
– exhibitions, group
    – (1981) #710
Johnson, Terence, Can sculptor, 1940-
– exhibitions
    – (1981) #5969
– exhibitions, group
    – (1978) #786
Johnstad, Byron, Can ceramicist, fl. 1970s- #2395
Johnston, Clifford M., Can photographer, 1897-1951
– exhibitions, group
    – (1970) #1675
Johnston, Frances-Anne
– see Arbuckle, Frances-Anne Johnston
Johnston, Francis Hans (Franz), Can artist, 1888-1949 #5971
– and Group of Seven #1732
– as father of Frances-Anne Johnston #5970
– book illustration and design #939
– exhibitions, group
    – (1972) #5972
    – (1973) #5973
– illustrations, Farmer's Magazine #1765
Johnston, James P., Amer architect, 1841-1893
– Brockville (Ont), Idlewild #8671
Johnston, Michael, Can artist, fl. 1950s-
– stage designs #472
Johnston, Robert Edwin, Can artist, 1885-1933
– illustrations #916
Joliette (Qué)
– churches #1287 8876

Joliette (Qué), Cégep de Joliette
– exhibitions
– *Lithographs/Lithographies* (1973) #825
Joliette (Qué), Chapel of the Novitiate of the
Clerics of Saint-Viateur
– stained glass, Marius Gérald Plamondon
#2447
– stained glass and cross, Marius Gérald
Plamondon #6888
Joliette (Qué), Church of Saint-Paul
– architecture and interior, Amable Gauthier
#241 242
Joliette (Qué), Church of Saint-Viateur
– architecture and interior, Amable Gauthier
#241 242
Joliette (Qué), Musée d'art de Joliette
– collection #3100 3101
– exhibitions
– *De la figuration à la non-figuration dans
l'art québécois* (1977) #1461
– *Rodolphe Duguay, 1891-1973* (1979) #5318
Joly, François, Can sculptor, 1951- #1630
Jolybois, Antoine
– *see* Jacson (*dit* Jolybois), Antoine
Jones, Barrie, Can photographer, 1950-
– exhibitions, group
– (1979) #2069
Jones, Brian Rendel, Can artist, 1950- #5975
– exhibitions
– (1978) #5974
Jones, Chilion, Can architect, 1835-1912
– Ottawa (Ont), Parliament Buildings #9054
Jones, Francis, Can furniture-maker,
1827-1894 #2580
Jones, Hugh Griffith, Can architect,
1872-1947
– Toronto (Ont), Union Station #9531 9536
– Winnipeg (Man), City Hall, competition
#8979
Jones, Jacobine, Can sculptor, 1898-1976
#739 5976
– exhibitions, group
– (1971), medals #772
– mural sculpture, Bank of Nova Scotia
(Toronto, Ont) #5977
Jones, Trevor Patrick Garwood
– *see* Garwood-Jones, Trevor Patrick
Jones, Wade, Can artist, 1945- #5978
– exhibitions
– (1976) #5979
– exhibitions, group
– (1976) #2060
– use of photography #1057
Jones, William (Bill), Can artist, 1946- #2053
Jones, William Harris, Amer artist in
Canada, fl. ca. 1825-1850s
– influence on Halifax (NS) art (1830s) #1226
Jones Fall (Ont), forge
– architecture #8019
Jong, Simon Leendert de, Can artist, 1942-
– exhibitions, group
– (1967) #1916
Jongers, Alphonse, Can artist, 1872-1945
#302
Jonquière (Qué), Centre national
d'expositions de Jonquière/National
Exhibition Centre
– exhibitions
– *Métiers d'art Ontario-Québec,
1979/1980/Quebec-Ontario Crafts,
1979/1980* (1980) #2138
– *Rodolphe Duguay, 1891-1973* (1980) #5318
Jonquière (Qué), Church of Saint-Raphaël
– architecture, St-Gelais & Tremblay #8765

Jopling, Frederick Waistell, Can artist,
1859-1945
– prints #822
Jordan & Over, Can architectural firm
– Winnipeg (Man), domestic architecture
#8493
Josakeed, Ojibwa #3492
Joslin, Paul, Can photographer, fl. 1977
– portfolio of photographs #1023
Jost, Edward R., Can artist, fl. 1864
– exhibitions (reviews) #964
Joubert family, Can ceramicists, fl.
1860s-1870s #2281
Jour, Le, Can newspaper
– and Antoine Désilets #5287 5288
Jourdain (*dit* Labrosse), Denis, Can sculptor,
1671-1743 #1572
Jourdain (*dit* Labrosse), Paul-Raymond, Can
sculptor, 1697-1769 #249 250 1572
Journal de Québec, Can periodical
– Plamondon, Antoine-Sébastien, treatise on
good and bad art #1348
*Journal of Canadian Art History/Annales
d'histoire de l'art canadien*, Can periodical
#111
journals
– *see* artists' diaries; periodicals
Jouvenet, Jean Baptiste, Fr artist, 1644-1717
– influence on Antoine-Sébastien
Plamondon #6886
Judah, Doris Minette, Can sculptor,
1887-1965
– exhibitions
– (1980) #5980
Judd, Donald, Amer sculptor, 1928-
– influence on André Lucien Fauteux #5413
judges
– portraits of, George Theodore Berthon
#4713
Judson, William Lee, Can artist, 1842-1928
– exhibitions, group
– (1888) #175
Jugendstil
– *see* Art Nouveau
jugs
– *see* pitchers
Julien, Henri, Can artist, 1852-1908 #1315
1323 5981 5984 5985 5986 5987 5988 5989
5993
– as artist, North-West Mounted Police
expedition (1874) #5990 5992
– cartoons, Fathers of Confederation and
Montreal Star #943
– Christmas scene #5982
– exhibitions
– (1938) #5983
– illustrations of legends #5991
– political cartoons #957
– revolutionary subjects #1351
Jullien, Philip M., Can architect, fl.
1912-1916
– Vancouver (BC), Terminal City Club #9061
Juneau, Denis, Can artist, 1925- #5994
– and Optical art #1445
– exhibitions, group
– (1959) #1414
– (1968) #1263
– (1981) #1471
– use of plastics #1442
Juneau (Alaska), Alaska State Museum
– screens, Tlingit #3916
Jung, Carl, Sw psychiatrist, 1875-1961
– Markgraf, Waltraud Erna Else, compared
with #6416

Junior League of Winnipeg (Winnipeg, Man)
– art education (1940s) #1889
junk sculpture
– Patterson, Dan #6779
Jutras, Albert, Can collector, 1900-
– collection, Canadian paintings #372
Jutras, Joseph, Can artist, 1894-
– and Montée Saint-Michel #1236

K

Kagan, Samuel Lazar (Sam), Can sculptor,
1906-
– portraits #581
Kahane, Anne, Can sculptor, 1924- #5995
5996
– drawings and sculptures #5997
– exhibitions
– (1981) #5999
– *Song of the Earth*, Place des Arts (Montréal,
Qué) #8233
– *The Sea*, Canadian Embassy (Islamabad,
Pakistan) #5998
– woodcarvings (1960s) #744
Kahn, Louis Isidore, Amer architect,
1901-1974
– influence on A.J. Diamond and Barton
Myers #9349
Kahnawake (Qué), Church of
Saint-François-Xavier
– architecture #8890
Kahnawake (Qué), Presbytery (1720)
– architecture #8569
Kakarook, Guy, Amer artist, b. ca. 1860
#4217
Kakegamic, Goyce, Can artist, 1948- #4157
4161
– and Triple K Co-operative #4158
– exhibitions, group
– (1977) #4151
– (1980) #4159
– interview #4155
Kakegamic, Joshim, Can artist, 1953- #4157
4161
– and Triple K Co-operative #4158
– exhibitions, group
– (1977) #4151
Kakige, Francis, Can artist, 1929- #4157
– (1980) #4159
Kakinuma, Thomas, Can sculptor, 1908-
– garden sculpture #1849
Kalm, Peter, Swedish botanist in Canada,
1716-1779
– on log and stone wall housing
construction, Québec, 18th c. #8527
Kamata, Takuro, Can textile artist, 1939-
#6000
Kamba
– art, compared with Inuit art #4215
Kamins, Jeannie, Can artist, 1941-
– fibrework #2775
Kamloops (BC), Kamloops Public Art
Gallery
– exhibitions
– *Artisan '78: The First National Travelling
Exhibition of Contemporary Canadian
Crafts/Artisan '78: première exposition
nationale itinérante d'artisanat canadien
contemporain* (1979) #2134
– *Images of the Inuit from the Simon Fraser
Collection* (1981) #4495

Kandinsky, Wassily, Russ artist, 1866-1944
– and abstract art #422
– Brooker, Bertram Richard, on #4927
– concept of space #1441
– influence on Bertram Richard Brooker #4925 4926
– influence on Guido Molinari #6588
– influence on Lawren Phillips Harris #5711
Kane, Paul, Can artist, 1810-1871 #5 9 221 241 242 1705 3386 3720 6001 6003 6004 6005 6006 6007 6012 6013 6014 6015 6016 6017
– and Canadian painting #18
– and Hudson's Bay Company #273
– exhibitions, group
    – (1955) #1845
    – (1973) #1953
– exhibitions (reviews) #1692
– landscapes #140 209
– on Indians of North America #6002
– paintings (1846-1847) #6018
– portrait, Wilson S. Conger #6008
– portraits, Mayor George Gurnett #3178
– sketchbooks #6009 6011
– works #6010
– writings #92
Kansas City (Mo), William Rockhill Nelson Gallery of Art and Mary Atkins Museum of Fine Arts
– exhibitions
    – Sacred Circles: Two Thousand Years of North American Indian Art (1977) #3463
Kant, Immanuel, Ger philosopher, 1724-1804
– concept of nature #4882
Kantaroff, Maryon, Can sculptor, 1933-
– on her art #596 6019
– on women artists #144
Kardos, Ladislas, Can artist, 1909- #6020 6021
Karkutt, Edith, Can photographer, fl. 1960s
– portfolio of photographs #987
Karnick, Irwin, Can photographer, 1938-
– exhibitions (reviews) #1008
Karsh, Malak, Can photographer, 1918- #995
Karsh, Yousuf, Can photographer, 1908- #6032 6034
– autobiography #6026
– exhibitions
    – (1968) #6029
– exhibitions, group
    – (1967) #486 487
    – (1970) #1675
– interview #6030 6033
– on his art #6027
– on photographs of women #6024
– portraits #6022 6023 6025 6028 6031 6035
– Tata, Sam, compared with #7329
Karuna, Peter, Can photographer, ca. 1949-
– portfolio of photographs #1032
Kashetsky, Herzl J., Can artist, 1950- #1184
Kashetsky, Joseph, Can artist, 1941-1974 #1121 1184
– exhibitions, group
    – (1966) #1123
    – (1973) #1182
Kaska Indians
– culture #4090 4092
    – (1920s) #4093
Kater, Wolfgang, Can harpsichord-maker, fl. 1979 #2940
Kauffman, William, Can architect, ca. 1821-1875
– Toronto (Ont) #8059
Kavik, John, Can sculptor, 1897- #6036

kayaks
– see also boats
kayaks, Inuit #3339
kayaks, Netsilik #4363
Kazimierski, Daniel, Can photographer, 1949- #992
– portfolio of photographs #1023
Keefer, Samuel, Can civil servant, 19th c.
– and Parliament Buildings (Ottawa, Ont) #8930
Keene, Caleb, Can furniture-maker, 1862-1954
– use of lacquer decoration #2548
Keevil, Roland, Can artist, 1887-1963
– exhibitions, group
    – (1958) #1846
Keewatin (NWT)
– sculpture #4196
    – (1960s) #4407
Keirstead, James Lorimer, Can artist, 1932-
– art and writings #6037
Kejimkujik National Park (Fairy Bay, NS)
– petroglyphs, Micmac Indians #3614
kekuli, Shuswap #3983
Kelly, Beverly
– see Lambert-Kelly, Beverly
Kelly, Kerry Joe, Can stained glass artist, 1945- #2455
Kelman, Ralf, Can artist, 1947-
– Lite Probe #6038
Kelowna (BC), Kelowna Art Gallery
– exhibitions
    – J.Frederic McCulloch 1905-1932: Works on Paper (1978) #6463
Kelsey, Charles William, Can stained glass artist, 1877-1975
– stained glass, Westmount Park United Church (Montréal, Qué) #2448
Kemble, Julie, Can artist, 1945- #2076
Kemble, Roger, Can architect, 1929-
– interview #8379
Kenderdine, Frederick Augustus (Gus), Can artist, 1870-1947
– exhibitions
    – (1974) #6039
– exhibitions, group
    – (1940) #350
Kennedy, David Johnston, Can artist, 1816-1898 #6040
– watercolours #6041
Kennedy, Garry Neill, Can artist, 1935- #6044 6045
– as president, Nova Scotia College of Art and Design (Halifax, NS) #3003
– exhibitions
    – (1978) #6043
– exhibitions, group
    – (1980) #703
– interview #6042
– museum theme #714
– on buildings, Nova Scotia College of Art and Design (Halifax, NS) #9409
Kennedy, Sir Arthur Edward, Brit statesman in Canada, 1810-1883
– and Frederick Dally #5250
Kennedy, Sybil, Can sculptor, 1899- #739
– on her art #6046
Kenojuak
– see Ashevak, Kenojuak
Kent, Edwin S., Amer architect, fl. 1929-1931
– Lucerne (Qué), Château Lucerne #9283
Kent, Rockwell, Amer artist, writer, 1882-1971
– influence on Thoreau MacDonald #6381

– MacDonald, Thoreau, compared with #6384
Kent (BC)
– architecture #8147
Kent (Ohio), Kent State University. School of Art
– architecture, John Andrews Architects #8323
Kenyon, J.J., Can artist, 1862-1937
– animal portraits #1727
– paintings and photographs #1681
Kéro
– see Beaudoin-Hansen, Kéro-Claire (Kéro)
Kerr, David, Can photographer, 1942-
– portfolio of photographs #997 999
Kerr, Estelle Muriel, Can artist, 1897-1971 #207
– illustrations #916
– on studying abroad #206
Kerr, Illingworth Holey, Can artist, 1905-
– as juror, Saskatchewan Arts Exhibition (1954) #1910
– exhibitions
    – (1973) #6049
– interview #1974
– on art #1944
– on his illustrations #6047 6048
– Prairie landscapes #6050
– travelling art exhibition program, Alberta (1980) #1972
Kerr, John, Can silversmith, fl. 1870s #2649
Kerr-Lawson, James, Can artist, 1864-1939
– as member, Canadian Art Club #193
– exhibitions (reviews) #211
Kerslake, Roger, Can ceramicist, 1938- #2395
Kertland, Douglas Edwin, Can architect, 1888-
– Toronto (Ont), Canadian National Exhibition. Automotive Building #9207
Kestenbaum, Lothar J., Amer artist, 1926-
– influence on Marcel Braitstein #4899
Ketchikan Totem Park (Alaska)
– totem poles #3873
Kettle, Horace Gerard, Can artist, 1906-
– and Picture Loan Society (Toronto, Ont) #1746
Keuken, Johan van der, Can photographer, 1938-
– portfolio of photographs #997 999
Keziere, Robert, Can photographer, 1937-
– interview #6051
– portfolio of photographs #998
Kiakshuk, Can artist, ca. 1886-1966 #4460
Kieffer, Daniel René, Can photographer, 1940- #1562
Kielbach, Joseph, Can glassmaker, fl. 1906-1913
– as founder, Manitoba Glass Company (Beauséjour, Man) #2403
Kihn, W.Langdon, Amer artist, 1898-1957
– paintings, Northwest Coast Indians #1840
Kilbourn, Rosemary Elizabeth, Can artist, 1931-
– on printmaking #817
Kilgour, J.W., furniture-making firm (Beauharnois, Qué) #2463
Kilpin, Legh Mulhall, Can artist, 1853-1919
– exhibitions
    – (1979) #6052
Kilvert, Benjamin Sayre Cory, Can artist, b. 1879
– illustrations #916

kinetic art #654
- Hayden, Michael #5755
- Kelman, Ralf #6038
- Poulin, Roland #6908
- Toronto (Ont), Electric Gallery #1798
- Vilder, Roger #7487 7488 7489
kinetics
- see motion in art
King, B.A., Can photographer, 1934-
- exhibitions, group
  - (1973) #1002
  - (1981) #1070
King, George William, Can architect,
  1863-1945
- Toronto (Ont)
  - Government House, competition #8748
  - John Ross Robertson and Glenholme
    schools, competition for #9437
King, Phillip, Brit sculptor, 1934-
- Winsor, Jackie, compared with #7597
King-ego, Can sculptor, fl. late 19th c.-1900
  #3862
King William Island
- Netsilik artifacts, early 20th c. #4366
Kingcrafts (King City, Ont)
- (1950-1967) #2244
kings and rulers
- Louis XIV and Louis XV, portraits of, in
  North America #1598
Kings Landing (NB)
- architecture #7810 7811
Kings Landing (NB), Hagerman House
- furniture, John Warren Moore #2512
Kingston (Ont)
- architecture
  - 19th c. #7995 8015
  - 19th c.-1920s #7961
  - (1673-1867) #7989
  - (1920s) #7656
  - Newlands, William #8392
- art #1680
- chairs, 19th c. #2575
- fortifications (1759-1838) #8453
- furniture (1800-1867) #2567
- Martello towers #8416
- university and college libraries (1930s)
  #9042
Kingston (Ont), Agnes Etherington Art
  Centre
- see Kingston (Ont), Queen's University.
  Agnes Etherington Art Centre
Kingston (Ont), asylum
- architecture, William H. Coverdale #258
  259
Kingston (Ont), Bellevue (Macdonald
  House)
- interior decoration #7758
Kingston (Ont), Canadian Forces Hospital
- architecture, Shore & Moffat #9031
Kingston (Ont), Canadian Shop
- exhibitions (reviews)
  - Aird, Neil Carrick #4503
Kingston (Ont), City Hall
- architecture, George Browne #8339
Kingston (Ont), Commercial Mart
- architecture, George Browne #8339
Kingston (Ont), Kingston Penitentiary
- architecture, Joseph William Powers #9058
Kingston (Ont), Macdonald House
- see Kingston (Ont), Bellevue (Macdonald
  House)
Kingston (Ont), Mowat Building
- architecture, George Browne #8339

Kingston (Ont), Queen's Theological College
- Chesterfield, Albert A., photographs #5102
Kingston (Ont), Queen's University
- architecture #9447
- Biéler, André Charles, as teacher #4725
- Conference of Canadian Artists (1941)
  #351
  - and André Charles Biéler #390
- Conference on Canadian-American Affairs
  (1937) #337
- exhibitions
  - Surrealism in Canadian Painting (1964)
    #463
- Roberts, Goodridge, as resident artist
  #7041
Kingston (Ont), Queen's University. Agnes
  Etherington Art Centre
- collection #3145
- exhibitions
  - 7 West Coast Painters (1959) #1997
  - A Retrospective Exhibition of the Work of
    André Biéler, 1925-1963 (1963) #4723
  - A Terrible Beauty: The Art of Canada at
    War (1979) #1111
  - André Biéler 50 Years: A Retrospective
    Exhibition 1920-1970 (1971) #4725
  - Ann Kipling: Recent Landscapes (1980)
    #6057
  - Barker Fairley: Landscapes and Portraits
    (1980) #5404
  - Beauté tragique: les deux conflits mondiaux
    vus par des artistes canadiens (1979) #1112
  - Carl Schaefer: Retrospective Exhibition;
    Paintings from 1926 to 1969 (1969) #7155
  - Celebration of the Body (1976) #6676
  - Centennial Exhibition of Quebec and
    Ontario Contemporary Painters, 1967
    (1967) #484
  - Christopher Pratt (1970) #6910
  - Daniel Fowler (1964) #5489
  - Daniel Fowler of Amherst Island,
    1810-1894 (1979) #5491
  - David Bolduc: Recent Work (1980) #4775
  - David Milne: 1882-1953 (1967) #6558
  - David Milne: The New York Years,
    1903-1916 (1982) #6567
  - Dennis Burton Retrospective (1978) #4961
  - Dessins inédits d'Ozias Leduc/Ozias Leduc
    the Draughtsman (1979) #6210
  - Douglas Bentham "Enclosures and Opens"
    1975/76 (1976) #4683
  - Drawings and Pastels c. 1930-1967 by
    Miller Gore Brittain (1969) #4917
  - E. Lindner: Drawings, 1969-1972 (1972)
    #6285
  - Esther Warkov (1971) #7517
  - Esther Warkov Drawings (1977) #7519
  - Frederic Marlett Bell-Smith
    (1846-1923),(1978) #4668
  - From Women's Eyes: Women Painters in
    Canada (1975) #117
  - George Harlow White, R.C.A., 1817-1887
    (1975) #7550
  - George Heriot: Painter of the
    Canadas/George Heriot: peintre des deux
    Canadas (1978) #5786
  - Gift from the Douglas M. Duncan
    Collection and the Milne-Duncan
    Bequest/Le Don provenant de la collection
    Douglas M. Duncan et le legs
    Milne-Duncan (1971) #541

  - Guido Molinari: Works on Paper (1981)
    #6594
  - Harold Town: The First Exhibition of New
    Work, 1969-1973 (1973) #7413
  - Heritage Kingston (1973) #1680
  - Horatio Walker, 1858-1938 (1977) #7503
  - Imprint '76 (1977) #833
  - Inuit Art in the 1970's: A Travelling
    Exhibition/L'Art inuit actuel, 1970-79:
    exposition itinérante (1979) #4287
  - J.W. Beatty, 1869-1941 (1981) #4638
  - Jock Macdonald: Retrospective
    Exhibition/Jock Macdonald: rétrospective
    (1969) #6375
  - Joe Fafard: Recent Sculpture (1980) #5401
  - KJB: Works 1977-1981 (1981) #4983
  - Lilias Torrance Newton, 1896-1980 (1981)
    #6693
  - Lillian Freiman: Paintings and Drawings
    (1978) #5518
  - Lithographs/Lithographies (1972) #825
  - Metamorphosis, Memories, Dreams and
    Reflections: The Work of Florence Vale
    (1980) #7453
  - Milly Ristvedt-Handerek: Paintings of a
    Decade (1979) #7034
  - Other Realities: The Legacy of Surrealism in
    Canadian Art (1978) #508
  - Painters Eleven in Retrospect (1980) #1785
  - Painting Now: 76/77 (1976-1977) #609
  - Pasted Paper: A Look at Canadian Collage
    1955-1965 (1979) #510
  - Pierre Gauvreau: The First Decade (1981)
    #5578
  - Realism: Emulsion and Omission (1972)
    #545
  - Réalités autres: le legs du surréalisme à l'art
    canadien (1978) #509
  - Sculpture Out of Doors (1978) #786
  - The Contemporary Arts Society: Montreal
    1939-1948/La Société d'art contemporain:
    Montréal 1939-1948 (1981) #1474
  - The Last "Lion" ... Rambles in Quebec with
    James Pattison Cockburn: Incorporating
    "Quebec and Its Environs," a Reproduction
    of the 1831 Guidebook Attributed to J.P.
    Cockburn (1978) #5129
  - The New Brunswick Landscape Print:
    1760-1880 (1981) #1189
  - The Ontario Community Collects: A Survey
    of Canadian Painting from 1766 to the
    Present (1977) #120
  - The Saidye and Samuel Bronfman
    Collection of Canadian Art/La collection
    Saidye et Samuel Bronfman (1966) #3087
  - The Society of Canadian Painter-Etchers
    and Engravers in Retrospect/La Société des
    peintres-graveurs canadiens: vue
    rétrospective (1982) #836
  - The St. Lawrence River: Views by
    Nineteenth Century Artists (1981) #282
  - Tradition Plus One: Patchwork Quilts from
    South Eastern Ontario/Tradition plus une:
    courtepointes piquées de l'Ontario du
    sud-est (1974) #2796
  - Ondaatje, Kim, on #2798
  - Trésors d'art populaire québécois/Folk Art
    Treasures of Quebec (1980) #1297
  - Viewpoint: Twenty-nine by Nine; An
    Exhibition of Twenty-nine Works by
    Ontario Artists, Selected by Nine Curators

(1982) #1838
- *W. Sawyer, Portrait Painter* (1978) #7145
- *William Blair Bruce* (1975) #4942
- *William Brymner, 1855-1925: A Retrospective/William Brymner, 1885-1925: aperçu rétrospectif de l'artiste* (1979) #4953
- *William Goodridge Roberts, 1904-1974: Drawings* (1977) #7047
- exhibitions (reviews)
  - *Daniel Fowler of Amherst Island, 1810-1894* (1979) #5493
  - *Horatio Walker, 1858-1938* (1977) #7504
- Indian and Inuit pipes (1971) #3358
- International Video Art Symposium (1979) #671
- Painters' Symposium (1977) #620
- Roussel, Claude, *Atlantic* #7088
- Saxe, Henry, on works exhibited (1976) #7147
Kingston (Ont), Queen's University. Douglas Library
- architecture, Shepard & Calvin #9445
Kingston (Ont), Queen's University. Women's Residence
- architecture, Shepard & Calvin #9445
Kingston (Ont), Rockwood Villa
- architecture, George Browne #8339
Kingston (Ont), Royal Military College of Canada
- war memorial, John MacIntosh Lyle #1083
Kingston (Ont), St. Andrew's Manse
- architecture, George Browne #8339
Kingston (Ont), Wilson's Buildings
- architecture, George Browne #8339
Kingston Mills (Ont)
- architecture #8020
Kingston Mills (Ont), blockhouse
- architecture #8019
Kinton, Ada Florence, Can artist, 1859-1905
- autobiography #6053
Kiopini, Christian (Chris), Can artist, 1949- #1544
- exhibitions
  - (1976) #6054
- exhibitions, group
  - (1977) #1532
  - (1981) #1565
- symposium, Musée du Nouveau-Monde (La Rochelle, France), (1980) #1559
Kipahigan Lake (Sask and Man)
- pictographs, Plains #3714
Kipling, Ann, Can artist, 1934-
- exhibitions
  - (1976) #6055
  - (1980) #6057
- exhibitions, group
  - (1980) #698
- interview #6056
Kirschbaum, Robert, Can artist, 1949-
- prints #1214
Kishpiox (BC)
- totem poles, Gitksan #3797
Kiss, Zoltan, Can architect, 1924-
- Burnaby (BC), Simon Fraser University, competition #9501
kitchen utensils, Canadian #2318
- (1940s) #2603 2604
- (pre-1867), English Canada #2470
- as folk art #2139
- earthenware, Ontario, 19th-early 20th cs. #2355
- ironwork #2703 2705
- Maritimes, 19th c. #2147
- Montréal (Qué), Macdonald-Stewart

Foundation #2203
- pewter and copper, 19th c. #2704
- Québec
  - 17th-18th cs. #2161 2210
  - 17th-19th cs., European influences #2221
- treenware #2590 2591 2594
  - Ontario, 18th-19th cs. #2588
- Washington (DC), Smithsonian Institution #2111
Kitchener (Ont), Kitchener-Waterloo Art Gallery
- exhibitions
  - *9 Out of 10: A Survey of Contemporary Canadian Art* (1975) #569
  - *Bachinski: A Decade* (1977) #4578
  - *Canadian Paintings in the University of Toronto: An Exhibition in Celebration of the Sesquicentennial of the University of Toronto* (1977) #3168
  - *Centennial Exhibition of Quebec and Ontario Contemporary Painters, 1967* (1967) #484
  - *David Milne: 1882-1953* (1967) #6558
  - *Ed Bartram: 10 Years* (1980) #4618
  - *Gordon Rayner Retrospective* (1979) #6966
  - *Graham Coughtry: Retrospective* (1977) #5190
  - *Humorist Walter Trier: Selections from the Trier-Fodor Foundation Gift* (1980) #7428
  - *Imprint '76* (1977) #833
  - *J.W. Beatty, 1869-1941* (1982) #4638
  - *Joe Plaskett and His Paris: In Search of Time Past* (1972) #6893
  - *Joe Plaskett et son Paris: à la recherche d'un temps passé* (1972) #6894
  - *Louis Comtois: Paintings, 1974-1979* (1981) #5164
  - *Louis de Niverville* (1978) #6709
  - *Mennonite Traditional Arts of the Waterloo Region and Southern Ontario: A Historical View* (1974) #2250
  - *Painters Eleven in Retrospect* (1981) #1785
  - *Riopelle: Jean-Paul Riopelle* (1980) #7030
  - *Surrealism in Canadian Painting* (1964) #463
  - *The Figure: A Sensual Response* (1975) #578
  - *The Heritage of Jack Bush: A Tribute* (1982) #722
  - *The Ontario Community Collects: A Survey of Canadian Painting from 1766 to the Present* (1977) #120
  - *The Saidye and Samuel Bronfman Collection of Canadian Art/La collection Saidye et Samuel Bronfman* (1967) #3087
  - *The Work of Art: Six Artists* (1979) #665
  - *Tony Urquhart: Twenty-five Years; Retrospective* (1978) #7448
  - *Viewpoint: Twenty-nine by Nine; An Exhibition of Twenty-nine Works by Ontario Artists, Selected by Nine Curators* (1981) #1838
  - *William Perehudoff: Ten Years, 1970-1980/William Perehudoff: une décennie, 1970-1980* (1982) #6838
Kitchener (Ont), Molsons Bank
- architecture #9173
kites
- as sculpture, Royal Canadian Aerial Theatre (RCAT) #2058
kitsch
- in Canadian heraldry #2951
Kitsilano (BC)
- architecture #8146

Kitwancool (BC)
- totem poles, Gitksan #3925
Kitwancool Indians
- totem poles #3906
Kiyooka, Harry Mitsuo, Can artist, 1928-
- exhibitions (reviews) #6058
Kiyooka, Roy Kenzie, Can artist, 1926- #6059
- and plasticiens #1439
- exhibitions
  - (1975) #6062
- exhibitions, group
  - (1965) #469
  - (1968) #1263
  - (1974) #2050
  - (1979) #2069
- exhibitions (reviews) #520
- interview #6060 6061
- writings #536
Klausen, Jorgen, Can photographer, ca. 1942-
- portfolio of photographs #991
Klawak Park (Alaska)
- totem poles #3873
Klee, Paul, Sw artist, 1879-1940
- Bolt, Ron, compared with #4778
- influence on Albert Dumouchel #5325
- influence on Alfred Pellan #6803
- influence on Francis Coutellier #5196
- influence on Paul Livernois #6309
- influence on Pierre Jean Clerk #5118
- influence on Ulysse Comtois #5165
- Tremblay, Gérard, compared with #7424
Klein, Maurice Dalvin, Can architect, 1896-
- Toronto (Ont), Memorial Fountain to Dr. D.W. Young #729
Kleinburg (Ont), McMichael Canadian Collection #3164
- collection #3172
- Group of Seven, paintings #1780 1781
- Group of Seven and Tom Thomson, paintings #1783
Kleyn, Robert, Can artist, 1948-
- and avant-garde art #600
- interview #6063
Klikitat Indians
- basketry #3777 3778
Kline, Franz, Amer artist, 1910-1962
- influence on Christian Marcel Barbeau disputed #4607
- Mongeau, Jean-Guy, compared with #6596
Klunder, Harold, Can artist, 1943- #6064
- exhibitions, group
  - (1980) #708
Knaff, Jean-Christian, Can artist, 1949-
- illustrations, record covers #6065
knitting, Canadian
- (1608-1867) #2120
- and knotting, 20th c. #2121
- Newfoundland #2744
- Nova Scotia, patterns (pre-1920) #2785
- Québec, 18th c. #2200
knitting, Cowichan #3882 3929 4027
knitting, Scottish
- 19th c., and Cowichan knitting #3929
knives, Canadian
- wooden handles, Ontario, 18th-19th cs. #2588
Knobel, Harry Edward, Brit photographer, b. ca. 1872 #1114
- photographs of World War I #1113
Knott, Tom, Can photographer, 1942- #2071
Knottenbelt, Marianna, Can photographer, 1948-
- exhibitions (reviews) #1018

Knowles, Dorothy, Can artist, 1927- #1880
   6066
– exhibitions
   – (1973) #6067
– exhibitions, group
   – (1967) #1916
   – (1971) #1920
   – (1975) #1867 1926
   – (1981) #1885
– exhibitions (reviews) #1883
– participant, Symposium on 20th Century
   Canadian Culture (Washington, DC),
   (1977) #621
Knowles, Elizabeth Annie McGillivray, Can
   artist, 1866-1928 #207 6068 6069
Knowles, Harry Percy, Amer architect,
   1817-1923
– Toronto (Ont), Masonic Temple,
   competition #9062
Knox & Thompson, furniture-makers (Saint
   John, NB)
   – (1840s-1870s) #2511
Knudsen, Christian
– see Knudsen, Neils Christian (Chris)
Knudsen, Neils Christian (Chris), Can artist,
   1945- 6070 6071
– exhibitions, group
   – (1978) #668
   – (1981) #1565
– interview #6072
Koenig, Théodore, Fr poet, 1922-
– and Surrealism #5598
Koerner, Walter Charles, Can collector,
   1898-, and Marianne, Can collector, 1901-
– collection, art, Northwest Coast Indians
   #3994
Kokoschka, Oscar, Aus artist, 1886-
– Bobak, Bruno Joseph, compared with
   #4760
Kolbenhier, Eric, Can collector, 20th c.
– collection, Ukrainian Bukovinian
   embroidery #2124
Kolisnyk, Peter Henry, Can artist, 1934-
– exhibitions
   – (1977) #6075
   – (1980) #6076
– exhibitions, group
   – (1971) #98
   – (1977) #784
   – (1978) #786
– interview #6074
Kollwitz, Käthe, Ger artist, 1867-1945
– Muhlstock, Louis, compared with #6653
Koochin, William, Can sculptor, 1929-
– exhibitions
   – (1980) #6073
Kooning, Willem de
– see de Kooning, Willem
Kootenay Indians
– basketry #3788
– photographs of
   – Curtis, Edward Sheriff #3399
– pictographs #3965
Kopmanis, Augustus Arnold, Can sculptor,
   1910-1976
– exhibitions, group
   – (1971), medals #772
Kopsa, Michael M., Can architect, 1922-
– Charlottetown (PEI), Confederation
   Centre, competition #9088 9089
– Saskatoon (Sask), Mendel Art Gallery,
   competition #9091
– Winnipeg (Man), City Hall, competition
   #8985 8986

Korea
– photographic views
   – Hammock, Virgil #5696
Korner, John Michael Anthony, Can artist,
   1913- #1996 6078
– exhibitions, group
   – (1959) #1997
– on his murals #6077
Kostyniuk, Ronald Peter (Ron), Can
   sculptor, 1941-
– exhibitions
   – (1972) #6079
   – (1978) #6080
Kosuth, Joseph, Amer artist, 1945-
– Baxter, Iain, compared with #4630
Kovalik, Peter, Can artist, 1956-
– paintings and drawings (1968-1978) #6081
Kovalik, Tibor, Can artist, 1935-
– paintings and drawings (1968-1978) #6081
Kowal, Roman, Can artist, 1922-
– stained glass windows #2450
Kowall, Earl, Can photographer, 1948-
– portfolio of photographs #997 999
Koyukon Indians
– culture #3368
Kozloski, John, Can furniture-maker, fl.
   1860s #2565
Kramer, Burton, Can artist, 1932-
– and Paul Arthur and Associates #873
– prints #897
Kraulis, Janis A., Can photographer, 1949-
– portfolio #1023
Krauss, Rosalind Epstein, Amer art
   historian, 1940-
– and Betty Roodish Goodwin #5631
Kreiger, Harmut, Can sculptor, fl. 1980
– fountain, Vancouver (BC) #2077
Kreyes, Marielouise, Can artist, 1925-
   #6082
Krieghoff, Cornelius, Can artist, 1815-1872
   #5 9 89 221 241 242 812 1312 1313 1323
   1334 1335 6083 6084 6085 6087 6088 6089
   6091 6093 6094 6097 6098 6099 6101 6103
– and Canadian painting #18
– and nationalism in art #143
– Boylen, M.J., collection #1
– exhibitions
   – (1934) #213 6086
   – (1971) #6095
   – (1972) #6096
– forgeries, Ward-Price Galleries (Toronto,
   Ont), (1962) #64
– landscapes #26 209 6436
– painting as a livelihood #6092
– paintings of life on Québec farms,
   National Gallery of Canada (Ottawa, Ont)
   #6100
– sketchbook, Royal Ontario Museum.
   Sigmund Samuel Collection (Toronto,
   Ont) #6090
– The Pets and the Materials #6102
Krieghoff, Emilie Gauthier, Can, 1821-1906
– portrait of, Cornelius Krieghoff #6093
Kroupa, Bohuslar, Can artist, fl. 1870s #6104
Ksan (Hazelton, BC)
– art #4132 4134
– Reid, Bill, on #6987
– serigraphy #4167
Kubota, Nobuo, Can sculptor, 1932-
– exhibitions, group
   – (1975) #1809
   – (1976) #779
Kudluk, Thomassie, Can artist, ca. 1910-
   #6105

Kuhn, Bob, Amer artist, 1920-
– influence on George E. McLean #6501
Kuiper, Lidi, Can artist, 1948-
– exhibitions, group
   – (1977) #1901
Kujundzic, Zeljko, Can sculptor, 1920-
– exhibitions, group
   – (1971), medals #772
Kulp, John, Can ceramicist, 1799-1874 #2290
Kun, Joseph, Can bow-maker, 1930- #2940
Kupczynski, Stanislav, Can artist, 1928-
   #6106
Kurelek, William, Can artist, 1927-1977
   #6107 6108 6112
– autobiography #6110 6115
– exhibitions
   – (1970) #6109
– illustrated books #6111
– on his art #6113
– The Ukrainian Pioneer, Niagara Falls Art
   Gallery (Niagara Falls, Ont) #6116
– themes #6114
Kurz, Rudolph Friedrich, Sw artist in
   Canada, 1818-1871
– sketches, Siouan Indians #3400
Kutchin Indians
– costume #4102
– culture (1930s) #4096 4099
Kuthan, George, Can artist, 1916-1966 #6117
Kuypers, Jan, Can designer, 1925-
– chairs #2471
Kuzyk, Ron, Can photographer, ca. 1953-
– portfolio of photographs #1032
Kwakiutl Indians
– architecture and totem poles #3936
– art #3060 3996 4037 4052
   – (1970s) #4145
   – serpent motif #3840
– blankets #3973
– culture #3935
   – (1880s-1890s) #3787
   – (1890s) #3764
– masks #3348 3920 3938 3945 3990 4030
– mythology #3883
– photographs of
   – Curtis, Edward Sheriff #3399
– pipes #3850
– potlatch #3956
– rattles #4026
– rites and ceremonies #3768 3838
– serigraphy #4120
– Thunderbird Dance #3867
– totem poles #3844 3848 3957 4115 4124
– whalebone war club #3813
Kyle, James Fergus, Can artist, 1876-1941
– cartoons, Toronto Globe #943
– illustrations #916
Kyle, John, Can artist, 1871-1958
– as teacher of women potters, Victoria (BC),
   (1920s) #2278
Kyoto (Japan)
– chapel, interior decoration, Gaston-Pierre
   Petit #6844

L

L'Acadie (Qué), church
– architecture, Odelin & Mailloux #8830
L'Anse-à-Maheu (Qué), Church of
   L'Anse-à-Maheu
– architecture and interior #8889

L'Assomption (Qué)
- *ceinture fléchée* #2813 2818 2819 2823 2824 2827 2864 2865 2873
L'Assomption (Qué), Church of L'Assomption
- sculptures, Gilles Bolvin #4781 4782
L'Islet (Qué), Church of Notre-Dame-de-Bon-Secours
- architecture and interior #8879
- chalices, François Ranvoyzé #2658 2673
L'Islet sur mer (Qué), Musée maritime
- exhibitions
  - *De la figuration à la non-figuration dans l'art québécois* (1977) #1461
La Canardière (Qué), Garneau House
- architecture, Paul Latouche and Isaac Dorion #8615
La Joue, François de, Fr architect in Canada, 1656-1718
- as teacher, Ecole des arts et métiers de Saint-Joachim (Saint-Joachim, Qué) #2992
La Palme, Robert, Can artist, 1908- #6119
- exhibitions (reviews) #6118
- on caricature #6120
- on studying in Europe #408
- *Orphée chez Dionysos*, Place des Arts (Montréal, Qué) #8233
- political cartoons #957
- works, Ayerst, McKenna and Harrison chemists' firm #852
La Pérade (Qué), church
- sculptures, Gilles Bolvin #4781
La Pierre, Thomas (Tom), Can artist, 1930- #6122
- exhibitions
  - (1976) #6121
La Pistole, Jacques
- *see* Varin (*dit* La Pistole), Jacques
La Prairie (Qué), Church of Saint-Isadore
- altar, Church of Saint-Isadore #241 242
La Rochelle (France), Musée du Nouveau-Monde
- symposium on Québec painting (1980) #1559
La Rochelle (France), Musée du Nouveau Monde. Chapelle du Lycée Fromentin
- exhibitions
  - *Mémoire d'une Amérique: cartographie, topographie et allégories d'une vision française du Nouveau Monde, objets ethnographiques, livres anciens, botanique et zoologie* (1980) #276
Labastrou, Roger, Can artist, fl. 1971
- and Jacques Guillon Designers Inc. #884
Labelle, Henri Sicotte, Can architect, 1896-
- Valleyfield (Qué), Cathedral of Salaberry #8843
Labelle, Paul, Can photographer, 1947- #1562
Labelle, Ronald, Can photographer, 1942-
- portfolio of photographs #997
Laberge, Albert, Can writer, 1871-1960
- exhibitions
  - (1971) #5604
Laberge, Jean-Marie, Can artist, 1933- #1551
Labor Arts Guild (Vancouver, BC)
- (1944-1945) #1985
Labouret, Auguste, Fr artist, 1871-1964
- mosaics, Saint Ann's Basilica (Sainte-Anne-de-Beaupré, Qué) #8859 8860
Labrador
- architecture #7782
- art, Art Association of Newfoundland and Labrador #1144

- culture (1910s) #4321
- decorative arts
  - 20th c. #2155
  - (1970s) #2149
- Dorset artifacts #4377 4379 4380
- grasswork #2945
- hooked and poked mats #2765 2767
- photographic views (1849-1949) #1160
- Trapper's tilt #8532
- views
  - Bradford, Robert William #4898
Labrèche, François, Can artist, fl. 1842 #1301
Labrosse, Antoine, Can sculptor, fl. 1738
- crucifix, Church of Notre-Dame. Chapel of Sacré-Coeur (Montréal, Qué) #6123
Labrosse, Denis
- *see* Jourdain (*dit* Labrosse), Denis
Labrosse, Paul-Raymond
- *see* Jourdain (*dit* Labrosse), Paul-Raymond
Labrosse family, Can sculptors, 18th c. #1300
- woodcarvings #1575
Lac Barrière (Qué)
- Algonquian Indians #3544
Lac Bouchette (Qué), Chapel of l'Ermitage
- paintings, Charles Edouard Huot #5877 5878 5882 5884
Lac Bouchette (Qué), Marial Chapel
- architecture, Henri Tremblay #8832
Lac La Ronge (Sask)
- beadwork, Cree #3696
Lac Saint-Jean (Qué)
- photographic views
  - Bull, W. #4956
LACAC
- *see* Local Architectural Conservation Advisory Committee (LACAC)
lace, Canadian
- Québec, 17th-18th cs. #2187 2200
Lachaise, Gaston, Fr sculptor, 1882-1935
- influence on Claude Roussel #7087
Lachance, Walter W., Can architect, b. 1869
- Beamsville (Ont), high school #9387
- Saskatoon (Sask), Flanagan Hotel #9263
Lachapelle, Edouard, Can artist, 1943-
- linocuts, Marie-Calumet dance troupe #6124
Lachenaie (Qué), Church of Saint-Charles
- architecture and interior #8808
- sculptures, Gilles Bolvin #4781
Laciserave, Michel
- *see* Lefebvre (*dit* Laciserave), Michel
lacquer
- decorations, Canadian furniture #2548
Lacroix, André, Can photographer, fl. 1970s #1534
Lacroix, Henriette, Can artist, 1928- #1551
Lacroix, Jacques, Can artist, 1944- #1551
Lacroix, Richard, Can artist, 1939- #6126 6127
- and Fusion des arts (Montréal, Qué) #1482 1483
- and Québec printmaking (1960s) #1641
- as founder of Atelier libre de recherches graphiques (Montréal, Qué) #1642 1653
- as founder of Guilde graphique (Montréal, Qué) #1647 1655 6128
- book illustrations #926
- exhibitions, group
  - (1967) #821
- on his art education #470
- prints #6125 6129
Ladouceur, Jean-Paul, Can artist, 1921- #6130
Lafitau, Joseph-François, Fr priest, writer,

1681-1746
- and nationalism in art #1373
- description of Indians of North America as headless figures #281
Laflamme, Carole Simard
- *see* Simard-Laflamme, Carole
Laflamme, M.A., Can artist, fl. 1842 #1301
Lafleur, Claude, Can artist, 1932- #1282
- and RACE #1536
Lafleur, François
- *see* Bailly (*dit* Lafleur), François
Lafleur, Jean M., Can architect, 1903-
- Valleyfield (Qué), Cathedral of Salaberry #8843
Lafleur, Pierre, Can artist, 1938- #6131 6132
Laford, John, Can artist, 1955-
- exhibitions, group
  - (1981) #4173
Laforge, Jean, Can artist, 1911- #6133
Lafortune, François, Can photographer, 1921-
- interview #6134
Lafrenière, J.L.D., Can architect, 1874-1929
- Montréal (Qué), City Hall #8980
Lagacé, Jean-Baptiste, Can stained glass artist, 1868-1946
- stained glass, Church of Notre-Dame (Montréal, Qué) #2444 8839
Lagacé, Paule, Can artist, 1951- #1538
Lagrave, Augustin, Can silversmith, fl. 1791-1797
- works, Detroit Institute of Arts (Detroit, Mich) #2691
Lagroix, Joseph
- *see* Huppé (*dit* Lagroix), Joseph
Lahaise, Guillaume, Can poet, 1888-1969
- influence on Ozias Leduc #6209
Lahr (West Germany), Ailla Luisen Schule
- exhibitions
  - *Contemporary Native Art of Canada: The Woodland Indians/Art contemporain des Indiens sylvicoles du Canada/Zeitgenössische Kunst der kanadischen Waldland Indianer* (1976) #4143
Laing, G.Blair, Can art dealer, 1911-
- autobiography #1686
Laing, William (Bill), Can artist, 1944- #6135
Laithwaite, George, Can sculptor, 1873-1956 #1792
- exhibitions, group
  - (1975) #1682
Lajeunie, Jean-Claude, Can artist, 1943- #1479 1480
- interview #1485
Lajoie, Guy Gérin
- *see* Gérin-Lajoie, Guy
Lajoie, Noël, Can artist, 1927-
- exhibitions, group
  - (1955) #1408
Lajoie, Paul, Can artist, 1932- #6136
Lake, Suzy, Can artist, 1947- #675 717 1512
- and avant-garde art #600
- compared with Raymonde April #1059
- exhibitions
  - (1975) #6138
  - (1980) #6140
- exhibitions, group
  - (1978) #668
- interview #6139
- self-portrait photographs #6137
- use of photography #1057
Lake Kejimkoojik (NS)
- petroglyphs, Micmac #3617

Lake Louise (Alta), Château Lake Louise
– architecture, Barott & Blackader #9279
Lake Louise (Alta), Skoki Lodge
– restoration #9296
Lake of Bays (Ont), Bigwin Inn
– architecture, John Wilson #9275
Lake Ontario
– fortifications #8457
Lake Simcoe (Ont)
– views
  – Smith, William St. Thomas #7236
Lake Superior (Ont)
– views
  – Fraser, John Arthur #5509
  – Harris, Lawren Stewart #5732
  – Hopkins, Frances Ann Beechy #5833
Lake Superior Provincial Park (Ont and
  Man)
– pictographs, Algonquian #3576
Lake Windermere (BC), Melchin summer
  houses
– architecture, Gordon L. Atkins #7694
Laliberté, Alfred, Can sculptor, 1878-1953
  #302 1315 1382 6142 6143 6149 6150
– as teacher of Doris Minette Judah #5980
– as teacher of Zénon Alary #4505
– bronzes, Musée du Québec (Québec, Qué)
  #6144
– exhibitions
  – (1978) #6146
– exhibitions, group
  – (1980) #1296
– influence of Bois-Francs #6151
– Légendes, coutumes, métiers series #6148
– monument, Maisonneuve market
  (Montréal, Qué) #6141
– monument to Dollard des Ormeaux
  (Montréal, Qué) #1623
– on Québec sculpture (1940s) #1580
– sculptures, National Gallery of Canada
  (Ottawa, Ont) #6147
– writings #6145
Laliberté, Guy, Can artist, 1930- #6152
Laliberté, Madeleine, Can artist, 1922- #6153
Laliberté, Norman, Can artist, 1925-
– interview, on his banners #6154
Lamanna, Carmen, Can art dealer, 1927-
  #628
– on Carmen Lamanna Gallery (Toronto,
  Ont) #1811
– at 3e Salon international de galeries pilotes:
  artistes et découvreurs de nos temps,
  exhibition (1970) #531
Lamarche, Ulric, Can artist, 1867-1921 #1382
  6155
Lamb, Harold Mortimer, Can artist, art
  critic, 1872-1970
– exhibitions
  – (1977) #6156
Lamb, Molly
– see Bobak, Molly Lamb
Lamb, Thomas L., Can designer, 1938- #2487
Lamb, Thomas White, Amer architect,
  1871-1942
– Hamilton (Ont), Loew's Theatre #9069
– Loew's theatres #9122 9123
– Montréal (Qué), Loew's Theatre #9069
– Toronto (Ont)
  – Loew's Uptown Theatre #9075
  – Loew's Yonge Street Theatre (Elgin and
    Wintergarden) #9064 9067
  – Pantages Theatre #9075
Lambart, Evelyn, Can filmmaker, 1914-

– and Norman McLaren, Spanish Civil War
  film #6498
Lambert, Jacques, Can artist, 1928- #1546
  1551
Lambert, John, Brit writer, fl. 1811
– on log and stone wall housing
  construction, Québec, early 19th c. #8527
Lambert, Lucie, Can artist, 1947-
– Album Frayère #6157
Lambert, Phyllis Bronfman, Can architect,
  curator, collector, 1927-
– Montréal (Qué), Le Havre South Seafront
  rehousing scheme #8512
– photographs, greystone buildings,
  Montréal (Qué) #7922
Lambert, Ronald (Ron), Can artist, 1927-
– as student of Hans Hofmann #402
Lambert (dit Saint-Paul), Paul, Can
  silversmith, 1691-1749 #249 250 2660 2668
– alms cups #2671
– and Samuel Payne, porringer, Montreal
  Museum of Fine Arts (Montréal, Qué)
  #2689
– compared with French silver #2688
– works, Detroit Institute of Arts (Detroit,
  Mich) #2691
– works, Musée du Québec (Québec, Qué)
  #2678
Lambert-Kelly, Beverley, Can artist, 1943-
– on visual perception #525
Lambeth, Michel, Can photographer,
  1923-1977 #6158 6159
Lambton Mills (Ont), school
– architecture, Ellis & Ellis #9388
Lamont Glass Co., glass manufacturer
  (Trenton, NS) #2398 2409 2417
Lamoureux, Gisèle, Can photographer, fl.
  1970s
– portfolio of photographs #991
Lamps, Can periodical #1667
lamps, Canadian
– 18th-19th cs. #2703 2920
– (1825-1925) #2404
– guide for collectors #2104 2125 2131
– Hookway, Elmer John #5828
– Ontario
  – 18th-19th cs. #2918
  – 19th c., wick lamps #2947
Lancaster County (Penn)
– Pennsylvania-German decorative arts
  #2263
land art
– see also earthworks (sculpture)
– Snow, Michael #7245
– Vazan, Bill #7471 7475
land use
– see also architecture
– Alberta ranches, late 19th-early 20th cs.
  #8720 8721
– Charlevoix (Qué) #8629
– Cornwall (Ont), Inverarden #8673
– Lower Fort Garry (Man) #8483
– Norfolk County (Ont), 19th c. #8656
– Nova Scotia, 17th-19th cs. #7814
– Ontario, 18th-19th cs. #7993
– Québec
  – late 16th c.-1950s #7855
  – seigneuries #8611
– Saint-Roch-de-l'Achigan (Qué) #7854
Landron, Jean-François, Can silversmith,
  1686-ca. 1760 #249 250
– works, Detroit Institute of Arts (Detroit,
  Mich) #2681 2691
Landry, Yvan, Can ceramicist, 1932- #6160

landscape, American
– see also Hudson River School
– compared with Canadian landscape
  painting #106
landscape, British
– 19th c., influence on Canadian landscape
  painting #66
landscape, Canadian
– 17th c.-1940s #29
– 18th-19th cs. #812
– 18th c.-1920s #14
– 18th-mid 20th cs. #88
– 19th-20th cs. #132
– 19th c. #178 241 242 266
– 19th c.-1910s #209
– 19th c.-1970s #140
– (1670-1930) #106
– (1670s) #1328
– (1750-1850) #279
– (1860-1890) #271 272
  – Montréal (Qué) and Toronto (Ont) #264
– (1890s) #6436
– (1900-1920) #309
– (1920s) #287 301 315
– (1930s) #338 344 347
– (1930s-1940s) #352
– (1930s-1960s) #496
– (1930s-1970s), and Canadian currency #759
– (1940s) #380
– (1970s) #595 617
– Alberta #1965
  – (1981) #1974
– and A.Y. Jackson #5915 5922
– and geography #26 41
– and nationalism #109 183 341
– British Columbia
  – 18th c.-1930s, forests #2008
  – (1840s-1970s) #2016
– Christmas greeting cards #844 845 863
– compared with Australian landscape #44
– early 20th c., compared with Barbizon
  school #497
– Eastern Townships (Qué), (1800-1950)
  #1296
– Group of Seven #1735 1764 1774 1782
– imaginary (1970s) #1960 2045
– Laurentian Mountains (Qué), 20th c. #1278
  1279
– New Brunswick, 19th c. #1180
– New York (NY), Canadian Club of New
  York #3211
– North American stoneware pottery #2309
– Northwest Coast, 18th c. #2002
– Ontario, 19th c. #1720
– photographs (1860-1900) #268
– Prairies #1855 1872 1882
  – (1960s) #1848 1862
  – and Illingworth Holey Kerr #6050
  – large-scale paintings #1885
– prints, 18th-19th cs. #839
– Québec #1265
  – (1800-1940) #1286
  – (1940s-1950s) #1426
– Royal Canadian Academy of Arts #153 283
– Saskatchewan #3202
  – (1905-1980) #1940
– St. Lawrence River (Ont and Qué), 19th c.
  #282
– western Canada #1863
– winter landscapes #285 1298
landscape architecture
– see also conservation and restoration,
  landscape architecture; gardens; parks
landscape architecture, Canadian #7768

– 19th c.-1950s #7677
– and domestic architecture (1930s) #8501
– and schools (1950s) #9391
– Charlottetown (PEI), Province House #8937
– Mawson, Thomas Hayton #8388 9405
– Montréal (Qué)
    – Expo '67 #9219 9222
    – Mount Royal Park #7903 7912 7924
– Niagara Parks (Ont) #7975
– Ottawa (Ont)
    – Earnscliffe #8652
    – Parliament Buildings #8048
– Victoria (BC), Crystal Gardens #9134 9146
– Winnipeg (Man) #8105
Landsley, Patrick Alfred, Can artist, 1926-
– exhibitions, group
    – (1977) #1278 1279
Lane, Albert, Can furniture-maker, b. ca. 1821 #2571
Lane, Henry Bowyer, Brit architect in Canada, b. 1787, fl. 1840s
– Toronto (Ont) #8075
    – City Hall #8993
    – Osgoode Hall #9002 9003
Lang, George Macdonald, Can architect, 1860-1930
– Halifax (NS) #7838
Langevin, Joseph, Can photographer, ca. 1830-1882 #6161
Langevin, Richard, Can sculptor, fl. 1978 #1540
Langford, Adelaide Elizabeth, Can artist, 1854-1939
– mural paintings, Canadian Pacific Railway station (Vancouver, BC) #9546
Langley, Henry, Can architect, 1836-1907
– Toronto (Ont), Yorkville Town Hall #8997
Langley & Howland, Can architectural firm
– Toronto (Ont)
    – Imperial Bank of Canada #9181
    – John Ross Robertson and Glenholme schools, competition for #9437
    – Molsons Bank #9159
Langley (BC)
– architecture #8147
Langley (BC), Langley Centennial Museum and National Exhibition Centre
– exhibitions
    – Creative Flight (1979) #147
Langlois, Denis, Can artist, 1945- #1540 6162
Langton, John, Can, auditor-general of Canada and vice-chancellor of University of Toronto, 1808-1894
– and architecture of University of Toronto. University College (Toronto, Ont) #9453
language and art
– see also words in art
– (1970s), Canada #574
– (1970s), Québec #1552
– (1980), Canada #1063
– Clark, Tim #5113
– Copithorne, Judith #5176
– Curnoe, Greg #78
– N.E. Thing Co. Ltd. #524 6677 6678
– Robert, Louise #695 7039
– W.O.R.K.S. #1955
Lankinen, Wayne, Can photographer, ca. 1932-
– portfolio of photographs #1032
Lansdowne, James Fenwick, Can artist, 1937- #6163 6165
– exhibitions
    – (1981) #6164

Lantier, Jean, Can artist, 1953- #6166
Lapalme, Dominique Janson, Can builder, 1701-1762 #7844
Lapalme, Pierre
– see Janson (dit Lapalme), Pierre
Lapierre, Viateur, Can artist, 1917- #6167
Lapointe, Conrad, Can artist, fl. 1974
– interview #1527
Lapointe, Esther, Can sculptor, 1947- #6168
Lapointe, Frank, Can artist, 1942- #1148 6170
– diaries #6169
Lapointe, Jean-Paul, Can artist, 1935- #1551
Lapointe, Paul-Marie, Can poet, 1929-
– poems, Vierge incendiée #4831
Laporte, Lucie, Can artist, 1946- #6171
– exhibitions, group
    – (1980) #1663
Lapoterie, Louis-Nicolas
– see Gaudin (dit Lapoterie), Louis-Nicolas
Lapoterie, Nicolas
– see Gaudin (dit Lapoterie), Nicolas
Larivée, Francine, Can artist, 1942-
– La chambre nuptiale #1634
Larivière, Paul, Can collector, 20th c.
– interview #3219
Larose & Larose, Can architectural firm
– Dorval (Qué), Montreal International Airport. Air Terminal Building #9515
Larouche (Qué), Church of Saint-Gérard Magella
– architecture, St-Gelais & Tremblay #8841
Larouche-Villeneuve, Jeanne, Can collector, 1925-
– collection, devotional images, Université Laval (Québec, Qué) #1662
– collection, prints of devotional images, Université Laval (Québec, Qué) #130
Larseneur, Charles, Can sculptor, fl. 1842 #1301
Larson, Doris Wall, Can artist, 1939-
– prints #1214
LaSalle (Qué), fort
– recommended for conservation (1881) #7754
LaSalle (Qué), manoir Ogilvie
– architecture, Alexander Cowper Hutchison #8636
LaSalle (Qué), Saint John Brébeuf Parish Church
– architecture, John Bird #8766
laser art
– laser holography, Jerry Pethick #6840
Lasnier, Raymond, Can artist, 1924-1968 #6172
Lasserre, Frederic (Fred), Can architect, 1911-1961
– Vancouver (BC), University of British Columbia. Gymnasium #7679
Last Supper
– see Jesus Christ, Last Supper
Latchford, Joan, Can photographer, 1926- #993
Laterrière (Qué), Church of Notre-Dame
– architecture and art #7882
Laterrière (Qué), windmill of père Honorat
– architecture #7882
Latouche, Paul, Can mason, fl. 1835
– La Canardière (Qué), Garneau House #8615
Latour, Jacques
– see Leblond (dit Latour), Jacques
Latour, Jean, Can sculptor, 1632-1677 #1572
Latour, Pierre
– see Huguet (dit Latour), Pierre

Latschaw, Abraham, Can fraktur artist, 1799-1870 #2255
– influence on Joseph Bauman #4628
Latvians in Canada
– art #49 475
– Manitoba, folk art #968
Latvis Society of Artists
– exhibitions
    – (1966) #475
Laufer, Murray Bernard, Can artist, 1929-
– stage designs #6173
Laurens, Jean-Paul, Fr artist, 1838-1921
– influence on Charles Edouard Huot #5878 5884
Laurens, Jean-Pierre, Fr artist, 1875-1932
– as teacher of Clarence Alphonse Gagnon #5544 5546 5547
– as teacher of Rodolphe Duguay #5317
Laurens, Paul-Albert, Fr artist, 1870-1934
– as teacher of Rodolph Duguay #5317
Laurentian Mountains (Qué)
– views
    – 20th c. #1278 1279
    – Borenstein, Sam #4853
    – Browne, Joseph Archibald #4939
    – Cullen, Maurice #5220
    – Gagen, Robert Ford #5530
    – Gransow, Helmut #5645
    – Harris, Lawren Stewart #5729
    – Pichet, Roland #6868
Laurier, Wilfrid, Can statesman, 1841-1919
– portrait of, Georges Delfosse #1385
Laurin, Serge, Can photographer, 1947-
– interview, on Groupe d'action photographique #1494
– portfolio of photographs #997 999
Lausanne (Switzerland), Musée cantonal des beaux-arts
– exhibitions
    – Canada: art d'aujourd'hui (1968) #518
– exhibitions (reviews)
    – 3e Salon international de galeries pilotes: artistes et découvreurs de nos temps (1970) #531
Lauzon, Jean, Can photographer, fl. 1970s #1556
Lauzon, Réal, Can sculptor, 1945-
– as member of Centre communautaire catholique Tour de David (Saint-Basile-le-Grand, Qué) #1510
– Laboratoire #1627
Laval, François de, Fr bishop in Canada, 1623-1708
– and Episcopal Palace (Québec, Qué) #8787
– as founder, Ecole des arts et métiers de Saint-Joachim (Saint-Joachim, Qué) #1327 2181 2992
Laval (Qué), André B. Papineau House
– architecture #8625
Laval (Qué), Church of Sainte-Rose
– architecture, Victor Bourgeau #8854
Laval (Qué), Laval Civic Centre
– architecture, Affleck, Desbarats, Dimakopoulos, Lebensold, Sise #8322
Lavallée, André
– see Paquet (dit Lavallée), André
Lavigne, Paul
– see Tessier (dit Lavigne), Paul
Lavoie, Raymond, Can artist, 1950-
– exhibitions
    – (1980) #685
law
– use of wampum as legal document #3567
Law, Anthony (Tony), Can artist, 1916-

#6174
Law, Ivan, Can sculptor, 1885-1979 #2596
law and architecture
– see also state and architecture
– and architectural materials, Québec (Qué),
  late 17th c.-1920s #7952
– and conservation
  – Canada (1950s) #7755
  – Canada (1970s) #7772 7833
  – Ontario (1970s) #8024
  – Ontario, religious properties (1970s)
    #8906
  – Québec (1970s) #7870
  – St. John's (Nfld), (1970s) #7789
  – Winnipeg (Man), (1970s) #8108
– and destruction of architecture, Montréal
  (Qué), (1970s) #8601
– and urban development (1960s-1970s)
  #9302
– Québec, 17th-18th cs. #8621
– Royal Architectural Institute of Canada
  survey (1960s) #8309
law and art
– see also copyright; forgeries; state and art
– Canada (1970s) #682
– protection of Inuit and Indian art #3347
– Québec (1961-1975) #3280
Law Society of Upper Canada
– headquarters, Osgoode Hall (Toronto,
  Ont) #9002 9003
Lawrence, Alexander, Can furniture-maker,
  1788-1843 #2500 2501 2511
Lawson, Ernest, Can artist in USA,
  1873-1939 #6175 6177
– as member, Canadian Art Club #193
– exhibitions
  – (1967) #6176
  – (1976) #6178
  – (1979) #6179
– exhibitions (reviews) #204 211
– winter landscapes #285
Lawson, James Kerr
– see Kerr-Lawson, James
Lawson & Little, Architects and Engineers,
  Can architectural firm
– Lucerne (Qué), Château Lucerne #9283
Le Ber, Jacques, Can, d. 1693
– household furnishings #2522
Le Ber, Jeanne, Can nun, artist, 1662-1724
  #2095 2778
Le Ber, Pierre, Can artist, 1669-1707 #234 235
  1363
– portrait, Marguerite Bourgeoys #1333 6180
Le Blanc, Michel, Can architect, 1930-
– Montréal (Qué), métro. Peel Station #9553
Le Corbusier, Charles Edouard Jeanneret, Fr
  architect, artist, 1887-1965
– art and architecture #8232
– influence on Marcel Parizeau #8397
Le Poitevin, Léonard
– see Paillard (dit Le Poitevin), Léonard
Le Rouge, Jean, Can builder, 1639-1712 #234
  235
Le Testu, Guillaume, Fr cartographer,
  1509-1572
– maps of Canada #875
Leadbeater, Roy, Can sculptor, jeweller,
  1928- #6181
Leaf Rapids (Man), National Exhibition
  Centre
– exhibitions
  – Canadians: A National Photography Show
    about People/Canadiens: exposition
    nationale de photographie ayant les gens

comme thème (1979) #1035
– Edward Curtis in the Collection of the
  Edmonton Art Gallery (1980) #3480
– Images of the Inuit from the Simon Fraser
  Collection (1981) #4495
– J.Frederic McCulloch 1905-1932: Works on
  Paper (1979) #6463
– Looking South (1978) #4278
Leaf Rapids (Man), Town Centre
– architecture, Leslie Stechesen #8409 8974
Leaning, John Dalton, Can architect, 1926-
– Ottawa (Ont), La Salle Academy #9480
  9481
Lear, Edward, Brit artist, writer, 1812-1888
– and Daniel Fowler #5491
– Lansdowne, James Fenwick, compared
  with #6163
Leathers, Winston Lyle, Can artist, 1932-
– exhibitions, group
  – (1981) #1907
leatherwork, Algonquian #3456 3672
leatherwork, Algonquin
– moccasins #3554
leatherwork, Blackfoot #3651 3654 3678 3686
leatherwork, Canadian
– 17th-19th cs. #2112
– 20th c. #2121 2142
– (1970s) #2936
– (1980) #2257
– Québec #2228 2953
  – 20th c. #2198
– Simard, René #7208
leatherwork, Carrier
– (1970s) #4145
leatherwork, Cree #3651
leatherwork, Delaware
– moccasins #3554
leatherwork, Gros Ventre #3651
leatherwork, Micmac
– arm bands #3572
leatherwork, Ojibwa #3557
leatherwork, Penobscot
– moccasins #3554
leatherwork, Plains #3456 3651 3658 3660
  3672 3684
– leggings #3697
– painting #3709
leatherwork, Salish
– (1970s) #4145
leatherwork, Siouan #3456 3651 3672
leatherwork, Tagish #4106
leatherwork, Tlingit #4106
leatherwork, Tutchone #4106
leaves in art
– see also plants in art; trees in art
– Canadian and American stoneware
  pottery #2309
– maple leaf, Canadian pottery #2312
Lebel, Maurice, Can artist, 1898-1963 #1382
  1393
Lebensold, D.Fred, Can architect, 1917-
– Montréal (Qué), Montreal Museum of Fine
  Arts #9124 9125 9133
Leblanc, Augustin, Can sculptor, 1799-1882
– influence of Baillairgé family #1582
Leblanc, Leo B., Can artist, 1914- #6182
LeBlanc, Pierre, Can builder, fl. 1830
– Lower Fort Garry (Man) #8475
Leblond, Jean
– see Jacquiés (dit Leblond), Jean
Leblond (dit Latour), Jacques, Can priest,
  artist, 1671-1715 #234 235 1233 1324 2992
– woodcarvings #1577
Lebredt, Gordon, Can artist, 1948-

– exhibitions, group
  – (1977) #1901
  – (1978) #669
Lebrun, Hughes and Jean-Camille, Can
  metalsmiths, fl. 1920s-1940s #2174 2179
  2693
Lebrun, Rico, Amer artist, 1900-1964
– Bachinski, Walter Joseph Gerard,
  compared with #4578
Leclair, Michel, Can artist, 1948- #6183
Leclerc, Eugène, Can sculptor, 1886-1968
  #2174 2179 2194 2209
Leclerc, père, Can furniture-maker, 19th c.
– rocking chairs #2535
Lecor, Paul (Tex), Can artist, 1933- #6184
Leduc, Fernand, Can artist, 1916- #1294 1453
  1504 1542 1543 6191
– and plasticiens #1439
– as artist and theorist (1941-1947) #1443
– Bénic, Lorraine, compared with #4678
– debate with Paul-Emile Borduas #6586
– exhibitions
  – (1970) #6185 6186
  – (1977) #6190
  – (1980) #6193
– exhibitions, group
  – (1955) #1408
  – (1959) #1414
  – (1981) #1471
– exhibitions (reviews) #6187 6192
– in Paris (France) #1434
– interview #6188 6189
– on Ozias Leduc #6199
– Refus global #1396
– writings #1449 6194
Leduc, Ozias, Can artist, 1864-1955 #302
  1240 1270 1393 6198 6199 6202 6205 6209
  6211
– as teacher of Paul-Emile Borduas #4811
  4814 4836 4843 4850
– Borduas, Paul-Emile, on #4839 6197
– exhibitions
  – (1955) #6200
  – (1974) #6206
  – (1978) #6210
– exhibitions (reviews) #283
– illustrations #918
– influence on Paul-Emile Borduas #4820
  4829 4830 4841
– interior, Bishop's Palace, Sherbrooke (Qué)
  #6208
– interior, Church of Saint-Enfant-Jésus du
  Mile-End. Chapel of Sacré-Coeur
  (Montréal, Qué) #6195
– paintings, Church of Notre-Dame de la
  Présentation (Shawinigan, Qué) #6201
– paintings, National Gallery of Canada
  (Ottawa, Ont) #1266
– preparatory studies #6203 6207
– religious paintings #1384
– works (1920s) #1231
– writings #6196
Lee, Abel Alexander, Can artist, 1918- #6212
Lee, Ann Dow, Can artist, fl. 1960s-
– exhibitions (reviews) #1167
Lee, Clifford E., Can collector, d. 1972
– Inuit prints of games and contests #4492
Lee, Lawrence, Brit stained glass artist,
  1909-
– and Master Stained Glass Workshop, Art
  Gallery at Harbourfront (Toronto, Ont)
  #2455
– stained glass, Saint Andrew and Saint
  Paul Church (Montréal, Qué) #2448

Lee-Nova, Gary, Can artist, 1943-
– exhibitions
  – (1969) #2039
– exhibitions, group
  – (1971) #2042
  – (1973) #2045
– exhibitions (reviews) #2051
– interview #6213
– on the sacred in art #94
– on visual perception #525
Lees, Samuel, Can artist, fl. 1847
– as member, Toronto Society of Arts #1689
Leeson, Benjamin W., Can photographer,
  1866-1948
– exhibitions, group
  – (1976) #2012
LeFébure, Jean, Can artist, 1930-
– exhibitions, group
  – (1962) #1420
Lefebvre, Nicolas, Fr artist, 1660-ca. 1740
– paintings, Calvary at Oka (Qué) #1355
  1356
Lefebvre, Oliver, Can sculptor, 1872-1962
– woodcarvings, Nettie Sharpe collection
  #1607
Lefebvre (dit Laciseraye), Michel, Can
  builder, 1654-1708 #234 235
Lefort, Agnès, Can artist, art dealer,
  1891-1973
– and Canadian art, Agnès Lefort Gallery
  (Montréal, Qué) #1424
Légaré, Joseph, Can artist, 1795-1855 #1318
  1336 6215 6216 6219
– and Québec painting #1353
– and Québec society #1375
– exhibitions
  – (1978) #6217 6218
– exhibitions, group
  – (1959) #219
– influence on Québec painting #6220
– Le choléra à Québec, National Gallery of
  Canada (Ottawa, Ont) #6214
– paintings, Université Laval (Québec, Qué)
  #3078
– paintings of Indians #6222
– Paysage au monument à Wolfe, and
  French-Canadian nationalism #1373
– support for national museum in Québec
  (Qué) #3120
– views of buildings, Québec (Qué) #6221
Legault, Jean-Onésime, Can artist, 1882-1944
– and Montée Saint-Michel #1236
legends
– see also folklore; mythology
legends, Algonquian
– and Samuel Ash #4558
legends, Canadian #2096
– New Brunswick, Legends on Tapestries
  (1962) #5296
– Québec #1290 2169 2171
  – and Georges Saint-Pierre #7118
  – and Henri Julien #5988 5991 5993
  – and Louis-Philippe Hébert #5767
legends, Indians of North America
– images of women #121
legends, Inuit
– and Davidialuk Alasua Amittu #4521
– and Jean-Paul Riopelle #7024
– Dorset #4379
– images of women #121
legends, Iroquois
– and Arthur Guindon #5665
legends, Kwakiutl
– and Mungo Martin #6429

legends, Ojibway
– and Norval Morrisseau #6646
Léger, Fernand, Fr artist, 1881-1955
– as teacher of Canadian artists (1940s) #384
– influence on Alfred Pellan #6826
– influence on Jeanne Leblanc Rhéaume
  #6994
Léger, Jeanne, Can artist, 20th c.
– as teacher of Marie-Hélène Allain #4508
Léger, Onésime-Aimé, Can artist, 1881-1924
  #1382
Legislative Council of Canada
– see Canada. Legislative Council of Canada
Legrady, George, Can photographer, 1950-
– portfolio of photographs #997 999 1053
Legrady, Miklos, Can photographer, 1951-
– portfolio of photographs #997 999
Legros, Enid Sharon, Can ceramicist, 1943-
  #6223
Legros, Jean-Pierre, Can sculptor, 1943-
– Continuum II #1627
Leiden (Netherlands), Rijksmuseum voor
  Volkenkunde
– tipi, Blackfoot #3718
Leier, Grant, Can artist, 1956- #6224
Leighton, Alfred Crocker, Can artist,
  1901-1965 #6225
– and Alberta Society of Artists #1942
– as husband of Barbara Leighton #3017
– as teacher of Marion F.S. Mackay Nicoll
  #6703
– exhibitions, group
  – (1940) #350
– travelling art exhibition program, Alberta
  (1980) #1972
Leighton, Barbara Harvey, Can artist, 1911-
  #3017
Leimanis, Andris, Can artist, 1938-
– illustrations #941
Lemay, J.Eudore, Can photographer,
  1874-1947 #1283
Lemay & Leclerc, Can architectural firm
– Montréal (Qué), Church of
  Saint-Jean-Baptiste #8766
Lemieux, Irénée, Can artist, 1931-
– interview #6226
Lemieux, Jean-Paul, Can artist, 1904- #97
  1392 1432 1453 1541 1542 1543 6227 6228
  6230 6233 6234 6235 6236 6237
– as teacher, Ecole des beaux-arts (Québec,
  Qué) #1404
– concept of space and time #6240
– Dumouchel, Albert, compared with #5328
– exhibitions
  – (1967) #6231
  – (1974) #6232
– exhibitions, group
  – (1958) #431
  – (1959) #438
  – (1964) #462
– illustrations, Maria Chapdelaine #6239
– Mercier, Monique, compared with #6512
– on Gérard Morisset #3305
– on Québec art #1386 1399
– on Société des arts plastiques #1411
– paintings (1956-1960) #6229
– photographs of #6238
– portraits #715
– Prévost, Antoine, compared with #6927
– Surrey, Philip Henry, compared with
  #7289
Lemieux, Lisette, Can sculptor, 1943- #6241
Lemieux, Lyse, Can artist, 1956-
– exhibitions, group

– (1978) #2067
Lemieux, Marguerite, Can artist, 1899- #1380
  1382
Lemieux, Maurice, Can sculptor, 1932- #6242
Lemire, Jean, Fr builder in Canada,
  1626-1685 #228 229
LeMoine, Edmond, Can artist, 1877-1922
  #6243
Lemoyne, Serge, Can artist, 1941- #1479 1480
– (1981) #1564
– interview #1485
LeMoyne, Suzanne Rivard, Can artist, 1928-
– and Art Bank #3276
Lemyre, Marcel, Can artist, 1948-
– and Betty Roodish Goodwin, Rue Mentana
  project #1558 5631
Lengauer, Karl W., Can stained glass artist,
  1928- #2460
Lenhardt, Molly, Can artist, 1920- #1881
Leningrad (USSR), Hermitage
– exhibitions
  – Sculpture of the Inuit: Masterworks of the
    Canadian Arctic/La sculpture chez les Inuit:
    chefs-d'oeuvre de l'Arctique canadien
    (1972) #4423 4440
Leningrad (USSR), Leningrad Museum of
  Anthropology and Ethnography
– art, Tlingit #3947 3978
Lennie, Beatrice, Can sculptor, 1905- #6244
Lennox, Edward James, Can architect,
  1855-1933
– Toronto (Ont)
  – Bank of Toronto #9151
  – Church of Saint Paul's #8897 8902
  – City Hall #8993
  – Excelsior Life Building #9333
  – McConkey's Lunch #9269
  – Stewart Building #9354
  – Wolseley Motor Car Company Building
    #9332
Lent, Benjamin, Can ceramicist, fl. late
  1820s-1841 #2367
Leon, Robert, Can sculptor, ca. 1943- #6245
Leon H. Lempert & Son, Can architectural
  firm
– Toronto (Ont), Shea's Hippodrome #9066
Leonard, John C., Can artist, 1944-
– exhibitions
  – (1981) #6246
Leonardo da Vinci, It artist, 1452-1519
– Cormier, Ernest, compared with #8346
leopards
– skin motif, Kate Craig and Eric Metcalfe
  #2070
Leprohon, Louis-Xavier, Can sculptor,
  1795-1876
– influence of Baillairgé family #1582
Leroux-Guillaume, Janine, Can artist, 1927-
  #6247
Leroy, Hugh Alexander, Can artist, 1932-
  #1479
– exhibitions, group
  – (1967) #490
Lery, Gaspard Chaussegros de, Fr architect
  in Canada, 1682-1752
– plan of façade, Church of Notre-Dame
  (Montréal, Qué) #3081
Les Sables-d'Olonnes (France), Musée de
  l'abbaye Sainte-Croix
– exhibitions
  – Louis Comtois: 4 tableaux récents grand
    format (1978) #5163
Leslie, John, Can silversmith, 1849-1939
– hallmarks #2635

Leslie R. Fairn & Associates, Can
architectural firm
– Halifax (NS)
– Dalhousie University. Killam Library
#9052
– Neptune Theatre #9097
Lespérance, Pierre, Can silversmith,
1819-1882 #6248
Letarte, Jean-Paul, Can jeweller, 1933- #6249
Letendre, Rita, Can artist, 1929- #1418 1542
1543 6250 6251
– exhibitions
– (1974) #6252
– exhibitions, group
– (1955) #1408
Lethbridge (Alta)
– architecture, Chinatown #8137
Lethbridge (Alta), Saint Michael's General
Hospital
– architecture, Henry William Meech; Benzie
& Bow, Associate Architects #9021
Lethbridge (Alta), Southern Alberta Art
Gallery
– exhibitions
– Alberta Society of Artists exhibition
(1979) #1942
– *Another Dimension/Une autre dimension*
(1977) #783
– *Artisan '78: The First National Travelling
Exhibition of Contemporary Canadian
Crafts/Artisan '78: première exposition
nationale itinérante d'artisanat canadien
contemporain* (1979) #2134
– *Canadians: A National Photography Show
about People/Canadiens: exposition
nationale de photographie ayant les gens
comme thème* (1980) #1035
– *Carol Fraser Paintings and Drawings:
1967-1977* (1978) #5507
– *David Craven: New Works* (1978) #5206
– *Dennis Burton Retrospective* (1977) #4961
– *Enns, Evans & Ulrich* (1977) #1956
– *Goodridge Roberts: Selected
Works/Goodridge Roberts: oeuvres choisies*
(1982) #7050
– *Gordon Rayner Retrospective* (1980) #6966
– *Joe Fafard: Recent Sculpture* (1980) #5401
– *Liz Magor* (1979) #6405
– *Otto Rogers: New Paintings and Sculpture,
1977-78* (1978) #7065
– *Real Sculpture: John McEwen* (1979) #6472
– *Ron Martin: Water on Paper* (1976) #6433
– *Yves Gaucher & Christopher Pratt* (1977)
#643
– exhibitions (reviews)
– Kennedy, Garry Neill #6042
Lethbridge (Alta), University of Lethbridge
– architecture, Arthur Charles Erickson
#8358 8361 9406 9497
– exhibitions
– *The University of Lethbridge Phase II
Sculpture Competition* (1981) #797
– *William Perehudoff: Ten Years,
1970-1980/William Perehudoff: une
décennie, 1970-1980* (1981) #6838
Lett/Smith, Can architectural firm
– London (Ont), Grand Theatre, restoration
#7776
lettering in art
– *see also* signs and sign-boards
– Curnoe, Greg #5228
– MacDonald, Thoreau #6385
Levasseur, François-Noël, Can sculptor,
1703-1794 #269 270

– interior, Church of Saint-François-de-Sales
(île d'Orléans, Qué) #8796
– tabernacles #1613
Levasseur, Michel, Can silversmith, fl.
1699-ca. 1709 #234 235 2669 2677
– works, Detroit Institute of Arts (Detroit,
Mich) #2681
Levasseur, Noël, Can sculptor, 1680-1740
#234 235 1324 1572 1592
– compared with David Fleury David #1596
– tabernacles #1613
Levasseur, Pierre-Noël, Can sculptor,
1690-1770 #249 250
– correspondence, François Filiau-Dubois
#6253 6255
– interior, Ursuline Convent. Chapel
(Québec, Qué) #8852
– sketch of chair, Archives nationales du
Québec (Québec, Qué) #6257
– tabernacles #1613
– works, churches, Charlesbourg (Qué)
#8851
Levasseur, René Michel, Can, fl. 1745-1758
– correspondence, on apprenticeship to
François Filiau-Dubois #6253 6255
Levasseur (*dit* Delor), Jean-Baptiste-Antoine,
Can sculptor, 1717-1775 #269 270
– tabernacles #1613
Levasseur family, Can sculptors, 18th c.
#6256
– interior, Church of Saint-Etienne
(Beaumont, Qué) #8809
– woodcarvings #1573 1575 6254
– Church of Saint-Pierre (île d'Orléans,
Qué) #8802
– Church of Sainte-Famille (île d'Orléans,
Qué) #1612
Lévesque, Paule, Can artist, 1947-
– television graphics #909
Lévi-Strauss, Claude, Fr anthropologist,
philosopher, 1908-
– collection, art, Northwest Coast Indians
#4005
– writings, and conceptual art #7473
Levine, Leslie Leopold (Les), Can artist,
1936- #535 536 6262
– art and writings #6273
– chair series #6258
– disposable sculpture #538
– etchings #6272
– exhibitions
– (1970) #6264
– (1971) #6265
– (1974) #6267
– exhibitions, group
– (1967) #480
– (1970) #771
– (1971) #98
– exhibitions (reviews) #6266
– imaginary works #530
– interview #6260
– on disposable art #6259
– on Inuit art #6269 6270 6271
– on *Red Tape* installation work, University
of Toronto. Hart House (Toronto, Ont)
#6263
– on work of art proposal for Government
of Canada building (Toronto, Ont) #6268
– sculptures, *Electric Shock* and *Process of
Elimination* #6261
– video art #616
Levine, Marilyn Ann, Can sculptor,
ceramicist, 1935-
– exhibitions, group

– (1974) #1925
– (1977) #781
– exhibitions (reviews) #2383
– interview #6274
Lévis (Qué), Church of
Notre-Dame-de-la-Victoire
– architecture and art #8789
Lewis, David, Can photographer, ca. 1946-
– portfolio of photographs #1032
Lewis, Glenn Alun, Can artist, 1935-
– exhibitions
– (1979) #6276
– exhibitions, group
– (1969) #2039
– (1974) #2050
– (1976) #2060
– (1979) #2070
– (1980) #696 8237
– imaginary works #530
– interview #6275
– portfolio of photographs #996
Lewis, Maude, Can artist, ca. 1903-1970
#6277
Lewis, Richard, Can architect, 1824-1875
– Victoria (BC) #8145
Lewis, Stanley, Can artist, 1930-
– sculptures #6278
Lewis, Wyndham, Brit artist in Canada,
1882-1957 #6279
Lewis and Clark Expedition (1804-1806)
– and related art works #3649
Lewiston (NY), Artpark
– Poulin, Roland, open-air sculpture #706
Lewitt, Sol, Amer sculptor, 1928-
– Winsor, Jackie, compared with #7597
Liaison, Can periodical
– and Géraldine Bourbeau #4877
Liang, Kar, Can artist, fl. 1969
– computer art #528
Liberty style
– *see* Art Nouveau
Libling, Michener & Associates, Can
architectural firm
– Saint-Boniface (Man), Chapel of
Saint-Louis-le-roi #8765
– Winnipeg (Man), Winnipeg Art Gallery,
competition #9102
libraries, American
– university and college libraries (1970s)
#9052
libraries, Canadian
– (1910s) #9039
– (1940s) #9043
– (1950s) #9044
– conversion of public buildings for #9147
9148
– Guelph (Ont), University of Guelph.
Library Building #9468
– Montréal (Qué), Canadian Centre for
Architecture #7749
– Niagara Falls (Ont), Earl W. Brydges
Public Library #9050
– Ontario (1955-1965) #9045
– Ottawa (Ont), National Science Library
#9049
– Scarborough (Ont), Albert Campbell
Library #9047
– Toronto (Ont)
– Metro Toronto Public Library #9051
– public libraries
– (1920s) #9040
– (1930s) #9041
– University of Toronto. John P. Robarts
Research Library #9048 9050

– University of Toronto. Victoria College.
  Library #9038
– university and college libraries
  – (1930s) #9042
  – (1960s) #9046
  – (1970s) #9052
– Vernon (BC), Vernon Civic Centre #8972
Liébert, Philippe, Can sculptor, 1732-1804
  #1592 6280 6281
– wooden chandelier, church (Oka, Qué)
  #8818
Liechtenstein, House of, collection
– acquisitions, National Gallery of Canada
  (Ottawa, Ont) #3035
Lieutenant-Governors of Canada
– medals #757
life
– stages, Jean-Paul Lemieux on #6233
Life, Amer periodical
– cartoons, Arthur George Racey #6952
life, tree of
– *see* tree of life
life drawing
– *see* drawing; nude in art
light
– electric light
  – Canadian sculpture (1960s) #767
  – Kelman, Ralf #6038
– fluorescent installations, Jeff Wall #7506
– in art
  – Bloore, Ronald Langley #4749
  – Chambers, Jack #516
  – Harris, Lawren Stewart #5726
  – Toronto (Ont), Electric Gallery #1798
lighthouses, American #9524
lighthouses, Canadian #9520 9521 9524
– 19th c. #9512
– Great Lakes (Ont) #9519
– Halifax (NS) #7818
– Newfoundland #9523
  – Cape Spear and Cape Bonavista #9525
– Nova Scotia #9522
– Pointe-des-Monts (Qué) #9526
lighting
– *see also* lamps
lighting, Canadian
– 18th-19th cs. #2703 2920
– (1940s) #2601 2604
– guide for collectors #2125 2131
– Ontario
  – 18th-19th cs. #2918
  – 19th c. #2245
– Winnipeg (Man), Royal Alexandra Hotel
  #2599
Liljefors, Bruno, Swedish artist, 1860-1939
– influence on George E. McLean #6501
– Lansdowne, James Fenwick, compared
  with #6165
Lillooet Indians
– basketry #3773 3927
– culture #3783
Limners (Victoria, BC) #2043
Lin, Chien-Shih, Can artist, 1922-
– influence on Jack Marlowe Wise #7602
Lincoln, A.H., Can photographer, fl. 1850s
  #1211
Lincoln (Mass), De Cordova and Dana
  Museum
– exhibitions
  – *Changing Visions: The Canadian
    Landscape/Aperçus divers: le paysage
    canadien* (1976) #617
Lincoln (Mass), De Cordova Museum
– exhibitions

– *Eleven Canadian Printmakers* (1967) #821
Lincoln County (Ont)
– pottery, 19th c. #2290
Lincoln G. Morris Studios, Can lighting firm
– interior, Royal Bank of Canada (Montréal,
  Qué) #9176
Lindgren, Charlotte, Can artist, 1931- #1126
  6283
– exhibitions
  – (1980) #6282
– exhibitions (reviews) #2771
Lindner, Ernest, Can artist, 1897- #6286
– and realism #110
– Cowley, Reta Madeline, compared with
  #5200
– drawings #6287
– exhibitions
  – (1970) #6284
  – (1972) #6285
  – (1977) #6288 6289
– exhibitions, group
  – (1967) #1916
  – (1971) #1920
  – (1975) #1926
  – (1980) #1940
– Hall, John, compared with #1860
– interview #6290
Lindoe, Luke Orton, Can artist, 1913-
– exhibitions, group
  – (1968) #2382
– interview #1974
Lindsay, Brydon & Greig, Can architectural
  firm
– Toronto (Ont), domestic architecture #8493
Lindsay, James (Jim), Can artist, 1944-
– on art #6291
Lindsay, Jeffrey, Can designer, ca. 1925-
– "shell truss" structural system #7674
Lindsay, T.D., Can photographer, 1926-
– exhibitions, group
  – (1972) #1952
Lindsay (Ont), Lindsay Gallery
– exhibitions
  – *John Howlin* (1979) #5852
line engraving
– *see* engraving
linen, Canadian
– 17th-19th cs. #2730 2736
– (1608-1867) #2120
– Ontario, 19th c. #2805
Lingwood, Daphne, Can leather sculptor, fl.
  1970s #2936
Lingwood, Rex, Can leather sculptor, 1946-
  #2936
Linnell, Henry R., Can architect, fl. 1915
– Winnipeg (Man), domestic architecture
  #8493
Lismer, Arthur, Can artist, 1885-1969 #6293
  6294 6295 6299 6300 6301 6303 6305 6307
– *A September Gale, Georgian Bay*, National
  Gallery of Canada (Ottawa, Ont) #6304
– and Edith Grace Coombs #5172
– and Group of Seven #286 1732
– and Louis Jobin #5964 5966
– as principal, Nova Scotia College of Art
  (Halifax, NS) #2993
– as teacher #1395 6302
  – Toronto (Ont), Art Gallery of Toronto
    #3020
– as teacher of Doris Jean McCarthy #6461
– book illustration and design #939
– correspondence, Homer Ransford Watson
  #7536
– exhibitions

– (1950) #6298
– exhibitions, group
  – (1968) #3224
– exhibitions (reviews) #1710 6296 6297
– illustrations, *Farmer's Magazine* #1765
– landscapes #6306
– murals, James MacCallum House,
  National Gallery of Canada (Ottawa, Ont)
  #1745
– on A.Y. Jackson #5914 5925
– on art education #2965 2966 2968 2971
  2974 2981 2984 2985 2987
  – Toronto (Ont), Art Gallery of Toronto
    #2975
– on Canadian art #6292
– on Frederick Horsman Varley #7463
– on Maurice Galbraith Cullen #5221
– on mural painting #15
– on Tom Thomson #7358
Literary and Philosophical Society (Toronto,
  Ont)
– support of museums #3152
literature
– *see also* authors; poetry
– children's literature, late 19th c.-1930s
  #2932
– compared with folk art #967
literature, Canadian #129
– (1880s-1920s) #10
– (1970s) #619
– (1975-1980) #1799
– and fashion (1882-1910) #2897
– and nationalism #327 341
– immigrant authors (1940s-1960s) #465
– New Brunswick #1178
– Newfoundland, 19th c.-1950s #1139
– Nova Scotia (1606-1950) #1196
– Québec
  – 19th c.-1930s #1382
  – 19th c.-1940s #1242
  – (1940s) #1391
  – (1960s) #529 1473
– Winnipeg (Man) #1891
– women authors, 20th c. #95 96
literature and art
– and Alex Colville #5141
– and Don Proch #6942
– and Francesca Vivenza #7495
– and Maxwell Bennett Bates #4621
– Canada #92 104
  – 19th c.-1930s #89
  – (1970s) #1529
  – and photography #1065 1066
  – and sociology #164
  – attitudes to wilderness #93
– Québec
  – and automatism #1449 4831
  – and Surrealism #1464
lithography, American
– (1940s) #810
lithography, Canadian
– 19th c. #812 925 1720
– (1940s) #810
– Halifax (NS), Nova Scotia College of Art
  and Design. Lithography Workshop
  (1970s) #825 830
– Heaviside, Lady Mary Love #258 259 1175
– Tazewell, Samuel Oliver #7339
– Wheatley, Willis Sifton #7548
Lithuanians in Canada
– costume #2892
Litteljohn, Bruce, Can photographer, 1935-
– exhibitions (reviews) #1009
Little, Harold Robert, Can architect,

1887-1948
- Montréal (Qué), McGill University.
  Athletic buildings, competition #9417
Little, John Geoffrey Caruthers, Can artist,
  1920-
- Ouellet, Angemil, compared with #1546
Little Bow (Alta), Little Bow Municipal
  Hospital
- architecture, Meech, Mitchell, Robins &
  Associates #9032
liturgical objects
- see also bells; chalices; ciboria (vessels);
  crosses; crucifixes; religious articles;
  tabernacles
liturgical objects, Canadian
- 17th-19th cs. #2627
- Québec
  - 17th-19th cs. #2681
  - (1950s) #1406
  - censers, 17th-18th cs. #2665
  - Jesuits #2192
  - pax, 17th-19th cs. #2666
Livernois, Jules-Benoît, Can photographer,
  1830-1865 #1275
- collection, photographs #6308
Livernois, Jules-Ernest, Can photographer,
  1858-1933 #1275
Livernois, Jules-Isaïe
- see Benoît (dit Livernois), Jules-Isaïe
Livernois, Paul, Can artist, 1948- #6309
Liverpool (NS), Simeon Perkins House
- architecture #7823 8536
Liverpool (NS), Simeon Perkins Museum
- exhibitions
  - Charles Wm. MacDonald: Seaman,
    Labourer, Artist, Manufacturer (1874-1967)
    (1981) #6355
Livick, Stephen, Can photographer, 1945-
  #1007
- exhibitions, group
  - (1981) #1070
livres d'artistes
- see also artists' books
livres d'artistes, Canadian
- Graff (Montréal, Qué) #1645
- Nantel, Michel #6684
- Québec (1967-1977) #1659
- women artists (1970s) #936
Loates, Glen, Can artist, 1945- #6310 6311
Lobchuk, William Harry (Bill), Can artist,
  1942-
- and Grand Western Canadian Screen Shop
  #1902
Local Architectural Conservation Advisory
  Committee (LACAC)
- conservation, Ontario #8022
Lochhead, Kenneth Campbell, Can artist,
  1926- #145 536 6312 6313 6314
- and Saskatchewan art (1950s) #1912
- Dallaire, Jean-Philippe, compared with
  #5238
- exhibitions
  - (1972) #6316
  - (1977) #6318
- exhibitions, group
  - (1958) #431
  - (1961) #1913
  - (1962) #1847
  - (1971) #98
  - (1981) #1907
- exhibitions (reviews) #520 6320
- interview #6317 6319
- on his art education #470
- use of spray gun (1970-1972) #6315

Lockport (Man), Saint Andrew's Church
- architecture and interior #8909
Lockport (Man), Saint Andrew's Parsonage
- architecture and land use #8716
locomotives
- steam-engine models, Walter H. Stansell
  #1792
Loder, Erik, Can artist, poet, 1933-
- on Jack Chambers #700
Lodge, Judith (Judy), Can artist, 1941- #2053
- The Walls of Eden series #6321
lodges (architecture), Blackfoot #3647
Loeb, Mr. and Mrs. Jules, Can collectors,
  20th c.
- collection, Canadian art #3231
Loew's, motion picture chain
- theatres, Canadian and American
  (1910s-1930s) #9122 9123
log cabins, Canadian
- Acadian #7804
- Arctic #8189
- British Columbia #8148
- Gaspé (Qué) #7896
- Labrador Trapper's tilt #8532
- maple sugar cabins, Québec, 17th-18th cs.
  #2217
- Ontario, 19th c. #7979 7990
- Ottawa Valley (Ont) #8029
- Prince Albert National Park (Sask), Grey
  Owl Cabin site #8719
- restoration #8526
- Ukrainian #8090
Logan, Robert Fulton, Can artist, 1889-1959
- exhibitions
  - (1928) #1732
Loire, Gabriel, Fr stained glass artist, 20th c.
- stained glass, Saint Antonin Church
  (Montréal, Qué) #2448
Lom d'Arce, Louis Armand de, Baron de La
  Hontan, Fr writer, army officer, 1666-ca.
  1716
- and nationalism in art #1373
London, George, Can stained glass artist, fl.
  1907-
- and Yvonne Williams #7589
London (England)
- blitzkrieg, impact on Jack Leonard
  Shadbolt #7189
- urban development #7902
London (England), Anthropos Gallery
- sculpture, Inuit #4289
London (England), Arthur Tooth & Sons
- exhibitions
  - J.-P. Riopelle: Paintings, 1949-1959 (1959)
    #7015
London (England), Arts Council of Great
  Britain
- exhibitions
  - Jack Bush: Paintings and Drawings,
    1955-1976 (1980) #4976
London (England), British Empire Exhibition
  (1910)
- Dyonnet, Edmond, on Canadian art
  exhibited #5347 5349
London (England), British Museum
- art, Indians of North America
  - Sloane, Sir Hans, collection #3397
- art, Inuit #4289 4360 4369
- art, Kwakiutl #3850
- art, Northwest Coast Indians #4062
- buffalo hair bag, Indians of North
  America #3398
- Catlin, George, illustrations of tobacco
  pipes #3478

- coffer, Northwest Coast Indians #3805
- exhibitions
  - Artificial Curiosities from the Northwest
    Coast of America (1981) #4064
  - Sculpture of the Inuit: Masterworks of the
    Canadian Arctic/La sculpture chez les Inuit:
    chefs-d'oeuvre de l'Arctique canadien
    (1972) #4423 4440
- pipes, Indians of North America #3470
- puffin-beak rattles, Northwest Coast
  Indians #3960
- White, John, drawings of North American
  Indians and Eskimos #7552
- winter count #3747
London (England), Burlington Gallery
- exhibitions
  - Australian and New Zealand, American and
    Canadian Oil Paintings and Water Colour
    Drawings (1888) #175
  - Exhibition of Australian, New Zealand,
    American and Canadian Oil Paintings and
    Water Colour Drawings (1890) #177
  - Exhibition of Water-color Drawings of
    Yellowstone Park, Yosemite Valley and
    Rocky Mountain Views, also Canadian and
    North Western Buffalo Hunts and Other
    Indian Sports,(1890) #1839
London (England), Canada House Gallery
- exhibitions
  - Bill Vazan: Recent Photoworks and
    Videotapes (1978) #7474
  - Canadians: A National Photography Show
    about People/Canadiens: exposition
    nationale de photographie ayant les gens
    comme thème (1978) #1035
  - Contemporary Native Art of Canada: The
    Woodland Indians/Art contemporain des
    Indiens sylvicoles du
    Canada/Zeitgenössische Kunst der
    kanadischen Waldland Indianer (1976)
    #4143
  - D.P. Brown, Ken Danby, Tom Forrestall,
    Christopher Pratt (1974) #573
  - Emily Carr: The Mature Years/Emily Carr:
    les années de maturité (1979) #5042
  - Exposition d'estampes en l'honneur de C.
    Krieghoff, 1815-1872/Exhibition of Prints
    in Honour of C. Krieghoff, 1815-1872
    (1972) #6096
  - General Idea's Reconstructing
    Futures/General Idea: reconstruction de
    l'avenir (1978) #5583
  - Group of Seven, Canadian Landscape
    Painters: A Travelling Exhibition from the
    McMichael Canadian Collection, Kleinburg,
    Ontario/Groupe des Sept: peintres
    canadiens de paysages: une exposition
    itinérante de la collection canadienne
    McMichael, de Kleinberg, Ontario
    (1977) #1780
  - Ivan Eyre Exposition (1982) #5394
  - Jack Chambers: Selection of Paintings and
    Drawings (1980) #5080
  - Leslie Reid (1980) #6981
  - Other Realities: The Legacy of Surrealism in
    Canadian Art (1979) #508
  - Réalités autres: le legs du surréalisme à l'art
    canadien (1979) #509
  - The Fabric of Their Lives: Hooked and
    Poked Mats of Newfoundland and
    Labrador/L'étoffe de leur vie: tapis crochetés
    et poinçonnés de Terre-Neuve et du
    Labrador (1980) #2765
  - Twelve Mile Creek: Exhibition/Exposition

(1975) #1808
- *Windows of Perception* (1977)
- Curnoe, Greg, on #5230
- exhibitions (reviews)
  - *Exposition d'estampes en l'honneur de C. Krieghoff, 1815-1872/Exhibition of Prints in Honour of C. Krieghoff, 1815-1872* (1972) #6099
  - *Jack Chambers: Selection of Paintings and Drawings* (1980) #5082
  - Young, Robert (1979) #7629
London (England), Carroll Gallery
- exhibitions
  - *Catalogue of an Exhibition of Water Colours Representing the "Canadian Rockies" by Charles John Collings* (1912) #5133
  - *The Art of Charles John Collings* (1914?) #5134
- exhibitions (reviews)
  - *Catalogue of an Exhibition of Water Colours Representing the "Canadian Rockies" by Charles John Collings* (1912) #5132
London (England), Chelsea School of Art
- Woolnough, Hilda Mary, as student #7616
London (England), Colonial and Indian Exhibition (1886)
- Canadian art #14 172 174
London (England), Commonwealth Art Gallery
- exhibitions
  - *Commonwealth Artists of Fame, 1952-1977* (1977) #633
London (England), Earls Court Exhibition
- exhibitions
  - *Catalogue of the Memorial Exhibition of Pictures Left by the Late Henry Sandham, Royal Canadian Academician* (1911) #7120
London (England), Frost and Reed's Art Galleries
- exhibitions
  - *Arthur Heming: Recorder of the Northland of Canada; Exhibition of Paintings at Frost & Reed's Art Galleries; Where Mr. Heming's Work is Shown for the First Time in Europe* (1934) #5776
London (England), Grafton Galleries
- exhibitions
  - *Catalogue of the Canadian Official War Photographs Exhibition for the Benefit of the Canadian War Memorials Fund* (1916) #1072
London (England), Grosvenor Life School
- Wrinch, Mary Evelyn, as student #7618
London (England), Hayward Gallery
- exhibitions
  - *Sacred Circles: Two Thousand Years of North American Indian Art* (1976) #3463
London (England), Horniman Museum
- Inuit artifacts and art #4289
London (England), Institute of Contemporary Arts Ltd.
- First International Sculpture Competition (1953) #5995
London (England), Leigh's Academy
- Verner, Frederick Arthur, as student #7484
London (England), London Mechanics' Institution
- Birkbeck, George, as president #3064
London (England), Marlborough Fine Art Gallery
- exhibitions
  - *Alex Colville* (1970) #5145
London (England), Molton Galleries

- exhibitions
  - *Gerald Gladstone* (1962) #5611
London (England), Redfern Gallery
- exhibitions (reviews)
  - Young, Robert (1979) #7629
London (England), Royal Academy of Arts
- Cruikshank, William, works exhibited #5212
- Hopkins, Frances Ann Beechy, works exhibited #5835
London (England), Royal Academy School of Architecture
- Carter, Alexander Scott, as student #5050
London (England), Royal College of Art
- Warren, Emily Mary Bibbens, as student #7524
London (England), Royal Institute Galleries
- exhibitions
  - *Artists of the British Empire Overseas* (1937) #339
London (England), Royal Institute of British Architects. Galleries
- Canadian architecture exhibited (ca. 1927) #8224
London (England), Serpentine Gallery
- exhibitions
  - *Jack Bush: Paintings and Drawings, 1955-1976* (1980) #4976
- exhibitions (reviews)
  - Bush, Jack Hamilton #4977
London (England), Slade School
- Blackstock, Hattie, as student #4738
- Grier, Edmund Wyly, as student #5660
London (England), South Kensington School of Art
- Forbes, John Colin, as student #5459
- Kinton, Ada Florence, as student #6053
- Pemberton, Sophia Theresa, as student #6828
London (England), Sunhill Sanatorium
- Carr, Emily, as patient #5018
London (England), Tate Gallery
- exhibitions
  - *A Century of Canadian Art* (1938) #19
  - *Canadian Painting, 1939-1963* (1964) #462
- exhibitions (reviews)
  - *A Century of Canadian Art* (1938) #22
London (England), Westminster School of Art
- Carr, Emily, as student #5018 5045
London (England), Whitechapel Gallery
- exhibitions
  - *Exhibition of Canadian Art* (1925) #290
  - *Robert Downing: Sculpture* (1969) #5304
  - *Yves Gaucher* (1970) #5563
London (England), Woodstock Gallery
- exhibitions
  - *Catalogue of an Exhibition of Paintings and Drawings by Walt Ruhman (Canada)* (1959) #7106
London (Ont)
- architecture
  - 19th c. #8003 8007 8010 8018
- art
  - (1940s-1970s) #1670
  - (1947-1979) #1828
  - (1960s) #90 1791
  - (1970s) #1813
  - (1970s), compared with Saskatoon (Sask) art #1932
- decorative arts (1970s) #2260
- graphic arts and photography (1970s) #1812
- pottery, 19th c. #2350

- video art #550
London (Ont), Aberdeen School
- architecture, Watt & Blackwell #9388
London (Ont), Eldon House
- architecture and interior #8660
London (Ont), Fanshawe College
- Eloul, Kosso, *Now* #5367
London (Ont), Grand Theatre
- restoration, Lett/Smith #7776
London (Ont), H.P. Beal Technical School
- influence on London (Ont) art (1960s) #1791
London (Ont), London Art Gallery
- *see also* London (Ont), London Public Library and Art Museum; London (Ont), London Regional Art Gallery
- exhibitions
  - *Another Dimension/Une autre dimension* (1977) #783
  - *Esther Warkov Drawings* (1977) #7519
  - *Frederic Marlett Bell-Smith (1846-1923)* (1978) #4668
  - *Graham Coughtry: Retrospective* (1976) #5190
  - *Graphics and Photographics: The Second of Four Major Survey Exhibitions of London Art* (1976) #1812
  - *Greg Curnoe: Some Lettered Works, 1961-1969* (1975) #5228
  - *London Saskatoon Exchange* (1977) #1932
  - *London Survey Number Four: Crafts* (1977) #2260
  - *R.L. Bloore: Sixteen Years, 1958-1974* (1975) #4751
  - *White Paintings: John Noestheden* (1977) #6715
  - *Young Contemporaries/Jeunes contemporains* (1975-1979) #584
- exhibitions (reviews)
  - *The Tony Urquhart Reunion* (1970) #7445
London (Ont), London Public Library and Art Museum
- *see also* London (Ont), London Art Gallery; London (Ont), London Regional Art Gallery
- collection #3153
- cultural services (1940s) #3133
- exhibitions
  - *7 West Coast Painters* (1959) #1997
  - *Alan C. Collier Retrospective* (1971) #5131
  - *André Biéler 50 Years: A Retrospective Exhibition 1920-1970* (1971) #4725
  - *Canadian Artists Abroad* (1956) #413 414
  - *Carl Schaefer: Retrospective Exhibition; Paintings from 1926 to 1969* (1969) #7155
  - *Centennial Exhibition of Quebec and Ontario Contemporary Painters, 1967* (1967) #484
  - *Changing Visions: The Canadian Landscape/Aperçus divers: le paysage canadien* (1977) #617
  - *Daniel Fowler* (1965) #5489
  - *David Milne: 1882-1953* (1967) #6558
  - *Drawings and Pastels c. 1930-1967 by Miller Gore Brittain* (1969) #4917
  - *Five Years of Robert Downing, 1966-1971* (1972) #5306
  - *Goodridge Roberts: A Retrospective Exhibition/Goodridge Roberts: une exposition rétrospective* (1970) #7045
  - *Harold Town: The First Exhibition of New Work, 1969-1973* (1973) #7413
  - *J.M. Barnsley (1861-1929), Retrospective Exhibition* (1964) #4611

– *Jock Macdonald: Retrospective Exhibition/Jock Macdonald: rétrospective* (1970) #6375
– *Joe Plaskett and His Paris: In Search of Time Past* (1972) #6893
– *Joe Plaskett et son Paris: à la recherche d'un temps passé* (1972) #6894
– *John Meredith: Fifteen Years* (1975) #6514
– *Léon Bellefleur* (1968) #4662
– *Lithographs/Lithographies* (1973) #825
– *London Collects* (1972, 1976) #100
– *London Painting Now: A Survey of London Painting* (1976) #1813
– *Neglected Aspects of Canadian Culture* (1973) #962
– *Ontario Society of Artists: 100 Years* (1973) #1678
– *Paterson Ewen Retrospective* (1976) #5384
– *Paul Peel, 1860-1892: Memorial Exhibition in the Art Gallery* (1970) #6792
– *Quebec* (1944) #12
– *Some Paintings, Drawings and Prints from the Douglas Duncan Collection* (1967) #3223
– *Surrealism in Canadian Painting* (1964) #463
– *The J.S. McLean Collection of Canadian Painting* (1969) #3228
– *The Ontario Community Collects: A Survey of Canadian Painting from 1766 to the Present* (1976) #120
– *Western Ontario Exhibition* (1941-1978) #1670
– *York Wilson Retrospective (1927-1973)* (1975) #7596
– exhibitions (reviews)
  – *Points of View* (1959) #432
  – Sculptors' Society of Canada (1944) #736
London (Ont), London Regional Art Gallery
– see also London (Ont), London Art Gallery; London (Ont), London Public Library and Art Museum
– architecture, Raymond Moriyama #3174 9145
– exhibitions
  – *Brian Jones* (1978) #5974
  – *Celebration: The Canadian Embroiderer's Guild* (1981) #2793
  – *Certain Traditions: Recent British and Canadian Art* (1979) #653
  – *Colette Whiten* (1978) #7561
  – *Ed Bartram: 10 Years* (1980) #4618
  – *Gordon Rayner Retrospective* (1979) #6966
  – *Greg Curnoe: rétrospective/Greg Curnoe: Retrospective* (1982) #5231
  – *Guido Molinari: Works on Paper* (1981) #6594
  – *Ivan Eyre Exposition* (1981) #5394
  – *Jack Chambers: The Last Decade* (1980) #5081
  – *London/Banff Exchange* (1978) #1964
  – *Louis de Niverville* (1978) #6709
  – *Mary Pratt* (1981) #6919
  – *Métiers d'art Ontario-Québec, 1979/1980/Quebec-Ontario Crafts, 1979/1980* (1981) #2138
  – *Nine Regional Nineteenth Century Artists* (1978) #1726
  – *Painters Eleven in Retrospect* (1980) #1785
  – *The Society of Canadian Painter-Etchers and Engravers in Retrospect/La Société des peintres-graveurs canadiens: vue rétrospective* (1981) #836

– *Trésors d'art populaire québécois/Folk Art Treasures of Quebec* (1981) #1297
– *Viewpoint: Twenty-nine by Nine; An Exhibition of Twenty-nine Works by Ontario Artists, Selected by Nine Curators* (1981) #1838
London (Ont), Lord Roberts School
– architecture, McBride & Gilbert; Arthur E. Nutter, Associate Architect #9388
London (Ont), McCormick Manufacturing Co.
– architecture, Watt & Blackwell #9234
London (Ont), McIntosh Art Gallery
– see London (Ont), University of Western Ontario. McIntosh Art Gallery
London (Ont), Northern Life of Canada Building
– Reid, Stuart, *Hudson Bay Triptych* #6983
London (Ont), Riverview School
– architecture, Lewis E. Carrothers and John Vicar Munro #9388
London (Ont), Ryerson School
– architecture, Watt & Blackwell; William G. Murray, Associate Architect #9386
London (Ont), Tecumseh School
– architecture, Watt & Blackwell #9388
London (Ont), Theo Waddington
– exhibitions
  – *Mathew Aqiggaaq: Recent Sculpture* (1979) #4534
London (Ont), University of Western Ontario
– and Fanshawe Pioneer Village (Ont) #8066
– architecture, John M. Moore & Company #9448
London (Ont), University of Western Ontario. McIntosh Art Gallery
– exhibitions
  – *Eskimo Wall Hangings* (1974) #4253
  – *Imprint '76* (1976) #833
  – *The Artist and the Critic: A Tribute to Lenore Crawford* (1974) #112
  – *The Image of Man in Canadian Painting: 1878-1978/L'image de l'homme dans la peinture canadienne: 1878-1978* (1978) #135
– exhibitions (reviews)
  – *The Mask of Objectivity/Subjective Images* (1981) #1067
London (Ont), University of Western Ontario. McIntosh Memorial Art Gallery
– exhibitions
  – *A Century of Pioneering* (1943) #12
  – *Sports and Pastimes* (1944) #12
  – *The Marine Collection* (1943) #12
London (Ont), University of Western Ontario. Science Building
– architecture, John M. Moore & Company #9442
London (Ont), University of Western Ontario. Student residence
– architecture, Tillmann & Lamb #9467
London (Ont), Western School of Art
– Griffiths, John Howard, as teacher and principal #2305
London (Ont), Womanspirit - Art Research and Learning Centre
– and Sasha Hayman #5756
London Crockery Mfg. Co., ceramic manufacturer (London, Ont) #2350
London Free Press, Can newspaper
– Crawford, Lenore, as art critic #112
Lonechild, Michael, Can artist, 1955- #6322

Long, J.W., & Associates, Can architectural firm
– Edmonton (Alta), Hillington Court #8744
Long, Jack W., Can architect, 1925-
– Calgary (Alta) #8381
– Calgary (Alta), Kelvin Grove Patio Apartments #8518
– on planning #7746
Long, Marion, Can artist, 1882-1970
– and Albert Angus Macdonald #6354
– exhibitions (reviews) #432
Longfellow, Henry Wadsworth, Amer poet, 1807-1882
– *Evangéline*, as inspiration for Henri Beau, *La dispersion des Acadiens* (1900) #4639
Longpré & Marchand, Can architectural firm
– Montréal (Qué), métro. Berri-de-Montigny Station #9549
Longueuil (Qué), Lamarre House
– architecture #8608
looms
– see also Jacquard weaving
looms, Canadian
– 19th c. #2735
looms, Indians of North America #3413
looms, Salish #3963
Lorcini, Gino, Can artist, 1923- #1479 6323
– and plasticiens #1439
– exhibitions, group
  – (1967) #490
– use of light #767
Lord, Daniel, Can silversmith, fl. 1840s-1860s #2649
Lordly, Albert James, Can furniture-maker, b. 1826 #2511
Lorenzetto, Adeline, Can weaver, fl. 1960s
– Salish weaving #3941
Lorette (Qué), Huron Mission
– altar frontal, mère Marie Le Maire des Anges #1328
Loretteville (Qué), Church of Notre-Dame-de-la-Jeune-Lorette
– architecture and interior #8804
Loring, Frances Norma, Can sculptor, 1887-1968 #739
– and Florence Wyle #758
– exhibitions, group
  – (1969) #754
Lorlie (Sask)
– views, George Campbell Tinning #7378
Lorne, John Douglas Sutherland, later 9th duke of Argyll, Marquess of, Brit statesman, artist in Canada, 1845-1914
– and Royal Canadian Academy of Arts #2 153 275 280
– as patron of Canadian art #168
Lorrain, Madeleine, Can artist, fl. 1950
– Christmas greeting cards #856
Lortie, Jocelyne, Can artist, fl. 1978 #6325
Lortie, Joseph Antoine François (Niska), Can artist, 1940- #6324
Los Angeles (Calif), Bunker Hill redevelopment
– architecture, competition for #8364
Los Angeles (Calif), Felix Landau Gallery
– exhibitions
  – *Etrog* (1964) #5376
Los Angeles (Calif), Museum of Natural History of Los Angeles County
– exhibitions
  – *Objects of Bright Pride: Northwest Coast Indian Art from the American Museum of Natural History* (1978) #4024

Los Angeles (Calif), Southwest Museum
- ivory carvings, Inuit #4382
- quill-decorated birchbark boxes, Ottawa Indians #3548
Los Angeles (Calif), University of California
- Peterson, Margaret, as student and teacher #6839
Lotbinière, Pierre-Gustave Joly de, Can photographer, d. 1865 #6326
Lotbinière (Qué)
- churches #8835
Lougheed, Robert Elmer, Can artist, 1910- #6327 6328
Louis, Morris, Amer artist, 1912-1962
- Christensen, Dan, compared with #5104
Louis, Pat, Can photographer, fl. 1970s-
- portfolio of photographs #991
Louis XVI style
- architecture
  - Calgary (Alta), Hotel Palliser #9271
  - Toronto (Ont)
    - Chorley Park #8749
    - Royal Alexandra Theatre #9059
Louisbourg (NS) #8419 8422 8439 8442
- artisans #2148
- costume
  - 18th c. #2868
  - female (1713-1758) #2855
- domestic architecture #8427
- earthenware #2368 2369
- fortifications #8426
  - barracks, King's Bastion #8435 8436
  - guardhouses #8428 8429
- furniture #2484
- glass, 18th c. #2427
- île du Quai, restoration #8423
- interior decoration #7758
- military uniforms (1713-1758) #2857 2866
- restoration #8425
- roofs, use of wooden shingles #7703
- statues, Louis XV #1598
Louisbourg (NS), Dugas House
- glass #2441 2442
Louisiana
- statues, Louis XIV #1598
- views by French explorers #276
Louisville (Ky), J.B. Speed Art Museum
- exhibitions
  - 19 Canadian Painters 1962 (1962) #450
Louy, Pierre, Can artist, fl. 1960s
- as member of Hampton Group #1177
Love, Lady
- see Heaviside, Mary (Lady Love)
love in art
- see also erotic art
- Pellan, Alfred #6822
  - L'amour fou #6820
Loveroff, Frederick Nicholas, Can artist, 1894-1960 #6329 6330
- exhibitions
  - (1981) #6331
Lowe, Frederic C., Can artist, fl. 1843-1856
- as member, Toronto Society of Arts #1689
Lower Fort Garry (Man)
- architecture #8094 8475 8483
  - men's house #8482
  - North-West Bastion and walls #8476
  - warehouse building #8480
Lozeau, Jean-Baptiste, Can metalworker, ca. 1694-1745 #249 250
Luc, frère
- see François, Claude (frère Luc)
Lucas, Gabriel, Can jeweller, 20th c.

- and Georges Delrue #2694
Lucerne (Qué), Château Lucerne
- architecture, Lawson & Little, Architects and Engineers; Edwin S. Kent and Geo. W. White Associates #9283
Lucerne (Switzerland), Kunstmuseum Luzern
- exhibitions
  - Michael Snow (1979) #7258
  - Michael Snow: Works 1969-1978, Films 1964-1976/Michael Snow: Werke 1969-1978, Filme 1964-1976 (1979) #7261
Luci & Associés #1502
Lucy
- see Qinnuayuak, Lucy
Lui, Andrew, Can artist, 1951- #6332
Luke, Alexandra, Can artist, 1901-1967
- as member, Canadian Group of Painters #324
- as student of Hans Hofmann #402 1850
- collection, Canadian art, Robert McLaughlin Gallery (Oshawa, Ont) #3169
- correspondence, Jock Macdonald #6376
- exhibitions
  - (1977) #6333
- exhibitions (reviews) #6334
Lum, Kay, Can photographer, ca. 1950-
- portfolio of photographs #1023
Lummi Indians
- totem poles #3967
Lund, Chris, Can photographer, 1923-
- portfolio of photographs #987
Lunenburg (NS)
- architecture #7836 7837
Lunenburg (NS), Lunenburg Art Gallery
- exhibitions
  - Charles Wm. MacDonald: Seaman, Labourer, Artist, Manufacturer (1874-1967) (1981) #6355
Lunenburg (NS), Soloman House
- architecture and interior #8549
Lurçat, Jean, Fr tapestry artist, 1892-1966
- as teacher of Roger Caron #5005
Lussier, Denis Lionel, Can architect, 1938-1975
- Saint-Boniface (Man), Precious Blood Church #8908
Lussier, Michel, Can sculptor, 1948-
- use of plastics #1603
Lussier, Paul, Can artist, 1944- #6335
- as founder of atelier Arachel (Montréal, Qué) #1657
Lutkenhaus, Almuth, Can sculptor, 1927-
- interview #6336
Lutterworth (England), Saint Mary's Parish Church
- influence on Lloyd Johnson's stone church (Saint John, NB) #8778
Luxembourg (Luxembourg), Musée de l'Etat
- exhibitions
  - 10 Canadian Artists in the 1970s (1981) #703
Luxfer Prism Co., stained glass studio (Toronto, Ont) #2450
Lyall, Laura Adeline Muntz, Can artist, 1860-1930 #207 6337 6338 6339
- and Mary Evelyn Wrinch #7617
Lyceum Club (Toronto, Ont)
- and Women's Art Association of Canada #176
- exhibitions
  - (1939) #1

Lyle, John MacIntosh, Can architect, 1872-1945
- architectural decorations, Canadian banks (1930s) #8226
- as teacher #8243
- Bank of Nova Scotia buildings #9186 9203
- exhibitions, group
  - (1933) #8224
- Halifax (NS), Bank of Nova Scotia #9182
- Kingston (Ont), war memorial, Royal Military College of Canada #1083
- on Canadian art #329
- plan, northwestern entrance to Hamilton (Ont) #7962
- Toronto (Ont)
  - Bank of Ottawa #9159
  - Dominion Bank #9188
  - Government House, competition #8748
  - Masonic Temple, competition #9062
  - Royal Alexandra Theatre #9059
  - Toronto Stock Exchange, competition #9161
  - Union Station #9531 9536
- use of stucco and brickwork #8052
Lyman, John Goodwin, Can artist, art critic, 1886-1967 #6340 6344
- and Contemporary Arts Society (Montréal, Qué) #1474
- and James Wilson Morrice #6634
- and Paul-Emile Borduas #4814
- as teacher of Kim Ondaatje #6733
- exhibitions
  - (1963) #6343
  - (1966) #6345
- exhibitions, group
  - (1977) #1278 1279
- exhibitions (reviews) #6341
- influence on Québec abstract art #1468
- interview #6342
- on James Wilson Morrice #6618 6619
- paintings (1930s) #502
- writings #6346 6347
Lynn, Washington Frank, Can artist, 1836-1906 #1896 6348
Lynn, William H., Irish architect in Canada, fl. 1860s-1870s
- Québec (Qué), fortifications #7946
Lyon, N.T., Can stained glass artist, fl. 1880-1890 #2450
lyrical abstraction
- British Columbia (1950s) #1990
- Montréal (Qué), (1950s) #1426 1437 1438
- Québec #1453
lyrical realism
- see realism
Lytle, Can photographer, fl. 1856-1867 #1724
Lyttleton, Westcott Whitchurch Lewis, Brit army officer, artist in Canada, 1818-1879
- Halifax Harbour Seen from McNab's Island, Royal Ontario Museum (Toronto, Ont) #6349

M

M, Can periodical #3097
M'Intyre, Thomas
- see McIntyre (M'Intyre), Thomas
MacAskill, Wallace R., Can photographer, 1890-1956 #6350 6351
MacAulay, John, Can collector, 1895-
- collection, Canadian and European art,

exhibited at National Gallery of Canada
(Ottawa, Ont), (1954) #3212
MacCallum, James Metcalfe, Can physician,
collector, 1860-1943
– and A.Y. Jackson #5917
– and Arthur Lismer #6300
– and G.Blair Laing, as dealer #1686
– and Group of Seven and Tom Thomson
#1745 3237
– correspondence, Norman I. Gurd #1776
– paintings, Tom Thomson and Group of
Seven, given to National Gallery of
Canada (Ottawa, Ont) #3229
MacCarthy, Hamilton Plantagenet, Can
sculptor, 1846-1939 #178 6352 6353
– on Canadian sculpture (1960s) #727
MacCormack, Terry, Can photographer, fl.
1970s-
– portfolio of photographs #991
Macdonald, Albert Angus, Can artist, 1909-
#6354
MacDonald, Charles William, Can artist,
1874-1967
– exhibitions
– (1980) #6355
Macdonald, Evan Weekes, Can artist,
1905-1972 #6357
– interview #6356
Macdonald, Grant Kenneth, Can artist, 1909-
#6358
Macdonald, Hugh John, Can statesman,
1850-1929
– residence, Dalnavert (Winnipeg, Man)
#8708
MacDonald, J.Blair/Barry V. Downs, Can
architectural firm
– Canadian Architect community art gallery
competition (1957) #9082
Macdonald, James Alexander Stirling, Can
artist, 1921- #6359
MacDonald, James Edward Hervey (J.E.H.),
Can artist, 1873-1932 #6329 6364 6365 6366
6367 6368 6372
– and Catharine Robb Whyte and Peter
Whyte #7571
– and Edith Grace Coombs #5172
– and Group of Seven #1732
– and Thoreau MacDonald #6384 6385
– art and writings, West Indies (1932) #6371
– book illustration and design #939
– bookplates #917
– correspondence, Tom Thomson #7356
– eulogy #6363
– exhibitions
– (1933) #294
– (1965) #6370
– exhibitions, group
– (1968) #3224
– exhibitions (reviews) #1710
– influence of Scandinavian art #1788
– influence on Charles William Jefferys
#5958
– interior, Saint Anne's Church (Toronto,
Ont) #1733
– landscapes #140
– murals, James MacCallum house, National
Gallery of Canada (Ottawa, Ont) #1745
– on artists and critics #6360
– on mural painting #6362
– on painting from a railroad car (1919)
#6361
– on Tom Thomson #7350
– Schaefer, Carl Fellman, compared with
#7157

– sketchbooks (1915-1922) #6373
– writings #92
Macdonald, James Williamson Galloway
(Jock), Can artist, 1897-1960 #6374 6377
– and British Columbia Society of Fine Arts
#1978
– and Marion F.S. Mackay Nicoll #6703
– and Vancouver (BC) painting (1950s)
#1992
– as member, Canadian Group of Painters
#324
– as student of Hans Hofmann #402 1850
– as teacher #2990 6378
– as teacher of Arthur McKay #6477
– correspondence from Europe (1954-1955)
#6376
– exhibitions
– (1969) #6375
– (1981) #6379
– exhibitions, group
– (1978) #133 508 509
– exhibitions (reviews) #1982
– influence on Kenneth Edison Danby #5251
– influence on William S. Ronald #7072
– Luke, Alexandra, on #6334
– on Frederick Horsman Varley #7463
– Vanderpant, John A., compared with
#7459
Macdonald, John A., Can prime minister,
1815-1891
– cartoons of #944
– Bengough, John Wilson #942
– painting of his house #964
– portrait sculpture of, Hamilton
Plantagenet McCarthy #727
MacDonald, Manly Edward, Can artist,
1889-1971
– exhibitions (reviews) #432
MacDonald, Thomas Reid, Can artist,
curator, 1908-1978
– exhibitions
– (1980) #6380
MacDonald, Thoreau, Can artist, 1901- #6381
6382 6383 6384
– designs and illustrations #6385
– illustrations, Canadian Forum #930
– on J.E.H. MacDonald #6366 6369
– on Tom Thomson #7364
MacDonald Stewart Foundation
– restoration, château Dufresne (Montréal,
Qué) #8617
MacEachern, Ian, Can photographer, 1942-
#6386
MacGee, Chris, Can artist, poet, 1951-
– on Jack Chambers #700
MacGregor, James Gamble, Can artist, 1898-
#1888
MacGregor, John, Can artist, 1944- #6387
– exhibitions, group
– (1978) #665
– interview #6388
machinery, Canadian
– (1940s) #2603
machinery in art
– Cournoyer, Serge, sculptures #5194
MacInnis, Garfield Allister (Gar), Can
architect, 1936-
– Charlottetown (PEI), Confederation
Centre, competition #9089
– Saskatoon (Sask), Mendel Art Gallery
#9091
Mack, T.A., Can furniture-maker, b. 1889
#2587
MacKay, Thomas, Can architect, 1792-1855

– Ottawa (Ont) #8038
MacKeeman, Karl, Can artist, 1948- #6389
Mackenzie, Alexander, Brit explorer in
Canada, 1763-1820
– expedition, natives of North America
#4097
Mackenzie, Cynthia, Can artist, 1952-
– interview #6390
Mackenzie, Hugh Seaforth, Can artist, 1928-
– and realism #110
Mackenzie, Norman, Can collector,
1869-1936
– collection, European and Asian art #1912
– collection, Norman Mackenzie Art Gallery
(Regina, Sask) #3197
MacKenzie, Robin, Can artist, 1938-
– exhibitions, group
– (1975) #1809
– (1976) #779
– landscape photographs, Scotland
(1975-1976) #6393
– map images #561
– sculptures #6391 6392
– use of photography #1057
MacLaughlan, Donald Shaw, Can artist,
1876-1938 #6394
MacLean, Robert, Can artist, 1942-1972
– tattoo drawings #2923
Maclean's, Can periodical
– illustrations, H.W. Cooper #5173
MacLeay, R.Scott, Can photographer, fl.
1977
– portfolio of photographs #1023
MacLennan, Toby Chapman, Can artist,
1939- #6395
– exhibitions, group
– (1974) #2050
– performance sculpture #658
MacLeod, Pegi Nicol, Can artist, 1904-1949
#336 6396 6398
– and genre painting #392
– exhibitions
– (1949) #6397
Maclure, Samuel, Can architect, artist,
1860-1929 #8384 8385
– compared with Francis Mawson
Rattenbury #8152
– domestic architecture #8494
– exhibitions
– (1971) #8383
– Saanich Peninsula (BC), Miraloma (now
Latch Restaurant) #8731
– Victoria (BC), Alexis Martin House #8682
MacMillan, Harvey Reginald, Can collector,
1885-1975
– collection, art, Kwakiutl Indians #3996
MacNab, Sir Allan, Can statesman,
1798-1862
– residence, Dundurn Castle (Hamilton,
Ont) #8650 8662
MacNamara, Gordon Robertson, Can artist,
1910- #6399
MacNevin, Brian, Can artist, fl. 1970s
– exhibitions, group
– (1979) #1157
MacPherson, Diane, Can stained glass artist,
fl. 1975
– stained glass #2452
Macpherson, Duncan Ian, Can artist, 1924-
– exhibitions
– (1980) #6401
– illustrations #855
– political cartoons #957 6400
Macri, Tommaso (Tom), Can sculptor, 1943-

#2076
MacTavish, Catharine, Can artist, 1952-
– exhibitions (reviews) #2081
Madahbee, Mel, Can artist, 1956-
– exhibitions, group
  – (1981) #4173
Maday, Helene Julia, Can sculptor, 1916-
– exhibitions, group
  – (1971), medals #772
Made in Kebec, Can comic strip #948
Madison (Wis), Elvehjem Art Center
– *see* Madison (Wis), University of
  Wisconsin. Elvehjem Art Center
Madison (Wis), University of Wisconsin.
  Elvehjem Art Center
– exhibitions
  – *Canadian Landscape Painting, 1670-1930:
    The Artist and the Land* (1973) #106
Madonna
– *see* Mary, Virgin
Madrid (Spain), Museo de America
– art, Inuit and Indians of North America
  #3372
Madrid (Spain), Real Academia de Bellas
  Artes
– Chambers, Jack, as student #5073
Magdalenian art
– compared with Inuit art #4341
Maggs, Arnaud, Can photographer, 1926-
– exhibitions, group
  – (1981) #1070
– record covers #862
magic realism
– *see* realism
Magog (Qué), Monastery of
  Saint-Benoît-du-Lac
– architecture, Dom Bellot #8332
Magor, Elizabeth (Liz), Can artist, 1948-
  #6402 6403
– *Compost Figures* and *A Concise History*
  #6404
– exhibitions
  – (1979) #6405
  – (1980) #6407
  – (1981) #6408
– exhibitions, group
  – (1976) #2060
  – (1978) #2066
– exhibitions (reviews) #622
– interview #6406
– natural constructions (1970s) #2065
Magrini, Alex, Can artist, 1951- #640
– exhibitions
  – (1980) #685
Maguire Partners, Amer architectural firm
– Los Angeles (Calif), Bunker Hill
  redevelopment, competition #8364
Mah, Tom, Can artist, 1951- #6409
Maher, Dean, Can photographer, fl. 1981
– portfolio of photographs #1023
Mahl-stick Club (Toronto, Ont)
– and Canadian Society of Graphic Art #801
Mahler, Gustav, Aus composer, 1860-1911
– portrait of, Virgil Hammock #5696
Mahon, Lilette, Can artist, d. 1956
– on Emily Carr, as teacher #5014
mail art
– Canada (1970s) #555
– Craig, Kate #2070
– in *File* periodical #544
– Lewis, Glenn Alun #2070
– Metcalfe, Eric #2070
Maillard, Charles, Can artist, 1887-1973 #302
– as director, Ecole des beaux-arts

(Montréal, Qué) #1456 2972
– as teacher of Jean-Paul Lemieux #6228
– on Ecole des beaux-arts (Montréal, Qué),
  (1924-1933) #2973
– on nationalism in art #4851
– paintings (1930s) #1460
Maillol, Aristide, Fr sculptor, 1861-1944
– influence on Claude Roussel #7087
Maillou (*dit* Desmoulins), Jean-Baptiste, Can
  architect, 1668-1753 #249 250
– architectural drawing, Chapel of Episcopal
  Palace of Mgr de Saint-Vallier (Québec,
  Qué) #8856
– Québec (Qué), Notre-Dame-des-Victoires
  #8858
Mailloux, Joseph, Can furniture-maker, fl.
  1920s-1940s #2184
– rocking chairs #2535
Mainguy, Lucien, Can architect, 1911-
– Québec (Qué), Les Prévoyants du Canada
  insurance building #7939
Maisonbasse, Jean-Baptiste
– *see* Deschevery (*dit* Maisonbasse),
  Jean-Baptiste
Maisonneuve, Paul de Chomedey de, Fr
  officer and governor in Canada, 1612-1676
– and history of Montréal (Qué) #7899
– monument, Louis-Philippe Hébert #1623
Maitland (Ont), Saint James Episcopal
  Church
– architecture, Arthur McClean #8382
Major, Laure, Can artist, 1930- #1418
Makah Indians
– culture (1870s) #4031
– wolf ritual #3885
Malabar, Can ship
– woodcarvings #1604
Malach, Lorraine, Can artist, 1933-
– exhibitions, group
  – (1975) #1867
Malaspina Expedition (1791)
– collection, art, Inuit and Indians of North
  America #3372
Malepart de Beaucourt, François
– *see* Beaucourt, François Malepart de
Malepart de Grand Maison (*dit* Beaucour),
  Paul, Can artist, 1700-1756 #249 250
Maler, Miroslav, Can sculptor, 1946-
– Symposium international de sculpture
  environnementale de Chicoutimi (Qué),
  (1980) #1639
Malevich, Kasimir Severinovich, Russ artist,
  1878-1935
– Gaucher, Yves, compared with #5567
– influence on Claude Tousignant #7401
– influence on Lionel LeMoine FitzGerald
  #5450
Malewotkuk, Florence Nupok, Amer artist,
  1910- #4217
Maligne Lake (Alta)
– photographic views
  – Warren, Mary Schaffer #7526
Maliseet Indians
– art #3634
– basketry #3637
– basketry and beadwork #3628
– costume #3641
Malkauskas, Algie, Can artist, fl. late 1960s-
– and Inuit whalebone carving, Spence Bay
  (NWT) #4436
Mallandaine, Edward, Can architect, ca.
  1827-1905
– Victoria (BC) #8145
Mallepart de Grand Maison (*dit* Beaucour),

Paul
– *see* Malepart de Grand Maison (*dit*
  Beaucour), Paul
Mallet, Denis, Can sculptor, ca. 1670-1704
  #234 235 1572
– as teacher, Ecole des arts et métiers de
  Saint-Joachim (Saint-Joachim, Qué) #2992
Mallorytown Glass Works, glass
  manufacturer (Mallorytown, Ont) #2401
  2416
– and William Godkin Beach #2396
Malo, André, Can artist, 1945-
– and RACE #1536
Malraux, André, Fr writer, 1901-1976
– Plaskett, Joe, on #6891
Maltais, Marcelle, Can artist, 1933- #1418
  6410 6412
– in Paris (France) #1434
– interview #6411
Malton (Ont), Toronto International Airport
– architecture #9517
  – John B. Parkin Associates, in association
    with William Alexander Ramsay #9516
Maltwood, Katharine Emma, Can artist,
  collector, 1878-1961
– exhibitions
  – (1981) #6413
– exhibitions, group
  – (1978) #3242
Mamalilicoola (BC)
– totem poles #3848
Manarey, Thelma Alberta, Can artist, 1913-
– interview #1974
Manchester (England), Manchester Museum
– gambling pegs, Haida Indians #3915
Manchester (NH), Currier Gallery of Art
– exhibitions
  – *Paul-Emile Borduas, 1905-1960: A Loan
    Exhibition* (1967) #4812
mandala in art
– Sawyer, Walter Michael #7144
– Wise, Jack Marlowe #7600 7602
Mandan Indians
– quillwork #3701
Manet, Edouard, Fr artist, 1832-1883
– influence on James Wilson Morrice #6633
Manitoba
– architecture #8083 8094 8098
  – 19th-early 20th cs. #8102
  – (1970s) #8087
– art #1895 1896
  – (1940s) #350
  – (1950s-1970s) #1884
  – (1964-1978), Red River Exhibition #1903
  – (1970s) #1860 1868 1899 1900
  – Ukrainian #1843
– art and architecture (1980) #1906
– art education (1940s) #1889 1890
– ceramic sculpture (1970s) #1864
– churches and decorative arts, Ukrainian
  #2270
– courthouses (pre-1930) #9007
– crosses #1625
– domestic architecture
  – 19th c. #8692
  – (1907-1927) #8689
  – Ukrainian #8691
– folk art
  – 20th c. #1897
  – Ukrainian and Latvian #968
– furniture
  – 19th c. #2584 2586
  – (1920s) #2463
– glass #2403 2415

– graphic arts
  – (1910-1940) #1898
– hospitals (1950s) #9029
– museums (1970s) #3193
– painting #1893
– photographic views
  – Hime, Humphrey Lloyd #5801
  – Horetzky, Charles George #5838
– photography
  – (1935-1943), Manitoba Camera Club #985
  – (1970s) #1879 1904
– post offices #9053
– pottery, 19th c. #2300
– pottery and quilts #2272
– railroad stations #9543 9545
– schools (1920s) #9389
– sepulchral monuments #733
– stained glass #2450
– stores (1940s) #9372
– views
  – Hind, William George Richardson #5807
  – Howarth, Edward J. #5853
  – Lynn, Washington Frank #6348
  – Rindisbacher, Peter #7003 7009
  – Verner, Frederick Arthur #7484
Manitoba. Architectural Historical Survey of Manitoba
– photographs, Manitoba architecture #8096 8098 8102
Manitoba Camera Club
– (1935-1943) #985
Manitoba Glass Works, glass manufacturer (Beauséjour, Man) #2403 2415
Manitou, Cree #3724 3726
Manitou, Ojibwa #3726
Manitou, Saulteaux #3726
Manitoulin Island (Ont)
– painting, 20th c. #4156
Manly, Charles MacDonald, Can artist, 1855-1924
– exhibitions
  – (1973) #6414
– exhibitions (reviews) #1703
Mann, Anthony, Can artist, 1927-
– design, Olympic coins (1976) #778
Manning, Les, Can ceramicist, 1944- #6415
mansions
– see castles and country houses
Manuge, Robert, Can art dealer, 1921-
– and Manuge Gallery (Halifax, NS) #3244
Manzù, Giacomo, It sculptor, 1908-
– Bachinski, Walter Joseph Gerard, compared with #4578
Maori
– art #3691
Maple Ridge (BC)
– architecture #8147
maple sugar
– Québec #1334 1335 1364
  – moulds #2592
maps
– Andrews, Stephen, as cartographer #4528
– in art
  – (1970s) #561
  – Vazan, Bill #7471
– of New France (1542-1550), animals on #831
maps, American
– Toronto (Ont), Royal Ontario Museum. Sigmund Samuel Collection #3135
maps, Canadian #125
– 16th-18th cs. #875
– 18th-19th cs. #812
– (1850s) #1692

– beaver motif #23 56
– Brant County (Ont), (1793-1930) #1684
– Gravelot, Hubert François #1323
– illustrations of canoes, 17th c. #841
– illustrations of Indians, Codex Canadiensis #1372
– Kingston (Ont) #1680
– Louisbourg (NS) #8422 8426
– Millen, Walter H., collection #21
– Montréal (Qué), 17th-18th cs. #1325
– Toronto (Ont), Royal Ontario Museum. Sigmund Samuel Collection #3135 3140
maps, French
– of the New World, 16th-18th cs. #276
Maquart, Laurent, Can artist, 1937-
– and Jacques Guillon Designers Inc. #884
Marani, Ferdinand Herbert, Can architect, 1893-
– on bank architecture #9191
Marani, Lawson & Morris, Can architectural firm
– Galt (Ont), Gore District Mutual Fire Insurance Company building #7973
– Ottawa (Ont), Bank of Canada head office #9337
Marani, Morris & Allan, Can architectural firm
– Toronto (Ont), Salvation Army Arthur Meighen Lodge #8516
Marani, Rounthwaite & Dick, Can architectural firm
– Ottawa (Ont), Bank of Canada head office #9199
Marani & Morris, Can architectural firm
– Toronto (Ont)
  – Bank of Montreal #9190
  – Canadian National Exhibition Grandstand #9208
  – Manufacturers Life Insurance Company building #9339
Marburg (West Germany), Philipps University
– architecture #9464
March, Peter, Can artist, fl. 1842-1851
– as member, Toronto Society of Arts #1689
Marchand, Jean Hippolyte, Fr artist, 1883-1940
– East, Benoît, compared with #5353
Marchand, Joseph-Omer, Can architect, 1872-1936
– and beaux-arts architecture #7923
– Montréal (Qué), City Hall #8980
– Ottawa (Ont), Parliament Buildings #8926 8927
Marcil, Joseph, Can sculptor, 1941-
– exhibitions, group
  – (1980) #1663
Marega, Charles, Can sculptor, 1875-1936
– exhibitions (reviews) #1982
– works, British Columbia Parliament Buildings (Victoria, BC) #8967
Margeson, James M., Can photographer, fl. 1850s-1860s #1211
Maria Chapdelaine, Can novel
– illustrations
  – Gagnon, Clarence Alphonse #5542 5546 5547
  – MacDonald, Thoreau #6384
Maricourt (Qué)
– graphic arts (1972-1975) #4475
– sculpture, Inuit #4405
Marie de l'Incarnation, Can nun, artist, 1599-1672
– embroidery #2791

– needlework #2788
– portrait, Mère de Saint-Joseph #1333
Marie Le Maire des Anges, Can nun, artist, fl. 1671-1690s
– landscapes, religious works #1328
marine architecture
– see naval architecture
marine painting
– see also boats; naval prints; ships in art
– views, Northwest Coast of America (1778-1793) #2017
marine painting, Canadian #139
– 18th-19th cs. #246
– (1600-1900) #225
– Adams, Loren D. #4501
– Bailly, Evern Earl #4595
– Barnsley, James Macdonald #4612
– Bolt, Ron #4779
– folk painting #965 966
– Gagen, Robert Ford #5530
– Gray, John Warren #5648 5649
– Law, Tony #6174
– Murphy, Rowley Walter #6665 6666
– Ottawa (Ont), Public Archives of Canada. William H. Coverdale Collection #12
– Redgrave, Felicity #1169
– Russell, Edward John #7110 7111
– Smith, William St. Thomas #7236 7238
– votive offerings, to Saint Ann #1292
– World War II #1106
Marino, Carol, Can photographer, 1943-
– exhibitions, group
  – (1981) #1070
Marinoff, Ivan A., Can architect, 1920-
– Saskatoon (Sask), Mendel Art Gallery, competition #9091
Marion, Gilbert, Can artist, 1933-
– and Québec printmaking (1960s) #1641
– exhibitions, group
  – (1967) #821
Marion, Israël, Can artist, d. 1899 #1319
Marion, Salomon, Can silversmith, 1782-1832
– Immaculate Conception statue, National Gallery of Canada (Ottawa, Ont) #2683
Maritime Art, Can periodical #25 349
Maritime Art Association
– (1930s-1960s) #1125
– exhibitions
  – (1959-1965) #1120
– periodical, Maritime Art #349
Maritime Art Glass Works, glass manufacturer (NB) #2400
Maritimes
– architecture #7779
  – (1950s) #7673
  – use of building and ornamental stones (1910s) #7646 7647
– art
  – 17th c.-1890s #185
  – (1830s-1930s) #28
  – (1930s-1960s) #1125
  – (1950s) #389 429 1172
  – (1959-1965) #1120
  – (1960s) #1122 1126
  – (1970s) #543
  – Acadian #1137 1181
– art and architecture #1119
  – 18th-19th cs. #7780
– bookplates, 18th-19th cs. #915
– costume, Acadian #2836 2840 2876 2877 2894
– decorative arts
  – 18th-19th cs. #2093

- 19th c. #2147
- Germanic tradition #2140
- domestic architecture
  - 19th c. #8528
  - (pre-1900) #8551
  - summer homes, 20th c. #8524
- furniture
  - 18th-19th cs. #2474 2475
  - Acadian, 18th-19th cs. #2516
- painting
  - 19th c. #197
  - 20th c. #1121
  - (1860s-1880s) #230
  - (1933-1970) #498
- photographic views
  - Jaycocks, T.G. #5950
- photography (1970s) #1134
- portrait photography, 19th c. #1171
- portraits, 18th-19th cs. #263
- pottery, 19th c. #2302 2318 2319
- silver
  - 17th-19th cs. #2627
  - 18th-19th cs. #2636 2646
- textiles, 18th c. #2727
- views
  - (1890s) #6436
  - Day, Mabel Killam #5273
  - Forrestall, Tom #5463
  - McLaughlin, Agnes #6500
Mark/Musselman/McIntyre/Combe, Can
  architectural firm
- Brantford (Ont), Evangel Pentecostal
  Church #8766
Markell, Jack, Can artist, 1919-
- exhibitions, group
  - (1962) #1847
markets, Canadian
- Charlottetown (PEI), (1813-1958) #7800
- Montréal (Qué) #7917
Markgraf, Waltraud Erna Else, Can artist,
  1937- #6416
Markham, Michael J., Can artist, 1946-
- interview #6417
Markham (Ont)
- fraktur #2254
- furniture, Mennonite #2568
Markle, Robert Nelson, Can artist, 1936-
  #6418
marks, artists'
- see artists' marks
Marks, Gerald Yanders (Gerry), Can artist,
  1951- #2706
- silkscreen prints #4148
marks, pottery
- see pottery marks
Markson, Jerome, Can architect, 1929-
- Etobicoke (Ont), Martin Grove Estate
  #8744
- Ontario #8387
- Sault Ste Marie (Ont), Group Health
  Centre #9033
- Toronto (Ont)
  - Jewish Community Centre #8078
  - Whitburn Apartments #8514
Marlatt, John, Can ceramicist, d. 1868
- as founder of Marlatt Pottery (Paris, Ont)
  #2330
Marlatt Pottery, ceramic manufacturer
  (Paris, Ont) #2330
Marois, Lauréat, Can artist, 1949- #6419
Marosan, Julius, Can sculptor, 1915-
- exhibitions, group
  - (1971), medals #772
Marquis, Robert, Can photographer, fl. 1971

#997
Marr, David, Can furniture-maker,
  1790-1871 #2573
Marsan, Jean-Claude, Can architect,
  architectural historian, 1938-
- on Québec architecture #7746
Marsh, Charles, Can artist, 1948-
- exhibitions, group
  - (1977) #1933
Marsh, Winifred Florence Petchy, Can artist,
  1905-
- watercolours, Caribou Eskimo, Eskimo
  Point (NWT) #4265
Marshall, David Franklin, Can sculptor,
  1928-
- exhibitions
  - (1978) #6420
- garden sculpture #1849
- stone sculpture, Van Dusen Gardens
  (Vancouver, BC) #775
Marshall, Patricia (Pat), Can artist, 1951-
- interview #6422
Marshall, Roz, Can artist, 1947-
- exhibitions (reviews) #2081
Marshall, Willard, Can photographer, fl.
  1856-1867 #1724
Marshall (Mars), Tanya, Can artist, 1948-
- on Codpiece exhibition, Powerhouse
  Gallery (Montréal, Qué) #6421
Marshalore, Can artist, 1946-
- performance and video art #655
Martel, Elisée, Can artist, 1881-1965
- and Montée Saint-Michel #1236
Martel, William M. (Bill), Can artist, fl.
  1950s-1960s #1121 1173
Martello towers, American #8415
Martello towers, Canadian #8415
- (1796-1846) #8416
- Carleton Martello tower (Saint John, NB)
  #8437
Martigues (France)
- views
  - Brymner, William #4950
Martin, Arthur N., Can architect, artist,
  1889-1961
- exhibitions
  - (1977) #6423
Martin, David, Can sculptor, ca. 1917-1959
- totem pole, Beacon Hill Park (Victoria, BC)
  #4115
Martin, Emma May, Can artist, 1865-1956
  #6425
- exhibitions
  - (1980) #6424
Martin, Félix, Can priest, architect,
  1804-1886
- plans, Church of Saint-François-Xavier
  (Kahnawake, Qué) #8890
Martin, Henry, Can artist, 1837-1902
- as father of Arthur N. Martin #6423
Martin, Henry Byam, Brit naval officer,
  artist in Canada, 1804-1865
- exhibitions
  - (1981) #6426
Martin, Ian, Can architect, 1922-
- Osaka (Japan), Expo '70. Canadian
  Pavilion, competition #9217
Martin, Jane, Can artist, 1943-
- exhibitions, group
  - (1979) #674
- on Jack Chambers #700
Martin, John (Jack), Can artist, 1904-1965
- as member, Canadian Group of Painters
  #324

Martin, Mungo, Can artist, 1880-1962 #3912
  6428 6430
- and Bill Reid #6984
- Great Killer Whale Copper, given to
  Provincial Museum of British Columbia
  (Vancouver, BC) #4054
- influence on Henry Hunt #5872
- paintings, University of British Columbia.
  Museum of Anthropology (Vancouver,
  BC) #6429
- totem poles #6427
  - Beacon Hill Park (Victoria, BC) #4115
  - Totem Park (Vancouver, BC) #4124
Martin, Ronald Albert (Ron), Can artist,
  1943- #6432
- and Toronto (Ont) art (1970s) #1796
- exhibitions
  - (1976) #6433 6434
- exhibitions, group
  - (1973) #557
  - (1977) #636
  - (1978) #661
  - (1979) #510
  - (1980) #703
  - (1981) #723
- interview #6431
Martin, Thomas Mower, Can artist,
  1838-1934 #6438
- and British Columbia Society of Fine Arts
  #1978
- as father of Emma May Martin #6424
- exhibitions, group
  - (1888) #175
  - (1961) #62
- on art #6437
- on Canadian scenery for artists #6436
- on trip through Rocky Mountains (1889)
  #6435
Martyn, H.H., & Co., woodcarvers
  (Cheltenham, England)
- works, British Columbia Parliament
  Buildings (Victoria, BC) #8967
Marxism
- influence on Surrealism #1466
Mary, Virgin
- and Child, Québec sculpture #1596
- annunciation, Québec sculpture, late
  17th-20th cs. #1633
- assumption, Canadian art #37
- Immaculate Conception statue, Salomon
  Marion #2683
- Québec art, 17th c. #1365
Mary Magdalen
- Québec art, 17th c. #1365
Masciuch, John Edward, Can sculptor, 1944-
- use of light #767
masks
- Pellan, Alfred #6816
- Proch, Don #6941
masks, Afikpo (Africa)
- compared with masks, Kwakiutl #3945
masks, Algonquian #3337 3529
- (1760s-early 20th c.) #3633
masks, Athapaskan #4083
masks, Bakuba (Africa)
- compared with masks, Kwakiutl #3920
masks, Bella Coola #3772
- Ottawa (Ont), National Museum of Man
  #4000
masks, Cree #3742
masks, Dorset
- Button Point (Bylot Island, NWT) #4356
  4357 4359
- Qikertaaluk Island (NWT), petroglyphs of

#4362
masks, Haida
- portrait #3794
- Queen Charlotte Islands (BC) #3961
masks, Huron #3519
masks, Ingalik #4083
masks, Inuit #3340 3940 4212
- Berkeley (Calif), University of California.
  Robert H. Lowie Museum of
  Anthropology #4349
- Labrador #3337 4178
masks, Iroquois #3337 3359 3489 3519 3570
  3598 3613 7346
- (1760s-early 20th c.) #3633
- False Face Society #3588 3595 3604 3632
- Midwinter ceremony #3606
masks, Japanese
- compared with masks, Northwest Coast
  Indians #3824
masks, Kwakiutl #3348 3768 4030
- Bokwus mythic figure #3990
- compared with masks of Afikpo (Africa)
  #3945
- compared with masks of Bakuba (Africa)
  #3920
- Milwaukee (Wis), Milwaukee Public
  Museum #3938
- Thunderbird Dance #3867
masks, natives of North America #3327
masks, Northwest Coast Indians #3340 3866
  3894 3940 4030
- compared with Japanese masks #3824
- New York (NY), American Museum of
  Natural History #3414
- portrait #3977 4038
masks, Onondaga #3588
masks, Salish #4013
masks, Seneca #3508 3563 3636
- False Face Society #3533 4113
masks, Squamish
- Vancouver (BC), City Archives #3864
masks, Sxwaywey #4033
masks, Tlingit #3976
- use of human hair #3917
masks, Tsimshian #4056 4069
- portrait #3794
masks, Woodlands
- (1760s-early 20th c.) #3633
masonry
- see also brick; cements, mortars, and
  plasters; stone; walls
masonry, Canadian
- brick, Aultsville region (Ont), 19th c. #7980
- clapboarded, Québec, 17th c. #7860
- hollow-wall construction, Ontario, 19th c.
  #8004
- Louisbourg (NS) #8427
- plankwall framing, 17th-19th cs. #7712
- Trois-Rivières (Qué), Forges of
  Saint-Maurice #7878
mass communication
- see mass media
mass media
- see also films; television
- Canada
  - American influences (1970s) #3279
  - and architecture (1970s) #7728
  - and the arts
    - (1950s) #3254 3255
    - (1960s) #529
    - (1970s) #542 551 583 1799 3267 3270
  - and women (1970s) #562
- General Idea #5583
Massé, Henriette Fauteux

- see Fauteux-Massé, Henriette
Masset (Queen Charlotte Islands, BC)
- totem poles, Haida #3765
Massey, Hart Parkin Vincent, Can architect,
  1918-
- Ottawa (Ont)
  - Carleton University #9455
  - War Memorial area #8041
Massey, John, Can artist, 1950- #6439
- exhibitions, group
  - (1980) #687 696
  - (1981) #723
- exhibitions (reviews) #697 794
Massey, Vincent, Can statesman, collector,
  1887-1967
- and Royal Commission on National
  Development in the Arts, Letters and
  Sciences (Massey Report) #3254 3255 3261
- as patron of Jack Weldon Humphrey
  #5865
- collection, Canadian paintings #3220
  - Ottawa (Ont), National Gallery of
    Canada #3227
- support of Canadian architecture #7737
- support of Canadian arts and sciences
  #3258
Massey & Flanders, Can architectural firm
- Ottawa (Ont), Tovell House #8519
Massey Awards for Excellence in the Urban
  Environment
- (1971) #8217
- (1975) #8218
Massey Medals for Architecture
- (1952) #8205
- (1955) #8206
- (1958) #8207
- (1961) #8208 8209 8210
- (1964) #8211
- (1967) #8212 8213 8214
- (1970) #8215 8216
- survey of architects on (1962) #8305
Massey Report
- see Canada. Royal Commission on
  National Development in the Arts, Letters
  and Sciences (Massey Report)
Massicotte, Edmond-Joseph, Can artist,
  1875-1929 #6441
- views of Québec #6440
- winter landscapes #1298
Masson, André, Fr artist, 1896-
- influence on Alfred Pellan #6822
Masson, Henri L., Can artist, 1907- #1392
  6443 6444 6445 6447 6448
- and genre painting #392
- exhibitions (reviews) #6442
- works (1950s) #6446
Matane (Qué), Galerie d'art du CEGEP de
  Matane
- exhibitions
  - De la figuration à la non-figuration dans
    l'art québécois (1977) #1461
mathematics and art
- Canadian paintings and sculptures, 20th c.
  #471
- Gnass, Peter #5619
- Rockburne, Dorothea #7060
Mathers, Charles Wesley, Can
  photographer, 1868-1950 #6451
- and Ernest Brown #4935
- photographs, Ernest Brown collection
  #1949
Mathers & Haldenby, Can architectural firm
- Toronto (Ont)
  - Bank of Nova Scotia #9192

- Imperial Oil Building #9340
- Toronto General Hospital #9032
- University of Toronto. John P. Robarts
  Research Library #9048 9050 9052
- William H. Wright Building #9338
Matheson, Roderick, Can army officer,
  1793-1873
- residence, Matheson House (now Perth
  Museum) (Perth, Ont) #8670
Mathieson, Hugh, Can furniture-maker, fl.
  1850s-1860s #2584
Mathieu, André, Can sculptor, 1952-
- use of wood #1634
Mathurin, Jacques, Can photographer, ca.
  1952-
- portfolio of photographs #1032
Matisse, Henri, Fr artist, 1869-1954
- as teacher of Canadian artists (1940s) #384
- Bush, Jack Hamilton, compared with
  #4977
- influence on Clark Holmes McDougall
  #6464
- influence on David Brown Milne #6567
- influence on Goodridge Roberts #7046
- influence on Jack Hamilton Bush #4972
  4973
- influence on James Wilson Morrice #6629
- influence on Jeanne Leblanc Rhéaume
  #6994
- influence on John Goodwin Lyman #6340
  6344
- influence on Paul-Emile Borduas #4841
- influence on Paul Fournier #5486
- influence on Pierre Jean Clerk #5118
- influence on Robert La Palme #6119
- Morrice, James Wilson, compared with
  #6631
- on James Wilson Morrice #6619
mats, Algonquian
- birchbark #3561 3571
mats, Canadian
- grasswork mats, Labrador #2945
mats, Northwest Coast Indians
- prehistoric #4017
mats, Ojibwa #3557 3585
Matsqui (BC)
- architecture #8147
Matsubara, Naoko, Can artist, 1937- #6450
- exhibitions, group
  - (1976) #6449
- exhibitions, group
  - (1980) #8237
Matta-Clark, Gordon, Amer artist, 1945-1978
Matthews, James S., Can archivist, fl.
  1930s-1970
- and J.A. Brock & Co. photographs,
  Vancouver City Archives (Vancouver, BC)
  #2021
Matthews, Marmaduke, Can artist,
  1837-1913
- and Thomas Mower Martin #6435 6438
- exhibitions (reviews) #186
Mauger, Jacques
- see Gadois (dit Mauger), Jacques
Maugham, William Somerset, Brit writer,
  1874-1965
- on James Wilson Morrice #6619
Maurault, Olivier, Can priest, 1886-1968
- and Ozias Leduc #6201 6203
Mavor, James, Can educator, 1854-1925
- collection #1713
Maw, Samuel Herbert, Can architect,
  1881-1952
- Toronto (Ont), Toronto Stock Exchange

#9187
Maw & Co., tile manufacturer (Broseley and
 Jackfield, England)
- tiles for Toronto (Ont) houses, 19th c.
 #2373
Maw & Drewitt, Can architectural firm
- Moose Jaw (Sask), City Hall, competition
 #8978
Mawson, Thomas Hayton, Brit landscape
 architect, city planner in Canada,
 1861-1933
- Canada, city planning and landscape
 architecture #8388 9405
- Halifax (NS), Dalhousie University #9408
- on Canadian architecture #7648
Max, John, Can photographer, 1936-
- portfolio of photographs #996
Max-Ingrand, Maurice, Fr stained glass
 artist, 1908-1969
- stained glass, Saint Arsène Church
 (Montréal, Qué) #2448
Maximilian II, king of Bavaria, 1811-1864
- and emergence of named Indian artists
 #3486
Maxwell, Edward, Can architect, 1867-1923
- Calgary (Alta), Hotel Palliser #9271
- Montréal (Qué)
  - Arts Club, renovation of house for
   #1314
  - Dominion Express Company Building
   #9306
  - Montreal Museum of Fine Arts #9063
   9065
  - oratory in house #8557
  - Windsor Station #9537
- Ottawa (Ont), Departmental and Justice
 Buildings, competition #8921
- Québec (Qué), Château Frontenac #9278
- Regina (Sask)
  - Legislative Buildings #8944 8945 8957
   8958 8959 8960 8961
  - War Memorial Museum, competition
   #9073
- Winnipeg (Man), Legislative and
 Executive Building, competition #8946
Maxwell, William Sutherland, Can architect,
 1874-1952
- Calgary (Alta), Hotel Palliser #9271
- Montréal (Qué)
  - Arts Club, renovation of house for
   #1314
  - Dominion Express Company Building
   #9306
  - Montreal Museum of Fine Arts #9063
   9065
  - oratory in house #8557
- Ottawa (Ont), Departmental and Justice
 Buildings, competition #8921
- Québec (Qué), Château Frontenac #9278
- Regina (Sask)
  - Legislative Buildings #8944 8945 8957
   8958 8959 8960 8961
  - War Memorial Museum, competition
   #9073
- Winnipeg (Man), Legislative and
 Executive Building, competition #8946
Maxwell & Pitts, Can architectural firm
- Québec (Qué), Château Frontenac #9278
May, Henrietta Mabel, Can artist, 1884-1971
- exhibitions (reviews) #283
May, Karl, Can artist, 1901-1975 #6452
- exhibitions
  - (1976) #6453
May, R.G., Can photographer, fl. 1880s

#1950
May, Walter (Wally), Can sculptor, 1950-
- exhibitions, group
  - (1978) #2066
Mayerovitch, Harry, Can architect, artist,
 1910-
- on his sculptures #6454
Mayhew, Elza Edith, Can sculptor, 1916-
 #6455
- as member of Limners #2043
Maynard, Hannah Hatherly, Can
 photographer, 1834-1918 #2018 6456 6457
 6458
- and the Victoria Theatre Photographic
 Gallery (Victoria, BC) #2027
- photographs, Northwest Coast Indians
 #2033
Maynard, Max, Can artist, 1903- #2011
Maynard, Richard, Can photographer,
 1832-1907
- photographs, Northwest Coast Indians
 #2033
Mayor, Robin, Can artist, 1937-
- exhibitions, group
  - (1979) #2075
- exhibitions (reviews) #2072
- interview #6459
McArthur, James J., Can photographer,
 1856-1925
- survey photographs #1014 1015
  - Rocky Mountains (1880s-1890s) #1874
- use of survey camera #989
McBride & Gilbert, Can architectural firm
- London (Ont), Lord Roberts School #9388
McCall, Helen, Can photographer, fl.
 1920s-1930s #2018 6460
McCall & Co., furniture-making firm (Ont)
- (1860s-1960s) #2573
McCargar, William C., Can artist, 1906-1980
 #1881
McCarter, Nairne & Partners, Can
 architectural firm
- Vancouver (BC) #9514
- Victoria (BC), B.C. Telephone Offices
 #9301
McCarter & Nairne, Can architectural firm
- Vancouver (BC), Marine Building #8171
 9356
McCarthy, Doris Jean, Can artist, 1910-
 #6461
McCausland, J., & Co., stained glass studio
 (Toronto, Ont)
- stained glass
  - Montréal (Qué) #2448
  - Toronto (Ont), Trinity College Chapel
   #2461
McCausland, Joseph, Can stained glass
 artist, 1829-1885
- as founder, Canada Stained Glass Works
 #2449
- stained glass, British Columbia Parliament
 Buildings (Victoria, BC) #8967
McCausland, Robert, Can stained glass
 artist, 1856-1923
- stained glass
  - Manitoba #2450
  - Toronto (Ont), City Hall #2449
McClallum village site (Agassiz, BC)
- architecture, Salish Indians #3872
McClean, Arthur, Can architect, 1779-1864
 #8382
McClure, Sir Robert John Le Mesurier, Brit
 navigator, explorer, 1807-1873
- expedition, Arctic (1851-1853) #278

McConnell, Clyde S., Can artist, 1944-
- interview #6462
McConnell, Newton, Can artist, 1877-1940
- cartoons, Toronto Daily News #943
McCord, David Ross, Can collector,
 1844-1930
- collection, McGill University. McCord
 Museum (Montréal, Qué) #222 223
McCormack, W.A., Can sculptor, fl. 1897
- on woodcarving and architecture #726
McCormick, Alexander, Can stained glass
 artist, fl. 1899-1913 #2450
McCulloch, James Frederic, Can artist,
 1905-1932
- exhibitions
  - (1978) #6463
McCurry, Harry Orr, Can curator, 1889-1964
 #3036
- and National Gallery of Canada (Ottawa,
 Ont) #3050
- as director, National Gallery of Canada
 (Ottawa, Ont) #3049
McDermott, Michaelin, Can photographer,
 1947-
- exhibitions, group
  - (1979) #1904
McDonald, John, Can fur trader, ca.
 1771-1866
- residence, Inverarden (Cornwall, Ont)
 #8673
McDonald, Robert, Amer collector, 20th c.
- collection, artifacts, Piegan Indians #3759
McDougall, Clark Holmes, Can artist,
 1921-1980 #6465
- exhibitions
  - (1977) #6464
McDougall, Ian, Can architect, 1939-
- Calgary (Alta), Ian McDougall House
 #8727
McDougall, Keith, Can photographer, ca.
 1948-
- portfolio of photographs #1032
McDougall, Smith & Fleming, Can
 architectural firm
- Montréal (Qué), Montreal General
 Hospital #9030
McEachern, Susan, Can photographer, 1951-
- exhibitions (reviews) #1067
McElcheran, William Hadd, Can sculptor,
 1927- #6466
McEwen, Jean Albert, Can artist, 1923-
 #6467 6468
- and Claude Monet #6470
- exhibitions
  - (1973) #6469
  - (1978) #6471
- exhibitions, group
  - (1955) #1408
  - (1964) #462
McEwen, John Alan, Can sculptor, 1945-
- exhibitions
  - (1979) #6472
- exhibitions (reviews) #697 794
- Western Channel, University of Lethbridge
 (Lethbridge, Alta) #797
McFarlane, Walter, Can artist, ca. 1917-
 #6473
McGill, James, Can merchant, 1744-1813
- and château de Ramezay (Montréal, Qué)
 #3082
- portrait of, Louis Dulongpré #5321
McGlade, Terry, Can artist, fl. 1970s
- exhibitions, group
  - (1979) #1157

McGlashen, Stewart, and Son, Brit sculpture
  firm (Edinburgh, Scotland)
- St. John's (Nfld), Sergeants' War Memorial
  #7783
McGowan, John, Can collector, 20th c.
- collection, Canadian glass #2424
McGrath, James Arthur (Jim), Amer artist,
  1928-
- cosmological concepts #554
McGrath, Jerry, Can artist, fl. 1980
- exhibitions, group
  - (1980) #1832
McGrath, Judy Waldner, Can artist, 1936-
- workshop, Spence Bay (NWT) #4249 6474
McGregor, Edward, Can artist, fl. 1847-1872
- as member, Toronto Society of Arts #1689
McGuire, Patrick (Pat), Can artist, 1943-1970
- influence on Pat Dixon #5294
McInnes, Harvey A., Can artist, 1904- #1881
McInnis, Robert F.M., Can artist, 1942-
- portraits #715
McIntyre (M'Intyre), Thomas, Can
  furniture-maker, fl. 1830s-1870s #2571
McKay, Arthur Fortescue, Can artist, 1926-
  #6475 6477
- exhibitions
  - (1961) #1913
  - (1968) #6476
  - (1979) #6478
- exhibitions, group
  - (1967) #490 1916
McKay, David, Can artist, 1945- #6479
McKee, John, Can artist, 1941-
- exhibitions, group
  - (1981) #1885
McKeen's Corner (NB), All Saints' Church
- architecture, Edward Shuttleworth Medley
  #8776
McKendry, Blake, Can collector, 1919-
- restoration, Tunis Snook Farm (near
  Kingston, Ont) #8681
McKendry, Ruth, Can collector, 1920-
- collection, Ontario quilts, 19th c. #2804
- restoration, Tunis Snook Farm (near
  Kingston, Ont) #8681
McKenzie, Jim, Can artist, 1953- #6480
McKenzie, Robert Tait, Can sculptor in
  USA, 1867-1938 #10 6481 6482 6483 6484
  6486 6487 6488
- Danby, Ken, compared with #5252
- on sculptures of athletes #6485
McKenzie, Tait
- see McKenzie, Robert Tait
McKim, Mead & White, Amer architectural
  firm
- influence on Canadian architecture #7652
- Montréal (Qué), Bank of Montreal #9168
- Winnipeg (Man), Bank of Montreal #9202
  9205
McKinley, Donald Lloyd, Can designer,
  furniture-maker, 1932- #6489
McKinley, Ruth Gowdy, Can ceramicist,
  1931-1981 #2395
McLagan Furniture Co., furniture-making
  firm (Stratford, Ont)
- (1920s) #2547
McLaren, Agnes Maud, Can artist, b. 1882
- illustrations #916
McLaren, John Wilson (Jack), Can artist,
  1896-
- wood engravings #804
McLaren, Norman, Can artist, filmmaker,
  1914- #6490 6491 6492 6493 6494 6498 6499

- drawings #6496
- exhibitions
  - (1965) #6495
- FitzGerald, Lionel LeMoine, compared
  with #5452
- interview #6497
McLaughlin, Agnes, Can artist, ca. 1913-
  #6500
McLaughlin, Isabel, Can artist, 1903- #309
McLaughlin, Samuel, Can photographer,
  1826-1914
- exhibitions, group
  - (1970) #1675
- photographs of buildings being built
  #1019
- *The Photographic Portfolio* #1048
McLean, George E., Can artist, 1939- #6501
McLean, James Stanley, Can collector,
  1876-1954
- collection, Canadian art, 20th c. #3210 3226
McLean, John, Brit artist, 1939-
- exhibitions, group
  - (1981) #722
McLean, Terry, Can artist, ca. 1935- #6502
McLean, Thomas Wesley (Tom), Can artist,
  1881-1951 #6503
McLeod, Barclay, Can architect, 1936-
- Vancouver (BC), Caulfield Cove
  Townhouses #8746
McLeod, Peter, Can statesman, d. 1852
- portrait of, Théophile Hamel #5690
McLuhan, Herbert Marshall, Can educator,
  writer, 1911-
- on technology and art #513
McMichael, Robert, Can collector, 1921-, and
  Signe Kirsten Sorensen McMichael, Can
  collector, 1921-
- and McMichael Canadian Collection
  (Kleinburg, Ont) #3172
McMillan, David, Can photographer, 1945-
  #1879
- exhibitions
  - (1980) #6504
- exhibitions, group
  - (1977) #1033
  - (1978) #669
  - (1979) #1037
- exhibitions (reviews) #1046 1060
McMordie, Michael, Can architect, 1935-
- on architecture #7746
McMurtie, William Birch, Amer artist in
  Canada, 1816-1872
- views of Vancouver Island (BC) #6505
McNally, Edwin (Ed), Can artist, 1916-1971
- illustrations #855
McNamara, Robert Strange, Amer
  statesman, 1916-
- portrait of, Art Green #5650
McNamee, Donald Keith (Don), Can artist,
  1938-
- exhibitions
  - (1968) #6506
McNicoll, Helen Galloway, Can artist,
  1879-1915
- exhibitions
  - (1974) #6507
McOnie, Alan, Can photographer, fl. 1970s
- portfolio of photographs #998
McQuesten family, Can, 19th-20th cs.
- residence, Whitehern (Hamilton, Ont)
  #8664
McRitchie, Donald (David), Can artist,
  1881-1948
- cartoons, *Montreal Daily Mail* #943

McWilliams, Allan, Can artist, 1944- #6508
- exhibitions, group
  - (1976) #2060
  - (1978) #2066
Meanwell, Jack, Can artist, 1919-
- exhibitions, group
  - (1977) #646
Meares, Hermina (Ina), Can artist, 1921-
  #6509
Meares, John, Brit naval officer, artist in
  Canada, ca. 1756-1809
- views of Nootka Sound, Vancouver Island
  (BC) #2002
mechanics' institutes, Canadian
- (1830s-1860s) #3064
- Ontario, 19th c. #2261
medallions
- see coins and medals
medals
- see coins and medals
Medalta Potteries, ceramic manufacturer
  (Medicine Hat, Alta)
- (1916-1954) #2325
- (1924-1952) #2371
- markings #2372
Medalta Stoneware, ceramic manufacturer
  (Medicine Hat, Alta)
- (1915-1924) #2371
- markings #2372
Mederschein, Charles, Can ceramicist, 19th
  c. #2298 2322
Medford (Mass), Tufts University.
  Behavioral Sciences Building
- architecture, John Andrews Architects
  #8323
media, mass
- see mass media
media and techniques, costume
- 19th c., female #2846
- (1780-1967) #2849
- (1800-1821), female #2860
- (1822-1839), female #2863
- (1840-1866), female #2885
- (1848-1868) #2887
- (1867-1898), female #2889
- (1870s) #2854 2859
- (1870s), female #2878
- (1920s), female #2906
- *ceinture fléchée* #2818 2827
- Lithuanian #2892
media and techniques, drawing
- Binning, B.C. #4730
- Séminaire des jésuites, 19th c. #2982
media and techniques, graphic arts
- colour drypoint, David Brown Milne
  #6546 6552 6563 6564
- lithography, Robert Allen Paterson #6778
- woodcut, Walter Joseph Phillips #6854
  6855
media and techniques, needlework #2785
- Ukrainian embroidery #2782
media and techniques, painting
- Biéler, André Charles #4720 4721
- *nihonga*, Miyuki Tanobe #7324 7325
media and techniques, photography
- Karsh, Yousuf #6025 6033
- Notman, William #6723
- Patterson, Freeman #6780 6781 6782
media and techniques, pottery #2280 2317
- 19th c. #2290 2367
- 20th c. #2390
media and techniques, quilts #2799
media and techniques, textiles
- dyeing #2745 2749

- hooked rugs #2750 2752
- weaving #2719 2721 2730
  - Jacquard #2740
  - Salish Indians #3963
medical illustration
- Blackstock, Hattie #4738
medicine
- domestic manufacture, 18th-19th cs. #2112
- in Canadian bottles #2432
Medicine Hat (Alta)
- art (1940s) #1943
- pottery, 20th c. #2371 2372
Medicine Hat (Alta), Medicine Hat Museum and Art Gallery
- exhibitions
  - *Ann Kipling: Recent Landscapes* (1980) #6057
  - *William Perehudoff: Ten Years, 1970-1980/William Perehudoff: une décennie, 1970-1980* (1982) #6838
Medicine Hat (Alta), National Exhibition Centre
- exhibitions
  - *Artisan '78: The First National Travelling Exhibition of Contemporary Canadian Crafts/Artisan '78: première exposition nationale itinérante d'artisanat canadien contemporain* (1979) #2134
  - *Canadians: A National Photography Show about People/Canadiens: exposition nationale de photographie ayant les gens comme thème* (1980) #1035
  - *Edward Curtis in the Collection of the Edmonton Art Gallery* (1980) #3480
Medicine Hat Potteries, ceramic manufacturer (Medicine Hat, Alta)
- (1937-1956) #2371
Medicine Hat Pottery, ceramic manufacturer (Medicine Hat, Alta)
- (1912-ca. 1914) #2371
medicine in art
- Inuit, therapeutic symbolism #4488
- Inuit and Indians of North America, therapeutic symbolism #3356
Medicine Pipe ceremony, Blackfoot #3681
Medley, Edward Shuttleworth, Can clergyman, architect, 1838-1910
- churches #8776
- Saint Stephen (NB), Christ Church #8774
Medway River (NS)
- petroglyphs, Micmac #3617
Meech, Henry William, Can architect, 1880-1947
- Lethbridge (Alta), Saint Michael's General Hospital #9021
Meech, Mitchell, Robins & Associates, Can architectural firm
- Little Bow (Alta), Little Bow Municipal Hospital #9032
- Picture Butte (Alta), Picture Butte Municipal Hospital #9032
meeting houses, Canadian
- Ontario
  - 19th c. #8006
  - Mennonite #2572
Mehta, Dilip, Can photographer, ca. 1953- #995
Meigs, Mary, Can artist, writer, 1917-
- autobiography #6510
Meikle, William, Can stained glass artist, 1870-1953 #2450
Meikle Studio, stained glass studio (Toronto, Ont)
- stained glass, Montréal (Qué) #2448

Meisterman, Ken, Can artist, 1953-
- exhibitions, group
  - (1979) #2075
- exhibitions (reviews) #2072
Melanson, Léo, Can builder, fl. 1903-1905
- Church Point (NS), Saint Mary's Parish Church #8779
Melbourne (Australia), National Gallery of Victoria
- exhibitions
  - *Contemporary Canadian Painters* (1957) #423
Melick, James C., Can photographer, d. 1885
- as teacher of William Herman Rulofson #7107
Melick, James Godfrey, Can silversmith, 1802-1885 #2649
Melville Peninsula (NWT)
- Iglulik, culture (1920s) #4326
memorials, war
- see war memorials
Memramcook (NB), Célestin Bourque House
- architecture #8543
Ménage, Pierre, Can builder, ca. 1648-1715 #234 235
Mendel, Frederick Salomon, Can collector, 1888-1976
- collection, Mendel Art Gallery (Saskatoon, Sask) #72 3187
- collection, paintings #1912
Mendelow & Keywan, Can architectural firm
- Don Mills (Ont), Beth-El Synagogue #8903
Menkès, René, Can architect, 1932-
- Montréal (Qué), Les Terrasses #7886
Mennonites in Canada
- and Nancy-Lou Patterson #6783
- decorative arts #2140 2246 2264 2267
  - Ontario #2250
  - Waterloo County (Ont) #2243
- dolls and costumes #2942
- domestic architecture #8715
- folk art #2268
- fraktur #2259
- furniture #2568 2572 2585
- paperwork #2265
- quilts #2729
Menomine Indians
- basketry #3620
Menses, Jan, Can artist, 1933- #6511
Menut, Jean-Baptiste, Can metalworker, fl. 1857-1868 #2704
Menut, Thomas, Can metalworker, fl. early 19th c. #2704
Menzies, Archibald, Brit naturalist in Canada, 1754-1842
- aesthetic response to Northwest Coast #2009
- expedition, Northwest Coast Indians #4062
Mercer, June, Can artist, fl. 1955
- jewellery #2695
Merchants Bank
- Ontario (1915-1919) #9170
Mercier, Monique, Can artist, 1934- #6512
Meredith, John, Can artist, 1933- #6513 6515
- exhibitions
  - (1974) #6514
  - (1980) #6516
- exhibitions, group
  - (1967) #480
  - (1971) #98
  - (1977) #636
Meriden Britannia, silversmithing firm (Hamilton, Ont) #2405

- (1879-1922) #2642
Merola, Mario Virgilio, Can artist, 1931-
  #6517 6519 6521
- and plasticiens #1439
- exhibitions
  - (1971) #6520
  - (1976) #6522
- mural, Canadian Pavilion, Universal and International Exhibition of 1958 (Brussels, Belgium) #6518
Merrett, Brian, Can photographer, 1945-
- portfolio of photographs #997 999
Merrett, Campbell, Can architect, 1909-
- Ottawa (Ont), Carleton University #9455
Merriam, D.H., Can furniture-maker, fl. 1840s-1850s #2571
Merriam, John H., Can furniture-maker, fl. 1840s-1850s #2571
Merriam, Joseph, Can furniture-maker, b. ca. 1780, fl. 1824-1829 #2571
Merrick, John, Can architect, fl. 1810-1820
- Halifax (NS), Mount Uniacke House #8528
Merrick, Paul McCarley, Can architect, 1938-
- restoration, Orpheum Theatre (Vancouver, BC) #9135
Mery, Daniel, Can artist, 1934-
- television graphics #909
Mesnard, Albert, Can architect, 1847-1909
- Oka (Qué), church #8818
Metal Arts Guild
- and Harold Stacey #7274
Metal Arts Guild of Nova Scotia
- exhibitions
  - (1951) #1192
metalwork
- see also tinsmithing
metalwork, Athapaskan
- (1970s), women artisans #3367
metalwork, Canadian #2089
- 20th c. #2121 2142
- (1837-1887) #253
- (1940s) #2601 2693
- (1960s) #2106
- (1964-1967) #2108 2109
- (1970s) #2706
- (1979-1980) #2138
- (1980) #2257
- and architecture
  - (1910s) #8222
  - (1960s) #8236
- Beau, Paul #4641
- Chaudron, Bernard #5099
- Chaudron, Bernard and Louise #5098
- guide for collectors #2104 2125 2131
- Lozeau, Jean-Baptiste #249 250
- pewter and copper, 19th c. #2704
- Québec #2183 2228 2711
  - 17th-18th cs., artisans #2214
  - 17th-19th cs. #1341
  - 20th c. #2198
  - (1940s) #8820
- Stuart, Don #7281
- tableware #2470
- Toronto (Ont)
  - Canadian Bank of Commerce #9180
  - T. Eaton Company department store #9368
- use of Canadian motifs (1930s) #8225
metalwork, Indians of North America
- beadwork #3457
- trade goods #3440
metalwork, Inuit
- (1970s), women artisans #3367
metalwork, Plains #3698

Metcalf, Eliab, Amer artist in Canada, 1785-1834 #1377

Metcalfe, Eric W. (Dr. Brute), Can artist, 1940-
– exhibitions, group
– (1979) #2070
– video art #2044

Meteghan (NS), Vieille Maison
– architecture and interior #8531

methodology
– see art history

Metiq Co-operative (Belcher Islands, NWT) #4459

Métis
– architecture #8102
– art #3731
– beadwork #3677
– embroidery #4110

Metro Toronto Board of Trade
– collection, Canadian art #3291

Metson, Graham, Can artist, 1934- #6523

Mexico
– influence on K.J. Butler #4982

Meyer, Henry Hoppner, Can artist, ca. 1782-1847
– as father of Hoppner Francis Meyer #6524

Meyer, Hoppner Francis, Can artist, fl. 1832-1863 #6524
– as member, Toronto Society of Arts #1689

Mezei, Lesley N., Can artist, fl. 1968
– on computer art #517

Mia and Klaus, Can photographers, fl. 1960s
– portfolio of photographs #987

Michaud, Jean, Can architect, 1919-
– Montréal (Qué), Town of Mount Royal Post Office #7857

Michaud, Pierre Joseph, Can priest, architect, 1823-1902 #1319

Michel, André, Can artist, 1945- #6525

Michel, Claude
– see Clodion

Michener, Robert, Can artist, 1935-
– exhibitions (reviews) #6526

Michener, Sally, Can artist, 1935- #6527
– ceramic sculptures (1970s) #2065
– exhibitions
– (1979) #6528

Micklethwaite, Frank W., Can photographer, 1849-1925 #1024

Micmac Indians
– arm bands #3572
– art #3528 3569 3634 3643
– basketry #3630
– basketry and beadwork #3628
– beadwork and quillwork #3624
– costume #3641
– fans and games #3500
– moccasins #3554
– petroglyphs #3614 3617
– pictographs #3494
– pipes #3565
– shamanism #3556
– stonework #3531
– wampum #3497

Middleton, W.E.K., Can photographer, ca. 1900-
– portfolio of photographs #991

Midewiwin, Algonquian #3580
– scrolls #3702

Midewiwin, Cree #3726
– influence on painting, 20th c. #4154

Midewiwin, Northwest Coast Indians
– masks #4038

Midewiwin, Ojibwa #3492 3602 3726

– and boulder monuments, Whiteshell (Man) #3578
– buffalo robes #3517
– influence on painting, 20th c. #4154
– scrolls #3539 3626 3661

Midewiwin, Saulteaux #3726

Midewiwin, Siouan
– scrolls #3702

Midwinter ceremony, Iroquois #3606
– masks #3598

Mies van der Rohe, Ludwig, Ger-Amer architect, 1886-1969
– integration of art into architecture #8232
– Montréal (Qué)
– Nun's Island #8587
– Westmount Square #9326
– Toronto (Ont), Toronto-Dominion Centre #9197 9301 9345 9348

Mignard, Pierre, Fr artist, 1612-1695
– influence on Antoine-Sébastien Plamondon #6886

Mihalcheon, Jean Lapointe, Can sculptor, ceramicist, 1929- #2392 6529

Mikkanen, Raili Marjatta, Can artist, 1950- #6530 6531

Mikutowski, Frank, Amer architect, fl. 1950s-
– Toronto (Ont), City Hall and Civic Square, competition #8981

Milan (Italy), Galleria Levi arte contemporanea
– exhibitions
– Borduas, Riopelle e la giovane pittura canadese (1962) #1420

Miles, John Christopher, Can artist, 1832-1911 #6532 6533
– exhibitions, group
– (1969) #1180
– Wilde, Oscar, on #238

Milette, Alexis, Can sculptor, architect, 1793-1869 #258 259 6947
– influence of Baillairgé family #1582
– interior, church, Berthierville (Qué) #8874

military architecture
– see also barracks; fortifications; Martello towers

military architecture, Canadian
– (1950s) #8414
– Halifax (NS) #7839
– 18th-19th cs. #7818
– Niagara-on-the-Lake (Ont)
– (1814-1837) #8470
– (1838-1871) #8471
– (1871-1978) #8472
– Québec
– 17th-18th cs. #1320 7845
– 17th-19th cs. #7853
– 18th c. #7861
– Québec (Qué) #7946
– Trois-Rivières (Qué), (1630s-1910s) #7883

military uniforms, American
– (1665-1970) #2867

military uniforms, Canadian #2881
– 18th-19th cs. #1309 2825
– (1665-1970) #2867 2910 2911
– (1742-1960) #2835
– (1770s-1812) #2848
– buttons #2882
– Canadian Militia dress regulations #2874
– Louisbourg (NS) #2866
– (1713-1758) #2857
– Saint John (NB), New Brunswick Museum #2900

Milk River region (Mon)

– pictographs #3706

Mill, Richard, Can artist, 1949- #1524 1544
– exhibitions
– (1978) #6534
– (1979) #6535
– exhibitions, group
– (1981) #1565

Millán, Gonzalo, Can artist, 1947-
– on his art #1552

Millar, C.Blakeway (Blake), Can architect, 1935-
– Georgian Bay (Ont)
– F.S. Eaton summer residence #8519
– summer residence #8745
– Toronto (Ont), Trolley Restaurant #8078

Millarville (Alta), Leighton Centre
– Leighton, Barbara, as teacher #3017

Miller, Alfred Jacob, Amer artist, 1810-1874
– in western Canada #1859
– paintings of Indians, Public Archives of Canada (Ottawa, Ont) #6536 6537

Miller, David G., Can photographer, 1949-
– documentary photographs #1556

Miller, Gary, Can artist, 1950- #6538
– on marketing Indian art #6539

Miller, George Martel, Can architect, 1854-1933
– Guelph (Ont), Macdonald Consolidated School #3176

Miller, John Bellamy, Can photographer, 1869-1906 #6540

Miller, Maria Frances Ann Morris, Can artist, 1813-1875 #241 242 1118 1219 6541 6542

Miller, Martha, Can photographer, fl. 1979
– exhibitions, group
– (1979) #2069

Millet, Jean-François, Fr artist, 1814-1875
– and Wyatt Eaton #5355 5357
– Huot, Charles Edouard, compared with #5876
– influence on Wyatt Eaton #5356
– Walker, Horatio, compared with #7498 7499 7500 7503

Millette, Claude, Can sculptor, 1957-
– concept of space #1631

Millikin, William, fl. 1840s
– cartoons, Québec society #6543

mills
– see also windmills

mills, American
– northeastern USA #9249

mills, Canadian #9248 9249
– Acadian #7804
– Conception Bay (Nfld), wood-processing mill (ca. 1620) #7718
– Kingston Mills (Ont) #8020
– Ontario #9239
– 19th c. #7745
– (1780s-1880s) #9259
– Pointe-du-Lac (Qué), "Garceau" Mill #9246
– Québec #9242 9252
– 17th-18th cs. #7845
– 17th-19th cs. #7852 9243
– 18th-19th cs. #8560 8561
– Trois-Rivières (Qué), Forges of Saint-Maurice #9253

Mills, Charles, Can architect, 1860-1934
– Hamilton (Ont)
– Bank of Hamilton #9160
– Hamilton Terminal Station #9527

Mills & Hutton, Can architectural firm
– domestic architecture #8494
– Hamilton (Ont), YWCA building #7957

Mills-Cockell, John, Can musician, 1943-
- and Intersystems #767
Milman, Adolf, Russ artist in France, fl.
  1920s
- as teacher of Edwin Headley Holgate
  #5818 5819
Milne, David Brown, Can artist, 1882-1953
  #336 461 6544 6547 6549 6550 6551 6554
  6555 6556
- and Douglas M. Duncan, as patron #119
  541 570 3223
- and G.Blair Laing, as dealer #1686
- and Paraskeva Clark #5112
- and Vincent Massey #3227
- as modernist #507
- correspondence #536
- exhibitions
  - (1955) #6552
  - (1967) #6558
  - (1971) #6559
  - (1976) #6561
  - (1980) #6563 6564 6566
  - (1981) #6567
- exhibitions, group
  - (1975) #589 592
- landscapes #347
  - (1930s) #338
- notes and correspondence (1920-1921)
  #6560
- on colour drypoint #6546
- on his art #6548 6553
- on his watercolours #6545
- Painting Place, National Gallery of Canada
  (Ottawa, Ont) #6562
- paintings
  - (1930s) #502
  - Massey, Vincent, collection #3220
  - McLean, J.S., collection #3228
  - McMichael Canadian Collection
    (Kleinburg, Ont) #3172
  - Venice Biennale (1952) #399
- prints #6565
- watercolours, World War I aftermath
  (1918-1919) #6557
Milne, Eleanor, Can artist, 1926-
- interview #6569
- sculptures, Parliament Buildings (Ottawa,
  Ont) #755
- sculptures and stained glass windows,
  Parliament Buildings (Ottawa, Ont) #6568
Milne, Gilbert Alexander, Can
  photographer, 1914-
- photographs of World War II #1107
- portfolio of photographs #995
Milne, Graham, Can photographer, fl. 1970s
- portfolio of photographs #998
Milojevic, Peter, Can artist, fl. 1969
- computer art #528
Milwaukee (Wis), Milwaukee Public
  Museum
- masks, Kwakiutl #3938
mimesis
- in Québec painting #1267
Minden, Robert, Can photographer, 1941-
- interview #6570
mine buildings, American
- western USA #8083
mine buildings, Canadian
- western Canada #8083
mines and mining
- argillite, for Haida sculpture #3944
- soapstone, for Inuit sculpture #4409 4416
miniatures, British
- 19th c., influence on Canadian painting

#1118
miniatures, Canadian
- (1760-1860), Montréal (Qué) #1377
- ceramic sculpture #2302
- Crist, Lela Gurnee #5209
- Field, Robert #5432 5433
- Montréal (Qué), (1760-1860) #1376
- Québec, as folk art #1291
- Rindisbacher, Peter #7007
- Wrinch, Mary Evelyn #7618
minimal art
- see also serial art
- and André Lucien Fauteux #5413
- and Colette Whiten #7561
- and David Bolduc #4774
- and David George Rabinowitch #6950
- and Guido Molinari #6585
- and Henry Saxe #7149
- and Mia Westerlund #7544
- and Peter Henry Kolisnyk #6075 6076
- and Pierre Jean Clerk #5118
- and Ronald Bladen #4740
- and Tim Zuck #7636
- and Walter Redinger #6970
- Canada #788
- Québec #1483
Minìpoka, Blackfoot #3749
ministère des Affaires culturelles
- see Québec. Ministère des Affaires
  culturelles
ministère des Travaux publics et de
  l'Approvisionnement
- see Québec. Ministère des Travaux publics
  et de l'Approvisionnement
Ministic Carvers Co-op (Garden Hill, Man)
  #4153
Ministry of Culture and Recreation
- see Canada. Ministry of Culture and
  Recreation
Minneapolis (Minn), Walker Art Center
- exhibitions
  - American Indian Art: Form and Tradition
    (1972) #3359
Minton porcelain
- china painting, James and John Howard
  Griffiths #2305
- tiles, in Toronto (Ont) houses, 19th c.
  #2373
Mirabel (Qué), Montreal International
  Airport. Passenger Terminal Building
- architecture, PGL Architects #9518
Miramichi (NB)
- Irish settlements #8523
Miró, Joan, Sp artist, 1893-
- influence on Alfred Pellan #6805 6822
- influence on Francis Coutellier #5196
- influence on Jack Hamilton Bush #4973
- influence on John Meredith #6516
- influence on Pierre Gendron #5581
- influence on Pierre Jean Clerk #5118
- influence on Robert La Palme #6119
Miron, Claire, Can artist, 1923- #6571
mirrors, Canadian
- Ontario (1790s-1857) #2558
mirrors, Niska #3804
mirrors, Tsimshian #3804
mirrors in art
- Canada #525
- Morris, Michael #6641
Mission (BC)
- architecture #8147
Mission (BC), Westminster Abbey
- stained glass #2460
missionaries, French

- and Indians of North America, 17th c.
  #1354 1358 1363
Mississauga (Ont), Sheridan College School
  of Crafts and Design
- handmade glass #2440
Mistassini Indians
- art #4080 4100
- hunting charms #4075
- quillwork #3701
Mistro, Walter del, Can artist, 1912-
- mosaics, Saint Ann's Basilica
  (Sainte-Anne-de-Beaupré, Qué) #6572 6573
  8865 8866
Mitchel, Owen, Can photographer, fl. 1970s
- portfolio of photographs #991
Mitchell, Janet, Can artist, 1915-
- exhibitions
  - (1977) #6574
- interview #1974
Mitchell, Louisette Gauthier
- see Gauthier-Mitchell, Louisette
Mitchell, Michael, Can photographer, 1943-
- exhibitions
  - (1978) #6575
- exhibitions (reviews) #6576
Mitchell, Thomas, Brit artist in Canada, ca.
  1833-1924
- photographs and watercolours, British
  Arctic Expedition (1875-1876) #240
Mitchell, Thomas Wilberforce, Can artist,
  1879-1958
- exhibitions (reviews) #1710
Mitchell & Creighton, Can architectural firm
- Montréal (Qué), Jacobs Building #9305
Mitchell & Raine, Brit architectural firm
- Regina (Sask), Legislative Buildings,
  competition #8955
Mitra, Shyamal, Can photographer, fl.
  1970s-
- portfolio of photographs #1023 1032
Mitton, Edward Stanley, Can architect, b.
  1880
- British Columbia, bungalows #8684
mobiles
- Trudeau, Yves #7435
moccasins, Algonquian #3631
- Lac Barrière (Qué) #3544
- quillwork #3652
moccasins, Arapaho #3554
moccasins, Blackfoot #3651
moccasins, Cree #3651
moccasins, Dakota
- symbolic designs #3648
moccasins, Gros Ventre #3651
moccasins, Huron
- moose hair embroidery #3513
moccasins, Indians of North America #2241
  2872 3424
moccasins, Iroquois #3489 3631
moccasins, Micmac #3554
moccasins, Ojibwa #3539 3554
- Parry Island Reservation (Ont) #3540
moccasins, Plains #3651 3656 3666
- quillwork #3652
moccasins, Potawatomi
- Parry Island Reservation (Ont) #3540
moccasins, Siouan #3651 3666
- decorated soles (1880s-1910s) #3740
- quillwork #3652
moccasins, Tête de Boule #4079
moccasins, Woodlands #3554 3631
model books, architecture
- see pattern books, architecture
modeling in wax

– *see* wax modeling
models
– *see* artists and models
modernism
– *see also* abstract art; post-modernism
– and Alfred Pellan #1448
– and Group of Seven #1767
– and James Wilson Morrice #6623
– and Jean-Paul Lemieux #6228
– and Paul-Emile Borduas #4851
– and Pierre Gauvreau #5576 5578
– and Royal Canadian Academy of Arts
  (1930s) #329
– Canada
  – (1920s) #289
  – (1920s-1940s), architecture #7668
  – (1930s) #319
– Plaskett, Joe, on #6889
– plasticiens and Painters Eleven #720
– Québec (1940s) #1462
– Saskatchewan (1940s-1950s) #1919
modernist art
– *see* modernism
Modigliani, Amedeo, It artist, 1884-1920
– influence on Gerald Gladstone #5612
– Macdonald, Grant Kenneth, compared
  with #6358
Moffat, Normand, Can artist, 1949- #1511
Mohammedan art
– *see* Islamic art
Mohawk Indians
– costume, 18th c. #3550
Moisan, Gatien, Can artist, 1939- #1549 1551
  6577
Moiseiwitsch, Tanya, Brit artist in Canada,
  1914-
– stage designs #472
Mol, Leo, Can artist, 1915- #6578
– exhibitions
  – (1975) #6579
– interview #6580
– stained glass #2450
Molinari, Guido, Can artist, 1933- #1294
  1542 1543 6582 6585 6591
– and Claude Tousignant #7398
– and minimal art #1483
– and Optical art #1445
– and plasticiens #1439
– compared with Piet Mondrian #1457
– concept of space #6589
– drawings #6593
– exhibitions
  – (1974) #6584
  – (1976) #6588
  – (1979) #6592
  – (1981) #6594
– exhibitions, group
  – (1955) #1408
  – (1959) #1414
  – (1967) #480 490
  – (1968) #522 1263
  – (1971) #98
  – (1973) #556
  – (1977) #636
  – (1980) #703
  – (1981) #1471
– interview #6581 6587
– on Canadian art
  – (1960s) #478
  – (1970s) #620
– on his art #6590
– paintings (1953-1956) #1454

– participant, Symposium on 20th Century
  Canadian Culture (Washington, DC),
  (1977) #621
– sculptures (1960s) #1484
– symposium, Musée du Nouveau-Monde
  (La Rochelle, France), (1980) #1559
– use of colour #468 1425
  – checkerboard paintings (1969-1970)
    #6583
– writings #6586
Mollise (Morris), Mâli Christianne Paul
  (Christina), Can artist, ca. 1804-1886
– as artist and model #6635
Molsons Bank
– architecture (1920s) #9173
monasteries
– *see also* convents
monasteries, Canadian
– Magog (Qué), Monastery of
  Saint-Benoît-du-Lac #8332
Moncornet, Baltasar, Fr artist, ca. 1600-1668
– portrait of Samuel de Champlain,
  misattributed #191
Moncton (NB), Aberdeen School
– architecture, F.Neil Brodie #9387
Moncton (NB), Bank of Nova Scotia
– architecture, Sharp & Horner #9174
Moncton (NB), Université de Moncton
– printmaking (1970s) #1185
– Roussel, Claude, as director, Department
  of Fine Arts #7088
Moncton (NB), Université de Moncton.
  Galerie d'art
– exhibitions
  – *Annie D. Savage: Drawings and
    Watercolours* (1975) #7129
  – *Claude Roussel* (1977) #7089
  – *Roger Savage* (1979) #7135
  – *The Murray and Marguerite Vaughan Inuit
    Print Collection/Collection d'estampes inuit*
    (1982) #4498
Mondou, Pierrette, Can tapestry artist, 1945-
  #1282 6595
Mondrian, Piet, Nl artist, 1872-1944
– and abstract art #422
– Borduas, Paul-Emile, compared with #4813
– concept of space #1441 4816
– influence on Claude Tousignant #7401
– influence on Fernand Leduc #6186
– influence on Guido Molinari #6588 6591
– influence on Pierre Jean Clerk #5118
– influence on Québec art #1483
– influence on Robert La Palme #6119
– influence on the plasticiens #1457
– use of colour, influence on Montréal (Qué)
  painting #1425
– Westerlund, Mia, compared with #7545
Monet, Claude, Fr artist, 1840-1926
– Christensen, Dan, compared with #5104
– influence on Jean Albert McEwen #6470
– influence on Lionel LeMoine FitzGerald
  #5450
Monette, Georges Alphonse, Can architect,
  1870-1941
– Montréal (Qué)
  – La Patrie Building #9303
  – Roman Catholic school on Côte des
    Neiges #9387
money
– *see also* coins and medals
money, Canadian
– landscape imagery (1930-1970) #759

Mongeau, Jean-Guy, Can artist, 1931- #6596
Mongrain, Claude, Can sculptor, 1948- #681
  6597
– exhibitions, group
  – (1977) #782
  – (1980) #706
– interview #6598
Monk, James, Can, 1745-1826
– crewelwork bed hangings, Royal Ontario
  Museum (Toronto, Ont) #2784
Monk, Lorraine Althea Constance Spurrell,
  Can curator, 1922- #993
– and National Film Board. Still
  Photography Division #1028
– interview #1020
monkeys
– as imagery, Brian Porter #6907
monograms
– on Canadian glass fruit jars #2413
Mont-Joli (Qué), Laberge Cottage
– and Canadian Heritage of Quebec #7871
Mont-Joli (Qué), Wexford Manor
– and Canadian Heritage of Quebec #7871
Mont Sainte-Marie (Qué), resort centre
– architecture, Eberhard Henrich Zeidler
  #7886
Montagnais Indians
– amulets #4075
– art #4082
– beadwork #4076 4103
– caribou skin #3622
– containers #4078 4086
– snowshoes #2812
Monte Carlo (Monaco)
– views, Franklin Milton Armington #4550
Montebello (Qué), Château Montebello
– architecture #9295
Montée Saint-Michel (Montréal, Qué) #1236
Montgomery, Stewart, Can artist, 1941-
– sculptures #1151
Montpetit, Guy, Can artist, 1938- #6600
– influence of plasticiens disputed #6599
– murals, Montréal (Qué) #6601
Montréal (Qué)
– architecture #7909 7913 7927 7930 7933
  8604
  – 16th c.-1840s #7898
  – 17th-19th cs. #7899
  – 18th c. #7861
  – 19th c. #7915 7916
  – 20th c., concept of space #7748
  – (1642-1970s) #7918 7934
  – (1850s) #7920
  – (1870s-1920s) #7843
  – (1880-1914) #7928 7929
  – (1880-1915) #7921
  – (1920s) #7656
  – (1950s) #7673
  – (1960s) #7693 7698 7862 8213 9220 9400
  – architectural materials, 19th-20th cs.
    #7926
  – downtown area
    – (1950s-1960s) #7901
    – (1960s-1970s) #7925
  – greystone buildings #7922
  – Old Montréal #7904 7905 7910 7911 7919
  – use of terra cotta (1880s-1920s) #7750
– architecture and art
  – 17th c.-1950s #7900
– architecture and urban development #7906
  7931
– art #1265
  – 20th c. #145 567
  – (1840s) #1301

– (1880-1910) #214
– (1880-1965) #1228
– (1890s) #1311
– (1908-1965) #1261
– (1910s) #1317
– (1940s) #1443
– (1940s-1950s) #1426
– (1940s-1960s) #1437
– (1940s-1970s) #571
– (1950) #1400
– (1950s) #389 429
– (1950s-1970s) #131
– (1960s) #90 441 519 1479 1480 1484
– (1968-1970) #1481
– (1970s) #1489 1504 1509 1541 1548
– (1976), *Corridart, Mosaicart,* and
  Artisanage street exhibitions #615
– (1976), *Corridart* street exhibition #1522
  1530 5091 5092
– automatism #1449
– Independent Art Association #1379
– métro stations #1531
– art galleries
  – (1945-1970) #1264
  – (1960s) #442
  – (1970s) #1495
– banks (1845-1933) #9201
– churches #8886
  – 19th c. #8821
  – (1960s) #1435
– conservation of architecture #7914
  – facades #7766
– costume
  – 17th c., male #2821
  – 19th c. #2837
  – (1890-1910) #2861
– crosses #1569
– decorative arts (1740-1760) #2218
– decorative arts and architecture
  (1880-1914) #1367
– domestic architecture #8576 8620
  – 17th-19th cs. #8505 8559
  – 19th c. #8612
  – (1698-1940s) #8570
  – (1910s) #8492 8493 8494 8496 8556
    – small houses #8555
  – (1920s) #8499 8562
  – brick houses, early 19th c. #8521
  – country houses #8572
  – late 19th c. #8610
  – seigneuries #8611
  – terrace houses, 19th c. #8653
– fortifications
  – Boisberthelot de Beaucours, Josué #8336
– furniture
  – 17th-18th cs. #2522
  – (1800-1850) #2538
– graphic arts
  – 20th c. #1648
  – (1940s-1960s) #1641
  – (1960s-1970s) #1652
  – (1970s) #1655
– hotels, 17th c.-1950s #9287
– landscape painting and photography
  (1860-1890) #271 272
– miniatures and silhouettes (1760-1860)
  #1376 1377
– monuments, late 19th c.-1920s #1623
– museums #3098 3108
– office buildings
  – (1950s-1960s) #9300
  – architects' offices (1940s) #9297
– painting
  – 20th c. #507 1463

– (1860-1890) #264
– (1860-1960) #1253
– (1870-1970) #97
– (1920s-1950s) #424
– (1930s) #589 592 1460
– (1933-1970) #498
– (1938-1948) #378
– (1940s) #1390 1397
– (1940s-1950s) #412 1416 1426 1432
– (1940s-1960s) #1438 1445
– (1950s) #1403 1752
– (1950s-1960s) #1263 1415 1425 1469
– (1953-1956) #1454
– (1954-1955) #1408
– (1955-1965) #1471
– (1960s) #520 1418
– photographic views
  – (1850-1900) #1061
  – Kieffer, Daniel #1562
  – Notman, William #6725
  – Szilasi, Gabor #7309
– photography (1970s) #992 1003 1494
– posters (1970s) #880
– pottery (1970s) #2331
– railroad stations #9538
– recreation buildings #9081
– rocking chairs #2535
– schools
  – 19th-20th cs. #9426
  – elementary schools
    – (1950-1968) #9422
    – (1950s) #9419
– sculpture #1572
  – (1890s) #727
  – (1960s) #767 1485
  – (1970s) #1624
– seminaries and convents (1642-1913) #7932
– silver #2197
  – 17th-19th cs. #2685 2686
  – 18th-19th cs. #2650
  – 18th c. #2677
  – 19th c. #2630 2674
  – Indian trade silver, late 18th-early 19th
    cs. #2634 2659
– skyscrapers (1960s) #9318
– stained glass #2448 2462
– universities (1960s) #9401
– urban development #7902
– video art #605 1498 1499 1537 1550
– views
  – 16th-19th cs. #927
  – 17th-18th cs. #1325
  – 19th c. #1337
  – (1803-1878) #7924
  – (1960s) #1427
  – Delfosse, Georges #5279
  – Hébert, Adrien #5761 5762
  – Kroupa, Bohuslar #6104
  – on tureen (ca. 1840) #2370
  – Surrey, Philip Henry #7286 7288 7289
  – Tanobe, Miyuki #7322 7323 7324 7325
– woodcarving #1573 1575
  – 18th-19th cs. #1593
Montréal (Qué), 1306 Amherst St.
– exhibitions
  – *03 23 03: premières rencontres
    internationales d'art contemporain,
    Montréal 1977* (1977) #634
Montréal (Qué), académie des Saints Noms
  de Jésus et de Marie
– architecture, Charles Aime Reeves #9388
Montréal (Qué), Aldred Building
– architecture #7933
  – Barott & Blackader #9313

Montréal (Qué), American Prudential
  Building
– tapestry, Andrée Beauregard #4653
Montréal (Qué), Architects Building
– architecture, Ross & Macdonald #9312
Montréal (Qué), Archives nationales du
  Québec
– Poirier, Conrad, photographs #6897
Montréal (Qué), Art Association of Montreal
  #1294 3114
– *see also* Montréal (Qué), Musée des
  beaux-arts de Montréal/Montreal Museum
  of Fine Arts
– (1847-1909) #3079
– (1847-1947) #1246
– (1860-1912) #1343
– (1879), museum opening #3075
– (1890s) #188
– (1908-1965), spring exhibitions #1261
– (1928-1929), exhibitions #307
– (1950), criticism of jury selections #1443
– and Benaiah Gibb #3110
– and Daniel Fowler #5488
– and Doris Minette Judah #5980
– and James Wilson Morrice #6634
– and Montreal Museum of Fine Arts #9063
– and William Brymner #4953
– exhibitions
  – *Exhibition of Paintings by Cornelius
    Krieghoff, 1815-1872* (1934) #6086
  – *Les arts du Canada français, 1613-1870*
    (1946) #1331
  – *The Arts of French Canada, 1613-1870*
    (1946) #1330
  – *The Development of Painting in Canada,
    1665-1945/Le développement de la peinture
    au Canada, 1665-1945* (1945) #34
– exhibitions (reviews)
  – (1864) #1303
  – (1865) #1304
  – (1880) #1308
  – (1883) #1310
  – (1892-1893) #179
  – (1913) #1316
  – *Arts and Crafts Exhibit* (1923) #2160
  – Canadian Group of Painters (1940) #348
  – Royal Canadian Academy of Arts
    – (1915) #210
    – (1917) #283
    – (1928) #303
    – (1929) #312
    – (1931) #323
    – (1935) #328
– Gagnon, Clarence Alphonse, as student
  #5544 5548
– Lismer, Arthur, as teacher #6295
– nationalism and landscape painting, late
  19th c. #271 272
– Pellan, Alfred, works exhibited (1942)
  #6801
– photographs and drawings of Québec
  buildings exhibited (1924) #7842
– Savage, Anne Douglas, as student #7130
  7132
– typography (1940s) #922
Montréal (Qué), atelier Arachel #1657
Montréal (Qué), Atelier libre de recherches
  graphiques #1495 1642
– and Richard Lacroix #6126
Montréal (Qué), Bank of British North
  America
– architecture, Barott, Blackader & Webster
  #9164
Montréal (Qué), Bank of Montreal

– architecture
 – Wells, John #9200
 – Wells, John; McKim, Mead & White
  #9168
– Coade stone plaques #7908
Montréal (Qué), Bank of Montreal. Head
 Office
– architecture #9183
Montréal (Qué), Bank of Toronto
– architecture, Hogle & Davis #9167
Montréal (Qué), Baron Byng High School
– Savage, Anne Douglas, as teacher #7130
Montréal (Qué), Basilica of
 Saint-Jacques-le-Majeur
– architecture #7899
Montréal (Qué), Bell Canada
– architecture, Barott & Blackader #9310
Montréal (Qué), Bibliothèque municipale
– architecture #7923
Montréal (Qué), Bibliothèque nationale du
 Québec
– exhibitions
 – *Livres d'artistes: le livre illustré québécois,*
  1967-1977 (1978) #1659
Montréal (Qué), bibliothèque Saint-Sulpice
– architecture, Eugène Payette #9039 9415
– Leduc, Ozias, works exhibited (1916)
  #6210
Montréal (Qué), Bigot House
– restoration #8567
Montréal (Qué), Bonaventure Station
– architecture, Edmund Phillips Hannaford
  #9538
Montréal (Qué), Canadian Bank of
 Commerce
– architecture, Darling & Pearson #9153
Montréal (Qué), Canadian Centre for
 Architecture
– *see* Montréal (Qué), Centre canadien
  d'architecture/Canadian Centre for
  Architecture
Montréal (Qué), Canadian Express
 Company Building
– architecture, Hutchison & Wood #9304
Montréal (Qué), Canadian Imperial Bank of
 Commerce
– architecture, Peter Dickinson #9194
Montréal (Qué), Casa Loma
– exhibitions
 – *Les moins de 35: du 22 janvier au 4 février*
  (1973) #1501
 – *Québec Underground: 1962-1972* (1973)
  #1502
– exhibitions (reviews)
 – *Québec Underground: 1962-1972* (1973)
  #1500
Montréal (Qué), Caserne centrale des
 pompiers
– architecture #7933
Montréal (Qué), Cathedral of
 Saint-Jacques-le-Majeur
– paintings, Georges Delfosse #5278
Montréal (Qué), Cathedral of Saint James
– baldachin #8826
Montréal (Qué), CEGEP du Vieux-Montréal
– Garnier, Jacques, *Vingt personnages* #5557
Montréal (Qué), Centaur Galleries #1004
Montréal (Qué), Central Station
– architecture, John Schofield #9535
Montréal (Qué), Centre canadien
 d'architecture/Canadian Centre for
 Architecture #7749
Montréal (Qué), Centre marial des pères
 Monfortains

– architecture, Roux & Morin #8840
Montréal (Qué), centre Saidye
 Bronfman/Saidye Bronfman Centre
– exhibitions
 – *Canadians: A National Photography Show*
  about People/Canadiens: exposition
  nationale de photographie ayant les gens
  comme thème (1979) #1035
 – *Changing Visions: The Canadian*
  Landscape/Aperçus divers: le paysage
  canadien (1976) #617
 – *Gift from the Douglas M. Duncan*
  Collection and the Milne-Duncan
  Bequest/Le Don provenant de la collection
  Douglas M. Duncan et le legs
  Milne-Duncan (1971) #541
 – *Imprint '76* (1976) #833
 – *Les moins de 35: du 22 janvier au 4 février*
  (1973) #1501
 – *The People Within/Les Gens de l'intérieur*
  (1976) #4266
Montréal (Qué), Cercle universitaire
– exhibitions (reviews)
 – Guité, Suzanne #1400
Montréal (Qué), Chapel of
 l'Invention-de-la-Sainte-Croix
– architecture #8862
Montréal (Qué), Chapel of
 Notre-Dame-de-Lourdes
– architecture and interior, Napoléon
 Bourassa #4866 8836
– paintings, Napoléon Bourassa #4865 4875
 8784
Montréal (Qué), Chateau Apartments
– architecture, Ross & Macdonald; Harold
 Lea Fetherstonhaugh, Associate Architect
 #8558
Montréal (Qué), château de Callière
– architecture #8565
Montréal (Qué), château de Ramezay #3108
 8566
– (1705-1950s) #3082 3083
– architecture
 – extension, Paul Tessier (*dit* Lavigne)
  #269 270
– collection #3076 3077
– cradles, Iroquois #3593
– moulds, Québec #2916
Montréal (Qué), château Dufresne (Musée
 des arts décoratifs/Museum of Decorative
 Arts) #1294
– architecture
 – Dufresne, Marius, and Jules Renard
  #8617 8618
Montréal (Qué), Christ Church Cathedral
– architecture, Frank Wills #8798
Montréal (Qué), Church of Mont
 Sainte-Famille
– mural painting, Napoléon Bourassa #4862
Montréal (Qué), Church of Notre-Dame
– architecture #8828
 – O'Donnell, James #1233 8780 8848
 – O'Donnell, James, and renovation,
  Victor Bourgeau #8849 8892
 architecture and interior #8839
– baptistry, paintings, Ozias Leduc #6203
– crucifix, Antoine Labrosse #6123
– stained glass, Jean-Baptiste Lagacé #2444
– Virgin Mary statue, influence on Salomon
 Marion #2683
Montréal (Qué), Church of Notre-Dame.
 Chapel of Sacré-Coeur
– paintings, Joseph-Charles Franchère #5497

Montréal (Qué), Church of Notre-Dame.
 Museum #3081
Montréal (Qué), Church of
 Notre-Dame-de-Bon-Secours
– architecture #7899
– architecture and interior #8788
Montréal (Qué), Church of
 Notre-Dame-de-Grâce
– architecture #7899
Montréal (Qué), Church of Sacré-Coeur
– altarpiece, Philippe Liébert #6280 6281
Montréal (Qué), Church of
 Saint-Enfant-Jésus du Mile-End
– baptistry, paintings, Ozias Leduc #6195
 6203 6204
Montréal (Qué), Church of Saint-Jacques
– architecture #7899 8781
 – and Université du Québec à Montréal
  building #9427
 – Bourgeau, Victor #8782
Montréal (Qué), Church of
 Saint-Jean-Baptiste
– architecture, Lemay & Leclerc #8766
Montréal (Qué), Church of Saint-Patrice
– architecture #7899
– mural painting, Napoléon Bourassa #4862
Montreal (Qué), Church of Saint-Rémi
– architecture, Roger D'Astous #8841
Montréal (Qué), Church of Saint-Viateur
– mural paintings, Guido Nincheri #1378
Montréal (Qué), Church of Sainte-Anne
– mural painting, Napoléon Bourassa #4862
Montréal (Qué), Church of Sainte-Catherine
– architecture, Joseph Sawyer #8407
Montréal (Qué), Church of
 Sainte-Catherine-d'Alexandrie
– conservation attempt #8867
Montréal (Qué), Church of Sault-au-Récollet
– sculptures, Philippe Liébert #6281
Montréal (Qué), cinéma Odéon Champlain
– architecture, Henry Eli Greenspoon #9078
Montréal (Qué), Cinémathèque canadienne
– exhibitions
 – *Norman McLaren* (1965) #6495
Montréal (Qué), Cinémathèque québécoise.
 Musée du cinéma
– exhibitions
 – *Michael Snow, rétrospective* (1975) #7253
Montréal (Qué), citadel
– architecture #8445
Montréal (Qué), City Hall
– *see* Montréal (Qué), hôtel de ville/City
 Hall
– Delfosse, Georges, works #5280
Montréal (Qué), collège Notre-Dame de
 Montréal
– Jérôme, frère, as teacher #6761
Montréal (Qué), complexe Desjardins
– architecture #7925 9327
– exhibitions
 – *Spectrum Canada* (1976) #610
Montréal (Qué), Concordia University
– *see also* Montréal (Qué), Sir George
 Williams University
Montréal (Qué), Concordia University. Sir
 George Williams Art Galleries
– collection #3096
– exhibitions
 – *Annie D. Savage: Drawings and*
  Watercolours (1974) #7129
 – *David Bolduc: Recent Work* (1979) #4775
 – *David Milne: The New York Years,*
  1903-1916 (1982) #6567
 – *Dennis Burton Retrospective* (1978) #4961

– *Dessins inédits d'Ozias Leduc/Ozias Leduc the Draughtsman* (1978) #6210
– *Edwy Cooke: aquarelles, 1942-1977* (1977) #5171
– *Gordon Rayner Retrospective* (1979) #6966
– *Graham Coughtry: Retrospective* (1977) #5190
– *Henry Sandham (1842-1912): The Mr. & Mrs. Leo J. Heaps Loan Collection/Henry Sandham (1842-1912): Collection empruntée de M. et Mme Léo J. Heaps* (1976) #7121
– *Ivan Eyre Exposition* (1981) #5394
– *John Fox: 10 New Paintings* (1980) #5495
– *Looking South* (1978) #4278
– *Painters Eleven in Retrospect* (1981) #1785
– *Peter Kolisnyk* (1977) #6075
– *The Heritage of Jack Bush: A Tribute* (1982) #722
– *The Queen Comes to New Brunswick: Paintings and Drawings by Molly Lamb Bobak* (1979) #4765
– *William Blair Bruce* (1975) #4942
– exhibitions (reviews)
   – Gagnon, Pnina #5550
Montréal (Qué), congrégation de Notre-Dame
– embroidery #2778
– liturgical objects, François Ranvoyzé #2658
Montréal (Qué), Cormier House
– architecture and interior, Ernest Cormier #8346 8347 8348
Montréal (Qué), Court House
– sculpture, Charles Daudelin #5263
Montréal (Qué), Court House Annex
– architecture, Louis A. Amos; Chas. Saxe; Ernest Cormier #9001
Montréal (Qué), Couvent des récollets
– architecture and interior #8855
Montréal (Qué), Crystal Palace
– exhibitions (reviews)
   – (1863) #1302
Montréal (Qué), Customs House
– architecture, John Ostell #7917
Montréal (Qué), David & David architects' office
– architecture and interior, David & David #9299
Montréal (Qué), Design Centre
– closure (1970) #2621
Montréal (Qué), Dominion Express Company Building
– architecture and interior, Edward and William Sutherland Maxwell #9306
Montréal (Qué), Dominion Gallery
– *see* Montréal (Qué), galerie Dominion/Dominion Gallery
Montréal (Qué), Drummond Military Convalescent Hospital (formerly Loyola College)
– architecture #9016
Montréal (Qué), Ecole de Montréal
– silversmithing #2670
Montréal (Qué), Ecole des beaux-arts #1231 1456
– (1922-1935) #2972
– (1960s), compared with Ontario College of Art (Toronto, Ont) #2990
– (1968) #2995
– Allain, Marie-Hélène, as student #4508
– architectural education
   – (1941) #8245
   – (1948) #8247
   – (1949) #8248

– (1950) #8249
– (1952) #8251 8252
– (1953) #8253
– (1954) #8255
– (1955) #8257
– (1956) #8259
– (1957) #8260 8261
– Ayotte, Léo, as student #4575
– Baril, Marcel, as student #4608
– Blier, Jean-Marc, as student #4743
– Borduas, Paul-Emile, as student #4827 4836
– Brault, Maurice, as student #4906
– Comtois, Ulysse, as teacher #1489
– Cosgrove, Stanley Morel, as her #5184
– Couturier, Pierre Charles Marie-Alain, as teacher #1407
– Dallaire, Jean-Philippe, as teacher #5241 5244
– Daoust, Sylvia Marie Emilienne, as student #5257
– Dumouchel, Albert, as teacher #1641 5325 5326 5327 5331
– Dyonnet, Edmond, as teacher #5347 5348 5349
– exhibitions
   – *Art abstrait* (1959) #1414
   – *Les anciens des Beaux-Arts de Montréal: premier grand salon* (1935) #2973
   – *The National Gallery of Canada Presents: 1958-59, Painters Eleven* (1958) #1751
– exhibitions (reviews)
   – Cullen, Maurice Galbraith #5216
   – *The National Gallery of Canada Presents: 1958-59, Painters Eleven* (1958) #1752
   – Walker, Horatio #306
– Filion, Armand, as teacher #5437
– Fournelle, André, as student #5484
– Legros, Enid Sharon, as student #6223
– Lemieux, Jean-Paul, as student #6228
– Lemieux, Jean-Paul, as teacher #6227
– MacLeod, Pegi Nicol, as student #6397
– Pellan, Alfred, as teacher #6809
– Raymond, Maurice, as teacher #6962
– Roberts, Goodridge, as student #7044
– Senécal, Irène, as teacher #3010
Montréal (Qué), Ecole du Conseil des arts et manufactures
– Dyonnet, Edmond, as teacher #5347 5349
Montréal (Qué), Ecole du meuble
– (1935-1950) #2980
– (1937) #2976
– (1940s) #2190
– and Québec furniture (1940s) #2523
– Borduas, Paul-Emile, as teacher #4819 4832 4843
– Couturier, Pierre Charles Marie-Alain, as teacher #1407
– Garnier, Jacques, as student #5557
– Gauvreau, Jean-Marie, as director #2176
– Jaque, Louis, as student #5940
– Lemieux, Jean-Paul, as teacher #6227
Montréal (Qué), école Louis-Hébert
– architecture, Charles David #7664
Montréal (Qué), Ecole technique de Montréal
– furniture #2970
Montréal (Qué), Editions Formart
– and René Derouin #5285
Montréal (Qué), Expo '67 (1967) #483
– architecture #7693 7709 7737 7862 9220
   – Erickson, Arthur Charles #8361
– architecture and art #9214
– architecture and site #9212 9213 9219 9221

9222
– art #1453
– Art Gallery #9223
– Canada Design '67 program #2616 2617
– exhibitions
   – *Sculpture canadienne: Expo 67/Canadian Sculpture: Expo 67* (1967) #752
– graphic arts #876
– industrial design #2615 2618
– pavilions #7686 9216 9218
   – Affleck, Desbarats, Dimakopoulos, Lebensold, Sise #9215
– sculpture #769 7691 7692
– sculpture, Canadian #751
Montréal (Qué), Expo '67 (1967). Administration and Press Building
– architecture, Irving Grossman #9301
Montréal (Qué), Expo '67 (1967). Canadian Government Pavilion/Pavillon du Canada
– architecture #7691 7692
– exhibitions
   – *Canadian Fine Crafts* (1967) #2108
   – *Canadian Prints and Drawings: With a Collection of Photographs by Yousuf Karsh* (1967) #486
   – *La peinture au Canada* (1967) #84
   – *Le dessin et la gravure au Canada: ainsi qu'une exposition de photographies de Yousuf Karsh* (1967) #487
   – *Les métiers d'art au Canada* (1967) #2109
   – *Painting in Canada* (1967) #83
   – *The Camera as Witness* #987
   – Smith, Gord, *Canada Screen* #7222
Montréal (Qué), Expo '67 (1967). Expo Stadium
– architecture, Victor Prus and Maurice Desnoyers #9101
Montréal (Qué), Expo '67 (1967). Pavillon de la France
– architecture, Jean Faugeron #1435
Montréal (Qué), Fraser Hickson Library
– sculpture, Louis Archambault #4542
Montréal (Qué), Galerie 13 #1495
Montréal (Qué), galerie Agnès Lefort
– and Mira Godard #161
– Lefort, Agnès, as art dealer #1424
Montréal (Qué), galerie Cartier
– exhibitions
   – *An Exhibition of Eskimo Sculpture, Eskimo Prints and Paintings of Norval Morrisseau* (1968) #3350
Montréal (Qué), galerie Curzi
– exhibitions
   – *Louise Robert* (1977) #7039
– exhibitions (reviews)
   – *Louise Robert* (1977) #7038
Montréal (Qué), galerie de la SAPQ #1495
Montréal (Qué), galerie de la Sauvegarde
– exhibitions (reviews)
   – Rousseau, Denis (1977) #7084
Montréal (Qué), galerie de Montréal
– exhibitions
   – *Kosso Eloul* (1973) #5368
– exhibitions (reviews)
   – Glass, Alan Frank #5615
Montréal (Qué), galerie Dominion/Dominion Gallery
– and Max Stern #1293 1431
– exhibitions (reviews)
   – Lyman, John Goodwin #6341
   – Scott, Marian Mildred Dale #7165
– western Canadian painting (1951) #1842
– Leduc, Fernand, on works exhibited (1943) #6189

Montréal (Qué), galerie Dresdnere
- exhibitions
  - *Etrog* (1964) #5376
Montréal (Qué), galerie Espace #1495
  - *Les moins de 35: du 22 janvier au 4 février* (1973) #1501
Montréal (Qué), galerie France Morin
- Massey, John, installation work #6439
Montréal (Qué), galerie Gilles Corbeil
- exhibitions (reviews)
  - Connolly, Reynald #5167
  - Gnass, Peter #5619
Montréal (Qué), galerie Gilles Gheerbrant
- exhibitions
  - *Jacques Palumbo: dessins, gravures, aquarelles/Jacques Palumbo: Drawings, Prints, Watercolours* (1975) #6754
  - *Suzy Lake* (1975) #6138
- exhibitions (reviews)
  - Palumbo, Jacques #662
  - Snow, Michael #7264
Montréal (Qué), galerie Godard Lefort
- exhibitions
  - *Christopher Pratt* (1970) #6910
  - *David Milne, 1882-1953: A Survey Exhibition/David Milne, 1882-1953: une exposition rétrospective* (1971) #6559
Montréal (Qué), galerie L'Actuelle
- and Guido Molinari #6588 6590
Montréal (Qué), galerie L'Art Français
- exhibitions
  - *Alfred Laliberté, 1878-1953* (1978) #6146
Montréal (Qué), galerie Lippel/Lippel Gallery
- exhibitions
  - *Ada Eyetoaq: Recent Sculpture/Ada Eyetoaq: sculpture récente* (1979) #5387
  - *Inuit Sculpture 1974/Sculpture inuit 1974* (1974) #4432
Montréal (Qué), Galerie lll #1495
Montréal (Qué), galerie Marlborough Godard/Marlborough Godard Gallery
- exhibition of Canadian artists, Marlborough Gallery, New York (1974) #572
Montréal (Qué), galerie Martal
- exhibitions (reviews)
  - Menses, Jan (1972) #6511
Montréal (Qué), galerie Mira Godard
- exhibitions
  - *Jean McEwen: Suite parisienne* (1979) #6471
Montréal (Qué), galerie Optica/Optica Gallery #1555
  - *Camerart: 24 artistes du Québec* (1974) #1507
- exhibitions (reviews)
  - *Destination: Europe* (1976) #1018
  - Sullivan, Françoise #7282
Montréal (Qué), galerie Powerhouse/Powerhouse Gallery #1554 1555 1557
- (1973-1975) #1516
- (1973-1979) #1553
- exhibitions
  - *Women's Bookworks/Livres d'artistes-femmes* (1979) #936
- fact sheet, on *Women in Art Systems* panel discussion (1980) #701
- Mars, Tanya, *Codpiece* exhibition (1974) #6421
Montréal (Qué), galerie Waddington/Waddington Gallery

- and Arthur Villeneuve #7490
Montréal (Qué), galerie Walter Klinkhoff/Walter Klinkhoff Gallery
- exhibitions
  - *Prudence Heward (1896-1947): An Introduction to Her Life and Work* (1980) #5796
Montréal (Qué), galerie Watson/Watson Gallery
- exhibitions (reviews)
  - Cullen, Maurice Galbraith #306
Montréal (Qué), galerie Yajima/Yajima Gallery
- exhibitions
  - *6 Young Canadian Photographers* (1976) #1018
  - *Clara Gutsche: paysages vitrés/Clara Gutsche: Inner Landscapes* (1980) #5673
- exhibitions (reviews)
  - Whittome, Irene #7567 7570
Montréal (Qué), George Etienne Cartier House
- architecture and interior #8619
Montréal (Qué), Gleneagles Apartments
- architecture #7933
Montréal (Qué), Graff #1495 1562 1645 1658
- exhibitions (reviews)
  - Wolfe, Robert (1979) #7606
Montréal (Qué), Graphia #1660
Montréal (Qué), Guilde graphique #1647 1653 1655
- and Tobie Thelma Steinhouse #7278
- Lacroix, Richard, as founder #6128
Montréal (Qué), Habitat '67
- architecture, Moshe Safdie #8403 8574 8575 8577 8578 8580 8583 8584 8585 8590 9215
  - and David, Barott, Boulva, Associated Architects #7694
Montréal (Qué), Hôpital-Général
- (1693-1871) #7932
- architecture, Victor Bourgeau #8862
Montréal (Qué), Hosmer House
- interior decoration #2110
Montréal (Qué), hôtel de ville/City Hall
- architecture, J.L.D. Lafrenière; Joseph-Omer Marchand, Consulting Architect #8980
- reconstruction #1231
Montréal (Qué), Hôtel-Dieu
- (1642-1861) #7932
Montréal (Qué), Hôtel-Dieu. Pavillon Jérôme Le Royer de la Dauversière
- architecture #9023
Montréal (Qué), Hurtubise House
- and Canadian Heritage of Quebec #7871
Montréal (Qué), Institut Canada
- and Alfred Boisseau #4769
Montréal (Qué), Institut d'art contemporain
- exhibitions
  - *Québec 75* (1975) #1515
Montréal (Qué), Institut des arts graphiques #1648
- Dumouchel, Albert, as teacher #1641 5325 5334
- Perrault, Gérard, as teacher #851
- typography (1940s) #922
Montréal (Qué), Institut national des beaux-arts, sciences, arts et métiers et industrie
- Chabert, Joseph, as director #3005
- Delfosse, Georges, as student #5279
Montréal (Qué), Jacobs Building
- architecture, Mitchell & Creighton #9305

Montréal (Qué), Jacques-Cartier Bridge #7933
Montréal (Qué), Jardin botanique
- exhibitions (reviews)
  - *Confrontation 65: exposition internationale de sculpture/Confrontation 65: International Exhibition of Sculpture* (1965) #1586
Montréal (Qué), Jewish General Hospital
- architecture, Fleming & Smith #9031
Montréal (Qué), L'Ermitage
- exhibitions (reviews)
  - Borduas, Paul-Emile #4798 4801
Montréal (Qué), La Patrie Building
- architecture, Georges Alphonse Monette and Joseph Ovide Turgeon #9303
Montréal (Qué), Le Havre South Seafront rehousing scheme
- architecture, Phyllis Bronfman Lambert #8512
Montréal (Qué), Les Ilots Saint-Martin, La Petite Bourgogne
- architecture, Ouellet Reeves Alain #8520
Montréal (Qué), Les Terrasses
- architecture, René Menkès #7886
- *Eclipse à trois éléments* sculpture, Maurice Lemieux #6242
Montréal (Qué), Lippel Gallery
- see Montréal (Qué), galerie Lippel/Lippel Gallery
Montréal (Qué), Loew's Theatre
- architecture, Thomas White Lamb #9069
Montréal (Qué), Loyola College. George P. Vanier Library
- architecture, Affleck, Desbarats, Dimakopoulos, Lebensold, Sise #8322
Montréal (Qué), Macdonald-Stewart Foundation
- collection, decorative arts #2203 2204
Montréal (Qué), maison mère de la Congrégation de Notre-Dame
- (1657-1913) #7932
Montréal (Qué), maison mère des Soeurs Grises
- architecture #8862
Montréal (Qué), Man and His World
- see Montréal (Qué), Terre des Hommes/Man and His World
Montréal (Qué), McCord Museum
- see Montréal (Qué), McGill University. McCord Museum
Montréal (Qué), McGill University
- architecture #9414
- Blackstock, Hattie, as medical illustrator (1920s) #4738
- Pen and Pencil Club, documents #1251
- Savage, Anne Douglas, as teacher #7130
Montréal (Qué), McGill University. Athletic buildings
- architecture, competition for #9417
Montréal (Qué), McGill University. Macdonald Engineering Building
- architecture, Percy Erskine Nobbs #9425
Montréal (Qué), McGill University. Macdonald Physics Building
- architecture, Sir Andrew Thomas Taylor #9411
Montréal (Qué), McGill University. McCord Museum #3098 3108
- and château de Ramezay (Montréal, Qué) #3082
- architecture, Percy Erskine Nobbs #9423 9425

– art, Haida Indians #4011
– Canadian intaglio prints #840
– exhibitions
  – *A Terrible Beauty: The Art of Canada at War* (1978) #1111
  – *An Exhibition of Canadian Gameboards of the 19th & 20th Centuries from Ontario, Quebec & Nova Scotia* (1981) #2597
  – *Beauté tragique: les deux conflits mondiaux vus par des artistes canadiens* (1978) #1112
  – *Canadian Hooked Rugs, 1860-1960/Le tapis crocheté canadien, 1860-1960* (1977) #2758
  – *De grandes espérances: la vision européenne en Nouvelle-Ecosse, 1749-1848* (1981) #1220
  – *Everyman's Canada: Paintings and Drawings from the McCord Museum of McGill University* (1962) #223
  – *Exposition d'estampes en l'honneur de C. Krieghoff, 1815-1872/Exhibition of Prints in Honour of C. Krieghoff, 1815-1872* (1972) #6096
  – *George Heriot: Painter of the Canadas/George Heriot: peintre des deux Canadas* (1979) #5786
  – *Great Expectations: The European Vision in Nova Scotia, 1749-1848* (1981) #1222
  – *Le réel et l'imaginaire: peinture et photographie canadiennes, 1860-1900/Fact and Fiction: Canadian Painting and Photography, 1860-1900* (1979) #268
  – *Mont-Royal Montréal/Mount Royal Montreal* (1977) #7924
  – *Ozias Leduc: peinture symboliste et religieuse/Ozias Leduc: Symbolist and Religious Painting* (1974) #6206
  – *Peter Pitseolak (1902-1973), chroniqueur inuit de Seekooseelak: photographies et dessins du Cap Dorset, terre de Baffin/Peter Pitseolak (1902-1973), Inuit Historian of Seekooseelak: Photographs and Drawings from Cape Dorset, Baffin Island* (1980) #6883
  – *Printmaking in Canada: The Earliest Views and Portraits/Les débuts de l'estampe imprimée au Canada: vues et portraits* (1980) #839
  – *Quillwork by Native Peoples in Canada/Travaux en piquants de porc-épic exécutés par les autochtones au Canada* (1978) #3475
  – *Quillwork by Native Peoples in Canada* (1977) #3474
  – *Silhouettes ca. 1840-1965* (1965) #2842
  – *The Art of Nunstins/L'art de Nunstins* (1981) #6934
  – *Une imagerie canadienne: peinture et dessins du musée McCord de l'Université McGill* (1962) #222
– exhibitions (reviews)
  – *George Heriot: Painter of the Canadas/George Heriot: peintre des deux Canadas* (1979) #5789
  – *Peter Pitseolak (1902-1973), chroniqueur inuit de Seekooseelak: photographies et dessins du Cap Dorset, terre de Baffin/Peter Pitseolak (1902-1973), Inuit Historian of Seekooseelak: Photographs and Drawings from Cape Dorset, Baffin Island* (1980) #6882
– Heriot, George, paintings #5785
– Hertel de Rouville family, portraits of #1345
– Macdonald, Jock, documents #6376

– McGill, James, portrait of #5321
– Québec folk art, 19th c. #1362
– Québec views, 18th-mid 19th cs. #1366
– Shanly, Charles Dawson, drawings #241 242
– silk-patchwork quilt (1726) #2803
Montréal (Qué), McGill University. McCord Museum. Notman Photographic Archives
– Baltzly, Benjamin, photographs #4598
– Henderson, Alexander, photographs and documents #5777
– Nakash, George, portrait photographs #6683
– Notman, William, photographs #6724 6725
– photographs of women, 19th c. #2908
Montréal (Qué), McGill University. McLennan and Redpath Library
– architecture, Dobush, Stewart, Bourke #9046
Montréal (Qué), McGill University. Medical Building
– architecture, Brown & Vallance #9412
Montréal (Qué), McGill University. Osler Library
– architecture, Percy Erskine Nobbs #9425
Montréal (Qué), McGill University. Pathological Institute
– architecture, Percy Erskine Nobbs #9423 9425
Montréal (Qué), McGill University. Pulp and Paper Research Institute of Canada
– architecture, Percy Erskine Nobbs #9425
Montréal (Qué), McGill University. Royal Victoria College extension
– architecture, Percy Erskine Nobbs #9425
Montréal (Qué), McGill University. School of Architecture
– architectural education
  – (1909) #8242
  – (1941) #8245
  – (1948) #8247
  – (1949) #8248
  – (1950) #8249
  – (1951) #8250
  – (1952) #8252
  – (1953) #8253
  – (1954) #8255
  – (1955) #8257
  – (1956) #8259
  – (1957) #8260
  – (1958) #8262
  – (1959) #8263
  – (1960) #8264
  – (1961) #8266 8267
  – (1962) #8268
  – (1963) #8270
  – (1964) #8271
  – (1965) #8273
  – (1966) #8274
  – (1967) #8275
  – (1970s) #8287
  – (1980) #8289
– student assistance to residents of low-income housing (1970s) #8283
Montréal (Qué), McGill University. Stephen Leacock Building
– architecture, Affleck, Desbarats, Dimakopoulos, Lebensold, Sise #8322
Montréal (Qué), McGill University. University Centre
– architecture, Affleck, Desbarats, Dimakopoulos, Lebensold, Sise #8322
Montréal (Qué), McGill University. University Library extension

– architecture, Percy Erskine Nobbs #9425
Montréal (Qué), Média
– (1970s) #1525
Montréal (Qué), Média-gravures
– exhibitions
  – *Les moins de 35: du 22 janvier au 4 février* (1973) #1501
Montréal (Qué), Média gravures et multiples #1495
Montréal (Qué), métro #9551
– architecture #9550 9552
Montréal (Qué), métro. Angrignon Station
– architecture, Jean-Louis Beaulieu #9555
Montréal (Qué), métro. Beaubien Station
– architecture, Roger D'Astous #9549
Montréal (Qué), métro. Berri-de-Montigny Station
– architecture, Longpré & Marchand #9549
Montréal (Qué), métro. Champ-de-Mars Station
– stained glass, Marcelle Ferron #5423 5424
Montréal (Qué), métro. Crémazie Station
– architecture, Victor Prus #9549
Montréal (Qué), métro. Jarry Station
– architecture, Bland, Lemoyne, Edwards, Shine #9549
Montréal (Qué), métro. LaSalle Station
– mural, Peter Gnass #5619
Montréal (Qué), métro. Mont-Royal Station
– architecture, Victor Prus #9549
Montréal (Qué), métro. Peel Station
– architecture and art #9553
Montréal (Qué), Molsons Bank
– architecture #9173
Montréal (Qué), Montreal Club
– architecture and interior, Edward and William Sutherland Maxwell #9306
Montréal (Qué), Montreal General Hospital
– architecture, McDougall, Smith & Fleming #9030
Montréal (Qué), Montreal Museum of Fine Arts
– see Montréal (Qué), Musée des beaux-arts de Montréal/Montreal Museum of Fine Arts
Montréal (Qué), Monument National
– Alary, Zénon, as student #4505
– Beaugrand, Gilles, as student #4650
Montréal (Qué), Mount Royal cemeteries
– landscape architecture #7933
Montréal (Qué), Mount Royal Hotel
– architecture, Ross & Macdonald #9276
Montréal (Qué), Mount Royal Park
– cross #7899
– landscape architecture, Frederick Law Olmsted #7903 7912 7924
Montréal (Qué), Musée d'art contemporain #1294 3091 3094 3105
– (1961-1967) #1453
– (1964-1968) #3093
– (1970s) #3102
– Borduas, Paul-Emile, paintings #4849
– Boyer, Jean-Pierre, video art #1498
– collection #3086
– dance presentation, Françoise Sullivan #7282
– exhibitions
  – *Albert Dumouchel: rétrospective de l'oeuvre gravé* (1974) #5332
  – *Automatisme et surréalisme en gravure*

québecoise: une exposition itinérante réalisée par le Musée d'art contemporain de Montréal à partir de sa collection permanente (1976) #1650
– Betty Goodwin (1976) #5629
– Bill Vazan: suites photographiques récentes et oeuvres sur le terrain/Bill Vazan: Recent Land and Photoworks (1980) #7476
– Borduas et les automatistes, Montréal 1942-1955 (1971) #1449
– Bruce Parsons: A Model of Reality/Bruce Parsons: un modèle de la réalité (1976) #6265
– Canadian Painting in the Thirties (1975) #592
– Chantal Dupont: histoires à voir debout (1979) #5341
– Charles Daudelin (1974) #5262
– Claude Tousignant: diptyques 1978-1980 (1980) #7402
– Conceptual Decorative: Prints by Les Levine, 1965-1970/Conceptuel décoratif: estampes de Les Levine, 1965-1970 (1971) #6265
– Constructions Mario Merola (1976) #6522
– De la figuration à la non-figuration dans l'art québécois (1976) #1461
– Dessin et surréalisme au Québec (1979) #1470
– Dessins de Lionel Lemoine FitzGerald et Bertram Brooker (1976) #503
– Dix ans de propositions géométriques: le Québec, 1955-1965 (1981) #1471
– Edmund Alleyn: une belle fin de journée (1974) #4512
– Fernand Leduc: dix ans de microchromies 1970/1980 (1980) #6193
– Fernand Leduc: rétrospective (1970) #6185
– Françoise Sullivan rétrospective (1981) #7283
– Gilles Boisvert: dessins (1975) #4770
– Graveurs du Québec (1967) #1643
– Guido Molinari: Quantificateur (1979) #6592
– Ivanhoë Fortier: inter-modulaires (1979) #5472
– Jack Bush: A Retrospective/Rétrospective: Jack Bush (1977) #4969
– Jacques Hurtubise (1981) #5890
– Jauran et les premiers plasticiens (1977) #1465
– Jean Dallaire (1979) #5244
– Jean-Paul Mousseau: aspects (1967) #6651
– Jean-Paul Riopelle: peinture, 1946-1977 (1982) #7032
– John Greer: Sculptural Objective, 1968-1981; Everything Always Changes but Something Still Remains (1982) #5654
– John Heward (1977) #5793
– John Lyman: hommage à John Lyman à l'occasion de ses 80 ans/John Lyman, Octogenarian: A Retrospective Tribute (1966) #6345
– La nouvelle tapisserie québécoise (1978) #2772
– La révolution automatiste (1980) #1475
– Le dessin de la jeune peinture (1981) #1565
– Léon Bellefleur (1968) #4662
– Lionel Lemoine FitzGerald, Bertram Brooker: Their Drawings (1976) #504
– Lithographs/Lithographies (1972) #825
– Louise Gadbois, 1936-1955: le portrait dans la peinture (1979) #5528
– Louise Robert et Michel Goulet (1980) #695

– Louisette Gauthier-Mitchell: oeuvres ouvertes, 1977/1980 (1980) #5574
– Luc Béland: études 1976 (1976) #4655
– Luc Béland, Lucio de Heusch, Jocelyn Jean, Christian Kiopini (1977) #1532
– Lucie Laporte: collaboration à l'oeuvre gravé: Joseph Marcil (1980) #1663
– Marcelle Ferron de 1945 à 1970 (1970) #5424
– Mark Prent 1970-1975 (1979) #6926
– McEwen: 1953-1973 (1973) #6469
– Melvin Charney: oeuvres 1970-1979 (1979) #5093
– Michael Morris: photographies (1980) #6641
– Miljenko Horvat: noir sur blanc (1980) #5843
– Mill (1978) #6534
– Nouvelle figuration en gravure québécoise (1977) #1651
– Oeuvres de Pierre Gauvreau (1979) #5577
– Panorama de la peinture au Québec, 1940-1966 (1967) #1440
– Panorama de la sculpture au Québec, 1945-1970 (1970) #1599
– Paul-Emile Borduas: esquisses et oeuvres sur papier, 1920-1940 (1977) #4836
– Peinture canadienne des années trente (1975) #589
– Périphéries (1974) #1508
– Philip Surrey, le peintre dans la ville (1971) #7289
– Pierre Ayot (1980) #4573
– Pouvoir du noir (1966) #5593
– Progressions, Peter Gnass (1977) #5620
– Progressions chromatiques 1975-1976: dessins de Christian Kiopini (1976) #6054
– Proliférations: C. Gagnon-Fortier (1978) #5552
– Québec 74 (1974) #1509
– Québec 75 (1975)
  – Charney, Melvin, on his Une histoire d'architecture - le trésor de Trois-Rivieres #5091
– R.L. Bloore: Sixteen Years, 1958-1974 (1975) #4751
– Regard sur l'oeuvre d'Albert Dumouchel (1916-1971) (1979) #5334
– Rétrospective: Jean Dallaire (1968) #5241
– Robert Roussil (1965) #7092
– Roger Vilder (1975) #7489
– Ronald: 25 Years (1975) #7073
– S. Guité: sculptures et tapisseries (1977) #5669
– Sculptures et dessins de Gunter Nolte (1978) #6717
– Serge Tousignant: dessins, photos, 1970-74 (1975) #7403
– Surfacentres Cozic (1977) #5204
– Tendances de la sculpture québécoise, 1960-1970 (1977) #1622
– The Canadian Canvas: A Travelling Exhibition of 85 Recent Paintings/Peintres canadiens actuels: exposition itinérante de 85 oeuvres récentes (1975) #588
– The Contemporary Arts Society: Montreal 1939-1948/La Société d'art contemporain: Montréal 1939-1948 (1981) #1474
– Trois générations d'art québécois, 1940, 1950, 1960 (1976) #1462
– Yves Gaucher: peintures et gravures: "perspective", 1963-1976 (1976) #5566
– Yves Trudeau (1978) #7436
– exhibitions (reviews)

– Borduas et les automatistes, Montréal, 1942-1955 (1971) #1447
– Cent onze dessins du Québec/One Hundred and Eleven Drawings from Quebec (1976)
  – Parent, Alain, on #1523
– Charles Daudelin (1974) #5263
– Dix ans de propositions géométriques: le Québec, 1955-1965 (1981) #720
– Fernand Leduc: dix ans de microchromies 1970/1980 (1980) #6192
– Fernand Leduc: rétrospective (1970) #6187
– Louise Gadbois, 1936-1955: le portrait dans la peinture (1979) #5529
– Mark Prent 1970-1975 (1979) #6925
– Québec 75 (1975) #1517 1518 1525
– Saxe, Henry #7146
– Szilasi, Gabor #7309
– The Canadian Canvas: A Travelling Exhibition of 85 Recent Paintings/Peintres canadiens actuels: exposition itinérante de 85 oeuvres récentes (1975) #582
– Tonnancour, Jacques Godefroy de #7388
– periodical, Ateliers #1493
– Québec art #1271
– Thériault, Normand, on Québec 75 exhibition (1975) #1528
Montréal (Qué), Musée des beaux-arts de Montréal/Montreal Museum of Fine Arts #1294 3084 3098 3099 3104 3106 3108 3114
– acquisition policy #3219
– and Art Association of Montreal #1246
– architecture #7709
  – Lebensold, Fred #9124 9125 9133
  – Maxwell, Edward, and William Sutherland Maxwell #9063 9065
– Benjamin-Constant, Jean-Joseph, paintings #243
– Brymner, William, works exhibited (1979) #4952
– Canadian presentation silver #2656
– collection #3112 3117 3118
– computerized inventory of collection #159
– exhibitions
  – 35 Painters of Today/35 peintres dans l'actualité (1957) #1413
  – Alfred Pellan (1960) #6807
  – Allan Harrison (1978) #5748
  – Anne Savage: sa vision de la beauté/Anne Savage: Her Expression of Beauty (1979) #7132
  – Art d'aujourd'hui: collection d'art canadien contemporain commanditée par Saidye et Samuel Bronfman/Art Today: Collection of Contemporary Canadian Art Sponsored by Saidye and Samuel Bronfman (1969) #526
  – Charles Gagnon (1979) #5540
  – Claude Tousignant (1973) #7401
  – Eleven Artists in Montreal, 1860-1960/Onze artistes à Montréal, 1860-1960 (1960) #1253
  – Emily Carr: A Centennial Exhibition Celebrating the One Hundredth Anniversary of Her Birth (1971) #5027
  – Emily Carr: exposition centenaire commémorant le centième anniversaire de sa naissance (1971) #5028
  – Espace 55: exposition groupant 11 peintres de Montréal/Espace 55: Exhibition Showing 11 Montreal Painters (1955) #1408
  – Exhibition of Works by Canadian Jewish Artists (1959) #435
  – F.H. Varley: A Centennial Exhibition/F.H. Varley: une exposition centenaire (1982) #7468

– *F.H. Varley: Paintings, 1915-1954* (1955) #7463
– *George Trakas Montreal* (1979) #7421
– *Goodridge Roberts: A Retrospective Exhibition/Goodridge Roberts: une exposition rétrospective* (1969) #7045
– *Greg Curnoe: rétrospective/Greg Curnoe: Retrospective* (1981) #5231
– *Guido Molinari* (1976) #6588
– *Guido Molinari: Works on Paper* (1981) #6594
– *Habitation sculpture de Robert Roussil exécutée pour la Société centrale d'hypothèques et de logement/Habitation Sculpture by Robert Roussil Commissioned by Central Mortgage and Housing Corporation* (1971) #7095
– *Hier & après/Yesterday & After* (1980) #696
– *Irene Whittome, 1975-1980* (1980) #7569
– *J.M. Barnsley (1861-1929), Retrospective Exhibition* (1964) #4611
– *J.W. Morrice, 1865-1924* (1965) #6625
– *James Bay Project - A River Drowned by Water/Projet de la baie James - une rivière qui se noie* (1981) #1566
– *Jean-Paul Lemieux* (1967) #6231
– *Jean-Paul Riopelle: Paintings and Sculpture/Jean-Paul Riopelle: peinture et sculpture* (1962) #7018
– *John Lyman* (1963) #6343
– *Joseph Légaré, 1795-1855: l'oeuvre* (1979) #6217
– *L'art de Tom Thomson* (1972) #7367
– *L'art du Québec au lendemain de la Conquête, 1760-1790* (1977) #1369
– *L'art graphique de Monique Charbonneau/The Graphic Art of Monique Charbonneau,*(1978) #5090
– *L'illustration de la chanson folklorique au Québec des origines à La bonne chanson/The Illustration of the Folksong in Québec from its Origins to La Bonne Chanson* (1980) #938
– *L.L. FitzGerald, 1890-1956: A Memorial Exhibition 1958* (1958) #5448
– *Les chroniques du Québec d'Arthur Villeneuve/Arthur Villeneuve's Quebec Chronicles* (1972) #7491
– *Louis de Niverville* (1979) #6709
– *Louis Jaque* (1977) #5942
– *Marius Dubois* (1979) #5311
– *Maurice Cullen, 1866-1934* (1956) #5221
– *Michael Snow* (1979) #7258
– *Montreal 1971: International Exhibition of Graphics/Montréal 1971: Salon international de la gravure* (1971) #824
– *Montréal plus ou moins?/Montreal Plus or Minus?* (1972) #7906
– *Paul-Emile Borduas 1905-1960* (1962) #4809
– *Peintres du Québec: collection Maurice et Andrée Corbeil/Painters of Quebec: Maurice and Andrée Corbeil Collection* (1973) #3234
– *Pellan* (1972) #6816
– *Prize Award Winners, 1908-1965, Spring Exhibitions/Lauréats 1908-1965, Salons de printemps* (1967) #1261
– *Robert W. Pilot Retrospective/Rétrospective Robert W. Pilot* (1968) #6872
– *Spring Exhibition*
  – (1880-1965) #1228
  – (1895) #1311
  – (1950) #1400
  – (1964) #1423
  – (1965) #1430
– *Survey/Sondage* (1968-1970) #1481
– *The Art of Tom Thomson* (1972) #7368
– *The Inuit Sea Goddess/La déesse inuit de la mer,*(1980) #4376
– *The Painter and the New World: A Survey of Painting from 1564 to 1867, Marking the Founding of Canadian Confederation, Exhibited from June 9 to July 30, 1967/Le peintre et le Nouveau Monde: étude sur la peinture de 1564 à 1867 pour souligner le centenaire de la Confédération canadienne, exposée du 9 juin au 30 juillet 1967* (1967) #231
– *The Saidye and Samuel Bronfman Collection of Canadian Art/La collection Saidye et Samuel Bronfman* (1966) #3087
– *The Works of Joseph Légaré: 1795-1855* (1979) #6218
– *Tom Forrestall Exhibition* (1972) #5461
– *William Brymner, 1855-1925: A Retrospective/William Brymner, 1855-1925: aperçu rétrospectif de l'artiste* (1979) #4953
– *William G.R. Hind (1833-1888): A Confederation Painter in Canada* (1967) #5806
– *Yousuf Karsh: visages contemporains/Yousuf Karsh: Men Who Make Our World* (1968) #6029
– exhibitions (reviews)
  – Archambault, Louis, and Jacques Godefroy de Tonnancour #1412
  – Barbeau, Christian Marcel #4607
  – Bastin, Michèle #4619
  – Charles Gagnon (1979) #5537 5538 5539
  – Fortin, Marc-Aurèle #5475
  – Greg Curnoe: rétrospective/Greg Curnoe: Retrospective (1981) #5232
  – Irene Whittome, 1975 (1980) #7570
  – Muhlstock, Louis #6654
  – Peintres du Québec: collection Maurice et Andrée Corbeil/Painters of Quebec: Maurice and Andrée Corbeil Collection (1973) #3233
  – Realism(e)s (1970) #533
  – The Painter and the New World: A Survey of Painting from 1564 to 1867, marking the Founding of Canadian Federation, Exhibited from June 9 to July 30, 1967/Le peintre et le Nouveau Monde: étude sur la peinture de 1564 à 1867 pour souligner le centenaire de la Confédération canadienne, exposée du 9 juin au 30 juillet 1967 (1967) #233
– extension program #3116
– furniture #2484
– Gagnon, Clarence Alphonse, *Boeufs au labeur/Oxen Ploughing Beaupré* #5548
– Gaspé crucifix #1605
– Gibb, Benaiah, as patron #3110
– graphic arts, Inuit #4474
– Inuit and Aztec art #3362
– Morrice, James Wilson, sketchbooks #6631
– periodical, *M* #3097
– photography collection #1051
– Plamondon, Antoine-Sébastien, *Chemin de la Croix* #6886
– Québec art, collections and exhibitions (1970s) #3115
– silver porringer, Paul Lambert (*dit* Saint-Paul) and Samuel Payne #2689
Montréal (Qué), Museum of Decorative Arts
– *see* Montréal (Qué), château Dufresne

(Musée des arts décoratifs/Museum of Decorative Arts)
Montréal (Qué), National Film Board of Canada/Office national du film du Canada
– and Norman McLaren #6490
– exhibitions (reviews)
  – Frank, Robert Louis #5505
Montréal (Qué), New Princess Theatre
– architecture, David Jerome Spence #9069
Montréal (Qué), New York Life Insurance Co. Building
– architecture #7933
– use of terra cotta #7750
Montréal (Qué), Northern Electric
– architecture, W.J. Carmichael #9234
Montreal (Qué), Notre-Dame-des-Neiges cemetery
– sepulchral monuments, 19th c. #1567
Montréal (Qué), Nun's Island
– architecture #8587
Montréal (Qué), Olympic Centre
– architecture #9128
Montréal (Qué), Olympic Stadium
– architecture
  – Daoust, André, Chief Architect; Roger Taillibert, Consulting Architect #9127
  – Taillibert, Roger #9130 9139
Montréal (Qué), Olympic Village
– architecture, Roger D'Astous and Luc Durand #9127
Montréal (Qué), oratoire Saint-Joseph/Saint Joseph's Oratory
– architecture #7923
  – Viau & Venne #8794
– influence of Dom Bellot #8332
– sculptures, Stations of the Cross, Louis Joseph Parent #6764
– stained glass, Marius Plamondon #2448
Montréal (Qué), Pied-du-Courant Prison
– architecture #9056
Montréal (Qué), Place Bonaventure
– architecture #7709
  – Affleck, Desbarats, Dimakopoulos, Lebensold, Sise #7694 9292 9319 9320 9321 9322 9323 9325
  – and urban development #9302
– exhibitions
  – Eskimo Canada (1968) #4414
  – Salon des métiers d'art du Québec (1970-1971) #1490
– interior decoration #9324
Montréal (Qué), Place d'Accueil
– architecture, Smith Carter Searle Associates #7686
Montréal (Qué), Place des Arts
– architecture, Affleck, Desbarats, Dimakopoulos, Lebensold, Michaud, Sise #9083 9092 9093 9096
– art #8233
– curtain, Micheline Beauchemin #4643
– interior decoration #9324
– sculptures, Pierre Rolland Dinel #5293
– stained-glass windows, Alfred Pellan #1442
Montréal (Qué), place Jacques-Cartier. Nelson Monument
– use of Coade stone #7908
Montréal (Qué), Place Victoria
– architecture #7709 9317
  – Moretti, Luigi; Pier Luigi Nervi; Greenspoon, Freedlander & Dunne, Associated Architects; Jacques Morin, Consulting Architect #9195

– Nervi, Pier Luigi, and Luigi Moretti
  #9316
Montréal (Qué), Place Ville-Marie
– architecture #7709 7901
  – and urban development #9302
  – I.M. Pei & Associates, Architects and
    Planners; Affleck, Desbarats,
    Dimakopoulos, Lebensold, Michaud,
    Sise, Associate Architects #9314 9315
Montréal (Qué), Powerhouse Gallery
– see Montréal (Qué), galerie
  Powerhouse/Powerhouse Gallery
Montréal (Qué), Protestant School Board of
  Greater Montreal
– elementary school buildings (1950s) #9419
Montréal (Qué), Queen Elizabeth Hotel
– architecture, George Drummond, Harold
  C. Greensides, John W. Wood #9286
– interior #8228
Montréal (Qué), Radio-Canada
– architecture #7925
Montréal (Qué), Ritz-Carlton Hotel
– architecture and interior, Warren &
  Wetmore #9267
Montréal (Qué), Roman Catholic school on
  Côte des Neiges
– architecture, Georges Alphonse Monette
  #9387
Montréal (Qué), Royal Bank of Canada
– architecture #7933
  – York & Sawyer; Sumner Godfrey
    Davenport, Associate Architect #9176
Montréal (Qué), Royal Victoria Hospital
– architecture #7933
Montréal (Qué), Royal Victoria Hospital.
  Ross Pavilion
– architecture; Stevens & Lee and Kenneth
  Guscotte Rea, Associated Architects #9017
Montréal (Qué), Saidye Bronfman Centre
– see Montréal (Qué), centre Saidye
  Bronfman/Saidye Bronfman Centre
Montréal (Qué), Saint Alphonse Church
– stained glass, Vincent Poggi #2448
Montréal (Qué), Saint Andrew and Saint
  Paul Church
– stained glass, Lawrence Lee #2448
Montréal (Qué), Saint Antonin Church
– stained glass, Gabriel Loire #2448
Montréal (Qué), Saint Arsène Church
– stained glass, Max Ingrand #2448
Montréal (Qué), Saint Gabriel's Church
– architecture, John Bird #8766
Montréal (Qué), Saint Gabriel House
– architecture and interior #8597
Montréal (Qué), Saint George's Greek
  Orthodox Cathedral
– architecture, Affleck, Desbarats,
  Dimakopoulos, Lebensold, Sise #8841 8846
Montréal (Qué), Saint Joseph's Oratory
– see Montréal (Qué), oratoire
  Saint-Joseph/Saint Joseph's Oratory
Montréal (Qué), Saint Leon's Church
– stained glass, Guido Nincheri Studios
  #2448
Montréal (Qué), Sainte-Justine Hospital
– architecture, Joseph Sawyer #8407
Montréal (Qué), Scott and Son Gallery
– exhibitions #1367
– support of James Wilson Morrice #6616
Montréal (Qué), Simon McTavish House
– architecture #8564
Montréal (Qué), Sir George Williams Art
  Galleries
– see Montréal (Qué), Concordia University.

Sir George Williams Art Galleries
Montréal (Qué), Sir George Williams
  University
– see also Montréal (Qué), Concordia
  University
– exhibitions
  – Adrien Hébert: trente ans de son oeuvre,
    1923-1953/Adrien Hébert: Thirty Years of
    His Art, 1923-1953 (1971) #5763
  – André Biéler 50 Years: A Retrospective
    Exhibition 1920-1970 (1970) #4725
  – Carl Schaefer: Retrospective Exhibition;
    Paintings from 1926 to 1969 (1969) #7155
  – Drawings and Pastels c. 1930-1967 by
    Miller Gore Brittain (1969) #4917
  – Esther Warkov (1971) #7517
  – Fritz Brandtner 1896-1969: A Retrospective
    Exhibition (1971) #4903
  – Robert Harris (1849-1919) (1973) #5743
  – The Mr. and Mrs. Jules Loeb Collection/La
    collection M. et Mme Jules Loeb (1970)
    #3231
Montréal (Qué), Sir William Van Horne
  Mansion
– destruction of architecture #8594 8601
Montréal (Qué), St. Denis Theatre
– architecture and interior, Barott, Blackader
  & Webster #9068
Montréal (Qué), Studio 23
– exhibitions (reviews)
  – Szilasi, Gabor #7308
Montréal (Qué), Sun Life Building
– architecture, Darling & Pearson #9308 9309
– exhibitions
  – Independent Art Association #1379
Montréal (Qué), T. Eaton Company
  Department Store
– architecture #7933
  – Ross & Macdonald; Sproatt & Rolph,
    Consulting Architects #9365
– interior, Jacques Carlu #9370
Montréal (Qué), Temple Emmanu-El
– architecture, Max W. Roth; Greenspoon,
  Freedlander & Dunne, Associated
  Architects #8840
Montréal (Qué), Terre des Hommes/Man
  and His World
– exhibitions
  – Art d'aujourd'hui: collection d'art canadien
    contemporain commanditée par Saidye et
    Samuel Bronfman/Art Today: Collection of
    Contemporary Canadian Art Sponsored by
    Saidye and Samuel Bronfman (1969) #526
  – Cultures du soleil et de la neige: l'art des
    Indiens et des Esquimaux du continent
    américain/Cultures of the Sun and the
    Snow: Indian and Eskimo Art of the
    Americas (1973) #3362
– Fortier, Ivanhoë, Environment #5471
Montréal (Qué), Terre des Hommes/Man
  and His World. Pavillon de la gravure
– exhibitions (reviews)
  – Dumouchel, Albert #5330
  – graphic arts, Canadian (1970s) #1644
Montréal (Qué), Terre des Hommes/Man
  and His World. Pavillon du Québec
– exhibitions
  – Les arts du Québec (1974) #1271
– exhibitions (reviews)
  – Artisanat-Design (1972) #2205 2211
Montréal (Qué), Théâtre du Nouveau
  Monde
– costumes, Alfred Pellan #6816
Montréal (Qué), Tifereth Jerusalem

Synagogue
– architecture, Affleck, Desbarats,
  Dimakopoulos, Lebensold, Sise #8846
Montréal (Qué), Town of Mount Royal Post
  Office
– architecture, Jean Michaud and Raymond
  Tait Affleck #7857
Montréal (Qué), Trafalgar Apartments
– architecture #7933
Montréal (Qué), Transportation Building
– architecture, Carrere & Hastings and
  Eustace G. Bird #9307
Montréal (Qué), Université de Montréal
– architecture #7900 9415
  – Cormier, Ernest #8345
– conference, on Québec painting (1970)
  #1267
– exhibitions
  – Une exposition d'art de la Province:
    céramique, sculpture, émail, joaillerie,
    orfèvrerie (1957) #2193
Montréal (Qué), Université de Montréal.
  Ecole d'architecture
– architectural education
  – (1958) #8262
  – (1959) #8263
  – (1960) #8264
  – (1960s) #8269
  – (1961) #8266
  – (1962) #8268
  – (1963) #8270
  – (1964) #8271
  – (1965) #8273
  – (1966) #8274
  – (1967) #8275
  – (1967), urban megastructure project
    #8276
  – (1968) #8277
  – (1976) #7728
  – (1980) #8289
Montréal (Qué), Université de Montréal.
  Ecole des hautes études commerciales
– architecture #7709
Montréal (Qué), Université du Québec à
  Montréal
– architecture #7925
– art (1962-1972) #1502
– Dumouchel, Albert, as teacher #5331
Montréal (Qué), Université du Québec à
  Montréal. Galerie UQAM
– exhibitions
  – Robert Wolfe: noir est l'espace blanc (1977)
    #7605
  – Rodolphe Duguay, 1891-1973 (1979) #5318
– exhibitions (reviews)
  – Lemieux, Lisette #6241
Montréal (Qué), Véhicule Art #1495 1503
  1525 1555
– (1970s) #641 1508
– exhibitions
  – Vehicule Art: In Transit (1975) #1512
Montréal (Qué), Vidéographe
– video art #605 1498 1499
Montréal (Qué), Waddington Gallery
– see Montréal (Qué), galerie
  Waddington/Waddington Gallery
Montréal (Qué), Walter Klinkhoff Gallery
– see Montréal (Qué), galerie Walter
  Klinkhoff/Walter Klinkhoff Gallery
Montréal (Qué), Watson Gallery
– see Montréal (Qué), galerie
  Watson/Watson Gallery
Montréal (Qué), Westmount Park United
  Church

- stained glass, C.W. Kelsey #2448
Montréal (Qué), Westmount Square
- architecture, Ludwig Mies van der Rohe
#9326
- architecture and urban development #9302
Montréal (Qué), Windsor Station
- architecture
  - Painter, Walter Scott #9532
  - Price, Bruce, and Edward Maxwell
  #9537
Montréal (Qué), Wiser's Museum
- collection, decorative arts #2469
Montréal (Qué), Yajima Gallery
- see Montréal (Qué), galerie Yajima/Yajima
  Gallery
Montréal (Qué), Youville Stables
- restoration #7905
Montreal Camera Club (Montréal, Qué)
- exhibitions (reviews) #978
Montreal Daily Mail, Can newspaper
- cartoons, David McRitchie #943
Montreal Estonian Society (Montréal, Qué)
- exhibition of Estonian art (1951) #118
Montreal Herald, Can newspaper
- cartoons, Ben Fitzmaurice #943
Montreal Society of Artists (Montréal, Qué)
#1246 3114
Montreal Star, Can newspaper
- cartoons
  - Julien, Henri #943
  - Racey, Arthur George #943 6952
- illustrations, Henri Julien #5984 5985 5986
  5987 5990 5993
- Lamb, Harold Mortimer, as art critic #6156
Montreal Theatre Ballet (Montréal, Qué)
- stage designs and costumes (1950s) #1410
monumental art
- Charney, Melvin, on #5091 5092
monuments
- see also historic sites; sepulchral
  monuments; war memorials
monuments, Canadian
- Allward, Walter Seymour #4516
  - Battle of Ypres (Ypres, France) #4518
- Carillon (Qué), Dollard des Ormeaux
  #1591
- Hahn, Emanuel Otto #5680
- Hébert, Louis-Philippe #5769
- Hill, George William #5799
- Laliberté, Alfred #6142 6143
- MacCarthy, Hamilton Plantagenet #6352
  6353
- Montréal (Qué), late 19th c.-1920s #1623
- Ottawa (Ont), National Capital Region
  #762
- Québec #1570 7887
  - late 19th c.-1920s #1606
  - revolutionary subjects #1351
- Québec (Qué) #7945
  - 17th-19th cs. #1309
  - General James Wolfe #1568 1600
- St. John's (Nfld) #7783
- Toronto (Ont), Memorial to Dr. D.W.
  Young #729
- World War I and World War II dead
  #1108 1109
- World War I dead #731 732
monuments, Plains
- medicine wheels #3748
Moodie, Geraldine, Can photographer,
1854-1946 #6602
Moody, Alan R., Can architect, 1924-1979
- Toronto (Ont), George Brown College of
  Applied Arts & Technology. Casa Loma

Campus #9479
Moody, Moore & Partners, Can architectural
firm
- Winnipeg (Man), University of Manitoba.
  Arts College #9399
Moody, Rufus, Can sculptor, 1923-
- argillite carving #3944
  - Vancouver (BC), Vancouver Centennial
  Museum #4006
Mooney, Terry, Can jeweller, fl. 1976 #2706
Moore, David, Can artist, 1943-
- exhibitions, group
  - (1976) #1529
Moore, Henry, Brit sculptor, 1898-
- sculpture, Vancouver (BC) #2080
- sculptures, Art Gallery of Ontario
  (Toronto, Ont) #3154 3158 9121
Moore, John Warren, Can furniture-maker,
1812-1893 #2500 2511 6603
- furniture, Hagerman House, Kings
  Landing (NB) #2512
Moorish art
- see Islamic art
Moose Factory (Ont)
- architecture #7976 7998 8032
moose hair
- embroidery
  - Athapaskan #4152
  - Huron and Algonquian #3513
  - Iroquois #3559
  - on birchbark, Indians of North America
  #3629
  - Penobscot #3537
Moose Jaw (Sask), City Hall
- architecture, competition for #8978
Moose Jaw (Sask), Moose Jaw Art Museum
- exhibitions
  - *Conceptual Decorative: Prints by Les
  Levine, 1965-1970/Conceptuel décoratif:
  estampes de Les Levine, 1965-1970* (1972)
  #6265
  - *Manitoba Mainstream: People's Art/Fine
  Art/Le Grand Courant du Manitoba: arts
  populaires, beaux-arts* (1972) #1897
  - *Saskatchewan: Art and Artists* (1971)
  #1919
  - *Watercolour Painters from
  Saskatchewan/Aquarellistes de la
  Saskatchewan* (1972) #1920
  - *William Perehudoff: Ten Years,
  1970-1980/William Perehudoff: une
  décennie, 1970-1980* (1982) #6838
Moose Jaw (Sask), National Exhibition
Centre
- exhibitions
  - *The Paintings of Frederick Nicholas
  Loveroff/Les peintures de Frederick Nicholas
  Loveroff* (1981) #6331
Moppett, Carroll, Can sculptor, 1948-
- exhibitions, group
  - (1978) #2066
- interview #788
morality and art
- see ethics and art
Morand, Paul, Can silversmith, 1775-1856
#6604
- works, Detroit Institute of Arts (Detroit,
  Mich) #2691
Morandi, Georgio, It artist, 1890-1964
- East, Benoît, compared with #5353
Morant, Nicholas (Nick), Can photographer,
1910- #6605
- portfolio of photographs #987 995
Morash, Barbara, Can artist, fl. 1969 #6606

Moreau, Gustave, Fr artist, 1826-1898
- influence on Graham Metson #6523
- influence on Ozias Leduc #6206
Morée, Michael de, Can photographer, fl.
1970s-
- portfolio of photographs #991
Morel, Octave, Can sculptor, b. 1837
- animal subjects #1579
Morelli, François, Can artist, 1953- #640
Morency, André, Can artist, 1910- #1393
Moretti, Luigi, It architect, 1907-1973
- Montréal (Qué), Place Victoria #9195 9316
Moretti, Pierre, Can artist, fl. 1969
- computer art #528
Moretti, Victor, artist, fl. 1890s
- works, British Columbia Parliament
  Buildings (Victoria, BC) #8967
Morgan, D., Can art dealer, 20th c.
- collection, Canadian textiles #2747 2748
Morgan, Earle Clifford, Can architect,
1903-1972
- Toronto (Ont), O'Keefe Centre for the
  Performing Arts #9087
Morgan, Peter, Can artist, 1951-
- stonecut prints #6607
Morier, Pauline, Can artist, 1942-
- exhibitions
  - (1975) #6608
Morin, Jacques, Can architect, 1911-
- Montréal (Qué), Place Victoria #9195
Morin, Jean, Can artist, 1938-
- prints #897
- typographic designs #932
Morin, Serge, Can photographer, fl. 1979
- portfolio of photographs #996
Morisset, Denys, Can artist, 1930-
- exhibitions (reviews) #6610
- interview #6609
- on art #6611
- on his art #6613
- photographs #6612
Morisset, Gérard, Can art historian, curator,
architect, 1898-1970 #3126 3305 3321
- and conservation of monuments #7897
- and Musée du Québec (Qué) #3095 3125
  3127
- and Québec culture #1477
- and the media #3323
- as architect #8891
- as art critic #3326
- as art historian #3322
- on art #3324
- on Michel Dessailliant (*dit* Richeterre)
  #5290
- on organs #2952
- on Québec silver #2692
- revival of *ceinture fléchée* #2864
Moriyama, Raymond, Can architect, 1929-
- Charlottetown (PEI), Confederation
  Centre, competition #9089
- Guelph (Ont), Macdonald Stewart Art
  Centre #3176
- interview, on relationship of artists and
  architects #8234
- London (Ont), London Regional Art
  Gallery #3174 9145
- on motel architecture #9288
- Scarborough (Ont), Scarborough Civic
  Centre #8973
- Toronto (Ont) #7733
  - architects' office #9346
  - Japanese Cultural Centre #9095
  - Metro Toronto Public Library #9051
  - Ontario Science Centre #9106

Morrell, Paul Luther, Can clergyman, 20th c.
- and J.E.H. MacDonald #6362
Morrice, James Wilson, Can artist, 1865-1924
  #10 24 89 192 6614 6615 6617 6618 6619
  6620 6622 6624 6626 6628 6629 6633
- and Canadian painting #18 1389
- and G.Blair Laing #1686
- and internationalism in art #354
- and Marc-Aurèle de Foy Suzor-Coté #7295
- and Maurice Galbraith Cullen #5221
- and modernism #27 383 6623
- as conservative artist (1930s) #322
- as member, Canadian Art Club #193
- Canadian press reaction (1886-1916) #6634
- compared with Emily Carr #352
- compared with Paul-Emile Borduas #4845
- exhibitions
  - (1965) #6625
  - (1968) #6627
- exhibitions, group
  - (1927) #299
  - (1975) #6630
- exhibitions (reviews) #204 211
- influence of French painting #1244
- influence on Edwin Headley Holgate
  #5818 5819
- influence on René-Jean Richard #6998
- paintings
  - Kleinburg (Ont), McMichael Canadian
    Collection #3172
  - Montréal (Qué), Montreal Museum of
    Fine Arts #3113
- sketchbooks #6621 6631
  - Ottawa (Ont), National Gallery of
    Canada #6632
- support from Scott and Son Gallery
  (Montréal, Qué) #6616
- winter landscapes #285
Morris, Christina
- see Mollise (Morris), Mâli Christianne Paul
  (Christina)
Morris, E.W., Company, design firm
  (London, England)
- works, British Columbia Parliament
  Buildings (Victoria, BC) #8967
Morris, Edmund Montague, Can artist,
  1871-1913 #6636 6638
- as member, Canadian Art Club #193
- exhibitions
  - (1909) #6637
Morris, Jerrold, Can artist, art dealer, 1911-
- autobiography #6639
Morris, John, Can civil servant, 19th c.
- and Parliament Buildings (Ottawa, Ont)
  #8930
Morris, Maria Frances Ann
- see Miller, Maria Frances Ann Morris
Morris, Marshall, Faulkner & Co., design
  firm (London, England)
- stained glass windows, Canada
  (1861-1874) #2453
Morris, Michael William, Can artist, 1942-
  #6640
- correspondence on 1971 Miss General Idea
  Pageant #546
- exhibitions
  - (1980) #6641
- exhibitions, group
  - (1969) #2039
  - (1971) #2042
  - (1974) #2050
  - (1979) #2070
- exhibitions (reviews) #520
- on visual perception #525

Morris, Robert, Amer sculptor, 1931-
- exhibitions, group
  - (1978) #790
- exhibitions (reviews) #787
Morris, Robert Schofield, Can architect,
  1898-1964
- award, Royal Institute of British Architects
  Royal Gold Medal (1958) #8389
Morris, William, Brit artist, writer, 1834-1896
- influence on Canadian Arts and Crafts
  movement #189
- influence on George Selkirk Gibson #5591
- influence on tapestry design #2774
Morris & Co. Ltd., design firm (London,
  England)
- stained glass
  - Canada (1874-1940) #2453
  - Montréal (Qué) #2462
Morris & Company (Art-Workers Ltd.),
  design firm (London, England)
- and John Henry and Duncan W. Dearle
  #2458
Morrison, Alfred L., Can artist, 1909-
- paintings of Prince Edward Island #6642
Morrisseau, Norval H., Can artist, 1932-
  #4136 4155 4157 4161 6643 6644 6647
  6649
- exhibitions
  - (1966) #6645
- exhibitions, group
  - (1968) #3350
  - (1977) #4151
- influence on Indian painting (1970s) #6648
- influence on Woodlands painting #4144
  4156
- Midewiwin images #4154
- Ojibwa legends #4122 6646
Morrow, Patrick, Can photographer, 1952-
- portfolio of photographs #1023
mortars (architecture)
- see cements, mortars, and plasters
mortars and pestles, Canadian
- wooden, Ontario, 18th-19th cs. #2588
Mortimer, Ann, Can ceramicist, 1934- #2395
Mortimer-Lamb, Harold
- see Lamb, Harold Mortimer
Morton, Douglas Gibb, Can artist, 1926-
- exhibitions
  - (1961) #1913
- exhibitions, group
  - (1967) #490 1916
Morton, James, Can photographer, fl.
  1856-1867 #1724
mosaics, Canadian
- murals (1950s) #4732
- Peterson, Margaret #6839
- Québec (1940s) #2199
- Sainte-Anne-de-Beaupré (Qué), Saint
  Ann's Basilica #6572 6573 8859 8860 8865
  8866
Moscow (USSR), Lomonosov State
  University. Anthropological Museum
- art, Tlingit #3947 3978
Moscow (USSR), Pushkin Fine Arts Museum
- exhibitions
  - Sculpture of the Inuit: Masterworks of the
    Canadian Arctic/La sculpture chez les Inuit:
    chefs-d'oeuvre de l'Arctique canadien
    (1972) #4423 4440
Moscow (USSR), Zagorsk History and Art
  Museum
- art, Inuit and Chukchi #4302
Moses, Gerald Milne (Gerry), Can artist,
  1913-

- as art director, Imperial Oil Review #924
- photographs of World War II #1107
Moss, Charles Eugene, Can artist, 1860-1901
- exhibitions (reviews) #186
motels, Canadian
- (1960s) #9288
Motherwell, Robert, Amer artist, 1915-
- influence on Douglas Hector Haynes
  #5758
Motherwell, William Richard, Can
  statesman, 1860-1943
- W.R. Motherwell Farmstead National
  Historic Park (Abernethy, Sask) #8723
  8724 9232
motion in art
- Canada (1970s) #783
Mott & Myles, Can architectural firm
- Saint John (NB), Saint John General
  Hospital #9031
Moulding, Fred, Can artist, 1897- #1881
moulds, Canadian
- Québec #2916
Mounsey, Yseult, Can photographer, fl.
  1970s-
- portfolio of photographs #991
Mount Uniake (NS), Uniake House
- architecture and interior #8534
Mountbatten, Louis Francis Albert Victor
  Nicholas, 1st earl of Burma, 1900-1979
- portrait of, Yousuf Karsh #6022
Mousseau, Jean-Paul Armand, Can artist,
  1927- #1502
- exhibitions
  - (1967) #6651
- exhibitions, group
  - (1955) #1408
  - (1958) #431
- interview #6650
- use of plastics #1442
movement
- see motion in art
movie houses
- see theatres
moving-pictures
- see films
Mowat, Grace Helen, Can weaver, 1875-1964
  #2144
Mowat, H.J., Can artist, fl. 1919-1931
- illustrations #916
Moyer, Harry, Can artist, b. 1884
- cartoons, Toronto Daily Star #943
Moyer, Samuel I., Can furniture-maker, b.
  1818 #2571
Mozino Suarez de Figueroa, José Mariano,
  Sp explorer in Canada, 1757-1819
- expedition, Nootka Indians #3966
Mud Bight Village (Alaska)
- totem poles #3873
Muhlstock, Louis, Can artist, 1904- #6653
  6655 6657 6659
- exhibitions
  - (1976) #6658
- exhibitions, group
  - (1977) #1278 1279
- exhibitions (reviews) #6654
- interview #6656
- on the nude in art #6652
Mulcaster, Wynona Croft, Can artist, 1915-
  #6660
- as teacher of Allen Sapp #7122 7123
- exhibitions, group
  - (1975) #1926
- exhibitions (reviews) #1883
Mulders, Gerard and Anne, Can collectors,

20th c.
– collection, Inuit sculpture #4443
Muller, Keith, Can designer, 1938- #2487
multiples
– and Michael Snow #7245
Munakata, Shiko, Ja artist, 1903-1975
– exhibitions, group
  – (1976) #6449
Munch, Edvard, Norwegian artist, 1863-1944
– influence on Tom La Pierre #6122
– Yerxa, Leo, compared with #7624
Munich (West Germany), Residenz
– exhibitions
  – *Group of Seven: Kanadische
  Landschafts-Maler: Eine Wanderausstellung
  der McMichael Canadian Collection,
  Kleinburg, Ontario, Kanada* (1977) #1781
Munich (West Germany), Städtische Galerie
  im Lenbachhaus
– exhibitions
  – *Michael Snow* (1979) #7258
  – *Michael Snow: Works 1969-1978, Films
  1964-1976/Michael Snow: Werke
  1969-1978, Filme 1964-1976* (1979) #7261
municipal art
– *see* public art
municipal buildings
– *see* public buildings
Munn, Kathleen Jean, Can artist, 1887-1974
  #309
Munnings, Alfred James, Brit artist,
  1878-1959
– exhibitions, group
  – (1926) #1084
Munro, John, Can silversmith, 1791-1875
  #2649
Munro, John Vicar, Can architect, 1872-1976
– London (Ont), Riverview School #9388
Muntz, Laura Adeline
– *see* Lyall, Laura Adeline Muntz
Murakami, Yoichi, Ja ceramicist, fl. 20th c.
– influence on Wayne G. Ngan #6695
mural painting
– *see also* conservation and restoration,
  mural painting
– Bourassa, Napoléon, on #4862 4870
– Challener, Frederick Sproston, on #5066
– Iliu, Josef, on #8229
– Korner, John Michael Anthony, on #6077
– Lismer, Arthur, on #15
– MacDonald, J.E.H., on #6362
– Reid, George Agnew, on #6974 6975 6979
mural painting, Canadian
– (1890-1900) #190
– (1890s), recommendations #8220
– (1938-1948) #379
– (1940s) #370
– (pre-1940) #28
– Calgary (Alta) #1959
– Challener, Frederick Sproston #5067
– Granville Ferry region (NS), Hall-Croscup
  House #1223
– Group of Seven #1774
– Montréal (Qué) and Toronto (Ont),
  exterior murals (1970s) #539
– western Canada (1950s) #1844
Murch, Walter Tandy, Can artist, 1907-1967
  #6662
– interview #6661
Murphy, Burland E., Can artist, fl. 1975-
  #6663
– prints #1214
Murphy, Patrick J., Can artist, 1917- #6664
Murphy, Rowley Walter, Can artist,

1891-1975 #6666
– on his art #6665
Murphy, Sean, Can collector, 1924-
– interview #3219
Murphy, Serge, Can artist, 1953-
– on his art #1552
Murray, Ian, Can artist, 1951-
– books #940
– exhibitions, group
  – (1981) #710
Murray, James Albert, Can architect, 1919-
– Cooksville (Ont), Applewood United
  Church #8763
– Don Mills (Ont)
  – Chatham Village #8511
  – South Mills Village #7679
– Ottawa (Ont), University of Ottawa #9458
  9465
Murray, Jim, Can photographer, ca. 1947-
– portfolio of photographs #1032
Murray, Robert Gray, Can sculptor in USA,
  1936- #6667 6669 6671 6672 6673 6674
– exhibitions
  – (1969) #6670
– exhibitions, group
  – (1967) #480 490
  – (1971) #98
  – (1976) #613
– interview #6668
– on Canadian art (1960s) #478
– on his art education #470
– on living in New York (1960s) #460
  sculpture, Vancouver (BC) #2080
Murray, William, Can architect, fl.
  1820s-1840s, d. ca. 1860 #8390
Murray, William G., Can architect,
  1876-1954
– London (Ont), Ryerson School #9386
Murray & Murray, Can architectural firm
– Ottawa (Ont), Saint-Maurice Roman
  Catholic Church #8766
Murray Bay (Qué)
– decorative arts (1930s) #2172
Murray Bay (Qué), Manoir Richelieu
– collection of Canadiana #12 3230
Murraygreen, Ryan, Can artist, 1947-
  exhibitions, group
  – (1981) #2084
museums, American
– collections, toys and dolls #2932
museums, Canadian
– 19th c.-1970s #3055
– (1830s-1860s), mechanics' institutes #3064
– (1898), recommendation for #1705
– (1908), recommendation for state aid #2963
– (1909), recommendation for #8242
– (1920s) #311
– (1930s) #3024
  – recommendations #3026
– (1940s) #3030
  – and Royal Canadian Academy of Arts
  #361
– (1950s) #3037
  – compared with American museums
  #3031
– (1953-1954) #3035
– (1960s) #87 3043 3045
  – galleries #442
  – support of Canadian artists #448 523
  – *The Simmons Report on Art Gallery
  Development in Canada* (1969) #3046
– (1960s-1970s), support of Canadian
  women artists #677
– (1970s) #542 551 682 3051 3059 3279

– and Canadian Museums Association
  #3054
– and women #562
– and women artists #701
– parallel galleries #641 660 1042
– photography galleries #1027
– public attitudes #3056
– support of Canadian artists #6747
– (1972-1974) #552
– (1980) #683
– Acadian #1137
– and art education
  – (1940s) #2984
  – (1940s-1980s) #2983
– and performance art #634
– architecture #9098
  – *Canadian Architect* community art gallery
  competition (1957) #9082
  – Charlottetown (PEI), Confederation
  Centre #9088 9089
  – conversion of public buildings for #9147
  9148
  – London (Ont), London Regional Art
  Gallery #9145
  – Montréal (Qué)
    – château Dufresne #8617 8618
    – Expo '67 Art Gallery #9223
    – Montreal Museum of Fine Arts #9063
    9065 9124 9125 9133
    – Saint Gabriel House #8597
  – Ottawa (Ont), National Gallery of
  Canada #9079 9136 9142
  – Perth (Ont), Perth Museum (formerly
  Matheson House) #8670
  – Queen Charlotte Islands (BC), Queen
  Charlotte Islands Museum #9129
  – Rimouski (Qué), Musée régional de
  Rimouski #9118
  – Saskatoon (Sask), Mendel Art Gallery
  #9091
  – Toronto (Ont)
    – Art Gallery of Ontario #8680 9121
    – Art Gallery of Toronto #3132 9076
    – Art Museum of Toronto #9070
    – Colborne Lodge #8659
    – Jenkins Art Galleries #8053
    – Ontario Science Centre #9106
  – Vancouver (BC)
    – University of British Columbia.
    Museum of Anthropology #9132 9137
    9138
    – Vancouver Art Gallery #9149
  – Vernon (BC), Vernon Civic Centre #8972
  – Winnipeg (Man)
    – Seven Oaks Museum (formerly Seven
    Oaks House) #8703
    – Winnipeg Art Gallery #9102 9111 9117
– Atlantic provinces
  – 20th c. #1130
  – (1960s) #1124 3053
  – (1970s) #1127 1131
– British Columbia
  – 19th c.-1940s #1986
  – and art education (1960s) #2989
– collections
  – Canadian art #3320
  – Canadian lamps #2920
  – Canadian quilts #2799
  – Canadian samplers #2792
  – furniture #2484
  – photography #1051
  – Québec decorative arts #2226
  – Québec furniture #2528
  – textiles #2739

– toys and dolls #2932
– Halifax (NS), (1970s) #1208
– Manitoba (1970s) #3193
– Montréal (Qué)
  – 19th-early 20th cs. #7899
  – galleries #1555
– Newfoundland #1142
– Ontario
  – 19th c.-early 20th c. #3152
  – (1970s) #1802
– periodicals #3313
  – *Canadian Museums Association. Gazette*
    #3042
– Québec #3098 3108
  – 19th c.-1940s #1242
  – (1833-1853), support for national
    museum #3120
  – (1940s-1950s) #1426
  – (1940s-1970s) #1269
  – (1970s) #3015 3102
– Saint John (NB), (1842-1945) #3065
– Saskatchewan #1919
– small galleries (1950s) #3034
– Vancouver (BC)
  – (1960s) #3190
  – Vancouver Museum #3180
museums in art
– (1970s-1980s) #714
– Whittome, Irene #7568
Musgrove, Alexander Johnston, Can artist,
  1890-1952
– exhibitions, group
  – (1940) #350
mushrooms in art
– Fournier, Paul #5487
– Jackson, Henry Alexander Carmichael
  #5926 5927 5928
music
– *see also* folk songs
music, Canadian #129
– (1970s) #693 3279
– Canadian Creative Music Collective
  (CCMC) #690
– New Brunswick #1178
– Newfoundland #1139
– periodical, *Canadian Review of Music and
  Art* #357
– Québec #1231 1235
  – (1870s) #1307
– Winnipeg (Man) #1891
music, Inuit #4317
music and art
– Andrews, Stephen #4528
– Bergeron, André #4702
– Bolt, Ron #4778
– Colville, Alex #5141
– Gaucher, Yves #5565 5568 5570
– Harris, Lawren Stewart #5721
– MacGregor, John #6388
– McDougall, Clark Holmes #6464
– McLaren, Norman #6493 6494 6497 6498
– Parent, Omer #6767
– performance art #634
– Rayner, Gordon #6965
– Tonnancour, Jacques Godefroy de #7383
  7390
– Trudeau, Yves #7433
– W.O.R.K.S. #1955
– Young, Robert #7628
musical instruments
– *see also* conservation and restoration,
  musical instruments
– for children, late 19th c.-1930s #2932
musical instruments, Blackfoot #3654

musical instruments, Canadian
– (1970s) #2940
– Ottawa (Ont), National Museum of Man.
  Canadian Centre for Folk Culture Studies
  #963
– Québec #1237
musical instruments, Cree #3402 3742
musical instruments, Indians of North
  America #3363
musical instruments, Saulteaux #3402
muskets
– *see* firearms
Muskoka (Ont)
– views, Mary Evelyn Wrinch #7617
Muslim art
– *see* Islamic art
Muybridge, Eadweard, Brit photographer,
  1830-1904
– Cohen, Sorel, compared with #5130
Myers, Barton, Can architect, 1934-
– Edmonton (Alta), Citadel Theatre #8091
– on architecture #7746
– on his architecture #8391
Myren, Ronald L., Can artist, 1937-
– exhibitions, group
  – (1981) #1885
mysticism
– and Charles Gagnon #5533
– and Lawren Stewart Harris #5726 5731
mythology
– *see also* folklore
– sculpture, British Columbia (1970s) #2066
mythology, Algonquian #3385
– Thunderbird #3493
– tree #3516
mythology, Bella Coola #3772
mythology, Blackfoot
– bear #3746
mythology, Canadian
– Wieland, Joyce, on #7576
mythology, Copper Eskimo #4330
mythology, Cree
– Manitou #3724
mythology, Haida #3780 3890
– moon image #4059
mythology, Indians of Central America
– serpents #3391
mythology, Indians of North America
– and shamanism #3361
– cardinal points #3498
– serpents #3391
– Thunderbird #3410
mythology, Inuit #4295 4315 4317 4320 4321
  4404 4433 4488
– influence on Jean-Paul Riopelle #7024
– Povungnituk (Qué) #4417 4437 4494
– Sea Goddess #4312 4376
mythology, Iroquois
– tree #3516
mythology, Kwakiutl #3883 4120
– Bokwus #3990
mythology, natives of North America #3334
mythology, Netsilik #4328
mythology, Northwest Coast Indians #4036
– Thunderbird and whale #3831
mythology, Ojibwa #4122
mythology, Sarcee
– bear #3746
mythology, Seneca
– masks #3508
mythology, Tlingit
– devilfish #4045
mythology, Tsimshian #3910

N

N.B. Crystal Glass Co.
– *see* Crystal, N.B., Glass Co.
N.E. Thing Co. Ltd. (Vancouver, BC) #536
– and avant-garde art #600
– and Iain Baxter #535
– exhibitions
  – (1969) #524 6675
  – (1974) #574
  – (1976) #2060 6676
  – (1977) #6678
– exhibitions, group
  – (1969) #2039
  – (1970) #534
  – (1980) #703
– sculptural photographs #994
– use of language #6677
– video art #550
Nadeau, Luis, Can photographer, 1951-
  #6679
– portfolio of photographs #991
Nadeau, Marc Antoine, Can artist, 1943-
– Pop art #1497
Nahani Indians
– beadwork #4077
Nahuas
– sacrificial stone, authenticity questioned
  #4094
Nairobi (Kenya), Sorsbie Gallery
– exhibitions
  – *Contemporary Canadian Art* (1962) #451
naive art
– *see* folk art
naive painting, Canadian #965 966
– 18th-19th cs., McGill University. McCord
  Museum (Montréal, Qué) #222 223
– 19th c. #252
– 20th c. #960
– Charlevoix (Qué), (1940s) #1243
– Newfoundland
  – 20th c. #1153 1155
  – (1970s) #1156
– Price, Ralph and Patricia, collection #971
– Saskatchewan, 20th c. #1927
– western Canada, 20th c. #1846
Nakamura, Kazuo, Can artist, 1926- #6680
  6681 6682
– influence on Toronto (Ont) painting #1749
  1760
Nakamura, Richard Yoshio, Can
  photographer, 1924-
– photographs of Canadian military forces
  #1107
Nakash, George, Can photographer,
  1892-1976 #6683
Nakashima, Hiro, Can architect, 1936-
– Toronto (Ont), St. Lawrence Housing
  #8078
Nakayama, Ja artist, 20th c.
– as teacher of Gaston-Pierre Petit #6844
Nanaimo (BC)
– photography, late 19th c. #2022
Nanaimo (BC), Malaspina College. Madrona
  Exposition Centre
– exhibitions
  – *J.Frederic McCulloch 1905-1932: Works on
    Paper* (1978) #6463
  – *Jack Wise: A Decade of Work* (1978) #7601
Nantel, Michel, Can artist, fl. 1976 #6684
Napanee Glass House, glass manufacturer
  (Napanee, Ont) #2401

– *see* Napanee Glass House
Narcissus
– as theme, Irene Whittome #7566
Nash, Chauncey C., Amer collector, 20th c.
– collection, Inuit art #4191
Nash, Paul, Brit artist, 1889-1946
– exhibitions, group
  – (1926) #1084
– Schaefer, Carl Fellman, compared with
  #7157
Naskapi Indians
– art #3554 4082 4149
– beadwork #4076 4103
– caribou skin #3622
– containers #4078
– costume #4098
– culture (1880s) #3379
– rattles #3363
– snowshoes #2812
Nasmith, Eric Anderson, Can artist, 1916-
  #6685
Nass River (BC)
– totem poles #3839 3852
National Association for Photographic
  Art/L'Association nationale d'art
  photographique
– periodical, *Camera Canada* #991
National Awards for Residential Design
– (1969) #8743
National Ballet of Canada
– and Ken Bell, as photographer #4657
– and St. Lawrence Hall (Toronto, Ont)
  #9103
National Capital Commission
– *see* Canada. National Capital Commission
National Design Council
– *see* Canada. National Design Council
National Film Board of Canada
– *see* Canada. National Film Board of
  Canada; Montréal (Qué), National Film
  Board of Canada/Office national du film
  du Canada
National Film Society of Canada
– founding, Donald William Buchanan
  #3325
*National Gallery of Canada. Annual
  Bulletin/Galerie nationale du Canada. Bulletin
  annuel*, Can periodical #69
National Home Monthly, Can periodical
– illustrations, Illingworth Holey Kerr #6048
National House Builders Association
– domestic architecture (1950s) #8512
National Industrial Design Committee
– *see* Canada. National Industrial Design
  Committee
National Industrial Design Council
– *see* Canada. National Industrial Design
  Council
National Museums Corporation
– *see* Canada. National Museums
  Corporation
National Parks Service
– *see* Canada. National Parks Service
National Research Council
– *see* Canada. National Research Council
National Transcontinental Railway
– railroad stations #9542
nationalism and architecture
– Canada #7728
  – 20th c. #7690 7731
  – (1910s) #7642 7644
  – (1920s) #7657
  – (1950s) #7675
  – Victorian architecture #7697 7725

– Québec #7848 7868
nationalism and art
– Boyle, John Bernard #4891
– Canada #67 68 76 77 143
  – 17th-19th cs. #187
  – 20th c. #29 58 59 61 297 482 4851
  – (1860-1890) #264 271 272
  – (1860s-1880s) #230
  – (1860s-1970s) #148 150
  – (1870s-1910s), compared with USA #196
  – (1890s) #183
  – (1890s-1970s) #102
  – (1910s) #205
    – compared with USA #203
  – (1910s-1940s) #354
  – (1920s) #289 1737
  – (1920s-1930s) #322
  – (1920s-1960s), compared with Latin
    America #495
  – (1930s) #338 1763
    – compared with Mexico and USA #337
  – (1938-1948) #378
  – (1940s) #368
  – (1950s) #52 387 401 439
  – (1950s-1960s) #511
  – (1960s) #529
  – (1970s) #574 619 620 629 3274 6747
  – folk painting, 17th-20th cs. #965
  – imagery on money #759
  – influence of World War II and the
    Depression #327
  – landscapes #109 341
  – photography #1056
  – political cartoons, 19th-20th cs. #957
  – stoneware, 19th c. #2309
– Curnoe, Greg #5231
– Dallaire, Jean-Philippe #5240
– Group of Seven #1741 1743 1747 1767 1768
  1774 1782 1789 1790
– Harris, Lawren Stewart #293 308 5729
– Jackson, A.Y. #5915
– Légaré, Joseph #6216 6219
– Lismer, Arthur #6292
– Montréal (Qué)
  – (1970s) #1548
  – monuments, late 19th c.-1920s #1623
– Québec
  – 17th-19th cs. #1373
  – (1759-1914) #1351
  – (1825-1850) #1368
  – (1930s) #334 1460 2170
  – (1940s) #1388
  – (1970s) #1528
  – monuments, late 19th c.-1920s #1606
– Roussel, Claude #7089
– Royal Canadian Academy of Arts #181
natives of North America
– *see also* Inuit, Indians of North America
– architecture #3353
– art #3334 3335 3336 3338 3341 3342 3346
  3349 3364 3369 3377 3378 3381 3435 3463
  3468 3479
  – (1980s) #4170
  – prehistoric #3375
– basketry #3411
– bows and arrows #3328
– masks #3327
– pipes #3358
– shamanism #3360
– tattooing #3330
nativity
– *see* Jesus Christ, nativity
natural history
– artifacts

– Edmonton (Alta), University of Alberta
  #3200
– Halifax (NS), Nova Scotia Museum
  #3071
– Québec (Qué), Musée du Québec #3095
– Toronto (Ont), Royal Ontario Museum
  #3141
Natural History Society of New Brunswick
  (Saint John, NB)
– (1862-1932) #3065
nature
– and Arthur Lismer #6294
– and Ernest Lindner #6287
– and Ernest Thompson Seton #7172
– and Gershon Iskowitz #5904
– and Jack Leonard Shadbolt #7177
– and Jean-Paul Riopelle #7018
– and Kenneth Campbell Lochhead #6314
– and Richard Prince #6937
– Canadian art #104 373
– Canadian art and literature #93
– Canadian photography #1062
Nauja
– *see* Angiju, Peter Nauja
Nauman, Bruce, Amer artist, 1941-
– and visual perception #525
– video art #651
naval architecture
– *see also* ships
naval architecture, Canadian
– New Brunswick, 19th c. #1190
– Nova Scotia, 19th c. #1201
– Québec, 19th c. #1334 1335
naval prints
– *see also* ships in art
naval prints, Canadian
– 18th-19th cs. #812
– Nootka Sound, Vancouver Island (BC),
  late 18th c. #2002
necklaces
– *see also* adornment
necklaces, Blackfoot
– Soumak, Washington State Museum
  (Seattle, Wash) #3685
necklaces, Montagnais
– natutshikan #4103
necklaces, Naskapi
– natutshikan #4103
needlework
– *see also* embroidery
needlework, Canadian
– 17th c.-1940s #2780
– Mennonite #2253 2264
– Newfoundland #2744
– Nova Scotia, patterns (pre-1920) #2785
– Québec, 17th-18th cs. #2200
– Ursuline #2788 2789
needlework technique
– *see* media and techniques, needlework
Neel, Ellen, Can artist, ca. 1910-1966 #4121
Neil, Allan, Can artist, 1924-
– exhibitions, group
  – (1971) #2042
Neil & Beggs, Can architectural firm
– Toronto (Ont)
  – Beaver Theatre #9066
  – Garden Theatre #9066
Neilson, Henry Ivan, Can artist, 1865-1931
– as member, Canadian Art Club #193
– etchings #799 800
– exhibitions (reviews) #211
Nelson, Horatio, Brit vice-admiral, 1758-1805
– monument, place Jacques-Cartier
  (Montréal, Qué) #7908

Nelson, John, Can photographer, fl.
  1840s-1850s
– portraits #1171
Nelson, Ronald Keith (Ron), Can architect,
  1932-
– restoration, Orpheum Theatre (Vancouver,
  BC) #9135
Nelson (BC)
– architecture #8155
Neo-Baroque architecture
– Québec, churches #8821
Neo-classical architecture
– Baillairgé, Thomas #8328
– Browne, George #8339
– Canada #7661
    – banks #9196
    – domestic architecture #7696
    – railroad stations #9539
– Kahnawake (Qué), Church of
  Saint-François-Xavier #8890
– Kingston and Frontenac County (Ont)
  #8015
– Montréal (Qué) #1367
– Ontario #7983 8654
    – churches #8904
– Ottawa (Ont) #8036
– Québec
    – and Jérôme Demers #7874
    – churches #8870
    – villas #8632
– Québec (Qué) #7892 7943
– Toronto (Ont)
    – Bank of Montreal #9155
    – Bank of Toronto #9151
– Winnipeg (Man)
    – Bank of Nova Scotia #9157
    – banks #9205
Neo-Gothic architecture
– see Gothic revival architecture
Neo-Plasticism
– influence on Québec painting #489
Neo-primitivism
– see naive painting
Neo-Romanticism
– domestic architecture, Ontario #8654
neon sculpture
– Toronto (Ont), Electric Gallery #1798
Nervi, Pier Luigi, It architect, 1891-1979
– Montréal (Qué), Place Victoria #9195 9316
Netsilik
– culture
    – (1903-1905) #4366
    – (1920s) #4328
– implements #4363
Networks Limited, Can communications
  firm (Halifax, NS)
– and Larry Wayne Richards #8402
Neumann, Alexander (Alex), Can artist,
  1949-
– exhibitions, group
    – (1976) #1529
Neumann, Ernst, Can artist, 1907-1956 #6686
Neutral Indians
– stonework #3503
Neuville (Qué)
– architecture #7875
– stone houses #8607
Neuville (Qué), church
– baldachin, Joseph Quintal and Gilles
  Bolvin #8826
Nevers, Edmond de, Can writer, 1862-1906
– writings, illustrated by Marc-Aurèle de
  Foy Suzor-Coté #7299
Nevitt, Richard Barrington, Can artist,

physician, 1850-1928 #6687 6688
New Brunswick
– architecture
    – 18th-19th cs. #7808
    – (1763-1930) #7659
    – Acadian #7804
    – Murray, William #8390
– architecture and decorative arts #2150
– art
    – (1750s-1970s) #1183
    – (1940s) #350
    – (1960s) #1177
    – (1970s) #1131
    – (pre-1867) #2110
    – Acadian #1181
    – (1960s-1980) #1136
– art and architecture, 18th-19th cs. #7780
– arts #1178
– bookplates, 18th-19th cs. #915
– churches, Edward Shuttleworth Medley
  #8776
– clocks #2925
– courthouses (pre-1914) #9004
– crosses #1625
– decorative arts (1940s) #2144
– domestic architecture, late 18th-early 19th
  cs. #8529
– furniture
    – 18th-19th cs. #2495 2500 2504
    – (1760s-1920s) #2511
    – (1783-1970s) #2503
    – (pre-1900) #2491
– glass #2400
– graphic arts (1970s) #1185
– photographic views
    – (1869-1918) #1186
    – Smith, Madge #7235
    – Taylor, George Thomas #7333
– pottery, 19th c. #2319
– quilts (1920s) #2794
– ship portraits, 19th c. #1190
– silver #2640 2649
    – late 18th-19th cs. #2646
– stoneware, 18th c. #2364 2365
– tapestries (1970s) #5296
– views
    – 19th c. #1180
    – (1760-1880), prints #1189
    – Cleveland, Xenophon #5119
    – Gagen, Robert Ford #5530
    – Gregory, Joan Steeves #5657
    – Heaviside, Lady Mary Love #1175
    – Leblanc, Leo B. #6182
    – Petley, Robert #5351
    – Russell, Edward John #7110
    – Taylor, George Thomas #7334
    – Woolford, John Elliott #258 259
– woodcarving, Graham family #1187
New Carlisle (Qué), palais de justice
– mural, Suzanne Guité #5667
New England
– architecture, 17th-18th cs., influence on
  Nova Scotia architecture #7823
– architecture, 18th c., influence on Nova
  Scotia architecture #7815
New Era Social Club
– and Glenn Alun Lewis #6275
New Hamburg Pottery, ceramic
  manufacturer (New Hamburg, Ont) #2336
– (1854-1916) #2348
New Haven (Conn), Yale University. Art
  Gallery
– exhibitions
    – Canadian Art, 1760-1943 (1944) #31

New Haven (Conn), Yale University. School
  of Art
– Aziz, Philip, as student #4576
– DeLauro, Joseph Nicola, as student #5276
New Maryland (NB), Church of Saint Mary
  the Virgin
– architecture, Edward Shuttleworth Medley
  #8776
New Westminster (BC)
– architecture #8147
New Westminster (BC), Courthouse
– architecture, George William Grant #9011
New York
– architecture, James O'Donnell #8848
– potters in Ontario, 19th c. #2309
New York (NY)
– art (1960s) #441
– views
    – Day, Mabel Killam #5273
New York (NY), 291 Gallery
– Lamb, Harold Mortimer, photographs
  exhibited #6156
New York (NY), 49th Parallel/49e Parallèle
  #712
– exhibitions
    – John Greer: Sculptural Objective,
      1968-1981; Everything Always Changes
      but Something Still Remains (1982) #5654
New York (NY), ACA Galleries
– exhibitions
    – Ernest Lawson Retrospective (1976) #6178
New York (NY), American Museum of
  Natural History
– art, Indians of North America #3452
– art, Northwest Coast Indians #4024
– art, Plains Indians #3668
– containers, Haida Indians #4066
New York (NY), Art Students League
– and Marion F.S. Mackay Nicoll #6703
– Brittain, Miller Gore, as student #4917
– Humphrey, Jack Weldon, as student #5865
– Lougheed, Robert Elmer, as student #6327
– Morris, Edmund Montague, as student
  #6636
– Roberts, Goodridge, as student #7044
– Steinhouse, Tobie Thelma, as student
  #7278
– Thibault, René, as student #7344
– Wrinch, Mary Evelyn, as student #7618
New York (NY), Artists Space
– exhibitions
    – 7 Toronto Artists (1980) #1832
New York (NY), Bonestell Gallery
– exhibitions (reviews)
    – La Palme, Robert #6118
New York (NY), Brooklyn Museum
– art, Dakota Indians #3705
New York (NY), Canadian Club of New
  York
– Canadian landscapes #3211
New York (NY), Carnegie Museum
– basketry, Abenaki #3596
New York (NY), Center for Inter-American
  Relations
– exhibitions
    – About 30 Works by Michael Snow/Autour
      de 30 oeuvres de Michael Snow (1972)
      #7248
    – Canada: Ron Martin, Henry Saxe (1978)
      #661
    – Objects of Bright Pride: Northwest Coast
      Indian Art from the American Museum of
      Natural History (1978) #4024
New York (NY), Cooper Union Art School

– Kahane, Anne, as student #5998
New York (NY), Davis & Long Co.
– exhibitions
  – *Charles Conder, Robert Henri, James Morrice, Maurice Prendergast: The Formative Years, Paris 1890s* (1975) #6630
New York (NY), Emmerich Gallery
– exhibitions (reviews)
  – Bush, Jack Hamilton #4965 4974
New York (NY), Exposition of Indian Tribal Arts, Inc.
– exhibitions
  – *Introduction to American Indian Art: To Accompany the First Exhibition of American Indian Art Selected Entirely with Consideration of Esthetic Value* (1931) #3412
New York (NY), Finch College. Museum of Art
– exhibitions (reviews)
  – Levine, Les #6266
New York (NY), Gallery of Modern Art
– Beny, Wilfred Roloff, *A Visual Odyssey* photography exhibition (1968) #4691
New York (NY), Grand Central Art Galleries
– exhibitions
  – *Canadiana* (1942) #12
New York (NY), James Yu Gallery
– exhibitions (reviews)
  – Niverville, Louis de (1975) #6708
New York (NY), Marlborough Gallery
– exhibitions
  – *Thirteen Artists from Marlborough Godard, Toronto-Montreal* (1974) #572
New York (NY), Martha Jackson Gallery
– exhibitions (reviews)
  – Iskowitz, Gershon #5906
New York (NY), Mead Library of Ideas
– exhibitions (reviews)
  – *Graphicanada 67* (1967) #877
New York (NY), Metropolitan Museum of Art
– exhibitions
  – *Masterworks from the Museum of the American Indian: Heye Foundation* (1973) #3450
New York (NY), Museum of Modern Art
– exhibitions
  – *Fifteen Canadian Artists* (1963) #453
  – *Information* (1970) #534
– exhibitions (reviews)
  – *Photography into Sculpture* (1970) #994
  – *The Responsive Eye* #468
New York (NY), Museum of the American Indian. Heye Foundation
– art, Cree, Dogrib, and Nahani #4077
– art, Indians of North America #3437 3450 3452
– beadwork, Indians of North America #3457
– birchbark containers, Algonquin #3542
– blankets, Salish #3818
– exhibitions
  – *Arctic Art: Eskimo Ivory* (1980) #4453
  – *The Ancestors: Native Artisans of the Americas* (1979) #4040
– ivory carvings, Inuit #4381 4458
– wampum belt, Algonquian #3541
– war club, Iroquois #3538
New York (NY), National Academy of Design

– Cruikshank, William, as student #5212
– Eaton, Wyatt, as student #5355
New York (NY), Riverside Museum
– exhibitions
  – *Canadian Women Artists* (1947) #377
New York (NY), Robert Elkon Gallery
– exhibitions
  – *Jack Bush, a Selection: 1961-65* (1980) #4978
New York (NY), Rockefeller Center
– architecture, compared with Bunker Hill redevelopment, Los Angeles (Calif) #8364
New York (NY), Seagram Building
– architecture, Ludwig Mies van der Rohe #9348
New York (NY), Theo Waddington Gallery
– exhibitions
  – *Aipellie Osuitok (Oshaweetok): Sculpture* (1980) #6745
  – *Kiawak Ashoona: Sculpture* (1980) #4565
New York (NY), Wade School of Photography
– MacAskill, Wallace R., as student #6350
New York (NY), Whitney Museum of American Art
– exhibitions
  – *Two Hundred Years of North American Indian Art* (1971) #3442
– exhibitions (reviews)
  – *22 Realists* exhibition, compared with *Realism(e)s* exhibition, Montreal Museum of Fine Arts (Montréal, Qué) #533
New York (NY), World's Fair (1939)
– exhibitions
  – *Exhibition of Canadian Art, New York World's Fair, 1939* (1939) #346
– Innes, Alice A., paintings #5900
New York Herald, Amer newspaper
– illustrations, Charles William Jefferys #5953
New York school
– and Hans Hofmann #1850
– and Kenneth Campbell Lochhead #6319
New Yorker, Amer periodical
– cartoons, Richard Taylor #7336
New Zealand, Pacific Rim Symposium
– Burrows, Tom, *Gas Works* #4960
Newark (NJ), Newark Museum
– art, Indians of North America #3425
– exhibitions
  – *Survival: Life and Art of the Alaskan Eskimo* (1977) #4272
Newcastle (NB)
– architecture, William Murray #8390
Newcastle (NB), Miramichi Valley High School
– exhibitions
  – *Colville, Pratt, Forrestall* (1974) #1129
Newcombe, Charles Frederick, Can collector, b. 1851
– collection, Emily Carr, paintings #5023
Newfeld, Frank, Can artist, 1928-
– interview #6689
Newfoundland
– architecture #7782 7792
  – 16th-19th cs. #7781
  – 18th-19th cs. #7779
– art #1154
  – (1867-1967) #1142
  – (1940s) #350
  – (1950s) #389
  – (1970s) #1131 1146 1149
  – (1980s) #1161

– Art Association of Newfoundland and Labrador #1144
– late 19th c.-1940s #1138
– arts, 19th c.-1950s #1139
– barrels #2151
– bells #2717
– churches (1850s) #8772
– courthouses (1830-1903) #9008
– decorative arts #2158 2159
  – 20th c. #2155
  – (1950s) #2146
  – (1970s) #2149 2152
– domestic architecture #7785 7791 8541
  – Newfoundland tilt #8535
– Dorset artifacts #4346 4377 4379 4380
– folk art #1155
– folk painting (1970s) #1153 1156
– furniture
  – 18th c.-1850s #2502
  – 19th c. #2520
  – 19th-early 20th c. #2519
– graphic arts
  – (1970s) #1148
  – (1980) #1159
– grasswork #2945
– hooked and poked mats #2765 2767
  – Belbin, Louise #2759
– hooked rugs (1940s-1970s) #2760
– hospitals (1950s) #9029
– lighthouses #9523 9525
– newspaper advertisements of services and commodities (1806-1900) #1158
– painting, late 19th c.-1970s #1147
– photographic views
  – (1849-1949) #1160
  – Holloway, Elsie #5820
– prehistoric artifacts #4332
– public buildings #7784
– sculpture (1970s) #1151
– sepulchral monuments, 18th c.-1860 #1163
– silver #2640
– stoneware, 18th c. #2364 2365
– textiles #2744
– views
  – 18th-19th cs., prints #1150
  – (1497-1887), prints and periodical illustrations #1145
  – (1970s), videoscapes #1157
  – Blackwood, David Lloyd #4739
  – Cullen, Maurice Galbraith #1143
  – Lapointe, Frank #6169 6170
  – Smith, William St. Thomas #7236
  – Squires, Gerald Leopold #7272
  – Williamson, Albert Curtis #7590
Newfoundland. Department of Education. Handicraft Centre
– support of Newfoundland handicrafts (1950s) #2146
Newfoundland Academy of Art #1142
Newfoundland Arts Council for the Province of Newfoundland
– founding, Newfoundland Conference of the Arts (1974) #1146
Newfoundland Historic Trust
– restoration, Christ Church (Quidi Vidi, Nfld) #7788
Newfoundland Society of Art #1138
– (1925-1936) #1141 1142
Newlan, Emery, Can sculptor, fl. 1955- #6690
Newlands, William, Can architect, 1853-1926 #8392
Newlyn Brotherhood
– and Edmund Wyly Grier #5660

Newman, Barnett, Amer artist, 1905-1970
- and Emma Lake Workshops (Emma Lake, Sask) #1915 1929
- as teacher of Arthur McKay #6477
- as teacher of Claude Tousignant #7400
- influence on Arthur Fortescue McKay #6476
- influence on Guido Molinari #6588
- Menses, Jan, compared with #6511
- use of colour, influence on Montréal (Qué) painting #1425
- Westerlund, Mia, compared with #7545
Newman, Brian, Can artist, 1943- #6691
Newman, Brian, Can photographer, ca. 1952-
- portfolio of photographs #1032
Newman, John Beatty, Can artist, 1918-
- portraits #715
Newport (RI), Art Association of Newport
- exhibitions
  - *An Exhibition of Eskimo Sculpture, Eskimo Prints and Paintings of Norval Morrisseau* (1968) #3350
Newport News (Va), Mariners' Museum
- exhibitions
  - *Ships of the Great Lakes* (1943) #12
newspapers
- *see also* periodicals
- (1870s), fashion news #2859
newspapers, Canadian
- (1886-1916), reaction to James Wilson Morrice #6634
- advertisements, late 19th-early 20th cs. #891
- on needlework (1940s) #2780
- political cartoons #943
- reaction to Royal Commission on National Development in the Arts, Letters and Sciences (Massey Report), (1951) #3257
- St. John's (Nfld), advertisements (1806-1900) #1158
Newton, Lilias Torrance, Can artist, 1896-1980 #6692
- exhibitions
  - (1981) #6693
Newton, Neil, Can photographer, 1933-
- exhibitions
  - (1978) #6694
Nez Percé Indians
- photographs of, Sir John Benjamin Stone #3717
Ngan, Wayne G., Can ceramicist, 1937- #2395
- exhibitions
  - (1978) #6695
- exhibitions (reviews) #6696
Niagara (Ont)
- art (1970s) #1795
- fraktur #2254
- furniture, 19th c. #2571
- furniture imports, 18th-19th cs. #2569
- views
  - (1697-1880), prints #1718
  - Jameson, Anna Brownell #5933
Niagara Artists' Co-operative (St. Catharines, Ont)
- and John Bernard Boyle #4892
- exhibitions
  - (1975) #1808
- unlimited print editions #834
Niagara Falls (NY), Buscaglia-Castellani Art Gallery
- *see* Niagara Falls (NY), Niagara University. Buscaglia-Castellani Art Gallery

Niagara Falls (NY), Native American Center for the Living Arts
- exhibitions
  - *American Indian Art in the 1980's* (1981) #4171
Niagara Falls (NY), Niagara University. Buscaglia-Castellani Art Gallery
- exhibitions
  - *Spirit of the Earth* (1980) #4163
Niagara Falls (NY and Ont)
- views
  - 18th-19th cs. #812
  - 18th c.-1960s #1673
  - late 19th c. #1839
Niagara Falls (Ont), Earl W. Brydges Public Library
- architecture, Paul Rudolph #9050
Niagara Falls (Ont), Greater Niagara General Hospital
- architecture, John B. Parkin Associates #9031
Niagara Falls (Ont), Niagara Falls Art Gallery
- Kurelek, William, *The Ukrainian Pioneer* #6116
Niagara-on-the-Lake (Ont)
- architecture
  - 19th c. #7986 7992 8655
  - late 18th-early 19th cs. #8000
- brick houses, early 19th c. #8521
- fortifications
  - (1814-1837) #8470
  - (1871-1978) #8472
- military architecture
  - (1838-1871) #8471
Niagara-on-the-Lake (Ont), Clench House
- architecture #7959
Niagara-on-the-Lake (Ont), Navy Hall
- architecture #8464 8465
Niagara-on-the-Lake (Ont), Saint Andrew's Church
- architecture #7959
  - Clyde, John Edward, and Saxton Burr #8901
Niagara-on-the-Lake (Ont), Shaw Festival Theatre
- architecture
  - Thom, Ron #9120
  - Thom, Ron, and Peter Smith #9119
Niagara Parks (Ont)
- architecture and historic sites #7975
Niagara Parks Commission
- *see* Ontario. Niagara Parks Commission
Niagara River (Ont)
- views, Claire Shuttleworth #7202
Nichol, Walter Cameron, Can, 1866-1928
- residence, Miraloma (Saanich Peninsula, BC) #8731
Nicholls, Ken, Can artist, 1949-
- on Jack Chambers #700
Nichols, Jack, Can artist, 1921- #6697 6698 6699
- and Ontario printmaking (1960s) #1756
- Gould, John Howard, compared with #5635
- in Paris (France) #426
- on printmaking #810 817 818
Nichols, T.R., Can bandura-maker, fl. 1979 #2940
Nicholson, Ben, Brit artist, 1894-
- influence on Lawren Phillip Harris #5711
Nicholson, John Hobson, Brit artist, 1911-
- as teacher of Toni Onley #6741

Nicol, Pegi
- *see* MacLeod, Pegi Nicol
Nicolaides, Kimon, Amer artist, 1892-1938
- as teacher of Will Ogilvie #6732
Nicolas, Louis, Fr priest, artist in Canada, 1634-after 1682
- *Codex Canadiensis* #1372
Nicolet (Qué), Saint-Grégoire de Nicolet
- altarpiece #1636
Nicoll, James McLaren (Jim), Can artist, 1892- #6701
- correspondence, Jock Macdonald #6376
- exhibitions
  - (1977) #6700
- interview #1974
- on art #1944
Nicoll, Marion F.S. Mackay, Can artist, 1909- #6701 6703
- correspondence, Jock Macdonald #6376
- exhibitions
  - (1975) #6702
- interview #1974
Nicomen (BC)
- architecture #8147
NIDC
- *see* Canadian Design Index-NIDC
night
- photographs of, Michael Mitchell #6575 6576
Nincheri, Guido, Can artist, 1885-1973
- as teacher of Umberto Bruni #4946
- paintings, Church of Saint-Viateur (Montréal, Qué) #1378
- stained glass, Saint Leon's Church (Montréal, Qué) #2448
Ninstints (BC)
- totem poles, Haida #4067
Nisbet, Thomas, Can furniture-maker, d. 1850 #2500 2501 2511
Niska
- *see* Lortie, Joseph Antoine François
Niska Indians
- mirrors #3804
- rattles #6788
- totem poles #3839 3895 4032
Niverville, Louis de, Can artist, 1933- #6704 6705 6706 6708 6710
- acrylic works (1970s) #6707
- exhibitions
  - (1978) #6709
- exhibitions (reviews)
  - (1978) #6711
Niviaksiak, Can artist, 1908-1959 #4460
Noah
- *see* Nuna, Noah
Nobbs, Percy Erskine, Can architect, 1875-1964
- Montréal (Qué), McGill University #9425
  - McGill University Union (now McCord Museum) and Pathological Institute #9423
- on architectural drawing #8241
- on Canadian domestic architecture #8499
- on plasterwork #8221
Nobbs & Hyde, Can architectural firm
- Edmonton (Alta), University of Alberta #9492 9493
- Montréal (Qué), schools #9413
- Regina (Sask), War Memorial Museum #9073
- Winnipeg (Man), Birks Building #9355
Noeich River (BC)
- petroglyphs, Bella Coola #3816
Noël, Jean, Can artist, 1940- #6713 6714

– interview #1485
Noestheden, John Theodore M., Can artist,
   1945-
– exhibitions
   – (1977) #6715
Noffke, Werner Ernest, Can architect,
   1878-1964
– Ottawa (Ont) #8393
Nokony, Denis, Can artist, 1951-
– exhibitions
   – (1981) #6716
– exhibitions, group
   – (1977) #1933
Noland, Kenneth, Amer artist, 1924-
– and Emma Lake Workshops (Emma Lake,
   Sask) #1929
– Bush, Jack Hamilton, compared with
   #4969
– influence on André Lucien Fauteux #5413
– influence on Arthur Fortescue McKay
   #6476
– Perehudoff, William, compared with #6837
Nolette, Joseph, Can builder, 18th c.
– bell, church, L'Acadie (Qué) #8830
Nolin, Alice, Can artist, 1896-1967 #1380
Nolte, Gunter, Can artist, 1938-
– exhibitions
   – (1978) #6717
Non-Figurative Artists' Association of
   Montreal/L'Association des artistes non
   figuratifs de Montréal (Montréal, Qué)
– (1956-1961) #1469 1478
– and Guido Molinari #6588
– exhibitions
   – (1960) #1415
non-objective art
– see abstract art
Nootka Indians
– art #3908
– basketry #3991
– canoes #3344
– culture #3764 3880 4020 4025
   – 18th c. #3966
– hats #3779
   – worn by chiefs #3829
– photographs of
   – Curtis, Edward Sheriff #3399
– rattles #4026
– serigraphy #4167
– wolf ritual #3885
Nootka Sound, Vancouver Island (BC)
– views, late 18th c. #2002
Nordbeck, Peter, Can silversmith, jeweller,
   1789-1861 #258 259
Norfolk County (Ont)
– domestic architecture, 19th c. #8656
– furniture, 19th c. #2573
– photography, 19th c. #1722
Norfolk County (Ont), Normandale Iron
   Works #2699
Nori, Angela, Can photographer, 1945-
– portfolio of photographs #991
Norman, Joseph van
– see Van Norman, Joseph
Norman architecture
– 17th–mid-18th cs., influence on Québec
   architecture #7847
Norman Hotson Architects, Can
   architectural firm
– Vancouver (BC), Granville Island #8170
Normandeau, Pierre-Aimé, 1906-1965
– as teacher of Jacques Garnier #5557
Normandin, Richard, Can artist, 1934- #6718
Norris, George A., Can sculptor, 1928- #6719

– fountain, Vancouver (BC) #2077
– public sculptures, Vancouver (BC) #2080
Norris, Joe, Can artist, 1924- #6721
– exhibitions
   – (1978) #6720
Norris, Leonard Matheson (Len), Can artist,
   1913- #6722
– political cartoons #957
North American Boundary Commission
– surveys (1858-1875) #1014 1015
North Hatley (Qué), Bradley House
– architecture, Peter Rose #7886
North Hatley (Qué), La Poterie
– Beaudin, Gaétan, as teacher #2381
North-West Company
– fur trade posts, Alberta, 18th-19th cs.
   #8129
– headquarters, Fort William (Ont),
   (1803-1821) #8460
– Nor'westers Museum (Williamstown, Ont)
   #3148
North-West Mounted Police
– and Henri Julien #5990 5992
– and Richard Barrington Nevitt #6687 6688
– and T.George Anderton #4525
– architecture, Fort Battleford (Battleford,
   Sask) #8484
– headquarters, Lower Fort Garry (Man)
   #8475
North York (Ont), Atria North
– architecture, Thom Partnership #8412
North York (Ont), Koffler Centre for the
   Arts. Leah Posluns Theatre
– architecture, Jerome Markson Architects
   #8386
Northampton (Mass), Smith College. Art
   Complex
– architecture, John Andrews Architects
   #8323
Northern Alberta Railway
– railroad stations #9545
Northgrave, Paul, Can architect, 1945-
– Toronto (Ont), Bedford Glen #8078
Northwest Coast
– views
   – 19th-early 20th cs. #1999
   – (1789-1791), Spanish artists #1998
   – Bacstrom, Sigismund #4581
Northwest Coast Indian Artists Guild
– silkscreen prints (1977) #4148
Northwest Coast Indians
– amulets #3853
– and Emily Carr #5013 5016 5021 5023 5030
   5038 5040 5044
– and Jack Leonard Shadbolt #7184 7189
   7191
– and Tom Price #6934
– antlerwork #3817
– architecture #3812 3939 8148
– art #19 299 1995 3172 3333 3342 3359 3370
   3414 3770 3799 3809 3827 3843 3854 3866
   3869 3871 3875 3905 3907 3918 3919 3921
   3922 3923 3928 3933 3937 3942 3948 3950
   3959 3969 3970 3974 3975 3987 3992 3998
   4002 4003 4022 4024 4034 4036 4041 4043
   4049 4055 5006
   – 18th c. #4062
   – 18th-early 19th cs. #4064
   – 20th c. #3199
   – (1940s) #4114
   – (1960s) #4117 4119 4121
   – (1970s) #4132 4145
   – woman subjects #3348
– art history, methodology (1930s-1970s)

   #4060
– atlatl #3951
– basketry #3888 3953 4004 4009 4029 4142
   – prehistoric #4017
– canoes #3339
– Carr, Emily, on #5007 5019 5031
– churches #8917 8918
– churches and cemetery art #8914
– containers #4015
– coppers #3924 4065 4071
– crests #3791 3858 3863
– culture #3810 3860 3897 3931 3989 4035
   – 18th c. #3445
   – (1880s) #3762
– earthworks, 13th c. #3955
– facial painting #3771
– graphic arts #4166
– graphic arts and sculpture #4162
– implements #4068
– in art #1999
   – 18th c. #3767
   – (1789-1791) #1998
   – (1845-1871) #2023
   – (1920s) #1840
   – Carr, Emily #5045
   – Webber, John #269 270
– masks #3340 3824 3894 3940 4030 4038
– painting #3415 3847
– petroglyphs #3814 3846 3971 3988 3997
   4050
– photographs of
   – Dally, Frederick #5250
   – late 19th early 20th cs. #2029 2033
– pictographs #3893 3952
– potlatch #3899 3911
– prehistoric art #3785 3861 3903 3914 4023
   4039
– quillwork #3811
– rattles #3960 3980 4014
– rock art #3859 3886 3999
– sculptors in society #3912
– sculpture #370 3377 3463 3831 3857 3877
   3892 3934 3954 3977
– serigraphy #4168
   – (1970s) #4148 4160
– shamanism and tree of life #3365
– stone sculpture #3887 3889 3900 4001
– stonework #4058
– Thunderbird #3410
– totem poles #2095 3766 3836 3837 3849
   3855 3791 3858 3863 3909 3930 3932 3972 3984 3993
   4057
– trade goods #3949
– weaving #3832
– winter counts #3728
– wolf ritual #3885
Northwest Institute of Sculpture. British
   Columbia Region
– exhibitions
   – (1956-1960) #1993
Northwest Rebellion
– photographs, by Canadian military
   photographers #1107
Northwest Territories
– photographic views
   – Moodie, Geraldine #6602
Northwood, George W., Can architect,
   1878-1959
– Edmonton and Calgary (Alta), Dominion
   Bank #9188
Norwegians in Canada
– Alberta, ethnocultural traditions #2273
Norwell, Graham Noble, Can artist,
   1901-1967

– exhibitions, group
  – (1978) #133
Notman, William, Can photographer,
  1826-1891 #6724 6725 6726
– and Benjamin Baltzly #4598
– and Canadian photography #986
– and J.Henry Sandham #7121
– and William James Topley #1001
– cabinet portraits #1026
– exhibitions, group
  – (1976) #3281
– influence on Canadian photography and
  painting #268
– on photography #6723
– photographs of buildings being built
  #1019
– photographs of women #2908 6024
– relation of photography and painting #245
Notre Dame (Ind), Saint Mary's College
– Laliberté, Norman, banners #6154
Notre Dame Bay (Nfld)
– artifacts, Beothuk Indians #3627
Nova, Gary Lee
– see Lee-Nova, Gary
Nova Scotia
– architecture #7779 7820 7821 7827
  – 17th-19th cs. #7687 7814
  – 18th c. #7815
  – 19th c. #7832
  – Harris, William Critchlow #8372
– architecture and historic sites #7830
– art #3072
  – 17th c.-1914 #1191
  – 18th c.-1867 #28
  – (1749-1848) #1215 1220 1222 1224 1225
  – (1900-1945) #1194
  – (1920s-1970s) #1192
  – (1940s) #350
  – (1970s) #1131
  – (pre-1867) #2110
– art and architecture, 18th-19th cs. #7780
– arts #1196
– board games, 19th-20th cs. #2597
– bookplates, 18th-19th cs. #915
– bottles #2409 2428
– chairs, 18th-19th cs. #2493 2509
– churches, late 18th-19th cs. #8775
– clocks #2925
– decorative arts #2156 2157
  – (1940s) #2145
  – (1970s) #2154
  – Germanic tradition #2135
– domestic architecture, 17th-18th cs. #7823
– engraving (1784-1897) #1198
– folk art, 20th c. #1206 1207 1210 1212 1213
– furniture #2521
  – 17th-19th cs. #2489
  – 17th c.-1840s #2494
  – 18th-19th cs. #2496 2497 2499
  – 19th c. #2515
  – 19th c., Pictou County #2513
  – (1920s) #2463
  – Holder, Thomas Cook, and Henry
    Arthur #2506
  – painted and carved decorations #2514
– glass #2114 2417
  – 19th c. #2398
  – (1881-1920) #2399
– gold and silver
  – 17th-19th cs. #2639
  – 18th-20th cs. #2632
– hats #2907
– libraries (1950s) #9044
– lighthouses #9522

– needlework #2785
– photographic views
  – MacAskill, Wallace R. #6351
– pottery
  – 19th c. #2308
  – (1780s-1925) #2307
– quilts and coverlets (1820-1930) #2807
– sepulchral monuments #733 1193 1216
– ship portraits, 19th c. #163 1201
– silver #2640 2648
– stoneware #2324
  – 18th c. #2364 2365
– textiles #2731
– views
  – 17th c.-1918 #1202
  – (1605-1878), prints #1203
  – (1749-1848) #1224 1225
  – Eagar, William H. #5351
  – Gray, John Warren #5648
  – Hammond, Charlotte Wilson #5697
  – Heriot, George #5785
  – Lawson, Ernest #6175
  – Lismer, Arthur #6294
  – Miles, John Christopher #6532
  – Petley, Robert #5351
  – Woolford, John Elliott #258 259
– women artists
  – (1830s-1840s) #1219
  – (1850s-1950s) #1204
  – (1970s) #1205
Nova Scotia Glass Co., glass manufacturer
  (Trenton, NS) #2398 2409 2421 2435
Nova Scotia Society of Artists #1119 1194
– exhibitions
  – (1923-1972) #1192
Nova Scotia Talent Trust
– support of arts #1199
Nowlan, Alden, Can poet, 1933-
– Shaped by This Land #5463
nuclear explosions
– Keziere, Robert, antinuclear photographs
  #6051
nude in art
– see also erotic art; human figure in art
– Brooker, Bertram Richard, on #317
– Canadian painting #101
– Muhlstock, Louis, on #6652
– Pellan, Alfred #6826
– Vilder, Roger #1489
Nugent, John, Can artist, 1921-
– exhibitions, group
  – (1972) #1922
Nulf, Frank Allen, Can artist, 1933-
– drawings #6729
– exhibitions
  – (1975) #6727
  – (1976) #6728
– exhibitions, group
  – (1977) #1933
  – (1979) #678
Number Ten Architectural Group, Can
  architectural firm
– Winnipeg (Man)
  – University of Manitoba. University
    Centre #9488
  – Winnipeg Art Gallery #9117
numerals in art
– Palumbo, Jacques #662
Numismatic and Antiquarian Society of
  Montreal
– see Antiquarian and Numismatic Society
  of Montreal (Montréal, Qué)
numismatics
– see coins and medals

Nuna, Noah, Can sculptor, 1900-
– interview #6712
Nunivak Island (Alaska)
– basketry #4180
nunneries
– see convents
Nutt, Elizabeth Styring, Can artist,
  1870-1946
– and Nova Scotia Society of Artists #1192
– as principal, Nova Scotia College of Art
  (Halifax, NS) #1194 2993
– exhibitions
  – (1981) #6730
Nutter, Arthur E., Can architect, 1874-1967
– London (Ont), Lord Roberts School #9388
Nymark, Victor, Can builder, fl. 1930s
– Montebello (Qué), Château Montebello
  #9295

O

O'Brien, Lucius Richard, Can artist,
  1832-1899 #178
– and Thomas Mower Martin #6438
– exhibitions, group
  – (1888) #175
  – (1890) #1839
– exhibitions (reviews) #174 186 1703
– house, converted into Jenkins Art Galleries
  (Toronto, Ont) #8053
– landscapes #2008
O'Brien, Paddy Gunn, Can artist, 1929-
– exhibitions, group
  – (1965) #473
O'Donnell, James, Amer architect, 1774-1830
  #8848
– and Québec architecture #7851
– Montréal (Qué), Church of Notre-Dame
  #1233 8780 8839 8849 8892
O'Donnell, William D., Can photographer,
  fl. 1850s-1860s #1211
O'Neil, Bruce William, Can artist, 1942-
  #6734
O'Neill, Louis, Can statesman, 1925-
– interview, on video art #1550
O'Reilly, Samuel F., Amer artist, fl. ca. 1900
– tattoos #2923
Oak Ridge (Ont), De La Salle Training
  School
– architecture, Hynes, Feldman & Watson
  #9386
Oakville (Ont)
– architecture #8025
Oakville (Ont), Oakville Centennial Gallery
– exhibitions
  – Alan C. Collier Retrospective (1971) #5131
  – Contemporary Native Arts of Ontario
    (1973) #4133
  – Ed Bartram: 10 Years (1980) #4618
  – Imprint '76 (1977) #833
  – Neil Newton Retrospective (1978) #6694
  – Of Human Bondage (1976) #611
  – The Heritage of Jack Bush: A Tribute (1981)
    #722
Oberheide, Heidi, Can artist, 1943- #1148
– and St. Michael's Printshop (St. John's,
  Nfld) #1159
Odelin & Mailloux, Can architectural firm
– L'Acadie (Qué), church #8830
Odjig, Daphne, Can artist, 1919- #4136 4155
  4157 6731

- exhibitions, group
  - (1972) #4131
  - (1975) #4141
  - (1981) #4173
- exhibitions (reviews) #1866
  - (1972) #4128
- influence of Midewiwin images #4154
Offenbach (West Germany), Deutsches Ledermuseum
- exhibitions
  - *Deutsches Ledermuseum: Katalog Heft 4: Indianer Nordamerikas, Zirkumpolare Völker* (1976) #3464
offerings
- *see* votive offerings
office buildings
- *see also* skyscrapers
office buildings, Canadian
- (1910s) #9332
- (1911-1912) #8295
- (1912) #7645
- (1950s-1960s) #9300
- (1960s) #9301
- and urban development (1950s-1970s) #9302
- architects' offices
  - (1940s) #9297
  - (1950s) #9299
  - (1960s) #9346
- Calgary (Alta), (1970s-1980s) #9362
- Halifax (NS), Bank of Nova Scotia Building #9182
- John B. Parkin Associates #8395
- Montréal (Qué) #7933 9318
  - Aldred Building #9313
  - Architects Building #9312
  - Bell Canada #9310
  - Canadian Express Company Building #9304
  - complexe Desjardins #9327
  - Dominion Express Company Building #9306
  - Jacobs Building #9305
  - La Patrie Building #9303
  - Place Bonaventure #9319 9320 9321 9322 9323 9325
  - Place Victoria #9195 9316 9317
  - Place Ville-Marie #9314
  - Royal Bank of Canada Building #9176
  - Sun Life Building #9308 9309
  - Transportation Building #9307
  - Westmount Square #9326
- Ottawa (Ont)
  - Bank of Canada Head Office Building (1938) #9337
  - Bank of Canada Head Office Building (1978) #9199
  - Northern Electric Research and Development Laboratories #9344
- Québec (Qué), Price House #9311
- telephone buildings, Ontario and Québec (1880s-1950s) #9298
- Toronto (Ont)
  - (1920s) #9367
  - (1960s-1970s) #8337
  - Bank of Montreal Building #9190
  - Bank of Nova Scotia Building #9192
  - C.P.R. Building #9329
  - Canada Life Building #9336
  - Canada Permanent Building #9177
  - Canadian Bank of Commerce Building #9178
  - Commerce Court #9350
  - Eaton Centre #9377 9378 9382

  - Excelsior Life Building #9333
  - Graphic Arts Building #9330
  - Hydro Place #9352
  - Imperial Oil Building #9340
  - Joseph E. Shephard Government of Canada Building #8975
  - Manufacturers Life Insurance Company Building #9339
  - Ontario Association of Architects headquarters #8300 9341
  - Ontario Medical Association #9349
  - Royal Bank Plaza #9198 9353
  - Stewart Building #9354
  - Sun Life Building #9342
  - Toronto-Dominion Centre #9197 9345 9348
  - Toronto Star Building #9334
  - Toronto Stock Exchange #9187
  - William H. Wright Building #9338
  - William Wrigley Junior Co. Ltd. Building #9343
- Vancouver (BC)
  - Block 51-61-71 project #7728
  - MacMillan Bloedel Building #9358
  - Marine Building #9356
  - office/retail complex, from renovation of Canadian Pacific Railway station #9546
  - Royal Bank Building #9179
  - Westcoast Building #9359
- Waterloo (Ont), Mutual Life Assurance Company Building #9331
- Winnipeg (Man)
  - 19th c.-1960s #8095
  - (1880s-1914) #8107
  - Birks Building #9355
  - Cauchon Block #9361
  - Monarch Life Building #9357
Ogilvie, William, Can photographer, 1846-1912
- survey photographs #1014 1015 1865 1874
Ogilvie, William Abernathy (Will), Can artist, 1901- #6732
- *Bombed Houses, Caen* #1115
Ogilvie, William Watson, Can businessman, 1835-1900
- summer residence, manoir Ogilvie (LaSalle, Qué) #8636
Ohe, Dorothy Katie von der, Can artist, 1937-
- exhibitions, group
  - (1975) #1867
Ojibwa Indians
- art #3540 3557 3560 3610 3755 4112
  - 20th c. #4173
  - (1600-1760) #3579
- basketry #3547
- birchbark #3551
- birdstones #3546
- boulder monuments #3578 3592
- bundles #3699
- burial site, Red Deer River (Man) #3615
- costume #3517
- culture #3539 4089
- culture (1820s) #3488
- drums #3363
- Manitou effigy #3726
- mats #3585
- Midewiwin #3492 3661
  - influence on painting, 20th c. #4154
  - scrolls #3626
- moccasins #3554
- mythology #4122
- painting, 20th c. #4156

- painting and sculpture (1970s) #4133
- petroglyphs #3568 3581 3591
- rattles #3363
- scrolls #3583
- shamanism #3602
- tattooing #3723
Ojibway (Ont)
- domestic architecture, post-World War I #8495
Ojibway Indians
- *see* Ojibwa Indians
Oka (Qué), Calvary
- architecture and art #1355 1356 8853
- crosses #1569
Oka (Qué), Church of Oka
- architecture and interior #8818 8885
Okanagan region (BC)
- art (1970s) #2048
Oklahoma City (Okla), John Deere Plow Company Warehouse
- architecture, Oscar A. Eckerman #9247
Okvik
- bonework #4340
- carvings #4364
- ivory carving figurine #4353
Old Bering Sea
- artifacts #4327
- prehistoric artifacts #4340
Old Colony Club (Nfld) #1138
Oldenburg, Claes, Amer sculptor, 1929-
- Ayot, Pierre, compared with #4572
Oldham (England), Museum and Art Gallery
- exhibitions
  - *Exhibition of Canadian Art* (1926) #290
Olier, Jean-Jacques, Fr priest, 1608-1657 #1365
Olitski, Jules, Amer artist, 1922-
- and Emma Lake Workshops (Emma Lake, Sask) #1929
- Christensen, Dan, compared with #5104
- influence on Jean Albert McEwen #6471
- influence on Kenneth Lochhead #6315
Oliver, Bobbie, Can artist, 1943- #675
- exhibitions, group
  - (1980) #698
Olmsted, Frederick Law, Amer landscape architect, 1822-1903
- and Calvert Vaux #8048
- Montréal (Qué), Mount Royal Park #7903 7912 7924
Olson, Wilfred Harold, Can photographer, 1922-
- photographs of Canadian military forces #1107
Olympic Games
- 1976, Montréal (Qué)
  - *Corridart, Mosaicart,* and *Artisanage* street exhibitions #615
  - *Corridart* street exhibition #1522 1530
  - Danby, Ken, paintings and drawings of athletes #5252
  - designs #898 901 902 2625 5858
  - Olympic coins #778
  - posters #900
Omaha (Nebr), John Deere Plow Company Warehouse
- architecture, Oscar A. Eckerman #9247
Ondaatje, Kim, Can artist, 1928- #6733
- and Niagara Artists' Co-operative #834
- on quilt-making #2796 2798
Oneida Indians
- rattles #3363
Onley, Toni, Can artist, 1928- #6740 6742

– collages #6735
– exhibitions
    – (1972) #6736
    – (1978) #6739
– exhibitions, group
    – (1976) #613
– on trip to Japan (1978) #6738
– prints (1963-1974) #6737
– watercolours (1974-1981) #6741
Only Paper Today, Can periodical #1799
Onondaga Indians
– masks #3588
Ontario
– architectural drawings #8028
– architectural education (1890s) #8239
– architecture #8017 8024
    – 17th-19th cs. #7687
    – 19th c. #5959 7959 7974 7993 8006 8015
      8023 8672
    – (1763-1930) #7659
    – (1800-1855) #8014
    – (1831-1861) #8009
    – (1901-1911), Ontario Association of
      Architects #7955
    – (1920s) #7657 8223
    – (pre-1880), Rideau Corridor #8008
    – and Ontario Heritage Foundation #8001
    – hollow-wall construction, 19th c. #8004
    – Jerome Markson Architects #8386 8387
    – log buildings, French-Canadian settlers,
      19th c. #7685
    – mid-19th–20th cs. #8030
    – Neo-classical #7983
    – polygonal buildings, 19th c. #7987
    – stone buildings, 19th c. #8011
    – use of building and ornamental stones
      (1910s) #7646 7647
    – wooden, 19th c. #7745
– architecture and decorative arts
  (1800-1850) #7965
– art #8943
    – (1840s-1870s) #28
    – (1850s) #1691
    – (1870s-1970s) #1666
    – (1880-1930s) #45
    – (1880s) #1698
    – (1940s) #350 381
    – (1940s-1970s) #1670
    – (1950s) #429
    – (1960s) #492
    – (1970s) #38 543 590 625 1806 1814 1816
      1825
    – (1979-1981), northern Ontario #1829
    – (1981) #1838
    – (pre-1867) #2110
    – French-speaking Ontario #1820 1821
    – late 19th c. #1726
– art education (1856) #3128
– art societies, 19th c. #1706
– artisans, 19th c. #2261
– barns, 19th c. #9227 9229
– beds, 19th c. #2562
– board games, 19th-20th cs. #2597
– books (1970s) #935
– chairs #2560
    – 19th c. #2575
    – (1790s-1850) #2553
    – (1790s-1870s) #2564
– chests #2554 2557
– churches #8906
    – 17th c.-1860s #8904
    – (1960s) #8765
    – (pre-1867) #8904
– clocks #2925

– conservation of architecture #7996
– costume
    – 19th c. #2888
    – (1780-1867), female #2839
    – (1784-1867) #2852
    – (1867-1907) #2871
    – (1867-1907), female #2843
– courthouses, 19th-early 20th cs. #9010
– cupboards #2574
– decorative arts
    – 19th c. #2099
    – (1900) #2240
    – (1920s-1960s), Canadian Handicrafts
      Guild #2118
    – (1970s) #2247 2596
    – (1970s-1980s) #2257
    – (1979-1980) #2138
    – artisans and sales outlets (1970s) #2256
    – Germanic tradition #2135 2140 2263
    – Mennonite #2251 2264 2267
– desks #2579
– domestic architecture #7968 8654
    – 19th c. #8002 8005 8656 8677 8678 8679
    – (1763-1860) #8527
    – (1784-1840) #7966
    – (1910s) #8642
    – (1920s) #8497 8646
    – (1930s) #8647
    – brick houses, early 19th c. #8521
    – early 19th c. #8648
    – plankwall framing, 19th c. #8046
    – summer homes (1940s) #8651
    – summer homes and resorts, 20th c.
      #8524
    – terrace houses (1850s-1950s) #8653
– farm buildings (1920s) #9225
– folk art #1682
    – (1960s) #1792
– fortifications #8454
– fraktur #2254 2255 2259
– furniture
    – 18th-19th cs. #2474 2475
    – 19th c. #2552 2556 2561 2570 2571 2573
    – 19th c.-1920s #2463
    – (1760-1840), Georgian #2477
    – (1790s-1850s) #2550
    – (1790s-1857) #2558
    – (1800-1837), Upper Canada Village
      (Morrisburg, Ont) #2549
    – (1800-1865) #2563
    – (1800-1867) #2567
    – (1850-1900) #2580
    – (1860s), Polish settlers #2565
    – (1920s) #2547
    – (1950s) #2467
    – imports, 18th-19th cs. #2569
    – Mennonite #2568 2572
– glass
    – 19th c. #2401 2416 2421
    – (1825-1948) #2399
– glass and pottery (1970s) #2262
– graphic arts
    – (1960s) #1756
    – Society of Painter-Etchers and Engravers
      #3
– hospitals (1950s) #9029
– ironwork
    – 19th c. #2703
    – German-Alsatian iron funeral crosses
      #2709
– lamps #2918
    – 19th c. #2947
– libraries
    – (1950s) #9044

– (1955-1965) #9045
– log cabins #7990
    – 19th c. #7979
– mills #9239
    – (1780s-1880s) #9259
– painting #1676
    – 19th c. #1705
    – (1846-1867), Upper Canada provincial
      exhibitions #1715
    – (1860s-1880s) #230
    – (1920s-1950s) #396
    – (1930s) #589 592
    – (1960s) #484
    – (1970s) #588
– paperwork, Mennonite, 19th-early 20th cs.
  #2265
– photographic views
    – Esson, James #5373
    – Jaycocks, T.G. #5950
– photography
    – 19th c. #1722 1730
    – (1856-1867) #1724
– pioneer and frontier life #2245
– portraits
    – 19th c. #263
– pottery #2249 2317
    – 18th-19th cs. #2318
    – 19th c. #2279 2284 2286 2290 2302 2303
      2309 2330 2334 2335 2348 2350 2356
    – 19th-early 20th cs. #2347 2355
    – (1750-1910) #3962
    – (1796-1930s) #2349
– quilts #2796 2797 2801 2806
    – 19th c. #2804 2805
– railroad stations #9541
– rugs, 19th c. #2754
– samplers #2787
– schools
    – (1920s) #9450
    – (1950s) #9391 9392
    – (1960s) #9395
– schools and universities (1960s) #9401
– sculpture
    – (1960s) #749
– sepulchral monuments
    – 18th c.-1930s #1669
    – 19th c.-1910s #1723
    – late 18th c.-19th cs. #1721
– shopping centres (1950s) #9373
– silver
    – 18th-19th cs. #2627 2636
    – 19th-20th cs. #2638
– stoneware #2324
– stores
    – 19th-20th cs. #9379
    – (1940s) #9372
– synagogues (1960s) #8903
– tables #2566
    – (1815-1845), drop-leaf tables #2555
– tapestry (1970s) #2768
– telephone buildings (1880s-1950s) #9298
– textiles #2249 2729
    – 19th c. #2723 2726
    – (1750-1900) #2727
– treenware #2590
– views
    – 18th-20th cs. #156
    – 19th c. #1720
    – (1890s) #6436
    – Armstrong, William #4552
    – Bartram, Ed #4618
    – Bouchard, Lorne Holland #4857
    – Brigden, Fred #4913
    – Brooks, Leonard #4929

- Lismer, Arthur #6298
- MacDonald, J.E.H. #6361
- Martin, Henry Byam #6426
- Nevitt, Richard Barrington #6688
- Price, Addison Winchell #6935
- Reynolds, Catherine #6993
- Schaefer, Carl Fellman #7151 7153 7157
- Shanly, Charles Dawson #241 242
- Simcoe, Elizabeth Posthuma Gwillim #7212
- Varley, Frederick Horsman #7462
- wreaths, 19th c. #2248
Ontario. Government of Ontario
- Morris, Edmund Montague, commissioned Indian portraits (1906-1907) #6636 6638
Ontario. Government of Ontario Art Collection #8943
- policies and purchases (1873-1914) #1728
Ontario. Niagara Parks Commission
- (1940s) #7975
Ontario. Royal Commission on Education in Ontario
- recommendations (1950) #9392
Ontario Advisory Committee on University Affairs
- and Ontario College of Art (Toronto, Ont), (1968) #2996 2997
Ontario Arts Council
- (1960s) #529
- Creative Artists in School program (1970s) #3004
- economic aspects of arts in Ontario report (1972) #1802
- report on French-speaking Ontario (1977) #1820 1821
Ontario Association of Architects
- (1889-1954) #8300
- (1890-1950) #8299
- (1908), convention proceedings #8292
- and architecture practice, Toronto (Ont), 19th c. #8070
- and National Gallery of Canada (Ottawa, Ont) competition (1975-1977) #9126
- and Toronto Society of Architects #7956
- exhibitions
    - (1930) #1
- exhibitions (reviews)
    - (1926) #7958
    - (1927) #7960
    - (1929) #7964
    - (1931) #7967
    - (1933) #7969
    - (1935) #7971 7972
    - (1937) #7973
- on architectural education (1890s) #8239
- Proceedings
    - (1901-1911) #7955
    - Construction: A Journal for the Architectural Engineering and Contracting Interests of Canada #7641
Ontario Craft, Can periodical #2257
Ontario Crafts Council
- periodical, Ontario Craft #2257
Ontario Government Housing Competition
- (1936) #8737
Ontario Handweavers and Spinners
- (1956-1979) #2743
Ontario Heritage Foundation
- and conservation #8001
Ontario Historical Society
- and conservation of Old Fort York (Toronto, Ont), (1905-1909) #8458
Ontario Housing Corporation Design Competition
- (1972) #8663
Ontario Hydro Golden Medallion "All Electric Home" Competition
- (1961) #8514
Ontario Institute of Painters
- exhibitions (reviews)
    - (1959) #432
Ontario Ministry of Natural Resources
- Fort William (Ont), restoration #8460
Ontario Pottery
- see Don Bridge Pottery
Ontario Society for Education through Art
- and Visual Arts Ontario #1806
Ontario Society of Artists #5 14
- (1872-1898) #1706
- (1872-1947) #1672
- (1872-1972) #1679
- (1890s) #188
- (1907) #3299
- and Albert Angus Macdonald #6354
- and Alice A. Innes #5900
- and Charlotte Mount Brook Morrell Schreiber #7164
- and Daniel Fowler #5488
- and Frederic Marlett Bell-Smith #4668
- and Helen Frances Gregor #5656
- and James Wilson Morrice #6634
- and Mary Hiester Reid #6982
- and Ronald York Wilson #7594
- and Visual Arts Ontario #1806
- exhibitions
    - (1873-1970s) #1666
    - (1882), and George Agnew Reid #6977
    - (1882-1948), Canadian National Exhibition (Toronto, Ont) #1
    - (1883) #166
    - (1900) #2240
    - (1972) #1678
- exhibitions (reviews)
    - (1873) #1693
    - (1875) #1695
    - (1876) #1696
    - (1877) #1697
    - (1890) #1700
    - (1892-1893) #179
    - (1896) #1703
    - (1898) #1707
    - (1899) #1708
    - (1900) #1709
    - (1913) #1710
    - (1919) #1731
    - (1953), Ontario arrow-back chair, as subject for paintings #1770
    - (1955) #1748
- nationalism and landscape painting, late 19th c. #271 272
- organization of non-Canadian art exhibitions, Canadian National Exhibition (Toronto, Ont), (1905-1938) #107
- works, purchased by Government of Ontario Art Collection (1873-1914) #1728
Ontario St. Lawrence Development Commission
- and Upper Canada Village (Ont) #7982
Ontario Student Housing Corporation
- and student residences (1960s) #9467
Oonark, Jessie, Can artist, 1906- #4242 4260 4460 6743 6744
- exhibitions, group
    - (1970) #4220
- tapestry #4304
Op art
- see Optical art
open-air sculpture, Canadian
- (1960s) #742 750 766 769
- (1970s) #771 784 786
- (1980s) #797 1639
- British Columbia
    - (1956-1960) #1993
    - (1977) #2057
- Garnier, Hubert #5556
- Montréal (Qué), Expo '67 #7691 7692 9213
- Murray, Robert Gray #6672
- Ontario (1960s) #1587
- Poulin, Roland #706
- Prince, Richard #6936
- Québec (1960s) #1587
- Regina (Sask), (1970s) #1924
- Roussil, Robert, on #7093
- Royal Canadian Aerial Theatre (RCAT) #2058
- Toronto (Ont) #1834
- Trudeau, Yves #7432
- Turner, Richard Julian #7440
- Vancouver (BC) #2080
- Yuristy, Russell #7632
Opération déclic #1502
Ophthalmia Company of Inglis, Asessippi, Manitoba
- and Don Proch #6940
Opinion publique, L', Can periodical
- illustrations
    - Julien, Henri #5987
    - Kroupa, Bohuslav #6104
Oppenheim, Dennis, Amer artist, 1938-
- map images #561
OPT, Can periodical #1799
Optical art #468
- and Denis Juneau #5994
- and Norman McLaren #6497
- Canada #1445 6586
Opus International Ltd., design firm (Toronto, Ont)
- furniture, Hugh Spencer #2551
oral history
- and Canadian art #608
- use of, and Napoléon Bourassa #4873
- use of, Charles Marius Barbeau #3309
oratories, Canadian
- Montréal (Qué), oratoire Saint-Joseph #8332 8794
- Montréal (Qué), residence #8557
Orban, Jeno F., Can photographer, fl. 1970s
- portfolio of photographs #998
Orchinsky, Peter, Can collector, 20th c.
- collection, Bukovynian shirts and jewellery for women (1865-1945) #2869
Order of Architects of Quebec
- see Ordre des architectes du Québec/Order of Architects of Quebec
Ordre des architectes du Québec/Order of Architects of Quebec
- and Royal Architectural Institute of Canada (1974) #8318
- prix d'excellence en architecture
    - (1978) #7886
    - (1979) #9555
Oregon
- views
    - Miller, Alfred Jacob #6536 6537
    - Warre, Henry James #7522
organs, Canadian
- Jourdain (dit Labrosse), Paul-Raymond #249 250
- Morisset, Gérard, on #2952

– Québec #1237
Oriental art
– and art, Northwest Coast Indians #3359
– and Jack Leonard Shadbolt #7192
– and Raymonde Godin #5623
– and Robert Savoie #7139
– and Tom Mah #6409
– and Wayne G. Ngan #6696
– and William Perehudoff #6837
– animal motifs #3460
– Chinese sculpture, compared with Inuit
    sculpture #4394
– Persian rugs, and Gordon Rayner #6964
Orillia (Ont), Dominion Gallery
– and Joseph Julius Hümme #5863
Orono (Ont), Clarke Public Library
– exhibitions
    – Arthur A. Drummond, 1975 (1975) #5309
Orozco, José Clemente, Mexican artist,
    1883-1949
– and Stanley Morel Cosgrove #5178 5181
– as teacher of Stanley Morel Cosgrove
    #5180 5182 5184
– influence on Carol Fraser #5508
Orpen, William Newenham Montague, Brit
    artist, 1878-1931
– exhibitions, group
    – (1926) #1084
– Newton, Lilias Torrance, compared with
    #6692
Orwell Corner (PEI)
– restoration #7795
Osage Indians
– containers #3744
Osaka (Japan), Expo '70 (1970). Canadian
    Pavilion
– architecture
    – competition for #9217
    – Erickson/Massey #9224
    – Erickson, Arthur Charles #8356 8361
Osborne, Robert, Can silversmith, fl.
    1852-1869 #2638
Oshawa (Ont)
– art (1970s) #1826
Oshawa (Ont), 45 Hillsdale Manor Home for
    the Aged
– architecture, John B. Parkin Associates
    #8516
Oshawa (Ont), R.S. McLaughlin House
– mural, Frederick Sproston Challener #5068
Oshawa (Ont), Robert McLaughlin Gallery
– collection #3169
– exhibitions
    – 'Twas Ever Thus: A Selection of Eastern
        Canadian Folk Art (1979) #971
    – A Terrible Beauty: The Art of Canada at
        War (1977) #1111
    – Alan C. Collier Retrospective (1971) #5131
    – Alexandra Luke: A Tribute (1977) #6333
    – André Biéler 50 Years: A Retrospective
        Exhibition 1920-1970 (1971) #4725
    – Arthur A. Drummond, 1975 (1975) #5309
    – Beauté tragique: les deux conflits mondiaux
        vus par des artistes canadiens (1977) #1112
    – Canadian Artists of the Second World War
        (1981) #1116
    – Canadian Paintings in the University of
        Toronto: An Exhibition in Celebration of
        the Sesquicentennial of the University of
        Toronto (1978) #3168
    – Carol Fraser Paintings and Drawings:
        1967-1977 (1978) #5507
    – Dennis Burton Retrospective (1977) #4961

– Fernand Leduc (1971) #6186
– Five Years of Robert Downing, 1966-1971
    (1972) #5306
– Fourteen Artists of Durham Region (1979)
    #1826
– Franz Johnston, Frances-Anne Johnston,
    Paul Rodrik (1972) #5972
– Frederic Marlett Bell-Smith (1846-1923)
    (1978) #4668
– George Harlow White, R.C.A., 1817-1887
    (1975) #7550
– Gift from the Douglas M. Duncan
    Collection and the Milne-Duncan
    Bequest/Le Don provenant de la collection
    Douglas M. Duncan et le legs
    Milne-Duncan (1971) #541
– Gordon Rayner Retrospective (1979) #6966
– Graham Coughtry: Retrospective (1976)
    #5190
– Harold Town: The First Exhibition of New
    Work, 1969-1973 (1973) #7413
– Impressionism in Canada, 1895-1935 (1974)
    #115
– Ivan Eyre Exposition (1980) #5394
– Jock Macdonald's Students (1981) #6378
– Joe Fafard: Recent Sculpture (1980) #5401
– John Fox: 10 New Paintings (1980) #5495
– Lithographs/Lithographies (1972) #825
– Louis de Niverville (1978) #6709
– Neil Newton Retrospective (1978) #6694
– Of Human Bondage (1976) #611
– Painters Eleven, 1953-1959 (1972) #1771
– Painters Eleven in Retrospect (1979) #1785
– Ronald: 25 Years (1975) #7073
– Roy K. Kiyooka: 25 Years (1976) #6062
– The Heritage of Jack Bush: A Tribute (1981)
    #722
– The Objective Object (1976) #4936
– The Ontario Community Collects: A Survey
    of Canadian Painting from 1766 to the
    Present (1976) #120
– The Queen Comes to New Brunswick:
    Paintings and Drawings by Molly Lamb
    Bobak (1978) #4765
– Twelve Canadian Artists (1980) #698
– Viewpoint: Twenty-nine by Nine; An
    Exhibition of Twenty-nine Works by
    Ontario Artists, Selected by Nine Curators
    (1981) #1838
– Water Colours by E.May Martin (1980)
    #6424
– William Blair Bruce (1975) #4942
– Windows and Doorways: Susan Scott,
    Denise Therrien, Victoria Walker (1979)
    #676
– York Wilson Retrospective (1927-1973)
    (1974) #7596
– exhibitions (reviews)
    – 'Twas Ever Thus: A Selection of Eastern
        Canadian Folk Art (1979) #972
    – Alexandra Luke: A Tribute (1977) #6334
    – Gordon Rayner Retrospective (1979) #6964
    – Painters Eleven in Retrospect (1979) #720
        1786 1787
– Macdonald, Jock, documents #6376
Oshawa (Ont), Saint George's Anglican
    Church
– architecture, Eden Smith #8899
Oshaweetok, Aipellie
– see Osuitok, Ipeelee
Oshaweetok, Ipeelee
– see Osuitok, Ipeelee
Oshaweetok, Tukiki

– see Osuitok, Tuqiqi
Osipov, Lou, Can collector, 20th c.
– collection, Inuit sculpture #4447
Oslo (Norway), Universitets Etnografiske
– Netsilik artifacts, Roald Amundsen
    collection #4366
Osstidcho #1502
Ostell, John, Can architect, 1813-1892
– Montréal (Qué)
    – Church of Notre-Dame #8839
    – Customs House #7917
Ostiguy, Jean-René, Can curator, 1925-
– on Ozias Leduc #6211
Ostrom, David Walter, Can ceramicist, 1944-
    #2395
Osuitok, Aipellie
– see Osuitok, Ipeelee
Osuitok, Ipeelee, Can sculptor, 1923-
– exhibitions
    – (1980) #6745
Osuitok, Tuqiqi, Can artist, 1952- #6746
Otis, Serge, Can artist, 1938-
– interview #1485
Ott, Günter, Can photographer, fl. 1981
– portfolio of photographs #1023
Ottawa (Ont)
– architecture #8036
    – (1920s) #7656
    – (1950s) #7673
    – (1960s) #7698
    – (pre-1914) #8047
    – building stone (1850s) #8033
    – early 19th c. #8038
    – Glebe district #8042
    – Noffke, Werner Ernest #8393
– architecture and urban planning, National
    Capital Region #7683 8034 8035 8037 8039
    8041 8045
– art (1960s) #441
– conservation of architecture, National
    Capital Region #8043 8044
– domestic architecture
    – plankwall framing, 19th c. #8046
    – terrace houses, 19th c. #8653
– galleries (1960s) #442
– photographic views
    – (1850-1900) #1061
    – Topley, William James #1001
– photography #1675
    – (1896) #1704
    – (1896-1970) #1677
– recreation buildings #9081
– sculpture
    – (1890s) #727
    – National Capital Region #762
– views
    – (1807-1882), prints #1716
Ottawa (Ont), Baldwin-Lafontaine Memorial
– Allward, Walter Seymour #4516
Ottawa (Ont), Bank of Canada head office
    (1938)
– architecture, Marani, Lawson & Morris;
    Sumner Godfrey Davenport, Associated
    Architects #9337
Ottawa (Ont), Bank of Canada head office
    (1978)
– architecture, Marani, Rounthwaite & Dick;
    Arthur Erickson, Associated Architects
    #9199
Ottawa (Ont), Bank of Nova Scotia
– architecture, John MacIntosh Lyle #9186
    9203
Ottawa (Ont), Canada Council. Art

Bank/Conseil des Arts du Canada.
  Banque d'oeuvres d'art #625
– (1970s) #3293
  – and corporations #3286
– (1972-1975) #3276
– acquisitions (1972-1975) #576
– exhibitions
  – *Transparent Things: The Artist's Use of the
    Photograph/Transparences: l'utilisation de
    la photographie par l'artiste* (1977) #635
– influence on Canadian art (1970s) #3277
– influence on Canadian art market (1970s)
  #3236
– purchase of Canadian art #3273
– purchasing policy #3287
Ottawa (Ont), Canadian Centre for Folk
  Culture Studies
– *see* Ottawa (Ont), National Museum of
  Man. Canadian Centre for Folk Culture
  Studies/Musée national de l'Homme.
  Centre canadien d'études sur la culture
  traditionelle
Ottawa (Ont), Canadian Government
  Conference Centre/Centre de conférences
  du gouvernement canadien
– exhibitions
  – *A Display of Contemporary Canadian
    Works of Art Organized by the National
    Gallery of Canada, on the Occasion of the
    Commonwealth Heads of Government
    Meeting, 2-10 August 1973 at the
    Canadian Government Conference Centre,
    Ottawa/Exposition d'oeuvres canadiennes
    contemporaines, organisée par la Galerie
    nationale du Canada, à l'occasion de la
    réunion des chefs de gouvernement du
    Commonwealth, du 2 au 10 août, 1973*
    (1973) #556
  – *An Exhibition of Canadian Photography
    Produced by the Still Photography
    Division, National Film Board of Canada
    on the Occasion of the Commonwealth
    Heads of Government Meeting, Aug 2-10,
    1973/Une exposition de photographies
    canadiennes présentée par le Service de la
    photographie de l'Office national du film du
    Canada, à l'occasion de la Conférence des
    chefs de gouvernement du Commonwealth,
    2-10 août, 1973* (1973) #1002
  – *Photo Festival '74* (1974) #1009
– exhibitions (reviews)
  – *Photo Festival '74* (1974) #1008
– Reeves, John #6972
Ottawa (Ont), Canadian Medical Association
– collection, Canadian art #138
Ottawa (Ont), Canadian Museum of
  Civilization/Musée canadien des
  civilisations
– *see* Ottawa (Ont), National Museum of
  Man/Musée national de l'Homme
Ottawa (Ont), Canadian War
  Museum/Musée canadien de la guerre
– aviation paintings, World War II #1110
– Colville, Alex, drawings #5156
– Cullen, Maurice Galbraith, paintings #5215
– exhibitions
  – *A Terrible Beauty: The Art of Canada at
    War* (1980) #1111
  – *Aviation Paintings from the Art Collection
    of the Canadian War Museum* (1972)
    #1104
  – *Beauté tragique: les deux conflits mondiaux
    vus par des artistes canadiens* (1980) #1112
  – *Four War Artists/Quatre artistes de guerre*

  (1981) #1117
  – *Naval Paintings of the Second World
    War/Tableaux navals de la Seconde Guerre
    mondiale* (1973) #1106
  – *Tableaux de l'aviation militaire, provenant
    de la collection d'art du Musée de guerre
    canadien* (1972) #1105
– military uniforms #2910 2911
Ottawa (Ont), Canterbury High School
– art education (1970s) #3004
Ottawa (Ont), Capitol Theatre
– architecture #9110 9131
  – Lamb, Thomas White #9122 9123
Ottawa (Ont), Carleton University
– architecture, Watson Balharrie, Hart
  Massey, Eric Arthur, John Bland, and
  Campbell Merrett #9455
– art collection #3144
– exhibitions
  – *Canadian Printmakers' Showcase*
    (1969-1974) #823
Ottawa (Ont), Carleton University. Henry
  Marshall Tory Science Building
– mosaic mural, Gerald Mathew Trottier
  #7429
Ottawa (Ont), Carleton University. School of
  Architecture
– architectural education (1980) #8289
– architecture, Carmen Corneil in
  association with Schoeler Heaton
  Menendez #8284
Ottawa (Ont), Central Station
– architecture
  – Gilbert, Bradford Lee #9529
  – Gilbert, Bradford Lee; Ross &
    Macfarlane #9528
  – Ross & Macfarlane #9264
Ottawa (Ont), Champagne Hotel
– architecture #9480 9481
Ottawa (Ont), Château Laurier
– architecture #9265
  – Archibald, John Smith, and John
    Schofield #9282
  – Gilbert, Bradford Lee #9529
  – Gilbert, Bradford Lee; Ross &
    Macfarlane #9528
Ottawa (Ont), City Hall
– architecture, Rother/Bland/Trudeau #7679
  8984
Ottawa (Ont), Design Centre
– Bush, Robin B., as director #4979
Ottawa (Ont), Dominion Art Exhibition
– exhibitions (reviews)
  – (1880) #167
Ottawa (Ont), Earnscliffe
– architecture and interior #8652
Ottawa (Ont), Fisheries Building
– and National Gallery of Canada #275
Ottawa (Ont), Hall of Commerce Building
– exhibitions
  – *Visual Arts Ottawa Survey Exhibition no.
    1: The First Comprehensive Survey of the
    Visual Arts in Ottawa-Outaouais and the
    Valley/Arts visuels outaouais
    Expo-Inventaire no 1: premier inventaire
    des ressources artistiques outaouaises*
    (1975) #590
Ottawa (Ont), Hanlon House
– architecture, James William Strutt #7984
Ottawa (Ont), Heritage Canada. Gallery
– exhibitions
  – *The Architecture of W.E. Noffke* (1976)
    #8393
Ottawa (Ont), La Salle Academy

– architecture #9480 9481
Ottawa (Ont), Loew's Theatre
– architecture #9099
Ottawa (Ont), Metropolitan Life Insurance
  Building
– Jaworska, Tamara Hans, *Stream of Life*
  #5949
Ottawa (Ont), National Air Photo Library
  #1017
Ottawa (Ont), National Archives of
  Canada/Archives nationales du Canada
– *see* Ottawa (Ont), Public Archives of
  Canada/Archives publiques du Canada
Ottawa (Ont), National Arts Centre/Centre
  national des arts
– architecture #7709
– architecture and art #9104 9105 9108
– exhibitions
  – *Oonark/Pangnark* (1970) #4220
– mural, William S. Ronald #7074
– sculpture, Charles Daudelin #5261
– theatre curtain, Micheline Beauchemin
  #4644
Ottawa (Ont), National Film Board of
  Canada. Photo Gallery/Office national du
  film du Canada. Galerie de l'Image
– exhibitions
  – *The Female Eye/Coup d'oeil féminin* (1975)
    #1011
  – *Words and Images/Mots et images* (1980)
    #1063
– exhibitions (reviews)
  – *13 Cameras* (1979) #1044
  – *From an Icicle, I Made Winter* (1974)
    #1008
  – *Glass Dreams* (1974) #1008
  – *People of the Gaspé* (1974) #1008
  – *The Female Eye/Coup d'oeil féminin* (1975)
    #1013
  – *Winter Mood* (1974) #1008
Ottawa (Ont), National Film Board of
  Canada. Still Photography Division/Office
  national du film du Canada. Service de la
  photographie
– (1916-1977) #1043
– and Lorraine Monk #1020 1028
Ottawa (Ont), National Gallery of
  Canada/Galerie nationale du Canada
– (1870s), plans for a National Gallery of
  Paintings #1693
– (1870s-1883), documents #166
– (1880-1913) #3021 3022
– (1880-1921) #3041
– (1880-1966) #3050
– (1880-1970) #3049
– (1880-1980) #3061
– (1880s-1890s), plans for a national gallery
  #184
– (1882-1979), exhibitions #3063
– (1890s) #188
– (1920s) #288
– (1924), dispute with Royal Canadian
  Academy of Arts #500
– (1928-1929), exhibitions #307
– (1930s) #3025
– (1940s) #3027 3028
  – and art education #2983
  – criticism of nudes in art exhibited #6652
– (1941), Conference of Canadian Artists
  #351
– (1951), Royal Commission on National
  Development in the Arts, Letters and
  Sciences (Massey Report) #3254 3255 3256
– (1960s) #3039 3044

– (1970s) #3048 3102
– support of photography #1038
– (1979-1980), travelling exhibitions, Maritime region #3062
– and A.Y. Jackson #5925
– and Donald William Buchanan #3325
– and Edmond Dyonnet #5348
– and Emily Carr #5034
– and Federation of Canadian Artists #364
– and Homer Ransford Watson #7533
– and National Industrial Design Committee #2609
– and Royal Canadian Academy of Arts #275
– and Sir Byron Edmund Walker #3206
– architecture
  – Green, Blankstein, Russell & Associates #3035
– architecture, competition for
  – (1954) #9079
  – (1975-1977) #7747 9126 9136 9142
– Baltzly, Benjamin, photographs #4598
– Barnsley, James Macdonald, works #4613
– Berczy, William von Moll, *Woolsey Family* #4700
– Borduas, Paul-Emile
  – paintings #1266
  – *Sous le vent de l'île* #4815
– Brown, Eric, as director #3029 3032 3040
– Canadian art #3273
  – compared with University of Toronto. Hart House (Toronto, Ont) #3137
– *Canadian Design Index-NIDC* #2604 2606
– Canadian landscape drawing, early 20th c. #497
– Canadian painting and sculpture #3038
– Carr, Emily, *Blunden Harbour* #5036
– Colville, Alex, paintings #5144
– computerized inventory of collection #159
– Coverdale, William H., collection #3230
– Design Centre and *Canadian Design Index-NIDC* (1953-1954) #3033
– directors #3058
– Duncan, Douglas M., collection #119 570
– exhibitions
  – *"Our Own Country Canada"/"Notre patrie le Canada"* (1978) #264
  – *03 23 03: premières rencontres internationales d'art contemporain, Montréal 1977* (1977) #634
  – *7 West Coast Painters* (1959) #1997
  – *A.Y. Jackson: Paintings, 1902-1953* (1953) #5914
  – *A Display of Contemporary Canadian Works of Art Organized by the National Gallery of Canada, on the Occasion of the Commonwealth Heads of Government Meeting, 2-10 August 1973 at the Canadian Government Conference Centre, Ottawa/Exposition d'oeuvres canadiennes contemporaines, organisée par la Galerie nationale du Canada, à l'occasion de la réunion des chefs de gouvernement du Commonwealth, du 2 au 10 août, 1973* (1973) #556
  – *A Pageant of Canada/Pages d'histoire du Canada* (1967) #232
  – *Adrien Hébert: trente ans de son oeuvre, 1923-1953/Adrien Hébert: Thirty Years of His Art, 1923-1953* (1971) #5763
  – *Albert H. Robinson: Retrospective Exhibition* (1955) #7055
  – *Alfred Pellan* (1960) #6807
  – *Annual Exhibition of Canadian Art*

(1926-1933) #294
  – *Another Dimension/Une autre dimension* (1977) #783
  – *Antoine Plamondon, 1802-1895; Théophile Hamel, 1817-1870: Two Painters of Quebec/Antoine Plamondon, 1802-1895; Théophile Hamel, 1817-1870: deux peintres du Québec* (1970) #1348
  – *Arte indio y esquimal del Canada/Indian and Eskimo Art of Canada/Art indien et esquimau du Canada/Die Kunst der Indianer und Eskimos in Kanada* (1969) #3352
  – *Arthur Lismer: Paintings, 1913-1949* (1950) #6298
  – *Artists of Atlantic Canada/Artistes de la côte atlantique du Canada* (1966) #1123
  – *Atlantic Coast: An Illustrated Journal/Côte de l'Atlantique: un journal illustré* (1976) #1132
  – *Biennial of Canadian Painting/Biennale de la peinture canadienne* (1953-1968) #400
  – *Boucherville, Montréal, Toronto, London: 1973* (1973) #557
  – *Canadian Army Art Exhibition, 1945* (1945) #1096
  – *Canadian Army Art Exhibition* (1944) #1092
  – *Canadian Fine Crafts, 1966-67/L'artisanat canadien, 1966-67* (1966) #2106
  – *Canadian Group of Painters* (1933-1968) #324
  – *Canadian Outdoor Sculpture Exhibition 1962/Exposition en plein air de sculpture canadienne* (1962) #742
  – *Canadian Painting, 1850-1950/La peinture canadienne, 1850-1950* #86
  – *Canadian Painting in the Thirties* (1975) #592
    – use of oral documentation #608
  – *Canadian Portraits of the 18th and 19th Centuries/Portraits canadiens du 18e et 19e siècles* (1959) #219
  – Canadian Society of Painters in Water Colour (1934-1947) #6
  – *Canadian War Memorials Exhibition, 1919* (1919) #1078
  – *Canadian War Memorials Exhibition, 1920* (1920) #1080
  – *Canadian Water Colours and Graphics Today* (1959) #437
  – *Cape Dorset: A Decade of Eskimo Prints and Recent Sculptures* (1967) #4211
  – *Charles Gagnon* (1979) #5540
  – *Clarence A. Gagnon, R.C.A., LL.D., 1881-1942: Memorial Exhibition* (1942) #5542
  – *Claude Tousignant* (1973) #7401
  – *Daniel Fowler* (1965) #5489
  – *Daniel Fowler of Amherst Island, 1810-1894* (1979) #5491
  – *David Milne 1955-56* (1955) #6552
  – *Emily Carr: Her Paintings and Sketches* (1945) #5012
  – *Ernest Lawson, 1873-1939* (1967) #6176
  – *Eskimo Sculpture* (1955) #4387
  – *Everyman's Canada: Paintings and Drawings from the McCord Museum of McGill University* (1962) #223
  – *Exhibition of Canadian Painting by a Group of Selected Artists* (1935) #17
  – *Exhibition of Canadian Painting to Celebrate the Coronation of Her Majesty Queen Elizabeth II* (1953) #50

  – *Exhibition of Canadian War Art* (1945) #1097
  – *Exhibition of Canadian War Art* (1946) #1099
  – *Exhibition of Canadian War Memorials* (1923) #1081
  – *Exhibition of Contemporary Canadian Painting* (1936) #335
  – *Exhibition of Paintings by Cornelius Krieghoff, 1815-1872* (1934) #6086
  – *Exposition médailles Massey en architecture, 1961* (1961) #8209
  – *F.H. Varley: A Centennial Exhibition/F.H. Varley: une exposition centenaire* (1982) #7468
  – *F.H. Varley: Paintings, 1915-1954* (1954) #7463
  – *Five Painters from Regina: Bloore, Godwin, Lochhead, McKay, Morton/Cinq peintres de Regina: Bloore, Godwin, Lochhead, McKay, Morton* (1961) #1913
  – *Folk Painters of the Canadian West* (1958) #1846
  – *Fortin* (1964) #5474
  – *Frederick Arthur Verner 1836-1928: Paintings, Watercolours, Drawings/Frederick Arthur Verner 1836-1928: tableaux, aquarelles, dessins* (1976) #7484
  – *George Heriot: Painter of the Canadas/George Heriot: peintre des deux Canadas* (1979) #5786
  – *Gift from the Douglas M. Duncan Collection and the Milne-Duncan Bequest/Le Don provenant de la collection Douglas M. Duncan et le legs Milne-Duncan* (1971) #541
  – *Goodridge Roberts: A Retrospective Exhibition/Goodridge Roberts: une exposition rétrospective* (1970) #7045
  – *Greg Curnoe: rétrospective/Greg Curnoe: Retrospective* (1981) #5231
  – *Guido Molinari* (1976) #6588
  – *Henri Julien, 1851-1908: Memorial Exhibition* #5983
  – *In Memoriam: Capt. G.D. Pepper, 1903-1962* (1964) #6832
  – *J.E.H. MacDonald, R.C.A., 1873-1932* (1966) #6370
  – *J.W. Morrice, 1865-1924* (1965) #6625
  – *Jack Bush: A Retrospective/Rétrospective: Jack Bush* (1977) #4969
  – *Jack Shadbolt* (1970) #7182
  – *Jean-Paul Lemieux* (1967) #6231
  – *Jean-Paul Riopelle: Paintings and Sculpture/Jean-Paul Riopelle: peinture et sculpture* (1962) #7018
  – *Jock Macdonald: Retrospective Exhibition/Jock Macdonald: rétrospective* (1969) #6375
  – *John Hall: Paintings and Auxiliary Works, 1969-1978/John Hall: peintures et oeuvres auxiliaires, 1969-1978* (1979) #5683
  – *John Lyman* (1963) #6343
  – *John Vanderpant Photographs/John Vanderpant photographies* (1976) #7459
  – *Joseph Légaré, 1795-1855: l'oeuvre* (1978) #6217
  – *Joyce Wieland: Drawings for "The Far Shore"/Joyce Wieland: dessins pour "The Far Shore"* (1978) #7583
  – *L'art des étoffes: le filage et le tissage traditionnels au Canada* (1981) #2747
  – *L.L. FitzGerald, 1890-1956: A Memorial*

Exhibition 1958 (1958) #5448
– *L'orfèvrerie en Nouvelle-France* (1974) #2685
– *Lawren Harris: Retrospective Exhibition, 1963/Lawren Harris: exposition rétrospective, 1963* (1963) #5725
– *Le calvaire d'Oka* (1974) #1355
– *Léon Bellefleur* (1968) #4662
– *Les arts du Canada français, 1613-1870* (1946) #1331
– *Les dessins d'Alfred Pellan* (1980) #6824
– *Massey Medals for Architecture, 1961* (1961) #8210
– *Masterpieces of Indian and Eskimo Art from Canada/Chefs-d'oeuvre des arts indiens et esquimaux du Canada* (1969) #3351
– *Maurice Cullen, 1866-1934* (1956) #5221
– *Mountain: A Lithograph by James B. Spencer/Montagne: une lithographie de James B. Spencer* (1974) #7270
– *N.E. Thing Co. Ltd.* (1969) #6675
– *Norman White* (1975) #7554
– *Ozias Leduc: peinture symboliste et religieuse/Ozias Leduc: Symbolist and Religious Painting* (1974) #6206
– *Ozias Leduc 1864-1955* (1955) #6200
– *Paintings and Drawings from the Collection of J.S. McLean* (1952) #3210
– *Paul-Emile Borduas 1905-1960* (1962) #4809
– *Peintres du Québec: collection Maurice et Andrée Corbeil/Painters of Quebec: Maurice and Andrée Corbeil Collection* (1973) #3234
– *Peinture canadienne des années trente* (1975) #589
– *Pellan* (1972) #6816
– *People's Art: Naïve Art in Canada/L'art populaire: l'art naïf au Canada* (1973) #966
– *Pluralities: 1980/Pluralités: 1980* (1980) #699
– *Prudence Heward, 1896-1947: Memorial Exhibition* (1948) #5795
– *Quarante gravures de Rodolphe Duguay/Forty Woodcuts by Rodolphe Duguay* (1975) #5314
– *Reflections in a Quiet Pool: The Prints of David Milne* (1980) #6564
– *Reflets dans un miroir d'eau: estampes de David Milne* (1980) #6563
– *Robert Harris (1849-1919)* (1973) #5743
– *Robert W. Pilot Retrospective/Rétrospective Robert W. Pilot* (1968) #6872
– *Royal Canadian Air Force: Exhibition of Paintings and Drawings* (1944) #1093
– *Sarah Robertson 1891-1948: Memorial Exhibition* (1951) #7054
– *Silver in New France* (1974) #2686
– *Some Canadian Women Artists/Quelques artistes canadiennes* (1975) #591
– *The Arts of French Canada, 1613-1870* (1946) #1330
– *The Calvary at Oka* (1974) #1356
– *The Canadian Society of Painters in Water Colour: Retrospective Exhibition, 1926-1951* (1951) #394
– *The Comfortable Arts: Traditional Spinning and Weaving in Canada* (1981) #2748
– *The Development of Painting in Canada, 1665-1945/Le développement de la peinture au Canada, 1665-1945* (1945) #34
– *The Drawings of Alfred Pellan* (1980) #6825
– *The MacCallum Bequest of Paintings by Tom Thomson and Other Canadian Painters & The Mr. and Mrs. H.R. Jackman Gift of the Murals from the Late Dr. MacCallum's Cottage Painted by Some of the Members of the Group of Seven/Le legs MacCallum, peintures par Tom Thomson et par d'autres peintres canadiens & le don de M. et Mme. H.R. Jackman de panneaux décoratifs du chalet de feu le Dr. MacCallum peints par quelques-uns des membres du Groupe des Sept* (1969) #3229
– *The Mr. and Mrs. Jules Loeb Collection/La collection M. et Mme Jules Loeb* (1970) #3231
– *The Non-Figurative Artists' Association of Montreal/L'Association des artistes non-figuratifs de Montréal* (1960) #1415
– *The Vincent Massey Bequest: The Canadian Paintings/Legs Vincent Massey, peintures canadiennes* (1968) #3227
– *The Works of Joseph Légaré: 1795-1855* (1978) #6218
– *Thomas Davies, c.1737-1812* (1972) #5272
– *Three Hundred Years of Canadian Art: An Exhibition Arranged in Celebration of the Centenary of Confederation/Trois cents ans d'art canadien: exposition organisée à l'occasion du centenaire de la Confédération* (1967) #85
– *Toronto Painting: 1953-1965/La Peinture torontoise 1953-1965* (1972) #1772
– *Traditional Landscape Painting in Canada/Le paysage dans la peinture canadienne* (1968) #88
– *Treasures from Quebec: An Exhibition of Paintings Assembled from Quebec and Its Environs/Trésors de Québec: exposition de peintures provenant de Québec et des environs* (1965) #1344
– *True Patriot Love/Veritable amour patriotique* (1971) #7577
– *Une imagerie canadienne: peinture et dessins du musée McCord de l'Université McGill* (1962) #222
– *Walter J. Phillips: A Selection of His Works and Thoughts/Walter J. Phillips: un choix de son oeuvre et de ses réflexions* (1978) #6860
– *Watercolour Painters from Saskatchewan/Aquarellistes de la Saskatchewan* (1971) #1920
– *William Brymner, 1855-1925: A Retrospective/William Brymner, 1855-1925: aperçu rétrospectif de l'artiste* (1979) #4953
– exhibitions (reviews)
– *300 Years of Canadian Art: An Exhibition Arranged in Celebration of the Centenary of Confederation/Trois cents ans d'art canadien: exposition organisée à l'occasion du centenaire de la Confédération* (1967) #488
– *Biennial Exhibition of Canadian Art* (1957) #420
– *Biennial Exhibition of Canadian Painting* (1955) #410
– *Canadian Army Art Exhibition* (1944) #1089
– *Cent onze dessins du Québec/One Hundred and Eleven Drawings from Québec* (1976) #1520
  – Parent, Alain, on #1523
– *Claude Tousignant* (1973) #7400
– *Design in Industry* (1947) #2602
– Dumouchel, Albert #5333
– Frenkel, Vera #5520
– *Greg Curnoe: rétrospective/Greg Curnoe: Retrospective* (1981) #5233
– *Guido Molinari* (1976) #6585
– *John Hall: Paintings and Auxiliary Works, 1969-1978/John Hall: peintures et oeuvres auxiliaires, 1969-1978* (1979) #5684
– *L'orfèvrerie en Nouvelle-France* (1974) #2688
– MacAulay, John, collection of Canadian and European art (1954) #3212
– *Maurice Cullen, 1866-1934* (1956) #5224
– *Ozias Leduc: peinture symboliste et religieuse/Ozias Leduc: Symbolist and Religious Painting* (1974) #6207
– *Peintres du Québec: collection Maurice et Andrée Corbeil/Painters of Quebec: Maurice and Andrée Corbeil Collection* (1973) #3233
– *People's Art: Naïve Art in Canada/L'art populaire: l'art naïf au Canada* #964
– *Pluralities: 1980/Pluralités: 1980* (1980) #691
– second annual exhibition of Canadian art (1927) #298
– *Second Exhibition of Canadian War Art* (1946) #1098
– *Some Canadian Women Artists/Quelques artistes canadiennes* (1975) #579
– *The Development of Painting in Canada, 1665-1945/Le développement de la peinture au Canada, 1665-1945* (1945) #32
– *The Drawings of Alfred Pellan* (1980) #6823
– *The Works of Joseph Légaré: 1795-1855* (1978) #6221
– *Three Hundred Years of Canadian Art: An Exhibition Arranged in Celebration of the Centenary of Confederation/Trois cents ans d'art canadien: exposition organisée à l'occasion du centenaire de la Confédération* (1967) #80
– *Toronto Painting: 1953-1965/La peinture torontoise 1953-1965* (1972) #1773 1775
– *True Patriot Love/Véritable amour patriotique* (1971) #7576
– Field, Robert, portrait of Provo William Parry Wallis #5430 5431
– Group of Seven and Tom Thomson, mural paintings, from James MacCallum house (near Go Home Bay, Ont) #1745
– Jackson, A.Y., sketchbook (1909) #5924
– Jackson, Henry Alexander Carmichael, watercolour paintings of mushrooms #5927 5928
– Krieghoff, Cornelius, paintings of life on Québec farms #6100
– Laliberté, Alfred, sculptures #6147
– Leduc, Ozias, paintings #1266
– Lewis, Wyndham, *A Canadian Gunpit* #6279
– Liechtenstein collection #3035
– Lismer, Arthur, *A September Gale, Georgian Bay* #6304
– MacDonald, J.E.H., sketchbooks #6373
– Marion, Salomon, Immaculate Conception statue #2683
– McCurry, Harry Orr, as director #3036
– Milne, David Brown, *Painting Place* #6562
– Montreal Museum of Fine Arts (Montréal, Qué), compared with #3099
– Morrice, James Wilson, sketchbooks #6632
– mural paintings, from Hall-Croscup House (near Granville Ferry, NS) #1223

– Patterson, Dan, Carnation Milk cans construction #962
– Pellan, Alfred, portraits #6814
– periodical, *National Gallery of Canada. Annual Bulletin/Galerie nationale du Canada. Bulletin annuel* #69
– Plamondon, Antoine-Sébastien, portrait of Sister Saint-Alphonse #6887
– Ranvoyzé, François, chalices #2680
– silver, Henry Birks Collection of Canadian Silver #2653
    – Canadian presentation silver #2656
– Suzor-Coté, Marc-Aurèle de Foy, *Paysage d'hiver* #7301
– Thomson, Tom, *The Jack Pine* #7369
– Viau, Guy, as assistant director #7485
– Wallis, Katherine Elizabeth, *La lutte pour la vie* #7512
– war art collections
    – World War I, Canadian
        – War Memorials Collection #1102
    – World War I and World War II #1101
    – World War II #1103
Ottawa (Ont), National Library of Canada/Bibliothèque nationale du Canada
– engraved glass panels, John Hutton #5894
– exhibitions
    – *Albert Laberge, 1871-1960; Charles Gill, 1871-1918* #5604
    – *Pictures to Share: Illustration in Canadian Children's Books: Annotated Catalogue/Images pour tous: illustration de livres canadiens pour enfants: catalogue annoté* (1979) #937
Ottawa (Ont), National Museum of Man/Musée national de l'Homme
– and Royal Commission on National Development in the Arts, Letters and Sciences (Massey Report) #3254 3255
– architecture, Thompson, Berwick, Pratt & Partners #8041
– art, Indians of North America #3408 3452
    – Speyer collection #3622
– art, Kwakiutl, returned to Kwakiutl Indians #3060
– art, Tsimshian Indians #3926
– artifacts, Dorset #4322
– artifacts, Thule #4372
– basketry, Micmac Indians #3630
– Canadian birdhouses #2593
– coppers, Northwest Coast Indians #3924
– coverlets, Charlevoix County (Qué) #2738
– exhibition spaces (1976) #3057
– exhibitions
    – *"Bo'jou, Neejee!": Profiles of Canadian Indian Art* (1976) #3466
    – *"Bo'jou, Neejee!": regards sur l'art indien du Canada* (1976) #3465
    – *Canadian Political Cartoons* (1977) #956
    – *Continuity and Change: The Ukrainian Folk Heritage in Canada* (1972) #961
    – *L'art assure notre survivance/We Still Live in Our Art* (1971) #2117
    – *La chaîne d'alliance: l'orfèvrerie de traite et de cérémonie chez les Indiens* (1980) #3645
    – *Les Athabascans, ces étrangers du Nord: une exposition itinérante formée des collections du Musée national de l'Homme (Canada) et du Royal Scottish Museum* (1974) #4104
    – *Quebec Furniture, 1700-1820/Le mobilier québécois, 1700-1820* (1973) #2537
    – *Sculpture of the Inuit: Masterworks of the Canadian Arctic/La sculpture chez les Inuit: chefs-d'oeuvre de l'Arctique canadien* (1973) #4423 4440
    – *The Art of Nunstins/L'art de Nunstins* (1981) #6934
    – *The Athapaskans: Strangers of the North; An International Travelling Exhibition from the Collection of the National Museum of Man, Canada, and the Royal Scottish Museum* (1974) #4105
    – *The Covenant Chain: Indian Ceremonial and Trade Silver* (1980) #3646
    – *The Inuit Print/L'estampe inuit* (1977) #4490
– exhibitions (reviews)
    – *The Inuit Print/L'estampe inuit* (1977) #4493
– furniture #2484
– Jesuit religious articles #2192
– Jobin, Louis, sculptures #5967
– mask, Tsimshian Indians #4069
– masks, Bella Coola Indians #4000
– Ontario quilts, Ruth McKendry collection #2804
– Pitseolak, Peter, watercolours #6875 6877
– puppets, Tsimshian Indians #3891
– Québec, moulds #2916
– sacrificial stone, Nahuas, authenticity questioned #4094
– sculpture, Inuit #4417 4437
– spinning wheels #2483
– St-Germain, Arthème, sculptures #962
Ottawa (Ont), National Museum of Man. Canadian Centre for Folk Culture Studies/Musée national de l'Homme. Centre canadien d'études sur la culture traditionnelle
– Canadian folk art #963 969
Ottawa (Ont), National Museums of Canada/Musées nationaux du Canada
– (1840-1969) #3047
– and Art Bank (1970s) #3277
Ottawa (Ont), National Science Library
– architecture and art #9049
Ottawa (Ont), Northern Electric Research and Development Laboratories
– architecture, Bland, Lemoyne & Edwards and Charles Elliott Trudeau #9344
Ottawa (Ont), Ottawa Civic Centre
– architecture, Gerald Hamilton & Associates; Craig & Kohler #9101
Ottawa (Ont), Ottawa International Airport. Air Terminal Building
– architecture, Gilleland & Strutt and William Alexander Ramsay #9515
Ottawa (Ont), Ottawa Public Library
– exhibitions
    – *Hooked Rugs: A Canadian Tradition* (1975) #2755
Ottawa (Ont), Parliament Buildings
– architecture #7695 8930 8931 8932
    – as national style #7697
    – Darling & Pearson; Joseph-Omer Marchand, Associate Architect #8926
    – Fuller, Thomas #7671 8366
        – influence on post offices, 19th c. #9054 9055
    – Fuller & Jones #8922
    – Pearson, John Andrew, and Joseph-Omer Marchand #8927
    – use of hollow-wall construction, 19th c. #8004
– architecture, competition for
    – Foulis, James #8923

– Sproatt & Rolph #8924
– Harris, Robert, *The Fathers of Confederation* #5736
– ironwork, Paul Beau #4640 4641
– landscape architecture, Calvert Vaux #8048
– photographs of buildings being built #1019
– sculptures #755
– sculptures and stained glass windows, Eleanor Milne #6568
– Soldiers' Memorial Windows, Gladys W. Allen and F.S.J. Hollister #2445
Ottawa (Ont), Parliament Buildings. Central Block
– destruction (1916) #8925
Ottawa (Ont), Parliament Buildings. Departmental and Justice Buildings
– architecture, competition for #8921
Ottawa (Ont), Parliament Buildings. East Block (formerly Departmental Buildings)
– architecture #8936
    – Stent & Laver #8922
    – architecture and interior #8933 8934
    – architecture and renovation #8935
Ottawa (Ont), Parliament Buildings. Peace Tower and Memorial Chamber
– architecture and interior, John Andrew Pearson #8928 8929
Ottawa (Ont), Place Bell Canada
– Jaworska, Tamara Hans, *Unity* #5949
Ottawa (Ont), Place de Ville
– architecture and urban development #9302
Ottawa (Ont), Public Archives of Canada/Archives publiques du Canada
– architectural archives #7738
– collection (1925) #3023
– Coverdale, William H., Collection of Canadiana #12 3230
– engraved glass panels, John Hutton #5894
– exhibitions
    – *City Blocks, City Spaces: Historical Photographs of Canada's Urban Growth, c.1850-1900/Espaces urbains: photographies historiques de la croissance urbaine au Canada, vers 1850-1900* (1980) #7744
        – Koltun, Lilly, on #1061
    – *Daily Smile/Sourire quotidien* (1980) #6401
    – *Dans le silence et la solitude: la photographie d'arpentage dans l'Ouest canadien (1858-1900)* (1975) #1014
    – *Exposition d'estampes en l'honneur de C. Krieghoff, 1815-1872/Exhibition of Prints in Honour of C. Krieghoff, 1815-1872* (1972) #6096
    – *Friendly Spies on the Northern Tour, 1815-1837: The Sketches of Henry Byam Martin/Aimables espions en Amérique du Nord, 1815-1837: croquis d'Henry Byam Martin* (1981) #6426
    – *Image of Canada: Documentary Watercolours and Drawings from the Permanent Collection of the Public Archives of Canada/Visage du Canada: aquarelles et dessins historiques tirés de la collection permanente des Archives publiques du Canada,* #244
    – *Into the Silent Land: Survey Photography in the Canadian West (1858-1900)* (1975) #1015
    – *Karl May Retrospective, 1948-1975/Rétrospective Karl May 1948-1975* (1976) #6453
    – *Napoléon Bourassa, 1827-1916* (1976) #4872

– *Neil Newton Retrospective* (1978) #6694
– *Printmaking in Canada: The Earliest Views and Portraits/Les débuts de l'estampe imprimée au Canada: vues et portraits* (1980) #839
– *Reflections on a Capital: 12 Ottawa Photographers, Selected from the National Photographic Collection in the Public Archives of Canada/Reflets d'une capitale: 12 photographes d'Ottawa, choix tiré de la Collection nationale de photographies aux Archives publiques du Canada* (1970) #1675
– *Seventy-five Years of Photography, 1896 to 1970* (1971) #1677
– *Ten Contemporary Canadian Medallists/Dix médailleurs canadiens contemporains* (1971) #772
– Heriot, George, works #5785
– Miller, Alfred Jacob, paintings #6536 6537
– Moodie, Geraldine, photographs #6602
– Warre, Henry James, works #7522
– watercolours and drawings (1750-1850) #239
Ottawa (Ont), Public Archives of Canada. National Photography Collection/Archives publiques du Canada. Collection nationale de photographies #3052
– as model for Yukon Archives photography collection #2087
– Baltzly, Benjamin, photographs #4598
– Fleming, Sandford, collection #1876
– Hime, Humphrey Lloyd, photographs #5803
– Mitchell, Thomas, and George Harlow White, photographs, British Arctic Expedition (1875-1876) #240
– Nakash, George, portrait photographs #6683
– photographs of immigrants (1908-1910) #1031
Ottawa (Ont), Public Archives of Canada. Picture Division/Archives publiques du Canada. Division de l'iconographie
– costume illustrations #2883 2884 2904
– standards for description of works of art #159
Ottawa (Ont), Rideau Canal Lock Station
– architecture #8019
Ottawa (Ont), Rideau Hall
– architecture #8755 8756
Ottawa (Ont), Robertson Galleries
– exhibitions
– *Eskimo Sculpture, '69* (1969) #4418
– exhibitions (reviews)
– Tagoona, Armand #7311
Ottawa (Ont), Royal Engineers' Office
– architecture #8019
Ottawa (Ont), Russell Opera House
– mural, Frederick Sproston Challener #5068
Ottawa (Ont), Saint Basil's Roman Catholic Church
– architecture, Bemi, Murray & Associates #8765
Ottawa (Ont), Saint-Maurice Roman Catholic Church
– architecture, Murray & Murray #8766
Ottawa (Ont), Saint Michael and All Angels Church
– architecture, Edward J. Cuhaci #8766
Ottawa (Ont), Sussex Annex Works
– exhibitions
– *Contemporary Canadian Poster Art from*

1960 to the Present (1976) #903
Ottawa (Ont), Thomas Donnelly House
– architecture #9480 9481
Ottawa (Ont), Tovell House
– architecture, Massey & Flanders #8519
Ottawa (Ont), University of Ottawa
– architecture, James A. Murray #9458 9465
Ottawa (Ont), University of Ottawa. School of Architecture
– architectural education (1976) #7728
Ottawa (Ont), Uplands Airport
– sculpture, Louis Archambault #4542
Ottawa (Ont), Veteran Affairs Building
– exhibitions
– *World War II Paintings from the War Collections of the National Gallery of Canada/Tableaux de la Seconde Guerre mondiale: collections de guerre de la Galerie nationale du Canada* (1970) #1103
Ottawa (Ont), Wallack Galleries
– exhibitions
– *New Paintings by Otto Rogers* (1974) #7062
Ottawa (Ont), War Memorial area
– architecture, Hart Massey #8041
Ottawa Camera Club (Ottawa, Ont)
– exhibitions
– (1971) #1677
– exhibitions (reviews)
– (1896) #1704
Ottawa Glass Works, glass manufacturer (Vaudreuil, Qué) #2418
Ottawa Indians
– art, 17th-18th cs. #3579
– basketry #3547
– quillwork #3548
– wampum #3501
Ottawa Little Theatre (Ottawa, Ont)
– stage designs, Stan White #7555
Ottawa Valley (Ont)
– art (1970s) #590
– views
– Masson, Henri L. #6442
– wooden architecture #8029
Otto, Frei, Ger architect, 1925-
– Montréal (Qué), Expo '67. West German Pavilion #9218
Ouellet, Angémil, Can artist, 1936- #1546
Ouellet, David, Can architect, 1844-1915
– architecture, Church of Saint-Augustin-de-Desmaures #8889
Ouellet, Gaétan, Can artist, 1948- #640
Ouellet, Jean, Can architect, 1922-
– on architecture #7746
Ouellet, Joseph-Pierre, Can architect, 1872-1959 #8394
Ouellet Reeves Alain, Can architectural firm
– Montréal (Qué), Les Ilots Saint-Martin, La Petite Bourgogne #8520
outdoor sculpture
– see open-air sculpture
Overbeck, Johann Friedrich, Ger artist, 1789-1869
– influence on Napoléon Bourassa #4874
Overton, George, Can artist, b. 1880
– influence on Caven Ernest Atkins #4570
OVO, Can periodical #997 999 3314
Owen Sound (Ont), Tom Thomson Memorial Gallery and Museum of Fine Art
– collection #3146
– exhibitions
– *Centennial Exhibition of Quebec and Ontario Contemporary Painters, 1967*

(1967) #484
– *Goodridge Roberts: Paintings from the 1950s and 60s* (1981) #7048
– *Of Human Bondage* (1976) #611
– *The Ontario Community Collects: A Survey of Canadian Painting from 1766 to the Present* (1976) #120
Owidzka, Jolanta, Polish artist, 1927-
– tapestry, National Arts Centre (Ottawa, Ont) #9108
Oxford (England), Oxford University. Ashmolean Museum
– art, Indians of North America #3422
– influence on Frederic William Cumberland #9475
Oxford (England), Oxford University. Pitt Rivers Museum
– buffalo hair bag, Indians of North America #3398
– Inuit art, 19th c. #4369
– Piegan leggings #3715
– totem poles, Haida Indians #3775

P

Pachter, Charles, Can artist, 1942-
– and Charles Pachter Graphics #834
– interview #6748
Pacific coast (Canada)
– views #139
Pacific Great Eastern Railway
– railroad stations #9545
Page, J.R., Can artist, fl. 1864-1865
– animal portraits #1727
Page, James Ritchey, Can photographer, 1938-
– portfolio of photographs #1023
Pagé, Lewis, Can sculptor, 1931-
– *Dispute philosophique* #6750
Page, Patricia Kathleen, Can artist, 1916- #6751
– exhibitions, group
– (1978) #649
Page, Robin, Can artist, 1932- #6752
Page & Steele, Can architectural firm
– Scarborough (Ont), University of Toronto. Scarborough College #9396 9462 9463 9464
– Toronto (Ont)
– Canadian Bank of Commerce #9351
– Commerce Court #9350
– O'Keefe Centre for the Performing Arts #9087
Page & Warrington, Can architectural firm
– Toronto (Ont)
– domestic architecture #8493
– National Cash Register #9234
Pagé (*dit* Quercy or Carcy), Jacques, Can silversmith, watchmaker, 1682-1742 #249 250 6749
– as apprentice of Michel Levasseur #2669
Paillard (*dit* Le Poitevin), Léonard, Can builder, 1647-1729 #234 235
Pailthorpe, Grace Winifred, Brit artist, psychiatrist, 1890-1971
– influence on Jock Macdonald #6377
Painchaud, Fabien, Can carriage-maker, fl. 1842 #1301
Paine, Arthur James Carman, Can architect, 1886-1965
– Montréal (Qué), McGill University. Athletic buildings, competition #9417

paint
– see pigments
Painter, Walter Scott, Can architect, b. 1877
– Montréal (Qué), Windsor Station #9532
– Québec (Qué), Château Frontenac,
    extension #9261
Painters Eleven #97 476 489 512 1752 1760
    1769 1787
– and Alexandra Luke #3169 6333 6334
– and Jack Hamilton Bush #4975
– and Jock Macdonald #6375
– and nationalism in art #495
– and Oscar Cahén #4986
– compared with plasticiens #720
– exhibitions
    – (1958) #429 1751
    – (1972) #1771
    – (1980) #1785
– exhibitions (reviews)
    – (1959) #432
    – (1979) #1786
– influence on Toronto (Ont) painting
    (1950s-1960s) #1772
painting
– see also china painting; genre; glass
    painting; hard-edge; history painting;
    landscape; lyrical abstraction; marine
    painting; media and techniques, painting;
    miniatures; mural painting; naive
    painting; portraits; Precisionism; Tachism;
    trompe-l'oeil; watercolour painting
– and photography, 20th c. #988
– and sculpture (1960s) #449
– and video art #651
– by artists in America (1564-1867) #231
– by Commonwealth artists (1950-1970s)
    #633
– European
    – 19th c., compared with Canadian
        painting #252
    – (1940s), compared with Canadian
        painting #358
    – in Canadian collections #63
    – Ottawa (Ont), National Gallery of
        Canada #3021 3022 3050
    – Québec (Qué), Université Laval #3078
painting, Algonquian #3672
– 20th c. #4157
painting, American
– see also Hudson River School
– (1860-1900), influence on Canadian
    painting #262
– (1880s), compared with Canadian painting
    #172
– (1930s), compared with Canadian painting
    #337
– (1932), Canadian National Exhibition
    (Toronto, Ont) #320
– (1940-1950), compared with Canadian
    painting #1458
– (1940s), compared with Canadian painting
    #358
– (1950s-1960s), influence on Québec
    painting #1453
– influence on Jack Hamilton Bush #4967
– New York (NY)
    – influence on automatistes #1448
    – influence on Canadian painting (1960s)
        #477 478
    – influence on Montréal (Qué) painting
        (1950s-1960s) #1263
    – influence on Painters Eleven #1785
    – influence on Toronto (Ont) painting

(1950s-1960s) #1772 1773
(1970s) #1803 1807
– Toronto (Ont), Royal Ontario Museum.
    Sigmund Samuel Collection #3135
painting, Australian
– (1880s), compared with Canadian painting
    #172
painting, Belgian
– (1927), Canadian National Exhibition
    (Toronto, Ont) #295
painting, Blackfoot #3669 3678 3686 3741
painting, Blood Indians
– buffalo hunt, University of Alberta
    (Edmonton, Alta) #3711
painting, British
– 19th c., influence on Canadian painting
    #178
– 19th c., influence on Ontario painting
    #1705
– (1927), Canadian National Exhibition
    (Toronto, Ont) #295
– (1940s), influence on Canadian painting
    #379
– (1970s), compared with Canadian painting
    #653
– Fredericton (NB), Beaverbrook Art Gallery
    #3066
– realism, influence on Canadian painting
    #110
– war subjects #1073 1080
    – Ottawa (Ont), National Gallery of
        Canada #1101 1102
painting, Canadian #9 35 39 43 46 57 58 59
    60 61 63 65 66 113 125 129 485 2096
– 17th-19th cs. #232 236
– 17th c.-1910s #205
– 18th-19th cs. #226 231 1338
– 18th c.-1930s #45
– 18th c.-1950s #50
– 19th c. #178 197 252
– 19th c.-1920s #11
– 19th c.-1930s #18
– 19th c.-1940s #36 1242
– 19th-early 20th cs. #7
– 20th c. #52 83 84 145 407 423 482 507 665
    – and engineering #471
– (1605-1867) #2110
– (1663-1912) #198
– (1665-1945) #32 34
– (1665-1960) #76 77
– (1665-1965) #108
– (1750s-1890s) #221
– (1800-1960) #99
– (1820-1940) #28
– (1821-1860), Hudson's Bay Company
    territory #273
– (1830s-1930s) #33
– (1837-1887) #253
– (1837-1900), Victorian #254
– (1850-1950) #86
– (1850s-1920s) #297
– (1860s-1880s) #230
– (1860s-1960s) #75
– (1867-1967) #82
– (1870-1970) #97
– (1874), Art Union of Canada (Toronto,
    Ont) #1694
– (1880) #167
– (1880-1910) #214
– (1880-1914) #265
– (1880s) #170 172
– (1880s-1930s) #17
– (1886), Colonial and Indian Exhibition

(London, England) #174
– (1890s), by artists in Paris (France) #180
– (1890s-1930s), influence of Impressionism
    #115 227
– (1890s-1940s) #27 367
– (1900-1920s) #309
– (1900-1949) #42
– (1910), Canadian National Exhibition
    (Toronto, Ont) #201
– (1910s) #284
– (1910s-1940s) #354 383
– (1910s-1950s) #427
– (1920-1950) #391
– (1920s) #293 315
– (1920s-1940s), Canadian Forum coverage
    #3301
– (1920s-1950s) #396 424
– (1920s-1960s), compared with Latin
    American painting #495
– (1927), Canadian National Exhibition
    (Toronto, Ont) #295
– (1930), Canadian National Exhibition
    (Toronto, Ont) #313
– (1930s) #314 335 336 338 340 342 502 589
    592
    – and nationalism #337
    – use of oral documentation #608
– (1931), Canadian National Exhibition
    (Toronto, Ont) #316
– (1932), Canadian National Exhibition
    (Toronto, Ont) #320 321
– (1933-1970) #498
– (1938-1948) #378 379
– (1939-1963) #462
– (1940-1960) #512
– (1940s) #355 358 370 371 374 386 1389
    – by artists in Paris (France) #384
– (1940s-1950s) #412 452 1426
– (1940s-1960s) #453 489
– (1945-1970) #499 501
– (1950s) #401 410 416 429 438
    – by artists abroad #413 414
    – by artists in Paris (France) #426
    – influence of Hans Hofmann #402
– (1950s-1960s) #400 455 476
– (1955-1971) #1453
– (1960s) #450 478 491 520 521
    – by Québec artists in Paris (France) #1434
– (1960s-1970s) #704
– (1970s) #565 582 588 609 618 620 653 684
    – large-scale paintings #644
– Alberta #1948 1970
    – (1970s) #1951
    – (1980) #1969
    – realism #1954
– and architecture
    – (1950s) #7670
    – (1960s) #8236
– and Cornelius Krieghoff #6087 6089 6094
– and Emily Carr #5030
– and imagination #104
– and Jack Hamilton Bush #722 4969
– and James Wilson Morrice #6622
– and Jean-Paul Riopelle #7018
– and Jean-Philippe Dallaire #5240
– and Jock Macdonald #6378
– and Marc-Aurèle de Foy Suzor-Coté #7293
– and photography
    – (1860-1900) #245 262 268
    – (1970s) #1007
– Art Deco #505
– attitudes to wilderness #93
– automatistes #1398 1420 1447 1448 1475
    1476

– Bell-Irving family #4665
– Brampton (Ont), Perkins Bull Collection #3208
– Brant County (Ont), (1793-1930) #1684
– British Columbia #1995 2000 2011
    – (1848-1890s) #2004
    – (1894-1932) #2007
    – (1940s) #1989
    – (1950s) #1990 1994 1997
– by Scottish-born artists #133
– Canadian Group of Painters #324 331 348 356 365 382
– Canadian railway companies, as patrons #3281
– Canadian Shield, 18th-20th cs. #156
– Charlevoix (Qué) #1280
– CIL Inc., collection #124
– Contemporary Arts Society #1459 1474
– Eastern Townships (Qué)
    – (1800-1950) #1296
    – (1815-1940) #1288
– Edmonton (Alta), Edmonton Art Gallery, Ernest Edward Poole Collection #3217 3222 3235
– figurative #71 101 103 578
    – (1878-1978) #135
– folk painting, 17th-20th cs. #965
– forgeries #64 70 73
– Fredericton (NB), Beaverbrook Art Gallery #3066 3067
– Garber, Bram, collection #3247
– Group of Seven #1735 1737 1738 1739 1740 1741 1743 1744 1745 1747 1754 1763 1764 1766 1767 1768 1774 1776 1777 1778 1779 1781 1782 1783 1784 1789
– guide for collectors #2252
– Halifax (NS)
    – (1815-1867) #1217
    – collections #47
– Hamilton (Ont), Art Gallery of Hamilton #3159
– influence of American painting #126
– Joliette (Qué), churches #8876
– Jutras, Albert, collection #372
– Kingston (Ont) #1680
– L'Islet (Qué), Church of Notre-Dame-de-Bon-Secours #8879
– landscapes #14 26 41 88 106 132 140 301 352 496 595
– London (Ont), (1970s) #1813
– MacAulay, John, collection #3212
– Manitoba #1893 1895
    – Doig, Mr. and Mrs. D.R., collection #3224
– Maritimes, 20th c. #1121
– Massey, Vincent, collection #3220
– McLean, J.S., collection #3228
– Montée Saint-Michel #1236
– Montréal (Qué) #7900
    – (1860-1960) #1253
    – (1940s) #1397
    – (1940s-1950s) #1416
    – (1940s-1960s) #1438
    – (1950s) #389 1403
    – (1950s-1960s) #1263 1425
    – (1954-1955) #1408
    – (1960s) #1418 1427 1484
    – and Alfred Pellan #6826
    – and Louis Muhlstock #6658
    – Church of Notre-Dame #8839
    – Grey Nuns #8862
    – McGill University. McCord Museum #222 223
    – Montreal Museum of Fine Arts #3113

– Optical art #1445
– New Brunswick #1178
    – ship portraits, 19th c. #1190
– Newfoundland #1139 1147 1154
    – (1970s) #1149
– Non-Figurative Artists' Association of Montreal #1415 1469 1478
– Nova Scotia
    – (1749-1958) #1196
    – (1970s) #1221
    – folk painting, 20th c. #1206 1207
    – ship portraits, 19th c. #163 1201
– Oka (Qué) #1356
    – Calvary at Oka #1355
– Ontario #1676
    – 19th c. #1705 1720
    – (1846-1867) #1715
    – animal portraits #1727
    – collections #120
    – Government of Ontario Art Collection #1728
– Ontario and Québec (1960s) #484
– Ontario Society of Artists #1770
– Ottawa (Ont)
    – Canada Council. Art Bank #636
    – National Gallery of Canada #3038
        – Massey, Vincent, bequest #3227
    – Public Archives of Canada. William H. Coverdale Collection #12 3230
– Painters Eleven #1752 1769 1771 1785 1786 1787
– Painters Eleven and plasticiens #720
– plasticiens #1439 1457 1465
– Prairies
    – (1950s-1970s) #1884
    – landscapes #1872 1882 1885
– Prince Edward Island, women artists (1970s) #1167
– Québec #1235 1237 1249 1258 1259 1265 1289 1294 1340 1344 1346 1393 1596 2183
    – 17th-18th cs. #2187
    – 17th-19th cs. #1305
    – 17th c. #1363
    – 17th c.-1920s #1229
    – 18th-19th cs. #1323
    – 18th-early 20th cs. #1339
    – 19th c. #1312 1318 1336
    – 19th c.-1930s #1382
    – 19th c.-1940s #1242 1248
    – 19th c.-1960s #1256 1262
    – 20th c. #1270 1392 1422 4877
    – (1760-1790) #1369
    – (1870s) #1307
    – (1875-1915) #1364
    – (1880-1914), influence of French painting #1371
    – (1920s) #302
    – (1920s-1970s) #1463
    – (1930s) #1460
    – (1930s), influence of French painting #1381
    – (1930s-1960s) #1421
    – (1939-1950s) #1461
    – (1940-1960) #1462
    – (1940-1966) #1440
    – (1940s) #1384 1390 1468
    – (1940s-1950s) #1432 1472
    – (1940s-1960s) #1436
    – (1940s-1970s) #1267 1269
    – (1950s) #1413 1414
    – (1950s-1960s) #1441
    – (1953-1956) #1454
    – (1955-1965) #1471
    – (1960s) #1419 1487

    – (1970s) #1542 1543 1544 1552 1560
    – and Alfred Pellan #6801
    – and Fernand Leduc #6191
    – and Joseph Légaré #6220
    – and Paul-Emile Borduas #4826
    – Corbeil, Maurice and Andrée, collection #3234
    – influence of Desjardins Collection #3207
    – landscapes, Laurentian Mountains (Qué), 20th c. #1278 1279
    – mid-17th c.–1908 #1353
    – Pop art #1497
    – review of literature #1295
    – Surrealism #1464
– Québec (Qué)
    – 17th c. #1352
    – Hôtel-Dieu #3119
    – Université Laval #3078 3080
– realism #110 716 1810
    – (1970s) #545
– Regina (Sask), (1960s) #1913
– religious subjects, 20th c. #479
– Saguenay-Lac-Saint-Jean (Qué), 20th c. #1551
– Saint John (NB)
    – 20th c. #1184
    – (1950s) #1173
– Saskatchewan #1919
    – (1883-1959) #1915
– Saskatoon (Sask)
    – Nutana Collegiate Institute. Memorial Art Gallery #3183
– seascapes #139 225
– small-scale paintings (1913-1914) #199
– Surrealism #463 508 509 1458
– Toronto (Ont)
    – 20th c. #1760
    – (1940s-1950s) #5171
    – (1950s) #1749
    – (1950s-1960s) #4961
    – (1953-1965) #1772 1773 1775
    – (1960s) #1753
    – (1970s) #1803 1807 1823 1831
    – Art Gallery of Ontario #3149
    – Colborne Lodge #3129
    – Royal Ontario Museum. Sigmund Samuel Collection #3135 3140
    – Saint Anne's Church #1733
    – University of Toronto #3168
        – Hart House #3137 3147
        – University College #3151
– Vancouver (BC)
    – (1950s) #1992
    – (1970s) #2075
– Varennes (Qué), churches #8813
– war subjects #1073 1074 1075 1076 1078 1080 1081 1085 1092 1093 1096 1097 1099 1110 1111 1112 1115
    – Ottawa (Ont), National Gallery of Canada #1077 1101 1102 1103
– western Canada
    – (1938-1948) #1841
    – (1950s) #1842
    – landscapes #1863
– Winnipeg (Man) #1891
    – (1960s) #1892
    – Legislative Building #8951
– Winnipeg Sketch Club #1894
– women artists, 17th-20th cs. #117
painting, Coast Salish #3878
painting, Cree
    – (1970s) #4133
painting, Dutch
    – 17th-19th cs., Desjardins collection #3207

– 17th c., influence on Cornelius Krieghoff #6101
– 17th c., influence on Henk Ykelenstam #7626
– 19th c., in Canadian private collections #194
– 19th c., influence on Canadian painting #39
– (1880-1910), influence on Canadian art #214
painting, Egyptian
– influence on Ronald Langley Bloore #4749
painting, Flemish
– 19th c., influence on Canadian painting #39
painting, French
– see also Impressionism
– 17th-19th cs., Desjardins collection #3207
– 17th c.-1930s, influence on Canadian painting #39
– 18th c., Calvary at Oka (Oka, Qué) #8853
– 19th c., influence on Canadian painting #178 265
– 19th c., influence on Ontario painting #1705
– (1867-1914) #274
– (1880-1914), influence on Québec painting #1371
– (1880s), influence on Canadian painting #172
– (1927), Canadian National Exhibition (Toronto, Ont) #295
– (1930s), influence on Québec painting #1381
– (1940s), influence on Canadian painting #379 496
– (1940s), influence on Québec painting #1256 1262 1390
– (1950s-1960s), influence on Montréal (Qué) painting #1263
painting, German
– realism, influence on Canadian painting #110
painting, Haida
– beaver motif #23
painting, Indians of North America #3381 3432 3462
– 20th c. #3441
– Tulsa (Okla), Philbrook Art Center #4165
– (1830-1970) #3451
– (1970s) #6648
– facial #3461
painting, Inuit #4202
painting, Iroquois
– (1970s) #4133
painting, Italian
– 17th-19th cs., Desjardins collection #3207
– Florence, Robert Harris, on #5737
– influence on Paul Kane #6003
painting, Japanese
– influence on Bruno Joseph Bobak #4756
– Nangan school, influence on Kazuo Hamasaki #5688
– sumi-e, influence on Gaston-Pierre Petit #6843 6844 6845
– sumi-e, influence on Takao Tanabe #7320 7321
– Ukiyo-e, influence on Miyuki Tanobe #7322
painting, Latin American
– (1920s-1960s), compared with Canadian painting #495
painting, Mexican

– (1930s), compared with Canadian painting #337
painting, Naskapi #4098
painting, natives of North America #3341
painting, Northwest Coast Indians
– facial #3771
– pigments and materials #3415 3847
painting, Ojibwa
– 20th c. #4156
– (1970s) #4133
painting, Plains #3672 3716 3751
– leatherwork #3709
– winter count motif #3728
painting, Quinault #3845
painting, Scottish #133
painting, Siouan #3672 3728
painting, Woodlands
– influence of Norval H. Morrisseau #4144
painting technique
– see media and techniques, painting
Paisley, Douglas A., Can photographer, 1949-
– portfolio of photographs #995
Paisley, James Ernest Harris, Can architect, 1890-1955
– Toronto (Ont), Helena Rubenstein Beauty Salon #9367
Paivio, Jules Peter, Can architect, 1917-
– Vancouver (BC), Vancouver Civic Auditorium, competition #9080
palaces
– see also castles and country houses
palaces, Italian
– Venice, influence on Royal Bank building (Toronto, Ont) #9152
Palchinski, Sylvia Scott, Can artist, 1946-
– on her art #6753
Palladian style architecture
– villas, Québec, 19th c. #8632
Palm Springs (Calif), Palm Springs Desert Museum
– exhibitions
– Rita Letendre (1974) #6252
Palmer, Herbert Franklin, Can artist, 1921-
– exhibitions, group
– (1962) #1847
Palmer, Herbert Sidney, Can artist, 1881-1970
– exhibitions (reviews) #1710
Palmer, Samuel, Brit artist, 1805-1881
– influence on Brian Rendel Jones #5974
Palumbo, Jacques, Can artist, 1939-
– exhibitions
– (1975) #6754
– use of colour #6755
– use of numbers #662
Panabaker, Frank Shirley, Can artist, 1904- #6756
– art and writings #6757
Panamick, Martin, Can artist, 1956-1977
– exhibitions, group
– (1981) #4173
Pangnark, Can artist, 1920-
– exhibitions, group
– (1970) #4220
Pangnirtung (NWT)
– graphic arts
– (1959-1976) #4490
– (1973-) #4485
– weaving #4237
– and Don Stuart #7281
– Pangnirtung weaving shop #4298 4308 4310
– whalebone carving #4413

Panko, William, Can artist, 1892-1948
– exhibitions, group
– (1958) #1846
– exhibitions (reviews) #964
Panneton, André, Can photographer, 1949- #1562
Panneton, Louise, Can tapestry artist, 1926- #6758
– exhibitions, group
– (1978) #2772
panoramas
– Burr, William and Elias Paul Barnes #218
panoramic photography
– Canada, city views (1850-1900) #1061
Panton, Lawrence Arthur Colley, Can artist, 1894-1954
– exhibitions
– (1974) #6759
papermaking, Canadian
– Ontario (1970s) #935
paperweights, Canadian
– glass (1880-1925) #2438
paperwork, Canadian
– 20th c. #2142
– Mennonite #2264
– 19th-early 20th cs. #2265
papier collé
– see collage
Papineau, André B., Can public servant, d. 1832
– residence, Laval (Qué) #8625
Papineau, Gérin-Lajoie, LeBlanc, Edwards, Can architectural firm
– Frobisher Bay (NWT), Frobisher Bay Academic and Occupational School #8188
– Mirabel (Qué), Montreal International Airport. Passenger Terminal Building #9518
Papineau, Louis J., Can architect, 1930-
– Montréal (Qué), métro. Peel Station #9553
Paquet, Edmond, Can sculptor, 18th c.
– sculptures, Church of Saint-Pierre (île d'Orléans, Qué) #6651
Paquet (dit Lavallée), André, Can sculptor, 1799-1860 #1324
– influence of Baillairgé family #1582
– sculptures
– Bellechasse (Qué), Church of Saint-Charles-Borromée #8803
– Charlesbourg (Qué), church #8851
– île d'Orléans (Qué)
– Church of Saint-François-de-Sales #8796
– Church of Saint-Pierre #8802
Paquin, Roger, Can sculptor, 1941- #6760
– interview #1485
Parachute, Can periodical #593
– (1970s) #3310
Parachute Center for Cultural Affairs (Calgary, Alta)
– Centerfold #603
Paradis, Claude, Can artist, 1937-
– interview #1485 1489
Paradis, Jérôme (frère Jérôme), Can artist, 1902- #6761 6762
– as teacher #6763
– as teacher of Jean-Paul Armand Mousseau #6651
Paradis, Jobson Emilian Henri, Can artist, 1871-1926 #1382
Paradis, Roland, Can silversmith, ca. 1696-1754 #249 250
– works, Detroit Institute of Arts (Detroit, Mich) #2691

paradise
– in art, Glenn Alun Lewis #6275 6276
Parallelogramme, Can periodical #612
– (1970s) #3310
Paré, Réjean, ceramicist, 1948- #1547
Pare, Richard, Brit photographer in Canada,
    1948-
– photographs, greystone buildings,
    Montréal (Qué) #7922
Parent, Louis Joseph, Can sculptor,
    1908-
– sculptures, Stations of the Cross, Saint
    Joseph's Oratory (Montréal, Qué) #6764
Parent, Michel, Can artist, 1938- #6765
Parent, Omer, Can artist, 1907- #6766
– as teacher, Ecole des beaux-arts (Québec,
    Qué) #1404
– exhibitions
    – (1976) #6767
Parent-Benoît, Mimi, Can artist, 1924-
– in Paris (France) #426
Parent Report
– *see* Québec. Rapport de la Commission
    d'enquête sur l'enseignement des arts au
    Québec (Rapport Parent)
Parfitt, Gilbert, Can architect, 1886-1966
– Winnipeg (Man), University of Manitoba.
    Science Building and Arts Building #9485
parfleche, Algonquian #3456 3672
parfleche, Plains #3456 3660 3672 3716
parfleche, Siouan #3456 3672
Paris (France)
– urban development #7902
– views, Franklin Milton Armington #4550
Paris (France), académie Colarossi
– Bell-Smith, Frederic Marlett, as student
    #4666
– Carr, Emily, as student #5045
– Reid, George Agnew, as student #6979
Paris (France), académie Julian
– Benjamin-Constant, Jean-Joseph, as teacher
    #243
– Brymner, William, as student #4948 4953
– Canadian artists, as students (1940s) #384
– Carlyle, Florence, as student #4999
– Duquet, Georges-Henri, as student #5343
– Forster, John Wycliffe Lowes, as student
    #5468
– Gagnon, Clarence Alphonse, as student
    #5544 5546 5547
– Hill, George William, as student #5799
– Pemberton, Sophia Theresa, as student
    #6828
– Reid, George Agnew, as student #6977
    6979
– Scovil, James Noel, as student #7167
Paris (France), Académie royale de peinture
    et sculpture de Paris
– Baillairgé, François, as student #4592
Paris (France), Atelier 17
– and Stanley William Hayter #1641
– influence on Canadian printmaking
    (1960s) #820
Paris (France), Ateliers d'art sacré
– Gilson, Jacqueline Marie-Charlotte, as
    student #5606
Paris (France), Canadian Cultural Centre
– *see* Paris (France), Centre culturel
    canadien/Canadian Cultural Centre
Paris (France), Centre culturel
    canadien/Canadian Cultural Centre
– (1970s) #647
– exhibitions
    – *Canadian West Coast Hermetics: The*

*Metaphysical Landscape/Les hermétiques
    canadiens de la côte ouest: le paysage
    métaphysique* (1973) #2045
– *Claude Goulet: multidimensionnels* (1971)
    #5639
– *Claude Tousignant* (1973) #7401
– *Contemporary Canadian Painters: An
    Exhibition of Works from the Canada
    Council Art Bank/Peintres canadiens
    contemporains: une exposition de la banque
    d'oeuvres d'art du Conseil des arts du
    Canada* (1977) #636
– *D.P. Brown, Ken Danby, Tom Forrestall,
    Christopher Pratt* (1974) #573
– *Emily Carr: The Mature Years/Emily Carr:
    les années de maturité* (1979) #5042
– *Exposition d'estampes en l'honneur de C.
    Krieghoff, 1815-1872/Exhibition of Prints
    in Honour of C. Krieghoff, 1815-1872*
    (1972) #6096
– *Fernand Leduc* (1970) #6186
– *Fernand Leduc: microchromie gris,
    puissance 6* (1977) #6190
– *General Idea's Reconstructing
    Futures/General Idea: reconstruction de
    l'avenir* (1978) #5583
– *Guido Molinari* (1974) #6584
– *Ivan Eyre Exposition* (1982) #5394
– *Jack Chambers: Selection of Paintings and
    Drawings* (1980) #5080
– *Jean McEwen: Suite parisienne* (1978)
    #6471
– *Joe Plaskett* (1977) #6895
– *L'art de Vittorio Fiorucci: affiches
    1964-1981* (1981) #5444
– *La tapisserie canadienne contemporaine:
    exposition/Canadian Contemporary
    Tapestry: Exhibition* (1980) #2774
– *Leslie Reid* (1980) #6981
– *Lithographs/Lithographies* (1973) #825
– *Louis Comtois: 4 tableaux récents grand
    format* (1978) #5163
– *Louis Jaque: les idiomes galactiques* (1978)
    #5943
– *Métiers d'art* (1973,1976,1979) #2215
– *Other Realities: The Legacy of Surrealism in
    Canadian Art* (1979) #508
– *Ozias Leduc: peinture symboliste et
    religieuse/Ozias Leduc: Symbolist and
    Religious Painting* (1974) #6206
– *Peter Gnass: installation-Chantier interdit
    au public* (1980) #5621
– *Philip Surrey, le peintre dans la ville* (1972)
    #7289
– *Pierre Clerk: oeuvres récentes, peintures et
    sculptures* (1981) #5118
– *Raymonde Godin: l'espace et les signes*
    (1979) #5623
– *Réalités autres: le legs du surréalisme à l'art
    canadien* (1979) #509
– *Réflexion sur un sentiment rural/Reflecting
    a Rural Consciousness* (1980) #700
– *Richard Mill: 5 tableaux récents* (1979)
    #6535
– *Riopelle: ficelles et autres jeux* (1972) #7025
– *Roger Vilder* (1973) #7488
– *Tendances actuelles* (1977) #637
– *Touchez! Yvon Cozic* (1974) #5203
– *Yves Trudeau: "murs fermés et ouverts";
    sculptures et pliages* (1975) #7434
– exhibitions (reviews)
    – Blanchette, Pierre #1563
    – *Les 7 jours de Fernand Leduc* (1973) #6188
    – *Ozias Leduc: peinture symboliste et*

*religieuse/Ozias Leduc: Symbolist and
    Religious Painting* (1974) #6205
– *Peter Gnass: installation - Chantier interdit
    au public* (1981) #1563
– Viau, Guy, as director #537 7485
Paris (France), Centre national d'art et de
    culture Georges Pompidou. Musée
    national d'art moderne
– exhibitions
    – *Canada: art d'aujourd'hui* (1968) #518
    – *Jean-Paul Riopelle: peinture, 1946-1977*
        (1981) #7032
    – *Michael Snow* (1978) #7258
– exhibitions (reviews)
    – *Michael Snow* (1978) #7263
Paris (France), Chez Léopold
– mural, Marc-Aurèle de Foy Suzor-Coté
    and Joseph Saint-Charles #7296
Paris (France), Ecole des beaux-arts
– architectural drawing #8241
– Chabert, Joseph, as student #3005
– compared with Ecole des beaux-arts
    (Montréal, Qué) #1456
– Franchère, Joseph-Charles, as student
    #5497
– Hill, George William, as student #5799
– influence on Québec architecture #7923
Paris (France), Exposition des arts décoratifs
    (1925)
– influence on Canadian art #1244
Paris (France), galerie Arnaud
– exhibitions
    – *Fernand Toupin* (1970) #7394
Paris (France), galerie Jacques Dubourg
– exhibitions
    – *La sculpture de peintre: bronzes de Riopelle*
        (1962) #7019
Paris (France), galeries Georges Petit
– exhibitions
    – *Exposition Frank M. Armington, peintures*
        (1921) #4550
    – *Exposition rétrospective de l'oeuvre de W.
        Blair Bruce* (1907) #4941
Paris (France), Grand Palais
– exhibitions
    – *Borduas et les automatistes, Montréal
        1942-1955* (1971) #1449
    – *L'Amérique vue par l'Europe* (1976) #255
    – *Sculpture of the Inuit: Masterworks of the
        Canadian Arctic/La sculpture chez les Inuit:
        chefs-d'oeuvre de l'Arctique canadien*
        (1972) #4423 4440
    – *The European Vision of America* (1976)
        #256
– exhibitions (reviews)
    – *Sculpture of the Inuit: Masterworks of the
        Canadian Arctic/La Sculpture chez les
        Inuit: chefs-d'oeuvre de l'Arctique canadien*
        (1972) #4239
Paris (France), La Grande Chaumière
– Canadian artists, as students (1940s) #384
Paris (France), Musée d'art moderne de la
    ville de Paris
– 11th Paris Biennale, Canadian art
    exhibited (1980) #687
– exhibitions
    – *Canada trajectoires 73* (1973) #558
        – Charney, Melvin, on *Quelques
            monuments nationaux* #5091
    – *Jean-Paul Lemieux* (1974) #6232
– exhibitions (reviews)
    – Beaulieu, Paul-Vanier #4651
    – Pellan, Alfred #6805
Paris (France), Musée de l'Homme

– exhibitions
   – *Arte indio y esquimal del Canada/Indian and Eskimo Art of Canada/Art indien et esquimau du Canada/Die Kunst der Indianer und Eskimos in Kanada* (1969) #3352
   – *Chefs-d'oeuvre des arts indiens et esquimaux du Canada/Masterpieces of Indian and Eskimo Art from Canada* (1969) #3351
– exhibitions (reviews)
   – *Chefs-d'oeuvre des arts indiens et esquimaux du Canada/Masterpieces of Indian and Eskimo Art from Canada* (1969) #3356 3954
– mask, Tsimshian Indians #4069
– moccasins and footgear, Indians of North America #3424
– totem poles, Northwest Coast Indians #3930
Paris (France), Musée du Jeu de paume
– exhibitions
   – *Exposition d'art canadien* (1927) #299
– Pellan, Alfred, works exhibited #6796
Paris (France), Musée national d'art moderne
– see Paris (France), Centre national d'art et de culture Georges Pompidou. Musée national d'art moderne
– exhibitions
   – *Pellan* (1955) #6804
Paris (France), musée Rodin
– exhibitions
   – *Panorama de la sculpture au Québec, 1945-1970* (1970) #1599
Paris (France), Paris Biennale (1969)
– exhibitions (reviews)
   – Levine, Les #6261
Paris (France), Paris Biennale (1980)
– Canadian art #687
Paris (France), Salon
– and Alexander Phimister Proctor #6943
– and Atha Haydock Caldwell #4991
– and Claire Shuttleworth #7202
– and Florence Carlyle #4999
– and Laura Adeline Muntz Lyall #6337 6339
– and Lilias Torrance Newton #6692
– and Mary Riter Hamilton #5694
– and Paul Peel #6790 6791
– and Sydney Strickland Tully #7438
Paris (France), Société nationale des beaux-arts
– and Maurice Galbraith Cullen #5220
– Cullen, Maurice Galbraith, as student #5219
Paris (Ont)
– pottery, 19th c. #2330
Paris Pottery
– see Ahrens Pottery
Parish, Isaac, Can photographer, fl. 1860s #1211
Parizad, Can photographer, fl. 1981
– portfolio of photographs #1023
Parizeau, Marcel, Can architect, 1898-1945 #8397
parkas, Inuit #4300
Parker, Blake, Can poet, 1943-
– and Intersystems #767
Parkin, Edmund, Can architect, 1912-
– and John B. Parkin Associates #8396
Parkin, John Burnett, Can architect, 1911-1975
– and John B. Parkin Associates #8396

Parkin, John C., Can architect, 1922-
– and John B. Parkin Associates #8396
– on architecture #7746
– on relationship of artists and architects #8234
– Ontario, summer houses #8651
– Toronto (Ont) #7733 8057
   – John C. Parkin House #9299
   – Salvation Army headquarters #8232
   – Sun Life Building #8232
   – Toronto International Airport #8232
Parkin Architects and Planners, Can architectural firm
– Ottawa (Ont), National Gallery of Canada, competition #9142
Parkin Partnership, Can architectural firm
– Toronto (Ont)
   – Art Gallery of Ontario #3163 9121
   – Art Gallery of Ontario. Henry Moore Centre #8078
parks
– see also amusement parks; landscape architecture
parks, Canadian
– landscape architecture #7677
– Montréal (Qué), Mount Royal Park #7924
– recreation buildings #9081
– Toronto (Ont) #5651
Parks Canada
– see Canada. Parks Canada
Parr, Nuna, Can artist, 1889-1969 #6768 6770
– exhibitions
   – (1979) #6769
Parry, Sir William Edward, Brit navigator, explorer, 1790-1855
– expedition, Arctic #278
Parry Island Reservation (Ont)
– art, Ojibwa and Potawatomi #3540
Parsons, Alison, Can textile artist, 1939-
– interview #6771
Parsons, Bruce, Can artist, 1937-
– exhibitions
   – (1976) #6772
– exhibitions, group
   – (1967) #1916
– map images #561
– prints #1214
Parsons, F.R., Can photographer in USA, fl. 1890s #6773
Parthenais, Louis-Anatole, Can sculptor, 1839-1864 #1319
– sculpture, Montréal (Qué) #727
Parti-pris #1502
Partridge, David Gerry, Can artist, 1919- #6775 6776
– on his art #6774
– on printmaking #817
Partz, Felix, Can artist, 1945-
– exhibitions, group
   – (1977) #5583
Paskievich, John, Can photographer, 1947- #1879 6777
   – (1979) #1904
Pasquin, Suzanne, Can artist, 1935- #1418
Passillé-Sylvestre, Micheline de, Can enameller, 1936- #2216
Paterson, Malcolm, Can photographer, fl. 1970s-
– portfolio of photographs #991
Paterson, Robert Allen, Can artist, 1936- #6778
Patrie, La, Can newspaper
– comic strips #954
– illustrations, Henri Julien #5988

Patriot, Can newspaper
– letters on Society of Artists and Amateurs of Toronto exhibition, Toronto (Ont) (1834) #1729
patronage of art
– see also collectors and collecting
– Canada #369
   – (1950s) #3253 3260
   – (1960s) #3263
   – (1970s) #693 3157 3275 3278 3286 3291 3293
– Canada Foundation #3262
– Toronto (Ont), (1890s) #1699
pattern
– see also design
– in art, Vancouver (BC), (1980s) #2081
pattern books, architecture
– schools, Henry Bernard #9384
pattern books, costume
– (1870s) #2878
pattern books, glass painting
– Vancouver (BC), (1890-1940) #2457
pattern books, textiles
– needlework, Nova Scotia (pre-1920) #2785
Patterson, Andrew Dickson, Can artist, 1854-1930
– portraits #1698
Patterson, Daniel (Dan), Can sculptor, 1886-1968
– Carnation Milk cans construction #1792 6779
   – Ottawa (Ont), National Gallery of Canada #962
– exhibitions, group
   – (1975) #1682
Patterson, Freeman, Can photographer, 1937-
– correspondence, Michael William Semak #1016
– exhibitions (reviews) #1009
– on his photography #6781
– on landscape photography #6780
– on photography #6782
– portfolio of photographs #995 1023
Patterson, Nancy-Lou, Can artist, art historian, 1929-
– interview #6783
Pattle, Colin, Can artist, 1922- #6784
Paul Arthur and Associates, Can graphic design firm #873
Pavelic, Myfanwy Spencer, Can artist, 1916- #6785
– as member of Limners #2043
– on Emily Carr #5043
Paxton, Maureen, Can artist, 1950- #6786
Payette, Eugène, Can architect, 1874-1959
– Montréal (Qué), bibliothèque Saint-Sulpice #9039 9415
Payne, Gordon MacEwan, Can artist, 1933-
– exhibitions, group
   – (1979) #2075
– exhibitions (reviews) #2072
Payne, Julia, Can sculptor, 20th c.
– as wife of William St. Thomas Smith #7236
Payne, Samuel, Can silversmith, 1696-1732 #234 235
– and Paul Lambert (*dit* Saint-Paul), porringer, Montreal Museum of Fine Arts (Montréal, Qué) #2689
Payne, Stephen, Can artist, 1953-
– exhibitions, group
   – (1979) #1157
Payne Bay (Qué)
– graphic arts (1972-1975) #4475

Payton, Evlyn B., Can artist, 1920- #6787
Peachey, James, Brit army officer, artist in
    Canada, fl. 1774-1797 #269 270 279 812
Peachy, Joseph Ferdinand, Can architect,
    1830-1903
– and Québec architecture #7851
Peacock, Graham, Can artist, 1945-
– exhibitions, group
    – (1974) #565
Pearson, Carol, Can artist, 1910-
– as student of Emily Carr #5020
Pearson, Cedric, Can photographer, 1949-
– photographic views, Disraëli (Qué), (1972)
    #1513
Pearson, John Andrew, Can architect,
    1867-1940 #8398
– Ottawa (Ont)
    – Parliament Buildings #8926 8927
        – Peace Tower and Memorial Chamber
            #8928 8929
– Toronto (Ont) #8055
Pédery-Hunt, Dora de
– see De Pédery-Hunt, Dora
pedigree
– see genealogy
Pednaud, Victoire, Can weaver, fl.
    1920s-1940s #2184
Peel, Bryan, Can sculptor, b. 1875
– beaver carving #6789
– raven rattle #6788
Peel, Paul, Can artist, 1860-1892 #10 178
    4999 6790 6791
– After the Bath paintings #6794
– and Florence Carlyle #5000
– exhibitions
    – (1970) #6792
– exhibitions, group
    – (1978) #1726
– exhibitions (reviews) #174
– paintings #6793
– relation of photography and painting #245
Peel County (Ont)
– views, Perkins Bull Collection #3208
Peene, Alfred W., Can architect, 1868-1940
– Hamilton (Ont)
    – Hamilton Public Library #7957
    – Royal Connaught Hotel #9274
Peggy's Cove (NS)
– views, Ernest Lawson #6175
Peguis, Indian chief, d. 1864
– portrait of, Peter Rindisbacher #7005
Pehap, Eric Konstantin, Can artist, 1912-
    #6795
Pei, I.M., & Associates, Amer architectural
    firm
– Montréal (Qué), Place Ville-Marie #9314
    9315
– Toronto (Ont), Commerce Court #9350
Pei, Ieoh Ming, Amer architect, 1917-
– influence on Montréal (Qué) architecture
    (1960s) #7901
– Toronto (Ont)
    – Canadian Bank of Commerce,
        restoration #9351
    – City Hall and Civic Square, competition
        #8981
Pel, Brian, Can photographer, ca. 1954-
– portfolio of photographs #1032
Pellan, Alfred, Can artist, 1906- #97 1294
    1392 1426 1432 1504 1542 1543 6796 6797
    6801 6802 6803 6808 6809 6810 6815 6817
    6818 6819
– and automatistes #1448
– and Contemporary Arts Society #1459

– and Jean-Paul Lemieux #6228
– and Paul-Emile Borduas #1451
– and Pierre Gauvreau #5578
– and Surrealism #1453 1464
– as teacher #482 1395
– dispute with Paul-Emile Borduas #4832
– Dumouchel, Albert, compared with #5332
– East, Benoît, compared with #5353
– exhibitions
    – (1955) #6804
    – (1960) #6807
    – (1972) #6816
    – (1980) #6824 6825
– exhibitions, group #509
    – (1958) #431
    – (1964) #462
    – (1978) #508
– exhibitions (reviews) #428 6823
– Gagnon-Fortier, C., compared with #5552
– heads, surrealistic traits #6822
– influence on Alan Glass #5614
– influence on Jean-Philippe Dallaire #5241
    5244
– influence on Madeleine Laliberté #6153
– influence on Montréal (Qué) painting
    #1416 1437
– influence on Québec abstract art #1468
– influence on Québec decorative arts #2199
– influence on Québec painting #489 1389
    6826
– international recognition (1950s) #425
– interview #6800 6806 6811 6812 6821
– L'amour fou #6820
– murals, Canadian Embassy (Rio de
    Janeiro, Brazil) #6798
– on Gérard Morisset #3305
– on his art education #470
– on Normand Hudon #5855
– Polychromées #1647
– portraits, National Gallery of Canada
    (Ottawa, Ont) #6814
– Scherzo, stained glass, Place des Arts
    (Montréal, Qué) #1442 8233
– stage design and costume, La nuit des rois
    #6799
– works (1946-1948) #6813
– works, exhibited at Musée d'art moderne
    de la ville de Paris (Paris, France) #6805
– works, Venice Biennale (1952) #399
Pellat, Sir Henry Mill, Can businessman,
    1859-1939
– residence, Casa Loma (Toronto, Ont)
    #8649
Pelletier, Didace (Claude) (frère Didace),
    Can artist, 1657-1699 #228 229
Pelletier, Marie-Louise Emilie (soeur
    Saint-Alphonse), Can nun, 1816-1846
– portrait of, Antoine-Sébastien Plamondon
    #6887
Pelletier, Pierre-Yves, Can artist, 1948-
– designs, Olympic Games (1976) #898
Pelly Bay (NWT)
– Inuit artists #4221
– ivory carving #4438
– Netsilik implements #4363
Pemberton, Sophia Theresa, Can artist,
    1869-1959 #6827 6829
– exhibitions
    – (1978) #6828
Pen and Pencil Club of Montreal (Montréal,
    Qué) #1254
– (1890-1955) #1251
– and Edmond Dyonnet #5346
Pender, William, Can photographer, fl.

1850s
– portraits #1171
Pender Bay (BC), Pearson College
– architecture, Thom Partnership #8412
penitentiaries
– see prisons
Penner, Marian
– see Bancroft, Marian Penner
Pennington, James Carlisle, Can architect,
    1885-1963
– Toronto (Ont), Park School #9388
– Windsor (Ont), Collegiate Institute #9388
Pennsylvania Germans
– decorative arts #2243 2250 2251 2263 2264
    2267
– earthenware (1750-1910) #3962
– fraktur #2254 2259
– furniture #2552 2568 2572
– pottery, 19th c. #2303
– treenware #2590
Penny, Edward, Brit artist, 1714-1791
– painting of death of Wolfe #220
Penobscot Indians
– art #3537
– birchbark #3510
– leatherwork #3554
Penticton (BC), Penticton Art Centre Gallery
– exhibitions
    – A Tribute to William Townsend: 1909 to
        1973 (1974) #7418
Pentland, Samuel, Can weaver, fl.
    1840s-1850s #2723
Pentz, Don, Can artist, 1940-
– exhibitions
    – (1979) #6830
Pépin, Arthur, Can artist, 1928-
– interview #6831
Pépin, Jean-Paul, Can artist, 1897-
– and Montée Saint-Michel #1236
Pépin, Joseph, Can sculptor, 1770-1842 #1300
    6947
– altarpiece, church, Berthierville (Qué)
    #8874
Pépin, Louis, Can photographer, 1956- #1562
Pépin, Yves, Can artist, 1943-
– exhibitions, group
    – (1977) #637
Pepper, George Douglas, Can army officer,
    artist, 1903-1962
– as member, Canadian Group of Painters
    #324
– exhibitions
    – (1964) #6832
Percé (Qué)
– views, Marc-Aurèle Fortin #5481
perception and art
– Indians of North America #3487
– Inuit #4294
– Molinari, Guido #6591
– Northwest Coast Indians #4001
– Snow, Michael #7245 7259
– Tousignant, Serge #7404
– use of mirrors and windows #525
– video art #651
Percival, Robert, Can artist, curator, 1924-
    #6833 6834
– exhibitions (reviews) #6835
Perehudoff, William (Bill), Can artist, 1919-
– exhibitions
    – (1977) #6836
    – (1978) #6837
    – (1981) #6838
– exhibitions, group
    – (1967) #1916

– (1975) #1926
– (1981) #722
– exhibitions (reviews) #1883
– mural paintings #1844
Peressutti, Enrico, It architect, 1908-
– Venice (Italy), Canadian Pavilion, 19th
Biennale #9210
performance art
– see also body art; conceptual art
– (1970s) #634 672 2046
   – and sculpture #654
   – tele-performance #603
– Berman, Michaele #4710
– Canada #1799
   – (1970s) #538 598 669 6676
      – sculpture #658
   – (1978), Fifth Network/Cinquième réseau
     #655
   – (1979-1981), Impressions #996
   – (1981) #709 713 718
– Clark, Tim #687
– Dean, Max #687
– Falk, Gathie #5410
– General Idea #5583
– Greyson, John #687
– Heward, John #5793
– Lewis, Glenn Alun #2070
– MacLennan, Toby Chapman #6395
– Montréal (Qué), Powerhouse Gallery
  (1970s) #1553
– Nokony, Denis #6716
– Robertson, Clive #7053
– Tomczak, Kim #687
– Vancouver (BC), Living Art Performance
  Festival (1979) #2073
– W.O.R.K.S. #1955
– Wong, Paul #7607
– Zuck, Tim #7636
performing arts, Canadian
– (1970s) #693
– Ontario (1970s) #1802
– Polish-Canadian artists #149
– women artists, 20th c. #95 96
performing arts centres, Canadian
– Alberta, Jubilee Auditoriums #9084
– Charlottetown (PEI), Confederation Centre
  #7683 9088 9089 9094
– Cobourg (Ont), Victoria Hall #8994 8995
– conversion of public buildings for #9147
  9148
– Montréal (Qué), Place des Arts #9083 9092
  9093 9096
– Ottawa (Ont), National Arts Centre #9104
  9105 9108
– Toronto (Ont)
   – O'Keefe Centre for the Performing Arts
     #9087
   – Ontario Place #9115
   – St. Lawrence Centre for the Arts #9109
   – St. Lawrence Hall #9103
– Vancouver (BC)
   – Orpheum Theatre #9141
   – Queen Elizabeth Theatre #9085
   – Vancouver Civic Auditorium #9080
– Winnipeg (Man), Manitoba Museum of
  Man and Nature. Concert Hall #9107
periodical illustration
– influence on Homer Ransford Watson
  #7536
periodical illustration, American
– views of western USA (1857-1900) #931
periodical illustration, Canadian #925 3313
– (1880s-1940s) #28
– (1967) #877

– (1981) #941
– Cahén, Oscar, on #4985
– Canadian Forum (1920-1951) #930
– Imperial Oil Review (1950s) #924
– views of British Columbia (1513-1891)
  #2006
– views of Canada, 18th-19th cs. #246
– views of Eastern Townships (Qué),
  (1832-1881) #1342
– views of Newfoundland (1497-1887) #1145
– views of Niagara Peninsula (Ont),
  17th-19th cs. #1718
– views of Nova Scotia (1605-1878) #1203
– views of Ottawa (Ont), (1807-1882) #1716
– views of Québec (Qué), (1608-1875) #1349
– views of Toronto (Ont), (1813-1882) #1717
– views of western Canada (1857-1900) #931
periodicals
– see also architectural periodicals; art
  periodicals; newspapers; photography
  periodicals
– 19th c., clothing patterns #2854 2871 2889
– (1870s), fashion news #2878
– (1920s), fashion news #2906
periodicals, Canadian
– advertisements, late 19th-early 20th cs.
  #891
– and art #3313
Perkins, Simeon, Can merchant, fl.
  1766-1812
– residence, Simeon Perkins House
  (Liverpool, NS) #8536
Perkins & Will, Amer architectural firm
– Toronto (Ont), City Hall and Civic Square,
  competition #8981
Perrault, Gérard, Can artist, 1903-
– on graphic design (1940s) #851
Perrault, Henri-Maurice, Can architect,
  1857-1909
– Oka (Qué), church #8818
Perrault, Jean Chrysostome, Can sculptor,
  1793-1829
– interior, Church of Saint-Jean-Baptiste
  (Saint-Jean-Port-Joli, Qué) #8812
Perrault, Pierre, Can artist, 1927-
– on state and art #3269
Perrault, Pierre, Can photographer, 1955-
– portfolio of photographs #1023
Perret, Auguste, Fr architect, writer,
  1874-1954
– influence on Marcel Parizeau #8397
Perrigard, Hal Ross, Can artist, 1891-1960
  #302 1382
Perron, Germain, Can artist, 1943- #1502
– in Paris (France) #1434
Perron, J.Eugène, Can architect, 1900-1969
– Valleyfield (Qué), Cathedral of Salaberry
  #8843
Perrot, André, Can artist, fl. 1956
– and Québec religious art (1950s) #1250
Perry, Arthur, Can art critic, 20th c.
– winner of critical writing on art
  competition (1979) #3312
Perth (Australia), Art Gallery of Western
  Australia
– exhibitions
   – Contemporary Canadian Painters (1957)
     #423
Perth (Ont)
– domestic architecture, 19th c. #8669
Perth (Ont), Inge-Va (formerly Radenhurst
  House)
– architecture #8669
Perth (Ont), McMartin House

– architecture #8669
Perth (Ont), Perth Museum (formerly
  Matheson House)
– architecture #8670
Peterborough (Ont)
– architecture (pre-1890) #8021
– Irish settlements #8523
– petroglyphs, Algonquian #3619
– petroglyphs, Ojibwa #3568 3581 3591
– wedding costume (1810-1938) #2909
Peterborough (Ont), Art Gallery of
  Peterborough
– exhibitions
   – David Bolduc: Recent Work (1980) #4775
   – Humorist Walter Trier: Selections from the
     Trier-Fodor Foundation Gift (1980) #7428
   – Manitoba Flashback (1981) #1907
   – The Heritage of Jack Bush: A Tribute (1982)
     #722
   – Water Colours by E.May Martin (1980)
     #6424
Peterborough (Ont), Artspace #700 1836
– (1970s) #641
Peterborough (Ont), Hutchison House
– architecture #8674
Peterborough (Ont), Peterborough
  Centennial Museum and Archives
– exhibitions
   – Dearly Beloved... Wedding Costumes and
     Customs from 1810-1930 (1981) #2909
Peterborough (Ont), Sir Sandford Fleming
  College
– and Haliburton School of Fine Arts
  (Haliburton, Ont) #2258
– exhibitions
   – Catalogue: Canadian Antique Pottery &
     Stoneware (1975) #2324
Peterborough (Ont), Trent University
– architecture
   – Thom, Ron #9470 9473 9478
   – Thom Partnership #8412
– conferences, on conserving Ontario's main
  streets (1978) #8024
Peterborough (Ont), Trent University.
  Champlain College
– architecture, Thompson, Berwick & Pratt
  #7694 9465 9474
– exhibitions
   – Rodrik/Johnston (1973) #5973
Peterborough (Ont), Trent University. Lady
  Eaton College
– architecture, Thompson, Berwick & Pratt
  #9474
Peterborough (Ont), Trent University.
  Mackenzie Gallery
– exhibitions
   – A Selection of Work: Contemporary Indian
     Art; The Trail from the Past to the Future
     (1977) #4150
Peterborough (Ont), Trent University.
  Student residence
– architecture, Fairfield & DuBois #9467
Peters, Barry, Can artist, 1938-
– exhibitions, group
   – (1977) #4151
Peters, James, Can photographer, 1853-1927
– photographs of Northwest Rebellion #1107
Peters, Kenneth M., Can artist, 1939-
– exhibitions, group
   – (1967) #1916
Peters, Mary, Can weaver, fl. 1960s
– Salish weaving #3941
Peters, Paddy, Can artist, 1956-
– exhibitions, group

– (1977) #4151
Peterson, Margaret, Can artist, 1902-
– exhibitions
– (1978) #6839
Peterson, Warren H., Can artist, 1935-
– exhibitions, group
– (1977) #1933
Pethick, Jerry, Can artist, 1936- #6842
– interview #6841
– on laser holography #6840
Petit, Gaston-Pierre, Can priest, artist, 1930-
#6843 6844 6845
Petit, Jean-Marc, Can photographer, fl. 1971
#997
Petite, Marion, artist, fl. 1970s
– video art #651
Petley, Robert, Brit army officer, artist in
Canada, ca. 1809-1869
– views of Nova Scotia and New Brunswick
#5351
Petrigo, Walter, Can photographer, 1932-
– portfolio of photographs #995
petroglyphs
– see also conservation and restoration,
petroglyphs; rock art
petroglyphs, Algonquian
– Peterborough (Ont) #3619
petroglyphs, Assiniboine #3673
petroglyphs, Bella Coola
– Noeich River (BC) #3816
petroglyphs, Chipewyan #3439
petroglyphs, Coast Salish #3870
petroglyphs, Cree #3439
petroglyphs, Dorset
– Qikertaaluk Island (NWT) #4362
petroglyphs, Iroquois #3599
petroglyphs, Micmac #3617
– Kejimkujik National Park (Fairy Bay, NS)
#3614
petroglyphs, Northwest Coast Indians #3785
3859 3971 3988 3997 3999 4058
– Aldridge Point (BC) #3814
– Columbia Valley (BC) #3903
– compared with pictographs #3886
– Gabriola Island (BC) #4050
– Prince Rupert (BC) #3846
petroglyphs, Ojibwa #3591
– Peterborough (Ont) #3568
– Peterborough and Stoney Lake (Ont)
#3581
petroglyphs, Plains
– boulder monuments #3689
petroglyphs, Tlingit #3786
petrol stations
– see gasoline stations
Petrucci, Aimé, Can sculptor, 1887-1950
– annunciation theme #1633
Petry, Nancy Wargin, Can artist, 1931-
– exhibitions, group
– (1976) #1529
pewter, Canadian
– 19th c. #2704
– guide for collectors #2104 2252
– Québec #2226 2228 2664 2700
– Volpi, Charles de, collection #3248
Pfeifer, Bodo, Can artist, 1936-
– exhibitions, group
– (1969) #2039
Pfeiffer, Gordon Edward, Can artist, 1899-
#6846 6847
Pfliger, Terry, Can artist, 1947-
– on Jack Chambers #700
Pflug, Christiane Sybille, Can artist,
1936-1972 #110 6848 6849

– exhibitions
– (1974) #6850
– (1979) #6851
PGL Architects (Papineau, Gérin-Lajoie,
LeBlanc), Can architectural firm
– Mirabel (Qué), Montreal International
Airport. Passenger Terminal Building
#9518
Phases (Paris, France)
– and Roland Giguère #5598
Philadelphia (Penn)
– views, David Johnston Kennedy #6040
Philadelphia (Penn), Moore College of Art.
Gallery
– Recorded Activities exhibition (1970), Les
Levine on #6265
Philadelphia (Penn), Olympia Galleries
– exhibitions
– Watercolors by Robert Murray and Toni
Onley (1976) #613
Philadelphia (Penn), Pennsylvania Academy
of Fine Arts
– Reid, George Agnew, as student #6979
– Reid, Mary Hiester, as student #6982
Philadelphia (Penn), Philadelphia Museum
of Art
– exhibitions
– Sculpture of the Inuit: Masterworks of the
Canadian Arctic/La sculpture chez les Inuit:
chefs-d'oeuvre de l'Arctique canadien
(1973) #4423 4440
Philadelphia (Penn), University of
Pennsylvania. Museum
– artifacts, Thule #4372
– engraved artifacts, Inuit #4323
– headgear, Tlingit Indians #3803
– shark helmet, Kaguanton Clan #3833
– shield, Plains Indians #3680
– shields, Dakota #3670
– wampum, Iroquois #3518
– wampum, Micmac #3497
Philadelphia Society of Etchers
– exhibition, Toronto (Ont), (1885) #798
Phillips, Walter Joseph, Can artist, 1884-1963
#6856 6857 6859 6861
– as teacher of Gerald Tailfeathers #7312
7313
– exhibitions
– (1978) #6860
– landscapes #2016
– woodcuts #802 804 6852 6853 6854 6855
6858
philosophy
– see also transcendentalism
philosophy, Oriental
– influence on Frederick Horsman Varley
#7461
– influence on Pierre Archambault #4545
philosophy and art
– and Group of Seven #1774
– and Paul-Emile Borduas #1455
philosophy of art
– see art theory and criticism; aesthetics
Phinney, Robert, Can sculptor, fl. 1959-
#6862
Phipps, Lynn, Can photographer, 1936-
– portfolio of photographs #998
phonograph record covers
– (1950s) #862
– Knaff, Jean-Christian #6065
phonorecord jackets
– see phonograph record covers
Photo Age, Can periodical #987
Photo Canada, Can periodical #1032

Photo Club of Canada (Toronto, Ont)
– exhibitions (reviews) #978
Photo Communiqué, Can periodical #1053
3314
Photo Fun, Can periodical #987
Photo Life, Can periodical #1023
Photo-realism
– and Mary Frances Pratt #6919
Photograms of [189-]: A Pictorial and Literary
Record of the Best Photographic Work of the
Year
– Canadian photography (1895-1898) #978
Photograms of the Year, Brit periodical
– Canadian photography (1905-1940) #978
photographers, Canadian
– Absil, Mickey #1023
– Achim, Normand #1534
– Altman, Gerry #1023
– Anderton, T.George #4525
– Appel, Brian #1904
– April, Raymonde #1059 1063 1556
– Astman, Barbara Anne #1010 1063
– Baber, Jack #987
– Baczynski, George #1023
– Bailey, Charles S. #2012 4583
– Bailey, Clayton #1033 4584
– Bailey, William #2012
– Balch, Reg #991
– Baltzly, Benjamin #1014 1015 4598
– Bancroft, Marian Penner #2018 2071
– Barbour, David #1904
– Bareket, Nir #1023
– Barnes, Elliott Chappel #4610
– Bates, Maxwell Bennett #4621
– Baturin, Jon #1023
– Baxter, Iain #1057
– Bayley, W.B. #977
– Beaudoin-Hansen, Kéro #4648
– Beaugrand-Champagne, Claire #1513 1556
1562
– Bedford, Michael #995
– Bell, Bert #1036
– Bell, Ken #995 4657
– Bendahan, Raphael #4670
– Benoît (dit Livernois), Jules-Isaïe #258 259
– Bentley, Percy #2012
– Beny, Wilfred Roloff #4688 4689 4690 4691
– Beube, Doug #991
– Beveridge, Karl John #1052 1063
– Bierwagen, Ottmar #995
– Bigger, Charles A. #1014 1015
– Biggs, Hugh Beynon #4728
– Bingham, John #1032
– Blahut, John #1007
– Bleyenberg, Harry #1023 4742
– Bluesinger, Taki #996
– Bohar, Dick #998
– Boisvert, Paul #1023
– Boland, Con #1023
– Boogaerts, Pierre #1018
– Boorne, William Hanson #4796 4797
– Borremans, Guy #997 999
– Bot, Marten #995
– Bourdeau, Robert Charles John #987 1002
1018 1023 1037 1046 1060 1070
– Boyd, Jerry #1023
– Boyd, W.H. #989
– Boyer, Michel #1023
– Bradley, Randy #2071
– Breukelman, Jim #2071
– Brown, Alisen #1023
– Brown, Bert #995
– Brown, Douglas #1023
– Brown, Ernest #6451

– Brown, Gordon F. #991
– Brown, Randy #1023 1032
– Brown, Thomas #1000
– Bruce, David #2071
– Bruenner, Ralph #991
– Bruno, Anthony #995
– Bryson, Joseph Vincent #1032
– Buchan, David #1067
– Buchanan, Donald William #3325
– Calnen, Robert F. #995
– Cameron, Duncan #1675
– Campbell, Paul #1067
– Campbell-Smith, Struan #995
– Campeau, Michel #997 999 1513
– Carey, David #1023
– Carr-Harris, Ian #1057
– Carruthers, Alan #995
– Cassidy, Eugene Haanel #5054
– Castonguay, J.Alex #1675
– Caton, Peter #624
– Cavoukian, Artin #624
– Chabot, J.E. #1283
– Chambers, Jack #5075
– Chaput, Yves #997 999
– Charbonneau, Roger #997 999 1513 1556
– Chechik, Jeremiah #992
– Chesterfield, Albert A. #5102
– Chrismas, Lawrence #991
– Christl, Rudi #1023
– Chu, T.K. #1023
– Clairrou, Jacques #997 999
– Clark, Tim #1556
– Clément, Serge #991
– Cloutier, Marcel #1283
– Cohen, Lynne #1018 1037 1046 1053 1060
  1067
– Cohen, Sorel #5130
– Condé, Carole #1052 1063
– Conner, Scott #1032
– Corman, Don #1063
– Corsault, Share #2071
– Coshof, Karen #995 1023
– Cossette, Marie Andrée #1556
– Cousineau, Sylvain P. #1018 1067
– Coutellier, Francis #996
– Crête, Alphida #1562
– Croydon, Peter #1036
– Cupit, William Henry #2071
– Curtin, Walter #1054
– Dally, Frederick #5249
– Danson, Andrew #1053
– Davies, Barbara #993
– Davis, Leonard #991
– Dawson, George Mercer #1014 1015
– De Carufel, René #1562
– Delbuguet, René #1023
– Demers, Claude #1065 1066
– Denniston, Stan #1067
– Désilets, Antoine #5287 5288
– Desmarais, Gaby #624
– Devenyi, Denes #987
– Deville, Edouard Gaston Daniel #989 1014
  1015 1875
– Devor, Holly #2018
– Dickey, Estelle #2018
– Dille, Lutz #987 990 5292
– Dillon, Gera #1023 1032
– Donovan, Duncan #5299
– Downing, Claire #2012
– Dubreuil, Michel #1562
– Durocher, Gabriel #997 999
– Erb, Isaac #1186
– Esson, James #5373
– Evans, David #1018

– Evans, John #995
– Fardon, George Robinson #5411
– Farnsworth, Miss #977
– Ferguson, Mary #991
– Fieguth, Menno #1023
– Fisher, Bob #995
– Fisher, Tom #1556
– Fitzgerald, Owen #991
– Fletcher, Kenneth #992
– Flomen, Michael #1018
– Foster, Janet Green #991 1009
– Foster, John #991 1009
– Foster, Stuart #1023
– Frank, Leonard #2012
– Gaettens, Marianne #993
– Gagné, Andrée #1023
– Gagné, Marc-André #991 997 999 1000
– Gagnon, Charles #997 999 1007 1018 1037
  1046 1060 1556 5539
– Gallozzi, Chuck #1023
– Gamble, Millie #5554
– Gano, John Henry #5555
– Gascon, Michel #1562
– Gaudard, Pierre Raymond #990 1556
– Gauthier, Michel #1283
– General Idea #1057 1063
– Gibson, Carol #1018
– Gibson, Tom #997 999 1018 1037 1046 1060
– Gilbert, Albert #995
– Gore, Tom #2071
– Goss, Arthur S. #5633 5634
– Grant, Ted #995
– Green, Harold #991 1032
– Greenhill, Ralph #5651
– Grégoire, Normand #987 990 997 999 1556
  1562 5655
– Grice, Art #991 996 998 5659
– Grice, Emily #5659
– Grierson, John #1056
– Guimons, Jean #997
– Gunterman, Mattie #2012 2018 5670 5671
  5672
– Gutsche, Clara #1053 1556 5673
– Haddon, Jim #1023
– Haeffely, Claude #5674
– Hammock, Virgil #5696
– Harmer, William Morell #1675
– Harmon, Byron #5707
– Haroutiun, Georges #5708
– Harris, Pamela #996
– Helfand, Fern #1010
– Henderson, Alexander #5777
– Herzog, Fred #998
– Heuvel, Francis van den #997 999
– Hicks, Bill #995
– Hildred, Philip #998
– Hilst, Robert van der #1023
– Hime, Humphrey Lloyd #1014 1015 5801
  5802 5803 5804
– Hines, Sherman #995
– Hinton, John Henry #5812
– Hlynsky, David #992 1070
– Hobden, Mark D. #991
– Hoferichter, Bert #991
– Holloway, Elsie #5820
– Holownia, Thaddeus #1070
– Horeis, William Richard #1070 5836
– Horetzky, Charles George #995 1014 1015
  5837 5838
– Horvath, Tibor #995
– Hume, Clare #991
– Hurni, Jean-Claude #997 999
– Hutchinson, Peter #991
– Ives, R.E. #991

– Janosi, Paul #1032
– Jarvis, Samuel J. #1675
– Jauvin, Serge #1562
– Jaycocks, T.G. #5950
– Jensen, Vicki #998
– Johnson, Joanne Jackson #1033
– Johnston, Clifford M. #1675
– Jones, Bill #1057
– Joslin, Paul #1023
– Karkutt, Edith #987
– Karnick, Irwin #1008
– Karsh, Malak #995
– Karsh, Yousuf #1675 6022 6023 6024 6025
  6026 6027 6028 6029 6030 6031 6032 6033
  6034 6035 7329
– Karuna, Peter #1032
– Kazimierski, Daniel #992 1023
– Kerr, David #997 999
– Keuken, Johan van der #997 999
– Keziere, Robert #998 6051
– Kieffer, Daniel René #1562
– King, B.A. #1002 1070
– Klausen, Jorgen #991
– Knott, Tom #2071
– Knottenbelt, Marianna #1018
– Knudsen, Chris #6070 6071
– Kowall, Earl #997 999
– Kraulis, Janis A. #1023
– Kuzyk, Ron #1032
– Labelle, Paul #1562
– Labelle, Ronald #997
– Lacroix, André #1534
– Lafortune, François #6134
– Lake, Suzy #675 1057 1059 6137 6138 6139
  6140
– Lamoureux, Gisèle #991
– Langevin, Joseph #6161
– Lankinen, Wayne #1032
– Latchford, Joan #993
– Laurin, Serge #997 999
– Lauzon, Jean #1556
– Leeson, Benjamin W. #2012
– Legrady, George #997 999 1053
– Legrady, Miklos #997 999
– Lemay, J.Eudore #1283
– Lewis, David #1032
– Lewis, Glenn Alun #996
– Litteljohn, Bruce #1009
– Livernois, Jules-Benoît #6308
– Livick, Stephen #1007 1070
– Lotbinière, Pierre-Gustave Joly de #6326
– Lougheed, Robert Elmer #6327
– Louis, Pat #991
– Lum, Kay #1023
– Lund, Chris #987
– MacAskill, Wallace R. #6350 6351
– MacCormack, Terry #991
– MacEachern, Ian #6386
– MacKenzie, Robin #1057
– MacLeay, R.Scott #1023
– Maggs, Arnaud #1070
– Maher, Dean #1023
– Marino, Carol #1070
– Marquis, Robert #997
– Mathers, Charles Wesley #6451
– Mathurin, Jacques #1032
– Max, John #996
– Maynard, Hannah Hatherly #2018 6456
  6457 6458
– McArthur, James J. #989 1014 1015
– McCall, Helen #2018 6460
– McDermott, Michaelin #1904
– McDougall, Keith #1032
– McEachern, Susan #1067

– McLaughlin, Samuel #1019 1675
– McMillan, David #1033 1037 1046 1060 6504
– McOnie, Alan #998
– Mehta, Dilip #995
– Merrett, Brian #997 999
– Mia and Klaus #987
– Micklethwaite, Frank W. #1024
– Middleton, W.E.K. #991
– Miller, David G. #1556
– Miller, John Bellamy #6540
– Miller, Martha #2069
– Milne, Gilbert Alexander #995
– Milne, Graham #998
– Minden, Robert #6570
– Mitchel, Owen #991
– Mitchell, Michael #6575 6576
– Mitra, Shyamal #1023 1032
– Moodie, Geraldine #6602
– Morant, Nick #987 995 6605
– Morée, Michael de #991
– Morin, Serge #996
– Morrow, Patrick #1023
– Mounsey, Yseult #991
– Murray, Jim #1032
– Nadeau, Luis #991 6679
– Nakash, George #6683
– Newman, Brian #1032
– Nori, Angela #991
– Notman, William #245 986 1001 1019 6723 6724 6725
– Ogilvie, William #1014 1015
– Orban, Jeno F. #998
– Ott, Günter #1023
– Page, James Ritchey #1023
– Paisley, Douglas A. #995
– Panneton, André #1562
– Parizad #1023
– Parsons, F.R. #6773
– Paskievich, John #1904 6777
– Paterson, Malcolm #991
– Patterson, Freeman #995 1009 1016 1023 6780 6781 6782
– Pearson, Cedric #1513
– Pel, Brian #1032
– Pépin, Louis #1562
– Perrault, Pierre #1023
– Petit, Jean-Marc #997
– Petrigo, Walter #995
– Phipps, Lynn #998
– Pickering, Dale #2071
– Pikulin, Michael #991
– Pilon, Michel #1562
– Piton, Bill #992
– Pittaway, Alfred G. #1675
– Pluta, Andrzej #1023
– Pocock, Philip J. #987 1023
– Poirier, Conrad #6897
– Pollard, Harry #6899
– Porter, Tim #998 2071
– Powell, John #991
– Preston, John F. #1018
– Prud'homme, Luc #1023
– Raginsky, Nina #1002 1007 1037 1046 1060
– Rajotte, Normand #1556
– Randall, Cliff #1023
– Ranford, Barry #991
– Rankin, Toby #995
– Raskin, Lawrie #1063
– Redivo, Hugo #995
– Reeves, John #991 1065 1066 1070
– Rémi, Daniel #997 999
– Renaud, François #997 999
– Riley, Jerry #1032

– Rivest, Gilles G. #995
– Robertson, Tom #2071
– Robideau, Henri #1063
– Rockett, Beverly #993
– Rockett, Paul #1036
– Rojik, Michael #1032
– Rosenberg, Fred #997 998 999
– Royal, Frank #991
– Rubin, Mark #1002
– Rulofson, William Herman #7107
– Ruskay, John #991
– Ryan, Cyril #1018
– Saint-Jean, Michel #991 999 1562
– Sasabuchi, Shun #1032
– Sauer, June #993
– Savard, Alphonse E. #2012
– Schiele, Bernard #997 999 1000
– Schiffer, Fred #624
– Schlichting, Leonard #1904
– Schubert, Marcus #1053
– Seding, Volker #1070
– Semak, Michael William #987 990 991 996 1016 1023 1063 7168 7169
– Semchishen, Orest #991 1037 1046 1060
– Sénécal, André #997 999
– Sénéchal, Gilles #1283
– Sévigny, Marc #1534
– Shames, Stephen #998
– Sharp, Vincent #1018 7193
– Siegel, Lois #1000
– Simon, Harold #991
– Simone, Joe #995
– Simpkins, Bill #1023
– Simpson, Richard #1032
– Smalley, Katherine #1023
– Smith, Harold Thomas Faulkner #2012
– Smith, Madge #7235
– Snow, Michael #1057 7240 7242 7243 7244 7245 7248 7251 7254 7255 7256 7257 7258 7259 7260 7262
– Sommerer, Karl #995 7266
– Sowdon, Michael #1070
– Spencer, Elihu #1675
– Spencer, Mary #2018
– Spiteri, Ed #991 1023
– Spremo, Boris #995
– Sproul, Wayne #995
– Staley, Bill #1023
– Starbuck, Fletcher #992 1007 7275 7276
– Steltzer, Ulli #2018
– Stiff, Philander S. #1675
– Stiff, Thomas P. #1675
– Stott, Gregg #1032
– Straiton, Ken #2071
– Sugino, Shin #991
– Sulcs, Ernie #991
– Swensson, Pete #991
– Szilasi, Gabor #997 999 1002 1556 7308 7309
– Taconis, Kryn #1054
– Taillefer, Robert Eugene #991
– Tata, Sam #999 1556 7329
– Taylor, George Thomas #1174 1186 7333 7334
– Taylor, Jeremy #987
– Taylor, John #991
– Tesiorowski, Carol #1032
– Tessler, Ronnie #2071
– Tester, Wayne #1032
– Thomas, George #991
– Thomas, Randy #1023
– Thompson, Stuart #2012
– Thomson, Harry S. #1952
– Timms, Phillip Thomas #2012

– Title, Robert #991 998 2071
– Tomlinson, Jim #2071
– Topley, William James #1001 1024 1675
– Torosian, Michael #996
– Tousignant, Serge #1057 1067
– Tremblay, Pierre-Paul #1562
– Trowsse, Pegi #991
– Trueman, Richard H. #7437
– Turcot, Guy #997 999 1562
– Turner, Jack #7439
– Tyrrell, Joseph Burr #1014 1015
– Vachon, Ginette #1032
– Vail, Floyd #977
– Valiquet, Carl #997 999
– Van Dusen, Ray #1070
– Vanderpant, John A. #7456 7458 7459
– Vazan, Bill #1057
– Vickers, Ron #987
– Vinet, Pierre #990
– Visser, John de #991
– Vittecoq, Arlette #1534
– Von Baich, Paul #1023
– Wadsworth, Lizzy #7496
– Walker, Harry #1023
– Walker, John Barras #991
– Wan, Theodore Saskatche #1067 7514
– Warren, Bill #991
– Warren, Mary Schaffer #7525 7526 7527
– Watson, Budd #995
– Webb, Tom #1032
– Webber, Ron #1008
– Weiss, Joe #7541
– Weissmann, Lawrence #997 999 1000
– Wells, William #1032
– Wertschek, John #2071
– Weyler, Rex #991 998
– Wheeler, Arthur Oliver #989
– Whiteside, George #991 1067
– Wiley, Matthew #995
– Williams, Al #1032
– Williams, Robin #991
– Williamson, Betty #987
– Wilson, James #991
– Wiseman, Nelson #7604
– Wishlaw, Robert #2071
– Wong, Paul #992
– Woodley, Charles #1032
– Woodruff, John #1675
– Wright, Richard Thomas #1023
– Wu, Allan #1032
– Würtele, Fred C. #7619
– Xavier, John #1023
– Yoshi #998
– Young, Ron #1023
– Zarov, Basil #987
– Zelkine, Alexandre #997
Photographic Association of Canada
– Canadian Convention (1895) #979
photography
– see also aerial photography; ambrotypes; architectural photography; cameras; daguerrotypes; documentary photography; panoramic photography; photomontage; portrait photography; stereoscopic photography
– as archival documentation #1040
– Canadian museum collections #1051
– Ottawa (Ont), National Gallery of Canada #3061
photography, Canadian #2 925 986 1041
– 19th c. #1006 1048
– 20th c. #988 1007
– (1837-1887) #253
– (1839-1920) #1039

– (1851-1878), collodian wet-plate method #1025
– (1860-1890), landscapes #271 272
– (1890s) #979 1886
– (1905-1940) #978
– (1909) #981
– (1910s) #982
– (1920s) #7456
– (1930), Canadian National Exhibition (Toronto, Ont) #313
– (1930s) #340
– (1970s) #610 997 999 1000 1002 1012 1018 1022 1027 1030 1033 1037 1044 1045 1046 1060
  – landscapes #1050
– (1974), *Photo Festival '74* (Ottawa, Ont) #1008
– (1975-1980) #1799
– (1980s) #912 1067 1070
– (1981), Federal Cultural Policy Review Committee #1068
– Alberta
  – (1970s) #1952
  – (1980) #1976
– and advertising, 19th-20th cs. #1024
– and art (1970s) #635 1057
– and language (1980) #1063
– and literature (1980) #1065 1066
– and painting
  – (1860-1900) #245 262 268
  – (1970s) #545
  – landscapes, late 19th c. #264
– and sculpture (1970s) #994
– archival collections #1029
– Art Director's Club of Toronto #854
– art market (1970s) #1038
– Atlantic provinces (1970s) #1132
– Boorne and May (1880s) #1950
– British Columbia
  – (1858-1888), landscapes #2015
  – (1858-1914) #2032
  – (1860-1978), women photographers #2018
  – (1890-1914) #2030
  – (1890-1940) #2012
  – (1970s) #2041 2056 2063 2071
– Brock, J.A., & Co. (1886-1888) #2021
– Brown, Ernest, collection #1949
– cabinet portraits (1860s) #1026
– conference (1979) #1047
– Dojc, Yuri #1023
– Eastern Townships (Qué), (1970s) #1534
– Fringe Research Inc. #1827 1905
– Great Eastern Photographic and Advertising Company #2022
– Grice, Art #991
– Groupe d'action photographique #1003 1494
– Halifax (NS), (1830s-1860s) #1211
– Hamilton (Ont), (1867-1900) #1719
– *Homemaker's* periodical (1980s) #5708
– *Image* series, National Film Board of Canada (Ottawa, Ont), (1967-1971) #990
– *Impressions* #996
– Karsh, Yousuf, on #486 487
– Kingston (Ont) #1680
– Livernois family (1857-1960) #1275
– London (Ont), (1970s) #1812
– Manitoba #1895 1904
– Manitoba Camera Club #985
– Maritimes (1970s) #1134
– military photography (1885-1970s) #1107

– Montréal (Qué), Centaur Galleries #1004
– nature photography #1062
– New Brunswick (1869-1918) #1186
– of Canadians (1970s) #1035 1055
– of immigrants, Québec (1908-1910) #1031
– of Inuit (1920s) #1021
– of Northwest Coast Indians, late 19th-early 20th cs. #2029 2033
– Ottawa (Ont) #1675
  – National Film Board. Still Photography Division #1028 1043
  – Public Archives of Canada. National Photography Collection #3052
– Ottawa Camera Club #1677 1704
– parallel galleries (1970s) #1042
– periodicals
  – (1970s) #3314
  – *BC Photographer* #998
  – *Camera Canada* #991
  – *Canadian Journal of Photography* #974
  – *Canadian Photographic Journal* #976
  – *Canadian Photography* #995
  – *Image Nation* #992
  – *Impressions* #996
  – *Impulse* #538
  – *OVO* #997 999
  – *Photo Age* #987
  – *Photo Canada* #1032
  – *Photo Communiqué* #1053
  – *Photo Life* #1023
– Prairies (1970s) #1879
– Québec
  – 19th c.-1940s #1242
  – (1970s) #1507 1556
  – (1980s) #1562
– realism #716
– Saguenay-Lac-Saint-Jean (Qué) #1283
– Simcoe and Norfolk County (Ont), 19th c. #1722
– Simcoe County (Ont), 19th c. #1730
– survey photography #989
  – 19th c., supported by railway companies #3281
  – (1850s), Assiniboine and Saskatchewan Exploring Expedition #5804
  – (1850s-1890s), western Canada #1865
  – (1858-1900), British Columbia #2028
  – (1870s), Canadian Pacific Railway #1876
  – (1880s-1890s), Rocky Mountains #1874
– Toronto (Ont)
  – (1839-1867) #1725
  – Baldwin Street Gallery of Photography #1794
  – Metro Toronto Public Library #3143
  – Ryerson Polytechnical Institute #1805
– Toronto Camera Club #1 975 977 980 983 984 1683 1702
– Vancouver (BC)
  – (1970s) #2064 2069
  – Gallery of Photography #2052
– views of Canadian cities (1850-1900) #1058 1061 7744
– views of Newfoundland and Labrador (1849-1949) #1160
– Wellington County (Ont), (1856-1867) #1724
– western Canada
  – (1858-1900) #1014 1015
  – (1964-1970) #872
– Western Photographic Circle #2019
– Whitehorse (Yukon), Yukon Archives #2087
– women artists #1005 1064

– (1840-1900) #1049
– (1970s) #993 1011 1013
– World War I #1072 1113 1114
– World War II #1095
photography periodicals, Canadian #3313
– (1970s) #3314
– *BC Photographer* #998
– *Camera Canada* #991
– *Canadian Journal of Photography* #974
– *Canadian Photographic Journal* #976
– *Canadian Photography* #995
– *Image Nation* #992
– *Impressions* #996
– *Impulse* #538
– *OVO* #997 999
– *Photo Age* #987
– *Photo Canada* #1032
– *Photo Communiqué* #1053
– *Photo Life* #1023
photography technique
– *see* media and techniques, photography
photomontage
– Guimond, Pierre #5664
– Notman, William #6726
physicians
– Canadian, portrait medals, Robert Tait McKenzie #6483
– residences, Ontario, 19th c. #8675
Pi, Lutz
– *see* Haufschild, Lutz
Piaget, Jean, Sw psychologist, 1896-1980
– theories, and N.E. Thing Co. Ltd. #6677
pianos, Canadian
– Nova Scotia #2489
Picabia, Francis, Fr artist, 1879-1953
– influence on Alfred Pellan #6822
Picard, Armand, Can sculptor, 1943- #1626
Picard, Edmond, Can builder, b. 1881 #6863
Picard, Louis-Alexandre, Can jeweller, silversmith, ca. 1728-1799 #269 270
Picasso, Pablo, Sp artist, 1881-1973
– Bates, Maxwell Bennett, compared with #4623
– influence on Alfred Pellan #6803 6805 6811 6821 6822 6826
– influence on Bill Reid #6985
– influence on Jacques de Tonnancour #7383
– influence on Paraskeva Clark #5110
– influence on Paul-Emile Borduas #4841
– influence on Robert La Palme #6119
– Pellan, Alfred, compared with #6814
Piccaluga, Aldo, Can designer, 1936-
– interior, CN Tower. Restaurant #9511
Piccaluga, Francesco, Can designer, 1932-
– interior, CN Tower. Restaurant #9511
Piccirilli brothers, Amer sculptors, fl. 1920s
– sculpture, Legislative Building (Winnipeg, Man) #8948 8952
Piché, Reynald, Can artist, 1929- #6864
Piché-Whissell, Aline, Can artist, 1919- #6865
Picher, Claude, Can artist, 1927- #6866 6867
Pichet, Roland, Can artist, 1936- #6868
– exhibitions, group
  – (1977) #1278 1279
Pickering, Dale, Can photographer, 1948- #2071
  – (1979) #2069
Pickering, David, Can sculptor, 1941-
– exhibitions, group
  – (1978) #786
pictographs
– *see also* rock art
pictographs, Algonquian #3385 3576

- Agawa River region (Ont) #3589
- birchbark #3571
- Great Lakes region (Ont) #3583
- Lac Wapizagonke region (Qué) #3600
- Quetico Park (Ont and Man) #3575
pictographs, Carrier #3965
pictographs, Cree #3760
pictographs, Dakota
- winter counts #3747
pictographs, Indians of North America
#3390 3392
pictographs, Inuit
- Alaska #4217
pictographs, Kootenay #3965
pictographs, Lillooet #3783
pictographs, Micmac
- Fairy Lake (NS) #3494
pictographs, Northwest Coast Indians #3859
3893 3952 3999
- compared with petroglyphs #3886
pictographs, Ojibwa #3539
- Midewiwin #3492
pictographs, Penobscot #3537
pictographs, Plains
- Kipahigan Lake region (Sask and Man)
#3714
- Milk River region (Mon) #3706
pictographs, Skeena
- Skeena River (BC) #3822
pictographs, Thompson Indians #3769
Picton (Ont)
- pottery, 19th c. #2286
Pictou (NS), Hector Centre Trust
- exhibitions
- *Nineteenth Century Pictou County
Furniture* (1977) #2513
Pictou County (NS)
- architecture #7821 7827
Picture Butte (Alta), Picture Butte Municipal
Hospital
- architecture, Meech, Mitchell, Robins &
Associates #9032
picture frames
- *see* frames
Picture Loan Society (Toronto, Ont) #1746
Picturesque
- and British Columbia views (1845-1871)
#2020
- and churches, Ontario #8904
- and George Heriot #5786
- and Northwest Coast views, 18th c. #2009
- and Nova Scotia views, 18th-19th cs. #1220
1222
- and William Henry Bartlett #4617
Piegan Indians
- art #3759
- costume #3414 3715
Pierce, Edith Chown, Can collector, d. 1954
- collection, Canadian glass #2397 2398 2399
Pieroway, Percy, Can artist, 1921- #1155
- exhibitions, group
- (1976) #1153
- (1977) #1156
Pierron, Jean, Fr priest, artist in Canada,
1631-1673 #198 1363
- devotional images #1354 1358
pigments
- *see also* dyes and dyeing
- from Québec soil, for painting (1820s) #165
Pikulin, Michael, Can photographer,
1945-1975
- portfolio of photographs #991
Pilon, Germain, Fr sculptor, 1535-1590
- Baillairgé, François, compared with #4589

Pilon, Michel, Can photographer, 1951-
#1562
Pilot, Robert Wakeham, Can artist,
1898-1967 #302 6869
- and Group of Seven #1732
- as stepson of Maurice Galbraith Cullen
#5222
- exhibitions
- (1968) #6872
- exhibitions, group
- (1977) #1278 1279
- interview #6871
- on Albert Henry Robinson #7057
- on Maurice Galbraith Cullen #1143 5219
5221
- on Québec (Qué) #6870
Pilote, Clode, Can artist, 1944- #1626
Pingerqalik (Foxe Basin, NWT)
- artifacts, Dorset #4335
pipes, Algonquian #3463 3511 3529
pipes, Blackfoot #3654 3678 3704
- Medicine Pipe ceremony #3681
- pipe bundles #3665
pipes, Canadian
- Bell, W. & D., Pottery #2298 2322
- ceramic, Québec, 17th-19th cs. #2313
pipes, Cayuga #3525
pipes, Cree
- and calumet ceremony #3662
pipes, Dogrib #4077
pipes, Haida #3782
- argillite carving #4047
pipes, Huron
- carved stone faces #3632
- Toronto (Ont), Royal Ontario Museum
#3504
pipes, Indians of North America #3329 3416
3444 3700
- illustrations, George Catlin #3478
- London (England), British Museum #3470
pipes, Iroquois #3489 3525 3555 3566 3618
- carved human figures #3642
- Toronto (Ont), Royal Ontario Museum
#3504 3644
pipes, Micmac #3565
pipes, Nahani #4077
pipes, natives of North America #3358
pipes, Ojibwa #3539
pipes, Seneca #3636
- carved human figures #3642
pipes, Tahltan
- (1910s) #4074
pipes, Woodlands #3491
Piqtoukun, David Ruben, Can sculptor,
1950- #6873
- stone sculpture, Van Dusen Gardens
(Vancouver, BC) #775
Piquette, Jean-Baptiste, Can silversmith, fl.
1781-1813
- works, Detroit Institute of Arts (Detroit,
Mich) #2691
Piranesi, Giovanni Battista, It architect,
artist, 1720-1778
- Cormier, Ernest, on #8346
Pissarro, Camille, Fr artist, 1830-1903
- influence on Robert Wakeham Pilot #6869
pitchers
- *see also* cruets
pitchers, American
- glass, 19th-early 20th cs. #2430
pitchers, Canadian
- glass, 19th-early 20th cs. #2430
- presentation jug, Cap-Rouge Pottery
(Québec, Qué) #2332

Piton, Bill, Can photographer, fl. 1970s #992
Pitseolak, Mary, Can artist, 1901- #4260
Pitseolak, Peter, Can artist, 1902-1973 #4242
4460 6874 6878 6880 6881
- autobiography #6876
- drawing #4202
- exhibitions
- (1980) #6883
- exhibitions (reviews) #6882
- photographs of Inuit #6879
- watercolour paintings, National Museum
of Man (Ottawa, Ont) #6875 6877
Pitsiulak, Lypa, Can artist, 1943-
- ceremonial mace, Northwest Territories
Council #4386
Pittaway, Alfred G., Can photographer,
1858-1930
- exhibitions, group
- (1970) #1675
Placentia (Nfld)
- architecture #7792
- fortifications (1662-1811) #8420 8421
Plains Indians #3660
- architecture #8102
- art #3359 3434 3463 3668 3690 3691 3720
3730 3751
- 19th c. #3737 3750
- prehistoric #3710
- beadwork #3682
- boulder monuments #3689
- buffalo robe #3664
- costume #3656 3657 3658 3692 3694 3697
- culture #3651 3684 3717 3756
- (1830s) #3738
- drawing and painting #3709
- equestrian trappings #3405
- feathered headdresses #3683
- ghost dance #3736
- horse sticks #3743
- leatherwork #3456
- medicine wheels #3748
- metalwork #3698
- moccasins #3666
- painting #3672 3716
- pictographs #3706 3714
- pony beads, 19th c. #3722
- quillwork #3443 3652 3745
- rites and ceremonies #3725
- secret societies #3727
- shields #3680 3732
- shields and tipis #3758
- Thunderbird #3410
- tipis #3675
- wampum #3521
- winter counts #3728
Plamondon, Antoine-Sébastien, Can artist,
1804-1895 #1315 1318 1323 1336 6884
- and Québec painting #1353
- and Québec society #1375
- as teacher of Théophile Hamel #5690
- *Chemin de la Croix*, Montreal Museum of
Fine Arts (Montréal, Qué) #6886
- compared with Théophile Hamel #5689
- exhibitions, group
- (1880) #1308
- (1959) #219
- (1970) #1348
- influence of French painting #1244
- *Le flûtiste* #6885
- *Soeur Saint-Alphonse*, National Gallery of
Canada (Ottawa, Ont) #6887
- works, Art Association of Montreal
(Montréal, Qué) #3075
Plamondon, Guy, Can curator, 20th c.

– as director of 49th Parallel (New York, NY) #712
Plamondon, Marius Gérald, Can artist, 1914-1976 #6888
– as teacher, Ecole des beaux-arts (Québec, Qué) #1404
– as teacher of Aline Piché-Whissell #6865
– stained glass
  – Joliette (Qué), Novitiate of the Clerics of Saint-Viateur #2447
  – Montréal (Qué)
    – Queen Elizabeth Hotel #8228
    – Saint Joseph's Oratory #2448
Plamondon, Maurice, Can, 20th c.
– on Gérard Morisset #3305
plants
– Ontario, 19th c. #2245
plants in art
– see also flowers in art; leaves in art; trees in art
– British Columbia botanical art, late 18th c.-1970s #2024
– Canadian architectural decoration (1930s) #8225 8226
– Canadian pottery, 17th-19th cs. #2302
– European artists in America, 16th-19th cs. #260
– Holmes, Robert #5823
– Pellan, Alfred #6818 6819
– Sinclair, Robert #7215
Plaskett, Joseph Francis (Joe), Can artist, 1918- #1996 6890
– and Molly Lamb Bobak #4766
– as student of Hans Hofmann #1850
– exhibitions
  – (1971) #6893 6894
  – (1977) #6895
– interview #6892
– on Herbert Edward Read #6891
– on influence of Hans Hofmann on Canadian painting #402
– on modernism #6889
– portraits #715
– stage design and costume, Pygmalion #1991
plaster casts
– of male models, Colette Whiten #7557 7558
plasters
– see cements, mortars, and plasters
plasticiens (Montréal, Qué) #145 476 536 1294 1426 1438 1439 1465 1472 1487 6586
– and Denis Juneau #5994
– and Fernand Leduc #6187
– and Guido Molinari #6590
– and Guy Montpetit #6599 6600
– and Optical art #1445
– and Pierre Gendron #5582
– compared with automatistes #7398
– compared with Painters Eleven #720
– hard-edge prints #832
– influence of Piet Mondrian #1457
– Manifeste des plasticiens, Fernand Toupin on #7396
plastics
– Canadian decorative arts, 20th c. #2121
– Canadian sculpture #768
– Québec art (1960s) #1442
– Québec sculpture (1970s) #1603
plastics, Canadian
– industrial design (1940s) #2601
Plateau Indians
– culture #3774
Platt, Charles Adams, Amer architect,

1861-1933
– influence on Northway Department Store (Toronto, Ont) #9366
Plattsburgh (NY), Clinton County Historical Museum
– exhibitions
  – Folk Art in Canada (1981) #973
Plaw, John, Can architect, 1745-1820 #8399
– Charlottetown (PEI), market building #7800
playing cards
– in art, David Brown Milne #6553
plazas
– see squares (cities)
Plear, Scott, Can artist, 1952-
– exhibitions, group
  – (1981) #2084
Ploethner, Frederick K., Can furniture-maker, weaver, b. 1826 #6896
Plotek, Leopold, Can artist, 1948-
– exhibitions, group
  – (1981) #1565
Pluta, Andrzej, Can photographer, fl. 1977
– portfolio of photographs #1023
Pocock, John (Jack), Can jeweller, 1912- #2696
Pocock, Philip J., Can photographer, 1954-
– exhibitions, group
  – (1981) #1069
– portfolio of photographs #987 1023
Podbielski, Marie, Can artist, fl. 1980s
– illustrations #941
poetry
– see also concrete poetry
poetry, Canadian
– after War of 1812 #327
poetry, Inuit #4317
poetry and art
– Canada
  – (1970s) #649 1529
  – automatism #1449
  – landscape theme #140
  – nature and humble dwellings themes #104
– Giguère, Roland #5593 5597
– Kiyooka, Roy Kenzie #6062
– Leduc, Ozias #6196
– Meredith, John #6514
– Nicoll, Jim #6700
– Nokony, Denis #6716
– Pellan, Alfred #6808 6815 6824 6825
– Pichet, Roland #6868
– Québec, Surrealism #1464
– Shadbolt, Jack Leonard #7183
– Wallace, Ian #7509
Poggi, Vincent, Can stained glass artist, fl. 1958
– stained glass, Saint Alphonse Church (Montréal, Qué) #2448
Point, Father, Can priest, 1799-1868
– and Blackfoot Indians #3721
Point Spencer (Alaska)
– prehistoric artifacts #4374
Pointe au Baril (Ont)
– views, Barker Fairley #5402
Pointe-aux-Trembles (Qué), Church of l'Enfant-Jésus
– interior, Antoine Cirier #269 270
Pointe-aux-Trembles (Qué), Church of pèlerinage de-la-Réparation
– architecture, André Blouin #8840
Pointe-Claire (Qué), Pointe-Claire Cultural Centre. Stewart Hall Art Gallery
– exhibitions

– Manitoba Mainstream: People's Art/Fine Art/Le Grand Courant du Manitoba: arts populaires, beaux-arts (1973) #1897
– Mountain: A Lithograph by James B. Spencer/Montagne: une lithographie de James B. Spencer (1974) #7270
– Watercolour Painters from Saskatchewan/Aquarellistes de la Saskatchewan (1972) #1920
Pointe-des-Monts (Qué), lighthouse
– architecture #9526
Pointe-du-Lac (Qué), "Garceau" Mill #9246
Pointe-Saint-Charles (Qué), Saint-Jean Parish Church
– sculptures, Charles Daudelin #5258
Pointon, Philip, Can ceramicist, fl. 1874 #2301
– presentation jug, Cap-Rouge Pottery (Québec, Qué) #2332
Poirier, Anne, Fr sculptor, 1942-
– exhibitions, group
  – (1980) #8237
Poirier, Conrad, Can photographer, 1913-1968 #6897
Poirier, Narcisse, Can artist, 1883-
– and Montée Saint-Michel #1236
Poirier, Patrick, Fr sculptor, 1941-
– exhibitions, group
  – (1980) #8237
Poisson, Renée, Can ceramicist, sculptor, 1944-
– interview #6898
Poitras, Jacques, Can sculptor, fl. 1842 #1301
Poland
– art #603
Poldaas, Jaan, Can artist, 1948-
– colour xerography #614
Poles in Canada
– art #642
– arts #149
police stations, Canadian
– Toronto (Ont), (1930s) #8970
political cartoons
– see also caricature
political cartoons, Canadian #943
– 19th-20th cs. #957
– (1759-1914), Québec, revolutionary subjects #1351
– (1770s-1970s) #956
– (1867-1967) #945
– (1874-1946), Canadian East-West discord #958
– Bengough, John Wilson #942
– Julien, Henri #5986
– Macpherson, Duncan Ian #6400 6401
– Norris, Len #6722
– prime ministers #944
– Racey, Arthur George #6952
politics and architecture
– and conservation #7767
politics and art
– Bengough, John Wilson #4676 4677
– Borduas, Paul-Emile #1466
– Canada #910 3910
  – (1960s) #87 447 529 3263
  – (1970s) #602 619 693
    – and parallel galleries #641
  – (1980), and museums #683
  – and fashion (1882-1910) #2897
– Clark, Kelly #5109
– Frenkel, Vera #5522
– Girouard, Jean-Joseph #5609
– Légaré, Joseph #6215
– Montpetit, Guy #6600

– Montréal (Qué)
  – (1968-1969) #1514
  – (1970s) #1489 1548
  – *Corridart* street exhibition (1976) #1530
  – Olympic Stadium #9139
– Québec
  – (1640-1840) #1329
  – (1760-1790) #1369
  – (1961-1975) #3280
  – (1970s) #1528
  – and video art #1499 1537 1550
– Russell, Edward John #7110
– W.O.R.K.S. #1955
– Walker, Robert #7505
– Wieland, Joyce #7579 7580
Polken, Jeffrey Ervin, Can artist, 1934-
– exhibitions, group
  – (1966) #1123
Pollard, Harry, Can photographer,
  1881-1968 #6899
Pollock, Jackson, Amer artist, 1912-1956
– Borduas, Paul-Emile, compared with #4847
– Borduas, Paul-Emile, on #4838
– influence on Guido Molinari #6585 6588
  6591
– influence on Jean-Paul Riopelle #7027
– influence on Paul-Emile Borduas #4846
– Ronald, William S., compared with #7076
Polonceau, Henri, Can silversmith,
  1766-1828
– pax #2666
– works, Detroit Institute of Arts (Detroit,
  Mich) #2681
Pommier, Hugues, Fr priest, artist in
  Canada, ca. 1637-1686 #228 229 1323 1363
– portraits of clergy #1333
Pond, Irving K., Amer architect, 1857-1939
– Saint John (NB), General Public Hospital
  #9020
Pond, Martin & Lloyd, Amer architectural
  firm
– Saint John (NB), General Public Hospital
  #9020
Ponoka (Alta)
– art (1940s) #1943
Pontbriand, Henri Marie Dubreuil de, Can
  bishop, 1708-1760
– art objects given to Church of
  Notre-Dame. Museum (Montréal, Qué)
  #3081
Ponte, Vincent, Can city planner, 1919-
– influence on Montréal architecture (1960s)
  #7901
Pontiac County (Qué)
– architecture #7894 7895
pony beads, Plains
– 19th c. #3722
Poole, Ernest Edward, Can collector,
  1884-1964
– collection, Canadian art #3217 3222 3235
Poole, Leslie Donald, Can artist, 1942- #2053
  6900 6901
– *Confessions* #6902
– exhibitions
  – (1979) #6903
Pootoogook, Kananginak, Can artist, 1935-
  #4460 6904
Pop art
– and Greg Curnoe #5231 5233
– and Guido Molinari #6591
– and Michael Snow #7245
– and Pierre Ayot #4573
– and Robert Percival #6835
– Canada #71 87 476

– Québec #1497
Pope, William, Can artist, 1811-1902 #6905
  6906
porcelain
– *see* pottery
porcelain painting
– *see* china painting
Porcepic, Can periodical #538
Port Alberni (BC), Alberni Valley Museum
– art, Nootka Indians #4020
Port Arthur (Ont), Thunder Bay Historical
  Society
– exhibitions
  – *The Far West* (1943) #12
Port-au-Choix (Nfld)
– artifacts, Dorset #4354
– burial sites, Beothuk #3611
Port-au-Persil (Qué)
– views, Jean-Paul Lemieux #6230
Port-Cartier (Qué)
– architecture, Rother/Bland/Trudeau #8184
Port Credit (Ont), J.P. Bickell House
– architecture, Murray Brown #8338
Port Hope (Ont), Batterwood House
– residence, Vincent Massey #3220
Port Hope (Ont), Carr Farm
– architecture #7959
Port Hope (Ont), Trinity College School. Art
  Gallery
– exhibitions
  – *David Blackwood: Paintings, Drawings,
    Prints* (1967) #4739
Port-Meunier (Qué)
– architecture #7869
Port-Nouveau-Québec (Qué)
– graphic arts (1972-1975) #4475
Porteous, Charles, Can businessman,
  collector, b. 1848
– as patron of William Brymner #4951
Porter, Brian, Can artist, 1948- #6907
– prints #1214
Porter, Edward Clark, Can artist, 1935-
– prints #1214
Porter, Katherine, Amer artist, 1941-
– drawings #532
Porter, Timothy Nichol (Tim), Can
  photographer, 1946- #2071
– portfolio of photographs #998
Portland (Oreg), Portland Art Museum
– art, Northwest Coast Indians, Rasmussen
  Collection #3875 3937
– exhibitions
  – *Prehistoric Stone Sculpture of the Pacific
    Northwest* (1952) #3887
  – *The Far North: 2000 Years of American
    Eskimo and Indian Art* (1973) #3366
Portneuf (Qué), Church of Rivière-à-Pierre
– interior, Gérard Morisset #8891
Portneuf (Qué), Church of Saint-Gilbert
– interior, Gérard Morisset #8891
Portneuf County (Qué)
– crosses #1621
Portneuf Pottery, Brit ceramic manufacturer
  #2306
portrait medals
– *see* coins and medals
portrait photography, Canadian
– (1860-1900), and painting #268
– (1970s), artists on #624
– Bailey, Clayton #4584
– Beaudoin-Hansen, Kéro #4648
– cabinet portraits (1860s) #1026
– Donovan, Duncan #5298 5299
– Halifax (NS), (1860s) #1211

– Holloway, Elsie #5820
– Karsh, Yousuf #486 487 6023 6026 6030
  6031 6032 6034 6035
  – famous men and women #6025 6028
    6029
  – government and military figures #6022
  – women #6024
– Maritimes, 19th c. #1171
– Nakash, George #6683
– Parsons, F.R. #6773
– Pollard, Harry #6899
– Reeves, John #6971 6972
  – Canadian authors #1065 1066
– Sawyer, William #7145
– Tata, Sam #7329
portrait sculpture, Canadian
– Hahn, Emanuel Otto #5679
– Hébert, Louis-Philippe #5767 5769
– Judah, Doris Minette #5980
– Liébert, Philippe #6281
– McKenzie, Robert Tait #6484
– Mol, Leo #6579 6580
– Wheeler, Orson Shorey #7549
portraits
– *see also* portrait photography; self-portraits;
  silhouettes
– Forster, John Wycliffe Lowes, on #5467
– Ottawa (Ont), Public Archives of Canada
  #3023
portraits, American
– 18th-early 19th c., influence on Canadian
  portraits #1197
– Eaton, Wyatt #5357
– Field, Robert #5432
portraits, Canadian #715
– 17th-19th cs. #173
– 18th-19th cs. #246
  – prints #839
– 18th-early 19th c. #1197
– 19th c. #66 178 1323
– 19th c.-1920s #8
  – (1780-1870) #263
  – (1860-1900), and photography #268
  – (1890s), recommendations #183
  – (1900-1940) #28
  – (1910s) #205
  – (1970s), artists on #624
– Beaucourt, François Malepart de #4646
– Berczy, William Bent #241 242
– Berczy, William von Moll #4701
  – *Woolsey Family* #4700
– Berthon, George Theodore, judges #4713
– Boisseau, Alfred #4769
– Borduas, Paul-Emile #4836
– Bourassa, Napoléon #4872
– Crist, Lela Gurnee #5209
– Field, Robert #5432
– Forbes, John Colin #5459
– Forster, John Wycliffe Lowes #5468 5469
  5470
– Foulis, Robert #258 259
– Girouard, Jean-Joseph, patriots of rebellion
  (1837-1838) #5609
– Halifax (NS), (1740s-1940s) #1195
– Hamel, Théophile #258 259 1348 5690
– Harris, Lawren Stewart #5733
– Harris, Robert #5743
  – *The Fathers of Confederation* #5736 5738
    5740
– Holman, James Henry #5821
– Kane, Paul #6010
– Krieghoff, Cornelius #241 242 6097
– Lyall, Laura Adeline Muntz, children
  #6339

– Macdonald, Evan Weekes #6356
– MacDonald, Thomas Reid #6380
– Montréal (Qué), miniatures and
  silhouettes (1760-1860) #1376 1377
– Newton, Lilias Torrance #6692 6693
– Ontario
  – 19th-20th cs., children #1687
  – 19th c. #267
– Plamondon, Antoine-Sébastien #1348 6884
  – nuns #6887
– Québec #959 1265
  – 17th-18th cs., portraits of clergy #1333
  – 17th c. #228 229
  – 18th-19th cs. #219
  – 19th c. #1336
– *Souvenirs canadiens* #1326
– Toronto (Ont)
  – City of Toronto Archives #3178
  – Metro Toronto Public Library. John Ross
    Robertson Historical Collection #3130
    3131
– Town, Harold Barling #7416
– Varley, Frederick Horsman #7466 7467
– war subjects, National Gallery of Canada
  (Ottawa, Ont) #1101
– Wright, Edith P. Stevenson #7279
ports
– *see* harbours
Post, Jordan, Can silversmith, fl. 1787-1840s
  #2638
Post-Impressionism
– and Group of Seven #1741
– and J.E.H. MacDonald #6366
– and James Wilson Morrice #6622
post-modernism
– Canadian architecture #7732
– Canadian art and architecture #8237
post offices, Canadian
– 19th c. #9054
– (1881-1896), Thomas Fuller #9055
– Manitoba #9053
postage stamps
– (1963-1974) #829
postage stamps, Canadian
– (1918-1940s) #807
– (1950s), Laurence Hyde on #811
– guide for collectors #2104
– Hahn, Emanuel Otto #5680
– MacAskill, Wallace R., *Bluenose* #6351
– Price, Art #6928
– Volpi, Charles de, collection #3248
postal cards, Canadian
– Image Bank (Vancouver, BC) #826
– McCall, Helen #6460
postal sculpture
– *see* mail art
Poste-de-la-Baleine (Qué)
– graphic arts (1972-1975) #4475
posters, Canadian #908 910 911
– (1940s) #353 374 851
– (1960s) #868
– Fiorucci, Vittorio #5442 5443
– Group of Seven #1774
– Kingston (Ont) #1680
– Montréal (Qué), (1970s) #880
– Olympic Games, 1976 (Montréal, Qué)
  #900
– Ontario and Québec (1960-1975) #903
– western Canada (1964-1970) #872
– World War I #916
– World War II #847 848
Potawatomi Indians
– art #3540
  – (1600-1760) #3579

potlatch, Bella Coola #3874
potlatch, Kwakiutl #3956 4052
potlatch, Northwest Coast Indians #3871
  3899 3911
  – masks #4038
potlatch, Tlingit #4012
pottery
– *see also* ceramic sculpture; china painting;
  Chinese export porcelain; pitchers;
  stoneware; tiles; tureens
– Louisbourg (NS) #2368 2369
pottery, Algonquian #3502 3529 3530 3545
pottery, American
– 19th c., influence on Canadian pottery
  #2281 2309
– (1750-1910), earthenware, Pennsylvania
  and Ontario compared #3962
– early 20th c., for Canadian market #2346
pottery, Athapaskan
– (1970s), women artisans #3367
pottery, Blackfoot #3678
  – 18th-19th cs. #3679
pottery, British
– *see also* Minton porcelain; Rockingham
  ware; Staffordshire ware
– 19th c., influence on Canadian pottery
  #2281 2339
– 19th c., views of Canada, Minton dessert
  service #2289
– for Canadian market #2297
  – 18th-19th cs. #2363
  – 19th c. #2288 2294 2315 2320 2354
  – (1750s-early 19th c.) #2316
  – (1830s-early 20th c.) #2357 2358
  – (1850s-1890s) #2361
  – (1880-1914) #2340
– Glasgow (Scotland), Britannia Pottery
  #2326
– Hudson's Bay Company #2351
– John Marshall & Co., sporting subjects
  #2360
– Portneuf Pottery #2285 2306
pottery, Canadian #2107
– 17th-19th cs. #2302 2318 2324
– 17th-early 20th cs. #2281
– 19th c. #2099 2288 2297
– 20th c. #2121 2142
– (1837-1887) #253
– (1880-1914) #2340
– (1910-1961), Canadian National Exhibition
  (Toronto, Ont) #1
– (1940s) #2601
– (1950s) #2380
– (1955-1971) #2379
– (1960s) #2106 2382
– (1964-1967) #2108 2109
– (1970s) #2387 2388
– (1979-1980) #2138
– (1980) #2394 2395
– Ahrens Pottery (Paris, Ont) #2328
– Alberta
  – (1900-1970s) #2337 2386
  – (1912-1981) #2371
  – (1970s) #1951
  – (1980) #2393
– and architecture (1960s) #8236
– Archambault, Louis #4539
– Ariss, Margot Phillips #4546
– Atlantic provinces (1970s) #1132
– Beaudin, Gaétan #2381
– beaver motif #56
– Belleau, Charles #2366
– Benjamin Lent Pottery (Lincoln County,
  Ont) #2367

– Bourbeau, Géraldine #4877
– Brantford Pottery (Brantford, Ont) #2295
  2335
– British Columbia (1970s) #2391
– Brothers Glass (London, Ont) #2350
– Cap-Rouge region (Qué) #2296 2301
– Cartier, Jean Bernard #5051 5052
– china painting (1890s) #2277
– Cournoyer, Georget #5192
– Deichmann, Erica and Kjeld #1170 2377
– Deichmann, Kjeld #2376
– Desrochers-Drolet, Françoise #5289
– Dion Pottery (Ancienne-Lorette, Qué)
  #2345
– Doucet, Louise #5303
– Ecanada Art Pottery (Hamilton, Ont)
  #2359
– education (1940s) #2375
– Egmondville Pottery (Huron County, Ont)
  #2323 2329
– Gagné-Dufresne, Hélène #5531
– Garnier, Jacques #5557
– Germanic tradition #2140 2263
– guide for collectors #2101 2104 2125 2131
  2252
– Hamilton Pottery (Hamilton, Ont) #2347
– Handy, Arthur #5701
– Hart Pottery (Picton and Belleville, Ont)
  #2286 2293
– Hilton, Charles #2392
– Humberstone Potteries (north of Toronto,
  Ont) #2338
– Indian motifs, Victoria (BC), (1920s) #2278
– Jacquet, François #269 270
– Landry, Yvan #6160
– Legros, Enid Sharon #6223
– Levine, Marilyn Ann #6274
– Lincoln County (Ont), 19th c. #2290
– Luke, Alexandra #6333
– Manitoba #2272
– Manning, Les #6415
– Medalta Potteries (Medicine Hat, Alta)
  #2325 2372
– Mihalcheon, Jean Lapointe #2392 6529
– moulds, Ontario, 19th c. #2334
– nativity theme #393
– New Brunswick #2150
  – 19th c. #2319
– New Hamburg Pottery (New Hamburg,
  Ont) #2336 2348
– Ngan, Wayne G. #6695 6696
– Nova Scotia
  – 19th c. #2308
  – (1780s-1925) #2307
– Ontario #2249 2317
  – 19th c. #2284 2303 2356 2374
  – 19th-early 20th cs. #2355
  – (1750-1910), earthenware #3962
  – (1796-1930s) #2349
  – (1970s) #2262
– Paré, Réjean #1547
– Paris (Ont), 19th c. #2330
– Poisson, Renée #6898
– Prairies (1880-1920s) #2431
– Prince Edward Island, 19th c. #2311
– Québec #2226 2228 2237 2331
  – 17th-18th cs. #2181
  – 17th-19th cs. #2095
  – 18th-19th cs. #2299 2321
  – 19th c. #1334 1335 2283
  – 20th c. #2198
  – (1650-1837) #2313
  – (1655-1916) #2344
  – (1840s-1900) #2298 2322

– (1940s) #2188 2199
– (1950s) #2193
– (1970s) #2384 2390
– Québec (Qué), place Royale #2201 2352
– Québec and Ontario, 19th c. #2279
– Rakine, Marthe #6956
– Regina (Sask), (1970s) #2383 2385
– Sadowska, Krystyna #7113
– Sadowski, Konrad Jagin #7113 7114
– Saint-Denis (Qué), (1785-1888) #2343
– Saskatchewan #1919
– Savoie, Maurice #7137
– Sherbrooke (Qué), (1970s) #2232
– Spénard, Jean-Jacques #2179
– St. Johns Stone Chinaware Company
  (Saint-Jean, Qué) #2327
    – porcelain bust #2314
– State dinner service of Canada (1898)
  #2333
– Sures, Jack #7285
– Taylor Pottery (Port Hope, Ont) #2292
– techniques #2280
– Thibault, René #7344
– Thomas views #2287
– Thornsbury, James #1926
– Toronto (Ont), Ontario College of Art
  #3009
– Tremblay, Alain #2216
– Tremblay, Michèle #2216
– Tremblay, Suzanne #1549
– Vermette, Claude #2378
– Victoria (BC) #2269
– views, ships, 19th c. #2341
– Volpi, Charles de, collection #3248
– W. & D. Bell Pottery (Québec, Qué) #2291
– William Eby Pottery (Conestogo, Ont)
  #2304
– Young, Helen Granger #7627
pottery, Cayuga #3525
pottery, Huron #3502 3520
pottery, Indians of North America #3329
pottery, Inuit
– (1970s), women artisans #3367
– Rankin Inlet (NWT)
    – Craft Development Program (1966)
      #4207
    – Eskimo Arts and Crafts Centre (1970s)
      #4226
pottery, Iroquois #3502 3520 3525 3545 3555
  3564 3566
pottery, Japanese
– influence on Louise Doucet #5303
pottery, Northwest Coast Indians #3866
– Carr, Emily, collection #3827
pottery, Ojibwa #3539
pottery, Salish #3841
pottery, Sarcee #3659
pottery, Siouan #3687
pottery, Woodlands #3491 3545
– Draper site (Ont) #3640
pottery marks, Canadian
– Medalta Stoneware and Medalta Potteries
  (Medicine Hat, Alta), (1916-1954) #2372
– Ontario, 19th-early 20th cs. #2355
pottery technique
– see media and techniques, pottery
Poulin, Julien, Can artist, 1940-
– exhibitions, group
    – (1980) #705
– on video art #1537
Poulin, Robert, Can sculptor, 1949- #681
  1630
Poulin, Roland, Can artist, 1940- #1512 6908
– exhibitions, group

– (1977) #782
– (1978) #786
– (1980) #706
– on his art #6909
Pouliot, Mario, Can artist, 1949-
– and RACE #1536
Poussin, Nicolas, Fr artist, 1594-1665
– Colville, Alex, compared with #5147
– Surrey, Philip Henry, compared with
  #7289
Povungnituk (Qué)
– art #4274
– graphic arts #4494
    – (1959-1972) #4478
    – (1959-1976) #4490
    – (1960s) #4496
    – (1962) #4460
    – (1962-) #4468
    – (1972-1975) #4475
    – (1976) #4489
– graphic arts and sculpture #4200 4219
– sculpture #4411 4417 4421 4437
    – (1960s) #4189
    – competition (1967) #4223 4240 4415
Powell, glass manufacturing firm (Leeds,
  England)
– works, British Columbia Parliament
  Buildings (Victoria, BC) #8967
Powell, John, Can photographer, fl. 1970s-
– portfolio of photographs #991
Powers, Joseph William, Can architect,
  1852-1925
– Kingston (Ont), Kingston Penitentiary
  #9058
Prack & Perrine, Can architectural firm
– Toronto (Ont), William Wrigley Jr. Factory
  #9234
Prague (Czechoslovakia), Národni Galerie
– exhibitions
    – Grafika Kanadských Eskymáku (1972)
      #4479
Prairies
– architecture #8080 8083 8088 8089
    – 20th c. #8084 8086
    – (1970s) #8087
    – Jewish #8081
    – Ukrainian #8085
    – use of building and ornamental stones
      (1910s) #7646 7647
– art
    – 20th c. #145
    – (1920s-1960s) #461
    – (1950s) #429
    – (1960s) #1848 1851
    – (1960s-1970s) #1862
    – (1970s) #1860 1880
– bottles #2431
– decorative arts, Germanic tradition #2140
– domestic architecture #8717
    – sod houses #8701 8706
    – Ukrainian #8710
– folk art
    – (1960s) #1852
    – (1970s) #1881
– grain elevators #9237
– painting
    – (1920s-1950s) #396
    – (1970s) #588
– photographic views
    – Hime, Humphrey Lloyd #5801
    – late 19th c. #1949
– photography (1970s) #996 1879
– sculpture
    – (1960s) #1853

– (1970s) #1873 1878
– views
    – 19th-20th cs. #1855 1872 1882 1953 1970
    – 20th c. #1885
    – Chester, Donovan T. #1858
    – Condon, Wanda #5166
    – Eyre, Ivan Kenneth #5390
    – FitzGerald, Lionel LeMoine #5448
    – Herreilers, John #5791
    – Hind, William George Richardson #5807
    – Hurley, Robert Newton #1918 5885
    – Jefferys, Charles William #5953 5958
    – Kerr, Illingworth Holey #6050
    – Knowles, Dorothy #6066 6067
    – Kurelek, William #6109 6114
    – Leighton, Alfred Crocker #6225
    – Lochhead, Kenneth Campbell #6312
      6313
    – Lonechild, Michael #6322
    – Mulcaster, Wynona Croft #6660
    – Nokony, Denis #6716
    – Perehudoff, William #6836
    – Proch, Don #6940
    – Rindisbacher, Peter #7009
    – Sheldon-Williams, Inglis #7195 7196
    – Sinclair, Robert #7214
    – Tanabe, Takao #7321
    – Tascona, Tony #7328
    – Tinning, George Campbell #7378
    – Wyers, Jan #1918
Prangnell, Peter, Can architect, 1930-
– experimental curriculum, University of
  Toronto. School of Architecture (Toronto,
  Ont), (1967-1975) #8286
– on architectural education, University of
  Toronto. School of Architecture (Toronto,
  Ont), (1970) #8313
Pratt, Christopher, Can artist, 1935- #6911
  6912 6915
– and Mary Pratt #6914
– and realism #110
– exhibitions
    – (1970) #6910
– exhibitions, group
    – (1966) #1123
    – (1974) #573 1129
    – (1977) #643
– Forrestall, Tom, compared with #5466
– interview #6913
Pratt, George, Can sculptor, 1939- #6916
Pratt, Mary Frances, Can artist, 1935- #675
– and Christopher Pratt #6914
– exhibitions
    – (1981) #6919
– exhibitions, group
    – (1975) #591
    – (1980) #698
– exhibitions (reviews) #579
– interview #6917 6918
Pratt & Ross, Can architectural firm
– Brandon (Man), Prince Edward Hotel and
  Canadian National Railway Station #9266
– Winnipeg (Man)
    – Deer Lodge #9260
    – Hotel at Silver Springs #9263
pre-Columbian art
– and Margaret Peterson #6839
– and Robin MacKenzie #6392
Pre-Raphaelitism
– and Carol Fraser #5508
– and William George Richardson Hind
  #5805
Precisionism
– and Carl Fellman Schaefer #7157

prefabricated buildings, Canadian
– Arctic houses (1960s) #8732
– Vancouver (BC), British Columbia Mills
   Timber and Trading Company (1904-1910)
   #8082
prehistoric art
– and Katharine Emma Maltwood #6413
– Roussil, Robert, compared with #7090
Prendergast, Maurice Brazil, Amer artist,
   1859-1924
– influence on David Brown Milne #6567
– influence on James Wilson Morrice #6626
   6630
– Morrice, James Wilson, compared with
   #6631
Prent, Mark, Can sculptor, 1947- #538 6920
   6923 6924
– exhibition closures #6922
– exhibitions
   – (1979) #6926
– exhibitions, group
   – (1981) #796
– exhibitions (reviews) #6925
– interview #6921
Prescott/Maitland region (Ont), Poplar Hall
– architecture #7959
Prescott, Charles Ramage, Can, 1772-1859
– Cornwallis Valley (NS), Acacia Grove
   House #8528
Prescott (Ont)
– fortifications #8454
preservation of works of art
– see conservation and restoration
Presse, La, Can newspaper
– comic strips #954
– photographs #1562
   – Désilets, Antoine #5287 5288
Preston, John F., Can photographer, 1954-
– exhibitions (reviews) #1018
Preston (Ont)
– photographic views
   – Esson, James #5373
Prévost, Antoine, Can artist, 1930- #6927
Prévost, Robert, Can artist, 1928-
– stage designs #472
Price, Addison Winchell, Can artist, 1907-
   #6935
Price, Arthur Donald (Art), Can artist, 1918-
   #6928 6929 6930
– and architecture #8231
Price, Bruce, Amer architect, 1845-1903
– Montréal (Qué), Windsor Station #9537
– Québec (Qué), Château Frontenac #9278
   9291
– railway hotels #9290
Price, Daniel (Danny), Can artist, 1947-
   #6931
Price, Henry Edward, Can photographer,
   1918-
– photographs of World War II #1107
Price, Norman Molls, Can artist, 1871-1951
– illustrations #916
Price, Ralph, Can collector, 1939-, and
   Patricia, Can collector, 20th c.
– collection, Canadian folk art #971 972
– interview, on collecting Canadian folk art
   #970
Price, Tom, Can artist, 1860-1927 #4169 6932
– drawings #6933
– exhibitions
   – (1981) #6934
primitive art #3333
– see also prehistoric art
– compared with folk art #1243

– Indians of North America #3428
– influence on Canadian sculpture (1970s)
   #789
– influence on Sorel Etrog #5378
– Inuit #4341
– natives of North America #3342 3377
– Northwest Coast Indians #3348
Prince, Richard, Can artist, 1949- #6936 6937
   6938
– exhibitions
   – (1979) #6939
– exhibitions, group
   – (1976) #2060
   – (1978) #2066
   – (1981) #796
– natural constructions (1970s) #2065
– use of space and scale #2062
Prince Albert (Sask), Grace Campbell
   Gallery
– exhibitions
   – Images of the Inuit from the Simon Fraser
      Collection (1981) #4495
Prince Albert National Park (Sask), Grey
   Owl Cabin site
– architecture #8719
Prince Edward County (Ont)
– art (1970s) #1816
Prince Edward Island
– architecture #7798 7799 7801
   – 17th c.-1930s #7796
   – Harris, William Critchlow #8372
   – Plaw, John #8399
– art #1164 1166
   – (1940s) #350
   – (1970s) #1131 1165 1168
– art and architecture, 18th-19th cs. #7780
– bookplates, 18th-19th cs. #915
– churches #8777
– courthouses (pre-1914) #9009
– decorative arts #2153
– domestic architecture
   – 18th-19th cs. #8530
   – (1880s-1930s) #8544
   – sandstone houses, early 19th c. #8552
– furniture #2508
   – 18th-19th cs. #2498 2507 2518
– photographic views
   – Gamble, Millie #5554
   – Turner, Jack #7439
– pottery, 19th c. #2311
– quilts
   – (1850s-1970s) #2802
   – (1920s) #2794
– silver #2640
– stoneware, 18th c. #2364 2365
– textiles, 18th-19th cs. #2734
– views
   – Hammond, Charlotte Wilson #1169
   – Morrison, Alfred L. #6642
   – Redgrave, Felicity #1169
   – women artists (1970s) #1167
Prince Edward Island Heritage Foundation
– restoration projects (1970s) #7795
Prince Edward Island Pottery, ceramic
   manufacturer (Charlottetown, PEI) #2302
Prince Rupert (BC)
– petroglyphs, Northwest Coast Indians
   #3846
– totem poles, Kwakiutl #3957
Princeton (NJ), Princeton University
– ceramics, Trumbull-Prime Collection #2363
Princeton (NJ), Princeton University. Art
   Museum
– exhibitions

– Art of the Northwest Coast (1969) #3959
Prindle, Harry Edward, Can architect, b.
   1873
– Québec (Qué), Union Station #9533
Print and Drawing Council of Canada #835
– and Canadian Society of Graphic Art #801
– and Society of Canadian Painter-Etchers
   and Engravers #3
printing
– see also books; colour printing; commercial
   art
printing, Canadian
– (1947), Carl Dair, on #920
– Ontario, private presses (1970s) #935
– Toronto (Ont), Bridgens Limited #883
– typography #910
   – (1940s) #922
   – (1950s) #860 929 5455
   – (1958-1964) #923
   – (1960s) #868
   – (1970s) #932
   – (1980s) #912
prints
– see graphic arts
priories
– see monasteries
Prisme d'yeux #1472
– and Alfred Pellan #6808 6809
– and Surrealism #1458
– manifesto #6810
prisoners
– political, portraits of, Jean-Joseph Girouard
   #5609
prisons, Canadian
– Halifax (NS), 18th-19th cs. #7818
– Kingston (Ont), Kingston Penitentiary
   #9058
– Montréal (Qué) #8336
   – Pied-du-Courant Prison #9056
– Ontario, polygonal buildings, 19th c. #7987
– Québec (Qué), Plains of Abraham Prison
   #9057
Priteca, Benjamin Marcus, Amer architect,
   1889-1971
– Vancouver (BC), Orpheum Theatre #9135
   9141
private collections
– see collectors and collecting
Prix nationaux aux constructeurs de
   maisons unifamiliales
– (1960) #8742
prizes
– see awards
procedural art
– see process art
process art
– see also performance art
– Canada, landscapes #617
– Whiten, Colette #7556 7557 7558 7561
Proch, Donald (Don), Can artist, 1944- #6940
   6942
– exhibitions, group
   – (1977) #1901
   – (1978) #2066
– Field #714
– masks #6941
Proctor, Alexander Phimister, Can artist,
   1862-1950 #6943
– as member, Canadian Art Club #193
– autobiography #6944
– exhibitions (reviews) #204
Professional Native Indian Artists
   Association
– and Daphne Odjig #6731

Professional Photographer, Amer periodical
– and *Canadian Photographic Journal* #976
projectile points, Northwest Coast Indians
– arrows and spearheads #3785
Proof Only, Can periodical #1799
– (1970s) #1804
Protestantism
– and Québec churches #8887
Proulx, J.-Octave, Amer artist in Canada, b.
  1890
– and Montée Saint-Michel #1236
Provence (France)
– views
    – Reid, Leslie Mary Margaret #6981
Providence (RI), Brown University.
  Haffenreffer Museum of Anthropology
– art, Plains Indians #3751
Providence (RI), Haffenreffer Museum of
  Anthropology
– *see* Providence (RI), Brown University.
  Haffenreffer Museum of Anthropology
Provincetown (Mass), Rhode Island School
  of Design
– Stacey, Harold, as student #7274
Prud'homme, Luc, Can photographer, fl.
  1981
– portfolio of photographs #1023
Prus, Victor, Can architect, 1917-
– Montréal (Qué)
    – Expo Stadium #9101
    – métro. Crémazie and Mont-Royal
      Stations #9549
– Québec (Qué), Grand Théâtre de Québec
  #9112
public art
– *see also* open-air sculpture; state and art
– Roussil, Robert, on #7093
public art, Canadian
– (1960s), and architecture #753
– (1970s) #773 4524
– Alberta #1973
– Calgary (Alta), (1970s) #1959
– Montréal (Qué), late 19th c.-1920s #1623
– Montréal (Qué) and Toronto (Ont), mural
  paintings (1972) #539
– Québec #1606
– Royal Canadian Aerial Theatre (RCAT)
  #2058
– St. Catharines (Ont), (1972) #1795
– Vancouver (BC) #2080
    – (1905-1971) #2005
public buildings
– *see also* post offices
public buildings, American
– Fitzpatrick, Francis W. #8365
– state capital buildings #8944
public buildings, Canadian #7689
– (1880-1914) #7736
– (1911-1912) #8295
– (1920s) #7656
– (1950s) #8227
– (1960-1970) #7710
– (pre-1924) #7652
– Alberta (1900-1930s) #8126
– Charlottetown (PEI), Province House
  #8937 8938 8939
– conversion to cultural facilities #9147 9148
– Dawson City (Yukon), (1899-1902) #8367
  8368
– Department of Public Works
    – (1840-1960s) #8976 8977
    – (1950s) #8971
    – (1954-1959) #7681
– Edmonton (Alta)

– (1900-1914) #8130
– Alberta Government Administrative
  Building #8963
– Legislative Buildings #8962
– Fredericton (NB), Legislative Building
  #8940 8941
– Gothic revival #7739 7740
– Guelph (Ont), 19th c. #7970
– Halifax (NS)
    – 18th-19th cs. #7818
    – Lang, George Macdonald #7838
– Hamilton (Ont), Victorian #7991
– Hooper, Thomas #8376
– John B. Parkin Associates #8395
– Kingston (Ont)
    – 17th-19th cs. #7989
    – 19th c. #7995
– London (Ont), 19th c. #8007 8010
– Manitoba, 19th-early 20th cs. #8102
– Montréal (Qué)
    – architectural drawings, Archives
      nationales du Québec à Montréal #8604
    – Customs House #7917
– Newfoundland #7784
– Niagara-on-the-Lake (Ont), Navy Hall
  #8464 8465
– Nova Scotia, 17th-19th cs. #7814
– Ontario, 19th c. #8006
– Ottawa (Ont)
    – Parliament and Departmental Buildings
      #8923
    – Parliament Buildings #7695 8921 8922
      8924 8925 8927 8928 8930 8931 8932
      8933 8934 8935 8936 9055
– Prairies, legislative buildings #8944 8945
– prefabricated buildings, western Canada,
  early 20th c. #8082
– Québec
    – 17th c.-1940s #7853
    – (1880-1914) #7929
    – (1960s) #7862
– Québec (Qué), National Assembly #8942
– Regina (Sask)
    – (1910s) #8111
    – Legislative Buildings #8954 8955 8956
      8957 8958 8959 8960 8961
– Second Empire #7741 7742
– Toronto (Ont)
    – 19th c.-1930s #8076
    – Joseph E. Shephard Government of
      Canada Building #8975
    – Parliament Buildings (1791-1893) #8943
– Trois-Rivières (Qué), (1630s-1910s) #7883
– Victoria (BC), British Columbia Parliament
  Buildings #8964 8965 8966 8967
– Winnipeg (Man) #8105
    – (1880s-1910s) #8101
    – (19th c.-1960) #8095
    – Legislative Building #8946 8947 8948
      8949 8950 8951 8952 8953
public gardens
– *see* gardens
public housing, Canadian
– (1960s) #8518
    – for the aged #8516
– (1970s) #8520
public monuments
– *see* monuments
public squares
– *see* squares (cities)
publishing, Canadian
– (1970s) #619 693 3279
– art periodicals (1970s) #3310
– exhibition catalogues #3311 3319

pubs
– *see* taverns
Pudlat, Pudlo, Can artist, 1916- #4460
Puffin Island (Nfld), lighthouse #9523
Pulford, Edward Berwyn, Can artist, 1914-
  #6945
Pullman (Wash), Washington State
  Historical Society Museum
– basketry, Northwest Coast Indians #4004
pulpits, Canadian
– Québec (1650-1925) #1592
Punch, Brit periodical
– cartoons, Arthur George Racey #6952
Punuk
– artifacts #4327
puppets, Tsimshian
– Ottawa (Ont), National Museum of Man
  #3891
Purdy, Henry Carl, Can sculptor, 1937-
– exhibitions
    – (1978) #6946
Puvis de Chavannes, Pierre, Fr artist,
  1824-1898
– influence on Ozias Leduc #6206
– influence on Paul-Emile Borduas #4841
Pyle, James W., Can photographer, 1915-
– exhibitions, group
    – (1972) #1952

Q

Qikertaaluk Island (NWT)
– petroglyphs, Dorset #4362
Qinnuayuak, Lucy, Can artist, 1915-1982
  #4260 4460
Qu'Appelle Valley (Sask)
– views, James Henderson #5778 5779
Québec
– architectural materials (1800-1870) #7947
– architecture #7848 7850 7851 7855 7868
  7936
    – 17th-18th cs. #7844 7845
    – 17th-19th cs. #7687 7841 7842 7852 7858
      7859 7866
    – 17th c.-1940s #7853
    – 17th c.-1970s #7711
    – 18th-19th cs. #8622
    – 18th c. #7861 7865
    – 20th c. #7731
    – (1608-1930) #7659
    – (1880-1914) #7929
    – (1920s) #7657
    – (1940s) #7846
    – (1950s) #7857
    – (1960s) #8307
    – (1980) #7893
    – archival sources #7863
    – Baillairgé, François #4586
    – beaux-arts #7923
    – influence of Ecole des beaux-arts #8265
    – influence of Jérôme Demers #7874
    – Parizeau, Marcel #8397
    – use of architectural models, 17th-19th cs.
      #7872
    – use of building and ornamental stones
      (1910s) #7646 7647
    – wooden, 17th-18th cs. #7717
– architecture and decorative arts, 17th-18th
  cs. #2181 2217
– architecture and historic sites #7887
– architecture and sculpture, 17th-19th cs.

#7849
– architecture and urban development #7867
– art #1238 1271 1294 3085 3109
  – 17th-18th cs. #2187
  – 17th-19th cs. #136 137 1245 1332 1347
    1581 2128 8224
  – 17th c.-1867 #2110
  – 17th c.-1890s #185
  – 17th c.-1920s #1229
  – 17th c.-1920s, French influences #1244
  – 17th c.-1930s #2169 2171
  – 17th c.-1967 #1260
  – 19th c.-1940s #1242
  – 20th c. #145
  – (1613-1870) #1330 1331
  – (1759-1914), revolutionary subjects #1351
  – (1820-1940) #28
  – (1825-1850) #1368
  – (1875-1915) #1364
  – (1880-1914) #1371
  – (1880-1930s) #45
  – (1900-1920s) #1231
  – (1910s) #1317
  – (1920s) #302
  – (1920s-1960s) #461
  – (1930s-1970s) #1299
  – (1940-1960) #1462
  – (1940s) #350 381 1383 1386 1387
  – (1940s-1960s) #1438
  – (1940s-1970s) #1269 1473 1521
  – (1950s) #425 1402
  – (1950s-1980s) #55
  – (1955-1971) #1453
  – (1960s) #492 1442 1487
  – (1960s-1970s) #1257 1496
  – (1962-1972) #1500 1502
  – (1963-1980) #1564
  – (1966-1976) #1527
  – (1970-1975) #1515
  – (1970s) #134 543 593 1486 1488 1491
    1493 1506 1508 1511 1517 1525 1526
    1528 1545
    – by artists under 35 #1501
  – (1975) #1518
– art and architecture #67 68 1234 1237 1249
  1258 1259 1265 1327
  – 17th-18th cs. #1320
  – 17th-19th cs. #1305 1324 1334 1335 1341
  – 17th c. #228 229
  – 17th c.-1930s #1235
  – 18th-19th cs. #1338
  – 18th c. #234 235 249 250 269 270
  – 18th c.-1820s #1300
  – 18th-early 20th cs. #1339
  – (1640-1840) #1329
  – (1760-1790) #1369
  – (1870s) #1307
  – (1925-1950) #1405
  – (1970s-1980) #1561
– art and literature, 20th c. #1391
– art history #1255
– artisans
  – 17th-18th cs. #2214
  – 18th-19th cs. #2206
  – (1660-1815), apprentices #2231
  – late 19th-early 20th cs. #2235
– banks (1910s) #9166
– barns, 17th-19th cs. #9230 9231
– basketry, 20th c. #2954
– board games, 19th-20th cs. #2597
– book illustration (1960s) #926
– bread ovens #2233 2234
– building, 17th-19th cs. #7864
– calvaries and crosses #1609

– chairs #2534
– churches #8806 8816 8819
  – 17th-18th cs. #8790 8827 8869
    – use of clapboarding and
      whitewashing #8829
  – 17th-19th cs. #1588
  – 17th c. #8817
  – 18th-19th cs. #8893
  – 19th c. #258 259
  – (1600-1850) #8870
  – (1608-1760s) #8825 8837
  – (1615-1665) #8822 8823
  – (1647-1800) #8792 8793
  – (1820s-1880s) #7856
  – (1900-1934) #8334
  – (1930-1952) #8831
  – (1940s) #8820
  – (1940s-1950s) #8838
  – (1950s-1960s) #8845
  – (1960s) #8840 8841 8846
  – Baillairgé, Thomas #8327 8328
  – Conefroy, Pierre #8834
  – Ouellet, Joseph-Pierre #8394
  – Protestant #8887 8888
– churches and woodcarving
  – 18th-19th cs. #8799
  – (1780-1850) #1232 1574
– clocks #2925
  – 17th-18th cs. #2914
– comic strips #948 952 953 954
  – (1970s) #950 951
– conservation of architecture #8595
– costume
  – 17th-18th cs. #2850
  – 17th-19th cs. #2822 2825 2832
  – 18th-19th cs., travellers and coureurs de
    bois #2826
  – 18th c. #2820
  – 19th c. #2828 2829 2896
  – (1605-1963), male #2838
  – (1840-1900) #2899
  – (1850s) #2834
  – in French-Canadian folk songs #2898
– coverlets, 17th-19th cs. #2746
– crosses #1569 1609 1619 1621 1625 1637
  1640
– crucifixes #1585 1638
– daguerreotypes (1839-1855) #1374
– dance and costume #2879
– decorative arts #1274 2197 2202 2208 2219
  2222 2223 2226 2228 2229 2237
  – 17th-18th cs. #2097 2200
  – 17th-19th cs. #2093 2111 2221
  – 18th c.-1930s #2177
  – 19th c. #2099
  – 20th c. #2179 2198
  – (1613-1870) #2191
  – (1870s-1930s) #2977
  – (1930s) #2163 2164 2166 2167 2172 2173
    2174 2176 2969
  – (1930s-1940s) #2185
  – (1940s) #357 2188 2190 2199
  – (1950s) #2193
  – (1960s) #2102 2195
  – (1970s) #2215 2216 2224 2225 2230
  – (1979-1980) #2138
– decorative arts and design (1970s) #2205
  2211
– domestic architecture #8568 8591 8592
  8599 8600
  – 17th-18th cs. #8586 8602 8603 8605 8606
    8621
  – 17th-19th cs. #8505 8559 8579 8593 8596
    8609 8623

  – 18th-19th cs. #8560 8561 8582
  – (1763-1860), travellers' descriptions
    #8527
  – (1920s) #8497
  – and Canadian Heritage of Quebec #7871
  – artisans' houses (1810-1819) #8616
  – country houses #8572
  – rural houses
    – 17th-18th cs. #8581
    – 17th-19th cs. #8624
    – (1600-1800) #8614
  – seigneuries #8611
  – use of stone, 17th-19th cs. #7891
– drawing, 20th c. #1520 1523
– embroidery, Ursulines #2778 2779 2781
  2783 2788 2789
– engraving (1958-1965) #1654
– farm buildings (1910s) #8554
– folk art #1268 1285 1291 1297 2183
  – 17th-19th cs. #1284
  – 19th c. #1362
  – (1920s-1940s) #2189
  – (1940s) #1243
  – (1960s) #1428 1429
– folk song illustrations #938
– furniture #2544
  – 17th-18th cs. #2525 2526 2529 2530 2531
    2539 2543
  – 17th-19th cs. #2464 2524 2541
  – 18th-19th cs. #2474 2532
  – 18th-19th cs., Anglo-Québec #2542
  – 18th c. #2488 2545
  – (1660-1760) #2540
  – (1700-1820) #2537
  – (1760-1840), Georgian #2477
  – (1920s) #2463
  – (1930-1935) #2970
  – (1940s) #2523
  – (1950s) #2467
  – (1970s) #2533
  – late 17th-mid 19th cs. #2527
– gilding #2930
– glass
  – 19th c. #2418 2421
  – (1847-1898) #2399
– graphic arts
  – 17th-18th cs. #1649
  – (1960s) #1643
  – (1970s) #893 1533 1644 1651 1656
  – automatism and Surrealism #1650
– hats
  – 17th-19th cs. #2815
  – (pre-1736) #2831
– hooked rugs #2751 2753
– hospitals (1950s) #9029
– iron funeral crosses #2716
– ironwork #2697 2702 2705 2707 2711 2712
  2713
  – 18th-19th cs. #2703
  – Cauchon family #5062
– jewellery (1970s) #2701
– kitchen utensils, 17th-18th cs. #2210
– landscape (1800-1940) #1286
– maple-sugar moulds #2592
– mills #9242 9252
  – 17th-19th cs. #9243
– monuments #1570
  – late 19th c.-1920s #1606
– moulds #2916
– museums #3098 3108
  – (1970s) #3102
– open-air sculpture (1960s) #1587
– painting #1289 1340 1344 1346
  – 17th c. #1363

– 18th-19th cs. #1323
– 19th c. #197 1312 1318 1336 3233
– 19th c.-1930s #1382
– 19th c.-1940s #1248
– 19th c.-(1960s) #1256 1262
– 20th c. #1270 1392 1422 1463
– (1860s-1880s) #230
– (1930s) #589 592 1460
– (1930s-1960s) #1421
– (1939-1950s) #1461
– (1940-1966) #1440
– (1940s) #355 1384 1389 1390 1393 1468
– (1940s-1950s) #412 1432 1472
– (1940s-1960s) #1436
– (1950s) #1413
– (1950s-1960s) #1441
– (1953-1956) #1454
– (1955-1965) #1471
– (1960s) #484 1419
– (1970s) #588 1542 1543 1544 1552 1560
– mid-17th c.-1908 #1353
– photographic views
  – Benoît (dit Livernois), Jules-Isaïe #258 259
  – Lafortune, François #6134
  – Würtele, Fred C. #7619
– photography #1283
  – (1857-1960), Livernois family #1275
  – (1970s) #996 1507 1556
  – (1980s) #1562
– Pop art #1497
– portraits, 18th-19th cs. #263
– posters (1940s) #851
– pottery #2324 2331
  – 17th-19th cs. #2301 2302 2313 2318
  – 18th-19th cs. #2299 2321 2343
  – 18th c. #2364 2365
  – 19th c. #2279 2283
    – Scottish potters #2339
  – (1655-1916) #2344
  – (1840s-1900) #2298 2322
  – (1960s) #2381
  – (1970s) #2384 2390
– prisons, 19th c. #9056
– quilts (1920s) #2794
– religion and art #1292
  – (1940s) #1394
  – (1950s) #1250 1406
  – (1960s) #1435
– rocking chairs, 18th-19th cs. #2536
– roofs, 17th-18th cs. #7703 7881
– schools #9420 9424
  – (1919-1923) #9416
  – (1950s) #9391 9392 9418
– sculpture #1590 1596 1617
  – 17th-19th cs. #1589 1594 1611
  – (1650-1925) #1592
  – (1945-1970) #1599
  – (1960s) #1586 1595 1622
  – (1960s-1970s) #1584
  – (1970s) #1603 1626 1627 1628 1630 1631 1634 1635
  – (1980) #685
  – annunciation theme, late 17th-20th cs. #1633
  – supper at Emmaus theme, 19th-20th cs. #1615
– sepulchral monuments #733
– shoes #2880
– signs and signboards, 17th-19th cs. #2919
– silver #2670
  – 17th-18th cs. #2657

– 17th-19th cs. #2095 2627 2636 2660 2662 2664 2666 2676 2681 2690 2691
– 18th-19th cs. #2644 2658 2672 2682 2687
– 18th c. #2673 2677
– (1534-1763) #2684
– stained glass #2448
– stoves (pre-1867) #2220
– Surrealism #1464 1470
– tabernacles, 17th-19th cs. #1613
– tableware, 17th-18th cs. #2161
– tapestry (1970s) #2772 2773
– telephone buildings (1880s-1950s) #9298
– textiles
  – 19th-early 20th cs. #2737
  – (1750-1900) #2727
  – (1930s), women artisans #2165
– theatres #9078
– toys #2924
  – 17th-19th cs. #2921 2933 2934
  – (1800-1925) #2937
– treenware #2590
– urban development, 17th-18th cs. #7885
– views
  – 18th-mid 19th cs. #1366
  – 19th c. #1298 2326
    – on pottery #2291 2306
    – Thomas pottery #2287
  – (1608-1875), prints #1349
  – (1890s) #6436
  – Banting, Frederick Grant #4600
  – Bouchard, Lorne Holland #4857
  – Cockburn, James Pattison #5126
  – Fortin, Marc-Aurèle #5474
  – French explorers #276
  – Heriot, George #5786
  – Hudon-Beaulac, Simone Marie Yvette #857 5856
  – Jackson, A.Y. #5919 5922
  – Krieghoff, Cornelius #241 242 6085 6091 6093 6099
  – Lougheed, Robert Elmer #6328
– villas, 19th c. #8632
– votive offerings #1370
– weathercocks #2589
– weaving and rugs (1930s-1940s) #2186
– weaving and spinning (1920s) #2718
– windmills #9255
– women artists
  – (1930s) #1380
  – (1930s-1970s) #1273
– woodcarving #1573 1576 1577 1614
  – 17th-19th cs. #1575 1583
  – 18th-19th cs. #6947
  – 18th-20th cs. #1616
  – Levasseur family #6254
Québec. Department of Agriculture
– (1930s), revival of handicrafts #2165
Québec. Ministère des Affaires culturelles. Direction générale du patrimoine
– conservation of architecture #7870
Québec. Ministère des Affaires culturelles. Service de l'Inventaire des biens culturels
– inventory of Québec art and architecture (1974-1977) #1277
Québec. Ministère des Travaux publics et de l'Approvisionnement
– art purchases #1561
Québec. Rapport de la Commission d'enquête sur l'enseignement des arts au Québec (Rapport Parent) (1968)
– and art (1960s) #1473
Québec. Rapport de la Commission royale d'enquête sur l'enseignement dans la province de Québec (Rapport Rioux)

(1963-1966)
– and art (1960s) #1473
Québec (Qué)
– architecture #7892 7938 7940
  – 16th-18th cs. #7935
  – 17th-19th cs. #7936 7949 7950
  – 18th c. #7861 7943
  – (1608-late 19th c.) #7944
  – (1870s-1920s) #7843
  – (1920s) #7656
  – (1950s) #7673
  – Baillairgé, Charles #8324
  – influence of Norman architecture, 17th-mid-18th cs. #7847
  – late 17th c.-1920s, destruction by fire #7952
– architecture and monuments #7945
– art #1399 6870
  – 17th c. #1352
  – (1950s) #1404
  – (1970s) #1509
– art and architecture #1233 7939
  – 17th-19th cs. #1306 1309
– art galleries
  – (1960s) #442
  – (1970s) #1519
– churches (1960s) #1435
– city gates #8444
– conservation of architecture #7937 7942
– decorative arts, early 20th c. #1313
– domestic architecture
  – 17th-19th cs. #7941 8505 8559
  – brick houses, early 19th c. #8521
  – country houses #8572
  – seigneuries #8611
  – terrace houses, 19th c. #8653
– fortifications #7946 8450
  – Boisberthelot de Beaucours, Josué #8336
– Martello towers #8416
– museums #3098 3108
– photographic views (1850-1900) #1061
– rocking chairs #2535
– sculpture (1890s) #727
– silver #2197
  – 17th-19th cs. #2674 2685 2686
  – 18th-19th cs. #2630 2634 2650
  – 18th c. #2677
– tapestry, 20th c. #2769
– views
  – Cockburn, James Pattison #5125 5127 5128
  – Légaré, Joseph #6221
  – Massicotte, Edmond-Joseph #6440
  – Pilot, Robert Wakeham #6871
  – Short, Richard #249 250
– woodcarving, 17th-19th cs. #1593
Québec (Qué), Archives municipales
– exhibitions
  – C. Baillairgé, Arct. Ing: dessins architecturaux (1979) #8324
Québec (Qué), Archives nationales du Québec
– artisans, documents (1810-1819) #8616
– Livernois family, photographs and documents #1275
Québec (Qué), Artillery Park
– fortifications #8449
Québec (Qué), Artillery Park. Redoute Dauphine
– architecture #8448 8452
Québec (Qué), Assemblée nationale/National Assembly

– architecture #8942
  – Baillairgé, Thomas #8325
  – Huot, Charles Edouard
    – *Débats sur les langues de 1793* #5878 5880 5881 5884
    – *Je me souviens* #5874 5875
    – mural paintings #5876
Québec (Qué), Atelier de réalisations graphiques (ARG) #1661
Québec (Qué), café du Parlement
– exhibitions
  – *L'art religieux contemporain au Canada* (1952) #1406
Québec (Qué), Campus intercommunautaire de Cap-Rouge
– architecture, Jean-Marie Roy #9421
Québec (Qué), Cathedral of the Holy Trinity #1305
– architecture #8786
Québec (Qué), Chalet des employés civils
– architecture, André Robitaille #7939
Québec (Qué), Chalmers-Wesley Church
– architecture, George Browne #7873
Québec (Qué), Chambre blanche
– exhibitions (reviews)
  – Jean, Marcel #5952
Québec (Qué), Chapel of Mgr Olivier Briand
– *see* Québec (Qué), Séminaire de Québec. Chapel of Mgr Olivier Briand
Québec (Qué), Chapel of the congrégation Notre-Dame de Québec
– architecture and interior, François Baillairgé, attributed to #8864
Québec (Qué), Château Frontenac
– architecture #9278 9291
  – Painter, Walter Scott #9261
Québec (Qué), château Saint-Louis
– architecture #8443 8754
Québec (Qué), church
– architecture, Gauthier & Guité #8766
Québec (Qué), Church of Notre-Dame-de-Grâce
– architecture, Gérard Morisset #8891
Québec (Qué), Church of Notre-Dame de Québec #8857
– architecture, Thomas Baillairgé #8325
– architecture and interior #8791
– paintings #1305
– tabernacle, François Baillairgé #4591
– vaults, use of plasters #1618
Québec (Qué), Church of Notre-Dame-des-Anges
– architecture #9022
Québec (Qué), Church of Notre-Dame-des-Victoires
– architecture and interior #8858
Québec (Qué), Church of Saint-Dominique
– sculptures, Lauréat Vallière #7455
Québec (Qué), Church of Saint-Jean-Baptiste
– paintings #1305
Québec (Qué), Church of Saint-Joachim de Montmorency
– interior, François and Thomas Baillairgé #8880
Québec (Qué), Church of Saint-Pascal-Baylon
– architecture, Gérard Morisset #8891
Québec (Qué), Church of Saint-Sauveur
– paintings, Charles Edouard Huot #5883
Québec (Qué), Church of Saint-Thomas d'Aquin
– sculptures, Lauréat Vallière #7455
Québec (Qué), Church of the Récollets
– architectural model #8869

Québec (Qué), Collège des jésuites
– architecture #7953
– church, architectural model #8869
Québec (Qué), Complex G
– sculpture, Charles Daudelin #5263
Québec (Qué), Couvent des ursulines/Ursuline Convent
– architecture and art #1352
– architecture and interior #8810
– chapel, architecture and interior #8852
– embroidery #2778 2788 2789
– paintings #1305
Québec (Qué), Ecole des arts domestiques de Québec/Quebec School of Handicrafts
– (1930-1935) #2167
– (1930s-1940s) #2185 2186
– (1940s) #2190
– revival of *ceinture fléchée* #2833
Québec (Qué), Ecole des beaux-arts
– (1950s) #1404
– architectural models of Québec (Qué) #7936
– Bourdeau, Micheline, as student #4879
– Caron, Roger, as student #5005
– Dallaire, Jean-Philippe, as teacher #5239
– Daoust, Sylvia Emilienne, as student #5257
– Desrochers-Drolet, Françoise, as student #5289
– East, Benoît, as teacher #5352
– Laliberté, Madeleine, as student #6153
– LeMoine, Edmond, as teacher #6243
– Maltais, Marcelle, as student #6412
– Pellan, Alfred, as student #6809 6811
– Thibault, René, as student and teacher #7344
Québec (Qué), école secondaire Marie-de-l'Incarnation
– architecture, Maurice Bouchard #7939
Québec (Qué), Episcopal Palace
– *see* Québec (Qué), Palais épiscopal/Episcopal Palace
Québec (Qué), Fornel House
– architecture #7953
Québec (Qué), Fort Saint-Louis
– architecture #8443
Québec (Qué), galerie Bénédek-Grenier
– exhibitions
  – *Michel Champagne* (1974) #5084
Québec (Qué), galerie de l'Anse-aux-Barques
– exhibitions (reviews)
  – Cantieni, Graham #4995
  – Roy, Mario #7099
Québec (Qué), Galerie de peinture de Québec
– (1830s-1850s) #3120
– (1838) #1368
Québec (Qué), galerie Jolliet
– exhibitions (reviews)
  – Gnass, Peter #5619
  – Morisset, Denys #6610
Québec (Qué), Grand Théâtre de Québec
– architecture #7709
  – Prus, Victor #9112
– columns, Marcel Jean #5951
– murals, Jordi Bonet #4786 4787 4788 4789 4791 4792
Québec (Qué), Grand Théâtre de Québec. Foyer de la salle Louis-Fréchette
– exhibitions
  – *Jordi Bonet* (1974) #4790
Québec (Qué), Hôpital-Général
– architecture #9022
– collection #3108
– gilding workshop, late 18th-early 19th cs.

#2930
– tabernacles #1359
Québec (Qué), Hôpital-Général. Windmill
– restoration #9245
Québec (Qué), Hôtel-Dieu #3108
– architecture and art #1352
– artificial flowers, 18th-19th cs. #1350
– paintings #1305 3119
Québec (Qué), hôtel Union
– architecture #9284
Québec (Qué), institut Valtemare
– and proposal for national museum in Québec, mid-19th c. #3120
Québec (Qué), Intendant's Palace
– architecture #8553
Québec (Qué), Jardins Mérici
– architecture
  – Gauthier, Paul #7886
  – Gauthier Guité Roy #8746
Québec (Qué), La Solidarité insurance building
– architecture, Robert Blatter and G.Fernand Caron #7939
Québec (Qué), Legislative Assembly
– *see* Québec (Qué), Assemblée nationale/National Assembly
Québec (Qué), Les Prévoyants du Canada insurance building
– architecture, Lucien Mainguy #7939
Québec (Qué), maison Maizerets
– architecture #8622
Québec (Qué), maison mère Mallet
– architecture, Charles Baillairgé #8884
Québec (Qué), Merchant's House, No. 92 Saint Peter Street
– architecture #8563
Québec (Qué), monastère de Notre-Dame-des-Anges
– paintings #1305
Québec (Qué), monastère des augustines de l'Hôtel-Dieu
– *see* Québec (Qué), Hôtel-Dieu
Québec (Qué), Monument of the Victims of 1837-1838 #1309
Québec (Qué), musée Chasseur
– and proposal for national museum in Québec #3120
Québec (Qué), Musée de la citadelle/Citadel Museum
– statue of General Wolfe #1600
Québec (Qué), Musée de la province de Québec/Museum of the Province of Quebec
– *see also* Québec (Qué), Musée du Québec
– exhibitions
  – *Alfred Pellan* (1960) #6807
  – *Canadian Portraits of the 18th and 19th Centuries/Portraits canadiens du 18e et 19e siècles* (1959) #219
  – *Catalogue of Memorial Exhibitions of the Work of Clarence Gagnon, R.C.A.; J.W. Beatty, R.C.A., O.S.A.* #359
  – *Exhibition of Edmond Dyonnet, R.C.A., Ozias Leduc, A.R.C.A., Joseph Saint-Charles, A.R.C.A., Elzéar Soucy* (1945) #1240
  – *Exposition rétrospective de l'art au Canada français/The Arts in French Canada* (1952) #1249
  – *John Lyman: hommage à John Lyman à l'occasion de ses 80 ans/John Lyman, Octogenarian: A Retrospective Tribute* (1966) #6345
  – *Les arts du Canada français, 1613-1870*

(1946) #1331
- *The Arts of French Canada, 1613-1870*
  (1946) #1330
- *The Development of Painting in Canada,
  1665-1945/Le développement de la peinture
  au Canada, 1665-1945* (1945) #34
- *Vieux Québec* (1942) #12
Québec (Qué), Musée des ursulines
- embroidery #2791
Québec (Qué), Musée du Québec #3092 3098
  3107 3108 3111 4790
- (1933-1960s) #3085
- (1970s) #3102
- and Gérard Morisset #3125 3126 3127
- Bouchard, Laurent, as director #3122
- collection #3095 3121
- Dulongpré, Louis, portrait of James McGill
  #5321
- exhibitions
  - *An Exhibition of Canadian Gameboards of
    the 19th & 20th Centuries from Ontario,
    Quebec & Nova Scotia* (1981) #2597
  - *Antoine Plamondon, 1802-1895; Théophile
    Hamel, 1817-1870: Two Painters of
    Quebec/Antoine Plamondon, 1802-1895;
    Théophile Hamel, 1817-1870: deux peintres
    du Québec* (1970) #1348
  - *Bill Vazan* (1974) #7472
  - *Carol Fraser Paintings and Drawings:
    1967-1977* (1978) #5507
  - *Charles Daudelin* (1974) #5262
  - *Cordonnerie traditionnelle* (1977) #2880
  - *Cornelius Krieghoff, 1815-1872* (1971)
    #6095
  - *David Milne: 1882-1953* (1967) #6558
  - *Dessins inédits d'Ozias Leduc/Ozias Leduc
    the Draughtsman* (1979) #6210
  - *Edmund Alleyn: une belle fin de journée*
    (1974) #4512
  - *Esquimaux, peuple du Québec: exposition
    d'art et d'objets d'usage courant des
    Esquimaux du Nouveau-Québec,*(1966)
    #4406
  - *Fernand Leduc* (1971) #6186
  - *Fernand Leduc: dix ans de microchromies
    1970/1980* (1981) #6193
  - *François Baillairgé et son oeuvre
    (1759-1830)* (1975) #4592
  - *François Ranvoyzé, orfèvre, 1739-1819*
    (1968) #6960
  - *Georges Saint-Pierre* (1975) #7118
  - *Goodridge Roberts: A Retrospective
    Exhibition/Goodridge Roberts: une
    exposition rétropective* (1969) #7045
  - *Graveurs du Québec* (1966) #1643
  - *Héritage vivant de l'orfèvrerie: vingt pièces
    de la collection du Musée du Québec* (1977)
    #2690
  - *Hier au Québec, 1875-1915* (1976) #1364
  - *Hommage à Jordi Bonet* (1980) #4793
  - *Jean-Paul Lemieux* (1967) #6231
  - *Jean-Paul Riopelle: peinture, 1946-1977*
    (1981) #7032
  - *Joseph Légaré, 1795-1855: l'oeuvre* (1979)
    #6217
  - *L'architecture et la nature à Québec au
    dix-neuvième siècle: les villas* (1980) #8632
  - *L'art du paysage au Québec,
    1800-1940/Landscape Painting in Québec,
    1800-1940* (1978) #1286
  - *L'art du Québec au lendemain de la
    Conquête, 1760-1790* (1977) #1369
  - *Le jouet dans l'univers de l'enfant,
    1800-1925* (1977) #2937
  - *Les chroniques du Québec d'Arthur
    Villeneuve/Arthur Villeneuve's Quebec
    Chronicles* (1972) #7491
  - *Les moins de 35: du 22 janvier au 4 février*
    (1973) #1501
  - *Louis-Pierre Bougie (dessins)* (1978) #4861
  - *Mario Merola* (1971) #6520
  - *Mill* (1978) #6534
  - *Norval Morrisseau* (1966) #6645
  - *Omer Parent* (1976) #6767
  - *Peinture traditionnelle du Québec* (1967)
    #1346
  - *Peinture vivante du Québec, 1966:
    vingt-cinq ans de libération de l'oeil et du
    geste* (1966) #1436
  - *Pellan* (1972) #6816
  - *Pouvoir du noir* (1966) #5593
  - *Profil de la sculpture québécoise
    XVIIe-XIXe siècles* (1969) #1594
  - *Rétrospective: Jean Dallaire* (1968) #5241
  - *Riopelle* (1967) #7021
  - *Rodolphe Duguay, 1891-1973* (1979) #5318
  - *S. Guité: sculptures et tapisseries* (1977)
    #5669
  - *Sculpture traditionnelle du Québec* (1967)
    #1589
  - *Tactile* (1978) #1545
  - *The Canadian Canvas: A Travelling
    Exhibition of 85 Recent Paintings/Peintres
    canadiens actuels: exposition itinérante de
    85 oeuvres récentes* (1975) #588
  - *The Saidye and Samuel Bronfman
    Collection of Canadian Art/La collection
    Saidye et Samuel Bronfman* (1967) #3087
  - *The Works of Joseph Légaré: 1795-1855*
    (1979) #6218
  - *Treasures from Québec: An Exhibition of
    Paintings Assembled from Quebec and Its
    Environs/Trésors de Québec: exposition de
    peintures provenant de Québec et des
    environs* (1965) #1344
  - *Trésors des communautés religieuses de la
    ville de Québec* (1973) #1352
  - *William Brymner, 1855-1925: A
    Retrospective/William Brymner, 1855-1925:
    aperçu rétrospectif de l'artiste* (1979) #4953
- exhibitions (reviews)
  - Daoust, Sylvia Marie Emilienne #5257
  - *François Baillairgé et son oeuvre
    (1759-1830)* (1975) #4593
  - *The Canadian Canvas: A Travelling
    Exhibition of 85 Recent Paintings/Peintres
    canadiens actuels: exposition itinérante de
    85 oeuvres récentes* (1975) #582
- furniture #2484
- Gagnon, Clarence Alphonse, prints #359
- Heriot, George, paintings #5785
- Laliberté, Alfred, bronzes #6144
- Massicotte, Edmond-Joseph, notebooks
  #6441
- Québec art #1271 1347
- Québec folk legends, illustrations of #1290
- Québec silver #2678
- Québec textiles, 19th-early 20th cs. #2737
- Soucy, Jean-Baptiste, as director #3103
- Viau, Guy, as director #7485
Québec (Qué), Museum of the Province of
  Quebec
- see Québec (Qué), Musée de la province de
  Québec/Museum of the Province of
  Quebec
Québec (Qué), National Assembly
- see Québec (Qué), Assemblée
  nationale/National Assembly

Québec (Qué), Palais épiscopal/Episcopal
  Palace
- architecture #8787
  - Baillairgé, Thomas #8325
- chapel, architectural model #8869
- chapel, architectural plan, Jean-Baptiste
  Maillou (*dit* Desmoulins) #8856
Québec (Qué), Palais Montcalm
- exhibitions (reviews)
  - Lemieux, Irénée #6226
Québec (Qué), place Royale
- domestic architecture #2201 8588 8589
- pottery #2352
- restoration #7948 7951
- statues, Louis XIV #1598
Québec (Qué), place Royale. Hazeur House
- architecture #8626
Québec (Qué), Price House
- architecture, Ross & Macdonald #9311
Québec (Qué), prison des plaines
  d'Abraham/Plains of Abraham Prison
- architecture, Charles Philippe Ferdinand
  Baillairgé #9057
Québec (Qué), Redoute Dauphine
- see Québec (Qué), Artillary Park. Redoute
  Dauphine
Québec (Qué), Royal Battery
- architecture and restoration #8451
Québec (Qué), Salon des artisans de Québec
- exhibitions
  - *Métiers d'art Ontario-Québec,
    1979/1980/Quebec-Ontario Crafts,
    1979/1980* (1979) #2138
Québec (Qué), Séminaire de
  Notre-Dame-des-Anges
- architecture #8785
Québec (Qué), Séminaire de Québec
- see also Québec (Qué), Université Laval
- architecture #1341 8844 8847
- architecture and art #1352 8842
- compared with Church of Saint-Joachim
  (Saint-Joachim, Qué) #7953
- influence on Québec architecture,
  18th-19th cs. #8622
- student uniforms #2809
Québec (Qué), Séminaire de Québec.
  Archives
- prints #3124
Québec (Qué), Séminaire de Québec. Chapel
- paintings #1305
Québec (Qué), Séminaire de Québec. Chapel
  of Mgr Jean-Olivier Briand
- architecture and interior #8800
- sculpture, Pierre Emond #5371
Québec (Qué), Séminaire de Québec. Musée
  du Séminaire #3098 3108
Québec (Qué), Séminaire des jésuites
- use of drawing manuals, 19th c. #2982
Québec (Qué), Union Station
- architecture, Harry Edward Prindle #9533
Québec (Qué), Université Laval
- see also Québec (Qué), Séminaire de
  Québec
- art, Indians of North America #3422
- collection #3080
- devotional images, Jeanne
  Larouche-Villeneuve collection #1662
- exhibitions
  - *Descriptive and Historical Catalogue of a
    Special Exhibition of Painting in the
    Gallery of Laval University, Quebec, Lately
    Restored/Musée des peintures, Université
    Laval, Québec* (1909) #3078
- paintings #1306

– prints of devotional images #130
Québec (Qué), Université Laval. Ecole
  d'architecture
– architectural education
  – (1964) #8271
  – (1965) #8273
  – (1966) #8274
  – (1967) #8275
  – (1968) #8277
  – (1980) #8289
Québec (Qué), Ursuline Convent
– see Québec (Qué), Couvent des
  ursulines/Ursuline Convent
Quebec Sculptors Association/Association
  des sculpteurs du Québec
– (1970s) #1490
– exhibitions
  – (1961-1977) #1584
  – (1977) #1622
– exhibitions (reviews)
  – (1965) #1586
Quebec Sculpture Council
– see Conseil de la Sculpture du
  Québec/Quebec Scupture Council
Queen Anne style
– architecture
  – LaSalle (Qué), manoir Ogilvie #8636
Queen Charlotte Islands (BC)
– masks, Haida #3961
– totem poles, Haida #3982 4008
Queen Charlotte Islands (BC), Queen
  Charlotte Islands Museum
– architecture, Henry Hawthorn #9129
– exhibitions
  – The Art of Nunstins/L'art de Nunstins
    (1981) #6934
Queenston (Ont), Prest House
– architecture #7959
Quercy, Jacques
– see Pagé (dit Quercy or Carcy), Jacques
Quetico Park (Ont and Man)
– pictographs, Algonquian #3575 3576
Quévillon, Louis-Amable, Can sculptor,
  1749-1823 #1233 1324 1592 6947
– altarpiece, church, Berthierville (Qué)
  #8874
– gilding #2930
– interior, Church of Saint-Etienne
  (Beaumont, Qué) #8809
– tabernacles #1613
– woodcarving #1571 1573
Quévillon School, Can sculptors, late
  18th-19th cs. #1300
– and origins of Québec woodcarving and
  architecture #1574
– influence on Québec architecture #7851
– woodcarving #1232 1571 1576
Quidi Vidi (Nfld), Christ Church
– restoration, Newfoundland Historic Trust
  #7788
quillwork, Algonquian #3443 3605
– beadwork #3635
– double-curve and floral motifs #3409
– moccasins #3652
– Toronto (Ont), Royal Ontario Museum
  #3471 3474 3475
quillwork, Arapaho
– New York (NY), American Museum of
  Natural History #3414
quillwork, Assiniboine #3653 3739
quillwork, Athapaskan #4152
– Toronto (Ont), Royal Ontario Museum
  #3471 3474 3475
quillwork, Blackfoot #3651 3654 3678 3686

3703 3739 3745 3754
quillwork, Blood #3739
quillwork, Cree #3651 3739 3745
quillwork, Dogrib #4089
quillwork, Gros Ventre #3651
– rosettes #3753
quillwork, Hidatsa #3701
quillwork, Indians of North America
– Ottawa (Ont), National Museum of Man
  #3465 3466
– Toronto (Ont), Royal Ontario Museum
  #3474 3475
quillwork, Iroquois #3559 3605
– beadwork #3635
quillwork, Mandan #3701
quillwork, Micmac #3569 3624 3643
quillwork, Mistassini #3701
quillwork, natives of North America #3341
quillwork, Northwest Coast Indians #3811
quillwork, Ojibwa #3551 3557 4089
quillwork, Ottawa
– containers, Los Angeles (Calif), Southwest
  Museum #3548
quillwork, Penobscot #3537
quillwork, Plains #3443 3651 3658 3684 3745
  3751
– moccasins #3652
– New York (NY), American Museum of
  Natural History #3668
quillwork, Sarcee #3739
quillwork, Siouan #3443 3651 3674 3745
– moccasins #3652 3666
– Toronto (Ont), Royal Ontario Museum
  #3471
quillwork, Slavey #4089
quillwork, Tanana #4095
quillwork, Woodlands #3443
– beadwork #3635
quilt technique
– see media and techniques, quilts
quilts
– see also coverlets
quilts, American
– 18th c., compared with Canadian quilt
  (1726), McGill University. McCord
  Museum (Montréal, Qué) #2803
quilts, Canadian #2107 2799 2800
– (1608-1867) #2120
– (1726), silk-patchwork quilt, McGill
  University. McCord Museum (Montréal,
  Qué) #2803
– (1920s) #2794
– Boyce, Eleanor #4890
– Cape Breton (NS) #2732
– Manitoba #2272
– Mennonite #2253 2264 2267
– Newfoundland #1154 1155 2744
– Nova Scotia #2731
  – (1820-1930) #2807
  – (1970s) #2154
  – patterns (pre-1920) #2785
– Ondaatje, Kim #2798
– Ontario #2729 2796 2801
  – 19th-20th cs. #1682 2806
  – 19th c. #2805
– Ottawa (Ont), National Museum of Man
  #2804
– Prince Edward Island (1850s-1970s) #2802
– Québec
  – 17th-18th cs. #2200
  – 17th-19th cs. #2746
  – (1875-1915) #1364
– Rosenberg, Gloria, collection #2808
– Simcoe County (Ont) #2795

– Toronto (Ont), Royal Ontario Museum
  #2797
– Wieland, Joyce #7581
quilts, Indians of North America #2799
Quinault Indians
– basketry #3773 3778
– culture #3845
  – (1870s) #4031
Quinn, William, Can glassmaker, 19th c.
  #2400
Quintal, Joseph (frère Augustin), Can priest,
  artist, architect, 1683-1776
– baldachin, Parish Church (Neuville, Qué)
  and Church (Trois-Rivières, Qué) #8826

R

Rabinowitch, David George, Can sculptor,
  1943- #1817
– and avant-garde art #600
– and Toronto (Ont) art (1970s) #1796
– drawings, The Construction of Vision series
  #6949
– exhibitions, group
  – (1971) #98
  – (1976) #779
  – (1977) #782
  – (1978) #790
  – (1980) #703
– exhibitions (reviews) #787
– on his sculptures #6948
– sculptures (1976-1977) #6950
– support of #123
Rabinowitch, Royden, Can sculptor, 1943-
  #1817
– and Toronto (Ont) art (1970s) #1796
– exhibitions, group
  – (1976) #779
  – (1977) #782
  – (1980) #703
– sculptures (1970-1975) #6951
RACAR (Revue d'art canadienne/Canadian Art
  Review), Can periodical #114
RACE
– see Regroupement des artistes des Cantons
  de l'Est (RACE)
Racey, Arthur George, Can artist, 1870-1941
  #6952
– cartoons, Montreal Star #943
Rackham, Arthur, Brit artist, 1867-1939
– influence on James Frederic McCulloch
  #6463
Rackus, George Keistus, Can artist, 1927-
– exhibitions
  – (1972) #6953
Radecki, Brigitte, Can artist, 1940-
– Symposium international de sculpture
  environnementale de Chicoutimi (Qué),
  (1980) #1639
radical realism
– see Photo-realism
Raginsky, Nina, Can photographer, 1941-
  #1007
– exhibitions, group
  – (1973) #1002
  – (1979) #1037
– exhibitions (reviews) #1046 1060
RAIC
– see Royal Architectural Institute of Canada
RAIC. Journal
– see Royal Architectural Institute of Canada.

Journal
railings
– *see also* balustrades
railings, Canadian
– Norfolk County (Ont), Normandale Iron
  Works #2699
railroad stations, American
– western USA #8083
railroad stations, British
– influence on Union Station (Toronto, Ont)
  #9536
railroad stations, Canadian
– 19th c. #9512
– (1880-1914) #7736
– Brandon (Man), Canadian National
  Railway #9266
– Grand Trunk Railway and Canadian
  Pacific Railway #9539
– Hamilton (Ont), Hamilton Terminal
  Station #9527
– Manitoba #9543
– Montréal (Qué)
  – Bonaventure Station (1888-1952) #9538
  – Central Station #9535
  – Windsor Station #9532 9537
– Ontario #9541
  – 19th c. #8006
– Ottawa (Ont), Central Station #9528 9529
– Québec (Qué), Union Station #9533
– Saskatchewan #9544
– Toronto (Ont)
  – 19th c.-1930s #8076
  – Union Station #9531 9536 9540
– Vancouver (BC)
  – Canadian Pacific Railway Station #9534
  – Canadian Pacific Railway stations
    (1887-1914) #9546
– western Canada #8083 9542 9545
– Winnipeg (Man), Fort Garry Terminal
  #9530
railroad stations, French
– influence on Union Station (Toronto, Ont)
  #9536
railroads
– *see also* locomotives; subways
railroads, Canadian
– buildings and structures, 19th c. #9512
– photographs of, Boorne and May #4797
Raine, Herbert, Can artist, architect,
  1875-1951
– etchings #800
Rajotte, Normand, Can photographer, fl.
  1970s #1556
Rajotte, Yves, Can artist, 1932-
– writings #6954
Rakine, Marthe, Can artist, 1926- #6955 6956
Raley, G.H., Can missionary and collector,
  fl. 1890s-1930s
– collection, art, Northwest Coast Indians
  #3996
Ralston, William, Can architect, b. 1886
– winner, Dominion Housing Act Small
  House Competition (1936) #8736
– winner, Ontario Government Housing
  Competition (1936) #8737
Ramage, John, Can artist, 1748-1802
– miniatures #1377
Ramezay, Claude de, Fr officer in Canada
  and acting governor of New France,
  1659-1724
– residence, château de Ramezay (Montréal,
  Qué) #3076 3077 3083
Ramsay, William Alexander, Can architect,
  1910-

– Dorval (Qué), Montreal International
  Airport. Air Terminal Building #9515
– Halifax (NS), Halifax International
  Airport. Air Terminal Building #9515
– Ottawa (Ont), Ottawa International
  Airport. Air Terminal Building #9515
– Toronto (Ont), Toronto International
  Airport. Air Terminal Building #9516
Rand, Paul, Can artist, 1896-1970 #2011
– exhibitions
  – (1980) #6957
Randall, Cliff, Can photographer, ca. 1953-
– portfolio of photographs #1023
Randy and Barneche
– performance art #655
Ranford, Barry, Can photographer, fl. 1970s-
– portfolio of photographs #991
Rankin, Joan Melvin, Can artist, 1927- #6958
Rankin, Toby, Can photographer, 1940-
– portfolio of photographs #995
Rankin Inlet (NWT)
– ceramic sculpture #4207 4210 4314
– ivory carving #4195
– tapestry #4253
Rankin Inlet (NWT), Eskimo Arts and Crafts
  Centre
– pottery (1970s) #4226
Ranvoyzé, François, Can silversmith,
  1739-1819 #2658 2660 2662 6959
– alms cups #2671
– analysis of silver composition #2682
– as apprentice of Ignace-François
  Delezenne #1620
– chalices #2679
  – L'Islet (Qué), Church of
    Notre-Dame-de-Bon-Secours #2673
  – Ottawa (Ont), National Gallery of
    Canada #2680
– exhibitions
  – (1968) #6960
– pax #2666
– works
  – Detroit (Mich), Detroit Institute of Arts
    #2681
  – Québec (Qué), Musée du Québec #2678
Raphael, William, Can artist, 1833-1914
– relation of photography and painting #245
Rapin, François-Xavier Aldéric, Can artist,
  1868-1901 #6961
Rapport de la Commission d'enquête sur
  l'enseignement des arts au Québec
– *see* Québec. Rapport de la Commission
  d'enquête sur l'enseignement des arts au
  Québec (Rapport Parent)
Rapport de la Commission royale d'enquête
  sur l'enseignement dans la province de
  Québec
– *see* Québec. Rapport de la Commission
  royale d'enquête sur l'enseignement dans
  la province de Québec (Rapport Rioux)
Rapport Parent
– *see* Québec. Rapport de la Commission
  d'enquête sur l'enseignement des arts au
  Québec (Rapport Parent)
Raquette, père
– *see* Jackson, Alexander Young (A.Y.)
Raskin, Lawrie, Can photographer, 1943-
– exhibitions, group
  – (1980) #1063
Rasmussen, Knud Johan Victor, Da explorer
  in Canada, 1879-1933
– expedition, Arctic #4324 4326 4328 4330
  4417 4437
Rattenbury, Francis Mawson, Can architect,

1867-1935 #8400
– compared with Samuel Maclure #8152
– drawings and correspondence #8401
– Mawson, Thomas Hayton, compared with
  #9405
– railway hotels #9290
– Vancouver (BC), Courthouse #9149
– Victoria (BC) #8175
  – British Columbia Parliament Buildings
    #8964 8965 8966 8967
  – Crystal Gardens #9134 9146
rattles, Bella Coola
– raven rattles #4026
rattles, Cree #3363
rattles, Haida
– raven rattles #4026
rattles, Iroquois #3489
– effigy rattle pipes, Royal Ontario Museum
  (Toronto, Ont) #3644
rattles, Kwakiutl
– raven rattles #4026
rattles, Naskapi #3363
rattles, Niska
– raven rattle, Bryan Peel #6788
rattles, Nootka
– raven rattles #4026
rattles, Northwest Coast Indians #3866 3977
– puffin-beak rattles #3960
– raven rattles #3980 4014
rattles, Ojibwa #3363 3539
– Parry Island Reservation (Ont) #3540
rattles, Oneida #3363
rattles, Potawatomi
– Parry Island Reservation (Ont) #3540
rattles, Saulteaux #3363
rattles, Tlingit #3363 3976
– raven rattles #4026
– use of human hair #3917
Rattray, William Jordan, Can writer,
  1835-1883
– Bengough, John Wilson, on #4673
Rauschenberg, Robert, Amer artist, 1925-
– Ayot, Pierre, compared with #4572
– influence on Alan Wood #7611
– influence on Chris Knudsen disputed
  #6070
Ravenhill, Alice, Can artist, fl. 1940s #4114
Rawe, James, Can photographer, fl.
  1856-1867 #1724
Ray, Carl, Can artist, 1943-1979 #4157 4161
  6648
Raymond, Maurice, Can artist, 1912- #6962
– Christmas greeting cards #856
Raymond Lee and Associates Ltd., Can
  graphic design firm #886
Raymond Moriyama & Associates
– motel #9288
Rayner, Gordon, Can artist, 1935- #6963
  6964 6965
– and Toronto (Ont) painting (1960s) #1753
– exhibitions
  – (1979) #6966
– exhibitions, group
  – (1965) #473
– on Canadian art (1960s) #478
Razutis, Al, Can artist, 1946-
– video art #605
RCAT
– *see* Royal Canadian Aerial Theatre (RCAT)
Rea, Kenneth Guscotte, Can architect,
  1878-1941
– Montréal (Qué), Royal Victoria Hospital.
  Ross Pavilion #9017
Read, Charles James, Can architect, d. 1920

- Toronto (Ont)
  - New Princess Theatre #9069
  - York Theatre #9066
Read, Herbert Edward, Brit critic, art historian, 1893-1968
- on Wilfred Roloff Beny #4690
- Plaskett, Joe, on art theories of #6891
- theories, related to Alex Colville #5149
Réal d'Anjou, publishing firm (Québec, Qué)
- Christmas greeting cards (1950) #856
realism
- see also Photo-realism; trompe-l'oeil
- Alberta #1954
- and Ernest Lindner #6286
- and Fred Ross #7079
- and Glenn Howarth #5851
- and Jack Chambers #5070 5071 5072 5073 5075 5078 5079 5080 5081
- and John C. Leonard #6246
- and Kenneth Edison Danby #5251
- and Mary Frances Pratt #6919
- and Tom Forrestall #5465
- and Vincent Beull #4719
- and William George Richardson Hind #5805 5810
- Atlantic provinces (1970s) #1129
- Canada
  - 20th c. #110 498 716
  - (1860-1900), influence of photography #262
  - (1860s-1880s) #230
  - (1950s) #151
  - (1960s) #496
  - (1970s) #545 573 606 694 1810
- magic realism
  - Alberta #1965
  - and Alex Colville #5143 5144
- Nova Scotia (1970s) #1221
- Sackville (NB), Mount Allison University #1130
- Saint John (NB), 20th c. #1184
Reaney, James Crerar, Can writer, 1926-
- regionalism, compared with Greg Curnoe #5225
Rebanks, Leslie, Can architect, 1927-
- Toronto (Ont) #7733
Rebel, The, Can periodical
- illustrations #930
Recklinghausen (West Germany), Städtische Kunsthalle
- exhibitions
  - 10 Canadian Artists in the 1970s (1981) #703
Recollets
- architecture, Montréal (Qué) #7932
- architecture and sculpture, Québec #8855
recreation buildings
- see also amusement parks; resorts
recreation buildings, Canadian
- (1950s) #9081
- Toronto (Ont)
  - Ontario Place #9113 9114
  - Sunnyside #8054
- Victoria (BC), Crystal Gardens #9134 9146
recreational surveys
- Canada (1974) #3056
rectories, Canadian
- Batiscan (Qué), Old Presbytery #8807
- Kahnawake (Qué), Presbytery (1720) #8569
- Lockport (Man), Saint Andrew's Parsonage #8716
Red Deer (Alta), City Hall

- architecture, James E. Secord and Saul Herzog #8990
Red Deer (Alta), Red Deer and District Museum
- exhibitions
  - Artisan '78: The First National Travelling Exhibition of Contemporary Canadian Crafts/Artisan '78: première exposition nationale itinérante d'artisanat canadien contemporain (1979) #2134
Red Deer (Alta), Red Deer Public Library
- exhibitions
  - Images of the Inuit from the Simon Fraser Collection (1981) #4495
Red Deer (Alta), Saint Mary's Church
- architecture, Douglas Joseph Cardinal #8343
Red Deer River (Man)
- burial site, Ojibwa #3615
Red Indian Lake (Nfld)
- artifacts, Beothuk Indians #3623
Red River Exhibition Association (Man)
- exhibitions (1964-1978) #1903
Red River Expedition (1870)
- and Frances Ann Beechy Hopkins #5833
Red River region (Man)
- domestic architecture, 19th c. #8692
Redbank (NB)
- artifacts, Algonquian #3561
Redcliff (Alta)
- pottery, 20th c. #2371
Redgrave, Felicity, Can artist, 1920-
- exhibitions
  - (1978) #6967
- exhibitions (reviews) #1169
Redinger, Walter, Can sculptor, 1940- #6968 6969
- exhibitions, group
  - (1970) #771
  - (1972) #548
- interview #6970
- sculptures (1960s) #1793
Redivo, Hugo, Can photographer, fl. 1950s-
- portfolio of photographs #995
Redman, Alvin James, Can artist, 1947-
- exhibitions, group
  - (1975) #4141
Redon, Odilon, Fr artist, 1840-1916
- influence on Tom La Pierre #6122
Reeves, Charles Aime, Can architect, 1872-1948
- Montréal (Qué), académie des Saints Noms de Jésus et de Marie #9388
Reeves, Gladys, Can photographer, 1890-1974
- and Ernest Brown #4935
Reeves, John, Can photographer, 1938-
- exhibitions, group
  - (1981) #1070
- portfolio of photographs #991
- portrait photographs #6971
  - Canadian authors #1065 1066
  - famous Canadian women #6972
Regency style
- architecture
  - churches, Ontario #8904
  - houses, Ontario #8654
  - St. John's (Nfld) #8542
  - Toronto (Ont), Colborne Lodge #8659
- chairs, Ontario #2553
- furniture
  - Canada #2101
  - New Brunswick #2501
  - Newfoundland #2502

- Québec #2542
Regina (Sask)
- architecture
  - (1909) #8109
  - (1910s) #8111
  - (1920s) #7656
- art
  - (1950s) #6284
  - (1950s-1970s) #1935
  - (1960s) #441 1848
  - (1960s-1970s) #1862
- ceramic sculpture
  - (1960s-1970s) #1939
  - (1970s) #1924
- city planning, Thomas Hayton Mawson #9405
- domestic architecture (1910s) #8687
- painting (1960s) #1913
- pottery (1970s) #2383 2385
- sculpture (1960s) #1853
Regina (Sask), 38 Saskatchewan Geriatric Centre
- architecture, Stock, Ramsey & Associates #8516
Regina (Sask), Grain Show Building
- mural, Fritz Brandtner #4900
Regina (Sask), Legislative Buildings
- architecture, competition for
  - Gilbert, Cass #8954
  - Mitchell & Raine #8955
  - Storey & Van Egmond #8956
- architecture, Edward and William Sutherland Maxwell #8944 8945 8957 8958 8959 8960 8961
Regina (Sask), Norman Mackenzie Art Gallery
- see Regina (Sask), University of Regina. Norman Mackenzie Art Gallery
Regina (Sask), RCMP Chapel
- architecture #8911
Regina (Sask), RCMP Museum
- Moodie, Geraldine, photographs #6602
Regina (Sask), Regina College. Norman Mackenzie Art Gallery
- see also Regina (Sask), University of Regina. Norman Mackenzie Art Gallery; Regina (Sask), University of Saskatchewan. Norman Mackenzie Art Gallery
- exhibitions
  - 7 West Coast Painters (1959) #1997
  - The Great West before White Settlement: 28 Paintings by Paul Kane, 1810-1871 and George Catlin, 1796-1872 (1955) #1845
Regina (Sask), Regina Public Library
- exhibitions
  - Russell Yuristy: Sculpture 1971-1981 in Photographs and Drawings (1981) #7632
  - Saskatchewan: Art and Artists (1971) #1919
  - Younger Vancouver Sculptors (1968) #2037
Regina (Sask), Regina Public Library. Dunlop Art Gallery
- exhibitions
  - Artisan '78: The First National Travelling Exhibition of Contemporary Canadian Crafts/Artisan '78: première exposition nationale itinérante d'artisanat canadien contemporain (1979) #2134
  - Dorothy Knowles (1973) #6067
  - Henry Saxe: "Two Works" (1977) #7148
  - John Greer: Sculptural Objective, 1968-1981; Everything Always Changes but Something Still Remains (1982) #5654

- *New Paintings by Otto Rogers* (1974)
  #7062
- *Sylvain P. Cousineau: Photographs and
  Paintings* (1980) #5195
- *The Group of Seven in the Rockies* (1974)
  #1861
Regina (Sask), Saint Anne's Church and
  Rectory
- architecture, Etienne J. Gaboury #8767
Regina (Sask), School of Art
- Lochhead, Kenneth Campbell, as director
  #6317
Regina (Sask), University of Regina.
  Norman Mackenzie Art Gallery
- *see also* Regina (Sask), Regina College.
  Norman Mackenzie Art Gallery; Regina
  (Sask), University of Saskatchewan.
  Norman Mackenzie Art Gallery
- exhibitions
  - *100 Years of Saskatchewan Indian Art,
    1830-1930* (1975) #3734
  - *A Terrible Beauty: The Art of Canada at
    War* (1979) #1111
  - *Beauté tragique: les deux conflits mondiaux
    vus par des artistes canadiens* (1979) #1112
  - *Bill Vazan: suites photographiques récentes
    et oeuvres sur le terrain/Bill Vazan: Recent
    Land and Photoworks* (1981) #7476
  - *Building a Collection: Part 1, Selections
    from the Mackenzie Bequest and Other
    Gifts; Part 2, Selections from Purchases
    Made 1953 to 1977* (1978) #3197
  - *Canadians: A National Photography Show
    about People/Canadiens: exposition
    nationale de photographie ayant les gens
    comme thème* (1980) #1035
  - *Changes: 11 Artists Working on the
    Prairies* (1975) #1867
  - *Chester: A Two-Person Exhibition with
    Marilyn Levine* (1974) #1925
  - *Dessins inédits d'Ozias Leduc/Ozias Leduc
    the Draughtsman* (1978) #6210
  - *Douglas Bentham: Getting to Now* (1980)
    #4686
  - *Drawings by Jack Weldon Humphrey: A
    Travelling Exhibition Organized by the
    Beaverbrook Art Gallery, Fredericton, New
    Brunswick, Canada, 1977-1979* (1979)
    #5871
  - *Esther Warkov Drawings* (1976) #7519
  - *Frank Nulf* (1976) #6728
  - *Gordon Rayner Retrospective* (1980) #6966
  - *Grassroots Saskatchewan* (1976) #1931
  - *Jack I. Cowin* (1975) #5198
  - *Jack Sures* (1976) #7285
  - *Joe Fafard: Recent Sculpture* (1981) #5401
  - *Kenneth Lochhead: An Exhibition of
    Paintings 1952-1975* (1978) #6318
  - *Making Marks: An Exhibition of Current
    Canadian Drawing* (1977) #638
  - *New Clay in Regina* (1974) #2385
  - *Obsessions, Rituals, Controls: An
    Exhibition of Sculptural Works* (1978)
    #2066
  - *Otto Rogers* (1977) #7064
  - *R.L. Bloore: Sixteen Years, 1958-1974*
    (1975) #4751
  - *Regina 25 Years, 1953-1978: An Exhibition
    in Honour of Regina's 75th Anniversary*
    (1978) #1935
  - *Reta Cowley* (1975) #5200
  - *Ric Gomez* (1977) #5626
  - *Takao Tanabe, 1972-1976: The Land* (1976)
    #7320

- *The Continental Clay Connection* (1980)
  #1939
- *The Jacqui and Morris Shumiatcher
  Collection of Inuit Art* (1981) #4311
- *The Paintings of Frederick Nicholas
  Loveroff/Les peintures de Frederick Nicholas
  Loveroff*, 1981 #6331
- *The Saskatchewan Arts Board Collection*
  (1978) #1936
- *The Society of Canadian Painter-Etchers
  and Engravers in Retrospect/La Société des
  peintres-graveurs canadiens: vue
  rétrospective* (1981) #836
- *William Perehudoff: Recent Paintings*
  (1978) #6837
Regina (Sask), University of Saskatchewan
- Bornstein, Eli, as teacher #4854
- Saunders, Leslie Gail, as teacher #7128
Regina (Sask), University of Saskatchewan.
  Central heating and cooling plant
- architecture, Clifford Wiens #7694
Regina (Sask), University of Saskatchewan.
  Norman Mackenzie Art Gallery
- *see also* Regina (Sask), University of
  Regina. Norman Mackenzie Art Gallery
- exhibitions
  - *A.F. McKay, Paintings and Drawings,
    1959-1967* (1968) #6476
  - *Diversity: Canada East* (1972) #543
  - *E. Lindner: Drawings, 1969-1972* (1972)
    #6285
  - *Early Building in Saskatchewan* (1967)
    #8113
  - *Eleven Saskatchewan Artists* (1967) #1916
  - *Emma Lake Workshops, 1955-1973* (1973)
    #1923
  - *Gift from the Douglas M. Duncan
    Collection and the Milne-Duncan
    Bequest/Le Don provenant de la collection
    Douglas M. Duncan et le legs
    Milne-Duncan* (1972) #541
  - *J.M. Barnsley (1861-1929), Retrospective
    Exhibition* (1964) #4611
  - *Jan Wyers, Robert N. Hurley: An
    Exhibition of Two Prairie Painters* (1970)
    #1918
  - *John Nugent and Ted Godwin* (1972) #1922
  - *L'art de Tom Thomson* (1972) #7367
  - *Maxwell Bates: Retrospective Exhibition*
    (1960) #4622
  - *Maxwell Bates in Retrospect, 1921-1971*
    (1973) #4624
  - *Painting in Saskatchewan, 1883-1959*
    (1967) #1915
  - *Robert Harris (1849-1919)* (1973) #5743
  - *Saskatchewan: Art and Artists* (1971)
    #1919
  - *Saskatoon: Thirteen Artists* (1969) #1917
  - *Statements: 18 Canadian Artists* (1967)
    #490
  - *The Art of Tom Thomson* (1972) #7368
  - *The J.S. McLean Collection of Canadian
    Painting* (1969) #3228
  - *William G.R. Hind (1833-1888): A
    Confederation Painter in Canada* (1967)
    #5806
- exhibitions (reviews)
  - *Six Regina Artists* (1973) #2383
Regina (Sask), War Memorial Museum
- architecture, competition for #9073
Regina Five (Regina, Sask) #1913 1919
- and Kenneth Campbell Lochhead #6317
  6320
regionalism and art

- Alberta, mid 19th c.-1960s #1953
- and Carl Fellman Schaefer #7157 7158
- and Greg Curnoe #5225 5233
- Canada
  - 17th c.-1970s, landscapes #140
  - 20th c. #507 567
  - (1750s-1890s) #221
  - (1930s) #379
  - (1940s) #381
  - (1940s-1950s) #57
  - (1950-1960) #511
  - (1960s) #65
  - (1970s) #629
- Prairies (1960s-1970s) #1862
- Québec (1940s) #1387
Regroupement des artistes des Cantons de
  l'Est (RACE) #1536 1539
Reichert, Donald Karl (Don), Can artist,
  1932-
- exhibitions, group
  - (1981) #1907
Reid, Archibald, Can furniture-maker, d.
  1888 #2573
Reid, George, Can artist, fl. 1840s-1850s
- as member, Toronto Society of Arts #1689
Reid, George Agnew, Can artist, 1860-1947
  #178 6976 6979
- and Charles MacDonald Manly #6414
- and Edith Grace Coombs #5172
- and Mary Evelyn Wrinch #7617
- and Royal Canadian Academy of Arts
  #152
- as husband of Mary Hiester Reid #6982
- as principal, Ontario College of Art
  (Toronto, Ont) #2964
- as teacher of Frederick Nicholas Loveroff
  #6329
- as teacher of Mary Evelyn Wrinch #7618
- exhibitions, group
  - (1935) #17
  - (1978) #1726
- exhibitions (reviews) #186
- interview #6977
- murals, Jarvis Collegiate Institute
  Auditorium (Toronto, Ont) #6978
- on his art #6973
- on mural painting #6974 6975
- on painting and sketching buildings #8219
- relation of photography and painting #245
Reid, Leslie Mary Margaret, Can artist,
  1947- #675 6980
- exhibitions
  - (1980) #6981
- exhibitions, group
  - (1975) #591
  - (1977) #637
- exhibitions (reviews) #579
Reid, Mary Evelyn Wrinch
- *see* Wrinch, Mary Evelyn
Reid, Mary Hiester, Can artist, 1854-1921
  #207
- as teacher of Hattie Blackstock #4738
- as wife of George Agnew Reid #6979
- exhibitions
  - (1922) #6982
Reid, Richard, Can artist, 1930-
- exhibitions, group
  - (1974) #2050
Reid, Robert Dow, Can artist, 1933-
- exhibitions (reviews) #860
- memorial, Toronto (Ont) #727
Reid, Stuart, Can artist, 1953- #6983
Reid, Terrence Edward, Can artist, 1947-
- exhibitions, group

– (1971) #2042
Reid, William Ronald (Bill), Can sculptor, jeweller, 1920- #4066 4121 4155 4162 6984 6988
– and Northwest Coast art #6986
– carvings, Totem Park (Vancouver, BC) #4118 4124
– exhibitions
– (1974) #6985
– influence on Robert Davidson #5269
– interview #6987
– jewellery #2695
– on copper objects, Northwest Coast Indians #4071
– on totem poles #3972
– *Raven and the First People*, University of British Columbia. Museum of Anthropology (Vancouver, BC) #6989
Reinblatt, Moses Martin (Moe), Can artist, 1917-1979
– on printmaking #817
Reitzenstein, Reinhard, Can artist, 1949-
– on art #594
Rejlander, Oscar Gustave, Swedish photographer in England, 1832-1875
– Notman, William, compared with #6726
religion
– *see also* mysticism
– Ontario, 19th-20th cs. #8906
religion and architecture
– British Columbia (1858-1925) #8916
– Québec (1950s) #1406
religion and art
– and George Sawchuk #7142 7143
– and Jordi Bonet #4784
– and Napoléon Bourassa #4870
– and Ozias Leduc #6204 6206
– and Paul-Emile Borduas #4820
– and Pierre Charles Marie-Alain Couturier #1407
– and William Kurelek #6110
– Canada
– 20th c. #479 1393
– (1960s) #457 459
– (1970s) #94
– folk art #965 966
– images of women #121
– Sunday Mass Book illustrations (1970s) #597
– Montréal (Qué), Ecole des beaux-arts #2972
– Québec
– 17th-18th cs. #66 2187
– 17th c. #1322 1358 1363 1365
– 17th c.-1950s #1247
– 19th c. #1336
– (1640-1840) #1329
– (1940s) #1384 1394
– (1950s) #1250 1402 1406
– (1960s) #1435
– crosses #1619 1637
– crucifixes #1638
– folk art #1292
– images of the Devil, 17th c.-1840 #1357
– ironwork #2713
– review of literature #1295
– Québec (Qué), 17th c. #1352
– Saint-Basile-le-Grand (Qué), Centre communautaire catholique Tour de David #1510
religious art objects
– *see* religious articles
religious articles
– *see also* liturgical objects

religious articles, Canadian
– (1964-1967) #2108 2109
– Québec
– 17th-18th cs. #2187
– 17th-19th cs. #1245
– 17th c., Jesuits #2192
– Québec (Qué), 17th c. #1352
religious ceremonies
– *see* rites and ceremonies
religious costume
– *see also* vestments
religious costume, Canadian #2825
– Québec #2779 2838
Rémi, Daniel, Can photographer, fl. 1973
– portfolio of photographs #997 999
Renaissance art
– compared with art revival, Northwest Coast Indians #6986
– France, influence on Québec woodcarving and architecture #1574
– influence on Marius Dubois #5310
– influence on William Perehudoff #6837
Renard, Jules, Fr architect, fl. 1916
– Montréal (Qué), château Dufresne #8617 8618
Renaud, François, Can photographer, fl. 1973
– portfolio of photographs #997 999
Renaud (*dit* Cannard), Pierre, Can builder, 1699-1774 #269 270
Renfrew County (Ont)
– furniture, Polish settlers #2565
Rennes (France), Musée de Rennes
– exhibitions
– *Art et artisanat des Indiens Iroquois* (1964) #3590
Renoir, Pierre Auguste, Fr artist, 1841-1919
– influence on Paul-Emile Borduas #4841
Renzins, Rudy, Swedish silversmith, fl. 1930s
– as teacher of Harold Stacey #7274
Repentigny, Marie Favery de, Can nun, d. 1675 #2212
– craft education #2979
Repentigny, Rodolphe de (Jauran), Can artist, art critic, 1926-1959
– as art critic #3318
– exhibitions, group
– (1977) #1465
– (1981) #1471
Repentigny (Qué)
– architecture #7888
Repentigny (Qué), church
– sculptures, Philippe Liébert #6281
Reppen, Jack, Can artist, 1933-1964 #6990
République des Beaux-Arts #1502
Repulse Bay (NWT)
– ivory carving #4438
– sculpture #4450
reredos
– *see* altarpieces
Resnais, Alain, Fr filmmaker, 1922-
– influence on Vera Frenkel #5526
resorts, American
– 20th c. #8524
resorts, Canadian
– 20th c. #8524
restaurants, Canadian
– Toronto (Ont), (1910s) #9269
restoration of works of art
– *see* conservation and restoration
Restoule, Tim, Can artist, 1960-
– exhibitions, group
– (1980) #4159

– (1981) #4173
Retable
– and Wilfrid Corbeil #1402
retables
– *see* altarpieces
Reusch, Astri, Can stained glass artist, 1945- #2455
Reusch, Kina, Can artist, 1940-
– ritual and cult elements #789
Reuter, William, Can artist, 1940-
– typographic designs #932
Revell, Viljo, Finnish architect, 1910-1964
– Toronto (Ont), City Hall and Civic Square #8981 8990 8991 8992 8993
– competition #8989
revolution and art
– automatistes, writings on #1443
– Québec (1759-1914) #1351
Revue d'art canadienne
– *see* RACAR (*Revue d'art canadienne/Canadian Art Review*)
Revue moderne, La, Can periodical
– and Ulric Lamarche #6155
Reynolds, Alan, Can sculptor, 1947-
– exhibitions (reviews) #6991
– techniques #792
Reynolds, Catherine, Can artist, 1784-1864 #6992
– exhibitions
– (1967) #6993
Rhéaume, Damase, Can sculptor, 1832-1903
– woodcarvings, Nettie Sharpe collection #1607
Rhéaume, Jeanne Leblanc, Can artist, 1915- #6994
Rhind, William Birnie, Brit sculptor, d. 1933
– sculpture, Legislative Building (Winnipeg, Man) #8948
Rho, Joseph-Adolphe, Can artist, 1835-1905 #1318 1323
Rhone & Iredale, Can architectural firm
– Burnaby (BC), Simon Fraser University, competition #9501
– Vancouver (BC)
– Fairview Place #8746
– University of British Columbia. Sedgewick Undergraduate Library #9052
– Westcoast Building #9359
RIBA
– *see* Royal Institute of British Architects (RIBA)
ribbon appliqué, Penobscot #3537
Rice, Gordon, Can artist, 1933- #6995
Richard, Damase, Can sculptor, 1852-1922
– woodcarvings, Nettie Sharpe collection #1607
Richard, Hélène Roy, Can artist, 1941- #1538
– and RACE #1536
Richard, Jean-Jules, Can writer, 1911-1975
– correspondence, Paul-Emile Borduas #1443
Richard, René-Jean, Can artist, 1895- #1393 6996 6998 6999
– interview #6997
Richard, Wilfrid, Can sculptor, b. ca. 1895 #7000
Richard Strong Associates-James Secord Consortium, Can landscape architects
– Montréal (Qué), Expo '67. La Ronde #9222
Richards, Cecil Clarence, Can sculptor, 1907-
– exhibitions, group
– (1978) #666
Richards, Larry Wayne, Can architect, 1944-

#8402
Richards, William, Can artist, ca. 1786-1811
#7001
Richardson, Henry Hobson, Amer architect,
1838-1886
- influence on Bruce Price #9537
- influence on Edward James Lennox #9354
- influence on Toronto (Ont) architecture
#8055
- influence on William Newlands #8392
Richelieu and Ontario Navigation Company,
S.S. *Kingston* (passenger ship)
- mural, Frederick Sproston Challener #5068
Richelieu Valley (Qué)
- pottery, 18th-19th cs. #2299 2321
Richeterre, Michel
- *see* Dessailliant (*dit* Richeterre), Michel
Richmond, Chris, Can artist, fl. 1976
- exhibitions, group
  - (1976) #1529
Ricketts, Charles, Brit artist, 1866-1931
- and National Gallery of Canada (Ottawa,
Ont) #3050
Rideau Canal region (Qué and Ont)
- architecture
  - 19th c. #8019
  - (1826-1832) #8012
Rideau Corridor (Ont)
- architecture (pre-1880) #8008
Rider-Rider, William, Brit photographer, b.
1889
- photographs of World War I #1107 1113
Ridgway, Morley, Wear & Co., ceramic
manufacturer (Hanley, England)
- views of Canada #2362
Riel, Louis, Métis leader, 1844-1885
- photograph of, Joseph Langevin #6161
Riggio, Mike, Can artist, 1946-
- exhibitions, group
  - (1979) #1157
Riley, Jerry, Can photographer, ca. 1949-
- portfolio of photographs #1032
Rimmer, David McLellan, Can artist, 1942-
- exhibitions, group
  - (1979) #2069
- films #626
Rimouski (Qué)
- churches and crosses #8872
Rimouski (Qué), Church of Sainte-Luce
- architecture, Thomas Baillairgé #1361
Rimouski (Qué), Ecole d'arts et métiers de
Rimouski
- *see* Rimouski (Qué), Séminaire de
Rimouski. Ecole d'arts et métiers de
Rimouski
Rimouski (Qué), Musée régional de
Rimouski #9118
- exhibitions
  - *De la figuration à la non-figuration dans
l'art québécois* (1977) #1461
  - *Dessins inédits d'Ozias Leduc/Ozias Leduc
the Draughtsman* (1979) #6210
Rimouski (Qué), National Exhibition Centre
- exhibitions
  - *Edward Curtis in the Collection of the
Edmonton Art Gallery* (1980) #3480
Rimouski (Qué), Séminaire de Rimouski.
Ecole d'arts et métiers de Rimouski
- (1942) #2978
Rindisbacher, Peter, Can artist, 1806-1834
#7003 7004 7006 7007 7008 7009 7010
- and Hudson's Bay Company #273
- in Minnesota #7002
- in western Canada #1859

- paintings of Indians and Eskimos, Saint
John's Cathedral (Winnipeg, Man) #7005
Ringness, Charles, Can artist, 1923- #7011
- exhibitions, group
  - (1977) #1933
  - (1979) #678
rings, Canadian
- episcopal ring, William Maurice
Carmichael #5003
Rio de Janeiro (Brazil)
- views
  - Tonnancour, Jacques Godefroy de #7382
Rio de Janeiro (Brazil), Canadian Embassy
- murals, Alfred Pellan #6798
Rio de Janeiro (Brazil), Museu de arte
moderna
- exhibitions
  - *Artistas canadenses* (1955) #1409
Rio de Janeiro (Brazil), Museu nacional de
belas artes
- exhibitions
  - *Artes graficas do Canada 1946* (1946) #806
  - *Pintura canadense contemporanea* (1944)
#367
Riopelle, Dominique, Can silversmith,
1787-1859
- works, Detroit Institute of Arts (Detroit,
Mich) #2691
Riopelle, Jean-Paul, Can artist, 1923- #1432
1453 1504 1541 1542 1543 7012 7013 7014
7016 7017 7020 7022 7023 7027 7033
- and Montréal (Qué) art (1940s-1960s)
#1437
- cover illustration, *Refus global* #1396
- exhibitions
  - (1959) #7015
  - (1962) #7018 7019
  - (1967) #7021
  - (1972) #7025
  - (1980) #7030
  - (1981) #7032
- exhibitions, group #1409
  - (1955) #411
  - (1958) #431
  - (1962) #1420
  - (1964) #462
  - (1977) #633 1278 1279
- exhibitions (reviews) #7024
- *Icebergs* series #7028
- influence on Pierre Gendron #5581
- international recognition (1950s) #425
- interview #7026
- paintings (1947-1950) #7031
- paintings and sculptures #7029
Rioux, Jules-Bernardin-Raoul, Can priest,
artist, 1835-1921 #1319
Rioux Report
- *see* Québec. Rapport de la Commission
royale d'enquête sur l'enseignement dans
la province de Québec (Rapport Rioux)
Ristvedt-Handerek, Milly, Can artist, 1942-
#7035
- exhibitions
  - (1979) #7034
- exhibitions, group
  - (1974) #565
Ritchie, Bill, Can artist, 1954-
- video art #616
Ritchie, James Edward, Can sculptor in
France, 1929-
- interview #7036
rites and ceremonies
- *see also* festivals
- sculpture, British Columbia (1970s) #2066

rites and ceremonies, Algonquian
- Midewiwin #3580 3702
- use of wampum #3521
rites and ceremonies, Athapaskan #4072
4073
- masks #4083
rites and ceremonies, Bella Coola #3874
rites and ceremonies, Beothuk #3528
rites and ceremonies, Blackfoot #3721
- Catchers Society #3665
- Medicine Pipe ceremony #3681
- Minìpoka #3749
rites and ceremonies, Copper Eskimo #4330
rites and ceremonies, Cree #3655 3742
- calumet ceremony #3662
rites and ceremonies, Delaware #3506
rites and ceremonies, Ingalik #4087
- masks #4083
rites and ceremonies, Inuit #4254 4315 4317
4320 4321 4404 4492
- bear cult #4355
- masks #4349
- Sea Goddess #4376
rites and ceremonies, Iroquois #3489
- False Face Society #3595
- masks #3570 3588 3613
- Midwinter ceremony #3606
- Six Nations Reserve (Ont) #3598
- use of tobacco #3618
- use of wampum #3521
rites and ceremonies, Kwakiutl #3768 3838
- masks #4030
- Thunderbird Dance #3867
rites and ceremonies, Makah
- wolf ritual #3885
rites and ceremonies, Micmac #3528 3569
rites and ceremonies, Mistassini #4080
rites and ceremonies, Montagnais #4082
rites and ceremonies, Naskapi #4082
rites and ceremonies, Netsilik #4328
rites and ceremonies, Nootka
- wolf ritual #3885
rites and ceremonies, Northwest Coast
Indians #3869 3871 3970 3989 4065
- masks #4030 4038
- potlatch #3911
- raven rattles #3980
- totem poles #3930
- wolf ritual #3885
rites and ceremonies, Ojibwa #3488 3539
3602
- Midewiwin #3492 3517 3626 3661
rites and ceremonies, Onondaga
- masks #3588
rites and ceremonies, Plains #3725 3727
- ghost dance #3736
rites and ceremonies, Salish #3838
rites and ceremonies, Seneca
- False Face Society #3533
- masks #3508
rites and ceremonies, Siouan #3725
- Midewiwin #3702
rites and ceremonies, Tlingit #3976
- potlatch #4012
ritual
- *see* rites and ceremonies
Rivard, Yvon, Can writer, 1945-
- and Lucie Lambert, *Album Frayère* #6157
Rivest, Gilles G., Can photographer, ca.
1936-
- portfolio of photographs #995
Rivière-du-Loup (Qué)
- art and architecture #1233
Rivière-du-Loup (Qué), Church of

Saint-Patrice
- paintings, Charles Edouard Huot #5878 5884
- sculptures, Louis Jobin #5967
Rivière-du-Loup (Qué), Musée d'archéologie de l'est du Québec
- exhibitions
 - *De la figuration à la non-figuration dans l'art québécois* (1976) #1461
Robb, Jim, Can artist, 1934- #7037
Robbe-Grillet, Alain, Fr writer, 1922-
- influence on Vera Frenkel #5526
Robbie, Roderick G., Can architect, 1928-
- as codirector, Toronto School Board Study of Educational Facilities (SEF) #9472
Robe, Sir William, Brit. army officer and architect in Canada, 1765-1820
- Québec (Qué), Cathedral of the Holy Trinity #8786
Robert, Guy, Can artist, art critic, poet, 1933-
- works, Venice Biennale (1952) #399
Robert, Louise, Can artist, 1941- #717 7038
- exhibitions
 - (1977) #7039
- exhibitions, group
 - (1980) #695 698
 - (1981) #1565
Robert Fairfield Associates, Can architectural firm
- Toronto (Ont), Central Technical School Art Centre #7684
Robert-Fleury, Tony, Fr artist, 1837-1912
- as teacher of William Blair Bruce #4941
- as teacher of William Brymner #4948
Robert McCausland Limited, stained glass studio (Toronto, Ont)
- stained glass #2399
Roberts, Goodridge
- see Roberts, William Goodridge
Roberts, Olive, Can photographer, fl. 1967
- exhibitions, group
 - (1967) #8113
Roberts, Sir Charles George Douglas, Can poet, 1860-1943
- Wilde, Oscar, on #238
Roberts, Tomtu H., Can artist, 1859-1938
- exhibitions
 - (1980) #7051
Roberts, William Goodridge, Can artist, 1904-1974 #7040 7041 7044
- autobiography #7043
- exhibitions
 - (1969) #7045
 - (1977) #7047
 - (1980) #7048
 - (1981) #7050
- exhibitions, group
 - (1958) #431
 - (1959) #438
 - (1964) #462
 - (1977) #1278 1279
- exhibitions (reviews) #7046
- influence on Alberta landscape painting (1930s-1940s) #1965
- influence on Jean-Paul Lemieux #6227
- influence on Robert Gray Murray #613
- influence on Toni Onley #613
- interview #7042
- late works #7049
- on studying in Europe #408
- Tonnancour, Jacques Godefroy de, compared with #7384
Roberts, William Griffith, Can artist, 1920- #7052

Robertson, Clive, Can artist, 1946-
- and W.O.R.K.S. #1955
- exhibitions
 - (1977) #7053
- exhibitions, group
 - (1977) #631
- performance art #655
Robertson, John Ross, Can collector, historian, publisher, 1841-1918
- collection #1713
- collection, Canadiana, Metro Toronto Public Library (Toronto, Ont) #3130 3131 3204
Robertson, Sarah Margaret Armour, Can artist, 1891-1948
- exhibitions
 - (1951) #7054
- exhibitions, group
 - (1928) #301
Robertson, Tom, Can photographer, fl. 1979 #2071
Robertson, William Francis, Can photographer, fl. 1863-1864
- and the Victoria Theatre Photographic Gallery (Victoria, BC) #2027
Robicheau, Louis, Can, 20th c.
- residence, Vieille Maison (Meteghan, NS) #8531
Robideau, Henri, Can photographer, 1946-
- exhibitions, group
 - (1980) #1063
Robillard, Yves, Can designer, art critic, 1939-
- and Fusion des arts (Montréal, Qué) #1482 1483
Robinson, Albert Henry, Can artist, 1881-1956 #7056 7057
- and Group of Seven #1732
- exhibitions
 - (1955) #7055
- exhibitions, group
 - (1928) #301
- works, McMichael Canadian Collection (Kleinburg, Ont) #3172
Robinson, Boardman, Can artist, 1876-1952 #1128
Robinson, George, Can photographer, 1825-1895
- and the Victoria Theatre Photographic Gallery (Victoria, BC) #2027
Robinson, Gerald, Can architect, 1930-
- Saskatoon (Sask), Mendel Art Gallery, competition #9091
- Winnipeg (Man), City Hall, competition #8985 8986 8987
Robinson, Joseph, Can silversmith, 1842-1880 #2649
Robinson, Percy James, Can artist, 1873-1953
- and Group of Seven #1732
Robinson & Heinrichs, Can architectural firm
- Toronto (Ont), St. Lawrence housing #8078
Robitaille, André, Can architect, 1922-
- Québec (Qué), Chalet des employés civils #7939
Robitaille, Louis, Can silversmith, 1755-1822
- works, Detroit Institute of Arts (Detroit, Mich) #2691
Robson, Albert Henry, Can art critic, artist, 1882-1939 #7058
- and Arthur Lismer #6300
Robson, John, Can artist, 20th c. #4169

Roch, Ernst, Can artist, 1928-
- and Design Collaborative Montreal Ltd. #878 882
- prints #897
- typographic designs #932
Rochdale (England), Corporation Art Gallery
- exhibitions
 - *Exhibition of Canadian Art* (1926) #290
Roche Percée (Sask)
- petroglyphs, Assiniboine Indians #3673
Rochester (NY), Rochester Memorial Art Gallery
- exhibitions
 - *Contemporary Canadian Painting and Sculpture* (1963) #455
Rochester (NY), Rochester Museum
- art, Inuit #4424
- art, Iroquois #3590
Rochette, Sylvie, Can sculptor, fl. 1979- #1626
rock art
- see also petroglyphs; pictographs
rock art, Blackfoot
- boulder monuments #3688
rock art, Cree
- boulder monuments #3688
rock art, Indians of North America #3329 3359 3433 3472 3481 3482 3484
rock art, Ojibwa
- boulder monuments (Whiteshell, Man) #3578 3592
rock art, Plains
- shield motif #3710
rock art, Siouan
- boulder monuments #3688
Rockburne, Dorothea, Can artist in USA, 1934- #7059 7060
Rockett, Beverly, Can photographer, fl. 1970 #993
Rockett, Paul, Can photographer, 1919- #1036
rocking chairs, Canadian
- île aux Coudres (Qué) #2178
- Québec #1334 1335
 - 18th-19th cs. #2535 2536
Rockingham ware, American
- imported into Canada, early 20th c. #2346
Rockingham ware, Canadian
- 19th c. #2302
- W. & D. Bell Pottery (Québec, Qué) #2291
- Welding, W.E., Brantford Pottery (Brantford, Ont) #2335
Rockman, Arnold, Can artist, 1930-
- as juror, *B.C. Artists Annual Exhibition*, Vancouver Art Gallery (Vancouver, BC), (1966) #1983
- on randomness in art #7061
Rocky Mountain House (Alta)
- fur trade posts #8129
Rocky Mountains (Canada)
- photographic views
 - (1880s-1890s) #1874
 - Gleason, Herbert Wendell #5617
 - Harmon, Byron #5707
 - Warren, Mary Schaffer #7526
 - Weiss, Joe #7541
- summer homes and resorts, 20th c. #8524
- views
 - Bell-Smith, Frederic Marlett #4666 4667 4668
 - Brown, Annora #4933
 - Collings, Charles John #5132 5133 5135 5136

– Fraser, John Arthur #5510
– Group of Seven #1861
– Harris, Lawren Stewart #5732 5734
– Hind, William George Richardson #5807
– Knowles, Dorothy #6067
– late 19th c. #271 272 1839
– Leighton, Alfred Crocker #6225
– MacDonald, J.E.H. #6370
– Martin, Thomas Mower #6435 6438
– Roper, Edward #7077
– Warre, Henry James #7521
– Warren, Mary Schaffer #7525
Rocky Mountains (USA)
– views
– Miller, Alfred Jacob #6536 6537
Rodchenko, Aleksandr Mihailovic, Russ
  artist, 1891-1956
– influence on Lionel LeMoine FitzGerald
  #5450
Roden Bros., Can silversmith firm
– (1890s-1920s) #2638
Rodier, Olivier, Can artist, fl. 1842 #1301
Rodin, Auguste, Fr sculptor, 1840-1917
– influence on Douglas Bentham #4686
Rodrik, Paul, Can artist, 1915-
– exhibitions, group
  – (1972) #5972
  – (1973) #5973
Roebuck (Grenville County, Ont)
– artifacts, Iroquois #3616
Rogers, Joseph S., Can photographer, fl.
  1860s #1211
Rogers, Otto Donald, Can artist, 1935- #7063
– exhibitions
  – (1973) #7062
  – (1977) #7064 7065
– exhibitions, group
  – (1967) #1916
  – (1975) #1926
  – (1977) #1933
– interview #7066
Rogers, Robert, Can artist, 1944-
– prints #1214
Rogerson, John, Can sculptor,
  furniture-maker, 1837-1925 #7067 7068
Rojik, Michael, Can photographer, fl. 1980
– portfolio of photographs #1032
Rolland, Dominique, Can sculptor, 1954-
– use of stone #1634
Rollin, Paul, Can sculptor, fl. 1812-1830
  #6947
Rolph, Joseph Thomas, Can artist, 1831-1916
– watercolour paintings, Art Gallery of
  Cobourg (Cobourg, Ont) #3162
Rolph, Smith & Co., publishing firm
  (Toronto, Ont)
– Christmas greeting cards #842 890
Roma Site (PEI)
– cutlery #2714 2715
– glass
  – 19th c. #2436 2437
Roman Stone Company (Toronto, Ont)
– influence on Canadian architecture
  (1903-1920s) #7734
Romanesque revival architecture
– New Brunswick #7808
– Newlands, William #8392
– Toronto (Ont) #8064
  – Stewart Building #9354
  – University of Toronto. University
    College #9429 9453
Romanticism
– Canada
  – 19th c. #66

– (1860s) #230
Rombout, Luke, Can curator, 1933-
– and Art Bank #3276
– on Miller Gore Brittain #4917
Rome (Italy)
– urban development #7902
Rome (Italy), Collegio di Propaganda Fide
– art, Indians of North America #3396
Rome (Italy), Free School of Art
– Grier, Edmund Wyly, as student #5660
Rome (Italy), Saint Peter's Cathedral
– baldachin, influence on baldachin, church,
  Neuville (Qué) #8826
Romney, George, Brit artist, 1734-1802
– painting of death of Wolfe #220
Romses, Kwan & Associates, Can
  architectural firm
– Vancouver (BC), Chinese Cultural Centre,
  competition #9144
Ronald, William S., Can artist, 1926- #7069
  7071 7072 7074 7075 7076
– and Toronto (Ont) painting (1960s) #1753
  1760
– exhibitions
  – (1975) #7073
– exhibitions, group
  – (1958) #431
– mural, Anglican rectory, Ward's Island
  (Toronto, Ont) #7070
– mural, National Arts Centre (Ottawa, Ont)
  #9108
– on living in New York (1960s) #460
rood screens, Canadian
– Québec (1650-1925) #1592
roofs, Canadian
– 17th-19th cs. #7703
– Montréal (Qué), stone roof frames #8598
– Québec
  – 17th-18th cs. #7881
  – 17th c., clapboard masonry #7860
  – 18th-19th cs. #8560 8561
  – 19th c. #8624
Roper, Edward, Brit artist in Canada,
  1857-1891 #7077
– supported by Canadian railway
  companies #3281
Rosa, Salvator, It artist, 1615-1673
– *Mercury Putting Argus to Sleep*, influence
  on Joseph Légaré #1373
Roscoe, Stanley M., Can architect, 1921-
– Hamilton (Ont), City Hall and Civic
  Square #8988
Rose, Jurgen, Can artist, ca. 1937-
– stage designs #472
Rose, Peter, Can architect, 1943-
– North Hatley (Qué), Bradley House #7886
– on architecture #7746
Rose, T.Bert, Can educator, fl. 1970s
– Broughton Island (NWT), wood and
  styrofoam dome house #8734
Rose Blanche Point (Nfld), lighthouse #9523
Rosebud Creek (Alta)
– photographic views
  – Biggs, Hugh Beynon #4728
Rosenberg, Fred, Can photographer, fl.
  1970s
– portfolio of photographs #997 998 999
Rosenberg, Gloria, Can art dealer, 1926-
– collection, quilts #2808
Rosenberg, Tanya
– *see* Marshall (Mars), Tanya
Rosenblatt, Joe, Can artist, 1933-
– exhibitions, group
  – (1978) #649

Rosenfield, Ethel, Can sculptor, 1910- #7078
Rosengarten, Morton, Can sculptor, 1933-
– clay sculptures (1960s) #743
Ross, Charles, Amer artist, 1937-
– on visual perception #525
Ross, David, Can ceramicist, 1925-1974
– and Hansen-Ross Pottery (Fort
  Qu'Appelle, Sask) #2389
Ross, Frederick Joseph (Fred), Can artist,
  1927- #1121 1173 1184
– and realism #110
– interview #7079
– on art, Saint John (NB) #1188
– portraits #715
Ross, Richard Bartlett (Rick), Can sculptor,
  1940-
– natural constructions (1970s) #2065
Ross, Rosie, Can artist, fl. 1964 #4121
Ross, Sir John, Brit naval officer, artist in
  Canada, 1777-1856
– expedition, Arctic #278
Ross & Macdonald, Can architectural firm
– Edmonton (Alta), Hotel Macdonald #9270
– Montréal (Qué)
  – Architects Building #9312
  – Chateau Apartments #8558
  – Mount Royal Hotel #9276
– Québec (Qué), Price House #9311
– T. Eaton Company department stores
  #9365
– Toronto (Ont)
  – Central Technical School #9434
  – Royal Bank #9165
  – Royal York Hotel #9280 9281
  – T. Eaton Company Department Store
    #9368
  – Union Station #9531 9536
– Winnipeg (Man), Fort Garry Hotel #9268
Ross & Macfarlane, Can architectural firm
– Ottawa (Ont), Central Station and Château
  Laurier #9264 9528
Roth, Evelyn, Can artist, 1936- #675
– exhibitions, group
  – (1980) #698
– fibrework #2775
Roth, Ghitta Caiserman
– *see* Caiserman-Roth, Ghitta
Roth, Max W., Can architect, 1913-
– Montréal (Qué), Temple Emmanu-El #8840
Rother/Bland/Trudeau, Can architectural
  firm
– Ottawa (Ont), City Hall #7679 8984
– Port-Cartier (Qué) #8184
Rothko, Mark, Amer artist, 1903-1970
– influence on Claude Tousignant #7401
– influence on Jean Albert McEwen #6471
– influence on Montréal (Qué) painting
  #1425
Rothmans of Pall Mall Canada, Can tobacco
  firm
– as art patron (1970s) #3275
– collection, Inuit sculpture #4257
Rothschild, Hanni, Can sculptor, 1921- #7080
Rotterdam (Netherlands), musée Boymans
  Van Beuningen
– exhibitions
  – *Michael Snow* (1979) #7258
Rouault, Georges, Fr artist, 1871-1958
– 1964 inaugural exhibition, Musée d'art
  contemporain (Montréal, Qué) #3094
– Bates, Maxwell Bennett, compared with
  #4623
– influence on Lillian Freiman #5517
Rouer, Louis, Sieur de Villeray, Can public

servant, 1629-1700
- residence, maison Fornel (Québec, Qué)
 #7953
Rougier, Roger, Can furniture manufacturer,
 fl. 1970s
- office furniture #7081
Rounthwaite & Associates, Can architectural
 firm
- Saskatoon (Sask), Mendel Art Gallery,
 competition #9091
Rounthwaite & Fairfield, Can architectural
 firm
- Stratford (Ont), Stratford Festival Theatre
 #7679
Rousseau, Albert, Can artist, 1908- #1393
 7082 7083
Rousseau, Denis, Can artist, 1951- #7084
- exhibitions, group
 - (1979) #674
Rousseau, François, Can architect, fl. 1964-
- and Fusion des arts (Montréal, Qué) #1482
Rousseau, Henri, Fr artist, 1844-1910
- Davies, Thomas, compared with #5272
- influence on Carol Fraser #5508
- influence on Homer Ransford Watson
 #7531
Rousseau, Michèle
- see Bernatchez-Rousseau, Michèle
Rousseau, Richard, Can artist, 1946-
- as member of Centre communautaire
 catholique Tour de David
 (Saint-Basile-le-Grand, Qué) #1510
Rousseau-Vermette, Mariette, Can tapestry
 artist, 1926- #7085
- exhibitions, group
 - (1978) #2772
 - (1981) #2776
- exhibitions (reviews) #2771
Roussel, Claude, Can artist, 1930- #7088
- exhibitions
 - (1977) #7089
- interview #7087
- on Acadian art (1960s) #1181
- prints #1185
- Royal Architectural Institute of Canada
 Allied Arts Medal winner (1963) #7086
Roussil, Robert, Can sculptor, 1925- #1502
 7090 7098
- as founder, artist's colony,
 Tourette-sur-Loup (France) #7091
- exhibitions
 - (1965) #7092
 - (1971) #7095
- exhibitions, group
 - (1977) #1622
- influence on Pierre Rolland Dinel #5293
- interview #3269 7093 7094 7097
- on his art #7096
Rouville, Hertel de, Can family, 18th-19th
 cs.
- portraits of #1345
Roux & Morin, Can architectural firm
- Montréal (Qué), Centre marial des pères
 Monfortains #8840
Rouyn (Qué), Comité des expositions
 artistiques de Rouyn-Noranda
- exhibitions
 - De la figuration à la non-figuration dans
 l'art québécois (1977) #1461
 - Métiers d'art Ontario-Québec,
 1979/1980/Quebec-Ontario Crafts,
 1979/1980 (1980) #2138
row houses, Canadian
- Montréal (Qué), Park Avenue #7933

Rowley, Frances Elswood Richards, Can
 artist, 1852-1934
- Wilde, Oscar, on #238
Roy, Jean-Marie, Can architect, 1925-
- Québec (Qué), Campus
 intercommunautaire de Cap-Rouge #9421
Roy, LeMoyne & Gordon Edwards, Can
 architectural firm
- Charlottetown (PEI), Confederation
 Centre, competition #9088
Roy, Mario, Can artist, 1953- #7099
Roy, Phillippe, Can artist, 1899-
- woodcarvings, Nettie Sharpe collection
 #1607
Roy, Ronald Hamilton (Ron), Can
 ceramicist, 1935-
- exhibitions, group
 - (1968) #2382
Roy-Audy, Jean-Baptiste, Can artist,
 1778-1848 #1336 7100 7102 7103
 - (1959) #219
- L'éducation de la Vierge and Saint-Joseph et
 l'Enfant-Jésus #7101
- portrait, Hertel de Rouville family
 member #1345
Royal, Frank, Can photographer, fl. 1960s-
- portfolio of photographs #991
Royal Architectural Institute of Canada
- (1920s) #8244
- (1950s-1960s) #8305
- (1959), annual meeting, reports of group
 discussions #8303
- (1960), Committee of Inquiry into the
 Design of the Residential Environment,
 report #8513
- (1960s), architects on #8311
- (1961), resolution to survey the profession
 #8309
- (1965), survey of architects on the
 profession #8308
- (1970s), survey of architects on #8314
- (1974), criticism of #8318 8319
- (1975-1977), and National Gallery of
 Canada (Ottawa, Ont) competition #9126
- Allied Arts Medal
 - (1956)
 - Thomas, Lionel Arthur John #7348
 - (1958)
 - Archambault, Louis #4540
 - (1960)
 - Mol, Leo #6578
 - (1961)
 - Daoust, Sylvia Marie Emilienne #5256
 - (1962)
 - Binning, B.C. #4733
 - (1963)
 - Roussel, Claude #7086
 - (1965)
 - Bonet, Jordi #4785
- awards
 - (1931) #7660
 - (1937) #7664
 - (1940) #7665
- Committee on the Preservation of Historic
 Buildings #7756
 - exhibitions
 - (1964-1966) #7688
 - exhibitions (reviews)
 - (1931) #323
 - (1933) #7662
- Honorary Fellowship Award, Walter
 Seymour Allward (1937) #4519
- housing designs (1950s) #8509

Royal Architectural Institute of Canada. Journal,
 Can periodical #7654
Royal Canadian Academy of Arts #5 16 28
 152 153 157
- 19th c.-1930s, and academies of art #343
- (1870s-1883), documents #166
- (1880-1910), influence on Canadian art
 #214
- (1880-1913) #3061
- (1880-1971) #2
- (1880-1979), exhibitions and members #162
- (1880s-1890s) #102 184 1706
- (1880s-1920s), and landscape painting #14
- (1880s-1930s), architects as members #8298
- (1890-1900) #190
- (1890s) #181 188
- (1890s-1910s), and National Gallery of
 Canada (Ottawa, Ont) #275 3041
- (1898), compared with Ontario Society of
 Artists #1707
- (1914-1918), World War I, National
 Patriotic Fund #208
- (1924), British Empire Exhibition
 (Wembley, England) #458 500
- (1940s), criticism of #366
- (1943), criticism of #361
- (1950s), and academies of art #434
- (1980) #689
- (1980s), criticism of #686
- and Alice A. Innes #5900
- and Canadian Society of Graphic Art #801
- and Charlotte Mount Brook Morrell
 Schreiber #7164
- and Doris Minette Judah #5980
- and Edmond Dyonnet #5346 5348
- and Florence Carlyle #4999
- and George Harlow White #7551
- and Helen Galloway McNicoll #6507
- and Homer Ransford Watson #7533
- and James Wilson Morrice #6634
- and Laura Adeline Muntz Lyall #6339
- and Lord Lorne #280
- and Marion F.S. Mackay Nicoll #6703
- and Mary Hiester Reid #6982
- and Ontario Society of Artists #1666 1679
- and Robert Wakeham Pilot #6869
- collection, National Gallery of Canada
 (Ottawa, Ont) #3044
- exhibitions
 - (1884) #170
 - (1939) #346
 - (1966) #474
 - (1980) #1906
- exhibitions (reviews)
 - (1881) #168
 - (1885) #171
 - (1892-1893) #179
 - (1898) #186
 - (1910) #195
 - (1912) #202
 - (1915) #210
 - (1916) #283
 - (1927) #296
 - (1928) #303 310
 - (1929) #312
 - (1930) #318
 - (1931) #323
 - (1933) #325
 - (1934) #326
 - (1935) #328
 - (1936) #329
 - (1947) #3304
- nationalism and landscape painting, late
 19th c. #271 272

Royal Canadian Aerial Theatre (RCAT)
(Vancouver, BC)
– balloon and kite sculptures #2058
Royal Canadian Air Force
– see Canada. Royal Canadian Air Force
Royal Canadian Institute
– (1884-1888), photographic section #975
Royal Canadian Navy
– see Canada. Royal Canadian Navy
Royal Commission on Education in Ontario
– see Ontario. Royal Commission on
Education in Ontario
Royal Commission on National
Development in the Arts, Letters and
Sciences (Massey Report)
– see Canada. Royal Commission on
National Development in the Arts, Letters
and Sciences (Massey Report)
Royal Engineers
– British Columbia, architecture and
planning #8150
– St. John's (Nfld), Commissariat House
#8538
Royal Institute of British Architects (RIBA)
– (1960s), survey of architectural profession
#8307
– and Royal Architectural Institute of
Canada (1920s) #8244
– architectural drawing, early 20th c. #8241
– Royal Gold Medal
– Darling, Frank (1915) #8349 8350
– Morris, Robert Schofield (1958) #8389
royalty
– see kings and rulers
Royle, Stanley, Can artist, 1886-1961
– on his art #7104
Roza, Gustavo da, Can architect, 1933-
– Winnipeg (Man)
– Winnipeg Art Gallery #9111 9117
– Winnipeg Art Gallery, competition
#9102
Rozaire, Arthur Dominique, Can artist,
1879-1922 #1382
Rozynska, Wanda, Can ceramicist, 1929-
#2232
Ruben, David
– see Piqtoukun, David Ruben
Rubin, Mark, Can photographer, fl. 1973
– exhibitions, group
– (1973) #1002
Rudolph, Paul Marvin, Amer architect, 1918-
– Niagara Falls (Ont), Earl W. Brydges
Public Library #9050
Ruelland, Ludger, Can artist, 1827-1896
– exhibitions, group
– (1959) #219
Rugh, Herbert Bell, Amer architect,
1888-1924
– Winnipeg (Man), houses #8493 8683
rugs
– see also conservation and restoration, rugs
rugs, Canadian #2725
– 17th-19th cs. #2730 2736
– 20th c. #2121
– (1608-1867) #2120
– beaver motif #56
– Belbin, Louise #2759
– Canadian Handicrafts Guild #2090
– from old clothing, 19th c. #2888
– Gagnon, Clarence Alphonse #5546 5547
– Germanic tradition #2140
– hooked and poked mats, Newfoundland
and Labrador #2765 2767
– hooked rugs #2107 2752 2755 2757 2766

– (1860-1960) #2758
– (1860-early 20th c.) #2761 2762
– Bluenose #2763
– MacDonald, Charles William, designs
#6355
– Mennonite #2264
– Newfoundland #1154 2744 2760
– Newfoundland and Labrador #2155
– Nova Scotia #2731
– Québec #2750 2751 2752 2753
– Tremblay, Georges-Edouard #2756
– île d'Orléans (Qué) #1252 2764
– Newfoundland #1155
– Nova Scotia, patterns (pre-1920) #2785
– Ontario, 19th c. #2754
– Price, Ralph and Patricia, collection #971
– Québec
– (1930s) #2164 2165
– (1930s-1940s) #2186
– (1940s) #2188
Ruhman, Walter, Can artist, 1899- #7105
– exhibitions
– (1959) #7106
rulers
– see kings and rulers
Rulofson, William Herman, Can
photographer, 1826-1878 #7107
– portrait photographs #1171
Rumball, Alma, Can artist, 1902-
– exhibitions
– (1978) #7108
Rungius, Carl Clemens Moritz, Can artist,
1869-1959
– influence on George E. McLean #6501
– Lansdowne, James Fenwick, compared
with #6165
rural architecture
– see bungalows; domestic architecture; farm
buildings
rural subjects
– Climo, Lindee #5120
– Fortin, Marc-Aurèle #5474 5479 5481
– Gagnon, Clarence Alphonse #5548
– Krieghoff, Cornelius #241 242 6097 6100
– Massicotte, Edmond-Joseph, Québec
scenes #6440
– Suzor-Coté, Marc-Aurèle de Foy #7299
– Watson, Homer Ransford #7529
– Wickson, Paul Giovanni #7573
Ruskay, John, Can photographer, fl. 1970s-
– portfolio of photographs #991
Ruskin, John, Brit critic, 1819-1900
– and Emily Mary Bibbens Warren #7524
– influence on Frederic William Cumberland
#9475
Russell, Charles Marion, Amer artist,
1863-1926
– influence on Gerald Tailfeathers #7313
Russell, Edward John, Can artist, 1832-1906
#7110 7111
Russell, George Horne, Can artist, 1861-1933
– exhibitions, group
– (1978) #133
– relation of photography and painting #245
Russell, Gyrth, Can artist, 1892-1970
– etchings #799
Russell, John Hamilton Gordon, Can
architect, 1863-1946
– Regina (Sask), War Memorial Museum,
competition #9073
– Winnipeg (Man), Marlborough Hotel
#9277
Russell, John Wentworth, Can artist,
1879-1959 #7109

– as member, Canadian Art Club #193
Russians in Canada
– Alberta, log buildings #8136
Russo, Silvio, Can artist, 1939- #2487
Ryan, Alonso, Can artist, b. ca. 1868
– La Caricature politique #943
Ryan, Cyril, Can photographer, 1946-
– exhibitions (reviews) #1018
Ryan, Frederick William, Can artist, 1907-
#1164
Ryan, Terrence, Can artist, 1931-
– and Peter Pitseolak #6880 6881
– on introduction of pencil drawing to the
Inuit, Baffin Island (NWT) #4194
Ryerson, Adolphus Egerton, Can educator,
1803-1882
– and Educational Museum of Upper
Canada (Toronto, Ont) #3150 3155
– and Royal Ontario Museum (Toronto,
Ont) #3152

S

S.B. Coon & Son
– see Coon, S.B., & Son
Saanich Peninsula (BC), Miraloma (now
Latch Restaurant)
– architecture, Samuel Maclure #8731
Saarniit, Joann-Woldemar (John), Can artist,
1909- #7112
Sackville (NB), Mount Allison University
– art education
– (1893-1977) #3013
– (1960s-1970s), emphasis on realism
#1130
– Burke, Rebecca, as teacher #717
– Harris, Lawren Phillips, as director #5709
– Harris, Lawren Phillips, as teacher #5713
– Pulford, Edward Berwyn, as teacher #6945
– Savage, Roger, as student #7136
Sackville (NB), Mount Allison University.
Owens Art Gallery
– and Alex Colville #5151
– Canadian art #3068
– exhibitions
– An Exhibition of Canadian Gameboards of
the 19th & 20th Centuries from Ontario,
Quebec & Nova Scotia (1981) #2597
– André Fauteux (1976) #5413
– Art at Mount Allison ... a History (1977)
#3013
– Claude Breeze (1978) #4911
– Claude Tousignant (1974) #7401
– David Bolduc: Recent Work (1980) #4775
– Douglas Bentham "Enclosures and Opens"
1975/76 (1977) #4683
– Drawings and Pastels c. 1930-1967 by
Miller Gore Brittain (1969) #4917
– Drawings by Jack Weldon Humphrey: A
Travelling Exhibition Organized by the
Beaverbrook Art Gallery, Fredericton, New
Brunswick, Canada, 1977-1979 (1978)
#5871
– Esther Warkov (1971) #7517
– Fritz Brandtner 1896-1969: A Retrospective
Exhibition (1971) #4903
– Investigations: Ian Carr-Harris, John Greer,
N.E. Thing Co., Ltd. (1974) #574
– J.Frederic McCulloch 1905-1932: Works on
Paper (1979) #6463
– John Fox: 10 New Paintings (1981) #5495

– *John Hammond, R.C.A., 1843-1939: Retrospective Exhibition* (1967) #5699
– *Looking South* (1978) #4278
– *Miller Brittain - Painter* (1981) #4922
– *Norman White* (1976) #7554
– *Roger Savage* (1981) #7135
– *The Carmen Lamanna Gallery at the Owens Art Gallery* (1975) #594
– *The Electric Show* (1973) #1800
– *The Murray and Marguerite Vaughan Inuit Print Collection/Collection d'estampes inuit* (1983) #4498
– *The Society of Canadian Painter-Etchers and Engravers in Retrospect/La Société des peintres-graveurs canadiens: vue rétrospective* (1982) #836
– *William Perehudoff: Ten Years, 1970-1980/William Perehudoff: une décennie, 1970-1980* (1982) #6837
– Saxe, Henry, on works exhibited (1976) #7147
Sackville (NB), Owens Art Gallery
– *see* Sackville (NB), Mount Allison University. Owens Art Gallery
Sackville (NB), Owens College of Fine Arts
– craft education (1904) #2979
Sackville (NB), Women's Academy #3013
Sadowska, Krystyna, Can artist, 1912- #7113
– ceramics #2380
– exhibitions
– (1977) #7115
Sadowski, Konrad Jagin, Can ceramicist, 1902-1960 #2380 7113 7114
Sadowski, Krystyna
– *see* Sadowska, Krystyna
Safdie, Moshe, Can architect, 1938- #8405
– Montréal (Qué), Habitat '67 #7694 8574 8575 8577 8578 8580 8583 8584 8585 8590 9215
– on domestic architecture #8406
– on his architecture #8403 8404
Sagard, Gabriel, Fr writer, ca. 1614-ca. 1636
– representations of Indians of North America as headless figures #281
Sager, Peter, Can sculptor, 1920- #7116
Sagittaires (Montréal, Qué) #1393
Saguenay (Qué)
– photographic views
– Bull, W. #4956
– views
– Gagnon, René #5551
– Huot, Charles Edouard #5877
Saguenay-Lac-Saint-Jean (Qué)
– art
– 20th c. #1551
– (1970s) #1538 1540 1546 1547 1549
– churches (1960s) #1435
– photography, 19th-20th cs. #1283
Saila, Pauta, Can artist, 1916- #4460
Saint
– *see also* St.
Saint-Alphonse, soeur
– *see* Pelletier, Marie-Louise Emilie (soeur Saint-Alphonse)
Saint Ann
– in art #1230 1323
– Sainte-Anne-de-Beaupré (Qué), Saint Ann's Basilica #1370 8859 8860 8865 8866
– votive offerings #1292
Saint-Augustin-de-Desmaures (Qué), Church of Saint-Augustin-de-Desmaures
– architecture and interior #8889
Saint-Barthélemi (Qué), Church of

Saint-Barthélemi
– pulpit, Amable Gauthier #241 242
Saint-Basile-le-Grand (Qué), Centre communautaire catholique Tour de David
– art (1970s) #1510
Saint-Boniface (Man), Cathedral of Saint-Boniface
– architecture #8094
Saint-Boniface (Man), Centre culturel franco-manitobain
– exhibitions
– *Hubert Garnier: la sculpture architecturale* (1976) #5556
– *Objets faits à la main au Manitoba français* (1976) #2275
– *Pauline Morier: images et arabesques* (1975) #6608
– *Réal Bérard* (1975) #4692
Saint-Boniface (Man), Chapel of Saint-Louis-le-roi
– architecture, Libling, Michener & Associates #8765
Saint-Boniface (Man), Precious Blood Church
– architecture
– Gaboury, Etienne J. #8091
– Gaboury, Etienne J.; Denis Lussier, Associate Architect #8908
Saint-Charles, Joseph A., Can artist, 1868-1956 #302 1240 1315 7117
– and Marc-Aurèle de Foy Suzor-Coté #7296
Saint-Charles region (Qué)
– pottery (1840s-1900) #2298 2322
Saint-Denis (Qué)
– pottery
– 18th-19th cs. #2299 2321
– (1785-1888) #2343
Saint-Denis-sur-Richelieu (Qué)
– churches #8811
Saint-Etienne de Lauzon (Qué), Moulin des arts
– Rousseau, Albert, artists' workshop #7082 7083
Saint-Eugène (Qué), Church of Saint-Eugène-de-Grantham
– architecture and art #8873
Saint Gaudens, Augustus, Amer artist, 1848-1907
– and Alexander Phimister Proctor #6943
– influence on Robert Tait McKenzie #6487
Saint-Germain, Léon, Can carriage-maker, fl. 1842 #1301
Saint-Henri (Qué), Church of Saint-Henri
– sculptures, Louis Jobin #5967
Saint-Hilaire (Qué)
– views
– Leduc, Ozias #6199 6206 6209
Saint-Hilaire (Qué), Centre artisanal de Saint-Hilaire
– exhibitions (reviews)
– (1941) #2182
Saint-Hilaire (Qué), manoir Campbell
– murals, Jordi Bonet #4787
Saint-Jean, Michel, Can photographer, 1937- #1562
– portfolio of photographs #991 997 999
Saint-Jean-Eudes
– in art, Québec, 17th c. #1365
Saint-Jean-Port-Joli (Qué)
– decorative arts #2209
– 20th c. #2194
– (1930s) #2174
– woodcarving #1597 1608 4883
Saint-Jean-Port-Joli (Qué), Church of

Saint-Jean-Baptiste
– architecture and interior #8812
Saint-Jean-Port-Joli (Qué), Church of Saint-Jean-Port-Joli #2194 8871
Saint-Jean-Port-Joli (Qué), La Vastringue
– Bourgault, Pier, as director #4889
Saint-Jean-Port-Joli (Qué), manoir d'Haberville #2194
Saint-Jérôme (Qué), Church of Saint-Jérôme
– paintings, Charles Edouard Huot #5878 5884
Saint-Joachim (Qué), château Bellevue
– architecture #8622
Saint-Joachim (Qué), Church of Saint-Joachim
– architecture #7953
– sculpture, François Baillairgé #4589
Saint-Joachim (Qué), Ecole des arts et métiers de Saint-Joachim #1233 1327 1334 1335 1363 2181 2967 2991 2992 3007 3008
– domestic architecture #8505
– furniture-making #2464
– Leblond (*dit* Latour), Jacques, as teacher #234 235
Saint John (NB)
– architecture #7807
– 18th-19th cs. #7808
– art
– 20th c. #1188
– (1940s) #1170
– (1950s) #1119 1172
– (1960s) #4994
– domestic architecture (1830s) #2490
– furniture (pre-1900) #2491
– Martello towers #8416
– painting
– 20th c. #1184
– (1950s) #1173
– portrait photography, 19th c. #1171
– views
– Comingo, Joseph #5161
– Humphrey, Jack Weldon #5867
– Smith, George Neilson #7221
Saint John (NB), Gallery Theatre
– exhibitions, and Robert Percival #6833
Saint John (NB), General Public Hospital
– architecture, Irving K. Pond #9020
Saint John (NB), Gesner's Museum
– (1842-1846) #3065
Saint John (NB), Gregory House
– architecture and interior #8545
Saint John (NB), hôtel de ville/City Hall
– sculpture, Claude Roussel #7088
Saint John (NB), Mechanics' Institute Museum
– (1846-1890) #3065
Saint John (NB), New Brunswick Museum
– (1842-1945) #3065
– (1940s) #1170
– (1960s) #1122
– and John Clarence Webster #3073
– and Saint John (NB) painting (1950s) #1173
– arm bands, Micmac Indians #3572
– art, Micmac Indians #3634
– Canadian pressed glass, exhibited (1969) #2407
– ceramic plates, 19th c. #2354
– exhibitions
– *Albert Franck (1899-1973) in Retrospect: A Small Selection from the Artist's Collection* (1973) #5500
– *Annie D. Savage: Drawings and Watercolours* (1975) #7129
– *Arctic Values '65/Valeurs septentrionales*

'65 (1965) #4195
– *Arthur F. McKay* (1980) #6478
– *Exhibition of Portraits of James Henry Holman, 1821-1891* (1959) #5821
– *Fritz Brandtner 1896-1969: A Retrospective Exhibition* (1971) #4903
– *George Rackus: Anodized Aluminum Works & Prints* (1973) #6953
– *Gordon Rayner Retrospective* (1979) #6966
– *Miller Brittain - Painter* (1981) #4922
– *New Brunswick Landscape Artists of the 19th Century* (1969) #1180
– *Seven Plus: A Selection of Works by the Group of Seven* (1976) #1778
– *The Electric Show* (1973) #1800
– *The Murray and Marguerite Vaughan Inuit Print Collection/Collection d'estampes inuit* (1982) #4498
– *The New Brunswick Landscape Print: 1760-1880* (1980) #1189
– *The Saidye and Samuel Bronfman Collection of Canadian Art/La collection Saidye et Samuel Bronfman* (1967) #3087
– *Watercolour Painters from Saskatchewan/Aquarellistes de la Saskatchewan* (1971) #1920
– exhibitions (reviews)
  – McLaughlin, Agnes (1980) #6500
  – Percival, Robert (1979) #6835
– female clothing, 19th c. #2875
– furniture #2484
– Graham family, woodcarvings #1187
– military uniforms #2900
– New Brunswick furniture, 18th-19th cs. #2504
– New Brunswick silver #2649
– Rogerson, John, works #7068
– Webster, John Clarence, Canadiana collection #3209
Saint John (NB), Owen Art Gallery
– exhibitions
  – *Art Loan Exhibition* (1884) #170
Saint John (NB), Provincial Exhibition
– exhibitions
  – *Catalogue of St. John Art Club Loan Exhibition: Paintings by Canadian Artists,* (1920) #286
Saint John (NB), Saint John General Hospital
– architecture, Allward & Gillies; Mott & Myles #9031
– mural cartoons, Miller Gore Brittain #4916
Saint John (NB), Saint John Vocational School
– art education (1940s) #1170
– Campbell, Ted, as teacher #1188
Saint John (NB), School of Arts
– Foulis, Robert, as director #258 259
Saint John (NB), stone church
– architecture, Lloyd Johnson #8778
Saint John Art Club (Saint John, NB)
– (1940s) #1170
– and Elizabeth Russell Holt #1173
– exhibitions
  – (1920) #286
Saint John Glass Co., glass manufacturer (Saint John, NB) #2400
Saint John River (NB)
– views
  – Miles, John Christopher #6532
Saint John Telegraph, Can newspaper
– illustrations, Edward John Russell #7110
Saint-Joseph, mère de, Can nun, d. 1652
– portrait of, Marie de l'Incarnation #1333
Saint-Joseph (NB), Université Saint-Joseph

– Beau, Henri, *La dispersion des Acadiens* (1900) #4639
Saint-Laurent (Qué), Collège de Saint-Laurent. Chapel
– architecture #8815
Saint-Laurent (Qué), Collège de Saint-Laurent. Galerie Nova et Vetera
– collection #3089
– exhibitions
  – *Images taillées du Québec* (1966) #3090
Saint-Laurent (Qué), Collège de Saint-Laurent. Musée d'art #3123
Saint-Laurent (Qué), Galerie Nova et Vetera
– see Saint-Laurent (Qué), Collège de Saint-Laurent. Galerie Nova et Vetera
Saint-Marc-des-Carrières (Qué)
– stone sculpture (1932) #1629
Saint-Martin, Fernande, Can art critic, curator, 1927-
– concept of pictorial space #4816
– on Québec art (1940s-1970s) #1521
Saint-Mathias-de-Rouville (Qué), Church of Saint-Mathias-de-Rouville
– architecture and interior #8878
Saint-Mathieu (Qué), Salle du Couvent de Saint-Mathieu
– exhibitions
  – *Le cercle de promotion humaine présente Yvon Héroux, peintre figuratif de St-Mathieu* (1972) #5790
Saint-Nicolas (Qué), Church of Saint-Nicolas
– architecture, André Gilbert #8766
Saint-Paul, Paul
– see Lambert (*dit* Saint-Paul), Paul
Saint-Pierre, Georges, Can artist, 1927-
– exhibitions
  – (1975) #7118
– interview #1527
Saint-Pierre (île d'Orléans, Qué)
– art and architecture #1252
– churches #8875
Saint-Rémi-de-Napierville (Qué)
– calvary #1569
Saint-Rémi-de-Napierville (Qué), cemetery
– iron funeral crosses #2716
Saint-Roch-de-l'Achigan (Qué)
– architecture #7854
Saint-Romuald (Qué), Ecole de sculpture
– and Lauréat Vallière #7455
Saint-Sauveur, André Grasset de, Can statesman, 1720-1794
– and history of Montréal (Qué) #7899
Saint-Sauveur (Qué), Church of Saint-Sauveur
– paintings, Charles Edouard Huot #5878 5884
Saint-Thomas de Montmagny (Qué), Bernatchez House
– architecture and interior #8630
Saint-Vallier, Jean-Baptiste de la Croix de Chevrières de, Can bishop, 1653-1727
– and Episcopal Palace, Québec (Qué) #8787
– and use of stone in Québec architecture #7859
Saint-Vincent-de-Paul (Qué), Ecole de Saint-Vincent-de-Paul #5108
Sainte-Anne-de-Beaupré (Qué)
– churches #8863 8877
Sainte-Anne-de-Beaupré (Qué), Musée de l'Historial de Sainte-Anne-de-Beaupré
– Boivin, Joseph, *Ex-voto de Dorval* #4771
Sainte-Anne-de-Beaupré (Qué), Saint Ann's Basilica
– architecture #8824 8863 8877

– interior #1601 1602
– mosaics
  – Gaudin, Jean, and August Labouret #8859 8860
  – Gaudin, Jean, and Walter del Mistro #8865 8866
  – Mistro, Walter del #6572 6573
– paintings #1321
– votive offerings #1370
Sainte-Anne-de-Bellevue (Qué), church
– architecture, Josué Boisberthelot de Beaucours #8336
Sainte-Anne-de-la-Pocatière (Qué)
– churches #8882
Sainte-Anne-de-la-Pocatière (Qué), musée François Pilote
– exhibitions
  – *De la figuration à la non-figuration dans l'art québécois* (1978) #1461
Sainte-Foy (Qué), Church of Saint-Louis-de-France
– architecture, Blatter, Caron & Côté #8841
Sainte-Foy (Qué), Falardeau House
– architecture #8627
Sainte-Foy (Qué), Parent House
– architecture #8627
Sainte-Foy (Qué), Routhier House
– architecture #8627
Sainte-Louise (Qué)
– views, A.Y. Jackson #5921
Sainte-Marie-de-Beauce (Qué), Church of Sainte-Marie-de-Beauce
– mère Marie Le Maire des Anges, *Madone druidique de la Nouvelle-France* #1328
Sainte-Rose (Qué)
– views
  – Hébert, Adrien #5763
Sainte-Scholastique (Qué), Sulpician seignory
– architecture #1341
saints in art
– Québec, 17th c. #1365
Salem (Mass), Peabody Museum of Salem
– exhibitions
  – *The Art of Nunstins/L'art de Nunstins* (1981) #6934
Salish Indians
– architecture #3807
– art (1970s) #4145
– basketry #3777 3801 3876 3991
– blankets #3469 3790 3818 3830
– costume #4013
– culture #3764
– jade #3331
– photographs of
  – Curtis, Edward Sheriff #3399
  – Stone, Sir John Benjamin #3717
– pottery #3841
– rites and ceremonies #3838
– weaving #3898 3963 4018 4044 4147
  – 20th c. #3964
  – (1960s) #3941
– weaving and basketry #4027
Salish Weavers' Guild
– (1970s) #4147
Sallirmiut
– artifacts #4324
Sallows, R.R., Can photographer, fl. 1909 #7119
Salon des métiers d'art du Québec
– exhibitions (reviews)
  – (1970) #1490
Salteri, Thomas A., Can photographer, fl. 1850s-1870s #1211

Saltmarche, Kenneth Charles, Can artist,
1920-
– exhibitions, group
– (1965) #473
Salvation Army
– and Ada Florence Kinton #6053
samplers, Canadian
– 18th-19th cs. #2792
– British Columbia (1860s) #2786
– Mennonite, 19th-20th cs. #2267
– Ontario #2787
– Robertson, Maria (1843) #2790
Samson, Olivier, Can sculptor, ca. 1830-ca.
1900
– interior, Church of Saint-François-de-Sales
(île d'Orléans, Qué) #8796
Samuel, Sigmund, Can collector, 1867-1962
– collection, Canadiana and Americana,
Royal Ontario Museum (Toronto, Ont)
#247 3135 3140
San Francisco (Calif), California School of
Design
– Carr, Emily, as student #5045
San Francisco (Calif), California School of
Fine Arts
– Smith, Gordon Appelbe, as student #7225
San Francisco (Calif), Embarcadero Plaza
– fountain, Armand Vaillancourt #7451
San Francisco (Calif), Golden Gate
International Exposition (1939)
– exhibitions
– Aboriginal Cultures of the Western
Hemisphere (1940) #3336
– Pacific Cultures (1939) #3854
San Francisco (Calif), Images of the North
– exhibitions
– George Arluk: The Song in the Stone (1979)
#4547
San Francisco (Calif), Mount Zion Hospital
– architecture #9026
San Francisco (Calif), San Francisco Art
Institute
– Hammock, Virgil as student #5696
San Francisco (Calif), San Francisco Museum
of Modern Art
– exhibitions
– James Bay Project - A River Drowned by
Water/Projet de la baie James - une rivière
qui se noie (1981) #1566
San Miguel de Allende (Mexico), San
Miguel de Allende Instituto
– Onley, Toni, as student #6740
– Woolnough, Hilda Mary, as student #7616
Sanavik Cooperative (Baker Lake, NWT)
– graphic arts #4480
– (1969-1973) #4481
– (1970-) #4472
Sandby, Paul, Brit artist, 1725-1809
– as teacher of James Pattison Cockburn
#5126
– influence on George Heriot #5786 5787
5788
– influence on James Pattison Cockburn
#5125
– influence on Thomas Davies #5272
Sandham, J.Henry, Can artist, 1842-1910
#178
– exhibitions
– (1911) #7120
– (1976) #7121
– relation of photography and painting #245
sandstone
– Calgary (Alta) architecture #8133
– Prince Edward Island houses, early 19th c.

#8552
Sandwich (Ont), Banwell House
– architecture #7685
Sangudo (Alta)
– art (1940s) #1943
Santa Ana (Calif), Charles W. Bowers
Memorial Museum
– exhibitions
– Indian Basketry of Western North America
from the Collection of the Bowers Museum,
Santa Ana, California (1974) #3991
Santa Barbara (Calif), University of
California. Art Galleries
– exhibitions
– Indian Art of the Northern Plains (1974)
#3730
– The New Art of Vancouver (1969) #2039
Santa Cruz (Calif), University of California
– architecture #9464
Santa Fe (NM), Institute of American Indian
Arts
– painting (1970s) #3462
Santa Fe (NM), Museum of New Mexico
– art, Inuit and Indians of North America
#3372
Santa Fe (NM), Wheelwright Museum of the
American Indian
– exhibition
– Lullabies from the Earth (1980) #3485
São Paulo (Brazil), Biblioteca Publica
Municipal
– exhibitions
– Artes graficas do Canada 1946 (1946) #806
São Paulo (Brazil), Bienal (1944)
– exhibitions (reviews)
– Exhibition of Contemporary Canadian
Painting/L'exposition de peinture
contemporaine du Canada (1944) #371
São Paulo (Brazil), Bienal (1955)
– exhibitions
– III Bienal (1955) #411
– exhibitions (reviews)
– Borduas, Paul-Emile #4843
São Paulo (Brazil), Bienal (1965)
– exhibitions
– O Canadá em São Paulo/Canada at São
Paulo 1965/Le Canada à São Paulo 1965
(1965) #469
São Paulo (Brazil), Bienal (1967)
– exhibitions
– Jacques Hurtubise; Jack Bush: O Canadá em
São Paulo/Le Canada à São Paulo/Canada
at São Paulo (1967) #491
São Paulo (Brazil), Bienal (1969)
– exhibitions
– Greg Curnoe: Canada (1969) #5227
– N.E. Thing Co. Ltd./La compagnie N.E.
Thing (1969) #6675
– Robert Murray (1969) #6670
São Paulo (Brazil), Museu de arte moderna
de São Paulo
– exhibitions
– III Bienal (1955) #411
Sapp, Allen, Can artist, 1929- #4125 4136
4161 7123 7124 7126
– autobiography #7125
– exhibitions
– (1969) #7122
– influence on Michael Lonechild #6322
Sarasota (Fla), Ringling Museum of Art
– exhibitions
– 49th Parallels: New Canadian Art (1971)
#98
– Oscar Cahén: First American Retrospective

Exhibition (1968) #4986
Sarcee Indians
– art, bear motif #3746
– costume #3739
– culture (1930s) #3671
– drums #3363
– photographs of
– Curtis, Edward Sheriff #3399
– pottery #3659
– tipis #3735
Sargent, John Singer, Amer artist, 1856-1925
– influence on Addison Winchell Price #6935
Sargent, Susan, Can artist, fl. 1970s
– exhibitions, group
– (1977) #1933
Sarnia (Ont), public school
– architecture, S.B. Coon & Son #9387
Sarnia (Ont), Sarnia Public Library and Art
Gallery
– Canadian art #3179
– exhibitions
– A Survey of Forty-five Years (1977) #6658
– A Terrible Beauty: The Art of Canada at
War (1978) #1111
– Alan C. Collier Retrospective (1971) #5131
– B.C. Currents (1981) #2082
– Beauté tragique: les deux conflits mondiaux
vus par des artistes canadiens (1978) #1112
– Centennial Exhibition of Quebec and
Ontario Contemporary Painters, 1967
(1967) #484
– David Milne: 1882-1953 (1967) #6558
– Indications: Paintings, Collage, Drawings,
Prints, Sculpture (1975) #7415
– John Leonard: 10 Years: An Exhibition of
Paintings and Drawings (1981) #6246
– John Meredith: Fifteen Years (1974) #6514
– Louis de Niverville (1978) #6709
– Ontario Society of Artists: 100 Years (1973)
#1678
– The Ontario Community Collects: A Survey
of Canadian Painting from 1766 to the
Present (1976) #120
– York Wilson Retrospective (1927-1973)
(1974) #7596
Sarnia Art Movement (Sarnia, Ont)
– support of Group of Seven #1776
Sarqaq
– artifacts #4342
Sasabuchi, Shun, Can photographer, 1951-
– portfolio of photographs #1032
sashes, Canadian
– ceinture fléchée #24 2089 2095 2165 2181
2718 2810 2813 2818 2819 2823 2824 2827
2833 2864 2865 2873 2901
– influence on Iroquois sashes #3534
sashes, French
– compared with ceinture fléchée #2901
sashes, Iroquois #3534
sashes, Ojibwa #3557
sashes, Scandinavian
– compared with ceinture fléchée #2865
Saskatchewan
– architecture #8083
– (1880s-1920s) #8113
– (1960s) #8112
– (1970s) #8087
– pioneer houses, late 19th-early 20th cs.
#8696
– art #1919 3187 3202
– 20th c. #145 536 1936
– (1940s) #350
– (1945) #1909
– (1950-1964) #1910

– (1950s) #1911 1912
– (1950s-1970s) #1884 1935
– (1960s) #1916 1917
– (1970s) #1860 1868 1926 1930 1932 1937
– ceramic sculpture (1970s) #1864
– churches, Ukrainian #8912 8915
– folk art, 20th c. #1931
– folk painting, 20th c. #1846 1927
– furniture (1800-1921) #2587
– painting
– (1883-1959) #1915
– (1930s-1970s) #1920
– (1950s-1960s) #476
– (1960s) #1913
– photographic views
– Hime, Humphrey Lloyd #5801 5802
5803 5804
– Horetzky, Charles George #5838
– photography
– (1930s-1940s) #985
– (1970s) #1879
– pottery (1970s) #2383 2385
– railroad stations #9544
– schools (1920s) #9389
– stores (1940s) #9372
– views
– Fisher, Sanford #5445
– Henderson, James #5778
– Hind, William George Richardson #5807
– Hurley, Robert Newton #5885
– Kenderdine, Gus #6039
– Kerr, Illingworth Holey #6047
– Lonechild, Michael #6322
– Sheldon-Williams, Inglis #7195 7196
– Tinning, George Campbell #7378
– watercolour painting (1905-1980) #1940
Saskatchewan Arts Board
– (1948-1960s) #1914
– (1948-1978) #1938
– (1950s) #1911 1912
– collection #1936
– exhibitions
– (1950-1964) #1910
– Saskatchewan: Art and Artists (1971)
#1919
Saskatchewan Association of Architects
#8312
Saskatoon (Sask)
– architecture #8114
– (1909) #8110
– art
– (1945) #1909
– (1960s) #1848 1917
– (1960s-1970s) #1862
– (1970s) #1932
– art galleries (1960s) #442
– sculpture (1960s) #1853
– women artists (1970s) #1928
Saskatoon (Sask), Bank of Nova Scotia
– exhibitions
– The Bank of Nova Scotia Fine Art
Collection, Saskatoon, Saskatchewan, 1980
(1980) #3245
Saskatoon (Sask), Flanagan Hotel
– architecture, Walter W. Lachance #9263
Saskatoon (Sask), Gallery One
– exhibitions
– Arthur F. McKay (1980) #6478
Saskatoon (Sask), Mendel Art Gallery
– architecture, competition for #9091
– exhibitions
– A Retrospective Exhibition of the Works of
Leo Mol (1975) #6579
– An Exhibition of Paintings by James

Henderson, 1871-1951 (1969) #5779
– Antique Canadian Glass from the John
McGowan Collection (1976) #2424
– Artisan '78: The First National Travelling
Exhibition of Contemporary Canadian
Crafts/Artisan '78: première exposition
nationale itinérante d'artisanat canadien
contemporain (1979) #2134
– Brian Wood: Photographic Works (1979)
#7612
– Canadian Painting in the Thirties (1975)
#592
– Carl Schaefer in Hanover (1980) #7157
– Certain Traditions: Recent British and
Canadian Art (1978) #653
– Changes: 11 Artists Working on the
Prairies (1976) #1867
– Christopher Pratt (1970) #6910
– David Craven: Recent Works (1977) #5205
– David Milne: The New York Years,
1903-1916 (1981) #6567
– Dennis Burton Retrospective (1978) #4961
– Don McNamee (1968) #6506
– Douglas Bentham: Six Steel Sculptures
1978 (1979) #4685
– Drawings and Pastels c. 1930-1967 by
Miller Gore Brittain (1969) #4917
– Drawings by Jack Weldon Humphrey: A
Travelling Exhibition Organized by the
Beaverbrook Art Gallery, Fredericton, New
Brunswick, Canada, 1977-1979 (1979)
#5871
– E. Lindner: Drawings, 1969-1972 (1972)
#6285
– E. Lindner in Retrospect: The Years
1963-1977 (1977) #6288
– Eleven Saskatchewan Artists (1967) #1916
– Ernest Lindner 1897-: A Retrospective
Exhibition (1970) #6284
– Esther Warkov (1971) #7517
– Fernand Leduc (1971) #6186
– Figure in Landscape: Drawings by Denis
Nokony (1981) #6716
– Frank Nulf: Charles Ringness: Recent Work
(1979) #678
– George Sawchuk (1980) #7142
– Gift from the Douglas M. Duncan
Collection and the Milne-Duncan
Bequest/Le Don provenant de la collection
Douglas M. Duncan et le legs
Milne-Duncan (1972) #541
– Goodridge Roberts: Selected
Works/Goodridge Roberts: oeuvres choisies
(1981) #7050
– Graham Coughtry: Retrospective (1976)
#5190
– Gus Kenderdine, 1870-1947, Pioneer (1974)
#6039
– Images of the Prairie (1979) #1882
– Impressionism in Canada, 1895-1935 (1974)
#115
– Ivan Eyre Exposition (1982) #5394
– Ivory Carvings from Repulse Bay and Pelly
Bay (1975) #4438
– Jack Shadbolt (1970) #7182
– Jeffrey Spalding Paintings (1981) #7269
– Joe Fafard: Recent Sculpture (1980) #5401
– Joe Plaskett and His Paris: In Search of
Time Past (1972) #6893
– Joe Plaskett et son Paris: à la recherche d'un
temps passé (1972) #6894
– John Hall: Paintings and Auxiliary Works
1979-1980 (1981) #5686
– Kenneth Lochhead: An Exhibition of

Paintings 1952-1975 (1978) #6318
– Lithographs/Lithographies (1973) #825
– Louis Comtois: Paintings, 1974-1979 (1981)
#5164
– Louis de Niverville (1979) #6709
– Major Saskatchewan Artists/Artistes
importants de la Saskatchewan (1975)
#1926
– Manitoba Mainstream: People's Art/Fine
Art/Le Grand Courant du Manitoba: arts
populaires, beaux-arts (1973) #1897
– Maxwell Bates in Retrospect, 1921-1971
(1973) #4624
– Oonark/Pangnark (1970) #4220
– Otto Rogers: New Paintings and Sculpture,
1977-78 (1978) #7065
– Painters Eleven in Retrospect (1981) #1785
– Painting in Saskatchewan, 1883-1959
(1967) #1915
– Peinture canadienne des années trente
(1975) #589
– Photographs by L.G. Saunders, 1895-1968:
A Memorial (1970) #7128
– Recent Paintings by Allen Sapp (1969)
#7122
– Robert Young: Prints/Robert Young:
gravures (1981) #7631
– Saskatchewan: Art and Artists (1971)
#1919
– Saskatchewan Primitives (1975) #1927
– Saskatoon Women Artists (1975) #1928
– Selected Saskatchewan Drawings (1977)
#1933
– Suzy Lake: Are You Talking to Me? (1980)
#6140
– Sylvain P. Cousineau: Photographs and
Paintings (1981) #5195
– Takao Tanabe, 1972-1976: The Land (1976)
#7320
– Terence Johnson: Forts (1982) #5969
– The Canadian Canvas: A Travelling
Exhibition of 85 Recent Paintings/Peintres
canadiens actuels: exposition itinérante de
85 oeuvres récentes (1975) #588
– The J.S. McLean Collection of Canadian
Painting (1969) #3228
– The Mendel Collection: Opening Exhibition
(1964) #72
– The Mr. and Mrs. Jules Loeb Collection/La
collection M. et Mme Jules Loeb (1971)
#3231
– The Paintings of Frederick Nicholas
Loveroff/Les peintures de Frederick Nicholas
Loveroff (1982) #6331
– The Private Eye (1979) #679
– The Railway: Patron of the Arts in Canada
(1976) #3281
– The Saidye and Samuel Bronfman
Collection of Canadian Art/La collection
Saidye et Samuel (1966) #3087
– Tim Zuck: Paintings (1981) #7636
– Tom Forrestall Exhibition (1971) #5461
– Tom La Pierre: Paintings, Drawings, Prints
(1977) #6121
– Watercolour Painting in Saskatchewan
1905-1980 (1980) #1940
– William Perehudoff: Ten Years,
1970-1980/William Perehudoff: une
décennie, 1970-1980 (1981) #6838
– exhibitions (reviews)
– Suzy Lake: Are You Talking To Me? (1980)
#717
– The Canadian Canvas: A Travelling
Exhibition of 85 Recent Paintings/Peintres

canadiens actuels: exposition itinérante de 85 oeuvres récentes (1975) #582
Saskatoon (Sask), Nutana Collegiate Institute. Memorial Art Gallery
– collection #3183
Saskatoon (Sask), Photographers Gallery #1042
– (1970s) #1879
– exhibitions
    – *The Photographs of Mattie Gunterman/Les photographies de Mattie Gunterman* (1977) #5671
Saskatoon (Sask), Saint John's Episcopal Church
– architecture, Thompson, Daniel & Colthurst #8907
Saskatoon (Sask), Saskatoon Gallery and Conservatory Corporation
– *see* Saskatoon (Sask), Mendel Art Gallery
Saskatoon (Sask), Saskatoon Public Library. Art Gallery
– exhibitions
    – *Eli Bornstein: Structurist Reliefs, 1966-1975* (1975) #4856
    – *Saskatchewan: Art and Artists* (1971) #1919
Saskatoon (Sask), T. Eaton Company Department Store
– architecture, Ross & Macdonald; Sproatt & Rolph, Consulting Architects #9365
Saskatoon (Sask), University of Saskatchewan
– architecture
    – Brown & Vallance #9489 9491
    – Izumi, Arnott & Sugiyama #9490
– art collection #3202
– exhibitions
    – *Saskatchewan: Art and Artists* (1971) #1919
– planning, Thomas Hayton Mawson #9405
Saskatoon (Sask), University of Saskatchewan. Art Department Gallery
– exhibitions
    – *Edward Curtis in the Collection of the Edmonton Art Gallery* (1980) #3480
Saskatoon (Sask), Western Development Museum
– exhibitions
    – *Canadians: A National Photography Show about People/Canadiens: exposition nationale de photographie ayant les gens comme thème* (1980) #1035
Sasseville, François, Can silversmith, 1797-1864 #258 259 2660 2672
– analysis of silver composition #2682
– censers #2665
– works
    – Cap-Santé (Qué), churches #8814
    – Detroit (Mich), Detroit Institute of Arts #2681 2691
Sasseville, Joseph, Can silversmith, 1790-1837 #2672
– works, Detroit Institute of Arts (Detroit, Mich) #2691
Satorelli, Jane, Can artist, fl. 1979 #7127
Satterli, Molly, Can ceramicist, fl. 1961 #2102
Saucier, Robert, Can sculptor, 1951-
– exhibitions
    – (1980) #685
Sauer, June, Can photographer, fl. 1970 #993
Sault-au-Récollet (Qué), Church of the Visitation
– architecture and interior #8797

Sault Ste Marie (Ont)
– views
    – Jameson, Anna Brownell #5933
    – Kane, Paul #6009
Sault Ste Marie (Ont), Algoma Fall Festival
– exhibitions
    – *Métiers d'art Ontario-Québec, 1979/1980/Quebec-Ontario Crafts, 1979/1980* (1980) #2138
Sault Ste Marie (Ont), Art Gallery of Algoma
– exhibitions
    – *Painters of the Shield* (1980) #156
Sault Ste Marie (Ont), Group Health Centre
– architecture, Jerome Markson #9033
Saulteaux Indians
– culture #3402 3549
– Manitou effigy #3726
– rattles #3363
Saunders, Leslie Gail, Can photographer, 1895-1968
– exhibitions
    – (1970) #7128
Saunders & Ryrie, Can architectural firm
– Toronto (Ont), Osgoode Hall #9002 9003
Sauvé, Paulette-Marie, Can artist, 1949-
– exhibitions, group
    – (1978) #2772
Savage, Anne Douglas, Can artist, 1897-1971 #7130 7131
– and Canadian painting #18
– exhibitions
    – (1974) #7129
    – (1979) #7132
– exhibitions, group
    – (1977) #1278 1279
Savage, Harry, Can artist, 1938- #1856 7133
– exhibitions (reviews) #1866
Savage, Roger, Can artist, 1941- #7134 7136
– exhibitions
    – (1979) #7135
– prints #1214
Savard, Alphonse E., Can photographer, 1864-1934
– exhibitions, group
    – (1976) #2012
Savoie, Maurice, Can ceramicist, 1930- #2395
– interview #7137
Savoie, Robert, Can artist, 1939- #7138 7139
Savoie, Roméo Albert, Can artist, 1928- #7140
Savory, Albert, Brit silversmith, fl. 1830s-1840s
– presentation silver tea service #2647
Savory, Joseph, Brit silversmith, fl. 1830s-1840s
– presentation silver tea service #2647
Sawchuk, George, Can sculptor, 1927- #7143
– exhibitions
    – (1980) #7142
– interview #7141
sawmills, American
– northeastern USA #9249
sawmills, Canadian #9248 9249
– Kingston Mills (Ont) #8020
Sawyer, Joseph, Can architect, 1874-1965 #8407
Sawyer, Walter Michael, Can artist, 1943-
– interview #7144
Sawyer, William, Can artist, 1820-1889
– exhibitions
    – (1978) #7145
– relation of photography and painting #245
Saxe, Charles Jewett, Can architect,

1870-1943
– Montréal (Qué), Court House Annex #9001
Saxe, Henry, Can artist, 1937- #1479 7146 7149
– and Fusion des arts (Montréal, Qué) #1482
– exhibitions
    – (1976) #7148
– exhibitions, group
    – (1973) #557
    – (1976) #779
    – (1977) #782
    – (1978) #661
– interview, on *Instrument Series* #7147
Saxe & Archibald, Can architectural firm
– Montréal (Qué), domestic architecture #8493
Saxman Totem Park (Alaska)
– totem poles #3873
Scandinavians in Canada
– Alberta, log buildings #8136
– furniture #2585
Scarborough (Ont), Albert Campbell Library
– architecture, Fairfield & DuBois #9047
Scarborough (Ont), North Bridlewood Junior Public School
– architecture, Howard Vincent Walker #9471
Scarborough (Ont), Scarborough Civic Centre
– architecture, Raymond Moriyama #8973
Scarborough (Ont), Scarborough College
– *see* Scarborough (Ont), University of Toronto. Scarborough College
Scarborough (Ont), Stephen Leacock Educational Complex
– architecture, Abram & Ingleson #9476
Scarborough (Ont), University of Toronto. Scarborough College
– architecture, John Andrews Architects #8323
– architecture, Page & Steele; John Hamilton Andrews #9396 9462 9463 9464
– interior design (1960s) #9402
scenography, Canadian
– (1960s) #472
– Kolisnyk, Peter Henry #6075
– Laufer, Murray Bernard #6173
– Montreal Theatre Ballet (1950s) #1410
– Pellan, Alfred #6799
– Plaskett, Joe #1991
– Price, Art #6929
– Shadbolt, Jack Leonard #1991
– White, Stan #7555
Schacter, William M., Can architect, 1926-
– Central Mortgage and Housing Corporation competition (1960) #8040
Schaefer, Carl Fellman, Can artist, 1903- #7151 7152 7153 7156
– and Charles Fraser Comfort, as war artists in Italy #1090
– and Toni Onley #6741
– correspondence, David Brown Milne #6563 6564
– exhibitions
    – (1969) #7155
    – (1980) #7157
– exhibitions, group
    – (1979) #147
– exhibitions (reviews) #7158
– interview #7154
– landscapes #347
– on his art #349
– on Iceland #7150

– paintings (1930s) #502
– Phillips, Walter Joseph, compared with
  #6858
Schantz, Karl, Can glassmaker, 1944- #7159
– and Sheridan College School of Crafts and
  Design (Mississauga, Ont) #2440
Schelle, Susan, Can artist, 1947-
– exhibitions
  – (1981) #7160
Schiele, Bernard, Can photographer, 1943-
  #1000
– portfolio of photographs #997 999
Schiffer, Fred, Can photographer, fl. 1970s
– on portraiture #624
Schindler, Joseph, Can silversmith, ca.
  1730-1792 #269 270
– works, Detroit Institute of Arts (Detroit,
  Mich) #2691
Schleicher, Edythe Hembroff
– see Hembroff-Schleicher, Edythe
Schlichting, Leonard, Can photographer, fl.
  1970s
– exhibitions, group
  – (1979) #1904
Schlienger, Oscar, Can artist, 1905-
– influence on James Lorimer Keirstead
  #6037
Schlieper, Heiko, Can artist, 1931-
– icon painting #7161
Schlombs, Wolfgang, Can collector, 20th c.
– collection, Canadian furniture #2485
Schluep, Walter, Can jeweller, 1931- #2696
Schmid-Esler, Annemarie, Can artist, 1930-
  #675
– ceramic sculpture #795
– exhibitions, group
  – (1980) #698
– interview #7162
– pottery #2395
Schmidt, Marianna, Can artist, 1918-
– exhibitions, group
  – (1967) #821
Schoeler Heaton Menendez, Can
  architectural firm
– Ottawa (Ont), Carleton University. School
  of Architecture #8284
Schoenauer, Norbert H., Can architect, 1923-
– Central Mortgage and Housing
  Corporation competition (1960) #8040
Schofield, John, Can architect, 1883-1971
– Montréal (Qué), Central Station #9535
– Ottawa (Ont), Château Laurier #9282
schools, American
– (1960s) #9394
– western USA #8083
schools, Canadian
– 17th-early 19th cs. #7841
– 18th c.-1950s #9392
– (1870s) #9384
– (1908) #9385
– (1910s) #9386 9387 9388
– (1920s) #7656
– (1950s) #9391 9393
  – recommendations #9390
– (1960-1970) #7710
– (1960s) #9394 9395 9397 9398 9401 9403 9420
– British Columbia, log buildings, 19th-20th
  cs. #8148
– Duncan (BC), Duncan Public School #9508
– Edmonton (Alta), (1900-1914) #8130
– Frobisher Bay (NWT), Frobisher Academic
  and Occupational School #8188
– Guelph (Ont), 19th c. #7970
– Hamilton (Ont)

– (1910s) #9436
– Victorian #7991
– Indian Education Centre (Alta) #9494
– Kingston (Ont), William Newlands #8392
– Manitoba, 19th-early 20th cs. #8102
– Montréal (Qué)
  – 19th-20th cs. #9426
  – (1910s) #9413
  – (1950-1968) #9422
  – (1950s) #9419
– Ontario
  – 19th c. #8006
  – (1920s) #9450
  – polygonal buildings, 19th c. #7987
– Prairies #8080
– Québec #9424
  – (1919-1923) #9416
  – (1950s) #9418
  – (1960s) #7862
– Scarborough (Ont)
  – North Bridlewood Junior Public School
    #9471
  – Stephen Leacock Educational Complex
    #9476
– Toronto (Ont)
  – (1920s) #9443
  – Central Technical School #9434
  – John Ross Robertson and Glenholme
    schools #9437
  – Study of Educational Facilities (SEF)
    – (1968) #9466
    – (1969) #9472
– Trois-Rivières (Qué), (1630s-1910s) #7883
– Vancouver (BC), elementary school design
  competition (1970) #9507
– western Canada #8083
  – (1920s) #9389
  – late 19th-early 20th cs. #9404
– Winnipeg (Man) #8105
  – (1831-1960) #8095
  – (1880s-1910s) #8101
  – (1908) #9484
Schoonover, Frank Earle, Amer artist in
  Canada, 1877-1972 #7163
Schreiber, Charlotte Mount Brook Morrell,
  Can artist, 1834-1922 #7164
Schubert, Marcus, Can photographer, 1955-
– portfolio of photographs #1053
Schwitters, Kurt, Ger artist, 1887-1948
– as teacher of Almuth Lutkenhaus #6336
Scie, La, Can newspaper
– cartoons, Jean-Baptiste Côté #5186 5187
Scotland
– photographic views, Robin MacKenzie
  #6393
Scots in Canada
– architecture, 19th c. #7977
– art, 19th-20th cs. #133
– pottery, 19th c. #2339
Scott, Adam Sheriff, Can artist, 1887-1980
– as teacher of Armand Tatossian #7330
– exhibitions, group
  – (1978) #133
– interior, Château Frontenac (Québec, Qué)
  #9278
– interior, Royal Bank of Canada (Montréal,
  Qué) #9176
Scott, Adrian Gilbert, Brit architect,
  1882-1963
– influence on Gothic revival architecture in
  Canada #7724
– Vancouver (BC), Saint James Anglican
  Church #8171
Scott, Charles Hepburn, Can artist,

1886-1964
– as director, Vancouver School of Art
  (Vancouver, BC) #3019
– exhibitions (reviews) #1982
Scott, George Gilbert, Brit architect,
  1837-1897
– influence on Gothic revival architecture in
  Canada #7724
Scott, Gilbert, Brit architect, 1811-1878
– London (England), Albert Memorial #725
– St. John's (Nfld), Saint John's Cathedral
  #8771
Scott, Giles Gilbert, Brit architect, 1880-1960
– influence on Gothic revival architecture in
  Canada #7724
Scott, J.D., Can medal engraver, fl. 1879
– temperance medals #724
Scott, John McBride, Can artist, 1950-
– exhibitions, group
  – (1980) #1832
Scott, Mackay Hugh Baillie, Brit architect,
  designer, 1865-1945
– furniture, Alexis Martin House (Victoria,
  BC) #8682
– influence on Samuel Maclure #8384
Scott, Marian Mildred Dale, Can artist, 1906-
  #7166
– non-figurative paintings (1950s) #7165
Scott, Susan, Can artist, 1949-
– exhibitions, group
  – (1979) #676
Scott, Thomas Seaton, Can architect,
  1836-1895
– Stratford (Ont), Post Office #9054
Scovil, James Noel, Can artist, b. 1876 #7167
scrap art
– see junk sculpture
screens, Tlingit
– Juneau (Alaska), Alaska State Museum
  #3916
scrimshaw #3419
scrolls, Algonquian
– Midewiwin #3702
scrolls, Ojibwa
– Midewiwin #3539 3583 3626
scrolls, Siouan
– Midewiwin #3702
Sculptors' Society of British Columbia
– exhibitions
  – (1977) #2057
Sculptors' Society of Canada #740
– (1920s) #735
– (1928-1958) #741
– and Emanuel Otto Hahn #5679
– and Visual Arts Ontario #1806
– exhibitions
  – (1928-) #734
  – (1929-1930) #294
  – (1939) #346
– exhibitions (reviews)
  – (1944) #736
sculpture
– see also bronzes; ceramic sculpture;
  conservation and restoration, sculpture;
  ivories; junk sculpture; mobiles; neon
  sculpture; open-air sculpture; plaster
  casts; portrait sculpture; sepulchral
  monuments; sound sculpture; wax
  modeling; woodcarving
– (1950s), Julien Hébert on #5765
– (1960s), and painting #449
– (1967), International Sculpture Symposium
  (Toronto, Ont) #765
– (1978), International Sculpture Conference

(Toronto, Ont) #791
sculpture, African
- Zimbabwe, influence on Ian Trowell #7431
sculpture, American
- (1960s) #787 790
sculpture, Bella Bella
- carved wooden containers, 19th c.,
  Smithsonian Institution (Washington, DC)
  #3985
sculpture, British
- (1880s), Canadian subjects #725
- (1970s) #653
sculpture, Canadian #57 58 59 61 63 129 761
- 17th-19th cs. #232
- 17th c.-1910s #205
- 18th c.-1930s #45
- 19th c.-1920s #11
- 19th c.-1940s #1242
- 20th c. #145
  - compared with engineering
    constructions #471
- (1750s-1890s) #221
- (1837-1887) #253
- (1867-1967) #82
- (1880s-1940s) #28
- (1890s) #727
- (1901-1912), Toronto Society of Architects
  exhibitions #7956
- (1910s) #205
- (1920s) #735
- (1920s-1940s) #737
- (1928-1958) #741
- (1929-1930) #294
- (1930), Canadian National Exhibition
  (Toronto, Ont) #313
- (1930s) #13 340
- (1938-1948) #379 738
- (1940s) #370 374 736
- (1940s-1960s) #453
- (1950s-1960s) #455
- (1955-1971) #1453
- (1960s) #478 521 743 744 745 746 747 748
  767 770 787 790 1793
- (1970s) #653 654 779 782 788 792 794
  - concept of motion #783
  - conservation of #793
- Alberta
  - (1970s) #1951
  - (1980) #1969
- and architecture
  - (1950s) #7670
  - (1960s) #753 8236
  - (1970s) #773
- and Emanuel Otto Hahn #5679
- and photography (1970s) #994
- Atlantic provinces (1970s) #1132
- Berthierville (Qué), church #8833 8874
- British Columbia #1995
  - (1950s) #1994
  - (1960s) #1854 2001
  - (1970s) #2049 2062 2065 2066
  - garden sculpture (1960s) #1849
- Calgary (Alta), 20th c. #1959
- Carillon (Qué), Dollard des Ormeaux
  #1591
- Charlesbourg (Qué), churches #8851
- Eastern Townships (Qué), (1815-1940)
  #1288
- electric, Electric Gallery (Toronto, Ont)
  #1800
- figurative works (1970s) #760
- île d'Orléans (Qué), Church of Saint-Pierre
  #8802
- influence of American sculpture #126

- Joliette (Qué), churches #8876
- Lachenaie (Qué), Church of Saint-Charles
  #8808
- Laterrière (Qué), Church of Notre-Dame
  #7882
- Lévis (Qué), Church of
  Notre-Dame-de-la-Victoire #8789
- Lotbinière (Qué), churches #8835
- Manitoba #1895
- Maritimes (1960s) #1126
- Montréal (Qué) #1572
  - (1940s-1950s) #1426
  - (1950s) #389 7900
  - (1960s) #1485
  - (1970s) #1624
  - Chapel of Notre-Dame-de-Lourdes
    #8836
  - Church of Notre-Dame #8839
  - Expo '67 #751 752 7691 7692 9214
  - Grey Nuns #8862
  - late 19th c.-1920s #1623
- Newfoundland
  - 19th c.-1950s #1139
  - (1970s) #1151
- Nova Scotia, folk sculpture, 20th c. #1206
  1207
- of Louis XIV and Louis XV #1598
- Ontario
  - (1970s) #1806
  - Government of Ontario Art Collection
    (1873-1941) #1728
- Ottawa (Ont)
  - National Capital Region #762
  - National Gallery of Canada #3038
  - Parliament Buildings #755
- performance sculpture (1970s) #658
- Prairies
  - (1950s-1970s) #1884
  - (1960s) #1848 1853
  - (1970s) #1873 1878
- Québec #1233 1234 1235 1237 1249 1258
  1259 1265 1324 1590 1596 1617 2184 2197
  7887
  - 17th-19th cs. #1341 1589 1594 2128 7852
  - 17th c.-1920s #1229
  - 18th-19th cs. #1338 7849
  - 18th-early 20th cs. #1339
  - (1640-1840) #1329
  - (1650-1925) #1592
  - (1760-1790) #1369
  - (1875-1915) #1364
  - (1880-1914), influence from Paris
    (France) #1371
  - (1920s) #302
  - (1930s), influence of French sculpture
    #1381
  - (1940s) #1580 8820
  - (1940s-1970s) #1269
  - (1945-1970) #1599
  - (1950s) #2193
  - (1960s) #1487 1586 1595 1622
  - (1960s-1970s) #1584
  - (1970s) #1626 1627 1630 1631 1634 1635
  - (1980) #685
  - annunciation theme, late 17th-20th cs.
    #1633
  - as folk art #1291
  - Confrérie des menuisiers de madame
    Sainte-Anne #1241 5965
  - Conseil de la sculpture du Québec
    (1978-1979) #1628
  - crucifixes #1585 1638
  - folk sculpture, 17th-19th cs. #1611
  - influence of Baillairgé family #1582

- late 19th c.-1920s #1606
- monuments #1570
- Recollets #8855
- review of literature #1295
- Soucy family #7267
- supper at Emmaus theme, 19th-20th cs.
  #1615
- use of plaster #1618
- use of plastics (1970s) #1603
- Québec (Qué)
  - 17th c. #1352
  - General James Wolfe monuments #1568
- realism #716
- ritual and cult elements (1970s) #789
- Saint-Marc-des-Carrières (Qué) #1629
- Saskatchewan #1919
- Sculptors' Society of Canada #346 734 740
- Sherbrooke (Qué), (1970s) #2232
- Toronto (Ont)
  - (1970s) #697 1817
  - Saint Anne's Church #1733
  - University of Toronto. University
    College #9482
- use of plastics (1960s) #768
- Vancouver (BC) #2026
  - (1960s) #2037
- Varennes (Qué), churches #8813
- war subjects #1081 1111 1112
  - Battle of Ypres (Ypres, France), Walter
    Seymour Allward #4518
  - Ottawa (Ont), National Gallery of
    Canada #1101
  - World War I #731 732
- Winnipeg (Man) #1891
  - Legislative Building #8951 8953
- women sculptors, 20th c. #739
sculpture, Carrier
- 'Ksan artists' cooperative #4129 4130
sculpture, Coast Salish #3896 4046
sculpture, Copper Eskimo
- antlerwork #4412
sculpture, Cree
- (1970s) #4133
sculpture, Dorset #4350
- Cape Dorset (NWT) #4322
- multiple human images #4429
sculpture, French
- (1930s), influence on Québec sculpture
  #1381
sculpture, Gitksan
- 'Ksan arts cooperative #4134
sculpture, Haida #4040
- (1970s) #4145
- and medicine #3904
- argillite carving #3761 3890 4016 4042 4051
  - (1820-1910) #3958 4010
  - (1910s-1950s) #4116
  - Bear Mother and shaman images #3901
  - Bear Mother images #3868
  - Chapman, Isaac #5088
  - Collison, Louis #5138
  - Edenshaw, Henry #5361
  - influence of scrimshaw #3419
  - Moody, Rufus #3944
  - Vancouver (BC), Vancouver Centennial
    Museum #4006
- carved wooden containers, 19th c.,
  Smithsonian Institution (Washington, DC)
  #3985
- late 19th c. #3862
- woodcarving #4041
sculpture, Indians of North America #761
3381
- Montréal (Qué), Montreal Museum of Fine

Arts #3362
sculpture, Inuit #761 1294 3359 3374 4198
 4200 4205 4229 4231 4232 4239 4261 4273
 4275 4388 4394 4395 4404 4406 4414 4418
 4419 4423 4426 4432 4440 4442 4444 4451
 4456
– (1940s-1960s) #4392
– (1950s) #4183 4311 4383 4384 4385 4387
 4390 4393
– (1960s-1970s) #4447
– (1970s) #4287 4422 4448
 – Baffin Island (NWT) #4420
– (1977-1980) #4269
– amautik subject #4300
– and mythology #4433
– art market #4396 4397
– Baker Lake (NWT) #4266 4402 4403 4408
 4434
 – (1950s-1960s) #4400
– Belcher Islands (NWT) #4459
– Cape Dorset (NWT) #4192 4211 4299 4425
 4441
 – mining quarries #4409
– ceramic sculpture, Rankin Inlet (NWT)
 #4207 4210 4314
– Churchill (Man), Eskimo Museum #4290
– exhibitions aimed at visually handicapped
 #4430
– Gjoa Haven (NWT) #4435
– guide for collectors #4431
– hand images #4439
– Holman (NWT) #3350
– Inoucdjouac (Qué) #4267 4279
– ivory carving #4175 4391
 – Alaska #4398
 – late 19th c. #4453
 – Los Angeles (Calif), Southwest Museum
 #4382
 – New York (NY), Museum of the
 American Indian. Heye Foundation
 #4381 4458
 – Rankin Inlet (NWT) #4195
 – Repulse Bay and Pelly Bay (NWT) #4438
– Keewatin (NWT) #4196 4407
– Maricourt (Qué) #4405
– Montréal (Qué), Montreal Museum of Fine
 Arts #3362
– multiple human images #4429
– Povungnituk (Qué) #4219 4240 4274 4411
 4417 4421 4437
 – competition (1967) #4415
– Povungnituk (Qué) and Cape Dorset
 (NWT) #4189
– Repulse Bay (NWT) #4450
– research methodology #4401
– Rothmans of Pall Mall Canada collection
 #4257
– soapstone carving #4214
 – symbolism #4234
– Spence Bay (NWT) #4416 4454
– Toronto (Ont), York University. Art
 Gallery of York University #4228
– Toronto-Dominion Bank collection #4201
 4248
– Vancouver (BC), Vancouver Art Gallery.
 Gallery Shop #4455
– walrus tusks, Eskimo Museum (Churchill,
 Man) #4446
– whalebone carving #4413
 – Holman (NWT) #4457
 – Spence Bay (NWT) #4436 4445
– Winnipeg (Man), Winnipeg Art Gallery
 #4285 4410 4427 4428 4443 4449
sculpture, Iroquois

– (1970s) #4133
– small human effigies #3553
sculpture, Kwakiutl #3787
– (1970s) #4145
sculpture, Nootka #3880
sculpture, Northwest Coast Indians #370
 3359 3377 3463 3857 3866 3892 3931 3954
 4043 4057
– (1950s-1970s) #4162
– antler prongs, Boundary Bay (BC) #3817
– prehistoric, Columbia River (BC) #3914
– protruding tongue and related motifs
 #3934
– sculptors in society #3912
– stone #3785 3887 3889 4001
 – Victoria (BC), Provincial Museum #3900
– Thunderbird and whale motifs #3831
– wood #3877
sculpture, Ojibwa
– (1970s) #4133
sculpture, Tlingit #3902 3976
– carved wooden containers, 19th c.,
 Smithsonian Institution (Washington, DC)
 #3985
– halibut fishing hooks #4061
– woodcarving #4041
sculpture, Tsimshian #3881
– (1970s) #4145
– argillite carving #3910
– carved wooden containers, 19th c.,
 Smithsonian Institution (Washington, DC)
 #3985
Sea Goddess, Inuit #4312 4376
Seaby, Allen William, Brit artist, 1867-1953
– and Walter Joseph Phillips #6860
Seagram, House of, Can distillers firm
– collection, Canadian art #403
seascape
– see marine painting
seasons in art
– see also winter
– Riopelle, Jean-Paul #7018
Seath, Ethel, Can artist, 1879-1963
– as member, Canadian Group of Painters
 #324
Seattle (Wash), Seattle Art Museum
– exhibitions
 – Objects of Bright Pride: Northwest Coast
 Indian Art from the American Museum of
 Natural History (1978) #4024
Seattle (Wash), Seattle World's Fair (1962).
 Fine Arts Pavilion
– exhibitions
 – Northwest Coast Indian Art (1962) #3919
Seattle (Wash), Thomas Burke Museum
– see Seattle (Wash), Washington State
 University. Thomas Burke Museum
Seattle (Wash), Washington State Museum
– Soumak necklaces, Blackfoot #3685
Seattle (Wash), Washington State University.
 Thomas Burke Museum
– art, Northwest Coast Indians #3974
Seavey, Julien Ruggles, Can artist, 1857-1940
– china painting #2277
– drawings of Wentworth County (Ont)
 buildings #7954
Seaweed, Willie, Can artist, 1873-1967
– engraving on Great Killer Whale Copper
 #4054
Sécal
– see Société d'électrolyse et de chimie Alcan
 Ltée (Sécal)
Second Empire architecture
– Canada #7741 7742

– domestic architecture #7696
– railroad stations #9539
Secord, James E., Can architect, 1917-1979
– Red Deer (Alta), City Hall #8990
secret societies, Kwakiutl #3768
secret societies, Northwest Coast Indians
 #3871
secret societies, Ojibwa #3492 3602
secret societies, Plains #3727
secret societies, Seneca #3508
Seding, Volker, Can photographer, 1943-
– exhibitions, group
 – (1981) #1070
Sedna festival, Inuit #4376
Seese, Wayne, Amer artist in Canada,
 1918-1980 #1282
– and RACE #1536
Segal, George, Amer sculptor, 1924-
– Whiten, Colette, compared with #7559
Séguin, Jean-Pierre, Can artist, 1951- #1526
Sekani Indians
– culture (1920s) #4084
self-love
– see Narcissus
self-portraits
– Bobak, Bruno Joseph #4760
– Lake, Suzy #6137 6138
– Maynard, Hannah Hatherly #6458
– Morris, Michael #6641
– Poole, Leslie Donald #6902 6903
– Snow, Michael #7243
– Vincent, Zacharie #7494
Selkirk, Lord
– on housing construction #8527
Selkirk Mountains (BC)
– views
 – Bell-Smith, Frederic Marlett #4667
 – Collings, Charles John #5133
Semak, Michael William, Can photographer,
 1934- #7168 7169
– correspondence, Freeman Patterson #1016
– exhibitions, group
 – (1980) #1063
– photographs of Ghana #990
– portfolio of photographs #987 991 996
 1023
Semchishen, Orest, Can photographer, 1932-
– exhibitions, group
 – (1979) #1037
– exhibitions (reviews) #1046 1060
– photographs of Alberta churches #8913
– portfolio of photographs #991
seminaries, Canadian
– Montréal (Qué) #7932
– Québec #7853 7861
– Québec (Qué)
 – Collège des jésuites #7953
 – Séminaire de Notre-Dame-des-Anges
 #8785
 – Séminaire de Québec #8842 8844 8847
Seminole Indians
– gorgets #3536
Sen, Ranjan, Can artist, 1941-
– exhibitions, group
 – (1979) #2075
– exhibitions (reviews) #2072
Seneca Indians
– basketry #3552
– combs #3587
– masks #3508 3533 3563 4113
– masks and pipes #3636
– pipes #3642
– war clubs #3535
Sénécal, André, Can photographer, fl. 1976

– portfolio of photographs #997 999
Senécal, Irène, Can artist, 1901-1978 #1380
– as teacher #2999 3010
Sénéchal, Gilles, Can photographer, fl. 1970s
#1283
Senft, Douglas, Can sculptor, 1950-
– *Aldergrove Valley* #7170
Senior, Raymond (Ray), Can tapestry artist,
1921-
– exhibitions, group
– (1978) #2772
– front curtain, Shaw Festival Theatre
(Niagara-on-the-Lake, Ont) #9119
Sept-Iles (Qué), Musée de Sept-Iles
– exhibitions
– *De la figuration à la non-figuration dans
l'art québécois* (1977) #1461
sepulchral monuments
– *see also* cemeteries
sepulchral monuments, British
– exported to Newfoundland, 18th c.-1860
#1163
sepulchral monuments, Canadian #733
– Hamilton (Ont), Hamilton Mausoleum
#8900
– iron crosses
– Ontario #2709
– Québec #2716
– Montréal (Qué), Notre-Dame-des-Neiges
cemetery #1567
– Newfoundland, 18th c.-1860 #1163
– Nova Scotia #1193 1216
– Ontario
– 18th c.-1930s #1669
– 19th c.-1910s #1723
– late 18th-19th cs. #1721
– Toronto (Ont), Mount Pleasant Cemetery
– Eaton Mausoleum #8895
– Senator Cox's Mausoleum #8894
sepulchral monuments, Haida #3995
sepulchral monuments, Indians of North
America #733
sepulchral monuments, Irish
– exported to Newfoundland, 18th c.-1860
#1163
sepulchral monuments, Northwest Coast
Indians #8914
serial art
– Molinari, Guido #6588 6590 6592
serigraphy
– Bornstein, Eli, on #4854
– Casson, Alfred Joseph, on #5055
serigraphy, Algonquian
– Triple K Co-operative (Red Lake, Ont)
#4151 4158
serigraphy, Kwakiutl #4120
serigraphy, Nootka #4167
serigraphy, Northwest Coast Indians #4168
– (1970s) #4160
– Northwest Coast Indian Artists Guild
(1977) #4148
serigraphy, Tsimshian #4167
Serpent Mound (Rice Lake, Ont)
– artifacts, Algonquian and Hopewell #3574
Serra, Richard, Amer sculptor, 1939-
– concrete sculpture, King City (Ont) #1796
– exhibitions, group
– (1978) #790
– exhibitions (reviews) #787
Sert, Jackson, Can architectural firm
– Guelph (Ont), University of Guelph. Arts
and Library buildings #9468
Sérusier, Paul, Fr artist, 1863-1927
– as teacher of André Charles Biéler #4725

service stations (automobile)
– *see* gasoline stations
Seton, Ernest Thompson, Can artist,
1860-1946 #7171 7172 7173
– exhibitions, group
– (1961) #62
Seurat, Georges Pierre, Fr artist, 1859-1891
– FitzGerald, Lionel LeMoine, compared
with #5452
– influence on Lionel LeMoine FitzGerald
#5450
Sévigny, Marc, Can photographer, ca. 1957-
#1534
sex in art
– *see also* erotic art
– by women artists (1970s) #596
Shaa, Aqjangajuk, Can sculptor, 1937-
– interview #7174
Shabaeff, Valentin, Can artist, 1891- #7175
Shadbolt, Doris, Can curator, art critic,
jeweller, 1918-
– jewellery #2695
– on Emily Carr #5043
Shadbolt, Jack Leonard, Can artist, 1909-
#476 1996 7184 7188 7191
– and Molly Lamb Bobak #4766
– and Vancouver (BC) painting #1992 6742
– as art critic #3308
– as juror, *Saskatchewan Arts Exhibition* (1954)
#1910
– as teacher of Arthur McKay #6477
– Dallaire, Jean-Philippe, compared with
#5238
– drawings and writings #7181 7183
– exhibitions
– (1969) #7182
– (1978) #7187
– (1980) #7189
– exhibitions, group
– (1958) #431
– (1959) #438 1997
– (1964) #462
– (1977) #633
– exhibitions (reviews) #2074 7176
– form and meaning #7179
– in Europe (1956-1957) #7180
– influence of nature #7177
– influence on Gordon Appelbe Smith #7232
– interview #7178
– mural paintings #1844
– on artistic experience #7186
– on Emily Carr #5043
– on image-making #7192
– on influences of history on his art #7185
– paintings (1970s) #7190
– participant, Symposium on 20th Century
Canadian Culture (Washington, DC),
(1977) #621
– stage design and costume, *Daphnis and
Chloe* #1991
– writings #92
Shahn, Ben, Amer artist, 1898-1969
– mentioned, in relation to Canadian culture
#6747
Shakespeare, Noah, Can photographer,
1839-1921
– and the Victoria Theatre Photographic
Gallery (Victoria, BC) #2027
shamanism
– and Jack Butler #4982
– and Jack Leonard Shadbolt #7190 7191
– and Karoo Ashevak #4562
– and Norval Morrisseau #6647
– sculpture, British Columbia (1970s) #2066

shamanism, Algonquian
– tree of life #3365
shamanism, Copper Eskimo #4330
shamanism, Dorset #4361
shamanism, Haida #3904
– and medicine #3904
– argillite carving #3901
shamanism, Huron
– pipes #3632
shamanism, Indians of North America #3361
3383
shamanism, Inuit #4243 4283 4488
– masks #4349
– tree of life #3365
shamanism, Iroquois
– pipes #3642
shamanism, Micmac #3556
shamanism, Montagnais
– natutshikan #4103
shamanism, Naskapi
– natutshikan #4103
shamanism, natives of North America #3360
shamanism, Netsilik #4328
shamanism, Northwest Coast Indians #4065
– and petroglyphs #3971
shamanism, Ojibwa #3492 3517 3602
shamanism, Seneca
– pipes #3642
shamanism, Tlingit
– and halibut fishing #4061
shamanism, Tsimshian
– masks #4056
Shames, Stephen, Can photographer, fl.
1970s
– portfolio of photographs #998
Shanly, Charles Dawson, Irish artist in
Canada, 1811-1875 #241 242
Sharon (Ont), Children of Peace Meeting
House (1810)
– architecture, David Willson #8352
Sharon (Ont), Temple of the Children of
Peace
– architecture #7959
– Willson, David #8351 8352
Sharp, Vincent, Can photographer, 1937-
#7193
– exhibitions (reviews) #1018
Sharp & Brown, Can architectural firm
– Calgary (Alta), Bank of Nova Scotia #8118
– Moose Jaw (Sask), City Hall, competition
#8978
– Winnipeg (Man), Legislative and
Executive Building, competition #8946
Sharp & Horner, Can architectural firm
– Bank of Nova Scotia buildings #9174
Sharp & Thompson, Berwick, Pratt, Can
architectural firm
– Vancouver (BC), Dal Grauer Substation
#8171
Sharp & Thompson, Can architectural firm
– Vancouver (BC)
– Saint James Anglican Church #8171
– University of British Columbia #9500
– University of British Columbia,
competition #9498 9509
Sharpe, Nettie, Can collector, 20th c.
– collection, Québec folk sculpture #1607
Shaughnessy, Arthur, Can sculptor,
1884-1945
– influence on Henry Hunt #5872
Shawinigan (Qué), Church of Notre-Dame
de la Présentation

– paintings, Ozias Leduc #6201
Sheeguapik
– *see* Sivuarapik, Charlie
Sheep Creek (Alta), Cottonwoods
– architecture #8720 8721
Sheep Creek (Alta), Gate Ranch House
– architecture #8720 8721
Sheep Creek (Alta), Viewfield Ranch House
– architecture #8720 8721
Sheffield (England), Sheffield School of Art
– Varley, Frederick Horsman, as student
 #7462
Shehu, Aferdita (Dita), Can artist, fl. 1970s
– interview #7194
Shelburne (NS), Christ Church
– architecture, Isaac Hildrith #8374 8375
Shelburne (NS), Ross Thompson House and
 Warehouse
– architecture #7823
Sheldon-Williams, Inglis, Can artist,
 1870-1940 #7195 7196
– exhibitions, group
 – (1980) #1940
– views, western Canada #931
Shell Canada Ltd., oil firm
– collection, Canadian art #3238 3240
shellwork, Algonquian #3505 3511
shellwork, Indians of North America #3388
– beadwork #3457
– wampum #3522
shellwork, Iroquois #3505 3607
shellwork, Northwest Coast Indians
– implements #4068
shellwork, Woodlands #3505
Shepard & Calvin, Can architectural firm
– Kingston (Ont), Queen's University.
 Douglas Library #9445
– Toronto (Ont), Oke Building #9335
Shepherd, Helen Parsons, Can artist, 1923-
– as cofounder, Newfoundland Academy of
 Art (St. John's, Nfld) #2988
Shepherd, Reginald, Can artist, 1924-
– as cofounder, Newfoundland Academy of
 Art (St. John's, Nfld) #2988
Shepley, Ellen Garde, Can collector, 20th c.
– collection, souvenir spoons, Royal Ontario
 Museum (Toronto, Ont) #2652
Sheppard, Earle Leonard, Can architect,
 1894-1957
– plan, northwestern entrance to Hamilton
 (Ont) #7962
Sheraton style furniture
– Newfoundland #2502
– Québec #2542
Sherbrooke (NS), Sherbrooke Village Exhibit
 Centre
– exhibitions
 – *Canadians: A National Photography Show
 about People/Canadiens: exposition
 nationale de photographie ayant les gens
 comme thème* (1979) #1035
Sherbrooke (Qué)
– decorative arts (1970s) #2232
– petroglyphs, Iroquois #3599
Sherbrooke (Qué), Bishop's Palace
– interior, Ozias Leduc #6208
Sherbrooke (Qué), Cathedral of Sherbrooke.
 Pauline Chapel
– paintings, Ozias Leduc #6204
Sherbrooke (Qué), Chapelle universitaire
 chrétienne
– architecture, Paul Faucher, Jacques
 Folch-Ribas #8841
Sherbrooke (Qué), Université de Sherbrooke.

Centre culturel
– exhibitions
 – *Claude Tousignant* (1974) #7401
 – *Concours d'estampe et de dessin*
 (1977,1979,1981) #1533
 – *Fernand Leduc* (1971) #6186
 – *Joe Plaskett and His Paris: In Search of
 Time Past* (1973) #6893
 – *Joe Plaskett et son Paris: à la recherche d'un
 temps passé* (1973) #6894
 – *L'art des Cantons de l'Est, 1800-1950*
 (1980) #1296
 – *Métiers d'art Ontario-Québec,
 1979/1980/Quebec-Ontario Crafts,
 1979/1980* (1980) #2138
 – *The Mr. and Mrs. Jules Loeb Collection/La
 collection M. et Mme Jules Loeb* (1971)
 #3231
– exhibitions (reviews)
 – *Les arts visuels des Cantons de l'Est
 1800-1950* (1978) #1282
Sherman, Tom, Can artist, 1947-
– exhibitions, group
 – (1977) #631
 – (1980) #705
– performance art #655
Sherwood, William Albert, Can artist,
 1855-1919
– exhibitions (reviews) #1703
Sherwood Park (Alta)
– public art #1973
Sherwood Park (Alta), County of Strathcona
 Building
– architecture, Peter Hemingway, and art,
 Alex Janvier #5937
shields, Algonquian #3672
shields, Dakota
– Philadelphia (Penn), University of
 Pennsylvania. Museum #3670
Shields, George S., Can artist, 1872-1952
– cartoons, *Toronto Evening Telegram* #943
shields, Plains #3672 3680 3732
– animal motifs #3758
shields, Siouan #3672
Shilling, Arthur, Can artist, 1941- #7197
– influence of Midewiwin images #4154
– interview #7198
– portraits #715
Shimaoka, Tatsuzo, Ja ceramicist, 20th c.
– as teacher of Québec ceramicists (1964)
 #2381
ship models, Canadian
– Bradford, John Locke #4895
– in bottles, Québec #2944
– Leclerc, Eugène #2174 2209
– Newfoundland #1155
– sailboats, île aux Coudres (Qué) #2178
– Saint-Jean-Port-Joli (Qué) #2194
– Toronto (Ont), Royal Ontario Museum.
 Sigmund Samuel Collection #3135
ships
– *see also* boats; figureheads of ships; ship
 models
ships, Canadian
– 19th c. #2095
– New Brunswick, 19th c. #2150
– Québec, 19th c. #1604
ships in art
– (1600-1900) #225
– (Ottawa, Ont), Public Archives of Canada.
 William H. Coverdale Collection #12
– Bluenose hooked rugs #2763
– Canadian folk painting #965 966
– Canadian pottery #2288

– 19th c. #2341
– MacAskill, Wallace R., photographic views
 #6351
– Murphy, Rowley Walter #6666
– New Brunswick, windjammers, 19th c.
 #1190
– Nova Scotia, 19th c. #163 1201
– Plamondon, Antoine-Sébastien, *Le flûtiste*
 #6885
– Russell, Edward John #7111
Shirley, James R., Can artist, 1944- #7199
– exhibitions (reviews) #1208
– prints #1214
Shives, Arnold, Can artist, 1943-
– exhibitions
 – (1976) #2059
shoes, Canadian
– (1850s) #2811
– and boots, Fort Beauséjour (NB),
 (1750s-1830s) #2858
– artisans (1608-1950) #2946
– female, Louisbourg (NS), (1713-1758)
 #2855
– Québec #2816
 – 17th-19th cs. #2814
 – 17th-20th cs. #2953
 – 19th-20th cs. #2880
 – artisans, 17th-18th cs. #2214
 – early 20th c. #1313
– skin boots, Newfoundland and Labrador,
 20th c. #2155
shoes, Indians of North America #2814 3424
shopping centres, Canadian
– (1950s) #9373
– Montréal (Qué)
 – complexe Desjardins #9327
 – Place Bonaventure #9319 9320 9321 9322
 9323 9325
 – Place Ville-Marie #9314
 – Westmount Square #9326
– Toronto (Ont)
 – Eaton Centre #9377 9378 9382
 – Yorkdale Shopping Centre #9374 9375
shops
– *see* stores
Shore, Henrietta Mary, Can artist in USA,
 1880-1963 #7200
Shore, Tilbe, Henschel, Irwin, Can
 architectural firm
– Toronto (Ont), Joseph E. Shephard
 Government of Canada Building #8975
Shore, Tilbe, Henschel, Irwin, Peters, Can
 architectural firm
– Toronto (Ont), Dundas Street police
 station #8078
Shore & Moffat, Can architectural firm
– Kingston (Ont), Canadian Forces Hospital
 #9031
Shore & Moffat and Partners, Can
 architectural firm
– Toronto (Ont), York University #9396 9469
Short, Richard, Brit naval officer, artist in
 Canada, fl. before 1754-after 1766 #249 250
Shortt, Stephen, Can artist, fl. 1970s
– exhibitions, group
 – (1976) #1529
Shortt, Terence Michael, Can artist, 1910-
 #7201
– and Frederick Horsman Varley #506
show business
– *see* performing arts
Shreveport (La), R.W. Norton Art Gallery
– exhibitions
 – *Loren D. Adams, Jr.: A Retrospective*

Exhibition (1979) #4501
Shubenacadie Canal (NS)
– survey of location, Isaac Hildrith #8374
Shufeldt, Robert Wilson, Amer curator,
  1850-1934
– and emergence of named Indian artists
  #3486
Shuldham Island (Labrador, Nfld)
– prehistoric artifacts #4377
Shum, Hilda, Can artist, 1957-
– exhibitions, group
  – (1981) #2084
Shumiatcher, Jacqui and Morris, Can
  collectors, 20th c.
– collection, Inuit art #4311
Shuswap Indians
– culture #3789
– kekuli #3983
Shuttleworth, Claire, Amer artist in Canada,
  1868-1930 #7202
Siberia (USSR)
– art (1900-1980) #4303
Sibley Brothers, furniture-making firm (NS)
  #2493
Sicily (Italy)
– views, World War II, Carl Fellman
  Schaefer #1090
Sickert, Walter Richard, Brit artist, 1860-1942
– Morrice, James Wilson, compared with
  #6631
Sicotte, Rolande, Can artist, fl. 1936 #1380
Siddall, Dennis & Associates, Can
  architectural firm
– Victoria (BC), University of Victoria.
  Centennial Stadium #9101
Siddall, John Wilson, Can architect,
  1861-1941
– Toronto (Ont)
  – Big Nickel Theatre #9066
  – theatres #9067
Siebens, Harold, Can collector, 20th c.
– collection of photographs by Wilfred
  Roloff Beny acquired for University of
  Calgary. Art Gallery (Calgary, Alta) #4691
Siebner, Herbert Johannes Joseph, Can artist,
  1925- #2061 7203
– as member of Limners #2043
– exhibitions
  – (1979) #7205
– interview #7204
Siegel, Lois, Can photographer, 1946- #1000
sign painting
– *see* signs and sign-boards
signs and sign-boards
– *see also* billboards; lettering in art
signs and signboards, Canadian
– Hébert, Julien #5766
– neon signs, Vancouver (BC) #2079
– Ottawa (Ont), National Arts Centre #9104
– Québec
  – 17th-19th cs. #2919 2922
  – (1759-1914), revolutionary subjects #1351
– Wallot, Jacques-Albert-François-Joseph
  #7513
Silcox, David, Can arts administrator, 1937-
– interview, on Canada Council art
  collection #3266
silhouettes, Canadian
– Halifax (NS), 18th-19th cs. #1195
– Julien, Henri #5981
– Montréal (Qué), (1760-1860) #1376 1377
silica

– in Vaudreuil (Qué), for glass
  manufacturing #2418
silk appliqué, Algonquian #3605
silk appliqué, Dogrib #4089
silk appliqué, Iroquois #3605
silk appliqué, Ojibwa #4089
silk appliqué, Slavey #4089
silk screen printing
– *see* serigraphy
Sillaste, Henno, Can architect, 1936-
– Toronto (Ont), St. Lawrence Housing
  #8078
Sillery (Qué)
– architecture, 17th-19th cs. #7879
Sillery (Qué), Bois de Coulonge (formerly
  Spencer Wood)
– architecture #8754
Sillery (Qué), Maison des jésuites
– architecture #8571
silver
– *see also* adornment; candlesticks;
  hallmarks; jewellery; spoons; tea services
silver, Algonquian #2101 3605
– adornment #3594 3608 3633
silver, American
– trade silver #2629 2634
silver, British
– for Canadian market, 19th c. #2645
– presentation tea service (1857) #2647
– trade silver #2629 2634
silver, Canadian #2630 2637 2651
– 17th-19th cs. #2128 2627
  – biographical sources #2633
  – Henry Birks and Sons Ltd., collection
    #2636
– 17th c.-1867 #2110
– 18th-19th cs. #1338 2641 2687
  – (1680s-1830s) #2628
  – (1700-1830) #2643
  – (1960s) #2102
– alms cups, Québec, 17th-18th cs. #2671
– Arnoldi family, 18th-19th cs. #2663
– Atlantic provinces #2640
– Baudry (*dit* Des Butes), Guillaume #234
  235
– Beaugrand, Gilles #2179 4650
– Bellechasse County (Qué), Church of
  Saint-Charles-Borromée #8803
– Berthierville (Qué), church #8833 8874
– Betteridge, Lois Etherington #4718
– Brault, Maurice #4906
– Cap-Santé (Qué), churches #8814
– Carmichael, William Maurice #5003 5004
– censers, Québec, 17th-18th cs. #2665
– Chambellan, François #2667
– Cotton, Michel #249 250
– crucifixes, Québec #1585
– Delezenne, Ignace-François #269 270
– Deschevery (*dit* Maisonbasse),
  Jean-Baptiste #249 250
– Edenshaw, Charles #5360
– Gadois (*dit* Mauger), Jacques #249 250
– Gaudin (*dit* Lapoterie), Louis-Nicolas
  #5571
– Gaudin (*dit* Lapoterie), Nicolas #5571 5572
– guide for collectors #2104 2252
– hallmarks, 18th-19th cs. #2635
– Hamilton (Ont), International Silver
  Company #2642
– île d'Orléans (Qué), Church of Saint-Pierre
  #8802
– influence on Canadian art, 20th c. #2093

– Jesuits, Québec #2192
– Joliette (Qué), churches #8876
– L'Islet (Qué), Church of
  Notre-Dame-de-Bon-Secours #8879
– Lambert (*dit* Saint-Paul), Paul #249 250
  2668
– Lambert (*dit* Saint-Paul), Paul, and Samuel
  Payne #2689
– Landron, Jean-François #249 250
– Lespérance, Pierre #6248
– Levasseur, Michel #234 235 2669
– Loretteville (Qué), Church of
  Notre-Dame-de-la-Jeune-Lorette #8804
– Lotbinière (Qué), churches #8835
– Marion, Salomon #2683
– Montréal (Qué)
  – Church of Notre-Dame #8839
  – Grey Nuns #8862
– Morand, Paul #6604
– New Brunswick #2150
  – late 18th-19th cs. #2646
  – Saint John (NB), New Brunswick
    Museum #2649
– Nordbeck, Peter #258 259
– Nova Scotia #2648
  – 17th-19th cs. #2639
  – 18th-20th cs. #2632
– Oka (Qué), church #8818
– Ontario, 19th-20th cs. #2638
– Ottawa (Ont), National Gallery of Canada.
  Henry Birks Collection of Canadian Silver
  #2653
– Pagé (*dit* Quercy or Carcy), Jacques #249
  250 6749
– Paradis, Roland #249 250
– pax, Québec, 17th-19th cs. #2666
– Payne, Samuel #234 235
– Picard, Louis-Alexandre #269 270
– presentation silver #2656
– Québec #1235 1237 1249 1324 1596 2169
  2171 2183 2197 2226 2228 2670
  – 17th-18th cs. #1320 2181 2187 2657
  – 17th-19th cs. #216 1330 1331 1589 2095
    2101 2660 2662 2664 2674 2676 2678
    2681 2685 2686 2690 2691
    – compared with French silver #2688
  – 18th-19th cs. #2644 2650 2661
    – compositional analysis #2682
  – 18th c. #1620 2673 2677 5277
  – 18th-early 20th cs. #1339
  – (1534-1763) #2684
  – (1613-1870) #2191
  – (1640-1840) #1329
  – (1760-1790) #1369
  – (1867-1871) #2675
  – (1940s) #2199
  – (1950s) #2193
  – apprentices (1660-1815) #2231
  – Carrier, Louis, collection #3213
  – Morisset, Gérard, on #2692
  – review of literature #1295
– Québec (Qué)
  – 17th c. #1352
  – Ursuline Convent #8810
– Ranvoyzé, François #2658 2679 2680 6959
  6960
– Saint John (NB), stone church #8778
– Sasseville, François #258 259 2672
– Schindler, Joseph #269 270
– souvenir spoons, Royal Ontario Museum.
  Shepley collection (Toronto, Ont) #2652
– Stacey, Harold #7273 7274
– Stuart, Don #7281
– Toronto (Ont), Ontario College of Art

#3009
- trade silver #2629 2634 2654 2659 3594 3645 3646
  - gorgets #2655
- Varennes (Qué), churches #8813
- Varin (*dit* La Pistole), Jacques #269 270
- Victoria (BC) #2269
silver, Delaware
- adornment #3506
silver, French
- 17th-18th cs., exported to Québec #2687
- 17th-19th cs., compared with Québec silver #2688
- 17th-19th cs., exported to Québec #2685 2686
- 17th-19th cs., influence on Québec silver #2676
- trade silver #2634
silver, Haida #5358
silver, Indians of North America #2630
- gorgets #2655
- trade silver #269 270 2101 2628 2629 2631 2633 2634 2651 2653 2654 2659 3440
silver, Iroquois #3605
- adornment #3633
- brooches #3509 3512
- gorgets #3536
- trade silver #3645 3646
Silver, Mr. and Mrs. Stanley S., Can collectors, 20th c.
- collection, glass bottles, 19th-20th cs. #2414
silver, Plains #3698
silver, Woodlands
- adornment #3633
Silverberg, David, Can artist, 1936- #7206
- exhibitions, group
  - (1973) #1182
silversmithing
- *see* goldsmithing; silver
Simard, Claude A., Can artist, 1943- #7207
Simard, Cyril, Can arts administrator, 1938-
- and Centrale d'artisanat du Québec #2213
Simard, Jean, Can artist, 1916-
- Christmas greeting cards #856
Simard, Léonard, Can artist, 1933- #1547 1551
Simard, René, Can leatherworker, 1896- #7208
Simard-Laflamme, Carole, Can tapestry artist, 1945- #7209
- exhibitions, group
  - (1978) #2772
Simcoe, Elizabeth Posthuma Gwillim, Brit artist in Canada, 1766-1850 #7211 7212
- autobiography #7210
Simcoe, John Graves, Can statesman, 1752-1806
- and William von Moll Berczy, founding of Toronto (Ont) #4699
Simcoe (Ont), Lynnwood Arts Centre
- exhibitions
  - *Goodridge Roberts: Paintings from the 1950s and 60s* (1980) #7048
Simcoe County (Ont)
- photography, 19th c. #1722 1730
- quilts #2795
Simcoe County Arts and Crafts Association (Simcoe County, Ont)
- quilts #2795
Simkins, Howard, Can artist, 1948- #1807
Simmerman, Henry, Can furniture-maker, b. ca. 1814 #2571
Simon, Ellen Rosalie, Can stained glass artist, 1916- #7589

Simon, Frank Worthington, Brit architect, 1863-1933
- Winnipeg (Man)
  - Legislative Building #8944 8945 8947 8948 8949 8950 8951 8952
  - Legislative Building, competition #8946
Simon, Harold, Can photographer, ca. 1952-
- portfolio of photographs #991
Simon, Lucien J., Fr artist, 1861-1945
- Pellan, Alfred, compared with #6814
Simonds, Charles Frederick, Amer sculptor, architect, 1945-
- exhibitions, group
  - (1980) #8237
Simone, Joseph (Joe), Can photographer, ca. 1943-
- portfolio of photographs #995
Simonin, Francine, Can artist, 1936- #7213
Simpkins, William Charles (Bill), Can photographer, 1945-
- portfolio of photographs #1023
Simpson, Charles Walter, Can artist, 1878-1942 #302
- illustrations #916
Simpson, Gregg Cairns, Can artist, 1947-
- exhibitions, group
  - (1971) #2042
  - (1973) #2045
- exhibitions (reviews) #2051
Simpson, Richard, Can photographer, fl. 1970s
- portfolio of photographs #1032
Simpson, Sir George, Brit governor in Canada of the Hudson's Bay Company, 1787-1860
- collection, Paul Kane paintings #6018
Sinclair, Robert, Can artist, 1939- #7214 7215
- exhibitions
  - (1976) #7216
Singer, Judy, Can artist, 1951- #711 717
- exhibitions, group
  - (1981) #722
Singleton, Rebecca (Becky), Can artist, 1952-
- exhibitions, group
  - (1981) #723
Siouan Indians
- art #3434 3649 3731
  - 19th c. #3737 3750
- boulder monuments #3688
- culture #3651
- equestrian trappings #3405
- gun cases #3713
- in art, Rudolph Friedrich Kurz #3400
- leatherwork #3456
- Midewiwin, scrolls #3702
- moccasins #3666 3740
- painting #3672
- pony beads, 19th c. #3722
- pottery #3687
- quillwork #3443 3471 3652 3745
- quillwork and beadwork #3674
- rites and ceremonies #3725
- winter counts #3728
Sisler, Rebecca Jean, Can sculptor, 1932-
- exhibitions, group
  - (1978) #666
Site Inc. Sculpture in the Environment
- exhibitions, group
  - (1980) #8237
Sitka (Alaska), Sheldon Jackson Museum
- art, Indians of North America #3370
Sivuarapik, Charlie, Can sculptor, 1911-1968 #7217
Siwinski, Stefan, Can designer, 1918-

- chairs #2471
Six Nations Reserve (Ont)
- Iroquois Indians, rites and ceremonies #3598
Skagit River (BC)
- atlatl, Northwest Coast Indians #3951
Skalnik, Pavel, Can artist, 1941- #7218
- prints #1185
Skedans (BC)
- totem poles, Northwest Coast Indians #3984
Skeena Indians
- pictographs #3822
- stone clubs #4053
Skeena River (BC)
- totem poles, Gitksan #3828
skeletons in art
- *see also* human figure in art
- from archaeological excavations, Frank Allen Nulf #6727
sketchbooks
- Brooke, Arthur Adair #4924
- Carr, Emily #5018
- Edson, Aaron Allan #5363
- Gemeinhardt, John #5579
- Jackson, A.Y. #5924
- Jackson, Henry Alexander Carmichael #5927 5928
- Jameson, Anna Brownell #5933
- Jarvis, Donald Alvin #5944
- Jefferys, Charles William #5957
- Kane, Paul #6006 6009 6011 6012
- Krieghoff, Cornelius #6090
- Leduc, Ozias #6210
- Lismer, Arthur #6305
- MacDonald, J.E.H. #6373
- Massicotte, Edmond-Joseph #6441
- Miller, Alfred Jacob #6536 6537
- Morrice, James Wilson #6621 6631 6632
- Pope, William #6906
- Simcoe, Elizabeth Posthuma Gwillim #7212
- Thomson, Tom #7370
Skidegate (BC), Queen Charlotte Islands Museum
- architecture, Hawthorn Mansfield Towers #8373
Skinner, Si Angelo, Can artist, fl. 1940s
- exhibitions, group
  - (1940) #350
Skokomish Indians
- culture #3835
skyscrapers, Canadian
- (1970s) #7733
- Montréal (Qué), (1960s) #9318
Slater, James, Can civil servant, 19th c.
- and Parliament Buildings (Ottawa, Ont) #8930
Slater, Norman, Can architect, artist, 1922- #8231
- mural, Canadian Pavilion, Universal and International Exhibition of 1958 (Brussels, Belgium) #419 4541
- mural, Place des Arts (Montréal, Qué) #9093
- wall screens, National Arts Centre (Ottawa, Ont) #9108
Slavey Indians
- culture #4088 4089
Sleep, Joseph (Joe), Can artist, 1914-1978
- exhibitions
  - (1981) #7219
- exhibitions (reviews) #1208
Sloane, Sir Hans, Brit physician, naturalist,

collector, 1660-1753
- collection, art, Indians of North America
  - London (England), British Museum
  #3397
Sloggett, Paul, Can artist, 1950- #1807
- exhibitions (reviews) #639
Smalley, Katherine, Can photographer, fl.
  1979
- portfolio of photographs #1023
Smellie, David, Can metalworker, 1780-1827
  #2704
Smeraldi, artist, fl. 1925
- interior, Château Frontenac (Québec, Qué)
  #9278
Smily, William, Brit silversmith, fl.
  1840s-1850s
- presentation silver tea service, for John S.
  Helmcken #2647
Smith, Ann, Can artist, 1946- #7220
Smith, Bill, Can beltsmith, fl. 1970s #2936
Smith, Daniel J., Can photographer, fl.
  1850s-1860s #1211
Smith, David, Amer sculptor, 1906-1965
- influence on Douglas Bentham #4683 4686
- influence on Henry Saxe #7149
Smith, Eden, Can architect, 1858-1949 #8408
- on Canadian architecture (1910s) #7644
  8491
- Oshawa (Ont), Saint George's Anglican
  Church #8899
- Toronto (Ont)
  - domestic architecture #8493
  - row houses #8492
Smith, Edith Agnes, Can artist, 1867-1954
- and Nova Scotia Society of Artists #1192
Smith, Frederick, Can glassmaker, fl. 1840S
- as founder, Canada Glass Works
  (Saint-Jean, Qué) #2420
Smith, Garfield Stuart (Gar), Can artist,
  1946-
- and realism #533
Smith, George Neilson, Can artist, 1789-1854
- views, Saint John (NB) #7221
Smith, Gordon Appelbe, Can artist, 1919-
  #1996 7223 7224 7230 7232
- and Vancouver (BC) painting #1992 6742
- exhibitions
  - (1976) #7229
- exhibitions, group
  - (1959) #438 1997
- exhibitions (reviews) #432 7227 7231
- interview #7225 7226
- on printmaking #817
- on teaching art #7228
Smith, Gordon Hammond (Gord), Can
  sculptor, 1937- #7222
- welded sculptures (1960s) #745
Smith, Harold Thomas Faulkner, Can
  photographer, 1893-
- exhibitions, group
  - (1976) #2012
Smith, Jean and Elizabeth, Can collectors,
  20th c.
- collection, Canadian decorative arts #2125
  2131
Smith, Jeremy, Can artist, 1946-
- and realism #110
Smith, John Ivor, Can sculptor, 1927-
- clay sculptures (1960s) #743
Smith, John Roxborough, Can architect,
  1881-1975
- restoration, Québec (Qué) #7936
Smith, Leslie Victor, Can artist, 1880-1952
- bookplates (1916-1946) #7234

Smith, Levi Alasua Pirti, Can artist, 1927-
  #4421
Smith, Madge, Can photographer, art dealer,
  fl. 1930s- #7235
Smith, Marjorie (Jori), Can artist, 1907-
  #7233
Smith, Morley, Can artist, 1938-
- and Jacques Guillon Designers Inc. #884
Smith, Munn, Carter, Katelnikoff & Ian M.
  Brown, Can architectural firm
- Ottawa (Ont), National Gallery of Canada,
  competition #9079
Smith, Muriel, Can beltsmith, fl. 1970s #2936
Smith, Peter John, Can architect, 1936-
- Niagara-on-the-Lake (Ont), Shaw Festival
  Theatre #9119
Smith, Richard, Brit artist, 1931-
- influence on Alan Wood #7610
Smith, Russell (Awasatlas), 1950-
- silkscreen prints #4148
Smith, Struan Campbell
- see Campbell-Smith, Struan
Smith, Thomas, Can photographer, fl.
  1856-1867 #1724
Smith, William St. Thomas, Can artist,
  1862-1947 #7236 7237 7238
- exhibitions, group
  - (1978) #1726
Smith & McCulloch, Can architectural firm
- Castlegar (BC), hospital #9031
- Invermere (BC), hospital #9031
Smith Carter Searle Associates, Can
  architectural firm
- Montréal (Qué), Place d'Accueil #7686
- Winnipeg (Man)
  - City Hall, competition #8985 8986
  - Monarch Life #9357
  - Pan-Am Pool #9101
  - Smith Carter Searle Associates
    architectural and engineering office
    #7683
  - University of Manitoba. School of
    Architecture #9487
Smithson, Robert I., Amer sculptor,
  1938-1973
- Prince, Richard, compared with #6937
Smolenski, Joseph, Can ceramicist, 19th c.
  #2298 2322
Smyth, Hervey, Brit army officer, artist in
  Canada, 1734-1811
- portrait of General James Wolfe #1568
Smyth, John Richard Coke, Brit artist in
  Canada, 1808-1882
- forgeries #4614
Snell, Don, Can sculptor, 1946-1978
- exhibitions, group
  - (1980) #1835
Snider, Gregory, Can sculptor, 1945-
- exhibitions, group
  - (1978) #786
Snider, Kenneth, Can architect, fl. 1965
- Vancouver (BC), University of British
  Columbia. Student Union #9503
Sninig, Bella Coola
- petroglyph of #3816
Snow, Charles, Can artist, 20th c.
- as teacher of Robert MacLean #2923
Snow, Michael, Can artist, 1929- #538 1762
- and art criticism #3315
- and avant-garde art #600
- books #940
  - Cover to Cover #7254 7255 7256
- drawings #532
- exhibitions

- (1970) #7243 7244
- (1972) #7248
- (1975) #7253
- (1978) #7258
- (1979) #7261
- exhibitions, group
  - (1967) #490
  - (1971) #98
  - (1973) #556
  - (1977) #783
  - (1979) #510
  - (1980) #690 703
- exhibitions (reviews) #520 7242 7245 7259
  7263 7264
- films #626
  - La région centrale #7247 7250
  - Wavelength #568 7241 7246
- films and photographs (1960s and 1970s)
  #7260
- influence on Toronto (Ont) painting #1749
- interview #7257
  - on his films #7249 7252
- on Canadian art (1960s) #478
- on Joyce Wieland #7577
- on living in New York (1960s) #460
- on visual perception #525
- outside Canadian art tradition #7239
- paintings and sculptures #449
- photographs as maps of perception #7251
- Plus tard #714 7262
- use of photography #1057
- uses and transformation of history #577
- video art #616
- Walking Woman series #7240
snowshoes, Algonquian #3523 3631
snowshoes, Canadian #2812
- influence on Canadian chair design #2464
- Newfoundland and Labrador, 20th c.
  #2155
snowshoes, Indians of North America #2812
  3515
snowshoes, Inuit #3515
snowshoes, Iroquois #3523 3631
snowshoes, Mistassini #4080
snowshoes, Ojibwa #3539
snowshoes, Woodlands #3631
Snuqualmi Indians
- culture #3835
social realism
- see realism
socialism and art
- see also Communism and art
- Canadian painting #113
- Hutchinson, Leonard, prints (1930-1940)
  #5893
- Taylor, Frederick Bourchier, Talking Union
  (1950) #7332
Société d'électrolyse et de chimie Alcan Ltée
  (Sécal) (Montréal, Qué)
- collection #3246
Société des artistes professionnels du
  Québec
- (1971-1975) #1488
- exhibitions (reviews)
  - (1970) #1490
Société des arts (Montréal, Qué)
- periodical, Vie des arts #55
Société des arts plastiques
- Lemieux, Jean-Paul, on #1411
Société des graphistes du Québec
- (1974-1981) #893
Société pour l'encouragement des arts et des
  sciences au Canada
- and Québec art (1827-1829) #1368

Société Radio-Canada
– see Canada. Société Radio-Canada
society and architecture
– British Columbia (1970s) #8146
– Canada #7728
  – 20th c. #7690 7731 7732
  – (1890-1944) #30
  – (1930s) #7658
  – (1960s) #8513
    – role of architects #8279 8280
  – archival and historical sources #7729
  – Victorian #7725
– Montréal (Qué), Bank of Montreal (1846)
  #9200
– Ontario, 19th c. #7745
– Prairies, 19th-20th cs. #8080
– Québec #7851
  – 17th-18th cs. #8586
  – (1970s) #7868
  – (1980) #7893
– Safdie, Moshe, on #8406
– Toronto (Ont), 19th-20th cs. #8060
– Trois-Rivières (Qué), Forges of
  Saint-Maurice #9257
society and art
– and A.Y. Jackson #5922
– and Bertram Richard Brooker #330
– and Charles William Jefferys #5957
– and Cornelius Krieghoff #6093 6101
– and Elizabeth Posthuma Gwillim Simcoe
  #7211
– and Gérard Morisset #1477 3321
– and Group of Seven #1735 1763 1764
– and John Wilson Bengough #4671 4676
  4677
– and Joseph Légaré #6215 6216
– and Lawren Stewart Harris #5722
– and Les Levine #6265
– and Michel Lambeth #6159
– and Napoléon Bourassa #4876
– and Neils Christian Knudsen #6072
– and Paul-Emile Borduas #1455 4811 4812
  4834 4837 4848 4849
– and Théophile Hamel #5692
– and William George Richardson Hind
  #5811
– and William Millikin #6543
– Atlantic provinces (1960s-1970s) #1130
– Calgary (Alta), (1970s) #1966
– Canada #104 327
  – 20th c. #567
  – (1760-1860) #251
  – (1882-1910), and fashion #2897
  – (1890-1900) #190
  – (1890s) #187
  – (1892-1908) #277
  – (1909) #194
  – (1920s) #305 311
  – (1920s-1960s) #495
  – (1930s), attitude to nudes in art #317
  – (1940s) #40 351 363 366 369
    – and Federation of Canadian Artists
      #360 376
    – attitude to nudes in art #6652
    – proposal for increasing public contact
      #368
  – (1950s) #3254 3255 3256
    – compared with France #436
  – (1950s-1970s), and government aid
    #3290
  – (1951), Royal Commission on National
    Development in the Arts, Letters and
    Sciences (Massey Report) #3257 3261
  – (1960s) #87 444 447 448 529 3265

– role of museums #3045
– (1970s) #583 586 587 599 602 621 693
  3056 3270 3279 6747
  – and government aid #3268 3278
  – role of museums #3059
– (1980) #683 3294 3295
– (1981) #3297 3298
– images of women, 17th-20th cs. #121
– photography, 19th-20th cs. #1024
– posters #910
– women artists #95 96
– (1970s) #701
– Eastern Townships (Qué), (1800-1950)
  #1296
– Halifax (NS), (1815-1867) #1217
– Maritimes (1950s) #1119
– Montréal (Qué) #1395
  – (1860-1912), and Art Association of
    Montreal #1343
  – (1940s-1950s) #1426
  – (1940s-1960s) #1438
  – (1968-1969) #1514
  – (1970s) #1489 1505 1548
– Newfoundland
  – 19th c.-1950s #1139
  – (1970s) #1154
– Nova Scotia, 18th-19th cs. #1215 1220 1222
– Ontario (1950s) #1748
– Ontario Society of Artists (1870s-1970s)
  #1678
– Québec #1237 1294 1444
  – 17th c.-1850 #1340
  – (1640-1840) #1329
  – (1759-1914) #1351
  – (1760-1790) #1369
  – (1780-1840) #1375
  – (1825-1850) #1368
  – (1870s) #1307
  – (1930s) #1460
  – (1930s-1970s), and women #1273
  – (1940s-1970s) #1269
  – (1960s) #1487
  – (1970s) #1446 1450
    – and predictions to 2001 #2225
    – and video art #1499 1537 1550
– western Canada (1950s) #1947
society and art, Indians of North America
  #3355
society and art, Inuit #3355 3377 4214 4215
  4232 4235 4245 4251 4254 4261 4262 4263
  4264 4275 4276 4378 4401 4433
  – (1960s) #4399
  – (1970s) #4281
society and art, Northwest Coast Indians
– role of sculptors #3912
Society for Art Publications
– periodical, Artscanada #25
Society for the Preservation of Architectural
  Resources (SPARC) (Calgary, Alta) #8133
Society for the Study of Architecture in
  Canada/Société pour l'étude de
  l'architecture au Canada
– periodical, Selected Papers #7721
Society of American Artists
– and Wyatt Eaton #5357
Society of Applied Arts (Toronto, Ont)
– exhibitions (reviews)
  – (1905) #2242
Society of Artists and Amateurs of Toronto
  (Toronto, Ont) #1706 1729
– exhibitions
  – (1834) #1688
Society of Canadian Artists
– and Visual Arts Ontario #1806

– nationalism and landscape painting, late
  19th c. #271 272
– periodical, Artmagazine #560
Society of Canadian Painter-Etchers and
  Engravers
– (1885-1976) #836
– (1916-1976) #3
– (1946-1947) #809
– and Canadian Society of Graphic Art #801
– and Visual Arts Ontario #1806
– and William Walker Alexander #4506
– as forerunner of Print and Drawing
  Council of Canada #835
– exhibitions
  – (1971) #824
Society of Estonian Artists (Toronto, Ont)
  #118
– (1955-1966) #1761
Society of Manitoba Artists
– (1928-1929), exhibitions #307
Society of Typographic Designers of Canada
– (1956-1964) #923
sociology of art
– Canada
  – (1760-1860) #251
  – and art history #164
– Québec (1970s) #1446 1450
sod
– use in Prairie domestic architecture #8701
  8706
– use in Saskatchewan pioneer houses, late
  19th-early 20th cs. #8696
Soeurs Grises
– see Grey Nuns
sofas, Canadian
– Montréal (Qué), (1800-1850) #2538
– Ontario
  – (1780-1900) #2577
  – (1790s-1857) #2558
– Québec, 18th-19th cs. #2536
Sole, Stelio, Can artist, 1932- #7265
Solomon, Daniel, Can artist, 1945- #1803
  1807
– exhibitions, group
  – (1974) #565
– participant, Symposium on 20th Century
  Canadian Culture (Washington, DC),
  (1977) #621
Somerville, William Lyon, Can architect,
  1886-1965
– Hamilton (Ont), McMaster University
  #9451
– Toronto (Ont), Red Cross Lodge #9027
Sommerer, Karl, Can photographer, 1931-
  #7266
– portfolio of photographs #995
Sonfist, Alan, Amer artist, 1946-
– exhibitions, group
  – (1980) #8237
songs, Iroquois
– Six Nations Reserve (Ont) #3598
songs, Ojibwa #3610
sonic sculpture
– see sound sculpture
Sontheim, Herman, Can metalsmith, fl. 1944
  #2693
Soogwilis, Kwakiutl #3883
Sorel (Qué)
– brick houses, early 19th c. #8521
Sorensen, Chris, Can designer, 1921- #2471
Soucy, Cléophas, Can sculptor, 1879-1950
  #7267
Soucy, Donat, Can sculptor, 1909- #7267
Soucy, Elzéar, Can sculptor, 1876-1970 #1240

2179 7267
- as teacher of Zénon Alary #4505
- woodcarving, Church of Notre-Dame (Montréal, Qué) #8839
Soucy, François, Can sculptor, 1929-
- and Fusion des arts (Montréal, Qué) #1482
- exhibitions (reviews) #7268
Soucy, Jean-Baptiste, Can curator, 1899-
- as director, Musée du Québec (Québec, Qué) #3103
Soulages, Pierre Jean Louis, Fr artist, 1919-
- Mongeau, Jean-Guy, compared with #6596
Soulis, George, Can designer, 1925-
- on furniture design #2468
Soullard, Jean, Can metalworker, 1642-1710 #234 235
Soumande, Jean, Can priest, artist, 1669-1716
- as director, Ecole des arts et métiers de Saint-Joachim (Saint-Joachim, Qué) #2992
sound sculpture
- (1970s) #776
soup tureens
- see tureens
South Africa
- photographs, by Canadian military photographers #1107
South America
- views by French explorers #276
Southam, Harry Stevenson, Can publisher, collector, 1875-1954
- and National Gallery of Canada (Ottawa, Ont) #3050
Southampton Island (NWT)
- art, Aivilik Eskimos #4184
- Inuit culture #4320
Southcott, J. and W., Can architects, fl. 1840s
- St. John's (Nfld), houses #8542
Southwell, George H., Can artist, 1865-1958
- exhibitions, group
  - (1961) #62
- works, British Columbia Parliament Buildings (Victoria, BC) #8967
Sowdon, Michael, Can photographer, 1948-
- exhibitions, group
  - (1979) #1905
  - (1981) #1070
- holograms, Fringe Research Inc. (Toronto, Ont) #1827
- map images #561
space
- in architecture, Canada, 20th c. #7748
- in art
  - Allen, Ralph #4509
  - Borduas, Paul-Emile #4816 4824 4835
  - Breeze, Claude Herbert #4910
  - Harris, Lawren Stewart #5732
  - Inuit art #4184 4185 4244 4341
  - Lemieux, Jean-Paul #6235 6236 6240
  - Québec painting (1950s-1960s) #1441
  - Québec sculpture (1970s) #1631
  - Snow, Michael #7240 7245
Spahnn, Justin, Can silversmith, 1803-1856 #2649
Spalding, Jeffrey John, Can artist, 1951-
- exhibitions
  - (1981) #7269
Spanish Civil War (1936-1939)
- McLaren, Norman, and Evelynn Lambart, film on #6498
Spanish in Canada
- Northwest Coast views (1789-1791) #1998
SPARC
- see Society for the Preservation of Architectural Resources (SPARC)

Speck, Henry, Can artist, 1908-1971 #4121
Speier, Matthew, Can artist, fl. 1973
- videos #2044
Speirs, Doris Huestis Mills, Can artist, 1894-
- correspondence, J.E.H. MacDonald #6371
Spénard, Jean-Jacques, Can ceramicist, 1913- #2179
Spence, David Jerome, Can architect, 1873-1955
- Montréal (Qué), New Princess Theatre #9069
Spence Bay (NWT)
- dye workshop, Judy McGrath #4249 6474
- photographic views
  - Pamela Harris #996
- sculpture #4445 4454
  - whalebone carving #4436
Spencer, Deirdre, Can jeweller, fl. 1975 #2706
Spencer, Elihu, Can photographer, fl. 1859-1869
- exhibitions, group
  - (1970) #1675
Spencer, Hugh, Can designer, fl. 1950s-
- furniture, Opus International Ltd. #2551
Spencer, James Burton, Can artist, 1940-
- exhibitions
  - (1974) #7270
- exhibitions, group
  - (1973) #557
  - (1980) #1221
Spencer, Mary, Can photographer, d. 1938 #2018
Spencer, Sam A., Can artist, 1898- #1881
  - (1975) #1927
Spencer, Stanley, Brit artist, 1891-1959
- influence on Brian Rendel Jones #5974
- influence on Tom La Pierre #6122
Spencer, Stephen Allen, Can photographer, ca. 1829-1911
- and the Victoria Theatre Photographic Gallery (Victoria, BC) #2027
Speyer, Arthur, Ger collector, 1894-1958
- collection, art, Indians of North America #3434 3465 3466 3622
Spickett, Ronald John, Can artist, 1926- #7271
- exhibitions, group
  - (1962) #1847
spinning, Canadian #2747 2748
- 17th-19th cs. #2112
- Cape Breton (NS) #2732
- Chamard, Emélie #2194 2209
- île aux Coudres (Qué) #2168
- Newfoundland and Labrador, 20th c. #2155
- Ontario
  - 19th c. #2726
  - (1784-1867) #2852
- Ontario Handweavers and Spinners (1956-1979) #2743
- Québec (1920s) #2718
- spinning wheels #2483
spinning, Cowichan #3796
spinning, Indians of North America #3413
spires, Canadian
- Québec, ironwork #2702 2705
spiritism
- see spiritualism
spiritualism
- and Lionel LeMoine FitzGerald #5453
Spiteri, Edward J. (Ed), Can photographer, 1939-
- exhibitions, group

- (1972) #1952
- (1978) #1962
- portfolio of photographs #991 1023
Spode and Copeland, ceramic manufacturer (Staffordshire, England)
- and Hudson's Bay Company #2300 2357 2358
Spokane (Wash), Cheney Cowles Memorial Museum
- exhibitions
  - Enns, Evans & Ulrich (1977) #1956
Spokane (Wash), Eastern Washington State Historical Society
- exhibitions
  - An Art Perspective of the Historic Pacific Northwest (1963) #1999
Spoleto (Italy), Palazzo Collicola
- exhibitions
  - La peinture canadienne moderne: 25 années de peinture au Canada-français: 5 festival dei due mondi (1962) #1421
Spooner, James, Can art dealer, artist, fl. 1867-1888
- correspondence, Homer Ransford Watson #7534
spoons, Canadian
- souvenir spoons, Royal Ontario Museum. Shepley collection (Toronto, Ont) #2652
spoons, Haida #3782
spoons, Iroquois
- carved antler spoons #3524
Sporting Magazine, Amer periodical
- illustrations, Peter Rindisbacher #7002
sporting subjects
- see also boats; hunting in art; wrestling
- (Ottawa, Ont), Public Archives of Canada. William H. Coverdale Collection #12
- athletes
  - Danby, Ken #5252
  - McKenzie, Robert Tait #6482 6484 6485 6486
- Canadian art
  - 18th-19th cs. #812
  - 19th c. #257
  - (1970s) #6676
- Canadian folk art #965 966
- Canadian posters #910
- Canadian pottery and greeting cards (1880s) #2360
- John Marshall & Co., pottery, Canadian Sport Series #2306
- Saskatoon (Sask), Mendel Art Gallery #3187
- Toronto (Ont), Metro Toronto Public Library. John Ross Robertson Historical Collection #3131
Sprachman, Mandel, Can architect, 1925-
- Charlottetown (PEI), Confederation Centre, competition #9088 9089
- St. Catharines (Ont), Pen Centre Cinemas #9100
Spreitz, Karl, Can artist, 1927- #2061
Spremo, Boris, Can photographer, 1935-
- portfolio of photographs #995
Spring Park Pottery, ceramic manufacturer (Charlottetown, PEI) #2311
Sproatt, Henry, Can architect, 1866-1934
- and Gothic revival architecture #7724
Sproatt & Rolph, Can architectural firm
- influence on Canadian architecture #7652
- Ottawa (Ont), Parliament Buildings, competition #8924
- T. Eaton Company department stores #9365

– Toronto (Ont)
  – Bishop Strachan School #9386
  – Canada Life #9336
  – Canada Permanent #9177
  – Jenkins Art Galleries #8053
  – Mount Pleasant Cemetery
    – Eaton Mausoleum #8895
    – Senator Cox's Mausoleum #8894
  – Oxford University Press Building #9335
  – Paterson Building #9335
  – Royal York Hotel #9280 9281
  – T. Eaton Company Department Store
    #9368
  – University of Toronto #9449
    – Emmanuel College #9452
    – Hart House #9433 9439 9440 9441
    – Victoria College. Library #9038
– use of stucco and brickwork #8052
Sproul, Wayne, Can photographer, fl. 1970s
– portfolio of photographs #995
Sproule, Robert Auchmaty, Can artist,
  1799-1845
– view of Montréal (Qué) #2370
Squamish Indians
– Xaixwai masks #3864
squares (cities)
– Hamilton (Ont), City Hall and Civic
  Square #8988
– Toronto (Ont), City Hall and Civic Square
  #8981 8983 8989
– Vancouver (BC), Robson Square #8362
Squires, Gerald Leopold, Can artist, 1937-
– exhibitions
  – (1979) #7272
– sculptures #1151
St.
– see also Saint
St. Andrew's Society (Saint John, NB)
– president's chair, John Rogerson #7067
  7068
St. Andrews (NB)
– architecture #7806 8550
– architecture (1920s) #7656
St. Andrews (NB), Sunbury Shores Arts and
  Nature Centre
– exhibitions
  – Colville, Pratt, Forrestall (1974) #1129
  – The Beaverbrook Art Gallery Presents Nine
    New Brunswick Artists/La Galerie d'art
    Beaverbrook présente neuf artistes du
    Nouveau-Brunswick (1973) #1182
  – The Murray and Marguerite Vaughan Inuit
    Print Collection/Collection d'estampes inuit
    (1982) #4498
St. Catharines (Ont)
– art (1970s) #1795
– domestic architecture (1920s) #8645
St. Catharines (Ont), Pen Centre Cinemas
– architecture, Mandel Sprachman #9100
St. Catharines (Ont), Rodman Hall Arts
  Centre
– exhibitions
  – A Governor General Looks at Canada: An
    Exhibition of Watercolours by the Rt. Hon.
    Sir Edmund Head, Bart., K.C.B., F.R.S.,
    and Lady Head (1978) #5760
  – A Survey of Forty-five Years (1977) #6658
  – A Terrible Beauty: The Art of Canada at
    War (1977) #1111
  – André Biéler 50 Years: A Retrospective
    Exhibition 1920-1970 (1971) #4725
  – Beauté tragique: les deux conflits mondiaux
    vus par des artistes canadiens (1977) #1112
  – Canadian Paintings in the University of

Toronto: An Exhibition in Celebration of
  the Sesquicentennial of the University of
  Toronto (1978) #3168
  – Canadian Political Cartoons (1977) #956
  – Centennial Exhibition of Quebec and
    Ontario Contemporary Painters, 1967
    (1967) #484
  – Daniel Fowler (1965) #5489
  – David Milne: 1882-1953 (1967) #6558
  – Dessins inédits d'Ozias Leduc/Ozias Leduc
    the Draughtsman (1979) #6210
  – Douglas Bentham "Enclosures and Opens"
    1975/76 (1977) #4683
  – Five Years of Robert Downing, 1966-1971
    (1972) #5306
  – Goodridge Roberts: Paintings from the
    1950s and 60s (1981) #7048
  – Gordon Rayner Retrospective (1979) #6966
  – Graham Coughtry: Retrospective (1976)
    #5190
  – Harold Town: The First Exhibition of New
    Work, 1969-1973 (1973) #7413
  – Humorist Walter Trier: Selections from the
    Trier-Fodor Foundation Gift (1981) #7428
  – Imprint '76 (1977) #833
  – Ivan Eyre Exposition (1980) #5394
  – Joe Plaskett and His Paris: In Search of
    Time Past (1973) #6893
  – Joe Plaskett et son Paris: à la recherche d'un
    temps passé (1973) #6894
  – John Meredith: Fifteen Years (1975) #6514
  – Lillian Freiman: Paintings and Drawings
    (1978) #5518
  – Lithographs/Lithographies (1971) #825
  – Louis de Niverville (1978) #6709
  – Metamorphosis, Memories, Dreams and
    Reflections: The Work of Florence Vale
    (1980) #7453
  – Métiers d'art Ontario-Québec,
    1979/1980/Quebec-Ontario Crafts,
    1979/1980 (1980) #2138
  – Niagara Now (1972) #1795
  – Ronald: 25 Years (1975) #7073
  – T.R. MacDonald, 1908-1978 (1981) #6380
  – The Drawn Image: Selected Works,
    1959-1979/John Gould (1979) #5637
  – The Figure: A Sensual Response (1975)
    #578
  – The Heritage of Jack Bush: A Tribute (1982)
    #722
  – The Ontario Community Collects: A Survey
    of Canadian Paintings from 1766 to the
    Present (1976) #120
  – The Railway: Patron of the Arts in Canada
    (1976) #3281
  – The Work of Art: Six Artists (1979) #665
  – Trésors d'art populaire québécois/Folk Art
    Treasures of Quebec (1981) #1297
  – Viewpoint: Twenty-nine by Nine; An
    Exhibition of Twenty-nine Works by
    Ontario Artists, Selected by Nine Curators
    (1982) #1838
  – Water Colours by E.May Martin (1980)
    #6424
  – William Perehudoff: Recent Paintings
    (1979) #6837
– Harris, Alfred Peter, as director #5735
St. Clair, Bruce, Can artist, 1945-
– exhibitions, group
  – (1976) #1810
St. Cloud (Minn), St. Cloud State University
– Ringness, Charles, as student #7011
St. David's (Ont), Locust Hall
– architecture #7959

St. John's (Nfld)
– architecture #7787 7790 7793 7794
  – (pre-1900) #7781 7786 7789
– architecture and monuments #7783
– newspaper advertisements of services and
  commodities (1806-1900) #1158
– photographic views
  – Holloway, Elsie #5820
St. John's (Nfld), Anglican Cathedral
– architecture #7783
St. John's (Nfld), Arts and Culture Centre
– architecture #7782
– exhibitions
  – Christopher Pratt (1970) #6910
St. John's (Nfld), Cabot Tower
– architecture #7783
St. John's (Nfld), Caribou Monument #7783
St. John's (Nfld), Carter Monument #7783
St. John's (Nfld), Colonial Building
– architecture #7783
St. John's (Nfld), Commissariat House
– architecture and interior #8538
St. John's (Nfld), Confederation Building
– architecture #7782
– mural, Harold Barwick Goodridge #1140
St. John's (Nfld), Custom House
– architecture #7783
St. John's (Nfld), Ethel Dickinson Memorial
  #7783
St. John's (Nfld), Father Morris Monument
  #7783
St. John's (Nfld), Fighting
  Newfoundlanders' Memorial
– sculpture, Basil Gotto #7783
St. John's (Nfld), Government House
– architecture #7783 8754
– architecture and interior #8751 8752
St. John's (Nfld), Gower Street Methodist
  Church
– architecture #7783
St. John's (Nfld), Masonic Temple
– architecture #7783
St. John's (Nfld), Memorial College
– art education (1940s) #1138
St. John's (Nfld), Memorial University of
  Newfoundland
– architecture #7782
– Extension Service, contribution to
  Newfoundland art (1970s) #1146 1149
  1154
– visual and performing arts (1980s) #1161
St. John's (Nfld), Memorial University of
  Newfoundland. Art Gallery
– exhibitions
  – 28 Women Artists in Newfoundland (1975)
    #1152
  – Albert Franck (1899-1973) in Retrospect: A
    Small Selection from the Artist's Collection
    (1974) #5500
  – Ann Kipling: Recent Landscapes (1980)
    #6057
  – Annie D. Savage: Drawings and
    Watercolours (1975) #7129
  – Canadians: A National Photography Show
    about People/Canadiens: exposition
    nationale de photographie ayant les gens
    comme thème (1978) #1035
  – Carol Fraser Paintings and Drawings:
    1967-1977 (1977) #5507
  – Certain Traditions: Recent British and
    Canadian Art (1979) #653
  – Claude Tousignant (1974) #7401
  – Colville, Pratt, Forrestall (1974) #1129
  – Conceptual Decorative: Prints by Les

Levine, 1965-1970/Conceptuel décoratif: estampes de Les Levine, 1965-1970 (1972) #6265
- *David Blackwood: Paintings, Drawings, Prints (1967)* #4739
- *David Bolduc: Recent Work (1980)* #4775
- *Dennis Burton Retrospective (1977)* #4961
- *Drawings and Pastels c. 1930-1967 by Miller Gore Brittain (1969)* #4917
- *Drawings by Jack Weldon Humphrey: A Travelling Exhibition Organized by the Beaverbrook Art Gallery, Fredericton, New Brunswick, Canada, 1977-1979 (1978)* #5871
- *Esther Warkov (1971)* #7517
- *Felicity Redgrave (1979)* #6967
- *Fernand Leduc (1971)* #6186
- *Folk Images '77: Arch Williams, Leonard Burt, Carl Barbour, Thomas Hudson, Percy Pieroway (1977)* #1156
- *Folk Memory: Three Newfoundland Painters (1976)* #1153
- *Fritz Brandtner 1896-1969: A Retrospective Exhibition (1971)* #4903
- *George Rackus: Anodized Aluminum Works & Prints (1972)* #6953
- *Gerald Squires: Ferryland Downs (1979)* #7272
- *Gift from the Douglas M. Duncan Collection and the Milne-Duncan Bequest/Le Don provenant de la collection Douglas M. Duncan et le legs Milne-Duncan (1971)* #541
- *Gordon Rayner Retrospective (1980)* #6966
- *Graham Coughtry: Retrospective (1976)* #5190
- *Grass Work of Labrador (1979)* #2945
- *Jack Shadbolt (1970)* #7182
- *John Fox: 10 New Paintings (1981)* #5495
- *John Greer: Sculptural Objective, 1968-1981; Everything Always Changes but Something Still Remains (1983)* #5654
- *Kostyniuk: Relief Structures, 1969-1972 (1973)* #6079
- *L'art du paysage au Québec, 1800-1940/Landscape Painting in Québec, 1800-1940 (1978)* #1286
- *Mountain: A Lithograph by James B. Spencer/Montagne: une lithographie de James B. Spencer (1974)* #7270
- *Roger Savage (1980)* #7135
- *Terence Johnson: Forts (1981)* #5969
- *The Fabric of Their Lives: Hooked and Poked Mats of Newfoundland and Labrador/L'étoffe de leur vie: tapis crochetés et poinçonnés de Terre-Neuve et du Labrador (1980)* #2765
- *The Queen Comes to New Brunswick: Paintings and Drawings by Mary Lamb Bobak, (1978)* #4765
- *Traditional Newfoundland Mats: Louise Belbin, Grand Bank, Burin Peninsula (1978)* #2759
- *Videoscape: Newfoundland Edition (1979)* #1157
- *William Blair Bruce (1975)* #4942
- *William Perehudoff: Recent Paintings (1978)* #6837
- exhibitions (reviews)
    - *Studies in Steel (1975)* #1151
St. John's (Nfld), Monroe Monument #7783
St. John's (Nfld), National War Memorial #7783
St. John's (Nfld), Newfoundland Academy of Art
- (1949-1958) #2988
St. John's (Nfld), Newfoundland Museum #3069
- artifacts, Beothuk Indians #3627
- exhibitions
    - *Edward Curtis in the Collection of the Edmonton Art Gallery (1980)* #3480
    - *Newfoundland Photography, 1849-1949 (1980)* #1160
    - *Spirits of Earth and Water: Ancient Dorset Eskimo Culture of Newfoundland and Labrador (1981)* #4380
- exhibitions (reviews)
    - *Spirits of Earth and Water: Ancient Dorset Eskimo Culture of Newfoundland and Labrador (1981)* #4379
- furniture #2484
- project, compilation of services and commodities available in St. John's (Nfld), (1806-1900) #1158
St. John's (Nfld), Peter Pan Monument #7783
St. John's (Nfld), Post Office
- architecture #7783
St. John's (Nfld), Queen's College
- Newfoundland Conference of the Arts (1974) #1146
St. John's (Nfld), Roman Catholic Cathedral
- architecture #7783
St. John's (Nfld), Saint John's Cathedral
- architecture, George Gilbert Scott #8771
- furniture #2586
St. John's (Nfld), Saint Patrick's Church
- architecture #7783
St. John's (Nfld), Saint Teresa's Church
- interior, William Hadd McElcheran #6466
St. John's (Nfld), Saint Thomas's Church
- architecture #7783
St. John's (Nfld), Sergeants' War Memorial
- sculpture, Stewart McGlashen and Son #7783
St. John's (Nfld), St. Michael's Printshop
- and Heidi Oberheide #1159
- and Karl MacKeeman #6389
St. John's (Nlfd), Arts and Culture Centre
- (1967) #1142
St. John's Art Club (St. John's, Nfld) #1138
St. Johns Stone Chinaware Company, ceramic manufacturer (Saint-Jean, Qué) #2288 2299 2302 2321 2327
- introduction of whiteware pottery (1873) #2339
- porcelain bust of Colonel de Charette #2314
St. Lawrence Glass Co., glass manufacturer (Montréal, Qué) #2410
St. Lawrence Island (Alaska)
- prehistoric artifacts #4327
St. Lawrence River (Ont and Qué)
- summer homes, 20th c. #8524
- views
    - 19th c. #282
    - Browne, Joseph Archibald #4939
    - Jackson, A.Y. #5919
    - Smith, William St. Thomas #7236
St. Louis (Mo), City Art Museum
- exhibitions
    - *An Exhibition of Paintings by Contemporary Canadian Artists: Catalogue (1930)* #315
    - *Exhibition of Paintings by Canadian Artists (1918)* #284
St. Louis (Mo), Forest Park Community College
- architecture #9464
St. Louis (Mo), John Deere Plow Company warehouse
- architecture, Oscar A. Eckerman #9247
St. Louis (Mo), St. Louis Purchase
- and Laura Adeline Muntz Lyall #6337
- Wickson, Paul Giovanni, works exhibited #7573
St. Paul (Minn), Science Museum of Minnesota
- exhibitions
    - *Straight Tongue: Minnesota Indian Art from the Bishop Whipple Collections (1980)* #3755
St. Paul (Minn), University of Minnesota
- architecture, John Andrews Architects #8323
St. Stephen (NB), Christ Church
- architecture
    - Butterfield, William; Edward Shuttleworth Medley #8774
    - Medley, Edward Shuttleworth #8776
St. Stephen (NB), St. Stephen High School
- exhibitions
    - *Colville, Pratt, Forrestall (1974)* #1129
St. Thomas (Ont)
- views, Anna Brownell Jameson #5933
St. Thomas (Ont), Art Gallery of St. Thomas-Elgin
- exhibitions
    - *Of Human Bondage (1976)* #611
St-Gelais & Tremblay, Can architectural firm
- Jonquière (Qué), Church of Saint-Raphaël #8765
- Larouche (Qué), Church of Saint-Gérard Magella #8841
St-Germain, Arthème, Can sculptor, 1896-1971 #962
St-James (*dit* Beauvais), René, Can sculptor, 1785-1837 #6947
- Immaculate Conception statue #2683
St-Pierre, Marc, Can artist, 1952-
- exhibitions, group
    - (1977) #1901
stables
- *see also* barns
stables, Canadian
- Montréal (Qué), Youville Stables #7905
- Québec, roofs, 17th-18th cs. #7881
Stacey, Harold, Can silversmith, 1912- #2638 7273 7274
Stackhouse, James C. (Jim), Can artist, 1924-
- on art, Saint John (NB) #1188
stadiums, American
- (1960s) #9101
stadiums, Canadian
- (1960s) #9101
- Montréal (Qué), Olympic Stadium #9127 9128 9130 9139
- Toronto (Ont), Canadian National Exhibition Grandstand #9208
stadiums, French
- Taillibert, Roger #9130
stadiums, Mexican
- (1960s) #9101
Staffordshire ware
- Canada, 19th c. #2339
- for Canadian market
    - 19th c. #2362
    - (1830s-early 20th c.) #2357 2358
    - (1850s-1890s) #2361
- Saint-Jean (Qué), 19th c. #2314
- tiles, Toronto (Ont) houses, 19th c. #2373
- views of Canada, 19th c. #2099 2282

stage setting and scenery
– see scenography
stained glass
– see glass painting
Staley, Bill, Can photographer, fl. 1976
– portfolio of photographs #1023
Stamford (Ont), house
– architecture #7959
Staniszkis, Joanna Kataszyna, Can tapestry artist, 1944-
– exhibitions, group
– (1981) #2776
Stansell, Walter H., Can artist, 1904-
– steam-engine models #1792
Staples, Owen, Can artist, 1866-1949
– on views, Peel County (Ont), William Perkins Bull Collection #3208
Starbuck, Fletcher, Can photographer, 1945-
#538 1007 7275
– and Image Nation #992
– exhibitions (reviews) #7276
state and architecture
– see also law and architecture
– Canada
– (1908), recommendations #2963
– (1950s) #7670
– (1970s) #7728 8975
– Department of Northern Affairs (1950s) #8184
– Department of Public Works
– (1840-1960s) #8976 8977
– (1954-1959) #7681
– domestic architecture (1960s) #8513
– Dominion image in post office buildings, late 19th c. #9054 9055
– office buildings (1970s) #9302
– public housing (1960s) #8518
– schools (1960s) #9395
– conservation
– Canada (1950s) #7755
– Canada (1970s) #7767 7771 8964
– Heritage Canada #7770
– Montréal (Qué) #7914
– Ontario #8906
– Québec #7870 7937
– Victoria (BC) #8149
– destruction of architecture, Montréal (Qué), (1970s) #8601
– Newfoundland #7784
– Ottawa (Ont), National Gallery of Canada, competition (1975-1977) #9126
– Québec, 17th-18th cs. #7858
state and art
– see also law and art
– and Royal Canadian Academy of Arts #275
– British Columbia
– (1970s) #3272
– British Columbia Art Collection #2078
– Canada #129 910
– 20th c. #567
– (1870s) #1693
– (1880s-1890s) #264
– (1940s) #363
– (1944), Brief Concerning the Cultural Aspects of Canadian Reconstruction #3250 3251
– (1950s) #3253
– (1950s-1970s) #3290
– (1951), Royal Commission on National Development in the Arts, Letters and Sciences (Massey Report) #391 398 1401 1405 3254 3255 3256 3257 3261
– (1960s) #443 448 529 3043 3263 3265

– graphic arts #868
– (1960s-1970s) #157
– (1970s) #542 551 571 625 693 897 3157 3267 3268 3269 3270 3273 3274 3275 3278 3282 3285 3286 3287 3292 3293
– (1974), proposal on business support for the arts by 1980 #3271
– (1975), predictions #585
– (1977), Cultural Property Export and Import Act #3283 3284 3296
– (1981), Federal Cultural Policy Review Committee #1068
– conservation #7767
– industrial design #2621 2624
– museums
– (1970s) #3059
– (1980) #683
– women artists (1980) #719
– Canada Council
– (1950s-1960s) #3264
– (1960s) #523
– (1970s) #586
– Art Bank #3276 3277
– Canadian Conference of the Arts
– (1980) #3294 3295
– (1981) #3297 3298
– Frenkel, Vera, on #5522
– Manitoba (1970s) #1899 3193
– municipal governments (1970s) #3288 3289
– Newfoundland
– (1970s) #1146 1154
– (1980s) #1161
– Nova Scotia (1940s) #2145
– Ontario #492
– and Ontario Society of Artists #1679 1728
– French-speaking Ontario (1970s) #1820 1821
– Québec
– 17th-18th cs. #2214
– (1825-1850) #1368
– (1940s) #2190 3252
– (1960s) #1473
– (1961-1975) #3280
– (1970s) #1521 2208 3015
– cultural centres #3088
– Department of Agriculture (1930s) #2165
– ministère des Travaux publics et de l'Approvisionnement #1561
– museums (1970s) #3102
– role of Centrale d'artisanat du Québec #2213 2238
– Saskatchewan Arts Board
– (1848-1960s) #1914
– (1948-1978) #1938
state and art, Indians of North America #6539
state and art, Inuit #4222 4397
– (1977-1980) #4269
– Alaska #4208
Stations of the Cross
– see also calvaries
– Montréal (Qué), Saint Joseph's Oratory #6764
– Plamondon, Antoine-Sébastien #6886
– Plamondon, Marius Gérald #6888
Stechesen, Leslie (Les), Can architect, 1934- #8409
– Leaf Rapids (Man), Town Centre #8974
steel
– use in Canadian architecture #7686 7695
– use in Manitoba architecture #8102
steel engraving
– see engraving

Steele, Lisa, Can artist, 1947-
– exhibitions, group
– (1977) #631
– (1980) #705
– video art #605 630 7277
steeples
– see spires
Steinberg, Saul, Amer artist, 1914-
– influence on Louis de Niverville #6704
Steiner, Michael, Amer sculptor, 1945-
– and Emma Lake Workshops (Emma Lake, Sask) #1929
– influence on Douglas Bentham #4683 4686
Steinhouse, Tobie Thelma, Can artist, 1925- #7278
Stella, Claudine
– see Bouzonnet-Stella, Claudine
Stella, Frank, Amer artist, 1936-
– influence on Graham Metson #6523
Stella, Jacques, Fr artist, 1596-1657
– influence on Antoine-Sébastien Plamondon #6886
Stellarton (NS), Bank of Nova Scotia
– architecture, Sharp & Horner #9174
Steltzer, Ulli, Can photographer, 1923- #2018
Stennett, William, Can silversmith, 1822-1847 #2638
Stent & Laver, Can architectural firm
– Ottawa (Ont), Parliament Buildings. East Block #8922 8930 8936
stereoscopic photography, Canadian
– city views #1058 1061
– Esson, James #5373
– Halifax (NS) #1211
– Toronto (Ont) #1725
Stern, Max, Can art dealer, 1904- #1431
– as owner, Dominion Gallery (Montréal, Qué) #1293
Stevens, Dorothy, Can artist, 1888-1966
– etchings #799 800
– illustrations #916
Stevens, Gerald, Can collector, 1909-1981
– collection, Canadian glass #2397 2398 2399
Stevens & Lee, Can architectural firm
– Montréal (Qué), Royal Victoria Hospital. Ross Pavilion #9017
– Toronto (Ont), Hospital for Sick Children #9015
Stevenson, Orlando John, Can educator, 1869-1950
– and acquisition, Canadian paintings, University of Guelph (Guelph, Ont) #3173
Stevenson, Sylvie, Can artist, 1943-
– exhibitions, group
– (1981) #2084
Stevenson, Thomas H., Can artist, fl. 1841-1858
– as member, Toronto Society of Arts #1689
Stevenson & Dewar, Can architectural firm
– Vancouver (BC), Vancouver Civic Auditorium, competition #9080
Stewart, Betty, Can artist, fl. 1965
– as partner of Paul Arthur and Associates #873
Stewart, Michael, Can designer, 1940- #2487
Stewart, W.N., Can artist, b. 1888
– exhibitions, group
– (1958) #1846
Stewart, William, Can printer, fl. 1870s
– zinc etching #4673
Stidworthy, William F., Can artist, 1889-
– exhibitions
– (1960) #1668
Stiff, Philander S., Can photographer, fl.

1860s-1870s
- exhibitions, group
  - (1970) #1675
Stiff, Thomas P., Can photographer, fl.
  1860s-1870s
- exhibitions, group
  - (1970) #1675
Stijl, de
- and Robert Gray Murray #6668
Still, Clyfford, Amer artist, 1904-1980
- influence on Jean Albert McEwen #6471
Stirling, David, Can architect, 1822-1877
- and William Critchlow #8372
- Halifax (NS) #7838
Stirton, Alexander Mackenzie, Can
  photographer, 1915-
- photographs of World War II #1107
Stitt, Donald Munroe, Can photographer,
  1924-
- photographs of Canadian military forces
  #1107
Stock, Ramsey & Associates, Can
  architectural firm
- Regina (Sask), 38 Saskatchewan Geriatric
  Centre #8516
stock exchanges, Canadian
- Toronto (Ont), Toronto Stock Exchange
  #9161 9187
Stockdale (Ont)
- photographic views, Lizzy Wadsworth
  #7496
Stockholm (Sweden), National Museum
- puffin-beak rattles, Northwest Coast
  Indians #3960
- totem pole, Kwakiutl #3844
Stoddard, S.P., Brit artist in Canada, fl. 1843
- views of Windsor (NS) #1218
Stodthard, J., Brit naval officer, artist in
  Canada, 18th c.
- views, Nootka Sound, Vancouver Island
  (BC) #2002
Stoke-on-Trent (England), Minton Works
  Museum
- Minton dessert service #2289
Stokes, Louis, Can sculptor, 1941-
- exhibitions, group
  - (1977) #784
Stokes, Peter John, Can architect, 1926-
- restoration, The Grange (Toronto, Ont)
  #8680
Stolfa, Lydia, Can weaver, fl. 1961 #2102
stone
- see also masonry
- building and ornamental stones, Canada
  (1910s) #7646 7647
- Coade stone, Montréal (Qué) #7908
- Ottawa region, 19th c. #8033
- quarries, Terrebonne (Qué), (1816-1820s)
  #7907
- use in Canadian Bank of Commerce
  (Montréal, Qué) #9153
- use in Canadian buildings (1867-1967)
  #7695
- use in Forges of Saint-Maurice
  (Trois-Rivières, Qué) #7878
- use in Kingston (Ont) buildings
  (1673-1867) #7989
- use in Manitoba buildings (pre-1900)
  #8102
- use in Ontario buildings (1831-1861) #8009
- use in Ontario houses (1920s) #8646
- use in Québec buildings, 17th-19th cs.
  #7859
- use in Québec houses

- 17th-18th cs. #8621
- 17th-19th cs. #7891 8559
- use in Saint John's Cathedral (St. John's,
  Nfld) #8771
- use in Waterloo County (Ont) buildings,
  19th c. #8011
Stone, Sir John Benjamin, Brit photographer
  in Canada, 1838-1914
- photographs, Flathead and Nez Percé
  Indians #3717
Stone, Sylvia, Can artist, 1927-
- on living in New York (1960s) #460
stoneware
- Ottawa (Ont), Parks Canada collection
  #2364 2365
stoneware, American
- beaver and maple-leaf motifs #2312
- decorations #2309
stoneware, British
- beaver and maple-leaf motifs #2312
stoneware, Canadian #2302
- 17th-19th cs. #2318 2324
- beaver and maple-leaf motifs #2312
- Brantford Pottery (Brantford, Ont) #2295
- decorations #2309
- Lincoln County (Ont), 19th c. #2290
- Toronto (Ont), 19th c. #2310
stonework, Algonquian #3406 3529
- birdstones #3499 3511 3577
stonework, Beothuk
- Port-au-Choix (Nfld) #3611
- Red Indian Lake (Nfld) #3623
stonework, Cayuga #3525
stonework, Huron
- pipes, Royal Ontario Museum (Toronto,
  Ont) #3504
stonework, Indians of North America
- beadwork #3457
- prehistoric #3401
stonework, Inuit
- inukshuks and inunguaks #4199
stonework, Iroquois #3525 3566
- pipes, Royal Ontario Museum (Toronto,
  Ont) #3504
stonework, Micmac #3643
- Clyde River (NS) #3531
stonework, natives of North America #3341
stonework, Neutral
- adornment #3503
stonework, Northwest Coast Indians
- arrows and spearheads #3785
- implements #4068
stonework, Ojibwa
- birdstones #3546
stonework, Penobscot #3537
stonework, Plains
- boulder effigies #3708
stonework, Tagish #4106
stonework, Tlingit #4106
stonework, Tutchone #4106
stonework, Woodlands #3491
Stoney Lake (Ont)
- petroglyphs, Ojibwa #3581
stores
- see also shopping centres
stores, Canadian
- (1940s) #9372
- British Columbia, wooden #8153
- Dawson City (Yukon)
  - Madame Tremblay's Store #9380 9381
  - Winaut's Store #9383
- John B. Parkin Associates #8395
- Montréal (Qué)
  - T. Eaton Company Department Store

#7933
- Montréal (Qué), T. Eaton Company
  Department Store #9370
- Ontario
  - 19th-20th cs. #9379
- T. Eaton Company department stores
  (1920s) #9365
- Toronto (Ont)
  - 19th c.-1930s #8076
  - (1920s) #9364
  - (1930s) #9371
  - Eaton Centre #9382
  - Fairweather's Store #9363
  - Mason & Risch Company Building
    #9328
  - Northway Department Store #9366
  - T. Eaton Company Department Store
    #9368 9369 9370
- Vancouver (BC), from renovation of
  Canadian Pacific Railway station #9546
Storey & Van Egmond, Can architectural
  firm
- Regina (Sask)
  - Legislative Buildings, competition #8956
  - War Memorial Museum, competition
    #9073
Storm, William George, Can architect,
  1826-1892
- Toronto (Ont) #8056 8059 8075
  - University of Toronto. University
    College #9428
Stott, Gregg, Can photographer, fl. 1980
- portfolio of photographs #1032
Stouf, Jean Baptiste, Fr sculptor, 1742-1826
- as teacher of François Baillairgé #4588
Stoughton, Arthur A., Can architect,
  1867-1955
- Winnipeg (Man), University of Manitoba.
  Science Building and Arts Building #9485
stoves, Canadian #2705
- bread ovens, Québec #2233 2234
- ceramic, Québec #2298 2313 2322
- Norfolk County (Ont), Normandale Iron
  Works #2699
- Québec (pre-1867) #2220
- Trois-Rivières (Qué), Forges of
  Saint-Maurice #2698 2708
Straiton, Ken, Can photographer, 1949-
  #2071
Straram, Patrick, Can writer, 1934- #1502
Stratford (Ont)
- art galleries (1960s) #442
Stratford (Ont), Rothmans Art Gallery of
  Stratford
- exhibitions
  - André Biéler 50 Years: A Retrospective
    Exhibition 1920-1970 (1971) #4725
  - Dan Christensen: Recent Paintings (1974)
    #5104
  - Five Years of Robert Downing, 1966-1971
    (1972) #5306
  - Gift from the Douglas M. Duncan
    Collection and the Milne-Duncan
    Bequest/Le Don provenant de la collection
    Douglas M. Duncan et le legs
    Milne-Duncan (1972) #541
  - Watercolour Painters from
    Saskatchewan/Aquarellistes de la
    Saskatchewan (1972) #1920
  - York Wilson Retrospective (1927-1973)
    (1974) #7596
- exhibitions (reviews)
  - Aspects of Realism (1976) #606
Stratford (Ont), Stratford Festival Art

Exhibition
- exhibitions
  - *25 Quebec Painters* (1961) #1419
  - *Painting at Stratford, 1962: Nine Prairie Province Painters* (1962) #1847
  - *Ten Canadians: The Stratford Festival Art Exhibition, 1959* (1959) #438
Stratford (Ont), Stratford Festival Theatre
- architecture #9086
  - Rounthwaite & Fairfield #7679
Stratford (Ont), Stratford Shakespearean Festival
- exhibitions
  - *First Open-air Sculpture Exhibition* (1965) #749
  - *La Deuxième Exposition champêtre de sculptures du festival Shakespearien de Stratford, 1966/Second Open-Air Sculpture Exhibition, Stratford Shakespearean Festival, 1966* (1966) #1587
Stratford (Ont), The Gallery/Stratford
- exhibitions
  - *20th Century Canadian Drawings* (1979) #146
  - *9 Out of 10: A Survey of Contemporary Canadian Art* (1975) #569
  - *A Survey of Forty-five Years* (1977) #6658
  - *A Terrible Beauty: The Art of Canada at War* (1978) #1111
  - *Ann Kipling: Recent Landscapes* (1981) #6057
  - *Beauté tragique: les deux conflits mondiaux vus par des artistes canadiens* (1978) #1112
  - *Coasts, the Sea, and Canadian Art* (1978) #139
  - *Ed Bartram: 10 Years* (1980) #4618
  - *Edward Curtis in the Collection of the Edmonton Art Gallery* (1980) #3480
  - *Eleven London Artists* (1979) #1828
  - *Frederic Marlett Bell-Smith (1846-1923)* (1978) #4668
  - *Humorist Walter Trier: Selections from the Trier-Fodor Foundation Gift* (1981) #7428
  - *John Fox: 10 New Paintings* (1980) #5495
  - *Metamorphosis, Memories, Dreams and Reflections: The Work of Florence Vale* (1980) #7453
  - *Métiers d'art Ontario-Québec, 1979/1980/Quebec-Ontario Crafts, 1979/1980* (1980) #2138
  - *Painters Eleven in Retrospect* (1980) #1785
  - *Roland Brener* (1979) #4912
  - *Sculpture: Limits, Lines, Projections: Recent Works by André Fauteux, Peter Kolisnyk, Louis Stokes, Patrick Thibert* (1977) #784
  - *The Heritage of Jack Bush: A Tribute* (1982) #722
  - *The Ontario Community Collects: A Survey of Canadian Painting from 1766 to the Present* (1976) #120
  - *Viewpoint: Twenty-nine by Nine; An Exhibition of Twenty-nine Works by Ontario Artists, Selected by Nine Curators* (1981) #1838
street art
- Montréal (Qué), *Corridart* (1976) #1522 1530
- Montréal (Qué), *Corridart, Mosaicart, and Artisanage* (1976) #615
streets
- highway imagery, Michael J. Markham #6417
streets, Canadian
- (1960s) #8231

- Halifax (NS), Granville Street #7817
- Ontario, 19th c. #8006 8024
- street names
  - London (Ont) #8007
  - Toronto (Ont) #8070
- Toronto (Ont)
  - 19th c.-1930s #8076
  - late 19th c. #8064
Strickland, Samuel, auteur can, 1804-1867
- on housing construction #8527
string figures, Inuit #4177
structuralism
- and Eli Bornstein #536 4856
- and Joyce Wieland #7580
Structurism #777
- and Ron Kostyniuk #6079
Strutt, James William, Can architect, 1924-
- Ottawa (Ont), Hanlon House #7984
Stryjek, Dmytro, Can artist, 1899-
- exhibitions, group
  - (1975) #1927
- interview #7280
Stuart, Donald A. (Don), Can artist, 1945- #7281
- and Pangnirtung weaving shop (Pangnirtung, NWT) #4308
stucco
- use in Canadian houses (1908) #8638
Studio, The, Brit periodical
- Lamb, Harold Mortimer, as Canadian correspondent #6156
Studio Club (Toronto, Ont)
- exhibitions (reviews) #978
studios, artists'
- *see* artists' studios
Stump, Sarrain, Can artist, 1945-1974 #4136
- cosmological concepts #554
Sturdy, Martha, Can artist, 1943-
- jewellery #2706
Stuttgart (West Germany), Linden Museum
- art, Plains Indians #3737 3750
Stuttgart (West Germany), Museum für Länder-und Völkerkunde
- exhibitions
  - *Indianische Malerei in Nordamerika, 1830-1970: Prärie und Plains, Sudwesten Neue Indianer* (1973) #3451
Style Moderne
- *see* Art Deco
Subarctic natives
- *see* Athapaskan Indians, Inuit
sublime
- and Robert Charles John Bourdeau #4882
- and William Henry Bartlett #4617
- views of Northwest Coast, 18th c. #2009
subways, Canadian
- Montréal (Qué) #1531 9549 9550 9551 9552
  - Angrignon Station #9555
  - Peel Station #9553
- Toronto (Ont) #9547 9548 9554
Sudbury (Ont)
- art (1970s) #1801
Sudbury (Ont), Laurentian University
- architecture #9461
Sudbury (Ont), Laurentian University. Museum and Arts Centre
- exhibitions
  - *Alan C. Collier Retrospective* (1971) #5131
  - *Canadian Paintings in the University of Toronto: An Exhibition in Celebration of the Sesquicentennial of the University of Toronto* (1978) #3168
  - *Goodridge Roberts: Paintings from the 1950s and 60s* (1980) #7048

- *Humorist Walter Trier: Selections from the Trier-Fodor Foundation Gift* (1980) #7428
- *Norart: Annual Juried Exhibition of Northern Ontario Art/Norart: exposition annuelle d'arts du Nord-Ontario* (1979-) #1829
- *The Ontario Community Collects: A Survey of Canadian Painting from 1766 to the Present* (1976) #120
- *The Work of Art: Six Artists* (1979) #665
- *Trésors d'art populaire québécois/Folk Art Treasures of Quebec* (1980) #1297
- *Viewpoint: Twenty-nine by Nine; An Exhibition of Twenty-nine Works by Ontario Artists, Selected by Nine Curators* (1982) #1838
Sugino, Shin, Can photographer, 1946-
- portfolio of photographs #991
Sugluk (Qué)
- graphic arts (1972-1975) #4475
Sukhachev, Ihor, Can artist, fl. 1970s
- frescoes, Church of Saint Nicholas (Toronto, Ont) #1822
Sulcs, Ernie, Can photographer, fl. 1970s-
- portfolio of photographs #991
Sullivan, Francis Conroy, Can architect, 1882-1929 #8410
Sullivan, Françoise, Can artist, 1928- #7282
- exhibitions
  - (1981) #7283
- exhibitions, group
  - (1976) #1529
- *Refus global* #1396
- writings #1449
Sulpicians
- architecture, Montréal (Qué) #7919 7932
- Montréal (Qué), Church of Notre-Dame #8849 8892
Summerside (PEI), Eptek Centre
- exhibitions
  - *Canadians: A National Photography Show about People/Canadiens: exposition nationale de photographie ayant les gens comme thème* (1979) #1035
Summerside (PEI), Green Park
- architecture and interior #8540
Sunderland, Maurice, Can architect, 1926-
- Vancouver (BC), Vancouver Civic Auditorium, competition #9080
sundials, Canadian
- Québec, 17th-18th cs. #2914
super realism
- *see* Photo-realism
Surcouf, Lorraine Joy, Can artist, 1933- #7284
Sures, Jack, Can artist, 1935- #2395
- as teacher of Marilyn Ann Levine #6274
- exhibitions
  - (1976) #7285
- exhibitions, group
  - (1968) #2382
Suria, Tomás de, Sp artist in Canada, 1761-1835
- views, Northwest Coast #1998
Surrealism #454
- and Alan Frank Glass #5614
- and Alex Colville #5144
- and Alfred Pellan #1453 6800 6808 6812 6820 6821 6822 6826
- and Arthur Handy #5702
- and Carol Fraser #5508
- and Esther Warkov #7518
- and Fernand Leduc #1443 6191
- and Gordon Rayner #6964

– and Jack Leonard Shadbolt #7188
– and Jean-Antoine Demers #5283
– and Jean-Philippe Dallaire #5242 5244
– and Jock Macdonald #6379
– and John Howard Gould #5636
– and Kenneth Campbell Lochhead #6313
– and Ladislav Guderna #5663
– and Léon Bellefleur #4660
– and Louis de Niverville #6709
– and Ludwig Zeller #7633
– and Norman McLaren #6497
– and Paul-Emile Borduas #1467 4839 4843
– and Pierre Gendron #5581
– and Robert Gray Murray #6668
– and Roland Giguère #5595 5598
– and Susana Wald #7633
– and Tibor and Peter Kovalik #6081
– British Columbia #2051
– Canada #463 508 509
  – war paintings, World War II #1115
– Canada and USA #1458
– Canadian National Exhibition (Toronto, Ont), (1938) #1
– influence of Kwakiutl Hawk mask #3361
– Montréal (Qué) #1426
  – (1954-1955) #1408
– Québec #1270 1464 1650
  – drawings #1470
Surrey, Philip Henry, Can artist, 1910- #7286 7290
– and genre painting #392
– cityscapes #7287 7288
– exhibitions
  – (1971) #7289
– on Canadian silkscreen prints, World War II #805
Surrey (BC)
– architecture #8147
Surrey (BC), Surrey Art Gallery
– exhibitions
  – An Exhibition of Works in Transparent Media: Sandy Arthur, Garry Cullen, Anna Gustafson, D'Arcy Henderson, Lyse Lemieux, Lynn Vardeman (1978) #2067
  – Creative Flight (1979) #147
  – Joe Fafard: Recent Sculpture (1980) #5401
  – Nora Blanck, Karen Chapnick: A Presentation of Current Work (1978) #663
  – Sculpture of the Inuit: Lorne Balshine Collection/Lou Osipov Collection/Dr. Harry Winrob Collection (1978) #4447
  – Sherry Grauer...So Far... (1980) #5647
  – The Inuit Sea Goddess (1981) #4312
  – The Surrey Art Gallery Permanent Collection (1979) #3201
Surrey (BC), Surrey Arts Centre
– architecture, Hawthorn Mansfield Towers #8373
Surrey (BC), Surrey Memorial Hospital
– architecture, Gardiner, Thornton, Gathe & Associates #9032
Surveyer, Arthur, Can, b. 1878
– and Royal Commission on National Development in the Arts, Letters and Sciences (Massey Report) #3261
Suscan, Charles, Can artist, 1932- #7291
Sussex (NB), Sussex Composite High School
– exhibitions
  – Colville, Pratt, Forrestall (1974) #1129
  – The Beaverbrook Art Gallery Presents Nine New Brunswick Artists/La Galerie d'art Beaverbrook présente neuf artistes du Nouveau-Brunswick (1973) #1182
Sutton, Carol, Can artist, 1945- #711 7292

– exhibitions, group
  – (1981) #722
– on Canadian painting (1970s) #620
Suzor-Coté, Marc-Aurèle de Foy, Can artist, 1869-1937 #10 302 1315 1392 1713 7293 7294 7295 7297 7298 7300 7302
– and, Canadian Art Club #193
– and Albert Henry Robinson #7057
– and Georges-Henri Duquet #5343
– and Royal Canadian Academy of Arts #152
– as teacher of Jean-Paul Lemieux #6228
– as teacher of Rodolphe Duguay #5317
– exhibitions, group
  – (1935) #17
  – (1980) #1296
– exhibitions (reviews) #204 211 1316
– in Paris (France) #7296
– influence of French painting #1244
– influence of Impressionism #227
– landscapes and rural subjects #7299
– Paysage d'hiver, National Gallery of Canada (Ottawa, Ont) #7301
– winter landscapes #285
Suzuki, Aiko, Can artist, 1937-
– exhibitions (reviews) #2771
Svarre, Grace, Can artist, 1936-
– in Mexico #7303
Svatina, Maria, Can artist, 1934-
– exhibitions, group
  – (1978) #2772
Swales, Francis S., Can architect, 1878-1962
– Vancouver (BC), Hotel Vancouver #9272 9273
Swanson, Herbert Andrew, Can architect, 1926-
– Central Mortgage and Housing Corporation competition (1960) #8040
Swarthmore (Penn), Swarthmore College
– Murray, Robert Gray, Garnet #6672
sweaters, Cowichan #3929
sweet grass
– use in Ojibwa basketry #3547
Swensson, Pete, Can photographer, fl. 1960s, d. 1976
– portfolio of photographs #991
Swibold, Susanne, Can artist, 1938- #7304
Swift, Joseph, Can artist, d. 1889
– animal portraits #1727
Swift Current (Sask), National Exhibition Centre
– exhibitions
  – Artisan '78: The First National Travelling Exhibition of Contemporary Canadian Crafts/Artisan '78: première exposition nationale itinérante d'artisanat canadien contemporain (1979) #2134
  – Roger Savage (1980) #7135
  – William Perehudoff: Ten Years, 1970-1980/William Perehudoff: une décennie, 1970-1980 (1983) #6838
Swinton, George, Can artist, art historian, collector, 1917-
– collection, Inuit art #4306
– exhibitions, group
  – (1962) #1847
– interview #7305
– on Winnipeg Art Gallery (Winnipeg, Man) #4449
Sxwaywey Indians
– masks #4033
Sydenham Glass Co., glass manufacturer (Wallaceburg, Ont) #2401
Sydney (Australia), Hooker Tower

– architecture, John Andrews Architects #8323
Sydney (Australia), National Art Gallery of New South Wales
– exhibitions
  – Contemporary Canadian Painters (1957) #423
Sydney (NS), Bank of Nova Scotia
– architecture, Sharp & Horner #9174
Sykes, John, Brit naval officer, artist in Canada, 1773-1858
– views, Nootka Sound, Vancouver Island (BC) #2002
Sylvestre, Micheline de Passillé
– see Passillé-Sylvestre, Micheline de
Syme, James, Can architect, 1832-1881
– Victoria (BC) #8145
Symons, Robert David, Can artist, 1898-1973
– exhibitions, group
  – (1971) #1920
Symons & Rae, Can architectural firm
– Toronto (Ont), Cathedral of Saint Alban the Martyr #8896
– Vancouver (BC), University of British Columbia, competition #9498
symposia
– see conferences
synagogues, Canadian
– (1950s) #8763 8764
– Montréal (Qué), Tifereth Jerusalem Synagogue #8846
– Ontario (1960s) #8903
Syverson, Terrence, Can artist, 1939-
– interview #460
Szabo, Zoltan, Can artist, 1928- #7306
Szaszkiewicz, Cécile, Can artist, 1935- #7307
Szebenyi, Imre, Can sculptor, 1923-
– exhibitions, group
  – (1971), medals #772
Szenes, Arpad, Fr artist, b. 1897
– as teacher of Tobie Thelma Steinhouse #7278
Szilasi, Gabor, Can photographer, 1928-
– documentary photographs #1556
– exhibitions, group
  – (1973) #1002
– exhibitions (reviews) #7308 7309
– portfolio of photographs #997 999

T

T. Eaton Company Limited
– see Eaton, T., Company Limited
tabernacles, Canadian
– Québec
  – 17th-18th cs. #1359
  – 17th-19th cs. #1613
tables, Canadian
– Nova Scotia (1740s-1850s) #2497
– Ontario #2566
  – (1780-1900) #2577
  – (1790s-1857) #2558
  – drop leaf (1815-1845) #2555
– Prince Edward Island #2508 2518
– Québec, 17th-18th cs. #2529 2530 2531
tableware
– see also pitchers; tureens
tableware, American
– beaver and maple-leaf motifs #2312
– glass, 19th-early 20th cs. #2430
tableware, British

– (1760-1840), Susannah Anne Weldon
   Collection, King's College (Windsor, NS)
   #2363
– beaver and maple-leaf motifs #2312
– for Canadian market, 19th c. #2315
– Spode and Copeland pottery #2357 2358
tableware, Canadian
– 17th-19th cs. #2318
– (pre-1867), English Canada #2470
– beaver and maple-leaf motifs #2312
– children's toys, late 19th c.-1930s #2932
– earthenware, Ontario, 19th-early 20th cs.
   #2355
– glass, 19th-early 20th cs. #2430
– pewter, Québec, 17th-19th cs. #2700
– Québec #2237
   – 17th-18th cs. #2161
– silver
   – 17th-18th cs. #2210
   – 17th-19th cs. #2637 2651
– State dinner service of Canada (1898)
   #2333
Taché, Eugène Etienne, Can architect,
   1836-1912
– Québec (Qué), National Assembly #8942
Tachism
– and Claude Tousignant #7401
– and Jean-Paul Riopelle #7020
Tack, Augustus Vincent, Amer artist,
   1870-1949
– murals, Legislative Building (Winnipeg,
   Man) #8948 8949 8952
Taçon, Edna Jeanette, Can artist, 1913-1980
   #7310
Taconis, Kryn, Can photographer, 1918-1979
   #1054
Tagish Indians
– culture #4106
Tagoona, Armand, Can artist, 1926-
– on his art #7311
Tahltan Indians
– culture (1910s) #4074 4093
Tailfeathers, Gerald, Can artist, 1925-1975
   #4125 4136 7312 7313
– exhibitions, group
   – (1961) #62
Taillefer, Robert Eugene, Can photographer,
   ca. 1947-
– portfolio of photographs #991
Taillibert, Roger, Fr architect, 1926-
– Montréal (Qué), Olympic Stadium #9127
– on his architecture #9139
– stadiums #9130
Tait, Norman, Can sculptor, 1941-
– exhibitions
   – (1977) #7314
Tait, Sylvia, Can artist, 1932-
– serigraphs #7315
Takashima, Shizueye Violet, Can artist,
   1928- #7316
Takrik, Bobby, Can sculptor, 1934- #7317
Talirunili, Joe, Can artist, 1906-1976 #7318
Tallin (Estonia), State College of Art
– Lee, Abel, as student #6212
Tampold & Wells, Can architectural firm
– Halifax (NS), Saint Mary's University.
   Student residence #8744
– Toronto (Ont), Tartu College #8744
– Toronto (Ont), University of Toronto.
   Student residence #9467
– Waterloo (Ont), University of Waterloo.
   Student residence #9467
Tanabe, Takao, Can artist, 1926- #7319
– as student of Hans Hofmann #402 1850

– exhibitions
   – (1976) #7320
– exhibitions, group
   – (1958) #431
   – (1959) #1997
– mural paintings #1844
– Prairie landscape drawings #7321
Tanaina Indians
– culture (1930s) #4085
Tanaka, Kazumi, Can photographer, 1948-
– exhibitions, group
   – (1979) #2069
Tanana Indians
– culture #4095
Tanguay, Michel, Can artist, 1937- #1551
Tanguay, Thérèse
– see Brassard, Thérèse Tanguay
Tanobe, Miyuki, Can artist, 1939- #7323 7324
   7325
– urban scenes #7322
tapestry
– see also textiles
tapestry, Canadian
– 20th c. #2774
– (1970s), from artists' designs #2770
– Arbour, Madeleine #4535 4536
– Beauchemin, Micheline #4642 4643 4644
   4645 8233
– Beauregard, Andrée #4653
– Blackburn, Jacques #4737
– Caron, Roger #5005
– Chamard, Emélie #5069
– Clerk, Pierre Jean #5118
– Corriveau, Jeanne d'Arc #5177
– Crowell, Ivan H. #5296
– Dallaire, Jean-Philippe #5244
– Donaldson, Margery Rogers #5296
– Dorsey, Fran #5302
– Gregor, Helen Frances #2776 5656
– Guité, Suzanne #5669
– Hayman, Sasha #5756
– Jaworska, Tamara Hans #5949
– Leduc, Fernand #6188
– Mondou, Pierrette #1282 6595
– Ontario (1970s) #2768
– Owidzka, Jolanta #9108
– Panneton, Louise #6758
– Pellan, Alfred #6804
– Québec (1970s) #2772 2773
– Québec (Qué), 20th c. #2769
– Rousseau-Vermette, Mariette #2776 7085
– Roussil, Robert #7097
– Sherbrooke (Qué), (1970s) #2232
– Simard-Laflamme, Carole #7209
– Staniszkis, Joanna Kataszyna #2776
– Stuart, Don #7281
– Van Ginhoven, Anke #1282
tapestry, Hungarian
– ceinture fléchée, compared with #2865
Tardif-Hébert, Jeannine, Can artist, 1934-
   #1538
Tardy, Henri, Can priest, fl. 1965-
– encouragement of Inuit graphic arts,
   Holman (NWT) #4197 4469
Tascona, Antonio (Tony), Can artist, 1926-
   #7326 7327 7328
– exhibitions, group
   – (1977) #1901
   – (1981) #1907
Tassie, James, Scot sculptor, 1735-1799
– influence on Robert Tait McKenzie #6487
taste (aesthetics)
– (1870s-1970s), influence of Ontario Society
   of Artists #1678

– (1880-1910), public attitudes to Canadian
   art, Montréal (Qué) and Toronto (Ont)
   #214
– (1950s), influence of art institutions,
   western Canada #1947
– Bourassa, Napoléon, on #4864
Tata, Sam, Can photographer, 1911- #7329
– documentary photographs #1556
– portfolio of photographs #997 999
Tatossian, Armand, Can artist, 1948- #7330
   7331
tattooing #2948
– see also body art
– MacLean, Robert #2923
tattooing, Assiniboine
– compared with Cree tattooing #3723
tattooing, Cree #3655 3723
tattooing, Haida #3761
tattooing, Indians of North America #3453
tattooing, Inuit #4209
tattooing, Lillooet #3783
tattooing, natives of North America #3330
tattooing, Ojibwa
– compared with Cree tattooing #3723
tattooing, Plains #3684
tattooing, Saulteaux
– Island Lake (Man) #3549
tattooing, Thompson Indians #3823
Tatty, Robert, Can artist, 1927-
– exhibitions, group
   – (1968) #3350
taverns, American
– 19th c. #9285
taverns, Canadian
– 19th c. #9285
taxation and art
– Canada
   – (1906) #3249
   – (1970s) #682 3286
      – and Canadian Artists' Representation
         #632
   – (1977), Cultural Property Export and
      Import Act #3283 3284 3296
Taylor, Frederick Bourchier, Can artist,
   1906-
– Talking Union #7332
Taylor, George Thomas, Can artist,
   1838-1913 #1186
– exhibitions
   – (1968) #7334
– photographs #7333
– view of Fredericton (NB) #1174
Taylor, James, Can ceramicist, b. 1867
– as founder of Taylor Pottery (Port Hope,
   Ont) #2292
Taylor, Jeremy, Can photographer, 1938-
– portfolio of photographs #987
Taylor, John, Can photographer, 1946-
– portfolio of photographs #991
Taylor, John Benjamin (Jack), Can artist,
   1917-1970 #1164
– exhibitions
   – (1973) #7335
– exhibitions, group
   – (1940) #350
Taylor, Joseph, Can builder, fl. 1890-1891
– Windsor (NS), Shand House #8546
Taylor, Mabel, Can basketmaker, fl. 1976
   #4142
Taylor, Richard, Can artist in USA,
   1902-1970 #7336 7337
Taylor, Sir Andrew Thomas, Can architect,
   1850-1937
– Montréal (Qué), McGill University.

Macdonald Physics Building #9411
Taylor, Thomas Grey (Tom), Can sculptor, 1919- #7338
Taylor Pottery, ceramic manufacturer (Port Hope, Ont) #2292
Tazewell, Samuel Oliver, Can lithographer, fl. 1823-1838 #7339
Tchelitchev, Pavel, Russ-Amer artist, scenographer, 1898-1957
– Markgraf, Waltraud Erna Else, compared with #6416
tea services, British
– Helmcken, John S., presentation silver (1857) #2647
teaching
– see education
Teague, John, Can architect, 1833-1902
– Victoria (BC) #8145 8175
technique
– see media and techniques
technology and architecture
– Canada
   – (1867-1967) #7695
   – (1930s) #7658
   – (1960s) #8280
   – Victorian #7725
technology and art
– Bornstein, Eli, on #4855
– Canada (1940s) #369
– Création #1492
– Fusion des arts (Montréal, Qué) #1482
– Levine, Les, on #6260 6265
– McLuhan, Marshall, on #513
– Québec, 17th-19th cs. #2221
teepees
– see tipis
Teevee, Jamasie, Can artist, 1910- #4460
Teit, James Alexander, Can ethnographer, 1864-1922 #3952
Teitelbaum, Mashel, Can artist, 1921-
– as teacher #7340
Tekakouitha, Catherine
– see Tekakwitha, Kateri
Tekakwitha, Kateri, Can Indian, 1656-1680
– commemorative cross #1569
Telegram, Can newspaper
– cartoons, Richard Taylor #7336
telephone buildings, Canadian
– (1880s-1950s) #9298
– Montréal (Qué), Bell Canada #9310
television
– see also video art
television, American
– graphics (1980) #913
television, Canadian
– (1950s), Royal Commission on National Development in the Arts, Letters and Sciences (Massey Report) #3261
– (1970s) #583 693 3279
– graphics
   – (1950s) #866 869
   – (1950s-1970s) #909
   – (1964-1970) #872
   – (1965-1968) #874
   – (1970s) #899
   – (1980) #913
   – Art Directors' Club of Toronto #854
   – Head, George Bruce #5759
television and art
– Canada (1960s) #867
– General Idea #5583
– MacEachern, Ian #6386
– Robertson, Clive #7053
– W.O.R.K.S. #1955

Temporali, Louis, Can sculptor, 1909-
– and Jacobine Jones, mural sculpture, Bank of Nova Scotia (Toronto, Ont) #5977
Temporali, Pete, Can sculptor, fl. 1951
– and Jacobine Jones, mural sculpture, Bank of Nova Scotia (Toronto, Ont) #5977
terra cotta
– Canada (1809-1930) #7704
– Montréal (Qué), (1880s-1920s) #7750
– Toronto (Ont)
   – Bank of Montreal #9155
   – Standard Bank #9158
– Winnipeg (Man), Birks Building #9355
Terrace (BC), Terrace and District Hospital
– architecture, Thompson, Berwick & Pratt #9032
Tesiorowski, Carol, Can photographer, ca. 1954-
– portfolio of photographs #1032
Tessier (dit Lavigne), Paul, Can builder, 1701-1773 #7844
Tessier (dit Lavigne), Paul, Can builder, 1701-1773 #269 270
Tessler, Ronnie, Can photographer, 1944- #2071
Tester, Wayne, Can photographer, ca. 1928-
– portfolio of photographs #1032
Tête de Boule Indians
– art #4079
– containers #4108
Tétreault, Denyse Gérin
– see Gérin-Tétreault, Denyse
Tétreault, Pierre-Léon, Can artist, 1947- #7341
– as member of Centre communautaire catholique Tour de David (Saint-Basile-le-Grand, Qué) #1510
Tettamanti, James R., Can architect, 1923-
– Vancouver (BC), Royal Trust, renovation #9301
textiles
– see also conservation and restoration, textiles; dyes and dyeing; embroidery; fibrework; lace; linen; needlework; pattern books, textiles; rugs; silk appliqué; spinning; tapestry; weaving; wool
– clothing
   – 17th-19th cs. #2825
   – (1870s) #2878
   – Louisbourg (NS), (1713-1758) #2855
   – Montréal (Qué), 17th c. #2821
textiles, Algonquian
– burial site, Redbank (NB) #3561
textiles, Blackfoot #3654
textiles, Canadian #2089 2725 2739 2747 2748
– 17th-19th cs. #2730 2736
– 20th c. #2142
– (1608-1867) #2120
– (1750-1900) #2727
– (1837-1887) #253
– (1886-1930), Eaton's catalogues #2851
– (1940s) #2601
– (1960s) #2106
– (1964-1967) #2108 2109
– (1980) #2257
– batik (1970s) #2741
– Brown, Annora #4933
– Cape Breton (NS) #2732
– Charlevoix (Qué), 17th-19th cs. #2733
– designs (1940s) #2722
– dyes #2745
– Germanic tradition #2140
– guide for collectors #2104 2125 2131 2252
– Hamilton, Mary Riter, painted fabrics

#5695
– Kamata, Takuro #6000
– Miron, Claire, designs for Dominion Textile Co. (Montréal, Qué) #6571
– Newfoundland #2744
– Nova Scotia #2731
   – 20th c. #1206 1207
– Ontario #2249 2729
   – 19th c. #2723 2726
   – Germanic tradition #2263
– Ottawa (Ont), National Museum of Man. Canadian Centre for Folk Culture Studies #963
– Pednaud, Victoire #2184
– Prince Edward Island, 18th-19th cs. #2734
– Québec #2223
   – 17th-18th cs. #2200 2850
   – 17th-19th cs., European influences #2221
   – 19th-early 20th cs. #2737
   – (1840-1900) #2899
   – (1930s) #2164
   – (1930s), women artisans #2165
   – (1940s) #2188
   – as folk art #1291
– textile patterning, 20th c. #2121
– Toronto (Ont), Ontario College of Art #3009
– weaving techniques #2719 2721
textiles, Great Basin Indians #3986
textiles, Indians of North America #2727 3381 3469 3476
textiles, Inuit
– Spence Bay (NWT) #4249
textiles, Micmac #3643
textiles technique
– see media and techniques, textiles
Thauberger, David Allan, Can artist, 1948- #1937
– exhibitions, group
   – (1976) #1930
theatre
– see also scenography
theatre, Canadian #129
– (1970s) #542 619
– Nova Scotia (1606-1930) #1196
– street theatre (1970s) #555
– Winnipeg (Man), (1960s) #1891
theatre and art
– see also festivals; scenography
– Canada, 20th c. #438
– Pellan, Alfred #6804 6816 6818 6819
– Percival, Robert #6834
– Plaskett, Joe #1991
– Shadbolt, Jack Leonard #1991
– Szaszkiewicz, Cécile #7307
– Toronto (Ont), Canadian National Exhibition (1939) #1
theatres, American
– (1910s-1930s) #9122 9123
theatres, Canadian
– (1910s) #9069
– (1910s-1930s) #9122 9123
– (1920-1966) #9099
– (1930s), recommendations #9077
– (1940s) #9078
– Calgary (Alta), (1910s) #8118
– conversion of public buildings for #9147 9148
– Dawson City (Yukon), Palace Grand Theatre #9090
– Edmonton (Alta)
   – (1906) #9143
   – Citadel Theatre #9140
– Halifax (NS), Neptune Theatre #9097

– Montréal (Qué), St. Denis Theatre #9068
– Niagara-on-the-Lake (Ont), Shaw Festival Theatre #9119 9120
– Ottawa (Ont), Capitol Theatre #9110 9131
– Québec (Qué), Grand Théâtre de Québec #9112
– St. Catharines (Ont), Pen Centre Cinemas #9100
– Toronto (Ont) #9067
  – (1910s) #9066
  – Allen's Bloor Street Theatre #9071
  – Allen's Danforth Theatre #9072
  – Gayety Theatre #9060
  – Loew's Yonge Street Theatre (Elgin and Wintergarden) #9064
  – Pantages and Loew's Uptown Theatres #9075
  – Royal Alexandra Theatre #9059
– Vancouver (BC)
  – Orpheum Theatre #9135 9141
  – Queen Elizabeth Theatre #9085
– Winnipeg (Man) #8105
  – Allen Theatre #9074
Théberge, Claude, Can artist, 1934- #7342 7343
Themarat, Jeanne Aline, Can artist, ca. 1893- #1881
theme parks
– see amusement parks
Thénot, Jean-Paul, Fr artist, 1943-
– museum theme #714
Theo Dimson, Can graphic design firm #886
theosophy
– and Group of Seven #1774
– and Lawren Stewart Harris #5716 5726 5731
Théroux, André, Can artist, 1938-
– television graphics #909
Therrien, Denise, Can artist, 1945-
– exhibitions, group
  – (1979) #676
theses, Canadian
– Allshouse, John Clayton. The Sculpture Arts of the Pacific Northwest Coast Indians #3857
– Astles, Allen Richard. The Evolution and Role of Historic and Architectural Preservation within the North American City #7761
– Barkham, Brian. The Development of Land Settlement and Rural Architecture in the Province of Quebec #7855
– Bebbington, Julia Marie. Porcupine Quillwork of the Central and Northern Plains Indians #3745
– Bédard, Rodrique. Napoléon Bourassa et l'enseignement des arts au XIXe siècle #4875
– Bélisle, Jean. Le mythe récollet: l'ensemble de Montréal #8855
– Bengle, Céline. Evolution picturale de l'oeuvre de Guido Molinari #6582
– Berleur, Paul. Les représentations du diable dans l'art religieux au Canada français des origines jusqu'à 1840 #1357
– Betcherman, Lita-Rose. William von Moll Berczy: His Career as an Artist in Lower Canada, 1805-1812 #4697
– Birkhans, Martin. The Life and Work of Francis C. Sullivan, Architect, 1882-1929 #8410
– Blodgett, Ruth Jean. Multiple Human Images in Eskimo Sculpture #4429
– Blouin-Sioui, Anne-Marie. Iconographie de l'Indien en Nouvelle-France: le Codex Canadiensis de Louis Nicolas #1372

– Bodnar, Diana Lynn. The Prairie Legislative Buildings of Canada #8944
– Braide, Janet Grace Mills. William Brymner (1855-1925): The Artist in Retrospect #4952
– Brosseau, Mathilde. Le pittoresque et le revitalisme architecturaux au Canada et leur application aux gares du Grand Tronc et du Canadien Pacifique #9539
– Brown, Sheila MacKenzie. The Church Bell Tradition in Newfoundland: A Reflection of Culture Change #2717
– Brunette, Michel. Paysage et paysan dans l'oeuvre de Suzor-Côté (Suzor-Côté et Edmond de Nevers) #7299
– Bryers, Joanne E. The Graphic Art of the Baker Lake Eskimos from July 1969 to July 1973 #4481
– Buck, Charles Spurgeon. The Origins and Character of the Early Architecture and Practical Arts of Ontario to 1850 #7965
– Burant, James K.P. The Development of the Visual Arts in Halifax, Nova Scotia from 1815 to 1867 as an Expression of Cultural Awakening #1217
– Buxton, Judith M. Earthworks of Southwestern British Columbia #3955
– Carpentier, Paul. Les croix de chemin: un phénomène de comportement en religion populaire #1637
– Cauchon, Michel. Jean-Baptiste Roy-Audy, peintre québécois du XIXe siècle #7103
– Champagne, Edith. Les vêtements dans les chansons énumératives #2898
– Clerk, Nathalie. La peinture de Borduas de 1941 à 1948: en quoi reste-t-elle encore attachée à la figuration? #4823
– Clermont, Ghislain. Alex Colville: une introduction à l'homme et à l'oeuvre #5146
– Cloutier-Cournoyer, Françoise. Structure de l'espace pictural dans l'oeuvre parisienne de Paul-Emile Borduas (1955-1960) #4824
– Cohen, Sorel. Feminist Art in the '70s #673
– Colton, Alfred Stanley. A Survey of Educational Resources in the Visual Arts in British Columbia #2989
– Croes, Dale Ross. Basketry from the Ozette Village Archaeological Site: A Technological, Functional, and Comparative Study #4017
– Crooker, Mervyn John Arthur. The Influence of French Impressionism on Canadian Painting #227
– Davidson, Margaret. The Group of Seven: A New Approach #1764
– Davis, Ann. An Apprehended Vision: The Philosophy of the Group of Seven #1774
– Day, Gordon H. The Life and Times of Aaron Allan Edson #5363
– Derome, Robert. Delezenne, les orfèvres, l'orfèvrerie (1740-1790) #5277
– Désy, Léopold. Lauréat Vallière sculpteur #7455
– Dinsmore, Cynthia K. An Historical Analysis, Documentary Summary and Teaching Proposal for "Referential Abstraction" in Canadian Painting, 1940-1960 #512
– Dion, Thérèse. Ascension de trois artistes canadiens sur le marché de l'art: Jack Bush, Yves Gaucher, David Rabinowitch #123
– Dorais, Lucie. James Wilson Morrice, peintre canadien (1865-1924): les années de formation #6633
– Douglass, Susan C. Kwakiutl Chilkat Blankets #3973

– Dumouchel, Suzanne Beaudoin. La fondation des arts graphiques #1648
– Dupont, Jean-Claude. Le forgeron et ses traditions #2697
– Dupont, Jean-Claude. Les traditions de l'artisan du fer dans la civilisation traditionnelle au Québec #2707
– Dusseault-Letocha, Louise. Les origines de l'art de l'estampe au Québec #1649
– Emerson, John Norman. The Archaeology of the Ontario Iroquois #3566
– Ennals, Peter M. The Development of Farm Barn Types in Southern Ontario during the Nineteenth Century #9227
– Field, Robin Wayne. The Graphic Images of Eskimo Prints #4478
– Fleming, John. Jack Shadbolt: A Study of a Canadian Painter #7188
– Forrest, Kevin A. The Prints of L.L. FitzGerald #5451
– Forsyth, Leslie Lerena. Images of Canadianism: A History of Currency as an Art Form #759
– Fournier, Jacques-Gilles. L'idée de tradition artistique dans l'historigraphie de l'art canadien (1760-1860): essai d'analyse sociologique #251
– Fraser, Mary. An Architecture of Expediency: Aspects of Horizontal Log Construction in Lanark, Ottawa-Carleton and Renfrew of the Ottawa Valley (1980) #8029
– French, Diana Elizabeth. An Analysis of the Tlingit Gravehouse in South east Alaska and North-west British Columbia #4007
– Galanti-Amiel, Mireille. Arthur Villeneuve: artiste-peintre #7492
– Gascon, France. Analyse formelle d'une tradition artisanale: la courtepointe (1977) #2800
– Glatthaar, Trisha Corliss. Tom Price (c. 1860-1927): The Art and Style of a Haida Artist #6932
– Gould, Jennifer Chambers. The Iconography of the Northwest Coast Raven Rattle #3980
– Gowans, Alan Wilbert. A History of Church Architecture in New France #8825
– Goyer, Michelle. Borduas et l'enseignement artistique, 1923-1943 #4827
– Grigsby, Jefferson Eugene. African and Indian Masks: A Comparative Study of Masks Produced by the Ba Kuba Tribe of the Congo and Masks Produced by the Kwakiutl Indians of the Northwest Pacific Coast of America #3920
– Gubbay, Aline. Three Montreal Monuments: An Expression of Nationalism #1623
– Guilbault, Nicole. Henri Julien illustrateur de légendes #5991
– Halpin, Marjorie, M. The Tsimshian Crest System: A Study Based on Museum Specimens and the Marius Barbeau and William Beynon Field Notes #3981
– Hannibal, Emmett Ronald. Existential Challenges: The Confluence and Expression of Art, Culture, and Education at the Winnipeg Art Gallery, 1975-1977 #3196
– Hardy, Jean-Pierre. L'apprentissage à Québec sous le régime français #2207
– Holdsworth, Deryck William. House and Home in Vancouver: The Emergence of a West Coast Urban Landscape, 1886-1929 #8730
– Hupman, Odessa Lenora. Nova Scotia Lighthouses to 1867 #9522

– Hurlich, Susan Marilyn. *Systems, Culture Change and Eskimo Art* #4245
– Jean, Suzanne. *Aménagement intérieur et fonctions de la maison rurale de l'île d'Orléans entre 1761 et 1767* #8613
– Jones, Joan Megan. *Northwest Coast Indian Basketry: A Stylistic Analysis* #4009
– Kaufmann, Carole Natalie. *Changes in Haida Indian Argillite Carvings, 1820 to 1910* #3958
– Kemp, Samuel James. *Some Relationships Between Style and Tool Form in Kwakiutl and Afikpo Carved Masks* #3945
– King, John D.H. *The Emma Lake Workshops, 1955-1970: A Documented Study of the Artists' Workshop at Emma Lake, Saskatchewan, of the School of Art, University of Saskatchewan, Regina, from 1955 to 1970* #1921
– Kollar, Kathryn L. *John Arthur Fraser (1838-1898)* #5511
– Kutcher, Stanley Paul. *John Wilson Bengough: Artist of Righteousness* #4676
– La Grenade, Monique. *Le costume civil à Louisbourg au XVIIIe siècle* #2868
– Lacroix, Laurier. *La décoration religieuse d'Ozias Leduc à l'évêché de Sherbrooke* #6204
– Laframboise, Yves. *Technologie traditionnelle de la taille de la pierre à Québec (XVIIIe et XIX siècles)* #7891
– Lamarche, Lise. *Armand Vaillancourt et la presse écrite* #7452
– Lambert, Margaret Anne May. *Women's Costume in Northwest North America During the 1890's: With a Time-lag Study of Fashion Diffusion* #2856
– Lamontagne, Laurence. *Méthodologie et présentation muséologique du "geste" dans quelques sculptures d'Alfred Laliberté* #6148
– Lapalme, Pierre. *Mondrian et les plasticiens* #1457
– Laurin, François. *Les gouaches de 1942 de Borduas* #4822
– Le Gris, Françoise. *Borduas et la peinture religieuse* #4820
– Lebel, Bertrand. *Sélection et carrière des artistes plastiques au Québec* #1446
– Leblanc, Pierre. *L'Association des artistes non-figuratifs de Montréal, 1956-1961* #1469
– Leduc, Pierre. *Les origines et le développement de l'Art Association de Montréal* #1343
– Lee, Roger. *The Theories of Hans Hofmann and Their Influence on His West-coast Canadian Students* #1850
– Lefebvre, Germain. *Alfred Pellan: sa vie et son imagerie* #6817
– Lemire, Suzanne. *Analyse formelle des oeuvres de Jacques Hurtubise de 1960 à 1980* #5888
– Léonidoff, Georges-Pierre. *L'architecture domestique de Charlevoix: le contexte évolutif et les granges-étables* #8629
– Lundy, Doris Marion. *The Rock Art of the Northwest Coast* #3999
– MacHardy, Carolyn Wynne. *The West Wind by Tom Thomson, 1877-1917* #7371
– MacKinnon, Joan. *Kingston Cabinetmakers, 1800-1867* #2567
– Malkin, Peter Grundy. *Gordon Smith: A Study of the Artist's Life and Career from 1919-1955* #7230
– Martin, Denis. *Les collections de gravures du Séminaire de Québec: histoire et destins culturels* #3124
– Martin, James Edward. *The Grand Trunk Railway's Bonaventure Station in Montreal* #9538
– Martin, Paul-Louis. *Origine et évolution de la berçante québécoise* #2535
– Martin,Thérèse. *La structure spatiale de l'oeuvre new-yorkaise de Paul-Emile Borduas (1953-1955)* #4835
– Martinsen, Hanna E.H. *The Scandinavian Artists Influence on the Canadian Painters in the Group of Seven* #1788
– Mathews, Zena Pearlstone. *The Relation of Seneca False Face Masks to Seneca and Ontario Archeology* #3636
– McCrea, Rosalie Smith. *James Wilson Morrice and the Canadian Press 1886-1916: His Role in Canadian Art* #6634
– McIntyre, William John. *Chairs and Chairmaking in Upper Canada* #2564
– McKinnon, Sarah M. *Traditional Rural Architecture in Northwest France and Québec 1600-1800* #8614
– McLaren, Carol Sheehan. *Unmasking Frontlet Headdresses: An Iconographic Study of Images in Northern Northwest Coast Ceremonial Headdresses* #4019
– Mendel, David. *Les crucifix du Québec: le sacré et le profane* #1638
– Mills, David B. *The Evolution of Folk House Forms in Trinity Bay, Newfoundland* #8541
– Moogk, Peter Nicholas. *The Craftsmen of New France* #2214
– Munroe, Doris C. *Public Art in Vancouver* #2005
– Murray, Charlotte C. *Rehabilitation of Inner City Buildings for Family Residential Use: Vancouver* #8725
– Needham, Harold G. *The Origins of the Royal Ontario Museum* #3152
– Noppen, Luc. *Le renouveau architectural proposé par Thomas Baillairgé au Québec de 1820 à 1850* #8328
– Pandev, Margaret. *Marchandises sèches 1840-1900: étude sociolinguistique* #2899
– Parent-Vidal, Louise. *L'éducation artistique et l'éducation par l'art, l'Ecole de Montréal 1940-1969: le travail d'Irène Senécal* #2999
– Perreault, Lise. *La Société d'art contemporain, 1939-1948* #1459
– Persson, Diane Iona. *Mask, Myth and Ritual: An Analysis of Interrelationships on the Northwest Coast* #3990
– Petel, Denise. *Le bestiaire dans la cartographie de la Nouvelle-France entre 1542 et 1550* #831
– Peters, Helen. *Sketches from the Colonial Period: Early Artistic Representations of British Columbia and Vancouver Island* #2020
– Potvin, Danielle. *La situation de l'artiste au Bas-Canada, de 1780 à 1840* #1375
– Proulx, Gilles. *Le costume et l'équipement militaires à la forteresse de Louisbourg* #2866
– Richard, Alain. *Espace et matière de l'architecture québécoise ancienne: recherche de l'oeuvre d'art* #7865
– Rosenfeld, Roslyn Margaret. *Miniatures and Silhouettes in Montreal, 1760-1860* #1377
– Saint-Pierre, Marcel. *L'oeuvre écrite et peinte de Roland Giguère ou l'espace du rêve* #5596
– Schiff, Marilyn A. *Guido Molinari: Works on Paper; Part I - The Text; Part II - Catalogue Raisonné* #6593
– Schwartz, Joan Marsha. *Images of Early British Columbia: Landscape Photography, 1858-1888* #2015
– Sens, Karen Linda. *A Discussion of the Stylistic Development in the Dated Oil Paintings of Lionel LeMoine FitzGerald, 1890-1956* #5449
– Shane, Audrey Patricia MacKay. *Shadow and Substance: A Computer Assisted Study of Niska and Gitksan Totem Poles* #4032
– Sibun, Piers Seton. *Ceramics in Quebec: Past, Present, Projected* #2331
– Sommer, Warren Frederick. *Upon Thy Holy Hill: A Historical Geography of the Early Vernacular Church Architecture of the Southern Interior of British Columbia* #8916
– Sparling, Mary Christine. *The British Vision in Nova Scotia, 1749-1848: What Views the Artists Reflected and Reinforced* #1215
– Sproull, Jane. *Towards a Definition of Styles and Patterns in Thule Eskimo Decorative Art* #4372
– St-Arnaud, Micheline. *Les diffuseurs de l'innovation artistique au Québec* #1450
– Steida, Sieglinde. *The Development of a Handbook of Bio-bibliographies of Canadian Artists who Illustrated Children's Books Published between 1815-1975* #934
– Stewart, Susan Jane Hopkins. *The Hudson's Bay Company's Contribution to the Work of Three Important Artists in Their Territory, 1821-1860* #273
– Théberge, Pierre. *La peinture optique et ses sources* #1445
– Thom, William Wylie. *The Fine Arts in Vancouver, 1886-1930: An Historical Survey* #2003
– Thomas, Ann. *The Role of Photography in Canadian Painting, 1860-1900: Relationships between the Photographic Image and a Style of Realism in Painting* #262
– Thomas, Christopher Alexander. *Dominion Architecture: Fuller's Canadian Post Offices, 1881-1896* #9055
– Todd, Patricia Ann. *James D. Duncan (1806-1881): Catalogue of Works and Introduction to His Art* #5336
– Tolmatch, Elaine. *L'esthétique du paysage chez Arthur Lismer* #6306
– Tremblay, Claire. *L'oeuvre profane de Joseph Légaré* #6215
– Tuele, Nicholas Craig. *Sophia Theresa Pemberton: Her Life and Art* #6829
– Tye, Diane. *A Contextual Study of a Newfoundland Folk Artist: Patrick J. Murphy, Bell Island* #6664
– Van Wyk, Dirk W. *Canadian Prairie Landscape Drawings* #1855
– Vastokas, Joan Marie. *Architecture of the Northwest Coast Indians of America* #3939
– Vincelli, Brendan MacLean. *The Symbolic Function of the Bank of Montreal Building on the Place d'Armes, 1846: An Image of the English Mercantile Aristocracy* #9200
– Wade, Catherine Jill. *Red River Architecture 1812-1870* #8097
– Wadland, John Henry. *Ernest Thompson Seton: Man in Nature and the Progressive Era, 1880-1915* #7172
– Walker, Doreen Elizabeth. *The Treatment of Nature in Canadian Art Since the Time of the Group of Seven* #496
– Wallot, Jacques-Albert. *La pédagogie de Borduas et celle de Dumouchel* #3001

– Wight, Darlene. *Watercolour and Landscape in Early Canada* #279
– Wong, Maureen Lansing. *A Study of the Painting of Lawren Harris* #5730
– Woodley, Virginia Anne. *Jack Bush 1909-1977: The Events Which Led to His International Reputation* #4975
– Wylie, Elizabeth. *The Development of Spirituality in the Work of Lionel LeMoine FitzGerald, 1890-1956* #5453

Thibault, René, Can sculptor, ceramicist, 1909- #7344

Thibert, Patrick, Can sculptor, 1943-
– exhibitions, group
 – (1977) #784
– exhibitions (reviews) #7345

Thibert, Ronald, Can sculptor, 1942- #1546
– concept of space #1631
– Symposium international de sculpture environnementale de Chicoutimi (Qué), (1980) #1639

Thom, Ronald James (Ron), Can architect, 1923-
– Niagara-on-the-Lake (Ont), Shaw Festival Theatre #9119 9120
– on his art education #470
– on university architecture #9478
– Peterborough (Ont), Trent University #9470 9473 9474
– Toronto (Ont)
 – M.S. Yolles Associates Offices #9346
 – University of Toronto. Massey College #9460
– Vancouver (BC)
 – domestic architecture (1960s) #8411
 – University of British Columbia. Student Union, competition #9503

Thom Partnership, Can architectural firm #8412
– Toronto (Ont), Pauline McGibbon Cultural Centre, restoration #7776

Thomas, Francis, Can china merchant, fl. 1880s
– Thomas views of Québec #2287 2291 2306 2326

Thomas, George, Can photographer, 1934-
– portfolio of photographs #991

Thomas, Gordon Evan, Can photographer, 1930-
– photographs of Canadian military forces #1107

Thomas, Jacob, Can artist, 1922-
– false face masks #7346

Thomas, Lionel Arthur John, Can artist, 1915- #7347 7348
– and Vancouver (BC) painting (1950s) #1992
– as student of Hans Hofmann #402 1850
– interview #7349

Thomas, Randolph William (Randy), Can photographer, 1948-
– portfolio of photographs #1023

Thomas, Roy, Can artist, 1949- #4157

Thomas, William, Can architect, artist, 1799-1860 #8413
– as member, Toronto Society of Arts #1689
– Toronto (Ont) #8055 8056 8059 8061 8075
 – St. Lawrence Hall #9103

Thomas, William Tutin, Can architect, 1828-1892
– as member, Toronto Society of Arts #1689

Thomas Bell, furniture-making firm (Southampton, Ont) #2463

Thomas De La Rue & Co., publishing firm

(London, England, and Paris, France)
– Christmas greeting cards #842

Thompson, Berwick, Pratt & Partners, Can architectural firm
– and Thom Partnership #8412
– Cloverdale (BC), Dogwood Gardens #8744
– Faro (Yukon), Faro Townsite Recreation Centre #8182
– Ottawa (Ont), National Museum of Man #8041
– Vancouver (BC)
 – Canadian Broadcasting Corporation Regional Broadcasting Centre #8171
 – False Creek #8170
 – IBM Building #9301

Thompson, Berwick & Pratt, Can architectural firm
– Peterborough (Ont), Trent University
 – Champlain College #7694 9465
 – Champlain College and Lady Eaton College #9474
– Terrace (BC), Terrace and District Hospital #9032
– Toronto (Ont), University of Toronto. Massey College #9460
– Vancouver (BC)
 – BC Electric Building #7679
 – Crown Life Insurance headquarters #7683
 – elementary school design award (1970) #9507
 – Orpheum Theatre, restoration #9141
 – University of British Columbia #9500
 – Fine Arts Building #9502
 – gymnasium #7679
 – Thea Koerner House #7683

Thompson, Charles, Can furniture-maker, fl. 1850s-1870s #2511

Thompson, Daniel & Colthurst, Can architectural firm
– Saskatoon (Sask), Saint John's Episcopal Church #8907

Thompson, Richard, Can silversmith, 1809-1890 #2649

Thompson, Stuart, Can photographer, 1881-1960
– exhibitions, group
 – (1976) #2012

Thompson Indians
– architecture #4063
– basketry #3773
– beadwork and embroidery #3808
– culture #3774
– pictographs #3769
– tattooing #3823

Thomson, Harry S., Can photographer, fl. 1970s
– exhibitions, group
 – (1972) #1952

Thomson, Tom, Can artist, 1877-1917 #5 10 24 289 7350 7351 7353 7355 7357 7358 7359 7360 7362 7363 7370
– and Arthur Lismer #6301
– and Canadian identity #327
– and G.Blair Laing, as dealer #1686
– and Group of Seven #1735 1744 1766 1768 1774 1789
– circumstances surrounding his death #7365
– compared with Horatio Walker #215
– correspondence, J.E.H. MacDonald #7356
– exhibitions
 – (1971) #7367 7368
– exhibitions, group

– (1927) #299
– (1969) #3229
– exhibitions (reviews) #283 292 1710
– forgeries #70
 – Toronto (Ont), Ward-Price Galleries (1962) #64
– in Algonquin Park (Ont), (1914-1917) #7364
– influence of French painting #1244
– MacCallum, James Metcalfe, as patron #3237
– nature in art #373
– obituary #7352
– paintings
 – Kleinburg (Ont), McMichael Canadian Collection #1783 3172
 – Owen Sound (Ont), Tom Thomson Memorial Gallery and Museum of Fine Art #3146
 – Vincent Massey collection #3220
– photographs and paintings compared #7366
– reminiscences #7361
– Richard, René-Jean, compared with #6996
– *The Jack Pine*, National Gallery of Canada (Ottawa, Ont) #7369
– *The West Wind* #7354 7371
– views, Georgian Bay (Ont) #1745

Thomson, William James, Can artist, 1858-1927 #7372
– etchings #800

Thorburn, Archibald, Can artist, 1860-1935
– exhibitions
 – (1974) #7373
– Lansdowne, James Fenwick, compared with #6165

Thoreau, Henry David, Amer naturalist and writer, 1817-1862
– Thomson, Tom, compared with #7360

Thorkelsson, Ione, Can glassmaker, 1947- #2440

Thorne, Joseph Bradshaw, Can artist, 1869-1963 #7374

Thornsbury, James, Can ceramicist, 1941-
– exhibitions, group
 – (1975) #1926

Thornton, Mildred Valley Stinson, Can artist, 1896-1967 #7375

Thornton, Peter M., Can architect, 1916-
– Vancouver (BC), University of British Columbia. Student Union, competition #9503

Thousand Islands
– summer homes and resorts, 20th c. #8524

Thresher, Eliza W. Morrison, Can artist, fl. 1821-1830 #1164

Thresher, George Godsell, Can artist, 1779-1859 #1164

Thule
– artifacts #4238 4324 4327 4331 4342 4345 4347 4370 4372 4373 4378
 – compared with Dorset artifacts #4333
 – Cumberland Sound (NWT) #4367
 – Pingerqalik (Foxe Basin, NWT) #4335
 – therapeutic symbolism #3356
– petroglyphs #4344
– pottery #4207

Thunder Bay (Ont)
– decorative arts #2266

Thunder Bay (Ont), National Exhibition Centre
– exhibitions
 – *Canadian Paintings in the University of Toronto: An Exhibition in Celebration of*

the Sesquicentennial of the University of Toronto (1978) #3168
– *Canadians: A National Photography Show about People/Canadiens: exposition nationale de photographie ayant les gens comme thème* (1979) #1035
– *Métiers d'art Ontario-Québec, 1979/1980/Quebec-Ontario Crafts, 1979/1980* (1980) #2138
– *Trésors d'art populaire québécois/Folk Art Treasures of Quebec* (1980) #1297
Thunderbird, Algonquian #3493
Thunderbird, Blackfoot #3676
Thunderbird, Indians of North America #3410
Thunderbird, Kwakiutl #3867
Thunderbird, Northwest Coast Indians #3831 3855
Thunderbird, Ojibwa #3699
Ti-pop #1502
Tiedemann, Herman Otto, Can architect, artist, 1821-1891
– Victoria (BC) #8145
Tiepolo, Giovanni Battista, It artist, 1696-1770
– influence on John Fox #5495
Tiessen, George, Can artist, 1935-
– exhibitions, group
 – (1966) #1123
 – (1967) #821
Tiffany, Louis Comfort, Amer artist, designer, 1848-1933
– stained glass windows, Montréal (Qué) #2462
Tignish (PEI)
– architecture, 19th c. #7801
Tiktak, John, Can artist, 1916-1981 #4407
– exhibitions
 – (1970) #7376
tiles, British
– in Toronto (Ont) houses, 19th c. #2373
Tillenius, Clarence, Can artist, 1913- #7377
Tillmann & Lamb, Can architectural firm
– London (Ont), University of Western Ontario. Student residence #9467
time in art
– Canada (1980) #699
– Goodwin, Betty Roodish #5627
– Inuit art #4244
– Lemieux, Jean-Paul #6235 6236 6240
– Snow, Michael #7245
Time-Life, publishing firm
– as art patron (1970s) #3275
Timmins (Ont), Timmins Museum Centre
– exhibitions
 – *Imprint '76* (1977) #833
Timms, Philip Thomas, Can photographer, 1874-1973
– exhibitions, group
 – (1976) #2012
Tinning, George Campbell, Can artist, 1910-
– on his art #7378
tinsmithing, Canadian
– guide for collectors #2252
– late 18th-19th cs. #2703
– Québec #2711
tinwork
– *see* tinsmithing
tipis, Algonquian #3672
tipis, Blackfoot #3669 3686 3735 3741 3754
– Leiden (Netherlands), Rijksmuseum voor Volkenkunde #3718
– Thunderbird motif #3676
– water monster motif #3757

tipis, Cree #3655 3663 3735 3742
tipis, Plains #3672 3675
– animal motifs #3758
tipis, Sarcee #3735
tipis, Siouan #3672
Title, Robert, Can photographer, 1936- #2071
– portfolio of photographs #991 998
Tlingit Indians
– amulets #4028
– art #3366 3917 3946 3947 3978
 – devilfish motif #4045
 – halibut hook motif #4061
– basketry #3776 3792 3806 3865 3991 4309
– basketry and weaving #4027
– blankets #3826
– carved wooden containers, 19th c. #3985
– culture #3976 4106
 – (1880s) #3763
– face painting #3968
– gravehouse #4007
– headgear #3803 4019
– jade #3331
– killer whale dance batons #3802
– petroglyphs #3786
– potlatch #4012
– rattles #3363 4026
– screens #3916
– sculpture #4041
– sculpture and weaving #3902
– shark helmet, Kaguanton Clan #3833
– totem poles #3781 3856 3873
– totem poles and coppers #3812
– weaving #4018
tobacco, Huron
– pouches #3514
tobacco, Indians of North America #3416
tobacco, Iroquois #3618
tobacco boxes
– *see* tobacco jars and boxes
tobacco jars and boxes, Canadian
– wooden, Ontario, 18th-19th cs. #2588
tobacco pipes
– *see* pipes
Tobey, Mark, Amer artist, 1890-1976
– influence on Emily Carr #5044 5046
– influence on Jack Marlowe Wise #7601
toboggans, Algonquian #3631
toboggans, Iroquois #3631
toboggans, Woodlands #3631
Toby, Russell & Buckwell, Can architectural firm
– Vancouver (BC), West Vancouver Municipal Hall #8990
Todd, Robert Clow, Can artist, 1809-1866 #258 259
Tofin, Frank Peter, Can architect, 1920-
– Vancouver (BC), University of British Columbia. Student Union, competition #9503
toilet articles, British
– Spode and Copeland pottery #2357 2358
Toit, Roger du
– *see* Du Toit, Roger
Tolchinsky & Goodz, Can architectural firm
– Dorval (Qué), Club 230 #7776
Tolgesy, Victor, Can sculptor, 1928-1980 #7380
– interview #7379
Tolmie, Kenneth, Can artist, 1941-
– exhibitions, group
 – (1980) #1221
Tom, Mrs. Mike, Can basketmaker, fl. 1976 #4142
tombs

– *see* sepulchral monuments
Tomczak, Kim, Can artist, 1953-
– exhibitions, group
 – (1980) #687
Tomlinson, Jim, Can photographer, fl. 1979 #2071
Tonnancour, Jacques Godefroy de, Can artist, 1917- #97 1453 1542 1543 7383 7384 7389 7390
– and Ecole des beaux-arts (Montréal, Qué), (1968) #2995
– compared with Louis Archambault #1412
– exhibitions
 – (1966) #7387
– exhibitions, group
 – (1959) #438
 – (1977) #1278 1279
– exhibitions (reviews) #428 7388
– furniture design #2608
– interview #7386
– on art #7381
– on art education #3018
– on Canadian art (1940s) #385
– on his art #7382 7385
– on nationalism in art #4851
– on Paul-Emile Borduas #4798
Tonpass (Alaska)
– totem poles, Tlingit #3856
tools
– *see also* agricultural implements
tools, Canadian
– as folk art #2139
 – Québec #1291
– Norfolk County (Ont), Normandale Iron Works #2699
– Ottawa (Ont), National Museum of Man. Canadian Centre for Folk Culture Studies #963
– potters' tools, 19th c. #2329
– wooden, 18th-19th cs. #2594
Topham, William Thurston, Can artist, 1888-1966
– illustrations #916
Topley, William James, Can photographer, 1845-1930 #1001 1024
– exhibitions, group
 – (1970) #1675
topographical illustration
– 16th-18th cs., views of America #276
– 16th-19th cs., views of Montréal (Qué) #927
– 18th-19th cs.
 – views of America #255 256 260
 – views of Canada #12 26 39 45 51 66 197 224 239 244 246 248 252 266 279 812 828 839 1366 1720 3230
 – views of Charlevoix (Qué) #1280
 – views of Halifax (NS) #1195
 – views of Montréal (Qué) #1325
 – views of New Brunswick #1183
 – views of Newfoundland #1145
 – views of Nova Scotia #1203 1215 1220 1222
 – views of Québec #1334 1335 1349
 – views of the Arctic #278
– 18th c., views of Nootka Sound, Vancouver Island (BC) #2002
– 19th-20th cs., views of Canada #132
– 19th c.
 – views of British Columbia #2004 2006 2020 2023
 – views of Eastern Townships (Qué) #1342
 – views of Niagara Peninsula (Ont) #1718
 – views of Ottawa (Ont) #1716

– views of St. Lawrence River (Ont and Qué) #282
– views of Toronto (Ont) #1717
– (1789-1791), views of Northwest Coast #1998
– Back, George #4580
– Cockburn, James Pattison #5125 5126 5127 5128 5129
– Davies, Thomas #5270 5271 5272
– Finlay, George E. #5439
– Heriot, George #5782 5783 5785 5786 5787 5788 5789
– Hood, Robert #5825
– Lyttleton, Westcott Whitchurch Lewis #6349
– Martin, Henry Byam #6426
– Peachey, James #269 270
– Short, Richard #249 250
– Smith, George Neilson #7221
– Warre, Henry James #7521
– Woolford, John Elliott #258 259
Toppings, Glenn, Can artist, 1930-1972 #7391
– exhibitions
– (1977) #7392
Torbett, Charles W., Can engraver, fl. 1812-1834
– engravings #1198
Toresdahl, David, Can artist, 1939-
– exhibitions, group
– (1981) #2084
Toronto (Ont)
– apartment houses
– (1910s) #8640
– (1920s) #8644
– architecture #8060 8070
– 19th c. #8051 8056 8059 8064 8073 8075
– 19th c.-1920s #7961
– 19th c.-1930s #8076
– 20th c., concept of space #7748
– (1794-1977) #8074
– (1810) #8058
– (1834-1934) #8055
– (1849) #8061
– (1850s) #8050
– (1890-1928), beaux-arts #8069
– (1910s), use of brickwork and stucco #8052
– (1920s) #7656
– (1950s) #7673 8057
– (1960s) #7693 7698
– Baker, Francis Spence #8330
– Chapman, Alfred Hirschfelder #8344
– Howard, John George #8378
– Martin, Arthur N. #6423
– Myers, Barton #8391
– Smith, Eden #8408
– Thomas, William #8413
– walking tours #8065
– art
– 20th c. #145 536 567
– (1847-1848), Toronto Society of Arts #1689
– (1880-1910) #214
– (1890s) #1699 6436
– (1908-1915), Canadian Art Club #193
– (1910s) #1712
– (1940s-1970s) #571
– (1950s) #1750
– (1950s-1970s) #131
– (1960s) #90 441 519 1757
– (1970s) #1804 1809 1818 1823
– (1977-1980) #1815
– (1980s) #1832 1837
– art galleries (1960s) #442

– banks
– (1910s) #9159
– Dominion Banks #9188
– Berczy, William von Moll, as cofounder #4699
– chairs, 19th c. #2575
– domestic architecture
– 19th-20th cs. #8077
– (1791-1882) #8676
– (1908), use of stucco #8638
– (1910s) #8492 8493 8494 8496 8639 8641
– (1920s) #8499
– (1930s) #8647 8737
– Watson, Harold R. #8643
– furniture (1800-1865) #2563
– government houses (pre-1867) #8754
– graphic arts
– (1960s) #1756
– Society of Painter-Etchers and Engravers #3
– installation works #1834
– landscape painting and photography (1860-1890) #271 272
– libraries
– public libraries
– (1920s) #9040
– (1930s) #9041
– university and college libraries (1930s) #9042
– office buildings
– (1910s) #9332
– (1950s-1960s) #9300
– (1960s-1970s) #8337
– architects' offices (1940s) #9297
– painting
– 20th c. #1760
– (1860-1890) #264
– (1870-1970) #97
– (1920s-1950s) #424
– (1930s) #589 592
– (1933-1970) #498
– (1938-1948) #378
– (1940s-1950s) #412
– (1950s) #1749 1752
– (1953-1965) #1772 1773 1775
– (1960s) #507 520 1753
– (1970s) #1803 1807 1831
– photographic views
– (1850-1900) #1061
– Goss, Arthur S. #5633 5634
– Greenhill, Ralph #5651
– Henrickson, Thomas Elton, and Martha Charlotte Henrickson #5781
– photography
– (1839-1867) #1725
– (1880s-1970s) #1683
– (1890s) #977 1702
– (1906) #980
– (1910s) #983
– (1920s) #984
– (1970s) #992 996
– Toronto Camera Club #975
– portraits of civic and elected officials #3178
– pottery, 19th c. #2310
– schools (1960s) #9403
– sculpture
– (1890s) #727
– (1960s) #767
– (1970s) #697 1817
– stained glass windows (1880s-1890s) #2451
– stores (1930s) #9371
– subways #9547
– synagogues (1960s) #8903

– tapestry (1970s) #2768
– tiles in houses, 19th c. #2373
– urban development #8067
– video art #550 605
– views
– 18th c.-1910s #3130 3143
– 19th c. #3204
– (1813-1882), prints #1717
– Brooks, Leonard #4929
– Franck, Albert Jacques #5500 5502
– Harris, Lawren Stewart #5734
– Pflug, Christiane Sybille #6848 6849 6850
– Ward, John #7515
– Winter, William Arthur #7599
– women artists (1970s) #1797
Toronto (Ont), 2nd International Toronto Art Fair
– Burnett, David, on his Toronto/New York exhibition (1981) #1837
Toronto (Ont), A Space #1042
– (1970s) #641 1804
– books #940
– periodical, Only Paper Today #1799
– videos (1981) #721
Toronto (Ont), Academy of Music
– exhibitions, Ontario Society of Artists, early 20th c. #1666
Toronto (Ont), Albert White Gallery
– exhibitions
– Legends (1967) #4633
Toronto (Ont), Allen's Bloor Street Theatre
– architecture, Hynes, Feldman & Watson #9071
Toronto (Ont), Allen's Danforth Theatre
– architecture, Hynes, Feldman & Watson #9072
Toronto (Ont), Allen Theatre
– architecture, C.Howard Crane; Hynes, Feldman & Watson, Associate Architects #9069
Toronto (Ont), Anglican rectory, Ward's Island
– mural, William Ronald #7070
Toronto (Ont), Archives of Ontario
– Donovan, Duncan, photographs #5298
– Horwood, John Charles Batstone, and Eric Crompton, Collection of Architectural Drawings #8028 8030
– Simcoe, Elizabeth Posthuma Gwillim, sketchbooks #7212
Toronto (Ont), Art Galleries, 165 King Street West
– exhibitions
– Applied Art Exhibition: Catalogue 1900, Held in the Art Galleries, 165 King Street West, Toronto (1900) #2240
Toronto (Ont), Art Gallery at Harbourfront
– (1976-1977) #3166
– exhibitions
– Felicity Redgrave (1978) #6967
– Open Studio: Ten Years (1980) #1833
– Viewpoint: Twenty-nine by Nine; An Exhibition of Twenty-nine Works by Ontario Artists, Selected by Nine Curators (1981) #1838
– exhibitions (reviews)
– fibrework (1978) #2771
– Open Space: Ten Years (1980) #1830
– stained glass (1970s) #2455
Toronto (Ont), Art Gallery of Ontario #3154 3177
– see also Toronto (Ont), Art Gallery of Toronto; Toronto (Ont), Art Museum of Toronto; Toronto (Ont), The Grange

- (1906-1966), exhibitions #3175
- (1973), annual meeting #3157
- and Ontario Society of Artists #1679
- and Sir Byron Edmund Walker #3206
- architecture #8680
  - Parkin Partnership #9121
- art education (1970s) #3004
- audio-visual collection, subject index #159
- Canadian art #3149
- Canadian wing #3163 3167 3171
- collection #3158
- Duncan, Douglas M., collection #119
- exhibitions
  - ...It's Still Privileged Art (1976) #602
  - 10 Canadian Artists in the 1970s (1980) #703
  - 100 Years: Evolution of the Ontario College of Art (1976) #3011
  - A.J. Casson (1978) #5060
  - A Canadian Survey: Selected Works from the Collection of Imperial Oil Limited/Tour d'horizon canadien: oeuvres choisies de la collection de la Compagnie Pétrolière Impériale Ltée (1978) #3241
  - A Tribute to Albert Franck (1973) #5501
  - Antoine Plamondon, 1802-1895; Théophile Hamel, 1817-1870: Two Painters of Quebec/Antoine Plamondon, 1802-1895; Théophile Hamel, 1817-1870: deux peintres du Québec (1970) #1348
  - Art and Engineering (1965) #471
  - Autobiography: Film/Video/Photography (1978) #664
  - Canadian Artists 68/Artistes canadiens 68 (1968) #521
  - Canadian Cartoon and Caricature (1969) #946
  - Canadian Painting in the Thirties (1975) #592
  - Canadian Paintings in the University of Toronto: An Exhibition in Celebration of the Sesquicentennial of the University of Toronto (1977) #3168
  - Canadian Political Cartoons (1977) #956
  - Canadian Society of Painters in Water Colour (1975) #6
  - Canadian Tapestries, 1977 (1977) #2770
  - Canadians in Paris, 1867-1914: An Educational Exhibition Using the Gallery's Collection and Long Term Loans (1979) #274
  - Carl Schaefer in Hanover (1981) #7157
  - Changing Visions: The Canadian Landscape/Aperçus divers: le paysage canadien (1976) #617
  - Charles Gagnon (1979) #5540
  - Daniel Fowler of Amherst Island, 1810-1894 (1979) #5491
  - Dennis Burton Retrospective (1978) #4961
  - Dessins inédits d'Ozias Leduc/Ozias Leduc the Draughtsman (1979) #6210
  - Drawings by Jack Weldon Humphrey: A Travelling Exhibition Organized by the Beaverbrook Art Gallery, Fredericton, New Brunswick, Canada, 1977-1979 (1979) #5871
  - E.Haanel Cassidy: Photographs, 1933-1945 (1981) #5054
  - F.H. Varley: A Centennial Exhibition/F.H. Varley: une exposition centenaire (1982) #7468
  - F.H. Varley: Paintings, 1915-1954 (1954) #7463
  - Fifty Years: The Canadian Society of

  - Painters in Water Colour, 1925-1975 (1975) #127
  - From Ocean to Ocean: Nineteenth Century Water Colour Painting in Canada (1978) #266
  - Garry Neill Kennedy: Recent Work (1978) #6043
  - Gerald Ferguson: Paintings (1977) #5420
  - Goodridge Roberts: Paintings from the 1950s and 60s (1980) #7048
  - Gordon Rayner Retrospective (1980) #6966
  - Greg Curnoe: rétrospective/Greg Curnoe: Retrospective (1982) #5231
  - Guido Molinari (1976) #6588
  - Humorist Walter Trier: Selections from the Trier-Fodor Foundation Gift (1980) #7428
  - Impressionism in Canada, 1895-1935 (1974) #115
  - Imprint '76 (1976) #833
  - In Video (1978) #631
  - J.W. Beatty, 1869-1941 (1981) #4638
  - Jack Bush: A Retrospective/Rétrospective: Jack Bush (1976) #4969
  - Jock Macdonald: The Inner Landscape: A Retrospective Exhibition/Jock Macdonald: le paysage intérieur: rétrospective (1981) #6379
  - John Meredith: Fifteen Years (1974) #6514
  - Joseph Légaré, 1795-1855: l'oeuvre (1978) #6217
  - L'art de Tom Thomson (1971) #7367
  - Lawren S. Harris: Urban Scenes and Wilderness Landscapes, 1906-1930 (1978) #5734
  - Les Laurentides: peintres et paysage (1977) #1279
  - Louis Comtois: Paintings, 1974-1979 (1980) #5164
  - Louis de Niverville (1979) #6709
  - Metamorphosis, Memories, Dreams and Reflections: The Work of Florence Vale (1980) #7453
  - Michael Snow: A Survey (1970) #7243
  - Nightlife: Photographs by Michael Mitchell (1978) #6575
  - Ontario Centennial Art Exhibition/L'exposition d'art de l'Ontario à l'occasion du Centenaire (1967) #492
  - Ontario Society of Artists: 100 Years (1972) #1678
  - Peinture canadienne des années trente (1975) #589
  - Perspective '67 (1967) #493
  - Pertaining to Space: An Exhibition of Works by Robert Sinclair (1976) #7216
  - Peter Kolisnyk (1977) #6075
  - Realism(e)s (1970) #1481
  - Robert Bourdeau & Philip Pocock (1981) #1069
  - Ron Martin: World Paintings (1976) #6434
  - Spring Hurlbut, Ron Martin, John Massey, Becky Singleton (1981) #723
  - Structures for Behaviour: New Sculptures by Robert Morris, David Rabinowitch, Richard Serra and George Trakas (1978) #790
  - Trakas, George, on #7420
  - The Art and Pictorial Press in Canada (1979) #3313
  - The Art of Tom Thomson (1971) #7368
  - The Canadian Canvas: A Travelling Exhibition of 85 Recent Paintings/Peintres canadiens actuels: exposition itinérante de 85 oeuvres récentes (1975) #588

  - The Image of Man in Canadian Painting: 1878-1978/L'image de l'homme dans la peinture canadienne: 1878-1978 (1978) #135
  - The J.S. McLean Collection of Canadian Painting (1968) #3228
  - The Laurentians: Painters in a Landscape (1977) #1278
  - The Ontario Community Collects: A Survey of Canadian Painting from 1766 to the Present (1975) #120
  - The People Within/Les Gens de l'intérieur (1976) #4266
  - The Work of Art: Six Artists (1978) #665
  - The Works of Joseph Légaré: 1795-1855 (1978) #6218
  - Tim Zuck: Paintings (1980) #7636
  - Toronto Painting: 1953-1965/La Peinture torontoise 1953-1965 (1972) #1772
  - Trésors d'art populaire québécois/Folk Art Treasures of Quebec (1980) #1297
  - Videoscape: An Exhibition of Video Art (1974) #575
  - Yves Gaucher: A Fifteen-Year Perspective, 1963-1978/Yves Gaucher: une perspective de quinze ans, 1963-1978 (1979) #5570
- exhibitions (reviews)
  - 100 Years: Evolution of the Ontario College of Art (1976) #3009
  - A Reconstruction of the First Exhibition of the Group of Seven (1970) #1767
  - colour xerography show (1976) #614
  - Exposure: Canadian Contemporary Photographers/Exposure: photographes canadiens contemporains (1975) #1012 1022
  - Garry Neill Kennedy: Recent Work (1978) #6044 6045
  - Jack Bush: A Retrospective/Rétrospective: Jack Bush (1976) #4968
  - John Meredith: Fifteen Years (1974) #6515
  - Michael Snow: A Survey (1970) #7245
  - Nightlife: Photographs by Michael Mitchell (1978) #6576
  - The Canadian Canvas: A Travelling Exhibition of 85 Recent Paintings/Peintres canadiens actuels: exposition itinérante de 85 oeuvres récentes (1975) #582
  - Videoscape: An Exhibition of Video Art (1974) #580
  - Winsor, Jackie #7597
  - Yves Gaucher: A Fifteen-Year Perspective, 1963-1978/Yves Gaucher: une perspective quinze ans, 1963-1978 (1979) #5568 5569
- Massey, John, installation work #6439
- Peel, Paul, After the Bath #6794
- photography collection #1051
- The Grange, restoration #8665 8666
Toronto (Ont), Art Gallery of Ontario. Henry Moore Centre
- architecture, Parkin Partnership #8078
Toronto (Ont), Art Gallery of Toronto
- see also Toronto (Ont), Art Gallery of Ontario; Toronto (Ont), Art Museum of Toronto; Toronto (Ont), The Grange
- (1906-1950) #3136
- (1919-1966), exhibitions #3175
- (1920s) #3132
- (1928-1929), exhibitions #307
- and Arthur Lismer #2975 2981 6295 6303
- architecture, Darling & Pearson #9076
- art education (1918-1980) #3020
- Canadian prints #799
- exhibitions

– *A.Y. Jackson: Paintings, 1902-1953* (1953) #5914
– Jackson, A.Y., on #5917
– *Alfred Pellan* (1960) #6807
– *Arthur Lismer: Paintings, 1913-1949* (1950) #6298
– Canadian Group of Painters (1933-1968) #324
– Canadian National Exhibition (1955-1961) #1
– Canadian Society of Graphic Art (1924-1963) #801
– Canadian Society of Painters in Water Colour (1926-1958) #6
– *Catalogue of an Exhibition of the Canadian War Memorials* (1926) #1084
– *Catalogue of Toronto Centennial Historical Exhibition; Paintings by Cornelius Krieghoff; Loan Collection of XVI and XVII Century Paintings; Flower Miniatures by Lorna Burgoyne* (1934) #213
– *Emily Carr: Her Paintings and Sketches* (1945) #5012
– *Exhibition of Architecture and the Allied Arts* (1927-1939) #8224
– *Exhibition of Canadian West Coast Art* (1928) #3827
– *Exhibition of Contemporary Canadian Arts* (1950) #388
– *Fifty Years of Painting in Canada* (1949) #42
– Group of Seven (1920-1922, 1925-1926, 1928, 1930-1931) #1732
– *J.E.H. MacDonald, R.C.A., 1873-1932* (1965) #6370
– *Jean-Paul Riopelle: Paintings and Sculpture/Jean-Paul Riopelle: peinture et sculpture* (1962) #7018
– *L.L. FitzGerald, 1890-1956: A Memorial Exhibition 1958* (1958) #5448
– *Lawren Harris: Paintings 1910-1948* (1948) #5720
– *Maurice Cullen, 1866-1934* (1956) #5221
– *Memorial Exhibition of Paintings by Mary Hiester Reid, A.R.C.A., O.S.A.* (1922) #6982
– Ontario Society of Artists (1918-) #1666
– *Paul-Emile Borduas 1905-1960* (1962) #4809
– *Prudence Heward, 1896-1947: Memorial Exhibition* (1948) #5795
– Society of Painter-Etchers and Engravers (1919-1932) #3
– *The Development of Painting in Canada, 1665-1945/Le développement de la peinture au Canada, 1665-1945* (1945) #34
– Toronto Camera Club, *Annual Spring Salon* (1926-1937) #975
– *Watercolours by Robert Holmes, 1861-1930, in the Collection of the Art Gallery of Toronto* (1964) #5823
– exhibitions (reviews)
– *A.Y. Jackson: Paintings, 1902-1953* (1953) #5915
– *Architectural and Allied Arts Exhibition* (1927) #8223
– *Arthur Lismer: Paintings, 1913-1949* (1950) #6296 6297
– Canadian Group of Painters
– (1936) #331
– (1942) #356
– (1944) #365
– *Exhibition of Architecture and the Allied Arts*
– (1927) #7960 8223

– (1929) #7964
– (1931) #7967
– (1933) #7969
– (1935) #7971 7972
– (1937) #7973
– *Exhibition of Contemporary Canadian Arts* (1950) #387
– Group of Seven (1926) #1734
– *International Exhibition of Modern Art Assembled by the Société Anonyme* (1927) #5714
– *Lawren Harris: Paintings 1910-1948* (1948) #5718
– Macpherson, Duncan Ian #6400
– Royal Canadian Academy of Arts
– (1927) #296
– (1928) #310
– (1930) #318
– (1934) #326
– (1936) #329
– (1947) #3304
– Sculptors' Society of Canada (1944) #736
– Women's Committee annual sales (1950s) #3260
Toronto (Ont), Art Metropole Galleries
– exhibitions
– *Sydney Strickland Tully, A.R.C.A.: Memorial Exhibition of Paintings and Drawings* (1911) #7438
Toronto (Ont), Art Museum of Toronto
– see also Toronto (Ont), Art Gallery of Ontario; Toronto (Ont), Art Gallery of Toronto; Toronto (Ont), The Grange
– (1906-1919), exhibitions #3175
– architecture, Darling & Pearson #9070
– exhibitions
– Ontario Society of Artists #1666
– exhibitions (reviews)
– Ontario Society of Artists (1919) #1731
Toronto (Ont), Ashley & Crippen Building
– architecture, Baldwin & Greene #9367
Toronto (Ont), B'nai Israel Beth David Synagogue
– architecture, Irving Grossman #8903
Toronto (Ont), Baldwin Street Gallery of Photography #1794
– exhibitions
– *Canadians: A National Photography Show about People/Canadiens: exposition nationale de photographie ayant les gens comme thème* (1979) #1035
– exhibitions (reviews)
– Szilasi, Gabor #7308
Toronto (Ont), Bank of British North America
– architecture, Ellis & Connery #9150
Toronto (Ont), Bank of Montreal (1910)
– architecture, Darling & Pearson #9155
Toronto (Ont), Bank of Montreal (1949)
– architecture, Chapman, Oxley & Facey and Marani & Morris, Architects; K.R. Blatherwick, Associate Architect #9190
Toronto (Ont), Bank of Montreal Tower
– Jaworska, Tamara Hans, *Quartet Moderne* #5949
Toronto (Ont), Bank of Nova Scotia (1922)
– architecture, Sharp & Horner #9174
Toronto (Ont), Bank of Nova Scotia (1951)
– architecture, Mathers & Haldenby, Architects; Beck & Eadie, Associate Architects #9192
– mural sculpture, Jacobine Jones #5977
Toronto (Ont), Bank of Nova Scotia (1958)
– architecture, Arthur Hunter Eadie #9193

Toronto (Ont), Bank of Ottawa
– architecture, John MacIntosh Lyle #9159
Toronto (Ont), Bank of Toronto (1908)
– architecture, Edward James Lennox #9151
Toronto (Ont), Bank of Toronto (1913)
– architecture, Carrere & Hastings; Eustace Godfrey Bird #8293 9162 9185
Toronto (Ont), Barton Myers's House
– architecture, Diamond & Myers #8071
Toronto (Ont), Basilican Seminary
– Gilson, Jacqueline Marie-Charlotte, *Chemin de la Croix* #5606
Toronto (Ont), Bau-Xi Gallery
– exhibitions (reviews)
– Hopkins, Elisabeth Margaret #5830
– Jarvis, Don #2074
– Kipling, Ann #6056
Toronto (Ont), Beaver Theatre
– architecture, Neil & Beggs #9066
Toronto (Ont), Bedford Glen housing
– architecture, Ernest Annau and Paul Northgrave #8078
Toronto (Ont), Bedford Theatre
– architecture, Murray Brown #8338
Toronto (Ont), Belsize Theatre
– architecture, Murray Brown #8338
Toronto (Ont), Big Nickel Theatre
– architecture, John Wilson Siddall #9066
Toronto (Ont), Bishop Strachan School
– architecture, Sproatt & Rolph #9386
Toronto (Ont), Blair Laing Gallery
– Town, Harold, works exhibited (1961) #445 446
Toronto (Ont), Bowles Lunch Room
– architecture, Hand, Harris & Merritt #9269
Toronto (Ont), Bruce House
– architecture, Armstrong & Molesworth #8746
Toronto (Ont), Canada Life
– architecture, Sproatt & Rolph #9336
Toronto (Ont), Canada Permanent
– architecture, F. Hilton Wilkes; Sproatt & Rolph, Consulting Architects #9177
Toronto (Ont), Canadian Art Club. Gallery
– exhibitions
– *Catalogue of the Morris Collection of Indian Portraits at the Gallery of the Canadian Art Club* (1909) #6637
Toronto (Ont), Canadian Bank of Commerce
– architecture
– Darling & Pearson, Architects; York & Sawyer, Consulting Architects #9178
– Darling & Pearson; restoration, Page & Steele #9351
Toronto (Ont), Canadian Bank of Commerce (1930)
– architecture, Darling & Pearson #9189
Toronto (Ont), Canadian Bank of Commerce (1931)
– architecture, V.D. Horsburgh #9181
– interior, bronze metalwork #9180
Toronto (Ont), Canadian Education Showplace
– exhibition (1965) #9398
Toronto (Ont), Canadian National Exhibition
– and Graphic Arts Club of Toronto (1913) #1711
– architecture, George Wallace Gouinlock #9206
– exhibitions
– (1904-1961) #1
– (1905-1938), non-Canadian art #107
– (1909-1923), Canadian Society of Graphic Art #801

– (1918-1939), Toronto Camera Club #975
– (1928-1929) #307
– (1932-1967), Canadian Guild of Crafts #2118
– *A Terrible Beauty: The Art of Canada at War* (1978) #1111
– *Beauté tragique: les deux conflits mondiaux vus par des artistes canadiens* (1978) #1112
– *Contemporary Art of Canada and Newfoundland: Collection of the International Business Machines Corporation* (1940) #350
– exhibitions (reviews)
  – (1913) #201
  – (1919), Canadian War Memorials Collection #1077
  – (1921), Toronto Camera Club #984
  – (1927) #295
  – (1928) #300
  – (1929) #304
  – (1930) #313
  – (1931) #316
  – (1932) #320 321
Toronto (Ont), Canadian National Exhibition. Automotive Building
– architecture, Douglas Edwin Kertland #9207
Toronto (Ont), Canadian National Exhibition. Grandstand
– architecture, Marani & Morris #9208
Toronto (Ont), Canadian Pacific Railway Building
– architecture, Darling & Pearson #9329
Toronto (Ont), Carmen Lamanna Gallery
– exhibitions
  – *General Idea's Reconstructing Futures/General Idea: reconstruction de l'avenir* (1977) #5583
– exhibitions (reviews)
  – Janitch, Mary #5935
– Lamanna, Carmen, on #1811
– support of Canadian artists (1970s) #628
Toronto (Ont), Carroll Fine Art Gallery
– exhibitions (reviews)
  – Broomfield, Adolphus George #4932
Toronto (Ont), Casa Loma
– architecture #8649
– exhibitions
  – *Three Centuries of Canadian History in Picture and Story, 1630-1930: Catalogue of the Walter H. Millen Collection of Canadiana* (1938) #21
Toronto (Ont), Cathedral of Saint Alban the Martyr
– architecture, Symons & Rae #8896
Toronto (Ont), Cemetery Chapel of Saint James the Less
– architecture, Frederic William Cumberland #8905
Toronto (Ont), Centennial Centre of Science & Technology
– see Toronto (Ont), Ontario Science Centre
Toronto (Ont), Central Ontario School of Art and Industrial Design
– (1890s) #188
– (1907) #3299
Toronto (Ont), Central Technical School
– architecture, Ross & Macdonald #9434
Toronto (Ont), Central Technical School Art Centre
– architecture, Robert Fairfield Associates; Macy DuBois, project associate #7684
Toronto (Ont), Centre for Experimental Art and Communication

– exhibitions
  – *Véhicule's Véhicule* (1976) #1529
Toronto (Ont), Chapman & Walker Building
– architecture, Chadwick & Beckett #9332
Toronto (Ont), Chewett Block
– architecture, James Grant Chewett #258 259
Toronto (Ont), Chief Justice Sir William Campbell House
– architecture and interior #8661
Toronto (Ont), Church of Saint Nicholas
– frescoes #1822
Toronto (Ont), Church of Saint Paul's
– architecture and interior, Edward James Lennox #8897 8902
Toronto (Ont), Church of Saint Simon the Apostle
– architecture, Eden Smith #8408
Toronto (Ont), City Hall
– exhibitions
  – *Beaux-arts Toronto: Permanence and Change in Early 20th Century Architecture* (1973) #8069
  – *Sculpture '67: An Open-air Exhibition of Canadian Sculpture/Sculpture 67: exposition en plein air de sculptures canadiennes* (1967) #766
– exhibitions (reviews)
  – *Sculpture '67: An Open-air Exhibition of Canadian Sculpture/Sculpture 67: exposition en plein air de sculptures canadiennes* (1967) #750 769
Toronto (Ont), City Hall (1832)
– architecture, James Grant Chewett #8993
Toronto (Ont), City Hall (1844)
– architecture, Henry Bowyer Lane #8993
Toronto (Ont), City Hall (1898)
– architecture, Edward James Lennox #8993
– stained glass, Robert McCausland #2449
Toronto (Ont), City Hall and Civic Square
– architecture #7709
  – competition for #8981 8983 8989
  – Revell, Viljo #8993
  – Revell, Viljo, and John B. Parkin Associates #8990 8991
Toronto (Ont), City of Toronto. Public Works Department
– Goss, Arthur S., as photographer #5633
Toronto (Ont), City of Toronto Archives
– Goss, Arthur S., photographs #5633
Toronto (Ont), City of Toronto Archives. Market Gallery #1806
– exhibitions
  – *Arthur S. Goss, City Photographer: Works by Toronto's Official Photographer, 1911-1940* (1980) #5633
  – *John George Howard, 1803-1890: A Tribute* (1979) #8378
  – *The Corporate Image: An Exhibition of 19th and 20th Century Portraiture from the City of Toronto's Permanent Collection* (1980) #3178
  – *Water Colours by E.May Martin* (1980) #6424
Toronto (Ont), Civic Garden Centre
– architecture, Jerome Markson Architects #8386
Toronto (Ont), Clintwood Maisonette Project
– architecture, Henry Fliess #8514
Toronto (Ont), CN Tower
– architecture #9510
  – John Andrews International; Roger du Toit; Webb Zerafa Menkès Housden Partnership; Edward R. Baldwin #9511

– paintings, Greg Curnoe #5230
Toronto (Ont), CN Tower. Restaurant
– interior, Aldo and Francesco Piccaluga #9511
Toronto (Ont), Colborne Lodge
– architecture and art, John George Howard #8659
Toronto (Ont), Commerce Court
– architecture, I.M. Pei & Associates; Page & Steele, Associated Architects #9350
Toronto (Ont), Confederation Square
– architecture, Thom Partnership #8412
Toronto (Ont), Cooper Cap Company Building
– architecture, Isadore Feldman #9332
Toronto (Ont), Crown Tailoring Co. Building
– architecture, Charles Frederick Wagner #9332
Toronto (Ont), D. & J. Ritchie Ltd.
– Canadian art auction prices (1975-1980) #160
Toronto (Ont), D.O. Roblin Warehouse
– architecture, Eden Smith & Sons #9234
Toronto (Ont), David Mirvish Gallery
– exhibitions (reviews)
  – Murray, Robert Gray #6669
Toronto (Ont), Design Centre #2613
– closure (1970) #2621
Toronto (Ont), Dominion Bank (1914)
– architecture, Darling & Pearson #9163
Toronto (Ont), Dominion Bank (1932)
– architecture, John MacIntosh Lyle #8226
Toronto (Ont), Dominion of Canada Industrial Exhibition (1903)
– Canadian art #1
Toronto (Ont), Don Valley Woods/Phase 1 project
– architecture, Jack Klein & Henry Sears #8518
Toronto (Ont), Dorothy Cameron Gallery
– exhibitions
  – *Canadian Printmaking Today* (1965) #820
  – *Canadian Sculpture Today* (1964) #748
– exhibitions (reviews)
  – *Canadian Sculpture Today* (1964) #747
  – Hedrick, Robert Burns #5773
Toronto (Ont), Dow Corning Silicones Ltd. head office building
– architecture, Fairfield & DuBois #9301
Toronto (Ont), Dundas Street police station
– architecture, Shore, Tilbe, Henschel, Irwin, Peters #8078
Toronto (Ont), Eaton Centre
– architecture, Bregman & Hamann and Zeidler Partnership #9377 9378 9382
Toronto (Ont), Eaton Centre. Henry Birks
– exhibitions
  – *Historic Canadian Silver from "The Henry Birks Collection"* (1978) #2650
Toronto (Ont), Edgeley in the Village
– architecture, Irving Grossman #8520
Toronto (Ont), Educational Museum of Upper Canada
– (1856) #3128
– and Adolphus Egerton Ryerson #3150 3152 3155
Toronto (Ont), Electric Gallery #1798
– sculpture (1970s) #1800
Toronto (Ont), Empire Club
– debate between A.Y. Jackson and Edmund Wyly Grier #5923
Toronto (Ont), Excelsior Life Building
– architecture, Edward James Lennox #9333

Toronto (Ont), Fairweather's Store
– architecture, Charles Sherman Cobb #9363
Toronto (Ont), Fine Arts on Markham
– see Toronto (Ont), York University. Fine Arts on Markham
Toronto (Ont), Fire Hall at Gerrard Street and Carlaw Avenue
– architecture, Toronto City Architect's Office #8970
Toronto (Ont), Fisher House
– timber framing, compared with Gleason House (Farmington, Conn) #8658
Toronto (Ont), Flemingdon Park
– architecture, Irving Grossman #7683 8370 8514 8657
Toronto (Ont), Fort York
– preservation, and Ontario Historical Society (1905-1909) #8458
Toronto (Ont), Four Seasons Sheraton Hotel
– architecture, John B. Parkin Associates #9294
Toronto (Ont), G.J. Foy Company Building
– architecture, Curry & Sparling #9332
Toronto (Ont), Galerie Dresdnere
– exhibitions
– Homage to Miller Brittain (1919-1968): A Survey: Drawing and Mixed Media, 1936-1967 (1972) #4918
– exhibitions (reviews)
– Homage to Miller Brittain (1919-1968): A Survey: Drawing and Mixed Media, 1936-1967 (1972) #4919
Toronto (Ont), Gallery Moos
– exhibitions
– Albert Franck (1899-1973) in Retrospect: A Small Selection from the Artist's Collection (1974) #5500
– Etrog (1964) #5376
– exhibitions (reviews)
– Iskowitz, Gershon #5905
Toronto (Ont), Gallery O
– exhibitions
– Arthur F. McKay (1979) #6478
– exhibitions (reviews)
– Thibert, Patrick (1979) #7345
Toronto (Ont), Gallery One
– exhibitions
– Parr, 1893-1969: A Print Retrospective (1979) #6769
– exhibitions (reviews)
– Clarke, Ann #5114
Toronto (Ont), Garden Theatre
– architecture, Neil & Beggs #9066
Toronto (Ont), Gayety Theatre
– architecture, George Wallace Gouinlock #9060
Toronto (Ont), George Brown College of Applied Arts & Technology. Casa Loma Campus
– architecture, Fairfield & DuBois; Alan R. Moody #9479
Toronto (Ont), Girl Guides of Canada headquarters
– architecture, Corneil & McBain #7984
Toronto (Ont), Glenholme School
– architecture, competition for #9437
Toronto (Ont), Government House (1866)
– architecture, Gundry & Langley #8753
Toronto (Ont), Government House (1911)
– architecture, competition for #8748
Toronto (Ont), Government House (Chorley Park)
– architecture, Francis Riley Heakes #8749
Toronto (Ont), Government of Canada

Building
– Levine, Les, on fine art project proposal #6268
Toronto (Ont), Graphic Arts Building
– architecture, Francis Spence Baker #9330
Toronto (Ont), Grierson & Walker architect's office
– architecture and interior, Grierson & Walker #9299
Toronto (Ont), Guild Shop
– exhibitions
– Davidialuk, 1977 (1977) #4521
– Tuna Iquliq: Recent Sculpture (1979) #5903
Toronto (Ont), Harbour City
– architecture, Craig, Zeidler & Strong #8062
Toronto (Ont), Harbourfront Art Gallery
– see Toronto (Ont), Art Gallery at Harbourfront
Toronto (Ont), Hart House
– see Toronto (Ont), University of Toronto. Hart House
Toronto (Ont), Hazelton Lanes
– architecture, Webb Zerafa Menkès Housden Partnership #8078
Toronto (Ont), Helena Rubenstein Beauty Salon
– architecture, James Ernest Harris Paisley #9367
Toronto (Ont), Hermant Building
– architecture, Bond & Smith #9332
Toronto (Ont), High School of Commerce and Finance
– architecture #9387
Toronto (Ont), Holly-Dunfield Apartments
– architecture, Burston, Wells & Tampold #7683 8514
Toronto (Ont), Holt Renfrew Store
– architecture, Crang & Boake #8078
Toronto (Ont), Holwood Mansion
– architecture, Frank Darling #8667
Toronto (Ont), Hospital for Sick Children
– architecture
– Govan, Ferguson, Lindsay, Kaminker, Maw, Langley, Keenleyside #9028
– Stevens & Lee #9015
Toronto (Ont), Hotel Mossop
– architecture, James Patrick Hynes #9262
Toronto (Ont), Humber College
– Stacey, Harold, as teacher #7274
Toronto (Ont), Hyatt Regency Hotel
– architecture, Webb Zerafa Menkès Housden Partnership #9293
Toronto (Ont), Hydro Place
– architecture, Kenneth R. Cooper; Kenneth H. Candy and Adamson Associates, Consulting Architects #9352
Toronto (Ont), Imperial Bank of Canada
– architecture, Langley & Howland #9181
Toronto (Ont), Imperial Oil Building
– architecture, Mathers & Haldenby #9340
Toronto (Ont), Inn on the Park
– architecture, Peter Webb #9289
Toronto (Ont), Innuit Gallery of Eskimo Art
– and Av Isaacs #4236
– exhibitions
– Baker Lake Sculpture (1974) #4434
– From the Bottom of the Kudlik: Carvings and Artifacts from Gjoa Haven, 1974/Du fond des âges: sculptures et objets de Gjoa Haven, 1974 (1974) #4435
– Spence Bay Sculpture: An Expressive Force (1980) #4454
– The Hand (1975) #4439

– exhibitions (reviews)
– Shaa, Aqjangajuk #7174
Toronto (Ont), Irving Grossman architect's office and apartment residence
– architecture and interior, Irving Grossman #9299
Toronto (Ont), Isaacs Gallery
– (1970s) #1804
– exhibitions
– "Les Levine Copies Everyone" (1970) #6264
– exhibitions (reviews)
– Coughtry, John Graham #5191
– Curnoe, Greg #5226
– Handy, Arthur (1964) #5701
– Kurelek, William #6113
– Paradise (1978) #6964
Toronto (Ont), Jane Corkin Gallery
– exhibitions
– Twelve Canadians: Contemporary Canadian Photography (1981) #1070
Toronto (Ont), Japanese Cultural Centre
– architecture, Raymond Moriyama #9095
Toronto (Ont), Jarvis Collegiate Institute
– architecture #9443
– murals, George Agnew Reid and Lorna Claire #6978
Toronto (Ont), Jenkins Art Galleries
– architecture, Sproatt & Rolph #8053
– exhibitions
– A Memorial Exhibition of the Paintings of the Late Florence Carlyle, A.R.C.A. (1925) #5000
– exhibitions (reviews)
– A Memorial Exhibition of the Paintings of the Late Florence Carlyle, A.R.C.A. (1925) #4999
– Watson, Homer Ransford #7529
Toronto (Ont), Jewish Community Centre
– architecture, Jerome Markson #8078
Toronto (Ont), John C. Parkin House
– architecture and interior, John C. Parkin #9299
Toronto (Ont), John Ross Robertson School
– architecture, competition for #9437
Toronto (Ont), Joseph E. Shephard Government of Canada Building
– architecture, DuBois, Strong, Bindhart; Shore, Tilbe, Henschel, Irwin, Associated Architects #8975
Toronto (Ont), Knox College
– see Toronto (Ont), University of Toronto. Knox College
Toronto (Ont), Lawrence Park Apartments
– architecture #8644
Toronto (Ont), legislative buildings
– architecture, James Grant Chewett #258 259
Toronto (Ont), Loew's Uptown Theatre
– architecture, Thomas White Lamb #9075
Toronto (Ont), Loew's Yonge Street Theatre (Elgin and Wintergarden)
– architecture, Thomas White Lamb #9064 9067
Toronto (Ont), M.S. Yolles Associates Offices
– architecture and interior, Ron Thom #9346
Toronto (Ont), Macdonald Galleries
– Macdonald, Albert Angus, as owner #6354
Toronto (Ont), Macdonald Gallery
– exhibitions
– Contemporary Art of Iroquoia (1980) #4164
– The Child in Ontario Art (1979) #1687
– The Living Image: Three Contemporary Visions: Barbara Howard, Cecil Richards,

Rebecca Sisler (1978) #666
- exhibitions (reviews)
  - Bloore, Ronald Langley #4752
Toronto (Ont), MacKenzie & Co. Art Galleries
- exhibitions
  - *Exhibition of Paintings by M.R. Hamilton* (1906) #5693
Toronto (Ont), Madison Apartments
- architecture #8486
Toronto (Ont), Manufacturers Life Insurance Company Building
- architecture and interior, Marani & Morris #9339
Toronto (Ont), Market Gallery
- see Toronto (Ont), City of Toronto Archives. Market Gallery
Toronto (Ont), Markleangelo Restaurant
- mural, Robert Nelson Markle #6418
Toronto (Ont), Marlborough Godard Gallery
- and Mira Godard #161
- exhibition, Canadian art, Marlborough Gallery, New York (NY), (1974) #572
- exhibitions
  - *David Milne: The Toronto Years, 1939-1940* (1976) #6561
Toronto (Ont), Mason & Risch Company Building
- architecture, Bond & Smith #9328
Toronto (Ont), Masonic Temple
- architecture, competition #9062
Toronto (Ont), Massey College
- see Toronto (Ont), University of Toronto. Massey College
Toronto (Ont), Massey Foundation
- collection #2142
Toronto (Ont), McConkey's Lunch
- architecture, Edward James Lennox #9269
Toronto (Ont), Mellors Art Gallery
- Laing, G.Blair, on #1686
Toronto (Ont), Memorial Fountain to Dr. D.W. Young
- design, Maurice D. Klein; sculpture, Florence Wyle #729
Toronto (Ont), Mercer Union
- exhibitions
  - *Locations: Outdoor Works by Toronto Artists* (1980) #1834
- exhibitions (reviews)
  - Cohen, Sorel #5130
Toronto (Ont), Metro Centre
- and Union Station (Toronto, Ont) #9540
- architecture, John Andrews Architects #8323
Toronto (Ont), Metro Toronto Public Library
- architecture, Raymond Moriyama #9051
- Robertson, John Ross, Historical Collection #3130 3131 3204
- Toronto and Early Canada Picture Collection #3143
Toronto (Ont), Metro Toronto Zoo
- architecture, Thom Partnership #8412
Toronto (Ont), Mira Godard Gallery
- exhibitions
  - *Ed Bartram: 10 Years* (1980) #4618
  - *Jean McEwen: Suite parisienne* (1979) #6471
  - *Otto Rogers: New Paintings and Sculpture, 1977-78* (1979) #7065
- exhibitions (reviews)
  - Bentham, Douglas,(1978) #785
  - Smith, Gordon Appelbe (1978) #7231
Toronto (Ont), Molsons Bank
- architecture, Langley & Howland #9159

Toronto (Ont), Montessori School
- children's letters on visit to Electric Gallery (Toronto, Ont) #1798
Toronto (Ont), Morris Gallery
- exhibitions
  - *Bertram Brooker, 1888-1955* (1971) #4925
  - *Helen McNicoll, 1879-1915: Oil Paintings from the Estate* (1974) #6507
  - *Tim Whiten: Sculpture and Drawings* (1972) #7562
Toronto (Ont), Mount Pleasant Cemetery. Eaton Mausoleum
- architecture, Sproatt & Rolph #8895
Toronto (Ont), Mount Pleasant Cemetery. Senator Cox's Mausoleum
- architecture, Sproatt & Rolph #8894
Toronto (Ont), Nancy Poole's Studio
- exhibitions (reviews)
  - Marshall, Pat (1979) #6422
Toronto (Ont), National Cash Register
- architecture, Page & Warrington #9234
Toronto (Ont), Native Friendship Centre
- exhibitions (reviews)
  - *First Native Art Auction* (1981) #4170
Toronto (Ont), New Princess Theatre
- architecture, C.Howard Crane; Charles James Read, Associate Architect #9069
Toronto (Ont), New School of Art
- (1960s) #2994
- (1970s) #3004
- Teitelbaum, Mashel, as teacher #7340
Toronto (Ont), Northway Department Store
- architecture, Horwood & White #9366
Toronto (Ont), O'Keefe Centre for the Performing Arts
- architecture, Earle C. Morgan; Page & Steele #9087
- exhibitions
  - Canadian Society of Painters in Water Colour (1974) #6
Toronto (Ont), Odeon Theatre
- architecture, Henry Eli Greenspoon #9078
Toronto (Ont), Oke Building
- architecture, Shepard & Calvin #9335
Toronto (Ont), Olympia Square
- architecture, Bregman & Hamann #9301
Toronto (Ont), Ontario Archaeological Museum
- stonework, Neutral Indians #3503
Toronto (Ont), Ontario Association of Architects headquarters
- architecture, John B. Parkin Associates #7679 8300 9341
Toronto (Ont), Ontario College of Art
- (1876-1976) #3009 3011 3012
- (1910-1920s) #309
- (1910s) #1712
- (1912) #2964
- (1960s), compared with Ecole des beaux-arts (Montréal, Qué) #2990
- (1968), dispute #2997
  - Ontario Advisory Committee on University Affairs, report #2996
- (1970s) #3004
- (1971-1972), controversy over policies #3002
- and Ontario Society of Artists #1679
- Bartram, Ed, as student #4618
- Coombs, Edith Grace, as teacher #5172
- Cruikshank, William, as teacher #5212
- Freifeld, Eric, as teacher #5516
- Hallam, Joseph Sydney, as student #5687
- Handy, Arthur, as teacher #5701
- Holmes, Robert

- as student #5822
- books from his library #5824
- Innes, Alice A., as student #5900
- Kurelek, William, as student #6110
- Lapointe, Frank, as student #6170
- Lismer, Arthur, as teacher #6295 6301
- Lougheed, Robert Elmer, as student #6327
- Loveroff, Frederick Nicholas, as student #6329 6330 6331
- Lui, Andrew, as student #6332
- Macdonald, Jock, as teacher #6378
- MacGregor, John, as teacher #6387
- Manly, Charles MacDonald, drawings #6414
- Nicoll, Marion F.S. Mackay, as student #6702 6703
- Paterson, Robert Allen, as student #6778
- Reid, George Agnew, as principal #6979
- Ronald, William S., as student #7071
- Schaefer, Carl Fellman, as teacher #7156
- Shepherd, Helen, as student #2988
- Shepherd, Reginald, as student #2988
- Stacey, Harold, as student #7273
- Whiten, Colette
  - as student #7560
  - *Untitled 1971-72 installation work* #7556
Toronto (Ont), Ontario Heritage Foundation
- Firestone Art Collection #3239
Toronto (Ont), Ontario Medical Association
- architecture
  - A.J. Diamond Associates #8078
  - Diamond, A.J., and Barton Myers #9349
  - Diamond & Myers #8071
Toronto (Ont), Ontario Place
- architecture, Craig, Zeidler & Strong #9113 9114 9115
Toronto (Ont), Ontario Provincial Museum
- works, from Educational Museum of Upper Canada (Toronto, Ont) #3155
Toronto (Ont), Ontario School of Art
- Reid, George Agnew, as student #6979
Toronto (Ont), Ontario School of Art and Design #3128
- and Charlotte Mount Brook Morrell Schreiber #7164
Toronto (Ont), Ontario Science Centre
- architecture #7709
- architecture, Raymond Moriyama #9106
- exhibitions
  - *Make (Mak) Contemporary Crafts, 1971: An Exhibit of Contemporary Crafts by Ontario's Leading Designer-Craftsmen* (1971) #2247
Toronto (Ont), Open Studio #1806
- (1970-1977) #1819
- (1970-1980) #1830 1833
Toronto (Ont), Osgoode Hall
- architecture, Hopkins, Lawson & Nelson; Henry Bowyer Lane; Cumberland & Storm; Saunders & Ryrie #9002 9003
Toronto (Ont), Oxford University Press Building
- architecture, Sproatt & Rolph #9335
Toronto (Ont), Palace of Government
- architecture #8943
Toronto (Ont), Pantages Theatre
- architecture, Thomas White Lamb #9075
Toronto (Ont), Park Gallery
- exhibitions
  - *The National Gallery of Canada Presents: 1958-59, Painters Eleven* (1958) #1751
Toronto (Ont), Park School
- architecture, James Carlisle Pennington #9388

Toronto (Ont), Parliament Buildings
- architecture (1791-1893) #8055 8943
Toronto (Ont), Paterson Building
- architecture, Sproatt & Rolph #9335
Toronto (Ont), Pauline McGibbon Cultural
  Centre
- exhibitions
  - *Twelve Canadian Artists* (1980) #698
- restoration, Thom Partnership #7776
Toronto (Ont), Picture Loan Society #1758
- and Douglas M. Duncan #570 3223 3232
Toronto (Ont), Police Station No 6
- architecture, Toronto City Architect's
  Office #8970
Toronto (Ont), Pollock Gallery
- exhibitions
  - *Frances Loring - Florence Wyle* (1969) #754
  - Ontario Society of Artists (1966) #1666
- exhibitions (reviews)
  - Morrisseau, Norval (1963) #6643
Toronto (Ont), Prince Hotel
- architecture, Thom Partnership #8412
Toronto (Ont), Provincial Exhibition
- exhibitions (reviews)
  - (1852) #1691 1692
Toronto (Ont), Provincial Lunatic Asylum
- architecture
  - Howard, John George #8378
  - Howard, John George, and Kivas Tully
    #9034
Toronto (Ont), Provincial Museum of
  Ontario
- periodical, *Archaeological Report* #3329
Toronto (Ont), Public Reference Library
- exhibitions
  - *Catalogue of Exhibition of Little Pictures by
    Canadian Artists at Art Galleries of the
    Public Reference Library: 1st-2nd*
    (1913-1914) #199
Toronto (Ont), Quan and King Gallery
- exhibitions (reviews)
  - Bloore, Ronald Langley #4754
Toronto (Ont), Raymond Moriyama.
  Architect's office
- architecture and interior, Raymond
  Moriyama #9346
Toronto (Ont), Red Cross Lodge
- architecture, William Lyon Somerville
  #9027
Toronto (Ont), Regent Park
- housing projects (1950s) #8511
Toronto (Ont), Registry Office
- architecture, Charles S. Cobb #8969
Toronto (Ont), Ridpath's Store
- architecture, Thom Partnership #8412
Toronto (Ont), Ridpath Building
- architecture, Mackenzie Waters #9335
Toronto (Ont), Riverdale Technical School
- architecture #9443
Toronto (Ont), Robert Simpson Gallery
- exhibitions
  - Ontario Society of Artists (1924) #1666
Toronto (Ont), Roberts Gallery
- exhibitions (reviews)
  - Roberts, Goodridge #7046
Toronto (Ont), Royal Alexandra Theatre
- architecture, John Lyle MacIntosh #9059
- mural, Frederick Sproston Challener #5068
Toronto (Ont), Royal Bank (1908)
- architecture, Carrere & Hastings; Eustace
  Godfrey Bird #9152
Toronto (Ont), Royal Bank (1915)
- architecture, Ross & Macdonald #9165
Toronto (Ont), Royal Bank Plaza

- architecture, Webb Zerafa Menkès
  Housden Partnership #9198 9353
Toronto (Ont), Royal Ontario Museum
  #3161 3170
- and Sir Byron Edmund Walker #3206
- Anglo-Québec furniture, 18th-19th cs.
  #2542
- art, Indians of North America #3382
- art, Northwest Coast Indians #4002
- as client of Burton Kramer Associates #889
- Canadian costume #2839 2844 2853
- Canadian crewel bed hangings, late 19th c.
  #2784
- Canadian glass, Edith Chown Pierce and
  Gerald Stevens collection #2397 2398 2399
- Canadian portraits (1780-1870) #263
- Canadian quilts #2797
- Canadian textiles #2723 2730
- Canadian watercolour paintings and
  drawings, 18th-19th cs. #247
- Canadiana picture collection #159
- collection 3141
- Currelly, Charles Trick, as director #3139
- effigy rattle pipes, Iroquois #3644
- exhibitions
  - *An Exhibition of Canadian Gameboards of
    the 19th & 20th Centuries from Ontario,
    Quebec & Nova Scotia* (1981) #2597
  - *Canadian Indian Art 74: An Exhibition of
    Contemporary Art and Traditional
    Crafts/L'art des Indiens du Canada 74: une
    exposition d'art contemporain et des
    traditions de l'artisanat* (1974) #4138
  - *Canadian Textiles, 1750-1900: An
    Exhibition* (1965) #2727
  - *Contemporary Native Art of Canada: Alex
    Janvier* (1978) #5939
  - *Contemporary Native Art of Canada:
    Manitoulin Island* (1978) #4156
  - *Contemporary Native Art of Canada: Silk
    Screens from the Triple K Co-operative, Red
    Lake, Ontario* (1977) #4151
  - *Contemporary Native Art of Canada: The
    Naskapi* (1977) #4149
  - *Contemporary Native Art of Canada: The
    Western Subarctic; Porcupine Quillwork;
    Moose Hair Tufting* (1977) #4152
  - *Contemporary Native Art of Canada: The
    Woodland Indians/Art contemporain des
    Indiens sylvicoles du
    Canada/Zeitgenössische Kunst der
    kanadischen Waldland Indianer* (1976)
    #4143
  - *Craft Dimensions Canada* (1969) #2115
  - *De grandes espérances: la vision européenne
    en Nouvelle-Ecosse, 1749-1848* (1981)
    #1220
  - *Emily Carr: A Centennial Exhibition
    Celebrating the One Hundredth
    Anniversary of Her Birth* (1972) #5027
  - *Emily Carr: exposition centenaire
    commémorant le centième anniversaire de
    sa naissance* (1972) #5028
  - *Exposition d'estampes en l'honneur de C.
    Krieghoff, 1815-1872/Exhibition of Prints
    in Honour of C. Krieghoff, 1815-1872*
    (1972) #6096
  - *George Heriot: Painter of the
    Canadas/George Heriot: peintre des deux
    Canadas* (1979) #5786
  - *Great Expectations: The European Vision in
    Nova Scotia, 1749-1848* (1981) #1222
  - *Modesty to Mod: Dress and Underdress in
    Canada, 1780-1967* (1967) #2849

  - *People's Art: Naïve Art in Canada/L'art
    populaire: l'art naïf au Canada* (1974) #966
  - *Printmaking in Canada: The Earliest Views
    and Portraits/Les débuts de l'estampe
    imprimée au Canada: vues et portraits*
    (1980) #839
  - *Quillwork by Native Peoples in
    Canada/Travaux en piquants de porc-épic
    exécutés par les autochtones au Canada*
    (1977) #3475
  - *Quillwork by Native Peoples in Canada*
    (1977) #3474
  - *Ryerson: A Community of Photographers*
    (1974) #1805
  - *Society of Painter-Etchers and Engravers*
    (1943-1959) #3
  - *The Arctic: Views of Early Explorations*
    (1980) #278
  - *The New Brunswick Landscape Print:
    1760-1880* (1981) #1189
- exhibitions (reviews)
  - *Contemporary Native Art of Canada: Alex
    Janvier* (1978) #5938
  - *Modesty to Mod: Dress and Underdress in
    Canada, 1780-1967* (1967) #2847
- furniture #2484
- Jacquard coverlets #2740
- Kane, Paul, works #3386 6004 6009 6012
- Krieghoff, Cornelius, sketchbook #6090
- Lyttleton, Westcott Whitchurch Lewis,
  Halifax Harbour Seen from McNab's Island
  #6349
- Montreal Museum of Fine Arts (Montréal,
  Qué), compared with #3099
- origins, 19th c. #3152
- Québec furniture #2527
- quillwork, Indians of North America
  #3471
- Rindisbacher, Peter, works exhibited
  (1970) #7008
- Samuel, Sigmund, Canadiana collection
  #812 3135 3140
- Shortt, Terence Michael, as Chief Display
  Biologist #7201
- souvenir spoons, Shepley collection #2652
- stone pipes, Huron and Iroquois #3504
- totem poles, Northwest Coast Indians
  #3895
- works, from Educational Museum of
  Upper Canada (Toronto, Ont) #3155
Toronto (Ont), Royal York Hotel
- architecture, Ross & Macdonald; Sproatt &
  Rolph, Associate Architects #9280 9281
Toronto (Ont), Ryerson Polytechnical
  Institute
- photographs, faculty and students (1970s)
  #1805
Toronto (Ont), Ryerson Polytechnical
  Institute. Department of Photography
- conference, *Canadian Perspectives* (1979)
  #1041
Toronto (Ont), Sable-Castelli Gallery
- exhibitions (reviews)
  - Fauteux, André Lucien (1978) #785
  - Klunder, Harold #6064
Toronto (Ont), Saint Anne's Church
- architecture and interior #1733
Toronto (Ont), Saint James Cathedral
- architecture, Frederic William Cumberland
  #8905
Toronto (Ont), Salvation Army Arthur
  Meighen Lodge
- architecture, Marani, Morris & Allan #8516
Toronto (Ont), Salvation Army headquarters

– architecture and art #8232
Toronto (Ont), Sawtooth Borders Inc.
– Rosenberg, Gloria, as owner #2808
Toronto (Ont), Shaarei Teffillah Synagogue
– architecture, Irving Grossman #8903
Toronto (Ont), Shea's Hippodrome
– architecture, Leon H. Lempert & Son #9066
Toronto (Ont), Sheridan School of Design
– Schantz, Karl, as teacher of glassmaking #7159
Toronto (Ont), Simpson's
– exhibitions (reviews)
– Painters Eleven (1953) #1769
Toronto (Ont), Sotheby & Co. (Canada) Ltd.
– Canadian art auction prices (1968-1975) #116
Toronto (Ont), South African Memorial
– Allward, Walter Seymour #4516
Toronto (Ont), St. Charles Hotel
– architecture, Hynes, Feldman & Watson #9269
Toronto (Ont), St. James Court Apartments
– architecture #8644
Toronto (Ont), St. James Town
– architecture and urban development #9302
Toronto (Ont), St. Lawrence Centre for the Arts
– architecture, Gordon S. Adamson & Associates #9109
Toronto (Ont), St. Lawrence Hall
– architecture, William Thomas #9103
Toronto (Ont), St. Lawrence Neighbourhood
– architecture, Robinson & Heinrichs; Sillaste Nakashima #8078
– architecture and urban planning #8079
Toronto (Ont), Standard Bank
– architecture, Darling & Pearson #9158
Toronto (Ont), Stewart Building
– architecture, Edward James Lennox #9354
Toronto (Ont), subway
– architecture #9548 9554
– compared with métro (Montréal, Qué) #9552
Toronto (Ont), Sun Life Building
– architecture, John B. Parkin Associates #9342
– architecture and art #8232
– sculpture, Louis Archambault #4542
Toronto (Ont), Sunnybrook Hospital
– architecture, Allward & Gouinlock #9027
– mural, Albert Angus Macdonald #6354
Toronto (Ont), Sunnyside
– architecture, Chapman, Oxley & Bishop #8054
Toronto (Ont), T. Eaton Company Department Store (College Street)
– architecture, Ross & Macdonald; Sproatt & Rolph, Consulting Architects #9365 9369
– interior
– Carlu, Jacques #9370
– ornamental metalwork #9368
– sales centre of Canadian Handicrafts Guild #2118
Toronto (Ont), T. Eaton Company Limited. Fine Art Galleries
– exhibitions
– Canadian art (1944) #5866
– *The Art of Philip Aziz: Retrospective Show of Paintings, Watercolours and Drawings* (1957) #4576
– Toronto Camera Club #975
– exhibitions (reviews)
– Canadian war paintings (1947) #1100

– Taçon, Edna Jeanette #7310
Toronto (Ont), Tartu College
– architecture, Tampold & Wells #8744
Toronto (Ont), Temple Emanu-El
– architecture, Irving Grossman #8903
Toronto (Ont), Temple-Pattison Building
– architecture, Denison & Stephenson #9332
Toronto (Ont), The Grange
– *see also* Toronto (Ont), Art Gallery of Ontario; Toronto (Ont), Art Gallery of Toronto; Toronto (Ont), Art Museum of Toronto
– architecture #8637
– architecture and restoration #8680
– restoration #3177 8665 8666
Toronto (Ont), Timothy Eaton Memorial Church
– architecture, Wickson & Gregg #8898
Toronto (Ont), Todmorden Mills
– architecture #8072
Toronto (Ont), Toronto Art Museum
– exhibitions (reviews)
– Toronto Camera Club (1918) #983
Toronto (Ont), Toronto Art School
– Kinton, Ada Florence, as teacher #6053
– Smith, William St. Thomas, as student #7236
Toronto (Ont), Toronto-Dominion Bank
– Inuit art #4201 4216 4248 4427
– Inuit art and Canadian paintings #3225
Toronto (Ont), Toronto-Dominion Centre
– architecture
– John B. Parkin Associates; Bregman & Hamann #7694
– John B. Parkin Associates; Bregman & Hamann; Ludwig Mies van der Rohe, Consulting Architect #9197 9301 9345
– Mies van der Rohe, Ludwig, Consulting Architect #9348
– architecture and urban development #9302
– exhibitions
– *A Visual Odyssey 1958-1968, Roloff Beny* (1971) #4690
– *Crafts from Arctic Canada/Artisanat de l'Arctique canadien* (1974) #4255
– *The Eskimo Art Collection of the Toronto-Dominion Bank* (1973) #4248
Toronto (Ont), Toronto General Hospital
– architecture
– Darling & Pearson #9012 9013
– Mathers & Haldenby #9032
Toronto (Ont), Toronto General Hospital. Private Patients' Building
– architecture, Darling & Pearson #9020
Toronto (Ont), Toronto Guild of Civic Art
– and Sir Byron Edmund Walker #3206
Toronto (Ont), Toronto Hilton Hotel
– architecture, Webb Zerafa Menkès #9292
Toronto (Ont), Toronto Industrial Exhibition
– (1879-1902), exhibitions #1
Toronto (Ont), Toronto International Airport
– architecture and art #8232
Toronto (Ont), Toronto Public Libraries
– architecture, branch libraries (1917) #9039
– exhibitions
– *Keewatin Eskimo Ceramics '67* (1967) #4210
– Ontario Society of Artists, early 20th c. #1666
– *William G.R. Hind (1833-1888): A Confederation Painter in Canada* (1967) #5806
– Pope, William, works #6905 6906
Toronto (Ont), Toronto Public Libraries.

Central Circulating Library
– architecture #9041
Toronto (Ont), Toronto Public Libraries. Danforth Branch Library
– architecture #9041
Toronto (Ont), Toronto Public Libraries. Parkdale Branch
– exhibitions
– *16 Polish-Canadian Artists: An Exhibition* (1977) #642
Toronto (Ont), Toronto Public Libraries. Runnymede Branch Library
– architecture #9041
Toronto (Ont), Toronto School Board
– Study of Educational Facilities (SEF) #9401 9466 9472 9479
Toronto (Ont), Toronto Star Building
– architecture, Chapman & Oxley #9334
Toronto (Ont), Toronto Stock Exchange
– architecture
– competition for #9161
– George & Moorhouse, Architects; Samuel Herbert Maw, Associate Architect #9187
Toronto (Ont), Traders Bank Apartments
– architecture #8486
Toronto (Ont), Trinity College
– *see* Toronto (Ont), University of Toronto. Trinity College
Toronto (Ont), Trinity College (King Street)
– architecture, Kivas Tully #9483
Toronto (Ont), Trolley Restaurant
– architecture, Blake Millar #8078
Toronto (Ont), Union Bank of Canada
– architecture, Henry Byran Gilbert #9159
Toronto (Ont), Union Station
– and Metro Centre (Toronto, Ont) #9540
– architecture, Ross & Macdonald; Hugh Griffith Jones; John MacIntosh Lyle #9531 9536
Toronto (Ont), University College
– *see* Toronto (Ont), University of Toronto. University College
Toronto (Ont), University of Toronto
– and Charles Trick Currelly #3139
– and Royal Ontario Museum (Toronto, Ont) #3152
– architecture #9477
– expansion plan (1950s) #9456
– interior design (1960s) #9402
Toronto (Ont), University of Toronto. Anatomy Building
– architecture, Darling & Pearson #9444
Toronto (Ont), University of Toronto. Convocation Hall
– architecture, Darling & Pearson #9430
Toronto (Ont), University of Toronto. Emmanuel College
– architecture, Sproatt & Rolph #9452
Toronto (Ont), University of Toronto. Engineering Building
– architecture, Robert William Anderson #9459
Toronto (Ont), University of Toronto. Hart House
– architecture #9438
– compared with University of Toronto. Massey College #9460
– Sproatt & Rolph #9433 9439 9440 9441
– collection #3134 3137 3147 3168
Toronto (Ont), University of Toronto. Hart House. Art Gallery
– exhibitions
– *7 West Coast Painters* (1959) #1997

- *A Governor General Looks at Canada: An Exhibition of Watercolours by the Rt. Hon. Sir Edmund Head, Bart., K.C.B., F.R.S., and Lady Head* (1979) #5760
- *Drawings and Pastels c. 1930-1967 by Miller Gore Brittain* (1969) #4917
- *Joe Plaskett and His Paris: In Search of Time Past* (1973) #6893
- *Joe Plaskett et son Paris: à la recherche d'un temps passé* (1973) #6894
- *L.A.C. Panton (1894-1954): A Retrospective* (1974) #6759
- *Monuments 70: An Exhibition of Recent Canadian Sculpture in the Quadrangles of Hart House and Trinity College, University of Toronto* (1970) #771
- *Painters Eleven in Retrospect* (1980) #1785
- *Romanesque Toronto: A Photographic Exhibition of Late Nineteenth Century Architecture* (1971) #8064
- exhibitions (reviews)
  - Bloore, Ronald Langley #4750
  - Iskowitz, Gershon #5905
- Levine, Les, *Red Tape* #6263
- MacDonald, Thoreau, drawings for *Maria Chapdelaine* #6383
Toronto (Ont), University of Toronto. John P. Robarts Research Library
- architecture, Mathers & Haldenby, principal architects; Warner, Burns, Toan, Lunde, design and schematic concepts #9048 9050 9052
Toronto (Ont), University of Toronto. Knox College
- architecture
  - Chapman & McGiffin #9435
  - competition for #9432
Toronto (Ont), University of Toronto. Massey College
- architecture
  - Thom Partnership #8412
  - Thompson, Berwick & Pratt; Architect-in-charge, Ronald James Thom #9460
Toronto (Ont), University of Toronto. Men's residence
- architecture, Eden Smith & Sons #9431
Toronto (Ont), University of Toronto. Ontario College of Education addition
- architecture, Darling & Pearson #9444
Toronto (Ont), University of Toronto. School of Architecture
- architectural education
  - (1930s) #8224
  - (1941) #8245
  - (1947) #8246
  - (1948) #8247
  - (1949) #8248
  - (1950) #8249
  - (1951) #8250
  - (1952) #8252
  - (1953) #8254
  - (1960s) #8282
  - (1967-1975), experimental curriculum program #8286
  - (1968), operational gaming teaching technique #8278
  - (1970), Peter Prangnell on #8313
  - (1980) #8289
- influence on Toronto architecture (1930s) #8055
Toronto (Ont), University of Toronto. Simcoe Hall
- architecture, Darling & Pearson #9444

Toronto (Ont), University of Toronto. Student residence
- architecture, Tampold & Wells #9467
Toronto (Ont), University of Toronto. Trinity College
- architecture, Darling & Pearson #9446 9483
- exhibitions
  - *Monuments 70: An Exhibition of Recent Canadian Sculpture in the Quadrangles of Hart House and Trinity College, University of Toronto* (1970) #771
Toronto (Ont), University of Toronto. Trinity College. Chapel
- stained glass, J. McCausland & Co. #2461
Toronto (Ont), University of Toronto. University College
- architecture, Frederic William Cumberland #7697 9428 9429 9453 9475
- collection #3151 3168
- restoration #9482
  - Wilson Newton Roberts Duncan and Eric R. Arthur #7776
Toronto (Ont), University of Toronto. Victoria College
- collection #3168
Toronto (Ont), University of Toronto. Victoria College. Library
- architecture, Sproatt & Rolph #9038
Toronto (Ont), University of Toronto. Victoria College. Wymilwood
- architecture, Fleury & Arthur #9454
Toronto (Ont), Victoria College
- see Toronto (Ont), University of Toronto. Victoria College
Toronto (Ont), Waddington's Auctioneers
- Inuit art auctions #4305
Toronto (Ont), Waddington Galleries
- exhibitions (reviews)
  - Sutton, Carol (1979) #7292
Toronto (Ont), Ward-Price Galleries
- forgeries, Canadian paintings (1962) #64
Toronto (Ont), Wembley Apartments
- architecture #8644
Toronto (Ont), Whitburn Apartments
- architecture, Jerome Markson; Jack Klein & Henry Sears #8514
Toronto (Ont), William H. Wright Building
- architecture, Mathers & Haldenby #9338
Toronto (Ont), William Wrigley Jr. Factory
- architecture, Prack & Perrine #9234
Toronto (Ont), William Wrigley Junior Co. Ltd. Building
- architecture, Gordon S. Adamson & Associates #9343
Toronto (Ont), Wolseley Motor Car Company Building
- architecture, Edward James Lennox #9332
Toronto (Ont), York Mechanics' Institute
- proposal for a society of architects (ca. 1835) #8306
Toronto (Ont), York Square
- architecture, Diamond & Myers #8071 9347
Toronto (Ont), York Theatre
- architecture, Charles James Read #9066
Toronto (Ont), York University
- architecture, Gordon S. Adamson & Associates; John B. Parkin Associates; Shore & Moffat and Partners #9396 9469
- Arts Administration program, Faculty of Administrative Studies (1970s) #3291
- Faculty of Fine Arts (1970s) #3004
- Hayden, Michael, *Escalator Piece* #5755
- interior design (1960s) #9402

- workshop, Inuit printmaking (1980) #4269
Toronto (Ont), York University. Art Gallery of York University
- exhibitions
  - *Art Deco Tendencies in Canadian Painting* (1977) #505
  - *Centennial Exhibition of Quebec and Ontario Contemporary Painters, 1967* (1967) #484
  - *Douglas Bentham "Enclosures and Opens" 1975/76* (1976) #4683
  - *E.J. Hughes* (1967) #5860
  - *Edward Curtis in the Collection of the Edmonton Art Gallery* (1980) #3480
  - *Ernest Lindner: Drawings, 1971-77* (1977) #6289
  - *Eskimo Carvings and Prints from the Collection of York University* (1971) #4228
  - *Esther Warkov Drawings* (1977) #7519
  - *Historic Canadian Silver from "The Henry Birks Collection"* (1978) #2650
  - *Kostyniuk: Relief Structures, 1969-1972* (1973) #6079
  - *The Automatic Drawings of Alma Rumball* (1978) #7108
  - *Tim Whiten: Sculpture and Drawings* (1972) #7562
Toronto (Ont), York University. Fine Arts on Markham
- exhibitions
  - *Guido Molinari: Quantificateur* (1979) #6592
Toronto (Ont), York University. Glendon Hall
- architecture, Thomas Howarth #9457
Toronto (Ont), Yorkdale Shopping Centre
- architecture #9374 9375
Toronto (Ont), Yorkville Town Hall
- architecture, William Hay and Henry Langley #8997
Toronto (Ont), Yorkville Village
- urban renewal (1960s) #9376
Toronto (Ont), Yorkwoods Village/Phase 1 project
- architecture, Jack Klein & Henry Sears #8518
Toronto (Ont), Young People's Theatre
- restoration, Zeidler Partnership #7776
Toronto Amateur Photographic Association (Toronto, Ont)
- (1888-1891) #975
Toronto Architectural Club (Toronto, Ont)
- and Toronto Architectural Eighteen Club #8299
Toronto Architectural Eighteen Club (Toronto, Ont)
- (1899-1907) #7956
- (1899-1908) #8299 8300
Toronto Art Students' League (Toronto, Ont) #28
- (1886-1890s) #1706
- (1886-1893) #2959
- (1886-1894) #2961
- (1886-1904) #1714
- (1890s) #188
- and Canadian Society of Graphic Art #801
- and Charles William Jefferys #5955 5956 5958
- book illustration and design #928
- *Exhibition of Modern Posters* (1896) #911
Toronto Board of Trade (Toronto, Ont)
- on historic preservation (1979) #8027
Toronto Camera Club (Toronto, Ont) #1039
- (1888-1976) #1683

– exhibitions
  – (1891-) #975
  – (1924-1940), Canadian National Exhibition (Toronto, Ont) #1
– exhibitions (reviews) #978
  – (1894) #977 1702
  – (1906) #980
  – (1918) #983
  – (1921) #984
Toronto City Architect's Office (Toronto, Ont)
– fire hall and police stations (1930s) #8970
Toronto Daily News, Can newspaper
– cartoons, Newton McConnell #943
Toronto-Dominion Bank
– architecture (1950s) #9193
Toronto Evening Telegram, Can newspaper
– cartoons, George Shields #943
Toronto Glass Co., glass manufacturer (Toronto, Ont) #2401
Toronto Globe, Can newspaper
– cartoons, James Fergus Kyle #943
– illustrations, Charles William Jefferys #5953
Toronto Guild of Civic Art (Toronto, Ont)
– (1890s) #188
  – and mural painting #6974
Toronto Lithographing Company, publishing firm (Toronto, Ont)
– and Charles William Jefferys #5955
Toronto Patriot, Can newspaper
– reviews of Society of Artists and Amateurs of Toronto exhibition (Toronto, Ont) (1834) #1729
Toronto Photographers Co-operative (Toronto, Ont)
– (1981), brief, Federal Cultural Policy Review Committee #1068
Toronto Pottery Company, ceramic importer (Toronto, Ont) #2346
Toronto Society of Architects (Toronto, Ont)
– (1907-1912) #7956
– and Ontario Association of Architects #7955
Toronto Society of Arts (Toronto, Ont) #1706
– (1847-1848) #1689
– and Society of Artists and Amateurs of Toronto (Toronto, Ont) #1729
– exhibitions (reviews)
  – (1847) #1690
Toronto Star, Can newspaper
– cartoons
  – Hunter, Samuel #943
  – Macpherson, Duncan #6401
  – Moyer, Harry #943
Toronto Theosophical Society (Toronto, Ont)
– and Bertram Richard Brooker #4926
– and Lawren Stewart Harris #5731
Torosian, Michael, Can photographer, 1952-
– portfolio of photographs #996
totem poles
– *see also* conservation and restoration, totem poles
totem poles, Bella Coola #3874
totem poles, Chilkat #3798
totem poles, Gitksan #3797 3815 3828 3834 3884 4032
– Kitwancool (BC) #3906 3925
totem poles, Haida #3766 3943 3982
– H'Kusam #3913
– Masset (Queen Charlotte Islands, BC) #3765
– Ninstints (BC) #4067

– Oxford (England), Oxford University. Pitt Rivers Museum #3775
– Queen Charlotte Islands (BC) #4008
– Vancouver (BC), Totem Park #4118 4124
totem poles, Kwakiutl #3848
– Alert Bay (BC) #3936
– Prince Rupert (BC) #3957
– Stockholm (Sweden), National Museum #3844
– Vancouver (BC), Totem Park #4124
– Victoria (BC), Beacon Hill Park #4115
totem poles, Lummi #3967
totem poles, natives of North America #3341
totem poles, Niska #4032
– Edinburgh (Scotland), Royal Scottish Museum #3839
– Toronto (Ont), Royal Ontario Museum #3895
totem poles, Northwest Coast Indians #2095 3766 3836 3849 3857 3866 3879 3909 3930 3977 3993 4057
– beaver motif #23
– Capilano totem pole #3837
– influence on Norman Tait #7314
– Martin, Mungo #6427
– Reid, Bill #3972 4162 6987
– Skedans (BC) #3984
– Vancouver (BC), Stanley Park #3932
totem poles, Tlingit #3781 3812
– Alaska #3873
– Tonpass (Alaska) #3856
totem poles, Tsimshian #3834
– Bear Mother #3868
– Nass River (BC) #3852
Toulouse-Lautrec, Henri Marie Raymond de, Fr artist, 1864-1901
– influence on Lillian Freiman #5517
Tounissoux, Françoise, Can artist, 1947- #1544
Toupin, Fernand, Can artist, 1930- #1541 7393 7395 7397
– exhibitions
  – (1970) #7394
– exhibitions, group
  – (1959) #1414
  – (1977) #1465
  – (1981) #1471
– interview #7396
Toupin, Gilles, Can art critic, 20th c.
– winner of critical writing on art competition (1979) #3312
Tourbin, Dennis, Can artist, 1946-
– on Jack Chambers #700
– performance art #655
Tourette-sur-Loup (France)
– Roussil, Robert, as founder of artist's colony #7091
Tousignant, Claude, Can artist, 1932- #7398 7400
– and minimal art #1483
– and Optical art #1445
– and plasticiens #1439
– drawings #6586
– exhibitions
  – (1973) #7401
  – (1980) #7402
– exhibitions, group
  – (1959) #1414
  – (1965) #469
  – (1967) #480
  – (1968) #1263
  – (1971) #98
  – (1973) #556
  – (1981) #1471

– interview #7399
– paintings (1953-1956) #1454
– symposium, Musée du Nouveau-Monde (La Rochelle, France), (1980) #1559
– use of colour #468 1425
Tousignant, Serge, Can artist, 1942- #1479 1480 1542 1543
– exhibitions
  – (1975) #7403
– exhibitions, group
  – (1981) #1564
– exhibitions (reviews) #1067
– interview #1485
– *Mona* and *Environment Transformé No 1, Dotscape* #7404
– on visual perception #525
– prints #7405
– use of light #767
– use of photography #1057
Tousley, Nancy, Can art critic, 1943-
– winner of critical writing on art competition (1979) #3312
Towdystan (BC)
– pictographs #3965
towers
– *see also* Martello towers; spires
towers, Canadian
– Toronto (Ont), CN Tower #9510 9511
– water towers, British Columbia #8153
Town, Harold Barling, Can artist, 1924- #7408 7409
– and Albert Jacques Franck #5501
– and Ontario printmaking (1960s) #1756
– and Toronto (Ont) painting (1960s) #1753
– drawings #7411
– exhibitions
  – (1973) #7413
  – (1975) #7415
  – (1980) #7416
– exhibitions, group
  – (1958) #431
  – (1959) #438
  – (1964) #462
  – (1967) #490 821
  – (1979) #510
– exhibitions (reviews) #520
– influence of Abstract-expressionism #1773
– influence of American painting #495
– influence on Toronto (Ont) painting (1960s) #1760
– interview #7407
– on comic strips #947
– on erotic art #7410
– on printmaking #817 818
– on relationship of artists and architects #8234
– on women in art #7414
– paintings and sculptures #449
– paintings on art market (1961) #445 446
– participant, Symposium on 20th Century Canadian Culture (Washington, DC), (1977) #621
– prints #7406
– stage designs #472
– works (1950s) #7412
– writings #92
town halls
– *see* city halls
town planning
– *see* city planning
townhouses
– *see* row houses
towns
– *see* cities and towns

Townsend, William, Brit artist in Canada, 1909-1973
- as juror, *Saskatchewan Arts Exhibition* (1963) #1910
- exhibitions
  - (1974) #7418
- works (1964-1968) #7417
toys
- 19th-early 20th cs., imported into Canada #2928
- Band, Percy, collection #2917
- late 19th c.-1930s #2932
toys, Blackfoot
- Minìpoka #3749
toys, Canadian #2938
- 18th-19th cs. #2594
- 19th-early 20th cs. #2928
- (1837-1887) #253
- ceramic miniatures and whimsys, 19th c. #2302
- Germanic tradition #2140
- guide for collectors #2125 2131
- Labrador #2955
- Ontario, 19th c. #2245
- Ottawa (Ont), National Museum of Man. Canadian Centre for Folk Culture Studies #963
- Québec #2226 2924
  - 17th-19th cs. #2921 2933 2934
  - (1800-1925) #2937
  - as folk art #1291
toys, Indians of North America #2934
toys, Ingalik #4087
toys, Inuit
- influence on Jean-Paul Riopelle #7025
Trace: A Canadian Review of Architecture, Can periodical #7753
trade, Algonquian
- silver and glass beads #3594
- trade silver #3608
trade, Haida
- argillite carving #4016
trade, Indians of North America #3440
trade, Iroquois
- trade silver #3645 3646
trade, Northwest Coast Indians #3949
trading posts, Canadian
- Alberta, 18th-19th cs. #8129
- Fort Langley (BC) #8477
- Lower Fort Garry (Man) #8483
trains
- *see* railroads
Trakas, George, Can sculptor, 1944- #1632 7422
- exhibitions
  - (1979) #7421
  - (1980) #7423
- exhibitions, group
  - (1978) #790
- exhibitions (reviews) #787
- interview #7420
- *Passage* and *Union Station* #7419
transcendentalism
- and Group of Seven #1774
transience
- and disposable art, Les Levine #6259
transportation
- Québec, 17th-19th cs., European influences #2221
transportation, Athapaskan #4104 4105
transportation, Blackfoot #3654
transportation, Cree #3402
transportation, Dogrib #4089
transportation, Han #4101

transportation, Huron #3514
transportation, Ingalik #4087
transportation, Ojibwa #3488 4089
transportation, Saulteaux #3402
transportation, Slavey #4089
transportation and architecture
- Canada
  - 19th c. #9512
  - (1938-1942) #7666
transportation in art
- Armstrong, William #4552
- Canadian posters #908 910
- Innes, John I. #5901
- Toronto (Ont), Metro Toronto Public Library. John Ross Robertson Historical Collection #3131
Trasov, Vincent (Mr. Peanut), Can artist, 1947-
- correspondence, on 1971 Miss General Idea Pageant #546
- exhibitions, group
  - (1971) #2042
  - (1979) #2070
travellers
- clothing, Canada, 18th-19th cs. #2826
tree of life
- German-Alsatian iron funeral crosses, Ontario #2709
- natives of North America #3365
trees in art
- *see also* leaves in art; plants in art
- British Columbia forests
  - 18th c.-1930s #2008
- Carr, Emily #5033
- myths and symbols, Iroquois and Algonquian #3516
Treherne, Harold J., Can artist, 1899-1975
- exhibitions, group
  - (1977) #1933
Tremblay, A. Henri, Can architect, fl. 1927-1954
- Lac Bouchette (Qué), Marial Chapel #8832
Tremblay, Alain, Can ceramicist, 1941- #2216
Tremblay, Denys, Can artist, 1951- #1540 1634
Tremblay, Esther, Can artist, 1927- #1551
Tremblay, Georges-Edouard, Can artist, 1907- #1428 1429
- hooked rug designs #2756
Tremblay, Gérard, Can artist, 1928- #1541 7424
- and Montréal (Qué) painting (1950s) #1403
Tremblay, Jean-Jacques, Can artist, 1926-
- paintings (1970s-1979) #7425
Tremblay, Michel, Can playwright, 1943-
- and Michel Leclair, *Chez Fada* album #6183
Tremblay, Michel-Thomas, Can artist, fl. 1974-
- as founder of Atelier de l'île (Val-David, Qué) #1664
Tremblay, Michèle, Can ceramicist, fl. 1960s-1970s #2216
Tremblay, Pierre-Paul, Can photographer, fl. 1981 #1562
Tremblay, Richard-Max, Can artist, 1952- #1526
Tremblay, Suzanne, Can ceramicist, fl. 1970s- #1549
Tremblay-Gagnon, Yvonne, Can artist, 1931- #1546
Tremblé, Léo-Paul, Can artist, 1924- #1547 1551
triangles

- in sculpture, Pierre Heyvaert #5797
Triaud, Louis-Hubert, Can artist, 1794-1836 #1336
Trier, Walter, Can artist, 1890-1951 #7426 7427
- exhibitions
  - (1980) #7428
Trinity (Nfld)
- architecture #7792
Trinity Bay (Nfld)
- domestic architecture #7785 7791 8541
Triple K Co-operative (Red Lake, Ont)
- serigraphy (1970s) #4151 4158
Trois-Rivières (Qué)
- architecture
  - 18th c. #7861
  - (1630s-1910s) #7883
- brick houses, early 19th c. #8521
- churches #8806
- decorative arts (1930s) #2174
- rocking chairs #2535
- seigneuries #8611
Trois-Rivières (Qué), Centre culturel de Trois-Rivières/Trois-Rivières Cultural Centre
- exhibitions
  - *Manitoba Mainstream: People's Art/Fine Art/Le Grand Courant du Manitoba: arts populaires, beaux-arts* (1973) #1897
Trois-Rivières (Qué), Chapel of the Recollets
- architecture and interior #8850
Trois-Rivières (Qué), church
- baldachin, Joseph Quintal (frère Augustin) and Gilles Bolvin #8826
- sculpture, Gilles Bolvin #4781
Trois-Rivières (Qué), Deschenaux House, also known as manoir de Tonnancour
- architecture and interior #8633
Trois-Rivières (Qué), Forges of Saint-Maurice #2698 2711 9238 9240
- architectural materials #7878
- architecture #9251 9256
- domestic architecture #8634 9250 9254
- historiography #9257
- mills #9253
- stoves #2708
Trois-Rivières (Qué), musée Pierre Boucher
- *see* Trois-Rivières (Qué), Université du Québec à Trois-Rivières. Musée Pierre Boucher
Trois-Rivières (Qué), Trois-Rivières Cultural Centre
- *see* Trois-Rivières (Qué), Centre culturel de Trois-Rivières/Trois-Rivières Cultural Centre
Trois-Rivières (Qué), Université du Québec à Trois-Rivières. Musée Pierre Boucher
- exhibitions
  - *De la figuration à la non-figuration dans l'art québécois* (1977) #1461
  - *Les moins de 35: du 22 janvier au 4 février* (1973) #1501
  - *Rodolphe Duguay, 1891-1973* (1979) #5318
trompe-l'oeil #525
Tropaco (Virgin Islands), Habitat
- architecture, Moshe Safdie #8404
Trottier, Gerald Mathew, Can artist, 1925-
- exhibitions, group
  - (1965) #469
- mosaic mural, Henry Marshall Tory Science Building, Carleton University (Ottawa, Ont) #7429
Trottier-Dufour, Gisèle, Can artist, fl. 1978 #1538

Trounce, Thomas, Can architect, 1813-1900
– Victoria (BC) #8145
Trowell, Ian, Can sculptor, 1930- #7431
– exhibitions
– (1980) #7430
Trowsse, Pegi, Can photographer, ca. 1952-
– portfolio of photographs #991
Trudeau, Angus, Can artist, 1908-
– exhibitions, group
– (1981) #4173
Trudeau, Charles Elliott, Can architect, 1922-
– Ottawa (Ont), Northern Electric Research
and Development Laboratories #9344
Trudeau, Randy, Can artist, 1954-
– exhibitions, group
– (1980) #4159
– (1981) #4173
Trudeau, Yves, Can sculptor, 1930- #7432
7435
– and Création #1492
– exhibitions
– (1975) #7434
– (1978) #7436
– sculptures (1960-1970) #7433
Trueman, Richard Henry, Can
photographer, 1856-1911 #7437
Truro (NS)
– architecture #7828
Tsimshian Indians
– art #3881 3926
– (1970s) #4145
– moon image #4059
– blankets #3826
– carved wooden containers, 19th c. #3985
– clubs #4048
– crests #3795 3981
– culture (1880s) #3763
– headgear #4019
– masks #4056 4069
– mirrors #3804
– mythology #3910
– portraits #3794
– puppets #3891
– serigraphy #4167
– stone clubs #4053
– totem poles #3834 3852 3868
Tsutakawa, George, Amer sculptor, 1910-
– fountain, Vancouver (BC) #2077
Tucson (Ariz), University of Arizona.
Museum of Art
– exhibitions
– Ernest Lawson 1873-1939 (1979) #6179
Tudor architecture
– influence on Vancouver (BC) houses
(1900-1930) #8730
Tudor-Hart, Ernest Percyval, Can artist,
1873-1954
– influence on Tony Law #6174
Tully, Kivas, Can architect, 1820-1905
– as member, Toronto Society of Arts #1689
– Cobourg (Ont), Victoria Hall #8994 8995
– Toronto (Ont) #8056
– Provincial Lunatic Asylum #9034
– Trinity College #9483
Tully, Sydney Strickland, Can artist,
1860-1911
– as teacher of Hattie Blackstock #4738
– exhibitions
– (1911) #7438
Tulsa (Okla), Philbrook Art Center
– exhibitions
– Magic Images: Contemporary Native
American Art (1981) #4172
– Native American Art at Philbrook (1980)

#4165
tumplines, Northwest Coast Indians
– prehistoric #4017
tunnels
– see also subways
tunnels, Canadian
– railroad tunnel, 19th c. (Ottawa, Ont)
#8019
Tunnillie, Ikayukta, Can artist, 1911-1980
#4460
Tupper, Sir Charles Andrew, Can statesman,
1821-1915
– correspondence, Frederic Marlett
Bell-Smith #4668
Turcot, Guy, Can photographer, 1950- #1562
– portfolio of photographs #997 999
tureens, British
– (ca. 1840), view of Montréal (Qué) #2370
Turgeon, Adélard, Can sculptor, 1883-1969
– woodcarvings, Nettie Sharpe collection
#1607
Turgeon, Joseph Ovide, Can architect,
1875-1933
– Montréal (Qué), La Patrie Building #9303
– Québec (Qué), Episcopal Palace #8787
Turner, E.R., Can harpsichord-maker can, fl.
1979 #2940
Turner, Jack, Can artist, 1934- #7439
Turner, Joseph Mallord William, Brit artist,
1775-1851
– Collings, Charles John, compared with
#5135
– influence on Gordon Appelbe Smith #7232
– influence on Lionel LeMoine FitzGerald
#5450
– influence on William Perehudoff #6837
– Verner, Frederick Arthur, compared with
#1696
Turner, Philip John, Can architect, 1876-1943
– Vancouver (BC), University of British
Columbia, competition #9498
Turner, Richard Julian, Can artist, 1936-
#7440
– exhibitions, group
– (1967) #490
Turner & Carless, Can architectural firm
– domestic architecture #8494
– Montréal (Qué) #8493 8556
turtles in art
– ceramic sculpture, Joe Fafard and students
#1924
Tutchone Indians
– culture #4106
Tuu'luq, Marion, Can artist, 1910- #4255
– exhibitions
– (1980) #7442
– exhibitions, group
– (1976) #4268
– exhibitions (reviews) #7441
Twana Indians
– culture (1870s) #4031
Tweedsmuir, Lord
– see Buchan, John, 1st Baron Tweedsmuir
Twillingate (Nfld)
– architecture #7792
Twomey, Jerry, Can collector, 1915-
– collection, Inuit art #4306 4427
Tyara site (Sugluk Island, Qué)
– Dorset artifacts #4351
Typographic Designers of Canada
– (1956) #923
typography
– see printing
Tyrrell, Joseph Burr, Can photographer,

1858-1957
– survey photographs #1014 1015 1865

U

Uhthoff, Ina D.D., Can artist, 1889-1971
#7443
Ukrainian Women's Association of Canada
– preservation and promotion of Ukrainian
handicrafts #2782
Ukrainians in Canada
– architecture #8085 8127 8713
– art #1843
– Bukovynian shirts and jewellery
(1865-1945) #2869
– churches #8768 8912 8915
– churches and decorative arts #2270
– domestic architecture #8691 8704 8709
8710
– Easter eggs #2132
– embroidery #2124 2782
– folk art #968 2117
– late 18th-20th cs. #961
– Kurelek, William, paintings of #6113 6114
6116
– log buildings #8090 8136
– needlework #2780
– sepulchral monuments #733
Ulrich, James (Jim), Can artist, 1944-
– exhibitions, group
– (1977) #1956
Umholtz, David, Can artist, 1943-
– exhibitions, group
– (1977) #1901
– (1978) #669
umiaks
– see also boats
umiaks, Inuit #3339
– compared with Nootka canoes #3344
Una
– see Oonark, Jessie
Unaaq
– see Oonark, Jessie
underground railroads
– see subways
UNESCO
– and Norman McLaren #6492
– and Royal Commission on National
Development in the Arts, Letters and
Sciences (Massey Report) #3261
Ungava District (Qué)
– Naskapi Indians and Inuit culture (1880s)
#3379
Uniake, Richard John, Can statesman,
1753-1830
– residence, Uniake House (Mount Uniake,
NS) #8534
universities and colleges, Canadian
– (1911-1912) #8295
– (1920s) #7656
– (1960-1970) #7710
– (1960s) #9396 9400 9401
– and government planning #9395
– (1970s) #9478
– and art education
– (1894), recommendations #2960
– Lismer, Arthur, on #2966
– and Royal Commission on National
Development in the Arts, Letters and
Sciences (Massey Report) #3261
– and study of Canadian art history

– (1930s-1960s) #3306
– (1980) #3316
– Burnaby (BC), Simon Fraser University #9406 9501 9504 9505 9506
– Edmonton (Alta), University of Alberta #9492 9493 9495
  – Students' Union Housing #9496
– Gothic revival #7671
– Guelph (Ont), University of Guelph. Arts and Library buildings #9468
– Halifax (NS)
  – Dalhousie University #9408
  – Nova Scotia College of Art and Design #9409 9410
– Hamilton (Ont), McMaster University #9451
– interior design (1960s) #9402
– Kingston (Ont), Queen's University #9447
  – Douglas Library #9445
  – Women's Residence #9445
– Lethbridge (Alta), University of Lethbridge #9406 9497
– libraries
  – (1930s) #9042
  – (1960s) #9046
  – (1970s) #9052
– London (Ont), University of Western Ontario #9442 9448
– Montréal (Qué)
  – McGill University #9414 9423
    – Athletic buildings #9417
    – Macdonald Physics Building #9411
    – Medical Building #9412
  – Université de Montréal #8345 9415
  – Université du Québec à Montréal #9427
– Ontario, museum collections (1850-1900) #3152
– Ottawa (Ont)
  – Carleton University #9455
    – School of Architecture #8284
  – University of Ottawa #9458 9465
– Peterborough (Ont), Trent University #9470 9473 9474
  – Champlain College #9465
– Québec (1960s) #7862
– Québec (Qué), Campus intercommunautaire de Cap-Rouge #9421
– Saskatoon (Sask), University of Saskatchewan #9489 9490 9491
– Scarborough (Ont), University of Toronto. Scarborough College #9462 9463 9464
– Sudbury (Ont), Laurentian University #9461
– Toronto (Ont)
  – George Brown College of Applied Arts & Technology. Casa Loma Campus #9479
  – University of Toronto #9444 9449 9459 9477
    – Convocation Hall #9430
    – Emmanuel College #9452
    – expansion program (1950s) #9456
    – Hart House #9433 9438 9439 9440 9441
    – Knox College #9432 9435
    – Massey College #9460
    – men's residence #9431
    – Trinity College #9446 9483
    – University College #9428 9429 9453 9475 9482
    – Victoria College. Wymilwood #9454
  – York University #9469
    – Glendon Hall #9457
– university housing (1960s) #9399 9467

– Vancouver (BC)
  – University of British Columbia #9498 9499 9500 9509
    – Fine Arts Building #9502
    – Student Union #9503
– Winnipeg (Man), University of Manitoba #9485 9486
  – School of Architecture #9487
  – University Centre #9488
– Wolfville (NS), Acadia University #9407
Universities Art Association of Canada
– conference session, on Canadian art funding (1979) #3293
– periodical, RACAR (Revue d'art canadienne/Canadian Art Review) #114
upholstery, Canadian
– Montréal (Qué), (1800-1850) #2538
– Québec
  – 17th-18th cs. #2530 2531
  – (1790-1890) #2536
Upper Canada Agricultural Society
– (1846-1867), exhibitions #1715
Upper Canada Village (Morrisburg, Ont) #7981 8031 8063
– architecture #7982 7988
– Cook, Nelson, portraits of Dickinson family #5170
– furniture #2484 2549
– spinning and weaving #2726
Upper Fort Garry (Man)
– architecture #8094
Urban, Colette, Can artist, 1952-
– exhibitions (reviews) #1227
urban development
– see also city planning
– Alberta, Chinatowns, 20th c. #8137
– British Columbia
  – (1950s) #8142
  – early 20th c., Royal Engineers #8150
– Calgary (Alta), (1970s) #8122 9362
– Canada
  – (1850-1900), photographic views #7744
  – (1867-1967) #7695
  – (1880-1914) #7736
  – (1950s) #8514
  – (1960s) #8231 8311 8518
  – and housing
    – (1960s) #8513 8515
    – (1970s) #7728
  – and office buildings
    – (1950s-1970s) #9302
    – (1960s) #9300 9301
– Edmonton (Alta), (1970s) #8123
– Faro (Yukon), (1970s) #8182
– Halifax (NS) #7835
– Kitsilano (BC), (1970s) #8146
– Massey Awards for Excellence in the Urban Environment (1975) #8218
– Montréal (Qué) #7914
  – 17th-20th cs. #7902 7906 7931
  – (1642-1970s) #7918 7934
  – (1803-1878) #7924
  – (1950s-1960s) #7901
  – Old Montréal (1970s) #7911
  – Place Bonaventure #9325
– Ontario (1970s) #8024
– Ottawa (Ont)
  – Glebe district #8042
  – National Capital Region #8035 8037 8039
  – Smyth Road Development Competition (1960) #8040
– Prairies, 20th c. #8089
– Québec #7867
  – 17th-18th cs. #7885 8603

– Québec (Qué) #7938
– Safdie, Moshe, on #8403 8405
– Toronto (Ont)
  – and housing (1970s) #8068
  – and subway system (1970s) #9554
  – Flemingdon Park (1960s) #8657
  – Harbour City (1970s) #8062
  – Regent Park (1950s) #8511
  – St. Lawrence Neighbourhood, progress report (1980) #8079
  – York Square (1960s) #9347
  – Yorkville Village (1960s) #9376
– Vancouver (BC) #8161
  – 20th c. #8171
  – (1960s) #8158
  – (1970s) #8162
  – and housing
    – (1886-1929) #8714 8730
    – (1980) #8725
  – False Creek (1920s-1980) #8169
– Victoria (BC), (1970s) #8146
– Winnipeg (Man)
  – (1870-1914) #8103
  – (1950s) #8514
  – (1970s) #8104 8108
urban planning
– see city planning
urbanism
– see city planning
Uritani, Giselle, Can stained glass artist, fl. 1975
– stained glass #2452
Urquhart, Tony, Can artist, 1934- #7444 7445
– and Toronto (Ont) painting (1960s) #1753
– archetypal imagery #7446
– death theme #1759
– drawings #7447
– exhibitions
  – (1978) #7448
– exhibitions, group
  – (1965) #473
  – (1978) #665
– landscapes #7449
– regionalism, compared with Greg Curnoe #5225
– sculptures (1960s) #1793
Ursulines
– art #1323 1334 1335
– art education #2979
– decorative arts #2174
– embroidery #1581 2169 2171 2777 2779 2780 2781 2783 2788 2789 2791 3629
  – Le Ber, Jeanne #2778
– gilding #2930
– Québec (Qué), Ursuline Convent #1352 8810
  – Chapel #8852
– silver, François Ranvoyzé #2658
– tabernacles #1359
– weaving #2212
Urushibara Mokuchu, Yoshijiro, Ja artist, 1888-1953
– and Walter Joseph Phillips #6860
Urwick Currie & Partners Ltd., management consultants
– study of Royal Architectural Institute of Canada (1974) #8318
USSR
– photographic views, Michael William Semak #7169
Utrecht (Netherlands), Utrecht Centraal Museum
– exhibitions
  – Moderne canadese schilderkunst (1958)

#431
Uu, David, Can artist, 1948-
- exhibitions, group
  - (1971) #2042
  - (1973) #2045
- exhibitions (reviews) #2051

V

Vachon, Ginette, Can photographer, ca.
  1949-
- portfolio of photographs #1032
Vadeboncoeur, F.Louis, Can sculptor,
  architect, 1831-1896 #1319
Vail, Floyd, Can photographer, fl. 1894 #977
Vaillancourt, Armand, Can sculptor, 1932-
  #1502 7450
- and André Fournelle #5484
- exhibitions, group
  - (1977) #1622
- fountain, Embarcadero Plaza (San
  Francisco, Calif) #7451
- influence on Pierre Rolland Dinel #5293
- press reaction #7452
- sculptures (1960s) #745 746
- Symposium international de sculpture
  environnementale de Chicoutimi (Qué),
  (1980) #1639
Vaillancourt, Paul-Gilles, Can artist, 1941-
- stage designs and costumes, Montreal
  Theatre Ballet #1410
Val-d'Or (Qué), Centre culturel de Val-d'Or
- exhibitions
  - De la figuration à la non-figuration dans
    l'art québécois (1977) #1461
Val-David (Qué), Atelier de l'île #1664
Valcourt (Qué), Centre culturel de Valcourt
- exhibitions
  - De la figuration à la non-figuration dans
    l'art québécois (1977) #1461
Vale, Florence Gertrude, Can artist, 1909-
- and Albert Jacques Franck #5499
- drawings, influence on Harold Barling
  Town #7413
- exhibitions
  - (1980) #7453
Valentine, Hugh Allen Inglis, Can architect,
  1904-1978
- Montréal (Qué), McGill University.
  Athletic buildings, competition #9417
Valentine, William, Can artist, 1798-1849
  #1191
- daguerreotype portraits #1211
- influence on Maria Frances Ann Morris
  Miller #6541
Valéry, Paul, Fr poet, 1871-1945
- Cormier, Ernest, compared with #8346
Valin, Jean, Can sculptor, 1691-1759
- tabernacles #1613
Valiquet, Carl, Can photographer, 1946-
- portfolio of photographs #997 999
Valius, Telesforas, Can artist, 1914-1977
- as teacher of Ed Bartram #4618
Vallery, Hugh J., Can, 20th c.
- as codirector, Toronto School Board Study
  of Educational Facilities (SEF) #9472
Valley City Seating Company, woodcarving
  firm (Dundas, Ont)
- altar and reredos, Church of Saint John
  the Evangelist (Hamilton, Ont) #730
Valleyfield (Qué), Cathedral of

Salaberry-de-Valleyfield
- architecture, Henri Sicotte Labelle in
  association with Jean M. Lafleur and J.
  Eugène Perron; L.N. Audet, Consulting
  Architect #8843
Valleyfield (Qué), Catholic Seminary
- (1950s) #3034
Vallière, Lauréat, Can sculptor, 1888-1973
  #7454 7455
- woodcarvings, Church of Sainte-Famille
  (île d'Orléans, Qué) #1612
Vallière, Phillipe, Can furniture-maker, 19th
  c. #2464
Van Den Heuvel, Francis
- see Heuvel, Francis van den
Van der Hilst, Robert
- see Hilst, Robert van der
Van der Keuken, Johan
- see Keuken, Johan van der
Van Dusen, Raymond (Ray), Can
  photographer, 1949-
- exhibitions, group
  - (1981) #1070
Van Ginhoven, Anke, Can artist, 1931- #1282
Van Gogh, Vincent
- see Gogh, Vincent van
Van Horne, Sir William Cornelius, Can
  railway official, collector, 1843-1915 #1713
- and James Wilson Morrice #6626
- and railway hotels #9290
- correspondence, Frederic Marlett
  Bell-Smith #4668
- residence, Sir William Van Horne Mansion
  (Montréal, Qué) #8594 8601
Van Norman, Joseph, Can ironmaster, fl.
  1813-1829
- and Normandale Iron Works (Norfolk
  County, Ont) #2699
Van Slyck, Winnifred (Wyn), Can artist,
  1910-
- and the Dugald Costume Collection
  (Dugald, Man) #2902
Vance, Dennis John, Can artist, 1940-
- exhibitions, group
  - (1976) #2060
Vancouver, George, Brit navigator, explorer
  in Canada, 1758-1798
- aesthetic response to Northwest Coast
  #2009
- expedition, Northwest Coast Indians #3445
  3767 4062
Vancouver (BC)
- apartment houses (1960s) #8699
- architecture #7762 8159 8164 8166 8170
  - (1886-1914) #8165
  - (1899-1901) #1977
  - (1910s-1970s), downtown area #8171
  - (1914) #8156
  - (1940s) #8141
  - (1950s) #7673 8144 8157
  - (1959-1961) #8158
  - (1960s) #7698
  - Art Deco #8167
  - Downs, Barry Vance #8353
  - Erickson, Arthur Charles #8357
  - Gastown #7772 8160 8163
  - Hooper, Thomas #8376
  - Kemble, Roger #8379
  - Robson Square #8172
  - walking and driving tours #8168
  - Whiteway, William Tuff #9508
- architecture and art (1950s) #1992
- art #547
  - 20th c. #536

- (1886-1930) #2003
- (1890s-1940s) #1984
- (1944-1955) #7230
- (1950s-1960s) #2039
- (1950s-1970s) #131
- (1960s) #90 441 519 2035 2036 2038
- (1970s) #1870 2040 2053
- (1980) #2076
- art galleries (1960s) #442
- comic strips (1970s) #955
- conservation of architecture #7761 8161
- domestic architecture
  - (1886-1929) #8714 8730
  - (1950-1960) #8697
  - rehabilitation proposal for inner city
    buildings (1980) #8725
  - Thom, Ron #8411
- fountains #2077
- museums #3190
- neon signs #2079
- office buildings
  - (1950s-1960s) #9300
  - architects' offices (1940s) #9297
- open-air sculpture #2080
- painting #2000
  - (1920s-1950s) #424
  - (1940s-1950s) #412
  - (1960s) #520
  - (1970s) #2075
- performance art #2073
- photographic views
  - (1886-1888), J.A. Brock & Co. #2021
  - Bailey, Charles S. #4583
- photography
  - (1880s-1890s) #2022
  - (1960s) #2019
  - (1970s) #998 2064 2069
- public art (1905-1971) #2005
- railroad stations #9545 9546
- recreation buildings #9081
- sculpture #2026
  - (1960s) #1854 2037
  - (1970s) #2049
- stained glass windows
  - (1890-1940) #2454 2456
  - Dearle, John Henry, and Duncan W.
    #2458
- urban development (1970s) #8162
- video art #605 2044
- views
  - (1845-1871) #2020
  - McMurtie, William Birch #6505
Vancouver (BC), Ace Space Company
- videos #2044
Vancouver (BC), Arthur Erickson House
- architecture, Arthur Charles Erickson
  #8357
Vancouver (BC), B.C. Binning House
- architecture #8694
Vancouver (BC), B.C. Electric Building
- architecture, Thompson, Berwick & Pratt
  #7679
Vancouver (BC), Bau-Xi Gallery
- exhibitions
  - Toni Onley: 10 Years of Painting, 1962-72
    (1972) #6736
- exhibitions (reviews)
  - Doray, Audrey Capel #5301
  - Shadbolt, Jack Leonard (1973) #7184
  - Smith, Gordon Appelbe (1978) #7231
Vancouver (BC), BC Art League. Gallery
- exhibitions
  - British Columbia Society of Fine Arts
    #1978

Vancouver (BC), Birks Building
- architecture and recommendation for
  conservation #7762
- proposed demolition #8146
Vancouver (BC), Block 51-61-71 project
- architecture #7728
Vancouver (BC), Brittania Community
  Services Centre
- architecture and planning #9116
Vancouver (BC), Canadian Broadcasting
  Corporation
- architecture, CBC Engineering
  Headquarters; Thompson, Berwick, Pratt
  & Partners, Associate Architects #8171
Vancouver (BC), Canadian Pacific Railway
  Station
- architecture, Barott, Blackader & Webster
  #9534
- architecture and recommendation for
  conservation #7762
Vancouver (BC), Caulfield Cove
  Townhouses
- architecture, Ronald Howard and Barclay
  McLeod #8746
Vancouver (BC), Charles H. Scott Gallery
- see Vancouver (BC), Emily Carr College of
  Art. Charles H. Scott Gallery
Vancouver (BC), Chinatown
- architecture #8171
- restoration, Birmingham & Wood #8159
Vancouver (BC), Chinatown freeway project
- architectural proposal, Arthur Charles
  Erickson #8360
Vancouver (BC), Chinese Cultural Centre
- architecture, competition for #9144
Vancouver (BC), Christ Church Cathedral
- architectural proposal, Arthur Charles
  Erickson #8360
- architecture, C.O. Wickenden #8171
- architecture and recommendation for
  conservation #7762 8910
Vancouver (BC), City Stage Theatre
- architecture, Hawthorn Mansfield Towers
  #8373
Vancouver (BC), Connexions
- videos #2044
Vancouver (BC), Coquitlam Centre
- stained glass #2459 2460
Vancouver (BC), Court House
- architecture and recommendation for
  conservation #7762
Vancouver (BC), Courthouse
- architecture, Arthur Charles Erickson
  #8362
Vancouver (BC), Crown Life Insurance
  headquarters
- architecture, Thompson, Berwick & Pratt
  #7683
Vancouver (BC), Dal Grauer Substation
- architecture, Sharp & Thompson, Berwick,
  Pratt #8171
Vancouver (BC), David Y.H. Lui Theatre
- architecture, Hawthorn Mansfield Towers
  #8373
Vancouver (BC), Dominion Hall
- exhibitions
  - British Columbia Society of Fine Arts
    (1909) #1978
Vancouver (BC), Eera Townhouses
- architecture, Hawthorn Mansfield Towers
  #8373
Vancouver (BC), Emily Carr College of Art.
  Charles H. Scott Gallery
- exhibitions

- The West Face, 1981 (1981) #2084
- Vancouver School of Art: The Early Years,
  1925-1939 (1980) #3019
- Wood, Alan, Ranch installation work
  (1981) #7611
Vancouver (BC), Eppich House
- architecture, Arthur Charles Erickson
  #8745
Vancouver (BC), Equinox Gallery
- exhibitions (reviews)
  - Michener, Robert (1974) #6526
Vancouver (BC), Eye Scream Restaurant
- exhibition, N.E. Thing Co. Ltd. (1977)
  #6678
Vancouver (BC), F.P. 18 (Champlain Place)
- architecture, Downs & Archambault #8744
Vancouver (BC), Fairview Place
- architecture, Rhone & Iredale #8746
Vancouver (BC), False Creek
- architecture and urban development #8169
  - Thompson, Berwick, Pratt & Partners
    #8170
Vancouver (BC), Finlayson House
- architecture, Samuel Maclure #8384
Vancouver (BC), Gallery of Photography
- Baykal, Erol, on #2052
Vancouver (BC), Goddamatch
- videos #2044
Vancouver (BC), Gordon Smith House
- architecture, Arthur Charles Erickson
  #8357
Vancouver (BC), Granville Island
- architecture, Norman Hotson Architects
  #8170
Vancouver (BC), Harbour Park
- architecture and urban development #9302
Vancouver (BC), Hauer House
- architecture, Erickson/Massey #8519
Vancouver (BC), Hodson Manor
- architecture #8707
Vancouver (BC), Hotel Vancouver
- architecture and interior, Francis S. Swales
  #9272 9273
- architecture and recommendation for
  conservation #7762
Vancouver (BC), Hudson's Bay Company.
  Vancouver Store
- exhibitions
  - The World of Emily Carr: A New
    Exhibition of Her Paintings from the
    Newcombe Collection, Recently Acquired by
    the Province of British Columbia (1962)
    #5023
Vancouver (BC), IBM Building
- architecture, Thompson, Berwick, Pratt &
  Partners #9301
Vancouver (BC), Imperial Bank
- mosaic mural, B.C. Binning #4732
Vancouver (BC), Imperial Bank of Canada
- architecture, Gerald Hamilton #9193
Vancouver (BC), Infinity Studio
- videos #2044
Vancouver (BC), Kenneth Heffel Gallery
- exhibitions (reviews)
  - Onley, Toni #6742
Vancouver (BC), Laurel Street Crossing
- architecture, Hawthorn Mansfield Towers
  #8373
Vancouver (BC), lodge for paraplegics
- architecture, Downs & Archambault #8744
Vancouver (BC), MacMillan Bloedel
  Building
- architecture, Arthur Charles Erickson
  #8357 8361 9358

Vancouver (BC), Maples Development
- architecture, Daniel E. White #8746
Vancouver (BC), Marine Building
- architecture, McCarter & Nairne #8171
  9356
Vancouver (BC), Metro Media
- videos #2044
Vancouver (BC), Nelson Towers
- architecture, Erickson/Massey #8744
Vancouver (BC), Nova Gallery
- exhibitions (reviews)
  - Allegorical Imperatives (1978) #7507
Vancouver (BC), Open Space
- (1970s) #641
Vancouver (BC), Orpheum Theatre
- architecture, Benjamin Marcus Priteca, and
  restoration, Thompson, Berwick & Pratt
  #9141
Vancouver (BC), Pender Street Gallery
- exhibitions (reviews)
  - Lodge, Judy (1977) #6321
Vancouver (BC), Petrov Restoration Gallery
- exhibitions
  - Tomtu H. Roberts: Early Canadian Artist
    (1859-1938) (1980) #7051
Vancouver (BC), Porter House
- architecture, Davison & Porter #7679
Vancouver (BC), Project 200
- architecture and urban development #9302
Vancouver (BC), Queen Elizabeth Theatre
- architecture, Affleck, Desbarats,
  Dimakopoulos, Lebensold, Michaud, Sise
  #7679 9085
- exhibitions
  - Centennial Sculpture '67 (1967) #2001
Vancouver (BC), Raymur Place Housing
- architecture, Duncan McNab & Partners
  #8520
Vancouver (BC), Robert M. Filberg House
- architecture, Arthur Charles Erickson
  #8354
Vancouver (BC), Robson Square
- architecture #8171
  - Erickson, Arthur Charles #8362
Vancouver (BC), Robson Square Complex
- exhibitions
  - Artisan '78: The First National Travelling
    Exhibition of Contemporary Canadian
    Crafts/Artisan '78: première exposition
    nationale itinérante d'artisanat canadien
    contemporain (1979) #2134
Vancouver (BC), Royal Bank
- architecture, Sumner Godfrey Davenport
  #8171 9179
Vancouver (BC), Royal Trust
- architecture, James Tettamanti #9301
Vancouver (BC), Saint James Anglican
  Church
- architecture, Adrian Gilbert Scott; Sharp &
  Thompson, Associate Architects #8171
Vancouver (BC), Saint Paul's Hospital.
  Surgical Wing
- Gardiner & Mercer #9021
Vancouver (BC), Saint Paul's Indian Mission
  Church
- architecture #8919
Vancouver (BC), Sam Kee Building
- architecture #8171
Vancouver (BC), Shannon Estate
- architecture, Arthur Charles Erickson
  #8360
Vancouver (BC), Stanley Park
- totem poles #3932
Vancouver (BC), Terminal City Club

– architecture and interior, Philip M. Jullien #9061

Vancouver (BC), University of British Columbia
– architecture #9499
  – competition for #9498 9509
  – Thompson, Berwick & Pratt #9500
– art, Kwakiutl Indians #4037
– art education
  – (1950s) #1992
  – (1970s) #3006
– Binning, B.C., as teacher #4734
– Martin, Mungo, totem poles #6427
– planning, Thomas Hayton Mawson #9405
– public art (1905-1971) #2005
– sculpture #2026

Vancouver (BC), University of British Columbia. Fine Arts Building
– architecture, Thompson, Berwick & Pratt #9502

Vancouver (BC), University of British Columbia. Fine Arts Gallery
– exhibitions
  – 477-74-7, An Exhibition of Work of 7 Professors in the Bachelor of Fine Arts Program, U.B.C. (1974) #2050
  – 7 West Coast Painters (1959) #1997
  – Ann Kipling: Recent Landscapes (1980) #6057
  – B.C. Binning: A Retrospective (1973) #4734
  – Canadian West Coast Hermetics: The Metaphysical Landscape/Les hermétiques canadiens de la côte ouest: le paysage métaphysique (1973) #2045
  – Contemporary Ceramic Sculpture from Alberta, Saskatchewan, British Columbia and Manitoba (1974) #1864
  – Four Canadian Artists: Arnold Shives, Wayne Eastcott, Pnina Granirer, James Felter (1976) #2059
  – Glenn Toppings Remembered (1978) #7392
  – Image Bank Post Card Show (1971) #826
  – Joe Plaskett and His Paris: In Search of Time Past (1971) #6893
  – Joe Plaskett et son Paris: à la recherche d'un temps passé (1971) #6894
  – Joy and Celebration (1967) #2036
  – Lithographs/Lithographies (1972) #825
  – Liz Magor (1979) #6405
  – Paintings from the Collection of Ernest E. Poole and Family (1959) #3217
  – The Collage Show (1971) #2042
  – The Mr. and Mrs. Jules Loeb Collection/La collection M. et Mme Jules Loeb (1971) #3231
  – Younger Vancouver Sculptors (1968) #2037
– exhibitions (reviews)
  – B.C. Binning: A Retrospective (1973) #4735
  – Canadian West Coast Hermetics: The Metaphysical Landscape/Les Hermétiques canadiens de la côte ouest: le paysage métaphysique (1973) #2051

Vancouver (BC), University of British Columbia. Grounds
– exhibitions
  – Open Air Sculpture Exhibition (1956,1958,1960) #1993

Vancouver (BC), University of British Columbia. Gymnasium
– architecture, Thompson, Berwick & Pratt and Fred Lasserre #7679

Vancouver (BC), University of British Columbia. Museum of Anthropology
– architecture, Arthur Charles Erickson

#8170 8360 9132 9137 9138
– art, Kwakiutl Indians #3996
– art, Northwest Coast Indians, Walter and Marianne Koerner collection #3994
– collections #3195
– exhibitions
  – Cycles, the Graphic Art of Robert Davidson, Haida (1979) #5268
  – Joe David (1978) #5266
  – Norman Tait, Nishga Carver (1977) #7314
  – Plantae Occidentalis: 200 Years of Botanical Art in British Columbia (1979) #2024
  – Pursuing the Past: A General Account of British Columbia Archaeology (1978) #4023
– Martin, Mungo, paintings #6429
– Reid, Bill, Raven and the First People #6989

Vancouver (BC), University of British Columbia. School of Architecture
– architectural education
  – (1947) #8246
  – (1948) #8247
  – (1949) #8248
  – (1950) #8249
  – (1951) #8250
  – (1952) #8252
  – (1955) #8258
  – (1960s) #8265
  – (1970s) #8146
  – (1980) #8289

Vancouver (BC), University of British Columbia. Sedgewick Undergraduate Library
– architecture, Rhone & Iredale #9052

Vancouver (BC), University of British Columbia. Student residence
– architecture, Vladimir Plavsic & Associates #9467

Vancouver (BC), University of British Columbia. Student Union
– architecture, competition for #9503

Vancouver (BC), University of British Columbia. Student Union. Art Gallery
– exhibitions
  – Dawn: An Exhibition by Women Artists of British Columbia (1975) #2054

Vancouver (BC), University of British Columbia. Thea Koerner House
– architecture, Thompson, Berwick & Pratt #7683

Vancouver (BC), University of British Columbia. Thunderbird Stadium
– architecture, Vladimir Plavsic & Associates #9101

Vancouver (BC), University of British Columbia. Totem Park #4118 4124

Vancouver (BC), Up Front
– videos #2044

Vancouver (BC), Van Dusen Gardens
– stone sculptures, International Stone Symposium (1975) #775

Vancouver (BC), Vancouver Airport. Air Terminal Building
– architecture, McCarter, Nairne & Partners #9514
– public art #2005

Vancouver (BC), Vancouver Art Gallery
– (1940s) #1841 3185
– (1950s) #1992
– (1980) #3203
– art education (1970s) #3006
– Carr, Emily, works #5039 5042
– carving, Haida Indians #3820
– collection #3186
– exhibitions

– 13 Cameras (1978) #2069
– 17 Canadian Artists: A Protean View (1976) #618
– Affinities: Ten Painters of This Region; Max Benjamin, Pierre Coupey, Laurie de Camillis, Sally Gregson, Robin Mayor, Ken Meisterman, Gordon Payne, Ranjan Sen, Ken Wallace, Robert E. Youds (1979) #2075
– An Exhibition of Paintings on Canvas and a Mural by Bill Featherston (1979) #5417
– Ann Kipling (1976) #6055
– Another Dimension/Une autre dimension (1977) #783
– Architectural References: Alice Aycock, Melvin Charney, General Idea, Glenn Lewis, Gordon Matta-Clark, Anne & Patrick Poirier, Charles Simonds, Site, Alan Sonfist (1980) #8237
– Art of the Raven: Masterworks by the Northwest Coast Indian, (1967) #3948
– B.C. Artists Annual Exhibition (1932-1968) #1983
– Baker Lake Drawings (1972) #4241
– Bewilderness: The Origins of Paradise (1978) #6276
– Bill Jones: A Survey (1976) #5979
– Bill Reid: A Retrospective Exhibition (1974) #6985
– Borduas and America/Borduas et l'Amérique (1977) #4838
– British Columbia Society of Artists (1909-1967) #1978
– Canadian Painting in the Thirties (1975) #592
– Canadian Tapestries, 1977 (1977) #2770
– Catalogue: Founders' Collection (1931) #3184
– Charles Gagnon (1979) #5540
– Christopher Pratt (1970) #6910
– Clark McDougall: Paintings Since 1953 (1977) #6464
– Claude Tousignant (1973) #7401
– Confrontations: Ian Carr-Harris, John McEwen, John Massey (1979) #794
– David Craven: Recent Works (1977) #5205
– de Tonnancour (1966) #7387
– Dessins inédits d'Ozias Leduc/Ozias Leduc the Draughtsman (1979) #6210
– Don Jarvis: A Twenty-Nine Year Retrospective (1977) #5947
– E.J. Hughes (1967) #5860
– Eleven Early British Columbian Photographers, 1890-1940 (1976) #2012
– Emily Carr: A Centennial Exhibition Celebrating the One Hundredth Anniversary of Her Birth (1971) #5027
– Emily Carr: exposition centenaire commémorant le centième anniversaire de sa naissance (1971) #5028
– Eric Cameron/Noel Harding: Two Audio-Visual Constructs/Eric Cameron/Noel Harding: deux installations audio-visuelles (1978) #667
– Eric Freifeld: Selected Works, 1938-1968 (1968) #5514
– For Suzy Lake, Chris Knudsen, and Robert Walker (1978) #668
– From This Point of View: 60 British Columbia Painters, Sculptors, Photographers, Graphic and Video Artists (1977) #2063
– Gordon Smith (1976) #7229
– Graham Coughtry: Retrospective (1977)

#5190
- *Group of Seven* (1954) #1747
- *Guido Molinari* (1976) #6588
- *Henry Saxe, Robin MacKenzie, Irene Whittome, David Rabinowitch, Nobuo Kubota, Royden Rabinowitch, Colette Whiten* (1976) #779
- *Ian Wallace: Work, 1979* (1979) #7509
- *Images for a Canadian Heritage* (1966) #79
- *Impressionism in Canada, 1895-1935* (1974) #115
- *Irene Whittome, 1975-1980* (1980) #7569
- *J.Fenwick Lansdowne* (1981) #6164
- *J.M. Barnsley (1861-1929), Retrospective Exhibition* (1964) #4611
- *Jack Bush: A Retrospective/Rétrospective: Jack Bush* (1976) #4969
- *Jack Chambers : A Retrospective* (1970) #5074
- *Jack Shadbolt* (1969) #7182
- *Jack Shadbolt: Seven Years* (1978) #7187
- *Jacques Hurtubise* (1981) #5890
- *Jock Macdonald: The Inner Landscape: A Retrospective Exhibition/Jock Macdonald: le paysage intérieur: rétrospective* (1982) #6379
- *John Meredith: Fifteen Years* (1975) #6514
- *Lawren Harris: Retrospective Exhibition, 1963/Lawren Harris: exposition rétrospective, 1963* (1963) #5725
- *Les chroniques du Québec d'Arthur Villeneuve/Arthur Villeneuve's Quebec Chronicles* (1972) #7491
- *Les Levine* (1974) #6267
- *Leslie Poole: Confessions* (1979) #6903
- *Lies & Truths: An Exhibition of Mixed Format Installations by Vera Frenkel* (1978) #5525
- *Liz Magor: Production/Reproduction* (1980) #6407
- *Maxwell Bates in Retrospect, 1921-1971* (1973) #4624
- *Mia Westerlund: Recent Work, Sculpture and Drawing* (1978) #7544
- *Montreal Tapes: Video as a Community or Political Tool* (1978) #1537 1550
- *N.E. Thing Co. Ltd: Another 2 Projects: People/Language, Eye Scream Restaurant* (1977) #6678
- *Norman White* (1975) #7554
- *Of Ships and the Sea, 1600-1900* (1963) #225
- *One Hundred Years of B.C. Art: An Exhibition Held at the Vancouver Art Gallery to Commemorate the British Columbia Centennial Year* (1958) #1995
- *Oonark/Pangnark* (1970) #4220
- *Pacific Vibrations* (1973) #2046
- *Paterson Ewen: Recent Works* (1977) #5386
- *Peinture canadienne des années trente* (1975) #589
- *People's Art: Naïve Art in Canada/L'art populaire: l'art naïf au Canada* (1974) #966
- *Pottery by Wayne Ngan* (1978) #6695
- *R. Fish* (1978) #5434
- *R.L. Bloore: Sixteen Years, 1958-1975* (1975) #4751
- *Roy K. Kiyooka: 25 Years* (1975) #6062
- *Sally Michener: Ceramic Sculpture* (1979) #6528
- *Saskatchewan: Art and Artists* (1971) #1919
- *Sculpture of the Inuit: Masterworks of the Canadian Arctic/La sculpture chez les Inuit: chefs-d'oeuvre de l'Arctique canadien* (1972) #4423 4440
- *Stephen Cruise* (1976) #5213
- *The Arts in French Canada/Les arts au Canada français* (1959) #1339
- *The Canadian Canvas: A Travelling Exhibition of 85 Recent Paintings/Peintres canadiens actuels: exposition itinérante de 85 oeuvres récentes* (1975) #588
- *The Image of Man in Canadian Painting: 1878-1978/L'image de l'homme dans la peinture canadienne: 1878-1978* (1978) #135
- *The J.S. McLean Collection of Canadian Painting* (1969) #3228
- *Toni Onley: A Retrospective Exhibition* (1978) #6739
- *Yves Gaucher* (1969) #5563
- *Yves Gaucher & Christopher Pratt* (1977) #643
- exhibitions (reviews)
  - *13 Cameras* (1978) #2064
  - *13 Cameras* (1979) #1044
  - *Affinities: Ten Painters of this Region; Max Benjamin, Pierre Coupey, Laurie de Camillis, Sally Gregson, Robin Mayor, Ken Meisterman, Gordon Payne, Ranjan Sen, Ken Wallace, Robert E. Youds* (1979) #2072
  - Amess, Frederick Arthur #4520
  - Breeze, Claude Herbert #4909
  - *Confrontations: Ian Carr-Harris, John McEwen, John Massey<u>* (1979) #697
  - *Current Pursuits* (1976) #1871
  - *Don Jarvis: A Twenty-Nine Year Retrospective* (1977) #5946
  - *Eric Cameron/Noel Harding: Two Audio-Visual Constructs/Eric Cameron/Noel Harding: deux installations audio-visuelles* (1978) #656
  - first exhibition (1932) #1982
  - *Four Places* (1977) #622
  - *Gordon Smith* (1976) #7227
  - *J.M. Barnsley (1861-1929), Retrospective Exhibition* (1964) #4612
  - *Jack Shadbolt: Seven Years* (1978) #2074
  - *Leslie Poole: Confessions* (1979) #6902
  - *Liz Magor: Production/Reproduction* (1980) #6406
  - *Maxwell Bates in Retrospect, 1921-1971* (1973) #4623
  - Ngan, Wayne G. #6696
  - *Paterson Ewen: Recent Works* (1977) #5385
  - Pethick, Jerry, *Krieghoff/Eskimo Proximity Device* (1979) #6841 6842
  - Shadbolt, Jack Leonard (1946) #7176
  - *The Canadian Canvas: A Travelling Exhibition of 85 Recent Paintings/Peintres canadiens actuels: exposition itinérante de 85 oeuvres récentes* (1975) #582
- Hughes, Lynn, *Rank Beginnings* #5862
- Kleyn, Robert, on works exhibited (1976) #6063
- Morris, Jerrold, as curator #6639
- photography collection #1051
- projected move to central Vancouver #3198
- renovation of Courthouse to house Vancouver Art Gallery #9149
- Wong, Paul, *in ten sity* performance #7607
Vancouver (BC), Vancouver Art Gallery. Gallery Shop
- Inuit art #4455
Vancouver (BC), Vancouver Centennial Museum
- argillite carving, Haida Indians, Ferna and George Cook collection #4006
- exhibitions
  - *Impression of an Age* (1969) #2004
  - *Made by Hand '76* (1979) #2276
  - *Rainbows in Our Walls: Art and Stained Glass in Vancouver, 1890-1940* (1978) #2456
  - *The Art of Nunstins/L'art de Nunstins* (1981) #6934
Vancouver (BC), Vancouver City Archives
- Brock, J.A., & Co., photographs (1886-1888) #2021
- masks, Squamish Indians #3864
Vancouver (BC), Vancouver Civic Auditorium
- architecture, competition for #9080
Vancouver (BC), Vancouver Museum
- (1894-1917) #3182
- collection (1908) #3180
Vancouver (BC), Vancouver School of Art
- (1925-1939) #3019
- (1940s) #1841
- (1950s) #145 1992
- (1970s) #3006
- Laing, Bill as teacher #6135
- Mayor, Robin, as principal #6459
- Yip, Chuck Wing, as teacher #7625
Vancouver (BC), Victory Square
- architecture #8171
Vancouver (BC), Video Inn
- and Mike Goldberg #5625
- video art #605 2044
Vancouver (BC), West Vancouver Municipal Hall
- architecture, Toby, Russell & Buckwell #8990
Vancouver (BC), Westcoast Building
- architecture, Rhone & Iredale #9359
Vancouver (BC), Woodcroft Estate
- architecture, Arthur Charles Erickson #8360
Vancouver Art Gallery. Bulletin, Can periodical #547
Vancouver Arts and Crafts Association (Vancouver, BC)
- (1900-1901) #1977
Vancouver Island (BC)
- photographic views
  - Dally, Frederick #5250
  - Fardon, George Robinson #5411
Vancouver Studio Club (Vancouver, BC)
- (1910s) #1979
Vancouver Sun, Can newspaper
- cartoons
  - Innis, Jack #943
  - Norris, Len #6722
Vanderpant, John A., Can photographer, 1884-1939 #7457 7458 7459
- on photography #7456
vanes, American
- on barns #9228
vanes, Canadian #1364
- beaver motif #56
- ironwork, Québec #2702 2705
- on barns #9228
- weathercocks
  - Price, Ralph and Patricia, collection #971
  - Québec #2589
Vanguard, Can periodical #547 3203
- (1970s) #3310
Vanier, Bernard, Can artist, 1927- #7460
- in Paris (France) #426

Vanier, Georges, Can statesman, collector, 1888-1967, and Pauline, Can collector, 1898-
- collection, Canadian art #3216
Vardeman, Lynn, Can artist, 1932-
- exhibitions, group
   - (1978) #2067
Varennes (Qué)
- churches #8813
Varin (dit La Pistole), Jacques, Can silversmith, jeweller, 1736-1791 #269 270
Varley, Frederick Horsman, Can artist, 1881-1969 #7461 7462 7465 7466 7467
- and Group of Seven #1732
- and Molly Lamb Bobak #4766
- and Terence Shortt #506
- Arctic trips #1779
- as teacher of Joseph Sydney Hallam #5687
- book illustration and design #939
- drawings of Inuit (1938) #4185
- exhibitions
   - (1954) #7463
   - (1981) #7468
- exhibitions, group
   - (1968) #3224
- exhibitions (reviews) #1982
- Gould, John Howard, compared with #5635
- influence on André Charles Biéler #4725
- influence on Edward John Hughes #5861
- influence on Evadna Chapman #5087
- influence on Tony Law #6174
- landscapes #7464
- Pellan, Alfred, compared with #6814
- war paintings #1075
   - Canadian War Memorials Collection #1077
Varney, Edwin (Ed), Can artist, 1944-
- exhibitions, group
   - (1971) #2042
   - (1973) #2045
- exhibitions (reviews) #2051
Varvarande, Robert Emile, Can artist, 1922- #7469
- influence on Toronto (Ont) painting #1749
Vasarely, Victor de, Fr artist, 1908-
- use of colour #468
Vastringue, La, toy manufacturer (Saint-Jean-Port-Joli, Qué) #2924
Vaudreuil (Qué)
- silica, for glass manufacturing #2418
Vaudreuil (Qué), church
- altarpiece, Philippe Liébert #6280 6281
Vaudreuil (Qué), Musée de Vaudreuil #3108
- collection #3109
Vaudreuil (Qué), Musée régional de Vaudreuil-Soulanges
- exhibitions
   - La couverture de lit du Québec ancien (1980) #2746
Vaughan, John William, Can photographer, fl. 1862-1865
- and the Victoria Theatre Photographic Gallery (Victoria, BC) #2027
Vaux, Calvert, Brit landscape architect in USA, 1824-1895
- Ottawa (Ont), Parliament Buildings #8048
Vauxcelles, Louis, Fr writer, art critic, b. 1870
- on James Wilson Morrice #6619
Vavasour, Mervin, Brit army officer in Canada, 1821-1866
- and Henry James Warre, expedition to Oregon (1845-1846) #7522

Vazan, William (Bill), Can artist, 1933- #1512 7475 7477
- and realism #533
- exhibitions
   - (1974) #7472
   - (1978) #7474
   - (1980) #7476
- exhibitions (reviews) #1517
- interview #7478
- land art #7471
- map images #561
- on conceptual art #7473
- on Worldline (1969-1971) #7470
- Symposium international de sculpture environnementale de Chicoutimi (Qué), (1980) #1639
- use of photography #1057
vedute
- see topographical illustration
Vegreville (Alta)
- art (1940s) #1943
vehicles, Canadian
- (1940s) #2603
Venice (Italy), Biennale (1952)
- Canadian art #399 401
Venice (Italy), Biennale (1956)
- exhibitions (reviews)
   - Town, Harold Barling #7406
Venice (Italy), Biennale (1958). Canadian Pavilion
- architecture, Enrico Peressutti #9210
Venice (Italy), Biennale (1962)
- exhibitions
   - Jean-Paul Riopelle: Paintings and Sculpture/Jean-Paul Riopelle: peinture et sculpture (1962) #7018
Venice (Italy), Biennale (1968)
- exhibitions
   - Ulysse Comtois, Guido Molinari (1968) #522
Venice (Italy), Biennale (1970)
- exhibitions
   - Michael Snow, XXXV International Biennial Exhibition of Art, Venice, 24 June-31 October 1970/Michael Snow, XXXV Exposition biennale internationale d'art, Venise, 24 juin-31 octobre, 1970 (1970) #7244
- exhibitions (reviews)
   - Michael Snow, XXXV International Biennial Exhibition of Art, Venice, 24 June-31 October 1970/Michael Snow, XXXV Exposition biennale internationale d'art, Venise, 24 juin-31 octobre, 1970 (1970) #7242
Venice (Italy), Biennale (1972)
- exhibitions
   - Canada: Gershon Iskowitz, Walter Redinger (1972) #548
Venice (Italy), Biennale (1976)
- exhibitions
   - Canada: Greg Curnoe (1976) #5229
Venice (Italy), Biennale (1978)
- exhibitions
   - Canada: Ron Martin, Henry Saxe (1978) #661
Venice (Italy), Biennale (1980)
- exhibitions
   - Canada Video: Colin Campbell, Pierre Falardeau/Julien Poulin, General Idea, Tom Sherman, Lisa Steele (1980) #705
Venne, Joseph, Can architect, 1859-1925
- Montréal (Qué), Université de Montréal #9415

Venning, William Norris, Can silversmith, 1795-1877 #2649
Venor, Robert, Can artist, 1931- #1418
Venturi, Robert, Amer architect, 1925-
- influence on A.J. Diamond and Barton Myers #9349
Verbist, Pascal Joseph, Can priest, 1829-1879
- proposal for fine arts academy in Montréal (Qué), (1873) #2957
Verchères (Qué)
- domestic architecture #8635
Verdun (Qué), Centre culturel de Verdun
- exhibitions
   - M.A. Fortin (1968) #5478
Vereydhen, Charles, Can architect, 1820-1872
- Victoria (BC) #8145
Vermette, Claude, Can artist, 1930- #2102 2378 7480 7481 7482 7483
- and architecture #8231
- and Québec religious art (1950s) #1250
- as husband of Mariette Rousseau-Vermette #7085
- ceramic tiles, Queen Elizabeth Hotel (Montréal, Qué) #8228
- murals #7479
Vermette, Mariette Rousseau
- see Rousseau-Vermette, Mariette
vernacular architecture, British
- 19th c., influence on Trinity Bay (Nfld) architecture #7791
vernacular architecture, Canadian
- British Columbia, churches (1858-1925) #8916
- Maritimes (pre-1900) #8551
- Newfoundland #7782
   - Newfoundland tilt #8535
- Ontario #8654
   - (pre-1867) #8904
- Québec
   - 17th-19th cs. #8559
   - (1880-1914) #7929
- Trinity Bay (Nfld) #7785 7791 8541
- Ukrainian #8090 8127 8710 8713
Verner, Frederick Arthur, Can artist, 1836-1928
- exhibitions
   - (1976) #7484
- exhibitions, group
   - (1888) #175
   - (1890) #177 1839
   - (1961) #62
- exhibitions (reviews) #1696
Vernon (BC), Vernon Civic Centre
- architecture, Allen, Gower, Huggins & Meiklejohn #8972
Verrier, Étienne, Fr engineer, artist in Canada, fl. 1724-1747
- Louisbourg (NS) #8419
Versailles (France), château de Versailles
- art, Indians of North America #3422
Versailles (France), Petit Trianon
- influence on château Dufresne (Montréal, Qué) #8618
Verville, Jean-François, Fr engineer in Canada, fl. 1717
- Louisbourg (NS) #8419
vestments, Canadian
- Jesuits, Québec #2192
- L'Islet (Qué), Church of Notre-Dame-de-Bon-Secours #8879
Vézina, Charles, Can sculptor, 1685-1755 #249 250
- works, churches, Charlesbourg (Qué)

#8851
Vezina, Emile, Can artist, 1876-1942 #1391
via crucis
– see Stations of the Cross
Viau, Guy, Can artist, critic, curator,
1920-1971 #7485
– drawings, late works #7486
– interview, on Centre culturel canadien
(Paris, France) #537
– interview, on National Arts Centre
(Ottawa, Ont) #9105
Viau & Venne, Can architectural firm
– Montréal (Qué), Saint Joseph's Oratory
#8794
Vickers, Ron, Can photographer, fl. 1960s
– portfolio of photographs #987
Vickers, Roy Henry, Can artist, 1946-
– silkscreen prints #4148
Victoria (BC)
– architecture #8146 8149 8173 8176 8177
8178
    – (1843-1929) #8180
    – (1843-1960s) #8174
    – (1850s-1890s) #8145
    – (1872-1912) #8175
    – (1899-1901) #1977
    – (1950s) #8144
    – Chinatown #8179 8181
    – Hooper, Thomas #8376
    – Rattenbury, Francis Mawson #8400
    – Whiteway, William Tuff #9508
– architecture and decorative arts #2269
– art
    – (1910-1941), Island Arts and Crafts
    Society #1980
    – (1970s) #1870 2053
– art galleries #442
– domestic architecture #8722
    – (1910s) #8494
– museums #3190
– painting #2000
– photographic views
    – (1850-1900) #1061
    – Dally, Frederick #5249
    – Maynard, Hannah Hatherly #6457
– photography, late 19th c. #2022
Victoria (BC), Alexis Martin House
– architecture, Samuel Maclure #8682
Victoria (BC), Art Gallery of Greater Victoria
– collection #3189
– exhibitions
    – Adrien Hébert: trente ans de son oeuvre,
    1923-1953/Adrien Hébert: Thirty Years of
    His Art, 1923-1953 (1972) #5763
    – Ann Kipling: Recent Landscapes (1980)
    #6057
    – B.C. Binning: Drawings (1979) #4736
    – Black & White Almost: Pat Martin Bates
    (1972) #4626
    – Carl Schaefer in Hanover (1980) #7157
    – Christopher Pratt (1971) #6910
    – Claude Mongrain; Roland Poulin (1980)
    #706
    – Conceptual Decorative: Prints by Les
    Levine, 1965-1970/Conceptuel décoratif:
    estampes de Les Levine, 1965-1970 (1972)
    #6265
    – Daniel Fowler of Amherst Island,
    1810-1894 (1979) #5491
    – Edward Curtis in the Collection of the
    Edmonton Art Gallery (1980) #3480
    – F.H. Varley: A Centennial Exhibition/F.H.
    Varley: une exposition centenaire (1981)
    #7468

    – Fired Sculpture (1974) #774
    – Franklin Carmichael Watercolours (1981)
    #5001
    – Frederic Marlett Bell-Smith (1846-1923)
    (1977) #4668
    – Gift from the Douglas M. Duncan
    Collection and the Milne-Duncan
    Bequest/Le Don provenant de la collection
    Douglas M. Duncan et le legs
    Milne-Duncan (1972) #541
    – Glenn Toppings Remembered (1977) #7392
    – Goodridge Roberts: Selected
    Works/Goodridge Roberts: oeuvres choisies
    (1982) #7050
    – H. Mortimer-Lamb: Paintings (1977) #6156
    – Images Stone B.C.: Thirty Centuries of
    Northwest Coast Indian Sculpture (1975)
    #4001
    – Ina D.D. Uhthoff: Memorial Exhibition
    (1972) #7443
    – Inuit Art in the 1970's: A Travelling
    Exhibition/L'Art inuit actuel, 1970-79:
    exposition itinérante (1980) #4287
    – Jack Shadbolt (1970) #7182
    – Jack Shadbolt: Early Watercolours (1980)
    #7189
    – Jack Wise: A Decade of Work (1977) #7601
    – Jeff Wall: Installation of Faking Death
    (1977), The Destroyed Room (1978), Young
    Workers (1978), Picture for Women (1979)
    (1979) #7506
    – John Dobereiner (1978) #5295
    – John Meredith: Drawings, 1957-1980
    (1980) #6516
    – L.M. Kilpin, 1855(sic)-1919 (1979) #6052
    – Liz Magor (1979) #6405
    – Manitoba Mainstream: People's Art/Fine
    Art/Le Grand Courant du Manitoba: arts
    populaires, beaux-arts (1973) #1897
    – Margaret Peterson: A Retrospective (1978)
    #6839
    – Mary Riter Hamilton, 1873-1954 (1978)
    #5695
    – Miller Brittain - Painter (1982) #4922
    – Milne: Watercolours (1980) #6566
    – Mokuhan: The Woodcuts of Munakata and
    Matsubara (1976) #6449
    – Nationalism in Canadian Art (1979) #148
    – Paintings from the Collection of Ernest E.
    Poole and Family (1959) #3217
    – Paul Rand (1980) #6957
    – Robert Young: Prints/Robert Young:
    gravures (1981) #7631
    – Sally Gregson: Paintings (1976) #5658
    – Salmon Harris (1978) #5745
    – Sophia Theresa Pemberton, 1869-1959
    (1978) #6828
    – Sophie Deane-Drummond (1967) #6827
    – Takao Tanabe, 1972-1976: The Land (1977)
    #7320
    – The Architecture of Samuel Maclure (1971)
    #8383
    – The Canadian Block Print: Woodcuts,
    Linocuts, Stonecuts and Wood Engravings
    (1978) #837
    – The Prints of Clarence Gagnon (1981)
    #5549
    – The Society of Canadian Painter-Etchers
    and Engravers in Retrospect/La Société des
    peintres-graveurs canadiens: vue
    rétrospective (1981) #836
    – Tom Forrestall Exhibition (1972) #5461
    – Victoria Kinesis '75 (1975) #2055
    – W.P. Weston (1980) #7546

    – Watercolours and Drawings of Emily Carr
    (1977) #5039
    – William G.R. Hind (1833-1888): A
    Confederation Painter in Canada (1967)
    #5806
    – Younger Vancouver: Cross Section'68
    (1968) #2038
– exhibitions (reviews)
    – Liz Magor (1979) #6404
    – Nationalism in Canadian Art (1979) #143
– Graham, Colin, as curator #5642
Victoria (BC), B.C. Telephone Offices
– architecture, McCarter, Nairne & Partners
#9301
Victoria (BC), Beacon Hill Park
– totem poles, Kwakiutl Indians #4115
Victoria (BC), British Columbia Parliament
Buildings
– architecture, Francis Mawson Rattenbury
#8967
– restoration, Alan James Hodgson #8964
8965 8966
Victoria (BC), City Hall
– architecture #8177
Victoria (BC), Craigdarroch Castle
– architecture #8176 8177
Victoria (BC), Craigflower Manor
– architecture #8176
Victoria (BC), Crystal Gardens
– architecture, Francis Mawson Rattenbury
and Percy Leonard James #9134 9146
Victoria (BC), Emily Carr Gallery
– see Victoria (BC), Provincial Archives of
British Columbia. Emily Carr Gallery
Victoria (BC), Emily Carr home
– architecture #8176 8177
Victoria (BC), Fardon's Photographic Gallery
– and George Robinson Fardon #5411
Victoria (BC), Fort Rodd Hill
– architecture #8479
Victoria (BC), Government House
– architecture #8754
Victoria (BC), Hudson's Bay Company.
Victoria Store
– exhibitions
    – The World of Emily Carr: A New
    Exhibition of Her Paintings from the
    Newcombe Collection, Recently Acquired by
    the Province of British Columbia (1962)
    #5023
Victoria (BC), Kyle Gallery
– exhibitions (reviews)
    – Graham, Colin (1980) #5642
Victoria (BC), Labatt's Brewery
– architecture #8177
Victoria (BC), Little Gallery
– exhibitions (reviews)
    – Pattle, Colin (1979) #6784
Victoria (BC), Maltwood Art Museum and
Gallery
– see Victoria (BC), University of Victoria.
Maltwood Art Museum and Gallery
Victoria (BC), Norwich House
– architecture #8177
Victoria (BC), Open Space #1042
– exhibitions
    – Mountain: A Lithograph by James B.
    Spencer/Montagne: une lithographie de
    James B. Spencer (1974) #7270
    – Tom La Pierre: Paintings, Drawings, Prints
    (1976) #6121
    – Vehicule Art: In Transit (1975) #1512
Victoria (BC), Point Ellice House
– architecture #8176

Victoria (BC), Provincial Archives of British
Columbia
– Maynard, Hannah Hatherly, photographs
#6457
– pictorial art collection #159
Victoria (BC), Provincial Archives of British
Columbia. Emily Carr Gallery
– exhibitions
– *The Modern Room* (1981) #2034
Victoria (BC), Provincial Government
Building
– architecture, Hawthorn Mansfield Towers
#8373
Victoria (BC), Provincial Museum
– Carmichael, William Maurice, silver #5003
– Martin, Mungo, *Great Killer Whale Copper*
#4054
– prehistoric stone sculpture, Northwest
Coast Indians #3900
– Price, Tom, drawings, Newcombe
collection #6934
– totem poles, Haida Indians #4008
Victoria (BC), Provincial Normal School
– architecture, William Charles Frederick
Gillam #9386
Victoria (BC), Salvation Army Matson
Lodge
– architecture, Wade, Stockdill & Armour
#8516
Victoria (BC), Scuby House
– architecture, Wade Williams Partnership
#8170
Victoria (BC), University of Victoria
– art education (1970s) #3006
– Poulin, Roland, open-air sculpture #706
Victoria (BC), University of Victoria.
Centennial Stadium
– architecture, Siddall, Dennis & Associates
#9101
Victoria (BC), University of Victoria.
Maltwood Art Museum and Gallery
– exhibitions
– *Canadians: A National Photography Show
about People/Canadiens: exposition
nationale de photographie ayant les gens
comme thème* (1980) #1035
– *Herbert Siebner: A Monograph* (1979)
#7205
– *Katharine Emma Maltwood, Artist,
1878-1961* (1981) #6413
– *Painting during the Colonial Period in
British Columbia, 1845-1871* (1979) #2023
– *The Maltwood Collection* (1978) #3242
– *The University Collection* (1978) #3199
Victoria (BC), University of Victoria.
Maltwood Museum of Historic Art
– exhibitions
– *Arts of the Forgotten Pioneers: Catalogue
for an Exhibition*, (1971) #2269
Victoria (BC), Victoria College of Art
– Wise, Jack Marlowe, as teacher #7602
Victoria (BC), Victoria Theatre Photographic
Gallery #2027
Victorian architecture
– Battleford (Sask), Fort Battleford #8484
– British Columbia #8150
– Canada #7652 7668 7769
– as national style #7697 7725
– Victorian Gothic #7739 7740
– Hamilton (Ont) #7991
– Montréal (Qué) #7918 7934 8620
– Ontario
– churches #8905
– domestic architecture #8677

– Ottawa (Ont) #8036
– Québec #7853
– villas #8632
– Québec (Qué), fortifications #7946
– St. John's (Nfld) #8542
– Toronto (Ont) #5651 8060
– Yorkville Town Hall #8997
– Vancouver (BC), domestic architecture
(1886-1929) #8730
– Winnipeg (Man), Dalnavert #8708
Victorian art
– and William George Richardson Hind
#5810
– Canada
– (1837-1887) #253
– (1837-1900) #254
– (1840-1918) #237
Victorian costume
– female, Canada #2847 2870 2885
Victorian furniture
– Canada #2472 2559
– Newfoundland #2502
Victorian interior decoration
– Canada, parlour (1870-1890) #2129
Victorian tiles
– in Toronto (Ont) houses, 19th c. #2373
Vidal, Claude, Can educator, fl. 1968
– and Ecole des beaux-arts (Montréal, Qué),
(1968) #2995
Vidal, Guy, Can jeweller, artist, 1938- #2216
2701
video art #538 604
– and performance art #2073
– and realism #716
– and sculpture #654
– British Columbia #2063
– Britton, Susan #687
– Cameron, Eric #651 656
– Campbell, Colin #630 705 4993
– Campus, Peter #651
– Canada #553 566 575 580 598 605 631 650
690 710 713 912 1799
– (1978), Canadian Video Open #603
– (1978), *Fifth Network/Cinquième réseau*
#655
– (1979-1981), *Impressions* #996
– Canada and United States #550
– Canada and USA #616 664
– Chitty, Elizabeth #687
– Cruise, Stephen #5213
– Dragu, Margaret #687
– Falardeau, Pierre #705
– Frenkel, Vera #5524 5525
– General Idea #630 692 705 5583
– Harding, Noel #651 656 687 5705
– International Video Art Symposium,
Kingston (Ont), (1979) #671
– Lake, Suzy #668
– Montréal (Qué) #1498 1537 1550
– Vidéographe #1499
– Nauman, Bruce #651
– Newfoundland #1157
– Palchinski, Sylvia Scott #6753
– Petite, Marion #651
– Poulin, Julien #705
– Québec
– (1970-1975) #1515
– women artists #1064
– Robertson, Clive #7053
– Sherman, Tom #705
– Steele, Lisa #630 7277
– Toronto (Ont), A Space #721
– Vancouver (BC) #2044
– Vancouver Art Gallery #3203

– W.O.R.K.S. #1955
– Werden, Rodney #630
Video Ring #550
Vie des arts, Can periodical #55
– (1970s) #3310
Viel, Nicolas, Fr priest in Canada, d. 1625
– commemorative cross #1569
Vienna (Austria), Museum für Völkerkunde
– exhibitions
– *Indianer Nordamerikas* (1968) #3436
view painting
– *see* topographical illustration
Viger, Jacques, Can statesman, collector,
1787-1858
– album #1337
– and citadel (Montréal, Qué) #8445
– correspondence, William von Moll Berczy
#4695
– *L'album des costumes de communautés
religieuses de femmes au Canada* #2834
– *Souvenirs canadiens* #1326
Vilder, Roger, Can artist, 1938- #7487
– exhibitions
– (1973) #7488
– (1975) #7489
– interview #1485 1489
– use of light #767
Village Jacques de Chambly (Qué)
– architecture #8573
villages
– *see* cities and towns
villas
– *see also* castles and country houses
villas, Canadian
– Québec, 19th c. #8632
villas, Italian
– influence on Lanark Place (Abernethy,
Sask) #8700
Ville-Marie (Qué), fort
– recommended for conservation (1881)
#7754
Villeneuve, Arthur, Can artist, 1910- #1428
1429 1551 7490 7492
– exhibitions
– (1972) #7491
Villeneuve, Jeanne Larouche
– *see* Larouche-Villeneuve, Jeanne
Villeneuve, Joseph, Can sculptor, 20th c.
– as teacher of Lauréat Vallière #7454
Villiers, Frederick, Brit artist in Canada,
1851-1922
– views, western Canada #931
Vimy (France), Vimy Memorial
– Allward, Walter Seymour #4519
Vincelette, Roméo, Can artist, 1902-
– and Montée Saint-Michel #1236
Vincennes, Vincent
– *see* Chartrand (*dit* Vincennes), Vincent
Vincent, Zacharie, Can artist, 1812-1886
#7493
– exhibitions, group
– (1959) #219
– self-portraits #7494
Vincent Rother Associates, Can architectural
firm
– Ottawa (Ont), National Gallery of Canada,
competition #9079
Vinet, Pierre, Can photographer, 1940- #990
Viollet-le-Duc, Eugène Emmanuel, Fr
architect, theorist, 1814-1879
– Cormier, Ernest, on #8346
– theories, influence on Québec church
architecture #8819
Virgin Mary

- redemption, with Jesus Christ, Ozias Leduc #6204
visionary art
- see fantastic art
Visser, John de, Can photographer, 1930-
- portfolio of photographs #991
Visual Arts Ontario
- periodical, ArtViews #1806
Visual Communications Association of Winnipeg (Winnipeg, Man)
- and Art Directors' Club of Winnipeg #872
Vitruvius, Roman writer, engineer, architect, late first c. B.C. - early first c. A.D.
- Cormier, Ernest, on #8346
Vittecoq, Arlette, Can photographer, fl. 1960s- #1534
Vivenza, Francesca, Can artist, 1941- #7495
Vladimir Plavsic & Associates, Can architectural firm
- Vancouver (BC)
 - University of British Columbia
  - Student residence #9467
  - Thunderbird Stadium #9101
Vogt, Adolphe, Can artist, 1843-1871 #10
Volgyesi, Andrew Stephen, Can architect, 1937-
- Toronto (Ont), house #8078
Volpi, Charles de, Can collector, 1910-1981 #3248
Von Baich, Paul, Can photographer, fl. 1980
- portfolio of photographs #1023
Von der Ohe, Dorothy Katie
- see Ohe, Dorothy Katie von der
Vorticism
- and Canadian war paintings, World War I #1075
votive offerings
- Boivin, Joseph, Ex-voto de Dorval #4771
- Québec #1341 1370
 - crosses #1621 1640
 - marine paintings and Saint Ann #1292
- Saint Ann #1230 1323
- Sainte-Anne-de-Beaupré (Qué), Saint Ann's Basilica #1321
Vouet, Simon, Fr artist, 1590-1649
- as teacher of frère Luc #5503
Voulkos, Peter, Amer sculptor, 1924-
- influence on Sally Michener #6527
voyagers
- see travellers
Voyer, Pierre, Can writer, 1949-
- poems, for drawings by Louis-Pierre Bougie #4861
Voysey, Charles Frances Annesley, Brit architect, designer, 1857-1941
- influence on Samuel Maclure #8384
Vroom Brothers, Can furniture-makers, fl. 1870s-1920s #2511

W

W. & D. Bell Pottery
- see Bell, W. & D., Pottery
W.O.R.K.S. #1955
- video art #550
Wabeno, Ojibwa #3492
Wade, Stockdill & Armour, Can architectural firm
- Victoria (BC), Salvation Army Matson Lodge #8516
Wade Williams Partnership, Can

architectural firm
- Victoria (BC), Scuby House #8170
Wadsworth, Elizabeth Jane (Lizzy), Can photographer, 1868-1944 #7496
Wagner, Charles Frederick, Can architect, 1862-1934
- Toronto (Ont), Crown Tailoring Co. Building #9332
Wainio, Carol, Can artist, 1955-
- exhibitions (reviews) #1227
Wainwright, Ruth, Can artist, 1902-
- interview #7497
Waisman, Ross & Associates, Can architectural firm
- Winnipeg (Man)
 - University of Manitoba. Crop Research Centre #7683
 - Winnipeg School Division #1 administration building #7683
Wakeham Bay (Qué)
- graphic arts (1972-1975) #4475
Wald, Susana, Can artist, 1937-
- and Surrealism #7633
Waldmann, Oscar, Sw sculptor, b. 1856
- influence on Katherine Elizabeth Wallis #7511 7512
Wales, Shirley, Can artist, 1931-
- and Québec printmaking (1960s) #1641
- exhibitions, group
 - (1967) #821
- on printmaking #817 818
Walker, Harry, Can photographer, fl. 1977
- portfolio of photographs #1023
Walker, Horatio, Can artist, 1858-1938 #10 302 1312 7498 7500 7501
- as member, Canadian Art Club #193
- compared with Homer Ransford Watson #217
- exhibitions
 - (1977) #7503
- exhibitions, group
 - (1935) #17
 - (1978) #1726
- exhibitions (reviews) #204 211 306 7504
- influence of Impressionism #227
- interview #7502
- Millet, Jean-François, compared with #7499
- Thomson, Tom, compared with #215
Walker, Howard Vincent, Can architect, 1927-
- Scarborough (Ont), North Bridlewood Junior Public School #9471
Walker, John Barras, Can photographer, fl. 1970s-
- portfolio of photographs #991
Walker, Joy, Can artist, 1942- #675
- exhibitions, group
 - (1980) #698
Walker, Robert, Can artist, 1945-
- exhibitions, group
 - (1978) #668
- interview #7505
Walker, Sir Byron Edmund, Can collector, banker, 1848-1924 #3206
- and National Gallery of Canada (Ottawa, Ont) #3050
- collection #1713 3205
Walker, Victoria, Can artist, 1943-
- exhibitions, group
 - (1979) #676
Wall, Jeffrey David (Jeff), Can artist, 1946-
- exhibitions
 - (1979) #7506

- exhibitions, group
 - (1970) #534
 - (1971) #2042
- imaginary works #530
Wallace, George Burton, Can artist, 1920-
- on Paul Fournier #5487
Wallace, Ian, Can artist, 1943-
- and Mike Banwell #4601
- exhibitions
 - (1979) #7509
- exhibitions, group
 - (1971) #2042
- exhibitions (reviews) #7507
- photographs (1973-1979) #7508
Wallace, Ken, Can artist, 1945- #2053
- exhibitions
 - (1980) #7510
- exhibitions, group
 - (1979) #2075
- exhibitions (reviews) #1883 2072
Wallbridge & Imrie, Can architectural firm
- Edmonton (Alta), row houses for Western Heritable Investment Co. (Canada) Ltd. #8511
Wallis, Adah, Can artist, fl. early 20th c.
- as sister of Katherine Elizabeth Wallis #7512
Wallis, Katherine Elizabeth, Can sculptor, 1861-1957 #7511 7512
Wallis, Provo William Parry, Brit naval officer in Canada, 1791-1892
- portraits of, Robert Field #5430 5431
Wallot, Jacques-Albert-François-Joseph, Can artist, 1938- #7513
wallpaper, American
- imported into Canada #2949 2950
wallpaper, British
- imported into Canada #2949 2950
- late 18th-19th cs., imported into Canada #2926 2929
wallpaper, Canadian
- 19th c. #2926 2929
- (1750s-1950s) #2949 2950
wallpaper, French
- imported into Canada #2949 2950
walls
- see also masonry; mural painting
walls, Canadian
- hollow-wall construction, Ontario, 19th c. #8004
- plankwall framing #7712
 - Ontario, 19th c. #8046
- use of paint, Ontario, 19th c. #8013
Walper, Ora C., Can artist, 1881-1961 #1681
Walter, G.P., Co., furniture-making firm (Bowmanville, Ont) #2556
wampum, Abenaki
- belts (1699) #3526
wampum, Algonquian #3505 3521
- beadwork #3635
- belts
 - Albany (NY), New York State Museum #3603
 - recording end of war with Iroquois (1670) #3541
- use as legal document #3567
wampum, Huron
- belts #3495 3514
 - (1674) #3526
wampum, Indians of North America #3387 3388 3457 3522 3612
- trade goods #3440
wampum, Iroquois #3505 3521 3607
- beadwork #3635

– belts #3532
  – Albany (NY), New York State Museum #3603
  – and Iroquois Confederacy #3496 3567
– Philadelphia (Penn), University of Pennsylvania. Museum #3518
wampum, Micmac
– belts #3497
wampum, Ottawa
– belts, representing peace treaties (1764-1852) #3501
wampum, Plains #3521
wampum, Woodlands #3505
  – beadwork #3635
  – belts, Albany (NY), New York State Museum #3603
Wan, Theodore Saskatche, Can photographer, 1953- #7514
– exhibitions (reviews) #1067
war in art
– Champlain, Samuel de, *Les voyages du sieur de Champlain* (1613) #933
– Proctor, Alexander Phimister, military sculptures #6943 6944
– Toronto (Ont), Metro Toronto Public Library. John Ross Robertson Historical Collection #3131
war memorials, Canadian
– Battle of Ypres (Ypres, France), Walter Seymour Allward #4518
– Jackson, A.Y., on #1076
– Kingston (Ont), John MacIntosh Lyle #1083
– MacCarthy, Hamilton Plantagenet #6353
– McKenzie, Robert Tait #6484
– Oshawa (Ont), Saint George's Anglican Church #8899
– Regina (Sask), War Memorial Museum #9073
– St. John's (Nfld) #7783
– Vimy Memorial (Vimy, France), Walter Seymour Allward #4519
– World War I #731 732 1073 1074 1078 1080 1082 1084 1085
  – architecture, recommendations for #1079
– World War I and World War II #1108 1109
Ward, Charles Caleb, Can artist, ca. 1831-1896
– exhibitions, group
  – (1969) #1180
Ward, John, Can artist, 1948-
– paintings of Toronto (Ont) #7515
Wardrop, Lanier Robert, Can architect, fl. 1912
– Calgary (Alta), Lougheed Building #8118
warehouses, American
– John Deere Plow Company #9247
warehouses, Canadian
– (1910s) #9234
– (1950s) #9241
– Hudson's Bay Company, 19th c. #8480
– John Deere Plow Company #9247
– Winnipeg (Man) #8106
  – (1880s-1914) #8107
Warhol, Andy, Amer artist, filmmaker, 1928- #544
– interview #996
– use of light #516
Waring, Stephanie E., Can artist, fl. 1979
– on her art #7516
Warkov, Esther, Can artist, 1941- #7518
– exhibitions
  – (1970) #7517
  – (1976) #7519

– exhibitions, group
  – (1975) #1867
  – (1981) #1907
– works (1970s) #7520
Warner, Burns, Toan, Lunde, Amer architectural firm
– Toronto (Ont), University of Toronto. John P. Robarts Research Library #9048 9050 9052
Warner, Ralph Malcolm, Australian artist, 1902-1966
– exhibitions, group
  – (1981) #1117
Warner, William E., Can ceramicist, fl. 1856-1860
– as founder of Warner & Co. (Toronto, Ont) #2310
Warner & Co., ceramic manufacturer (Toronto, Ont) #2310
Warre, Henry James, Brit army officer, artist in Canada, 1819-1898 #279 2020 7521
– and Hudson's Bay Company #273
– exhibitions, group
  – (1979) #2023
– expedition to Oregon (1845-1846) #7522
Warren, Bill, Can photographer, ca. 1932-
– portfolio of photographs #991
Warren, Emily Mary Bibbens, Can artist, 1870-1956 #7523 7524
Warren, Mary Schaffer, Can artist, 1861-1939 #7525 7526 7527
Warren & Wetmore, Amer architectural firm
– Montréal (Qué), Ritz-Carlton Hotel #9267
– Winnipeg (Man), Fort Garry Terminal #9530
Warsaw (Poland), Muzeum Narodowe
– exhibitions
  – *Nowoczesne, Malarstwo, Kanadyjskie* (1962) #452
Warshaw, Leonard, Can architect, 1933-
– Osaka (Japan), Expo '70. Canadian Pavilion, competition #9217
Warwick, Septimus, Can architect, 1881-1953
– domestic architecture #8496
  – Montréal (Qué) #8556
Washington (DC), Corcoran Gallery of Art
– exhibitions
  – *An Exhibition of Paintings by Contemporary Canadian Artists: Catalogue* (1930) #315
– exhibitions (reviews)
  – *An Exhibition of Paintings by Contemporary Canadian Artists: Catalogue* (1930) #314
Washington (DC), Joseph H. Hirshhorn Museum and Sculpture Garden
– see Washington (DC), Smithsonian Institution. Joseph H. Hirshhorn Museum and Sculpture Garden
Washington (DC), National Gallery of Art
– exhibitions
  – *Canadian Painting* (1950) #46
  – *L'Amérique vue par l'Europe* (1975) #255
  – *The European Vision of America* (1975) #256
  – *The Far North: 2000 Years of American Eskimo and Indian Art* (1973) #3366
Washington (DC), Phillips Collection
– exhibitions
  – *Group of Seven: Canadian Landscape Painters* (1977) #1782
Washington (DC), Renwick Gallery
– see Washington (DC), Smithsonian Institution. Renwick Gallery

Washington (DC), Smithsonian Institution
– art, Northwest Coast Indians #3763
– basketry, Indians of North America #3389
– bonework, Inuit #4319
– decorative arts, Canadian #2111
– masks, natives of North America #3327
– pottery, British, with views of North America #2294
Washington (DC), Smithsonian Institution. Joseph H. Hirshhorn Museum and Sculpture Garden
– exhibitions
  – *14 Canadians: A Critic's Choice* (1977) #644
    – Hudson, Andrew, on works selected #623
– exhibitions (reviews)
  – *14 Canadians: A Critic's Choice* (1977) #621 627 645
Washington (DC), Smithsonian Institution. Renwick Gallery
– exhibitions
  – *Boxes and Bowls: Decorated Containers by Nineteenth-Century Haida, Tlingit, Bella Bella and Tsimshian Indian Artists* (1973) #3985
Washington (DC), Washington Gallery of Modern Art
– exhibitions
  – *Seven Montreal Artists* (1968) #1263
watches
– see also clocks
watches, Canadian
– 18th-19th cs. #2925
– (1700-1900), watchmakers #2931
– Québec, 17th-18th cs. #1320 2914
  – silversmiths #2657
Water Colour Society (Montréal, Qué)
– exhibitions (reviews)
  – (1950) #1400
watercolour painting, British
– (1927), Canadian National Exhibition (Toronto, Ont) #295
– influence on Toni Onley #6741
watercolour painting, Canadian
– 18th-19th cs. #246 248
  – Toronto (Ont), Royal Ontario Museum #247
– 19th c. #266
– (1750-1850) #279
– (1750s-1940s) #51
– (1890s-1940s) #367
– (1940s) #362 374
– (1950s) #437
– Bell-Irving family #4665
– British Columbia (1845-1871) #2020 2023
– Canadian Society of Painters in Water Colour #6 127 332 346 394
– late 19th c. #1839
– Maritimes, by women artists, 19th c. #1118
– Ontario, 19th c. #1720
– Saskatchewan
  – (1905-1980) #1940
  – (1930s-1970s) #1920
Waterloo (Ont), Mutual Life Assurance Company Building
– architecture, Darling & Pearson #9331
Waterloo (Ont), University of Waterloo
– architectural education (1980) #8289
– interior design (1960s) #9402
Waterloo (Ont), University of Waterloo. Arts Centre Gallery
– exhibitions
  – *Roger Savage* (1981) #7135

Waterloo (Ont), University of Waterloo.
   Museum and Archive of Games
 - exhibitions
   - *An Exhibition of Canadian Gameboards of
     the 19th & 20th Centuries from Ontario,
     Quebec & Nova Scotia* (1981) #2597
Waterloo (Ont), University of Waterloo.
   Student residence
 - architecture #9467
Waterloo County (Ont)
 - cemeteries, German-Alsatian crosses #2709
 - decorative arts #2243 2246 2264
 - folk art #1681
 - fraktur #2254 2255
 - furniture #2570
 - paperwork #2265
 - pottery, mid 19th-early 20th cs. #2348
 - pottery and textiles #2249
 - stone buildings, 19th c. #8011
Waters, Mackenzie, Can architect, 1894-1968
 - Toronto (Ont), Ridpath Building #9335
Watson, Budd, Can photographer, 1930-
 - portfolio of photographs #995
Watson, Harold R., Can architect, fl.
   1915-1928
 - Toronto (Ont) #8643
Watson, Homer Ransford, Can artist,
   1855-1936 #10 178 221 1713 7532 7533 7535
   7536 7537
 - and Royal Canadian Academy of Arts
   #152
 - as member, Canadian Art Club #193
 - compared with Horatio Walker #217
 - correspondence, James Spooner (1887)
   #7534
 - exhibitions
   - (1936) #7531
 - exhibitions, group
   - (1935) #17
   - (1978) #1726
 - exhibitions (reviews) #168 174 186 204 210
   7529
 - influence of Impressionism #227
 - interview #7528
 - landscapes #140
 - reminiscences #7530
 - Wilde, Oscar, on #238
Watson, Mrs. Homer Ransford, Can, 19th c.
 - correspondence, Homer Ransford Watson
   #7533
Watson, Susan, Can artist, 1949-
 - exhibitions (reviews) #2771
Watson, William Arthur, Can architect,
   1903-1977
 - plan, northwestern entrance to Hamilton
   (Ont) #7962
Watson, William R., Can art dealer,
   1887-1973
 - autobiography #1272
Watt & Blackwell, Can architectural firm
 - London (Ont)
   - Aberdeen School #9388
   - McCormick Manufacturing Co. #9234
   - Ryerson School #9386
   - Tecumseh School #9388
Watts, Fraser, Can architect, 1926-
 - Central Mortgage and Housing
   Corporation competition (1960) #8040
wax modelling, Canadian
 - Québec #2183
Way of the Cross
 - *see* Stations of the Cross
weapons
 - *see also* firearms

weapons, Athapaskan #4104 4105
weapons, Beothuk #3528
weapons, Cree #3742
weapons, Huron #3519
weapons, Indians of North America
 - prehistoric #3401
 - shellwork #3388
weapons, Micmac #3528
weapons, Netsilik #4363
weapons, Northwest Coast Indians
 - atlatl #3951
weapons, Ojibwa
 - Parry Island Reservation (Ont) #3540
weapons, Plains
 - secret societies #3727
weapons, Potawatomi
 - Parry Island Reservation (Ont) #3540
weapons, Seneca
 - war clubs #3535
weapons, Tahltan
 - (1910s) #4074
weather vanes
 - *see* vanes
weaving
 - *see also* beadwork; Jacquard weaving
weaving, Algonquian #3374 3605
 - fibre bags #3638 3744
weaving, Athapaskan
 - (1970s), women artisans #3367
weaving, Blackfoot
 - Soumak necklaces #3685
weaving, Canadian #2719 2721 2747 2748
 - 17th-19th cs. #2112 2730 2736
 - 17th c.-1940s #2720
 - 20th c. #2121 2142 2774
 - (1608-1867) #2120
 - (1867) #2735
 - (1960s) #2106
 - Cape Breton (NS) #2728 2732
   - tartan weaving #2724
 - *ceinture fléchée* #2818 2824 2827 2873
 - Chamard, Emélie #2209
 - Charlevoix (Qué)
   - 17th-19th cs. #2733
   - blankets #2738
 - Fredericks, Beany #5513
 - île aux Coudres (Qué) #2168
 - île d'Orléans (Qué) #1252
 - influence on Canadian art, 20th c. #2093
 - Lindgren, Charlotte #6282 6283
 - New Brunswick #2150
 - Nova Scotia #2731
   - (pre-1920) #2785
 - Ontario
   - 19th c. #2723 2726
   - Germanic tradition #2263
 - Ontario Handweavers and Spinners
   (1956-1979) #2743
 - Ploethner, Frederick K. #6896
 - Prince Edward Island, 18th-19th cs. #2734
 - Québec #1327 2223
   - 17th-18th cs. #2181 2187 2200
   - 17th-19th cs., European influences #2221
   - 20th c. #2198
   - (1920s) #2718
   - (1930s-1940s) #2186
   - (1940s) #2199
   - women artisans #2212
 - Saint-Jean-Port-Joli (Qué) #2194
weaving, Chilkat #3784
 - influence of Salish weaving #3898
weaving, Coast Salish #3851 3896
weaving, Cree #3402
weaving, Gitksan

 - 'Ksan #4134
weaving, Great Basin Indians #3986
weaving, Indians of Central America
 - compared with weaving, Northwest Coast
   Indians #3832
weaving, Indians of North America #2739
   2747 2748 3413 3476
 - *ceinture fléchée* #2818 2823 2824 2827 2873
 - influence on Canadian weaving #2774
weaving, Indians of South America
 - influence on Canadian weaving #2774
weaving, Inuit
 - (1970s), women artisans #3367
 - Pangnirtung (NWT) #4237 4298 4308 4310
weaving, Iroquois #3605
 - fibre bags #3638 3744
 - sashes #3534
weaving, Kwakiutl #3787
weaving, Lillooet #3783
weaving, Maliseet #2144
weaving, Nootka #3880
weaving, Northwest Coast Indians #3832
   3931
weaving, Ojibwa #3539 3557
 - mats #3585
weaving, Osage
 - fibre bags #3744
weaving, Quinault #3845
weaving, Salish #3963 4018 4027 4044
 - 20th c. #3964
 - (1960s) #3941
 - (1960s-1970s) #4147
 - influence on Chilkat weaving #3898
weaving, Saulteaux #3402
weaving, Shuswap #3789
weaving, Skokomish #3835
weaving, Snuqualmi #3835
weaving, Tlingit #3826 3902 3976 4018 4027
weaving, Tsimshian #3826
weaving, Woodlands
 - fibre bags #3638 3744
Webb, Peter John, Can architect, 1927-
 - Toronto (Ont), Inn on the Park #9289
Webb, Tom, Can photographer, fl. 1950s-
 - portfolio of photographs #1032
Webb Zerafa Menkès, Can architectural firm
 - Toronto (Ont), Toronto Hilton Hotel #9292
 - Waterloo (Ont), University of Waterloo.
   Student residence #9467
Webb Zerafa Menkès Housden Partnership,
   Can architectural firm
 - Calgary (Alta), office buildings #9362
 - Toronto (Ont)
   - CN Tower #9511
   - Hazelton Lanes #8078
   - Hyatt Regency Hotel #9293
   - Royal Bank Plaza #9198 9353
   - Union Station #9540
Webber, Gordon McKinley, Can artist,
   1909-1965
 - as member, Canadian Group of Painters
   #324
 - interview #7538
Webber, John, Brit artist in Canada,
   1751-1793 #269 270
 - views of Nootka Sound, Vancouver Island
   (BC) #2002
Webber, Ron, Can photographer, 1944-
 - exhibitions (reviews) #1008
Weber, Anna, Can fraktur artist, 1814-1888
   #7539
Weber, George, Can artist, 1907- #7540
Weber, Rudolph, Amer artist, 1858-1933
 - drawings, Thompson Indians #3774

Webern, Anton, Aus composer, 1883-1945
– influence on Yves Gaucher #5560 5562 5565 5568
Webster, David, Can architect, 1866-1952
– Regina (Sask), War Memorial Museum, competition #9073
Webster, John Clarence, Can collector, 1863-1950
– collection, Canadiana, New Brunswick Museum (Saint John, NB) #3073 3209
Weisman, Gustav Oswald, Can stained glass artist, 1926- #7589
Weiss, Joseph (Joe), Can photographer, 1895- #7541
Weissmann, Lawrence, Can photographer, 1943- #1000
– exhibitions, group
  – (1973) #1002
– portfolio of photographs #997 999
Welch, Roger, Amer artist, 1946-
– Lapointe, Frank, compared with #6170
Welcome (Ont), Oke House
– architecture #7959
Welding, William E., ceramicist, fl. 1867-1894 #2335
Weldon, Susannah Anne, Can collector, b. 1817
– collection, British and Chinese ceramics, King's College (Windsor, NS) #2363
Welland (Ont), Welland County General Hospital
– architecture, Agnew, Ludlow & Scott #9031
Welland Canal (Ont)
– views, William James Thomson #7372
Weller, Walter J., Can architect, 1936-
– Charlottetown (PEI), Confederation Centre, competition #9089
Wellington County (Ont)
– photography (1856-1867) #1724
wells, Canadian
– (1608-1867) #2120
Wells, John, Can architect, 1789-1864
– Montréal (Qué), Bank of Montreal #9168 9200
Wells, William, Can photographer, ca. 1956-
– portfolio of photographs #1032
Wembley (England), British Empire Exhibition (1924)
– and Clarence Alphonse Gagnon #5546 5547
– and Eric Brown #458
– and National Gallery of Canada (Ottawa, Ont) #3040
– dispute on Canadian institutional sponsorship and participation #500
  – and Royal Canadian Academy of Arts #157
– exhibitions
  – Canadian Section of Fine Arts (1924) #14 299
– exhibitions (reviews)
  – Canadian Section of Fine Arts (1924) #287 288 291 322
Wembley (England), British Empire Exhibition (1925)
– exhibitions
  – Exhibition of Canadian Art (1925) #14 290 299
– exhibitions (reviews)
  – Exhibition of Canadian Art (1925) #291 292
Wentworth, Sir John, Brit statesman in Canada, 1737-1820

– as first occupant of Government House (Halifax, NS) #8750
Wentworth, Thomas Hanford, Can artist, 1781-1849
– portraits #1171
Wentworth County (Ont)
– architecture #7954
Wentworth-Fitzwilliam, William, Viscount Milton, Brit nobleman, 1839-1877
– Minton dessert service #2289
Werde Point (Nfld), lighthouse #9523
Werden, Rodney, Can artist, 1946-
– exhibitions, group
  – (1977) #631
  – (1978) #650
– video art #630
Werlich, Mr., Can weaver, fl. 1840s-1850s #2723
Werner, Bernhard, Can builder, fl. 1981
– restoration, Skoki Lodge (Lake Louise, Alta) #9296
Wertheimer, Esther, Can sculptor, 1926- #7542
Wertschek, John, Can photographer, fl. 1979 #2071
Wescoupe, Clemence, Can artist, 1951- #4157
West, Benjamin, Amer artist, 1738-1820
– Christ Healing the Sick #1323
– The Death of Wolfe #220
West, John, Can architect, fl. 1820
– protestant church, Red River settlement (1820) #7005
West, W. Richard (Dick), Amer artist, 1912-
– use of water monster motif #3757
West Baffin Eskimo Co-operative (Cape Dorset, NWT) #4192 4460
– and Peter Pitseolak #6880 6881
West Bay (Ont), Ojibwa Cultural Foundation
– exhibitions
  – Anishnabe Mee-Kun: A Circulating Exhibition of Art by Anishnabe Artists of the Manitoulin Island Area (1981) #4173
West End Dresden Pottery, ceramic manufacturer (Montréal, Qué) #2410
West Indies
– views
  – by French explorers, 16th c. #276
– views,
  – J.E.H. MacDonald #6371
West Vancouver (BC), Woyat-Bowie Building. Architects' offices
– architecture and interior, Fred Thornton Hollingsworth and Barry Vance Downs #9346
Westerlund, Mia, Can sculptor, 1942- #675 7543 7545
– exhibitions
  – (1978) #7544
– exhibitions, group
  – (1975) #1809
  – (1981) #797
– interview #788
Westermann, Horace Clifford, Amer artist, 1922-
– influence on John Meredith #6516
Western Art Glass, glass firm (Winnipeg, Man) #2450
Western Front (Vancouver, BC)
– and Glenn Alun Lewis #6275
– exhibitions
  – (1979) #2070
– video art #605
Western Photographic Circle (Vancouver, BC)

– (1964-1967) #2019
Westfield Pioneer Village (Ont) #8063
Westmount (Qué)
– architecture #7930
Weston, William Percival, Can artist, 1879-1967
– and British Columbia Society of Fine Arts #1978
– exhibitions
  – (1980) #7546
Wetherell, Robert Charles, Can architect, d. 1845
– Hamilton (Ont), Dundurn Castle #8662
Weyler, Rex, Can photographer, 1947-
– portfolio of photographs #991 998
Whale, Robert Reginald, Can artist, 1805-1887 #221 7547
– exhibitions, group
  – (1978) #1726
Whalen, Robert, Can designer, 1939- #2487
Wheatley, Willis Sifton, Can artist, 1910-
– on lithography #7548
Wheeler, Arthur Oliver, Can photographer, 1860-1945
– use of survey camera #989
Wheeler, Charles Henry, Can architect, 1838-1917
– Winnipeg (Man), Dalnavert #8708
Wheeler, Dennis, Can, d. 1977
– commemorative photographic series, by Marian Penner Bancroft #4599
Wheeler, Orson Shorey, Can sculptor, 1902- #7549
Wheeler, Thomas, Can engraver, watchmaker, b. ca. 1809, fl. 1847-1871
– as member, Toronto Society of Arts #1689
Whipple, Henry Benjamin, Amer bishop, 1822-1901
– collection, art, Ojibwa and Dakota Indians #3755
Whissell, Aline Piché
– see Piché-Whissell, Aline
Whistler, James Abbott McNeill, Amer artist, 1834-1903
– and Homer Ransford Watson #7533
– and Wyatt Eaton #5355
– Hammond, John A., on #5699
– influence on David Brown Milne #6567
– influence on James Wilson Morrice #6624 6626 6633
Whitby (Ont)
– architecture, 19th c. #8016
Whitby (Ont), Lynde House
– architecture and interior #8668
Whitby (Ont), Station Gallery
– exhibitions
  – John Leonard: 10 Years: An Exhibition of Paintings and Drawings (1981) #6246
White, Daniel Evan, Can architect, 1933-
– Vancouver (BC), Maples Development #8746
White, Edward, Can army officer, b. 1811
– residence, St. John's (Nfld) #8542
White, Frederick, Can ceramicist, 1838-1919 #2319
White, George, Amer architect, 1874-1964
– Lucerne (Qué), Château Lucerne #9283
White, George Harlow, Can artist, 1817-1887 #7551
– exhibitions
  – (1975) #7550
– photographs and watercolours, British Arctic Expedition (1875-1876) #240
White, James, Can ceramicist, 1841-1928

#2319
White, John, Brit statesman, artist in Canada, b. ca. 1540-1550 #228 229
– drawings of Eskimos #7553
– drawings of Indians and Eskimos #7552
White, John Clayton, Brit army officer, architect, artist in Canada, 1835-1907 #2020
– exhibitions, group
  – (1979) #2023
– Victoria (BC) #8145
White, John P., Brit furniture-maker, fl. early 20th c.
– furniture, Alexis Martin House (Victoria, BC) #8682
White, Joseph, Can ceramicist, 1799-1870 #2319
White, Michael, Can photographer, 1946-
– interview, on Groupe d'action photographique #1494
White, Minor, Amer photographer, writer, 1908-1976
– influence on Robert Charles John Bourdeau #4880
White, Norman, Can sculptor, 1938-
– exhibitions
  – (1975) #7554
– exhibitions, group
  – (1977) #783
White, Peter, Can art critic, 1950-
– winner of critical writing on art competition (1979) #3312
White, Stan, Can architect, artist, theatre critic, 1926-
– on stage design #7555
White Pottery, ceramic manufacturer (Courtenay Bay and Saint John, NB) #2319
Whitefield, Edwin, Amer artist in Canada, 1816-1892 #812
Whitehorse (Yukon), Yukon Archives
– photography collection #2087
Whiten, Colette, Can sculptor, 1945- #675 7559 7560
– exhibitions
  – (1978) #7561
– exhibitions, group
  – (1975) #591 1809
  – (1976) #779
  – (1981) #796
– exhibitions (reviews) #579 7556
– interview #788
– performance sculpture #658
– process art #7557 7558
Whiten, Tim, Can artist, 1941-
– cosmological concepts #554
– drawings #532 7563
– exhibitions
  – (1972) #7562
Whiteshell Provincial Park (Man)
– boulder monuments, Ojibwa Indians #3578 3592
Whiteside, George, Can photographer, 1958-
– exhibitions (reviews) #1067
– portfolio of photographs #991
Whiteway, William Tuff, Can architect, 1856-1940
– Duncan (BC), Duncan Public School #9508
Whitlock, An, Can artist, 1944-
– exhibitions, group
  – (1975) #591
– exhibitions (reviews) #579 622
– interview #788 7564
– performance sculpture #658
Whitman, Walt, Amer poet, 1819-1892

– Thomson, Tom, compared with #7357 7360
Whitman Fellowship of Toronto (Toronto, Ont)
– and Lawren Stewart Harris #5731
Whittaker, E.J., Can art dealer, 20th c.
– on Alex Simeon Janvier #5936
Whittome, Irene, Can artist, 1942-
– exhibitions
  – (1980) #7569
– exhibitions, group
  – (1976) #779
  – (1977) #637
  – (1981) #710
– exhibitions (reviews) #7567 7568 7570
– Le musée blanc/White Museum #714 7565
– theme of Narcissus #7566
Whymper, Frederick, Brit army officer, artist in Canada, 1838-1908 #2020
– exhibitions, group
  – (1979) #2023
Whyte, Catharine Robb, Can artist, 1906-1979
– art and writings #7572
– interview #7571
– travelling art exhibition program, Alberta (1980) #1972
Whyte, Peter, Can artist, 1905-1966 #7572
– and Catharine Robb Whyte #7571
– travelling art exhibition program, Alberta (1980) #1972
Wickenden, Charles Osborn, Can architect, 1851-1934
– Vancouver (BC), Christ Church Cathedral #8171 8910
Wickenden, Robert J., Can artist, 1861-1931 #1312 1382
Wickey, Harry H., Amer artist, 1892-
– influence on Miller Gore Brittain #4917
Wickson, Paul Giovanni, Can artist, 1860-1922 #7573
Wickson & Gregg, Can architectural firm
– domestic architecture #8494
– Toronto (Ont), Timothy Eaton Memorial Church #8898
– use of stucco and brickwork #8052
Wied, Maximilian, prince of, Ger naturalist, 1782-1867
– collection, artifacts, Plains Indians #3737 3750
– expedition, Plains Indians #3738
Wieland, Joyce, Can artist, 1931- #657 675
– and nationalism in art #143
– and Toronto (Ont) painting (1960s) #1753
– books #940
– exhibitions
  – (1971) #7577
– exhibitions, group
  – (1971) #98
  – (1973) #556
  – (1979) #147 510
– exhibitions (reviews) #7576
– films #626 7574 7575 7579
  – Reason over Passion #568
  – The Far Shore #7581 7583
  – True Patriot Love #7578
– interview #7580 7582
  – on living in New York (1960s) #460
– on Gordon Rayner #6965
– on Jack Chambers #700
– on Michel Lambeth #6159
Wiens, Clifford, Can architect, 1926-
– and Prairie architecture #8084
– on architecture #7746
– Regina (Sask) #7733

– University of Saskatchewan. Central heating and cooling plant #7694
Wiitasalo, Shirley, Can artist, 1949- #7584
– exhibitions, group
  – (1975) #591
  – (1980) #1832
– exhibitions (reviews) #579
Wilber, A.Rutherford, Can artist, 1869-1949
– exhibitions, group
  – (1969) #1180
Wilby, Robert, Can artist, fl. 1973-
– stoneware and batik, Flat River Crafts Studio #2153
Wilby, Roslynn, Can artist, fl. 1973-
– stoneware and batik, Flat River Crafts Studio #2153
Wilby, Susan, Can artist, fl. 1973-
– stoneware and batik, Flat River Crafts Studio #2153
Wilde, Oscar, Irish writer, 1854-1900
– and Homer Ransford Watson #7533
– in USA and Canada (1882) #238
Wiley, Matthew, Can photographer, fl. 1970s
– portfolio of photographs #995
Wilhelm, Paul, duke of Württemberg, 1797-1860
– collection, artifacts, Plains Indians #3737 3750
Wilkes, Elizabeth
– see Hoey, Elizabeth Wilkes
Wilkes, Francis Hilton, Can architect, 1891-
– Toronto (Ont), Canada Permanent #9177
Wilkin, Rick L., Can architect, 1938-
– Edmonton (Alta)
  – Citadel Theatre #8091 9140
  – University of Alberta. Students' Union Housing #9496
Will, John, Can artist, 1939-
– exhibitions
  – (1980) #7585
Will, Mary Shannon, Can sculptor, ceramicist, 1933-
– ceramic sculpture #795
– interview #7586
Willar, Fred, Can artist, 1939- #1126
William Eby Pottery, ceramic manufacturer (Conestoga, Ont)
– (1855-1907) #2304
William Thomas and Sons, Can architectural firm
– Halifax (NS) #9410
Williams, Al, Can photographer, fl. 1981
– portfolio of photographs #1032
Williams, Alyn, Brit artist, 1865-1955
– and Mary Evelyn Wrinch #7617
– as teacher of Mary Evelyn Wrinch #7618
Williams, Arch, Can artist, 1909- #1155
– exhibitions, group
  – (1976) #1153
  – (1977) #1156
Williams, Francis, Can artist, 1936-
– interview #7587
– silkscreen prints #4148
Williams, Judith (Judy), Can artist, 1940- #7588
Williams, Paul, Can leather sculptor, 1949- #2936
Williams, Robin, Can photographer, 1946-
– portfolio of photographs #991
Williams, Saul, Can artist, 1954- #4157
– exhibitions, group
  – (1977) #4151
Williams, Warren Heywood, Amer architect,

1844-1888
– Victoria (BC) #8175
Williams, William Frederick, Can architect, 1904-1947
– winner, T. Eaton Company Architectural Competition for House Designs (1936) #8738
Williams, Yvonne, Can stained glass artist, 1901- #2455 7589
– on stained glass (1944) #2446
– stained glass #2445
– Montréal (Qué) #2448
Williams & Ferguson, Can architectural firm
– Toronto (Ont), Toronto Stock Exchange, competition #9161
Williamsburg (Ont), Molsons Bank
– architecture #9173
Williamson, Albert Curtis, Can artist, 1867-1944 #7590
– as member, Canadian Art Club #193
– exhibitions (reviews) #204 211
Williamson, Beatrice (Betty) Lyell, Can photographer, 1916-
– portfolio of photographs #987
Williamson, James D. (Jim), Can artist, 1924-
– as teacher, Art Gallery of Toronto (Toronto, Ont) #3020
Williamstown (Ont)
– architecture #7997
Williamstown (Ont), Nor'westers Museum #3148
Willmott, Elizabeth, Can sculptor, 1928-
– relief structures #777
Willoughby, Linda, Can artist, fl. 1981
– fibrework #2775
Willowdale (Ont), Koffler Gallery
– exhibitions
– The Heritage of Jack Bush: A Tribute (1981) #722
Willowdale (Ont), North York Public Library
– exhibitions
– Reader, Lover of Books, Lover of Heaven: A Catalogue Based on an Exhibition of the Book Arts in Ontario (1978, 1981) #935
Willowdale (Ont), Regis College
– exhibitions
– Canadian Religious Art Today: An Exhibition of Contemporary Art/L'art religieux canadien d'aujourd'hui: une exposition d'art contemporain (1966) #479
Wills, Frank, Can architect, 1822-1857
– Fredericton (NB), chapel #8770
– Montréal (Qué), Christ Church Cathedral #8798
Willson, David, Can architect, ca. 1778/1780-1866
– Sharon (Ont)
– Temple of Peace #8351
– Temple of Peace and Children of Peace Meeting House #8352
Wilson, Bunnell & Borgstrom Ltd., Can consulting engineers and landscape architects
– plan, northwestern entrance to Hamilton (Ont) #7962
Wilson, Don, Can artist, fl. 1980 #7592
Wilson, James, Can photographer, ca. 1950-
– portfolio of photographs #991
Wilson, John, Can architect, 1863-1952
– Lake of Bays (Ont), Bigwin Inn #9275
Wilson, Richard D., Can artist, 1920-
– views, Montréal (Qué) #7919
Wilson, Ronald York, Can artist, 1907- #7594 7595

– and architecture #8231
– exhibitions
– (1974) #7596
– exhibitions, group
– (1959) #438
– exhibitions (reviews) #432
– in Mexico #4931
– on art and architecture #8235
Wilson, Sir Daniel, Can educator, artist, 1816-1892 #7591
Wilson, William F., Can artist, fl. 1842-1854 #7593
Wilson Newton Roberts Duncan, Can architectural firm
– Toronto (Ont), University of Toronto. University College, restoration #7776
wind
– in sculptures, Richard Prince #6936
windmills, American
– northeastern USA #9249
windmills, Canadian #9244 9248 9249
– 17th-early 19th cs. #7841
– Québec #9255
– Québec (Qué), Hôpital-Général #9245
windows, Canadian
– conservation #7778
– glass manufacturing, 19th-20th cs. #7752
– guide to conservation #7777
– Halifax (NS), Halifax Citadel #8441
– Saint-Jean (Qué), Canada Glass Works #2420
windows in art
– and perception #525
– Gutsche, Clara, photographs of store-window displays #5673
Windsor (NS)
– views
– Bartlett, William Henry #1218
Windsor (NS), King's College
– pottery, British and Chinese, 17th-19th cs., Susannah Anne Weldon Collection #2363
Windsor (NS), Martock House
– architecture #8528
Windsor (NS), Shand House
– architecture and interior, Joseph Taylor #8546
Windsor (Ont)
– art #1668
– log buildings, French-Canadian settlers, 19th c. #7685
Windsor (Ont), Art Gallery of Windsor
– collection #3156
– exhibitions
– A.J. Casson (1978) #5060
– A Retrospective Exhibition of Selected Works by Caven Atkins Spanning Fifty Years of the Artist's Life (1979) #4569
– A Survey of Forty-five Years (1976) #6658
– André Biéler 50 Years: A Retrospective Exhibition 1920-1970 (1970) #4725
– Canadian Paintings in the University of Toronto: An Exhibition in Celebration of the Sesquicentennial of the University of Toronto (1978) #3168
– Carl Schaefer: Retrospective Exhibition; Paintings from 1926 to 1969 (1969) #7155
– Certain Traditions: Recent British and Canadian Art (1978) #653
– Changing Visions: The Canadian Landscape/Aperçus divers: le paysage canadien (1976) #617
– Charles Fraser Comfort: Fifty Years (1973) #5159
– David Bolduc: Recent Work (1980) #4775
– Dessins inédits d'Ozias Leduc/Ozias Leduc

the Draughtsman (1979) #6210
– Don Snell and Nancy Hazelgrove: Sculpture and Painting (1980) #1835
– Esther Warkov Drawings (1977) #7519
– Frederic Marlett Bell-Smith (1846-1923) (1978) #4668
– George Heriot: Painter of the Canadas/George Heriot: peintre des deux Canadas (1979) #5786
– Goodridge Roberts: Selected Works/Goodridge Roberts: oeuvres choisies (1981) #7050
– Gordon Rayner Retrospective (1979) #6966
– Graham Coughtry: Retrospective (1977) #5190
– Guido Molinari: Works on Paper (1981) #6594
– Indications: Paintings, Collage, Drawings, Prints, Sculpture (1975) #7415
– Inuit Art in the 1970's: A Travelling Exhibition/L'Art inuit actuel, 1970-79: exposition itinérante (1980) #4287
– Ivan Eyre Exposition (1981) #5394
– J.W. Beatty, 1869-1941 (1981) #4638
– Jack Wise: A Decade of Work (1978) #7601
– Jock Macdonald: The Inner Landscape: A Retrospective Exhibition/Jock Macdonald: le paysage intérieur: rétrospective (1981) #6379
– Joe de Angelis, Bob Ferraro (1978) #1824
– Joe Plaskett and His Paris: In Search of Time Past (1972) #6893
– Joe Plaskett et son Paris: à la recherche d'un temps passé (1972) #6894
– John Fox: 10 New Paintings (1980) #5495
– John Meredith: Fifteen Years (1975) #6514
– Joseph Nicola DeLauro: Sculpture (1981) #5276
– Kenneth Lochhead: An Exhibition of Paintings 1952-1975 (1977) #6318
– Lochhead, Kenneth Campbell, on #6319
– Krystyna Sadowska: Sculptures, Drawings, Collages, Batiks, Paintings (1977) #7115
– Louis de Niverville (1978) #6709
– Mary Celestino: Recent Paintings (1980) #5063
– Ontario Society of Artists: 100 Years (1973) #1678
– Otto Rogers: New Paintings and Sculpture, 1977-78 (1979) #7065
– Painters Eleven in Retrospect (1980) #1785
– Peter Harris: A Survey of Fifteen Years (1977) #5735
– Peter Kolisnyk (1977) #6075
– Poets and Other People: Drawings by Harold Town (1980) #7416
– R.L. Bloore: Sixteen Years, 1958-1974 (1975) #4751
– Ronald: 25 Years (1976) #7073
– Roy K. Kiyooka: 25 Years (1976) #6062
– Southwest (1970-) #1668
– T.R. MacDonald, 1908-1978 (1981) #6380
– Ted Hodgkinson, Jack Meanwell (1977) #646
– The Contemporary Arts Society: Montreal 1939-1948/La Société d'art contemporain: Montréal 1939-1948 (1981) #1474
– The Heritage of Jack Bush: A Tribute (1983) #722
– The Mr. and Mrs. Jules Loeb Collection/La collection M. et Mme Jules Loeb (1971) #3231
– The Ontario Community Collects: A Survey of Canadian Painting from 1766 to the

Present (1976) #120
- *The Work of Art: Six Artists* (1979) #665
- *Tom Forrestall Exhibition* (1972) #5461
- *Traditional Arts of French Canada* (1975) #2128
- *Trésors d'art populaire québécois/Folk Art Treasures of Quebec* (1981) #1297
- *Viewpoint: Twenty-nine by Nine; An Exhibition of Twenty-nine Works by Ontario Artists, Selected by Nine Curators* (1981) #1838
- *William Perehudoff: Recent Paintings* (1979) #6837
- exhibitions (reviews)
  - *Kenneth Lochhead: An Exhibition of Paintings 1952-1975* (1977) #6320
Windsor (Ont), Carnegie Library
- Heller, Clair, sculpture demonstration #5775
Windsor (Ont), Collegiate Institute
- architecture, James Carlisle Pennington #9388
Windsor (Ont), Dominion Bank
- architecture, Carrere & Hastings; Eustace G. Bird #9188
Windsor (Ont), Imperial Bank of Canada
- architecture, Charles S. Cobb #9175
Windsor (Ont), University of Windsor. School of Visual Arts
- Angelis, Joe de, as teacher #1824
- DeLauro, Joseph Nicola, as founder and head #5276
- Ferraro, Bob, as teacher #1824
Windsor (Ont), Willistead Art Gallery
- exhibitions
  - *7 West Coast Painters* (1959) #1997
  - *Centennial Exhibition of Quebec and Ontario Contemporary Painters, 1967* (1967) #484
  - *David Milne: 1882-1953* (1967) #6558
  - *Essex County Artists (1940-1968)* #1668
  - *Fakir Art Club (1930-1940)* #1668
  - *Some Canadians in Spain* (1965) #473
  - *Some Paintings, Drawings and Prints from the Douglas Duncan Collection* (1967) #3223
  - *The Saidye and Samuel Bronfman Collection of Canadian Art/La collection Saidye et Samuel Bronfman* (1968) #3087
  - *William G.R. Hind (1833-1888): A Confederation Painter in Canada* (1967) #5806
- Heriot, George, paintings of Indians #5784
Windsor furniture
- chairs #2476
  - Ontario #2553 2560
- rocking chairs, Québec #2536
Winnipeg (Man)
- apartment houses (1910s) #8686
- architects' offices (1940s) #9297
- architecture #8092 8096 8105 8256
  - 19th c.-1909 #8093
  - 19th c.-1910s #8099
  - (1831-1960) #8095
  - (1881-1912) #8101
  - (1950s) #7673
  - (1960s) #7698
  - Barber & Barber #8331
  - downtown area #8108
    - (1970s) #8104
  - Stechesen, Leslie #8409
  - warehouse area #8106
- architecture and urban development (1870-1917) #8103

- art
  - (1950s-1970s) #131
  - (1960s) #1848
  - (1960s-1980s) #1907
  - (1970s) #1856
- art and architecture #1891
- art education (1940s) #1889 1890
- art galleries (1960s) #442
- banks
  - (1898-1914) #9205
  - (1910s) #9202
- city halls (1876-1962) #8996
- domestic architecture
  - 19th c. #8702
  - (1910s) #8493 8688
  - (1950s) #8514
  - Rugh, Herbert Bell #8683
- graphic arts
  - (1970s) #1901
  - (1981) #1908
- office buildings and warehouses (1880s-1914) #8107
- painting
  - (1940s-1950s) #412
  - (1960s) #1892
- photographic views
  - (1850-1900) #1061
  - Paskievich, John #6777
- photography
  - (1890s) #1886
  - (1970s) #1030 1879
- schools
  - (1908) #9484
  - (1920s) #9389
- sculpture (1960s) #1853
Winnipeg (Man), Allen Theatre
- architecture, C.Howard Crane #9074
Winnipeg (Man), Assiniboine Block
- architecture, Louise Arsene Desy #9361
Winnipeg (Man), Bank of Commerce
- architecture, Darling & Pearson #9202
Winnipeg (Man), Bank of Hamilton
- architecture, John D. Atchison & Co.; H.C. Ingalls and F.B. Hoffman, Associate Architects #9171
Winnipeg (Man), Bank of Montreal
- architecture, McKim, Mead & White #9202 9205
Winnipeg (Man), Bank of Nova Scotia
- architecture, Darling & Pearson #9157 9202
Winnipeg (Man), Birks Building
- architecture, Nobbs & Hyde #9355
Winnipeg (Man), Cauchon Block
- architecture, Louis Arsene Desy #9361
Winnipeg (Man), Chapel of Christ the King
- *see* Winnipeg (Man), University of Manitoba. Chapel of Christ the King
Winnipeg (Man), Chase Gallery
- exhibitions (reviews)
  - Winnipeg photographers (1977) #1030
Winnipeg (Man), City Hall
- architecture, competition for
  - (1913) #8979
  - (1960) #8985 8986 8987
Winnipeg (Man), City Hall (1883-1886)
- architecture, Barber & Barber #8331 8996
Winnipeg (Man), Dalnavert
- architecture, Charles Henry Wheeler #8708
Winnipeg (Man), Deer Lodge
- architecture, Pratt & Ross #9260
Winnipeg (Man), Dominion Bank
- architecture, Darling & Pearson #9188
Winnipeg (Man), Empire Hotel
- architecture, Louis Arsene Desy #9361

Winnipeg (Man), Etienne Gaboury House
- architecture, Etienne J. Gaboury #8519
Winnipeg (Man), Fleet Gallery
- exhibitions (reviews)
  - *Povungnituk 1976 Prints/Estampes* (1977) #4489
Winnipeg (Man), Fort Garry Hotel
- architecture, Ross & Macdonald #9268
Winnipeg (Man), Fort Garry Terminal
- architecture, Warren & Wetmore #9530
Winnipeg (Man), Grand Western Canadian Screen Shop
- (1968-1977) #1902
Winnipeg (Man), Green, Blankstein, Russell & Associates architects' office
- architecture and interior, Green, Blankstein, Russell & Associates #9299
Winnipeg (Man), Hotel at Silver Springs
- architecture, Pratt & Ross #9263
Winnipeg (Man), Ikoy Partnership architects' office
- architecture, Ikoy Partnership #8091
Winnipeg (Man), Legislative Building
- architecture
  - competition for #8946
  - Simon, Frank Worthington #8944 8945 8947 8948 8949 8950 8951 8952
- architecture and sculpture #8953
- exhibitions
  - *150 Years of Art in Manitoba: Struggle for a Visual Civilization; An Exhibition for the Manitoba Centennial, 1970* (1970) #1895
  - *Eskimo Sculpture* (1967) #4410
- exhibitions (reviews)
  - *150 Years of Art in Manitoba: Struggle for a Visual Civilization; An Exhibition for the Manitoba Centennial, 1970* (1970) #1893
Winnipeg (Man), Lombard Plaza
- architecture and urban development #9302
Winnipeg (Man), Manitoba Archives Building
- exhibitions
  - *Twenty-Seven Artists and the Manitoba Arts Council* (1976) #1899
Winnipeg (Man), Manitoba Museum
- art education (1940s) #1889
Winnipeg (Man), Manitoba Museum of Man and Nature
- exhibitions
  - *Artisan '78: The First National Travelling Exhibition of Contemporary Canadian Crafts/Artisan '78: première exposition nationale itinérante d'artisanat canadien contemporain* (1979) #2134
Winnipeg (Man), Manitoba Museum of Man and Nature. Concert Hall
- architecture #9107
Winnipeg (Man), Marlborough Hotel
- architecture, James Chisolm & Son and John Hamilton Gordon Russell #9277
Winnipeg (Man), Monarch Life Building
- architecture, Smith Carter Searle Associates #9357
Winnipeg (Man), Pan-Am Pool
- architecture, Smith Carter Searle Associates #9101
Winnipeg (Man), Plug In Gallery
- exhibitions
  - *John Greer: Sculptural Objective, 1968-1981; Everything Always Changes but Something Still Remains* (1982) #5654
Winnipeg (Man), Royal Alexandra Hotel
- lights #2599
- mural, Frederick Sproston Challener #5068

Winnipeg (Man), Saint John's Cathedral
– Rindisbacher, Peter, paintings #7005
Winnipeg (Man), Saint Paul's College
– see Winnipeg (Man), University of
  Manitoba. Saint Paul's College
Winnipeg (Man), Seven Oaks House (now
  Seven Oaks Museum)
– architecture and interior #8703
Winnipeg (Man), Smith Carter Searle
  Associates, architectural and engineering
  office
– architecture, Smith Carter Searle
  Associates #7683
Winnipeg (Man), Thomas Gallery
– exhibitions (reviews)
  – Fafard, Joe #5399
  – Sheila Butler: Recent Paintings, Drawings
    and Prints (1977) #4984
Winnipeg (Man), Ukrainian Canadian
  Committee
– exhibitions
  – Program of the First Ukrainian Display of
    Fine Arts in Winnipeg (1951) #1843
Winnipeg (Man), University of Manitoba.
  Art and Adult Education Centre
  (proposed)
– architecture #8250
Winnipeg (Man), University of Manitoba.
  Arts Building
– architecture, Arthur A. Stoughton and
  Gilbert Parfitt #9485
Winnipeg (Man), University of Manitoba.
  Arts College
– architecture, Moody, Moore & Partners
  #9399
Winnipeg (Man), University of Manitoba.
  Chapel of Christ the King
– architecture, Gardiner, Thornton, Gathe &
  Associates; Green, Blankstein, Russell &
  Associates #9486
Winnipeg (Man), University of Manitoba.
  Crop Research Centre
– architecture, Waisman, Ross & Associates
  #7683
Winnipeg (Man), University of Manitoba.
  Freshwater Research Institute
– works, Tony Tascona #7326
Winnipeg (Man), University of Manitoba.
  Saint Paul's College
– architecture, Gardiner, Thornton, Gathe &
  Associates; Green, Blankstein, Russell &
  Associates #9486
Winnipeg (Man), University of Manitoba.
  School of Architecture
– architectural education
  – (1941) #8245
  – (1947) #8246
  – (1948) #8247
  – (1949) #8248
  – (1950) #8249
  – (1950s) #8256
  – (1951) #8250
  – (1952) #8252
  – (1964) #8272
  – (1968), environmental studies program
    #8281
  – (1980) #8289
Winnipeg (Man), University of Manitoba.
  School of Architecture Building
– architecture, Smith Carter Searle
  Associates #9487
Winnipeg (Man), University of Manitoba.
  School of Art
– (1950-1970s) #3006

Winnipeg (Man), University of Manitoba.
  School of Art. Gallery III
– exhibitions
  – Eskimo Fantastic Art (1972) #4240
  – Henry Saxe: "Two Works" (1976) #7148
  – Kenneth Lochhead: Recent Works on Paper
    (1972) #6316
  – Tiktak: Sculptor from Rankin Inlet, N.W.T.:
    A Retrospective Exhibition (1970) #7376
  – Younger Vancouver Sculptors (1968) #2037
Winnipeg (Man), University of Manitoba.
  Science Building
– architecture, Arthur A. Stoughton and
  Gilbert Parfitt #9485
Winnipeg (Man), University of Manitoba.
  University Centre
– architecture, Number Ten Architectural
  Group #9488
Winnipeg (Man), Upstairs Gallery
– exhibitions
  – Marion Tuu'luq: Wallhangings (1980)
    #7442
– exhibitions (reviews)
  – Marion Tuu'luq: Wallhangings (1980)
    #7441
Winnipeg (Man), Walker Theatre
– curtain, Frederick Sproston Challener
  #5068
Winnipeg (Man), Wardlow Apartments
– architecture #8486
Winnipeg (Man), Winnipeg Art Gallery
– (1912) #3181
– (1912-1962) #3188
– (1971) #9111
– (1975-1977) #3196
– architecture
  – competition for #9102
  – Roza, Gustavo da, and Number Ten
    Architectural Group #9117
– art education (1940s) #1889
– collection #3192
– Dobush, Peter, collection #3221
– exhibitions
  – 150 Years of Art in Manitoba: Struggle for
    a Visual Civilization; An Exhibition for the
    Manitoba Centennial, 1970 (1970) #1895
  – 7 West Coast Painters (1959) #1997
  – A Terrible Beauty: The Art of Canada at
    War (1979) #1111
  – Adrien Hébert: trente ans de son oeuvre,
    1923-1953/Adrien Hébert: Thirty Years of
    His Art, 1923-1953 (1972) #5763
  – André Biéler 50 Years: A Retrospective
    Exhibition 1920-1970 (1971) #4725
  – Artists' Prints and Multiples (1977) #1901
  – Baker Lake Drawings (1972) #4241
  – Barbeau,(1969) #4605
  – Beauté tragique: les deux conflits mondiaux
    vus par des artistes canadiens (1979) #1112
  – Belcher Islands/Sanikiluaq (1981) #4459
  – Bill Vazan: suites photographiques récentes
    et oeuvres sur le terrain/Bill Vazan: Recent
    Land and Photoworks (1981) #7476
  – Canadian Art of Our Time (1967) #494
  – Canadian Political Cartoons (1977) #956
  – Canadian Tapestries, 1977 (1977) #2770
  – Canvas, Quill, Brush and Hide: An
    Exploration of Manitoba Indian Art (1975)
    #4141
  – Cape Dorset (1980) #4299
  – Cape Dorset: Selected Sculpture from the
    Collections of the Winnipeg Art Gallery
    (1975) #4441
  – Changing Visions: The Canadian

  Landscape/Aperçus divers: le paysage
    canadien (1976) #617
  – Charles Fraser Comfort: Fifty Years (1972)
    #5159
  – Charles Gagnon (1979) #5540
  – Christiane Pflug, 1936-1972 (1974) #6850
  – Claude Tousignant (1973) #7401
  – Conceptual Decorative: Prints by Les
    Levine, 1965-1970/Conceptuel décoratif:
    estampes de Les Levine, 1965-1970 (1972)
    #6265
  – David Craven/Harold Klunder (1980) #708
  – David McMillan: Recent Photographs
    (1980) #6504
  – David Milne: 1882-1953 (1967) #6558
  – Dessins de Lionel LeMoine FitzGerald et
    Bertram Brooker (1975) #503
  – Drawings and Pastels c. 1930-1967 by
    Miller Gore Brittain (1969) #4917
  – E. Lindner: Drawings, 1969-1972 (1972)
    #6285
  – E. Lindner in Retrospect: The Years
    1963-1977 (1977) #6288
  – Eight from Toronto (1975) #1809
  – Eskimo Narrative (1979) #4285
  – Five Manitoba Photographers: John
    Paskievich, Michaelin McDermott, Leonard
    Schlichting, David Barbour, Brian Appel
    (1979) #1904
  – Form & Performance (1978) #669
  – Fritz Brandtner 1896-1969: A Retrospective
    Exhibition (1971) #4903
  – Frontiers of Our Dreams: Quebec Painting
    in the 1940's and 1950's (1979) #1472
  – Gambling on the Future: Holography,
    Photography and Painting from Fringe
    Research Inc. (1979) #1905
  – Gift from the Douglas M. Duncan
    Collection and the Milne-Duncan
    Bequest/Le Don provenant de la collection
    Douglas M. Duncan et le legs
    Milne-Duncan (1972) #541
  – Images of Woman (1975) #121
  – In Video (1978) #631
  – Irene Whittome, 1975-1980 (1980) #7569
  – Ivan Eyre: A Retrospective Show (1969)
    #5389
  – Ivan Eyre: Recent Paintings and Sculpture
    (1974) #5390
  – Jack Shadbolt (1970) #7182
  – Jock Macdonald: The Inner Landscape: A
    Retrospective Exhibition/Jock Macdonald: le
    paysage intérieur: rétrospective (1981)
    #6379
  – John Meredith: Fifteen Years (1975) #6514
  – K.J. Butler: Paintings (1977) #4982
  – Karoo Ashevak (1977) #4562
  – Kenneth Lochhead: An Exhibition of
    Paintings 1952-1975 (1977) #6318
  – L'art de Tom Thomson (1972) #7367
  – L.L. FitzGerald, 1890-1956: A Memorial
    Exhibition 1958 (1958) #5448
  – Lionel Lemoine FitzGerald, Bertram
    Brooker: Their Drawings (1975) #504
  – Lionel LeMoine FitzGerald (1890-1956):
    The Development of an Artist (1978) #5450
  – Lithographs/Lithographies (1973) #825
  – Looking South (1978) #4278
  – Manitoba Etchings - 1910 to 1940 (1973)
    #1898
  – Manitoba Mainstream: People's Art/Fine
    Art/Le Grand Courant du Manitoba: arts
    populaires, beaux-arts (1973) #1897
  – Manitoba Quilts and Ceramics (1972)

#2272
- *Maxwell Bates: Retrospective Exhibition* (1961) #4622
- *Ministic Sculpture* (1977) #4153
- *Oonark/Pangnark* (1970) #4220
- *Photographs: Clayton Bailey, Joanne Jackson Johnson, David McMillan* (1977) #1033
- *Port Harrison/Inoucdjouac* (1976) #4267
- *Povungnituk* (1977) #4274
- *R.L. Bloore: Sixteen Years, 1958-1974* (1975) #4751
- *Rankin Inlet/Kangirllniq* (1981) #4314
- *Repulse Bay* (1979) #4450
- *Robert Harris (1849-1919)* (1974?) #5743
- *Sculpture on the Prairies* (1977) #1873
- *Selections from the Twomey Collection* (1972) #4427
- *The Art of Tom Thomson* (1972) #7368
- *The Artists' Proof* (1981) #1908
- *The Bessie Bulman Collection: An Exhibition of Contemporary Eskimo Sculpture* (1973) #4428
- *The Birds of America by John James Audubon* (1944) #12
- *The Canadian Canvas: A Travelling Exhibition of 85 Recent Paintings/Peintres canadiens actuels: exposition itinérante de 85 oeuvres récentes* (1976) #588
- *The Coming and Going of the Shaman: Eskimo Shamanism and Art* (1978) #4283
- *The Development of Canadian Silver: A Winnipeg Centennial Exhibition* (1974) #2644
- *The Drawings of Christiane Pflug* (1979) #6851
- *The Inuit Amautik: "I Like My Hood To Be Full"* (1980) #4300
- *The J.S. McLean Collection of Canadian Painting* (1969) #3228
- *The Mr. and Mrs. Jules Loeb Collection/La collection M. et Mme Jules Loeb* (1971) #3231
- *The Mulders' Collection of Eskimo Sculpture* (1976) #4443
- *The R.C.A. Exhibition* (1980) #1906
- *The Railway: Patron of the Arts in Canada* (1976) #3281
- *The Temptation of Aquarius: Paintings by Robert Ralph Carmichael* (1972) #5002
- *The Winnipeg Show* (1955-1970) #54
- *The Zazelenchuk Collection of Eskimo Art* (1978) #4284
- *Tom Forrestall Exhibition* (1972) #5461
- *Treaty Numbers 23, 287, 1171: Three Indian Painters of the Prairies* (1972) #4131
- *Tuu'luq/Anguhadluq: An Exhibition of Works by Marion Tuu'luq and Luke Anguhadluq of Baker Lake* (1976) #4268
- *Waiting: Photographs by Clayton Bailey* (1978) #4584
- *Watercolour Painters from Saskatchewan/Aquarellistes de la Saskatchewan* (1972) #1920
- *West Coast Waves* (1976) #2060
- *Western Canadian Salon of Photography (1935-1943)* #985
- *William Blair Bruce* (1976) #4942
- *Winnipeg Perspective* (1978-) #54
- *Woman as Viewer* (1975) #596
- *Yves Gaucher & Christopher Pratt* (1978) #643
- exhibitions (reviews)
 - *150 Years of Art in Manitoba: Struggle for a Visual Civilization; An Exhibition for the Manitoba Centennial, 1970* (1970) #1893
 - Condon, Wanda (1976) #5166
 - *Exposure: Contemporary Canadian Photographers/Exposure: photographes canadiens contemporains* (1977) #1030
 - *Manitoba 1976 Juried Exhibitions* (1977) #1030
 - Manitoba art (1977) #1900
 - *Sculpture on the Prairies* (1977) #1878
 - *The Canadian Canvas: A Travelling Exhibition of 85 Recent Paintings/Peintres canadiens actuels: exposition itinérante de 85 oeuvres récentes* (1976) #582
 - *The Temptation of Aquarius: Paintings by Robert Ralph Carmichael* (1972) #1866
 - *The Winnipeg Show* (1956) #416
 - *Treaty Numbers 23, 287, 1171: Three Indian Painters of the Prairies* (1972) #1866 4128
 - *West Coast Waves* (1976) #1871
 - *Woman as Viewer* (1975) #601 1877
- Inuit art #4306
- Inuit sculpture #4449
- photography collection #1051
- Proch, Don, *Asessippi* mixed-media event (1972) #6941
Winnipeg (Man), Winnipeg Convention Centre
- work, Dale Amundson #4524
Winnipeg (Man), Winnipeg International Airport
- architecture #9517
- exhibitions
 - *Eskimo Carvers of Keewatin, N.W.T.* (1964) #4402
Winnipeg (Man), Winnipeg School Division #1 administration building
- architecture, Waisman, Ross & Associates #7683
Winnipeg (Man), Winnipeg School of Art
- (1913-1950) #3006
- and Winnipeg Sketch Club #1887
Winnipeg (Man), Winnipeg Square
- Head, George Bruce, *The Wall* #5759
Winnipeg (Man), Woodsworth Building
- Dale Amundson, relief sculpture #4524
- Head, George Bruce, "shapescapes" #5759
- Howarth, Edward J., *Stratoscape* #5853
Winnipeg Camera Club (Winnipeg, Man)
- (1890s) #1886
Winnipeg Paint and Glass Company, glass firm (Winnipeg, Man) #2450
Winnipeg Sketch Club (Winnipeg, Man)
- (1914-) #1887
- (1914-1970) #1894
Winnipeg Tribune, Can newspaper
- and Walter Joseph Phillips #6857
Winrob, Harry, Can physician, collector, 20th c.
- collection, Inuit art #4312 4445 4447
Winsor, Jacqueline (Jackie), Can sculptor, 1941- #7598
- exhibitions (reviews) #7597
winter
- Canadian Christmas cards #863
- Canadian landscapes #285 1298
- Cullen, Maurice Galbraith, landscapes #5214
- Suzor-Coté, Marc-Aurèle de Foy, *Paysage d'hiver* #7301
- Tremblay, Georges-Edouard, hooked rugs #2756
Winter, William Arthur, Can artist, 1909-
#7599
winter clothing
- Québec, 17th-19th cs. #2832
winter counts, Blackfoot #3707
winter counts, Dakota
- London (England), British Museum #3747
winter counts, Plains
- in art #3728
winter counts, Siouan
- in art #3728
Winton, Jan, Can artist, 1954-
- *Syncopation* #1833
Wise, Jack Marlowe, Can artist, 1928- #7600
- exhibitions
 - (1977) #7601
- exhibitions, group
 - (1973) #2045
- exhibitions (reviews) #2051
- interview #7602
Wiseman, James Lovell, Can artist, 1897-1912 #7603
Wiseman, Nelson, Can photographer, fl. 1981
- on his photographs in photo booths #7604
Wishlaw, Robert, Can photographer, fl. 1979 #2071
Witmer, Joseph, Can furniture-maker, 1812-1896 #2578
Wittenborn, Rainer, Ger artist, 1941-
- views of James Bay (Qué) #1566
Wittgenstein, Ludwig Josef Johann, Aus philosopher, 1889-1951
- art theory, and Inuit art #4294
- *Tractatus Logico-Philosophicus*, influence on John Heward #5793
Witton & Walsh, Can architectural firm
- Hamilton (Ont), Church of Saint John the Evangelist #730
Wolfe, James, Brit army officer in Canada, 1727/1728-1759
- portraits of #212 1568
- statues, Québec (Qué) #1309 1600
Wolfe, Robert, Can artist, 1935- #7606
- exhibitions
 - (1977) #7605
Wolfe County (Qué), Church of Saint-Gérard Majella
- architecture, Affleck, Desbarats, Dimakopoulos, Lebensold, Sise #8846
Wolff, Louis-Augustin, Can artist, fl. 1760-1818
- gilding #2930
Wolfville (NS)
- architects' offices (1940s) #9297
- domestic architecture, 19th c. #8533
Wolfville (NS), Acadia University
- architecture, Leslie Raymond Fairn #9407
Wolfville (NS), Acadia University. Art Gallery
- exhibitions
 - *Charles Wm. MacDonald: Seaman, Labourer, Artist, Manufacturer (1874-1967)* (1981) #6355
Wolfville (NS), Acadia University. Fine Arts Department
- (1940s) #1194
Wolhaupter, Benjamin, Can silversmith, 1800-1857 #2649
Women's Art Association of Canada
- (1889-1901) #176
- (1890s) #1706
- and Canadian Handicrafts Guild #2090
- art education (1910s) #1712
- commission, State dinner service of

Canada (1898) #2333
– exhibitions
  – (1904) #2241
  – (1939) #1
Women's Art Association of Hamilton
  (Hamilton, Ont)
– (1894-) #1701
women's movement
– *see* feminism
women architects
– Canada #7678
women artist #4935
women artists
– 17th-18th cs., Québec, decorative arts
  #2200
– 17th-20th cs., Canada #117
– 17th c.-1910s, Québec, household crafts
  #2212
– 19th c., Nova Scotia #1215 1220 1222
– 19th c.-1920s, Canada #5
– 19th c.-1970s, Canada, basketmakers #2943
– 19th c.-1970s, Canada, photographers
  #1005 1064
– 20th c., Canada #53 95 96 121 739
– 20th c., Canada, artisans #2107
– (1790s-19th c.), Canada #7164
– (1830s), Toronto (Ont) #1688
– (1830s-1840s), Nova Scotia #1219
– (1830s-1860s), Toronto (Ont),
  photographers #1725
– (1840-1900), Canada, photographers #1049
– (1850-1950), Nova Scotia #1204
– (1880s-1926), Montréal (Qué), china
  painting #1228
– (1889-1901), Women's Art Association of
  Canada #176
– (1890s), Montréal (Qué) #1311
– (1894-), Women's Art Association of
  Hamilton #1701
– (1904), decorative arts #2241
– (1910s), Canada #202 207 209
– (1910s), Canada, students abroad #206
– (1920s), Canada #14
– (1920s), Victoria (BC), potters #2278
– (1920s-1950s), Inuit, basketmakers #4180
– (1930s), Québec #1380
– (1930s), Québec, artisans #2165
– (1930s-1970s), Québec #1273
– (1939-1945), Canada, war subjects #1116
– (1940s), Canada #377
– (1960s-1970s), Canada #677
– (1960s-1970s), Inuit, weavers #4298
– (1960s-1970s), Salish, weavers #4147
– (1960s-1980s), Canada #717
– (1970s), British Columbia #2054
– (1970s), Canada #542 562 579 591 601 625
  675 698 701 1877
  – "Women's Work" project #659
  – bookworks #936
  – video art #550
  – views of sensuality and sexuality #596
– (1970s), Canada, photographers #1011 1013
– (1970s), Durham region (Ont) #1826
– (1970s), Inuit #4258 4260
– (1970s), Inuit, embroidery #4259
– (1970s), Inuit, Spence Bay (NWT) #6474
– (1970s), Inuit and Athapaskan, artisans
  #3367
– (1970s), Mennonite #2253
– (1970s), Montréal (Qué), Powerhouse
  Gallery #1516 1553 1554 1555 1557
– (1970s), Newfoundland #1152
– (1970s), Nova Scotia #1205
– (1970s), Nova Scotia, artisans #2154

– (1970s), photographers #992
– (1970s), Prince Edward Island #1168
– (1970s), Québec #2773
– (1970s), Québec, tapestry artists #2773
– (1970s), Saskatoon (Sask) #1928
– (1970s), Toronto (Ont) #1797
– (1980), Canada #603 719
– (1980), Inuit #1294
– (1980), Inuit, weavers, Pangnirtung (NWT)
  #4308
– Aarons, Anita #2696
– Adelaide, Mary Ann #1210
– Akulukjuk, Malaya #4298
– Allain, Marie-Hélène #4508
– Allen, Gladys W. #2445
– Allen, Marguerite Buller #916
– Alloucherie, Jocelyne #4514
– Alpert, Laura #1867
– Anderson, Carol #2706
– Anderson, Tobey C. #700
– Andrews, Sybil #4529
– April, Raymonde #1059 1063 1556
– Arbour, Madeleine #4535 4536
– Arbuckle, Frances-Anne Johnston #4538
  5970 5972
– Ariss, Margot Phillips #473 4546
– Arkell, Robin #941
– Armington, Caroline Helena #4548 4549
  4550
– Arthur, Sandy #2067
– Ashevak, Kenojuak #4260 4460 4559 4563
  4564
– Askren, Pat #674 1972
– Astman, Barbara Anne #614 700 1010 1063
  4567
– Aubin, Régine #2954
– Back, Süzel #2741
– Badani, Pat #4582
– Bain, Freda Guttman #4596
– Balint, Gerrie #2394
– Bancroft, Marian Penner #2018 2069 2071
  4599
– Barot, Cécile #2833
– Bastin, Michèle #4619
– Bates, Pat Martin #821 4626 4627
– Baxter, Ingrid #574
– Bayfield, Fanny Amelia Wright #1164
– Beauchemin, Micheline #2102 2772 4642
  4643 4644 4645 8233 9108
– Beaudin, Denise #2772
– Beaudoin-Hansen, Kéro #4648
– Beaugrand-Champagne, Claire #1513 1556
  1562
– Beauregard, Andrée #4653
– Beck, Claire #1551
– Belbin, Louise #2759
– Bénic, Lorraine #4678
– Berczy, Jean-Charlotte Allamand #4694
– Bergeron, Suzanne #426 4706 4707
– Berman, Michaele #4710
– Bernatchez-Rousseau, Michèle #2769
– Bessonett, Cecilia Augusta #1118
– Betteridge, Lois Etherington #4718
– Beveridge, Eleanor #1199
– Birdsall, Pam #2395
– Blackstock, Hattie #4738
– Blanck, Nora #663 2065 2081
– Bobak, Molly Lamb #1123 1182 1910 4755
  4759 4761 4762 4763 4764 4765 4766 4767
– Bolduc, Blanche #4772
– Bond, Eleanor #1908
– Bouchard, Edith #1428 1429
– Bouchard, Marie-Cécile #1428 1429
– Bouchard, Mary Simone #1428 1429

– Bourbeau, Géraldine #4877 4878
– Bourdeau, Micheline #4879
– Boyce, Eleanor #4890
– Brandl, Eva #1512 1529
– Brassard, Thérèse Tanguay #2102 4905
– Briansky, Rita #817
– Britton, Susan #631 650 687 1832
– Brown, Alisen #1023
– Brown, Annora #1944 4933 4934
– Bruneau, Kittie #1647 4943 4944
– Buell, Katrina S.D. #309
– Bujold, Françoise #4955
– Burden, Eve #4957
– Bureau, Monique #2174
– Burgess, Catherine #717
– Burke, Rebecca #717
– Burnett, Moyra Theresa #2452
– Butler, Sheila #4984
– Cain, Maryanne #4987
– Caiserman-Roth, Ghitta #1660 4989 4990
– Caldwell, Atha Haydock #4991
– Caldwell, Dorothy #700
– Camillis, Laurie de #2072 2075
– Carlyle, Florence #186 207 4999 5000
– Carr, Emily #18 92 140 294 309 350 352 404
  461 1840 1978 1982 1986 1995 2011 2016
  3308 3827 5006 5007 5008 5009 5010 5011
  5012 5013 5014 5015 5016 5017 5018 5019
  5020 5021 5022 5023 5024 5025 5026 5027
  5028 5029 5030 5031 5033 5034 5035 5036
  5037 5038 5039 5040 5041 5042 5043 5044
  5045 5046 5861
– Carrier, Louise #5049
– Carroll, Jane #1211
– Celestino, Mary #5063
– Chamard, Emélie #2194 2209 5069
– Chaplin, Millicent Mary #1219
– Chapman, Evadna #5087
– Chapnick, Karen #663 2081
– Charbonneau, Monique #5089 5090
– Chaudron, Louise #5098
– Chitty, Elizabeth #655 687
– Claire, Lorna #6978
– Clark, Paraskeva #5110 5111 5112
– Clarke, Ann #565 698 722 1867 5114
– Clayton, Edith #2935
– Climo, Lindee #5120 5121
– Cohen, Lynne #1018 1037 1046 1053 1060
  1067
– Cohen, Sorel #673 5130
– Condé, Carole #602 1063
– Condon, Wanda #669 698 5166
– Cook, Mrs. Nelson #5170
– Coombs, Edith Grace #5172
– Cooper, Heather #897 904 905 941 5174
  5175
– Copithorne, Judith #5176
– Corne, Sharon #1877
– Corriveau, Jeanne d'Arc #2102 2769 5177
– Corsault, Share #2071 2084
– Coshof, Karen #995 1023
– Cossette, Marie Andrée #1556
– Cournoyer, Georget #5192
– Cournoyer, Michèle #5193
– Covit, Linda #1557
– Cowley, Reta Madeline #1920 5201
– Craig, Kate #687 1157 2070
– Crawford, Julia Tilley #1173
– Crête, Alphida #1562
– Crist, Lela Gurnee #5209
– Crone-Findlay, Noreen #5211
– Currelly, Judith #5234
– Cutting, Lorna #1933
– Danis, Monique Laguerre #1547

– Daoust, Sylvia Marie Emilienne #739 1380 5254 5255 5256 5257 5856
– Davies, Barbara #993
– Davis, Olea Marion Montgomery #1849
– Davison, Betty #674
– Day, Mabel Killam #350 5273
– De Pédery-Hunt, Dora #772 778 5275
– Deichmann, Erica #1170 2144 2376 2377 2380
– Denéchaud, Simone #350 1380
– Dennis, Eva A. #1881 1927
– Denny, Marion #2706
– DesClayes, Berthe #133
– DesClayes, Gertrude #133
– Desrochers-Drolet, Françoise #2378 5289
– Desrosiers, Madeleine #1380
– Devlin, Joyce #624
– Devor, Holly #2018
– Dickey, Estelle #2018
– Dickson, Jennifer #5291
– Dignam, Mary Ella #2333 2958 3208
– Dillon, Gera #1023 1032
– Dionne, Rose #1380
– Donaldson, Margery Rogers #5296
– Donoghue, Lynn #665
– Doray, Audrey Capel #5300 5301
– Dorsey, Fran #5302
– Doucet, Louise #5303
– Doull, Mary Allison #1164
– Dragu, Margaret #687
– Drouin, Michèle #5308
– Drum, Sydney Maria #698
– Duck, Adele #717
– Dukes, Caroline #1867
– Dumouchel, Suzanne #5335
– Duncan, Helen #2102
– Duplessis, Jacqueline #5339
– Dupont, Chantal #5341
– Dupuis, Luce #1632
– Dupuis-Maillet, Corinne #5342
– Duquet, Suzanne #2995 5344
– Egan, Alice Mary #2333
– Enns, Maureen #1956 5372
– Essex, Margaret Mary #916
– Eyetoaq, Ada #5387
– Falk, Gathie #579 591 622 658 781 2039 2060 2065 2081 2382 5408 5409 5410
– Farnsworth, Miss #977
– Fat, Dulcie Foo #1867 5412
– Fauteux-Massé, Henriette #5414
– Ferguson, Mary #991
– Ferron, Marcelle #426 817 1420 1434 5421 5422 5423 5424 5425 5426
– Ferron, Monique Bourbonnais #2395
– Fichaud, Gwen Johnston #1167 5427 5428
– Filer, Mary Harris #2440
– Fleisher, Pat #5454
– Forrest, Nita Osborne #2043
– Foster, Janet Green #991 1009
– Frame, Statira Elizabeth #2011 2016
– Franks, Rhonda #4159
– Fraser, Carol Lucille Hoorn #1123
– Fraser, Judith Margaret Williams #2042
– Fredericks, Beany #5513
– Freiman, Lillian #336 5517 5518
– Frenkel, Vera #713 4618 5519 5522 5524
– Frick, Joan #5527
– Furse, Barbara #1177
– Fyshe, Avis Selina #849
– Gadbois, Louise Landry #1433
– Gaettens, Marianne #993
– Gagné, Andrée #1023
– Gagné-Dufresne, Hélène #2995
– Gagnon, Pnina #5550
– Gagnon-Fortier, C. #5552

– Gambioli, Joan #775
– Gamble, Millie #5554
– Gauthier-Charlebois, Alyne #1380
– Gauthier-Mitchell, Louisette #1511 5574
– Généreux, Marie Arline #1380
– Gérin-Tétreault, Denyse #1282 1536
– Gervais, Lise #5586 5587
– Gibson, Carol #1018
– Gibson, Susan #1221
– Giguère, Denise #5598
– Gilbert, Ina Elaine #5600
– Gillett, Violet Amy #1173 5605
– Gilson, Jacqueline Marie-Charlotte #5606
– Gingras, Micheline #5607
– Godin, Raymonde #426 5622 5623
– Goodwin, Betty Roodish #658 714 1504 1558 5627 5628 5629 5630 5631
– Gordon, Hortense #1850
– Gordon, Lee #993
– Gordon, Mary #2695
– Goss, Sandra #2706
– Gougeon, Diane #685 1631
– Gow, Isobel Dowler #1512 1529
– Graham, Kay M. #565 722 1803 1807 5643
– Granirer, Pnina #2059 5644
– Graser, Toby #5646
– Grauer, Sherry #579 591 2053 2060 5647
– Grauerholz, Angela #1067
– Greenstone, Marion #5652
– Gregor, Helen Frances #2771 2776 5656
– Gregory, Joan Steeves #5657
– Gregson, Sally #2072 2075 5658
– Gricc, Emily #5659
– Guité, Suzanne #1400 5666 5667 5668 5669
– Guité, Thérèse #2741
– Gunterman, Mattie #2012 2018 5670 5671 5672
– Gustafson, Anna #2067 2459
– Gutsche, Clara #1053 1556 5673
– Haeseker, Sandy #674 698 1867 5675
– Hagarty, Clara Sophia #1703
– Hale, Catherine #5682
– Hall, Joice #717 1867
– Hamilton, Mary Riter #1887 1978 5693 5694 5695
– Hammond, Charlotte Wilson #1169 5697
– Harburn, Flora #2695
– Harbuz, Ann Alexandra #1881 1927
– Hardman, Trish #2044
– Harris, Bess Larkin Housser #301
– Harris, Pamela #996
– Hayman, Sasha #5756
– Hazelgrove, Nancy Ann #1835
– Head, Lady Anna Maria Yorke #5760
– Heaviside, Lady Mary Love #258 259 1175
– Helfand, Fern #1010
– Heller, Clair #5775
– Hendershot, Janet #675 698 717
– Henrickson, Martha Charlotte #5781
– Herman, Lorraine #2395
– Heward, Efa Prudence #5794 5795 5796
– Hicklin, Barbara Jane #5798
– Hoey, Elizabeth Wilkes #5816 6354
– Holbrook, Elizabeth M. Bradford #772
– Holloway, Elsie #5820
– Holt, Elizabeth Russell #1173
– Hooker, Marion Hope Nelson #1896
– Hooper, Kathy #1177 1182
– Hopkins, Elisabeth Margaret #1883 5830 5831 5832
– Hopkins, Frances Ann Beechy #175 5830 5833 5834 5835
– Housser, Muriel Yvonne McKague #309 5845

– Howard, Barbara #666
– Hower, Else #9278
– Hudon-Beaulac, Simone Marie Yvette #806 857 1380 5856
– Hudson, Susan Mary #1660
– Hughes, Lynn #2065 5862
– Hummer Sisters #655
– Huntress, Judith Allsopp #717 1867
– Hurlbut, Spring #723
– Hutchinson, Mrs. Richard Ernest #1118
– Innes, Alice A. #5900
– Ireland, Denise #700
– Irving, Daphne #1167
– Ishulutaq, Elisapee #4260
– Itter, Carole #2053
– Jackson, Naomi #5929
– Jackson, Sarah Jeanette #5930 5931 5932
– Jacques, Sylvie #2954
– James, Ann #2383
– Jameson, Anna Brownell #5933 5934
– Janitch, Mary #1811 5935
– Jarvis, Joan #2394
– Jaworska, Tamara Hans #2771 5949
– Jeffery, Alicia Anne #1219
– Jensen, Vicki #998
– Johnson, Esther #2445
– Johnson, Joanne Jackson #1033
– Johnson, Nancy #710
– Jones, Jacobine #739 772 5976 5977
– Judah, Doris Minette #5980
– Kahane, Anne #744 5995 5996 5997 5998 5999 8233
– Kamins, Jeannie #2775
– Kantaroff, Maryon #144 6019
– Karkutt, Edith #987
– Kemble, Julie #2076
– Kennedy, Sybil #739 6046
– Kerr, Estelle Muriel #206 207 916
– Kilbourn, Rosemary Elizabeth #817
– Kinton, Ada Florence #6053
– Kipling, Ann #698 6055 6056
– Knottenbelt, Marianna #1018
– Knowles, Dorothy #1867 1880 1885 1916 1920 1926 6066 6067
– Knowles, Elizabeth Annie McGillivray #207 6068 6069
– Kreyes, Marielouise #6082
– Lacroix, Henriette #1551
– Lagacé, Paule #1538
– Lake, Suzy #600 668 675 717 1057 1059 1512 6137 6138 6139 6140
– Laliberté, Madeleine #6153
– Lambert, Lucie #6157
– Lambert-Kelly, Beverley #525
– Lamoureux, Gisèle #991
– Langford, Adelaide #9546
– Lapointe, Esther #6168
– Laporte, Lucie #1663 6171
– Larivée, Francine #1634
– Larson, Doris Wall #1214
– Latchford, Joan #993
– Le Ber, Jeanne #2095 2778
– Lee, Ann #1167
– Léger, Jeanne #4508
– Legros, Enid Sharon #6223
– Leighton, Barbara #3017
– Lemieux, Lisette #6241
– Lemieux, Lyse #2067
– Lemieux, Marguerite #1380 1382
– LeMoyne, Suzanne Rivard #3276
– Lenhardt, Molly #1881
– Lennie, Beatrice #6244
– Leroux-Guillaume, Janine #6247
– Letendre, Rita #1408 1418 1542 1543 6250

6251 6252
– Lévesque, Paule #909
– Levine, Marilyn Ann #781 1925 2383 6274
– Lewis, Maude #6277
– Lindgren, Charlotte #1126 2771 6282 6283
– Lingwood, Daphne #2936
– Lodge, Judy #2053 6321
– Long, Marion #432 6354
– Lorenzetto, Adeline #3941
– Loring, Frances Norma #739 754 758
– Lortie, Jocelyne #6325
– Luke, Alexandra #324 402 1850 3169 6376
– Lum, Kay #1023
– Lutkenhaus, Almuth #6336
– Lyall, Laura Adeline Muntz #207 6337 6338
– Mackenzie, Cynthia #6390
– MacLennan, Toby Chapman #658 2050 6395
– MacLeod, Pegi Nicol #336 392 6396 6397 6398
– MacPherson, Diane #2452
– MacTavish, Catharine #2081
– Maday, Helene Julia #772
– Magor, Liz #622 2060 2065 2066 6402 6403 6404 6405 6406 6407 6408
– Mahon, Lilette #5014
– Major, Laure #1418
– Malach, Lorraine #1867
– Maltais, Marcelle #1418 1434 6410 6411 6412
– Maltwood, Katharine Emma #3242 6413
– Manarey, Thelma Alberta #1974
– Marie de l'Incarnation, mère #2788 2791
– Marie Le Maire des Anges, mère #1328
– Marino, Carol #1070
– Markgraf, Waltraud Erna Else #6416
– Marsh, Winifred Florence Petchy #4265
– Marshall, Pat #6422
– Marshall (Mars), Tanya #6421
– Marshalore #655
– Marshall, Roz #2081
– Martin, Emma May #6424 6425
– Martin, Jane #674 700
– Matsubara, Naoko #6449 6450
– May, Henrietta Mabel #283
– Mayhew, Elza Edith #2043 6455
– Maynard, Hannah Hatherly #2018 2027 2033 6456 6457 6458
– McCall, Helen #2018 6460
– McCarthy, Doris Jean #6461
– McDermott, Michaelin #1904
– McEachern, Susan #1067
– McGrath, Judy #6474
– McKinley, Ruth Gowdy #2395
– McLaren, Agnes Maud #916
– McLaughlin, Agnes #6500
– McLaughlin, Isabel #309
– McNicoll, Helen Galloway #6507
– Meares, Ina #6509
– Meigs, Mary #6510
– Mercer, June #2695
– Mercier, Monique #6512
– Michener, Sally #2065 6527 6528
– Mihalcheon, Jean Lapointe #2392 6529
– Mikkanen, Raili Marjatta #6531
– Miller, Maria Frances Ann Morris #241 242 1118 1219 6541 6542
– Miller, Martha #2069
– Milne, Eleanor #755 6568 6569
– Miron, Claire #6571
– Mitchell, Janet #1974 6574
– Mollise, Mâli Christianne Paul #6635
– Mondou, Pierrette #1282 6595

– Moodie, Geraldine #6602
– Moppett, Carroll #788 2066
– Morash, Barbara #6606
– Morier, Pauline #6608
– Mortimer, Ann #2395
– Mounsey, Yseult #991
– Mowat, Grace Helen #2144
– Mulcaster, Wynona Croft #1883 1926 6660 7123
– Munn, Kathleen Jean #309
– Neel, Ellen #4121
– Newton, Lilias Torrance #6692 6693
– Nicoll, Marion F.S. Mackay #1974 6376 6701 6702 6703
– Nolin, Alice #1380
– Nori, Angela #991
– Nutt, Elizabeth Styring #1192 1194 2993 6730
– Oberheide, Heidi #1148 1159
– Odjig, Daphne #1866 4128 4131 4136 4141 4154 4155 4173 6731
– Ohe, Dorothy Katie von der #1867
– Oliver, Bobbie #675 698
– Ondaatje, Kim #2796 2798 6733
– Oonark, Jessie #4220 4260 4304 4460 6743 6744
– Owidzka, Jolanta #9108
– Page, Patricia Kathleen #649 6751
– Palchinski, Sylvia Scott #6753
– Panneton, Louise #2772 6758
– Parent-Benoît, Mimi #426
– Parizad #1023
– Parsons, Alison #6771
– Pasquin, Suzanne #1418
– Passillé-Sylvestre, Micheline de #2216
– Patterson, Nancy-Lou #6783
– Pavelic, Myfanwy Spencer #6785
– Paxton, Maureen #6786
– Payton, Evlyn B. #6787
– Pearson, Carol #5020
– Pednaud, Victoire #2184
– Pemberton, Sophia Theresa #6827 6828 6829
– Peters, Mary #3941
– Peterson, Margaret #6839
– Petite, Marion #651
– Petry, Nancy Wargin #1529
– Pflug, Christiane Sybille #110 6848 6849 6850 6851
– Phipps, Lynn #998
– Piché-Whissell, Aline #6865
– Pitseolak, Mary #4260
– Podbielski, Marie #941
– Poisson, Renée #6898
– Pratt, Mary Frances #579 591 675 698 6914 6917 6918 6919
– Qinnuayuak, Lucy #4260 4460
– Radecki, Brigitte #1639
– Raginsky, Nina #1002 1037 1046 1060
– Rakine, Marthe #6955 6956
– Rankin, Joan Melvin #6958
– Ravenhill, Alice #4114
– Redgrave, Felicity #1169 6967
– Reeves, Gladys #4935
– Reid, Leslie Mary Margaret #579 591 637 675 6980 6981
– Reid, Mary Hiester #207 6979 6982
– Reusch, Astri #2455
– Reusch, Kina #789
– Reynolds, Catherine #6992 6993
– Rhéaume, Jeanne Leblanc #6994
– Richard, Hélène Roy #1536 1538
– Richards, Cecil Clarence #666
– Ristvedt-Handerek, Milly #565 7034 7035

– Robert, Louise #695 698 717 1565 7038 7039
– Roberts, Olive #8113
– Robertson, Sarah Margaret Armour #301 7054
– Rochette, Sylvie #1626
– Rockburne, Dorothea #7059 7060
– Rockett, Beverly #993
– Rolland, Dominique #1634
– Rosenfield, Ethel #7078
– Ross, Rosie #4121
– Roth, Evelyn #675 698 2775
– Rothschild, Hanni #7080
– Rousseau-Vermette, Mariette #2771 2772 2776 7085
– Rowley, Frances Elswood Richards #238
– Rozynska, Wanda #2232
– Rumball, Alma #7108
– Sadowska, Krystyna #2380 7113 7115
– Sargent, Susan #1933
– Satorelli, Jane #7127
– Satterly, Molly #2102
– Sauer, June #993
– Sauvé, Paulette-Marie #2772
– Savage, Anne Douglas #18 1278 1279 7131 7132
– Schelle, Susan #7160
– Schmid-Esler, Annemarie #675 698 795 2395 7162
– Schmidt, Marianna #821
– Schreiber, Charlotte Mount Brook Morrell #7164
– Scott, Marian Mildred Dale #7165 7166
– Scott, Susan #676
– Seath, Ethel #324
– Senécal, Irène #1380 3010
– Shadbolt, Doris #2695
– Shehu, Dita #7194
– Shepherd, Helen Parsons #2988
– Shore, Henrietta Mary #7200
– Shum, Hilda #2084
– Shuttleworth, Claire #7202
– Sicotte, Rolande #1380
– Siegel, Lois #1000
– Simard-Laflamme, Carole #2772 7209
– Simcoe, Elizabeth Posthuma Gwillim #7210 7211 7212
– Simon, Ellen Rosalie #7589
– Simonin, Francine #7213
– Singer, Judy #711 717 722
– Singleton, Becky #723
– Sisler, Rebecca Jean #666
– Smalley, Katherine #1023
– Smith, Ann #7220
– Smith, Edith Agnes #1192
– Smith, Jori #7233
– Smith, Madge #7235
– Smith, Muriel #2936
– Speirs, Doris Huestis Mills #6371
– Spencer, Deirdre #2706
– Spencer, Mary #2018
– Staniszkis, Joanna Kataszyna #2776
– Steele, Lisa #605 630 631 705 7277
– Steinhouse, Tobie Thelma #7278
– Steltzer, Ulli #2018
– Stevens, Dorothy #799 800 916
– Stevenson, Sylvie #2084
– Stewart, Betty #873
– Stolfa, Lydia #2102
– Stone, Sylvia #460
– Sturdy, Martha #2706
– Sullivan, Françoise #1396 1449 1529 7282 7283
– Surcouf, Lorraine Joy #7284

- Sutton, Carol #620 711 722 7292
- Suzuki, Aiko #2771
- Svarre, Grace #7303
- Svatina, Maria #2772
- Swibold, Susanne #7304
- Szaszkiewicz, Cécile #7307
- Taçon, Edna Jeanette #7310
- Tait, Sylvia #7315
- Takashima, Shizueye Violet #7316
- Tanobe, Miyuki #7322 7323 7324 7325
- Tardif-Hébert, Jeannine #1538
- Tesiorowski, Carol #1032
- Themarat, Jeanne Aline #1881
- Therrien, Denise #676
- Thorkelsson, Ione #2440
- Thornton, Mildred Valley Stinson #7375
- Thresher, Eliza W. Morrison #1164
- Tounissoux, Françoise #1544
- Tremblay, Esther #1551
- Tremblay, Michèle #2216
- Tremblay, Suzanne #1549
- Tremblay-Gagnon, Yvonne #1546
- Trottier-Dufour, Gisèle #1538
- Trowsse, Pegi #991
- Tully, Sydney Strickland #7438
- Tuu'luq, Marion #4255 4268 7441 7442
- Uhthoff, Ina D.D. #7443
- Urban, Colette #1227
- Uritani, Giselle #2452
- Vachon, Ginette #1032
- Vale, Florence Gertrude #5499 7413
- Van Ginhoven, Anke #1282
- Van Slyck, Wyn #2902
- Vardeman, Lynn #2067
- Vittecoq, Arlette #1534
- Vivenza, Francesca #7495
- Wadsworth, Lizzy #7496
- Wainio, Carol #1227
- Wainwright, Ruth #7497
- Wald, Susana #7633
- Wales, Shirley #817 818 821 1641
- Walker, Joy #675 698
- Walker, Victoria #676
- Wallis, Adah #7512
- Wallis, Katherine Elizabeth #7511 7512
- Waring, Stephanie E. #7516
- Warkov, Esther #1867 7517 7518 7519 7520
- Warren, Emily Mary Bibbens #7523 7524
- Warren, Mary Schaffer #7525 7526 7527
- Watson, Susan #2771
- Weber, Anna #7539
- Wertheimer, Esther #7542
- Westerlund, Mia #675 788 797 1809 7543 7544 7545
- Whiten, Colette #579 591 658 675 779 788 796 1809 7556 7559 7560 7561
- Whitlock, An #579 591 622 658 788 7564
- Whittome, Irene #637 710 714 779 7565 7566 7567 7568 7569 7570
- Whyte, Catharine Robb #1972 7571 7572
- Wieland, Joyce #98 143 147 460 510 556 568 626 657 675 700 940 1753 7574 7575 7576 7577 7578 7579 7580 7581 7582 7583
- Wiitasalo, Shirley #579 591 1832 7584
- Wilby, Roslynn #2153
- Wilby, Susan #2153
- Will, Mary Shannon #795 7586
- Williams, Judy #7588
- Williams, Yvonne #2445 2446 2448 2455 7589
- Williamson, Betty #987
- Willmott, Elizabeth #777
- Willoughby, Linda #2775
- Winsor, Jackie #7597 7598

- Wood, Elizabeth Wyn #368 739 5677 5678 7613
- Wood, Faith #581
- Woolnough, Hilda Mary #7616
- Wright, Edith P. Stevenson #7279
- Wrinch, Mary Evelyn #207 1710 6979 7617 7618
- Wyle, Florence #729 739 754 758
- Young, Helen Granger #7627
- Young, Hester #2723
- Young, Rosanna #2723
- Zack, Badanna Bernice #657
- Zellinger, Jean #7634
women in art
- Bleyenberg, Harry #4742
- Brymner, William #4954
- Canadian art #53 121
- Gunterman, Mattie #5670
- Heward, Efa Prudence #5796
- Karsh, Yousuf #6024
- Lindner, Ernest #6285 6287
- Northwest Coast Indians #3348 3377
- Prince, Richard #6939
- Reeves, John #6972
- Town, Harold Barling #7414
Wong, Paul, Can artist, 1954- #992
- exhibitions, group
  - (1979) #2069
- in ten sity, performance, Vancouver Art Gallery (Vancouver, BC) #7607
wood
- Alberta architecture #8136
  - late 19th -early 20th cs. #8120
- architectural decoration
  - (1930s) #8225
  - Montréal (Qué), 19th c. #8612
  - Ontario, 19th c. #8002 8005
- British Columbia architecture #8148 8153
- British Columbia churches and cemetery art (1880-1910) #8914
- Canadian and American architecture, 17th-18th cs. #7717
- Canadian architecture #7695
  - (1910s) #8494
  - (1950s) #7680
- Canadian decorative arts (1970s) #2596
- Canadian domestic architecture #7722
- Canadian roofs, 17th-19th cs. #7703
- framing
  - comparison of two houses (1650 and 1836) #8658
  - plankwall #7712
- Hudson's Bay buildings, 19th c. #8100
- Manitoba architecture #8102
- Ontario architecture
  - 19th c. #7745
  - (1831-1861) #8009
- Ontario cedar log cabins, early 19th c. #7990
- Ontario domestic architecture
  - 19th c. #8677
  - (1920s) #8646
- Ontario log buildings, French-Canadian settlers, 19th c. #7685
- Québec architecture, 17th-19th cs. #7859
- Québec domestic architecture, 17th-18th cs. #8621
- Saskatchewan pioneer houses, late 19th-early 20th cs. #8696
- Ukrainian architecture #8090
- Vancouver (BC) architecture #8159
- wood-processing industry
  - Canada and USA (1607-1623) #7718
  - documents, 18th-19th cs. #7720

Wood, Alan, Can artist, 1935- #2053 7609 7610
- exhibitions
  - (1977) #7608
- natural constructions (1970s) #2065
- Ranch, Emily Carr College of Art (Vancouver, BC) #7611
- use of space and scale #2062
Wood, Brian, Can photographer, 1948-
- exhibitions
  - (1979) #7612
Wood, Elizabeth Wyn, Can sculptor, 1903-1966 #739 5677 7613
- as wife of Emanuel Hahn #5678
- on nationalism and art #368
Wood, Enoch, Brit ceramicist, 1759-1840
- Staffordshire ware, views of Canada #2288
Wood, Faith, Can artist, 1917-
- portraits #581
Wood, John W., Can architect, b. 1885
- Montréal (Qué), Queen Elizabeth Hotel #9286
Wood, Marshall, Brit sculptor, d. 1882
- sculpture, Ottawa (Ont) #727
Wood, William John, Can artist, 1877-1954 #309
- obituary #7614
wood engraving
- Hyde, Lawrence, on #5895
wood engraving, Canadian #925
- (1930s) #802 804
wood engraving, Japanese
- influence on Monique Charbonneau #5089
woodcarving, American
- folk sculpture #756
woodcarving, Canadian #2089 2107
- (1890s), and architecture #726
- (1960s) #744
- (1970s) #2596
- Association des artisans Saint-Jean-Port-Joli (Saint-Jean-Port-Joli, Qué) #1608
- Baillairgé, François and Thomas, Church of Saint-Joachim de Montmorency (Québec, Qué) #8880
- Baillairgé, Thomas #8326
- Beaumont (Qué), Church of Saint-Etienne #8809
- Bellechasse County (Qué), Church of Saint-Charles-Borromée #8803
- Bourgault family #4884 4886
- Charlesbourg (Qué), churches #8851
- crucifixes, Québec #1585
- figureheads of ships
  - Nova Scotia, 19th c. #1200
- folk sculpture #756 966
- Hamilton (Ont), Church of Saint John the Evangelist #730
- île d'Orléans (Qué) #1238
  - Church of Saint-François-de-Sales #8796
  - Church of Saint-Jean #8801
  - Church of Saint-Pierre #8802
  - Church of Sainte-Famille #1612 8795
- influence on Canadian art, 20th c. #2093
- Joliette (Qué), churches #8876
- Lachenaie (Qué), Church of Saint-Charles #8808
- Laterrière (Qué), Church of Notre-Dame #7882
- Loretteville (Qué), Church of Notre-Dame-de-la-Jeune-Lorette #8804
- Lotbinière (Qué), churches #8835
- Montréal (Qué), Chapel of Notre-Dame-de-Lourdes #8836

– New Brunswick
  – (pre-1900) #2491
  – Graham family #1187
– Newfoundland #1155
– Nova Scotia, Atlantic Woodcarvers' Guild #1194
– Oka (Qué)
  – Calvary at Oka #1355 1356
  – church #8818
– Ottawa (Ont)
  – National Museum of Man. Canadian Centre for Folk Culture Studies #963
  – Parliament Buildings #8928
– Price, Ralph and Patricia, collection #971
– Québec #19 761 1233 1235 1327 1573 1576 1577 1614 2169 2171 2183
  – 17th-18th cs. #2181 2187
  – 17th-19th cs. #1575 1581 1583 1588 1593
  – 18th-19th cs. #1338 6947 8799
  – 18th-20th cs. #1616
  – 18th c. #234 235 249 250 269 270
  – 18th c.-1820s #1300
  – 20th c. #2179 2198
  – (1640-1840) #1329
  – (1650-1925) #1592
  – (1780-1850) #1232 1574
  – animal subjects (1940s) #1579
  – apprentices (1660-1815) #2231
  – Baillairgé, François #4589
  – figureheads of ships, 18th-19th cs. #1604
  – folk sculpture, Nettie Sharpe collection #1607
  – Levasseur family #6254
  – Soucy family #7267
  – tabernacles #1613
  – Washington (DC), Smithsonian Institution #2111
– Québec (Qué), Ursuline Convent #8810
  – Chapel #8852
– Saint-Jean-Port-Joli (Qué) #1597 2194 2209 4883
  – Church of Saint-Jean-Baptiste #8812
– Saint John (NB), stone church #8778
– Sault-au-Récollet (Qué), Church of the Visitation #8797
– Varennes (Qué), churches #8813
woodcarving, French
– influence on Québec woodcarving, 17th-19th cs. #1583
Woodchuck Press (Toronto, Ont)
– and Thoreau MacDonald #6384
Woodcock, Percy Franklin, Can artist, 1855-1936 #178
– *Abandoned Nest* #172
woodcuts
– Duguay, Rodolphe #5314 5315 5316
– Munakata, Shiko, and Naoko Matsubara #6449
– Phillips, Walter Joseph, on #6853 6855
Woodlands Indians
– art #3172 3359 3434 3633 3639
  – 20th c. #4143 4150
  – (1970s-1980s) #4139
  – (1980) #4159
– basketry #3562 3625
– beadwork #3635
– birchbark #3527
– containers #3638 3744
– culture #3631
– moccasins #3554
– painting, 20th c. #4144
– pottery #3545 3640
– prehistoric artifacts #3491
– quillwork #3443

– shellwork #3505
– Thunderbird #3410
– wampum #3603
Woodley, Charles D., Can photographer, ca. 1911-
– portfolio of photographs #1032
Woodman & Carey, Can architectural firm
– Winnipeg (Man), City Hall, competition #8979
Woodrow, Paul, Can artist, 1941-
– and W.O.R.K.S. #1955
– *Bureau of Imaginary Exchange* #714
Woodruff, John, Can photographer, 1859-1917
– exhibitions, group
  – (1970) #1675
Woods, Chris, Can sculptor, 1949- #7615
Woodside, Henry Joseph, Can photographer, 1858-1929
– military photographs, Yukon and South Africa #1107
Woodstock (NB), Carleton County Vocational School
– exhibitions
  – *Colville, Pratt, Forrestall* (1974) #1129
  – *The Beaverbrook Art Gallery Presents Nine New Brunswick Artists/La Galerie d'art Beaverbrook présente neuf artistes du Nouveau-Brunswick* (1973) #1182
Woodstock (Ont), Oxford County Art Association
– exhibitions
  – *Centennial Exhibition of Quebec and Ontario Contemporary Painters, 1967* (1967) #484
Woodstock (Ont), Woodstock Public Library and Art Gallery
– exhibitions
  – *Alan C. Collier Retrospective* (1971) #5131
  – *Ed Bartram: 10 Years* (1980) #4618
  – *Imprint '76* (1976) #833
  – *William Blair Bruce* (1976) #4942
Woodville, Richard Caton, Brit artist in Canada, 1856-1927
– views, western Canada #931
woodwork, Algonquian #3605
– containers #3507
woodwork, Canadian
– 18th-19th cs. #2112 2594
– 20th c. #2121 2142
– (1940s) #2601
– (1960s) #2106
– (1964-1967) #2108 2109
– (1980) #2257
– decoys #2595
– guide for collectors #2104 2125 2131
– Mennonite, Waterloo County (Ont) #2264
– New Brunswick #2150
– Ontario, 18th-19th cs. #2588
– Ottawa (Ont), National Museum of Man. Canadian Centre for Folk Culture Studies #963
– Picard, Edmond #6863
– Québec #2223 2226 2237
  – 17th-18th cs. #2530 2531
  – 20th c. #2198
  – apprentices (1660-1815) #2231
– treenware #2252 2470 2590 2591
woodwork, Huron #3519
woodwork, Iroquois #3519 3605
woodwork, Micmac #3569 3643
woodwork, Ojibwa #3557
woodwork, Penobscot #3537
wool

– Canada, 17th-19th cs. #2096 2120
– dyes
  – Nova Scotia #2749
  – Ontario, 19th c. #2742
– Québec, 18th c. #2200
Woolford, John Elliott, Brit army officer, artist, architect in Canada, 1778-1866 #258 259 279
Woolnough, Hilda Mary, Can artist, 1934- #7616
Woolsey, John William, Can businessman, 1767-1852
– family portrait, William von Moll Berczy #4700
Woolwich (England), Royal Military Academy
– and George Heriot #5789
– and Thomas Davies #5272
Worcester (Mass), Clark University. Goddard Library
– architecture, John M. Johansen #9046
words in art
– *see also* concrete poetry
– Ariss, Margot Phillips #4546
– Curnoe, Greg #5226
– Fischl, Eric #662
workers' housing, Canadian
– post-World War I #8495
workers in art
– devotional images #1662
– Featherston, Bill #5418
– Gaudard, Pierre #990
– Labor Arts Guild #1985
– Magor, Liz, nonexistent occupations #6402
– Rand, Paul #6957
– unemployment subjects, Atlantic provinces (1970s) #1133 1135
World Crafts Council
– (1979), recommendations to #2136 2137
World War I (1914-1918)
– and A.Y. Jackson #1077 5913 5919
– and André Charles Biéler #4725
– and David Brown Milne #6551 6557 6566
– and Florence Carlyle #5000
– and Frederick Horsman Varley #1077 7466 7467 7468
– and H.W. Cooper #5173
– and Homer Ransford Watson #210
– and Inglis Sheldon-Williams #7196
– and Jack Turner #7439
– and James Wilson Morrice #6626
– and Mary Riter Hamilton #5695
– and Maurice Galbraith Cullen #5215 5217 5220 5222
– and Robert Wakeham Pilot #6869
– and Royal Canadian Academy of Arts #208
– and Tom Thomson #7356
– and Walter Seymour Allward #4518 4519
– and William Brymner #4953
– and Wyndham Lewis #6279
– art #1071
– aviation paintings #1104 1105
– Canadian art #1075 1111 1112 1667
– Canadian posters #910 911
– Canadian war memorial buildings, recommendations #1079
– Canadian War Memorials #284 1073 1074 1076 1078 1080 1081 1082 1084 1085
  – Ottawa (Ont), National Gallery of Canada #1077 1101 1102 3044
– Canadian War Memorials competition #731 732
– cemeteries and war memorials, Canadian

soldiers #1108 1109
- photographic views #1072 1107 1113 1114
- workers' housing, post-World War I #8495
World War II (1939-1945)
- (1940-1941), failure to employ Canadian
  war artists #1087
- and Albert-Edouard Cloutier #1117
- and Alex Colville #5146 5151 5156
- and Bruno Joseph Bobak #4759
- and Canadian Committee #3262
- and Carl Fellman Schaefer #1090 7150
  7152 7153 7155 7156
- and Charles Fraser Comfort #1090 5158
- and Charles Goldhamer #1091 1117
- and Donald William Buchanan #3325
- and Edward John Hughes #5859 5861
- and George Adolphus Broomfield #4932
- and George Douglas Pepper #6832
- and Gershon Iskowitz #5906
- and Gordon Appelbe Smith #7229
- and Group of Seven #1768 1789
- and Jack Leonard Shadbolt #7176 7189
- and Jack Nichols #6697
- and Jan Menses #6511
- and Jean-Philippe Dallaire #5239
- and Jerrold Morris #1110 6639
- and John Saarniit #7112
- and John William Beatty #4637
- and Ken Bell #4657
- and Lawren Phillip Harris #5713
- and Leonard Brooks #4930
- and Louis Muhlstock #6658
- and Maxwell Bennett Bates #4620
- and Miller Gore Brittain #4921
- and Molly Lamb Bobak #4759 4761 4764
  4765 4766 4767
- and Nick Morant #6605
- and Oscar Cahén #4986
- and Pegi Nicol MacLeod #6396 6397
- and Ralph Malcolm Warner #1117
- and Robert Marshall Buckhan #1117
- and Robert Wakeham Pilot #6869
- and Rowley Walter Murphy #6665 6666
- and Tobie Thelma Steinhouse #7278
- and Tony Law #6174
- and Walter Ruhman #7105
- and Wilfred Roloff Beny #4687
- aviation paintings #1104 1105
- Canadian Air Force art #1093
- Canadian architecture #7666
- Canadian Army, Navy, and Air Force art
  #1097 1099
- Canadian Army art #1092 1094 1096
- Canadian art #151 370 498 1088 1098 1111
  1112 1116
  - and Surrealism #1115
  - Ottawa (Ont), Canadian War Museum
    #1103
  - Ottawa (Ont), National Gallery of
    Canada #1101 3044
- Canadian artistic identity #327
- Canadian comic strips #947
- Canadian paintings #1100
- Canadian paintings and drawings #1089
- Canadian posters #847 848 908 910 911
- Canadian sculptures #738
- Canadian silkscreen prints #805
- Canadian Society of Painters in Water
  Colour #127
- Canadian War Arts Programme #379 1086
- cemeteries and war memorials, Canadian
  soldiers #1108 1109
- naval paintings, Canadian War Museum
  (Ottawa, Ont) #1106

- needlework for Canadian soldiers #2780
- photographic views #1095 1107
- Wartime Housing Limited #8506
Worthington, Timothy (Tim), Can
  ceramicist, 1950- #2395
Wray, John, Can designer, fl. 1950s-
- Halifax (NS), Nepture Theatre #9097
wreaths, Canadian
- Ontario, 19th c. #2248
wrestling
- Cohen, Sorel, photographic series #5130
Wright, Don, Can artist, 1931- #1148
Wright, Douglas, Can artist, ca. 1918-
- illustrations #855
Wright, Edith P. Stevenson, Can artist, fl.
  1869-1950 #7279
Wright, Frank Lloyd, Amer architect,
  1867-1959
- as teacher of Francis Conroy Sullivan
  #8410
- as teacher of James William Strutt #7984
- influence on architecture, Trent University
  (Peterborough, Ont), #9474
- influence on Canadian architecture #7680
Wright, John, Can architect, 1830-1915
- Victoria (BC) #8145
Wright, Richard Thomas, Can photographer,
  fl. 1977
- portfolio of photographs #1023
Wrinch, Mary Evelyn, Can artist, 1877-1969
  #207 7617
- as wife of George Agnew Reid #6979
- exhibitions
  - (1980) #7618
- exhibitions (reviews) #1710
writers
- see authors
writing desks
- see desks
wrought iron
- see ironwork
Wu, Allan, Can photographer, ca. 1947-
- portfolio of photographs #1032
Würtele, Frederick C. (Fred), Can
  photographer, 1843-1920 #7619
Wyers, Jan G., Can artist, 1888-1973 #1852
  7620
- exhibitions, group
  - (1958) #1846
  - (1970) #1918
Wyeth, Andrew Newell, Amer artist, 1917-
- Colville, Alex, compared with #5151
- Forrestall, Tom, compared with #5466
- Prévost, Antoine, compared with #6927
Wyle, Florence, Can sculptor, 1881-1968
  #739
- and Frances Norma Loring #758
- exhibitions, group
  - (1969) #754
- Memorial Fountain to Dr. D.W. Young
  (Toronto, Ont) #729

X

Xavier, John, Can photographer, fl. 1981
- portfolio of photographs #1023
Xerox art
- see copy art

Y

Yakuglas
- see James, Charlie
Yale (BC)
- views, 19th c. #2031
Yamachiche (Qué), Church of Sainte-Anne
- architecture and art #8783
Yamazaki & Ridpath, Can architectural firm
- Beamsville (Ont), Nipponia Home for the
  Aged #8516
Yarmouth (NS), Yarmouth County Museum
- collection, ship portraits #163
Yarwood, Walter Hawley, Can sculptor,
  1917-
- interview #7621
- sculptures (1960s) #745 746
Yates, Edward Norman, Can artist, 1923-
  #1880 7622 7623
Yates, Richard, Can leatherworker, 1949-
  #2936
Yecny, Vaclav, Can furniture-maker, d. 1921
  #2587
Yellowknife Indians
- culture (1920s) #4081
Yellowstone Park (USA)
- views, late 19th c. #1839
Yeo, James, Can shipbuilder, merchant,
  farmer, 1789-1868
- residence, Green Park (Summerside
  region, PEI) #8540
Yerxa, Leo, Can artist, 1947- #4140 7624
- design, Olympic coins (1976) #778
Yip, Chuck Wing, Can artist, 1923- #7625
Ykelenstam, Henk, Can artist, fl. 1981 #7626
York & Sawyer, Can architectural firm
- Montréal (Qué), Royal Bank of Canada
  #9176
- Toronto (Ont), Canadian Bank of
  Commerce #9178
York Factory (Man)
- men's house #8482
Yosemite Valley (USA)
- views, late 19th c. #1839
Yoshi, Can photographer, fl. 1975
- portfolio of photographs #998
Youds, Robert E., Can artist, 1954-
- exhibitions, group
  - (1979) #2075
- exhibitions (reviews) #2072
Young, D.W., Can physician, 20th c.
- Memorial Fountain (Toronto, Ont) #729
Young, Helen Granger, Can ceramicist,
  1923- #7627
Young, Hester, Can weaver, fl. 1840s-1850s
  #2723
Young, Mahonri MacIntosh, Amer artist,
  1877-1957
- influence on Miller Gore Brittain #4917
Young, Robert, Can artist, 1938- #7628 7629
  7630
- exhibitions
  - (1981) #7631
Young, Ron, Can photographer, fl. 1978
- portfolio of photographs #1023
Young, Rosanna, Can weaver, fl.
  1840s-1850s #2723
Young, Thomas, Can architect, artist, ca.
  1810-1860
- as member, Toronto Society of Arts #1689
Youngblood, Gene, Amer writer, 1942-
- on the sacred in art #94

Ypres (France)
– Battle of Ypres, Walter Seymour Allward
    #4518
Yukon
– architecture #8083
– art (1970s) #2086 2088
– photographic views
    – (1880s-1890s) #1874
    – Canadian military photographers #1107
– views
    – Harrison, Ted #5749 5750 5751
    – Robb, Jim #7037
Yuristy, Russell, Can artist, 1936- #1937
– exhibitions
    – (1981) #7632
– exhibitions, group
    – (1976) #1930
– exhibitions (reviews) #2383

Z

Zach, Jan, Can sculptor, 1914-
– as teacher of Elza Mayhew #6455
Zack, Badanna Bernice, Can artist, 1943-
    #657
– on Jack Chambers #700
Zadow, J. Albert, Can furniture-maker,
    1854-1941 #2582
Zander, Dick, Can artist, 1943-
– and Intersystems #767
Zarov, Basil, Can photographer, ca. 1918-
– portfolio of photographs #987
Zazelenchuk, Stanley, Can collector, 1941-,
    and Patricia Jean, Can collector, 1943-
– collection, Inuit art #4284 4306
Zeidler, Eberhard Henrich, Can architect,
    1926-
– Mont Sainte-Marie (Qué), resort centre
    #7886
– on architecture #7746
– on McMaster University Health Sciences
    Centre (Hamilton, Ont) #9037
Zeidler Partnership, Can architectural firm
– Toronto (Ont)
    – Eaton Centre #9377 9378 9382
    – Young People's Theatre, restoration
        #7776
Zeldin, Gerald, Can artist, 1943-
– exhibitions, group
    – (1976) #1810
Zelenak, Edward (Ed), Can sculptor, 1940-
– and Walter Redinger #6968
– exhibitions, group
    – (1970) #771
    – (1971) #98
    – (1978) #786
– on art #594
Zelkine, Alexandre, Can photographer, fl.
    1971 #997
Zeller, Ludwig, Can artist, 1927-
– and Surrealism #7633
Zellinger, Jean, Can sculptor, fl. 1960- #7634
Zen Buddhism
– influence on Gaston-Pierre Petit #6843
– influence on Kazuo Hamasaki #5688
– influence on Kenneth Campbell Lochhead
    #6319
– influence on Robert Savoie #7139
Zontal, Jorge, Can artist, 1944-
– exhibitions, group
    – (1977) #5583

Zuck, Tim, Can artist, 1947- #7635
– exhibitions
    – (1980) #7636
– interview #7637
Zurich (Switzerland), André Emmerich
    Gallery
– exhibitions (reviews)
    – Bush, Jack (1974) #4967
Zurich (Switzerland), Feldstrasse Secondary
– art, Indians of North America #3455

Index des sujets traités

A

A.J. Diamond Associates
– *voir* Diamond, A.J., Associates
Aarons, Anita, conservatrice, critique d'art
et artiste can, 1912-
– bijoux #2696
– directrice, Art Gallery at Harbourfront
(Toronto, Ont) #3166
Abbott, A.C., collectionneur can, XXe s., et
Eileen, collectionneuse can, 1896-1980
– collection, art inuit #4306
Abénaquis
– vannerie #3596
– wampum #3526
Abernethy (Sask), Lanark Place
– architecture #8700
Abernethy (Sask), parc historique national
W.R. Motherwell Farmstead #8723 8724
9232
Abitibi (Qué)
– vues photographiques
– Szilasi, Gabor #7309
About Arts and Crafts/L'Art et l'artisanat,
périodique can #4269
Abram, George S., architecte can, 1923-
– Winnipeg (Man), hôtel de ville, concours
#8985 8986
Abram & Ingleson, agence can
d'architecture
– Scarborough (Ont), Stephen Leacock
Educational Complex #9476
Absil, Mickey, photographe can, ca 1950-
– catalogue de photographies #1023
abstraction géométrique
– Canada (années 1950) #832
– et Guido Molinari #6591
– Montréal (Qué), (années 1950-1960) #1437
– Québec (1955-1965) #1471
abstraction lyrique
– Colombie-Britannique (années 1950) #1990
– Montréal (Qué), (années 1950) #1426 1437
1438
– Québec #1453
Abverdjar (Foxe Basin, TNO)
– artefacts dorsétiens #4333 4358
Académie royale des arts du Canada #5 16
28 152 153 157

– (1880-1910), influence sur art canadien
#214
– (1880-1913) #3061
– (1880-1971) #2
– (1880-1979), expositions et membres #162
– (1890-1900) #190
– (1898), en comparaison avec Ontario
Society of Artists #1707
– (1914-1918), Première Guerre mondiale,
aide aux femmes des combattants #208
– (1924), British Empire Exhibition
(Wembley, Angleterre) #458 500
– (1943), critique #361
– (1980) #689
– (années 1870-1883), documents #166
– (années 1880-1890) #102 184 1706
– (années 1880-1920), et peinture de
paysages #14
– (années 1880-1930), architectes membres
de l'Académie #8298
– (années 1890) #181 188
– (années 1890-1910), et Galerie nationale du
Canada (Ottawa, Ont) #275 3041
– (années 1940), critique #366
– (années 1950), et académies artistiques
#434
– (années 1980), critique #686
– collection, Galerie nationale du Canada
(Ottawa, Ont) #3044
– et Alice A. Innes #5900
– et Charlotte Mount Brook Morrell
Schreiber #7164
– et Doris Minette Judah #5980
– et Edmond Dyonnet #5346 5348
– et Florence Carlyle #4999
– et George Harlow White #7551
– et Helen Galloway McNicoll #6507
– et Homer Ransford Watson #7533
– et James Wilson Morrice #6634
– et Laura Adeline Muntz Lyall #6339
– et Lord Lorne #280
– et Marion F.S. Mackay Nicoll #6703
– et Mary Hiester Reid #6982
– et Ontario Society of Artists #1666 1679
– et Robert Wakeham Pilot #6869
– et Société canadienne des arts graphiques
#801
– expositions
– (1884) #170

– (1939) #346
– (1966) #474
– (1980) #1906
– expositions, critiques
– (1881) #168
– (1885) #171
– (1892-1893) #179
– (1898) #186
– (1910) #195
– (1912) #202
– (1915) #210
– (1916) #283
– (1927) #296
– (1928) #303 310
– (1929) #312
– (1930) #318
– (1931) #323
– (1933) #325
– (1934) #326
– (1935) #328
– (1936) #329
– (1947) #3304
– nationalisme et peinture de paysages, fin
XIXe s. #271 272
– XIXe s.-années 1930, et académies
artistiques #343
académies artistiques
– (années 1950), et Académie royale des arts
du Canada #434
– XIXe s., et Académie royale des arts du
Canada #16 153 181
– XIXe s.-années 1930, Canada, critique #343
– XXe s., et Académie royale des arts du
Canada #326
Achard, Maurice, céramiste can, 1942-
– expositions de groupe
– (1968) #2382
Achim, André, sculpteur can, 1793-1843
#1578
Achim, Normand, photographe can, ca
1948- #1534
Achtemichuk, Robert Brian, artiste can,
1948-
– expositions de groupe
– (1977) #1901
– (1978) #669
acier
– dans architecture canadienne #7686 7695
– dans architecture manitobaine #8102

acoustique
- Montréal (Qué), Place des Arts #9092 9096
- Ottawa (Ont), Centre national des arts.
  Opéra. #9104
Acs, Joe, artiste can, 1936- #1880
Adams, Loren Dean, artiste can, 1945-
- expositions
  - (1979) #4501
Adamson, Anthony, architecte can, 1906-
- Edmonton (Alta), Canada Packers Limited
  #7973
Adamson, Gerald (Jerry), designer can,
  1937- #2487
- sièges (mobilier) #2471
Adamson Associates, agence can
  d'architecture
- Toronto (Ont), Hydro Place #9352
Adaskin, Gordon, artiste can, 1931- #4502
Adelaide, Mary Ann, artiste can, 1910-1973
- expositions, critiques #1210
Adelaide (Australie), Art Gallery of South
  Australia
- expositions
  - Contemporary Canadian Painters (1957)
    #423
Adirondacks (montagnes), (NY)
- vues
  - Browne, Joseph Archibald #4939
Adoian, Vosdanig Manoog
- voir Gorky, Arshile (Vosdanig Manoog
  Adoian)
aéroports canadiens
- (années 1950) #9513 9514 9515
- (années 1960) #9517
- Mirabel (Qué), Aéroport international de
  Montréal #9518
- Toronto (Ont), Aéroport international de
  Toronto #9516
affaires
- et art
  - Levine, Les #6262
  - Lorcini, Gino #6323
affiches . Canada #908 910 911
- (années 1940) #353 374 851
- (années 1960) #868
- Fiorucci, Vittorio #5442 5443
- Groupe des Sept #1774
- Jeux olympiques, 1976 (Montréal, Qué)
  #900
- Kingston (Ont) #1680
- Montréal (Qué), (années 1970) #880
- Ontario et Québec (1960-1975) #903
- Première Guerre mondiale #916
- provinces de l'Ouest (1964-1970) #872
- Seconde Guerre mondiale #847 848
Affleck, Desbarats, Dimakopoulos,
  Lebensold, Michaud, Sise, agence can
  d'architecture
- Montréal (Qué)
  - Place des Arts #9083 9092 9093 9096
  - Place Ville-Marie #9314 9315
- Vancouver (CB)
  - Queen Elizabeth Theatre #7679 9085
  - Vancouver Civic Auditorium, concours
    #9080
Affleck, Desbarats, Dimakopoulos,

Lebensold, Sise, agence can d'architecture
- Charlottetown (IPE)
  - Confederation Centre #9094
- Chomedey (Qué)
  - hôtel de ville #8990
- comté de Wolfe (Qué)
  - église Saint-Gérard Majella #8846
- Montréal (Qué) #8322
  - Expo 67, pavillons thématiques #7686
    9215
  - Place Bonaventure #7694 9292 9319 9320
    9321 9322 9323 9325
  - Saint George, cathédrale orthodoxe
    grecque #8841 8846
  - synagogue Tifereth Jerusalem #8846
- Osaka (Japon)
  - Expo 70. Pavillon du Canada, concours
    #9217
- Ottawa (Ont)
  - Centre national des arts #9104 9105
Affleck, Desbarats, Dimakopoulos,
  Lebensold, Sise & Schoenauer, agence can
  d'architecture
- Charlottetown (IPE)
  - Confederation Centre #7683
    - concours #9088 9089
Affleck, Raymond Tait (Ray), architecte can,
  1922-
- Montréal (Qué), bureau de poste de Ville
  Mont-Royal #7857
- théories sur l'architecture #7746
Afikpo (Afrique)
- masques #3945
Afrique du Sud
- photographies prises par photographes de
  l'armée canadienne #1107
Agnew, Ludlow & Scott, agence can
  d'architecture
- Welland (Ont), Welland County General
  Hospital #9031
Agniers
- costume, XVIIIe s. #3550
Ahrens, Carl Henry, artiste can, 1863-1936
- et Homer Ransford Watson #7533
Ahrens, Jacob Henry, céramiste can,
  1828-1905
- fondateur, Ahrens Pottery, Paris (Ont)
  #2328
Ahrens Pottery (connu également sous Paris
  Pottery), fabricants de céramique (Paris,
  Ont) #2328
Ahvakana, Laurence, artiste amér, actif 1977
  #4272
Aicher, Otl, artiste all, 1922-
- graphisme, Jeux olympiques (Munich,
  Allemagne de l'Ouest) #898
Aide-Créquy, Jean-Antoine, prêtre et artiste
  can, 1749-1780 #269 270 1233 1323
Aipelee, Oshaweetuk, artiste can, 1923-
- masse de cérémonie, Conseil des
  Territoires du Nord-Ouest #4386
Aird, Neil Carrick, joaillier can, 1945- #4503
Ajax (Ont), Ajax Municipal Building
- architecture, Craig, Zeidler & Strong #7694
Akeeaktashook
- voir Akeeaktashuk

Akeeaktashuk, sculpteur can, 1896-1954
  #4504
Akkanarshoonak
- voir Arnasungnaaq, Barnabus
Akulukjuk, Malaya, artiste can, 1941-
- motifs de tissage #4298
Alabama
- vues photographiques, Walker Evans
  #1513
Alary, Zénon, sculpteur can, 1894-1974
  #2179
- entretien #4505
Alaska
- Inuit
  - art #4208 4280 4424
    - (années 1970) #4233
    - début XIXe s. #4369
  - artefacts préhistoriques #4327 4348
  - arts graphiques #4217
  - culture #4272 4318
  - objets en os #4319
  - sculpture d'ivoire #4382 4398
- vues
  - Jackson, A.Y. #5911
Alaska Native Arts and Crafts Association
  #4208
Albany (NY), Albany Institute of History
  and Art
- expositions
  - Les arts du Canada français, 1613-1870
    (1946) #1331
  - Painting in Canada: A Selective Historical
    Survey (1946) #35
  - The Arts of French Canada, 1613-1870
    (1946) #1330
Albany (NY), New York State Museum
- art iroquois #3586
- wampum, Indiens des forêts du Nord-Est
  #3603
Albers, Josef, artiste amér, 1888-1976
- utilisation de la couleur #468
Alberta
- architecture #8083
  - (1900-années 1930) #8126
  - (années 1950) #8119
  - (années 1970) #8087
  - architecture ukrainienne #8127
  - bois #8120 8136
  - quartiers chinois #8137
- architecture domestique
  - architecture ukrainienne #8704 8709
  - ranches, fin XIXe-début XXe s. #8720
    8721
- art #1953 1967 1972
  - (1980) #1969
  - (1981) #1974
  - (années 1920-1980) #1941
  - (années 1930-1940) #1943
  - (années 1930-1970) #1942
  - (années 1940) #350 1841
  - (années 1940-1960) #1944
  - (années 1950) #1946 1947
  - (années 1950-1970) #1884
  - (années 1970) #1860 1868 1963
  - réalisme #1954
  - tradition huttérite #1962

– tradition norvégienne #2273
– art public (i.e. art dans les lieux publics) #1973
– arts graphiques
    – (1959-1973) #815
    – (années 1970) #1958
– dessin #1968
– écoles (années 1950) #9392
– églises #8913
– enseignement de l'art (années 1940) #2981
– palais de justice (avant 1930) #9005
– peinture #1948 1970
– photographie
    – (1980) #1971 1976
    – (années 1930-1940) #985
    – (années 1970) #1879 1952
– poterie #2337 2371 2372 2386 2393
– sculpture de céramique (années 1970) #1864
– vues #1965 1970
    – Anderton, T.George #4525
    – Barker, Charles Edward #4609
    – Brown, Annora #4933
    – Hind, William George Richardson #5807
    – Kerr, Illingworth Holey #6049
    – Savage, Harry #7133
    – Warren, Mary Schaffer #7527
    – Weber, George #7540
– vues photographiques
    – Biggs, Hugh Beynon #4728
    – Horetzky, Charles George #5838
    – Warren, Mary Schaffer #7526
Alberta. Department of Public Works
– Jubilee Auditoriums (1957) #9084
Alberta. Ministère de l'Education
– architecture des écoles #9404
Alberta. Ministère des Travaux publics
– Edmonton (Alta), Alberta Government Administrative Building #8963
Alberta Association of Architects
– siège social, Duggan House (Edmonton, Alta) #8729
Alberta Community Arts Clubs Association
– programme d'expositions itinérantes (1980) #1972
Alberta Culture. Service des lieux historiques
– conservation de l'architecture, Calgary (Alta), (1974-1980) #8134
Alberta Potteries, fabricants de céramique (Alta) #2371
Alberta Potters' Association
– (1980) #2393
Alberta Society of Artists
– et Alfred Crocker Leighton #6225
– expositions
    – (1931-) #1942
– périodique, Highlights, Quarterly Newsletter of the Alberta Society of Artists #1944
Albright, Ivan Le Lorraine, artiste amér, 1897-
– influence sur Tom La Pierre #6122
Aldridge Point (CB)
– pétroglyphes, Indiens de la côte nord-ouest #3814
Aldworth, Roger, artiste can, 1941-

– sculptures #1151
Aléoutes
– art #3370 4360
– artefacts préhistoriques #4340
– culture, XVIIIe s. #3445
– jade #3331
Alert Bay (CB)
– maison communautaire et totems, Kwakiutls #3936
Alert Bay (CB), U'Mista Cultural Museum
– art kwakiutl #4052
– expositions
    – The Art of Nunstins/L'art de Nunstins (1981) #6934
Alexander, William Walker, artiste can, 1869-1948
– ex-libris #917 4506
Alexie, Frederick (Fred), artiste can, 1853-1939 #4507
– expositions
    – (1928) #3827
Alfred (NY), New York State College of Ceramics
– McKinley, Donald Lloyd, élève #6489
Algoma (Ont)
– vues
    – Groupe des Sept #1768 1789
    – Jackson, A.Y. #5907
    – MacDonald, J.E.H. #6366 6370
Algonquiens
– arbre, mythes et symboles #3516
– art #3374 3385 3403 3404 3434 3558 3574 3605 3621 3633
    – (1980) #4159
    – (années 1970-1980) #4139
    – XIXe s. #3737 3750
    – XXe s. #4143 4150
– broderie en poil d'orignal #3513
– chamanisme et arbre de vie #3365
– coiffures (costume) #3417
– costume #3580 3739
– culture #3490 3529 3631 4097
– écorce de bouleau #3483 3510 3571
– harnachement #3405
– masques #3337
– Midéwiwins, parchemins #3702
– mocassins et récipients #3544
– nattes #3561
– Oiseau-Tonnerre #3493
– orfèvrerie #2101
– orfèvrerie de traite #3594 3608
– ouvrages en piquants de porc-épic #3443 3471 3474 3475 3652
– ouvrages perlés #3582 3635
– peinture #3672 4144 4157
– pétroglyphes #3619
– pictogrammes #3575 3576 3583 3589 3600
– pierres aviformes #3499 3511 3577
– pipes #3463
– poterie #3502 3530 3545
– raquettes #2812 3523
– récipients #3507 3638 3744
– sérigraphie #4151 4158
– travail de la pierre #3406
– travail du cuir #3456
– vannerie #3562 3625

– wampum #3521 3541 3567 3603
Algonquin Legend Painters
– et Jackson Beardy #4161
– et Norval Morrisseau #4161
Algonquin Park (Ont)
– monument à Tom Thomson #7350
– vues, Tom Thomson #7351 7364
Algonquins
– art #3601
– mocassins #3554
– ouvrages en coquillages #3505
– récipients #3542 4078
aliments
– boulangerie et pâtisserie, Québec #2187
– décoration, mennonites #2264
– décoration, oeufs de Pâques, tradition ukrainienne #2132
– fabrication domestique, XVIIIe-XIXe s. #2112
– moules, Musée national de l'Homme, Centre canadien d'études sur la culture traditionnelle #963
– Ontario, XIXe s. #2245 7981
– Québec, influence européenne #2221
Allain, Marie-Hélène, sculpteure can, 1939-
– entretien #4508
Allan, George & Moorhouse, agence can d'architecture
– Toronto (Ont), architecture domestique #8493
Allan, George William, collectionneur can, 1822-1901
– protecteur de Paul Kane #6004
Allan, Marguerite Buller, artiste can, active 1905-1919
– illustrations #916
Allemands au Canada
– Alberta, constructions en bois rond #8136
– architecture, XIXe s.-années 1970 #7735
– Nouvelle-Ecosse et Ontario, arts décoratifs #2135
– Ontario
    – arts décoratifs #2243
    – mennonites, arts décoratifs #2250 2251 2263 2264 2267
    – poterie #2318 3962
– provinces maritimes, Ontario et Prairies, arts décoratifs #2140
Allemands en Pennsylvanie
– arts décoratifs #2243 2250 2251 2263 2264 2267
– faïence (1750-1910) #3962
– mobilier #2552 2568 2572
– objets en bois #2590
– poterie, XIXe s. #2303
– style "fraktur" #2254 2259
Allen, Gladys W., artiste can (vitrail), active années 1920-1940
– vitraux
    – Oshawa (Ont), Saint George's Anglican Church #8899
    – Ottawa (Ont), édifices du Parlement. Tour de la Paix. Fenêtres commémoratives en l'honneur des soldats #2445
Allen, Gower, Huggins & Meiklejohn, agence can d'architecture

– Vernon (CB), Vernon Civic Centre #8972
Allen, Ralph, artiste can, 1926-
– concept d'espace #4509
Alleyn, George Edmund, artiste can, 1931-
　#1542 1543 4510 4511 4513
– à Paris (France) #426 1434
– entretien #1527
– expositions
　– (1974) #4512
– expositions de groupe
　– (1962) #1420
Alliance graphique internationale (AGI)
– (années 1970) #897
Allison, Frank Drummond, artiste can,
　1883-1951
– expositions de groupe
　– (1940) #350
Alloucherie, Jocelyne, artiste can, 1945-
– entretien #4514
Allukpik, John, artiste can, 1935- #4202
Allward, John Raphael, artiste can (vitrail),
　1856-1929 #2450 4515
Allward, Walter Seymour, sculpteur can,
　1876-1955 #10 1231 1713 4517
– bataille d'Ypres, monument aux disparus
　(Ypres, France) #4518
– expositions, critiques #204
– membre du Canadian Art Club #193
– Mémorial de Vimy (Vimy, France) #4519
– monuments #4516
Allward & Gillies, agence can d'architecture
– Saint-Jean (NB), Hôpital général de
　Saint-Jean #9031
Allward & Gouinlock, agence can
　d'architecture
– Toronto (Ont), Sunnybrook Hospital #9027
Allward and McCormick, atelier de vitraux
　(Winnipeg, Man) #2450
Almanach du peuple, L', périodique can
– illustrations, Henri Julien #5987
Alpert, Laura, artiste can, 1948-
– expositions de groupe
　– (1975) #1867
Alpes
– vues, Robert Ford Gagen #5530
Alpine Club of Canada
– et A.Y. Jackson #5919
– et Byron Harmon #5707
Altman, Gerry, photographe can, actif 1976
– catalogue de photographies #1023
aluminium . Canada
– XXe s., et baisse du marché #2704
Amarook, Michael, sculpteur can, 1941-
– expositions, critiques #4403 4408
Amarouk
– voir Amarook, Michael
amautik inuit
– dans l'art #4300
Amaya, Mario, conservateur can, 1933-
– et exposition Realism(e)s, Musée des
　beaux-arts (Montréal, Qué) #533
ambrotypes canadiens
– Halifax (NE) #1211
– portraits, provinces maritimes #1171
– Toronto (Ont) #1725
Américains au Canada

– (années 1750-1970) #126
American Institute of Architects (AIA)
– étude sur la profession d'architecte
　(années 1960) #8307
American Turf Register, périodique amér
– illustrations, Peter Rindisbacher #7002
Amérindiens
– voir aussi Abénaquis; Agniers;
　Algonquiens; Algonquins; Arapahos;
　Assiniboines; Athapascans; Bella-Coolas;
　Béothuks; Carriers; Chilcotins; Chilkats;
　Clallams; Couteaux-Jaunes; Cowichans;
　Cris; Cris de l'Est; Crows; Dakotas;
　Delawares; Flancs-de-Chien; Folles
　Avoines; Gens-du-Sang; Gitksans;
　Goyogouins; Gros-Ventres; Haidas; Hans;
　Hidatsas; Hurons; Indiens de la côte
　nord-ouest; Indiens des forêts du
　Nord-Est; Indiens des plaines; Indiens du
　bassin; Indiens du plateau; Ingaliks;
　Iroquois; Kaskas; Klikitats; Kootenays;
　Koyukons; Kutchins; Kwakiutls; Lillooets;
　Lièvres; Lummis; Makahs; Malécites;
　Mandans; Micmacs; Mistassins;
　Montagnais; Nahanis; Naskapis; Neutres;
　Nez-Percé; Niskas; Nootkas; Onneiouts;
　Onontagués; Osages; Outaouais;
　Pentaguets; Pesmacodys; Pieds-Noirs;
　Piégans; Potéouatamis; Quinaults; Salish
　de la côte ; Salish de l'intérieur;
　Salishiens; Sarcis; Saulteux;
　Saulteux/Ojibwa; Sékanis; Shuswaps;
　Siouens; Skeenas; Skokomish; Slaveys;
　Snuqualmis; Squamish; Tagish; Tahltans;
　Tanainas; Tananas; Têtes-de-Boule;
　Thompsons; Tlingits; Tsimshians;
　Tsonnontouans; Tutchonis; Twanas
– architecture #7722
　– et Douglas Joseph Cardinal #8341
　– influence du climat #7701
– art #5 45 63 129 136 137 485 2093 2096
　3117 3118 3148 3329 3351 3352 3354 3355
　3357 3359 3366 3372 3382 3395 3397 3400
　3408 3412 3418 3421 3422 3423 3425 3428
　3430 3431 3436 3438 3442 3448 3450 3452
　3454 3455 3458 3459 3460 3463 3464 3465
　3466 3467 3473 3477 4126 4127 4146 4165
　– (années 1950) #151
　– (années 1960) #4125 4136
　– (années 1970) #3376 4138 4140 4155
　– (années 1980) #4161 4171
　– et art inuit #3332 4325
　– symbolisme thérapeutique #3356
　– XIXe s. #3486
　– XXe s. #4163 4172
– art pariétal #3433 3472 3481 3482 3484
– artefacts préhistoriques #3371 3380 3401
　– région arctique #4373
– articles de traite #3440
– arts décoratifs #2089 2104 2107 2125 2131
　– (1964-1967) #2108 2109
　– Québec (années 1970) #2230
　– XXe s. #2143
– arts graphiques (années 1970) #3373
– berceaux #3407 3485
– bijoux, XXe s. #2143

– broderie #2783
　– XVIIIe s. #2169 2171
– Cardinal, Douglas J.H., commentaire #8342
– chamanisme #3361 3383
– chaussures #2814 3424
– conservation de l'art et de l'architecture
　#7767
– cosmologie #3498
– costume #3453
　– influence sur costume canadien #2841
　2849
　– XVIIe-XIXe s. #2825
– courtepointes #2799
– culture #3343
– dans l'art #12
　– Armstrong, William #4552
　– Brown, Annora #4933
　– Carr, Emily #5011
　– Catlin, George #1845 3384 3426
　– Chauchetière, Claude #234 235
　– figures sans tête #281
　– fin XIXe s. #1839
　– Hébert, Louis-Philippe #5767
　– Henderson, James #5778 5779
　– Heriot, George #5783 5784
　– Hooker, Marion Hope Nelson #1896
　– Housser, Muriel Yvonne McKague
　　#5845
　– images de la femme #121
　– Jefferys, Charles William #5953
　– Kane, Paul #1845 3386 6002 6003 6004
　　6005 6006 6011 6012 6014 6015 6016
　　6018
　– Krieghoff, Cornelius #6091 6093 6097
　　6436
　– Légaré, Joseph #6222
　– Lynn, Washington Frank #6348
　– Miller, Alfred Jacob #6536 6537
　– Morris, Edmund Montague #6636 6637
　　6638
　– Nicolas, Louis #1372
　– Phillips, Walter Joseph #6854
　– Proctor, Alexander Phimister #6943 6944
　– Rindisbacher, Peter #7003 7005 7006
　　7007
　– Roper, Edward #7077
　– Shilling, Arthur #7197
　– Simcoe, Elizabeth Posthuma Gwillim
　　#7210
　– Thornton, Mildred Valley Stinson #7375
　– Verner, Frederick Arthur #7484
　– Vincent, Zacharie #7493
　– White, John #7552
　– XVIe-XIXe s. #255 256 260
　– XVIe-XVIIIe s. #276
　– XVIIe s. #1363
　– XVIIe-XIXe s. #3427
– droit, art et #3347
– esthétique #3487
　– (années 1970) #4137
– et religion, XVIIe s. #1354 1358
– instruments de musique #3363
– instruments préhistoriques #3393
– jouets #2917 2934
– médailles, signature de traités #763
– métier à tisser #3413

– mocassins #2241 2872
– monuments funéraires #733
– motifs, thèmes amérindiens, poterie (années 1920) #2278
– objets religieux, missionnaires jésuites #2192
– Oiseau-Tonnerre #3410
– orfèvrerie #2630
– orfèvrerie de traite #269 270 728 2101 2628 2629 2631 2633 2634 2651 2653 2654 2655 2659 2664
– ouvrages en coquillages #3388
– ouvrages en piquants de porc-épic #3474 3475
– ouvrages perlés #3420 3449 3457
   – XXe s. #2143
– peinture #165 3432 3451 3462
   – (années 1970) #6648
   – XXe s. #3441
– peinture faciale #3461
– photographies d'Amérindiens
   – Boorne, William Hanson #4796
   – Boorne et May #1950 4797
   – Chesterfield, Albert A. #5102
   – Curtis, Edward Sheriff #3399 3480
   – Hime, Humphrey Lloyd #5801 5803
   – Jauvin, Serge #1562
   – Mathers, Charles Wesley #6451
   – Moodie, Geraldine #6602
   – Pollard, Harry #6899
– pictogrammes #3390 3392
– pipes #3470 3700
   – dessins, George Catlin #3478
– pipes et tabac #3416 3444
– poupées, XXe s. #2143
– raquettes #2812 3515
– sculpture #761 3362
– serpents #3391
– textiles et tissus #2727 2739 3469
– thème décoratif du castor #23 56
– tissage #2747 2748 3476
   – ceinture fléchée #2818 2823 2824 2827 2873
– vannerie #2943 3389 3394 3446 3447 3991
   – XXe s. #2143
– wampum #3387 3522 3612
Amérique
– dans l'art
   – (1564-1867) #231 233
   – XVIe-XIXe s., vue par des artistes européens #255 256 260
Amérique du Sud
– vues, explorateurs français #276
Amess, Frederick Arthur, artiste can, 1909-1971
– aquarelles #4520
Amherst (Mass), University of Massachusetts. University Gallery
– expositions
   – George Trakas: Log Mass: Mass Carving (1980) #7423
Amittu, Davidialuk Alasua, artiste can, 1910-1976 #4468 4521 4522 4523
   – (1977) #4521
Amos, Louis A., architecte can, 1869-1948
– Montréal (Qué), palais de justice, annexe #9001

amour dans l'art
– voir aussi art érotique
– Pellan, Alfred #6822
amulettes . Algonquiens
– orfèvrerie de traite #3608
– ouvrages en pierre #3406
– pierres aviformes #3499 3511 3577
amulettes . Amérindiens #3329
amulettes . Canada
– Ottawa (Ont), Musée national de l'Homme. Centre canadien d'études sur la culture traditionnelle #963
amulettes . Dorsétiens
– cuivre #4365
– os et ivoire #4354
amulettes . Indiens de la côte nord-ouest
– capteurs d'âmes #3853
amulettes . Indiens des forêts du Nord-Est #3491
amulettes . Inuit #4453
amulettes . Micmacs #3556
amulettes . Mistassins
– chasse #4075
amulettes . Montagnais #4075 4082
amulettes . Naskapis #4082
amulettes . Saulteux/Ojibwa #3539
amulettes . Tlingits #3976
– loutre #4028
amulettes . Tsonnontouans
– dessins représentant masques #3533
Amundsen, Roald Engelbert Gravning, explorateur norvégien, 1872-1928
– expédition, King William Island #4366
Amundson, Dale, artiste can, 1940-
– et art public (i.e. art dans les lieux publics) #4524
Amyot, Laurent, orfèvre can, 1764-1839 #2660 2662
– analyse de la composition de l'argent #2682
– encensoirs #2665
– et François Ranvoyzé #2658 2679 6959
– et François Sasseville #2672
– influence sur orfèvrerie française #1244
– oeuvres
   – Cap-Santé (Qué), église #8814
   – Detroit (Mich), Detroit Institute of Arts #2681 2691
   – Québec (Qué), Musée du Québec #2678
– paix #2666
Anchorage (Alaska), Anchorage Historical and Fine Arts Museum
– expositions
   – The Far North: 2000 Years of American Eskimo and Indian Art (1973) #3366
Anchorage (Alaska), University of Alaska. Native Arts Center
– Anghik, Abe, élève #4530
Anderson, Carol, joaillière can, active 1975 #2706
Anderson, Laurie, artiste amér, 1947-
– United States: Part II: A Performance #718
Anderson, Robert William, architecte can, 1924-
– Toronto (Ont), University of Toronto. Engineering Building #9459

Anderson, Tobey C., artiste can, 1946-
– commentaire sur Jack Chambers #700
Anderton, T.George, photographe can, actif années 1870-1890 #4525
Andover (Mass), Phillips Academy. Addison Gallery of American Art
– expositions
   – Aspects of Contemporary Painting in Canada (1942) #355
– expositions, critiques
   – Aspects of Contemporary Painting in Canada (1942) #358
André, Paul, artiste can, 1933- #4526
Andrew Malcolm Furniture Co., fabricants de meubles (Kincardine et Listowel, Ont) #2463
Andrew Malcolm Furniture Co., fabricants de meubles (Kincardine et Southampton, Ont)
– (années 1920) #2547
Andrews, John Hamilton, architecte can, 1933-
– Toronto (Ont)
   – hôtel de ville et Civic Square, concours #8981
   – University of Toronto. Scarborough College #9396 9462 9463 9464
– Vancouver (CB)
   – University of British Columbia. Student Union Building, concours #9503
Andrews, Stephen, artiste can, 1922- #4528
– commentaire sur ses études à Londres #4527
Andrews, Sybil, artiste can, 1898- #4529
Angelis, Joseph R. (Joe) de, artiste can, 1939-
– expositions de groupe
   – (1978) #1824
Anghik, Abraham Apakark (Abe), artiste can, 1951- #4530
Angiju, Peter Nauja, artiste can, 1932- #4202 4531
anglicans
– Sisters of St. John, ouvrages à l'aiguille #2780
Angokwazhuk (Happy Jack), sculpteur can, né 1873 #4398
Angotiawak, artiste can, actif 1956
– dessin représentant célébration de la "kaitemayoh" #4532
Anguhadluq, Luke, artiste can, 1895-
– estampes (1969-1977) #4533
– expositions de groupe
   – (1976) #4268
animation (cinématographie)
– Canada (années 1940) #370
– Doray, Audrey Capel #5301
– McLaren, Norman #6490 6491 6492 6493 6494 6495 6496 6497 6499
– Price, Art #6928
animaux
– cheptel, Québec, apport de l'Europe #2221
– dans création artistique, Arnold Rockman, commentaire #7061
animaux dans l'art
– voir aussi chasse dans l'art; oiseaux dans l'art

– Alary, Zénon #4505
– amulettes, Montagnais et Mistassins #4075
– art canadien #549
– art primitif #3333
– artistes européens en Amérique,
  XVIe-XIXe s. #260
– artistes français en Amérique, XVIe-XVIIIe
  s. #276
– baleines, Indiens de la côte nord-ouest
  #3831 3883
– Beetz, Johan #4654
– Bella-Coolas #3772
– bison
  – art canadien et art américain, fin
    XVIIIe-XXe s. #62
  – Gens-du-Sang #3711
– Bradford, John Locke #4897
– Carr, Emily #5010 5019
– cartes de la Nouvelle-France (1542-1550)
  #831
– castor
  – art canadien #23
  – art canadien et art amérindien #56
  – poterie canadienne #2302 2312
– chevaux
  – Cameron, Walter Graham #4992
  – effigies de chevaux . Indiens des plaines
    #3743
  – Kenyon, J.J. #1681
  – Richard, Wilfrid #7000
  – Todd, Robert Clow #258 259
  – Wickson, Paul Giovanni #7573
– chien, Sandy Haeseker #5675
– Clarke, Fred #5115
– coiffure tlingit #3803
– Côté, Jean-Baptiste #5187 5188
– décoration architecturale canadienne
  (années 1930) #8226
– Fafard, Joe #5397
– Fournier, Paul #5487
– grenouilles, David James Gilhooly #5601
  5602
– gros animaux, Joe Fafard et élèves #1924
– Hood, Robert #5825 5826 5827
– Indiens de la côte nord-ouest #3770 3890
  4036
– Indiens des plaines #3758
– Kerr, Illingworth Holey #6049
– Loates, Glen #6310
– Lougheed, Robert Elmer #6327
– loutres, amulettes, Tlingits #4028
– MacDonald, Thoreau #6381
– McLean, George E. #6501
– monuments funéraires, Ontario, XIXe
  s.-années 1910 #1723
– Muhlstock, Louis #6656
– Ontario, XIXe s. #1727
– ours
  – Inuit #4355
  – Pieds-Noirs #3746
– Parr, Nuna #6768
– pieuvre, Tlingits #4045
– pipes, Iroquois et Hurons #3504
– poisson, Tommy Brayshaw #4907
– Pope, William #6906
– poterie de grès, Canada et Etats-Unis

#2309
– Pratt, George #6916
– Proctor, Alexander Phimister #6943 6944
– Riopelle, Jean-Paul #7029
– Roussil, Robert #7090
– Savage, Harry #7133
– sculpture inuit #4404
– sculpture sur bois québécoise (années
  1940) #1579
– serpents
  – Indiens de l'Amérique du Nord
    (Amérindiens) et de l'Amérique centrale
    #3391
  – Kwakiutls #3840
– Seton, Ernest Thompson #7171 7172 7173
– style animalier
  – Amérindiens #3460
  – Inuit #4334
– Tillenius, Clarence #7377
– tortues, Indiens des plaines #3708
– Waldmann, Oscar #7511
Annacis Island (CB), Annacis Industrial
  Estate
– architecture, Francis Donaldson #7679
  9241
Annapolis Royal (NE), maison Banks
– architecture #7823
Annau, Ernest, architecte can, 1931-
– Toronto (Ont), Bedford Glen #8078
anneaux et bagues . Canada
– anneau épiscopal, William Maurice
  Carmichael #5003
Annecy (France), Journées internationales
  du cinéma d'animation (1965)
– expositions
  – Norman McLaren (1965) #6495
Annonciation, l'
– voir Marie, Vierge, l'Annonciation
Antigonish (NE), Saint Francis Xavier
  University
– conférence, mouvement artisanal en
  Nouvelle-Ecosse (1942) #2145
Antilles
– vues
  – explorateurs français, XVIe s. #276
  – J.E.H. MacDonald #6371
appareils ménagers . Canada
– (années 1940) #2603
appareils photographiques
– Deville, Edouard Gaston Daniel, appareil
  photogrammétrique #989 1874 1875
appartements
– voir immeubles d'habitation
appâts (chasse) . Canada
– guide pour collectionneurs #2595
– Price, Ralph et Patricia, collection #971
Appel, Brian, photographe can, actif années
  1970
– expositions de groupe
  – (1979) #1904
appliques de ruban . Pentaguets #3537
appliques de soie . Algonquiens #3605
appliques de soie . Flancs-de-Chien #4089
appliques de soie . Iroquois #3605
appliques de soie . Saulteux/Ojibwa #4089
appliques de soie . Slaveys #4089

appréciation de l'art
– Borduas, Paul-Emile, commentaire #4799
  4821 4839
– Brooker, Bertram Richard, commentaire
  #317
– Lismer, Arthur, commentaire #311 2965
apprentis
– Ontario, XIXe s. #2261
– Québec #2222
  – (1660-1815) #2231
  – (années 1740) #6253 6255
  – ébénistes, XVIIe-XVIIIe s. #2530 2531
  – forgerons, XVIIe-XIXe s. #2697
  – potiers
    – (1655-1916) #2344
    – (années 1850-1920) #2345
  – XVIIe-XIXe s. #2236
  – XVIIe-XVIIIe s. #2214
– Québec (Qué), XVIIe-XIXe s. #2207
April, Raymonde, photographe can, 1953-
– en comparaison avec Suzy Lake #1059
– expositions de groupe
  – (1980) #1063
– photographies comme mode d'expression
  personnelle #1556
Aqiggaaq, Mathew, sculpteur can, 1940-
– expositions
  – (1979) #4534
aquarelle . Canada
– (1750-1850) #279
– (années 1750-1940) #51
– (années 1890-1940) #367
– (années 1940) #362 374
– (années 1950) #437
– Colombie-Britannique (1845-1871) #2020
  2023
– famille Bell-Irving #4665
– fin XIXe s. #1839
– Ontario, XIXe s. #1720
– provinces maritimes, femmes artistes,
  XIXe s. #1118
– Saskatchewan
  – (1905-1980) #1940
  – (années 1930-1970) #1920
– Société canadienne des aquarellistes #6 127
  332 346 394
– XIXe s. #266
– XVIIIe-XIXe s. #246 248
  – Toronto (Ont), Royal Ontario Museum
    #247
aquarelle . Grande-Bretagne
– (1927), Canadian National Exhibition
  (Toronto, Ont) #295
– influence sur Toni Onley #6741
aquatinte . Canada
– Cotton, John Wesley #822
Arapahos
– mocassins #3554
– ouvrages perlés et ouvrages en piquants
  de porc-épic #3414
Arbour, Léo, sculpteur can, 1912- #2174 2179
Arbour, Madeleine, artiste can, 1923- #4535
– entretien #4536
arbre de vie
– autochtones #3365
– croix funéraires germano-alsaciennes en

fer, Ontario #2709
arbres dans l'art
– *voir aussi* feuilles dans l'art; plantes dans
     l'art
– forêts, Colombie-Britannique
     – Carr, Emily #5033
     – XVIIIe s.-années 1930 #2008
– mythes et symboles, Iroquois et
     Algonquiens #3516
Arbuckle, Frances-Anne Johnston, artiste
     can, 1910-
– expositions de groupe
     – (1972) #5972
– réflexion sur son oeuvre #5970
– réminiscences #4538
Arbuckle, Franklin, artiste can, 1909- #4537
– mari de Frances-Anne Johnston #5970
– réminiscences #4538
*Arcadia: A Journal devoted exclusively to Music,
     Art and Literature*, périodique can #179
Archaeological Report, périodique can #3329
Archambault, Louis, artiste can, 1915- #1504
     4539 4541 4543 4544
– en comparaison avec Jacques Godefroy de
     Tonnancour #1412
– entretien #4542
– et architecture #8231
– et peinture montréalaise (années 1950)
     #1403
– études en Europe #408
– expositions de groupe
     – (1977) #1622
– lauréat, médaille des arts connexes de
     l'Institut royal d'architecture du Canada
     (1958) #4540
– murale, pavillon du Canada, Exposition
     universelle et internationale de 1958
     (Bruxelles, Belgique) #419
– *Winged Personnages*, Place des Arts
     (Montréal, Qué) #8233
Archambault, Pierre, artiste can, 1943- #4545
archéologie
– dans l'art, Frank Allen Nulf #6727
Archibald, John Smith, architecte can,
     1872-1934
– Ottawa (Ont)
     – Château Laurier #9282
Archipenko, Alexander, sculpteur russe aux
     Etats-Unis, 1887-1964
– professeur de Sybil Kennedy #6046
architectes #8303
– *voir aussi* femmes architectes
– (1749-1973), émergence comme groupe
     professionnel, Halifax (NE) #8317
– (1835), création d'une société d'architectes
     #8306
– (1888-1908), nécrologie #7639
– (1901-1912) #7956
– (1911-1912) #8295
– (1945), recommandations #8380
– (1974), critique de l'Institut royal
     d'architecture du Canada #8319
– (années 1870) #8290
– (années 1880-1930), membres de
     l'Académie royale des arts du Canada
     #8298

– (années 1880-1950), Ontario #8300
– (années 1910) #8294
     – concurrence des architectes américains
          #8296
– (années 1920), normes professionnelles
     d'admission #8244
– (années 1940), perspectives de carrière
     pour les diplômés #8247
– (années 1950)
     – (Don Mills, Ont), et constructeurs #8301
     – architecture des écoles #9393
– (années 1960) #8267 8307
     – en comparaison avec architectes
          britanniques #7693
     – et artistes #8234
     – et conditions du logement #8513
     – et constructeurs, et clients #8310
     – et société #8279 8280
     – et urbanisme #8304
     – théorie sur l'architecture #8311
– (années 1970) #7728 7835 8315
     – attitudes envers profession #8316
– bureaux d'architectes
     – (années 1940) #9297
     – (années 1960) #9346
– *Canadian Architect*, études
     – (1958) #8302
     – (1972) #8314 8316
     – (1974-1976) #8320
     – (1976) #8321
– Institut royal d'architecture du Canada,
     étude
     – (1965) #8308
     – (1966) #8309
– résidences, design d'architectes (années
     1970) #8525
– Toronto (Ont), XIXe-début XXe s. #8070
architectes . correspondance
– Harris, William Critchlow #8372
– Rattenbury, Francis Mawson #8401
architectes . écrits
– Bellot, Dom #8333
– Cardinal, Douglas Joseph #8340 8342
– Chapman, Alfred Hirschfelder #8344
– Demers, Jérôme #7874
– Erickson, Arthur Charles #8354 8356 8361
– Myers, Barton #8391
– Plaw, John #8399
– Richards, Larry Wayne #8402
– Safdie, Moshe #8403 8406
– Taillibert, Roger #9139
– Thom, Ron #8412
– Zeidler, Eberhard Henrich #9037
architectes . notes personnelles
– Thomas, William #9103
Architectural Draughtsmen's Club (Toronto,
     Ont)
– (1886-1889) #8299
– (1886-1896) #8300
Architectural Guild of Toronto (Toronto,
     Ont)
– (1887-1898) #8297 8299 8300
Architectural Historical Survey of Manitoba
– *voir* Manitoba. Architectural Historical
     Survey of Manitoba
Architectural Institute of British Columbia

#3186 8142
Architectural League of America
– et Toronto Society of Architects #7956
Architectural Record, périodique amér
– prix et récompenses, Record Houses of
     1975 (concours) #8745
architecture
– *voir aussi* architecture à l'italienne;
     architecture baroque; architecture
     byzantine; architecture commerciale;
     architecture . destruction; architecture
     domestique; architecture georgienne;
     architecture grecque; architecture
     industrielle; architecture militaire;
     architecture navale; architecture
     néo-baroque; architecture néo-classique;
     architecture néo-gothique; architecture
     néo-grecque; architecture néo-romane;
     architecture normande; architecture . style
     art déco; architecture . style beaux-arts;
     architecture . style Tudor; architecture
     vernaculaire; architecture victorienne;
     banques; bâtiments agricoles;
     bibliothèques; brasseries; catalogues de
     modèles . architecture; centres
     administratifs; centres commerciaux;
     centres d'arts d'interprétation; centres
     récréatifs; châteaux et maisons de
     campagne; clochers; construction; écoles;
     édifices préfabriqués; édifices publics;
     églises; élévateurs à grain; entrepôts;
     expositions . bâtiments; façades; gares;
     granges; gratte-ciel; hôpitaux; hôtels;
     hôtels de ville; huttes; iglous; immeubles à
     bureaux; lieux historiques; magasins;
     mines . constructions; monastères;
     moulins; oratoires; palais; palais de
     justice; phares; postes d'essence; postes de
     police; prisons; restaurants; stades;
     synagogues; tavernes; théâtres et cinémas;
     tipis; toits; tours; usines; villas;
     villégiature
– et art
     – (années 1890) #8220
     – (années 1950) #8227
     – (années 1960) #8232 8236
     – (années 1980) #8237
     – British American Oil Company, édifices
          #8230
     – Clerk, Pierre Jean, commentaire #5116
     – Harris, Lawren Stewart, commentaire
          #5721
     – Iliu, Josef, commentaire #8229
     – Korner, John Michael Anthony,
          commentaire #6077
     – Reid, George Agnew, commentaire
          #8219
     – Thomas, Lionel Arthur John,
          commentaire #7349
– et céramique, Claude Vermette #7480
– et peinture murale
     – (années 1930) #15
     – (années 1950), provinces de l'Ouest
          #1844
– et photographie documentaire #1019
– et sculpture habitable, Robert Roussil

#7094 7095 7096 7098
architecture, catalogues de modèles
– *voir* catalogues, de modèles . architecture
architecture, concours d'
– *voir* concours d'architecture
architecture, conservation de l'
– *voir* conservation de l'architecture
architecture . Algonquiens
– écorce de bouleau #3571
architecture . Amérindiens
– conservation #7767
– et Douglas Joseph Cardinal #8341
– Manitoba #8102
architecture . Assiniboines #3653
architecture . Athapascans #4073
architecture . autochtones #3353
architecture . Chilkats #3793 3798
architecture . Cris #3402 3742
architecture . destruction
– Calgary (Alta), (1875-1914) #8121
– églises québécoises #8790 8893
– Montréal (Qué)
  – (années 1960) #8576
  – (années 1970) #7914
  – maison Van-Horne #8594 8601
– Ottawa (Ont), édifices du Parlement.
  Edifice du Centre (1916) #8925
– Québec (Qué), incendies, fin XVIIe
  s.-années 1920 #7952
– Toronto (Ont)
  – (1849) #8061
  – Government House #8753
architecture . enseignement
– Canada
  – (années 1960) #8265
architecture . Flancs-de-Chien #4089
architecture . Haidas #3763 3982 4021
– H'Kusam #3913
– influence sur Arthur Charles Erickson
  #8359
– longues-maisons #3979
– reconstruction, Totem Park (Vancouver,
  CB) #4118
architecture . Hans #4101
architecture . Indiens de la côte nord-ouest
  #3866
– constructions en bois rond #8148
– et architecture précolombienne #3810
– fosses de maisons semi-souterraines #3812
architecture . Ingaliks #4087
architecture . Kwakiutls #3787
– maison communautaire, Alert Bay (CB)
  #3936
architecture . Métis #8102
architecture . Micmacs #3569
architecture . modèles . Canada
– (1927-1939), *Exhibition of Architecture and
  the Allied Arts* (Toronto, Ont) #8224
– (1969) #7700
– (1970) #7702
– Nouveau-Brunswick, églises #7873
– Québec
  – églises, XVIIe-XVIIIe s. #8869
  – XVIIe-XIXe s. #7872
– Québec (Qué) #7936
architecture . périodiques . Canada #3313

– *Architecture concept* #7667
– *Canadian Architect* #7672
– *Canadian Architect & Builder* #7639
– *Canadian Heritage* #7764
– *Construction: A Journal for the Architectural
  Engineering and Contracting Interests of
  Canada* #7641
– *Royal Architectural Institute of Canada.
  Journal* #7654
– *Selected Papers from the Society for the Study
  of Architecture in Canada* #7721
– *Trace: A Canadian Review of Architecture*
  #7753
architecture . Pieds-Noirs #3654
architecture . Quinaults #3845
architecture . Salish de la côte #3851 3896
– site archéologique de McClallum (CB)
  #3872
architecture . Salishiens #3807
architecture . Sallirmiuts #4324
architecture . Saulteux/Ojibwa #3402 4089
– Island Lake (Man) #3549
architecture . Slaveys #4089
architecture . style Art déco
– Montréal (Qué), maison Cormier #8347
– Vancouver (CB) #8167
architecture . style beaux-arts
– Canada #7740
  – et néo-gothique en architecture #7724
    7739
  – gares #9539
– Lyle, John MacIntosh, Banque de
  Nouvelle-Ecosse, édifices #9203
– Prairies, édifices du Parlement #8945
– provinces des Prairies, édifices du
  Parlement #8944
– Québec #7923 8265
– Toronto (Ont) #8069
architecture . style Tudor
– influence sur architecture résidentielle,
  Vancouver (CB), (1900-1930) #8730
architecture . Tagish #4106
architecture . Tahltans
– (années 1910) #4074
architecture . Tanainas #4085
architecture . Tananas #4095
architecture . théorie et critique
– Bellot, Dom #8333
– Charney, Melvin #5095
– Cormier, Ernest #8346
– Demers, Jérôme #7874
– Gaboury, Etienne J. #8369
– Nobbs, Percy Erskine #7642
– Safdie, Moshe #8403 8404 8406
architecture . Thompsons
– habitations hivernales #4063
architecture . Thuléens #4324
architecture . Tlingits #3763 4106
– caveaux funéraires #4007
– potlatch #4012
architecture . Tsimshians #3763
architecture . Tutchonis #4106
architecture à l'italienne
– Albernethy (Sask), Lanark Place #8700
– Canada
  – architecture domestique #7696

– gares de chemins de fer #9539
– Ontario, églises #8904
architecture allemande
– XIXe-XXe s., influence sur architecture
  canadienne #7735
architecture américaine
– (1880-1914), influence sur architecture
  montréalaise #7928 7929
– (1901-1909), Toronto Society of Architects,
  expositions #7956
– (années 1850), influence sur architecture
  montréalaise #7920
– (années 1910), influence sur architecture
  canadienne #7648
– (années 1920), influence sur architecture
  canadienne #7653
– (années 1930), influence sur architecture
  canadienne #7658 7661
– (années 1960-1970), en comparaison avec
  architecture canadienne #8315
– architecture Second Empire, influence sur
  architecture canadienne #7741 7742
– bois, XVIIe-XVIIIe s. #7717
– début XIXe s., influence sur Government
  House (Halifax, NE) #8750
– fin XIXe-milieu XXe s., influence sur
  architecture canadienne #7724
– Ouest américain #8083
– région nord-ouest du Pacifique (avant
  1860) #8140
– style beaux-arts, influence sur architecture
  québécoise #7923
– utilisation de béton (années 1910) #7643
– XIXe-début XXe s., influence sur
  architecture canadienne #7652
– XIXe s., influence sur architecture
  québécoise #7850
– XVIIe-XIXe s., influence sur architecture
  canadienne #7687
– XVIIIe s., influence sur architecture de la
  Nouvelle-Ecosse #7815
– XVIIIe s., style national, en comparaison
  avec style national canadien (1860-1890)
  #7697
architecture baroque
– Québec, églises #8817 8821
Architecture-Bâtiment-Construction, périodique
  can #7667
architecture britannique #8494
– (1880-1914), influence sur architecture
  montréalaise #7929
– architecture Second Empire, influence sur
  architecture canadienne #7741 7742
– fin XIXe-milieu XXe s., influence sur
  architecture canadienne #7724
– style national, néo-gothique, en
  comparaison avec style national, Canada
  (1860-1890) #7697
– XIXe s., influence sur architecture
  canadienne #7650 7652
– XIXe s., influence sur architecture
  manitobaine #8097
– XIXe s., influence sur architecture
  québécoise #7850 7892
– XVIIe-XIXe s., influence sur architecture
  canadienne #7687

– XVIIIe s., influence sur architecture de la
  Nouvelle-Ecosse #7815
architecture byzantine
– influence sur architecture des églises
  albertaines #8913
– influence sur architecture des églises
  orthodoxes ukrainiennes, Saskatchewan
  #8912
Architecture Canada, périodique can #7654
Architecture Canada Newsmagazine,
  périodique can #7654
architecture canadienne #30 57 58 59 61 129
  7668 7688 7689 7714 7728 8523
– (1608-1867) #2120
– (1608-1930) #7659
– (1850-1900) #7744
– (1867-1967) #7695
– (1880-1914) #7736
– (1890-1900) #190
– (1900-1940) #28
– (1918-années 1920) #7958
– (1919), concurrence des architectes
  américains #8296
– (1927-1939), *Exhibition of Architecture and
  the Allied Arts* (Toronto, Ont) #8224
– (1938-1942) #7666
– (1945), recommandations #8380
– (1945-années 1960) #7682
– (1945-années 1970) #7737
– (1959-1969) #7700
– (1960-1970) #7710
– (1967) #7694
– (1967-1970) #7709
– (1970), modèles de constructions #7702
– (1981), commentaires d'architectes #7746
– (années 1850), recommandations #7638
– (années 1870) #8290
– (années 1880), recommandations #8238
– (années 1880-1930), Académie royale des
  arts du Canada, expositions #8298
– (années 1890) #7640 8291
  – en comparaison avec architecture
    américaine #7640
– (années 1910) #7644 7648 7649 8294
– (années 1920) #7653 7656 7657 7960 7964
  8223
– (années 1930) #1 340 7658 7663 7967 7969
  7971 7972 7973
– (années 1940) #370 7669
– (années 1940-1960), architectes d'origine
  étrangère #465
– (années 1950) #388 7670 7673 7675 7680
– (années 1960) #7683 7691 7692 7698 8311
  9400
– (années 1960-1970), en comparaison avec
  architecture américaine #8315
– (années 1970) #610 7731
  – commentaires d'architectes #7733
– Académie royale des arts du Canada #2
– Alberta
  – (1900-années 1930) #8126
  – (années 1950) #8119
  – (années 1970) #1951
  – architecture ukrainienne #8127 8713
  – bois #8136
  – quartiers chinois #8137

– XVIIIe-XIXe s., postes de traite des
  fourrures #8129
– architectes d'origine polonaise #149
– architecture estonienne #7723
– architecture géorgienne #8522
– architecture néo-gothique #7671 7724 7739
  7740
– architecture Second Empire #7741 7742
– architecture ukrainienne #8085
– architecture victorienne #7697 7725 7769
– archives et sources historiques #7729
– Arctique #8184 8185 8186 8187
  – milieu XIXe-milieu XXe s., bois #8189
– Association pour l'avancement des
  méthodes de préservation #7757
– Aylmer (Qué), (1800-1921) #7889
– Barkerville (CB) #8151
– bâtiments préfabriqués, provinces de
  l'Ouest (1904-1910) #8082
– Batoche (Sask) #8115
– Beauport (Qué) #7880
– Bedeque Bay (IPE) #7798
– béton
  – (années 1910) #7643
  – Concours pour ouvrages en béton #7706
– béton décoratif (1903-années 1920) #7734
– béton préfabriqué (années 1960) #7684
– bibliographies (années 1960-1970) #7713
– bois
  – XIXe s., Compagnie de la baie
    d'Hudson, établissement de la rivière
    Rouge #8100
  – XVIIe-XVIIIe s. #7717
– Boucherville (Qué), XVIIe-XIXe s. #7890
– Calgary (Alta) #8124 8134
  – (1875-1914) #8121 8128
  – (1880-1980) #8138
  – (1909) #8116
  – (1910) #8118
  – centre-ville (années 1970) #8122
  – couloirs suspendus #8132 8135 8139
  – édifices de grès #8133
– Calgary (Alta), University of Calgary.
  Canadian Architectural Archives #7730
  7751
– Calixa-Lavallée (Qué) #7877
– *Canadian Architect*, prix et récompenses
  #8190 8191 8192 8193 8194 8195 8196 8197
  8198 8199 8200 8201 8202 8203 8204
– Charlottetown (IPE) #7797 7802
– Colombie-Britannique #8142 8146
  – (1895-1914) #8152
  – (1899-1901) #1977
  – (années 1940) #8141
  – (années 1950) #8144
  – (avant 1860) #8140
  – architecture chinoise #8154
  – bois #8153
  – et Royal Engineers #8150
  – vallée du Fraser #8147
  – Whiteway, William Tuff #9508
– comté de Bellechasse (Qué) #1281
– comté de Haliburton (Ont), John Billing
  #8335
– comté de Pictou (NE) #7821 7827
– comté de Pontiac (Qué) #7894 7895

– comté de Waterloo (Ont), édifices en
  pierre, XIXe s. #8011
– comté de Wentworth (Ont) #7954
– conservation de l'architecture #7767 7772
– construction en acier (années 1960) #7686
– Cormier, Ernest #8345
– corridor du canal Rideau (Ont), (avant
  1880) #8008
– Dawson City (Yukon), (1897-1903) #8183
– Denison's Mills (Qué) #7884
– Dundas (Ont), (1813-années 1850) #7994
– Edmonton (Alta)
  – (1800 1914) #8130
  – (1909) #8117
  – (années 1910) #8131
  – centre-ville (années 1970) #8123
– et architecture paysagiste, fin XIXe
  s.-années 1950 #7677
– et art
  – (années 1960) #753 8235
– et art public (i.e. art dans les lieux
  publics), Vancouver (CB) #2005
– et arts décoratifs (années 1960) #8231
– et Héritage Canada #7770
– et moyens de transport, XIXe s. #9512
– et sculpture
  – (années 1970) #773
  – Québec #1234
– et sculpture sur bois (années 1890) #726
– et vitrail (années 1940) #2446 2447
– Expo 67 #483
– femmes architectes #7678
– Fredericton (NB) #7809
  – XIXe s. #7803
– Georgetown (IPE) #7799
– Guelph (Ont), XIXe s. #7970
– Halifax (NE) #7816 7833 8317
  – (années 1750-1930) #7839
  – édifices portuaires, XIXe s. #7822 7834
  – Lang, George Macdonald #7838
  – rue Barrington #7840
  – rue Granville #7817
  – XIXe s. #7826
  – XVIIIe-XIXe s. #7818
– Hamilton (Ont) #7978 7985
  – (années 1910) #7957
  – architecture victorienne #7991
– Heritage Park (Alta) #8125
– île d'Anticosti (Qué) #7869
– île d'Orléans (Qué) #1252
– Ile-du-Prince-Edouard, XVIIe s.-années
  1930 #7796
– influence du climat #7701
– Institut royal d'architecture du Canada,
  prix et récompenses #7660 7662 7664 7665
– Inventaire canadien des bâtiments
  historiques #7707 7708 7716
  – inventaire informatisé #159
– inventaire des archives de l'architecture
  avant 1950, Ottawa (Ont), collections
  privées #8049
– Kings Landing (NB) #7810 7811
– Kingston (Ont) #1680
  – (1673-1867) #7989
  – Browne, George #8339
  – XIXe s. #7995

- Kingston et comté de Frontenac (Ont), XIXe s. #8015
- Kingston et Toronto (Ont), XIXe s.-années 1920 #7961
- Kingston Mills (Ont) #8020
- Laterrière (Qué), XIXe s. #7882
- London (Ont) #8003 8007 8010 8018
- Lunenburg (NE) #7836 7837
- Manitoba #8094 8098
  - (1812-1870) #8097
  - (1980) #1906
  - Stechesen, Leslie #8409
  - XIXe-début XXe s. #8102
- médailles Massey en architecture #8205 8206 8207 8208 8209 8210 8211 8212 8213 8214 8215 8216
- Montréal (Qué) #7906 7909 7913 7927 7930 7931 7933
  - (1642-années 1970) #7918 7934
  - (1880-1914) #1367 7928
  - (1880-1915) #7921
  - (années 1850) #7920
  - (années 1960) #9220
  - centre-ville (années 1950-1960) #7901
  - centre-ville (années 1960-1970) #7925
  - édifices en pierres grises #7922
  - Vieux-Montréal #7904 7905 7910 7911 7919
  - XIXe-début XXe s. #7914
  - XIXe s. #7915 7916
  - XVIe s.-années 1840 #7898
  - XVIIe s.-années 1950 #7900
  - XVIIe-XIXe s. #7899
- Montréal (Qué) et Québec (Qué), (années 1870-1920) #7843
- Montréal (Qué) et Toronto (Ont), (années 1960) #7693
- Moose Factory (Ont) #7976 8032
- Nelson (CB) #8155
- Neuville (Qué) #7875
- Niagara-on-the-Lake (Ont)
  - fin XVIIIe-début XIXe s. #8000
  - XIXe s. #7986 7992 8655
- Nouveau-Brunswick #1178 2150
  - Murray, William #8390
  - XVIIIe-XIXe s. #7808
- Nouvelle-Ecosse #7820
  - (1605-1850) #1196
  - XIXe s. #7832
  - XVIIe-XIXe s. #7814
  - XVIIIe s. #7815
  - XVIIIe-XIXe s. #7829
- Oakville (Ont) #8025
- Ontario #8017 8024
  - (1800-1850) #7965
  - (1800-1855) #8014
  - (1831-1861) #8009
  - architecture néo-classique #7983
  - construction à murs creux, XIXe s. #8004
  - constructions polygonales, XIXe s. #7987
  - et Fondation du patrimoine ontarien #8001
  - influence de l'architecture écossaise, XIXe s. #7977
  - Jerome Markson Architects #8386 8387
  - Ontario Association of Architects #7955

- Thomas, William #8413
- villages de pionniers #8063
- vues, Charles William Jefferys #5959
- XIXe s. #7959 7993 8006 8023 8672
- Ordre des architectes du Québec, prix d'excellence en architecture #7886
- Ottawa (Ont) #8036
  - (avant 1914) #8047
  - Académie de La Salle #9480 9481
  - Archives publiques du Canada, archives de l'architecture #7738
  - début XIXe s. #8038
  - district de Glebe #8042
  - Noffke, Werner Ernest #8393
  - Région de la capitale nationale #8035 8037 8039 8043 8044
- périodiques
  - *Architecture concept* #7667
  - *Canadian Architect* #7672
  - *Canadian Architect & Builder* #7639
  - *Canadian Heritage* #7764
  - *Construction: A Journal for the Architectural Engineering and Contracting Interests of Canada* #7641
  - *Royal Architectural Institute of Canada. Journal* #7654
  - *Selected Papers from the Society for the Study of Architecture in Canada* #7721
  - *Trace: A Canadian Review of Architecture* #7753
- Peterborough (Ont), (avant 1890) #8021
- pierre à bâtir et pierre d'ornement #7646 7647
- Prairies #8080 8088 8089
  - (années 1970) #8084 8086 8087
  - architecture juive #8081
- prix Vincent Massey pour l'aménagement urbain #8217 8218
- provinces maritimes #1119 7779
  - XVIIIe-XIXe s. #7780
- Québec #1233 1235 1237 1249 1258 1259 1265 1327 1596 2183 2184 7850 7851 7867 7868 7887
  - (1640-1840) #1329
  - (1760-1790) #1369
  - (1780-1850) #1232 1574
  - (1880-1914) #7929
  - (1925-1950) #1405
  - (1980) #7893
  - (années 1870) #1307
  - (années 1930), influence de l'architecture française #1381
  - (années 1940) #7846
  - (années 1950) #7857
  - (années 1960) #7862
  - archives #7863
  - art traditionnel #1291
  - Baillairgé, François #4586
  - Baillairgé, Thomas #8326 8328
  - Baillif, Claude #8329
  - Confrérie des menuisiers de madame Sainte-Anne #1241
  - et art (années 1970-1980) #1561
  - et colonisation #7855
  - et nationalisme #7848
  - et sculpture (années 1970) #1628

- influence de l'Ecole des beaux-arts #8265
- ministère des Affaires culturelles du Québec. Service de l'Inventaire des biens culturels #1277
- Morisset, Gérard #8891
- Parizeau, Marcel #8397
- récollets #8855
- Roussil, Robert, commentaire #7097
- utilisation de modèles architecturaux, XVIIe-XIXe s. #7872
- utilisation de plâtre #1618
- XVIIe s. #228 229
- XVIIe s.-années 1940 #7853
- XVIIe-XIXe s. #1334 1335 1341 7842 7852 7858 7859
  - influence européenne #2221
- XVIIe-XVIIIe s. #1320 2181 7844 7845
- XVIIIe-début XXe s. #1339
- XVIIIe s. #234 235 269 270 7861
- XVIIIe s.-années 1820 #1300
- XVIIIe-XIXe s. #1338
- Québec (Qué) #7892 7938 7939 7940 7942 7945
  - (1608-fin XIXe s.) #7944
  - Baillairgé, Charles #8324
  - Baillairgé, Thomas #8325
  - destruction par le feu (fin XVIIe s.-années 1920) #7952
  - place Royale #7948
  - XVIIe s. #1352
  - XVIIe-XIXe s. #1306 1309 7936 7949 7950
  - XVIIe-XVIIIe s. #7935
  - XVIIIe s. #7943
- Québec (Qué) et île d'Orléans (Qué) #7847
- Regina (Sask)
  - (1909) #8109
  - (années 1910) #8111
- région d'Aultsville (Ont) #7980
- région du canal Rideau (Qué et Ont) #8012
- Repentigny (Qué) #7888
- Saint-Jean (NB) #7807
- Saint-Roch-de-l'Achigan (Qué) #7854
- Saskatchewan
  - (années 1880-1920) #8113
  - (années 1960) #8112
- Saskatoon (Sask) #8114
  - (1909) #8110
- Sillery (Qué), XVIIe-XIXe s. #7879
- St. Andrews (NB) #7806 8550
- St. John's (TN) #7783 7787 7789 7790 7793 7794
  - (avant 1900) #7786
- structure à voiles minces, Québec et Colombie-Britannique (années 1950) #7674
- Terre-Neuve #7792
  - XVIe-XIXe s. #7781
- Terre-Neuve et Labrador #7782
- Tignish (IPE) #7801
- Toronto (Ont) #5651 8060 8065 8067
  - (1794-1977) #8074
  - (1810) #8058
  - (1834-1934) #8055
  - (1849) #8061
  - (1890-1928) #8069
  - (années 1850) #8050

– (années 1950) #8057
– architecture néo-romane #8064
– Archives publiques de l'Ontario. John
  Charles Batstone and Eric Crompton
  Horwood Collection of Architectural
  Drawings #8028 8030
– Baker, Francis Spence #8330
– brique et stuc (années 1910) #8052
– Brown, Murray #8338
– Chapman, Alfred Hirschfelder #8344
– Diamond & Myers #8071
– fin XVIIIe-début XXe s. #8070
– Howard, John George #8378
– Martin, Arthur N. #6423
– Smith, Eden #8408
– Todmorden Mills #8072
– XIXe s. #8051 8056 8059 8073 8075
– XIXe s.-années 1930 #8076
– Toronto Society of Architects #7956
– Toronto Society of Arts #1690
– tradition germanique #2140 7735
– tradition norvégienne #2273
– Trois-Rivières (Qué), (années 1630-1910)
  #7883
– Truro (NE) #7828
– Upper Canada Village (Morrisburg, Ont)
  #7981 7982 7988 8031
– utilisation de terre cuite (1809-1930) #7704
– vallée de l'Outaouais (Ont), contructions
  en bois rond #8029
  Vancouver (CB) #7761 8159 8161 8164 8166
  8168 8170
  – (1886-1914) #8165
  – (1914) #8156
  – (1959-1961) #8158
  – (années 1950) #1992 8157
  – (années 1970) #8162
  – centre-ville #7762 8171
  – Downs, Barry Vance #8353
  – Erickson, Arthur Charles #8357
  – Gastown #8160 8163
  – Kemble, Roger #8379
  – Robson Square #8172
– Victoria (CB) #2269 8149 8173 8176 8177
  8178
  – (1843-1929) #8180
  – (1843-années 1960) #8174
  – (1872-1912) #8175
  – quartier chinois #8179 8181
  – Rattenbury, Francis Mawson #8400
– Village Canadiana (Rawdon, Qué) #7876
– Village Historique Acadien (Caraquet, NB)
  #7805
– Whitby (Ont) #8016
– Williamstown (Ont) #7997
– Winnipeg (Man) #1891 8092 8096 8105
  8256
  – (1831-1960) #8095
  – (1870-1914) #8103
  – (1881-1912) #8101
  – (années 1970) #8104
  – Barber & Barber #8331
  – centre-ville #8108
  – XIXe s.-1909 #8093
  – XIXe s.-années 1910 #8099
– XIXe s. #258 259 7974

– XVIIe-début XIXe s. #7841
– XVIIe s.-années 1910 #7650
– XVIIe s.-années 1920 #7651 7652
– XVIIe s.-années 1930 #7661
– XVIIe s.-années 1940 #7676
– XVIIe s.-années 1970 #7711
– XVIIe-XIXe s. #67 68
  – influence européenne et influence
    américaine #7687
– XVIIIe-début XXe s. #7719 7727
– XVIIIe s. #249 250
– XVIIIe s.-années 1930 #45
– XXe s.
  – concept d'espace #7748
  – et société #7732
  – expression culturelle #7690
architecture commerciale . Canada
– (1880-1914) #7736
– (1911-1912) #8295
– (1938-1942) #7666
– (1960-1970) #7710
– (années 1910) #9332
– (années 1920) #7656
– architecture néo-gothique #7739 7740
– architecture Second Empire #7741 7742
– bâtiments préfabriqués, provinces de
  l'Ouest, début XXe s. #8082
– Calgary (Alta)
  – (1909) #8116
– Colombie-Britannique
  – (années 1970) #9360
  – Hooper, Thomas #8376
– Halifax (NE) #7819
  – rues Prince et Hollis, édifices, XIXe s.
    #7831
  – XVIIIe-XIXe s. #7818
– Hamilton (Ont)
  – architecture victorienne #7991
– John B. Parkin Associates #8395
– Kingston (Ont)
  – (années 1670-fin X1Xe s.) #7989
  – XIXe s. #7995
– London (Ont)
  – XIXe s. #8007
– Manitoba
  – XIXe-début XXe s. #8102
– Montréal (Qué)
  – dessins d'architecture, Archives
    nationales du Québec à Montréal #8604
– Nouvelle-Ecosse
  – XVIIe-XIXe s. #7814
– Ontario
  – XIXe s. #8006
– Québec
  – (années 1960) #7862
– Regina (Sask)
  – (1909) #8109
– St. John's (TN)
  – (avant 1900) #7786
– Toronto (Ont)
  – (années 1920) #9335 9367
  – XIXe s. #8059
– Trois-Rivières (Qué)
  – (années 1630-1910) #7883
– Winnipeg (Man) #8105 8106
  – (1831-1960) #8095

– (années 1880-1910) #8101
– XVIIe s.-années 1960 #7689
Architecture concept, périodique can #7667
architecture dans l'art
– Canada, habitations modestes #104
architecture domestique
– voir aussi bungalows; cabanes en bois
  rond; immeubles d'habitation; logements
  subventionnés; logements subventionnés
  pour travailleurs; immeubles en bandes;
  pavillons de chasse
– Erickson, Arthur Charles, commentaire
  #8354
– Safdie, Moshe, commentaire #8406
architecture domestique . Amérindiens
– bois #7722
architecture domestique . Béothuks #3528
architecture domestique . Canada
– (1608-1867) #2120
– (1880-1914) #7736
– (1909) #8488
– (1938-1942) #7666
– (1960-1970) #7710
– (années 1770-1870) #7696
– (années 1890) #8485
– (années 1910) #8489 8491 8492 8493 8494
  – maisons de banlieue #8490
– (années 1920) #7656 8499
– (années 1930) #8500 8502
  – et jardins #8501
  – maisonnettes #8503 8504
– (années 1940), maisonnettes #8507
– (années 1950) #8227 8508 8509 8510 8512
  – immeubles en bande #8511
– (années 1960) #8231 8513 8517 8519
– (années 1970) #8525
– Abernethy (Sask)
  – Lanark Place #8700
  – parc historique national W.R.
    Motherwell Farmstead #8723 8724 9232
– Acadie #7804
– Alberta
  – (1900-années 1930) #8126
  – architecture ukrainienne #8713
  – bois #8120
  – ranches, fin XIXe-début XXe s. #8720
    8721
– Architectural Record Record Houses
  (concours), (1975) #8745
– architecture géorgienne #8498 8522
– architecture néo-gothique #7739 7740
– architecture Second Empire #7741 7742
– architecture ukrainienne #8085 8691 8704
  8709 8710
– Arctique
  – (années 1960) #8732
  – (années 1970) #8733
– bâtiments préfabriqués, provinces de
  l'Ouest, début XXe s. #8082
– bois #7722
– Brigus (TN), Hawthorne Cottage #8539
– Brockville (Ont), Idlewild #8671
– Broughton Island (TNO), habitation en
  forme de dôme, bois et polyéthylène
  #8734
– bungalows (1908) #8487

– cabane en rondins verticaux #8535
– Calgary (Alta)
  – (1875-1914) #8711
  – (1909) #8116
  – (1975-1980) #8728
  – Jenkins, Dan #8726
  – Long, Jack #8381
  – résidence d'Ian McDougall #8727
– Calixa-Lavallée (Qué) #7877
– Charlevoix (Qué) #8629
– Colombie-Britannique #8143
  – (années 1850-début XXe s.) #8712
  – (années 1910), bungalows #8685
  – (années 1940) #1987 8693
  – bois #8153
  – Maclure, Samuel #8383 8384 8385
  – résidences estivales #8698
  – XIXe s.-années 1920 #8690
– Comox (CB), résidence Filberg #8355
– comté de Norfolk (Ont), XIXe s. #8656
– Conseil national de l'habitation
  – (1957-) #8741
– Cornwall (Ont), Inverarden #8673
– Cowichan (île de Vancouver, CB),
  Marshall House #8695
– Don Mills (Ont), rapports entre architectes
  et constructeurs (années 1950) #8301
– Edmonton (Alta)
  – (1900-1914) #8130
  – (années 1920-1970), maisons à deux
    étages #8705
  – Duggan House #8729
  – maison Holgate #8718
– Erickson, Arthur Charles #8356
– Fanshawe Pioneer Village (Ont) #8066
– finis en stuc de ciment (1908) #8638
– Fredericton (NB), XIXe s. #7803
– Georgeville (Qué), maison Joshua-Copp
  #8628
– Grand Digue (NB), maison
  Hélène-et-Roma-Bourgeois #8547
– Guelph (Ont), XIXe s. #6040 7970
– guide pour la restauration #7760
– habitations à prix modique, après
  Première Guerre mondiale #8495
– Halifax (NE)
  – Black-Binney House #8548
  – maison West, rue Brunswick #8537
  – XVIIIe-XIXe s. #7818
– Hamilton (Ont)
  – architecture victorienne #7991
  – Dundurn Castle #8650 8662
  – Whitehern #8664
– île d'Orléans (Qué) #1252
  – (1761-1767) #8613
– Ile-du-Prince-Edouard
  – (années 1880-1930) #8544
  – habitations en grès, début XIXe s. #8552
  – XVIIIe-XIXe s. #8530
– Kings Landing (NB) #7810 7811
– Kingston (Ont)
  – Newlands, William #8392
  – XIXe s. #7995
  – XVIIe-XIXe s. #7989
– Kingston Mills (Ont) #8020
– La Canardière (Qué), maison Garneau

#8615
– LaSalle (Qué), manoir Ogilvie #8636
– Laval (Qué), maison André B.-Papineau
  #8625
– Liverpool (NE), résidence de Simeon
  Perkins #8536
– Lockport (Man), Saint Andrew's
  Parsonage #8716
– London (Ont)
  – Eldon House #8660
  – XIXe s. #8007 8010
– Longueuil (Qué), maison Lamarre #8608
– Louisbourg (NE) #8419 8422 8427
– Lunenburg (NE), Soloman House #8549
– Manitoba
  – (1812-1870) #8097
  – (1907-1927) #8689
  – XIXe-début XXe s. #8102
  – XIXe s. #8098 8692
– Memramcook (NB), maison
  Célestin-Bourque #8543
– mennonites #2268 2572 8715
– Meteghan (NE), Vieille Maison #8531
– Montréal (Qué) #8576 8620
  – (1698-années 1940) #8570
  – (années 1880-1890) #8610
  – (années 1910) #8556
  – (années 1910), maisonnettes #8555
  – (années 1920) #8562
  – (années 1970), étudiants en architecture,
    Université McGill, assistance aux
    locataires à faible revenu #8283
  – Arts Club #1314
  – château de Callière #8565
  – château Dufresne #8617 8618
  – construction en pierre #8598
  – dessins d'architecture, Archives
    nationales du Québec à Montréal #8604
  – île des Soeurs #8587
  – maison Bigot #8567
  – maison Cormier #8347 8348
  – maison George-Etienne-Cartier #8619
  – maison Saint-Gabriel #8597
  – maison Simon-McTavish #8564
  – maison Van-Horne #8594 8601
  – XIXe s. #8612
– Mount Uniake (NE), Uniake House #8534
– Neuville (Qué) #7875 8607
– Niagara-on-the-Lake (Ont)
  – fin XVIIIe-début XIXe s. #8000
  – XIXe s. #7986 8655
– Nouveau-Brunswick, fin XVIIIe-début
  XIXe s. #8529
– Nouvelle-Ecosse #7820
  – XVIIe-XIXe s. #7814
  – XVIIe-XVIIIe s. #7823
  – XVIIIe s. #7815
– Ontario #7968 8654
  – (1784-1840) #7966
  – (1800-1855) #8014
  – (années 1850-1950), maisons en terrasses
    #8653
  – (années 1910) #8642
  – (années 1920) #8646
  – (années 1930) #8647
  – architecture géorgienne #8648

  – charpente en madriers, XIXe s. #8046
  – constructions polygonales, XIXe s. #7987
  – influence de l'architecture écossaise,
    XIXe s. #7977
  – résidences estivales (années 1940) #8651
  – sud de l'Ontario, XIXe s. #8679
  – XIXe-début XXe s. #8002
  – XIXe s. #2245 8005 8006 8672 8677 8678
– Ontario et Québec
  – (années 1910) #8496
  – (années 1920) #8497
  – maisons en brique (années 1790-1810)
    #8521
– Ontario et Québec, récits de voyageurs
  (1763-1860) #8527
– Perth (Ont)
  – Matheson House (maintenant Perth
    Museum) #8670
  – XIXe s. #8669
– Peterborough (Ont), Hutchison House
  #8674
– Prairies #8080 8717
  – huttes en tourbe #8701 8706
– presbytères
  – Batiscan (Qué), Vieux Presbytère #8807
– prix et récompenses
  – Canadian Small House Competition
    (1946) #8740
  – Conseil canadien de l'habitation
    – (1972) #8744
    – (1974) #8746
    – (1979) #8747
  – Dominion Housing Act Competition
    (1938) #8739
  – Dominion Housing Act Small House
    Competition (1936) #8736
  – Ontario Government Housing
    Competition (1936) #8737
  – Ontario Housing Corporation Design
    Competition (1972) #8663
  – Ontario Hydro Golden Medallion "All
    Electric Home" Competition (1961)
    #8514
  – Prix nationaux aux constructeurs de
    maisons unifamiliales (1960) #8742
  – Prix nationaux aux constructeurs de
    maisons unifamiliales (1969) #8743
  – T. Eaton Company Architectural
    Competition for House Designs (1936)
    #8738
  – T. Eaton Company Ideal Ontario Home
    Competition (1930) #8735
– provinces maritimes
  – (avant 1900) #8551
  – XIXe s. #8528
– Québec #7868 8568 8591 8592 8599 8600
  8603
  – (1880-1914) #7929
  – (années 1960) #7862
  – et Héritage canadien du Québec #7871
  – habitations rurales
    – (1600-1800) #8614
    – XVIIe-XIXe s. #8624
    – XVIIe-XVIIIe s. #8581
  – maisons de campagne #8572
  – maisons de ferme (années 1910) #8554

- résidences d'artisans (1810-1819) #8616
- seigneuries #8611
- utilisation de la pierre, XVIIe-XIXe s. #7891
- villas, XIXe s. #8632
- XVIIe s.-années 1940 #7853
- XVIIe-XIXe s. #7852 7866 8505 8559 8579 8593 8596 8609 8623
- XVIIe-XVIIIe s. #2217 7655 7845 8602 8605 8606 8621
- XVIIIe s. #7861 7865
- XVIIIe-XIXe s. #8560 8561 8582
- Québec (Qué) #8631
  - maison d'un marchand, no 92 rue Saint-Pierre #8563
  - maison Fornel #7953
  - palais de l'intendant #8553
  - place Royale #8588 8589
  - place Royale. Maison Hazeur #8626
  - XVIIe-XIXe s. #7941
- Regina (Sask)
  - (1909) #8109
  - (années 1910) #8687
- région de Summerside (IPE), Green Park #8540
- Repentigny (Qué) #7888
- résidences d'architectes
  - (années 1950) #9299
- résidences de médecins, Ontario, XIXe s. #8675
- résidences estivales, XXe s. #8524
- résidences officielles
  - (avant 1867) #8754
  - Colombie-Britannique (1849-1871) #8757
  - Halifax (NE), Government House #8750
  - Montréal (Qué), château de Ramezay #3076 3077 8566
  - Niagara-on-the-Lake (Ont), Navy Hall #8464 8465
  - Ottawa (Ont)
    - Earnscliffe #8652
    - Rideau Hall #8755 8756
  - St. John's (TN) #8751 8752
  - Toronto (Ont)
    - Chorley Park #8749
    - Government House (1866) #8753
    - Government House (1911) #8748
- Saanich Peninsula (CB), Miraloma #8731
- Saint-Jean (NB), maison Gregory #8545
- Saint-Jean (TN) #8542
- Saint-Thomas de Montmagny (Qué), maison Bernatchez #8630
- Sainte-Foy (Qué), XVIIIe s. #8627
- Sandwich (Ont), Banwell House #7685
- Saskatchewan, habitations temporaires de colons, fin XIXe-début XXe s. #8696
- Sillery (Qué), Maison des jésuites #8571
- St. Catharines (Ont), (années 1920) #8645
- St. John's (TN)
  - (avant 1900) #7786
  - Commissariat House #8538
- Toronto (Ont)
  - (1791-1882) #8676
  - (1920), Harold R. Watson #8643
  - (années 1910) #8639 8641
  - (années 1970), rénovation de secteurs

résidentiels en milieu urbain #8068
  - Casa Loma #8649
  - Flemingdon Park #8370 8657
  - Harbour City #8062
  - Holwood Mansion #8667
  - résidence du juge en chef Sir William Campbell #8661
  - The Grange #8637 8665 8666
  - Thom Partnership #8412
  - XIXe-début XXe s. #8077
  - XIXe s.-années 1930 #8076
- tradition irlandaise, XIXe s. #8523
- Trinity Bay (TN) #7785 7791 8541
- Trois-Rivières (Qué)
  - (années 1630-1910) #7883
  - maison Deschenaux dite manoir de Tonnancour #8633
- Trois-Rivières (Qué), Forges du Saint-Maurice #8634 9250 9254
- Tunis Snook Farm (près de Kingston, Ont) #8681
- Vancouver (CB)
  - (1886-1929) #8714 8730
  - (1950-1960) #8697
  - (années 1950) #1992
  - Erickson, Arthur Charles #8357 8361
  - False Creek #8169
  - Hodson Manor #8707
  - proposition, réhabilitation des édifices du centre-ville (1980) #8725
  - résidence de B.C. Binning #8694
  - Thom, Ron #8411
- Verchères (Qué) #8635
- Victoria (CB) #8722
  - résidence d'Alexis Martin #8682
- Village Jacques de Chambly (Qué) #8573
- Wartime Housing Limited, Seconde Guerre mondiale #8506
- Whitby (Ont), Lynde House #8668
- Windsor (NE), maison Shand #8546
- Winnipeg (Man) #8096 8105
  - (1831-1960) #8095
  - (années 1880-1910) #8101
  - (années 1910) #8688
  - Dalnavert #8708
  - Rugh, Herbert Bell #8683
  - Seven Oaks House (maintenant Seven Oaks Museum) #8703
  - XIXe s. #8702
- Wolfville (NE) #8533
- XIXe s. #7974
- XIXe s.-années 1960 #8515
- XVIIe-début XIXe s. #7841
- XVIIe s.-années 1960 #7689
- XVIIe-XIXe s. #7687
- XVIIe-XVIIIe s. #8586
architecture domestique . Cris de l'Est
- huttes en tourbe #3609
architecture domestique . Etats-Unis
- (1745-1845), influence sur architecture domestique canadienne #8522
- (1908), architecture domestique hispano-américaine, influence sur architecture domestique canadienne #8638
- (années 1910), bungalows californiens, influence sur architecture résidentielle

(bungalows), Colombie-Britannique #8685
- (années 1950) #8509
- architecture géorgienne #8498
- résidences estivales, XXe s. #8524
- XVIIe-XVIIIe s., influence sur architecture de la Nouvelle-Ecosse #7823
- XVIIIe-XIXe s., influence sur architecture domestique québécoise #8592
- XXe s., influence sur architecture domestique québécoise #8591
architecture domestique . France
- XVIIe-XVIIIe s., influence sur architecture domestique québécoise #8581 8592 8602
- XVIIIe s., influence sur architecture domestique, île d'Orléans (Qué) #8613
architecture domestique . Grande-Bretagne
- (1900-1930), cottages et maisons de ferme, style Tudor, influence sur architecture résidentielle, Vancouver (CB) #8730
- (années 1950) #8509
- maisons de campagne, influence sur habitation canadienne (années 1910) #8490
- XIXe s., influence sur architecture canadienne, banques et maisons de campagne #9200
- XIXe s., influence sur architecture domestique, Ile-du-Prince-Edouard #8552
- XVIIIe-XIXe s., influence sur architecture domestique québécoise #8592
architecture domestique . Hurons #3519
architecture domestique . Inuit #7728
- (années 1950) #8184
- bois #7722
architecture domestique . Iroquois #3519
architecture domestique . Micmacs #3528
architecture domestique . Potéouatamis
- Parry Island Reservation (Ont) #3540
architecture domestique . Saulteux/Ojibwa
- Parry Island Reservation (Ont) #3540
architecture écossaise
- XIXe s., influence sur architecture manitobaine #8097
- XIXe s., influence sur architecture ontarienne #7977
architecture et droit
- voir droit, architecture et
architecture et Etat
- voir Etat, architecture et
architecture et photographie #7922
- édifices historiques canadiens #7688
- villes canadiennes (1850-1900) #7744
architecture et politique
- voir politique, architecture et
architecture et religion
- voir religion, architecture et
architecture et societé
- voir societé, architecture et
architecture et technologie
- voir technologie, architecture et
architecture fictive
- voir architecture dans l'art
architecture française
- (années 1930), influence sur architecture québécoise #1381
- architecture Second Empire, influence sur architecture canadienne #7741 7742

– influence sur architecture canadienne #7650 7652 7658
– influence sur architecture québécoise #7843 7892
– XIXe s., influence sur architecture québécoise #7850
– XVIIe-XIXe s., influence sur architecture canadienne #7661 7687
architecture géorgienne
– Canada #7661 7687 7696 8522
– Canada et Etats-Unis #8498
– Nouvelle-Ecosse #7839
– Ontario #7959 8648 8654 8677
– Perth (Ont), Matheson House (maintenant Perth Museum) #8670
– Saint-Jean (NB) #2490
– St. John's (TN), Commissariat House #8538
– Toronto (Ont) #5651 8060
    – The Grange #8637
– Whitby (Ont), Lynde House #8668
architecture grecque
– influence sur William Perehudoff #6837
architecture industrielle
– *voir aussi* brasseries; entrepôts; moulins; usines
architecture industrielle . Canada
– (1938-1942) #7666
– (1960-1970) #7710
– (années 1950) #9241
– Alberta (1900-années 1930) #8126
– Montréal (Qué)
    – (années 1950) #7900
    – dessins d'architecture, Archives nationales du Québec à Montréal #8604
– Nouvelle-Ecosse, XVIIe-XIXe s. #7814
– Ontario, XIXe s. #8006
– Québec (années 1960) #7862
– région du canal Rideau (Qué et Ont) #8019
– Winnipeg (Man) #8105
architecture japonaise
– influence sur Arthur Charles Erickson #8359
architecture marine
– *voir* architecture navale
architecture militaire
– *voir aussi* casernes; fortifications; tours Martello
architecture militaire . Canada
– (années 1950) #8414
– Halifax (NE) #7839
    – XVIIIe-XIXe s. #7818
– Niagara-on-the-Lake (Ont)
    – (1814-1837) #8470
    – (1838-1871) #8471
    – (1871-1978) #8472
– Québec
    – XVIIe-XIXe s. #7853
    – XVIIe-XVIIIe s. #1320 7845
    – XVIIIe s. #7861
– Québec (Qué) #7946
– Trois-Rivières (Qué), (années 1630-1910) #7883
architecture navale
– *voir aussi* bateaux
architecture navale . Canada

– Nouveau-Brunswick, XIXe s. #1190
– Nouvelle-Ecosse, XIXe s. #1201
– Québec, XIXe s. #1334 1335
architecture néo-baroque
– Québec, églises #7856 8821
architecture néo-classique
– Baillairgé, Thomas #8328
– Browne, George #8339
– Canada #7661
    – architecture domestique #7696
    – banques #9196
    – gares #9539
– Kahnawake (Qué), église Saint-François-Xavier #8890
– Kingston et comté de Frontenac (Ont) #8015
– Montréal (Qué) #1367
– Ontario #7983 8654
    – églises #8904
– Ottawa (Ont) #8036
– Québec
    – églises #8870
    – et Jérôme Demers #7874
    – villas #8632
– Québec (Qué) #7892 7943
– Toronto (Ont)
    – Bank of Toronto #9151
    – Banque de Montréal #9155
– Winnipeg (Man)
    – Banque de Nouvelle-Ecosse #9157
    – banques #9205
architecture néo-gothique
– architecture domestique
    – Canada #7696
    – Ontario #8677
– Battleford (Sask), Fort Battleford #8484
– Belleville (Ont), Institution for the Deaf and Dumb #8968
– Canada #7652 7668 7671 7724 7739 7740
– églises, Ontario #8904
– Fuller, Thomas #8366
– Harris, William Critchlow #8372
– Kingston et comté de Frontenac (Ont) #8015
– London (Ont), University of Western Ontario #9442
– Medley, Edward Shuttleworth #8776
– Montréal (Qué) #1367
    – église Notre-Dame #8828 8848
– Nouveau-Brunswick #7808
– Ottawa (Ont) #8036
    – édifices du Parlement #8921 8922 8925
– Regina (Sask), édifices du Parlement #8954
– Saint-Jean (NB), église en pierre #8778
– Saskatoon (Sask), University of Saskatchewan #9491
– St. Stephen (NB), Christ Church #8774
– Toronto (Ont)
    – Cathedral of Saint Alban the Martyr #8896
    – Church of Saint Paul's #8897 8902
    – University of Toronto
        – Hart House #9433 9438
        – Knox College #9435
    – Yorkville Town Hall #8997
architecture néo-grecque

– Ontario, églises #8904
architecture néo-romane
– Newlands, William #8392
– Nouveau-Brunswick #7808
– Toronto (Ont) #8064
    – Stewart Building #9354
    – University of Toronto. University College #9429 9453
architecture normande
– XVIIe-milieu XVIIIe s., influence sur architecture québécoise #7847
architecture palladienne
– villas, Québec, XIXe s. #8632
architecture paysagiste
– *voir aussi* conservation et restauration, architecture paysagiste; jardins; parcs
architecture paysagiste . Canada #7768
– Charlottetown (IPE), Province House #8937
– et architecture domestique (années 1930) #8501
– et écoles (années 1950) #9391
– Mawson, Thomas Hayton #8388 9405
– Montréal (Qué)
    – Expo 67 #9219 9222
    – parc du Mont-Royal #7903 7912 7924
– Niagara Parks (Ont) #7975
– Ottawa (Ont)
    – Earnscliffe #8652
    – édifices du Parlement #8048
– Victoria (CB), Crystal Gardens #9134 9146
– Winnipeg (Man) #8105
– XIXe s.-années 1950 #7677
architecture rurale
– *voir* bungalows; architecture domestique; bâtiments agricoles
architecture scandinave
– constructions en bois rond, influence sur architecture de la Colombie-Britannique #8148
architecture Second Empire
– Canada #7741 7742
    – architecture domestique #7696
    – gares #9539
architecture traditionnelle
– *voir* architecture vernaculaire
architecture vernaculaire . Canada
– architecture ukrainienne #8090 8127 8710 8713
– Colombie-Britannique, églises (1858-1925) #8916
– Ontario #8654
    – (avant 1867) #8904
– provinces maritimes (avant 1900) #8551
– Québec
    – (1880-1914) #7929
    – XVIIe-XIXe s. #8559
– Terre-Neuve #7782
    – cabane en rondins verticaux #8535
– Trinity Bay (TN) #7785 7791 8541
architecture vernaculaire . Grande-Bretagne
– XIXe s., influence sur architecture, Trinity Bay (TN) #7791
architecture victorienne
– Battleford (Sask), Fort Battleford #8484
– Canada #7652 7668 7769

– et style national #7697 7725
– gothique victorien #7739 7740
– Colombie-Britannique #8150
– Hamilton (Ont) #7991
– Montréal (Qué) #7918 7934 8620
– Ontario
  – architecture domestique #8677
  – églises #8905
– Ottawa (Ont) #8036
– Québec #7853
  – villas #8632
– Québec (Qué), fortifications #7946
– St.-John's (TN) #8542
– Toronto (Ont) #5651 8060
  – Yorkville Town Hall #8997
– Vancouver (CB), architecture domestique
  (1886-1929) #8730
– Winnipeg (Man), Dalnavert #8708
archives canadiennes
– Calgary (Alta), University of Calgary.
  Canadian Architectural Archives #7730
  7751
– collections de photographie #1029 1040
– Montréal (Qué), Centre canadien
  d'architecture #7749
– Ottawa (Ont), Archives publiques du
  Canada, archives d'architecture #7738
– Ottawa (Ont), collections privées, archives
  de l'architecture avant 1950 #8049
– Toronto (Ont), Archives publiques de
  l'Ontario. John Charles Batstone and Eric
  Crompton Horwood Collection of
  Architectural Drawings #8028 8030
arcs et flèches, Assiniboines #3693
arcs et flèches, autochtones #3328
arcs et flèches, Hurons #3519
arcs et flèches, Inuit #4316
arcs et flèches, Iroquois #3489 3519
Arctique
– architecture #7728 8185 8186 8187
– architecture domestique
  – (années 1960) #8732
  – (années 1970) #8733
– art
  – (années 1960) #441
– artefacts préhistoriques #4371 4373
– églises #8920
– vues
  – Angiju, Peter Nauja #4531
  – Back, George #241 242 4580
  – Banting, Frederick Grant #4600
  – Bouchard, Lorne Holland #4858
  – Bradford, Robert William #4898
  – Bruce, Robert Donald #4940
  – Constantineau, Fleurimond #5168
  – Cresswell, Samuel Gurney #258 259
  – Harris, Lawren Stewart #308 1779 5732
    5734
  – Haycock, Maurice Hall #5754
  – Hood, Robert #5825 5827
  – Jackson, A.Y. #1779 5907 5919
  – Kudluk, Thomassie #6105
  – McCarthy, Doris Jean #6461
  – McGrath, Judy #6474
  – Paterson, Robert Allen #6778
  – Richard, René-Jean #6997

– Shortt, Terence Michael #506
– Varley, Frederick Horsman #506 1779
  7461 7466 7467
– XVIIIe-XIXe s. #278
– vues photographiques
  – Mitchell, Thomas et George White #240
ARG
– voir Québec (Qué), Atelier de réalisations
  graphiques (ARG)
argent
– voir monnaie
Argosy, périodique can
– commentaire sur John A. Hammond,
  Owens Art Gallery, et Sackville (NB)
  #5699
Ariss, Herbert Joshua (Herb), artiste can,
  1918-
– expositions de groupe
  – (1965) #473
Ariss, Margot Phillips, artiste can, 1929-
– écriture dans l'art #4546
– expositions de groupe
  – (1965) #473
Arkell, Robin, artiste can, active années 1980
– illustrations #941
Arluk, George, sculpteur can, 1949-
– expositions
  – (1979) #4547
Armée du Salut
– et Ada Florence Kinton #6053
armes
– voir aussi armes à feu
armes . Amérindiens
– armes préhistoriques #3401
– ouvrages en coquillages #3388
armes . Athapascans #4104 4105
armes . Béothuks #3528
armes . Cris #3742
armes . Hurons #3519
armes . Indiens de la côte nord-ouest
– atlatl #3951
armes . Indiens des plaines
– sociétés secrètes #3727
armes . Micmacs #3528
armes . Netsilik #4363
armes . Potéouatamis
– Parry Island Reservation (Ont) #3540
armes . Saulteux/Ojibwa
– Parry Island Reservation (Ont) #3540
armes . Tahltans
– (années 1910) #4074
armes . Tsonnontouans
– masses d'armes #3535
armes à feu
– voir aussi armes
armes à feu . Canada
– guide pour collectionneurs #2104
– Québec, XVIIe-XIXe s. #2221
– XIXe s. #2099
armes à feu . Indiens des plaines
– étuis à fusils #3713
Armington, Caroline Helena, artiste can,
  1875-1939 #4548 4549
– femme de Franklin Milton Armington
  #4550
Armington, Franklin Milton, artiste can,

  1876-1941 #4548
– expositions
  – (1921) #4550
armoires canadiennes
– Ontario
  – (1780-1900) #2577
– Québec
  – XVIIe-XVIIIe s. #2525 2530 2531
armoiries
– voir héraldique; signes héraldiques
Armstrong, Beere & Hime, imprimerie
  (Toronto, Ont)
– catalogue de photographies, vues de
  Toronto (Ont) #7744
Armstrong, Geoffrey, artiste et architecte
  can, 1928- #4551
Armstrong, James G., artiste can, actif
  1879-1890
– expositions, critiques #1692
Armstrong, W.J., Ltd., fabricants de meubles
  (Guelph, Ont)
– (années 1920) #2547
Armstrong, William, artiste et ingénieur can,
  1822-1914 #4552
Armstrong, William Walton, artiste can,
  1916- #4553
Armstrong & Molesworth, agence can
  d'architecture
– Toronto (Ont), résidence Bruce #8746
Arn, Robert, artiste can, 1942-
– xérographie en couleurs #614
Arnasungnaaq, Barnabus, sculpteur can,
  1924- #4554
– expositions, critiques #4403 4408
Arnault, Jean-Marie, graveur de médailles fr
  au Canada, actif années 1830-1840
– médailles de tempérance #724
Arnold, J., artiste can, actif 1852
– expositions, critiques #1692
Arnoldi, Charles, horloger et joaillier can,
  1779-1817 #2663
Arnoldi, Johann Peter, orfèvre can,
  1769-1808 #2663
Arnoldi, Michael, orfèvre can, 1763-1807
  #2663
Arsenault, Réal, artiste can, 1931- #4555 4556
  4557
– à Paris (France) #1434
art
– voir aussi art abstrait; Art brut; art
  byzantin; art cinétique; art d'amateurs; art
  dans la rue; art enfantin; art fantastique;
  art minimal; art monumental; art oriental;
  art pré-colombien; art préhistorique; art
  primitif; art publicitaire; art traditionnel;
  art victorien; conservation et restauration;
  pop'art; renaissance . art
– (1905-1938), Canadian National Exhibition
  (Toronto, Ont) #107
– (années 1970) #696
  – nouvelle génération d'artistes #534
– art européen
  – Québec (Qué), communautés religieuses
    #1352
  – vues de l'Amérique, XVIe-XIXe s. #255
    256 260

– Calgary (Alta), Glenbow-Alberta Institute #3194
– Charlottetown (IPE), Confederation Centre Art Gallery and Museum #3070
– Cobourg (Ont), Art Gallery of Cobourg #3162
– début XXe s., Canadian National Exhibition (Toronto, Ont) #1
– et architecture
    – (1980) #8237
    – (années 1960) #8232 8236
    – Clerk, Pierre Jean, commentaire #5116
    – Iliu, Josef, commentaire #8229
    – Ottawa (Ont), Bibliothèque scientifique nationale #9049
– et photographie (années 1910) #982
– Guelph (Ont), University of Guelph #3173
– Halifax (NE), Mount Saint Vincent University #3072
– Hamilton (Ont), Art Gallery of Hamilton #3142 3160
– Joliette (Qué), Musée d'art de Joliette #3100 3101
– Kingston (Ont), Queen's University. Agnes Etherington Art Centre #3145
– London (Ont), London Public Library and Art Museum #3153
– Montréal (Qué)
    – église Notre-Dame. Musée #3081
    – Expo 67. Pavillon des beaux-arts #9223
    – galerie Dominion #1293
    – Musée des beaux-arts de Montréal #1343 3104 3112 3117 3118 9133
    – Université Concordia. Galeries d'art Sir George Williams #3096
– Oshawa (Ont), Robert McLaughlin Gallery #3169
– Ottawa (Ont)
    – Carleton University #3144
    – Galerie nationale du Canada #3061
– Québec (Qué)
    – Musée du Québec #3107 3111 3121
    – Université Laval #3080
– Saint-Laurent (Qué)
    – Collège de Saint-Laurent. Galerie Nova et Vetera #3089
– Saskatoon (Sask)
    – Mendel Art Gallery #72 3187
    – University of Saskatchewan #3202
– Toronto (Ont)
    – Art Gallery of Ontario #3136 3158
    – Royal Ontario Museum #3139 3141 3170
       – collection du Educational Museum of Upper Canada #3155
– Vancouver (CB)
    – Vancouver Art Gallery #3184 3185 3186
    – Vancouver Museum #3180
       – (1917) #3182
– Victoria (CB)
    – Art Gallery of Greater Victoria #3189
    – University of Victoria. Maltwood Art Museum and Gallery #3199
– Windsor (Ont), Art Gallery of Windsor #3156
– Winnipeg (Man), Winnipeg Art Gallery #3188 3192

– XIXe s., Art Association of Montreal (Montréal, Qué), exposition (1865) #1304
Art, Historical and Scientific Association of Vancouver (Vancouver, CB)
– (1894-1944) #1984
– (années 1910) #1979
Art, périodique can #560
art . Aléoutes
– Londres (Angleterre), British Museum #4360
– Sitka (Alaska), Sheldon Jackson Museum #3370
– XVIIIe s. #3445
art . Algonquiens #3385 3605 3621
– (1760-1860) #3434
– (1980) #4159
– (années 1970-1980) #4139
– arbre, mythes et symboles #3516
– écorce de bouleau #3571
– en comparaison avec art hopewell #3558
– motif de la double courbe #3403 3404 3409
– motif floral #3543
– Serpent Mound, Rice Lake (Ont) #3574
– Stuttgart (Allemagne de l'Ouest), Linden Museum #3737 3750
– XXe s. #4143 4150
art . Algonquins
– caractéristiques formelles #3601
art . Amérindiens #136 137 3351 3352 3354 3357 3359 3366 3395 3412 3418 3422 3427 3428 3442 3448 3452 3458 3467 4126 4127 4146 4692
– (1972-1974) #4138
– (1980) #4161
– (années 1960) #4125 4136
– (années 1970) #3376 4140 4155
– (années 1980) #4171
– (avant 1850) #3431
– Belfast (Irlande du Nord), Ulster Museum #3477
– Berlin (Allemagne de l'Ouest), Berliner Museum für Völkerkunde #3421 3423
– Berne (Suisse), Historisches Museum #3400 3473
– Calgary (Alta), Glenbow-Alberta Institute #3438
– Cincinnati (Ohio), Cincinnati Art Museum #3459
– collection Malaspina #3372
– collections italiennes #3396
– comté de Wentworth (Ont) #7954
– conservation #7767
– dans la décoration architecturale canadienne (années 1930) #8225
– Dresden (Allemagne de l'Est), Indianer Museum Radebeul #3430
– et chamanisme #3361 3383
– Exeter (Angleterre), Royal Albert Memorial Museum #3454
– influence sur sculpture, Colombie-Britannique (années 1970) #2066
– Londres (Angleterre), British Museum
    – Sloane, Sir Hans, collection #3397
– Montréal (Qué), Musée des beaux-arts de Montréal #3117 3118

– motif pointillé #3332 4325
– New York (NY), American Museum of Natural History #3414
– New York (NY), Museum of the American Indian. Heye Foundation #3437 3450
– Newark (NJ), Newark Museum #3425
– Offenbach (Allemagne de l'Ouest), Deutsches Ledermuseum #3464
– Oiseau-Tonnerre #3410
– Ottawa (Ont), Musée national de l'Homme #3408 3465 3466 3622
– protection juridique #3347
– serpents #3391
– symbolisme thérapeutique #3356
– Toronto (Ont), Royal Ontario Museum #3382
– Tulsa (Okla), Philbrook Art Center #4165
– Vienne (Autriche), Museum für Völkerkunde #3436
– Williamstown (Ont), Nor'westers Museum #3148
– XIXe s., émergence d'artistes reconnus #3486
– XXe s. #4163 4172
– Zurich (Suisse), Feldstrasse Secondary School #3455
art . Assiniboines
– motif floral #3731
art . Athapascans #3366 4104 4105
– Sitka (Alaska), Sheldon Jackson Museum #3370
– XVIIIe s. #3445
art . autochtones #3334 3335 3336 3342 3346 3349 3364 3369 3377 3381 3435 3463 3468
– (années 1980) #4170
– art préhistorique #3375
– Claremont (Calif), Claremont College #3378
– Copenhagen (Danemark), Nationalmuseet #3338
– Denver (Colo), Denver Art Museum #3479
– et chamanisme #3360
art . Bella-Coolas
– Ottawa (Ont), Musée national de l'Homme #4000
art . Béothuks
– lieux de sépulture, Port-au-Choix (TN) #3611
– Red Indian Lake (TN) #3623
– St. John's (TN), Newfoundland Museum #3627
art . Chukchis
– Moscou (URSS), Musée historique et artistique de Zagorsk #4302
– Sibérie (URSS)
    – (1900-1980) #4303
art . Cris
– (1830-1930) #3734
– motif floral #3731
art . Dakotas
– esprit protecteur, dessins #3650
– New York (NY), Brooklyn Museum #3705
– St. Paul (Minn), Science Museum of Minnesota #3755
art . Delawares #3506
art . Flancs-de-Chien #4089

art . Haidas #3946
– attributions #4169
– et Tom Price #6934
– influence sur Bill Reid #6986
– Montréal (Qué), Université McGill. Musée McCord #4011
– représentation de la lune #4059
– représentations de l'homme blanc #4070
– Washington (DC), Smithsonian Institution #3763
art . Hurons
– (1600-1760) #3579
art . Indiens d'Amérique centrale #3427 3435
– serpents #3391
art . Indiens de l'Amérique du Sud #3412 3427
art . Indiens de la côte nord-ouest #19 299 1995 3333 3342 3799 3809 3827 3854 3869 3871 3907 3911 3919 3921 3923 3928 3933 3942 3948 3950 3959 3969 3970 3989 3992 3998 4022 4034 4036 4043 4049 4055
– (1940-1943), BC Society for the Furtherance of Indian Arts and Crafts #4114
– (années 1960) #4117 4119 4121
– (années 1970) #4132 4145
– Anchorage (Alaska), Alaska International Art Institute #3987
– art préhistorique #3861 4039
– Berlin (Allemagne de l'Ouest), Royal Berlin Ethnological Museum #3762
– Carr, Emily, commentaire #5006
– collections californiennes #4041
– dédoublement de représentation #3905 3922
– Denver (Colo), Denver Art Museum #3918
– en comparaison avec art chinois #3843 3975
– et art précolombien #3810
– et Wilson Duff #4003
– influence sur art canadien #24
– influence sur Elford Bradley Cox #5202
– influence sur Jack Leonard Shadbolt #7184 7189 7191
– influence sur Margaret Peterson #6839
– influence sur Nancy-Lou Patterson #6783
– Kleinburg (Ont), McMichael Canadian Collection #3172
– Londres (Angleterre), British Museum #4062 4064
– New York (NY), American Museum of Natural History #3860 4024
– Portland (Oreg), Portland Art Museum #3875 3937
– recherche, méthodologie (années 1930-1970) #4060
– Reid, Bill, commentaire #6985
– représentation d'animaux #3770
– représentations de la femme #3348
– Seattle (Wash), Washington State University. Thomas Burke Museum. Sidney Gerber Memorial Collection #3974
– Sitka (Alaska), Sheldon Jackson Museum #3370
– sources asiatiques #3359
– Toronto (Ont), Royal Ontario Museum #4002

– Vancouver (CB), University of British Columbia. Museum of Anthropology #3994
– Victoria (CB), University of Victoria. Maltwood Art Museum and Gallery #3199
– XVIIIe s. #3445
– Vancouver, George, expédition #3767
art . Indiens des forêts du Nord-Est #3359
– (1760-1860) #3434
– (1980) #4159
– (années 1970-1980) #4139
– caractéristiques formelles #3639
– Kleinburg (Ont), McMichael Canadian Collection #3172
– XXe s. #4143 4150
art . Indiens des plaines #3359 3463 3691 3720 3725 3730
– (1760-1860) #3434
– Bismarck (ND), State Historical Society of North Dakota #3690
– bouclier, motif #3710
– Providence (RI), Brown University. Haffenreffer Museum of Anthropology #3751
– Stuttgart (Allemagne de l'Ouest), Linden Museum #3737 3750
art . Indiens du plateau #3774
art . Inuit #25 136 137 3351 3352 3354 3357 3366 3374 3377 4179 4181 4182 4188 4190 4216 4223 4231 4238 4254 4255 4278 4295 4317 4338 4368
– (années 1950-1970) #4246
– (années 1960) #4193 4204
– (années 1970) #3376 4247 4256 4263
– artisanes #4258
– Alaska #4208 4280
– art fantastique #4240
– art préhistorique #3380 4339
– Cambridge (Mass), Harvard University. Peabody Museum #4191
– Cape Dorset (TNO)
– (années 1960) #4187
– Levine, Les, commentaire #6270 6271
– Churchill (Man), Eskimo Museum #4227 4313
– collection Malaspina #3372
– concept d'espace #4341
– concept d'espace et de temps #4244
– dans églises et édifices publics, Arctique #4304
– déesse de la mer #4312 4376
– et chamanisme #4243 4283
– et esthétique #4282 4297
– et James Archibald Houston #4449 4452 5846 5847
– et société #4232
– fin XVIIIe s.-années 1940 #4286
– Frobisher Bay (TNO), The Museum of Things from the Land #4224
– Groenland #4206 4315
– Guilde canadienne des métiers d'art (Québec) #4292 4293
– influence européenne #4176
– influence sociale et influence économique #4215 4245 4277
– influence sur Art Price #6930

– influence sur K.J. Butler #4982
– Kleinburg (Ont), McMichael Canadian Collection #3172
– Londres (Angleterre)
– British Museum #4360
– collections de musées #4289
– Montréal (Qué), Musée des beaux-arts de Montréal #3117 3118
– Moscou (URSS), Musée historique et artistique de Zagorsk #4302
– motif pointillé #3332 4325
– murales #4253
– Baker Lake (TNO) #4230 4266
– Pangnirtung (TNO) #4237
– nalunaikutanga #4264
– Offenbach (Allemagne de l'Ouest), Deutsches Ledermuseum #3464
– Oxford (Angleterre), Oxford University. Pitt Rivers Museum #4369
– périodiques
– About Arts and Crafts/L'Art et l'artisanat #4269
– Arts and Culture of the North #4270
– Povungnituk (Qué) #4274
– Producteurs de l'Arctique canadien #4222 4291
– protection juridique #3347
– Québec #4296
– recherche, méthodologie #4225
– Rochester (NY), Rochester Museum #4424
– Sitka (Alaska), Sheldon Jackson Museum #3370
– sources biographiques #4252 4301
– Pelly Bay (TNO) #4221
– Southampton Island (TNO), (années 1950) #4184
– style animalier eurasien #4334
– Winnipeg (Man), Winnipeg Art Gallery #3188 4284 4306
art . Iroquois #3559 3566 3605
– (1760-1860) #3434
– (1980) #4159
– (années 1970-1980) #4139
– Albany (NY), New York State Museum #3586
– arbre, mythes et symboles #3516
– caractéristiques formelles #3601 3639
– cérémonie du Milieu de l'Hiver #3606
– Rochester (NY), Rochester Museum #3590
– XXe s. #4143 4150 4164
art . Kwakiutls #3935 4037
– Ottawa (Ont), Musée national de l'Homme #3060
– Vancouver (CB), University of British Columbia. Museum of Anthropology #3996
art . Malécites
– Saint-Jean (NB), Musée du Nouveau-Brunswick #3634
art . Maoris
– figure à la langue pendante et motifs connexes #3934
art . Métis
– motif floral #3731
art . Micmacs
– Saint-Jean (NB), Musée du

Nouveau-Brunswick #3634
art . Mistassins #4080 4100
art . Montagnais #3409 4082
art . Naskapis #3409 3554 4082 4149
art . Nootkas #3908 4025
art . Outaouais
– (1600-1760) #3579
art . périodiques
– (années 1950-1960), influence sur peinture
  torontoise #1773
art . périodiques . Canada #3313
– (années 1970) #707 3310
  – et critique d'art #3308
– *Annales d'histoire de l'art canadien/Journal of
  Canadian Art History* #111
– *Arcadia: A Journal devoted exclusively to
  Music, Art and Literature* #179
– *Archaeological Report* #3329
– *Artisan* #2133
– *Artisan, L'/Craftsman, The* #2113
– *Artists Review* #1815
– *Artmagazine* #560
– *Arts Bulletin* #551
– *Arts West* #1868
– *ArtsAtlantic* #128
– *Artscanada* #25
– *ArtViews* #1806
– *Ateliers* #1493
– *Canada Crafts* #2126
– *Canadian Antiques and Art Review* #141
– *Canadian Collector* #74
– *Canadian Design/Design canadien* #2625
– *Canadian Museums Association. Gazette*
  #3042
– *Canadian Review of Music and Art* #357
– *CAR/FAC News* #625
– *Collectionneur, Le* #134
– *Communiqué* #542
– *Craft Dimensions Artisanales* #2116
– *Creative Source* #912
– *Criteria* #564
– *Culture vivante* #1257
– *File* #544
– *Fuse: The Cultural News Magazine* #603
– *Galerie nationale du Canada. Bulletin
  annuel/National Gallery of Canada. Annual
  Bulletin* #69
– *Highlights, Quarterly Newsletter of the
  Alberta Society of Artists* #1944
– *Impulse* #538
– *Lamps* #1667
– *M* #3097
– *Maritime Art* #349
– *Only Paper Today* #1799
– *Ontario Craft* #2257
– *Parachute* #593
– *Parallelogramme* #612
– *RACAR (Revue d'art canadienne/Canadian
  Art Review)* #114
– *Vanguard* #547
– *Vie des arts* #55
art . périodiques . Inuit
– *About Arts and Crafts/L'Art et l'artisanat*
  #4269
– *Arts and Culture of the North* #4270
art . Pieds-Noirs

– monstre marin, thème décoratif #3757
– ours, motif #3746
art . Piégans
– fin XIXe-début XXe s., Glenbow-Alberta
  Institute (Calgary, Alta) #3759
art . Potéouatamis
– (1600-1760) #3579
art . Sarcis
– ours, motif #3746
art . Saulteux/Ojibwa #3539 3557 3610 4089
– (1600-1760) #3579
– (années 1930) #4112
– dessins, motifs #3560
– St. Paul (Minn), Science Museum of
  Minnesota #3755
– XXe s. #4173
art . Siouens #3725
– (1760-1860) #3434
– Boston (Mass), Harvard University.
  Peabody Museum #3649
– motif floral #3731
– Stuttgart (Allemagne de l'Ouest), Linden
  Museum #3737 3750
art . Slaveys #4089
art . Tagish #4106
art . Tahltans
– (années 1910) #4074
art . Tanainas #4085
art . Têtes-de-Boule #4079
art . théorie et critique
– *voir aussi* esthétique
– art non figuratif (années 1950) #421
– Barbeau, Charles Marius #3309
– Bates, Maxwell Bennett #405 4621
– Bellot, Dom #8333
– Bloore, Ronald Langley #4748
– Borduas, Paul-Emile #4799 4803 4839
  – *Projections libérantes*, réaction de la
    presse #4819
  – *Refus global* et *Projections libérantes*,
    réaction de la presse #1452
– Bourassa, Napoléon #4869 4871
– Bourbeau, Géraldine #4877
– Brooker, Bertram Richard #330 4927
– Brymner, William #4947
– Buchanan, Donald William #3325
– Bush, Jack Hamilton #4975
– Caiserman-Roth, Ghitta #4989
– Canada
  – (1907) #3299
  – (1980) #3315 3316
  – (années 1890) #1705
  – (années 1910) #3300
  – (années 1920) #1231
  – (années 1920-1940), *Canadian Forum*
    #3301
  – (années 1940) #380 3302 3304
  – (années 1960) #87
  – (années 1970) #598 620 3308 3312 6747
    – catalogues d'expositions #3311
    – revues d'art canadiennes #3310
– Carr, Emily #5030 5032
– catalogues d'expositions #3319
– Colville, Alex #5140
– Comfort, Charles Fraser #5157
– Coombs, Edith Grace #5172

– Cosgrove, Stanley Morel #3307
– Crawford, Lenore #112
– Frenkel, Vera #5522 5523
– Groupe des Sept #1739 1744
– Harper, John Russell #3317
– Harris, Lawren Stewart #5714 5721 5722
  5724 5725 5726 5729
– Hodgson, Tom #5814
– Hofmann, Hans #1850
– impressionnisme (1881) #169
– Laliberté, Alfred #6145
– Leduc, Ozias #6211
– Levine, Les #6260
– Lindsay, Jim #6291
– Lyman, John Goodwin #6343 6346 6347
– Martin, Thomas Mower #6437
– Milne, David Brown #6548 6556
– Molinari, Guido #6586 6587
– Montréal (Qué), (années 1940-1950) #1426
– Morisset, Gérard #3305 3321 3324 3326
– Morrice, James Wilson, réaction de la
  presse (1886-1916) #6634
– Peterson, Margaret #6839
– Plamondon, Antoine-Sébastien #1348
– Plaskett, Joe #6889 6891
– Québec #1255 7117
  – (1920-1945) #1456
– Reid, George Agnew #6973
– Repentigny, Rodolphe de #1465 3318
– Rockman, Arnold #7061
– Shadbolt, Jack Leonard #7181 7185 7186
  7188 7192
– Swinton, George #7305
– Tonnancour, Jacques Godefroy de #385
  7381
– Vaillancourt, Armand #7452
– Villeneuve, Arthur #7492
– Wertheimer, Esther #7542
art . Thompsons #3774
art . Tlingits #3946
– motif de pieuvre #4045
– musées russes, collections #3947 3978
– Washington (DC), Smithsonian Institution
  #3763
art . Tsimshians #3926
– représentation de la lune #4059
– Washington (DC), Smithsonian Institution
  #3763
art . Tutchonis #4106
art abstrait
– *voir aussi* abstraction géométrique;
  modernisme
– Association des artistes non figuratifs de
  Montréal #1415 1469
– Borduas, Paul-Emile, commentaire #4803
– Canada #498
  – (années 1930) #338
  – (années 1940) #151
  – (années 1950) #416 417
– Colombie-Britannique (années 1950) #1990
– et art canadien (années 1950) #422
– et Painters Eleven #1785
– Harris, Lawren Stewart, commentaire
  #5714 5721 5723 5724 5725
– Masson, Henri L., commentaire #6444
– Montréal (Qué), (années 1940) #1395

– Prairies (années 1960) #1848 1862
– Québec
– (années 1940) #1468
– (années 1950) #1414
– (années 1950-1960) #1441
– (années 1970) #1544
– Taçon, Edna Jeanette, commentaire #7310
– Toronto (Ont)
– (1953-1965) #1772 1773
art africain
– en comparaison avec art inuit #4225
art américain
– (1870-1910), en comparaison avec art canadien #196
– (1950-1970), influence sur art canadien #98
– (années 1910), en comparaison avec art canadien #203
– (années 1950), en comparaison avec art canadien #397
– (années 1960), influence sur art canadien #515 519
– (années 1970), influence sur art des provinces de l'Ouest #1857
– (années 1970), influence sur art torontois #1796
– Los Angeles (Calif), en comparaison avec art, Vancouver (CB) #2035
– New York (années 1980), en comparaison avec art torontois #1837
– XVIIIe-XIXe s., influence sur art de la Nouvelle-Ecosse #1220 1222
art arabe
– voir art islamique
Art Association of Montreal
– voir Montréal (Qué), Art Association of Montreal
Art Association of Newfoundland and Labrador
– (1967-1979) #1144
Art Association of Ottawa (Ottawa, Ont)
– (années 1890) #188
Art Association of Vancouver (Vancouver, CB)
– (1889-1894) #1981
art au laser
– holographie au laser, Jerry Pethick #6840
art australien
– (1888) #175
– (1890) #177
– en comparaison avec art canadien #44
art britannique
– (1928), Canadian National Exhibition (Toronto, Ont) #300
– (1929), Canadian National Exhibition (Toronto, Ont) #304
– scènes de guerre #1082 1084
– XVIIIe-XIXe s., influence sur art de la Nouvelle-Ecosse #1215 1220 1222
Art brut
– voir aussi art d'amateurs
– et Francine Simonin #7213
art byzantin
– influence sur icônes et fresques, Church of Saint Nicholas (Toronto, Ont) #1822
– influence sur John Bernard Boyle #4894
art canadien #5 19 24 29 30 45 58 59 63 79 80

85 369
– (1564-1867) #233
– (1760-1943) #31
– (1815-1965) #122
– (1820-1940) #28
– (1867-1930) #13
– (1879-1961), Canadian National Exhibition (Toronto, Ont) #1
– (1880-années 1930) #20
– (1890-1900) #190
– (1901), Pan-American Exposition (Buffalo, NY) #189
– (1907), critique #3299
– (1909) #194
– (1924), British Empire Exhibition (Wembley, Angleterre) #287 288 291 458 5546 5547
– (1925), British Empire Exhibition (Wembley, Angleterre) #290 291 292
– (1926-1933) #294
– (1928), Canadian National Exhibition (Toronto, Ont) #300
– (1928-1929) #307
– (1929), Canadian National Exhibition (Toronto, Ont) #304
– (1930-1980) #151
– (1935) #333
– (1938-1939) #345
– (1938-1948) #379
– (1939), Exposition universelle (New York, NY) #346
– (1950-1960) #511
– (1950-1970) #98
– (1952), Biennale de Venise (Venise, Italie) #399
– (1958), Exposition universelle et internationale (Bruxelles, Belgique) #428 430
– (1967) #488
– (1968-1970) #1481
– (1975), prédictions #585
– (1975-1976) #627 645
– (1980) #690 691 699
– 11e Biennale de Paris (Paris, France) #687
– (années 1840-1920) #4
– (années 1850) #1692
– (années 1860) #1302
– (années 1870-1910) #196 200
– (années 1880) #175
– (années 1880-1920) #10
– (années 1890) #177 188
– (années 1890), recommandations aux artistes canadiens #182
– (années 1910) #203 1713
– (années 1910-1960) #494
– (années 1920) #288 289 298 299
– (années 1920-1930) #322
– (années 1920-1940), Canadian Forum #3301
– (années 1920-1960) #461
– (années 1930) #22 339 340
– (années 1930-1940) #395
– (années 1940) #363 380 381 385 3250 5866
– et Galerie nationale du Canada (Ottawa, Ont) #3027
– (années 1940-1960) #451 485 536

– artistes d'origine étrangère #465
– (années 1940-1970) #571
– (années 1950) #387 388 389 406 415 420 429 432 433 439
– en comparaison avec art américain #397
– (années 1950-1960) #455
– (années 1950-1970) #54 131 6586
– (années 1960) #87 441 443 456 469 477 478 480 481 490 493 514 515 518 519 529
– artistes new-yorkais #460
– conservation #527
– (années 1960-1970) #3274
– (années 1970) #531 552 555 558 594 610 619 621 637 680 696 702 703 707
– artistes de moins de 30 ans #584
– commentaires d'artistes #648
– Est du Canada #543
– galerie Marlborough Godard, Toronto (Ont) et Montréal (Qué) #572
– oeuvres de grand format #644
– sauf Ontario #569
– (années 1980) #912
– Académie royale des arts du Canada #2 16 152 153 157 162 166 168 171 181 184 186 195 202 210 280 283 296 303 310 312 318 323 325 326 328 329 361 366 434 474 500 686
– Acadie #1137 1181
– (années 1960-1980) #1136
– Alberta #1947 1953 1967 1972
– (1980) #1969
– (1981) #1974
– (années 1920-1980) #1941
– (années 1930-1940) #1943
– (années 1950) #1946
– (années 1970) #1963
– Edmonton (Alta), Alberta Art Foundation #1957
– périodiques
– Highlights, Quarterly Newsletter of the Alberta Society of Artists #1944
– Alberta Society of Artists #1942
– Art Association of Newfoundland and Labrador #1144
– art estonien #118 1761
– Art in Living Group (Vancouver, CB) #1988
– art letton #49 475
– art ukrainien #1843
– artistes canadiens d'origine polonaise #149 642
– artistes juifs #435
– Arts and Letters Club (Toronto, Ont) #1671
– Arts Club of Montreal (Montréal, Qué) #1254
– automatistes #1443
– avant-garde (années 1960) #600
– aviation, thèmes #147
– Banff (Alta) #1964
– Banque de Nouvelle-Ecosse, collection d'oeuvres d'art #3245
– Boucherville (Qué), église de la Sainte-Famille #8868
– British Columbia Society of Artists #1978
– Calgary (Alta)

– (années 1970) #1966
– Glenbow-Alberta Institute #3191 3194
– Canada, musées et galeries d'art, collections #3320
– Canadian Art Club (Toronto, Ont) #193 204 211
– Cantons de l'Est (Qué)
  – (années 1970) #1282 1535
  – Regroupement des artistes des Cantons de l'Est (RACE) #1539
– Charlottetown (IPE), Confederation Centre Art Gallery and Museum #3070
– Châteauguay (Qué), église Saint-Joachim #8861
– Chicoutimi (Qué), Université du Québec (années 1970) #3016
– Cobourg (Ont), Art Gallery of Cobourg #3162
– Colombie-Britannique #1986 1987 1995 2010 3827
  – (1793-1886) #2025
  – (1932-1968) #1983
  – (1981) #2084
  – (années 1910) #1979
  – (années 1930) #1982
  – (années 1950) #1994
  – (années 1950-1970) #2013
  – (années 1970) #2047 2050 2053 2060 2063 2067 2068 2078
    – région de l'Okanagan #2048
  – (années 1970-1980) #2082
  – femmes artistes (années 1970) #2054
– comté de Bellechasse (Qué) #1281
– Création (Montréal, Qué) #1492
– Duncan, Douglas M., collection #119 3218 3232
– Edmonton (Alta)
  – (années 1960-1980) #1975
  – collections privées #105
  – University of Alberta #3200
– Emma Lake (Sask), Emma Lake Workshops #1921 1923
– en comparaison avec art australien #44
– entreprises, collections #3243 3259 3291
– Essex County Artists #1668
– et architecture (années 1960) #753 8231 8235
– et art abstrait (années 1950) #422
– et Arthur Lismer #6292 6293 6297 6300
– et collectionneurs (années 1960) #3219
– et histoire canadienne, John Bernard Boyle, commentaire #4893
– et identité canadienne #327
– et John Russell Harper #3317
– et Lenore Crawford #112
– et mode (1882-1910) #2897
– et nationalisme #102 143
– et photographie (années 1970) #635
– Expo 67 #483
– Fédération des artistes canadiens #360 364 376
– femmes artistes #95 96
  – (années 1910) #207
  – (années 1940) #377
  – (années 1960-1970) #677
  – (années 1960-1980) #717

– (années 1970) #579 591 659 675 698 1877
  – Montréal (Qué), galerie Powerhouse #1557
– Fredericton (NB)
  – collections privées #142
  – XIXe s. #1174
– Fredericton Art Club (Fredericton, NB) #1176
– Fusion des arts (Montréal, Qué) #1482
– General Idea #5583 5584
– Groupe des Sept #375 1732 1780 1790
– Guelph (Ont)
  – (années 1850-1970) #1685
  – University of Guelph #3173
– guerre, images, thèmes #1082 1084 1088 1094 1098 1116 1117
  – Ottawa (Ont), Musée canadien de la guerre #1106
– guide pour collectionneurs #2104
– Halifax (NE)
  – (1749-1949) #1195
  – (1980) #1227
  – (années 1830) #1226
  – Mount Saint Vincent University #3072
– Hamilton (Ont) #1674 7978
  – Art Gallery of Hamilton #3138 3142 3160
    – exposition annuelle (1948-) #38
  – Women's Art Association of Hamilton #1701
– Hampton Group (Hampton, NB) #1177
– île d'Orléans (Qué) #1238
– Ile-du-Prince-Edouard #1164 1166
  – (années 1970) #1165
  – femmes artistes (années 1970) #1168
– Imperial Oil Ltd. #3241
– Independent Art Association #1379
– inventaire informatisé, normes pour oeuvres d'art #159
– Island Arts and Crafts Society (Victoria, CB) #2034
– Joliette (Qué), Musée d'art de Joliette #3100 3101
– Kingston (Ont), Queen's University. Agnes Etherington Art Centre #3145
– Kleinburg (Ont), McMichael Canadian Collection #3172
– Labor Arts Guild (Vancouver, CB) #1985
– Limners (Victoria, CB) #2043
– Loeb, M. et Mme. Jules, collection #3231
– London (Ont)
  – (1947-1979) #1828
  – (années 1960) #1759 1791
  – fin XIXe s. #1726
  – London Public Library and Art Museum #3153
– Manitoba #1895 1896
  – (1964-1978), Red River Exhibition #1903
  – (1980) #1906
  – (années 1970) #1899 1900
– McLean, James Stanley, collection #3210 3226
– Millen, Walter H., collection #21
– Montréal (Qué)
  – (1922-1935) #2972
  – (1950), expositions #1400

– (1968-1969) #1514
– (années 1840) #1301
– (années 1910) #1317
– (années 1940-1960) #1437
– (années 1960) #1430 1479 1480 1484
– (années 1970) #1489 1495 1504 1541 1555
– Art Association of Montreal #1246 1308 1310 1316
– château de Ramezay #3076 3077 3083
– Ecole des beaux-arts (1925-1932) #2973
– église Notre-Dame #8849 8892
– hôtel Reine-Elizabeth #8228
– Musée d'art contemporain #3086 3091 3093 3094
– Musée des beaux-arts de Montréal #3104 3112 3113 3114 3117 3118
  – Bronfman, Saidye et Samuel, collection #526 3087
– Place des Arts #8233 9092 9093 9096
– *Salon de printemps*
  – (1880-1965) #1228
  – (1895) #1311
  – (1908-1965) #1261
  – (1964) #1423
– Société d'électrolyse et de chimie Alcan Ltée (Sécal), collection #3246
– stations de métro #1531
– Université Concordia. Galerie d'art Sir George Williams #3096
– Université McGill. Musée McCord #1366
– Véhicule Art #1503
– XVIIe-XVIIIe s. #1325
– New York (NY), 49e Parallèle #712
– Newfoundland Society of Art #1141
– Niagara (Ont), (années 1970) #1795
– Nouveau-Brunswick #1183
  – XXe s. #1182
– Nouvelle-Ecosse #1191 1202
  – (1749-1848) #1215 1220 1222 1224 1225
  – (1900-1945) #1194
  – (années 1970) #1208
  – femmes artistes
    – (1850-1950) #1204
    – (années 1830-1840) #1219
    – (années 1970) #1205
– Nova Scotia Talent Trust #1199
– Nova Scotia Society of Artists #1192
– oeuvres de l'imaginaire #530
– Ontario #8943
  – (1881), Art Union #1698
  – (1979-1981), Nord de l'Ontario #1829
  – (1981) #1838
  – (années 1850) #1691
  – (années 1940-1970) #1670
  – (années 1970) #590 1814 1816 1825
  – Government of Ontario Art Collection (1873-1914) #1728
  – Ontario, francophones (années 1970) #1820 1821
  – périodiques
    – *Art Views* #1806
– Ontario et Québec (années 1960) #492
– Ontario Society of Artists #1666 1672 1679 1693 1695 1697 1700 1703 1707 1708 1709 1710 1731 1748
– Oshawa (Ont), Robert McLaughlin Gallery

#3169
- Ottawa (Ont)
  - Association médicale canadienne, siège
    social #138
  - Bibliothèque scientifique nationale #9049
  - Carleton University #3144
  - Centre national des arts #9104 9105 9108
  - Conseil des Arts du Canada #90 3266
  - Conseil des Arts du Canada. Banque
    d'oeuvres d'art #576 3276
  - Galerie nationale du Canada #3044
    - Duncan, Douglas M., collection, et
      legs Milne-Duncan #541
- Owen Sound (Ont), Tom Thomson
  Memorial Gallery and Museum of Fine
  Art #3146
- Paris (France), Centre culturel canadien
  #537 647
- Pen and Pencil Club (Montréal, Qué)
  #1251
- périodiques
  - Annales d'histoire de l'art canadien/Journal
    of Canadian Art History #111
  - Arcadia: A Journal devoted exclusively to
    Music, Art and Literature #179
  - Artisan, L'/Craftsman, The #2113
  - Artists Review #1815
  - Artmagazine #560
  - Arts Bulletin #551
  - Arts West #1868
  - Artscanada #25
  - Ateliers #1493
  - Canadian Collector #74
  - Canadian Museums Association. Gazette
    #3042
  - Canadian Review of Music and Art #357
  - CAR/FAC News #625
  - Collectionneur, Le #134
  - Communiqué #542
  - Criteria #564
  - Culture vivante #1257
  - Fuse: The Cultural News Magazine #603
  - Galerie nationale du Canada. Bulletin
    annuel/National Gallery of Canada. Annual
    Bulletin #69
  - Lamps #1667
  - M #3097
  - Maritime Art #349
  - Only Paper Today #1799
  - Parachute #593
  - Parallelogramme #612
  - RACAR (Revue d'art canadienne/Canadian
    Art Review) #114
  - Vanguard #547
  - Vie des arts #55
- Peterborough (Ont), Artspace #1836
- Picture Loan Society (Toronto, Ont) #1746
- Prairies
  - (années 1950-1970) #1884
  - (années 1960) #1848 1851
  - (années 1960-1970) #1862
  - (années 1970) #1860 1880
  - femmes artistes (années 1970) #1867
- provinces de l'Atlantique #1123
  - (années 1960) #1124
  - (années 1960-1970) #1130

  - (années 1970) #1127 1131 1132 1133 1135
  - Atlantic Provinces Art Circuit
    (1964-1971) #3053
  - périodiques
    - ArtsAtlantic #128
- provinces de l'Ouest
  - (années 1970) #1857 1866 1869 1870 1871
    1883
  - influence de Hans Hofmann #1850
- provinces maritimes #1119
  - (1959-1965) #1120
  - (années 1930-1960) #1125
  - (années 1950) #1172
  - (années 1960) #1122 1126
  - XVIIIe-XIXe s. #7780
- Québec #1233 1234 1237 1239 1271 1294
  1444
  - (1520-1880) #216
  - (1613-1870) #1330 1331
  - (1825-1850) #1368
  - (1900-1934) #8334
  - (1925-1950) #1405
  - (1962-1972) #1500 1502
  - (1963-1980) #1564
  - (1966-1976) #1527
  - (1970-1975) #1515
  - (1975) #1518
  - (1977) #1532
  - (années 1930-1970) #1299
  - (années 1940) #1383 1386 1387
  - (années 1940-1960) #1462
  - (années 1940-1970) #1269 1473 1521
  - (années 1950) #425
  - (années 1960) #1487
  - (années 1960-1970) #1496
  - (années 1970) #1486 1488 1490 1491 1506
    1508 1509 1511 1517 1525 1526 1528
    1545 3115
    - artistes de moins de 35 ans #1501
  - centres culturels #3088
  - Corbeil, Maurice et Andrée, collection
    #3233
  - et femmes (années 1930-1970) #1273
  - et Gérard Morisset #3305
  - femmes artistes (années 1930) #1380
  - illustrations de légendes populaires
    #1290
  - images du diable, XVIIe s.-1840 #1357
  - ministère des Affaires culturelles du
    Québec. Service de l'Inventaire des
    biens culturels #1277
  - ministère des Travaux publics et de
    l'Approvisionnement #1561
  - thème de la rébellion (1759-1914) #1351
  - utilisation du plastique (années 1960)
    #1442
  - XIXe s.-années 1920 #1231
  - XIXe s.-années 1940 #1242
  - XVIIe s. #228 229 1365
  - XVIIe s.-1967 #1260
  - XVIIe s.-années 1930 #1235 2169 2171
  - XVIIe-XIXe s. #1245 1305 1332 1334 1335
    1341 1347 1581
  - XVIIIe-début XXe s. #1339
  - XVIIIe s. #234 235 269 270
  - XVIIIe s.-années 1820 #1300

  - XXe s. #1391
- Québec (Qué) #1399
  - Assemblée nationale #8942
  - église Notre-Dame de Québec #8791
  - Musée du Québec #3085 3092 3095 3107
    3111 3121 3122
  - Séminaire de Québec #8842
  - Université Laval #3080
  - XVIIe-XIXe s. #1306 1309
- réalisme #694
  - (années 1970) #606
- Regina (Sask)
  - (années 1950) #6284
  - University of Regina. Norman
    Mackenzie Art Gallery #3197
- région de Durham (Ont), (années 1970)
  #1826
- Sackville (NB), Mount Allison University
  #3068
- Saguenay-Lac-Saint-Jean (Qué) #1549
  - (années 1970) #1538 1540 1546 1547
- Saint-Basile-le-Grand (Qué), Centre
  communautaire catholique Tour de David
  #1510
- Saint-Jean (NB)
  - (années 1940) #1170
  - Musée du Nouveau-Brunswick.
    Collection Canadiana de John Clarence
    Webster #3073 3209
  - XXe s. #1188
- Saint John Art Club (Saint-Jean, NB) #286
- Saint-Laurent (Qué)
  - Collège de Saint-Laurent. Galerie Nova
    et Vetera #3089 3090
  - Collège de Saint-Laurent. Musée d'art
    #3123
- Sarnia (Ont), Sarnia Public Library and
  Art Gallery #3179
- Saskatchewan #1919
  - (1945) #1909
  - (1950-1964) #1910
  - (années 1950) #1912
  - (années 1950-1970) #1935
  - (années 1960) #1916
  - (années 1970) #1926 1930 1937
- Saskatchewan Arts Board #1914
  - (années 1950) #1911
  - collection #1936
- Saskatoon (Sask)
  - (années 1960) #1917
  - (années 1970) #1932
  - collections privées #679
  - femmes artistes (années 1970) #1928
  - Mendel Art Gallery #72 3187
- Shell Canada Ltée, collection #3238 3240
- Society of Artists and Amateurs of
  Toronto (Toronto, Ont) #1688 1729
- sources biographiques #81
- style victorien #237
- Sudbury (Ont), (années 1970) #1801
- synagogues (années 1950) #8763
- Terre-Neuve #1147 1154
  - (1867-1967) #1142
  - (années 1970) #1146 1149
  - (années 1980) #1161
  - femmes artistes (années 1970) #1152

– fin XIXe s.-années 1940 #1138
– Toronto (Ont)
  – (1980) #1832
  – (années 1890) #1699
  – (années 1910) #1712
  – (années 1950) #1750
  – (années 1960) #1757
  – (années 1970) #1804 1809 1818
  – (années 1980), en comparaison avec art
    new-yorkais #1837
  – Art Gallery of Ontario #3149 3158 3163
    3167 3171
  – Art Gallery of Toronto #3132
  – femmes artistes (années 1970) #1797
  – Fondation du patrimoine ontarien.
    Collection d'art Firestone #3239
  – Metro Toronto Public Library #3143
    – John Ross Robertson Historical
      Collection #3130 3131 3204
  – Place de l'Ontario #9113
  – Royal Ontario Museum #3139 3141
  – University of Toronto. Hart House
    #3134
– Toronto Art Students' League (Toronto,
  Ont) #1714 2959 2961
– Toronto Society of Arts (Toronto, Ont)
  #1689 1690
– utilisation de documentation orale #608
– Vancouver (CB)
  – (1886-1930) #2003
  – (1901) #1977
  – (1980) #2076
  – (années 1950-1960) #2039
  – (années 1960) #2035 2036 2038 8158
  – (années 1970) #2040
  – Vancouver Art Gallery #3184 3185 3186
  – Vancouver School of Art (1925-1939)
    #3019
– Vanier, Georges et Pauline, collection
  #3216
– Vaudreuil (Qué), Musée de Vaudreuil
  #3109
– Victoria (CB)
  – (années 1970) #2055
  – Art Gallery of Greater Victoria #3189
  – Island Arts and Crafts Society #1980
– W.O.R.K.S. #1955
– Walker, sir Byron Edmund, collection
  #3205
– Windsor (Ont), Art Gallery of Windsor
  #3156
– Winnipeg (Man)
  – (années 1960-1980) #1907
  – Palais législatif #8948 8949 8950
  – Winnipeg Art Gallery #3188 3192
    – Dobush, Peter, collection #3221
– Winnipeg Sketch Club (Winnipeg, Man)
  #1887
– Women's Art Association of Canada #176
– XIXe s. #241 242 258 259
  – et Napoléon Bourassa #4872 4876
  – expositions universelles #261
– XIXe s.-années 1970 #100
– XIXe-XXe s. #136 137
– XVIIe s.-années 1890 #185
– XVIIe s.-années 1910 #205

– XVIIe s.-années 1940 #40
– XVIIe s.-années 1960 #67 68
– XVIIe-XIXe s., influence française #2180
– XVIIIe s. #249 250
– XVIIIe-XIXe s. #812
– XXe s. #567
  – influence des arts décoratifs, XVIIe-XIXe
    s. #2093
– Yukon (années 1970) #2086 2088
art chinois
– en comparaison avec art amérindien de la
  côte nord-ouest #3843 3975
– figure à la langue pendante et motifs
  connexes #3934
art cinétique #654
– Hayden, Michael #5755
– Kelman, Ralf #6038
– Poulin, Roland #6908
– Toronto (Ont), Electric Gallery #1798
– Vilder, Roger #7487 7488 7489
art corporel
– voir aussi tatouage
– Canada #6676
– Sullivan, Françoise #7282
art d'amateurs
– voir aussi Art brut
art d'amateurs . Canada
– (1750-1850), Archives publiques du
  Canada (Ottawa, Ont) #239
– (1900-années 1920) #309
– Aviation royale du Canada (années 1940)
  #1091
– en comparaison avec peinture
  traditionnelle #960
– Ontario, sociétés d'artistes, XIXe s. #343
– Saint John Art Club (Saint-Jean, NB) #286
– Terre-Neuve #1154
art danois
– (1929), Canadian National Exhibition
  (Toronto, Ont) #304
art dans la rue
– Montréal (Qué), Corridart (1976) #1522
  1530
– Montréal (Qué), Corridart, Mosaicart, et
  Artisanage (1976) #615
art de performance
– voir aussi art corporel; conceptualisme
– (années 1970) #634 672 2046
  – et sculpture #654
  – tele-performance #603
– Berman, Michaele #4710
– Canada #1799
  – (1978), Fifth Network/Cinquième réseau
    #655
  – (1979-1981), Impressions #996
  – (1981) #709 713 718
  – (années 1970) #538 598 669 6676
    – sculpture #658
– Clark, Tim #687
– Dean, Max #687
– Falk, Gathie #5410
– General Idea #5583
– Greyson, John #687
– Heward, John #5793
– Lewis, Glenn Alun #2070
– MacLennan, Toby Chapman #6395

– Montréal (Qué), galerie Powerhouse
  (années 1970) #1553
– Nokony, Denis #6716
– Robertson, Clive #7053
– Tomczak, Kim #687
– Vancouver (CB), Living Art Performance
  Festival (1979) #2073
– W.O.R.K.S. #1955
– Wong, Paul #7607
– Zuck, Tim #7636
Art déco
– affiches, Canada #911
– Canada #505
– et Paul-Emile Borduas #4828
Art Directors' Club of Montreal (Montréal,
Qué)
– expositions
  – (1965) #874
– expositions, critiques
  – (1952) #860
Art Directors' Club of Toronto (Toronto,
Ont)
– (années 1940) #853
– (années 1950) #858
– expositions
  – (1949-) #854
  – (1968) #874
– expositions, critiques
  – (1952) #860
  – (1973) #894
  – (1974) #888
Art Directors' Club of Winnipeg (Winnipeg,
Man)
– expositions
  – (1964-1970) #872
art électronique
– voir art vidéo
art enfantin
– et enseignement de l'art
  – Borduas, Paul-Emile #4827
  – Brandtner, Fritz #4901
  – Colombie-Britannique #1995
  – Fredericton (NB), Fredericton Art Club
    #1176
  – Lismer, Arthur #2966 2968 2971 2974
    2975 2981 2984 2985 2987 6301 6302
    6303
  – Vancouver (CB), Vancouver Art Gallery
    #3186
– et frère Jérôme #6761
– Rockman, Arnold, commentaire #7061
– Ruhman, Walter, dessins d'enfants #7106
art environnemental
– voir aussi art nature (sculpture)
– Snow, Michael #7245
– Vazan, Bill #7471 7475
art érotique
– voir aussi amour dans l'art; nu dans l'art;
  sexualité dans l'art
– Burton, Dennis Eugene Norman #4961
  4962
– Canada #467
– fantasmes féminins #601
– Hall, Joice #717
– Town, Harold Barling #7410
art espagnol

– (1928), Canadian National Exhibition (Toronto, Ont) #300

art et communisme
– *voir* communisme, art et

art et droit
– *voir* droit, art et

art et économie
– *voir* économie, art et

art et Etat
– *voir* Etat, art et

art et éthique
– *voir* éthique, art et

art et fiscalité
– *voir* fiscalité, art et

art et guerre
– *voir* guerre, art et

art et histoire
– *voir* histoire, art et

art et langage
– *voir* langage, art et

art et littérature
– *voir* littérature, art et

art et mathématiques
– *voir* mathématiques, art et

art et musique
– *voir* musique, art et

art et poésie
– *voir* poésie, art et

art et politique
– *voir* politique, art et

art et religion
– *voir* religion, art et

art et socialisme
– *voir* socialisme, art et

art et société
– *voir* société, art et

art et techonologie
– *voir* technologie, art et

art et théâtre
– *voir* théâtre, art et

art fantastique
– Inuit #4240
– paysages, Colombie-Britannique #2045

art français
– vues du Nouveau Monde, XVIe-XVIIIe s. #276
– XVIIe s.-années 1920, influence sur art canadien #1244
– XVIIe-XIXe s., influence sur art canadien #2180

Art Gallery Association of Newfoundland #1142

art grec
– en comparaison avec art préhistorique, Indiens de la côte nord-ouest #3861

art hopewell
– en comparaison avec art algonquien #3558
– Serpent Mound, Rice Lake (Ont) #3574

Art in Living Group (Vancouver, CB) #1841
– (années 1940) #1988

art islamique
– influence sur Pat Bates #4627

art japonais
– influence sur Paterson Ewen #5383
– influence sur Walter Joseph Phillips #6856

art magdalénien

– en comparaison avec l'art inuit #4341

art mahométan
– *voir* art islamique

art mauresque
– *voir* art islamique

art minimal
– *voir aussi* composition sérielle
– Canada #788
– et André Lucien Fauteux #5413
– et Colette Whiten #7561
– et David Bolduc #4774
– et David George Rabinowitch #6950
– et Guido Molinari #6585
– et Henry Saxe #7149
– et Mia Westerlund #7544
– et Peter Henry Kolisnyk #6075 6076
– et Pierre Jean Clerk #5118
– et Ronald Bladen #4740
– et Tim Zuck #7636
– et Walter Redinger #6970
– Québec #1483

art moderne
– *voir* Art déco

art moderniste
– *voir* modernisme

art monumental
– Charney, Melvin, commentaire #5091 5092

art municipal
– *voir* art public (i.e. art dans les lieux publics)

art musulman
– *voir* art islamique

art naïf
– *voir* art traditionnel

art nature (sculpture)
– Canada #617
– Sawchuk, George #7141 7143
– Vazan, Bill #7477

art néo-zélandais
– (1888) #175
– (1890) #177

art non figuratif
– *voir* art abstrait

Art nouveau
– et Bruno Joseph Bobak #4756
– et Katharine Emma Maltwood #3242
– et Kenneth Campbell Lochhead #6314
– et tapisserie canadienne #2774
– Montréal (Qué) #1367

art optique
– *voir* op'art

art oriental
– dessins d'animaux #3460
– et art amérindien de la côte nord-ouest #3359
– et Jack Leonard Shadbolt #7192
– et Raymonde Godin #5623
– et Robert Savoie #7139
– et Tom Mah #6409
– et Wayne G. Ngan #6696
– et William Perehudoff #6837
– sculpture chinoise, en comparaison avec sculpture inuit #4394
– tapis de Perse, et Gordon Rayner #6964

art par correspondance
– *voir* art postal

art par ordinateur
– (années 1960) Canada #517
– (années 1960) Québec #528
– Duquet, Suzanne #5344
– Hushlak, Gerald #1961 5891 5892

art pariétal
– *voir aussi* pétroglyphes; pictogrammes

art pariétal . Amérindiens #3329 3359 3433 3472 3481 3482 3484

art pariétal . Cris
– assemblages de rochers #3688

art pariétal . Indiens des plaines
– bouclier, motif #3710

art pariétal . Pieds-Noirs
– assemblages de rochers #3688

art pariétal . Saulteux/Ojibwa
– assemblages de rochers (Whiteshell, Man) #3578 3592

art pariétal . Siouens
– assemblages de rochers #3688

art populaire
– *voir* art traditionnel

art postal
– Canada (années 1970) #555
– Craig, Kate #2070
– dans *File*, périodique #544
– Lewis, Glenn Alun #2070
– Metcalfe, Eric #2070

art pré-colombien
– et Margaret Peterson #6839
– et Robin MacKenzie #6392

art préhistorique
– et Katharine Emma Maltwood #6413
– Roussil, Robert, comparaison #7090

art primitif
– *voir aussi* art préhistorique

art primitif #3333
– Amérindiens #3428
– autochtones #3342 3377
– en comparaison avec l'art traditionnel #1243
– Indiens de la côte nord-ouest #3348
– influence sur la sculpture canadienne (années 1970) #789
– influence sur Sorel Etrog #5378
– Inuit #4341

art public (i.e. art dans les lieux publics)
– *voir aussi* Etat, art et; sculpture en plein air
– (années 1960), et architecture #753
– (années 1970) #773 4524
– Alberta #1973
– Calgary (Alta), (années 1970) #1959
– Montréal (Qué), fin XIXe s.-années 1920 #1623
– Montréal (Qué) et Toronto (Ont), peintures murales (1972) #539
– Québec #1606
– Roussil, Robert, commentaire #7093
– Royal Canadian Aerial Theatre (RCAT) #2058
– St. Catharines (Ont), (1972) #1795
– Vancouver (CB) #2080
– (1905-1971) #2005

art publicitaire
– Fleming, Allan Robb, commentaire #5456

art publicitaire . Canada

– (années 1930) #340
– Halifax (NE), Nova Scotia College of Art
#2993
art romain
– en comparaison avec art préhistorique,
Indiens de la côte nord-ouest #3861
art rupestre
– *voir* art pariétal
art scandinave
– (1912-1913), Exposition d'art scandinave,
influence sur Groupe des Sept #1788
– influence sur J.E.H. MacDonald #6370
Art Students' Club (St. John's, TN) #1142
Art Students' League (Hamilton, Ont)
– (années 1890) #1706
art traditionnel . Canada #369 966 1562 2094
– (années 1970) #962
– Acadie (années 1960-1980) #1136
– appâts (chasse) #2595
– art letton #49
– art ukrainien #2117 2270
– fin XVIIIe-XXe s. #961
– oeufs de Pâques #2132
– ornementation peinte sur édifices #8090
– castor, thème décoratif #23
– Charlevoix (Qué), (années 1940) #1243
– documentation orale #608
– en comparaison avec art régional #959
– granges, ornementation #9228
– héraldique #2951
– instruments et ustensiles #2139
– Labrador, ouvrage de vannerie, XXe s.
#2945
– Manitoba, XXe s. #1897
– mennonites #2243 2246 2264 2268
– nichoirs d'oiseaux #2593
– Nouvelle-Ecosse
– mobilier #2514
– XXe s. #1206 1207 1210 1212 1213
– Ontario
– (années 1960) #1792
– (années 1970) #1682
– croix funéraires germano-alsaciennes en
fer #2709
– Ottawa (Ont), Musée national de
l'Homme. Centre canadien d'études sur la
culture traditionnelle #963 969
– peinture #964 965
– poterie de grès, ornementation #2309
– Prairies #1852
– (années 1970) #1881
– Price, Ralph et Patricia, collection #970 971
972
– provinces de l'Ouest, XXe s. #1846
– Québec #1235 1268 1276 1285 1297 2183
2184
– (1875-1915) #1364
– (années 1920-1940) #2189
– (années 1960) #1428 1429 2195
– artisanes, XVIIe-XVIIIe s. #2200
– croix funéraires en fer #2716
– crucifix #1638
– dessin d'oiseau #1284
– en comparaison avec littérature #967
– girouettes #2589
– inventaire #1291

– miniatures en bois dans bouteilles #2944
– Montréal (Qué), Université McGill.
Musée McCord #1362
– motifs #1274
– ouvrages de ferronnerie #2702 2712
– publications #1295
– sculpture ancienne (art populaire)
– Sharpe, Nettie, collection #1607
– XVIIe-XIXe s. #1589 1611
– Saint-Marc-des-Carrières (Qué), sculpture
en pierre #1629
– Saskatchewan, XXe s. #1927 1931
– sculptures sur bois #756
– tapis crochetés #2757
– Bluenose #2763
– Terre-Neuve #1155
– (années 1970) #1146 1153 1156
– et Patrick J. Murphy #6664
– Terre-Neuve et Labrador, XXe s. #2155
– tradition germanique #2140
– tradition norvégienne #2273
– tradition ukrainienne et tradition lettonne,
comparaison #968
– traditions ethniques #2122
– XIXe-XXe s. #973
art traditionnel . Etats-Unis
– granges, ornementations #9228
– poterie de grès, ornementation #2309
– sculptures sur bois #756
Art Union of Canada
– (années 1870) #1706
– expositions, critiques
– (1874) #1694
– (1881) #1698
art victorien
– Canada
– (1837-1887) #253
– (1837-1900) #254
– (1840-1918) #237
– et William George Richardson Hind #5810
art vidéo #538 604
– Britton, Susan #687
– Cameron, Eric #651 656
– Campbell, Colin #630 705 4993
– Campus, Peter #651
– Canada #553 566 575 580 598 605 631 650
690 710 713 912 1799
– (1978), Canadian Video Open #603
– (1978), *Fifth Network/Cinquième réseau*
#655
– (1979-1981), *Impressions* #996
– Canada et Etats-Unis #550 616 664
– Chitty, Elizabeth #687
– Colombie-Britannique #2063
– Cruise, Stephen #5213
– Dragu, Margaret #687
– et art de performance #2073
– et réalisme #716
– et sculpture #654
– Falardeau, Pierre #705
– Frenkel, Vera #5524 5525
– General Idea #630 692 705 5583
– Harding, Noel #651 656 687 5705
– International Video Art Symposium,
Kingston (Ont), (1979) #671
– Lake, Suzy #668

– Montréal (Qué) #1498 1537 1550
– Vidéographe #1499
– Nauman, Bruce #651
– Palchinski, Sylvia Scott #6753
– Petite, Marion #651
– Poulin, Julien #705
– Québec
– (1970-1975) #1515
– femmes artistes #1064
– Robertson, Clive #7053
– Sherman, Tom #705
– Steele, Lisa #630 7277
– Terre-Neuve #1157
– Toronto (Ont), A Space #721
– Vancouver (CB) #2044
– Vancouver Art Gallery #3203
– W.O.R.K.S. #1955
– Werden, Rodney #630
Arthabaska (Qué)
– vues, Marc-Aurèle de Foy Suzor-Coté
#7301
Arthur, Eric Ross, architecte can, 1898-
– Edmonton (Alta), Canada Packers Limited
#7973
– influence sur architecture domestique de
l'Ontario #8646
– Ottawa (Ont)
– Carleton University #9455
– Toronto (Ont)
– University of Toronto. University
College, restauration #7776
Arthur, Paul, artiste can, 1924-
– associé, Paul Arthur and Associates #873
– commentaire sur la publicité #859 865
– et *Canadian Art* #25
Arthur, Sandy, artiste can, 1947-
– expositions de groupe
– (1978) #2067
Arthur Pequegnat Clock Company,
horlogers (Kitchener, Ont) #2912 2927
2956
articles de toilette . Grande-Bretagne
– Spode and Copeland, poterie #2357 2358
Artisan, périodique can #2133
Artisan nouvelles/Artisan News, périodique
can #2133
artisanat
– *voir* arts décoratifs
artisans
– *voir aussi* apprentis
– Louisbourg (NE) #2148
– Ontario, XIXe s. #2261
– Québec #2208 2222 2229
– (1660-1815) #2231
– (1810-1819) #8616
– (années 1940) #2190
– articles de luxe, fin XVIIe-début XVIIIe
s. #2162
– fin XIXe-début XXe s. #2235
– habitations, XVIIe-XVIIIe s. #8621
– XVIIe-XIXe s. #2236
– XVIIe-XVIIIe s. #2200 2214
– XVIIIe-XIXe s. #2206
– Québec (Qué), (1608-1950), cordonniers
#2946
artistes

– Lapointe, Frank #6169
– Lyman, John Goodwin #6347
– McKenzie, Robert Tait #6488
– Milne, David Brown (1920-1921) #6560
– Onley, Toni #6738
– Pope, William #6905 6906
– Schoonover, Frank Earle #7163
– Simcoe, Elizabeth Posthuma Gwillim #7210 7211 7212
– Warre, Henry James (1845-1846) #7522
– Whyte, Catharine Robb #7572
artistes amérindiens
– Alexie, Fred #3827 4507
– Ash, Samuel #4161 4558
– Ashkewe, Del #4159 6648
– Beam, Carl #4155 4173
– Beardy, Henry #4649
– Beardy, Jackson #1866 4128 4131 4161 4634 4635 4636
– Bell, Leland #4173
– Brown, Charles #3856
– Chapman, Isaac #5088
– Chee Chee, Benjamin #5100 5101 6648
– Clutesi, George C. #3956 5122
– Cranmer, Doug #4121
– Cross, John #4169
– Crow, James #4113
– David, Joe #4148 5266
– Davidson, Robert #4006 4132 4162 5267 5268 5269
– Davidson, Robert Charles #4148
– Debassige, Blake #4173
– Dixon, Pat #5294
– Edenshaw, Albert Edward #5358
– Edenshaw, Charles #3820 3995 4006 4042 4169 5358 5359 5360 6985
– Edenshaw, Henry #5361
– Ense, Don #4155 4173
– Fisher, Sanford #5445
– Franks, Rhonda #4159
– Gwaytihl #3862 4169
– Hamilton, Ron #4132 4148
– Hanuse, Roy James #4148
– Hill, Stan #5800
– Hill, Tom #4155
– Houle, Robert James #5844
– Hunt, Henry #4115 4132 5872
– Hunt, Richard #4148
– James, Charlie #3848
– Janvier, Alex Simeon #1866 4128 4131 5936 5937 5938 5939
– John, Chauncey Johnny #4113
– Kakegamic, Goyce #4151 4155 4158 4159 4161
– Kakegamic, Joshim #4151 4158 4161
– Kakige, Francis #4159
– King-ego #3862
– Laford, John #4173
– Lonechild, Michael #6322
– Lorenzetto, Adeline #3941
– Madahbee, Mel #4173
– Marks, Gerald Yanders #2706 4148
– Martin, David #4115
– Martin, Mungo #3912 4054 4115 5872 6427 6428 6429 6430 6984
– McGrath, Jim #554

– McGuire, Pat #5294
– Miller, Gary #6538 6539
– Moody, Rufus #4006
– Morris, Christina #6635
– Morrisseau, Norval #3350 4122 4144 4151 4154 4155 4156 4161 6643 6644 6645 6646 6647 6649
– Neel, Ellen #4121
– Odjig, Daphne #1866 4128 4131 4154 4173 6731
– Panamick, Martin #4173
– Peel, Bryan #6788 6789
– Peters, Barry #4151
– Peters, Mary #3941
– Peters, Paddy #4151
– Price, Art #6928 6929 6930
– Price, Tom #4169 6932 6933 6934
– Ravenhill, Alice #4114
– Ray, Carl #4161 6648
– Reid, Bill #2695 4121 4155 4162 6984 6985 6986 6987 6988 6989
– Restoule, Tim #4159 4173
– Robson, John #4169
– Ross, Rosie #4121
– Sapp, Allen #4125 4161 7122 7123 7125
– Seaweed, Willie #4054
– Shaughnessy, Arthur #5872
– Shilling, Arthur #4154 7198
– Smith, Awasatlas #4148
– Speck, Henry #4121
– Tailfeathers, Gerald #4125 7312 7313
– Tait, Norman #7314
– Thomas, Jacob #7346
– Trudeau, Angus #4173
– Trudeau, Randy #4159 4173
– Vickers, Roy Henry #4148
– Vincent, Zacharie #7493 7494
– Williams, Francis #4148 7587
– Williams, Saul #4151
– Yerxa, Leo #4140 7624
artistes et modèles
– Mollise, Mâli Christianne Paul, modèle #6635
– Whiten, Colette, emploi de modèles masculins #7556 7557 7558
artistes étrangers au Canada
– (années 1940-1960) #465
– (années 1970) #3287
– Ontario, XIXe s. #2261
artistes inuit
– Aipelee, Oshaweetuk #4386
– Akeeaktashuk #4504
– Akulukjuk, Malaya #4298
– Allukpik, John #4202
– Amarook, Michael #4403 4408
– Amittu, Davidialuk Alasua #4468 4521 4522 4523
– Anghik, Abe #4530
– Angiju, Peter Nauja #4202 4531
– Angokwazhuk #4398
– Angotiawak #4532
– Anguhadluq, Luke #4268 4533
– Aqiggaaq, Mathew #4534
– Arluk, George #4547
– Arnasungnaaq, Barnabus #4403 4408 4554
– Ashevak, Johnniebo #4559 4563

– Ashevak, Karoo #4560 4561 4562
– Ashevak, Kenojuak #4260 4460 4563 4564
– Ashoona, Kiawak #4565
– Echalook, Thomasee #4487
– Erkoolik, Tuna #4407
– Etook, Tivi #4468 5374 5375
– Etungat, Abraham #5382
– Eyetoaq, Ada #5387
– Iksik, Francis #5897
– Ikutaaq, David #4407 5898
– Inukpuk, Daniel #4487
– Ipellie, Alootook #5902
– Iquliq, Tuna #5903
– Ishulutaq, Elisapee #4260
– Kavik, John #6036
– Kiakshuk #4460
– Kudluk, Thomassie #6105
– Malkauskas, Algie #4436
– Morgan, Peter #6607
– Nuna, Noah #6712
– Oonark, Jessie #4220 4242 4260 4460 6743 6744
– Osuitok, Ipeelee #6745
– Osuitok, Tuqiqi #6746
– Parr, Nuna #6768 6769 6770
– Piqtoukun, David Ruben #775 6873
– Pitseolak, Mary #4260
– Pitseolak, Peter #4202 4242 4460 6874 6875 6877 6880 6881 6883
– Pitsiulak, Lypa #4386
– Pootoogook, Kananginak #4460 6904
– Pudlat, Pudlo #4460
– Qinnuayuak, Lucy #4260 4460
– Saila, Pauta #4460
– Shaa, Aqjangajuk #7174
– Sivuarapik, Charlie #7217
– Smith, Levi Alasua Pirti #4421
– Tagoona, Armand #7311
– Takrik, Bobby #7317
– Talirunili, Joe #7318
– Tatty, Robert #3350
– Teevee, Jamasie #4460
– Tiktak, John #4407 7376
– Tunnillie, Ikayukta #4460
– Tuu'luq, Marion #4255 4268 7441 7442
artistes traditionnels . Canada
– Barbour, Carl #1155 1156
– Barker, Sydney Herbert #1846
– Berggren, Nels #1852
– Bissonette, Héliodore #1428 1429
– Bouchard, Edith #1428 1429
– Bouchard, Marie-Cécile #1428 1429
– Bouchard, Mary Simone #1428 1429
– Burt, Leonard #1153 1156
– Cauchon, Robert #964 1428 1429
– Côté, Jean-Baptiste #1607
– Dahlstrom, Eugene W. #1846
– Dennis, Eva A. #1881 1927
– Dennis, Wes #1881 1927
– Eisenhauer, Collins #1213
– Harbuz, Ann Alexandra #1881 1927
– Hopkins, Elisabeth Margaret #5830 5831 5832
– Hudson, Tom #1155 1156
– Jost, Edward R. #964
– Keevil, Roland #1846

– Lachapelle, Edouard #6124
– Laithwaite, George #1792
– Leblanc, Leo B. #6182
– Lefebvre, Oliver #1607
– Lenhardt, Molly #1881
– Lewis, Maude #6277
– MacDonald, Charles William #6355
– Macdonald, John A. #964
– McCargar, William C. #1881
– McInnes, Harvey A. #1881
– McLaughlin, Agnes #6500
– Moulding, Fred #1881
– Murphy, Patrick J. #6664
– Norris, Joe #6720 6721
– Panko, William #964 1846
– Patterson, Dan #962
– Pieroway, Percy #1153 1155 1156
– Rhéaume, Damase #1607
– Richard, Wilfrid #7000
– Spencer, Sam A. #1881 1927
– St. Germain, Arthème #962
– Stansell, Walter H. #1792
– Stewart, W.N. #1846
– Stryjek, Dmytro #1927 7280
– Themarat, Jeanne Aline #1881
– Tremblay, Georges-Edouard #1428 1429
– Turgeon, Adélard #1607
– Villeneuve, Arthur #1428 1429 7490 7491
  7492
– Williams, Arch #1153 1155 1156
– Wyers, Jan G. #1846 1852 7620
Artists' Cooperative Toronto (ACT)
  (Toronto, Ont)
– périodique, *Artists Review* #1815
Artists' Union of Toronto (Toronto, Ont)
– (années 1930) #1742
Artists Review, périodique can #1815
Artmagazine, périodique can #560 3314
– (années 1970) #3310
Arts, périodique can #551
Arts and Crafts, mouvement artisanal
– Californie, influence sur architecture
  domestique, Vancouver (CB), (1910-années
  1920) #8730
– Canada #189
– et George Selkirk Gibson #5591
– et Katharine Emma Maltwood #3242 6413
– Montréal (Qué) #1367
– Vancouver (CB) #1977
– Victoria (CB) #1980 2269
Arts and Crafts Association (Hamilton, Ont)
– (années 1890) #1706
– expositions, critiques
  – (1895) #2239
Arts and Crafts Society of Canada
– expositions
  – (1904) #2241
Arts and Culture of the North, périodique
  amér #4270
Arts and Letters Club (Toronto, Ont)
– (1908-1944) #1671
– appui du Groupe des Sept #1763
– périodique, *Lamps* #1667
arts appliqués
– *voir* arts décoratifs
Arts Bulletin, périodique can #551

Arts Club of Montreal (Montréal, Qué)
  #1254
– rénovation domiciliaire, 51, rue Victoria
  #1314
arts d'interprétation . Canada
– (années 1970) #693
– artistes canadiens d'origine polonaise #149
– femmes artistes, XXe s. #95 96
– Ontario (années 1970) #1802
arts décoratifs
– *voir aussi* conservation et restauration, arts
  décoratifs; objets liturgiques
– objets domestiques, et Les Levine #6258
arts décoratifs . Amérindiens #2089 2107
– (1964-1967) #2108 2109
– guide pour collectionneurs #2104 2125
  2131
– influence sur art canadien, XXe s. #2093
– Québec, sources biographiques #2230
– XXe s. #2143
arts décoratifs . Canada #30 45 57 58 59 61
  63 485 2089 2094 2096 2097 8228
– (1608-1867) #2120
– (1901-1912), Toronto Society of Architects,
  expositions #7956
– (1904), Arts and Crafts Society of Canada
  #2241
– (1910-1961), Canadian National Exhibition
  (Toronto, Ont) #1
– (1964-1967) #2108 2109
– (1967-1969) #2115
– (1979), recommandations #2136 2137
– (1979-1980) #2138
– (années 1750-1890) #221
– (années 1850) #1692
– (années 1920) #2160 7960 8223
– (années 1920-1930) #8224
– (années 1920-1940) #28
– (années 1930) #340
– (années 1940) #370 374 2601 2603
  – Est du Canada #2098
  – et industrie #2092
  – objets domestiques #2604
– (années 1950) #387 388 2100
– (années 1960) #2102 2103 2105 2106 2196
– (années 1970) #2123 2130 2134
– Académie royale des arts du Canada #2
– Acadie #1137
– Alberta (années 1970) #1951
– arts décoratifs ukrainiens, Manitoba #2270
– bois (années 1970) #2596
– British American Oil Company, édifices
  #8230
– Cantons de l'Est (Qué), (années 1970)
  #1535
– Cap-Santé (Qué), église de la
  Sainte-Famille #8883
– Chicoutimi (Qué), Ecole d'arts et métiers
  #2175
– Colombie-Britannique #2271
  – (années 1970) #2274 2276
– Corporation canadienne de l'artisanat
  #2090 2118
  – (années 1930) #2091
– enseignement (1639-années 1940) #2979
– et architecture

– (années 1950) #8227
– (années 1960) #8231
– femmes artistes (années 1970) #1877
– Groupe des Sept #1774
– guide pour collectionneurs #2101 2114
  2119 2125 2127 2131 2141 2252
– Haliburton (Ont) #2258
– Halifax (NE), Nova Scotia Museum #3071
– Hamilton (Ont), Arts and Crafts
  Association (1895) #2239
– huttérites #1962
– île aux Coudres (Qué) #2168 2178
– île d'Orléans (Qué) #1252
  – XVIIIe s. #8613
– Ile-du-Prince-Edouard #2153
– Independent Art Association #1379
– influence sur art canadien, XXe s. #2093
– Kingcrafts (King City, Ont) #2244
– Kingston (Ont) #1680
– La Malbaie (Qué), (années 1930) #2172
– London (Ont), (années 1970) #2260
– Lotbinière (Qué), églises #8835
– Louisbourg (NE) #2148
– Manitoba, Franco-Manitobains #2275
– mennonites #2246 2253
  – comté de Waterloo (Ont) #2243
  – Ontario #2250 2267
– Montréal (Qué)
  – (1740-1760) #2218
  – (1880-1914) #1367
  – (années 1840) #1301
  – (années 1950) #389 7900
  – Fondation Macdonald-Stewart #2203
    2204
  – Musée Wiser #2469
– Norvège #2273
– Nouveau-Brunswick #1178 2150
  – (années 1940) #2144
  – et Pegi Nicol MacLeod #6398
– Nouvelle-Ecosse #2156 2157
  – (1942), proposition pour la création
    d'une ligue d'artisanat #2145
  – (années 1970) #2154
– objets en bois #2591
– Ontario
  – (1800-1850) #7965
  – (1900) #2240
  – (années 1850) #1691
  – (années 1970) #2247
  – artisans, XIXe s. #2261
  – artisans et points de vente (années 1970)
    #2256
  – XIXe s. #2245
– Ottawa (Ont), Musée national de
  l'Homme. Centre canadien d'études sur la
  culture traditionnelle #963 969
– périodiques
  – *Artisan* #2133
  – *Artisan, L'/Craftsman, The* #2113
  – *Canada Crafts* #2126
  – *Canadian Antiques and Art Review* #141
  – *Canadian Collector* #74
  – *Canadian Review of Music and Art* #357
  – *Construction: A Journal for the
    Architectural Engineering and Contracting
    Interests of Canada* #7641

- *Craft Dimensions Artisanales* #2116
- *Ontario Craft* #2257
- petit salon, style victorien (1870-1890) #2129
- provinces maritimes
  - XIXe s. #2147
  - XXe s. #1119
- Québec #1235 1237 1249 1258 1259 1265 1276 1297 1327 2183 2184 2197 2202 2208 2219 2222 2223 2228 2229 2237 5069
  - (1613-1870), style provincial français #2191
  - (1640-1840) #1329
  - (1872-1939), écoles d'artisanat #2977
  - (1875-1915) #1364
  - (1908) #1313
  - (années 1920-1940) #2189
  - (années 1930) #2163 2164 2167 2173 2174 2176
  - (années 1930-1940) #2186
  - (années 1940) #2188 2199
  - (années 1940-1970) #1269
  - (années 1950) #2193
  - (années 1960) #2195
  - (années 1970) #1490 2205 2211 2215 2216 2224
    - projections pour l'an 2001 #2225
    - sources biographiques #2230
  - apprentis (1660-1815) #2231
  - art traditionnel #1291
  - artisanes, XVIIe-XVIIIe s. #2200
  - artisans, XVIIe-XVIIIe s. #2214
  - Centrale d'artisanat du Québec #2213 2238
  - Confrérie des menuisiers de madame Sainte-Anne #1241
  - Ecole des arts domestiques de Québec
    - (années 1930) #2166 2969
  - Ecole des arts domestiques de Québec
    - (années 1930-1940) #2185
  - Est du Québec, fin XIXe-début XXe s. #2235
  - et Gérard Morisset #3305
  - guide pour collectionneurs #2226
  - motifs, thèmes décoratifs #1274
  - objets de luxe, fin XVIIe-début XVIIIe s. #2162
  - ouvrages de ferronnerie #2712
  - XIXe s., enseignement des arts et métiers #343
  - XVIIe-XIXe s. #1334 1335 2128
    - influence européenne #2221
  - XVIIe-XVIIIe s. #1320 2181 2217
  - XVIIIe-début XXe s. #1339
  - XVIIIe s.-années 1930 #2177
  - XVIIIe-XIXe s. #2206
  - XXe s. #2179 2198
- Québec (Qué)
  - XVIIe s. #1352
- Saint-Basile-le-Grand (Qué), Centre communautaire catholique Tour de David #1510
- Saint-Hilaire (Qué), Centre artisanal de Saint-Hilaire #2182
- Saint-Jean-Port-Joli (Qué) #2194 2209

- Sherbrooke (Qué), (années 1970) #2232
- Society of Applied Arts (1905) #2242
- Terre-Neuve #2146 2158 2159
  - (années 1970) #1149 2152
- Terre-Neuve et Labrador
  - (années 1970), recommandations #2149
  - XXe s. #2155
- Thunder Bay (Ont) #2266
- Toronto (Ont), Ontario College of Art #3009
- tradition germanique #2140
  - Nouvelle-Ecosse et Ontario #2135
  - Ontario #2251 2263
- traditions ethniques #2122
- Vaudreuil (Qué), Musée de Vaudreuil #3109
- Victoria (CB) #2269
  - Island Arts and Crafts Society #1980
- Washington (DC), Smithsonian Institution #2111
- Women's Art Association of Canada #176
- XIXe s. #2099
- XVIIe-XIXe s. #2112
- XXe s. #2121 2142
arts décoratifs . France
- XVIIe-XVIIIe s., influence sur arts décoratifs au Québec #2191
arts décoratifs . Inuit #2089
- (1964-1967) #2108 2109
- (1977-1980) #4269
arts décoratifs . Iroquois
- (années 1960) #4123
arts décoratifs . Scandinavie
- (années 1940), influence sur arts décoratifs au Québec #2186
arts décoratifs . Suède
- influence sur Jean Bernard Cartier #5052
arts graphiques
- *voir aussi* affiches; aquatinte; art publicitaire; eau-forte; gravure; gravure sur bois debout; impression en couleurs; imprimerie; lithographie; scènes marines (estampes)
- (années 1970) #824
- Arthur, Paul, commentaire #859
- Fleming, Allan Robb, commentaire #5456
- Ottawa (Ont), Galerie nationale du Canada #3061
- Québec (Qué), Séminaire de Québec #3124
arts graphiques, techniques
- *voir* matériaux et techniques . arts graphiques
arts graphiques . Amérindiens #3381
- (1975-1977) #3373
arts graphiques . Canada #925
- (1792-1850) #839
- (1900-1940) #28
- (1910-années 1960), Canadian National Exhibition (Toronto, Ont) #1
- (1927), Canadian National Exhibition (Toronto, Ont) #295
- (1930), Canadian National Exhibition (Toronto, Ont) #313
- (1931), Société canadienne des arts graphiques #803
- (1938-1948) #379 809

- (1939), Société canadienne des arts graphiques #346
- (1965-1968) #874
- (1966-1968) #881
- (1967) #877
- (1969-1974) #823
- (années 1840-1920) #4
- (années 1880) #170
- (années 1910) #916
- (années 1930) #340
- (années 1940) #374 806 808 851
- (années 1950) #429 437 813 814 855 860 869
- (années 1950-1960) #821
- (années 1960) #486 487 817 818 819 820 867 868
- (années 1960-1970) #816
- (années 1970) #610 827 833 895 897 907
- (années 1980) #912
- Alberta
  - (années 1950-1973) #815
  - (années 1970) #1951 1958
  - Edmonton (Alta), Alberta Art Foundation #1957
- art graphique, cinéma et télévision (années 1970) #899
- arts graphiques télédiffusés
  - (1980) #913
  - (années 1950) #866
  - (années 1950 1970) #909
- comté de Brant (Ont), (1793-1930) #1684
- Conseil canadien de gravure et de dessin #835
- éditions à tirage illimité (années 1970) #834
- femmes artistes (années 1970) #936 1877
- Groupe des Sept #930
- guide pour collectionneurs #2101 2252
- Halifax (NE), (1749-1949) #1195
- hard-edge #832
- impression sur cliché #837
- Kingston (Ont) #1680
- London (Ont), (années 1970) #1812
- Manitoba #1895
- Montréal (Qué)
  - (années 1940-1960) #1641
  - (années 1960-1970) #1652
  - atelier Arachel #1657
  - Atelier libre de recherches graphiques #1642
  - Design Collaborative Montreal Ltd. #878 882 885
  - Expo 67 #876
  - Graff #1645 1658
  - Graphia #1660
  - Groupe Média Gravures et Multiples #1646
  - Guilde graphique #1647 1653 1655
  - Jeux olympiques (1976) #898 901 902 5858
  - Musée McCord. Université McGill #840
  - XXe s. #1648
- Nouveau-Brunswick
  - (1760-1880) #1189
  - (années 1970) #1185
- Nouvelle-Ecosse (années 1970) #1214

– Ontario
  – (années 1960) #1756
  – (années 1970) #1806
  – XIXe s. #1720
– Ottawa (Ont), Archives publiques du
  Canada. Collection William H. Coverdale
  #12 3230
– paysages #132
  – (années 1970) #595
– provinces de l'Ouest
  – (1964-1970) #872
  – (années 1970) #2059
– publicité
  – (1890-1940) #846
  – (années 1940) #850 853
  – (années 1950) #858 861 865
  – (années 1960) #870
  – (années 1970) #886 888 894
  – années 1880-début XXe s. #891
  – Art Directors' Club of Toronto #854
  – Burns, Cooper, Hynes Ltd. #905 906
  – Burns & Cooper Ltd. #892 896
  – Burton Kramer Associates #889
  – Carlton Studio (Londres, Angleterre)
    #843
  – Cooper and Beatty Ltd. #5297
  – Gerald Bern Agency #871
  – Gottschalk & Ash #879 887
  – Jacques Guillon Designers Inc. #884
    2623
  – Paul Arthur and Associates #873
– Québec #1249 1258 1259
  – (1940-1980) #1665
  – (1967-1977), livres d'artistes #1659
  – (1974-1981), Société des graphistes du
    Québec #893
  – (1977-1981) #1533
  – (années 1940-1970) #1269
  – (années 1960) #1643
  – (années 1970) #1644 2228
    – oeuvres figuratives #1651
  – art traditionnel #1291
  – automatisme et surréalisme #1650
  – et Albert Dumouchel #5325
  – et Rodolphe Duguay #5320
  – marché de l'art (années 1970) #1656
  – XVIIe-XVIIIe s. #1320 1649
– Québec (Qué), Atelier de réalisations
  graphiques #1661
– réalisme #716 1810
– Société canadienne des arts graphiques
  #801
– Société canadienne des peintres-graveurs
  #3
– Terre-Neuve
  – (1980) #1159
  – (années 1970) #1148 1149
  – XIXe s.-années 1950 #1139
– thème décoratif du castor #23
– Toronto (Ont)
  – (1980) #1830
  – Brigdens Limited #883
  – Graphic Arts Club of Toronto #1711
  – Metro Toronto Public Library #3143
    – John Ross Robertson Historical
      Collection #3130 3131

– Open Studio #1819 1833
– Royal Ontario Museum. Collection
  Sigmund Samuel #3135 3140
– Val-David (Qué), Atelier de l'île #1664
– vues d'Ottawa (Ont), (1807-1882) #1716
– vues de la Colombie-Britannique
  (1513-1891) #2006
– vues de la Nouvelle-Ecosse (1605-1878)
  #1203
– vues de la péninsule du Niagara (Ont),
  (1697-1880) #1718
– vues de Montréal (Qué), XVI-XIXe s. #927
– vues de Québec (Qué), (1608-1875) #1349
– vues de Terre-Neuve
  – (1497-1887) #1145
  – XVIIIe-XIXe s. #1150
– vues de Toronto (Ont), (1813-1882) #1717
– vues des Cantons de l'Est (Qué),
  (1832-1881) #1342
– Winnipeg (Man)
  – (1981) #1908
  – (années 1970) #1901
  – Grand Western Canadian Screen Shop
    #1902
– XIXe s. #838
  – Volpi, Charles de, collection #3248
– XIXe s.-années 1920 #11 14
– XIXe-XXe s. #48
– XVIIe-XIXe s. #236
– XVIIIe-XIXe s. #812 828
arts graphiques . Carriers
– 'Ksan (coopérative d'artistes) #4129 4130
arts graphiques . Etats-Unis
– graphisme télédiffusé (1980) #913
– Toronto (Ont), Royal Ontario Museum.
  Collection Sigmund Samuel #3135
arts graphiques . Gitksans
– 'Ksan (coopérative d'artistes) #4134
arts graphiques . Haidas
– et Tom Price #6932
arts graphiques . Indiens de la côte
  nord-ouest #5269
– (années 1950-1970) #4162
– (années 1960-1970) #4166
arts graphiques . Inuit #1294 3374 4200 4214
  4229 4239 4465 4482 4493
– (1959-1968) #4479
– (1959-1969) #4471
– (1959-1972) #4478
– (1959-1976) #4490
– (1959-1980) #4498
– (1977-1980) #4269
– (années 1950) #4311
– (années 1960) #4463 4467
– (années 1970) #4287
– Alaska #4217
– Baker Lake (TNO) #4241 4266 4473 4480
  – (1969-1973) #4481
  – (1970-) #4472
  – (1975-1977) #3373
  – et Sheila et Jack Butler #4486
– Cape Dorset (TNO) #4192 4211 4299 4460
  4461 4466 4476 4477 4483 4484 4500
  – (1976-1977) #4491
  – (années 1960) #4464
– Burnaby (CB), Simon Fraser University.

  Simon Fraser Gallery #4495
– et James Archibald Houston #4186 4462
  4470
– Collection de la Banque
  Toronto-Dominion #4201 4248
– et chamanisme #4488
– et Robert Allen Paterson #6778
– femmes artistes (années 1970) #4260
– Holman (TNO) #3350 4197 4469
  – (années 1960) #4195
– île de Baffin (TNO), Iqutaq Group, Clyde
  River #4499
– Inoucdjouac (Qué) #4267 4279 4487
– Montréal (Qué), Musée des beaux-arts de
  Montréal #4474
– Pangnirtung (TNO), (1973-) #4485
– Povungnituk (Qué) #4219 4494
  – (1962-) #4468
  – (1976) #4489
  – (années 1960) #4496
– Québec #4475
– scènes de jeu #4492
– sources biographiques #4497
– symbolisme #4234
– thème de l'amautik #4300
– Toronto (Ont), York University. Art
  Gallery of York University #4228
– Winnipeg (Man), Winnipeg Art Gallery
  #4285
Arts West, périodique can #1868 3310
ArtsAtlantic, périodique can #128
Artscanada, périodique can #25
– (années 1970) #3310
– symposium de sculpture (1974) #773
ArtViews, périodique can #1806
Arvida (Qué), centrale électrique de
  Shipshaw
– murale, André Charles Biéler #4721
ascendance
– *voir* généalogie
Ascott, Roy, artiste brit et éducateur au
  Canada, 1934-
– directeur, Ontario College of Art (Toronto,
  Ont) #3002
Ash, Samuel, artiste can, 1951- #4157 4161
– peintures illustrant légendes algonquines
  #4558
Ash, Stuart B., artiste can, 1942-
– design typographique #932
– estampes #897
Ashevak, Johnniebo, artiste can, 1923-1972
  #4559 4563
Ashevak, Karoo, artiste can, 1940-1974 #4560
  4561
– expositions
  – (1977) #4562
Ashevak, Kenojuak, artiste can, 1927- #4260
  4460 4563
– entretien #4564
– et Johnniebo Ashevak, erreurs
  d'attribution #4559
Ashkewe, Delmer (Del), artiste can, 1947-
  #6648
– expositions de groupe
  – (1980) #4159
Ashley, Benedict, prêtre amér, actif 1971

- commentaire sur le sacré dans l'art #94
Ashoona, Kiawak, artiste can, 1933-
- expositions
 – (1980) #4565
Askevold, David Marius, artiste can, 1940-
- art vidéo #605
- entretien #4566
- et art d'avant-garde #600
- expositions de groupe
 – (1970) #534
 – (1980) #690
Askren, Patricia Alice (Pat), artiste can,
 1951-
- expositions de groupe
 – (1979) #674
- programme d'expositions itinérantes,
 Alberta (1980) #1972
Aspell, Peter Noel Lawson, artiste can, 1918-
- expositions de groupe
 – (1959) #1997
Assekikuk, chef amérindien
- voir Assiginack, Jean-Baptiste
Asselin, Denis, artiste can, 1943- #1524 1544
- expositions de groupe
 – (1981) #1565
Assiginack, Jean-Baptiste, chef de tribu
 amérindienne, ca 1768-1865
- wampum représentant traités de paix
 (1764-1852) #3501
Assiniboine (rivière)
- vues photographiques
 – Hime, Humphrey Lloyd #5801 5802
 5803 5804
Assiniboines
- arcs et flèches #3693
- art #3731
- costume #3739
- culture #3653
- étuis à fusils #3713
- pétroglyphes #3673
- tatouage #3723
- vues photographiques
 – Curtis, Edward Sheriff #3399
Association canadienne d'urbanisme
- modèles d'habitations (années 1950) #8509
Association canadienne de photographes et
 illustrateurs de publicité
- (1981), rapport, Comité fédéral d'études
 d'une politique culturelle #1068
Association canadienne des professeurs
 d'université
- et Ontario College of Art (1968) #2997
Association d'art des universités du Canada
- conférence, financement de l'art canadien
 (1979) #3293
- périodique, RACAR (Revue d'art
 canadienne/Canadian Art Review) #114
Association des architectes de la province de
 Québec (AAPQ)
- (années 1960) #8307
Association des artisans de
 Saint-Jean-Port-Joli
- sculptures sur bois #1608
Association des artisans du
 Canada/Canadian Craftsman's
 Association
- périodique, L'Artisan/The Craftsman #2113

Association des artistes non figuratifs de
 Montréal/Non-Figurative Artists'
 Association of Montreal (Montréal, Qué)
- (1956-1961) #1469 1478
- et Guido Molinari #6588
- expositions
 – (1960) #1415
Association des centres nationaux d'artistes
 à but non lucratif #683
- (1976-1981) #598
- et Artspace (Peterborough, Ont) #1836
- périodique, Parallelogramme #612
Association des designers industriels du
 Canada
- (1948-1958) #2612
- (1949) #2604
Association des métiers d'art du Québec
- (années 1970) #1490
Association des musées canadiens
- (années 1960) #3045
- (années 1970) #3054
- et Harry Orr McCurry #3036
- périodique, Canadian Museums Association.
 Gazette #3042
Association des sculpteurs du
 Québec/Quebec Sculptors Association
- (années 1970) #1490
- expositions
 – (1961-1977) #1584
 – (1977) #1622
- expositions, critiques
 – (1965) #1586
Association nationale d'art photographique,
 L'/National Association for Photographic
 Art
- périodique, Camera Canada #991
Association nationale des constructeurs
 d'habitations
- architecture domestique (années 1950)
 #8512
Association of Canadian Etchers
- expositions
 – (1885) #798
Association pour l'avancement des méthodes de
 préservation/Association for Preservation
 Technology. Bulletin (APT Bulletin),
 périodique can #7757
associations canadiennes
- (1860-1890) #264
- (1880-1914) #265
- (1890-1900) #190
- (1949-1951), Commission royale d'enquête
 sur l'avancement des arts, lettres et
 sciences (Rapport Massey) #3254 #3255
 3256 3261
- (années 1860-1930) #28
- (années 1870-1910) #200
- (années 1880-1930) #45
- (années 1890) #187 188
- (années 1910) #205
- (années 1930) #502
- (années 1940) #363
 – et Académie royale des arts du Canada
 #361
- (années 1960) #447
- (années 1970) #682 707 3278 3279
- association nationale d'architectes,

recommandation (1897) #8291
- associations d'artisans québécois #2227
- Colombie-Britannique
 – (années 1880-1940) #1986
 – (années 1890-1930) #2007
 – (années 1910) #1979
 – (années 1940) #1987
 – (années 1960) #2989
 – (années 1970) #3272
- et musées
 – (années 1960) #3043
 – XIXe s.-années 1970 #3055
- Nouvelle-Ecosse (1900-1945) #1194
- Ontario
 – (années 1870) #1693
 – (années 1970) #1802 1825
 – XIXe s. #1706
- provinces de l'Ouest (années 1940) #1841
- Québec
 – (1825-1850) #1368
 – (années 1940-1970) #1269
 – XVIIe-XVIIIe s. #2214
- Saskatchewan, fin XIXe s.-années 1950
 #1919
- Terre-Neuve #1138 1142 1147
 – (années 1950) #2146
- Toronto (Ont)
 – (années 1880) #3129
 – XIXe s. #7956
- Vancouver (CB) #1977
 – (1886-1930) #2003
 – (1889-1894) #1981
 – XIXe s. #153 185 275
 – XIXe s.-années 1920 #11
 – XVIIIe s.-années 1930 #343
Assomption
- voir Marie, Vierge, l'Assomption
Astman, Barbara Anne, artiste can, 1950-
 #4567
- commentaire sur Jack Chambers #700
- en comparaison avec Fern Helfand #1010
- expositions de groupe
 – (1980) #1063
- xérographie en couleurs #614
Atchison, John Danley, architecte can,
 1870-1959
- Moose Jaw (Sask), hôtel de ville, concours
 #8978
- Winnipeg (Man)
 – architecture domestique #8493
 – Bank of Hamilton #9171
 – hôtel de ville, concours #8979
Atelier libre de recherches graphiques
 (Montréal, Qué) #1653
Ateliers, périodique can #1493
ateliers d'artistes
- Ayotte, Léo #4574
- Campbell, Ted #4994
- Carr, Emily #5020
- Chaudron, Bernard #5099
- Chaudron, Bernard et Louise #5098
- Jobin, Louis #5962 5964
- Lemieux, Jean-Paul #6238
- Muhlstock, Louis #6658
- Plaskett, Joe #6890 6895
- Watson, Homer Ransford #7528
Athapascans

– art #3366 3370 4091 4104 4105
– arts décoratifs (années 1970) #3367
– broderie #4110 4152
– costume #4102 4111
– culture #4072 4073 4097
  – XVIIIe s. #3445
– masques #4083
– ouvrages en piquants de porc-épic #3471
  3474 3475
– ouvrages perlés #4107
– raquettes #2812
athlètes dans l'art
– Clarke, Fred #5115
– McKenzie, Robert Tait #6481
Atkins, Caven Ernest, artiste can, 1907-
  #4568 4570
– expositions
  – (1979) #4569
Atkins, Gordon L., architecte can, 1937-
– Lake Windermere (CB), Melchin,
  résidences estivales #7694
Atkinson, William Edwin, artiste can,
  1862-1926 #4571
– expositions, critiques #204 211 1703
– membre du Canadian Art Club #193
Atlantic Provinces Art Circuit (APAC)
  – (1964-1971) #3053
  – (années 1960) #1124
Atlantic Woodcarver's Guild #1194
atriums . Canada
  – (années 1970-1980) #7743
Aubin, Ernest, artiste can, 1893-1963
– et Montée Saint-Michel #1236
Aubin, Régine, artisane can (vannerie),
  active 1981 #2954
Auclair, André, sculpteur can, 1803-1865
  #1301 1578
Audet, Louis-Napoléon, architecte can,
  1881-1971
– et Ozias Leduc #6204
– Valleyfield (Qué)
  – cathédrale de Salaberry-de-Valleyfield
    #8843
Audubon, John James, artiste et
  ornithologiste amér, 1785-1851
– expositions
  – (1944) #12
– influence sur Glen Loates #6310
– Lansdowne, James Fenwick, comparaison
  #6163
– Pope, William, comparaison #6905
augustines
– Québec (Qué), Hôtel-Dieu #1352 3119
– tabernacles, Québec #1359
Austin (Texas), University Art Museum
– expositions
  – Canadian Landscape Painting, 1670-1930:
    The Artist and the Land (1973) #106
auteurs canadiens
– portraits, John Reeves #1065 1066
autochtones
– voir aussi Amérindiens; Inuit
– architecture #3353
– arcs et flèches #3328
– art #3334 3335 3336 3338 3341 3342 3346
  3349 3364 3369 3377 3378 3381 3435 3463

3468 3479
  – (années 1980) #4170
  – préhistoire #3375
– chamanisme #3360
– masques #3327
– pipes #3358
– tatouages #3330
– vannerie #3411
automatisme #1467
– Canada #6586
– et Alfred Pellan #6815
– et Christian Marcel Barbeau #4602 4606
– et Fernand Leduc #6187 6189 6190 6191
  6194
– et Guido Molinari #6591
– et Jean-Paul Armand Mousseau #6650
  6651
– et Jean-Paul Riopelle #7012 7022 7031
– et Jock Macdonald #6377 6379
– et Léon Bellefleur #4660
– et Louis Jaque #5942
– et Marcelle Ferron #5421 5424 5425
– et Paterson Ewen #5384
– et Paul-Emile Borduas #1270 1417 1453
  1455 4809 4810 4811 4815 4821 4829 4830
  4832 4833 4843 4849 7026
– et Pierre Gauvreau #5575 5576 5577 5578
– et Pierre Gendron #5582
– et René Derouin #5285
– et Rita Letendre #6251
– et Roland Giguère #5598
– Montréal (Qué) #1398 1420 1426 1437 1448
  1449 1475 1476
  – (1954-1955) #1408
– oeuvres littéraires #4831
– Québec #1294
– Québec, estampes #1650
automatistes (Montréal, Qué) #512 1472 1475
– écrits #1443
– en comparaison avec plasticiens #7398
– et Alfred Pellan #1451
– et Paul-Emile Borduas #1462
– et Refus global #1396 1447 1466
– et surréalisme #1458 1464 1467
– expositions, critiques
  – (1950) #1400
autoportraits
– Bobak, Bruno Joseph #4760
– Lake, Suzy #6137 6138
– Maynard, Hannah Hatherly #6458
– Morris, Michael #6641
– Poole, Leslie Donald #6902 6903
– Snow, Michael #7243
– Vincent, Zacharie #7494
auvents . Canada
– Québec
  – (1650-1925) #1592
  – XVIIe-XIXe s. #8826
avions dans l'art #147
– Bennett, Geoffrey #4680
– Pattle, Colin #6784
– peinture d'avions, Musée canadien de la
  guerre (Ottawa, Ont) #1104 1105 1110
Awasatlas
– voir Smith, Russell (Awasatlas)
Axangayu

– voir Shaa, Aqjangajuk
Aycock, Alice, sculpteure amér, 1946-
– expositions de groupe
  – (1980) #8237
Ayerst, McKenna et Harrison chimistes
  (Montréal, Qué)
– collection, art canadien #852
Aylmer (Qué)
– architecture (1800-1921) #7889
Ayot, Pierre, artiste can, 1943- #4572
– directeur, Graff (Montréal, Qué) #1645
– expositions
  – (1980) #4573
– expositions de groupe
  – (1981) #1564
– gravures #1654
– pop'art #1497
Ayotte, Léo, artiste can, 1909-1976 #1393
  4574 4575
Ayr (Ont), Molsons Bank
– architecture #9173
Ayre, Robert, critique d'art can, 1900-
– commentaire sur Albert Henry Robinson
  #7056
– commentaire sur Marc-Aurèle Fortin
  #5475
Aziz, Philip John Andrew Ferris, artiste can,
  1923- #4577
– expositions
  – (1957) #4576

B

Baber, Jack, photographe can, actif années
  1960
– photographies #987
Bach, Johann Christian, musicien et
  compositeur all, 1735-1782
– La Toccata, influence sur oeuvre
  cinématographique de Michèle Cournoyer
  #5193
Bachelard, Gaston, philosophe fr, 1884-1962
– influence sur Albert Dumouchel #5333
Bachinski, Walter Joseph Gerard, artiste can,
  1939-
– expositions
  – (1977) #4578
  – (1981) #4579
Back, George, officier de la marine brit,
  artiste au Canada, 1796-1878 #241 242 279
  4580
– et expédition de Franklin dans l'Arctique
  (1819-1821) #5825
Back, Süzel, artiste can, 1956-
– batik #2741
Bacon, Francis, artiste brit, 1909-
– Bates, Maxwell Bennett, comparaison
  #4623
– Cohen, Sorel, comparaison #5130
– influence sur Joe Plaskett #6889
– influence sur Louis de Niverville #6711
– Markgraf, Waltraud Erna Else,
  comparaison #6416
– Niverville, Louis de, comparaison #6707

Bacstrom, Sigismund, artiste, médecin et scientifique all au Canada, actif années 1763-1795
- vues, côte nord-ouest #4581
Baczynski, George, photographe can, ca 1951-
- catalogue de photographies #1023
Badani, Pat, artiste can, 1951- #4582
bagues
- *voir* anneaux et bagues
bahà'isme (religion)
- influence sur Otto Rogers #7063 7064
Bahamas
- vues
  - Gagen, Robert Ford #5530
  - Panabaker, Frank Shirley #6756
Baich, Paul von
- *voir* Von Baich, Paul
Baie-Comeau (Qué), Centre sportif
- expositions
  - *Un siècle et demi d'art canadien (Collection du Musée de la province de Québec)/A Century and a Half of Canadian Art (Collection of the Museum of the Province of Quebec)* (1951) #1248
Baie James (Qué)
- vues (1981) #1566
- vues photographiques
  - Turcot, Guy #1562
Baie-Saint-Paul (Qué)
- vues
  - Bolduc, Blanche #4772
  - Gagnon, Clarence Alphonse #5545
  - Richard, René-Jean #6996 6999
Baie-Saint-Paul (Qué), église
- architecture et intérieur, François Baillairgé #7849
Bailey, Charles S., photographe can, 1869-1896 #4583
- expositions de groupe
  - (1976) #2012
Bailey, Clayton George (Cal), photographe can, 1947- #1879
- expositions
  - (1978) #4584
- expositions de groupe
  - (1977) #1033
Bailey, William, photographe can, 1865-1936/1937
- expositions de groupe
  - (1976) #2012
Baillairgé, Charles Philippe Ferdinand, architecte can, 1826-1906
- Cap-Rouge (Qué), Henry Howison Pottery #2301
- et André-Raphaël Giroux #5610
- expositions
  - (1979) #8324
- Québec (Qué)
  - maison Mère-Mallet #8884
  - prison des plaines d'Abraham #9057
Baillairgé, famille, architectes et sculpteurs can, XVIIIe-XIXe s. #1233 1300
- influence sur architecture québécoise #7851
- sculptures sur bois #1573 1575 1576

Baillairgé, François, architecte et artiste can, 1759-1830 #1232 1592 4585 4586 4588 4589 4590 4593 6947
- Baie-Saint-Paul (Qué), architecture et sculpture #7849
- chevaux à bascule #2934
- emploi de modèles architecturaux #7872
- et origines de l'architecture et de la sculpture sur bois au Québec #1574
- et société québécoise #1375
- expositions
  - (1975) #4592
- expositions de groupe
  - (1959), portraits #219
- frère de Pierre-Florent Baillairgé #4594
- influence de la peinture française #1244
- influence sur Thomas Baillairgé #8328
- peinture #4587
- professeur #1582
- Québec (Qué)
  - chapelle de la congrégation Notre-Dame de Québec #8864
  - église Saint-Joachim de Montmorency, intérieur #8880
  - Notre-Dame-des-Victoires #8858
- sculptures #1324
- tabernacles #1613 4591
Baillairgé, Jean, sculpteur can, 1726-1805 #4585
- intérieur, église Saint-Jean-Baptiste (Saint-Jean-Port-Joli, Qué) #8812
- père de François Baillairgé #4590
- père de Pierre-Florent Baillairgé #4594
- professeur #1582
- professeur de Pierre Emond #5371
- sculptures #1324
- tabernacles #1613
Baillairgé, Pierre-Florent, sculpteur can, 1761-1812 #1324 4594
- intérieur, église de la Sainte-Famille (île d'Orléans, Qué) #8795
- intérieur, église Saint-Jean-Baptiste (Saint-Jean-Port-Joli, Qué) #8812
- professeur #1582
- tabernacles #1613
- travaux, églises, Charlesbourg (Qué) #8851
Baillairgé, Thomas, architecte et sculpteur can, 1791-1859 #1232 1324 1592 8325 8326 8327 8328
- Charlesbourg (Qué), église #8851
- emploi de modèles architecturaux #7872
- et architecture religieuse au Québec #8821
- intérieur, église de la Sainte-Famille (île d'Orléans, Qué) #8795
- intérieur, église Saint-Joachim de Montmorency (Québec, Qué) #8880
- professeur #1582
- professeur de André-Raphaël Giroux #5610
- Québec (Qué), Palais épiscopal #8787
- tabernacles #1613
- thème du souper d'Emmaüs #1615
Baillif, Claude, architecte can, 1635-1698 #228 229 8329
- professeur, Ecole des arts et métiers de Saint-Joachim (Saint-Joachim, Qué) #2992

- Québec (Qué), Notre-Dame-des-Victoires #8858
Bailly, Evern Earl, artiste can, 1903-1977 #4595
Bailly (dit Lafleur), François, constructeur au Canada, ca 1627-1690 #228 229 7844
Bain, Freda Guttman, artiste can, 1934-
- estampes #4596
Baird, George, architecte can, 1939-
- commentaire sur l'architecture torontoise #7746
Baird, Nini, administratrice des arts can, active 1977
- Livre vert *Twenty Plus Five*, Conseil des Arts du Canada #3285
Baird, Ronald Arnott (Ron), sculpteur can, 1940-
- commentaire sur l'art canadien (années 1960) #478
- sculptures architecturales #4597
Baker, Francis Spence, architecte can, 1867-1926
- Toronto (Ont) #8330
  - Graphic Arts Building #9330
Baker, Isaac Bennett, constructeur et ébéniste can, 1833-1925 #2581
Baker Lake (TNO)
- art #4266
- arts graphiques #4473
  - (1959-1972) #4478
  - (1959-1976) #4490
  - (1969-1973) #4481
  - (1970-) #4472
  - (1975-1977) #3373
  - et Sheila et Jack Butler #4486
- femmes artistes (années 1970) #4260
- murales #4230 4253
- sculpture #4402 4403 4408 4434
  - (années 1950-1960) #4400
Baker Lake (TNO), Coopérative Sanavick
- estampes, d'après dessins de Luke Anguhadluq #4533
Bakken, Haakon, joaillier can, 1932- #2706
Bakuba (Afrique)
- masques, en comparaison avec masques, Kwakiutls #3920
Balboa (Calif), Newport Harbour Art Museum
- expositions
  - *The New Art of Vancouver* (1969) #2039
Balch, Reg, photographe can, 1894-
- catalogue de photographies #991
Baldwin, Edward R., architecte can, 1935-
- Toronto (Ont), Tour du CN #9511
Baldwin, Lee, artiste can (vitrail), actif 1975
- vitrail #2452
Baldwin, William Warren, architecte can, 1775-1844
- proposition pour la création d'une société d'architectes (ca 1835) #8306
Baldwin & Greene, agence can d'architecture
- Toronto (Ont), Ashley & Crippen Building #9367
Bâle (Suisse), Kunsthalle
- expositions

– *General Idea's Reconstructing Futures/General Idea: reconstruction de l'avenir* (1978) #5583
– expositions, critiques
 – Snow, Michael #7263
Balharrie, James Watson, architecte can, 1910-
– Ottawa (Ont), Carleton University #9455
Balint, Gerrie, céramiciste can, 1928- #2394
ballet
– *voir aussi* scénographie
– Canada #129
– influence sur Norman McLaren #6497
– Winnipeg (Man) #1891
Ballet national du Canada
– et Ken Bell, photographe #4657
– et St. Lawrence Hall (Toronto, Ont) #9103
ballons
– en tant que sculptures, Royal Canadian Aerial Theatre (RCAT) #2058
Balshine, Lorne, collectionneur can, XXe s.
– collection, art inuit #4312 4447
Baltimore (Md), Baltimore Museum of Art
– expositions
 – *"And Eagles Sweep Across the Sky": Indian Textiles of the North American West* (1977) #4015
 – *An Exhibition of Paintings by Contemporary Canadian Artists: Catalogue* (1930) #315
Baltzly, Benjamin, photographe can, 1835-1883
– photographies d'arpentage #1014 1015 1865 1876
– photographies et journal, expédition en Colombie-Britannique (1871) #4598
balustrades . Canada
– comté de Norfolk (Ont), Normandale Iron Works #2699
– Québec #2702
Bancroft, Marian Penner, photographe can, 1947- #2018 2071 4599
– expositions de groupe
 – (1979) #2069
Band, Charles Shaw, collectionneur can, 1885-1969
– entretien #3219
Band, Charles Shaw, collectionneur can, 1885-1969, et Helen, collectionneuse can, XXe s.
– collection, peintures et dessins canadiens, XXe s. #3215
Band, Helen, collectionneuse can, XXe s.
– commentaire sur Alex Simeon Janvier #5936
Band, Percy, collectionneur can, XXe s.
– collection, jouets et jeux, XIXe s. #2917
bandes dessinées
– et Greg Curnoe #5233
bandes dessinées . Canada
– (1939-1945) #947
– Cantons de l'Est (Qué), (années 1970) #1535
– Québec #948 952 953 954
 – (années 1970) #950 951 1502
– Vancouver (CB), (années 1970) #955

Banff (Alta)
– architecture
 – (années 1920) #7656
– art #1964
 – (années 1970) #1870 1960
– urbanisme, Thomas Hayton Mawson #9405
– vues photographiques
 – Harmon, Byron #5707
Banff (Alta), Banff Centre. School of Fine Arts
– (années 1970) #3006
– expositions
 – *Dennis Burton Retrospective* (1978) #4961
Banff (Alta), Banff Centre. Walter Phillips Gallery
– expositions
 – *Artisan '78: The First National Travelling Exhibition of Contemporary Canadian Crafts/Artisan '78: première exposition nationale itinérante d'artisanat canadien contemporain* (1978) #2134
 – *Enns, Evans & Ulrich* (1977) #1956
 – *Joe Fafard: Recent Sculpture* (1980) #5401
 – *Louis de Niverville* (1980) #6709
 – *Sylvain P. Cousineau: Photographs and Paintings* (1980) #5195
 – *The Banff Purchase: An Exhibition of Photography in Canada* (1979) #1037
– expositions, critiques
 – Andrews, Stephen #4528
 – *The Banff Purchase: An Exhibition of Photography in Canada* (1979) #1046 1060
– expositions de photographie (années 1970) #1879
Banff (Alta), Banff School of Fine Arts
– (années 1940) #1841
– Cameron, Donald, directeur #3000
– Tailfeathers, Gerald, étudiant #7312
– Townsend, William, professeur #7418
Banff (Alta), Peter Whyte Gallery
– expositions
 – *A Tribute to William Townsend: 1909 to 1973* (1974) #7418
 – *Beyond Exceptional Pass* (1978) #1960
 – *Canadian Political Cartoons* (1977) #956
 – *H.G. Glyde in Canada* (1975) #5618
 – *The Group of Seven in the Rockies* (1974) #1861
 – *The Railway: Patron of the Arts in Canada* (1976) #3281
 – *The Temptation of Aquarius: Paintings by Robert Ralph Carmichael* (1972) #5002
Banff (Alta), Peter Whyte Gallery. Archives of the Canadian Rockies
– expositions
 – *Joe Plaskett and His Paris: In Search of Time Past* (1972) #6893
 – *Joe Plaskett et son Paris: à la recherche d'un temps passé* (1972) #6894
– Harmon, Byron, photographies #5707
Banfield, A.F., & Company, fabricants can d'ameublement
– mobilier, Deer Lodge (Winnipeg, Man) #9260

Bank of Toronto
– banques (années 1930) #9185
bannières et drapeaux #2939
– Laliberté, Norman #6154
– Wainwright, Ruth #7497
Bannister, Edward M., artiste can aux EU, 1833-1901
– expositions de groupe
 – (1969) #1180
Banque canadienne de commerce
– architecture
 – (années 1920) #9172
 – (années 1930) #9189
 – Horsburgh, V.D. #9169
– bâtiments préfabriqués, provinces de l'Ouest, début XXe s. #8082
Banque de Montréal
– banques (années 1930) #9183
Banque de Nouvelle-Ecosse
– banques
 – (années 1920) #9174
 – (années 1930) #9186
– collection, art canadien #3245
Banque Toronto-Dominion
– architecture (1950s) #9193
banques canadiennes
– (1867-1967) #9196
– (1911-1912) #8295
– (1912) #7645
– (années 1910) #9156 9166 9169
– (années 1930) #9184
– (années 1940-1950) #9191
– (années 1950) #9193
– Bank of Toronto (années 1930) #9185
– Banque canadienne de commerce
 – (années 1920) #9172
 – (années 1930) #9189
– Banque de Montréal (années 1930) #9183
– Banque de Nouvelle-Ecosse
 – (années 1920) #9174
 – (années 1930) #9186
 – et John MacIntosh Lyle #9203
– Dominion Bank (années 1870-1930) #9188
– Edmonton (Alta), Imperial Bank of Canada #9154
– Halifax (NE), Banque de Nouvelle-Ecosse #9182
– Hamilton (Ont), Bank of Hamilton #9160
– London (Ont), XIXe s. #8010
– Molsons Bank (années 1920) #9173
– Montréal (Qué)
 – (1845-1933) #9201
 – Bank of British North America #9164
 – Bank of Toronto #9167
 – Banque canadienne de commerce #9153
 – Banque de commerce canadienne impériale #9194
 – Banque de Montréal (1846) #9200
 – Banque de Montréal (1918) #9168
 – Banque Royale du Canada #7933 9176
– Ontario (1915-1919) #9170
– Ottawa (Ont)
 – Banque du Canada, siège social (1938) #9337
 – Banque du Canada, siège social (1978) #9199

– provinces de l'Ouest, bâtiments préfabriqués, début XXe s. #8082
– restauration (années 1980) #9204
– style victorien #7769
– thèmes d'inspiration canadienne dans décoration architecturale (années1930) #8226
– Toronto (Ont)
    – (années 1910) #9159
    – (années 1930) #9181
    – Bank of British North America #9150
    – Bank of Toronto (1908) #9151
    – Bank of Toronto (1913) #8293 9162
    – Banque canadienne de commerce #9178 9180 9351
    – Banque de Montréal (1910) #9155
    – Banque de Montréal (1949) #9190
    – Banque de Nouvelle-Ecosse #9192
    – Banque Royale (1908) #9152
    – Banque Royale (1915) #9165
    – Dominion Bank #9163
    – Royal Bank Plaza #9198 9353
    – Standard Bank #9158
    – Toronto-Dominion Centre #9197 9348
    – XIXe s.-années 1930 #8076
– Vancouver (CB), Banque Royale #9179
– Windsor (Ont), Imperial Bank of Canada #9175
– Winnipeg (Man)
    – (1898-1914) #9205
    – (années 1910) #9202
    – Bank of Hamilton #9171
    – Banque de Nouvelle-Ecosse #9157
Banting, Frederick Grant, médecin et artiste can, 1891-1941 #4600
– peintures, Association médicale canadienne (Ottawa, Ont) #138
Banwell, Michael (Mike), sculpteur can, 1943-
– expositions de groupe
    – (1981) #797
– installation #4601
baptistère
– voir fonts baptismaux
Barbeau, Charles Marius, anthropologue can, 1883-1969 #3303 3309
– ceinture fléchée, renouveau #2833 2864
– commentaire sur les Tsimshians #3981
– et Emily Carr #5021 5024 5034 5040
– et Gordon Edward Pfeiffer #6847
– influence sur Tony Law #6174
Barbeau, Christian Marcel, artiste can, 1925- #1282 1453 4606
– entretien #4604
– et op'art #1445
– et plasticiens #1439
– expositions, critiques #4607
– expositions de groupe
    – (1967) #480
    – (1968) #1263
– peinture (années 1950-1961) #4602 4603
Barbeau, Jean-Guy, artiste can, 1925- #1549 1551
Barbeau, Marius
– voir Barbeau, Charles Marius
Barber, Charles Arnold, architecte can,

1848-1915 #8331
Barber, Earle William, architecte can, 1855-1915
– Winnipeg (Man) #8331
Barber & Barber, agence can d'architecture
– Winnipeg (Man) #8331
    – hôtel de ville #8996
Barber & Ellis, éditeurs (Toronto, Ont)
– cartes de Noël #890
Barbin, Raoul, artiste, actif 1925
– intérieur, Château Frontenac (Québec, Qué) #9278
Barbour, Carl, artiste can, 1908- #1155
– expositions de groupe
    – (1977) #1156
Barbour, David, photographe can, 1952- #1879
    – (1979) #1904
Bardon, Lynn, auteur can, 1947-
– Suttles and Seawinds, industrie à domicile (New Germany, NE) #2154
Bareket, Nir, photographe can, 1939-
– catalogue de photographies #1023
Baril, Marcel, artiste can, 1929- #4608
Barker, Charles Edward, artiste can, 1900-1974
– expositions
    – (1975) #4609
Barker, Sydney Herbert, artiste can, 1893-1970
– expositions de groupe
    – (1958) #1846
Barkerville (CB)
– architecture #8151
Barnard, Henry, éducateur amér, 1811-1900
– guides sur l'architecture de maisons d'enseignement #9384
Barnes, Elias Paul, artiste amér, 1840-1865
– panorama du fleuve Saint-Laurent et des Grands Lacs #218
Barnes, Elliott Chappel, photographe can, actif 1905-1919 #4610
Barnes, Robert Percy, architecte can, 1857-1926
– Edmonton (Alta), Imperial Bank of Canada #9154
Barnet, Will, artiste amér, 1911-
– et Marion F.S. Mackay Nicoll #6701 6703
Barnett, David, artiste can, 1933-
– expositions de groupe
    – (1979) #674
Barnsley, James Macdonald, artiste can, 1861-1929 #4612
– expositions
    – (1964) #4611
– influence de l'impressionnisme #227
– oeuvres, Galerie nationale du Canada (Ottawa, Ont) #4613
Barot, Cécile, tisserande can, m. 1958
– ceinture fléchée #2833
Barott, Blackader & Webster, agence can d'architecture
– Montréal (Qué)
    – Bank of British North America #9164
    – théâtre Saint-Denis #9068
– Vancouver (CB), gare du Canadien

Pacifique #9534
Barott & Blackader, agence can d'architecture
– Lake Louise (Alta), Château Lake Louise #9279
– Montréal (Qué)
    – Bell Canada #9310
    – édifice Aldred #9313
Barr, David John, artiste amér, 1939-
– structures en relief #777
Barraud, Cyril, artiste can, 1877-1965
– et Walter Joseph Phillips #6856
Barrett, Joel, architecte can, actif 1956
– Vancouver (CB), Vancouver Civic Auditorium, concours #9080
Barrett, Samuel A., collectionneur amér, XXe s.
– collection, masques kwakiutls #3938
Barrington (NE), Meeting House
– architecture #7823
Barry, James, artiste irlandais, 1741-1806
– peinture, mort de Wolfe #220
Barry, John, orfèvre can, né 1815, actif 1838-1857 #2649
bars
– voir tavernes
Bartlett, Bob, officier de la marine brit au Canada, 1875-1946
– résidence, Brigus (TN) #8539
Bartlett, William Henry, artiste brit au Canada, 1809-1854 #812 1323
– art et écrits #4617
– Canadian Scenery #4615 4616
    – vues sur poterie #2282 2288 2362
– faux #4614
– Windsor, Nova Scotia #1218
Barton Myers Associates, agence can d'architecture
– Edmonton (Alta), Citadel Theatre #9140
– Los Angeles (Calif), revitalisation du quartier Bunker Hill #8364
Bartram, Edward John (Ed), artiste can, 1938-
– expositions
    – (1979) #4618
Basin Head (IPE)
– restauration de cabanes de pêcheurs #7795
Bastien, Jean-Marie, artiste can, 1934- #2769
Bastin, Michèle, artiste can, 1944-
– expositions, critiques #4619
bateaux
– voir aussi bateaux miniatures; canots; kayaks; figures de proue; umiaks
bateaux . Canada
– confection de voiles, Nouvelle-Ecosse #2157
– Nouveau-Brunswick, XIXe s. #2150
– Nouvelle-Ecosse, vues
    – Gray, John Warren #5648
    – Lismer, Arthur #6294
– Québec, XIXe s. #1604
– XIXe s. #2095
bateaux dans l'art
– (1600-1900) #225
– (Ottawa, Ont), Archives publiques du Canada. Collection William H. Coverdale

#12
– Bluenose, tapis crocheté #2763
– MacAskill, Wallace R., vues
  photographiques #6351
– Murphy, Rowley Walter #6666
– Nouveau-Brunswick, grands voiliers, XIXe
  s. #1190
– Nouvelle-Ecosse, XIXe s. #163 1201
– peinture canadienne traditionnelle #965
  966
– Plamondon, Antoine-Sébastien, *Le flûtiste*
  #6885
– poterie canadienne #2288
    – XIXe s. #2341
– Russell, Edward John #7111
bateaux miniatures . Canada
– Bradford, John Locke #4895
– en bouteilles, Québec #2944
– Leclerc, Eugène #2174 2209
– Saint-Jean-Port-Joli (Qué) #2194
– Terre-Neuve #1155
– Toronto (Ont), Royal Ontario Museum.
  Collection Sigmund Samuel #3135
– voiliers, île aux Coudres (Qué) #2178
Bates, Maxwell Bennett, artiste et architecte
  can, 1906-1980 #4620 4625
– commentaire sur l'art, la littérature, et la
  photographie #4621
– commentaire sur la gravure #817
– correspondance, Jock Macdonald #6376
– expositions
    – (1960) #4622
    – (1973) #4624
– expositions, critiques #4623
– expositions de groupe
    – (1962) #1847
– membre du groupe Limners #2043
– portraits #715
– théories sur l'art #1944
Bates, Patricia (Pat) Martin, artiste can, 1927-
  #4627
– expositions
    – (1972) #4626
– expositions de groupe
    – (1967) #821
Bath (Angleterre), Bath Festival. Holburne of
  Menstrie Museum
– expositions
    – *James Wilson Morrice 1865-1924* (1968)
      #6627
Bathurst (NB), Nepisiguit Centennial
  Library
– expositions
    – *Colville, Pratt, Forrestall* (1974) #1129
    – *The Beaverbrook Art Gallery Presents Nine
      New Brunswick Artists/La Galerie d'art
      Beaverbrook présente neuf artistes du
      Nouveau-Brunswick* (1973) #1182
Bathurst Island (TNO)
– artefacts dorsétiens #4375
bâtiments agricoles
– *voir aussi* écuries; élévateurs à grains;
  granges
bâtiments agricoles . Canada
– (1938-1942) #7666
– Charlevoix (Qué) #8629

– Colombie-Britannique #8153
– mennonites #8715
– Nouvelle-Ecosse, XVIIIe s. #7815
– Ontario #9225
– Prairies, décorations peintes #1852
– provinces de l'Ouest #8083
– Québec #8572
    – (années 1910) #8554
    – XVIIe-XVIIIe s. #2217 8581
– tradition irlandaise, XIXe s. #8523
– Tunis Snook Farm (près de Kingston, Ont)
  #8681
bâtiments agricoles . Etats-Unis
– Ouest américain #8083
Batiscan (Qué), Vieux Presbytère
– architecture et intérieur #8807
Batoche (Sask)
– architecture et utilisation du sol #8115
Battleford (Sask), Fort Battleford
– architecture #8481 8484
Baturin, Jon, photographe can, actif 1980-
– catalogue de photographies #1023
Baudot, Jean, artiste can, 1929-
– art par ordinateur #528
Baudry (dit Des Butes), Guillaume, orfèvre
  can, 1657-1732 #234 235
Bauhaus
– influence sur architecture canadienne
  #7735
– influence sur Fritz Brandtner #4904
– influence sur tapisserie canadienne #2774
Bauman, Joseph, artiste can de style
  "fraktur", 1815-1899 #2255 4628
Baxter, Brian, artiste can (vitrail), actif 1981
  #2460
Baxter, Iain, artiste can, 1936- #4629 4630
– commentaire sur N.E. Thing Co. Ltd.
  #6675
– et George Sawchuk #7143
– et N.E. Thing Co. Ltd. #535
– expositions, critiques #520
– expositions de groupe
    – (1967) #490
    – (1971) #98
    – (1974) #574
    – (1979) #2069
    – (1980) #703
    – (1981) #797
– oeuvres de l'imaginaire #530
– utilisation de la photographie #1057
Baxter, Ingrid (Elaine) Hieber, artiste can,
  1938-
– et George Sawchuk #7143
– expositions de groupe
    – (1974) #574
Baxter, Robert W., architecte can, 1936-
– Vancouver (CB), University of British
  Columbia. Student Union, concours #9503
Bayefsky, Aba, artiste can, 1923-
– en Inde #4631
– expositions
    – (1967) #4633
– murale, *Out of Bondage*, Beth-El Synagogue
  (Don Mills, Ont) #4632
Bayfield, Fanny Amelia Wright, artiste can,
  1814-1891 #1164

Baykal, Erol, photographe can, actif 1975
– et Gallery of Photography (Vancouver,
  CB) #2052
Bayley, W.B., photographe can, 1857-1939
  #977
Bazaine, Jean-René, artiste fr, 1904-
– influence sur Fernand Leduc #6186
BC Photographer, périodique can #998
BC Society for the Furtherance of Indian
  Arts and Crafts
– (1940-1943) #4114
Beach, William Godkin, artisan verrier can,
  1839-1902 #2396
Beaconsfield (Qué), église Saint Edmund of
  Canterbury
– architecture, Roger D'Astous #8840
Bealy, Allan, artiste can, 1951- #1512
Beam, Carl, artiste can, 1943-
– entretien #4155
– expositions de groupe
    – (1981) #4173
Beamsville (Ont), école secondaire
– architecture, Walter W. Lachance #9387
Beamsville (Ont), Nipponia Home for the
  Aged
– architecture, Henry Fliess, et Yamazaki &
  Ridpath #8516
Beardsley, Aubrey Vincent, artiste et auteur
  brit, 1872-1898
– influence sur James Frederic McCulloch
  #6463
– influence sur Louis de Niverville #6705
Beardy, Jackson, artiste can, 1944- #4157
  4161 4634 4635 4636
– expositions, critiques #1866
    – (1972) #4128
– expositions de groupe
    – (1972) #4131
Beatty, John William, artiste can, 1869-1941
  #4637
– correspondance, J.E.H. MacDonald #6371
– et Edith Grace Coombs #5172
– expositions
    – (1981) #4638
– expositions, critiques #1710
– expositions de groupe
    – (1942) #359
– professeur d'Addison Winchell Price
  #6935
– professeur d'Alice A. Innes #5900
– professeur de Frederick Nicholas Loveroff
  #6329 6330
– professeur de Joseph Sydney Hallam
  #5687
Beau, Henri, artiste can, 1863-1949 #1382
– *La dispersion des Acadiens* (1900) #4639
Beau, Paul, orfèvre can, 1871-1949 #2693
  4640 4641
Beauce (Qué)
– costume féminin (ca 1875) #2828
– croix et calvaires #1292
Beauchemin, Micheline, artiste can, 1930-
  #2102 4642 4643 4644 4645
– expositions de groupe
    – (1978) #2772
– *La chute d'Icare*, tapisserie et rideau de

scène, Place des Arts (Montréal, Qué)
#8233
– rideau de scène, Centre national des arts
(Ottawa, Ont) #9108
Beaucour, Paul
– *voir* Malepart de Grand Maison (dit
Beaucour), Paul
Beaucourt, François Malepart de, artiste can,
1740-1794 #269 270 1300 4646 4647
– et société québécoise #1375
– expositions de groupe
– (1959) #219
– influence de la peinture française #1244
Beaudin, Denise, artiste can, 1930-
– expositions de groupe
– (1978) #2772
Beaudin, Gaétan, céramiste can, 1924- #2395
– professeur #2381
Beaudoin-Hansen, Kéro-Claire (Kéro),
photographe can, 1940- #4648
Beaudry, Henry, artiste can, 1921- #4649
Beaugrand, Gilles, orfèvre can, 1906- #2179
2693 4650
– et art religieux québécois (années 1950)
#1250
Beaugrand, Honoré, homme d'Etat can,
1849-1906
– portrait, Alfred Boisseau #4769
Beaugrand-Champagne, Claire, photographe
can, 1948- #1556 1562
– vues photographiques, Disraëli (Qué),
(1972) #1513
Beaulac, Henri, artiste et designer can, 1914-
#2174
– cartes de Noël #856
– et Simone Marie Yvette Hudon-Beaulac
#5856
– intérieur, Place des Arts (Montréal, Qué)
#8233
Beaulac, Simone Marie Yvette Hudon
– *voir* Hudon-Beaulac, Simone Marie Yvette
Beaulieu, Jean-Louis, architecte can, 1943-
– Montréal (Qué), station de métro
Angrignon #9555
Beaulieu, Paul Vanier, artiste can, 1910-
#4651 4652
– illustrations de livres #926
Beaumont, Serge, sculpteur can, 1951-
– Symposium international de sculpture
environnementale de Chicoutimi (Qué),
(1980) #1639
– utilisation de la pierre #1634
Beaumont (Qué), église Saint-Etienne
– architecture et intérieur #8809
Beauport (Qué)
– architecture (1625-1975) #7880
Beauport (Qué), Asile des aliénés
– vue, XIXe s., sur bol en faïence #2342
Beaupré (Qué)
– architecture domestique, XVIIIe-XIXe s.
#8582
Beauregard, Andrée, artiste can (tapisserie),
1927- #4653
beauté
– et art
– Borduas, Paul-Emile, commentaire #4799

– Harris, Lawren Stewart, commentaire
#5716
Beauvais, René
– *voir* St-James (dit Beauvais), René
Beaver Flint Glass Co., fabricants de verre
(Toronto, Ont) #2401
Beaver Hall Group #589 592
– et Anne Douglas Savage #7131 7132
– et Edwin Headley Holgate #5818 5819
Beaverbrook, William Maxwell Aitken,
baron, éditeur can en Angleterre,
1879-1964
– et Beaverbrook Art Gallery (Fredericton,
NB) #3067
– et Canadian War Memorials, collection
#1102
– portrait, Yousuf Karsh #6022
Beck, Hélène Boily (Claire), artiste can, 1932-
#1551
Beck & Eadie, agence can d'architecture
– Toronto (Ont), Banque de Nouvelle-Ecosse
#9192
Beckett, Samuel, auteur irlandais, 1906-
– Kennedy, Garry Neill, comparaison #6043
Beckett, Samuel G., architecte can, 1869-1917
– Toronto (Ont), résidences #8639
Beckington, Alice J., artiste amér, 1868-1942
– professeure de Mary Evelyn Wrinch #7617
7618
Beckmann, Max, artiste all, 1884-1950
– influence sur Ivan Kenneth Eyre #5394
Bédard, Jean-Baptiste, charpentier et
arpenteur can, 1761-1818 #1300
Bedeque Bay (IPE)
– architecture #7798
Bedford, Michael, photographe can, actif
années 1970
– catalogue de photographies #995
Bedford (Ont), Molsons Bank
– architecture #9173
Bedini, Cajetan, prêtre it au Canada, actif
années 1850
– *L'album des costumes de communautés
religieuses de femmes au Canada en 1853*
#2834
Bedwell, Edward Parker, officier de la
marine brit, artiste au Canada, actif
1851-1862, m. 1919 #2020
– expositions de groupe
– (1979) #2023
Beechey, Frederick William, officier de la
marine brit, artiste au Canada, 1796-1856
– expédition, Alaska (Nord-Ouest) #4369
Beetz, Johan, artiste can, 1874-1949 #4654
Beggs, Neil G., architecte can, 1871-1935
– Toronto (Ont), théâtres et cinémas #9067
Beil, Charlie, sculpteur can, 1894-
– programme d'expositions itinérantes,
Alberta (1980) #1972
Béland, Luc, artiste can, 1951- #1544
– expositions
– (1976) #4655
– expositions de groupe
– (1977) #1532
– (1981) #1565
– symposium, Musée du Nouveau-Monde
(La Rochelle, France), (1980) #1559

Bélanger, Gérard, artiste can, 1932-
– entretien #1527
Belbin, Louise, artiste can, 1898-
– expositions
– (1978) #2759
Belcher, Edward, officier de la marine brit,
artiste au Canada, 1799-1877
– expédition, Alaska (Nord-Ouest) #4369
Belcher Islands (TNO)
– sculpture #4459
Belfast (Irlande du Nord), Ulster Museum
– art amérindien #3477
Belkin, Arnold, artiste can, 1930- #4656
Bell, Alistair Macready, artiste can, 1913-
– commentaire sur la gravure #817
Bell, Bert, photographe can, 1938- #1036
Bell, Clive, critique brit, 1881-1964
– commentaire sur James Wilson Morrice
#6619
Bell, George Kenneth (Ken), photographe
can, 1914-
– catalogue de photographies #995
– entretien #4657
– photographies de la Seconde Guerre
mondiale #1107
Bell, Leland, artiste can, 1953-
– expositions de groupe
– (1981) #4173
Bell, Mathew, maître de forges can, actif
1793-1845
– et Forges du Saint-Maurice (Trois-Rivières,
Qué) #2698
Bell, W. & D., Pottery, fabricants de
céramique (Québec, Qué)
– (années 1850-ca 1900) #2291 2298 2322
– paysages québécois dits "de Thomas"
#2287
Bell-Irving, Henry Ogle, artiste et architecte
can, 1856-1931
– expositions de groupe
– (1980) #4665
Bell-Smith, Frederic Marlett, artiste can,
1846-1923 #221 4666
– commentaire sur dessins faits en
expédition, Rocheuses et chaîne Selkirk
(1887-1889) #4667
– et British Columbia Society of Fine Arts
#1978
– et Thomas Mower Martin #6435 6438
– expositions
– (1977) #4668
– expositions, critiques #174
– expositions de groupe
– (1978) #1726
Bella-Bellas
– récipients #3985
Bella-Coolas
– crécelles #4026
– culture #3874
– masques #4000
– mythologie #3772
– pétroglyphes #3816
Belle, Charles Ernest de, artiste can,
1873-1939 #1382 4658
– en comparaison avec Georges Delfosse
#1385

Belleau, Charles, céramiste can, 1799-1889 #2366

Bellefleur, Léon, artiste can, 1910- #1541 1542 1543 4659 4660 4661
– à Paris (France) #1434
– entretien #4663
– et peinture, Montréal (Qué), (années 1950) #1403
– expositions
   – (1968) #4662
– expositions de groupe
   – (1962) #1420
– influence sur Janine Leroux-Guillaume #6247

Bellerive, Marcel, artiste can, 1934- #4664

Belleval, Jean Fournier de, décorateur can, 1922-
– décors et costumes, Montreal Theatre Ballet #1410

Belleville, François
– voir Guernon (dit Belleville), François

Belleville (Ont)
– maisons en brique, début XIXe s. #8521
– poterie, XIXe s. #2286

Belleville (Ont), Belleville Public Library
– expositions
   – Quinte Arts Council: Survey 1977 (1977) #1816

Belleville (Ont), Institut des sourds et muets
– architecture #8968

Belley, René, artiste can, 1951-
– membre du Centre communautaire catholique Tour de David (Saint-Basile-le-Grand, Qué) #1510

Belli, Flavio, artiste can, 1950-
– xérographie en couleurs #614

Bellingham (Wash), Whatcom Museum of Natural History and Art
– expositions
   – Arts of a Vanished Era: An Exhibition of the Whatcom Museum of History and Art, Bellingham, Washington (1968) #3950

Bellot, Paul (Dom), prêtre et architecte can, 1878-1944
– architecture religieuse au Québec #8831
– églises #8838
– influence sur architecture religieuse au Québec #8334 8820
– Magog (Qué), monastère de Saint-Benoît-du-Lac #8332
– théories sur l'art et l'architecture #8333

Belzile, Louis, artiste can, 1929- #4669
– expositions de groupe
   – (1959) #1414
   – (1977) #1465
   – (1981) #1471

Bemi, Murray & Associates, agence can d'architecture
– Ottawa (Ont), Saint Basil's Roman Catholic Church #8765

Bendahan, Raphael, photographe can, 1944- #4670

Bengough, John Wilson, artiste can, 1851-1923 #4674 4676 4677
– art et écrits #4671
– au Québec (1887) #4675

– autobiographie #4673
– dessins humoristiques et politiques #942 957
   – The Grip #943
– réflexion sur son oeuvre #4672

Bénic, Lorraine, artiste can, 1937- #4678

Benjamin, Anthony, artiste can, 1931- #4679

Benjamin, Max, artiste can, 1928-
– expositions, critiques #2072
– expositions de groupe
   – (1979) #2075

Benjamin-Constant, Jean-Joseph, artiste fr, 1845-1902
– enseignement aux artistes canadiens #243

Benjamin Lent Pottery, fabricants de céramique (comté de Lincoln, Ont)
– (1836-1841) #2367

Bennet & Co., éditeur (Montréal, Qué)
– cartes de souhaits
   – Noël, thème décoratif #890
   – scènes sportives #2360

Bennett, Arnold, écrivain brit, 1867-1931
– commentaire sur James Wilson Morrice #6619

Bennett, Geoffrey, artiste can, actif années 1960
– entretien #4680

Benoît, Jacques, artiste can, 1946-
– et RACE (Regroupement des artistes des Cantons de l'Est) #1536

Benoît, Jean, artiste can, 1922-
– à Paris (France) #426

Benoît, Mimi Parent
– voir Parent-Benoît, Mimi

Benoît (dit Livernois), Jules-Isaïe, photographe can, 1830-1865 #258 259 1275

Benson & Hedges Company, compagnie de tabac
– murales, Montréal (Qué) et Toronto (Ont) #539

Bentham, Douglas, sculpteur can, 1947- #145 4681 4682 4684
– en comparaison avec André Fauteux #785
– entretien, Emma Lake Workshops (Emma Lake, Sask) #1934
– expositions
   – (1973) #1858
   – (1976) #4683
   – (1979) #4685
   – (1980) #4686
– expositions de groupe
   – (1975) #1926
   – (1977) #782
   – (1981) #797
– techniques #792

Bentley, Percy, photographe can, 1882-1968
– expositions de groupe
   – (1976) #2012

Beny, Wilfred Roloff, artiste can, 1924- #4688
– commentaire sur la mise en pages artistique #921
– expositions
   – (1971) #4690
– photographies, University of Calgary. Art Gallery (Calgary, Alta) #4691
– théories sur l'art #4687

Benzie & Bow, agence can d'architecture
– Lethbridge (Alta), Saint Michael's General Hospital #9021

Béothuks
– art #3528 3611 3623 3627
– costume #3584
– culture #3597
– dans l'art #1162

Bequette, Jean-Baptiste, orfèvre can, actif ca 1817-ca 1846
– oeuvres, Detroit Institute of Arts (Detroit, Mich) #2691

Bérard, François, carrossier can, actif 1842 #1301

Bérard, Réal, artiste can, 1935-
– expositions
   – (1975) #4692

berceaux . Amérindiens #3407 3485

berceaux . Canada
– Ontario
   – (1780-1900) #2577
   – (années 1790-1857) #2558
– Québec, XVIIe-XVIIIe s. #2530 2531

berceaux . Hurons #3519

berceaux . Indiens de la côte nord-ouest
– préhistoire #4017

berceaux . Ingaliks #4087

berceaux . Iroquois #3519
– Montréal (Qué), château de Ramezay #3593

berceaux . Saulteux/Ojibwa
– Island Lake (Man) #3549

berceaux . Tagish #4106

berceaux . Têtes-de-Boule #4079

berceaux . Tlingits #4106

berceaux . Tutchonis #4106

berceuses . Canada
– île aux Coudres (Qué) #2178
– Québec #1334 1335
   – XVIIIe-XIXe s. #2535 2536

Bercovitch, Aleksandre (Alexander), artiste can, 1891-1951 #4693

Berczy, Jean-Charlotte Allamand, artiste can, 1760-1839
– correspondance avec son mari (1798-1812) #4696
– mère et professeure de William Bent Berczy #4694

Berczy, William Bent, artiste can, 1791-1873 #241 242 4694
– correspondance avec son père #4700

Berczy, William von Moll, artiste can, 1748-1813 #4695 4697 4698 4699 4701
– correspondance avec sa femme (1798-1812) #4696
– peintures, Université Laval (Québec, Qué) #3078
– père et professeur de William Bent Berczy #4694
– portrait d'un membre de la famille Hertel de Rouville #1345
– Woolsey Family, Galerie nationale du Canada (Ottawa, Ont) #4700

Bergeron, André, artiste can, 1937- #4703
– lithographies, Le Cantique spirituel #4702

Bergeron, Fernand, artiste can, 1942-

- gravures, *Pour les nuits blanches de Nini de Saint-H la petite* #4704
Bergeron, Germain, sculpteur can, 1933- #4705
Bergeron, Jean-Baptiste, sculpteur et émailleur can, 1919- #2378
Bergeron, Suzanne, artiste can, 1930- #4706 4707
- à Paris (France) #426
Berggren, Nels, artiste can, 1910-
- Imperial (Sask), Centennial Fountain #1852
Bergman, Henry Eric, artiste can, 1893-1958 #4708
- expositions
  - (1980) #4709
- gravure sur bois de fil #802
- oeuvres, Ayerst, McKenna and Harrison, entreprise de produits chimiques #852
Bériau, Oscar-Alphonse, administrateur des arts can, né 1883
- directeur, Ecole des arts domestiques de Québec (Québec, Qué) #2186 2969
Béringiens anciennes
- artefacts #4327
- artefacts préhistoriques #4340
Berkeley (Calif), University of California. Robert H. Lowie Museum of Anthropology
- expositions
  - *Art of the Northwest Coast* (1965) #3928
- masques inuit #4349
Berlin (Allemagne de l'Ouest), Akademie der Künste
- expositions
  - *Group of Seven: Kanadische Landschafts-Maler: Eine Wanderausstellung der McMichael Canadian Collection, Kleinburg, Ontario, Kanada* (1977) #1781
Berlin (Allemagne de l'Ouest), Berlin Free University
- architecture #9464
Berlin (Allemagne de l'Ouest), Berliner Museum für Völkerkunde
- art amérindien #3421 3423
- art amérindien de la côte nord-ouest #3762
Berlin (Allemagne de l'Ouest), Nationalgalerie
- architecture, Ludwig Mies van der Rohe #9348
Berlinguet, Louis-Thomas, architecte et sculpteur can, 1790-1863 #6947
- île d'Orléans (Qué), église Saint-Jean #8801
- thème du souper d'Emmaüs #1615
Berman, Michaele, artiste can, 1947-
- entretien #4710
Bernatchez-Rousseau, Michèle, artiste can (tapisserie), 1939- #2769
Berne (Suisse), Historisches Museum
- art amérindien #3400 3473
Bernini, Gian Lorenzo, artiste it, 1598-1680
- baldaquin de la cathédrale Saint-Pierre-de-Rome (Italie), inspiration pour le baldaquin de l'église de Neuville (Qué) #8826
Berry, Martha, collectionneuse amér, 1866-1942

- collection, coffrets en écorce de bouleau ornés de piquants de porc-épic, Outaouais #3548
Bersudsky, Sid, designer can, 1919- #4711
Berthier (Qué), église Sainte-Elisabeth
- architecture et intérieur, Amable Gauthier #241 242
Berthier-en-Haut (Qué), église
- sculptures sur bois, Gilles Bolvin #4781
Berthierville (Qué), chapelle Cuthbert
- architecture #8881
Berthierville (Qué), église
- architecture #8833
- architecture et art #8874
Berthon, George Theodore, artiste can, 1806-1892 #1705 4713
- portrait, sir Isaac Brock #4712
Bertounesque, André, artiste can, 1937- #4714
Bérulle, Pierre de, cardinal, prêtre fr, 1575-1619 #1365
Besant, Derek Michael, artiste can, 1950- #4715
- expositions, critiques #1883
Besner, Jacques, sculpteur can, 1919- #4716 4717
- utilisation du plastique #1442
Bessonett, Cecilia Augusta, artiste can, active années 1850 #1118
béton
- architecture canadienne (1867-1967) #7695
- architecture canadienne et architecture américaine (années 1910) #7643
- architecture manitobaine, XIXe-début XXe s. #8102
- béton préfabriqué
  - (années 1960) #7684 9401
  - Montréal (Qué), Habitat 67 #8578
- Concours pour ouvrages en béton (1971) #7706
- édifice Jacobs (Montréal, Qué) #9305
- Hamilton Terminal Station (Hamilton, Ont) #9527
- Toronto (Ont), Roman Stone Company (années 1903-1920) #7734
Betteridge, Lois Etherington, orfèvre can, 1928- #4718
Beube, Douglas S. (Doug), photographe can, 1950-
- catalogue de photographies #991
Beug, Lorne, artiste can, 1948- #2076
- expositions de groupe
  - (1977) #781
- sculpture en céramique #795
Beull, Vincent, artiste can, 1953- #4719
Beuys, Joseph, artiste all, 1921-
- Frenkel, Vera, commentaire #713
Bevan & Moore, agence can d'architecture
- Toronto (Ont), Government House, concours #8748
Beveridge, Eleanor, céramiste can, 1920- #1199
Beveridge, Karl John, artiste can, 1945-
- commentaire sur la politique et l'art #602
- expositions de groupe
  - (1971) #98

- (1977) #782
- (1980) #1063
- *Maybe Wendy's Right* #1052
Beynon, William, ethnologue can, 1888-1958
- commentaire sur les Tsimshians #3981
bibliothèques . Canada
- (années 1910) #9039
- (années 1940) #9043
- (années 1950) #9044
- bibliothèques, universités et collèges
  - (années 1930) #9042
  - (années 1960) #9046
  - (années 1970) #9052
- Guelph (Ont), University of Guelph. Library Building #9468
- Montréal (Qué), Centre canadien d'architecture #7749
- Niagara Falls (Ont), Earl W. Brydges Public Library #9050
- Ontario (1955-1965) #9045
- Ottawa (Ont), Bibliothèque scientifique nationale #9049
- Scarborough (Ont), Albert Campbell Library #9047
- Toronto (Ont)
  - bibliothèques publiques
    - (années 1920) #9040
    - (années 1930) #9041
  - Metro Toronto Public Library #9051
  - University of Toronto. John P. Robarts Research Library #9048 9050
  - University of Toronto. Victoria College. Bibliothèque #9038
- transformation d'édifices publics en bibliothèque #9147 9148
- Vernon (CB), Vernon Civic Centre #8972
bibliothèques . Etats-Unis
- bibliothèques, universités et collèges (années 1970) #9052
Bice, Clare, artiste can, 1909-1976
- commentaire sur ses études en Europe #408
Bick, Walter, collectionneur can, XXe s.
- bocaux à marinades #2405
Bidner, Michael Thomas, artiste can, 1944-
- xérographie en couleurs #614
Biederman, Charles Joseph, artiste amér, 1906-
- et structurisme #6079
- structures en relief #777
Biegert, Claus, écrivain all, 1947-
- commentaire sur la baie James (Qué) #1566
Biéler, André Charles, artiste can, 1896- #1392 4722 4726 4727
- commentaire sur l'art canadien (1941-1951) #390
- commentaire sur le nationalisme dans l'art canadien (années 1930) #337
- et Gordon Edward Pfeiffer #6847
- et peinture de genre #392
- expositions
  - (1963) #4723
  - (1970) #4725
- expositions de groupe
  - (1977) #1278 1279

– gravures en relief #4724
– gravures sur bois debout #804
– réflexion sur sa technique #4720 4721
– réflexion sur son oeuvre #349
Bieler, André Charles Théodore (Ted),
    sculpteur can, 1938-
– sculptures (années 1960) #1793
– sculptures d'argile (années 1960) #743
– théories sur l'art et l'architecture #8235
Bieler, Ted A.
– *voir* Bieler, André Charles Théodore (Ted)
Bierk, David, artiste can, 1944-
– commentaire sur Jack Chambers #700
Bierstadt, Albert, artiste amér, 1830-1902
– dans provinces de l'Ouest #1859
– et Thomas Mower Martin #6435
Bierwagen, Ottmar, photographe can, actif
    années 1970
– catalogue de photographies #995
Bigger, Charles A., photographe can,
    1853-1923
– photographies d'arpentage #1014 1015
Biggs, Hugh Beynon, photographe can,
    1876-1941 #4728
bijoux
– *voir aussi* anneaux et bagues; broches
    (bijoux); orfèvrerie
bijoux . Amérindiens
– orfèvrerie de traite #2634
– XXe s. #2143
bijoux . Canada
– (1837-1887) #253
– (1964-1967) #2108 2109
– (1979-1980) #2138
– (années 1960) #2696
– (années 1970) #2706
– Aird, Neil Carrick #4503
– Alberta (années 1970) #1951
– Arnoldi, Charles #2663
– bijoux ukrainiens (1865-1945) #2869
– Colombie-Britannique (années 1950) #2695
– Delrue, Georges #2694 5281 5282
– Gaudin (dit Lapoterterie), Nicolas #5572
– guide pour collectionneurs #2125 2131
– Leadbeater, Roy #6181
– Letarte, Jean-Paul #6249
– Nicoll, Marion F.S. Mackay #6702
– Nordbeck, Peter #258 259
– Ottawa (Ont), Musée national de
    l'Homme. Centre canadien d'études sur la
    culture traditionnelle #963
– Picard, Louis-Alexandre #269 270
– Price, Art #6928
– Québec #2228
    – (années 1950) #2193
    – (années 1970) #2701
    – dans les chansons traditionnelles
        canadiennes-françaises #2898
    – XVIIe-XVIIIe s. #2657
– Reid, Bill #6985 6987
– Toronto (Ont), Ontario College of Art
    #3009
– Varin (dit La Pistole), Jacques #269 270
– Vidal, Guy #2216
– XXe s. #2142
Bill, Edward B., artiste can, actif 1885-1903

– professeur de Georges Delfosse #5279
Billing, John H., maçon can, actif années
    1880-début XXe s.
– comté de Haliburton (Ont) #8335
Bingham, John, photographe can, actif 1979
– catalogue de photographies #1032
Binning, Bertram Charles (B.C.), artiste can,
    1909-1976 #1996 4731
– commentaire sur l'enseignement du dessin
    #4730
– commentaire sur sa mosaïque murale,
    Imperial Bank, Vancouver (CB) #4732
– dessins #4729
– expositions
    – (1973) #4734
    – (1979) #4736
– expositions, critiques #4735
– expositions de groupe
    – (1958) #431
– lauréat, médaille des arts connexes de
    l'Institut royal d'architecture du Canada
    (1962) #4733
– professeur de Donald Alvin Jarvis #5947
– résidence, West Vancouver (CB) #8694
Bird, Eustace Godfrey, architecte can,
    1870-1950
– Montréal (Qué), Transportation Building
    #9307
– Toronto (Ont)
    – Bank of Toronto #8293 9162 9185
    – Banque Royale #9152
– Windsor (Ont), Dominion Bank #9188
Bird, John, architecte can, 1923-
– LaSalle (Qué), Saint John Brébeuf Parish
    Church #8766
– Montréal (Qué), Saint Gabriel's Church
    #8766
Bird, Wallace S., collectionneur can, 1917-
– collection, art canadien, provinces de
    l'Atlantique, XXe s. #1130
Birdsall, Pam, céramiste can, active 1980
    #2395
Birkbeck, George, médecin brit, 1776-1841
– rôle dans le développement des
    Mechanic's Institutes, Angleterre et
    Canada #3064
Birks, Henry Gifford, orfèvre can, 1892-1979
– collection, orfèvrerie, Galerie nationale du
    Canada (Ottawa, Ont) #2653
Birmingham & Wood, agence can
    d'architecture
– restauration, quartier chinois, Vancouver
    (CB) #8159
Birmingham (Ala), Birmingham Festival of
    the Arts
– expositions
    – *Eskimo Narrative* (1979) #4285
Birmingham (Angleterre), Ikon Gallery
– expositions
    – *Canada in Birmingham* (1981) #710
    – *Jack Bush: Paintings and Drawings,
        1955-1976* (1980) #4976
Birnie, Ian, conservateur can, actif 1974
– entretien sur l'exposition *Videoscape*, Art
    Gallery of Ontario (Toronto, Ont), (1974)
    #566

Birnirk
– artefacts préhistoriques #4327 4345
Birnstihl, Adam, céramiste can, mort 1900
    #2356
Bischoff, Elmer Nelson, artiste amér, 1916-
– influence sur Gordon Appelbe Smith
    #7232
– professeur de Gordon Appelbe Smith
    #7225
Bishop, G., graveur de médailles can, actif
    1878
– médailles de tempérance #724
Bismarck (ND), State Historical Society of
    North Dakota
– art, Indiens des plaines #3690
bison
– art canadien et art américain, fin
    XVIIIe-XXe s. #62
Bissett, Bill, artiste can, 1939-
– expositions de groupe
    – (1971) #2042
Bissonette, Héliodore, artiste can, 1890-1966
    #1428 1429
Bittdorf-Holland-Christianson Architects,
    agence can d'architecture
– restauration, Duggan House (Edmonton,
    Alta) #8729
Black Creek Pioneer Village (Toronto, Ont)
    #8063
– atelier de tissage #2735
– résidence de médecin #8675
Blackburn, Jacques, artiste can (tapisserie),
    1945- #4737
Blackstock, Hattie, artiste can, 1894-
– entretien #4738
Blackwood, David Lloyd, artiste can, 1941-
– expositions
    – (1967) #4739
Bladen, Ronald, sculpteur can, 1918- #4741
– commentaire sur la vie à New York
    (années 1960) #460
– entretien #4740
Blahut, John, photographe can, 1950- #1007
Blais, Marie-Claire, auteure can, 1939-
– et Mary Meigs #6510
Blake, William, artiste et poète brit,
    1757-1827
– influence sur Bertram Richard Brooker
    #4925
– influence sur Graham Metson #6523
Blakey, Richard Palin, architecte can,
    1879-1963
– Edmonton (Alta), édifices du Parlement
    #8944 8945
Blanchette, Pierre, artiste can, 1953-
– *Ispaham* #1563
Blanck, Nora, artiste can, 1947-
– constructions en matériaux bruts (années
    1970) #2065
– expositions, critiques #2081
– expositions de groupe
    – (1978) #663
Bland, John, architecte can, 1911-
– Charlottetown (IPE), Confederation
    Centre, concours #9088
– Ottawa (Ont), Carleton University #9455

Bland, Lemoyne, Edwards, Shine, agence
    can d'architecture
– Montréal (Qué), station de métro Jarry
    #9549
Bland, Lemoyne & Edwards, agence can
    d'architecture
– Charlottetown (IPE), Confederation
    Centre, concours #9089
– Ottawa (Ont), Northern Electric Research
    and Development Laboratories #9344
Bland, Salem Goldworth, médecin can,
    1859-1950
– portrait, Lawren Stewart Harris #5733
Blankstein, Coop & Gillmor, agence can
    d'architecture
– Saskatoon (Sask), Mendel Art Gallery,
    concours #9091
Blatherwick, Kater R., architecte can, 1890-
– Toronto (Ont), Banque de Montréal #9190
Blatter, Caron & Côté, agence can
    d'architecture
– Sainte-Foy (Qué), église
    Saint-Louis-de-France #8841
Blatter, Robert, architecte can, 1899-
– Québec (Qué), édifice de la compagnie
    d'assurance La Solidarité #7939
Blazeje, Zbigniew, sculpteur can, 1942-
– expositions de groupe
    – (1967) #490
– sculptures (années 1960) #1793
– utilisation de la lumière #767
Bleyenberg, Harry, photographe can, ca
    1947-
– catalogue de photographies #1023
– collection *Woman and World* #4742
Blier, Jean-Marc, artiste can, 1921- #4743
    4744
Blin, Claude, artiste can, 1931- #4745
Bloch, Martin, artiste brit, 1883-1954
– influence sur Stephen Andrews #4527
Blomfield (né Bloomfield), James Jerris,
    artiste can (vitrail), 1872-1951
– vitraux #1977
    – Hamilton (Ont), Hamilton Mausoleum
        #8900
    – Vancouver (CB) #2456
    – Victoria (CB), édifices du Parlement
        #8966
Bloomfield, Charles Ernest, artiste can
    (vitraux), 1877-1954
– vitraux, Vancouver (CB) #2456
Bloomfield, James Jerris
– *voir* Blomfield, James Jerris
Bloomfield Hills (Mich), Cranbrook
    Academy of Art
– Betteridge, Lois Etherington, élève #4718
– Pachter, Charles, élève #6748
Bloomfield Hills (Mich), Cranbrook
    Academy of Art. Musée
– expositions
    – *Beads: Their Use by Upper Great Lakes
        Indians* (1977) #3635
    – *Eight from Toronto* (1975) #1809
Bloore, Ronald Langley, artiste can, 1925-
    #4753
– commentaire sur l'art canadien (années

1960) #478
– commentaire sur le sacré dans l'art #94
– dessins #532
– entretien #4749
– esthétique #4746
– et critique formaliste (années 1960) #4747
– expositions
    – (1961) #1913
    – (1975) #4751
– expositions, critiques #4750 4752 4754
– expositions de groupe
    – (1962) #1847
    – (1964) #462
    – (1967) #490
– influence sur Arthur Fortescue McKay
    #6476
– références et transformations historiques
    #577
– théories sur l'art #4748
Blouin, André, architecte can, 1920-
– églises #7857
– Pointe-aux-Trembles (Qué), église de
    pèlerinage de-la-Réparation #8840
Blue Eagle, Acee, artiste amér, 1907-1959
– thème décoratif du monstre marin #3757
Bluenose (navire)
– vues photographiques, Wallace R.
    MacAskill #6351
Bluesinger, Taki, photographe can, 1943-
– catalogue de photographies #996
– et Glenn Alun Lewis #6275 6276
– expositions de groupe
    – (1979) #2069
Blum, Michel, artiste can, actif 1977
– et Marcelle Ferron #5422
Blunden Harbour (CB)
– vues, Emily Carr #5036
Boas, Franz, anthropologue amér, 1858-1942
– influence sur Charles Marius Barbeau
    #3309
Bobak, Bruno Joseph, artiste can, 1923-
    #1996 4756 4757 4758
– commentaire sur l'art canadien (années
    1960) #448
– commentaire sur la gravure #817
– en comparaison avec Molly Lamb Bobak
    #4755
– et Molly Lamb Bobak #4759 4762 4766
– et peinture, Vancouver (CB), (années 1950)
    #1992
– expositions de groupe
    – (1966) #1123
    – (1973) #1182
– mari de Molly Lamb Bobak #4764
– oeuvres figuratives #4760
Bobak, Molly Lamb, artiste can, 1922- #1996
    4763 4767
– autobiographie #4766
– commentaire sur la vie militaire #4761
– commentaire sur un séjour en Angleterre
    #4762
– en comparaison avec Bruno Joseph Bobak
    #4755
– entretien #4764
– et Bruno Joseph Bobak #4759
– et peinture, Vancouver (CB), (années 1950)

#1992
– expositions
    – (1977) #4765
– expositions de groupe
    – (1966) #1123
    – (1973) #1182
– membre du jury, *Saskatchewan Arts
    Exhibition* (1955) #1910
Bodmer, Karl, artiste suisse au Canada,
    1809-1893
– aquarelles, Indiens des plaines #3738
– et émergence d'artistes amérindiens
    reconnus #3486
Bodolai, Joseph Stephen (Joe), artiste can,
    1947-
– et art vidéo #550
Bodor, Andrew Steven, sculpteur can, 1947-
– entretien #788
Boehler, Valentine, céramiste can, 1852-1876
    #2323
Boehler, Xavier, céramiste can, actif
    1851-1874 #2348
Bogardi, George, artiste can, 1943-
– art québécois, commentaire (années
    1940-1970) #1521
– expositions de groupe
    – (1977) #637
Boggs, Jean Sutherland, conservatrice de
    musée et historienne d'art can, 1922-
– commentaire sur Louis Muhlstock #6657
– directeur, Galerie nationale du Canada
    (Ottawa, Ont) #3049 3050 3058
Bohar, Dick, photographe can, actif années
    1970
– catalogue de photographies #998
Boiestown (NB), Upper Miramichi Regional
    High School
– expositions
    – *The Beaverbrook Art Gallery Presents Nine
        New Brunswick Artists/La Galerie d'art
        Beaverbrook présente neuf artistes du
        Nouveau-Brunswick* (1973) #1182
Boileau, Philip, artiste can, 1863-1917
– illustrations #916
bois
– architecture, Colombie-Britannique #8148
    8153
– architecture, Vancouver (CB) #8159
– architecture albertaine #8136
    – fin XIXe-début XXe s. #8120
– architecture canadienne #7695
    – (années 1910) #8494
    – (années 1950) #7680
– architecture domestique canadienne #7722
– architecture domestique ontarienne
    – (années 1920) #8646
    – XIXe s. #8677
– architecture domestique québécoise,
    XVIIe-XVIIIe s. #8621
– architecture manitobaine #8102
– architecture ontarienne
    – (1831-1861) #8009
    – XIXe s. #7745
– architecture québécoise, XVIIe-XIXe s.
    #7859
– architecture ukrainienne #8090

– architecture canadienne et américaine,
XVIIe-XVIIIe s. #7717
– arts décoratifs canadiens (années 1970)
#2596
– bâtiments de style baie d'Hudson, XIXe s.
#8100
– charpente
– comparaison de deux maisons (1650 et
1836) #8658
– madriers #7712
– décoration architecturale
– (années 1930) #8225
– Montréal (Qué), XIXe s. #8612
– Ontario, XIXe s. #8002 8005
– églises et art funéraire,
Colombie-Britannique (1880-1910) #8914
– industrie de transformation du bois
– Canada et E.-U. (1607-1623) #7718
– documents, XVIIIe-XIXe s. #7720
– Ontario, cabanes en bois rond, cèdre,
début XIXe s. #7990
– Ontario, constructions en bois rond, colons
canadiens-français, XIXe s. #7685
– Saskatchewan, habitations temporaires de
colons, fin XIXe-début XXe s #8696
– toits canadiens, XVIIe-XIXe s. #7703
Bois-Francs (Qué)
– églises protestantes, XIXe s. #8888
– vues, Alfred Laliberté #6151
Boisberthelot de Beaucours, Josué, officier
de l'armée fr, architecte au Canada,
1662-1750 #7844 8336
Boisseau, Alfred, artiste can, 1823-1901
#4768 4769
Boisvert, Gilles, artiste can, 1940- #1479 1480
1542 1543
– entretien #1485
– expositions
– (1975) #4770
– expositions de groupe
– (1981) #1564
– pop'art #1497
Boisvert, Paul, photographe can, actif 1977
– catalogue de photographies #1023
Boisvert, Pierre, artiste can, actif 1950
– cartes de Nöel #856
Boivin, François, architecte fr au Canada,
1612/1616-ca 1675 #228 229
Boivin, Joseph, artiste can, 1874-1960
– *Ex-voto de Dorval*, Musée de l'Historial de
Sainte-Anne-de-Beaupré (Qué) #4771
Boivin, Louis-Philippe, orfèvre can, actif
1842-1857
– oeuvres, Detroit Institute of Arts (Detroit,
Mich) #2691
Bokwus . Kwakiutls #3990
Boland, Con, photographe can, ca 1948-
– catalogue de photographies #1023
Bolduc, Blanche, artiste can, 1907- #4772
Bolduc, David, artiste can, 1945- #1803 1807
4773 4776
– expositions
– (1979) #4775
– expositions de groupe
– (1974) #565
– (1977) #637

– (1981) #722
– participant, Symposium on 20th Century
Canadian Culture (Washington, DC),
(1977) #621
– peinture (1976-1981) #4777
– peinture (1977-1979) #4774
Boller, Harry, artiste amér au Canada, 1938-
– et Paul Arthur and Associates #873
Bollivar, Samuel, artiste can, né 1884
– expositions, critiques #1210
bols
– *voir aussi* récipients
bols . Canada
– bois, Ontario, XVIIIe-XIXe s. #2588
– verre, XIXe-début XXe s. #2430
bols . Etats-Unis
– verre, XIXe-début XXe s. #2430
bols . Indiens de la côte nord-ouest
– préhistoire, ouvrage en pierre #3900
Bolt, Beranek & Newman, firme can
d'ingénierie
– acoustique, Place des Arts (Montréal, Qué)
#9092
Bolt, Ron, artiste can, 1938- #4778 4779
Bolvin, Gilles, sculpteur can, 1711-1766 #249
250 1324 4780 4781
– baldaquins, église paroissiale de Neuville
(Qué) et église de Trois-Rivières (Qué)
#8826
– influence sur Philippe Liébert #6281
– retable, église de Berthierville (Qué) #8874
– retable, église de L'Assomption
(L'Assomption, Qué) #4782
– sculptures, église Saint-Charles (Lachenaie,
Qué) #8808
– tabernacles #1613
Bonan, Mino, artiste can, 1943-
– art graphique télédiffusé #909
Bonavista (TN)
– architecture #7792
Bond, Eleanor, artiste can, 1948-
– expositions de groupe
– (1981) #1908
Bond & Smith, agence can d'architecture
– Toronto (Ont)
– Hermant Building #9332
– Mason & Risch Company Building
#9328
Bonet, Jordi, artiste can, 1932-1979 #4783
4784 4786 4787 4791 4792
– entretien #1527
– expositions
– (1974) #4790
– (1980) #4793
– lauréat, médaille des arts connexes de
l'Institut royal d'architecture du Canada
(1965) #4785
– murale, Grand Théâtre (Québec, Qué)
#4788 4789
– murale, Place des Arts (Montréal, Qué)
#8233
Bonham, Don, sculpteur can, 1940-
– thème du corps humain et de la machine
#4794
Bonin, Raoul, artiste can, 1904-1949 #4795
Bonn (Allemagne de l'Ouest), Rheinisches

Landesmuseum
– expositions
– *Michael Snow* (1979) #7258
– *Michael Snow: Works 1969-1978, Films
1964-1976/Michael Snow: Werke
1969-1978, Filme 1964-1976* (1979) #7261
Bonnard, Pierre, artiste fr, 1867-1947
– influence sur Alfred Pellan #6811
– Morrice, James Wilson, comparaison #6631
Bonnat, Léon-Joseph-Florentin, artiste fr,
1834-1923
– professeur de Robert Harris #5739
Boogaerts, Pierre, photographe can, 1946-
– expositions, critiques #1018
– expositions de groupe
– (1976) #1529
Boorne, William Hanson, photographe can,
1859-1945 #1950
– commentaire sur photographies
d'Amérindiens #4796
– et Boorne and May #4797
Boorne and May, studio de photographie
(Calgary, Alta) #4797
– (1886-1889) #1950
– et Charles Wesley Mathers #6451
Bordeaux (France), Académie de Bordeaux
– Beaucourt, François Malepart de, élève
#269 270
Bordeaux (France), Musée de Bordeaux
– expositions
– *L'art au Canada* (1962) #63
Borduas, Paul-Emile, artiste can, 1905-1960
#97 1270 1294 1432 4800 4801 4806 4810
4811 4813 4814 4817 4821 4829 4830 4837
4843 4845 4849 4850
– à New York (NY), (1953-1955) #4835
– à Paris (France) #426 4846
– *Abstraction verte* #4852
– Alleyn, George Edmund, comparaison
#4511
– Bush, Jack Hamilton, comparaison #1753
– chronologie #4842
– commentaire sur le nationalisme dans l'art
#4851
– commentaire sur Ozias Leduc #6197 6199
– concept d'espace #1441 4816
– peintures, Paris (1955-1960) #4824
– correspondance, Claude Gauvreau #4804
4805 4807
– correspondance, Fernand Leduc #6194
– désaccord avec Fernand Leduc #6586
– Dumouchel, Albert, comparaison #5332
– écrits #92 1443 4839
– entretien #4802
– et Alfred Pellan #1451
– et Art déco #4828
– et art montréalais (années 1940-1960)
#1437
– et automatisme #1417 1453 1455 1476 4832
– et automatistes #1447
– et frère Jérôme #6761
– et Guy Viau #7485
– et internationalisme dans l'art #567
– et Jacques Godefroy de Tonnancour #4798
– et nationalisme dans l'art #495
– et Paraskeva Clark #5112

– et Pierre Gauvreau #5576 5578
– et séparatisme québécois #4834 4848
– et Société d'art contemporain #1459
– et surréalisme #1464 1467
– expositions
   – (1962) #4809
   – (1967) #4812
   – (1971) #1449
   – (1977) #4836 4838
– expositions, critiques #428
– expositions de groupe
   – (1955) #411 1409
   – (1958) #431
   – (1962) #1420
   – (1964) #462
   – (1976) #1462
   – (1978) #508 509
   – (1979) #1472
   – (1981) #1471
– Gagnon-Fortier, C., comparaison #5552
– gouaches (1942) #4822 4825
– influence sur art abstrait québécois #1468
– influence sur Christian Marcel Barbeau
   #4607
– influence sur Fernand Leduc #6186
– influence sur Jean Albert McEwen #6470
   6471
– influence sur Jean-Paul Armand Mousseau
   #6651
– influence sur John Meredith #6516
– influence sur Marcelle Ferron #5421 5426
– influence sur peinture américaine (années
   1950) #4826
– influence sur peinture québécoise #145
– influence sur Rita Letendre #6251
– La cité absurde #4833
– Molinari, Guido, comparaison #6584
– peinture
   – (1941-1948) #4823
   – (1953-1956) #1454
   – (1955-1960) #4844
   – (années 1930) #1460
   – (avant 1946) #4841
   – Ottawa (Ont), Galerie nationale du
      Canada #1266
– peinture religieuse #1384
   – (1922-1932) #4820
– professeur #1395 2990 3001 4827
– professeur d'André Jasmin #4808
– Projections libérantes #4818 4819
– reconnaissance internationale (années
   1950) #425
– Refus global #1396 1466 1475 4840
   – en comparaison avec autres oeuvres
      littéraires automatistes #4831
   – influence sur Françoise Sullivan #7282
   – influence sur Le Manifeste des plasticiens
      #1465
   – Leduc, Fernand, commentaire #6189
   – Mousseau, Jean-Paul Armand,
      commentaire #6650
– Refus global et Projections libérantes,
   réactions de presse (1948-1949) #1452
– Riopelle, Jean-Paul, commentaire #7026
– signe, images, symboles #4847
– Sous le vent de l'île, Galerie nationale du

Canada (Ottawa, Ont) #4815
– théories sur l'art #4799 4803
Borenstein, Sam, artiste can, 1908-1969 #4853
– expositions de groupe
   – (1977) #1278 1279
Borges, Jorge Luis, écrivain argentin, 1899-
– A Personal Anthology, influence sur John
   Heward #5793
– influence sur Michael Brodie #4923
Bornstein, Eli, sculpteur can, 1922-
– commentaire sur l'art et la technologie
   #4855
– commentaire sur la sérigraphie #4854
– commentaire sur le structuralisme dans
   l'art #536
– expositions
   – (1975) #4856
– expositions de groupe
   – (1967) #490 1916
– sculptures (années 1960) #746
– structures en relief #777
Borremans, Guy, photographe can, 1934-
– catalogue de photographies #997 999
Bosch, Hieronymus (Hieronymus van
   Aken), artiste néerlandais, ca 1450-1516
– influence sur Tom La Pierre #6122
– influence sur Tony Urquhart #7446
Boston (Mass), Boston Museum of Fine Arts
– expositions
   – Forty Years of Canadian Painting: From
      Tom Thomson and the Group of Seven to
      the Present Day (1949) #383
   – Jack Bush (1972) #4966
– Humphrey, Jack Weldon, élève #5865
– McMurtie, William Birch, vues, île de
   Vancouver (CB) #6505
Boston (Mass), Institute of Contemporary
   Art
– expositions
   – Nine Canadians (1967) #480
Boszin, Andrew (Endre), sculpteur can,
   1923-
– expositions de groupe
   – (1971) #772
Bot, Marten, photographe can, actif 1978
   #995
Bouchard, Edith, artiste can, 1924- #1428
   1429
Bouchard, Laurent, artiste et conservateur
   can, 1931-
– entretien sur le Musée du Québec
   (Québec, Qué) #3122
Bouchard, Lorne Holland, artiste can,
   1913-1978 #1393 4857 4858
Bouchard, Marie-Cécile, artiste can,
   1920-1973 #1428 1429
Bouchard, Mary Simone, artiste can,
   1912-1945 #1428 1429
Bouchard, Maurice René, architecte can,
   1909-
– Québec (Qué), école secondaire
   Marie-de-l'Incarnation #7939
Boucher, Maximilien, prêtre et artiste can,
   1918-1975 #4860
Boucher, Wayne, artiste can, 1943-
– expositions de groupe

   – (1980) #1221
Boucher (dit Belleville), Alexis Charles,
   artiste can, 1808-1885 #4859
Boucherville (Qué)
– architecture, XVIIe-XIXe s. #7890
Boucherville (Qué), église Sainte-Famille
– architecture et intérieur #8868
– tabernacle, Gilles Bolvin #249 250 4781
Bouclier canadien
– vues, XVIIIe-XXe s. #156
boucliers . Algonquiens #3672
boucliers . Dakotas
– Philadelphie (Penn), University of
   Pennsylvania. Museum #3670
boucliers . Indiens des plaines #3672 3680
   3732
– motifs d'animaux #3758
boucliers . Siouens #3672
bouddhisme zen
– influence sur Gaston-Pierre Petit #6843
– influence sur Kazuo Hamasaki #5688
– influence sur Kenneth Campbell Lochhead
   #6319
– influence sur Robert Savoie #7139
Boudreau, Pierre de Ligny, artiste can, 1923-
– à Paris (France) #426
Bougie, Louis-Pierre, artiste can, 1946-
– expositions
   – (1978) #4861
Bouguercau, Adolphe William, artiste fr,
   1825-1905
– professeur de John Wycliffe Lowes Forster
   #5469
– professeur de William Blair Bruce #4941
Boultbee, Alfred, artiste can, 1863-1928
   #2085
Boulton, D'Arcy, fils, avocat can, 1785-1846
– résidence, The Grange (Toronto, Ont)
   #8680
Boundary Bay (CB)
– sculptures sur ramure, Indiens de la côte
   nord-ouest #3817
Bourassa, Anne, Can, 1906-
– entretien sur Napoléon Bourassa #4873
   4874
Bourassa, Napoléon, artiste, architecte et
   auteur can, 1827-1916 #1231 1315 1318
   1323 4863 4866 4867 4869 4870 4871 4874
   4875 4876
– commentaire sur le goût dans l'art #4864
– commentaire sur ses peintures murales
   #4862
– écrits #4868
– et peinture québécoise #1353
– expositions
   – (1976) #4872
– expositions de groupe
   – (1880) #1308
– influence de Théophile Hamel #5690
– oeuvres, Art Association of Montreal
   (Montréal, Qué) #3075
– peintures, chapelle
   Notre-Dame-de-Lourdes (Montréal, Qué)
   #4865 8784 8836
– professeur de Louis-Philippe Hébert #5768
   5769 5771

– sources de l'histoire orale #4873
Bourassa, Robert, homme d'Etat can, 1933-
– et Stade olympique (Montréal, Qué) #9139
Bourbeau, Géraldine, artiste et critique d'art can, 1906-1953 #4877 4878
Bourdeau, Micheline, artiste can, active 1969 #4879
Bourdeau, Robert Charles John, photographe can, 1931- #4880 4881 4882
– catalogue de photographies #987 1023
– expositions, critiques #1018 1046 1060
– expositions de groupe
  – (1973) #1002
  – (1979) #1037
  – (1981) #1069 1070
Bourdieu, Pierre, professeur de sciences sociales fr, 1930-
– cité dans une étude sur l'art montréalais (1968-1969) #1514
Bourgault, André, sculpteur can, 1898-1958 #4884 4886
Bourgault, famille, sculpteurs can, XXe s.
– et art religieux, Québec (années 1950) #1250
– influence sur Zénon Alary #4505
Bourgault, Jean-Julien, sculpteur can, 1910- #2194 2209 4884 4886
Bourgault, Médard, sculpteur can, 1897-1967 #2174 2179 2194 2209 4883 4884 4885 4886 4887 4888
– et art religieux, Québec (années 1950) #1250
Bourgault, Pier, sculpteur can, 1942- #4889
– et école de sculpture sur bois, Saint-Jean-Port-Joli (Qué) #1597
– Symposium international de sculpture environnementale de Chicoutimi (Qué), (1980) #1639
Bourgeau, Victor, architecte can, 1809-1888
– et architecture québécoise néo-baroque #7856
– Laval (Qué), église de Sainte-Rose #8854
– Montréal (Qué)
  – église Notre-Dame #8849 8892
  – église Saint-Jacques #8782
  – Hôpital-Général #8862
Bourgeault, Victor
– voir Bourgeau, Victor
Bourgeois, Albéric, artiste can, 1876-1962 #1382
Bourgeois, Hélène et Joseph-Romain (Roma), Can, XIXe s.
– résidence, Grand Digue (NB) #8547
Bourgeois, Marguerite
– voir Bourgeoys, Marguerite
Bourgeoys, Marguerite, religieuse can, 1620-1700 #2212
– et Notre-Dame-de-Bon-Secours (Montréal, Qué) #8788
– portrait, Pierre Le Ber #1333 6180
Bourne, Adolphus, artiste can, 1795-1886
– gravure d'après View of Montreal from St. Helen's Island de Robert Auchmaty Sproule #2370
Bourque, Célestin, Can, né 1786
– résidence, Memramcook (NB) #8543

bourse . Canada
– Toronto (Ont), Bourse de Toronto #9161 9187
bouteilles et flacons
– voir aussi pots à condiments
bouteilles et flacons . Canada #2425 2427
– (1825-1931) #2419
– bouteilles de lait #2412
– flacons de médicaments #2432
– Nouvelle-Ecosse #2409 2428
– Prairies (1880-années 1920) #2431
– Saint-Jean (Qué), Canada Glass Works #2420
– Silver, M. et Mme. Stanley S., collection, XIXe-XXe s. #2414
Boutilier, Ralph, artiste can, 1906-
– expositions, critiques #1210
boutiques
– voir magasins
boutons . Canada
– insignes militaires #2874 2882
Bouzonnet-Stella, Claudine, artiste fr, 1636-1697
– influence sur Antoine-Sébastien Plamondon #6886
Bow, Douglas Scott, architecte can, actif 1913
– Vancouver (CB), University of British Columbia, concours #9498
Bowen Island (CB)
– paysages, Lionel LeMoine FitzGerald #5446
Bowers, Robert, artiste can, 1943-
– cartes géographiques, illustrations #561
Bowmanville (Ont)
– mobilier, XIXe s. #2556
Bowmanville (Ont), Bowmanville Public Library
– expositions
  – Arthur A. Drummond, 1975 (1975) #5309
Bowmanville (Ont), The Photography Gallery
– expositions
  – Neil Newton Retrospective (1978) #6694
Bowmanville Furniture Manufacturing Co., fabricants de meubles (Bowmanville, Ont) #2556
Boyce, Eleanor, Can, confectionneuse de courtepointes, 1918-1980
– entretien #4890
Boyd, Douglas, orfèvre can, actif années 1960 #2638
Boyd, James Henderson, artiste can, 1928-
– commentaire sur la gravure #817 818
– et gravure ontarienne (années 1960) #1756
Boyd, Jerry, photographe can, actif 1979
– catalogue de photographies #1023
Boyd, W.H., ingénieur can, actif 1927
– utilisation d'appareils photogrammétriques #989
Boyer, Jean-Pierre, artiste can, 1950-
– vidéos, Musée d'art contemporain (Montréal, Qué) #1498
Boyer, Michel, photographe can, actif 1977
– catalogue de photographies #1023
Boyle, John Bernard, artiste can, 1941- #4891

– commentaire sur Jack Chambers #700
– commentaire sur l'art canadien et l'histoire canadienne #4893
– Elsinore Editions #834
– entretien #4892
– et nationalisme dans l'art #102 143
– et régionalisme dans l'art #567
– expositions, critiques #4894
Boylen, M.J., collectionneur can, 1907-1970
– collection, peintures de Cornelius Krieghoff #1
Bradford, John Locke, sculpteur can, 1897-1919 #4897
– commentaire sur la sculpture sur bois #4895 4896
Bradford, Robert William, artiste amér, 1923- #4898
Bradley, Randy, photographe can, 1948- #2071
Braitstein, Marcel, sculpteur can, 1935-
– sculptures (1959-1969) #4899
– sculptures soudées (années 1960) #745
Brancusi, Constantin, artiste roum, 1876-1957
– influence sur Douglas Bentham #4686
– Westerlund, Mia, comparaison #7545
Brandl, Eva, artiste can, 1951- #1512
– expositions de groupe
  – (1976) #1529
Brandon (Man), Brandon Allied Arts Centre
– expositions
  – Canadians: A National Photography Show about People/Canadiens: exposition nationale de photographie ayant les gens comme thème (1980) #1035
Brandon (Man), Brandon Art Club
– (années 1950) #3034
Brandon (Man), Brandon University
– expositions
  – Doig Collection of Canadian Paintings, Featuring the Group of Seven (1968) #3224
Brandon (Man), gare du Canadien National
– architecture, Pratt & Ross #9266
Brandon (Man), Hospital for the Insane
– architecture, Victor William Horwood #9014
Brandon (Man), Prince Edward Hotel
– architecture, Pratt & Ross #9266
Brandtner, Fritz, artiste can, 1896-1969 #1294 4900 4901 4904
– commentaire sur la linogravure #4902
– expositions
  – (1971) #4903
– expositions de groupe
  – (1977) #1278 1279
– influence sur Caven Ernest Atkins #4570
Brangwyn, Frank, artiste brit, 1867-1956
– murale, Palais législatif (Winnipeg, Man) #8952
Bransom, Paul, artiste amér, 1885-1979
– influence sur George E. McLean #6501
Brantford (Ont)
– architecture domestique, après Première Guerre mondiale #8495
Brantford (Ont), Art Gallery of Brant
– expositions

– *Alan C. Collier Retrospective* (1971) #5131
– *Ed Bartram: 10 Years* (1979) #4618
– *Four Ontario Realists: D.P. Brown, Ken Danby, Bruce St. Clair, Gerald Zeldin; Paintings, Drawings and Prints* (1976) #1810
– *Grand River Pottery and Textiles, Past and Present* (1974) #2249
– *Graphex* (1973-1979, 1981-) #827
– *Heritage of Brant: A Retrospective Exhibition of Paintings, Maps and Prints from Brant County Selected to Commemorate Brantford's Centennial* (1977) #1684
– *The Figure: A Sensual Response* (1975) #578
– expositions, critiques
– Whale, Robert Reginald (1969) #7547
Brantford (Ont), Bell Memorial
– Allward, Walter Seymour #4516
Brantford (Ont), Brantford and District Civic Centre
– architecture, Brooks & Van Poorten #9101
Brantford (Ont), Evangel Pentecostal Church
– architecture, Mark/Musselman/McIntyre/Combe #8766
Brantford (Ont), Woodland Indian Cultural Educational Centre
– expositions
– *Indian Art* (1975-1981) #4139
Brantford Pottery, fabricants de céramique (Brantford, Ont) #2295 2302 2335
Braque, Georges, artiste fr, 1882-1963
– Borduas, Paul-Emile, comparaison #4813
– Brooker, Bertram Richard, commentaire #4927
– East, Benoît, comparaison #5353
– influence sur Robert La Palme #6119
Brassard, Thérèse Tanguay, émailleuse can, 1930- #2102 4905
brassards micmacs #3572
brasseries canadiennes
– bouteilles de verre (1825-1931) #2419
– Nouvelle-Ecosse (1836-1947) #2428
Brault, Maurice, orfèvre et émailleur can, 1930-1958 #4906
Brauner, Victor, artiste roum, 1902-1966
– influence sur Francis Coutellier #5196
Brayshaw, Thomas (Tommy), artiste can, ca 1886-1967 #4907
Brazilia (Brésil), Ambassade du Canada
– expositions
– *Lacos de tradiçao: uma exibiçao de arte canadense indigena contemorânea/Links to a Tradition: An Exhibition of Contemporary Canadian Indian Art/Liens du passé: une exposition d'art contemporain des Indiens du Canada* (1977) #4146
Breeze, Claude Herbert, artiste can, 1938- #145
– collection *Canadian Atlas* #4910
– commentaire sur les établissements artistiques (années 1970) #620
– dessins #532
– expositions

– (1978) #4911
– expositions, critiques #520 4909
– expositions de groupe
– (1977) #636
– oeuvres figuratives #71
– *Sunday Afternoon (from an Old American Photograph)* #4908
Bregman, Sidney (Sid), architecte can, 1922-
– et Bregman & Hamann #8337
Bregman & Hamann, agence can d'architecture
– Calgary (Alta), immeubles à bureaux #9362
– Toronto (Ont) #8337
– Eaton Centre #9377 9378 9382
– Olympia Square #9301
– Toronto-Dominion Centre #7694 9197 9301 9345
Brener, Roland, sculpteur can, 1942-
– entretien #4912
Brésil
– vues, explorateurs français, XVIe s. #276
Brest (France), Musée municipal de Brest
– expositions
– *Fernand Leduc: microchromie gris, puissance 6* (1977) #6190
– *Louis Comtois: 4 tableaux récents grand format* (1978) #5163
Breton, André, auteur fr, 1896-1966
– correspondance, Fernand Leduc #6194
– et Alfred Pellan #6821
– et Fernand Leduc #6189
– et Roland Giguère #5598
– influence du masque de faucon kwakiutl #3361
– influence sur Jean-Paul Riopelle #7014 7027
– influence sur Paul-Emile Borduas #4814 4850
– influence sur peinture québécoise #1270
– Riopelle, Jean-Paul, commentaire #7026
Breukelman, Jim, photographe can, 1941- #2071
Briand, Jean-Olivier, évêque can, 1715-1794
– chapelle, Séminaire de Québec (Québec, Qué) #5371 8800
Briansky, Rita, artiste can, 1925-
– commentaire sur la gravure (procédé) #817
Bridgewater (NE), DesBrisay Museum/National Exhibition Centre
– Hebb, Howard D., exposition de meubles (1977) #2510
Bridgman, John Wesley, artiste can, actif 1861-1907 #5469
– professeur de Tomtu H. Roberts #7051
Brief Concerning the Cultural Aspects of Canadian Reconstruction
– *voir* Canada. Brief Concerning the Cultural Aspects of Canadian Reconstruction
Brien (dit Desrochers), Urbain, artiste can, 1780-1860
– calvaire, Varennes (Qué) #1585
Brigden, Frederick, artiste can, 1841-1917
– fondateur, Brigdens Limited (Toronto, Ont) #883
Brigden, Frederick Henry (Fred), artiste can,

1871-1956 #4913
– commentaire sur Walter Joseph Phillips #6856
– et Frank Shirley Panabaker #6757
– expositions, critiques #1710
Brigdens Limited, éditeur (Toronto, Ont) #883
– et Robert Elmer Lougheed #6327
Brighton (Ont), Union School
– architecture, Ellis & Ellis #9387
Brigus (TN)
– architecture #7792
Brigus (TN), Hawthorne Cottage
– architecture et intérieur #8539
brique
– *voir aussi* maçonnerie
– architecture, région d'Aultsville (Ont), XIXe s. #7980
– architecture canadienne (1867-1967) #7695
– architecture domestique, Ontario
– (années 1920) #8646
– XIXe s. #8677
– architecture manitobaine, XIXe-début XXe s. #8102
– architecture ontarienne (1831-1861) #8009
– brique dichromatique, Ontario (années 1870-1880) #8026
– brique polychromatique, Yorkville Town Hall (Toronto, Ont) #8997
– et constructions en stuc, Toronto (Ont), (années 1910) #8052
– industrie
– Canada (1885-1915) #7726
– Québec (1650-1837) #2313
– Toronto (Ont), The Grange #8680
Brisbane (Australie), Queensland National Art Gallery
– expositions
– *Contemporary Canadian Painters* (1957) #423
Briscoe, Barrie, designer can, actif années 1960 #4914
Brisley, Stuart, artiste brit, 1933-
– *The one and the other in the attic of poverty* #718
Bristol's Hope (TN)
– architecture #7792
Britannia Pottery, fabricants de céramique (Glasgow, Ecosse)
– vues de la ville de Québec #2306 2326
Britanniques au Canada
– XVIIIe-XIXe s. #231 244
– Nouvelle-Ecosse #1215 1220 1222
British American Oil Company
– édifices, décoration intérieure, arts décoratifs canadiens #8230
British Columbia Art Collection
– acquisitions (1974-1980) #2078
British Columbia Ballet (Vancouver, CB)
– décors et costumes (1953) #1991
British Columbia Mills Timber and Trading Company (Vancouver, CB)
– bâtiments préfabriqués (1904-1910) #8082
British Columbia Society of Artists
– (1949-1967) #1978
British Columbia Society of Fine Arts #1841

2003
– (1909-1948) #1978
– (années 1910) #1979
Brittain, Miller Gore, artiste can, 1912-1968
#1121 1128 1173 1179 1184 4915 4919 4920
4921
– et peinture de genre #392
– et situation de l'art, Saint-Jean (NB),
(années 1940) #1170
– expositions
– (1968) #4917
– (1972) #4918
– (1981) #4922
– expositions de groupe
– (1966) #1123
– (1973) #1182
– murale (dessins humoristiques), Hôpital
général de Saint-Jean (Saint-Jean, NB)
#4916
Britton, Susan, artiste can, 1952-
– expositions de groupe
– (1977) #631
– (1978) #650
– (1980) #687 1832
Brochard, Armand, joaillier can, 1931- #2701
2706
broches (bijoux)
– *voir aussi* parure
broches (bijoux) . Algonquiens
– broches en argent #3608
broches (bijoux) . Ecossais
– Luckenbooth, influence sur art iroquois,
broches (bijoux) #3509 3512
broches (bijoux) . Haidas
– Reid, Bill #6984
broches (bijoux) . Iroquois
– broches en argent #3509 3512 3645 3646
Brock, J.A., & Co., studio de photographie
(Vancouver, CB)
– vues de Vancouver (1886-1888) #2021
Brock, John Allan, photographe can, actif
1886-1889
– et J.A. Brock & Co. (Vancouver, CB) #2021
Brock, sir Isaac, homme d'Etat et officier de
l'armée brit résidant au Canada,
1769-1812
– portrait, George Theodore Berthon #4712
Brockville (Ont), Idlewild
– architecture, James P. Johnston #8671
Brockville (Ont), Saint Peter's Anglican
Church
– architecture, Arthur McClean #8382
Brockville (Ont), Sherwood Park Manor
Nursing Home
– architecture, Jerome Markson Architects
#8386
broderie
– *voir aussi* ouvrages à l'aiguille; ouvrages
perlés; tapisserie à l'aiguille
broderie . Algonquiens
– ouvrages perlés #3635
– poil d'orignal #3513
broderie . Amérindiens
– poil d'orignal #2783 3629
– XVIIIe s. #2169 2171
broderie . Athapascans #4110

broderie . Canada
– (1608-1867) #2120
– broderie ukrainienne #2782
– Brown, Annora #4933
– Canadian Embroiderer's Guild #2793
– influence sur art canadien, XXe s. #2093
– Le Ber, Jeanne #2778
– mennonites #2267 2729
– Nouvelle-Ecosse #2731
– poil d'orignal, XVIIIe s. #3629
– influence sur broderie européenne #2783
– points de croix ukrainiens bukoviniens
#2124
– Québec #1235 1324 1327 2169 2171 2183
2184
– XVIIe-XVIIIe s. #1320 2181 2200 2779
– ursuline #1581 2777 2781 2783 2788 2789
2791
– XXe s. #2121
broderie . Hurons
– poil d'orignal #3513
broderie . Indiens des forêts du Nord-Est
– ouvrages perlés #3635
broderie . Inuit #4259
broderie . Iroquois
– ouvrages perlés #3635
– poil d'orignal #3559
broderie . Métis #4110
broderie . Montagnais
– motifs floraux #4076
broderie . Naskapis
– motifs floraux #4076
broderie . Pentaguets #3537
broderie . Thompsons #3808
broderie de perles
– *voir* ouvrages perlés
Brodie, F.Neil, architecte can, ca 1870-1926
– Moncton (NB), Aberdeen School #9387
Brodie, Michael, artiste can, ca 1950- #4923
Bromley, Valentine Walter, artiste brit au
Canada, 1848-1877
– vues, provinces de l'Ouest #931
Brompton (Qué)
– pétroglyphes, Iroquois #3599
Bromsgrove Guild (Montréal, Qué)
– médaillons et statuettes #1
Bromsgrove Guild (Worcestershire,
Angleterre)
– oeuvres, Victoria College. Library
(Toronto, Ont) #9038
Bronfman, Samuel, collectionneur can,
1891-1971
– oeuvres commandées pour exposition *The
Seagram Collection of Paintings of Cities of
Canada* (1953) #403
Bronfman, Samuel, collectionneur can,
1891-1971, et Saidye, collectionneuse can,
1896-
– don, Musée des beaux-arts de Montréal,
acquisition d'oeuvres d'art canadiennes,
XXe s. #526 3087
Bronson, A.A., artiste can, 1946-
– expositions de groupe
– (1977) #5583
bronze
– Toronto (Ont), façades de magasins

(années 1920) #9364
bronzes . Canada
– (années 1910) #6141
– Colombie-Britannique (années 1980) #2083
Brooke, Arthur Adair, artiste can, 1874-1959
– carnet à dessins #4924
Brooker, Bertram Richard, artiste can,
1888-1955 #309 4926 4928
– commentaire sur l'art et la société #330
– commentaire sur le nu dans l'art #317
– expositions
– (1971) #4925
– expositions de groupe
– (1929) #1666
– (1975) #503 504
– oeuvres (années 1920-1940) #4927
– paysages (années 1930) #338
Brooks, Leonard, artiste can, 1911-
– commentaire sur le Mexique #4931
– entretien #4929
– réflexion sur son oeuvre #4930
Brooks & Van Poorten, agence can
d'architecture
– Brantford (Ont), Brantford and District
Civic Centre #9101
Broomfield, Adolphus George, artiste can,
1906- #4932
Brossard, Urbain, constructeur can,
1633/1634-1710 #234 235 7844
Brossin, Jean-François, Can, actif 1968
– et Ecole des beaux-arts (Montréal, Qué),
(1968) #2995
Brothers Glass, fabricants de céramique
(London, Ont) #2350
Broughton Island (TNO), habitation, dôme
en bois et polyéthylène
– architecture, T.Bert Rose #8734
Brown, Alisen, photographe can, active 1977
– catalogue de photographies #1023
Brown, Annora, artiste can, 1899- #4933
– autobiographie #4934
– théories sur l'art #1944
Brown, Arthur William, artiste can,
1881-1966
– illustrations #916
Brown, Bert, photographe can, actif 1979
– catalogue de photographies #995
Brown, Charles, sculpteur amér, actif années
1890
– totem #3856
Brown, Daniel Price Ericksen (D.P.), artiste
can, 1939-
– et réalisme #110
– expositions de groupe
– (1974) #573
– (1976) #1810
Brown, Douglas, photographe can, actif
1956-
– catalogue de photographies #1023
Brown, E.B., artiste can, actif 1898 #2085
Brown, Eric, conservateur can, 1877-1939
– directeur, Galerie nationale du Canada
(Ottawa, Ont) #3021 3022 3029 3032 3040
3041 3049 3050
– et British Empire Exhibition (Wembley,
Angleterre), (1924) #458

– et Emily Carr #5021 5034
Brown, Ernest, photographe can, 1877-1951
#4935
– collection, photographies #1949
– et Charles Wesley Mathers #6451
Brown, Francis Bruce, architecte can,
1899-
– Hamilton (Ont), McMaster University
#9451
Brown, Gordon F., photographe can, 1943-
– catalogue de photographies #991
– expositions de groupe
– (1972) #1952
Brown, Huntley, artiste can, 1932-
– illustrations #941
Brown, John Francis, architecte can,
1866-1942
– Hamilton (Ont), McMaster University
#9451
Brown, Murray, architecte can, 1885-1958
#8338
Brown, Peter, sculpteur can, 1947-
– expositions
– (1976) #4936
Brown, Randy, photographe can, 1943-
– catalogue de photographies #1023 1032
Brown, Thomas, photographe can, 1945-
#1000
Brown & Vallance, agence can d'architecture
– Montréal (Qué), Université McGill.
Medical Building #9412
– Regina (Sask), War Memorial Museum,
concours #9073
– Saskatoon (Sask), University of
Saskatchewan #9489 9491
– Winnipeg (Man)
– hôtel de ville, concours #8979
– Legislative and Executive Building,
concours #8946
Browne, George, architecte can, 1811-1885
– Kingston (Ont) #8339
– Québec (Qué), Chalmers-Wesley Church
#7873
Browne, Joseph Archibald, artiste can,
1864/1866-1948 #302 1713 4937 4938 4939
– et Homer Ransford Watson #7533
– expositions, critiques #204 211
– membre du Canadian Art Club #193
Brownell, Peleg Franklin, artiste can,
1857-1946
– expositions, critiques #186 211
– expositions de groupe
– (1935) #17
– membre du Canadian Art Club #193
– professeur de Pegi Nicol MacLeod #6397
Browning (Mon), Museum of the Plains
Indian
– expositions
– The Buffalo in Western American Art: An
Exhibition from the Collections of the
Glenbow Foundation, Calgary (1961) #62
Bruce, Brad, artiste can, ca 1952-
– expositions, critiques #1227
Bruce, David, photographe can, actif 1979
#2071
Bruce, Robert Donald, artiste can, 1911-

– commentaire sur l'expédition Exercise
Muskox (1946) #4940
Bruce, William Blair, artiste can, 1859-1906
– expositions
– (1907) #4941
– (1975) #4942
Bruce Brown & Brisley, agence can
d'architecture
– Hamilton (Ont), McMaster Divinity
College #8765
Brücke, Die
– et Karl May #6452
– et Philip Henry Surrey #7290
Bruegel, Pieter, l'aîné, artiste flam, m. 1569
– Eyre, Ivan Kenneth, comparaison #5394
Bruenner, Ralph, photographe can, actif
années 1970-
– catalogue de photographies #991
Bruneau, Kittie, artiste can, 1929- #4943 4944
4945
– Entre chien et loup #1647
Brunet, Joseph, sculpteur can, né 1899
– monuments funéraires, cimetière
Notre-Dame-des-Neiges, Montréal (Qué)
#1567
Bruni, Umberto, artiste can, 1914- #4946
Bruno, Anthony, photographe can, actif
années 1970
– catalogue de photographies #995
Brute, Dr.
– voir Metcalfe, Eric W. (Dr. Brute)
Bruxelles (Belgique), Ambassade du
Canada/Canadian Embassy
– expositions
– Exposition d'estampes en l'honneur de C.
Krieghoff, 1815-1872/Exhibition of Prints
in Honour of C. Krieghoff, 1815-1872
(1972) #6096
Bruxelles (Belgique), Centre culturel et
d'information canadien
– expositions
– D.P. Brown, Ken Danby, Tom Forrestall,
Christopher Pratt (1974) #573
– Ozias Leduc: peinture symboliste et
religieuse/Ozias Leduc: Symbolist and
Religious Painting (1974) #6206
– Peter Gnass: installation-Chantier interdit
au public (1981) #5621
– Richard Mill: 5 tableaux récents (1980)
#6535
Bruxelles (Belgique), Exposition universelle
et internationale de 1958. Pavillon du
Canada
– architecture #9209
– Greenberg, Charles #9211
– architecture et art #419 430
– art #428
– murale, Louis Archambault #4541 4542
– murale, Mario Virgilio Merola #6518 6521
Bruxelles (Belgique), galerie Isy Brachot
– expositions
– Exposition d'art esquimau: sculptures
(1977) #4444
Bruxelles (Belgique), Palais des beaux-arts
– expositions
– Canada: art d'aujourd'hui (1968) #518

– Yves Trudeau: "murs fermés et ouverts";
sculptures et pliages (1976) #7434
Bry, Theodore de, graveur néerlandais,
1528-1598
– America, estampes illustrant Amérindiens
et Inuit d'après dessin de John White
#7552
Brymner, William, artiste can, 1855-1925
#178 4948 4952
– à Martigues (France), (1908) #4950
– artiste traditionnel (années 1930) #322
– et Académie royale des arts du Canada
#152
– et Edmond Dyonnet #5347 5349
– expositions
– (1979) #4953
– expositions, critiques #174 186 204 211
– expositions de groupe
– (1935) #17
– (1978) #133
– influence de l'impressionnisme #227
– influence sur Robert Wakeman Pilot #6872
– membre du Canadian Art Club #193
– peintures murales, maison Charles
Porteous, île d'Orléans (Qué) #4951
– professeur #4949
– professeur d'Anne Douglas Savage #7130
7132
– professeur d'Arthur George Racey #6952
– professeur d'Edwin Headley Holgate
#5818 5819
– professeur de Lilias Torrance Newton
#6693
– professeur de Sarah Margaret Armour
Robertson #7054
– sujets féminins #4954
– théories sur l'art #4947
Bryson, Joseph Vincent, photographe can,
1953-
– catalogue de photographies #1032
Buchan, David, artiste can, 1950-
– art de performance #655
– expositions, critiques #1067
– expositions de groupe
– (1980) #1832
Buchan, John, baron Tweedsmuir, 1er,
auteur brit, gouverneur général au
Canada, 1875-1940
– mécène de Peter Pitseolak #6875 6877
Buchanan, Donald William, historien d'art
et conservateur can, 1908-1966 #3325
– correspondance, David Brown Milne
#6550 6553
– critique d'art, Prairies #1851
Bucke, Richard Maurice, psychiatre et
auteur can, 1837-1902
– croyances mystiques dans Cosmic
Consciousness, influence sur Lawren
Stewart Harris #5731
Buckhan, Robert Marshall, artiste can, 1918-
– expositions de groupe
– (1981) #1117
Budden, John Sherring, directeur d'enchères
can, 1825-1918
– mécène de Cornelius Krieghoff #6092
Buell, Katrina S.D., artiste can, active

1890-1926 #309
Buff, Richard, artiste can, 1947-
– commentaire sur Jack Chambers #700
Buffalo (NY), Albright-Knox Art Gallery
– exposition, vues des chutes du Niagara
(1964) #1673
Buffalo (NY), Buffalo Fine Arts Academy.
Albright Art Gallery
– expositions
– *Exhibition of Paintings by Canadian Artists*
(1928) #301
– *The Collection of Mr. and Mrs. Charles S.
Band: Contemporary Canadian Painting
and Drawing* (1958) #3215
Buffalo (NY), Pan-American Exposition
(1901)
– et Laura Adeline Muntz Lyall #6337
– expositions, critiques
– art canadien #189
buffets . Canada
– Ile-du-Prince-Edouard #2508 2518
– Nouvelle-Ecosse, XVIIe-XIXe s. #2489 2499
– Ontario #2574
– (1780-1900) #2577
– (années 1790-1857) #2558
– XIXe s. #2573
– Québec, XVIIe-XVIIIe s. #2530 2531
Bujold, Françoise, artiste can, 1933-1981
– entretien #4955
Bukovyna (Ukraine)
– costume, collection Peter Orchinsky #2869
Bull, Edward Claxton, artiste can, actif
1847-1851
– membre de la Toronto Society of Arts
#1689
Bull, Perkins, collectionneur can, 1870-1948
– collection, peinture canadienne #3208
Bull, W., photographe can, actif 1894
– commentaire sur une expédition de
photographie #4956
Bulman, Bessie, collectionneuse can,
1915-1971
– collection, sculpture inuit #4306 4428
bungalows
– *voir aussi* architecture domestique
bungalows . Canada
– (1908) #8487
– Colombie-Britannique (années 1910) #8684
8685
bungalows . Etats-Unis
– Californie
– (années 1910) #8685
– influence sur architecture résidentielle,
Vancouver (CB), (1910-années 1920)
#8730
Bunyard, Richard Geoffrey, architecte can,
1883-1973
– Régina (Sask), War Memorial Museum,
concours #9073
Burchfield, Charles Ephraim, artiste amér,
1893-1967
– Schaefer, Carl Fellman, commentaire #7158
– Schaefer, Carl Fellman, comparaison #7157
Burden, Eve, orfèvre can, ca 1953- #4957
Burden, John, orfèvre can, actif années 1960-
#4957

Bureau, Monique, artiste can, active 1937
#2174
bureaux (mobilier) . Canada
– Ontario #2579
– (1780-1900) #2577
– (années 1790-1857) #2558
– Québec
– XVIIe-XVIIIe s. #2530 2531
bureaux de poste . Canada
– (1881-1896), Thomas Fuller #9055
– Manitoba #9053
– XIXe s. #9054
Buren, Daniel, artiste fr, 1938-
– étude sur le musée #714
Burgess, Catherine, sculpteure can, 1953-
#717
Burgess, Cecil Scott, architecte can,
1870-1971
– Edmonton (Alta), Alberta Government
Administrative Building #8963
Burgess, William, photographe can, actif
1856-1867 #1724
Burka, Jan, artiste can, 1924-
– art et poésie #4958
– commentaire sur ses études en art #470
Burke, Horwood & White, agence can
d'architecture
– architecture domestique #8496
– Calgary (Alta), magasin La Baie #8118
– Toronto (Ont), architecture domestique
#8493
Burke, Rebecca, artiste can, 1946- #717
Burlington (Ont), Burlington Cultural Centre
#1806
– expositions
– *Ed Bartram: 10 Years* (1980) #4618
– *Goodridge Roberts: Paintings from the
1950s and 60s* (1981) #7048
– *Ivan Eyre Exposition* (1982) #5394
– *Lillian Freiman: Paintings and Drawings*
(1978) #5518
– *Métiers d'art Ontario-Québec,
1979/1980/Quebec-Ontario Crafts,
1979/1980* (1981) #2138
– *Realism: Structure and Illusion: Toward a
Definition of Representational Art* (1981)
#716
– *The Heritage of Jack Bush: A Tribute* (1982)
#722
– *Water Colours by E.May Martin* (1980)
#6424
Burlington Glass Works, fabricants de verre
(Hamilton, Ont) #2401 2406 2416 2421
2434
Burman, Irving, artiste can, 1928-
– commentaire sur l'art canadien (années
1960) #478
– sculptures sur bois (années 1960) #744
Burnaby (CB)
– vues
– Lamb, Harold Mortimer #6156
Burnaby (CB), Burnaby Art Gallery
– expositions
– *10th Anniversart Show: Burnaby Art
Gallery,*(1977) #2013
– *A Terrible Beauty: The Art of Canada at*

War (1979) #1111
– *A Tribute to William Townsend: 1909 to
1973* (1974) #7418
– *Artists from the Sea 1778-1793: A Visual
Documentation of British Columbia* (1978)
#2017
– *Artists Overland: A Visual Record of
British Columbia 1793-1886* (1980) #2025
– *Beauté tragique: les deux conflits mondiaux
vus par des artistes canadiens* (1979) #1112
– *Bill Koochin* (1980) #6073
– *Burnaby Print Show* (1967-1977) #816
– *Carol Fraser Paintings and Drawings:
1967-1977* (1977) #5507
– *Charles John Collings, 1848-1931* (1978)
#5137
– *David Marshall Sculpture* (1978) #6420
– *E. Lindner: Drawings, 1969-1972* (1972)
#6285
– *Eskimo Fantastic Art* (1972) #4240
– *H.Eric Bergman, 1893-1958* (1980) #4709
– *Jock Macdonald: Retrospective
Exhibition/Jock Macdonald: rétrospective*
(1970) #6375
– *Ken Wallace 1980* (1980) #7510
– *Mountain: A Lithograph by James B.
Spencer/Montagne: une lithographie de
James B. Spencer* (1974) #7270
– *Mystic Circle* (1973) #559
– *Northwest Renaissance* (1980) #4160
– *Okanagan Energy, An Exhibition of the
Work of a Selected Group of Okanagan
Artists* (1974) #2048
– *Richard Prince: Figure Structures* (1979)
#6939
– *Ronald: 25 Years* (1976) #7073
– *The Bell-Irvings of British Columbia* (1980)
#4665
– *Three Poet Artists* (1978) #649
– *Tom La Pierre: Paintings, Drawings, Prints*
(1976) #6121
– *Watercolour Painters from
Saskatchewan/Aquarellistes de la
Saskatchewan* (1972) #1920
– Hushlak, Gerald, art par ordinateur #5891
Burnaby (CB), Burnaby Centennial Pavilion
– expositions
– *Burnaby National Print Show* (1961, 1963)
#816
Burnaby (CB), Simon Fraser University
– architecture
– Erickson/Massey #8360 9396 9467 9504
9505 9506
– concours #9501
– Erickson, Arthur Charles #8358 8361
9406
– décoration intérieure (années 1960) #9402
– enseignement de l'art (années 1970) #3006
Burnaby (CB), Simon Fraser University.
Bibliothèque
– architecture, Robert F. Harrison #9046
Burnaby (CB), Simon Fraser University.
Centre for Communication and the Arts
– expositions
– *Kenneth Lochhead: Recent Works on Paper*
(1972) #6316

Burnaby (CB), Simon Fraser University.
Simon Fraser Gallery
– expositions
– *Artists' Stamps and Images: An
International Invitational Exhibition* (1974)
#829
– *Canadians: A National Photography Show
about People/Canadiens: exposition
nationale de photographie ayant les gens
comme thème* (1980) #1035
– *Changing Visions: The Canadian
Landscape/Aperçus divers: le paysage
canadien* (1977) #617
– *Contemporaries of Emily Carr in British
Columbia* (1974) #2007
– *Dessins de Lionel LeMoine FitzGerald et
Bertram Brooker* (1975) #503
– *Esther Warkov Drawings* (1977) #7519
– *Images of the Inuit from the Simon Fraser
Collection* (1979) #4495
– *J.Frederic McCulloch 1905-1932: Works on
Paper* (1978) #6463
– *Jack Wise: A Decade of Work* (1978) #7601
– *Lionel Lemoine FitzGerald, Bertram
Brooker: Their Drawings* (1975) #504
– *The Art of the Eskimo* (1971) #4223
– *Vehicule Art: In Transit* (1975) #1512
– *White Sculpture of the Inuit* (1977) #4445
– expositions, critiques
– photographes de la
Colombie-Britannique, exposition
– (1971) #2041
– (1974) #2056
Burnaby (CB), Simon Fraser University.
Théâtre
– expositions
– *Burnaby National Print Show* (1966) #816
Burnaby Art Gallery Association (Burnaby,
CB) #2013
Burnaby Art Society (Burnaby, CB) #2013
– (1961-1977), *Burnaby National Print Show*
#816
Burne-Jones, Edward, artiste brit, 1833-1898
– influence sur Graham Metson #6523
– influence sur Ozias Leduc #6206
Burnett, Moyra Theresa, artiste can (vitrail),
1927-
– vitrail #2452
Burnett, William Dudley, artiste can,
1879-1935
– illustrations #916
Burns, Cooper, Donoahue, Fleming &
Company Ltd., studio can de graphisme
#904
Burns, Cooper, Hynes Ltd., studio can de
graphisme #905
– expositions
– (1979) #906
Burns, Robert, artiste can, 1942-
– co-fondateur de Burns, Cooper, Hynes
Ltd. #905
– estampes #897
– et Burns, Cooper, Donoahue, Fleming &
Company Ltd. #904
Burns, T.M., céramiste can, actif 1862-1865
– fondateur de Spring Park Pottery

(Charlottetown, IPE) #2311
Burns & Cooper Ltd., studio can de
graphisme #892 896
Burnt Cove (TN), imprimerie #1148
Burr, Saxton, constructeur can, actif 1831
– Niagara-on-the-Lake (Ont), Saint
Andrew's Church #8901
Burr, William, artiste amér, 1810-1875/1876
– panorama du fleuve Saint-Laurent et des
Grands-Lacs #218
Burritt's Rapids (Ont), Christ's Church
– architecture, Arthur McClean #8382
Burrows, Thomas Carl (Tom), artiste can,
1940-
– entretien #4959
– expositions de groupe
– (1974) #2050
– *Gas Works* #4960
Burston, Wells & Tampold, agence can
d'architecture
– Toronto (Ont), Holly-Dunfield Apartments
#7683 8514
Burt, Leonard, artiste can, ca 1928- #1155
– expositions de groupe
– (1976) #1153
– (1977) #1156
Burton, Dennis Eugene Norman, artiste can,
1933- #1762
– commentaire sur Frederick Hagan #5676
– commentaire sur Gordon Rayner #6965
– commentaire sur la peinture torontoise
(1953-1965) #1773
– commentaire sur ses études en art #470
– entretien #4962
– expositions
– (1977) #4961
– expositions de groupe
– (1979) #510
Burton Kramer Associates, studio can de
graphisme #889
Burwash, Lachan T., officier de l'armée
canadienne, 1874-1940
– commentaires sur les Inuit (1928) #1021
Bury (Angleterre), Corporation Art Gallery
– expositions
– *Exhibition of Canadian Art* (1926) #290
Bush, Jack Hamilton, artiste can, 1909-1977
#1803 4963 4970 4973
– entretien #536
– et art torontois
– (années 1960) #1753
– (années 1970) #1796
– et internationalisme dans l'art #567
– expositions
– (1972) #4966
– (1976) #4969
– (1980) #4976 4978
– expositions, critiques #4965 4967 4968 4971
4972 4974 4977
– expositions de groupe
– (1967) #480 490 491
– (1971) #98
– (1980) #703
– (1981) #722
– influence sur Douglas Hector Haynes
#5758

– influence sur peinture torontoise #1807
– reconnaissance de l'artiste #123 4975
– utilisation de la couleur #4964
Bush, Robin B., designer can, 1921- #4979
4980
– commentaire sur le design de meubles
#2468
– et architecture #8231
– sièges (mobilier) #2471
bustes
– *voir* sculpture canadienne . portrait
Butcher, Mark, architecte can, actif 1867
– Charlottetown (IPE), marché public #7800
Butler, Kenneth John (Jack/K.J.), artiste can,
1937- #4981
– collection, art inuit #4243
– débuts de la gravure, Baker Lake (TNO)
#4241 4486
– et coopérative Sanavik, Baker Lake (TNO)
#4480
– expositions
– (1977) #4982
– (1981) #4983
– expositions de groupe
– (1977) #1901
Butler, Sheila, artiste can, 1938-
– débuts de la gravure, Baker Lake (TNO)
#4241 4486
– expositions, critiques #4984
Butterfield, William, architecte brit,
1814-1900
– Fredericton (NB), cathédrale #8770
– St. Stephen (NB), Christ Church #8774
Button Point (Bylot Island, TNO)
– artefacts dorsétiens #4359 4361
– masque dorsétien #4356 4357 4362

C

C.A. Fowler and Company
– *voir* Fowler, C.A., and Company
Cabanel, Alexandre, artiste fr, 1823-1889
– professeur de Charles Edouard Huot
#5878 5884
cabanes en bois rond . Canada
– Acadie #7804
– Arctique #8189
– cabanes en rondins verticaux #8532
– Colombie-Britannique #8148
– érablière, Québec, XVIIe-XVIIIe s. #2217
– Gaspé (Qué) #7896
– Ontario, XIXe s. #7979 7990
– parc national de Prince Albert (Sask),
cabane Grey Owl #8719
– restauration #8526
– Ukrainiens #8090
– vallée de l'Outaouais (Ont) #8029
cachots
– *voir* prisons
Cadillac Fairview Corporation, agence can
d'architecture
– Los Angeles (Calif), revitalisation du
quartier Bunker Hill, concours #8364
cadrans solaires . Canada

– expositions, critiques #639
– expositions de groupe
  – (1981) #722
Cameron, Alexander W., homme d'affaires, actif 1906-1909
– et théâtres, Edmonton (Alta), (1906) #9143
Cameron, Donald, administrateur des arts, 1901-
– directeur, Banff School of Fine Arts (Banff, Alta) #3000
Cameron, Duncan, photographe can, 1930-
– expositions de groupe
  – (1970) #1675
Cameron, Eric, artiste can, 1935-
– commentaire sur l'art vidéo #580 616 651
– expositions, critiques #656
– expositions de groupe
  – (1977) #631
  – (1978) #667
Cameron, Walter Graham, sculpteur et forgeron can, 1894- #4992
Cameron & Ralston, agence can d'architecture
– Hamilton (Ont), Hamilton Mausoleum #8900
Camillis, Laurie de, artiste can, 1951-
– expositions, critiques #2072
– expositions de groupe
  – (1979) #2075
Camp, Garry, ébéniste can, actif 1818 #2571
Campbell, Colin, artiste can, 1942-
– art vidéo #605 630 4993
– expositions de groupe
  – (1977) #631
  – (1980) #690 705
– Peripheral Blur #718
Campbell, Daniel Edwin (Ted), artiste can, 1904- #1173 1184
– atelier #4994
– influence sur art, Saint-Jean (NB) #1188
Campbell, John, artisan-tisserand can, actif 1860 #2723
Campbell, Keith Thomas, céramiste can, 1947- #2395
Campbell, Paul, photographe can, 1949-
– expositions, critiques #1067
– expositions de groupe
  – (1980) #1832
Campbell, William, architecte can, actif années 1840-1870
– Saint-Jean (TN), résidence #8542
Campbell, William, juge en chef can, 1758-1834
– résidence, Toronto (Ont) #8661
Campbell-Smith, Struan, photographe can, actif 1979 #995
Campbellton (NB), galerie Restigouche/Restigouche Gallery
– expositions
  – Canadians: A National Photography Show about People/Canadiens: exposition nationale de photographie ayant les gens comme thème (1978) #1035
  – Diversité: Diane Gougeon, Raymond Lavoie, Alex Magrini, Robert Saucier (1980) #685
  – George Rackus: Anodized Aluminum Works

  & Prints (1973) #6953
  – Miller Brittain - Painter (1981) #4922
  – Roger Savage (1980) #7135
  – The Beaverbrook Art Gallery Presents Nine New Brunswick Artists/La Galerie d'art Beaverbrook présente neuf artistes du Nouveau-Brunswick (1973) #1182
Campbellton (NB), Restigouche Senior High School
– expositions
  – Colville, Pratt, Forrestall (1974) #1129
Campeau, Michel, photographe can, 1948- #997
– catalogue de photographies #997 999
– entretien sur le Groupe d'action photographique #1494
– vues photographiques, Disraëli (Qué), (1972) #1513
Campeau Corporation (Calgary, Alta)
– transformation de McKay Farm House en bureau commercial #8133
camps de concentration
– vues
  – Menses, Jan #6511
  – Saarniit, John #7112
  – Shadbolt, Jack Leonard #7189
Campus, Peter, artiste amér, 1937-
– art vidéo #651
Canada
– cartes géographiques
  – XVIIe s. #841
  – XVIIe-XVIIIe s. #875
– dans sculpture britannique (années 1880) #725
– dessins humoristiques et politiques
  – dissensions Est-Ouest au Canada (1874-1946) #958
  – Union de 1841 #942
  – XIXe s.-années 1970 #957
– vues
  – (1750-1850) #279
  – (années 1890) #6436
  – (années 1890), service de table officiel, Canada #2333
  – (années 1910) #1710
  – (années 1950) #403
  – art traditionnel #965 966
  – Bartlett, William Henry #4615 4616
  – Davies, Thomas #5270 5271
  – Groupe des Sept #1744 1774
  – Heriot, George #5785
  – Hind, William George Richardson #5807 5808 5809
  – Hopkins, Frances Ann Beechy #5835
  – Julien, Henri #5983
  – Krieghoff, Cornelius #6091 6101
  – Martin, Henry Byam #6426
  – Martin, Thomas Mower #6438
  – Morrice, James Wilson #6622
  – poterie, XIXe s. #2288 2294 2309
  – poterie de Portneuf #2285
  – poterie Staffordshire #2099 2282
  – Roper, Edward #7077
  – Russell, Edward John #7111
  – service à dessert Minton #2289
  – Simcoe, Elizabeth Posthuma Gwillim

  #7210
  – Volpi, Charles de, collection #3248
  – Warre, Henry James #7522
  – White, George Harlow #7551
  – XIXe s. #224 241 242 266 840 1326 1337 2362
  – XIXe s.-années 1970 #132
  – XVIe-XIXe s., vues, artistes européens #255 256 260
  – XVIIe-XIXe s. #231
  – XVIIIe s. #269 270
  – XVIIIe s.-années 1910 #3130 3131 3143 3204
  – XVIIIe s.-années 1940 #26
  – XVIIIe-XIXe s. #12 222 223 239 244 246 247 812 828 839 1220 1222 1224 1225 1366 3230
  – XXe s. #41
– vues photographiques
  – Jaycocks, T.G. #5950
  – Notman, William #6725
Canada. Aviation royale du Canada
– artistes de guerre, Seconde Guerre mondiale #4761
– et Charles Goldhamer #1091
Canada. Brief Concerning the Cultural Aspects of Canadian Reconstruction (1944)
– rapport #3251
– réactions #3250
Canada. Canadian Broadcasting Corporation (CBC)
– art graphique télédiffusé
  – (années 1950) #866 869
  – (années 1950-1970) #909
  – (années 1970) #899
– et le public canadien #447
– et Louis de Niverville #6704 6706
Canada. Comité fédéral d'études d'une politique culturelle (Commission Applebaum-Hébert)
– commentaire sur la photographie #1068
– Conférence canadienne des arts, rapport
  – (1980) #3294 3295
  – (1981) #3297 3298
– femmes artistes canadiennes, rapport (1980) #719
Canada. Commission de la capitale nationale
– (années 1960) #7683
– et région de la capitale nationale (Ottawa, Ont) #8037 8039 8044
Canada. Commission royale d'enquête sur l'avancement des arts, lettres et sciences (Rapport Massey) #3254 3255
– commentaire sur l'art québécois (1925-1950) #1405
– commentaire sur la construction de centres d'arts d'interprétation #9086
– commentaire sur la peinture canadienne (1920-1950) #391
– commentaire sur le marché de l'art #3260
– critique #398
– et Alberta Society of Artists #1944
– et artistes québécois #1401
– et conférence de l'institut canadien des

affaires publiques (Lake Couchiching, Ont), (1976) #619
– et Conference of Canadian Artists (1941) #390
– et Conseil des Arts du Canada (1951-années 1960) #3264
– et *Exhibition of Contemporary Canadian Arts* (1950) #387
– et Vincent Massey #3258
– extraits #3256
– influence sur culture canadienne (années 1950-1970) #3278 3290
– Milne, David Brown, commentaire #6550
– réactions de presse #3257
– résumé des recommandations #3261
– théories sur l'architecture #7670 7673
Canada. Conseil de recherches pour la défense
– architecture militaire, recherches sur le bâtiment (années 1950) #8414
Canada. Conseil législatif du Canada
– Krieghoff, Cornelius, pétition visant à promouvoir scènes canadiennes dans la peinture (1856) #6091
Canada. Conseil national de l'esthétique
– (1961-1973) #2624
– Concours pour ouvrages en béton
  – (1971) #7706
Canada. Conseil national de l'esthétique industrielle
– (1944), recommandation #2600
– (années 1950) #2605 2609
– conférence sur la conception d'ameublement (1954) #2468
– prix et récompenses, critique
  – (1951) #2608
  – (1958) #2610
– rapport sur la fabrication d'ameublement (1950) #2467
Canada. Conseil national de recherches
– (1916-1961), et le public canadien #447
– recherche sur le bâtiment (années 1960) #7683
Canada. Conseil national de recherches. Division des recherches sur le bâtiment #7715
Canada. Corporation des musées nationaux
– conception de musées, devis #9129
Canada. Institut canadien du film
– McLaren, Norman, films #6498
Canada. Inventaire canadien des bâtiments historiques #7707 7708 7716 7771
– inventaire informatisé #159
Canada. Marine royale du Canada
– et Rowley Walter Murphy #6665
Canada. Ministère de la Culture et des Loisirs
– protection des arts (années 1950-1970) #3278
Canada. Ministère de la Défense nationale
– architecture militaire (années 1950) #8414
– collection, photographies #1024
Canada. Ministère des Affaires du Nord
– habitations, Arctique
  – (années 1950) #8184
  – (années 1960) #8732

Canada. Ministère des Affaires extérieures
– Murray, Robert Gray, *Haida* #6672
Canada. Ministère des Affaires indiennes et du Nord canadien
– collection, art inuit #4246
– expositions de sculpture inuit pour handicapés visuels #4430
Canada. Ministère des Transports
– aérogares
  – (années 1950) #9514
  – (années 1960) #9517
Canada. Ministère des Travaux publics
– (1840-années 1960) #8976 8977
– architecture
  – (1954-1959) #7681
  – (années 1950) #8227 8971
  – (années 1970) #7728
  – Second Empire #7741 7742
– et Banque d'oeuvres d'art (années 1970) #3277
– et Galerie nationale du Canada (Ottawa, Ont), concours (1975-1977) #9126
– Fort Battleford (Battleford, Sask) #8484
– Fuller, Thomas, architecte en chef #8366 9055
– Fuller, Thomas William, architecte en chef #8367 8368
– programme d'études en art (années 1970) #9049
– rapport présenté à l'Institut royal d'architecture du Canada (1966) #8309
Canada. National Industrial Design Committee
– (1948-1953) #2609
– (1951) #2606
– (années 1940) #2604
Canada. Office national du film du Canada #626
– art graphique au cinéma (années 1970) #899
– et Commission royale d'enquête sur l'avancement des arts, lettres et sciences (Rapport Massey) #3254 3255 3261 9906
– et Jean-Philippe Dallaire #5238 5239
– et Norman McLaren #6492 6493 6498
– Minden, Robert, photographies #6570
– publications, collection *Image* (1967-1971) #990
– soutien à la photographie canadienne (années 1970) #1038
Canada. Parcs Canada
– politique de reconstruction d'habitations historiques #7758
Canada. Service des parcs nationaux
– édifices récréatifs #9081
Canada. Service féminin de l'Armée canadienne
– et Molly Lamb Bobak #4761 4766
Canada. Société centrale d'hypothèques et de logement
– (années 1940) #8507
– Demonstration Program (années 1970) #7728
– logement subventionné (années 1960) #8518
– modèles d'habitations (années 1950) #8509

– Roussil, Robert, sculpture habitable #7096
– Smyth Road Development Competition (1960) #8040
Canada. Société Radio-Canada
– collection d'art canadien #3273
Canada Clock Company, horlogers (Whitby et Hamilton, Ont) #2927
Canada Crafts, périodique can #2126
Canada Glass Works, fabricants de verre (Saint-Jean, Qué) #2420
Canada Glass Works, fabricants de verre (Vaudreuil, Qué) #2418
Canada Publishing Co., éditeur (Toronto, Ont)
– cartes de Noël #842
Canada Stained Glass Works, fabricants de verre (Toronto, Ont)
– (années 1850-1960) #2449
Canada Steamship Lines
– Coverdale, William H., Collection Canadiana #12 3230
Canadian Antiques and Art Review, périodique can #141
Canadian Antiques Collector, périodique can #74
Canadian Architect, périodique can #7672
– organisateurs, galerie d'art communautaire, concours (1957) #9082
– prix et récompenses
  – (1968) #8190
  – (1969) #8191
  – (1970) #8192
  – (1971) #8193
  – (1972) #8194
  – (1973) #8195
  – (1974) #8196
  – (1975) #8197
  – (1976) #8198
  – (1977) #8199
  – (1978) #8200
  – (1979) #8201 8202
  – (1980) #8203
  – (1981) #8204
– sondages auprès des architectes
  – (1958) #8302
  – (1972) #8314 8316
  – (1974-1976) #8320
  – (1976) #8321
Canadian Architect & Builder, périodique can #7639
Canadian Architect Yearbook, périodique can #7672
Canadian Architectural Students' Association #8250
Canadian Art, périodique can #25 349
Canadian Art Club (Toronto, Ont) #14 28
– (1907-1915) #193
– et James Wilson Morrice #6634
– et Laura Adeline Muntz Lyall #6339
– expositions, critiques
  – (1909) #194
  – (1913) #204
  – (1916) #211
– influence sur art canadien (1907-1910) #214
Canadian Art Glass Limited, fabricants de vitraux (Calgary, Alta) #2455

Canadian Broadcasting Corporation
– *voir* Canada. Canadian Broadcasting
    Corporation (CBC)
Canadian Collector, périodique can #74
Canadian Correspondent, journal can
– lettres concernant exposition de la Society
    of Artists and Amateurs of Toronto #1729
Canadian Creative Music Collective (CCMC)
– expositions
    – (1980) #690
Canadian Design Index–NIDC
– (1950-1957) #2605
– (1953-1954) #3033
– et Galerie nationale du Canada (Ottawa,
    Ont) #2604 2606
Canadian Dimension, périodique can
– illustrations, Kelly Clark #5109
Canadian Embroiderer's Guild (London,
    Ont)
– expositions
    – (1981) #2793
Canadian Forum, périodique can
– commentaire sur l'art canadien (années
    1920-1940) #3301
– commentaire sur le Groupe des Sept #1739
    1763
– et Barker Fairley #5403 5404 5405
– et Thoreau MacDonald #6381 6383
– illustrations (1920-1951) #930
Canadian Guild of Potters
– expositions, critiques
    – (1957) #2380
– expositions (1955-1971) #2379
Canadian Heritage, périodique can #7764
Canadian Illustrated News, périodique can
    #5990
– illustrations
    – Julien, Henri #5992
    – Kroupa, Bohuslar #6104
    – Russell, Edward John #7110
    – Taylor, George Thomas #7334
– photographies #1006
Canadian Industrial Photography, périodique
    can #995
Canadian Journal, périodique can
– et Paul Kane #6003
Canadian Journal of Photography, périodique
    can #974
Canadian Magazine, périodique can
– illustrations
    – Brigden, Fred #4913
    – Julien, Henri #5987
Canadian Northern Railway
– gares #9542 9545
    – Manitoba #9543
Canadian Photo Journal, périodique can #1032
Canadian Photographer, périodique can #987
Canadian Photographic Journal, périodique can
    #976
Canadian Photography, périodique can #995
Canadian Professional Indian Artists
    Association
– et Alex Simeon Janvier #5936
Canadian Professional Photography, périodique
    can #995
Canadian Review of Music and Art, périodique

can #357
Canadian Rock Art Research Associates
– conférence, Victoria (CB), (1977) #3481
Canadian Small House Competition
– (1946) #8740
Canadian Society for Creative Leathercraft
– (années 1970) #2936
Canadien National
– et Allan Robb Fleming #5457
– gares #9542 9545
    – Montréal (Qué), gare Centrale #9535
– Montréal (Qué), hôtel Reine-Elizabeth
    #8228 9286
– sociétés ferroviaires, hôtels, style château
    #9290 9291
Canadien Pacifique
– architecture
    – Victoria (CB) #8175
        – Crystal Gardens #9146
– architecture et art #3281
– et Alfred Crocker Leighton #6225
– et Charles George Horetzky #1014 1015
    5837 5838
– et Edward Roper #7077
– et Frederic Marlett Bell-Smith #4668
– et Harry Pollard #6899
– et John A. Hammond #5698
– et John Colin Forbes #5459
– et Nick Morant #6605
– et Richard H. Trueman #7437
– gares #9538 9539 9545
    – Manitoba #9543
    – Saskatchewan #9544
    – Vancouver (CB) #9546
– photographies d'arpentage (années (1870)
    #1876
– sociétés ferroviaires, hôtels, style château
    #9290 9291
Canadiens à Taiwan
– Onley, Toni #6738
Canadiens au Brésil
– (années 1950) #413 414
– Rio de Janeiro
    – Pellan, Alfred #6798
    – Tonnancour, Jacques Godefroy de #7382
Canadiens au Ghana
– Semak, Michael William #990
Canadiens au Japon
– Cassidy, Eugene Haanel #5054
– Knudsen, Chris #6070
– Kyoto
    – Beauchemin, Micheline #4644
– Ngan, Wayne G. #6695
– Onley, Toni #6738
– Petit, Gaston-Pierre #6843 6844 6845
Canadiens au Mexique
– (années 1950) #413 414
– Brooks, Leonard #4931
– Cosgrove, Stanley Morel #5178 5180 5181
    5184
– Glass, Alan Frank #5614
– Lewis, Stanley #6278
– Mulcaster, Wynona Croft #6660
– Onley, Toni #6740 6741
– Reppen, Jack #6990
– Svarre, Grace #7303

– Wilson, Ronald York #4931 7595
Canadiens au Moyen-Orient
– Currelly, Charles Trick #3139
Canadiens au Proche-Orient
– Kane, Paul #6005
– Lotbinière, Pierre-Gustave Joly de #6326
Canadiens aux Antilles
– MacDonald, J.E.H. #6371
– Morrice, James Wilson #6617 6626
– Suzor-Coté, Marc-Aurèle de Foy #7297
    7300
Canadiens aux Etats-Unis
– (1759-années 1970) #126
– (années 1850), architectes montréalais
    #7920
– (années 1890), architectes #7640
– (années 1910), graphistes #916
– (années 1940-1960) #485
– Boisseau, Alfred #4768
– Boston (Mass)
    – Harris, Lawren Phillips #5713
    – Harris, Robert #5737
    – Karsh, Yousuf #6026
    – Miles, John Christopher #6533
    – Sandham, J.Henry #7121
    – Wilson, William F. #7593
– Californie
    – Levine, Marilyn Ann #6274
    – Rulofson, William Herman #7107
    – Zuck, Tim #7635
– Carlyle, Florence #5000
– Carr, Emily #5023
– Cassidy, Eugene Haanel #5054
– Christin, Léopold #5105
– Cincinnati (Ohio)
    – Meanwell, Jack #646
– Colorado
    – Proctor, Alexander Phimister #6944
– Cooke, Edwy Francis #5171
– Cranbrook (Mich)
    – Betteridge, Lois Etherington #4718
    – Pachter, Charles #6748
– Day, Mabel Killam #5273
– Duncanson, Robert Stuart #241 242
– Eaton, Wyatt #5355
– Field, Robert #5429 5432 5433
– Fraser, John Arthur #5511
– Garnier, Hubert #5556
– Gordon, Hortense Mattice #1850
– Hammond, John A. #5700
– Harrison, Allan #5746
– Humphrey, Jack Weldon #5865 5870
– Jarvis, Donald Alvin #1850
– Kane, Paul #6005
– Kennedy, Sybil #6046
– Lawson, Ernest #6176 6177 6178 6179
– Levine, Les #6262
– Livernois, Jules-Benoît #6308
– Luke, Alexandra #1850
– Macdonald, Jock #1850
– McKenzie, Robert Tait #6482 6484 6485
    6486 6487 6488
– New York (NY)
    – (années 1910), femmes artistes #206
    – (années 1960) #460
    – (années 1970) #555

– Barnsley, James Macdonald #4612
– Bladen, Ronald #4741
– Borduas, Paul-Emile #4803 4810 4826
  4835 4839 4843 4846 4849
– Brittain, Miller Gore #4917
– Cardinal, Marcel #4997
– Clerk, Pierre Jean #5118
– Coburn, Frederick Simpson #5124
– Cruikshank, William #5212
– Dumouchel, Albert #5325
– Fauteux-Massé, Henriette #5415
– FitzGerald, Lionel LeMoine #5449
– Freiman, Lillian #5517
– Gagnon, Charles #5533 5540
– Harrison, Allan #862 5747
– Hümme, Joseph Julius #5863
– Jarvis, Donald Alvin #5947
– Jefferys, Charles William #5953 5956
– Jobin, Louis #5962
– Kahane, Anne #5998
– Kerr, Estelle Muriel #206
– Laliberté, Madeleine #6153
– Lawson, Ernest #6175
– MacAskill, Wallace R. #6350
– MacLeod, Pegi Nicol #6397
– Maggs, Arnaud #862
– Milne, David Brown #6554 6555 6560
  6566 6567
– Morris, Edmund Montague #6636
– Mousseau, Jean-Paul Armand #6650
– Nicoll, Marion F.S. Mackay #6703
– Ogilvie, Will #6732
– Oliver, Bobbie #675
– Pavelic, Myfanwy Spencer #6785
– Riopelle, Jean-Paul #7029
– Roberts, Goodridge #7044
– Steinhouse, Tobie Thelma #7278
– Taylor, Richard #7336 7337
– Tousignant, Claude #7400
– Tully, Sydney Strickland #7438
– Westerlund, Mia #675
– Wrinch, Mary Evelyn #7618
– Parsons, F.R. #6773
– Philadelphie (Penn)
  – Reid, George Agnew #6977 6979
  – Reid, Mary Hiester #6982
– Plaskett, Joe #1850
– Provincetown (Mass)
  – Borduas, Paul-Emile #4843
  – Stacey, Harold #7274
– Ringness, Charles #7011
– San Francisco (Calif)
  – Carr, Emily #5045
  – Hammock, Virgil #5696
  – Smith, Gordon Appelbe #7225
– Suzor-Coté, Marc-Aurèle de Foy #7297
  7300
– Tanabe, Takao #1850
– Thomas, Lionel Arthur John #1850
Canadiens aux Pays-Bas
– Coburn, Frederick Simpson #5124
– Hammond, John A. #5699
– Jackson, A.Y. #5924
Canadiens en Afrique
– Morrice, James Wilson #6617 6623 6626
  6629

– Phillips, Walter Joseph #6857 6860
Canadiens en Allemagne
– Coburn, Frederick Simpson #5124
– Dresden
  – Wallis, Katherine Elizabeth #7512
– Harris, Lawren Stewart #5734
– Hümme, Joseph Julius #5863
– Munich
  – Humphrey, Jack Weldon #5870
Canadiens en Amérique du Sud
– Bruni, Umberto #4946
– Harrison, Allan #5746
Canadiens en Asie
– Currelly, Charles Trick #3139
– Hammond, John A. #5700
– Mah, Tom #6409
– Wolfe, Robert #7606
Canadiens en Belgique
– Brault, Maurice #4906
– Jackson, A.Y. #5924
Canadiens en Chine
– McLaren, Norman #6492
– Onley, Toni #6738
Canadiens en Ecosse
– MacKenzie, Robert #6393
Canadiens en Espagne
– Ariss, Herb #473
– Ariss, Margot Phillips #473
– Bonet, Jordi #4784
– Chambers, Jack #473 5070 5071 5073
– Coughtry, John Graham #473
– Gould, John Howard #473
– Hedrick, Robert Burns #473
– Lafleur, Pierre #6132
– Lambart, Evelynn #6498
– McLaren, Norman #6498
– O'Brien, Paddy Gunn #473
– Rayner, Gordon #473
– Saltmarche, Kenneth Charles #473
– Urquhart, Tony #473
Canadiens en Europe
– (années 1930) #13
– Archambault, Louis #408
– Arthur, Paul #859
– Barnsley, James Macdonald #4612
– Berczy, William von Moll #4699
– Bice, Clare #408
– Bourassa, Napoléon #4868 4875
– Broomfield, Adolphus George #4932
– Bruni, Umberto #4946
– Brymner, William #4948
– Carlyle, Florence #207 5000
– Carr, Emily #5023
– Cormier, Ernest #8345
– Cullen, Maurice Galbraith #5220
– Currelly, Charles Trick #3139
– Dumouchel, Albert #5325
– Dyonnet, Edmond #5347 5349
– Eaton, Wyatt #5356
– Forster, John Wycliffe #5469
– Fowler, Daniel #5491
– Gagen, Robert Ford #5530
– Gagnon, Clarence Alphonse #5546 5547
– Glass, Alan Frank #5614
– Grier, Edmund Wyly #5660
– Hamel, Théophile #5690

– Hamilton, Mary Riter #5694 5695
– Hammond, John A. #5700
– Harris, Robert #5737
– Harrison, Allan #5746
– Humphrey, Jack Weldon #5865
– Kane, Paul #6003 6005 6007 6010
– Kerr, Estelle Muriel #207
– Knowles, Elizabeth Annie McGillivray
  #207
– Krieghoff, Cornelius #6093
– La Palme, Robert #408
– Leduc, Ozias #6209
– Lemieux, Jean-Paul #6227 6230
– LeMoine, Edmond #6243
– Lismer, Arthur #6301
– Livernois, Jules-Benoît #6308
– Lyall, Laura Adeline Muntz #207 6339
– Lyman, John Goodwin #6347
– Macdonald, Jock #6376
– MacLaughlan, Donald Shaw #6394
– McCulloch, James Frederic #6463
– McNicoll, Helen Galloway #6507
– Mercier, Monique #6512
– Molinari, Guido #6588
– Morrice, James Wilson #6617 6619 6628
– Morris, Jerrold #6639
– Mulcaster, Wynona Croft #6660
– Palchinski, Sylvia Scott #6753
– Parizeau, Marcel #8397
– Peel, Paul #6792
– Pflug, Christiane Sybille #6849
– Pilot, Robert Wakeham #6869
– Plaskett, Joe #6889
– Reid, Leslie Mary Margaret #6980
– Reid, Mary Hiester #207
– Roberts, Goodridge #408
– Ryerson, Adolphus Egerton #3150 3155
– Sandham, J.Henry #7121
– Shadbolt, Jack Leonard #7180
– Smith, William St. Thomas #7236
– Suzor-Coté, Marc-Aurèle de Foy #7295
  7297 7298 7300
– Tanobe, Miyuki #7324 7325
– Wheeler, Orson Shorey #7549
– Wrinch, Mary Evelyn #207
– XIXe s. #197
– XIXe s.-années 1920 #14
Canadiens en France
– (années 1880), et Jean-Joseph
  Benjamin-Constant #243
– (années 1950) #413 414
– Allward, Walter Seymour #4519
– Amyot, Laurent #1244
– Arsenault, Réal #4556
– Ayotte, Léo #4575
– Baillairgé, François #1244
– Beaucourt, François Malepart de #269 270
  1244
– Bergeron, André #4703
– Bruce, William Blair #4941
– Carr, Emily #5027 5028 5044
– Dallaire, Jean-Philippe #5241 5244 5246
  5247
– Daoust, Sylvia Marie Emilienne #5257
– Duguay, Rodolphe #5317
– Eaton, Wyatt #5355 5357

– Kleyn, Robert #6063
– Morrice, James Wilson #6617 6623 6632
– Peterson, Margaret #6839
– Sole, Stelio #7265
– Sullivan, Françoise #7282
– Venise
  – Binning, B.C. #4732
Canadiens en Jamaïque
– Field, Robert #5429 5432
Canadiens en Norvège
– Brault, Maurice #4906
Canadiens en Scandinavie
– Brassard, Thérèse Tanguay #4905
Canadiens en Suède
– Cartier, Jean Bernard #5052
– Janvier, Alex Simeon #5938
– Stacey, Harold #7273
– Stockholm
  – Bruce, William Blair #4941
Canadiens en Suisse
– Arthur, Paul #865
– Bergeron, André #4703
Canadiens en Tunisie
– Tunis
  – Pflug, Christiane Sybille #6850
Canadiens en URSS
– Semak, Michael William #7169
canal Welland (Ont)
– William James Thomson, vues #7372
canaux . Canada
– constructions, Ottawa (Ont) #8019
– écluses et ponts, XIXe s. #9512
Canberra (Australie), Belconnen
  Government Office Complex
– architecture, John Andrews Architects
  #8323
Canberra (Australie), National Gallery of
  Australia
– expositions
  – *Contemporary Canadian Painters* (1957)
    #423
Candy, Kenneth H., architecte can, 1914-
– Toronto (Ont), Hydro Place #9352
Cannard, Pierre
– *voir* Renaud (dit Cannard), Pierre
Cannon, John R., photographe can,
  1861-1931 #1724
Cannon, Thomas, photographe can,
  1832-1899 #1724
canons . Canada
– Terre-Neuve, XXe s. #2151
– Terre-Neuve et Labrador, XXe s. #2155
canots
– *voir aussi* bateaux
– scènes de voyages en canot, Frances Ann
  Beechy Hopkins #5834
canots . Algonquiens #3571
canots . Amérindiens
– sur cartes géographiques, XVIIe s. #841
canots . Haidas
– ailerons de canots cérémoniels #3825
canots . Indiens de la côte nord-ouest #3339
canots . Nootkas
– en comparaison avec umiaks inuit #3344
canots . Quinaults #3845
canots . Salish de la côte #3851 3896
Cantieni, Graham, artiste can, 1938- #4996
– et RACE (Regroupement des artistes des
  Cantons de l'Est) #1536
– expositions, critiques #4995
Cantin, Jean-François, artiste can, 1958-
– art de performance #655
Cantons de l'Est (Qué)
– art

– (1800-1950) #1296
– (1815-1940) #1288
– (années 1970) #1282 1535 1539
– églises protestantes, XIXe s. #8888
– vues
  – (1832-1881) #1342
  – Edson, Aaron Allan #5362
– vues photographiques
  – (années 1970) #1534
Cap-Breton (NE)
– tartan, tissage #2724
– textiles et tissus #2732
– tissage #2728
Cap-Breton (NE), Gaelic College of St. Ann's
– tartan, tissage #2724
Cap-Rouge, atelier de poterie de (Québec,
  Qué) #2302
– (1860-1890) #2296 2298 2301 2322
– pièce-souvenir, cruche, Philip Pointon
  #2332
Cap-Santé (Qué)
– églises #8814
Cap-Santé (Qué), église
– architecture, Pierre Renaud (dit Cannard)
  #269 270
– peintures, Paul Malepart de Grand Maison
  (dit Beaucour) #249 250
Cap-Santé (Qué), église Sainte-Famille #8883
Cap-Tourmente (Qué), Ecole du
  Cap-Tourmente
– *voir* Saint-Joachim (Qué), Ecoles des arts et
  métiers de Saint-Joachim
Cape Bonavista (TN), phare #9523 9525
Cape Dorset (TNO)
– art #6904
  – (années 1960) #4187
  – (années 1970) #6270 6271
– artefacts dorsétiens #4322
– arts graphiques #4461 4466 4476 4477 4484
  4500
  – (1959-1972) #4478
  – (1959-1974) #4483
  – (1959-1976) #4490
  – (1960-) #4460
  – (1976-1977) #4491
  – (années 1960) #4464
  – Burnaby (CB), Simon Fraser University.
    Simon Fraser Gallery #4495
  – et James Archibald Houston #4186 4462
    4470
– arts graphiques et sculpture #4200 4299
  – (1957-1967) #4211
  – (années 1960) #4192
– aspect social, Les Levine, commentaire
  #6269
– colonie d'artistes, Peter Pitseolak,
  commentaire #6880 6881
– femmes artistes (années 1970) #4260
– sculpture #4425 4441
  – mines, carrières #4409
– sculpture et dessin (années 1960) #4189
– vues
  – Pitseolak, Peter #6883
Cape Mudge (CB), Cape Mudge Kwakiutl
  Museum
– art kwakiutl #4052
Cape Spear (TN), phare #9525
capitonnage
– *voir* rembourrage
Cappello, Luigi, artiste it au Canada, actif
  1874-1892
– peintures, église Sainte-Anne (Yamachiche,
  Qué) #8783
CAR/FAC

– *voir* Front des artistes canadiens/Canadian
  Artists' Representation (CAR/FAC)
CAR/FAC News, périodique can #625
CAR News/RAC Journal, périodique can #625
Caraquet (NB), école polyvalente Louis
  Mailloux
– expositions
  – *Colville, Pratt, Forrestall* (1974) #1129
  – *The Beaverbrook Art Gallery Presents Nine
    New Brunswick Artists/La Galerie d'art
    Beaverbrook présente neuf artistes du
    Nouveau-Brunswick* (1973) #1182
Carbonear (TN)
– architecture #7792
Carcy, Jacques
– *voir* Pagé (dit Quercy ou Carcy), Jacques
Cardero, José (Pepe), artiste esp, 1768-après
  1808
– expédition, côte nord-ouest #1998
Cardinal, Douglas Joseph, architecte can,
  1934- #8084 8341 8343
– écrits #8342
– Edmonton (Alta), résidence #8091
– Indian Education Centre #9494
– réflexion sur son oeuvre architecturale
  #8340
– théories sur l'architecture #7746
Cardinal, Marcelin (Marcel), artiste can,
  1920- #4997 4998
Carey, David, photographe can, ca 1947-
– catalogue de photographies #1023
caricature
– *voir aussi* politique et dessins
  humoristiques
– La Palme, Robert, commentaire #6120
caricature . Canada #925 946
– (1792-1850) #839
– Art Directors' Club of Toronto #854
– Bengough, John Wilson #4671 4673 4675
  4676 4677
– Côté, Jean-Baptiste #5186 5187 5188
– Fay-Génot, Jean-Etienne-Achille #5416
– Fiorucci, Vittorio #5442
– Forrestall, Tom #5464
– Hudon, Normand #5854
– Innes, John I. #5901
– Julien, Henri #5981 5983 5986 5987 5990
  5993
– La Palme, Robert #6119
– Macpherson, Duncan Ian #6400
– Millikin, William #6543
– Robinson, Albert Henry #7056
– Scovil, James Noel #7167
– Taylor, Richard #7337
– Trier, Walter #7428
– XVIIIe-XIXe s. #812 949
Carillon (Qué)
– monument à Dollard des Ormeaux #1591
Carli, Thomas, sculpteur can, 1838-1906
– thème de l'Annonciation #1633
– thème du souper d'Emmaüs #1615
Carlton Studio, studio de graphisme
  (Londres, Angleterre)
– (1903-1915) #843
Carlu, Jacques, architecte fr, 1890-1976
– design des magasins Eaton #9370
Carlu, Natacha, artiste fr, active 1931
– murales, magasins Eaton #9370
Carlyle, Florence, artiste can, 1864-1923 #207
  4999
– expositions
  – (1925) #5000
– expositions, critiques #186
Carmichael, Franklin, artiste can, 1890-1945

– et Alfred Joseph Casson #5056
– et Groupe des Sept #1732
– expositions
  – (1981) #5001
– illustration de livres et mise en page
  artistique #939
Carmichael, Maurice
– *voir* Carmichael, William Maurice
Carmichael, Robert Ralph, artiste can, 1938-
– expositions
  – (1972) #5002
– expositions, critiques #1866
Carmichael, William John, architecte can,
  1867-1927
– Montréal (Qué), Northern Electric #9234
Carmichael, William Maurice, orfèvre can,
  1892-1954 #5003 5004
carnets à dessins
– Brooke, Arthur Adair #4924
– Carr, Emily #5018
– Edson, Aaron Allan #5363
– Gemeinhardt, John #5579
– Jackson, A.Y. #5924
– Jackson, Henry Alexander Carmichael
  #5927 5928
– Jameson, Anna Brownell #5933
– Jarvis, Donald Alvin #5944
– Jefferys, Charles William #5957
– Kane, Paul #6006 6009 6011 6012
– Krieghoff, Cornelius #6090
– Leduc, Ozias #6210
– Lismer, Arthur #6305
– MacDonald, J.E.H. #6373
– Massicotte, Edmond-Joseph #6441
– Miller, Alfred Jacob #6536 6537
– Morrice, James Wilson #6621 6631 6632
– Pope, William #6906
– Simcoe, Elizabeth Posthuma Gwillim
  #7212
– Thomson, Tom #7370
Caro, Anthony, sculpteur brit, 1924-
– entretien, Emma Lake Workshops (Emma
  Lake, Sask) #1934
– influence sur Alan Wood #7610 7611
– influence sur André Lucien Fauteux #5413
– influence sur Douglas Bentham #4684 4686
– influence sur Robert Murray #6669
Caron, G.Fernand, architecte can, 1905-1963
– Québec (Qué), édifice de la compagnie
  d'assurance La Solidarité #7939
Caron, Louis, architecte can, 1848-1917
– Saint-Eugène (Qué), église
  Saint-Eugène-de-Grantham #8873
Caron, Paul Archibald, artiste can, 1874-1941
– gravure sur bois de fil #802
Caron, Roger, artiste can (tapisserie), 1925-
  #5005
CAROT, périodique can #625
Carpenter, Edmund Snow, anthropologue
  can aux E-U, 1922-
– commentaire sur le sacré dans l'art #94
Carr, Emily, artiste can, 1871-1945 #309 461
  1986 2011 5008 5016 5021 5022 5024 5026
  5033 5034 5035 5037 5040 5045
– appui du public #5032
– art et écrits #5019 5044
– autobiographie #5009 5010 5013 5017
– *Blunden Harbour*, Galerie nationale du
  Canada (Ottawa, Ont) #5036
– commentaire sur l'art amérindien de la
  côte nord-ouest #5006
– commentaire sur les Indiens de la côte
  nord-ouest #5007 5031
– commentaire sur un séjour (1902-1903) au

Sunhill Sanatorium (Londres, Angleterre)
  #5018
– correspondance, Ruth Humphrey
  (1937-1944) #5029
– critique d'art #3308
– écrits #92
  – (1927-1941) #5025
– en comparaison avec Jack Weldon
  Humphrey #404
– et British Columbia Society of Fine Arts
  #1978
– et Max Stern #1431
– et peinture canadienne #18
– et peinture en Colombie-Britannique
  (1894-1932) #2007
– et ses soeurs #5015
– expositions
  – (1945) #5012
  – (1962) #5023
  – (1971) #5027 5028
  – (1977) #5039
  – (1979) #5042 5046
– expositions, critiques #1982
– expositions de groupe
  – (1928) #294 3827
  – (1940) #350
  – (1947) #377
  – (1958) #1995
– Hughes, Edward John, comparaison #5861
– huiles sur papier (années 1930-1940) #5041
– influence sur art en Colombie-Britannique
  #2003
– influence sur Jack Leonard Shadbolt #7178
– *Klee Wyck* #5038
– MacLeod, Pegi Nicol, comparaison #6398
– oeuvres, Biennale de Venise (1952) #399
– oeuvres, McMichael Canadian Collection
  (Kleinburg, Ont) #3172
– paysages #140 2016
  – en comparaison avec James Wilson
    Morrice #352
– peintre moderniste #507
– peintures, Indiens de la côte nord-ouest
  #1840
– peintures (années 1930) #502
– poterie, motifs amérindiens #2278
– professeure #5014 5020
– réminiscences #5011 5043
– résidence, Victoria (CB) #8176 8177
– Shadbolt, Jack Leonard, comparaison
  #7191
– théories sur l'art #5030
Carr-Harris, Ian, artiste can, 1941-
– entretien #5048
– expositions, critiques #697 794
– expositions de groupe
  – (1974) #574
  – (1981) #710
– réflexion sur son oeuvre #5047
– sculpture, art de performance #658
– utilisation de la photographie #1057
carreaux de céramique . Grande-Bretagne
– dans habitations torontoises, XIXe s. #2373
carreaux de céramique . style victorien
– dans habitations torontoises, XIXe s. #2373
Carrere & Hastings, agence amér
  d'architecture
– Montréal (Qué), Transportation Building
  #9307
– Toronto (Ont)
  – Bank of Toronto #8293 9162 9185
  – Banque Royale #9152
– Windsor (Ont), Dominion Bank #9188
Carrier, Louis, collectionneur can, né 1898

– collection, orfèvrerie québécoise #3213
Carrier, Louise, artiste can, 1925-1976 #5049
Carriers
– 'Ksan (coopérative d'artistes) #4129 4130
– art
  – (années 1970) #4145
– pictogrammes #3965
Carroll, Jane, photographe can, active
  années 1850 #1211
Carrothers, Lewis E., architecte can, né 1878
– London (Ont), Riverview School #9388
Carruthers, Alan, photographe can, actif
  1980
– catalogue de photographies #995
Carter, Alexander Scott, artiste et architecte
  can, 1881-1968 #5050
Carter, Gerald Gordon, sculpteur can, 1930-
– sculpture de jardin #1849
cartes à jouer
– dans l'art, David Brown Milne #6553
cartes de souhaits . Canada
– (années 1920) #4
– Noël, thèmes décoratifs
  – (années 1920) #845
    – *Canadian Artists' Series* #844
  – (années 1920-1950) #863
    – thème de la nativité #393
  – (années 1940), Avis Selina Fyshe,
    commentaire #849
  – fin XIXe s. #842 890
– scènes sportives, Bennet & Co. #2360
cartes géographiques
– Andrews, Stephen, cartographe #4528
– dans l'art
  – (années 1970) #561
  – Vazan, Bill #7471
– Nouvelle-France (1542-1550), animaux
  #831
cartes géographiques . Canada #125
– (années 1850) #1692
– *Codex Canadiensis*, dessins représentant
  Amérindiens #1372
– comté de Brant (Ont), (1793-1930) #1684
– Gravelot, Hubert François #1323
– illustrations de canots, XVIIe s. #841
– Kingston (Ont) #1680
– Louisbourg (NE) #8422 8426
– Millen, Walter H., collection #21
– Montréal (Qué), XVIIe-XVIIIe s. #1325
– Nouveau-Monde, XVIe-XVIIIe s. #276
– thème décoratif du castor #23 56
– Toronto (Ont), Royal Ontario Museum.
  Collection Sigmund Samuel #3135 3140
– XVIe-XVIIIe s. #875
– XVIIIe-XIXe s. #812
cartes géographiques . Etats-Unis
– Toronto (Ont), Royal Ontario Museum.
  Collection Sigmund Samuel #3135
cartes postales . Canada
– Image Bank (Vancouver, CB) #826
– McCall, Helen #6460
Cartier, Jean Bernard, céramiste can, 1915-
  #5051
– correspondance de Suède #5052
Cartier, Sir Georges-Etienne, homme d'Etat
  can, 1814-1873
– monument, George Hill #1623
Cartierville (Qué),
  Notre-Dame-du-Bel-Amour
– architecture, Roger D'Astous #8763
cartographie
– *voir* cartes géographiques
Cartoon, The, périodique can
– et Edward John Russell #7110

Carufel, René de
- *voir* De Carufel, René
Cas 1970) #8414
casernes
- *voir aussi* fortifications
casernes . Canada
- Fort Malden (Amherstburg, Ont) #8456
- Louisbourg (NE), bastion du Roi #8435
  8436
- Québec (Qué), Parc de l'Artillerie. Caserne
  Saint-Jean #8449
casernes de pompiers . Canada
- Toronto (Ont), (années 1930) #8970
- Vernon (CB), Vernon Civic Centre #8972
casques
- *voir aussi* costume; coiffures (costume)
casques . Tlingits
- casques en peau de requin, clan des
  Kaguantons, University of Pennsylvania.
  Musée (Philadelphia, Penn) #3833
Cassan, Vital, artiste can, né 1852 #5053
Cassidy, Eugene Haanel, photographe can,
  1903-1980
- expositions
  - (1981) #5054
Casson, Alfred Joseph, artiste can, 1898-
  #5057 5059 5061
- commentaire sur la sérigraphie #5055
- et Groupe des Sept #1732 1774
- expositions
  - (1975) #5058
  - (1978) #5060
- expositions de groupe
  - (1940) #350
- illustration de livres et mise en pages
  artistique #939
- influence sur Alan Caswell Collier #5131
Castle, William Ivor, photographe brit, né ca
  1877
- photographies de la Première Guerre
  mondiale #1113 1114
Castle and Sons, artistes (vitrail), (Montréal,
  Qué)
- vitraux #2462
Castlegar (CB), Centre national
  d'expositions
- expositions
  - *Canadians: A National Photography Show
    about People/Canadiens: exposition
    nationale de photographie ayant les gens
    comme thème* (1980) #1035
  - *Looking South* (1978) #4278
Castlegar (CB), hôpital
- architecture, Smith & McCulloch #9031
Castonguay, J.Alex, photographe can,
  1877-après 1949
- expositions de groupe
  - (1970) #1675
castor
- art canadien #23
- emblème canadien #56
- poterie canadienne #2302
Castro, Robert de, sculpteur can, 1923-
- membre du groupe Limners #2043
Caswell, Thomas Jefferson, ébéniste can,
  1806-1894 #2511
catalogues
- catalogues d'expositions
  - (années 1970) #3311
  - Ontario #3319
- vente par correspondance, catalogues, T.
  Eaton Company Limited (1886-1930)
  #2851
catalogues de mode . costume

- (années 1870) #2878
catalogues de modèles . architecture
- modèles d'écoles, Henry Bernard,
  commentaire #9384
catalogues de patrons . peinture sur verre
- Vancouver (CB), (1890-1940) #2457
catalogues de patrons . textiles
- ouvrages à l'aiguille, Nouvelle-Ecosse
  (avant 1920) #2785
Catlin, George, artiste amér, 1796-1872
- art et écrits #3384 3426
- dessins de pipes à tabac, British Museum
  (Londres, Angleterre) #3478
- et émergence d'artistes amérindiens
  reconnus #3486
- expositions de groupe
  - (1955) #1845
- Kane, Paul, comparaison #6004 6013
Caton, Peter, photographe can, actif années
  1970
- commentaire sur l'art du portrait #624
Cauchon, Alfred, carrossier can, actif 1933
  #5062
Cauchon, Henri, orfèvre can, actif 1933
  #5062
Cauchon, Joseph, orfèvre can, ca 1856- #5062
Cauchon, Robert, artiste can, 1897-1969
  #1428 1429
- expositions, critiques #964
Caughnawaga (Qué)
- *voir* Kahnawake (Qué)
Cavoukian (Cavouk), Artin, photographe
  can, 1915-
- commentaire sur l'art du portrait #624
Cayley, William, homme d'Etat can,
  1807-1890
- Toronto (Ont), The Grange #8637
ceinture fléchée
- *voir* ceintures (de tissu)
ceintures (de tissu) . Canada
- ceinture fléchée #24 2089 2095 2165 2181
  2718 2810 2813 2818 2819 2823 2824 2827
  2833 2864 2865 2873 2901
  - influence sur ceintures (de tissu)
    iroquoises #3534
ceintures (de tissu) . France
- en comparaison avec ceinture fléchée
  #2901
ceintures (de tissu) . Iroquois #3534
ceintures (de tissu) . Saulteux/Ojibwa #3557
ceintures (de tissu) . Scandinavie
- en comparaison avec ceinture fléchée
  #2865
célébrations
- *voir* festivals; rites et cérémonies
Celestino, Mary, artiste can, 1935-
- expositions
  - (1980) #5063
Celle (Allemagne de l'Ouest), Schloss Celle
- expositions
  - *Indianer Nordamerikas* (1956) #3423
Cène
- *voir* Jésus-Christ, Cène
censure de l'art
- Canada (années 1970) #625 693
- et Mark Prent #6922 6924
- Montréal (Qué), démantèlement de
  l'exposition *Corridart*, 1976 #1530
- nus dans l'art #317 6652
Centerfold, périodique can #603
Centrale d'artisanat du Québec #2213 2238
centres administratifs . Canada
- Faro (Yukon), Faro Townsite Recreation
  Centre #8182

- Leaf Rapids (Man), centre municipal #8409
  8974
- Scarborough (Ont), Scarborough Civic
  Centre #8973
- Vancouver (CB), Britannia Community
  Services Centre #9116
- Vernon (CB), Vernon Civic Centre #8972
centres commerciaux . Canada
- (années 1950) #9373
- Montréal (Qué)
  - complexe Desjardins #9327
  - Place Bonaventure #9319 9320 9321 9322
    9323 9325
  - Place Ville-Marie #9314
  - Westmount Square #9326
- Toronto (Ont)
  - Eaton Centre #9377 9378 9382
  - Yorkdale Shopping Centre #9374 9375
centres culturels . Canada
- Québec (années 1960) #3088
centres d'arts d'interprétation . Canada
- Alberta, Jubilee Auditoriums #9084
- Charlottetown (IPE), Confederation Centre
  #7683 9088 9089 9094
- Cobourg (Ont), Victoria Hall #8994 8995
- Montréal (Qué), Place des Arts #9083 9092
  9093 9096
- Ottawa (Ont), Centre national des arts
  #9104 9105 9108
- Toronto (Ont)
  - O'Keefe Centre for the Performing Arts
    #9087
  - Ontario Place #9115
  - St. Lawrence Centre for the Arts #9109
  - St. Lawrence Hall #9103
- transformation d'édifices publics en centre
  d'arts d'interprétation #9147 9148
- Vancouver (CB)
  - Orpheum Theatre #9141
  - Queen Elizabeth Theatre #9085
  - Vancouver Civic Auditorium #9080
- Winnipeg (Man), Manitoba Museum of
  Man and Nature. Concert Hall #9107
centres de loisirs
- *voir* centres récréatifs
Century, périodique amér
- illustrations, Henri Julien #5984
Century Pioneer Village (Ont) #8063
céramique
- *voir* poterie
Cercle des fermières
- encouragement des arts domestiques
  #2212
cercles
- dans art nord-américain #559
cérémonie de la Pipe-Médecine . Pieds-Noirs
  #3681
cérémonie du Milieu de l'Hiver . Iroquois
  #3606
- masques #3598
cérémonies
- *voir* rites et cérémonies
cérémonies religieuses
- *voir* rites et cérémonies
cerfs-volants
- sculpture, Royal Canadian Aerial Theatre
  (RCAT) #2058
céroplastique . Canada
- Québec #2183
Cetin, Anton, artiste can, 1936- #5065
- expositions
  - (1978) #5064
Cézanne, Paul, artiste fr, 1839-1906
- Bates, Maxwell Bennett, comparaison

#4623
- Carr, Emily, commentaire #5030
- East, Benoît, comparaison #5353
- influence sur David Brown Milne #6567
- influence sur Goodridge Roberts #7046
- influence sur Lawren Phillip Harris #5711
- influence sur Lionel LeMoine FitzGerald #5450
- influence sur Louise Landry Gadbois #5529
- influence sur Paraskeva Clark #5110
- influence sur Paul-Emile Borduas #1468 4841
- influence sur Paul Fournier #5486
- influence sur Pierre Jean Clerk #5118
Chabert, Joseph, prêtre et artiste can, 1832-1894
- directeur, Institut national des beaux-arts, sciences, arts et métiers et industrie (Montréal, Qué) #3005
- professeur de François-Xavier Aldéric Rapin #6961
Chabot, J.E., photographe can, 1897-1976 #1283
Chaboulié (Chaboillez), Charles, sculpteur can, ca 1638-1708 #234 235 1572
Chadwick & Beckett, agence can d'architecture
- Toronto (Ont)
  - architecture domestique #8493
  - Chapman & Walker Building #9332
  - Government House, concours #8748
  - habitations #8639
Chagall, Marc, artiste russe, 1887-
- influence sur Walter Joseph Gerard Bachinski #4578
Chagnon, Alain, photographe can, 1948-
- catalogue de photographies #997 999
chaires . Canada
- Québec (1650-1925) #1592
chaise (mobilier) . Canada
- Ontario
  - fauteuil "arrow-back", thème pictural #1770
Chalitmiut (Alaska)
- objet en os, Okvik #4340
Chalke, John, sculpteur et céramiste can, 1940- #2395
Challener, Frederick Sproston, artiste can, 1869-1959 #4638 5067
- commentaire sur la peinture murale #5066
- expositions de groupe
  - (1935) #17
- peintures murales #5068
Chalmers, John, ingénieur can, actif 1909
- Edmonton (Alta), édifices du Parlement #8962
chamanisme
- et Jack Butler #4982
- et Jack Leonard Shadbolt #7190 7191
- et Karoo Ashevak #4562
- et Norval Morrisseau #6647
- sculpture, Colombie-Britannique (années 1970) #2066
chamanisme . Algonquiens
- arbre de vie #3365
chamanisme . Amérindiens #3361 3383
chamanisme . autochtones #3360
chamanisme . Dorsétiens #4361
chamanisme . Esquimaux du cuivre #4330
chamanisme . Haidas #3904
- et médecine #3904
- sculpture d'argilite #3901
chamanisme . Hurons

- pipes #3632
chamanisme . Indiens de la côte nord-ouest #4065
- et pétroglyphes #3971
chamanisme . Inuit #4243 4283 4488
- arbre de vie #3365
- masques #4349
chamanisme . Iroquois
- pipes #3642
chamanisme . Micmacs #3556
chamanisme . Montagnais
- natutshikan #4103
chamanisme . Naskapis
- natutshikan #4103
chamanisme . Netsilik #4328
chamanisme . Saulteux/Ojibwa #3492 3517 3602
chamanisme . Tlingits
- et pêche au flétan #4061
chamanisme . Tsimshians
- masques #4056
chamanisme . Tsonnontouans
- pipes #3642
Chamard, Emélie, tisserande can, née 1887 #2194 2209 5069
Chambellan, François, orfèvre can, ca 1688-1747 #2667
Chambers, John Richard (Jack), artiste can, 1931-1978 #5073 5078
- autobiographie #5079
- commentaire sur la perception visuelle #525
- commentaire sur le Front des artistes canadiens (FAC) #563
- commentaire sur le réalisme perceptuel #5071
- dessins #532 5077
- écrits #92
- entretien #5070 5075
- et critique d'art #3315
- et réalisme #110 533
- expositions
  - (1970) #5074
  - (1980) #700 5080 5081
- expositions, critiques #5082
- expositions de groupe
  - (1965) #473
  - (1971) #98
  - (1979) #674
- influence sur art, London (Ont), (années 1960) #1791
- influence sur Brian Rendel Jones #5974
- oeuvres cinématographiques #626
  - *Hart of London* #5076
- régionalisme, en comparaison avec Greg Curnoe #5225
- thème de la mort #1759
- utilisation de la lumière #516
- utilisation de la photographie #5072
chambre claire
- dans peinture et photographie canadiennes, XIXe s. #268
- dans portraits, provinces maritimes, XIXe s. #1171
- utilisation, James Pattison Cockburn #5125
Chambre de commerce de Toronto (Toronto, Ont)
- collection, art canadien #3291
- commentaire sur conservation d'édifices historiques (1979) #8027
chambre noire
- dans peinture et photographie canadiennes, XIXe s. #268
Champagne, Jean-Serge, sculpteur can, 1947-

#5083
- expositions de groupe
  - (1977) #637 782
Champagne, Louis
- *voir* Foureur (dit Champagne), Louis
Champagne, Michel, artiste can, 1940- #5084 5085
Champagne, Pierre
- *voir* Foureur (dit Champagne), Pierre
Champaign (Ill), University of Illinois
- architecture #9464
Champeau, André, artiste can, 1934-
- à Paris (France) #426
champignons dans l'art
- Fournier, Paul #5487
- Jackson, Henry Alexander Carmichael #5926 5927 5928
Champlain, Samuel de, explorateur fr au Canada, 1567-1635
- Habitation Port-Royal (Granville Ferry, NE) #7655 7813
- illustrations, *Les voyages du sieur de Champlain* (1613) #933
- portraits #191
- vues de la Nouvelle-Ecosse (ca 1605) #1202
Champlain (Qué), église
- sculptures sur bois, Gilles Bolvin #4781
chance
- dans l'art
  - Hudson, Andrew #5857
  - Rockman, Arnold #7061
chandeliers . Canada
- Ontario, XVIIIe-XIXe s. #2918
- Ontario et provinces de l'Atlantique, XVIIIe-XIXe s. #2475
Chandler Kennedy Architectural Group, agence can d'architecture
- Calgary (Alta), immeubles à bureaux #9362
chansons folkloriques canadiennes #2096
- île d'Orléans (Qué) #1238
- illustrations, Joseph-Charles Franchère #5497
- Québec #1234 1258 1259
  - illustrations #938
  - références au costume #2898
- tradition norvégienne #2273
chants iroquois
- Six Nations Reserve (Ont) #3598
chants ojibwa #3610
chapeaux
- *voir aussi* costume; coiffures (costume)
chapeaux . Canada
- (avant 1736) #2831
- chapeaux de paille, XVIIIe s. #2200
- Huppé (dit Lagroix), Joseph #269 270
- Montréal (Qué), XIXe s. #2837
- Nouvelle-Ecosse, fin XVIIIe-XIXe s. #2907
- Québec, XVIIe-XIXe s. #2815
chapeaux . Nootkas
- Cambridge (Mass), Harvard University. Peabody Museum #3779
- portés par chefs de tribus #3829
chapeaux . Tlingits #3865
Chaplin, Carl, artiste can, 1946- #5086
Chaplin, Millicent Mary, artiste can, active 1838-1844 #1219
Chapman, Alfred Hirschfelder, architecte can, 1879-1949 #8344
Chapman, Evadna, artiste can, 1933-
- entretien #5087
Chapman, Isaac, sculpteur can, ca 1880-ca 1908
- sculpture d'argilite #5088

Chapman, Oxley & Bishop, agence can
d'architecture
- Toronto (Ont), Sunnyside #8054
Chapman, Oxley & Facey, agence can
d'architecture
- Toronto (Ont), Banque de Montréal #9190
Chapman & McGiffin, agence can
d'architecture
- architecture domestique #8494
- Toronto (Ont)
  - Bourse de Toronto, concours #9161
  - University of Toronto. Knox College
    #9435 9449
    - concours #9432
Chapman & Oxley, agence can
d'architecture
- Toronto (Ont), Toronto Star Building
  #9334
Chapnick, Karen, artiste can, 1950-
- expositions, critiques #2081
- expositions de groupe
  - (1978) #663
Chaput, Yves, photographe can, actif 1973
- catalogue de photographies #997 999
Charbonneau, Jean-Guy, poète, actif 1978
- poèmes, dessins de Louis-Pierre Bougie
  #4861
Charbonneau, Monique, artiste can, 1928-
  #5089
- expositions
  - (1978) #5090
Charbonneau, Roger, photographe can,
1947- #1556
- catalogue de photographies #997 999
- entretien sur le Groupe d'action
  photographique #1494
- vues photographiques, Disraëli (Qué),
  (1972) #1513
Chardin, Jean Baptiste Siméon, artiste fr,
1699-1779
- Leduc, Ozias, comparaison #6200
Charette, colonel Athanase-Charles-Marie
de, officier de l'armée fr, 1832-1911
- buste en porcelaine, St. Johns Stone
  Chinaware Company (Saint-Jean, Qué)
  #2314
Charlebois, Alyne Gauthier
- voir Gauthier-Charlebois, Alyne
Charlebois, Joseph Charles Théophile, artiste
can, 1872-1935 #1382
Charles Pachter Graphics, éditeur (Toronto,
Ont)
- et Charles Pachter #834
Charlesbourg (Qué)
- églises #8851
Charlevoix (Qué)
- architecture domestique #8629
- art et architecture #1233
- art traditionnel #1243
- costume
  - fin XIXe-début XXe s. #2890
  - XIXe s. #2829
- couvertures #2738
- teinture, XVIIe-XIXe s. #2733
- tissage #1327
- vues
  - (années 1750-1970) #1280
  - Jackson, A.Y. #5910
- vues photographiques
  - Szilasi, Gabor #7308
Charlottetown (IPE)
- architecture #7797 7802
- marchés (1813-1958) #7800
Charlottetown (IPE), Banque de

Nouvelle-Ecosse
- architecture, Sharp & Horner #9174
Charlottetown (IPE), Confederation Centre
- architecture
  - Affleck, Desbarats, Dimakopoulos,
    Lebensold, Sise #9094
  - Affleck, Desbarats, Dimakopoulos,
    Lebensold, Sise & Schoenauer #7683
  - concours #9088 9089
Charlottetown (IPE), Confederation Centre
Art Gallery and Museum
- (années 1960) #1122
- collection #3070
- expositions
  - A Century of Colonial Painting: The Seven
    Years War to Confederation: An Exhibition
    Organized for the Inauguration of the
    Fathers of Confederation Building,
    Charlottetown, P.E.I./Un siècle de peinture,
    l'époque coloniale: de la guerre de Sept Ans
    à la Confédération: exposition organisée
    pour l'inauguration de l'édifice des Pères de
    la Confédération, I.P.E. (1964) #226
  - A Country Painter's Harvest: Lindee Climo:
    Paintings and Drawings (1978) #5120
  - A Nineteenth Century Look: The Victorian
    Parlour (1976) #2129
  - A Terrible Beauty: The Art of Canada at
    War (1978) #1111
  - André Biéler 50 Years: A Retrospective
    Exhibition 1920-1970 (1970) #4725
  - Annie D. Savage: Drawings and
    Watercolours (1975) #7129
  - Beauté tragique: les deux conflits mondiaux
    vus par des artistes canadiens (1978) #1112
  - Canadian Political Cartoons (1977) #956
  - Canadian Tapestries, 1977 (1977) #2770
  - Carl Schaefer in Hanover (1980) #7157
  - Carol Fraser Paintings and Drawings:
    1967-1977 (1977) #5507
  - Charles Fraser Comfort: Fifty Years (1973)
    #5159
  - Christopher Pratt (1971) #6910
  - Claude Tousignant (1974) #7401
  - David Bolduc: Recent Work (1980) #4775
  - Directors' Choice (1967) #481
  - Douglas Bentham "Enclosures and Opens"
    1975/76 (1977) #4683
  - Drawings and Pastels c. 1930-1967 by
    Miller Gore Brittain (1969) #4917
  - Drawings by Jack Weldon Humphrey: A
    Travelling Exhibition Organized by the
    Beaverbrook Art Gallery, Fredericton, New
    Brunswick, Canada, 1977-1979 (1979)
    #5871
  - Esther Warkov (1971) #7517
  - Felicity Redgrave (1979) #6967
  - Fritz Brandtner 1896-1969: A Retrospective
    Exhibition (1971) #4903
  - Goodridge Roberts: A Retrospective
    Exhibition/Goodridge Roberts: une
    exposition rétrospective (1969) #7045
  - Goodridge Roberts: Selected
    Works/Goodridge Roberts: oeuvres choisies
    (1982) #7050
  - Henry Purdy: A Personal Decade
    1968-1978 (1978) #6946
  - Impressionism in Canada, 1895-1935 (1974)
    #115
  - J.M. Barnsley (1861-1929), Retrospective
    Exhibition (1964) #4611
  - Jack Shadbolt (1970) #7182
  - Jack Wise: A Decade of Work (1978) #7601
  - Joe Fafard: Recent Sculpture (1980) #5401

  - John Fox: 10 New Paintings (1980) #5495
  - L'art de Tom Thomson (1972) #7367
  - Lithographs/Lithographies (1972) #825
  - Louis de Niverville (1979) #6709
  - Manitoba Mainstream: People's Art/Fine
    Art/Le Grand Courant du Manitoba: arts
    populaires, beaux-arts (1973) #1897
  - Metamorphosis, Memories, Dreams and
    Reflections: The Work of Florence Vale
    (1981) #7453
  - Miller Brittain - Painter (1982) #4922
  - Plains and Northwest Coast Indians: Indian
    Art and Crafts from Glenbow-Alberta
    Institute, Calgary (1970) #3438
  - Robert Harris, 1849-1919 (1967) #5739
  - Robert Harris (1849-1919) (1973) #5743
  - Robert Young: Prints/Robert Young:
    gravures (1981) #7631
  - Roger Savage (1980) #7135
  - Ronald: 25 Years (1975) #7073
  - Sunshine and Shadows: A Look at Island
    Quilts and Quilting (1978) #2802
  - Terence Johnson: Forts (1981) #5969
  - The Academy in Retrospect (1966) #474
  - The Art of Tom Thomson (1972) #7368
  - The J.S. McLean Collection of Canadian
    Painting (1968) #3228
  - The Murray and Marguerite Vaughan Inuit
    Print Collection/Collection d'estampes inuit
    (1982) #4498
  - The Poole Collection: An Exhibition of
    Canadian Paintings from Krieghoff to
    Riopelle (1965) #3222
  - The Queen Comes to New Brunswick:
    Paintings and Drawings by Molly Lamb
    Bobak (1978) #4765
  - The Railway: Patron of the Arts in Canada
    (1976) #3281
  - The Saidye and Samuel Bronfman
    Collection of Canadian Art/La collection
    Saidye et Samuel Bronfman (1967) #3087
  - The Society of Canadian Painter-Etchers
    and Engravers in Retrospect/La Société des
    peintres-graveurs canadiens: vue
    rétrospective (1981) #836
  - The Trowell Touch, 1965-1980 (1980)
    #7430
  - The Work of Art: Six Artists (1979) #665
  - William Perehudoff: Recent Paintings
    (1979) #6837
  - Women Artists of P.E.I.: A Survey of
    Female Artistic Activity on the Island
    (1977) #1168
- expositions, critiques
  - Three Painters of Prince Edward Island
    (1976) #1167
- influence sur art, Ile-du-Prince-Edouard
  (1964-1974) #1165
Charlottetown (IPE), EPTEK. Centre national
d'expositions
- expositions
  - Looking South (1978) #4278
Charlottetown (IPE), Government House
- architecture #8754
Charlottetown (IPE), Holland College School
of Visual Arts
- Purdy, Henry Carl, directeur #6946
Charlottetown (IPE), Islander Motor Inn
- murale, Gwen Johnston Fichaud #5428
Charlottetown (IPE), Prince Edward Island
Heritage Foundation
- mobilier #2484
Charlottetown (IPE), Province House
- architecture #8937

– mobilier (1864) #8938
– plans architecturaux #8939
Charlottetown (IPE), Saint Dunstan's
  University
– expositions
    – *Contemporary Sacred Art in Canada/L'art
      sacré contemporain au Canada* (1964) #459
Charney, Melvin, architecte et artiste can,
  1935- #5094 5095
– commentaire sur l'architecture canadienne
  (années 1960) #9400
– commentaire sur les "monuments" dans
  ses réalisations architecturales #5091
– entretien #5092
– expositions
    – (1972) #7906
    – (1979) #5093
– expositions de groupe
    – (1980) #8237
– organisateur, exposition *Corridart*,
  Montréal (Qué), (1976) #1522 1530
– théories sur l'architecture #7746
Charpentier, Louis, artiste can, 1947- #1511
Charron, Amable, sculpteur can, 1785-1844
– intérieur, église Saint-Jean-Baptiste
  (Saint-Jean-Port-Joli, Qué) #8812
Charron, François, artiste can, 1952-
– réflexion sur son oeuvre #1552
Chartier, Gilles, artiste can, 1940- #1504 5096
Chartrand (dit Vincennes), Vincent, artiste
  can, actif 1822-1863 #6947
chartreuses
– *voir* monastères
Chase, Wellington, photographe can, actif
  1860-1870 #1211
chasse dans l'art
– *voir aussi* scènes sportives
– Etook, Tivi #5375
– Parr, Nuna #6768
Châteauguay (Qué), église Saint-Joachim
– architecture et intérieur #8861
Châteauguay (Qué), maison Lepailleur
  McFarlane
– et Héritage canadien du Québec #7871
châteaux
– *voir* châteaux et maisons de campagne
châteaux et maisons de campagne
– *voir aussi* palais; villas
– France, influence sur hôtels canadiens de
  style château #9291
Chater, Leslie, artiste can, XXe s. .
– et Albert Angus Macdonald #6354
Chatham (NB), James M. Hill Memorial
  High School
– expositions
    – *Colville, Pratt, Forrestall* (1974) #1129
    – *The Beaverbrook Art Gallery Presents Nine
      New Brunswick Artists/La Galerie d'art
      Beaverbrook présente neuf artistes du
      Nouveau-Brunswick* (1973) #1182
Châtigny, Edmond, sculpteur can, 1895-
  #5097
Chauchetière, Claude, prêtre et artiste can,
  1645-1709 #234 235 1363
– et nationalisme dans l'art #1373
– images pieuses #1354 1358
Chaudron, Bernard, orfèvre et joaillier can,
  1931- #5098 5099
Chaudron, Louise, orfèvre can, active
  années 1960-1970 #5098
Chaulette, frères, sculpteurs can, XVIIIe s.
– statue du général James Wolfe, Québec
  (Qué) #1568 1600
chaussures . Amérindiens #2814 3424

chaussures . Canada
– (années 1850) #2811
– artisans (1608-1950) #2946
– bottes en peau, Terre-Neuve et Labrador,
  XXe s. #2155
– chaussures de femme, Louisbourg (NE),
  (1713-1758) #2855
– et bottes, Fort Beauséjour (NB), (années
  1750-1830) #2858
– Québec #2816
    – artisans, XVIIe-XVIIIe s. #2214
    – début XXe s. #1313
    – XIXe-XXe s. #2880
    – XVIIe-XIXe s. #2814
    – XVIIe-XXe s. #2953
Chauvin, Jean, auteur can, 1895-1958
– et Ozias Leduc #6211
Chavignaud, George, artiste can, 1865-1944
– directeur, Nova Scotia College of Art
  (Halifax, NE) #2993
Chechik, Jeremiah, artiste can, 1951- #992
Chee Chee, Benjamin, artiste can, 1944-1977
  #5100 5101 6648
chemins de croix
– *voir aussi* calvaires
– Montréal (Qué), oratoire Saint-Joseph
  #6764
– Plamondon, Antoine-Sébastien #6886
– Plamondon, Marius Gérald #6888
chemins de fer
– *voir aussi* locomotives; métros,
  constructions
chemins de fer . Canada
– bâtiments et structures, XIXe s. #9512
– photographies, Boorne & May #4797
Cheney, Gordon Lewis, architecte can, 1934-
– Charlottetown (IPE), Confederation
  Centre, concours #9088 9089
Cheney, Nan Lawson, artiste can, 1897-
– commentaire sur Emily Carr #5043
Cheng, James K.M., architecte can, 1947-
– Vancouver (CB), Chinese Cultural Centre,
  concours #9144
Chequamegon Bay (Ont)
– vues
    – Fraser, John Arthur #5509
Chernavitch, Ken, sculpteur can, 1945-
– sculpture en céramique #795
Cherria, François, prêtre, actif 1792
– et église, Saint-Denis-sur-Richelieu (Qué)
  #8811
Cherry, Sheldon, Can, XXe s.
– entretien sur le déménagement projeté,
  Vancouver Art Gallery (Vancouver, CB)
  #3198
Chester, Donovan T. (Don), artiste can,
  1940-
– expositions
    – (1973) #1858
– expositions de groupe
    – (1974) #565 1925
    – (1975) #1926
Chesterfield, Albert A., photographe can,
  1877-1959 #5102
chevaux dans l'art
– Cameron, Walter Graham #4992
– Hill, George William #5799
– Kenyon, J.J. #1681
– Richard, Wilfrid #7000
– Todd, Robert Clow #258 259
– Wickson, Paul Giovanni #7573
cheveux
– cheveux humains, dans le chamanisme et
  l'art tlingit #3917

Chewett, James Grant, architecte can,
  1793-1862 #258 259
– Toronto (Ont), hôtel de ville #8993
Chicago (Ill), Art Institute of Chicago
– expositions
    – *The Native American Heritage: A Survey of
      North American Indian Art* (1977) #3468
    – *Yakutat South Indian Art of the Northwest
      Coast* (1964) #3923
– Loring, Frances Norma, élève #758
– Wyle, Florence, élève #758
Chicago (Ill), Chicago Tribune Building
– Toronto Star Building (Toronto, Ont),
  comparaison #9334
Chicago (Ill), Field Museum of Natural
  History
– costume athapascan #4111
– masques haidas #3961
Chicago (Ill), Museum of Contemporary Art
– expositions
    – *49th Parallels: New Canadian Art* (1971)
      #98
Chicoutimi (Qué), Ecole d'arts et métiers
– (années 1930) #2175
Chicoutimi (Qué), Hôtel-Dieu Saint-Vallier
– peintures, Charles Edouard Huot #5878
  5884
Chicoutimi (Qué), Musée du
  Saguenay-Lac-Saint-Jean
– expositions
    – *James Bay Project - A River Drowned by
      Water/Projet de la baie James - une rivière
      qui se noie* (1982) #1566
Chicoutimi (Qué), Societé des arts de
  Chicoutimi
– expositions
    – *De la figuration à la non-figuration dans
      l'art québécois* (1978) #1461
Chicoutimi (Qué), Université du Québec
– enseignement de l'art (années 1960) #3016
Chiendent, illustrateurs de bandes dessinées
  can #948 952 1502
chiens dans l'art
– Haeseker, Sandy #5675
– Krieghoff, Cornelius, *The Pets and the
  Materials* #6102
Chignecto (NB)
– architecture et arts décoratifs #2150
Chigot, Francis, artiste fr (vitrail), actif 1932
– vitraux, église Notre-Dame (Montréal,
  Qué) #2444
Chigot de Limoges, atelier fr (vitrail),
  (Limoges, France)
– vitraux, église Notre-Dame (Montréal,
  Qué) #8839
Chilcotins
– culture #3789
Chilkats
– architecture #3793
– architecture et totems #3798
– couvertures #3784 3821 3826 3898 3973
– couvertures et vannerie #3333
– ouvrages en piquants de porc-épic #3811
Chillas, Robert, ébéniste can, actif années
  1780-1820 #2511
Chilliwack (CB)
– architecture #8147
Chine
– vues photographiques
    – Hinton, John Henry #5812
Chinois au Canada
– Alberta, architecture #8137
– Colombie-Britannique, architecture #8154
– Victoria (CB), architecture #8179 8181

Chirico, Giorgio de, artiste it, 1888-1978
- Colville, Alex, comparaison #1115
- influence sur Alfred Pellan #6820 6822
- influence sur Kenneth Campbell Lochhead #6319
Chisasibi (Qué), école de Chisasibi
- expositions
  - *James Bay Project - A River Drowned by Water/Projet de la baie James - une rivière qui se noie* (1981) #1566
Chitty, Elizabeth, artiste can, 1953-
- art vidéo #655
- expositions de groupe
  - (1980) #687
Chodorow, Neil, artiste can, 1946-
- entretien #5103
choléra
- Légaré, Joseph, *Le choléra à Québec* #6214
Chomedey (Qué), église Saint-Pie X
- architecture, Des Rochers & Dumont #8840
Chomedey (Qué), hôtel de ville
- architecture, Affleck, Desbarats, Dimakopoulos, Lebensold, Sise #8990
Chrismas, Lawrence, photographe can, 1941-
- catalogue de photographies #991
Christensen, Dan, artiste can, 1942-
- expositions
  - (1973) #5104
- expositions de groupe
  - (1981) #722
Christie, Robert E., artiste can, 1946-
- expositions de groupe
  - (1974) #565
  - (1975) #1926
  - (1981) #722
Christin, Léopold, artiste et musicien can, né 1877 #5105
Christl, Rudi, photographe can, ca 1946-
- catalogue de photographies #1023
Christopher, Ken, artiste can, 1942-
- expositions de groupe
  - (1981) #1885
chronique en images . Dakotas
- Londres (Angleterre), British Museum #3747
chronique en images . Indiens des plaines
- dans l'art #3728
chronique en images . Pieds-Noirs #3707
chronique en images . Siouens
- dans l'art #3728
Chu, T.K., photographe can, actif 1977
- catalogue de photographies #1023
Chukchis
- art #4302 4303
Church Point (NE), église Sainte-Marie
- architecture, Léo Melanson #8779
Churchill (Man), Eskimo Museum #4290 4313
- art inuit et artefacts #4227
- sculptures inuit, défenses de morse #4446
chutes du Niagara (NY et Ont)
- vues
  - fin XIXe s. #1839
  - XVIIIe s.-années 1960 #1673
  - XVIIIe-XIXe s. #812
ciboires . Canada
- XVIIe-XIXe s.
  - Québec #2681
  - Québec et Ontario #2627
Cicansky, Victor (Vic), sculpteur et céramiste can, 1935- #1937
- expositions, critiques #2383
- expositions de groupe
  - (1976) #1930

- (1977) #781
- sculpture en céramique #795
Ciccimarra, Richard Matthew, artiste can, 1924-1973 #5106
- expositions
  - (1974) #5107
- membre du groupe Limners #2043
Cigoli (Ludovico Cardi), artiste it, 1559-1613
- influence sur Antoine-Sébastien Plamondon #6886
CIL Inc., fabricants et distributeurs de produits chimiques
- collection, peinture canadienne #124
ciment, mortier et plâtre
- *voir aussi* maçonnerie
- plâtre dans sculpture québécoise #1618
cimetières
- *voir aussi* monuments funéraires
cimetières canadiens
- Montréal (Qué), cimetière du Mont-Royal #7933
- Première et Seconde Guerres mondiales #1108 1109
- Québec (Qué), XVIIe-XVIIIe s. #1306
Cinader, Bernard, collectionneur can, 1919-
- collection, art amérindien des forêts du Nord-Est #4150
Cincinnati (Ohio), Cincinnati Art Museum
- expositions
  - *Art of the First Americans* (1976) #3459
  - *Robert S. Duncanson: A Centennial Exhibition* (1972) #5338
cinéma
- *voir aussi* animation (cinématographie)
- (années 1970) #634
- autobiographie, Canada et Etats-Unis (années 1970) #664
cinéma canadien #2 129 626
- (années 1940) #374
- (années 1960) #521
- (années 1970) #555 598 610 3279
- (années 1980) #690 912
- Berman, Michaele #4710
- Chambers, Jack #5072 5074 5076 5081
- Cournoyer, Michèle #5193
- Dallaire, Jean-Philippe #5238 5239
- Doray, Audrey Capel #5301
- Fiorucci, Vittorio #5442
- Gagnon, Charles #5533 5534 5535 5537
- Gordon, Lee #993
- Gould, John Howard #5636
- graphisme
  - (années 1950) #866
  - (années 1970) #899
- Harmon, Byron #5707
- Lee-Nova, Gary #6213
- McLaren, Norman #6491 6492 6493 6494 6495 6496 6497 6498 6499
- Niverville, Louis de #6704 6706
- Price, Art #6928
- Québec
  - (1970-1975) #1515
  - réalisatrices #1064
- Snow, Michael #568 7241 7243 7245 7246 7247 7249 7250 7252 7253 7255 7256 7257 7260 7261 7263
- Wieland, Joyce #568 7574 7575 7576 7577 7578 7579 7580 7581 7582 7583
cinétique
- *voir* mouvement dans l'art
Cinq-Mars, Alonzo, artiste can, 1881-1969 #1391
Cirier, Antoine, sculpteur can, 1718-1798 #269 270 5108

- influence sur Philippe Liébert #6281
Cirier, Martin, constructeur et sculpteur can, 1678-1751 #5108
Cizek, Albert Franz, sculpteur et orfèvre autr, 1866-1943
- oeuvres, édifices du Parlement (Victoria, CB) #8967
Cizek, Franz, artiste tchèque, 1865-1946
- influence sur Fritz Brandtner #4904
Claire, Lorna, artiste can, active années 1920-
- murales, Jarvis Collegiate Institute Auditorium (Toronto, Ont) #6978
Clairrou, Jacques, photographe can, actif 1972
- catalogue de photographies #997 999
Clallams
- culture
  - (années 1870) #4031
  - (années 1920) #3819
Clam Harbour (NE)
- vues, Charlotte Wilson Hammond #5697
Clapp, William Henry, artiste can, 1879-1954
- membre du Canadian Art Club #193
Claremont (Calif), Claremont College
- expositions
  - *Native American Art from the Permanent Collection* (1979) #3378
Clark, John Arthur, artiste can, 1943- #1227
Clark, Kelvin William David (Kelly), artiste can, 1935- #5109
Clark, Paraskeva, artiste can, 1898- #5110 5112
- entretien #5111
Clark, Tim, artiste can, 1945-
- expositions de groupe
  - (1980) #687
- photographies, comme mode d'expression personnelle #1556
- réflexion sur son oeuvre photographique #5113
Clarke, Ann, artiste can, 1944- #5114
- expositions de groupe
  - (1974) #565
  - (1975) #1867
  - (1980) #698
  - (1981) #722
- situation de l'art à Edmonton (Alta), (1981) #1975
Clarke, Fred, sculpteur can, ca 1902- #5115
Clarke, James, artiste amér, 1885-1969
- correspondance, David Brown Milne #6560
Clarke, Stanley, H. (Stan), artiste can, 1914-
- bijoux #2695
Clarke, W.J., & Co., éditeur (Montréal, Qué)
- cartes de Noël #890
Class, Gerhard Hans, sculpteur can, 1924-
- fontaine, Vancouver (CB) #2077
- sculpture, Vancouver (CB) #2080
- sculpture de jardin #1849
classe ouvrière dans l'art
- chômage, thème pictural, provinces de l'Atlantique (années 1970) #1133 1135 8414
- Featherston, Bill #5418
- Gaudard, Pierre #990
- images pieuses #1662
- Labor Arts Guild #1985
- Magor, Liz, occupations inexistantes #6402
- Rand, Paul #6957
Claude Neon Ltée., entreprise d'enseignes lumineuses (Montréal, Qué)
- entreprises, image de marque, Gottschalk & Ash #887

Clayton, Edith, artisane (vannerie) can, 1920-
#2935
Clayton & Bond, agence can d'architecture
– Vancouver (CB), Vancouver Civic
Auditorium, concours #9080
Clazie, John, artiste can, actif 1956
– bijoux #2695
Clemens, Isaac, artiste can, actif années
1770-1790
– gravures #1198
Clément, Serge, photographe can, 1950-
– catalogue de photographies #991
Clemesha & Portnall, agence can
d'architecture
– Winnipeg (Man)
– hôtel de ville, concours #8979
– Legislative and Executive Building,
concours #8946
Clerk, Pierre Jean, artiste can, 1928- #5117
– entretien #5116
– expositions
– (1981) #5118
Cleveland, Xenophon, artiste can, 1839-1899
#5119
Cleveland (Ohio), Cleveland Museum of Art
– expositions
– L'Amérique vue par l'Europe (1976) #255
– Les arts du Canada français, 1613-1870
(1946) #1331
– Objects of Bright Pride: Northwest Coast
Indian Art from the American Museum of
Natural History (1978) #4024
– The Arts of French Canada, 1613-1870
(1946) #1330
– The European Vision of America (1976)
#256
Cleverdon, Thomas A., photographe can,
actif années 1840-1850 #1211
climat
– influence sur architecture canadienne
#7648 7652 7658 7701
– influence sur architecture domestique des
Prairies #8717
– influence sur architecture domestique
québécoise #8592
Climo, Lindee, artiste can, 1948- #5121
– expositions
– (1978) #5120
clochers . Canada
– Québec, ouvrage de ferronerie #2702 2705
cloches . Canada
– Terre-Neuve #2717
Clodion (Claude Michel), sculpteur fr,
1738-1814
– influence sur François Baillairgé #4589
Closse, Lambert, officier de l'armée can, m.
1662
– articles de maison #2522
clôtures . Canada #9226 9233
– clôtures en bois, XVIIIe-XIXe s. #2594
– Colombie-Britannique, clôtures en bois,
XIXe-XXe s. #8148
– Québec, ouvrage de ferronerie #2702
Cloutier, Albert-Edouard, artiste can,
1900-1965
– expositions de groupe
– (1981) #1117
– murale, hôtel Reine-Elizabeth. Salle
Bonaventure #9286
– murale, hôtel Reine-Elizabeth (Montréal,
Qué) #8228
Cloutier, Eugène, auteur can, 1921-
– Blanc-seing, estampes de Claude Vermette
#7482

Cloutier, Marcel, photographe can, 1949-
#1283
Cloutier, Pierre, sculpteur can, 1945-
– et école de sculpture sur bois,
Saint-Jean-Port-Joli (Qué) #1597
Cloverdale (CB), Dogwood Gardens
– architecture, Thompson, Berwick, Pratt &
Partners #8744
Clow, Clephen John, artiste can, actif
1831-ca 1850
– portraits #1171 1211
clowns
– imagerie, Brian Porter #6907
Club Graphica de Montréal (Montréal, Qué)
– expositions
– (1967) #874
clubs . Canada
– Montréal (Qué), Montreal Club #9306
– Vancouver (CB), Terminal City Club #9061
Clutesi, George C., artiste can, 1905- #5122
– potlatch #3956
Clyde, John Edward, constructeur can, actif
1831
– Niagara-on-the-Lake (Ont), Saint
Andrew's Church #8901
Clyde River (NE)
– travail de la pierre, Micmacs #3531
Clymer, John Ford, artiste can, 1907-
– expositions de groupe
– (1961) #62
Coach House Press, éditeur (Toronto, Ont)
– (années 1960) #488
– (années 1970) #1804
Coade, entreprise (Londres, Angleterre)
– et Coade (pierre), Banque de Montréal
(Montréal, Qué) #7908
Coade, pierre
– plaques et monuments, Montréal (Qué)
#7908
Coaticook (Qué), église Saint-Edmond
– peintures, Ozias Leduc #6204
Cobb, Andrew Randall, architecte can,
1876-1943
– Halifax (NE)
– Banque de Nouvelle-Ecosse #9182
– Dalhousie University #9408
Cobb, Charles Sherman, architecte can,
1882-1964
– Moose Jaw (Sask), hôtel de ville, concours
#8978
– Toronto (Ont)
– habitations #8496
– magasin Fairweather #9363
– Registry Office #8969
– Windsor (Ont), Imperial Bank of Canada
#9175
Cobb, Henry N., architecte amér, 1926-
– Montréal (Qué) #7901
Cobourg (Ont), Art Gallery of Cobourg
– collection #3162
– expositions
– Alan C. Collier Retrospective (1971) #5131
– Arthur N. Martin, 1889-1961 (1977) #6423
– C.M. Manly A.R.C.A., 1855-1924 (1973)
#6414
– Goodridge Roberts: Paintings from the
1950s and 60s (1980) #7048
– Neil Newton Retrospective (1978) #6694
Cobourg (Ont), Ontario Military
Convalescent Hospital (autrefois Old
Victoria College)
– architecture #9016
Cobourg (Ont), Victoria Hall
– architecture, Kivas Tully #8994 8995

– Thomas, William, contracteurs pour les
sculptures décoratives #8413
Cobra
– et Albert Dumouchel #5325
Coburn, Frederick Simpson, artiste can,
1871-1960 #302 5124
– dessins, Art Gallery of Cobourg (Cobourg,
Ont) #3162
– illustrations #916 5123
– Farmer's Magazine #1765
Cockburn, James Patterson
– voir Cockburn, James Pattison
Cockburn, James Pattison, officier de
l'armée brit, artiste au Canada, 1779-1847
#812 5125 5126
– expositions
– (1978) #5129
– paysages #26
– paysages d'hiver #1298
– vues, Québec (Qué) #5127 5128
coffres . Canada
– coffre à lingerie
– Ile-du-Prince-Edouard #2507 2508
– Ontario #2554
– Ontario #2557
– (1780-1900) #2577
– (années 1790-1857) #2558
– Québec
– bahuts #2528
– XVIIe-XVIIIe s. #2529 2530 2531
coffres . Haidas
– Londres (Angleterre), British Museum
#3805
coffres . Tsimshians
– Londres (Angleterre), British Museum
#3805
Cohen, Lynne, photographe can, 1944-
– catalogue de photographies #1053
– expositions, critiques #1018 1046 1060 1067
– expositions de groupe
– (1979) #1037
Cohen, Sorel, artiste can, 1936-
– commentaire sur l'art féministe #673
– entretien #5130
Cohn, Norman, artiste can, 1946-
– expositions de groupe
– (1979) #1157
Cohos Evamy & Partners, agence can
d'architecture
– Calgary (Alta), immeubles à bureaux
#9362
coiffures (costume)
– ouvrages en ramure, Asie et Amérique du
Nord #3460
coiffures (costume) . Algonquiens
– coiffure en forme d'éventail #3417
coiffures (costume) . Amérindiens #3453
coiffures (costume) . Assiniboines #3739
coiffures (costume) . Cris #3739
coiffures (costume) . Gens-du-Sang #3739
coiffures (costume) . Haidas #4019
coiffures (costume) . Indiens de la côte
nord-ouest #3977
– préhistoire #4017
coiffures (costume) . Indiens des plaines
– coiffure à plumes #3683
– sociétés secrètes #3727
coiffures (costume) . Pieds-Noirs #3739
coiffures (costume) . Sarcis #3739
coiffures (costume) . Saulteux/Ojibwa #3539
coiffures (costume) . Tlingits #4019
– Philadelphie (Penn), University of
Pennsylvania. Museum #3803
coiffures (costume) . Tsimshians #4019

Colborne, Lew, artiste can, 1952-
– expositions de groupe
– (1981) #1908
Cole, James, ébéniste can, actif 1816-1827
#2493
Coleman, M.E., évêque can, 1902-
– croix pectorale et anneau épiscopal,
William Maurice Carmichael #5003
Colgate, William George, auteur et historien
d'art can, né 1882
– réflexion sur architecture canadienne
#7697
collage
– Bourdeau, Micheline #4879
– Canada (1955-1965) #510
– Colombie-Britannique (années 1970) #2042
– Craven, David #5206 5208
collection Desjardins
– dans établissements religieux et collections
privées du Québec #3207
– et Joseph Légaré #6217 6218
– influence sur Jean-Baptiste Roy-Audy
#7103
– influence sur peinture québécoise, XIXe s.
#1244 7102
Collectionneur, Le, périodique can #134
collectionneurs et collections
– voir aussi entreprises . collections d'art;
protection des arts
– (1880-1912), Montréal (Qué) #1343
– (1890-1900), Canada #190
– (années 1930-1970), Toronto (Ont) #1686
– Abbott, art inuit #4306
– Balshine, Lorne, art inuit #4312 4447
– Band, Charles S., art canadien #3219
– Band, Charles S. et Helen, art canadien
#3215
– Band, Percy, jouets et jeux, XIXe s. #2917
– Bick, Walter, bocaux à marinades #2405
– Bird, Wallace S., art, provinces de
l'Atlantique, XXe s. #1130
– Boylen, M.J., Cornelius Krieghoff,
peintures #1
– Bronfman, Samuel, art canadien #403
– Brown, Ernest, photographies
canadiennes, fin XIXe s. #1949
– Bull, Perkins, peinture canadienne #3208
– Bulman, Bessie, sculpture inuit #4306 4428
– Butler, Jack/K.J., art inuit #4243
– Carr, Emily, poterie, Indiens de la côte
nord-ouest #3827
– Carrier, Louis, orfèvrerie québécoise #3213
– Collison, W.H., art, Indiens de la côte
nord-ouest #3996
– Cook, Ferna et George, sculptures
d'argilite #4006
– Corbeil, Maurice et Andrée, peinture
québécoise #3233 3234
– Coverdale, William H., collection
Canadiana #12 3230
– Currelly, Charles Trick, oeuvres d'art et
artefacts, Royal Ontario Museum
(Toronto, Ont) #3139
– Dobush, Peter, art canadien #3221
– Doig, M. et Mme D.R., peinture
canadienne #3224
– Duncan, Douglas M., art canadien, XXe s.
#119 541 570 3218 3219 3232
– Firestone, Jack, art canadien #3239
– Fleming, Sandford, photographies
d'arpentage canadiennes #1876
– Garber, Bram, peinture canadienne, XXe s.
#3247
– Gerber, Sidney, art, Indiens de la côte

nord-ouest #3974
– Gibb, Benaiah, art européen et art
canadien #3075 3110
– Hooper, James, art des autochtones du
Pacifique, d'Afrique et du continent
américain #3369
– Howard, John George, peintures #3129
– Jaffe, Lilly Weil, art inuit #4223
– Jutras, Albert, peinture canadienne #372
– Koerner, Walter et Marianne, art, Indiens
de la côte nord-ouest #3994
– Kolbenhier, Eric, broderie ukrainienne
bukovinienne #2124
– Larouche-Villeneuve, Jeanne, images
pieuses, estampes #130 1662
– Lee, Clifford E., estampes inuit #4492
– Livernois, Jules-Benoît, photographies
#6308
– Loeb, M. et Mme Jules, art canadien #3231
– Luke, Alexandra, art canadien #3169
– MacAulay, John, art canadien et art
européen #3212
– MacCallum, James Metcalfe, Tom
Thomson et Groupe des Sept #3229
– Mackenzie, Norman, art européen,
asiatique et canadien #1912 3197
– MacMillan, Harvey Reginald, art, Indiens
de la côte nord-ouest #3996
– Maltwood, Katharine Emma, art canadien,
art européen et art oriental #3242 6413
– Manuge, Robert, art canadien #3244
– Massey, Vincent, peinture canadienne
#3220 3227
– Mavor, James #1713
– McCord, David Ross, art canadien #222
223
– McGowan, John, verre canadien #2424
– McKendry, Ruth, courtepointes, Ontario,
XIXe s. #2804
– McKendry, Ruth et Blake, mobilier #8681
– McLean, James Stanley, art canadien, XXe
s. #3210 3226 3228
– Mendel, Frederick Salomon, art européen
et art canadien #72 1912 3187
– Millen, Walter H., collection Canadiana
#21
– Morgan, D., textiles et tissus, Canada
#2747 2748
– Mulders, Gerard et Anne, sculpture inuit
#4443
– Newcombe, famille, oeuvres d'Emily Carr
#5023
– Orchinsky, Peter, chemises et bijoux
bukoviniens #2869
– Osipov, Lou, sculpture inuit #4447
– Pierce, Edith Chown, verre canadien #2397
2398 2399
– Poole, Ernest Edward, peintures
canadiennes et européennes #3217 3222
3235
– Price, Ralph et Patricia, art traditionnel
canadien #970 971 972
– Raley, G.H., art, Indiens de la côte
nord-ouest #3996
– Robertson, John Ross, collection
Canadiana #1713 3130 3131 3204
– Rosenberg, Gloria, courtepointes #2808
– Ryerson, Adolphus Egerton, objets d'art et
artefacts, Educational Museum of Upper
Canada (Toronto, Ont) #3150
– Samuel, Sigmund, collection Canadiana et
collection Americana #247 3135 3140
– Schlombs, Wolfgang, mobilier canadien
#2485

– Sharpe, Nettie, sculpture traditionnelle
québécoise #1607
– Shepley, cuillers à l'emblème du Canada
#2652
– Shumiatcher, Jacqui et Morris, art inuit
#4311
– Silver, M. et Mme Stanley S., bouteilles et
flacons en verre, Canada et
Grande-Bretagne, XIXe-XXe s. #2414
– Sloane, Sir Hans, art amérindien #3397
– Smith, Jean et Elizabeth, arts décoratifs
canadiens #2125 2131
– Stevens, Gerald, verre canadien #2397 2398
2399
– Swinton, George, art inuit #4306
– Twomey, Jerry, art inuit #4306
– Van Horne, Sir William Cornelius #1713
– Vanier, Georges et Pauline, art canadien
#3216
– Viger, Jacques, art canadien #1326 1337
2834 4695 8445
– Volpi, Charles de, collection Canadiana
#3248
– Walker, sir Byron Edmund, art canadien
et européen #3205 3206
– Walker, Sir Byron Edmund, art canadien
et européen #1713
– Webster, John Clarence, collection
Canadiana #3073 3209
– Weldon, Susannah Anne, céramique
anglaise et céramique chinoise,
XVIIe-XIXe s. #2363
– Winrob, Harry, art inuit #4312 4445 4447
– XVIIIe-XXe s., art, Indiens de la côte
nord-ouest #4005
– Zazelenchuk, Stanley et Patricia Jean, art
inuit #4284 4306
collections privées
– voir collectionneurs et collections
Collier, Alan Caswell, artiste can, 1911-
– expositions
– (1971) #5131
colliers
– voir aussi parure
colliers . Montagnais
– natutshikan #4103
colliers . Naskapis
– natutshikan #4103
colliers . Pieds-Noirs
– Soumak, Washington State Museum
(Seattle, Wash) #3685
Collings, Charles John, artiste can, 1848-1931
#2011 5132 5135 5136
– expositions
– (1912) #5133
– (1914?) #5134
– (1978) #5137
– paysages #2016
Collison, Louis, sculpteur can, né 1898
– sculptures d'argilite #5138
Collison, W.E., missionnaire et
collectionneur can, actif années 1890
– années 1950 #3996
Collison, W.H., collectionneur can,
1847-1922
– collection, art, Indiens de la côte
nord-ouest #3996
Collyer, Robin John, artiste can, 1949- #5139
– expositions de groupe
– (1973) #557
– (1977) #782
– (1980) #1832
Cologne (Allemagne de l'Ouest),
Rautenstrauch-Joest-Museum

– expositions
  – *Indianer Nordamerikas: Schätze des Museum of the American Indian - Heye Foundation - New York* (1969) #3437
Cologne (Allemagne de l'Ouest), Wallraf-Richartz-Museum
– expositions
  – *Zeitgenössische Kunst in Kanada* (1959) #433
Colombie-Britannique
– architecture #8083 8142 8146
  – (1895-1914) #8152
  – (années 1940) #8141
  – (années 1950) #8144
  – (avant 1860) #8140
  – bois #8148 8153
  – chinoise #8154
  – utilisation de pierres à bâtir et de pierres d'ornementation (années 1910) #7646 7647
  – vallée du Fraser #8147
  – Whiteway, William Tuff #9508
– architecture commerciale (années 1970) #9360
– architecture domestique #8143 8698
  – (années 1850-début XXe s.) #8712
  – (années 1910) #8685
  – (années 1940) #8693
  – Maclure, Samuel #8385
  – résidences des lieutenants-gouverneurs (1849-1871) #8757
  – résidences estivales, XXe s. #8524
  – XIXe s.-années 1920 #8690
– art #547 1986 1987 1995 2010
  – (1793-1886) #2025
  – (1909-1967) #1978
  – (1932-1968) #1983
  – (1981) #2084
  – (années 1870-1940) #28
  – (années 1910) #1979
  – (années 1920-1960) #461
  – (années 1930) #1982
  – (années 1940) #350 1841
  – (années 1950) #429 1994
  – (années 1950-1970) #145
  – (années 1970) #1868 2040 2047 2050 2053 2063 2067 2068 2078
  – (années 1970), région de l'Okanagan #2048
  – (années 1970-1980) #2082
  – XXe s. #3199
– arts décoratifs #2271
  – (années 1970) #2274 2276
– arts graphiques (années 1970) #2059
– bibliothèques (années 1950) #9044
– bijoux (années 1950) #2695
– bungalows (années 1910) #8684
– conserveries #9258
– écoles
  – (années 1920) #9389
  – (années 1950) #9391 9392
– écoles et universités (années 1960) #9401
– églises
  – (1789-début XXe s.) #8918
  – (1858-1925) #8916
– enseignement de l'art (années 1960) #2989
– femmes artistes (années 1970) #2054
– hôpitaux (années 1950) #9029
– illustrations, de plantes #2024
– magasins (années 1940) #9372
– mobilier (années 1920) #2463
– modèles de broderie #2786
– monuments funéraires #733
– palais de justice (1849-1930) #9006

– peinture #2011
  – (1848-années 1890) #2004
  – (1894-1932) #2007
  – (années 1930) #589 592
  – (années 1940) #1989
  – (années 1940-1950) #412
  – (années 1950) #1990
  – (années 1960) #489
– photographie
  – (1858-1900) #2028
  – (1858-1914) #2032
  – (1860-1978), femmes photographes #2018
  – (1890-1940) #2012
  – (années 1930-1940) #985
  – (années 1970) #990 996 998 2041 2056 2071
  – XIXe s., Great Eastern Photographic and Advertising Company #2022
– poterie (années 1970) #2391
– sculpture
  – (années 1960) #1849 2001
  – (années 1970) #2049 2062 2065 2066
– sculpture en céramique (années 1970) #1864
– sculpture en plein air
  – (1956-1960) #1993
  – (1977) #2057
– vitraux #2452
– vues
  – (1513-1891) #2006
  – (1778-1793), côte nord-ouest #2017
  – (1845-1871) #2020 2023
  – (années 1840-1970) #2016
  – Carr, Emily #5033 5045
  – Hind, William George Richardson #5807 5810 5811
  – Innes, John I. #5901
  – Kipling, Ann #6057
  – McCall, Helen #6460
  – Varley, Frederick Horsman #7462
  – Weber, George #7540
  – Weston, William Percival #7546
  – Wood, Alan #7608 7609
  – XVIIIe s.-années 1930 #2008
– vues photographiques #1039
  – (1858-1871) #2014
  – (1858-1888) #2015
  – (1890-1914) #2030
  – Bailey, Charles S. #4583
  – Baltzly, Benjamin #4598
  – Brock, J.A., & Co. (1886-1888) #2021
  – Dally, Frederick #5249 5250
  – Gunterman, Mattie #5670 5672
  – Horetzky, Charles George #5837 5838
  – Trueman, Richard H. #7437
colonisation
– Britanniques au Canada
  – et Joseph Légaré #6216
  – et William George Richardson Hind #5811
Colonna, Edward, architecte amér, 1862-1948
– Montréal (Qué), maison Van-Horne #8594
Colophon, The, périodique brit
– Milne, David Brown, *Painting Place* #6562
colorants et teinture . Canada
– (1608-1867) #2120
– Cap-Breton (NE) #2732
– Charlevoix (Qué), XVIIe-XIXe s. #2733
– Nouvelle-Ecosse #2749
– Ontario #2742
– Québec #2745
  – (années 1820) #165
– Terre-Neuve #2744

colorants et teinture . Hurons
– XIXe s. #165
colorants et teinture . Indiens de la côte nord-ouest #3415
colorants et teinture . Inuit
– et Judy McGrath #4249 4255 6474
Colour and Form Society (Toronto, Ont)
– art estonien, soutien #118
Colville, Alexander (Alex), artiste can, 1920-
#5141 5142 5146 5148 5150 5151 5152 5155
– commentaire sur la gravure #817
– dessins et estampes, Seconde Guerre mondiale #5156
– en comparaison avec Nicolas Poussin #5147
– entretien #5154
– estampes #1214
– et réalisme #110
– et réalisme magique #5143
– expositions
  – (1977) #5153
  – (1979) #5145
– expositions de groupe
  – (1958) #431
  – (1959) #438
  – (1964) #462
  – (1966) #1123
  – (1967) #490
  – (1974) #1129
  – (1977) #633
  – (1978) #665
  – (1979) #147
  – (1980) #1221
– Forrestall, Tom, comparaison #5462 5466
– *Horse and Train*, Art Gallery of Hamilton (Hamilton, Ont) #38
– imagerie #5149
– *Infantry near Nijmegen* #1115
– influence sur Jim McKenzie #6480
– nus #5140
– peintures, Galerie nationale du Canada (Ottawa, Ont) #5144
– Prévost, Antoine, comparaison #6927
Combe, Lawrence W., architecte can, 1932-
– lauréat du concours, Ontario Hydro Golden Medallion "All Electric Home" (1961) #8514
Comfort, Charles Fraser, artiste et conservateur can, 1900- #5160
– commentaire sur l'art du portrait #624
– commentaire sur Louis Muhlstock #6657
– *Dieppe Raid* #1115
– directeur, Galerie nationale du Canada (Ottawa, Ont) #3049 3050
– expositions
  – (1972) #5159
– expositions de groupe
  – (1978) #133
– gravure sur bois de fil #802
– *Parliament Buildings*, Canadian Club of New York (New York, NY) #3211
– professeur de Gerald Tailfeathers #7312 7313
– Seconde Guerre mondiale, campagne d'Italie (1943-1944) #1090 5158
– théories sur l'art #5157
Comingo, Joseph Brown, artiste can, né 1784, actif jusqu'en 1820
– portrait, enfants de William Hazen #5161
Comité consultatif local pour la conservation de l'architecture/Local Architectural Conservation Advisory Committee (LACAC)
– conservation, Ontario #8022

commerce . Algonquiens
– orfèvrerie de traite #3608
– orfèvrerie et perles en verre #3594
commerce . Amérindiens #3440
commerce . Haidas
– sculpture d'argilite #4016
commerce . Indiens de la côte nord-ouest
#3949
commerce . Iroquois
– orfèvrerie de traite #3645 3646
commerce des fourrures
– artefacts, Nor'westers Museum
(Williamstown, Ont) #3148
– comptoirs commerciaux (postes de traite)
– Alberta, XVIIIe-XIXe s. #8129
– Canada, XVIIe s. #7655
– Compagnie de la baie d'Hudson #8100
– Fort Langley (CB) #8477
– et architecture d'Edmonton (Alta),
(1800-1870) #8130
– et articles de traite amérindiens #3440
– et ceinture fléchée #2818 2824 2827
– et orfèvrerie de traite amérindienne #2659
3594 3608 3645 3646
Commercial Gazette, journal can
– et James Lovell Wiseman #7603
Commission des parcs du Niagara
– voir Ontario. Commission des parcs du
Niagara
Commission frontalière internationale
– études (1886-1900) #1014 1015
Commission frontalière nord-américaine
– études (1858-1875) #1014 1015
Commission géologique du Canada
– (1871), et Benjamin Baltzly #1014 1015
4598
– (1875-1900), George Mercer Dawson et
Joseph Burr Tyrrell #1014 1015
Committee to Strengthen Canadian Culture
– (années 1970), et Michel Lambeth #6159
communications de masse
– voir mass media
Communiqué, périodique can #542 551
communisme, art et
– voir aussi socialisme, art et
– Canada #1393
– Sawchuk, George #7143
Community Design Workshop
– assistance aux résidents d'habitations à
loyer modique, Montréal (Qué), (années
1970) #8283
Comox (CB), résidence Filberg
– architecture et intérieur, Arthur Charles
Erickson #8355
Compagnie de la baie d'Hudson
– architecture
– Alberta, comptoirs commerciaux #8129
– charpente en madriers #7712
– entrepôts #8480
– établissement de la rivière Rouge (Man)
#8097 8100
– Fort Langley (CB), comptoir commercial
#8477
– Manitoba #8094
– Moose Factory (Ont) #7976 7998 8032
– Petit Fort Garry (Man) #8483
– caserne #8482
– Victoria (CB) #8175
– ceinture fléchée #2818 2819 2824 2827
– et Edward Hopkins #5835
– importations de poteries fabriquées par
Spode and Copeland #2300 2357 2358
– poterie #2351
– soutien aux artistes canadiens (1821-1860)

#273
– verrières, John Allward #4515
Compagnie du Nord-Ouest
– Nor'westers Museum (Williamstown, Ont)
#3148
– poste de traite des fourrures, Alberta,
XVIIIe-XIXe s. #8129
– quartier général, Fort William (Ont),
(1803-1821) #8460
Compagnons, Les, troupe de théâtre can
– Pellan, Alfred, costumes et décors pour La
nuit des rois #6799
composition sérielle
– Molinari, Guido #6588 6590 6592
comté d'Albert (NB)
– vues, Joan Steeves Gregory #5657
comté d'Elgin (Ont), Hall-Baker-Stewart
House
– architecture, Isaac Bennett Baker #2581
comté d'Essex (Ont)
– art #1668
comté de Bellechasse (Qué)
– art et architecture #1281
comté de Bellechasse (Qué), église
Saint-Charles-Borromée
– architecture et intérieur #8803
comté de Brant (Ont)
– art (1793-1930) #1684
– poterie et textiles #2249
comté de Bruce (Ont)
– cimetières, croix germano-alsaciennes
#2709
comté de Colchester (NE)
– mobilier, XIXe s. #2515
comté de Frontenac (Ont)
– architecture, XIXe s. #8015
comté de Haliburton (Ont)
– architecture, John H. Billing #8335
comté de Lancaster (Penn)
– arts décoratifs, tradition germanique en
Pennsylvanie #2263
comté de Lincoln (Ont)
– poterie, XIXe s. #2290
comté de Norfolk (Ont)
– architecture domestique, XIXe s. #8656
– mobilier, XIXe s. #2573
– photographie, XIXe s. #1722
comté de Norfolk (Ont), Normandale Iron
Works #2699
comté de Peel (Ont)
– vues, collection Perkins Bull #3208
comté de Pictou (NE)
– architecture #7821 7827
comté de Pontiac (Qué)
– architecture #7894 7895
comté de Portneuf (Qué)
– croix #1621
comté de Prince Edward (Ont)
– art (années 1970) #1816
comté de Renfrew (Ont)
– mobilier, colons polonais #2565
comté de Simcoe (Ont)
– courtepointes #2795
– photographie, XIXe s. #1722 1730
comté de Waterloo (Ont)
– art traditionnel #1681
– arts décoratifs #2243 2246 2264
– bâtiments en pierre, XIXe s. #8011
– cimetières, croix germano-alsaciennes
#2709
– fraktur #2254 2255
– mobilier #2570
– ouvrages en papier #2265
– poterie, milieu XIXe-début XXe s. #2348

– poterie et textiles #2249
comté de Wellington (Ont)
– photographie (1856-1867) #1724
comté de Wentworth (Ont)
– architecture #7954
comté de Wolfe (Qué), église Saint-Gérard
Majella
– architecture, Affleck, Desbarats,
Dimakopoulos, Lebensold, Sise #8846
Comtois, Louis, artiste can, 1945- #1544 5162
– expositions
– (1978) #5163
– (1980) #5164
– expositions de groupe
– (1981) #1565
Comtois, Ulysse, artiste can, 1931- #5165
– entretien #1489
– expositions de groupe
– (1955) #1408
– (1968) #522
– (1973) #556
Conacher, John, artiste can, actif 1919
– illustrations #916
Conception Bay (TN)
– transformation du bois, moulin (ca 1620)
#7718
conceptualisme
– Canada #540 574
– paysages #617
– et Bill Vazan #7473
– et Garry Neill Kennedy #6043
– et George Sawchuk #7143
– et Thomas Elton Henrickson et Martha
Charlotte Henrickson #5781
– et Tim Zuck #7636
– W.O.R.K.S. #1955
concours d'architecture
– (années 1950-1960), Canada #7682
– (années 1960), Canada #7683
– (années 1970), sondage auprès des
architectes #8314
– Burnaby (CB), Simon Fraser University
#9501
– Canadian Architect, concours, galerie d'art
communautaire (1957) #9082
– Canadian Small House Competition (1946)
#8740
– Charlottetown (IPE)
– Confederation Centre #9088 9089 9094
– Province House #8937
– Dominion Housing Act Competition
– (1938) #8739
– Edmonton (Alta), hôtel de ville #8998 8999
9000
– Hamilton (Ont), accès nord-ouest #7962
– Los Angeles (Calif), revitalisation du
quartier Bunker Hill #8364
– Montréal (Qué), Université McGill.
Athletic buildings #9417
– Moose Jaw (Sask), hôtel de ville #8978
– Ontario Hydro Golden Medallion "All
Electric Home" Competition (1961) #8514
– Osaka (Japon), Expo 70. Pavillon du
Canada #9217
– Ottawa (Ont)
– Departmental and Justice Buildings
#8921
– édifices du Parlement #8922 8923 8924
– Galerie nationale du Canada
– (1954) #9079
– (1975-1977) #9126 9136 9142
– Regina (Sask)
– édifices du Parlement #8954 8955 8956
8961

– War Memorial Museum #9073
– Saskatoon (Sask), Mendel Art Gallery #9091
– T. Eaton Company Ideal Ontario Home Competition (1930) #8735
– Toronto (Ont)
  – Bank of Toronto #8293
  – Bourse de Toronto #9161
  – édifices du Parlement #8943
  – Government House (1911) #8748
  – hôtel de ville et Civic Square #8981 8983 8989
  – John Ross Robertson School et Glenholme School #9437
  – Masonic Temple #9062
  – University of Toronto. Knox College #9432
– Vancouver (CB)
  – architecture des écoles primaires (1970) #9507
  – Chinese Cultural Centre #9144
  – University of British Columbia #9498 9500 9509
    – Student Union #9503
  – Vancouver Civic Auditorium #9080
– Winnipeg (Man)
  – édifices du Parlement #8946 8949 8950
  – hôtel de ville (1913) #8979
  – hôtel de ville (1960) #8985 8986 8987
  – Winnipeg Art Gallery #9102
– XXe s., Canada #7747
concours de sculpture
– Hamilton (Ont), Art Gallery of Hamilton (1976) #780
– Lethbridge (Alta), University of Lethbridge (1980-1981) #797
– monuments aux disparus, concours, Première Guerre mondiale #731 732
Concours pour ouvrages en béton
– (1971) #7706
Condé, Carole, artiste can, 1940-
– commentaire sur la politique et l'art #602
– expositions de groupe
  – (1980) #1063
– Maybe Wendy's Right #1052
Conder, Charles, artiste brit, 1868-1909
– influence sur James Wilson Morrice #6630
Condon, Wanda, artiste can, 1951-
– expositions, critiques #5166
– expositions de groupe
  – (1978) #669
  – (1980) #698
Condron, Brian, photographe can, 1949-
– catalogue de photographies #1053
Conefroy, Pierre, prêtre et architecte can, 1752-1816 #8834
– églises, plans
  – Berthierville (Qué) #8833
  – L'Acadie (Qué) #8830
Conférence canadienne des arts
– (1961) #444
– (années 1960) #447
– (années 1970) #3270
– Comité fédéral d'études d'une politique culturelle, rapport
  – (1980) #3294 3295
  – (1981) #3297 3298
– périodiques
  – Arts Bulletin #551
  – Communiqué #542
Conference of Canadian Artists
– (1941) #351 379
– (1941-1951) #390
conférences

– 20th Century Canadian Culture: A Symposium (Washington, DC) (1977) #621 627
– Conférence canadienne des arts (1961) #444
– Conférence de l'Institut canadien des affaires publiques (Lake Couchiching, Ont) (1976) #619
– Conference of Canadian Artists (1941) #351 379 390
– Conference on Canadian-American Affairs (Kingston, Ont) (1937) #337
– Fédération des artistes canadiens (1941 et 1947) #376
– Painters' Symposium (Kingston, Ont) (1977) #620
– Preserving the Canadian Heritage/La préservation du patrimoine canadien (1975) #7767
Confrérie des menuisiers de madame Sainte-Anne #1241 5965
Confrérie des poursuivants. Pieds-Noirs
– étuis à pipes #3665
Conger, Wilson S., politicien can, m. 1864
– portrait, Paul Kane #6008
congrès
– voir conférences
Conner, Bruce, artiste amér, 1933-
– et Gary Lee-Nova #6213
Conner, Scott, photographe can, ca 1952-
– catalogue de photographies #1032
Connolly, Reynald, artiste can, 1944- #1479 5167
Conseil canadien de gravure et de dessin #835
– et Société canadienne des arts graphiques #801
– et Société canadienne des peintres-graveurs #3
Conseil canadien de l'artisanat
– périodique, L'Artisan/The Craftsman #2113 2133
Conseil canadien de l'habitation
– prix et récompenses
  – (1957-) #8741
  – (1972) #8744
  – (1974) #8746
  – (1979) #8747
Conseil canadien des arts
– fondation (1945) #379
Conseil canadien des arts de l'espace
– (1965) #2105
Conseil de la sculpture du Québec/Quebec Sculpture Council
– (1978-1979) #1628
Conseil de recherches pour la défense
– voir aussi Canada. Conseil de recherches pour la défense
Conseil des arts de l'Ontario
– (années 1960) #529
– Creative Artists in School, programme scolaire (années 1970) #3004
– rapport sur les arts dans la vie franco-ontarienne (1977) #1820 1821
– rapport sur les aspects économiques de l'art en Ontario (1972) #1802
Conseil des Arts du Canada
– 1974, proposition pour l'encouragement des arts par le milieu des affaires d'ici 1980 #3271
– (années 1950-1960) #3264
– (années 1960) #529
– (années 1970) #586 693 3278 3293
– collection, art canadien #90 3266

– et Commission royale d'enquête sur l'avancement des arts, lettres et sciences (Rapport Massey) #3254 3255 3261 9906
– photographie, soutien (années 1970) #1038
– politique de financement (1978) #3287
– projet "Directors' Choice" (1962-1967) #481
– Twenty Plus Five, livre vert (1977) #3285
Conseil des arts et manufactures/Council of Arts and Manufactures
– Québec, fin XIXe s. #2962
– rapport, enseignement des arts industriels (1876) #2598
Conseil des universités de l'Ontario
– recommandations, enseignement de l'architecture en Ontario (années 1970) #8288
conservation de l'architecture
– Association pour l'avancement des méthodes de préservation #7757
– banques #9204
– Barkerville (CB) #8151
– Brockville (Ont), Idlewild #8671
– bureaux d'architectes (années 1950) #9299
– Calgary (Alta) #8121 8133 8134 8138
– Canada #7767 7772
  – (1959), Institut royal d'architecture du Canada. Comité pour la préservation des édifices historiques #7756
  – (1980) #7776
  – (années 1880) #7754
  – (années 1930-1940) #7666
  – (années 1950), droit et législation #7755
  – (années 1960) #7759
  – (années 1970) #7705 7765 7771 8964
    – conservation de l'architecture, formation #7773
  – (années 1970-1980) #7764
  – transformation d'édifices publics en établissements culturels #9147 9148
– Canada et Etats-Unis, XIXe s.-années 1970 #7761
– Charlottetown (IPE), Province House #8938 8939
– Colombie-Britannique, églises amérindiennes en bois #8917
– comté de Pontiac (Qué) #7894 7895
– Cormier, Ernest, commentaire #8346
– Dawson City (Yukon), Palace Grand Theatre #9090
– Edmonton (Alta) #8131
  – maison Duggan #8729
  – maison Holgate #8718
– façades #7766
– Fanshawe Pioneer Village (Ont) #8066
– Fondation du patrimoine ontarien #8001
– Fort George (Niagara-on-the-Lake, Ont) #8459
– Fort Langley (CB) #8474
– Fort Saint James (CB) #8478
– Fort William (Ont) #8460
– Granville Ferry (NE), Habitation Port-Royal #7812 7813
– guide #7774 7775
– Halifax (NE) #7830 7834
  – bord de l'eau, édifices #7822 7824 7825
  – centre-ville #7819
  – citadelle de Halifax #8430 8434 8440
  – conservation du patrimoine, critères d'évaluation #7833
  – édifices des rues Prince et Hollis #7831
  – maison West, rue Brunswick #8537
  – Neptune Theatre #9097
  – Nova Scotia College of Art and Design #9409 9410

- rue Granville #7817
- Héritage Canada #7763 7770
- Heritage Park (Alta) #8125
- Inventaire canadien des bâtiments historiques #7707 7708 7716
- Kings Landing (NB) #7810 7811
- Kingston (Ont) #7995
- Lake Louise (Alta), Skoki Lodge #9296
- Laval (Qué), maison André B.-Papineau #8625
- Louisbourg (NE) #8423 8425 8439 8442
- Lunenburg (NE), Soloman House #8549
- maisons en bois rond #8526
- Midland (Ont), Sainte-Marie among the Hurons #7999
- Montréal (Qué) #7911 7914
  - château Dufresne #8617 8618
  - église Sainte-Catherine-d'Alexandrie #8867
  - habitations à loyer modique (années 1970) #8283
  - maison Bigot #8567
  - maison Saint-Gabriel #8597
  - Vieux-Montréal #7905 7910 7919
- Moose Factory (Ont) #7998
- moulins #9248
- Nelson (CB) #8155
- Oka (Qué), calvaire d'Oka #8853
- Ontario #8024
  - (1971), programme gouvernemental de préservation #7996
  - (années 1930) #7966
  - cabanes en bois rond #7990
  - Comité consultatif pour la conservation de l'architecture #8022
  - constructions en bois, XIXe s. #7745
  - églises #8906
- Ottawa (Ont) #8935
  - Académie de La Salle #9480 9481
  - quartier de Glebe #8042
  - région de la capitale nationale #8043 8044
- Peterborough (Ont) #8021
  - Hutchison House #8674
- Prince Edward Island Heritage Foundation #7795
- Québec #1324 7870 8595
  - architecture domestique #7760 8592 8600 8624
  - églises #1247
  - et Gérard Morisset #7897
  - Héritage canadien du Québec #7871
  - ministère des Affaires culturelles du Québec. Service de l'Inventaire des biens culturels #1277
- Québec (Qué) #7936 7937 7938 7940 7941 7942
  - Batterie Royale #8451
  - Hôpital-Général. Moulin à vent #9245
  - place Royale #7948 7951
- Quidi Vidi (TN), Christ Church #7788
- Rimouski (Qué), Musée régional de Rimouski #9118
- Saint-Jean (NB) #7807
- Saskatoon (Sask) #8114
- St. Andrews (NB) #8550
- St. John's (TN) #7789 7790 7793 7794
- style victorien #7769
- théâtres et cinémas #9131
- Toronto (Ont) #8073
  - Banque canadienne de commerce #9351
  - centre-ville, secteurs résidentiels (années 1970) #8068
  - Chambre de commerce,

recommandations (1979) #8027
  - Colborne Lodge #8659
  - Fort York #8458
  - Osgoode Hall #9003
  - quartier St. Lawrence #8079
  - résidence du juge en chef Sir William Campbell #8661
  - St. Lawrence Hall #9103
  - Stewart Building #9354
  - The Grange #8665 8666 8680
  - Todmorden Mills #8072
  - University of Toronto. University College #9482
  - Yorkville Village #9376
- Trois-Rivières (Qué), maison Deschenaux dite manoir de Tonnancour #8633
- Tunis Snook Farm (près de Kingston, Ont) #8681
- Upper Canada Village (Morrisburg, Ont) #7981 7982 7988 8031
- Vancouver (CB) #7762 8161 8164 8166
  - (années 1970) #8162
  - Gastown #8163
  - Hodson Manor #8707
  - Orpheum Theatre #9135
  - transformation d'édifices urbains en immeubles résidentiels (1980) #8725
- Victoria (CB) #8149 8173 8176 8177 8178
  - architecture domestique #8722
  - édifices du Parlement, Colombie-Britannique #8965 8966
- Village Canadiana (Rawdon, Qué) #7876
- Village Historique Acadien (Caraquet, NB) #7805
- Village Jacques de Chambly (Qué) #8573
- Winnipeg (Man) #8103 8108
  - entrepôts et immeubles à bureaux #8106 8107

conservation et restauration
- Canada #7767
- Québec
  - (années 1970) #3015
  - et Gérard Morisset #3125 3127 3305
- Québec (Qué), Musée du Québec #3092
conservation et restauration, architecture paysagiste #7768
conservation et restauration, art
- (années 1960), matériel d'artistes #527
conservation et restauration, arts décoratifs #2252
conservation et restauration, instruments de musique
- Morisset, Gérard #2952
conservation et restauration, livres #935
conservation et restauration, mobilier
- Québec, XVIIe-XVIIIe s. #2530 2531
conservation et restauration, peinture murale
- région de Granville Ferry (NE), Hall-Croscup House #1223
conservation et restauration, pétroglyphes
- Amérindiens #3481
- Indiens de la côte nord-ouest #3988
conservation et restauration, sculpture
- (années 1970), recommandations #793
conservation et restauration, tapis
- tapis crochetés #2756
conservation et restauration, textiles
- Amérindiens #3476
conservation et restauration, totems #3884 3925 4119
conservation et restauration, verre
- verre à fenêtres #7777 7778
conserveries . Canada

- Colombie-Britannique #9258
- provinces de l'Ouest #8083
conserveries . Etats-Unis
- Ouest américain #8083
consommateurs
- Canada (1885-1925) #2851
Constable, John, artiste brit, 1776-1837
- influence sur Homer Ransford Watson #7531
- influence sur J.E.H. MacDonald #6370
Constantineau, Fleurimond, artiste can, 1905-1981 #5168
construction #9901
- voir aussi murs
- bâtiments préfabriqués, province de l'Ouest (1904-1910) #8082
- Canada. Conseil national de recherches. Division des recherches sur le bâtiment #7715
- charpente en bois d'oeuvre
  - Canada et Etats-Unis, XVIIe-XVIIIe s. #7717
  - comparaison entre deux types d'habitations (1650 et 1836) #8658
- charpente en madriers #7712
  - Ontario, XIXe s. #8046
- Colombie-Britannique #8142
- conception de murs-rideaux, immeubles à bureaux (années 1950-1960) #9300
- construction à murs creux, Ontario, XIXe s. #8004
- construction en bois #7722 7745
- construction en bois rond
  - Alberta, fin XIXe-début XXe s. #8120
  - colons canadiens-français en Ontario, XIXe s. #7685
  - Ontario, XIXe s. #7979
  - vallée de l'Outaouais #8029
- Dawson City (Yukon), (1897-1903) #8183
- élévateurs à grain (années 1920) #9236
- et architecture
  - (années 1960) #8310
  - Canadian Architect, étude (1974-1976) #8320
  - Don Mills (Ont), logement (années 1950) #8301
  - Institut royal d'architecture du Canada, étude (années 1960) #8309
- établissements industriels (années 1950) #9241
- habitations de la Saskatchewan, fin XIXe-début XXe s. #8696
- habitations ontariennes, XIXe s. #8677
- habitations québécoises (années 1960) #8279
- industrie de transformation du bois
  - Canada et Etats-Unis (1607-1623) #7718
  - XVIIIe-XIXe s. #7720
- Lindsay, Jeffrey, structure à voiles minces #7674
- Louisbourg (NE) #8426 8427 8435 8436
- pierre
  - comté de Waterloo (Ont), XIXe s. #8011
  - région d'Ottawa (Ont), XIXe s. #8033
  - Terrebonne (Qué), (années 1816-1820) #7907
- Québec
  - XIXe-XXe s. #7926
  - XVIIe-XIXe s. #7864
- toitures, matériaux et techniques, XVIIe-XIXe s. #7703
- Trois-Rivières (Qué), Forges du Saint-Maurice #7878
- Vancouver (CB), (1888-1913) #8165

Construction: A Journal for the Architectural Engineering and Contracting Interests of Canada, périodique can #7641
constructivisme
– Canada, sculpture en plein-air (années 1970) #784
– et art vidéo #654
– et Lawren Phillip Harris #5711
– et Peter Henry Kolisnyk #6075 6076
– et Robert Gray Murray #6668
– et Roger Vilder #7489
– et structurisme #777
– et Tim Zuck #7636
constructivistes de la côte ouest
– et Alan Wood #7608 7610
Contant, Gabriel, artiste can, 1931- #5169
contes traditionnels
– *voir* folklore; légendes
Cook, Ferna et George, collectionneurs can, XXe s.
– collection, sculptures d'argilite #4006
Cook, James, navigateur brit, explorateur au Canada, 1728-1779
– collection, art indien de la côte nord-ouest #4005
– expédition, Indiens de la côte nord-ouest #269 270 3445 4062 4064
– expédition dans l'Arctique #278
Cook, Mme. Nelson, artiste can, active années 1830-1850 #5170
Cook, Nelson, artiste can, 1817-1892
– portraits de la famille Dickinson #5170
Cooke, Edwy Francis, artiste can, 1926-
– expositions
– (1977) #5171
Cooksville (Ont), Applewood United Church
– architecture, James A. Murray #8763
Coombs, Edith Grace, artiste can, 1890- #5172
Coon, S.B., & Son, agence can d'architecture
– Sarnia (Ont), école publique #9387
Cooper, H.W., artiste can, actif 1914-1919
– art et écrits, Première Guerre mondiale #5173
– illustrations #916
Cooper, Heather, artiste can, 1945- #5175
– co-fondatrice de Burns, Cooper, Hynes Ltd. #905
– estampes #897 941
– et Burns, Cooper, Donoahue, Fleming & Company Ltd. #904
– peintures et illustrations #5174
Cooper, Kenneth R., architecte can, 1928-
– Toronto (Ont), Hydro Place #9352
Cooper, Lynda, artiste can, 1952-
– dessin de monnaie olympique (1976) #778
Cooper and Beatty Ltd., studio can de graphisme
– et Jim Donoahue #5297
– expositions, critiques #860
Coopération des petits dessins, illustrateurs de bandes dessinées can #952
Coopérative de l'Arctique canadien
– (1977-1980) #4269
coopératives d'artistes amérindiens
– 'Ksan (Hazelton, CB) #4129 4130
– Garden Hill (Man), Ministic Carvers Co-op #4153
– Island Lake (Man), Garden Hill Cooperative #4135
– Red Lake (Ont), Triple K Co-operative #4151 4158
coopératives d'artistes inuit #4231 4288

– Baker Lake (TNO), Sanavik Cooperative #4480 4481
– Belcher Islands (TNO), Metiq Co-operative #4459
– Cape Dorset (TNO) #4187 4464 6270
– West Baffin Eskimo Co-operative #4192 4299 4460
– et industrie de l'art #4262
– Inoucdjouac (Qué) #4267
– Povungnituk (Qué) #4274
Cooperstown (NY), New York State Historical Association
– expositions
– *The Marine Collection* (1943) #12
Copenhague (Danemark), Ethnografish Samling
– artefacts thuléens #4372
Copenhague (Danemark), Nationalmuseet
– art autochtone #3338
– expositions
– *Sculpture of the Inuit: Masterworks of the Canadian Arctic/La sculpture chez les Inuit: chefs-d'oeuvre de l'Arctique canadien* (1972) #4423 4440
Copithorne, Judith, artiste can, 1939-
– poésie visuelle #5176
Copley, John Singleton, artiste amér, 1738-1815
– portraits d'habitants de la Nouvelle-Ecosse #1197
Corbeil, Maurice et Andrée, collectionneurs can, XXe s.
– collection, peinture québécoise #3233 3234
Corbeil, Wilfrid, prêtre, architecte et artiste can, 1893-1979
– commentaire sur la peinture québécoise (années 1950) #1402
– églises #8838
Cordeau, Bagbaria, architecte can, actif années 1980
– Edmonton (Alta), hôtel de ville #8998
Cordner, Andrew, artiste can (vitrail), 1935- #2450
Corée
– vues photographiques
– Hammock, Virgil #5696
Corkan, Juan (Corky), architecte can, 1927-
– restauration, Duggan House (Edmonton, Alta) #8729
Corman, Don, photographe can, 1951-
– expositions de groupe
– (1980) #1063
Cormier, Bruno M., psychiatre et auteur can, 1919-
– écrits #1449
– *Refus global* #1396
Cormier, Ernest, architecte et artiste can, 1885-1980 #302 8345
– entretien #8346
– expositions de groupe
– (1933) #8224
– Montréal (Qué)
– maison Cormier #8347 8348
– palais de justice, annexe #9001
Cormon, Fernand Anne Piestre, artiste fr, 1845-1924
– influence sur Charles Edouard Huot #5878 5884
Corne, Sharon Joy, artiste can, 1936-
– commentaire sur l'exposition, *Woman as Viewer*, Winnipeg Art Gallery (Winnipeg, Man), (1975) #596 1877

Corneil, Carmen, architecte can, 1933-
– Ottawa (Ont), Carleton University. School of Architecture #8284
Corneil & McBain, agence can d'architecture
– Toronto (Ont), Guides du Canada, siège social #7984
Cornell, Joseph, sculpteur amér, 1903-1972
– influence sur Alan Frank Glass #5616
Cornellier, Pierre, artiste can, 1943- #1479 1480
Cornwall (Ont), Institut de formation de Transports Canada
– architecture, Thom Partnership #8412
Cornwall (Ont), Inverarden (résidence de John McDonald of Garth)
– architecture #8673
Cornwallis Valley (NE), Acacia Grove House
– architecture #8528
Corot, Jean Baptiste Camille, artiste fr, 1796-1875
– East, Benoît, comparaison #5353
– influence sur Robert Wakeham Pilot #6869
Corporation canadienne de l'artisanat
– (1894-1929) #2090
– (1929-1967) #2118
– (années 1920) #2089
– (années 1930) #2091
– (années 1950) #7900
– (années 1960) #2103
– art inuit #4397
– expositions, critiques
– (1957) #2380
correspondance
– *voir* artistes, correspondance
corridor du canal Rideau (Ont)
– architecture (avant 1880) #8008
Corriveau, Jeanne d'Arc, artiste can (tapisserie), 1931- #2102 2769 5177
Corsault, Share, photographe can, 1947- #2071
– expositions de groupe
– (1981) #2084
Cosgrove, Stanley Morel, artiste can, 1911- #5180 5182 5183 5184 5185
– et critique d'art #3307
– oeuvres
– (1944) #5178
– (1944-1950) #5181
– (années 1940) #5179
Coshof, Karen, photographe can, 1945- #995
– catalogue de photographies #1023
cosmologie . Amérindiens
– points cardinaux #3498
cosmologie . Haidas #3780
cosmologie . Indiens de la côte nord-ouest
– pétroglyphes #3988
cosmologie . Indiens des plaines
– Roue-Médecine #3748
Cossette, Marie Andrée, photographe can, active années 1970 #1556
costume
– *voir aussi* boutons; brassards; casques; catalogues de modes. costume; ceintures (de tissu); chapeaux; chaussures; mode; uniformes militaires; vêtements sacerdotaux
– Pellan, Alfred #6804
– *La nuit des rois* #6799
costume . Agniers
– XVIIIe s. #3550
costume . Algonquiens #3374 3605 3672
– (années 1760-début XXe s.) #3633

– broderie en poil d'orignal #3513
– ouvrages perlés #3582 3635
– tournures #3580
– wampum #3521
costume . Amérindiens #2849 3453
– illustrations, Archives publiques du
  Canada. Division de l'iconographie
  (Ottawa, Ont) #2883 2884
– influence sur costume canadien #2841
– ouvrages perlés #3449
– peintures, George Catlin #3384
– XVIIe-XIXe s. #2825
costume . Assiniboines #3653 3739
costume . Athapascans #4073 4102 4104 4105
– XIXe s. #4111
costume . Béothuks #3528 3584
costume . Canada #2730 2825
– (1608-1867) #2120
– (1780-1967) #2849
– (1848-1868) #2887
– (1867) #2844
– (1886-1930), catalogues du magasin Eaton
  #2851
– (1890-1910), Montréal (Qué) #2861
– (années 1870) #2854 2859
– Acadie
  – (années 1870) #2840
  – XIXe s. #2877
  – XVIIIe-XIXe s. #2836 2876 2894
– chemises bukoviniennes (1865-1945) #2869
– costume féminin
  – (1713-1758), Louisbourg (NE) #2855
  – (1780-1867), Ontario #2839
  – (1800-1821) #2860
  – (1800-1867), sous-vêtements #2886
  – (1803), Québec #2830
  – (1822-1839) #2863
  – (1840-1866) #2885
  – (1840-1965), robes de soirée, Montréal
    (Qué) #2842
  – (1867-1898) #2889
  – (1867-1907), Ontario #2843
  – (1909-1919) #2905
  – (années 1830-1880) #2870
  – (années 1840-1850) #2847
  – (années 1870) #2829 2878
    – Beauce (Qué) #2828
  – (années 1890), Amérique du Nord
    (Nord-Ouest) #2856
  – (années 1920) #2906
  – XIXe s. #2846 2875 2908
  – XVIIIe-XIXe s. #2903
– costume féminin, style victorien #2847
  2870 2885
– costume lithuanien #2892
– costume masculin
  – (1605-1963), Québec #2838
  – XIXe s. #2845
    – Québec #2896
  – XVIIe s., Montréal (Qué) #2821
– costume norvégien #2273
– costume paysan
  – Ontario, XIXe s. #2888
  – Québec, XVIIe-XVIIIe s. #2217
– costume religieux, Québec #2779 2838
– costume ukrainien #2117
– Dugald (Man), Dugald Costume Collection
  #2902
– Edmonton (Alta), University of Alberta
  #3200
– General Idea #5583
– groupes ethniques #2893
– île d'Orléans (Qué)
  – XVIIe s. #2895

– XVIIe-XIXe s. #1252
– illustrations #1326
– illustrations, Archives publiques du
  Canada. Division de l'iconographie
  (Ottawa, Ont) #2883 2884 2904
– influence du costume amérindien #2841
– Marshall, Pat #6422
– mennonites #2264
– Montréal (Qué), XIXe s. #2837
– Montreal Theatre Ballet (années 1950)
  #1410
– Ontario
  – (1784-1867) #2852
  – (1867-1907) #2871
– Ottawa (Ont), Musée national de
  l'Homme. Centre canadien d'études sur la
  culture traditionnelle #963
– Pellan, Alfred #6816
– Québec #2879
  – (1840-1900) #2899
  – (années 1850) #2834
  – art traditionnel #1291
  – dans chansons folkloriques
    canadiennes-françaises #2898
  – manchon #2817
  – tailleurs, XVIIIe s. #2820
  – XVIIe-XIXe s. #2822
    – influence européenne #2221
  – XVIIe-XVIIIe s. #2850
  – XVIIIe s. #2200
– Québec (Qué), Séminaire de Québec #2809
– robes et costumes de marié(e)s,
  Peterborough (Ont), (1810-1938) #2909
– sports et jeux, XIXe s. #257
– vêtements d'enfants
  – (1780-1930) #2862
  – (1820-1890) #2853
  – fin XIXe s.-années 1930 #2932
– vêtements d'hiver
  – Charlevoix (Qué), fin XIXe-début XXe s.
    #2890
  – XIXe s. #2891
– voyageurs et coureurs de bois,
  XVIIIe-XIXe s. #2826
– XVIIe-XIXe s. #2825
– XVIIIe s. #2868
costume . Chilkats #3811
costume . Cris #3402 3739 3742
costume . Dakotas
– St. Paul (Minn), Science Museum of
  Minnesota #3755
costume . Esquimaux du caribou #4265
costume . Flancs-de-chien #4089
costume . France
– costume féminin, noblesse (1659) #2830
costume . Gens-du-Sang #3739
– New York (NY), American Museum of
  Natural History #3414
costume . Gros-Ventres #3753
costume . Haidas
– Washington (DC), Smithsonian Institution
  #3763
costume . Hans #4101
costume . Hurons #3514
– broderie en poil d'orignal #3513
costume . Indiens de la côte nord-ouest
– jambières ornées de piquants de porc-épic
  #3811
costume . Indiens des forêts du Nord-Est
– (années 1760-début XXe s.) #3633
– ouvrages perlés #3635
costume . Indiens des plaines #3656 3657
  3672 3684 3716 3717
– costume féminin #3658

– danse #3694
– jambières #3697
– New York (NY), American Museum of
  Natural History #3668
– sociétés secrètes #3727
– tournures #3692
– wampum #3521
costume . Ingaliks #4087
costume . Inuit
– amautik #4300
costume . Iroquois #3489 3559 3605
– (années 1760-début XXe s.) #3633
– ouvrages perlés #3635
– Six Nations Reserve (Ont) #3598
– wampum #3521
costume . Kutchins #4102
costume . Kwakiutls #3787
costume . Malécites #3641
costume . Métis #4110
costume . Micmacs #3528 3569 3641 3643
costume . Mistassins #4080 4100
costume . Naskapis
– peinture sur costume #4098
costume . Pieds-Noirs #3654 3686 3739
– (1910-1960) #3712
– costume féminin #3695
– Minìpoka #3749
– New York (NY), American Museum of
  Natural History #3414
costume . Piégans
– jambières #3715
– New York (NY), American Museum of
  Natural History #3414
costume . Salish de la côte #3851 3896
costume . Salishiens #4013
costume . Sarcis #3739
costume . Saulteux/Ojibwa #3402 3488 3539
  3557 4089
– chaman, société des Midéwiwins, tuniques
  en peaux de bison #3517
– Island Lake (Man) #3549
– St. Paul (Minn), Science Museum of
  Minnesota #3755
costume . Shuswaps #3789
costume . Siouens #3672
costume . Skokomish #3835
costume . Slaveys #4089
costume . Snuqualmis #3835
costume . Tagish #4106
costume . Tahltans
– (années 1910) #4074
costume . Tanainas #4085
costume . Tanana #4095
costume . Têtes-de-Boule #4079
costume . Thompsons
– ouvrages perlés et broderie #3808
costume . Tlingits #3976 4106
– Washington (DC), Smithsonian Institution
  #3763
costume . Tsimshians #3763 3795
costume . Tutchonis #4106
Côté, Dom Claude-Marie, prêtre et
  architecte can, 1908-
– églises québécoises #8334
Côté, Jean-Baptiste, sculpteur can, 1834-1907
  #1334 1335 2169 2171 5186 5187 5188
– influence sur Henri Julien #5993
– Jobin, Louis, comparaison #5968
– représentation d'animaux #1579
– sculptures sur bois #756 1577
  – Québec (Qué), Musée du Québec #1612
  – Sharpe, Nettie, collection #1607
– statue du général Wolfe, Québec (Qué)
  #1600

– thème du souper d'Emmaüs #1615
côte atlantique (Canada)
– vues #139
côte nord-ouest
– vues
– (1789-1791), artistes espagnols #1998
– Bacstrom, Sigismund #4581
– XIXe-début XXe s. #1999
Cotton, John Wesley, artiste can, 1869-1931
– estampes #822
Cotton, Michel, orfèvre et cordonnier can,
    1700-après 1747 #249 250
Coubertin, Baron Pierre de, homme d'Etat
    fr, 1863-1937
– et Jeux olympiques #1364
Couchiching, Conférence de l'Institut
    canadien des affaires publiques (Lake
    Couchiching, Ont)
– (1976), mémoires et comptes rendus #619
Coughtry, John Graham, artiste can, l931-
– commentaire sur Gordon Rayner #6965
– commentaire sur ses études en art #470
– et peinture torontoise
    – (années 1950) #1749
    – (années 1960) #1753
– expositions
    – (1976) #5190
– expositions, critiques #5191
– expositions de groupe
    – (1964) #462
    – (1965) #473
– peintures (1957-1959) #5189
– peintures et sculptures #449
couleur
– Bush, Jack Hamilton #4964
– Comtois, Louis #5163 5164
– Gaucher, Yves #5570
– Giguère, Roland, commentaire #5599
– Lindner, Ernest #6286
– Molinari, Guido #6590 6591
– peinture montréalaise (années 1950-1960)
    #1425
– symbolisme et cosmologie chez
    Amérindiens #3498
Coulombe, Jacques, sculpteur can, 1941-
    #1630
Coulson, Harry W., artiste can, actif
    1894-1897
– peinture sur porcelaine #2277
coupes . Canada
– verre moulé #2430
coupes . Etats-Unis
– verre moulé #2430
Coupey, Pierre, artiste can, 1942-
– expositions, critiques #2072
– expositions de groupe
    – (1979) #2075
Courbet, Gustave, artiste fr, 1819-1877
– Boyle, John Bernard, comparaison #4891
– influence sur Marc-Aurèle de Foy
    Suzor-Coté #7297 7300
Courchesne, Edgar, architecte can, 1903-1979
– églises québécoises #8334
Courcy, Michael John de, artiste can, 1944-
– cartes géographiques, illustrations #561
– expositions de groupe
    – (1976) #2060
    – (1979) #2069
coureurs de bois
– habillement #2826 2841
Cournoyer, Georget, céramiste can, 1931-
    #5192
Cournoyer, Michèle, artiste can, 1943- #5193
Cournoyer, Serge, sculpteur can, 1943-

– "oeuvres-machines" #5194
– entretien #1485
– utilisation de la lumière #767
couronnes . Canada
– Ontario, XIXe s. #2248
courroies porte-fardeaux . Indiens de la côte
    nord-ouest
– préhistoire #4017
courtepointes
– voir aussi couvre-lits
courtepointes, techniques
– voir matériaux et techniques .
    courtepointes
courtepointes . Amérindiens #2799
courtepointes . Canada #2107 2799 2800
– (1608-1867) #2120
– (1726), courtepointe piquée en soie,
    Université McGill. Musée McCord
    (Montréal, Qué) #2803
– (années 1920) #2794
– Boyce, Eleanor #4890
– Cap-Breton (NE) #2732
– comté de Simcoe (Ont) #2795
– Ile-du-Prince-Edouard (années 1850-1970)
    #2802
– Manitoba #2272
– mennonites #2253 2264 2267
– Nouvelle-Ecosse #2731
    – (1820-1930) #2807
    – (années 1970) #2154
    – motifs (avant 1920) #2785
– Ondaatje, Kim #2798
– Ontario #2729 2796 2801
    – XIXe s. #2805
    – XIXe-XXe s. #1682 2806
– Ottawa (Ont), Musée national de l'Homme
    #2804
– Québec
    – (1875-1915) #1364
    – XVIIe-XIXe s. #2746
    – XVIIe-XVIIIe s. #2200
– Rosenberg, Gloria, collection #2808
– Terre-Neuve #1154 1155 2744
– Toronto (Ont), Royal Ontario Museum
    #2797
– Wieland, Joyce #7581
courtepointes . Etats-Unis
– XVIIIe s., en comparaison avec
    courtepointe, Canada (1726), Université
    McGill. Musée McCord (Montréal, Qué)
    #2803
Cousineau, Sylvain P., artiste can, 1949-
– expositions
    – (1980) #5195
– expositions, critiques #1018 1067
couteaux . Canada
– poignées en bois, Ontario, XVIIIe-XIXe s.
    #2588
Couteaux-Jaunes
– culture (années 1920) #4081
coutellerie et ustensiles de table
– site archéologique de Roma (IPE) #2714
    2715
Coutellier, Francis, artiste can, 1945- #5196
– catalogue de photographies #996
– estampes #1185
– expositions de groupe
    – (1973) #1182
Couturier, Pierre, constructeur can, actif
    1700-1715, m. 1715 #7844
Couturier, Pierre Charles Marie-Alain,
    prêtre et artiste fr au Canada, 1897-1954
    #1407
– et art québécois (années 1940) #1402 1436

1474
– influence sur Paul-Emile Borduas #4850
– Québec, églises #8838
couvents
– voir aussi monastères
couvents . Canada
– Montréal (Qué) #7932
    – maison mère des Soeurs Grises #8862
– Québec
    – XVIIe-début XIXe s. #7841 7853
    – XVIIe-XVIIIe s. #7845
– Québec (Qué)
    – Couvent des ursulines #8810
    – Hôpital-Général #9022
    – maison Mère-Mallet #8884
– Trois-Rivières (Qué), (années 1630-1910)
    #7883
couvert . Canada
– (avant 1867), Canada anglais #2470
couvert . Etats-Unis
– motifs du castor et de la feuille d'érable
    #2312
– verre, XIXe-début XXe s. #2430
couvert . Grande-Bretagne
– (1760-1840), collection Susannah Anne
    Weldon, King's College (Windsor, NE)
    #2363
– motifs du castor et de la feuille d'érable
    #2312
– pour le marché canadien, XIXe s. #2315
– Spode and Copeland, poterie #2357 2358
couvertures . Carriers
– (années 1970) #4145
couvertures . Chilkats #3333 3784 3821 3826
    3898 3973
couvertures . Cowichans
– (années 1970) #4145
couvertures . Crows
– rosace (motif) #3752
couvertures . Kwakiutls #3973
couvertures . Salish de la côte
– poil de chien #3800
couvertures . Salishiens #3830
– New York (NY), Museum of the American
    Indian. Heye Foundation #3818
– XIXe s. #3790
couvertures . Tlingits #3826
couvertures . Tsimshians #3826
couvre-lits
– voir aussi courtepointes
couvre-lits . Canada
– Cap-Breton (NE) #2728
– Charlevoix (Qué) #2738
– île aux Coudres (Qué) #2178
– Nouvelle-Ecosse (1820-1930) #2807
– Ontario #2729
    – jacquard, artisans tisserands #2740
    – XIXe s. #2805
– Québec
    – XVIIe-XIXe s. #2221 2746
– XVIIe-XIXe s. #2730 2736
couvre-lits . Salishiens #3469 4018
couvre-lits . Tlingits #4018
Couvreur, Daniel, sculpteur can, 1944- #5197
Coverdale, William H., ingénieur et
    collectionneur can, 1801-1865 #258 259
– collection, Archives publiques du Canada
    (Ottawa, Ont) #12 3230
Covit, Linda, artiste et conservatrice can,
    1948-
– entrevue sur la galerie Powerhouse
    (Montréal, Qué) #1557
Cowichan (Ile de Vancouver, CB), Marshall
    House

– architecture #8695
Cowichans
– filage #3796
– tricot #3882 3929
– tricot et vannerie #4027
Cowin, Jack I., artiste can, 1947- #5199
– expositions
– (1975) #5198
Cowley, Reta Madeline, artiste can, 1910-
#5200 5201
– expositions de groupe
– (1971) #1920
Cox, Elford Bradley, sculpteur can, 1914-
#5202
– professeur de George Pratt #6916
– théories sur l'art et l'architecture #8235
Cox, George Albertus, homme d'Etat can,
1840-1914
– Senator Cox's Mausoleum, Mount Pleasant
Cemetery (Toronto, Ont) #8894
Cox, Palmer, artiste can aux EU, 1840-1924
– illustrations #916
Coyne, Michael, artiste can, 1950-
– expositions de groupe
– (1980) #1221
Cozic, Yvon, artiste can, 1942-
– entretien #1485
– expositions
– (1974) #5203
– (1977) #5204
– expositions de groupe
– (1981) #1564
Craft Dimensions Artisanales, périodique can
#2116
Craftsman, périodique can #2257
Craftsman, The/Artisan, L', périodique can
#2113
Craig, John, artiste can, 1804-1854
– membre de la Toronto Society of Arts
#1689
Craig, Kate, artiste can, 1947-
– expositions de groupe
– (1979) #1157 2070
– (1980) #687
Craig, Zeidler & Strong, agence can
d'architecture
– Ajax (Ont), Ajax Municipal Building #7694
– Hamilton (Ont), McMaster University
Health Sciences Centre #9035 9036 9037
– Toronto (Ont)
– Harbour City #8062
– Place de l'Ontario #9113 9114 9115
Craig & Kohler, agence can d'architecture
– Ottawa (Ont), Centre municipal d'Ottawa
#9101
Cram, Goodhue & Ferguson, agence amér
d'architecture
– Halifax (NE), All Saints' Cathedral #8773
Cram, Ralph Adams, architecte amér,
1863-1942
– influence sur architecture néo-gothique au
Canada #7724
Crane, C.Howard, architecte amér,
1885-1952
– Toronto (Ont)
– Allen Theatre #9069
– New Princess Theatre #9069
– Winnipeg (Man), Allen Theatre #9074
Crang & Boake, agence can d'architecture
– Toronto (Ont), magasin Holt Renfrew
#8078
– Waterloo (Ont), University of Waterloo.
Résidence des étudiants #9467
Cranmer, Doug, sculpteur can, 1927- #4121

– sculptures, Totem Park (Vancouver, CB)
#4118 4124
Craven, David, artiste can, 1946-
– collages #5208
– expositions
– (1977) #5205
– (1978) #5206
– expositions, critiques #639
– expositions de groupe
– (1975) #1809
– (1977) #637
– (1980) #687 708
– (1981) #710
– oeuvres (1975-1978) #5207
Crawford, Julia Tilley, artiste can, 1896-1968
#1173
Crawford, Lenore, critique d'art can, 1909-
– commentaire sur l'art canadien #112
Création (Montréal, Qué) #1492
Creative Source, périodique can #912
créativité
– artistes canadiens, XXe s. #594 665
– Frenkel, Vera, commentaire #5522
– Harris, Lawren Stewart, commentaire
#5715 5722
– Hodgson, Tom, commentaire #5814
– Shadbolt, Jack Leonard, commentaire
#7181
crécelles . Bella-Coolas
– crécelles en forme de corbeau #4026
crécelles . Cris #3363
crécelles . Haidas
– crécelles en forme de corbeau #4026
crécelles . Indiens de la côte nord-ouest
#3866 3977
– crécelles en forme de bec de macareux
#3960
– crécelles en forme de corbeau #3980 4014
crécelles . Iroquois #3489
– pipes-crécelles, Royal Ontario Museum
(Toronto, Ont) #3644
crécelles . Kwakiutls
– crécelles en forme de corbeau #4026
crécelles . Naskapis #3363
crécelles . Niskas
– crécelles en forme de corbeau, Bryan Peel
#6788
crécelles . Nootkas
– crécelles en forme de corbeau #4026
crécelles . Onneiouts #3363
crécelles . Potéouatamis
– Parry Island Reservation (Ont) #3540
crécelles . Saulteux #3363
crécelles . Saulteux/Ojibwa #3363 3539 3540
crécelles . Tlingits #3363 3976
– crécelles en forme de corbeau #4026
– utilisation de cheveux humains #3917
Crespin, Antoine, prêtre can, XVIIIe s.
– inventaires des maisons de l'île d'Orléans
(1761-1767) #8613
Cresswell, Samuel Gurney, officier de la
marine brit, artiste au Canada, 1827-1867
#258 259
Cresswell, William Nichol, artiste can,
1822-1888
– expositions de groupe
– (1978) #1726
Crête, Alphida, photographe can, actif 1981
#1562
Crichton, Daniel, artisan verrier can, 1946-
– et Sheridan College School of Crafts and
Design (Mississauga, Ont) #2440
crin de cheval . Hidatsas
– ouvrages en piquants de porc-épic #3701

crin de cheval . Mandans
– ouvrages en piquants de porc-épic #3701
Cris
– art #3731 4141
– (1830-1930) #3734
– assemblages de rochers #3688
– costume #3739
– culture #3402 3651 3655 3742
– écorce de bouleau #3573
– effigie du Grand Manitou #3724 3726
– étuis à fusils #3713
– instruments de musique #3363
– ouvrages en piquants de porc-épic #3745
– ouvrages perlés #3696 3719 3729 4077
– peinture, XXe s. #4154
– peinture et sculpture (années 1970) #4133
– peintures, Sanford Fisher #5445
– pétroglyphes #3439
– photographies, Edward Sheriff Curtis
#3399
– pictogrammes #3760
– pipes #3662
– raquettes #2812
– récipients #4078
– tatouage #3723
– tipis #3663 3735
Cris de l'Est
– huttes en tourbe #3609
Crisp, Arthur Watkins, artiste can, 1881-1974
– expositions, critiques #211
– illustrations #916
Crist, Lela Gurnee, artiste can, active années
1950- #5209
Criteria, périodique can #564
– (années 1970) #3310
critique d'art
– voir art . théorie et critique
critiques d'art
– voir historiens et critiques d'art
Croft, Lewis Scott, artiste can, 1911-
– réflexion sur son oeuvre #5210
croix
– voir aussi calvaires; crucifix
croix . Canada
– croix funéraires en fer
– Ontario #2709
– Québec #2716
– croix pectorale, William Maurice
Carmichael #5003
– Montréal (Qué), Mont-Royal #7899
– Ottawa (Ont), Musée national de
l'Homme. Centre canadien d'études sur la
culture traditionnelle #963
– Québec #1292 1569 1609 1619 1637 1640
– offrande votive #1621
– ouvrages de ferronnerie #2702
– XVIIe-XVIIIe s. #1320
– Québec, Nouveau-Brunswick, Manitoba,
oeuvres d'artistes canadiens-français
#1625
– Rimouski (Qué) #8872
Crone-Findlay, Noreen, artiste can, active
1981
– entretien #5211
Cross, John, artiste can, XXe s. #4169
Crow, James, sculpteur amér, actif 1940
– masques de la Société des Faux Visages
#4113
Crowell, Ivan Herbert, tisserand can, actif
années 1940-1960
– Legends on Tapestries, série d'expositions
#5296
Crows
– couvertures #3752

Croydon, Peter, photographe can, 1924-
#1036
crucifix
– *voir aussi* croix
crucifix . Canada
– Montréal (Qué), église Notre-Dame #6123
– Québec #1585 1638
  – XIXe s. #1605
crucifixion
– *voir* Jésus-Christ, crucifixion
Cruickshank, Robert, orfèvre can, 1748-1808
– oeuvres, Detroit Institute of Arts (Detroit, Mich) #2681 2691
Cruikshank, William, artiste can, 1849-1922 #178 5212
– expositions, critiques #186
– expositions de groupe
  – (1978) #133
– professeur de Frederick Nicholas Loveroff #6329
Cruise, Stephen, artiste can, 1949-
– expositions
  – (1976) #5213
– expositions de groupe
  – (1975) #1809
Crystal, N.B., Glass Co., fabricants de verre (Saint-Jean, NB) #2400
Crystal Glass Co., fabricants de verre (Sapperton, CB) #2423
cubisme
– et Alfred Pellan #6815
– et art vidéo #654
– et Bertram Richard Brooker #4925
– et David Craven #5207
– et Jack Leonard Shadbolt #7188
– et Jean-Philippe Dallaire #5238
– et Jock Macdonald #6379
– et Lawren Phillips Harris #5711
– et Paul-Vanier Beaulieu #4652
– et peinture canadienne, Première Guerre mondiale #1075
– et Pierre Gendron #5581
– et Raymonde Godin #5623
– et Robert Gray Murray #6668
cubiste-réalisme
– *voir* précisionnisme
Cuhaci, Edward J., architecte can, 1930-
– Ottawa (Ont), Saint Michael and All Angels Church #8766
cuillers . Canada
– cuiller-souvenir, Royal Ontario Museum. Collection Shepley (Toronto, Ont) #2652
cuillers . Haidas #3782
cuillers . Iroquois
– cuillers en ramure sculptée #3524
cuivre . Canada
– façades de magasins (années 1920) #9364
– guide pour collectionneurs #2252
– XIXe s. #2704
cuivres . Amérindiens
– préhistoire #3401
cuivres . Haidas
– *Great Killer Whale Copper* #4054
– monstre marin #3821
cuivres . Indiens de la côte nord-ouest #4065 4071
– Ottawa (Ont), Musée national de l'Homme #3924
cuivres . Skeenas
– pictogramme, Skeena River (CB) #3822
cuivres . Tagish #4106
cuivres . Tlingits #3812 4106
cuivres . Tutchonis #4106
Cullen, Garry, photographe can, 1954-

– expositions de groupe
  – (1978) #2067
Cullen, Maurice Galbraith, artiste can, 1866-1934 #302 1143 1382 5215 5217 5218 5219 5220 5222 5224
– et Académie royale des arts du Canada #152
– et Arts Club (Montréal, Qué) #1314
– et Edmond Dyonnet #5347 5349
– et Marc-Aurèle de Foy Suzor-Coté #7295
– et modernisme #27 383
– et nationalisme dans l'art #143
– et peinture canadienne #18
– et Robert Wakeham Pilot #6869
– expositions
  – (1956) #5221
– expositions, critiques #204 211 306 1316 5216
– expositions de groupe
  – (1935) #17
  – (1977) #1278 1279
– influence de l'impressionnisme #227
– influence sur André Charles Biéler #4725
– influence sur Groupe des Sept #5223
– influence sur Robert Wakeman Pilot #6872
– membre du Canadian Art Club #193
– Morrice, James Wilson, commentaire #6622
– paysages d'hiver #285 5214
– professeur d'Anne Douglas Savage #7130
Culture Hero, journal can
– et Les Levine #6267
culture populaire
– *voir* culture traditionnelle
Culture vivante, périodique can #1257
Cumberland, Frederic William, architecte can, 1821-1881
– églises ontariennes #8905
– Toronto (Ont) #8056 8059 8075
  – University of Toronto. University College #7697 9428 9429 9449 9453 9475 9482
Cumberland & Storm, agence can d'architecture
– Ottawa (Ont), édifices du Parlement #8930
– Toronto (Ont) #8055
  – Osgoode Hall #9002 9003
Cumberland Sound (TNO)
– artefacts thuléens #4367
– culture inuit #4320
Cupit, William Henry, photographe can, 1946- #2071
Curnoe, Gregory Richard (Greg), artiste can, 1936- #5226
– cartes géographiques, illustrations #561
– commentaire sur ses études en art #470
– écrits #92 536
– emploi de documentation orale #608
– entretien #5230
– et nationalisme dans l'art #102 143
– et régionalisme dans l'art #567 5225
– expositions
  – (1969) #5227
  – (1975) #5228
  – (1976) #5229
  – (1981) #5231
– expositions, critiques #520 5233
– expositions de groupe
  – (1967) #490
  – (1979) #510
– images verbales #78
– influence sur art, London (Ont), (années 1960) #1791
– oeuvres (années 1960-1980) #5232
– perception visuelle #525

– réflexion sur l'art canadien
  – (années 1960) #478
  – (années 1970) #620
– thème de la mort #1759
Currelly, Charles Trick, conservateur can, 1876-1957
– autobiographie #3139
– directeur, Royal Ontario Museum (Toronto, Ont) #3170
Currelly, Judith, artiste can, 1946- #5234
Curry & Sparling, agence can d'architecture
– Toronto (Ont), G.J. Foy Company Building #9332
Curtin, Walter, photographe can, 1911- #1054
Curtis, Edward Sheriff, photographe amér, 1868-1952
– expositions
  – (1979) #3480
– photographies et écrits, Amérindiens #3399
Cusack, Stephen, artiste (vitrail), XIXe s.
– vitraux, maison Gregory (Saint-Jean, NB) #8545
Cuthbert, James, Can, m. 1798
– Berthierville (Qué), chapelle Cuthbert #8881
Cuthbertson, George Adrian, artiste amér, 1900-1969
– peintures, navires et combats navals sur les Grands Lacs (1680-1835) #12
Cutter and Power, ébénistes (NE) #2493
Cutting, Lorna, artiste can, 1933-
– expositions de groupe
  – (1977) #1933

D

D'Astous, Roger, architecte can, 1926-
– Beaconsfield (Qué), église Saint Edmund of Canterbury #8840
– Cartierville (Qué), Notre-Dame-du-Bel-Amour #8763
– Laval-sur-le-lac (Qué), habitation #7857
– Montréal (Qué)
  – église Saint-Rémi #8841
  – station de métro Beaubien #9549
  – Village olympique #9127
Dada
– et David Craven #5207
– et Greg Curnoe #5232 5233
– et Jan Burka #4958
– et Ulysse Comtois #5165
Daglish, Peter William, artiste can, 1930- #1418 5235
daguerréotypes . Canada #1039
– Lotbinière, Pierre-Gustave Joly de #6326
– portraits
  – Halifax (NE) #1211
  – provinces maritimes #1171
– Québec #1374
– Toronto (Ont) #1725
– vues urbaines #1061
Dahl, Chris, artiste can, 1948-
– expositions de groupe
  – (1979) #2069
Dahlstrom, Eugene W., artiste can, 1885-1971
– expositions de groupe
  – (1958) #1846
Dair, Carl, artiste can, 1912-1967

– commentaire sur la typographie
  industrielle canadienne (1947) #920
Dakotas
– art #3650 3705 3755
– boucliers #3670
– chronique en images et pictogrammes
  #3747
– écorce de bouleau #3483
– mocassins #3648
– poupées #3733
Dale, Archibald (Archie), artiste can,
  1882-1962
– dessins humoristiques et politiques #957
Dale, Jack, artiste can, 1928-
– entretien #5236
– photographies sculpturales #994
Dale, William S.A. (Bill), conservateur can,
  1921-
– directeur, Galerie nationale du Canada
  (Ottawa, Ont) #3049
Dali, Salvador, artiste esp, 1904-
– Comfort, Charles Fraser, comparaison
  #1115
– influence sur Alfred Pellan #6811 6822
– influence sur Fernand Leduc #6186
Dallaire, François, artiste can, 1947- #5237
Dallaire, Jean-Philippe, artiste can, 1916-1965
  #97 5238 5242 5245 5246 5247
– entretien #5239
– et peinture canadienne #5240
– expositions
  – (1968) #5241
  – (1979) #5244
– expositions de groupe
  – (1958) #431
– murale, hôtel Reine-Elizabeth (Montréal,
  Qué) #8228
– peintures religieuses (1936-1937) #5243
– père de François Dallaire #5237
Dallas (Tex), Dallas Museum for
  Contemporary Arts
– expositions
  – A Canadian Portfolio: The Dallas Museum
    for Contemporary Arts Looks at Art in
    Canada (1958) #429
Dallégret, François, sculpteur can, 1938-
  #1502 5248
– utilisation de la lumière #767
Dally, Frederick, photographe can,
  1838-1914 #5249
– et Victoria Theatre Photographic Gallery
  (Victoria, CB) #2027
– photographies, Indiens de la côte
  nord-ouest #2033 5250
Damoreau, Charles F., artiste amér au
  Canada, actif 1856-1871
– peintures d'animaux #1727
Danby, Kenneth Edison (Ken), artiste can,
  1940- #5251
– athlètes #5252
– dessin de monnaie olympique (1976) #778
– et réalisme #110
– expositions
  – (1980) #5253
– expositions de groupe
  – (1974) #573
  – (1976) #1810
Daniel Knechtel, fabricants de meubles
  (Hanover, Ont) #2463
Danis, Monique Laguerre, artiste can, 1948-
  #1547
danse
– voir aussi ballet
– Canada

– costumes folkloriques #2893
– et art (années 1970) #6676
– et art de performance (années 1970)
  #634
– et Bruce Parsons #6772
– Québec #1258 1259 2879
danse . Algonquiens
– danse du Rêve #3580
danse . Indiens de la côte nord-ouest
– danse du Soleil, photographies, William
  Hanson Boorne #4796
danse . Iroquois
– Six Nations Reserve (Ont) #3598
danse de l'Ours Grizzly . Pieds-Noirs #3681
danse des Esprits . Indiens des plaines
  #3736
danse du Rêve . Algonquiens #3580
Danson, Andrew, photographe can, 1945-
– catalogue de photographies #1053
Daoust, André, architecte can, 1919-
– Montréal (Qué), Stade olympique #9127
Daoust, Sylvia Marie Emilienne, sculpteure
  can, 1902-1974 #739 1380 5254 5257
– entretien #5255
– et Simone Marie Yvette Hudon-Beaulac
  #5856
– influence sur René Thibault #7344
– lauréate, médaille des arts connexes de
  l'Institut royal d'architecture du Canada
  (1961) #5256
Daquin, Pierre, artiste fr (tapisserie), 1936-
– influence sur Andrée Beauregard #4653
Darling, Frank, architecte can, 1850-1923
– Edmonton (Alta), University of Alberta
  #9493
– et John Andrew Pearson #8398
– Halifax (NE), Dalhousie University #9408
– lauréat, Royal Institute of British
  Architects Royal Gold Medal (1915) #8349
  8350 8389
– Toronto (Ont) #8055
  – Holwood Mansion #8667
  – University of Toronto. Trinity College
    #9446 9483
Darling & Pearson, agence can
  d'architecture
– Montréal (Qué)
  – Banque canadienne de commerce #9153
  – édifice Sun Life #9308 9309
– Ottawa (Ont)
  – Departmental and Justice Buildings,
    concours #8921
  – édifices du Parlement #8926
– Toronto (Ont)
  – Art Gallery of Toronto #9076
  – Art Museum of Toronto #9070
  – Banque canadienne de commerce #9178
    9180 9189 9351
  – Banque de Montréal #9155
  – Dominion Bank #9163 9188
  – édifice du Canadien Pacifique #9329
  – Standard Bank #9158
  – Toronto General Hospital #9012 9013
  – Toronto General Hospital. Private
    Patients' Building #9020
  – University of Toronto #9444 9449
    – Convocation Hall #9430
    – Trinity College #9446 9483
– Waterloo (Ont), Mutual Life Assurance
  Company Building #9331
– Winnipeg (Man)
  – Bank of Commerce #9202
  – Banque de Nouvelle-Ecosse #9157 9202
  – Dominion Bank #9188

Darmstadt (Allemagne de l'Ouest),
  Hessisches Landesmuseum
– art amérindien #3464
Dartmouth (NE), Dartmouth Heritage
  Museum
– expositions
  – Albert Franck (1899-1973) in Retrospect: A
    Small Selection from the Artist's Collection
    (1974) #5500
  – Annie D. Savage: Drawings and
    Watercolours (1975) #7129
Daubigny, Charles François, artiste fr,
  1817-1878
– Walker, Horatio, comparaison #306
Daudelin, Charles, artiste can, 1920- #1541
  5259 5260 5263
– entretien #1527
– expositions
  – (1974) #5262
– expositions de groupe
  – (1977) #1622
– sculpture, Centre national des arts
  (Ottawa, Ont) #5261 9108
– sculptures, église paroissiale Saint-Jean
  (Pointe-Saint-Charles, Qué) #5258
Daudelin, Eric, photographe can, 1920-
– entretien #5264
Daudelin, Fernand, artiste can, 1920- #5265
Davenport, Sumner Godfrey, architecte can,
  1877-1956
– Montréal (Qué), Banque Royale du
  Canada #9176
– Ottawa (Ont), Banque du Canada, siège
  social #9337
– Vancouver (CB), Banque Royale #8171
  9179
David, Athanase, fonctionnaire can,
  1882-1953
– fondateur de l'Ecole des beaux-arts #2973
David, Barott, Boulva, architectes associés,
  agence can d'architecture
– Montréal (Qué), Habitat 67 #7694 8575
David, Charles, architecte can, 1890-1962
– Montréal (Qué), école Louis-Hébert #7664
David, David Fleury, sculpteur can,
  1780-1841
– en comparaison avec Noël Levasseur
  #1596
David, Jacques, sculpteur can, 1946-
– emploi du plastique #1603
– Octa #1627
David, Joseph (Joe), artiste can, 1946-
– expositions
  – (1978) #5266
– sérigraphies #4148
David, Louis Basile, sculpteur can, actif 1812
– intérieur, église Saint-Jean (île d'Orléans,
  Qué) #8801
David, Théophile, artiste can, actif 1842
  #1301
David & David, agence can d'architecture
– Montréal (Qué), David & David, bureau
  d'architectes #9299
David Burns Pottery, fabricants de
  céramique (Holmesville, Ont)
– moules #2334
Davidialuk
– voir Amittu, Davidialuk Alasua
Davidson, Beatrice, collectionneuse can, XXe
  s.
– entretien #3219
Davidson, C.D., & Co., agence can
  d'architecture
– Halifax (NE), Aéroport international de

Halifax. Aérogare #9515
Davidson, Robert, artiste can, 1923- #4132
4162 5267 5269
- et Bill Reid #6987
- expositions
 – (1979) #5268
- sculptures d'argilite, Vancouver
 Centennial Museum (Vancouver, CB)
 #4006
Davidson, Robert Charles, artiste can, 1946-
- sérigraphies #4148
Davies, Archibald, artiste, actif 1925
- décoration intérieure, Château Frontenac
 (Québec, Qué) #9278
Davies, Barbara, photographe can, active
 1970 #993
Davies, Thomas, officier de l'armée brit,
 artiste au Canada, 1737-1812 #279 812
 5270 5271
- expositions
 – (1972) #5272
Davis, Leonard, photographe can, 1906-
- catalogue de photographies #991
Davis, Olea Marion Montgomery, sculpteur
 can, 1899-
- sculpture de jardin #1849
Davis, Theodore Russell, artiste amér au
 Canada, 1840-1894
- dans provinces de l'Ouest #1859
Davis, William L., collectionneur can, 1905-
- protecteur d'Albert Henry Robinson #7057
Davis (Calif), University of California.
 Richard L. Nelson Gallery
- expositions
 – *Northwest Coast Indian Art from California
 Collections* (1980) #4041
Davison, Betty, artiste can, 1909-
- expositions de groupe
 – (1979) #674
Davison & Porter, agence can d'architecture
- Vancouver (CB), résidence Porter #7679
Dawson, George Mercer, photographe can,
 1849-1901
- collection, art haida #4011
- photographies d'arpentage #1014 1015
 1865
Dawson City (Yukon)
- architecture
 – (1897-1903) #8183
 – Fuller, Thomas William #8367 8368
Dawson City (Yukon), magasin de Madame
 Tremblay
- architecture #9380 9381
Dawson City (Yukon), magasin Winaut
- architecture #9383
Dawson City (Yukon), Palace Grand Theatre
- architecture #9090
Dawson-Watson, John, artiste brit au
 Canada, actif ca 1900 #1312
Day, Bill, artiste can, actif 1973
- art vidéo #2044
Day, Mabel Killam, artiste can, 1884-1961
 #5273
- expositions de groupe
 – (1940) #350
De Angelis, Joseph R. (Joe)
- *voir* Angelis, Joseph R. (Joe) de
De Appel Foundation
- appui au groupe General Idea, bande
 vidéo *Test Tube* (1979) #692
De Belleval, Jean Fournier
- *voir* Belleval, Jean Fournier de
De Camillis, Laurie
- *voir* Camillis, Laurie de

De Carufel, René, photographe can, 1954-
 #1562
De Casson, Dollier
- *voir* Dollier de Casson
De Charette, colonel
 Athanase-Charles-Marie
- *voir* Charette, colonel
 Athanase-Charles-Marie de
De Chirico, Giorgio
- *voir* Chirico, Giorgio de
De Courcy, Michael John
- *voir* Courcy, Micheal John de
De Fer, Nicholas
- *voir* Fer, Nicholas de
De Heer, Louis-Chrétien
- *voir* Heer, Louis-Chrétien de
De Heusch, Lucio
- *voir* Heusch, Lucio de
De Jong, Simon Leendert
- *voir* Jong, Simon Leendert de
de Kooning, Willem, artiste amér, 1904-
- Ronald, William S., comparaison #7076
De La Joue, François
- *voir* La Joue, François de
De Lery, Gaspard Chaussegros
- *voir* Lery, Gaspard Chaussegros de
De Lotbinière, Pierre Gustave Joly
- *voir* Lotbinière, Pierre Gustave Joly de
De Maisonneuve, Paul de Chomedey
- *voir* Maisonneuve, Paul de Chomedey de
De Morée, Michael
- *voir* Morée, Michael de
De Nevers, Edmond
- *voir* Nevers, Edmond de
De Niverville, Louis
- *voir* Niverville, Louis de
De Passillé-Sylvestre, Micheline
- *voir* Passillé-Sylvestre, Micheline de
De Pédery-Hunt, Dora, sculpteure can, 1913-
 #5275
- dessin de monnaie olympique (1976) #778
- expositions de groupe
 – (1971), médailles #772
De Ramezay, Claude
- *voir* Ramezay, Claude de
De Repentigny, Marie Favery
- *voir* Repentigny, Marie Favery de
De Repentigny, Rodolphe
- *voir* Repentigny, Rodolphe de (Jauran)
De Rouville, Hertel
- *voir* Rouville, Hertel de
De Stijl
- *voir* Stijl, de
De Suria, Tomás
- *voir* Suria, Tomás de
De Tonnancour, Jacques Godefroy
- *voir* Tonnancour, Jacques Godefroy de
De Vasarely, Victor
- *voir* Vasarely, Victor de
De Visser, John
- *voir* Visser, John de
De Volpi, Charles
- *voir* Volpi, Charles de
Deacon, Peter, artiste can, 1945-
- expositions de groupe
 – (1978) #1961
Dean, Max, artiste can, 1949- #5274
- *A Work* et *Pass It On* #714
- expositions de groupe
 – (1977) #1901
 – (1978) #669 2066
 – (1980) #687
Dean, Tom, artiste can, 1947-
- entretien #1489

Deane-Drummond, Sophie
- *voir* Pemberton, Sophia Theresa
Dearle, Duncan W., artiste brit (vitrail), m.
 1954
- verrière, Vancouver (CB) #2458
Dearle, John Henry, artiste brit (vitrail),
 1860-1932
- verrière, Vancouver (CB) #2458
Debassige, Blake, artiste can, 1956- 4157
- expositions de groupe
 – (1981) #4173
décoration architecturale
- *voir aussi* balustrades; clôtures
décoration architecturale . Canada
- Montréal (Qué)
 – architecture domestique #8620
 – XIXe s. #8612
- motifs, thèmes canadiens
 – (années 1930) #8225
 – édifices de la Banque de
 Nouvelle-Ecosse (années 1930) #9186
- Ontario, style tarabiscoté, XIXe s. #8002
 8005
- Québec (1650-1925) #1592
- Toronto (Ont), façades de magasins
 (années 1920) #9364
- utilisation de la peinture, Ontario XIXe s.
 #8013
- utilisation de thèmes canadiens, motifs
 (années 1930) #8226
- utilisation du bronze et d'ouvrages de
 ferronnerie (années 1910) #8222
- utilisation du plâtre, début XXe s. #8221
- Winnipeg (Man), Birks Building #9355
décoration intérieure
- *voir aussi* décoration intérieure . Art
 nouveau; décoration intérieure . style
 victorien; draperies; papier peint;
 rembourrage
décoration intérieure . Canada
- (1890-1900) #190
- (années 1920) #7960
- (années 1960), décorateurs-ensembliers et
 fabricants #9324
- Colombie-Britannique, habitations #8712
- Direction des parcs nationaux, politique
 de reconstruction de bâtiments historiques
 #7758
- trains, gares et hôtels #3281
- universités (années 1960) #9402
décoration intérieure . style Art nouveau
- Canada, sociétés ferroviaires, hôtels #3281
décoration intérieure . style victorien
- petit salon canadien (1870-1890) #2129
décors
- *voir* scénographie
déesse de la mer . Inuit #4312 4376
Degas, Hilaire Germain Edgar, artiste fr,
 1834-1917
- influence sur Lillian Freiman #5517
DeGeay, Jacques, prêtre can, 1717-1774
- correspondance, Gilles Bolvin #4782
Deguise (dit Flamand), Jacques, constructeur
 can, 1697-1780 #269 270
Deichmann, Erica, céramiste can, 1914-
 #2144 2376 2377 2380
- et art, Saint-Jean (NB), (années 1940) #1170
Deichmann, Kjeld, céramiste can, 1900-1963
 #2144 2376 2377 2380
- et situation de l'art à Saint-Jean (NB),
 (années 1940) #1170
- réflexion sur son oeuvre #349
Del Mistro, Walter
- *voir* Mistro, Walter del

Delacroix, Eugène, artiste fr, 1798-1863
– influence sur Marc-Aurèle de Foy
  Suzor-Coté #7297 7300
Delahaye, Guy
– *voir* Lahaise, Guillaume
Delamarre, Elzéar, prêtre can, ca 1854-1925
– et Charles Edouard Huot #5877
Delaroche, Paul, artiste fr, 1797-1856
– professeur d'Alfred Boisseau #4768 4769
Delaunay, Jules Elie, artiste fr, 1828-1891
– professeur de Maurice Galbraith Cullen
  #5217
Delaunay, Robert, artiste fr, 1885-1941
– Curnoe, Greg, comparaison #5233
– Pellan, Alfred, comparaison #6814
DeLauro, Joseph Nicola, sculpteur can, 1916-
– expositions
  – (1981) #5276
Delavalle, Jean-Marie, artiste can, 1944-
– entretien #1485
– expositions de groupe
  – (1973) #557
Delawares
– art #3506
– travail du cuir #3554
Delay, Emile E., architecte can, 1875-1939
– Regina (Sask), War Memorial Museum,
  concours #9073
Delbuguet, René, photographe can, ca 1931-
– catalogue de photographies #1023
Delezenne, Ignace-François, orfèvre can,
  1718-1790 #269 270 5277
– oeuvres, en comparaison avec orfèvrerie
  française #2688
– professeur de François Ranvoyzé #1620
Delfosse, Georges, artiste can, 1869-1939
  #302 5279 5280
– en comparaison avec Charles de Belle
  #1385
– peintures, cathédrale
  Saint-Jacques-le-Majeur (Montréal, Qué)
  #5278
Delor, Jean-Baptiste-Antoine
– *voir* Levasseur (dit Delor),
  Jean-Baptiste-Antoine
Delrue, Georges, joaillier can, 1920- #2694
  2701 5281 5282
Delta (CB)
– architecture #8147
Delvaux, Paul, artiste belge, 1897-
– influence sur Alex Colville #5151
Delville, Jean, artiste belge, 1867-1953
– influence sur Graham Metson #6523
Demaine, Martin, artisan verrier can, ca
  1943- #2440
Demasso, Michel-François, artiste fr,
  1654-1679/1702
– influence sur Antoine-Sébastien
  Plamondon #6886
Demers, Claude, photographe can, actif 1981
– photographies et poèmes #1065 1066
Demers, Jean-Antoine, artiste can, 1931-
  #5283
Demers, Jérôme, prêtre et artiste can,
  1774-1853 #1231
– écrits, influence sur François et Thomas
  Baillairgé #8880
– influence sur architecture québécoise
  #7874
– influence sur Thomas Baillairgé #8327
  8328
Demers, Maurice, artiste can, 1936- #1502
  5284
Denault, Pierre, artiste can, actif 1974

– membre du Centre communautaire
  catholique Tour de David
  (Saint-Basile-le-Grand, Qué) #1510
Denéchaud, Simone, artiste can, 1905-1974
  #1380
– expositions de groupe
  – (1940) #350
Denis, Maurice, artiste et auteur fr,
  1870-1943
– cité dans une étude sur la peinture
  religieuse au Québec (années 1940) #1384
– professeur d'André Charles Biéler #4725
– professeur de Paul-Emile Borduas #4841
  4843 4850
Denison's Mills (Qué)
– architecture #7884
Denison & Stephenson, agence can
  d'architecture
– Toronto (Ont), Temple-Pattison Building
  #9332
Dennis, Eva A., artiste can, 1904- #1881
– expositions de groupe
  – (1975) #1927
Dennis, Wesley Clare (Wes), artiste can,
  1899- #1881 1927
Denniston, Stan, photographe can, 1953-
– expositions, critiques #1067
Denny, Marion, joaillière can, active 1975
  #2706
Dent, J.M., éditeur
– illustrations, Illingworth Holey Kerr #6048
dentelle . Canada
– Québec, XVIIe-XVIIIe s. #2187 2200
Denver (Colo), Denver Art Museum
– art, Indiens de la côte nord-ouest #3918
– art autochtone #3479
– expositions
  – *American Indian Art Before 1850* (1965)
    #3431
  – *Objects of Bright Pride: Northwest Coast
    Indian Art from the American Museum of
    Natural History* (1978) #4024
– *Robes of White Shell and Sunrise* (1974) #3453
Derouin, René, artiste can, 1936- #5285
Déry, François, artiste can, 1941-
– utilisation de la lumière #767
Des Rochers & Dumont, agence can
  d'architecture
– Chomedey (Qué), église Saint-Pie X #8840
Desaulniers, Gilles, artisan verrier can, 1935-
  #5286
Desbarats Company, imprimerie (Montréal,
  Qué)
– et Henri Julien #5985 5990
DesBarres, Joseph Frederick Wallet, officier
  de l'armée brit, artiste au Canada,
  1722-1824 #812
Descartes, René, philosophe fr, 1596-1650
– Kennedy, Garry Neill, comparaison #6043
Deschevery (dit Maisonbasse), Jean-Baptiste,
  orfèvre can, ca 1695-ca 1745 #249 250
– oeuvres, en comparaison avec orfèvrerie
  française #2688
DesClayes, Berthe, artiste can, 1877-1968
– expositions de groupe
  – (1978) #133
DesClayes, Gertrude, artiste can, 1879-1949
– expositions de groupe
  – (1978) #133
design
– Buchanan, Donald William, commentaire
  #3325
– Fleming, Allan Robb, commentaire #5456
Design Awards, périodique can

– (1953-1958) #2609
design canadien
– (années 1920), et art amérindien #3408
– (années 1940) #851 2604
– (années 1950) #2607
– (années 1960) #867 2613 2619 9324
– (années 1970) #907 2620 2622
– Art Directors' Club of Toronto #854
– et Donald William Buchanan #3325
– périodiques
  – *Canadian Design/Design canadien* #2625
– publicité #904
  – (années 1950) #860
  – (années 1960) #868
– Québec (années 1970) #2205 2211
– textiles et tissus (années 1940) #2722
– Toronto (Ont), Ontario College of Art
  #3009
Design canadien/Canadian Design, périodique
  can #2625
Design Collaborative Montreal Ltd., studio
  can de graphisme #878 882 885
design industriel . Canada
– (1947) #2602
– (1948-1958) #2611
  – Association des designers industriels du
    Canada #2612
– (1961-1973), Conseil national de
  l'esthétique #2624
– (1967), opération Esthétique-Canada 67
  #2616 2617
– (1970), Centre d'esthétique industrielle,
  fermeture (Montréal, Qué, et Toronto,
  Ont) #2621
– (années 1940) #2600 2601 2603 2604
  – recommandations #353
– (années 1950) #2605 2606 2607 2608 2609
  2610
– (années 1960) #2614 2615
  – articles de maison #2619
  – influence de la Galerie nationale du
    Canada (Ottawa, Ont) #3039
– (années 1970) #610 2620 2622 2626
– Académie royale des arts du Canada #2
– Alberta (1970s) #1951
– Bersudsky and Associates #4711
– et architecture (années 1960) #8231
– et Donald William Buchanan #3325
– Montréal (Qué), Expo '67 #2618
– Ottawa (Ont), Galerie nationale du
  Canada. Centre d'esthétique industrielle
  (1953-1954) #3033
– Québec #2190
  – (années 1960) #2195
  – fin XIXe s. #2598
Désilets, Antoine, photographe can, 1927-
  #5287 5288
Desmarais, Gabriel (Gaby), photographe
  can, 1927-
– commentaire sur l'art du portrait #624
Desmoulins, Jean-Baptiste
– *voir* Maillou (dit Desmoulins),
  Jean-Baptiste
Desnoyers, Charles, sculpteur can, 1806-1902
  #1578
Desnoyers, Maurice, architecte can, 1927-
– Montréal (Qué), Autostade #9101
Desrochers-Drolet, Françoise, céramiste et
  émailleuse can, 1921- #2378 5289
Desrosiers, Madeleine, artiste can, active
  1936 #1380
Dessaillant (dit Richeterre), Michel, artiste
  can, actif 1701-1723 #234 235 1323 1363
  5290

– portraits de membres du clergé #1333
dessin
– *voir aussi* carnets à dessins; graffiti
– Ottawa (Ont), Galerie nationale du
   Canada #3061
dessin, techniques
– *voir* matériaux et techniques . dessin
dessin . Canada
– (années 1850) #1692
– (années 1890-1940) #367
– (années 1950) #429
– (années 1960) #464 486 487
– (années 1960-1970) #532
– (années 1970) #595 607 638
– Alberta #1954 1968
– Colombie-Britannique (1845-1871) #2020
   2023
– début XXe s., en comparaison avec école
   de Barbizon #497
– Groupe des Sept #1736 1755
– Montréal (Qué)
   – (années 1960) #1427
   – Université McGill. musée McCord #222
      223
– Ottawa (Ont), Archives publiques du
   Canada. collection William H. Coverdale
   #12 3230
– Prairies #1855
– Québec
   – (1975-1980) #1565
   – surréalisme #1470
   – XXe s. #1520 1523
– Québec (Qué), Séminaire des jésuites
   #2982
– réalisme #1810
– Saskatchewan (années 1970) #1933
– scènes de guerre #1092 1093 1096 1097
   1099 1111 1112
– Toronto (Ont), Royal Ontario Museum,
   XVIIIe-XIXe s. #247
– Winnipeg Sketch Club #1887
– XIXe s.-années 1920 #11
– XIXe-XXe s. #48 154 155
– XVIIe-XIXe s. #232
– XVIIIe-XIXe s. #246
– XXe s. #146
dessin . Etats-Unis
– (années 1960-1970) #532
dessin . Indiens des plaines #3709
dessin . Inuit
– (1964), Baffin Island (TNO) #4194
– (années 1960), Cape Dorset (TNO) #4189
dessin d'après nature
– *voir* dessin; nu dans l'art
dessin d'architecture
– et monuments, Melvin Charney,
   commentaire #5091 5092
– Montréal (Qué), Centre canadien
   d'architecture #7749
– Nobbs, Percy Erskine, commentaire #8241
dessin d'architecture . Canada
– (1927-1939), *Exhibition of Architecture and
   the Allied Arts* (Toronto, Ont) #8224
– (1930), Canadian National Exhibition
   (Toronto, Ont) #313
– (années 1850) #1692
– (années 1960) #7984
– Baillairgé, Charles #8324
– Calgary (Alta), University of Calgary.
   Canadian Architectural Archives #7730
   7751
– expositions
   – Independent Art Association #1379
   – *Salon de printemps*, Musée des beaux-arts

(Montréal, Qué), fin XIXe-début XXe s.
   #1228
– Harris, William Critchlow #8372
– Montréal (Qué)
   – Archives nationales du Québec à
      Montréal #8604
   – Ecole des beaux-arts (années 1930) #2973
– Ottawa (Ont), collections privées #8049
– Rattenbury, Francis Mawson #8401
– Toronto (Ont), Archives publiques de
   l'Ontario. John Charles Batstone and Eric
   Crompton Horwood Collection of
   Architectural Drawings #8028 8030
– Toronto Society of Arts #1689
dessins animés
– *voir* animation (cinématographie)
destruction de l'architecture
– *voir* architecture . destruction
Desvallières, Georges, artiste fr, 1861-1950
– influence sur Paul-Emile Borduas #4850
Desy, Louis Arsene, architecte can,
   1856-1924
– Winnipeg (Man), Edifice Cauchon #9361
Detheridge, Allan, artiste can, 1943-
– expositions, critiques #622
Detroit (Mich), Detroit Institute of Arts
– expositions
   – *Les arts du Canada français, 1613-1870*
      (1946) #1331
   – *The Arts of French Canada, 1613-1870*
      (1946) #1330
   – *The French in America, 1520-1880* (1951)
      #216
   – *Traditional Arts of French Canada* (1975)
      #2128
– expositions, critiques
   – *The Arts of French Canada, 1613-1870*
      (1946) #1332
– orfèvrerie québécoise, XVIIe-XIXe s. #2691
– Trakas, George, *Passage*, installation (1972)
   #7419
détroit de Béring (Alaska)
– culture inuit #4318
détroit de Nootka, Vancouver Island (CB)
– vues, fin XVIIIe s. #2002
Deutscher Werkbund
– influence sur architecture canadienne
   #7735
Devenyi, Denes, photographe can, ca 1932-
– catalogue de photographies #987
Deville, Edouard Gaston Daniel,
   photographe can, 1849-1924
– photographies d'arpentage #1014 1015
   1865
– techniques de photogrammétrie en
   arpentage #989 1874 1875
Devine, Harry Torkington, photographe can,
   1865-1938
– et J.A. Brock & Co. (Vancouver, CB) #2021
Devlin, Joyce, artiste can, 1932-
– commentaire sur l'art du portrait #624
Devor, Holly, photographe can, active
   années 1970 #2018
Dewar & Stirling, agence can d'architecture
– et William Critchlow Harris #8371
Dewdney, Edgar, collectionneur et homme
   d'Etat can, 1835-1916
– collection, art amérindien #3454
Dewdney (CB)
– architecture #8147
Dewey, E.H., artiste can, XIXe s.
– peintures d'animaux #1727
diable
– dans art québécois, XVIIe s.-1840 #1357

Diamond, A.J., Associates, agence can
   d'architecture
– Toronto (Ont), Ontario Medical
   Association #8078
Diamond, Jack, architecte can, 1932-
– théories sur l'architecture #7746
Diamond & Myers, agence can
   d'architecture
– Edmonton (Alta)
   – University of Alberta #9495
   – University of Alberta. Students' Union
      Housing #9496
– Toronto (Ont) #8071
   – Ontario Medical Association #9349
   – rénovation des secteurs résidentiels en
      milieu urbain (années 1970) #8068
   – York Square #9347
Diamond Glass Co., fabricant de verre
   (Montréal, Qué)
– acquisition d'autres fabricants de verre
   #2429
– verre, motifs (1902-années 1930) #2411
Diamond Glass Co., fabricant de verre (NE)
   #2409 2416
Diaz de la Pena, Narcisse Virgile, artiste fr,
   1807-1876
– influence sur Homer Ransford Watson
   #7531
Dickey, Estelle, photographe can, née ca
   1898 #2018
Dickinson, Anson, artiste can, 1779-1852
– miniatures #1377
Dickinson, famille can, XIXe s.
– portraits, Nelson Cook #5170
Dickinson, Peter Allgood Rastall, architecte
   can, 1923-1961
– Montréal (Qué), Banque de commerce
   canadienne impériale #9194
– Toronto (Ont) #8057
Dickson, Alan, sculpteur can, 1937-
– expositions de groupe
   – (1978) #786
Dickson, Jennifer, artiste can, 1936- #5291
dictionnaires et encyclopédies
– artistes canadiens #81
– artistes inuit #4252 4301
   – Pelly Bay (TNO) #4221
– graphistes inuit #4497
– peintres et graveurs canadiens, XVIIe-XIXe
   s. #236
Dieudonné, Jacques, sculpteur can, 1949-
   #1626
Dignam, Mary Ella, artiste can, 1860-1938
– commentaire sur l'enseignement de l'art
   #2958
– commentaire sur vues de Peel County
   (Ont), collection William Perkins Bull
   #3208
– peinture sur porcelaine, service de table
   officiel du Canada (1898) #2333
Dikeakos, Christos, artiste can, 1946-
– expositions de groupe
   – (1971) #2042
Dille, Lutz, photographe can, 1922- #990
   5292
– catalogue de photographies #987
Dillon, Gera, photographe can, 1945-
– catalogue de photographies #1023 1032
Dilworth, Ira, auteur can, 1894-1962
– et Emily Carr #5045
Dimson, Theo, artiste can, 1930-
– commentaire sur ses études en art #470
– design typographique #932
Dine, Jim, artiste amér, 1935-

– Ayot, Pierre, comparaison #4572
Dineen Construction Ltd.
– Halifax (NE), maison West, rue Brunswick #8537
Dinel, Pierre Rolland, sculpteur can, 1919-
– sculptures, Place des Arts (Montréal, Qué) #5293
Dinsmore, Edward Jackson, artiste can, 1885-1936
– illustrations #916
Dion, Antoine, céramiste can, actif années 1850-1890 #2345
Dion, Daniel, artiste can, 1958-
– art de performance #655
Dion, famille, céramistes can, années 1850-1920
– et atelier de poterie Dion (L'Ancienne-Lorette, Qué) #2298 2322 2345
Dion, Jean-Baptiste, céramiste can, actif années 1850-1890 #2345
Dionne, Rose, artiste can, active 1936 #1380
Disney, Walt, cinéaste amér, 1901-1960
– influence sur Glen Loates #6310
Disraëli (Qué)
– vues photographiques #1513
Disraëli (Qué), Comité culturel de Disraëli
– expositions
– *De la figuration à la non-figuration dans l'art québécois* (1977) #1461
dissertations
– *voir* thèses
district d'Ungava (Qué)
– Naskapis et culture Inuit (années 1880) #3379
Dixon, Pat, sculpteur can, actif 1978
– entretien #5294
Doan, Ebenezer, constructeur et ébéniste can, 1772-1866 #8351 8352
Doan, John, constructeur et ébéniste can, 1768-1852 #8351 8352
Dobereiner, John Philip, artiste can, 1920-
– expositions
– (1978) #5295
Dobush, Peter, collectionneur can, 1908-
– collection, Winnipeg Art Gallery (Winnipeg, Man) #3221
Dobush, Stewart, Bourke, agence can d'architecture
– Montréal (Qué), Université McGill. McLennan and Redpath Library #9046
documents canadiens
– XVIIe-XIXe s. #232
Dodgson, Campbell, historien d'art et administrateur de musée brit, 1867-1948
– commentaire sur Walter Joseph Phillips #6856
Doerrié, Gerhard, artiste can, 1936-
– associé, Paul Arthur and Associates #873
– commentaire sur ses études en art #470
Doig, M. et Mme D.R., collectionneurs can, XXe s.
– collection, peinture canadienne #3224
Dojc, Yuri, photographe can, 1946-
– catalogue de photographies #1023
Dollard des Ormeaux, Adam, officier de l'armée française au Canada, 1635-1660
– monument, Alfred Laliberté #1623
– monument, Carillon (Qué) #1591
Dollier de Casson, François, prêtre et historien can, 1636-1701
– et Claude Baillif #8329
– et histoire de Montréal (Qué) #7899
domaines
– *voir* châteaux et maisons de campagne

Dominicains
– et Jean-Philippe Dallaire #5243 5247
Dominion Bank
– banques (années 1870-1930) #9188
Dominion Glass Co., fabricants de verre (Wallaceburg, Ont) #2401
Dominion Grocery and Fruit Journal, périodique can
– et James Lovell Wiseman #7603
Dominion Housing Act Competition
– prix et récompenses (1938) #8739
Dominion Housing Act Small House Competition
– prix et récompenses (1936) #8736
Dominion Textile Co., fabricants de textile (Montréal, Qué)
– textiles et tissus, motifs, Claire Miron #6571
Domville, Paul, architecte can aux Etats-Unis, actif 1914-1922
– architecture domestique #8496
Don Bridge Pottery, fabricant de céramique (Toronto, Ont) #2310
Don Mills (Ont)
– construction de logements, relations entre architectes et constructeurs (années 1950) #8301
Don Mills (Ont), Beth-El Synagogue
– architecture, Mendelow & Keywan and Henry Fliess #8903
– murale, *Out of Bondage*, Aba Bayefsky #4632
Don Mills (Ont), centre commercial
– architecture, John B. Parkin Associates #7679
Don Mills (Ont), Chatham Village
– architecture, James A. Murray et Henry Fliess #8511
Don Mills (Ont), Ortho Pharmaceutical, usines et bureaux
– architecture, John B. Parkin Associates #7679
Don Mills (Ont), South Mills Village
– architecture, James A. Murray et Henry Fliess #7679
Donaldson, Francis, architecte can, 1921-
– Annacis Island (CB), Annacis Industrial Estate #7679 9241
Donaldson, Margery Rogers, artiste can, 1926-
– *Legends on Tapestries*, série d'expositions #5296
Donoahue, James Thomas (Jim), artiste can, 1934-
– design typographique #932
– directeur artistique, Cooper and Beatty Ltd. #5297
– et Burns, Cooper, Donoahue, Fleming & Company Ltd. #904
Donoghue, Lynn, artiste can, 1953-
– expositions de groupe
– (1978) #665
Donovan, Duncan, photographe can, 1857-1933 #5298 5299
Doon (Ont), Doon School of Art
– Onley, Toni, étudiant #6741
Doon Pioneer Village (Ont) #8063
Doray, Audrey Capel, artiste can, 1931- #5300
– entretien #5301
Dorion, Isaac, entrepreneur can, actif 1835
– La Canardière (Qué), maison Garneau #8615
Dorrance, David, céramiste et sculpteur can,

1946-
– expositions de groupe
– (1977) #781
Dorsétiens
– amulettes
– Gulf Hazard (TNO) #4365
– Port-au-Choix (TN) #4354
– artefacts #4238 4331 4336 4342 4346 4347 4351 4373 4377 4378
– Abverdjar (Foxe Basin, TNO) #4333
– Bathurst Island (TNO) #4375
– Button Point (Bylot Island, TNO) #4359
– Cape Dorset (TNO) #4322
– et chamanisme #4361
– Igloolik (TNO) #4337
– Pingerqalik (Foxe Basin, TNO) #4335
– Point Spencer (Alaska) #4374
– symbolisme thérapeutique #3356
– Terre-Neuve #4332
– culture #4379 4380
– masques en bois, Button Point (Bylot Island, TNO) #4356 4357
– pétroglyphes #4344 4362
– sculptures #4350 4358 4364
Dorsey, Frances (Fran), artiste can (tapisserie), 1948-
– entretien #5302
dorure . Canada
– Québec #2930
Dorval (Qué), Aéroport internationale de Montréal. Aérogare
– architecture #9517
– Illsely, Templeton & Archibald; Larose & Larose; William Alexander Ramsay #9515
– murale, Greg Curnoe #5227
Dorval (Qué), Club 230
– restauration, Tolchinsky & Goodz #7776
Dorval (Qué), restaurant La Lanterna Verde
– murale, Giuseppe Fiore #5440
Dostaler, Martin d'Angeville, architecte can, 1846-1915 #1319
Doucet, Louise, céramiste can, 1938- #5303
Doukhobors au Canada
– et Frederick Nicholas Loveroff #6330
– mobilier #2585
– monuments funéraires #733
– ouvrages à l'aiguille #2780
– photographies, Robert Minden #6570
Doull, Mary Allison, artiste can, 1866-1953 #1164
Douville, Raymond, auteur can, 1905-
– commentaire sur Gérard Morisset #3305
Dowler & Michie, agence can d'architecture
– Calgary (Alta) #8116
Downing, Andrew Jackson, architecte amér, 1815-1852
– et Calvert Vaux #8048
Downing, Claire, photographe can, née 1887
– expositions de groupe
– (1976) #2012
Downing, Robert James, sculpteur can, 1935- #5305
– expositions
– (1969) #5304
– (1972) #5306
Downs, Barry Vance, architecte can, 1930-
– entretien #8353
– théories sur l'architecture #7746
– West Vancouver (CB), Woyat-Bowie Building. Bureaux d'architectes #9346
Downs & Archambault, agence can d'architecture
– Vancouver (CB) #8353

– Chinese Cultural Centre, concours #9144
– F.P. 18 (Champlain Place) #8744
– foyer pour paraplégiques #8744
Dr. Brute
– *voir* Metcalfe, Eric W. (Dr. Brute)
Dragu, Margaret, artiste can, 1953-
– expositions de groupe
  – (1980) #687
Drapeau, Jean, homme d'Etat can, 1916-
– commentaire sur la restauration du
  Vieux-Montréal (Montréal, Qué) #7905
– et Stade olympique (Montréal, Qué) #9139
drapeaux
– *voir* bannières et drapeaux
Drapell, Joseph, artiste can, 1940- #711 5307
– expositions de groupe
  – (1981) #722
Draper, Edward, ébéniste can, actif 1749
  #2488
draperies . Canada #2725
Drenters, Yosef G., sculpteur can, 1929-
– sculptures (années 1960) #744 746
Dresden (Allemagne de l'Est), Indianer
  Museum Radebeul
– art amérindien #3430
Drewry, W.S., photographe can, actif
  1880-1890
– photographies d'arpentage, Montagnes
  Rocheuses (années 1880-1890) #1874
droit
– wampum, utilisation comme document
  juridique #3567
droit, architecture et
– *voir aussi* Etat, architecture et
– et conservation
  – Canada (années 1970) #7833
  – Canada (années 1950) #7755
  – Canada (années 1970) #7772
  – Ontario, propriétés de l'Eglise (années
    1970) #8906
  – Ontario (années 1970) #8024
  – Québec (années 1970) #7870
  – St. John's (TN), (années 1970) #7789
  – Winnipeg (Man), (années 1970) #8108
– et destruction de l'architecture, Montréal
  (Qué), (années 1970) #8601
– et matériaux architecturaux, Québec (Qué),
  fin XVIIe s.-années 1920 #7952
– et urbanisme (années 1960-1970) #9302
– Institut royal d'architecture du Canada,
  étude (années 1960) #8309
– Québec, XVIIe-XVIIIe s. #8621
droit, art et
– *voir aussi* droit d'auteur; Etat, art et; faux .
  peinture
– Canada (années 1970) #682
– protection de l'art inuit et de l'art
  amérindien #3347
– Québec (1961-1975) #3280
droit d'auteur
– Canada
  – droits des artistes (années 1970) #682
  – et Front des artistes canadiens #563 632
Drolet, Françoise Desrochers
– *voir* Desrochers-Drolet, Françoise
Drouin, Michèle, artiste can, 1933- #5308
Drué, Juconde, prêtre fr, architecte et artiste
  au Canada, 1664-ca 1739 #234 235
Druik, Don, artiste can, 1945-
– art vidéo #605
– expositions de groupe
  – (1977) #631
Drum, Sydney Maria, artiste can, 1952-
– expositions de groupe

– (1980) #698
Drummond, Arthur Alexander, artiste can,
  1891-
– expositions
  – (1975) #5309
Drummond, George Fairly, architecte can,
  1891-
– Montréal (Qué), hôtel Reine-Elizabeth
  #9286
Drummond, William Henry, poète can,
  1854-1907
– illustrations de poèmes, Frederick
  Simpson Coburn #5123
Drury, Charles Mills, politicien can, 1912-
– et Galerie nationale du Canada (Ottawa,
  Ont) concours (1975-1977) #9126
Du Mond, Frank Vincent, artiste amér,
  1865-1951
– professeur de Robert Elmer Lougheed
  #6327
Du Toit, Roger, architecte can, 1939-
– Toronto (Ont)
  – gare Union #9540
  – Tour du CN #9511
Dub, Eugene N. (Gene), architecte can, 1943-
– Edmonton (Alta), hôtel de ville #8998
– Edmonton (Alta), hôtel de ville, concours
  #8999 9000
Dubois, Jean Baptiste
– *voir* Filiau (dit Dubois), Jean Baptiste
DuBois, Macy, architecte can, 1929-
– théories sur l'architecture #7746
– Toronto (Ont), Central Technical School
  Art Centre #7684
Dubois, Marius, artiste can, 1944- #5310
– expositions
  – (1979) #5311
Dubois, Pierre Gilles, artiste can, 1938- #5312
DuBois, Strong, Bindhart, agence can
  d'architecture
– Toronto (Ont), Joseph E. Shephard
  Government of Canada Building #8975
Dubreuil, Michel, photographe can, 1953-
  #1562
Dubuc, Jacques, artiste can, actif 1974
– membre du Centre communautaire
  catholique Tour de David
  (Saint-Basile-le-Grand, Qué) #1510
Dubuffet, Jean, artiste fr, 1901-
– Simonin, Francine, comparaison #7213
Duburou, prêtre can, XVIIIe s.
– portrait, François Malepart de Beaucourt
  #4646
Duchamp, Marcel, artiste fr, 1887-1968
– influence sur Alan Frank Glass #5616
Duck, Adele, artiste can, 1948- #717
Ducornet, Louis-Joseph-César, artiste fr,
  1806-1856
– portrait de Samuel de Champlain #191
Duff, Wilson, ethnologue can, 1925-1976
– commentaire sur Indiens de la côte
  nord-ouest #4003
– mélange #4049
Dufferin, Lady Harriot Georgiana, brit au
  Canada, 1843-1902
– collection, photographies canadiennes,
  XIXe s. #1048
Dufferin et Ava, Frederick Temple
  Blackwood, 1er marquis de, homme d'Etat
  brit au Canada, 1826-1902
– plans, fortifications de la ville de Québec
  (Qué), (1875) #7946
Duffus, Allan, architecte can, 1915-
– Halifax (NE) #7733

Duffus, Romans, Kundzins & Rounsefell,
  agence can d'architecture
– Halifax (NE), Nova Scotia Technical
  College. Résidence des étudiants #9467
Dufour, Claude, artiste can, 1925- #1546
  1551
Dufour, Gisèle Trottier
– *voir* Trottier-Dufour, Gisèle
Dufour, Marcellin, artiste can, 1946- #1547
Dufresne, Adrien, architecte can, 1904-
– églises québécoises #8334
Dufresne, Hélène Gagné
– *voir* Gagné-Dufresne, Hélène
Dufresne, Marius, ingénieur et arpenteur
  can, 1883-1945
– Montréal (Qué), château Dufresne #1294
  8617 8618
Dufresne, Oscar, industriel can,
  1875-1935/1936
– Montréal (Qué), château Dufresne #1294
  8617
Dugald (Man), Dugald Costume Collection
  #2902
Dugas, Marc, artiste can, 1945-
– fondateur, Atelier de réalisations
  graphiques (Québec, Qué) #1661
Duguay, Raoul, musicien can, 1939-
– poèmes, dessins de Louis-Pierre Bougie
  #4861
Duguay, Rodolphe, artiste can, 1891-1973
  #1393 5313 5315 5316 5319 5320
– autobiographie (1907-1927) #5317
– et Marcel Baril #4608
– expositions
  – (1979) #5318
– gravure sur bois de fil #5314
Dukes, Caroline, artiste can, 1929-
– expositions de groupe
  – (1975) #1867
Dulongpré, Louis, artiste can, 1754-1843
  #1323
– et société québécoise #1375
– expositions de groupe
  – (1959) #219
– influence de la peinture française #1244
– peintures, église de Berthierville (Qué)
  #8874
– portraits
  – Hertel de Rouville, membre de la
    famille #1345
  – McGill, James #5321
Dumas, Antoine, artiste can, 1932- #5322
Dumouchel, Albert, artiste can, 1916-1971
  #824 1453 1665 5323 5324 5325 5326 5329
  5331 5333
– Dallaire, Jean-Philippe, comparaison #5238
– et Jean-Paul Lemieux #5328
– et peinture montréalaise (Qué), (années
  1950) #1403
– et Serge Tousignant #7405
– expositions
  – (1974) #5332
  – (1979) #5334
– expositions, critiques #860 5330
– expositions de groupe
  – (1967) #821
– gravures #1654
– influence sur Janine Leroux-Guillaume
  #6247
– professeur #1641 3001 5327
  – Ecole des arts graphiques (Montréal,
    Qué) #1648
– professeur de Robert Wolfe #7606
Dumouchel, Suzanne, artiste can, 1920-

#5335
Dunbar, Frederick Alexander Turner, artiste
can, 1849-1921
– Wilde, Oscar, commentaire #238
Duncan, Douglas M., artiste, marchand
d'oeuvres d'art et collectionneur can,
1902-1968 #570 3232
– collection, art canadien, XXe s. #119 541
3223
– commentaire sur collections d'oeuvres
d'art canadiennes #3218
– entretien #3219
– et Picture Loan Society (Toronto, Ont)
#1746 1758
Duncan, Helen, céramiste can, active années
1950-1960 #2102
Duncan, James D., artiste can, 1806-1881
#5336
– illustrations, L'album des costumes de
communautés religieuses de femmes au
Canada en 1853 #2834
– relation entre photographie et peinture
#245
Duncan (CB), école publique
– architecture, William Tuff Whiteway #9508
Duncan McNab & Partners, agence can
d'architecture
– Vancouver (CB), Raymur Place Housing
#8520
Duncan S. McNab & Associates, agence can
d'architecture
– Burnaby (CB), Simon Fraser University,
concours #9501
Duncanson, Robert Stuart, artiste can,
1821-1872 #241 242 5337
– expositions
– (1972) #5338
Dundas (Ont)
– (1813-années 1850) #7994
Dunington, Lorrie Alfreda, architecte
paysagiste can, m. 1945
– plan, accès nord-ouest de Hamilton (Ont)
#7962
Dunington-Grubb, Howard Burlingham,
architecte paysagiste can, 1880-1965
– plan, accès nord-ouest de Hamilton (Ont)
#7962
Duplessis, Jacqueline, artiste can (textiles),
1920-
– batik #5339
Dupond, Marcel Jules René, émailleur can,
1907-1954 #5340
Dupont, Chantal, artiste can, 1942-
– expositions
– (1979) #5341
Dupont, Marcel, artiste can, actif 1974
– membre du Centre communautaire
catholique Tour de David
(Saint-Basile-le-Grand, Qué) #1510
Dupras, Robert, artiste can, 1928-
– expositions de groupe
– (1955) #1408
Dupré, Jules, artiste fr, 1811-1889
– professeur d'Atha Haydock Caldwell
#4991
Dupuis, Luce, sculpteure can, 1940- #1632
Dupuis-Maillet, Corinne, artiste can, 1895-
#5342
Duquet, Georges-Henri, artiste can, né 1889
#5343
Duquet, Suzanne, artiste can, 1916- #5344
– et Ecole des beaux-arts (Montréal, Qué),
(1968) #2995
– professeur d'Aline Piché-Whissell #6865

Durand, Luc, architecte can, 1929-
– Montréal (Qué), Village olympique #9127
Durham (Ont), Durham Art Gallery
– expositions
– The Prints of Mary Wrinch (1980) #7618
Durocher, Gabriel, photographe can, actif
1973
– catalogue de photographies #997 999
Düsseldorf (Allemagne de l'Ouest),
Kunsthalle
– expositions
– Alex Colville: Paintings and Drawings,
1970-1977/Alex Colville: Bilder und
Zeichnungen, 1970-1977 (1977) #5153
Dutkewytch, Andrew, artiste can, 1944-
#1512
– expositions de groupe
– (1976) #1529
Dyens, Georges, sculpteur can, 1932- #5345
Dyky, Ivan, artiste can, actif 1918-
– fresques, Church of Saint Nicholas
(Toronto, Ont) #1822
Dynes, Joseph, artiste can, 1825-1897
– et Samuel C. Hawksett #5753
– membre de la Toronto Society of Arts
#1689
Dyonnet, Edmond, artiste can, 1859-1954
#302 1240 5346 5348
– autobiographie #5347 5349
– et Pen and Pencil Club (Montréal, Qué)
#1251
– professeur de Orson Shorey Wheeler
#7549
Dyson, Brian, artiste can, 1944- #5350
– étude sur le musée (institution) #714
e #9900 9901

E

E.B. Eddy Company
– voir Eddy, E.B., Company
E.J. Gaboury and Associates
– voir Gaboury, E.J., and Associates
E.W. Morris Company
– voir Morris, E.W., Company
Eadie, Arthur Hunter, architecte can,
1897-1956
– Toronto (Ont), Banque de Nouvelle-Ecosse
#9193
Eagar, William H., artiste can, 1796-1839
#5351
Eakins, Thomas, artiste amér, 1844-1916
– scènes sportives #5252
East, Benoît, artiste can, 1915- #5352 5353
Eastcott, Robert Wayne, artiste can, 1943-
– entretien #5354
– expositions
– (1976) #2059
Eastlake, Charles Locke, designer et auteur
brit, 1836-1906
– influence sur Jacques & Hay Co. #2559
Eaton, T., Company Limited, magasin can à
grande surface
– Architectural Competition for House
Designs (1936) #8738
– Ideal Ontario Home Competition (1930)
#8735
– magasins (années 1920) #9365
– poupées #2941
– vente par correspondance, catalogues
#2851

– illustrations, Fred Brigden #4913
Eaton, Timothy, homme d'affaires can,
1834-1907
– Eaton Mausoleum, Mount Pleasant
Cemetery (Toronto, Ont) #8895
Eaton, Wyatt, artiste can, 1849-1896 #5355
5356 5357
eau-forte . Canada
– (1885), Association of Canadian Etchers
#798
– (1910), Canadian National Exhibition
(Toronto, Ont) #1
– (années 1910) #799 800
– début XXe s. #28
– Manitoba (1910-1940) #1898
Eberhardt, Nicholas, céramiste can, né 1834,
actif 1863-1879 #2310
Ebring, Axel, céramiste can, XXe s. #2391
Eby, William, céramiste can, 1831-1910
#2356
Ecanada Art Pottery, fabricants de
céramique (Hamilton, Ont) #2359
– (1945-1952) #2353
Echalook, Thomasee, artiste can, 1935-
– gravures sur pierre #4487
Echaluk, Thomassie
– voir Echalook, Thomasee
Echeverria y Godoy, Atanasio, artiste esp au
Canada, actif années 1780-1790
– expédition, côte nord-ouest #1998
Eckerman, Oscar A., architecte amér,
1873-1950
– John Deere Plow Company, entrepôts
#9247
éclairage
– voir aussi lampes
éclairage . Canada
– (années 1940) #2601 2604
– guide pour collectionneurs #2125 2131
– Ontario
– XIXe s. #2245
– XVIIIe-XIXe s. #2918
– Winnipeg (Man), Royal Alexandra Hotel
#2599
– XVIIIe-XIXe s. #2703 2920
éclairage électrique
– voir éclairage
Eco, Umberto, écrivain it, 1932-
– et Max Dean #5274
école d'Ashcan
– voir Eight, The (groupe américain)
école de Barbizon
– et Clarence Alphonse Gagnon #5548
– et dessins paysagistes canadiens, début
XXe s. #497
– et Horatio Walker #7503 7504
– et J.E.H. MacDonald #6370
– et Marc-Aurèle de Foy Suzor-Coté #7299
7302
– et peinture paysagiste canadienne
(1880-1910) #214
– et Robert Harris #5739
– et Tom Forrestall #5466
– peinture, dans collections privées au
Canada #194
école de New York
– et Hans Hofmann #1850
– et Kenneth Campbell Lochhead #6319
Ecole des arts domestiques de
Québec/Quebec School of Handicrafts
(années 1930) #2969
école Quévillon, sculpteurs can, fin
XVIIIe-XIXe s. #1300
– et origines de la sculpture sur bois et de

l'architecture québécoises #1574
– influence sur l'architecture québécoise #7851
– sculpture sur bois #1232 1571 1576
écoles . Canada
– (1908) #9385
– (1960-1970) #7710
– (années 1870) #9384
– (années 1910) #9386 9387 9388
– (années 1920) #7656
– (années 1950) #9391 9393
– recommandations #9390
– (années 1960) #9394 9395 9397 9398 9401 9403 9420
– Colombie-Britannique, bâtiments en bois rond, XIXe-XXe s. #8148
– Duncan (CB), Duncan Public School #9508
– Edmonton (Alta) (1900-1914) #8130
– Frobisher Bay (TNO), Frobisher Academic and Occupational School #8188
– Guelph (Ont), XIXe s. #7970
– Hamilton (Ont)
– (années 1910) #9436
– style victorien #7991
– Indian Education Centre (Alta) #9494
– Kingston (Ont), William Newlands #8392
– Manitoba, XIXe-début XXe s. #8102
– Montréal (Qué)
– (1950-1968) #9422
– (années 1910) #9413
– (années 1950) #9419
– XIXe-XXe s. #9426
– Ontario
– (années 1920) #9450
– bâtiments polygonaux, XIXe s. #7987
– XIXe s. #8006
– Prairies #8080
– provinces de l'Ouest #8083
– (années 1920) #9389
– fin XIXe-début XXe s. #9404
– Québec #9424
– (1919-1923) #9416
– (années 1950) #9418
– (années 1960) #7862
– Scarborough (Ont)
– North Bridlewood Junior Public School #9471
– Stephen Leacock Educational Complex #9476
– Toronto (Ont)
– (années 1920) #9443
– Central Technical School #9434
– John Ross Robertson and Glenholme schools #9437
– Study of Educational Facilities (SEF)
– (1968) #9466
– (1969) #9472
– Trois-Rivières (Qué), (années 1630-1910) #7883
– Vancouver (CB), design d'école élémentaires, concours (1970) #9507
– Winnipeg (Man) #8105
– (1831-1960) #8095
– (1908) #9484
– (années 1880-1910) #8101
– XVIIe-début XIXe s. #7841
– XVIIIe s.-années 1950 #9392
écoles . Etats-Unis
– (années 1960) #9394
– Ouest des Etats-Unis #8083
écologie
– et art, Canada (années 1970) #617
– Seton, Ernest Thompson, commentaire #7172

économie, art et
– Canada
– (1974), Conseil des Arts du Canada, proposition pour l'encouragement des arts par le milieu des affaires d'ici 1980 #3271
– (années 1940) #353
– (années 1960) #529 3265
– (années 1970) #586 619 682 3267 3275 3278 3286 3293
– et Front des artistes canadiens #632
– Inuit #3345 4215 4245 4262 4276 4277 4288
– Ontario (années 1970) #1802
– Québec (années 1970) #2211 2224
écorce de bouleau . Algonquiens #3571 3605
– découpes #3483
– Midéwiwins, parchemins #3702
– récipients #3510 3544
écorce de bouleau . Algonquins
– motif de la double courbe et motif floral #3409
– récipients #3542 4078
écorce de bouleau . Amérindiens
– dessins, motifs #3429
– et poterie amérindienne #3545
– support pour broderie en poil d'orignal #3629
écorce de bouleau . Cris #3573
écorce de bouleau . Dakotas
– découpes #3483
écorce de bouleau . Folles Avoines
– vannerie #3620
écorce de bouleau . Indiens des forêts du Nord-Est
– (années 1760-début XXe s.) #3633
– dessins sur arbres #3527
écorce de bouleau . Iroquois #3605
écorce de bouleau . Micmacs #3643
– récipients #3569
écorce de bouleau . Montagnais
– récipients #4086
écorce de bouleau . Outaouais
– récipients, Southwest Museum (Los Angeles, Calif) #3548
écorce de bouleau . Pentaguets #3537
– récipients #3510
écorce de bouleau . Saulteux/Ojibwa #3539 3551 3557
– Island Lake (Man) #3549
– parchemins #3492 3583 3626
écorce de bouleau . Siouens
– Midéwiwins, parchemins #3702
écorce de bouleau . Têtes-de-Boule
– récipients #4079 4108
Ecossais au Canada
– architecture, XIXe s. #7977
– art, XIXe-XXe s. #133
– poterie, XIXe s. #2339
Ecosse
– vues photographiques, Robin MacKenzie #6393
écriture dans l'oeuvre d'art
– voir aussi poésie visuelle
– Ariss, Margot Phillips #4546
– Curnoe, Greg #5226
– Fischl, Eric #662
écrivains
– voir auteurs
écuries
– voir aussi granges
écuries . Canada
– Montréal (Qué), écuries d'Youville #7905
– Québec, toits, XVIIe-XVIIIe s. #7881
Eddy, E.B., Companie, imprimerie (Hull,

Qué)
– typographie (années 1940) #922
Eden Smith & Sons, agence can d'architecture
– Toronto (Ont)
– D.O. Roblin Warehouse #9234
– University of Toronto. Résidence des hommes #9431
Edenshaw, Albert Edward, artiste can, XIXe s.
– orfèvrerie #5358
Edenshaw, Charles, artiste can, 1839-1920 #4042 4169 5359 5360
– influence sur Bill Reid #6985 6987
– influence sur Robert Davidson #5269
– orfèvrerie #5358
– pierres tombales, figures héraldiques #3995
– sculpture, Vancouver Art Gallery (Vancouver, CB) #3820
– sculptures d'argilite, Vancouver Centennial Museum (Vancouver, CB) #4006
Edenshaw, Charles, artiste can, XXe s. #5358
Edenshaw, Henry, sculpteur can, début XXe s.
– coffrets d'argilite #5361
édifices gouvernementaux
– voir édifices publics
édifices municipaux
– voir édifices publics
édifices préfabriqués . Canada
– Arctic houses (années 1960) #8732
– Vancouver (CB), British Columbia Mills Timber and Trading Company (1904-1910) #8082
édifices publics
– voir aussi bureaux de poste
édifices publics . Canada #7689
– (1880-1914) #7736
– (1911-1912) #8295
– (1960-1970) #7710
– (années 1920) #7656
– (années 1950) #8227
– (avant 1924) #7652
– Alberta (1900-années 1930) #8126
– Charlottetown (IPE), Province House #8937 8938 8939
– Dawson City (Yukon) (1899-1902) #8367 8368
– édifices préfabriqués, provinces de l'Ouest, début XXe s. #8082
– Edmonton (Alta)
– (1900-1914) #8130
– Alberta Government Administrative Building #8963
– édifices du Parlement #8962
– Fredericton (NB), édifice de l'Assemblée #8940 8941
– Guelph (Ont), XIXe s. #7970
– Halifax (NE)
– Lang, George Macdonald #7838
– XVIIIe-XIXe s. #7818
– Hamilton (Ont), style victorien #7991
– Hooper, Thomas #8376
– John B. Parkin Associates #8395
– Kingston (Ont)
– XIXe s. #7995
– XVIIe-XIXe s. #7989
– London (Ont), XIXe s. #8007 8010
– Manitoba, XIXe-début XXe s. #8102
– ministère des travaux publics
– (1840-années 1960) #8976 8977
– (1954-1959) #7681

– (années 1950) #8971
– Montréal (Qué)
– Customs House #7917
– dessins d'architecture, Archives nationales du Québec à Montréal #8604
– Niagara-on-the-Lake (Ont), Navy Hall #8464 8465
– Nouvelle-Ecosse, XVIIe-XIXe s. #7814
– Ontario, XIXe s. #8006
– Ottawa (Ont)
– édifices du Parlement #7695 8921 8922 8924 8925 8927 8928 8930 8931 8932 8933 8934 8935 8936 9055
– édifices du Parlement et édifices connexes #8923
– provinces des Prairies, édifices du Parlement #8944 8945
– Québec
– (1880-1914) #7929
– (années 1960) #7862
– XVIIe s.-années 1940 #7853
– Québec (Qué), Assemblée nationale #8942
– Regina (Sask)
– (années 1910) #8111
– édifices du Parlement #8954 8955 8956 8957 8958 8959 8960 8961
– style néo-gothique #7739 7740
– style Second Empire #7741 7742
– Terre-Neuve #7784
– Toronto (Ont)
– édifices du Parlement (1791-1893) #8943
– Joseph E. Shephard Government of Canada Building #8975
– XIXe s.-années 1930 #8076
– transformation d'édifices publics en établissements culturels #9147 9148
– Trois-Rivières (Qué), (1630s-1910s) #7883
– Victoria (CB), édifices du Parlement #8964 8965 8966 8967
– Winnipeg (Man) #8105
– (années 1880-1910) #8101
– (XIXe s.-1960) #8095
– Palais législatif #8946 8947 8948 8949 8950 8951 8952 8953
édifices publics . Etats-Unis
– édifices de la capitale nationale #8944
– Fitzpatrick, Francis W. #8365
édifices récréatifs
– voir aussi parcs d'amusement; villégiature . bâtiments
édifices récréatifs . Canada
– (années 1950) #9081
– Toronto (Ont)
– Place de l'Ontario #9113 9114
– Sunnyside #8054
– Victoria (CB), Crystal Gardens #9134 9146
Edimbourg (Ecosse), Edinburgh International Festival (1968)
– expositions
– Canada 101 (1968) #514
– expositions, critiques
– Canada 101 (1968) #519 520
Edimbourg (Ecosse), Edinburgh International Festival (1980)
– expositions
– The Legacy: Continuing Traditions of Canadian Northwest Coast Indian Art (1980) #4043
Edimbourg (Ecosse), Royal Scottish Academy
– Cruikshank, William, élève #5212
Edimbourg (Ecosse), Royal Scottish Museum
– artefacts athapascans #4091
– expositions

– Les Athabascans, ces étrangers du Nord: une exposition itinérante formée des collections du Musée national de l'Homme (Canada) et du Royal Scottish Museum (1974) #4104
– The Athapaskans: Strangers of the North; An International Travelling Exhibition from the Collection of the National Museum of Man, Canada, and the Royal Scottish Museum (1974) #4105
– totem, Niskas #3839
édition canadienne
– (années 1970) #619 693 3279
– catalogues d'expositions #3311 3319
– périodiques d'art (années 1970) #3310
Editions Erta, éditeur (Montréal, Qué) #926
– et Roland Giguère #1641
Editions Formart, éditeur (Montréal, Qué)
– expositions, critiques
– (1970) #1490
Editions Goglin, éditeur #926
Editions Lacia, éditeur (Québec, Qué)
– cartes de Nöel #857
Edmond, Pierre, sculpteur can, 1738-1800
– tabernacles #1613
Edmonton (Alta)
– architecture
– (1800-1914) #8130
– (1909) #8117
– centre-ville (années 1970) #8123
– Myers, Barton #8391
– quartier chinois #8137
– architecture domestique, maisons à deux étages (années 1920-1970) #8705
– art
– (années 1920-1980) #1941
– (années 1950-1970) #131
– (années 1960) #441 1848
– (années 1960-1980) #1975
– (années 1970) #1856
– art public (i.e. art dans les lieux publics) #1973
– arts graphiques (années 1970) #1958
– sculpture (années 1960) #1853
– théâtres (1906) #9143
– vues photographiques, Ernest Brown #4935
Edmonton (Alta), aéroport international d'Edmonton
– architecture #9517
Edmonton (Alta), Alberta Government Administrative Building
– architecture, Department of Public Works of the Province of Alberta; Cecil S. Burgess, architecte-conseil #8963
Edmonton (Alta), Archives provinciales de l'Alberta
– photographies, XIXe s., collection Ernest Brown #1949
Edmonton (Alta), Canada Packers Limited
– architecture, Eric Ross Arthur et Anthony Adamson #7973
Edmonton (Alta), Canadiana Galleries
– expositions
– Holman: Recent Sculpture (1981) #4457
Edmonton (Alta), Citadel Theatre
– architecture, Barton Myers; Rick L. Wilkin #8091 9140
Edmonton (Alta), Dominion Bank
– architecture, George W. Northwood #9188
Edmonton (Alta), Duggan House
– restauration, Juan Corkan et Mickey Holland #8729
Edmonton (Alta), édifices du Parlement

– architecture
– Jeffers, Allan Merrick, et John Chalmers #8962
– Jeffers, Allan Merrick, et R.P. Blakey #8944 8945
Edmonton (Alta), Edmonton Art Gallery
– collection de photographies #1051
– expositions
– Alberta '73 (1973) #1942
– Alberta Now (1980) #1969
– Alberta Realists (1974) #1954
– Art in Alberta: Paul Kane to the Present (1973) #1953
– Baker Lake Prints/Estampes (1970) #4473
– Canada X Ten (1974) #565
– Canadian Painting in the Thirties (1975) #592
– Carl Schaefer in Hanover (1980) #7157
– Certain Traditions: Recent British and Canadian Art (1978) #653
– Changing Visions: The Canadian Landscape/Aperçus divers: le paysage canadien (1976) #617
– Chester & Bentham: An Exhibition of Recent Paintings by D.T. Chester and Recent Sculpture by Douglas Bentham (1973) #1858
– Christopher Pratt (1971) #6910
– Claude Tousignant (1974) #7401
– Conceptual Decorative: Prints by Les Levine, 1965-1970/Conceptuel décoratif: estampes de Les Levine, 1965-1970 (1972) #6265
– Dan Christensen: Recent Paintings (1973) #5104
– David Craven: Recent Works (1978) #5205
– David Milne: The New York Years, 1903-1916 (1981) #6567
– Diversity: Canada East (1972) #543
– Dorothy Knowles (1973) #6067
– Drawings and Pastels c. 1930-1967 by Miller Gore Brittain (1969) #4917
– Drawings by Jack Weldon Humphrey: A Travelling Exhibition Organized by the Beaverbrook Art Gallery, Fredericton, New Brunswick, Canada, 1977-1979 (1979) #5871
– Edmonton Collects: l: Canadian Art (1973) #105
– Edward Curtis in the Collection of the Edmonton Art Gallery (1979) #3480
– Emily Carr: Oil on Paper Sketches (1979) #5046
– Environment '70 (1970) #1951
– F.H. Varley: A Centennial Exhibition/F.H. Varley: une exposition centenaire (1981) #7468
– Gift from the Douglas M. Duncan Collection and the Milne-Duncan Bequest/Le Don provenant de la collection Douglas M. Duncan et le legs Milne-Duncan (1972) #541
– H.G. Glyde in Canada (1974) #5618
– Impressionism in Canada, 1895-1935 (1974) #115
– J.B. Taylor: Landscapes (1973) #7335
– Jack Bush: A Retrospective/Rétrospective: Jack Bush (1977) #4969
– Jack Shadbolt (1970) #7182
– Jock Macdonald: Retrospective Exhibition/Jock Macdonald: rétrospective (1969) #6375
– Jock Macdonald: The Inner Landscape: A Retrospective Exhibition/Jock Macdonald: le

– (années 1960) #8765 8766 8767
– (années 1960-1970) #7710
– Acadie #1137
– Alberta
  – (1900-années 1930) #8126
  – églises byzantines #8913
– Arctique #8920
– Beaumont (Qué), église Saint-Etienne #8809
– Bellechasse (Qué), église Saint-Charles-Borromée #8803
– Berthierville (Qué) #8833 8874
  – chapelle Cuthbert #8881
– Boucherville (Qué), église de la Sainte-Famille #8868
– Cap-Santé (Qué) #8814
  – église de la Sainte-Famille #8883
– Charlesbourg (Qué) #8851
– Châteauguay (Qué), église Saint-Joachim #8861
– Church Point (NE), église Sainte-Marie #8779
– Colombie-Britannique
  – (1789-début XXe s.) #8918
  – (1858-1925) #8916
  – églises amérindiennes, bois #8914 8917
  – églises en bois #8148 8153
– églises anglicanes #8761
– églises ukrainiennes #8085 8768
  – Alberta #8704
  – Manitoba #2270
  – Saskatchewan #8912 8915
– Fredericton (NB) #8770
– Fuller, Thomas (1858-1867) #8366
– Guelph (Ont), XIXe s. #7970
– Halifax (NE)
  – All Saints' Cathedral #8773
  – XVIIIe-XIXe s. #7818
– Hamilton (Ont)
  – Church of Saint John the Evangelist #730
  – style victorien #7991
– île d'Orléans (Qué) #1238
  – église Saint-François-de-Sales #8796
  – église Saint-Jean #8801
  – église Saint-Pierre #8802
  – église Sainte-Famille #8795
– Ile-du-Prince-Edouard #8777
– île Perrot (Qué)
  – église Sainte-Jeanne-Françoise-de-Chantal #8805
– Joliette (Qué) #1287 8876
– Kahnawake (Qué), église Saint-François-Xavier #8890
– Kingston (Ont)
  – Newlands, William #8392
  – XIXe s. #7995
  – XVIIe-XIXe s. #7989
– L'Acadie (Qué) #8830
– L'Islet (Qué), église Notre-Dame-de-Bon-Secours #8879
– Lac Bouchette (Qué), Chapelle mariale #8832
– Lachenaie (Qué), église Saint-Charles #8808
– Laterrière (Qué), XIXe s. #7882
– Laval (Qué), église de Sainte-Rose #8854
– Lévis (Qué), église Notre-Dame-de-la-Victoire #8789
– Lockport (Man), Saint Andrew's Church #8909
– London (Ont), XIXe s. #8007 8010

– Loretteville (Qué), église Notre-Dame-de-la-Jeune-Lorette #8804
– Lotbinière (Qué) #8835
– Manitoba #8098
  – (1812-1870) #8097
  – verrières #2450
  – XIXe-début XXe s. #8102
– Midland (Ont), Sainte-Marie among the Hurons #7999
– Montréal (Qué) #8886
  – chapelle de l'Invention-de-la-Sainte-Croix #8862
  – chapelle Notre-Dame-de-Lourdes #8784 8836
  – Christ Church Cathedral #8798
  – dessins d'architecture, Archives nationales du Québec à Montréal #8604
  – église Notre-Dame #8780 8828 8839 8848 8849 8892
  – église Saint-Jacques #8781 8782
  – église Sainte-Catherine #8407
  – église Sainte-Catherine-d'Alexandrie #8867
  – Notre-Dame-de-Bon-Secours #8788
  – oratoire Saint-Joseph #8794
  – verrières #2462
  – XVIIe-XIXe s. #7899
– Niagara-on-the-Lake (Ont)
  – Saint Andrew's Church #8901
  – XIXe s. #7986
– Nicolet (Qué), Saint-Grégoire de Nicolet #1636
– Nouveau-Brunswick
  – Medley, Edward Shuttleworth #8776
  – utilisation de modèles architecturaux, XIXe s. #7873
– Nouvelle-Ecosse
  – fin XVIIIe-XIXe s. #8775
  – XVIIIe s. #7815
– Oka (Qué)
  – église #8818 8885
  – église de l'Annonciation #1355 1356
– Ontario #8906
  – (1800-1855) #8014
  – (avant 1867) #8904
  – bâtiments polygonaux, XIXe s. #7987
  – bois, XIXe s. #7745
  – Cumberland, Frederic William #8905
  – influence sur architecture écossaise, XIXe s. #7977
  – McClean, Arthur #8382
  – mennonites #2572
  – XIXe s. #8006 8672
– Oshawa (Ont), Saint George's Anglican Church #8899
– provinces de l'Ouest #8083
– provinces des Prairies #1852 8080
– Québec #1233 1324 8816 8819
  – (1600-1850) #8870
  – (1608-années 1760) #8825 8837
  – (1615-1665) #8822 8823
  – (1647-1800) #8792 8793
  – (1880-1914) #7929
  – (1900-1934) #8334
  – (1930-1952) #8831
  – (années 1820-1880), néo-baroque #7856
  – (années 1930) #1381
  – (années 1940) #8820
  – (années 1940-1950) #8838
  – (années 1950-1960) #8845
  – (années 1960) #1435 7862 8840 8841 8846
  – Baillairgé, Thomas #8327 8328
  – Borduas, Paul-Emile #4836
  – Conefroy, Pierre #8834

– décors intérieurs, école Quévillon #1571
– églises protestantes #8887 8888
– Morisset, Gérard #8891
– Ouellet, Joseph-Pierre #8394
– publications #1295
– sculpture sur bois et décor intérieur, fin XVIIe-XIXe s. #1588
– utilisation de bardeaux et de blanc de chaux #8829
– XVII-XIXe s. #7866
– XVIIe-début XXe s. #8821
– XVIIe s. #228 229 8817 8823
– XVIIe s.-années 1940 #7853
– XVIIe-XIXe s. #1305 7852
– XVIIe-XVIIIe s. #1320 2181 7655 7845 8790 8827 8869
– XVIIIe s. #269 270 7861 7865 8799
– XVIIIe-XIXe s. #1338 8893
– Québec (Qué)
  – Cathedral of the Holy Trinity #8786
  – chapelle de la congrégation Notre-Dame de Québec #8864
  – Couvent des ursulines. Chapelle #8852
  – église Notre-Dame de Québec #8791 8857
  – église Notre-Dame-des-Anges #9022
  – église Saint-Augustin-de-Desmaures #8889
  – église Saint-Joachim de Montmorency #8880
  – Notre-Dame-des-Victoires #8858
  – Séminaire de Québec. Chapelle de Mgr Jean-Olivier Briand #8800
– Quidi Vidi (TN), Christ Church #7788
– Red Deer (Alta), Saint Mary's Church #8343
– Regina (Sask), RCMP Chapel #8911
– Repentigny (Qué) #7888
– Rimouski (Qué) #1361 8872
– Rivière-du-Sud (Qué), église Saint-Pierre de la Rivière-du-Sud #8875
– Saint-Boniface (Man), Precious Blood Church #8908
– Saint-Denis-sur-Richelieu (Qué) #8811
– Saint-Eugène (Qué), église Saint-Eugène-de-Grantham #8873
– Saint-Jean (NB), église en pierre #8778
– Saint-Jean-Port-Joli (Qué)
  – église Saint-Jean-Baptiste #8812
  – église Saint-Jean-Port-Joli #8871
– Saint-Joachim (Qué), église Saint-Joachim #7953
– Saint-Laurent (Qué), Collège de Saint-Laurent. Chapelle #8815
– Saint-Mathias-de-Rouville (Qué), église de Saint-Mathias-de-Rouville #8878
– Sainte-Anne-de-Beaupré (Qué) #8863 8877
  – basilique Sainte-Anne #1601 1602 6572 6573 8824 8859 8860 8865 8866
– Sainte-Anne-de-Bellevue (Qué), église #8336
– Sainte-Anne-de-la-Pocatière (Qué) #8882
– Saskatoon (Sask), Saint John's Episcopal Church #8907
– Sault-au-Récollet (Qué), église de la Visitation #8797
– St. John's (TN), Saint John's Cathedral #8771
– St. Stephen (NB), Christ Church #8774
– style néo-gothique #7739 7740
– Terre-Neuve #8772
– Toronto (Ont)
  – Cathedral of Saint Alban the Martyr #8896

– Church of Saint Paul's #8897 8902
– Saint Anne's Church #1733
– Thomas, William #8413
– Timothy Eaton Memorial Church #8898
– XIXe s.-années 1930 #8076
– Trois-Rivières (Qué) #8806
– (années 1630-1910) #7883
– Valleyfield (Qué), cathédrale de Salaberry-de-Valleyfield #8843
– Vancouver (CB)
– Christ Church Cathedral #8910
– Saint Paul's Indian Mission Church #8919
– Varennes (Qué) #8813
– Winnipeg (Man) #8096 8105
– (1831-1960) #8095
– (années 1880-1910) #8101
– University of Manitoba. Chapel of Christ the King #9486
– XVIIe-début XIXe s. #7841
– XVIIe s.-années 1960 #7689
– XVIIe s.-1867, influence européenne et influence américaine #7687
– Yamachiche (Qué), église Sainte-Anne #8783
églises . Etats-Unis
– Ouest américain #8083
– XVIIIe s., influence sur architecture des églises canadiennes #8904
églises . France
– (années 1930), influence sur architecture des églises québécoises #1381
– XVIIe-XVIIIe s., influence sur architecture des églises québécoises #8821 8869 8870
églises . Grande-Bretagne
– XIXe s., influence sur Frederic William Cumberland #8905
– XVIIIe-XIXe s., influence sur architecture des églises québécoises #8821 8870
églises amérindiennes
– Colombie-Britannique #8914 8917 8918
– Ontario #8904
Egmondville Pottery, fabricants de céramique (comté d'Huron, Ont) #2329
– (1852-1910) #2323
égotisme
– voir Narcisse
Eight, The (groupe américain)
– influence sur David Brown Milne #6567
– influence sur Ernest Lawson #6178
Eisenhauer, Collins, sculpteur can, 1898- #5364
– expositions, critiques #1210 1213
El Al Airlines
– Odjig, Daphne, oeuvres commandées #6731
Elbaz, André, artiste can, 1934- #5365
Eleanor Le Maire Associates, agence can de décoration intérieur
– Toronto (Ont), magasin Holt Renfrew #8078
électricité dans l'art
– panneaux lumineux (Vancouver, CB) #2079
– sculptures, Electric Gallery (Toronto, Ont) #1800
élévateurs à grains . Canada #9237
– (1880-1914) #7736
– (années 1920) #7657 9236
– dans l'art, Robert Newton Hurley #5885
– Manitoba, XIXe-début XXe s. #8102
Elie, Robert, auteur et administrateur des arts can, 1915-1973
– correspondance, Paul-Emile Borduas #1270

4834
Elizabeth II, reine du Royaume-Uni de Grande-Bretagne et d'Irlande du Nord, 1926
– peintures commémorant visite au Nouveau-Brunswick (1976), Molly Lamb Bobak #4765
Ellingson, William John, artiste amér, 1929-
– professeur de Charles Ringness #7011
Elliot Lake (Ont)
– travaux de mise en valeur (années 1950) #8184
Elliot Lake (Ont), Centre for Continuing Education
– Frenkel, Vera, professeure #5519
Elliott, Alfred J., artiste can, actif 1977
– design typographique #932
Ellis, Francis Dean, artiste can, 1948- #5366
– constructions en matériaux bruts (années 1970) #2065
– expositions de groupe
– (1976) #2060
Ellis, James E., orfèvre can, actif 1848-1871 #2638
Ellis & Connery, agence can d'architecture
– Toronto (Ont), Bank of British North America #9150
Ellis & Ellis, agence can d'architecture
– Brighton (Ont), Union School #9387
– Lambton Mills (Ont), école #9388
– Toronto (Ont), John Ross Robertson School et Glenholme School, concours #9437
Elmsdale Pottery, fabricants de céramique can (Halifax, NE)
– poterie Staffordshire #2339
Elora (Ont)
– photographie (1856-1867) #1724
Eloul, Kosso, sculpteur can, 1920- #5370
– Canadac, Art Gallery of Hamilton (Hamilton, Ont) #780
– éléments reliés au culte et au rituel #789
– expositions
– (1973) #5368
– (1980) #5369
– Now, Fanshawe College (London, Ont) #5367
Elsinore Editions, éditeur (Elsinore, Ont)
– et John Bernard Boyle #834
Eluard, Paul, poète fr, 1895-1952
– poèmes, dessins d'Alfred Pellan #6824 6825
émaux . Canada
– (1964-1967) #2108 2109
– (années 1950) #2378
– Brassard, Thérèse Tanguay #4905
– Brault, Maurice #4906
– Dupond, Marcel Jules René #5340
– Passillé-Sylvestre, Micheline de #2216
– Québec
– (années 1950) #2193
– (années 1970) #2228
emblèmes et devises
– voir aussi héraldique
emblèmes et devises . Canada #2939
– castor #56
Emerging Arts West, périodique can #1868
Emerson, Ralph Waldo, auteur amér, 1803-1882
– Atkins, Caven Ernest, comparaison #4570
Emery, Alban S., ébéniste can, actif 1910- #2511
Emery, George E., céramiste can, 1881-1959
– fondateur, Ecanada Art Pottery (Hamilton, Ont) #2353 2359

Emilson, Bruce, artiste can, 1944-
– art vidéo #605
Emma Lake (Sask), Emma Lake Workshops #507
– (1955-1970) #1921
– (1955-1973) #1923
– (années 1950-1970) #145
– estampes de style hard-edge #832
– et Anthony Caro #1934
– et Douglas Bentham #4686
– et Ernest Lindner #6284
– et Judith Allsopp #717
– et Kenneth Campbell Lochhead #6317 6319
– et Marion F.S. Mackay Nicoll #6701 6703
– influence sur l'art en Saskatchewan #1862 1915 1932 1935
– paysages #1855
Emmons, George Thornton, collectionneur amér, 1852-1945
– collection, art, Indiens de la côte nord-ouest #4005
Emond, Philippe, artiste can, 1930-
– expositions de groupe
– (1955) #1408
Emond, Pierre, sculpteur can, 1738-1808 #5371
encadrements . Canada
– formes diverses
– Forrestall, Tom #5461 5465
– Zellinger, Jean #7634
– guide pour collectionneurs #2252
encensoirs . Canada
– orfèvrerie, Québec, XVIIe-XVIIIe s. #2665
encyclopédies
– voir dictionnaires et encyclopédies
enfance
– voir enfants
enfants
– emploi particulier du langage, et N.E. Thing Co. Ltd. #6677
– habillement (1780-1930) #2862
– thèmes reliés à l'enfance, art canadien (années 1970) #674
enfants dans l'art
– art ontarien #1687
– Heward, Efa Prudence #5796
– Kupczynski, Stanislav #6106
– Lyall, Laura Adeline Muntz #6339
– Peel, Paul #6790
– Wallis, Katherine Elizabeth #7511 7512
Enns, Maureen, artiste can, 1943- #5372
– expositions de groupe
– (1977) #1956
Ens, Frank, sculpteur can, actif 1978 #2596
Ense, Don, artiste can, 1953- #4155
– (1981) #4173
enseignement
– voir aussi éducation
enseignement de l'architecture
– Baillairgé, Thomas #8325
– Canada
– (1900-années 1920) #7652
– (1901), recommandations #8240
– (1902-1908) #7955
– (1908) #8292
– (1909) #8242
– (1980) #8289
– (années 1880), recommandations #8238
– (années 1890) #8239
– (années 1920) #8244
– (années 1930) #7658
– (années 1940) #8245 8246 8247 8248
– (années 1950) #7670 8249 8250 8252
– (années 1950-1960) #7682

– (années 1960) #8280
  – Institut royal d'architecture du
    Canada, étude #8309
  – (années 1970) #7728 8316
    – sondage auprès des architectes #8314
– Colombie-Britannique (années 1950) #8142
– conservation de l'architecture, formation
  (années 1970) #7773
– Demers, Jérôme #7874
– Halifax (NE), Nova Scotia Technical
  College. School of Architecture (années
  1970) #8285
– Montréal (Qué)
  – Ecole des beaux-arts
    – (1952) #8251
    – (1953) #8253
    – (1954) #8255
    – (1955) #8257
    – (1956) #8259
    – (1957) #8260 8261
  – Université de Montréal. Ecole
    d'architecture #8269
    – (1958) #8262
    – (1959) #8263
    – (1960) #8264
    – (1961) #8266
    – (1962) #8268
    – (1963) #8270
    – (1964) #8271
    – (1965) #8273
    – (1966) #8274
    – (1967) #8275
    – (1968) #8277
  – Université McGill. Ecole d'architecture
    – (1953) #8253
    – (1954) #8255
    – (1955) #8257
    – (1956) #8259
    – (1957) #8260
    – (1958) #8262
    – (1959) #8263
    – (1960) #8264
    – (1961) #8266 8267
    – (1962) #8268
    – (1963) #8270
    – (1964) #8271
    – (1965) #8273
    – (1966) #8274
    – (1967) #8275
    – (1968) #8277
    – (années 1970) #8287
  – XIXe s. #7900
– Ontario
  – (années 1970) #8288
– Ottawa (Ont), Carleton University. School
  of Architecture (années 1970) #8284
– Québec
  – (années 1960) #8307
  – et architecture domestique (années 1960)
    #8279
– Québec (Qué), Université Laval. Ecole
  d'architecture #8271
  – (1965) #8273
  – (1966) #8274
  – (1967) #8275
  – (1968) #8277
– Toronto (Ont)
  – (années 1910), et John MacIntosh Lyle
    #8243
  – University of Toronto. School of
    Architecture
    – (1967-1975), programme d'études
      expérimental #8286
    – (1968), mise en situation, technique

pédagogique #8278
– (1970) #8313
– (années 1950) #8254
– (années 1960) #8282
– Vancouver (CB), University of British
  Columbia. School of Architecture (années
  1950) #8258
– Winnipeg (Man), University of Manitoba.
  School of Architecture
  – (1968), programme d'études sur
    l'environnement #8281
  – (années 1950) #8256
  – (années 1960) #8272
enseignement de l'art
– voir aussi académies artistiques
– (1894), recommandations #2960
– (années 1910), femmes artistes à l'étranger
  #206
– Académie royale des arts du Canada #275
– Alberta #1946 1953
– artisanat pour enfants (années 1970) #2136
  2137
– arts graphiques (années 1960) #867
– Askevold, David, commentaire #4566
– Banff (Alta), Banff School of Fine Arts
  #3000
– Beaudin, Gaétan #2381
– Benjamin-Constant, Jean-Joseph,
  professeur d'artistes canadiens #243
– Biéler, André Charles #4725 4726
– Binning, B.C. #4730
– Borduas, Paul-Emile #2990 3001 4803 4811
  4818 4821 4827 4836 4843
– Bourassa, Napoléon #4864 4875
– Braitstein, Marcel #4899
– Brandtner, Fritz #4904
– Brooker, Bertram Richard #317
– Brymner, William #4949 4953
– Calgary (Alta), Calgary Art Centre (1947)
  #1945
– Cameron, Donald #3000
– Canada
  – (1890-1900) #190
  – (1908), recommandations #2963
  – (1938-1948) #379
  – (1975), prédictions #585
  – (années 1890) #182 184
    – artistes canadiens à Paris (France)
      #180
  – (années 1930) #7658
  – (années 1940) #370 384
    – et Académie royale des arts du
      Canada #361
    – poterie #2375
  – (années 1940-1980) #2983
  – (années 1960) #448
  – (années 1970) #542 625 682 2998 3270
    – commentaires d'artistes #648
    – provinces de l'Ouest #3006
  – (années 1970), et femmes #701
  – XIXe s. #343
  – XVIIe s.-années 1940, arts décoratifs
    #2097 2979
  – XXe s. #470
– Carr, Emily #5014
– Chabert, Joseph #3005
– Chicoutimi (Qué)
  – Ecole d'arts et métiers #2175
  – Université du Québec (années 1970)
    #3016
– Colombie-Britannique (années 1960) #2989
– Corporation canadienne de l'artisanat
  #2090
– Couturier, Pierre Charles Marie-Alain

#1407
– Cruikshank, William #5212
– Cullen, Maurice Galbraith #5219 5220
– Dignam, Mary Ella #2958
– Dumouchel, Albert #3001 5325 5330 5333
– Dyonnet, Edmond #5346 5347 5349
– Eagar, William H. #5351
– Edmonton (Alta), University of Alberta.
  Department of Extension (années
  1930-1940) #1943
– Emma Lake (Sask), Emma Lake
  Workshops #1921 1923
– Foulis, Robert #258 259
– Frenkel, Vera #5519
– Gaitskell, Charles #2986
– Halifax (NE), Nova Scotia College of Art
  and Design #2993 3003 3014
– Hofmann, Hans, enseignement aux artistes
  canadiens #1850
– Holgate, Edwin Headley #5818 5819
– Holmes, Robert #5822
– Jérôme, frère #6761 6762 6763
– Jones, William Harris #1226
– Kinton, Ada Florence #6053
– Leighton, Alfred Crocker #6225
– Leighton, Barbara #3017
– Lemieux, Jean-Paul #6227 6228 6235 6236
– Lismer, Arthur #9 311 2965 2966 2968 2971
  2974 2975 2981 2984 2985 2987 6293 6295
  6296 6297 6298 6299 6301 6302 6303 6305
– Macdonald, Jock #2990 6375 6378
– MacLeod, Pegi Nicol #6397
– Manitoba (années 1940) #1889 1890
– May, Karl #6453
– Miller, Maria Frances Ann Morris #6541
– Montréal (Qué)
  – (années 1940) #1395
  – Ecole des beaux-arts #2973 2995
    – (1922-1935) #2972
  – Ecole du meuble (1935-1950) #2980
  – Institut national des beaux-arts, sciences,
    arts et métiers et industrie #3005
– Nouveau-Brunswick #1137
  – arts décoratifs (années 1940) #2144
  – écoles (années 1960) #1177
– Nutt, Elizabeth Styring #6730
– Ontario
  – (1856) #3128
  – (années 1970) #3004
  – arts dans la vie franco-ontarienne #1820
    1821
– Ontario Society of Artists (années 1940)
  #1666
– provinces de l'Atlantique
  – (années 1960) #1124
  – (années 1960-1970) #1130
  – (années 1970) #1127 1131
– provinces maritimes (années 1950) #1119
– Pulford, Edward Berwyn #6945
– Québec #1231
  – (1872-1939), arts décoratifs #2977
  – (années 1930), arts décoratifs #2166 2969
  – (années 1930-1940), arts décoratifs #2185
  – (années 1940) #1390
  – Conseil des arts et manufactures, fin
    XIXe s. #2598 2962
  – et femmes (années 1930-1970) #1273
– Québec (Qué), Ecole des arts domestiques
  de Québec #2167 2186
– Rimouski (Qué), Séminaire de Rimouski.
  Ecole d'arts et métiers de Rimouski #2978
– Roberts, Goodridge #7041 7048
– Sackville (NB), Mount Allison University
  (1893-1977) #3013

– Saint-Joachim (Qué), Ecole des arts et
  métiers de Saint-Joachim #1233 1327 1363
  2967 2991 2992 3007 3008
– Saskatchewan #1919 1935
– Savage, Anne Douglas #7129 7130 7132
– Schaefer, Carl Fellman #7154 7155
– Scott, Charles Hepburn #3019
– Senécal, Irène #2999 3010
– Smith, Gordon Appelbe #7228 7230
– Suzor-Coté, Marc-Aurèle de Foy #7293
– Teitelbaum, Mashel #7340
– Terre-Neuve #1142 1147
   – (années 1970) #1146
– Tonnancour, Jacques Godefroy de #3018
  7386
– Toronto (Ont)
   – (années 1910) #1712
   – (années 1960) #1757
   – (avant 1912) #2964
   – Art Gallery of Toronto #3020
   – New School of Art #2994
   – Ontario College of Art
      – (1876-1976) #3009 3011 3012
      – (1971-1972) #3002
      – (années 1960) #2996 2997
– Toronto (Ont) et Montréal (Qué), (années
  1960) #2990
– Toronto Art Students' League
   – (1886-1893) #2959
   – (1886-1894) #2961
– Tully, Sydney Strickland #7438
– Vancouver (CB), Vancouver School of Art
  (1925-1939) #3019
– Verbist, P.J. #2957
– Winnipeg (Man), Winnipeg Art Gallery
  #3196
enseignes et panneaux d'affichage
– voir aussi lettrage dans l'art; panneaux
  d'affichage
enseignes et panneaux d'affichage . Canada
– enseignes lumineuses (CB) #2079
– Hébert, Julien #5766
– Ottawa (Ont), Centre national des arts
  #9104
– Québec
   – (1759-1914), thème de la rébellion #1351
   – XVIIe-XIXe s. #2919 2922
– Wallot, Jacques-Albert-François-Joseph
  #7513
entrepôts . Canada
– (années 1910) #9234
– (années 1950) #9241
– Compagnie de la Baie d'Hudson, XIXe s.
  #8480
– John Deere Plow Company #9247
– Winnipeg (Man) #8106
   – (années 1880-1914) #8107
entrepôts . Etats-Unis
– John Deere Plow Company #9247
entreprises . collections d'art
– Association médicale canadienne #138
– Ayerst, McKenna et Harrison #852
– Banque de Nouvelle-Ecosse #3245
– Banque Toronto-Dominion #3225 4201
  4216 4427
– Canada #3243
   – (années 1950) #3259
   – et Banque d'oeuvres d'art #3286
– Chambre de commerce de Toronto #3291
– CIL Inc. #124
– Fondation Macdonald-Stewart #2203 2204
– Henry Birks & Sons Ltd #2636 2637 2650
  2651 2656
– Imperial Oil Ltd. #3241

– International Business Machines
  Corporation (IBM) #350
– Rothmans of Pall Mall Canada #4257
– Seagram #403
– Shell Canada Ltée #1966 3238 3240
– Société d'électrolyse et de chimie Alcan
  Ltée (Sécal) #3246
Enukso Point (TNO)
– inukshuks et inunguaks, Inuit #4199
environnement
– voir écologie
environnementalisme
– Canada #617
– Demers, Maurice #5284
– Senft, Douglas #7170
– Thibert, Patrick #7345
– Vazan, Bill #7478
– Waring, Stephanie E. #7516
envois
– voir art postal
éphémère
– et art jetable, Les Levine #6259
Erb, Isaac, photographe can, 1846-1924
  #1186
Erdesz, Otto, luthier can, actif 1979 #2940
Erickson/Massey, agence can d'architecture
  #8360
– Burnaby (CB), Simon Fraser University
  #9396 9504 9505 9506
   – concours #9501
   – résidence des étudiants #9467
– Osaka (Japon), Expo 70. Pavillon du
  Canada #9224
   – concours #9217
– Vancouver (CB)
   – Hauer House #8519
   – Nelson Towers #8744
   – prix, conception d'école élémentaire
     (1970) #9507
Erickson, Arthur Charles, architecte can,
  1924- #8356 8358 8359 8360 8363
– Burnaby (CB), Simon Fraser University
  #9406
– commentaire sur Gordon Appelbe Smith
  #7227
– commentaire sur l'architecture domiciliaire
  #8354
– Comox (CB), résidence Filberg #8355
– entretien #8357
– Lethbridge (Alta), University of
  Lethbridge #9406 9497
– Los Angeles (Calif), revitalisation du
  quartier Bunker Hill #8364
– Ottawa (Ont), Banque du Canada, siège
  social #9199
– réflexion sur son oeuvre architecturale
  #8361
– théories sur l'architecture #7746
– Vancouver (CB) #7733
   – Eppich House #8745
   – MacMillan Bloedel Building #9358
   – University of British Columbia. Museum
     of Anthropology #8170 9132 9137 9138
Erindale (Ont), résidence de Adamson
– architecture #7959
Erkoolik, Tuna, sculpteur can, 1935- #4407
Ernst, Max, artiste all, 1891-1976
– influence sur Alfred Pellan #6803 6821
– Lee-Nova, Gary, comparaison #2051
– Letarte, Jean-Paul, comparaison #6249
– Pellan, Alfred, comparaison #6820
Esenwein & Johnson, agence amér
  d'architecture

– Hamilton (Ont), Royal Connaught Hotel
  #9274
Eskimo Point (TNO)
– Esquimaux du caribou #4265
– tapisserie #4253
Eskimos
– voir Inuit
Esler, Annemarie Schmid
– voir Schmid-Esler, Annemarie
Esler, John Kenneth, artiste can, 1933-
– expositions de groupe
   – (1967) #821
espace
– dans l'architecture canadienne, XIXe s.
  #7748
– dans l'art
   – Allen, Ralph #4509
   – art inuit #4184 4185 4244 4341
   – Borduas, Paul-Emile #4816 4824 4835
   – Breeze, Claude Herbert #4910
   – Harris, Lawren Stewart #5732
   – Lemieux, Jean-Paul #6235 6236 6240
   – peinture québécoise (années 1950-1960)
     #1441
   – sculpture québécoise (années 1970)
     #1631
   – Snow, Michael #7240 7245
Espagnols au Canada
– vues de la côte nord-ouest (1789-1791)
  #1998
Esquimaux du Caribou
– culture #4265
Esquimaux du cuivre
– culture
   – (1903-1905) #4366
   – (années 1920) #4330
– ouvrages en ramure #4412
Essex, Margaret Mary, artiste can, née 1891
– illustrations #916
Essex County Artists (Windsor, Ont)
– (1940-) #1668
Esson, James, photographe can, 1854-1933
– vues stéréoscopiques #5373
estampes
– voir arts graphiques
Estevan (Sask), Centre national
  d'expositions
– expositions
   – Edward Curtis in the Collection of the
     Edmonton Art Gallery (1981) #3480
   – The Paintings of Frederick Nicholas
     Loveroff/Les peintures de Frederick Nicholas
     Loveroff (1981) #6331
esthétique
– voir aussi art . théorie et critique; beauté;
  goût (esthétique); sublime
esthétique amérindienne #3487
– (années 1970) #4137
esthétique autochtone #3351
esthétique inuit #4263 4282 4295 4297 4420
  4422 4426 4442
Estoniens au Canada
– architecture #7723
– art #118 1761
étain . Canada
– guide pour collectionneurs #2104 2252
– Québec #2226 2228 2664 2700
– Volpi, Charles de, collection #3248
– XIXe s. #2704
Etat, architecture et
– voir aussi droit, architecture et
– Canada

– (1908), recommandations #2963
– (années 1950) #7670
– (années 1970) #7728 8975
– architecture domestique (années 1960) #8513
– écoles (années 1960) #9395
– édifices à bureaux (années 1970) #9302
– image du Dominion dans les bureaux de poste, fin XIXe s. #9054 9055
– logement subventionné (années 1960) #8518
– ministère des Affaires du Nord (années 1950) #8184
– ministère des Travaux publics
  – (1840-années 1960) #8976 8977
  – (1954-1959) #7681
– conservation
  – Canada (années 1950) #7755
  – Canada (années 1970) #7767 7771 8964
  – Heritage Canada #7770
  – Montréal (Qué) #7914
  – Ontario #8906
  – Québec #7870 7937
  – Victoria (CB) #8149
– destruction de l'architecture, Montréal (Qué), (années 1970) #8601
– Ottawa (Ont), Galerie nationale du Canada, concours (1975-1977) #9126
– Québec, XVIIe-XVIIIe s. #7858
– Terre-Neuve #7784
Etat, art et
– voir aussi droit, art et
– administrations municipales (années 1970) #3288 3289
– Canada #129 910
  – (1944), Brief Concerning the Cultural Aspects of Canadian Reconstruction #3250 3251
  – (1951), Commission royale d'enquête sur l'avancement des arts, lettres et sciences (Rapport Massey) #391 398 1401 1405 3254 3255 3256 3257 3261
  – (1974), proposition pour l'encouragement des arts par le milieu des affaires d'ici 1980 #3271
  – (1975), prédictions #585
  – (1977), Loi sur l'exportation et l'importation de biens culturels #3283 3284 3296
  – (1981), Comité fédéral d'études d'une politique culturelle #1068
  – (années 1870) #1693
  – (années 1880-1890) #264
  – (années 1940) #363
  – (années 1950) #3253
  – (années 1950-1970) #3290
  – (années 1960) #443 448 529 3043 3263 3265
    – arts graphiques #868
  – (années 1960-1970) #157
  – (années 1970) #542 551 571 625 693 897 3157 3267 3268 3269 3270 3273 3274 3275 3278 3282 3285 3286 3287 3292 3293
  – conservation #7767
  – design industriel #2621 2624
  – femmes artistes (1980) #719
  – musées
    – (1980) #683
    – (années 1970) #3059
  – XXe s. #567
– Colombie-Britannique
  – (années 1970) #3272
  – British Columbia Art Collection #2078

– Conférence canadienne des arts
  – (1980) #3294 3295
  – (1981) #3297 3298
– Conseil des Arts du Canada
  – (années 1950-1960) #3264
  – (années 1960) #523
  – (années 1970) #586
  – Banque d'oeuvres d'art #3276 3277
– et Académie royale des arts du Canada #275
– Frenkel, Vera, commentaire #5522
– Manitoba (années 1970) #1899 3193
– Nouvelle-Ecosse (années 1940) #2145
– Ontario #492
  – art dans la vie franco-ontarienne (années 1970) #1820 1821
  – et Ontario Society of Artists #1679 1728
– Québec
  – (1825-1850) #1368
  – (1961-1975) #3280
  – (années 1940) #2190 3252
  – (années 1960) #1473
  – (années 1970) #1521 2208 3015
  – centres culturels #3088
  – ministère de l'Agriculture (années 1930) #2165
  – ministère des Travaux publics et de l'Approvisionnement #1561
  – musées (années 1970) #3102
  – rôle de la Centrale d'artisanat du Québec #2213 2238
  – XVIIe-XVIIIe s. #2214
– Saskatchewan Arts Board
  – (1848-années 1960) #1914
  – (1948-1978) #1938
– Terre-Neuve
  – (années 1970) #1146 1154
  – (années 1980) #1161
Etat, art et . Amérindiens #6539
Etat, art et . Inuit #4222 4397
– (1977-1980) #4269
– Alaska #4208
Etherington, A.Bruce, architecte can, 1924-
– architecture des banques #9193
éthique, art et
– Harris, Lawren Stewart #5731
– Prent, Mark #6924
Etobicoke (Ont), Martin Grove Estate
– architecture, Jerome Markson #8744
étoffes
– voir textiles et tissus
Etook, Tivi, artiste can, 1928- #5374 5375
– entretien #4468
Etrog, Sorel, sculpteur can, 1933- #5377 5378 5380 5381
– constructions peintes (1952-1960) #5379
– éléments reliés au culte et au rituel #789
– expositions
  – (1964) #5376
– sculptures (années 1960) #1793
Etungat, Abraham, sculpteur can, 1911- #5382
Evans, David, photographe can, 1948-
– expositions, critiques #1018
Evans, Emrys, relieur can, 1944- #2936
Evans, John, architecte can, 1872-1944
– Galt (Ont), école publique #9387
Evans, John, photographe can, actif 1975
– catalogue de photographies #995
Evans, Roger T., artiste can, 1940-
– expositions de groupe
  – (1977) #1956
Evans, Walker, photographe amér, 1903-1975

– vues photographiques, Alabama (1936) #1513
évantails . Micmacs #3500
Eve
– Cetin, Anton, représentations symboliques #5064
– Lodge, Judy, collection, The Walls of Eden #6321
évolutionnisme
– voir aussi art de performance
– Canada, paysages #617
– Whiten, Colette #7556 7557 7558 7561
Ewen, Paterson, artiste can, 1925-
– commentaire sur Jack Chambers #700
– entretien #5383
– et plasticiens #1439
– expositions
  – (1976) #5384
  – (1977) #5386
– expositions, critiques #5385
– expositions de groupe
  – (1955) #1408
  – (1977) #636
  – (1980) #703
– peintures (années 1960) #1484
Ewing, Bill, conservateur can, actif 1973
– directeur, Centaur Galleries (Montréal, Qué) #1004
ex-libris . Canada #917
– Alexander, William Walker #4506
– Carter, Alexander Scott #5050
– provinces maritimes, XVIIIe-XIXe s. #915
– Smith, Leslie Victor #7234
– XVIIIe-début XXe s. #28
ex-votos
– voir offrande votive
excavations
– voir archéologie
Exeter (Angleterre), Royal Albert Memorial Museum
– art amérindien #3454
expansion urbaine
– voir aussi urbanisme
– Alberta, quartier chinois, XXe s. #8137
– Calgary (Alta) (années 1970) #8122 9362
– Canada
  – (1850-1900), vues photographiques #7744
  – (1867-1967) #7695
  – (1880-1914) #7736
  – (années 1950) #8514
  – (années 1960) #8231 8311 8518
  – et immeubles à bureaux
    – (années 1950-1970) #9302
    – (années 1960) #9300 9301
  – et logement
    – (années 1960) #8513 8515
    – (années 1970) #7728
– Colombie-Britannique
  – (années 1950) #8142
  – début XXe s., Royal Engineers #8150
– Edmonton (Alta), (années 1970) #8123
– Faro (Yukon), (années 1970) #8182
– Halifax (NE) #7835
– Kitsilano (CB), (années 1970) #8146
– Montréal (Qué) #7914
  – (1642-années 1970) #7918 7934
  – (1803-1878) #7924
  – (années 1950-1960) #7901
  – Place Bonaventure #9325
  – Vieux-Montréal (années 1970) #7911
  – XVIIe-XXe s. #7902 7906 7931
– Ontario (années 1970) #8024
– Ottawa (Ont)

– quartier de Glebe #8042
– Région de la capitale nationale #8035
   8037 8039
– Smyth Road Development Competition
   (1960) #8040
– Prix Vincent Massey pour l'aménagement
   urbain (1975) #8218
– provinces des Prairies, XXe s. #8089
– Québec #7867
   – XVIIe-XVIIIe s. #7885 8603
– Québec (Qué) #7938
– Safdie, Moshe, commentaire #8403 8405
– Toronto (Ont)
   – et logement (années 1970) #8068
   – et réseau du métro (années 1970) #9554
   – Flemingdon Park (années 1960) #8657
   – Harbour City (années 1970) #8062
   – quartier St. Lawrence, états des travaux
      (1980) #8079
   – Regent Park (années 1950) #8511
   – York Square (années 1960) #9347
   – Yorkville Village (années 1960) #9376
– Vancouver (CB) #8161
   – (années 1960) #8158
   – (années 1970) #8162
   – et logement
      – (1886-1929) #8714 8730
      – (1980) #8725
   – False Creek (années 1920-1980) #8169
   – XXe s. #8171
– Victoria (CB), (années 1970) #8146
– Winnipeg (Man)
   – (1870-1914) #8103
   – (années 1950) #8514
   – (années 1970) #8104 8108
expédition britannique dans l'Arctique
(1875-1876)
– Mitchell, Thomas et George White,
   photographies et aquarelles #240
expédition de la rivière Rouge (1870)
– et Frances Ann Beechy Hopkins #5833
expédition Lewis et Clark
– et oeuvres d'arts #3649
expédition Malaspina (1791)
– collection, art amérindien et art inuit
   #3372
exploitation minière
– voir mines et exploitation minière; mines
   d'or et exploitation minière
exploration de l'Assiniboine et de la
Saskatchewan (1858)
– et Humphrey Lloyd Hime #1014 1015 1865
   5801 5802 5803 5804
explosions nucléaires
– Keziere, Robert, photographies dénonçant
   le nucléaire #6051
expositions
– Académie royale des arts du Canada
   – (1880-1971) #2
   – (1880-1979) #162
– Art Association of Newfoundland and
   Labrador (1967-1979) #1144
– Art Directors' Club of Toronto (Toronto,
   Ont), (1949-) #854
– art international, Canadian National
   Exhibition (Toronto, Ont), (1905-1938)
   #107
– Association des sculpteurs du Québec
   (1961-1977) #1584
– Brantford (Ont), Art Gallery of Brant.
   Graphex (1973-1979, 1981-) #827
– British Columbia Society of Artists
   (1909-1967) #1978
– Burnaby Art Society. Burnaby National Print
   Show (Burnaby, CB), (1961-1977) #816

– Calgary (Alta), Alberta College of Art. Art
   Gallery. Calgary Graphics Exhibition
   (1959-1974) #815
– Canada
   – (1928-1929) #307
   – (1972-1974) #552
   – (1976-), centres d'artistes à but non
      lucratif #612
   – (1978-) #114
   – (années 1970) #682
   – femmes artistes (années 1960-1970) #677
– Canadian Art Club (1908-1915) #193
– Canadian Guild of Potters (1955-1971)
   #2379
– Canadian National Exhibition (1879-1961)
   #1
– Corporation canadienne de l'artisanat
   #2090
– Ecole des beaux-arts (Montréal, Qué),
   (1925-1932) #2973
– Edmonton Art Club (Edmonton, Alta),
   (1921-) #1941
– Essex County Artists (1940-) #1668
– Exhibition of Architecture and Allied Arts
   (Toronto, Ont), (1927-1939) #8224
– expositions universelles, XIXe s.,
   participation canadienne #261
– Groupe des peintres canadiens (1933-1968)
   #324
– Groupe des Sept (1920-1922, 1925-1926,
   1928, 1930-1931) #1732
– Hamilton (Ont), Art Gallery of Hamilton,
   exposition annuelle (1948-) #38
– Independent Art Association (Montréal,
   Qué), (1932-1963) #1379
– Island Arts and Crafts Club (Victoria, CB),
   (1910-1941) #1980
– London (Ont), London Art Gallery, Young
   Contemporaries/Jeunes contemporains
   (1975-1979) #584
– Maritime Art Association (1959-1965)
   #1120
– Montréal (Qué), Musée des beaux-arts de
   Montréal
   – Salon de printemps (1880-1965) #1228
   – Survey/Sondage (1968-1970) #1481
– Norart (Nord de l'Ontario), (1979-) #1829
– Nouvelle-Ecosse (1830-1913) #1191
– Nova Scotia Society of Artists (1923-1972)
   #1192
– Ontario Society of Artists (1873-) #1666
– Ottawa (Ont), Galerie nationale du
   Canada
   – (1882-1979) #3063
   – (1926-1933) #294
   – (1953-1968. Biennale) #400
– Québec, XIXe s.-années 1940 #1242
– Saskatchewan Art Exhibition (1950-1964)
   #1910
– Société canadienne des aquarellistes
   (1926-) #6
– Société canadienne des peintres-graveurs
   (1919-1974) #3
– Société des artistes professionnels du
   Québec (1971-1975) #1488
– Société des sculpteurs Canada (1928-) #734
– Society of Typographic Designers of
   Canada (1958-1964) #923
– The Winnipeg Show (Winnipeg, Man),
   (1955-1970) #54
– Toronto (Ont), (1977-1980), galeries d'art et
   ateliers d'artistes #1815
– Toronto (Ont), Art Gallery of Ontario
   (1906-1966) #3175
– Toronto Camera Club (Toronto, Ont),

   (1891-) #975
– Toronto Society of Architects (Toronto,
   Ont), (1901-1912) #7956
– Toronto Society of Arts (Toronto, Ont),
   (1847-1848) #1689
– Upper Canada Agricultural Society
   (1846-1867) #1715
– Vancouver (CB), Vancouver Art Gallery
   (1932-1968) #1983
– Western Ontario Exhibition (London, Ont),
   (1941-1978) #1670
– Winnipeg Sketch Club (Winnipeg, Man),
   (1914-) #1887
– Women's Art Association of Hamilton
   (Hamilton, Ont), (1894-) #1701
expositions . bâtiments
– Montréal (Qué), Expo 67 #9212 9213 9214
   9218 9219 9221 9222
expositions . bâtiments . Canada #9211
– Bruxelles (Belgique), Exposition
   universelle et internationale (1958).
   Pavillon du Canada #430 9209
– Montréal (Qué), Expo 67 #9215 9216 9220
– Osaka (Japon), Expo 70 #8356 9217 9224
– Toronto (Ont)
   – Canadian National Exhibition #1 9206
      – Automotive Building #9207
   – Place de l'Ontario #9115
– Vancouver (CB), Crystal Gardens #9146
– Venise (Italie), XIXe Biennale #9210
– Victoria (CB), Crystal Gardens #9134
expressionisme abstrait
– voir aussi tachisme
– Borduas, Paul-Emile, commentaire #4838
– Canada #52 489
   – dessins #638
   – paysages #496
– en comparaison avec automatisme #1476
– et Emma Lake Workshops (Emma Lake,
   Sask) #1929
– et Gordon Appelbe Smith #7225
– et John Graham Coughtry #5191
– et Norman McLaren #6497
– et Paterson Ewen #5384
– et Paul-Emile Borduas #4826 4829 4830
– et Pierre Gendron #5582
– et Robert Percival #6835
– Ontario #1748
– Québec #1487
– Toronto (Ont) #1773
Eyetoaq, Ada, artiste can, 1934-
– expositions
   – (1979) #5387
Eyre, Ivan Kenneth, artiste can, 1935- #1856
   5388 5391 5395
– entretien #5392 5393
– expositions
   – (1969) #5389
   – (1974) #5390
   – (1980) #5394
– expositions, critiques #1883
– expositions de groupe
   – (1981) #1885

F

Fablo, Serge Ventadour, artiste can, 1937-
– entretien #5396
fabrication de papier . Canada
– Ontario (années 1970) #935
façades . Canada
– conservation #7766

Fafard, Joseph (Joe), sculpteur et céramiste
can, 1942- #1937 5397 5398 5400
– et étudiants, sculptures en céramique
#1924
– expositions
– (1979) #5401
– expositions, critiques #2383 5399
– expositions de groupe
– (1976) #1930
– (1979) #674
faïence
– voir poterie
Fairfield & DuBois, agence can
d'architecture
– Peterborough (Ont), Trent University.
Résidence des étudiants #9467
– Scarborough (Ont), bibliothèque Albert
Campbell #9047
– Toronto (Ont)
– Dow Corning Silicones Ltd., siège social
#9301
– George Brown College of Applied Arts
& Technology. Campus Casa Loma
#9479
Fairley, Barker, artiste et auteur can, 1887-
#5403
– commentaire sur la présence humaine
dans l'art canadien #344
– commentaire sur le Groupe des peintres
canadiens (1940) #348
– correspondance, Norman I. Gurd #1776
– dessins, baie georgienne (Ont) #5402
– expositions
– (1980) #5404
– portraits #5405
– réflexion sur l'art canadien #380
Fairn, Leslie Raymond, architecte can,
1875-1971
– Wolfville (NE), Acadia University #9407
Fairy Lake (NE)
– pictogrammes, Micmacs #3494
Fakir Art Club (Windsor, Ont)
– (1930-1940) #1668
Falardeau, Antoine-Sébastien, artiste can,
1822-1889 #1318 1323 5406 5407
– expositions de groupe
– (1880) #1308
– oeuvres, Art Association of Montreal
(Montréal, Qué) #3075
– peintures, Université Laval (Québec, Qué)
#3078
Falardeau, Pierre, artiste can, 1946-
– commentaire sur l'art vidéo #1537
– expositions de groupe
– (1979) #1157
– (1980) #705
Falk, Gathie, artiste can, 1928- #5408
– art de performance #5410
– entretien #5409
– expositions, critiques #579 622 2081
– expositions de groupe
– (1968) #2382
– (1969) #2039
– (1975) #591
– (1976) #2060
– (1977) #781
– sculpture, art de performance #658
– sculptures en céramique (années 1970)
#2065
False Creek (CB), immeuble d'habitation
– proposition architecturale, Arthur Charles
Erickson #8360
Fanshawe, Hubert Valentine, artiste can,
1878-1940
– gravures sur bois de fil #802

Fanshawe Pioneer Village (Ont) #8063 8066
fantaisie
– Milne, David Brown, commentaire #6556
Fardon, George Robinson, photographe can,
1807-1886 #5411
Farmer's Magazine, périodique can
– illustrations (1910-1921) #1765
Farmington (Conn), Gleason House
– charpente en bois, en comparaison avec
Fisher House (Toronto, Ont) #8658
Farnsworth, Mademoiselle, photographe
can, active 1894 #977
Faro (Yukon), Faro Townsite Recreation
Centre
– architecture, Thompson, Berwick, Pratt &
Partners #8182
Farrar, famille, céramistes can, actifs années
1840-1927 #2288 2299 2321
Fat, Dulcie Foo, artiste can, 1946-
– entretien #5412
– expositions de groupe
– (1975) #1867
Faucher, Paul, architecte can, actif années
1960
– Sherbrooke (Qué), Chapelle universitaire
chrétienne #8841
Faugeron, Jean, architecte fr, actif années
1960-
– Montréal (Qué), Expo 67. Pavillon de la
France #1435
Fauteux, André Lucien, sculpteur can, 1946-
#1817
– en comparaison avec Douglas Bentham
#785
– entretien #788
– expositions
– (1976) #5413
– expositions de groupe
– (1975) #1809
– (1977) #782 784
– (1978) #786
– (1981) #797
– techniques #792
Fauteux-Massé, Henriette, artiste can, 1924-
#5414 5415
fauvisme
– et Clark Holmes McDougall #6464
– et David Brown Milne #6552 6567
faux
– objets anciens, Canada #2127
faux . dessin
– Bartlett, William Henry #4614
faux . peinture
– Krieghoff, Cornelius #6101
– peintures canadiennes #64 70 73
– peintures québécoises, début XXe s. #1313
Favro, Murray, artiste can, 1940-
– expositions de groupe
– (1973) #557
– (1977) #783
– (1980) #703
– influence sur Ron Martin #6431
– oeuvres, Carmen Lamanna Gallery
(Toronto, Ont) #1811
– régionalisme, en comparaison avec Greg
Curnoe #5225
– théories sur l'art #594
Fawcett, George, artiste can, 1877-1944
– eaux-fortes #800
Fay-Génot, Jean-Etienne-Achille, acteur et
artiste fr au Canada, 1823-1879 #5416
Fear, Jeffery, designer can, actif 1981 #2487
Featherston, William (Bill), artiste can, 1927-
– expositions
– (1979) #5417

– peintures, ouvriers Squamish #5418
Fédération canadienne de la nature
– expositions
– (1973-) #549
Fédération des artistes canadiens #390 502
– (1941), fondation #379
– (années 1940) #360 363 376 386
– Harris, Lawren Stewart, commentaire #364
Fédération des caisses Desjardins
– protecteur des arts (années 1970) #3275
Fédération des coopératives du Nouveau
Québec
– (1977-1980) #4269
Feininger, Andreas, photographe amér,
1906-
– et Wilfred Roloff Beny #4690
Feist, Harold Elmer, artiste can, 1945-
– expositions de groupe
– (1974) #565
– (1975) #1926
Feldman, Isadore, architecte can, 1887-1919
– Toronto (Ont), Cooper Cap Company
Building #9332
Felter, James Warren, artiste can, 1943-
– expositions
– (1976) #2059
féminisme
– et art, Canada (années 1970) #121 601 673
– et Freda Guttman Bain #4596
– et Maryon Kantaroff #6019
– et Maureen Paxton #6786
femmes architectes
– Canada #7678
femmes artistes #4935
– (1840-1900), Canada, photographes #1049
– (1850-1950), Nouvelle-Ecosse #1204
– (1889-1901), Women's Art Association of
Canada #176
– (1894-), Women's Art Association of
Hamilton #1701
– (1904), arts décoratifs #2241
– (1939-1945), Canada, scènes de guerre
#1116
– (1980), Canada #603 719
– (1980), Inuit #1294
– (1980), tisserandes inuit, Pangnirtung
(TNO) #4308
– (années 1790-X1Xe s.), Canada #7164
– (années 1830), Toronto (Ont) #1688
– (années 1830-1840), Nouvelle-Ecosse #1219
– (années 1830-1860), Toronto (Ont),
photographes #1725
– (années 1880-1926), Montréal (Qué),
peinture sur porcelaine #1228
– (années 1890), Montréal (Qué) #1311
– (années 1910), Canada #202 207 209
– (années 1910), Canada, étudiantes à
l'étranger #206
– (années 1920), Canada #14
– (années 1920), Victoria (CB), potières
#2278
– (années 1920-1950), artisanes inuit
(vannerie) #4180
– (années 1930), Québec #1380
– (années 1930), Québec, artisanes #2165
– (années 1930-1970), Québec #1273
– (années 1940), Canada #377
– (années 1960-1970), artisans tisserands
inuit #4298
– (années 1960-1970), artisans tisserands
salishiens #4147
– (années 1960-1970), Canada #677
– (années 1960-1980), Canada #717
– (années 1970), artisanes inuit et
athapascans #3367

7566 7567 7568 7569 7570
– Whyte, Catharine Robb #1972 7571 7572
– Wieland, Joyce #98 143 147 460 510 556
    568 626 657 675 700 940 1753 7574 7575
    7576 7577 7578 7579 7580 7581 7582
    7583
– Wiitasalo, Shirley #579 591 1832 7584
– Wilby, Roslynn #2153
– Wilby, Susan #2153
– Will, Mary Shannon #795 7586
– Williams, Judy #7588
– Williams, Yvonne #2445 2446 2448 2455
    7589
– Williamson, Betty #987
– Willmott, Elizabeth #777
– Willoughby, Linda #2775
– Winsor, Jackie #7597 7598
– Wood, Elizabeth Wyn #368 739 5677 5678
    7613
– Wood, Faith #581
– Woolnough, Hilda Mary #7616
– Wright, Edith P. Stevenson #7279
– Wrinch, Mary Evelyn #207 1710 6979 7617
    7618
– Wyle, Florence #729 739 754 758
– XIXe s., Nouvelle-Ecosse #1215 1220 1222
– XIXe s.-années 1920, Canada #5
– XIXe s.-années 1970, Canada, artisanes
    (vannerie) #2943
– XIXe s.-années 1970, Canada,
    photographes #1005 1064
– XVIIe s.-années 1910, Québec, artisanat
    domestique #2212
– XVIIe-XVIIIe s., arts décoratifs québécois
    #2200
– XVIIe-XXe s., Canada #117
– XXe s., Canada #53 95 96 121 739
– XXe s., Canada, artisanes #2107
– Young, Helen Granger #7627
– Young, Hester #2723
– Young, Rosanna #2723
– Zack, Badanna Bernice #657
– Zellinger, Jean #7634
femmes dans l'art
– art canadien #53 121
– Bleyenberg, Harry #4742
– Brymner, William #4954
– Gunterman, Mattie #5670
– Heward, Efa Prudence #5796
– Indiens de la côte nord-ouest #3348
    3377
– Karsh, Yousuf #6024
– Lindner, Ernest #6285 6287
– Prince, Richard #6939
– Reeves, John #6972
– Town, Harold Barling #7414
fenêtres . Canada
– conservation #7778
– fabrication de vitres, XIXe-XXe s. #7752
– guide pour la conservation #7777
– Halifax (NE), citadelle d'Halifax #8441
– Saint-Jean (Qué), Canada Glass Works
    #2420
fenêtres dans l'art
– et perception #525
– Gutsche, Clara, photographies de vitrines
    #5673
Fenton, Terry, artiste et conservateur can,
    1940-
– entretien lors des Emma Lake Workshops
    (Emma Lake, Sask) #1934
– expositions de groupe
    – (1967), photographies #8113
– influence sur Douglas Bentham #4683

– participant, Symposium on 20th Century
    Canadian Culture (Washington, DC),
    (1977) #621
– soutien de l'art à Edmonton (Alta) #1975
fer
– dans architecture canadienne #7695
– industrie, Québec et Ontario, fin
    XVIIIe-moitié XIXe s. #2703
Fer, Nicholas de, cartographe fr, 1646-1720
– vue de Terre-Neuve #1150
fer forgé
– voir ouvrages de ferronerie
ferblanterie canadienne
– fin XVIIIe-XIXe s. #2703
– guide pour collectionneurs #2252
– Québec #2711
Fergus (Ont)
– photographie (1856-1867) #1724
Ferguson, Gerald, artiste can, 1937- #5419
– expositions
    – (1977) 5420
– expositions de groupe
    – (1970) #534
Ferguson, Mary, photographe can, active
    années 1970-
– catalogue de photographies #991
fermes
– voir scènes rurales
– voir vie des premiers colons
Fernandes, Michael, artiste can, 1944-
– estampes #1214
Ferraro, Robert (Bob), artiste can, 1936-
– expositions de groupe
    – (1978) #1824
Ferron, Marcelle, artiste can, 1924- #5421
    5422 5423 5425 5426
– à Paris (France) #426 1434
– et Création #1492
– expositions
    – (1970) #5424
– expositions de groupe
    – (1962) #1420
– procédé de la gravure #817
Ferron, Monique Bourbonnais, céramiste
    can, 1924- #2395
Ferryland (TN)
– architecture #7792
Ferryland Downs (TN)
– vues
    – Squires, Gerald Leopold #7272
Ferryland Head (TN), phare #9523
festivals
– voir aussi théâtre
– festivals norvégiens #2273
– Nouvelle-Ecosse, Joseph Howe Festival
    #2887
– Toronto (Ont), Latvian Song Festival #49
– Vancouver (CB)
    – Living Art Performance Festival (1979)
        #2073
    – Pacific Vibrations (1973) #2046
fêtes
– voir festivals
Fetherstonhaugh, Harold Lea, architecte can,
    1887-1971
– Montréal (Qué), Appartements Château
    #8558
feuillage
– voir feuilles dans l'art
feuilles dans l'art
– voir aussi arbres dans l'art; plantes dans
    l'art
– Canada et Etats-Unis, poterie de grès
    #2309

– feuille d'érable, poterie canadienne #2312
Fichaud, Gwen Johnston, artiste can, 1915-
    #5427 5428
– expositions, critiques #1167
Fieguth, Menno, photographe can, ca 1952-
– catalogue de photographies #1023
Field, Robert, artiste can, 1769-1819 #1191
    5429 5433
– expositions
    – (1978) #5432
– gravures #1198
– influence sur Maria Frances Ann Morris
    Miller #6541
– portraits, Provo William Parry Wallis,
    Galerie nationale du Canada (Ottawa,
    Ont) #5430 5431
Field (Fish), Robert, artiste can, 1948-
– expositions
    – (1978) #5434
– expositions de groupe
    – (1980) #687
Fiertel, Neil, sculpteur can, 1941-
– expositions de groupe
    – (1978) #2066
figure humaine dans l'art
– voir aussi femmes dans l'art; mains; nu
    dans l'art; squelettes dans l'art; têtes
– art haida #4070
– Bobak, Bruno Joseph #4760
– Bonham, Don #4794
– Brooker, Bertram Richard #317
– Canada #71 103
    – (1878-1978), peinture #135
    – (années 1940) #380
    – (années 1960), sculpture sur bois #744
    – (années 1970) #578 611 6676
        – sculpture en céramique #774
    – (années 1980), sculpture #796
    – XIXe-XXe s., sculpture #760
– Coughtry, John Graham #5190
– Cox, Elford Bradley #5202
– Fairley, Barker #344
– Lemieux, Jean-Paul #6233
– MacEachern, Ian #6386
– Montréal (Qué)
    – (années 1940-1950) #1426
    – (années 1950-1960) #1438
– Nichols, Jack #6698
– Pellan, Alfred #6822
– Québec (années 1970), estampes #1651
– Saint-Jean (NB), XXe s. #1184
figures de proue
– Canada, XVIIIe-XIXe s. #1604
– Côté, Jean-Baptiste #1577 5186
– Nouvelle-Ecosse, XIXe s. #1200
– Rogerson, John #7067 7068
filage . Amérindiens #3413
filage . Canada #2747 2748
– Cap-Breton (NE) #2732
– Chamard, Emélie #2194 2209
– île aux Coudres (Qué) #2168
– Ontario
    – (1784-1867) #2852
    – XIXe s. #2726
– Ontario Handweavers and Spinners
    (1956-1979) #2743
– Québec (années 1920) #2718
– rouets #2483
– Terre-Neuve et Labrador, XXe s. #2155
– XVIIe-XIXe s. #2112
filage . Cowichan #3796
File, périodique can #544
– (années 1970) #3310
Filer, Mary Harris, artisane can (verre),

1920- #2440
Filiau (dit Dubois), Jean Baptiste, horloger
can, 1699-1772 #5435
Filiau-Dubois, François, constructeur can, né
1700
– correspondance, Pierre-Noël Levasseur
(1745) #6253 6255
Filion, Armand, sculpteur can, 1910- #5436
5437 5438
Filipovic, Augustin, sculpteur can, 1931-
– sculptures d'argile (années 1960) #743
Finlay, George E., officier de l'armée brit,
artiste au Canada, actif 1834-1848 #5439
Fiore, Giuseppe, artiste can, 1931- #5441
– murale, restaurant La Lanterna Verde
(Dorval, Qué) (1963) #5440
Fiorucci, Vittorio, artiste can, 1932- #5442
– affiches #5443
– expositions
– (1981) #5444
Firestone, Otto John (Jack), collectionneur
can, 1913-
– collection, art canadien, Fondation du
patrimoine ontarien (Toronto, Ont) #3239
fiscalité, art et
– Canada
– (1906) #3249
– (1977), Loi sur l'exportation et
l'importation de biens culturels #3283
3284 3296
– (années 1970) #682 3286
– et Front des artistes canadiens #632
Fischer, Hervé, artiste fr, 1941-
– étude sur le musée (institution) #714
Fischl, Eric, artiste amér au Canada, 1948-
– écriture dans l'art #662
– sculpture, art de performance #658
Fiset, Edouard, architecte can, 1910-
– Montréal (Qué), Expo 67 #9213
Fish, R.
– voir Field (Fish), Robert
Fisher, Bob, photographe can, ca 1945- #995
Fisher, Brian Richard, artiste can, 1939-
– commentaire sur la peinture canadienne
(années 1970) #620
– dessins #532
– expositions, critiques #520
– expositions de groupe
– (1967) #490
– (1969) #2039
– (1971) #98
Fisher, Jeff, photographe amér, actif années
1970 #1000
Fisher, Sanford, artiste can, 1927- #5445
Fisher, Tom, photographe can, actif années
1970
– photographies comme moyen d'expression
#1556
Fiske, John, constructeur can, actif 1977
– restauration, Nova Scotia College of Art
and Design (Halifax, NE) #9409
FitzGerald, Lionel LeMoine, artiste can,
1890-1956 #309 1891 1896 5449 5453
– estampes #5451
– et Bertram Richard Brooker #4925 4926
– et Douglas M. Duncan, protecteur des arts
#119 541
– et enseignement de l'art aux enfants
(années 1940) #1889 1890
– expositions
– (1958) #5448
– (1978) #5450
– expositions de groupe
– (1962) #1847

– (1975) #503 504 589 592
– influence sur Caven Ernest Atkins #4570
– membre, Groupe des peintres canadiens
#324
– membre, Winnipeg Sketch Club #1887
– paysages #1855
– Bowen Island (CB) #5446
– peinture
– (années 1930) #502
– Winnipeg (Man), Winnipeg Art Gallery
#3188
– professeur de Stephen Andrews #4528
– technique #5447 5452
Fitzgerald, Owen, photographe can, actif
années 1970-
– catalogue de photographies #991
Fitzmaurice, J.Ben, artiste can, ca 1873-1924
– dessins humoristiques, Montreal Herald
#943
Fitzpatrick, Francis W., architecte amér,
1864-1931 #8365
flacons
– voir bouteilles et flacons
Flaherty, Robert, photographe amér,
1884-1951
– collection, sculpture inuit #4185
Flamand, Jacques
– voir Deguise (dit Flamand), Jacques
Flancs-de-Chien
– culture #4089
– (années 1920) #4081
– pipes #4077
Flandrin, Jean Hippolyte, artiste fr,
1809-1864
– influence sur Napoléon Bourassa #4874
Flat River Crafts Studio (IPE) #2153
Flavelle, Sir Joseph Wesley, homme
d'affaires can, 1858-1939
– résidence, Holwood Mansion (Toronto,
Ont) #8667
Fleisher, Pat, artiste et critique d'art can,
1930- #5454
– directeur de la revue Artmagazine #560
Fleming, Allan Robb, artiste can, 1929-1977
#5456
– commentaire sur la typographie #5455
– et Burns, Cooper, Donoahue, Fleming &
Company Ltd. #904
– graphismes #897 5457
Fleming, Erik, designer suédois, 1894-
– professeur de Harold Stacey #7273 7274
Fleming, John, artiste can, actif 1976
– art vidéo #616
Fleming, John, photographe can, 1836-1876
– photographie d'arpentage #1865
Fleming, Sandford, ingénieur, scientifique et
artiste can, 1827-1915
– collection, photographies d'arpentage,
Canadien Pacifique #1876
– et Charles George Horetzky #5837
Fleming & Smith, agence can d'architecture
– Montréal (Qué), Hôpital général juif #9031
Fletcher, Kenneth, photographe can, actif
1970- #992
fleurs
– fleurs artificielles
– Québec, XVIIIe s. #1320
– Québec (Qué), Hôtel-Dieu, XVIIIe-XIXe
s. #1350
fleurs dans l'art
– voir aussi plantes dans l'art
– Algonquins #3543
– autochtones #3378
– Brown, Annora #4933

– Ciccimarra, Richard Matthew #5107
– décoration architecturale canadienne
(années 1930) #8225 8226
– Gillett, Violet Amy #5605
– Griffiths, James, et John Howard #2305
– Holmes, Robert #5822
– Miller, Maria Frances Ann Morris #241
242 1219 6542
– monuments funéraires, Ontario, XIXe
s.-années 1910 #1723
– Pellan, Alfred #6818 6819
– poterie de grès, Canada et Etats-Unis
#2309
– Rakine, Marthe #6956
– Warren, Mary Schaffer #7526 7527
Fleury, Arthur & Barclay, agence can
d'architecture
– Hamilton (Ont), hôtel de ville et Civic
Square #8988
Fleury & Arthur, agence can d'architecture
– Toronto (Ont), University of Toronto.
Victoria College. Wymilwood #9454
fleuve Columbia (CB)
– pétroglyphes #3870 3903
– sculpture, préhistoire #3914
– vannerie, préhistoire #3842
fleuve Niagara (Ont)
– vues, Claire Shuttleworth #7202
Fliess, Henry, architecte can, 1921-
– Beamsville (Ont), Nipponia Home for the
Aged #8516
– Don Mills (Ont)
– Beth-El Synagogue #8903
– Chatham Village #8511
– South Mills Village #7679
– Toronto (Ont), Clintwood Maisonette
Project #8514
Flomen, Michael, photographe can, 1952-
– expositions, critiques #1018
Florence (Italie), Museo nazionale di
antropologia ed etnologia
– art amérindien #3396
Floride (EU)
– vues, explorateurs français, XVIe s. #276
Fogo (TN)
– architecture #7792
Foisy, Dennis, ébéniste can, 1946- #5458
Foisy, Gilles, artiste can, 1948-
– expositions, critiques #2051
– expositions de groupe
– (1971) #2042
– (1973) #2045
Folch-Ribas, Jacques, architecte can, 1928-
– Carillon (Qué), monument à Dollard des
Ormeaux #1591
– Sherbrooke (Qué), Chapelle universitaire
chrétienne #8841
Foley, Herbert C., artiste can, 1935-
– membre du Hampton Group #1177
folklore
– voir aussi légendes; mythologie
folklore . Canada
– Québec #2169 2171
– et Georges Saint-Pierre #7118
Folles Avoines
– vannerie #3620
Fondation canadienne
– (1946-1959) #3262
Fondation des arts de l'Alberta/Alberta Art
Foundation
– collection #1963
Fondation du patrimoine ontarien
– et conservation #8001
Fondation MacDonald Stewart

- restauration, château Dufresne (Montréal, Qué) #8617
fontaines . Canada
- Laliberté, Alfred #6141
- San Francisco (Calif), Embarcadero Plaza, Armand Vaillancourt #7451
- Toronto (Ont), Dr. D.W. Young, monument #729
- Vancouver (CB) #2077
fonte
- façade, Cauchon Block (connu plus tard sous Empire Hotel) (Winnipeg, Man) #9361
fonts baptismaux . Canada
- Québec (1650-1925) #1592
Forbes, John Colin, artiste can, 1846-1925 #5459
Forbes, Kenneth Keith, artiste can, 1892-1980
- expositions, critiques #432
forçats
- voir prisonniers
Forest, Fred, artiste fr, 1933-
- étude sur le musée (institution) #714
forges . Canada
- comté de Norfolk (Ont), Normandale Iron Works #2699
- Jones Falls (Ont) #8019
- Trois-Rivières (Qué), Forges du Saint-Maurice #2698 2708 2711 7878 9238 9240 9250 9251 9253 9254 9256 9257
Forget, Robert, artiste can, 1943-
- commentaire sur l'art vidéo #1537
- et Vidéographe (Montréal, Qué) #1498
Forget, Sylvain, artiste can, 1962- #5460
formalisme
- et David Bolduc #4774
- et David Craven #5207
- et Michael Snow #7260
- et paysage canadien (années 1960) #496
- et peinture canadienne (années 1970) #620
- et Ronald Langley Bloore #4747
Forrest, Charles Ramus, officier de l'armée brit, artiste au Canada, actif 1821-1823, m. 1827 #279
Forrest, Nita Osborne, artiste can, 1926-
- membre du groupe Limners #2043
Forrestall, Thomas De Vany (Tom), artiste can, 1936- #5464 5465 5466
- en comparaison avec Alex Colville #5462
- et réalisme #110
- expositions
  - (1971) #5461
- expositions de groupe
  - (1966) #1123
  - (1974) #573 1129
  - (1980) #1221
- Shaped by This Land #5463
Forster, John Wycliffe Lowes, artiste can, 1850-1938 #5469
- commentaire sur l'art du portrait #5467 5470
- commentaire sur l'enseignement de l'art #2960
- commentaire sur vues, comté de Peel (Ont), collection William Perkins Bull #3208
- entretien #5468
- professeur de Tomtu H. Roberts #7051
Forsyth, Douglas, artiste can, actif années 1970-
- estampes #1214
Fort Amherst (TN), phare #9523
Fort Anne (NE)
- architecture, magasin sud #8424

Fort Battleford (Sask)
- architecture #8481 8484
Fort Beauséjour (NB)
- souliers et bottes (années 1750-1830) #2858
Fort de Chambly (Qué)
- architecture
  - Boisberthelot de Beaucours, Josué #8336
  - corps de garde #8446
Fort Erie (Ont), Mather Park
- et Commission des parcs du Niagara #7975
Fort Frontenac (Ont)
- architecture #8454
Fort Garry (Man)
- architecture #8094
- décoration intérieure #7758
- vues
  - Hind, William George Richardson #5807
Fort Garry (Man), University of Manitoba
- oeuvres, Tony Tascona #7326
Fort George (Niagara-on-the-Lake, Ont)
- architecture #8454 8457 8463 8472 8473
  - corps de garde #8459 8461 8462
- et Commission des parcs du Niagara #7975
Fort Henry (Kingston, Ont)
- architecture #8454 8455 8457
Fort Langley (CB)
- architecture #8477
- décoration intérieure #7758
- restauration #8474
Fort Lennox (Qué)
- architecture #8447
Fort Malden (Amherstburg, Ont)
- architecture #8456
- décoration intérieure #7758
Fort Mississauga (Toronto, Ont)
- architecture #8454 8457 8472
Fort Niagara (Youngstown, NY)
- architecture #8454 8457
Fort Ontario (Oswego, NY)
- architecture #8457
Fort Portchartrain (Qué)
- conservation, recommandation (1881) #7754
Fort Prince-de-Galles (Man)
- architecture #8094
Fort Rouille (Ont)
- architecture #8457
Fort Saint James (CB)
- architecture #8478
Fort Saint Joseph (Ont)
- architecture #8468 8469
Fort Simpson (TNO)
- caserne #8482
Fort Smith (TNO), Northern Life Museum and National Exhibition Centre
- expositions
  - Images of the Inuit from the Simon Fraser Collection (1980) #4495
Fort Ste Marie (Ont)
- architecture #8454
Fort Toronto (Ont)
- architecture #8454
Fort Wellington (Ont)
- architecture #8454 8466 8467
- décoration intérieure #7758
Fort William (Ont)
- architecture #8460
Fort William (Ont), Thunder Bay Historical Society
- expositions
  - The Far West (1943) #12
Fort Worth (Tex), Amon Carter Museum of

Western Art
- expositions
  - The Artist was a Young Man: The Life Story of Peter Rindisbacher (1970) #7009
  - The Far North: 2000 Years of American Eskimo and Indian Art (1973) #3366
Fort York (Toronto, Ont)
- architecture #8457
forteresses
- voir architecture militaire
Fortier, Ivanhoë, sculpteur can, 1931- #5471
- expositions
  - (1979) #5472
Fortier, Michel, artiste can, 1943-
- pop'art #1497
fortifications
- voir aussi portes . villes; tours Martello
- dans l'art, Terence Johnson #5969
fortifications . Canada
- Alberta, XVIIIe-XIXe s. #8129
- blockhaus (1749-1841) #8417 8418
- Boisberthelot de Beaucours, Josué #8336
- Fort Anne (NE) #8424
- Fort Battleford (Sask) #8481 8484
- Fort Chambly (Qué) #8446
- Fort George (Niagara-on-the-Lake, Ont) #8461 8462 8463 8473
  - corps de garde #8459
- Fort Henry (Kingston, Ont) #8455
- Fort Langley (CB) #8474
- Fort Lennox (Qué) #8447
- Fort Malden (Amherstburg, Ont) #8456
- Fort Rodd Hill (Victoria, CB), batteries supérieures et inférieures #8479
- Fort Saint James (CB) #8478
- Fort Saint Joseph (Ont) #8468 8469
- Fort Wellington (Ont) #8466 8467
- Fort William (Ont) #8460
- Fort York (Toronto, Ont) #8458
- Halifax (NE), citadelle d'Halifax #8430 8431 8432 8433 8434 8438 8440 8441
- Kingston (Ont)
  - (1759-1838) #8453
- Kingston Mills (Ont) #8020
  - blockhaus #8019
- lac Ontario #8457
- Louisbourg (NE) #8419 8422 8423 8425 8426 8439 8442
  - corps de garde #8428 8429
- Manitoba #8094
- Montréal (Qué), citadelle #8445
- Niagara-on-the-Lake (Ont)
  - (1814-1837) #8470
  - (1871-1978) #8472
  - Navy Hall #8464 8465
- Ontario #8454
- Petit Fort Garry (Man) #8475 8476 8480 8482 8483
- Placentia (TN), (1662-1811) #8420 8421
- Québec, moulins transformés en forteresses #9242
- Québec (Qué) #269 270 1306 8450
  - Batterie Royale #8451
  - fort et château Saint-Louis #8443
  - Parc de l'Artillerie #8449
  - Parc de l'Artillerie. Redoute Dauphine #8448 8452
- XVIIe-début XIXe s. #7841
Fortin, Marc-Aurèle, artiste can, 1888-1970 #302 1391 1392 1393 1432 5473 5477 5479 5480 5482
- en Gaspésie #5481
- expositions
  - (1964) #5474

– (1968) #5478
– expositions, critiques #5475
– expositions de groupe
    – (1977) #1278 1279
– peintures de maisons #5476
Fortin, Yvan, artiste can, 1950- #1526
Forton, Michel, orfèvre can, 1754-ca 1816
– oeuvres, Detroit Institute of Arts (Detroit,
    Mich) #2691
Fosbery, Ernest George, artiste can,
    1874-1958
– critique, exposition d'art canadien (1927)
    #298
Foster, Janet Green, photographe can, 1940-
– catalogue de photographies #991
– expositions, critiques #1009
Foster, John, photographe can, 1933-
– catalogue de photographies #991
– expositions, critiques #1009
Foster, Stuart, photographe can, ca 1953-
– catalogue de photographies #1023
Foster Brothers Glass Works, fabricants de
    verre (Saint-Jean, Qué)
– et Canada Glass Works #2420
Foulem, Leopold L., sculpteur can, 1945-
– expositions de groupe
    – (1977) #781
Foulis, James, architecte can, 1882-1932
– Ottawa (Ont), édifices du Parlement et
    édifices connexes, concours #8923
Foulis, Robert, artiste can, 1796-1866 #258
    259
– gravures #1198
– portraits #1171
Fouré, Raoul-Jean, couturier can, actif 1956
– costumes, Piano Concerto, Montreal Theatre
    Ballet #1410
Foureur (dit Champagne), Louis, ébéniste et
    sculpteur can, 1720-1789 #269 270
Foureur (dit Champagne), Pierre, orfèvre
    can, 1756-ca 1795
– oeuvres, Detroit Institute of Arts (Detroit,
    Mich) #2691
Fournelle, André, sculpteur can, 1939- #5483
    5484
Fournier, Arthur, ébéniste, sculpteur et
    collectionneur can, 1863-1931 #5485
Fournier, François-Marie, sculpteur can,
    1790-1864
– influence de la famille Baillairgé #1582
Fournier, Paul, artiste can, 1939- #1807 5486
    5487
– en comparaison avec Tony Calzetta #670
Fowler, C.A., and Company, agence can
    d'architecture
– Halifax (NE), Saint Mary's University.
    Bibliothèque #9046
Fowler, Daniel, artiste can, 1810-1894 #1705
    5488 5490
– correspondance et testament #5492
– expositions
    – (1964) #5489
    – (1979) #5491
– expositions, critiques #5493
Fowler, Orson Squire, auteur et phrénologue
    amér, 1809-1887
– constructions polygonales #7987
Fox, John Richard, artiste can, 1927- #5494
    5496
– expositions
    – (1980) #5495
Fox River (Wis)
– vues, Paul Kane #6009
foyers (âtre) . Canada

– instruments, Québec, XVIIe-XVIIIe s.
    #2210
– manteaux de cheminée, Québec,
    XVIIe-XVIIIe s. #2530 2531
– ouvrages de ferronnerie #2703 2705
fractur
– voir fraktur
fraktur
– Bauman, Joseph #4628
– Hoover, Christian #5829
– Ontario #2250 2253 2254 2255 2264 2267
– Ontario et Pennsylvanie #2259
– Weber, Anna #7539
Frame, Statira Elizabeth, artiste can,
    1870-1935 #2011
– paysages #2016
Français au Canada
– (1520-1880) #216
– (1564-1867) #231
Francastel, Pierre, historien d'art fr,
    1900-1970
– sociologie de l'art, théories appliquées à
    l'art canadien (1760-1860) #251
Franchère, Joseph-Charles, artiste can,
    1866-1921 #1315 1391 5497 5498
– et François-Xavier Aldéric Rapin #6961
Francis, Sam, artiste amér, 1923-
– influence sur Claude Tousignant #7401
– influence sur Jean Albert McEwen #6471
Francis Clementson & Co., fabricants de
    céramique (Saint-John, NB) #2361
Franck, Albert Jacques, artiste can, 1899-1973
    #5502
– et Florence Gertrude Vale #5499
– expositions
    – (1973) #5500 5501
– mari de Florence Gertrude Vale #7453
François, Claude (frère Luc), artiste fr au
    Canada, 1614-1685 #228 229 1323 1363
    5503 5504
– et Claude Baillif #8329
– et peinture québécoise #1353
– La France apportant la Foi aux Sauvages de la
    Nouvelle-France #1328
– peintures, basilique Sainte-Anne
    (Sainte-Anne-de-Beaupré, Qué) #1321
Frank, Leonard, photographe can, 1871-1944
– expositions de groupe
    – (1976) #2012
Frank, Robert Louis, photographe amér au
    Canada, 1924- #5506
– entretien #664
– expositions, critiques #5505
Frankford (Ont)
– vues photographiques, Lizzy Wadsworth
    #7496
Frankfurt am Main (Allemagne de l'Ouest),
    Städtische Museum für Völkerkunde
– art amérindien #3464
Franklin, David Randall, architecte can,
    1882-1948
– Toronto (Ont), John Ross Robertson School
    et Glenholme School #9437
Franklin, Sir John, officier de la marine brit,
    explorateur au Canada, 1786-1847
– expédition dans l'Arctique #278
    – et George Back #241 242 4580
    – et Robert Hood #5825 5826 5827
Franks, Rhonda, artiste can, 1959-
– expositions de groupe
    – (1980) #4159
Franquelin, Jean-Baptiste-Louis, cartographe
    fr, artiste au Canada, 1651/1653-1718
– cartes géographiques du Canada #875

Fraser, Carol Lucille Hoorn, artiste can,
    1930- #5508
– expositions
    – (1977) #5507
– expositions de groupe
    – (1966) #1123
Fraser, John Arthur, artiste can, 1838-1898
    #178 5511
– commentaire sur voyage à Chequamegon
    Bay (Ont) #5509
– commentaire sur voyage dans les
    Rocheuses (Canada) #5510
– et Ontario Society of Artists #1666
– et peinture canadienne #18
– expositions, critiques #174
Fraser, Judith Margaret Williams, artiste can,
    1940-
– commentaire sur le collage #2042
Fréchette, Louis Honoré, poète can,
    1839-1908
– Wilde, Oscar, commentaire #238
Frédéric, Frédéric, artiste can, 1938- #5512
Fredericks, Beany, artisane tisserande can,
    active 1966 #5513
Fredericton (NB)
– architecture #7809
    – XIXe s. #7803
– art (1960s) #441
– vues, XIXe s. #1174
– vues photographiques
    – Smith, Madge #7235
    – Taylor, George Thomas #7334
Fredericton (NB), Archives provinciales du
    Nouveau-Brunswick
– expositions
    – George Thomas Taylor, 1838-1913: An
      Exhibition of Photographs, Paintings, and
      Memorabilia to Mark the Official Opening
      of the New Brunswick Provincial Archives
      on May 29th, 1968 (1968) #7334
– Smith, Madge, photographies #7235
Fredericton (NB), Assemblée législative
– architecture #8940 8941
Fredericton (NB), cathédrale
– architecture, William Butterfield #8770
Fredericton (NB), chapelle
– architecture, Frank Wills #8770
Fredericton (NB), Fredericton National
    Exhibition Centre
– expositions
    – Canadians: A National Photography Show
      about People/Canadiens: exposition
      nationale de photographie ayant les gens
      comme thème (1979) #1035
Fredericton (NB), galerie d'art Beaverbrook
    #1178
– (années 1960) #1122
– acquisitions (jusqu'en juillet 1959) #3066
– expositions
    – Canadian Painting: Yesterday and Today,
      1800-1960: From the Collection of the
      Beaverbrook Art Gallery/La peinture
      canadienne hier et aujourd'hui, 1800-1960:
      collection de la Galerie d'art Beaverbrook
      (1972) #99
    – Carol Fraser Paintings and Drawings:
      1967-1977 (1977) #5507
    – Claude Tousignant (1973) #7401
    – Colville, Pratt, Forrestall (1974) #1129
    – Conceptual Decorative: Prints by Les
      Levine, 1965-1970/Conceptuel décoratif:
      estampes de Les Levine, 1965-1970 (1971)
      #6265
    – David Bolduc: Recent Work (1979) #4775

- *Dennis Burton Retrospective* (1977) #4961
- *Drawings and Pastels c. 1930-1967 by Miller Gore Brittain* (1968) #4917
- *Drawings by Jack Weldon Humphrey: A Travelling Exhibition Organized by the Beaverbrook Art Gallery, Fredericton, New Brunswick, Canada, 1977-1979* (1978) #5871
- *E. Lindner: Drawings, 1969-1972* (1972) #6285
- *Edwy Cooke: aquarelles, 1942-1977* (1978) #5171
- *Esther Warkov* (1970) #7517
- *Fernand Leduc* (1971) #6186
- *Fredericton Collects* (1979) #142
- *Goodridge Roberts: Selected Works/Goodridge Roberts: oeuvres choisies* (1981) #7050
- *Gordon Rayner Retrospective* (1980) #6966
- *Greg Curnoe: rétrospective/Greg Curnoe: Retrospective* (1982) #5231
- *Inuit Art in the 1970's: A Travelling Exhibition/L'Art inuit actuel, 1970-79: exposition itinérante* (1979) #4287
- *Ivan Eyre Exposition* (1981) #5394
- *Jack Humphrey: A Retrospective Exhibition/Jack Humphrey: une exposition* (1970) #5870
- *Joe Plaskett and His Paris: In Search of Time Past* (1972) #6893
- *Joe Plaskett et son Paris: à la recherche d'un temps passé* (1972) #6894
- *John Fox: 10 New Paintings* (1980) #5495
- *Kostyniuk: Relief Structures, 1969-1972* (1973) #6079
- *L'art du paysage au Québec, 1800-1940/Landscape Painting in Québec, 1800-1940* (1978) #1286
- *Maritime Art Exhibition* (1959-1965) #1120
- *Miller Brittain - Painter* (1981) #4922
- *Painters Eleven in Retrospect* (1981) #1785
- *Ronald: 25 Years* (1975) #7073
- *The Beaverbrook Art Gallery Presents Nine New Brunswick Artists/La Galerie d'art Beaverbrook présente neuf artistes du Nouveau-Brunswick* (1973) #1182
- *The Figure in Canadian Painting: From the Collection of the Beaverbrook Art Gallery/La peinture figurative canadienne: collection de la galerie d'art Beaverbrook* (1972) #103
- *The Image of Man in Canadian Painting: 1878-1978/L'image de l'homme dans la peinture canadienne: 1878-1978* (1978) #135
- *The J.S. McLean Collection of Canadian Painting* (1969) #3228
- *The Mr. and Mrs. Jules Loeb Collection/La collection M. et Mme Jules Loeb* (1971) #3231
- *The Murray and Marguerite Vaughan Inuit Print Collection/Collection d'estampes inuit* (1981) #4498
- *The New Brunswick Landscape Print: 1760-1880* (1980) #1189
- *The Queen Comes to New Brunswick: Paintings and Drawings by Molly Lamb Bobak* (1977) #4765
- *The Railway: Patron of the Arts in Canada* (1976) #3281
- *The Saidye and Samuel Bronfman Collection of Canadian Art/La collection Saidye et Samuel Bronfman* (1966) #3087
- *The Society of Canadian Painter-Etchers and Engravers in Retrospect/La Société des peintres-graveurs canadiens: vue rétrospective* (1981) #836
- *The Work of Art: Six Artists* (1979) #665
- *Tom Forrestall Exhibition* (1971) #5461
- *Wallace S. Bird Memorial Collection: An Exhibition of the Work of Artists from Atlantic Canada* (1975) #1130
- *William G.R. Hind (1833-1888): A Confederation Painter in Canada* (1967) #5806
- *William Perehudoff: Recent Paintings* (1979) #6837

Fredericton (NB), Government House
- architecture #8754
  - Woolford, John Elliott #258 259

Fredericton (NB), Kings Landing Historical Settlement
- mobilier #2484

Fredericton (NB), University of New Brunswick
- Bobak, Bruno Joseph, artiste résident (1960-1961) #4757
- Taylor, George Thomas, photographes #7333

Fredericton (NB), University of New Brunswick. Art Centre
- expositions
  - *Albert Franck (1899-1973) in Retrospect: A Small Selection from the Artist's Collection* (1974) #5500
  - *Annie D. Savage: Drawings and Watercolours* (1975) #7129
  - *Fritz Brandtner 1896-1969: A Restrospective Exhibition* (1971) #4903
  - *George Rackus: Anodized Aluminum Works & Prints* (1973) #6953

Fredericton (NB), University of New Brunswick. King's College
- architecture, John Elliott Woolford #258 259

Fredericton Art Club (Fredericton, NB)
- (1936-1961) #1176

Fredericton Society of Artists (Fredericton, NB) #1176

Freedman, Adele, critique d'art can, 1946-
- lauréate, concours de critique d'art (1979) #3312

Freifeld, Eric, artiste can, 1919- #5515
- entretien #5516
- et réalisme #110
- expositions
  - (1968) #5514

Freiman, Lillian, artiste can, 1908- #336 5517
  - (1978) #5518

Frémont (Qué)
- urbanisme #7728

Frenière, F. Daunais, artiste can, actif 1833-1843 #1301

Frenière, F.X., artiste can, actif 1842 #1301

Frenkel, Vera, artiste can, 1938- #5521 5526
  - commentaire sur l'art, l'amour et la politique #5522
  - commentaire sur l'art de performance et l'art vidéo #713
  - commentaire sur l'enseignement de l'art à des élèves de l'école secondaire (1969) #5519
  - élève d'Albert Dumouchel #5327
  - expositions
    - (1978) #5525
  - expositions, critiques #5520
  - professeure d'Ed Bartram #4618
  - théories sur l'art #5523

- vidéo, *No Solution - A Suspense Thriller* #5524

fresques
- *voir* peinture murale

Freud, Sigmund, psychiatre aut, 1856-1939
- théories
  - et art préhistorique, Indiens de la côte nord-ouest #3861
  - influence sur surréalisme #1466

Frick, Joan, artiste can, 1942-
- expositions, critiques #5527

Friend, Ray, artiste can (vitrail), actif 1980
- vitraux, Coquitlam Centre (Vancouver, CB) #2459

Friend, Washington, artiste amér, ca 1820-ca 1886
- expositions de groupe
  - (1888) #175
  - (1890) #177 1839

Fringe Research Inc., agence de photographie (Toronto, Ont)
- expositions
  - (1979) #1905
- hologrammes #1827

Fripp, Charles Edward, artiste brit au Canada, 1854-1906
- vues, Ouest canadien #931

Fripp, Robert Mackay, architecte can, 1858-1917
- Vancouver (CB), maisons #8685

Fripp, Thomas William, artiste can, 1864-1931 #1986 2011

Frise, James Llewellyn, artiste can, 1891-1948
- illustrations #855

Frobisher, Sir Martin, explorateur brit au Canada, 1535-1594
- expédition dans l'Arctique #228 229
- Inuit capturés, portraits, John White #7553

Frobisher Bay (TNO)
- projet d'aménagement (années 1950) #8184

Frobisher Bay (TNO), Frobisher Bay Academic and Occupational School
- architecture, Papineau, Gérin-Lajoie, LeBlanc, Edwards #8188

Frobisher Bay (TNO), The Museum of Things from the Land
- art inuit #4224

Front des artistes canadiens/Canadian Artists' Representation (CAR/FAC)
- (années 1970) #632 1804 3278
- conditions d'adhésion (1978) #3287
- et Jack Chambers #563 5081
- et Michel Lambeth #6159
- et Niagara Artists' Co-operative #834
- influence sur la perception de l'art du public (années 1970) #6748
- périodique, *CAR/FAC News* #625

Fry, George, artiste can, actif années 1960
- membre du Hampton Group #1177

Fry, Samuel, tisserand can, 1812-1881 #2723

Fuertes, Louis Agassiz, artiste amér, 1874-1927
- Lansdowne, James Fenwick, comparaison #6165

Fuller, Richard Buckminster, architecte amér, 1895-
- Montréal (Qué), Expo 67. Pavillon des Etats-Unis #9218

Fuller, Thomas, architecte can, 1823-1898 #8366
- bureaux de poste #9054 9055
- Ottawa (Ont), édifices du Parlement #7671
- père de Thomas William Fuller #8367 8368

Fuller, Thomas William, architecte can,

1865-1951 #8367 8368
Fuller & Jones, agence can d'architecture
– Ottawa (Ont), édifices du Parlement #8922 8930
Fulton, Christopher, photographe can, actif 1862-1864
– et Victoria Theatre Photographic Gallery (Victoria, CB) #2027
Furihata, artiste jap, XXe s.
– professeur de Gaston-Pierre Petit #6844
Furse, Barbara, artiste can, active années 1960
– membre du Hampton Group #1177
Furse, Peter Reynolds, cartographe can, m. 1970
– membre du Hampton Group #1177
Fuse: The Cultural News Magazine, périodique can #603
fusils
– voir armes à feu
Fusion des arts (Montréal, Qué) #1483 1502
– (1964-1968) #1482
– et Richard Lacroix #6126
– utilisation du plastique #1442
futurisme
– Canada (années 1910) #1071
– et art vidéo #654
Fyshe, Avis Selina, artiste can, née 1886
– commentaire sur cartes de Noël, Canada #849

G

Gabo, Naum, sculpteur russe, 1890-1977
– utilisation du plastique #768
Gaboury, E.J., and Associates, agence can d'architecture
– Saskatoon (Sask), Mendel Art Gallery, concours #9091
Gaboury, Etienne J., architecte can, 1930- #8084
– Regina (Sask), Saint Anne's Church et presbytère #8767
– Saint-Boniface (Man), Precious Blood Church #8091 8908
– théories sur l'architecture #7746 8369
– verrières #2450
– Winnipeg (Man), Etienne Gaboury House #8519
Gabriel, Pier, sculpteur can, actif 1979 #1626
Gabriola Island (CB)
– pétroglyphes, Indiens de la côte nord-ouest #4050
Gadbois, Louise Landry, artiste can, 1896- #5529
– expositions
  – (1979) #5528
– peinture montréalaise (1939-1950) #1433
Gaddi, Taddeo, artiste it, ca 1300-1366
– influence sur David Brown Milne #6567
Gadois (dit Mauger), Jacques, orfèvre can, 1686-1750 #249 250
Gaettens, Marianne, photographe can, active 1970 #993
Gagen, Robert Ford, artiste can, 1847-1926
– correspondance, John William Beatty (1918) #4638
– entretien #5530
– expositions de groupe
  – (1978) #1726
Gagné, Andrée, photographe can, 1951-

– catalogue de photographies #1023
Gagné, Marc-André, photographe can, 1939- #991 997 999 1000
Gagné, Marcel, architecte can, 1926-1973
– Osaka (Japon), Expo 70. Pavillon du Canada, concours #9217
Gagné-Dufresne, Hélène, sculpteure et céramiste can, 1931- #5531
– et Ecole des beaux-arts (Montréal, Qué), (1968) #2995
Gagnier, H., Ltd., éditeur (Toronto, Ont)
– siège social, Graphic Arts Building #9330
Gagnon, Charles, artiste can, 1934- #1007 1484 1542 1543 5533 5535
– catalogue de photographies #997 999
– collages (fin des années 1950) #5532
– entretien #5534
– et art minimal #1483
– et critique d'art #3315
– expositions
  – (1979) #5540
– expositions, critiques #1018 1046 1060 5537 5538 5539
– expositions de groupe
  – (1977) #636
  – (1979) #510 1037
– participant, Symposium on 20th Century Canadian Culture (Washington, DC), (1977) #621
– peintures et photographies #5536
– photographies comme moyen d'expression #1556
Gagnon, Clarence Alphonse, artiste can, 1881-1942 #302 1315 1392 5541 5543 5544 5546 5547
– à Baie-Saint-Paul (Qué) #5545
– Boeufs au labeur/Oxen Ploughing Beaupré #5548
– eaux-fortes #799
– et Albert Henry Robinson #7057
– et Maurice Galbraith Cullen #5221
– et peinture canadienne #18
– et peinture québécoise #1270
– expositions
  – (1942) #5542
  – (1981) #5549
– expositions de groupe
  – (1942) #359
– illustrations, Maria Chapdelaine #1
– influence sur René-Jean Richard #6997 6998 6999
– membre, Canadian Art Club #193
– oeuvres, McMichael Canadian Collection (Kleinburg, Ont) #3172
Gagnon, Edmond, artisan vannier can, actif 1981 #2954
Gagnon, Maurice, auteur can, 1904-
– écrits #1393
– et Paul-Emile Borduas #4814
Gagnon, Pnina, artiste can, 1940- #5550
Gagnon, René, artiste can, 1927- #5551
Gagnon, Yvonne Tremblay
– voir Tremblay-Gagnon, Yvonne
Gagnon-Fortier, C., artiste can, 1938-
– expositions
  – (1978) #5552
Gaitskell, Charles Dudley, artiste et éducateur can, 1908-
– réflexion sur l'enseignement de l'art dans les écoles canadiennes #2986
Galerie nationale du Canada. Bulletin annuel/National Gallery of Canada. Annual Bulletin, périodique can #69
Gallagher, Chris, photographe can, 1951-

– expositions de groupe
  – (1979) #2069
Gallie, Tommie J., artiste can, 1946-
– expositions
  – (1981) #5553
– expositions de groupe
  – (1978) #2066
Gallop, John Frederick, architecte can, actif années 1960
– Osaka (Japon), Expo 70. Pavillon du Canada, concours #9217
– sièges (mobilier) #2471
Gallozzi, Chuck, photographe can, actif 1977
– catalogue de photographies #1023
Galt (Ont), école publique
– architecture, John Evans #9387
Galt (Ont), Gore District Mutual Fire Insurance Company building
– architecture, Marani, Lawson & Morris #7973
Gambioli, Joan, sculpteure can, 1920-
– The Family, Van Dusen Gardens (Vancouver, BC) #775
Gamble, Eric, artiste can, 1950-
– expositions, critiques #639
Gamble, Millie, photographe can, née 1887 #5554
Gammon, George, ébéniste canadien, actif années 1830-1859 #2493
Gano, John Henry, photographe can, 1873-1947 #5555
GAP
– voir Groupe d'action photographique (GAP)
Garber, Bram, collectionneur can, XXe s.
– collection, peinture canadienne, XXe s. #3247
Gard, Thomas Dapleton, orfèvre can, actif 1856-1877 #2649
Gard, W.Tremaine, orfèvre can, 1867-1914 #2649
Garden Hill Cooperative (Island Lake, Man) #4135
Garden McMillan, agence can d'architecture
– Calgary (Alta), Brae Glen #8746
Gardet, Georges, sculpteur fr, 1863-1939
– sculpture, Palais législatif (Winnipeg, Man) #8948 8949 8952
Gardiner, Frederick, artiste can, 1898-1905 #2085
Gardiner, Thornton, Gathe, Davidson, Garrett, Masson & Associates, agence can d'architecture
– Osaka (Japon), Expo 70. Pavillon du Canada, concours #9217
Gardiner, Thornton, Gathe & Associates, agence can d'architecture
– Surrey (CB), Surrey Memorial Hospital #9032
– Winnipeg (Man), University of Manitoba. Saint Paul's College et Chapel of Christ the King #9486
Gardiner & Mercer, agence can d'architecture
– Vancouver (CB), Saint Paul's Hospital. Surgical Wing #9021
gares . Canada
– (1880-1914) #7736
– Brandon (Man), Canadien National #9266
– Grand Trunk Railway et Canadien Pacifique #9539
– Hamilton (Ont), Hamilton Terminal Station #9527
– Manitoba #9543

– Montréal (Qué)
  – gare Bonaventure (1888-1952) #9538
  – gare Centrale #9535
  – gare Windsor #9532 9537
– Ontario #9541
  – XIXe s. #8006
– Ottawa (Ont), gare Centrale #9528 9529
– provinces de l'Ouest #8083 9542 9545
– Québec (Qué), gare Union #9533
– Saskatchewan #9544
– Toronto (Ont)
  – gare Union #9531 9536 9540
  – XIXe s.-années 1930 #8076
– Vancouver (CB)
  – gare du Canadien Pacifique #9534
  – gares du Canadien Pacifique (1887-1914) #9546
– Winnipeg (Man), Fort Garry Terminal #9530
– XIXe s. #9512
gares . Etats-Unis
– Ouest des Etats-Unis #8083
gares . France
– influence sur gare Union (Toronto, Ont) #9536
gares . Grande-Bretagne
– influence sur gare Union (Toronto, Ont) #9536
Garneau, François-Xavier, historien can, 1809-1866
– résidence, maison Garneau (La Canardière, Qué) #8615
Garnier, Hubert, sculpteur can, 1903-
– expositions
  – (1976) #5556
Garnier, Jacques, céramiste can, 1943- #5557
garnitures de perles . Amérindiens
– motifs floraux #3449
Garrett, R.Michael, architecte can, 1931-
– Vancouver (CB), University of British Columbia. Student Union, concours #9503
Garstang-Hodgson, Wilfred, sculpteur can, 1885-1971 #5815
Garthwaite, Ernest Paul, artiste can, 1946-
– expositions, critiques #5558
Garwood-Jones, Trevor Patrick, architecte can, 1928-
– Hamilton (Ont), Art Gallery of Hamilton #3165
Gascon, Michel, photographe can, 1948- #1562
Gaspé (Qué)
– cabanes en bois rond #7896
– vues
  – Fortin, Marc-Aurèle #5481
– vues photographiques
  – Karnick, Irwin #1008
Gathe, Asbjorn R., architecte can, 1921-
– Vancouver (CB), University of British Columbia. Student Union, concours #9503
Gaucher, Yves, artiste can, 1934- #536 1542 1543 5561 5562 5564 5567 5568
– commentaire sur ses études en art #470
– dessins #532
– entretien #5560
– estampes (années 1960) #1654 5559
– et art minimal #1483
– et gravure québécoise (années 1960) #1641
– et op'art #1445
– expositions
  – (1969) #5563
  – (1976) #5566
– expositions, critiques #5569 5570

– expositions de groupe
  – (1967) #480 490 821
  – (1977) #643
– juge, B.C. Artists Annual Exhibition, Vancouver Art Gallery (Vancouver, BC), (1967) #1983
– peintures (1963-1973) #5565
– reconnaissance de l'artiste #123
Gaudard, Pierre Raymond, photographe can, 1927-
– photographies d'ouvriers #990
– photographies documentaires #1556
Gaudin, Jean, artiste fr, 1879-1954
– mosaïques, basilique Sainte-Anne (Sainte-Anne-de-Beaupré, Qué) #8859 8860 8865 8866
Gaudin (dit Lapoterie), Louis-Nicolas, orfèvre can, 1725-1809 #5571
Gaudin (dit Lapoterie), Nicolas, orfèvre can, ca 1695-ca 1743 #5572
– père de Louis-Nicolas Gaudin (dit Lapoterie) #5571
Gauguin, Paul, artiste fr, 1848-1903
– influence sur Mary Evelyn Wrinch #7617
Gauthier, Amable, sculpteur et architecte can, 1792-1873 #241 242 6947
– intérieur, église de Berthierville (Qué) #8874
Gauthier, Claude-Paul, sculpteur can, 1951- #1630
Gauthier, Michel, photographe can, actif années 1970 #1283
Gauthier, Paul, architecte can, 1935-
– Québec (Qué) #7733
  – Jardins Mérici #7886
Gauthier, Robert, artiste can, 1951- #5573
Gauthier & Guité, agence can d'architecture
– Québec (Qué), église #8766
Gauthier-Charlebois, Alyne, artiste can, active 1932 #1380
Gauthier Guité Roy, agence can d'architecture
– Québec (Qué), Jardins Mérici #8746
Gauthier-Mitchell, Louisette, artiste can, 1941- #1511
– expositions
  – (1980) #5574
Gautier, Théophile, auteur fr, 1811-1872
– théories sur l'art #405
Gauvreau, Claude, artiste et auteur can, 1925-1971 #1502
– commentaire sur Ozias Leduc #6199
– correspondance, Paul-Emile Borduas #4804 4805 4807 4834
– écrits #1449
– écrits et correspondance #1443
– Refus global #1396
Gauvreau, Jean-Marie, ébéniste can, 1903-1970
– directeur, Ecole du meuble (Montréal, Qué) #2176 2976
– et Centrale d'artisanat du Québec #2238
Gauvreau, Pierre, architecte can, 1813-1884
– Québec (Qué), Assemblée nationale #8942
Gauvreau, Pierre, artiste can, 1922-
– entretien #5576
– et automatisme #5575
– et peinture montréalaise (années 1950) #1403
– expositions
  – (1979) #5577
  – (1981) #5578
– expositions de groupe
  – (1955) #1408

Geisel, Albert, artiste can, 1889-1973
– expositions de groupe
  – (1975) #1682
Gelin, Denis, sculpteur fr, actif 1931
– oeuvres, T. Eaton Company, magasin à grande surface (Montréal, Qué, et Toronto, Ont) #9370
Gemeinhardt, John, ébéniste can, 1826-1912 #5579
Gendron, Ernest, artiste can, 1912- #5580
Gendron, Pierre, artiste can, 1934- #5581 5582
– commentaire sur la gravure #817
généalogie
– voir aussi héraldique
– Bourassa, Napoléon #4872 4874
– famille Bourgault #4886
– Hamel, Théophile #5692
– utilisation de modèles de broderie #2790
General Idea (Toronto, Ont) #5584
– art de performance #655
– art vidéo #605 630
– Conversation Pierre: Three Booths for the Miss General Idea Pavilion #714
– correspondance sur le concours Mademoiselle General Idea (1971) #546
– et art d'avant-garde #600
– expositions
  – (1977) #5583
  – (1980) #690
– expositions de groupe
  – (1977) #631
  – (1980) #705 1063 8237
– livres #940
– périodique, File #544
– Test Tube #692
– utilisation de la photographie #1057
Généreux, Marie Arline, artiste can, 1897- #1380
Genn, Robert, artiste can, 1936-
– autobiographie #5585
Génot, Achille
– voir Fay-Génot, Achille
Gens-du-Sang
– costume #3414 3739
– peau de bison peinte #3711
Gentile, Charles, photographe can, 1835-1893
– et Victoria Theatre Photographic Gallery (Victoria, CB) #2027
Geoffrey Massey/E.J. Watkins/R.B. Archambault/C.D. Rowett, agence can d'architecture
– Canadian Architect, concours, galerie d'art communautaire (1957) #9082
Geoffroy, André, sculpteur can, 1946-
– Symposium international de sculpture environnementale de Chicoutimi (Qué), (1980) #1639
géographie
– et paysage québécois #26 41
géologie
– et Paterson Ewen #5383
géométrie
– dans l'art
  – Bloore, Ronald Langley #4749
  – Dubois, Marius #5310
  – Rockburne, Dorothea #7060
George & Moorhouse, agence can d'architecture
– Toronto (Ont), Bourse de Toronto #9187
George II, roi de Grande-Bretagne et d'Irlande, 1683-1760
– statut, Cambridge University. Senate

House (Cambridge, Angleterre) #725
Georgetown (IPE)
– architecture #7799
Georgeville (Qué), maison Joshua Copp
– architecture et intérieur #8628
Georgian Bay (Ont)
– vues
  – Fairley, Barker #5402
  – Groupe des Sept #1745
  – Jackson, A.Y. #5919
  – Lismer, Arthur #6304
Georgian Bay (Ont), résidence d'été
– architecture, Blake Millar #8745
Georgian Bay (Ont), résidence d'été de F.S. Eaton
– architecture, Blake Millar #8519
Gerald Bern Agency, agence can de graphisme #871
Gerald Hamilton & Associates, agence can d'architecture
– Ottawa (Ont), Centre municipal d'Ottawa #9101
Gerber, Sidney, collectionneur amér, m. 1965
– collection, art, Indiens de la côte nord-ouest #3974
Gérin-Lajoie, Guy, architecte can, 1928-
– Montréal (Qué), métro. Station Peel #9553
Gérin-Tétreault, Denyse, artiste can, 1940- #1282
– et RACE (Regroupement des artistes des Cantons de l'Est) #1536
Gérôme, Jean-Léon, artiste fr, 1824-1904
– professeur de François-Xavier Aldéric Rapin #6961
– professeur de Joseph-Charles Franchère #5497
– professeur de Wyatt Eaton #5357
Gervais, Lise, artiste can, 1933- #5586
– entretien #5587
Gervais, Raymond, artiste can, 1946-
– expositions de groupe
  – (1977) #637
  – (1980) #687 696
– sculpture, art de performance #658
Geske, Allan, artiste can, 1945-
– expositions de groupe
  – (1981) #1908
geste
– dans la peinture, Gordon Appelbe Smith #7223
Ghana
– vues photographiques
  – Semak, Michael William #990
Ghent (Belgique), Museum van Hedendaagse Kunst
– expositions
  – Prospekt 80/2: Canada; CCMC, David Askevold, Colin Campbell, Dan Graham, Noel Harding, General Idea, Michael Snow (1980) #690
Giacometti, Alberto, artiste suisse, 1901-1966
– influence sur Joe Plaskett #6889
Gibb, Benaiah, collectionneur can, m. 1877
– et Art Association of Montreal (Montréal, Qué) #3075 3110
Gibbard, W.T., fabricants de meubles (Beauharnois, Qué) #2463
Gibbs, Leonard (Len), artiste can, 1929- #5589 5590
– entretien #5588
Gibson, Carol, photographe can, 1945-
– expositions, critiques #1018
Gibson, George, sculpteur can, 1915-
– oeuvres, travaux, édifices du Parlement

(Victoria, CB) #8967
Gibson, George Selkirk, artiste can, 1867-1942 #5591
Gibson, Susan, artiste can, 1947-
– expositions de groupe
  – (1980) #1221
Gibson, Thomas Kent Hamilton (Tom), photographe can, 1930- #5592
– catalogue de photographies #997 999
– expositions, critiques #1018 1046 1060
– expositions de groupe
  – (1979) #1037
Gibson's Landing (CB), Elphinstone Pioneer Museum
– McCall, Helen, photographies #6460
Giddings, J.Louis, archéologue amér, 1909-1964
– expédition dans l'Arctique #4371
Giguère, Denise, céramiste can, 1926-
– entretien #5598
Giguère, Roland, artiste et auteur can, 1929- #1541 5594 5595
– commentaire sur Léon Bellefleur #4662
– commentaire sur procédé de la gravure #818
– écrits #4831
– entretien #1527
– et Editions Erta #926 1641
– expositions
  – (1966) #5593
– peintures et poèmes #5597 5599
– procédé de la gravure #817
– réflexion sur son oeuvre #5598
– visions du rêve #5596
Gilbert, Albert, photographe can, actif 1973
– catalogue de photographies #995
Gilbert, André, architecte can, 1919-
– Saint-Nicolas (Qué), église Saint-Nicolas #8766
Gilbert, Bradford Lee, architecte amér, 1853-1911
– Ottawa (Ont), gare Centrale et Château Laurier #9528 9529
Gilbert, Cass, architecte amér, 1858-1934
– Regina (Sask), édifices du Parlement, concours #8954
Gilbert, Henry Byran, architecte can, 1885-
– Toronto (Ont), Union Bank of Canada #9159
Gilbert, Ina Elaine, artiste can, 1932- #5600
Gilbert, William Herbert (Herb), artiste can, 1926-
– expositions de groupe
  – (1959) #1997
  – (1974) #2050
Giles, William, artiste brit, né 1872
– et Walter Joseph Phillips #6860
Gilhooly, David James, sculpteur et céramiste can, 1943- #538 5601 5602
– et Joe Fafard #5398
– et l'art torontois (Ont), (années 1970) #1796
– expositions, critiques #2383
– expositions de groupe
  – (1977) #781
Gill, Charles Ignace Adélard, artiste et auteur can, 1871-1918 #89 1231 1382 5603
– et François-Xavier Aldéric Rapin #6961
– expositions
  – (1971) #5604
Gill, Dennis, artiste can, 1950-
– estampes #1214
– expositions, critiques #1227
Gillam, William Charles Frederick, architecte can, né 1867

– Victoria (CB), Provincial Normal School #9386
Gilleland & Strutt, agence can d'architecture
– Halifax (NE), Aéroport international de Halifax. Aérogare #9515
– Ottawa (Ont), Aéroport international d'Ottawa. Aérogare #9515
Gilles, Albert, artiste can, 1895-1979
– et art religieux au Québec (années 1950) #1250
Gillespie, J.H., artiste can, né 1793, actif années 1820-1840 #1171
Gillett, Violet Amy, artiste can, 1898- #1173 5605
Gilson, Jacqueline Marie-Charlotte, artiste can, 1912- #5606
Gingras, André, sculpteur can, XIXe s.
– intérieur, église Saint-Jean-Baptiste (Saint-Jean-Port-Joli, Qué) #8812
Gingras, Micheline, artiste can, 1947- #5607
Gingras, Ulric-Louis, poète can, 1894-1954
– Du soleil sur l'étang noir, illustrations, Rodolphe Duguay #5320
Girard, Claude, artiste can, 1938- #5608
Girouard, Jean-Joseph, homme d'Etat et artiste can, 1795-1855 #5609
girouettes . Canada #1364
– fixées aux granges #9228
– girouettes en forme de coq
  – Price, Ralph et Patricia, collection #971
  – Québec #2589
– ouvrages de ferronerie, Québec #2702 2705
– thème décoratif du castor #56
girouettes . Etats-Unis
– fixées aux granges #9228
Giroux, André-Raphaël, sculpteur et architecte can, 1815-1869 #258 259 5610
– emploi de modèles architecturaux #7872
– influence de la famille Baillairgé #1582
– intérieur, Cap-Santé (Qué) #8814
– Québec (Qué), Notre-Dame-des-Victoires #8858
Giroux, Raphäel
– voir Giroux, André-Raphaël
Gitksans
– 'Ksan (coopérative d'artistes) #4134
– totems #3797 3815 3828 3834 3884 3925 4032
Gjoa Haven (TNO)
– sculpture inuit #4435
Glackens, William James, artiste amér, 1870-1938
– influence sur James Wilson Morrice #6626
Gladstone, Gerald, sculpteur can, 1929- #5612
– commentaire sur la perception visuelle #525
– commentaire sur les relations entre artistes et architectes #8234
– entretien #5613
– expositions
  – (1962) #5611
– sculptures (années 1960) #745 746
Gladu, Arthur, artiste can, 1918-
– expositions, critiques #860
Glasgow (Ecosse), Glasgow School of Art
– McLaren, Norman, élève #6492 6493
Glass, Alan Frank, artiste can, 1932- #5614 5615 5616
– à Paris (France) #426
Gleason, Herbert Wendell, photographe amér, 1855-1937
– vues photographiques, Ouest canadien et Ouest américain #5617

Glengarry (Ont)
– cabanes en bois rond #7990
Globe and Mail, journal can
– siège social, William H. Wright Building
(Toronto, Ont) #9338
Glyde, Henry George, artiste can, 1906-
– expositions
– (1974) #5618
– professeur de Gerald Tailfeathers #7312
– programme d'expositions itinérantes,
Alberta (1980) #1972
Gnass, Peter, sculpteur can, 1936- #5619
– *Chantier interdit au public* #1563
– expositions
– (1977) #5620
– (1980) #5621
Gnosill, Albert E., artiste can, 1895-
– expositions
– (1960) #1668
Gobeil, Lucien, sculpteur can, 1946-
– utilisation de plastiques #1603
gobelins
– Jaworska, Tamara Hans #5949
Goblin, périodique can
– dessins humoristiques, Richard Taylor
#7336
Godard, Mira, marchande d'oeuvres d'art
can, 1932- #161
Godin, Raymonde, artiste can, 1930-
– à Paris (France) #426
– entretien #5622
– expositions
– (1979) #5623
Godwin, Ted, artiste can, 1933- #5624
– entretien sur l'Académie royale des arts
du Canada #689
– expositions
– (1961) #1913
– expositions de groupe
– (1962) #1847
– (1967) #1916
– (1972) #1922
– (1981) #1885
Goethals, Gregor, artiste et historien d'art
amér, 1926-
– commentaire sur le sacré dans l'art #94
Gogh, Vincent van, artiste néerlandais,
1853-1890
– influence sur Alfred Pellan #6803
– influence sur Emily Carr #5046
– influence sur John Bernard Boyle #4894
Goguen, Jean, artiste can, 1927-
– expositions de groupe
– (1959) #1414
– (1968) #1263
– (1981) #1471
Goldberg, Michael (Mike), cinéaste can,
1945-
– entretien, sur les vidéos #5625
Goldhamer, Charles, artiste can, 1903-
– emploi comme artiste commissionné,
Aviation royale du Canada #1091
– expositions de groupe
– (1981) #1117
Gomez, Ricardo Vincente José (Ric),
sculpteur can, 1942-
– expositions
– (1977) #5626
Gonor, Allan B., médecin can, XXe s.
– et Allen Sapp #7123
Goodridge, Harold Barwick, artiste can,
1901-
– murale, Confederation Building (St. John's,
TN) #1140

Goodwin, Betty Roodish, artiste can, 1923-
#1504
– entretien #5630
– expositions
– (1976) #5629
– *Passage in a Red Field* #714
– projet de la rue Mentana #1558 5631
– sculpture, art de performance #658
– *Vest* et *Tarpaulin*, collection #5627 5628
Goold, F.P., & Co., fabricants de céramique
(Brantford, Ont)
– dessins d'oiseaux #2335
Gordon, Hortense Mattice, artiste can,
1889-1961
– élève de Hans Hofmann #1850
Gordon, John Sloan, artiste can, 1868-1940
– illustrations #916
Gordon, Lee, cinéaste can, 1926- #993
Gordon, Mary, artiste can, active 1955
– bijoux #2695
Gordon, Ronald, artiste can, actif 1956
– décors et costumes, *Pantomime*, Montreal
Theatre Ballet #1410
Gordon S. Adamson & Associates, agence
can d'architecture
– Toronto (Ont)
– St. Lawrence Centre for the Arts #9109
– William Wrigley Junior Co. Ltd.
Building #9343
– York University #9396 9469
– Winnipeg (Man), Winnipeg Art Gallery,
competition #9102
Gore, Tom, photographe can, 1946- #2071
Gorin, Jean, artiste fr, 1899-
– structures en relief #777
Goring, Trevor, artiste can, 1949-
– expositions de groupe
– (1976) #1529
Gorky, Arshile (Vosdanig Manoog Adoian),
artiste amér, 1904-1948
– influence sur John Meredith #6516
– influence sur Walter Tandy Murch #6662
Gorman, Richard Borthwick, artiste can,
1935- #5632
– commentaire sur Gordon Rayner #6965
– et gravure ontarienne (années 1960) #1756
– expositions de groupe
– (1967) #821
Goss, Andrew, joaillier can, 1944- #2706
Goss, Arthur S., photographe can, 1911-1940
#5634
– expositions
– (1980) #5633
Goss, Sandra, joaillière can, 1946- #2706
Gosselin, F.Xavier, armurier can, actif 1842
#1301
Gosselin, Félix, artisan can, actif 1842 #1301
Gosselin, Gabriel, orfèvre can, 1690-1769
– sculptures, église Saint-Pierre (île
d'Orléans, Qué) #8802
Gosselin, Gabriel, artisan can, actif 1842
#1301
Gosselin, Gérard, artiste can, actif 1974
– membre du Centre communautaire
catholique Tour de David
(Saint-Basile-le-Grand, Qué) #1510
Gosselin, Pierre, artiste can, 1953-
– réflexion sur son oeuvre #1552
Gottlieb, Adolph, artiste amér, 1903-1974
– influence sur Douglas Hector Haynes
#5758
– influence sur Jack Hamilton Bush #4972
Gotto, Basil, sculpteur brit, 1866-1954
– St. John's (TN), Fighting

Newfoundlanders' Memorial #7783
Gottschalk, Fritz, artiste can, 1937-
– design typographique #932
– estampes #897
– projets de design, Jeux olympiques (1976)
#898
Gottschalk & Ash, agence can de graphisme
#879 886
– image de marque, Claude Neon Ltée #887
Gougeon, Diane, sculpteure can, 1955-
– concept d'espace #1631
– expositions
– (1980) #685
Gouinlock, George Wallace, architecte can,
1861-1932
– Toronto (Ont)
– Canadian National Exhibition, bâtiments
d'exposition #1 9206
– écoles John Ross Robertson et
Glenholme, concours #9437
– Gayety Theatre #9060
– Government House, concours #8748
Gould, John, artiste et ornithologiste brit,
1804-1881
– Lansdowne, James Fenwick, comparaison
#6163
Gould, John Howard, artiste can, 1929-
#5635
– expositions
– (1979) #5637
– expositions de groupe
– (1965) #473
– (1978) #665
– films et dessins #5636
Gould & Harvey, agence amér
d'architecture
– Toronto (Ont), Masonic Temple, concours
#9062
Goulet, Claude, artiste can, 1925- #1542 1543
5638 5640
– expositions
– (1971) #5639
Goulet, Michel, sculpteur can, 1944-
– expositions
– (1980) #695
– *Leur instable XVI* #1627
– Symposium international de sculpture
environnementale de Chicoutimi (Qué),
(1980) #1639
goût (esthétique)
– (1880-1910), réactions du public face à l'art
canadien, Montréal (Qué) et Toronto (Ont)
#214
– (années 1870-1970), influence de l'Ontario
Society of Artists #1678
– (années 1950), influence des écoles d'arts
plastiques, provinces de l'Ouest #1947
– Bourassa, Napoléon, commentaire #4864
Gouthro, Frederick Stephen (Steve), artiste
can, 1951-
– expositions de groupe
– (1981) #1908
gouverneurs généraux du Canada
– médailles #764
Govan, Ferguson, Lindsay, Kaminker, Maw,
Langley, Keenleyside, agence can
d'architecture
– Toronto (Ont), Hospital for Sick Children
#9028
Government of Ontario Art Collection
– *voir* Ontario. Government of Ontario Art
Collection
Gow, Isobel Dowler, artiste can, 1933- #1512
– expositions de groupe

– (1976) #1529
Gowans, Kent and Co., fabricants de verre (Toronto, Ont)
– verre, motifs (ca 1914) #2411
Goya y Lucientes, Francisco José de, artiste esp, 1746-1828
– Chambers, Jack, comparaison #516
– influence sur Tony Urquhart #7446
– influence sur Walter Joseph Gerard Bachinski #4578
Goyoguins
– culture #3525
– masses d'armes #3535
Graff, Leslie Frederick (Les), artiste can, 1936-
– entretien #5641
graffiti
– sur sculptures, Yves Trudeau #7435
Grafton (Ont), résidence de Barnum
– architecture #7959
Graham, Albert W., graveur can, actif 1858-1871
– gravure d'après portrait de James McGill #5321
Graham, Colin, artiste et conservateur can, 1915- #5642
Graham, Dan, artiste can, 1942-
– expositions de groupe
– (1977) #631
– (1980) #690
Graham, John, sculpteur can, actif 1827-1880
– sculptures sur bois, Musée du Nouveau-Brunswick (Saint-Jean, NB) #1187
Graham, Kay M., artiste can, 1913- #1803 1807 5643
– expositions de groupe
– (1974) #565
– (1981) #722
Graham, Kent, ébéniste can, actif 1978 #2596
Graham, Robert, fils, sculpteur can, actif fin XIXe-début XXe s.
– sculptures sur bois, Musée du Nouveau-Brunswick (Saint-Jean, NB) #1187
Graham, Robert, sculpteur can, actif milieu XIXe-fin XIXe s.
– sculptures sur bois, Musée du Nouveau-Brunswick (Saint-Jean, NB) #1187
graminées
– en tant que médium artistique, Labrador (TN), XXe s. #2945
Granby (Qué), galerie d'art
– (années 1950) #3034
Granche, Pierre, sculpteur can, 1948-
– concept d'espace #1631
– Symposium international de sculpture environnementale de Chicoutimi (Qué), (1980) #1639
Grand Bank (TN)
– architecture #7792
Grand Digue (NB), maison Hélène et Roma Bourgeois
– architecture #8547
Grand Falls (NB), Thomas Albert Senior High School
– expositions
– The Beaverbrook Art Gallery Presents Nine New Brunswick Artists/La Galerie d'art Beaverbrook présente neuf artistes du Nouveau-Brunswick (1973) #1182
Grand Falls (TN), Newfoundland Government Centre

– architecture #7782
Grand Maison, Paul Malepart de
– voir Malepart de Grand Maison (dit Beaucour), Paul
Grand Manitou . Cris #3724 3726
Grand Manitou . Saulteux/Ojibwa #3726
Grand Pré (NE), Old Covenanter's House
– architecture #7823
Grand Rapids (Mich), Grand Rapids Public Museum
– expositions
– Beads: Their Use by Upper Great Lakes Indians (1977) #3635
Grand Trunk Pacific Railway
– gares #9542 9545
– gares, Manitoba #9543
Grand Trunk Railway
– gares #9538 9539
– Ottawa (Ont), gare centrale et Château Laurier #9528
Grandbois, Alain, poète can, 1900-1975
– influence sur Alfred Pellan #6826
Grande Prairie (Alta)
– architecture, Douglas Joseph Cardinal #8341
Grands Lacs (Ont et Mich)
– phares #9519
– pictogrammes algonquiens #3583
– vues
– Armstrong, William #4552
– XVIIIe-XIXe s., Ottawa (Ont), Archives publiques du Canada. Collection William H. Coverdale #12
granges
– voir aussi écuries
granges . Canada #9228
– (1608-1867) #2120
– Abernethy (Sask), parc historique national W.R. Motherwell Farmstead #9232
– Acadie #7804
– Alberta #8120
– Colombie-Britannique #8148 8153
– Manitoba #8098
– XIXe-début XXe s. #8102
– mennonites #8715
– Niagara-on-the-Lake (Ont), XIXe s. #7986
– Ontario
– bâtiments polygonaux, XIXe s. #7987
– XIXe s. #7745 9227 9229
– Prairies #8080
– Québec
– toitures, XVIIe-XVIIIe s. #7881
– XVIIe-XIXe s. #9230 9231
– XVIIe-XVIIIe s. #2217
– Winnipeg (Man) #8096
granges . Etats-Unis #9228
Granirer, Pnina, artiste can, 1935- #5644
– expositions
– (1976) #2059
Gransow, Helmut, artiste can, 1921- #5645
Grant, George William, architecte can, 1852-1925
– New Westminster (CB), palais de justice #9011
Grant, Ted, photographe can, 1929-
– catalogue de photographies #995
Grant, Thomas J., officier de l'armée can, actif années 1860-1870
– collection, vues photographiques du Canada, XIXe s. #1048
Granville (NE), Amberman House
– architecture #7823
Granville Ferry (NE), Habitation Port-Royal #7655 7823 7849

– restauration #7812 7813
Granville Ferry (NE), Hall-Croscup House
– peintures murales, restauration #1223
Graphic, périodique brit et amér
– illustrations, Henri Julien #5983 5984
Graphic Arts Club of Toronto (Toronto, Ont)
– et Canadian National Exhibition (Toronto, Ont), (1913) #1711
Graphis, périodique suisse
– et Paul Arthur #865
Graser, Toby, artiste can, 1937-
– entretien #5646
Grassby, Percy, artiste brit au Canada, actif 1915
– eaux-fortes #799
gratte-ciel . Canada
– (années 1970) #7733
– Montréal (Qué), (années 1960) #9318
Grauer, Sherry, artiste can, 1939- #2053
– expositions
– (1980) #5647
– expositions, critiques #579
– expositions de groupe
– (1975) #591
– (1976) #2060
Grauerholz, Angela, photographe can, 1952-
– expositions, critiques #1067
Gravel, Charles, sculpteur can, XVIIIe s.
– oeuvres, églises, Charlesbourg (Qué) #8851
Gravelot, Hubert François, artiste fr, 1699-1773
– cartes du Canada #1323
gravure
– voir aussi gravure sur bois debout
– pointes sèches en couleurs, David Brown Milne, commentaire #6563 6564
gravure . Canada
– début XXe s. #28
– Nouvelle-Ecosse (1784-1897) #1198
– Québec (1958-1965) #1654
– Société canadienne des peintres-graveurs (1885-1976) #836
gravure sur acier
– voir gravure
gravure sur bois de fil
– Duguay, Rodolphe #5314 5315 5316
– Munakata, Shiko, et Naoko Matsubara #6449
– Phillips, Walter Joseph, commentaire #6853 6855
gravure sur bois debout
– Hyde, Lawrence, commentaire #5895
gravure sur bois debout . Canada #925
– (années 1930) #802 804
gravure sur bois debout . Japon
– influence sur Monique Charbonneau #5089
Gray, John Warren, artiste can, 1824-1912 #5648
– expositions de groupe
– (1969) #1180
– peintures, marine #5649
Gray & Betts, fabricants de céramique (London, Ont) #2350
Great Eastern Photographic and Advertising Company (Vancouver, Nanaimo, et Victoria, CB)
– (années 1880) #2022
Gréber, Jacques, architecte fr, 1917-1962
– plan, Région de la capitale nationale, Ottawa (Ont) #8034 8035 8039 8041 8045
Greco, El, artiste grec en Espagne, 1541-1614
– influence sur Jacques Godefroy de Tonnancour #7388

Green, Art, artiste can, 1941- #2053
– entretien #5650
Green, Blankstein, Russell & Associates,
  agence can d'architecture
– Ottawa (Ont), Galerie nationale du
  Canada #3035
  – concours #9079
– Winnipeg (Man)
  – Green, Blankstein, Russell & Associates,
    bureaux #9299
  – hôtel de ville, concours #8985 8986 8987
  – University of Manitoba. Saint Paul's
    College et Chapel of Christ the King
    #9486
Green, Daniel, ébéniste can, actif 1813-1821
  #2517
Green, Frederick Walter, architecte can,
  1821-1877
– Victoria (CB) #8145
Green, Harold, photographe can, 1917-
– catalogue de photographies #991 1032
Greenberg, Charles, architecte can, 1922-
– Bruxelles (Belgique), Pavillon du Canada,
  Exposition universelle et internationale
  (1958) #419 430 9209 9211
Greenberg, Clement, critique amér, 1909-
– commentaire sur Marion F.S. Mackay
  Nicoll #6702
– commentaire sur Red River Exhibition
  (1978) #1903
– et Emma Lake Workshops (Emma Lake,
  Sask) #1929 6317 6319
– et Painters Eleven #1785
– et William S. Ronald #7072
– influence sur Jack Hamilton Bush #123
  4970 4972 4975
– Luke, Alexandra, commentaire #6334
– théorie de l'imaginaire, et art canadien
  (années 1960) #515
Greene, Thomas Garland, artiste can,
  1875-1955
– illustrations #916
Greenhill, Ralph, photographe can, 1924-
– vues photographiques, Toronto (Ont)
  #5651
Greenhow famille, artistes can, XXe s.
– expositions de groupe
  – (1961) #1668
Greenshields, Charles Glass, collectionneur
  can, 1882-1974
– fondateur, Elizabeth T. Greenshields
  Memorial Foundation #466
Greensides, Harold C., architecte can,
  1904-1969
– lauréat, Ontario Government Housing
  Competition (1936) #8737
– Montréal (Qué), Hôtel Reine Elizabeth
  #9286
Greenspoon, Freedlander & Dunne, agence
  can d'architecture
– Montréal (Qué)
  – Place Victoria #9195
  – Temple Emmanu-El #8840
Greenspoon, Henry Eli, architecte can, 1909-
– Montréal (Qué) et Toronto (Ont), cinémas
  Odeon #9078
Greenstone, Marion, artiste can, 1925- #5652
Greer, John Sydney, artiste can, 1944-
– estampes #1214
– expositions
  – (1974) #5653
  – (1981) #5654
– expositions, critiques #1208 1227
– expositions de groupe

– (1974) #574
Grégoire, Normand, photographe et cinéaste
  can, 1944- #990 997 999 1556 1562 5655
– catalogue de photographies #987
Gregor, Helen Frances, artiste can
  (tapisserie), 1921- #5656
– expositions, critiques #2771
– expositions de groupe
  – (1981) #2776
Gregory, J.Fraser, marchand de bois can, né
  ca 1841
– résidence, Saint-Jean (NB) #8545
Gregory, Joan Steeves, artiste can, active
  1977
– dessins, comté d'Albert (NB), bâtiments
  #5657
Gregson, Sally, artiste can, 1939-
– expositions
  – (1976) #5658
– expositions, critiques #2072
– expositions de groupe
  – (1979) #2075
grenouilles dans l'art
– Fafard, Joe, et étudiants #1924
– Gilhooly, David James #5601 5602
grès
– Calgary (Alta) architecture #8133
– Ile-du-Prince-Edouard, maisons, début
  XIXe s. #8552
Grey Glass, fabricant de céramique (London,
  Ont) #2350
Greyson, John, artiste can, 1960-
– expositions de groupe
  – (1980) #687
– livres #940
Grice, Arthur D. (Art), photographe can,
  1942- #5659
– catalogue de photographies #991 996 998
Grice, Emily, photographe can, active 1976
  #5659
Grier, Edmund Wyly, artiste can, 1862-1957
  #17 1713 5660 5661
– commentaires sur vues, comté de Peel
  (Ont), collection William Perkins Bull
  #3208
– débat avec A.Y. Jackson, Empire Club
  (Toronto, Ont) #5923
– expositions, critiques #1703 1710
Grier, Eldon Brockwill, artiste can, 1917-
– expositions de groupe
  – (1978) #649
Grierson, John, cinéaste can, 1898-1972
– et photographie documentaire #1056
– influence sur Norman McLaren #6493
Grierson & Walker, agence can
  d'architecture
– Charlottetown (IPE), Confederation
  Centre, concours #9088
– Toronto (Ont), Grierson & Walker, bureau
  d'architectes #9299
Griffith, Julius Edward Lindsay, artiste can,
  1912-
– commentaire sur la gravure #817
Griffiths, James, artiste can, 1814-1896 #2305
Griffiths, John Howard, artiste can,
  1826-1897 #2305
grilles
– dans l'art
  – Knudsen, Chris #6070
  – Martin, Ron #6432
  – Smith, Gordon Appelbe #7227
Grimsby (Ont), Grimsby Public Library and
  Art Gallery
– expositions

– Of Human Bondage (1976) #611
Grip, journal can
– et John Wilson Bengough #942 943 4673
  4674 4677
– illustrations #14
Grip Limited, éditeur (Toronto, Ont)
– et le Groupe des Sept #1766
– siège social, Graphic Arts Building
  (Toronto, Ont) #9330
Grobb, John, ébéniste can, né 1800 #2571
Grobb, Moses, artisan tisserand can, né
  1806, actif 1853-1872 #2723
Groenland
– Inuit
  – culture #4315
  – sculpture #4206
Grondin, Jean-Luc, artiste can, 1938- #5662
Groningue (Pays-Bas), Groningen Museum
– expositions
  – Moderne canadese schilderkunst (1959)
    #431
Gros-Ventres
– costume #3753
– culture #3651
Grossman, Irving, architecte can, 1926-
– Montréal (Qué), Administration et Presse,
  édifices, Expo 67 #9301
– Toronto (Ont)
  – bureau d'architectes et immeuble
    résidentiel #9299
  – Edgeley in the Village #8520
  – Flemingdon Park #7683 8370 8514 8657
Grossman, Irving, Can architect, 1926-
– Toronto (Ont)
  – synagogues #8903
grotesque dans l'art
– Prent, Mark #6920
Groupe d'action photographique (GAP)
  (Montréal, Qué)
– (années 1970) #1003 1494
Groupe des peintres canadiens
– (1933-1970) #498
– (années 1930) #336 502 589 592 1768 1789
– (années 1940) #382
– expositions
  – (1939) #346
– expositions, critiques
  – (1936) #331
  – (1940) #348
  – (1942) #356
  – (1944) #365
  – (1962) #456
Groupe des Sept #5 14 24 28 45 52 66 97 289
  374 412 461 507 1667 1735 1738 1740 1743
  1760 1766 1768 1774 1777 1784 1789 1790
– (1924), British Empire Exhibition
  (Wembley, Angleterre) #458
– (années 1920) #309 1737
– (années 1930) #336 502 1234
– affiches #911
– appui #1763 1764
  – Gurd, Norman I., et Sarnia Art
    Movement #1776
– Bergeron, Suzanne, comparaison #4707
– Carr, Emily et Morrice, James Wilson,
  comparaison #352
– dessins #1736 1755
– et A.Y. Jackson #5912 5915 5917 5918 5923
– et Alan Caswell Collier #5131
– et Alexandra Luke #6333 6334
– et Alfred Joseph Casson #5056 5058 5060
– et Alice A. Innes #5900
– et Anne Douglas Savage #7131
– et art canadien (années 1940) #375

– et Arthur Lismer #6293 6296 6298 6300
  6301
– et Barker Fairley #5404 5405
– et Bertram Richard Brooker #4925 4926
  4927
– et Canadian Art Club #214
– et Carl Fellman Schaefer #7155 7156
– et Catharine Robb Whyte et Peter Whyte
  #7571
– et Charles William Jefferys #5956 5958
– et David Brown Milne #6551
– et Emily Carr #5025 5030 5034
– et Franklin Carmichael #5001
– et Frederick Horsman Varley #7462 7463
– et Galerie nationale du Canada (Ottawa,
  Ont) #3025
– et Goodridge Roberts #7050
– et Groupe des peintres canadiens #324
– et impressionnisme #227
– et J.E.H. MacDonald #6361 6369
– et Jock Macdonald #6375 6379
– et Lawren Stewart Harris #1744 1754 5720
– et Lionel LeMoine FitzGerald #5450
– et Marion F.S. Mackay Nicoll #6703
– et Maurice Galbraith Cullen #5223
– et modernisme #319
– et nationalisme dans l'art #102 109 327 338
  354 378 495
– et nature dans l'art #496
– et peinture canadienne #456
– et peinture québécoise (années 1930) #1460
– et Picture Loan Society (Toronto, Ont)
  #1758
– et Robert Gray Murray #613
– et Thoreau MacDonald #6384
– et Tom Thomson #7357 7363 7369
– et Toni Onley #613
– Ewen, Paterson, comparaison #5385
– expositions
  – (1920) #286
  – (1920-1922, 1925-1926, 1928, 1930-1931)
    #1732
  – (1954) #1747
  – (1958) #429
  – (1969) #3229
  – (1974) #1861
  – (1976) #1778
  – (1977) #1780 1781 1782
  – (1980) #156
– expositions, critiques
  – (1920) #1767
  – (1926) #1734
  – (1927) #298
  – (1932) #1739
– faux, Ward-Price Galleries (Toronto, Ont),
  (1962) #64
– Heidelberg (Australie) artistes,
  comparaison #44
– illustration de livres et mise en pages
  artistique #928 939
– illustrations
  – Canadian Forum #930
  – Farmer's Magazine #1765
– influence de l'art scandinave #1788
– influence sur peinture canadienne #57 300
  342 345 379 380 397 406 424
– Lecor, Tex, comparaison #6184
– Loveroff, Frederick Nicholas, comparaison
  #6331
– MacCallum, James Metcalfe, protecteur
  des arts #3237
– McLean, Tom, comparaison #6503
– Milne, David Brown, comparaison #6549
– oeuvres

– Doig Art Collection of Manitoba #3224
– Kleinburg (Ont), McMichael Canadian
  Collection #1783 3164
– McLean, J.S., collection #3228
– Poole, Ernest Edward, collection #3217
– Toronto (Ont)
  – Fondation du patrimoine ontarien.
    Collection d'art Firestone #3239
  – University of Toronto. Hart House
    #3134 3137
  – University of Toronto. University
    College #3151
– Phillips, Walter Joseph, comparaison #6858
– utilisation de la couleur #347
– voyages dans l'Arctique #1779
– vues
  – Charlevoix (Qué) #1280
  – Georgian Bay (Ont) #1745
Groupe Média Gravures et Multiples
  (Montréal, Qué)
– (1969-1973) #1646
– expositions, critiques
  – (1970) #1490
Groupes du Nouvel-Age #1502
groupes ethniques au Canada
– Alberta, constructions en bois rond #8136
– art traditionnel #2122
– arts décoratifs #2107
– costume #2893
– églises #8769
– filage et tissage #2747 2748
– granges #9228
– mobilier, fin XIXe-début XXe s. #2585
– ouvrages à l'aiguille #2780
– vannerie #2943
Grünewald, Matthias, artiste all, ca
  1480-1528
– influence sur Tom La Pierre #6122
Guderna, Ladislav, artiste can, 1921- #5663
Guelph (Ont)
– architecture, XIXe s. #7970
– art #1685
– photographie (1856-1867) #1724
– vues
  – Kennedy, David Johnston #6040 6041
Guelph (Ont), Guelph General Hospital
– architecture #9029
Guelph (Ont), Guelph Military Convalescent
  Hospital (autrefois Ontario Reformatory)
– architecture #9016
Guelph (Ont), hôtel de ville
– architecture, William Thomas #8413
Guelph (Ont), Macdonald Consolidated
  School (maintenant Macdonald Stewart
  Art Centre)
– architecture, George Martel Miller #3176
Guelph (Ont), Macdonald Stewart Art
  Centre
– architecture, George Martel Miller;
  rénovation, Raymond Moriyama #3176
– expositions
  – Ivan Eyre Exposition (1981) #5394
  – Painters Eleven in Retrospect (1981) #1785
  – Realism: Structure and Illusion: Toward a
    Definition of Representational Art (1981)
    #716
  – Water Colours by E.May Martin (1980)
    #6424
Guelph (Ont), University of Guelph
– expositions
  – Lithographs/Lithographies (1972) #825
Guelph (Ont), University of Guelph. Art
  Gallery
– art vidéo, professeurs et étudiants (1973)

  #553
– collection #3173
– expositions
  – Canada in the Victorian Image, 1837-1887
    (1975) #253
  – Centennial Exhibition of Quebec and
    Ontario Contemporary Painters, 1967
    (1967) #484
  – Ed Bartram: 10 Years (1980) #4618
  – Five Years of Robert Downing, 1966-1971
    (1972) #5306
  – Imprint '76 (1977) #833
  – Lillian Freiman: Paintings and Drawings
    (1978) #5518
  – Realism: Emulsion and Omission (1972) #545
  – The Ontario Community Collects: A Survey
    of Canadian Painting from 1766 to the
    Present (1976) #120
  – Trésors d'art populaire québécois/Folk Art
    Treasures of Quebec (1981) #1297
  – Visitors, Exiles and Residents: Guelph
    Artists Since 1827 (1977) #1685
Guelph (Ont), University of Guelph. Arts
  Building
– architecture, Hancock, Little, Calvert
  Associates; Sert, Jackson #9468
Guelph (Ont), University of Guelph. Library
  Building
– architecture, Hancock, Little, Calvert
  Associates; Sert, Jackson #9468
Guelph (Ont), University of Guelph.
  McLaughlin Library
– expositions
  – 19th and 20th Century Canadian Paintings
    from the Art Gallery of Hamilton (1974)
    #3159
  – Video Circuits: An Exhibition on the Theme
    of Videotape as Art (1973-1974) #553
Guernon (dit Belleville), François, sculpteur
  can, ca 1755-ca 1789
– sculptures sur bois, calvaire d'Oka (Oka,
  Qué) #1355 1356
guerre, art et
– Champlain, Samuel de, Les voyages du sieur
  de Champlain (1613) #933
– Proctor, Alexander Phimister, sculptures
  militaires #6943 6944
– Toronto (Ont), Metro Toronto Public
  Library. John Ross Robertson Historical
  Collection #3131
Guerre civile espagnole (1936-1939)
– film de McLaren, Norman, et d'Evelynn
  Lambart #6498
Guerre des Boers
– et John Innes #5901
Guerre mondiale, 1re (1914-1918)
– affiches canadiennes #910 911
– art #1071
– art canadien #1075 1111 1112 1667
– aviation, peintures #1104 1105
– cimetières et monuments aux morts,
  soldats canadiens #1108 1109
– collection d'art canadien en souvenir de la
  guerre #284 1073 1074 1076 1078 1080
  1081 1082 1084 1085
  – Ottawa (Ont), Galerie nationale du
    Canada #1077 1101 1102 3044
– édifices en souvenir des soldats canadiens
  morts au combat, recommandations #1079
– et A.Y. Jackson #1077 5913 5919
– et Académie royale des arts du Canada
  #208
– et André Charles Biéler #4725
– et David Brown Milne #6551 6557 6566

– et Florence Carlyle #5000
– et Frederick Horsman Varley #1077 7466
    7467 7468
– et H.W. Cooper #5173
– et Homer Ransford Watson #210
– et Inglis Sheldon-Williams #7196
– et Jack Turner #7439
– et James Wilson Morrice #6626
– et Mary Riter Hamilton #5695
– et Maurice Galbraith Cullen #5215 5217
    5220 5222
– et Robert Wakeham Pilot #6869
– et Tom Thomson #7356
– et Walter Seymour Allward #4518 4519
– et William Brymner #4953
– et Wyndham Lewis #6279
– logement subventionné pour travailleurs,
    après-guerre #8495
– monuments aux morts, concours #731 732
– vues photographiques #1072 1107 1113 1114
Guerre mondiale, 2e (1939-1945)
– (1940-1941), impossibilité d'engager des
    peintres de guerre canadiens #1087
– affiches canadiennes #847 848 908 910 911
– architecture canadienne #7666
– art canadien #151 370 498 1088 1098 1111
    1112 1116
        – et surréalisme #1115
        – Ottawa (Ont), Galerie nationale du
            Canada #1101 3044
        – Ottawa (Ont), Musée canadien de la
            guerre #1103
– aviation, peintures #1104 1105
– bandes dessinées canadiennes #947
– cimetières et monuments aux morts,
    soldats canadiens #1108 1109
– et Albert-Edouard Cloutier #1117
– et Alex Colville #5146 5151 5156
– et Bruno Joseph Bobak #4759
– et Canadian Committee #3262
– et Carl Fellman Schaefer #1090 7150 7152
    7153 7155 7156
– et Charles Fraser Comfort #1090 5158
– et Charles Goldhamer #1091 1117
– et Donald William Buchanan #3325
– et Edward John Hughes #5859 5861
– et George Adolphus Broomfield #4932
– et George Douglas Pepper #6832
– et Gershon Iskowitz #5906
– et Gordon Appelbe Smith #7229
– et Groupe des Sept #1768 1789
– et Jack Leonard Shadbolt #7176 7189
– et Jack Nichols #6697
– et Jan Menses #6511
– et Jean-Philippe Dallaire #5239
– et Jerrold Morris #1110 6639
– et John Saarniit #7112
– et John William Beatty #4637
– et Ken Bell #4657
– et Lawren Phillip Harris #5713
– et Leonard Brooks #4930
– et Louis Muhlstock #6658
– et Maxwell Bennett Bates #4620
– et Miller Gore Brittain #4921
– et Molly Lamb Bobak #4759 4761 4764
    4765 4766 4767
– et Nick Morant #6605
– et Oscar Cahén #4986
– et Pegi Nicol MacLeod #6396 6397
– et Ralph Malcolm Warner #1117
– et Robert Marshall Buckhan #1117
– et Robert Wakeham Pilot #6869
– et Rowley Walter Murphy #6665 6666
– et Tobie Thelma Steinhouse #7278

– et Tony Law #6174
– et Walter Ruhman #7105
– et Wilfred Roloff Beny #4687
– identité artistique canadienne #327
– oeuvres d'art, armée, marine et aviation
    canadienne #1097 1099
– oeuvres d'art, armée canadienne #1092
    1094 1096
– oeuvres d'art, Aviation royale du Canada
    #1093
– ouvrages à l'aiguille pour soldats
    canadiens #2780
– peintures canadiennes #1100
– peintures et dessins canadiens #1089
– programme pour favoriser l'art en temps
    de la guerre #379 1086
– scènes navales, Musée canadien de la
    guerre (Ottawa, Ont) #1106
– sculptures canadiennes #738
– sérigraphies canadiennes #805
– Société canadienne des aquarellistes #127
– vues photographiques #1095 1107
– Wartime Housing Limited #8506
guides
– *Quebec and Its Environs* (1831), attribué à
    James Pattison Cockburn #5129
Guilde canadienne des métiers d'art
– autrefois Corporation canadienne de
    l'artisanat #2118
– périodique, *Craft Dimensions Artisanales*
    #2116
Guilde canadienne des métiers d'art
(Ontario)
– et Visual Arts Ontario #1806
Guilde canadienne des métiers d'art
(Québec)/Canadian Guild of Crafts
(Québec)
– art inuit #4292 4293
Guillaume, Janine Leroux
– *voir* Leroux-Guillaume, Janine
Guillon, Jacques S., designer can, 1922-
    #2471
– et Jacques Guillon Designers Inc. #884
Guimond, Daniel, artiste can, actif 1978
– art de performance #655
Guimond, Pierre, photographe can, 1946-
    #5664
Guimons, Jean, photographe can, actif 1971
    #997
Guindon, Arthur, artiste can, 1864-1923
– peintures illustrant légendes iroquoises
    #5665
Guité, Suzanne, sculpteure can, 1927-1981
    #5666 5668
– expositions
    – (1977) #5669
– expositions, critiques #1400
– murale, palais de justice, New Carlisle
    (Qué) #5667
Guité, Thérèse, artiste can, 1930-1981
– batik #2741
Gulf Hazard (TNO)
– amulette dorsétienne en cuivre #4365
Gundry & Langley, agence can
    d'architecture
– Toronto (Ont), Government House #8753
Gunnlogsson & Nielsen, agence danoise
    d'architecture
– Toronto (Ont), hôtel de ville et Civic
    Square, concours #8981
Gunterman, Ida Madeline Warner (Mattie),
    photographe can, 1872-1945 #2018 5670
    5672
– expositions

– (1977) #5671
– expositions de groupe
    – (1976) #2012
Gurd, Norman I., protecteur des arts can,
    1870-1943
– et Sarnia Art Movement #1776
Gurdjieff, Georgei Ivanovitch, mystique
    russe, ca 1877-1949
– influence sur Alexandra Luke #6334
Gurnett, George, homme d'Etat et magistrat
    can, ca 1792-1861
– portrait, Paul Kane #3178
Gusella, Ernest, artiste can, 1941-
– art vidéo #616
Gustafson, Anna, artiste can, 1952-
– expositions de groupe
    – (1978) #2067
– vitraux, Coquitlam Centre (Vancouver,
    CB) #2459
Gutiérrez, José, artiste mexicain, 1900-1968
– professeur de Réal Bérard #4692
Gutsche, Clara, photographe can, 1949-
– catalogue de photographies #1053
– expositions
    – (1980) #5673
– photographies documentaires #1556
Guyanes
– vues, explorateurs français #276
Guyon, Jean, prêtre fr, artiste au Canada,
    1659-1687 #228 229 1363
Gwaytihl, sculpteur can, m. 1912 #3862 4169

H

H. Gagnier Ltd.
– *voir* Gagnier, H., Ltd.
H.H. Martyn & Co.
– *voir* Martyn, H.H., & Co.
H'Kusam (CB)
– architecture et totems, Haidas #3913
Haacke, Hans Christoph, artiste all, 1936-
– étude sur le musée (institution) #714
habitations
– *voir* architecture domestique
Haddon, Jim, photographe can, actif 1981
– catalogue de photographies #1023
Hadley, Glen, architecte can, 1934-
– Charlottetown (IPE), Confederation
    Centre, concours #9088
Haeffely, Claude, photographe can, 1927-
    #5674
– poèmes, dessins de Louis-Pierre Bougie
    #4861
Haeseker, Alexandra (Sandy), artiste can,
    1945-
– entretien #5675
– expositions de groupe
    – (1975) #1867
    – (1979) #674
    – (1980) #698
Hagan, Frederick, artiste can, 1918- #5676
Hagarty, Clara Sophia, artiste can, 1871-1958
– expositions, critiques #1703
Hahn, Emanuel Otto, sculpteur can,
    1881-1957 #5677 5679 5680
– dessin, dollar canadien en argent, 1935
    #5681
– et sculpture canadienne #741
– mari de Elizabeth Wyn Wood #5678
Haidas
– architecture #4021

– architecture et totems #3913 3979 3982 4118
– art #3946 4011 4169
  – (années 1970) #4145
  – représentation de la lune #4059
  – XIXe s. #4070
– art funéraire #3995
– arts graphiques #6932
– canots #3825
– coiffure #4019
– crécelles #4026
– cuivres #3821 4054
– culture
  – (1905-1909) #3780
  – (années 1870) #3761
  – (années 1880) #3763
– masques #3794 3961
– orfèvrerie #5358
– photographies, Edward Sheriff Curtis #3399
– pièces de jeu, XIXe s. #3915
– pipes #4047
– pipes et cuillers #3782
– récipients #4066
  – XIXe s. #3985
– sculpture #3904 4040 4041 4116
  – fin XIXe s. #3862
– sculpture d'argilite #3419 3868 3890 3901 3958 4006 4010 4016 4042 4051 5088 5138 5361
– totems #3765 3766 3775 3943 4008 4067 4124
Hale, Catherine, sculpteure can, 1927-
– ouvrages en fibres textiles #5682
Haliburton, Thomas Chandler, auteur et juge can, 1796-1865
– commentaire sur articles de maison et ameublement, provinces maritimes #2147
Haliburton (Ont)
– arts décoratifs #2258
Haliburton (Ont), Haliburton School of Fine Arts #2258
Halifax (NE)
– architecture #7816 8317
  – (années 1750-1930) #7839
  – (années 1960) #7698
  – bâtiments du port, XIXe s. #7822 7824 7825 7834
  – centre-ville #7819
  – Lang, George Macdonald #7838
  – région d'Hydrostone (années 1920) #7839
  – rue Granville #7817
  – rues Prince et Hollis, édifices, XIXe s. #7831
  – XIXe s. #7826
  – XVIIIe-XIXe s. #7818
– architecture et sites historiques #7830
– art
  – (1749-1949) #1195
  – (années 1830) #1226
  – (années 1950-1970) #131
  – (années 1970) #1208
  – (années 1980) #1227
– art vidéo #605
– bouteilles et flacons (1836-1947) #2428
– conservation architecturale #7833
– développement urbain #7835
– galeries d'art (années 1960) #442
– peinture (1815-1867) #1217
– photographie (années 1830-1860) #1211
– tours Martello #8416
– urbanisme #1119
– vues

– Lyttleton, Westcott Whitchurch Lewis #6349
– Short, Richard #249 250
– vues photographiques (1850-1900) #1061
Halifax (NE), Aéroport international de Halifax. Aérogare
– architecture, Gilleland & Strutt; C.D. Davidson & Co.; William Alexander Ramsay #9515
Halifax (NE), All Saints' Cathedral
– architecture, Cram, Goodhue & Ferguson #8773
– proposition architecturale, William Critchlow Harris #8371
Halifax (NE), Anna Leonowens Gallery
– voir Halifax (NE), Nova Scotia College of Art and Design. Anna Leonowens Gallery
Halifax (NE), Art Gallery of Nova Scotia
– expositions
  – Acadia Nova - 15 Artists (1980) #1136
  – An Exhibition of Canadian Gameboards of the 19th & 20th Centuries from Ontario, Quebec & Nova Scotia (1981) #2597
  – Annapolis Valley; Seven Artists 1980 (1980) #1221
  – Art populaire de la Nouvelle-Ecosse: une exposition itinérante d'art populaire de la Nouvelle-Ecosse du XXe siècle (1977) #1206
  – Charles Wm. MacDonald: Seaman, Labourer, Artist, Manufacturer (1874-1967) (1980) #6355
  – Charlotte Lindgren: Fibre Structures (1980) #6282
  – Claude Breeze (1978) #4911
  – David Bolduc: Recent Work (1980) #4775
  – Don Pentz: An Exhibition of Paintings and Drawings (1979) #6830
  – Felicity Redgrave (1979) #6967
  – Folk Art of Nova Scotia: A Travelling Exhibition of 20th Century Folk Art of Nova Scotia (1976) #1207
  – Joe Sleep Retrospective (1981) #7219
  – John Greer: Sculptural Objective, 1968-1981; Everything Always Changes but Something Still Remains (1981) #5654
  – Looking South (1978) #4278
  – Miller Brittain - Painter (1981) #4922
  – Painters Eleven in Retrospect (1981) #1785
  – Robert Field 1769-1819 (1978) #5432
  – Roger Savage (1979) #7135
  – Scottish Painting Canada (1978) #133
  – The Murray and Marguerite Vaughan Inuit Print Collection/Collection d'estampes inuit (1982) #4498
  – The New Brunswick Landscape Print: 1760-1880 (1980) #1189
  – Yves Gaucher & Christopher Pratt (1977) #643
– expositions, critiques
  – Folk Art of Nova Scotia: A Travelling Exhibition of 20th Century Folk Art of Nova Scotia (1976) #1210 1213
  – MacKeeman, Karl (1977) #6389
Halifax (NE), Banque de Nouvelle-Ecosse
– architecture #7839
  – Lyle, John MacIntosh #8226 9186 9203
  – Lyle, John MacIntosh; Cobb, Andrew Randall, Associate Architect #9182
Halifax (NE), Black-Binney House
– architecture et intérieur #8548
Halifax (NE), Cambridge Library
– architecture #7839
Halifax (NE), Centennial Art Gallery

– expositions
  – A Selection of Works by Women Artists in Nova Scotia, 1850-1950 (1975) #1204
  – Adrien Hébert: trente ans de son oeuvre, 1923-1953/Adrien Hébert: Thirty Years of His Art, 1923-1953 (1972) #5763
  – Albert Franck (1899-1973) in Retrospect: A Small Selection from the Artist's Collection (1973) #5500
  – Watercolour Painters from Saskatchewan/Aquarellistes de la Saskatchewan (1972) #1920
Halifax (NE), citadelle de Halifax
– architecture #8431 8432 8438 8440
  – (1906-1951) #8430
  – façade ouest #8434
  – magasin sud #8433
  – portes et fenêtres #8441
Halifax (NE), Crimean Memorial
– architecture #7839
Halifax (NE), Dalhousie Art Gallery
– voir Halifax (NE), Dalhousie University. Dalhousie Art Gallery
Halifax (NE), Dalhousie University
– architecture #7830
  – Darling, Frank, Thomas Hayton Mawson, Andrew Randall Cobb #9408
– planification, Thomas Hayton Mawson #9405
Halifax (NE), Dalhousie University. Dalhousie Art Gallery
– expositions
  – Bruce Parsons: A Model of Reality/Bruce Parsons: un modèle de la réalité (1976) #6772
  – Carl Schaefer in Hanover (1980) #7157
  – Carol Fraser Paintings and Drawings: 1967-1977 (1977) #5507
  – Claude Tousignant (1974) #7401
  – Dalhousie Drawing Exhibition (1976-) #607
  – Daniel Fowler of Amherst Island, 1810-1894 (1979) #5491
  – Decorated Nova Scotia Furnishings (1978) #2514
  – Douglas Bentham "Enclosures and Opens" 1975/76 (1976) #4683
  – Drawings by Jack Weldon Humphrey: A Travelling Exhibition Organized by the Beaverbrook Art Gallery, Fredericton, New Brunswick, Canada, 1977-1979 (1979) #5871
  – Early Nova Scotia Quilts and Coverlets (1981) #2807
  – Elizabeth S. Nutt: Heart and Head and Hand; Paintings from Nova Scotia Collections (1981) #6730
  – Frank Nulf (1975) #6727
  – Fritz Brandtner 1896-1969: A Retrospective Exhibition (1971) #4903
  – Gerald Ferguson: Paintings (1977) #5420
  – Gift from the Douglas M. Duncan Collection and the Milne-Duncan Bequest/Le Don provenant de la collection Douglas M. Duncan et le legs Milne-Duncan (1971) #541
  – Graham Coughtry: Retrospective (1976) #5190
  – In Video (1977) #631
  – J.W. Beatty, 1869-1941 (1981) #4638
  – Joe Norris: Paintings and Furniture (1978) #6720
  – Joe Plaskett and His Paris: In Search of Time Past (1973) #6893
  – Joe Plaskett et son Paris: à la recherche d'un

temps passé (1973) #6894
- *Kostyniuk: Relief Structures, 1969-1972* (1973) #6079
- *Lawren P. Harris 37/72* (1972) #5711
- *Louis Comtois: Paintings, 1974-1979* (1980) #5164
- *Louis de Niverville* (1978) #6709
- *Messages from Southern Saskatchewan* (1976) #1930
- *Metamorphosis, Memories, Dreams and Reflections: The Work of Florence Vale* (1981) #7453
- *Peter Kolisnyk* (1977) #6075
- *Sceptical Art Works at the Killam* (1974) #5653
- *Stephen Cruise* (1976) #5213
- *Susan Schelle: Recent Work* (1981) #7160
- *Terence Johnson: Forts* (1981) #5969
- *The Canadian Canvas: A Travelling Exhibition of 85 Recent Paintings/Peintres canadiens actuels: exposition itinérante de 85 oeuvres récentes* (1975) #588
- *The Contemporary Arts Society: Montreal 1939-1948/La Société d'art contemporain: Montréal 1939-1948* (1981) #1474
- expositions, critiques
  - Fischl, Eric #662
  - Hammock, Virgil (1978) #5696
  - *Lawren P. Harris 37/72* (1972) #5712
  - *Louis de Niverville* (1978) #6711
  - Shirley, James #1208
  - *Six from Halifax* (1981) #1227
  - *The Canadian Canvas: A Travelling Exhibition of 85 Recent Paintings/Peintres canadiens actuels: exposition itinérante de 85 oeuvres récentes* (1975) #582
Halifax (NE), Dalhousie University. Killam Library
- architecture, Leslie R. Fairn & Associates #9052
- expositions, critiques
  - Sleep, Joseph #1208
Halifax (NE), Eye Level Gallery
- (1975-1976) #1209
- expositions, critiques
  - Cohen, Sorel #5130
Halifax (NE), Gorsebrook House
- architecture #8528
Halifax (NE), Government House
- architecture #7839
  - Hildrith, Isaac #8374 8750 8754
Halifax (NE), Grand Parade
- architecture #7839
Halifax (NE), Halifax Memorial Library
- expositions
  - Nova Scotia Society of Artists #1192
  - *The Development of Canadian Painting: As Illustrated by Pictures Lent by Individuals and Institutions* (1951) #47
Halifax (NE), Halifax Public Gardens
- ferronnerie décorative, fin XIXe s. #2710
Halifax (NE), Little Dutch Church
- architecture #7839
Halifax (NE), Lord Nelson Hotel
- expositions
  - Nova Scotia Society of Artists #1192
Halifax (NE), maison West, rue Brunswick
- architecture #8537
Halifax (NE), Manuge Gallery
- (1975-1979) #3244
Halifax (NE), Maritime Museum of the Atlantic #3074
Halifax (NE), Mechanics' Institute
- et Nova Scotia Museum #3071

Halifax (NE), Mount Saint Vincent University. Art Gallery
- collection #3072
- expositions
  - *A Terrible Beauty: The Art of Canada at War* (1978) #1111
  - *Ann Kipling: Recent Landscapes* (1980) #6057
  - *Beauté tragique: les deux conflits mondiaux vus par des artistes canadiens* (1978) #1112
  - *Canadian Political Cartoons* (1977) #956
  - *Canadians: A National Photography Show about People/Canadiens: exposition nationale de photographie ayant les gens comme thème* (1978) #1035
  - *De grandes espérances: la vision européenne en Nouvelle-Ecosse, 1749-1848* (1980) #1220
  - *Great Expectations: The European Vision in Nova Scotia, 1749-1848* (1980) #1222
  - *L'art du paysage au Québec, 1800-1940/Landscape Painting in Québec, 1800-1940* (1978) #1286
  - *Manitoba Mainstream: People's Art/Fine Art/Le Grand Courant du Manitoba: arts populaires, beaux-arts* (1973) #1897
  - *Some Nova Scotia Women Artists* (1975) #1205
  - *Survival Atlantic Style: Works by 16 Artists from the Atlantic Provinces* (1979) #1133
  - *The Portrait Sculpture of Doris M. Judah* (1980) #5980
  - *Tim Zuck: Paintings* (1981) #7636
- expositions, critiques
  - *Canadians: A National Photography Show about People/Canadiens: exposition nationale de photographie ayant les gens comme thème* (1978) #1055
  - *Great Expectations: The European Vision in Nova Scotia, 1749-1848* (1980) #1224 1225
  - Greer, John #1208
  - *Survival Atlantic Style: Works by 16 Artists from the Atlantic Provinces* (1979) #1135
Halifax (NE), Mount Uniacke House
- architecture, John Merrick #8528
Halifax (NE), Neptune Theatre (autrefois Garrick Theatre)
- architecture et restauration, John Wray #9097
Halifax (NE), Nova Scotia College of Art
- (années 1880-1960) #2993
- expositions
  - Nova Scotia Society of Artists #1192
  - Nutt, Elizabeth Styring, directrice #1194
  - Savage, Roger, élève #7136
Halifax (NE), Nova Scotia College of Art and Design
- (1887-1977) #3014
- (années 1970) #3003
- architecture #9409 9410
- art vidéo #550
  - (1973), professeurs et étudiants #553
  - (années 1970) #575
- Askevold, David, professeur #4566
- atelier sur le financement de l'art canadien (1979) #3293
- et Art Green #5650
- expositions
  - *Conceptual Decorative: Prints by Les Levine, 1965-1970/Conceptuel décoratif: estampes de Les Levine, 1965-1970* (1971) #6265

- *Lithographs/Lithographies* (1972) #825
- *Trans VSI Connection NSCAD-NETCO* (1969) #524
- atelier de lithographie #830
- photographie (années 1970) #1134
Halifax (NE), Nova Scotia College of Art and Design. Anna Leonowens Gallery
- expositions
  - *The Canadian Canvas: A Travelling Exhibition of 85 Recent Paintings/Peintres canadiens actuels: exposition itinérante de 85 oeuvres récentes* (1975) #588
- expositions, critiques
  - *The Canadian Canvas: A Travelling Exhibition of 85 Recent Paintings/Peintres canadiens actuels: exposition itinérante de 85 oeuvres récentes* (1975) #582
Halifax (NE), Nova Scotia Museum #3071
- expositions
  - *Elitekey: Micmac Material Culture from 1600 A.D. to the Present* (1980) #3643
  - Holder, Thomas Cook, et Henry Arthur, mobilier #2505
  - mobilier #2484
Halifax (NE), Nova Scotia Technical College. Résidences des étudiants
- architecture, Duffus, Romans, Kundzins & Rounsefell #9467
Halifax (NE), Nova Scotia Technical College. School of Architecture
- enseignement de l'architecture (années 1970) #8285
Halifax (NE), Point Pleasant Park
- ferronnerie décorative, fin XIXe s. #2710
Halifax (NE), Prince's Lodge. Music Room
- architecture #7839
Halifax (NE), Province House
- architecture #7839
Halifax (NE), Queen Elizabeth High School
- expositions
  - *200 Years of Art in Halifax: An Exhibition Prepared in Honour of the Bicentenary of the Founding of the City of Halifax, N.S., 1749-1949* (1949) #1195
Halifax (NE), Royal Artillery Park
- architecture #7839
Halifax (NE), rue Barrington
- architecture #7840
Halifax (NE), Saint George's Church
- architecture #7839
Halifax (NE), Saint Mary's University. Bibliothèque
- architecture, C.A. Fowler and Company #9046
Halifax (NE), Saint Mary's University. Galerie d'art
- expositions
  - *George Rackus: Anodized Aluminum Works & Prints* (1973) #6953
- expositions, critiques
  - Society of Canadian Artists (1976) #1208
Halifax (NE), Saint Mary's University. Résidence des étudiants
- architecture, Tampold & Wells #8744
Halifax (NE), Saint Paul's Burial Ground
- architecture #7839
Halifax (NE), Scotia Square
- architecture et développement urbain #9302
Halifax (NE), State Building of Nova Scotia
- expositions, critiques
  - Académie royale des arts du Canada (1881) #168
Halifax (NE), Technical University of Nova

- architecture, Witton & Walsh #730
Hamilton (Ont), Church of the Ascension
- architecture, Frederic William Cumberland #8905
Hamilton (Ont), cinéma Loew
- architecture, Thomas White Lamb #9069
Hamilton (Ont), Dundurn Castle
- architecture, Robert Charles Wetherell #8650 8662
Hamilton (Ont), édifice du YWCA
- architecture, Mills & Hutton #7957
Hamilton (Ont), First Methodist Church
- architecture, William E.N. Hunter #7957
Hamilton (Ont), Hamilton Art School
- Robinson, Albert Henry, professeur et directeur #7056
Hamilton (Ont), Hamilton Mausoleum
- architecture #8900
Hamilton (Ont), Hamilton Public Library
- architecture, Alfred W. Peene #7957
Hamilton (Ont), Hamilton Technical School
- architecture #9436
Hamilton (Ont), Hamilton Terminal Station
- architecture, Charles Mills #9527
Hamilton (Ont), hôtel de ville et Civic Square
- architecture, Stanley M. Roscoe; Fleury, Arthur & Barclay, Consulting Architects #8988
Hamilton (Ont), McMaster Divinity College
- architecture, Bruce Brown & Brisley #8765
Hamilton (Ont), McMaster University
- architecture, W.L. Somerville; John Francis Brown & Francis Bruce Brown, Associated Architects #9451
- enseignement de l'histoire de l'art au Canada (1933) #3306
- expositions
  - David Blackwood: Paintings, Drawings, Prints (1967) #4739
Hamilton (Ont), McMaster University. Galerie d'art
- expositions
  - A.J. Casson: Retrospective (1975) #5058
  - Anne Kahane: Sculpture, Prints and Drawings, 1953-1976 (1981) #5999
  - Gift from the Douglas M. Duncan Collection and the Milne-Duncan Bequest/Le Don provenant de la collection Douglas M. Duncan et le legs Milne-Duncan (1971) #541
  - Mennonite Decorative Art (1981) #2267
Hamilton (Ont), McMaster University. Student Centre
- architecture, John Andrews Architects #8323
Hamilton (Ont), McMaster University Health Sciences Centre
- architecture, Craig, Zeidler & Strong #9035 9036 9037
Hamilton (Ont), Memorial School
- architecture #9436
Hamilton (Ont), Molsons Bank
- architecture #9173
Hamilton (Ont), Royal Connaught Hotel
- architecture, Esenwein & Johnson; Alfred W. Peene, Associate Architect #9274
Hamilton (Ont), Whitehern
- architecture et mobilier #8664
Hamilton Camera Club (Hamilton, Ont)
- expositions
  - (1967) #1719
- expositions, critiques #978
Hamilton Glass Works, fabricants de verre

(Hamilton, Ont) #2401
Hamilton Pottery, fabricants de céramique (Hamilton, Ont) #2347
Hammock, Virgil, artiste can, 1938- #5696
Hammond, Charlotte Wilson, artiste can, 1941- #1169 5697
Hammond, John A., artiste can, 1843-1939 #178 5698 5700
- expositions
  - (1967) #5699
- expositions, critiques #186
- expositions de groupe
  - (1969) #1180
Hampton Group (Hampton, NB)
- (années 1960) #1177
Hance, James B., artiste can, 1847-1915 #1312
Hancock, Little, Calvert Associates, agence can d'architecture
- Guelph (Ont), University of Guelph. Pavillon des arts et bibliothèque #9468
Hand, Harris & Merritt, agence can d'architecture
- Toronto (Ont), Bowles Lunch Room #9269
Handy, Arthur, artiste can, 1933- #5701 5702
- commentaire sur l'art canadien (années 1960) #478
- sculptures (années 1960) #1793
Hanford, Robert Gilmore, architecte can, né 1885, actif 1911-1914
- Winnipeg (Man), architecture domestique #8493
Hankes, Jarvis, artiste amér au Canada, né 1799, actif 1827-1834 #1377
Hannaford, Edmund Phillips, architecte can, 1834-1902
- Montréal (Qué), gare Bonaventure #9538
Hanover (NH), Dartmouth College. Hopkins Center. Jaffe-Friede Gallery
- expositions
  - Paul-Emile Borduas, 1905-1960: A Loan Exhibition (1967) #4812
Hanover (NH), Dartmouth College. Hopkins Center Art Galleries
- expositions
  - Canadian Landscape Painting, 1670-1930: The Artist and the Land (1973) #106
  - Eleven Canadian Printmakers (1967) #821
Hanover (NH), Hopkins Center Art Galleries
- voir Hanover (NH), Dartmouth College. Hopkins Center Art Galleries
Hanover (NH), Jaffe-Friede Gallery
- voir Hanover (NH), Dartmouth College. Hopkins Center. Jaffe-Friede Gallery
Hanover (Ont)
- vues
  - Schaefer, Carl Fellman #7153 7157
Hans
- culture #4101
Hansen, Folmer, céramiste can, 1930-
- Hansen-Ross Pottery (Fort Qu'Appelle, Sask) #2389
Hansen, James Colin, artiste can, 1939- #5703
Hansen-Ross Pottery, fabricants de céramique (Fort Qu'Appelle, Sask) #2389
Hanuse, Roy James, artiste can, 1943-
- sérigraphies #4148
Haohao . Bella-Coolas
- pétroglyphe #3816
Harbour Grace (TN)
- architecture #7792
Harbour Grace (TN), phare #9523
Harburn, Flora, artiste can, active 1955

- bijoux #2695
Harbuz, Ann Alexandra, artiste can, 1908- #1881
- expositions de groupe
  - (1975) #1927
hard-edge
- estampes canadiennes (années 1960-1970) #832
- et Gordon Appelbe Smith #7226 7227 7229
- et Pierre Jean Clerk #5118
Harder, Rolf, artiste can, 1929- #5704
- estampes #897
- et Design Collaborative Montreal Ltd. #878 882
Hardie, Martin, Brit artist, 1875-1952
- commentaire sur Walter Joseph Phillips #6856
Harding, James Duffield, artiste brit, 1798-1863
- professeur de Daniel Fowler #5491
Harding, Noel, artiste can, 1945-
- art vidéo #651 5705
- expositions, critiques #656
- expositions de groupe
  - (1977) #631
  - (1978) #667
  - (1980) #687 690
- sculpture, art de performance #658
Hardman, Jack Nelson, sculpteur can, 1923-
- sculpture de jardin #1849
Hardman, Trish, artiste can, active 1973
- art vidéo #2044
Hardy, Jean-Baptiste, sculpteur can, 1731-après 1758 #1592
Harman, Jack Kenneth, sculpteur can, 1927- #5706
- fonderie pour moulage de bronze (Vancouver, CB) #2083
Harmer, William Morell, photographe can, 1859-1949
- expositions de groupe
  - (1970) #1675
Harmon, Byron, photographe can, 1880-1942 #5707
harnachement . Algonquiens #3405
harnachement . Indiens des Prairies #3405
harnachement . Siouens #3405
Harold, Alexander, artiste can, m. ca 1923
- expositions de groupe
  - (1978) #133
Haroutiun, Georges, photographe can, 1945-
- entretien #5708
Harper, John, officier de la marine brit au Canada, XIXe s.
- portrait, incorrectement identifié #5430 5431
Harper, John Russell, historien d'art can, 1914- #3317
- livre, Painting in Canada #488
Harper's, périodique amér
- illustrations, Henri Julien #5984
Harpignies, Henri Joseph, artiste fr, 1819-1916
- influence sur James Wilson Morrice #6626
Harris, Alfred Peter, artiste can, 1932-
- expositions
  - (1977) #5735
Harris, Bess Larkin Housser, artiste can, 1890-1969
- et G.Blair Laing #1686
- expositions de groupe
  - (1928) #301
Harris, famille, XIXe-XXe s.
- résidence, Eldon House (London, Ont)

#8660
Harris, James Edward, architecte can,
1886-1954
– et William Critchlow Harris #8372
Harris, Lawren Phillips, artiste can, 1910-
#5709 5710 5712 5713
– *Battleground before Ortona* #1115
– expositions
– (1972) #5711
– expositions de groupe
– (1966) #1123
– (1973) #1182
Harris, Lawren Stewart, artiste can,
1885-1970 #24 1996 5719 5727 5730 5732
– Breeze, Claude Herbert, comparaison
#4910
– commentaire sur A.Y. Jackson #5925
– commentaire sur Arthur Lismer #6298
– commentaire sur Emily Carr #5012
– commentaire sur l'art abstrait #5721 5723
– commentaire sur l'art moderne #5714
– commentaire sur la créativité et l'art
canadien #5715
– commentaire sur la critique d'art #3300
– commentaire sur la Fédération des artistes
canadiens #364
– commentaire sur la peinture canadienne
#293
– commentaire sur la société et l'art #5722
– commentaire sur la théosophie et l'art
#5716
– commentaire sur le Groupe des Sept #1744
1747 1754
– commentaire sur le Nord canadien dans
l'art #308
– écrits #92
– et A.Y. Jackson #5912
– et Bertram Richard Brooker #4925 4926
– et Brief Concerning the Cultural Aspects
of Canadian Reconstruction (1944) #3251
– et G.Blair Laing #1686
– et Groupe des Sept #1732
– et nationalisme dans l'art #143 5729
– expositions
– (1948) #5720
– (1963) #5725
– (1978) #5734
– expositions, critiques #1710 5717 5718
– expositions de groupe
– (1968) #3224
– (1975) #589 592
– (1979) #147
– illustration et mise en pages artistique
#939
– influence de l'art scandinave #1788
– influence sur Alan Caswell Collier #5131
– influence sur Emily Carr #5021 5044
– influence sur peinture de paysages en
Alberta #1965
– influences mystiques #5726 5731
– McCarthy, Doris Jean, comparaison #6461
– paysages (1908-1930) #5728
– paysages d'hiver #285
– portraits #5733
– Schaefer, Carl Fellman, comparaison #7157
– théories sur l'art abstrait #5724
– voyages dans l'Arctique #1779
Harris, Pamela, photographe can, 1940-
– catalogue de photographies #996
Harris, Peter
– *voir* Harris, Alfred Peter
Harris, Robert, artiste can, 1849-1919 #178
221 5738 5741 5744
– dessins et portraits disparus #5742

– écrits #5737
– expositions
– (1967) #5739
– (1973) #5743
– expositions, critiques #174 186
– expositions de groupe
– (1976) #3281
– (1978) #665
– portraits #1698
– relation entre photographie et peinture
#245
– *The Fathers of Confederation* #5736 5740
Harris, Robert Harold, artiste can, 1878-1948
– linogravures, couvertures de catalogues
d'expositions, Winnipeg Sketch Club
#1887
Harris, Salmon, artiste can, 1948- #2053
– expositions
– (1978) #5745
Harris, William Critchlow, architecte can,
1854-1913 #8372
– Charlottetown (IPE), marché public #7800
– et Dewar & Stirling (Halifax, NE) #8371
– Ile-du-Prince-Edouard, églises #8777
Harrison, Allan, artiste can, 1911- #5746
5747
– expositions
– (1978) #5748
– pochettes de disques #862
Harrison, Birge Lovell, artiste can, 1854-1911
#1312
Harrison, Mark Robert, artiste can,
1819-1894
– membre de la Toronto Society of Arts
#1689
Harrison, Robert F., architecte can, 1925-
– Burnaby (CB)
– Simon Fraser University, bibliothèque
#9046
– Simon Fraser University, concours #9501
Harrison, Ted, artiste can, 1926- #5750 5751
– entretien #5749
Hart, Ernest H., ébéniste can, XXe s. #2493
Hart Pottery, fabricants de céramique
(Picton et Belleville, Ont)
– (1848-1914) #2286 2293
Hartung, Hans, artiste all, 1904-
– et Mario Roy #7099
Hastenteufel, Dieter, artiste can, 1939- #5752
Hauer, Jacob, artiste can, actif 1847
– membre de la Toronto Society of Arts
#1689
Haufschild, Lutz, artiste can, 1943- #2460
– fontaine, Vancouver (CB) #2077
– vitraux, Coquitlam Centre (Vancouver,
CB) #2459
hausse-cols
– *voir aussi* parure
hausse-cols . Algonquiens
– ouvrages en pierre #3406
hausse-cols . Amérindiens
– orfèvrerie de traite #3440
– ouvrages en coquillages #3388
hausse-cols . Iroquois
– orfèvrerie de traite #3536
hausse-cols . Séminoles
– orfèvrerie de traite #3536
Havre-Aubert (îles de la Madeleine), Musée
des îles
– expositions
– *De la figuration à la non-figuration dans
l'art québécois* (1977) #1461
Hawes, James, ébéniste can, actif années
1820-1850 #2511

Hawksett, Samuel C., artiste can, 1837-1910
#5753
– peintures, Université Laval (Québec, Qué)
#3078
– relation entre photographie et peinture
#245
Haworth, Peter, artiste can (vitrail), 1889-
– vitraux, Montréal (Qué) #2448
Hawthorn, Audrey, collectionneuse can, XXe
s.
– et University of British Columbia.
Museum of Anthropology (Vancouver,
CB) #3195
Hawthorn, Harry Bertram, anthropologue
can, 1910-
– et University of British Columbia.
Museum of Anthropology (Vancouver,
CB) #3195
Hawthorn, Henry Gilbert John, architecte
can, 1939-
– archipel de la reine Charlotte (CB), Queen
Charlotte Islands Museum #9129
– Vancouver (CB), rénovation, gare du
Canadien Pacifique, complexe, bureaux et
boutiques #9546
Hawthorn Mansfield Towers, agence can
d'architecture #8373
Hawthorne, Charles Webster, artiste amér,
1872-1930
– professeur de Jack Weldon Humphrey
#5865
Hay, Pierre, sculpteur can, 1661-1708 #1572
1578
Hay, Robert, ébéniste can, 1808-1890 #2463
Hay, William, architecte can, 1818-1888
– commentaire sur l'architecture torontoise
#8050
– Toronto (Ont) #8055 8056 8059
– Yorkville, hôtel de ville #8997
Haycock, Maurice Hall, artiste can, 1900-
#5754
Hayden, Michael, sculpteur can, 1943-
– *Escalator Piece* #5755
– et Intersystems #767
– expositions de groupe
– (1970) #771
– sculptures (années 1960) #1793
– xérographie en couleurs #614
Hayman, Sasha, artiste can (tapisserie),
1947- #5756
Haynes, Douglas Hector, artiste can, 1936-
#5758
– commentaire sur l'art, Edmonton (Alta),
(1981) #1975
– expositions
– (1974) #5757
– expositions de groupe
– (1981) #722
Hayter, Stanley William, artiste brit, 1901-
– enseignement de la gravure aux artistes
québécois #1641
– influence sur gravure canadienne (année
1960) #820
– professeur de David Silverberg #7206
Hayward, William B., architecte amér, actif
années 1950-
– Toronto (Ont), hôtel de ville et Civic
Square, concours #8981
Hazelgrove, Nancy Ann, artiste can, 1945-
– expositions de groupe
– (1980) #1835
Hazelton (CB)
– totems, Gitksans #3797
Hazelton (CB), 'Ksan

– expositions
  – 'Ksan, Breath of our Grandfathers: An
    Exhibition of 'Ksan Art (1972) #4130
  – 'Ksan: le souffle des ancêtres, une exposition
    de l'art de 'Ksan (1972) #4129
Hazen, William, Can, XVIIIe s.
– portrait de ses enfants, Joseph Comingo
  #5161
Head, George Bruce, artiste can, 1931- #5759
– expositions de groupe
  – (1962) #1847
  – (1981) #1907
Head, Lady Anna Maria Yorke, artiste brit
  au Canada, 1808-1890
– expositions de groupe
  – (1978) #5760
Head, Sir Edmund Walker, homme d'Etat et
  artiste brit au Canada, 1805-1868
– et édifices du Parlement (Ottawa, Ont),
  architecture #8930
– et University of Toronto. University
  College (Toronto, Ont), architecture #9453
– expositions de groupe
  – (1978) #5760
Heakes, Francis Riley, architecte can,
  1858-1930
– Toronto (Ont), Chorley Park #8749
Heaps, M. et Mme Leo J., collectionneurs
  brit, XXe s.
– collection, oeuvres d'art de J.Henry
  Sandham #7121
Heaviside, Mary (Lady Love), artiste can,
  1806-1866 #258 259
– lithographies, Nouveau-Brunswick (1830)
  #1175
Hebb, Howard D., ébéniste can, 1860-1939
  #2510
Hébert, Adrien, artiste can, 1890-1967 #302
  1392 1393
– expositions
  – (1971) #5763
– oeuvres (1909-1923) #5764
– Port de Montréal #5762
– réflexion sur son oeuvre #5761
Hébert, Anne, auteure can, 1916-
– Prévost, Antoine, comparaison #6927
Hébert, Henri, sculpteur can, 1884-1950 #302
  1315
– commentaire sur l'art québécois (années
  1940) #1383
Hébert, Jeannine Tardif
– voir Tardif-Hébert, Jeannine
Hébert, Julien, artiste can, 1917- #5766
– commentaire sur thèmes sculpturaux
  #5765
– fontaine, Centre national des arts (Ottawa,
  Ont) #9108
– oeuvres, Place des Arts (Montréal, Qué)
  #8233
– portes d'ascenseur en bronze, hôtel Reine
  Elizabeth (Montréal, Qué) #8228
Hébert, Louis-Philippe, sculpteur can,
  1850-1917 #1315 5767 5768 5769 5770 5771
– expositions, critiques #204
– Laliberté, Alfred, comparaison #6142
– monument à Paul de Chomedey de
  Maisonneuve, Montréal (Qué) #1623
– oeuvres, Art Association of Montreal
  (Montréal, Qué) #3075
– pierre tombale, cimetière, L'Acadie (Qué)
  #8830
– professeur de Maurice Galbraith Cullen
  #5217
– sculptures, Montréal (Qué) et Ottawa

(Ont) #727
Hébert, Marie Pollet, Can, XVIIe s.
– et artisanat domestique #2212
Hébert, Philippe
– voir Hébert, Louis-Philippe
Hébert, Pierre, artiste can, 1944-
– art par ordinateur #528
Hedges, Jack, orfèvre can, actif 1944 #2693
Hedrick, Robert Burns, artiste can, 1930-
  #5772 5774
– commentaire sur Gordon Rayner #6965
– commentaire sur l'art canadien #478
– expositions, critiques #5773
– expositions de groupe
  – (1965) #473
– peintures et sculptures #449
Heer, Louis-Chrétien de, artiste can,
  1755-1807 #1323
– et société québécoise #1375
– expositions de groupe
  – (1959) #219
– influence de la peinture française #1244
Held, Robert D.M., artisan verrier can, 1943-
– et Sheridan College School of Crafts and
  Design (Mississauga, Ont) #2440
– fondateur, Skookum Art Glass (Calgary,
  Alta) #2439
Helena (Mon), Montana Historical Society
– expositions
  – An Art Perspective of the Historic Pacific
    Northwest (1963) #1999
Helfand, Fern, photographe can, 1952-
– en comparaison avec Barbara Anne
  Astman #1010
Heller, Mary Ida Clair, sculpteure can, 1909-
  #5775
Helmcken, John S., médecin can, actif 1857
– cadeau, service à thé en argent #2647
Helmer Associates, agence can
  d'architecture
– Ottawa (Ont), Académie de La Salle #9480
  9481
Helsinki (Finlande), Institute of Crafts and
  Design
– McKinley, Donald Lloyd, élève #6489
Hembroff-Schleicher, Edythe, artiste can,
  1906-
– commentaire sur Emily Carr #5043
– correspondance, Emily Carr (1930-1940)
  #5026
Heming, Arthur Henry Howard, artiste can,
  1870-1940
– expositions
  – (1934) #5776
– illustrations #916
Hemingway, Peter, architecte can, 1929-
  #8084
– commentaire sur Alex Simeon Janvier
  #5936
– Edmonton (Alta) #7733
– Edmonton (Alta), Muttart Conservatory
  #8091
– Sherwood Park (Alta), County of
  Strathcona Building #5937
– théories sur l'architecture #7746
Hémon, Louis, auteur fr au Canada,
  1880-1913
– Maria Chapdelaine, illustrations
  – Gagnon, Clarence A. #1
  – Lemieux, Jean-Paul #6239
Hénault, Gilles, poète, conservateur et
  critique d'art can, 1920-
– commentaire sur Charles Daudelin #5262
– commentaire sur Léon Bellefleur #4662

Hendershot, Janet, artiste can, 1945- #675
  717
– expositions de groupe
  – (1980) #698
Henderson, Alexander, ébéniste can, actif
  1866-1906 #2511
Henderson, Alexander, photographe can,
  1831-1913 #5777
– photographies d'arpentage, Canadien
  Pacifique (années 1870) #1876
Henderson, D'Arcy S., artiste can, 1940-
– expositions de groupe
  – (1978) #2067
Henderson, J.T., imprimerie (Montréal, Qué)
– cartes de Noël #890
Henderson, James, artiste can, 1871-1951
  #5778
– expositions
  – (1969) #5779
– expositions de groupe
  – (1928) #294
  – (1978) #133
Henderson, Tom, sculpteur can, 1936- #5780
Hendery, Robert, orfèvre can, 1820-après
  1895 #2638
– et orfèvrerie québécoise #2675
– oeuvres, Detroit Institute of Arts (Detroit,
  Mich) #2691
– poinçons #2635
Hennessey, Frank Charles, artiste can,
  1894-1941
– influence sur Tony Law #6174
– paysages, tapis crochetés #2750
Henri, Robert, artiste amér, 1865-1929
– influence sur James Wilson Morrice #6626
  6630 6633
– professeur de Mabel Killam Day #5273
Henrickson, Martha Charlotte, photographe
  can, 1944-
– Awakenings #5781
Henrickson, Thomas Elton, photographe
  can, 1944-
– Awakenings #5781
Henriquez, Richard G., architecte can, 1941-
– théories sur l'art et l'architecture #7746
Henriquez & Todd, agence can
  d'architecture
– Vancouver (CB), prix, architecture, école
  élémentaire (1970) #9507
Henry Birks & Fils Ltée
– collection, orfèvrerie canadienne #2636
  2637 2650 2651 2656
Henry Bloomfield and Sons, atelier de
  vitraux (Vancouver, CB)
– vitraux, édifices du Parlement (Victoria,
  CB) #8966
héraldique
– voir aussi emblèmes et devises; généalogie;
  insignes; signes héraldiques
héraldique . Canada #2913 2915 2939
– Alexander, William Walker #4506
– art traditionnel et art kitsch #2951
– Carter, Alexander Scott #5050
– thème décoratif du castor #56
– vitraux héraldiques, Vancouver (CB),
  (1890-1940) #2454
Heriot, George, receveur des postes brit,
  artiste au Canada, 1766-1844 #279 5782
  5785 5787 5788 5789
– expositions
  – (1978) #5786
– peintures d'Amérindiens #5783
  – Windsor (Ont), Willistead Art Gallery
    #5784

Héritage Canada
– conservation de l'architecture
    – (1973) #7763
    – (1973-1977) #7770
– périodique, *Canadian Heritage* #7764
– préservation de l'architecture #7771
Heritage Canada/Héritage Canada, périodique can #7764
Héritage canadien du Québec
– et conservation de l'architecture #7871
Héritage Ottawa
– inventaire des archives de l'architecture avant l950, Ottawa (Ont), collections privées #8049
Heritage Park (Alta)
– architecture #8125
Herman, Jack, céramiste can, 1927- #2395
Herman, Josef, artiste brit, 1911-
– influence sur Stephen Andrews #4527
Herman, Lorraine, céramiste can, 1929- #2395
héroïnes
– *voir* héros et heroïnes
héros et héroïnes canadiens
– Boyle, John Bernard #4892 4893 4894
– Hébert, Louis-Philippe #5767
– Jefferys, Charles William #5957
Héroux, Yvon, artiste can, actif 1972
– expositions
    – (1972) #5790
Herreilers, John, artiste can, actif 1975
– entretien #5791
Herring, John, artisan verrier can, 1818-1898 #2396
Herring Glass Works, fabricants de verre (Mallorytown, Ont)
– et John Herring #2396
Hersey, John A., orfèvre can, actif 1823-1850 #2649
Hertel, François, prêtre jésuite, professeur et auteur can, 1905-
– et Paul-Emile Borduas #4814
Herzog, Fred, photographe can, 1930-
– catalogue de photographies #998
Herzog, Saul, architecte can, 1933-
– Red Deer (Alta), hôtel de ville #8990
Hesse, Eva, artiste amér, 1936-1970
– Westerlund, Mia, comparaison #7545
Hesse, Hermann, auteur all, 1877-1962
– influence sur Vera Frenkel #5526
Heusch, Lucio de, artiste can, 1946- #1544
– expositions de groupe
    – (1977) #1532
    – (1981) #1565
– symposium, Musée du Nouveau-Monde (La Rochelle, France), (1980) #1559
Heuvel, Francis van den, photographe can, 1949-
– catalogue de photographies #997 999
Heward, Efa Prudence, artiste can, 1896-1947 #5794
– expositions
    – (1948) #5795
    – (1980) #5796
Heward, John, artiste can, 1934- #5792
    – (1977) #5793
Hewett, M., médecin brit, collectionneur, XVIIIe s.
– collection, artefacts, Indiens de la côte nord-ouest #3767
Hewton, Randolph Stanley, artiste can, 1888-1960
– et Albert Henry Robinson #7057
– et Groupe des Sept #1732

– membre du Groupe des peintres canadiens #324
Heyer, Paul, anthropologue can, 1946-
– commentaire sur le conceptualisme #7473
Heyvaert, Pierre, sculpteur can, 1934-1974 #5797
Hicklin, Barbara Jane, artiste can, 1918- #5798
Hicks, Bill, photographe can, ca 1945-
– catalogue de photographies #995
Hidai, Nankoku, artiste jap, XXe s.
– professeur de Gaston-Pierre Petit #6844
Hidatsas
– ouvrages en piquants de porc-épic #3701
Hide, Peter, sculpteur can, 1944-
– expositions de groupe
    – (1981) #797
– techniques #792
hiérochloé odorante
– utilisation dans vannerie, Saulteux/Ojibwa #3547
Higgins, Steve, artiste can, 1946-
– expositions de groupe
    – (1977) #1901
Highlands (Ecosse)
– vues, Robert Ford Gagen #5530
Highlights, Quarterly Newsletter of the Alberta Society of Artists, périodique can #1944
Hildred, Philip, photographe can, actif 1971
– catalogue de photographies #998
Hildrith, Isaac, architecte can, 1741-1807 #8374 8375
– Halifax (NE), Government House #8750
Hill, George William, sculpteur can, 1862-1934 #192 5799
– monument à sir Georges-Etienne Cartier, Montréal (Qué) #1623
Hill, James Thomas, artiste can, 1930-
– illustrations #941
Hill, Stanley R. (Stan), sculpteur can, 1921- #5800
Hill, Tom, artiste can, 1943-
– entretien #4155
Hilst, Robert van der, photographe can, ca 1940-
– catalogue de photographies #1023
Hilton, Charles, sculpteur et céramiste can, 1937- #2392
Hime, Humphrey Lloyd, photographe can, 1833-1903 #5802 5803
– photographies, exploration de l'Assiniboine et de la Saskatchewan (1858) #1865 5801 5804
– photographies d'arpentage #1014 1015
Hind, William George Richardson, artiste can, 1833-1888 #5805 5808 5809
– artiste de style victorien #5810
– expositions
    – (1967) #5806
– expositions, critiques #1692
– paysages #1855
– peintre, expédition Fort Garry-Victoria (1862) #5807
– scènes de la ruée vers l'or, Colombie-Britannique #5811
Hines, Sherman, photographe can, ca 1942-
– catalogue de photographies #995
Hinge (Vancouver, CB) #2040
Hinton, John Henry, photographe can, 1875-1948
– expositions
    – (1977) #5812
Hiroshige, artiste jap, 1797-1858
– Tanobe, Miyuki, comparaison #7322

Hirschberg, Martin, sculpteur can, 1937-
– sculptures (années 1960) #1793
– utilisation de la lumière #767
histoire, art et
– Boyle, John Bernard, commentaire #4893
histoire de l'architecture
– Canada #7699
histoire de l'art
– Canada
    – (1980) #3316
    – (années 1930-1960) #3306
    – et sociologie de l'art #164
– femmes artistes #144
– méthodologie
    – art inuit #4205 4225 4282 4401 4426 4442
    – Indiens de la côte nord-ouest #4041 4060
– Québec #1255
    – Morisset, Gérard #3322
histoire et art
– Shadbolt, Jack Leonard, commentaire #7185
histoire naturelle
– artefacts
    – Edmonton (Alta), University of Alberta #3200
    – Halifax (NE), Nova Scotia Museum #3071
    – Québec (Qué), Musée du Québec #3095
    – Toronto (Ont), Royal Ontario Museum #3141
histoire orale
– et art canadien #608
– utilisation, et Charles Marius Barbeau #3309
– utilisation, et Napoléon Bourassa #4873
historiens et critiques d'art
– Canada
    – (1907) #3299
    – (années 1940) #380
    – (années 1970) #3312
– MacDonald, J.E.H., commentaire #6360
hiver
– cartes de Noël canadiennes #863
– Cullen, Maurice Galbraith, paysages #5214
– paysages canadiens #285 1298
– Suzor-Coté, Marc-Aurèle de Foy, *Paysage d'hiver* #7301
– Tremblay, Georges-Edouard, tapis crochetés #2756
Hlynsky, David, photographe can, 1947-
– et *Image Nation* #992
– expositions de groupe
    – (1979) #1905
    – (1981) #1070
– hologrammes, Fringe Research Inc. (Toronto, Ont) #1827
Hobart (Australie), Tasmanian Museum and Art Gallery
– expositions
    – *Contemporary Canadian Painters* (1957) #423
Hobden, Mark D., photographe can, 1947-
– catalogue de photographies #991
– expositions de groupe
    – (1972) #1952
Hobson Pottery, fabricants de céramique (Sainte-Angèle, Qué)
    – (années 1890) #2298 2322
hochets
– *voir* crécelles
Hodge, Albert Hemstock, sculpteur brit, 1875-1918
– sculpture, Palais législatif (Winnipeg, Man) #8948 8949

Hodgins, John George, éducateur can,
    1821-1912
– commentaire sur l'architecture des
    maisons d'enseignement #9384
Hodgkinson, Edward Allen, artiste can, 1918-
– expositions
    – (1963) #1668
– expositions de groupe
    – (1977) #646
Hodgson, Alan James, architecte can, 1928-
– Victoria (CB), édifice du Parlement,
    restauration #8964 8965 8966
Hodgson, Bates & Beattie, agence can
    d'architecture
– Calgary (Alta), Burns Building #8118
Hodgson, Thomas Sherlock (Tom), artiste
    can, 1924- #5813
– art et écrits #5814
Hodgson, Wilfred Garstang
– voir Garstang-Hodgson, Wilfred
Hodler, Ferdinand, artiste suisse, 1853-1918
– influence sur John Bernard Boyle #4894
Hoey, Elizabeth Wilkes, artiste can, active
    années 1930- #5816
– et Albert Angus Macdonald #6354
Hoferichter, Bert, photographe can, ca 1939-
– catalogue de photographies #991
Hoffman, F. Burrall, fils, architecte amér,
    actif 1914-1946
– Winnipeg (Man), Bank of Hamilton #9171
Hoffman, Fred G., sculpteur can, 1845-1926
    #5817
Hoffman, Louis, ébéniste can, 1818-1900
    #2573
Hofmann, Hans, artiste amér, 1880-1966
– influence sur Jack Hamilton Bush #4970
– professeur d'Alexandra Luke #6333
– professeur d'artistes canadiens #402 1850
– professeur de Donald Alvin Jarvis #5947
– professeur de Ruth Wainwright #7497
Hogle & Davis, agence can d'architecture
– Montréal (Qué), Bank of Toronto #9167
Holbrook, Elizabeth M. Bradford, sculpteure
    can, 1913-
– expositions de groupe
    – (1971) #772
Holder, Henry Arthur, ébéniste can,
    1853-1935 #2505 2506
Holder, Thomas Cook, ébéniste can,
    1821-1894 #2505 2506
Holgate, Bidwell A., promoteur de
    construction can, né 1878
– résidence, Edmonton (Alta) #8718
Holgate, Edwin Headley, artiste can,
    1892-1977 #302 309 5818 5819
– Cullen, Maurice Galbraith, comparaison
    #5216
– et Albert Henry Robinson #7057
– et le Groupe des Sept #1732 1774
– expositions de groupe
    – (1977) #1278 1279
– gravures sur bois de fil #802
– illustration et mise en pages artistique
    #939
– professeur de Jean-Paul Lemieux #6228
Holiwell, Charles E., éditeur officiel de
    l'armée brit au Canada, actif années 1870
– vues de la ville de Québec #2326
Holland, Michael (Mickey), architecte can,
    1929-
– restauration, Duggan House (Edmonton,
    Alta) #8729
Hollett, John, tonnelier can, 1888- #2151
Hollingsworth, Fred Thornton, architecte

can, 1917-
– West Vancouver (CB), Woyat-Bowie
    Building, Bureaux d'architectes #9346
Hollister, F.S.J., artiste can (vitrail), actif
    1924-
– Oshawa (Ont), Saint George's Anglican
    Church #8899
– Ottawa (Ont), édifices du Parlement. Tour
    de la Paix. Fenêtres commémoratives
    en l'honneur des soldats #2445
Holloway, Elsie, photographe can, active
    1908-1946 #5820
Holm, Bill, anthropologue can, 1925-
– et Bill Reid #6987
– influence sur Pat Dixon #5294
Holman, Donald (Don), artiste can, 1946-
– et James Burton Spencer, collaboration à
    l'exécution d'une lithographie #7270
Holman, James Henry, artiste can, 1821-1891
– expositions
    – (1959) #5821
Holman (TNO)
– arts graphiques #4197
    – (1959-1972) #4478
    – (1959-1976) #4490
    – (1966-) #4469
    – (années 1960) #4195
– arts graphiques et sculpture #3350 4200
    – sculpture en os de baleine #4457
Holmes, Robert, artiste can, 1861-1930 #5822
– Coombs, Edith Grace, comparaison #5172
– et Charles MacDonald Manly #6414
– et Mary Evelyn Wrinch #7617
– expositions
    – (1964) #5823
– livres tirés de sa bibliothèque #5824
hologramme
– voir holographie
holographie
– Canada (années 1970) #1827
– Pethick, Jerry #6840 6841
Holownia, Thaddeus, photographe can,
    1949-
– expositions de groupe
    – (1981) #1070
Holt, Elizabeth Russell, artiste can, active
    années 1920-1960
– et Saint John Art Club (Saint-Jean, NB)
    #1173
Holyoke, Rich, compositeur can, actif années
    1970
– et W.O.R.K.S. #1955
Homemaker's, périodique can
– Haroutiun, Georges, directeur artistique
    #5708
Honsberger, Henry, Can, actif 1850
– habitation, région de St. Catharines (Ont)
    #2485
Hood, Robert, officier de la marine brit,
    artiste au Canada, 1796-1821 #5826
– expédition de Franklin dans l'Arctique
    (1819-1821), journal #5825 5827
Hooker, Marion Hope Nelson, artiste can,
    1886-1946
– portraits d'Amérindiens #1896
Hookway, Elmer John, artisan verrier can,
    1889-1974 #5828
Hooper, James, collectionneur brit, XXe s.
– collection, art autochtone #3369
Hooper, John, sculpteur can, 1926-
– membre du Hampton Group #1177
Hooper, Katherine B. (Kathy), artiste can,
    1934-
– expositions de groupe

    – (1973) #1182
– membre du Hampton Group #1177
Hooper, Thomas, architecte can, 1859-1935
    #8376
– Vancouver (CB), University of British
    Columbia, concours #9509
Hoover, Christian, artiste can de style
    fraktur, 1835-1918 #5829
Hope, William R., artiste can, 1865-1931
– membre du Canadian Art Club #193
hôpitaux . Canada
– (1911-1912) #8295
– (1914-1917), hôpitaux militaires #9016
– (1919-1920) #9018
– (années 1920), hôpitaux militaires #9019
– (années 1930) #9020 9021
– (années 1940) #9024 9026
    – sanatoriums #9025
– (années 1950) #9029 9031
– (années 1960) #9032
– Brandon (Man), Hospital for the Insane
    #9014
– Hamilton (Ont), McMaster University
    Health Sciences Centre #9035 9036 9037
– Kingston (Ont), (avant 1867) #7989
– Montréal (Qué)
    – Hôpital général de Montréal #9030
    – hôpital Royal Victoria. Pavillon Ross
        #9017
    – hôpital Sainte-Justine #8407
    – Hôtel-Dieu. Pavillon Jérôme Le Royer
        de la Dauversière #9023
– Sault Ste Marie (Ont), Group Health
    Centre #9033
– Toronto (Ont)
    – Hospital for Sick Children #9015
    – Provincial Lunatic Asylum #8378 9034
    – Sunnybrook Hospital #9027
    – Toronto General Hospital #9012 9013
– XVIIIe s. #7861
Hopkins, Edward Martin, Brit, employé de
    la Compagnie de la baie d'Hudson au
    Canada, 1820-1893
– collection, jambières, Piégans #3715
– voyages au Canada #5835
Hopkins, Elisabeth Margaret, artiste can,
    1894- #5831 5832
– commentaire sur Frances Ann Beechy
    Hopkins #5830
– expositions, critiques #1883
Hopkins, Frances Ann Beechy, artiste brit au
    Canada, 1838-1918 #5830 5833 5834 5835
– expositions de groupe
    – (1888) #175
Hopkins, Lawson & Nelson, agence can
    d'architecture
– Toronto (Ont), Osgoode Hall #9002 9003
Hopper, Robin, céramiste can, 1939- #2395
Horeis, William Richard, photographe can,
    1945-
– entretien #5836
– expositions de groupe
    – (1981) #1070
Horetzky, Charles George, photographe can,
    1838-1900 #5838
– catalogue de photographies #995
– photographies d'arpentage, Canadien
    Pacifique (années 1870) #1014 1015 1865
    1876 5837
horloges
– voir aussi montres
horloges . Canada
– (1700-1900), horlogers #2931
– (années 1730-milieu XIXe s.) #2925

– Arthur Pequegnat Clock Co. #2912 2956
– Filiau (dit Dubois), Jean Baptiste #5435
– guide pour collectionneurs #2101
– île aux Coudres (Qué) #2178
– Montréal (Qué), église Notre-Dame #8839
– Nouvelle-Ecosse
   – XVIIe-XIXe s. #2489 2499
   – XVIIIe-XIXe s. #2496 2497
– Ontario
   – (1780-1900) #2577
   – (années 1790-1857) #2558
– orfèvres québécois, XVIIe-XVIIIe s. #2657
– Québec
   – XVIIe-XVIIIe s. #1320 2530 2531 2914
– XIXe s. #2927
horloges . Etats-Unis
– XIXe s. exportation au Canada #2927
Horne, Cleeve, artiste can, 1912-
– commentaire sur l'art du portrait #624
Horne, David Ernest, architecte can, 1929-
– Toronto (Ont), hôtel de ville et Civic
   Square, concours #8981
Horning, Isaac, photographe can, actif
   1850-1870
– vues, Simcoe (Ont) #1722
Hornyansky, Nicholas, artiste can, 1896-1965
– commentaire sur la gravure à l'eau-forte
   #5839
Horsburgh, Victor D., architecte can,
   1866-1947
– Banque canadienne de commerce, édifices
   #9169
– Toronto (Ont), Banque canadienne de
   commerce #9181
Horsfall, Arthur, artiste can, 1915-
– expositions de groupe
   – (1981) #1907
Horst, David B., sculpteur can, 1873-1965
   #5840
Horvat, Miljenko, artiste can, 1935- #5841
– entretien #5842
– expositions
   – (1980) #5843
Horvath, Tibor, photographe can, actif
   années 1950-
– catalogue de photographies #995
Horwood, Eric Crompton, architecte can,
   1900-1984
– dessins d'architecture, Archives publiques
   de l'Ontario (Toronto, Ont) #8028 8030
Horwood, Harold A., artiste can (vitrail),
   actif 1867-années 1890
– illustrations d'animaux #1727
– vitraux, Smithsonian Institution
   (Washington, DC) #2111
Horwood, John Charles Batstone, architecte
   can, 1864-1938
– commentaire sur l'architecture canadienne
   #7640
– dessins d'architecture, Archives publiques
   de l'Ontario (Toronto, Ont) #8028 8030
Horwood, Victor William, architecte can,
   1878-1939
– Brandon (Man), Hospital for the Insane
   #9014
Horwood & White, agence can
   d'architecture
– Toronto (Ont), Northway Department
   Store #9366
hospitalières de l'Hôtel-Dieu
– broderie #2779
hôtels
– voir aussi motels
hôtels . Canada

– (1880-1914) #7736
– Brandon (Man), Prince Edward Hotel
   #9266
– Calgary (Alta)
   – (1875-1914) #8711
   – Hotel Palliser #9271
– Edmonton (Alta), Hotel Macdonald #9270
– et sociétés ferroviaires canadiennes #3281
– Guelph (Ont), XIXe s. #7970
– Hamilton (Ont), Royal Connaught Hotel
   #9274
– lac Louise (Alta), Skoki Lodge #9296
– Lucerne (Qué), Château Lucerne #9283
– Manitoba #8098
– Montebello (Qué), Château Montebello
   #9295
– Montréal (Qué)
   – hôtel Mont-Royal #9276
   – hôtel Reine-Elizabeth #8228 9286
   – hôtel Ritz-Carlton #9267
   – Place Bonaventure #9292 9319 9320 9321
     9322 9323 9325
   – XVIIe s.-années 1950 #9287
– Ottawa (Ont), Château Laurier #9264 9265
   9282 9528 9529
– Québec (Qué)
   – Château Frontenac #9261 9278
   – hôtel Union #9284
– Saskatoon (Sask), Flanagan Hotel #9263
– sociétés ferroviaires, hôtels, style "château"
   #7652 9290 9291
– Toronto (Ont)
   – Four Seasons Sheraton Hotel #9294
   – Hotel Mossop #9262
   – Hyatt Regency Hotel #9293
   – Inn on the Park #9289
   – Royal York Hotel #9280 9281
   – St. Charles Hotel #9269
   – Toronto Hilton Hotel #9292
– Vancouver (CB), Hotel Vancouver #9272
   9273
– Winnipeg (Man)
   – (1831-1960) #8095
   – Deer Lodge #9260
   – Empire Hotel #9361
   – Fort Garry Hotel #9268
   – Hotel at Silver Springs #9263
   – Marlborough Hotel #9277
   – Royal Alexandra Hotel #2599
– XIXe s. #9512
   – auberges #9285
hôtels . Etats-Unis
– XIXe s., auberges #9285
hôtels de ville . Canada
– (années 1950) #8982
– (années 1960) #8990
– Cobourg (Ont), Victoria Hall #8994 8995
– Edmonton (Alta), hôtel de ville #8998 8999
   9000
– Hamilton (Ont), hôtel de ville et Civic
   Square #8988
– Leaf Rapids (Man), centre municipal #8974
– Montréal (Qué), hôtel de ville #1231 8980
– Moose Jaw (Sask), hôtel de ville #8978
– Niagara-on-the-Lake (Ont), XIXe s. #7986
– Ottawa (Ont), hôtel de ville #8984
– Scarborough (Ont), Scarborough Civic
   Centre #8973
– style victorien #7769
– Toronto (Ont)
   – hôtel de ville et Civic Square #8981 8983
     8989 8991 8992
   – Yorkville Town Hall #8997
– Vernon (CB), Vernon Civic Centre #8972

– Winnipeg (Man)
   – (1876-1962) #8996
   – hôtel de ville, concours (1913) #8979
   – hôtel de ville (1883-1886) #8331
   – hôtel de ville (1960) #8985 8986 8987
hôtels de ville . Grande-Bretagne #8944
Houle, Robert James, artiste et conservateur
   can, 1947-
– entretien #5844
Housser, Frederick Broughton, auteur can,
   1889-1936
– correspondance, Norman I. Gurd #1776
Housser, Muriel Yvonne McKague, artiste
   can, 1898- #309 5845
– commentaire sur Alexandra Luke #6333
Houston, James Archibald, artiste can, 1921-
   #5846
– entretien #5847
– et Kenojuak Ashevak #4564
– et la sculpture inuit #4392 4449
– et Peter Pitseolak #6880 6881
– initiation des Inuit à la gravure #4186 4201
   4461 4462 4470
– soutien de l'art inuit #4397 4452
Houston (Tex), Museum of Fine Arts
– expositions
   – The Eskimo (1969) #4216
Hovadik, Jaroslov, artiste can, 1935- #5848
Howard, Barbara, artiste can, 1926-
– expositions de groupe
   – (1978) #666
Howard, Jemima Frances Meikle (Mme
   John), artiste can, m. 1877 #3129
   – (1834) #1688
Howard, John, agriculteur, photographe et
   ébéniste can, né 1877 #2587
Howard, John George, architecte, artiste et
   collectionneur can, 1803-1890
– écrits #8377
– expositions
   – (1979) #8378
– membre de la Toronto Society of Arts
   #1689
– peintures, Colborne Lodge (Toronto, Ont)
   #3129
– Toronto (Ont) #8056 8075
   – Colborne Lodge #8659
   – Provincial Lunatic Asylum #9034
Howard, Ronald, architecte can, 1933-
– Vancouver (CB), Caulfield Cove Town
   Houses #8746
Howard, Sidney, sculpteur can, 1913- #2596
– expositions, critiques #1210
Howarth, Edward J., artiste can, 1943-
– Stratoscape (Woodsworth Building,
   Winnipeg, Man) #5853
Howarth, Glenn, artiste can, 1946- #2053
   5849 5850 5851
Howarth, Thomas, architecte can, 1914-
– Toronto (Ont), York University. Glendon
   Hall #9457
Howe, John Donallen, ébéniste can, né ca
   1841 #2511
– buffet et escalier, maison Gregory
   (Saint-Jean, NB) #8545
Howe, Jonas, ébéniste can, né ca 1844 #2511
Howe, Joseph, homme d'Etat can, 1804-1873
– Festival Joseph Howe (NE), costumes
   #2887
Hower, Else, artiste can, active 1925
– intérieur, Château Frontenac (Québec,
   Qué) #9278
Howison, Henry, céramiste can, actif années
   1860 #2301

Howlin, John, artiste can, 1941-
- expositions
  - (1979) #5852
HP (Anonyme), orfèvre can, XIXe s. #2691
Hudon, Normand, artiste can, 1929- #5854
5855
Hudon-Beaulac, Simone Marie Yvette,
  artiste can, 1905- #1380 5856
- cartes de Noël #857
- expositions, critiques #806
Hudson, Andrew, artiste et critique d'art
  can, 1935-
- oeuvres choisies, *14 Canadians: A Critic's
  Choice* (1977) #623 627 645
- réflexion sur son oeuvre #5857
Hudson, Susan Mary, artiste can, 1941-
- cofondatrice de Graphia (Montréal, Qué)
  #1660
Hudson, Thomas (Tom), artiste can, 1886-
  #1155
- expositions de groupe
  - (1977) #1156
Hudson River School
- et Aaron Allan Edson #5362
- et Robert Stuart Duncanson #5338
Huel, Georges, artiste can, 1930- #5858
- projets de design, Jeux olympiques (1976)
  #898 901 902
Hughes, Edward John, artiste can, 1913-
  #1996 5859 5861
- et réalisme #110
- expositions
  - (1976) #5860
Hughes, Lynn, sculpteure can, 1941-
- *Rank Beginnings* #5862
- sculptures en céramique (années 1970)
  #2065
Hughto, Darryl, artiste amér, 1943-
- expositions de groupe
  - (1981) #722
Huguet (dit Latour), Pierre, orfèvre can,
  1748-1817
- oeuvres, Detroit Institute of Arts (Detroit,
  Mich) #2691
- paix #2666
- professeur de Paul Morand #6604
Hull (Qué)
- édifices récréatifs #9081
Hull (Qué), région de la capital nationale
- statues et monuments #762
Humberstone Potteries, fabricants de
  céramique (au nord de Toronto, Ont)
  #2288
  - (1798-1918) #2338
Hume, Clare, photographe can, actif années
  1970-
- catalogue de photographies #991
Humeston, Jay, ébéniste can, actif 1798-1815
  #2493
Humlebaek (Danemark), Louisiana Museum
  of Modern Art
- expositions
  - *10 Canadian Artists in the 1970s* (1980)
    #703
Hümme, Joseph Julius, artiste can, 1825-1889
  #5863
Humphrey, Jack Weldon, artiste can,
  1901-1967 #336 1121 1128 1173 1179 1184
  5864 5865 5867 5868
- commentaire sur l'art canadien (années
  1940) #5866
- commentaire sur l'art des provinces
  maritimes (années 1950) #1172
- en comparaison avec Emily Carr #404

- entretien #5869
- et peintures des Maritimes (années 1960)
  #1122
- expositions
  - (1970) #5870
  - (1978) #5871
- expositions de groupe
  - (1966) #1123
  - (1973) #1182
- membre du Groupe des peintres
  canadiens #324
Humphrey, Ruth, éducatrice can, 1898-
- correspondance, Emily Carr (1937-1944)
  #5029
Humphreys Glass Works, fabricants de
  verre (Trenton, NE) #2398 2400 2409 2417
Humphries, Henry, officier de la marine
  brit, artiste au Canada, m. 1799
- vues, détroit de Nootka, Vancouver Island
  (CB) #2002
Hunsicker, Isaac, artiste can de style fraktur,
  1803-1870 #2255
Hunt, Henry, sculpteur can, 1923- #4132
  5872
- totem, Beacon Hill Park (Victoria, CB)
  #4115
Hunt, Richard, artiste can, 1951- #4148
Hunt, William Edward, artiste can, actif
  1916 #1391
Hunter, Samuel, artiste can, 1858-1939
- dessins humoristiques, *Toronto Star* #943
Hunter, William E.N., architecte amér,
  1868-1947
- Hamilton (Ont), First Methodist Church
  #7957
Huntress, Judith Allsopp, artiste can, 1943-
  #717
- expositions de groupe
  - (1975) #1867
Huot, Charles Edouard, artiste can,
  1855-1930 #302 1312 1315 1323 5873 5875
  5876 5878 5884
- *Débats sur les langues de 1793*, Assemblée
  nationale (Québec, Qué) #5880 5881
- et Elzéar Delamarre #5877
- *Je me souviens*, Assemblée nationale
  (Québec, Qué) #5874
- peintures
  - (1873) #5879
  - chapelle de l'Ermitage (Lac Bouchette,
    Qué) #5882
  - église Saint-Sauveur (Québec, Qué)
    #5883
- professeur de Edmond LeMoine #6243
- professeur de Georges-Henri Duquet
  #5343
Huppé (dit Lagroix), Joseph, constructeur et
  chapelier can, 1696-après 1776 #269 270
Huret, Grégoire, artiste fr, 1606-1670
- et nationalisme dans l'art #1373
Hurlbut, Spring, artiste can, 1931-
- expositions de groupe
  - (1981) #723
Hurley, Robert Newton, artiste can,
  1894-1980 #5885 5886
- Cowley, Reta Madeline, comparaison
  #5200
- expositions de groupe
  - (1970) #1918
  - (1971) #1920
Hurni, Jean-Claude, photographe can, 1936-
- catalogue de photographies #997 999
Huron Pottery, fabricants de céramique
  (Egmondville, Ont)

- moules #2334
Hurons
- art
  - (1600-1760) #3579
- colorants et teinture #165
- culture (1910s) #3514
- pipes #3504 3632
- poterie #3502 3520
- travail sur bois #3519
- wampum #3495 3526
Hurst, Patrick Russell, artiste can, 1947-
- expositions de groupe
  - (1977) #781
Hurtubise, Jacques, artiste can, 1939- #1418
  1542 1543 5887 5889
- et art minimal #1483
- et op'art #1445
- et plasticiens #1439
- expositions
  - (1981) #5890
- expositions de groupe
  - (1965) #469
  - (1967) #480 491
  - (1968) #1263
- Gagnon-Fortier, C., comparaison #5552
- peintures (1960-1980) #5888
- symposium, Musée du Nouveau-Monde
  (La Rochelle, France), (1980) #1559
Hushlak, Gerald, artiste can, 1944- #5892
- entretien #5891
- expositions de groupe
  - (1978) #1961
Hutchinson, Leonard, artiste can, 1896-1980
- estampes (1930-1940) #5893
Hutchinson, Mme Richard Ernest, artiste
  can, active années 1850 #1118
Hutchinson, Peter, photographe can, 1946-
- catalogue de photographies #991
Hutchison, Alexander Cowper, architecte
  can, 1838-1922
- LaSalle (Qué), manoir Ogilvie #8636
Hutchison, Wood & Miller, agence can
  d'architecture
- Montréal (Qué), construction domiciliaire
  #8556
- Toronto (Ont), Masonic Temple, concours
  #9062
Hutchison & Wood, agence can
  d'architecture
- Montréal (Qué), Canadian Express
  Company Building #9304
- Toronto (Ont), John Ross Robertson School
  et Glenholme School, concours #9437
Hutner, Paul, artiste can, 1948- #1807
- expositions de groupe
  - (1974) #565
  - (1975) #1809
huttérites au Canada
- art #1962
- arts décoratifs #2140
- mobilier #2585
huttes . Pieds-Noirs #3647
Hutton, Gordon Johnston, architecte can,
  1881-1942
- architecture domestique #8496
Hutton, John, artiste brit, 1906-
- gravures sur panneaux de verre,
  vestibules, Bibliothèque nationale du
  Canada et Archives publiques du Canada
  (Ottawa, Ont) #5894
Hyde, C., artiste can, actif 1847-1848
- membre de la Toronto Society of Arts
  #1689
Hyde, Laurence, artiste can, 1914-

– commentaire sur la gravure sur bois
debout #5895
– commentaire sur le dessin de timbres #811
Hynes, Feldman & Watson, agence can
d'architecture
– Oak Ridge (Ont), De La Salle Training
School #9386
– Toronto (Ont)
– Allen's Bloor Street Theatre #9071
– Allen's Danforth Theatre #9072
– Allen Theatre #9069
– Saint Charles Hotel #9269
Hynes, James Patrick, architecte can,
1868-1953
– Toronto (Ont), Hotel Mossop #9262

I

I.M. Pei & Associates
– voir Pei, I.M., & Associates
Iacurto, Francesco, artiste can, 1908- #5896
IBM
– voir International Business Machines
Corporation (IBM)
IBM (International Business Machines
Corporation)
– collection, art canadien, XXe s. #350
icônes
– Schlieper, Heiko #7161
Igloolik (TNO)
– artefacts dorsétiens #4337 4342
iglous #4213 4271 8733
Iglulik
– culture
– (années 1920) #4326
– début XXe s. #4366
Ikoy Partnership, agence can d'architecture
– Winnipeg (Man), Ikoy Partnership, bureau
d'architectes #8091
Iksik, Francis, sculpteur can, 1920- #5897
Ikutaaq, David, sculpteur can, 1929- #4407
– expositions
– (1981) #5898
île à la Crosse (Sask), école et centre
communautaire
– architecture, Douglas Joseph Cardinal
#8341
île aux Coudres (Qué)
– arts décoratifs #2178 2184
– (années 1930) #2168
île Bélair (Qué)
– vues
– Hébert, Adrien #5764
île d'Anticosti (Qué)
– architecture #7869
île d'Orléans (Qué)
– architecture #7847
– architecture domestique #8624
– (1761-1767) #8613
– XVIIIe-XIXe s. #8582
– art #1323
– art et architecture #1233 1238
– costume, XVIIe s. #2895
– tapis #2764
– tissage #1327
île d'Orléans (Qué), église de la
Sainte-Famille
– architecture et intérieur #8795
– modèle architectural #8869
– sculptures, Lauréat Vallière #7455
– sculptures sur bois #1612

île d'Orléans (Qué), église Saint-François
– modèle architectural #8869
île d'Orléans (Qué), église
Saint-François-de-Sales
– architecture et intérieur #8796
île d'Orléans (Qué), église Saint-Jean
– architecture et intérieur #8801
île d'Orléans (Qué), église Saint-Pierre
– architecture et intérieur #8802
île d'Orléans (Qué), maison Charles
Porteous
– peintures murales, William Brymner #4951
île de Baffin (TNO)
– arts graphiques #4499
– culture #4320
– (années 1920) #4326
– dessins (1964) #4194
– sculpture (années 1970) #4420
– vues, A.Y. Jackson #5919
– vues photographiques, Peter Pitseolak
#6876
île de Qikertaaluk (Qué)
– pétroglyphes #4344
Ile-du-Prince-Edouard
– architecture #7798 7799 7801
– Harris, William Critchlow #8372
– Plaw, John #8399
– XVIIe s.-années 1930 #7796
– architecture domestique
– (années 1880-1930) #8544
– maisons en grès, début XIXe s. #8552
– XVIIIe-XIXe s. #8530
– art #1164 1166
– (années 1940) #350
– (années 1970) #1131 1165 1168
– art et architecture, XVIIIe-XIXe s. #7780
– arts décoratifs #2153
– courtepointes
– (années 1850-1970) #2802
– (années 1920) #2794
– églises #8777
– ex-libris, XVIIIe-XIXe s. #915
– femmes artistes (années 1970) #1167
– mobilier #2508
– XVIIIe-XIXe s. #2498 2507 2518
– orfèvrerie #2640
– palais de justice (avant 1914) #9009
– poterie, XIXe s. #2311
– poterie de grès, XVIIIe s. #2364 2365
– textiles et tissus, XVIIIe-XIXe s. #2734
– vues
– Hammond, Charlotte Wilson #1169
– Morrison, Alfred L. #6642
– Redgrave, Felicity #1169
– vues photographiques
– Gamble, Millie #5554
– Turner, Jack #7439
île Perrot (Qué), église
Sainte-Jeanne-Françoise-de-Chantal
– architecture et intérieur #8805
îles de la Madeleine (Qué)
– architecture domestique #8624
– courtepointes (années 1920) #2794
– granges, XIXe s. #9230
– vues photographiques
– Beaudoin-Hansen, Kéro #4648
Iliu, Josef, artiste fr, 1914- #5899
– réflexion sur son oeuvre #8229
Illsely, Templeton & Archibald, agence can
d'architecture
– Dorval (Qué), Aéroport international de
Montréal. Aérogare #9515
Illustrated London News, périodique brit
– illustrations, Edward John Russell #7110
Illustration, L', périodique fr

– illustrations, Henri Julien #5983 5984
illustration . Canada #925
– (1759-1914), Québec, thème de la rébellion
#1351
– (1910-1921), Farmer's Magazine #1765
– (1930), Canadian National Exhibition
(Toronto, Ont) #313
– (1945), manuels divers #919
– (1965-1968) #874
– (1967) #877
– (1981) #941
– (années 1880-1940) #28
– (années 1890-1940) #928
– (années 1910) #205 916
– (années 1940) #374
– Beny, Wilfred Roloff, commentaire #921
– (années 1950) #855 860
– (années 1960) #867 868
– Québec #926
– (années 1970) #907
– (années 1980) #912
– Art Directors' Club of Toronto #854
– Barnsley, James Macdonald #4612
– Bérard, Réal #4692
– Brigden, Fred #4913
– Bush, Jack Hamilton #4963
– Cain, Maryanne #4987
– Cassan, Vital #5053
– Clark, Kelly #5109
– Coburn, Frederick Simpson #5123
– Cooper, Heather #5174 5175
– Cruikshank, William #5212
– Curnoe, Greg #5230
– Duguay, Rodolphe #5314 5316
– Duncan, James D. #2834
– Eager, William H. #5351
– Franchère, Joseph-Charles #5497
– Gagnon, Clarence Alphonse #1 359 5541
5543 5546 5547
– Groupe des Sept #939 1774
– illustrations de costumes, Archives
publiques du Canada. Division de
l'iconographie (Ottawa, Ont) #2904
– Innes, John I. #5901
– Jefferys, Charles William #5954 5955 5957
5959
– Jopling, Frederick Waistell #822
– Julien, Henri #5981 5983 5984 5985 5986
5987 5988 5990 5991
– Kerr, Illingworth Holey #6047 6048
– Kroupa, Bohuslar #6104
– Kurelek, William #6111
– Leduc, Ozias #918
– Lemieux, Jean-Paul #6239
– Macdonald, Evan Weekes #6356
– MacDonald, Thoreau #6381 6382 6383 6384
6385
– Massicotte, Edmond-Joseph #6441
– Millen, Walter H., collection #21
– Murphy, Rowley Walter #6666
– Phillips, Walter Joseph #6856
– Picturesque Canada: The Country As It Was
and Is (1882) #914
– Price, Art #6929
– publicité
– (années 1940) #850
– (années 1960) #870
– (années 1970) #888 894
– Robinson, Albert Henry #7056
– Russell, Edward John #7110 7111
– Sandham, J.Henry #7121
– Seton, Ernest Thompson #7172 7173
– Suzor-Coté, Marc-Aurèle de Foy #7299
– Thomson, Tom #7367 7368

– Tillenius, Clarence #7377
– Tremblay, Jean-Jacques #7425
– Trier, Walter #7428
– Varley, Frederick Horsman #7466 7467
– Wiseman, James Lovell #7603
– XIXe s.-années 1940, et chansons
  folkloriques québécoises #938
– XIXe s.-années 1960 #925
– XIXe-XXe s., livres pour enfants #934 937
– XVIIIe-XIXe s. #246 812
illustration . Indiens des forêts du Nord-Est
– (années 1970-1980) #4139
illustration botanique
– *voir aussi* fleurs dans l'art; plantes dans
  l'art
illustration botanique . Canada
– Colombie-Britannique #2024
– Jackson, Henry Alexander Carmichael
  #5927 5928
– Miller, Maria Frances Ann Morris #241
  242
illustration botanique . France
– Nouveau-Monde, XVIe-XVIIIe s. #276
illustration médicale
– Blackstock, Hattie #4738
illustration topographique
– (1789-1791), vues de la côte nord-ouest
  #1998
– Back, George #4580
– Cockburn, James Pattison #5125 5126 5127
  5128 5129
– Davies, Thomas #5270 5271 5272
– Finlay, George E. #5439
– Heriot, George #5782 5783 5785 5786 5787
  5788 5789
– Hood, Robert #5825
– Lyttleton, Westcott Whitchurch Lewis
  #6349
– Martin, Henry Byam #6426
– Peachey, James #269 270
– Short, Richard #249 250
– Smith, George Neilson #7221
– Warre, Henry James #7521
– Woolford, John Elliott #258 259
– XIXe s.
  – vues d'Ottawa (Ont) #1716
  – vues de la Colombie-Britannique #2004
    2006 2020 2023
  – vues de la péninsule du Niagara (Ont)
    #1718
  – vues de Toronto (Ont) #1717
  – vues des Cantons de l'Est (Qué) #1342
  – vues du fleuve Saint-Laurent (Qué et
    Ont) #282
– XIXe-XXe s., vues du Canada #132
– XVIe-XIXe s., vues de Montréal (Qué) #927
– XVIe-XVIIIe s., vues de l'Amérique #276
– XVIIIe s., vues du détroit de Nootka,
  Vancouver Island (CB) #2002
– XVIIIe-XIXe s.
  – vues de Charlevoix (Qué) #1280
  – vues de Halifax (NE) #1195
  – vues de l'Amérique #255 256 260
  – vues de l'Arctique #278
  – vues de la Nouvelle-Ecosse #1203 1215
    1220 1222
  – vues de Montréal (Qué) #1325
  – vues de Québec #1334 1335 1349
  – vues de Terre-Neuve #1145
  – vues du Canada #12 26 39 45 51 66 197
    224 239 244 246 248 252 266 279 812 828
    839 1366 1720 3230
  – vues du Nouveau-Brunswick #1183
Image Bank (Vancouver, CB) #2040

– cartes postales #826
– correspondance, Miss General Idea
  Pageant (1971) #546
Image et Verbe #1502
Image Nation, périodique can #992 3314
imagerie
– Shadbolt, Jack Leonard, commentaire
  #7183 7192
images de dévotion
– Québec
  – XVIIe s. #1322 1354 1365
– Québec (Qué), Université Laval. Collection
  Jeanne Larouche-Villeneuve #130 1662
images pieuses
– ouvriers et paysans, thème pictural #1662
imagination
– *voir aussi* créativité; fantaisie
– dans la littérature et l'art canadiens #104
Immaculée Conception
– *voir* Marie, Vierge, Immaculée Conception
immeubles à bureaux
– *voir aussi* gratte-ciel
immeubles à bureaux . Canada
– (1911-1912) #8295
– (1912) #7645
– (années 1910) #9332
– (années 1950-1960) #9300
– (années 1960) #9301
– bureaux d'architectes
  – (années 1940) #9297
  – (années 1950) #9299
  – (années 1960) #9346
  Calgary (Alta), (années 1970-1980) #9362
– édifice de la Banque de Montréal #9190
– et expansion urbaine (années 1950-1970)
  #9302
– Halifax (NE), Bank of Nova Scotia
  Building #9182
– John B. Parkin Associates #8395
– Montréal (Qué) #7933
  – (années 1960) #9318
  – Architects Building #9312
  – Bell Canada #9310
  – Canadian Express Company Building
    #9304
  – complexe Desjardins #9327
  – Dominion Express Company Building
    #9306
  – édifice Aldred #9313
  – édifice de la Banque Royale du Canada
    #9176
  – édifice Jacobs #9305
  – édifice La Patrie #9303
  – édifice Sun Life #9308 9309
  – Place Bonaventure #9319 9320 9321 9322
    9323 9325
  – Place Victoria #9195 9316 9317
  – Place Ville-Marie #9314
  – Transportation Building #9307
  – Westmount Square #9326
– Ottawa (Ont)
  – Banque du Canada, siège social (1938)
    #9337
  – Banque du Canada, siège social (1978)
    #9199
  – Northern Electric Research and
    Development Laboratories #9344
– Québec (Qué), maison Price #9311
– téléphone, constructions, Ontario et
  Québec (années 1880-1950) #9298
– Toronto (Ont)
  – (années 1920) #9367
  – (années 1960-1970) #8337
  – Banque de Nouvelle-Ecosse #9192

– Bourse de Toronto #9187
– Canada Life Building #9336
– Canada Permanent Building #9177
– Commerce Court #9350
– Eaton Centre #9377 9378 9382
– édifice de la Banque canadienne de
  commerce #9178
– édifice du Canadien Pacifique #9329
– Excelsior Life Building #9333
– Graphic Arts Building #9330
– Hydro Place #9352
– Imperial Oil Building #9340
– Joseph E. Shephard Government of
  Canada Building #8975
– Manufacturers Life Insurance Company
  Building #9339
– Ontario Association of Architects, siège
  social #8300 9341
– Ontario Medical Association #9349
– Royal Bank Plaza #9198 9353
– Stewart Building #9354
– Sun Life Building #9342
– Toronto-Dominion Centre #9197 9345
  9348
– Toronto Star Building #9334
– William H. Wright Building #9338
– William Wrigley Junior Co. Ltd.
  Building #9343
– Vancouver (CB)
  – Block 51-61-71 #7728
  – complexe, bureaux et boutiques,
    rénovation, gare du Canadien Pacifique
    #9546
  – édifice de la Banque Royale #9179
  – MacMillan Bloedel Building #9358
  – Marine Building #9356
  – Westcoast Building #9359
– Waterloo (Ont), Mutual Life Assurance
  Company Building #9331
– Winnipeg (Man)
  – (années 1880-1914) #8107
  – Birks Building #9355
  – Cauchon Block #9361
  – Monarch Life Building #9357
  – XIX s.-années 1960 #8095
immeubles d'habitation
– Safdie, Moshe, commentaire #8403 8404
  8406
immeubles d'habitation . Canada
– (1907) #8486
– (1972), Conseil canadien de l'habitation,
  prix et récompenses #8744
– (1974), Conseil canadien de l'habitation,
  prix et récompenses #8746
– (années 1950) #8508 8514
– (années 1960) #8517 8518
  – pour personnes âgées #8516
– (années 1970) #8512
  – habitations à loyer modique #8520
– Calgary (Alta)
  – (1875-1914) #8711
– Manitoba
  – XIXe-début XXe s. #8102
– Montréal (Qué) #7933
  – Appartements Château #8558
  – Habitat 67 #8574 8575 8578 8580 8584
    8585 8590 9215
  – île des Soeurs #8587
– Toronto (Ont)
  – (années 1910) #8640
  – (années 1920) #8644
  – Diamond & Myers #8071
– Vancouver (CB)
  – (années 1960) #8699

– Winnipeg (Man)
– (années 1910) #8686
– Assiniboine Block #9361
immeubles en bandes . Canada
– Montréal (Qué), avenue du Parc #7933
immigrants dans l'art
– photographies, Québec (1908-1910) #1031
Imperial Oil Ltd.
– collection, art canadien #3241
– Jefferys, Charles William, peintures et dessins #5956
Imperial Oil Review, périodique can #924
– illustrations #3241
impression en couleurs
– Milne, David Brown, commentaire #6546 6552 6563 6564
impression en creux
– voir aussi imprimerie
impression en creux . Canada
– Montréal (Qué), Université McGill. Musée McCord #840
impressionnisme
– Canada #39
– (1890-1900) #190
– (1895-1935) #115
– (1895-années 1930) #227
– Canada et France (1867-1914) #274
– critique (1881) #169
– et Albert Henry Robinson #7055
– et Alfred Pellan #6815
– et Donald Shaw MacLaughlan #6394
– et Ernest Lawson #6176 6178
– et Helen Galloway McNicoll #6507
– et J.E.H. MacDonald #6366
– et James Wilson Morrice #6618 6622 6633
– et John Wentworth Russell #7109
– et le Groupe des Sept #354
– et Lionel LeMoine FitzGerald #5450
– et Marc-Aurèle de Foy Suzor-Coté #7297 7299 7300 7301
– et Maurice Galbraith Cullen #5214 5218 5224
– et Ozias Leduc #6200
Impressions, périodique can #996 3314
– (années 1970) #3310
imprimerie
– voir aussi art publicitaire; impression en couleurs; livres
imprimerie canadienne
– (1947), Carl Dair, commentaire #920
– Ontario, imprimeries particulières (années 1970) #935
– Toronto (Ont), Bridgens Limited #883
– typographie #910
– (1958-1964) #923
– (années 1940) #922
– (années 1950) #860 929 5455
– (années 1960) #868
– (années 1970) #932
– (années 1980) #912
Impulse, périodique can #538
– (années 1970) #3310
Imredy, Elek, sculpteur can, 1912-
– expositions de groupe
– (1971), médailles #772
– sculpture de jardin #1849
INCA
– voir International Native American Council of Arts (INCA)
Incite, périodique can #992
Independent Art Association (Montréal, Qué)
– (1932-1963) #1379
Indian Carry, Saranac Lake (NY), Habitat

– architecture, Moshe Safdie #8404
Indian Education Centre (Alta)
– architecture et intérieur, Douglas Joseph Cardinal #9494
Indiens de l'Amérique centrale
– art #3435
– dans l'art #3427
– et Indiens de la côte nord-ouest #3810
– serpents #3391
– tissage #3832
Indiens de l'Amérique du Sud
– art #3355 3412
– dans l'art #3427
– tissage, influence sur tissage au Canada #2774
Indiens de la côte nord-ouest
– amulettes #3853
– architecture #3812 3939 8148
– art #19 299 1995 3172 3333 3342 3359 3370 3414 3770 3799 3809 3827 3843 3854 3866 3869 3871 3875 3905 3907 3918 3919 3921 3922 3923 3928 3933 3937 3942 3948 3950 3959 3969 3970 3974 3975 3987 3992 3998 4002 4003 4022 4024 4034 4036 4041 4043 4049 4055 5006
– (années 1940) #4114
– (années 1960) #4117 4119 4121
– (années 1970) #4132 4145
– représentations de la femme #3348
– XVIIIe-début XIXe s. #4064
– XVIIIe s. #4062
– XXe s. #3199
– art de la préhistoire #3785 3861 3903 3914 4023 4039
– art pariétal #3859 3886 3999
– articles de traite #3949
– arts graphiques #4166
– arts graphiques et sculpture #4162
– canots #3339
– Carr, Emily, commentaire #5007 5019 5031
– chamanisme et arbre de vie #3365
– chronique en images #3728
– crécelles #3960 3980 4014
– cuivres #3924 4065 4071
– culture #3810 3860 3897 3931 3989 4035
– (XVIIIe 1880) #3762
– XVIIIe s. #3445
– dans l'art #1999
– (1789-1791) #1998
– (1845-1871) #2023
– (années 1920) #1840
– Carr, Emily #5045
– Webber, John #269 270
– XVIIIe s. #3767
– églises #8917 8918
– églises et art funéraire #8914
– et Emily Carr #5013 5016 5021 5023 5030 5038 5040 5044
– et Jack Leonard Shadbolt #7184 7189 7191
– et Tom Price #6934
– histoire de l'art, méthodologie (années 1930-1970) #4060
– instruments #4068
– lance-javelines #3951
– masques #3340 3824 3894 3940 4030 4038
– objets en pierre #4058
– Oiseau-Tonnerre #3410
– ouvrage en ramure #3817
– ouvrages en piquants de porc-épic #3811
– peinture #3415 3847
– peinture faciale #3771
– pétroglyphes #3814 3846 3971 3988 3997 4050
– photographies

– Dally, Frederick #5250
– fin XIXe-début XXe s. #2029 2033
– pictogrammes #3893 3952
– potlatch #3899 3911
– récipients #4015
– rituel du Loup #3885
– sculpteurs et société #3912
– sculpture #370 3377 3463 3831 3857 3877 3892 3934 3954 3977
– sculpture sur pierre #3887 3889 3900 4001
– sérigraphie #4168
– (années 1970) #4148 4160
– signes héraldiques #3791 3858 3863
– terrassement, XIIIe s. #3955
– tissage #3832
– totems #2095 3766 3836 3837 3849 3855 3879 3909 3930 3932 3972 3984 3993 4057
– vannerie #3888 3953 4004 4009 4029 4142
– préhistoire #4017
Indiens des forêts du Nord-Est
– art #3172 3359 3434 3633 3639
– (1980) #4159
– (années 1970-1980) #4139
– XXe s. #4143 4150
– artefacts préhistoriques #3491
– culture #3631
– écorce de bouleau #3527
– mocassins #3554
– Oiseau-Tonnerre #3410
– ouvrages en coquillages #3505
– ouvrages en piquants de porc-épic #3443
– ouvrages perlés #3635
– peinture, XXe s. #4144
– poterie #3545 3640
– récipients #3638 3744
– vannerie #3562 3625
– wampum #3603
Indiens des plaines #3660
– architecture #8102
– art #3359 3434 3463 3668 3690 3691 3720 3730 3751
– préhistoire #3710
– XIXe s. #3737 3750
– assemblage de rochers #3689
– boucliers #3680 3732
– boucliers et tipis #3758
– chronique en images #3728
– coiffure à plumes #3683
– costume #3656 3657 3658 3692 3694 3697
– culture #3651 3684 3717 3756
– (années 1830) #3738
– danse de l'Esprit #3736
– dessin et peinture #3709
– effigies de chevaux #3743
– grosses perles, type "pony", XIXe s. #3722
– harnachement #3405
– mocassins #3666
– Oiseau-Tonnerre #3410
– ouvrages en piquants de porc-épic #3443 3652 3745
– ouvrages perlés #3682
– peinture #3672 3716
– pictogrammes #3706 3714
– rites et cérémonies #3725
– robe en peau de bison peinte #3664
– Roue-Médecine #3748
– sociétés secrètes #3727
– tipis #3675
– travail des métaux #3698
– travail du cuir #3456
– wampum #3521
Indiens du bassin
– culture #3986
Indiens du plateau

– culture #3774
Indiens hopewell
– art #3558 3574
Infonie #1502
Ingaliks
– culture #4087
– masques #4083
Ingalls, Harry Creighton, architecte amér,
    1876-1936
– Winnipeg (Man), Bank of Hamilton #9171
ingénierie
– *voir aussi* maçonnerie
– et architecture (années 1960) #8234
– photographies de constructions, en
    comparaison avec art canadien #471
Inglis, James, photographe can, actif
    1864-1884
– et Frederic Marlett Bell-Smith #4666
Inkster, John, marchand et agriculteur can,
    1799-1874
– résidence, Seven Oaks House (Winnipeg,
    Man) #8703
Innes, Alice A., artiste can, 1890-1970 #5900
Innes, John I. (Jack), artiste can, 1863-1941
    #5901
– dessins humoristiques, *Vancouver Sun* #943
– expositions de groupe
    – (1961) #62
Inoucdjouac (Qué)
– art #4452
– arts graphiques
    – (1972-1975) #4475
    – (années 1970) #4487
– arts graphiques et sculpture #4267 4279
insectes dans l'art
– Berczy, William Bent #241 242
insignes
– *voir aussi* emblèmes et devises; masses de
    cérémonie
insignes canadiens
– insignes militaires #2900
installations
– (1980), Canada #691 699
– (1980), Toronto (Ont) #1834
– Banwell, Mike #4601
– Cameron, Eric #656 667
– Carr-Harris, Ian #710
– Craven, David #687 710
– Cruise, Stephen #5213
– Dean, Max #5274
– Fish, Robert #687
– Frenkel, Vera #5521 5525
– Gallie, Tommie J. #5553
– Gervais, Raymond #687
– Gnass, Peter #1563 5620 5621
– Goodwin, Betty Roodish #5631
– Grauer, Sherry #5647
– Harding, Noel #656 667
– Hughes, Lynn #5862
– Johnson, Nancy #710
– Johnson, Terence #5969
– Levine, Les #6263
– Massey, John #687 723 6439
– Murray, Ian #710
– Singleton, Becky #723
– Trakas, George #7419 7420 7421
– Wall, Jeff #7506
– Whiten, Colette #7556
– Whittome, Irene #710 7565 7568 7569 7570
– Wood, Alan #7611
Institut canadien du film
– *voir* Canada. Institut canadien du film
Institut des artisans
– et l'art québécois (1830) #1368

Institut des artisans et association
    bibliophile du comté de Drummond
    (L'Avenir, Qué)
– (1856-1890) #1360
Institut royal d'architecture du Canada
– (1959), rencontre annuelle, comptes rendus
    des plénières #8303
– (1960), Comité d'enquête sur les
    conditions de l'habitation, rapport #8513
– (1961), résolution, sondage auprès des
    architectes #8309
– (1965), sondage, profession d'architecte
    #8308
– (1974), critique #8318 8319
– (1975-1977), et Galerie nationale du
    Canada (Ottawa, Ont), concours #9126
– (années 1920) #8244
– (années 1950-1960) #8305
– (années 1960), commentaires d'architectes
    #8311
– (années 1970), enquête auprès des
    architectes #8314
– Comité pour la préservation des édifices
    historiques #7756
    – expositions
        – (1964-1966) #7688
– expositions, critiques
    – (1931) #323
    – (1933) #7662
– Honorary Fellowship Award, Walter
    Seymour Allward (1937) #4519
– Médaille des arts connexes
    – (1956)
        – Thomas, Lionel Arthur John #7348
    – (1958)
        – Archambault, Louis #4540
    – (1960)
        – Mol, Leo #6578
    – (1961)
        – Daoust, Sylvia Marie Emilienne #5256
    – (1962)
        – Binning, B.C. #4733
    – (1963)
        – Roussel, Claude #7086
    – (1965)
        – Bonet, Jordi #4785
– modèles d'habitations (années 1950) #8509
– prix et récompenses
    – (1931) #7660
    – (1937) #7664
    – (1940) #7665
instruments . Algonquiens #3529
– ouvrages perlés #3635
instruments . Amérindiens
– articles de traite #3440
– ouvrages en coquillages #3388
– préhistoire #3393 3401
instruments . Athapascans #4073 4104 4105
instruments . Béothuks
– Red Indian Lake (TN) #3623
instruments . Dorsétiens
– Cape Dorset (TNO) #4322
instruments . Flancs-de-Chien #4089
instruments . Hans #4101
instruments . Hurons #3514
instruments . Indiens de la côte nord-ouest
    #4068
instruments . Indiens des forêts du Nord-Est
    #3491
– ouvrages perlés #3635
instruments . Indiens des plaines
– New York (NY), American Museum of
    Natural History #3668
instruments . Indiens du bassin #3986

instruments . Ingaliks #4087
instruments . Inuit
– sculpture d'ivoire #4453
instruments . Iroquois
– ouvrages perlés #3635
instruments . Micmacs #3569
instruments . Mistassins #4080
instruments . Netsilik #4363
instruments . Pieds-Noirs #3654
instruments . Potéouatamis
– Parry Island Reservation (Ont) #3540
instruments . Quinaults #3845
instruments . Saulteux #4089
instruments . Saulteux/Ojibwa
– Parry Island Reservation (Ont) #3540
instruments . Slaveys #4089
instruments . Tanainas #4085
instruments . Tananas #4095
instruments . Tlingits #3976
instruments agricoles . Canada #2095
– (1886-1930), catalogues du magasin Eaton
    #2851
– art traditionnel #2139
– bois, Ontario, XVIIIe-XIXe s. #2588
instruments de musique
– *voir aussi* conservation et restauration,
    instruments de musique
– pour enfants, fin XIXe s.-années 1930
    #2932
instruments de musique . Amérindiens
    #3363
instruments de musique . Canada
– (années 1970) #2940
– Ottawa (Ont), Musée national de
    l'Homme. Centre canadien d'études
    traditionnelles #963
– Québec #1237
instruments de musique . Cris #3402 3742
instruments de musique . Pieds-Noirs #3654
instruments de musique . Saulteux/Ojibwa
    #3402
Insurrection Art Co.
– et Robert Walker #7505
Interdesign Ltd., agence can de design
– et Robin B. Bush #4980
Intermedia (Vancouver, CB) #2040
– et Glenn Alun Lewis #6275
International Calvert House Competition
– (1954) #8510
International Grenfell Association
– soutien de l'artisanat à Terre-Neuve
    (années 1950) #2146
International Native American Council of
    Arts (INCA) #4163
International Silver Company, orfèvres
    (Hamilton, Ont) #2642
Intersystems (Toronto, Ont)
– sculptures, utilisation de la lumière #767
Inuit
– *voir aussi* Béringiens anciennes; Birnirk;
    Chukchis, Dorsétiens; Esquimaux du
    Caribou; Esquimaux du cuivre; Iglulik;
    Ipiutak; Labradors; Netsilik; Okvik;
    Punuk; Sallirmiuts; Sarqaq; Thuléens
– architecture
    – (années 1950) #8184
    – (années 1970) #7728
    – bois #7722
    – influence du climat #7701
– arcs #4316
– art #25 63 136 137 1294 3117 3118 3172
    3188 3329 3351 3354 3355 3357 3366 3370
    3372 3374 3377 3463 3464 4179 4181 4182
    4188 4190 4193 4200 4216 4218 4223 4224

4227 4231 4232 4235 4245 4255 4258 4262
4264 4276 4278 4284 4289 4290 4292 4293
4295 4296 4302 4306 4313 4338 4339 4360
4368
– (années 1940-1970) #4277
– (années 1950) #151
– (années 1950-1970) #4246
– (années 1960) #4204 4215
– (années 1970) #3376 4247 4256 4263 4270
4281 4287
– Alaska #4208 4280 4369 4424
– (années 1970) #4233
– Baker Lake (TNO) #4266
– Cape Dorset (TNO) #4187 6270 6271
6880 6881
– concept d'espace #4341
– concept d'espace et de temps #4244
– culte de l'ours #4355
– dans églises et édifices publics de
l'Arctique #4304
– et chamanisme #4283
– et James Archibald Houston #4452 5846
5847
– et perception #4294
– et valeurs #4251
– influences européennes #4176
– méthodologie de recherche #4205 4225
4401
– motif de l'arbre de vie #3365
– motif pointillé #3332 4325
– Povungnituk (Qué) #4274
– Producteurs de l'Arctique canadien
#4222 4291
– sources biographiques #4221 4252 4301
– Southampton Island (TNO) #4184
– style animalier eurasien #4334
– symbolisme #4234
– symbolisme thérapeutique #3356
– XVIIIe s.-années 1940 #4286
– art fantastique #4240
– artefacts gravés #4323
– artefacts préhistoriques #3371 3380 4331
4336 4343 4347 4352 4370 4371 4373 4378
– Alaska #4340 4348
– en comparaison avec artefacts, période
paléolithique #4329
– Groenland #4206
– Terre-Neuve et Labrador #4377
– arts décoratifs #2089
– (1964-1967) #2108 2109
– (années 1970) #3367
– arts graphiques #451 3345 4465 4466 4471
4474 4482 4493 4500
– (1959-1968) #4479
– (1959-1972) #4478
– (1959-1976) #4490
– (1959-1980) #4498
– (1960-) #4460
– (1972-1975) #4475
– (années 1960) #4463 4467
– (années 1970) #3373
– Alaska #4217
– Baker Lake (TNO) #4241 4472 4473 4480
4481 4486
– Cape Dorset (TNO) #4461 4462 4464
4470 4476 4477 4483 4484 4491 4495
– et chamanisme #4488
– et Terrence Ryan #4194
– Holman (TNO) #4197
– île de Baffin (TNO) #4499
– Inoucdjouac (Qué) #4487
– Povungnituk (Qué) #4468 4489 4494
4496
– scènes de jeu #4492

– sources biographiques #4497
– arts graphiques et sculpture #4191 4201
4228 4229 4239 4285
– (années 1950) #4311
– (années 1960) #4189
– Cape Dorset (TNO) #4192 4211 4299
– Holman (TNO) #3350
– Inoucdjouac (Qué) #4267 4279
– Povungnituk (Qué) #4219
– représentations de l'amautik #4300
– broderie #4259
– colorants et teinture #4249
– coopératives d'artistes #4288
– culture #3343 3368 4254 4317 4320
– (années 1840) #4174
– (années 1880) #3379
– (années 1930) #4185
– (années 1960) #4399
– Alaska #4272
– détroit de Béring (Alaska) #4318
– Groenland #4315
– Labrador (TN), (années 1910) #4321
– Levine, Les, commentaire #6269
– Pitseolak, Peter, commentaire #6876
– XVIIIe s. #4097
– dans l'art
– Back, George #4580
– Bruce, Robert Donald #4940
– Constantineau, Fleurimond #5168
– images de la femme #121
– Rindisbacher, Peter #7005
– White, John #228 229 7552 7553
– déesse de la mer #4312 4376
– esthétique #4282 4297
– femmes artistes (années 1970) #4260
– iglous #4213 4271 8733
– inukshuks et inunguaks #4199
– jeux de ficelle #4177
– kayaks et umiaks #3339
– loi, art et #3347
– marché de l'art #4236 4238 4242 4305 4396
4397
– masques #3337 3340 3940 4178 4212 4349
– masse de cérémonie, Conseil des
Territoires du Nord-Ouest #4386 4389
– murales #4253
– Baker Lake (TNO) #4230
– peinture #4202
– photographies
– (années 1920) #1021
– Chesterfield, Albert A. #5102
– Mathers, Charles Wesley #6451
– Pitseolak, Peter #6879
– poterie, Rankin Inlet (TNO) #4226
– raquettes #2812 3515
– sculpture #761 3359 3362 4183 4198 4257
4261 4275 4381 4388 4390 4394 4395 4404
4406 4410 4414 4418 4419 4423 4426 4427
4428 4430 4431 4432 4433 4440 4442 4443
4444 4446 4447 4449 4451 4455 4456
– (années 1940-1960) #4392
– (années 1950) #4383 4384 4385 4387 4393
– (années 1960) #4407
– (années 1970) #4273 4420 4422 4448
– Baker Lake (TNO) #4400 4402 4403 4408
4434
– Belcher Islands (TNO) #4459
– Cape Dorset (TNO) #4425 4441
– carrières #4409
– Keewatin (TNO) #4196
– mains #4439
– Maricourt (Qué) #4405
– Povungnituk (Qué) #4411 4415 4417
4421 4437

– Rankin Inlet (TNO) #4203 4207 4210
4314
– Repulse Bay (TNO) #4450
– sculpture d'ivoire #4175 4391 4438 4453
4458
– sculpture en os de baleine #4413 4436
4445 4457
– sculpture en stéatite #4214
– Spence Bay (TNO) #4416 4454
– sculpture sur os #4319
– signatures d'artistes #4250
– tambours #3363
– tatouage #4209
– tissage, Pangnirtung (TNO) #4237 4298
4308 4310
– umiaks #3344
– vannerie #4180 4307 4309
Inukpuk, Daniel, artiste can, 1942-
– gravures sur pierre #4487
inukshuks . Inuit
– Enukso Point (TNO) #4199
inukshuks . Netsilik #4363
inunguaks . Inuit
– Enukso Point (TNO) #4199
Inventaire canadien des bâtiments
historiques
– voir Canada. Inventaire canadien des
bâtiments historiques
inventaires
– art canadien et architecture canadienne
#159
Invermere (CB), hôpital
– architecture, Smith & McCulloch #9031
Iowa City (Iowa), University of Iowa.
Museum of Art
– expositions
– The Art of the Shaman (1973) #3361
Ipellie, Alootook, artiste can, 1952-
– entretien #5902
Ipiutak
– artefacts
– en comparaison avec artefacts dorsétiens
#4361
– Point Spencer (Alaska) #4374
Iquliq, Tuna, sculpteur can, 1935-
– expositions
– (1979) #5903
Iqutaq Group, Clyde River (île de Baffin,
TNO)
– arts graphiques #4499
Ireland, Denise, artiste can, 1949-
– et Jack Chambers #700
Irlandais au Canada
– XIXe s. #8523
Iroquois
– arbre, mythes et symboles #3516
– art #3434 3559 3566 3586 3601 3605 3633
3639
– (1980) #4159
– (années 1970-1980) #4139
– XXe s. #4143 4150 4164
– artefacts #3616
– arts décoratifs (années 1960) #4123
– berceau #3593
– broches #3509 3512
– ceintures (de tissu) #3534
– cérémonie du Milieu de l'Hiver #3606
– cuillers en ramure #3524
– culture #3489 3490 3525 3631
– danses et chants rituels #3598
– et Arthur Guindon #5665
– hausse-cols #3536
– instruments de musique #3363
– masques #3337 3570 3588 3595 3604 3613

7346
- masses d'armes #3538
- orfèvrerie de traite #3645 3646
- ouvrages en coquillages #3505
- ouvrages perlés #3635
- peignes #3587
- peinture, XXe s. #4144
- peinture et sculpture (années 1970) #4133
- pétroglyphes #3599
- pipes #3504 3618 3642 3644
- poterie #3502 3520 3545 3555 3564
- raquettes #3523
- récipients #3638 3744
- sculpture #3553
- travail sur bois #3519
- vannerie #3552 3562 3625
- wampum #3496 3518 3521 3532 3567 3603 3607
Irving, Daphne, artiste can, 1933-
- expositions, critiques #1167
Irving, Mary, Can, XIXe s.
- modèles de broderie (années 1860) #2786
Irving, Susan, Can, XIXe s.
- modèles de broderie (années 1860) #2786
Irving, William, architecte can, 1830-1883
- Toronto (Ont) #8059
  - Dominion Bank #9188
Isaacs, Avrom (Av), marchand d'oeuvres
  d'art, 1926-
- commentaire sur le marché de l'art inuit
  #4236
Ishulutaq, Elisapee, artiste can, 1925- #4260
Iskowitz, Gershon, artiste can, 1921- #5905
- entretien #5904
- expositions, critiques #5906
- expositions de groupe
  - (1972) #548
  - (1973) #556
  - (1977) #636
Islamabad (Pakistan), ambassade
  canadienne
- Kahane, Anne, The Sea #5998
Island Arts and Crafts Club (Victoria, CB)
- (1912-1922) #1980
Island Arts and Crafts Society (Victoria, CB)
- (1910-1941) #1980
- (années 1930) #2034
Island Arts Club (Victoria, CB)
- (1910-1912) #1980
- (années 1910) #1979
Island Lake (Man)
- culture, Saulteux/Ojibwa #3549
- Garden Hill Cooperative #4135
Islande
- (1946), Carl Fellman Schaefer,
  commentaire #7150
Isle of Man (Angleterre), Douglas School of
  Art
- Onley, Toni, élève #6741
Islet (Qué)
- voir L'Islet (Qué)
Istanbul (Turquie), église Sainte-Sophie
- murales, J.E.H. MacDonald, commentaire
  #6362
Itter, Carole, artiste can, 1939- #2053
Ives, R.E., photographe can, actif années
  1970-
- catalogue de photographies #991
Iveson, Robert, sculpteur can, 1951-
- expositions de groupe
  - (1978) #2066
ivoires . Canada
- Québec, XVIIe-XVIIIe s. #1320
ivoires . Inuit #4453

Ivujivik (Qué)
- arts graphiques (1972-1975) #4475
Izumi, Arnott & Sugiyama, agence can
  d'architecture
- Saskatoon (Sask), University of
  Saskatchewan #9490

J

J. McCausland & Co.
- voir McCausland, J., & Co.
J.M. Dent
- voir Dent, J.M.
Jack, Richard, artiste can, 1886-1952
- Mount Eisenhower, Canadian Club of New
  York (New York, NY) #3211
Jack Klein & Henry Sears, agence can
  d'architecture
- Toronto (Ont)
  - projet Don Valley Wood/Phase 1 #8518
  - projet Yorkwoods Village/Phase 1 #8518
  - Whitburn Apartments #8514
Jackson, Alexander Young (A.Y.), artiste
  can, 1882-1974 #24 309 373 5909 5915 5919
  5922 5923 5925
- à l'atelier de Louis Jobin (1925) #5966
- art et écrits #5908
- autobiographie #5916 5918
- carnet à dessins (1909), Galerie nationale
  du Canada (Ottawa, Ont) #5924
- commentaire sur Arthur Lismer #6297
  6300
- commentaire sur Canadian War
  Memorials exhibition, Burlington House
  (London, England) #1076
- commentaire sur Frederick Grant Banting
  #4600
- commentaire sur Frederick Horsman
  Varley #7463
- commentaire sur J.E.H. MacDonald #6364
- commentaire sur James Wilson Morrice
  #6622 6626
- commentaire sur la vie militaire #5913
- commentaire sur Lawren Stewart Harris
  #5720
- commentaire sur Maurice Galbraith Cullen
  #5221
- commentaire sur ses dessins effectués à
  Algoma (Ont) #5907
- commentaire sur ses dessins effectués sur
  l'autoroute de l'Alaska #5911
- correspondance, Anne Douglas Savage
  #7130
- critique d'art #3308
- dessins #5920
  - Sainte-Louise (Qué) #5921
- écrits #92
- entretien #5917
- et Albert Henry Robinson #7057
- et le Groupe des Sept #1732
- et Louis Jobin #5964
- et Maurice Hall Haycock #5754
- et Molly Lamb Bobak #4766
- et Paraskeva Clark #5112
- et sérigraphies canadiennes, Seconde
  Guerre mondiale #805
- et Tom Thomson #7351 7352
- expositions
  - (1953) #5914
- Georgian Bay, November, University of
  Toronto. Hart House (Toronto, Ont) #3134

- illustration et mise en page artistique #939
- l'art de guerre #1098
- peintures, collection d'art canadien en
  souvenir de la guerre #1077
- reminiscences #5912
- voyages dans l'Arctique #1779
- vues, Charlevoix (Qué) #5910
Jackson, George, ébéniste can, 1822-1901
  #2573
Jackson, Henry, orfèvre can, 1837-1869 #2638
Jackson, Henry Alexander Carmichael,
  artiste can, 1877-1961 #5926
- aquarelles, natures mortes (champignons),
  Galerie nationale du Canada (Ottawa,
  Ont) #5927 5928
Jackson, J.Anthony, architecte can, 1940-
- théories sur l'architecture #7746
Jackson, John, ébéniste can, 1818-1898 #2573
Jackson, Naomi, artiste can, 1910-
- commentaire sur les dessins d'enfants,
  Finlande (1946) #5929
Jackson, Sarah Jeanette, artiste can, 1924-
  #5931
- entretien #5930
- estampes #1214
- reprographie, art #5932
Jackson, William H., artiste amér au
  Canada, né 1832 #1164
Jacobsen, Johan, explorateur all, 1853-1947
- commentaire sur la culture matérielle,
  Indiens de la côte nord-ouest #3762
Jacovleff, Alexandre, artiste russe en France,
  1887-1938
- professeur de Lilias Torrance Newton
  #6692 6693
Jacques, John, ébéniste can, 1804-1880 #2463
Jacques, Louis, sculpteur can, 1664-1735
- oeuvres, églises, Charlesbourg (Qué) #8851
Jacques, Sylvie, artisane can (vannerie),
  active 1981 #2954
Jacques & Hay Co., fabricants de meubles
  (Toronto, Ont) #2463 2559
- (1835-années 1880) #2546
Jacques Guillon Designers Inc., agence can
  de graphisme #884 2623
Jacquet, François, céramiste can, ca
  1731-après 1777 #269 270
Jacquiés (dit Leblond), Jean, artiste can,
  1688-1724 #234 235 1572
- tabernacle de Saint-Maurice, Chapelle des
  récollets (Trois-Rivières, Qué) #8850
Jacson (dit Jolybois), Antoine, sculpteur can,
  1725-ca 1805
- sculptures, église Saint-Charles (Lachenaie,
  Qué) #8808
- sculptures, église Saint-Pierre (île
  d'Orléans, Qué) #8802
jade . Aléoutes #3331
jade . Salish de l'intérieur #3331
jade . Salishiens #3331
jade . Tlingits #3331
Jaffe, Lilly Weil, collectionneuse can, XXe s.
- collection, art inuit #4223
Jakobshavan (Groenland)
- artéfacts préhistoriques #4342
Jamaïque
- vues, Charles William Jefferys #5958
James, Ann, artiste can, 1925-
- expositions, critiques #2383
James, Charlie, sculpteur can, ca 1870-1938
- totems #3848
James, Percy Leonard, architecte can,
  1880-1970
- Victoria (CB), Crystal Gardens #9134 9146

James, Ralph, ébéniste can, actif 1926 #2583
James Campbell & Son, éditeur (Toronto, Ont)
– cartes de Noël #842 890
James Chisolm & Son, agence can d'architecture
– Winnipeg (Man), Marlborough Hotel #9277
James Secord & Saul Herzog, agence can d'architecture
– Charlottetown (IPE), Confederation Centre, concours #9088
Jameson, Anna Brownell, artiste brit, auteure au Canada, 1794-1860 #5934
– art et écrits #5933
Janitch, Mary, artiste can, 1949- #5935
– oeuvres, Carmen Lamanna Gallery (Toronto, Ont) #1811
Janosi, Paul, photographe can, ca 1954-
– catalogue de photographies #1032
Janson (dit Lapalme), Pierre, constructeur can, m. 1743 #7844
Janvier, Alex Simeon, artiste can, 1935- #4136 5936 5938
– expositions
– (1978) #5939
– expositions, critiques #1866
– (1972) #4128
– expositions de groupe
– (1972) #4131
– peintures, County of Strathcona Building (Sherwood Park, Alta) #5937
Jaque, Louis, artiste can, 1919- #1542 1543 5940 5941
– expositions
– (1977) #5942
– (1978) #5943
Jarden, Richard, artiste can, 1947-
– expositions de groupe
– (1970) #534
– oeuvres de l'imaginaire #530
jardins
– voir aussi architecture paysagiste; ornements et mobilier de jardin
– dans l'art
– Pellan, Alfred #6815 6818 6819
– Sawyer, Walter Michael #7144
– Vivenza, Francesca #7495
– et architecture domestique, Moshe Safdie, commentaire #8406
jardins . Canada
– (années 1950), et architecture #7677
– (années 1970), toits-jardins et architecture #7728
– Ontario, XIXe s. #2245
Jarvis, Alan, administrateur can des arts, 1915-1972
– correspondance, David Brown Milne #6563 6564
– directeur, Galerie nationale du Canada (Ottawa, Ont) #3049 3050
Jarvis, Donald Alvin (Don), artiste can, 1923- #5945
– carnets #5944
– élève de Hans Hofmann #402 1850
– entretien #5946
– et peinture de Vancouver (CB), (années 1950) #1992
– expositions
– (1977) #5947
– expositions, critiques #2074
– expositions de groupe
– (1959) #1997
Jarvis, Joan D., céramiste can, active années

1980 #2394
Jarvis, Nathan Sturges, collectionneur amér, 1801-1862
– collection, art dakota #3705
Jarvis, Samuel J., photographe can, 1863-1952
– expositions de groupe
– (1970) #1675
Jasmin, André, artiste can, 1922- #5948
– commentaire sur la gravure #817
– élève de Paul-Emile Borduas #4808
Jasmin, Claude, auteur can, 1930-
– commentaire sur Marc-Aurèle Fortin #5475
Jauran
– voir Repentigny, Rodolphe de (Jauran)
Jauvin, Serge, photographe can, actif 1981 #1562
Jaworska, Tamara Hans, artiste can (tapisserie), 1926- #5949
– expositions, critiques #2771
Jaycocks, T.G., photographe can, né 1889
– photographies et écrits #5950
Jean, Jocelyn, artiste can, 1947-
– expositions de groupe
– (1977) #1532
Jean, Marcel, artiste can, 1937- #5952
– colonnes, Grand Théâtre de Québec (Québec, Qué) #5951
Jean-Louis, Donald (Don), artiste can, 1937- #1762
Jeffers, Allan Merrick, architecte can, 1875-1926
– Edmonton (Alta), édifices du Parlement #8944 8945 8962
Jefferson Glass Co., fabricants de verre (Toronto, Ont) #2401
– verre, motifs (1915-années 1940) #2411
Jeffery, Alicia Anne, artiste can, née 1808 #1219
Jefferys, Charles William, artiste can, 1869-1951 #10 5953 5954 5955 5956 5957
– commentaire sur vues, comté de Peel (Ont), collection William Perkins Bull #3208
– expositions
– (1976) #5958
– expositions, critiques #1703 1710
– expositions de groupe
– (1935) #17
– illustrations #916
– bâtiments historiques ontariens #5959
– Farmer's Magazine #1765
Jenkins, Dan, architecte can, 1948-
– Calgary (Alta) #8726
Jensen, Vicki, photographe can, active années 1970
– catalogue de photographies #998
Jenson, L.B., artiste can, 1921-
– dessins, bâtiments de Halifax (NE) #7816
– dessins, bâtiments du comté de Pictou (NE) #7827
Jérôme, frère
– voir Paradis, Jérôme (frère Jérôme)
Jérôme, Jean-Paul, artiste can, 1928- #1541 5960
– expositions de groupe
– (1977) #1465
– (1981) #1471
Jerome Markson Architects, agence can d'architecture
– Ontario #8386 8387
Jérusalem (Israël), Habitat Israël
– architecture, Moshe Safdie #8404

jésuites
– Midland (Ont), Sainte-Marie among the Hurons #7999
– Montréal (Qué), édifices (1692-1791) #7932
– Québec, XVIIe s. #1354 1358 1363 2192
– Québec (Qué), Séminaire de Notre-Dame-des-Anges #8785
– Sillery (Qué), Maison des jésuites #8571
Jesup North Pacific Expedition #3771 3772 3773 3774 3780 3783 3785 3787 3789 3969
Jésus-Christ
– art québécois, XVIIe s. #1365
– bon Pasteur, sculpture québécoise, XVIIe-XIXe s. #1594
– Cène, Jean Baptiste Côté #5188
– crucifixion, sculpture québécoise #1638
– Leduc, Ozias #6195
– nativité
– art canadien #393
– Côté, Jean-Baptiste #5188
– peinture canadienne #864
– Passion, en bouteilles, Québec #2944
– Rédempteur, et la Vierge Marie, Ozias Leduc #6204
– souper d'Emmaüs, sculpture québécoise, XIXe-XXe s. #1615
jeux
– voir aussi Jeux olympiques
– Band, Percy, collection #2917
– dans l'art, David Askevold #4566
– jeux d'enfant, fin XIXe-années 1930 #2932
– XIXe-début XXe s., importation au Canada #2928
jeux . Canada
– jeux de société, XIXe-XXe s. #2597
– Labrador #2955
– Québec, dans l'art traditionnel #1291
– XIXe-début XXe s. #2928
jeux . Cris #3402
jeux . Ingaliks #4087
jeux . Inuit
– estampes #4492
jeux . Iroquois #3489
jeux . Micmacs #3500
jeux . Saulteux/Ojibwa #3402 3539
jeux de ficelle . Inuit #4177
Jeux olympiques
– 1976, Montréal (Qué)
– affiches #900
– Corridart, Mosaicart et Artisanage, art dans la rue #615
– Danby, Ken, peintures et dessins d'athlètes #5252
– exposition Corridart #1522 1530
– monnaies olympiques #778
– projets de design #898 901 902 2625 5858
Jewell, Milton, artiste can, 1938- #5961
Jobin, Gilles, artiste can, 1942- #1551
Jobin, Louis, sculpteur can, 1845-1928 #24 1233 1334 1335 1600 5962 5963 5965 5966 5967
– Côté, Jean-Baptiste, comparaison #5186 5187
– crucifixs #1585 1605
– entretien #2169 2171 5964
– La Sainte Famille #5968
– sculptures sur bois #756 1576 1577
– utilisation de plâtre #1618
Joe, Mathilde, artiste can (vannerie), active 1976 #4142
Johansen, John M., architecte amér, 1916-
– Worcester (Mass), Clark University. Goddard Library #9046
John, Augustus Edwin, artiste brit,

1878-1961
- Varley, Frederick Horsman, comparaison #7463
John, Chauncey Johnny, sculpteur amér, actif 1940
- masques de la société des Faux-Visages #4113
John Andrews Architects, agence can d'architecture #8323
John Andrews International, agence can d'architecture
- Toronto (Ont)
  - gare Union #9540
  - tour du CN #9511
John B. Parkin Associates, agence can d'architecture #8395 8396
- Charlottetown (IPE), Confederation Centre, concours #9088 9089
- Don Mills (Ont)
  - centre commercial #7679
  - Ortho Pharmaceutical, usine et bureaux #7679
- Malton (Ont), aéroport international de Toronto #9516
- Niagara Falls (Ont), Greater Niagara General Hospital #9031
- Oshawa (Ont), 45 Hillsdale Manor Home for the Aged #8516
- Ottawa (Ont), région de la capitale nationale, propositions #8041
- Toronto (Ont)
  - Four Seasons Sheraton Hotel #9294
  - hôtel de ville et Civic Square #8990 8991 8992
    - concours #8989
  - hôtel sur la rue Queen, proposition #9292
  - Ontario Association of Architects, siège social #7679 8300 9341
  - Sun Life Building #9342
  - Toronto-Dominion Centre #7694 9197 9301 9345
  - York University #9396 9469
John C. Spence and Sons, atelier de vitraux (Montréal, Qué)
- vitraux #2399 2462
John Deere Plow Company
- entrepôts #9247
John E. Garrett Co., dessinateurs de patrons (NE)
- tapis crochetés, motif Bluenose #2763
John M. Dayton & Roy Jessiman, agence can d'architecture
- Winnipeg (Man), hôtel de ville, concours #8985 8986 8987
John M. Moore & Company, agence can d'architecture
- London (Ont), University of Western Ontario #9442 9448
John Marshall & Co., fabricants de céramique (Bo'ness, Ecosse)
- série illustrant sports canadiens #2306 2360
Johnniebo
- voir Ashevak, Johnniebo
Johns, Jasper, artiste amér, 1930-
- influence sur Arthur Fortescue McKay #6476
Johnson, Bruce Henderson, artiste can, 1926-
- illustrations #941
Johnson, Burton Glenwood, photographe can, 1912-1965
- photographies de la Seconde Guerre mondiale #1107

Johnson, Esther, artiste can (vitrail), active années 1920-1940
- vitraux #2445
Johnson, Joanne Jackson, photographe can, 1936-
- expositions de groupe
  - (1977) #1033
Johnson, Johnson & Roy, agence amér d'architecture
- Montréal (Qué), île des Soeurs #8587
Johnson, Lloyd, architecte can, 1767-1842
- Saint-Jean (NB), église en pierre #8778
Johnson, Nancy, artiste can, 1951-
- expositions de groupe
  - (1981) #710
Johnson, Terence, sculpteur can, 1940-
- expositions
  - (1981) #5969
- expositions de groupe
  - (1978) #786
Johnstad, Byron, céramiste can, actif années 1970- #2395
Johnston, Clifford M., photographe can, 1897-1951
- expositions de groupe
  - (1970) #1675
Johnston, Frances-Anne
- voir Arbuckle, Frances-Anne Johnston
Johnston, Francis Hans (Franz), artiste can, 1888-1949 #5971
- et le Groupe des Sept #1732
- expositions de groupe
  - (1972) #5972
  - (1973) #5973
- illustration et mise en page artistique #939
- illustrations, Farmer's Magazine #1765
- père de Frances-Anne Johnston #5970
Johnston, James P., architecte amér, 1841-1893
- Brockville (Ont), Idlewild #8671
Johnston, Michael, artiste can, actif années 1950-
- décors #472
Johnston, Robert Edwin, artiste can, 1885-1933
- illustrations #916
Joliette (Qué)
- églises #1287 8876
Joliette (Qué), Cégep de Joliette
- expositions
  - Lithographs/Lithographies (1973) #825
Joliette (Qué), chapelle du noviciat des Clercs de Saint-Viateur
- vitraux, Marius Gérald Plamondon #2447
- vitraux et croix, Marius Gérald Plamondon #6888
Joliette (Qué), église Saint-Paul
- architecture et intérieur, Amable Gauthier #241 242
Joliette (Qué), église Saint-Viateur
- architecture et intérieur, Amable Gauthier #241 242
Joliette (Qué), Musée d'art de Joliette
- collection #3100 3101
- expositions
  - De la figuration à la non-figuration dans l'art québécois (1977) #1461
  - Rodolphe Duguay, 1891-1973 (1979) #5318
Joly, François, sculpteur can, 1951- #1630
Jolybois, Antoine
- voir Jacson (dit Jolybois), Antoine
Jones, Barrie, photographe can, 1950-
- expositions de groupe
  - (1979) #2069

Jones, Brian Rendel, artiste can, 1950- #5975
- expositions
  - (1978) #5974
Jones, Chilion, architecte can, 1835-1912
- Ottawa (Ont), édifices du Parlement #9054
Jones, Francis, ébéniste can, 1827-1894 #2580
Jones, Hugh Griffith, architecte can, 1872-1947
- Toronto (Ont), gare Union #9531 9536
- Winnipeg (Man), hôtel de ville, concours #8979
Jones, Jacobine, sculpteur can, 1898-1976 #739 5976
- expositions de groupe
  - (1971), médailles #772
- sculpture murale, Banque de Nouvelle-Ecosse (Toronto, Ont) #5977
Jones, Trevor Patrick Garwood
- voir Garwood-Jones, Trevor Patrick
Jones, Wade, artiste can, 1945- #5978
Jones, William (Bill), artiste can, 1946- #2053
- expositions
  - (1976) #5979
- expositions de groupe
  - (1976) #2060
- utilisation de la photographie #1057
Jones, William Harris, artiste amér au Canada, actif ca 1825-années 1850
- influence sur l'art de Halifax (NE), (années 1830) #1226
Jones Fall (Ont), forge
- architecture #8019
Jong, Simon Leendert de, artiste can, 1942-
- expositions de groupe
  - (1967) #1916
Jongers, Alphonse, artiste can, 1872-1945 #302
Jonquière (Qué), Centre national d'expositions de Jonquière/National Exhibition Centre
- expositions
  - Métiers d'art Ontario-Québec, 1979/1980/Quebec-Ontario Crafts, 1979/1980 (1980) #2138
  - Rodolphe Duguay, 1891-1973 (1980) #5318
Jonquière (Qué), église Saint-Raphaël
- architecture, St-Gelais & Tremblay #8765
Jopling, Frederick Waistell, artiste can, 1859-1945
- estampes #822
Jordan & Over, agence can d'architecture
- Winnipeg (Man), architecture domestique #8493
Josakeed (société secrète) . Saulteux/Ojibwa #3492
Joslin, Paul, photographe can, actif 1977
- catalogue de photographies #1023
Jost, Edward R., artiste can, actif 1864
- expositions, critiques #964
Joubert, famille, céramistes can, actifs années 1860-1870 #2281
jouets
- Band, Percy, collection #2917
- fin XIXe s.-années 1930 #2932
- XIXe-début XXe s., importation au Canada #2928
jouets . Amérindiens #2934
jouets . Canada #2938
- (1837-1887) #253
- guide pour collectionneurs #2125 2131
- Labrador #2955
- miniatures en céramique et fantaisies, XIXe s. #2302
- Ontario, XIXe s. #2245

– Ottawa (Ont), Musée national de l'homme.
  Centre canadien d'études sur la culture
  traditionnelle #963
– Québec #2226 2924
  – (1800-1925) #2937
  – dans l'art traditionnel #1291
  – XVIIe-XIXe s. #2921 2933 2934
– tradition germanique #2140
– XIXe-début XXe s. #2928
– XVIIIe-XIXe s. #2594
jouets . Ingaliks #4087
jouets . Inuit
– influence sur Jean-Paul Riopelle #7025
jouets . Pieds-Noirs
– Minìpoka #3749
Jour,Le, journal can
– et Antoine Désilets #5287 5288
Jourdain (dit Labrosse), Denis, sculpteur
  can, 1671-1743 #1572
Jourdain (dit Labrosse), Paul-Raymond,
  sculpteur can, 1697-1769 #249 250 1572
Journal de Québec, périodique can
– Plamondon, Antoine-Sébastien, traité, bons
  et mauvais tableaux #1348
*Journal of Canadian Art History/Annales
  d'histoire de l'art canadien*, périodique can
  #111
journaux
– *voir aussi* artistes . notes personnelles;
  périodiques
– (années 1870), articles sur la mode #2859
journaux canadiens
– (1886-1916), réaction envers l'oeuvre de
  James Wilson Morrice #6634
– commentaire sur les ouvrages à l'aiguille
  (années 1940) #2780
– dessins humoristiques et politiques #943
– publicités, fin XIXe-début XXe s. #891
– réaction envers la Commission royale
  d'enquête sur l'avancement des arts,
  lettres et sciences (Rapport Massey),
  (1951) #3257
– St. John's (TN), publicités (1806-1900)
  #1158
Jouvenet, Jean Baptiste, artiste fr, 1644-1717
– influence sur Antoine-Sébastien
  Plamondon #6886
jubés . Canada
– Québec (1650-1925) #1592
Judah, Doris Minette, sculpteure can,
  1887-1965
– expositions
  – (1980) #5980
Judd, Donald, sculpteur amér, 1928-
– influence sur André Lucien Fauteux #5413
Judson, William Lee, artiste can, 1842-1928
– expositions de groupe
  – (1888) #175
Jugendstil
– *voir* Art Nouveau
juges
– portraits, George Theodore Berthon #4713
Juifs au Canada
– art #435
– Prairies, architecture #8081
Julien, Henri, artiste can, 1852-1908 #1315
  1323 5981 5984 5985 5986 5987 5988 5989
  5993
– artiste lors de l'expédition de la
  North-West Mounted Police (1874) #5990
  5992
– dessins humoristiques, Pères de la
  Confédération et *Montreal Star* #943
– dessins humoristiques et politiques #957

– expositions
  – (1938) #5983
– illustrations de légendes #5991
– scènes de Noël #5982
– thème de la rébellion #1351
Jullien, Philip M., architecte can, actif
  1912-1916
– Vancouver (CB), Terminal City Club #9061
Juneau, Denis, artiste can, 1925- #5994
– et op'art #1445
– expositions de groupe
  – (1959) #1414
  – (1968) #1263
  – (1981) #1471
– utilisation de plastiques #1442
Juneau (Alaska), Alaska State Museum
– panneaux muraux, Tlingit #3916
Jung, Carl, psychiatre suisse, 1875-1961
– Markgraf, Waltraud Erna Else,
  comparaison #6416
Junior League of Winnipeg (Winnipeg, Man)
– enseignement de l'art (années 1940) #1889
Jutras, Albert, collectionneur can, 1900-
– collection, peinture canadienne #372
Jutras, Joseph, artiste can, 1894-
– et Montée Saint-Michel #1236

K

Kagan, Samuel Lazar (Sam), sculpteur can,
  1906-
– portraits #581
Kahane, Anne, sculpteure can, 1924- #5995
  5996
– dessins et sculptures #5997
– expositions
  – (1981) #5999
– sculpture sur bois (années 1960) #744
– *Song of the Earth*, Place des Arts (Montréal,
  Qué) #8233
– *The Sea*, ambassade canadienne
  (Islamabad, Pakistan) #5998
Kahn, Louis Isidore, architecte amér,
  1901-1974
– influence sur A.J. Diamond et Barton
  Myers #9349
Kahnawake (Qué), église
  Saint-François-Xavier
– architecture #8890
Kahnawake (Qué), presbytère (1720)
– architecture #8569
Kakarook, Guy, artiste amér, né ca 1860
  #4217
Kakegamic, Goyce, artiste can, 1948- #4157
  4161
– entretien #4155
– et coopérative Triple K #4158
– expositions de groupe
  – (1977) #4151
  – (1980) #4159
Kakegamic, Joshim, artiste can, 1953- #4157
  4161
– et coopérative Triple K #4158
– expositions de groupe
  – (1977) #4151
Kakige, Francis, artiste can, 1929- #4157
  – (1980) #4159
Kakinuma, Thomas, sculpteur can, 1908-
– sculpture de jardin #1849
Kalm, Peter, botaniste suédois au Canada,
  1716-1779

– commentaire sur maisons en bois rond et
  maisons en pierre, Québec, XVIIIe s.
  #8527
Kamata, Takuro, artiste can (textiles), 1939-
  #6000
Kamba (tribu africaine)
– art kamba, en comparaison avec art inuit
  #4215
Kamins, Jeannie, artiste can, 1941-
– ouvrages en fibres textiles #2775
Kamloops (CB), Kamloops Public Art
  Gallery
– expositions
  – *Artisan '78: The First National Travelling
    Exhibition of Contemporary Canadian
    Crafts/Artisan '78: première exposition
    nationale itinérante d'artisanat canadien
    contemporain* (1979) #2134
  – *Images of the Inuit from the Simon Fraser
    Collection* (1981) #4495
Kandinsky, Wassily, artiste russe, 1866-1944
– Brooker, Bertram Richard, commentaire
  #4927
– concept d'espace #1441
– et art abstrait #422
– influence sur Bertram Richard Brooker
  #4925 4926
– influence sur Guido Molinari #6588
– influence sur Lawren Phillips Harris #5711
Kane, Paul, artiste can, 1810-1871 #5 9 221
  241 242 1705 3386 3720 6001 6003 6004
  6005 6006 6007 6012 6013 6014 6015 6016
  6017
– carnets à dessins #6009 6011
– commentaire sur les Amérindiens #6002
– écrits #92
– et Compagnie de la Baie d'Hudson's #273
– et peinture canadienne #18
– expositions, critiques #1692
– expositions de groupe
  – (1955) #1845
  – (1973) #1953
– oeuvres #6010
– paysages #140 209
– peintures (1846-1847) #6018
– portrait, Wilson S. Conger #6008
– portraits, Mayor George Gurnett #3178
Kansas City (Mo), William Rockhill Nelson
  Gallery of Art et Mary Atkins Museum of
  Fine Arts
– expositions
  – *Sacred Circles: Two Thousand Years of
    North American Indian Art* (1977) #3463
Kant, Immanuel, philosophe all, 1724-1804
– concept de la nature #4882
Kantaroff, Maryon, sculpteure can, 1933-
– commentaire sur femmes artistes #144
– réflexion sur son oeuvre #596 6019
Kardos, Ladislas, artiste can, 1909- #6020
  6021
Karkutt, Edith, photographe can, active
  années 1960
– catalogue de photographies #987
Karnick, Irwin, photographe can, 1938-
– expositions, critiques #1008
Karsh, Malak, photographe can, 1918- #995
Karsh, Yousuf, photographe can, 1908-
  #6032 6034
– autobiographie #6026
– commentaire sur photographies de
  femmes #6024
– entretien #6030 6033
– expositions
  – (1968) #6029

– expositions de groupe
  – (1967) #486 487
  – (1970) #1675
– portraits #6022 6023 6025 6028 6031 6035
– réflexion sur son oeuvre #6027
– Tata, Sam, comparaison #7329
Karuna, Peter, photographe can, ca 1949-
– catalogue de photographies #1032
Kashetsky, Herzl J., artiste can, 1950- #1184
Kashetsky, Joseph, artiste can, 1941-1974 #1121 1184
– expositions de groupe
  – (1966) #1123
  – (1973) #1182
Kaskas
– culture #4090 4092
  – (années 1920) #4093
Kater, Wolfgang, facteur de clavecins can, actif 1979 #2940
Kauffman, William, architecte can, ca 1821-1875
– Toronto (Ont) #8059
Kavik, John, sculpteur can, 1897- #6036
kayaks
– voir aussi bateaux
kayaks . Inuit #3339
kayaks . Netsilik #4363
Kazimierski, Daniel, photographe can, 1949- #992
– catalogue de photographies #1023
Keefer, Samuel, fonctionnaire can, XIXe s.
– et édifices du Parlement (Ottawa, Ont) #8930
Keene, Caleb, ébéniste can, 1862-1954
– utilisation de décorations laquées #2548
Keevil, Roland, artiste can, 1887-1963
– expositions de groupe
  – (1958) #1846
Keewatin (TNO)
– sculpture #4196
  – (années 1960) #4407
Keirstead, James Lorimer, artiste can, 1932-
– art et écrits #6037
kekuli . Shuswaps #3983
Kelly, Beverly
– voir Lambert-Kelly, Beverly
Kelly, Kerry Joe, artiste can (vitrail), 1945- #2455
Kelman, Ralf, artiste can, 1947-
– Lite Probe #6038
Kelowna (CB), Kelowna Art Gallery
– expositions
  – J.Frederic McCulloch 1905-1932: Works on Paper (1978) #6463
Kelsey, Charles William, artiste can (vitrail), 1877-1975
– vitraux, Westmount Park United Church (Montréal, Qué) #2448
Kemble, Julie, artiste can, 1945- #2076
Kemble, Roger, architecte can, 1929-
– entretien #8379
Kenderdine, Frederick Augustus (Gus), artiste can, 1870-1947
– expositions
  – (1974) #6039
– expositions de groupe
  – (1940) #350
Kennedy, David Johnston, artiste can, 1816-1898 #6040
– aquarelles #6041
Kennedy, Garry Neill, artiste can, 1935- #6044 6045
– commentaire sur les édifices, Nova Scotia College of Art and Design (Halifax, NE)

#9409
– directeur, Nova Scotia College of Art and Design (Halifax, NE) #3003
– entretien #6042
– étude sur le musée (institution) #714
– expositions
  – (1978) #6043
– expositions de groupe
  – (1980) #703
Kennedy, Sir Arthur Edward, homme d'Etat brit au Canada, 1810-1883
– et Frederick Dally #5250
Kennedy, Sybil, sculpteure can, 1899- #739
– réflexion sur son oeuvre #6046
Kenojuak
– voir Ashevak, Kenojuak
Kent, Edwin S., architecte amér, actif 1929-1931
– Lucerne (Qué), Château Lucerne #9283
Kent, Rockwell, artiste et auteur amér, 1882-1971
– influence sur Thoreau MacDonald #6381
– MacDonald, Thoreau, comparaison #6384
Kent (CB)
– architecture #8147
Kent (Ohio), Kent State University. School of Art
– architecture, John Andrews Architects #8323
Kenyon, J.J., artiste can, 1862-1937
– peintures d'animaux #1727
– peintures et photographie #1681
Kerr, David, photographe can, 1942-
– catalogue de photographies #997 999
Kerr, Estelle Muriel, artiste can, 1897-1971 #207
– commentaire sur ses études à l'étranger #206
– illustrations #916
Kerr, Illingworth Holey, artiste can, 1905-
– commentaire sur ses illustrations #6047 6048
– entretien #1974
– expositions
  – (1973) #6049
– membre du jury, Saskatchewan Arts Exhibition (1954) #1910
– paysages des Prairies #6050
– programme d'expositions itinérantes, Alberta (1980) #1972
– théories sur l'art #1944
Kerr, John, orfèvre can, actif années 1870 #2649
Kerr-Lawson, James, artiste can, 1864-1939
– expositions, critiques #211
– membre du Canadian Art Club #193
Kerslake, Roger, céramiste can, 1938- #2395
Kertland, Douglas Edwin, architecte can, 1888-
– Toronto (Ont), Canadian National Exhibition. Automotive Building #9207
Kestenbaum, Lothar J., artiste amér, 1926-
– influence sur Marcel Braitstein #4899
Ketchikan Totem Park (Alaska)
– totems #3873
Kettle, Horace Gerard, artiste can, 1906-
– et Picture Loan Society (Toronto, Ont) #1746
Keuken, Johan van der, photographe can, 1938-
– catalogue de photographies #997 999
Keziere, Robert, photographe can, 1937-
– catalogue de photographies #998
– entretien #6051
Kiakshuk, artiste can, ca 1886-1966 #4460

Kieffer, Daniel René, photographe can, 1940- #1562
Kielbach, Joseph, artisan verrier can, actif 1906-1913
– fondateur, Manitoba Glass Company (Beauséjour, Man) #2403
Kihn, W.Langdon, artiste amér, 1898-1957
– peintures, Indiens de la côte nord-ouest #1840
Kilbourn, Rosemary Elizabeth, artiste can, 1931-
– commentaire sur la gravure #817
Kilgour, J.W., fabricants de meubles (Beauharnois, Qué) #2463
Kilpin, Legh Mulhall, artiste can, 1853-1919
– expositions
  – (1979) #6052
Kilvert, Benjamin Sayre Cory, artiste can, né 1879
– illustrations #916
King, B.A., photographe can, 1934-
– expositions de groupe
  – (1973) #1002
  – (1981) #1070
King, George William, architecte can, 1863-1945
– Toronto (Ont)
  – Government House, concours #8748
  – John Ross Robertson School et Glenholme School, concours #9437
King, Phillip, sculpteur brit, 1934-
– Winsor, Jackie, comparaison #7597
King-ego, sculpteur can, actif fin XIXe s.-1900 #3862
King William Island
– artefacts netsilik, début XXe s. #4366
Kingcrafts (King City, Ont)
  – (1950-1967) #2244
Kings Landing (NB)
– architecture #7810 7811
Kings Landing (NB), maison Hagerman
– mobilier, John Warren Moore #2512
Kingston (Ont)
– architecture
  – (1673-1867) #7989
  – (années 1920) #7656
  – Newlands, William #8392
  – XIXe s. #7995 8015
  – XIXe s.-années 1920 #7961
– art #1680
– bibliothèques, université et collège #9042
– fortifications (1759-1838) #8453
– mobilier (1800-1867) #2567
– sièges (mobilier), XIXe s. #2575
– tours Martello #8416
Kingston (Ont), Agnes Etherington Art Centre
– voir Kingston (Ont), Queen's University. Agnes Etherington Art Centre
Kingston (Ont), asile
– architecture, William H. Coverdale #258 259
Kingston (Ont), Bellevue (Macdonald House)
– décoration intérieure #7758
Kingston (Ont), Canadian Forces Hospital
– architecture, Shore & Moffat #9031
Kingston (Ont), Canadian Shop
– expositions, critiques
  – Aird, Neil Carrick #4503
Kingston (Ont), Commercial Mart
– architecture, George Browne #8339
Kingston (Ont), hôtel de ville
– architecture, George Browne #8339

the Sesquicentennial of the University of
Toronto (1977) #3168
– Centennial Exhibition of Quebec and
Ontario Contemporary Painters, 1967
(1967) #484
– David Milne: 1882-1953 (1967) #6558
– Ed Bartram: 10 Years (1980) #4618
– Gordon Rayner Retrospective (1979) #6966
– Graham Coughtry: Retrospective (1977)
#5190
– Humorist Walter Trier: Selections from the
Trier-Fodor Foundation Gift (1980) #7428
– Imprint '76 (1977) #833
– J.W. Beatty, 1869-1941 (1982) #4638
– Joe Plaskett and His Paris: In Search of
Time Past (1972) #6893
– Joe Plaskett et son Paris: à la recherche d'un
temps passé (1972) #6894
– Louis Comtois: Paintings, 1974-1979 (1981)
#5164
– Louis de Niverville (1978) #6709
– Mennonite Traditional Arts of the Waterloo
Region and Southern Ontario: A Historical
View (1974) #2250
– Painters Eleven in Retrospect (1981) #1785
– Riopelle: Jean-Paul Riopelle (1980) #7030
– Surrealism in Canadian Painting (1964)
#463
– The Figure: A Sensual Response (1975)
#578
– The Heritage of Jack Bush: A Tribute (1982)
#722
– The Ontario Community Collects: A Survey
of Canadian Painting from 1766 to the
Present (1977) #120
– The Saidye and Samuel Bronfman
Collection of Canadian Art/La collection
Saidye et Samuel Bronfman (1967) #3087
– The Work of Art: Six Artists (1979) #665
– Tony Urquhart: Twenty-five Years;
Retrospective (1978) #7448
– Viewpoint: Twenty-nine by Nine; An
Exhibition of Twenty-nine Works by
Ontario Artists, Selected by Nine Curators
(1981) #1838
– William Perehudoff: Ten Years,
1970-1980/William Perehudoff: une
décennie, 1970-1980 (1982) #6838
Kitchener (Ont), Molsons Bank
– architecture #9173
kitsch
– dans les signes héraldiques canadiens
#2951
Kitsilano (CB)
– architecture #8146
Kitwancool (CB)
– totems, Gitksans #3925
Kitwancools
– totems #3906
Kiyooka, Harry Mitsuo, artiste can, 1928-
– expositions, critiques #6058
Kiyooka, Roy Kenzie, artiste can, 1926-
#6059
– écrits #536
– entretien #6060 6061
– et plasticiens #1439
– expositions
– (1975) #6062
– expositions, critiques #520
– expositions de groupe
– (1965) #469
– (1968) #1263
– (1974) #2050
– (1979) #2069

Klausen, Jorgen, photographe can, ca 1942-
– catalogue de photographies #991
Klawak Park (Alaska)
– totems #3873
Klee, Paul, artiste suisse, 1879-1940
– Bolt, Ron, comparaison #4778
– influence sur Albert Dumouchel #5325
– influence sur Alfred Pellan #6803
– influence sur Francis Coutellier #5196
– influence sur Paul Livernois #6309
– influence sur Pierre Jean Clerk #5118
– influence sur Ulysse Comtois #5165
– Tremblay, Gérard, comparaison #7424
Klein, Maurice Dalvin, architecte can, 1896-
– Toronto (Ont), Dr. D.W. Young,
monument #729
Kleinburg (Ont), McMichael Canadian
Collection #3164
– collection #3172
– Groupe des Sept, peintures #1780 1781
– Groupe des Sept et Tom Thomson,
peintures #1783
Kleyn, Robert, artiste can, 1948-
– entretien #6063
– et art d'avant-garde #600
Klikitats
– vannerie #3777 3778
Kline, Franz, artiste amér, 1910-1962
– Mongeau, Jean-Guy, comparaison #6596
– remise en question de l'influence sur
Christian Marcel Barbeau #4607
Klunder, Harold, artiste can, 1943- #6064
– expositions de groupe
– (1980) #708
Knaff, Jean-Christian, artiste can, 1949-
– pochettes de disques, illustrations #6065
Knobel, Harry Edward, photographe brit, né
ca 1872 #1114
– photographies de la Première guerre
mondiale #1113
Knott, Tom, photographe can, 1942- #2071
Knottenbelt, Marianna, photographe can,
1948-
– expositions, critiques #1018
Knowles, Dorothy, artiste can, 1927- #1880
6066
– expositions
– (1973) #6067
– expositions, critiques #1883
– expositions de groupe
– (1967) #1916
– (1971) #1920
– (1975) #1867 1926
– (1981) #1885
– participant, Symposium on 20th Century
Canadian Culture (Washington, DC),
(1977) #621
Knowles, Elizabeth Annie McGillivray,
artiste can, 1866-1928 #207 6068 6069
Knowles, Harry Percy, architecte amér,
1817-1923
– Toronto (Ont), Masonic Temple, concours
#9062
Knox & Thompson, ébénistes (Saint-Jean,
NB)
– (années 1840-1870) #2511
Knudsen, Christian
– voir Knudsen, Neils Christian (Chris)
Knudsen, Neils Christian (Chris), artiste can,
1945- #6070 6071
– entretien #6072
– expositions de groupe
– (1978) #668
– (1981) #1565

Koenig, Théodore, poète fr, 1922-
– et surréalisme #5598
Koerner, Walter Charles, collectionneur can,
1898-, et Marianne, collectionneuse can,
1901-
– collection, art, Indiens de la côte
nord-ouest #3994
Kokoschka, Oscar, artiste autr, 1886-
– Bobak, Bruno Joseph, comparaison #4760
Kolbenhier, Eric, collectionneur can, XXe s.
– collection, broderie ukrainienne
bukovinienne #2124
Kolisnyk, Peter Henry, artiste can, 1934-
– entretien #6074
– expositions
– (1977) #6075
– (1980) #6076
– expositions de groupe
– (1971) #98
– (1977) #784
– (1978) #786
Kollwitz, Käthe, artiste all, 1867-1945
– Muhlstock, Louis, comparaison #6653
Koochin, William, sculpteur can, 1929-
– expositions
– (1980) #6073
Kooning, Willem de
– voir de Kooning, Willem
Kootenays
– photographies
– Curtis, Edward Sheriff #3399
– pictogrammes #3965
– vannerie #3788
Kopmanis, Augustus Arnold, sculpteur can,
1910-1976
– expositions de groupe
– (1971), médailles #772
Kopsa, Michael M., architecte can, 1922-
– Charlottetown (IPE), Confederation
Centre, concours #9088 9089
– Saskatoon (Sask), Mendel Art Gallery,
concours #9091
– Winnipeg (Man), hôtel de ville, concours
#8985 8986
Korner, John Michael Anthony, artiste can,
1913- #1996 6078
– commentaire sur ses murales #6077
– expositions de groupe
– (1959) #1997
Kostyniuk, Ronald Peter (Ron), sculpteur
can, 1941-
– expositions
– (1972) #6079
– (1978) #6080
Kosuth, Joseph, artiste amér, 1945-
– Baxter, Iain, comparaison #4630
Kovalik, Peter, artiste can, 1956-
– peintures et dessins (1968-1978) #6081
Kovalik, Tibor, artiste can, 1935-
– peintures et dessins (1968-1978) #6081
Kowal, Roman, artiste can, 1922-
– verrières #2450
Kowall, Earl, photographe can, 1948-
– catalogue de photographies #997 999
Koyukons
– culture #3368
Kozloski, John, ébéniste can, actif années
1860 #2565
Kramer, Burton, artiste can, 1932-
– estampes #897
– et Paul Arthur and Associates #873
Kraulis, Janis A., photographe can, 1949-
– catalogues de photographies #1023
Krauss, Rosalind Epstein, historienne d'art

amér, 1940-
– et Betty Roodish Goodwin #5631
Kreiger, Harmut, sculpteur can, actif 1980
– fontaine, Vancouver (CB) #2077
Kreyes, Marielouise, artiste can, 1925- #6082
Krieghoff, Cornelius, artiste can, 1815-1872
   #5 9 89 221 241 242 812 1312 1313 1323
   1334 1335 6083 6084 6085 6087 6088 6089
   6091 6093 6094 6097 6098 6099 6101 6103
– Boylen, M.J., collection #1
– carnets à dessins, Royal Ontario Museum.
   Collection Sigmund Samuel (Toronto,
   Ont) #6090
– et nationalisme dans l'art #143
– et peinture canadienne #18
– expositions
   – (1934) #213 6086
   – (1971) #6095
   – (1972) #6096
– faux, Ward-Price Galleries (Toronto, Ont),
   (1962) #64
– paysages #26 209 6436
– peintures, vie sur une ferme au Québec,
   Galerie nationale du Canada (Ottawa,
   Ont) #6100
– The Pets and the Materials #6102
– vivre de sa peinture #6092
Krieghoff, Emilie Gauthier, Can, 1821-1906
– portrait, Cornelius Krieghoff #6093
Kroupa, Bohuslar, artiste can, actif années
   1870 #6104
Ksan (Hazelton, CB)
– art #4132 4134
– Reid, Bill, commentaire #6987
– sérigraphie #4167
Kubota, Nobuo, sculpteur can, 1932-
– expositions de groupe
   – (1975) #1809
   – (1976) #779
Kudluk, Thomassie, artiste can, ca 1910-
   #6105
Kuhn, Bob, artiste amér, 1920-
– influence sur George E. McLean #6501
Kuiper, Lidi, artiste can, 1948-
– expositions de groupe
   – (1977) #1901
Kujundzic, Zeljko, sculpteur can, 1920-
– expositions de groupe
   – (1971), médailles #772
Kulp, John, céramiste can, 1799-1874 #2290
Kun, Joseph, fabricant d'archets can, 1930-
   #2940
Kupczynski, Stanislav, artiste can, 1928-
   #6106
Kurelek, William, artiste can, 1927-1977
   #6107 6108 6112
– autobiographie #6110 6115
– expositions
   – (1970) #6109
– livres illustrés #6111
– réflexion sur son oeuvre #6113
– The Ukrainian Pioneer, Niagara Falls Art
   Gallery (Niagara Falls, Ont) #6116
– themes #6114
Kurz, Rudolph Friedrich, artiste suisse au
   Canada, 1818-1871
– croquis, Siouens #3400
Kutchins
– costume #4102
– culture (années 1930) #4096 4099
Kuthan, George, artiste can, 1916-1966
   #6117
Kuypers, Jan, designer can, 1925-
– sièges (mobilier) #2471

Kuzyk, Ron, photographe can, ca 1953-
– catalogue de photographies #1032
Kwakiutls
– architecture et totems #3936
– art #3060 3996 4037 4052
   – (années 1970) #4145
   – motif du serpent #3840
– couvertures #3973
– crécelles #4026
– culture #3935
   – (années 1880-1890) #3787
   – (années 1890) #3764
– danse de l'Oiseau-Tonnerre #3867
– masques #3348 3920 3938 3945 3990 4030
– masse d'armes en fanon #3813
– mythologie #3883
– photographies
   – Curtis, Edward Sheriff #3399
– pipes #3850
– potlatch #3956
– rites et cérémonies #3768 3838
– sérigraphie #4120
– totems #3844 3848 3957 4115 4124
Kyle, James Fergus, artiste can, 1876-1941
– dessins humoristiques, Toronto Globe #943
– illustrations #916
Kyle, John, artiste can, 1871-1958
– enseignement de la poterie, femmes
   artistes, Victoria (CB), (années 1920) #2278
Kyoto (Japon)
– chapelle, décor intérieur, Gaston-Pierre
   Petit #6844

L

L'Acadie (Qué), église
– architecture, Odelin & Mailloux #8830
L'Anse-à-Maheu (Qué), église de
   L'Anse-à-Maheu
– architecture et intérieur #8889
L'Assomption (Qué)
– ceinture fléchée #2813 2818 2819 2823 2824
   2827 2864 2865 2873
L'Assomption (Qué), église de
   L'Assomption
– sculptures, Gilles Bolvin #4781 4782
L'Islet (Qué), église
   Notre-Dame-de-Bon-Secours
– architecture et intérieur #8879
– calices, François Ranvoyzé #2658 2673
L'Islet sur mer (Qué), Musée maritime
– expositions
   – De la figuration à la non-figuration dans
      l'art québécois (1977) #1461
La Canardière (Qué), maison Garneau
– architecture, Paul Latouche et Isaac Dorion
   #8615
La Joue, François de, architecte fr au
   Canada, 1656-1718
– professeur, Ecole des arts et métiers de
   Saint-Joachim (Saint-Joachim, Qué) #2992
La Malbaie (Qué)
– arts décoratifs (années 1930) #2172
La Malbaie (Qué), Manoir Richelieu
– collection Canadiana #12 3230
La Palme, Robert, artiste can, 1908- #6119
– commentaire sur la caricature #6120
– commentaire sur ses études en Europe
   #408
– dessins humoristiques et politiques #957
– expositions, critiques #6118

– oeuvres, Ayerst, McKenna & Harrison,
   entreprise de produits chimiques #852
– Orphée chez Dionysos, Place des Arts
   (Montréal, Qué) #8233
La Pérade (Qué), église
– sculptures, Gilles Bolvin #4781
La Pierre, Thomas (Tom), artiste can, 1930-
   #6122
– expositions
   – (1976) #6121
La Pistole, Jacques
– voir Varin (dit La Pistole), Jacques
La Prairie (Qué), église Saint-Isadore
– autel, église Saint-Isadore #241 242
La Rochelle (France), Musée du
   Nouveau-Monde
– symposium sur la peinture québécoise
   (1980) #1559
La Rochelle (France), Musée du Nouveau
   Monde. Chapelle du Lycée Fromentin
– expositions
   – Mémoire d'une Amérique: cartographie,
      topographie et allégories d'une vision
      française du Nouveau Monde, objets
      ethnographiques, livres anciens, botanique
      et zoologie (1980) #276
Labastrou, Roger, artiste can, actif 1971
– et Jacques Guillon Designers Inc. #884
Labelle, Henri Sicotte, architecte can, 1896-
– Valleyfield (Qué), cathédrale de
   Salaberry-de-Valleyfield #8843
Labelle, Paul, photographe can, 1947- #1562
Labelle, Ronald, photographe can, 1942-
– catalogue de photographies #997
Laberge, Albert, auteur can, 1871-1960
– expositions
   – (1971) #5604
Laberge, Jean-Marie, artiste can, 1933- #1551
Labor Arts Guild (Vancouver, CB)
– (1944-1945) #1985
Labouret, Auguste, artiste fr, 1871-1964
– mosaïques, basilique Sainte-Anne
   (Sainte-Anne-de-Beaupré, Qué) #8859 8860
Labrador
– architecture #7782
– art, Art Association of Newfoundland and
   Labrador #1144
– artefacts dorsétiens #4377 4379 4380
– arts décoratifs
   – (années 1970) #2149
   – XXe s. #2155
– cabane en rondins verticaux #8532
– ouvrage de vannerie #2945
– tapis crochetés et tapis poinçonnés #2765
   2767
– vues
   – Bradford, Robert William #4898
– vues photographiques (1849-1949) #1160
Labradors
– culture (années 1910) #4321
Labrèche, François, artiste can, actif 1842
   #1301
Labrosse, Antoine, sculpteur can, actif 1738
– crucifix, église Notre-Dame. Chapelle du
   Sacré-Coeur (Montréal, Qué) #6123
Labrosse, Denis
– voir Jourdain (dit Labrosse), Denis
Labrosse, famille, sculpteurs can, XVIIIe s.
   #1300
– sculptures sur bois #1575
Labrosse, Paul-Raymond
– voir Jourdain (dit Labrosse),
   Paul-Raymond
Lac Barrière (Qué)

– Algonquiens #3544
Lac-Bouchette (Qué), Chapelle mariale
– architecture, Henri Tremblay #8832
Lac-Bouchette (Qué), église de l'Ermitage
– peintures, Charles Edouard Huot #5877
  5878 5882 5884
Lac La Ronge (Sask)
– ouvrages perlés, Cris #3696
Lac Ontario
– fortifications #8457
Lac Saint-Jean (Qué)
– vues photographiques
  – Bull, W. #4956
Lac Supérieur (Ont)
– vues
  – Fraser, John Arthur #5509
  – Harris, Lawren Stewart #5732
  – Hopkins, Frances Ann Beechy #5833
LACAC
– voir Comité consultatif local pour la
  conservation de l'architecture/Local
  Architectural Conservation Advisory
  Committee (LACAC)
Lachaise, Gaston, sculpteur can, 1882-1935
– influence sur Claude Roussel #7087
Lachance, Walter W., architecte can, né 1869
– Beamsville (Ont), école secondaire #9387
– Saskatoon (Sask), Flanagan Hotel #9263
Lachapelle, Edouard, artiste can, 1943-
– linogravures, troupe de danse
  Marie-Calumet #6124
Lachenaie (Qué), église Saint-Charles
– architecture et intérieur #8808
– sculptures, Gilles Bolvin #4781
Laciseraye, Michel
– voir Lefebvre (dit Laciseraye), Michel
Lacroix, André, photographe can, actif
  années 1970 #1534
Lacroix, Henriette, artiste can, 1928- #1551
Lacroix, Jacques, artiste can, 1944- #1551
Lacroix, Richard, artiste can, 1939- #6126
  6127
– commentaire sur ses études en art #470
– estampes #6125 6129
– et Fusion des arts (Montréal, Qué) #1482
  1483
– et gravure québécoise (années 1960) #1641
– expositions de groupe
  – (1967) #821
– fondateur de l'Atelier libre de recherches
  graphiques (Montréal, Qué) #1642 1653
– fondateur de la Guilde graphique
  (Montréal, Qué) #1647 1655 6128
– illustrations de livre #926
Ladouceur, Jean-Paul, artiste can, 1921-
  #6130
Lafitau, Joseph-François, prêtre et auteur fr,
  1681-1746
– description des Amérindiens, thème de
  l'homme sans tête #281
– et nationalisme dans l'art #1373
Laflamme, Carole Simard
– voir Simard-Laflamme, Carole
Laflamme, M.A., artiste can, actif 1842 #1301
Lafleur, Claude, artiste can, 1932- #1282
– et RACE (Regroupement des artistes des
  Cantons de l'Est) #1536
Lafleur, Jean M., architecte can, 1903-
– Valleyfield (Qué), cathédrale de
  Salaberry-de-Valleyfield #8843
Lafleur, Pierre, artiste can, 1938- #6131 6132
Laford, John, artiste can, 1955-
– expositions de groupe
  – (1981) #4173

Laforge, Jean, artiste can, 1911- #6133
Lafortune, François, photographe can, 1921-
– entretien #6134
Lafrenière, J.L.D., architecte can, 1874-1929
– Montréal (Qué), hôtel de ville #8980
Lagacé, Jean-Baptiste, artiste can (vitrail),
  1868-1946
– vitraux, église Notre-Dame (Montréal,
  Qué) #2444 8839
Lagacé, Paule, artiste can, 1951- #1538
Lagrave, Augustin, orfèvre can, actif
  1791-1797
– oeuvres, Detroit Institute of Arts (Detroit,
  Mich) #2691
Lagroix, Joseph
– voir Huppé (dit Lagroix), Joseph
Lahaise, Guillaume, poète can, 1888-1969
– influence sur Ozias Leduc #6209
Lahr (Allemagne de l'Ouest), Ailla Luisen
  Schule
– expositions
  – Contemporary Native Art of Canada: The
    Woodland Indians/Art contemporain des
    Indiens sylvicoles du
    Canada/Zeitgenössische Kunst der
    kanadischen Waldland Indianer (1976)
    #4143
laine
– Canada, XVIIe-XIXe s. #2096 2120
– colorants
  – Nouvelle-Ecosse #2749
  – Ontario, XIXe s. #2742
– Québec, XVIIIe s. #2200
Laing, G.Blair, marchand d'oeuvres d'art
  can, 1911-
– autobiographie #1686
Laing, William (Bill), artiste can, 1944- #6135
Laithwaite, George, sculpteur can, 1873-1956
  #1792
– expositions de groupe
  – (1975) #1682
Lajeunie, Jean-Claude, artiste can, 1943-
  #1479 1480
– entretien #1485
Lajoie, Guy Gérin
– voir Gérin-Lajoie, Guy
Lajoie, Noël, artiste can, 1927-
– expositions de groupe
  – (1955) #1408
Lajoie, Paul, artiste can, 1932- #6136
Lake, Suzy, artiste can, 1947- #675 717 1512
– en comparaison avec Raymonde April
  #1059
– entretien #6139
– et art d'avant-garde #600
– expositions
  – (1975) #6138
  – (1980) #6140
– expositions de groupe
  – (1978) #668
– photographies autoportraits #6137
– utilisation de la photographie #1057
Lake Kejimkoojik (NE)
– pétroglyphes, Micmacs #3617
Lake Louise (Alta), Château Lake Louise
– architecture, Barott & Blackader #9279
Lake Louise (Alta), Skoki Lodge
– restauration #9296
Lake of Bays (Ont), Bigwin Inn
– architecture, John Wilson #9275
Lake Simcoe (Ont)
– vues
  – Smith, William St. Thomas #7236
Lake Superior Provincial Park (Ont et Man)

– pictogrammes algonquiens #3576
Lake Windermere (CB), Melchin, pavillons
– architecture, Gordon L. Atkins #7694
Laliberté, Alfred, sculpteur can, 1878-1953
  #302 1315 1382 6142 6143 6149 6150
– bronzes, Musée du Québec (Québec, Qué)
  #6144
– commentaire sur la sculpture québécoise
  (années 1940) #1580
– écrits #6145
– expositions
  – (1978) #6146
– expositions de groupe
  – (1980) #1296
– influence des Bois-Francs #6151
– Légendes, coutumes, métiers, séries #6148
– monument, marché Maisonneuve
  (Montréal, Qué) #6141
– monument à Dollard des Ormeaux
  (Montréal, Qué) #1623
– professeur de Doris Minette Judah #5980
– professeur de Zénon Alary #4505
– sculptures, Galerie nationale du Canada
  (Ottawa, Ont) #6147
Laliberté, Guy, artiste can, 1930- #6152
Laliberté, Madeleine, artiste can, 1922- #6153
Laliberté, Norman, artiste can, 1925-
– entretien, commentaire sur ses bannières
  #6154
Lamanna, Carmen, marchande d'oeuvres
  d'art can, 1927- #628
– au 3e Salon international de galeries pilotes:
  artistes et découvreurs de nos temps,
  exposition (1970) #531
– commentaire, Carmen Lamanna Gallery
  (Toronto, Ont) #1811
Lamarche, Ulric, artiste can, 1867-1921 #1382
  6155
Lamb, Harold Mortimer, artiste can, critique
  d'art, 1872-1970
– expositions
  – (1977) #6156
Lamb, Thomas L., designer can, 1938- #2487
Lamb, Thomas White, architecte amér,
  1871-1942
– cinémas Loew's #9122 9123
– Hamilton (Ont), cinéma Loew #9069
– Montréal (Qué), cinémas Loew #9069
– Toronto (Ont)
  – cinéma Loew's, rue Yonge (Elgin et
    Wintergarden) #9064 9067
  – cinéma Loew's, Uptown #9075
  – Pantages Theatre #9075
Lambart, Evelynn, cinéaste can, 1914-
– et Norman McLaren, film sur la guerre
  civile espagnole #6498
Lambert, Jacques, artiste can, 1928- #1546
  1551
Lambert, John, auteur brit, actif 1811
– commentaire sur maisons en bois rond et
  maisons en pierre, Québec, début XIXe s.
  #8527
Lambert, Lucie, artiste can, 1947-
– Album Frayère #6157
Lambert, Phyllis Bronfman, architecte,
  conservatrice et collectionneuse can, 1927-
– Montréal (Qué), Le Havre South Seafront,
  projet de "reconstruction domiciliaire"
  #8512
– photographies, édifices en pierre grise,
  Montréal (Qué) #7922
Lambert, Ronald (Ron), artiste can, 1927-
– élève de Hans Hofmann #402
Lambert (dit Saint-Paul), Paul, orfèvre can,

1691-1749 #249 250 2660 2668
– en comparaison avec l'orfèvrerie française #2688
– et Samuel Payne, écuelle, Musée des beaux-arts de Montréal (Montréal, Qué) #2689
– oeuvres, Detroit Institute of Arts (Detroit, Mich) #2691
– oeuvres, Musée du Québec (Québec, Qué) #2678
– tasse à quêter #2671
Lambert-Kelly, Beverley, artiste can, 1943-
– commentaire sur la perception visuelle #525
Lambeth, Michel, photographe can, 1923-1977 #6158 6159
Lambton Mills (Ont), école
– architecture, Ellis & Ellis #9388
Lamont Glass Co., fabricants de verre (Trenton, NE) #2398 2409 2417
Lamoureux, Gisèle, photographe can, active années 1970-
– catalogue de photographies #991
lampes . Canada
– (1825-1925) #2404
– guide pour collectionneurs #2104 2125 2131
– Hookway, Elmer John #5828
– Ontario
– XIXe s., lampes à l'huile #2947
– XVIIIe-XIXe s. #2918
– XVIIIe-XIXe s. #2703 2920
Lamps, périodique can #1667
Landron, Jean-François, orfèvre can, 1686-ca 1760 #249 250
– oeuvres, Detroit Institute of Arts (Detroit, Mich) #2681 2691
Landry, Yvan, céramiste can, 1932- #6160
Landsley, Patrick Alfred, artiste can, 1926-
– expositions de groupe
– (1977) #1278 1279
Lane, Albert, ébéniste can, né ca 1821 #2571
Lane, Henry Bowyer, architecte brit au Canada, né 1787, actif années 1840
– Toronto (Ont) #8075
– hôtel de ville #8993
– Osgoode Hall #9002 9003
Lang, George Macdonald, architecte can, 1860-1930
– Halifax (NE) #7838
langage, art et
– voir aussi écriture dans l'oeuvre d'art
– (1980), Canada #1063
– (années 1970), Canada #574
– (années 1970), Québec #1552
– Clark, Tim #5113
– Copithorne, Judith #5176
– Curnoe, Greg #78
– N.E. Thing Co. Ltd. #524 6677 6678
– Robert, Louise #695 7039
– W.O.R.K.S. #1955
Langevin, Joseph, photographe can, ca 1830-1882 #6161
Langevin, Richard, sculpteur can, actif 1978 #1540
Langford, Adelaide Elizabeth, artiste can, 1854-1939
– peintures murales, gare du Canadien Pacifique (Vancouver, CB) #9546
Langley, Henry, architecte can, 1836-1907
– Toronto (Ont), Yorkville Town Hall #8997
Langley & Howland, agence can d'architecture
– Toronto (Ont)

– Banque impériale du Canada #9181
– John Ross Robertson School et Glenholme School, concours #9437
– Molsons Bank #9159
Langley (CB)
– architecture #8147
Langley (CB), Langley Centennial Museum et National Exhibition Centre
– expositions
– Creative Flight (1979) #147
Langlois, Denis, artiste can, 1945- #1540 6162
Langton, John, Can, vérificateur général du Canada et vice-recteur de University of Toronto, 1808-1894
– et University of Toronto. University College (Toronto, Ont), architecture #9453
Lankinen, Wayne, photographe can, ca 1932-
– catalogue de photographies #1032
Lansdowne, James Fenwick, artiste can, 1937- #6163 6165
– expositions
– (1981) #6164
Lantier, Jean, artiste can, 1953- #6166
Lapalme, Dominique Janson, constructeur can, 1701-1762 #7844
Lapalme, Pierre
– voir Janson (dit Lapalme), Pierre
Lapierre, Viateur, artiste can, 1917- #6167
Lapointe, Conrad, artiste can, actif 1974
– entretien #1527
Lapointe, Esther, sculpteure can, 1947- #6168
Lapointe, Frank, artiste can, 1942- #1148 6170
– journal intime #6169
Lapointe, Jean-Paul, artiste can, 1935- #1551
Lapointe, Paul-Marie, poète can, 1929-
– poèmes, Vierge incendiée #4831
Laporte, Lucie, artiste can, 1946- #6171
– expositions de groupe
– (1980) #1663
Lapoterie, Louis-Nicolas
– voir Gaudin (dit Lapoterie), Louis-Nicolas
Lapoterie, Nicolas
– voir Gaudin (dit Lapoterie), Nicolas
laque
– décorations, mobilier canadien #2548
Larivée, Francine, artiste can, 1942-
– La chambre nuptiale #1634
Larivière, Paul, collectionneur can, XXe s.
– entretien #3219
Larose & Larose, agence can d'architecture
– Dorval (Qué), Aéroport international de Montréal. Aérogare #9515
Larouche (Qué), église Saint-Gérard Magella
– architecture, St-Gelais & Tremblay #8841
Larouche-Villeneuve, Jeanne, collectionneuse can, 1925-
– collection, images pieuses, Université Laval (Québec, Qué) #130 1662
Larseneur, Charles, sculpteur can, actif 1842 #1301
Larson, Doris Wall, artiste can, 1939-
– estampes #1214
LaSalle (Qué), fort
– recommandé pour conservation (1881) #7754
LaSalle (Qué), manoir Ogilvie
– architecture, Alexander Cowper Hutchison #8636
LaSalle (Qué), Saint John Brébeuf Parish Church
– architecture, John Bird #8766
Lasnier, Raymond, artiste can, 1924-1968 #6172

Lasserre, Frederic (Fred), architecte can, 1911-1961
– Vancouver (CB), University of British Columbia. Gymnase #7679
Latchford, Joan, photographe can, 1926- #993
Laterrière (Qué), église Notre-Dame
– architecture et art #7882
Laterrière (Qué), moulin du père Honorat
– architecture #7882
Latouche, Paul, maçon can, actif 1835
– La Canardière (Qué), maison Garneau #8615
Latour, Jacques
– voir Leblond (dit Latour), Jacques
Latour, Jean, sculpteur can, 1632-1677 #1572
Latour, Pierre
– voir Huguet (dit Latour), Pierre
Latschaw, Abraham, artiste can (style fraktur), 1799-1870 #2255
– influence sur Joseph Bauman #4628
Latvis Society of Artists
– expositions
– (1966) #475
Laufer, Murray Bernard, artiste can, 1929-
– décors #6173
Laurens, Jean-Paul, artiste fr, 1838-1921
– influence sur Charles Edouard Huot #5878 5884
Laurens, Jean-Pierre, artiste fr, 1875-1932
– professeur de Clarence Alphonse Gagnon #5544 5546 5547
– professeur de Rodolphe Duguay #5317
Laurens, Paul-Albert, artiste fr, 1870-1934
– professeur de Rodolphe Duguay #5317
Laurentides (chaîne de montagnes), (Qué)
– vues
– Borenstein, Sam #4853
– Browne, Joseph Archibald #4939
– Cullen, Maurice #5220
– Gagen, Robert Ford #5530
– Gransow, Helmut #5645
– Harris, Lawren Stewart #5729
– Pichet, Roland #6868
– XXe s. #1278 1279
Laurier, Wilfrid, homme d'Etat can, 1841-1919
– portrait, Georges Delfosse #1385
Laurin, Serge, photographe can, 1947-
– catalogue de photographies #997 999
– Groupe d'action photographique #1494
Lausanne (Suisse), Musée cantonal des beaux-arts
– expositions
– Canada: art d'aujourd'hui (1968) #518
– expositions, critiques
– 3e Salon international de galeries pilotes: artistes et découvreurs de nos temps (1970) #531
Lauzon, Jean, photographe can, actif années 1970 #1556
Lauzon, Réal, sculpteur can, 1945-
– Laboratoire #1627
– membre du Centre communautaire catholique Tour de David (Saint-Basile-le-Grand, Qué) #1510
Laval, François de, évêque fr au Canada, 1623-1708
– et Palais épiscopal (Québec, Qué) #8787
– fondateur, Ecole des arts et métiers de Saint-Joachim (Saint-Joachim, Qué) #1327 2181 2992
Laval (Qué), centre administratif
– architecture, Affleck, Desbarats,

Dimakopoulos, Lebensold, Sise #8322
Laval (Qué), église Sainte-Rose
– architecture, Victor Bourgeau #8854
Laval (Qué), maison André-B.-Papineau
– architecture #8625
Lavallée, André
– *voir* Paquet (dit Lavallée), André
Lavigne, Paul
– *voir* Tessier (dit Lavigne), Paul
Lavoie, Raymond, artiste can, 1950-
– expositions
  – (1980) #685
Law, Anthony (Tony), artiste can, 1916-
  #6174
Law, Ivan, sculpteur can, 1885-1979 #2596
Law Society of Upper Canada
– siège social, Osgoode Hall (Toronto, Ont)
  #9002 9003
Lawrence, Alexander, ébéniste can,
  1788-1843 #2500 2501 2511
Lawson, Ernest, artiste can aux EU,
  1873-1939 #6175 6177
– expositions
  – (1967) #6176
  – (1976) #6178
  – (1979) #6179
– expositions, critiques #204 211
– membre du Canadian Art Club #193
– paysages d'hiver #285
Lawson, James Kerr
– *voir* Kerr-Lawson, James
Lawson & Little, architectes et ingénieurs,
  agence can d'architecture
– Lucerne (Qué), Château Lucerne #9283
Le Ber, Jacques, Can, m. 1693
– articles de maison #2522
Le Ber, Jeanne, religieuse et artiste can,
  1662-1724 #2095 2778
Le Ber, Pierre, artiste can, 1669-1707 #234
  235 1363
– portrait, Marguerite Bourgeoys #1333 6180
Le Blanc, Michel, architecte can, 1930-
– Montréal (Qué), métro. Station Peel #9553
Le Corbusier, Charles Edouard Jeanneret,
  architecte et artiste fr, 1887-1965
– art et architecture #8232
– influence sur Marcel Parizeau #8397
Le Poitevin, Léonard
– *voir* Paillard (dit Le Poitevin), Léonard
Le Rouge, Jean, constructeur can, 1639-1712
  #234 235
Le Testu, Guillaume, cartographe fr,
  1509-1572
– cartes du Canada #875
Leadbeater, Roy, sculpteur et joaillier can,
  1928- #6181
Leaf Rapids (Man), centre municipal
– architecture, Leslie Stechesen #8409 8974
Leaf Rapids (Man), National Exhibition
  Centre
– expositions
  – *Canadians: A National Photography Show
    about People/Canadiens: exposition
    nationale de photographie ayant les gens
    comme thème* (1979) #1035
  – *Edward Curtis in the Collection of the
    Edmonton Art Gallery* (1980) #3480
  – *Images of the Inuit from the Simon Fraser
    Collection* (1981) #4495
  – *J.Frederic McCulloch 1905-1932: Works on
    Paper* (1979) #6463
  – *Looking South* (1978) #4278
Leaning, John Dalton, architecte can, 1926-
– Ottawa (Ont), Académie de La Salle #9480

9481
Lear, Edward, artiste et auteur brit,
  1812-1888
– et Daniel Fowler #5491
– Lansdowne, James Fenwick, comparaison
  #6163
Leathers, Winston Lyle, artiste can, 1932-
– expositions de groupe
  – (1981) #1907
Lebel, Maurice, artiste can, 1898-1963 #1382
  1393
Lebensold, D.Fred, architecte can, 1917-
– Montréal (Qué), Musée des beaux-arts de
  Montréal #9124 9125 9133
Leblanc, Augustin, sculpteur can, 1799-1882
– influence de la famille Baillairgé #1582
Leblanc, Leo B., artiste can, 1914- #6182
LeBlanc, Pierre, constructeur can, actif 1830
– Petit Fort Garry (Man) #8475
Leblond, Jean
– *voir* Jacquiés (dit Leblond), Jean
Leblond (dit Latour), Jacques, prêtre et
  artiste can, 1671-1715 #234 235 1233 1324
  2992
– sculptures sur bois #1577
Lebredt, Gordon, artiste can, 1948-
– expositions de groupe
  – (1977) #1901
  – (1978) #669
Lebrun, Hughes et Jean-Camille, orfèvres
  can, actifs années 1920-1940 #2174 2179
  2693
Lebrun, Rico, artiste amér, 1900-1964
– Bachinski, Walter Joseph Gerard,
  comparaison #4578
Leclair, Michel, artiste can, 1948- #6183
Leclerc, Eugène, sculpteur can, 1886-1968
  #2174 2179 2194 2209
Leclerc, père, ébéniste can, XIXe s.
– berceuses #2535
Lecor, Paul (Tex), artiste can, 1933- #6184
Leduc, Fernand, artiste can, 1916- #1294
  1453 1504 1542 1543 6191
– à Paris (France) #1434
– artiste et théoricien (1941-1947) #1443
– Bénic, Lorraine, comparaison #4678
– commentaire sur Ozias Leduc #6199
– débat avec Paul-Emile Borduas #6586
– écrits #1449 6194
– entretien #6188 6189
– et plasticiens #1439
– expositions
  – (1970) #6185 6186
  – (1977) #6190
  – (1980) #6193
– expositions, critiques #6187 6192
– expositions de groupe
  – (1955) #1408
  – (1959) #1414
  – (1981) #1471
– *Refus global* #1396
Leduc, Ozias, artiste can, 1864-1955 #302
  1240 1270 1393 6198 6199 6202 6205 6209
  6211
– Borduas, Paul-Emile, commentaire #4839
  6197
– dessins préparatoires #6203 6207
– écrits #6196
– expositions
  – (1955) #6200
  – (1974) #6206
  – (1978) #6210
– expositions, critiques #283
– illustrations #918

– influence sur Paul-Emile Borduas #4820
  4829 4830 4841
– intérieur, église Saint-Enfant-Jésus du
  Mile-End. Chapelle Sacré-Coeur
  (Montréal, Qué) #6195
– intérieur, Palais épiscopal, Sherbrooke
  (Qué) #6208
– oeuvres (années 1920) #1231
– peinture religieuse #1384
– peintures, église Notre-Dame de la
  Présentation (Shawinigan, Qué) #6201
– peintures, Galerie nationale du Canada
  (Ottawa, Ont) #1266
– professeur de Paul-Emile Borduas #4811
  4814 4836 4843 4850
Lee, Abel Alexander, artiste can, 1918- #6212
Lee, Ann Dow, artiste can, active années
  1960-
– expositions, critiques #1167
Lee, Clifford E., collectionneur can, m. 1972
– estampes inuit représentant jeux et
  concours #4492
Lee, Lawrence, artiste brit (vitrail), 1909-
– et Master Stained Glass Workshop, Art
  Gallery at Harbourfront (Toronto, Ont)
  #2455
– vitraux, Saint Andrew et Saint Paul
  Church (Montréal, Qué) #2448
Lee-Nova, Gary, artiste can, 1943-
– commentaire sur la perception visuelle
  #525
– commentaire sur le sacré dans l'art #94
– entretien #6213
– expositions
  – (1969) #2039
– expositions, critiques #2051
– expositions de groupe
  – (1971) #2042
  – (1973) #2045
Lees, Samuel, artiste can, actif 1847
– membre de la Toronto Society of Arts
  #1689
Leeson, Benjamin W., photographe can,
  1866-1948
– expositions de groupe
  – (1976) #2012
LeFébure, Jean, artiste can, 1930-
– expositions de groupe
  – (1962) #1420
Lefebvre, Nicolas, artiste fr, 1660-ca 1740
– peintures, calvaire d'Oka (Qué) #1355 1356
Lefebvre, Oliver, sculpteur can, 1872-1962
– sculpture sur bois, collection Nettie Sharpe
  #1607
Lefebvre (dit Laciseraye), Michel,
  constructeur can, 1654-1708 #234 235
Lefort, Agnès, artiste can, marchande
  d'oeuvres d'art, 1891-1973
– et art canadien, galerie Agnès Lefort
  (Montréal, Qué) #1424
Légaré, Joseph, artiste can, 1795-1855 #1318
  1336 6215 6216 6219
– appui, création d'un musée national à
  Québec (Qué) #3120
– et peinture québécoise #1353
– et société québécoise #1375
– expositions
  – (1978) #6217 6218
– expositions de groupe
  – (1959) #219
– influence sur la peinture québécoise #6220
– *Le choléra à Québec*, Galerie nationale du
  Canada (Ottawa, Ont) #6214
– *Paysage au monument à Wolfe*, et

nationalisme canadien-français #1373
– peintures, Université Laval (Québec, Qué) #3078
– peintures d'Amérindiens #6222
– vues de bâtiments, Québec (Qué) #6221
Legault, Jean-Onésime, artiste can, 1882-1944
– et Montée Saint-Michel #1236
légendes
– *voir aussi* folklore; mythologie
légendes algonquines
– et Samuel Ash #4558
légendes amérindiennes
– images de la femme #121
légendes canadiennes #2096
– Nouveau-Brunswick, *Legends on Tapestries* (1962) #5296
– Québec #1290 2169 2171
– et Georges Saint-Pierre #7118
– et Henri Julien #5988 5991 5993
– et Louis-Philippe Hébert #5767
légendes inuit
– Dorsétiens #4379
– et Davidialuk Alasua Amittu #4521
– et Jean-Paul Riopelle #7024
– images de la femme #121
légendes iroquoises
– et Arthur Guindon #5665
légendes kwakiutls
– et Mungo Martin #6429
légendes saulteuses/ojibwa
– et Norval Morrisseau #6646
Léger, Fernand, artiste fr, 1881-1955
– enseignement de l'art aux artistes canadiens (années 1940) #384
– influence sur Alfred Pellan #6826
– influence sur Jeanne Leblanc Rhéaume #6994
Léger, Jeanne, artiste can, XXe s.
– professeure de Marie-Hélène Allain #4508
Léger, Onésime-Aimé, artiste can, 1881-1924 #1382
Legrady, George, photographe can, 1950-
– catalogue de photographies #997 999 1053
Legrady, Miklos, photographe can, 1951-
– catalogue de photographies #997 999
Legros, Enid Sharon, céramiste can, 1943- #6223
Legros, Jean-Pierre, sculpteur can, 1943-
– *Continuum II* #1627
Leiden (Pays-Bas), Rijksmuseum voor Volkenkunde
– tipi, Pieds-Noirs #3718
Leier, Grant, artiste can, 1956- #6224
Leighton, Alfred Crocker, artiste can, 1901-1965 #6225
– et Alberta Society of Artists #1942
– expositions de groupe
– (1940) #350
– mari de Barbara Leighton #3017
– professeur de Marion F.S. Mackay Nicoll #6703
– programme d'expositions itinérantes, Alberta (1980) #1972
Leighton, Barbara Harvey, artiste can, 1911- #3017
Leimanis, Andris, artiste can, 1938-
– illustrations #941
Lemay, J.Eudore, photographe can, 1874-1947 #1283
Lemay & Leclerc, agence can d'architecture
– Montréal (Qué), église Saint-Jean-Baptiste #8766
Lemieux, Irénée, artiste can, 1931-
– entretien #6226

Lemieux, Jean-Paul, artiste can, 1904- #97 1392 1432 1453 1541 1542 1543 6227 6228 6230 6233 6234 6235 6236 6237
– commentaire sur Gérard Morisset #3305
– commentaire sur l'art québécois #1386 1399
– commentaire sur la Société des arts plastiques #1411
– concept d'espace et de temps #6240
– Dumouchel, Albert, comparaison #5328
– expositions
– (1967) #6231
– (1974) #6232
– expositions de groupe
– (1958) #431
– (1959) #438
– (1964) #462
– illustrations, *Maria Chapdelaine* #6239
– Mercier, Monique, comparaison #6512
– peintures (1956-1960) #6229
– photographies #6238
– portraits #715
– Prévost, Antoine, comparaison #6927
– professeur à l'Ecole des beaux-arts (Québec, Qué) #1404
– Surrey, Philip Henry, comparaison #7289
Lemieux, Lisette, sculpteure can, 1943- #6241
Lemieux, Lyse, artiste can, 1956-
– expositions de groupe
– (1978) #2067
Lemieux, Marguerite, artiste can, 1899- #1380 1382
Lemieux, Maurice, sculpteur can, 1932- #6242
Lemire, Jean, constructeur fr au Canada, 1626-1685 #228 229
LeMoine, Edmond, artiste can, 1877-1922 #6243
Lemoyne, Serge, artiste can, 1941- #1479 1480
– entretien #1485
– expositions de groupe
– (1981) #1564
LeMoyne, Suzanne Rivard, artiste can, 1928-
– et Banque d'oeuvres d'art #3276
Lemyre, Marcel, artiste can, 1948-
– et Betty Roodish Goodwin, projet de la rue Mentana #1558 5631
Lengauer, Karl W., artiste can (vitrail), 1928- #2460
Lenhardt, Molly, artiste can, 1920- #1881
Leningrad (URSS), Musée d'anthropologie et d'ethnographie de Leningrad
– art tlingit #3947 3978
Leningrad (URSS), musée l'Ermitage
– expositions
– *Sculpture of the Inuit: Masterworks of the Canadian Arctic/La sculpture chez les Inuit: chefs-d'oeuvre de l'Arctique canadien* (1972) #4423 4440
Lennie, Beatrice, sculpteure can, 1905- #6244
Lennox, Edward James, architecte can, 1855-1933
– Toronto (Ont)
– Bank of Toronto #9151
– Church of Saint Paul's #8897 8902
– Excelsior Life Building #9333
– hôtel de ville #8993
– McConkey's Lunch #9269
– Stewart Building #9354
– Wolseley Motor Car Company Building #9332
Lent, Benjamin, céramiste can, actif fin années 1820-1841 #2367

Leon, Robert, sculpteur can, ca 1943- #6245
Leon H. Lempert & Son, agence can d'architecture
– Toronto (Ont), Shea's Hippodrome #9066
Leonard, John C., artiste can, 1944-
– expositions
– (1981) #6246
Léonard de Vinci, artiste it, 1452-1519
– Cormier, Ernest, comparaison #8346
léopards
– motif, Kate Craig et Eric Metcalfe #2070
Leprohon, Louis-Xavier, sculpteur can, 1795-1876
– influence de la famille Baillairgé #1582
Leroux-Guillaume, Janine, artiste can, 1927- #6247
Leroy, Hugh Alexander, artiste can, 1932- #1479
– expositions de groupe
– (1967) #490
Lery, Gaspard Chaussegros de, architecte fr au Canada, 1682-1752
– plan de la façade, église Notre-Dame (Montréal, Qué) #3081
Les Sables-d'Olonnes (France), Musée de l'abbaye Sainte-Croix
– expositions
– *Louis Comtois: 4 tableaux récents grand format* (1978) #5163
Leslie, John, orfèvre can, 1849-1939
– poinçons #2635
Leslie R. Fairn & Associates, agence can d'architecture
– Halifax (NE)
– Dalhousie University. Killam Library #9052
– Neptune Theatre #9097
Lespérance, Pierre, orfèvre can, 1819-1882 #6248
Letarte, Jean-Paul, joaillier can, 1933- #6249
Letendre, Rita, artiste can, 1929- #1418 1542 1543 6250 6251
– expositions
– (1974) #6252
– expositions de groupe
– (1955) #1408
Lethbridge (Alta)
– architecture, quartier chinois #8137
Lethbridge (Alta), Saint Michael's General Hospital
– architecture, Henry William Meech; Benzie & Bow, Associate Architects #9021
Lethbridge (Alta), Southern Alberta Art Gallery
– expositions
– Alberta Society of Artists, exposition (1979) #1942
– *Another Dimension/Une autre dimension* (1977) #783
– *Artisan '78: The First National Travelling Exhibition of Contemporary Canadian Crafts/Artisan '78: première exposition nationale itinérante d'artisanat canadien contemporain* (1979) #2134
– *Canadians: A National Photography Show about People/Canadiens: exposition nationale de photographie ayant les gens comme thème* (1980) #1035
– *Carol Fraser Paintings and Drawings: 1967-1977* (1978) #5507
– *David Craven: New Works* (1978) #5206
– *Dennis Burton Retrospective* (1977) #4961
– *Enns, Evans & Ulrich* (1977) #1956
– *Goodridge Roberts: Selected*

Works/Goodridge Roberts: oeuvres choisies
(1982) #7050
– *Gordon Rayner Retrospective* (1980) #6966
– *Joe Fafard: Recent Sculpture* (1980) #5401
– *Liz Magor* (1979) #6405
– *Otto Rogers: New Paintings and Sculpture,
   1977-78* (1978) #7065
– *Real Sculpture: John McEwen* (1979) #6472
– *Ron Martin: Water on Paper* (1976) #6433
– *Yves Gaucher & Christopher Pratt* (1977)
   #643
– expositions, critiques
– Kennedy, Garry Neill #6042
Lethbridge (Alta), University of Lethbridge
– architecture, Arthur Charles Erickson
   #8358 8361 9406 9497
– expositions
   – *The University of Lethbridge Phase II
      Sculpture Competition* (1981) #797
   – *William Perehudoff: Ten Years,
      1970-1980/William Perehudoff: une
      décennie, 1970-1980* (1981) #6838
Lett/Smith, agence can d'architecture
– London (Ont), Grand Theatre, restauration
   #7776
Lettons au Canada
– art #49 475
– Manitoba, art traditionnel #968
lettrage dans l'art
– *voir aussi* enseignes et panneaux
   d'affichage
– Curnoe, Greg #5228
– MacDonald, Thoreau #6385
Levasseur, famille, sculpteurs can, XVIIIe s.
   #6256
– intérieur, église Saint-Etienne (Beaumont,
   Qué) #8809
– sculptures sur bois #1573 1575 6254
   – église Saint-Pierre (île d'Orléans, Qué)
      #8802
   – église Sainte-Famille (île d'Orléans, Qué)
      #1612
Levasseur, François-Noël, sculpteur can,
   1703-1794 #269 270
– intérieur, église Saint-François-de-Sales (île
   d'Orléans, Qué) #8796
– tabernacles #1613
Levasseur, Michel, orfèvre can, actif 1699-ca
   1709 #234 235 2669 2677
– oeuvres, Detroit Institute of Arts (Detroit,
   Mich) #2681
Levasseur, Noël, sculpteur can, 1680-1740
   #234 235 1324 1572 1592
– en comparaison avec David Fleury David
   #1596
– tabernacles #1613
Levasseur, Pierre-Noël, sculpteur can,
   1690-1770 #249 250
– correspondance, François Filiau-Dubois
   #6253 6255
– dessin de chaire, Archives nationales du
   Québec (Québec, Qué) #6257
– intérieur, couvent des ursulines. Chapelle
   (Québec, Qué) #8852
– oeuvres, églises, Charlesbourg (Qué) #8851
– tabernacles #1613
Levasseur, René Michel, can, actif 1745-1758
– correspondance, commentaire sur son
   apprentissage avec François Filiau-Dubois
   #6253 6255
Levasseur (dit Delor), Jean-Baptiste-Antoine,
   sculpteur can, 1717-1775 #269 270
– tabernacles #1613
Lévesque, Paule, artiste can, 1947-

– art graphique télédiffusé #909
Lévi-Strauss, Claude, anthropologue et
   philosophe fr, 1908-
– collection, art amérindien de la côte
   nord-ouest #4005
– écrits, et conceptualisme #7473
Levine, Leslie Leopold (Les), artiste can,
   1936- #535 536 6262
– art et écrits #6273
– art vidéo #616
– collection de chaises #6258
– commentaire sur l'art inuit #6269 6270
   6271
– commentaire sur l'art jetable #6259
– commentaire sur l'installation *Red Tape*,
   University of Toronto. Hart House
   (Toronto, Ont) #6263
– commentaire sur proposition d'oeuvre
   d'art, édifice, gouvernement du Canada
   (Toronto, Ont) #6268
– eaux-fortes #6272
– entretien #6260
– expositions
   – (1970) #6264
   – (1971) #6265
   – (1974) #6267
– expositions, critiques #6266
– expositions de groupe
   – (1967) #480
   – (1970) #771
   – (1971) #98
– oeuvres de l'imaginaire #530
– sculpture jetable #538
– sculptures, *Electric Shock* et *Process of
   Elimination* #6261
Levine, Marilyn Ann, sculpteure et
   céramiste can, 1935-
– entretien #6274
– expositions, critiques #2383
– expositions de groupe
   – (1974) #1925
   – (1977) #781
Lévis (Qué), église
   Notre-Dame-de-la-Victoire
– architecture et art #8789
Lewis, David, photographe can, ca 1946-
– catalogue de photographies #1032
Lewis, Glenn Alun, artiste can, 1935-
– catalogue de photographies #996
– entretien #6275
– expositions
   – (1979) #6276
– expositions de groupe
   – (1969) #2039
   – (1974) #2050
   – (1976) #2060
   – (1979) #2070
   – (1980) #696 8237
– oeuvres de l'imaginaire #530
Lewis, Maude, artiste can, ca 1903-1970
   #6277
Lewis, Richard, architecte can, 1824-1875
– Victoria (CB) #8145
Lewis, Stanley, artiste can, 1930-
– sculptures #6278
Lewis, Wyndham, artiste brit au Canada,
   1882-1957 #6279
Lewiston (NY), Artpark
– Poulin, Roland, sculpture en plein air #706
Lewitt, Sol, sculpteur amér, 1928-
– Winsor, Jackie, comparaison #7597
Liaison, périodique can
– et Géraldine Bourbeau #4877
Liang, Kar, artiste can, actif 1969

– art par ordinateur #528
Libling, Michener & Associates, agence can
   d'architecture
– Saint-Boniface (Man), chapelle
   Saint-Louis-le-roi #8765
– Winnipeg (Man), Winnipeg Art Gallery,
   concours #9102
Liébert, Philippe, sculpteur can, 1732-1804
   #1592 6280 6281
– lustre en bois, église (Oka, Qué) #8818
Liechtenstein, maison de, collection
– acquisitions, Galerie nationale du Canada
   (Ottawa, Ont) #3035
lieutenant-gouverneurs du Canada
– médailles #757
lieux de sépulture
– *voir* cimetières
lieux de sépulture . Algonquiens
– Redbank (NB) #3561
lieux de sépulture . Béothuks
– Port-au-Choix (TN) #3611
lieux de sépulture . Hurons
– poterie #3520
lieux de sépulture . Iroquois
– poterie #3520
– sculpture #3553
lieux de sépulture . Saulteux/Ojibwa
– Red Deer River (Man) #3615
lieux historiques
– *voir aussi* monuments aux morts
lieux historiques . Canada
– et conservation (années 1880) #7754
– Halifax (NE) #7830
– London (Ont) #8010
– Québec #7887
– Toronto (Ont) #5651
Lièvres
– culture
   – (années 1920) #4081
   – (années 1960) #4109
Life, périodique amér
– dessins humoristiques, Arthur George
   Racey #6952
Liljefors, Bruno, artiste suédois, 1860-1939
– influence sur George E. McLean #6501
– Lansdowne, James Fenwick, comparaison
   #6165
Lillooets
– culture #3783
– vannerie #3773 3927
Limners (Victoria, CB) #2043
Lin, Chien-Shih, artiste can, 1922-
– influence sur Jack Marlowe Wise #7602
lin . Canada
– (1608-1867) #2120
– Ontario, XIXe s. #2805
– XVIIe-XIXe s. #2730 2736
Lincoln, A.H., photographe can, actif années
   1850 #1211
Lincoln (Mass), De Cordova and Dana
   Museum
– expositions
   – *Changing Visions: The Canadian
      Landscape/Aperçus divers: le paysage
      canadien* (1976) #617
Lincoln (Mass), De Cordova Museum
– expositions
   – *Eleven Canadian Printmakers* (1967) #821
Lincoln G. Morris Studios, entreprise can
   d'appareils d'éclairage
– intérieur, Banque Royale du Canada
   (Montréal, Qué) #9176
Lindgren, Charlotte, artiste can, 1931- #1126
   6283

– expositions
  – (1980) #6282
– expositions, critiques #2771
Lindner, Ernest, artiste can, 1897- #6286
– Cowley, Reta Madeline, comparaison
  #5200
– dessins #6287
– entretien #6290
– et réalisme #110
– expositions
  – (1970) #6284
  – (1972) #6285
  – (1977) #6288 6289
– expositions de groupe
  – (1967) #1916
  – (1971) #1920
  – (1975) #1926
  – (1980) #1940
– Hall, John, comparaison #1860
Lindoe, Luke Orton, artiste can, 1913-
– entretien #1974
– expositions de groupe
  – (1968) #2382
Lindsay, Brydon & Greig, agence can
  d'architecture
– Toronto (Ont), architecture domestique
  #8493
Lindsay, James (Jim), artiste can, 1944-
– théories sur l'art #6291
Lindsay, Jeffrey, designer can, ca 1925-
– structure à voiles minces #7674
Lindsay, T.D., photographe can, 1926-
– expositions de groupe
  – (1972) #1952
Lindsay (Ont), Lindsay Gallery
– expositions
  – John Howlin (1979) #5852
Lingwood, Daphne, sculpteure can (cuir),
  active années 1970 #2936
Lingwood, Rex, sculpteur can (cuir), 1946-
  #2936
Linnell, Henry R., architecte can, actif 1915
– Winnipeg (Man), architecture domestique
  #8493
Lismer, Arthur, artiste can, 1885-1969 #6293
  6294 6295 6299 6300 6301 6303 6305 6307
– A September Gale, Georgian Bay, Galerie
  nationale du Canada (Ottawa, Ont) #6304
– commentaire sur A.Y. Jackson #5914 5925
– commentaire sur Frederick Horsman
  Varley #7463
– commentaire sur l'enseignement de l'art
  #2965 2966 2968 2971 2974 2981 2984 2985
  2987
  – Toronto (Ont), Art Gallery of Toronto
    #2975
– commentaire sur la peinture murale #15
– commentaire sur Maurice Galbraith Cullen
  #5221
– commentaire sur Tom Thomson #7358
– correspondance, Homer Ransford Watson
  #7536
– directeur, Nova Scotia College of Art
  (Halifax, NE) #2993
– et Edith Grace Coombs #5172
– et le Groupe des Sept #286 1732
– et Louis Jobin #5964 5966
– expositions
  – (1950) #6298
– expositions, critiques #1710 6296 6297
– expositions de groupe
  – (1968) #3224
– illustration et mise en page artistique #939
– illustrations, Farmer's Magazine #1765

– murales, maison James MacCallum,
  Galerie nationale du Canada (Ottawa,
  Ont) #1745
– paysages #6306
– professeur #1395 6302
  – Toronto (Ont), Art Gallery of Toronto
    #3020
– professeur de Doris Jean McCarthy #6461
– réflexion sur l'art canadien #6292
Literary and Philosophical Society (Toronto,
  Ont)
– aide apportée aux musées #3152
lithographie américaine
– (années 1940) #810
lithographie canadienne
– (années 1940) #810
– Halifax (NE), Nova Scotia College of Art
  and Design. Atelier de lithographie
  (années 1970) #825 830
– Heaviside, Lady Mary Love #258 259 1175
– Tazewell, Samuel Oliver #7339
– Wheatley, Willis Sifton #7548
– XIXe s. #812 925 1720
Lithuaniens au Canada
– costume #2892
lits . Canada #2473
– comté de Norfolk (Ont), Normandale Iron
  Works #2699
– Ontario
  – (1780-1900) #2577
  – (années 1790-1857) #2558
  – XIXe s. #2562
– Québec
  – XVIIe-XVIIIe s. #2530 2531
– tapisserie à l'aiguille, rideaux de lit, fin
  XVIIIe s. #2784
Litteljohn, Bruce, photographe can, 1935-
– expositions, critiques #1009
littérature
– voir aussi auteurs; poésie
– en comparaison avec art traditionnel #967
– littérature enfantine, fin XIXe s.-années
  1930 #2932
littérature, art et
– Canada #92 104
  – (années 1970) #1529
  – et photographie #1065 1066
  – et sociologie #164
  – représentation des grands espaces,
    réaction du public #93
  – XIXe s.-années 1930 #89
– et Alex Colville #5141
– et Don Proch #6942
– et Francesca Vivenza #7495
– et Maxwell Bennett Bates #4621
– Québec
  – et automatisme #1449 4831
  – et surréalisme #1464
littérature canadienne #129
– (1975-1980) #1799
– (années 1880-1920) #10
– (années 1970) #619
– auteures, XXe s. #95 96
– auteurs immigrants (années 1940-1960)
  #465
– et la mode (1882-1910) #2897
– et le nationalisme #327 341
– Nouveau-Brunswick #1178
– Nouvelle-Ecosse (1606-1950) #1196
– Québec
  – (années 1940) #1391
  – (années 1960) #529 1473
  – XIX s.-années 1940 #1242
  – XIXe s-années 1930 #1382

– Terre-Neuve, XIXe s.-années 1950 #1139
– Winnipeg (Man) #1891
Little, Harold Robert, architecte can,
  1887-1948
– Montréal (Qué), Université McGill.
  Athletic buildings, concours #9417
Little, John Geoffrey Caruthers, artiste can,
  1920-
– Ouellet, Angemil, comparaison #1546
Little Bow (Alta), Little Bow Municipal
  Hospital
– architecture, Meech, Mitchell, Robins &
  Associates #9032
Livernois, Jules-Benoît, photographe can,
  1830-1865 #1275
– collection de photographies #6308
Livernois, Jules-Ernest, photographe can,
  1858-1933 #1275
Livernois, Paul, artiste can, 1948- #6309
Liverpool (NE), résidence de Simeon
  Perkins
– architecture #7823 8536
Liverpool (NE), Simeon Perkins Museum
– expositions
  – Charles Wm. MacDonald: Seaman,
    Labourer, Artist, Manufacturer (1874-1967)
    (1981) #6355
Livick, Stephen, photographe can, 1945-
  #1007
– expositions de groupe
  – (1981) #1070
livres
– voir aussi catalogues de mode;
  conservation et restauration; guides; livres
  d'artistes; livres pour enfants
– Holmes, Robert, collection, Ontario
  College of Art (Toronto, Ont) #5824
livres canadiens
– guide pour collectionneurs #2104
– Ontario (années 1970) #935
– thème décoratif du castor #56
– théorie sur l'art canadien (1967) #488
– Toronto (Ont), Royal Ontario Museum.
  Collection Sigmund Samuel #3140
livres d'artistes
– femmes artistes, Canada (années 1970)
  #936
– Guilde graphique (Montréal, Qué) #1647
– Leclair, Michel, et Michel Tremblay #6183
– Morris, Michael William #6640
– Snow, Michael #7254
  – Cover to Cover #7255 7256
– Wieland, Joyce #7577
livres d'artistes canadiens #940
– Editions Erta (Montréal, Qué) #1641
– femmes artistes (années 1970) #936
– Graff (Montréal, Qué) #1645
– Nantel, Michel #6684
– Québec (1967-1977) #1659
livres pour enfants . Canada
– illustrations
  – Houston, James Archibald #5846
  – Newfeld, Frank #6689
  – Odjig, Daphne #6731
  – XIXe-XXe s. #934 937
Loates, Glen, artiste can, 1945- #6310 6311
Lobchuk, William Harry (Bill), artiste can,
  1942-
– et Grand Western Canadian Screen Shop
  #1902
Lochhead, Kenneth Campbell, artiste can,
  1926- #145 536 6312 6313 6314
– commentaire sur ses études en art #470
– Dallaire, Jean-Philippe, comparaison #5238

– entretien #6317 6319
– et l'art en Saskatchewan (années 1950) #1912
– expositions
  – (1972) #6316
  – (1977) #6318
– expositions, critiques #520 6320
– expositions de groupe
  – (1958) #431
  – (1961) #1913
  – (1962) #1847
  – (1971) #98
  – (1981) #1907
– technique du pistolet (1970-1972) #6315
Lockport (Man), Saint Andrew's Church
– architecture et intérieur #8909
Lockport (Man), Saint Andrew's Parsonage
– architecture et utilisation du terrain #8716
locomotives
– modèles à vapeur, Walter H. Stansell #1792
Loder, Erik, artiste et poète can, 1933-
– commentaire sur Jack Chambers #700
Lodge, Judith (Judy), artiste can, 1941- #2053
– collection *The Walls of Eden* #6321
Loeb, M. et Mme Jules, collectionneurs can, XXe s.
– collection, art canadien #3231
Logan, Robert Fulton, artiste can, 1889-1959
– expositions
  – (1928) #1732
logement subventionné . Canada
– (années 1960) #8518
  – logements pour personnes âgées #8516
– (années 1970) #8520
logement subventionné pour travailleurs . Canada
– après la Première Guerre mondiale #8495
Loire, Gabriel, artiste fr (vitrail), XXe s.
– vitraux, église Saint-Antonin (Montréal, Qué) #2448
loisirs, études
– Canada (1974) #3056
Lom d'Arce, Louis Armand de, Baron de La Hontan, auteur et officier de l'armée fr, 1666-ca 1716
– et nationalisme dans l'art #1373
London, George, artiste can (vitrail), actif 1907-
– et Yvonne Williams #7589
London (Ont)
– architecture
  – XIXe s. #8003 8007 8010 8018
– art
  – (1947-1979) #1828
  – (années 1940-1970) #1670
  – (années 1960) #90 1791
  – (années 1970) #1813
  – (années 1970), et situation de l'art à Saskatoon (Sask) #1932
– art vidéo #550
– arts décoratifs (années 1970) #2260
– arts graphiques et photographie (années 1970) #1812
– poterie, XIXe s. #2350
London (Ont), Aberdeen School
– architecture, Watt & Blackwell #9388
London (Ont), Eldon House
– architecture et intérieur #8660
London (Ont), Fanshawe College
– Eloul, Kosso, *Now* #5367
London (Ont), Grand Theatre
– restauration, Lett/Smith #7776
London (Ont), H.P. Beal Technical School

– influence sur l'art, London (Ont), (années 1960) #1791
London (Ont), London Art Gallery
– *voir aussi* London (Ont), London Public Library and Art Museum; London (Ont), London Regional Art Gallery
– expositions
  – *Another Dimension/Une autre dimension* (1977) #783
  – *Esther Warkov Drawings* (1977) #7519
  – *Frederic Marlett Bell-Smith (1846-1923)* (1978) #4668
  – *Graham Coughtry: Retrospective* (1976) #5190
  – *Graphics and Photographics: The Second of Four Major Survey Exhibitions of London Art* (1976) #1812
  – *Greg Curnoe: Some Lettered Works, 1961-1969* (1975) #5228
  – *London Saskatoon Exchange* (1977) #1932
  – *London Survey Number Four: Crafts* (1977) #2260
  – *R.L. Bloore: Sixteen Years, 1958-1974* (1975) #4751
  – *White Paintings: John Noestheden* (1977) #6715
  – *Young Contemporaries/Jeunes contemporains* (1975-1979) #584
– expositions, critiques
  – *The Tony Urquhart Reunion* (1970) #7445
London (Ont), London Public Library and Art Museum
– *voir aussi* London (Ont), London Art Gallery; London (Ont), London Regional Art Gallery
– collection #3153
– expositions
  – *7 West Coast Painters* (1959) #1997
  – *Alan C. Collier Retrospective* (1971) #5131
  – *André Biéler 50 Years: A Retrospective Exhibition 1920-1970* (1971) #4725
  – *Canadian Artists Abroad* (1956) #413 414
  – *Carl Schaefer: Retrospective Exhibition; Paintings from 1926 to 1969* (1969) #7155
  – *Centennial Exhibition of Quebec and Ontario Contemporary Painters, 1967* (1967) #484
  – *Changing Visions: The Canadian Landscape/Aperçus divers: le paysage canadien* (1977) #617
  – *Daniel Fowler* (1965) #5489
  – *David Milne: 1882-1953* (1967) #6558
  – *Drawings and Pastels c. 1930-1967 by Miller Gore Brittain* (1969) #4917
  – *Five Years of Robert Downing, 1966-1971* (1972) #5306
  – *Goodridge Roberts: A Retrospective Exhibition/Goodridge Roberts: une exposition rétrospective* (1970) #7045
  – *Harold Town: The First Exhibition of New Work, 1969-1973* (1973) #7413
  – *J.M. Barnsley (1861-1929), Retrospective Exhibition* (1964) #4611
  – *Jock Macdonald: Retrospective Exhibition/Jock Macdonald: rétrospective* (1970) #6375
  – *Joe Plaskett and His Paris: In Search of Time Past* (1972) #6893
  – *Joe Plaskett et son Paris: à la recherche d'un temps passé* (1972) #6894
  – *John Meredith: Fifteen Years* (1975) #6514
  – *Léon Bellefleur* (1968) #4662
  – *Lithographs/Lithographies* (1973) #825
  – *London Collects* (1972, 1976) #100

  – *London Painting Now: A Survey of London Painting* (1976) #1813
  – *Neglected Aspects of Canadian Culture* (1973) #962
  – *Ontario Society of Artists: 100 Years* (1973) #1678
  – *Paterson Ewen Retrospective* (1976) #5384
  – *Paul Peel, 1860-1892: Memorial Exhibition in the Art Gallery* (1970) #6792
  – *Quebec* (1944) #12
  – *Some Paintings, Drawings and Prints from the Douglas Duncan Collection* (1967) #3223
  – *Surrealism in Canadian Painting* (1964) #463
  – *The J.S. McLean Collection of Canadian Painting* (1969) #3228
  – *The Ontario Community Collects: A Survey of Canadian Painting from 1766 to the Present* (1976) #120
  – *Western Ontario Exhibition* (1941-1978) #1670
  – *York Wilson Retrospective (1927-1973)* (1975) #7596
– expositions, critiques
  – *Points of View* (1959) #432
  – *Société des sculpteurs du Canada* (1944) #736
– services culturels (années 1940) #3133
London (Ont), London Regional Art Gallery
– *voir aussi* London (Ont), London Art Gallery; London (Ont), London Public Library and Art Museum
– architecture, Raymond Moriyama #3174 9145
– expositions
  – *Brian Jones* (1978) #5974
  – *Celebration: The Canadian Embroiderer's Guild* (1981) #2793
  – *Certain Traditions: Recent British and Canadian Art* (1979) #653
  – *Colette Whiten* (1978) #7561
  – *Ed Bartram: 10 Years* (1980) #4618
  – *Gordon Rayner Retrospective* (1979) #6966
  – *Greg Curnoe: rétrospective/Greg Curnoe: Retrospective* (1982) #5231
  – *Guido Molinari: Works on Paper* (1981) #6594
  – *Ivan Eyre Exposition* (1981) #5394
  – *Jack Chambers: The Last Decade* (1980) #5081
  – *London/Banff Exchange* (1978) #1964
  – *Louis de Niverville* (1978) #6709
  – *Mary Pratt* (1981) #6919
  – *Métiers d'art Ontario-Québec, 1979/1980/Quebec-Ontario Crafts, 1979/1980* (1981) #2138
  – *Nine Regional Nineteenth Century Artists* (1978) #1726
  – *Painters Eleven in Retrospect* (1980) #1785
  – *The Society of Canadian Painter-Etchers and Engravers in Retrospect/La Société des peintres-graveurs canadiens: vue rétrospective* (1981) #836
  – *Trésors d'art populaire québécois/Folk Art Treasures of Quebec* (1981) #1297
  – *Viewpoint: Twenty-nine by Nine; An Exhibition of Twenty-nine Works by Ontario Artists, Selected by Nine Curators* (1981) #1838
London (Ont), Lord Roberts School
– architecture, McBride & Gilbert; Arthur E. Nutter, Associate Architect #9388

London (Ont), McCormick Manufacturing
Co.
– architecture, Watt & Blackwell #9234
London (Ont), McIntosh Art Gallery
– *voir* London (Ont), University of Western
Ontario. McIntosh Art Gallery
London (Ont), Northern Life of Canada
Building
– Reid, Stuart, *Hudson Bay Triptych* #6983
London (Ont), Riverview School
– architecture, Lewis E. Carrothers et John
Vicar Munro #9388
London (Ont), Ryerson School
– architecture, Watt & Blackwell; William G.
Murray, Associate Architect #9386
London (Ont), Tecumseh School
– architecture, Watt & Blackwell #9388
London (Ont), Theo Waddington
– expositions
– *Mathew Aqiggaaq: Recent Sculpture* (1979)
#4534
London (Ont), University of Western
Ontario
– architecture, John M. Moore & Company
#9448
– et Fanshawe Pioneer Village (Ont) #8066
London (Ont), University of Western
Ontario. McIntosh Art Gallery
– expositions
– *Eskimo Wall Hangings* (1974) #4253
– *Imprint '76* (1976) #833
– *The Artist and the Critic: A Tribute to
Lenore Crawford* (1974) #112
– *The Image of Man in Canadian Painting:
1878-1978/L'image de l'homme dans la
peinture canadienne: 1878-1978* (1978)
#135
– expositions, critiques
– *The Mask of Objectivity/Subjective Images*
(1981) #1067
London (Ont), University of Western
Ontario. McIntosh Memorial Art Gallery
– expositions
– *A Century of Pioneering* (1943) #12
– *Sports and Pastimes* (1944) #12
– *The Marine Collection* (1943) #12
London (Ont), University of Western
Ontario. Résidence des étudiants
– architecture, Tillmann & Lamb #9467
London (Ont), University of Western
Ontario. Science Building
– architecture, John M. Moore & Company
#9442
London (Ont), Western School of Art
– Griffiths, John Howard, professeur et
directeur #2305
London (Ont), Womanspirit - Art Research
and Learning Centre
– et Sasha Hayman #5756
London Crockery Mfg. Co., fabricants de
céramique (London, Ont) #2350
London Free Press, journal can
– Crawford, Lenore, critique d'art #112
Londres (Angleterre)
– développement urbain #7902
– guerre-éclair, influence sur Jack Leonard
Shadbolt #7189
Londres (Angleterre), Anthropos Gallery
– sculpture inuit #4289
Londres (Angleterre), Arthur Tooth & Sons
– expositions
– *J.-P. Riopelle: Paintings, 1949-1959* (1959)
#7015

Londres (Angleterre), Arts Council of Great
Britain
– expositions
– *Jack Bush: Paintings and Drawings,
1955-1976* (1980) #4976
Londres (Angleterre), British Empire
Exhibition (1910)
– Dyonnet, Edmond, exposition d'art
canadien, commentaire #5347 5349
Londres (Angleterre), British Museum
– art, Indiens de la côte nord-ouest #4062
– art amérindien
– Sloane, Sir Hans, collection #3397
– art inuit #4289 4360 4369
– art kwakiutl #3850
– Catlin, George, illustrations de pipes à
tabac #3478
– chroniques en images #3747
– coffre, Indiens de la côte nord-ouest #3805
– crécelles en forme de bec de macareux,
Indiens de la côte nord-ouest #3960
– expositions
– *Artificial Curiosities from the Northwest
Coast of America* (1981) #4064
– *Sculpture of the Inuit: Masterworks of the
Canadian Arctic/La sculpture chez les Inuit:
chefs-d'oeuvre de l'Arctique canadien*
(1972) #4423 4440
– pipes, Amérindiens #3470
– sac en poil de bison, Amérindiens #3398
– White, John, dessins d'Amérindiens et
d'Inuit #7552
Londres (Angleterre), Burlington Gallery
– expositions
– *Australian and New Zealand, American and
Canadian Oil Paintings and Water Colour
Drawings* (1888) #175
– *Exhibition of Australian, New Zealand,
American and Canadian Oil Paintings and
Water Colour Drawings* (1890) #177
– *Exhibition of Water-color Drawings of
Yellowstone Park, Yosemite Valley and
Rocky Mountain Views, also Canadian and
North Western Buffalo Hunts and Other
Indian Sports,*(1890) #1839
Londres (Angleterre), Canada House Gallery
– expositions
– *Bill Vazan: Recent Photoworks and
Videotapes* (1978) #7474
– *Canadians: A National Photography Show
about People/Canadiens: exposition
nationale de photographie ayant les gens
comme thème* (1978) #1035
– *Contemporary Native Art of Canada: The
Woodland Indians/Art contemporain des
Indiens sylvicoles du
Canada/Zeitgenössische Kunst der
kanadischen Waldland Indianer* (1976)
#4143
– *D.P. Brown, Ken Danby, Tom Forrestall,
Christopher Pratt* (1974) #573
– *Emily Carr: The Mature Years/Emily Carr:
les années de maturité* (1979) #5042
– *Exposition d'estampes en l'honneur de C.
Krieghoff, 1815-1872/Exhibition of Prints
in Honour of C. Krieghoff, 1815-1872*
(1972) #6096
– *General Idea's Reconstructing
Futures/General Idea: reconstruction de
l'avenir* (1978) #5583
– *Group of Seven, Canadian Landscape
Painters: A Travelling Exhibition from the
McMichael Canadian Collection, Kleinburg,*

*Ontario/Groupe des Sept: peintres
canadiens de paysages: une exposition
itinérante de la collection canadienne
McMichael, de Kleinberg, Ontario*
(1977) #1780
– *Ivan Eyre Exposition* (1982) #5394
– *Jack Chambers: Selection of Paintings and
Drawings* (1980) #5080
– *Leslie Reid* (1980) #6981
– *Other Realities: The Legacy of Surrealism in
Canadian Art* (1979) #508
– *Réalités autres: le legs du surréalisme à l'art
canadien* (1979) #509
– *The Fabric of Their Lives: Hooked and
Poked Mats of Newfoundland and
Labrador/L'étoffe de leur vie: tapis crochetés
et poinçonnés de Terre-Neuve et du
Labrador* (1980) #2765
– *Twelve Mile Creek: Exhibition/Exposition*
(1975) #1808
– *Windows of Perception* (1977)
– Curnoe, Greg, commentaire #5230
– expositions, critiques
– *Exposition d'estampes en l'honneur de C.
Krieghoff, 1815-1872/Exhibition of Prints
in Honour of C. Krieghoff, 1815-1872*
(1972) #6099
– *Jack Chambers: Selection of Paintings and
Drawings* (1980) #5082
– Young, Robert (1979) #7629
Londres (Angleterre), Carroll Gallery
– expositions
– *Catalogue of an Exhibition of Water
Colours Representing the "Canadian
Rockies" by Charles John Collings* (1912)
#5133
– *The Art of Charles John Collings* (1914?)
#5134
– expositions, critiques
– *Catalogue of an Exhibition of Water Colours
Representing the "Canadian Rockies" by
Charles John Collings* (1912) #5132
Londres (Angleterre), Chelsea School of Art
– Woolnough, Hilda Mary, élève #7616
Londres (Angleterre), Colonial and Indian
Exhibition (1886)
– art canadien #14 172 174
Londres (Angleterre), Commonwealth Art
Gallery
– expositions
– *Commonwealth Artists of Fame, 1952-1977*
(1977) #633
Londres (Angleterre), Earls Court Exhibition
– expositions
– *Catalogue of the Memorial Exhibition of
Pictures Left by the Late Henry Sandham,
Royal Canadian Academician* (1911) #7120
Londres (Angleterre), Frost and Reed's Art
Galleries
– expositions
– *Arthur Heming: Recorder of the Northland
of Canada; Exhibition of Paintings at Frost
& Reed's Art Galleries; Where Mr.
Heming's Work is Shown for the First
Time in Europe* (1934) #5776
Londres (Angleterre), Grafton Galleries
– expositions
– *Catalogue of the Canadian Official War
Photographs Exhibition for the Benefit of
the Canadian War Memorials Fund* (1916)
#1072
Londres (Angleterre), Grosvenor Life School

– Wrinch, Mary Evelyn, élève #7618
Londres (Angleterre), Hayward Gallery
– expositions
  – *Sacred Circles: Two Thousand Years of North American Indian Art* (1976) #3463
Londres (Angleterre), Horniman Museum
– artefacts et art inuit #4289
Londres (Angleterre), Institute of Contemporary Arts Ltd.
– First International Sculpture Competition (1953) #5995
Londres (Angleterre), Leigh's Academy
– Verner, Frederick Arthur, élève #7484
Londres (Angleterre), London Mechanics' Institution
– Birkbeck, George, président #3064
Londres (Angleterre), Marlborough Fine Art Gallery
– expositions
  – *Alex Colville* (1970) #5145
Londres (Angleterre), Molton Galleries
– expositions
  – *Gerald Gladstone* (1962) #5611
Londres (Angleterre), Redfern Gallery
– expositions, critiques
  – Young, Robert (1979) #7629
Londres (Angleterre), Royal Academy of Arts
– Cruikshank, William, exposition #5212
– Hopkins, Frances Ann Beechy, oeuvres #5835
Londres (Angleterre), Royal Academy School of Architecture
– Carter, Alexander Scott, élève #5050
Londres (Angleterre), Royal College of Art
– Warren, Emily Mary Bibbens, élève #7524
Londres (Angleterre), Royal Institute Galleries
– expositions
  – *Artists of the British Empire Overseas* (1937) #339
Londres (Angleterre), Royal Institute of British Architects. Galeries
– exposition, architecture canadienne (ca 1927) #8224
Londres (Angleterre), Serpentine Gallery
– expositions
  – *Jack Bush: Paintings and Drawings, 1955-1976* (1980) #4976
– expositions, critiques
  – Bush, Jack Hamilton #4977
Londres (Angleterre), Slade School
– Blackstock, Hattie, élève #4738
  Grier, Edmund Wyly, élève #5660
Londres (Angleterre), South Kensington School of Art
– Forbes, John Colin, élève #5459
– Kinton, Ada Florence, élève #6053
– Pemberton, Sophia Theresa, élève #6828
Londres (Angleterre), Sunhill Sanatorium
– Carr, Emily, séjour #5018
Londres (Angleterre), Tate Gallery
– expositions
  – *A Century of Canadian Art* (1938) #19
  – *Canadian Painting, 1939-1963* (1964) #462
– expositions, critiques
  – *A Century of Canadian Art* (1938) #22
Londres (Angleterre), Westminster School of Art
– Carr, Emily, élève #5018 5045
Londres (Angleterre), Whitechapel Gallery
– expositions
  – *Exhibition of Canadian Art* (1925) #290
  – *Robert Downing: Sculpture* (1969) #5304

  – *Yves Gaucher* (1970) #5563
Londres (Angleterre), Woodstock Gallery
– expositions
  – *Catalogue of an Exhibition of Paintings and Drawings by Walt Ruhman (Canada)* (1959) #7106
Lonechild, Michael, artiste can, 1955- #6322
Long, J.W., & Associates, agence can d'architecture
– Edmonton (Alta), Hillington Court #8744
Long, Jack W., architecte can, 1925-
– Calgary (Alta) #8381
– Calgary (Alta), Kelvin Grove Patio Apartments #8518
– commentaire sur la planification #7746
Long, Marion, artiste can, 1882-1970
– et Albert Angus Macdonald #6354
– expositions, critiques #432
Longfellow, Henry Wadsworth, poète amér, 1807-1882
– *Evangéline*, source d'inspiration pour *La dispersion des Acadiens* de Henri Beau (1900) #4639
Longpré & Marchand, agence can d'architecture
– Montréal (Qué), métro. Station Berri-de-Montigny #9549
Longueuil (Qué), maison Lamarre
Lorcini, Gino, artiste can, 1923- #1479 6323
– et plasticiens #1439
– expositions de groupe
  – (1967) #490
– utilisation de la lumière #767
Lord, Daniel, orfèvre can, actif années 1840-1860 #2649
Lordly, Albert James, ébéniste can, né 1826 #2511
Lorenzetto, Adeline, artisane tisserande can, active années 1960
– tissage salishiens #3941
Lorette (Qué), mission huronne
– parement d'autel, mère Marie Le Maire des Anges #1328
Loretteville (Qué), église Notre-Dame-de-la-Jeune-Lorette
– architecture et intérieur #8804
Loring, Frances Norma, sculpteure can, 1887-1968 #739
– et Florence Wyle #758
– expositions de groupe
  – (1969) #754
Lorlie (Sask)
– vues, George Campbell Tinning #7378
Lorne, John Douglas Sutherland, plus tard 9e duc d'Argyll, marquis de, homme d'Etat et artiste brit au Canada, 1845-1914
– et Académie royale des arts du Canada #2 153 275 280
– protecteur de l'art canadien #168
Lorrain, Madeleine, artiste can, active 1950
– cartes de Noël #856
Lortie, Jocelyne, artiste can, active 1978 #6325
Lortie, Joseph Antoine François (Niska), artiste can, 1940- #6324
Los Angeles (Calif), Bunker Hill, revitalisation du quartier
– architecture, concours #8364
Los Angeles (Calif), Felix Landau Gallery
– expositions
  – *Etrog* (1964) #5376
Los Angeles (Calif), Museum of Natural History of Los Angeles County

– expositions
  – *Objects of Bright Pride: Northwest Coast Indian Art from the American Museum of Natural History* (1978) #4024
Los Angeles (Calif), Southwest Museum
– boîtes en écorce de bouleau décorées de piquants de porc-épic, Outaouais #3548
– sculptures en ivoire, Inuit #4382
Los Angeles (Calif), University of California
– Peterson, Margaret, élève et professeure #6839
Lotbinière, Pierre-Gustave Joly de, photographe can, m. 1865 #6326
Lotbinière (Qué)
– églises #8835
Lougheed, Robert Elmer, artiste can, 1910- #6327 6328
Louis, Morris, artiste amér, 1912-1962
– Christensen, Dan, comparaison #5104
Louis, Pat, photographe can, actif années 1970-
– catalogue de photographies #991
Louisbourg (NE) #8442
– architecture #8419 8422 8439
  – toits, utilisation de bardeaux en bois #7703
– architecture domestique #8427
– artisans #2148
– costume
  – costume féminin (1713-1758) #2855
  – XVIIIe s. #2868
– décoration intérieure #7758
– faïence #2368 2369
– fortifications #8426
  – casernes, bastion du Roi #8435 8436
  – corps de garde #8428 8429
– île du Quai, restauration #8423
– mobilier #2484
– restauration #8425
– statues, Louis XV #1598
– uniformes militaires (1713-1758) #2857 2866
– verre, XVIIIe s. #2427
Louisbourg (NE), maison Dugas
– verre #2441 2442
Louisiane
– statues, Louis XIV #1598
– vues, explorateurs français #276
Louisville (Ky), J.B. Speed Art Museum
– expositions
  – *19 Canadian Painters 1962* (1962) #450
Louy, Pierre, artiste can, actif années 1960
– membre du Hampton Group #1177
Love, Lady
– *voir* Heaviside, Mary (Lady Love)
love in art
– Pellan, Alfred
  – *L'amour fou* #6820
Loveroff, Frederick Nicholas, artiste can, 1894-1960 #6329 6330
– expositions
  – (1981) #6331
Lowe, Frederic C., artiste can, actif 1843-1856
– membre de la Toronto Society of Arts #1689
Lozeau, Jean-Baptiste, ferronnier can, ca 1694-1745 #249 250
Luc, frère
– *voir* François, Claude (frère Luc)
Lucas, Gabriel, joaillier can, XXe s.
– et Georges Delrue #2694
Lucerne (Qué), Château Lucerne
– architecture, Lawson & Little, architectes

et ingénieurs; Edwin S. Kent & Geo. W.
White Associates #9283
Lucerne (Suisse), Kunstmuseum Luzern
– expositions
  – *Michael Snow* (1979) #7258
  – *Michael Snow: Works 1969-1978, Films
    1964-1976/Michael Snow: Werke
    1969-1978, Filme 1964-1976* (1979) #7261
Luci & Associés #1502
Lucy
– *voir* Qinnuayuak, Lucy
luges et toboggans . Algonquiens #3631
luges et toboggans . Indiens des forêts du
  Nord-Est #3631
luges et toboggans . Iroquois #3631
Lui, Andrew, artiste can, 1951- #6332
Luke, Alexandra, artiste can, 1901-1967
– collection, art canadien, Robert
  McLaughlin Gallery (Oshawa, Ont) #3169
– correspondance, Jock Macdonald #6376
– élève de Hans Hofmann #402 1850
– expositions
  – (1977) #6333
– expositions, critiques #6334
– membre du Groupe des peintres
  canadiens #324
Lum, Kay, photographe can, ca 1950-
– catalogue de photographies #1023
lumière
– *voir* éclairage
– dans l'art
  – Bloore, Ronald Langley #4749
  – Chambers, Jack #516
  – Harris, Lawren Stewart #5726
  – Toronto (Ont), Electric Gallery #1798
– installations fluorescentes, Jeff Wall #7506
– lumière électrique
  – Kelman, Ralf #6038
  – sculpture canadienne (années 1960) #767
Lummis
– totems #3967
Lund, Chris, photographe can, 1923-
– catalogue de photographies #987
Lunenburg (NE)
– architecture #7836 7837
Lunenburg (NE), Lunenburg Art Gallery
– expositions
  – *Charles Wm. MacDonald: Seaman,
    Labourer, Artist, Manufacturer (1874-1967)*
    (1981) #6355
Lunenburg (NE), Soloman House
– architecture et intérieur #8549
Lurçat, Jean, artiste fr (tapisserie), 1892-1966
– professeur de Roger Caron #5005
Lussier, Denis Lionel, architecte can,
  1938-1975
– Saint-Boniface (Man), Precious Blood
  Church #8908
Lussier, Michel, sculpteur can, 1948-
– utilisation du plastique #1603
Lussier, Paul, artiste can, 1944- #6335
– fondateur, atelier Arachel (Montréal, Qué)
  #1657
Lutkenhaus, Almuth, sculpteur can, 1927-
– entretien #6336
lutte
– Cohen, Sorel, série de photographies #5130
Lutterworth (Angleterre), Saint Mary's
  Parish Church
– influence sur architecture de Lloyd
  Johnson, église en pierre (Saint Jean, NB)
  #8778
Luxembourg (Luxembourg), Musée de l'Etat
– expositions

– *10 Canadian Artists in the 1970s* (1981)
  #703
Luxfer Prism Co., atelier de vitraux
  (Toronto, Ont) #2450
Lyall, Laura Adeline Muntz, artiste can,
  1860-1930 #207 6337 6338 6339
– et Mary Evelyn Wrinch #7617
Lyceum Club (Toronto, Ont)
– et Women's Art Association of Canada
  #176
– expositions
  – (1939) #1
Lyle, John MacIntosh, architecte can,
  1872-1945
– décorations architecturales, banques
  canadiennes (années 1930) #8226
– édifices de la Banque Nouvelle-Ecosse
  #9186 9203
– expositions de groupe
  – (1933) #8224
– Halifax (NE), Banque de Nouvelle-Ecosse
  #9182
– Kingston (Ont), mémorial, Royal Military
  College of Canada #1083
– plan, accès nord-ouest de Hamilton (Ont)
  #7962
– professeur #8243
– réflexion sur l'art canadien #329
– Toronto (Ont)
  – Bank of Ottawa #9159
  – Bourse de Toronto, concours #9161
  – Dominion Bank #9188
  – Government House, concours #8748
  – Masonic Temple, concours #9062
  – Royal Alexandra Theatre #9059
  – Union Station #9531 9536
– utilisation de brique et de stuc #8052
Lyman, John Goodwin, artiste et critique
  d'art can, 1886-1967 #6340 6344
– commentaire sur James Wilson Morrice
  #6618 6619
– écrits #6346 6347
– entretien #6342
– et James Wilson Morrice #6634
– et la Société d'art contemporain (Montréal,
  Qué) #1474
– et Paul-Emile Borduas #4814
– expositions
  – (1963) #6343
  – (1966) #6345
– expositions, critiques #6341
– expositions de groupe
  – (1977) #1278 1279
– influence sur l'art abstrait québécois #1468
– peintures (années 1930) #502
– professeur de Kim Ondaatje #6733
Lynn, Washington Frank, artiste can,
  1836-1906 #1896 6348
Lynn, William H., architecte irlandais au
  Canada, actif années 1860-1870
– Québec (Qué), fortifications #7946
Lyon, N.T., artiste can (vitrail), actif
  1880-1890 #2450
Lytle, photographe can, actif 1856-1867
  #1724
Lyttleton, Westcott Whitchurch Lewis,
  officier de l'armée brit, artiste au Canada,
  1818-1879
– *Halifax Harbour Seen from McNab's Island*,
  Royal Ontario Museum (Toronto, Ont)
  #6349

M

M, périodique can #3097
M'Intyre, Thomas
– *voir* McIntyre (M'Intyre), Thomas
MacAskill, Wallace R., photographe can,
  1890-1956 #6350 6351
MacAulay, John, collectionneur can, 1895-
– collection, art canadien et art européen,
  exposition, Galerie nationale du Canada
  (Ottawa, Ont), (1954) #3212
MacCallum, James Metcalfe, médecin et
  collectionneur can, 1860-1943
– correspondance, Norman I. Gurd #1776
– et A.Y. Jackson #5917
– et Arthur Lismer #6300
– et G.Blair Laing, marchand d'oeuvres d'art
  #1686
– et le Groupe des Sept et Tom Thomson
  #1745 3237
– peintures, Tom Thomson et le Groupe des
  Sept, dons à la Galerie nationale du
  Canada (Ottawa, Ont) #3229
MacCarthy, Hamilton Plantagenet, sculpteur
  can, 1846-1939 #178 6352 6353
– réflexion sur la sculpture canadienne
  (années 1960) #727
MacCormack, Terry, photographe can, actif
  années 1970-
– catalogue de photographies #991
Macdonald, Albert Angus, artiste can, 1909-
  #6354
MacDonald, Charles William, artiste can,
  1874-1967
– expositions
  – (1980) #6355
Macdonald, Evan Weekes, artiste can,
  1905-1972 #6357
– entretien #6356
Macdonald, Grant Kenneth, artiste can,
  1909- #6358
Macdonald, Hugh John, homme d'Etat can,
  1850-1929
– résidence, Dalnavert (Winnipeg, Man)
  #8708
MacDonald, J.Blair/Barry V. Downs, agence
  can d'architecture
– *Canadian Architect*, concours, galerie d'art
  communautaire (1957) #9082
Macdonald, James Alexander Stirling, artiste
  can, 1921- #6359
MacDonald, James Edward Hervey (J.E.H.),
  artiste can, 1873-1932 #6329 6364 6365
  6366 6367 6368 6369 6372
– art et écrits, Antilles (1932) #6371
– carnets à dessin (1915-1922) #6373
– commentaire sur la peinture murale #6362
– commentaire sur les artistes et les critiques
  #6360
– commentaire sur peintures faites à bord
  d'un train (1919) #6361
– commentaire sur Tom Thomson #7350
– correspondance, Tom Thomson #7356
– écrits #92
– et Catharine Robb Whyte et Peter Whyte
  #7571
– et Edith Grace Coombs #5172
– et le Groupe des Sept #1732
– et Thoreau MacDonald #6384 6385
– ex-libris #917
– expositions

– (1933) #294
– (1965) #6370
– expositions, critiques #1710
– expositions de groupe
– (1968) #3224
– illustration et mise en page artistique #939
– influence de l'art scandinave #1788
– influence sur Charles William Jefferys #5958
– intérieur, Saint Anne's Church (Toronto, Ont) #1733
– murales, résidence de James MacCallum, Galerie nationale du Canada (Ottawa, Ont) #1745
– panégyrique #6363
– paysages #140
– Schaefer, Carl Fellman, comparaison #7157
Macdonald, James Williamson Galloway (Jock), artiste can, 1897-1960 #6374 6377
– commentaire sur Frederick Horsman Varley #7463
– correspondance d'Europe (1954-1955) #6376
– élève de Hans Hofmann #402 1850
– et British Columbia Society of Fine Arts #1978
– et Marion F.S. Mackay Nicoll #6703
– et peinture de Vancouver (CB), (années 1950) #1992
– expositions
– (1969) #6375
– (1981) #6379
– expositions, critiques #1982
– expositions de groupe
– (1978) #133 508 509
– influence sur Kenneth Edison Danby #5251
– influence sur William S. Ronald #7072
– Luke, Alexandra, commentaire #6334
– membre, Groupe des peintres canadiens #324
– professeur #2990 6378
– professeur d'Arthur McKay #6477
– Vanderpant, John A., comparaison #7459
Macdonald, John A., premier ministre can, 1815-1891
– dessins humoristiques #944
– Bengough, John Wilson #942
– peinture représentant sa maison #964
– statue, Hamilton Plantagenet McCarthy #727
MacDonald, Manly Edward, artiste can, 1889-1971
– expositions, critiques #432
MacDonald, Thomas Reid, artiste et conservateur can, 1908-1978
– expositions
– (1980) #6380
MacDonald, Thoreau, artiste can, 1901- #6381 6382 6383 6384
– commentaire sur J.E.H. MacDonald #6366 6369
– commentaire sur Tom Thomson #7364
– dessins et illustrations #6385
– illustrations, *Canadian Forum* #930
MacEachern, Ian, photographe can, 1942- #6386
MacGee, Chris, artiste et poète can, 1951-
– commentaire sur Jack Chambers #700
MacGregor, James Gamble, artiste can, 1898- #1888
MacGregor, John, artiste can, 1944- #6387
– entretien #6388
– expositions de groupe

– (1978) #665
machines . Canada
– (années 1940) #2603
machines dans l'art
– Cournoyer, Serge, sculptures #5194
MacInnis, Garfield Allister (Gar), architecte can, 1936-
– Charlottetown (IPE), Confederation Centre, concours #9089
– Saskatoon (Sask), Mendel Art Gallery #9091
Mack, T.A., ébéniste can, né 1889 #2587
MacKay, Thomas, architecte can, 1792-1855
– Ottawa (Ont) #8038
MacKeeman, Karl, artiste can, 1948- #6389
Mackenzie, Alexander, explorateur brit au Canada, 1763-1820
– expédition, autochtones #4097
Mackenzie, Cynthia, artiste can, 1952-
– entretien #6390
Mackenzie, Hugh Seaforth, artiste can, 1928-
– et réalisme #110
Mackenzie, Norman, collectionneur can, 1869-1936
– collection, art européen et art asiatique #1912
– collection, Norman Mackenzie Art Gallery (Regina, Sask) #3197
MacKenzie, Robin, artiste can, 1938-
– cartes géographiques, illustration #561
– expositions de groupe
– (1975) #1809
– (1976) #779
– photographies de paysages, Ecosse (1975-1976) #6393
– sculptures #6391 6392
– utilisation de la photographie #1057
MacLaughlan, Donald Shaw, artiste can, 1876-1938 #6394
MacLean, Robert, artiste can, 1942-1972
– tatouage, dessins #2923
Maclean's, périodique can
– illustrations, H.W. Cooper #5173
MacLeay, R.Scott, photographe can, actif 1977
– catalogue de photographies #1023
MacLennan, Toby Chapman, artiste can, 1939- #6395
– expositions de groupe
– (1974) #2050
– sculpture, art de performance #658
MacLeod, Pegi Nicol, artiste can, 1904-1949 #336 6396 6398
– et peinture de genre #392
– expositions
– (1949) #6397
Maclure, Samuel, architecte et artiste can, 1860-1929 #8384 8385
– architecture domestique #8494
– en comparaison avec Francis Mawson Rattenbury #8152
– expositions
– (1971) #8383
– Saanich Peninsula (CB), Miraloma (maintenant Latch Restaurant) #8731
– Victoria (CB), résidence d'Alexis Martin #8682
MacMillan, Harvey Reginald, collectionneur can, 1885-1975
– collection, art kwakiutl #3996
MacNab, sir Allan, homme d'Etat can, 1798-1862
– résidence, Dundurn Castle (Hamilton, Ont) #8650 8662

MacNamara, Gordon Robertson, artiste can, 1910- #6399
MacNevin, Brian, artiste can, actif années 1970
– expositions de groupe
– (1979) #1157
maçonnerie
– *voir aussi* brique; ciment, mortier et plâtre; murs; pierre
maçonnerie . Canada
– bardeaux, Québec, XVIIe s. #7860
– brique, région d'Aultsville (Ont), XIXe s. #7980
– charpente en madriers, XVIIe-XIXe s. #7712
– construction à murs creux, Ontario, XIXe s. #8004
– Louisbourg (NE) #8427
– Trois-Rivières (Qué), Forges du Saint-Maurice #7878
MacPherson, Diane, artiste can (vitrail), active 1975
– vitraux #2452
Macpherson, Duncan Ian, artiste can, 1924-
– dessins humoristiques et politiques #957 6400
– expositions
– (1980) #6401
– illustrations #855
Macri, Tommaso (Tom), sculpteur can, 1943- #2076
MacTavish, Catharine, artiste can, 1952-
– expositions, critiques #2081
Madahbee, Mel, artiste can, 1956-
– expositions de groupe
– (1981) #4173
Maday, Helene Julia, sculpteure can, 1916-
– expositions de groupe
– (1971), médailles #772
Made in Kebec, bande dessinée can #948
Madison (Wis), Elvehjem Art Center
– *voir* Madison (Wis), University of Wisconsin. Elvehjem Art Center
Madison (Wis), University of Wisconsin. Elvehjem Art Center
– expositions
– *Canadian Landscape Painting, 1670-1930: The Artist and the Land* (1973) #106
Madonne
– *voir* Marie, Vierge
Madrid (Espagne), Museo de America
– art inuit et art amérindien #3372
Madrid (Espagne), Real Academia de Bellas Artes
– Chambers, Jack, élève #5073
magasins
– *voir aussi* centres commerciaux
magasins . Canada
– (années 1940) #9372
– Colombie-Britannique, magasins en bois #8153
– Dawson City (Yukon)
– magasin de Madame Tremblay #9380 9381
– magasin Winaut #9383
– John B. Parkin Associates #8395
– magasin Eaton (années 1920) #9365
– Montréal (Qué), magasin Eaton #7933 9370
– Ontario
– XIXe-XXe s. #9379
– Toronto (Ont)
– (années 1920) #9364
– (années 1930) #9371
– Eaton Centre #9382

– Fairweather's Store #9363
– magasin Eaton #9368 9369 9370
– Mason & Risch Company Building #9328
– Northway Department Store #9366
– XIXe s.-années 1930 #8076
– Vancouver (CB), gare du Canadien Pacifique, rénovation #9546
Maggs, Arnaud, photographe can, 1926-
– expositions de groupe
  – (1981) #1070
– pochettes de disque #862
Magog (Qué), monastère de Saint-Benoît-du-Lac
– architecture, Dom Bellot #8332
Magor, Elizabeth (Liz), artiste can, 1948- #6402 6403
– *Compost Figures* et *A Concise History* #6404
– constructions en matériaux bruts (années 1970) #2065
– entretien #6406
– expositions
  – (1979) #6405
  – (1980) #6407
  – (1981) #6408
– expositions, critiques #622
– expositions de groupe
  – (1976) #2060
  – (1978) #2066
Magrini, Alex, artiste can, 1951- #640
– expositions
  – (1980) #685
Maguire Partners, agence amér d'architecture
– Los Angeles (Calif), revitalisation du quartier Bunker Hill, concours #8364
Mah, Tom, artiste can, 1951- #6409
Maher, Dean, photographe can, actif 1981
– catalogue de photographies #1023
Mahl-stick Club (Toronto, Ont)
– et Société canadienne des arts graphiques #801
Mahler, Gustav, compositeur autr, 1860-1911
– portrait, Virgil Hammock #5696
Mahon, Lilette, artiste can, m. 1956
– commentaire sur Emily Carr, professeure #5014
Maillard, Charles, artiste can, 1887-1973 #302
– commentaire sur l'Ecole des beaux-arts (Montréal, Qué), (1924-1933) #2973
– directeur, Ecole des beaux-arts (Montréal, Qué) #1456 2972
– nationalisme dans l'art #4851
– peintures (années 1930) #1460
– professeur de Jean-Paul Lemieux #6228
Maillol, Aristide, sculpteur fr, 1861-1944
– influence sur Claude Roussel #7087
Maillou (dit Desmoulins), Jean-Baptiste, architecte can, 1668-1753 #249 250
– dessin d'architecture, chapelle du Palais épiscopal de Mgr de Saint-Vallier (Québec, Qué) #8856
– Québec (Qué), Notre-Dame-des-Victoires #8858
Mailloux, Joseph, ébéniste can, actif années 1920-1940 #2184
– berceuses #2535
Mainguy, Lucien, architecte can, 1911-
– Québec (Qué), édifice de la compagnie d'assurance Les Prévoyants du Canada #7939
mains
– dessins, Ernest Lindner #6287

– sculpture inuit #4439
maison de Liechtenstein
– *voir* Liechtenstein, maison de
Maisonbasse, Jean-Baptiste
– *voir* Deschevery (dit Maisonbasse), Jean-Baptiste
Maisonneuve, Paul de Chomedey de, officier fr et gouverneur au Canada, 1612-1676
– et histoire de Montréal (Qué) #7899
– monument, Louis-Philippe Hébert #1623
maisons d'artistes
– Falk, Gathie #5408
– Morash, Barbara #6606
– Norris, Joe #6721
maisons de campagne
– *voir* châteaux et maisons de campagne
Maitland (Ont), Saint James Episcopal Church
– architecture, Arthur McClean #8382
Major, Laure, artiste can, 1930- #1418
Makahs
– culture (années 1870) #4031
– rituel du Loup #3885
Malabar, navire can
– sculptures sur bois #1604
Malach, Lorraine, artiste can, 1933-
– expositions de groupe
  – (1975) #1867
Malécites
– art #3634
– costume #3641
– vannerie #3637
– vannerie et ouvrages perlés #3628
Malepart de Grand Maison (dit Beaucour), Paul, artiste can, 1700-1756 #249 250
Maler, Miroslav, sculpteur can, 1946-
– Symposium international de sculpture environnementale de Chicoutimi (Qué), (1980) #1639
Malevich, Kasimir Severinovich, artiste russe, 1878-1935
– Gaucher, Yves, comparaison #5567
– influence sur Claude Tousignant #7401
– influence sur Lionel LeMoine FitzGerald #5450
Malewotkuk, Florence Nupok, artiste amér, 1910- #4217
Maligne Lake (Alta)
– vues photographiques
  – Warren, Mary Schaffer #7526
Malkauskas, Algie, artiste can, actif fin années 1960-
– et sculpture inuit, os de baleine, Spence Bay (TNO) #4436
Mallandaine, Edward, architecte can, ca 1827-1905
– Victoria (CB) #8145
Mallepart de Grand Maison (dit Beaucour), Paul
– *voir* Malepart de Grand Maison (dit Beaucour), Paul
Mallet, Denis, sculpteur can, ca 1670-1704 #234 235 1572
– professeur, Ecole des arts et métiers de Saint-Joachim (Saint-Joachim, Qué) #2992
Mallorytown Glass Works, fabricants de verre (Mallorytown, Ont) #2401 2416
– et William Godkin Beach #2396
Malo, André, artiste can, 1945-
– et RACE (Regroupement des artistes des Cantons de l'Est) #1536
Malraux, André, auteur fr, 1901-1976
– Plaskett, Joe, commentaire #6891

Maltais, Marcelle, artiste can, 1933- #1418 6410 6412
– à Paris (France) #1434
– entretien #6411
Malton (Ont), Aéroport international de Toronto
– architecture #9517
  – John B. Parkin Associates, avec l'aide de William Alexander Ramsay #9516
Maltwood, Katharine Emma, artiste et collectionneuse can, 1878-1961
– expositions
  – (1981) #6413
– expositions de groupe
  – (1978) #3242
Mamalilicoolas (CB)
– totems #3848
Manarey, Thelma Alberta, artiste can, 1913-
– entretien #1974
Manchester (Angleterre), Manchester Museum
– pièces de jeu, Haidas #3915
Manchester (NH), Currier Gallery of Art
– expositions
  – *Paul-Emile Borduas, 1905-1960: A Loan Exhibition* (1967) #4812
mandalas dans l'art
– Sawyer, Walter Michael #7144
– Wise, Jack Marlowe #7600 7602
Mandans
– ouvrages en piquants de porc-épic #3701
Manet, Edouard, artiste fr, 1832-1883
– influence sur James Wilson Morrice #6633
Manitoba
– architecture #8083 8094 8098
  – (années 1970) #8087
  – XIXe-début XXe s. #8102
– architecture domestique
  – (1907-1927) #8689
  – tradition ukrainienne #8691
  – XIXe s. #8692
– art #1895 1896
  – (1964-1978), Red River Exhibition #1903
  – (années 1940) #350
  – (années 1950-1970) #1884
  – (années 1970) #1860 1868 1899 1900
  – tradition ukrainienne #1843
– art et architecture (1980) #1906
– art traditionnel
  – art traditionnel ukrainien et letton #968
  – XXe s. #1897
– arts graphiques
  – (1910-1940) #1898
– bureaux de poste #9053
– croix #1625
– écoles (années 1920) #9389
– églises et arts décoratifs, tradition ukrainienne #2270
– enseignement de l'art (années 1940) #1889 1890
– gares #9543 9545
– hôpitaux (années 1950) #9029
– magasins (années 1940) #9372
– mobilier
  – (années 1920) #2463
  – XIXe s. #2584 2586
– monuments funéraires #733
– musées (années 1970) #3193
– palais de justice (avant 1930) #9007
– peinture #1893
– photographie
  – (1935-1943), Manitoba Camera Club #985
  – (années 1970) #1879 1904

– poterie, XIXe s. #2300
– poterie et ouvrages en piquants de porc-épic #2272
– sculpture en céramique (années 1970) #1864
– verre #2403 2415
– vitraux #2450
– vues
  – Hind, William George Richardson #5807
  – Howarth, Edward J. #5853
  – Lynn, Washington Frank #6348
  – Rindisbacher, Peter #7003 7009
  – Verner, Frederick Arthur #7484
– vues photographiques
  – Hime, Humphrey Lloyd #5801
  – Horetzky, Charles George #5838
Manitoba. Architectural Historical Survey of Manitoba
– photographies, architecture manitobaine #8096 8098 8102
Manitoba Camera Club
– (1935-1943) #985
Manitoba Glass Works, fabricants de verre (Beauséjour, Man) #2403 2415
Manitoulin Island (Ont)
– peinture, XXe s. #4156
Manly, Charles MacDonald, artiste can, 1855-1924
– expositions
  – (1973) #6414
– expositions, critiques #1703
Mann, Anthony, artiste can, 1927-
– dessin de monnaie olympique (1976) #778
Manning, Les, céramiste can, 1944- #6415
manoirs
– voir châteaux et maisons de campagne
Manuge, Robert, marchand d'oeuvres d'art can, 1921-
– et Manuge Gallery (Halifax, NE) #3244
Manzù, Giacomo, sculpteur it, 1908-
– Bachinski, Walter Joseph Gerard, comparaison #4578
Maoris
– art #3691
Maple Ridge (CB)
– architecture #8147
Maquart, Laurent, artiste can, 1937-
– et Jacques Guillon Designers Inc. #884
Marani, Ferdinand Herbert, architecte can, 1893-
– commentaire sur l'architecture des banques #9191
Marani, Lawson & Morris, agence can d'architecture
– Galt (Ont), Gore District Mutual Fire Insurance Company, édifice #7973
– Ottawa (Ont), Banque du Canada, siège social #9337
Marani, Morris & Allan, agence can d'architecture
– Toronto (Ont), Armée du Salut, Arthur Meighen Lodge #8516
Marani, Rounthwaite & Dick, agence can d'architecture
– Ottawa (Ont), Banque du Canada, siège social #9199
Marani & Morris, agence can d'architecture
– Toronto (Ont)
  – Banque de Montréal #9190
  – Canadian National Exhibition Grandstand #9208
  – Manufacturers Life Insurance Company building #9339
Marburg (Allemagne de l'Ouest), Philipps University
– architecture #9464
March, Peter, artiste can, actif 1842-1851
– membre de la Toronto Society of Arts #1689
Marchand, Jean Hippolyte, artiste fr, 1883-1940
– East, Benoît, comparaison #5353
Marchand, Joseph-Omer, architecte can, 1872-1936
– et architecture, style beaux-arts #7923
– Montréal (Qué), hôtel de ville #8980
– Ottawa (Ont), édifices du Parlement #8926 8927
marchands d'oeuvres d'art
– voir marché de l'art
marché de l'art
– Amérindiens
  – art #6539
    – (années 1970) #4155
  – paniers #3625
  – textiles et tissus (années 1970) #3476
– antiquités canadiennes #2114 2127 2252 2271
– antiquités canadiennes-françaises #2226 2237
– art amérindien de la côte nord-ouest (années 1960) #4121
– art amérindien et art inuit (années 1970) #3376
– art inuit #3377 4189 4200 4218 4231 4236 4238 4242 4262 4270 4276 4305 4388 4466 6270
  – Producteurs de l'Arctique canadien #4222 4291
– arts décoratifs, Iroquois (années 1960) #4123
– arts décoratifs, Thunder Bay (Ont) #2266
– Bush, Jack Hamilton #4975
– Calgary (Alta), (années 1970) #1966
– Canada
  – (1970-1974) #91
  – (1972-1974) #552
  – (1975), prédictions #585
  – (1976), étude #599
  – (1980) #688
  – (années 1950) #151 409 3214 3260
  – (années 1960) #445 446 448 529
    – galeries d'art #442
    – marchands d'oeuvres d'art #3219
  – (années 1960-1970) #123
  – (années 1970) #619 625 682 693 3236 3291 3293
    – et les femmes #562
    – Front des artistes canadiens #632
  – (années 1980) #603
– Collectionneur, Le, périodique #134
– et Max Stern #1293 1431
– et Mira Godard #161
– et William R. Watson #1272
– galeries commerciales, Robert Percival, commentaire #6834
– gravure inuit #4483
– gravure québécoise (années 1970) #1656
– Harris, Lawren Stewart, commentaire #5722
– jouets et jeux, Canada #2928
– Laing, G.Blair, commentaire #1686
– mobilier, Terre-Neuve #2520
– mobilier canadien (années 1970) #7081
– Montréal (Qué), galeries d'art
  – (1945-1970) #1264
  – (années 1970) #1495
– Montréal (Qué) et Québec (Qué), (années 1970) #1509
– Muhlstock, Louis, commentaire #6657
– Nouvelle-Ecosse, mobilier rural #2521
– Ontario, mobilier, XIXe s. #2564
– Ontario (années 1970) #1825
– peinture canadienne et peinture européenne (années 1950) #418
– peinture québécoise #1289
– photographie canadienne (années 1970) #1038
– prix des oeuvres d'art canadiennes
  – (1968-1975) #116
  – (1975-1980) #160
  – (1980) #158
– protection juridique de l'art et de l'artisanat inuit et amérindiens #3347
– Québec #1269 1340
  – et religion (années 1950) #1406
– Québec (Qué), galeries d'art (années 1970) #1519
– sculpture inuit #4396 4397 4455
  – et Alma Houston #4425
– sculpture québécoise (années 1970) #1628
– Toronto (Ont)
  – (années 1970) #1803
  – et Artists' Union of Toronto #1742
marchés d'art
– Charlottetown (IPE), (1813-1958) #7800
– Montréal (Qué) #7917
Marcil, Joseph, sculpteur can, 1941-
– expositions de groupe
  – (1980) #1663
Marega, Charles, sculpteur can, 1875-1936
– expositions, critiques #1982
– oeuvres, édifices du Parlement (Victoria, CB) #8967
Margeson, James M., photographe can, actif années 1850-1860 #1211
Maria Chapdelaine, roman can
– illustrations
  – Gagnon, Clarence Alphonse #5542 5546 5547
  – MacDonald, Thoreau #6384
Maricourt (Qué)
– arts graphiques (1972-1975) #4475
– sculpture inuit #4405
Marie, Vierge
– art québécois, XVIIe s. #1365
– et l'Enfant-Jésus dans la sculpture québécoise #1596
– l'Annonciation, sculpture québécoise, fin XVIIe-XXe s. #1633
– l'Assomption, art canadien #37
– rédemption et Jésus-Christ, Ozias Leduc #6204
– statue de l'Immaculée Conception, Salomon Marion #2683
Marie de l'Incarnation, religieuse et artiste can, 1599-1672
– broderie #2791
– ouvrages à l'aiguille #2788
– portrait, mère de Saint-Joseph #1333
Marie Le Maire des Anges, religieuse et artiste can, active années 1671-1690
– paysages, oeuvres religieuses #1328
Marie-Madeleine
– art québécois, XVIIe s. #1365
marines (peinture)
– voir scènes marines (peinture)
Marino, Carol, photographe can, 1943-
– expositions de groupe
  – (1981) #1070
Marinoff, Ivan A., architecte can, 1920-
– Saskatoon (Sask), Mendel Art Gallery,

concours #9091
Marion, Gilbert, artiste can, 1933-
– et gravure québécoise (années 1960) #1641
– expositions de groupe
– (1967) #821
Marion, Israël, artiste can, m. 1899 #1319
Marion, Salomon, orfèvre can, 1782-1832
– statue de l'Immaculée-Conception, Galerie nationale du Canada (Ottawa, Ont) #2683
Maritime Art, périodique can #25 349
Maritime Art Association
– (années 1930-1960) #1125
– expositions
– (1959-1965) #1120
– périodique, *Maritime Art* #349
Maritime Art Glass Works, fabricants de verre (NB) #2400
Mark/Musselman/McIntyre/Combe, agence can d'architecture
– Brantford (Ont), Evangel Pentecostal Church #8766
Markell, Jack, artiste can, 1919-
– expositions de groupe
– (1962) #1847
Markgraf, Waltraud Erna Else, artiste can, 1937- #6416
Markham, Michael J., artiste can, 1946-
– entretien #6417
Markham (Ont)
– fraktur #2254
– mobilier mennonite #2568
Markle, Robert Nelson, artiste can, 1936- #6418
Marks, Gerald Yanders (Gerry), artiste can, 1951- #2706
– sérigraphies #4148
Markson, Jerome, architecte can, 1929-
– Etobicoke (Ont), Martin Grove Estate #8744
– Ontario #8387
– Sault Ste Marie (Ont), Group Health Centre #9033
– Toronto (Ont)
– Jewish Community Centre #8078
– Whitburn Apartments #8514
Marlatt, John, céramiste can, m. 1868
– fondateur, Marlatt Pottery (Paris, Ont) #2330
Marlatt Pottery, fabricants de céramique (Paris, Ont) #2330
Marois, Lauréat, artiste can, 1949- #6419
Marosan, Julius, sculpteur can, 1915-
– expositions de groupe
– (1971), médailles #772
marques d'artistes
– *voir* signatures d'artistes
Marquis, Robert, photographe can, actif 1971 #997
Marr, David, ébéniste can, 1790-1871 #2573
Marsan, Jean-Claude, architecte et historien de l'architecture can, 1930-
– commentaire sur l'architecture québécoise #7746
Marsh, Charles, artiste can, 1948-
– expositions de groupe
– (1977) #1933
Marsh, Winifred Florence Petchy, artiste can, 1905-
– aquarelles, Esquimaux du caribou, Eskimo Point (TNO) #4265
Marshall, David Franklin, sculpteur can, 1928-
– expositions
– (1978) #6420

– sculpture de jardin #1849
– sculpture en pierre, Van Dusen Gardens (Vancouver, CB) #775
Marshall, Patricia (Pat), artiste can, 1951-
– entretien #6422
Marshall, Roz, artiste can, 1947-
– expositions, critiques #2081
Marshall, Willard, photographe can, actif 1856-1867 #1724
Marshall (Mars), Tanya, artiste can, 1948-
– commentaire sur l'exposition *Codpiece*, galerie Powerhouse (Montréal, Qué) #6421
Marshalore, artiste can, 1946-
– art de performance et art vidéo #655
Martel, Elisée, artiste can, 1881-1965
– et Montée Saint-Michel #1236
Martel, William M. (Bill), artiste can, actif années 1950-1960 #1121 1173
Martigues (France)
– vues
– Brymner, William #4950
Martin, Arthur N., architecte et artiste can, 1889-1961
– expositions
– (1977) #6423
Martin, David, sculpteur can, ca 1917-1959
– totem, Beacon Hill Park (Victoria, CB) #4115
Martin, Emma May, artiste can, 1865-1956 #6425
– expositions
– (1980) #6424
Martin, Félix, prêtre et architecte can, 1804-1886
– plans, église Saint-François-Xavier (Kahnawake, Qué) #8890
Martin, Henry, artiste can, 1837-1902
– père d'Arthur N. Martin #6423
Martin, Henry Byam, officier de la marine brit, artiste au Canada, 1804-1865
– expositions
– (1981) #6426
Martin, Ian, architecte can, 1922-
– Osaka (Japon), Expo 70. Pavillon du Canada, concours #9217
Martin, Jane, artiste can, 1943-
– commentaire sur Jack Chambers #700
– expositions de groupe
– (1979) #674
Martin, John (Jack), artiste can, 1904-1965
– membre du Groupe des peintres canadiens #324
Martin, Mungo, artiste can, 1880-1962 #3912 6428 6430
– et Bill Reid #6984
– *Great Killer Whale Copper*, don, Provincial Museum of British Columbia (Vancouver, CB) #4054
– influence sur Henry Hunt #5872
– peintures, University of British Columbia. Museum of Anthropology (Vancouver, CB) #6429
– totems #6427
– Beacon Hill Park (Victoria, CB) #4115
– Totem Park (Vancouver, CB) #4124
Martin, Ronald Albert (Ron), artiste can, 1943- #6432
– entretien #6431
– et l'art torontois (Ont), (années 1970) #1796
– expositions
– (1976) #6433 6434
– expositions de groupe
– (1973) #557
– (1977) #636

– (1978) #661
– (1979) #510
– (1980) #703
– (1981) #723
Martin, Thomas Mower, artiste can, 1838-1934 #6438
– commentaire sur un voyage dans les Rocheuses (1889) #6435
– et British Columbia Society of Fine Arts #1978
– expositions de groupe
– (1888) #175
– (1961) #62
– père d'Emma May Martin #6424
– réflexion sur le paysage canadien dans la peinture #6436
– théories sur l'art #6437
Martyn, H.H., & Co., sculpteurs sur bois (Cheltenham, Angleterre)
– oeuvres, édifices du Parlement (Victoria, CB) #8967
marxisme
– influence sur surréalisme #1466
Masciuch, John Edward, sculpteur can, 1944-
– utilisation de la lumière #767
masques
– Pellan, Alfred #6816
– Proch, Don #6941
masques . Algonquiens #3337 3529
– (années 1760-début XXe s.) #3633
masques . Athapascans #4083
masques . autochtones #3327
masques . Bella-Coolas #3772
– Ottawa (Ont), Musée national de l'Homme #4000
masques . Cris #3742
masques . Dorsétiens
– Button Point (Bylot Island, TNO) #4356 4357 4359
– Qikertaaluk Island (TNO), pétroglyphes #4362
masques . Haidas
– portrait #3794
– Queen Charlotte Islands (CB) #3961
masques . Hurons #3519
masques . Indiens de la côte nord-ouest #3340 3866 3894 3940 4030
– en comparaison avec masques japonais #3824
– New York (NY), American Museum of Natural History #3414
– portrait #3977 4038
masques . Indiens des forêts du Nord-Est
– (années 1760-début XXe s.) #3633
masques . Ingaliks #4083
masques . Inuit #3340 3940 4212
– Berkeley (Calif), University of California. Robert H. Lowie Museum of Anthropology #4349
– Labrador #3337 4178
masques . Iroquois #3337 3359 3489 3519 3570 3598 3613 7346
– (années 1760-début XXe s.) #3633
– cérémonie du Milieu de l'Hiver #3606
– Société des Faux Visages #3588 3595 3604 3632
masques . Kwakiutls #3348 3768 4030
– Bokwus, personnage mythique #3990
– danse de l'Oiseau-Tonnerre #3867
– en comparaison avec masques afikpos (Afrique) #3945
– en comparaison avec masques bakubas (Afrique) #3920

– Milwaukee (Wis), Milwaukee Public
    Museum #3938
masques . Onontagués #3588
masques . Salishiens #4013
masques . Squamish
– Vancouver (CB), Archives municipales
    #3864
masques . Swaihwés #4033
masques . Tlingits #3976
– utilisation de cheveux humains #3917
masques . Tsimshians #4056 4069
– portrait #3794
masques . Tsonnontouans #3508 3563 3636
– Société des Faux Visages #3533 4113
masques afikpos (Afrique)
– en comparaison avec masques kwakiutls
    #3945
masques bakubas (Afrique)
– en comparaison avec masques kwakiutls
    #3920
masques japonais
– en comparaison avec masques
    amérindiens de la côte nord-ouest #3824
mass media
– voir aussi cinéma; télévision
– Canada
    – (années 1970), et femmes #562
    – et architecture (années 1970) #7728
    – et les arts
        – (années 1950) #3254 3255 9906
        – (années 1960) #529
        – (années 1970) #542 551 583 1799 3267
            3270
    – influences américaines (années 1970)
        #3279
– General Idea #5583
Massé, Henriette Fauteux
– voir Fauteux-Massé, Henriette
masses de cérémonie . Inuit
– Conseil des Territoires du Nord-Ouest
    #4304 4386 4389
Masset (Queen Charlotte Islands, CB)
– totems, Haidas #3765
Massey, Hart Parkin Vincent, architecte can,
    1918-
– Ottawa (Ont)
    – Carleton University #9455
    – secteur des monuments aux disparus
        #8041
Massey, John, artiste can, 1950- #6439
– expositions, critiques #697 794
– expositions de groupe
    – (1980) #687 696
    – (1981) #723
Massey, Vincent, homme d'Etat et
    collectionneur can, 1887-1967
– appui à Jack Weldon Humphrey #5865
– appui à l'architecture canadienne #7737
– appui aux sciences et aux arts canadiens
    #3258
– collection, peinture canadienne
    – Ottawa (Ont), Galerie nationale du
        Canada #3227
– collection, peintures canadiennes #3220
– et Commission royale d'enquête sur
    l'avancement des arts, lettres et sciences
    (Rapport Massey) #3254 3255 3261 9906
Massey & Flanders, agence can
    d'architecture
– Ottawa (Ont), Tovell House #8519
Massicotte, Edmond-Joseph, artiste can,
    1875-1929 #6441
– paysages d'hiver #1298
– vues de Québec #6440

Masson, André, artiste fr, 1896-
– influence sur Alfred Pellan #6822
Masson, Henri L., artiste can, 1907- #1392
    6443 6444 6445 6447 6448
– et peinture de genre #392
– expositions, critiques #6442
– oeuvres (années 1950) #6446
massues . Goyoguins
– masses d'armes #3535
massues . Indiens de la côte nord-ouest
    #3785
massues . Iroquois #3489 3519 3538
massues . Kwakiutls
– masses d'armes en os de baleine #3813
massues . Skeenas #4053
massues . Tsimshians #4053
– Londres (Angleterre), British Museum
    #4048
Matane (Qué), Galerie d'art du cégep de
    Matane
– expositions
    – De la figuration à la non-figuration dans
        l'art québécois (1977) #1461
matériaux d'architecture
– voir aussi béton; bois; brique; ciment,
    mortier et plâtre; fonte; maçonnerie;
    pierre; stuc
– Calgary (Alta), (1875-1914) #8121
– Canada
    – (1867-1967) #7695
    – début XXe s. #7652
– Charlevoix (Qué), habitations #8629
– Conseil national de recherches. Division
    des recherches sur le bâtiment #7715
– Halifax (NE), XIXe s. #7822
– Kingston et comté de Frontenac (Ont),
    XIXe s. #8015
– Manitoba, XIXe-début XXe s. #8102
– Nouvelle-Ecosse, XVIIIe s. #7815
– Ontario
    – (1831-1861) #8009
    – habitations (années 1920) #8646
– Québec
    – (1800-1870) #7947
    – habitations, XVIIe-XIXe s. #8614
    – habitations, XVIIe-XVIIIe s. #8581 8603
        8621
    – XIXe-XXe s. #7926
– Québec et Ontario (1763-1860),
    descriptions faites par voyageurs #8527
– toitures, XVIIe-XIXe s. #7703
– Trois-Rivières (Qué), Forges du
    Saint-Maurice #7878
matériaux de construction
– voir matériaux d'architecture
matériaux et techniques . arts graphiques
– gravures sur bois de fil, Walter Joseph
    Phillips #6854 6855
– lithographie, Robert Allen Paterson #6778
– pointes sèches en couleurs, David Brown
    Milne #6546 6552 6563 6564
matériaux et techniques . costume
– (1780-1967) #2849
– (1800-1821), costume féminin #2860
– (1822-1839), costume féminin #2863
– (1840-1866), costume féminin #2885
– (1848-1868) #2887
– (1867-1898), costume féminin #2889
– (années 1870) #2854 2859
– (années 1870), costume féminin #2878
– (années 1920), costume féminin #2906
– ceinture fléchée #2818 2827
– costume lithuanien #2892
– XIXe s., costume féminin #2846

matériaux et techniques . courtepointes
    #2799
matériaux et techniques . dessin
– Binning, B.C. #4730
– Séminaire des jésuites, XIXe s. #2982
matériaux et techniques . peinture
– Biéler, André Charles #4720 4721
– nihonga, Miyuki Tanobe #7324 7325
matériaux et techniques . photographie
– Karsh, Yousuf #6025 6033
– Notman, William #6723
– Patterson, Freeman #6780 6781 6782
matériaux et techniques . poterie #2280 2317
– XIXe s. #2290 2367
– XXe s. #2390
matériaux et techniques . textiles
– tapis crochetés #2750 2752
– teinture #2745 2749
– tissage #2719 2721 2730
    – jacquard #2740
    – Salishiens #3963
matériaux et techniques . travaux à l'aiguille
    #2785
– broderie ukrainienne #2782
mathématiques, art et
– Gnass, Peter #5619
– peintures et sculptures canadiennes, XXe
    s. #471
– Rockburne, Dorothea #7060
Mathers, Charles Wesley, photographe can,
    1868-1950 #6451
– et Ernest Brown #4935
– photographies, collection Ernest Brown
    #1949
Mathers & Haldenby, agence can
    d'architecture
– Toronto (Ont)
    – Banque de Nouvelle-Ecosse #9192
    – Imperial Oil Building #9340
    – Toronto General Hospital #9032
    – University of Toronto. John P. Robarts
        Research Library #9048 9050 9052
    – William H. Wright Building #9338
Matheson, Roderick, officier de l'armée can,
    1793-1873
– résidence, Matheson House (maintenant
    Perth Museum), (Perth, Ont) #8670
Mathieson, Hugh, ébéniste can, actif années
    1850-1860 #2584
Mathieu, André, sculpteur can, 1952-
– utilisation du bois #1634
Mathurin, Jacques, photographe can, ca
    1952-
– catalogue de photographies #1032
Matisse, Henri, artiste fr, 1869-1954
– Bush, Jack Hamilton, comparaison #4977
– commentaire sur James Wilson Morrice
    #6619
– enseignement de l'art aux artistes
    canadiens (années 1940) #384
– influence sur Clark Holmes McDougall
    #6464
– influence sur David Brown Milne #6567
– influence sur Goodridge Roberts #7046
– influence sur Jack Hamilton Bush #4972
    4973
– influence sur James Wilson Morrice #6629
– influence sur Jeanne Leblanc Rhéaume
    #6994
– influence sur John Goodwin Lyman #6340
    6344
– influence sur Paul-Emile Borduas #4841
– influence sur Paul Fournier #5486
– influence sur Pierre Jean Clerk #5118

– influence sur Robert La Palme #6119
– Morrice, James Wilson, comparaison #6631
Matsqui (CB)
– architecture #8147
Matsubara, Naoko, artiste can, 1937- #6450
– expositions de groupe
– (1976) #6449
Matta-Clark, Gordon, artiste amér,
    1945-1978
– expositions de groupe
– (1980) #8237
Matthews, James S., archiviste can, actif
    années 1930-1970
– et photographies de J.A. Brock & Co.,
    Archives municipales de Vancouver
    (Vancouver, CB) #2021
Matthews, Marmaduke, artiste can,
    1837-1913
– et Thomas Mower Martin #6435 6438
– expositions, critiques #186
Mauger, Jacques
– voir Gadois (dit Mauger), Jacques
Maugham, William Somerset, auteur brit,
    1874-1965
– commentaire sur James Wilson Morrice
    #6619
Maurault, Olivier, prêtre can, 1886-1968
– et Ozias Leduc #6201 6203
Mavor, James, éducateur can, 1854-1925
– collection #1713
Maw, Samuel Herbert, architecte can,
    1881-1952
– Toronto (Ont), Bourse de Toronto #9187
Maw & Co., fabricants de carreaux (Broseley
    et Jackfield, Angleterre)
– carreaux de céramique, habitations,
    Toronto (Ont), XIXe s. #2373
Maw & Drewitt, agence can d'architecture
– Moose Jaw (Sask), hôtel de ville, concours
    #8978
Mawson, Thomas Hayton, architecte
    paysagiste brit, urbaniste au Canada,
    1861-1933
– architecture canadienne #7648
– Canada, urbanisme et architecture
    paysagiste #8388 9405
– Halifax (NE), Dalhousie University #9408
Max, John, photographe can, 1936-
– catalogue de photographies #996
Max-Ingrand, Maurice, artiste fr (vitrail),
    1908-1969
– vitraux, église Saint-Arsène (Montréal,
    Qué) #2448
Maximilien II, roi de Bavière, 1811-1864
– et émergence d'artistes amérindiens
    reconnus #3486
Maxwell, Edward, architecte can, 1867-1923
– Calgary (Alta), Hotel Palliser #9271
– Montréal (Qué)
– Arts Club, rénovation d'habitation pour
    #1314
– Dominion Express Company Building
    #9306
– gare Windsor #9537
– Musée des beaux-arts de Montréal #9063
    9065
– oratoire privé #8557
– Ottawa (Ont), Departmental and Justice
    Buildings, concours #8921
– Québec (Qué), Château Frontenac #9278
– Regina (Sask)
– édifices du Parlement #8944 8945 8957
    8958 8959 8960 8961
– War Memorial Museum, concours #9073

– Winnipeg (Man), Legislative and
    Executive Building, concours #8946
Maxwell, William Sutherland, architecte can,
    1874-1952
– Calgary (Alta), Hotel Palliser #9271
– Montréal (Qué)
– Arts Club, rénovation d'habitation pour
    #1314
– Dominion Express Company Building
    #9306
– Musée des beaux-arts de Montréal #9063
    9065
– oratoire privé #8557
– Ottawa (Ont), Departmental and Justice
    Buildings, concours #8921
– Québec (Qué), Château Frontenac #9278
– Regina (Sask)
– édifices du Parlement #8944 8945 8957
    8958 8959 8960 8961
– War Memorial Museum, concours #9073
– Winnipeg (Man), Legislative and
    Executive Building, competition #8946
Maxwell & Pitts, agence can d'architecture
– Québec (Qué), Château Frontenac #9278
May, Henrietta Mabel, artiste can, 1884-1971
– expositions, critiques #283
May, Karl, artiste can, 1901-1975 #6452
– expositions
– (1976) #6453
May, R.G., photographe can, actif années
    1880 #1950
May, Walter (Wally), sculpteur can, 1950-
– expositions de groupe
– (1978) #2066
Mayerovitch, Harry, architecte et artiste can,
    1910-
– réflexion sur ses sculptures #6454
Mayhew, Elza Edith, sculpteure can, 1916-
    #6455
– membre du groupe Limners #2043
Maynard, Hannah Hatherly, photographe
    can, 1834-1918 #2018 6456 6457 6458
– et Victoria Theatre Photographic Gallery
    (Victoria, CB) #2027
– photographies, Indiens de la côte
    nord-ouest #2033
Maynard, Max, artiste can, 1903- #2011
Maynard, Richard, photographe can,
    1832-1907
– photographies, Indiens de la côte
    nord-ouest #2033
Mayor, Robin, artiste can, 1937-
– entretien #6459
– expositions, critiques #2072
– expositions de groupe
– (1979) #2075
McArthur, James J., photographe can,
    1856-1925
– photographies d'arpentage #1014 1015
– Montagnes Rocheuses (années
    1880-1890) #1874
– utilisation de l'appareil
    photogrammétrique #989
McBride & Gilbert, agence can
    d'architecture
– London (Ont), Lord Roberts School #9388
McCall, Helen, photographe can, active
    années 1920-1930 #2018 6460
McCall & Co., fabricants de meubles (Ont)
– (années 1860-1960) #2573
McCargar, William C., artiste can, 1906-1980
    #1881
McCarter, Nairne & Partners, agence can
    d'architecture

– Vancouver (CB) #9514
– Victoria (CB), B.C. Telephone, bureaux
    #9301
McCarter & Nairne, agence can
    d'architecture
– Vancouver (CB), Marine Building #8171
    9356
McCarthy, Doris Jean, artiste can, 1910-
    #6461
McCausland, J., & Co., atelier de vitraux
    (Toronto, Ont)
– vitraux
– Montréal (Qué) #2448
– Toronto (Ont), Trinity College Chapel
    #2461
McCausland, Joseph, artiste can (vitrail),
    1829-1885
– fondateur, Canada Stained Glass Works
    #2449
– vitraux, édifices du Parlement (Victoria,
    CB) #8967
McCausland, Robert, artiste can (vitrail),
    1856-1923
– vitraux
– Manitoba #2450
– Toronto (Ont), hôtel de ville #2449
McClean, Arthur, architecte can, 1779-1864
    #8382
McClure, sir Robert John Le Mesurier,
    navigateur et explorateur brit, 1807-1873
– expédition dans l'Arctique (1851-1853)
    #278
McConnell, Clyde S., artiste can, 1944-
– entretien #6462
McConnell, Newton, artiste can, 1877-1940
– dessins humoristiques, Toronto Daily News
    #943
McCord, David Ross, collectionneur can,
    1844-1930
– collection, Université McGill. Musée
    McCord (Montréal, Qué) #222 223
McCormack, W.A., sculpteur can, actif 1897
– commentaire sur la sculpture sur bois et
    l'architecture #726
McCormick, Alexander, artiste can (vitrail),
    actif 1899-1913 #2450
McCulloch, James Frederic, artiste can,
    1905-1932
– expositions
– (1978) #6463
McCurry, Harry Orr, conservateur can,
    1889-1964 #3036
– directeur, Galerie nationale du Canada
    (Ottawa, Ont) #3049
– et Galerie nationale du Canada (Ottawa,
    Ont) #3050
McDermott, Michaelin, photographe can,
    1947-
– expositions de groupe
– (1979) #1904
McDonald, John, commerçant de fourrures,
    ca 1771-1866
– résidence, Inverarden (Cornwall, Ont)
    #8673
McDonald, Robert, collectionneur amér, XXe
    s.
– collection, artefacts, Piégans #3759
McDougall, Clark Holmes, artiste can,
    1921-1980 #6465
– expositions
– (1977) #6464
McDougall, Ian, architecte can, 1939-
– Calgary (Alta), résidence d'Ian McDougall
    #8727

McDougall, Keith, photographe can, ca
1948-
– catalogue de photographies #1032
McDougall, Smith & Fleming, agence can
d'architecture
– Montréal (Qué), Hôpital général de
Montréal #9030
McEachern, Susan, photographe can, 1951-
– expositions, critiques #1067
McElcheran, William Hadd, sculpteur can,
1927- #6466
McEwen, Jean Albert, artiste can, 1923-
#6467 6468
– et Claude Monet #6470
– expositions
– (1973) #6469
– (1978) #6471
– expositions de groupe
– (1955) #1408
– (1964) #462
McEwen, John Alan, sculpteur can, 1945-
– expositions
– (1979) #6472
– expositions, critiques #697 794
– *Western Channel*, University of Lethbridge
(Lethbridge, Alta) #797
McFarlane, Walter, artiste can, ca 1917-
#6473
McGill, James, marchand can, 1744-1813
– et château de Ramezay (Montréal, Qué)
#3082
– portrait, Louis Dulongpré #5321
McGlade, Terry, artiste can, actif années
1970
– expositions de groupe
– (1979) #1157
McGlashen, Stewart, and Son, agence brit de
sculpture (Edimbourg, Ecosse)
– St. John's (TN), Sergeants' War Memorial
#7783
McGowan, John, collectionneur can, XXe s.
– collection, objets en verre, Canada #2424
McGrath, James Arthur (Jim), artiste amér,
1928-
– concepts cosmologiques #554
McGrath, Jerry, artiste can, actif 1980
– expositions de groupe
– (1980) #1832
McGrath, Judy Waldner, artiste can, 1936-
– atelier, Spence Bay (TNO) #4249 6474
McGregor, Edward, artiste can, actif
1847-1872
– membre de la Toronto Society of Arts
#1689
McGuire, Patrick (Pat), artiste can, 1943-
1970
– influence sur Pat Dixon #5294
McInnes, Harvey A., artiste can, 1904-
#1881
McInnis, Robert F.M., artiste can, 1942-
– portraits #715
McIntyre (M'Intyre), Thomas, ébéniste can,
actif années 1830-1870 #2571
McKay, Arthur Fortescue, artiste can, 1926-
#6475 6477
– expositions
– (1961) #1913
– (1968) #6476
– (1979) #6478
– expositions de groupe
– (1967) #490 1916
McKay, David, artiste can, 1945- #6479
McKee, John, artiste can, 1941-
– expositions de groupe

– (1981) #1885
McKeen's Corner (NB), All Saints' Church
– architecture, Edward Shuttleworth Medley
#8776
McKendry, Blake, collectionneur can, 1919-
– restauration, Tunis Snook Farm (près de
Kingston, Ont) #8681
McKendry, Ruth, collectionneuse can, 1920-
– collection, courtepointes, Ontario, XIXe s.
#2804
– restauration, Tunis Snook Farm (près de
Kingston, Ont) #8681
McKenzie, Jim, artiste can, 1953- #6480
McKenzie, Robert Tait, sculpteur can aux
E-U, 1867-1938 #10 6481 6482 6483 6484
6486 6487 6488
– commentaire sur statues d'athlètes #6485
– Danby, Ken, comparaison #5252
McKenzie, Tait
– *voir* McKenzie, Robert Tait
McKim, Mead & White, agence amér
d'architecture
– influence sur architecture canadienne
#7652
– Montréal (Qué), Banque de Montréal
#9168
– Winnipeg (Man), Banque de Montréal
#9202 9205
McKinley, Donald Lloyd, designer et
ébéniste can, 1932- #6489
McKinley, Ruth Gowdy, céramiste can,
1931-1981 #2395
McLagan Furniture Co., fabricants de
meubles (Stratford, Ont)
– (années 1920) #2547
McLaren, Agnes Maud, artiste can, née 1882
– illustrations #916
McLaren, John Wilson (Jack), artiste can,
1896-
– gravures sur bois debout #804
McLaren, Norman, artiste et cinéaste can,
1914- #6490 6491 6492 6493 6494 6498 6499
– dessins #6496
– entretien #6497
– expositions
– (1965) #6495
– FitzGerald, Lionel LeMoine, comparaison
#5452
McLaughlin, Agnes, artiste can, ca 1913-
#6500
McLaughlin, Isabel, artiste can, 1903- #309
McLaughlin, Samuel, photographe can,
1826-1914
– expositions de groupe
– (1970) #1675
– photographies, construction d'édifices
#1019
– *The Photographic Portfolio* #1048
McLean, George E., artiste can, 1939- #6501
McLean, James Stanley, collectionneur can,
1876-1954
– collection, art canadien, XXe s. #3210 3226
McLean, John, artiste brit, 1939-
– expositions de groupe
– (1981) #722
McLean, Terry, artiste can, ca 1935- #6502
McLean, Thomas Wesley (Tom), artiste can,
1881-1951 #6503
McLeod, Barclay, architecte can, 1936-
– Vancouver (CB), Caulfield Cove Town
Houses #8746
McLeod, Peter, homme d'Etat can, m. 1852
– portrait, Théophile Hamel #5690
McLuhan, Herbert Marshall, éducateur et

auteur can, 1911-
– réflexion sur l'art et la technologie #513
McMichael, Robert, collectionneur can,
1921-, et Signe Kirsten Sorensen
McMichael, collectionneuse can, 1921-
– et McMichael Canadian Collection
(Kleinburg, Ont) #3172
McMillan, David, photographe can, 1945-
#1879
– expositions
– (1980) #6504
– expositions, critiques #1046 1060
– expositions de groupe
– (1977) #1033
– (1978) #669
– (1979) #1037
McMordie, Michael, architecte can, 1939-
– théories sur l'architecture #7746
McMurtie, William Birch, artiste amér au
Canada, 1816-1872
– vues de l'île de Vancouver (CB) #6505
McNally, Edwin (Ed), artiste can, 1916-1971
– illustrations #855
McNamara, Robert Strange, homme d'Etat
amér, 1916-
– portrait, Art Green #5650
McNamee, Donald Keith (Don), artiste can,
1938-
– expositions
– (1968) #6506
McNicoll, Helen Galloway, artiste can,
1879-1915
– expositions
– (1974) #6507
McOnie, Alan, photographe can, actif
années 1970
– catalogue de photographies #998
McQuesten, famille, Can, XIXe-XXe s.
– résidence, Whitehern (Hamilton, Ont)
#8664
McRitchie, Donald (David), artiste can,
1881-1948
– dessins humoristiques, *Montreal Daily Mail*
#943
McWilliams, Allan, artiste can, 1944- #6508
– expositions de groupe
– (1976) #2060
– (1978) #2066
Meanwell, Jack, artiste can, 1919-
– expositions de groupe
– (1977) #646
Meares, Hermina (Ina), artiste can, 1921-
#6509
Meares, John, officier de la marine brit,
artiste au Canada, ca 1756-1809
– vues du détroit de Nootka, Vancouver
Island (CB) #2002
mécénat
– *voir* protection des arts
Mechanic's Institute . Canada
– (années 1830-1860) #3064
– Ontario, XIXe s. #2261
médailles
– *voir* monnaies et médailles
médailles Massey en architecture
– (1952) #8205
– (1955) #8206
– (1958) #8207
– (1961) #8208 8209 8210
– (1964) #8211
– (1967) #8212 8213 8214
– (1970) #8215 8216
– sondage auprès des architectes (1962)
#8305

– Shane, Audrey Patricia MacKay. *Shadow and Substance: A Computer Assisted Study of Niska and Gitksan Totem Poles* #4032
– Sibun, Piers Seton. *Ceramics in Quebec: Past, Present, Projected* #2331
– Sommer, Warren Frederick. *Upon Thy Holy Hill: A Historical Geography of the Early Vernacular Church Architecture of the Southern Interior of British Columbia* #8916
– Sparling, Mary Christine. *The British Vision in Nova Scotia, 1749-1848: What Views the Artists Reflected and Reinforced* #1215
– Sproull, Jane. *Towards a Definition of Styles and Patterns in Thule Eskimo Decorative Art* #4372
– St-Arnaud, Micheline. *Les diffuseurs de l'innovation artistique au Québec* #1450
– Steida, Sieglinde. *The Development of a Handbook of Bio-bibliographies of Canadian Artists who Illustrated Children's Books Published between 1815-1975* #934
– Stewart, Susan Jane Hopkins. *The Hudson's Bay Company's Contribution to the Work of Three Important Artists in Their Territory, 1821-1860* #273
– Théberge, Pierre. *La peinture optique et ses sources* #1445
– Thom, William Wylie. *The Fine Arts in Vancouver, 1886-1930: An Historical Survey* #2003
– Thomas, Ann. *The Role of Photography in Canadian Painting, 1860-1900: Relationships between the Photographic Image and a Style of Realism in Painting* #262
– Thomas, Christopher Alexander. *Dominion Architecture: Fuller's Canadian Post Offices, 1881-1896* #9055
– Todd, Patricia Ann. *James D. Duncan (1806-1881): Catalogue of Works and Introduction to His Art* #5336
– Tolmatch, Elaine. *L'esthétique du paysage chez Arthur Lismer* #6306
– Tremblay, Claire. *L'oeuvre profane de Joseph Légaré* #6215
– Tuele, Nicholas Craig. *Sophia Theresa Pemberton: Her Life and Art* #6829
– Tye, Diane. *A Contextual Study of a Newfoundland Folk Artist: Patrick J. Murphy, Bell Island* #6664
– Van Wyk, Dirk W. *Canadian Prairie Landscape Drawings* #1855
– Vastokas, Joan Marie. *Architecture of the Northwest Coast Indians of America* #3939
– Vincelli, Brendan MacLean. *The Symbolic Function of the Bank of Montreal Building on the Place d'Armes, 1846: An Image of the English Mercantile Aristocracy* #9200
– Wade, Catherine Jill. *Red River Architecture 1812-1870* #8097
– Wadland, John Henry. *Ernest Thompson Seton: Man in Nature and the Progressive Era, 1880-1915* #7172
– Walker, Doreen Elizabeth. *The Treatment of Nature in Canadian Art Since the Time of the Group of Seven* #496
– Wallot, Jacques-Albert. *La pédagogie de Borduas et celle de Dumouchel* #3001
– Wight, Darlene. *Watercolour and Landscape in Early Canada* #279
– Wong, Maureen Lansing. *A Study of the Painting of Lawren Harris* #5730
– Woodley, Virginia Anne. *Jack Bush 1909-1977: The Events Which Led to His International Reputation* #4975

– Wylie, Elizabeth. *The Development of Spirituality in the Work of Lionel LeMoine FitzGerald, 1890-1956* #5453
Memramcook (NB), maison Célestin-Bourque
– architecture #8543
Ménage, Pierre, constructeur can, ca 1648-1715 #234 235
Mendel, Frederick Salomon, collectionneur can, 1888-1976
– collection, Mendel Art Gallery (Saskatoon, Sask) #72 3187
– collection, peintures #1912
Mendelow & Keywan, agence can d'architecture
– Don Mills (Ont), Beth-El Synagogue #8903
Menkès, René, architecte can, 1932-
– Montréal (Qué), Les Terrasses #7886
mennonites au Canada
– architecture domestique #8715
– art traditionnel #2268
– arts décoratifs #2140 2246 2264 2267
  – comté de Waterloo (Ont) #2243
  – Ontario #2250
– courtepointes #2729
– et Nancy-Lou Patterson #6783
– fraktur #2259
– mobilier #2568 2572 2585
– ouvrages en papier #2265
– poupées et costumes #2942
Menses, Jan, artiste can, 1933- #6511
Menut, Jean-Baptiste, ferronnier can, actif 1857-1868 #2704
Menut, Thomas, ferronnier can, actif début XIXe s. #2704
Menzies, Archibald, naturaliste brit au Canada, 1754-1842
– expédition, Indiens de la côte nord-ouest #4062
– réaction à l'art de la côte nord-ouest #2009
Mercer, June, artiste can, active 1955
– bijoux #2695
Merchants Bank
– Ontario (1915-1919) #9170
Mercier, Monique, artiste can, 1934- #6512
Mère des Ours . Haidas #3868
– sculpture d'argilite #3862 3901
Mère des Ours . Tsimshians #3868
Meredith, John, artiste can, 1933- #6513 6515
– expositions
  – (1974) #6514
  – (1980) #6516
– expositions de groupe
  – (1967) #480
  – (1971) #98
  – (1977) #636
Meriden Britannia, atelier d'orfèvrerie (Hamilton, Ont) #2405
– (1879-1922) #2642
Merola, Mario Virgilio, artiste can, 1931- #6517 6519 6521
– et plasticiens #1439
– expositions
  – (1971) #6520
  – (1976) #6522
– murale, Pavillon canadien, Exposition universelle et internationale, 1958 (Bruxelles, Belgique) #6518
Merrett, Brian, photographe can, 1945-
– catalogue de photographies #997 999
Merrett, Campbell, architecte can, 1909-
– Ottawa (Ont), Carleton University #9455
Merriam, D.H., ébéniste can, actif années 1840-1850 #2571

Merriam, John H., ébéniste can, actif années 1840-1850 #2571
Merriam, Joseph, ébéniste can, né ca 1780, actif 1824-1829 #2571
Merrick, John, architecte can, actif 1810-1820
– Halifax (NE), Mount Uniacke House #8528
Merrick, Paul McCarley, architecte can, 1938-
– restauration, Orpheum Theatre (Vancouver, CB) #9135
Mery, Daniel, artiste can, 1934-
– art graphique télédiffusé #909
Mesnard, Albert, architecte can, 1847-1909
– Oka (Qué), église #8818
métal anglais
– voir étain
Metal Arts Guild
– et Harold Stacey #7274
Metal Arts Guild of Nova Scotia
– expositions
  – (1951) #1192
Metcalf, Eliab, artiste amér au Canada, 1785-1834 #1377
Metcalfe, Eric W. (Dr. Brute), artiste can, 1940-
– art vidéo #2044
– expositions de groupe
  – (1979) #2070
Meteghan (NE), Vieille Maison
– architecture et intérieur #8531
méthodologie
– voir histoire de l'art
métier de forgeron
– voir aussi ouvrages de ferronnerie
métier de forgeron . Canada
– boutiques de forgerons représentées dans sculptures sur bois #4992
– Québec #2697 2705 2707 2711
métiers à tisser
– voir aussi tissage jacquard
métiers à tisser . Amérindiens #3413
métiers à tisser . Canada
– XIXe s. #2735
métiers à tisser . Salishiens #3963
Metiq Co-operative (Belcher Islands, TNO) #4459
Métis
– architecture #8102
– art #3731
– broderie #4110
– ouvrages perlés #3677
métros, constructions . Canada
– Montréal (Qué) #1531 9549 9550 9551 9552
  – station Angrignon #9555
  – station Peel #9553
– Toronto (Ont) #9547 9548 9554
Metson, Graham, artiste can, 1934- #6523
Mexique
– influence sur K.J. Butler #4982
Meyer, Henry Hoppner, artiste can, ca 1782-1847
– père de Hoppner Francis Meyer #6524
Meyer, Hoppner Francis, artiste can, actif 1832-1863 #6524
– membre de la Toronto Society of Arts #1689
Mezei, Lesley N., artiste can, actif 1968
– art par ordinateur #517
Mia et Klaus, photographes can, actifs années 1960
– catalogue de photographies #987
Michaud, Jean, architecte can, 1919-
– Montréal (Qué), bureau de poste de Ville Mont-Royal #7857

Michaud, Pierre Joseph, prêtre et architecte can, 1823-1902 #1319
Michel, André, artiste can, 1945- #6525
Michener, Robert, artiste can, 1935-
– expositions, critiques #6526
Michener, Sally, artiste can, 1935- #6527
– expositions
– (1979) #6528
– sculptures en céramique (années 1970) #2065
Micklethwaite, Frank W., photographe can, 1849-1925 #1024
Micmacs
– art #3528 3569 3634 3643
– brassards #3572
– chamanisme #3556
– costume #3641
– éventails et jeux #3500
– mocassins #3554
– ouvrages perlés et ouvrages en piquants de pors-épic #3624
– pétroglyphes #3614 3617
– pictogrammes #3494
– pipes #3565
– travail de la pierre #3531
– vannerie #3630
– vannerie et ouvrages perlés #3628
– wampum #3497
Middleton, W.E.K., photographe can, ca 1900-
– catalogue de photographies #991
Midéwiwins . Algonquiens #3580
– parchemins #3702
Midéwiwins . Cris #3726
– influence sur peinture du XXe s. #4154
Midéwiwins . Indiens de la côte nord-ouest
– masques #4038
Midéwiwins . Saulteux/Ojibwa #3492 3602 3726
– et assemblages de rochers, Whiteshell (Man) #3578
– influence sur la peinture, XXe s. #4154
– parchemins #3539 3626 3661
– robes en peau de bison #3517
Midéwiwins . Siouens
– parchemins #3702
Mies van der Rohe, Ludwig, architecte germano-américain, 1886-1969
– intégration de l'art à l'architecture #8232
– Montréal (Qué)
– île des Soeurs #8587
– Westmount Square #9326
– Toronto (Ont), Toronto-Dominion Centre #9197 9301 9345 9348
Mignard, Pierre, artiste fr, 1612-1695
– influence sur Antoine-Sébastien Plamondon #6886
Mihalcheon, Jean Lapointe, sculpteur et céramiste can, 1929- #2392 6529
Mikkanen, Raili Marjatta, artiste can, 1950- #6530 6531
Mikutowski, Frank, architecte amér, actif années 1950-
– Toronto (Ont), hôtel de ville et Civic Square, concours #8981
Milan (Italie), Galleria Levi arte contemporanea
– expositions
– Borduas, Riopelle e la giovane pittura canadese (1962) #1420
Miles, John Christopher, artiste can, 1832-1911 #6532 6533
– expositions de groupe
– (1969) #1180

– Wilde, Oscar, commentaire #238
Milette, Alexis, sculpteur et architecte can, 1793-1869 #258 259 6947
– influence de la famille Baillairgé #1582
– intérieur, église, Berthierville (Qué) #8874
Mill, Richard, artiste can, 1949- #1524 1544
– expositions
– (1978) #6534
– (1979) #6535
– expositions de groupe
– (1981) #1565
Millán, Gonzalo, artiste can, 1947-
– réflexion sur son oeuvre #1552
Millar, C.Blakeway (Blake), architecte can, 1935-
– Georgian Bay (Ont)
– F.S. Eaton, résidence estivale #8519
– résidence estivale #8745
– Toronto (Ont), Trolley Restaurant #8078
Millarville (Alta), Leighton Centre
– Leighton, Barbara, professeur #3017
Mille-Iles
– résidences estivale, XXe s. #8524
Miller, Alfred Jacob, artiste amér, 1810-1874
– dans les provinces de l'Ouest #1859
– peintures représentant Amérindiens, Archives publiques du Canada (Ottawa, Ont) #6536 6537
Miller, David G., photographe can, 1949-
– photographies documentaires #1556
Miller, Gary, artiste can, 1950- #6538
– commentaire sur la mise en marché de l'art amérindien #6539
Miller, George Martel, architecte can, 1854-1933
– Guelph (Ont), Macdonald Consolidated School #3176
Miller, John Bellamy, photographe can, 1869-1906 #6540
Miller, Maria Frances Ann Morris, artiste can, 1813-1875 #241 242 1118 1219 6541 6542
Miller, Martha, photographe can, active 1979
– expositions de groupe
– (1979) #2069
Millet, Jean-François, artiste fr, 1814-1875
– et Wyatt Eaton #5355 5357
– Huot, Charles Edouard, comparaison #5876
– influence sur Wyatt Eaton #5356
– Walker, Horatio, comparaison #7498 7499 7500 7503
Millette, Claude, sculpteur can, 1957-
– concept d'espace #1631
Millikin, William, actif années 1840
– dessins humoristiques et société québécoise #6543
Mills, Charles, architecte can, 1860-1934
– Hamilton (Ont)
– Bank of Hamilton #9160
– Hamilton Terminal Station #9527
Mills & Hutton, agence can d'architecture
– architecture domestique #8494
– Hamilton (Ont), YWCA, édifice #7957
Mills-Cockell, John, musicien can, 1943-
– et Intersystems #767
Milman, Adolf, artiste russe en France, actif années 1920
– professeur de Edwin Headley Holgate #5818 5819
Milne, David Brown, artiste can, 1882-1953 #336 461 6544 6547 6549 6550 6551 6554 6555 6556
– aquarelles, conséquences de la Première

Guerre mondiale (1918-1919) #6557
– artiste moderniste #507
– commentaire sur la pointe sèche en couleurs #6546
– commentaire sur ses aquarelles #6545
– correspondance #536
– estampes #6565
– et Douglas M. Duncan, protecteur des arts #119 541 570 3223
– et G.Blair Laing, marchand d'oeuvres d'art #1686
– et Paraskeva Clark #5112
– et Vincent Massey #3227
– expositions
– (1955) #6552
– (1967) #6558
– (1971) #6559
– (1976) #6561
– (1980) #6563 6564 6566
– (1981) #6567
– expositions de groupe
– (1975) #589 592
– notes et correspondance (1920-1921) #6560
– Painting Place, Galerie nationale du Canada (Ottawa, Ont) #6562
– paysages #347
– (années 1930) #338
– peinture
– (années 1930) #502
– Biennale de Venise (1952) #399
– Massey, Vincent, collection #3220
– McLean, J.S., collection #3228
– McMichael Canadian Collection (Kleinburg, Ont) #3172
– réflexion sur son oeuvre #6548 6553
Milne, Eleanor, artiste can, 1926-
– entretien #6569
– sculptures, édifices du Parlement (Ottawa, Ont) #755
– sculptures et vitraux, édifices du Parlement (Ottawa, Ont) #6568
Milne, Gilbert Alexander, photographe can, 1914-
– catalogue de photographies #995
– photographies de la Seconde Guerre mondiale #1107
Milne, Graham, photographe can, actif années 1970
– catalogue de photographies #998
Milojevic, Peter, artiste can, actif 1969
– art par ordinateur #528
Milwaukee (Wis), Milwaukee Public Museum
– masques kwakiutls #3938
mimêsis
– dans la peinture québécoise #1267
Minden, Robert, photographe can, 1941-
– entretien #6570
mines . constructions . Canada
– provinces de l'Ouest #8083
mines . constructions . Etats-Unis
– Ouest américain #8083
mines d'or et exploitation minière
– vues
– Colombie-Britannique
– (années 1860) #2004
– Hind, William George Richardson #5811
– Klondike, ruée vers l'or, 1898 #2085
– vues photographiques, Colombie-Britannique, Charles Wesley Mathers #6451
mines et exploitation minière
– extraction de l'argilite pour la sculpture

haida #3944
- extraction de la stéatite pour la sculpture inuit #4409 4416
miniatures . Canada
- (1760-1860), Montréal (Qué) #1377
- Crist, Lela Gurnee #5209
- Field, Robert #5432 5433
- Montréal (Qué), (1760-1860) #1376
- Québec, art traditionnel #1291
- Rindisbacher, Peter #7007
- sculpture en céramique #2302
- Wrinch, Mary Evelyn #7618
miniatures . Grande-Bretagne
- XIXe s., influence sur peinture canadienne #1118
Minìpoka . Pieds-Noirs #3749
ministère des Affaires culturelles
- voir Québec. Ministère des Affaires culturelles
ministère des Affaires du Nord
- voir Canada. Ministère des Affaires du Nord
ministère des Affaires extérieures
- voir Canada. Ministère des Affaires extérieures
ministère des Affaires indiennes et du Nord
- voir Canada. Ministère des Affaires indiennes et du Nord
ministère des Travaux publics et de l'Approvisionnement
- voir Québec. Ministère des Travaux publics et de l'Approvisionnement
Ministic Carvers Co-op (Garden Hill, Man) #4153
Minneapolis (Minn), Walker Art Center
- expositions
    - American Indian Art: Form and Tradition (1972) #3359
minoteries
- voir moulins
Mirabel (Qué), Aéroport international de Montréal. Aérogare
- architecture, PGL Architectes #9518
Miramichi (NB)
- villages irlandais #8523
Miró, Joan, artiste esp, 1893-
- influence sur Alfred Pellan #6805 6822
- influence sur Francis Coutellier #5196
- influence sur Jack Hamilton Bush #4973
- influence sur John Meredith #6516
- influence sur Pierre Gendron #5581
- influence sur Pierre Jean Clerk #5118
- influence sur Robert La Palme #6119
miroirs . Canada
- Ontario (années 1790-1857) #2558
miroirs . Niskas #3804
miroirs . Tsimshians #3804
miroirs dans l'art
- Canada #525
- Morris, Michael #6641
Miron, Claire, artiste can, 1923- #6571
Mission (CB)
- architecture #8147
Mission (CB), Westminster Abbey
- vitraux #2460
missionnaires français
- et Amérindiens, XVIIe s. #1354 1358 1363
Mississauga (Ont), Sheridan College School of Crafts and Design
- fabrication artisanale du verre #2440
Mistassins
- art #4080 4100
- chasse, talismans #4075
- ouvrages en piquants de porc-épic #3701

Mistro, Walter del, artiste can, 1912-
- mosaïques, basilique Sainte-Anne (Sainte-Anne-de-Beaupré, Qué) #6572 6573 8865 8866
Mitchel, Owen, photographe can, actif années 1970
- catalogue de photographies #991
Mitchell, Janet, artiste can, 1915-
- entretien #1974
- expositions
    - (1977) #6574
Mitchell, Louisette Gauthier
- voir Gauthier-Mitchell, Louisette
Mitchell, Michael, photographe can, 1943-
- expositions
    - (1978) #6575
- expositions, critiques #6576
Mitchell, Thomas, artiste brit au Canada, ca 1833-1924
- photographies et aquarelles, expédition britannique dans l'Arctique (1875-1876) #240
Mitchell, Thomas Wilberforce, artiste can, 1879-1958
- expositions, critiques #1710
Mitchell & Creighton, agence can d'architecture
- Montréal (Qué), édifices Jacobs #9305
Mitchell & Raine, agence brit d'architecture
- Regina (Sask), édifices du Parlement, concours #8955
Mitra, Shyamal, photographe can, actif années 1970-
- catalogue de photographies #1023 1032
Mitton, Edward Stanley, architecte can, né 1880
- Colombie-Britannique, bungalows #8684
mobiles
- Trudeau, Yves #7435
mobilier
- voir aussi armoires; berceaux; buffets; bureaux (mobilier); coffres; conservation et restauration, mobilier; lits; miroirs; mobilier de style géorgien; mobilier de style Sheraton; mobilier de style Windsor; ornements et mobilier de jardin; rembourrage; sièges (mobilier); sofas; style Chippendale; tables; travail du bois
- dans collections appartenant aux musées canadiens #2484
- mobilier pour enfants, fin XIXe s.-années 1930 #2932
mobilier . Allemagne
- XIXe s., influence sur mobilier ontarien #2576 2577
mobilier . Canada #63 2107
- (1608-1867) #2120
- (1837-1887) #253
- (1910-1961), Canadian National Exhibition (Toronto, Ont) #1
- (1967-1969) #2115
- (années 1850) #1692
- (années 1920) #2465 2547
- (années 1930) #2466
- (années 1940) #2602 2603 2604
- (années 1950) #2467 2468 2610
    - et National Industrial Design Committee #2606
- (années 1970) #2224 7081
- (années 1980) #2487
- (avant 1867), Canada anglais #2470
- Acadie #7804
    - sièges (mobilier) #2492
    - XVIIIe-XIXe s. #2516

- Baker, Isaac Bennett #2581
- Barker, Charles Edward #4609
- Bersudsky, Sid #4711
- Bowmanville (Ont), XIXe s. #2556
- Bush, Robin B. #4979 4980
- Charlottetown (IPE), Province House #8937 8938
- comté de Colchester (NE), XIXe s. #2515
- Cormier, Ernest #8347
- Côté, Jean-Baptiste #5187 5188
- Direction des parcs nationaux. Politique de reconstruction de bâtiments historiques #7758
- Doan, John et Ebenezer #8351 8352
- Foisy, Dennis #5458
- Fournier, Arthur #5485
- Gemeinhardt, John #5579
- Graham, Kent #2596
- Green, Daniel #2517
- guide pour collectionneurs #2101 2104 2125 2131 2252 2486
- Hamilton (Ont), Whitehern #8664
- Hebb, Howard D. #2510
- Hébert, Julien #5766
- Holder, Thomas Cook, et Henry Arthur #2505 2506
- île aux Coudres (Qué) #2168
- île d'Orléans (Qué) #1252
- Ile-du-Prince-Edouard, XVIIIe-XIXe s. #2498 2508 2518
- Jacques & Hay Co. #2546 2559
- James, Ralph #2583
- Kingston (Ont) #1680
    - (1800-1867) #2567
- Kleyn, Robert #6063
- Levasseur (dit Delor), Jean-Baptiste-Antoine, et François-Noël Levasseur #269 270
- MacGregor, John #6388
- Manitoba, XIXe s. #2584 2586
- Maritimes, XIXe s. #2147
- McKinley, Donald Lloyd #6489
- mennonites #2568 2572
- mobilier de Vilnius, comté de Renfrew (Ont), (années 1860) #2565
- Montréal (Qué)
    - (1800-1850) #2538
    - Ecole du meuble (années 1930) #2976
    - maison Cormier #8347
    - maison Saint-Gabriel #8597
    - Place des Arts #9092
    - Soeurs Grises #8862
    - XVIIe-XVIIIe s. #2522
- Moore, John Warren #2512 6603
- Mount Uniake (NE), Uniake House #8534
- musées, techniques d'identification #2478
- Niagara (Ont) #2569 2571
- Nouveau-Brunswick #2150 2491 2503
    - (années 1760-1920) #2511
    - XIXe s. #2501
    - XVIIIe-XIXe s. #2495 2500
        - Saint-Jean (NB), Musée du Nouveau-Brunswick #2504
- Nouvelle-Ecosse #2521
    - décorations #1206 1207 2514
    - XIXe s. #2513
    - XVIIe s.-années 1840 #2494
    - XVIIe-XIXe s. #2489
    - XVIIIe-XIXe s. #2496 2499
- Ontario #2570
    - (1780-1900) #2577
    - (1800-1837), Upper Canada Village (Morrisburg, Ont) #2549
    - (1850-1900) #2580

– (années 1790-1850) #2550
– (années 1790-1857) #2558
– tradition germanique #2263
– utilisation de la peinture, XIXe s. #8013
– XIXe s. #2245 2552 2561 2573 2576
– Ontario et Provinces de l'Atlantique, XVIIIe-XIXe s. #2475
– Ottawa (Ont)
  – Earnscliffe #8652
  – Musée national de l'Homme. Centre canadien d'études sur la culture traditionnelle #963
– Ouest canadien, traditions ethniques, fin XIXe-début XXe s. #2585
– Perth (Ont), Matheson House (maintenant Perth Museum) #8670
– Petit Fort Garry (Man), caserne #8482
– Ploethner, Frederick K. #6896
– Québec #1327 2237 2544
  – (1613-1870), style provincial français #2191
  – (1660-1760) #2540
  – (1700-1820) #2537
  – (1875-1915) #1364
  – (1930-1935), Ecole technique de Montréal (Montréal, Qué) #2970
  – (années 1940) #2523
  – (années 1970) #2533
  – fin XVIIe-milieu XIXe s. #2527
  – XVIIe-XIXe s. #2128 2524 2541
    – influence européenne #2221
  – XVIIe-XVIIIe s. #1320 2181 2217 2526 2529 2530 2531 2539 2543
  – XVIIIe s. #2545
  – XVIIIe-XIXe s. #2532 2536
    – mobilier anglais #2542
– Québec (Qué)
  – Couvent des ursulines #8810
  – Hôpital-Général #9022
– Saskatchewan, fin XIXe s.-1921 #2587
– Schlombs, Wolfgang, collection #2485
– Spencer, Hugh #2551
– style géorgien #2477 2479 2480 2481 2482 2488
– style victorien #2472
– Terre-Neuve #1155 2520
  – XIXe-début XXe s. #2519
  – XVIIIe s.-années 1850 #2502
– thème décoratif du castor #56
– Tonnancour, Jacques Godefroy de #2608
– Toronto (Ont), (1800-1865) #2563
– tradition germanique #2140 2251
– Tunis Snook Farm (près de Kingston, Ont) #8681
– utilisation de décorations laquées #2548
– Victoria (CB) #2269
– Windsor (NE), maison Shand #8546
– Winnipeg (Man)
  – Deer Lodge #9260
  – Palais législatif #8951
– Witmer, Joseph #2578
– XIXe s. #2099
– XIXe s.-années 1920 #2463
– XVIIe s.-1867 #2110
– XVIIe-XIXe s. #2464
– XVIIIe-XIXe s. #2474 2594
– Zadow, J. Albert #2582
mobilier . Etats-Unis
– (1760-1840), influence sur mobilier canadien #2477
– (1780-1900), influence sur mobilier ontarien #2577
– (années 1780), influence sur mobilier du Nouveau-Brunswick #2495

– (années 1970), en comparaison avec mobilier québécois #2533
– fin XVIIIe s., influence sur mobilier québécois #2537 2543
– style géorgien, en comparaison avec mobilier canadien #2479 2481 2482
– XIXe s., exportation en Ontario #2575
– XIXe s., influence sur mobilier ontarien #2549 2552 2576
– XVIIIe-XIXe s., exportation dans la région de Niagara (Ont) #2569
– XVIIIe-XIXe s., influence sur mobilier ontarien #2550
mobilier . France
– (1660-1760), influence sur mobilier québécois #2540
– XIXe s., influence sur mobilier ontarien #2549
– XVIIe-XVIIIe s., en comparaison avec mobilier québécois #2530 2531
– XVIIe-XVIIIe s., influence sur mobilier québécois #2529 2539 2543
mobilier . Grande-Bretagne
– (1760-1840), influence sur mobilier canadien #2477
– (1780-1900), influence sur mobilier ontarien #2577
– (années 1810), influence sur mobilier du Nouveau-Brunswick #2495
– fin XVIIIe s., influence sur mobilier québécois #2537 2543
– style géorgien, en comparaison avec mobilier canadien #2481
– XIXe s., influence sur mobilier ontarien #2552
– XVIIIe-XIXe s., influence sur mobilier ontarien #2550 2576
– XVIIIe-XIXe s., mobilier apporté dans la région de Niagara (Ont) par officiers militaires #2569
mobilier . Italie
– (années 1970), en comparaison avec mobilier québécois #2533
mobilier . Pologne
– XIXe s., influence sur mobilier ontarien #2576 2577
mobilier . Suède
– (années 1970), en comparaison avec mobilier québécois #2533
mobilier baroque
– Ontario (années 1860), mobilier fabriqué par immigrants polonais #2565
mobilier d'église
– voir aussi balustrades; retables; tabernacles
mobilier d'église . Canada
– Joliette (Qué) #1287 8876
– L'Islet (Qué), église Notre-Dame-de-Bon-Secours #8879
– Lockport (Man), Saint Andrew's Church #8909
– Montréal (Qué), église Notre-Dame #8839
– Québec (1650-1925) #1592
– Sainte-Anne-de-Beaupré (Qué), basilique Sainte-Anne #1601 1602
mobilier de style géorgien
– Canada #2477 2479 2480 2481 2482 2488
– Ontario, sièges (mobilier) #2553
– Saint-Jean (NB) #2490
mobilier de style Sheraton
– Québec #2542
– Terre-Neuve #2502
mobilier de style victorien
– Canada #2472 2559
– Terre-Neuve #2502

mobilier de style Windsor
– berceuses, Québec #2536
– sièges (mobilier) #2476
  – Ontario #2553 2560
mocassins . Algonquiens #3631
– Lac Barrière (Qué) #3544
– ouvrages en piquants de porc-épic #3652
mocassins . Amérindiens #2241 2872 3424
mocassins . Arapahos #3554
mocassins . Cris #3651
mocassins . Dakotas
– dessins symboliques #3648
mocassins . Gros-Ventres #3651
mocassins . Hurons
– broderie en poil d'orignal #3513
mocassins . Indiens des forêts du Nord-Est #3554 3631
mocassins . Indiens des plaines #3651 3656 3666
– ouvrages en piquants de porc-épic #3652
mocassins . Iroquois #3489 3631
mocassins . Micmacs #3554
mocassins . Pieds-Noirs #3651
mocassins . Potéouatamis
– Parry Island Reservation (Ont) #3540
mocassins . Saulteux/Ojibwa #3539 3540 3554
mocassins . Siouens #3651 3666
– ouvrages en piquants de porc-épic #3652
– semelles décorées (années 1880-1910) #3740
mocassins . Têtes-de-Boule #4079
mode
– voir aussi costume
– (1882-1910) #2897
– (années 1870)
  – dans journaux #2859
  – dans revues #2878
– (années 1920), dans revues et catalogues #2906
– (années 1920-1930), Eaton's Weekly News #2851
modèles
– voir artistes et modèles
modèles de broderie . Canada
– Colombie-Britannique (années 1860) #2786
– mennonite, XIXe-XXe s. #2267
– Ontario #2787
– Robertson, Maria (1843) #2790
– XVIIIe-XIXe s. #2792
modernisme
– voir aussi art abstrait; post-modernisme
– Canada
  – (années 1920) #289
  – (années 1920-1940), architecture #7668
  – (années 1930) #319
– et Alfred Pellan #1448
– et James Wilson Morrice #6623
– et Jean-Paul Lemieux #6228
– et l'Académie royale des arts du Canada (années 1930) #329
– et le Groupe des Sept #1767
– et Paul-Emile Borduas #4851
– et Pierre Gauvreau #5576 5578
– Plaskett, Joe, commentaire #6889
– plasticiens et Painters Eleven #720
– Québec (années 1940) #1462
– Saskatchewan (années 1940-1950) #1919
Modigliani, Amedeo, artiste it, 1884-1920
– influence sur Gerald Gladstone #5612
– Macdonald, Grant Kenneth, comparaison #6358
Moffat, Normand, artiste can, 1949- #1511
Moisan, Gatien, artiste can, 1939- #1549 1551

6577
Moiseiwitsch, Tanya, artiste brit au Canada,
  1914-
– décors #472
Mol, Leo, artiste can, 1915- #6578
– entretien #6580
– expositions
    – (1975) #6579
– vitraux #2450
Molinari, Guido, artiste can, 1933- #1294
  1542 1543 6582 6585 6591
– concept d'espace #6589
– dessins #6593
– écrits #6586
– en comparaison avec Piet Mondrian #1457
– entretien #6581 6587
– et art minimal #1483
– et Claude Tousignant #7398
– et op'art #1445
– et plasticiens #1439
– expositions
    – (1974) #6584
    – (1976) #6588
    – (1979) #6592
    – (1981) #6594
– expositions de groupe
    – (1955) #1408
    – (1959) #1414
    – (1967) #480 490
    – (1968) #522 1263
    – (1971) #98
    – (1973) #556
    – (1977) #636
    – (1980) #703
    – (1981) #1471
– participant, Symposium on 20th Century
  Canadian Culture (Washington, DC),
  (1977) #621
– peintures (1953-1956) #1454
– réflexion sur l'art canadien
    – (années 1960) #478
    – (années 1970) #620
– réflexion sur son oeuvre #6590
– sculptures (années 1960) #1484
– symposium, Musée du Nouveau-Monde
  (La Rochelle, France), (1980) #1559
– utilisation de la couleur #468 1425
    – peintures en damiers (1969-1970) #6583
Mollise (Morris), Mâli Christianne Paul
  (Christina), artiste can, ca 1804-1886
– artiste et modèle #6635
Molsons Bank
– architecture (années 1920) #9173
monastères
– voir aussi couvents
monastères canadiens
– Magog (Qué), monastère de
  Saint-Benoît-du-Lac #8332
Moncornet, Baltasar, artiste fr, ca 1600-1668
– portrait de Samuel de Champlain, erreur
  d'attribution #191
Moncton (NB), Aberdeen School
– architecture, F.Neil Brodie #9387
Moncton (NB), Banque de Nouvelle-Ecosse
– architecture, Sharp & Horner #9174
Moncton (NB), Université de Moncton
– gravure (années 1970) #1185
– Roussel, Claude, directeur, Département
  des beaux-arts #7088
Moncton (NB), Université de Moncton.
  Galerie d'art
– expositions
    – Annie D. Savage: Drawings and
      Watercolours (1975) #7129

    – Claude Roussel (1977) #7089
    – Roger Savage (1979) #7135
    – The Murray and Marguerite Vaughan Inuit
      Print Collection/Collection d'estampes inuit
      (1982) #4498
Mondou, Pierrette, artiste can (tapisserie),
  1945- #1282 6595
Mondrian, Piet, artiste holl, 1872-1944
– Borduas, Paul-Emile, comparaison #4813
– concept d'espace #1441 4816
– et l'art abstrait #422
– influence sur art Québécois #1483
– influence sur Claude Tousignant #7401
– influence sur Fernand Leduc #6186
– influence sur Guido Molinari #6588 6591
– influence sur les plasticiens #1457
– influence sur Pierre Jean Clerk #5118
– influence sur Robert La Palme #6119
– utilisation de la couleur, influence sur la
  peinture montréalaise (Qué) #1425
– Westerlund, Mia, comparaison #7545
Monet, Claude, artiste fr, 1840-1926
– Christensen, Dan, comparaison #5104
– influence sur Jean Albert McEwen #6470
– influence sur Lionel LeMoine FitzGerald
  #5450
Monette, Georges Alphonse, architecte can,
  1870-1941
– Montréal (Qué)
    – école catholique, boulevard
      Côte-des-Neiges #9387
    – édifice La Patrie #9303
Mongeau, Jean-Guy, artiste can, 1931- #6596
Mongrain, Claude, sculpteur can, 1948- #681
  6597
– entretien #6598
– expositions de groupe
    – (1977) #782
    – (1980) #706
Monk, James, Can, 1745-1826
– tapisserie à l'aiguille, rideaux de lit, Royal
  Ontario Museum (Toronto, Ont) #2784
Monk, Lorraine Althea Constance Spurrell,
  conservatrice can, 1922- #993
– entretien #1020
– et Office national du film. Service de la
  photographie #1028
monnaie
– voir aussi monnaies et médailles
monnaie canadienne
– représentation du paysage (1930-1970)
  #759
monnaies et médailles
– hausse-cols #2634 2655
– médailles amérindiennes #728 763 2101
  3645 3646
monnaies et médailles . Canada
– (années 1680-1830) #2628
– Colville, Alex #5145 5148 5150
– De Pédery-Hunt, Dora #5275
– gouverneurs généraux du Canada,
  médailles #764
– guide pour collectionneurs #2104
– Hahn, Emanuel Otto #5680
    – pièce d'un dollar en argent, 1935 #5681
– lieutenant-gouverneurs du Canada,
  médailles #757
– MacAskill, Wallace R., Bluenose, dessin
  #6351
– McKenzie, Robert Tait #6483 6484 6487
– médailles de tempérance (années 1870)
  #724
– médailles militaires #2900
– milice canadienne #2874

– monnaie, imagerie #759
– monnaie olympique (1976) #778
– Ottawa (Ont), Archives publiques du
  Canada. Collection nationale de médailles
  #772
– thème décoratif du castor #23 56
– Toronto (Ont), Royal Ontario Museum.
  Collection Sigmund Samuel #3135
– XVIIe-XIXe s. #232
monnaies et médailles . Etats-Unis
– Toronto (Ont), Royal Ontario Museum.
  Collection Sigmund Samuel #3135
monnaies et médailles . France
– portraits, Louis XIV et Louis XV #1598
monogrammes
– bocaux de fruits, Canada #2413
Mont-Joli (Qué), cottage Laberge
– et Héritage canadien du Québec #7871
Mont-Joli (Qué), manoir Wexford
– et Héritage canadien du Québec #7871
mont Sainte-Marie (Qué), centre de
  villégiature
– architecture, Eberhard Henrich Zeidler
  #7886
Montagnais
– amulettes #4075
– art #4082
– ouvrages perlés #4076 4103
– peau de caribou #3622
– raquettes #2812
– récipients #4078 4086
Monte-Carlo (Monaco)
– vues, Franklin Milton Armington #4550
Montebello (Qué), Château Montebello
– architecture #9295
Montée Saint-Michel (Montréal, Qué) #1236
Montgomerie, Stewart, artiste can, 1941-
– sculptures #1151
Montpetit, Guy, artiste can, 1938- #6600
– murales, Montréal (Qué) #6601
– remise en question de l'influence des
  artistes plasticiens #6599
Montréal (Qué)
– affiches (années 1970) #880
– architecture #7909 7913 7927 7930 7933 8604
    – (1642-années 1970) #7918 7934
    – (1880-1914) #7928 7929
    – (1880-1915) #7921
    – (années 1850) #7920
    – (années 1870-1920) #7843
    – (années 1920) #7656
    – (années 1950) #7673
    – (années 1960) #7693 7698 7862 8213 9220
      9400
    – centre-ville
        – (années 1950-1960) #7901
        – (années 1960-1970) #7925
    – édifices en pierre grise #7922
    – matériaux d'architecture, XIXe-XXe s.
      #7926
    – utilisation de terre cuite (années
      1880-1920) #7750
    – Vieux-Montréal #7904 7905 7910 7911
      7919
    – XIXe s. #7915 7916
    – XVIe s.-années 1840 #7898
    – XVIIe-XIXe s. #7899
    – XVIIIe s. #7861
    – XXe s., concept d'espace #7748
– architecture domestique #8576 8620
    – (1698-années 1940) #8570
    – (années 1910) #8492 8493 8494 8496 8556
        – maisonnettes #8555
    – (années 1920) #8499 8562

– fin XIXe s. #8610
– maisons de campagne #8572
– maisons en brique, début XIXe s. #8521
– maisons en terrasses, XIXe s. #8653
– seigneuries #8611
– XIXe s. #8612
– XVIIe-XIXe s. #8505 8559
– architecture et art
  – XVIIe s.-années 1950 #7900
– architecture et expansion urbaine #7906
  7931
– art #1265
  – (1880-1910) #214
  – (1880-1965) #1228
  – (1908-1965) #1261
  – (1950) #1400
  – (1968-1970) #1481
  – (1976), *Corridart*, art dans la rue,
    exposition #1522 5091 5092
  – (1976), *Corridart*, *Mosaicart* et *Artisanage*,
    art dans la rue, expositions #615
  – (1976), exposition *Corridart* #1530
  – (années 1840) #1301
  – (années 1890) #1311
  – (années 1910) #1317
  – (années 1940) #1443
  – (années 1940-1950) #1426
  – (années 1940-1960) #1437
  – (années 1940-1970) #571
  – (années 1950) #389 429
  – (années 1950-1970) #131
  – (années 1960) #90 441 519 1479 1480
    1484
  – (années 1970) #1489 1504 1509 1541 1548
  – automatisme #1449
  – Independent Art Association #1379
  – stations de métro #1531
  – XXe s. #145 567
– art vidéo #605 1498 1499 1537 1550
– arts décoratifs (1740-1760) #2218
– arts décoratifs et architecture (1880-1914)
  #1367
– arts graphiques
  – (années 1940-1960) #1641
  – (années 1960-1970) #1652
  – (années 1970) #1655
  – XXe s. #1648
– banques (1845-1933) #9201
– berceuses #2535
– conservation de l'architecture #7914
  – façades #7766
– costume
  – (1890-1910) #2861
  – XIXe s. #2837
  – XVIIe s., costume masculin #2821
– croix #1569
– écoles
  – écoles élémentaires
    – (1950-1968) #9422
    – (années 1950) #9419
  – XIXe-XXe s. #9426
– édifices récréatifs #9081
– églises #8886
  – (années 1960) #1435
  – XIXe s. #8821
– expansion urbaine #7902
– fortifications
  – Boisberthelot de Beaucours, Josué #8336
– galeries d'art
  – (1945-1970) #1264
  – (années 1960) #442
  – (années 1970) #1495
– gares #9538
– gratte-ciel (années 1960) #9318

– hôtels, XVIIe s.-années 1950 #9287
– immeubles à bureaux
  – (années 1950-1960) #9300
  – bureaux d'architectes (années 1940)
    #9297
– miniatures et silhouettes (1760-1860) #1376
  1377
– mobilier
  – (1800-1850) #2538
  – XVIIe-XVIIIe s. #2522
– monuments, fin XIXe s.-années 1920 #1623
– musées #3098 3108
– orfèvrerie #2197
  – orfèvrerie de traite amérindienne, fin
    XVIIIe-début XIXe s. #2634 2659
  – XIXe s. #2630 2674
  – XVIIe-XIXe s. #2685 2686
  – XVIIIe s. #2677
  – XVIIIe-XIXe s. #2650
– peinture
  – (1860-1890) #264
  – (1860-1960) #1253
  – (1870-1970) #97
  – (1933-1970) #498
  – (1938-1948) #378
  – (1953-1956) #1454
  – (1954-1955) #1408
  – (1955-1965) #1471
  – (années 1920-1950) #424
  – (années 1930) #589 592 1460
  – (années 1940) #1390 1397
  – (années 1940-1950) #412 1416 1426 1432
  – (années 1940-1960) #1438 1445
  – (années 1950) #1403 1752
  – (années 1950-1960) #1263 1415 1425 1469
  – (années 1960) #520 1418
  – XXe s. #507 1463
– peinture et photographie de paysages
  (1860-1890) #271 272
– photographie (années 1970) #992 1003
  1494
– poterie (années 1970) #2331
– sculpture #1572
  – (années 1890) #727
  – (années 1960) #767 1485
  – (années 1970) #1624
– sculpture sur bois #1573 1575
  – XVIIIe-XIXe s. #1593
– séminaires et couvents (1642-1913) #7932
– universités (années 1960) #9401
– vitraux #2448 2462
– vues
  – (1803-1878) #7924
  – (années 1960) #1427
  – Delfosse, Georges #5279
  – Hébert, Adrien #5761 5762
  – Kroupa, Bohuslar #6104
  – sur soupière (ca 1840) #2370
  – Surrey, Philip Henry #7286 7288 7289
  – Tanobe, Miyuki #7322 7323 7324 7325
  – XIXe s. #1337
  – XVIe-XIXe s. #927
  – XVIIe-XVIIIe s. #1325
– vues photographiques
  – (1850-1900) #1061
  – Kieffer, Daniel #1562
  – Notman, William #6725
  – Szilasi, Gabor #7309
Montréal (Qué), 1306, rue Amherst
– expositions
  – *03 23 03: premières rencontres
    internationales d'art contemporain,
    Montréal 1977* (1977) #634
Montréal (Qué), académie des Saints Noms

de Jésus et de Marie
– architecture, Charles Aime Reeves #9388
Montréal (Qué), American Prudential
  Building
– tapisserie, Andrée Beauregard #4653
Montréal (Qué), Appartements Château
– architecture, Ross & Macdonald; Harold
  Lea Fetherstonhaugh, architecte associé
  #8558
Montréal (Qué), Appartements Gleneagles
– architecture #7933
Montréal (Qué), Appartements Trafalgar
– architecture #7933
Montréal (Qué), Architects Building
– architecture, Ross & Macdonald #9312
Montréal (Qué), Archives nationales du
  Québec
– Poirier, Conrad, photographies #6897
Montréal (Qué), Art Association of Montreal
  #1294 3114
– *voir aussi* Montréal (Qué), Musée des
  beaux-arts/Montreal Museum of Fine
  Arts
– (1847-1909) #3079
– (1847-1947) #1246
– (1860-1912) #1343
– (1879), ouverture du musée #3075
– (1908-1965), Salons de printemps #1261
– (1928-1929), expositions #307
– (1950), critique du choix et du
  fonctionnement du jury #1443
– (années 1890) #188
– et Benaiah Gibb #3110
– et Daniel Fowler #5488
– et Doris Minette Judah #5980
– et James Wilson Morrice #6634
– et Musée des beaux-arts de Montréal
  #9063
– et William Brymner #4953
– exposition, photographies et dessins
  d'édifices québécois (1924) #7842
– expositions
  – *Exhibition of Paintings by Cornelius
    Krieghoff, 1815-1872* (1934) #6086
  – *Les arts du Canada français, 1613-1870*
    (1946) #1331
  – *The Arts of French Canada, 1613-1870*
    (1946) #1330
  – *The Development of Painting in Canada,
    1665-1945/Le développement de la peinture
    au Canada, 1665-1945* (1945) #34
– expositions, critiques
  – (1864) #1303
  – (1865) #1304
  – (1880) #1308
  – (1883) #1310
  – (1892-1893) #179
  – (1913) #1316
  – Académie royale des arts du Canada
    – (1915) #210
    – (1917) #283
    – (1928) #303
    – (1929) #312
    – (1931) #323
    – (1935) #328
  – *Arts and Crafts Exhibit* (1923) #2160
  – Groupe des peintres canadiens (1940)
    #348
– Gagnon, Clarence Alphonse, élève #5544
  5548
– Lismer, Arthur, professeur #6295
– nationalisme et peinture de paysages, fin
  XIXe s. #271 272
– Pellan, Alfred, exposition de ses oeuvres

(1942) #6801
– Savage, Anne Douglas, élève #7130 7132
– typographie (années 1940) #922
Montréal (Qué), atelier Arachel #1657
Montréal (Qué), Atelier libre de recherches graphiques #1495 1642
– et Richard Lacroix #6126
Montréal (Qué), Bank of British North America
– architecture, Barott, Blackader & Webster #9164
Montréal (Qué), Bank of Toronto
– architecture, Hogle & Davis #9167
Montréal (Qué), Banque canadienne de Commerce
– architecture, Darling & Pearson #9153
Montréal (Qué), Banque de commerce canadienne impériale
– architecture, Peter Dickinson #9194
Montréal (Qué), Banque de Montréal
– architecture
    – Wells, John #9200
    – Wells, John; McKim, Mead & White #9168
– plaques en pierre Coade #7908
Montréal (Qué), Banque de Montréal. Siège social
– architecture #9183
Montréal (Qué), Banque Royale du Canada
– architecture #7933
    – York & Sawyer; Sumner Godfrey Davenport, architecte associé #9176
Montréal (Qué), Baron Byng High School
– Savage, Anne Douglas, professeur #7130
Montréal (Qué), basilique Saint-Jacques-le-Majeur
– architecture #7899
Montréal (Qué), Bell Canada
– architecture, Barott & Blackader #9310
Montréal (Qué), Bibliothèque municipale
– architecture #7923
Montréal (Qué), Bibliothèque nationale du Québec
– expositions
    – Livres d'artistes: le livre illustré québécois, 1967-1977 (1978) #1659
Montréal (Qué), bibliothèque Saint-Sulpice
– architecture, Eugène Payette #9039 9415
– Leduc, Ozias, exposition de ses oeuvres (1916) #6210
Montréal (Qué), bureau de la douane
– architecture, John Ostell #7917
Montréal (Qué), bureau de poste de Ville Mont-Royal
– architecture, Jean Michaud et Raymond Tait Affleck #7857
Montréal (Qué), Canadian Express Company Building
– architecture, Hutchison & Wood #9304
Montréal (Qué), Casa Loma
– expositions
    – Les moins de 35: du 22 janvier au 4 février (1973) #1501
    – Québec Underground: 1962-1972 (1973) #1502
– expositions, critiques
    – Québec Underground: 1962-1972 (1973) #1500
Montréal (Qué), Caserne centrale des pompiers
– architecture #7933
Montréal (Qué), cathédrale Saint-Jacques
– baldaquin #8826
Montréal (Qué), cathédrale

Saint-Jacques-le-Majeur
– peintures, Georges Delfosse #5278
Montréal (Qué), cégep du Vieux-Montréal
– Garnier, Jacques, Vingt personnages #5557
Montréal (Qué), Centaur Galleries #1004
Montréal (Qué), Centre canadien d'architecture/Canadian Centre for Architecture #7749
Montréal (Qué), Centre d'esthétique industrielle
– fermeture (1970) #2621
Montréal (Qué), Centre marial des pères Monfortains
– architecture, Roux & Morin #8840
Montréal (Qué), Centre olympique
– architecture #9128
Montréal (Qué), centre Saidye Bronfman/Saidye Bronfman Centre
– expositions
    – Canadians: A National Photography Show about People/Canadiens: exposition nationale de photographie ayant les gens comme thème (1979) #1035
    – Changing Visions: The Canadian Landscape/Aperçus divers: le paysage canadien (1976) #617
    – Gift from the Douglas M. Duncan Collection and the Milne-Duncan Bequest/Le Don provenant de la collection Douglas M. Duncan et le legs Milne-Duncan (1971) #541
    – Imprint '76 (1976) #833
    – Les moins de 35: du 22 janvier au 4 février (1973) #1501
    – The People Within/Les Gens de l'intérieur (1976) #4266
Montréal (Qué), Cercle universitaire
– expositions, critiques
    – Guité, Suzanne #1400
Montréal (Qué), chapelle de l'Invention-de-la-Sainte-Croix
– architecture #8862
Montréal (Qué), chapelle Notre-Dame-de-Lourdes
– architecture et intérieur, Napoléon Bourassa #4866 8836
– peintures, Napoléon Bourassa #4865 4875 8784
Montréal (Qué), château de Callière
– architecture #8565
Montréal (Qué), château de Ramezay #3108 8566
– (années 1705-1950) #3082 3083
– architecture
    – agrandissement, Paul Tessier (dit Lavigne) #269 270
– berceaux, Iroquois #3593
– collection #3076 3077
– moules, Québec #2916
Montréal (Qué), château Dufresne (Musée des arts décoratifs/Museum of Decorative Arts) #1294
– architecture
    – Dufresne, Marius, et Jules Renard #8617 8618
Montréal (Qué), Christ Church Cathedral
– architecture, Frank Wills #8798
Montréal (Qué), cimetière Notre-Dame-des-Neiges
– monuments funéraires, XIXe s. #1567
Montréal (Qué), cimetières du Mont-Royal
– architecture paysagiste #7933
Montréal (Qué), cinéma Loew
– architecture, Thomas White Lamb #9069

Montréal (Qué), cinéma Odéon Champlain
– architecture, Henry Eli Greenspoon #9078
Montréal (Qué), Cinémathèque canadienne
– expositions
    – Norman McLaren (1965) #6495
Montréal (Qué), Cinémathèque québécoise. Musée du cinéma
– expositions
    – Michael Snow, rétrospective (1975) #7253
Montréal (Qué), citadelle
– architecture #8445
Montréal (Qué), Collège Loyola. Bibliothèque George P. Vanier
– architecture, Affleck, Desbarats, Dimakopoulos, Lebensold, Sise #8322
Montréal (Qué), collège Notre-Dame de Montréal
– Jérôme, frère, professeur #6761
Montréal (Qué), Commission des écoles protestantes du grand Montréal
– écoles élémentaires (années 1950) #9419
Montréal (Qué), complexe Desjardins
– architecture #7925 9327
– expositions
    – Spectrum Canada (1976) #610
Montréal (Qué), congrégation de Notre-Dame
– broderie #2778
– objects liturgiques, François Ranvoyzé #2658
Montréal (Qué), Couvent des récollets
– architecture et intérieur #8855
Montréal (Qué), David & David, bureau d'architectes
– architecture et intérieur, David & David #9299
Montréal (Qué), Dominion Express Company Building
– architecture et intérieur, Edward et William Sutherland Maxwell #9306
Montréal (Qué), Drummond Military Convalescent Hospital (auparavant Collège Loyola)
– architecture #9016
Montréal (Qué), école catholique, boulevard Côte-des-Neiges
– architecture, Georges Alphonse Monette #9387
Montréal (Qué), Ecole de Montréal
– orfèvrerie #2670
Montréal (Qué), Ecole des beaux-arts #1231 1456
– (1922-1935) #2972
– (1968) #2995
– (années 1960), en comparaison avec Ontario College of Art (Toronto, Ont) #2990
– Allain, Marie-Hélène, élève #4508
– architecture, enseignement
    – (1941) #8245
    – (1948) #8247
    – (1949) #8248
    – (1950) #8249
    – (1952) #8251 8252
    – (1953) #8253
    – (1954) #8255
    – (1955) #8257
    – (1956) #8259
    – (1957) #8260 8261
– Ayotte, Léo, élève #4575
– Baril, Marcel, élève #4608
– Blier, Jean-Marc, élève #4743
– Borduas, Paul-Emile, élève #4827 4836
– Brault, Maurice, élève #4906

– Comtois, Ulysse, professeur #1489
– Cosgrove, Stanley Morel, professeur #5184
– Couturier, Pierre Charles Marie-Alain,
  professeur #1407
– Dallaire, Jean-Philippe, professeur #5241
  5244
– Daoust, Sylvia Marie Emilienne, élève
  #5257
– Dumouchel, Albert, professeur #1641 5325
  5326 5327 5331
– Dyonnet, Edmond, professeur #5347 5348
  5349
– expositions
  – Art abstrait (1959) #1414
  – Les anciens des Beaux-Arts de Montréal:
    premier grand salon (1935) #2973
  – The National Gallery of Canada Presents:
    1958-59, Painters Eleven (1958) #1751
– expositions, critiques
  – Cullen, Maurice Galbraith #5216
  – The National Gallery of Canada Presents:
    1958-59, Painters Eleven (1958) #1752
  – Walker, Horatio #306
– Filion, Armand, professeur #5437
– Fournelle, André, élève #5484
– Legros, Enid Sharon, élève #6223
– Lemieux, Jean-Paul, élève #6228
– Lemieux, Jean-Paul, professeur #6227
– MacLeod, Pegi Nicol, élève #6397
– Pellan, Alfred, professeur #6809
– Raymond, Maurice, professeur #6962
– Roberts, Goodridge, élève #7044
– Senécal, Irène, professeur #3010
Montréal (Qué), Ecole du Conseil des arts et
  manufactures
– Dyonnet, Edmond, professeur #5347 5349
Montréal (Qué), Ecole du meuble
– (1935-1950) #2980
– (1937) #2976
– (années 1940) #2190
– Borduas, Paul-Emile, professeur #4819
  4832 4843
– Couturier, Pierre Charles Marie-Alain,
  professeur #1407
– et mobilier québécois (années 1940) #2523
– Garnier, Jacques, élève #5557
– Gauvreau, Jean-Marie, directeur #2176
– Jaque, Louis, élève #5940
– Lemieux, Jean-Paul, professeur #6227
Montréal (Qué), école Louis-Hébert
– architecture, Charles David #7664
Montréal (Qué), Ecole technique de
  Montréal
– mobilier #2970
Montréal (Qué), écuries d'Youville
– restauration #7905
Montréal (Qué), édifice Aldred
– architecture #7933
  – Barott & Blackader #9313
Montréal (Qué), édifice Jacobs
– architecture, Mitchell & Creighton #9305
Montréal (Qué), édifice La Patrie
– architecture, Georges Alphonse Monette et
  Joseph Ovide Turgeon #9303
Montréal (Qué), édifice Sun Life
– architecture, Darling & Pearson #9308 9309
– expositions
  – Independent Art Association #1379
Montréal (Qué), Editions Formart
– et René Derouin #5285
Montréal (Qué), église du Mont
  Sainte-Famille
– peinture murale, Napoléon Bourassa #4862
Montréal (Qué), église du Sacré-Coeur

– retable, Philippe Liébert #6280 6281
Montréal (Qué), église du Sault-au-Récollet
– sculptures, Philippe Liébert #6281
Montréal (Qué), église Notre-Dame
– architecture #8828
  – O'Donnell, James #1233 8780 8848
  – O'Donnell, James, et rénovation, Victor
    Bourgeau #8849 8892
– architecture et intérieur #8839
– baptistère, peintures d'Ozias Leduc #6203
– crucifix, Antoine Labrosse #6123
– statue de la Vierge Marie, influence sur
  Salomon Marion #2683
– vitraux, Jean-Baptiste Lagacé #2444
Montréal (Qué), église Notre-Dame.
  Chapelle du Sacré-Coeur
– peintures, Joseph-Charles Franchère #5497
Montréal (Qué), église Notre-Dame. Musée
  #3081
Montréal (Qué), église
  Notre-Dame-de-Bon-Secours
– architecture #7899
– architecture et intérieur #8788
Montréal (Qué), église Notre-Dame-de-Grâce
– architecture #7899
Montréal (Qué), église Saint-Alphonse
– vitraux, Vincent Poggi #2448
Montréal (Qué), église Saint-Antonin
– vitraux, Gabriel Loire #2448
Montréal (Qué), église Saint-Arsène
– vitraux, Max Ingrand #2448
Montréal (Qué), église Saint-Enfant-Jésus du
  Mile-End
– baptistère, peintures d'Ozias Leduc #6195
  6203 6204
Montréal (Qué), église Saint-Jacques
– architecture #7899 8781
  – Bourgeau, Victor #8782
  – et Université du Québec à Montréal
    #9427
Montréal (Qué), église Saint-Jean-Baptiste
– architecture, Lemay & Leclerc #8766
Montréal (Qué), église Saint-Léon
– vitraux, Guido Nincheri Studios #2448
Montréal (Qué), église Saint-Patrice
– architecture #7899
– peinture murale, Napoléon Bourassa #4862
Montréal (Qué), église Saint-Rémi
– architecture, Roger D'Astous #8841
Montréal (Qué), église Saint-Viateur
– peintures murales, Guido Nincheri #1378
Montréal (Qué), église Sainte-Anne
– peinture murale, Napoléon Bourassa #4862
Montréal (Qué), église Sainte-Catherine
– architecture, Joseph Sawyer #8407
Montréal (Qué), église
  Sainte-Catherine-d'Alexandrie
– effort de conservation #8867
Montréal (Qué), Expo 67 (1967) #483
– architecture #7693 7709 7737 7862 9220
  – Erickson, Arthur Charles #8361
– architecture et art #9214
– architecture et emplacement #9212 9213
  9219 9221 9222
– art #1453
– arts graphiques #876
– design industriel #2615 2618
– expositions
  – Sculpture canadienne: Expo 67/Canadian
    Sculpture: Expo 67 (1967) #752
– opération Esthétique-Canada 67 #2616
  2617
– Pavillon des beaux-arts #9223
– pavillons #7686 9216 9218

– Affleck, Desbarats, Dimakopoulos,
  Lebensold, Sise #9215
– sculpture #769 7691 7692
– sculpture canadienne #751
Montréal (Qué), Expo 67 (1967).
  Administration et Presse
– architecture, Irving Grossman #9301
Montréal (Qué), Expo 67 (1967). Autostade
– architecture, Victor Prus et Maurice
  Desnoyers #9101
Montréal (Qué), Expo 67 (1967). Pavillon de
  la France
– architecture, Jean Faugeron #1435
Montréal (Qué), Expo 67 (1967). Pavillon du
  Canada/Canadian Government Pavilion
– architecture #7691 7692
– expositions
  – Canadian Fine Crafts (1967) #2108
  – Canadian Prints and Drawings: With a
    Collection of Photographs by Yousuf Karsh
    (1967) #486
  – La peinture au Canada (1967) #84
  – Le dessin et la gravure au Canada: ainsi
    qu'une exposition de photographies de
    Yousuf Karsh (1967) #487
  – Les métiers d'art au Canada (1967) #2109
  – Painting in Canada (1967) #83
  – The Camera as Witness #987
– Smith, Gord, Canada Screen #7222
Montréal (Qué), Fondation
  Macdonald-Stewart
– collection, arts décoratifs #2203 2204
Montréal (Qué), Fraser Hickson Library
– sculpture, Louis Archambault #4542
Montréal (Qué), Galerie 13 #1495
Montréal (Qué), galerie Agnès Lefort
– et Mira Godard #161
– Lefort, Agnès, marchande d'oeuvres d'art
  #1424
Montréal (Qué), galerie Cartier
– expositions
  – An Exhibition of Eskimo Sculpture, Eskimo
    Prints and Paintings of Norval Morrisseau
    (1968) #3350
Montréal (Qué), galerie Curzi
– expositions
  – Louise Robert (1977) #7039
– expositions, critiques
  – Louise Robert (1977) #7038
Montréal (Qué), galerie de la SAPQ #1495
– expositions
  – Les moins de 35: du 22 janvier au 4 février
    (1973) #1501
Montréal (Qué), galerie de la Sauvegarde
– expositions, critiques
  – Rousseau, Denis (1977) #7084
Montréal (Qué), galerie de Montréal
– expositions
  – Kosso Eloul (1973) #5368
– expositions, critiques
  – Glass, Alan Frank #5615
Montréal (Qué), galerie
  Dominion/Dominion Gallery
– et Max Stern #1293 1431
– expositions, critiques
  – Lyman, John Goodwin #6341
  – peinture, provinces de l'Ouest (1951)
    #1842
  – Scott, Marian Mildred Dale #7165
– Leduc, Fernand, commentaire sur ses
  oeuvres exposées (1943) #6189
Montréal (Qué), galerie Dresdnere
– expositions
  – Etrog (1964) #5376

Montréal (Qué), galerie Espace #1495
 – *Les moins de 35: du 22 janvier au 4 février* (1973) #1501
Montréal (Qué), galerie France Morin
– Massey, John, installation #6439
Montréal (Qué), galerie Gilles Corbeil
– expositions, critiques
 – Connolly, Reynald #5167
 – Gnass, Peter #5619
Montréal (Qué), galerie Gilles Gheerbrant
– expositions
 – *Jacques Palumbo: dessins, gravures, aquarelles/Jacques Palumbo: Drawings, Prints, Watercolours* (1975) #6754
 – *Suzy Lake* (1975) #6138
– expositions, critiques
 – Palumbo, Jacques #662
 – Snow, Michael #7264
Montréal (Qué), galerie Godard Lefort
– expositions
 – *Christopher Pratt* (1970) #6910
 – *David Milne, 1882-1953: A Survey Exhibition/David Milne, 1882-1953: une exposition rétrospective* (1971) #6559
Montréal (Qué), galerie L'Actuelle
– et Guido Molinari #6588 6590
Montréal (Qué), galerie L'Art Français
– expositions
 – *Alfred Laliberté, 1878-1953* (1978) #6146
Montréal (Qué), galerie Lippel/Lippel Gallery
– expositions
 – *Ada Eyetoaq: Recent Sculpture/Ada Eyetoaq: sculpture récente* (1979) #5387
 – *Inuit Sculpture 1974/Sculpture inuit 1974* (1974) #4432
Montréal (Qué), Galerie lll #1495
Montréal (Qué), galerie Marlborough Godard/Marlborough Godard Gallery
– exposition, artistes canadiens, Marlborough Gallery, New York (1974) #572
Montréal (Qué), galerie Martal
– expositions, critiques
 – Menses, Jan (1972) #6511
Montréal (Qué), galerie Mira Godard
– expositions
 – *Jean McEwen: Suite parisienne* (1979) #6471
Montréal (Qué), galerie Optica/Optica Gallery #1555
 – *Camerart: 24 artistes du Québec* (1974) #1507
– expositions, critiques
 – *Destination: Europe* (1976) #1018
 – Sullivan, Françoise #7282
Montréal (Qué), galerie Powerhouse/Powerhouse Gallery #1554 1555 1557
– (1973-1975) #1516
– (1973-1979) #1553
– expositions
 – *Women's Bookworks/Livres d'artistes-femmes* (1979) #936
– Mars, Tanya, *Codpiece* exposition (1974) #6421
– rapport, sur la situation des femmes dans l'art (1980) #701
Montréal (Qué), galerie Waddington/Waddington Gallery
– et Arthur Villeneuve #7490
Montréal (Qué), galerie Walter Klinkhoff/Walter Klinkhoff Gallery
– expositions

 – *Prudence Heward (1896-1947): An Introduction to Her Life and Work* (1980) #5796
Montréal (Qué), galerie Watson/Watson Gallery
– expositions, critiques
 – Cullen, Maurice Galbraith #306
Montréal (Qué), galerie Yajima/Yajima Gallery
– expositions
 – *6 Young Canadian Photographers* (1976) #1018
 – *Clara Gutsche: paysages vitrés/Clara Gutsche: Inner Landscapes* (1980) #5673
– expositions, critiques
 – Whittome, Irene #7567 7570
Montréal (Qué), Galeries d'art Sir George Williams
– *voir* Montréal (Qué), Université Concordia. Galeries d'art Sir George Williams
Montréal (Qué), gare Bonaventure
– architecture, Edmund Phillips Hannaford #9538
Montréal (Qué), gare Centrale
– architecture, John Schofield #9535
Montréal (Qué), gare Windsor
– architecture
 – Painter, Walter Scott #9532
 – Price, Bruce, et Edward Maxwell #9537
Montréal (Qué), Graff #1495 1562 1645 1658
– expositions, critiques
 – Wolfe, Robert (1979) #7606
Montréal (Qué), Graphia #1660
Montréal (Qué), Guilde graphique #1647 1653 1655
– et Tobie Thelma Steinhouse #7278
– Lacroix, Richard, fondateur #6128
Montréal (Qué), Habitat 67
– architecture, Moshe Safdie #8403 8574 8575 8577 8578 8580 8583 8584 8585 8590 9215
 – et David, Barott, Boulva, architectes associés #7694
Montréal (Qué), Hôpital-Général
– (1693-1871) #7932
– architecture, Victor Bourgeau #8862
Montréal (Qué), Hôpital général de Montréal
– architecture, McDougall, Smith & Fleming #9030
Montréal (Qué), Hôpital général juif
– architecture, Fleming & Smith #9031
Montréal (Qué), hôpital Royal Victoria
– architecture #7933
Montréal (Qué), hôpital Royal Victoria. Pavillon Ross
– architecture; Stevens & Lee and Kenneth Guscotte Rea, architectes associés #9017
Montréal (Qué), hôpital Sainte-Justine
– architecture, Joseph Sawyer #8407
Montréal (Qué), hôtel de ville
– architecture, J.L.D. Lafrenière; Joseph-Omer Marchand, architectes-conseils #8980
– Delfosse, Georges, oeuvres #5280
– reconstruction #1231
Montréal (Qué), Hôtel-Dieu
– (1642-1861) #7932
Montréal (Qué), Hôtel-Dieu. Pavillon Jérôme Le Royer de la Dauversière
– architecture #9023
Montréal (Qué), hôtel Mont-Royal
– architecture, Ross & Macdonald #9276
Montréal (Qué), hôtel Reine-Elizabeth
– architecture, George Drummond, Harold

 C. Greensides, John W. Wood #9286
– intérieur #8228
Montréal (Qué), hôtel Ritz-Carlton
– architecture et intérieur, Warren & Wetmore #9267
Montréal (Qué), île des Soeurs
– architecture #8587
Montréal (Qué), Institut Canada
– et Alfred Boisseau #4769
Montréal (Qué), Institut d'art contemporain
– expositions
 – *Québec 75* (1975) #1515
Montréal (Qué), Institut des arts graphiques #1648
– Dumouchel, Albert, professeur #1641 5325 5334
– Perrault, Gérard, professeur #851
– typographie (années 1940) #922
Montréal (Qué), Institut national des beaux-arts, sciences, arts et métiers et industrie
– Chabert, Joseph, directeur #3005
– Delfosse, Georges, élève #5279
Montréal (Qué), Jardin botanique
– expositions, critiques
 – *Confrontation 65: exposition internationale de sculpture/Confrontation 65: International Exhibition of Sculpture* (1965) #1586
Montréal (Qué), L'Ermitage
– expositions, critiques
 – Borduas, Paul-Emile #4798 4801
Montréal (Qué), Le Havre South Seafront, projet de "reconstruction domiciliaire"
– architecture, Phyllis Bronfman Lambert #8512
Montréal (Qué), Les Ilots Saint-Martin, La Petite Bourgogne
– architecture, Ouellet Reeves Alain #8520
Montréal (Qué), Les Terrasses
– architecture, René Menkès #7886
– *Eclipse à trois éléments*, sculpture, Maurice Lemieux #6242
Montréal (Qué), magasin Eaton
– architecture #7933
 – Ross & Macdonald; Sproatt & Rolph, architectes-conseils #9365
– intérieur, Jacques Carlu #9370
Montréal (Qué), maison Bigot
– restauration #8567
Montréal (Qué), maison Cormier
– architecture et intérieur, Ernest Cormier #8346 8347 8348
Montréal (Qué), maison George-Etienne-Cartier
– architecture et intérieur #8619
Montréal (Qué), maison Hosmer
– décoration intérieure #2110
Montréal (Qué), maison Hurtubise
– et Héritage canadien du Québec #7871
Montréal (Qué), maison mère de la Congrégation de Notre-Dame
– (1657-1913) #7932
Montréal (Qué), maison mère des Soeurs Grises
– architecture #8862
Montréal (Qué), maison Saint-Gabriel
– architecture et intérieur #8597
Montréal (Qué), maison Simon-McTavish
– architecture #8564
Montréal (Qué), maison Van-Horne
– architecture, destruction #8594 8601
Montréal (Qué), Média
– (années 1970) #1525
Montréal (Qué), Média-gravures

– Viau & Venne #8794
– influence de Dom Bellot #8332
– sculptures, Chemin de la Croix, Louis
  Joseph Parent #6764
– vitraux, Marius Plamondon #2448
Montréal (Qué), Palais de Cristal
– expositions, critiques
  – (1863) #1302
Montréal (Qué), palais de justice
– sculpture, Charles Daudelin #5263
Montréal (Qué), palais de justice, annexe
– architecture, Louis A. Amos; Chas. Saxe;
  Ernest Cormier #9001
Montréal (Qué), parc du Mont-Royal
– architecture paysagiste, Frederick Law
  Olmsted #7903 7912 7924
– croix #7899
Montréal (Qué), Place Bonaventure
– architecture #7709
  – Affleck, Desbarats, Dimakopoulos,
    Lebensold, Sise #7694 9292 9319 9320
    9321 9322 9323 9325
  – et expansion urbaine #9302
– décoration intérieure #9324
– expositions
  – Eskimo Canada (1968) #4414
  – Salon des métiers d'art du Québec
    (1970-1971) #1490
Montréal (Qué), Place d'Accueil
– architecture, Smith Carter Searle
  Associates #7686
Montréal (Qué), Place des Arts
– architecture, Affleck, Desbarats,
  Dimakopoulos, Lebensold, Michaud, Sise
  #9083 9092 9093 9096
– art #8233
– décoration intérieure #9324
– rideau de scène, Micheline Beauchemin
  #4643
– sculptures, Pierre Rolland Dinel #5293
– verrières, Alfred Pellan #1442
Montréal (Qué), place Jacques-Cartier.
  Monument Nelson
– utilisation de pierre Coade #7908
Montréal (Qué), Place Victoria
– architecture #7709 9317
  – Moretti, Luigi; Pier Luigi Nervi;
    Greenspoon, Freedlander & Dunne,
    architectes associés; Jacques Morin,
    architecte-conseil #9195
  – Nervi, Pier Luigi, et Luigi Moretti #9316
Montréal (Qué), Place Ville-Marie
– architecture #7709 7901
  – et expansion urbaine #9302
  – I.M. Pei & associés, architectes et
    urbanistes; Affleck, Desbarats,
    Dimakopoulos, Lebensold, Michaud,
    Sise, architectes associés #9314 9315
Montréal (Qué), pont Jacques-Cartier #7933
Montréal (Qué), prison du Pied-du-Courant
– architecture #9056
Montréal (Qué), Radio-Canada
– architecture #7925
Montréal (Qué), Saint Andrew et Saint Paul
  Church
– vitraux, Lawrence Lee #2448
Montréal (Qué), Saint Gabriel's Church
– architecture, John Bird #8766
Montréal (Qué), Saint George's Greek
  Orthodox Cathedral
– architecture, Affleck, Desbarats,
  Dimakopoulos, Lebensold, Sise #8841 8846
Montréal (Qué), Scott and Son Gallery
– expositions #1367

– soutien de James Wilson Morrice #6616
Montréal (Qué), Stade olympique
– architecture
  – Daoust, André, architecte en chef; Roger
    Taillibert, architecte-conseil #9127
  – Taillibert, Roger #9130 9139
Montréal (Qué), Studio 23
– expositions, critiques
  – Szilasi, Gabor #7308
Montréal (Qué), Temple Emmanu-El
– architecture, Max W. Roth; Greenspoon,
  Freedlander & Dunne, architectes associés
  #8840
Montréal (Qué), Terre des Hommes/Man
  and His World
– expositions
  – Art d'aujourd'hui: collection d'art canadien
    contemporain commanditée par Saidye et
    Samuel Bronfman/Art Today: Collection of
    Contemporary Canadian Art Sponsored by
    Saidye and Samuel Bronfman (1969) #526
  – Cultures du soleil et de la neige: l'art des
    Indiens et des Esquimaux du continent
    américain/Cultures of the Sun and the
    Snow: Indian and Eskimo Art of the
    Americas (1973) #3362
  – Fortier, Ivanhoë, Environment #5471
Montréal (Qué), Terre des Hommes/Man
  and His World. Pavillon de la gravure
– expositions, critiques
  – arts graphiques, Canada (années 1970)
    #1644
  – Dumouchel, Albert #5330
Montréal (Qué), Terre des Hommes/Man
  and His World. Pavillon du Québec
– expositions
  – Les arts du Québec (1974) #1271
– expositions, critiques
  – Artisanat-Design (1972) #2205 2211
Montréal (Qué), théâtre du Nouveau Monde
– costumes, Alfred Pellan #6816
Montréal (Qué), théâtre Saint-Denis
– architecture et intérieur, Barott, Blackader
  & Webster #9068
Montréal (Qué), Tifereth Jerusalem
  Synagogue
– architecture, Affleck, Desbarats,
  Dimakopoulos, Lebensold, Sise #8846
Montréal (Qué), Transportation Building
– architecture, Carrere & Hastings et
  Eustace G. Bird #9307
Montréal (Qué), Université Concordia
– voir aussi Montréal (Qué), Université Sir
  George Williams
Montréal (Qué), Université Concordia.
  Galeries d'art Sir George Williams
– collection #3096
– expositions
  – Annie D. Savage: Drawings and
    Watercolours (1974) #7129
  – David Bolduc: Recent Work (1979) #4775
  – David Milne: The New York Years,
    1903-1916 (1982) #6567
  – Dennis Burton Retrospective (1978) #4961
  – Dessins inédits d'Ozias Leduc/Ozias Leduc
    the Draughtsman (1978) #6210
  – Edwy Cooke: aquarelles, 1942-1977 (1977)
    #5171
  – Gordon Rayner Retrospective (1979) #6966
  – Graham Coughtry: Retrospective (1977)
    #5190
  – Henry Sandham (1842-1912): The Mr. &
    Mrs. Leo J. Heaps Loan Collection/Henry
    Sandham (1842-1912): Collection

empruntée de M. et Mme Léo J. Heaps
    (1976) #7121
  – Ivan Eyre Exposition (1981) #5394
  – John Fox: 10 New Paintings (1980) #5495
  – Looking South (1978) #4278
  – Painters Eleven in Retrospect (1981) #1785
  – Peter Kolisnyk (1977) #6075
  – The Heritage of Jack Bush: A Tribute (1982)
    #722
  – The Queen Comes to New Brunswick:
    Paintings and Drawings by Molly Lamb
    Bobak (1979) #4765
  – William Blair Bruce (1975) #4942
– expositions, critiques
  – Gagnon, Pnina #5550
Montréal (Qué), Université de Montréal
– architecture #7900 9415
  – Cormier, Ernest #8345
– conférence sur la peinture québécoise
  (1970) #1267
– expositions
  – Une exposition d'art de la Province:
    céramique, sculpture, émail, joaillerie,
    orfèvrerie (1957) #2193
Montréal (Qué), Université de Montréal.
  Ecole d'architecture
– architecture, enseignement
  – (1958) #8262
  – (1959) #8263
  – (1960) #8264
  – (1961) #8266
  – (1962) #8268
  – (1963) #8270
  – (1964) #8271
  – (1965) #8273
  – (1966) #8274
  – (1967) #8275
  – (1967), projet de mégastructure urbaine
    #8276
  – (1968) #8277
  – (1976) #7728
  – (1980) #8289
  – (années 1960) #8269
Montréal (Qué), Université de Montréal.
  Ecole des hautes études commerciales
– architecture #7709
Montréal (Qué), Université du Québec à
  Montréal
– architecture #7925
– art (1962-1972) #1502
– Dumouchel, Albert, professeur #5331
Montréal (Qué), Université du Québec à
  Montréal. Galerie UQAM
– expositions
  – Robert Wolfe: noir est l'espace blanc (1977)
    #7605
  – Rodolphe Duguay, 1891-1973 (1979) #5318
– expositions, critiques
  – Lemieux, Lisette #6241
Montréal (Qué), Université McGill
– architecture #9414
  – Blackstock, Hattie, illustration médicale
    (années 1920) #4738
  – Pen and Pencil Club, documents #1251
  – Savage, Anne Douglas, professeure #7130
Montréal (Qué), Université McGill. Athletic
  buildings
– architecture, concours #9417
Montréal (Qué), Université McGill. Ecole
  d'architecture
– architecture, enseignement
  – (1909) #8242
  – (1941) #8245
  – (1948) #8247

– (1949) #8248
– (1950) #8249
– (1951) #8250
– (1952) #8252
– (1953) #8253
– (1954) #8255
– (1955) #8257
– (1956) #8259
– (1957) #8260
– (1958) #8262
– (1959) #8263
– (1960) #8264
– (1961) #8266 8267
– (1962) #8268
– (1963) #8270
– (1964) #8271
– (1965) #8273
– (1966) #8274
– (1967) #8275
– (1980) #8289
– (années 1970) #8287
– assistance aux résidents d'habitations à loyer modique (années 1970) #8283
Montréal (Qué), Université McGill. Institut canadien de recherches sur les pâtes et papiers
– architecture, Percy Erskine Nobbs #9425
Montréal (Qué), Université McGill. Macdonald Engineering Building
– architecture, Percy Erskine Nobbs #9425
Montréal (Qué), Université McGill. Macdonald Physics Building
– architecture, sir Andrew Thomas Taylor #9411
Montréal (Qué), Université McGill. McLennan and Redpath Library
– architecture, Dobush, Stewart, Bourke #9046
Montréal (Qué), Université McGill. Medical Building
– architecture, Brown & Vallance #9412
Montréal (Qué), Université McGill. Musée McCord #3098 3108
– architecture, Percy Erskine Nobbs #9423 9425
– art haida #4011
– art traditionnel québécois, XIXe s. #1362
– courtepointe piquée en soie (1726) #2803
– estampes en creux, Canada #840
– et château de Ramezay (Montréal, Qué) #3082
– expositions
  – A Terrible Beauty: The Art of Canada at War (1978) #1111
  – An Exhibition of Canadian Gameboards of the 19th & 20th Centuries from Ontario, Quebec & Nova Scotia (1981) #2597
  – Beauté tragique: les deux conflits mondiaux vus par des artistes canadiens (1978) #1112
  – Canadian Hooked Rugs, 1860-1960/Le tapis crocheté canadien, 1860-1960 (1977) #2758
  – De grandes espérances: la vision européenne en Nouvelle-Écosse, 1749-1848 (1981) #1220
  – Everyman's Canada: Paintings and Drawings from the McCord Museum of McGill University (1962) #223
  – Exposition d'estampes en l'honneur de C. Krieghoff, 1815-1872/Exhibition of Prints in Honour of C. Krieghoff, 1815-1872 (1972) #6096
  – George Heriot: Painter of the Canadas/George Heriot: peintre des deux Canadas (1979) #5786

  – Great Expectations: The European Vision in Nova Scotia, 1749-1848 (1981) #1222
  – Le réel et l'imaginaire: peinture et photographie canadiennes, 1860-1900/Fact and Fiction: Canadian Painting and Photography, 1860-1900 (1979) #268
  – Mont-Royal Montréal/Mount Royal Montreal (1977) #7924
  – Ozias Leduc: peinture symboliste et religieuse/Ozias Leduc: Symbolist and Religious Painting (1974) #6206
  – Peter Pitseolak (1902-1973), chroniqueur inuit de Seekooseelak: photographies et dessins du Cap Dorset, terre de Baffin/Peter Pitseolak (1902-1973), Inuit Historian of Seekooseelak: Photographs and Drawings from Cape Dorset, Baffin Island (1980) #6883
  – Printmaking in Canada: The Earliest Views and Portraits/Les débuts de l'estampe imprimée au Canada: vues et portraits (1980) #839
  – Quillwork by Native Peoples in Canada/Travaux en piquants de porc-épic exécutés par les autochtones au Canada (1978) #3475
  – Quillwork by Native Peoples in Canada (1977) #3474
  – Silhouettes ca. 1840-1965 (1965) #2842
  – The Art of Nunstins/L'art de Nunstins (1981) #6934
  – Une imagerie canadienne: peinture et dessins du musée McCord de l'Université McGill (1962) #222
– expositions, critiques
  – George Heriot: Painter of the Canadas/George Heriot: peintre des deux Canadas (1979) #5789
  – Peter Pitseolak (1902-1973), chroniqueur inuit de Seekooseelak: photographies et dessins du Cap Dorset, terre de Baffin/Peter Pitseolak (1902-1973), Inuit Historian of Seekooseelak: Photographs and Drawings from Cape Dorset, Baffin Island (1980) #6882
– Heriot, George, peintures #5785
– Hertel de Rouville, famille, portraits #1345
– Macdonald, Jock, documents #6376
– McGill, James, portrait #5321
– Québec, vues, XVIIIe-milieu XIXe s. #1366
– Shanly, Charles Dawson, dessins #241 242
Montréal (Qué), Université McGill. Musée McCord. Archives photographiques Notman
– Baltzly, Benjamin, photographies #4598
– Henderson, Alexander, photographies et documents #5777
– Nakash, George, portraits photographiques #6683
– Notman, William, photographies #6724 6725
– photographies de femmes, XIXe s. #2908
Montréal (Qué), Université McGill. Osler Library
– architecture, Percy Erskine Nobbs #9425
Montréal (Qué), Université McGill. Pathological Institute
– architecture, Percy Erskine Nobbs #9423 9425
Montréal (Qué), Université McGill. Royal Victoria College. Annexe
– architecture, Percy Erskine Nobbs #9425
Montréal (Qué), Université McGill. Stephen Leacock Building

– architecture, Affleck, Desbarats, Dimakopoulos, Lebensold, Sise #8322
Montréal (Qué), Université McGill. University Centre
– architecture, Affleck, Desbarats, Dimakopoulos, Lebensold, Sise #8322
Montréal (Qué), Université McGill. University Library. Annexe
– architecture, Percy Erskine Nobbs #9425
Montréal (Qué), Université Sir George Williams
– voir aussi Montréal (Qué), Université Concordia
– expositions
  – Adrien Hébert: trente ans de son oeuvre, 1923-1953/Adrien Hébert: Thirty Years of His Art, 1923-1953 (1971) #5763
  – André Biéler 50 Years: A Retrospective Exhibition 1920-1970 (1970) #4725
  – Carl Schaefer: Retrospective Exhibition; Paintings from 1926 to 1969 (1969) #7155
  – Drawings and Pastels c. 1930-1967 by Miller Gore Brittain (1969) #4917
  – Esther Warkov (1971) #7517
  – Fritz Brandtner 1896-1969: A Retrospective Exhibition (1971) #4903
  – Robert Harris (1849-1919) (1973) #5743
  – The Mr. and Mrs. Jules Loeb Collection/La collection M. et Mme Jules Loeb (1970) #3231
Montréal (Qué), Véhicule Art #1495 1503 1525 1555
– (années 1970) #641 1508
– expositions
  – Vehicule Art: In Transit (1975) #1512
Montréal (Qué), Vidéographe
– art vidéo #605 1498 1499
Montréal (Qué), Village olympique
– architecture, Roger D'Astous et Luc Durand #9127
Montréal (Qué), Westmount Park United Church
– vitraux, C.W. Kelsey #2448
Montréal (Qué), Westmount Square
– architecture, Ludwig Mies van der Rohe #9326
– architecture et expansion urbaine #9302
Montréal (Qué), Wiser's Museum
– collection, decorative arts #2469
Montreal Camera Club (Montréal, Qué)
– expositions, critiques #978
Montreal Daily Mail, journal can
– dessins humoristiques, David McRitchie #943
Montreal Estonian Society (Montréal, Qué)
– exposition, art estonien (1951) #118
Montreal Herald, journal can
– dessins humoristiques, Ben Fitzmaurice #943
Montreal Society of Artists (Montréal, Qué) #1246 3114
Montreal Star, journal can
– dessins humoristiques
  – Julien, Henri #943
  – Racey, Arthur George #943 6952
– illustrations, Henri Julien #5984 5985 5986 5987 5990 5993
– Lamb, Harold Mortimer, critique d'art #6156
Montreal Theatre Ballet (Montréal, Qué)
– décors et costumes (années 1950) #1410
montres
– voir aussi horloges
montres . Canada

– (1700-1900), horlogers #2931
– Québec, XVIIe-XVIIIe s. #1320 2914
  – orfèvre #2657
– XVIIIe-XIXe s. #2925
monuments
– *voir aussi* lieux historiques; monuments
  aux morts; monuments funéraires
monuments . Canada
– Allward, Walter Seymour #4516
  – bataille d'Ypres (Ypres, France) #4518
– Carillon (Qué), Dollard des Ormeaux
  #1591
– Hahn, Emanuel Otto #5680
– Hébert, Louis-Philippe #5769
– Hill, George William #5799
– Laliberté, Alfred #6142 6143
– MacCarthy, Hamilton Plantagenet #6352
  6353
– Montréal (Qué), fin XIXe s.-années 1920
  #1623
– monuments aux morts, Première et
  Seconde Guerres mondiales #1108 1109
– monuments aux morts, Première Guerre
  mondiale #731 732
– Ottawa (Ont), région de la capitale
  nationale #762
– Québec #1570 7887
  – fin XIXe s.-années 1920 #1606
  – thème de la rébellion #1351
– Québec (Qué) #7945
  – général James Wolfe #1568 1600
  – XVIIe-XIXe s. #1309
– St. John's (TN) #7783
– Toronto (Ont), Dr. D.W. Young #729
monuments . Indiens des plaines
– Roue-Médecine #3748
monuments aux morts . Canada
– bataille d'Ypres (Ypres, France), Walter
  Seymour Allward #4518
– Jackson, A.Y., commentaire #1076
– Kingston (Ont), John MacIntosh Lyle
  #1083
– MacCarthy, Hamilton Plantagenet #6353
– McKenzie, Robert Tait #6484
– Mémorial de Vimy (Vimy, France), Walter
  Seymour Allward #4519
– Oshawa (Ont), Saint George's Anglican
  Church #8899
– Première et Seconde Guerres mondiales
  #1108 1109
– Première Guerre mondiale #731 732 1073
  1074 1078 1080 1082 1084 1085
  – architecture, recommandations #1079
– Regina (Sask), War Memorial Museum
  #9073
– St. John's (TN) #7783
monuments commémoratifs
– *voir* monuments
monuments funéraires
– *voir aussi* cimetières
monuments funéraires . Amérindiens #733
monuments funéraires . Canada #733
– croix en fer
  – Ontario #2709
  – Québec #2716
– Hamilton (Ont), Hamilton Mausoleum
  #8900
– Montréal (Qué), cimetière de
  Notre-Dame-des-Neiges #1567
– Nouvelle-Ecosse #1193 1216
– Ontario
  – fin XVIIIe-XIXe s. #1721
  – XIXe s.-années 1910 #1723
  – XVIIIe s.-années 1930 #1669

– Terre-Neuve, XVIIIe s.-1860 #1163
– Toronto (Ont), Mount Pleasant Cemetery
  – Eaton Mausoleum #8895
  – Senator Cox's Mausoleum #8894
monuments funéraires . Grande-Bretagne
– exportations à Terre-Neuve, XVIIIe s.-1860
  #1163
monuments funéraires . Haidas #3995
monuments funéraires . Indiens de la côte
  nord-ouest #8914
monuments funéraires . Irlande
– exportations à Terre-Neuve, XVIIIe s.-1860
  #1163
monuments historiques
– *voir* monuments
Moodie, Geraldine, photographe can,
  1854-1946 #6602
Moody, Alan R., architecte can, 1924-1979
– Toronto (Ont), George Brown College of
  Applied Arts & Technology. Casa Loma
  Campus #9479
Moody, Moore & Partners, agence can
  d'architecture
– Winnipeg (Man), University of Manitoba.
  Arts College #9399
Moody, Rufus, sculpteur can, 1923-
– sculpture d'argilite #3944
  – Vancouver (CB), Vancouver Centennial
    Museum #4006
Mooney, Terry, joaillier can, actif 1976 #2706
Moore, David, artiste can, 1943-
– expositions de groupe
  – (1976) #1529
Moore, Henry, sculpteur brit, 1898-
– sculpture, Vancouver (CB) #2080
– sculptures, Art Gallery of Ontario
  (Toronto, Ont) #3154 3158 9121
Moore, John Warren, ébéniste can, 1812-1893
  #2500 2511 6603
– mobilier, maison Hagerman, Kings
  Landing (NB) #2512
Moose Factory (Ont)
– architecture #7976 7998 8032
Moose Jaw (Sask), Centre national
  d'expositions
– expositions
  – *The Paintings of Frederick Nicholas
    Loveroff/Les peintures de Frederick Nicholas
    Loveroff* (1981) #6331
Moose Jaw (Sask), hôtel de ville
– architecture, concours #8978
Moose Jaw (Sask), Moose Jaw Art Museum
– expositions
  – *Conceptual Decorative: Prints by Les
    Levine, 1965-1970/Conceptuel décoratif:
    estampes de Les Levine, 1965-1970* (1972)
    #6265
  – *Manitoba Mainstream: People's Art/Fine
    Art/Le Grand Courant du Manitoba: arts
    populaires, beaux-arts* (1972) #1897
  – *Saskatchewan: Art and Artists* (1971)
    #1919
  – *Watercolour Painters from
    Saskatchewan/Aquarellistes de la
    Saskatchewan* (1972) #1920
  – *William Perehudoff: Ten Years,
    1970-1980/William Perehudoff: une
    décennie, 1970-1980* (1982) #6838
Moppett, Carroll, sculpteure can, 1948-
– entretien #788
– expositions de groupe
  – (1978) #2066
moquette
– *voir* tapis

moralité, art et
– *voir* éthique, art et
Morand, Paul, orfèvre can, 1775-1856 #6604
– oeuvres, Detroit Institute of Arts (Detroit,
  Mich) #2691
Morandi, Georgio, artiste it, 1890-1964
– East, Benoît, comparaison #5353
Morant, Nicholas (Nick), photographe can,
  1910- #6605
– catalogue de photographies #987 995
Morash, Barbara, artiste can, active 1969
  #6606
Moreau, Gustave, artiste fr, 1826-1898
– influence sur Graham Metson #6523
– influence sur Ozias Leduc #6206
Morée, Michael de, photographe can, actif
  années 1970-
– catalogue de photographies #991
Morel, Octave, sculpteur can, né 1837
– représentation d'animaux #1579
Morelli, François, artiste can, 1953- #640
Morency, André, artiste can, 1910- #1393
Moretti, Luigi, architecte it, 1907-1973
– Montréal (Qué), Place Victoria #9195 9316
Moretti, Pierre, artiste can, actif 1969
– art par ordinateur #528
Moretti, Victor, artiste, actif années 1890
– oeuvres, édifices du Parlement (Victoria,
  CB) #8967
Morgan, D., marchand d'oeuvres d'art can,
  XXe s.
– collection, tissus et textiles, Canada #2747
  2748
Morgan, Earle Clifford, architecte can,
  1903-1972
– Toronto (Ont), O'Keefe Centre for the
  Performing Arts #9087
Morgan, Peter, artiste can, 1951-
– gravures sur pierre #6607
Morier, Pauline, artiste can, 1942-
– expositions
  – (1975) #6608
Morin, Jacques, architecte can, 1911-
– Montréal (Qué), Place Victoria #9195
Morin, Jean, artiste can, 1938-
– design typographique #932
– estampes #897
Morin, Serge, photographe can, actif 1979
– catalogue de photographies #996
Morisset, Denys, artiste can, 1930-
– entretien #6609
– expositions, critiques #6610
– photographies #6612
– réflexion sur son oeuvre #6613
– théories sur l'art #6611
Morisset, Gérard, historien d'art,
  conservateur et architecte can, 1898-1970
  #3126 3305 3321
– architecte #8891
– commentaire sur l'orfèvrerie québécoise
  #2692
– commentaire sur les orgues #2952
– commentaire sur Michel Dessailliant (dit
  Richeterre) #5290
– critique d'art #3326
– et conservation de monuments #7897
– et culture québécoise #1477
– et les médias #3323
– et Musée du Québec (Qué) #3095 3125
  3127
– historien d'art #3322
– renouveau de la ceinture fléchée #2864
– théories sur l'art #3324
Moriyama, Raymond, architecte can, 1929-

– Charlottetown (IPE), Confederation Centre, concours #9089
– commentaire sur l'architecture de motels #9288
– entretien, relations entre artistes et architectes #8234
– Guelph (Ont), Macdonald Stewart Art Centre #3176
– London (Ont), London Regional Art Gallery #3174 9145
– Scarborough (Ont), Scarborough Civic Centre #8973
– Toronto (Ont) #7733
  – bureau d'architectes #9346
  – Japanese Cultural Centre #9095
  – Metro Toronto Public Library #9051
  – Ontario Science Centre #9106
Morrell, Paul Luther, pasteur can, XXe s.
– et J.E.H. MacDonald #6362
Morrice, James Wilson, artiste can, 1865-1924 #10 24 89 192 6614 6615 6617 6618 6619 6620 6622 6624 6626 6628 6629 6633
– artiste conservateur (années 1930) #322
– carnets à dessins #6621
  – Montréal (Qué), Musée des beaux-arts de Montréal #6631
  – Ottawa (Ont), Galerie nationale du Canada #6632
– en comparaison avec Emily Carr #352
– en comparaison avec Paul-Emile Borduas #4845
– et G.Blair Laing #1686
– et internationalisme dans l'art #354
– et la peinture canadienne #18 1389
– et Marc-Aurèle de Foy Suzor-Coté #7295
– et Maurice Galbraith Cullen #5221
– et modernisme #27 383 6623
– expositions
  – (1965) #6625
  – (1968) #6627
– expositions, critiques #204 211
– expositions de groupe
  – (1927) #299
  – (1975) #6630
– influence de la peinture française #1244
– influence sur Edwin Headley Holgate #5818 5819
– influence sur René-Jean Richard #6998
– membre du Canadian Art Club #193
– paysages d'hiver #285
– peinture
  – Kleinburg (Ont), McMichael Canadian Collection #3172
  – Montréal (Qué), Musée des beaux-arts de Montréal #3113
– réaction de la presse canadienne (1886-1916) #6634
– soutien donné par Scott and Son Gallery (Montréal, Qué) #6616
Morris, Christina
– voir Mollise (Morris), Mâli Christianne Paul (Christina)
Morris, E.W., Company, studio de design (Londres, Angleterre)
– oeuvres, édifices du Parlement (Victoria, CB) #8967
Morris, Edmund Montague, artiste can, 1871-1913 #6636 6638
– expositions
  – (1909) #6637
– membre du Canadian Art Club #193
Morris, Jerrold, artiste et marchand d'oeuvres d'art can, 1911-

– autobiographie #6639
Morris, John, fonctionnaire can, XIXe s.
– et édifices du Parlement (Ottawa, Ont) #8930
Morris, Maria Frances Ann
– voir Miller, Maria Frances Ann Morris
Morris, Marshall, Faulkner & Co., studio de design (Londres, Angleterre)
– verrières, Canada (1861-1874) #2453
Morris, Michael William, artiste can, 1942- #6640
– commentaire sur la perception visuelle #525
– correspondance, Miss General Idea (1971) #546
– expositions
  – (1980) #6641
– expositions, critiques #520
– expositions de groupe
  – (1969) #2039
  – (1971) #2042
  – (1974) #2050
  – (1979) #2070
Morris, Robert, sculpteur amér, 1931-
– expositions, critiques #787
– expositions de groupe
  – (1978) #790
Morris, Robert Schofield, architecte can, 1898-1964
– prix, Royal Institute of British Architects Royal Gold Medal (1958) #8389
Morris, William, artiste et auteur brit, 1834-1896
– influence sur art de la tapisserie #2774
– influence sur George Selkirk Gibson #5591
– influence sur mouvement artistique canadien, Arts and Crafts #189
Morris & Co. Ltd., studio de design (Londres, Angleterre)
– vitraux
  – Canada (1874-1940) #2453
  – Montréal (Qué) #2462
Morris & Company (Art-Workers Ltd.), studio de design (Londres, Angleterre)
– John Henry et Duncan W. Dearle #2458
Morrison, Alfred L., artiste can, 1909-
– peintures, scènes de l'Ile-du-Prince-Edouard #6642
Morrisseau, Norval H., artiste can, 1932- #4136 4155 4157 4161 6643 6644 6647 6649
– expositions
  – (1966) #6645
– expositions de groupe
  – (1968) #3350
  – (1977) #4151
– images, Midéwiwins #4154
– influence sur peinture, Indiens des forêts du Nord-Ouest #4144 4156
– influence sur peinture amérindienne (années 1970) #6648
– légendes, Saulteux/Ojibwa #4122 6646
Morrow, Patrick, photographe can, 1952-
– catalogue de photographies #1023
mort
– Dickson, Jennifer, Sweet Death and Other Pleasures #5291
– peintures, London (Ont), (années 1960) #1759
– scènes de combat, Canada, XVIIIe-XIXe s. #812
mortier (architecture)
– voir ciment, mortier et plâtre
mortiers et pilons . Canada
– sculpture sur bois, Ontario, XVIIIe-XIXe s.

#2588
Mortimer, Ann, céramiste can, 1934- #2395
Mortimer-Lamb, Harold
– voir Lamb, Harold Mortimer
Morton, Douglas Gibb, artiste can, 1926-
– expositions
  – (1961) #1913
– expositions de groupe
  – (1967) #490 1916
Morton, James, photographe can, actif 1856-1867 #1724
mosaïques . Canada
– murales (années 1950) #4732
– Peterson, Margaret #6839
– Québec (années 1940) #2199
– Sainte-Anne-de-Beaupré (Qué), basilique Sainte-Anne #6572 6573 8859 8860 8865 8866
Moscou (URSS), Musée des beaux-arts Pouchkine
– expositions
  – Sculpture of the Inuit: Masterworks of the Canadian Arctic/La sculpture chez les Inuit: chefs-d'oeuvre de l'Arctique canadien (1972) #4423 4440
Moscou (URSS), Musée historique et artistique de Zagorsk
– art inuit et Chukchi #4302
Moscou (URSS), Université Lomonosov. Musée d'anthropologie
– art tlingit #3947 3978
Moses, Gerald Milne (Gerry), artiste can, 1913-
– directeur artistique, Imperial Oil Review #924
– photographies de la Seconde Guerre mondiale #1107
Moss, Charles Eugene, artiste can, 1860-1901
– expositions, critiques #186
motels . Canada
– (années 1960) #9288
Motherwell, Robert, artiste amér, 1915-
– influence sur Douglas Hector Haynes #5758
Motherwell, William Richard, homme d'Etat can, 1860-1943
– parc historique national W.R. Motherwell Farmstead (Abernethy, Sask) #8723 8724 9232
motifs
– dans l'art, Vancouver (CB), (années 1980) #2081
Mott & Myles, agence can d'architecture
– Saint-Jean (NB), Hôpital général de Saint-Jean #9031
moulage
– voir plâtres
Moulding, Fred, artiste can, 1897- #1881
moules . Canada
– Québec #2916
moulins
– voir aussi moulins à vent
moulins . Canada #9248 9249
– Acadie #7804
– Conception Bay (TN), scierie (ca 1620) #7718
– Kingston Mills (Ont) #8020
– Ontario #9239
  – (années 1780-1880) #9259
  – XIXe s. #7745
– Pointe-du-Lac (Qué), moulin "Garceau" #9246
– Québec #9242 9252
  – XVIIe-XIXe s. #7852 9243

– XVIIe-XVIIIe s. #7845
– XVIIIe-XIXe s. #8560 8561
– Trois-Rivières (Qué), Forges du
  Saint-Maurice #9253
moulins . Etats-Unis
– Etats-Unis (Nord-Est) #9249
moulins à vent . Canada #9244 9248 9249
– Québec #9255
– Québec (Qué), Hôpital-Général #9245
– XVIIe-début XIXe s. #7841
moulins à vent . Etats-Unis
– Etats-Unis (Nord-Est) #9249
Mounsey, Yseult, photographe can, active
  années 1970-
– catalogue de photographies #991
Mount Uniake (NE), Uniake House
– architecture et intérieur #8534
Mountbatten, Louis Francis Albert Victor
  Nicholas, 1er comte de Burma, 1900-1979
– portrait, Yousuf Karsh #6022
mousquets
– voir armes à feu
Mousseau, Jean-Paul Armand, artiste can,
  1927- #1502
– entretien #6650
– expositions
  – (1967) #6651
– expositions de groupe
  – (1955) #1408
  – (1958) #431
– utilisation du plastique #1442
mouvement dans l'art
– Canada (années 1970) #783
mouvements féministes
– voir féminisme
Mowat, Grace Helen, artisane tisserande
  can, 1875-1964 #2144
Mowat, H.J., artiste can, actif 1919-1931
– illustrations #916
moyens de transport
– Québec, XVIIe-XIXe s., influences
  européennes #2221
moyens de transport . Athapascans #4104
  4105
moyens de transport . Cris #3402
moyens de transport . Flancs-de-Chien
  #4089
moyens de transport . Hans #4101
moyens de transport . Hurons #3514
moyens de transport . Ingaliks #4087
moyens de transport . Pieds-Noirs #3654
moyens de transport . Saulteux/Ojibwa
  #3402 3488 4089
moyens de transport . Slaveys #4089
moyens de transport dans l'art
– affiches canadiennes #908 910
– Armstrong, William #4552
– Innes, John I. #5901
– Toronto (Ont), Metro Toronto Public
  Library. John Ross Robertson Historical
  Collection #3131
Moyer, Harry, artiste can, né 1884
– dessins humoristiques, Toronto Daily Star
  #943
Moyer, Samuel I., ébéniste can, né 1818
  #2571
Mozino Suarez de Figueroa, José Mariano,
  explorateur esp au Canada, 1757-1819
– expédition, Nootkas #3966
Mud Bight Village (Alaska)
– totems #3873
Muhlstock, Louis, artiste can, 1904- #6653
  6655 6657 6659
– commentaire sur le nu dans l'art #6652

– entretien #6656
– expositions
  – (1976) #6658
– expositions, critiques #6654
– expositions de groupe
  – (1977) #1278 1279
Mulcaster, Wynona Croft, artiste can, 1915-
  #6660
– expositions, critiques #1883
– expositions de groupe
  – (1975) #1926
– professeure d'Allen Sapp #7122 7123
Mulders, Gerard et Anne, collectionneurs
  can, XXe s.
– collection, sculpture inuit #4443
Muller, Keith, designer can, 1938- #2487
multiples
– et Michael Snow #7245
Munakata, Shiko, artiste jap, 1903-1975
– expositions de groupe
  – (1976) #6449
Munch, Edvard, artiste norvégien, 1863-1944
– influence sur Tom La Pierre #6122
– Yerxa, Leo, comparaison #7624
Munich (Allemagne de l'Ouest), Residenz
– expositions
  – Group of Seven: Kanadische
    Landschafts-Maler: Eine Wanderausstellung
    der McMichael Canadian Collection,
    Kleinburg, Ontario, Kanada (1977) #1781
Munich (Allemagne de l'Ouest), Städtische
  Galerie im Lenbachhaus
– expositions
  – Michael Snow (1979) #7258
  – Michael Snow: Works 1969-1978, Films
    1964-1976/Michael Snow: Werke
    1969-1978, Filme 1964-1976 (1979) #7261
Munn, Kathleen Jean, artiste can, 1887-1974
  #309
Munnings, Alfred James, artiste brit,
  1878-1959
– expositions de groupe
  – (1926) #1084
Munro, John, orfèvre can, 1791-1875 #2649
Munro, John Vicar, architecte can, 1872-1976
– London (Ont), Riverview School #9388
Muntz, Laura Adeline
– voir Lyall, Laura Adeline Muntz
Murakami, Yoichi, céramiste jap, actif XXe s.
– influence sur Wayne G. Ngan #6695
Murch, Walter Tandy, artiste can, 1907-1967
  #6662
– entretien #6661
Murphy, Burland E., artiste can, actif 1975-
  #6663
– estampes #1214
Murphy, Patrick J., artiste can, 1917- #6664
Murphy, Rowley Walter, artiste can,
  1891-1975 #6666
– réflexion sur son oeuvre #6665
Murphy, Sean, collectionneur can, 1924-
– entretien #3219
Murphy, Serge, artiste can, 1953-
– réflexion sur son oeuvre #1552
Murray, Ian, artiste can, 1951-
– expositions de groupe
  – (1981) #710
– livres #940
Murray, James Albert, architecte can, 1919-
– Cooksville (Ont), Applewood United
  Church #8763
– Don Mills (Ont)
  – Chatham Village #8511
  – South Mills Village #7679

– Ottawa (Ont), Université d'Ottawa #9458
  9465
Murray, Jim, photographe can, ca 1947-
– catalogue de photographies #1032
Murray, Robert Gray, sculpteur can aux
  Etat-Unis, 1936- #6667 6669 6671 6672
  6673 6674
– commentaire sur ses études en art #470
– commentaire sur son séjour à New York
  (années 1960) #460
– entretien #6668
– expositions
  – (1969) #6670
– expositions de groupe
  – (1967) #480 490
  – (1971) #98
  – (1976) #613
– réflexion sur l'art canadien (années 1960)
  #478
– sculpture, Vancouver (CB) #2080
Murray, William, architecte can, actif années
  1820-1840, m. ca 1860 #8390
Murray, William G., architecte can,
  1876-1954
– London (Ont), Ryerson School #9386
Murray & Murray, agence can d'architecture
– Ottawa (Ont), église Saint-Maurice #8766
Murraygreen, Ryan, artiste can, 1947-
– expositions de groupe
  – (1981) #2084
murs
– voir aussi maçonnerie; peinture murale
murs . Canada
– charpente en madriers #7712
  – Ontario, XIXe s. #8046
– construction à murs creux, Ontario, XIXe
  s. #8004
– utilisation de la peinture, Ontario, XIXe s.
  #8013
musées . Canada
– (1898), recommandation #1705
– (1908), recommandation, assistance
  gouvernementale #2963
– (1909), recommandation #8242
– (1953-1954) #3035
– (1972-1974) #552
– (1980) #683
– (années 1830-1860), Mechanic's Institute
  #3064
– (années 1920) #311
– (années 1930) #3024
  – recommandations #3026
– (années 1940) #3030
  – et Académie royale des arts du Canada
    #361
– (années 1950) #3037
  – en comparaison avec musées américains
    #3031
– (années 1960) #87 3043 3045
  – appui aux artistes canadiens #448 523
  – galeries d'art #442
  – The Simmons Report on Art Gallery
    Development in Canada (1969) #3046
– (années 1960-1970), soutien aux femmes
  artistes canadiennes #677
– (années 1970) #542 551 682 3051 3059 3279
  – appui aux artistes canadiens #6747
  – et Association des musées canadiens
    #3054
  – et femmes artistes #701
  – et les femmes #562
  – galeries de photographie #1027
  – galeries parallèles #641 660 1042
  – réaction du public #3056

– Acadie #1137
– architecture #9098
  – *Canadian Architect*, galerie d'art communautaire, concours (1957) #9082
  – Charlottetown (IPE), Confederation Centre #9088 9089
  – London (Ont), London Regional Art Gallery #9145
  – Montréal (Qué)
    – château Dufresne #8617 8618
    – Expo 67, Pavillon des beaux-arts #9223
    – maison Saint-Gabriel #8597
    – Musée des beaux-arts de Montréal #9063 9065 9124 9125 9133
  – Ottawa (Ont), Galerie nationale du Canada #9079 9136 9142
  – Perth (Ont), Perth Museum (auparavent Matheson House) #8670
  – Queen Charlotte Islands (CB), Queen Charlotte Islands Museum #9129
  – Rimouski (Qué), Musée régional de Rimouski #9118
  – Saskatoon (Sask), Mendel Art Gallery #9091
  – Toronto (Ont)
    – Art Gallery of Ontario #8680 9121
    – Art Gallery of Toronto #3132 9076
    – Art Museum of Toronto #9070
    – Colborne Lodge #8659
    – Jenkins Art Galleries #8053
    – Ontario Science Centre #9106
  – transformation d'édifices publics en musées #9147 9148
  – Vancouver (CB)
    – University of British Columbia. Museum of Anthropology #9132 9137 9138
    – Vancouver Art Gallery #9149
  – Vernon (CB), Vernon Civic Centre #8972
  – Winnipeg (Man)
    – Seven Oaks Museum (auparavent Seven Oaks House) #8703
    – Winnipeg Art Gallery #9102 9111 9117
– collections
  – art canadien #3320
  – arts décoratifs québécois #2226
  – courtepointes canadiennes #2799
  – jouets et poupées #2932
  – lampes canadiennes #2920
  – mobilier #2484
  – mobilier québécois #2528
  – modèles de broderie, Canada #2792
  – photographie #1051
  – textiles et tissus #2739
– Colombie-Britannique
  – et enseignement de l'art (années 1960) #2989
  – XIX s.-années 1940 #1986
– et art de performance #634
– et enseignement de l'art
  – (années 1940) #2984
  – (années 1940-1980) #2983
– Halifax (NE), (années 1970) #1208
– Manitoba (années 1970) #3193
– Montréal (Qué)
  – galeries #1555
  – XIXe-début XXe s. #7899
– Ontario
  – (années 1970) #1802
  – XIXe-début XXe s. #3152
– périodiques #3313
  – *Canadian Museums Association. Gazette* #3042

– petites galeries d'art (années 1950) #3034
– provinces de l'Atlantique
  – (années 1960) #1124 3053
  – (années 1970) #1127 1131
  – XXe s. #1130
– Québec #3098 3108
  – (1833-1853), appui, création d'un musée national #3120
  – (années 1940-1950) #1426
  – (années 1940-1970) #1269
  – (années 1970) #3015 3102
  – XIXe s.-années 1940 #1242
– Saint-Jean (NB), (1842-1945) #3065
– Saskatchewan #1919
– Terre-Neuve #1142
– Vancouver (CB)
  – (années 1960) #3190
  – Vancouver Museum #3180
– XIX s.-années 1970 #3055
musées . Etats-Unis
– collections, jouets et poupées #2932
musées dans l'art
– (années 1970-1980) #714
– Whittome, Irene #7568
Musgrove, Alexander Johnston, artiste can, 1890-1952
– expositions de groupe
  – (1940) #350
musique
– *voir aussi* chansons folkloriques
musique, art et
– Andrews, Stephen #4528
– art de performance #634
– Bergeron, André #4702
– Bolt, Ron #4778
– Colville, Alex #5141
– Gaucher, Yves #5565 5568 5570
– Harris, Lawren Stewart #5721
– MacGregor, John #6388
– McDougall, Clark Holmes #6464
– McLaren, Norman #6493 6494 6497 6498
– Parent, Omer #6767
– Rayner, Gordon #6965
– Tonnancour, Jacques Godefroy de #7383 7390
– Trudeau, Yves #7433
– W.O.R.K.S. #1955
– Young, Robert #7628
musique . Canada #129
– (années 1970) #693 3279
– Canadian Creative Music Collective (CCMC) #690
– Nouveau-Brunswick #1178
– périodique, *Canadian Review of Music and Art* #357
– Québec #1231 1235
  – (années 1870) #1307
– Terre-Neuve #1139
– Winnipeg (Man) #1891
musique . Inuit #4317
Muskoka (Ont)
– vues, Mary Evelyn Wrinch #7617
Muybridge, Eadweard, photographe brit, 1830-1904
– Cohen, Sorel, comparaison #5130
Myers, Barton, architecte can, 1934-
– commentaire sur son oeuvre architecturale #8391
– Edmonton (Alta), Citadel Theatre #8091
– théories sur l'architecture #7746
Myren, Ronald L., artiste can, 1937-
– expositions de groupe
  – (1981) #1885
mysticisme

– et Charles Gagnon #5533
– et Lawren Stewart Harris #5726 5731
mythologie
– *voir aussi* folklore
– sculpture, Colombie Britannique (années 1970) #2066
mythologie . Algonquiens #3385
– arbre #3516
– Oiseau-Tonnerre #3493
mythologie . Amérindiens
– et chamanisme #3361
– Oiseau-Tonnerre #3410
– points cardinaux #3498
– serpents #3391
mythologie . autochtones #3334
mythologie . Bella-Coolas #3772
mythologie . Canada
– Wieland, Joyce, commentaire #7576
mythologie . Cris
– Grand Manitou #3724
mythologie . Esquimaux du cuivre #4330
mythologie . Haidas #3780 3890
– représentation de la lune #4059
mythologie . Indiens de l'Amérique Centrale
– serpents #3391
mythologie . Indiens de la côte nord-ouest #4036
– Oiseau-Tonnerre et baleine #3831
mythologie . Inuit #4295 4315 4317 4320 4321 4404 4433 4488
– déesse de la mer #4312 4376
– influence sur Jean-Paul Riopelle #7024
– Povungnituk (Qué) #4417 4437 4494
mythologie . Iroquois
– arbre #3516
mythologie . Kwakiutls #3883 4120
– Bokwus #3990
mythologie . Netsilik #4328
mythologie . Pieds-Noirs
– ours #3746
mythologie . Sarcis
– ours #3746
mythologie . Saulteux/Ojibwa #4122
mythologie . Tlingits
– pieuvre #4045
mythologie . Tsimshians #3910
mythologie . Tsonnontouans
– masques #3508

N

N.E. Thing Co. Ltd. (Vancouver, CB) #536
– art vidéo #550
– et Iain Baxter #535
– et l'art d'avant-garde #600
– expositions
  – (1969) #524 6675
  – (1974) #574
  – (1976) #2060 6676
  – (1977) #6678
– expositions de groupe
  – (1969) #2039
  – (1970) #534
  – (1980) #703
– photographies sculpturales #994
– utilisation du langage #6677
Nadeau, Luis, photographe can, 1951- #6679
– catalogue de photographies #991
Nadeau, Marc Antoine, artiste can, 1943-
– pop'art #1497

Nahanis
- ouvrages perlés #4077
Nahuas
- pierre sacrificielle, remise en question de
  son authenticité #4094
Nairobi (Kenya), Sorsbie Gallery
- expositions
  - *Contemporary Canadian Art* (1962) #451
Nakamura, Kazuo, artiste can, 1926- #6680
  6681 6682
- influence sur la peinture torontoise #1749
  1760
Nakamura, Richard Yoshio, photographe
  can, 1924-
- photographies, Forces armées canadiennes
  #1107
Nakash, George, photographe can,
  1892-1976 #6683
Nakashima, Hiro, architecte can, 1936-
- Toronto (Ont), habitations St. Lawrence
  #8078
Nakayama, artiste jap, XXe s.
- professeur de Gaston-Pierre Petit #6844
Nanaimo (CB)
- photographie, fin XIXe s. #2022
Nanaimo (CB), Malaspina College. Madrona
  Exposition Centre
- expositions
  - *J.Frederic McCulloch 1905-1932: Works on
    Paper* (1978) #6463
  - *Jack Wise: A Decade of Work* (1978) #7601
Nantel, Michel, artiste can, actif 1976 #6684
Napanee Glass House, fabricants de verre
  (Napanee, Ont) #2401
Napanee Glass Works
- *voir* Napanee Glass House
nappes d'autel . Canada
- broderie, ursulines #2777
Narcisse
- thème dans l'oeuvre d'Irene Whittome
  #7566
Nash, Chauncey C., collectionneur amér,
  XXe s.
- collection, art inuit #4191
Nash, Paul, artiste brit, 1889-1946
- expositions de groupe
  - (1926) #1084
- Schaefer, Carl Fellman, comparaison #7157
Naskapis
- art #3554 4082 4149
- costume #4098
- crécelles #3363
- culture (1880s) #3379
- ouvrages perlés #4076 4103
- peau de caribou #3622
- raquettes #2812
- récipients #4078
Nasmith, Eric Anderson, artiste can, 1916-
  #6685
Nass River (CB)
- totems #3839 3852
National Film Society of Canada
- fondation, Donald William Buchanan
  #3325
National Home Monthly, périodique can
- illustrations, Illingworth Holey Kerr #6048
National Transcontinental Railway
- gares #9542
nationalisme, architecture et
- Canada #7728
  - (années 1910) #7642 7644
  - (années 1920) #7657
  - (années 1950) #7675

- architecture victorienne #7697 7725
- XXe s. #7690 7731
- Québec #7848 7868
nationalisme, art et
- Académie royale des arts du Canada #181
- Boyle, John Bernard #4891
- Canada #67 68 76 77 143
  - (1860-1890) #264 271 272
  - (1938-1948) #378
  - (années 1860-1880) #230
  - (années 1860-1970) #148 150
  - (années 1870-1910), en comparaison
    avec Etats-Unis #196
  - (années 1890) #183
  - (années 1890-1970) #102
  - (années 1910) #205
    - en comparaison avec Etats-Unis #203
  - (années 1910-1940) #354
  - (années 1920) #289 1737
  - (années 1920-1930) #322
  - (années 1920-1960), en comparaison
    avec Amérique latine #495
  - (années 1930) #338 1763
    - en comparaison avec Mexique et
      Etats-Unis #337
  - (années 1940) #368
  - (années 1950) #52 387 401 439
  - (années 1950-1960) #511
  - (années 1960) #529
  - (années 1970) #574 619 620 629 3274
    6747
  - dessins humoristiques et politiques,
    XIXe-XXe s. #957
  - grès, XIXe s. #2309
  - influence de la Seconde Guerre
    mondiale et de la Dépression #327
  - monnaie, imagerie #759
  - paysages #109 341
  - peinture traditionnelle, XVIIe-XXe s.
    #965
  - photographie #1056
  - XVIIe-XIXe s. #187
  - XXe s. #29 58 59 61 297 482 4851
- Curnoe, Greg #5231
- Dallaire, Jean-Philippe #5240
- Groupe des Sept #1741 1743 1747 1767
  1768 1774 1782 1789 1790
- Harris, Lawren Stewart #293 308 5729
- Jackson, A.Y. #5915
- Légaré, Joseph #6216 6219
- Lismer, Arthur #6292
- Montréal (Qué)
  - (années 1970) #1548
  - monuments, fin XIXe s.-années 1920
    #1623
- Québec
  - (1759-1914) #1351
  - (1825-1850) #1368
  - (années 1930) #334 1460 2170
  - (années 1940) #1388
  - (années 1970) #1528
  - monuments, fin XIXe s.-années 1920
    #1606
  - XVIIe-XIXe s. #1373
- Roussel, Claude #7089
nativité
- *voir* Jésus-Christ, nativité
nattes
- *voir* tapis
nattes . Algonquiens
- écorce de bouleau #3561
nattes . Algonquins
- écorce de bouleau #3571

nattes . Canada
- Labrador #2945
nattes . Indiens de la côte nord-ouest
- préhistoire #4017
nattes . Saulteux/Ojibwa #3557 3585
nature
- art canadien #104 373
- et Arthur Lismer #6294
- et Ernest Lindner #6287
- et Ernest Thompson Seton #7172
- et Gershon Iskowitz #5904
- et Jack Leonard Shadbolt #7177
- et Jean-Paul Riopelle #7018
- et Kenneth Campbell Lochhead #6314
- et Richard Prince #6937
- littérature et art canadien #93
- photographie canadienne #1062
Nauja
- *voir* Angiju, Peter Nauja
Nauman, Bruce, artiste amér, 1941-
- art vidéo #651
- et perception visuelle #525
Neel, Ellen, artiste can, ca 1910-1966 #4121
Neil, Allan, artiste can, 1924-
- expositions de groupe
  - (1971) #2042
Neil & Beggs, agence can d'architecture
- Toronto (Ont)
  - Beaver Theatre #9066
  - Garden Theatre #9066
Neilson, Henry Ivan, artiste can, 1865-1931
- eaux-fortes #799 800
- expositions, critiques #211
- membre du Canadian Art Club #193
Nelson, Horatio, vice-amiral brit, 1758-1805
- monument, place Jacques-Cartier
  (Montréal, Qué) #7908
Nelson, John, photographe can, actif années
  1840-1850
- portraits #1171
Nelson, Ronald Keith (Ron), architecte can,
  1932-
- restauration, Orpheum Theatre
  (Vancouver, CB) #9135
Nelson (CB)
- architecture #8155
néo-plasticisme
- influence sur peinture québécoise #489
néo-primitivisme
- *voir* peinture naïve
néo-romantisme
- architecture domestique, Ontario #8654
Nervi, Pier Luigi, architecte it, 1891-1979
- Montréal (Qué), Place Victoria #9195 9316
Netsilik
- culture
  - (1903-1905) #4366
  - (années 1920) #4328
- instruments #4363
Networks Limited, agence can de
  communication (Halifax, NE)
- et Larry Wayne Richards #8402
Neumann, Alexander (Alex), artiste can,
  1949-
- expositions de groupe
  - (1976) #1529
Neumann, Ernst, artiste can, 1907-1956
  #6686
Neutres
- travail de la pierre #3503
Neuville (Qué)
- architecture #7875
- maisons en pierre #8607

Neuville (Qué), église
– baldaquin, Joseph Quintal et Gilles Bolvin #8826
Nevers, Edmond de, auteur can, 1862-1906
– écrits, illustrations de Marc-Aurèle de Foy Suzor-Coté #7299
Nevitt, Richard Barrington, artiste et médecin can, 1850-1928 #6687 6688
New Carlisle (Qué), palais de justice
– murale, Suzanne Guité #5667
New Era Social Club
– et Glenn Alun Lewis #6275
New Hamburg Pottery, fabricants de céramique (New Hamburg, Ont) #2336
– (1854-1916) #2348
New Haven (Conn), Yale University. Art Gallery
– expositions
– *Canadian Art, 1760-1943* (1944) #31
New Haven (Conn), Yale University. School of Art
– Aziz, Philip, élève #4576
– DeLauro, Joseph Nicola, élève #5276
New Maryland (NB), Church of Saint Mary the Virgin
– architecture, Edward Shuttleworth Medley #8776
New Westminster (CB)
– architecture #8147
New Westminster (CB), palais de justice
– architecture, George William Grant #9011
New York
– architecture, James O'Donnell #8848
– potiers de New York en Ontario, XIXe s. #2309
New York (NY)
– art (années 1960) #441
– vues
– Day, Mabel Killam #5273
New York (NY), 291 Gallery
– Lamb, Harold Mortimer, exposition de photographies #6156
New York (NY), 49th Parallel/49e Parallèle #712
– expositions
– *John Greer: Sculptural Objective, 1968-1981; Everything Always Changes but Something Still Remains* (1982) #5654
New York (NY), ACA Galleries
– expositions
– *Ernest Lawson Retrospective* (1976) #6178
New York (NY), American Museum of Natural History
– art, Indiens de la côte nord-ouest #4024
– art, Indiens des plaines #3668
– art amérindien #3452
– récipients haidas #4066
New York (NY), Art Students League
– Brittain, Miller Gore, élève #4917
– et Marion F.S. Mackay Nicoll #6703
– Humphrey, Jack Weldon, élève #5865
– Lougheed, Robert Elmer, élève #6327
– Morris, Edmund Montague, élève #6636
– Roberts, Goodridge, élève #7044
– Steinhouse, Tobie Thelma, élève #7278
– Thibault, René, élève #7344
– Wrinch, Mary Evelyn, élève #7618
New York (NY), Artists Space
– expositions
– *7 Toronto Artists* (1980) #1832
New York (NY), Bonestell Gallery
– expositions, critiques
– La Palme, Robert #6118
New York (NY), Brooklyn Museum

– art dakota #3705
New York (NY), Canadian Club of New York
– paysages canadiens #3211
New York (NY), Carnegie Museum
– vannerie, Abénaquis #3596
New York (NY), Center for Inter-American Relations
– expositions
– *About 30 Works by Michael Snow/Autour de 30 oeuvres de Michael Snow* (1972) #7248
– *Canada: Ron Martin, Henry Saxe* (1978) #661
– *Objects of Bright Pride: Northwest Coast Indian Art from the American Museum of Natural History* (1978) #4024
New York (NY), Cooper Union Art School
– Kahane, Anne, élève #5998
New York (NY), Davis & Long Co.
– expositions
– *Charles Conder, Robert Henri, James Morrice, Maurice Prendergast: The Formative Years, Paris 1890s* (1975) #6630
New York (NY), Emmerich Gallery
– expositions, critiques
– Bush, Jack Hamilton #4965 4974
New York (NY), Exposition internationale (1939)
– expositions
– *Exhibition of Canadian Art, New York World's Fair, 1939* (1939) #346
– Innes, Alice A., peintures #5900
New York (NY), Exposition of Indian Tribal Arts, Inc.
– expositions
– *Introduction to American Indian Art: To Accompany the First Exhibition of American Indian Art Selected Entirely with Consideration of Esthetic Value* (1931) #3412
New York (NY), Finch College. Museum of Art
– expositions, critiques
– Levine, Les #6266
New York (NY), Gallery of Modern Art
– Beny, Wilfred Roloff, *A Visual Odyssey*, exposition de photographies (1968) #4691
New York (NY), Grand Central Art Galleries
– expositions
– *Canadiana* (1942) #12
New York (NY), James Yu Gallery
– expositions, critiques
– Niverville, Louis de (1975) #6708
New York (NY), Marlborough Gallery
– expositions
– *Thirteen Artists from Marlborough Godard, Toronto-Montreal* (1974) #572
New York (NY), Martha Jackson Gallery
– expositions, critiques
– Iskowitz, Gershon #5906
New York (NY), Mead Library of Ideas
– expositions, critiques
– *Graphicanada 67* (1967) #877
New York (NY), Metropolitan Museum of Art
– expositions
– *Masterworks from the Museum of the American Indian: Heye Foundation* (1973) #3450
New York (NY), Museum of Modern Art
– exhibitions, critiques
– *Photography into Sculpture* (1970) #994

– expositions
– *Fifteen Canadian Artists* (1963) #453
– *Information* (1970) #534
– expositions, critiques
– *The Responsive Eye* #468
New York (NY), Museum of the American Indian. Heye Foundation
– art, Cris, Flancs-de-Chien, et Nahanis #4077
– art amérindien #3437 3450 3452
– couvertures salishiens #3818
– expositions
– *Arctic Art: Eskimo Ivory* (1980) #4453
– *The Ancestors: Native Artisans of the Americas* (1979) #4040
– masse d'armes, Iroquois #3538
– ouvrages perlés, Amérindiens #3457
– récipients en écorce de bouleau, Algonquins #3542
– sculptures d'ivoire inuit #4381 4458
– wampum, Algonquiens #3541
New York (NY), National Academy of Design
– Cruikshank, William, élève #5212
– Eaton, Wyatt, élève #5355
New York (NY), Riverside Museum
– expositions
– *Canadian Women Artists* (1947) #377
New York (NY), Robert Elkon Gallery
– expositions
– *Jack Bush, a Selection: 1961-65* (1980) #4978
New York (NY), Rockefeller Center
– architecture, en comparaison avec revitalisation du quartier Bunker Hill, Los Angeles (Calif) #8364
New York (NY), Seagram Building
– architecture, Ludwig Mies van der Rohe #9348
New York (NY), Theo Waddington Gallery
– expositions
– *Aipellie Osuitok (Oshaweetok): Sculpture* (1980) #6745
– *Kiawak Ashoona: Sculpture* (1980) #4565
New York (NY), Wade School of Photography
– MacAskill, Wallace R., élève #6350
New York (NY), Whitney Museum of American Art
– expositions
– *Two Hundred Years of North American Indian Art* (1971) #3442
– expositions, critiques
– exposition *22 Realists*, en comparaison avec l'exposition *Realism(e)s*, Musée des beaux-arts de Montréal (Montréal, Qué) #533
New York Herald, journal amér
– illustrations, Charles William Jefferys #5953
New Yorker, périodique amér
– dessins humoristiques, Richard Taylor #7336
Newark (NJ), Newark Museum
– art amérindien #3425
– expositions
– *Survival: Life and Art of the Alaskan Eskimo* (1977) #4272
Newcastle (NB)
– architecture, William Murray #8390
Newcastle (NB), Miramichi Valley High School
– expositions
– *Colville, Pratt, Forrestall* (1974) #1129

Newcombe, Charles Frederick,
collectionneur can, né 1851
- collection, peintures d'Emily Carr #5023
Newfeld, Frank, artiste can, 1928-
- entretien #6689
Newfoundland Academy of Art #1142
Newfoundland Arts Council for the
Province of Newfoundland
- fondation, Newfoundland Conference of
the Arts (1974) #1146
Newfoundland Historic Trust
- restauration, Christ Church (Quidi Vidi,
TN) #7788
Newfoundland Society of Art #1138
- (1925-1936) #1141 1142
Newlan, Emery, sculpteur can, actif 1955-
#6690
Newlands, William, architecte can,
1853-1926 #8392
Newlyn Brotherhood
- et Edmund Wyly Grier #5660
Newman, Barnett, artiste amér, 1905-1970
- et Emma Lake Workshops (Emma Lake,
Sask) #1915 1929
- influence sur Arthur Fortescue McKay
#6476
- influence sur Guido Molinari #6588
- Menses, Jan, comparaison #6511
- professeur d'Arthur McKay #6477
- professeur de Claude Tousignant #7400
- utilisation de la couleur, influence sur la
peinture montréalaise (Qué) #1425
- Westerlund, Mia, comparaison #7545
Newman, Brian, artiste can, 1943- #6691
Newman, Brian, photographe can, ca 1952-
- catalogue de photographies #1032
Newman, John Beatty, artiste can, 1918-
- portraits #715
Newport (RI), Art Association of Newport
- expositions
- An Exhibition of Eskimo Sculpture, Eskimo
Prints and Paintings of Norval Morrisseau
(1968) #3350
Newport News (Va), Mariners' Museum
- expositions
- Ships of the Great Lakes (1943) #12
Newton, Lilias Torrance, artiste can,
1896-1980 #6692
- (1981) #6693
Newton, Neil, photographe can, 1933-
- expositions
- (1978) #6694
Nez-Percés
- photographies, Sir John Benjamin Stone
#3717
Ngan, Wayne G., céramiste can, 1937-
#2395
- expositions
- (1978) #6695
- expositions, critiques #6696
Niagara (Ont)
- art (années 1970) #1795
- fraktur #2254
- mobilier, XIXe s. #2571
- mobilier importé, XVIIIe-XIXe s. #2569
- vues
- (1697-1880), estampes #1718
- Jameson, Anna Brownell #5933
Niagara Artists' Co-operative (St.
Catharines, Ont)
- éditions à tirage illimité #834
- et John Bernard Boyle #4892
- expositions
- (1975) #1808

Niagara Falls (NY), Buscaglia-Castellani Art
Gallery
- voir Niagara Falls (NY), Niagara
University. Buscaglia-Castellani Art
Gallery
Niagara Falls (NY), Native American Center
for the Living Arts
- expositions
- American Indian Art in the 1980's (1981)
#4171
Niagara Falls (NY), Niagara University.
Buscaglia-Castellani Art Gallery
- expositions
- Spirit of the Earth (1980) #4163
Niagara Falls (Ont), Earl W. Brydges Public
Library
- architecture, Paul Rudolph #9050
Niagara Falls (Ont), Greater Niagara
General Hospital
- architecture, John B. Parkin Associates
#9031
Niagara Falls (Ont), Niagara Falls Art
Gallery
- Kurelek, William, The Ukrainian Pioneer
#6116
Niagara-on-the-Lake (Ont)
- architecture
- fin XVIIIe-début XIXe s. #8000
- XIXe s. #7986 7992 8655
- architecture militaire
- (1838-1871) #8471
- fortifications
- (1814-1837) #8470
- (1871-1978) #8472
- maisons en brique, début XIXe s. #8521
Niagara-on-the-Lake (Ont), Navy Hall
- architecture #8464 8465
Niagara-on-the-Lake (Ont), résidence de
Clench
- architecture #7959
Niagara-on-the-Lake (Ont), Saint Andrew's
Church
- architecture #7959
- Clyde, John Edward, et Saxton Burr
#8901
Niagara-on-the-Lake (Ont), Shaw Festival
Theatre
- architecture
- Thom, Ron #9120
- Thom, Ron, et Peter Smith #9119
Niagara Parks (Ont)
- architecture et lieux historiques #7975
nichoirs d'oiseaux . Canada #2593
Nichol, Walter Cameron, Can, 1866-1928
- résidence, Miraloma (Saanich Peninsula,
CB) #8731
Nicholls, Ken, artiste can, 1949-
- commentaire sur Jack Chambers #700
Nichols, Jack, artiste can, 1921- #6697 6698
6699
- à Paris (France) #426
- commentaire sur la gravure #810 817 818
- et gravure ontarienne (années 1960) #1756
- Gould, John Howard, comparaison #5635
Nichols, T.R., fabricant de banduras can,
actif 1979 #2940
Nicholson, Ben, artiste brit, 1894-
- influence sur Lawren Phillip Harris #5711
Nicholson, John Hobson, artiste brit, 1911-
- professeur de Toni Onley #6741
Nicol, Pegi
- voir MacLeod, Pegi Nicol
Nicolaides, Kimon, artiste amér, 1892-1938
- professeur de Will Ogilvie #6732

Nicolas, Louis, prêtre fr, artiste au Canada,
1634-après 1682
- Codex Canadiensis #1372
Nicolet (Qué), Saint-Grégoire de Nicolet
- retable #1636
Nicoll, James McLaren (Jim), artiste can,
1892- #6701
- correspondance, Jock Macdonald #6376
- entretien #1974
- expositions
- (1977) #6700
- théories sur l'art #1944
Nicoll, Marion F.S. Mackay, artiste can,
1909- #6701 6703
- correspondance, Jock Macdonald #6376
- entretien #1974
- expositions
- (1975) #6702
Nicomen (CB)
- architecture #8147
Nincheri, Guido, artiste can, 1885-1973
- peintures, église Saint-Viateur (Montréal,
Qué) #1378
- professeur d'Umberto Bruni #4946
- vitraux, église Saint-Léon (Montréal, Qué)
#2448
Ninstints (CB)
- totems, Haidas #4067
Nisbet, Thomas, ébéniste can, m. 1850 #2500
2501 2511
Niska
- voir Lortie, Joseph Antoine François
Niskas
- crécelles #6788
- miroirs #3804
- totems #3839 3895 4032
Niverville, Louis de, artiste can, 1933- #6704
6705 6706 6708 6710
- expositions
- (1978) #6709
- expositions, critiques
- (1978) #6711
- oeuvres à l'acrylique (années 1970) #6707
Niviaksiak, artiste can, 1908-1959 #4460
Noah
- voir Nuna, Noah
Nobbs, Percy Erskine, architecte can,
1875-1964
- commentaire sur l'architecture domestique
canadienne #8499
- commentaire sur le dessin d'architecture
#8241
- commentaire sur le plâtre #8221
- Montréal (Qué), Université McGill #9425
- McGill University Union (maintenant
musée McCord) et Pathological Institute
#9423
Nobbs & Hyde, agence can d'architecture
- Edmonton (Alta), University of Alberta
#9492 9493
- Montréal (Qué), écoles #9413
- Regina (Sask), War Memorial Museum
#9073
- Winnipeg (Man), Birks Building #9355
Noeich River (CB)
- pétroglyphes, Bella-Coolas #3816
Noël
- cartes de souhaits, Canada
- (années 1880) #842
- Bennet & Co. #2360
- (années 1880-1890) #890
- (années 1920) #845
- Canadian Artists' Series #844
- (années 1920-1950) #863

– (années 1940), Avis Selina Fyshe, commentaire #849
– (années 1960) #868
– Editions Lacia (années 1950) #857
– Québec (1950) #856
– dans l'art
– Julien, Henri #5982
– peintures canadiennes #864
Noël, Jean, artiste can, 1940- #6713 6714
– entretien #1485
Noestheden, John Theodore M., artiste can, 1945-
– expositions
– (1977) #6715
Noffke, Werner Ernest, architecte can, 1878-1964
– Ottawa (Ont) #8393
Nokony, Denis, artiste can, 1951-
– expositions
– (1981) #6716
– expositions de groupe
– (1977) #1933
Noland, Kenneth, artiste amér, 1924-
– Bush, Jack Hamilton, comparaison #4969
– et Emma Lake Workshops (Emma Lake, Sask) #1929
– influence sur André Lucien Fauteux #5413
– influence sur Arthur Fortescue McKay #6476
– Perehudoff, William, comparaison #6837
Nolette, Joseph, charpentier can, XVIIIe s.
– clocher, église de l'Acadie (Qué) #8830
Nolin, Alice, artiste can, 1896-1967 #1380
Nolte, Gunter, artiste can, 1938-
– expositions
– (1978) #6717
nombres dans l'art
– Palumbo, Jacques #662
Nootkas
– art #3908
– canots #3344
– coiffures #3779
– coiffures de chefs #3829
– crécelles #4026
– culture #3764 3880 4020 4025
– XVIIIe s. #3966
– photographies
– Curtis, Edward Sheriff #3399
– rituel du Loup #3885
– sérigraphie #4167
– vannerie #3991
Nordbeck, Peter, orfèvre et joaillier can, 1789-1861 #258 259
Nori, Angela, photographe can, 1945-
– catalogue de photographies #991
Norman, Joseph van
– voir Van Norman, Joseph
Norman Hotson Architects, agence can d'architecture
– Vancouver (CB), Granville Island #8170
Normandeau, Pierre-Aimé, 1906-1965
– professeur de Jacques Garnier #5557
Normandin, Richard, artiste can, 1934- #6718
Norris, George A., sculpteur can, 1928- #6719
– fontaine, Vancouver (CB) #2077
– sculptures, lieux publics, Vancouver (CB) #2080
Norris, Joe, artiste can, 1924- #6721
– expositions
– (1978) #6720
Norris, Leonard Matheson (Len), artiste can, 1913- #6722
– dessins humoristiques et politiques #957

North Hatley (Qué), La Poterie
– Beaudin, Gaétan, professeur #2381
North Hatley (Qué), maison Bradley
– architecture, Peter Rose #7886
North York (Ont), Atria North
– architecture, Thom Partnership #8412
North York (Ont), Koffler Centre for the Arts. Leah Posluns Theatre
– architecture, Jerome Markson Architects #8386
Northampton (Mass), Smith College. Art Complex
– architecture, John Andrews Architects #8323
Northern Alberta Railway
– gares #9545
Northgrave, Paul, architecte can, 1945-
– Toronto (Ont), Bedford Glen #8078
Northwest Coast Indian Artists Guild
– sérigraphies (1977) #4148
Northwest Institute of Sculpture. British Columbia Region
– expositions
– (1956-1960) #1993
Northwood, George W., architecte can, 1878-1959
– Edmonton et Calgary (Alta), Dominion Bank #9188
Norvégiens au Canada
– Alberta, traditions ethnoculturelles #2273
Norwell, Graham Noble, artiste can, 1901-1967
– expositions de groupe
– (1978) #133
Notman, William, photographe can, 1826-1891 #6724 6725 6726
– et Benjamin Baltzly #4598
– et J.Henry Sandham #7121
– et photographie canadienne #986
– et William James Topley #1001
– expositions de groupe
– (1976) #3281
– influence sur la peinture et la photographie canadiennes #268
– photographie format album #1026
– photographies de bâtiments en construction #1019
– photographies de femmes #2908 6024
– réflexion sur la photographie #6723
– relation entre photographie et peinture #245
Notre Dame (Ind), Saint Mary's College
– Laliberté, Norman, bannières #6154
Notre Dame Bay (TN)
– artefacts béothuks #3627
Nouveau-Brunswick
– architecture
– (1763-1930) #7659
– Acadie #7804
– Murray, William #8390
– XVIIIe-XIXe s. #7808
– architecture domestique, fin XVIIIe-début XIXe s. #8529
– architecture et arts décoratifs #2150
– art
– (années 1750-1970) #1183
– (années 1940) #350
– (années 1960) #1177
– (années 1970) #1131
– (avant 1867) #2110
– Acadie #1181
– (années 1960-1980) #1136
– art et architecture, XVIIIe-XIXe s. #7780
– arts #1178

– arts décoratifs (années 1940) #2144
– arts graphiques (années 1970) #1185
– courtepointes (années 1920) #2794
– croix #1625
– églises, Edward Shuttleworth Medley #8776
– ex-libris, XVIIIe-XIXe s. #915
– horloges #2925
– mobilier
– (1783-années 1970) #2503
– (années 1760-1920) #2511
– (avant 1900) #2491
– XVIIIe-XIXe s. #2495 2500 2504
– orfèvrerie #2640 2649
– fin XVIIIe-XIXe s. #2646
– palais de justice (avant 1914) #9004
– poterie, XIXe s. #2319
– poterie de grès, XVIIIe s. #2364 2365
– scènes représentant bateaux, XIXe s. #1190
– sculpture sur bois, famille Graham #1187
– tapisseries (années 1970) #5296
– verre #2400
– vues
– (1760-1880), estampes #1189
– Cleveland, Xenophon #5119
– Gagen, Robert Ford #5530
– Gregory, Joan Steeves #5657
– Heaviside, Lady Mary Love #1175
– Leblanc, Leo B. #6182
– Petley, Robert #5351
– Russell, Edward John #7110
– Taylor, George Thomas #7334
– Woolford, John Elliott #258 259
– XIXe s. #1180
– vues photographiques
– (1869-1918) #1186
– Smith, Madge #7235
– Taylor, George Thomas #7333
Nouvelle-Angleterre
– architecture, XVIIe-XVIIIe s., influence sur architecture de la Nouvelle-Ecosse #7823
– architecture, XVIIIe s., influence sur architecture de la Nouvelle-Ecosse #7815
Nouvelle-Ecosse
– architecture #7779 7820 7821 7827
– Harris, William Critchlow #8372
– XIXe s. #7832
– XVIIe-XIXe s. #7687 7814
– XVIIIe s. #7815
– architecture domestique, XVIIe-XVIIIe s. #7823
– architecture et sites historiques #7830
– art #3072
– (1749-1848) #1215 1220 1222 1224 1225
– (1900-1945) #1194
– (années 1920-1970) #1192
– (années 1940) #350
– (années 1970) #1131
– (avant 1867) #2110
– XVIIe s.-1914 #1191
– XVIIIe s.-1867 #28
– art et architecture, XVIIIe-XIXe s. #7780
– art traditionnel, XXe s. #1206 1207 1210 1212 1213
– arts #1196
– arts décoratifs #2156 2157
– (années 1940) #2145
– (années 1970) #2154
– tradition germanique #2135
– bibliothèques (années 1950) #9044
– bouteilles et flacons #2409 2428
– chapeaux #2907
– courtepointes et couvre-lits (1820-1930) #2807

– églises, fin XVIIIe-XIXe s. #8775
– ex-libris, XVIIIe-XIXe s. #915
– femmes artistes
   – (années 1830-1840) #1219
   – (années 1850-1950) #1204
   – (années 1970) #1205
– gravure (1784-1897) #1198
– horloges #2925
– jeux de société, XIXe-XXe s. #2597
– mobilier #2521
   – (années 1920) #2463
   – décorations peintes et sculptées #2514
   – Holder, Thomas Cook, et Henry Arthur #2506
   – XIXe s. #2515
   – XIXe s., comté de Pictou #2513
   – XVIIe s.-années 1840 #2494
   – XVIIe-XIXe s. #2489
   – XVIIIe-XIXe s. #2496 2497 2499
– monuments funéraires #733 1193 1216
– or et argent
   – XVIIe-XIXe s. #2639
   – XVIIIe-XXe s. #2632
– orfèvrerie #2640 2648
– ouvrages à l'aiguille #2785
– phares #9522
– poterie
   – (années 1780-1925) #2307
   – XIXe s. #2308
– poterie de grès #2324
   – XVIIIe s. #2364 2365
– scènes représentant bateaux, XIXe s. #163 1201
– sièges (mobilier), XVIIIe-XIXe s. #2493 2509
– textiles et tissus #2731
– verre #2114 2417
   – (1881-1920) #2399
   – XIXe s. #2398
– vues
   – (1605-1878), estampes #1203
   – (1749-1848) #1224 1225
   – Eagar, William H. #5351
   – Gray, John Warren #5648
   – Hammond, Charlotte Wilson #5697
   – Heriot, George #5785
   – Lawson, Ernest #6175
   – Lismer, Arthur #6294
   – Miles, John Christopher #6532
   – Petley, Robert #5351
   – Woolford, John Elliott #258 259
   – XVIIe s.-1918 #1202
– vues photographiques
   – MacAskill, Wallace R. #6351
Nouvelle-Zélande, Pacific Rim Symposium
– Burrows, Tom, *Gas Works* #4960
Nova, Gary Lee
– *voir* Lee-Nova, Gary
Nova Scotia Glass Co., fabricants de verre (Trenton, NE) #2398 2409 2421 2435
Nova Scotia Society of Artists #1119 1194
– expositions
   – (1923-1972) #1192
Nova Scotia Talent Trust
– protection des arts #1199
Nowlan, Alden, poète can, 1933-
– *Shaped by This Land* #5463
nu dans l'art
– *voir aussi* art érotique; figure humaine dans l'art
– Brooker, Bertram Richard, commentaire #317
– Muhlstock, Louis, commentaire #6652
– peinture canadienne #101

– Pellan, Alfred #6826
– Vilder, Roger #1489
Nugent, John, artiste can, 1921-
– expositions de groupe
   – (1972) #1922
nuit
– photographies, Michael Mitchell #6575 6576
Nulf, Frank Allen, artiste can, 1933-
– dessins #6729
– expositions
   – (1975) #6727
   – (1976) #6728
– expositions de groupe
   – (1977) #1933
   – (1979) #678
Number Ten Architectural Group, agence can d'architecture
– Winnipeg (Man)
   – University of Manitoba. University Centre #9488
   – Winnipeg Art Gallery #9117
Numismatic and Antiquarian Society of Montreal
– *voir* Société d'archéologie et de numismatique de Montréal (Montréal, Qué)
numismatique
– *voir* monnaies et médailles
Nuna, Noah, sculpteur can, 1900-
– entretien #6712
Nunivak Island (Alaska)
– vannerie #4180
Nutt, Elizabeth Styring, artiste can, 1870-1946
– directrice, Nova Scotia College of Art (Halifax, NE) #1194 2993
– et Nova Scotia Society of Artists #1192
– expositions
   – (1981) #6730
Nutter, Arthur E., architecte can, 1874-1967
– London (Ont), Lord Roberts School #9388
Nymark, Victor, constructeur can, actif années 1930
– Montebello (Qué), Château Montebello #9295

O

O'Brien, Lucius Richard, artiste can, 1832-1899 #178
– aménagement de sa résidence en galerie d'art, Jenkins Art Galleries (Toronto, Ont) #8053
– et Thomas Mower Martin #6438
– expositions, critiques #174 186 1703
– expositions de groupe
   – (1888) #175
   – (1890) #1839
– paysages #2008
O'Brien, Paddy Gunn, artiste can, 1929-
– expositions de groupe
   – (1965) #473
O'Donnell, James, architecte amér, 1774-1830 #8848
– et architecture québécoise #7851
– Montréal (Qué), église Notre-Dame #1233 8780 8839 8849 8892
O'Donnell, William D., photographe can, actif années 1850-1860 #1211
O'Neil, Bruce William, artiste can, 1942-

#6734
O'Neill, Louis, homme d'Etat can, 1925-
– art vidéo #1550
O'Reilly, Samuel F., artiste amér, actif ca 1900
– tatouages #2923
Oak Ridge (Ont), De La Salle Training School
– architecture, Hynes, Feldman & Watson #9386
Oakville (Ont)
– architecture #8025
Oakville (Ont), Oakville Centennial Gallery
– expositions
   – *Alan C. Collier Retrospective* (1971) #5131
   – *Contemporary Native Arts of Ontario* (1973) #4133
   – *Ed Bartram: 10 Years* (1980) #4618
   – *Imprint '76* (1977) #833
   – *Neil Newton Retrospective* (1978) #6694
   – *Of Human Bondage* (1976) #611
   – *The Heritage of Jack Bush: A Tribute* (1981) #722
Oberheide, Heidi, artiste can, 1943- #1148
– et St. Michael's Printshop (St. John's, TN) #1159
objets d'art
– *voir* arts décoratifs
objets liturgiques
– *voir aussi* calices; ciboires; cloches; croix; crucifix; objets religieux; tabernacles
objets liturgiques . Canada
– Québec
   – (années 1950) #1406
   – encensoirs, XVIIe-XVIIIe s. #2665
   – jésuites #2192
   – paix, XVIIe-XIXe s. #2666
   – XVIIe-XIXe s. #2681
– XVIIe-XIXe s. #2627
objets religieux
– *voir aussi* objets liturgiques
objets religieux . Canada
– (1964-1967) #2108 2109
– Québec
   – XVIIe s., jésuites #2192
   – XVIIe-XIXe s. #1245
   – XVIIe-XVIIIe s. #2187
– Québec (Qué), XVIIe s. #1352
Odelin & Mailloux, agence can d'architecture
– L'Acadie (Qué), église #8830
Odjig, Daphne, artiste can, 1919- #4136 4155 4157 6731
– expositions, critiques #1866
   – (1977) #4128
– expositions de groupe
   – (1972) #4131
   – (1975) #4141
   – (1981) #4173
– influence des images de la société des Midéwiwins #4154
Offenbach (Allemagne de l'Ouest), Deutsches Ledermuseum
– expositions
   – *Deutsches Ledermuseum: Katalog Heft 4: Indianer Nordamerikas, Zirkumpolare Völker* (1976) #3464
offrande votive
– Boivin, Joseph, *Ex-voto de Dorval* #4771
– Québec #1341 1370
   – croix #1621 1640
   – scènes marines et sainte Anne #1292
– sainte Anne #1230 1323
– Sainte-Anne-de-Beaupré (Qué), basilique

Sainte-Anne #1321
Ogilvie, William, photographe can,
   1846-1912
– photographies d'arpentage #1014 1015
   1865 1874
Ogilvie, William Abernathy (Will), artiste
   can, 1901- #6732
– *Bombed Houses, Caen* #1115
Ogilvie, William Watson, homme d'affaires
   can, 1835-1900
– résidence d'été, manoir Ogilvie (LaSalle,
   Qué) #8636
Ohe, Dorothy Katie von der, artiste can,
   1937-
– expositions de groupe
   – (1975) #1867
Oiseau-Tonnerre . Algonquiens #3493
Oiseau-Tonnerre . Amérindiens #3410
Oiseau-Tonnerre . Indiens de la côte
   nord-ouest #3831 3855
Oiseau-Tonnerre . Kwakiutls #3867
Oiseau-Tonnerre . Pieds-Noirs #3676
Oiseau-Tonnerre . Saulteux/Ojibwa #3699
oiseaux dans l'art
– Archambault, Louis #4539
– art traditionnel québécois #1284 1362
– Carr, Emily #5019
– corbeau
   – Kwakiutls #3883
   – Tlingits #3786
– crécelles en forme de corbeau, Indiens de
   la côte nord-ouest #3980 4026
– décoration architecturale canadienne
   (années 1930) #8226
– girouettes, Québec #2589
– Grondin, Jean-Luc #5662
– Hood, Robert #5826
– Lansdowne, James Fenwick #6163 6164
   6165
– Loates, Glen #6310
– MacDonald, Thoreau #6381
– Murphy, Burland E. #6663
– Nasmith, Eric Anderson #6685
– Newlan, Emery #6690
– Oiseau-Tonnerre
   – Algonquiens #3493
   – Amérindiens #3410
   – Indiens de la côte nord-ouest #3831 3855
   – Indiens des plaines #3758
   – Pieds-Noirs #3676
   – Saulteux/Ojibways #3699
– Phinney, Robert #6862
– Picher, Claude #6867
– Pootoogook, Kananginak #6904
– Pope, William #6905 6906
– poterie canadienne #2309
   – Goold, F.P., & Co. (Brantford, Ont)
      #2335
– Pratt, George #6916
– Roussil, Robert #7090
– Savage, Harry #7133
– sculpture inuit #4404 4459
– Shortt, Terence Michael #506 7201
– Thorburn, Archibald #7373
Ojibway (Ont)
– architecture domestique, après Première
   Guerre mondiale #8495
Oka (Qué), calvaire
– architecture et art #1355 1356 8853
– croix #1569
Oka (Qué), église d'Oka
– architecture et intérieur #8818 8885
Oklahoma City (Okla), John Deere Plow
   Company, entrepôts

– architecture, Oscar A. Eckerman #9247
Okvik
– figurine d'ivoire #4353
– sculptures #4364
– sculptures sur os #4340
Old Colony Club (TN) #1138
Oldenburg, Claes, sculpteur amér, 1929-
– Ayot, Pierre, comparaison #4572
Oldham (Angleterre), Museum and Art
   Gallery
– expositions
   – *Exhibition of Canadian Art* (1926) #290
Olier, Jean-Jacques, prêtre fr, 1608-1657
   #1365
Olitski, Jules, artiste amér, 1922-
– Christensen, Dan, comparaison #5104
– et Emma Lake Workshops (Emma Lake,
   Sask) #1929
– influence sur Jean Albert McEwen #6471
– influence sur Kenneth Lochhead #6315
Oliver, Bobbie, artiste can, 1943- #675
– expositions de groupe
   – (1980) #698
Olmsted, Frederick Law, architecte
   paysagiste amér, 1822-1903
– et Calvert Vaux #8048
– Montréal (Qué), parc du Mont-Royal
   #7903 7912 7924
Olson, Wilfred Harold, photographe can,
   1922-
– photographies, Forces armées canadiennes
   #1107
Omaha (Nebr), John Deere Plow Company,
   entrepôts
– architecture, Oscar A. Eckerman #9247
Ondaatje, Kim, artiste can, 1928- #6733
– commentaire sur la confection de
   courtepointes #2796 2798
– et Niagara Artists' Co-operative #834
Onley, Toni, artiste can, 1928- #6740 6742
– aquarelles (1974-1981) #6741
– collages #6735
– commentaire sur son voyage au Japon
   (1978) #6738
– estampes (1963-1974) #6737
– expositions
   – (1972) #6736
   – (1978) #6739
– expositions de groupe
   – (1976) #613
Only Paper Today, périodique can #1799
Onneiouts
– crécelles #3363
Onontagués
– masques #3588
Ontario
– architecture #8017 8024
   – (1763-1930) #7659
   – (1800-1855) #8014
   – (1831-1861) #8009
   – (1901-1911), Ontario Association of
      Architects #7955
   – (années 1920) #7657 8223
   – (avant 1880), corridor du canal Rideau
      #8008
   – bâtiments en bois, XIXe s. #7745
   – bâtiments en bois rond, colons
      canadiens-français, XIXe s. #7685
   – bâtiments en pierre, XIXe s. #8011
   – bâtiments polygonaux, XIXe s. #7987
   – construction à murs creux, XIX e s.
      #8004
   – et Fondation du patrimoine ontarien
      #8001

   – Jerome Markson Architects #8386 8387
   – milieu XIXe-XXe s. #8030
   – style néo-classique #7983
   – utilisation de pierre à bâtir et de pierre
      d'ornement (années 1910) #7646 7647
   – XIXe s. #5959 7959 7974 7993 8006 8015
      8023 8672
   – XVIIe-XIXe s. #7687
– architecture domestique #7968 8654
   – (1763-1860) #8527
   – (1784-1840) #7966
   – (années 1910) #8642
   – (années 1920) #8497 8646
   – (années 1930) #8647
   – charpente en madriers, XIXe s. #8046
   – début XIXe s. #8648
   – maisons en brique, début XIXe s. #8521
   – maisons en terrasses (années 1850-1950)
      #8653
   – résidences estivales, XXe s. #8524
   – résidences estivales (années 1940) #8651
   – XIXe s. #8002 8005 8656 8677 8678 8679
– architecture et arts décoratifs (1800-1850)
   #7965
– art #8943
   – (1880-années 1930) #45
   – (1979-1981), Nord de l'Ontario #1829
   – (1981) #1838
   – (années 1840-1870) #28
   – (années 1850) #1691
   – (années 1870-1970) #1666
   – (années 1880) #1698
   – (années 1940) 350 381
   – (années 1940-1970) #1670
   – (années 1950) #429
   – (années 1960) #492
   – (années 1970) #38 543 590 625 1806 1814
      1816 1825
   – (avant 1867) #2110
   – fin XIXe s. #1726
   – Ontario, francophones #1820 1821
– art traditionnel #1682
   – (années 1960) #1792
– artisans, XIXe s. #2261
– arts décoratifs
   – (1900) #2240
   – (1979-1980) #2138
   – (années 1920-1960), Corporation
      canadienne de l'artisanat #2118
   – (années 1970) #2247 2596
   – (années 1970-1980) #2257
   – artisans et points de vente (années 1970)
      #2256
   – mennonites #2251 2264 2267
   – tradition germanique #2135 2140 2263
   – XIXe s. #2099
– arts graphiques
   – (années 1960) #1756
   – Société canadienne des
      peintres-graveurs #3
– associations artistiques, XIXe s. #1706
– bâtiments agricoles (années 1920) #9225
– bibliothèques
   – (1955-1965) #9045
   – (années 1950) #9044
– buffets #2574
– bureaux (mobilier) #2579
– cabanes en bois rond #7990
   – XIXe s. #7979
– centres commerciaux (années 1950) #9373
– coffres #2554 2557
– conservation de l'architecture #7996
– costume
   – (1780-1867), costume féminin #2839

– (1784-1867) #2852
– (1867-1907) #2871
– (1867-1907), costume féminin #2843
– XIXe s. #2888
– couronnes, XIXe s. #2248
– courtepointes #2796 2797 2801 2804 2805 2806
– dessins d'architecture #8028
– écoles
  – (années 1920) #9450
  – (années 1950) #9391 9392
  – (années 1960) #9395
– écoles et universités (années 1960) #9401
– églises #8765 8906
  – (avant 1867) #8904
  – XVIIe s.-années 1860 #8904
– enseignement de l'architecture (années 1890) #8239
– enseignement de l'art (1856) #3128
– fortifications #8454
– fraktur #2254 2255 2259
– gares #9541
– granges, XIXe s. #9227 9229
– hôpitaux (années 1950) #9029
– horloges #2925
– jeux de société, XIXe-XXe s. #2597
– lampes #2918
  – XIXe s. #2947
– lits, XIXe s. #2562
– livres (années 1970) #935
– magasins
  – (années 1940) #9372
  – XIXe-XXe s. #9379
– mobilier
  – (1760-1840), style géorgien #2477
  – (1800-1837), Upper Canada Village (Morrisburg, Ont) #2549
  – (1800-1865) #2563
  – (1800-1867) #2567
  – (1850-1900) #2580
  – (années 1790-1850) #2550
  – (années 1790-1857) #2558
  – (années 1860), immigrants polonais #2565
  – (années 1920) #2547
  – (années 1950) #2467
  – importations de mobilier, XVIIIe-XIXe s. #2569
  – mennonites #2568 2572
  – XIXe s. #2552 2556 2561 2570 2571 2573
  – XIXe s.-années 1920 #2463
  – XVIIIe-XIXe s. #2474 2475
– modèles de broderie #2787
– monuments funéraires
  – fin XVIIIe-XIXe s. #1721
  – XIXe s.-années 1910 #1723
  – XVIIIe s.-années 1930 #1669
– moulins #9239
  – (années 1780-1880) #9259
– objets en bois #2590
– orfèvrerie
  – XIXe-XXe s. #2638
  – XVIIIe-XIXe s. #2627 2636
– ouvrages de ferronnerie
  – croix funéraires en fer, germano-alsaciennes #2709
  – XIXe s. #2703
– ouvrages en papier, mennonites, XIXe-début XXe s. #2265
– palais de justice, XIXe s.-début XXe s. #9010
– peinture #1676
  – (1846-1867), Haut-Canada, expositions provinciales #1715

– (années 1860-1880) #230
– (années 1920-1950) #396
– (années 1930) #589 592
– (années 1960) #484
– (années 1970) #588
– XIXe s. #1705
– photographie
  – (1856-1867) #1724
  – XIXe s. #1722 1730
– portraits
  – XIXe s. #263
– poterie #2249 2317
  – (1750-1910) #3962
  – (1796-années 1930) #2349
  – XIXe-début XXe s. #2347 2355
  – XIXe s. #2279 2284 2286 2290 2302 2303 2309 2330 2334 2335 2348 2350 2356
  – XVIIIe-XIXe s. #2318
– poterie de grès #2324
– sculpture
  – (années 1960) #749
– sièges (mobilier) #2560
  – (années 1790-1850) #2553
  – (années 1790-1870) #2564
  – XIXe s. #2575
– synagogues (années 1960) #8903
– tables #2566
  – (1815-1845), tables à battants #2555
– tapis, XIXe s. #2754
– tapisserie (années 1970) #2768
– téléphone, construction (années 1880-1950) #9298
– textiles et tissus #2249 2729
  – (1750-1900) #2727
  – XIXe s. #2723 2726
– verre
  – (1825-1948) #2399
  – XIXe s. #2401 2416 2421
– verre et poterie (années 1970) #2262
– vie des premiers colons #2245
– vues
  – (années 1890) #6436
  – Armstrong, William #4552
  – Bartram, Ed #4618
  – Bouchard, Lorne Holland #4857
  – Brigden, Fred #4913
  – Brooks, Leonard #4929
  – Lismer, Arthur #6298
  – MacDonald, J.E.H. #6361
  – Martin, Henry Byam #6426
  – Nevitt, Richard Barrington #6688
  – Price, Addison Winchell #6935
  – Reynolds, Catherine #6993
  – Schaefer, Carl Fellman #7151 7153 7157
  – Shanly, Charles Dawson #241 242
  – Simcoe, Elizabeth Posthuma Gwillim #7212
  – Varley, Frederick Horsman #7462
  – XIXe s. #1720
  – XVIIIe-XXe s. #156
– vues photographiques
  – Esson, James #5373
  – Jaycocks, T.G. #5950
Ontario. Commission des parcs du Niagara
– (années 1940) #7975
Ontario. Gouvernement de l'Ontario
– Morris, Edmund Montague, portraits d'Amérindiens, oeuvres commandées (1906-1907) #6636 6638
Ontario. Government of Ontario Art Collection #8943
– politiques d'achat (1873-1914) #1728
Ontario. Ministère des Richesses naturelles
– Fort William (Ont), restauration #8460

Ontario. Royal Commission on Education in Ontario
– recommandations (1950) #9392
Ontario Advisory Committee on University Affairs
– et Ontario College of Art (Toronto, Ont), (1968) #2996 2997
Ontario Association of Architects
– (1889-1954) #8300
– (1890-1950) #8299
– (1908), mémoires et comptes rendus #8292
– et Galerie nationale du Canada (Ottawa, Ont) concours (1975-1977) #9126
– et pratique de l'architecture, Toronto (Ont), XIXe s. #8070
– et Toronto Society of Architects #7956
– expositions
  – (1930) #1
– expositions, critiques
  – (1926) #7958
  – (1927) #7960
  – (1929) #7964
  – (1931) #7967
  – (1933) #7969
  – (1935) #7971 7972
  – (1937) #7973
– mémoires et comptes rendus
  – (1901-1911) #7955
  – *Construction: A Journal for the Architectural Engineering and Contracting Interests of Canada* #7641
– réflexion sur l'enseignement de l'architecture (années 1890) #8239
Ontario Craft, périodique can #2257
Ontario Crafts Council
– périodique, *Ontario Craft* #2257
Ontario Government Housing Competition
– (1936) #8737
Ontario Handweavers and Spinners
– (1956-1979) #2743
Ontario Historical Society
– et conservation du vieux fort York (Toronto, Ont), (1905-1909) #8458
Ontario Housing Corporation Design Competition
– (1972) #8663
Ontario Hydro Golden Medallion "All Electric Home" Competition
– (1961) #8514
Ontario Institute of Painters
– expositions, critiques
  – (1959) #432
Ontario Pottery
– *voir* Don Bridge Pottery
Ontario Society of Artists #5 14
– (1872-1898) #1706
– (1872-1947) #1672
– (1872-1972) #1679
– (1907) #3299
– (années 1890) #188
– et Albert Angus Macdonald #6354
– et Alice A. Innes #5900
– et Charlotte Mount Brook Morrell Schreiber #7164
– et Daniel Fowler #5488
– et Frederic Marlett Bell-Smith #4668
– et Helen Frances Gregor #5656
– et James Wilson Morrice #6634
– et Mary Hiester Reid #6982
– et Ronald York Wilson #7594
– et Visual Arts Ontario #1806
– expositions
  – (1873-années 1970) #1666
  – (1882), et George Agnew Reid #6977

– (1882-1948), Canadian National Exhibition (Toronto, Ont) #1
– (1883) #166
– (1900) #2240
– (1972) #1678
– expositions, critiques
– (1873) #1693
– (1875) #1695
– (1876) #1696
– (1877) #1697
– (1890) #1700
– (1892-1893) #179
– (1896) #1703
– (1898) #1707
– (1899) #1708
– (1900) #1709
– (1913) #1710
– (1919) #1731
– (1953), Ontario, fauteuil "arrow-back", thème pictural #1770
– (1955) #1748
– nationalisme et peinture de paysages, fin XIXe s. #271 272
– oeuvres, achetées par Government of Ontario Art Collection (1873-1914) #1728
– organisation d'expositions d'art étranger/Canadian National Exhibition (Toronto, Ont), (1905-1938) #107
Ontario St. Lawrence Development Commission
– et Upper Canada Village (Ont) #7982
Ontario Student Housing Corporation
– et résidences pour étudiants (années 1960) #9467
Oonark, Jessie, artiste can, 1906- #4242 4260 4460 6743 6744
– expositions de groupe
– (1970) #4220
– tapisserie #4304
op'art #468
– Canada #1445 6586
– et Denis Juneau #5994
– et Norman McLaren #6497
Opération déclic #1502
Ophthalmia Company of Inglis, Asessippi, Manitoba
– et Don Proch #6940
Opinion publique, L', périodique can
– illustrations
– Julien, Henri #5987
– Kroupa, Bohuslar #6104
Oppenheim, Dennis, artiste amér, 1938-
– cartes géographiques, illustration #561
OPT, périodique can #1799
Opus International Ltd., studio de design (Toronto, Ont)
– mobilier, Hugh Spencer #2551
oratoires . Canada
– Montréal (Qué), oratoire Saint-Joseph #8332 8794
– Montréal (Qué), résidence #8557
Orban, Jeno F., photographe can, actif années 1970
– catalogue de photographies #998
Orchinsky, Peter, collectionneur can, XXe s.
– collection, chemises bukoviniennes et bijoux féminins (1865-1945) #2869
ordinateurs
– et architecture des bibliothèques (années 1960) #9046
– et art, Arnold Rockman, commentaire #7061
– et inventaires des oeuvres d'art et de l'architecture au Canada #159

Ordre des architectes du Québec/Order of Architects of Quebec
– et l'Institut royal d'architecture du Canada (1974) #8318
– prix d'excellence en architecture
– (1978) #7886
– (1979) #9555
Oregon
– vues
– Miller, Alfred Jacob #6536 6537
– Warre, Henry James #7522
orfèvrerie
– voir aussi bijoux; chandeliers; cuillers; parure; poinçons; services de thé; squelettes dans l'art
– voir aussi bijoux; dorure
orfèvrerie . Algonquiens #2101 3605
– parure #3594 3608 3633
orfèvrerie . Amérindiens #2630
– hausse-cols #2655
– orfèvrerie de traite #269 270 2101 2628 2629 2631 2633 2634 2651 2653 2654 2659 3440
orfèvrerie . Canada #2628 2630 2637 2651
– (1700-1830) #2643
– (années 1680-1830) #2628
– (années 1960) #2102
– Baudry (dit Des Butes), Guillaume #234 235
– Beaugrand, Gilles #2179 4650
– Berthierville (Qué), église #8833 8874
– Betteridge, Lois Etherington #4718
– Brault, Maurice #4906
– Burden, Eve et John #4957
– Cap-Santé (Qué), églises #8814
– Carmichael, William Maurice #5003 5004
– Chambellan, François #2667
– comté de Bellechasse (Qué), église Saint-Charles-Borromée #8803
– Cotton, Michel #249 250
– crucifix, Québec #1585
– cuillers-souvenirs, Royal Ontario Museum. Collection Shepley (Toronto, Ont) #2652
– Delezenne, Ignace-François #269 270
– Deschevery (dit Maisonbasse), Jean-Baptiste #249 250
– Edenshaw, Charles #5360
– encensoirs, Québec, XVIIe-XVIIIe s. #2665
– famille Arnoldi, XVIIIe-XIXe s. #2663
– Gadois (dit Mauger), Jacques #249 250
– Gaudin (dit Lapoterie), Louis-Nicolas #5571
– Gaudin (dit Lapoterie), Nicolas #5571 5572
– guide pour collectionneurs #2104 2252
– Hamilton (Ont), International Silver Company #2642
– île d'Orléans (Qué), église Saint-Pierre #8802
– influence sur l'art canadien, XXe s. #2093
– jésuites, Québec #2192
– Joliette (Qué), églises #8876
– L'Islet (Qué), église Notre-Dame-de-Bon-Secours #8879
– Lambert (dit Saint-Paul), Paul #249 250 2668
– Lambert (dit Saint-Paul), Paul, et Samuel Payne #2689
– Landron, Jean-François #249 250
– Lespérance, Pierre #6248
– Levasseur, Michel #234 235 2669
– Loretteville (Qué), église Notre-Dame-de-la-Jeune-Lorette #8804
– Lotbinière (Qué), églises #8835
– Marion, Salomon #2683

– Montréal (Qué)
– église Notre-Dame #8839
– Soeurs Grises #8862
– Morand, Paul #6604
– Nordbeck, Peter #258 259
– Nouveau-Brunswick #2150
– fin XVIIIe s.-XIXe s. #2646
– Saint-Jean (NB), Musée du Nouveau-Brunswick #2649
– Nouvelle-Ecosse #2648
– XVIIe-XIXe s. #2639
– XVIIIe s.-années 1940 #2632
– XVIIIe-XXe s. #2632
– Oka (Qué), église #8818
– Ontario, XIXe-XXe s. #2638
– orfèvrerie de traite #2629 2634 2654 2659 3594 3645 3646
– hausse-cols #2655
– Ottawa (Ont), Galerie nationale du Canada. Collection Henry Birks d'orfèvrerie canadienne #2653
– Pagé (dit Quercy ou Carcy), Jacques #249 250 6749
– paix, Québec, XVIIe-XIXe s. #2666
– Paradis, Roland #249 250
– Payne, Samuel #234 235
– Picard, Louis-Alexandre #269 270
– pièce commémorative en argent #2656
– poinçons, XVIIIe-XIXe s. #2635
– provinces de l'Atlantique #2640
– Québec #1235 1237 1249 1324 1596 2169 2171 2183 2197 2226 2228 2670
– (1534-1763) #2684
– (1613-1870) #2191
– (1640-1840) #1329
– (1760-1790) #1369
– (1867-1871) #2675
– (années 1940) #2199
– (années 1950) #2193
– apprentis (1660-1815) #2231
– Carrier, Louis, collection #3213
– Morisset, Gérard, commentaire #2692
– publications #1295
– XVIIe-XIXe s. #216 1330 1331 1589 2095 2101 2660 2662 2664 2674 2676 2678 2681 2685 2686 2690 2691
– en comparaison avec orfèvrerie française #2688
– XVIIe-XVIIIe s. #1320 1327 2181 2187 2657 2664
– XVIIIe-début XXe s. #1339
– XVIIIe s. #1620 2673 2677 5277
– XVIIIe-XIXe s. #2644 2650 2661
– composition, analyse #2682
– Québec (Qué)
– Couvent des ursulines #8810
– XVIIe s. #1352
– Ranvoyzé, François #2658 2679 2680 6959 6960
– Saint-Jean (NB), église en pierre #8778
– Sasseville, François #258 259 2672
– Schindler, Joseph #269 270
– Stacey, Harold #7273 7274
– Stuart, Don #7281
– tasses à quêter, Québec, XVIIe-XVIIIe s. #2671
– Toronto (Ont), Ontario College of Art #3009
– Varennes (Qué), églises #8813
– Varin (dit La Pistole), Jacques #269 270
– Victoria (CB) #2269
– XVIIe s.-1867 #2110
– XVIIe-XIXe s. #2128 2627
– Henry Birks et fils Ltée., collection #2636

– maisons en terrasses, XIXe s. #8653
– architecture et urbanisme, Région de la capitale nationale #7683 8034 8035 8037 8039 8041 8045
– art (années 1960) #441
– conservation de l'architecture, Région de la capitale nationale #8043 8044
– édifices récréatifs #9081
– galeries (années 1960) #442
– photographie #1675
  – (1896) #1704
  – (1896-1970) #1677
– sculpture
  – (années 1890) #727
  – Région de la capitale nationale #762
– vues
  – (1807-1882), estampes #1716
– vues photographiques
  – (1850-1900) #1061
  – Topley, William James #1001
Ottawa (Ont), Académie de La Salle
– architecture #9480 9481
Ottawa (Ont), aéroport d'Uplands
– sculpture, Louis Archambault #4542
Ottawa (Ont), Aéroport international d'Ottawa. Aérogare
– architecture, Gilleland & Strutt et William Alexander Ramsay #9515
Ottawa (Ont), Archives nationales du Canada/National Archives of Canada
– voir Ottawa(Ont), Archives publiques du Canada/Public Archives of Canada
Ottawa (Ont), Archives publiques du Canada/Public Archives of Canada
– aquarelles et dessins (1750-1850) #239
– archives de l'architecture #7738
– collection (1925) #3023
– Coverdale, William H., Collection Canadiana #12 3230
– expositions
  – City Blocks, City Spaces: Historical Photographs of Canada's Urban Growth, c.1850-1900/Espaces urbains: photographies historiques de la croissance urbaine au Canada, vers 1850-1900 (1980) #7744
    – Koltun, Lilly, commentaire #1061
  – Daily Smile/Sourire quotidien (1980) #6401
  – Dans le silence et la solitude: la photographie d'arpentage dans l'Ouest canadien (1858-1900) (1975) #1014
  – Exposition d'estampes en l'honneur de C. Krieghoff, 1815-1872/Exhibition of Prints in Honour of C. Krieghoff, 1815-1872 (1972) #6096
  – Friendly Spies on the Northern Tour, 1815-1837: The Sketches of Henry Byam Martin/Aimables espions en Amérique du Nord, 1815-1837: croquis d'Henry Byam Martin (1981) #6426
  – Image of Canada: Documentary Watercolours and Drawings from the Permanent Collection of the Public Archives of Canada/Visage du Canada: aquarelles et dessins historiques tirés de la collection permanente des Archives publiques du Canada, #244
  – Into the Silent Land: Survey Photography in the Canadian West (1858-1900) (1975) #1015
  – Karl May Retrospective, 1948-1975/Rétrospective Karl May 1948-1975 (1976) #6453
  – Napoléon Bourassa, 1827-1916 (1976) #4872

  – Neil Newton Retrospective (1978) #6694
  – Printmaking in Canada: The Earliest Views and Portraits/Les débuts de l'estampe imprimée au Canada: vues et portraits (1980) #839
  – Reflections on a Capital: 12 Ottawa Photographers, Selected from the National Photographic Collection in the Public Archives of Canada/Reflets d'une capitale: 12 photographes d'Ottawa, choix tiré de la Collection nationale de photographies aux Archives publiques du Canada (1970) #1675
  – Seventy-five Years of Photography, 1896 to 1970 (1971) #1677
  – Ten Contemporary Canadian Medallists/Dix médailleurs canadiens contemporains (1971) #772
– gravures sur panneaux de verre, John Hutton #5894
– Heriot, George, oeuvres #5785
– Miller, Alfred Jacob, peintures #6536 6537
– Moodie, Geraldine, photographies #6602
– Warre, Henry James, oeuvres #7522
Ottawa (Ont), Archives publiques du Canada. Collection nationale de photographies/Public Archives of Canada. National Photography Collection #3052
– Baltzly, Benjamin, photographies #4598
– Fleming, Sandford, collection #1876
– Hime, Humphrey Lloyd, photographies #5803
– Mitchell, Thomas, et George Harlow White, photographies, expédition britannique dans l'Arctique (1875-1876) #240
– modèle, collection de photographies des archives du Yukon #2087
– Nakash, George, portraits photographiques #6683
– photographies d'immigrants (1908-1910) #1031
Ottawa (Ont), Archives publiques du Canada. Division de l'iconographie/Public Archives of Canada. Picture Division
– illustrations de costumes #2883 2884 2904
– normes pour descriptions d'oeuvres d'art #159
Ottawa (Ont), Association médicale canadienne
– collection, art canadien #138
Ottawa (Ont), Banque de Nouvelle-Ecosse
– architecture, John MacIntosh Lyle #9186 9203
Ottawa (Ont), Banque du Canada, siège social (1938)
– architecture, Marani, Lawson & Morris; Sumner Godfrey Davenport, Associated Architects #9337
Ottawa (Ont), Banque du Canada, siège social (1978)
– architecture, Marani, Rounthwaite & Dick; Arthur Erickson, Associated Architects #9199
Ottawa (Ont), Bibliothèque nationale du Canada/National Library of Canada
– expositions
  – Albert Laberge, 1871-1960; Charles Gill, 1871-1918 #5604
  – Pictures to Share: Illustration in Canadian Children's Books: Annotated Catalogue/Images pour tous: illustration de

livres canadiens pour enfants: catalogue annoté (1979) #937
– gravures sur panneaux de verre, John Hutton #5894
Ottawa (Ont), Bibliothèque publique d'Ottawa
– expositions
  – Hooked Rugs: A Canadian Tradition (1975) #2755
Ottawa (Ont), Bibliothèque scientifique nationale
– architecture et art #9049
Ottawa (Ont), Canterbury High School
– enseignement de l'art (années 1970) #3004
Ottawa (Ont), Carleton University
– architecture, Watson Balharrie, Hart Massey, Eric Arthur, John Bland, et Campbell Merrett #9455
– collection d'oeuvres d'art #3144
– expositions
  – Canadian Printmakers' Showcase (1969-1974) #823
Ottawa (Ont), Carleton University. Henry Marshall Tory Science Building
– mosaïque murale, Gerald Mathew Trottier #7429
Ottawa (Ont), Carleton University. School of Architecture
– architecture, Carmen Corneil avec l'aide de Schoeler Heaton Menendez #8284
– enseignement de l'architecture (1980) #8289
Ottawa (Ont), Centre canadien d'études sur la culture traditionnelle
– voir Ottawa (Ont), Musée national de l'Homme. Centre canadien d'études sur la culture traditionnelle/National Museum of Man. Canadian Centre for Folk Culture Studies
Ottawa (Ont), Centre de conférences du gouvernement canadien/Canadian Government Conference Centre
– expositions
  – A Display of Contemporary Canadian Works of Art Organized by the National Gallery of Canada, on the Occasion of the Commonwealth Heads of Government Meeting, 2-10 August 1973 at the Canadian Government Conference Centre, Ottawa/Exposition d'oeuvres canadiennes contemporaines, organisée par la Galerie nationale du Canada, à l'occasion de la réunion des chefs de gouvernement du Commonwealth, du 2 au 10 août, 1973 (1973) #556
  – An Exhibition of Canadian Photography Produced by the Still Photography Division, National Film Board of Canada on the Occasion of the Commonwealth Heads of Government Meeting, Aug 2-10, 1973/Une exposition de photographies canadiennes présentée par le Service de la photographie de l'Office national du film du Canada, à l'occasion de la Conférence des chefs de gouvernement du Commonwealth, 2-10 août, 1973 (1973) #1002
  – Photo Festival '74 (1974) #1009
– expositions, critiques
  – Photo Festival '74 (1974) #1008
– Reeves, John #6972
Ottawa (Ont), Centre municipal d'Ottawa
– architecture, Gerald Hamilton & Associates; Craig & Kohler #9101
Ottawa (Ont), Centre national des

arts/National Arts Centre
- architecture #7709
- architecture et art #9104 9105 9108
- expositions
  - *Oonark/Pangnark* (1970) #4220
- murale, William S. Ronald #7074
- rideau de scène, Micheline Beauchemin #4644
- sculpture, Charles Daudelin #5261
Ottawa (Ont), Château Laurier
- architecture #9265
  - Archibald, John Smith, et John Schofield #9282
  - Gilbert, Bradford Lee #9529
  - Gilbert, Bradford Lee; Ross & Macfarlane #9528
Ottawa (Ont), cinéma Capitol
- architecture #9110 9131
  - Lamb, Thomas White #9122 9123
Ottawa (Ont), cinéma Loew
- architecture #9099
Ottawa (Ont), Conseil des Arts du Canada. Banque d'oeuvres d'art/Canada Council. Art Bank #625
- (1972-1975) #3276
- (années 1970) #3293
  - et entreprises #3286
- achat d'oeuvres d'art canadiennes #3273
- acquisitions (1972-1975) #576
- expositions
  - *Transparent Things: The Artist's Use of the Photograph/Transparences: l'utilisation de la photographie par l'artiste* (1977) #635
- influence sur art canadien (années 1970) #3277
- influence sur le marché de l'art canadien (années 1970) #3236
- politique d'achat #3287
Ottawa (Ont), Design Centre
- Bush, Robin B. #4979
Ottawa (Ont), Dominion Art Exhibition
- expositions, critiques
  - (1880) #167
Ottawa (Ont), Earnscliffe
- architecture et intérieur #8652
Ottawa (Ont), édifice des Affaires des anciens combattants
- expositions
  - *World War II Paintings from the War Collections of the National Gallery of Canada/Tableaux de la Seconde Guerre mondiale: collections de guerre de la Galerie nationale du Canada* (1970) #1103
Ottawa (Ont), édifice des Pêcheries
- et Galerie nationale du Canada #275
Ottawa (Ont), édifices du Parlement
- architecture #7695 8930 8931 8932
  - Darling & Pearson; Joseph-Omer Marchand, Associate Architect #8926
  - Fuller, Thomas #7671 8366
    - influence sur l'architecture des bureaux de poste, XIXe s. #9054 9055
  - Fuller & Jones #8922
  - Pearson, John Andrew, et Joseph-Omer Marchand #8927
  - style national #7697
  - utilisation de construction à murs creux, XIXe s. #8004
- architecture, concours
  - Foulis, James #8923
  - Sproatt & Rolph #8924
- architecture paysagiste, Calvert Vaux #8048
- fenêtres commémoratives en l'honneur des

soldats, Gladys W. Allen et F.S.J. Hollister #2445
- Harris, Robert, *The Fathers of Confederation* #5736
- ouvrage de ferronnerie, Paul Beau #4640 4641
- photographies de bâtiments en construction #1019
- sculptures #755
- sculptures et verrières, Eleanor Milne #6568
Ottawa (Ont), édifices du Parlement. Departmental and Justice Buildings
- architecture, concours #8921
Ottawa (Ont), édifices du Parlement. Edifice de l'Est (autrefois Departmental Buildings)
- architecture #8936
  - Stent & Laver #8922
- architecture et intérieur #8933 8934
- architecture et rénovation #8935
Ottawa (Ont), édifices du Parlement. Edifice du Centre
- destruction (1916) #8925
Ottawa (Ont), édifices du Parlement. Tour de la Paix et Chapelle du Souvenir
- architecture et intérieur, John Andrew Pearson #8928 8929
Ottawa (Ont), église St-Maurice
- architecture, Murray & Murray #8766
Ottawa (Ont), Galerie nationale du Canada/National Gallery of Canada
- (1880-1913) #3021 3022
- (1880-1921) #3041
- (1880-1966) #3050
- (1880-1970) #3049
- (1880-1980) #3061
- (1882-1979), expositions #3063
- (1924), conflit avec Académie royale des arts du Canada #500
- (1928-1929), expositions #307
- (1941), Conference of Canadian Artists #351
- (1951), Commission royale d'enquête sur l'avancement des arts, lettres et sciences (Rapport Massey) #3254 3255 3256
- (1979-1980), expositions itinérantes, provinces maritimes #3062
- (années 1870), plans pour la création d'une galerie nationale de peintures #1693
- (années 1870-1883), documents #166
- (années 1880-1890), plans pour la contruction d'une galerie nationale #184
- (années 1890) #188
- (années 1920) #288
- (années 1930) #3025
- (années 1940) #3027 3028
  - critique, nu dans l'art #6652
  - et enseignement de l'art #2983
- (années 1960) #3039 3044
- (années 1970) #3048 3102
  - photographie, appui #1038
- architecture
  - Green, Blankstein, Russell & Associates #3035
- architecture, concours
  - (1954) #9079
  - (1975-1977) #7747 9126 9136 9142
- art canadien #3273
  - en comparaison avec University of Toronto. Hart House (Toronto, Ont) #3137
- Baltzly, Benjamin, photographies #4598
- Barnsley, James Macdonald, oeuvres #4613
- Berczy, William von Moll, *Woolsey Family*

#4700
- Borduas, Paul-Emile
  - peintures #1266
  - *Sous le vent de l'île* #4815
- Brown, Eric, directeur #3029 3032 3040
- *Canadian Design Index-NIDC* #2604 2606
- Carr, Emily, *Blunden Harbour* #5036
- Centre d'esthétique industrielle et *Canadian Design Index-NIDC* (1953-1954) #3033
- collection Liechtenstein #3035
- Colville, Alex, peintures #5144
- Coverdale, William H., collection #3230
- dessins de paysages, Canada, début XXe s. #497
- directeurs #3058
- Duncan, Douglas M., collection #119 570
- et A.Y. Jackson #5925
- et Académie royale des arts du Canada #275
- et Donald William Buchanan #3325
- et Edmond Dyonnet #5348
- et Emily Carr #5034
- et Fédération des artistes canadiens #364
- et Homer Ransford Watson #7533
- et National Industrial Design Committee #2609
- et sir Byron Edmund Waker #3206
- expositions
  - *"Our Own Country Canada"/"Notre patrie le Canada"* (1978) #264
  - *03 23 03: premières rencontres internationales d'art contemporain, Montréal 1977* (1977) #634
  - *7 West Coast Painters* (1959) #1997
  - *A.Y. Jackson: Paintings, 1902-1953* (1953) #5914
  - *A Display of Contemporary Canadian Works of Art Organized by the National Gallery of Canada, on the Occasion of the Commonwealth Heads of Government Meeting, 2-10 August 1973 at the Canadian Government Conference Centre, Ottawa/Exposition d'oeuvres canadiennes contemporaines, organisée par la Galerie nationale du Canada, à l'occasion de la réunion des chefs de gouvernement du Commonwealth, du 2 au 10 août, 1973* (1973) #556
  - *A Pageant of Canada/Pages d'histoire du Canada* (1967) #232
  - *Adrien Hébert: trente ans de son oeuvre, 1923-1953/Adrien Hébert: Thirty Years of His Art, 1923-1953* (1971) #5763
  - *Albert H. Robinson: Retrospective Exhibition* (1955) #7055
  - *Alfred Pellan* (1960) #6807
  - *Annual Exhibition of Canadian Art* (1926-1933) #294
  - *Another Dimension/Une autre dimension* (1977) #783
  - *Antoine Plamondon, 1802-1895; Théophile Hamel, 1817-1870: Two Painters of Quebec/Antoine Plamondon, 1802-1895; Théophile Hamel, 1817-1870: deux peintres du Québec* (1970) #1348
  - *Arte indio y esquimal del Canada/Indian and Eskimo Art of Canada/Art indien et esquimau du Canada/Die Kunst der Indianer und Eskimos in Kanada* (1969) #3352
  - *Arthur Lismer: Paintings, 1913-1949* (1950) #6298
  - *Artists of Atlantic Canada/Artistes de la*

Montreal/L'Association des artistes non-figuratifs de Montréal (1960) #1415
- *The Vincent Massey Bequest: The Canadian Paintings/Legs Vincent Massey: peintures canadiennes (1968)* #3227
- *The Works of Joseph Légaré: 1795-1855 (1978)* #6218
- *Thomas Davies, c.1737-1812 (1972)* #5272
- *Three Hundred Years of Canadian Art: An Exhibition Arranged in Celebration of the Centenary of Confederation/Trois cents ans d'art canadien: exposition organisée à l'occasion du centenaire de la Confédération (1967)* #85
- *Toronto Painting: 1953-1965/La Peinture torontoise 1953-1965 (1972)* #1772
- *Traditional Landscape Painting in Canada/Le paysage dans la peinture canadienne (1968)* #88
- *Treasures from Quebec: An Exhibition of Paintings Assembled from Quebec and Its Environs/Trésors de Québec: exposition de peintures provenant de Québec et des environs (1965)* #1344
- *True Patriot Love/Véritable amour patriotique (1971)* #7577
- *Une imagerie canadienne: peinture et dessins du musée McCord de l'Université McGill (1962)* #222
- *Walter J. Phillips: A Selection of His Works and Thoughts/Walter J. Phillips: un choix de son oeuvre et de ses réflexions (1978)* #6860
- *Watercolour Painters from Saskatchewan/Aquarellistes de la Saskatchewan (1971)* #1920
- *William Brymner, 1855-1925: A Retrospective/William Brymner, 1855-1925: aperçu rétrospectif de l'artiste (1979)* #4953
- expositions, critiques
  - *2e exposition annuelle d'art canadien (1927)* #298
  - *300 Years of Canadian Art: An Exhibition Arranged in Celebration of the Centenary of Confederation/Trois cents ans d'art canadien: exposition organisée à l'occasion du centenaire de la Confédération (1967)* #488
  - *Biennial Exhibition of Canadian Art (1957)* #420
  - *Biennial Exhibition of Canadian Painting (1955)* #410
  - *Canadian Army Art Exhibition (1944)* #1089
  - *Cent onze dessins du Québec/One Hundred and Eleven Drawings from Québec (1976)* #1520
    - Parent, Alain, commentaire #1523
  - *Claude Tousignant (1973)* #7400
  - *Design in Industry (1947)* #2602
  - *Dumouchel, Albert* #5333
  - *Frenkel, Vera* #5520
  - *Greg Curnoe: rétrospective/Greg Curnoe: Retrospective (1981)* #5233
  - *Guido Molinari (1976)* #6585
  - *John Hall: Paintings and Auxiliary Works, 1969-1978/John Hall: peintures et oeuvres auxiliaires, 1969-1978 (1979)* #5684
  - *L'orfèvrerie en Nouvelle-France (1974)* #2688
  - MacAulay, John, collection d'art canadien et d'art européen (1954) #3212
  - *Maurice Cullen, 1866-1934 (1956)* #5224
  - *Ozias Leduc: peinture symboliste et religieuse/Ozias Leduc: Symbolist and Religious Painting (1974)* #6207
  - *Peintres du Québec: collection Maurice et Andrée Corbeil/Painters of Quebec: Maurice and Andrée Corbeil Collection (1973)* #3233
  - *People's Art: Naïve Art in Canada/L'art populaire: l'art naïf au Canada* #964
  - *Pluralities: 1980/Pluralités: 1980 (1980)* #691
  - *Second Exhibition of Canadian War Art (1946)* #1098
  - *Some Canadian Women Artists/Quelques artistes canadiennes (1975)* #579
  - *The Development of Painting in Canada, 1665-1945/Le développement de la peinture au Canada, 1665-1945 (1945)* #32
  - *The Drawings of Alfred Pellan (1980)* #6823
  - *The Works of Joseph Légaré: 1795-1855 (1978)* #6221
  - *Three Hundred Years of Canadian Art: An Exhibition Arranged in Celebration of the Centenary of Confederation/Trois cents ans d'art canadien: exposition organisée à l'occasion du centenaire de la Confédération (1967)* #80
  - *Toronto Painting: 1953-1965/La peinture torontoise 1953-1965 (1972)* #1773 1775
  - *True Patriot Love/Véritable amour patriotique (1971)* #7576
- Field, Robert, portrait de Provo William Parry Wallis #5430 5431
- Groupe des Sept et Tom Thomson, peintures murales, maison de James MacCallum (près de Go Home Bay, Ont) #1745
- guerre, collections d'oeuvres d'art
  - Première et Seconde Guerres mondiales #1101
  - Première Guerre mondiale #1103
  - Première Guerre mondiale, Canadian War Memorials, collection #1102
- inventaire informatisé de la collection #159
- Jackson, A.Y., carnet à dessins (1909) #5924
- Jackson, Henry Alexander Carmichael, aquarelles, natures mortes (champignons) #5927 5928
- Krieghoff, Cornelius, peintures, vie rurale au Québec #6100
- Laliberté, Alfred, sculptures #6147
- Leduc, Ozias, peintures #1266
- Lewis, Wyndham, *A Canadian Gunpit* #6279
- Lismer, Arthur, *A September Gale, Georgian Bay* #6304
- MacDonald, J.E.H., carnets à dessins #6373
- Marion, Salomon, statue de l'Immaculée Conception #2683
- McCurry, Harry Orr, directeur #3036
- Milne, David Brown, *Painting Place* #6562
- Morrice, James Wilson, carnets à dessins #6632
- Musée des beaux-arts de Montréal (Montréal, Qué), comparaison #3099
- orfèvrerie, Collection Henry Birks d'argenterie canadienne
  - pièces commémoratives en argent #2656
- orfèvrerie, Collection Henry Birks d'orfèvrerie canadienne #2653
- Patterson, Dan, sculpture, boîtes de lait Carnation #962
- peinture et sculpture canadiennes #3038

- peintures murales, Hall-Croscup House (près de Granville Ferry, NE) #1223
- Pellan, Alfred, portraits #6814
- périodique, *Galerie nationale du Canada. Bulletin annuel/National Gallery of Canada. Annual Bulletin* #69
- Plamondon, Antoine-Sébastien, portrait de soeur Saint-Alphonse #6887
- Ranvoyzé, François, calices #2680
- Suzor-Coté, Marc-Aurèle de Foy, *Paysage d'hiver* #7301
- Thomson, Tom, *Le pin* #7369
- Viau, Guy, directeur adjoint #7485
- Wallis, Katherine Elizabeth, *La lutte pour la vie* #7512
Ottawa (Ont), gare Centrale
- architecture
  - Gilbert, Bradford Lee #9529
  - Gilbert, Bradford Lee; Ross & Macfarlane #9528
  - Ross & Macfarlane #9264
Ottawa (Ont), Hall of Commerce Building
- expositions
  - *Visual Arts Ottawa Survey Exhibition no. 1: The First Comprehensive Survey of the Visual Arts in Ottawa-Outaouais and the Valley/Arts visuels outaouais Expo-Inventaire no 1: premier inventaire des ressources artistiques outaouaises (1975)* #590
Ottawa (Ont), Héritage Canada. Galerie d'art
- expositions
  - *The Architecture of W.E. Noffke (1976)* #8393
Ottawa (Ont), hôtel Champagne
- architecture #9480 9481
Ottawa (Ont), hôtel de ville
- architecture, Rother/Bland/Trudeau #7679 8984
Ottawa (Ont), maison Hanlon
- architecture, James William Strutt #7984
Ottawa (Ont), Metropolitan Life Insurance Building
- Jaworska, Tamara Hans, *Stream of Life* #5949
Ottawa (Ont), monument Baldwin-Lafontaine
- Allward, Walter Seymour #4516
Ottawa (Ont), Musée canadien de la guerre/Canadian War Museum
- aviation, peintures, Seconde Guerre mondiale #1110
- Colville, Alex, dessins #5156
- Cullen, Maurice Galbraith, peintures #5215
- expositions
  - *A Terrible Beauty: The Art of Canada at War (1980)* #1111
  - *Aviation Paintings from the Art Collection of the Canadian War Museum (1972)* #1104
  - *Beauté tragique: les deux conflits mondiaux vus par des artistes canadiens (1980)* #1112
  - *Four War Artists/Quatre artistes de guerre (1981)* #1117
  - *Naval Paintings of the Second World War/Tableaux navals de la Seconde Guerre mondiale (1973)* #1106
  - *Tableaux de l'aviation militaire, provenant de la collection d'art du Musée de guerre canadien (1972)* #1105
- uniformes militaires #2910 2911
Ottawa (Ont), Musée canadien des civilisations/Canadian Museum of

Civilization
– *voir* Ottawa (Ont), Musée national de l'Homme/National Museum of Man
Ottawa (Ont), Musée des beaux-arts du Canada/National Gallery of Canada
– *voir* Ottawa (Ont), Galerie nationale du Canada/National Gallery of Canada
Ottawa (Ont), Musée national de l'Homme/National Museum of Man
– architecture, Thompson, Berwick, Pratt & Partners #8041
– art amérindien #3408 3452
– collection Speyer #3622
– art kwakiutl, oeuvres retournés aux Kwakiutls #3060
– art tsimshian #3926
– artefacts dorsétiens #4322
– artefacts thuléens #4372
– courtepointes ontariennes, collection Ruth McKendry #2804
– couvre-lits, comté de Charlevoix (Qué) #2738
– cuivres, Indiens de la côte nord-ouest #3924
– et Commission royale d'enquête sur l'avancement des arts, lettres et sciences (Rapport Massey) #3254 3255 9906
– expositions
  – *"Bo'jou, Neejee!": Profiles of Canadian Indian Art* (1976) #3466
  – *"Bo'jou, Neejee!": regards sur l'art indien du Canada* (1976) #3465
  – *Canadian Political Cartoons* (1977) #956
  – *Continuity and Change: The Ukrainian Folk Heritage in Canada* (1972) #961
  – *L'art assure notre survivance/We Still Live in Our Art* (1971) #2117
  – *La chaîne d'alliance: l'orfèvrerie de traite et de cérémonie chez les Indiens* (1980) #3645
  – *Les Athabascans, ces étrangers du Nord: une exposition itinérante formée des collections du Musée national de l'Homme (Canada) et du Royal Scottish Museum* (1974) #4104
  – *Quebec Furniture, 1700-1820/Le mobilier québécois, 1700-1820* (1973) #2537
  – *Sculpture of the Inuit: Masterworks of the Canadian Arctic/La sculpture chez les Inuit: chefs-d'oeuvre de l'Arctique canadien* (1973) #4423 4440
  – *The Art of Nunstins/L'art de Nunstins* (1981) #6934
  – *The Athapaskans: Strangers of the North; An International Travelling Exhibition from the Collection of the National Museum of Man, Canada, and the Royal Scottish Museum* (1974) #4105
  – *The Covenant Chain: Indian Ceremonial and Trade Silver* (1980) #3646
  – *The Inuit Print/L'estampe inuit* (1977) #4490
– expositions, critiques
  – *The Inuit Print/L'estampe inuit* (1977) #4493
– jésuites, objets religieux #2192
– Jobin, Louis, sculptures #5967
– masque, Tsimshians #4069
– masques, Bella-Coolas #4000
– mobilier #2484
– nichoirs d'oiseaux, Canada #2593
– pantins, Tsimshians #3891
– pierre sacrificielle, Nahuas, remise en question de son authenticité #4094
– Pitseolak, Peter, aquarelles #6875 6877

– Québec, moules #2916
– rouets #2483
– salles d'exposition (1976) #3057
– sculpture inuit #4417 4437
– St-Germain, Arthème, sculptures #962
– vannerie, Micmacs #3630
Ottawa (Ont), Musée national de l'Homme. Centre canadien d'études sur la culture traditionnelle/National Museum of Man. Canadian Centre for Folk Culture Studies
– art traditionnel canadien #963 969
Ottawa (Ont), Musées nationaux du Canada/National Museums of Canada
– (1840-1969) #3047
– et Banque d'oeuvres d'art (années 1970) #3277
Ottawa (Ont), Northern Electric Research and Development Laboratories
– architecture, Bland, Lemoyne & Edwards and Charles Elliott Trudeau #9344
Ottawa (Ont), Office national du film du Canada. Galerie de l'Image/National Film Board of Canada. Photo Gallery
– expositions
  – *The Female Eye/Coup d'oeil féminin* (1975) #1011
  – *Words and Images/Mots et images* (1980) #1063
– expositions, critiques
  – *13 Cameras* (1979) #1044
  – *From an Icicle, I Made Winter* (1974) #1008
  – *Glass Dreams* (1974) #1008
  – *People of the Gaspé* (1974) #1008
  – *The Female Eye/Coup d'oeil féminin* (1975) #1013
  – *Winter Mood* (1974) #1008
Ottawa (Ont), Office national du film du Canada. Service de la photographie/National Film Board of Canada. Still Photography Division
– (1916-1977) #1043
– et Lorraine Monk #1020 1028
Ottawa (Ont), Ottawa Little Theatre
– décors, Stan White #7555
Ottawa (Ont), Photothèque nationale de l'air #1017
Ottawa (Ont), Place Bell Canada
– Jaworska, Tamara Hans, *Unity* #5949
Ottawa (Ont), Place de Ville
– architecture et urbanisme #9302
Ottawa (Ont), Rideau Hall
– architecture #8755 8756
Ottawa (Ont), Robertson Galleries
– expositions
  – *Eskimo Sculpture, '69* (1969) #4418
– expositions, critiques
  – Tagoona, Armand #7311
Ottawa (Ont), Royal Engineers, bureaux
– architecture #8019
Ottawa (Ont), Russell Opera House
– murale, Frederick Sproston Challener #5068
Ottawa (Ont), Saint Basil's Roman Catholic Church
– architecture, Bemi, Murray & Associates #8765
Ottawa (Ont), Saint Michael and All Angels Church
– architecture, Edward J. Cuhaci #8766
Ottawa (Ont), secteur des monuments aux disparus
– architecture, Hart Massey #8041
Ottawa (Ont), station d'éclusage d'Ottawa

– architecture #8019
Ottawa (Ont), Sussex Annex Works
– expositions
  – *Contemporary Canadian Poster Art from 1960 to the Present* (1976) #903
Ottawa (Ont), Thomas Donnelly House
– architecture #9480 9481
Ottawa (Ont), Tovell House
– architecture, Massey & Flanders #8519
Ottawa (Ont), Université d'Ottawa
– architecture, James A. Murray #9458 9465
Ottawa (Ont), Université d'Ottawa. Ecole d'architecture
– enseignement de l'architecture (1976) #7728
Ottawa (Ont), Wallack Galleries
– expositions
  – *New Paintings by Otto Rogers* (1974) #7062
Ottawa Camera Club (Ottawa, Ont)
– expositions
  – (1971) #1677
– expositions, critiques
  – (1896) #1704
Ottawa Glass Works, fabricants de verre (Vaudreuil, Qué) #2418
Otto, Frei, architecte all, 1925-
– Montréal (Qué), Expo 67. Pavillon de la République fédérale allemande #9218
Ouellet, Angémil, artiste can, 1936- #1546
Ouellet, David, architecte can, 1844-1915
– architecture, église Saint-Augustin-de-Desmaures #8889
Ouellet, Gaétan, artiste can, 1948- #640
Ouellet, Jean, architecte can, 1922-
– théories sur l'architecture #7746
Ouellet, Joseph-Pierre, architecte can, 1872-1959 #8394
Ouellet Reeves Alain, agence can d'architecture
– Montréal (Qué), Les Ilots Saint-Martin, La Petite Bourgogne #8520
Ouest américain
– art
  – (1804-1930) #5783
  – fin XVIIIe-début XXe s. #1859
  – illustrations de périodiques (1857-1900) #931
  – Kane, Paul, et George Catlin #1845
  – région nord-ouest du Pacifique, XIXe-début XXe s. #1999
Ouest canadien
– architecture #8083
– art
  – (années 1940) #381
  – fin XVIIIe-début XXe s. #1859
  – illustrations de périodiques (1857-1900) #931
– peinture
  – (1933-1970) #498
  – (années 1970) #588
– peinture traditionnelle, XXe s. #1846
– vues
  – (1804-1930) #5783
  – fin XIXe s. #271 272
  – Julien, Henri #5990
  – Kane, Paul #6007 6009 6011 6014 6016 6018
  – Kane, Paul, et George Catlin #1845
  – McCarthy, Doris Jean #6461
  – McLean, Terry #6502
  – Nevitt, Richard Barrington #6687 6688
  – Phillips, Walter Joseph #6857
  – XIX s.-années 1970 #1863

– XIXe-début XXe s. #1999
– vues photographiques
  – (1858-1900) #1014 1015
  – (années 1850-1890) #1865
  – (années 1870) #1876
  – (années 1880-1890) #1874
  – Barnes, Elliott Chappel #4610
  – Boorne and May #1950 4797
  – Curtis, Edward Sheriff #3480
  – Hime, Humphrey Lloyd #5801
Outaouais
– art, XVIIe-XVIIIe s. #3579
– ouvrages en piquants de porc-épic #3548
– vannerie #3547
– wampum #3501
outils
– voir aussi instruments agricoles
outils . Canada
– art traditionnel #2139
  – Québec #1291
– bois, XVIIIe-XIXe s. #2594
– comté de Norfolk (Ont), Normandale Iron
  Works #2699
– Ottawa (Ont), Musée national de l'homme.
  Centre canadien d'études traditionnelles
  #963
– outils de potier, XIXe s. #2329
ouvrages à l'aiguille
– voir aussi broderie
ouvrages à l'aiguille . Canada
– mennonites #2253 2264
– Nouvelle-Ecosse, patrons (avant 1920) #2785
– Québec, XVIIe-XVIIIe s. #2200
– Terre-Neuve #2744
– ursulines #2788 2789
– XVIIe s.-années 1940 #2780
ouvrages de ferronnerie
– voir aussi fonte; métier de forgeron
ouvrages de ferronnerie . Canada
– Beau, Paul #4640 4641
– comté de Norfolk (Ont), Normandale Iron
  Works #2699
– décoration architecturale (années 1910)
  #8222
– façade, Cauchon Block (plus tard Empire
  Hotel) (Winnipeg, Man) #9361
– famille Cauchon #5062
– guide pour collectionneurs #2252
– Nouveau-Brunswick #2150
– Ontario, croix funéraires
  germano-alsaciennes #2709
– Price, Ralph et Patricia, collection #971
– Québec #2226 2228 2702 2711 2712
  – croix funéraires #2716
  – dans l'art religieux #2713
  – XVIIe-XVIIIe s. #2530 2531
– Trois-Rivières (Qué), Forges du
  Saint-Maurice #2698 2708 9238 9240
– XVIIe-XIXe s. #2705
– XVIIIe-XIXe s. #2703
ouvrages de ferronnerie . Etats-Unis
– fin XIXe s., Halifax (NE), parcs #2710
ouvrages de ferronnerie . Grande-Bretagne
– fin XIXe s., Halifax (NE), parcs #2710
ouvrages en coquillages . Algonquiens #3511
ouvrages en coquillages . Algonquins #3505
ouvrages en coquillages . Amérindiens
  #3388
– ouvrages perlés #3457
– wampum #3522
ouvrages en coquillages . Indiens de la côte
  nord-ouest
– instruments #4068

ouvrages en coquillages . Indiens des forêts
  du Nord-Est #3505
ouvrages en coquillages . Iroquois #3505
  3607
ouvrages en papier
– mennonites #2264
  – XIXe-début XXe s. #2265
  – XXe s. #2142
ouvrages en piquants de porc-épic .
  Algonquiens #3443 3605
– mocassins #3652
– ouvrages perlés #3635
– Toronto (Ont), Royal Ontario Museum
  #3471 3474 3475
ouvrages en piquants de porc-épic .
  Algonquins
– motif de la double courbe et motif floral
  #3409
ouvrages en piquants de porc-épic .
  Amérindiens
– Ottawa (Ont), Musée national de l'Homme
  #3465 3466
– Toronto (Ont), Royal Ontario Museum
  #3474 3475
ouvrages en piquants de porc-épic .
  Arapahos
– New York (NY), American Museum of
  Natural History #3414
ouvrages en piquants de porc-épic .
  Assiniboines #3653 3739
ouvrages en piquants de porc-épic .
  Athapascans #4152
– Toronto (Ont), Royal Ontario Museum
  #3471 3474 3475
ouvrages en piquants de porc-épic .
  autochtones #3341
ouvrages en piquants de porc-épic . Cris
  #3651 3739 3745
ouvrages en piquants de porc-épic .
  Flancs-de-Chien #4089
ouvrages en piquants de porc-épic .
  Gens-du-Sang #3739
ouvrages en piquants de porc-épic .
  Gros-Ventres #3651
– rosettes #3753
ouvrages en piquants de porc-épic .
  Hidatsas #3701
ouvrages en piquants de porc-épic . Indiens
  de la côte nord-ouest #3811
ouvrages en piquants de porc-épic . Indiens
  des forêts du Nord-Est #3443
– ouvrages perlés #3635
ouvrages en piquants de porc-épic . Indiens
  des plaines #3443 3651 3658 3684 3745
  3751
– mocassins #3652
– New York (NY), American Museum of
  Natural History #3668
ouvrages en piquants de porc-épic . Iroquois
  #3559 3605
– ouvrages perlés #3635
ouvrages en piquants de porc-épic .
  Mandans #3701
ouvrages en piquants de porc-épic .
  Micmacs #3569 3624 3643
ouvrages en piquants de porc-épic .
  Mistassins #3701
ouvrages en piquants de porc-épic .
  Outaouais
– containers, Los Angeles (Calif), Southwest
  Museum #3548
ouvrages en piquants de porc-épic .
  Pentaguets #3537

ouvrages en piquants de porc-épic .
  Pieds-Noirs #3651 3654 3678 3686 3703
  3739 3745 3754
ouvrages en piquants de porc-épic . Sarcis
  #3739
ouvrages en piquants de porc-épic .
  Saulteux/Ojibwa #3551 3557 4089
ouvrages en piquants de porc-épic . Siouens
  #3443 3651 3674 3745
– mocassins #3652 3666
– Toronto (Ont), Royal Ontario Museum
  #3471
ouvrages en piquants de porc-épic . Slaveys
  #4089
ouvrages en piquants de porc-épic . Tananas
  #4095
ouvrages en plumes . Indiens des plaines
– coiffures #3683
ouvrages en plumes . Pieds-Noirs #3654
  3678
ouvrages perlés . Algonquiens #3374 3582
  3605 3635
– (années 1760-début XXe s.) #3633
– Albany (NY), New York State Museum
  #3603
ouvrages perlés . Algonquins
– motif de la double courbe et motif floral
  #3409
ouvrages perlés . Amérindiens #2739 3329
  3420
– articles de traite #3440
– New York (NY), Museum of the American
  Indian. Heye Foundation #3457
– Ottawa (Ont), Musée national de l'Homme
  #3465 3466
– ouvrages en coquillages #3388
– XXe s. #2143
ouvrages perlés . Arapahos
– New York (NY), American Museum of
  Natural History #3414
ouvrages perlés . Assiniboines #3653 3739
ouvrages perlés . Athapascans #4107 4110
ouvrages perlés . autochtones #3341
ouvrages perlés . Carriers
– (années 1970) #4145
ouvrages perlés . Cris #3651 3729 3739 4077
– (années 1960) #3719
– Lac La Ronge (Sask) #3696
ouvrages perlés . Delawares #3506
ouvrages perlés . Flancs-de-Chien #4089
ouvrages perlés . Gens-du-Sang #3739
ouvrages perlés . Gros-Ventres #3651
ouvrages perlés . Huron
– wampum #3495
ouvrages perlés . Indiens des forêts du
  Nord-Est #3635
– Albany (NY), New York State Museum
  #3603
– années 1760-début XXe s. #3633
– mocassins #3554
ouvrages perlés . Indiens des plaines #3651
  3666 3682 3684 3751
– New York (NY), American Museum of
  Natural History #3668
– XIXe s. #3722
ouvrages perlés . Iroquois #3559 3605 3635
– Albany (NY), New York State Museum
  #3603
– années 1760-début XXe s. #3633
– wampum #3496
ouvrages perlés . Malécites #3628 3641
ouvrages perlés . Métis #3677 4110
ouvrages perlés . Micmacs #3624 3628 3641
ouvrages perlés . Montagnais

– natutshikan #4103
– plantes et animaux, motifs #4076
ouvrages perlés . Nahanis #4077
ouvrages perlés . Naskapis
– natutshikan #4103
– plantes et animaux, motifs #4076
ouvrages perlés . Pieds-Noirs #3651 3654
   3678 3686 3739
ouvrages perlés . Salishiens
– (années 1970) #4145
ouvrages perlés . Sarcis #3739
ouvrages perlés . Saulteux/Ojibwa #3539
   3551 3557 4089
ouvrages perlés . Siouens #3651 3674
– mocassins #3666
   – années 1880-1910 #3740
– XIXe s. #3722
ouvrages perlés . Slaveys #4089
ouvrages perlés . Tananas #4095
ouvrages perlés . Thompsons #3808
Overbeck, Johann Friedrich, artiste all,
   1789-1869
– influence sur Napoléon Bourassa #4874
Overton, George, artiste can, né 1880
– influence sur Caven Ernest Atkins #4570
OVO, périodique can #997 999 3314
Owen Sound (Ont), Tom Thomson
   Memorial Gallery and Museum of Fine
   Art
– collection #3146
– expositions
   – Centennial Exhibition of Quebec and
      Ontario Contemporary Painters, 1967
      (1967) #484
   – Goodridge Roberts: Paintings from the
      1950s and 60s (1981) #7048
   – Of Human Bondage (1976) #611
   – The Ontario Community Collects: A Survey
      of Canadian Painting from 1766 to the
      Present (1976) #120
Owidzka, Jolanta, artiste polonaise, 1927-
– tapisserie, Centre national des arts
   (Ottawa, Ont) #9108
Oxford (Angleterre), Oxford University.
   Ashmolean Museum
– art amérindien #3422
– influence sur Frederic William
   Cumberland #9475
Oxford (Angleterre), Oxford University. Pitt
   Rivers Museum
– art inuit, XIXe s. #4369
– jambières, Piégans #3715
– sac en poil de bison, Amérindiens #3398
– totems, Haidas #3775

P

Pachter, Charles, artiste can, 1942-
– entretien #6748
– et Charles Pachter Graphics #834
Pacific Great Eastern Railway
– gares #9545
Pacifique, côte du (Canada)
– vues #139
pagaies de cérémonie . Tlingits
– utilisation de cheveux humains #3917
Page, J.R., artiste can, actif 1864-1865
– peintures d'animaux #1727
Page, James Ritchey, photographe can, 1938-
– catalogue de photographies #1023
Pagé, Lewis, sculpteur can, 1931-

– Dispute philosophique #6750
Page, Patricia Kathleen, artiste can, 1916-
   #6751
– expositions de groupe
   – (1978) #649
Page, Robin, artiste can, 1932- #6752
Page & Steele, agence can d'architecture
– Scarborough (Ont), University of Toronto.
   Scarborough College #9396 9462 9463 9464
– Toronto (Ont)
   – Banque canadienne de commerce #9351
   – Commerce Court #9350
   – O'Keefe Centre for the Performing Arts
      #9087
Page & Warrington, agence can
   d'architecture
– Toronto (Ont)
   – architecture domestique #8493
   – National Cash Register #9234
Pagé (dit Quercy ou Carcy), Jacques, orfèvre
   et horloger can, 1682-1742 #249 250 6749
– apprentissage chez Michel Levasseur
   #2669
Paillard (dit Le Poitevin), Léonard,
   constructeur can, 1647-1729 #234 235
Pailthorpe, Grace Winifred, artiste et
   psychiatre brit, 1890-1971
– influence sur Jock Macdonald #6377
pain
– fours, Québec #2233 2234
Painchaud, Fabien, carrossier can, actif 1842
   #1301
Paine, Arthur James Carman, architecte can,
   1886-1965
– Montréal (Qué), Université McGill.
   Athletic buildings, concours #9417
Painter, Walter Scott, architecte can, né 1877
– Montréal (Qué), gare Windsor #9532
– Québec (Qué), Château Frontenac, travaux
   d'agrandissement #9261
Painters Eleven #97 476 489 512 1752 1760
   1769 1787
– en comparaison avec les plasticiens #720
– et Alexandra Luke #3169 6333 6334
– et Jack Hamilton Bush #4975
– et Jock Macdonald #6375
– et nationalisme dans l'art #495
– et Oscar Cahén #4986
– expositions
   – (1958) #429 1751
   – (1972) #1771
   – (1980) #1785
– expositions, critiques
   – (1959) #432
   – (1979) #1786
– influence sur peinture torontoise (Ont),
   (années 1950-1960) #1772
painting, Canadian
– Brampton (Ont), Perkins Bull Collection
   #3208
Paisley, Douglas A., photographe can, 1949-
– catalogue de photographies #995
Paisley, James Ernest Harris, architecte can,
   1890-1955
– Toronto (Ont), Helena Rubenstein Beauty
   Salon #9367
Paivio, Jules Peter, architecte can, 1917-
– Vancouver (BC), Vancouver Civic
   Auditorium, concours #9080
palais
– voir aussi châteaux et maisons de
   campagne
palais de justice . Canada
– Alberta (avant 1930) #9005

– Colombie-Britannique (1849-1930) #9006
– Ile-du-Prince-Edouard (avant 1914) #9009
– Manitoba (avant 1930) #9007
– Montréal (Qué), palais de justice, annexe
   #9001
– New Westminster (CB) #9011
– Nouveau-Brunswick (avant 1914) #9004
– Ontario
   – influence de l'architecture écossaise,
      XIXe s. #7977
   – XIXe-début XXe s. #9010
– Terre-Neuve (1830-1903) #9008
– Toronto (Ont), Osgoode Hall #9002 9003
– Vancouver (CB), palais de justice #8362
   9149
palais épiscopaux . Canada
– Québec (Qué), Palais épiscopal #8787
palais italiens
– Venise, influence sur l'édifice de la
   Banque Royale (Toronto, Ont) #9152
Palchinski, Sylvia Scott, artiste can, 1946-
– réflexion sur son oeuvre #6753
Palm Springs (Calif), Palm Springs Desert
   Museum
– expositions
   – Rita Letendre (1974) #6252
Palmer, Herbert Franklin, artiste can, 1921-
– expositions de groupe
   – (1962) #1847
Palmer, Herbert Sidney, artiste can,
   1881-1970
– expositions, critiques #1710
Palmer, Samuel, artiste brit, 1805-1881
– influence sur Brian Rendel Jones #5974
Palumbo, Jacques, artiste can, 1939-
– expositions
   – (1975) #6754
– utilisation de la couleur #6755
– utilisation de symboles numériques #662
Panabaker, Frank Shirley, artiste can, 1904-
   #6756
– art et écrits #6757
Panamick, Martin, artiste can, 1956-1977
– expositions de groupe
   – (1981) #4173
Pangnark, artiste can, 1920-
– expositions de groupe
   – (1970) #4220
Pangnirtung (TNO)
– arts graphiques
   – (1959-1976) #4490
   – (1973-) #4485
– sculpture en os de baleine #4413
– tissage #4237
   – et Don Stuart #7281
   – Pangnirtung, atelier de tissage #4298
      4308 4310
Panko, William, artiste can, 1892-1948
– expositions, critiques #964
– expositions de groupe
   – (1958) #1846
panneaux d'affichage . Canada #910
panneaux muraux . Tlingits
– Juneau (Alaska), Alaska State Museum
   #3916
Panneton, André, photographe can, 1949-
   #1562
Panneton, Louise, artiste can (tapisserie),
   1926- #6758
– expositions de groupe
   – (1978) #2772
panoramas
– Burr, William et Elias Paul Barnes #218
pantins . Tsimshians

– Ottawa (Ont), Musée national de l'Homme #3891
Panton, Lawrence Arthur Colley, artiste can, 1894-1954
– expositions
– (1974) #6759
papier collé
– *voir* collage
papier peint . Canada
– (années 1750-1950) #2949 2950
– XIXe s. #2926 2929
papier peint . Etats-Unis
– importé au Canada #2949 2950
papier peint . France
– importé au Canada #2949 2950
papier peint . Grande-Bretagne
– fin XVIIIe-XIXe s., importé au Canada #2926 2929
– importé au Canada #2949 2950
Papineau, André B., fonctionnaire can, m. 1832
– résidence, Laval (Qué) #8625
Papineau, Gérin-Lajoie, LeBlanc, Edwards, agence can d'architecture
– Frobisher Bay (TNO), Frobisher Bay Academic and Occupational School #8188
– Mirabel (Qué), Aéroport international de Montréal. Aérogare #9518
Papineau, Louis J., architecte can, 1930-
– Montréal (Qué), station de métro Peel #9553
Pâques
– oeufs
– Ottawa (Ont), Musée national de l'Homme. Centre canadien d'études traditionnelles #963
– ukrainiens #2132
Paquet, Edmond, sculpteur can, XVIIIe s.
– sculptures, église Saint-Pierre (île d'Orléans, Qué) #8802
Paquet (dit Lavallée), André, sculpteur can, 1799-1860 #1324
– influence de la famille Baillairgé #1582
– sculptures
– Bellechasse (Qué), église Saint-Charles-Borromée #8803
– Charlesbourg (Qué), église #8851
– île d'Orléans (Qué)
– église Saint-François-de-Sales #8796
– église Saint-Pierre #8802
Paquin, Roger, sculpteur can, 1941- #6760
– entretien #1485
Parachute, périodique can #593
– (années 1970) #3310
Parachute Center for Cultural Affairs (Calgary, Alta)
– *Centerfold* #603
paradis
– dans l'art, Glenn Alun Lewis #6275 6276
Paradis, Claude, artiste can, 1937-
– entretien #1485 1489
Paradis, Jérôme (frère Jérôme), artiste can, 1902- #6761 6762
– professeur #6763
– professeur de Jean-Paul Armand Mousseau #6651
Paradis, Jobson Emilian Henri, artiste can, 1871-1926 #1382
Paradis, Roland, orfèvre can, ca 1696-1754 #249 250
– oeuvres, Detroit Institute of Arts (Detroit, Mich) #2691
Parallelogramme, périodique can #612
– (années 1970) #3310

parc national Buffalo (Sask)
– vues photographiques, John Henry Gano #5555
parc national de Banff (Alta), Village Lake Louise, construction domiciliaire (projet)
– proposition architecturale, Arthur Charles Erickson #8360
parc national de Prince-Albert (Sask), cabane Grey Owl
– architecture #8719
parc national Kejimkujik (Fairy Bay, NE)
– pétroglyphes, Micmacs #3614
parchemins . Algonquiens
– Midéwiwins #3702
parchemins . Saulteux/Ojibwa
– Midéwiwins #3539 3583 3626
parchemins . Siouens
– Midéwiwins #3702
parcs
– *voir aussi* architecture paysagiste; parcs d'amusement
parcs . Canada
– architecture paysagiste #7677
– édifices récréatifs #9081
– Montréal (Qué), parc du Mont-Royal #7924
– Toronto (Ont) #5651
parcs d'amusement
– *voir aussi* centres récréatifs
parcs d'amusement . Canada
– Montréal (Qué), Expo 67. La Ronde #9212 9214
parcs thématiques
– *voir* parcs d'amusement
Paré, Réjean, céramiste, 1948- #1547
Pare, Richard, photographe brit au Canada, 1948-
– photographies, édifices en pierre grise, Montréal (Qué) #7922
Parent, Louis Joseph, sculpteur can, 1908-
– sculptures, Chemin de la Croix, oratoire Saint-Joseph (Montréal, Qué) #6764
Parent, Michel, artiste can, 1938- #6765
Parent, Omer, artiste can, 1907- #6766
– expositions
– (1976) #6767
– professeur, Ecole des beaux-arts (Québec, Qué) #1404
Parent-Benoît, Mimi, artiste can, 1924-
– à Paris (France) #426
Parent Report
– *voir* Québec. Rapport de la Commission d'enquête sur l'enseignement des arts au Québec (Rapport Parent)
Parfitt, Gilbert, architecte can, 1886-1966
– Winnipeg (Man), University of Manitoba. Science Building and Arts Building #9485
parflèche . Algonquiens #3456 3672
parflèche . Indiens des plaines #3456 3660 3672 3716
parflèche . Siouens #3456 3672
Paris (France)
– expansion urbaine #7902
– vues, Franklin Milton Armington #4550
Paris (France), académie Colarossi
– Bell-Smith, Frederic Marlett, élève #4666
– Carr, Emily, élève #5045
– Reid, George Agnew, élève #6979
Paris (France), académie Julian
– artistes canadiens, élèves (années 1940) #384
– Benjamin-Constant, Jean-Joseph, professeur #243

– Brymner, William, élève #4948 4953
– Carlyle, Florence, élève #4999
– Duquet, Georges-Henri, élève #5343
– Forster, John Wycliffe Lowes, élève #5468
– Gagnon, Clarence Alphonse, élève #5544 5546 5547
– Hill, George William, élève #5799
– Pemberton, Sophia Theresa, élève #6828
– Reid, George Agnew, élève #6977 6979
– Scovil, James Noel, élève #7167
Paris (France), Académie royale de peinture et sculpture de Paris
– Baillairgé, François, élève #4592
Paris (France), Atelier 17
– et Stanley William Hayter #1641
– influence sur la gravure canadienne (années 1960) #820
Paris (France), Ateliers d'art sacré
– Gilson, Jacqueline Marie-Charlotte, élève #5606
Paris (France), Biennale de Paris (1969)
– expositions, critiques
– Levine, Les #6261
Paris (France), Biennale de Paris (1980)
– art canadien #687
Paris (France), Centre culturel canadien/Canadian Cultural Centre
– (années 1970) #647
– expositions
– *Canadian West Coast Hermetics: The Metaphysical Landscape/Les hermétiques canadiens de la côte ouest: le paysage métaphysique* (1973) #2045
– *Claude Goulet: multidimensionnels* (1971) #5639
– *Claude Tousignant* (1973) #7401
– *Contemporary Canadian Painters: An Exhibition of Works from the Canada Council Art Bank/Peintres canadiens contemporains: une exposition de la banque d'oeuvres d'art du Conseil des arts du Canada* (1977) #636
– *D.P. Brown, Ken Danby, Tom Forrestall, Christopher Pratt* (1974) #573
– *Emily Carr: The Mature Years/Emily Carr: les années de maturité* (1979) #5042
– *Exposition d'estampes en l'honneur de C. Krieghoff, 1815-1872/Exhibition of Prints in Honour of C. Krieghoff, 1815-1872* (1972) #6096
– *Fernand Leduc* (1970) #6186
– *Fernand Leduc: microchromie gris, puissance 6* (1977) #6190
– *General Idea's Reconstructing Futures/General Idea: reconstruction de l'avenir* (1978) #5583
– *Guido Molinari* (1974) #6584
– *Ivan Eyre Exposition* (1982) #5394
– *Jack Chambers: Selection of Paintings and Drawings* (1980) #5080
– *Jean McEwen: Suite parisienne* (1978) #6471
– *Joe Plaskett* (1977) #6895
– *L'art de Vittorio Fiorucci: affiches 1964-1981* (1981) #5444
– *La tapisserie canadienne contemporaine: exposition/Canadian Contemporary Tapestry: Exhibition* (1980) #2774
– *Leslie Reid* (1980) #6981
– *Lithographs/Lithographies* (1973) #825
– *Louis Comtois: 4 tableaux récents grand format* (1978) #5163
– *Louis Jaque: les idiomes galactiques* (1978) #5943

– *Métiers d'art* (1973,1976,1979) #2215
– *Other Realities: The Legacy of Surrealism in Canadian Art* (1979) #508
– *Ozias Leduc: peinture symboliste et religieuse/Ozias Leduc: Symbolist and Religious Painting* (1974) #6206
– *Peter Gnass: installation-Chantier interdit au public* (1980) #5621
– *Philip Surrey, le peintre dans la ville* (1972) #7289
– *Pierre Clerk: oeuvres récentes, peintures et sculptures* (1981) #5118
– *Raymonde Godin: l'espace et les signes* (1979) #5623
– *Réalités autres: le legs du surréalisme à l'art canadien* (1979) #509
– *Réflexion sur un sentiment rural/Reflecting a Rural Consciousness* (1980) #700
– *Richard Mill: 5 tableaux récents* (1979) #6535
– *Riopelle: ficelles et autres jeux* (1972) #7025
– *Roger Vilder* (1973) #7488
– *Tendances actuelles* (1977) #637
– *Touchez! Yvon Cozic* (1974) #5203
– *Yves Trudeau: "murs fermés et ouverts"; sculptures et pliages* (1975) #7434
– expositions, critiques
– Blanchette, Pierre #1563
– *Les 7 jours de Fernand Leduc* (1973) #6188
– *Ozias Leduc: peinture symboliste et religieuse/Ozias Leduc: Symbolist and Religious Painting* (1974) #6205
– *Peter Gnass: installation - Chantier interdit au public* (1981) #1563
– Viau, Guy, directeur #537 7485
Paris (France), Centre national d'art et de culture Georges Pompidou. Musée national d'art moderne
– expositions
– *Canada: art d'aujourd'hui* (1968) #518
– *Jean-Paul Riopelle: peinture, 1946-1977* (1981) #7032
– *Michael Snow* (1978) #7258
– expositions, critiques
– *Michael Snow* (1978) #7263
Paris (France), Chez Léopold
– murale, Marc-Aurèle de Foy Suzor-Coté et Joseph Saint-Charles #7296
Paris (France), Ecole des beaux-arts
– Chabert, Joseph, élève #3005
– dessin d'architecture #8241
– en comparaison avec l'Ecole des beaux-arts (Montréal, Qué) #1456
– Franchère, Joseph-Charles, élève #5497
– Hill, George William, élève #5799
– influence sur l'architecture québécoise #7923
Paris (France), Exposition des arts décoratifs (1925)
– influence sur l'art canadien #1244
Paris (France), galerie Arnaud
– expositions
– *Fernand Toupin* (1970) #7394
Paris (France), galerie Jacques Dubourg
– expositions
– *La sculpture de peintre: bronzes de Riopelle* (1962) #7019
Paris (France), galeries Georges Petit
– expositions
– *Exposition Frank M. Armington, peintures* (1921) #4550
– *Exposition rétrospective de l'oeuvre de W. Blair Bruce* (1907) #4941
Paris (France), Grand Palais

– expositions
– *Borduas et les automatistes, Montréal 1942-1955* (1971) #1449
– *L'Amérique vue par l'Europe* (1976) #255
– *Sculpture of the Inuit: Masterworks of the Canadian Arctic/La sculpture chez les Inuit: chefs-d'oeuvre de l'Arctique canadien* (1972) #4423 4440
– *The European Vision of America* (1976) #256
– expositions, critiques
– *Sculpture of the Inuit: Masterworks of the Canadian Arctic/La sculpture chez les Inuit: chefs-d'oeuvre de l'Arctique canadien* (1972) #4239
Paris (France), La Grande Chaumière
– artistes canadiens, élèves (années 1940) #384
Paris (France), Musée d'art moderne de la ville de Paris
– 11e Biennale de Paris, exposition d'art canadien (1980) #687
– expositions
– *Canada trajectoires 73* (1973) #558
– Charney, Melvin, *Quelques monuments nationaux*, commentaire #5091
– *Jean-Paul Lemieux* (1974) #6232
– expositions, critiques
– Beaulieu, Paul-Vanier #4651
– Pellan, Alfred #6805
Paris (France), Musée de l'Homme
– expositions
– *Arte indio y esquimal del Canada/Indian and Eskimo Art of Canada/Art indien et esquimau du Canada/Die Kunst der Indianer und Eskimos in Kanada* (1969) #3352
– *Chefs-d'oeuvre des arts indiens et esquimaux du Canada/Masterpieces of Indian and Eskimo Art from Canada* (1969) #3351
– expositions, critiques
– *Chefs-d'oeuvre des arts indiens et esquimaux du Canada/Masterpieces of Indian and Eskimo Art from Canada* (1969) #3356 3954
– masque, Tsimshians #4069
– mocassins et chaussures, Amérindiens #3424
– totems, Indiens de la côte nord-ouest #3930
Paris (France), Musée du Jeu de paume
– expositions
– *Exposition d'art canadien* (1927) #299
– Pellan, Alfred, exposition de ses oeuvres #6796
Paris (France), Musée national d'art moderne
– *voir* Paris (France), Centre national d'art et de culture Georges Pompidou. Musée national d'art moderne
– expositions
– *Pellan* (1955) #6804
Paris (France), musée Rodin
– expositions
– *Panorama de la sculpture au Québec, 1945-1970* (1970) #1599
Paris (France), Salon
– et Alexander Phimister Proctor #6943
– et Atha Haydock Caldwell #4991
– et Claire Shuttleworth #7202
– et Florence Carlyle #4999
– et Laura Adeline Muntz Lyall #6337 6339
– et Lilias Torrance Newton #6692

– et Mary Riter Hamilton #5694
– et Paul Peel #6790 6791
– et Sydney Strickland Tully #7438
Paris (France), Société nationale des beaux-arts
– Cullen, Maurice Galbraith, élève #5219
– et Maurice Galbraith Cullen #5220
Paris (Ont)
– poterie, XIXe s. #2330
Paris Pottery
– *voir* Ahrens Pottery
Parish, Isaac, photographe can, actif années 1860 #1211
Parizad, photographe can, actif 1981
– catalogue de photographies #1023
Parizeau, Marcel, architecte can, 1898-1945 #8397
parkas, Inuit #4300
Parker, Blake, poète can, 1943-
– et Intersystems #767
Parkin, Edmund, architecte can, 1912-
– et John B. Parkin Associates #8396
Parkin, John Burnett, architecte can, 1911-1975
– et John B. Parkin Associates #8396
Parkin, John C., architecte can, 1922-
– commentaire sur relations entre artistes et architectes #8234
– et John B. Parkin Associates #8396
– Ontario, résidences estivales #8651
– théories sur l'architecture #7746
– Toronto (Ont) #7733 8057
– Aéroport international de Toronto #8232
– Armée du Salut, siège social #8232
– résidence de John C. Parkin #9299
– Sun Life Building #8232
Parkin Architects and Planners, agence can d'architecture
– Ottawa (Ont), Galerie nationale du Canada, concours #9142
Parkin Partnership, agence can d'architecture
– Toronto (Ont)
– Art Gallery of Ontario #3163 9121
– Art Gallery of Ontario. Henry Moore Centre #8078
Parr, Nuna, artiste can, 1889-1969 #6768 6770
– expositions
– (1979) #6769
Parry, Sir William Edward, navigateur et explorateur brit, 1790-1855
– expédition dans l'Arctique #278
Parry Island Reservation (Ont)
– art, Ojibwa et Potéouatamis #3540
Parsons, Alison, artiste can (textiles), 1939-
– entretien #6771
Parsons, Bruce, artiste can, 1937-
– cartes géographiques, illustration #561
– estampes #1214
– expositions
– (1976) #6772
– expositions de groupe
– (1967) #1916
Parsons, F.R., photographe can aux EU, actif années 1890 #6773
Parthenais, Louis-Anatole, sculpteur can, 1839-1864 #1319
– sculpture, Montréal (Qué) #727
Parti-pris #1502
Partridge, David Gerry, artiste can, 1919- #6775 6776
– commentaire sur la gravure #817
– réflexion sur son oeuvre #6774

Partz, Felix, artiste can, 1945-
- expositions de groupe
  - (1977) #5583
parure
- *voir aussi* bijoux; broches; colliers;
  hausse-cols; orfèvrerie
parure . Algonquiens #3605 3633
- orfèvrerie de traite #3594 3608
- ouvrages perlés #3635
- wampum #3521
parure . Algonquins
- ouvrages en coquillages #3505
parure . Amérindiens #3453
- orfèvrerie de traite #2631
- ouvrages en coquillages #3388
- ouvrages perlés #3457
- préhistoire #3393
parure . Assiniboines #3653 3739
parure . Athapascans #4073
parure . autochtones #3334 3341
parure . Cris #3402 3739 3742
parure . Esquimaux du caribou #4265
parure . Flancs-de-Chien #4089
parure . Gens-du-Sang #3739
parure . Haidas #3763
parure . Indiens des forêts du Nord-Est
  #3633
- ouvrages en coquillages #3505
- ouvrages perlés #3635
parure . Indiens des plaines
- sociétés secrètes #3727
- travail des métaux #3698
- wampum #3521
parure . Ingaliks #4087
parure . Iroquois #3605 3633
- orfèvrerie de traite #3645 3646
- ouvrages en coquillages #3505
- ouvrages perlés #3635
- peignes #3587
- wampum #3521
parure . Kwakiutls #3787
parure . Malécites #3641
parure . Micmacs #3569 3641
parure . Mistassins #4080
parure . Neutres
- travail de la pierre #3503
parure . Pieds-Noirs #3654 3739
parure . Salish de la Côte #3896
parure . Sarcis #3739
parure . Saulteux/Ojibwa #3402 3539 4089
parure . Skokomish #3835
parure . Slaveys #4089
parure . Tagish #4106
parure . Tahltans
- (années 1910) #4074
parure . Tananas #4095
parure . Têtes-de-Boule #4079
parure . Tlingits #3763 3976 4106
parure . Tsimshians #3763
parure . Tsonnontouans
- peignes #3587
parure . Tutchonis #4106
Paskievich, John, photographe can, 1947-
  #1879 6777
- expositions de groupe
  - (1979) #1904
Pasquin, Suzanne, artiste can, 1935- #1418
Passillé-Sylvestre, Micheline de, émailleuse
  can, 1936- #2216
Paterson, Malcolm, photographe can, actif
  années 1970-
- catalogues de photographies #991
Paterson, Robert Allen, artiste can, 1936-

#6778
Patrie, La, journal can
- bandes dessinées #954
- illustrations, Henri Julien #5988
Patriot, journal can
- lettres concernant l'exposition de la
  Society of Artists and Amateurs of
  Toronto, Toronto (Ont) (1834) #1729
Patterson, Andrew Dickson, artiste can,
  1854-1930
- portraits #1698
Patterson, Daniel (Dan), sculpteur can,
  1886-1968
- expositions de groupe
  - (1975) #1682
- sculpture, boîtes de lait Carnation #1792
  6779
  - Ottawa (Ont), Galerie nationale du
    Canada #962
Patterson, Freeman, photographe can, 1937-
- catalogue de photographies #995 1023
- commentaire sur la photographie de
  paysages #6780
- correspondance, Michael William Semak
  #1016
- expositions, critiques #1009
- réflexion sur la photographie #6782
- réflexion sur son oeuvre photographique
  #6781
Patterson, Nancy-Lou, artiste et historienne
  d'art can, 1929-
- entretien #6783
Pattle, Colin, artiste can, 1922- #6784
Paul Arthur and Associates, studio can de
  graphisme #873
Pavelic, Myfanwy Spencer, artiste can, 1916-
  #6785
- et Emily Carr #5043
- membre du groupe Limners #2043
pavillons de chasse . Canada
- Gaspé (Qué), cabanes en bois rond #7896
Paxton, Maureen, artiste can, 1950- #6786
Payette, Eugène, architecte can, 1874-1959
- Montréal (Qué), bibliothèque Saint-Sulpice
  #9039 9415
Payne, Gordon MacEwan, artiste can, 1933-
- expositions, critiques #2072
- expositions de groupe
  - (1979) #2075
Payne, Julia, sculpteure can, XXe s.
- femme de William St. Thomas Smith
  #7236
Payne, Samuel, orfèvre can, 1696-1732 #234
  235
- et Paul Lambert (dit Saint-Paul), écuelle,
  Musée des beaux-arts de Montréal
  (Montréal, Qué) #2689
Payne, Stephen, artiste can, 1953-
- expositions de groupe
  - (1979) #1157
Payne Bay (Qué)
- arts graphiques (1972-1975) #4475
paysage américain
- *voir aussi* Hudson River School
- en comparaison avec peinture de
  paysages, Canada #106
paysage britannique
- XIXe s., influence sur peinture de
  paysages, Canada #66
paysage canadien
- (1670-1930) #106
- (1750-1850) #279
- (1860-1890) #271 272
  - Montréal (Qué) et Toronto (Ont) #264

- (1900-1920) #309
- (années 1670) #1328
- (années 1890) #6436
- (années 1920) #287 301 315
- (années 1930) #338 344 347
- (années 1930-1940) #352
- (années 1930-1960) #496
- (années 1930-1970), et monnaie canadienne
  #759
- (années 1940) #380
- (années 1970) #595 617
- Académie royale des arts du Canada #153
  283
- Alberta #1965
  - (1981) #1974
- Cantons de l'Est (Qué), (1800-1950) #1296
- cartes de Noël #844 845 863
- Colombie-Britannique
  - (années 1840-1970) #2016
  - XVIIIe s.-années 1930, forêts #2008
- côte nord-ouest, XVIIIe s. #2002
- début XXe s., en comparaison avec l'école
  de Barbizon #497
- en comparaison avec paysages australiens
  #44
- estampes, XVIIIe-XIXe s. #839
- et A.Y. Jackson #5915 5922
- et géographie #26 41
- et nationalisme #109 183 341
- fleuve Saint-Laurent (Ont et Qué), XIXe s.
  #282
- Groupe des Sept #1735 1764 1774 1782
- imaginaire (années 1970) #1960 2045
- Laurentides (Qué), XXe s. #1278 1279
- New York (NY), Canadian Club de New
  York #3211
- Nouveau-Brunswick, XIXe s. #1180
- Ontario, XIXe s. #1720
- paysages d'hiver #285 1298
- photographies (1860-1900) #268
- poterie en grès, Amérique du Nord #2309
- Prairies #1855 1872 1882
  - (années 1960) #1848 1862
  - et Illingworth Holey Kerr #6050
  - peintures de grand format #1885
- provinces de l'Ouest #1863
- Québec #1265
  - (1800-1940) #1286
  - (années 1940-1950) #1426
- Saskatchewan #3202
  - (1905-1980) #1940
- XIX s.-années 1970 #140
- XIXe s. #178 241 242 266
- XIXe s.-années 1910 #209
- XIXe-XXe s. #132
- XVIIe s.-années 1940 #29
- XVIIIe-milieu XXe s. #88
- XVIIIe s.-années 1920 #14
- XVIIIe-XIXe s. #812
Payton, Evlyn B., artiste can, 1920- #6787
Peachey, James, officier de l'armée brit,
  artiste au Canada, actif 1774-1797 #269 270
  279 812
Peachy, Joseph Ferdinand, architecte can,
  1830-1903
- et architecture québécoise #7851
Peacock, Graham, artiste can, 1945-
- expositions de groupe
  - (1974) #565
Pearson, Carol, artiste can, 1910-
- élève d'Emily Carr #5020
Pearson, Cedric, photographe can, 1949-
- vues photographiques, Disraëli (Qué),
  (1972) #1513

Pearson, John Andrew, architecte can, 1867-1940 #8398
- Ottawa (Ont)
  - édifices du Parlement #8926 8927
    - Tour de la Paix et Chapelle du Souvenir #8928 8929
  - Toronto (Ont) #8055
Pédery-Hunt, Dora de
- voir De Pédery-Hunt, Dora
Pednaud, Victoire, artisane tisserande can, active années 1920-1940 #2184
Peel, Bryan, sculpteur can, né 1875
- hochet en forme de corbeau #6788
- sculpture représentant un castor #6789
Peel, Paul, artiste can, 1860-1892 #10 178 4999 6790 6791
- After the Bath, peintures #6794
- et Florence Carlyle #5000
- expositions
  - (1970) #6792
- expositions, critiques #174
- expositions de groupe
  - (1978) #1726
- peinture #6793
- relation entre photographie et peinture #245
Peene, Alfred W., architecte can, 1868-1940
- Hamilton (Ont)
  - Hamilton Public Library #7957
  - Royal Connaught Hotel #9274
Peggy's Cove (NE)
- vues, Ernest Lawson #6175
Peguis, chef amérindien, m. 1864
- portrait, Peter Rindisbacher #7005
Pehap, Eric Konstantin, artiste can, 1912- #6795
Pei, I.M., & Associates, agence amér d'architecture
- Montréal (Qué), Place Ville-Marie #9314 9315
- Toronto (Ont), Commerce Court #9350
Pei, Ieoh Ming, architecte amér, 1917-
- influence sur architecture montréalaise (années 1960) #7901
- Toronto (Ont)
  - Banque canadienne de Commerce, restauration #9351
  - hôtel de ville et Civic Square, concours #8981
peignes . Iroquois #3587
peignes . Tsonnontouans #3587
peinture
- voir aussi abstraction lyrique; aquarelle; hard-edge; miniatures; paysage; peinture d'histoire; peinture de genre; peinture murale; peinture naïve; peinture sur porcelaine; peinture sur verre; portrait; précisionnisme; scènes marines (peinture); tachisme; trompe-l'oeil
- artistes des pays membres du Commonwealth (1950-années 1970) #633
- artistes en Amérique (1564-1867) #231
- et art vidéo #651
- et photographie, XXe s. #988
- et sculpture (années 1960) #449
- peinture européenne
  - (années 1940), en comparaison avec peinture canadienne #358
  - dans collections canadiennes #63
  - Ottawa (Ont), Galerie nationale du Canada 3021 3022 3050
  - Québec (Qué), Université Laval #3078
  - XIXe s., en comparaison avec peinture canadienne #252

peinture . Algonquiens #3672
- XXe s. #4157
peinture . Amérindiens #3381 3432 3462
- (1830-1970) #3451
- (années 1970) #6648
- peinture faciale #3461
- XXe s. #3441
  - Tulsa (Okla), Philbrook Art Center #4165
peinture . autochtones #3341
peinture . Canada
- XIXe s.-années 1930 #18
peinture . Cris
- (années 1970) #4133
peinture . Gens-du-Sang
- chasse au bison, University of Alberta (Edmonton, Alta) #3711
peinture . Haidas
- thème décoratif du castor #23
peinture . Indiens de la côte nord-ouest
- peinture faciale #3771
- pigments et matériaux #3415 3847
peinture . Indiens des forêts du Nord-Est
- influence de Norval H. Morrisseau #4144
peinture . Indiens des plaines #3672 3716 3751
- chronique en images, motifs #3728
- travail du cuir #3709
peinture . Inuit #4202
peinture . Iroquois
- (années 1970) #4133
peinture . Naskapis #4098
peinture . Pieds-Noirs #3669 3678 3686 3741
peinture . Quinaults #3845
peinture . Salish de la côte #3878
peinture . Saulteux/Ojibwa
- (années 1970) #4133
- XXe s. #4156
peinture . Siouens #3672
- chronique en images, motifs #3728
peinture (produit chimique)
- voir aussi pigments
- pigments tirés du sol québécois (années 1820) #165
peinture allemande
- réalisme, influence sur peinture canadienne #110
peinture américaine
- voir aussi Hudson River School
- (1860-1900), influence sur peinture canadienne #262
- (1932), Canadian National Exhibition (Toronto, Ont) #320
- (1940-1950), en comparaison avec peinture canadienne #1458
- (années 1880), en comparaison avec peinture canadienne #172
- (années 1930), en comparaison avec peinture canadienne #337
- (années 1940), en comparaison avec peinture canadienne #358
- (années 1950-1960), influence sur peinture québécoise #1453
- influence sur Jack Hamilton Bush #4967
- New York (NY)
  - influence sur les automatistes #1448
  - influence sur Painters Eleven #1785
  - influence sur peinture canadienne (années 1960) #477 478
  - influence sur peinture montréalaise (Qué), (années 1950-1960) #1263
  - influence sur peinture torontoise (Ont), (années 1950-1960) #1772 1773
  - influence sur peinture torontoise (Ont),

(années 1970) #1803 1807
  - Toronto (Ont), Royal Ontario Museum. Collection Sigmund Samuel #3135
peinture australienne
- (années 1880), en comparaison avec peinture canadienne #172
peinture belge
- (1927), Canadian National Exhibition (Toronto, Ont) #295
peinture britannique
- (1927), Canadian National Exhibition (Toronto, Ont) #295
- (années 1940), influence sur peinture canadienne #379
- (années 1970), en comparaison avec peinture canadienne #653
- Fredericton (NB), galerie d'art Beaverbrook #3066
- réalisme, influence sur peinture canadienne #110
- scènes de guerre #1073 1080
  - Ottawa (Ont), Galerie nationale du Canada #1101 1102
- XIXe s., influence sur peinture canadienne #178
- XIXe s., influence sur peinture ontarienne #1705
peinture canadienne #9 35 39 43 46 57 58 59 60 61 63 65 66 113 125 129 485 2096
- (1605-1867) #2110
- (1663-1912) #198
- (1665-1945) #32 34
- (1665-1960) #76 77
- (1665-1965) #108
- (1800-1960) #99
- (1820-1940) #28
- (1821-1860), territoire de la Compagnie de la Baie d'Hudson #273
- (1837-1887) #253
- (1837-1900), style victorien #254
- (1850-1950) #86
- (1867-1967) #82
- (1870-1970) #97
- (1874), Art Union of Canada (Toronto, Ont) #1694
- (1880) #167
- (1880-1910) #214
- (1880-1914) #265
- (1886), Colonial and Indian Exhibition (London, England) #174
- (1900-1949) #42
- (1900-années 1920) #309
- (1910), Canadian National Exhibition (Toronto, Ont) #201
- (1920-1950) #391
- (1927), Canadian National Exhibition (Toronto, Ont) #295
- (1930), Canadian National Exhibition (Toronto, Ont) #313
- (1931), Canadian National Exhibition (Toronto, Ont) #316
- (1932), Canadian National Exhibition (Toronto, Ont) #320 321
- (1933-1970) #498
- (1938-1948) #378 379
- (1939-1963) #462
- (1940-1960) #512
- (1945-1970) #499 501
- (1955-1971) #1453
- (années 1750-1890) #221
- (années 1830-1930) #33
- (années 1850-1920) #297
- (années 1860-1880) #230
- (années 1860-1960) #75

– (années 1880) #170 172
– (années 1880-1930) #17
– (années 1890), artistes à Paris (France) #180
– (années 1890-1930), influence de l'impressionnisme #115 227
– (années 1890-1940) #27 367
– (années 1910) #284
– (années 1910-1940) #354 383
– (années 1910-1950) #427
– (années 1920) #293 315
– (années 1920-1940), dans *Canadian Forum* #3301
– (années 1920-1950) #396 424
– (années 1920-1960), en comparaison avec peinture latino-américaine #495
– (années 1930) #314 335 336 338 340 342 502 589 592
  – et nationalisme #337
  – utilisation de documentation orale #608
– (années 1940) #355 358 370 371 374 386 1389
  – artistes à Paris (France) #384
– (années 1940-1950) #412 452 1426
– (années 1940-1960) #453 489
– (années 1950) #401 410 416 429 438
  – artistes à l'étranger #413 414
  – artistes à Paris (France) #426
  – influence de Hans Hofmann #402
– (années 1950-1960) #400 455 476
– (années 1960) #450 478 491 520 521
  – artistes québécois à Paris (France) #1434
– (années 1960-1970) #704
– (années 1970) #565 582 588 609 618 620 653 684
  – peintures de grand format #644
– Alberta #1948 1970
  – (1980) #1969
  – (années 1970) #1951
  – réalisme #1954
– Art déco #505
– artistes écossais #133
– Association des artistes non-figuratifs de Montréal #1415 1469 1478
– automatistes #1398 1420 1447 1448 1475 1476
– Bouclier canadien, XVIIIe-XXe s. #156
– Cantons de l'Est (Qué)
  – (1800-1950) #1296
  – (1815-1940) #1288
– Charlevoix (Qué) #1280
– CIL Inc., collection #124
– Colombie-Britannique #1995 2000 2011
  – (1848-années 1890) #2004
  – (1894-1932) #2007
  – (années 1940) #1989
  – (années 1950) #1990 1994 1997
– comté de Brant (Ont), (1793-1930) #1684
– Edmonton (Alta), Edmonton Art Gallery, collection Ernest Edward Poole #3217 3222 3235
– et architecture
  – (années 1950) #7670
  – (années 1960) #8236
– et Cornelius Krieghoff #6087 6089 6094
– et Emily Carr #5030
– et Jack Hamilton Bush #722 4969
– et James Wilson Morrice #6622
– et Jean-Paul Riopelle #7018
– et Jean-Philippe Dallaire #5240
– et Jock Macdonald #6378
– et l'imagination #104
– et Marc-Aurèle de Foy Suzor-Coté #7293
– et photographie

– (1860-1900) #245 262 268
– (années 1970) #1007
– famille Bell-Irving #4665
– faux #64 70 73
– femmes artistes, XVIIe-XXe s. #117
– Fredericton (NB), galerie d'art Beaverbrook #3066 3067
– Garber, Bram, collection #3247
– Groupe des peintres canadiens #324 331 348 356 365 382
– Groupe des Sept #1735 1737 1738 1739 1740 1741 1743 1744 1745 1747 1754 1763 1764 1766 1767 1768 1774 1776 1777 1778 1779 1781 1782 1783 1784 1789
– guide pour collectionneurs #2252
– Halifax (NE)
  – (1815-1867) #1217
  – collections #47
– Hamilton (Ont), Art Gallery of Hamilton #3159
– Ile-du-Prince-Edouard, femmes artistes (années 1970) #1167
– influence de la peinture américaine #126
– Joliette (Qué), églises #8876
– Jutras, Albert, collection #372
– Kingston (Ont) #1680
– L'Islet (Qué), église Notre-Dame-de-Bon-Secours #8879
– London (Ont), (1970s) #1813
– MacAulay, John, collection #3212
– Manitoba #1893 1895
  – Doig, M. et Mme D.R., collection #3224
– marines #139 225
– Maritimes, XXe s. #1121
– Massey, Vincent, collection #3220
– McLean, J.S., collection #3228
– Montée Saint-Michel #1236
– Montréal (Qué) #7900
  – (1860-1960) #1253
  – (1954-1955) #1408
  – (années 1940) #1397
  – (années 1940-1950) #1416
  – (années 1940-1960) #1438
  – (années 1950) #389 1403
  – (années 1950-1960) #1263 1425
  – (années 1960) #1418 1427 1484
  – église Notre-Dame #8839
  – et Alfred Pellan #6826
  – et Louis Muhlstock #6658
  – Musée des beaux-arts de Montréal #3113
  – op'art #1445
  – Soeurs Grises #8862
  – Université McGill. Musée McCord #222 223
Nouveau-Brunswick #1178
– scènes représentant bateaux, XIXe s. #1190
– Nouvelle-Ecosse
  – (1749-1958) #1196
  – (années 1970) #1221
  – peinture traditionnelle, XXe s. #1206 1207
  – scènes représentant bateaux, XIXe s. #163 1201
– Oka (Qué) #1356
  – calvaire d'Oka #1355
– Ontario #1676
  – (1846-1867) #1715
  – collections #120
  – Government of Ontario Art Collection #1728
  – peintures d'animaux #1727
  – XIXe s. #1705 1720
– Ontario et Québec (années 1960) #484

– Ontario Society of Artists #1770
– Ottawa (Ont)
  – Archives publiques du Canada. Collection William H. Coverdale #12 3230
  – Conseil des Arts du Canada. Banque d'oeuvres d'art #636
  – Galerie nationale du Canada #3038
    – Massey, Vincent, legs #3227
– Painters Eleven #1752 1769 1771 1785 1786 1787
– Painters Eleven et plasticiens #720
– paysages #14 26 41 88 106 132 140 301 352 496 595
– peinture figurative #71 101 103 578
  – (1878-1978) #135
– peinture traditionnelle #965
– peintures de petite dimension (1913-1914) #199
– plasticiens #1439 1457 1465
– Prairies
  – (années 1950-1970) #1884
  – paysages #1872 1882 1885
– provinces de l'Ouest
  – (1938-1948) #1841
  – (années 1950) #1842
  – paysages #1863
– Québec #1235 1237 1249 1258 1259 1265 1289 1294 1340 1344 1346 1393 1596 2183
  – (1760-1790) #1369
  – (1875-1915) #1364
  – (1880-1914), influence de la peinture française #1371
  – (1939-années 1950) #1461
  – (1940-1960) #1462
  – (1940-1966) #1440
  – (1953-1956) #1454
  – (1955-1965) #1471
  – (années 1870) #1307
  – (années 1920) #302
  – (années 1920-1970) #1463
  – (années 1930) #1460
  – (années 1930), influence de la peinture française #1381
  – (années 1930-1960) #1421
  – (années 1940) #1384 1390 1468
  – (années 1940-1950) #1432 1472
  – (années 1940-1960) #1436
  – (années 1940-1970) #1267 1269
  – (années 1950) #1413 1414
  – (années 1950-1960) #1441
  – (années 1960) #1419 1487
  – (années 1970) #1542 1543 1544 1552 1560
  – Corbeil, Maurice et Andrée, collection #3234
  – et Alfred Pellan #6801
  – et Fernand Leduc #6191
  – et Joseph Légaré #6220
  – et Paul-Emile Borduas #4826
  – influence de la collection Desjardins #3207
  – milieu XVIIe s.-1908 #1353
  – paysages, Laurentides (Qué), XXe s. #1278 1279
  – pop'art #1497
  – publications #1295
  – surréalisme #1464
  – XIX s.-années 1940 #1242 1248
  – XIX s.-années 1960 #1256 1262
  – XIXe s. #1312 1318 1336
  – XIXe s.-années 1930 #1382
  – XVIIe s. #1363
  – XVIIe s.-années 1920 #1229
  – XVIIe-XIXe s. #1305

– XVIIe-XVIIIe s. #2187
– XVIIIe-début XXe s. #1339
– XVIIIe-XIXe s. #1323
– XXe s. #1270 1392 1422 4877
– Québec (Qué)
  – Hôtel-Dieu #3119
  – Université Laval #3078 3080
  – XVIIe s. #1352
– réalisme #110 716 1810
  – (années 1970) #545
– Regina (Sask), (1960s) #1913
– représentation des grands espaces,
  réaction du public #93
– Saguenay-Lac-Saint-Jean (Qué), XXe s.
  #1551
– Saint-Jean (NB)
  – (années 1950) #1173
  – XXe s. #1184
– Saskatchewan #1919
  – (1883-1959) #1915
– Saskatoon (Sask)
  – Nutana Collegiate Institute. Memorial
    Art Gallery #3183
– scènes de guerre #1073 1074 1075 1076
  1078 1080 1081 1085 1092 1093 1096 1097
  1099 1110 1111 1112 1115
  – Ottawa (Ont), Galerie nationale du
    Canada #1077 1101 1102 1103
– Société d'art contemporain #1459 1474
– sociétés ferroviaires canadiennes,
  protecteur des arts #3281
– surréalisme #463 508 509 1458
– Terre-Neuve #1139 1147 1154
  – (années 1970) #1149
– thèmes religieux, XXe s. #479
– Toronto (Ont)
  – (1953-1965) #1772 1773 1775
  – (années 1940-1950) #5171
  – (années 1950) #1749
  – (années 1950-1960) #4961
  – (années 1960) #1753
  – (années 1970) #1803 1807 1823 1831
  – Art Gallery of Ontario #3149
  – Colborne Lodge #3129
  – Royal Ontario Museum. Collection
    Sigmund Samuel #3135 3140
  – Saint Anne's Church #1733
  – University of Toronto #3168
    – Hart House #3137 3147
    – University College #3151
  – XXe s. #1760
– Vancouver (CB)
  – (années 1950) #1992
  – (années 1970) #2075
– Varennes (Qué), églises #8813
– Winnipeg (Man) #1891
  – (années 1960) #1892
  – Palais législatif #8951
– Winnipeg Sketch Club #1894
– XIX s.-années 1940 #36 1242
– XIXe-début XXe s. #7
– XIXe s. #178 197 252
– XIXe s.-années 1920 #11
– XVIIe s.-années 1910 #205
– XVIIe-XIXe s. #232 236
– XVIIIe s.-années 1930 #45
– XVIIIe s.-années 1950 #50
– XVIIIe-XIXe s. #226 231 1338
– XXe s. #52 83 84 145 407 423 482 507 665
  – et génie #471
peinture d'histoire . Canada
– Beau, Henri #4639
– Berczy, William Bent #241 242
– Bourassa, Napoléon #4872 4874

– Delfosse, Georges #5280
– Harris, Robert #5736 5740
– Huot, Charles Edouard #5876 5878 5880
  5881 5884
– Innes, John I. #5901
– Jefferys, Charles William #5954 5956
– Légaré, Joseph #6214 6216 6219
– Montréal (Qué), Ecole des beaux-arts
  #2972
– Morrison, Alfred L. #6642
– Québec #1344
– Reid, George Agnew #6978
– Rindisbacher, Peter #7006 7009
– verrières, église Notre-Dame (Montréal,
  Qué) #2444
– XVIIe-XIXe s. #187
– XVIIIe-XIXe s. #247 812
peinture de genre . Canada
– (années 1890) #183
– (années 1950) #392
– Hébert, Louis-Philippe #5767
– Hind, William George Richardson #5811
– Krieghoff, Cornelius #6097
– Québec, XVIIe s.-années 1960 #1344
– Reid, George Agnew #6973
– XVIIIe-XIXe s. #812
  – Montréal (Qué), Université McGill.
    Musée McCord #222 223 1366
peinture écossaise #133
peinture égyptienne
– influence sur Ronald Langley Bloore #4749
peinture flamande
– XIXe s., influence sur peinture canadienne
  #39
peinture française
– voir aussi impressionisme
– (1867-1914) #274
– (1880-1914), influence sur peinture
  québécoise #1371
– (1927), Canadian National Exhibition
  (Toronto, Ont) #295
– (années 1880), influence sur peinture
  canadienne #172
– (années 1930), influence sur peinture
  québécoise #1381
– (années 1940), influence sur peinture
  canadienne #379 496
– (années 1940), influence sur peinture
  québécoise #1256 1262 1390
– (années 1950-1960), influence sur peinture
  montréalaise #1263
– XIXe s., influence sur peinture canadienne
  #178 265
– XIXe s., influence sur peinture ontarienne
  #1705
– XVIIe s.-années 1930, influence sur
  peinture canadienne #39
– XVIIe-XIXe s., collection Desjardins #3207
– XVIIIe s., calvaire d'Oka (Oka, Qué) #8853
peinture hollandaise
– (1880-1910), influence sur art canadien
  #214
– XIXe s., dans collections privées
  canadiennes #194
– XIXe s., influence sur peinture canadienne
  #39
– XVIIe s., influence sur Cornelius Krieghoff
  #6101
– XVIIe s., influence sur Henk Ykelenstam
  #7626
– XVIIe-XIXe s., collection Desjardins #3207
peinture italienne
– Florence, Robert Harris, commentaire
  #5737

– influence sur Paul Kane #6003
– XVIIe-XIXe s., collection Desjardins #3207
peinture japonaise
– école de Nangan, influence sur Kazuo
  Hamasaki #5688
– influence sur Bruno Joseph Bobak #4756
– sumi-é, influence sur Gaston-Pierre Petit
  #6843 6844 6845
– sumi-é, influence sur Takao Tanabe #7320
  7321
– Ukiyo-e, influence sur Miyuki Tanobe
  #7322
peinture latino-américaine
– (années 1920-1960), en comparaison avec
  peinture canadienne #495
peinture mexicaine
– (années 1930), en comparaison avec
  peinture canadienne #337
peinture murale
– voir aussi conservation et restauration,
  peinture murale
– Bourassa, Napoléon, commentaire #4862
  4870
– Challener, Frederick Sproston,
  commentaire #5066
– Iliu, Josef, commentaire #8229
– Korner, John Michael Anthony,
  commentaire #6077
– Lismer, Arthur, commentaire #15
– MacDonald, J.E.H., commentaire #6362
– Reid, George Agnew, commentaire #6974
  6975 6979
peinture murale . Canada
– (1890-1900) #190
– (1938-1948) #379
– (années 1890), recommandations #8220
– (années 1940) #370
– (avant 1940) #28
– Calgary (Alta) #1959
– Challener, Frederick Sproston #5067
– Groupe des Sept #1774
– Montréal (Qué) et Toronto (Ont), murales
  extérieures (années 1970) #539
– provinces de l'Ouest (années 1950) #1844
– région de Granville Ferry (NE),
  Hall-Croscup House #1223
peinture naïve . Canada #965 966
– Charlevoix (Qué), (années 1940) #1243
– Price, Ralph et Patricia, collection #971
– provinces de l'Ouest, XXe s. #1846
– Saskatchewan, XXe s. #1927
– Terre-Neuve
  – (années 1970) #1156
  – XXe s. #1153 1155
– XIXe s. #252
– XVIIIe-XIXe s., Université McGill. Musée
  McCord (Montréal, Qué) #222 223
– XXe s. #960
peinture populaire
– voir peinture traditionnelle
peinture sur porcelaine
– Canada
  – (années 1850-1890) #2305
  – (années 1890) #2277
  – XIXe s. #2288
– Montréal (Qué), Musée des beaux-arts de
  Montréal, Salon de printemps #1228 1311
– service de table officiel, Canada (1898)
  #2333
peinture sur verre . Canada #2455
– (1901-1912), Toronto Society of Architects,
  expositions #7956
– (1910-1961), Canadian National Exhibition
  (Toronto, Ont) #1

– (années 1880) #2443
– (années 1940)
   – Plamondon, Marius Gérald, commentaire #2447
   – Williams, Yvonne, commentaire #2446
– (années 1960) #2106
– Allward, John Raphael #4515
– Blomfield, James Jerris #1977 8900 8966
– Colombie-Britannique #2452
– églises, influence de la peinture sur verre française #1435
– et architecture (années 1960) #8236
– femmes artistes (années 1920-1940) #2445
– Ferron, Marcelle #5422 5423 5424 5425 5426
– Horwood, H. #2111
– Huot, Charles Edouard #5876
– Lockport (Man), Saint Andrew's Church #8909
– Louy, Pierre #1177
– Manitoba #2450
– May, Karl #6452 6453
– milieu XIXe-début XXe s. #2399
– Milne, Eleanor #6569
   – Ottawa (Ont), édifices du Parlement #6568
– Montréal (Qué) #2448
   – Bibliothèque Saint-Sulpice #9039
   – église Notre-Dame #2444 8839
   – fin XIXe s. #2462
– Morris, William #2453
– Murphy, Rowley Walter #6666
– Oshawa (Ont), Saint George's Anglican Church #8899
– Ottawa (Ont), édifices du Parlement. Tour de la Paix et Chapelle du Souvenir #8929
– Patterson, Nancy-Lou #6783
– Pellan, Alfred #1442 8233
– Piché-Whissell, Aline #6865
– Plamondon, Marius Gérald #1404 6888
– provinces de l'Ouest (années 1980) #2460
– Québec (années 1940) #2199 8820
– Reid, Stuart #6983
– Toronto (Ont)
   – (années 1880-1890) #2451
   – hôtel de ville (1898) #2449
   – Trinity College Chapel #2461
– Vancouver (CB)
   – (1890-1940) #2456
      – thèmes héraldiques #2454
      – utilisation de catalogues de patrons #2457
   – Coquitlam Centre #2459
   – Dearle, John Henry, et Duncan W. #2458
– Victoria (CB) #2269
– Williams, Yvonne #7589
– Winnipeg (Man), Marlborough Hotel #9277
peinture sur verre . France
– influence sur peinture sur verre, Canada #1435
peintures, technique
– voir matériaux et techniques . peinture
Peirron, Jean, prêtre fr, artiste au Canada, 1631-1673 #198
Pel, Brian, photographe can, ca 1954-
– catalogue de photographies #1032
Pellan, Alfred, artiste can, 1906- #97 1294 1392 1426 1432 1504 1542 1543 6796 6797 6801 6802 6803 6808 6809 6810 6815 6817 6818 6819
– commentaire sur Gérard Morisset #3305
– commentaire sur Normand Hudon #5855
– commentaire sur ses études en art #470

– décors et costumes, La nuit des rois #6799
– Dumouchel, Albert, comparaison #5332
– East, Benoît, comparaison #5353
– entretien #6800 6806 6811 6812 6821
– et automatistes #1448
– et Jean-Paul Lemieux #6228
– et Paul-Emile Borduas #1451
– et Pierre Gauvreau #5578
– et Société d'art contemporain #1459
– et surréalisme #1453 1464
– exposition de ses oeuvres, Musée d'art moderne de la ville de Paris (Paris, France) #6805
– expositions
   – (1955) #6804
   – (1960) #6807
   – (1972) #6816
   – (1980) #6824 6825
– expositions, critiques #428 6823
– expositions de groupe #509
   – (1958) #431
   – (1964) #462
   – (1978) #508
– Gagnon-Fortier, C., comparaison #5552
– influence sur Alan Glass #5614
– influence sur art abstrait québécois #1468
– influence sur arts décoratifs québécois #2199
– influence sur Jean-Philippe Dallaire #5241 5244
– influence sur Madeleine Laliberté #6153
– influence sur peinture montréalaise #1416 1437
– influence sur peinture québécoise #489 1389 6826
– L'amour fou #6820
– murales, ambassade canadienne (Rio de Janeiro, Brésil) #6798
– oeuvres (1946-1948) #6813
– Polychromées #1647
– portraits, Galerie nationale du Canada (Ottawa, Ont) #6814
– professeur #482 1395
– querelle avec Paul-Emile Borduas #4832
– reconnaissance internationale (années 1950) #425
– Scherzo, vitrail, Place des Arts (Montréal, Qué) #1442 8233
– têtes, traits surréalistes #6822
– works, Venice Biennale (1952) #399
Pellat, Sir Henry Mill, homme d'affaires, 1859-1939
– résidence, Casa Loma (Toronto, Ont) #8649
Pelletier, Didace (Claude) (frère Didace), artiste can, 1657-1699 #228 229
Pelletier, Marie-Louise Emilie (soeur Saint-Alphonse), religieuse can, 1816-1846
– portrait, Antoine-Sébastien Plamondon #6887
Pelletier, Pierre-Yves, artiste can, 1948-
– projets de design, Jeux olympiques (1976) #898
Pelly Bay (TNO)
– artistes inuit #4221
– instruments netsilik #4363
– sculpture d'ivoire #4438
Pemberton, Sophia Theresa, artiste can, 1869-1959 #6827 6829
– expositions
   – (1978) #6828
Pen and Pencil Club of Montreal (Montréal, Qué) #1254
– (1890-1955) #1251

– et Edmond Dyonnet #5346
Pender, William, photographe can, actif années 1850
– portraits #1171
Pender Bay (CB), Pearson College
– architecture, Thom Partnership #8412
péninsule d'Avalon (TN)
– villages irlandais #8523
péninsule de Saanich (CB), Miraloma (maintenant Latch Restaurant)
– architecture, Samuel Maclure #8731
pénitenciers
– voir prisons
Pennington, James Carlisle, architecte can, 1885-1963
– Toronto (Ont), Park School #9388
– Windsor (Ont), Collegiate Institute #9388
Penny, Edward, artiste brit, 1714-1791
– peinture, mort de Wolfe #220
Pentaguets
– art #3537
– écorce de bouleau #3510
– travail du cuir #3554
Penticton (CB), Penticton Art Centre Gallery
– expositions
   – A Tribute to William Townsend: 1909 to 1973 (1974) #7418
Pentland, Samuel, artisan tisserand can, années 1840-1850 #2723
Pentz, Don, artiste can, 1940-
– expositions
   – (1979) #6830
Pépin, Arthur, artiste can, 1928-
– entretien #6831
Pépin, Jean-Paul, artiste can, 1897-
– et Montée Saint-Michel #1236
Pépin, Joseph, sculpteur can, 1770-1842 #1300 6947
– retable, église Berthierville (Qué) #8874
Pépin, Louis, photographe can, 1956- #1562
Pépin, Yves, artiste can, 1943-
– expositions de groupe
   – (1977) #637
Pepper, George Douglas, artiste et officier de l'armée can, 1903-1962
– expositions
   – (1964) #6832
– membre du Groupe des peintres canadiens #324
Percé (Qué)
– vues, Marc-Aurèle Fortin #5481
perception et art
– Amérindiens #3487
– art vidéo #651
– Indiens de la côte nord-ouest #4001
– Inuit #4294
– Molinari, Guido #6591
– Snow, Michael #7245 7259
– Tousignant, Serge #7404
– utilisation de miroirs et fenêtres #525
Percival, Robert, artiste et conservateur can, 1924- #6833 6834
– expositions, critiques #6835
Perehudoff, William (Bill), artiste can, 1919-
– expositions
   – (1977) #6836
   – (1978) #6837
   – (1981) #6838
– expositions, critiques #1883
– expositions de groupe
   – (1967) #1916
   – (1975) #1926
   – (1981) #722
– peintures murales #1844

Peressutti, Enrico, architecte it, 1908-
– Venise (Italie), Pavillon canadien, XIXe Biennale #9210
périodiques
– *voir aussi* architecture . périodiques; art . périodiques; journaux; photographie . périodiques
– (années 1870), articles sur la mode #2878
– (années 1920), articles sur la mode #2906
– XIXe s., patrons de vêtements #2854 2871 2889
périodiques . illustration
– influence sur Homer Ransford Watson #7536
périodiques américains . illustration
– vues de l'Ouest américain (1857-1900) #931
périodiques canadiens
– et art #3313
– publicité, fin XIXe-début XXe s. #891
périodiques canadiens . illustration #925 3313
– (1967) #877
– (1981) #941
– (années 1880-1940) #28
– Cahén, Oscar, commentaire #4985
– *Canadian Forum* (1920-1951) #930
– *Imperial Oil Review* (années 1950) #924
– vues d'Ottawa (Ont), (1807-1882) #1716
– vues de la Colombie-Britannique (1513-1891) #2006
– vues de la Nouvelle-Ecosse (1605-1878) #1203
– vues de la péninsule du Niagara (Ont), XVIIe-XIXe s. #1718
– vues de Québec (Qué), (1608-1875) #1349
– vues de Terre-Neuve (1497-1887) #1145
– vues de Toronto (Ont), (1813-1882) #1717
– vues des Cantons de l'Est (Qué), (1832-1881) #1342
– vues des provinces de l'Ouest (1857-1900) #931
– vues du Canada, XVIIIe-XIXe s. #246
Perkins, Simeon, marchand can, actif 1766-1812
– résidence (Liverpool, NE) #8536
Perkins & Will, agence amér d'architecture
– Toronto (Ont), hôtel de ville et Civic Square, concours #8981
perles, type "pony" . Indiens des plaines
– XIXe s. #3722
Perrault, Gérard, artiste can, 1903-
– réflexion sur le graphisme (années 1940) #851
Perrault, Henri-Maurice, architecte can, 1857-1909
– Oka (Qué), église #8818
Perrault, Jean Chrysostome, sculpteur can, 1793-1829
– intérieur, église Saint-Jean-Baptiste (Saint-Jean-Port-Joli, Qué) #8812
Perrault, Pierre, artiste can, 1927-
– réflexion sur l'Etat et l'art #3269
Perrault, Pierre, photographe can, 1955-
– catalogue de photographies #1023
Perret, Auguste, architecte, auteur fr, 1874-1954
– influence sur Marcel Parizeau #8397
Perrigard, Hal Ross, artiste can, 1891-1960 #302 1382
Perron, Germain, artiste can, 1943- #1502
– à Paris (France) #1434
Perron, J.Eugène, architecte can, 1900-1969
– Valleyfield (Qué), cathédrale de Salaberry-de-Valleyfield #8843

Perrot, André, artiste can, actif 1956
– et l'art religieux québécois (années 1950) #1250
Perry, Arthur, critique d'art canadien, XXe s.
– lauréat, concours de critique d'art (1979) #3312
Perth (Australie), Art Gallery of Western Australia
– expositions
– *Contemporary Canadian Painters* (1957) #423
Perth (Ont)
– architecture domestique, XIXe s. #8669
Perth (Ont), Inge-Va (autrefois Radenhurst House)
– architecture #8669
Perth (Ont), McMartin House
– architecture #8669
Perth (Ont), Perth Museum (autrefois Matheson House)
– architecture #8670
Peterborough (Ont)
– architecture (avant-1890) #8021
– colonisation irlandaise #8523
– pétroglyphes algonquiens #3619
– pétroglyphes ojibwa #3568 3581 3591
– robes et costumes de marié(e)s (1810-1938) #2909
Peterborough (Ont), Art Gallery of Peterborough
– expositions
– *David Bolduc: Recent Work* (1980) #4775
– *Humorist Walter Trier: Selections from the Trier-Fodor Foundation Gift* (1980) #7428
– *Manitoba Flashback* (1981) #1907
– *The Heritage of Jack Bush: A Tribute* (1982) #722
– *Water Colours by E.May Martin* (1980) #6424
Peterborough (Ont), Artspace #700 1836
– (années 1970) #641
Peterborough (Ont), Hutchison House
– architecture #8674
Peterborough (Ont), Peterborough Centennial Museum and Archives
– expositions
– *Dearly Beloved... Wedding Costumes and Customs from 1810-1930* (1981) #2909
Peterborough (Ont), Sir Sandford Fleming College
– et Haliburton School of Fine Arts (Haliburton, Ont) #2258
– expositions
– *Catalogue: Canadian Antique Pottery & Stoneware* (1975) #2324
Peterborough (Ont), Trent University
– architecture
– Thom, Ron #9470 9473 9478
– Thom Partnership #8412
– conférences, conservation des grands-rues de l'Ontario (1978) #8024
Peterborough (Ont), Trent University. Champlain College
– architecture, Thompson, Berwick & Pratt #7694 9465 9474
– expositions
– *Rodrik/Johnston* (1973) #5973
Peterborough (Ont), Trent University. Lady Eaton College
– architecture, Thompson, Berwick & Pratt #9474
Peterborough (Ont), Trent University. Mackenzie Gallery
– expositions

– *A Selection of Work: Contemporary Indian Art; The Trail from the Past to the Future* (1977) #4150
Peterborough (Ont), Trent University. Résidence des étudiants
– architecture, Fairfield & DuBois #9467
Peters, Barry, artiste can, 1938-
– expositions de groupe
– (1977) #4151
Peters, James, photographe can, 1853-1927
– photographies de la rébellion du Nord-Ouest #1107
Peters, Kenneth M., artiste can, 1939-
– expositions de groupe
– (1967) #1916
Peters, Mary, artisane tisserande can, active années 1960
– tissage salishiens #3941
Peters, Paddy, artiste can, 1956-
– expositions de groupe
– (1977) #4151
Peterson, Margaret, artiste can, 1902-
– expositions
– (1978) #6839
Peterson, Warren H., artiste can, 1935-
– expositions de groupe
– (1977) #1933
Pethick, Jerry, artiste can, 1936- #6842
– commentaire sur l'holographie au laser #6840
– entretien #6841
Petit, Gaston-Pierre, prêtre et artiste can, 1930- #6843 6844 6845
Petit, Jean-Marc, photographe can, actif 1971 #997
Petit Fort Garry (Man)
– architecture #8094 8475 8483
– caserne #8482
– entrepôts #8480
– North-West Bastion and walls #8476
Petite, Marion, artiste, active années 1970
– art vidéo #651
Petley, Robert, officier de l'armée brit, artiste au Canada, ca 1809-1869
– vues de la Nouvelle-Ecosse et du Nouveau-Brunswick #5351
Petrigo, Walter, photographe can, 1932-
– catalogue de photographies #995
pétroglyphes
– *voir aussi* art pariétal; conservation et restauration, pétroglyphes
pétroglyphes . Algonquiens
– Peterborough (Ont) #3619
pétroglyphes . Assiniboines #3673
pétroglyphes . Bella-Coolas
– Noeich River (CB) #3816
pétroglyphes . Cris #3439
pétroglyphes . Dorsétiens
– Qikertaaluk Island (TNO) #4362
pétroglyphes . Indiens de la côte nord-ouest #3785 3859 3971 3988 3999 4058
– Aldridge Point (CB) #3814
– Columbia Valley (CB) #3903
– en comparaison avec pictogrammes #3886
– Gabriola Island (CB) #4050
– Prince Rupert (CB) #3846
pétroglyphes . Indiens des plaines
– assemblage de rochers #3689
pétroglyphes . Iroquois #3599
pétroglyphes . Micmacs #3617
– parc national Kejimkujik (Fairy Bay, NE) #3614
pétroglyphes . Salish de la côte #3870
pétroglyphes . Saulteux/Ojibwa #3591

- Peterborough (Ont) #3568
- Peterborough et Stoney Lake (Ont) #3581
pétroglyphes . Tchippewayans #3439
pétroglyphes . Tlingits #3786
Petrucci, Aimé, sculpteur can, 1887-1950
- thème de l'Annonciation #1633
Petry, Nancy Wargin, artiste can, 1931-
- expositions de groupe
  - (1976) #1529
Pfeifer, Bodo, artiste can, 1936-
- expositions de groupe
  - (1969) #2039
Pfeiffer, Gordon Edward, artiste can, 1899-
  #6846 6847
Pfliger, Terry, artiste can, 1947-
- commentaire sur Jack Chambers #700
Pflug, Christiane Sybille, artiste can,
  1936-1972 #110 6849
- expositions
  - (1974) #6850
  - (1979) #6851
PGL Architectes (Papineau, Gérin-Lajoie,
  LeBlanc), agence can d'architecture
- Mirabel (Qué), Aéroport international de
  Mirabel. Aérogare #9518
phares . Canada #9520 9521 9524
- Grands Lacs (Ont) #9519
- Halifax (NE) #7818
- Nouvelle-Ecosse #9522
- Pointe-des-Monts (Qué) #9526
- Terre-Neuve #9523
  - Cape Spear et Cape Bonavista #9525
- XIXe s. #9512
phares . Etats-Unis #9524
Phases (Paris, France)
- et Roland Giguère #5598
Philadelphia Society of Etchers
- exhibition, Toronto (Ont), (1885) #798
Philadelphie (Penn)
- vues, David Johnston Kennedy #6040
Philadelphie (Penn), Moore College of Art.
  Gallery
- exposition Recorded Activities (1970), Les
  Levine, commentaire #6265
Philadelphie (Penn), Olympia Galleries
- expositions
  - Watercolors by Robert Murray and Toni
    Onley (1976) #613
Philadelphie (Penn), Pennsylvania Academy
  of Fine Arts
- Reid, George Agnew, élève #6979
- Reid, Mary Hiester, élève #6982
Philadelphie (Penn), Philadelphia Museum
  of Art
- expositions
  - Sculpture of the Inuit: Masterworks of the
    Canadian Arctic/La sculpture chez les Inuit:
    chefs-d'oeuvre de l'Arctique canadien
    (1973) #4423 4440
Philadelphie (Penn), University of
  Pennsylvania. Museum
- artefacts gravés, Inuit #4323
- artefacts thuléens #4372
- boucliers, Dakotas #3670
- boucliers, Indiens des plaines #3680
- casques en peau de requin, clan des
  Kaguanton #3833
- coiffure, Tlingits #3803
- wampum, Iroquois #3518
- wampum, Micmacs #3497
Phillips, Walter Joseph, artiste can,
  1884-1963 #6856 6857 6859 6861
- expositions
  - (1978) #6860

- gravures sur bois de fil #802 804 6852 6853
  6854 6855 6858
- paysages #2016
- professeur de Gerald Tailfeathers #7312
  7313
philosophie
- voir aussi transcendentalisme
philosophie de l'art
- voir esthétique
philosophie et art
- et Groupe des Sept #1774
- et Paul-Emile Borduas #1455
philosophie orientale
- influence sur Frederick Horsman Varley
  #7461
- influence sur Pierre Archambault #4545
Phinney, Robert, sculpteur can, actif 1959-
  #6862
Phipps, Lynn, photographe can, 1936-
- catalogue de photographies #998
Photo Age, périodique can #987
Photo Canada, périodique can #1032
Photo Club of Canada (Toronto, Ont)
- expositions, critiques #978
Photo Communiqué, périodique can #1053
  3314
Photo Fun, périodique can #987
Photo Life, périodique can #1023
Photograms of [189-]: A Pictorial and Literary
  Record of the Best Photographic Work of the
  Year
- photographie canadienne (1895-1898) #978
Photograms of the Year, périodique brit
- photographie canadienne (1905-1940) #978
photographes canadiens
- Absil, Mickey #1023
- Achim, Normand #1534
- Altman, Gerry #1023
- Anderton, T.George #4525
- Appel, Brian #1904
- April, Raymonde #1059 1063 1556
- Astman, Barbara Anne #1010 1063
- Baber, Jack #987
- Baczynski, George #1023
- Bailey, Charles S. #2012 4583
- Bailey, Clayton #1033 4584
- Bailey, William #2012
- Balch, Reg #991
- Baltzly, Benjamin #1014 1015 4598
- Bancroft, Marian Penner #2018 2071
- Barbour, David #1904
- Bareket, Nir #1023
- Barnes, Elliott Chappel #4610
- Bates, Maxwell Bennett #4621
- Baturin, Jon #1023
- Baxter, Iain #1057
- Bayley, W.B. #977
- Beaudoin-Hansen, Kéro #4648
- Beaugrand-Champagne, Claire #1513 1556
  1562
- Bedford, Michael #995
- Bell, Bert #1036
- Bell, Ken #995 4657
- Bendahan, Raphael #4670
- Benoît (dit Livernois), Jules-Isaïe #258 259
- Bentley, Percy #2012
- Beny, Wilfred Roloff #4688 4689 4690 4691
- Beube, Doug #991
- Beveridge, Karl John #1052 1063
- Bierwagen, Ottmar #995
- Bigger, Charles A. #1014 1015
- Biggs, Hugh Beynon #4728
- Bingham, John #1032
- Blahut, John #1007

- Bleyenberg, Harry #1023 4742
- Bluesinger, Taki #996
- Bohar, Dick #998
- Boisvert, Paul #1023
- Boland, Con #1023
- Boogaerts, Pierre #1018
- Boorne, William Hanson #4796 4797
- Borremans, Guy #997 999
- Bot, Marten #995
- Bourdeau, Robert Charles John #987 1002
  1018 1023 1037 1046 1060 1070
- Boyd, Jerry #1023
- Boyd, W.H. #989
- Boyer, Michel #1023
- Bradley, Randy #2071
- Breukelman, Jim #2071
- Brown, Alisen #1023
- Brown, Bert #995
- Brown, Douglas #1023
- Brown, Ernest #6451
- Brown, Gordon F. #991
- Brown, Randy #1023 1032
- Brown, Thomas #1000
- Bruce, David #2071
- Bruenner, Ralph #991
- Bruno, Anthony #995
- Bryson, Joseph Vincent #1032
- Buchan, David #1067
- Buchanan, Donald William #3325
- Calnen, Robert F. #995
- Cameron, Duncan #1675
- Campbell, Paul #1067
- Campbell-Smith, Struan #995
- Campeau, Michel #997 999 1513
- Carey, David #1023
- Carr-Harris, Ian #1057
- Carruthers, Alan #995
- Cassidy, Eugene Haanel #5054
- Castonguay, J.Alex #1675
- Caton, Peter #624
- Cavoukian, Artin #624
- Chabot, J.E. #1283
- Chagnon, Alain #997 999
- Chambers, Jack #5075
- Chaput, Yves #997 999
- Charbonneau, Roger #997 999 1513 1556
- Chechik, Jeremiah #992
- Chesterfield, Albert A. #5102
- Chrismas, Lawrence #991
- Christl, Rudi #1023
- Chu, T.K. #1023
- Clairrou, Jacques #997 999
- Clark, Tim #1556
- Clément, Serge #991
- Cloutier, Marcel #1283
- Cohen, Lynne #1018 1037 1046 1053 1060
  1067
- Cohen, Sorel #5130
- Condé, Carole #1052 1063
- Conner, Scott #1032
- Corman, Don #1063
- Corsault, Share #2071
- Coshof, Karen #995 1023
- Cossette, Marie Andrée #1556
- Coutellier, Francis #996
- Cousineau, Sylvain P. #1018 1067
- Crête, Alphida #1562
- Croydon, Peter #1036
- Cupit, William Henry #2071
- Curtin, Walter #1054
- Dally, Frederick #5249
- Danson, Andrew #1053
- Davies, Barbara #993
- Davis, Leonard #991

– collection *Image*, Office national du film du Canada (Ottawa, Ont), (1967-1971) #990
– Colombie-Britannique
    – (1858-1888), paysages #2015
    – (1858-1914) #2032
    – (1860-1978), femmes photographes #2018
    – (1890-1914) #2030
    – (1890-1940) #2012
    – (années 1970) #2041 2056 2063 2071
– comté de Simcoe (Ont), XIXe s. #1730
– comté de Simcoe et Norfolk (Ont), XIXe s. #1722
– comté de Wellington (Ont), (1856-1867) #1724
– conference (1979) #1047
– et art (années 1970) #635 1057
– et langage (1980) #1063
– et littérature (1980) #1065 1066
– et peinture
    – (1860-1900) #245 262 268
    – (années 1970) #545
    – paysages, fin XIXe s. #264
– et publicité, XIXe-XXe s. #1024
– et sculpture (années 1970) #994
– famille Livernois (1857-1960) #1275
– femmes artistes #1005 1064
    – (1840-1900) #1049
    – (années 1970) #993 1011 1013
– Fringe Research Inc. #1827 1905
– galeries parallèles (années 1970) #1042
– Great Eastern Photographic and Advertising Company #2022
– Groupe d'action photographique #1003 1494
– Halifax (NE), (années 1830-1860) #1211
– Hamilton (Ont), (1867-1900) #1719
– *Homemaker's* périodique (années 1980) #5708
– *Impressions* #996
– Karsh, Yousuf, commentaire #486 487
– Kingston (Ont) #1680
– London (Ont), (années 1970) #1812
– Manitoba #1895 1904
– Manitoba Camera Club #985
– marché de l'art (années 1970) #1038
– Maritimes (années 1970) #1134
– Montréal (Qué), Centaur Galleries #1004
– Nouveau-Brunswick (1869-1918) #1186
– Ottawa (Ont) #1675
    – Archives publiques du Canada. Collection nationale de photographies #3052
    – Office national du film. Service de la photographie #1028 1043
– Ottawa Camera Club #1677 1704
– périodiques
    – (années 1970) #3314
    – *BC Photographer* #998
    – *Camera Canada* #991
    – *Canadian Journal of Photography* #974
    – *Canadian Photographic Journal* #976
    – *Canadian Photography* #995
    – *Image Nation* #992
    – *Impressions* #996
    – *Impulse* #538
    – *OVO* #997 999
    – *Photo Age* #987
    – *Photo Canada* #1032
    – *Photo Communiqué* #1053
    – *Photo Life* #1023
– photographie d'arpentage #989
    – (1858-1900), Colombie-Britannique #2028
    – (années 1850), exploration de

l'Assiniboine et de la Saskatchewan #5804
    – (années 1850-1890), provinces de l'Ouest #1865
    – (années 1870), Canadien Pacifique #1876
    – (années 1880-1890), Montagnes Rocheuses #1874
    – XIXe s., soutien aux compagnies ferroviaires #3281
– photographie de la nature #1062
– photographie militaire (1885-années 1970s) #1107
– photographies d'immigrants, Québec (1908-1910) #1031
– photographies d'Indiens de la côte nord-ouest, fin XIXe-début XXe s. #2029 2033
– photographies d'Inuit (années 1920) #1021
– photographies de Canadiens (années 1970) #1035 1055
– photographies format album (années 1860) #1026
– Prairies (années 1970) #1879
– Première Guerre mondiale #1072 1113 1114
– provinces de l'Atlantique (années 1970) #1132
– provinces de l'Ouest
    – (1858-1900) #1014 1015
    – (1964-1970) #872
– Québec
    – (années 1970) #1507 1556
    – (années 1980) #1562
    – XIX s.-années 1940 #1242
– réalisme #716
– Saguenay-Lac-Saint-Jean (Qué) #1283
– Seconde Guerre mondiale #1095
– Toronto (Ont)
    – (1839-1867) #1725
    – Baldwin Street Gallery of Photography #1794
    – Metro Toronto Public Library #3143
    – Ryerson Polytechnical Institute #1805
– Toronto Camera Club #1 975 977 980 983 984 1683 1702
– Vancouver (CB)
    – (années 1970) #2064 2069
    – Gallery of Photography #2052
– vues de Terre-Neuve et du Labrador (1849-1949) #1160
– vues de villes canadiennes (1850-1900) #1058 1061 7744
– Western Photographic Circle #2019
– Whitehorse (Yukon), Yukon Archives #2087
– XIXe s. #1006 1048
– XXe s. #988 1007
photographie canadienne . portrait
– (1860-1900), et peinture #268
– (années 1970), commentaires d'artistes #624
– Bailey, Clayton #4584
– Beaudoin-Hansen, Kéro #4648
– Donovan, Duncan #5298 5299
– Halifax (NS), (1860s) #1211
– Holloway, Elsie #5820
– Karsh, Yousuf #486 487 6023 6026 6030 6031 6032 6034 6035
    – femmes #6024
    – hommes et femmes célèbres #6025 6028 6029
    – hommes politiques et militaires #6022
– Maritimes, XIXe s. #1171
– Nakash, George #6683

– Parsons, F.R. #6773
– photographies format album (années 1860) #1026
– Pollard, Harry #6899
– Reeves, John #6971 6972
    – auteurs canadiens #1065 1066
– Sawyer, William #7145
– Tata, Sam #7329
photographie documentaire
– Minden, Robert, commentaire #6570
– vues, édifices publics #1019
photographie documentaire . Canada
– (années 1850-1910) #1034
– (années 1950-1970) #1056
– Alberta (1980) #1971
– Colombie-Britannique (1858-1871) #2014
– début XXe s. #1039
– vues urbaines (1850-1900) #1061
photographie stéréoscopique . Canada
– Esson, James #5373
– Halifax (NE) #1211
– Toronto (Ont) #1725
– vues urbaines #1058 1061
photographies de bâtiments
– *voir* architecture et photographie
photomontage
– Guimond, Pierre #5664
– Notman, William #6726
photoréalisme
– et Mary Frances Pratt #6919
Piaget, Jean, psychologue suisse, 1896-1980
– théories et N.E. Thing Co. Ltd. #6677
pianos . Canada
– Nouvelle-Ecosse #2489
Picabia, Francis, artiste fr, 1879-1953
– influence sur Alfred Pellan #6822
Picard, Armand, sculpteur can, 1943- #1626
Picard, Edmond, constructeur can, né 1881 #6863
Picard, Louis-Alexandre, joaillier et orfèvre can, ca 1728-1799 #269 270
Picasso, Pablo, artiste esp, 1881-1973
– Bates, Maxwell Bennett, comparaison #4623
– influence sur Alfred Pellan #6803 6805 6811 6821 6822 6826
– influence sur Bill Reid #6985
– influence sur Jacques de Tonnancour #7383
– influence sur Paraskeva Clark #5110
– influence sur Paul-Emile Borduas #4841
– influence sur Robert La Palme #6119
– Pellan, Alfred, comparaison #6814
Piccaluga, Aldo, designer can, 1936-
– intérieur, Tour du CN. Restaurant #9511
Piccaluga, Francesco, designer can, 1932-
– intérieur, Tour du CN. Restaurant #9511
Piccirilli, frères, sculpteurs amér, actifs années 1920
– sculpture, Legislative Building (Winnipeg, Man) #8948 8952
Piché, Reynald, artiste can, 1929- #6864
Piché-Whissell, Aline, artiste can, 1919- #6865
Picher, Claude, artiste can, 1927- #6866 6867
Pichet, Roland, artiste can, 1936- #6868
– expositions de groupe
    – (1977) #1278 1279
pichets
– *voir aussi* pots à condiments
pichets . Canada
– pièce-souvenir, cruche, atelier de poterie de Cap-Rouge #2332
– verre, XIXe-début XXe s. #2430

pichets . Etats-Unis
– verre, XIXe-début XXe s. #2430
Pickering, Dale, photographe can, 1948-
#2071
– expositions de groupe
– (1979) #2069
Pickering, David, sculpteur can, 1941-
– expositions de groupe
– (1978) #786
pictogrammes
– *voir aussi* art pariétal
pictogrammes . Algonquiens #3385 3576
– écorce de bouleau #3571
– Quetico Park (Ont et Man) #3575
– région de Agawa River (Ont) #3589
– région de Lac Wapizagonke (Qué) #3600
– région des Grands Lacs (Ont) #3583
pictogrammes . Amérindiens #3390 3392
pictogrammes . Carriers #3965
pictogrammes . Cris #3760
pictogrammes . Dakotas
– chronique en images #3747
pictogrammes . Indiens de la côte
nord-ouest #3859 3893 3952 3999
– en comparaison avec pétroglyphes #3886
pictogrammes . Indiens des plaines
– région de Kipahigan Lake (Sask et Man)
#3714
– région de Milk River (Mon) #3706
pictogrammes . Inuit
– Alaska #4217
pictogrammes . Kootenays #3965
pictogrammes . Lillooets #3783
pictogrammes . Micmacs
– Fairy Lake (NE) #3494
pictogrammes . Pentaguets #3537
pictogrammes . Saulteux/Ojibwa #3539
– Midéwiwin #3492
pictogrammes . Skeenas
– Skeena River (CB) #3822
pictogrammes . Thompsons #3769
Picton (Ont)
– poterie, XIXe s. #2286
Pictou (NE), Hector Centre Trust
– expositions
– *Nineteenth Century Pictou County
Furniture* (1977) #2513
Picture Butte (Alta), Picture Butte Municipal
Hospital
– architecture, Meech, Mitchell, Robins &
Associates #9032
Picture Loan Society (Toronto, Ont) #1746
Pieds-Noirs
– art #3654 3678 3686 3754 3757
– ours, motif #3746
– assemblage de rochers #3688
– cérémonie de la Pipe-Médicine #3681
– chronique en images #3707
– colliers soumak #3685
– costume #3414 3695 3739
– (1910-1960) #3712
– culture #3651 3667
– étuis à fusils #3713
– huttes #3647
– Minìpoka #3749
– ouvrages en piquants de porc-épic #3703
3745
– pipes #3704
– pipes et sac à pipes #3665
– poterie, XVIIIe-XIXe s. #3679
– rites et cérémonies #3721
– tipis #3669 3676 3718 3735 3741
Piégans
– art #3759

– costume #3414 3715
Pierce, Edith Chown, collectionneuse can, m.
1954
– collection, verre canadien #2397 2398 2399
Pieroway, Percy, artiste can, 1921- #1155
– expositions de groupe
– (1976) #1153
– (1977) #1156
pierre
– *voir aussi* maçonnerie
– Banque canadienne de commerce
(Montréal, Qué) #9153
– bâtiments canadiens (1867-1967) #7695
– bâtiments du comté de Waterloo (Ont),
XIXe s. #8011
– bâtiments manitobains (avant 1900) #8102
– bâtiments ontariens (1831-1861) #8009
– bâtiments québécois, XVIIe-XIXe s. #7859
– carrières, Terrebonne (Qué), (1816-années
1820) #7907
– Forges du Saint-Maurice (Trois-Rivières,
Qué) #7878
– habitations ontariennes (années 1920)
#8646
– habitations québécoises
– XVIIe-XIXe s. #7891 8559
– XVIIe-XVIIIe s. #8621
– Kingston (Ont), bâtiments (1673-1867)
#7989
– pierre à bâtir et pierre d'ornement,
Canada (années 1910) #7646 7647
– pierre Coade, Montréal (Qué) #7908
– région d'Ottawa, XIXe s. #8033
– Saint John's Cathedral (St. John's, TN)
#8771
pierres aviformes
– *voir aussi* travail de la pierre
pierres aviformes . Algonquiens #3406 3491
3499 3511 3577
pierres aviformes . Saulteux/Ojibwa #3546
pierres tombales
– *voir* monuments funéraires
Pierron, Jean, prêtre fr, artiste résidant au
Canada, 1631-1673 #1363
– images pieuses #1354 1358
pieuvre . Tlingits #4045
pigments
– *voir aussi* colorants et teinture; peinture
(produit chimique)
– tirés du sol québécois, pour peinture
(années 1820) #165
Pikulin, Michael, photographe can,
1945-1975
– catalogue de photographies #991
Pilon, Germain, sculpteur fr, 1535-1590
– Baillairgé, François, comparaison #4589
pilons
– *voir* mortiers et pilons
Pilot, Robert Wakeham, artiste can,
1898-1967 #302 6869
– beau-fils de Maurice Galbraith Cullen
#5222
– commentaire sur Albert Henry Robinson
#7057
– commentaire sur Maurice Galbraith Cullen
#1143
– commentaire sur Québec (Qué) #6870
– entretien #6871
– et le Groupe des Sept #1732
– et Maurice Galbraith Cullen #5219 5221
– expositions
– (1968) #6872
– expositions de groupe

– (1977) #1278 1279
Pilote, Clode, artiste can, 1944- #1626
Pingerqalik (Foxe Basin, TNO)
– artefacts dorsétiens #4335
pipes, Iroquois
– Toronto (Ont), Royal Ontario Museum
#3504
pipes . Algonquiens #3463 3511 3529
pipes . Amérindiens #3329 3416 3444 3700
– illustrations, George Catlin #3478
– Londres (Angleterre), British Museum
#3470
pipes . autochtones #3358
pipes . Canada
– Bell, W. & D., Pottery #2298 2322
– céramique, Québec, XVIIe-XIXe s. #2313
pipes . Cris
– et cérémonie du calumet de paix #3662
pipes . Flancs-de-Chien #4077
pipes . Goyoguins #3525
pipes . Haidas #3782
– sculpture d'argilite #4047
pipes . Hurons
– Toronto (Ont), Royal Ontario Museum
#3504
– visages sculptés dans la pierre #3632
pipes . Indiens des forêts du Nord-Est #3491
pipes . Iroquois #3489 3525 3555 3566 3618
– figures humaines sculptées #3642
– Toronto (Ont), Royal Ontario Museum
#3644
pipes . Micmacs #3565
pipes . Nahanis #4077
pipes . Pieds-Noirs #3654 3678 3704
– cérémonie de la Pipe-Médicine #3681
– sacs à pipes #3665
pipes . Saulteux/Ojibwa #3539
pipes . Tahltans
– (années 1910) #4074
pipes . Tsonnontouans #3636
– figures humaines sculptées #3642
Piqtoukun, David Ruben, sculpteur can,
1950- #6873
– sculpture de pierre, Van Dusen Gardens
(Vancouver, CB) #775
Piquette, Jean-Baptiste, orfèvre can, actif
1781-1813
– oeuvres, Detroit Institute of Arts (Detroit,
Mich) #2691
Piranesi, Giovanni Battista, architecte et
artiste it, 1720-1778
– Cormier, Ernest, commentaire #8346
Pissarro, Camille, artiste fr, 1830-1903
– influence sur Robert Wakeham Pilot #6869
Piton, Bill, photographe can, actif années
1970 #992
Pitseolak, Mary, artiste can, 1901- #4260
Pitseolak, Peter, artiste can, 1902-1973 #4242
4460 6874 6878 6880 6881
– aquarelles, Musée national de l'Homme
(Ottawa, Ont) #6875 6877
– autobiographie #6876
– dessin #4202
– expositions
– (1980) #6883
– expositions, critiques #6882
– photographies d'Inuit #6879
Pitsiulak, Lypa, artiste can, 1943-
– masse de cérémonie, Conseil des
Territoires du Nord-Ouest #4386
Pittaway, Alfred G., photographe can,
1858-1930
– expositions de groupe
– (1970) #1675

pittoresque
– et églises ontariennes #8904
– et George Heriot #5786
– et vues de la Colombie-Britannique (1845-1871) #2020
– et vues de la côte nord-ouest, XVIIIe s. #2009
– et William Henry Bartlett #4617
– vues de la Nouvelle-Ecosse, XVIIIe-XIXe s. #1220 1222
placards . Canada #910
Placentia (TN)
– architecture #7792
– fortifications (1662-1811) #8420 8421
places
– voir squares (villes)
Plamondon, Antoine-Sébastien, artiste can, 1804-1895 #1315 1318 1323 1336 6884
– Chemin de la Croix, Musée des beaux-arts de Montréal (Montréal, Qué) #6886
– en comparaison avec Théophile Hamel #5689
– et peinture québécoise #1353
– et société québécoise #1375
– expositions de groupe
– (1880) #1308
– (1959) #219
– (1970) #1348
– influence de la peinture française #1244
– Le flûtiste #6885
– oeuvres, Art Association of Montreal (Montréal, Qué) #3075
– professeur de Théophile Hamel #5690
– Soeur Saint-Alphonse, Galerie nationale du Canada (Ottawa, Ont) #6887
Plamondon, Guy, conservateur can, XXe s.
– directeur, 49e Parallèle (New York, NY) #712
Plamondon, Marius Gérald, artiste can, 1914-1976 #6888
– professeur, Ecole des beaux-arts (Québec, Qué) #1404
– professeur d'Aline Piché-Whissell #6865
– vitraux
– Joliette (Qué), Noviciat des clercs de Saint-Viateur #2447
– Montréal (Qué)
– hôtel Reine-Elizabeth #8228
– oratoire Saint-Joseph #2448
Plamondon, Maurice, Can, XXe s.
– commentaire sur Gérard Morisset #3305
planchers . Canada
– Ontario, utilisation de peinture, XXe s. #8013
plantes
– Ontario, XIXe s. #2245
plantes dans l'art
– voir aussi arbres dans l'art; feuilles dans l'art; fleurs dans l'art
– artistes européens en Amérique, XVIe-XIXe s. #260
– Colombie-Britannique, illustration de plantes, fin XVIIIe s.-années 1970 #2024
– décoration architecturale, Canada (années 1930) #8225 8226
– Holmes, Robert #5823
– Pellan, Alfred #6818 6819
– poterie canadienne, XVIIe-XIXe s. #2302
– Sinclair, Robert #7215
Plaskett, Joseph Francis (Joe), artiste can, 1918- #1996 6890
– commentaire sur Herbert Edward Read #6891
– commentaire sur l'influence de Hans

Hofmann sur la peinture canadienne #402
– commentaire sur modernisme #6889
– décors et costumes, Pygmalion #1991
– élève de Hans Hofmann #1850
– entretien #6892
– et Molly Lamb Bobak #4766
– expositions
– (1971) #6893 6894
– (1977) #6895
– portraits #715
plasticiens (Montréal, Qué) #145 476 536 1294 1426 1438 1439 1465 1472 1487 6586
– en comparaison avec les automatistes #7398
– en comparaison avec Painters Eleven #720
– estampes hard-edge #832
– et Denis Juneau #5994
– et Fernand Leduc #6187
– et Guido Molinari #6590
– et Guy Montpetit #6599 6600
– et Pierre Gendron #5582
– influence de Piet Mondrian #1457
– Manifeste des plasticiens, Fernand Toupin, commentaire #7396
– op'art #1445
plastiques
– art québécois (années 1960) #1442
– arts décoratifs canadiens, XXe s. #2121
– sculpture canadienne #768
– sculpture québécoise (années 1970) #1603
plastiques . Canada
– design industriel (années 1940) #2601
plâtre
– voir ciment, mortier et plâtre
plâtres
– modèles masculins, Colette Whiten #7557 7558
Platt, Charles Adams, architecte amér, 1861-1933
– influence sur Northway Department Store (Toronto, Ont) #9366
Plattsburgh (NY), Clinton County Historical Museum
– expositions
– Folk Art in Canada (1981) #973
Plaw, John, architecte can, 1745-1820 #8399
– Charlottetown (IPE), marché public #7800
Plear, Scott, artiste can, 1952-
– expositions de groupe
– (1981) #2084
Ploethner, Frederick K., ébéniste et artisan tisserand can, né 1826 #6896
Plotek, Leopold, artiste can, 1948-
– expositions de groupe
– (1981) #1565
Pluta, Andrzej, photographe can, actif 1977
– catalogue de photographies #1023
pochettes de disques
– (années 1950) #862
– Knaff, Jean-Christian #6065
Pocock, John (Jack), joaillier can, 1912- #2696
Pocock, Philip J., photographe can, 1954-
– catalogue de photographies #987 1023
– expositions de groupe
– (1981) #1069
Podbielski, Marie, artiste can, active années 1980
– illustrations #941
poêles, fours . Canada #2705
– céramique, Québec #2298 2313 2322
– comté de Norfolk (Ont), Normandale Iron Works #2699
– fours à pain, Québec #2233 2234
– Québec (avant-1867) #2220

– Trois-Rivières (Qué), Forges du Saint-Maurice #2698 2708
poésie
– voir aussi poésie visuelle
poésie, art et
– Canada
– (années 1970) #649 1529
– automatisme #1449
– nature et habitations modestes, thème pictural #104
– paysage, thème pictural #140
– Giguère, Roland #5593 5597
– Kiyooka, Roy Kenzie #6062
– Leduc, Ozias #6196
– Meredith, John #6514
– Nicoll, Jim #6700
– Nokony, Denis #6716
– Pellan, Alfred #6808 6815 6824 6825
– Pichet, Roland #6868
– Québec, surréalisme #1464
– Shadbolt, Jack Leonard #7183
– Wallace, Ian #7509
poésie canadienne
– après guerre de 1812 #327
poésie inuit #4317
poésie visuelle
– Copithorne, Judith #5176
– Frenkel, Vera #5521
– Palchinski, Sylvia Scott #6753
Poggi, Vincent, artiste can (vitrail), actif 1958
– vitraux, église Saint Alphonse (Montréal, Qué) #2448
poignées de sacs . Inuit
– Washington (DC), Smithsonian Institution #4319
poil d'orignal
– broderie
– Athapascans #4152
– Hurons et Algonquiens #3513
– Iroquois #3559
– Pentaguets #3537
– sur écorce de bouleau, Amérindiens #3629
poil de bison
– sacs, Amérindiens #3398
poinçons
– orfèvrerie de traite amérindienne #2629
poinçons . Canada
– orfèvrerie #2627
– provinces de l'Atlantique #2640
– sur pièces d'orfèvrerie en argent #2633 2635
– Québec #2664
– sur pièces d'orfèvrerie en or et en argent, Nouvelle-Ecosse #2632
Point, père, prêtre can, 1799-1868
– et Pieds-Noirs #3721
Point Spencer (Alaska)
– artefacts préhistoriques #4374
Pointe au Baril (Ont)
– vues, Barker Fairley #5402
Pointe-aux-Trembles (Qué), église de l'Enfant-Jésus
– intérieur, Antoine Cirier #269 270
Pointe-aux-Trembles (Qué), sanctuaire de-la-Réparation
– architecture, André Blouin #8840
Pointe-Claire (Qué), Centre culturel de Pointe-Claire. Galerie d'art Stewart Hall
– expositions
– Manitoba Mainstream: People's Art/Fine Art/Le Grand Courant du Manitoba: arts populaires, beaux-arts (1973) #1897
– Mountain: A Lithograph by James B.

Spencer/Montagne: une lithographie de James B. Spencer (1974) #7270
– *Watercolour Painters from Saskatchewan/Aquarellistes de la Saskatchewan* (1972) #1920
Pointe-des-Monts (Qué), phare
– architecture #9526
Pointe-du-Lac (Qué), moulin "Garceau" #9246
Pointe-Saint-Charles (Qué), église paroissiale Saint-Jean
– sculptures, Charles Daudelin #5258
pointes de projectiles . Indiens de la côte nord-ouest
– flèches et pointes de lance #3785
Pointon, Philip, céramiste can, actif 1874 #2301
– pièce-souvenir, cruche, atelier de poterie de Cap-Rouge (Québec, Qué) #2332
Poirier, Anne, sculpteure fr, 1942-
– expositions de groupe
– (1980) #8237
Poirier, Conrad, photographe can, 1913-1968 #6897
Poirier, Narcisse, artiste can, 1883-
– et Montée Saint-Michel #1236
Poirier, Patrick, sculpteur fr, 1941-
– expositions de groupe
– (1980) #8237
poisson
– dans l'art, Tommy Brayshaw #4907
Poisson, Renée, céramiste et sculpteure can, 1944-
– entretien #6898
Poitras, Jacques, sculpteur can, actif 1842 #1301
Poldaas, Jaan, artiste can, 1948-
– xérographie en couleurs #614
police à cheval du Nord-Ouest
– architecture, Fort Battleford (Battleford, Sask) #8484
– et Henri Julien #5990 5992
– et Richard Barrington Nevitt #6687 6688
– et T.George Anderton #4525
– quartiers généraux, Petit Fort Garry (Man) #8475
politique, architecture et
– et conservation #7767
politique, art et
– Bengough, John Wilson #4676 4677
– Borduas, Paul-Emile #1466
– Canada #910 3290
– (1980), et musées #683
– (années 1960) #87 447 529 3263
(années 1970) #602 619 693
– et galeries parallèles #641
– et mode (1882-1910) #2897
– Clark, Kelly #5109
– Frenkel, Vera #5522
– Girouard, Jean-Joseph #5609
– Légaré, Joseph #6215
– Montpetit, Guy #6600
– Montréal (Qué)
– (1968-1969) #1514
– (années 1970) #1489 1548
– exposition *Corridart* (1976) #1530
– Stade olympique #9139
– Québec
– (1640-1840) #1329
– (1760-1790) #1369
– (1961-1975) #3280
– (années 1970) #1528
– et art vidéo #1499 1537 1550
– Russell, Edward John #7110

– W.O.R.K.S. #1955
– Walker, Robert #7505
– Wieland, Joyce #7579 7580
politique et dessins humoristiques
– *voir aussi* caricature
politique et dessins humoristiques . Canada #943
– (1759-1914), Québec, thème de la rébellion #1351
– (1867-1967) #945
– (1874-1946), Canada, dissensions Est-Ouest #958
– (années 1770-1970) #956
– Bengough, John Wilson #942
– Julien, Henri #5986
– Macpherson, Duncan Ian #6400 6401
– Norris, Len #6722
– premiers ministres #944
– Racey, Arthur George #6952
– XIXe-XXe s. #957
Polken, Jeffrey Ervin, artiste can, 1934-
– expositions de groupe
– (1966) #1123
Pollard, Harry, photographe can, 1881-1968 #6899
Pollock, Jackson, artiste amér, 1912-1956
– Borduas, Paul-Emile, commentaire #4838
– Borduas, Paul-Emile, comparaison #4847
– influence sur Guido Molinari #6585 6588 6591
– influence sur Jean-Paul Riopelle #7027
– influence sur Paul-Emile Borduas #4846
– Ronald, William S., comparaison #7076
Pologne
– art #603
Polonais au Canada
– art #149 642
Polonceau, Henri, orfèvre can, 1766-1828
– oeuvres, Detroit Institute of Arts (Detroit, Mich) #2681
– paix #2666
Pommier, Hugues, prêtre fr, artiste au Canada, ca 1637-1686 #228 229 1323 1363
– portraits de membres du clergé #1333
Pond, Irving K., architecte amér, 1857-1939
– Saint-Jean (NB), General Public Hospital #9020
Pond, Martin & Lloyd, agence amér d'architecture
– Saint-Jean (NB), General Public Hospital #9020
Ponoka (Alta)
– art (années 1940) #1943
Pontbriand, Henri Marie Dubreuil de, évêque can, 1708-1760
– don d'objets d'art à l'église Notre-Dame. Musée (Montréal, Qué) #3081
Ponte, Vincent, urbaniste can, 1919-
– influence sur architecture montréalaise (années 1960) #7901
ponts . Canada
– bois
– Colombie-Britannique #8153
– Ontario, XIXe s. #7745
– Montréal (Qué), pont Jacques-Cartier #7933
– ponts de chemin de fer (1880-1914) #7736
– Québec, XVIIe-XVIIIe s. #1320
– XIXe s. #9512
ponts . Hurons #3519
ponts . Iroquois #3519
Poole, Ernest Edward, collectionneur can, 1884-1964
– collection, art canadien #3217 3222 3235

Poole, Leslie Donald, artiste can, 1942- #2053 6900 6901
– *Confessions* #6902
– expositions
– (1979) #6903
Pootoogook, Kananginak, artiste can, 1935- #4460 6904
pop'art
– Canada #71 87 476
– et Greg Curnoe #5231 5233
– et Guido Molinari #6591
– et Michael Snow #7245
– et Pierre Ayot #4573
– et Robert Percival #6835
– Québec #1497
Pope, William, artiste can, 1811-1902 #6905 6906
porcelaine
– *voir* poterie
porcelaine Bristol
– importation des Etats-Unis au Canada, début XXe s. #2346
porcelaine d'importation chinoise
– (1610-1790), collection Susannah Anne Weldon, King's College (Windsor, NE) #2363
porcelaine Minton
– carreaux de céramique, dans habitations de Toronto (Ont), XIXe s. #2373
– peinture sur porcelaine, John Howard Griffiths #2305
Porcepic, périodique can #538
Port Alberni (CB), Alberni Valley Museum
– art, Nootkas #4020
Port Arthur (Ont), Thunder Bay Historical Society
– expositions
– *The Far West* (1943) #12
Port-au-Choix (TN)
– artefacts dorsétiens #4354
– lieux de sépulture, Béothuks #3611
Port-au-Persil (Qué)
– vues, Jean-Paul Lemieux #6230
Port-Cartier (Qué)
– architecture, Rother/Bland/Trudeau #8184
Port Credit (Ont), J.P. Bickell House
– architecture, Murray Brown #8338
Port Hope (Ont), Batterwood House
– résidence, Vincent Massey #3220
Port Hope (Ont), ferme de Carr
– architecture #7959
Port Hope (Ont), Trinity College School. Art Gallery
– expositions
– *David Blackwood: Paintings, Drawings, Prints* (1967) #4739
Port-Meunier (Qué)
– architecture #7869
Port-Nouveau-Québec (Qué)
– arts graphiques (1972-1975) #4475
Porteous, Charles, homme d'affaires et collectionneur can, né 1848
– mécène de William Brymner #4951
Porter, Brian, artiste can, 1948- #6907
– estampes #1214
Porter, Edward Clark, artiste can, 1935-
– estampes #1214
Porter, Katherine, artiste amér, 1941-
– dessins #532
Porter, Timothy Nichol (Tim), photographe can, 1946- #2071
– catalogue de photographies #998
portes
– dans l'art

– Laporte, Lucie, et Joseph Marcil #1663
portes . Canada
– Halifax (NE), citadelle de Halifax #8441
– Ontario (avant 1840) #7963
– Québec, XVIIe-XVIIIe s. #2530 2531
portes . villes canadiennes
– Québec (Qué) #8444
Portland (Oreg), Portland Art Museum
– art, Indiens de la côte nord-ouest,
   collection Rasmussen #3875 3937
– expositions
   – *Prehistoric Stone Sculpture of the Pacific
      Northwest* (1952) #3887
   – *The Far North: 2000 Years of American
      Eskimo and Indian Art* (1973) #3366
Portneuf (Qué), église de Rivière-à-Pierre
– intérieur, Gérard Morisset #8891
Portneuf (Qué), église Saint-Gilbert
– intérieur, Gérard Morisset #8891
portrait
– *voir aussi* autoportraits; photographie .
   portrait; silhouettes
portrait américain
– Eaton, Wyatt #5357
– Field, Robert #5432
– XVIIIe-début XIXe s., influence sur
   portrait, Canada #1197
portrait canadien #715
– (1780-1870) #263
– (1860-1900), et photographie #268
– (1900-1940) #28
– (années 1890), recommandations #183
– (années 1910) #205
– (années 1970), commentaires d'artistes
   #624
– Beaucourt, François Malepart de #4646
– Berczy, William Bent #241 242
– Berczy, William von Moll #4701
   – *Woolsey Family* #4700
– Berthon, George Theodore, juges #4713
– Boisseau, Alfred #4769
– Borduas, Paul-Emile #4836
– Bourassa, Napoléon #4872
– Crist, Lela Gurnee #5209
– Field, Robert #5432
– Forbes, John Colin #5459
– Forster, John Wycliffe Lowes #5468 5469
   5470
– Foulis, Robert #258 259
– Girouard, Jean-Joseph, patriotes, Rébellion
   de 1837-1838 #5609
– Halifax (NE), (années 1740-1940) #1195
– Hamel, Théophile #258 259 1348 5690
– Harris, Lawren Stewart #5733
– Harris, Robert #5743
   – *The Fathers of Confederation* #5736 5738
      5740
– Holman, James Henry #5821
– Kane, Paul #6010
– Krieghoff, Cornelius #241 242 6097
– Lyall, Laura Adeline Muntz, enfants #6339
– Macdonald, Evan Weekes #6356
– MacDonald, Thomas Reid #6380
– Montréal (Qué), miniatures et silhouettes
   (1760-1860) #1376 1377
– Newton, Lilias Torrance #6692 6693
– Ontario
   – XIXe s. #267
   – XIXe-XXe s., enfants #1687
– Plamondon, Antoine-Sébastien #1348 6884
   – portraits de religieuses #6887
– Québec #959 1265
   – XIXe s. #1336
   – XVIIe s. #228 229

– XVIIe-XVIIIe s., portraits de membres
   du clergé #1333
– XVIIIe-XIXe s. #219
– scènes de guerre, Galerie nationale du
   Canada (Ottawa, Ont) #1101
– *Souvenirs canadiens* #1326
– Toronto (Ont)
   – City of Toronto Archives #3178
   – Metro Toronto Public Library. John Ross
      Robertson Historical Collection #3130
      3131
– Town, Harold Barling #7416
– Varley, Frederick Horsman #7466 7467
– Wright, Edith P. Stevenson #7279
– XIXe s. #66 178 1323
– XIXe s.-années 1920 #8
– XVIIe-XIXe s. #173
– XVIIIe-début XIXe s. #1197
– XVIIIe-XIXe s. #246
   – estampes #839
portraits
– Forster, John Wycliffe Lowes,
   commentaire #5467
– Ottawa (Ont), Archives publiques du
   Canada #3023
ports . Canada
– édifices portuaires, Halifax (NE), XIXe s.
   #7822 7824 7825 7834
– Montréal (Qué) #7917
Post, Jordan, orfèvre can, actif 1787-années
   1840 #2618
post-impressionnisme
– et J.E.H. MacDonald #6366
– et James Wilson Morrice #6622
– et le Groupe des Sept #1741
post-modernisme
– architecture canadienne #7732
– art et architecture, Canada #8237
Poste-de-la-Baleine (Qué)
– arts graphiques (1972-1975) #4475
postes d'essence . Canada
– (1919) #9235
postes de police . Canada
– Toronto (Ont), (années 1930) #8970
postes de traite . Canada
– Alberta, XVIIIe-XIXe s. #8129
– Fort Langley (CB) #8477
– Petit Fort Garry (Man) #8483
Potéouatamis
– art #3540
   – (1600-1760) #3579
poterie
– *voir aussi* carreaux de céramique; peinture
   sur porcelaine; pichets; porcelaine
   d'importation chinoise; poterie de grès;
   sculpture en céramique; soupières
– Louisbourg (NE) #2368 2369
poterie, techniques
– *voir* matériaux et techniques . poterie
poterie . Algonquiens #3463 3502 3529 3530
   3545
poterie . Amérindiens #3329
poterie . Athapascans
– (années 1970), artisanes #3367
poterie . Etats-Unis
– (1750-1910), faïence, Pennsylvanie et
   Ontario, comparaison #3962
– début XXe s., poterie destinée au marché
   canadien #2346
– XIXe s., influence sur poterie canadienne
   #2281 2309
poterie . Goyoguins #3525
poterie . Hurons #3502 3520
poterie . Indiens de la côte nord-ouest #3866

– Carr, Emily, collection #3827
– XIIIe s. #3955
poterie . Indiens des forêts du Nord-Est
   #3491 3545
– site archéologique de Draper (Ont) #3640
poterie . Inuit
– (années 1970), artisanes #3367
– Rankin Inlet (TNO)
   – Eskimo Arts and Crafts Centre (années
      1970) #4226
   – Programme de développement des
      métiers d'art (1966) #4207
poterie . Iroquois #3502 3520 3525 3545 3555
   3564 3566
poterie . Pieds-Noirs #3678
– XVIIIe-XIXe s. #3679
poterie . Salishiens #3841
poterie . Sarcis #3659
poterie . Saulteux/Ojibwa #3539
poterie . Siouens #3687
poterie (de) Staffordshire
– pour le marché canadien
   – (années 1830-début XXe s.) #2357 2358
   – (années 1850-années 1890) #2361
   – XIXe s. #2362
– vues du Canada, XIXe s. #2099 2282
poterie anglaise
– *voir aussi* porcelaine Minton; poterie
   Rockingham; poterie Staffordshire
– Compagnie de la Baie d'Hudson #2351
– Glasgow (Ecosse), Britannia Pottery #2326
– John Marshall & Co., scènes sportives
   #2360
– poterie de Portneuf #2285 2306
– pour le marché canadien #2297
   – (1880-1914) #2340
   – (années 1750-début XIXe s.) #2316
   – (années 1830-début XXe s.) #2357 2358
   – (années 1850-1890) #2361
   – XIXe s. #2288 2294 2315 2320 2354
   – XVIIIe-XIXe s. #2363
– XIXe s., influence sur poterie canadienne
   #2281 2339
– XIXe s., vues du Canada, service à dessert
   Minton #2289
poterie canadienne #2107
– (1837-1887) #253
– (1880-1914) #2340
– (1910-1961), Canadian National Exhibition
   (Toronto, Ont) #1
– (1955-1971) #2379
– (1964-1967) #2108 2109
– (1979-1980) #2138
– (1980) #2394 2395
– (années 1940) #2601
– (années 1950) #2380
– (années 1960) #2106 2382
– (années 1970) #2387 2388
– Ahrens Pottery (Paris, Ont) #2328
– Alberta
   – (1900-années 1970) #2337 2386
   – (1912-1981) #2371
   – (1980) #2393
   – (années 1970) #1951
– Archambault, Louis #4539
– Ariss, Margot Phillips #4546
– atelier de poterie Dion (Ancienne-Lorette,
   Qué) #2345
– Beaudin, Gaétan #2381
– Belleau, Charles #2366
– Benjamin Lent Pottery (comté de Lincoln,
   Ont) #2367
– Bourbeau, Géraldine #4877
– Brantford Pottery (Brantford, Ont) #2295

2335
– Brothers Glass (London, Ont) #2350
– Cartier, Jean Bernard #5051 5052
– Colombie-Britannique (années 1970) #2391
– comté de Lincoln (Ont), XIXe s. #2290
– Cournoyer, Georget #5192
– Deichmann, Erica et Kjeld #1170 2377
– Deichmann, Kjeld #2376
– Desrochers-Drolet, Françoise #5289
– Doucet, Louise #5303
– Ecanada Art Pottery (Hamilton, Ont)
  #2359
– Egmondville Pottery (comté de Huron,
  Ont) #2323 2329
– enseignement (années 1940) #2375
– et architecture (années 1960) #8236
– Gagné-Dufresne, Hélène #5531
– Garnier, Jacques #5557
– guide pour collectionneurs #2101 2104
  2125 2131 2252
– Hamilton Pottery (Hamilton, Ont) #2347
– Handy, Arthur #5701
– Hart Pottery (Picton et Belleville, Ont)
  #2286 2293
– Hilton, Charles #2392
– Humberstone Potteries (au nord de
  Toronto, Ont) #2338
– Ile-du-Prince-Edouard, XIXe s. #2311
– Jacquet, François #269 270
– Landry, Yvan #6160
– Legros, Enid Sharon #6223
– Levine, Marilyn Ann #6274
– Luke, Alexandra #6333
– Manitoba #2272
– Manning, Les #6415
– Medalta Potteries (Medicine Hat, Alta)
  #2325 2372
– Mihalcheon, Jean Lapointe #2392 6529
– motifs amérindiens, Victoria (CB), (années
  1920) #2278
– moules, Ontario, XIXe s. #2334
– New Hamburg Pottery (New Hamburg,
  Ont) #2336 2348
– Ngan, Wayne G. #6695 6696
– Nouveau-Brunswick #2150
  – XIXe s. #2319
– Nouvelle-Ecosse
  – (années 1780-1925) #2307
  – XIXe s. #2308
– Ontario #2249 2317
  – (1750-1910), faïence #3962
  – (1796-années 1930) #2349
  – (années 1970) #2262
  – XIXe-début XXe s. #2355
  – XIXe s. #2284 2303 2356 2374
– Paré, Réjean #1547
– Paris (Ont), XIXe s. #2330
– paysages québécois dits "de Thomas"
  #2287
– peinture sur porcelaine (années 1890)
  #2277
– Poisson, Renée #6898
– Prairies (1880-années 1920) #2431
– provinces de l'Atlantique (années 1970)
  #1132
– Québec #2226 2228 2237 2331
  – (1650-1837) #2313
  – (1655-1916) #2344
  – (années 1840-1900) #2298 2322
  – (années 1940) #2188 2199
  – (années 1950) #2193
  – (années 1970) #2384 2390
  – XIXe s. #1334 1335 2283
  – XVIIe-XIXe s. #2095

– XVIIe-XVIIIe s. #2181
– XVIIIe-XIXe s. #2299 2321
– XXe s. #2198
– Québec (Qué), place Royale #2201 2352
– Québec et Ontario, XIXe s. #2279
– Rakine, Marthe #6956
– Regina (Sask), (années 1970) #2383 2385
– région de Cap-Rouge (Qué) #2296 2301
– Sadowska, Krystyna #7113
– Sadowski, Konrad Jagin #7113 7114
– Saint-Denis (Qué), (1785-1888) #2343
– Saskatchewan #1919
– Savoie, Maurice #7137
– service de table officiel, Canada (1898)
  #2333
– Sherbrooke (Qué), (années 1970) #2232
– Spénard, Jean-Jacques #2179
– St. Johns Stone Chinaware Company
  (Saint-Jean, Qué) #2327
  – buste en porcelaine #2314
– Sures, Jack #7285
– Taylor Pottery (Port Hope, Ont) #2292
– techniques #2280
– thème de la nativité #393
– thème décoratif du castor #56
– Thibault, René #7344
– Thornsbury, James #1926
– Toronto (Ont), Ontario College of Art
  #3009
– tradition germanique #2140 2263
– Tremblay, Alain #2216
– Tremblay, Michèle #2216
– Tremblay, Suzanne #1549
– Vermette, Claude #2378
– Victoria (CB) #2269
– Volpi, Charles de, collection #3248
– vues représentant bateaux, XIXe s. #2341
– W. & D. Bell Pottery (Québec, Qué) #2291
– William Eby Pottery (Conestogo, Ont)
  #2304
– XIXe s. #2099 2288 2297
– XVIIe-début XXe s. #2281
– XVIIe-XIXe s. #2302 2318 2324
– XXe s. #2121 2142
– Young, Helen Granger #7627
poterie canadienne . marques
– Medalta Stoneware et Medalta Potteries
  (Medicine Hat, Alta), (1916-1954) #2372
– Ontario, XIXe-début XXe s. #2355
poterie de grès
– Ottawa (Ont), Parcs Canada, collection
  #2364 2365
poterie de grès . Canada #2302
– Brantford Pottery (Brantford, Ont) #2295
– comté de Lincoln (Ont), XIXe s. #2290
– décorations #2309
– motifs du castor et de la feuille d'érable
  #2312
– Toronto (Ont), XIXe s. #2310
– XVIIe-XIXe s. #2318 2324
poterie de grès . Etats-Unis
– décorations #2309
– motifs du castor et de la feuille d'érable
  #2312
poterie de grès . Grande-Bretagne
– motifs du castor et de la feuille d'érable
  #2312
poterie de Portneuf (Ecosse et
  Grande-Bretagne) #2306
poterie japonaise
– influence sur Louise Doucet #5303
poterie Rockingham . Canada
– W. & D. Bell Pottery (Québec, Qué) #2291
– Welding, W.E., Brantford Pottery

(Brantford, Ont) #2335
– XIXe s. #2302
poterie Rockingham . Etats-Unis
– importation au Canada, début XXe s.
  #2346
poterie Staffordshire
– Canada, XIXe s. #2339
– carreaux, habitations torontoises (Ont),
  XIXe s. #2373
– Saint-Jean (Qué), XIXe s. #2314
potlatch . Bella-Coolas #3874
potlatch . Indiens de la côte nord-ouest
  #3871 3899 3911
– masques #4038
potlatch . Kwakiutls #3956 4052
potlatch . Tlingits #4012
pots à condiments . Canada
– bocaux à marinades, collection Walter Bick
  #2405
Poulin, Julien, artiste can, 1940-
– expositions de groupe
  – (1980) #705
– réflexion sur l'art vidéo #1537
Poulin, Robert, sculpteur can, 1949- #681
  1630
Poulin, Roland, artiste can, 1940- #1512 6908
– expositions de groupe
  – (1977) #782
  – (1978) #786
  – (1980) #706
– réflexion sur son oeuvre #6909
Pouliot, Mario, artiste can, 1949-
– et RACE #1536
poupées
– fin XIXe s.-années 1930 #2932
poupées . Algonquiens
– (années 1760-début XXe s.) #3633
poupées . Amérindiens
– XXe s. #2143
poupées . Canada
– (1886-1930), catalogues du magasin Eaton
  #2851
– guide pour collectionneurs #2938 2941
– mennonites #2264 2942
– Québec (1800-1925) #2937
poupées . Dakotas #3733
poupées . Indiens des forêts du Nord-Est
– (années 1760-début XXe s.) #3633
poupées . Iroquois
– (années 1760-début XXe s.) #3633
Poussin, Nicolas, artiste fr, 1594-1665
– Colville, Alex, comparaison #5147
– Surrey, Philip Henry, comparaison #7289
Povungnituk (Qué)
– art #4274
– arts graphiques #4494
  – (1959-1972) #4478
  – (1959-1976) #4490
  – (1962) #4460
  – (1962-) #4468
  – (1972-1975) #4475
  – (1976) #4489
  – (années 1960) #4496
– arts graphiques et sculpture #4200 4219
– sculpture #4189 4411 4417 4421 4437
  – concours (1967) #4223 4240 4415
Powell, fabricants de verre (Leeds,
  Angleterre)
– oeuvres, édifices du Parlement, Victoria
  (CB) #8967
Powell, John, photographe can, actif années
  1970-
– catalogue de photographies #991
Powers, Joseph William, architecte can,

1852-1925
– Kingston (Ont), pénitencier de Kingston #9058
Prack & Perrine, agence can d'architecture
– Toronto (Ont), William Wrigley Jr. Factory #9234
Prague (Tchécoslovaquie), Národni Galerie
– expositions
– *Grafika Kanadskych Eskymáku* (1972) #4479
Prairies
– architecture #8080 8083 8088 8089
– (années 1970) #8087
– tradition juive #8081
– tradition ukrainienne #8085
– utilisation de pierre à bâtir et de pierre d'ornement (années 1910) #7646 7647
– XXe s. #8084 8086
– architecture domestique #8717
– huttes en tourbe #8701 8706
– tradition ukrainienne #8710
– art
– (années 1920-1960) #461
– (années 1950) #429
– (années 1960) #1848 1851
– (années 1960-1970) #1862
– (années 1970) #1860 1880
– XXe s. #145
– art traditionnel
– (années 1960) #1852
– (années 1970) #1881
– arts décoratifs, tradition germanique #2140
– bouteilles et flacons #2431
– élévateurs à grain #9237
– peinture
– (années 1920-1950) #396
– (années 1970) #588
– photographie (années 1970) #996 1879
– sculpture
– (années 1960) #1853
– (années 1970) #1873 1878
– vues
– Chester, Donovan T. #1858
– Condon, Wanda #5166
– Eyre, Ivan Kenneth #5390
– FitzGerald, Lionel LeMoine #5448
– Herreilers, John #5791
– Hind, William George Richardson #5807
– Hurley, Robert Newton #1918 5885
– Jefferys, Charles William #5953 5958
– Kerr, Illingworth Holey #6050
– Knowles, Dorothy #6066 6067
– Kurelek, William #6109 6114
– Leighton, Alfred Crocker #6225
– Lochhead, Kenneth Campbell #6312 6313
– Lonechild, Michael #6322
– Mulcaster, Wynona Croft #6660
– Nokony, Denis #6716
– Perehudoff, William #6836
– Proch, Don #6940
– Rindisbacher, Peter #7009
– Sheldon-Williams, Inglis #7195 7196
– Sinclair, Robert #7214
– Tanabe, Takao #7321
– Tascona, Tony #7328
– Tinning, George Campbell #7378
– Wyers, Jan #1918
– XIXe-XXe s. #1855 1872 1882 1953 1970
– XXe s. #1885
– vues photographiques
– fin XIXe s. #1949
– Hime, Humphrey Lloyd #5801
Prangnell, Peter, architecte can, 1930-

– commentaire sur l'enseignement de l'architecture, University of Toronto. School of Architecture (Toronto, Ont), (1970) #8313
– programme d'études expérimental, University of Toronto. School of Architecture (Toronto, Ont), (1967-1975) #8286
Pratt, Christopher, artiste can, 1935- #6911 6912 6915
– entretien #6913
– et Mary Pratt #6914
– et réalisme #110
– expositions
– (1970) #6910
– expositions de groupe
– (1966) #1123
– (1974) #573 1129
– (1977) #643
– Forrestall, Tom, comparaison #5466
Pratt, George, sculpteur can, 1939- #6916
Pratt, Mary Frances, artiste can, 1935- #675
– entretien #6917 6918
– et Christopher Pratt #6914
– expositions
– (1981) #6919
– expositions, critiques #579
– expositions de groupe
– (1975) #591
– (1980) #698
Pratt & Ross, agence can d'architecture
– Brandon (Man), Prince Edward Hotel et gare du Canadien National #9266
– Winnipeg (Man)
– Deer Lodge #9260
– Hotel at Silver Springs #9263
précisionnisme
– et Carl Fellman Schaefer #7157
Prendergast, Maurice Brazil, artiste amér, 1859-1924
– influence sur David Brown Milne #6567
– influence sur James Wilson Morrice #6626 6630
– Morrice, James Wilson, comparaison #6631
Prent, Mark, sculpteur can, 1947- #538 6920 6923 6924
– entretien #6921
– expositions
– (1979) #6926
– expositions, critiques #6925
– expositions de groupe
– (1981) #796
– interdictions d'exposer ses oeuvres #6922
préraphaélitisme
– et Carol Fraser #5508
– et William George Richardson Hind #5805
presbytères . Canada
– Batiscan (Qué), vieux Presbytère #8807
– Kahnawake (Qué), presbytère (1720) #8569
– Lockport (Man), Saint Andrew's Parsonage #8716
Prescott, Charles Ramage, Can, 1772-1859
– Cornwallis Valley (NE), Acacia Grove House #8528
Prescott (Ont)
– fortifications #8454
préservation d'oeuvres d'art
– *voir* conservation et restauration
presqu'île de Melville (TNO)
– Iglulik, culture (années 1920) #4326
Presse, La, journal can
– bandes dessinées #954
– photographies #1562
– Désilets, Antoine #5287 5288

presse-papiers . Canada
– verre (1880-1925) #2438
Preston, John F., photographe can, 1954-
– expositions, critiques #1018
Preston (Ont)
– vues photographiques
– Esson, James #5373
Prévost, Antoine, artiste can, 1930- #6927
Prévost, Robert, artiste can, 1928-
– décors #472
Price, Addison Winchell, artiste can, 1907- #6935
Price, Arthur Donald (Art), artiste can, 1918- #6928 6929 6930
– et architecture #8231
Price, Bruce, architecte amér, 1845-1903
– hôtels appartenant aux sociétés ferroviaires #9290
– Montréal (Qué), gare Windsor #9537
– Québec (Qué), Château Frontenac #9278 9291
Price, Daniel (Danny), artiste can, 1947- #6931
Price, Henry Edward, photographe can, 1918-
– photographies de la Seconde Guerre mondiale #1107
Price, Norman Molls, artiste can, 1871-1951
– illustrations #916
Price, Ralph, collectionneur can, 1939-, et Patricia, collectionneuse can, XXe s.
– collection, art traditionnel canadien #971 972
– entretien, sur collection d'art traditionnel canadien #970
Price, Tom, artiste can, 1860-1927 #4169 6932
– dessins #6933
– expositions
– (1981) #6934
prieurés
– *voir* monastères
Prince, Richard, artiste can, 1949- #6936 6937 6938
– constructions en matériaux bruts (années 1970) #2065
– expositions
– (1979) #6939
– expositions de groupe
– (1976) #2060
– (1978) #2066
– (1981) #796
– utlisation de l'espace #2062
Prince Albert (Sask), Grace Campbell Gallery
– expositions
– *Images of the Inuit from the Simon Fraser Collection* (1981) #4495
Prince Edward Island Heritage Foundation
– travaux de restauration (années 1970) #7795
Prince Edward Island Pottery, fabricants de céramique (Charlottetown, IPE) #2302
Prince Rupert (CB)
– pétroglyphes . Indiens de la côte nord-ouest #3846
– totems . Kwakiutls #3957
Princeton (NJ), Princeton University
– céramiques, collection Trumbull-Prime #2363
Princeton (NJ), Princeton University. Art Museum
– expositions
– *Art of the Northwest Coast* (1969) #3959
Prindle, Harry Edward, architecte can, né

1873
– Québec (Qué), gare Union #9533
Prisme d'yeux #1472
– et Alfred Pellan #6808 6809
– et surréalisme #1458
– manifeste #6810
prisonniers
– portraits de prisonniers politiques,
  Jean-Joseph Girouard #5609
prisons canadiennes
– Halifax (NE), XVIIIe-XIXe s. #7818
– Kingston (Ont), pénitencier de Kingston
  #9058
– Montréal (Qué) #8336
  – prison du Pied-du-Courant #9056
– Ontario, bâtiments polygonaux, XIXe s.
  #7987
– Québec (Qué), prison des plaines
  d'Abraham #9057
Priteca, Benjamin Marcus, architecte amér,
  1889-1971
– Vancouver (CB), Orpheum Theatre #9135
  9141
prix et récompenses
– Canadian Design Index-NIDC #2605 3033
– Conseil national de l'esthétique
  industrielle #2608 2610
– Design Awards #2609
– prix Jessie Dow, Art Association of
  Montreal (1908-1965) #1261
– Red River Exhibition (1964-1978) #1903
prix et récompenses, architecture
– Canadian Architect #7672
  – (1968) #8190
  – (1969) #8191
  – (1970) #8192
  – (1971) #8193
  – (1973) #8195
  – (1974) #8196
  – (1975) #8197
  – (1976) #8198
  – (1977) #8199
  – (1978) #8200
  – (1979) #8201 8202
  – (1980) #8203
  – (1981) #8204
– Concours pour ouvrages en béton (1971)
  #7706
– Conseil canadien de l'habitation
  – (1957-) #8741
  – (1972) #8744
  – (1974) #8746
  – (1979) #8747
– Dominion Housing Act Small House
  Competition (1936) #8736
– Eaton, T., Company Architectural
  Competition for House Designs (1936)
  #8738
– Institut royal d'architecture du Canada
  – (1931) #7660
  – (1937) #7664
  – (1940) #7665
– International Calvert House Competition
  (1954) #8510
– médailles Massey en architecture
  – (1952) #8205
  – (1955) #8206
  – (1958) #8207
  – (1961) #8208 8209 8210
  – (1962), sondage auprès des architectes
    #8305
  – (1964) #8211
  – (1967) #8212 8213 8214
  – (1970) #8215 8216

– Ontario Government Housing
  Competition (1936) #8737
– Ontario Housing Corporation Design
  Competition (1972) #8663
– Ordre des architectes du Québec (1978)
  #7886
– Prix nationaux aux constructeurs de
  maisons unifamiliales (1960) #8742
– Prix nationaux de modèles d'habitations
  (1969) #8743
– prix Vincent Massey pour l'aménagement
  urbain
  – (1971) #8217
  – (1975) #8218
– Royal Institute of British Architects Royal
  Gold Medal
  – Darling, Frank (1915) #8349 8350
  – Morris, Robert Schofield (1958) #8389
– Société centrale d'hypothèques et de
  logement (1960) #8040
Prix nationaux aux constructeurs de
  maisons unifamiliales
– (1960) #8742
Prix nationaux de modèles d'habitations
– (1969) #8743
prix Vincent Massey pour l'aménagement
  urbain
– (1971) #8217
– (1975) #8218
Proch, Donald (Don), artiste can, 1944-
  #6940 6942
– expositions de groupe
  – (1977) #1901
  – (1978) #2066
– Field #714
– masques #6941
Proctor, Alexander Phimister, artiste can,
  1862-1950 #6943
– autobiographie #6944
– expositions, critiques #204
– membre du Canadian Art Club #193
Producteurs de l'Artique canadien
– (1977-1980) #4269
– et art inuit #4222 4231 4291
Professional Native Indian Artists
  Association
– et Daphne Odjig #6731
Professional Photographer, périodique amér
– et Canadian Photographic Journal #976
Proof Only, périodique can #1799
– (années 1970) #1804
protection des arts
– voir aussi collectionneurs et collections
– Canada #369
  – (années 1950) #3253 3260
  – (années 1960) #3263
  – (années 1970) #693 3157 3275 3278 3286
    3291 3293
– Fondation canadienne #3262
– Toronto (Ont), (années 1890) #1699
Protestantisme
– et églises québécoises #8887
Proulx, J.-Octave, artiste amér résidant au
  Canada, né 1890
– et Montée Saint-Michel #1236
Provence (France)
– vues
  – Reid, Leslie Mary Margaret #6981
Providence (RI), Brown University.
  Haffenreffer Museum of Anthropology
– art, Indiens des plaines #3751
Providence (RI), Haffenreffer Museum of
  Anthropology
– voir Providence (RI), Brown University.

  Haffenreffer Museum of Anthropology
provinces de l'Atlantique
– art #128 1123
  – (années 1960) #1124
  – (années 1970) #1127 1131 1132 1133 1135
– orfèvrerie #2640
– peinture
  – (années 1970) #588
provinces maritimes
– architecture #7779
  – (années 1950) #7673
  – utilisation de pierre à bâtir et de pierre
    d'ornement (années 1910) #7646 7647
– architecture domestique
  – (avant 1900) #8551
  – résidences estivales et bâtiments de
    villégiature, XXe s. #8524
  – XIXe s. #8528
– art
  – (1959-1965) #1120
  – (années 1830-1930) #28
  – (années 1930-1960) #1125
  – (années 1950) #389 429 1172
  – (années 1960) #1122 1126
  – (années 1970) #543
  – Acadie #1137 1181
  – XVIIe s.-années 1890 #185
– art et architecture #1119
  – XVIIIe-XIXe s. #7780
– arts décoratifs
  – tradition germanique #2140
  – XIXe s. #2147
  – XVIIIe-XIXe s. #2093
– costume acadien #2836 2840 2876 2877
  2894
– ex-libris, XVIIIe-XIXe s. #915
– mobilier
  – Acadie, XVIIIe-XIXe s. #2516
  – XVIIIe-XIXe s. #2474 2475
– orfèvrerie
  – XVIIe-XIXe s. #2627
  – XVIIIe-XIXe s. #2636 2646
– peinture
  – (1933-1970) #498
  – (années 1860-1880) #230
  – XIXe s. #197
  – XXe s. #1121
– photographie (années 1970) #1134
– portrait photographique, XIXe s. #1171
– portraits, XVIIIe-XIXe s. #263
– poterie, XIXe s. #2302 2318 2319
– textiles et tissus, XVIIIe s. #2727
– vues
  – (années 1890) #6436
  – Day, Mabel Killam #5273
  – Forrestall, Tom #5463
  – McLaughlin, Agnes #6500
– vues photographiques
  – Jaycocks, T.G. #5950
Provincetown (Mass), Rhode Island School
  of Design
– Stacey, Harold, élève #7274
Prud'homme, Luc, photographe can, actif
  1981
– catalogue de photographies #1023
Prus, Victor, architecte can, 1917-
– Montréal (Qué)
  – Autostade #9101
  – stations de métro Crémazie et
    Mont-Royal #9549
– Québec (Qué), Grand Théâtre de Québec
  #9112
publicité
– voir aussi affiches

– Arthur, Paul, commentaire #859
– Elbaz, André, commentaire #5365
– et architecture
   – (années 1950) #8302
   – (années 1960) #8267
– utilisation de la photographie #1024
publicité canadienne
– (1890-1940) #846
– (1965-1968) #874
– (1981) #941
– (années 1940) #850 851 853 2603
– (années 1950) #855 858 860 861 865
– (années 1960) #867 868 870
– (années 1970) #886 888 894 907
– affiches #903 910
– Art Directors' Club of Toronto #854
– Art Directors' Club of Winnipeg
   (1964-1970) #872
– Burns, Cooper, Donoahue, Fleming &
   Company Ltd. #904
– Burns, Cooper, Hynes Ltd. #905 906
– Burns & Cooper Ltd. #892 896
– Burton Kramer Associates #889
– Bush, Jack Hamilton #4963
– Cooper and Beatty Ltd. #5297
– Design Collaborative Montreal Ltd. #878
   882 885
– Gerald Bern Agency #871
– Gottschalk & Ash #879 887
– Jacques Guillon Designers Inc. #2623
– journaux, St. John's (TN), (1806-1900)
   #1158
– journaux et revues, fin XIXe-début 20e s.
   #891
– Paul Arthur and Associates #873
– photographies, promotion de la
   Colombie-Britannique (1890-1914) #2030
pubs
– *voir* tavernes
Pudlat, Pudlo, artiste can, 1916- #4460
Puffin Island (TN), phare #9523
puits . Canada
– (1608-1867) #2120
Pulford, Edward Berwyn, artiste can, 1914-
   #6945
Pullman (Wash), Washington State
   Historical Society Museum
– vannerie, Indiens de la côte nord-ouest
   #4004
Punch, périodique brit
– dessins humoristiques, Arthur George
   Racey #6952
Punuk
– artefacts #4327
Purdy, Henry Carl, sculpteur can, 1937-
– expositions
   – (1978) #6946
Puvis de Chavannes, Pierre, artiste fr,
   1824-1898
– influence sur Ozias Leduc #6206
– influence sur Paul-Emile Borduas #4841
Pyle, James W., photographe can, 1915-
– expositions de groupe
   – (1972) #1952

Q

Qikertaaluk Island (TNO)
– pétroglyphes dorsétiens #4362
Qinnuayuak, Lucy, artiste can, 1915-1982
   #4260 4460

Qu'Appelle Valley (Sask)
– vues, James Henderson #5778 5779
Québec
– affiches (années 1940) #851
– architecture #7848 7850 7851 7855 7868
   7936
   – (1608-1930) #7659
   – (1880-1914) #7929
   – (1980) #7893
   – (années 1920) #7657
   – (années 1940) #7846
   – (années 1950) #7857
   – (années 1960) #8307
   – archives #7863
   – Baillairgé, François #4586
   – beaux-arts #7923
   – bois, XVIIe-XVIIIe s. #7717
   – emploi de modèles architecturaux,
     XVIIe-XIXe s. #7872
   – influence de Jérôme Demers #7874
   – influence de l'Ecole des beaux-arts
     #8265
   – Parizeau, Marcel #8397
   – utilisation de pierre à bâtir et de pierre
     d'ornement (années 1910) #7646 7647
   – XVII-XIXe s. #7866
   – XVIIe-années 1940 #7853
   – XVIIe s.-années 1970 #7711
   – XVIIe-XIXe s. #7687 7841 7842 7852 7858
     7859
   – XVIIe-XVIIIe s. #7844 7845
   – XVIIIe s. #7861 7865
   – XVIIIe-XIXe s. #8622
   – XXe s. #7731
– architecture domestique #8568 8591 8592
   8599 8600
   – (1763-1860), récits de voyageurs #8527
   – (années 1920) #8497
   – et Héritage canadien du Québec #7871
   – habitations rurales
     – (1600-1800) #8614
     – XVIIe-XIXe s. #8624
     – XVIIe-XVIIIe s. #8581
   – intérieurs domestiques d'artisans
     (1810-1819) #8616
   – maisons de campagne #8572
   – seigneuries #8611
   – utilisation de la pierre, XVIIe-XIXe s.
     #7891
   – XVIIe-XIXe s. #8505 8559 8579 8593 8596
     8609 8623
   – XVIIe-XVIIIe s. #8586 8602 8603 8605
     8606 8621
   – XVIIIe-XIXe s. #8560 8561 8582
– architecture et arts décoratifs, XVIIe-XVIIIe
   s. #2181 2217
– architecture et expansion urbaine #7867
– architecture et lieux historiques #7887
– architecture et sculpture, XVII-XIX s. #7849
– art #1238 1271 1294 3085 3109
   – (1613-1870) #1330 1331
   – (1759-1914), thème de la rébellion #1351
   – (1820-1940) #28
   – (1825-1850) #1368
   – (1875-1915) #1364
   – (1880-1914) #1371
   – (1880-années 1930) #45
   – (1900-années 1920) #1231
   – (1940-1960) #1462
   – (1955-1971) #1453
   – (1962-1972) #1500 1502
   – (1963-1980) #1564
   – (1966-1976) #1527
   – (1970-1975) #1515

   – (1975) #1518
   – (années 1910) #1317
   – (années 1920) #302
   – (années 1920-1960) #461
   – (années 1930-1970) #1299
   – (années 1940) #350 381 1383 1386 1387
   – (années 1940-1960) #1438
   – (années 1940-1970) #1269 1473 1521
   – (années 1950) #425 1402
   – (années 1950-1980) #55
   – (années 1960) #492 1442 1487
   – (années 1960-1970) #1257 1496
   – (années 1970) #134 543 593 1486 1488
     1491 1493 1506 1508 1511 1517 1525
     1526 1528 1545
     – artistes de moins de 35 ans #1501
   – XIX s.-années 1940 #1242
   – XVIIe s.-1867 #2110
   – XVIIe s.-1967 #1260
   – XVIIe s.-années 1890 #185
   – XVIIe s.-années 1920 #1229
   – XVIIe s.-années 1920, influence française
     #1244
   – XVIIe s.-années 1930 #2169 2171
   – XVIIe-XIXe s. #136 137 1245 1332 1347
     1581 2128 8224
   – XVIIe-XVIIIe s. #2187
   – XXe s. #145
– art décoratif et design (années 1970) #2205
– art et architecture #67 68 1234 1237 1249
   1258 1259 1265 1327
   – (1640-1840) #1329
   – (1760-1790) #1369
   – (1925-1950) #1405
   – (années 1870) #1307
   – (années 1970-1980) #1561
   – XVIIe s. #228 229
   – XVIIe s.-années 1930 #1235
   – XVIIe-XIXe s. #1305 1324 1334 1335 1341
   – XVIIe-XVIIIe s. #1320
   – XVIIIe-début XXe s. #1339
   – XVIIIe s. #234 235 249 250 269 270
   – XVIIIe s.-années 1820 #1300
   – XVIIIe-XIXe s. #1338
– art et littérature, XXe s. #1391
– art traditionnel #1268 1285 1291 1297 2183
   – (années 1920-1940) #2189
   – (années 1940) #1243
   – (années 1960) #1428 1429
   – XIXe s. #1362
   – XVIIe-XIXe s. #1284
– artisans
   – (1660-1815), apprentis #2231
   – fin XIXe-début XXe s. #2235
   – XVIIe-XVIIIe s. #2214
   – XVIIe-XIXe s. #2206
– arts décoratifs #1274 2197 2202 2208 2219
   2222 2223 2226 2228 2229 2237
   – (1613-1870) #2191
   – (1979-1980) #2138
   – (années 1870-1930) #2977
   – (années 1930) #2163 2164 2166 2167 2172
     2173 2174 2176 2969
   – (années 1930-1940) #2185
   – (années 1940) #357 2188 2190 2199
   – (années 1950) #2193
   – (années 1960) #2102 2195
   – (années 1970) #2215 2216 2224 2225 2230
   – XIXe s. #2099
   – XVIIe-XIXe s. #2093 2111 2221
   – XVIIe-XVIIIe s. #2097 2200
   – XVIIIe s.-années 1930 #2177
   – XXe s. #2179 2198
– arts décoratifs et design (années 1970)

#2211
- arts graphiques
  - (années 1960) #1643
  - (années 1970) #893 1533 1644 1651 1656
  - automatisme et surréalisme #1650
  - XVIIe-XVIIIe s. #1649
- bandes dessinées #948 952 953 954
  - (années 1970) #950 951
- banques (années 1910) #9166
- bâtiments agricoles (années 1910) #8554
- berceuses, XVIIIe-XIXe s. #2536
- bijoux (années 1970) #2701
- broderie, ursulines #2778 2779 2781 2783 2788 2789
- calvaires et croix #1609
- chapeaux
  - (avant 1736) #2831
  - XVIIe-XIXe s. #2815
- chaussures #2880
- cinémas #9078
- conservation de l'architecture #8595
- construction, XVIIe-XIXe s. #7864
- costume
  - (1605-1963), costume masculin #2838
  - (1840-1900) #2899
  - (années 1850) #2834
  - dans chansons folkloriques canadiennes #2898
  - XIXe s. #2828 2829 2896
  - XVIIe-XIXe s. #2822 2825 2832
  - XVIIe-XVIIIe s. #2850
  - XVIIIe s. #2820
  - XVIIIe-XIXe s., voyageurs et coureurs de bois #2826
- courtepointes (années 1920) #2794
- couvre-lits, XVIIe-XIXe s. #2746
- croix #1569 1609 1619 1621 1625 1637 1640
- croix funéraires en fer #2716
- crucifix #1585 1638
- daguerréotypes (1839-1855) #1374
- danse et costume #2879
- dessin, XXe s. #1520 1523
- dorure #2930
- écoles #9420 9424
  - (1919-1923) #9416
  - (années 1950) #9391 9392 9418
- églises #8806 8816 8819
  - (1600-1850) #8870
  - (1608-années 1760) #8825 8837
  - (1615-1665) #8822 8823
  - (1647-1800) #8792 8793
  - (1900-1934) #8334
  - (1930-1952) #8831
  - (années 1820-1880) #7856
  - (années 1940) #8820
  - (années 1940-1950) #8838
  - (années 1950-1960) #8845
  - (années 1960) #8840 8841 8846
  - Baillairgé, Thomas #8327 8328
  - Conefroy, Pierre #8834
  - Ouellet, Joseph-Pierre #8394
  - protestantes #8887 8888
  - revêtement en bardeaux et blanchissement à la chaux, XVIIe s. #8817
  - XIXe s. #258 259
  - XVIIe-XIXe s. #1588
  - XVIIe-XVIIIe s. #8790 8827 8869
    - revêtement en bardeaux et blanchissement à la chaux #8829
  - XVIIIe-XIXe s. #8893
- églises et sculpture sur bois
  - (1780-1850) #1232 1574
  - XVIIIe-XIXe s. #8799

- enseignes et panneaux d'affichage, XVIIe-XIXe s. #2919
- ex-voto #1370
- expansion urbaine, XVIIe-XVIIIe s. #7885
- femmes artistes
  - (années 1930) #1380
  - (années 1930-1970) #1273
- fours à pain #2233 2234
- girouettes #2589
- granges, XVIIe-XIXe s. #9230 9231
- gravure (1958-1965) #1654
- histoire de l'art #1255
- hôpitaux (années 1950) #9029
- horloges #2925
  - XVIIe-XVIIIe s. #2914
- illustration de chansons folkloriques #938
- illustration de livres (années 1960) #926
- jeux de société, XIXe-XXe s. #2597
- jouets #2924
  - (1800-1925) #2937
  - XVIIe-XIXe s. #2921 2933 2934
- jouets en bois #2590
- matériaux d'architecture (1800-1870) #7947
- mobilier #2544
  - (1660-1760) #2540
  - (1700-1820) #2537
  - (1760-1840), style géorgien #2477
  - (1930-1935) #2970
  - (années 1920) #2463
  - (années 1940) #2523
  - (années 1950) #2467
  - (années 1970) #2533
  - fin XVIIe-milieu XIXe s. #2527
  - XVIIe-XIXe s. #2464 2524 2541
  - XVIIe-XVIIIe s. #2525 2526 2529 2530 2531 2539 2543
  - XVIIIe s. #2488 2545
  - XVIIIe-XIXe s. #2474 2532
  - XVIIIe-XIXe s., mobilier anglais du Québec #2542
- monuments #1570
  - fin XIXe s.-années 1920 #1606
- monuments funéraires #733
- moules #2916
- moules à sucre d'érable #2592
- moulins #9242 9252
  - XVIIe-XIXe s. #9243
- moulins à vent #9255
- musées #3098 3108
  - (années 1970) #3102
- orfèvrerie #2670
  - (1534-1763) #2684
  - XVIIe-XIXe s. #2095 2627 2636 2660 2662 2664 2666 2676 2681 2690 2691
  - XVIIe-XVIIIe s. #2657
  - XVIIIe s. #2673 2677
  - XVIIIe-XIXe s. #2644 2658 2672 2682 2687
- ouvrages de ferronnerie #2697 2702 2705 2707 2711 2712 2713
  - Cauchon, famille #5062
  - XVIIIe-XIXe s. #2703
- paysage (1800-1940) #1286
- peinture #1289 1340 1344 1346
  - (1939-années 1950) #1461
  - (1940-1966) #1440
  - (1953-1956) #1454
  - (1955-1965) #1471
  - (années 1860-1880) #230
  - (années 1930) #589 592 1460
  - (années 1930-1960) #1421
  - (années 1940) #355 1384 1389 1390 1393 1468
  - (années 1940-1950) #412 1432 1472

  - (années 1940-1960) #1436
  - (années 1950) #1413
  - (années 1950-1960) #1441
  - (années 1960) #484 1419
  - (années 1970) #588 1542 1543 1544 1552 1560
  - milieu XVIIe s.-1908 #1353
  - XIXe s. #197 1312 1318 1336 3233
  - XIXe s.-années 1930 #1382
  - XIXe s.-années 1940 #1248
  - XIXe s.-années 1960 #1256 1262
  - XVIIe s. #1363
  - XVIIIe-XIXe s. #1323
  - XXe s. #1270 1392 1422 1463
- photographie #1283
  - (1857-1960), famille Livernois #1275
  - (années 1970) #996 1507 1556
  - (années 1980) #1562
- poêles (avant-1867) #2220
- pop'art #1497
- portraits, XVIII-XIXe s. #263
- poterie #2324 2331
  - (1655-1916) #2344
  - (années 1840-1900) #2298 2322
  - (années 1960) #2381
  - (années 1970) #2384 2390
  - XIXe s. #2279 2283
    - potiers écossais #2339
  - XVIIe-XIXe s. #2301 2302 2313 2318
  - XVIIIe s. #2364 2365
  - XVIIIe-XIXe s. #2299 2321 2343
- prisons, XIXe s. #9056
- religion, art et #1292
  - (années 1940) #1394
  - (années 1950) #1250 1406
  - (années 1960) #1435
- sculpture #1590 1596 1617
  - (1650-1925) #1592
  - (1945-1970) #1599
  - (1980) #685
  - (années 1960) #1586 1595 1622
  - (années 1960-1970) #1584
  - (années 1970) #1603 1626 1627 1628 1630 1631 1634 1635
  - thème de l'Annonciation, fin XVIIe-XXe s. #1633
  - thème du souper d'Emmaüs, XIXe-XXe s. #1615
  - XVIIe-XIXe s. #1589 1594 1611
- sculpture en plein air (années 1960) #1587
- sculpture sur bois #1573 1576 1577 1614
  - famille Levasseur #6254
  - XVIIe-XIXe s. #1575 1583
  - XVIIIe-XIXe s. #6947
  - XVIIIe-XXe s. #1616
- sièges (mobilier) #2534
- surréalisme #1464 1470
- tabernacles, XVIIe-XIXe s. #1613
- tapis crochetés #2751 2753
- tapisserie (années 1970) #2772 2773
- téléphone, constructions (années 1880-1950) #9298
- textiles et tissus
  - (1750-1900) #2727
  - (années 1930), artisanes #2165
  - XIXe-début XXe s. #2737
- tissage et filage (années 1920) #2718
- tissage et tapis (années 1930-1940) #2186
- toits, XVIIe-XVIIIe s. #7703 7881
- ustensiles de cuisine, XVIIe-XVIIIe s. #2210
- vaisselle, XVIIe-XVIIIe s. #2161
- vannerie, XXe s. #2954
- verre
  - (1847-1898) #2399

– XIXe s. #2418 2421
– villas, XIXe s. #8632
– vitraux #2448
– vues
– (1608-1875), estampes #1349
– (années 1890) #6436
– Banting, Frederick Grant #4600
– Bouchard, Lorne Holland #4857
– Cockburn, James Pattison #5126
– explorateurs français #276
– Fortin, Marc-Aurèle #5474
– Heriot, George #5786
– Hudon-Beaulac, Simone Marie Yvette #857 5856
– Jackson, A.Y. #5919 5922
– Krieghoff, Cornelius #241 242 6085 6091 6093 6099
– Lougheed, Robert Elmer #6328
– XIXe s. #1298 2326
– poterie #2291 2306
– poterie Thomas #2287
– XVIIIe-milieu XIXe s. #1366
– vues photographiques
– Benoît (dit Livernois), Jules-Isaïe #258 259
– Lafortune, François #6134
– Würtele, Fred C. #7619
Québec. Ministère de l'Agriculture
– (années 1930), renouveau dans l'artisanat #2165
Québec. Ministère des Affaires culturelles. Direction générale du patrimoine
– conservation de l'architecture #7870
Québec. Ministère des Affaires culturelles. Service de l'Inventaire des biens culturels
– inventaire des oeuvres d'art et des édifices (1974-1977) #1277
Québec. Ministère des Travaux publics et de l'Approvisionnement
– achats d'oeuvres d'art #1561
Québec. Rapport de la Commission d'enquête sur l'enseignement des arts au Québec (Rapport Parent) (1968)
– et art (années 1960) #1473
Québec. Rapport de la Commission royale d'enquête sur l'enseignement dans la province de Québec (Rapport Rioux) (1963-1966)
– et art (années 1960) #1473
Québec (Qué)
– architecture #7892 7938 7940
– (1608-fin X1Xe s.) #7944
– (années 1870-1920) #7843
– (années 1920) #7656
– (années 1950) #7673
– Baillairgé, Charles #8324
– fin XVIIe-années 1920, destruction par le feu #7952
– influence de l'architecture normande, XVIIe-milieu XVIIIe s. #7847
– XVIe-XVIIIe s. #7935
– XVIIe-XIXe s. #7936 7949 7950
– XVIIIe s. #7861 7943
– architecture domestique #8631
– maisons de campagne #8572
– maisons en brique, début XIXe s. #8521
– maisons en terrasses, XIXe s. #8653
– seigneuries #8611
– XVIIe-XIXe s. #7941 8505 8559
– architecture et monuments #7945
– art #1399 6870
– (années 1950) #1404
– (années 1970) #1509
– XVIIe s. #1352

– art et architecture #1233 7939
– XVIIe-XIXe s. #1306 1309
– arts décoratifs, début XXe s. #1313
– berceuses #2535
– conservation de l'architecture #7937 7942
– églises (années 1960) #1435
– fortifications #7946 8450
– Boisberthelot de Beaucours, Josué #8336
– galeries d'art
– (années 1960) #442
– (années 1970) #1519
– musées #3098 3108
– orfèvrerie #2197
– XVIIe-XIXe s. #2674 2685 2686
– XVIIIe s. #2677
– XVIIIe-XIXe s. #2630 2634 2650
– portes de la ville #8444
– sculpture (années 1890) #727
– sculpture sur bois, XVIIe-XIXe s. #1593
– tapisserie, XXe s. #2769
– tours Martello #8416
– vues
– Cockburn, James Pattison #5125 5127 5128
– Légaré, Joseph #6221
– Massicotte, Edmond-Joseph #6440
– Pilot, Robert Wakeham #6871
– Short, Richard #249 250
– vues photographiques (1850-1900) #1061
Québec (Qué), Archives municipales
– expositions
– C. Baillairgé, Arct. Ing: dessins architecturaux (1979) #8324
Québec (Qué), Archives nationales du Québec
– artisans, documents (1810-1819) #8616
– famille Livernois, photographies et documents #1275
Québec (Qué), Assemblée nationale
– architecture #8942
– Baillairgé, Thomas #8325
– Huot, Charles Edouard
– Débats sur les langues de 1793 #5878 5880 5881 5884
– Je me souviens #5874 5875
– peintures murales #5876
Québec (Qué), Atelier de réalisations graphiques (ARG) #1661
Québec (Qué), Batterie Royale
– architecture et restauration #8451
Québec (Qué), café du Parlement
– expositions
– L'art religieux contemporain au Canada (1952) #1406
Québec (Qué), Campus intercommunautaire de Cap-Rouge
– architecture, Jean-Marie Roy #9421
Québec (Qué), Cathedral of the Holy Trinity #1305
– architecture #8786
Québec (Qué), Chalet des employés civils
– architecture, André Robitaille #7939
Québec (Qué), Chalmers-Wesley Church
– architecture, George Browne #7873
Québec (Qué), Chambre blanche
– expositions, critiques
– Jean, Marcel #5952
Québec (Qué), chapelle de la congrégation Notre-Dame de Québec
– architecture et intérieur, attribués à François Baillairgé #8864
Québec (Qué), Chapelle de Mgr Olivier Briand
– voir Québec (Qué), Séminaire de Québec.

Chapelle de Mgr Olivier Briand
Québec (Qué), Château Frontenac
– architecture #9278 9291
– Painter, Walter Scott #9261
Québec (Qué), château Saint-Louis
– architecture #8443 8754
Québec (Qué), Collège des jésuites
– architecture #7953
– église, modèle architectural #8869
Québec (Qué), Complexe G
– sculpture, Charles Daudelin #5263
Québec (Qué), Couvent des ursulines
– architecture et art #1352
– architecture et intérieur #8810
– broderie #2778 2788 2789
– chapelle, architecture et intérieur #8852
– peinture #1305
Québec (Qué), Ecole des arts domestiques de Québec
– (1930-1935) #2167
– (années 1930) #2166
– (années 1930-1940) #2185 2186
– (années 1940) #2190
– renouveau de la ceinture fléchée #2833
Québec (Qué), Ecole des beaux-arts
– (années 1950) #1404
– Bourdeau, Micheline, élève #4879
– Caron, Roger, élève #5005
– Dallaire, Jean-Philippe, professeur #5239
– Daoust, Sylvia Emilienne, élève #5257
– Desrochers-Drolet, Françoise, élève #5289
– East, Benoît, professeur #5352
– Laliberté, Madeleine, élève #6153
– LeMoine, Edmond, professeur #6243
– Maltais, Marcelle, élève #6412
– modèles, architecture du Québec (Qué) #7936
– Pellan, Alfred, élève #6809 6811
– Thibault, René, professeur et élève #7344
Québec (Qué), école secondaire Marie-de-l'Incarnation
– architecture, Maurice Bouchard #7939
Québec (Qué), édifice de la compagnie d'assurance La Solidarité
– architecture, Robert Blatter et G.Fernand Caron #7939
Québec (Qué), édifice de la compagnie d'assurance Les Prévoyants du Canada
– architecture, Lucien Mainguy #7939
Québec (Qué), église
– architecture, Gauthier & Guité #8766
Québec (Qué), église des récollets
– modèle architectural #8869
Québec (Qué), église Notre-Dame-de-Grâce
– architecture, Gérard Morisset #8891
Québec (Qué), église Notre-Dame de Québec #8857
– architecture, Thomas Baillairgé #8325
– architecture et intérieur #8791
– peinture #1305
– tabernacle, François Baillairgé #4591
– voûte, utilisation du plâtre #1618
Québec (Qué), église Notre-Dame-des-Anges
– architecture #9022
Québec (Qué), église Notre-Dame-des-Victoires
– architecture et intérieur #8858
Québec (Qué), église Saint-Dominique
– sculptures, Lauréat Vallière #7455
Québec (Qué), église Saint-Jean-Baptiste
– peinture #1305
Québec (Qué), église Saint-Joachim de Montmorency
– intérieur, François et Thomas Baillairgé

*peintures provenant de Québec et des
environs* (1965) #1344
– *Trésors des communautés religieuses de la
ville de Québec* (1973) #1352
– *William Brymner, 1855-1925: A
Retrospective/William Brymner, 1855-1925:
aperçu rétrospectif de l'artiste* (1979) #4953
– expositions, critiques
– Daoust, Sylvia Marie Emilienne #5257
– *François Baillairgé et son oeuvre
(1759-1830)* (1975) #4593
– *The Canadian Canvas: A Travelling
Exhibition of 85 Recent Paintings/Peintres
canadiens actuels: exposition itinérante de
85 oeuvres récentes* (1975) #582
– Gagnon, Clarence Alphonse, estampes
#359
– Heriot, George, peintures #5785
– illustration de légendes folkloriques
québécoises #1290
– Laliberté, Alfred, bronzes #6144
– Massicotte, Edmond-Joseph, carnets de
notes #6441
– mobilier #2484
– orfèvrerie québécoise #2678
– Soucy, Jean-Baptiste, directeur #3103
– textiles québécois, XIXe -début XXe s.
#2737
– Viau, Guy, directeur #7485
Québec (Qué), Palais de l'intendant
– architecture #8553
Québec (Qué), Palais épiscopal/Episcopal
Palace
– architecture #8787
– Baillairgé, Thomas #8325
– chapelle, modèle architectural #8869
– chapelle, plan architectural, Jean-Baptiste
Maillou (dit Desmoulins) #8856
Québec (Qué), Palais Montcalm
– expositions, critiques
– Lemieux, Irénée #6226
Québec (Qué), Parc de l'Artillerie
– fortifications #8449
Québec (Qué), Parc de l'Artillerie. Redoute
Dauphine
– architecture #8448 8452
Québec (Qué), place Royale
– architecture domestique #2201 8588 8589
– poterie #2352
– restauration #7948 7951
– statues, Louis XIV #1598
Québec (Qué), place Royale. Maison Hazeur
– architecture #8626
Québec (Qué), prison des plaines
d'Abraham/Plains of Abraham Prison
– architecture, Charles Philippe Ferdinand
Baillairgé #9057
Québec (Qué), Redoute Dauphine
– *voir* Québec (Qué), Parc de l'Artillerie.
Redoute Dauphine
Québec (Qué), Salon des artisans de Québec
– expositions
– *Métiers d'art Ontario-Québec,
1979/1980/Quebec-Ontario Crafts,
1979/1980* (1979) #2138
Québec (Qué), Séminaire de
Notre-Dame-des-Anges
– architecture #8785
Québec (Qué), Séminaire de Québec
– *voir aussi* Québec (Qué), Université Laval
– architecture #1341 8844 8847
– architecture et art #1352 8842
– en comparaison avec l'église Saint-Joachim
(Saint-Joachim, Qué) #7953

– influence sur l'architecture québécoise,
XVIIIe-XIXe s. #8622
– uniforme des écoliers #2809
Québec (Qué), Séminaire de Québec.
Archives
– estampes #3124
Québec (Qué), Séminaire de Québec.
Chapelle
– peinture #1305
Québec (Qué), Séminaire de Québec.
Chapelle de Mgr Jean-Olivier Briand
– architecture et intérieur #8800
– sculpture, Pierre Emond #5371
Québec (Qué), Séminaire de Québec. Musée
du Séminaire #3098 3108
Québec (Qué), Séminaire des jésuites
– utilisation de manuels de dessin, XIXe s.
#2982
Québec (Qué), Université Laval
– *voir aussi* Québec (Qué), Séminaire de
Québec
– art amérindien #3422
– collection #3080
– estampes, images pieuses #130
– expositions
– *Descriptive and Historical Catalogue of a
Special Exhibition of Painting in the
Gallery of Laval University, Quebec, Lately
Restored/Musée des peintures, Université
Laval, Québec* (1909) #3078
– images de dévotion, collection Jeanne
Larouche-Villeneuve #1662
– peinture #1306
Québec (Qué), Université Laval. Ecole
d'architecture
– architecture, enseignement
– (1964) #8271
– (1965) #8273
– (1966) #8274
– (1967) #8275
– (1968) #8277
– (1980) #8289
Queen Charlotte Islands (CB)
– masques, Haidas #3961
– totems, Haidas #3982 4008
Queen Charlotte Islands (CB), Queen
Charlotte Islands Museum
– architecture, Henry Hawthorn #9129
– expositions
– *The Art of Nunstins/L'art de Nunstins*
(1981) #6934
Queenston (Ont), résidence de Prest
– architecture #7959
Quercy, Jacques
– *voir* Pagé (dit Quercy or Carcy), Jacques
Quetico Park (Ont et Man)
– pictogrammes . Algonquiens #3575 3576
Quévillon, Louis-Amable, sculpteur can,
1749-1823 #1233 1324 1592 6947
– dorure #2930
– intérieur, église Saint-Etienne (Beaumont,
Qué) #8809
– retable, église Berthierville (Qué) #8874
– sculpture sur bois #1571 1573
– tabernacles #1613
Quidi Vidi (TN), Christ Church
– restauration, Newfoundland Historic Trust
#7788
quillwork, Siouan
– mocassins #3652 3666
Quinaults
– culture #3845
– (années 1870) #4031
– vannerie #3773 3778

quincaillerie
– *voir aussi* outils
quincaillerie . Canada
– fin XVIIIe-moitié XIXe s. #2703
– quincaillerie de bâtiment, XVIIe-XIXe s.
#2705
Quinn, William, artisan verrier can, XIXe s.
#2400
Quintal, Joseph (frère Augustin), prêtre,
artiste, architecte can, 1683-1776
– baldaquin, église paroissiale de Neuville
(Qué) et église de Trois-Rivières (Qué)
#8826

R

Rabinowitch, David George, sculpteur can,
1943- #1817
– dessins, séries *The Construction of Vision*
#6949
– et l'art d'avant-garde #600
– et l'art torontois (Ont), (années 1970) #1796
– expositions, critiques #787
– expositions de groupe
– (1971) #98
– (1976) #779
– (1977) #782
– (1978) #790
– (1980) #703
– réflexion sur ses sculptures #6948
– sculptures (1976-1977) #6950
– soutien #123
Rabinowitch, Royden, sculpteur can, 1943-
#1817
– et l'art torontois (Ont), (années 1970) #1796
– expositions de groupe
– (1976) #779
– (1977) #782
– (1980) #703
– sculptures (1970-1975) #6951
*RACAR (Revue d'art canadienne/Canadian Art
Review)*, périodique can #114
RACE
– *voir* Regroupement des artistes des
Cantons de l'Est (RACE)
Racey, Arthur George, artiste can, 1870-1941
#6952
– dessins humoristiques *Montreal Star* #943
Rackham, Arthur, artiste brit, 1867-1939
– influence sur James Frederic McCulloch
#6463
Rackus, George Keistus, artiste can, 1927-
– expositions
– (1972) #6953
Radecki, Brigitte, artiste can, 1940-
– Symposium international de sculpture
environnementale de Chicoutimi (Qué),
(1980) #1639
radiotélédiffusion canadienne #129
– (années 1950), et Commission royale
d'enquête sur l'avancement des arts,
lettres et sciences (Rapport Massey) #3254
3255 3261 9906
– (années 1970) #583 3279
Raginsky, Nina, photographe can, 1941-
#1007
– expositions, critiques #1046 1060
– expositions de groupe
– (1973) #1002
– (1979) #1037
RAIC

– *voir* Institut royal d'architecture du
Canada
RAIC. Journal
– *voir Royal Architectural Institute of Canada.
Journal*
Raine, Herbert, artiste et architecte can,
1875-1951
– eaux-fortes #800
Rajotte, Normand, photographe can, actif
années 1970 #1556
Rajotte, Yves, artiste can, 1932-
– écrits #6954
Rakine, Marthe, artiste can, 1926- #6955 6956
Raley, G.H., missionnaire et collectionneur
can, actif années 1890-1930
– collection, art, Indiens de la côte
nord-ouest #3996
Ralston, William, architecte can, né 1886
– lauréat, Dominion Housing Act Small
House Competition (1936) #8736
– lauréat, Ontario Government Housing
Competition (1936) #8737
Ramage, John, artiste can, 1748-1802
– miniatures #1377
Ramezay, Claude de, officier fr au Canada
et gouverneur par intérim de la
Nouvelle-France, 1659-1724
– résidence, château de Ramezay (Montréal,
Qué) #3076 3077 3083
Ramsay, William Alexander, architecte can,
1910-
– Dorval (Qué), Aéroport international de
Montréal. Aérogare #9515
– Halifax (NE), Aéroport international
d'Halifax. Aérogare #9515
– Ottawa (Ont), Aéroport international
d'Ottawa. Aérogare #9515
– Toronto (Ont), Aéroport international de
Toronto. Aérogare #9516
ramure . Esquimaux du cuivre
– sculpture #4412
ramure . Indiens de la côte nord-ouest #3817
– instruments #4068
ramure . Iroquois
– cuillers sculptées #3524
– petites effigies humaines #3553
Rand, Paul, artiste can, 1896-1970 #2011
– expositions
– (1980) #6957
Randall, Cliff, photographe can, ca 1953-
– catalogue de photographies #1023
Randy et Barneche
– art de performance #655
Ranford, Barry, photographe can, actif
années 1970-
– catalogue de photographies #991
Rankin, Joan Melvin, artiste can, 1927- #6958
Rankin, Toby, photographe can, 1940-
– catalogue de photographies #995
Rankin Inlet (TNO)
– sculpture d'ivoire #4195
– sculpture en céramique #4207 4210 4314
– tapisserie #4253
Rankin Inlet (TNO), Eskimo Arts and Crafts
Centre
– poterie (années 1970) #4226
Ranvoyzé, François, orfèvre can, 1739-1819
#2658 2660 2662 6959
– analyse de la composition de l'argent
#2682
– apprentissage chez Ignace-François
Delezenne #1620
– calices #2679
– L'Islet (Qué), église

Notre-Dame-de-Bon-Secours #2673
– Ottawa (Ont), Galerie nationale du
Canada #2680
– expositions
– (1968) #6960
– oeuvres
– Detroit (Mich), Detroit Institute of Arts
#2681
– Québec (Qué), Musée du Québec #2678
– paix #2666
– tasses à quêter #2671
Raphael, William, artiste can, 1833-1914
– relation entre photographie et peinture
#245
Rapin, François-Xavier Aldéric, artiste can,
1868-1901 #6961
Rapport de la Commission d'enquête sur
l'enseignement des arts au Québec
– *voir* Québec. Rapport de la Commission
d'enquête sur l'enseignement des arts au
Québec (Rapport Parent)
Rapport de la Commission royale d'enquête
sur l'enseignement dans la province de
Québec
– *voir* Québec. Rapport de la Commission
royale d'enquête sur l'enseignement dans
la province de Québec (Rapport Rioux)
Rapport Parent
– *voir* Québec. Rapport de la Commission
d'enquête sur l'enseignement des arts au
Québec (Rapport Parent)
Rapport Rioux
– *voir* Québec. Rapport de la Commission
royale d'enquête sur l'enseignement dans
la province de Québec (Rapport Rioux)
Raquette, père
– *voir* Jackson, Alexander Young (A.Y.)
raquettes . Algonquiens #3523 3631
raquettes . Amérindiens #2812 3515
raquettes . Canada #2812
– influence sur les modèles de chaises
canadiennes #2464
– Terre-Neuve et Labrador, XXe s. #2155
raquettes . Indiens des forêts du Nord-Est
#3631
raquettes . Inuit #3515
raquettes . Iroquois #3523 3631
raquettes . Mistassins #4080
raquettes . Saulteux/Ojibwa #3539
Raskin, Lawrie, photographe can, 1943-
– expositions de groupe
– (1980) #1063
Rasmussen, Knud Johan Victor, explorateur
danois au Canada, 1879-1933
– expédition dans l'Arctique #4324 4326
4328 4330 4417 4437
Rattenbury, Francis Mawson, architecte can,
1867-1935 #8400
– dessins et correspondance #8401
– en comparaison avec Samuel Maclure
#8152
– hôtels appartenant à sociétés ferroviaires
#9290
– Mawson, Thomas Hayton, comparaison
#9405
– Vancouver (CB), palais de justice #9149
– Victoria (CB) #8175
– Colombie-Britannique, édifices du
Parlement #8964 8965 8966 8967
– Crystal Gardens #9134 9146
Rattray, William Jordan, écrivain can,
1835-1883
– Bengough, John Wilson, commentaire
#4673

Rauschenberg, Robert, artiste amér, 1925-
– Ayot, Pierre, comparaison #4572
– influence sur Alan Wood #7611
– influence sur Chris Knudsen, remise en
question #6070
Ravenhill, Alice, artiste can, active années
1940 #4114
Rawe, James, photographe can, actif
1856-1867 #1724
Ray, Carl, artiste can, 1943-1979 #4157 4161
6648
Raymond, Maurice, artiste can, 1912- #6962
– cartes de Noël #856
Raymond Lee and Associates Ltd., agence
can de graphisme #886
Raymond Moriyama & Associates
– motel #9288
Rayner, Gordon, artiste can, 1935- #6963
6964 6965
– et peinture torontoise (années 1960) #1753
– expositions
– (1979) #6966
– expositions de groupe
– (1965) #473
– réflexion sur l'art canadien (années 1960)
#478
Razutis, Al, artiste can, 1946-
– art vidéo #605
RCAT
– *voir* Royal Canadian Aerial Theatre
(RCAT)
Rea, Kenneth Guscotte, architecte can,
1878-1941
– Montréal (Qué), Hôpital Royal Victoria.
Pavillon Ross #9017
Read, Charles James, architecte can, m. 1920
– Toronto (Ont)
– New Princess Theatre #9069
– York Theatre #9066
Read, Herbert Edward, critique et historien
d'art brit, 1893-1968
– et Wilfred Roloff Beny #4690
– Plaskett, Joe, réflexion sur les théories
artistiques de, #6891
– théories concernant Alex Colville #5149
Réal d'Anjou, éditeur (Québec, Qué)
– cartes de Noël (1950) #856
réalisme
– *voir aussi* photoréalisme; trompe-l'oeil
– Alberta #1954
– Canada
– (1860-1900), influence de la
photographie #262
– (années 1860-1880) #230
– (années 1950) #151
– (années 1960) #496
– (années 1970) #545 573 606 694 1810
– XXe s. #110 498 716
– et Ernest Lindner #6286
– et Fred Ross #7079
– et Glenn Howarth #5851
– et Jack Chambers #5070 5071 5072 5073
5075 5078 5079 5080 5081
– et John C. Leonard #6246
– et Kenneth Edison Danby #5251
– et Mary Frances Pratt #6919
– et Tom Forrestall #5465
– et Vincent Beull #4719
– et William George Richardson Hind #5805
5810
– Nouvelle-Ecosse (années 1970) #1221
– provinces de l'Atlantique (années 1970)
#1129
– réalisme magique

– Alberta #1965
– et Alex Colville #5143 5144
– Sackville (NB), Mount Allison University #1130
– Saint Jean (NB), XXe s. #1184
réalisme lyrique
– *voir* réalisme
réalisme magique
– *voir* réalisme
réalisme radical
– *voir* photoréalisme
réalisme social
– *voir* réalisme
Reaney, James Crerar, auteur can, 1926-
– régionalisme, en comparaison avec Greg Curnoe #5225
Rebanks, Leslie, architecte can, 1927-
– Toronto (Ont) #7733
Rebel, The, périodique can
– illustrations #930
rébellion du Nord-Ouest
– photographies, photographes militaires canadiens #1107
récipients
– *voir aussi* bols
– dans l'art
– Lee-Nova, Gary #6213
– McWilliams, Allan #6508
– Prince, Richard #6938
– Urquhart, Tony #7448
récipients . Algonquiens
– bois, XVIIIe s. #3507
– écorce de bouleau #3571
– Lac Barrière (Qué) #3544
– ouvrages perlés #3635
– sacs en fibre textile #3638 3744
récipients . Algonquins
– écorce de bouleau #3542 4078
– ouvrages en coquillages #3505
récipients . Amérindiens
– sacs en poil de bison #3398
récipients . Athapascans #4104 4105
récipients . Bella-Bellas
– bols et coffrets en bois sculpté, XIXe s. #3985
récipients . Béothuks #3528
récipients . Canada
– bois, XVIIIe-XIXe s. #2594
– cuir (années 1970) #2936
– ouvrages de vannerie, Labrador, XXe s. #2945
récipients . Cris #3402 3655 3742
– éclisses de bouleau #4078
récipients . Delawares
– sacs à médecines des chamans #3506
récipients . Flancs-de-Chien #4089
récipients . Haidas
– bols et coffrets en bois sculpté, XIXe s. #3985
– New York (NY), American Museum of Natural History #4066
récipients . Hurons #3514 3519
récipients . Indiens de la côte nord-ouest #3866 4015
– cuivre #4071
récipients . Indiens des forêts du Nord-Est
– ouvrages en coquillages #3505
– ouvrages perlés #3635
– sacs en fibre textile #3638 3744
récipients . Indiens des plaines
– New York (NY), American Museum of Natural History #3668
récipients . Indiens du bassin #3986
récipients . Ingaliks #4087

récipients . Iroquois #3519
– ouvrages en coquillages #3505
– ouvrages perlés #3635
– sacs en fibre textile #3638 3744
récipients . Micmacs #3528 3569
récipients . Mistassins #4080
récipients . Montagnais
– éclisses de bouleau #4078
– écorce de bouleau #4086
récipients . Naskapis
– éclisses de bouleau #4078
récipients . Osages
– sacs en fibre textile #3744
récipients . Pentaguets
– écorce de bouleau #3510
récipients . Pieds-Noirs #3654
récipients . Saulteux/Ojibwa #3402 3488 3549 3557 4089
récipients . Slaveys #4089
récipients . Tanainas #4085
récipients . Têtes-de-Boule
– écorce de bouleau #4079 4108
récipients . Tlingits
– bols et coffrets en bois sculpté, XIXe s. #3985
récipients . Tsimshians
– bols et coffrets en bois sculpté, XIXe s. #3985
récipients eucharistiques
– *voir* objets liturgiques
Recklinghausen (Allemagne de l'Ouest), Städtische Kunsthalle
– expositions
– *10 Canadian Artists in the 1970s* (1981) #703
récollets
– architecture, Montréal (Qué) #7932
– architecture et sculpture, Québec #8855
récompenses
– *voir* prix et récompenses
Red Deer (Alta), hôtel de ville
– architecture, James E. Secord et Saul Herzog #8990
Red Deer (Alta), Red Deer and District Museum
– expositions
– *Artisan '78: The First National Travelling Exhibition of Contemporary Canadian Crafts/Artisan '78: première exposition nationale itinérante d'artisanat canadien contemporain* (1979) #2134
Red Deer (Alta), Red Deer Public Library
– expositions
– *Images of the Inuit from the Simon Fraser Collection* (1981) #4495
Red Deer (Alta), Saint Mary's Church
– architecture, Douglas Joseph Cardinal #8343
Red Deer River (Man)
– lieu de sépulture, Saulteux/Ojibwa #3615
Red Indian Lake (TN)
– artefacts, Béothuks #3623
Red River Exhibition Association (Man)
– expositions (1964-1978) #1903
Redbank (NB)
– artefacts algonquiens #3561
Redcliff (Alta)
– poterie, XXe s. #2371
Redgrave, Felicity, artiste can, 1920-
– expositions
– (1978) #6967
– expositions, critiques #1169
Redinger, Walter, sculpteur can, 1940- #6968 6969

– entretien #6970
– expositions de groupe
– (1970) #771
– (1972) #548
– sculptures (années 1960) #1793
Redivo, Hugo, photographe can, actif 1974
– catalogue de photographies #995
Redman, Alvin James, artiste can, 1947-
– expositions de groupe
– (1975) #4141
Redon, Odilon, artiste fr, 1840-1916
– influence sur Tom La Pierre #6122
Reeves, Charles Aime, architecte can, 1872-1948
– Montréal (Qué), académie des Saints Noms de Jésus et de Marie #9388
Reeves, Gladys, photographe can, 1890-1974
– et Ernest Brown #4935
Reeves, John, photographe can, 1938-
– catalogue de photographies #991
– expositions de groupe
– (1981) #1070
– portraits photographiques #6971
– auteurs canadiens #1065 1066
– femmes canadiennes célèbres #6972
Regina (Sask)
– architecture
– (1909) #8109
– (années 1910) #8111
– (années 1920) #7656
– architecture domestique (années 1910) #8687
– art
– (années 1950) #6284
– (années 1950-1970) #1935
– (années 1960) #441 1848
– (années 1960-1970) #1862
– peinture (années 1960) #1913
– poterie (années 1970) #2383 2385
– sculpture (années 1960) #1853
– sculpture en céramique
– (années 1960-1970) #1939
– (années 1970) #1924
– urbanisme, Thomas Hayton Mawson #9405
Regina (Sask), 38 Saskatchewan Geriatric Centre
– architecture, Stock, Ramsey & Associates #8516
Regina (Sask), édifices du Parlement
– architecture, concours
– Gilbert, Cass #8954
– Mitchell & Raine #8955
– Storey & Van Egmond #8956
Regina (Sask), Grain Show Building
– murale, Fritz Brandtner #4900
Regina (Sask), Legislative Buildings
– architecture, Edward et William Sutherland Maxwell #8944 8945 8957 8958 8959 8960 8961
Regina (Sask), Norman Mackenzie Art Gallery
– *voir* Regina (Sask), University of Regina. Norman Mackenzie Art Gallery
Regina (Sask), RCMP Chapel
– architecture #8911
Regina (Sask), RCMP Museum
– Moodie, Geraldine, photographies #6602
Regina (Sask), Regina College. Norman Mackenzie Art Gallery
– *voir aussi* Regina (Sask), University of Regina. Norman Mackenzie Art Gallery; Regina (Sask), University of Saskatchewan. Norman Mackenzie Art

Reid, George Agnew, artiste can, 1860-1947 #178 6976 6979
– commentaire, peinture et dessin de bâtiments #8219
– commentaire sur la peinture murale #6974 6975
– directeur, Ontario College of Art (Toronto, Ont) #2964
– entretien #6977
– et Académie royale des arts du Canada #152
– et Charles MacDonald Manly #6414
– et Edith Grace Coombs #5172
– et Mary Evelyn Wrinch #7617
– expositions, critiques #186
– expositions de groupe
  – (1935) #17
  – (1978) #1726
– mari de Mary Hiester Reid #6982
– murales, Jarvis Collegiate Institute Auditorium (Toronto, Ont) #6978
– professeur de Frederick Nicholas Loveroff #6329
– professeur de Mary Evelyn Wrinch #7618
– réflexion sur son oeuvre #6973
– relation entre photographie et peinture #245
Reid, Leslie Mary Margaret, artiste can, 1947- #675 6980
– expositions
  – (1980) #6981
– expositions, critiques #579
– expositions de groupe
  – (1975) #591
  – (1977) #637
Reid, Mary Evelyn Wrinch
– voir Wrinch, Mary Evelyn
Reid, Mary Hiester, artiste can, 1854-1921 #207
– expositions
  – (1922) #6982
– femme de George Agnew Reid #6979
– professeur de Hattie Blackstock #4738
Reid, Richard, artiste can, 1930-
– expositions de groupe
  – (1974) #2050
Reid, Robert Dow, artiste can, 1933-
– expositions, critiques #860
– monument commémoratif, Toronto (Ont) #727
Reid, Stuart, artiste can, 1953- #6983
Reid, Terrence Edward, artiste can, 1947-
– expositions de groupe
  – (1971) #2042
Reid, William Ronald (Bill), sculpteur et joaillier can, 1920- #4066 4121 4155 4162 6984 6988
– bijoux #2695
– commentaire sur les objets en cuivre, Indiens de la côte nord-ouest #4071
– commentaire sur les totems #3972
– entretien #6987
– et art de la côte nord-ouest #6986
– expositions
  – (1974) #6985
– influence sur Robert Davidson #5269
– Raven and the First People, University of British Columbia. Museum of Anthropology (Vancouver, CB) #6989
– sculptures, Totem Park (Vancouver, CB) #4118 4124
Reinblatt, Moses Martin (Moe), artiste can, 1917-1979
– réflexion sur la gravure #817

Reitzenstein, Reinhard, artiste can, 1949-
– théories sur l'art #594
Rejlander, Oscar Gustave, photographe suédois en Angleterre, 1832-1875
– Notman, William, comparaison #6726
religion
– voir aussi mysticisme
– Ontario, XIXe-XXe s. #8906
religion, architecture et
– Colombie-Britannique (1858-1925) #8916
– Québec (années 1950) #1406
religion, art et
– Canada
  – (années 1960) #457 459
  – (années 1970) #94
  – art traditionnel #965 966
  – images de femmes #121
  – livre de messe dominical, illustrations (années 1970) #597
  – XXe s. #479 1393
– et George Sawchuk #7142 7143
– et Jordi Bonet #4784
– et Napoléon Bourassa #4870
– et Ozias Leduc #6204 6206
– et Paul-Emile Borduas #4820
– et Pierre Charles Marie-Alain Couturier #1407
– et William Kurelek #6110
– Montréal (Qué), Ecole des beaux-arts #2972
– Québec
  – (1640-1840) #1329
  – (années 1940) #1384 1394
  – (années 1950) #1250 1402 1406
  – (années 1960) #1435
  – art traditionnel #1292
  – croix #1619 1637
  – crucifix #1638
  – images du diable, XVIIe s.-1840 #1357
  – ouvrages de ferronnerie #2713
  – publications #1295
  – XIXe s. #1336
  – XVIIe s. #1322 1358 1363 1365
  – XVIIe s.-années 1950 #1247
  – XVIIe-XVIIIe s. #66 2187
– Québec (Qué), XVIIe s. #1352
– Saint-Basile-le-Grand (Qué), Centre communautaire catholique Tour de David #1510
reliure . Canada
– (1964-1967) #2108 2109
– (années 1850) #1692
– Montréal (Qué), (années 1930-1940) #1648
– Ontario (années 1970) #935
– Québec #2183 2187 2228
rembourrage . Canada
– Montréal (Qué), (1800-1850) #2538
– Québec
  – (1790-1890) #2536
  – XVIIe-XVIIIe s. #2530 2531
Rémi, Daniel, photographe can, actif 1973
– catalogue de photographies #997 999
Renaissance . art
– en comparaison avec renouveau des arts, Indiens de la côte nord-ouest #6986
– France, influence sur l'architecture et la sculpture sur bois québécoises #1574
– influence sur Marius Dubois #5310
– influence sur William Perehudoff #6837
Renard, Jules, architecte fr, actif 1916
– Montréal (Qué), château Dufresne #8617 8618
Renaud, François, photographe can, actif 1973

– catalogue de photographies #997 999
Renaud (dit Cannard), Pierre, constructeur can, 1699-1774 #269 270
Rennes (France), Musée de Rennes
– expositions
  – Art et artisanat des Indiens Iroquois (1964) #3590
Renoir, Pierre Auguste, artiste fr, 1841-1919
– influence sur Paul-Emile Borduas #4841
Renzins, Rudy, orfèvre suédois, actif années 1930
– professeur d'Harold Stacey #7274
Repentigny, Marie Favery de, religieuse can, m. 1675 #2212
– enseignement de l'artisanat #2979
Repentigny, Rodolphe de (Jauran), artiste, critique d'art can, 1926-1959
– critique d'art #3318
– expositions de groupe
  – (1977) #1465
  – (1981) #1471
Repentigny (Qué)
– architecture #7888
Repentigny (Qué), église
– sculptures, Philippe Liébert #6281
Reppen, Jack, artiste can, 1933-1964 #6990
reprographie (art)
– Canada (années 1970) #614
– Eastcott, Robert Wayne #5354
– Jackson, Sarah Jeanette #5932
– N.E. Thing Co. Ltd. #524
– télécopieur #652
– Walker, Robert #668
République des Beaux-Arts #1502
Repulse Bay (TNO)
– sculpture #4450
– sculpture d'ivoire #4438
Resnais, Alain, cinéaste fr, 1922-
– influence sur Vera Frenkel #5526
restaurants . Canada
– Toronto (Ont), (années 1910) #9269
restauration d'oeuvres d'art
– voir conservation et restauration
Restoule, Tim, artiste can, 1960-
– expositions de groupe
  – (1980) #4159
  – (1981) #4173
Retable
– et Wilfrid Corbeil #1402
retables . Canada
– Baillairgé, François, église Notre-Dame de Québec (Québec, Qué) #4591
– Baillairgé, Thomas, Charlesbourg (Qué) #8851
– Bolvin, Gilles #4782 8874
– Gauthier, Amable #8874
– Levasseur, Pierre-Noël, Couvent des ursulines. Chapelle (Québec, Qué) #8852
– Liébert, Philippe #6280 6281
– Loretteville (Qué), église Notre-Dame-de-la-Jeune-Lorette #8804
– Montréal (Qué), Couvent des récollets #8855
– Nicolet (Qué), église Saint-Grégoire de Nicolet #1636
– Pépin, Joseph #8874
– Québec (1650-1925) #1592
– Quévillon, Louis-Amable #8874
Reusch, Astri, artiste can (vitrail), 1945- #2455
Reusch, Kina, artiste can, 1940-
– éléments reliés au culte et au rituel #789
Reuter, William, artiste can, 1940-
– design typographique #932

Revell, Viljo, architecte finnois, 1910-1964
– Toronto (Ont), hôtel de ville et Civic
  Square #8981 8990 8991 8992 8993
  – concours #8989
rêves
– dans l'art
  – Crone-Findlay, Noreen #5211
  – Giguère, Roland #5596
  – Granirer, Pnina #5644
  – Lodge, Judy #6321
  – Pellan, Alfred #6808 6815
révolution, art et
– automatistes, écrits #1443
– Québec (1759-1914) #1351
Revue d'art canadienne
– voir RACAR (Revue d'art
  canadienne/Canadian Art Review)
Revue moderne, La, périodique can
– et Ulric Lamarche #6155
revues d'architecture
– voir architecture . périodiques
revues d'art
– voir art . périodiques
revues d'art inuit
– voir art . périodiques . Inuit
Reynolds, Alan, sculpteur can, 1947-
– expositions, critiques #6991
– techniques #792
Reynolds, Catherine, artiste can, 1784-1864
  #6992
– expositions
  – (1967) #6993
Rhéaume, Damase, sculpteur can, 1832-1903
– sculptures sur bois, collection Nettie
  Sharpe #1607
Rhéaume, Jeanne Leblanc, artiste can, 1915-
  #6994
Rhind, William Birnie, sculpteur brit, m.
  1933
– sculpture, Palais législatif (Winnipeg,
  Man) #8948
Rho, Joseph-Adolphe, artiste can, 1835-1905
  #1318 1323
Rhone & Iredale, agence can d'architecture
– Burnaby (CB), Simon Fraser University,
  concours #9501
– Vancouver (CB)
  – Fairview Place #8746
  – University of British Columbia.
    Sedgewick Undergraduate Library
    #9052
  – Westcoast Building #9359
RIBA
– voir Royal Institute of British Architects
  (RIBA)
Rice, Gordon, artiste can, 1933- #6995
Richard, Damase, sculpteur can, 1852-1922
– sculptures sur bois, collection Nettie
  Sharpe #1607
Richard, Hélène Roy, artiste can, 1941-
  #1538
– et RACE #1536
Richard, Jean-Jules, auteur can, 1911-1975
– correspondance, Paul-Emile Borduas #1443
Richard, René-Jean, artiste can, 1895- #1393
  6996 6998 6999
– entretien #6997
Richard, Wilfrid, sculpteur can, né ca 1895
  #7000
Richard Strong Associates-James Secord
  Consortium, architectes paysagistes can
– Montréal (Qué), Expo 67. La Ronde #9222
Richards, Cecil Clarence, sculpteur can,
  1907-

– expositions de groupe
  – (1978) #666
Richards, Larry Wayne, architecte can, 1944-
  #8402
Richards, William, artiste can, ca 1786-1811
  #7001
Richardson, Henry Hobson, architecte amér,
  1838-1886
– influence sur architecture torontoise #8055
– influence sur Bruce Price #9537
– influence sur Edward James Lennox #9354
– influence sur William Newlands #8392
Richelieu and Ontario Navigation Company,
  S.S. Kingston (paquebot)
– murale, Frederick Sproston Challener
  #5068
Richeterre, Michel
– voir Dessailliant (dit Richeterre), Michel
Richmond, Chris, artiste can, actif 1976
– expositions de groupe
  – (1976) #1529
Ricketts, Charles, artiste brit, 1866-1931
– et Galerie nationale du Canada (Ottawa,
  Ont) #3050
rideaux
– voir draperies
Rider-Rider, William, photographe brit, né
  1889
– photographies de la Première Guerre
  mondiale #1107 1113
Ridgway, Morley, Wear & Co., fabricants de
  céramique (Hanley, Angleterre)
– vues du Canada #2362
Riel, Louis, dirigeant des métis, 1844-1885
– photographie, Joseph Langevin #6161
Riggio, Mike, artiste can, 1946-
– expositions de groupe
  – (1979) #1157
Riley, Jerry, photographe can, ca 1949-
– catalogue de photographies #1032
Rimmer, David McLellan, artiste can, 1942-
– expositions de groupe
  – (1979) #2069
– films #626
Rimouski (Qué)
– églises et croix #8872
Rimouski (Qué), Centre national
  d'expositions
– expositions
  – Edward Curtis in the Collection of the
    Edmonton Art Gallery (1980) #3480
Rimouski (Qué), Ecole d'arts et métiers de
  Rimouski
– voir Rimouski (Qué), Séminaire de
  Rimouski. Ecole d'arts et métiers de
  Rimouski
Rimouski (Qué), église de Sainte-Luce
– architecture, Thomas Baillairgé #1361
Rimouski (Qué), Musée régional de
  Rimouski #9118
– expositions
  – De la figuration à la non-figuration dans
    l'art québécois (1977) #1461
  – Dessins inédits d'Ozias Leduc/Ozias Leduc
    the Draughtsman (1979) #6210
Rimouski (Qué), Séminaire de Rimouski.
  Ecole d'arts et métiers de Rimouski
– (1942) #2978
Rindisbacher, Peter, artiste can, 1806-1834
  #7003 7004 7006 7007 7008 7009 7010
– au Minnesota #7002
– dans l'Ouest canadien #1859
– et Compagnie de la Baie d'Hudson #273
– peintures d'Amérindiens et d'Inuit, Saint

John's Cathedral (Winnipeg, Man) #7005
Ringness, Charles, artiste can, 1923- #7011
– expositions de groupe
  – (1977) #1933
  – (1979) #678
Rio de Janeiro (Brésil)
– vues
  – Tonnancour, Jacques Godefroy de #7382
Rio de Janeiro (Brésil), Ambassade du
  Canada
– murales, Alfred Pellan #6798
Rio de Janeiro (Brésil), Museu de arte
  moderna
– expositions
  – Artistas canadenses (1955) #1409
Rio de Janeiro (Brésil), Museu nacional de
  belas artes
– expositions
  – Artes graficas do Canada 1946 (1946) #806
  – Pintura canadense contemporanea (1944)
    #367
Riopelle, Dominique, orfèvre can, 1787-1859
– oeuvres, Detroit Institute of Arts (Detroit,
  Mich) #2691
Riopelle, Jean-Paul, artiste can, 1923- #1432
  1453 1504 1541 1542 1543 7012 7013 7014
  7016 7017 7020 7022 7023 7027 7033
– entretien #7026
– et l'art montréalais (Qué), (années
  1940-1960) #1437
– expositions
  – (1959) #7015
  – (1962) #7018 7019
  – (1967) #7021
  – (1972) #7025
  – (1980) #7030
  – (1981) #7032
– expositions, critiques #7024
– expositions de groupe #1409
  – (1955) #411
  – (1958) #431
  – (1962) #1420
  – (1964) #462
  – (1977) #633 1278 1279
– illustration de la page couverture, Refus
  global #1396
– influence sur Pierre Gendron #5581
– peintures (1947-1950) #7031
– peintures et sculptures #7029
– reconnaissance internationale (années
  1950) #425
– série Icebergs #7028
Rioux, Jules-Bernardin-Raoul, prêtre et
  artiste can, 1835-1921 #1319
rises . collections d'art
– Banque Toronto-Dominion #4248
Ristvedt-Handerek, Milly, artiste can, 1942-
  #7035
– expositions
  – (1979) #7034
– expositions de groupe
  – (1974) #565
Ritchie, Bill, artiste can, 1954-
– art vidéo #616
Ritchie, James Edward, sculpteur can en
  France, 1929-
– entretien #7036
rites et cérémonies
– voir aussi festivals
– sculpture, Colombie-Britannique (années
  1970) #2066
rites et cérémonies . Algonquiens
– Midéwiwin #3580 3702
– utilisation du wampum #3521

rites et cérémonies . Athapascans #4072 4073
– masques #4083
rites et cérémonies . Bella-Coolas #3874
rites et cérémonies . Béothuks #3528
rites et cérémonies . Cris #3655 3742
– cérémonie du calumet de paix #3662
rites et cérémonies . Delawares #3506
rites et cérémonies . Esquimaux du cuivre #4330
rites et cérémonies . Indiens de la côte nord-ouest #3869 3871 3970 3989 4065
– crécelles en forme de corbeau #3980
– masques #4030 4038
– potlatch #3911
– rituel du Loup #3885
– totems #3930
rites et cérémonies . Indiens des plaines #3725 3727
– danse des Esprits #3736
rites et cérémonies . Ingaliks #4087
– masques #4083
rites et cérémonies . Inuit #4254 4315 4317 4320 4321 4404 4492
– culte de l'Ours #4355
– déesse de la mer #4376
– masques #4349
rites et cérémonies . Iroquois #3489
– cérémonie du Milieu de l'Hiver #3606
– masques #3570 3588 3613
– Six Nations Reserve (Ont) #3598
– Société des Faux Visages #3595
– utilisation du tabac #3618
– utilisation du wampum #3521
rites et cérémonies . Kwakiutls #3768 3838
– danse de l'Oiseau-Tonnerre #3867
– masques #4030
rites et cérémonies . Makahs
– rituel du Loup #3885
rites et cérémonies . Micmacs #3528 3569
rites et cérémonies . Mistassins #4080
rites et cérémonies . Montagnais #4082
rites et cérémonies . Naskapis #4082
rites et cérémonies . Netsilik #4328
rites et cérémonies . Nootkas
– rituel du Loup #3885
rites et cérémonies . Onontagués
– masques #3588
rites et cérémonies . Pieds-Noirs #3721
– cérémonie de la Pipe-Médecine #3681
– Confrérie des poursuivants #3665
– Minìpoka #3749
rites et cérémonies . Salishiens #3838
rites et cérémonies . Saulteux/Ojibwa #3488 3539 3602
– Midéwiwin #3492 3517 3626 3661
rites et cérémonies . Siouens #3702 3725
rites et cérémonies . Tlingits #3976
– potlatch #4012
rites et cérémonies . Tsonnontouans
– masques #3508
– Société des Faux Visages #3533
Rivard, Yvon, auteur can, 1945-
– et Lucie Lambert, *Album Frayère* #6157
Rivest, Gilles G., photographe ca,, ca 1936-
– catalogue de photographies #995
Rivière-du-Loup (Qué)
– art et architecture #1233
Rivière-du-Loup (Qué), église Saint-Patrice
– peintures, Charles Edouard Huot #5878 5884
– sculptures, Louis Jobin #5967
Rivière-du-Loup (Qué), Musée d'archéologie de l'est du Québec
– expositions

– *De la figuration à la non-figuration dans l'art québécois* (1976) #1461
rivière George (Qué)
– arts graphiques (1972-1975) #4475
rivière Saint-Jean (NB)
– vues
– Miles, John Christopher #6532
Robb, Jim, artiste can, 1934- #7037
Robbe-Grillet, Alain, auteur fr, 1922-
– influence sur Vera Frenkel #5526
Robbie, Roderick G., architecte can, 1928-
– co-directeur, Toronto School Board Study of Educational Facilities (SEF) #9472
robe
– *voir* costume; mode
Robe, Sir William, officier de l'armée brit et architecte au Canada, 1765-1820
– Québec (Qué), Cathedral of the Holy Trinity #8786
Robert, Guy, artiste, critique d'art et poète can, 1933-
– oeuvres, Biennale de Venise (1952) #399
Robert, Louise, artiste can, 1941- #717 7038
– expositions
– (1977) #7039
– expositions de groupe
– (1980) #695 698
– (1981) #1565
Robert Fairfield Associates, agence can d'architecture
– Toronto (Ont), Central Technical School Art Centre #7684
Robert-Fleury, Tony, artiste fr, 1837-1912
– professeur de William Blair Bruce #4941
– professeur de William Brymner #4948
Robert McCausland Limited, atelier de vitraux (Toronto, Ont)
– vitraux #2399
Roberts, Goodridge
– *voir* Roberts, William Goodridge
Roberts, Olive, photographe can, active 1967
– expositions de groupe
– (1967) #8113
Roberts, Sir Charles George Douglas, poète can, 1860-1943
– Wilde, Oscar, commentaire #238
Roberts, Tomtu H., artiste can, 1859-1938
– expositions
– (1980) #7051
Roberts, William Goodridge, artiste can, 1904-1974 #7040 7041 7044
– autobiographie #7043
– commentaire sur ses études en Europe #408
– entretien #7042
– expositions
– (1969) #7045
– (1977) #7047
– (1980) #7048
– (1981) #7050
– expositions, critiques #7046
– expositions de groupe
– (1958) #431
– (1959) #438
– (1964) #462
– (1977) #1278 1279
– influence sur Jean-Paul Lemieux #6227
– influence sur peinture de paysages en Alberta (années 1930-1940) #1965
– influence sur Robert Gray Murray #613
– influence sur Toni Onley #613
– oeuvres tardives #7049
– Tonnancour, Jacques Godefroy de, comparaison #7384

Roberts, William Griffith, artiste can, 1920- #7052
Robertson, Clive, artiste can, 1946-
– art de performance #655
– et W.O.R.K.S. #1955
– expositions
– (1977) #7053
– expositions de groupe
– (1977) #631
Robertson, John Ross, collectionneur, historien et éditeur can, 1841-1918
– collection #1713
– collection Canadiana, Metro Toronto Public Library (Toronto, Ont) #3130 3131 3204
Robertson, Sarah Margaret Armour, artiste can, 1891-1948
– expositions
– (1951) #7054
– expositions de groupe
– (1928) #301
Robertson, Tom, photographe can, actif 1979 #2071
Robertson, William Francis, photographe can, actif 1863-1864
– et la Victoria Theatre Photographic Gallery (Victoria, CB) #2027
Robicheau, Louis, Can, XXe s.
– résidence, Vieille Maison (Meteghan, NE) #8531
Robideau, Henri, photographe can, 1946-
– expositions de groupe
– (1980) #1063
Robillard, Yves, designer et critique d'art can, 1939-
– et Fusion des arts (Montréal, Qué) #1482 1483
Robinson, Albert Henry, artiste can, 1881-1956 #7056 7057
– et le Groupe des Sept #1732
– expositions
– (1955) #7055
– expositions de groupe
– (1928) #301
– oeuvres, McMichael Canadian Collection (Kleinburg, Ont) #3172
Robinson, Boardman, artiste can, 1876-1952 #1128
Robinson, George, photographe can, 1825-1895
– et la Victoria Theatre Photographic Gallery (Victoria, CB) #2027
Robinson, Gerald, architecte can, 1930-
– Saskatoon (Sask), Mendel Art Gallery, competition #9091
– Winnipeg (Man), hôtel de ville, concours #8985 8986 8987
Robinson, Joseph, orfèvre can, 1842-1880 #2649
Robinson, Percy James, artiste can, 1873-1953
– et le Groupe des Sept #1732
Robinson & Heinrichs, agence can d'architecture
– Toronto (Ont), habitations St. Lawrence #8078
Robitaille, André, architecte can, 1922-
– Québec (Qué), Chalet des employés civils #7939
Robitaille, Louis, orfèvre can, 1755-1822
– oeuvres, Detroit Institute of Arts (Detroit, Mich) #2691
Robson, Albert Henry, critique d'art et artiste can, 1882-1939 #7058

– et Arthur Lismer #6300
Robson, John, artiste can, XXe s. #4169
Roch, Ernst, artiste can, 1928-
– design typographique #932
– estampes #897
– et Design Collaborative Montreal Ltd.
 #878 882
Rochdale (Angleterre), Corporation Art
 Gallery
– expositions
 – *Exhibition of Canadian Art* (1926) #290
Roche Percée (Sask)
– pétroglyphes Assiniboines #3673
Rochester (NY), Rochester Memorial Art
 Gallery
– expositions
 – *Contemporary Canadian Painting and
  Sculpture* (1963) #455
Rochester (NY), Rochester Museum
– art inuit #4424
– art iroquois #3590
Rochette, Sylvie, sculpteure can, active 1979-
 #1626
Rocheuses (montagnes), (Canada)
– résidences estivales et lieux de
 villégiature, XXe s. #8524
– vues
 – Bell-Smith, Frederic Marlett #4666 4667
  4668
 – Brown, Annora #4933
 – Collings, Charles John #5132 5133 5135
  5136
 – fin XIXe s. #271 272 1839
 – Fraser, John Arthur #5510
 – Groupe des Sept #1861
 – Harris, Lawren Stewart #5732 5734
 – Hind, William George Richardson #5807
 – Knowles, Dorothy #6067
 – Leighton, Alfred Crocker #6225
 – MacDonald, J.E.H. #6370
 – Martin, Thomas Mower #6435 6438
 – Roper, Edward #7077
 – Warre, Henry James #7521
 – Warren, Mary Schaffer #7525
– vues photographiques
 – (années 1880-1890) #1874
 – Gleason, Herbert Wendell #5617
 – Harmon, Byron #5707
 – Warren, Mary Schaffer #7526
 – Weiss, Joe #7541
Rocheuses (montagnes), (EU)
– vues
 – Miller, Alfred Jacob #6536 6537
Rockburne, Dorothea, artiste can aux EU,
 1934- #7059 7060
Rockett, Beverly, photographe can, active
 1970 #993
Rockett, Paul, photographe can, 1919- #1036
Rockman, Arnold, artiste can, 1930-
– commentaire sur le hasard dans l'art
 #7061
– juré, *B.C. Artists Annual Exhibition,*
 Vancouver Art Gallery (Vancouver, CB),
 (1966) #1983
Rocky Mountain House (Alta)
– poste de traite des fourrures #8129
Rodchenko, Aleksandr Mihailovic, artiste
 russe, 1891-1956
– influence sur Lionel LeMoine FitzGerald
 #5450
Roden Bros., atelier d'orfèvrerie can
– (années 1890-1920) #2638
Rodier, Olivier, artiste can, actif 1842 #1301
Rodin, Auguste, sculpteur fr, 1840-1917

– influence sur Douglas Bentham #4686
Rodrik, Paul, artiste can, 1915-
– expositions de groupe
 – (1972) #5972
 – (1973) #5973
Roebuck (comté de Grenville, Ont)
– artefacts iroquois #3616
Rogers, Joseph S., photographe can, actif
 années 1860 #1211
Rogers, Otto Donald, artiste can, 1935- #7063
– entretien #7066
– expositions
 – (1973) #7062
 – (1977) #7064 7065
– expositions de groupe
 – (1967) #1916
 – (1975) #1926
 – (1977) #1933
Rogers, Robert, artiste can, 1944-
– estampes #1214
Rogerson, John, sculpteur et ébéniste can,
 1837-1925 #7067 7068
rois et souverains
– Louis XIV et Louis XV, portraits,
 Amérique du Nord #1598
Rojik, Michael, photographe can, actif 1980
– catalogue de photographies #1032
Rolland, Dominique, sculpteur can, 1954-
– utilisation de la pierre #1634
Rollin, Paul, sculpteur can, actif 1812-1830
 #6947
Rolph, Joseph Thomas, artiste can, 1831-1916
– aquarelles, Art Gallery of Cobourg
 (Cobourg, Ont) #3162
Rolph, Smith & Co., éditeur (Toronto, Ont)
– cartes de Noël #842 890
Roman Stone Company (Toronto, Ont)
– influence sur l'architecture canadienne
 (1903-années 1920) #7734
romantisme
– Canada
 – (années 1860) #230
 – XIXe s. #66
Rombout, Luke, conservateur can, 1933-
– et la Banque d'oeuvres d'art #3276
– et Miller Gore Brittain #4917
Rome (Italie)
– expansion urbaine #7902
Rome (Italie), cathédrale
 Saint-Pierre-de-Rome
– baldaquin, influence sur baldaquin, église
 de Neuville (Qué) #8826
Rome (Italie), Collegio di Propaganda Fide
– art amérindien #3396
Rome (Italie), Free School of Art
– Grier, Edmund Wyly, élève #5660
Romney, George, artiste brit, 1734-1802
– peinture, mort de Wolfe #220
Romses, Kwan & Associates, agence can
 d'architecture
– Vancouver (CB), Chinese Cultural Centre,
 concours #9144
Ronald, William S., artiste can, 1926- #7069
 7071 7072 7074 7075 7076
– commentaire sur séjour à New York
 (années 1960) #460
– et peinture torontoise (années 1960) #1753
 1760
– expositions
 – (1975) #7073
– expositions de groupe
 – (1958) #431
– murale, centre national des arts (Ottawa,
 Ont) #9108

– murale, presbytère anglican, Ward's Island
 (Toronto, Ont) #7070
Roper, Edward, artiste brit au Canada,
 1857-1891 #7077
– soutien des sociétés ferroviaires
 canadiennes #3281
Rosa, Salvator, artiste it, 1615-1673
– *Mercury Putting Argus to Sleep*, influence
 sur Joseph Légaré #1373
Roscoe, Stanley M., architecte can, 1921-
– Hamilton (Ont), hôtel de ville et Civic
 Square #8988
Rose, Jurgen, artiste can, ca 1937-
– décors #472
Rose, Peter, architecte can, 1943-
– North Hatley (Qué), maison Bradley #7886
– théories sur l'architecture #7746
Rose, T.Bert, éducateur can, actif années
 1970
– Broughton Island (TNO), habitation, dôme
 en bois et polyéthylène #8734
Rose Blanche Point (TN), phare #9523
Rosebud Creek (Alta)
– vues photographiques
 – Biggs, Hugh Beynon #4728
Rosenberg, Fred, photographe can, actif
 années 1970
– catalogue de photographies #997 998 999
Rosenberg, Gloria, marchande can d'oeuvres
 d'art, 1926-
– collection, courtepointes #2808
Rosenberg, Tanya
– *voir* Marshall (Mars), Tanya
Rosenblatt, Joe, artiste can, 1933-
– expositions de groupe
 – (1978) #649
Rosenfield, Ethel, sculpteure can, 1910-
 #7078
Rosengarten, Morton, sculpteur can, 1933-
– sculptures d'argile (années 1960) #743
Ross, Charles, artiste amér, 1937-
– commentaire sur la perception visuelle
 #525
Ross, David, céramiciste can, 1925-1974
– et Hansen-Ross Pottery (Fort Qu'Appelle,
 Sask) #2389
Ross, Frederick Joseph (Fred), artiste can,
 1927- #1121 1173 1184
– entretien #7079
– et réalisme #110
– portraits #715
– réflexion sur l'art de Saint-Jean (NB) #1188
Ross, Richard Bartlett (Rick), sculpteur can,
 1940-
– constructions en matériaux bruts (années
 1970) #2065
Ross, Rosie, artiste can, active 1964 #4121
Ross, Sir John, artiste et officier de la marine
 brit au Canada, 1777-1856
– expédition dans l'Arctique #278
Ross & Macdonald, agence can
 d'architecture
– Edmonton (Alta), Hotel Macdonald #9270
– magasin Eaton #9365
– Montréal (Qué)
 – Appartements Château #8558
 – Architects Building #9312
 – hôtel Mont-Royal #9276
– Québec (Qué), maison Price #9311
– Toronto (Ont)
 – Banque Royale #9165
 – Central Technical School #9434
 – gare Union #9531 9536
 – magasin Eaton #9368

– Royal York Hotel #9280 9281
– Winnipeg (Man), Fort Garry Hotel #9268
Ross & Macfarlane, agence can d'architecture
– Ottawa (Ont), gare centrale et Château Laurier #9264 9528
Roth, Evelyn, artiste can, 1936- #675
– expositions de groupe
  – (1980) #698
– ouvrages en fibres textiles #2775
Roth, Max W., architecte can, 1913-
– Montréal (Qué), Temple Emmanu-El #8840
Rother/Bland/Trudeau, agence can d'architecture
– Ottawa (Ont), hôtel de ville #7679 8984
– Port-Cartier (Qué) #8184
Rothko, Mark, artiste amér, 1903-1970
– influence sur Claude Tousignant #7401
– influence sur Jean Albert McEwen #6471
– influence sur peinture montréalaise (Qué) #1425
Rothmans, compagnie can de tabac
– collection, sculpture Inuit #4257
– protecteurs des arts (années 1970) #3275
Rothschild, Hanni, sculpteure can, 1921- #7080
Rotterdam (Pays-Bas), musée Boymans Van Beuningen
– expositions
  – Michael Snow (1979) #7258
Rouault, Georges, artiste fr, 1871-1958
– 1964, exposition inaugurale, Musée d'art contemporain (Montréal, Qué) #3094
– Bates, Maxwell Bennett, comparaison #4623
– influence sur Lillian Freiman #5517
Rouer, Louis, Sieur de Villeray, fonctionnaire can, 1629-1700
– résidence, maison Fornel (Québec, Qué) #7953
Rougier, Roger, fabricants de meubles can, actif années 1970
– mobilier de bureau #7081
Rounthwaite & Associates, agence can d'architecture
– Saskatoon (Sask), Mendel Art Gallery, concours #9091
Rounthwaite & Fairfield, agence can d'architecture
– Stratford (Ont), Stratford Festival Theatre #7679
Rousseau, Albert, artiste can, 1908- #1393 7082 7083
Rousseau, Denis, artiste can, 1951- #7084
– expositions de groupe
  – (1979) #674
Rousseau, François, architecte can, actif 1964-
– et Fusion des arts (Montréal, Qué) #1482
Rousseau, Henri, artiste fr, 1844-1910
– Davies, Thomas, comparaison #5272
– influence sur Carol Fraser #5508
– influence sur Homer Ransford Watson #7531
Rousseau, Richard, artiste can, 1946-
– membre du Centre communautaire catholique Tour de David (Saint-Basile-le-Grand, Qué) #1510
Rousseau-Vermette, Mariette, artiste can (tapisserie), 1926- #7085
– expositions, critiques #2771
– expositions de groupe
  – (1978) #2772
  – (1981) #2776

Roussel, Claude, artiste can, 1930- #7088
– entretien #7087
– estampes #1185
– expositions
  – (1977) #7089
– lauréat, médaille des arts connexes de l'Institut royal d'architecture du Canada (1963) #7086
– réflexion sur l'art acadien (années 1960) #1181
Roussil, Robert, sculpteur can, 1925- #1502 7090 7098
– entretien #3269 7093 7094 7097
– expositions
  – (1965) #7092
  – (1971) #7095
– expositions de groupe
  – (1977) #1622
– fondateur, centre artistique, Tourette-sur-Loup (France) #7091
– influence sur Pierre Rolland Dinel #5293
– réflexion sur son oeuvre #7096
Rouville, Hertel de, famille can, XVIIIe-XIXe s.
– portraits #1345
Roux & Morin, agence can d'architecture
– Montréal (Qué), Centre marial des pères Monfortains #8840
Rouyn (Qué), Comité des expositions artistiques de Rouyn-Noranda
– expositions
  – De la figuration à la non-figuration dans l'art québécois (1977) #1461
  – Métiers d'art Ontario-Québec, 1979/1980/Quebec-Ontario Crafts, 1979/1980 (1980) #2138
Rowley, Frances Elswood Richards, artiste can, 1852-1934
– Wilde, Oscar, commentaire #238
Roy, Jean-Marie, architecte can, 1925-
– Québec (Qué), Campus intercommunautaire de Cap-Rouge #9421
Roy, LeMoyne & Gordon Edwards, agence can d'architecture
– Charlottetown (IPE), Confederation Centre, concours #9088
Roy, Mario, artiste can, 1953- #7099
Roy, Phillippe, artiste can, 1899-
– sculptures sur bois, collection Nettie Sharpe #1607
Roy, Ronald Hamilton (Ron), céramiciste can, 1935-
– expositions de groupe
  – (1968) #2382
Roy-Audy, Jean-Baptiste, artiste can, 1778-1848 #1336 7100 7102 7103
– (1959) #219
– L'éducation de la Vierge et Saint-Joseph et l'Enfant-Jésus #7101
– portrait, membre de la famille Hertel de Rouville #1345
Royal, Frank, photographe can, actif années 1960-
– catalogue de photographies #991
Royal Architectural Institute of Canada. Journal, périodique can #7654
Royal Canadian Aerial Theatre (RCAT) (Vancouver, CB)
– ballons et cerfs-volants, sculpture #2058
Royal Canadian Institute
– (1884-1888), division de la photographie #975
Royal Commission on Education in Ontario

– voir Ontario. Royal Commission on Education in Ontario
Royal Engineers
– Colombie-Britannique, architecture et urbanisme #8150
– St. John's (TN), Commissariat House #8538
Royal Institute of British Architects (RIBA)
– (années 1960), sondage, profession d'architecte #8307
– dessin d'architecture, début XXe s. #8241
– et Institut royal d'architecture du Canada (années 1920) #8244
– Royal Gold Medal
  – Darling, Frank (1915) #8349 8350
  – Morris, Robert Schofield (1958) #8389
royauté
– voir rois et souverains
Royle, Stanley, artiste can, 1886-1961
– réflexion sur son oeuvre #7104
Roza, Gustavo da, architecte can, 1933-
– Winnipeg (Man)
  – Winnipeg Art Gallery #9111 9117
  – Winnipeg Art Gallery, concours #9102
Rozaire, Arthur Dominique, artiste can, 1879-1922 #1382
Rozynska, Wanda, céramiciste can, 1929- #2232
Ruben, David
– voir Piqtoukun, David Ruben
Rubin, Mark, photographe can, actif 1973
– expositions de groupe
  – (1973) #1002
Rudolph, Paul Marvin, architecte amér, 1918-
– Niagara Falls (Ont), Earl W. Brydges Public Library #9050
Ruelland, Ludger, artiste can, 1827-1896
– expositions de groupe
  – (1959) #219
ruelles
– voir rues
rues
– imagerie de l'autoroute, Michael J. Markham #6417
rues . Canada
– (années 1960) #8231
– Halifax (NE), rue Granville #7817
– noms de rues
  – London (Ont) #8007
  – Toronto (Ont) #8070
– Ontario, XIXe s. #8006 8024
– Toronto (Ont)
  – fin XIXe s. #8064
  – XIXe s.-années 1930 #8076
Rugh, Herbert Bell, architecte amér, 1888-1924
– Winnipeg (Man), habitations #8493 8683
Ruhman, Walter, artiste can, 1899- #7105
– expositions
  – (1959) #7106
Rulofson, William Herman, photographe can, 1826-1878 #7107
– portraits photographiques #1171
Rumball, Alma, artiste can, 1902-
– expositions
  – (1978) #7108
Rungius, Carl Clemens Moritz, artiste can, 1869-1959
– influence sur George E. McLean #6501
– Lansdowne, James Fenwick, comparaison #6165
Ruskay, John, photographe can, actif années 1970-

– catalogue de photographies #991
Ruskin, John, critique brit, 1819-1900
– et Emily Mary Bibbens Warren #7524
– influence sur Frederic William
  Cumberland #9475
Russell, Charles Marion, artiste amér,
  1863-1926
– influence sur Gerald Tailfeathers #7313
Russell, Edward John, artiste can, 1832-1906
  #7110 7111
Russell, George Horne, artiste can,
  1861-1933
– expositions de groupe
  – (1978) #133
– relation entre photographie et peinture
  #245
Russell, Gyrth, artiste can, 1892-1970
– eaux-fortes #799
Russell, John Hamilton Gordon, architecte
  can, 1863-1946
– Regina (Sask), War Memorial Museum,
  concours #9073
– Winnipeg (Man), Marlborough Hotel
  #9277
Russell, John Wentworth, artiste can,
  1879-1959 #7109
– membre du Canadian Art Club #193
Russes au Canada
– Alberta, bâtiments en bois rond #8136
Russo, Silvio, artiste can, 1939- #2487
Ryan, Alonso, artiste can, né ca 1868
– La Caricature politique #943
Ryan, Cyril, photographe can, 1946-
– expositions, critiques #1018
Ryan, Frederick William, artiste can, 1907-
  #1164
Ryan, Terrence, artiste can, 1931-
– commentaire sur l'introduction du dessin
  au crayon auprès des Inuit, île de Baffin
  (TNO) #4194
– et Peter Pitseolak #6880 6881
Ryerson, Adolphus Egerton, éducateur can,
  1803-1882
– et Educational Museum of Upper Canada
  (Toronto, Ont) #3150 3155
– et Royal Ontario Museum (Toronto, Ont)
  #3152

S

Saarniit, Joann-Woldemar (John), artiste can,
  1909- #7112
sabliers . Canada
– XVIIe-XVIIIe s. #2914
Sackville (NB), Mount Allison University
– Burke, Rebecca, professeure #717
– enseignement de l'art
  – (1893-1977) #3013
  – (années 1960-1970), importance du
    réalisme #1130
– Harris, Lawren Phillips, directeur #5709
– Harris, Lawren Phillips, professeur #5713
– Pulford, Edward Berwyn, professeur #6945
– Savage, Roger, élève #7136
Sackville (NB), Mount Allison University.
  Owens Art Gallery
– art canadien #3068
– et Alex Colville #5151
– expositions
  – An Exhibition of Canadian Gameboards of
    the 19th & 20th Centuries from Ontario,

Quebec & Nova Scotia (1981) #2597
– André Fauteux (1976) #5413
– Art at Mount Allison...a History (1977)
  #3013
– Claude Breeze (1978) #4911
– Claude Tousignant (1974) #7401
– David Bolduc: Recent Work (1980) #4775
– Douglas Bentham "Enclosures and Opens"
  1975/76 (1977) #4683
– Drawings and Pastels c. 1930-1967 by
  Miller Gore Brittain (1969) #4917
– Drawings by Jack Weldon Humphrey: A
  Travelling Exhibition Organized by the
  Beaverbrook Art Gallery, Fredericton, New
  Brunswick, Canada, 1977-1979 (1978)
  #5871
– Esther Warkov (1971) #7517
– Fritz Brandtner 1896-1969: A Retrospective
  Exhibition (1971) #4903
– Investigations: Ian Carr-Harris, John Greer,
  N.E. Thing Co., Ltd. (1974) #574
– J.Frederic McCulloch 1905-1932: Works on
  Paper (1979) #6463
– John Fox: 10 New Paintings (1981) #5495
– John Hammond, R.C.A., 1843-1939:
  Retrospective Exhibition (1967) #5699
– Looking South (1978) #4278
– Miller Brittain - Painter (1981) #4922
– Norman White (1976) #7554
– Roger Savage (1981) #7135
– The Carmen Lamanna Gallery at the Owens
  Art Gallery (1975) #594
– The Electric Show (1973) #1800
– The Murray and Marguerite Vaughan Inuit
  Print Collection/Collection d'estampes inuit
  (1983) #4498
– The Society of Canadian Painter-Etchers
  and Engravers in Retrospect/La Société des
  peintres-graveurs canadiens: vue
  rétrospective (1982) #836
– William Perehudoff: Ten Years,
  1970-1980/William Perehudoff: une
  décennie, 1970-1980 (1982) #6837
– Saxe, Henry, commentaire sur ses oeuvres
  en exposition (1976) #7147
Sackville (NB), Owens Art Gallery
– voir Sackville (NB), Mount Allison
  University. Owens Art Gallery
Sackville (NB), Owens College of Fine Arts
– enseignement de l'artisanat (1904) #2979
Sackville (NB), Women's Academy #3013
sacs . Pieds-Noirs
– sacs à médecine #3754
– sacs à pipes #3665
sacs . Saulteux #3699
Sadowska, Krystyna, artiste can, 1912- #7113
– céramiques #2380
– expositions
  – (1977) #7115
Sadowski, Konrad Jagin, céramiciste can,
  1902-1960 #2380 7113 7114
Sadowski, Krystyna
– voir Sadowska, Krystyna
Safdie, Moshe, architecte can, 1938- #8405
– Montréal (Qué), Habitat 67 #7694 8574
  8575 8577 8578 8580 8583 8584 8585 8590
  9215
– réflexion sur l'architecture domestique
  #8406
– réflexion sur son oeuvre architecturale
  #8403 8404
Sagard, Gabriel, auteur fr, ca 1614-ca 1636
– description des Amérindiens, thème de
  l'homme sans tête #281

Sager, Peter, sculpteur can, 1920- #7116
Sagittaires (Montréal, Qué) #1393
Saguenay (Qué)
– vues
  – Gagnon, René #5551
  – Huot, Charles Edouard #5877
– vues photographiques
  – Bull, W. #4956
Saguenay-Lac-Saint-Jean (Qué)
– art
  – (années 1970) #1538 1540 1546 1547 1549
  – XXe s. #1551
– églises (années 1960) #1435
– photographie, XIXe-XXe s. #1283
Saila, Pauta, artiste can, 1916- #4460
Saint
– voir aussi St.
Saint-Alphonse, soeur
– voir Pelletier, Marie-Louise Emilie (soeur
  Saint-Alphonse)
Saint-Augustin-de-Desmaures (Qué), église
  Saint-Augustin-de-Desmaures
– architecture et intérieur #8889
Saint-Barthélemi (Qué), église
  Saint-Barthélemi
– chaire, Amable Gauthier #241 242
Saint-Basile-le-Grand (Qué), Centre
  communautaire catholique Tour de David
– art (années 1970) #1510
Saint-Boniface (Man), cathédrale de
  Saint-Boniface
– architecture #8094
Saint-Boniface (Man), Centre culturel
  franco-manitobain
– expositions
  – Hubert Garnier: la sculpture architecturale
    (1976) #5556
  – Objets faits à la main au Manitoba français
    (1976) #2275
  – Pauline Morier: images et arabesques (1975)
    #6608
  – Réal Bérard (1975) #4692
Saint-Boniface (Man), chapelle
  Saint-Louis-le-roi
– architecture, Libling, Michener &
  Associates #8765
Saint-Boniface (Man), église du
  Précieux-Sang
– architecture
  – Gaboury, Etienne J. #8091
  – Gaboury, Etienne J.; Denis Lussier,
    architecte associé #8908
Saint-Charles, Joseph A., artiste can,
  1868-1956 #302 1240 1315 7117
– et Marc-Aurèle de Foy Suzor-Coté #7296
Saint-Denis (Qué)
– poterie
  – (1785-1888) #2343
  – XVIIIe-XIXe s. #2299 2321
Saint-Denis-sur-Richelieu (Qué)
– églises #8811
Saint-Etienne de Lauzon (Qué), Moulin des
  arts
– Rousseau, Albert, atelier d'artistes #7082
  7083
Saint-Eugène (Qué), église
  Saint-Eugène-de-Grantham
– architecture et art #8873
Saint Gaudens, Augustus, artiste amér,
  1848-1907
– et Alexander Phimister Proctor #6943
– influence sur Robert Tait McKenzie #6487
Saint-Germain, Léon, carrossier can, actif
  1842 #1301

Saint-Henri (Qué), église Saint-Henri
– sculptures, Louis Jobin #5967
Saint-Hilaire (Qué)
– vues
  – Leduc, Ozias #6199 6206 6209
Saint-Hilaire (Qué), Centre artisanal de
  Saint-Hilaire
– expositions, critiques
  – (1941) #2182
Saint-Hilaire (Qué), manoir Campbell
– murales, Jordi Bonet #4787
Saint-Jean, Michel, photographe can, 1937-
  #1562
– catalogue de photographies #991 997 999
Saint-Jean (NB)
– architecture #7807
  – XVIIIe-XIXe s. #7808
– architecture domestique (années 1830)
  #2490
– art
  – (années 1940) #1170
  – (années 1950) #1119 1172
  – (années 1960) #4994
  – XXe s. #1188
– mobilier (avant 1900) #2491
– peinture
  – (années 1950) #1173
  – XXe s. #1184
– portrait photographique, XIXe s. #1171
– tours Martello #8416
– vues
  – Comingo, Joseph #5161
  – Humphrey, Jack Weldon #5867
  – Smith, George Neilson #7221
Saint-Jean (NB), église en pierre
– architecture, Lloyd Johnson #8778
Saint-Jean (NB), Gallery Theatre
– expositions, et Robert Percival #6833
Saint-Jean (NB), General Public Hospital
– architecture, Irving K. Pond #9020
Saint-Jean (NB), Gesner's Museum
– (1842-1846) #3065
Saint-Jean (NB), Hôpital général de
  Saint-Jean
– architecture, Allward & Gillies; Mott &
  Myles #9031
– murales (dessins), Miller Gore Brittain
  #4916
Saint-Jean (NB), hôtel de ville/City Hall
– sculpture, Claude Roussel #7088
Saint-Jean (NB), maison Gregory
– architecture et intérieur #8545
Saint-Jean (NB), Mechanics' Institute
  Museum
– (1846-1890) #3065
Saint-Jean (NB), Musée du
  Nouveau-Brunswick/New Brunswick
  Museum
– (1842-1945) #3065
– (années 1940) #1170
– (années 1960) #1122
– art, Micmacs #3634
– assiettes en céramique, XIXe s. #2354
– brassards, Micmacs #3572
– costume féminin, XIXe s. #2875
– et John Clarence Webster #3073
– et peinture à Saint-Jean (NB), (années
  1950) #1173
– exposition de verre moulé canadien (1969)
  #2407
– expositions
  – Albert Franck (1899-1973) in Retrospect: A
    Small Selection from the Artist's Collection
    (1973) #5500

  – Annie D. Savage: Drawings and
    Watercolours (1975) #7129
  – Arctic Values '65/Valeurs septentrionales
    '65 (1965) #4195
  – Arthur F. McKay (1980) #6478
  – Exhibition of Portraits of James Henry
    Holman, 1821-1891 (1959) #5821
  – Fritz Brandtner 1896-1969: A Retrospective
    Exhibition (1971) #4903
  – George Rackus: Anodized Aluminum Works
    & Prints (1973) #6953
  – Gordon Rayner Retrospective (1979) #6966
  – Miller Brittain - Painter (1981) #4922
  – New Brunswick Landscape Artists of the
    19th Century (1969) #1180
  – Seven Plus: A Selection of Works by the
    Group of Seven (1976) #1778
  – The Electric Show (1973) #1800
  – The Murray and Marguerite Vaughan Inuit
    Print Collection/Collection d'estampes inuit
    (1982) #4498
  – The New Brunswick Landscape Print:
    1760-1880 (1980) #1189
  – The Saidye and Samuel Bronfman
    Collection of Canadian Art/La collection
    Saidye et Samuel Bronfman (1967) #3087
  – Watercolour Painters from
    Saskatchewan/Aquarellistes de la
    Saskatchewan (1971) #1920
– expositions, critiques
  – McLaughlin, Agnes (1980) #6500
  – Percival, Robert (1979) #6835
– famille Graham, sculptures sur bois #1187
– mobilier #2484
– mobilier, Nouveau-Brunswick,
  XVIIIe-XIXe s. #2504
– orfèvrerie, Nouveau-Brunswick #2649
– Rogerson, John, oeuvres #7068
– uniformes militaires #2900
– Webster, John Clarence, collection
  Canadiana #3209
Saint-Jean (NB), Owen Art Gallery
– expositions
  – Art Loan Exhibition (1884) #170
Saint-Jean (NB), Provincial Exhibition
– expositions
  – Catalogue of St. John Art Club Loan
    Exhibition: Paintings by Canadian
    Artists,(1920) #286
Saint-Jean (NB), Saint John Vocational
  School
– Campbell, Ted, professeur #1188
– enseignement de l'art (années 1940) #1170
Saint-Jean (NB), School of Arts
– Foulis, Robert, directeur #258 259
Saint-Jean-Eudes
– dans l'art québécois, XVIIe s. #1365
Saint-Jean-Port-Joli (Qué)
– arts décoratifs #2209
  – (années 1930) #2174
  – XXe s. #2194
– sculpture sur bois #1597 1608 4883
Saint-Jean-Port-Joli (Qué), église de
  Saint-Jean-Port-Joli #2194
– architecture et intérieur #8871
Saint-Jean-Port-Joli (Qué), église
  Saint-Jean-Baptiste
– architecture et intérieur #8812
Saint-Jean-Port-Joli (Qué), La Vastringue
– Bourgault, Pier, directeur #4889
Saint-Jean-Port-Joli (Qué), manoir
  d'Haberville #2194
Saint-Jérôme (Qué), église de Saint-Jérôme
– peintures, Charles Edouard Huot #5878

  5884
Saint-Joachim (Qué), château Bellevue
– architecture #8622
Saint-Joachim (Qué), Ecole des arts et
  métiers de Saint-Joachim #1233 1327 1334
  1335 1363 2181 2967 2991 2992 3007 3008
– architecture domestique #8505
– fabrication de meubles #2464
– Leblond (dit Latour), Jacques, professeur
  #234 235
Saint-Joachim (Qué), église de Saint-Joachim
– architecture #7953
– sculpture, François Baillairgé #4589
Saint John Art Club (Saint-Jean, NB)
– (années 1940) #1170
– et Elizabeth Russell Holt #1173
– expositions
  – (1920) #286
Saint John Glass Co., fabricants de verre
  (Saint-Jean, NB) #2400
Saint John Telegraph, journal can
– illustrations, Edward John Russell #7110
Saint-Joseph, mère de, religieuse can, m.
  1652
– portrait, Marie de l'Incarnation #1333
Saint-Joseph (NB), Université Saint-Joseph
– Beau, Henri, La dispersion des Acadiens
  (1900) #4639
Saint-Laurent (fleuve), (Ont et Qué)
– résidences estivales et lieux de
  villégiature, XXe s. #8524
– vues
  – Browne, Joseph Archibald #4939
  – Jackson, A.Y. #5919
  – Smith, William St. Thomas #7236
  – XIXe s. #282
Saint-Laurent (Qué), Collège de
  Saint-Laurent. Chapelle
– architecture #8815
Saint-Laurent (Qué), Collège de
  Saint-Laurent. Galerie Nova et Vetera
– collection #3089
– expositions
  – Images taillées du Québec (1966) #3090
Saint-Laurent (Qué), Collège de
  Saint-Laurent. Musée d'art #3123
Saint-Laurent (Qué), Galerie Nova et Vetera
– voir Saint-Laurent (Qué), Collège de
  Saint-Laurent. Galerie Nova et Vetera
Saint-Marc-des-Carrières (Qué)
– sculpture en pierre (1932) #1629
Saint-Martin, Fernande, critique d'art et
  conservatrice can, 1927-
– concept de l'espace pictural #4816
– réflexion sur l'art québécois (années
  1940-1970) #1521
Saint-Mathias-de-Rouville (Qué), église de
  Saint-Mathias-de-Rouville
– architecture et intérieur #8878
Saint-Mathieu (Qué), salle du couvent de
  Saint-Mathieu
– expositions
  – Le cercle de promotion humaine présente
    Yvon Héroux, peintre figuratif de
    St-Mathieu (1972) #5790
Saint-Nicolas (Qué), église Saint-Nicolas
– architecture, André Gilbert #8766
Saint-Paul, Paul
– voir Lambert (dit Saint-Paul), Paul
Saint-Pierre, Georges, artiste can, 1927-
– entretien #1527
– expositions
  – (1975) #7118
Saint-Pierre (île d'Orléans, Qué)

– art et architecture #1252
– églises #8875
Saint-Rémi-de-Napierville (Qué)
– calvaire #1569
Saint-Rémi-de-Napierville (Qué), cimetière
– croix funéraires en fer #2716
Saint-Roch-de-l'Achigan (Qué)
– architecture #7854
Saint-Romuald (Qué), Ecole de sculpture
– et Lauréat Vallière #7455
Saint-Sauveur, André Grasset de, homme
d'Etat can, 1720-1794
– et histoire de Montréal (Qué) #7899
Saint-Sauveur (Qué), église de Saint-Sauveur
– peintures, Charles Edouard Huot #5878
5884
Saint-Thomas de Montmagny (Qué), maison
Bernatchez
– architecture et intérieur #8630
Saint-Vallier, Jean-Baptiste de la Croix de
Chevrières de, évêque can, 1653-1727
– et Palais épiscopal, Québec (Qué) #8787
– et utilisation de la pierre dans
l'architecture québécoise #7859
Saint-Vincent-de-Paul (Qué), Ecole de
Saint-Vincent-de-Paul #5108
sainte Anne
– dans l'art #1230 1323
– Sainte-Anne-de-Beaupré (Qué), basilique
Sainte-Anne #1370 8859 8860 8865 8866
– offrandes votives #1292
Sainte-Anne-de-Beaupré (Qué)
– églises #8863 8877
Sainte Anne de Beaupré (Qué), basilique
Sainte-Anne
– architecture #8824 8863 8877
– ex-voto #1370
– intérieur #1601 1602
– mosaïques
– Gaudin, Jean, et August Labouret #8859
8860
– Gaudin, Jean, et Walter del Mistro #8865
8866
– Mistro, Walter del #6572 6573
– peinture #1321
Sainte-Anne-de-Beaupré (Qué), Musée de
l'Historial de Sainte-Anne-de-Beaupré
– Boivin, Joseph, Ex-voto de Dorval #4771
Sainte-Anne-de-Bellevue (Qué), église
– architecture, Josué Boisberthelot de
Beaucours #8336
Sainte-Anne-de-la-Pocatière (Qué)
– églises #8882
Sainte-Anne-de-la-Pocatière (Qué), musée
François Pilote
– expositions
– De la figuration à la non-figuration dans
l'art québécois (1978) #1461
sainte Famille
– Jobin, Louis #5968
Sainte-Foy (Qué), église
Saint-Louis-de-France
– architecture, Blatter, Caron & Côté #8841
Sainte-Foy (Qué), maison Falardeau
– architecture #8627
Sainte-Foy (Qué), maison Parent
– architecture #8627
Sainte-Foy (Qué), maison Routhier
– architecture #8627
Sainte-Louise (Qué)
– vues, A.Y. Jackson #5921
Sainte-Marie-de-Beauce (Qué), église de
Sainte-Marie-de-Beauce
– mère Marie Le Maire des Anges, Madone

druidique de la Nouvelle-France #1328
Sainte-Rose (Qué)
– vues
– Hébert, Adrien #5763
Sainte-Scholastique (Qué), seigneurie des
Sulpiciens
– architecture #1341
saints dans l'art
– Québec, XVIIe s. #1365
saisons dans l'art
– voir aussi hiver
– Riopelle, Jean-Paul #7018
Salem (Mass), Peabody Museum of Salem
– expositions
– The Art of Nunstins/L'art de Nunstins
(1981) #6934
Salish de l'intérieur
– architecture #3872
– jade #3331
Salish de la côte
– architecture #3872
– couvertures #3800
– culture #3851 3896
– peinture #3878
– pétroglyphes #3870
– sculpture #4046
Salish Weavers' Guild
– (années 1970) #4147
Salishiens
– architecture #3807
– art (années 1970) #4145
– costume #4013
– couvertures #3469 3790 3818 3830
– culture #3764
– jade #3331
– photographies
– Curtis, Edward Sheriff #3399
– Stone, Sir John Benjamin #3717
– poterie #3841
– rites et cérémonies #3838
– tissage #3898 3963 4018 4044 4147
– (années 1960) #3941
– XXe s. #3964
– tissage et vannerie #4027
– vannerie #3777 3801 3876 3991
salles de cinéma Loew
– cinémas, Canada et Etats-Unis (années
1910-1930) #9122 9123
Sallirmiuts
– artefacts #4324
Sallows, R.R., photographe can, actif 1909
#7119
Salon des métiers d'art du Québec
– expositions, critiques
– (1970) #1490
Salteri, Thomas A., photographe can, actif
années 1850-1870 #1211
Saltmarche, Kenneth Charles, artiste can,
1920-
– expositions de groupe
– (1965) #473
Samson, Olivier, sculpteur can, ca 1830-ca
1900
– intérieur, église Saint-François-de-Sales (île
d'Orléans, Qué) #8796
Samuel, Sigmund, collectionneur can,
1867-1962
– collection Canadiana et Americana, Royal
Ontario Museum (Toronto, Ont) #247 3135
3140
San Francisco (Calif), California School of
Design
– Carr, Emily, élève #5045
San Francisco (Calif), California School of

Fine Arts
– Smith, Gordon Appelbe, élève #7225
San Francisco (Calif), Embarcadero Plaza
– fontaine, Armand Vaillancourt #7451
San Francisco (Calif), Golden Gate
International Exposition (1939)
– expositions
– Aboriginal Cultures of the Western
Hemisphere (1940) #3336
– Pacific Cultures (1939) #3854
San Francisco (Calif), Images of the North
– expositions
– George Arluk: The Song in the Stone (1979)
#4547
San Francisco (Calif), Mount Zion Hospital
– architecture #9026
San Francisco (Calif), San Francisco Art
Institute
– Hammock, Virgil, élève #5696
San Francisco (Calif), San Francisco Museum
of Modern Art
– expositions
– James Bay Project - A River Drowned by
Water/Projet de la baie James - une rivière
qui se noie (1981) #1566
San Miguel de Allende (Mexique), San
Miguel de Allende Instituto
– Onley, Toni, élève #6740
– Woolnough, Hilda Mary, élève #7616
Sanavik Cooperative (Baker Lake, TNO)
– arts graphiques #4480
– (1969-1973) #4481
– (1970-) #4472
Sandby, Paul, artiste brit, 1725-1809
– influence sur George Heriot #5786 5787
5788
– influence sur James Pattison Cockburn
#5125
– influence sur Thomas Davies #5272
– professeur de James Pattison Cockburn
#5126
Sandham, J.Henry, artiste can, 1842-1910
#178
– expositions
– (1911) #7120
– (1976) #7121
– relation entre photographie et peinture
#245
Sandwich (Ont), Banwell House
– architecture #7685
Sangudo (Alta)
– art (années 1940) #1943
Santa Ana (Calif), Charles W. Bowers
Memorial Museum
– expositions
– Indian Basketry of Western North America
from the Collection of the Bowers Museum,
Santa Ana, California (1974) #3991
Santa Barbara (Calif), University of
California. Art Galleries
– expositions
– Indian Art of the Northern Plains (1974)
#3730
– The New Art of Vancouver (1969) #2039
Santa Cruz (Calif), University of California
– architecture #9464
Santa Fe (NM), Institute of American Indian
Arts
– peinture (années 1970) #3462
Santa Fe (NM), Museum of New Mexico
– art Inuit et art amérindien #3372
Santa Fe (NM), Wheelwright Museum of the
American Indian
– exposition

– *Lullabies from the Earth* (1980) #3485
São Paulo (Brésil), Biblioteca Publica
Municipal
– expositions
– *Artes graficas do Canada 1946* (1946) #806
São Paulo (Brésil), Bienal (1944)
– expositions, critiques
– *Exhibition of Contemporary Canadian
Painting/L'exposition de peinture
contemporaine du Canada* (1944) #371
São Paulo (Brésil), Bienal (1955)
– expositions
– *III Bienal* (1955) #411
– expositions, critiques
– Borduas, Paul-Émile #4843
São Paulo (Brésil), Bienal (1965)
– expositions
– *O Canadá em São Paulo/Canada at São
Paulo 1965/Le Canada à São Paulo 1965*
(1965) #469
São Paulo (Brésil), Bienal (1967)
– expositions
– *Jacques Hurtubise; Jack Bush: O Canadá em
São Paulo/Le Canada à São Paulo/Canada
at São Paulo* (1967) #491
São Paulo (Brésil), Bienal (1969)
– expositions
– *Greg Curnoe: Canada* (1969) #5227
– *N.E. Thing Co. Ltd./La compagnie N.E.
Thing* (1969) #6675
– *Robert Murray* (1969) #6670
São Paulo (Brésil), Museu de arte moderna
de São Paulo
– expositions
– *III Bienal* (1955) #411
Sapp, Allen, artiste can, 1929- #4125 4136
4161 7123 7124 7126
– autobiographie #7125
– expositions
– (1969) #7122
– influence sur Michael Lonechild #6322
Sarasota (Fla), Ringling Museum of Art
– expositions
– *49th Parallels: New Canadian Art* (1971)
#98
– *Oscar Cahén: First American Retrospective
Exhibition* (1968) #4986
Sarcis
– costume #3739
– culture (années 1930) #3671
– ours, motif #3746
– photographies
– Curtis, Edward Sheriff #3399
– poterie #3659
– tambours #3363
– tipis #3735
Sargent, John Singer, artiste amér, 1856-1925
– influence sur Addison Winchell Price
#6935
Sargent, Susan, artiste can, active années
1970-
– expositions de groupe
– (1977) #1933
Sarnia (Ont), école publique
– architecture, S.B. Coon & Son #9387
Sarnia (Ont), Sarnia Public Library and Art
Gallery
– art canadien #3179
– expositions
– *A Survey of Forty-five Years* (1977) #6658
– *A Terrible Beauty: The Art of Canada at
War* (1978) #1111
– *Alan C. Collier Retrospective* (1971) #5131
– *B.C. Currents* (1981) #2082

– *Beauté tragique: les deux conflits mondiaux
vus par des artistes canadiens* (1978) #1112
– *Centennial Exhibition of Quebec and
Ontario Contemporary Painters, 1967*
(1967) #484
– *David Milne: 1882-1953* (1967) #6558
– *Indications: Paintings, Collage, Drawings,
Prints, Sculpture* (1975) #7415
– *John Leonard: 10 Years: An Exhibition of
Paintings and Drawings* (1981) #6246
– *John Meredith: Fifteen Years* (1974) #6514
– *Louis de Niverville* (1978) #6709
– *Ontario Society of Artists: 100 Years* (1973)
#1678
– *The Ontario Community Collects: A Survey
of Canadian Painting from 1766 to the
Present* (1976) #120
– *York Wilson Retrospective (1927-1973)*
(1974) #7596
Sarnia Art Movement (Sarnia, Ont)
– soutien apporté au Groupe des Sept #1776
Sarqaq
– artefacts #4342
Sasabuchi, Shun, photographe can, 1951-
– catalogue de photographies #1032
Saskatchewan
– aquarelle (1905-1980) #1940
– architecture #8083
– (années 1880-1920) #8113
– (années 1960) #8112
– (années 1970) #8087
– habitations temporaires de colons, fin
XIXe-début XXe s. #8696
– art #1919 3187 3202
– (1945) #1909
– (1950-1964) #1910
– (années 1940) #350
– (années 1950) #1911 1912
– (années 1950-1970) #1884 1935
– (années 1960) #1916 1917
– (années 1970) #1860 1868 1926 1930 1932
1937
– XXe s. #145 536 1936
– art traditionnel, XXe s. #1931
– écoles (années 1920) #9389
– églises ukrainiennes #8912 8915
– gares #9544
– magasins (années 1940) #9372
– mobilier (1800-1921) #2587
– peinture
– (1883-1959) #1915
– (années 1930-1970) #1920
– (années 1950-1960) #476
– (années 1960) #1913
– peinture traditionnelle, XXe s. #1846 1927
– photographie
– (années 1930-1940) #985
– (années 1970) #1879
– poterie (années 1970) #2383 2385
– sculpture en céramique (années 1970)
#1864
– vues
– Fisher, Sanford #5445
– Henderson, James #5778
– Hind, William George Richardson #5807
– Hurley, Robert Newton #5885
– Kenderdine, Gus #6039
– Kerr, Illingworth Holey #6047
– Lonechild, Michael #6322
– Sheldon-Williams, Inglis #7195 7196
– Tinning, George Campbell #7378
– vues photographiques
– Hime, Humphrey Lloyd #5801 5802
5803 5804

– Horetzky, Charles George #5838
Saskatchewan Arts Board
– (1948-1978) #1938
– (1948-années 1960) #1914
– (années 1950) #1911 1912
– collection #1936
– expositions
– (1950-1964) #1910
– *Saskatchewan: Art and Artists* (1971)
#1919
Saskatchewan Association of Architects
#8312
Saskatoon (Sask)
– architecture #8114
– (1909) #8110
– art
– (1945) #1909
– (années 1960) #1848 1917
– (années 1960-1970) #1862
– (années 1970) #1932
– femmes artistes (années 1970) #1928
– galeries d'art (années 1960) #442
– sculpture (années 1960) #1853
Saskatoon (Sask), Banque de
Nouvelle-Ecosse
– expositions
– *The Bank of Nova Scotia Fine Art
Collection, Saskatoon, Saskatchewan, 1980*
(1980) #3245
Saskatoon (Sask), Flanagan Hotel
– architecture, Walter W. Lachance #9263
Saskatoon (Sask), Gallery One
– expositions
– *Arthur F. McKay* (1980) #6478
Saskatoon (Sask), magasin Eaton
– architecture, Ross & Macdonald; Sproatt &
Rolph, architectes-conseils #9365
Saskatoon (Sask), Mendel Art Gallery
– architecture, concours #9091
– expositions
– *A Retrospective Exhibition of the Works of
Leo Mol* (1975) #6579
– *An Exhibition of Paintings by James
Henderson, 1871-1951* (1969) #5779
– *Antique Canadian Glass from the John
McGowan Collection* (1976) #2424
– *Artisan '78: The First National Travelling
Exhibition of Contemporary Canadian
Crafts/Artisan '78: première exposition
nationale itinérante d'artisanat canadien
contemporain* (1979) #2134
– *Brian Wood: Photographic Works* (1979)
#7612
– *Canadian Painting in the Thirties* (1975)
#592
– *Carl Schaefer in Hanover* (1980) #7157
– *Certain Traditions: Recent British and
Canadian Art* (1978) #653
– *Changes: 11 Artists Working on the
Prairies* (1976) #1867
– *Christopher Pratt* (1970) #6910
– *David Craven: Recent Works* (1977) #5205
– *David Milne: The New York Years,
1903-1916* (1981) #6567
– *Dennis Burton Retrospective* (1978) #4961
– *Don McNamee* (1968) #6506
– *Douglas Bentham: Six Steel Sculptures
1978* (1979) #4685
– *Drawings and Pastels c. 1930-1967 by
Miller Gore Brittain* (1969) #4917
– *Drawings by Jack Weldon Humphrey: A
Travelling Exhibition Organized by the
Beaverbrook Art Gallery, Fredericton, New
Brunswick, Canada, 1977-1979* (1979)

– Midéwiwins #3492 3661
  – influence sur la peinture, XXe s. #4154
  – parchemins #3626
– mocassins #3554
– mythologie #4122
– paquetages #3699
– parchemins #3583
– peinture, XXe s. #4156
– peinture et sculpture (années 1970) #4133
– pétroglyphes #3568 3581 3591
– tambours #3363
– tapis #3585
– tatouage #3723
– vannerie #3547
Saunders, Leslie Gail, photographe can, 1895-1968
– expositions
  – (1970) #7128
Saunders & Ryrie, agence can d'architecture
– Toronto (Ont), Osgoode Hall #9002 9003
Sauvé, Paulette-Marie, artiste can, 1949-
– expositions de groupe
  – (1978) #2772
Savage, Anne Douglas, artiste can, 1897-1971 #7130 7131
– et peinture canadienne #18
– expositions
  – (1974) #7129
  – (1979) #7132
– expositions de groupe
  – (1977) #1278 1279
Savage, Harry, artiste can, 1938- #1856 7133
– expositions, critiques #1866
Savage, Roger, artiste can, 1941- #7134 7136
– estampes #1214
– expositions
  – (1979) #7135
Savard, Alphonse E., photographe can, 1864-1934
– expositions de groupe
  – (1976) #2012
Savoie, Maurice, céramiste can, 1930- #2395
– entretien #7137
Savoie, Robert, artiste can, 1939- #7138 7139
Savoie, Roméo Albert, artiste can, 1928-#7140
Savory, Albert, orfèvre brit, actif années 1830-1840
– pièce commémorative, service à thé en argent #2647
Savory, Joseph, orfèvre brit, actif années 1830-1840
– pièce commémorative, service à thé en argent #2647
Sawchuk, George, sculpteur can, 1927- #7143
– entretien #7141
– expositions
  – (1980) #7142
Sawyer, Joseph, architecte can, 1874-1965 #8407
Sawyer, Walter Michael, artiste can, 1943-
– entretien #7144
Sawyer, William, artiste can, 1820-1889
– expositions
  – (1978) #7145
– relation entre photographie et peinture #245
Saxe, Charles Jewett, architecte can, 1870-1943
– Montréal (Qué), palais de justice, annexe #9001
Saxe, Henry, artiste can, 1937- #1479 7146 7149
– entretien, Instrument Series #7147

– et Fusion des arts (Montréal, Qué) #1482
– expositions
  – (1976) #7148
– expositions de groupe
  – (1973) #557
  – (1976) #779
  – (1977) #782
  – (1978) #661
Saxe & Archibald, agence can d'architecture
– Montréal (Qué), architecture domestique #8493
Saxman Totem Park (Alaska)
– totems #3873
Scandinaves au Canada
– Alberta, bâtiments en bois rond #8136
– mobilier #2585
Scarborough (Ont), Albert Campbell Library
– architecture, Fairfield & DuBois #9047
Scarborough (Ont), North Bridlewood Junior Public School
– architecture, Howard Vincent Walker #9471
Scarborough (Ont), Scarborough Civic Centre
– architecture, Raymond Moriyama #8973
Scarborough (Ont), Scarborough College
– voir Scarborough (Ont), University of Toronto. Scarborough College
Scarborough (Ont), Stephen Leacock Educational Complex
– architecture, Abram & Ingleson #9476
Scarborough (Ont), University of Toronto. Scarborough College
– architecture, John Andrews Architects #8323
– architecture, Page & Steele; John Hamilton Andrews #9396 9462 9463 9464
– décoration intérieure (années 1960) #9402
scènes de plage dans l'art
– Alleyn, George Edmund #4512
– Peel, Paul, série After the Bath #6790 6794
scènes marines (estampes)
– voir aussi bateaux dans l'art
scènes marines (estampes). Canada
– Détroit de Nootka, Vancouver Island (CB), fin XVIIIe s. #2002
– XVIIIe-XIXe s. #812
scènes marines (peinture)
– voir aussi bateaux; bateaux dans l'art; scènes marines (estampes)
scènes marines (peinture). Canada #139
– (1600-1900) #225
– Adams, Loren D. #4501
– Bailly, Evern Earl #4595
– Barnsley, James Macdonald #4612
– Bolt, Ron #4779
– Gagen, Robert Ford #5530
– Gray, John Warren #5648 5649
– Law, Tony #6174
– Murphy, Rowley Walter #6665 6666
– offrandes votives faites à sainte Anne #1292
– Ottawa (Ont), Archives publiques du Canada. Collection William H. Coverdale #12
– peinture traditionnelle #965 966
– Redgrave, Felicity #1169
– Russell, Edward John #7110 7111
– Seconde Guerre mondiale #1106
– Smith, William St. Thomas #7236 7238
– vues, côte nord-ouest (1778-1793) #2017
– XVIIIe-XIXe s. #246
scènes rurales
– Climo, Lindee #5120

– Fortin, Marc-Aurèle #5474 5479 5481
– Gagnon, Clarence Alphonse #5548
– Krieghoff, Cornelius #241 242 6097 6100
– Massicotte, Edmond-Joseph, scènes de la campagne québécoise #6440
– Suzor-Coté, Marc-Aurèle de Foy #7299
– Watson, Homer Ransford #7529
– Wickson, Paul Giovanni #7573
scènes sportives
– voir aussi bateaux; chasse dans l'art; lutte
– (Ottawa, Ont), Archives publiques du Canada. Collection William H. Coverdale #12
– affiches canadiennes #910
– art canadien
  – (années 1970) #6676
  – XIXe s. #257
  – XVIIIe-XIXe s. #812
– art traditionnel canadien #965 966
– athletes
  – Danby, Ken #5252
  – McKenzie, Robert Tait #6482 6484 6485 6486
– John Marshall & Co., poterie, série illustrant sports canadiens #2306
– poterie et cartes de voeux canadiennes (années 1880) #2360
– Saskatoon (Sask), Mendel Art Gallery #3187
– Toronto (Ont), Metro Toronto Public Library. John Ross Robertson Historical Collection #3131
scénographie canadienne
– (années 1960) #472
– Kolisnyk, Peter Henry #6075
– Laufer, Murray Bernard #6173
– Montreal Theatre Ballet (années 1950) #1410
– Pellan, Alfred #6799
– Plaskett, Joe #1991
– Price, Art #6929
– Shadbolt, Jack Leonard #1991
– White, Stan #7555
Schacter, William M., architecte can, 1926-
– Société centrale d'hypothèques et de logement, concours (1960) #8040
Schaefer, Carl Fellman, artiste can, 1903- #7151 7152 7153 7156
– commentaire sur l'Islande #7150
– correspondance, David Brown Milne #6563 6564
– entretien #7154
– et Charles Fraser Comfort, artistes de guerre en Italie #1090
– et Toni Onley #6741
– expositions
  – (1969) #7155
  – (1980) #7157
– expositions, critiques #7158
– expositions de groupe
  – (1979) #147
– paysages #347
– peintures (années 1930) #502
– Phillips, Walter Joseph, comparaison #6858
– réflexion sur son oeuvre #349
Schantz, Karl, artisan verrier can, 1944- #7159
– et Sheridan College School of Crafts and Design (Mississauga, Ont) #2440
Schelle, Susan, artiste can, 1947-
– expositions
  – (1981) #7160
Schiele, Bernard, photographe can, 1943- #1000

– catalogue de photographies #997 999
Schiffer, Fred, photographe can, actif années
    1970
– réflexion sur l'art du portrait #624
Schindler, Joseph, orfèvre can, ca 1730-1792
    #269 270
– oeuvres, Detroit Institute of Arts (Detroit,
    Mich) #2691
Schleicher, Edythe Hembroff
– voir Hembroff-Schleicher, Edythe
Schlichting, Leonard, photographe can, actif
    années 1970
– expositions de groupe
    – (1979) #1904
Schlienger, Oscar, artiste can, 1905-
– influence sur James Lorimer Keirstead
    #6037
Schlieper, Heiko, artiste can, 1931-
– peinture d'icônes #7161
Schlombs, Wolfgang, collectionneur can,
    XXe s.
– collection, mobilier canadien #2485
Schluep, Walter, joaillier can, 1931- #2696
Schmid-Esler, Annemarie, artiste can, 1930-
    #675
– entretien #7162
– expositions de groupe
    – (1980) #698
– poterie #2395
– sculpture en céramique #795
Schmidt, Marianna, artiste can, 1918-
– expositions de groupe
    – (1967) #821
Schoeler Heaton Menendez, agence can
    d'architecture
– Ottawa (Ont), Carleton University. School
    of Architecture #8284
Schoenauer, Norbert H., architecte can,
    1923-
– Société centrale d'hypothèques et de
    logement, concours (1960) #8040
Schofield, John, architecte can, 1883-1971
– Montréal (Qué), gare Centrale #9535
– Ottawa (Ont), Château Laurier #9282
Schoonover, Frank Earle, artiste amér au
    Canada, 1877-1972 #7163
Schreiber, Charlotte Mount Brook Morrell,
    artiste can, 1834-1922 #7164
Schubert, Marcus, photographe can, 1955-
– catalogue de photographies #1053
Schwitters, Kurt, artiste all, 1887-1948
– professeur d'Almuth Lutkenhaus #6336
Scie, La, journal can
– dessins humoristiques, Jean-Baptiste Côté
    #5186 5187
scieries . Canada #9248 9249
– Kingston Mills (Ont) #8020
scieries . Etats-Unis
– Nord-Est des Etats-Unis #9249
Scott, Adam Sheriff, artiste can, 1887-1980
– expositions de groupe
    – (1978) #133
– intérieur, Banque Royale du Canada
    (Montréal, Qué) #9176
– intérieur, Château Frontenac (Québec,
    Qué) #9278
– professeur d'Armand Tatossian #7330
Scott, Adrian Gilbert, architecte brit,
    1882-1963
– influence sur architecture néo-gothique au
    Canada #7724
– Vancouver (CB), Saint James Anglican
    Church #8171
Scott, Charles Hepburn, artiste can,

1886-1964
– directeur, Vancouver School of Art
    (Vancouver, CB) #3019
– expositions, critiques #1982
Scott, George Gilbert, architecte brit,
    1837-1897
– influence sur architecture néo-gothique au
    Canada #7724
Scott, Gilbert, architecte brit, 1811-1878
– Londres (Angleterre), Albert Memorial
    #725
– St. John's (TN), Saint John's Cathedral
    #8771
Scott, Giles Gilbert, architecte brit, 1880-1960
– influence sur architecture néo-gothique au
    Canada #7724
Scott, J.D., graveur de médailles can, actif
    1879
– médailles de tempérance #724
Scott, John McBride, artiste can, 1950-
– expositions de groupe
    – (1980) #1832
Scott, Mackay Hugh Baillie, architecte et
    designer brit, 1865-1945
– influence sur Samuel Maclure #8384
– mobilier, résidence d'Alexis Martin
    (Victoria, CB) #8682
Scott, Marian Mildred Dale, artiste can,
    1906- #7166
– peintures non-figuratives (années 1950)
    #7165
Scott, Susan, artiste can, 1949-
– expositions de groupe
    – (1979) #676
Scott, Thomas Seaton, architecte can,
    1836-1895
– Stratford (Ont), bureau de poste #9054
Scovil, James Noel, artiste can, né 1876
    #7167
scrimshaw #3419
Sculptors' Society of British Columbia
– expositions
    – (1977) #2057
sculpture
– voir aussi bronzes; céroplastique;
    conservation et restauration, sculpture;
    ivoires; mobiles; monuments funéraires;
    plâtres; sculpture . portrait; sculpture au
    néon; sculpture en céramique; sculpture
    en plein air; sculpture-rebut; sculpture
    sonore; sculpture sur bois
– (1967), International Sculpture Symposium
    (Toronto, Ont) #765
– (1978), International Sculpture Conference
    (Toronto, Ont) #791
– (années 1950), Julien Hébert, commentaire
    #5765
– (années 1960), et peinture #449
sculpture . Amérindiens #761 3381
– Montréal (Qué), Musée des beaux-arts de
    Montréal #3362
sculpture . Bella-Bellas
– récipients en bois sculpté, XIXe s.,
    Smithsonian Institution (Washington, DC)
    #3985
sculpture . Carriers
– 'Ksan (coopérative d'artistes) #4129 4130
sculpture . Cris
– (années 1970) #4133
sculpture . Dorsétiens #4350
– Cape Dorset (TNO) #4322
– représentations de visages humains #4429
sculpture . Esquimaux du cuivre
– ouvrages en ramure #4412

sculpture . Gitksans
– 'Ksan (coopérative d'artistes) #4134
sculpture . Haidas #4040
– (années 1970) #4145
– et médecine #3904
– fin XIXe s. #3862
– récipients en bois sculptés, XIXe s.,
    Smithsonian Institution (Washington, DC)
    #3985
– sculpture d'argilite #3761 3890 4016 4042
    4051
    – (1820-1910) #3958 4010
    – (années 1910-1950) #4116
    – Chapman, Isaac #5088
    – Collison, Louis #5138
    – Edenshaw, Henry #5361
    – images, Mère des Ours #3868
    – images, Mère des Ours et Chaman
        #3901
    – influence de scrimshaw #3419
    – Moody, Rufus #3944
    – Vancouver (CB), Vancouver Centennial
        Museum #4006
– sculpture en bois #4041
sculpture . Indiens de la côte nord-ouest
    #370 3359 3377 3463 3857 3866 3892 3931
    3954 4043 4057
– (années 1950-1970) #4162
– bois #3877
– figure à la langue pendante et motifs
    connexes #3934
– motifs de l'Oiseau-Tonnerre et de la
    baleine #3831
– pierre #3785 3887 3889 4001
    – Victoria (CB), Provincial Museum #3900
– pointes de ramure, Boundary Bay (CB)
    #3817
– préhistoire, fleuve Colombia (CB) #3914
– sculpteurs et société #3912
sculpture . Inuit #761 1294 3359 3374 4198
    4200 4205 4229 4231 4232 4239 4261 4273
    4275 4388 4394 4395 4404 4406 4414 4418
    4419 4423 4426 4432 4440 4442 4444 4451
    4456
– (1977-1980) #4269
– (années 1940-1960) #4392
– (années 1950) #4183 4311 4383 4384 4385
    4387 4390 4393
– (années 1960-1970) #4447
– (années 1970) #4287 4422 4448
    – île de Baffin (TNO) #4420
– Baker Lake (TNO) #4266 4402 4403 4408
    4434
    – (années 1950-1960) #4400
– Belcher Islands (TNO) #4459
– Cape Dorset (TNO) #4192 4211 4299 4425
    4441
    – mines, carrières #4409
– Churchill (Man), Eskimo Museum #4290
– collection de la Banque Toronto-Dominion
    #4201 4248
– collection Rothmans #4257
– défenses de morse, Eskimo Museum
    (Churchill, Man) #4446
– et mythologie #4433
– expositions destinées aux handicapés
    visuels #4430
– Gjoa Haven (TNO) #4435
– guide pour collectionneurs #4431
– Holman (TNO) #3350
– Inoucdjouac (Qué) #4267 4279
– Keewatin (TNO) #4196 4407
– marché de l'art #4396 4397
– Maricourt (Qué) #4405

– méthodologie de recherche #4401
– Montréal (Qué), Musée des beaux-arts de Montréal #3362
– Povungnituk (Qué) #4219 4240 4274 4411 4417 4421 4437
  – concours (1967) #4415
– Povungnituk (Qué) et Cape Dorset (TNO) #4189
– représentations de visages humains #4429
– Repulse Bay (TNO) #4450
– sculpture d'ivoire #4175 4391
  – Alaska #4398
  – fin XIXe s. #4453
  – Los Angeles (Calif), Southwest Museum #4382
  – New York (NY), Museum of the American Indian. Heye Foundation #4381 4458
  – Rankin Inlet (TNO) #4195
  – Repulse Bay et Pelly Bay (TNO) #4438
– sculpture en céramique, Rankin Inlet (TNO) #4207 4210 4314
– sculpture en os de baleine #4413
  – Holman (TNO) #4457
  – Spence Bay (TNO) #4436 4445
– sculpture en stéatite #4214
  – symbolisme #4234
– sculptures représentant des mains #4439
– Spence Bay (TNO) #4416 4454
– thème de l'amautik #4300
– Toronto (Ont), York University. Art Gallery of York University #4228
– Vancouver (CB), Vancouver Art Gallery. Gallery Shop #4455
– Winnipeg (Man), Winnipeg Art Gallery #4285 4410 4427 4428 4443 4449
sculpture . Iroquois
– (années 1970) #4133
– petites effigies humaines #3553
sculpture . Kwakiutls #3787
– (années 1970) #4145
sculpture . Nootkas #3880
sculpture . Salish de la côte #3896 4046
sculpture . Saulteux/Ojibwa
– (années 1970) #4133
sculpture . Tlingits #3902 3976
– hameçons sur la pêche au flétan #4061
– récipients en bois sculpté, XIXe s., Smithsonian Institution (Washington, DC) #3985
– sculpture sur bois #4041
sculpture . Tsimshians #3881
– (années 1970) #4145
– récipients en bois sculpté, XIXe s., Smithsonian Institution (Washington, DC) #3985
– sculpture d'argilite #3910
sculpture africaine
– Zimbabwe, influence sur Ian Trowell #7431
sculpture américaine
– (années 1960) #787 790
sculpture au néon
– Toronto (Ont), Electric Gallery #1798
sculpture britannique
– (années 1880), thèmes d'inspiration canadienne #725
– (années 1970) #653
sculpture canadienne #57 58 59 61 63 129 761
– (1837-1887) #253
– (1867-1967) #82
– (1901-1912), Toronto Society of Architects, expositions #7956

– (1928-1958) #741
– (1929-1930) #294
– (1930), Canadian National Exhibition (Toronto, Ont) #313
– (1938-1948) #379 738
– (1955-1971) #1453
– (années 1750-1890) #221
– (années 1880-1940) #28
– (années 1890) #727
– (années 1910) #205
– (années 1920) #735
– (années 1920-1940) #737
– (années 1930) #13 340
– (années 1940) #370 374 736
– (années 1940-1960) #453
– (années 1950-1960) #455
– (années 1960) #478 521 743 744 745 746 747 748 767 770 787 790 1793
– (années 1970) #653 654 779 782 788 792 794
  – concept de mouvement #783
  – conservation #793
– Alberta
  – (1980) #1969
  – (années 1970) #1951
– Berthierville (Qué), église #8833 8874
– Calgary (Alta), XXe s. #1959
– Cantons de l'Est (Qué), (1815-1940) #1288
– Carillon (Qué), Dollard des Ormeaux #1591
– Charlesbourg (Qué), églises #8851
– Colombie-Britannique #1995
  – (années 1950) #1994
  – (années 1960) #1854 2001
  – (années 1970) #2049 2062 2065 2066
  – sculpture de jardin (années 1960) #1849
– éléments reliés au rituel et au culte (années 1970) #789
– et architecture
  – (années 1950) #7670
  – (années 1960) #753 8236
  – (années 1970) #773
– et Emanuel Otto Hahn #5679
– et photographie (années 1970) #994
– île d'Orléans (Qué), église Saint-Pierre #8802
– influence de la sculpture américaine #126
– Joliette (Qué), églises #8876
– Lachenaie (Qué), église Saint-Charles #8808
– Laterrière (Qué), église Notre-Dame #7882
– Lévis (Qué), église Notre-Dame-de-la-Victoire #8789
– Lotbinière (Qué), églises #8835
– Louis XIV et Louis XV #1598
– Manitoba #1895
– Maritimes (années 1960) #1126
– Montréal (Qué) #1572
  – (années 1940-1950) #1426
  – (années 1950) #389 7900
  – (années 1960) #1485
  – (années 1970) #1624
  – Chapelle Notre-Dame-de-Lourdes #8836
  – église Notre-Dame #8839
  – Expo 67 #751 752 7691 7692 9214
  – fin XIXe-années 1920 #1623
  – Soeurs Grises #8862
– Nouvelle-Écosse, sculpture traditionnelle, XXe s. #1206 1207
– oeuvres figuratives (années 1970) #760
– Ontario
  – (années 1970) #1806
  – Government of Ontario Art Collection (1873-1941) #1728

– Ottawa (Ont)
  – édifices du Parlement #755
  – Galerie nationale du Canada #3038
  – Région de la capitale nationale #762
– Prairies
  – (années 1950-1970) #1884
  – (années 1960) #1848 1853
  – (années 1970) #1873 1878
– provinces de l'Atlantique (années 1970) #1132
– Québec #1233 1234 1235 1237 1249 1258 1259 1265 1324 1590 1596 1617 2184 2197 7887
  – (1640-1840) #1329
  – (1650-1925) #1592
  – (1760-1790) #1369
  – (1875-1915) #1364
  – (1880-1914), influence parisienne #1371
  – (1945-1970) #1599
  – (1980) #685
  – (années 1920) #302
  – (années 1930), influence de la sculpture française #1381
  – (années 1940) #1580 8820
  – (années 1940-1970) #1269
  – (années 1950) #2193
  – (années 1960) #1487 1586 1595 1622
  – (années 1960-1970) #1584
  – (années 1970) #1626 1627 1630 1631 1634 1635
  – art traditionnel #1291
  – Confrérie des menuisiers de madame Sainte-Anne #1241 5965
  – Conseil de la sculpture du Québec (1978-1979) #1628
  – crucifix #1585 1618
  – famille Soucy #7267
  – fin XIXe-années 1920 #1606
  – influence de la famille Baillairgé #1582
  – monuments #1570
  – publications #1295
  – récollets #8855
  – sculpture traditionnelle, XVIIe-XIXe s. #1611
  – thème de l'Annonciation, fin XVIIe-XXe s. #1633
  – thème du souper d'Emmaüs, XIXe-XXe s. #1615
  – utilisation du plastique (années 1970) #1603
  – utilisation du plâtre #1618
  – XVIIe s.-années 1920 #1229
  – XVIIe-XIXe s. #1341 1589 1594 2128 7852
  – XVIIIe-début XXe s. #1339
  – XVIIIe-XIXe s. #1338 7849
– Québec (Qué)
  – général James Wolfe #1568
  – XVIIe s. #1352
– réalisme #716
– Saint-Marc-des-Carrières (Qué) #1629
– Saskatchewan #1919
– scènes de guerre #1081 1111 1112
  – bataille d'Ypres (Ypres, France), Walter Seymour Allward #4518
  – Ottawa (Ont), Galerie nationale du Canada #1101
  – Première Guerre mondiale #731 732
– sculpteures, XXe s. #739
– sculpture, art de performance (années 1970) #658
– sculpture électrique, Electric Gallery (Toronto, Ont) #1800
– Sherbrooke (Qué), (années 1970) #2232
– Société des sculpteurs du Canada #346 734

740
- Terre-Neuve
  - (années 1970) #1151
  - XIXe s.-années 1950 #1139
- Toronto (Ont)
  - (années 1970) #697 1817
  - Saint Anne's Church #1733
  - University of Toronto. University
    College #9482
- utilisation du plastique (années 1960) #768
- Vancouver (CB) #2026
  - (années 1960) #2037
- Varennes (Qué), églises #8813
- Winnipeg (Man) #1891
  - Palais législatif #8951 8953
- XIXe s.-années 1920 #11
- XIXe s.-années 1940 #1242
- XVIIe s.-années 1910 #205
- XVIIe-XIXe s. #232
- XVIIIe s.-années 1930 #45
- XXe s. #145
  - en comparaison avec constructions
    techniques #471
sculpture canadienne . portrait
- Hahn, Emanuel Otto #5679
- Hébert, Louis-Philippe #5767 5769
- Judah, Doris Minette #5980
- Liébert, Philippe #6281
- McKenzie, Robert Tait #6484
- Mol, Leo #6579 6580
- Wheeler, Orson Shorey #7549
sculpture en céramique
- voir aussi terre cuite
sculpture en céramique . Canada
- (années 1970) #781
- buste en porcelaine du colonel de
  Charette, St. Johns Stone Chinaware
  Company (Saint-Jean, Qué) #2314
- miniatures #2302
- oeuvres figuratives (années 1970) #774
- provinces de l'Ouest (années 1970) #1864
- Regina (Sask)
  - (années 1960-1970) #1939
  - (années 1970) #1924
- XXe s. #795
sculpture en céramique . Etats-Unis
- Californie, comparaison avec sculpture en
  céramique de Regina (Sask), (années 1970)
  #1939
sculpture en céramique . Inuit
- Rankin Inlet (TNO) #4203
sculpture en plein air . Canada
- (années 1960) #742 750 766 769
- (années 1970) #771 784 786
- (années 1980) #797 1639
- Colombie-Britannique
  - (1956-1960) #1993
  - (1977) #2057
- Garnier, Hubert #5556
- Montréal (Qué), Expo 67 #7691 7692 9213
- Murray, Robert Gray #6672
- Ontario (années 1960) #749
- Poulin, Roland #706
- Prince, Richard #6936
- Québec (années 1960) #1587
- Regina (Sask), (années 1970) #1924
- Roussil, Robert, commentaire #7093
- Royal Canadian Aerial Theatre (RCAT)
  #2058
- Toronto (Ont) #1834
- Trudeau, Yves #7432
- Turner, Richard Julian #7440
- Vancouver (CB) #2080
- Yuristy, Russell #7632

sculpture française
- (années 1930), influence sur sculpture
  québécoise #1381
sculpture grecque
- athlètes, Robert Tait McKenzie,
  commentaire #6485
sculpture populaire
- voir sculpture traditionnelle
sculpture-rebut
- Patterson, Dan #6779
sculpture sonore
- (années 1970) #776
sculpture sur bois . Canada #2089 2107
- (années 1890), et architecture #726
- (années 1960) #744
- (années 1970) #2596
- Association des artisans
  Saint-Jean-Port-Joli (Saint-Jean-Port-Joli,
  Qué) #1608
- Baillairgé, François et Thomas, église
  Saint-Joachim de Montmorency (Québec,
  Qué) #8880
- Baillairgé, Thomas #8326
- Beaumont (Qué), église Saint-Etienne
  #8809
- Charlesbourg (Qué), églises #8851
- comté de Bellechasse (Qué), église
  Saint-Charles-Borromée #8803
- crucifix, Québec #1585
- famille Bourgault #4884 4886
- figures de proue
  - Nouvelle-Ecosse, XIXe s. #1200
- Hamilton (Ont), Church of Saint John the
  Evangelist #730
- île d'Orléans (Qué) #1238
  - église Saint-François-de-Sales #8796
  - église Saint-Jean #8801
  - église Saint-Pierre #8802
  - église Sainte-Famille #1612 8795
- influence sur l'art canadien, XXe s. #2093
- Joliette (Qué), églises #8876
- Lachenaie (Qué), église Saint-Charles
  #8808
- Laterrière (Qué), église Notre-Dame #7882
- Loretteville (Qué), église
  Notre-Dame-de-la-Jeune-Lorette #8804
- Lotbinière (Qué), églises #8835
- Montréal (Qué), chapelle
  Notre-Dame-de-Lourdes #8836
- Nouveau-Brunswick
  - (avant 1900) #2491
  - Graham, famille #1187
- Nouvelle-Ecosse, Atlantic Woodcarvers'
  Guild #1194
- Oka (Qué)
  - calvaire d'Oka #1355 1356
  - église #8818
- Ottawa (Ont)
  - édifices du Parlement #8928
  - Musée national de l'Homme. Centre
    canadien sur la culture traditionnelle
    #963
- Price, Ralph et Patricia, collection #971
- Québec #19 761 1233 1235 1327 1573 1576
  1577 1614 2169 2171 2183
  - (1640-1840) #1329
  - (1650-1925) #1592
  - (1780-1850) #1232 1574
  - apprentis (1660-1815) #2231
  - Baillairgé, François #4589
  - figures de proue, XVIIIe-XIXe s. #1604
  - Levasseur, famille #6254
  - représentation d'animaux (années 1940)
    #1579

- sculpture traditionnelle, collection Nettie
  Sharpe #1607
- Soucy, famille #7267
- tabernacles #1613
- Washington (DC), Smithsonian
  Institution #2111
- XVIIe-XIXe s. #1575 1581 1583 1588 1593
- XVIIe-XVIIIe s. #2181 2187
- XVIIIe s. #234 235 249 250 269 270
- XVIIIe s.-années 1820 #1300
- XVIIIe-XIXe s. #1338 6947 8799
- XVIIIe-XXe s. #1616
- XXe s. #2179 2198
- Québec (Qué), Couvent des ursulines
  #8810
  - chapelle #8852
- Saint-Jean (NB), église en pierre #8778
- Saint-Jean-Port-Joli (Qué) #1597 2194 2209
  4883
  - église Saint-Jean-Baptiste #8812
- Sault-au-Récollet (Qué), église de la
  Visitation #8797
- sculpture traditionnelle #756 966
- Terre-Neuve #1155
- Varennes (Qué), églises #8813
sculpture sur bois . Etats-Unis
- sculpture traditionnelle #756
sculpture sur bois . France
- influence sur sculpture sur bois québécois,
  XVIIe-XIXe s. #1583
sculpture sur os . Goyoguins #3525
sculpture sur os . Indiens de la côte
  nord-ouest
- flèches et pointes de lance #3785
- instruments #4068
sculpture sur os . Indiens des forêts du
  Nord-Est #3491
sculpture sur os . Inuit
- Washington (DC), Smithsonian Institution
  #4319
sculpture sur os . Iroquois #3525 3566
- petites effigies humaines #3553
sculpture sur os . Micmacs #3643
sculpture sur os . Pentaguets #3537
sculpture sur os . Tagish #4106
sculpture sur os . Tlingits #4106
sculpture sur os . Tutchonis #4106
Seaby, Allen William, artiste brit, 1867-1953
- et Walter Joseph Phillips #6860
Seagram, Maison, distillerie can
- collection, art canadien #403
Seath, Ethel, artiste can, 1879-1963
- membre du Groupe des peintres
  canadiens #324
Seattle (Wash), Seattle Art Museum
- expositions
  - Objects of Bright Pride: Northwest Coast
    Indian Art from the American Museum of
    Natural History (1978) #4024
Seattle (Wash), Seattle World's Fair (1962).
  Fine Arts Pavilion
- expositions
  - Northwest Coast Indian Art (1962) #3919
Seattle (Wash), Thomas Burke Museum
- voir Seattle (Wash), Washington State
  University. Thomas Burke Museum
Seattle (Wash), Washington State Museum
- colliers soumak, Pieds-Noirs #3685
Seattle (Wash), Washington State University.
  Thomas Burke Museum
- art, Indiens de la côte nord-ouest #3974
Seavey, Julien Ruggles, artiste can,
  1857-1940
- dessins de bâtiments, comté de

Wentworth (Ont) #7954
– peinture sur porcelaine #2277
Seaweed, Willie, artiste can, 1873-1967
– cuivres, *Great Killer Whale Copper* #4054
Sécal
– *voir* Société d'électrolyse et de chimie Alcan Ltée (Sécal)
Secord, James E., architecte can, 1917-1979
– Red Deer (Alta), hôtel de ville #8990
Seding, Volker, photographe can, 1943-
– expositions de groupe
  – (1981) #1070
Sedna, festival de . Inuit #4376
Seese, Wayne, artiste amér au Canada, 1918-1980 #1282
– et RACE #1536
Segal, George, sculpteur amér, 1924-
– Whiten, Colette, comparaison #7559
Séguin, Jean-Pierre, artiste can, 1951- #1526
Sékanis
– culture (années 1920) #4084
Selkirk, Lord
– commentaire sur la construction d'habitations #8527
Selkirk (montagnes), (CB)
– vues
  – Bell-Smith, Frederic Marlett #4667
  – Collings, Charles John #5133
Semak, Michael William, photographe can, 1934- #7168 7169
– catalogue de photographies #987 991 996 1023
– correspondance, Freeman Patterson #1016
– expositions de groupe
  – (1980) #1063
– photographies du Ghana #990
Semchishen, Orest, photographe can, 1932-
– catalogue de photographies #991
– expositions, critiques #1046 1060
– expositions de groupe
  – (1979) #1037
– photographies d'églises albertaines #8913
séminaires . Canada
– Montréal (Qué) #7932
– Québec #7853 7861
– Québec (Qué)
  – Collège des jésuites #7953
  – Séminaire de Notre-Dame-des-Anges #8785
  – Séminaire de Québec #8842 8844 8847
Séminoles
– hausse-cols #3536
Sen, Ranjan, artiste can, 1941-
– expositions, critiques #2072
– expositions de groupe
  – (1979) #2075
Sénécal, André, photographe can, actif 1976
– catalogue de photographies #997 999
Senécal, Irène, artiste can, 1901-1978 #1380
– professeure #2999 3010
Sénéchal, Gilles, photographe can, actif années 1970 #1283
Senft, Douglas, sculpteur can, 1950-
– *Aldergrove Valley* #7170
Senior, Raymond (Ray), artiste can (tapisserie), 1921-
– expositions de groupe
  – (1978) #2772
– rideau de scène, Shaw Festival Theatre (Niagara-on-the-Lake, Ont) #9119
Sept-Iles (Qué), Musée de Sept-Iles
– expositions
  – *De la figuration à la non-figuration dans l'art québécois* (1977) #1461

sérigraphie
– Bornstein, Eli, commentaire #4854
– Casson, Alfred Joseph, commentaire #5055
sérigraphie . Algonquiens
– Triple K Co-operative (Red Lake, Ont) #4151 4158
sérigraphie . Indiens de la côte nord-ouest #4168
– (années 1970) #4160
– Northwest Coast Indian Artists Guild (1977) #4148
sérigraphie . Kwakiutls #4120
sérigraphie . Nootkas #4167
sérigraphie . Tsimshians #4167
Serpent Mound (Rice Lake, Ont)
– artefacts, Algonquiens et Hopewell #3574
Serra, Richard, sculpteur amér, 1939-
– expositions, critiques #787
– expositions de groupe
  – (1978) #790
– sculpture en béton, King City (Ont) #1796
Sert, Jackson, agence can d'architecture
– Guelph (Ont), University of Guelph. Arts and Library buildings #9468
Sérusier, Paul, artiste fr, 1863-1927
– professeur d'André Charles Biéler #4725
Service féminin de l'Armée canadienne
– *voir* Canada. Service féminin de l'Armée canadienne
services à thé . Grande-Bretagne
– Helmcken, John S., pièce commémorative en argent (1857) #2647
Seton, Ernest Thompson, artiste can, 1860-1946 #7171 7172 7173
– expositions de groupe
  – (1961) #62
Seurat, Georges Pierre, artiste fr, 1859-1891
– FitzGerald, Lionel LeMoine, comparaison #5452
– influence sur Lionel LeMoine FitzGerald #5450
Sévigny, Marc, photographe can, ca 1957- #1534
sexualité dans l'art
– *voir aussi* art érotique
– femmes artistes (années 1970) #596
Shaa, Aqjangajuk, sculpteur can, 1937-
– entretien #7174
Shabaeff, Valentin, artiste can, 1891- #7175
Shadbolt, Doris, conservatrice, critique d'art et joaillière can, 1918-
– bijoux #2695
– et Emily Carr #5043
Shadbolt, Jack Leonard, artiste can, 1909- #476 1996 7184 7188 7191
– commentaire sur Emily Carr #5043
– commentaire sur son expérience artistique #7186
– critique d'art #3308
– Dallaire, Jean-Philippe, comparaison #5238
– décors et costumes, *Daphnis and Chloe* #1991
– dessins et écrits #7181 7183
– écrits #92
– en Europe (1956-1957) #7180
– entretien #7178
– et Molly Lamb Bobak #4766
– et peinture de Vancouver (CB) #1992 6742
– expositions
  – (1969) #7182
  – (1978) #7187
  – (1980) #7189
– expositions, critiques #2074 7176
– expositions de groupe

– (1958) #431
– (1959) #438 1997
– (1964) #462
– (1977) #633
– influence de la nature #7177
– influence sur Gordon Appelbe Smith #7232
– juré, *Saskatchewan Arts Exhibition* (1954) #1910
– le fond et la forme #7179
– participant, Symposium on 20th Century Canadian Culture (Washington, DC), (1977) #621
– peintures (années 1970) #7190
– peintures murales #1844
– professeur d'Arthur McKay #6477
– réflexion sur l'influences de l'histoire sur son oeuvre #7185
– réflexion sur le processus de création #7192
Shahn, Ben, artiste amér, 1898-1969
– cité dans un article sur la culture canadienne #6747
Shakespeare, Noah, photographe can, 1839-1921
– et la Victoria Theatre Photographic Gallery (Victoria, CB) #2027
Shames, Stephen, photographe can, actif années 1970
– catalogue de photographies #998
Shanly, Charles Dawson, artiste irlandais au Canada, 1811-1875 #241 242
Sharon (Ont), Children of Peace Meeting House (1810)
– architecture, David Willson #8352
Sharon (Ont), Temple of the Children of Peace
– architecture #7959
– Willson, David #8351 8352
Sharp, Vincent, photographe can, 1937- #7193
– expositions, critiques #1018
Sharp & Brown, agence can d'architecture
– Calgary (Alta), Banque de Nouvelle-Ecosse #8118
– Moose Jaw (Sask), hôtel de ville, concours #8978
– Winnipeg (Man), Legislative and Executive Building, concours #8946
Sharp & Horner, agence can d'architecture
– Banque de Nouvelle-Ecosse, édifices #9174
Sharp & Thompson, agence can d'architecture
– Vancouver (CB)
  – Saint James Anglican Church #8171
  – University of British Columbia #9500
  – University of British Columbia, concours #9498 9509
Sharp & Thompson, Berwick, Pratt, agence can d'architecture
– Vancouver (CB), Dal Grauer Substation #8171
Sharpe, Nettie, collectionneuse can, XXe s.
– collection, sculpture traditionnelle québécoise #1607
Shaughnessy, Arthur, sculpteur can, 1884-1945
– influence sur Henry Hunt #5872
Shawinigan (Qué), église Notre-Dame de la Présentation
– peintures, Ozias Leduc #6201
Sheeguapik
– *voir* Sivuarapik, Charlie
Sheep Creek (Alta), Cottonwoods

- architecture #8720 8721
Sheep Creek (Alta), Gate Ranch House
- architecture #8720 8721
Sheep Creek (Alta), Viewfield Ranch House
- architecture #8720 8721
Sheffield (Angleterre), Sheffield School of
  Art
- Varley, Frederick Horsman, élève #7462
Shehu, Aferdita (Dita), artiste can, active
  années 1970
- entretien #7194
Shelburne (NE), Christ Church
- architecture, Isaac Hildrith #8374 8375
Shelburne (NE), Ross Thompson . Maison et
  entrepôt
- architecture #7823
Sheldon-Williams, Inglis, artiste can,
  1870-1940 #7195 7196
- expositions de groupe
  - (1980) #1940
- vues, provinces de l'Ouest #931
Shell Canada Ltée, société pétrolière
- collection, art canadien #3238 3240
Shepard & Calvin, agence can d'architecture
- Kingston (Ont), Queen's University.
  Douglas Library #9445
- Toronto (Ont), Oke Building #9335
Shepherd, Helen Parsons, artiste can, 1923-
- co-fondatrice, Newfoundland Academy of
  Art (St. John's, TN) #2988
Shepherd, Reginald, artiste can, 1924-
- co-fondateur, Newfoundland Academy of
  Art (St. John's, TN) #2988
Shepley, Ellen Garde, collectionneuse can,
  XXe s.
- collection, cuillers-souvenirs, Royal
  Ontario Museum (Toronto, Ont) #2652
Sheppard, Earle Leonard, architecte can,
  1894-1957
- plan, accès nord-ouest de Hamilton (Ont)
  #7962
Sherbrooke (NE), Sherbrooke Village Exhibit
  Centre
- expositions
  - Canadians: A National Photography Show
    about People/Canadiens: exposition
    nationale de photographie ayant les gens
    comme thème (1979) #1035
Sherbrooke (Qué)
- arts décoratifs (années 1970) #2232
- pétroglyphes iroquois #3599
Sherbrooke (Qué), Cathédrale de
  Sherbrooke. Chapelle Pauline
- peintures, Ozias Leduc #6204
Sherbrooke (Qué), Chapelle universitaire
  chrétienne
- architecture, Paul Faucher, Jacques
  Folch-Ribas #8841
Sherbrooke (Qué), Palais épiscopal
- intérieur, Ozias Leduc #6208
Sherbrooke (Qué), Université de Sherbrooke.
  Centre culturel
- expositions
  - Claude Tousignant (1974) #7401
  - Concours d'estampe et de dessin
    (1977,1979,1981) #1533
  - Fernand Leduc (1971) #6186
  - Joe Plaskett and His Paris: In Search of
    Time Past (1973) #6893
  - Joe Plaskett et son Paris: à la recherche d'un
    temps passé (1973) #6894
  - L'art des Cantons de l'Est, 1800-1950
    (1980) #1296
  - Métiers d'art Ontario-Québec,

1979/1980/Quebec-Ontario Crafts,
  1979/1980 (1980) #2138
- The Mr. and Mrs. Jules Loeb Collection/La
  collection M. et Mme Jules Loeb (1971)
  #3231
- expositions, critiques
  - Les arts visuels des Cantons de l'Est
    1800-1950 (1978) #1282
Sherman, Tom, artiste can, 1947-
- art de performance #655
- expositions de groupe
  - (1977) #631
  - (1980) #705
Sherwood, William Albert, artiste can,
  1855-1919
- expositions, critiques #1703
Sherwood Park (Alta)
- art public (i.e. art dans les lieux publics)
  #1973
Sherwood Park (Alta), County of Strathcona
  Building
- architecture, Peter Hemingway, et art,
  Alex Janvier #5937
Shields, George S., artiste can, 1872-1952
- dessins humoristiques, Toronto Evening
  Telegram #943
Shilling, Arthur, artiste can, 1941- #7197
- entretien #7198
- influence des images Midéwiwins #4154
- portraits #715
Shimaoka, Tatsuzo, céramiste jap, XXe s.
- professeur de céramistes québécois (1964)
  #2381
Shirley, James R., artiste can, 1944- #7199
- estampes #1214
- expositions, critiques #1208
Shives, Arnold, artiste can, 1943-
- expositions
  - (1976) #2059
Shore, Henrietta Mary, artiste can au EU,
  1880-1963 #7200
Shore, Tilbe, Henschel, Irwin, agence can
  d'architecture
- Toronto (Ont), Joseph E. Shephard
  Government of Canada Building #8975
Shore, Tilbe, Henschel, Irwin, Peters, agence
  can d'architecture
- Toronto (Ont), Dundas Street, poste de
  police #8078
Shore & Moffat, agence can d'architecture
- Kingston (Ont), Canadian Forces Hospital
  #9031
Shore & Moffat and Partners, agence can
  d'architecture
- Toronto (Ont), York University #9396 9469
Short, Richard, officier de la marine brit,
  artiste au Canada, actif avant 1754-après
  1766 #249 250
Shortt, Stephen, artiste can, actif années 1970
- expositions de groupe
  - (1976) #1529
Shortt, Terence Michael, artiste can, 1910-
  #7201
- et Frederick Horsman Varley #506
Shreveport (La), R.W. Norton Art Gallery
- expositions
  - Loren D. Adams, Jr.: A Retrospective
    Exhibition (1979) #4501
Shubenacadie Canal (NE)
- arpentage, Isaac Hildrith #8374
Shufeldt, Robert Wilson, conservateur amér,
  1850-1934
- et émergence d'artistes amérindiens
  reconnus #3486

Shuldham Island (Labrador, TN)
- artefacts préhistoriques #4377
Shum, Hilda, artiste can, 1957-
- expositions de groupe
  - (1981) #2084
Shumiatcher, Jacqui et Morris,
  collectionneurs can, XXe s.
- collection, art inuit #4311
Shuswaps
- culture #3789
- kekuli #3983
Shuttleworth, Claire, artiste amér au
  Canada, 1868-1930 #7202
Sibérie (URSS)
- art (1900-1980) #4303
Sibley Brothers, fabricants de mobilier (NE)
  #2493
Sicile (Italie)
- vues, Seconde Guerre mondiale, Carl
  Fellman Schaefer #1090
Sickert, Walter Richard, artiste brit,
  1860-1942
- Morrice, James Wilson, comparaison #6631
Sicotte, Rolande, artiste can, active 1936
  #1380
Siddall, Dennis & Associates, agence can
  d'architecture
- Victoria (BC), University of Victoria.
  Centennial Stadium #9101
Siddall, John Wilson, architecte can,
  1861-1941
- Toronto (Ont)
  - Big Nickel Theatre #9066
  - cinémas et théâtres #9067
Siebens, Harold, collectionneur can, XXe s.
- collection de photographies de Wilfred
  Roloff Beny, acquisition pour University
  of Calgary. Art Gallery (Calgary, Alta)
  #4691
Siebner, Herbert Johannes Joseph, artiste
  can, 1925- #2061 7203
- entretien #7204
- expositions
  - (1979) #7205
- membre du groupe Limners #2043
Siegel, Lois, photographe can, 1946- #1000
sièges (mobilier)
- voir aussi berceuses; mobilier de style
  Windsor
- sculptures, Les Levine #6258
sièges (mobilier) . Canada
- (années 1790-1850) #2553
- (années 1960) #2471
- Acadie #2492
- croquis attribué à Pierre-Noël Levasseur
  #6257
- Green, Daniel #2517
- Hébert, Julien #5766
- Mailloux, Joseph #2184
- Manitoba, XIXe s. #2584
- Montréal (Qué), (1800-1850) #2538
- Nouveau-Brunswick, XVIIIe-XIXe s. #2500
- Nouvelle-Ecosse #2496
  - (années 1740-1850) #2497
  - XVIIIe-XIXe s. #2493 2499 2509
- Ontario #2560
  - (1780-1900) #2577
  - (années 1790-1857) #2558
  - (années 1790-1870) #2564
  - XIXe s. #2575
- Québec #2534
  - XVIIe-XVIIIe s. #2529
- Rogerson, John, président, St. Andrew's

Society (Saint-Jean, NB) #7067 7068
- Toronto (Ont), (1800-1865) #2563
- Windsor #2476
- XVIIe-XIXe s. #2489
sièges (mobilier) . Ecosse
- XIXe s., influence sur mobilier canadien, sièges #2553
sièges (mobilier) . Etats-Unis
- XIXe s., influence sur mobilier canadien, sièges #2553 2564
- XVIIIe-XIXe s., influence sur berceuses, Québec #2536
sièges (mobilier) . Grande-Bretagne
- Windsor, influence sur berceuses, Québec #2536
- XIXe s., influence sur mobilier canadien, sièges #2553
signatures d'artistes inuit #4250 4431 4462
- igloo, marque de commerce #4213
signes héraldiques . Haidas #3780
- représentation de la lune #4059
signes héraldiques . Indiens de la côte nord-ouest #3791 3858 3863 3928
signes héraldiques . Tsimshians #3795 3981
Silcox, David, Can, administrateur des arts, 1937-
- entretien, collection d'oeuvres d'arts du Conseil des Arts #3266
silhouette humaine dans l'art
- sculpture inuit #4404
silhouettes . Canada
- Halifax (NE), XVIIIe-XIXe s. #1195
- Julien, Henri #5981
- Montréal (Qué), (1760-1860) #1376 1377
silice
- de Vaudreuil (Qué), dans fabrication de verre #2418
Sillaste, Henno, architecte can, 1936-
- Toronto (Ont), habitations St. Lawrence #8078
Sillery (Qué)
- architecture, XVIIe-XIXe s. #7879
Sillery (Qué), Bois de Coulonge (autrefois Spencer Wood)
- architecture #8754
Sillery (Qué), Maison des jésuites
- architecture #8571
silos à grains
- voir élévateurs à grains
Silver, M. et Mme Stanley S., collectionneurs can, XXe s.
- collection, bouteille en verre, XIXe-XXe s. #2414
Silverberg, David, artiste can, 1936- #7206
- expositions de groupe
    - (1973) #1182
Simard, Claude A., artiste can, 1943- #7207
Simard, Cyril, administrateur des arts can, 1938-
- et Centrale d'artisanat du Québec #2213
Simard, Jean, artiste can, 1916-
- cartes de Noël #856
Simard, Léonard, artiste can, 1933- #1547 1551
Simard, René, maroquinier can, 1896- #7208
Simard-Laflamme, Carole, artiste can (tapisserie), 1945- #7209
- expositions de groupe
    - (1978) #2772
Simcoe, Elizabeth Posthuma Gwillim, artiste brit au Canada, 1766-1850 #7211 7212
- autobiographie #7210
Simcoe, John Graves, homme d'Etat can, 1752-1806

- et William von Moll Berczy, fondation de Toronto (Ont) #4699
Simcoe (Ont), Lynnwood Arts Centre
- expositions
    - Goodridge Roberts: Paintings from the 1950s and 60s (1980) #7048
Simcoe County Arts and Crafts Association (comté de Simcoe, Ont)
- courtepointes #2795
Simkins, Howard, artiste can, 1948- #1807
Simmerman, Henry, ébéniste can, né ca 1814 #2571
Simon, Ellen Rosalie, artiste can (vitrail), 1916- #7589
Simon, Frank Worthington, architecte brit, 1863-1933
- Winnipeg (Man)
    - Palais législatif #8944 8945 8947 8948 8949 8950 8951 8952
    - Palais législatif, concours #8946
Simon, Harold, photographe can, ca 1952-
- catalogue de photographies #991
Simon, Lucien J., artiste fr, 1861-1945
- Pellan, Alfred, comparaison #6814
Simonds, Charles Frederick, sculpteur et architecte amér, 1945-
- expositions de groupe
    - (1980) #8237
Simone, Joseph (Joe), photographe can, ca 1943-
- catalogue de photographies #995
Simonin, Francine, artiste can, 1936- #7213
Simpkins, William Charles (Bill), photographe can, 1945-
- catalogue de photographies #1023
Simpson, Charles Walter, artiste can, 1878-1942 #302
- illustrations #916
Simpson, Gregg Cairns, artiste can, 1947-
- expositions, critiques #2051
- expositions de groupe
    - (1971) #2042
    - (1973) #2045
Simpson, Richard, photographe can, actif années 1970
- catalogue de photographies #1032
Simpson, Sir George, Brit résidant au Canada, administrateur de la Compagnie de la Baie d'Hudson, 1787-1860
- collection, peintures de Paul Kane #6018
Sinclair, Robert, artiste can, 1939- #7214 7215
- expositions
    - (1976) #7216
Singer, Judy, artiste can, 1951- #711 717
- expositions de groupe
    - (1981) #722
singes
- dans l'imagerie de Brian Porter #6907
Singleton, Rebecca (Becky), artiste can, 1952-
- expositions de groupe
    - (1981) #723
Siouens
- art #3434 3649 3731
    - XIXe s. #3737 3750
- assemblages de rochers #3688
- chronique en images #3728
- culture #3651
- et art, Rudolph Friedrich Kurz #3400
- étuis à fusils #3713
- grosses perles, type "pony", XIXe s. #3722
- harnachement #3405
- mocassins #3666 3740
- ouvrages en piquants de porc-épic #3443 3471 3652 3745

- ouvrages en piquants de porc-épic et ouvrages perlés #3674
- parchemins, Midéwiwins #3702
- peinture #3672
- poterie #3687
- rites et cérémonies #3725
- travail du cuir #3456
Sisler, Rebecca Jean, sculpteure can, 1932-
- expositions de groupe
    - (1978) #666
site archéologique d'Arnapik (Mansel Island, TNO)
- artefacts prédorsétiens #4351
site archéologique de Draper (Ont)
- poterie, Indiens des forêts du Nord-Est #3640
site archéologique de Roma (IPE)
- coutellerie et ustensiles de table #2714 2715
- verre
    - XIXe s. #2436 2437
site archéologique de Tyara (Sugluk Island, Qué)
- artefacts dorsétiens #4351
site archéologique du village de McClallum (Agassiz, CB)
- architecture, Salish #3872
Site Inc. Sculpture in the Environment
- expositions de groupe
    - (1980) #8237
Sitka (Alaska), Sheldon Jackson Museum
- art amérindien #3370
Sivuarapik, Charlie, sculpteur can, 1911-1968 #7217
Siwinski, Stefan, designer can, 1918-
- sièges #2471
Six Nations Reserve (Ont)
- Iroquois, rites et cérémonies #3598
Skagit River (CB)
- atlatl, Indiens de la côte nord-ouest #3951
Skalnik, Pavel, artiste can, 1941- #7218
- estampes #1185
Skedans (CB)
- totems . Indiens de la côte nord-ouest #3984
Skeena River (CB)
- totems . Gitksans #3828
Skeenas
- massues en pierre #4053
- pictogrammes #3822
Skidegate (CB), Queen Charlotte Islands Museum
- architecture, Hawthorn Mansfield Towers #8373
Skinner, Si Angelo, artiste can, actif années 1940
- expositions de groupe
    - (1940) #350
Skokomish
- culture #3835
Slater, James, fonctionnaire can, XIXe s.
- et édifices du Parlement (Ottawa, Ont) #8930
Slater, Norman, architecte, artiste can, 1922-
- murale, Pavillon du Canada, Exposition universelle et internationale (1958), (Bruxelles, Belgique) #419 4541
- murale, Place des Arts (Montréal, Qué) #9093
- panneaux muraux, Centre national des arts (Ottawa, Ont) #9108
Slater, Norman, architecte et artiste can, 1922- #8231
Slaveys

– culture #4088 4089
Sleep, Joseph (Joe), artiste can, 1914-1978
– expositions
 – (1981) #7219
– expositions, critiques #1208
Sloane, Sir Hans, médecin, naturaliste et
 collectionneur brit, 1660-1753
– collection, art amérindien
 – Londres (Angleterre), British Museum
  #3397
Sloggett, Paul, artiste can, 1950- #1807
– expositions, critiques #639
Smalley, Katherine, photographe can, active
 1979
– catalogue de photographies #1023
Smellie, David, ferronnier can, 1780-1827
 #2704
Smeraldi, artiste, actif 1925
– intérieur, Château Frontenac (Québec,
 Qué) #9278
Smily, William, orfèvre brit, actif années
 1840-1850
– pièce commémorative pour John S.
 Helmcken, service à thé en argent #2647
Smith, Ann, artiste can, 1946- #7220
Smith, Bill, maroquinier can, actif années
 1970 #2936
Smith, Daniel J., photographe can, actif
 années 1850-1860 #1211
Smith, David, sculpteur amér, 1906-1965
– influence sur Douglas Bentham #4683 4686
– influence sur Henry Saxe #7149
Smith, Eden, architecte can, 1858-1949 #8408
– Oshawa (Ont), Saint George's Anglican
 Church #8899
– réflexion sur l'architecture canadienne
 (années 1910) #7644 8491
– Toronto (Ont)
 – architecture domestique #8493
 – habitations en bande #8492
Smith, Edith Agnes, artiste can, 1867-1954
– et Nova Scotia Society of Artists #1192
Smith, Frederick, artisan verrier can, actif
 années 1840
– fondateur, Canada Glass Works
 (Saint-Jean, Qué) #2420
Smith, Garfield Stuart (Gar), artiste can,
 1946-
– et réalisme #533
Smith, George Neilson, artiste can,
 1789-1854
– vues, Saint-Jean (NB) #7221
Smith, Gordon Appelbe, artiste can, 1919-
 #1996 7223 7224 7230 7232
– commentaire sur l'enseignement de l'art
 #7228
– commentaire sur la gravure #817
– entretien #7225 7226
– et peinture de Vancouver (CB) #1992 6742
– expositions
 – (1976) #7229
– expositions, critiques #432 7227 7231
– expositions de groupe
 – (1959) #438 1997
Smith, Gordon Hammond (Gord), sculpteur
 can, 1937- #7222
– sculptures soudées (années 1960) #745
Smith, Harold Thomas Faulkner,
 photographe can, 1893-
– expositions de groupe
 – (1976) #2012
Smith, Jean et Elizabeth, collectionneuses
 can, XXe s.
– collection, arts décoratifs canadiens #2125

2131
Smith, Jeremy, artiste can, 1946-
– et réalisme #110
Smith, John Ivor, sculpteur can, 1927-
– sculptures d'argile (années 1960) #743
Smith, John Roxborough, architecte can,
 1881-1975
– restauration, Québec (Qué) #7936
Smith, Leslie Victor, artiste can, 1880-1952
– ex-libris (1916-1946) #7234
Smith, Levi Alasua Pirti, artiste can, 1927-
 #4421
Smith, Madge, photographe et marchande
 d'oeuvres d'art can, active années 1930-
 #7235
Smith, Marjorie (Jori), artiste can, 1907-
 #7233
Smith, Morley, artiste can, 1938-
– et Jacques Guillon Designers Inc. #884
Smith, Munn, Carter, Katelnikoff & Ian M.
 Brown, agence can d'architecture
– Ottawa (Ont), Galerie nationale du
 Canada, concours #9079
Smith, Muriel, artisane (cuir), active années
 1970 #2936
Smith, Peter John, architecte can, 1936-
– Niagara-on-the-Lake (Ont), Shaw Festival
 Theatre #9119
Smith, Richard, artiste brit, 1931-
– influence sur Alan Wood #7610
Smith, Russell (Awasatlas), 1950-
– sérigraphies #4148
Smith, Thomas, photographe can, actif
 1856-1867 #1724
Smith, William St. Thomas, artiste can,
 1862-1947 #7236 7237 7238
– expositions de groupe
 – (1978) #1726
Smith & McCulloch, agence can
 d'architecture
– Castlegar (CB), hôpital #9031
– Invermere (CB), hôpital #9031
Smith Carter Searle Associates, agence can
 d'architecture
– Montréal (Qué), Place d'Accueil #7686
– Winnipeg (Man)
 – hôtel de ville, concours #8985 8986
 – Monarch Life #9357
 – Pan-Am Pool #9101
 – Smith Carter Searle Associates, bureau
  d'architectes et d'ingénieurs #7683
 – University of Manitoba. School of
  Architecture #9487
Smithson, Robert I., sculpteur amér,
 1938-1973
– Prince, Richard, comparaison #6937
Smolenski, Joseph, céramiste can, XIXe s.
 #2298 2322
Smyth, Hervey, officier de l'armée brit,
 artiste au Canada, 1734-1811
– portrait du général James Wolfe #1568
Smyth, John Richard Coke, artiste brit au
 Canada, 1808-1882
– faux #4614
Snell, Don, sculpteur can, 1946-1978
– expositions de groupe
 – (1980) #1835
Snider, Gregory, sculpteur can, 1945-
– expositions de groupe
 – (1978) #786
Snider, Kenneth, architecte can, actif 1965
– Vancouver (CB), University of British
 Columbia. Student Union #9503
Sninig, Bella-Coolas

– pétroglyphe #3816
Snow, Charles, artiste can, XXe s.
– professeur de Robert MacLean #2923
Snow, Michael, artiste can, 1929- #538 1762
– à l'extérieur de la tradition artistique
 canadienne #7239
– art vidéo #616
– collection Walking Woman #7240
– commentaire sur Joyce Wieland #7577
– commentaire sur la perception visuelle
 #525
– commentaire sur un séjour à New York
 (années 1960) #460
– dessins #532
– entretien #7257
 – oeuvre cinématographique #7249 7252
– et l'art d'avant-garde #600
– et la critique d'art #3315
– expositions
 – (1970) #7243 7244
 – (1972) #7248
 – (1975) #7253
 – (1978) #7258
 – (1979) #7261
– expositions, critiques #520 7242 7245 7259
 7263 7264
– expositions de groupe
 – (1967) #490
 – (1971) #98
 – (1973) #556
 – (1977) #783
 – (1979) #510
 – (1980) #690 703
– films #626
 – la région centrale #7247 7250
 – Wavelength #568 7241 7246
– films et photographies (années 1960 et
 1970) #7260
– influence sur la peinture torontoise #1749
– livres #940
 – Cover to Cover #7254 7255 7256
– peintures et sculptures #449
– photographies, cartes de la perception
 #7251
– Plus tard #714 7262
– références et transformations historiques
 #577
– réflexion sur l'art canadien (années 1960)
 #478
– utilisation de la photographie #1057
Snuqualmis
– culture #3835
socialisme, art et
– voir aussi communisme, art et
– Hutchinson, Leonard, estampes
 (1930-1940) #5893
– peinture canadienne #113
– Taylor, Frederick Bourchier, Talking Union
 (1950) #7332
société, architecture et
– Canada #7728
 – (1890-1944) #30
 – (années 1930) #7658
 – (années 1960) #8513
  – rôle des architectes #8279 8280
 – archives et sources historiques #7729
 – style victorien #7725
 – XXe s. #7690 7731 7732
– Colombie-Britannique (années 1970) #8146
– Montréal (Qué), Banque de Montréal
 (1846) #9200
– Ontario, XIXe s. #7745
– Prairies, XIXe-XXe s. #8080
– Québec #7851

– (1980) #7893
– (années 1970) #7868
– XVIIe-XVIIIe s. #8586
– Safdie, Moshe, commentaire #8406
– Toronto (Ont), XIXe-XXe s. #8060
– Trois-Rivières (Qué), Forges du Saint-Maurice #9257
société, art et
– Calgary (Alta), (années 1970) #1966
– Canada #104 327
    – (1760-1860) #251
    – (1882-1910), et mode #2897
    – (1890-1900) #190
    – (1892-1908) #277
    – (1909) #194
    – (1951), Commission royale d'enquête sur l'avancement des arts, lettres et sciences (Rapport Massey) #3257 3261
    – (1980) #3294 3295
        – rôle des musées #683
    – (1981) #3297 3298
    – (années 1890) #187
    – (années 1920) #305 311
    – (années 1920-1960) #495
    – (années 1930), attitude envers le nu dans l'art #317
    – (années 1940) #40 351 363 366 369
        – attitude envers le nu dans l'art #6652
        – et Fédération des artistes canadiens #360 376
        – proposition en vue d'accroître les contacts entre le public et l'art #368
    – (années 1950) #3255 3256 9906
        – en comparaison avec la France #436
    – (années 1950-1970), et aide gouvernementale #3290
    – (années 1960) #87 444 447 448 529 3265
        – rôle des musées #3045
    – (années 1970) #583 586 587 599 602 621 693 3056 3270 3279 6747
        – et aide gouvernementale #3268 3278
        – rôle des musées #3059
    – affiches #910
    – femmes artistes #95 96
        – (années 1970) #701
    – images des femmes, XVIIe-XXe s. #121
    – photographie, XIXe-XXe s. #1024
    – XXe s. #567
– Cantons de l'Est (Qué), (1800-1950) #1296
– et A.Y. Jackson #5922
– et Bertram Richard Brooker #330
– et Charles William Jefferys #5957
– et Cornelius Krieghoff #6093 6101
– et Elizabeth Posthuma Gwillim Simcoe #7211
– et Gérard Morisset #1477 3321
– et John Wilson Bengough #4671 4676 4677
– et Joseph Légaré #6215 6216
– et Lawren Stewart Harris #5722
– et le Groupe des Sept #1735 1763 1764
– et Les Levine #6265
– et Michel Lambeth #6159
– et Napoléon Bourassa #4876
– et Neils Christian Knudsen #6072
– et Paul-Emile Borduas #1455 4811 4812 4834 4837 4848 4849
– et Théophile Hamel #5692
– et William George Richardson Hind #5811
– et William Millikin #6543
– Halifax (NE), (1815-1867) #1217
– Maritimes (années 1950) #1119
– Montréal (Qué) #1395
    – (1860-1912), et Art Association of Montreal #1343

– (1968-1969) #1514
– (années 1940-1950) #1426
– (années 1940-1960) #1438
– (années 1970) #1489 1505 1548
– Nouvelle-Ecosse, XVIIIe-XIXe s. #1215 1220 1222
– Ontario (années 1950) #1748
– Ontario Society of Artists (années 1870-1970) #1678
– provinces de l'Atlantique (années 1960-1970) #1130
– provinces de l'Ouest (années 1950) #1947
– Québec #1237 1294 1444
    – (1640-1840) #1329
    – (1759-1914) #1351
    – (1760-1790) #1369
    – (1780-1840) #1375
    – (1825-1850) #1368
    – (années 1870) #1307
    – (années 1930) #1460
    – (années 1930-1970), et femmes #1273
    – (années 1940-1970) #1269
    – (années 1960) #1487
    – (années 1970) #1446 1450
        – et art vidéo #1499 1537 1550
        – et prédictions pour l'an 2001 #2225
    – XVIIe s.-1850 #1340
– Terre-Neuve
    – (années 1970) #1154
    – XIXe s.-années 1950 #1139
société, art et . Amérindiens #3355
société, art et . Indiens de la côte nord-ouest
– rôle des sculpteurs #3912
société, art et . Inuit #3355 3377 4214 4215 4232 4235 4245 4251 4254 4261 4262 4263 4264 4275 4276 4378 4401 4433
    – (années 1960) #4399
    – (années 1970) #4281
Société canadienne des aquarellistes
– (1925-) #6
– (1926-1936) #332
– et Visual Arts Ontario #1806
– expositions
    – (1939) #346
    – (1951) #394
    – (1976) #127
– oeuvres, appui aux artistes amateurs de l'Aviation royale du Canada (années 1940) #1091
Société canadienne des arts graphiques
– (1931), répertoire #803
– et Société canadienne des peintres-graveurs #3
– et Visual Arts Ontario #1806
– expositions
    – (1939) #346
    – (1971) #824
– expositions, critiques
    – (1947) #809
– précède Conseil canadien de gravure et de dessin #835
Société canadienne des peintres-graveurs
– (1885-1976) #836
– (1916-1976) #3
– (1946-1947) #809
– et Société canadienne des arts graphiques #801
– et Visual Arts Ontario #1806
– et William Walker Alexander #4506
– expositions
    – (1971) #824
– précède Conseil canadien de gravure et dessin #835
Société canadiennne des arts graphiques

– (1904-1976) #801
Société centrale d'hypothèques et de logement
– voir Canada. Société centrale d'hypothèques et de logement
Société d'archéologie et de numismatique de Montréal (Montréal, Qué)
– (1887) #173
– et château de Ramezay (Montréal, Qué) #3076 3077 3083
Société d'art contemporain (Montréal, Qué) #589 592 1393 1451 1459 1474
– et Louise Landry Gadbois #1433
– et Paul-Emile Borduas #4809 4843
– influence sur peinture de paysages, Alberta #1965
Société d'électrolyse et de chimie Alcan Ltée (Sécal) (Montréal, Qué)
– collection #3246
Société d'histoire naturelle du Nouveau-Brunswick (Saint-Jean, NB)
– (1862-1932) #3065
Société des artistes professionnels du Québec
– (1971-1975) #1488
– expositions, critiques
    – (1970) #1490
Société des arts (Montréal, Qué)
– périodique, Vie des arts #55
Société des arts plastiques
– Lemieux, Jean-Paul, commentaire #1411
Société des Faux Visages . Iroquois #3595
– masques #3337 3588 3604 7346
Société des Faux Visages . Tsonnontouans
– masques #3533 3636 4113
Société des graphistes du Québec
– (1974-1981) #893
Société des sculpteurs du Canada #740
– (1928-1958) #741
– (années 1920) #735
– et Emanuel Otto Hahn #5679
– et Visual Arts Ontario #1806
– expositions
    – (1928-) #734
    – (1929-1930) #294
    – (1939) #346
– expositions, critiques
    – (1944) #736
Société ontarienne d'éducation par l'art
– et Visual Arts Ontario #1806
Société pour l'encouragement des arts et des sciences au Canada
– et l'art québécois (1827-1829) #1368
Société pour l'étude de l'architecture au Canada/Society for the Study of Architecture in Canada
– périodique, Selected Papers #7721
Société Radio-Canada
– voir Canada. Société Radio-Canada (CBC)
sociétés secrètes . Indiens de la côte nord-ouest #3871
sociétés secrètes . Indiens des plaines #3727
sociétés secrètes . Kwakiutls #3768
sociétés secrètes . Saulteux/Ojibwa #3492 3602
sociétés secrètes . Tsonnontouans #3508
Society for Art Publications
– périodique, Artscanada #25
Society for the Preservation of Architectural Resources (SPARC) (Calgary, Alta) #8133
Society of American Artists
– et Wyatt Eaton #5357
Society of Applied Arts (Toronto, Ont)
– expositions, critiques

– (1905) #2242
Society of Artists and Amateurs of Toronto
(Toronto, Ont) #1706 1729
– expositions
– (1834) #1688
Society of Canadian Artists
– et Visual Arts Ontario #1806
– nationalisme et peinture de paysages, fin
XIXe s. #271 272
– périodique, *Artmagazine* #560
Society of Estonian Artists (Toronto, Ont)
#118
– (1955-1966) #1761
Society of Manitoba Artists
– (1928-1929), expositions #307
Society of Typographic Designers of Canada
– (1956-1964) #923
sociologie de l'art
– Canada
– (1760-1860) #251
– et histoire de l'art #164
– Québec (années 1970) #1446 1450
Soeurs Grises
– Montréal (Qué), art et architecture #8862
soeurs Hummer
– art de performance #655
sofas . Canada
– Montréal (Qué), (1800-1850) #2538
– Ontario
– (1780-1900) #2577
– (années 1790-1857) #2558
– Québec, XVIIIe-XIXe s. #2536
sol, utilisation du
– *voir aussi* architecture
– Alberta, ranchs, fin XIXe-début XXe s.
#8720 8721
– Charlevoix (Qué) #8629
– comté de Norfolk (Ont), XIXe s. #8656
– Cornwall (Ont), Inverarden #8673
– Nouvelle-Ecosse, XVIIe-XIXe s. #7814
– Ontario, XVIIIe-XIXe s. #7993
– Petit Fort Garry (Man) #8483
– Québec
– fin XVIe s.-années 1950 #7855
– seigneuries #8611
– Saint-Roch-de-l'Achigan (Qué) #7854
Sole, Stelio, artiste can, 1932- #7265
Solomon, Daniel, artiste can, 1945- #1803
1807
– expositions de groupe
– (1974) #565
– participant, Symposium on 20th Century
Canadian Culture (Washington, DC),
(1977) #621
Somerville, William Lyon, architecte can,
1886-1965
– Hamilton (Ont), McMaster University
#9451
– Toronto (Ont), Red Cross Lodge #9027
Sommerer, Karl, photographe can, 1931-
#7266
– catalogue de photographies #995
Sonfist, Alan, artiste amér, 1946-
– expositions de groupe
– (1980) #8237
Sontheim, Herman, orfèvre can, actif 1944
#2693
Soogwilis, Kwakiutls #3883
Sorel (Qué)
– maisons en brique, début XIX s. #8521
Sorensen, Chris, designer can, 1921- #2471
Soucy, Cléophas, sculpteur can, 1879-1950
#7267
Soucy, Donat, sculpteur can, 1909- #7267

Soucy, Elzéar, sculpteur can, 1876-1970
#1240 2179 7267
– professeur de Zénon Alary #4505
– sculpture sur bois, église Notre-Dame
(Montréal, Qué) #8839
Soucy, François, sculpteur can, 1929-
– et Fusion des arts (Montréal, Qué) #1482
– expositions, critiques #7268
Soucy, Jean-Baptiste, conservateur can, 1899-
– directeur, Musée du Québec (Québec,
Qué) #3103
Soulages, Pierre Jean Louis, artiste fr, 1919-
– Mongeau, Jean-Guy, comparaison #6596
Soulis, George, designer can, 1925-
– commentaire sur création de meubles
#2468
Soullard, Jean, ferronnier can, 1642-1710
#234 235
Soumande, Jean, prêtre et artiste can,
1669-1716
– directeur, Ecole des arts et métiers de
Saint-Joachim (Saint-Joachim, Qué) #2992
soupières anglaises
– (ca 1840), vue de Montréal (Qué) #2370
Southam, Harry Stevenson, éditeur et
collectionneur can, 1875-1954
– et Galerie nationale du Canada (Ottawa,
Ont) #3050
Southampton Island (TNO)
– art, Aivilik Eskimos #4184
– culture inuit #4320
Southcott, J. et W., architectes can, actifs
années 1840
– Saint-Jean (TN), maisons #8542
Southwell, George H., artiste can, 1865-1958
– expositions de groupe
– (1961) #62
– oeuvres, édifices du Parlement,
Colombie-Britannique (Victoria, CB) #8967
souverains
– *voir* rois et souverains
Sowdon, Michael, photographe can, 1948-
– cartes géographiques, illustration #561
– expositions de groupe
– (1979) #1905
– (1981) #1070
– hologrammes, Fringe Research Inc.
(Toronto, Ont) #1827
Spahnn, Justin, orfèvre can, 1803-1856 #2649
Spalding, Jeffrey John, artiste can, 1951-
– expositions
– (1981) #7269
SPARC
– *voir* Society for the Preservation of
Architectural Resources (SPARC)
Speck, Henry, artiste can, 1908-1971 #4121
spectacle
– *voir* arts d'interprétation
Speier, Matthew, artiste can, actif 1973
– vidéos #2044
Speirs, Doris Huestis Mills, artiste can, 1894-
– correspondance, J.E.H. MacDonald #6371
Spénard, Jean-Jacques, céramiste can, 1913-
#2179
Spence, David Jerome, architecte can,
1873-1955
– Montréal (Qué), New Princess Theatre
#9069
Spence Bay (TNO)
– atelier de teinture, Judy McGrath #4249
6474
– sculpture #4445 4454
– sculpture sur os de baleine #4436
– vues photographiques

– Pamela Harris #996
Spencer, Deirdre, joaillière can, active 1975
#2706
Spencer, Elihu, photographe can, actif
1859-1869
– expositions de groupe
– (1970) #1675
Spencer, Hugh, designer can, actif années
1750-
– mobilier, Opus International Ltd. #2551
Spencer, James Burton, artiste can, 1940-
– expositions
– (1974) #7270
– expositions de groupe
– (1973) #557
– (1980) #1221
Spencer, Mary, photographe can, m. 1938
#2018
Spencer, Sam A., artiste can, né 1898 #1881
– (1975) #1927
Spencer, Stanley, artiste brit, 1891-1959
– influence sur Brian Rendel Jones #5974
– influence sur Tom La Pierre #6122
Spencer, Stephen Allen, photographe can, ca
1829-1911
– et la Victoria Theatre Photographic Gallery
(Victoria, CB) #2027
Speyer, Arthur, collectionneur all, 1894-1958
– collection, art amérindien #3434 3465 3466
3622
Spickett, Ronald John, artiste can, 1926-
#7271
– expositions de groupe
– (1962) #1847
spiritisme
– *voir* spiritualisme
spiritualisme
– et Lionel LeMoine FitzGerald #5453
Spiteri, Edward J. (Ed), photographe can,
1939-
– catalogue de photographies #991 1023
– expositions de groupe
– (1972) #1952
– (1978) #1962
Spode and Copeland, fabricants de
céramique (Staffordshire, Angleterre)
– et Compagnie de la baie d'Hudson #2300
2357 2358
Spokane (Wash), Cheney Cowles Memorial
Museum
– expositions
– *Enns, Evans & Ulrich* (1977) #1956
Spokane (Wash), Eastern Washington State
Historical Society
– expositions
– *An Art Perspective of the Historic Pacific
Northwest* (1963) #1999
Spoleto (Italie), Palazzo Collicola
– expositions
– *La peinture canadienne moderne: 25 années
de peinture au Canada-français: 5 festival
dei due mondi* (1962) #1421
Spooner, James, marchand d'oeuvres d'art et
artiste can, actif 1867-1888
– correspondance, Homer Ransford Watson
#7534
Sporting Magazine, périodique amér
– illustrations, Peter Rindisbacher #7002
Sprachman, Mandel, architecte can, 1925-
– Charlottetown (IPE), Confederation
Centre, concours #9088 9089
– St. Catharines (Ont), Pen Centre Cinemas
#9100
Spreitz, Karl, artiste can, 1927- #2061

Staniszkis, Joanna Kataszyna, artiste can (tapisserie), 1944-
– expositions de groupe
– (1981) #2776
Stansell, Walter H., artiste can, 1904-
– modèles de locomotives à vapeur #1792
Staples, Owen, artiste can, 1866-1949
– réflexion sur vues du comté de Peel (Ont), collection William Perkins Bull #3208
Starbuck, Fletcher, photographe can, 1945- #538 1007 7275
– et *Image Nation* #992
– expositions, critiques #7276
Stechesen, Leslie (Les), architecte can, 1934- #8409
– Leaf Rapids (Man), centre municipal #8974
Steele, Lisa, artiste can, 1947-
– art vidéo #605 630 7277
– expositions de groupe
– (1977) #631
– (1980) #705
Steinberg, Saul, artiste amér, 1914-
– influence sur Louis de Niverville #6704
Steiner, Michael, sculpteur amér, 1945-
– et Emma Lake Workshops (Emma Lake, Sask) #1929
– influence sur Douglas Bentham #4683 4686
Steinhouse, Tobie Thelma, artiste can, 1925- #7278
Stella, Frank, artiste amér, 1936-
– influence sur Graham Metson #6523
Stella, Jacques, artiste fr, 1596-1657
– influence sur Antoine-Sébastien Plamondon #6886
Stellarton (NE), Banque de Nouvelle-Ecosse
– architecture, Sharp & Horner #9174
Steltzer, Ulli, photographe can, 1923- #2018
Stennett, William, orfèvre can, 1822-1847 #2638
Stent & Laver, agence can d'architecture
– Ottawa (Ont), édifices du Parlement. Edifice de l'Est #8922 8930 8936
Stern, Max, marchand d'oeuvres d'art can, 1904- #1431
– propriétaire, galerie Dominion (Montréal, Qué) #1293
Stevens, Dorothy, artiste can, 1888-1966
– eaux-fortes #799 800
– illustrations #916
Stevens, Gerald, collectionneur can, 1909-1981
– collection, verre canadien #2397 2398 2399
Stevens & Lee, agence can d'architecture
– Montréal (Qué), hôpital Royal Victoria. Pavillon Ross #9017
– Toronto (Ont), Hospital for Sick Children #9015
Stevenson, Orlando John, éducateur can, 1869-1950
– et acquisition de peintures canadiennes, University of Guelph (Guelph, Ont) #3173
Stevenson, Sylvie, artiste can, 1943-
– expositions de groupe
– (1981) #2084
Stevenson, Thomas H., artiste can, actif 1841-1858
– membre de la Toronto Society of Arts #1689
Stevenson & Dewar, agence can d'architecture
– Vancouver (BC), Vancouver Civic Auditorium, competition #9080
Stewart, Betty, artiste can, active 1965
– associé, Paul Arthur and Associates #873

Stewart, Michael, designer can, 1940- #2487
Stewart, W.N., artiste can, né 1888
– expositions de groupe
– (1958) #1846
Stewart, William, imprimeur can, actif années 1870
– eau-forte sur zinc #4673
Stidworthy, William F., artiste can, 1889-
– expositions
– (1960) #1668
Stiff, Philander S., photographe can, actif années 1860-1870
– expositions de groupe
– (1970) #1675
Stiff, Thomas P., photographe can, actif années 1860-1870
– expositions de groupe
– (1970) #1675
Stijl, de
– et Robert Gray Murray #6668
Still, Clyfford, artiste amér, 1904-1980
– influence sur Jean Albert McEwen #6471
Stirling, David, architecte can, 1822-1877
– et William Critchlow #8372
– Halifax (NE) #7838
Stirton, Alexander Mackenzie, photographe can, 1915-
– photographies de la Seconde Guerre mondiale #1107
Stitt, Donald Munroe, photographe can, 1924-
– photographies, Forces armées canadiennes #1107
Stock, Ramsey & Associates, agence can d'architecture
– Regina (Sask), 38 Saskatchewan Geriatric Centre #8516
Stockdale (Ont)
– vues photographiques, Lizzy Wadsworth #7496
Stockholm (Suède), Musée national
– crécelles en forme de bec de macareux, Indiens de la côte nord-ouest #3960
– totem, Kwakiutl #3844
Stoddard, S.P., artiste brit au Canada, actif 1843
– vues de Windsor (NE) #1218
Stodthard, J., officier de la marine brit, artiste au Canada, XVIIIe s.
– vues, détroit de Nootka, Vancouver Island (CB) #2002
Stoke-on-Trent (Angleterre), Minton Works Museum
– service à dessert Minton #2289
Stokes, Louis, sculpteur can, 1941-
– expositions de groupe
– (1977) #784
Stokes, Peter John, architecte can, 1926-
– restauration, The Grange (Toronto, Ont) #8680
Stolfa, Lydia, artisane tisserande can, active 1961 #2102
Stone, Sir John Benjamin, photographe brit au Canada, 1838-1914
– photographies, Têtes Plates et Nez-Percés #3717
Stone, Sylvia, artiste can, 1927-
– commentaire sur séjour à New York (années 1960) #460
Stoney Lake (Ont)
– pétroglyphes, Saulteux/Ojibwa #3581
Storey & Van Egmond, agence can d'architecture
– Regina (Sask)

– édifices du Parlement, concours #8956
– War Memorial Museum, competition #9073
Storm, William George, architecte can, 1826-1892
– Toronto (Ont) #8056 8059 8075
– University of Toronto. University College #9428
Stott, Gregg, photographe can, actif 1980
– catalogue de photographies #1032
Stouf, Jean Baptiste, sculpteur fr, 1742-1826
– professeur de François Baillairgé #4588
Stoughton, Arthur A., architecte can, 1867-1955
– Winnipeg (Man), University of Manitoba. Science Building et Arts Building #9485
Straiton, Ken, photographe can, 1949- #2071
Straram, Patrick, auteur can, 1934- #1502
Stratford (Ont)
– galeries d'art (années 1960) #442
Stratford (Ont), Rothmans Art Gallery of Stratford
– expositions
– *André Biéler 50 Years: A Retrospective Exhibition 1920-1970* (1971) #4725
– *Dan Christensen: Recent Paintings* (1974) #5104
– *Five Years of Robert Downing, 1966-1971* (1972) #5306
– *Gift from the Douglas M. Duncan Collection and the Milne-Duncan Bequest/Le Don provenant de la collection Douglas M. Duncan et le legs Milne-Duncan* (1972) #541
– *Watercolour Painters from Saskatchewan/Aquarellistes de la Saskatchewan* (1972) #1920
– *York Wilson Retrospective (1927-1973)* (1974) #7596
– expositions, critiques
– *Aspects of Realism* (1976) #606
Stratford (Ont), Stratford Festival Art Exhibition
– expositions
– *25 Quebec Painters* (1961) #1419
– *Painting at Stratford, 1962: Nine Prairie Province Painters* (1962) #1847
– *Ten Canadians: The Stratford Festival Art Exhibition, 1959* (1959) #438
Stratford (Ont), Stratford Festival Theatre
– architecture #9086
– Rounthwaite & Fairfield #7679
Stratford (Ont), Stratford Shakespearean Festival
– expositions
– *First Open-air Sculpture Exhibition* (1965) #749
– *La Deuxième Exposition champêtre de sculptures du festival Shakespearien de Stratford, 1966/Second Open-Air Sculpture Exhibition, Stratford Shakespearean Festival, 1966* (1966) #1587
Stratford (Ont), The Gallery/Stratford
– expositions
– *20th Century Canadian Drawings* (1979) #146
– *9 Out of 10: A Survey of Contemporary Canadian Art* (1975) #569
– *A Survey of Forty-five Years* (1977) #6658
– *A Terrible Beauty: The Art of Canada at War* (1978) #1111
– *Ann Kipling: Recent Landscapes* (1981) #6057
– *Beauté tragique: les deux conflits mondiaux*

vus par des artistes canadiens (1978) #1112
- *Coasts, the Sea, and Canadian Art* (1978) #139
- *Ed Bartram: 10 Years* (1980) #4618
- *Edward Curtis in the Collection of the Edmonton Art Gallery* (1980) #3480
- *Eleven London Artists* (1979) #1828
- *Frederic Marlett Bell-Smith (1846-1923)* (1978) #4668
- *Humorist Walter Trier: Selections from the Trier-Fodor Foundation Gift* (1981) #7428
- *John Fox: 10 New Paintings* (1980) #5495
- *Metamorphosis, Memories, Dreams and Reflections: The Work of Florence Vale* (1980) #7453
- *Métiers d'art Ontario-Québec, 1979/1980/Quebec-Ontario Crafts, 1979/1980* (1980) #2138
- *Painters Eleven in Retrospect* (1980) #1785
- *Roland Brener* (1979) #4912
- *Sculpture: Limits, Lines, Projections: Recent Works by André Fauteux, Peter Kolisnyk, Louis Stokes, Patrick Thibert* (1977) #784
- *The Heritage of Jack Bush: A Tribute* (1982) #722
- *The Ontario Community Collects: A Survey of Canadian Painting from 1766 to the Present* (1976) #120
- *Viewpoint: Twenty-nine by Nine; An Exhibition of Twenty-nine Works by Ontario Artists, Selected by Nine Curators* (1981) #1838

Strickland, Samuel, écrivain can, 1804-1867
- commentaire sur construction d'habitation #8527
structuralisme
- et Eli Bornstein #536 4856
- et Joyce Wieland #7580
structurisme #777
- et Ron Kostyniuk #6079
Strutt, James William, architecte can, 1924-
- Ottawa (Ont), maison Hanlon #7984
Stryjek, Dmytro, artiste can, 1899-
- entretien #7280
- expositions de groupe
  - (1975) #1927
Stuart, Donald A. (Don), artiste can, 1945- #7281
- et atelier de tissage de Panghirtung (Pangnirtung, TNO) #4308
stuc
- utilisation dans habitations canadiennes (1908) #8638
Studio, The, périodique brit
- Lamb, Harold Mortimer, correspondant canadien #6156
Studio Club (Toronto, Ont)
- expositions, critiques #978
Stump, Sarrain, artiste can, 1945-1974 #4136
- concepts cosmologiques #554
stupéfiants
- influence sur Arthur Fortescue McKay #6475 6477
Sturdy, Martha, artiste can, 1943-
- bijoux #2706
Stuttgart (Allemagne de l'Ouest), Linden Museum
- art, Indiens des plaines #3737 3750
Stuttgart (West Germany), Museum für Länder-und Völkerkunde
- expositions
  - *Indianische Malerei in Nordamerika, 1830-1970: Prärie und Plains, Südwesten Neue Indianer* (1973) #3451

style Chippendale
- mobilier
  - Québec #2542
  - Terre-Neuve #2502
style Hepplewhite
- mobilier québécois #2542
style international (architecture, XXe s.)
- Canada #7680
  - architecture domestique #8502
  - banques #9196
- Prairies #8084 8086
style Liberty
- *voir* Art nouveau
style Louis XVI
- architecture
  - Calgary (Alta), Hotel Palliser #9271
  - Toronto (Ont)
    - Chorley Park #8749
    - Royal Alexandra Theatre #9059
style moderne
- *voir* Art déco
style Queen Anne
- architecture
  - LaSalle (Qué), manoir Ogilvie #8636
style Regency
- architecture
  - églises, Ontario #8904
  - maisons, Ontario #8654
  - Saint-Jean (TN) #8542
  - Toronto (Ont), Colborne Lodge #8659
- mobilier
  - Canada #2101
  - Nouveau-Brunswick #2501
  - Québec #2542
  - Terre-Neuve #2502
  - sièges, Ontario #2553
sublime
- et Robert Charles John Bourdeau #4882
- et William Henry Bartlett #4617
- vues de la côte nord-ouest, XVIIIe s. #2009
sucre d'érable
- Québec #1334 1335 1364
  - moules #2592
Sudbury (Ont)
- art (années 1970) #1801
Sudbury (Ont), Université Laurentienne
- architecture #9461
Sudbury (Ont), Université Laurentienne. Musée et Centre d'art
- expositions
  - *Alan C. Collier Retrospective* (1971) #5131
  - *Canadian Paintings in the University of Toronto: An Exhibition in Celebration of the Sesquicentennial of the University of Toronto* (1978) #3168
  - *Goodridge Roberts: Paintings from the 1950s and 60s* (1980) #7048
  - *Humorist Walter Trier: Selections from the Trier-Fodor Foundation Gift* (1980) #7428
  - *Norart: Annual Juried Exhibition of Northern Ontario Art/Norart: exposition annuelle d'arts du Nord-Ontario* (1979-) #1829
  - *The Ontario Community Collects: A Survey of Canadian Painting from 1766 to the Present* (1976) #120
  - *The Work of Art: Six Artists* (1979) #665
  - *Trésors d'art populaire québécois/Folk Art Treasures of Quebec* (1980) #1297
  - *Viewpoint: Twenty-nine by Nine; An Exhibition of Twenty-nine Works by Ontario Artists, Selected by Nine Curators* (1982) #1838
Sugino, Shin, photographe can, 1946-

- catalogue de photographies #991
Sugluk (Qué)
- arts graphiques (1972-1975) #4475
Sukhachev, Ihor, artiste can, actif années 1970
- fresques, Church of Saint Nicholas (Toronto, Ont) #1822
Sulcs, Ernie, photographe can, actif années 1970-
- catalogue de photographies #991
Sullivan, Francis Conroy, architecte can, 1882-1929 #8410
Sullivan, Françoise, artiste can, 1928- #7282
- écrits #1449
- expositions
  - (1981) #7283
- expositions de groupe
  - (1976) #1529
- *Refus global* #1396
sulpiciens
- architecture, Montréal (Qué) #7919 7932
- Montréal (Qué), église Notre-Dame #8849 8892
Summerside (IPE), Eptek Centre
- expositions
  - *Canadians: A National Photography Show about People/Canadiens: exposition nationale de photographie ayant les gens comme thème* (1979) #1035
Summerside (IPE), Green Park
- architecture et intérieur #8540
Sunderland, Maurice, architecte can, 1926-
- Vancouver (CB), Vancouver Civic Auditorium, concours #9080
Surcouf, Lorraine Joy, artiste can, 1933- #7284
Sures, Jack, artiste can, 1935- #2395
- expositions
  - (1976) #7285
- expositions de groupe
  - (1968) #2382
- professeur de Marilyn Ann Levine #6274
Suria, Tomás de, artiste esp au Canada, 1761-1835
- vues, côte nord-ouest #1998
surréalisme #454
- Canada #463 508 509
  - scènes de guerre, Seconde Guerre mondiale #1115
- Canada et Etats-Unis #1458
- Canadian National Exhibition (Toronto, Ont), (1938) #1
- Colombie-Britannique #2051
- et Alan Frank Glass #5614
- et Alex Colville #5144
- et Alfred Pellan #1453 6800 6808 6812 6820 6821 6822 6826
- et Arthur Handy #5702
- et Carol Fraser #5508
- et Esther Warkov #7518
- et Fernand Leduc #1443 6191
- et Gordon Rayner #6964
- et Jack Leonard Shadbolt #7188
- et Jean-Antoine Demers #5283
- et Jean-Philippe Dallaire #5242 5244
- et Jock Macdonald #6379
- et John Howard Gould #5636
- et Kenneth Campbell Lochhead #6313
- et Ladislav Guderna #5663
- et Léon Bellefleur #4660
- et Louis de Niverville #6709
- et Ludwig Zeller #7633
- et Norman McLaren #6497
- et Paul-Emile Borduas #1467 4839 4843

– et Pierre Gendron #5581
– et Robert Gray Murray #6668
– et Roland Giguère #5595 5598
– et Susana Wald #7633
– et Tibor et Peter Kovalik #6081
– influence du masque de faucon kwakiutl #3361
– Montréal (Qué) #1426
– (1954-1955) #1408
– Québec #1270 1464 1650
– dessins #1470
Surrey, Philip Henry, artiste can, 1910-#7286 7290
– et peinture de genre #392
– expositions
– (1971) #7289
– paysages urbains #7287 7288
– réflexion sur sérigraphies canadiennes, Seconde Guerre mondiale #805
Surrey (CB)
– architecture #8147
Surrey (CB), Surrey Art Gallery
– expositions
– An Exhibition of Works in Transparent Media: Sandy Arthur, Garry Cullen, Anna Gustafson, D'Arcy Henderson, Lyse Lemieux, Lynn Vardeman (1978) #2067
– Creative Flight (1979) #147
– Joe Fafard: Recent Sculpture (1980) #5401
– Nora Blanck, Karen Chapnick: A Presentation of Current Work (1978) #663
– Sculpture of the Inuit: Lorne Balshine Collection/Lou Osipov Collection/Dr. Harry Winrob Collection (1978) #4447
– Sherry Grauer...So Far... (1980) #5647
– The Inuit Sea Goddess (1981) #4312
– The Surrey Art Gallery Permanent Collection (1979) #3201
Surrey (CB), Surrey Arts Centre
– architecture, Hawthorn Mansfield Towers #8373
Surrey (CB), Surrey Memorial Hospital
– architecture, Gardiner, Thornton, Gathe & Associates #9032
Surveyer, Arthur, Can, né 1878
– et Commission royale d'enquête sur l'avancement des arts, lettres et sciences (Rapport Massey) #3261
Suscan, Charles, artiste can, 1932- #7291
Sussex (NB), Sussex Composite High School
– expositions
– Colville, Pratt, Forrestall (1974) #1129
– The Beaverbrook Art Gallery Presents Nine New Brunswick Artists/La Galerie d'art Beaverbrook présente neuf artistes du Nouveau-Brunswick (1973) #1182
Sutton, Carol, artiste can, 1945- #711 7292
– expositions de groupe
– (1981) #722
– réflexion sur peinture canadienne (années 1970) #620
Suzor-Coté, Marc-Aurèle de Foy, artiste can, 1869-1937 #10 302 1315 1392 1713 7293 7294 7295 7297 7298 7300 7302
– à Paris (France) #7296
– et Académie royale des arts du Canada #152
– et Albert Henry Robinson #7057
– et Canadian Art Club #193
– et Georges-Henri Duquet #5343
– expositions, critiques #204 211 1316
– expositions de groupe
– (1935) #17
– (1980) #1296

– influence de l'impressionisme #227
– influence de la peinture française #1244
– Paysage d'hiver, Galerie nationale du Canada (Ottawa, Ont) #7301
– paysages d'hiver #285
– paysages et scènes rurales #7299
– professeur de Jean-Paul Lemieux #6228
– professeur de Rodolphe Duguay #5317
Suzuki, Aiko, artiste can, 1937-
– expositions, critiques #2771
Svarre, Grace, artiste can, 1936-
– au Mexique #7303
Svatina, Maria, artiste can, 1934-
– expositions de groupe
– (1978) #2772
Swaihwés
– masques #4033
Swales, Francis S., architecte can, 1878-1962
– Vancouver (CB), Hotel Vancouver #9272 9273
Swanson, Herbert Andrew, architecte can, 1926-
– Société centrale d'hypothèques et de logement, concours (1960) #8040
Swarthmore (Penn), Swarthmore College
– Murray, Robert Gray, Garnet #6672
Swensson, Pete, photographe can, actif années 1960, m. 1976
– catalogue de photographies #991
Swibold, Susanne, artiste can, 1938- #7304
Swift, Joseph, artiste can, m. 1889
– peintures d'animaux #1727
Swift Current (Sask), National Exhibition Centre
– expositions
– Artisan '78: The First National Travelling Exhibition of Contemporary Canadian Crafts/Artisan '78: première exposition nationale itinérante d'artisanat canadien contemporain (1979) #2134
– Roger Savage (1980) #7135
– William Perehudoff: Ten Years, 1970-1980/William Perehudoff: une décennie, 1970-1980 (1983) #6838
Swinton, George, artiste, historien d'art et collectionneur can, 1917-
– collection, art inuit #4306
– commentaire sur Winnipeg Art Gallery (Winnipeg, Man) #4449
– entretien #7305
– expositions de groupe
– (1962) #1847
Sydenham Glass Co., fabricants de verre (Wallaceburg, Ont) #2401
Sydney (Australie), Hooker Tower
– architecture, John Andrews Architects #8323
Sydney (Australie), National Art Gallery of New South Wales
– expositions
– Contemporary Canadian Painters (1957) #423
Sydney (NE), Banque de Nouvelle-Ecosse
– architecture, Sharp & Horner #9174
Sykes, John, officier de la marine brit, artiste au Canada, 1773-1858
– vues, détroit de Nootka, Vancouver Island (CB) #2002
Sylvestre, Micheline de Passillé
– voir Passillé-Sylvestre, Micheline de
Syme, James, architecte can, 1832-1881
– Victoria (CB) #8145
Symons, Robert David, artiste can, 1898-1973
– expositions de groupe

– (1971) #1920
Symons & Rae, agence can d'architecture
– Toronto (Ont), Cathedral of Saint Alban the Martyr #8896
– Vancouver (BC), University of British Columbia, concours #9498
symposium
– voir conférences
synagogues . Canada
– (années 1950) #8763 8764
– Montréal (Qué), Tifereth Jerusalem Synagogue #8846
– Ontario (années 1960) #8903
Syverson, Terrence, artiste can, 1939-
– entretien #460
Szabo, Zoltan, artiste can, 1928- #7306
Szaszkiewicz, Cécile, artiste can, 1935- #7307
Szebenyi, Imre, sculpteur can, 1923-
– expositions de groupe
– (1971), médailles #772
Szenes, Arpad, artiste fr, né 1897
– professeur de Tobie Thelma Steinhouse #7278
Szilasi, Gabor, photographe can, 1928-
– catalogue de photographies #997 999
– expositions, critiques #7308 7309
– expositions de groupe
– (1973) #1002
– photographies documentaires #1556

T

T. Eaton Company Limited
– voir Eaton, T., Company Limited
tabac . Amérindiens #3416
tabac . Hurons
– blagues à tabac #3514
tabac . Iroquois #3618
tabac . pots et boîtes . Canada
– bois, Ontario, XVIIIe-XIXe s. #2588
tabatières
– voir tabac . pots et boîtes
tabernacles . Canada
– Québec
– XVIIe-XIXe s. #1613
– XVIIe-XVIIIe s. #1359
tables . Canada
– Ile-du-Prince-Edouard #2508 2518
– Nouvelle-Ecosse (années 1740-1850) #2497
– Ontario #2566
– (1780-1900) #2577
– (années 1790-1857) #2558
– table à battants (1815-1845) #2555
– Québec, XVIIe-XVIIIe s. #2529 2530 2531
Taché, Eugène Etienne, architecte can, 1836-1912
– Québec (Qué), Assemblée nationale #8942
tachisme
– et Claude Tousignant #7401
– et Jean-Paul Riopelle #7020
Tack, Augustus Vincent, artiste amér, 1870-1949
– murales, Palais législatif (Winnipeg, Man) #8948 8949 8952
Taçon, Edna Jeanette, artiste can, 1913-1980 #7310
Taconis, Kryn, photographe can, 1918-1979 #1054
Tagish
– culture #4106
Tagoona, Armand, artiste can, 1926-

– réflexion sur son oeuvre #7311
Tahltans
– culture (années 1910) #4074 4093
Tailfeathers, Gerald, artiste can, 1925-1975
#4125 4136 7312 7313
– expositions de groupe
– (1961) #62
taille-douce
– *voir* gravure
Taillefer, Robert Eugene, photographe can,
ca 1947-
– catalogue de photographies #991
Taillibert, Roger, architecte fr, 1926-
– Montréal (Qué), Stade olympique #9127
– réflexion sur son oeuvre architecturale
#9139
– stades #9130
Tait, Norman, sculpteur can, 1941-
– expositions
– (1977) #7314
Tait, Sylvia, artiste can, 1932-
– sérigraphies #7315
Takashima, Shizueye Violet, artiste can,
1928- #7316
Takrik, Bobby, sculpteur can, 1934- #7317
Talirunili, Joe, artiste can, 1906-1976 #7318
Tallin (Estonie), State College of Art
– Lee, Abel, élève #6212
tambours . Iroquois #3489
tambours . Kwakiutls
– danse de l'Oiseau-Tonnerre #3867
tambours . Micmacs #3556
tambours . Saulteux/Ojibwa #3539
tambours . Tlingits #3976
Tampold & Wells, agence can d'architecture
– Halifax (NE), Saint Mary's University.
Résidence des étudiants #8744
– Toronto (Ont), Tartu College #8744
– Toronto (Ont), University of Toronto.
Résidence des étudiants #9467
– Waterloo (Ont), University of Waterloo.
Résidence des étudiants #9467
Tanabe, Takao, artiste can, 1926- #7319
– dessins de paysages, Prairies #7321
– élève de Hans Hofmann #402 1850
– expositions
– (1976) #7320
– expositions de groupe
– (1958) #431
– (1959) #1997
– peintures murales #1844
Tanainas
– culture (années 1930) #4085
Tanaka, Kazumi, photographe can, 1948-
– expositions de groupe
– (1979) #2069
Tananas
– culture #4095
Tanguay, Michel, artiste can, 1937- #1551
Tanobe, Miyuki, artiste can, 1939- #7323
7324 7325
– scènes urbaines #7322
tapis
– *voir aussi* conservation et restauration,
tapis
– *voir* nattes
tapis . Canada #2725
– (1608-1867) #2120
– Belbin, Louise #2759
– Corporation canadienne de l'artisanat
#2090
– fait à partir de vieux vêtements, XIXe s.
#2888
– Gagnon, Clarence Alphonse #5546 5547

– île d'Orléans (Qué) #1252 2764
– Nouvelle-Ecosse, patrons (avant 1920)
#2785
– Ontario, XIXe s. #2754
– Price, Ralph et Patricia, collection #971
– Québec
– (années 1930) #2164 2165
– (années 1930-1940) #2186
– (années 1940) #2188
– tapis crochetés #2107 2752 2755 2757 2766
– (1860-1960) #2758
– (1860-début XXe s.) #2761 2762
– Bluenose #2763
– MacDonald, Charles William, dessins
#6355
– mennonites #2264
– Nouvelle-Ecosse #2731
– Québec #2750 2751 2752 2753
– Terre-Neuve #1154 2744 2760
– Terre-Neuve et Labrador #2155
– Tremblay, Georges-Edouard #2756
– tapis crochetés et tapis poinçonnés,
Terre-Neuve et Labrador #2765 2767
– Terre-Neuve #1155
– thème décoratif du castor #56
– tradition germanique #2140
– XVIIe-XIXe s. #2730 2736
– XXe s. #2121
tapisserie
– *voir aussi* textiles et tissus
tapisserie . Canada
– (années 1970), motifs conçus par des
artistes #2770
– Arbour, Madeleine #4535 4536
– Beauchemin, Micheline #4642 4643 4644
4645 8233
– Beauregard, Andrée #4653
– Blackburn, Jacques #4737
– Caron, Roger #5005
– Chamard, Emélie #5069
– Clerk, Pierre Jean #5118
– Corriveau, Jeanne d'Arc #5177
– Crowell, Ivan H. #5296
– Dallaire, Jean-Philippe #5244
– Donaldson, Margery Rogers #5296
– Dorsey, Fran #5302
– Gregor, Helen Frances #2776 5656
– Guité, Suzanne #5669
– Hayman, Sasha #5756
– Jaworska, Tamara Hans #5949
– Leduc, Fernand #6188
– Mondou, Pierrette #1282 6595
– Ontario (années 1970) #2768
– Owidzka, Jolanta #9108
– Panneton, Louise #6758
– Pellan, Alfred #6804
– Québec (années 1970) #2772 2773
– Québec (Qué), XXe s. #2769
– Rousseau-Vermette, Mariette #2776 7085
– Roussil, Robert #7097
– Sherbrooke (Qué), (années 1970) #2232
– Simard-Laflamme, Carole #7209
– Staniszkis, Joanna Kataszyna #2776
– Stuart, Don #7281
– Van Ginhoven, Anke #1282
– XXe s. #2774
tapisserie . Hongrie
– ceinture fléchée, comparaison #2865
tapisserie à l'aiguille . Canada
– rideaux de lits, Royal Ontario Museum
(Toronto, Ont) #2784
Tardif-Hébert, Jeannine, artiste can, 1934-
#1538
Tardy, Henri, prêtre can, actif 1965-

– encouragement des arts graphiques inuit,
Holman (TNO) #4197 4469
Tascona, Antonio (Tony), artiste can, 1926-
#7326 7327 7328
– expositions de groupe
– (1977) #1901
– (1981) #1907
tasses . Canada
– tasses à quêter en argent, Québec,
XVIIe-XVIIIe s. #2671
Tassie, James, sculpteur écossais, 1735-1799
– influence sur Robert Tait McKenzie #6487
tat, art et . Inuit #4397
Tata, Sam, photographe can, 1911- #7329
– catalogue de photographies #997 999
– photographies documentaires #1556
Tatossian, Armand, artiste can, 1948- #7330
7331
tatouage #2948
– *voir aussi* art corporel
– MacLean, Robert #2923
tatouage . Amérindiens #3453
tatouage . Assiniboines
– en comparaison avec tatouage cri #3723
tatouage . autochtones #3330
tatouage . Cris #3655 3723
tatouage . Haidas #3761
tatouage . Indiens des plaines #3684
tatouage . Inuit #4209
tatouage . Lillooets #3783
tatouage . Saulteux/Ojibwa
– en comparaison avec tatouage cri #3723
– Island Lake (Man) #3549
tatouage . Thompsons #3823
Tatty, Robert, artiste can, 1927-
– expositions de groupe
– (1968) #3350
tavernes . Canada
– XIXe s. #9285
tavernes . Etats-Unis
– XIXe s. #9285
Taylor, Frederick Bourchier, artiste can,
1906-
– *Talking Union* #7332
Taylor, George Thomas, artiste can,
1838-1913 #1186
– expositions
– (1968) #7334
– photographes #7333
– vues de Fredericton (NB) #1174
Taylor, James, céramiste can, né 1867
– fondateur, Taylor Pottery (Port Hope, Ont)
#2292
Taylor, Jeremy, photographe can, 1938-
– catalogue de photographies #987
Taylor, John, photographe can, 1946-
– catalogue de photographies #991
Taylor, John Benjamin (Jack), artiste can,
1917-1970 #1164
– expositions
– (1973) #7335
– expositions de groupe
– (1940) #350
Taylor, Joseph, constructeur can, actif
1890-1891
– Windsor (NE), maison Shand #8546
Taylor, Mabel, artisane can (vannerie),
active 1976 #4142
Taylor, Richard, artiste can aux Etats-Unis,
1902-1970 #7336 7337
Taylor, sir Andrew Thomas, architecte can,
1850-1937
– Montréal (Qué), Université McGill.
Macdonald Physics Building #9411

Taylor, Thomas Grey (Tom), sculpteur can, 1919- #7338

Taylor Pottery, fabricants de céramique (Port Hope, Ont) #2292

Tazewell, Samuel Oliver, lithographe can, actif 1823-1838 #7339

Tchécoslovaquie, *Second Triennial of Naive Art*
– Patterson, Dan, sculpture, boîtes de lait Carnation #6779

Tchelitchev, Pavel, artiste et scénographe soviéto-américain, 1898-1957
– Markgraf, Waltraud Erna Else, comparaison #6416

Tchippewayans
– *voir aussi* Athapascans; Couteaux-Jaunes; Flancs-de-Chien; Slaveys
– pétroglyphes #3439
– photographies
– Curtis, Edward Sheriff #3399

Teague, John, architecte can, 1833-1902
– Victoria (CB) #8145 8175

techniques
– *voir* matériaux et techniques

technologie, architecture et
– Canada
– (1867-1967) #7695
– (années 1930) #7658
– (années 1960) #8280
– style victorien #7725

technologie, art et
– Bornstein, Eli, commentaire #4855
– Canada (années 1940) #369
– Création #1492
– Fusion des arts (Montréal, Qué) #1482
– Levine, Les, commentaire #6260 6265
– McLuhan, Marshall, commentaire #513
– Québec, XVIIe-XIXe s. #2221

teepees
– *voir* tipis

Teevee, Jamasie, artiste can, 1910- #4460

Teit, James Alexander, ethnographe can, 1864-1922 #3952

Teitelbaum, Mashel, artiste can, 1921-
– professeur #7340

Tekakouitha, Catherine
– *voir* Tekakwitha, Kateri

Tekakwitha, Kateri, Amérindienne can, 1656-1680
– croix commémorative #1569

Telegram, journal can
– dessins humoristiques, Richard Taylor #7336

téléphone . construction . Canada
– (années 1880-1950) #9298
– Montréal (Qué), Bell Canada #9310

télévision
– *voir aussi* art vidéo

télévision, art et
– Canada (années 1960) #867
– General Idea #5583
– MacEachern, Ian #6386
– Robertson, Clive #7053
– W.O.R.K.S. #1955

télévision américaine
– graphisme (1980) #913

télévision canadienne
– (années 1950), Commission royale d'enquête sur l'avancement des arts, lettres et sciences (Rapport Massey) #3261
– (années 1970) #583 693 3279
– graphisme
– (1964-1970) #872
– (1965-1968) #874

– (1980) #913
– (années 1950) #866 869
– (années 1950-1970) #909
– (années 1970) #899
– Art Directors' Club of Toronto #854
– Head, George Bruce #5759

Temporali, Louis, sculpteur can, 1909-
– et Jacobine Jones, sculpture murale, Banque de Nouvelle-Écosse (Toronto, Ont) #5977

Temporali, Pete, sculpteur can, actif 1951
– et Jacobine Jones, sculpture murale, Banque de Nouvelle-Écosse (Toronto, Ont) #5977

temps dans l'art
– art inuit #4244
– Canada (1980) #699
– Goodwin, Betty Roodish #5627
– Lemieux, Jean-Paul #6235 6236 6240
– Snow, Michael #7245

tentures
– *voir* draperies

Terrace (CB), Terrace and District Hospital
– architecture, Thompson, Berwick & Pratt #9032

terre cuite
– Canada (1809-1930) #7704
– Montréal (Qué), (années 1880-1920) #7750
– Toronto (Ont)
– Banque de Montréal #9155
– Standard Bank #9158
– Winnipeg (Man), Birks Building #9355

Terre-Neuve
– annonces dans les journaux, services et marchandises (1806-1900) #1158
– architecture #7782 7792
– XVIe-XIXe s. #7781
– XVIIIe-XIXe s. #7779
– architecture domestique #7785 7791 8541
– cabanes en rondins verticaux #8535
– art #1154
– (1867-1967) #1142
– (années 1940) #350
– (années 1950) #389
– (années 1970) #1131 1146 1149
– (années 1980) #1161
– Art Association of Newfoundland and Labrador #1144
– fin XIXe s.-années 1940 #1138
– art traditionnel #1155
– artefacts dorsétiens #4346 4377 4379 4380
– artefacts préhistoriques #4332
– arts, XIXe s.-années 1950 #1139
– arts décoratifs #2158 2159
– (années 1950) #2146
– (années 1970) #2149 2152
– XXe s. #2155
– arts graphiques
– (1980) #1159
– (années 1970) #1148
– cloches #2717
– édifices publics #7784
– églises (années 1850) #8772
– hôpitaux (années 1950) #9029
– mobilier
– XIXe-début XXe s. #2519
– XIXe s. #2520
– XVIIIe s.-années 1850 #2502
– monuments funéraires, XVIIIe s.-1860 #1163
– orfèvrerie #2640
– ouvrage de vannerie #2945
– palais de justice (1830-1903) #9008
– peinture, fin XIXe s.-années 1970 #1147

– peinture traditionnelle (années 1970) #1153 1156
– phares #9523 9525
– poterie de grès, XVIIIe s. #2364 2365
– sculpture (années 1970) #1151
– tapis crochetés (années 1940-1970) #2760
– tapis crochetés et tapis poinçonnés #2765 2767
– Belbin, Louise #2759
– textiles et tissus #2744
– tonneaux #2151
– vues
– (1497-1887), estampes et illustrations de périodiques #1145
– (années 1970), art vidéo, paysages #1157
– Blackwood, David Lloyd #4739
– Cullen, Maurice Galbraith #1143
– Lapointe, Frank #6169 6170
– Smith, William St. Thomas #7236
– Squires, Gerald Leopold #7272
– Williamson, Albert Curtis #7590
– XVIIIe-XIXe s., estampes #1150
– vues photographiques
– (1849-1949) #1160
– Holloway, Elsie #5820

Terre-Neuve. Ministère de l'Éducation. Handicraft Centre
– Terre-Neuve, métiers d'arts, appui (années 1950) #2146

Territoires du Nord-Ouest
– vues photographiques
– Moodie, Geraldine #6602

Tesiorowski, Carol, photographe can, ca 1954-
– catalogue de photographies #1032

Tessier (dit Lavigne), Paul, constructeur can, 1701-1773 #269 270 7844

Tessler, Ronnie, photographe can, 1944- #2071

Tester, Wayne, photographe can, ca 1928-
– catalogue de photographies #1032

têtes
– sculpture inuit et sculpture dorsétienne, représentations de visages humains #4429

Têtes-de-Boule
– art #4079
– récipients #4108

Tétreault, Denyse Gérin
– *voir* Gérin-Tétreault, Denyse

Tétreault, Pierre-Léon, artiste can, 1947- #7341
– membre du Centre communautaire catholique Tour de David (Saint-Basile-le-Grand, Qué) #1510

Tettamanti, James R., architecte can, 1923-
– Vancouver (CB), Trust Royal, rénovation #9301

textiles et tissus
– *voir aussi* appliqués de soie; broderie; catalogues de patrons . textiles; colorants et teinture; conservation et restauration, textiles; dentelle; filage; laine; lin; ouvrages à l'aiguille; tapis; tapisserie; tissage; travail des fibres
– vêtements
– (années 1870) #2878
– Louisbourg (NE), (1713-1758) #2855
– Montréal (Qué), XVIIe s. #2821
– XVIIe-XIXe s. #2825

textiles et tissus, techniques
– *voir* matériaux et techniques . textiles

textiles et tissus . Algonquiens
– lieux de sépulture, Redbank (NB) #3561

textiles et tissus . Amérindiens #2727 3381

3469 3476
textiles et tissus . Canada #2089 2725 2739
    2747 2748
– (1608-1867) #2120
– (1750-1900) #2727
– (1837-1887) #253
– (1886-1930), catalogues du magasin Eaton
    #2851
– (1964-1967) #2108 2109
– (1980) #2257
– (années 1940) #2601
– (années 1960) #2106
– batik (années 1970) #2741
– Brown, Annora #4933
– Cap-Breton (NE) #2732
– Charlevoix (Qué), XVIIe-XIXe s. #2733
– guide pour collectionneurs #2104 2125
    2131 2252
– Hamilton, Mary Riter, peinture sur étoffe
    #5695
– Ile-de-Prince-Edouard, XVIIIe-XIXe s.
    #2734
– Kamata, Takuro #6000
– Miron, Claire, motifs, Dominion Textile
    Co. (Montréal, Qué) #6571
– motifs, XXe s. #2121
– motifs (années 1940) #2722
– Nouvelle-Ecosse #2731
    – XXe s. #1206 1207
– Ontario #2249 2729
    – tradition germanique #2263
    – XIXe s. #2723 2726
– Ottawa (Ont), Musée national de
    l'Homme. Centre canadien d'études sur la
    culture traditionelle #963
– Pednaud, Victoire #2184
– Québec #2223
    – (1840-1900) #2899
    – (années 1930) #2164
    – (années 1930), artisanes #2165
    – (années 1940) #2188
    – art traditionnel #1291
    – XIXe-début XXe s. #2737
    – XVIIe-XIXe s., influence européenne
        #2221
    – XVIIe-XVIIIe s. #2200 2850
– techniques de tissage #2719 2721
– teintures #2745
– Terre-Neuve #2744
– Toronto (Ont), Ontario College of Art
    #3009
– tradition germanique #2140
– XVIIe-XIXe s. #2730 2736
– XXe s. #2142
textiles et tissus . Indiens du bassin #3986
textiles et tissus . Inuit
– Spence Bay (TNO) #4249
textiles et tissus . Micmacs #3643
textiles et tissus . Pieds-Noirs #3654
Thauberger, David Allan, artiste can, 1948-
    #1937
– expositions de groupe
    – (1976) #1930
théâtre
– voir aussi scénographie
théâtre, art et
– voir aussi festivals; scénographie
– Canada, XXe s. #438
– Pellan, Alfred #6804 6816 6818 6819
– Percival, Robert #6834
– Plaskett, Joe #1991
– Shadbolt, Jack Leonard #1991
– Szaszkiewicz, Cécile #7307
– Toronto (Ont), Canadian National

Exhibition (1939) #1
théâtre canadien #129
– (années 1970) #542 619
– Nouvelle-Ecosse (1606-1930) #1196
– théâtre de rue (années 1970) #555
– Winnipeg (Man), (années 1960) #1891
théâtres et cinémas . Canada
– (1920-1966) #9099
– (années 1910) #9069
– (années 1910-1930) #9122 9123
– (années 1930), recommandations #9077
– (années 1940) #9078
– Calgary (Alta), (années 1910) #8118
– Dawson City (Yukon), Palace Grand
    Theatre #9090
– Edmonton (Alta)
    – (1906) #9143
    – Citadel Theatre #9140
– Halifax (NE), Neptune Theatre #9097
– Montréal (Qué), théâtre Saint-Denis #9068
– Niagara-on-the-Lake (Ont), Shaw Festival
    Theatre #9119 9120
– Ottawa (Ont), cinéma Capitol #9110 9131
– Québec (Qué), Grand Théâtre de Québec
    #9112
– St. Catharines (Ont), Pen Centre Cinemas
    #9100
– Toronto (Ont) #9067
    – (années 1910) #9066
    – Allen's Bloor Street Theatre #9071
    – Allen's Danforth Theatre #9072
    – cinéma Loew, rue Yonge (Elgin et
        Wintergarden) #9064
    – Gayety Theatre #9060
    – Pantages Theatre et cinéma Loew
        (Uptown) #9075
    – Royal Alexandra Theatre #9059
– transformation d'édifices publics en
    théâtres #9147 9148
– Vancouver (CB)
    Orpheum Theatre #9135 9141
    – Queen Elizabeth Theatre #9085
– Winnipeg (Man) #8105
    – Allen Theatre #9074
théâtres et cinémas . Etats-Unis
– (années 1910-1930) #9122 9123
Théberge, Claude, artiste can, 1934- #7342 7343
Themarat, Jeanne Aline, artiste can, ca 1893-
    #1881
Thénot, Jean-Paul, artiste fr, 1943-
– étude sur le musée #714
Theo Dimson, studio can de graphisme #886
théosophie
– et Lawren Stewart Harris #5716 5726 5731
– et le Groupe des Sept #1774
Théroux, André, artiste can, 1938-
– art graphique télédiffusé #909
Therrien, Denise, artiste can, 1945-
– expositions de groupe
    – (1979) #676
Thibault, René, sculpteur et céramiste can,
    1909- #7344
Thibert, Patrick, sculpteur can, 1943-
– expositions, critiques #7345
– expositions de groupe
    – (1977) #784
Thibert, Ronald, sculpteur can, 1942- #1546
– concept d'espace #1631
– Symposium international de sculpture
    environnementale de Chicoutimi (Qué),
    (1980) #1639
Thom, Ronald James (Ron), architecte can,
    1923-
– commentaire sur l'architecture des

universités #9478
– commentaire sur ses études en art #470
– Niagara-on-the-Lake (Ont), Shaw Festival
    Theatre #9119 9120
– Peterborough (Ont), Trent University
    #9470 9473 9474
– Toronto (Ont)
    – M.S. Yolles Associates. Bureaux #9346
    – University of Toronto. Massey College
        #9460
– Vancouver (CB)
    – architecture domestique (années 1960)
        #8411
    – University of British Columbia. Student
        Union, concours #9503
Thom Partnership, agence can d'architecture
    #8412
– Toronto (Ont), Pauline McGibbon Cultural
    Centre, restauration #7776
Thomas, Francis, marchand de porcelaine
    can, actif années 1880
– paysages québécois dits "de Thomas"
    #2287 2291 2306 2326
Thomas, George, photographe can, 1934-
– catalogue de photographies #991
Thomas, Gordon Evan, photographe can,
    1930-
– photographies, Forces armées canadiennes
    #1107
Thomas, Jacob, artiste can, 1922-
– masques de la Société des Faux Visages
    #7346
Thomas, Lionel Arthur John, artiste can,
    1915- #7347 7348
– élève de Hans Hofmann #402 1850
– entretien #7349
– et peinture de Vancouver (CB), (années
    1950) #1992
Thomas, Randolph William (Randy),
    photographe can, 1948-
– catalogue de photographies #1023
Thomas, Roy, artiste can, 1949- #4157
Thomas, William, architecte et artiste can,
    1799-1860 #8413
– membre de la Toronto Society of Arts
    #1689
– Toronto (Ont) #8055 8056 8059 8061 8075
    – St. Lawrence Hall #9103
Thomas, William Tutin, architecte can,
    1828-1892
– membre de la Toronto Society of Arts
    #1689
Thomas Bell, fabricants de meubles
    (Southampton, Ont) #2463
Thomas De La Rue & Co., éditeur (Londres,
    Angleterre, et Paris, France)
– cartes de Noël #842
Thompson, Berwick, Pratt & Partners,
    agence can d'architecture
– Cloverdale (CB), Dogwood Gardens #8744
– et Thom Partnership #8412
– Faro (Yukon), Faro Townsite Recreation
    Centre #8182
– Ottawa (Ont), Musée national de l'Homme
    #8041
– Vancouver (CB)
    – Canadian Broadcasting Corporation.
        Centre régional de radiotélévision #8171
    – False Creek #8170
    – IBM Building #9301
Thompson, Berwick & Pratt, agence can
    d'architecture
– Peterborough (Ont), Trent University
    – Champlain College #7694 9465

– Champlain College et Lady Eaton College #9474
– Terrace (CB), Terrace and District Hospital #9032
– Toronto (Ont), University of Toronto. Massey College #9460
– Vancouver (CB)
  – BC Electric Building #7679
  – Crown Compagnie d'assurance-vie, siège social #7683
  – Orpheum Theatre, restauration #9141
  – prix, modèle d'école élémentaire (1970) #9507
  – University of British Columbia #9500
    – Fine Arts Building #9502
    – gymnase #7679
    – résidence Thea Koerner #7683
Thompson, Charles, ébéniste can, actif années 1850-1870 #2511
Thompson, Daniel & Colthurst, agence can d'architecture
– Saskatoon (Sask), Saint John's Episcopal Church #8907
Thompson, Richard, orfèvre can, 1809-1890 #2649
Thompson, Stuart, photographe can, 1881-1960
– expositions de groupe
  – (1976) #2012
Thompsons
– architecture #4063
– broderie et ouvrages perlés #3808
– culture #3774
– pictogrammes #3769
– tatouage #3823
– vannerie #3773
Thomson, Harry S., photographe can, actif années 1970
– expositions de groupe
  – (1972) #1952
Thomson, Tom, artiste can, 1877-1917 #5 10 24 289 7350 7351 7353 7355 7357 7358 7359 7360 7362 7363 7370
– au Algonquin Park (Ont), (1914-1917) #7364
– circonstances entourant sa mort #7365
– comparaison entre photographies et peintures #7366
– correspondance, J.E.H. MacDonald #7356
– en comparaison avec Horatio Walker #215
– et Arthur Lismer #6301
– et G.Blair Laing, marchand d'oeuvres d'art #1686
– et l'identité canadienne #327
– et le Groupe des Sept #1735 1744 1766 1768 1774 1789
– expositions
  – (1971) #7367 7368
– expositions, critiques #283 292 1710
– expositions de groupe
  – (1927) #299
  – (1969) #3229
– faux #70
– forgeries
  – Toronto (Ont), Ward-Price Galleries (1962) #64
– influence de la peinture française #1244
– Le pin, Galerie nationale du Canada (Ottawa, Ont) #7369
– MacCallum, James Metcalfe, mécène #3237
– nature dans l'art #373
– notice nécrologique #7352
– peinture
  – collection Vincent Massey #3220

– Kleinburg (Ont), McMichael Canadian Collection #1783 3172
– Owen Sound (Ont), Tom Thomson Memorial Gallery and Museum of Fine Art #3146
– réminiscences #7361
– Richard, René-Jean, comparaison #6996
– The West Wind #7354 7371
– vues, Georgian Bay (Ont) #1745
Thomson, William James, artiste can, 1858-1927 #7372
– eaux-fortes #800
Thorburn, Archibald, artiste can, 1860-1935
– expositions
  – (1974) #7373
– Lansdowne, James Fenwick, comparaison #6165
Thoreau, Henry David, auteur et naturaliste amér, 1817-1862
– Thomson, Tom, comparaison #7360
Thorkelsson, Ione, artiste can (verre), 1947- #2440
Thorne, Joseph Bradshaw, artiste can, 1869-1963 #7374
Thornsbury, James, céramiste can, 1941-
– expositions de groupe
  – (1975) #1926
Thornton, Mildred Valley Stinson, artiste can, 1896-1967 #7375
Thornton, Peter M., architecte can, 1916-
– Vancouver (CB), University of British Columbia. Student Union, concours #9503
Thresher, Eliza W. Morrison, artiste can, active 1821-1830 #1164
Thresher, George Godsell, artiste can, 1779-1859 #1164
Thuléens
– artefacts #4238 4324 4327 4331 4342 4345 4347 4370 4372 4373 4378
  – Cumberland Sound (TNO) #4367
  – en comparaison avec artefacts dorsétiens #4333
  – Pingerqalik (Foxe Basin, TNO) #4335
  – symbolisme thérapeutique #3356
– pétroglyphes #4344
– poterie #4207
Thunder Bay (Ont)
– arts décoratifs #2266
Thunder Bay (Ont), Centre national d'expositions
– expositions
  – Canadian Paintings in the University of Toronto: An Exhibition in Celebration of the Sesquicentennial of the University of Toronto (1978) #3168
  – Canadians: A National Photography Show about People/Canadiens: exposition nationale de photographie ayant les gens comme thème (1979) #1035
  – Métiers d'art Ontario-Québec, 1979/1980/Quebec-Ontario Crafts, 1979/1980 (1980) #2138
  – Trésors d'art populaire québécois/Folk Art Treasures of Quebec (1980) #1297
Ti-pop #1502
Tiedemann, Herman Otto, architecte et artiste can, 1821-1891
– Victoria (CB) #8145
Tiepolo, Giovanni Battista, artiste it, 1696-1770
– influence sur John Fox #5495
Tiessen, George, artiste can, 1935-
– expositions de groupe
  – (1966) #1123

– (1967) #821
Tiffany, Louis Comfort, artiste et designer amér, 1848-1933
– verrières, Montréal (Qué) #2462
Tignish (IPE)
– architecture, XIXe s. #7801
Tiktak, John, artiste can, 1916-1981 #4407
– expositions
  – (1970) #7376
Tillenius, Clarence, artiste can, 1913- #7377
Tillmann & Lamb, agence can d'architecture
– London (Ont), University of Western Ontario. Résidence des étudiants #9467
timbres-poste
– (1963-1974) #829
timbres-poste canadiens
– (1918-années 1940) #807
– (années 1950), Laurence Hyde, commentaire #811
– guide pour collectionneurs #2104
– Hahn, Emanuel Otto #5680
– MacAskill, Wallace R., Bluenose #6351
– Price, Art #6928
– Volpi, Charles de, collection #3248
Time-Life, éditeur
– protecteur des arts (années 1970) #3275
Timmins (Ont), Timmins Museum Centre
– expositions
  – Imprint '76 (1977) #833
Timms, Philip Thomas, photographe can, 1874-1973
– expositions de groupe
  – (1976) #2012
Tinning, George Campbell, artiste can, 1910-
– réflexion sur son oeuvre #7378
tipis . Algonquiens #3672
tipis . Cris #3655 3663 3735 3742
tipis . Indiens des plaines #3672 3675
– animaux, motifs #3758
tipis . Pieds-Noirs #3669 3686 3735 3741 3754
– Leiden (Pays-Bas), Rijksmuseum voor Volkenkunde #3718
– monstre marin, motif #3757
– Oiseau-Tonnerre, motif #3676
tipis . Sarcis #3735
tipis . Siouens #3672
tissage
– voir aussi ouvrages perlés; tissage jacquard
tissage . Algonquiens #3374 3605
– sacs en fibre textile #3638 3744
tissage . Amérindiens #2739 2747 2748 3413 3476
– ceinture fléchée #2818 2823 2824 2827 2873
– influence sur tissage canadien #2774
tissage . Athapascans
– (années 1970), artisanes #3367
tissage . Canada #2719 2721 2747 2748
– (1608-1867) #2120
– (1867) #2735
– (années 1960) #2106
– Cap-Breton (NE) #2728 2732
  – tartan, tissage #2724
– ceinture fléchée #2818 2824 2827 2873
– Chamard, Émilie #2209
– Charlevoix (Qué)
  – couvertures #2738
  – XVIIe-XIXe s. #2733
– Fredericks, Beany #5513
– île aux Coudres (Qué) #2168
– île d'Orléans (Qué) #1252
– Ile-du-Prince-Edouard, XVIIIe-XIXe s. #2734
– influence sur l'art canadien, XXe s. #2093

– Lindgren, Charlotte #6282 6283
– Nouveau-Brunswick #2150
– Nouvelle-Ecosse #2731
  – (avant 1920) #2785
– Ontario
  – tradition germanique #2263
  – XIXe s. #2723 2726
– Ontario Handweavers and Spinners (1956-1979) #2743
– Ploethner, Frederick K. #6896
– Québec #1327 2223
  – (années 1920) #2718
  – (années 1930-1940) #2186
  – (années 1940) #2199
  – artisanes #2212
  – XVIIe-XIXe s., influence européenne #2221
  – XVIIe-XVIIIe s. #2181 2187 2200
  – XXe s. #2198
– Saint-Jean-Port-Joli (Qué) #2194
– XVIIe s.-années 1940 #2720
– XVIIe-XIXe s. #2112 2730 2736
– XXe s. #2121 2142 2774
tissage . Chilkats #3784
– influence sur tissage salish #3898
tissage . Cris #3402
tissage . Gitksans
– 'Ksan #4134
tissage . Indiens de l'Amérique centrale
– en comparaison avec tissage, Indiens de la côte nord-ouest #3832
tissage . Indiens de l'Amérique du Sud
– influence sur tissage canadien #2774
tissage . Indiens de la côte nord-ouest #3832 3931
tissage . Indiens des fôrets du Nord-Est
– sacs en fibre textile #3638 3744
tissage . Indiens du bassin #3986
tissage . Inuit
– (années 1970), artisanes #3367
– Pangnirtung (TNO) #4237 4298 4308 4310
tissage . Iroquois #3605
– ceintures (de tissu) #3534
– sacs en fibre textile #3638 3744
tissage . Kwakiutls #3787
tissage . Lillooets #3783
tissage . Malécites #2144
tissage . Nootkas #3880
tissage . Pieds-Noirs
– colliers soumak #3685
tissage . Quinaults #3845
tissage . Salish de la côte #3851 3896
tissage . Salishiens #3963 4018 4027 4044
– (années 1960) #3941
– (années 1960-1970) #4147
– influence sur tissage chilkat #3898
– XXe s. #3964
tissage . Saulteux/Ojibwa #3402 3539 3557
– nattes #3585
tissage . Shuswaps #3789
tissage . Skokomish #3835
tissage . Snuqualmis #3835
tissage . Tlingits #3826 3902 3976 4018 4027
tissage . Tsimshians #3826
tissage jacquard
– Ontario, XIXe s. #2740
tissages . Osages
– sacs en fibre textile #3744
tissus
– voir textiles et tissus
Title, Robert, photographe can, 1936- #2071
– catalogue de photographies #991 998
Tlingits
– amulettes #4028

– art #3366 3917 3946 3947 3978
  – hameçon pour la pêche au flétan, motif #4061
  – pieuvre, motif #4045
– bâton de danse représentant un orque #3802
– casque en peau de requin, clan des Kaguanton #3833
– caveau funéraire #4007
– coiffure #3803 4019
– couvertures #3826
– crécelles #3363 4026
– culture #3976 4106
  – (années 1880) #3763
– jade #3331
– panneaux muraux #3916
– peinture faciale #3968
– pétroglyphes #3786
– potlatch #4012
– récipients en bois sculpté, XIXe s. #3985
– sculpture #4041
– sculpture et tissage #3902
– tissage #4018
– totems #3781 3856 3873
– totems et cuivres #3812
– vannerie #3776 3792 3806 3865 3991 4309
– vannerie et tissage #4027
Tobey, Mark, artiste amér, 1890-1976
– influence sur Emily Carr #5044 5046
– influence sur Jack Marlowe Wise #7601
Toby, Russell & Buckwell, agence can d'architecture
– Vancouver (CB), West Vancouver Municipal Hall #8990
Todd, Robert Clow, artiste can, 1809-1866 #258 259
Tofin, Frank Peter, architecte can, 1920-
– Vancouver (CB), University of British Columbia. Student Union, concours #9503
Toit, Roger du
– voir Du Toit, Roger
toits . Canada
– Montréal (Qué), structures de toits en pierre #8598
– Québec
  – XIXe s. #8624
  – XVIIe s., maçonnerie en bardeaux #7860
  – XVIIe-XVIIIe s. #7881
  – XVIIIe-XIXe s. #8560 8561
  – XVIIe-XIXe s. #7703
Tolchinsky & Goodz, agence can d'architecture
– Dorval (Qué), Club 230 #7776
Tolgesy, Victor, sculpteur can, 1928-1980 #7380
– entretien #7379
Tolmie, Kenneth, artiste can, 1941-
– expositions de groupe
  – (1980) #1221
Tom, Mme Mike, artisane can (vannerie), active 1976 #4142
tombes
– voir cimetières
– voir monuments funéraires
Tomczak, Kim, artiste can, 1953-
– expositions de groupe
  – (1980) #687
Tomlinson, Jim, photographe can, actif 1979 #2071
Tonnancour, Jacques Godefroy de, artiste can, 1917- #97 1453 1542 1543 7383 7384 7389 7390
– commentaire sur le nationalisme dans l'art #4851

– commentaire sur Paul-Emile Borduas #4798
– design de meubles #2608
– en comparaison avec Louis Archambault #1412
– entretien #7386
– et Ecole des beaux-arts (Montréal, Qué), (1968) #2995
– expositions
  – (1966) #7387
– expositions, critiques #428 7388
– expositions de groupe
  – (1959) #438
  – (1977) #1278 1279
– réflexion sur l'art canadien (années 1940) #385
– réflexion sur l'enseignement de l'art #3018
– réflexion sur son oeuvre #7382 7385
– théories sur l'art #7381
Tonpass (Alaska)
– totems, Tlingit #3856
Topham, William Thurston, artiste can, 1888-1966
– illustrations #916
Topley, William James, photographe can, 1845-1930 #1001 1024
– expositions de groupe
  – (1970) #1675
Toppings, Glenn, artiste can, 1930-1972 #7391
– expositions
  – (1977) #7392
Torbett, Charles W., graveur can, actif 1812-1834
– gravures #1198
Toresdahl, David, artiste can, 1939-
– expositions de groupe
  – (1981) #2084
Toronto (Ont)
– architecture #8060 8070
  – (1794-1977) #8074
  – (1810) #8058
  – (1834-1934) #8055
  – (1849) #8061
  – (1890-1928), style beaux-arts #8069
  – (années 1850) #8050
  – (années 1910), utilisation de brique et de stuc #8052
  – (années 1920) #7656
  – (années 1950) #7673 8057
  – (années 1960) #7693 7698
  – Baker, Francis Spence #8330
  – Chapman, Alfred Hirschfelder #8344
  – Howard, John George #8378
  – Martin, Arthur N. #6423
  – Myers, Barton #8391
  – promenades guidées #8065
  – Smith, Eden #8408
  – Thomas, William #8413
  – XIXe s. #8051 8056 8059 8064 8073 8075
  – XIXe s.-années 1920 #7961
  – XIXe s.-années 1930 #8076
  – XXe s., concept d'espace #7748
– architecture domestique
  – (1791-1882) #8676
  – (1908), utilisation de stuc #8638
  – (années 1910) #8492 8493 8494 8496 8639 8641
  – (années 1920) #8499
  – (années 1930) #8647 8737
  – Watson, Harold R. #8643
  – XIXe-XXe s. #8077
– art
  – (1847-1848), Toronto Society of Arts

#1689
- (1880-1910) #214
- (1908-1915), Canadian Art Club #193
- (1977-1980) #1815
- (années 1890) #1699 6436
- (années 1910) #1712
- (années 1940-1970) #571
- (années 1950) #1750
- (années 1950-1970) #131
- (années 1960) #90 441 519 1757
- (années 1970) #1804 1809 1818 1823
- (années 1980) #1832 1837
- XXe s. #145 536 567
- art vidéo #550 605
- arts graphiques
  - (années 1960) #1756
  - Société canadienne des peintres-graveurs #3
- banques
  - (années 1910) #9159
  - Dominion Banks #9188
- Berczy, William von Moll, cofondateur #4699
- bibliothèques
  - bibliothèques publiques
    - (années 1920) #9040
    - (années 1930) #9041
  - collèges et universités, bibliothèques (années 1930) #9042
- carreaux de céramique dans habitations, XIXe s. #2373
- écoles (années 1960) #9403
- expansion urbaine #8067
- femmes artistes (années 1970) #1797
- galeries d'art (années 1960) #442
- immeubles à bureaux
  - (années 1910) #9332
  - (années 1950-1960) #9300
  - (années 1960-1970) #8337
  - bureaux d'architectes (années 1940) #9297
- immeubles d'habitation
  - (années 1910) #8640
  - (années 1920) #8644
- installations #1834
- magasins (années 1930) #9371
- métros #9547
- mobilier (1800-1865) #2563
- peinture
  - (1860-1890) #264
  - (1870-1970) #97
  - (1933-1970) #498
  - (1938-1948) #378
  - (1953-1965) #1772 1773 1775
  - (années 1920-1950) #424
  - (années 1930) #589 592
  - (années 1940-1950) #412
  - (années 1950) #1749 1752
  - (années 1960) #507 520 1753
  - (années 1970) #1803 1807 1831
  - XXe s. #1760
- peinture et photographie de paysages (1860-1890) #271 272
- photographie
  - (1839-1867) #1725
  - (1906) #980
  - (années 1880-1970) #1683
  - (années 1890) #977 1702
  - (années 1910) #983
  - (années 1920) #984
  - (années 1970) #992 996
  - Toronto Camera Club #975
- portraits de représentants municipaux #3178

- poterie, XIXe s. #2310
- résidences des lieutenants-gouverneurs (avant 1867) #8754
- sculpture
  - (années 1890) #727
  - (années 1960) #767
  - (années 1970) #697 1817
- sièges, XIXe s. #2575
- synagogues (années 1960) #8903
- tapisserie (années 1970) #2768
- verrières (années 1880-1890) #2451
- vues
  - (1813-1882), estampes #1717
  - Brooks, Leonard #4929
  - Franck, Albert Jacques #5500 5502
  - Harris, Lawren Stewart #5734
  - Pflug, Christiane Sybille #6849 6850
  - Ward, John #7515
  - Winter, William Arthur #7599
  - XIXe s. #3204
  - XVIIIe s.-années 1910 #3130 3143
- vues photographiques
  - (1850-1900) #1061
  - Goss, Arthur S. #5633 5634
  - Greenhill, Ralph #5651
  - Henrickson, Thomas Elton, et Martha Charlotte Henrickson #5781
Toronto (Ont), 2nd International Toronto Art Fair
- Burnett, David, commentaire sur son exposition *Toronto/New York* (1981) #1837
Toronto (Ont), A Space #1042
- (années 1970) #641 1804
- livres #940
- périodique, *Only Paper Today* #1799
- vidéos (1981) #721
Toronto (Ont), Academy of Music
- expositions, Ontario Society of Artists, début XXe s. #1666
Toronto (Ont), Aéroport international de Toronto
- architecture et art #8232
Toronto (Ont), Albert White Gallery
- expositions
  - *Legends* (1967) #4633
Toronto (Ont), Allen's Bloor Street Theatre
- architecture, Hynes, Feldman & Watson #9071
Toronto (Ont), Allen's Danforth Theatre
- architecture, Hynes, Feldman & Watson #9072
Toronto (Ont), Allen Theatre
- architecture, C.Howard Crane; Hynes, Feldman & Watson, architectes associés #9069
Toronto (Ont), Archives publiques de l'Ontario
- Donovan, Duncan, photographies #5298
- Horwood, John Charles Batstone, et Eric Crompton, Collection of Architectural Drawings #8028 8030
- Simcoe, Elizabeth Posthuma Gwillim, carnets à dessins #7212
Toronto (Ont), Armée du Salut. Arthur Meighen Lodge
- architecture, Marani, Morris & Allan #8516
Toronto (Ont), Armée du Salut. Siège social
- architecture et art #8232
Toronto (Ont), Art Galleries, 165, rue King Ouest
- expositions
  - *Applied Art Exhibition: Catalogue 1900, Held in the Art Galleries, 165 King Street West, Toronto* (1900) #2240

Toronto (Ont), Art Gallery at Harbourfront
- (1976-1977) #3166
- expositions
  - *Felicity Redgrave* (1978) #6967
  - *Open Studio: Ten Years* (1980) #1833
  - *Viewpoint: Twenty-nine by Nine; An Exhibition of Twenty-nine Works by Ontario Artists, Selected by Nine Curators* (1981) #1838
- expositions, critiques
  - *Open Space: Ten Years* (1980) #1830
  - ouvrage en fibre textile (1978) #2771
- vitraux (années 1970) #2455
Toronto (Ont), Art Gallery of Ontario #3154 3177
- *voir aussi* Toronto (Ont), Art Gallery of Toronto; Toronto (Ont), Art Museum of Toronto; Toronto (Ont), The Grange
- (1906-1966), expositions #3175
- (1973), rencontre annuelle #3157
- architecture #8680
  - Parkin Partnership #9121
- art canadien #3149
- collection #3158
- collection audio-visuelle, index des matières #159
- collection de photographie #1051
- Duncan, Douglas M., collection #119
- enseignement de l'art (années 1970) #3004
- et Ontario Society of Artists #1679
- et sir Byron Edmund Walker #3206
- expositions
  - *...It's Still Privileged Art* (1976) #602
  - *10 Canadian Artists in the 1970s* (1980) #703
  - *100 Years: Evolution of the Ontario College of Art* (1976) #3011
  - *A.J. Casson* (1978) #5060
  - *A Canadian Survey: Selected Works from the Collection of Imperial Oil Limited/Tour d'horizon canadien: oeuvres choisies de la collection de la Compagnie Pétrolière Impériale Ltée* (1978) #3241
  - *A Tribute to Albert Franck* (1973) #5501
  - *Antoine Plamondon, 1802-1895; Théophile Hamel, 1817-1870: Two Painters of Quebec/Antoine Plamondon, 1802-1895; Théophile Hamel, 1817-1870: deux peintres du Québec* (1970) #1348
  - *Art and Engineering* (1965) #471
  - *Autobiography: Film/Video/Photography* (1978) #664
  - *Canadian Artists 68/Artistes canadiens 68* (1968) #521
  - *Canadian Cartoon and Caricature* (1969) #946
  - *Canadian Painting in the Thirties* (1975) #592
  - *Canadian Paintings in the University of Toronto: An Exhibition in Celebration of the Sesquicentennial of the University of Toronto* (1977) #3168
  - *Canadian Political Cartoons* (1977) #956
  - *Canadian Tapestries, 1977* (1977) #2770
  - *Canadians in Paris, 1867-1914: An Educational Exhibition Using the Gallery's Collection and Long Term Loans* (1979) #274
  - *Carl Schaefer in Hanover* (1981) #7157
  - *Changing Visions: The Canadian Landscape/Aperçus divers: le paysage canadien* (1976) #617
  - *Charles Gagnon* (1979) #5540
  - *Daniel Fowler of Amherst Island,*

peintres-graveurs (1919-1932) #3
- *The Development of Painting in Canada, 1665-1945/Le développement de la peinture au Canada, 1665-1945* (1945) #34
- Toronto Camera Club, *Annual Spring Salon* (1926-1937) #975
- *Watercolours by Robert Holmes, 1861-1930, in the Collection of the Art Gallery of Toronto* (1964) #5823
- expositions, critiques
  - *A.Y. Jackson: Paintings, 1902-1953* (1953) #5915
  - Académie royale des arts du Canada
    - (1927) #296
    - (1928) #310
    - (1930) #318
    - (1934) #326
    - (1936) #329
    - (1947) #3304
  - *Arthur Lismer: Paintings, 1913-1949* (1950) #6296 6297
  - *Exhibition of Architecture and the Allied Arts*
    - (1927) #7960 8223
    - (1929) #7964
    - (1931) #7967
    - (1933) #7969
    - (1935) #7971 7972
    - (1937) #7973
  - *Exhibition of Contemporary Canadian Arts* (1950) #387
  - Groupe des peintres canadiens
    - (1936) #331
    - (1942) #356
    - (1944) #365
  - Groupe des Sept (1926) #1734
  - *International Exhibition of Modern Art Assembled by the Société Anonyme* (1927) #5714
  - *Lawren Harris: Paintings 1910-1948* (1948) #5718
  - Macpherson, Duncan Ian #6400
  - Société des sculpteurs du Canada (1944) #736
Toronto (Ont), Art Metropole Galleries
- expositions
  - *Sydney Strickland Tully, A.R.C.A.: Memorial Exhibition of Paintings and Drawings* (1911) #7438
Toronto (Ont), Art Museum of Toronto
- *voir aussi* Toronto (Ont), Art Gallery of Ontario; Toronto (Ont), Art Gallery of Toronto; Toronto (Ont), The Grange
- (1906-1919), expositions #3175
- architecture, Darling & Pearson #9070
- expositions
  - Ontario Society of Artists #1666
- expositions, critiques
  - Ontario Society of Artists (1919) #1731
Toronto (Ont), Ashley & Crippen Building
- architecture, Baldwin & Greene #9367
Toronto (Ont), B'nai Israel Beth David Synagogue
- architecture, Irving Grossman #8903
Toronto (Ont), Baldwin Street Gallery of Photography #1794
- expositions
  - *Canadians: A National Photography Show about People/Canadiens: exposition nationale de photographie ayant les gens comme thème* (1979) #1035
- expositions, critiques
  - Szilasi, Gabor #7308
Toronto (Ont), Bank of British North America

- architecture, Ellis & Connery #9150
Toronto (Ont), Bank of Ottawa
- architecture, John MacIntosh Lyle #9159
Toronto (Ont), Bank of Toronto (1908)
- architecture, Edward James Lennox #9151
Toronto (Ont), Bank of Toronto (1913)
- architecture, Carrere & Hastings; Eustace Godfrey Bird #8293 9162 9185
Toronto (Ont), Banque canadienne de commerce
- architecture
  - Darling & Pearson, architectes; York & Sawyer, architectes-conseils #9178
  - Darling & Pearson; restauration, Page & Steele #9351
Toronto (Ont), Banque canadienne de commerce (1930)
- architecture, Darling & Pearson #9189
Toronto (Ont), Banque canadienne de commerce (1931)
- architecture, V.D. Horsburgh #9181
- intérieur, décoration en bronze #9180
Toronto (Ont), Banque de Montréal. Tour
- Jaworska, Tamara Hans, *Quartet Moderne* #5949
Toronto (Ont), Banque de Montréal (1910)
- architecture, Darling & Pearson #9155
Toronto (Ont), Banque de Montréal (1949)
- architecture, Chapman, Oxley & Facey et Marani & Morris, architectes; K.R. Blatherwick, architecte associé #9190
Toronto (Ont), Banque de Nouvelle-Ecosse (1922)
- architecture, Sharp & Horner #9174
Toronto (Ont), Banque de Nouvelle-Ecosse (1951)
- architecture, Mathers & Haldenby, architectes; Beck & Eadie, architectes associés #9192
- sculpture murale, Jacobine Jones #5977
Toronto (Ont), Banque de Nouvelle-Ecosse (1958)
- architecture, Arthur Hunter Eadie #9193
Toronto (Ont), Banque Royale (1908)
- architecture, Carrere & Hastings; Eustace Godfrey Bird #9152
Toronto (Ont), Banque Royale (1915)
- architecture, Ross & Macdonald #9165
Toronto (Ont), Banque Toronto-Dominion
- art inuit #4201 4216 4248 4427
- art inuit et peintures canadiennes #3225
Toronto (Ont), Bau-Xi Gallery
- expositions, critiques
  - Hopkins, Elisabeth Margaret #5830
  - Jarvis, Don #2074
  - Kipling, Ann #6056
Toronto (Ont), Beaver Theatre
- architecture, Neil & Beggs #9066
Toronto (Ont), Bedford Glen
- architecture, Ernest Annau et Paul Northgrave #8078
Toronto (Ont), Bedford Theatre
- architecture, Murray Brown #8338
Toronto (Ont), Belsize Theatre
- architecture, Murray Brown #8338
Toronto (Ont), Big Nickel Theatre
- architecture, John Wilson Siddall #9066
Toronto (Ont), Bishop Strachan School
- architecture, Sproatt & Rolph #9386
Toronto (Ont), Blair Laing Gallery
- Town, Harold, exposition de ses oeuvres (1961) #445 446

Toronto (Ont), Bourse de Toronto
- architecture
  - concours #9161
  - George & Moorhouse, architectes; Samuel Herbert Maw, architecte associé #9187
Toronto (Ont), Bowles Lunch Room
- architecture, Hand, Harris & Merritt #9269
Toronto (Ont), bureau d'enregistrement
- architecture, Charles S. Cobb #8969
Toronto (Ont), Canada Life
- architecture, Sproatt & Rolph #9336
Toronto (Ont), Canada Permanent
- architecture, F. Hilton Wilkes; Sproatt & Rolph, architectes-conseils #9177
Toronto (Ont), Canadian Art Club. Gallery
- expositions
  - *Catalogue of the Morris Collection of Indian Portraits at the Gallery of the Canadian Art Club* (1909) #6637
Toronto (Ont), Canadian Education Showplace
- exhibition (1965) #9398
Toronto (Ont), Canadian National Exhibition
- architecture, George Wallace Gouinlock #9206
- et Graphic Arts Club of Toronto (1913) #1711
- expositions
  - (1904-1961) #1
  - (1905-1938), art international #107
  - (1909-1923), Société canadienne des arts graphiques #801
  - (1918-1939), Toronto Camera Club #975
  - (1928-1929) #307
  - (1932-1967), Guilde canadienne des métiers d'art #2118
  - *A Terrible Beauty: The Art of Canada at War* (1978) #1111
  - *Beauté tragique: les deux conflits mondiaux vus par des artistes canadiens* (1978) #1112
  - *Contemporary Art of Canada and Newfoundland: Collection of the International Business Machines Corporation* (1940) #350
- expositions, critiques
  - (1913) #201
  - (1919), Canadian War Memorials Collection #1077
  - (1921), Toronto Camera Club #984
  - (1927) #295
  - (1928) #300
  - (1929) #304
  - (1930) #313
  - (1931) #316
  - (1932) #320 321
Toronto (Ont), Canadian National Exhibition. Automotive Building
- architecture, Douglas Edwin Kertland #9207
Toronto (Ont), Canadian National Exhibition. Grandstand
- architecture, Marani & Morris #9208
Toronto (Ont), Canadian Pacific Railway Building
- architecture, Darling & Pearson #9329
Toronto (Ont), Carmen Lamanna Gallery
- aide aux artistes canadiens (années 1970) #628
- expositions
  - *General Idea's Reconstructing Futures/General Idea: reconstruction de l'avenir* (1977) #5583

– expositions, critiques
– Janitch, Mary #5935
– Lamanna, Carmen, commentaire #1811
Toronto (Ont), Carroll Fine Art Gallery
– expositions, critiques
– Broomfield, Adolphus George #4932
Toronto (Ont), Casa Loma
– architecture #8649
– expositions
– *Three Centuries of Canadian History in Picture and Story, 1630-1930: Catalogue of the Walter H. Millen Collection of Canadiana* (1938) #21
Toronto (Ont), caserne de pompiers, rue Gerrard et avenue Carlaw
– architecture, Toronto City Architect's Office #8970
Toronto (Ont), Cathedral of Saint Alban the Martyr
– architecture, Symons & Rae #8896
Toronto (Ont), Cemetery Chapel of Saint James the Less
– architecture, Frederic William Cumberland #8905
Toronto (Ont), Centennial Centre of Science & Technology
– *voir* Toronto (Ont), Ontario Science Centre
Toronto (Ont), Central Ontario School of Art and Industrial Design
– (1907) #3299
– (années 1890) #188
Toronto (Ont), Central Technical School
– architecture, Ross & Macdonald #9434
Toronto (Ont), Central Technical School Art Centre
– architecture, Robert Fairfield Associates; Macy DuBois, architecte associé #7684
Toronto (Ont), Centre d'esthétique industrielle #2613
– fermeture (1970) #2621
Toronto (Ont), Centre for Experimental Art and Communication
– expositions
– *Véhicule's Véhicule* (1976) #1529
Toronto (Ont), Chapman & Walker Building
– architecture, Chadwick & Beckett #9332
Toronto (Ont), Chewett Block
– architecture, James Grant Chewett #258 259
Toronto (Ont), Church of Saint Nicholas
– fresques #1822
Toronto (Ont), Church of Saint Paul's
– architecture et intérieur, Edward James Lennox #8897 8902
Toronto (Ont), Church of Saint Simon the Apostle
– architecture, Eden Smith #8408
Toronto (Ont), cinéma Loew, rue Yonge (Elgin et Wintergarden)
– architecture, Thomas White Lamb #9064 9067
Toronto (Ont), cinéma Loew (Uptown)
– architecture, Thomas White Lamb #9075
Toronto (Ont), cinéma Odéon
– architecture, Henry Eli Greenspoon #9078
Toronto (Ont), City of Toronto Archives
– Goss, Arthur S., photographies #5633
Toronto (Ont), City of Toronto Archives. Market Gallery #1806
– expositions
– *Arthur S. Goss, City Photographer: Works by Toronto's Official Photographer, 1911-1940* (1980) #5633
– *John George Howard, 1803-1890: A Tribute* (1979) #8378
– *The Corporate Image: An Exhibition of 19th and 20th Century Portraiture from the City of Toronto's Permanent Collection* (1980) #3178
– *Water Colours by E.May Martin* (1980) #6424
Toronto (Ont), Civic Garden Centre
– architecture, Jerome Markson Architects #8386
Toronto (Ont), Clintwood Maisonette Project
– architecture, Henry Fliess #8514
Toronto (Ont), Colborne Lodge
– architecture et art, John George Howard #8659
Toronto (Ont), Commerce Court
– architecture, I.M. Pei & Associates; Page & Steele, architectes associés #9350
Toronto (Ont), Confederation Square
– architecture, Thom Partnership #8412
Toronto (Ont), Cooper Cap Company Building
– architecture, Isadore Feldman #9332
Toronto (Ont), Crown Tailoring Co. Building
– architecture, Charles Frederick Wagner #9332
Toronto (Ont), D. & J. Ritchie Ltd.
– vente aux enchères, prix des oeuvres d'art canadiennes (1975-1980) #160
Toronto (Ont), D.O. Roblin Warehouse
– architecture, Eden Smith & Sons #9234
Toronto (Ont), David Mirvish Gallery
– expositions, critiques
– Murray, Robert Gray #6669
Toronto (Ont), Dominion Bank (1914)
– architecture, Darling & Pearson #9163
Toronto (Ont), Dominion Bank (1932)
– architecture, John MacIntosh Lyle #8226
Toronto (Ont), Dominion of Canada Industrial Exhibition (1903)
– art canadien #1
Toronto (Ont), Don Valley Woods/Phase 1
– architecture, Jack Klein & Henry Sears #8518
Toronto (Ont), Dorothy Cameron Gallery
– expositions
– *Canadian Printmaking Today* (1965) #820
– *Canadian Sculpture Today* (1964) #748
– expositions, critiques
– *Canadian Sculpture Today* (1964) #747
– Hedrick, Robert Burns #5773
Toronto (Ont), Dow Corning Silicones Ltd., siège social
– architecture, Fairfield & DuBois #9301
Toronto (Ont), Dr. D.W. Young, monument
– conception, Maurice D. Klein; sculpture, Florence Wyle #729
Toronto (Ont), Eaton Centre
– architecture, Bregman & Hamann et Zeidler Partnership #9377 9378 9382
Toronto (Ont), Eaton Centre. Henry Birks
– expositions
– *Historic Canadian Silver from "The Henry Birks Collection"* (1978) #2650
Toronto (Ont), Edgeley in the Village
– architecture, Irving Grossman #8520
Toronto (Ont), édifices du Parlement
– architecture (1791-1893) #8055 8943
– architecture, James Grant Chewett #258 259
Toronto (Ont), Educational Museum of Upper Canada
– (1856) #3128
– et Adolphus Egerton Ryerson #3150 3152 3155
Toronto (Ont), Electric Gallery #1798
– sculpture (années 1970) #1800
Toronto (Ont), Empire Club
– débat entre A.Y. Jackson et Edmund Wyly Grier #5923
Toronto (Ont), Excelsior Life Building
– architecture, Edward James Lennox #9333
Toronto (Ont), Fine Arts on Markham
– *voir* Toronto (Ont), York University. Fine Arts on Markham
Toronto (Ont), Fisher House
– charpente en bois d'oeuvre, en comparaison avec Gleason House (Farmington, Conn) #8658
Toronto (Ont), Flemingdon Park
– architecture, Irving Grossman #7683 8370 8514 8657
Toronto (Ont), Fondation du patrimoine ontarien
– collection d'art Firestone #3239
Toronto (Ont), Fort York
– conservation et Ontario Historical Society (1905-1909) #8458
Toronto (Ont), Four Seasons Sheraton Hotel
– architecture, John B. Parkin Associates #9294
Toronto (Ont), G.J. Foy Company Building
– architecture, Curry & Sparling #9332
Toronto (Ont), Galerie Dresdnere
– expositions
– *Homage to Miller Brittain (1919-1968): A Survey: Drawing and Mixed Media, 1936-1967* (1972) #4918
– expositions, critiques
– *Homage to Miller Brittain (1919-1968): A Survey: Drawing and Mixed Media, 1936-1967* (1972) #4919
Toronto (Ont), Gallery Moos
– expositions
– *Albert Franck (1899-1973) in Retrospect: A Small Selection from the Artist's Collection* (1974) #5500
– *Etrog* (1964) #5376
– expositions, critiques
– Iskowitz, Gershon #5905
Toronto (Ont), Gallery O
– expositions
– *Arthur F. McKay* (1979) #6478
– expositions, critiques
– Thibert, Patrick (1979) #7345
Toronto (Ont), Gallery One
– expositions
– *Parr, 1893-1969: A Print Retrospective* (1979) #6769
– expositions, critiques
– Clarke, Ann #5114
Toronto (Ont), Garden Theatre
– architecture, Neil & Beggs #9066
Toronto (Ont), gare Union
– architecture, Ross & Macdonald; Hugh Griffith Jones; John MacIntosh Lyle #9531 9536
– et Metro Centre (Toronto, Ont) #9540
Toronto (Ont), Gayety Theatre
– architecture, George Wallace Gouinlock #9060
Toronto (Ont), George Brown College of Applied Arts & Technology. Casa Loma Campus
– architecture, Fairfield & DuBois; Alan R. Moody #9479

Toronto (Ont), Glenholme School
- architecture, concours #9437
Toronto (Ont), Government House (1866)
- architecture, Gundry & Langley #8753
Toronto (Ont), Government House (1911)
- architecture, concours #8748
Toronto (Ont), Government House (Chorley Park)
- architecture, Francis Riley Heakes #8749
Toronto (Ont), Government of Canada Building
- Levine, Les, commentaire sur proposition d'oeuvre d'art #6268
Toronto (Ont), Graphic Arts Building
- architecture, Francis Spence Baker #9330
Toronto (Ont), Grierson & Walker, bureau d'architectes
- architecture et intérieur, Grierson & Walker #9299
Toronto (Ont), Guides du Canada, siège social
- architecture, Corneil & McBain #7984
Toronto (Ont), Guild Shop
- expositions
    - Davidialuk, 1977 (1977) #4521
    - Tuna Iquliq: Recent Sculpture (1979) #5903
Toronto (Ont), Harbour City
- architecture, Craig, Zeidler & Strong #8062
Toronto (Ont), Harbourfront Art Gallery
- voir Toronto (Ont), Art Gallery at Harbourfront
Toronto (Ont), Hart House
- voir Toronto (Ont), University of Toronto. Hart House
Toronto (Ont), Hazelton Lanes
- architecture, Webb Zerafa Menkès Housden Partnership #8078
Toronto (Ont), Helena Rubenstein Beauty Salon
- architecture, James Ernest Harris Paisley #9367
Toronto (Ont), Hermant Building
- architecture, Bond & Smith #9332
Toronto (Ont), High School of Commerce and Finance
- architecture #9387
Toronto (Ont), Holly-Dunfield Apartments
- architecture, Burston, Wells & Tampold #7683 8514
Toronto (Ont), Holwood Mansion
- architecture, Frank Darling #8667
Toronto (Ont), Hospital for Sick Children
- architecture
    - Govan, Ferguson, Lindsay, Kaminker, Maw, Langley, Keenleyside #9028
    - Stevens & Lee #9015
Toronto (Ont), hôtel de ville
- expositions
    - Beaux-arts Toronto: Permanence and Change in Early 20th Century Architecture (1973) #8069
    - Sculpture '67: An Open-air Exhibition of Canadian Sculpture/Sculpture 67: exposition en plein air de sculptures canadiennes (1967) #766
- expositions, critiques
    - Sculpture '67: An Open-air Exhibition of Canadian Sculpture/Sculpture 67: exposition en plein air de sculptures canadiennes (1967) #750 769
Toronto (Ont), hôtel de ville (1832)
- architecture, James Grant Chewett #8993
Toronto (Ont), hôtel de ville (1844)
- architecture, Henry Bowyer Lane #8993

Toronto (Ont), hôtel de ville (1898)
- architecture, Edward James Lennox #8993
- vitraux, Robert McCausland #2449
Toronto (Ont), hôtel de ville et Civic Square
- architecture #7709
    - concours #8981 8983 8989
    - Revell, Viljo #8993
    - Revell, Viljo, et John B. Parkin Associates #8990 8991
Toronto (Ont), Hotel Mossop
- architecture, James Patrick Hynes #9262
Toronto (Ont), Humber College
- Stacey, Harold, professeur #7274
Toronto (Ont), Hyatt Regency Hotel
- architecture, Webb Zerafa Menkès Housden Partnership #9293
Toronto (Ont), Hydro Place
- architecture, Kenneth R. Cooper; Kenneth H. Candy et Adamson Associates, architectes-conseils #9352
Toronto (Ont), Imperial Bank of Canada
- architecture, Langley & Howland #9181
Toronto (Ont), Imperial Oil Building
- architecture, Mathers & Haldenby #9340
Toronto (Ont), Inn on the Park
- architecture, Peter Webb #9289
Toronto (Ont), Innuit Gallery of Eskimo Art
- et Av Isaacs #4236
- expositions
    - Baker Lake Sculpture (1974) #4434
    - From the Bottom of the Kudlik: Carvings and Artifacts from Gjoa Haven, 1974/Du fond des âges: sculptures et objets de Gjoa Haven, 1974 (1974) #4435
    - Spence Bay Sculpture: An Expressive Force (1980) #4454
    - The Hand (1975) #4439
- expositions, critiques
    - Shaa, Aqjangajuk #7174
Toronto (Ont), Irving Grossman. Bureaux et appartement
- architecture et intérieur, Irving Grossman #9299
Toronto (Ont), Isaacs Gallery
- (années 1970) #1804
- expositions
    - "Les Levine Copies Everyone" (1970) #6264
- expositions, critiques
    - Coughtry, John Graham #5191
    - Curnoe, Greg #5226
    - Handy, Arthur (1964) #5701
    - Kurelek, William #6113
    - Paradise (1978) #6964
Toronto (Ont), Jane Corkin Gallery
- expositions
    - Twelve Canadians: Contemporary Canadian Photography (1981) #1070
Toronto (Ont), Japanese Cultural Centre
- architecture, Raymond Moriyama #9095
Toronto (Ont), Jarvis Collegiate Institute
- architecture #9443
- murales, George Agnew Reid et Lorna Claire #6978
Toronto (Ont), Jenkins Art Galleries
- architecture, Sproatt & Rolph #8053
- expositions
    - A Memorial Exhibition of the Paintings of the Late Florence Carlyle, A.R.C.A. (1925) #5000
- expositions, critiques
    - A Memorial Exhibition of the Paintings of the Late Florence Carlyle, A.R.C.A. (1925) #4999
    - Watson, Homer Ransford #7529

Toronto (Ont), Jewish Community Centre
- architecture, Jerome Markson #8078
Toronto (Ont), John Ross Robertson School
- architecture, concours #9437
Toronto (Ont), Joseph E. Shephard Government of Canada Building
- architecture, DuBois, Strong, Bindhart; Shore, Tilbe, Henschel, Irwin, Associated Architects #8975
Toronto (Ont), Knox College
- voir Toronto (Ont), University of Toronto. Knox College
Toronto (Ont), Lawrence Park Apartments
- architecture #8644
Toronto (Ont), M.S. Yolles Associates Offices
- architecture et intérieur, Ron Thom #9346
Toronto (Ont), Macdonald Galleries
- Macdonald, Albert Angus, propriétaire #6354
Toronto (Ont), Macdonald Gallery
- expositions
    - Contemporary Art of Iroquoia (1980) #4164
    - The Child in Ontario Art (1979) #1687
    - The Living Image: Three Contemporary Visions: Barbara Howard, Cecil Richards, Rebecca Sisler (1978) #666
- expositions, critiques
    - Bloore, Ronald Langley #4752
Toronto (Ont), MacKenzie & Co. Art Galleries
- expositions
    - Exhibition of Paintings by M.R. Hamilton (1906) #5693
Toronto (Ont), Madison Apartments
- architecture #8486
Toronto (Ont), magasin Eaton (rue College)
- architecture, Ross & Macdonald; Sproatt & Rolph, architectes-conseils #9365 9369
- comptoir de la Corporation canadienne de l'artisanat #2118
- intérieur
    - Carlu, Jacques #9370
    - ouvrages en fer d'ornement #9368
Toronto (Ont), magasin Fairweather
- architecture, Charles Sherman Cobb #9363
Toronto (Ont), magasin Holt Renfrew
- architecture, Crang & Boake #8078
Toronto (Ont), magasin Simpson
- expositions, critiques
    - Painters Eleven (1953) #1769
Toronto (Ont), Manufacturers Life Insurance Company Building
- architecture et intérieur, Marani & Morris #9339
Toronto (Ont), Market Gallery
- voir Toronto (Ont), City of Toronto Archives. Market Gallery
Toronto (Ont), Markleangelo Restaurant
- murale, Robert Nelson Markle #6418
Toronto (Ont), Marlborough Godard
- et Mira Godard #161
- exposition, art canadien, Marlborough Gallery, New York (NY), (1974) #572
- expositions
    - David Milne: The Toronto Years, 1939-1940 (1976) #6561
Toronto (Ont), Mason & Risch Company Building
- architecture, Bond & Smith #9328
Toronto (Ont), Masonic Temple
- architecture, concours #9062
Toronto (Ont), Massey College
- voir Toronto (Ont), University of Toronto. Massey College

Toronto (Ont), Massey Foundation
– collection #2142
Toronto (Ont), McConkey's Lunch
– architecture, Edward James Lennox #9269
Toronto (Ont), Mellors Art Gallery
– Laing, G.Blair, commentaire #1686
Toronto (Ont), Mercer Union
– expositions
 – *Locations: Outdoor Works by Toronto Artists* (1980) #1834
– expositions, critiques
 – Cohen, Sorel #5130
Toronto (Ont), métro
– architecture #9548 9554
– en comparaison avec métro de Montréal (Montréal, Qué) #9552
Toronto (Ont), Metro Centre
– architecture, John Andrews Architects #8323
– et gare Union (Toronto, Ont) #9540
Toronto (Ont), Metro Toronto Public Library
– architecture, Raymond Moriyama #9051
– Robertson, John Ross, Historical Collection #3130 3131 3204
– Toronto and Early Canada Picture Collection #3143
Toronto (Ont), Metro Toronto Zoo
– architecture, Thom Partnership #8412
Toronto (Ont), Mira Godard Gallery
– expositions
 – *Ed Bartram: 10 Years* (1980) #4618
 – *Jean McEwen: Suite parisienne* (1979) #6471
 – *Otto Rogers: New Paintings and Sculpture, 1977-78* (1979) #7065
– expositions, critiques
 – Bentham, Douglas (1978) #785
 – Smith, Gordon Appelbe (1978) #7231
Toronto (Ont), Molsons Bank
– architecture, Langley & Howland #9159
Toronto (Ont), Montessori School
– lettres d'enfants, réponses aux questions concernant Electric Gallery (Toronto, Ont) #1798
Toronto (Ont), Morris Gallery
– expositions
 – *Bertram Brooker, 1888-1955* (1971) #4925
 – *Helen McNicoll, 1879-1915: Oil Paintings from the Estate* (1974) #6507
 – *Tim Whiten: Sculpture and Drawings* (1972) #7562
Toronto (Ont), Mount Pleasant Cemetery. Eaton Mausoleum
– architecture, Sproatt & Rolph #8895
Toronto (Ont), Mount Pleasant Cemetery. Senator Cox's Mausoleum
– architecture, Sproatt & Rolph #8894
Toronto (Ont), Musée des beaux-arts de l'Ontario
– *voir* Toronto (Ont), Art Gallery of Ontario
Toronto (Ont), Nancy Poole's Studio
– expositions, critiques
 – Marshall, Pat (1979) #6422
Toronto (Ont), National Cash Register
– architecture, Page & Warrington #9234
Toronto (Ont), Native Friendship Centre
– expositions, critiques
 – *First Native Art Auction* (1981) #4170
Toronto (Ont), New Princess Theatre
– architecture, C.Howard Crane; Charles James Read, architecte associé #9069
Toronto (Ont), New School of Art
– (années 1960) #2994
– (années 1970) #3004

– Teitelbaum, Mashel, professeur #7340
Toronto (Ont), Northway Department Store
– architecture, Horwood & White #9366
Toronto (Ont), O'Keefe Centre for the Performing Arts
– architecture, Earle C. Morgan; Page & Steele #9087
– expositions
 – Société canadienne des aquarellistes (1974) #6
Toronto (Ont), Oke Building
– architecture, Shepard & Calvin #9335
Toronto (Ont), Olympia Square
– architecture, Bregman & Hamann #9301
Toronto (Ont), Ontario Archaeological Museum
– ouvrages en pierre, Neutres #3503
Toronto (Ont), Ontario Association of Architects, siège social
– architecture, John B. Parkin Associates #7679 8300 9341
Toronto (Ont), Ontario College of Art
– (1876-1976) #3009 3011 3012
– (1910-années 1920) #309
– (1912) #2964
– (1968), débat #2997
 – Ontario Advisory Committee on University Affairs, rapport #2996
– (1971-1972), politique controversée #3002
– (années 1910) #1712
– (années 1960), en comparaison avec Ecole des beaux-arts (Montréal, Qué) #2990
– (années 1970) #3004
– Bartram, Ed, élève #4618
– Coombs, Edith Grace, professeure #5172
– Cruikshank, William, professeur #5212
– et Ontario Society of Artists #1679
– Freifeld, Eric, professeur #5516
– Hallam, Joseph Sydney, élève #5687
– Handy, Arthur, professeur #5701
– Holmes, Robert
 – élève #5822
 – livres de sa bibliothèque #5824
– Innes, Alice A., élève #5900
– Kurelek, William, élève #6110
– Lapointe, Frank, élève #6170
– Lismer, Arthur, professeur #6295 6301
– Lougheed, Robert Elmer, élève #6327
– Loveroff, Frederick Nicholas, élève #6329 6330 6331
– Lui, Andrew, élève #6332
– Macdonald, Jock, professeur #6378
– MacGregor, John, professeur #6387
– Manly, Charles MacDonald, dessins #6414
– Nicoll, Marion F.S. Mackay, élève #6702 6703
– Paterson, Robert Allen, élève #6778
– Reid, George Agnew, directeur #6979
– Ronald, William S., élève #7071
– Schaefer, Carl Fellman, professeur #7156
– Shepherd, Helen, élève #2988
– Shepherd, Reginald, élève #2988
– Stacey, Harold, élève #7273
– Whiten, Colette
 – élève #7560
 – *Untitled 1971-72*, installation #7556
Toronto (Ont), Ontario Medical Association
– architecture
 – A.J. Diamond Associates #8078
 – Diamond, A.J., et Barton Myers #9349
 – Diamond & Myers #8071
Toronto (Ont), Ontario Provincial Museum
– oeuvres d'art appartenant au Educational Museum of Upper Canada (Toronto, Ont)

#3155
Toronto (Ont), Ontario School of Art
– Reid, George Agnew, élève #6979
Toronto (Ont), Ontario School of Art and Design #3128
– et Charlotte Mount Brook Morrell Schreiber #7164
Toronto (Ont), Ontario Science Centre
– architecture #7709
– architecture, Raymond Moriyama #9106
– expositions
 – *Make (Mak) Contemporary Crafts, 1971: An Exhibit of Contemporary Crafts by Ontario's Leading Designer-Craftsmen* (1971) #2247
Toronto (Ont), Open Studio #1806
– (1970-1977) #1819
– (1970-1980) #1830 1833
Toronto (Ont), Osgoode Hall
– architecture, Hopkins, Lawson & Nelson; Henry Bowyer Lane; Cumberland & Storm; Saunders & Ryrie #9002 9003
Toronto (Ont), Oxford University Press Building
– architecture, Sproatt & Rolph #9335
Toronto (Ont), Palace of Government
– architecture #8943
Toronto (Ont), Pantages Theatre
– architecture, Thomas White Lamb #9075
Toronto (Ont), Park Gallery
– expositions
 – *The National Gallery of Canada Presents: 1958-59, Painters Eleven* (1958) #1751
Toronto (Ont), Park School
– architecture, James Carlisle Pennington #9388
Toronto (Ont), Paterson Building
– architecture, Sproatt & Rolph #9335
Toronto (Ont), Pauline McGibbon Cultural Centre
– expositions
 – *Twelve Canadian Artists* (1980) #698
– restauration, Thom Partnership #7776
Toronto (Ont), Picture Loan Society #1758
– et Douglas M. Duncan #570 3223 3232
Toronto (Ont), Place de l'Ontario
– architecture, Craig, Zeidler & Strong #9113 9114 9115
Toronto (Ont), Pollock Gallery
– expositions
 – *Frances Loring - Florence Wyle* (1969) #754
 – Ontario Society of Artists (1966) #1666
– expositions, critiques
 – Morrisseau, Norval (1963) #6643
Toronto (Ont), poste de police, rue Dundas
– architecture, Shore, Tilbe, Henschel, Irwin, Peters #8078
Toronto (Ont), poste de police No 6
– architecture, Toronto City Architect's Office #8970
Toronto (Ont), presbytère anglican, Ward's Island
– murale, William Ronald #7070
Toronto (Ont), Prince Hotel
– architecture, Thom Partnership #8412
Toronto (Ont), Provincial Exhibition
– expositions, critiques
 – (1852) #1691 1692
Toronto (Ont), Provincial Lunatic Asylum
– architecture
 – Howard, John George #8378
 – Howard, John George, et Kivas Tully #9034
Toronto (Ont), Provincial Museum of

Toronto Society of Architects (Toronto, Ont)
– (1907-1912) #7956
– et Ontario Association of Architects #7955
Toronto Society of Arts (Toronto, Ont) #1706
– (1847-1848) #1689
– et Society of Artists and Amateurs of
  Toronto (Toronto, Ont) #1729
– expositions, critiques
  – (1847) #1690
Toronto Star, journal can
– dessins humoristiques
  – Hunter, Samuel #943
  – Macpherson, Duncan #6401
Toronto Theosophical Society (Toronto, Ont)
– et Bertram Richard Brooker #4926
– et Lawren Stewart Harris #5731
Torosian, Michael, photographe can, 1952-
– catalogue de photographies #996
tortues dans l'art
– sculpture en céramique, Joe Fafard et
  élèves #1924
totems
– *voir aussi* conservation et restauration,
  totems
totems . autochtones #3341
totems . Bella-Coolas #3874
totems . Chilkats #3798
totems . Gitksans #3797 3815 3828 3834 3884
  4032
– Kitwancool (CB) #3906 3925
totems . Haidas #3766 3943 3982
– H'Kusam #3913
– Masset (Queen Charlotte Islands, CB)
  #3765
– Ninstints (CB) #4067
– Oxford (Angleterre), Oxford University.
  Pitt Rivers Museum #3775
– Queen Charlotte Islands (CB) #4008
– Vancouver (CB), Totem Park #4118 4124
totems . Indiens de la côte nord-ouest #2095
  3766 3836 3849 3857 3866 3879 3909 3930
  3977 3993 4057
– influence sur Norman Tait #7314
– Martin, Mungo #6427
– Reid, Bill #3972 4162 6987
– Skedans (CB) #3984
– thème décoratif du castor #23
– totem de Joe Capilano #3837
– Vancouver (CB), Stanley Park #3932
totems . Kwakiutls #3848
– Alert Bay (CB) #3936
– Prince Rupert (CB) #3957
– Stockholm (Suède), Musée national #3844
– Vancouver (CB), Totem Park #4124
– Victoria (CB), Beacon Hill Park #4115
totems . Lummis #3967
totems . Niskas #4032
– Edimbourg (Ecosse), Royal Scottish
  Museum #3839
– Toronto (Ont), Royal Ontario Museum
  #3895
totems . Tlingits #3781 3812
– Alaska #3873
– Tonpass (Alaska) #3856
totems . Tsimshians #3834
– Mère des Ours #3868
– Nass River (CB) #3852
Toulouse-Lautrec, Henri Marie Raymond de,
  artiste fr, 1864-1901
– influence sur Lillian Freiman #5517
Tounissoux, Françoise, artiste can, 1947-
  #1544
Toupin, Fernand, artiste can, 1930- #1541
  7393 7395 7397

– entretien #7396
– expositions
  – (1970) #7394
– expositions de groupe
  – (1959) #1414
  – (1977) #1465
  – (1981) #1471
Toupin, Gilles, critique d'art can, XXe s.
– lauréat, concours de critique d'art (1979)
  #3312
tour Carleton Martello
– architecture #8437
tourbe
– dans architecture domestique, Prairies
  #8701 8706
– dans habitations temporaires, colons de la
  Saskatchewan, fin XIXe-début XXe s.
  #8696
Tourbin, Dennis, artiste can, 1946-
– art de performance #655
– commentaire sur Jack Chambers #700
Tourette-sur-Loup (France)
– Roussil, Robert, fondateur d'un centre
  artistique #7091
tours
– *voir aussi* clochers; tours Martello
tours . Canada
– châteaux d'eau, Colombie-Britannique
  #8153
– Toronto (Ont), Tour du CN #9510 9511
tours Martello . Canada #8415
– (1796-1846) #8416
– tour Carleton Martello (Saint-Jean, NB)
  #8437
tours Martello . Etats-Unis #8415
Tousignant, Claude, artiste can, 1932- #7398
  7400
– dessins #6586
– entretien #7399
– et art minimal #1483
– et op'art #1445
– et plasticiens #1439
– expositions
  – (1973) #7401
  – (1980) #7402
– expositions de groupe
  – (1959) #1414
  – (1965) #469
  – (1967) #480
  – (1968) #1263
  – (1971) #98
  – (1973) #556
  – (1981) #1471
– peintures (1953-1956) #1454
– symposium, Musée du Nouveau-Monde
  (La Rochelle, France), (1980) #1559
– utilisation de la couleur #468 1425
Tousignant, Serge, artiste can, 1942- #1479
  1480 1542 1543
– commentaire sur la perception visuelle
  #525
– entretien #1485
– estampes #7405
– expositions
  – (1975) #7403
– expositions, critiques #1067
– expositions de groupe
  – (1981) #1564
– *Mona* et *Environnement Transformé No 1,
  Dotscape* #7404
– utilisation de la lumière #767
– utilisation de la photographie #1057
Tousley, Nancy, critique d'art can, 1943-
– lauréate, concours de critique d'art (1979)

#3312
Towdystan (CB)
– pictogrammes #3965
Town, Harold Barling, artiste can, 1924-
  #947 7408 7409
– commentaire sur l'art érotique #7410
– commentaire sur la gravure #817 818
– commentaire sur les femmes dans l'art
  #7414
– commentaire sur les rapports entre artistes
  et architectes #8234
– décors #472
– dessins #7411
– écrits #92
– entretien #7407
– estampes #7406
– et Albert Jacques Franck #5501
– et gravure ontarienne (années 1960) #1756
– et peinture torontoise (années 1960) #1753
– expositions
  – (1973) #7413
  – (1975) #7415
  – (1980) #7416
– expositions, critiques #520
– expositions de groupe
  – (1958) #431
  – (1959) #438
  – (1964) #462
  – (1967) #490 821
  – (1979) #510
– influence de l'expressionisme abstrait
  #1773
– influence de la peinture américaine #495
– influence sur peinture torontoise (années
  1960) #1760
– oeuvres (années 1950) #7412
– participant, Symposium on 20th Century
  Canadian Culture (Washington, DC),
  (1977) #621
– peintures et sculptures #449
– peintures sur le marché de l'art (1961)
  #445 446
Townsend, William, artiste brit résidant au
  Canada, 1909-1973
– expositions
  – (1974) #7418
– juré, *Saskatchewan Arts Exhibition* (1963)
  #1910
– oeuvres (1964-1968) #7417
Trace: A Canadian Review of Architecture,
  périodique can #7753
traite des fourrures
– *voir* commerce des fourrures
Trakas, George, sculpteur can, 1944- #1632
  7422
– entretien #7420
– expositions
  – (1979) #7421
  – (1980) #7423
– expositions, critiques #787
– expositions de groupe
  – (1978) #790
– *Passage* et *Union Station* #7419
transcendentalisme
– et le Groupe des Sept #1774
transport, architecture et
– Canada
  – (1938-1942) #7666
  – XIXe s. #9512
Trasov, Vincent (Mr. Peanut), artiste can,
  1947-
– correspondance, Miss General Idea (1971)
  #546
– expositions de groupe

– (1971) #2042
– (1979) #2070
travail de la pierre . Algonquiens #3406 3529
– pierres aviformes #3499 3511 3577
travail de la pierre . Amérindiens
– ouvrages perlés #3457
– préhistoire #3401
travail de la pierre . autochtones #3341
travail de la pierre . Béothuks
– Port-au-Choix (TN) #3611
– Red Indian Lake (TN) #3623
travail de la pierre . Goyoguins #3525
travail de la pierre . Hurons
– pipes, Royal Ontario Museum (Toronto, Ont) #3504
travail de la pierre . Indiens de la côte nord-ouest
– flèches et pointes de lance #3785
– instruments #4068
travail de la pierre . Indiens des forêts du Nord-Est #3491
travail de la pierre . Indiens des plaines
– assemblages de rochers #3708
travail de la pierre . Inuit
– inukshuks et inunguaks #4199
travail de la pierre . Iroquois #3525 3566
– pipes, Royal Ontario Museum (Toronto, Ont) #3504
travail de la pierre . Micmacs #3643
– Clyde River (NE) #3531
travail de la pierre . Neutres
– parure #3503
travail de la pierre . Pentaguets #3537
travail de la pierre . Saulteux/Ojibwa
– pierres aviformes #3546
travail de la pierre . Tagish #4106
travail de la pierre . Tlingits #4106
travail de la pierre . Tutchonis #4106
travail des fibres
– voir aussi textiles et tissus
travail des fibres . Canada
– (1979-1980) #2138
– (1980) #2257
– (années 1970) #2771
– mennonites #2264
– Vancouver (CB), (années 1980) #2775
– XXe s. #2142
travail des métaux
– voir aussi ferblanterie
travail des métaux . Amérindiens
– articles de traite #3440
– ouvrages perlés #3457
travail des métaux . Athapascans
– (années 1970), artisanes #3367
travail des métaux . Canada #2089
– (1837-1887) #253
– (1964-1967) #2108 2109
– (1979-1980) #2138
– (1980) #2257
– (années 1940) #2601 2693
– (années 1960) #2106
– (années 1970) #2706
– Beau, Paul #4641
– Chaudron, Bernard #5099
– Chaudron, Bernard et Louise #5098
– couvert #2470
– et architecture
– (années 1910) #8222
– (années 1960) #8236
– étain et cuivre, XIXe s. #2704
– guide pour collectionneurs #2104 2125 2131
– Lozeau, Jean-Baptiste #249 250
– Québec #2183 2228 2711

– (années 1940) #8820
– XVIIe-XIXe s. #1341
– XVIIe-XVIIIe s., artisans #2214
– XXe s. #2198
– Stuart, Don #7281
– Toronto (Ont)
– Banque canadienne de commerce #9180
– magasin Eaton #9368
– utilisation de motifs canadiens (années 1930) #8225
– XXe s. #2121 2142
travail des métaux . Indiens des plaines #3698
travail des métaux . Inuit
– (années 1970), artisanes #3367
travail du bois . Algonquiens #3605
– récipients #3507
travail du bois . Canada
– (1964-1967) #2108 2109
– (1980) #2257
– (années 1940) #2601
– (années 1960) #2106
– appâts (chasse) #2595
– guide pour collectionneurs #2104 2125 2131
– mennonites, comté de Waterloo (Ont) #2264
– Nouveau-Brunswick #2150
– objets en bois #2252 2470 2590 2591
– Ontario, XVIIIe-XIXe s. #2588
– Ottawa (Ont), Musée national de l'Homme. Centre canadien d'études sur la culture traditionnelle #963
– Picard, Edmond #6863
– Québec #2223 2226 2237
– apprentis (1660-1815) #2231
– XVIIe-XVIIIe s. #2530 2531
– XXe s. #2198
– XVIIIe-XIXe s. #2112 2594
– XXe s. #2121 2142
travail du bois . Hurons #3519
travail du bois . Iroquois #3519 3605
travail du bois . Micmacs #3569 3643
travail du bois . Pentaguets #3537
travail du bois . Saulteux/Ojibwa #3557
travail du cuir . Algonquiens #3456 3672
travail du cuir . Algonquins
– mocassins #3554
travail du cuir . Canada
– (1980) #2257
– (années 1970) #2936
– Québec #2198 2228 2953
– Simard, René #7208
– XVIIe-XIXe s. #2112
– XXe s. #2121 2142
travail du cuir . Carriers
– (années 1970) #4145
travail du cuir . Cris #3651
travail du cuir . Delawares
– mocassins #3554
travail du cuir . Gros Ventres #3651
travail du cuir . Indiens des plaines #3456 3651 3658 3660 3672 3684
– jambières #3697
– peinture #3709
travail du cuir . Micmacs
– brassards #3572
travail du cuir . Pentaguets
– mocassins #3554
travail du cuir . Pieds-Noirs #3651 3654 3678 3686
travail du cuir . Salishiens
– (années 1970) #4145
travail du cuir . Saulteux/Ojibwa #3557

travail du cuir . Siouens #3456 3651 3672
travail du cuir . Tagish #4106
travail du cuir . Tlingits #4106
travail du cuir . Tutchonis #4106
travaux à l'aiguille, techniques
– voir matériaux et techniques . travaux à l'aiguille
Treherne, Harold J., artiste can, 1899-1975
– expositions de groupe
– (1977) #1933
Tremblay, A. Henri, architecte can, actif 1927-1954
– Lac-Bouchette (Qué), Chapelle mariale #8832
Tremblay, Alain, céramiste can, 1941- #2216
Tremblay, Denys, artiste can, 1951- #1540 1634
Tremblay, Esther, artiste can, 1927- #1551
Tremblay, Georges-Edouard, artiste can, 1907- #1428 1429
– tapis crocheté, motifs #2756
Tremblay, Gérard, artiste can, 1928- #1541 7424
– et peinture montréalaise (années 1950) #1403
Tremblay, Jean-Jacques, artiste can, 1926-
– peintures (années 1970-1979) #7425
Tremblay, Michel, dramaturge can, 1943-
– et Michel Leclair, album Chez Fada #6183
Tremblay, Michel-Thomas, artiste can, actif 1974-
– fondateur de l'Atelier de l'île (Val-David, Qué) #1664
Tremblay, Michèle, céramiste can, active années 1960-1970 #2216
Tremblay, Pierre-Paul, photographe can, actif 1981 #1562
Tremblay, Richard-Max, artiste can, 1952- #1526
Tremblay, Suzanne, céramiste can, active années 1970- #1549
Tremblay-Gagnon, Yvonne, artiste can, 1931- #1546
Tremblé, Léo-Paul, artiste can, 1924- #1547 1551
triangles
– dans sculpture, Pierre Heyvaert #5797
Triaud, Louis-Hubert, artiste can, 1794-1836 #1336
tricot . Canada
– (1608-1867) #2120
– et macramé, XXe s. #2121
– Nouvelle-Ecosse, patrons (avant 1920) #2785
– Québec, XVIIIe s. #2200
– Terre-Neuve #2744
tricot . Cowichans #3882 3929 4027
tricot . Ecosse
– XIXe s., et tricot cowichan #3929
tricots (vêtements) . Cowichans #3929
Trier, Walter, artiste can, 1890-1951 #7426 7427
– expositions
– (1980) #7428
Trinity (TN)
– architecture #7792
Trinity Bay (TN)
– architecture domestique #7785 7791 8541
Triple K Co-operative (Red Lake, Ont)
– sérigraphie (années 1970) #4151 4158
Trois-Rivières (Qué)
– architecture
– (années 1630-1910) #7883
– XVIIIe s. #7861

– arts décoratifs (années 1930) #2174
– berceuses #2535
– églises #8806
– maisons en brique, début XIXe s. #8521
– seigneuries #8611
Trois-Rivières (Qué), Centre culturel de
  Trois-Rivières/Trois-Rivières Cultural
  Centre
– expositions
  – *Manitoba Mainstream: People's Art/Fine
    Art/Le Grand Courant du Manitoba: arts
    populaires, beaux-arts* (1973) #1897
Trois-Rivières (Qué), Chapelle des récollets
– architecture et intérieur #8850
Trois-Rivières (Qué), église
– baldaquin, Joseph Quintal (frère Augustin)
  et Gilles Bolvin #8826
– sculpture, Gilles Bolvin #4781
Trois-Rivières (Qué), Forges du
  Saint-Maurice #2698 2711 9238 9240
– architecture #9251 9256
– architecture domestique #8634 9250 9254
– historiographie #9257
– matériaux d'architecture #7878
– moulins #9253
– poêles #2708
Trois-Rivières (Qué), maison Deschenaux
  dite manoir de Tonnancour
– architecture et intérieur #8633
Trois-Rivières (Qué), musée Pierre Boucher
– *voir* Trois-Rivières (Qué), Université du
  Québec à Trois-Rivières. Musée Pierre
  Boucher
Trois-Rivières (Qué), Université du Québec
  à Trois-Rivières. Musée Pierre Boucher
– expositions
  – *De la figuration à la non-figuration dans
    l'art québécois* (1977) #1461
  – *Les moins de 35: du 22 janvier au 4 février*
    (1973) #1501
  – *Rodolphe Duguay, 1891-1973* (1979) #5318
trompe-l'oeil #525
Tropaco (Iles Vierges), Habitat
– architecture, Moshe Safdie #8404
Trottier, Gerald Mathew, artiste can, 1925-
– expositions de groupe
  – (1965) #469
– mosaïque murale, Henry Marshall Tory
  Science Building, Carleton University
  (Ottawa, Ont) #7429
Trottier-Dufour, Gisèle, artiste can, active
  1978 #1538
Trounce, Thomas, architecte can, 1813-1900
– Victoria (CB) #8145
Trowell, Ian, sculpteur can, 1930- #7431
– expositions
  – (1980) #7430
Trowsse, Pegi, photographe can, ca 1952-
– catalogue de photographies #991
Trudeau, Angus, artiste can, 1908-
– expositions de groupe
  – (1981) #4173
Trudeau, Charles Elliott, architecte can,
  1922-
– Ottawa (Ont), Northern Electric Research
  and Development Laboratories #9344
Trudeau, Randy, artiste can, 1954-
– expositions de groupe
  – (1980) #4159
  – (1981) #4173
Trudeau, Yves, sculpteur can, 1930- #7432
  7435
– et Création #1492
– expositions

– (1975) #7434
– (1978) #7436
– sculptures (1960-1970) #7433
Trueman, Richard Henry, photographe can,
  1856-1911 #7437
Truro (NE)
– architecture #7828
Tsimshians
– art #3881 3926
  – (années 1970) #4145
  – représentation de la lune #4059
– coiffure #4019
– couvertures #3826
– culture (années 1880) #3763
– masques #4056 4069
– massues #4048
– massues en pierre #4053
– miroirs #3804
– mythologie #3910
– pantins #3891
– portraits #3794
– récipients en bois sculpté, XIXe s. #3985
– sérigraphie #4167
– signes héraldiques #3795 3981
– totems #3834 3852 3868
Tsonnontouans
– masques #3508 3533 3563 4113
– masques et pipes #3636
– masses d'armes #3535
– peignes #3587
– pipes #3642
– vannerie #3552
Tsutakawa, George, sculpteur amér, 1910-
– fontaine, Vancouver (CB) #2077
Tucson (Ariz), University of Arizona.
  Museum of Art
– expositions
  – *Ernest Lawson 1873-1939* (1979) #6179
Tudor-Hart, Ernest Percyval, artiste can,
  1873-1954
– influence sur Tony Law #6174
Tully, Kivas, architecte can, 1820-1905
– Cobourg (Ont), Victoria Hall #8994 8995
– membre de la Toronto Society of Arts
  #1689
– Toronto (Ont) #8056
  – Provincial Lunatic Asylum #9034
  – Trinity College #9483
Tully, Sydney Strickland, artiste can,
  1860-1911
– expositions
  – (1911) #7438
– professeur de Hattie Blackstock #4738
Tulsa (Okla), Philbrook Art Center
– expositions
  – *Magic Images: Contemporary Native
    American Art* (1981) #4172
  – *Native American Art at Philbrook* (1980)
    #4165
tunnels
– *voir aussi* métros, constructions
tunnels . Canada
– tunnels de chemins de fer, XIXe s.
  (Ottawa, Ont) #8019
Tunnillie, Ikayukta, artiste can, 1911-1980
  #4460
Tupper, sir Charles Andrew, homme d'Etat
  can, 1821-1915
– correspondance, Frederic Marlett
  Bell-Smith #4668
Turcot, Guy, photographe can, 1950- #1562
– catalogue de photographies #997 999
Turgeon, Adélard, sculpteur can, 1883-1969
– sculpture sur bois, collection Nettie Sharpe

#1607
Turgeon, Joseph Ovide, architecte can,
  1875-1933
– Montréal (Qué), édifice La Patrie #9303
– Québec (Qué), Palais épiscopal #8787
Turner, E.R., facteur de clavecins can, actif
  1979 #2940
Turner, Jack, artiste can, 1934- #7439
Turner, Joseph Mallord William, artiste brit,
  1775-1851
– Collings, Charles John, comparaison #5135
– influence sur Gordon Appelbe Smith
  #7232
– influence sur Lionel LeMoine FitzGerald
  #5450
– influence sur William Perehudoff #6837
– Verner, Frederick Arthur, comparaison
  #1696
Turner, Philip John, architecte can,
  1876-1943
– Vancouver (CB), University of British
  Columbia, concours #9498
Turner, Richard Julian, artiste can, 1936-
  #7440
– expositions de groupe
  – (1967) #490
Turner & Carless, agence can d'architecture
– architecture domestique #8494
  – Montréal (Qué) #8493 8556
Tutchonis
– culture #4106
Tuu'luq, Marion, artiste can, 1910- #4255
– expositions
  – (1980) #7442
  – expositions, critiques #7441
– expositions de groupe
  – (1976) #4268
Twanas
– culture (années 1870) #4031
Tweedsmuir, baron
– *voir* Buchan, John, baron Tweedsmuir
Twillingate (TN)
– architecture #7792
Twomey, Jerry, collectionneur can, 1915-
– collection, art inuit #4306 4427
Typographic Designers of Canada
– (1956) #923
typographie
– *voir* imprimerie
Tyrrell, Joseph Burr, photographe can,
  1858-1957
– photographies d'arpentage #1014 1015
  1865

U

Uhthoff, Ina D.D., artiste can, 1889-1971
  #7443
Ukrainian Women's Association of Canada
– conservation et promotion des métiers
  d'art ukrainiens #2782
Ukrainiens au Canada
– architecture #8085 8127 8713
– architecture domestique #8691 8704 8709
  8710
– art #1843
– art traditionnel #968 2117
  – fin XVIIIe-XXe s. #961
– broderie #2124 2782
– chemises et bijoux bukoviniens (1865-1945)
  #2869

– construction en bois rond #8090 8136
– églises #8768 8912 8915
– églises et arts décoratifs #2270
– Kurelek, William, peintures #6113 6114
  6116
– monuments funéraires #733
– oeufs de Pâques #2132
– ouvrages à l'aiguille #2780
Ulrich, James (Jim), artiste can, 1944-
– expositions de groupe
  – (1977) #1956
Umholtz, David, artiste can, 1943-
– expositions de groupe
  – (1977) #1901
  – (1978) #669
umiaks
– voir aussi bateaux
umiaks . Inuit #3339
– en comparaison avec canots nootkas #3344
Una
– voir Oonark, Jessie
Unaaq
– voir Oonark, Jessie
UNESCO
– et Commission royale d'enquête sur
  l'avancement des arts, lettres et sciences
  (Rapport Massey) #3261
– et Norman McLaren #6492
Uniake, Richard, homme d'Etat can,
  1753-1830
– résidence (Mount Uniake, NE) #8534
uniformes militaires . Canada #2867 2881
  2910 2911
– (1742-1960) #2835
– (années 1770-1812) #2848
– boutons #2882
– Louisbourg (NE) #2866
  – (1713-1758) #2857
– milice canadienne, règlements concernant
  les vêtements #2874
– Saint-Jean (NB), Musée du
  Nouveau-Brunswick #2900
– XVIIIe-XIXe s. #1309 2825
uniformes militaires . Etats-Unis
– (1665-1970) #2867
universités et collèges canadiens
– (1911-1912) #8295
– (1960-1970) #7710
– (années 1920) #7656
– (années 1960) #9396 9400 9401
  – et planification gouvernementale #9395
– (années 1970) #9478
– bibliothèques
  – (années 1930) #9042
  – (années 1960) #9046
  – (années 1970) #9052
– Burnaby (CB), Simon Fraser University
  #9406 9501 9504 9505 9506
– design intérieur (années 1960) #9402
– Edmonton (Alta), University of Alberta
  #9492 9493 9495
  – Students' Union Housing #9496
– et Commission royale d'enquête sur
  l'avancement des arts, lettres et sciences
  (Rapport Massey) #3261
– et enseignement de l'art
  – (1894), recommandations #2960
  – Lismer, Arthur commentaire #2966
– et étude de l'histoire de l'art au Canada
  – (1980) #3316
  – (années 1930-1960) #3306
– Guelph (Ont), University of Guelph. Arts
  and Library Buildings #9468
– Halifax (NE)

– Dalhousie University #9408
– Nova Scotia College of Art and Design
  #9409 9410
– Hamilton (Ont), McMaster University
  #9451
– Kingston (Ont), Queen's University #9447
  – Douglas Library #9445
  – résidence des femmes #9445
– Lethbridge (Alta), University of
  Lethbridge #9406 9497
– London (Ont), University of Western
  Ontario #9442 9448
– Montréal (Qué)
  – Université de Montréal #8345 9415
  – Université du Québec à Montréal #9427
  – Université McGill #9414 9423
    – Athletic buildings #9417
    – Macdonald Physics Building #9411
    – Medical Building #9412
– Ontario, collections d'oeuvres d'art dans
  universités (1850-1900) #3152
– Ottawa (Ont)
  – Carleton University #9455
    – School of Architecture #8284
  – Université d'Ottawa #9458 9465
– Peterborough (Ont), Trent University
  #9470 9473 9474
  – Champlain College #9465
– Québec (années 1960) #7862
– Québec (Qué), Campus
  intercommunautaire de Cap-Rouge #9421
– résidences pour étudiants (années 1960)
  #9399 9467
– Saskatoon (Sask), University of
  Saskatchewan #9489 9490 9491
– Scarborough (Ont), University of Toronto.
  Scarborough College #9462 9463 9464
– style néo-gothique #7671
– Sudbury (Ont), Université Laurentienne
  #9461
– Toronto (Ont)
  – George Brown College of Applied Arts
    & Technology. Campus Casa Loma
    #9479
  – University of Toronto #9444 9449 9459
    9477
    – Convocation Hall #9430
    – Emmanuel College #9452
    – Hart House #9433 9438 9439 9440
      9441
    – Knox College #9432 9435
    – Massey College #9460
    – programme d'agrandissement (années
      1950) #9456
    – résidence des hommes #9431
    – Trinity College #9446 9483
    – University College #9428 9429 9453
      9475 9482
    – Victoria College. Wymilwood #9454
  – York University #9469
    – Glendon Hall #9457
– Vancouver (CB)
  – University of British Columbia #9498
    9499 9500 9509
    – Fine Arts Building #9502
    – Student Union #9503
– Winnipeg (Man), University of Manitoba
  #9485 9486
  – School of Architecture #9487
  – University Centre #9488
– Wolfville (NE), Acadia University #9407
Upper Canada Agricultural Society
– (1846-1867), expositions #1715
Upper Canada Village (Morrisburg, Ont)

  #7981 8031 8063
– architecture #7982 7988
– Cook, Nelson, portraits de la famille
  Dickinson #5170
– filage et tissage #2726
– mobilier #2484 2549
Urban, Colette, artiste can, 1952-
– expositions, critiques #1227
urbanisme
– voir aussi expansion urbaine; squares
  (villes)
– Arctique
  – (années 1950) #8184
  – (années 1960) #8186
  – (années 1970) #8187
– Calgary (Alta), (années 1970) #8122
– Canada
  – (1867-1967) #7695
  – (1880-1914) #7736
  – (années 1950) #7675
  – (années 1960) #7682 8304
  – début XXe s. #7955
  – Mawson, Thomas Hayton #9405
– Colombie-Britannique, fin XIXe s. #8150
– Edmonton (Alta), (années 1970) #8123
– Halifax (NE) #1119
– Montréal (Qué) #7931
– Nouvelle-Ecosse, XVIIe-XIXe s. #7814
– Ontario #8024
– Ottawa (Ont), région de la capitale
  nationale #8035 8037
– provinces maritimes #7779
– Québec, XVIIe-XVIIIe s. #1320 7885 8603
– St. John's (TN) #7786
– Toronto (Ont), hôtel de ville et Civic
  Square #8983
– Vancouver (CB)
  – (1886-1929) #8730
  – (1914) #8156
  – (années 1960) #8158
– Winnipeg (Man) #1891
  – (années 1970) #8104
Uritani, Giselle, artiste can (vitrail), active
  1975
– vitraux #2452
Urquhart, Tony, artiste can, 1934- #7444
  7445
– dessins #7447
– et peinture torontoise (années 1960) #1753
– expositions
  – (1978) #7448
– expositions de groupe
  – (1965) #473
  – (1978) #665
– imagerie archétype #7446
– paysages #7449
– régionalisme, en comparaison avec Greg
  Curnoe #5225
– sculptures (années 1960) #1793
– thème de la mort #1759
URSS
– vues photographiques, Michael William
  Semak #7169
ursulines
– art #1323 1334 1335
– arts décoratifs #2174
– broderie #1581 2169 2171 2777 2779 2780
  2781 2783 2788 2789 2791 3629
  – Le Ber, Jeanne #2778
– dorure #2930
– enseignement de l'art #2979
– orfèvrerie, François Ranvoyzé #2658
– Québec (Qué), Couvent des ursulines
  #1352 8810

– chapelle #8852
– tabernacles #1359
– tissage #2212
Urushibara Mokuchu, Yoshijiro, artiste jap, 1888-1953
– et Walter Joseph Phillips #6860
Urwick Currie & Partners Ltd., conseillers en gestion
– étude de l'Institut royale d'architecture du Canada (1974) #8318
usines
– voir aussi moulins
usines . Canada
– (années 1910) #9234
ustensiles de cuisine . Canada #2318
– (années 1940) #2603 2604
– (avant 1867), Canada anglais #2470
– art traditionnel #2139
– étain et cuivre, XIXe s. #2704
– Maritimes, XIXe s. #2147
– Montréal (Qué), Fondation Macdonald-Stewart #2203
– Ontario, XIXe-début XXe s. #2355
– ouvrages de ferronnerie #2703 2705
– Québec
– XVIIe-XIXe s., influence européenne #2221
– XVIIe-XVIIIe s. #2161 2210
– ustensiles en bois #2590 2591 2594
– Ontario, XVIIIe-XIXe s. #2588
– Washington (DC), Smithsonian Institution #2111
Utrecht (Pays-Bas), Utrecht Centraal Museum
– expositions
– Moderne canadese schilderkunst (1958) #431
Uu, David, artiste can, 1948-
– expositions, critiques #2051
– expositions de groupe
– (1971) #2042
– (1973) #2045

V

Vachon, Ginette, photographe can, ca 1949-
– catalogue de photographies #1032
Vadeboncoeur, F.Louis, sculpteur et architecte can, 1831-1896 #1319
Vail, Floyd, photographe can, actif 1894 #977
Vaillancourt, Armand, sculpteur can, 1932- #1502 7450
– et André Fournelle #5484
– expositions de groupe
– (1977) #1622
– fontaine, Embarcadero Plaza (San Francisco, Calif) #7451
– influence sur Pierre Rolland Dinel #5293
– réaction de la presse #7452
– sculptures (années 1960) #745 746
– Symposium international de sculpture environnementale de Chicoutimi (Qué), (1980) #1639
Vaillancourt, Paul-Gilles, artiste can, 1941-
– décors et costumes, Montreal Theatre Ballet #1410
vaisselle
– voir aussi couvert; pichets; soupières
vaisselle . Canada
– étain, Québec, XVIIe-XIXe s. #2700
– faïence, Ontario, XIXe s.-début XXe s.

#2355
– jouets d'enfant, fin XIXe s.-années 1930 #2932
– motifs du castor et de la feuille d'érable #2312
– orfèvrerie
– XVIIe-XIXe s. #2637 2651
– XVIIe-XVIIIe s. #2210
– Québec #2161 2237
– service de table officiel, Canada (1898) #2333
– verre, XIXe-début XXe s. #2430
– XVIIe-XIXe s. #2318
Val-d'Or (Qué), Centre culturel de Val-d'Or
– expositions
– De la figuration à la non-figuration dans l'art québécois (1977) #1461
Val-David (Qué), Atelier de l'île #1664
Valcourt (Qué), Centre culturel de Valcourt
– expositions
– De la figuration à la non-figuration dans l'art québécois (1977) #1461
Vale, Florence Gertrude, artiste can, 1909-
– dessins, influence sur Harold Barling Town #7413
– et Albert Jacques Franck #5499
– expositions
– (1980) #7453
Valentine, Hugh Allen Inglis, architecte can, 1904-1978
– Montréal (Qué), Université McGill. Athletic buildings, concours #9417
Valentine, William, artiste can, 1798-1849 #1191
– daguerréotype #1211
– influence sur Maria Frances Ann Morris Miller #6541
Valéry, Paul, poète fr, 1871-1945
– Cormier, Ernest, comparaison #8346
Valin, Jean, sculpteur can, 1691-1759
– tabernacles #1613
Valiquet, Carl, photographe can, 1946-
– catalogue de photographies #997 999
Valius, Telesforas, artiste can, 1914-1977
– professeur d'Ed Bartram #4618
vallée de l'Outaouais
– architecture, bois #8029
– art (années 1970) #590
– vues
– Masson, Henri L. #6442
vallée du Richelieu (Qué)
– poterie, XVIIIe-XIXe s. #2299 2321
Vallery, Hugh J., Can, XXe s.
– codirecteur, Toronto School Board Study of Educational Facilities (SEF) #9472
Valley City Seating Company, graveurs sur bois (Dundas, Ont)
– retables, Church of Saint John the Evangelist (Hamilton, Ont) #730
Valleyfield (Qué), cathédrale de Salaberry-de-Valleyfield
– architecture, Henri Sicotte Labelle avec l'aide de Jean M. Lafleur et de J. Eugène Perron; L.N. Audet, architecte-conseil #8843
Valleyfield (Qué), séminaire catholique
– (années 1950) #3034
Vallière, Lauréat, sculpteur can, 1888-1973 #7454 7455
– sculptures sur bois, église Sainte-Famille (île d'Orléans, Qué) #1612
Vallière, Phillipe, ébéniste can, XIXe s. #2464
Van Den Heuvel, Francis
– voir Heuvel, Francis van den

Van der Hilst, Robert
– voir Hilst, Robert van der
Van der Keuken, Johan
– voir Keuken, Johan van der
Van Dusen, Raymond (Ray), photographe can, 1949-
– expositions de groupe
– (1981) #1070
Van Ginhoven, Anke, artiste can, 1931- #1282
Van Gogh, Vincent
– voir Gogh, Vincent van
Van Horne, Sir William Cornelius, directeur de société ferroviaire et collectionneur can, 1843-1915 #1713
– correspondance, Frederic Marlett Bell-Smith #4668
– et hôtels appartenant à sociétés ferroviaires #9290
– et James Wilson Morrice #6626
– résidence, maison Van-Horne (Montréal, Qué) #8594 8601
Van Norman, Joseph, maître de forges can, actif 1813-1829
– et Normandale Iron Works (comté de Norfolk, Ont) #2699
Van Slyck, Winnifred (Wyn), artiste can, 1910-
– et Dugald Costume Collection (Dugald, Man) #2902
Vance, Dennis John, artiste can, 1940-
– expositions de groupe
– (1976) #2060
Vancouver, George, navigateur, explorateur brit résidant au Canada, 1758-1798
– expédition, Indiens de la côte nord-ouest #3445 3767 4062
– réaction à l'art de la côte nord-ouest #2009
Vancouver (CB)
– architecture #7762 8159 8164 8166 8170
– (1886-1914) #8165
– (1899-1901) #1977
– (1914) #8156
– (1959-1961) #8158
– (années 1910-1970), centre-ville #8171
– (années 1940) #8141
– (années 1950) #7673 8144 8157
– (années 1960) #7698
– art déco #8167
– Downs, Barry Vance #8353
– Erickson, Arthur Charles #8357
– Gastown #7772 8160 8163
– Hooper, Thomas #8376
– Kemble, Roger #8379
– Robson Square #8172
– visites guidées #8168
– Whiteway, William Tuff #9508
– architecture domestique
– (1886-1929) #8714 8730
– (1950-1960) #8697
– proposition, réhabilitation des édifices du centre-ville (1980) #8725
– Thom, Ron #8411
– architecture et art (années 1950) #1992
– art #547
– (1886-1930) #2003
– (1944-1955) #7230
– (1980) #2076
– (années 1890-1940) #1984
– (années 1950-1960) #2039
– (années 1950-1970) #131
– (années 1960) #90 441 519 2035 2036 2038
– (années 1970) #1870 2040 2053

– XXe s. #536
– art de performance #2073
– art public (i.e. art dans les lieux publics), (1905-1971) #2005
– art vidéo #605 2044
– bandes dessinées (années 1970) #955
– conservation de l'architecture #7761 8161
– édifices récréatifs #9081
– expansion urbaine (années 1970) #8162
– fontaines #2077
– galeries d'art (années 1960) #442
– gares #9545 9546
– immeubles à bureaux
  – (années 1950-1960) #9300
  – bureaux d'architectes (années 1940) #9297
– immeubles d'habitation (années 1960) #8699
– musées #3190
– panneaux lumineux #2079
– peinture #2000
  – (années 1920-1950) #424
  – (années 1940-1950) #412
  – (années 1960) #520
  – (années 1970) #2075
– photographie
  – (années 1880-1890) #2022
  – (années 1960) #2019
  – (années 1970) #998 2064 2069
– sculpture #2026
  – (années 1960) #1854 2037
  – (années 1970) #2049
– sculpture en plein air #2080
– verrières
  – (1890-1940) #2454 2456
  – Dearle, John Henry, et Duncan W. #2458
– vues
  – (1845-1871) #2020
  – McMurtie, William Birch #6505
– vues photographiques
  – (1886-1888), J.A. Brock & Co. #2021
  – Bailey, Charles S. #4583
Vancouver (CB), Ace Space Company
– vidéos #2044
Vancouver (CB), Aéroport de Vancouver. Aérogare
– architecture, McCarter, Nairne & Partners #9514
– art public (i.e. art dans les lieux publics) #2005
Vancouver (CB), B.C. Electric Building
– architecture, Thompson, Berwick & Pratt #7679
Vancouver (CB), Banque Royale
– architecture, Sumner Godfrey Davenport #8171 9179
Vancouver (CB), Bau-Xi Gallery
– expositions
  – Toni Onley: 10 Years of Painting, 1962-72 (1972) #6736
– expositions, critiques
  – Doray, Audrey Capel #5301
  – Shadbolt, Jack Leonard (1973) #7184
  – Smith, Gordon Appelbe (1978) #7231
Vancouver (CB), BC Art League. Gallery
– expositions
  – British Columbia Society of Fine Arts #1978
Vancouver (CB), Birks Building
– architecture et conservation #7762
– démolition, suggestion #8146
Vancouver (CB), Block 51-61-71 project
– architecture #7728
Vancouver (CB), Brittania Community

Services Centre
– architecture et planification #9116
Vancouver (CB), Canadian Broadcasting Corporation
– architecture, Siège de l'Ingénierie de Canadian Broadcating Corporation; Thompson, Berwick, Pratt & Partners, Associate Architects #8171
Vancouver (CB), Caulfield Cove Townhouses
– architecture, Ronald Howard et Barclay McLeod #8746
Vancouver (CB), Charles H. Scott Gallery
– voir Vancouver (CB), Emily Carr College of Art. Charles H. Scott Gallery
Vancouver (CB), Chinese Cultural Centre
– architecture, concours #9144
Vancouver (CB), Christ Church Cathedral
– architecture, C.O. Wickenden #8171
– architecture et conservation #7762 8910
– proposition architecturale, Arthur Charles Erickson #8360
Vancouver (CB), City Stage Theatre
– architecture, Hawthorn Mansfield Towers #8373
Vancouver (CB), Connexions
– vidéos #2044
Vancouver (CB), Coquitlam Centre
– vitraux #2459 2460
Vancouver (CB), Crown Compagnie d'assurance-vie, siège social
– architecture, Thompson, Berwick & Pratt #7683
Vancouver (CB), Dal Grauer Substation
– architecture, Sharp & Thompson, Berwick, Pratt #8171
Vancouver (CB), David Y.H. Lui Theatre
– architecture, Hawthorn Mansfield Towers #8373
Vancouver (CB), Dominion Hall
– expositions
  – British Columbia Society of Fine Arts (1909) #1978
Vancouver (CB), Eera Townhouses
– architecture, Hawthorn Mansfield Towers #8373
Vancouver (CB), Emily Carr College of Art. Charles H. Scott Gallery
– expositions
  – The West Face, 1981 (1981) #2084
  – Vancouver School of Art: The Early Years, 1925-1939 (1980) #3019
– Wood, Alan, Ranch, installation (1981) #7611
Vancouver (CB), Eppich House
– architecture, Arthur Charles Erickson #8745
Vancouver (CB), Equinox Gallery
– expositions, critiques
  – Michener, Robert (1974) #6526
Vancouver (CB), Eye Scream Restaurant
– exposition, N.E. Thing Co. Ltd. (1977) #6678
Vancouver (CB), F.P. 18 (Champlain Place)
– architecture, Downs & Archambault #8744
Vancouver (CB), Fairview Place
– architecture, Rhone & Iredale #8746
Vancouver (CB), False Creek
– architecture et croissance urbaine #8169
  – Thompson, Berwick, Pratt & Partners #8170
Vancouver (CB), Finlayson House
– architecture, Samuel Maclure #8384
Vancouver (CB), foyer pour paraplégiques

– architecture, Downs & Archambault #8744
Vancouver (CB), Gallery of Photography
– Baykal, Erol, commentaire #2052
Vancouver (CB), gare du Canadien Pacifique
– architecture, Barott, Blackader & Webster #9534
– architecture et conservation #7762
Vancouver (CB), Goddamatch
– vidéos #2044
Vancouver (CB), Granville Island
– architecture, Norman Hotson Architects #8170
Vancouver (CB), Harbour Park
– architecture et croissance urbaine #9302
Vancouver (CB), Hodson Manor
– architecture #8707
Vancouver (CB), hôtel de ville. Vancouver Ouest
– architecture, Toby, Russell & Buckwell #8990
Vancouver (CB), Hotel Vancouver
– architecture et conservation #7762
– architecture et intérieur, Francis S. Swales #9272 9273
Vancouver (CB), IBM Building
– architecture, Thompson, Berwick, Pratt & Partners #9301
Vancouver (CB), Imperial Bank
– mosaïque murale, B.C. Binning #4732
Vancouver (CB), Imperial Bank of Canada
– architecture, Gerald Hamilton #9193
Vancouver (CB), Infinity Studio
– vidéos #2044
Vancouver (CB), Kenneth Heffel Gallery
– expositions, critiques
  – Onley, Toni #6742
Vancouver (CB), Laurel Street Crossing
– architecture, Hawthorn Mansfield Towers #8373
Vancouver (CB), MacMillan Bloedel Building
– architecture, Arthur Charles Erickson #8357 8361 9358
Vancouver (CB), magasin La Baie
– expositions
  – The World of Emily Carr: A New Exhibition of Her Paintings from the Newcombe Collection, Recently Acquired by the Province of British Columbia (1962) #5023
Vancouver (CB), Maples Development
– architecture, Daniel E. White #8746
Vancouver (CB), Marine Building
– architecture, McCarter & Nairne #8171 9356
Vancouver (CB), Metro Media
– vidéos #2044
Vancouver (CB), Nelson Towers
– architecture, Erickson/Massey #8744
Vancouver (CB), Nova Gallery
– expositions, critiques
  – Allegorical Imperatives (1978) #7507
Vancouver (CB), Open Space
– (années 1970) #641
Vancouver (CB), Orpheum Theatre
– architecture, Benjamin Marcus Priteca, et restauration, Thompson, Berwick & Pratt #9141
Vancouver (CB), palais de justice
– architecture, Arthur Charles Erickson #8362
– architecture et conservation #7762
Vancouver (CB), Pender Street Gallery
– expositions, critiques

– Lodge, Judy (1977) #6321
Vancouver (CB), Petrov Restoration Gallery
– expositions
– *Tomtu H. Roberts: Early Canadian Artist (1859-1938)* (1980) #7051
Vancouver (CB), Project 200
– architecture et croissance urbaine #9302
Vancouver (CB), projet d'autoroute, quartier chinois
– proposition architecturale, Arthur Charles Erickson #8360
Vancouver (CB), quartier chinois
– architecture #8171
– restauration, Birmingham & Wood #8159
Vancouver (CB), Queen Elizabeth Theatre
– architecture, Affleck, Desbarats, Dimakopoulos, Lebensold, Michaud, Sise #7679 9085
– expositions
– *Centennial Sculpture '67* (1967) #2001
Vancouver (CB), Raymur Place Housing
– architecture, Duncan McNab & Partners #8520
Vancouver (CB), résidence d'Arthur Erickson
– architecture, Arthur Charles Erickson #8357
Vancouver (CB), résidence de B.C. Binning
– architecture #8694
Vancouver (CB), résidence de Gordon Smith
– architecture, Arthur Charles Erickson #8357
Vancouver (CB), résidence de Robert M. Filberg
– architecture, Arthur Charles Erickson #8354
Vancouver (CB), résidence des Hauer
– architecture, Erickson/Massey #8519
Vancouver (CB), résidence Porter
– architecture, Davison & Porter #7679
Vancouver (CB), Robson Square
– architecture #8171
– Erickson, Arthur Charles #8362
Vancouver (CB), Robson Square Complex
– expositions
– *Artisan '78: The First National Travelling Exhibition of Contemporary Canadian Crafts/Artisan '78: première exposition nationale itinérante d'artisanat canadien contemporain* (1979) #2134
Vancouver (CB), Saint James Anglican Church
– architecture, Adrian Gilbert Scott; Sharp & Thompson, Associate Architects #8171
Vancouver (CB), Saint Paul's Hospital. Aile de chirurgie
– Gardiner & Mercer #9021
Vancouver (CB), Saint Paul's Indian Mission Church
– architecture #8919
Vancouver (CB), Sam Kee Building
– architecture #8171
Vancouver (CB), Shannon Estate
– architecture, Arthur Charles Erickson #8360
Vancouver (CB), Stanley Park
– totems #3932
Vancouver (CB), Terminal City Club
– architecture et intérieur, Philip M. Jullien #9061
Vancouver (CB), Trust Royal
– architecture, James Tettamanti #9301
Vancouver (CB), University of British Columbia

– architecture #9499
– concours #9498 9509
– Thompson, Berwick & Pratt #9500
– art, Kwakiutls #4037
– art public (ie. art dans les lieux publics), (1905-1971) #2005
– Binning, B.C., professeur #4734
– enseignement de l'art
– (années 1950) #1992
– (années 1970) #3006
– Martin, Mungo, totems #6427
– plans de l'université, Thomas Hayton Mawson #9405
– sculpture #2026
Vancouver (CB), University of British Columbia. Fine Arts Building
– architecture, Thompson, Berwick & Pratt #9502
Vancouver (CB), University of British Columbia. Fine Arts Gallery
– expositions
– *477-74-7, An Exhibition of Work of 7 Professors in the Bachelor of Fine Arts Program, U.B.C.* (1974) #2050
– *7 West Coast Painters* (1959) #1997
– *Ann Kipling: Recent Landscapes* (1980) #6057
– *B.C. Binning: A Retrospective* (1973) #4734
– *Canadian West Coast Hermetics: The Metaphysical Landscape/Les hermétiques canadiens de la côte ouest: le paysage métaphysique* (1973) #2045
– *Contemporary Ceramic Sculpture from Alberta, Saskatchewan, British Columbia and Manitoba* (1974) #1864
– *Four Canadian Artists: Arnold Shives, Wayne Eastcott, Pnina Granirer, James Felter* (1976) #2059
– *Glenn Toppings Remembered* (1978) #7392
– *Image Bank Post Card Show* (1971) #826
– *Joe Plaskett and His Paris: In Search of Time Past* (1971) #6893
– *Joe Plaskett et son Paris: à la recherche d'un temps passé* (1971) #6894
– *Joy and Celebration* (1967) #2036
– *Lithographs/Lithographies* (1972) #825
– *Liz Magor* (1979) #6405
– *Paintings from the Collection of Ernest E. Poole and Family* (1959) #3217
– *The Collage Show* (1971) #2042
– *The Mr. and Mrs. Jules Loeb Collection/La collection M. et Mme Jules Loeb* (1971) #3231
– *Younger Vancouver Sculptors* (1968) #2037
– expositions, critiques
– *B.C. Binning: A Retrospective* (1973) #4735
– *Canadian West Coast Hermetics: The Metaphysical Landscape/Les Hermétiques canadiens de la côte ouest: le paysage métaphysique* (1973) #2051
Vancouver (CB), University of British Columbia. Gymnase
– architecture, Thompson, Berwick & Pratt et Fred Lasserre #7679
Vancouver (CB), University of British Columbia. Museum of Anthropology
– architecture, Arthur Charles Erickson #8170 8360 9132 9137 9138
– art, Indiens de la côte nord-ouest, collection Walter et Marianne Koerner #3994
– art, Kwakiutls #3996
– collections #3195
– expositions

– *Cycles, the Graphic Art of Robert Davidson, Haida* (1979) #5268
– *Joe David* (1978) #5266
– *Norman Tait, Nishga Carver* (1977) #7314
– *Plantae Occidentalis: 200 Years of Botanical Art in British Columbia* (1979) #2024
– *Pursuing the Past: A General Account of British Columbia Archaeology* (1978) #4023
– Martin, Mungo, peintures #6429
– Reid, Bill, *Raven and the First People* #6989
Vancouver (CB), University of British Columbia. Résidence des étudiants
– architecture, Vladimir Plavsic & Associates #9467
Vancouver (CB), University of British Columbia. Résidence Thea Koerner
– architecture, Thompson, Berwick & Pratt #7683
Vancouver (CB), University of British Columbia. School of Architecture
– architecture, enseignement
– (1947) #8246
– (1948) #8247
– (1949) #8248
– (1950) #8249
– (1951) #8250
– (1952) #8252
– (1955) #8258
– (1980) #8289
– (années 1960) #8265
– (années 1970) #8146
Vancouver (CB), University of British Columbia. Sedgewick Undergraduate Library
– architecture, Rhone & Iredale #9052
Vancouver (CB), University of British Columbia. Student Union
– architecture, concours #9503
Vancouver (CB), University of British Columbia. Student Union. Art Gallery
– expositions
– *Dawn: An Exhibition by Women Artists of British Columbia* (1975) #2054
Vancouver (CB), University of British Columbia. Terrain environnant
– expositions
– *Open Air Sculpture Exhibition* (1956,1958,1960) #1993
Vancouver (CB), University of British Columbia. Thunderbird Stadium
– architecture, Vladimir Plavsic & Associates #9101
Vancouver (CB), University of British Columbia. Totem Park #4118 4124
Vancouver (CB), Up Front
– vidéos #2044
Vancouver (CB), Van Dusen Gardens
– sculptures en pierre, International Stone Symposium (1975) #775
Vancouver (CB), Vancouver Art Gallery
– (1980) #3203
– (années 1940) #1841 3185
– (années 1950) #1992
– Carr, Emily, oeuvres #5039 5042
– collection #3186
– collection de photographie #1051
– déménagement probable vers le centre-ville de Vancouver #3198
– enseignement de l'art (années 1970) #3006
– expositions
– *13 Cameras* (1978) #2069
– *17 Canadian Artists: A Protean View* (1976) #618
– *Affinities: Ten Painters of This Region; Max*

#2456
– *The Art of Nunstins/L'art de Nunstins*
 (1981) #6934
– sculpture en argilite, Haidas, collection
 Ferna et George Cook #4006
Vancouver (CB), Vancouver City Archives
– Brock, J.A., & Co., photographies
 (1886-1888) #2021
– masques, Squamish #3864
Vancouver (CB), Vancouver Civic
 Auditorium
– architecture, concours #9080
Vancouver (CB), Vancouver Museum
– (1894-1917) #3182
– collection (1908) #3180
Vancouver (CB), Vancouver School of Art
– (1925-1939) #3019
– (années 1940) #1841
– (années 1950) #145 1992
– (années 1970) #3006
– Laing, Bill, professeur #6135
– Mayor, Robin, directeur #6459
– Yip, Chuck Wing, professeur #7625
Vancouver (CB), Victory Square
– architecture #8171
Vancouver (CB), Video Inn
– art vidéo #605 2044
– et Mike Goldberg #5625
Vancouver (CB), Westcoast Building
– architecture, Rhone & Iredale #9359
Vancouver (CB), Woodcroft Estate
– architecture, Arthur Charles Erickson
 #8360
Vancouver Art Gallery. Bulletin, périodique
 can #547
Vancouver Arts and Crafts Association
 (Vancouver, CB)
– (1900-1901) #1977
Vancouver Island (CB)
– vues photographiques
 – Dally, Frederick #5250
 – Fardon, George Robinson #5411
Vancouver Studio Club (Vancouver, CB)
– (années 1910) #1979
Vancouver Sun, journal can
– dessins humoristiques
 – Innis, Jack #943
 – Norris, Len #6722
Vanderpant, John A., photographe can,
 1884-1939 #7457 7458 7459
– réflexion sur la photographie #7456
Vanguard, périodique can #547 3203
– (années 1970) #3310
Vanier, Bernard, artiste can, 1927- #7460
– à Paris (France) #426
Vanier, Georges, homme d'Etat,
 collectionneur can, 1888-1967, et Pauline,
 collectionneuse can, 1898-
– collection, art canadien #3216
vannerie . Abénaquis #3596
vannerie . Algonquiens #3374 3605 3625
– (années 1760-début XXe s.) #3633
– ornamentation estampée #3562
vannerie . Amérindiens #2739 3394 3447
– Coachella Valley (Calif) #3378
– technique #3446
– Washington (DC), Smithsonian Institution
 #3389
– XXe s. #2143
vannerie . autochtones #3411
vannerie . Canada #2089
– corbeilles à ouvrages, XIXe s.-années 1970
 #2943
– éclisses, Nouvelle-Ecosse #2935

– Labrador, XXe s. #2945
– Nouvelle-Ecosse #2157
– Québec, XXe s. #2954
vannerie . Carriers
– (années 1970) #4145
vannerie . Chilcotins #3789
vannerie . Cowichans #4027
vannerie . Delawares #3506
vannerie . Flancs-de-Chien #4089
vannerie . Folles Avoines
– écorce de bouleau #3620
vannerie . Haidas
– Santa Ana (Calif), Charles W. Bowers
 Memorial Museum #3991
vannerie . Hurons #3519
vannerie . Indiens de la côte nord-ouest
 #3888 3953 4009 4015 4029 4142
– et art précolombien #3810
– motifs, chronique en images #3728
– préhistoire #4017
– Pullman (Wash), Washington State
 Historical Society Museum #4004
vannerie . Indiens des forêts du Nord-Est
 #3625
– (années 1760-début XXe s.) #3633
– ornementation estampée #3562
vannerie . Indiens du bassin #3986
vannerie . Indiens du fleuve Columbia
– préhistoire #3842
vannerie . Inuit #4307
– en comparaison avec vannerie tlingit
 #4309
– Nunivak Island (Alaska) #4180
vannerie . Iroquois #3519 3605 3625
– (années 1760-début XXe s.) #3633
– et vannerie tsonnontouan #3552
– ornementation estampée #3562
vannerie . Klikitats #3778
– vannerie en spirale #3777
vannerie . Kootenays
– vannerie en spirale #3788
vannerie . Kwakiutls #3787
vannerie . Lillooets #3773 3783 3927
vannerie . Malécites #2144 3628 3637
vannerie . Micmacs #3569 3628 3630 3643
vannerie . Mistassins #4080
vannerie . Nootkas #3880 4025
– Santa Ana (Calif), Charles W. Bowers
 Memorial Museum #3991
vannerie . Outaouais
– utilisation de l'hiérochloé odorante #3547
vannerie . Quinaults #3773 3778
vannerie . Salish de la côte #3896
vannerie . Salishiens #3876 4027
– (années 1970) #4145
– Santa Ana (Calif), Charles W. Bowers
 Memorial Museum #3991
– vannerie en spirale #3777 3801
vannerie . Saulteux/Ojibwa #3539 3557 4089
– emploi de l'hiérochloé odorante #3547
vannerie . Shuswaps #3789
vannerie . Skokomish #3835
vannerie . Slaveys #4089
vannerie . Snuqualmis #3835
vannerie . Thompsons #3773
vannerie . Tlingits #3776 3792 3806 3865
 3976 4027
– en comparaison avec vannerie, Inuit du
 Pacifique #4309
– Santa Ana (Calif), Charles W. Bowers
 Memorial Museum #3991
vannerie . Tsonnontouans #3552
Vardeman, Lynn, artiste can, 1932-
– expositions de groupe

– (1978) #2067
Varennes (Qué)
– églises #8813
Varin (dit La Pistole), Jacques, orfèvre et
 joaillier can, 1736-1791 #269 270
Varley, Frederick Horsman, artiste can,
 1881-1969 #7461 7462 7465 7466 7467
– dessins d'Inuit (1938) #4185
– et le Groupe des Sept #1732
– et Molly Lamb Bobak #4766
– et Terence Shortt #506
– expositions
 – (1954) #7463
 – (1981) #7468
– expositions, critiques #1982
– expositions de groupe
 – (1968) #3224
– Gould, John Howard, comparaison #5635
– illustration et mise en pages artistique
 #939
– influence sur André Charles Biéler #4725
– influence sur Edward John Hughes #5861
– influence sur Evadna Chapman #5087
– influence sur Tony Law #6174
– paysages #7464
– peintures, scènes de guerre #1075
 – Canadian War Memorials Collection
 #1077
– Pellan, Alfred, comparaison #6814
– professeur de Joseph Sydney Hallam
 #5687
– voyages dans l'Arcticque #1779
Varney, Edwin (Ed), artiste can, 1944-
– expositions, critiques #2051
– expositions de groupe
 – (1971) #2042
 – (1973) #2045
Varsovie (Pologne), Muzeum Narodowe
– expositions
 – *Nowoczesne, Malarstwo, Kanadyjskie* (1962)
 #452
Varvarande, Robert Emile, artiste can, 1922-
 #7469
– influence sur peinture torontoise #1749
Vasarely, Victor de, artiste fr, 1908-
– utilisation de la couleur #468
Vastringue, La, fabricants de jouets
 (Saint-Jean-Port-Joli, Qué) #2924
Vaudreuil (Qué)
– silice, pour fabrication du verre #2418
Vaudreuil (Qué), église
– retable, Philippe Liébert #6280 6281
Vaudreuil (Qué), Musée de Vaudreuil #3108
– collection #3109
Vaudreuil (Qué), Musée régional de
 Vaudreuil-Soulanges
– expositions
 – *La couverture de lit du Québec ancien*
 (1980) #2746
Vaughan, John William, photographe can,
 actif 1862-1865
– et la Victoria Theatre Photographic Gallery
 (Victoria, CB) #2027
Vaux, Calvert, architecte paysagiste brit
 résidant aux Etats-Unis, 1824-1895
– Ottawa (Ont), édifices du Parlement #8048
Vauxcelles, Louis, auteur et critique d'art fr,
 né 1870
– commentaire sur James Wilson Morrice
 #6619
Vavasour, Mervin, officier de l'armée brit
 résidant au Canada, 1821-1866
– et Henry James Warre, expédition en
 Orégon (1845-1846) #7522

Vazan, William (Bill), artiste can, 1933-
#1512 7475 7477
– art environnemental #7471
– cartes géographiques, illustrations #561
– commentaire sur l'art conceptuel #7473
– commentaire sur *Worldline* (1969-1971)
#7470
– entretien #7478
– et réalisme #533
– expositions
– (1974) #7472
– (1978) #7474
– (1980) #7476
– expositions, critiques #1517
– Symposium international de sculpture
environnementale de Chicoutimi (Qué),
(1980) #1639
– utilisation de la photographie #1057
Vegreville (Alta)
– art (années 1940) #1943
véhicules . Canada
– (années 1940) #2603
Venise (Italie), Biennale (1952)
– art canadien #399 401
Venise (Italie), Biennale (1956)
– expositions, critiques
– Town, Harold Barling #7406
Venise (Italie), Biennale (1958). Pavillon du
Canada
– architecture, Enrico Peressutti #9210
Venise (Italie), Biennale (1962)
– expositions
– *Jean-Paul Riopelle: Paintings and
Sculpture/Jean-Paul Riopelle: peinture et
sculpture* (1962) #7018
Venise (Italie), Biennale (1968)
– expositions
– *Ulysse Comtois, Guido Molinari (1968)*
#522
Venise (Italie), Biennale (1970)
– expositions
– *Michael Snow, XXXV International
Biennial Exhibition of Art, Venice, 24
June-31 October 1970/Michael Snow,
XXXV Exposition biennale internationale
d'art, Venise, 24 juin-31 octobre, 1970*
(1970) #7244
– expositions, critiques
– *Michael Snow, XXXV International
Biennial Exhibition of Art, Venice, 24
June-31 October 1970/Michael Snow,
XXXV Exposition biennale internationale
d'art, Venise, 24 juin-31 octobre, 1970*
(1970) #7242
Venise (Italie), Biennale (1972)
– expositions
– *Canada: Gershon Iskowitz, Walter Redinger*
(1972) #548
Venise (Italie), Biennale (1976)
– expositions
– *Canada: Greg Curnoe (1976)* #5229
Venise (Italie), Biennale (1978)
– expositions
– *Canada: Ron Martin, Henry Saxe (1978)*
#661
Venise (Italie), Biennale (1980)
– expositions
– *Canada Video: Colin Campbell, Pierre
Falardeau/Julien Poulin, General Idea, Tom
Sherman, Lisa Steele (1980)* #705
Venne, Joseph, architecte can, 1859-1925
– Montréal (Qué), Université de Montréal
#9415
Venning, William Norris, orfèvre can,

1795-1877 #2649
Venor, Robert, artiste can, 1931- #1418
vent
– dans sculptures, Richard Prince #6936
ventes aux enchères
– *voir* marché de l'art
Venturi, Robert, architecte amér, 1925-
– influence sur A.J. Diamond et Barton
Myers #9349
Verbist, Pascal Joseph, prêtre can, 1829-1879
– projet, création d'une académie des
beaux-arts à Montréal (Qué), (1873) #2957
Verchères (Qué)
– architecture domestique #8635
Verdun (Qué), Centre culturel de Verdun
– expositions
– *M.A. Fortin* (1968) #5478
Vereydhen, Charles, architecte can,
1820-1872
– Victoria (CB) #8145
Vermette, Claude, artiste can, 1930- #2102
2378 7480 7481 7482 7483
– carreaux en céramique, hôtel
Reine-Elizabeth (Montréal, Qué) #8228
– et architecture #8231
– et l'art religieux québécois (années 1950)
#1250
– mari de Mariette Rousseau-Vermette #7085
– murales #7479
Vermette, Mariette Rousseau
– *voir* Rousseau-Vermette, Mariette
Verner, Frederick Arthur, artiste can,
1836-1928
– expositions
– (1976) #7484
– expositions, critiques #1696
– expositions de groupe
– (1888) #175
– (1890) #177 1839
– (1961) #62
Vernon (CB), Vernon Civic Centre
– architecture, Allen, Gower, Huggins &
Meiklejohn #8972
verre
– *voir aussi* bouteilles et flacons;
conservation et restauration, verre;
peinture sur verre
– bouteilles et flacons (1600-1903) #2427
– Louisbourg (NE), maison Dugas #2441
2442
– site archéologique de Roma (IPE)
– XIXe s. #2436 2437
verre . Algonquiens
– ouvrages perlés #3635
verre . Canada #2402 2408
– (1800-1940) #2433
– (1825-1920) #2399
– (1825-1925) #2404
– (1837-1887) #253
– (1979-1980) #2138
– (années 1940) #2601
– (années 1960-1980) #2440
– (années 1970) #2224
– Beach, William Godkin #2396
– Beauséjour (Man), Manitoba Glass Works
#2415
– bocaux à marinades, collection Walter Bick
#2405
– bocaux de fruits #2413 2426
– bouteilles de lait #2412
– bouteilles et flacons #2425
– (1825-1931) #2419
– Nouvelle-Ecosse #2409 2428
– Prairies (1880-années 1920) #2431

– Silver, M. et Mme Stanley S., collection
#2414
– XIXe-debut XXe s. #2427
– Calgary (Alta), Skookum Art Glass #2439
– Desaulniers, Gilles #5286
– et argenterie #2637
– flacons de médicaments #2432
– guide pour collectionneurs #2104 2252
2422 2429
– Hamilton (Ont), Burlington Glass Works
#2406 2434
– Hookway, Elmer John #5828
– McGowan, John, collection #2424
– Montréal (Qué), St. Lawrence Glass Co.
#2410
– motifs (1902-1940) #2411
– Nouveau-Brunswick #2150 2400
– Nouvelle-Ecosse #2114 2398 2417
– Ontario
– (1825-1948) #2401
– (années 1970) #2262
– XIXe s. #2416
– Pierce, Edith Chown, et Gerald Stevens,
collection #2397
– presse-papiers (1880-1925) #2438
– Québec #2226 2228 2237 2418
– XXe s. #2198
– Québec (Qué), place Royale #2201
– Saint-Jean (Qué), Canada Glass Works
#2420
– Sapperton (BC), Crystal Glass Co. #2423
– Schantz, Karl #7159
– Trenton (NE), Nova Scotia Glass Co. #2435
– verre à vitre, XIXe-XXe s. #7752
– verre moulé #2407 2430
– XIXe s. #2099 2421
– XXe s. #2121 2142
verre . Etats-Unis
– (1800-1940), au Canada #2433
– verre moulé #2430
– XIXe s., influence sur verre, Canada #2434
verre . Grande-Bretagne
– (1800-1940), au Canada #2433
– bouteilles et flacons, collection de M. et
Mme Stanley S. Silver #2414
verre . Indiens des forêts du Nord-Est
– ouvrages perlés #3635
verre . Iroquois
– ouvrages perlés #3635
Verrier, Etienne, ingénieur et artiste fr au
Canada, actif 1724-1747
– Louisbourg (NE) #8419
Versailles (France), château de Versailles
– art amérindien #3422
Versailles (France), Petit Trianon
– influence sur château Dufresne (Montréal,
Qué) #8618
Verville, Jean-François, ingénieur fr au
Canada, actif année 1717
– Louisbourg (NE) #8419
vêtements d'hiver
– Québec, XVIIe-XIXe s. #2832
vêtements sacerdotaux . Canada
– jésuites, Québec #2192
– L'Islet (Qué), église
Notre-Dame-de-Bon-Secours #8879
Vézina, Charles, sculpteur can, 1685-1755
#249 250
– oeuvres, églises, Charlesbourg (Qué) #8851
Vezina, Emile, artiste can, 1876-1942 #1391
Viau, Guy, artiste, critique et conservateur
can, 1920-1971 #7485
– dessins, dernières oeuvres #7486
– entretien sur le Centre culturel canadien

#8373
Victoria (CB), Provincial Museum
- Carmichael, William Maurice, orfèvrerie #5003
- Martin, Mungo, *Great Killer Whale Copper* #4054
- Price, Tom, dessins, collection Newcombe #6934
- sculpture préhistorique en pierre, Indiens de la côte nord-ouest #3900
- totems, haidas #4008
Victoria (CB), Provincial Normal School
- architecture, William Charles Frederick Gillam #9386
Victoria (CB), résidence d'Alexis Martin
- architecture, Samuel Maclure #8682
Victoria (CB), Salvation Army Matson Lodge
- architecture, Wade, Stockdill & Armour #8516
Victoria (CB), Scuby House
- architecture, Wade Williams Partnership #8170
Victoria (CB), University of Victoria
- enseignement de l'art (années 1970) #3006
- Poulin, Roland, sculpture en plein air #706
Victoria (CB), University of Victoria. Centennial Stadium
- architecture, Siddall, Dennis & Associates #9101
Victoria (CB), University of Victoria. Maltwood Art Museum and Gallery
- expositions
   - *Canadians: A National Photography Show about People/Canadiens: exposition nationale de photographie ayant les gens comme thème* (1980) #1035
   - *Herbert Siebner: A Monograph* (1979) #7205
   - *Katharine Emma Maltwood, Artist, 1878-1961* (1981) #6413
   - *Painting during the Colonial Period in British Columbia, 1845-1871* (1979) #2023
   - *The Maltwood Collection* (1978) #3242
   - *The University Collection* (1978) #3199
Victoria (CB), University of Victoria. Maltwood Museum of Historic Art
- expositions
   - *Arts of the Forgotten Pioneers: Catalogue for an Exhibition*, (1971) #2269
Victoria (CB), Victoria College of Art
- Wise, Jack Marlowe, professeur #7602
Victoria (CB), Victoria Theatre Photographic Gallery #2027
Vidal, Claude, éducateur can, actif 1968
- et Ecole des beaux-arts (Montréal, Qué), (1968) #2995
Vidal, Guy, joaillier, artiste can, 1938- #2216 2701
Video Ring #550
vie
- cycles, Jean-Paul Lemieux, commentaire #6233
Vie des arts, périodique can #55
- (années 1970) #3310
vie des premiers colons
- Black Creek Pioneer Village (Ont) #8675
- Canada #2112 2120
- Fanshawe Pioneer Village (Ont) #8066
- Heritage Park (Alta) #8125
- Kings Landing (NB) #7810 7811
- Louisbourg (NE) #8442

- Ontario, XIXe s. #2245
- Québec #2217
   - femmes #2212
   - XVIIe-XVIIIe s. #2200
- Upper Canada Village (Morrisburg, Ont) #7981 7982 8031
- Village Canadiana (Rawdon, Qué) #7876
- villages de pionniers, musées, sud de l'Ontario #8063
Viel, Nicolas, prêtre fr au Canada, m. 1625
- croix commémorative #1569
Vienne (Autriche), Museum für Völkerkunde
- expositions
   - *Indianer Nordamerikas* (1968) #3436
Viger, Jacques, homme d'Etat et collectionneur can, 1787-1858
- album #1337
- correspondance, William von Moll Berczy #4695
- et citadelle (Montréal, Qué) #8445
- *L'album des costumes de communautés religieuses de femmes au Canada* #2834
- *Souvenirs canadiens* #1326
Vilder, Roger, artiste can, 1938- #7487
- entretien #1485 1489
- expositions
   - (1973) #7488
   - (1975) #7489
- utilisation de la lumière #767
Village Canadiana (Rawdon, Qué)
- architecture #7876
Village Historique Acadien (Caraquet, NB)
- architecture #7805
Village Jacques de Chambly (Qué)
- architecture #8573
villas
- *voir aussi* châteaux et maisons de campagne
villas . Canada
- Québec, XIXe s. #8632
villas . Italie
- influence sur Lanark Place (Abernethy, Sask) #8700
Ville-Marie (Qué), fort
- conservation, recommandation (1881) #7754
villégiature . bâtiments . Canada
- XXe s. #8524
villégiature . bâtiments . Etats-Unis
- XXe s. #8524
Villeneuve, Arthur, artiste can, 1910- #1428 1429 1551 7490 7492
- expositions
   - (1972) #7491
Villeneuve, Jeanne Larouche
- *voir* Larouche-Villeneuve, Jeanne
Villeneuve, Joseph, sculpteur can, XXe s.
- professeur de Lauréat Vallière #7454
villes et villages . Canada
- conservation de l'architecture, XIXe s.-années 1970 #7761
- peintures traditionnelles #965 966
- provinces de l'Ouest #8083
- vues
   - (années 1950) #403
   - XVIIIe-XIXe s. #839
- vues photographiques (1850-1900) #1058 1061 7744
villes et villages . Etats-Unis
- conservation de l'architecture, XIXe s.-années 1970 #7761

- Ouest américain #8083
Villiers, Frederick, artiste brit au Canada, 1851-1922
- vues, provinces de l'Ouest #931
Vimy (France), Mémorial de Vimy
- Allward, Walter Seymour #4519
Vincelette, Roméo, artiste can, 1902-
- et Montée Saint-Michel #1236
Vincent, Zacharie, artiste can, 1812-1886 #7493
- autoportraits #7494
- expositions de groupe
   - (1959) #219
Vincent Rother Associates, agence can d'architecture
- Ottawa (Ont), Galerie nationale du Canada, concours #9079
Vinet, Pierre, photographe can, 1940- #990
Viollet-le-Duc, Eugène Emmanuel, architecte et théoricien fr, 1814-1879
- Cormier, Ernest, commentaire #8346
- théories, influence sur l'architecture religieuse du Québec #8819
Visser, John de, photographe can, 1930-
- catalogue de photographies #991
Visual Arts Ontario
- périodique, *ArtViews* #1806
Visual Communications Association of Winnipeg (Winnipeg, Man)
- et Art Directors' Club of Winnipeg #872
vitraux
- *voir* peinture sur verre
Vitruvius, auteur, ingénieur et architecte romain, fin 1er s. av. J.-C.-début 1er s.
- Cormier, Ernest, commentaire #8346
Vittecoq, Arlette, photographe can, active années 1960- #1534
Vivenza, Francesca, artiste can, 1941- #7495
Vladimir Plavsic & Associates, agence can d'architecture
- Vancouver (CB)
   - University of British Columbia
      - résidence des étudiants #9467
      - Thunderbird Stadium #9101
Vogt, Adolphe, artiste can, 1843-1871 #10
Volgyesi, Andrew Stephen, architecte can, 1937-
- Toronto (Ont), maison #8078
Volpi, Charles de, collectionneur can, 1910-1981 #3248
Von Baich, Paul, photographe can, actif 1980
- catalogue de photographies #1023
Von der Ohe, Dorothy Katie
- *voir* Ohe, Dorothy Katie von der
vorticisme
- et peinture canadienne, scènes de guerre, Première Guerre mondiale #1075
Vouet, Simon, artiste fr, 1590-1649
- professeur du frère Luc #5503
Voulkos, Peter, sculpteur amér, 1924-
- influence sur Sally Michener #6527
voyageurs
- vêtements, Canada, XVIIIe-XIXe s. #2826
Voyer, Pierre, auteur can, 1949-
- poèmes, dessins de Louis-Pierre Bougie #4861
Voysey, Charles Frances Annesley, architecte, designer brit, 1857-1941
- influence sur Samuel Maclure #8384
Vroom, frères, ébénistes can, actifs années 1870-1920 #2511

W

W.O.R.K.S. #1955
– art vidéo #550
Wabeno . Saulteux/Ojibwa #3492
Wade, Stockdill & Armour, agence can
  d'architecture
– Victoria (CB), Salvation Army Matson
  Lodge #8516
Wade Williams Partnership, agence can
  d'architecture
– Victoria (CB), Scuby House #8170
Wadsworth, Elizabeth Jane (Lizzy),
  photographe can, 1868-1944 #7496
Wagner, Charles Frederick, architecte can,
  1862-1934
– Toronto (Ont), Crown Tailoring Co.
  Building #9332
Wainio, Carol, artiste can, 1955-
– expositions, critiques #1227
Wainwright, Ruth, artiste can, 1902-
– entretien #7497
Waisman, Ross & Associates, agence can
  d'architecture
– Winnipeg (Man)
  – University of Manitoba. Crop Research
    Centre #7683
  – Winnipeg School Division #1. Edifice
    administratif #7683
Wald, Susana, artiste can, 1937-
– et surréalisme #7633
Waldmann, Oscar, sculpteur suisse, né 1856
– influence sur Katherine Elizabeth Wallis
  #7511 7512
Wales, Shirley, artiste can, 1931-
– commentaire sur la gravure #817 818
– et gravure québécoise (années 1960) #1641
– expositions de groupe
  – (1967) #821
Walker, Harry, photographe can, actif 1977
– catalogue de photographies #1023
Walker, Horatio, artiste can, 1858-1938 #10
  302 1312 7498 7500 7501
– en comparaison avec Homer Ransford
  Watson #217
– entretien #7502
– expositions
  – (1977) #7503
– expositions, critiques #204 211 306 7504
– expositions de groupe
  – (1935) #17
  – (1978) #1726
– influence de l'impressionnisme #227
– membre du Canadian Art Club #193
– Millet, Jean-François, comparaison #7499
– Thomson, Tom, comparaison #215
Walker, Howard Vincent, architecte can,
  1927-
– Scarborough (Ont), North Bridlewood
  Junior Public School #9471
Walker, John Barras, photographe can, actif
  années 1970-
– catalogue de photographies #991
Walker, Joy, artiste can, 1942- #675
– expositions de groupe
  – (1980) #698
Walker, Robert, artiste can, 1945-
– entretien #7505
– expositions de groupe
  – (1978) #668
Walker, sir Byron Edmund, collectionneur et
  banquier can, 1848-1924 #3206

– collection #1713 3205
– et Galerie nationale du Canada (Ottawa,
  Ont) #3050
Walker, Victoria, artiste can, 1943-
– expositions de groupe
  – (1979) #676
Wall, Jeffrey David (Jeff), artiste can, 1946-
– expositions
  – (1979) #7506
– expositions de groupe
  – (1970) #534
  – (1971) #2042
– oeuvres de l'imaginaire #530
Wallace, George Burton, artiste can, 1920-
– commentaire sur Paul Fournier #5487
Wallace, Ian, artiste can, 1943-
– et Mike Banwell #4601
– expositions
  – (1979) #7509
– expositions, critiques #7507
– expositions de groupe
  – (1971) #2042
– photographies (1973-1979) #7508
Wallace, Ken, artiste can, 1945- #2053
– expositions
  – (1980) #7510
– expositions, critiques #1883 2072
– expositions de groupe
  – (1979) #2075
Wallbridge & Imrie, agence can
  d'architecture
– Edmonton (Alta), row houses for Western
  Heritable Investment Co. (Canada) Ltd.
  #8511
Wallis, Adah, artiste can, active début XXe
  s.
– soeur de Katherine Elizabeth Wallis #7512
Wallis, Katherine Elizabeth, sculpteure can,
  1861-1957 #7511 7512
Wallis, Provo William Parry, officier de la
  marine brit au Canada, 1791-1892
– portraits, Robert Field #5430 5431
Wallot, Jacques-Albert-François-Joseph,
  artiste can, 1938- #7513
Walper, Ora C., artiste can, 1881-1961 #1681
Walter, G.P., Co., fabricants d'ameublement
  (Bowmanville, Ont) #2556
wampum . Abénakis
– ceintures (1699) #3526
wampum . Algonquiens #3521
– ceintures
  – Albany (NY), New York State Museum
    #3603
  – enregistrement de la fin de la guerre
    contre les Iroquois #3541
– ouvrages perlés #3635
– utilisation comme document juridique
  #3567
wampum . Algonquins #3505
wampum . Amérindiens #3387 3388 3457
  3522 3612
– articles de traite #3440
wampum . Hurons
– ceintures #3495 3514
  – (1674) #3526
wampum . Indiens des forêts du Nord-Est
  #3505
– ceintures, Albany (NY), New York State
  Museum #3603
– ouvrages perlés #3635
wampum . Indiens des plaines #3521
wampum . Iroquois #3505 3521 3607
– belts
  – et Iroquois Confederacy #3567

– ceintures #3532
  – Albany (NY), New York State Museum
    #3603
  – et Iroquois Confederacy #3496
– ouvrages perlés #3635
– Philadelphie (Penn), University of
  Pennsylvania. Museum #3518
wampum . Micmacs
– ceintures #3497
wampum . Outaouais
– ceintures représentant traités de paix
  (1764-1852) #3501
Wan, Theodore Saskatche, photographe can,
  1953- #7514
– expositions, critiques #1067
Ward, Charles Caleb, artiste can, ca
  1831-1896
– expositions de groupe
  – (1969) #1180
Ward, John, artiste can, 1948-
– peintures de Toronto (Ont) #7515
Wardrop, R., architecte can, actif 1912
– Calgary (Alta),ary (Alta), Lougheed
  Building #8118
Warhol, Andy, artiste et cinéaste amér,
  1928- #544
– entretien #996
– utilisation de la lumière #516
Waring, Stephanie E., artiste can, active 1979
– réflexion sur son oeuvre #7516
Warkov, Esther, artiste can, 1941- #7518
– expositions
  – (1970) #7517
  – (1976) #7519
– expositions de groupe
  – (1975) #1867
  – (1981) #1907
– oeuvres (années 1970) #7520
Warner, Burns, Toan, Lunde, agence amér
  d'architecture
– Toronto (Ont), University of Toronto. John
  P. Robarts Research Library #9048 9050
  9052
Warner, Ralph Malcolm, artiste austr,
  1902-1966
– expositions de groupe
  – (1981) #1117
Warner, William E., céramiste can, actif
  1856-1860
– fondateur de Warner & Co. (Toronto, Ont)
  #2310
Warner & Co., fabricants de céramique
  (Toronto, Ont) #2310
Warre, Henry James, officier de l'armée brit,
  artiste au Canada, 1819-1898 #279 2020
  7521
– et Compagnie de la baie d'Hudson #273
– expédition en Orégon (1845-1846) #7522
– expositions de groupe
  – (1979) #2023
Warren, Bill, photographe can, ca 1932-
– catalogue de photographies #991
Warren, Emily Mary Bibbens, artiste can,
  1870-1956 #7523 7524
Warren, Mary Schaffer, artiste can,
  1861-1939 #7525 7526 7527
Warren & Wetmore, agence amér
  d'architecture
– Montréal (Qué), hôtel Ritz-Carlton #9267
– Winnipeg (Man), Fort Garry Terminal
  #9530
Warshaw, Leonard, architecte can, 1933-
– Osaka (Japon), Expo 70. Pavillon canadien,
  concours #9217

Warwick, Septimus, architecte can,
1881-1953
– architecture domestique #8496
– Montréal (Qué) #8556
Washington (DC), Corcoran Gallery of Art
– expositions
– *An Exhibition of Paintings by
Contemporary Canadian Artists: Catalogue*
(1930) #315
– expositions, critiques
– *An Exhibition of Paintings by
Contemporary Canadian Artists: Catalogue*
(1930) #314
Washington (DC), Joseph H. Hirshhorn
Museum and Sculpture Garden
– *voir* Washington (DC), Smithsonian
Institution. Joseph H. Hirshhorn Museum
and Sculpture Garden
Washington (DC), National Gallery of Art
– expositions
– *Canadian Painting* (1950) #46
– *L'Amérique vue par l'Europe* (1975) #255
– *The European Vision of America* (1975)
#256
– *The Far North: 2000 Years of American
Eskimo and Indian Art* (1973) #3366
Washington (DC), Phillips Collection
– expositions
– *Group of Seven: Canadian Landscape
Painters* (1977) #1782
Washington (DC), Renwick Gallery
– *voir* Washington (DC), Smithsonian
Institution. Renwick Gallery
Washington (DC), Smithsonian Institution
– art, Indiens de la côte nord-ouest #3763
– arts décoratifs, Canada #2111
– masques, autochtones #3327
– objets en os, Inuit #4319
– poterie anglaise, vues de l'Amérique du
Nord #2294
– vannerie, Amérindiens #3389
Washington (DC), Smithsonian Institution.
Joseph H. Hirshhorn Museum and
Sculpture Garden
– expositions
– *14 Canadians: A Critic's Choice* (1977)
#644
– Hudson, Andrew, commentaire sur le
choix des oeuvres exposées #623
– expositions, critiques
– *14 Canadians: A Critic's Choice* (1977)
#621 627 645
Washington (DC), Smithsonian Institution.
Renwick Gallery
– expositions
– *Boxes and Bowls: Decorated Containers by
Nineteenth-Century Haida, Tlingit, Bella
Bella and Tsimshian Indian Artists* (1973)
#3985
Washington (DC), Washington Gallery of
Modern Art
– expositions
– *Seven Montreal Artists* (1968) #1263
Water Colour Society (Montréal, Qué)
– expositions, critiques
– (1950) #1400
Waterloo (Ont), Mutual Life Assurance
Company Building
– architecture, Darling & Pearson #9331
Waterloo (Ont), University of Waterloo
– décoration intérieure (années 1960) #9402
– enseignement de l'architecture (1980)
#8289
Waterloo (Ont), University of Waterloo. Arts

Centre Gallery
– expositions
– *Roger Savage* (1981) #7135
Waterloo (Ont), University of Waterloo.
Museum and Archive of Games
– expositions
– *An Exhibition of Canadian Gameboards of
the 19th & 20th Centuries from Ontario,
Quebec & Nova Scotia* (1981) #2597
Waterloo (Ont), University of Waterloo.
Résidence des étudiants
– architecture #9467
Waters, Mackenzie, architecte can, 1894-1968
– Toronto (Ont), Ridpath Building #9335
Watson, Budd, photographe can, 1930-
– catalogue de photographies #995
Watson, Harold R., architecte can, actif
1915-1928
– Toronto (Ont) #8643
Watson, Homer Ransford, artiste can,
1855-1936 #10 178 221 1713 7532 7533 7535
7536 7537
– correspondance, James Spooner (1887)
#7534
– en comparaison avec Horatio Walker #217
– entretien #7528
– et Académie royale des arts du Canada
#152
– expositions
– (1936) #7531
– expositions, critiques #168 174 186 204 210
7529
– expositions de groupe
– (1935) #17
– (1978) #1726
– influence de l'impressionisme #227
– membre du Canadian Art Club #193
– paysages #140
– réminiscences #7530
– Wilde, Oscar, commentaire #238
Watson, Mme Homer Ransford, Can, XIXe s.
– correspondance, Homer Ransford Watson
#7533
Watson, Susan, artiste can, 1949-
– expositions, critiques #2771
Watson, William Arthur, architecte can,
1903-1977
– plan, accès nord-ouest d'Hamilton (Ont)
#7962
Watson, William R., marchand d'oeuvres
d'art can, 1887-1973
– autobiographie #1272
Watt & Blackwell, agence can d'architecture
– London (Ont)
– Aberdeen School #9388
– McCormick Manufacturing Co. #9234
– Ryerson School #9386
– Tecumseh School #9388
Watts, Fraser, architecte can, 1926-
– Société centrale d'hypotèques et de
logement, concours (1960) #8040
Webb, Peter John, architecte can, 1927-
– Toronto (Ont), Inn on the Park #9289
Webb, Tom, photographe can, actif années
1950-
– catalogue de photographies #1032
Webb Zerafa Menkès, agence can
d'architecture
– Toronto (Ont), Toronto Hilton Hotel #9292
– Waterloo (Ont), University of Waterloo.
Résidence des étudiants #9467
Webb Zerafa Menkès Housden Partnership,
agence can d'architecture
– Calgary (Alta), édifices à bureaux #9362

– Toronto (Ont)
– gare Union #9540
– Hazelton Lanes #8078
– Hyatt Regency Hotel #9293
– Royal Bank Plaza #9198 9353
– Tour du CN #9511
Webber, Gordon McKinley, artiste can,
1909-1965
– entretien #7538
– membre du Groupe des peintres
canadiens #324
Webber, John, artiste brit au Canada,
1751-1793 #269 270
– vues, Nootka Sound, Vancouver Island
(CB) #2002
Webber, Ron, photographe can, 1944-
– expositions, critiques #1008
Weber, Anna, artiste can, style fraktur,
1814-1888 #7539
Weber, George, artiste can, 1907- #7540
Weber, Rudolph, artiste amér, 1858-1933
– dessins, Thompsons #3774
Webern, Anton, compositeur autr, 1883-1945
– influence sur Yves Gaucher #5560 5562
5565 5568
Webster, David, architecte can, 1866-1952
– Regina (Sask), War Memorial Museum,
concours #9073
Webster, John Clarence, collectionneur can,
1863-1950
– collection Canadiana, Musée du
Nouveau-Brunswick (Saint-Jean, NB)
#3073 3209
Weisman, Gustav Oswald, artiste can
(vitrail), 1926- #7589
Weiss, Joseph (Joe), photographe can, 1895-
#7541
Weissmann, Lawrence, photographe can,
1943- #1000
– catalogue de photographies #997 999
– expositions de groupe
– (1973) #1002
Welch, Roger, artiste amér, 1946-
– Lapointe, Frank, comparaison #6170
Welcome (Ont), résidence de Oke
– architecture #7959
Welding, William E., céramiste, actif
1867-1894 #2335
Weldon, Susannah Anne, collectionneuse
can, née 1817
– collection, céramique anglaise et
céramique chinoise, King's College
(Windsor, NE) #2363
Welland (Ont), Welland County General
Hospital
– architecture, Agnew, Ludlow & Scott
#9031
Weller, Walter J., architecte can, 1936-
– Charlottetown (IPE), Confederation
Centre, concours #9089
Wells, John, architecte can, 1789-1864
– Montréal (Qué), Banque de Montréal
#9168 9200
Wells, William, photographe can, ca 1956-
– catalogue de photographies #1032
Wembley (Angleterre), British Empire
Exhibition (1924)
– désaccord concernant la participation de
l'Etat #500
– et Académie royale des arts du Canada
#157
– et Clarence Alphonse Gagnon #5546 5547
– et Eric Brown #458
– et Galerie nationale du Canada (Ottawa,

Ont) #3040
- expositions
  - *Canadian Section of Fine Arts* (1924) #14
    299
- expositions, critiques
  - *Canadian Section of Fine Arts* (1924) #287
    288 291 322
Wembley (Angleterre), British Empire
  Exhibition (1925)
- expositions
  - *Exhibition of Canadian Art* (1925) #14 290
    299
- expositions, critiques
  - *Exhibition of Canadian Art* (1925) #291
    292
Wentworth, sir John, homme d'Etat brit au
  Canada, 1737-1820
- premier occupant, Government House
  (Halifax, NE) #8750
Wentworth, Thomas Hanford, artiste can,
  1781-1849
- portraits #1171
Wentworth-Fitzwilliam, William, vicomte
  Milton, noble brit, 1839-1877
- service à dessert Minton #2289
Werde Point (TN), phare #9523
Werden, Rodney, artiste can, 1946-
- art vidéo #630
- expositions de groupe
  - (1977) #631
  - (1978) #650
Werlich, Mr., artisan tisserand can, actif
  années 1840-1850 #2723
Werner, Bernhard, constructeur can, actif
  1981
- restauration, Skoki Lodge (Lake Louise,
  Alta) #9296
Wertheimer, Esther, sculpteure can, 1926-
  #7542
Wertschek, John, photographe can, actif
  1979 #2071
Wescoupe, Clemence, artiste can, 1951-
  #4157
West, Benjamin, artiste amér, 1738-1820
- *Christ Healing the Sick* #1323
- *The Death of Wolfe* #220
West, John, architecte can, actif 1820
- église protestante, colonie de Red River
  (1820) #7005
West, W.Richard (Dick), artiste amér, 1912-
- utilisation du motif du monstre marin
  #3757
West Baffin Eskimo Co-operative (Cape
  Dorset, TNO) #4192 4460
- et Peter Pitseolak #6880 6881
West Bay (Ont), Ojibwa Cultural Foundation
- expositions
  - *Anishnabe Mee-Kun: A Circulating
    Exhibition of Art by Anishnabe Artists of
    the Manitoulin Island Area* (1981) #4173
West End Dresden Pottery, fabricants de
  céramique (Montréal, Qué) #2410
West Vancouver (CB), Woyat-Bowie
  Building. Bureaux d'architectes
- architecture et intérieur, Fred Thornton
  Hollingsworth et Barry Vance Downs
  #9346
Westerlund, Mia, sculpteure can, 1942- #675
  7543 7545
- entretien #788
- expositions
  - (1978) #7544
- expositions de groupe
  - (1975) #1809

- (1981) #797
Westermann, Horace Clifford, artiste amér,
  1922-
- influence sur John Meredith #6516
Western Art Glass, fabricants de verre
  (Winnipeg, Man) #2450
Western Front (Vancouver, CB)
- art vidéo #605
- et Glenn Alun Lewis #6275
- expositions
  - (1979) #2070
Western Photographic Circle (Vancouver,
  CB)
- (1964-1967) #2019
Westfield Pioneer Village (Ont) #8063
Weston, William Percival, artiste can,
  1879-1967
- et British Columbia Society of Fine Arts
  #1978
- expositions
  - (1980) #7546
Wetherell, Robert Charles, architecte can, m.
  1845
- Hamilton (Ont), Dundurn Castle #8662
Weyler, Rex, photographe can, 1947-
- catalogue de photographies #991 998
Whale, Robert Reginald, artiste can,
  1805-1887 #221 7547
- expositions de groupe
  - (1978) #1726
Whalen, Robert, designer can, 1939- #2487
Wheatley, Willis Sifton, artiste can, 1910-
- commentaire sur la lithographie #7548
Wheeler, Arthur Oliver, photographe can,
  1860-1945
- appareils photogrammétriques #989
Wheeler, Charles Henry, architecte can,
  1838-1917
- Winnipeg (Man), Dalnavert #8708
Wheeler, Dennis, Can, m. 1977
- collection de photographies
  commémoratives, Marian Penner Bancroft
  #4599
Wheeler, Orson Shorey, sculpteur can, 1902-
  #7549
Wheeler, Thomas, graveur et horloger can,
  né ca 1809, actif 1847-1871
- membre de la Toronto Society of Arts
  #1689
Whipple, Henry Benjamin, évêque amér,
  1822-1901
- collection, art, Saulteux/Ojibwa et Dakotas
  #3755
Whissell, Aline Piché
- *voir* Piché-Whissell, Aline
Whistler, James Abbott McNeill, artiste
  amér, 1834-1903
- et Homer Ransford Watson #7533
- et Wyatt Eaton #5355
- Hammond, John A., commentaire #5699
- influence sur David Brown Milne #6567
- influence sur James Wilson Morrice #6624
  6626 6633
Whitby (Ont)
- architecture, XIXe s. #8016
Whitby (Ont), maison Lynde
- architecture et intérieur #8668
Whitby (Ont), Station Gallery
- expositions
  - *John Leonard: 10 Years: An Exhibition of
    Paintings and Drawings* (1981) #6246
White, Daniel Evan, architecte can, 1933-
- Vancouver (CB), Maples Development
  #8746

White, Edward, officier de l'armée
  canadienne, né 1811
- résidence, Saint-Jean (TN) #8542
White, Frederick, céramiste can, 1838-1919
  #2319
White, George, architecte amér, 1874-1964
- Lucerne (Qué), Château Lucerne #9283
White, George Harlow, artiste can,
  1817-1887 #7551
- expositions
  - (1975) #7550
- photographies et aquarelles, expédition
  britannique dans l'Arctique (1875-1876)
  #240
White, James, céramiste can, 1841-1928
  #2319
White, John, homme d'Etat brit et artiste au
  Canada, né ca 1540-1550 #228 229
- dessins d'Amérindiens et d'Inuit #7552
- dessins d'Inuit #7553
White, John Clayton, officier de l'armée brit,
  architecte et artiste au Canada, 1835-1907
  #2020
- expositions de groupe
  - (1979) #2023
- Victoria (CB) #8145
White, John P., ébéniste brit, actif début XX
  s.
- mobilier, résidence d'Alexis Martin
  (Victoria, CB) #8682
White, Joseph, céramiste can, 1799-1870
  #2319
White, Michael, photographe can, 1946-
- entretien sur le Groupe d'action
  photographique #1494
White, Minor, photographe et auteur amér,
  1908-1976
- influence sur Robert Charles John
  Bourdeau #4880
White, Norman, sculpteur can, 1938-
- expositions
  - (1975) #7554
- expositions de groupe
  - (1977) #783
White, Peter, critique d'art can, 1950-
- lauréat, concours de critique d'art (1979)
  #3312
White, Stan, architecte, artiste et critique
  théâtral can, 1926-
- commentaire sur les décors #7555
White Pottery, fabricants de céramique
  (Courtenay Bay et Saint-Jean, NB) #2319
Whitefield, Edwin, artiste amér au Canada,
  1816-1892 #812
Whitehorse (Yukon), Yukon Archives
- collection de photographie #2087
Whiten, Colette, sculpteure can, 1945- #675
  7559 7560
- entretien #788
- évolutionnisme #7557 7558
- expositions
  - (1978) #7561
- expositions, critiques #579 7556
- expositions de groupe
  - (1975) #591 1809
  - (1976) #779
  - (1981) #796
- sculpture, art de performance #658
Whiten, Tim, artiste can, 1941-
- concepts cosmologiques #554
- dessins #532 7563
- expositions
  - (1972) #7562
Whiteshell Provincial Park (Man)

– assemblage de rochers, Saulteux/Ojibwa #3578 3592

Whiteside, George, photographe can, 1958-
– catalogue de photographies #991
– expositions, critiques #1067

Whiteway, William Tuff, architecte can, 1856-1940
– Duncan (CB), Duncan Public School #9508

Whitlock, An, artiste can, 1944-
– entretien #788 7564
– expositions, critiques #579 622
– expositions de groupe
 – (1975) #591
– sculpture, art de performance #658

Whitman, Walt, poète amér, 1819-1892
– Thomson, Tom, comparaison #7357 7360

Whitman Fellowship of Toronto (Toronto, Ont)
– et Lawren Stewart Harris #5731

Whittaker, E.J., marchand d'oeuvres d'art can, XXe s.
– commentaire sur Alex Simeon Janvier #5936

Whittome, Irene, artiste can, 1942-
– expositions
 – (1980) #7569
– expositions, critiques #7567 7568 7570
– expositions de groupe
 – (1976) #779
 – (1977) #637
 – (1981) #710
– Le musée blanc/White Museum #714 7565
– thème de Narcisse #7566

Whymper, Frederick, officier de l'armée brit et artiste au Canada, 1838-1908 #2020
– expositions de groupe
 – (1979) #2023

Whyte, Catharine Robb, artiste can, 1906-1979
– art et écrits #7572
– entretien #7571
– programme d'expositions itinérantes, Alberta (1980) #1972

Whyte, Peter, artiste can, 1905-1966 #7572
– et Catharine Robb Whyte #7571
– programme d'expositions itinérantes, Alberta (1980) #1972

Wickenden, Charles Osborn, architecte can, 1851-1934
– Vancouver (CB), Christ Church Cathedral #8171 8910

Wickenden, Robert J., artiste can, 1861-1931 #1312 1382

Wickey, Harry H., artiste amér, 1892-
– influence sur Miller Gore Brittain #4917

Wickson, Paul Giovanni, artiste can, 1860-1922 #7573

Wickson & Gregg, agence can d'architecture
– architecture domestique #8494
– Toronto (Ont), Timothy Eaton Memorial Church #8898
– utilisation de stuc et de brique #8052

Wied, Maximilian, prince de, naturaliste all, 1782-1867
– collection, artefacts, Indiens des plaines #3737 3750
– expédition, Indiens des plaines #3738

Wieland, Joyce, artiste can, 1931- #657 675
– commentaire sur Gordon Rayner #6965
– commentaire sur Jack Chambers #700
– commentaire sur Michel Lambeth #6159
– entretien #7580 7582
 – séjour à New York (années 1960) #460
– et nationalisme dans l'art #143

– et peinture torontoise (années 1960) #1753
– expositions
 – (1971) #7577
– expositions, critiques #7576
– expositions de groupe
 – (1971) #98
 – (1973) #556
 – (1979) #147 510
– films #626 7574 7575 7579
 – Reason over Passion #568
 – The Far Shore #7581 7583
 – True Patriot Love #7578
– livres #940

Wiens, Clifford, architecte can, 1926-
– et architecture des Prairies #8084
– Regina (Sask) #7733
 – University of Saskatchewan. Chaufferie #7694
– théories sur l'architecture #7746

Wiitasalo, Shirley, artiste can, 1949- #7584
– expositions, critiques #579
– expositions de groupe
 – (1975) #591
 – (1980) #1832

Wilber, A.Rutherford, artiste can, 1869-1949
– expositions de groupe
 – (1969) #1180

Wilby, Robert, artiste can, actif 1973-
– poterie de grès et batik, Flat River Crafts Studio #2153

Wilby, Roslynn, artiste can, active 1973-
– poterie de grès et batik, Flat River Crafts Studio #2153

Wilby, Susan, artiste can, active 1973-
– poterie de grès et batik, Flat River Crafts Studio #2153

Wilde, Oscar, auteur irlandais, 1854-1900
– aux Etats-Unis et au Canada (1882) #238
– et Homer Ransford Watson #7533

Wiley, Matthew, photographe can, actif années 1970
– catalogue de photographies #995

Wilhelm, Paul, duc de Württemberg, 1797-1860
– collection, artefacts, Indiens des plaines #3737 3750

Wilkes, Elizabeth
– voir Hoey, Elizabeth Wilkes

Wilkes, Francis Hilton, architecte can, 1891-
– Toronto (Ont), Canada Permanent #9177

Wilkin, Rick L., architecte can, 1938-
– Edmonton (Alta)
 – Citadel Theatre #8091 9140
 – University of Alberta. Students' Union Housing #9496

Will, John, artiste can, 1939-
– expositions
 – (1980) #7585

Will, Mary Shannon, sculpteure et céramiste can, 1933-
– entretien #7586
– sculpture en céramique #795

Willar, Fred, artiste can, 1939- #1126

William Eby Pottery, fabricants de céramique (Conestoga, Ont)
– (1855-1907) #2304

William Thomas and Sons, agence can d'architecture
– Halifax (NE) #9410

Williams, Al, photographe can, actif 1981
– catalogue de photographies #1032

Williams, Alyn, artiste brit, 1865-1955
– et Mary Evelyn Wrinch #7617
– professeur de Mary Evelyn Wrinch #7618

Williams, Arch, artiste can, 1909- #1155
– expositions de groupe
 – (1976) #1153
 – (1977) #1156

Williams, Francis, artiste can, 1936-
– entretien #7587
– sérigraphies #4148

Williams, Judith (Judy), artiste can, 1940- #7588

Williams, Paul, sculpteur can (cuir), 1949- #2936

Williams, Robin, photographe can, 1946-
– catalogue de photographies #991

Williams, Saul, artiste can, 1954- #4157
– expositions de groupe
 – (1977) #4151

Williams, Warren Heywood, architecte amér, 1844-1888
– Victoria (CB) #8175

Williams, William Frederick, architecte can, 1904-1947
– lauréat, T. Eaton Company Architectural Competition for House Designs (1936) #8738

Williams, Yvonne, artiste can (vitrail), 1901- #2455 7589
– commentaire sur l'art du vitrail (1944) #2446
– vitraux #2445
 – Montréal (Qué) #2448

Williams & Ferguson, agence can d'architecture
– Toronto (Ont), Bourse de Toronto, concours #9161

Williamsburg (Ont), Molsons Bank
– architecture #9173

Williamson, Albert Curtis, artiste can, 1867-1944 #7590
– expositions, critiques #204 211
– membre du Canadian Art Club #193

Williamson, Beatrice (Betty) Lyell, photographe can, 1916-
– catalogue de photographies #987

Williamson, James D. (Jim), artiste can, 1924-
– professeur, Art Gallery of Toronto (Toronto, Ont) #3020

Williamstown (Ont)
– architecture #7997

Williamstown (Ont), Nor'westers Museum #3148

Willmott, Elizabeth, sculpteure can, 1928-
– structures en relief #777

Willoughby, Linda, artiste can, active 1981
– ouvrages en fibre textile #2775

Willowdale (Ont), Koffler Gallery
– expositions
 – The Heritage of Jack Bush: A Tribute (1981) #722

Willowdale (Ont), North York Public Library
– expositions
 – Reader, Lover of Books, Lover of Heaven: A Catalogue Based on an Exhibition of the Book Arts in Ontario (1978, 1981) #935

Willowdale (Ont), Regis College
– expositions
 – Canadian Religious Art Today: An Exhibition of Contemporary Art/L'art religieux canadien d'aujourd'hui: une exposition d'art contemporain (1966) #479

Wills, Frank, architecte can, 1822-1857
– Fredericton (NB), chapelle #8770
– Montréal (Qué), Christ Church Cathedral

#8798
Willson, David, architecte can, ca
   1778/1780-1866
- Sharon (Ont)
   - Temple of Peace #8351
   - Temple of the Children of Peace et
      Children of Peace Meeting House #8352
Wilson, Bunnell & Borgstrom Ltd.,
   ingénieurs-conseil et architectes
   paysagistes can
- plan, accès nord-ouest d'Hamilton (Ont)
   #7962
Wilson, Don, artiste can, actif 1980 #7592
Wilson, James, photographe can, ca 1950-
- catalogue de photographies #991
Wilson, John, architecte can, 1863-1952
- Lake of Bays (Ont), Bigwin Inn #9275
Wilson, Richard D., artiste can, 1920-
- vues, Montréal (Qué) #7919
Wilson, Ronald York, artiste can, 1907-
   #7594 7595
- au Mexique #4931
- et architecture #8231
- expositions
   - (1974) #7596
- expositions, critiques #432
- expositions de groupe
   - (1959) #438
- théories sur l'art et l'architecture #8235
Wilson, sir Daniel, éducateur et artiste can,
   1816-1892 #7591
Wilson, William F., artiste can, actif
   1842-1854 #7593
Wilson Newton Roberts Duncan, agence can
   d'architecture
- Toronto (Ont), University of Toronto.
   University College, restauration #7776
Windsor (NE)
- vues
   - Bartlett, William Henry #1218
Windsor (NE), King's College
- céramique anglaise et céramique chinoise,
   XVIIe-XIXe s., collection Susannah Anne
   Weldon #2363
Windsor (NE), maison Martock
- architecture #8528
Windsor (NE), maison Shand
- architecture et intérieur, Joseph Taylor
   #8546
Windsor (Ont)
- art #1668
- bâtiments en bois rond, colons
   canadiens-français, XIXe s. #7685
Windsor (Ont), Art Gallery of Windsor
- collection #3156
- expositions
   - A.J. Casson (1978) #5060
   - A Retrospective Exhibition of Selected
      Works by Caven Atkins Spanning Fifty
      Years of the Artist's Life (1979) #4569
   - A Survey of Forty-five Years (1976) #6658
   - André Biéler 50 Years: A Retrospective
      Exhibition 1920-1970 (1970) #4725
   - Canadian Paintings in the University of
      Toronto: An Exhibition in Celebration of
      the Sesquicentennial of the University of
      Toronto (1978) #3168
   - Carl Schaefer: Retrospective Exhibition;
      Paintings from 1926 to 1969 (1969) #7155
   - Certain Traditions: Recent British and
      Canadian Art (1978) #653
   - Changing Visions: The Canadian
      Landscape/Aperçus divers: le paysage
      canadien (1976) #617

   - Charles Fraser Comfort: Fifty Years (1973)
      #5159
   - David Bolduc: Recent Work (1980) #4775
   - Dessins inédits d'Ozias Leduc/Ozias Leduc
      the Draughtsman (1979) #6210
   - Don Snell and Nancy Hazelgrove:
      Sculpture and Painting (1980) #1835
   - Esther Warkov Drawings (1977) #7519
   - Frederic Marlett Bell-Smith (1846-1923)
      (1978) #4668
   - George Heriot: Painter of the
      Canadas/George Heriot: peintre des deux
      Canadas (1979) #5786
   - Goodridge Roberts: Selected
      Works/Goodridge Roberts: oeuvres choisies
      (1981) #7050
   - Gordon Rayner Retrospective (1979) #6966
   - Graham Coughtry: Retrospective (1977)
      #5190
   - Guido Molinari: Works on Paper (1981)
      #6594
   - Indications: Paintings, Collage, Drawings,
      Prints, Sculpture (1975) #7415
   - Inuit Art in the 1970's: A Travelling
      Exhibition/L'Art inuit actuel, 1970-79:
      exposition itinérante (1980) #4287
   - Ivan Eyre Exposition (1981) #5394
   - J.W. Beatty, 1869-1941 (1981) #4638
   - Jack Wise: A Decade of Work (1978) #7601
   - Jock Macdonald: The Inner Landscape: A
      Retrospective Exhibition/Jock Macdonald: le
      paysage intérieur: rétrospective (1981)
      #6379
   - Joe de Angelis, Bob Ferraro (1978) #1824
   - Joe Plaskett and His Paris: In Search of
      Time Past (1972) #6893
   - Joe Plaskett et son Paris: à la recherche d'un
      temps passé (1972) #6894
   - John Fox: 10 New Paintings (1980) #5495
   - John Meredith: Fifteen Years (1975) #6514
   - Joseph Nicola DeLauro: Sculpture (1981)
      #5276
   - Kenneth Lochhead: An Exhibition of
      Paintings 1952-1975 (1977) #6318
      - Lochhead, Kenneth Campbell,
         commentaire #6319
   - Krystyna Sadowska: Sculptures, Drawings,
      Collages, Batiks, Paintings (1977) #7115
   - Louis de Niverville (1978) #6709
   - Mary Celestino: Recent Paintings (1980)
      #5063
   - Ontario Society of Artists: 100 Years (1973)
      #1678
   - Otto Rogers: New Paintings and Sculpture,
      1977-78 (1979) #7065
   - Painters Eleven in Retrospect (1980) #1785
   - Peter Harris: A Survey of Fifteen Years
      (1977) #5735
   - Peter Kolisnyk (1977) #6075
   - Poets and Other People: Drawings by
      Harold Town (1980) #7416
   - R.L. Bloore: Sixteen Years, 1958-1974
      (1975) #4751
   - Ronald: 25 Years (1976) #7073
   - Roy K. Kiyooka: 25 Years (1976) #6062
   - Southwest (1970-) #1668
   - T.R. MacDonald, 1908-1978 (1981) #6380
   - Ted Hodgkinson, Jack Meanwell (1977)
      #646
   - The Contemporary Arts Society: Montreal
      1939-1948/La Société d'art contemporain:
      Montréal 1939-1948 (1981) #1474
   - The Heritage of Jack Bush: A Tribute (1983)
      #722

   - The Mr. and Mrs. Jules Loeb Collection/La
      collection M. et Mme Jules Loeb (1971)
      #3231
   - The Ontario Community Collects: A Survey
      of Canadian Painting from 1766 to the
      Present (1976) #120
   - The Work of Art: Six Artists (1979) #665
   - Tom Forrestall Exhibition (1972) #5461
   - Traditional Arts of French Canada (1975)
      #2128
   - Trésors d'art populaire québécois/Folk Art
      Treasures of Quebec (1981) #1297
   - Viewpoint: Twenty-nine by Nine; An
      Exhibition of Twenty-nine Works by
      Ontario Artists, Selected by Nine Curators
      (1981) #1838
   - William Perehudoff: Recent Paintings
      (1979) #6837
- expositions, critiques
   - Kenneth Lochhead: An Exhibition of
      Paintings 1952-1975 (1977) #6320
Windsor (Ont), Carnegie Library
- Heller, Clair, démonstration de sculpture
   #5775
Windsor (Ont), Collegiate Institute
- architecture, James Carlisle Pennington
   #9388
Windsor (Ont), Dominion Bank
- architecture, Carrere & Hastings; Eustace
   G. Bird #9188
Windsor (Ont), Imperial Bank of Canada
- architecture, Charles S. Cobb #9175
Windsor (Ont), University of Windsor.
   School of Visual Arts
- Angelis, Joe de, professeur #1824
- DeLauro, Joseph Nicola, fondateur et
   directeur #5276
- Ferraro, Bob, professeur #1824
Windsor (Ont), Willistead Art Gallery
- expositions
   - 7 West Coast Painters (1959) #1997
   - Centennial Exhibition of Quebec and
      Ontario Contemporary Painters, 1967
      (1967) #484
   - David Milne: 1882-1953 (1967) #6558
   - Essex County Artists (1940-1968) #1668
   - Fakir Art Club (1930-1940) #1668
   - Some Canadians in Spain (1965) #473
   - Some Paintings, Drawings and Prints from
      the Douglas Duncan Collection (1967)
      #3223
   - The Saidye and Samuel Bronfman
      Collection of Canadian Art/La collection
      Saidye et Samuel Bronfman (1968) #3087
   - William G.R. Hind (1833-1888): A
      Confederation Painter in Canada (1967)
      #5806
- Heriot, George, peintures d'Amér #5784
Winnipeg (Man)
- architecture #8092 8096 8105 8256
   - (1831-1960) #8095
   - (1881-1912) #8101
   - (années 1950) #7673
   - (années 1960) #7698
   - Barber & Barber #8331
   - centre-ville #8108
      - (années 1970) #8104
   - Stechesen, Leslie #8409
   - XIXe s.-1909 #8093
   - XIXe s.-années 1910 #8099
   - zone des entrepôts #8106
- architecture domestique
   - (années 1910) #8493 8688
   - (années 1950) #8514

- Rugh, Herbert Bell #8683
- XIXe s. #8702
- architecture et croissance urbaine (1870-1917) #8103
- art
  - (années 1950-1970) #131
  - (années 1960) #1848
  - (années 1960-1980) #1907
  - (années 1970) #1856
- art et architecture #1891
- arts graphiques
  - (1981) #1908
  - (années 1970) #1901
- banques
  - (1898-1914) #9205
  - (années 1910) #9202
- bureaux d'architectes (années 1940) #9297
- écoles
  - (1908) #9484
  - (années 1920) #9389
- enseignement de l'art (années 1940) #1889 1890
- galeries d'art (années 1960) #442
- hôtel de ville (1876-1962) #8996
- immeubles à bureaux et entrepôts (années 1880-1914) #8107
- immeubles d'habitation (années 1910) #8686
- peinture
  - (années 1940-1950) #412
  - (années 1960) #1892
- photographie
  - (années 1890) #1886
  - (années 1970) #1030 1879
- sculpture (années 1960) #1853
- vues photographiques
  - (1850-1900) #1061
  - Paskievich, John #6777
Winnipeg (Man), aéroport international de Winnipeg
- architecture #9517
- expositions
  - Eskimo Carvers of Keewatin, N.W.T. (1964) #4402
Winnipeg (Man), Allen Theatre
- architecture, C.Howard Crane #9074
Winnipeg (Man), Assiniboine Block
- architecture, Louise Arsene Desy #9361
Winnipeg (Man), Bank of Hamilton
- architecture, John D. Atchison & Co.; H.C. Ingalls and F.B. Hoffman, Associate Architects #9171
Winnipeg (Man), Banque de commerce
- architecture, Darling & Pearson #9202
Winnipeg (Man), Banque de Montréal
- architecture, McKim, Mead & White #9202 9205
Winnipeg (Man), Banque de Nouvelle-Ecosse
- architecture, Darling & Pearson #9157 9202
Winnipeg (Man), Birks Building
- architecture, Nobbs & Hyde #9355
Winnipeg (Man), Cauchon Block
- architecture, Louis Arsene Desy #9361
Winnipeg (Man), Chapel of Christ the King
- voir Winnipeg (Man), University of Manitoba. Chapel of Christ the King
Winnipeg (Man), Chase Gallery
- expositions, critiques
  - photographes de Winnipeg (1977) #1030
Winnipeg (Man), Dalnavert
- architecture, Charles Henry Wheeler #8708
Winnipeg (Man), Deer Lodge
- architecture, Pratt & Ross #9260

Winnipeg (Man), Dominion Bank
- architecture, Darling & Pearson #9188
Winnipeg (Man), Empire Hotel
- architecture, Louis Arsene Desy #9361
Winnipeg (Man), Fleet Gallery
- expositions
  - Povungnituk 1976 Prints/Estampes (1977) #4489
Winnipeg (Man), Fort Garry Hotel
- architecture, Ross & Macdonald #9268
Winnipeg (Man), Fort Garry Terminal
- architecture, Warren & Wetmore #9530
Winnipeg (Man), Grand Western Canadian Screen Shop
- (1968-1977) #1902
Winnipeg (Man), Green, Blankstein, Russell & Associates. Bureaux d'architectes
- architecture et intérieur, Green, Blankstein, Russell & Associates #9299
Winnipeg (Man), Hotel at Silver Springs
- architecture, Pratt & Ross #9263
Winnipeg (Man), hôtel de ville
- architecture, concours
  - (1913) #8979
  - (1960) #8985 8986 8987
Winnipeg (Man), hôtel de ville (1883-1886)
- architecture, Barber & Barber #8331 8996
Winnipeg (Man), Ikoy Partnership. Bureaux d'architectes
- architecture, Ikoy Partnership #8091
Winnipeg (Man), Lombard Plaza
- architecture et croissance urbaine #9302
Winnipeg (Man), maison d'Etienne Gaboury
- architecture, Etienne J. Gaboury #8519
Winnipeg (Man), Manitoba Archives Building
- expositions
  - Twenty-Seven Artists and the Manitoba Arts Council (1976) #1899
Winnipeg (Man), Manitoba Museum
- enseignement de l'art (années 1940) #1889
Winnipeg (Man), Manitoba Museum of Man and Nature
- expositions
  - Artisan '78: The First National Travelling Exhibition of Contemporary Canadian Crafts/Artisan '78: première exposition nationale itinérante d'artisanat canadien contemporain (1979) #2134
Winnipeg (Man), Manitoba Museum of Man and Nature. Concert Hall
- architecture #9107
Winnipeg (Man), Marlborough Hotel
- architecture, James Chisolm & Son et John Hamilton Gordon Russell #9277
Winnipeg (Man), Monarch Life Building
- architecture, Smith Carter Searle Associates #9357
Winnipeg (Man), Palais législatif
- architecture
  - concours #8946
  - Simon, Frank Worthington #8944 8945 8947 8948 8949 8950 8951 8952
- architecture et sculpture #8953
- expositions
  - 150 Years of Art in Manitoba: Struggle for a Visual Civilization; An Exhibition for the Manitoba Centennial, 1970 (1970) #1895
  - Eskimo Sculpture (1967) #4410
- expositions, critiques
  - 150 Years of Art in Manitoba: Struggle for a Visual Civilization; An Exhibition for the Manitoba Centennial, 1970 (1970) #1893
Winnipeg (Man), Pan-Am Pool

- architecture, Smith Carter Searle Associates #9101
Winnipeg (Man), Plug In Gallery
- expositions
  - John Greer: Sculptural Objective, 1968-1981; Everything Always Changes but Something Still Remains (1982) #5654
Winnipeg (Man), Royal Alexandra Hotel
- éclairage #2599
- murale, Frederick Sproston Challener #5068
Winnipeg (Man), Saint John's Cathedral
- Rindisbacher, Peter, peintures #7005
Winnipeg (Man), Saint Paul's College
- voir Winnipeg (Man), University of Manitoba. Saint Paul's College
Winnipeg (Man), Seven Oaks House (maintenant Seven Oaks Museum)
- architecture et intérieur #8703
Winnipeg (Man), Smith Carter Searle Associates, bureau d'architectes et d'ingénieurs
- architecture, Smith Carter Searle Associates #7683
Winnipeg (Man), Thomas Gallery
- expositions, critiques
  - Fafard, Joe #5399
  - Sheila Butler: Recent Paintings, Drawings and Prints (1977) #4984
Winnipeg (Man), Ukrainian Canadian Committee
- expositions
  - Program of the First Ukrainian Display of Fine Arts in Winnipeg (1951) #1843
Winnipeg (Man), University of Manitoba. Art and Adult Education Centre (proposition)
- architecture #8250
Winnipeg (Man), University of Manitoba. Arts Building
- architecture, Arthur A. Stoughton et Gilbert Parfitt #9485
Winnipeg (Man), University of Manitoba. Arts College
- architecture, Moody, Moore & Partners #9399
Winnipeg (Man), University of Manitoba. Chapel of Christ the King
- architecture, Gardiner, Thornton, Gathe & Associates; Green, Blankstein, Russell & Associates #9486
Winnipeg (Man), University of Manitoba. Crop Research Centre
- architecture, Waisman, Ross & Associates #7683
Winnipeg (Man), University of Manitoba. Freshwater Research Institute
- oeuvres, Tony Tascona #7326
Winnipeg (Man), University of Manitoba. Saint Paul's College
- architecture, Gardiner, Thornton, Gathe & Associates; Green, Blankstein, Russell & Associates #9486
Winnipeg (Man), University of Manitoba. School of Architecture
- architecture, enseignement
  - (1941) #8245
  - (1947) #8246
  - (1948) #8247
  - (1949) #8248
  - (1950) #8249
  - (1951) #8250
  - (1952) #8252
  - (1964) #8272

– *Watercolour Painters from Saskatchewan/Aquarellistes de la Saskatchewan* (1972) #1920
– *West Coast Waves* (1976) #2060
– *Western Canadian Salon of Photography* (1935-1943) #985
– *William Blair Bruce* (1976) #4942
– *Winnipeg Perspective* (1978-) #54
– *Woman as Viewer* (1975) #596
– *Yves Gaucher & Christopher Pratt* (1978) #643
– expositions, critiques
– *150 Years of Art in Manitoba: Struggle for a Visual Civilization; An Exhibition for the Manitoba Centennial, 1970* (1970) #1893
– art, Manitoba (1977) #1900
– Condon, Wanda (1976) #5166
– *Exposure: Contemporary Canadian Photographers/Exposure: photographes canadiens contemporains* (1977) #1030
– *Manitoba 1976 Juried Exhibitions* (1977) #1030
– *Sculpture on the Prairies* (1977) #1878
– *The Canadian Canvas: A Travelling Exhibition of 85 Recent Paintings/Peintres canadiens actuels: exposition itinérante de 85 oeuvres récentes* (1976) #582
– *The Temptation of Aquarius: Paintings by Robert Ralph Carmichael* (1972) #1866
– *The Winnipeg Show* (1956) #416
– *Treaty Numbers 23, 287, 1171: Three Indian Painters of the Prairies* (1972) #1866 4128
– *West Coast Waves* (1976) #1871
– *Woman as Viewer* (1975) #601 1877
– Proch, Don, *Asessippi*, oeuvres mixtes (1972) #6941
– sculpture inuit #4449
Winnipeg (Man), Winnipeg Convention Centre
– oeuvre, Dale Amundson #4524
Winnipeg (Man), Winnipeg School Division #1. Edifice administratif
– architecture, Waisman, Ross & Associates #7683
Winnipeg (Man), Winnipeg School of Art
– (1913-1950) #3006
– et Winnipeg Sketch Club #1887
Winnipeg (Man), Winnipeg Square
– Head, George Bruce, *The Wall* #5759
Winnipeg (Man), Woodsworth Building
– Dale Amundson, sculpture #4524
– Head, George Bruce, sculpture circulaire en béton #5759
– Howarth, Edward J., *Stratoscape* #5853
Winnipeg Camera Club (Winnipeg, Man)
– (années 1890) #1886
Winnipeg Paint and Glass Company, fabricants de verre (Winnipeg, Man) #2450
Winnipeg Sketch Club (Winnipeg, Man)
– (1914-) #1887
– (1914-1970) #1894
Winnipeg Tribune, journal can
– et Walter Joseph Phillips #6857
Winrob, Harry, médecin et collectionneur can, XXe s.
– collection, art inuit #4312 4445 4447
Winsor, Jacqueline (Jackie), sculpteure can, 1941- #7598
– expositions, critiques #7597
Winter, William Arthur, artiste can, 1909- #7599
winter counts
– *voir* chroniques en images

Winton, Jan, artiste can, 1954-
– *Syncopation* #1833
Wise, Jack Marlowe, artiste can, 1928- #7600
– entretien #7602
– expositions
– (1977) #7601
– expositions, critiques #2051
– expositions de groupe
– (1973) #2045
Wiseman, James Lovell, artiste can, 1897-1912 #7603
Wiseman, Nelson, photographe can, actif 1981
– réflexion sur photographies prises dans cabines téléphoniques #7604
Wishlaw, Robert, photographe can, actif 1979 #2071
Witmer, Joseph, ébéniste can, 1812-1896 #2578
Wittenborn, Rainer, artiste all, 1941-
– vues de la baie James (Qué) #1566
Wittgenstein, Ludwig Josef Johann, philosophe autr, 1889-1951
– théorie de l'art et art inuit #4294
– *Tractatus Logico-Philosophicus*, influence sur John Heward #5793
Witton & Walsh, agence can d'architecture
– Hamilton (Ont), Church of Saint John the Evangelist #730
Wolfe, James, officier de l'armée brit au Canada, 1727/1728-1759
– portraits #212 1568
– statues, Québec (Qué) #1309 1600
Wolfe, Robert, artiste can, 1935- #7606
– expositions
– (1977) #7605
Wolff, Louis-Augustin, artiste can, actif 1760-1818
– dorure #2930
Wolfville (NE)
– architecture domestique, XIXe s. #8533
– bureaux d'architectes (années 1940) #9297
Wolfville (NE), Acadia University
– architecture, Leslie Raymond Fairn #9407
Wolfville (NE), Acadia University. Art Gallery
– expositions
– *Charles Wm. MacDonald: Seaman, Labourer, Artist, Manufacturer (1874-1967)* (1981) #6355
Wolfville (NE), Acadia University. Fine Arts Department
– (années 1940) #1194
Wolhaupter, Benjamin, orfèvre can, 1800-1857 #2649
Women's Art Association of Canada
– (1889-1901) #176
– (années 1890) #1706
– commande, service de table officiel, Canada (1898) #2333
– enseignement de l'art (années 1910) #1712
– et Corporation canadienne de l'artisanat #2090
– expositions
– (1904) #2241
– (1939) #1
Women's Art Association of Hamilton (Hamilton, Ont)
– (1894-) #1701
Wong, Paul, artiste can, 1954- #992
– expositions de groupe
– (1979) #2069
– présentation de *in ten sity*, Vancouver Art Gallery (Vancouver, CB) #7607

Wood, Alan, artiste can, 1935- #2053 7609 7610
– constructions en matériaux bruts (années 1970) #2065
– expositions
– (1977) #7608
– *Ranch*, Emily Carr College of Art (Vancouver, CB) #7611
– utilisation de l'espace #2062
Wood, Brian, photographe can, 1948-
– expositions
– (1979) #7612
Wood, Elizabeth Wyn, sculpteure can, 1903-1966 #739 5677 7613
– femme d'Emanuel Hahn #5678
– réflexion sur le nationalisme et l'art #368
Wood, Enoch, céramiste brit, XIXe s.
– poterie de Staffordshire, vues du Canada #2288
Wood, Faith, artiste can, 1917-
– portraits #581
Wood, John W., architecte can, né 1885
– Montréal (Qué), hôtel Reine-Elizabeth #9286
Wood, Marshall, sculpteur brit, m. 1882
– sculpture, Ottawa (Ont) #727
Wood, William John, artiste can, 1877-1954 #309
– notice nécrologique #7614
Woodchuck Press (Toronto, Ont)
– et Thoreau MacDonald #6384
Woodcock, Percy Franklin, artiste can, 1855-1936 #178
– *Abandoned Nest* #172
Woodley, Charles D., photographe can, ca 1911-
– catalogue de photographies #1032
Woodman & Carey, agence can d'architecture
– Winnipeg (Man), hôtel de ville, concours #8979
Woodrow, Paul, artiste can, 1941-
– *Bureau of Imaginary Exchange* #714
– et W.O.R.K.S. #1955
Woodruff, John, photographe can, 1859-1917
– expositions de groupe
– (1970) #1675
Woods, Chris, sculpteur can, 1949- #7615
Woodside, Henry Joseph, photographe can, 1858-1929
– photographies militaires, Yukon et Afrique du Sud #1107
Woodstock (NB), Carleton County Vocational School
– expositions
– *Colville, Pratt, Forrestall* (1974) #1129
– *The Beaverbrook Art Gallery Presents Nine New Brunswick Artists/La Galerie d'art Beaverbrook présente neuf artistes du Nouveau-Brunswick* (1973) #1182
Woodstock (Ont), Oxford County Art Association
– expositions
– *Centennial Exhibition of Quebec and Ontario Contemporary Painters, 1967* (1967) #484
Woodstock (Ont), Woodstock Public Library and Art Gallery
– expositions
– *Alan C. Collier Retrospective* (1971) #5131
– *Ed Bartram: 10 Years* (1980) #4618
– *Imprint '76* (1976) #833
– *William Blair Bruce* (1976) #4942
Woodville, Richard Caton, artiste brit au

Canada, 1856-1927
- vues, Ouest canadien #931
Woolford, John Elliott, officier de l'armée
  brit, artiste et architecte au Canada,
  1778-1866 #258 259 279
Woolnough, Hilda Mary, artiste can, 1934-
  #7616
Woolsey, John William, homme d'affaires
  can, 1767-1852
- portrait de famille, William von Moll
  Berczy #4700
Woolwich (Angleterre), Royal Military
  Academy
- et George Heriot #5789
- et Thomas Davies #5272
Worcester (Mass), Clark University.
  Goddard Library
- architecture, John M. Johansen #9046
World Crafts Council
- (1979), recommandations #2136 2137
Worthington, Timothy (Tim), céramiste can,
  1950- #2395
Wray, John, designer can, actif années 1950-
- Halifax (NE), Nepture Theatre #9097
Wright, Don, artiste can, 1931- #1148
Wright, Douglas, artiste can, ca 1918-
- illustrations #855
Wright, Edith P. Stevenson, artiste can,
  active 1869-1950 #7279
Wright, Frank Lloyd, architecte amér,
  1867-1959
- influence sur l'architecture canadienne
  #7680
- influence sur l'architecture de Trent
  University (Peterborough, Ont), #9474
- professeur de Francis Conroy Sullivan
  #8410
- professeur de James William Strutt #7984
Wright, John, architecte can, 1830-1915
- Victoria (CB) #8145
Wright, Richard Thomas, photographe can,
  actif 1977
- catalogue de photographies #1023
Wrinch, Mary Evelyn, artiste can, 1877-1969
  #207 7617
- expositions
  - (1980) #7618
- expositions, critiques #1710
- femme de George Agnew Reid #6979
Wroclaw (Pologne), Ecole des beaux-arts
- Kupczynski, Stanislav, élève #6106
Wu, Allan, photographe can, ca 1947-
- catalogue de photographies #1032
Würtele, Frederick C. (Fred), photographe
  can, 1843-1920 #7619
Wyers, Jan G., artiste can, 1888-1973 #1852
  7620
- expositions de groupe
  - (1958) #1846
  - (1970) #1918
Wyeth, Andrew Newell, artiste amér, 1917-
- Colville, Alex, comparaison #5151
- Forrestall, Tom, comparaison #5466
- Prévost, Antoine, comparaison #6927
Wyle, Florence, sculpteure can, 1881-1968
  #739
- Dr. D.W. Young (Toronto, Ont),
  monument #729
- et Frances Norma Loring #758
- expositions de groupe
  - (1969) #754

X

Xavier, John, photographe can, actif 1981
- catalogue de photographies #1023

Y

Yakuglas
- voir James, Charlie
Yale (CB)
- vues, XIXe s. #2031
Yamachiche (Qué), église Sainte-Anne
- architecture et art #8783
Yamazaki & Ridpath, agence can
  d'architecture
- Beamsville (Ont), Nipponia Home for the
  Aged #8516
Yarmouth (NE), Yarmouth County Museum
- collection, scènes représentant bateaux
  #163
Yarwood, Walter Hawley, sculpteur can,
  1917-
- entretien #7621
- sculptures (années 1960) #745 746
Yates, Edward Norman, artiste can, 1923-
  #1880 7622 7623
Yates, Richard, maroquinier can, 1949- #2936
Yecny, Vaclav, ébéniste can, m. 1921 #2587
Yellowstone Park (EU)
- vues, fin XIXe s. #1839
Yeo, James, constructeur de navire,
  marchand et fermier can, 1789-1868
- résidence, Green Park (région de
  Summerside, IPE) #8540
Yerxa, Leo, artiste can, 1947- #4140 7624
- dessin de monnaie olympique (1976) #778
Yip, Chuck Wing, artiste can, 1923- #7625
Ykelenstam, Henk, artiste can, actif 1981
  #7626
York & Sawyer, agence can d'architecture
- Montréal (Qué), Banque Royale du
  Canada #9176
- Toronto (Ont), Banque canadienne de
  Commerce #9178
York Factory (Man)
- caserne #8482
Yosemite Valley (EU)
- vues, fin XIXe s. #1839
Yoshi, photographe can, actif 1975
- catalogue de photographies #998
Youds, Robert E., artiste can, 1954-
- expositions, critiques #2072
- expositions de groupe
  - (1979) #2075
Young, D.W., médecin can, XXe s.
- monument (Toronto, Ont) #729
Young, Helen Granger, céramiste can, 1923-
  #7627
Young, Hester, artisane tisserande can,
  active années 1840-1850 #2723
Young, Mahonri MacIntosh, artiste amér,
  1877-1957
- influence sur Miller Gore Brittain #4917
Young, Robert, artiste can, 1938- #7628 7629
  7630
- expositions
  - (1981) #7631
Young, Ron, photographe can, actif 1978
- catalogue de photographies #1023

Young, Rosanna, artisane tisserande can,
  active années 1840-1850 #2723
Young, Thomas, architecte et artiste can, ca
  1810-1860
- membre de la Toronto Society of Arts
  #1689
Youngblood, Gene, auteur amér, 1942-
- réflexion sur le sacré dans l'art #94
Ypres (France)
- bataille d'Ypres, Walter Seymour Allward
  #4518
Yukon
- architecture #8083
- art (années 1970) #2086 2088
- vues
  - Harrison, Ted #5749 5750 5751
  - Robb, Jim #7037
- vues photographiques
  - (années 1880-1890) #1874
  - photographes militaires canadiens #1107
Yuristy, Russell, artiste can, 1936- #1937
- expositions
  - (1981) #7632
- expositions, critiques #2383
- expositions de groupe
  - (1976) #1930

Z

Zach, Jan, sculpteur can, 1914-
- professeur d'Elza Mayhew #6455
Zack, Badanna Bernice, artiste can, 1943-
  #657
- commentaire sur Jack Chambers #700
Zadow, J. Albert, ébéniste can, 1854-1941
  #2582
Zander, Dick, artiste can, 1943-
- et Intersystems #767
Zarov, Basil, photographe can, ca 1918-
- catalogue de photographies #987
Zazelenchuk, Stanley, collectionneur can,
  1941-, et Patricia Jean, collectionneuse can,
  1943-
- collection, art inuit #4284 4306
Zeidler, Eberhard Henrich, architecte can,
  1926-
- commentaire, McMaster University Health
  Sciences Centre (Hamilton, Ont) #9037
- mont Sainte-Marie (Qué), centre de
  villégiature #7886
- théories sur l'architecture #7746
Zeidler Partnership, agence can
  d'architecture
- Toronto (Ont)
  - Eaton Centre #9377 9378 9382
  - Young People's Theatre, restauration
    #7776
Zeldin, Gerald, artiste can, 1943-
- expositions de groupe
  - (1976) #1810
Zelenak, Edward (Ed), sculpteur can, 1940-
- et Walter Redinger #6968
- expositions de groupe
  - (1970) #771
  - (1971) #98
  - (1978) #786
- théories sur l'art #594
Zelkine, Alexandre, photographe can, actif
  1971 #997
Zeller, Ludwig, artiste can, 1927-
- et surréalisme #7633